World Trade Almanac

1996-1997

Economic, Marketing, Trade, Cultural, Legal, & Travel Surveys for the World's Top 100 Countries

WORLD TRADE PRESS
PUBLICATIONS

General References

Importers Manual USA

Exporting to the USA

World Trade Almanac

A Basic Guide to Exporting

Dictionary of International Trade

Country Business Guides

ARGENTINA Business   KOREA Business

AUSTRALIA Business   MEXICO Business

CANADA Business   PHILIPPINES Business

CHINA Business   SINGAPORE Business

HONG KONG Business   TAIWAN Business

JAPAN Business   USA Business

Passport to the World Series

Passport Argentina   Passport Korea

Passport Brazil   Passport Mexico

Passport China   Passport Philippines

Passport France   Passport Singapore

Passport Hong Kong   Passport Taiwan

Passport India   Passport Thailand

Passport Israel   Passport UK

Passport Japan   Passport USA

Passport Vietnam

CD-ROMs

Importers Manual USA CD-ROM

Exporting to the USA CD-ROM

World Trade Almanac CD-ROM

World Trade Almanac
1996-1997

Economic, Marketing, Trade, Cultural, Legal, & Travel Surveys for the World's Top 100 Countries

Molly E. Thurmond, J.D.

Joe Reif

Peter G. Jones   Janet Whittle

Alexandra Woznick

Cathy Baehler   Christopher Mahon

Douglas Baughman   Laurie Mayhew

Dan Blacharski   Bobbie Miller

John Broderick   Kristen Montgomery

Jeffrey Byrd   Paul Nicholes

Karen Fitzgerald   Cary Pepper

Andrew Grzeskowiak   Ken Presti

Jack Handley   Sonja Rothko

Edward G. Hinkelman   Michelle Tovar

Kay Johnson   Laurie Wiegler

Commercial Law Affiliates
Magellan Geographix^{sm}
Ernst & Young

WORLD
TRADE
PRESS®

San Rafael, California

WORLD TRADE ALMANAC
1996-97 Edition

World Trade Press
1505 Fifth Avenue
San Rafael, CA 94901, USA
Tel (415) 454-9934
Fax (415) 453-7980
Email WorldPress@aol.com
Order Line (800) 833-8586

Maps: Magellan^{sm} Geographix, Peter G. Jones, Phil Seiresen, David Baker
Cover design: Brad Greene, Peter G. Jones
Text design: Edward G. Hinkelman, Peter G. Jones, Molly E. Thurmond

ACKNOWLEDGEMENTS

We owe many leaders in the international business community a debt of gratitude. Hundreds of trade and reference experts have brought this book to life. We are indebted to numerous business consultants, researchers, travel advisors, embassy and trade mission officers, attorneys, and others who answered our incessant inquiries and volunteered facts, figures, and expert opinions. It would be impossible to name them all. But, to all these many individuals, named and unnamed, we extend our thanks.

The professional talents of many researchers, authors, and editors have been combined to created the *World Trade Almanac*. At the top of the list is Bobbie Miller, who spent endless hours finding information, translating it into coherent sentences, filling empty spaces, and generally completing tasks others left undone. We all relied heavily on her ability to follow through and keep it all straight. Her unending assistance in this endeavor was invaluable.

Andrew Grzeskowiak wrote most of the marketing sections, several economy sections, and various other portions of the book. John Broderick toiled away on the economy sections, and plowed through a great number of them. He also undertook to put it all together and summarize the information we presented for each country. His understanding of the big picture is noted and appreciated.

Kay Johnson, Douglas Baughman, Jack Handley, Ken Presti, and Dan Blacharski all contributed several sections with tremendous insight and thoroughness. Their knowledge of international trade is impressive, and their ability to convey it clearly and in understandable language was always appreciated.

Cathy Baehler, Laurie Mayhew, and Sonja Rothko used their extensive travel experiences to write the travel sections. Karen Fitzgerald, Cary Pepper, and Paul Nicholes dug into the different cultures of the various countries and came up with interesting and little known insights.

Christopher Mahon sorted through a mass of trade data to come up with the opportunities for importing and exporting for each country. Kristen Montgomery and Laurie Mayhew compiled demographic, geographic, and miscellaneous data on each country for the At a Glance sections. Their research skills are noted.

Laurie Wiegler and Jeffrey Byrd, who joined the team near the end, did an excellent job finding information and writing about those difficult countries that everybody else left undone. We are grateful.

Joan Alexander and Jackie Luman found and typed addresses and more, and we appreciate their assistance. The special research skills of Patrick Sullivan were essential to compiling the Internet sites. Peter Jones used his impressive artistic and design talents to present all the information in a visually pleasing, logical manner.

Commercial Law Affiliates rose to the occasion by gathering its impressive cadre of experienced attorneys all over the world. They are the world's largest organization of independent business and commercial litigation law firms, and provide access to the expertise normally associated with the world's largest law firms. Unlike other legal networks, the CLA has strict membership criteria and an ongoing satisfaction monitoring system, all designed to provide high levels of professional service and instill client confidence. We would not have had a legal section without their timely assistance. To each of the individuals who contributed, we are grateful. (Commercial Law Affiliates, 420 North Fifth Street, Suite 970, Minneapolis, MN 55401; Tel: (612) 339–8680, Fax: (612) 337–5783)

We are also indebted to Ernst & Young, who unhesitatingly allowed us to use information from their *Worldwide Corporate Tax Guide and Directory*. Their expertise in international tax matters is unmatched.

We relied heavily on the reference librarians and resources available at the libraries of the University of California at Berkeley, San Rafael Public Library, Oakland City Library, Marin County Civic Center Library, and the Marin County and University of California at Berkeley Law Libraries. Many thanks to all of the librarians who steered us to obscure data on countries large and small.

DISCLAIMER

Material for this publication has been obtained from information supplied by U.S. government agencies, foreign government embassies, consulates and agencies, industry and trade organizations, from personal interview and by telephone and correspondence. We have diligently tried to ensure the accuracy of all of the information in this publication and to present as comprehensive a reference work as space would permit. The fluidity and fast pace of today's business world makes the task of keeping data current and accurate an extremely difficult one. Our purpose is to give you information so that you can become aware of important issues and can discover resources most useful for your particular business. As you contact the resources within this book, you will no doubt learn of new and exciting business opportunities and of additional trading requirements that have arisen even within the short time since we published this edition. If we find errors, we will strive to correct them in preparing future editions. The publishers take no responsibility for inaccurate or incomplete information that may have been submitted to them in the course of research for this publication. The facts published indicate the result of those inquiries and no warranty as to their accuracy is given.

Table of Contents

Overview

In the world's complex and rapidly changing business environment, enterprises of all sorts and sizes are increasingly called upon to explore new markets–often in distant and foreign lands. Although we can't expect to be experts in every subject, a little bit of general knowledge about the countries and people we may be called upon to do business with will help tremendously in accomplishing our objectives.

The *World Trade Almanac* is designed to provide international traders with a blueprint for success in foreign markets. The *Almanac* provides useful information on a variety of subjects–from economics to travel–for 100 of the world's leading trading nations. It is structured in a logical, easy-to-follow format which allows ready comparison of the business environments of different countries so traders can gain a good understanding of the overall conditions and requirements of doing business in these countries.

Economy

The Economy section provides an overall perspective on each country's economic development, foreign trade, economic sectors, and future prospects. It gives a historical perspective on the economic development of each country and examines the major forces that have shaped each nation, and the trends that will impact its future economic development.

Foreign Trade

The Foreign Trade section takes a closer look at each country's main trading partners and primary imports and exports. It provides lists of opportunities for trading with that country, including importing, exporting, special growth sectors, and government procurement projects. This section also contains a digest of some of the rules and regulations relating to foreign trade with each nation.

Marketing

An overview of marketing in each country is presented, along with specific information about distribution channels, agents, selling techniques and advertising. Special marketing tips are offered, and nearly all contain lists of local advertising agencies or market research firms.

Business Culture

The information in this section will help foreign traders understand the cultural environment of each country so they will know how best to approach businesspeople in or from that culture. Common greetings and courtesies, business ethics, women in business, attire, negotiations and decision-making are all covered, as are special cultural hints and cautions to help foreign traders avoid costly social faux pas.

Legal

International traders will often run into issues about intellectual property rights, business licensing and registration, contracts, dispute resolution and labor relations. While it may be necessary to engage local legal counsel to address these matters, the *Almanac* does provide general information to give traders knowledge they can use to compare how these matters are dealt with in the different countries. Local legal contacts are also provided for each country.

Money

This section highlights each country's currency, exchange mechanisms, and policies on capital transfers and foreign investment. It includes an "At a Glance" look at the country's taxation structure, excerpted from the Ernst & Young International Business Series, *Worldwide Corporate Tax Guide and Directory*, 1995 edition.

Travel

Business visits to foreign markets are an essential part of international trade and good preparation is important to ensure a successful trip. The Business Travel section provides useful information on visa and passport requirements, departure formalities, immunization requirements, workweeks and holidays, air travel times, and the available communications systems in each country. Telephone numbers of important sources of information are provided and the best travel books on each country are listed.

Contacts

Each country listing also includes important local contact addresses and telephone numbers, such as government agencies, market research firms, banks, trade associations, and media sources.

Additional Features

Each country listing contains an "At a Glance" section which provides diverse information designed to give traders a quick overview of the country, its demographics, infrastructure, politics, and environment. The *Almanac* also includes a map of each country, with features such as major roads, railways, waterways, borders, capital and major cities, and some ports and airports.

Ten Tips to International Success

1. **Think like a global citizen** In order to successfully trade in foreign markets, it is important to start thinking on a global level. Devote continuing attention to your international business, even if your domestic business is booming. Look for trends in other countries that might indicate an emerging market for your product. Look for ways your product could be adapted to suit the needs of a foreign market.

2. **Conduct detailed research** Entering the unknown can be a daunting task and the more you can find out about prospective markets the more confident you will be in your business transactions. Read foreign trade publications, keep your eyes and ears tuned to news coverage of international current events; seek out other international traders–hopefully you will find somebody with experience in your target market. Although it will cost more, you can gain invaluable information by conducting in-country market research, possibly through a local research firm.

3. **Develop a marketing approach** Each market will require a different approach if you want to present your product in the best light. Before engaging in international trade obtain qualified expert counseling to develop your goals and objectives and identify the problems you anticipate; then plan solutions to them. Know your market before you get there, and learn about distribution alternatives (and problems).

4. **Adapt to the country** Do not assume that a given product or marketing technique will automatically be successful in all countries. Be willing to modify products to meet regulations or cultural preferences in other countries.

5. **Stay in touch with economic trends** World markets are continually evolving, making it essential to stay in touch with market trends. As one market matures and begins to show signs of slowing, or even depression, another will be on the verge of a boom. Careful attention to these details could reveal early opportunities for new markets, and can also alert you to signs of trouble on the horizon.

6. **Stay in touch with political trends** Political events have a big impact on a country's economics. Political instability can be devastating to a country's markets, while a stable government can be a great asset, even if other economic indicators have yet to register positive. Also keep in touch with government regulation of markets. There is a general trend in the world toward liberalization and reducing barriers to foreign trade. Regulations are being continually relaxed and this presents lots of new opportunities for astute traders.

7. **Know the law** You will be subject to many different laws once you enter the foreign trade arena. Be aware of them and be prepared to hire local legal counsel when necessary.

8. **Be aware of trade agreements** Many countries have trade agreements that confer special status on foreign traders.

9. **Learn the culture** The importance of culture must not be underestimated. Your success in foreign trade often depends on your awareness of and sensitivity to other cultures.

10. **Prepare for your travels** International trade usually entails a lot of travel and detailed preparation will ensure that everything goes smoothly when you are abroad. Learn something about the country, the climate, business hours and holidays, and available services.

Economic Trends

A New World Order

International trade is becoming increasingly important to every nation's prosperity. While a few countries will continue to attempt to go it alone, most governments have come to recognize the need to develop and refine their global economic strategies. Today, more than ever, international commerce is an important way for most nations of the world to develop and maintain a strong economy. As the economies of the world become more integrated, traditional national boundaries, while still in place, are losing their former significance. Already, economic borders have for the most part disappeared. A new world order is emerging; one focusing on markets wherever they are found, regardless of a government's attempts to protect them from foreign influences.

Economic Trends

New and challenging foreign trade opportunities continue to arise all over the world. Commerce is no longer confined to domestic markets or traditional trading patterns. Just as old markets begin to decline, new ones emerge, and as the economic pie grows larger, so does competition for each slice. Intense competition from more diverse sources is making it increasingly difficult for traders to prevail on international markets. Success often depends on a trader's ability to remain well-informed of economic trends, to analyze their significance, and to apply appropriate business strategies to each trading area in the global market. Specific economic trends that have brought about recent changes, and how these trends will influence markets in the future, are important bits of information traders should seek.

Though there are many new markets and opportunities, success is far from guaranteed. Current statistics show that new businesses have only a 10 percent chance of achieving long-term success in China–and the success rates are not much higher in a well-developed market such as Japan. Traders should acquire as much knowledge as they can before they do business in any foreign country.

While many businesspeople throughout the world understand this, only some will attempt to make use of the information available. Although there is no universal remedy for the inherent difficulties of trading with foreign countries, one thing is certain–the more traders know about the economic trends in current or prospective markets, the better equipped they will be to meet the inherent challenges of international trade. Understanding the significance of these trends and why they are inextricably linked to a trader's performance in foreign markets is a major step on the road to success.

Gaining Global Vision

Although exporting and importing play a central role in many companies' business strategies, there are many others who view trading on international markets simply as an aside, or bonus, to the main transactions that take place in their home markets. This mentality is largely understandable, but the evolution of a true world market is forcing many businesses to reconsider their positions, especially in light of increased foreign competition in their own domestic markets.

The obvious benefit to traders who adopt a global approach to business is knowledge of a wider marketplace, and the opportunity to gain access to markets where growth rates dramatically exceed those at home. Traders who maintain a truly global vision will spot opportunities arising from the wide discrepancies both in levels and rates of development throughout the world. Astute traders will often be able to revive a product that is suffering from diminishing returns in one market and extend its shelf life in other global outlets where demand is on an upturn. Knowledge and analysis of the main import and export opportunities in each country will reveal the wide diversity of needs from one market to the next–traders who can take advantage of these needs will see their returns increase accordingly.

Assessing Global Opportunities

Once a trader has started to think globally and has identified possible outlets for products, the trader must be able to effectively gauge the market potential for products in any given economy. Even though world markets are becoming increasingly integrated, it is of vital importance to remember that market opportunities need to be assessed on an individual basis. The conditions enabling you to make a successful entry into one market are unlikely to be replicated in another. Making positive or negative assumptions about markets for any reason without adequate knowledge is a pitfall to be avoided at all costs.

Statistics With Meaning

Trade and economic statistics are important indicators of trends that will affect the performance of products in the marketplace. Trade statistics on particular countries are usually broken down into product categories which provide specific information, such as the total volume of certain goods sold in any one country over a particular period of time and how much of that total is accounted for by imports. Traders can thus assess the relative strength of domestic industries and the level of competition they are likely to

Trade Fundamentals
ECONOMIC TERMS

While analyzing the main trends of each country it is important to be conversant with some of the economic terms regularly referred to in this book.

External value The purchasing power of a currency abroad, converted using the exchange rate.

Gross domestic product (GDP) The total market value of the goods and services produced within a country during a given period, excluding income derived from investments abroad.

GDP per capita Gross domestic product divided by a nation's population. This measurement gives an indication of the relative wealth of a country and, especially, the purchasing power of its citizens.

Life-cycle processing An accounting approach in which a company sets product prices based on recovering costs over the entire life cycle of the product. This is especially important in international trade as profits are often not generated for several years after entering a foreign market. Traders looking to recoup their costs immediately, rather than factoring costs over a longer period, will miss many valuable opportunities.

Services Economic activities that are usually of an intangible character and often consumed as they are produced. Services include everything from retail sales, to government services, to tourism, to sophisticated international banking transactions.

Trade balance The *balance of trade* refers to the difference in value between the total exports and imports of a nation. In general, a positive balance occurs when a nation's exports exceed its imports.

Current balance The value of all exports (goods and services) less all imports of a country over a specific period of time, equal to the sum of the trade balance plus net receipts of interest, profits and dividends from abroad.

Balance of payments A statement of all the economic and financial transactions between companies, banks, private households, and public authorities of one nation with those of other nations over a specific time period.

Current account That portion of a country's balance of payments that records current (as opposed to capital) transactions, including visible trade (exports and imports), invisible trade (income and expenditures from services), profits earned from foreign operations, interest and transfer payments.

Trade surplus The amount by which a nation's exports exceed its imports.

Trade deficit The amount by which a nation's imports exceed its exports. Analysis of the trade surplus or trade deficit can provide you with crucial information on the prevailing economic climate, living standards, distribution of wealth, import and export policies, and growth patterns of various countries.

Inflation Loss of purchasing power of money, caused by growth of the amount of money in circulation which, if the supply of goods stays the same or only increases at a slower rate, leads to an increase in prices.

Liberalization In general, a relative freeing of import controls or restraints, and/or a preference for reducing existing barriers to trade, often contrasted with the protectionist preference for retaining or raising barriers to imports, or imposing other governmental restraints on trade.

Infrastructure The basic structure of a nation's economy, including transportation, communications, and other public services, on which the country's economic activity relies.

Import substitution A strategy which emphasizes the replacement of imports with domestically produced goods, rather than the production of goods for export. Governments generally implement such a policy to encourage the development of domestic industry.

encounter from other foreign producers. In addition to studying trends for company products, traders can also study trends for related products that could indirectly influence demand. Analysis of this type of information will reveal the relative size of markets in different countries, and help traders to make comparisons that will lead to more informed decisions.

A study of growth rates in particular industries of interest can reveal much about a product's prospects in a given market. Trends in growth rates can measure a product's susceptibility to economic change, and traders can spot markets which may be on the verge of rapid growth. Important factors to consider include whether the rate of growth has been steady over a long period of time and if so, whether it has remained constant or declined during times of recession. Overall trends in growth rates will assist traders in identifying the best markets for their products and in pinpointing markets that should be avoided.

Agriculture

Despite all the technological advances of the past 50 years and the rising worldwide importance of manufacturing industries, agriculture is still one of the mainstays of a country's economy. For some countries, the agricultural sector dominates GDP; for others, it is barely a blip on the graph. In all cases, it strongly influences a country's position in the international trade arena. The term agriculture can actually mean a number of different fields, including (but not limited to) crops, livestock, forestry and aquaculture. When trading internationally, it is important to know how dominant the agriculture sector is in a country's economy, and to have some idea of the policies and trends that influence this sector.

Industry

Industry and manufacturing used to be the darlings of technologically advanced countries only; now they are a major economic force the world over. Industry is often the driving force behind a country's development into a sophisticated economy. Third World countries that just a few years ago knew nothing of technology and manufacturing are now world economic heavyweights, thanks to a strong industrial base. An understanding of each country's industrial development, and its dominant industries, will help traders make rational decisions about markets and trading opportunities around the world.

Services

A country's services can actually mean a host of different fields, including (but not limited to) government services and tourism. Most countries around the world have a large services sector. In many less developed countries, most service providers are local and can serve only small retail market segments; in others, like Macau, the service sector represents virtually the entire GDP. Some countries have highly developed financial service industries which cater to businesses and governments the world over. In all cases a country's service sector has a tremendous impact on the ability of foreigners to undertake business ventures in that particular country. A country's service sector should be reviewed, therefore, and its strengths and weaknesses understood, before any investment is made therein.

The Political Arena

Politics and business are inextricably intertwined, necessitating a comprehensive understanding of the prevailing political trends and the influences they exert over a given economy. Markets are continually evolving and a historical perspective of both political and economic trends influencing a given market will help traders protect themselves from sudden changes that could adversely affect their businesses. It will help them make decisions about the viability of current and prospective markets, and will better equip them overall to meet the challenges of international trade. Knowledge of a country's political climate can provide a trader with invaluable answers as to whether the present government can provide the political stability and business support that traders need to thrive.

Most governments apply regulations in the form of tariffs or non-tariff barriers to restrict the level of imports and protect domestic industries from foreign competition. Many also provide domestic producers with export subsidies which make that country's goods more competitive on world markets. Other trade regulations are often imposed to enforce compliance with local environmental controls, or to boycott goods emanating from certain countries. Because these regulations can represent serious barriers to trade and because they differ from country to country, it is essential to study the regulatory framework as it pertains to current economic conditions and to be aware of potential changes in trade regulations before making a commitment to do business in a particular market.

In Summary

International markets are in a constant state of change and require continual surveillance of the economic and political trends which might impact them. The best way for traders to ensure that they are entering a profitable trading environment and to minimize costly business errors is to learn as much as possible about each country they intend to do business in—or with.

Basics of Importing

The Import Process

Every country processes imports. In some, the import process is minimal; in others, delays for paperwork and official authorizations can be significant. Some countries offer accelerated customs clearance, but a trader must still file proof of source and destination, complete certificates and forms, and satisfy local customs officials. Even for products subject to no import restrictions, certain data is usually furnished to a customs authority so the government can compile trade statistics and assess fees and taxes.

Importing is always evolving. To decrease border delays, many countries are consolidating departments, revamping reporting requirements, and implementing computerized systems. Some allow for preshipment inspections and pre-entry filings. Traders should keep checking for new options.

Government Regulation

Import requirements depend on the laws and regulations of the importer's own country, not those of the exporting country. In general, a country has one authority that is primarily responsible for administering its import laws. Depending on the type of product, a number of other authorities may indirectly control the process, as well. These may include agencies that enforce health, agricultural, environmental, transport, navigation, construction, and consumer laws. Thus, traders must comply not only with import laws, but also with all other laws specifically regulating the consumption or use of the product within the importing country. For some products, government regulations are so complex that traders typically retain customs brokers or freight forwarders to assist in compliance.

Preshipment Considerations

Costly delays or rejections at the border can usually be kept to a minimum with advance planning. Licenses, permits, duty payments, inspections, shipping, packaging, and insurance can usually be arranged before shipment.

Licenses and permits For goods that may be imported only with government authorization, the importer may have to obtain a permit or license before entry. In some countries, all importers must be licensed regardless of the product. Permits and licenses are usually issued for a fee, and periodic renewals may also be necessary, again for a fee.

Intellectual and industrial property rights If a patent, trademark, service mark, copyright, or other similar right in a product is to be protected wherever sold, that right may need to be registered in a country before the product is distributed there. Otherwise, it may be irretrievably lost. Registration procedures differ substantially, and so does processing time.

Entry of Goods

Type of entry When goods reach a port of entry, they are held until the entry process is complete, after which they are released into that country. Many countries allow for different types of entries depending on the purpose for importing. A standard entry is one for *consumption*—the products will be sold or otherwise used in the importing country. Some countries offer temporary entry for test, trade fair, or market samples. A few countries offer incentives, such as free trade zones or bonded warehouse facilities, to encourage in-country processing of goods for re-export or later entry. Other entry requirements apply to products sent through international mail.

Customs Clearance

Depending on such factors as the nature of the product, size of shipment, country of import, available automation, and shipper's reputation, the entry process may require hours, days, weeks, or even months. Most shipments can be immediately released for transport into the country. Goods not immediately released are held at the border or transferred to storage facilities in bond, if available, to await processing. Officials may also reject goods for noncompliance and return them to the shipper. A trader can usually keep border delays to a minimum by preparing in advance to meet the following requirements:

- Standard documentation
- Product compliance
- Payment of assessed duties and other charges

Standard Documentation

At entry, a customs official will require the importer to present documents describing the goods and indicating that all entry requirements have been met. In general, if import documents have not already been filed, importers are allowed a certain amount of time to prepare and present the proper documentation. Although these documents differ from country to country, the following are fairly standard.

Reasons To Import

1. To obtain raw materials unavailable in your own country.
2. To acquire products not manufactured in your own country.
3. To buy directly from the source of supply when that source is located in a foreign country.
4. To exercise better control over the supply of foreign-made products, rather than depend on a domestic source.
5. To pay a lower price than is offered domestically.
6. To contract for overseas manufacture of products when the cost is lower or specialized labor is unavailable domestically.
7. To have a foreign supplier provide made-to-order products according to your specifications.
8. To follow up specific business connections in other countries.
9. To take advantage of incentive programs and subsidies offered by other countries to investors producing exports.
10. To earn a living while traveling.
11. To expand your established business line by offering foreign products or services.
12. To expand an established domestic business into a global operation.

Importing Success

1. **Business knowledge and experience** The experience and ability to operate a business effectively.
2. **Knowledge of the import process** Experience with, or knowledge of the entire import process from finding suppliers to customs entry and clearance.
3. **Knowledge of product** Thorough knowledge of the products you plan to import, based on experience or knowledge gained from being a broker, designer, manufacturer, retailer, wholesaler, or other international trade professional.
4. **Knowledge of costs** Knowledge of all costs of obtaining and bringing the product to market.
5. **Access to low cost supply** Ability to obtain quality products or commodities at the source for the lowest possible price.
6. **Relationship with suppliers** Ability to establish and maintain a good working relationship with suppliers.
7. **Ability to establish a market** Ability to find or develop a market for the goods.
8. **Knowledge of price structure** Knowledge of the pricing structure for the imported goods that enables you to know how much to pay and how much to charge.
9. **Knowledge of the market** Specialized knowledge of the wholesale, retail, mail order, or other market for the product, based on actual experience or special knowledge.
10. **Ability to sell to a specific market efficiently** Past experience or special knowledge that enables you to sell your product or commodity for the highest possible price once you have imported it.
11. **Working capital** An appropriate amount of working capital for the size and type of import operation you envision.
12. **Use professionals** Your ability to establish and maintain good working relationships with your professional partners:
    - Customs broker
    - Freight forwarder
    - Banker
    - Attorney
    - Customs lawyer
    - Accountant

Application for entry Typically an importer is required to file a brief form to inform the customs authority about the importer's identity and the type and quantity of goods being imported.

Invoice Nearly every country requires some form of *commercial invoice,* or a *pro forma* invoice. The commercial invoice is usually fairly detailed, describing the products being imported (such as name, type, classification, quantity, grade, value, markings, labels, packaging) as well as certain aspects of the transaction (such as price per unit and total price).

Bill of lading or air waybill An international carrier usually issues this document to the shipper. It sets forth the conditions of transport and serves as a receipt and evidence of ownership for the goods.

Packing list Shippers commonly enclose or attach a list naming the goods and quantities included.

Declarations or certificates Various declarations or certificates may be required as proof of compliance with import requirements. For example, certificates or declarations may be needed to show ownership, consulate approval, government authorization, quality control, country of origin, treatment for pest infestation, sanitary production, quarantine compliance, and inspection.

Bond or other guarantee In some countries, customs authorities may agree to release goods for entry into the country before the importer has paid all assessed amounts, provided that the importer posts a bond or other guarantee sufficient to cover the amount owed.

Product Compliance

Inspections While import documentation is being completed, customs officials will most likely review the goods for compliance with import laws. This process may include examination of the entire shipment or samples from it, as well as its outer and inner packaging. The shipment may be counted and weighed and, for some products, may be subject to laboratory testing. Inspectors will verify that the shipment complies with the country's laws and matches the invoice description. To reduce freight congestion at the border, some countries have established preshipment or bonded post-shipment inspection programs.

Marking and labeling Goods may be rejected if their marking and labeling fail to meet legal requirements. Common mandatory markings include country of origin and name of manufacturer. Labels must usually state product components and adherence to applicable technical standards (such as flammability, energy efficiency, or hazardous emissions). In some countries, goods may be stored while bringing them into conformance, in which case release is delayed for a fixed time after which the goods are rejected if still not properly marked or labelled.

Prohibitions and Restrictions

Quotas To exercise control over the quantity of certain imports, some governments impose absolute or tariff-rate quotas. An *absolute quota* prohibits additional imports once a fixed number have been entered within a certain period. Under a *tariff-rate quota,* a fixed amount of goods can be entered at a reduced duty rate during a certain period. Goods imported in excess of that amount are subject to a higher duty rate.

Restricted imports Every country restricts imports of certain products, and customs officials will reject such imports if presented for entry without strict adherence to the law. Imports commonly prohibited or restricted include articles that are perceived as a significant threat to the country's public health and welfare, environment, national interest, and economic interest.

Import Duties

Dutiable status In countries that impose duties (or tariffs) on imports, the customs official's examination of the documents and products in a shipment usually leads to a determination of dutiable status. This is typically a two-step process: classification and valuation. If duties are assessed, the goods are released from customs only after payment is made or, if permitted, after a bond is presented to secure later payment.

Classification In an effort to impose duties uniformly, most countries classify imported goods into categories of a duty schedule. For this purpose, many countries have adopted a version of the international Harmonized System (HS), dividing nearly all products into about 100 product groups.

Valuation If duties are based on an ad valorem rate (a percentage of value), a value must be fixed for the goods. Valuation formulas differ from country to country. Some countries use FOB (free onboard), others use CIF (cost plus insurance plus freight), and still others use transaction value.

Other Assessments

Customs fee Many countries charge a customs processing fee to cover the costs of inspection and approval. It may be levied as a flat charge or a percentage of the value of the goods.

Value-added tax (VAT) Some countries impose a value-added tax on imports. This tax is assessed on the amount by which the value of goods has been increased because of importing. The value is considered to increase, for example, by the tariff assessed, any customs fee paid, and the shipping, insurance, and related transport charges.

Importing

DIFFICULT-TO-IMPORT PRODUCTS

- aerospace products
- animals (live)
- animal products (nonfood)
- beverages
- chemicals
- combustibles
- cosmetics
- drugs
- explosives
- foods
- radioactive materials
- radiation-producing products
- radio frequency devices
- used merchandise
- vehicles
- weapons

EASY-TO-IMPORT PRODUCTS

- artwork
- brushes
- crafts
- flowers (artificial)
- gems and gemstones
- glass and glass products
- household appliances (electronic or mechanical)
- jewelry
- leather goods (not from endangered species)
- lighting fixtures
- metals (base)
- musical instruments
- optics and optical products
- paper and paper products
- pearls
- plastics and plastic products
- rubber and rubber products
- saddlery
- sporting goods
- tools (hand implements, utensils, machine tools)

COMMONLY PROHIBITED ITEMS

- food products raised or processed in pest-invested or disease-ridden regions
- products derived from endangered species if the country is a member of the Convention on International Trade in Endangered Species (CITES)
- products that violate intellectual or industrial rights laws
- materials considered pornographic
- national treasures, including archaeological finds

Basics of Exporting

Methods of Exporting and Channels of Distribution

The most common methods of exporting are indirect selling and direct selling. In indirect selling, an export intermediary such as an export management company (EMC) or an export trading company (ETC) usually assumes responsibility for finding overseas buyers, shipping products, and getting paid. The principal advantage of indirect exporting for most companies is that it provides a way to penetrate foreign markets without the complexities and risks of direct exporting.

Direct selling occurs when the producer deals directly with a foreign buyer. This approach has the advantages of providing more control over the export process, having a potential for higher profits, and allowing a closer relationship to the overseas buyer and marketplace. However, the company must spend more time, personnel, and corporate resources than with indirect exporting.

The paramount consideration in determining which method to use is the amount of resources a company is willing to devote to its international marketing effort. Other important factors to consider are the size of the firm, the nature of its products, previous export experience and expertise, and business conditions in the selected overseas markets.

Export Licenses

Many countries require export licenses to be obtained before exporting certain products therefrom. Export licenses can be required for a number of reasons, but usually apply to products dealing with natural resources, national security, or health and safety. Export licenses are also sometimes required to ensure compliance with international treaties or conventions.

Preparing Products for Export

Selecting and preparing a product for export requires not only product knowledge but also knowledge of the unique characteristics of each market being targeted. Before the sale can occur, a product may need to be modified to satisfy buyer tastes or needs in foreign markets.

Product adaptation To achieve success in a foreign market, a product may have to be modified in order to conform it to foreign government regulations, geographic and climatic conditions, buyer preferences, or standards of living. A product may also need to be modified to facilitate shipment or compensate for possible differences in engineering or design standards.

Foreign government product regulations are common in international trade and are expected to expand in the future. These regulations can take the form of high tariffs or of non-tariff barriers, such as tough product standards.

Engineering and redesign Fundamental aspects of a product may require redesign. For example, electrical standards in many foreign countries differ. It is not unusual to find phases, cycles, or voltages that would damage or impair the operating efficiency of equipment designed for use in other countries.

Branding, labeling, and packaging Some of the considerations that an exporter should undertake regarding the branding and labeling of products are:

- Are international brand names important to promote and distinguish a product, or should local brands or private labels be employed to heighten local interest?
- Can labels be produced in official or customary languages if required by law or practice?
- Must information on product content and country of origin be provided?
- Are weights and measures stated in the local units of measurement?
- Are local tastes and customs considered?

Companies may find that building international recognition for a brand is expensive, and piracy of the company's brand names and counterfeiting of its products are widespread in some countries. The level of protection for brand names varies from one country to another, and in some developing countries, barriers to the use of foreign brands or trademarks may exist. It may be a costly and lengthy process to register a trademark, copyright, or patent, which can delay entry into the market by several years.

Installation An exporter should also consider the ease of installing the product overseas. If technicians or engineers are needed overseas to assist in installation, it is wise to preassemble or pretest the product before shipping in order to minimize the time in the field. If a product is sent disassembled, there may be savings in shipping costs, but there also may be a delay in payment if completion of the sale is contingent on the delivery of an assembled product. If trained personnel are not sent to install the product, all product information, such as training manuals, installation instructions, and parts lists, may need to be provided in the local language. It is also advisable to provide a quickly accessible line of communication—telephone, fax, or other—for customer service if you do not have a representative on site.

Warranties In some instances, companies should include a warranty on their products, particularly

Choosing a Foreign Distributor

SIZE OF SALES FORCE

- How many field sales personnel does the representative or distributor have?
- What are its short and long range expansion plans, if any?
- Would it need to expand to accommodate your account properly? If so, would it be willing to do so?

SALES RECORD

- Has its sales growth been consistent? If not, why not? Try to determine sales volume for the past five years.
- What is its sales volume per outside salesperson?
- What are its sales objectives for next year? How were they determined?

TERRITORIAL ANALYSIS

- What territory does it now cover?
- Is it consistent with the coverage you desire? If not, is it able and willing to expand?
- Does it have any branch offices in the territory to be covered?
- If so, are they located where your sales prospects are greatest?
- Does it have any plans to open additional offices?

PRODUCT MIX

- How many product lines does it represent?
- Are these product lines compatible with yours?
- Would there be any conflict of interest?
- Does it represent any other firms from your country? If so, which ones?
- If necessary, would it be willing to alter its present product mix to accommodate yours?
- What would be the minimum sales volume needed to justify its handling your lines? Do its sales projections reflect this minimum figure? From what you know of the territory and the prospective representative or distributor, is its projection realistic?

FACILITIES AND EQUIPMENT

- Does it have adequate warehouse facilities?
- What is its method of stock control?
- Does it use computers? Are they compatible with yours?
- What communications facilities does it have (fax, modem, telex, etc.)?
- If your product requires servicing, is it equipped and qualified to do so?
- If necessary and customary, is it willing to inventory repair parts and replacement items?

CUSTOMER PROFILE

- What kinds of customers is it currently contacting?
- Are its interests compatible with your product line?
- Who are its key accounts?
- What percentage of its total gross receipts do these key accounts represent?
- How many principals is it currently representing?
- Would you be its primary supplier?
- If not, what percentage of its total business would you represent?

PROMOTIONAL THRUST

- Can it help you compile market research information to be used in making forecasts?
- What media does it use, if any, to promote sales?
- How much of its budget is allocated to advertising? How is it distributed among various principals?

if the buyer is likely to expect a specific level of performance and a guarantee that it will be achieved. However, consumer expectations for warranties vary from country to country depending on the level of development, competitive practices, activism of consumer groups, local standards of production quality, and other similar factors. If a warranty is not expected, the exporter generally need not provide one; to do so might cause production costs to be higher than a competitor's. Exporters should keep in mind that servicing warranties is more expensive and troublesome in foreign markets. It is usually desirable to arrange warranty service locally with the assistance of a representative or distributor.

Preparing a Product for Shipping

When preparing to ship a product overseas, the exporter needs to ensure that the merchandise is packed correctly so that it arrives in good condition; labeled correctly to ensure that the goods are handled properly and will arrive on time and at the right place; documented correctly to meet government requirements, as well as proper collection standards; and insured against damage, loss, and pilferage and, in some cases, delay.

Freight forwarders The international freight forwarder acts as an agent for the exporter in moving cargo to the overseas destination. The freight forwarder can assist with an order from the start by advising the exporter of the freight costs, port charges, consular fees, cost of special documentation, and insurance costs, as well as the freight forwarder's handling fees—all of which help in preparing price quotations. The freight forwarder may also recommend the type of packing for best protecting the merchandise in transit and can arrange to have the merchandise packed at the port or placed into containers.

Packing In packing an item for export, the shipper should be aware of the demands that transport puts on a package, namely, breakage, weight, moisture, and pilferage. Because proper packing is essential in exporting, the buyer often specifies packing requirements. One popular method of shipment is the use of containers obtained from carriers or private leasing concerns. These containers vary in size, material, and construction, and can accommodate most cargo. Refrigerated and liquid bulk containers are readily available as well.

Labeling Specific markings and labeling are used on export shipping cartons and containers to meet shipping regulations, ensure proper handling, conceal the identity of the contents, and help receivers identify shipments. The overseas buyer usually specifies which export marks should appear on the cargo for easy identification by receivers.

Documentation Exporters should seriously consider having the freight forwarder handle the formidable amount of documentation that exporting requires, because freight forwarders are specialists in this process. Documentation must be precise. Slight discrepancies or omissions may prevent merchandise from being exported, result in firms not getting paid, or even result in the seizure of the exporter's goods by foreign government customs.

Shipping The export marks should be added to the standard information shown on the domestic bill of lading and should show the name of the exporting carrier and the latest permissible arrival date at the port of export. The exporter should also include instructions for the inland carrier to notify the international freight forwarder by telephone on arrival.

Insurance Export shipments are usually insured by cargo insurance against loss, damage, and delay in transit. For international shipments, the carrier's liability is frequently limited by international agreements, and the coverage is substantially different from domestic coverage. Arrangements for cargo insurance may be made by either the buyer or seller, depending on the terms of sale. Exporters are advised to consult with international insurance carriers or freight forwarders for more information.

Damaging weather conditions, rough handling by carriers, and other common hazards to cargo make marine insurance important protection for exporters. If the terms of sale make the firm responsible for insurance, it should either obtain its own policy or insure cargo under a freight forwarder's policy for a fee. If the terms of sale make the foreign buyer responsible, the exporter should make sure via examination of documentation (not assume or even take the buyer's word) that adequate insurance has been obtained. If the buyer neglects to obtain coverage or obtains too little, damage to the cargo may cause a major financial loss to the exporter.

Additional information on exporting can be found in "International Marketing" on page 14 and "International Payments" on page 27.

Ten Tips to Export Success

1. **Develop a plan.** Before starting an export business, obtain qualified expert counseling and develop a master international marketing plan that clearly defines your goals and objectives and identifies the problems you anticipate, plus potential solutions.

2. **Get commitments.** If necessary, secure a commitment from top management to overcome the initial difficulties and meet the financial requirements of exporting.

3. **Pick distributors with care.** Take sufficient care in selecting overseas distributors, because they will generally operate much more independently than their domestic counterparts.

4. **Create a successful pattern.** Establish a basis for profitable operations and orderly growth, and do not simply rely on unsolicited trade leads.

5. **Devote attention to exporting.** Devote continuing attention to your export business, even if your domestic market is also booming.

6. **Consider international distributors equal to domestic ones.** Treat international distributors on an equal basis with domestic counterparts by offering such things as institutional advertising campaigns, special discount offers, sales incentive programs, special credit term programs, and warranty offers that are appropriate to their situation.

7. **Different markets require different plans.** Do not assume that a given market technique and product will automatically be successful in all countries.

8. **Don't be afraid to change products for markets.** Be willing to modify products to meet regulations or cultural preferences in other countries.

9. **Adhere to language changes.** Print service, sale, and warranty messages in locally understood languages.

10. **Provide reliable service.** Provide readily available servicing for the product, since an otherwise successful product may acquire a bad reputation if it lacks the necessary service support.

Trade Agreements

General Agreement on Tariffs and Trade (GATT)

GATT is designed to provide a standard framework for global trade by ensuring that a fair multilateral trading system exists. Founded in 1947 with 23 members, GATT has passed through eight series of negotiations, known as rounds. The most recent is the Uruguay Round, begun in 1986. The Final Uruguay Agreement was signed in December 1993 by 124 member countries. Several other countries outside of GATT, including China, Russia, and Taiwan, have since applied for membership.

Effects

The successful conclusion of the Uruguay Round involved new or more efficient protocols in a number of areas, including agriculture, services and intellectual property. As the provisions of the agreement come into effect it should provide a substantial boost to international business–GATT experts estimate that the increase in international merchandise trade could increase by US$745 billion by 2005. All international traders should benefit from either improved returns resulting from major direct savings on duties, or from increased trade volumes generated by lower trade barriers.

Agreements

- **Agriculture** This agreement includes provisions which encourage the use of less trade-distorting domestic support policies to maintain the rural economy, and that allow actions to be taken to ease any adjustment burden. In the area of market access, non-tariff border measures are replaced by tariffs that provide substantially the same level of protection to a country's agricultural industries. Tariffs resulting from this "tariffication" process, as well as other tariffs on agricultural products, are to be reduced by an average 36 percent in the case of developed countries and 24 percent in the case of developing countries. Reductions are to be undertaken over six years in the case of developed countries and over ten years in the case of developing countries. Least-developed countries are not required to reduce their tariffs. Members are required to reduce the value of direct export subsidies to a level 36 percent below the 1986-90 base period level over the six-year implementation period, and the quantity of subsidized exports by 21 percent over the same period. In the case of developing countries, the reductions are two-thirds those of developed countries over a ten-year period. There are no reduction requirements applying to the least developed countries.
- **Textiles and clothing** This agreement aims for the eventual integration into GATT of the textiles and clothing sector, where much of the trade is currently subject to bilateral quotas negotiated under the Multifiber Arrangement (MFA). During a phased integration period extending until January 1, 2005, all MFA restrictions in place on December 31, 1994 will be carried over into the new agreement and maintained until such time as the restrictions are removed or the products integrated into GATT. While this agreement focuses largely on the phasing-out of MFA restrictions, it also recognizes that some members maintain non-MFA restrictions not justified under a GATT provision. These would also be brought into conformity with GATT or phased out progressively during the phase-out period to 2005.
- **Technical barriers to trade** This agreement extends and clarifies the existing agreement reached in the Tokyo Round. It seeks to ensure that technical negotiations and standards, as well as testing and certification procedures, do not create unnecessary obstacles to trade. It does, however, recognize the right of countries to establish protections at levels they consider appropriate, for human, animal or plant life or health, or the environment. It allows countries to take measures necessary to ensure that reasonable domestic levels of protection are met. It encourages countries to use international standards where these are appropriate, but it does not require them to change their levels of protection as a result of standardization.
- **Anti-dumping** GATT provides for the right of contracting parties to apply anti-dumping measures–measures against imports of a product at an export price below its "normal value" (usually the price of the product in the domestic market of the exporting country) if such dumped imports cause injury to a domestic industry in the territory of the importing country. The agreement contains rules to ensure that a fair comparison is made between the export price and the normal value of a product so as not to arbitrarily create or inflate margins of dumping. It strengthens the requirement for the importing country to establish a clear causal relationship between dumped imports and injury to the domestic industry. Clear-cut procedures have been established on how anti-dumping cases are to be initiated and how such investigations are to be conducted. It also requires the immediate termination of an anti-dumping investigation in cases where the authorities determine that the margin of dumping is de minimis (which is defined as less than two percent of the export price of the product), or that the volume dumped is negligible (generally, when the volume of dumped imports from an individual country accounts for less than three percent of the imports of the product in question into the importing country).
- **Preshipment Inspection** Preshipment inspection (PSI) is the practice of employing specialized private companies to check shipment details–essentially price, quantity, quality–of goods

In General

International trade agreements are usually based on the reciprocal extension of trade privileges between the nationals of sovereign parties to the specific agreement. They generally serve to lower tariffs, eliminate quota restrictions, or otherwise remove protectionist barriers to cross-border trade. Most international trade agreements are either between several different countries, a few countries or only two. There are also international conventions which sovereign nations can sign and agree to adhere to.

HISTORICAL PERSPECTIVE

- **Early 20th century** Trade policies in the first two decades of the 20th century emphasized stable tariffs, which led to equality in international trade. After the Great Depression of 1929, however, many countries came under economic pressure resulting in the adoption of restrictive import controls to protect domestic economies. As a result, international trade ground to a halt, which in turn caused the depression to actually worsen.
- **A change of heart** Following World War II, it was generally recognized that international trade was a benefit to all the nations of the world and the protectionist policies of the 1930s were regarded as counterproductive.
- **The United Nations** The founders of the United Nations agreed that future prosperity depended on increased international trade. They recommended that more liberalized conditions should be put in place in order to facilitate trade.
- **Some resistance** This trade normalization did not, of course, embrace the entire world. China prohibited foreign trade after the revolution, Eastern Europe was not able to trade freely due to the influence of the Soviet Union and trade in Southeast Asia was seriously disrupted due to war. Nonetheless, trade relations between many of the world's nations were vastly improved, which led to a steady increase in global trade that continues today.
- **Looking back** Although the total value of international trade has increased in the past few decades, governments continue to adopt trade policies today that act as barriers to international trade. It is quite clear that national economic interests still take precedence over international concerns but this reality is now tempered by a recognition that mutually beneficial agreements can be reached between trading nations.

TYPES OF TRADE AGREEMENTS

- **International** The United Nations, through its conference on Trade and Development; the Organization for Economic Cooperation and Development (OECD); and especially the General Agreement on Tariffs and Trade (GATT)/World Trade Organization (WTO) are all examples of international trade agreements to which most trading nations of the world belong. In general, the terms of these large agreements are designed more to provide guidelines for members than they are specific dictates on trade policies and procedures.
- **Multilateral** World trade has recently seen a trend toward groupings of three or more countries into trading blocs which together have more economic power than any one of the individual members. Multilateral trade agreements usually provide for a free-trade or a customs union between member countries through which people and products may pass freely–or with greatly reduced restrictions. The members of multilateral trade agreement will generally present a unified position in international trade negotiations such as GATT or OECD.
- **Bilateral** Bilateral trade agreements provide for preferential terms of trade and commerce between two sovereign nations. They can range from narrowly defined or informal arrangements to comprehensive agreements which provide for an essentially free trade zone between the two countries, such as the Common Economic Region of Australia and New Zealand.

ordered overseas. Used by governments of developing countries, the purpose is to safeguard national financial interests (prevention of capital flight and commercial fraud as well as customs duty evasion, for instance) and to compensate for inadequacies in administrative infrastructures. This agreement places obligations on PSI-user governments of non-discrimination, transparency, protection of confidential business information, avoidance of unreasonable delay, the use of specific guidelines for conducting price verification and the avoidance of conflicts of interest of the PSI agencies.

- **Rules of origin** The agreement aims at long-term harmonization of rules of origin, other than rules of origin relating to the granting of tariff preferences, and ensurance that such rules do not themselves create unnecessary obstacles to trade. Upon completion of a harmonization program set up by committee, contracting parties would be expected to ensure that their rules of origin are transparent; that they do not have restricting, distorting or disruptive effects on international trade; that they are administered in a consistent, uniform, impartial and reasonable manner; and that they are based on a positive standard (i.e. that they state what does confer origin rather than what does not).

- **Subsidies and countervailing measures** This agreement contains a definition of subsidy and introduces the concept of a "specific" subsidy–for the most part, a subsidy available only to an enterprise or industry or group of enterprises or industries within the jurisdiction of the authority granting the subsidy. Subsidies which are contingent in whole or in part on export performance and those contingent upon the use of domestic over imported goods are prohibited. Subsidies which adversely effect the interests of other signatories must be withdrawn or their adverse effects removed. Non-specific or specific subsidies involving assistance to industrial research and pre-competitive development activity, assistance to disadvantaged regions, or certain types of assistance for adapting existing facilities to new environmental requirements imposed by law or regulations are not specifically actionable, although if their application results in serious adverse effects to a domestic industry appropriate action may be taken.

- **Trade in services** The agreement regarding trade in services requires most favored nation treatment for like services and service providers from member nations, although it does allow for some limited specific exemptions. It also requires member countries to publish all relevant laws and regulations regarding services and services providers. The agreement contains obligations with respect to recognition requirements (educational background for instance) for the purpose of securing authorizations, licenses or certification in the services area. It encourages recognition requirements achieved through harmonization and internationally-agreed criteria. In short, it aims to progressively eliminate limitations on numbers of service providers, on the total value of service transactions or on the total number of service operations or people employed. It also restricts the kind of legal entity or joint venture through which a service is provided or any foreign capital limitations relating to maximum levels of foreign participation are to be progressively eliminated.

Areas of Disagreement

Several areas of disagreement were specifically excluded from GATT due to a failure of the major parties to reach accord, including aircraft, entertainment, financial services, shipping, steel, and telecommunications. The main antagonists over most of these issues were the US and the EU.

World Trade Organization (WTO)

The WTO is the embodiment of the results of the Uruguay Round trade negotiations and the successor to the GATT. The WTO was established on January 1, 1995, to set in motion a substantially expanded multilateral trading system, greater in scope and strength than the current system which has been operating as GATT since 1948. The Uruguay Round produced some 28 agreements with provisions to establish about 20 bodies to administer them, under the WTO as the common institutional framework for the conduct of trade relations among members. WTO members commit themselves not to take unilateral action against perceived violations of the trade rules but to seek recourse in the multilateral dispute settlement system and to abide by its rules and findings. The WTO extends and clarifies previous GATT rules that laid down the basis on which governments could impose compensating duties on two forms of "unfair" competition: dumping and subsidies.

An important aspect of the WTO's mandate is to cooperate with the International Monetary Fund, the World Bank and other multilateral institutions to achieve greater coherence in global economic policy-making.

The essential functions of the WTO are:
- administering and implementing the multilateral and plurilateral trade agreements which together make up the WTO;
- acting as a forum for multilateral trade negotiations;
- seeking to resolve trade disputes;
- overseeing national trade policies; and
- cooperating with other international institutions involved in global economic policy-making.

Other Regional Trade Agreements

CARIBBEAN COMMUNITY AND COMMON MARKET (CARICOM)

This attempt by 17 Caribbean nations to create a Caribbean Common Market, including common external tariff, has to date not met with much success. The economic difficulties of the individual members, and their inability to agree even on common or complementary tariff levels, has resulted in more frustration than practical implementation of stated policies. The members do, however, continue to meet regularly in an effort to increase trade relations between themselves and with neighboring nations.

CENTRAL AMERICAN COMMON MARKET (CACM)

Costa Rica, Guatemala, El Salvador, Honduras, and Nicaragua decided in 1960 to liberalize intraregional trade and establish a free-trade area and a customs union. Economic integration in the region, however, has been hampered by ideological differences between governments, difficulties in internal supply, protectionist measures by overseas markets, external and inter-regional debates, adverse rates of exchange and high interest rates.

COOPERATION COUNCIL FOR THE ARAB STATES OF THE GULF

The Cooperation Council consists of Bahrain, Kuwait, Oman, Qatar, Saudi Arabia, and the UAE. In economic matters it operates under a "unified economic agreement" which covers freedom of movement of residents and capital between member states, abolition of customs duties, technical cooperation, unified banking regulations, and financial and monetary coordination. Most of these objectives have been accomplished. In addition, many trade activities between residents of member states have been liberalized.

COUNCIL OF ARAB ECONOMIC UNITY

This agreement anticipates an eventual customs union between the member states–Egypt, Iraq, Jordan, Kuwait, Libya, Mauritania, PLO, Somalia, Sudan, Syria, UAE, and Yemen–and a full Arab Common Market consisting of Egypt, Iraq, Jordan, Libya, Mauritania, Syria and Yemen. The group promotes the ideal of faster economic development through joint ventures between members and many such enterprises have been established.

THE FRANC ZONE

The Franc Zone includes all those countries and groups of countries whose currencies are linked with the French franc at a fixed rate of exchange and who agree to hold their reserves mainly in the form of French francs. This monetary union is based on agreements concluded between France and each country or group of countries. Currencies of the Franc Zone are freely convertible into the French franc at a fixed rate, through "operations accounts". These accounts in local banks are backed fully by the French Treasury, which also provides the issuing banks with overdraft facilities.

OTHER TRADE AGREEMENTS

- **Cairns Group** Established in 1986 by major agricultural exporting countries which do not subsidize these exports, The Cairns Group agreement strives to bring about reforms in international agricultural trade, including reductions in export subsidies, in barriers to access, and in internal support measures. Members include Argentina, Australia, Brazil, Canada, Chile, Colombia, Fiji, Hungary, Indonesia, New Zealand, Philippines, Thailand, and Uruguay.

- **The Caribbean Basin Initiative (CBI)** is a program providing for the duty-free entry into the United States of merchandise from designated beneficiary countries or territories in the Caribbean basin. The program is meant to increase the economic aid and trade preferences for 28 states of the Caribbean region.

The North American Free Trade Agreement (NAFTA)

NAFTA has created an economic bloc consisting of the US, Canada, and Mexico, with a combined GDP greater than US$7 trillion. The agreement calls for the gradual elimination of tariff and non-tariff barriers in a variety of areas and removes numerous impediments to investment, such as performance requirements and exclusionary approval procedures.

NAFTA requires the parties to adopt, maintain, and enforce rules against anticompetitive business practices. Government enterprises–federal, state, and local–will be required to abide by NAFTA non-discrimination principles when exercising their authority, including the granting of licenses.

Rules and Principles

Dispute resolution NAFTA provides several methods for the resolution of disputes. The NAFTA Trilateral Trade Commission will monitor trade relations among the parties and establish bilateral or trilateral panels of private sector trade experts to resolve specific disputes. If the recommendations regarding the resolution of particular disputes are not carried out, the aggrieved nation is authorized to withdraw "equivalent trade concessions".

Government procurement NAFTA eliminates such discriminatory practices as requiring the use of domestic purchasers or suppliers in government procurement. The agreement opens a significant portion of the government procurement market to non-discriminatory bidding.

Intellectual property rights NAFTA provides a high standard of protection for copyrights, patents, trademarks, trade secrets, plant breeders' rights, industrial designs, and integrated circuits (semiconductor chips). Copyright provisions provide protection for 50 years. NAFTA provides for strong enforcement, including provisions for damages, injunctive relief, and due process.

Investment NAFTA specifically reduces the need for prior government approval of foreign investments by member nationals; and provides for the elimination of various investment distortions, including the requirements that foreign investors use domestic suppliers, export a given amount of product, limit imports to a certain percentage of exports, or require the transfer of technology. NAFTA also prohibits discrimination against investors who seek to acquire, establish, or operate a business in the member countries. Under NAFTA, the members agree to eliminate screening of new foreign investments in most sectors and to limit the nature of official review in takeovers of existing enterprises. The agreement establishes procedural guidelines for the resolution of investment disputes through arbitration, including binding international arbitration. NAFTA does not cover investment in maritime concerns, government sponsored technology consortia, or research and development programs.

Market access NAFTA covers numerous areas relevant to market access, including tariffs, quotas, and import licenses. Most significantly, the NAFTA countries have agreed to remove most import and export restrictions. Under specified circumstances each NAFTA nation may establish restrictions directly related to health, safety, and welfare as long as these are not designed as barriers to market entry. The parties have also agreed not to impose additional customs user fees.

Tariffs NAFTA provides for the gradual elimination of tariffs on US, Mexican, and Canadian products by the member nations based on the Harmonized Commodity Description and Coding system (HS) classification. The reduction in tariffs is occurring at different stages on a variety of products. Some tariffs were eliminated when the agreement became effective, while tariffs on other products will be removed over periods of five to 10 years. Tariffs on some sensitive products will not be completely removed for 15 years.

Rules of origin Two explicit and strict rules of origin mechanisms are established under NAFTA: tariff-shift and value-content. Tariff-shift rules require that all non-NAFTA inputs must be transformed into a product with a different HS chapter heading or tariff item number from that under which they were admitted. A set percentage of the value of the product must be of North American origin. A de minimis rule allows NAFTA origin treatment for items containing as much as seven percent non-NAFTA content. NAFTA establishes specific rules of origin for various trade sectors. For example, light trucks and passenger vehicles ultimately will have to demonstrate 62.5 percent North American content to obtain preferential treatment. In the textiles sector, NAFTA requires that eligible garments be made from North American fabric and yarn. In order for computers to qualify under NAFTA, the motherboard (accounting for 20 to 40 percent of the value of a computer) must be manufactured in North America.

Technical standards NAFTA affirms the rights of each party to adopt, apply, and enforce its own standards designed to promote safety and protect people, animals, plants, and the environment. However, the agreement stipulates that standards-related measures must provide both national treatment and most-favored nation treatment for all members.

Generalized System of Preferences (GSP)

GSP programs have been set up by many industrialized nations to assist developing nations by granting selective waivers or reductions of tariffs on imports of products from developing nations. GSP programs in the US, Japan, Canada, Australia and the EU countries promote growth in and exports from developing countries while also reducing the cost to national consumers of many imported products. More than 4,400 products from some 146 beneficiary entities are eligible for duty free entry under the GSP program.

There are 117 independent countries, 26 non-independent countries and territories, and three association of countries treated for customs purposes as single entities eligible for GSP treatment. Countries excluded as eligible for GSP treatment include:

- Socialist countries that are not members of GATT or the International Monetary Fund (IMF)

- Members of the Organization of Petroleum Exporting Countries (OPEC), or other countries withholding supplies of vital commodities from trade or otherwise raising the price of such commodities through artificial manipulation.

- Countries failing to take adequate steps to prevent traffic in illegal drugs.

- Countries supporting terrorists or terrorism.

BASIC GSP REQUIREMENTS

There are seven basic requirements for importing goods duty free under the GSP.

1. The product must be imported from a designated beneficiary developing country (BDC) to one of the GSP grantee countries. This means that it must be shipped directly from the BDC to the grantee country, or if, when shipped through another country, it does not enter into the commerce of that country, and the invoices, bills of lading, and other documents show the grantee country as the final destination.

2. The product must be on the GSP eligible products list. The many products eligible for GSP treatment include a wide range of manufactured and semi-manufactured products, as well as certain agricultural, fishery, and industrial products. Raw materials and similar unprocessed commodities are not generally eligible, although even basic processing qualifies many commodities as semi-manufactured. Approximately 2,750 product categories are eligible for entry duty free under the terms of GSP programs, and these categories often include multiple individual product types, which will all be eligible.

3. The product must be entirely grown, produced, or manufactured in the BDC, or it must be primarily the product of the BDC with a minimum of 35 percent of its value coming from the cost of materials and/or direct costs of processing in the BDC. This country of origin requirement is designed to prevent the granting of preferential treatment to products which actually originate elsewhere and receive only insubstantial processing in the eligible country without substantially benefiting that BDC.

4. Proper documentation, including a certified UN Conference on Trade and Development (UNCTAD) Certificate of Origin Form A, must be submitted in addition to normal customs entry documentation. In most cases the seller will have the responsibility for obtaining, filling out, and certifying Form A. Most grantee countries require that Form A must be certified by a designated official authority in the BDC.

5. The product must be imported directly from the BDC to the grantee country, except as explained in item #1 above.

6. The importer must formally request GSP status.

7. The product must meet the competitive needs limitations, which can be used to limit preferential treatment for specific products from particular countries. The purpose of GSP programs is to make eligible products competitive in the grantee markets, but not to the point that they seriously undersell comparable domestic goods. To protect domestic industry, an overly competitive product from a specific country loses its eligibility at least temporarily.

Goods and Services

Agricultural products Mexican tariffs on certain sensitive products originating in the US and Canada will be phased out over a period of up to 15 years. All US and Mexican non-tariff barriers–such as licensing–will be converted to either tariff-rate quotas or ordinary tariffs during a phase-in period.

Automobiles NAFTA is intended to liberalize and integrate the North American automotive sector by reducing barriers, increasing competitiveness, creating employment opportunities, and reducing prices paid by consumers. Mexican tariff and non-tariff restrictions on foreign sales to and participation in the Mexican market will be phased out over a 10-year period.

Energy Implementation of NAFTA immediately reduced trade and investment restrictions in many areas of the Mexican energy market. While retaining the national monopoly in the core energy production sector, it allows firms to negotiate supply contracts directly with Mexican natural gas and basic petrochemicals entities.

Environment NAFTA creates a series of mutual standards, protections, and procedures, as well as many opportunities for environmental equipment firms and services. It should in particular increase US exports of environmental control and mitigation technology to Mexico and Canada. Existing environmental accords, such as the Montreal Protocol on Substances that Deplete the Ozone Layer, have primacy over conflicting NAFTA provisions. NAFTA requires the maintenance of stringent health, safety, and environmental standards, requiring national treatment for investments.

Financial services NAFTA provides a comprehensive approach to the regulation of providers of various financial services. The agreement contains definitive liberalization commitments and transition periods for the opening of markets. A key benefit of the agreement is that those involved in transactions in one member country will be able to use the same financial service providers for both domestic and international operations and allow foreign member operations in one country to process their financial materials in their home country. NAFTA also stipulates the need for transparency in applications procedures for the creation of financial institutions, and subjects the financial services sector to the agreement's dispute settlement mechanism.

Sanitary and phytosanitary measures NAFTA establishes standards for the protection of human, animal, and plant life, as well as standards for health risks due to animal pests or plant diseases, food additives, or food contaminants. While providing that each NAFTA country may establish its own sanitary and phytosanitary rules, the agreement stipulates that such regulations must be based on scientific principle and risk assessment and must be applied only to the extent necessary to meet the country's chosen level of protection. Such regulations may not be designed to restrict trade.

Services NAFTA improves access to Canada's huge market, opens Mexico's largely closed services market, and further opens the US services market to providers from the other member countries. In addition to requiring national and most favored nation treatment, NAFTA also eliminates the requirement that a service provider establish a local presence and resident status.

Telecommunications While NAFTA does not open basic telecommunications services, such as local and long-distance telephone services, it does open up services such as advanced data-processing and other enhancements.

Textiles and apparel NAFTA covers a wide range of products, including fibers, yarns, textiles, and clothing, and it has been agreed that NAFTA has primacy over other existing textile agreements. The signatories immediately removed–or will phase out over a maximum period of 10 years–customs duties on textiles and apparel that satisfy NAFTA rules of origin. The US will initially remove import quotas on such goods produced in Mexico, and will gradually remove import quotas on other Mexican textiles and apparel that do not meet NAFTA rules of origin. Both Canada and Mexico will phase out tariffs on apparel over 10 years and tariffs on other textile products over eight years. NAFTA minimally increases most quotas on textiles and apparel by two percent per year for five years. The agreement does permit the use of unilaterally imposed tariff or quota increases should serious damage to domestic markets result from the greater volume of imports. It provides strict rules of origin, including provisions covering yarn and fiber content, and establishes tariff rate quotas on many products.

Transportation NAFTA removes barriers to various land transport services and establishes a framework for compatible land transport technical and safety standards. Member nation charter and tour bus operators will acquire full access to regular bus routes in the signatory countries by the end of 1996. NAFTA will also allow foreign member bus and trucking firms to carry international passengers and cargo throughout the bloc on a phased in schedule.

NAFTA Supplemental Agreements

NAFTA members have agreed on supplemental accords designed to ensure enforcement of certain laws and standards. The accords prohibit the signatories from lowering existing labor or environmental standards, although member states are allowed to make such standards more stringent.

Most Favored Nation (MFN)

MFN = THE NORM

MFN status represents what has come to be seen as the norm in bilateral trade relationships between countries rather than the special preferential status the name implies. Under MFN status both parties agree not to extend to any third party nation any trade preferences which are more favorable than those available under the agreement concluded between them, unless they simultaneously make the same provisions available to each other. MFN status is reciprocal, with each party agreeing to grant the status to the other. MFN must be negotiated on a separate basis with each and every country. Most MFN agreements require that all such agreements include provisions for national security exceptions, intellectual property rights protections, a dispute settlement framework, a plan for mutual trade promotion, and various other safeguards.

Because of the cumulative availability of such provisions to all parties, MFN effectively becomes the international standard. Because of this, the withholding of MFN status becomes a punitive, political act generally reserved only for outlaw states. In fact, even such states as Iran, Iraq, and Libya formally enjoy MFN status from only a handful of communist and formerly communist countries, including Cuba, North Korea, and Vietnam, and bilateral negotiations are underway with both Vietnam and North Korea.

SPECIAL PREFERENCES

Despite the assumption that because MFN status requires equivalent treatment no greater preferential treatment is allowed, international law and practice recognizes that specific countries may make additional arrangements granting special preferences to other nationals without violating MFN precepts. Such arrangements include free trade areas between two or more countries and commodity-specific and /or country-specific preferences. International canons approve such arrangements provided that the agreement contains explicit rules of origin specifying limits to the benefits and that the special rate preferences are achieved by lowering internal rates among the participants rather than by raising external tariffs.

The European Union (EU)

What is now the European Union (EU) began in 1951 as the European Coal and Steel Community (ECSC), consisting of Belgium, France, Germany, Italy, Luxembourg and the Netherlands. The ECSC was, even then, envisioned as the first step toward a United Europe.

The ECSC was followed by the European Economic Community (EEC) and European Atomic Energy Community (EUROTOM) in 1957. The common institutions of these three Communities were formalized by a treaty signed in 1965, and together they came to be known as the European Community.

The Treaty on European Union (The Maastricht Agreement), effective November 1, 1993, formally established a European Union, which introduced citizenship thereof and aimed to increase inter-governmental cooperation in economic and monetary affairs; to establish a common foreign and security policy; and to introduce cooperation in justice and home affairs.

The EU does not supersede any of the premises or provisions of the EC; rather, it broadens their scope and formalizes many of the informal arrangements existing between the parties. Consisting of 15 members (Austria, Belgium, Denmark, Finland, France, Germany, Greece, Ireland, Italy, Luxembourg, the Netherlands, Portugal, Spain, Sweden, and the United Kingdom) the EU's stated objectives are to create an area without internal frontiers by strengthening economic and social ties between member countries. The EU seeks to establish a full economic and monetary union, including a single currency. The EU also envisions the implementation of a common foreign and security policy, including a common defense policy, leading ultimately to the introduction of a citizenship of the EU.

European Commission

The EU is governed by the European Commission (EC) which ensures application of the provisions of the Treaties, and formulates recommendations and opinions in matters regarding the EU.

The EU has diplomatic relations in its own right and participates as a body in international conferences on trade and development. Agreements have been signed with numerous countries allowing for cooperation in trade and other matters.

Foreign Trade Agreements

Eastern Europe The EU maintains "Europe Agreements," under which markets are opened and customs duties reduced or eliminated, with Bulgaria, the Czech Republic, Hungary, Poland, Romania, and Slovakia. The "Europe Agreements" envision the eventual establishment of free trade areas between the parties. The EU has also entered into trade and cooperation agreements with Estonia, Latvia and Lithuania, and has agreed to pursue closer economic and political relations with the Ukraine. An economic partnership and cooperation agreement with Russia has been signed, but remains to be implemented due to the instability and economic uncertainty which continues to prevail in Russia.

Middle East The EU has entered into agreements with Turkey, Malta, and Cyprus, establishing free access to its markets for most industrial products, and reducing tariffs on many agricultural products.These agreements are intended to lead to the establishment of a full customs union or, (as did a similar one with Greece) to EU assession. Cooperation agreements covering free access to the EU's market for industrial products, customs preferences for certain agricultural products, and financial aid are in force with Israel, Algeria, Morocco, Tunisia, Egypt, Jordan, Lebanon, and Syria.

Latin America The EU and MERCOSUR have entered into an agreement aimed at promoting trade liberalization and greater political cooperation between the groups, and which also confirms their commitment to establish a free-trade area in the future. The EU also maintains a cooperation agreement with the Andean Group (Bolivia, Colombia, Ecuador, Peru, and Venezuela) to broaden the scope of economic and development cooperation and enhance trade relations.

Asia and Australasia Cooperation agreements are in force between the EU and Australia, India, Bangladesh, Sri Lanka, Pakistan, and Macau, as well as between the EU and ASEAN.

North America Although trade levels are high and trade relations remain good, the EU does not maintain any specific free-trade agreements with the US, although it does maintain a wide-ranging trade preference and cooperation agreement with Canada.

Association of Southeast Asian Nations (ASEAN)

Founded in 1967 with the signing of the Bangkok Declaration by the foreign ministers of Indonesia, Malaysia, the Philippines, Singapore, and Thailand (Brunei was added a member in 1984, and Vietnam in 1995), ASEAN seeks to strengthen regional cohesion and self-reliance through economic, social and cultural cooperation. The objectives of ASEAN are to accelerate economic growth, social progress, and cultural development in the region through joint endeavors in order to strengthen the foundation for a prosperous and peaceful community of Southeast Asian nations; to promote regional peace and stability; to promote active collaboration and mutual assistance in matters of common interest; and to collaborate more effectively for the greater utilization of agricultural and industrial resources, the expansion of trade,

EU Provisions

AGRICULTURE

Cooperation in the EU is at its most highly organized in the area of agriculture. The objectives of the Common Agricultural Policy (CAP) are primarily 1) the increase of agricultural productivity by developing technical progress and by ensuring the rational development of agricultural production and the optimum utilization of the factors of production, particularly labor; 2) the ensurance thereby of a fair standard of living for the agricultural population; 3) the stabilization of markets; 4) regular supplies; and 5) reasonable prices in supplies to consumers.

Implementation of these objectives has often been hindered, however, by unstable monetary situations, which required the introduction of a "monetary compensatory amount" system (MCA). MCAs were added or deducted in agricultural exchanges between member states to take into account fluctuations between the reference rate of exchange and the real rate. Thus a subsidy was paid to the supplier in a country whose currency had appreciated against a reference rate of exchange, and a tax was paid by the supplier where the currency had depreciated or not appreciated as much. In practice, however, the MCA system led to wide variations in prices within the Community, and proved disadvantageous to any country which was a net food exporter with a weak currency. In 1989 the relative stability of currencies made it possible to abolish MCAs for all countries that were full members of the European Monetary System. The system was completely dismantled in 1992.

Agricultural prices are, in theory, fixed each year at a common level for the community as a whole, taking into account the rate of inflation and the need to discourage surplus production of certain commodities. Export subsidies are paid to enable farmers to sell produce at the lower world market prices without loss. These subsidies account for some 50 percent of agricultural spending.

When market prices for certain agricultural products fall below a designated level the Community intervenes, and buys a certain quantity which is then stored until prices recover. Agriculture is by far the largest item in the Community budget, accounting for about two-thirds of annual expenditure, mainly for supporting prices.

The CAP has come under attack in GATT, with the US especially demanding huge reductions in the EU's agricultural subsidies.

FISHERIES

The Common Fisheries Policy (CFP) came into effect in January 1983 after seven years of negotiations, particularly concerning the problem of access to fishing grounds. This agreement confirmed a previously set 200-mile (370-km) fishing zone around its coastline (excluding the Mediterranean) within which all members have access to fishing. The agreement also allows exclusive national zones of six miles with access between six and 121 miles from the shore for other countries according to specified "historic rights."

INDUSTRY

Industrial cooperation was the earliest activity of the EU, and it continues to support its coal and steel industries.

The European textile and clothing industry has recently been affected by overseas competition, and the EU participates in the Multi-fiber Arrangement to limit imports from low-cost suppliers overseas. The European Regional Development Fund gives particular support to regions where textiles formerly provided a large proportion of industrial employment, while the European Social Fund also assists in retraining displaced textile workers.

The Commission has made a number of proposals on a joint strategy for developing the information technology industry in Europe, particularly in view of the superiority of Japan and the US in the market for advanced electronic circuits. The ESPRIT research program aims to build the technological foundations for a fully competitive European industry. The EC has issued a directive requiring member states to liberalize their rules on the supply of telecommunications terminal equipment, thus ending the monopolies enjoyed by national tele-

and improvement of transportation and communications throughout the region. Although the diverse economic interests of its members caused ASEAN to develop slowly at first, it now represents itself as a powerful, more unified bargaining interest group within international organizations.

The ASEAN nations are mainly committed to market and export oriented economic growth strategies. Although some achievements have occurred in all areas contemplated under ASEAN, the agreement has been unable to stimulate economic growth to the extent envisioned by the founders. ASEAN is currently trying to increase its intra-organization activity, relying heavily on private sector initiatives. Indeed, the private sectors of all the member nations are playing an increasingly active role in ASEAN cooperation.

ASEAN Free Trade Area (AFTA) AFTA was created in January 1992, and covers several areas of cooperation, including the harmonization of standards, the reciprocal recognition of testing and certification, the removal of barriers to foreign investments, macroeconomic consultations, rules for fair competition, and the promotion of venture capital formation. When fully implemented, it will encompass a market of 425 million people that can draw foreign investment and compete more effectively with other Asian economies.

At the heart of AFTA is the Common Effective Preferential Tariff (CEPT) scheme, under which member countries agreed to reduce tariffs on products traded among themselves to a maximum of 20 percent within a period of five to eight years, and then to zero to five percent by the year 2008.

ASEAN External Relations ASEAN holds regular dialogues on trade and other matters with the EU, US, Japan, Australia, Canada, Korea, and New Zealand; it maintains preferential trade agreements with the EU, Japan, the US and Indochina.

Mercado Comun del Sur (Mercosur)

In December 1994 Argentina, Brazil, Paraguay, and Uruguay signed the Protocol of Ouro Preto, implementing Mercosur, which was created by the Treaty of Asuncion in March 1991. Under the Treaty, a full common market was established among the members, effective January 1, 1995. The agreement required a gradual elimination of all tariffs on goods originating in and traded among the member states and the formation of a Common External Tariff (CET). Mercosur operates within the context of larger groupings, including GATT/WTO, of which it is a part. As of January 1, 1995, approximately 80 percent of all products traded–about 8,000 categories of goods–began to be traded duty-free within the bloc. Exceptions include textiles, steel, automobiles, and petrochemicals, which will remain protected by domestic tariffs for a period of four years.

Mercosur is still far from being a true common market, but the members have managed to achieve a customs union and continue negotiations aimed at full common market status by 2006. As such, members will be expected to harmonize their standards, establish a supranational bureaucracy with considerable power to affect the policy-making decisions of each country's government, and implement fully a common external tariff structure.

Mercosur has helped to lock in the liberalizing changes already made by its members during the past few years, and the momentum that such change has created will prove very difficult to halt or reverse. Mercosur may be small compared to NAFTA or the EU, but its effects will be felt beyond its immediate borders. The wide variety of topographies, climates, and resources it encompasses provide substantial opportunities for expansion and complementation in production; as well as plenty of room for new members to join the agreement.

Australia-New Zealand Closer Economic Relations (CER)

The CER entered into force in January 1983, expanding upon a history of bilateral preferential trade agreements between the two countries dating back to 1922. While previous agreements had resulted in the removal of tariffs and quantitative restrictions on more than 80 percent of trans-Tasman trade, there were no provisions for further liberalizations, nor for broadening the scope of preferences between the two countries. The CER provides a framework for the progressive and automatic accomplishment of a full free trade area between the two countries. The CER provides generally for the removal of all tariffs, quantitative import restrictions and tariff quotas; the removal of monopoly import arrangements on fresh fruits; free and fair trade in dairy products between the two countries; the abolition of anti-dumping procedures for goods originating in the free trade area; and the elimination of export subsidies.

Andean Group

Created by the Cartagena Agreement in 1969, and consisting of Bolivia, Colombia, Ecuador, and Venezuela, the Andean Group aims to accelerate the harmonious development of the member states through economic and social integration. The agreement covers about 100 million inhabitants. Since its inception, trade between the member countries has increased significantly in response to substantial tariff reductions, although the ultimate goal of a full customs union including common external tariff remains in the distant future.

communications authorities. It has also adopted a plan for the gradual introduction of a competitive market in satellite communications.

Harmonization of national company law to form a common legal structure had led by the end of 1991 to the adoption of directives concerning disclosure of information, company capital, internal mergers, the accounts of companies and of financial institutions, division of companies, the qualification of auditors, and single-member private limited companies.

FINANCIAL SERVICES AND CAPITAL MOVEMENTS

The EC has laid down common prudential criteria for the establishment and operation of banks in member states. As of 1993, a single community license for banking was issued, whereby a bank established in one member country can automatically and without further authorization open branches in any other. There are also measures ensuring the capital adequacy of credit institutions, and the prevention of "money laundering" by criminals.

Insurance companies in one member state may now have free access to customers in other member states without having to establish a base in the other member states.

ECONOMIC AND MONETARY UNION

The EU intends to establish an Economic and Monetary Union (EMU) with a common monetary and exchange rate policy no later than 1999. During the second stage of EMU, which began on January 1, 1994, the member states continue to coordinate their exchange rate policies through the European Monetary System (EMS) and, specifically, its Exchange Rate Mechanism (ERM). Member states retain full authority to set monetary policies during the second stage of EMU.

The EU aims to promote monetary, price, and exchange rage stability in Europe by limiting the fluctuations of participating currencies within a certain range around bilateral central parity rates. However, pressures in foreign exchange markets in September 1992 led the UK and Italy to suspend their participation in the ERM, and compelled adjustment of the parities for other currencies in subsequent months.

TAX POLICY

Tax policy remains the prerogative of the member states, who must approve by unanimity any EU legislation in this domain. EU legislation to date in this area has been aimed at eliminating tax-induced distortions of competition within the Union. As such, it has focused on harmonizing value-added and excise taxes; eliminating double taxation of corporate profits, interest and dividends; and facilitating cross-border mergers and asset transfers.

EXPORT SUBSIDIES

Export subsidies (also known as export restitutions or refunds) are widely used by the EU to offset competitive disadvantages of EU agricultural exports caused by high EU internal support prices. Export subsidies enable the EU to dispose of its surplus production at prices that match, and often undersell, other developed countries' exports to foreign markets. These export subsidies, however, were subject to disciplines as a result of the Uruguay Round. As that agreement is implemented, there will be progressive reductions in the value and volume of subsidized agricultural exports.

INTELLECTUAL PROPERTY RIGHTS

The EC is committed to securing a high level of protection for intellectual property rights (IPR) in the EU. It aims to harmonize the scope of IPR protection so that trade and investment within the Union will not be distorted based on differences in the scope of intellectual property protection among the member states. Especially in the areas of biotechnology and data bases, where current IPR protection is seen as hindering development of EU industry, the EC has adopted directives providing greater protection to software, pharmaceuticals, and semiconductor topologies.

In the copyright area, the EC has adopted directives establishing rental and lending rights, and harmonizing neighboring rights and the term of protection, and creating a system for protecting works transmitted by satellite and cable retransmission.

International Marketing

The Importance of Marketing

Once a company decides to expand its business horizons by engaging in foreign trade, attention turns to potential markets–wherever in the world they may be–and the necessary steps to establish a strong foundation on which to trade successfully. The main goal of any company's domestic business plan should be the production of quality goods with enough unique attributes to give them a crucial competitive edge in the marketplace. An additional goal when planning to sell internationally should be a marketing campaign that is specifically suited to the target market. While products may have to be modified somewhat to make them saleable in foreign markets, those sales will, quite simply, not materialize if the trader fails to adapt a marketing strategy to suit the market. Some of the most important determinants of success in foreign markets are the marketing techniques a company employs.

Marketing Trends: A Trader's Perspective

Since marketing plays such a vital role in international trade, it is important to preface any discussion on the subject with some useful observations on prerequisites to success in this field. Although it is true that as we move toward a more integrated international marketplace a greater degree of global homogeneity can be seen, it is absolutely essential to bear in mind that each nation retains distinguishing characteristics that sets it apart from even its closest neighbors. All around the globe self-determination, nationalism and cultural pride are as important today as ever. Before engaging in foreign sales, traders need to be committed to their markets, sensitive to differences, and flexible enough to adjust to varied sets of circumstances in order to succeed.

Commitment Because of the comparatively greater complexity involved in international trade, traders need to be aware of the time frame to which they are committing themselves in order to achieve a profitable return on their investment. Most successful companies have prevailed in foreign markets because of a commitment to the long haul. In fact, many successful companies initially concentrate their efforts on gaining market share before even contemplating profitability. There is no such thing as a short-term fix, and there are very, very few get-rich-quick schemes that will work. The fact that foreign traders are often perceived as being motivated by the desire to make a quick killing makes it especially important that companies work twice as hard to allay these perceptions by showing a level of commitment sufficient to sustain the long haul.

Sensitivity The onus on traders to become intimately acquainted with their markets is very great. It has long been noted that one of the biggest single errors of international traders is not getting to know their customers. In light of the commitment and effort involved it is perhaps understandable why this should be the case. Getting to know the customer requires analyzing trade and economic statistics, studying demographics and buying patterns, and keeping informed of world events that influence the international marketplace. However, it is absolutely essential that some effort be made to understand these issues and to focus your marketing strategies accordingly.

Creating a Presence

It is also essential that traders be willing and able to make personal visits to their foreign markets. Many cultures highly value personal relationships and will not even consider entering into a business arrangement with someone whom they do not know personally. This approach requires a substantial investment of time and money but the rewards will justify the effort. A trader's presence in a foreign country will send a strong message of commitment to local business, in addition to giving the trader a true feel for the nuances of a particular market and ultimately to really get to know the customer base.

Gauging the Best Markets

Market research is essential to discover both where the customer is and what the customer wants. Foreign traders can and should carry out primary and secondary market research in pursuit of this data. Primary research, the most effective and costly method, involves collecting information directly from the foreign markets through surveys, interviews, and personal contact with potential buyers. Secondary research is conducted by keeping informed of economic trends, studying reports on the performance of a specific sector, analyzing trade statistics, or consulting international experts. In each case the goal is to become informed of the fastest growing markets for certain products, the main sources of competition, and any particular challenges that may affect entry to or operation in these markets.

Discovering the Best Distribution Channels

Once you have decided to do business in a foreign market, the next consideration should be how the goods will be distributed in that market. Distribution channels are of paramount importance because they

Keys to Success

LEARNING TO LOVE MARKETING

1. **Eliminate as much guesswork as possible.** You cannot successfully market in a country by accident. A well thought out marketing plan is needed, and you may find that the use of expert consultants represents time and money well spent. A plan is the best way to uncover hidden traps and costs before you get overly involved and end up in a mess. You may see an opportunity, but you need to know how to exploit it successfully. To do that, you must plot, plan, and prepare.

2. **Just go for it.** Planning is important and should never be forgotten, but sometimes the best plan is to use a shotgun approach—just blast away and see if you hit anything. You can narrow your options later. If your product is new to the market, there may be almost no preexisting marketing information, and you may essentially have no choice other than just to dive in.

3. **Be patient.** International marketing consultants report that many companies invariably cut their international trade budgets when the results in the first few months are anything less than wonderful; these cuts represent premature decisions and produce unnecessary failures. The hard fact is that exports do not bring in money as quickly as domestic sales. Be patient, keep a close but not suffocating watch on international marketing efforts, and give your venture a chance to develop.

4. **Avoid an internal tug-of-war.** Export marketing requires support and teamwork within your own company. Allowing internal conflicts to dominate the planning process will amount to creating your own obstacles to exporting success.

5. **Stick with exporting even if business booms at home.** Exporting is not something to allow to surface only when domestic markets falter and then to submerge when business at home increases. It is difficult to move into exporting; a clear commitment needs to be made right at the start. Any other attitude is likely to doom the venture from the beginning.

YOUR MARKET

One of the first major issues you must face is deciding who exactly your market is. What type of individual and what type of business constitutes the natural target audience for the product you seek to import and sell?

- **Is the individual of a particular age, social, or economic group?**

- **Is the individual more interested in fashion or more interested in quality and durability?**

- **Is the person interested in a bargain?**

- **Is the person interested in the "story" that goes along with the item?**

- **Is the person already buying the product or do you have to educate them to buy either a new product or your product specifically?**

- **What needs are you filling with the product?**

Another question you must answer for a marketing plan is: Where is your market located? You will have to define the geographic location of your potential market.

- **Who needs your product and why?**

- **What makes your product different and desirable?**

- **Where do you find the people who need your product?**

- **What other product criteria lead to acceptance or rejection?**

- **List prospective market areas which could support a sales program for your product. Tease the various prospective markets to determine where your marketing efforts will be most effective.**

represent the lifeline between the seller and the buyer. The problem of finding suitable channels of distribution is often complicated by a foreign environment, but it is still critical to find the best means for your needs. Most countries support many trade services such as export management companies, export trading companies, commission agents, and export remarketers.

The degree of challenge in finding effective distribution channels will largely depend on whether a trader sells directly or indirectly to the end user. If a trader decides to sell indirectly the risks and complexities associated with foreign trade are somewhat less, but the level of control over and contact with foreign markets is also reduced. By selling directly, the exporter retains greater control over the process, can personally meet customers, and need not pay out a percentage of the sale price. As one would expect, with the potential for greater dividends comes greater responsibility–and risk. Selling directly to the market requires a trader to select the best channels of distribution and this can be a difficult task. The channels of distribution generally include agents, distributors, sales representatives, retailers and partners. In some countries they perform identical or overlapping functions; in others their roles are quite different. It is important to know the role each plays in a particular country.

Agents and Agencies

Many businesspeople find that selling in foreign markets is much easier through a local agent or representative. Many countries actually require that sales of imports be made this way. An agent will generally represent and act on behalf of a company in a foreign country. In some countries, agencies are broadly defined and agents are protected by law both as to compensation and termination. In this case especially, it is imperative that a foreign seller choose its local agent wisely and that a good relationship be maintained at all times. Dealing with agencies can be very risky; they can be very successful, but they can also destroy a foreign business.

Selling Techniques

Every nation has individual characteristics that distinguish its markets from any others in the world. The important issue when it comes to determining the best sales techniques is whether or not the techniques employed are appropriate to the market in which trade is being conducted. Some markets require a high level of personal contact between buyer and seller, others do not; some markets impose serious restrictions on certain types of promotional campaigns, others do not. What is clear is that sales strategies that work well on the domestic market may not have the same impact on foreign markets.

Adjusting the Advertising Message

Advertising is one of the most powerful marketing tools ever, but unless it is used wisely it can do untold damage to a trader's reputation in foreign markets. Advertising generally reflects cultural characteristics in a given nation—values, beliefs, trends, and taboos—and these need to be clearly understood in order to ensure the specific message is heard and understood in the way a trader intends it to be. Styles and methods that work in a trader's domestic market are unlikely to achieve the same effect in a foreign market and adjustment is usually needed. Linguistic factors may dictate the renaming of a product to avoid offense or ridicule and due attention must be paid even to the color schemes of product packaging which may have a particular meaning in a given market. In addition selection of the most effective sectors of the media to best convey your message is a formidable task in itself.

Adding Value: Customer Service and Support

Traders who plan to enter or expand into a foreign market must address the question of customer satisfaction. Customers who are considering the purchase of foreign goods, particularly high-tech products, are likely to be especially concerned with the level of service support they are going to receive after the sale. In addition, a good service and customer support network will not only enhance a foreign trader's reputation, but will also be used as an important feature in making the sale in the first place.

Providing a high level of service requires the careful selection of distributors and a prior commitment that they will make the necessary investment to create adequate product service capabilities. In addition, considerable product training is required and routine personal visits to distributors are usually necessary. However, noteworthy customer service and support can in itself distinguish a foreign product from its competitors. Investment in this regard may be well worth the expense and effort.

In Summary

In an ideal world, marketing begins with detailed research from diverse sources. Application of the knowledge gained should culminate in profitable results in the marketplace. International trade is complex, however, and, despite the best market research methods, mistakes will be made. A certain amount of trial and error will be required to fine-tune foreign marketing strategies once a product has come to market. Still, good marketing techniques can help overcome what may otherwise appear to be insurmountable obstacles.

Boosting Your Sales

TWELVE TIPS

Even after having some success in foreign markets, a trader needs to reevaluate regularly not only whether a product is selling, but whether it is being exposed to the most ideal market. These tips suggest ways to test the success of your market strategies and to explore new pathways.

1. **Keep in contact with your most important customers and contacts.** Personal contact—by telephone or in-country visits—can be critical to building a commercial relationship. For many businesses, telephone contact is considered sufficient, for others, face-to-face contact is a necessity.

2. **Offer to demonstrate or send samples of your products.** The value of a presentation—with or without your physical presence—can be a key to acceptance. This is a highly effective—and usually inexpensive—sales booster.

3. **Distribute catalogs, brochures, flyers, and technical data to potential buyers and associations.** These potential customers will be able to evaluate the material on their own and will understand who you are when you approach them. Follow up the materials with telephone calls and additional promotional materials that focus on new releases and product improvements.

4. **Respect language and cultural differences, and adapt your product and marketing as needed.** Your products and marketing techniques need to be suited to your target market. They must also be in line with government regulations. Learn the differences, respect them, adapt to them, and avoid mistakes. Products may need to be modified for sale in different regions or to customers with diverse characteristics.

5. **Focus your product promotion.** Concentrate your time, money, and efforts on a specific market or region, work to build lasting relationships and repeat business there, and then expand as your products gain reputation and market share.

6. **Follow up on initial sales inquiries.** Pursue a lead. Establish a liaison for major accounts—a single person who will be responsible for working with a client from the start of a transaction, through delivery, to after-sales support.

7. **Price your product to fit the market.** Don't get greedy and try to generate maximum profits. At the same time, don't underprice your merchandise. There are many bargain hunters, but there are also many who question the quality of products that come with a low price tag. Price your product to match the market.

8. **Always provide quality products.** Consumers are used to having quality products, and they are used to returning items and demanding their money back when their purchase doesn't work, breaks, or otherwise doesn't live up to the intended purpose.

9. **Establish a direct feedback system.** From the start, you should have a plan in place to measure the effectiveness of your marketing efforts. This may be as simple as the collection of sales receipt data, brief surveys of new customers, or postcard customer registration forms.

10. **Promote repeat business.** Some companies are now sending personalized thank you notes, reminder cards, and holiday greetings to their more treasured or large-ticket item purchasers. Some electronic tracking systems offer the option of processing a customer's preferences and issuing discounts, advertising, or special offers to the customer on the spot or through the mail.

11. **Deliver on time.** If you don't, someone else will. Failure to deliver on time can destroy a carefully built reputation.

12. **Emphasize customer service.** Marketing becomes more effective if customers reached once return to buy again. Customer service is essential in developing repeat business; the treatment of your customers is as important as the quality of the product.

Business Culture

Interactive World Dynamics

International commerce presents countless challenges to traders that they simply do not encounter in their domestic markets. Much of what makes a foreign country "foreign" and what exerts a strong influence on foreign trade is culture. While it is imperative that you know your customer, it is equally important that you know the environment in which that customer operates, i.e. the culture. From a business point of view, culture can be looked upon as a set of rules that govern the way business transactions are conducted with nationals of particular nations. These rules will dictate the etiquette, traditions, values, communication, and negotiating styles of the particular culture to which they apply.

It should also be noted that culture does not necessarily refer to a whole country but rather to connected groups of people. Thus a country may have a distinctive overall culture but within this framework many subcultures may exist. In addition, cultures are not fixed in stone–they are continually evolving and are flexible by nature. Cultures are not impervious to outside influences and younger generations, in particular, may not have the same cultural precepts as their elders.

Cultural Norms: A Trader's Perspective

All traders conduct business transactions in their own domestic markets in accordance with the rules and requirements of the prevailing culture; they understand what is and is not acceptable behavior. When conducting business abroad, however they are faced with a different set of rules which govern their associates' behavior, and with which they are often not familiar.

In order to be successful in global trade, businesspeople need to be aware of their own cultural influences and be sensitive to those of the nations with whom they intend to trade. They must also be sensitive to any particular biases or practices within their own culture that may lead to inappropriate judgments or assumptions about another culture; and they must try to understand the particular biases of the foreign culture within which they are operating. Failure to do this can lead to serious misunderstandings that could adversely affect cross-border business.

Practicing Common Business Courtesies

Business practices vary from culture to culture and the proper protocol should be followed when operating in foreign environments–at least to the extent you can do so within the constraints of your own cultural background. Nobody expects you to behave exactly as they do; indeed it would probably be looked upon as less than sincere if you tried to become "one of them." To have some understanding of a country's cultural background, to be sensitive to the ways that your own culture may cause offense, and to adapt accordingly, should suffice. But, while there are many ways in which business practices differ, it should also be remembered that certain practices are common to all cultures—being polite and courteous, personally signing all correspondence, and responding to requests promptly will be appreciated anywhere.

Gaining Cultural Awareness

Rules of etiquette differ from culture to culture and what is acceptable in your own country may be considered rude elsewhere. As initial impressions are vital in establishing business relationships it is important to know what is expected of you when first meeting potential business partners from another culture. Some cultures demand the use of respectful titles when addressing people while others are more informal. For example, in Japan the accepted form of greeting is the bow; subordinates bow more deeply than their superiors, though it is not common to make physical contact. In many Middle Eastern countries, however, there is much hugging, kissing, and extended hand holding upon greeting. In Middle Eastern countries, it is socially unacceptable to inquire about a colleague's wife and family, while in Mexico this practice is entirely appropriate and indeed expected. There are a host of social courtesies that accompany any relationship, and it is important to have some idea of those which might apply to the people with whom you do business.

Language

Language is central to the communication process and as such it can be a significant barrier to international trade. Being clearly understood by your business partners is of paramount importance whether you are negotiating a deal, drafting a contract or issuing instructions from your home base. While English is probably the most commonly used language in international trade it is not spoken everywhere. Even where it is used there may be differing levels of comprehension, and different meanings may be attributed to certain words. Knowledge of the language of the market in which you are trading may be necessary in the long term, although in general the use of well trained interpreters will suffice for most purposes.

Cultural Fundamentals

TEN TIPS FOR SUCCESS

1. **Empathize with foreign cultures.** It is important to understand the cultural framework within which you are operating. If you can see things from the point of view of another culture it will help you to be more tolerant of the differences in approach. It is also necessary to recognize that your own cultural background is influencing how you look at and approach situations, and that your foreign associate may not be familiar with your culture. Recognizing and understanding these things can make the whole business process a lot easier–and more enjoyable.

2. **Be flexible.** Cultural practices vary widely even within one country. Therefore it is necessary to be flexible enough to be able to adapt your behavior to a particular situation. You will probably need a different approach for every country you trade with, and in many countries you will need to at least make some adaptations between industries or regions.

3. **Do not push your identity on others.** When in a foreign culture do not insist on doing things the way you do them at home. At the same time, do not try to become "one of them". Nobody expects a foreigner to be a part of their culture, only to respect it and its values and traditions.

4. **Show respect for etiquette.** Etiquette is deeply entrenched in many cultures and by showing respect for social and business etiquette you are showing respect for your trading partners. It is therefore necessary to learn at least something about the local etiquette of both business and social occasions. Such things as personal space, physical contact, gestures, gifts and basic pleasantries differ from country to country; but everybody will appreciate it if you know about and make an effort to accommodate their particular preferences in these matters.

5. **Suspend unnecessary judgments.** There may be things about another culture you do not like or agree with. To the extent they are based on personal experience or first-hand knowledge, you must deal with them with the same tact you would utilize with domestic business associates you do not particularly care for. But, to the extent your perceptions are based on unfounded biases or prejudices, you should make every effort to overcome them.

6. **Language is important.** Language can be one of the biggest barriers to business for foreign traders. Learn a little bit of the language if possible (your efforts will probably be appreciated), and use the services of competent interpreters for most business dealings. Be aware of the ambiguity of language - what you say and what is understood are not always the same thing.

7. **Don't overlook gestures.** Gestures and body language are important means of communicating, and some familiarity with the local ways of expression will go far in recognizing and interpreting unspoken messages.

8. **Develop trust.** It is often difficult to do business in foreign cultures because there can be a certain built-in mistrust of outsiders. Establish trust with your business partners by demonstrating respect and professionalism, and a commitment to their markets.

9. **Participate.** Be an active participant in your foreign business dealings and make an effort to interact with your foreign associates. You will gain an understanding not otherwise available and will develop closer working relationships with your partners abroad.

10. **Travel.** While research is an important way to learn about another culture there is no substitute for visiting a country to experience its culture in person.

Communication

Communication includes both spoken language and non-verbal expressions. Business relationships, and negotiations in particular, are highly dependent on the communication styles of the participants. While an interpreter can help with verbal expressions, success will often depend on your ability to pick up non-verbal cues, and respond accordingly. Nationals of some countries tend to be very emotional, and relationships and negotiations can get volatile; others rely on very subtle body language to communicate their feelings. It is wise, and may well avoid misunderstandings, to have some idea of the general communication style of a country before you go.

Important Cultural Issues

The cultural issues you will face in your international business dealings will vary from country to country. In some, issues like punctuality and the protocol of business meetings will vary even within the country. Some countries maintain very rigid structures, and you must follow certain rules if you want any hope of success; in others, almost anything goes. There are certain aspects of business relationships where cultural issues become particularly important. Some examples include:

Greetings and Courtesies

There are a million different ways to greet people. In some countries, businesspeople are very open and informal, while in others, formality is a key and you must always use a person's title when referring to them. Some countries prefer a handshake to greet people but others shy away from any physical contact. There are also cultural norms surrounding gift giving; some countries have extensive rules and laws defining "gift," limiting their legality, while in others lavish gifts are expected–and necessary.

Business Ethic and Framework

The level of formality also changes drastically from country to country. Some countries are very informal, and appointments can be made any time; you may be able to simply walk in without an appointment and make a deal. In other countries, meetings require months of preparation with appointments made and confirmed far in advance.

Decision Making

Do you expect to make a sale on your first trip to that foreign country? In some places, this is possible; some countries are very open and focus more on the deal than the relationship. In others, even a tentative decision will not be made until a personal relationship is established, and after consensus is reached at all levels of the hierarchy. This could, understandably, take months or even years.

Women

How are women treated in the country in which you wish to do business? This is a touchy subject and is becoming a major issue in many countries. In some countries, women and men are treated equally, in many others, women simply cannot effectively conduct business. It could be devastating to any business relationship to overlook this issue–or to enter a relationship unprepared.

Meetings

Meetings are a crucial part of doing business in some countries. In some places, meetings are very informal, with constant interruptions and a tone that may seem more like a social gathering. Others are much more rigid, and you may need to send an agenda and a list of everyone from your company who will be present. In some countries, punctuality is very important, and you must be on time if not somewhat early; in other places, you may be kept waiting for your host for an hour or more.

Business Attire

Your attire can also have an impact on the success or failure of your foreign endeavor. Appropriate business attire ranges from very casual as in many businesses in Israel, to extremely formal and subdued, as you will find in Japan. While it is always best to wear clothes in which you feel comfortable, your attire may need to be modified somewhat to suit a foreign environment.

In Summary

To some extent cultural faux pas are unavoidable and are usually laughed off by all concerned. However, they can also sometimes lead to a total failure of business purpose and irreparable loss of profitable relationships. If you are aware of another's cultural background, and have made an attempt to understand its influences, you will be better equipped to adjust your behavior and expectations without patronizing your foreign associates. When cultures collide, as they inevitably will, the damage can be greatly reduced with knowledge, understanding, and appreciation of what caused the collision.

Cultural Cautions

DO'S

Sometimes seemingly minor issues can have a major impact and even the slightest attempt to get along will bring disproportionately positive results. Pay attention to such things as

- **Level of eye and physical contact**
- **Posture**
- **Gifts to bring to parties and other social occasions**
- **Knowing something about the country you are visiting**

DON'TS

Many things that are commonplace at home are totally unacceptable elsewhere. It is easy to make little mistakes that have large repercussions. Following a few simple rules of courtesy and politeness will go far in foreign countries. Things to especially avoid include:

- **Do not litter**
- **Do not discuss politics or religion**
- **Do not criticize**
- **Do not assert your own sense of time**

CUSTOMS

Customs are more than just do's and don'ts, they are deeply rooted cultural issues that are quite important to nationals of certain countries. It is important to understand some of the customs of the place you intend to do business. Some things to be aware of include:

- **Eating habits and mealtimes vary significantly from culture to culture and people can be offended by habits different from their own**
- **Work hours and holidays**
- **Drinking and toasting rules and issues when attending parties or social gatherings**
- **The role of women**

OBSERVATIONS

There are many peculiarities about different cultures that are not quite rules, and not quite traditions or customs, but are nonetheless noticeable similarities in the way nationals act or approach problems or situations. You don't need to be in a country long to recognize some of these cultural differences. Some observations might include:

- **How much business takes place at the first meeting, and how important business cards are**
- **Whether business continues during a meal after a meeting, or whether you should just enjoy the social occasion**
- **National pride**
- **Gestures and non-verbal body language**

NEGOTIATIONS

Negotiations and negotiating styles are absolutely critical to the success or failure of a foreign business endeavor. Yet these vary so widely even within cultures it is difficult to pinpoint specific rules or recommendations. There are, however, some important issues to remember when negotiating, including:

- **Avoid outright conflict with foreign business associates**
- **Avoid shifts in conversation tone or in negotiating style**
- **Follow the host's lead on the level of formality of the negotiations**

International Travel

The Shrinking Globe

The growth of global trade in the past five decades has resulted in a dramatic increase in the number of business trips international traders make each year. Business travel may be expensive and time consuming, but it is also the most effective way to develop strong business relationships. First-hand experience of the countries and the people with whom they do business give traders a better understanding of particular business cultures, and also demonstrates to their foreign associates a high level of commitment to a foreign market.

Traveling Productively

The key to making a successful business trip is preparation. Good preparation will help you to focus on the purpose of your trip and maximize your productive time in a foreign country. Simply hoping for the best when you get there is a recipe for certain disaster. When preparing for a business trip it is important to establish your particular goals to ensure that your trip is a productive one. You may be in the initial stages of market research, you may want to make contact with potential distributors for your product, or you may want to return home with a signed and sealed business contract. Whatever your goals are, only after they have been established can you set about planning the best way to achieve them.

Getting in Touch with Other Business Worlds

The first step in planning your trip is thorough research. There are many published sources of information on countries all over the world, and important information can also be gleaned from other traders familiar with the territory. This type of research will help you to focus on many important travel issues you may not have yet considered.

The time of year in which business trips are made is an important issue that is often overlooked by business travelers. National and religious holidays are different wherever you go and it may be necessary to confirm these in order to avoid arriving at inopportune times. In Saudi Arabia, for example, people fast for a month before the Ramadan religious festival, and this makes it more difficult to conduct business at this time of year. Workweeks and daily hours of operation also vary from country to country and you will need to be aware of these in order to properly structure your visit.

Getting in touch with potential foreign business contacts before you go will help you plan your schedule and will save you a lot of time when you get there. Information on local business contacts may be available at your country's local embassy or consulate. Confirming appointments in writing before a trip will help to ensure that you get the attention you deserve when you arrive.

Passing the Border

Visa requirements vary from country to country and it is important to obtain all the necessary documents well in advance of your trip. If you are traveling to more than one country you should establish whether or not having the visa of one country will preclude you from entering another country.

If you are bringing product samples on your trip these may be subject to import duties and lengthy customs procedures. These can be avoided by obtaining an international customs document called an ATA Carnet. Many countries already adhere to the ATA Carnet conventions, and new countries are continually being added to the system so it is important to get the most current list before traveling.

You may be required to produce proof of vaccination against certain diseases before entering some countries, and it may be advisable to get yourself vaccinated even when it is not required by law. In addition, it is important to ascertain whether or not there are any other significant health hazards in the country you are visiting. If you have a particular medical condition it may be necessary to seek precautionary advice from your doctor before departing. There are many private organizations who provide lists of suitably qualified doctors in foreign countries in the event of an emergency.

Putting Safety First

While abroad, all travelers are subject to the local law and it is important to know about the laws of the country you are visiting. Actions that are perfectly legal in your own country may land you in trouble in a foreign country. Also, it is advisable to ascertain if there are any public safety concerns in the country you intend to visit. This information should be easily obtained from the relevant government departments before traveling. Once you arrive at your destination it is recommended you visit your local embassy to obtain further information that will be of help to you on your trip.

Keys to Success

PACKING FOR PERSONAL TRAVEL

- Travel light.
- High-quality molded suitcases will last longer and are worth the money, especially if you plan to travel frequently.
- Leave enough room for articles purchased overseas and brought back with you. Consider packing a foldable canvas bag in your other baggage to handle the overflow on the way home.
- If your suitcases use keys, be sure to keep one set on your person and another in your briefcase.
- Pack clothing that is appropriate for the trip.
- Be sure your medical kit is appropriate for the destination.
- Prescriptions to be filled while traveling:
  - Vitamins
  - Prescriptions
  - Anti-diarrhea pills
  - Anti-malarial pills
  - Extra eyeglasses
  - Extra pair of contact lenses plus accessories
  - Water purification tablets
  - Medical bracelet if appropriate
- Documents to remember:
  - Passport
  - International health certificate
  - Visas
  - Driver's license/international driver's license
  - Travelers checks and personal checks
  - Credit cards
  - Extra passport photos
  - Refund locations for travelers checks
  - Travelers check numbers
  - Birth certificate (if necessary)
  - Address book (leave photo copy at home!)
  - Letters of introduction from major institutions
  - Tickets and vouchers
  - Business cards
  - Business brochures

MANAGING YOUR ABSENCE

- If appropriate, give power of attorney to your attorney, accountant, business associate, or family member before you leave.
- Pay existing bills and prepay bills that will come due during your absence, especially telephone, utilities, and payable-upon-presentation bills such as American Express and Diners Club.
- Notify police, post office, and newspaper delivery services of your absence.
- Leave your itinerary with several people in your organization and/or family.
- Leave a list of credit cards, travelers checks, passport information, and suitcase combination lock numbers with someone accessible by telephone.

TRAVEL SAFETY TIPS

- Be conservative in your dress and manners. Consider that you may be wearing items worth 10 years' earnings to a local laborer. Don't flaunt your wealth.
- Leave your flashy jewelry at home. If you must take it, cover it up in public and display it only at appropriate social events.
- Don't carry large amounts of cash on your person.
- Know where you are going. Those who appear confused and indecisive are prime targets for con artists and muggers.
- Beware of pickpockets in crowded situations.
- If you use a shoulder bag, keep it on the side away from the street and hold it with your hand. Robbers on motorbikes grab bags as they speed by.

Time Zone Map

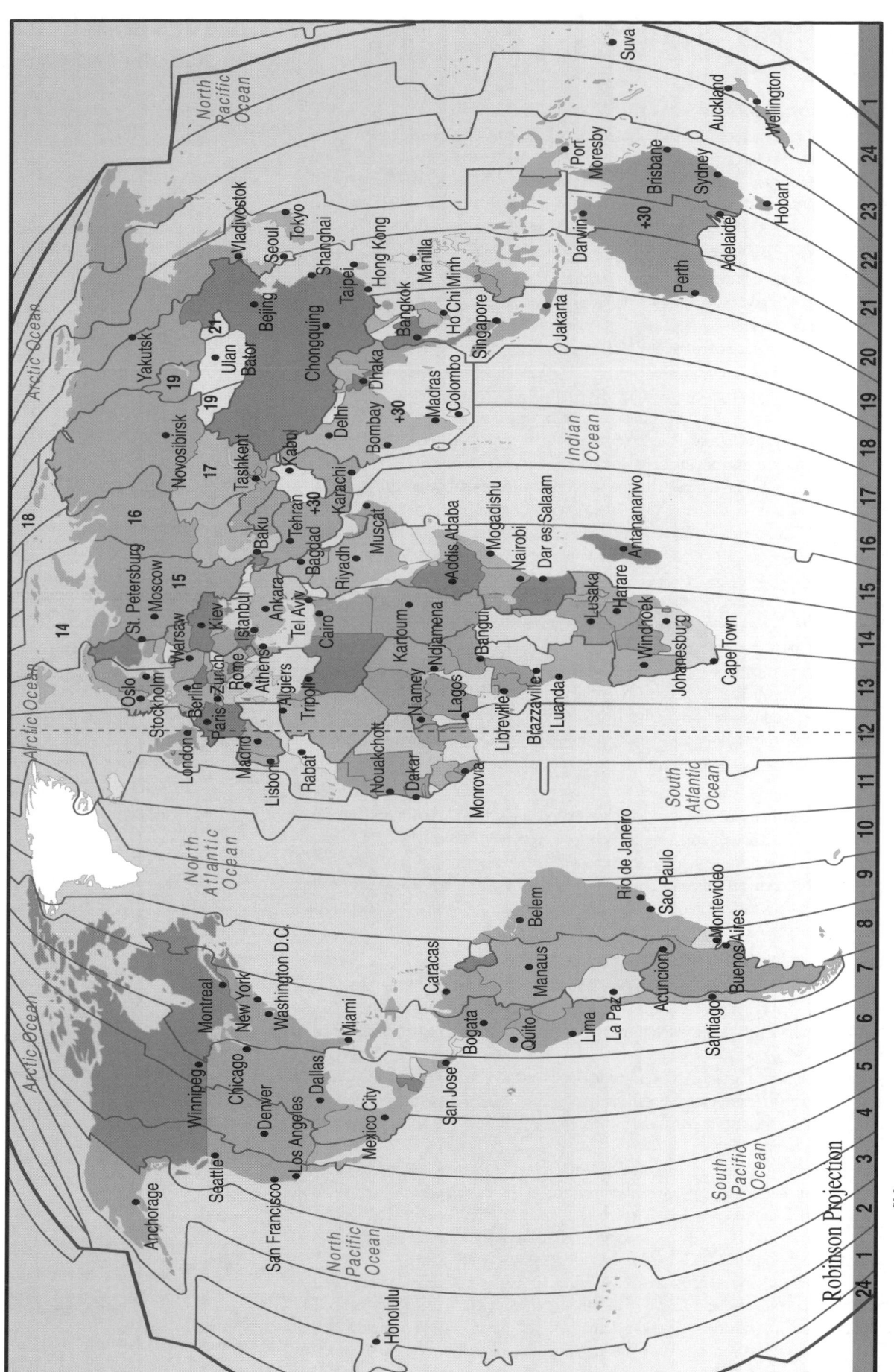

Robinson Projection

©1994 Magellan Geographix,SM Santa Barbara, CA

To use the time zone map, simply add or subtract the difference in the hours shown at the bottom from the time at your location. For example, if it is noon in London, it is 8 pm in Perth, Australia (Perth is eight hours ahead of London), and 9 am in Rio de Janeiro, Brazil (Brazil is three hours behind London).

Country Legal Trends

Law in the International Arena

Traders entering the international arena must be prepared to deal with a wide array of laws with which they are often unfamiliar. As has been stressed so often with reference to foreign trade, it is important that traders recognize they are dealing with individual countries with distinct requirements regarding the conduct of business. Each foreign country has its own legal system, commercial laws, and trade regulations, all of which have a strong impact on the way business is conducted therein.

Legal Trends: A Trader's Perspective

Traders engaging in international trade are confronted with many important legal issues including domestic laws as they pertain to imports and exports, contracts, arbitration, intellectual property rights, labor, taxation, and the influence of national governments in trade matters. It is important to bear in mind that traders are subject to the laws of each country they trade with and they may be subject to these laws even if they do not physically enter the country.

Throughout the world national governments regulate domestic economic activities to varying degrees. Some governments exert minimal economic influence, preferring a laissez-faire approach, while other economies are dominated by the state, and the government exerts considerable influence over all economic activity. In cases where the government has a strong influence over business it usually follows that there are more legal barriers for traders to deal with and government approval may have to be directly sought before sealing any business contract. In order to successfully conduct business in a given market, traders need to know the economic goals and priorities of a particular government and how prevailing legislation furthers those goals. Armed with this knowledge they can tailor their business approach accordingly.

Legal matters are further complicated for international traders by virtue of the fact that they are operating simultaneously under two or more legal systems–their own and that of the country or countries with which they are trading. This is important when it comes to agreeing to contracts with foreign businesses. For example, the exact nature of the business relationship between a trader and the foreign distributor or supplier will differ depending on which law governs this relationship. In some countries agents are considered employees and are entitled to the rights and benefits conferred thereby. In others, their relationship is limited by the terms of the contract. This simple difference could have serious ramifications for traders who terminate a relationship with an agent in ignorance of the law.

Plan Ahead

There are a host of legal requirements that a trader must comply with or avoid when trading with foreign countries and therefore the issue of obtaining reliable local legal advice becomes an important one. In the event a trader feels he is being unfairly discriminated against under the law it may even be possible to enlist the help of his own government. This will be especially effective if the country with which he is conducting business has entered into trade agreements guaranteeing "national treatment" of traders from his own country.

Gaining Property Protection

Traders also need to ascertain the extent to which their patents, copyrights and trademarks will be protected under intellectual property rights laws. Some issues to consider with intellectual properties are the amount of protection a country will give to such property, and whether local registration is valid in other countries.

Patents A patent is a grant from a country's government to an inventor of the right to exclude others from making, using, or selling an invention for a specific term of years. A patent application describing the invention in detail and stating specifically what the inventor believes is new and patentable usually must be filed with a country's patent office.

Copyrights A copyright is a granted right to protect the expressions of an author or originator of a literary or artistic work from unauthorized copying or performance. In some countries, a copyright automatically arises when a work is created, while in others registration is required. Another copyright issue that varies from country to country is how long the copyright remains in effect. Most copyrights last for the life of the creator; in some countries, they extend until long after his death.

Trademarks A trademark (or service mark) is usually defined as "any word, name, symbol, or device, or any combination thereof, adopted and used by a manufacturer or merchant to identify its goods and distinguish them from those manufactured or sold by others." Trademarks and service marks identify goods and services, respectively, as coming from a single source, and consumers rely on these marks to purchase goods (or services) with which they are familiar. Again, every country regards trademarks

International Contracts

BASICS OF A ONE-TIME SALE

Many traders anticipating a small, or one-time international transaction may want to negotiate the deal and draft the contract without the services of professional legal counsel. There are several things to be aware of, and clauses which must be included, in any such deal.

- **Contract date** Specify the date when the contract is signed. This date is particularly important if payment or delivery times are fixed in reference to it–for example, "shipment within 30 days of the contract date."

- **Identification of parties** Name the parties, describe their relation to each other, and designate any persons who are authorized to act for each party. The persons designated should also be the ones who sign the contract.

- **Description, quantity and price of goods** *Description:* You may simply indicate a model number or you may have to attach detailed lists, plans, drawings, or other specifications. This clause should be clear enough that both parties fully understand the specifications and have no discretion in interpreting them. *Quantity:* Specify the number of units, or other measure of quantity, of the goods. If the goods are measured by weight, the goods are prepackaged and are subject to weight restrictions in the end market, you may want to ensure that the seller will provide goods packaged to comply with those restrictions. *Price:* Indicate the price per unit or other measure, such as per pound or ton, and the extended price.

- **Packaging arrangements** Set forth packaging specifications, especially for goods that could be damaged in transit. At a minimum, this provision should require the seller to package the goods in such a way as to withstand transportation. If special packaging requirements are necessary to meet consumer and product liability standards in the end market, you should specify them also.

- **Transportation arrangements** *Carrier:* Name a preferred carrier for transporting the goods. You should designate a particular carrier if, for example, a carrier offers you special pricing or is better able than others to transport the product. *Storage:* Specify any particular requirements for storage of the goods before or during shipment, such as security arrangements, special climate demands, and weather protection needs. *Notice provisions:* Require the seller to notify the buyer when the goods are ready for delivery or pickup, particularly if the goods are perishable or fluctuate in value. If your transaction is time-sensitive, you could even provide for several notices to allow the buyer to track the goods and take steps to minimize damages if delivery is delayed. *Shipping time:* State the exact date for shipping or provide for shipment within a reasonable time from the contract date. If this clause is included and the seller fails to ship on time, the buyer may claim a right to cancel the contract, even if the goods have been shipped, provided that the buyer has not yet accepted delivery.

- **Costs and charges** Specify which party is to pay any additional costs and charges related to the sale, including duties and taxes, insurance costs, and handling and transport charges.

- **Insurance or risk of loss protection** Specify the insurance required, the beneficiary of the policy, the party who will obtain the insurance and the date by which it will have been obtained.

- **Payment provisions** In a one-time transaction, the seller will typically seek the most secure form of payment before committing to shipment, while a buyer will want the goods cleared through customs and delivered in satisfactory condition before remitting full payment. In any event, the payment provision should include method of payment, medium of exchange, and a designated exchange rate.

- **Indemnity** Agree that one or both parties will hold the other harmless from damages arising from specific causes, such as the manufacture of a product.

differently, and substantial research should be given to how best to protect one.

Trade secrets Generally, a trade secret is any formula, pattern, device, or compilation of information used in a business which gives the owner a competitive advantage in the business, and which has been maintained by its owner as a secret. In some countries, trade secrets may include customer lists, sources of supply, pricing information, and other similar business information. Many countries still view trade secret protection as a novelty, but more and more are beginning to draft legislation to protect trade secrets.

Contracts

Contracts are governed by the laws developed in each country and modified by country statutes. For countries following common law, elements of a contract in its simplest form are: (1) an offer; (2) an acceptance of that offer; and (3) transfer of payment or some item of value in connection with the offer and acceptance (known as consideration). Although oral contracts may be legally binding in some countries, a precisely drafted, written contract will help to eliminate misunderstandings between parties. At the very least, you should have a written contract whenever you pay for or take possession of goods. Contracts sometimes can be voided (that is, considered to have no effect) if they were based, for example, upon a mistake of law or if they were entered into by someone deemed to lack decision-making capability.

Some important contract issues include:

Terms of payment In international business transactions, you will use different methods of payment, and possibly different currency, than you do in domestic transactions. You will have to become familiar with different currencies, currency restrictions, and exchange rates. Contact your international banker for information about foreign exchange and currency restrictions.

Terms of transport and delivery In any sales agreement, definitions of transport and delivery terms are essential. The terms commonly used in international business transactions often sound similar to those used in domestic contracts, but they frequently have different meanings in global transactions. Confusion over these terms can result in a lost sale or a financial loss on a sale. For this reason, you must know, understand and agree upon the meaning of these terms before completing your agreement.

Dispute Resolution

It is inevitable that misunderstandings rising to the level of legal disputes will arise in international transactions. Different cultures have different ways of dealing with business disputes. Americans, for example, are quick to resort to legal action, while the Japanese are absolutely loath to do so. Some countries favor legally binding arbitration; others informal conciliation. In any event, it is wise to know the options available for dispute resolution, and their effect, in each country in which you do business.

Immediate and temporary relief Communication between you and your foreign business partners is essential to keeping the relationship smooth. For minor discrepancies, or even major calamities, your business relationships and reputation will benefit if you approach the problem with understanding and a view toward finding a resolution that will satisfy everyone involved. A good rule to remember: create a working relationship with your foreign business partners, not an adversarial one. Negotiation, followed by a written confirmation of any modified contract terms, is the most effective means of resolution in terms of cost and time. If a dispute continues despite your informal attempts to resolve it, you should take steps to protect your rights. Your most imminent concern will probably be to recover your own property quickly or to find an immediate replacement supplier so that you can honor your commitments to third parties.

Arbitration The parties to a commercial transaction may provide in their contract that any disputes over interpretation or performance of the agreement will be resolved through arbitration. In the domestic context, arbitration may be appealing for a number of reasons. Approach arbitration in an international setting with caution, however. In many countries, arbitration is unavailable or is just being developed. Although less adversarial than a court trial, arbitration is still viewed in many cultures with suspicion, if not abhorrence. A request for arbitration may be viewed as a personal insult to your foreign counterpart, and instead of being a means of dispute resolution, it may destroy the potential for settlement through private negotiation. Because of the complexity of the subject, legal advice should be obtained for specific transactions.

Litigation At best, litigation is costly, time consuming and even if ultimately resolved in your favor still does not address a primary concern: collection of money owed or specific performance of the contract terms. In reality, undertaking litigation proceedings in foreign courts does not often result in a favorable outcome–even after all the time and expense. The courts of many countries are biased in favor of their own nationals, and foreigners rarely, if ever, obtain satisfaction. The best advice is to avoid litigation altogether. If you do become embroiled in a legal battle abroad obtain the best local counsel available as soon as possible.

Law Fundamentals

TEN TIPS TO PROTECT YOUR LEGAL RIGHTS

1. **Be prepared.** Traders must be prepared to deal with a wide array of laws when trading internationally. Make an effort to know something about the particular country's policies regarding business registration, labor benefits and protections, intellectual property rights, extra payments which may be required or expected by governmental authorities (and the legal implications of making these payments), and foreign investment laws.

2. **Do not make assumptions.** Every country has different legal systems and commercial laws and traders should never assume that these systems are the same as their own. Foreign traders should also not assume that a particular country's laws will not apply to them if they are not physically present in that country–often times the law applies regardless of physical presence.

3. **Agree on one set of laws to govern a contract.** When negotiating contracts it is important that one set of laws governs the deal and that both parties agree on this. This will help to prevent future disputes.

4. **Clarify meanings of words in contracts.** Cultural differences may result in the attribution of different meanings to certain words and it is important that all ambiguities are clarified before signing a contract. While this may result in unduly lengthy contracts, this is sometimes better than engaging in later disputes over the meaning of words.

5. **Consider all the ramifications of a contract.** It is important to understand the extent to which your interests are protected and the liabilities you may be subject to under the terms of your contract. If you do not personally understand every provision in the contract you should engage legal counsel to explain them to you before you sign.

6. **Seek out reliable foreign legal advice.** Considering that traders are often dealing with unfamiliar laws it is important to seek out well informed local foreign legal advice–especially if you anticipate a long, multi-deal relationship.

7. **Understand national priorities.** Governments can exert a strong influence over trade and related legislation. Familiarity with governmental policies can aid foreign traders in anticipating future problem areas in a contract–and making timely provision to deal with them. Be aware of trade agreements.

8. **Be aware of trade agreements.** Trade agreements between countries often extend national treatment to traders of each country, or allow for tariff reductions or duty free entry of goods. Some trade agreements specifically address dispute resolution and offer protections or guarantees that foreigners would otherwise not be entitled to.

9. **Select an appropriate form of business entity.** Selection of the most appropriate form of business entity is one of the most important decisions facing a foreign enterprise. There are several ways to do business in different countries, and each has different ramifications regarding legality, financial and personal liability and taxation. Although selection of the proper entity format cannot assure the success of the venture, a wrong choice may contribute to a venture's failure.

10. **Learn the procedures.** Registration and documentation requirements and procedures must be complied with to ensure protection of your investment and to make sure that you will be protected in the event of later dispute.

International Banking

Banking Services

If you are planning to engage in trade or invest in foreign markets, it is important to cultivate your banking relationships early on. The foreign trader who views this relationship as integral to his company's overseas business tends to be significantly more successful than those who do not.

There are over fifty international US banks with truly global operational scope, and about three hundred foreign banks maintain a presence in the United States. In addition to financing, major international banks are in a position to provide the trader with critical information on overseas markets, currency exchange regulations, movement of funds, securing overseas credit, potential suppliers, and the creditworthiness of foreign firms. Other foreign banks run agencies in the United States. These banks can lend, handle trade bills, issue letters of credit, act as an intermediary for the trader, and offer payment services, but they cannot accept deposits. In addition, hundreds of other state and federally chartered institutions have more limited relationships with overseas correspondent banks. At the very least, a local bank can provide the foreign trader with a letter of introduction for a local bank officer in the destination country.

Capital Transfers

Any firm doing business overseas needs to have a knowledge of the basic principles of international accounting and taxation, including accounting for international transactions, translation of income, and consolidation of financial sheets. Currency exchange exposure (translation exposure, transaction exposure, and economic exposure) in ongoing operations needs to be factored into bottom line operating expectations. Legal regulations of the country of origin for the import/export of specific commodities, specific currency exchange regulations and specific customs regulations all need careful consideration as well.

International Payments

Although open account terms can be made available to exporters and importers who are known to each other, it is far more likely that another, more secure method of payment will be required. Customs brokers, bankers, and international attorneys can provide assistance in this area. There are four basic methods of international payment: prepayment (cash payment or order); documentary letter of credit; documentary collection or draft; and open account or other terms. Terms in the transaction that will need to be finalized through written contractual agreement are: merchandise, including quality and

amount; price paid as stipulated in a certain currency; freight charges and insurance for each portion of the journey; shipment deadline; required documentation format; and other specialized contractual terms.

Investing in a Country

Most countries offer some type of incentive to companies planning to invest there, including tax rebates, sales tax concessions, and exemptions from customs duties. The government will also often offer grants for projects, usually for those that offer job creation potential, have some degree of local sourcing, and that have good export potential. Countries also have various restrictions for companies, usually in certain sectors upon which the government has a monopoly. Some restrictions include high taxes and bureaucratic red tape. Investors should also be concerned about issues like inadequate infrastructure, political instability, and corruption. Although these aren't government imposed restrictions, they can nonetheless create barriers to foreign investment.

Foreign Exchange

The issue of dealing with many different currencies and monetary systems throughout the world is one of vital importance to foreign traders. Business transactions in the international trade arena are more complicated due to the use of different currencies and the influence of national governments in matters concerning foreign exchange and investment procedures. It is imperative that traders familiarize themselves with the problems and risks associated with the currency or monetary system of the country with which they are trading. There are many techniques that traders can use to protect themselves, and the advice of trade experts or fellow traders should be sought so that the best plan is put in place.

Buyers and sellers from different countries seldom use the same currency and the problem of which currency to use can become a serious barrier to completing a deal. The relative value of currencies is constantly changing, and some are quite volatile; if this value changes between the time a deal is made and the time payment is received it could have a serious impact on the profitability of a deal. For example, if a trader has made a deal and the foreign currency devalues before payment is made he will receive less money for his goods than originally anticipated. Of course it is also true that extra profits could be made if the foreign currency increases in value, but this is a risk that most traders would prefer to avoid.

The Difficulties of Converting Currency

Traders also need to be aware of the fact that most of the world's currencies are not readily convertible. For a variety of reasons national governments use their powers to set exchange controls that curtail the movement of currency to and from their countries. Foreign traders are thus totally reliant on the government for all their foreign exchange needs. It is important to understand the exchange control system in a particular country so that steps can be taken to ensure the availability of hard currency. In addition to foreign exchange controls, each country has different rules and regulations with regard to investment procedures, tax relief to avoid double taxation, export exemptions and stock market operations.

Foreign Exchange Risk

There are many ways of dealing with foreign exchange risk and the simplest is insisting on payment in your own currency. This strategy lays the risk at the buyer's door but it may not always be a viable option, and traders may have to accept payment in foreign currency in order to make the sale. If full agreement cannot be reached it may be possible for traders to share the risk by arranging for a portion of the payment to be made in one currency and the remainder in another. Alternatively it may be possible for payment to be made in a unit of account such as a special drawing right (SDR) which is made up of a number of currencies. In this case increases in one currency are likely to be balanced by corresponding decreases in other currencies.

If it is absolutely necessary to take on the foreign exchange risk, traders can protect themselves in a number of ways. They can build the estimated cost of a currency fluctuation into the deal to guard against potential losses. However, as this is simply an estimate it does not fully protect the trader. A safer but more costly method is the use of a system called factoring. Factoring allows the trader to transfer title to his foreign accounts receivable on a discounted basis to a factoring house or factor. The factor assumes responsibility for the credit, collection, and record keeping functions for the client, and the seller is guaranteed his–albeit somewhat lower–price. Another method, called hedging, is an attractive option for those stout of heart. While it ensures a set exchange rate and eliminates the risk of a currency moving in the wrong direction, it involves the use of forward and options contracts (at no small cost) and professional advice should be sought before entering into any such contracts.

Foreign Exchange

Exchange Uncertainties

One of the added uncertainties of conducting international trade is the fluctuation in exchange rates among currencies. The relative value between the buyer's currency and the seller's currency may change between the time the deal is made and the time payment is received. A devaluation or rise in one currency against another causes either a windfall or a loss to one party or the other involved in the transaction.

For example, if an importer in the United States has agreed to pay 200,000 French francs (F) for a shipment and the franc is valued at US$0.19 (its approximate value in late1994), the buyer would expect to pay US$38,000. If the franc later rose in value to 19.5 cents—an increase of just over 2.5%, a not unlikely occurrence in the volatile short-term foreign exchange market—payment at the new rate would require US$39,000, for an added cost of US$1,000 to the importer. On the other hand, if the foreign currency fell in value to 18.5 cents, the importer would have to pay only US$37,000, saving US$1,000. Most traders prefer to avoid such risk rather than speculate on fluctuations in foreign exchange markets.

One of the simplest ways for a trader to avoid this type of risk is to quote prices and establish payment in the currency of one's own country; this places the burden and risk on the other party. This is practical when one's own currency is freely convertible and stable. Typically, the currency of a major trading country is used. Therefore, US dollars, German marks, English pounds, Japanese yen, French francs, and Swiss francs are often quoted.

If the exporter/seller asks to receive payment in a foreign currency, the importer should consult an international banker before negotiating the purchase contract. Banks can offer advice on foreign exchange trends and risks. Many international banks can also help the importer hedge against such a risk.

Terms and Concepts

International trade and other transactions involving cross-border flows of funds require the participants to enter the world of foreign exchange. Foreign exchange is defined as claims payable in a foreign country in a foreign currency. (Foreign exchange is often referred to as forex or simply abbreviated as FX.) As a rule, businesses and individuals operate using their own national currencies—money recognized and legally acceptable for transactions (legal tender) within the particular currency zone (the territorial area in which a given currency is recognized, usually coinciding with national boundaries).

For example, a seller/exporter in Japan usually wants to be paid in his or her own currency—the yen (¥)—rather than in that of the importer, who, if he is from the US, may want to use U.S. dollars (US$). However, the seller may on occasion prefer to be paid in Deutsche Marks (DM) in order to pay off obligations due to a German firm in that currency. And the French business traveler going to Montreal to negotiate a deal needs to pay expenses in Canadian dollars (Can$) rather than in French francs (F). A British investor may need to convert English pounds sterling (£) into Dutch guilders (G) to put funds into a venture in that country. All of these scenarios require the participants to convert a home currency into one or more foreign currencies or vice versa.

Currencies

A currency which can be readily exchanged for another is known as a convertible currency. If it can be fully, readily, and legally converted under virtually all circumstances, a currency is referred to as being unrestricted. Many countries maintain restricted convertibility on their currencies, often allowing full convertibility only for nonresidents while limiting the ability of residents to exchange domestic for foreign currencies. Other countries have inconvertible currencies, which cannot legally be taken out of the country or exchanged for foreign currencies at all. Yet other countries distinguish between foreign exchange involving current transactions (for goods and services) and those involving capital investments, with freedom of convertibility being restricted to some degree for one category or the other. This situation often results in what is known as a two-tier market, in which access to restricted currency is rationed and those who need it must obtain special authorization to acquire it. Such exchange controls ration the availability of foreign currency, which can block imports into the country. These limitations often result in a thriving illicit black market trade in currencies and commodities.

Hard currencies are those of large, strong economies which have few if any restrictions on the use and exchange of their currencies, while soft currencies are those for which there is little or no demand due to restrictions on free exchange (this is usually also a function of a limited or weak economy). International financial operations are usually transacted using key currencies, that is those which are relatively strong, broadly convertible, and generally accepted. Such currencies, sometimes referred to as reserve currencies, and most international business is transacted using–or at least with reference to–these currencies.

Key Terms

Arbitrage The simultaneous buying and selling of identical currencies or commodities in two or more markets in order to take advantage of price differentials.

Basket of currencies A means of establishing value for a composite unit consisting of the currencies of designated nations. Each currency is represented in proportion to its value in relation to the total.

Call option The right (but not the obligation) to buy a fixed amount of a currency from the option writer (seller) at a predetermined rate and/or exercise price within a specified time limit.

Cross rate Exchange rate parities which are not quoted against the dollar.

European currency unit (ECU) A weighted average of the currencies of the European Community member nations, used as a unit of value in transactions among businesses in the member countries.

Exchange rate The price of one currency expressed in terms of another, i.e., the number of units of one currency that may be exchanged for one unit of another currency.

Fixed exchange rate An exchange rate in which the value of a currency is linked to a commodity, such as gold, or to another strong currency, such as the US$.

Floating exchange rate An exchange rate which is determined through market fluctuations against a variety of other currencies.

Foreign exchange Current or liquid claims payable in foreign currency and in a foreign country (bank balances, checks, bills of exchange). Foreign bank notes and coin are not included in this definition.

Forward foreign exchange An agreement to purchase foreign exchange (currency) at a future date at a predetermined rate of exchange. Forward foreign exchange contracts are often purchased by international buyers of goods who wish to hedge against foreign exchange fluctuations between the time the contract is negotiated and the time payment is to be made.

Hard currency Currency that is relatively strong, broadly convertible, and universally accepted internationally. Examples are: the US and Canadian dollar ($), Japanese yen (¥), British pound (£), German Deutsche Mark (DM), French franc (F), Dutch guilder (G or f.), and Swiss franc (SwF).

Options Contracts which allow foreign exchange traders the right to buy (call) or sell (put) specified quantities of currencies at a point in the future.

Pips The last decimal places of a foreign exchange price quotation. In futures trading the smallest possible price fluctuation upwards or downwards (1 pip) is called a tick. Professionals are assumed to know the base rates and deal only in the marginal fluctuations.

Put option A contract which entitles one party, at his option, to sell a specified amount of a commodity, security or foreign exchange to another party, at the price fixed in the contract, during the life of the contract.

Spot exchange The purchase and sale of foreign exchange for delivery and payment at the time of the transaction.

Spot market The market for foreign exchange available for immediate delivery (usually one or two days after the transaction date).

Spot/next Swap transaction, the spot side of which has the normal spot value date while the forward side becomes due one business day later.

Spot price A price quotation for immediate sale and delivery of a commodity or currency.

Swap Sale of one currency against another currency at a specific maturity and the simultaneous repurchase from the same counterparty at a different maturity. Normally, one of the maturity dates will be that of spot operations.

Tick *See pips.*

Tom/next Swap transaction where the spot side becomes due on the business day following the day on which the contract was concluded and where the forward side becomes due on the day after, i.e. on the normal spot value date.

Rates of Exchange

The exchange rate is simply the amount of a nation's currency that can be bought at a given time for a specified amount of the currency of another country. For example, as of September 30, 1994, $/¥=98.48, meaning that one US dollar was equal to 98.48 Japanese yen. The exchange rate is given either as a direct quote—expressed as the number of units of a foreign currency per US$ (1.547DM/$), or as an indirect quote, expressed as the number of US$ per unit of foreign currency (.646$/DM), which is the reciprocal of the first quote. Because the US$ is the most commonly traded currency, international foreign exchange transactions are usually quoted directly using the US$ as the reference point. Thus an inquiry from a Swiss bank to a German bank about their rates would be quoted not in SwF/DM but in DM/US$, even though both parties understand that the Swiss bank is interested in the rate of the DM against the SwF, not the US$.

This necessitates the use of cross-rates, in which currencies are not compared directly with each other but in terms of a reference currency which serves as a common denominator. For example, in order to find the rate for the SwF/DM, you must first have quotes on both currencies in US$ (1.2845SwF/US$ and 1.547DM/US$), then use them to calculate the rate for SwF/DM with reference to the common dollar rates of each (1.2845/1.547=.83SwF/DM).

Forex traders quote bid and ask price ranges, with the first figure always that at which they stand ready to buy currencies and the second (always higher) figure that at which they are willing to sell. This difference is conceptually similar to buying wholesale and selling retail, and constitutes the spread, or base profit margin for the institution. Professional traders deal not in full quotes but in a shorthand, referred to as pips or ticks. These are the last decimal places in a quote, usually 1/100th, or .01, of a percent (professionals are assumed to know the base rates and deal only in the marginal fluctuations).

The necessary series of conversions allows for the possibility of arbitrage, which involves taking advantage of temporal and spatial anomalies in pricing in the international currency markets. If, as in the example above, the German bank's price on SwF is less than the Swiss bank can get for them in Hong Kong, it will buy SwF from the German bank and immediately sell them to the Hong Kong bank to make a profit on the price differential. However, because virtually all international currency transactions are quoted against the US$ and because instant communications and 24-hour trading compensate for distance and time differences, the opportunities for such arbitrage are few. Professional traders now generally use the term to refer to trading for the institution's own ac-count rather than for that of a client.

The actual amount received in a conversion, or the effective exchange rate, usually differs from the stated rate because it takes into account all taxes, commissions, and other costs that the public must pay to complete the transaction and actually receive the foreign funds.

Setting Exchange Rates

The relative value of one currency against another depends on a variety of economic and political factors, but ultimately it boils down to supply and demand. The main economic factor is the equilibrium rate, or purchasing power parity, at which goods would cost the same in each country. This ignores many important factors, such as quality, exportability, and long-term capital flow issues, but serves as a useful approximation of the relative strength of currencies against each other. If the same amount of currency in country A buys the same goods as an equivalent amount of currency in country B, the currencies are at parity. If the same amount of currency buys more goods in country A than in country B, then the currency of country A is undervalued and/or that of country B is overvalued.

A nation's account balance (the sum of the value of goods and services it has exported during a given period netted against the value of those imported during the same period plus any transfer payments remitted abroad) can be used as a barometer of a country's economic strength. If the economy is consistently in a surplus position, that is it has received more than it has paid out, its currency can be expected to strengthen, or appreciate (rise in value) over time. Conversely, in a deficit position—one in which it spends more than it takes in—its currency will be expected to weaken, or depreciate (lose value) with respect to that of partners maintaining a surplus. Most countries keep foreign currency reserves to pay for current needs and serve as a cushion for fluctuations in the international income and outgo of funds.

Nations generally try to manage their currencies to maintain stable exchange rates against those of their trading partners. This can be done in a number of ways. The authorities may attempt to maintain a fixed exchange rate in which the value of their currency is linked to a commodity, such as gold, or to another strong currency, such as the US$. When a currency is linked directly to that of a stronger country (usually its main trading partner), it is said to be pegged to that of the stronger country whose lead it follows. The nations of the world have generally been unable to maintain such fixed rates in the volatile and increasingly integrated global economy of the 20th century, leading to the use of floating rates. Since the 1970s, most national currencies have floated, allowing their value to be determined through fluctuations against a variety of other currencies.

Floats can be clean, that is, determined solely by market forces without official interference (a situation that never really occurs in the real world), or dirty—managed to a greater or lesser extent by government authorities. Although some governments arbitrarily set exchange rates and policies to enforce them, such management usually involves intervention, or attempts to influence markets. This is accomplished primarily through open market operations in which the government buys or sells large quantities of its own or another country's currency or securities in an attempt to influence the relationship between the two by altering supply and demand factors. Because foreign exchange markets are so large and active, it has become virtually impossible for any government or international agency to effectively exercise control over exchange rates.

In practice, floating exchange systems rely on a variety of mechanisms to set actual prices. The main ones involve trade-weighted rates which hinge on the degree of importance of a given country's trade with the nation. A variation of this is to use a basket of currencies in which the exchange rate is figured in proportion to the value of the various currencies among the designated countries. This has been implemented by such schemes as the snake, a system in which northern European countries agreed to keep their currencies within a certain proportional relationship to each other (because adjustments occurred serially rather than simultaneously, the effect of such changes as they worked through the system was thought to resemble the undulations of a snake). The crawling peg—in which a country with a subsidiary currency commits to adjust by incremental stages to maintain its agreed upon level with respect to the stronger currency that it tracks—represents a further variation on this theme. Often the pegged currency will have a daily or weekly limit on how much it can rise or fall to adapt to the target currency. The fixed band within which a currency is allowed to fluctuate is called the grid.

On occasion a currency cannot move either rapidly or far enough by using such mechanisms to reach an equilibrium point. The authorities must then realign, or change the official value of, the currency. Such realignments may require officials to devalue—officially reduce its value relative to that of the currency of another country—or revalue—officially raise its value relative to that of another country. In devaluation, the country's currency buys less, hurting imports (but also perhaps boosting sales of its now-cheaper exports). Upward revaluation allows the country to buy more abroad with its more valuable currency, but usually cuts into overseas sales of its now more expensive exports.

The Mechanics of Foreign Exchange Operations

Most foreign exchange trading stems from the need to acquire foreign currency for a specific transaction. If the conversion is for use in a current transaction, it occurs in the spot market at the current price, or spot rate, for immediate delivery (actually within two business days). If the foreign exchange is required for a future transaction, it occurs in the forward market for future delivery. The basic difference between the prices in the spot and forward markets is due to the relative levels of interest rates in the two countries. If a currency is actually held by the party, it can earn interest between now and when it is needed at prevailing money market rates. Or, conversely, it must be borrowed at a cost commensurate with the value of the interest earnings foregone by the lender. So the forward price will include the amount of interest which could be earned during the period, usually making forward rates higher than spot rates due to this premium.

Hedging Risks

The ability to buy forward foreign exchange allows businesses to hedge their risks by counterbalancing a current transaction through a similar future transaction to offset the effects of price changes during the interim. In currency trading this is often accomplished through a swap—the spot purchase (or sale) of foreign exchange and a simultaneous forward sale (or purchase) of the same currency. A spot purchase coupled with a future sale is known as an outward swap, while a spot sale linked to a forward purchase is an inward swap. A forward purchase or sale not covered by an offsetting spot transaction is known as an outright transaction. Actual holdings of a currency are known as long positions, while those with uncovered future positions, that is with net indebtedness, are said to be short of exchange.

It is possible to buy forward (or futures) contracts for set amounts of major currency deliverable at a specified future date. These can vary from short-term spot/next swaps (in which the spot side is the current price and the offsetting closeout position is the price on the next business day) and tom/next swaps (in which the current price is that for the next business day and the offsetting position is valued at the price for the next business day after that) to positions as far out as one year.

Options

While futures—contracts to buy or sell a specified quantity of foreign currency at a stated date in the future, the basis of forward transactions—are useful for hedging risks, options are largely speculative instruments. Options contracts allow foreign exchange traders the right to buy (call) or sell (put) specified quantities of currencies at a point in the future. If an option is in the money—that is the actual price is above the exercise price and therefore the option is profitable—it can be exercised. If it is out of the money (the exercise price being below the actual price and therefore unprofitable to exercise), it can be allowed to expire. Options traders seldom if ever take delivery of the actual currencies but simply close out the profitable contracts for the amount of the profit. Contracts known as American options can be exercised at any time during the life of the contract, while European options can only be exercised on the expiration date.

Markets

Despite the growth of trade and an increasingly interdependent global economy, most foreign exchange trading involves financial institutions trading for their own accounts rather than straight business transactions on behalf of clients. Such activity serves to add depth and liquidity to the forex market. Because of the high turnover in self-liquidating transactions—many of which are highly leveraged—the nominal dollar value of the volume of such trade far outstrips that of the underlying economic and monetary base that supports it. Major foreign exchange markets are run out of New York, London, Frankfurt, Amsterdam, Singapore, Hong Kong, and Tokyo, but traders can operate anywhere thanks to modern communications links. Trading is most active during the business hours in these respective locations, but can occur anytime.

Euromarkets—consisting of informal markets to deal in transactions involving a currency outside of its country of origin—provide offshore international access to funds unencumbered by governmental regulation. London, Frankfurt, Zurich, and Amsterdam are the main centers of this trade. The US$ accounts for about two-thirds of the Euromarket, with the DM, SwF, and ¥ collectively making up as much as one-quarter of the remainder. The Asian dollar market, operating primarily out of Singapore, is also growing rapidly. Again the US$ is the primary currency, but use of the ¥ is increasing. By some accounts, more US$ are traded in such markets than in the domestic market. For example, the average daily turnover in the Singapore Asian dollar market was nearly US$75 billion in 1990.

Within the U.S., futures contracts are handled through the International Monetary Market of the Chicago Mercantile Exchange. Standard foreign exchange options are traded through the Philadelphia Stock Exchange and the Chicago Board Options Exchange. Many large, internationally-oriented banks will write specific nonstandard futures contracts to cover the needs of clients.

Ten Tips for Currency Transactions

1. **Monitor change.** The relative value of currencies is continually changing. Familiarity with currency trends can avert potentially costly mistakes. There are several readily available international media sources which provide up to date information on the relative values of several currencies. The Wall Street Journal, The Economist, and the International Herald Tribune are all available in large cities throughout the world and quote currency rates as well as report relevant news from around the world.

2. **Understand the implications of dealing in a particular currency.** A decision to use one currency over another can have serious implications for your profit margins. Some currencies are readily convertible on the open market, though many have restrictions attached to their exchange. Some countries have wholly inconvertible currencies, which cannot legally be taken out of the country or exchanged for foreign currencies at all. Before finalizing payment terms, make certain that they can be carried out in accordance with the contract.

3. **Understand the mechanics of foreign exchange.** There are many ways to protect yourself against foreign currency fluctuations. It is essential to become familiar with these methods. If the conversion is for use in a current transaction, it occurs in the spot market at the current price, or spot rate, for immediate delivery (actually within two business days).

4. **Hedge your risks.** The spot purchase (or sale) of foreign exchange and a simultaneous forward sale (or purchase) of the same currency is called a swap, and allows businesses to hedge their risks by counterbalancing a current transaction through a similar future transaction to offset the effects of price changes during the interim.

5. **Options for risk-takers.** Options contracts allow foreign exchange traders the right to buy (call) or sell (put) specified quantities of currencies at a point in the future. Options traders seldom if ever take delivery of the actual currencies but simply close out the profitable contracts for the amount of the profit.

6. **Seek expert advice.** Banks can offer advice on the foreign exchange risks that exist and can help you analyze the best methods and terms of payment regarding your business abroad.

7. **Factor your transaction costs.** Many methods for dealing with foreign exchange risks have fairly substantial transaction costs associated with them. These costs are generally proportional to the amount of risk and/or complexity associated with the transaction method.

8. **Understand exchange controls.** Exchange control systems differ from country to country. While some governments do not interfere at all with currency exchange transactions, many others impose restrictions to various degrees. It is important to know and understand the regulations in effect in the country in which you intend to do business prior to finalizing any agreement. You many not get paid otherwise.

9. **Be alert to change.** especially in countries where the government maintains heavy controls on the exchange system. In some cases, a government may even make changes in exchange regulations retroactive, which can obviously have serious ramifications on an agreed transaction.

10. **Look for incentives.** Many governments offer attractive financial incentives to lure foreign investment, especially in underdeveloped regions or industries pegged for export growth. Tax exemptions, rent rebates, preferential financing, and production subsidies are some common incentives that can make countries more attractive for investment. Currencies are used as a store of liquid wealth by other countries, which keep their international reserves in these hard currencies. The US$, ¥, £, DM, F, Can$, G (also abbreviated as "f," for Dutch florin), and Swiss franc (SwF) are considered to be key or reserve currencies, and most international business is transacted using—or at least with reference to these currencies.

The International Chamber of Commerce (ICC)

The International Chamber of Commerce is a non-governmental organization serving as a policy advocate for world business. Members in 110 countries comprise tens of thousands of companies and business organizations. The ICC aims to facilitate world trade, investment, and an international free market economy through consultation with other inter-governmental organizations.

The ICC was founded in Atlantic City in 1919. It now encompasses associations and companies from all branches of industry. As an institution of international economic self-administration, it operates through expert commissions, sub-committees and working groups to address questions which are of importance for the international business community. These include, for example, contract and delivery clauses (Incoterms); standardization of means of payment, (Uniform Rules for Collection, Uniform Customs and Practice for Documentary Credits, Uniform Rules for Demand Guarantees); arbitral jurisdiction (Rules of Conciliation and Arbitration); questions relating to such issues as competition, foreign investments, and transportation.

The ICC also offers various services to the business community such as the ATA Carnet system.

The ICC publishes many books and references which are valuable to the international trade community. The following is a select list of publications available from the ICC.

ICC Guide to Documentary Credit Operations

Offers a complete explanation of the documentary credit process including international trade considerations; a list of political, legal and economic issues; documentary requirements; role of issuing and advising banks; and types and uses of documentary credits. ICC publication No. 515, 1994 Edition, 122 pages.

Uniform Customs and Practice for Documentary Credits

These are the official rules governing the use of documentary credits. The 49 articles of the UCP 500 are a comprehensive and practical working aid to bankers, lawyers, transport executives, educators, and those involved in international trade transactions. ICC publication No. 500, 1993 Edition, 60 pages.

UCP 500 and 400 Compared

An article-by-article comparison study between the 1993 revision and the 1983 revision to the UCP. This study also incorporates commentaries on the rationale for rewrite of the articles. ICC Publication No. 511, 1993 Edition, 135 pages.

Incoterms 1990

Defines the 13 Incoterms and specifies the respective rights and obligations of buyer and seller in an international transaction. ICC publication No. 460, 1990 Edition, 216 pages.

ICC publications are available in the United States from:
ICC Publishing, Inc.
156 Fifth Avenue, Suite 308
New York, NY 10010 USA
Tel: +1 (212) 206-1150
Fax: +1 (212) 633-6025

and in France from:
ICC Publishing S.A.
38, Cours Albert 1er
75008 Paris, France
Tel: +33-1-49-53-28-28
Fax: +33-1-42-25-36-23

International Payments

Documentary Collections & Documentary Letters of Credit

Overview of Payment Methods

There are four common methods of international payment, each providing the buyer and the seller with varying degrees of protection for getting paid and for guaranteeing shipment of the goods. Ranked in order of most security for the seller to most security for the buyer, they are:

1. **Cash in Advance,**
2. **Documentary Letters of Credit (L/C),**
3. **Documentary Collections (D/P and D/A),**
4. **Open Account.**

Cash in Advance

✔ Greatest security for seller

✔ Greatest risk for buyer

In cash in advance terms, the buyer simply prepays the seller prior to shipment of goods. Cash in advance terms are generally used in new relationships where transactions are small and the buyer has no choice but to prepay. These terms give maximum security to the seller but leave the buyer at great risk. Because the buyer has no guarantee that the goods will be shipped, there must be a high degree of trust in the seller's ability and willingness to follow through. The buyer must also consider the economic, political, and social stability of the seller's country, as these conditions may make it impossible for the seller to ship as promised.

Documentary Letters of Credit

✔ Excellent security and equal risk for both buyer and seller

✔ Added costs to buyer

✔ More involved than a Documentary Collection

A letter of credit is a bank's promise to pay a seller on behalf of the buyer so long as the seller meets certain terms and conditions stated in the credit. Documents are the key issue in letter of credit transactions. Banks act as intermediaries and have nothing to do with the goods themselves.

Letters of credit are the most common form of international payment because they provide a high degree of protection for both the buyer and the seller. The buyer specifies the documentation required from the seller before the bank is to make payment, and the seller is given assurance that payment will be received after shipping the goods so long as the documentation is in order.

Documentary Collections

✔ Good security and almost equal risk for buyer and seller

✔ Less costly than a L/C

✔ Easier to use than a L/C

A documentary collection is like an international cash on delivery (COD), but with a few twists. The exporter ships goods to the importer, but forwards shipping documents (including title document) to the buyer's bank. The buyer's bank is instructed not to transfer the documents to the buyer until payment is made (Documents against Payment, D/P) or upon guarantee that payment will be made within a specified period of time (Documents against Acceptance, D/A). Once in possession of the documentation, the buyer may take ownership of the shipment.

D/P and D/A terms are commonly used in ongoing business relationships and provide a measure of protection for both parties. The buyer and seller both assume risk in the transaction, however, ranging from refusal on the part of the buyer to pay for the documents, to the seller's shipping of unacceptable goods.

Open Account

✔ Least risk for buyer

✔ Greatest risk for seller

This is an agreement by the buyer to pay for goods within a designated time after the shipment, usually in 30, 60, or 90 days. Open account terms give maximum security to the buyer and greatest risk to the seller. This form of payment is used only when the seller has significant trust and faith in the buyer's ability and willingness to pay once the goods have been shipped. The seller must also consider the economic, political, and social stability of the buyer's country as these conditions may make it impossible for the buyer to pay as promised.

Choosing the right payment method can be the key to a transaction's feasibility and profitability.

Documentary Collections (D/P, D/A)

A documentary collection

is a good method of

payment for buyers and

sellers who require

low risk, have fundamental

trust in each other,

and wish to avoid the more

cumbersome letter of credit

process.

In a documentary collection banks act as intermediaries to collect payment from the buyer in exchange for the transfer of documents which enable the holder to take possession of the goods. The procedure is easier than a letter of credit and bank charges are lower.

Basic Procedure

The documentary collection procedure has been standardized by a set of rules published by the International Chamber of Commerce (ICC). These are called the Uniform Rules for Collections (URC). The basic procedure involves the step-by-step exchanging of documents giving title to the goods for either cash or a contracted promise to pay at a later time.

The seller (also called the remitter) ships the goods and presents the documents (such as the bill of lading, invoices, and certificate of origin) to his bank (also called the remitting bank), which then forwards them to the buyer's bank (also called the collecting bank). The buyer then pays his bank the sum due, receives the documents, and takes possession of the goods.

Types of Collections

There are three types of documentary collections. The basic procedure is the same for all except that the buyer has different payment options which the seller must agree to before shipment. In each case the buyer may take possession of the goods only by presenting the documentation including the bill of lading to customs and shipping authorities.

Documents against Payment (D/P)

In D/P terms the buyer receives the title documents only after making payment at the bank.

Documents against Acceptance (D/A)

In D/A terms the buyer receives the title and other documents after signing a time draft at the bank promising to pay at a later date.

Acceptance Documents against Payment (Acceptance D/P)

In Acceptance D/P terms the buyer signs a time draft for payment at a later date. However, the documents are transferred only after the time draft reaches maturity. In essence, the goods remain in escrow until payment has been made.

Risks for Buyers

The main risk for buyers is that the goods shipped might not conform to the goods specified. In such a case the buyer will have to seek recourse with the seller, because banks deal only in documents and not in goods.

Risks for Sellers

Risks to the seller center around the fact that payment is not made until after the goods are shipped. Specific risks are as follows:

1. The seller assumes insurance and storage liability while the goods are in transit until payment/acceptance takes place.
2. The buyer may not pay for the documents. While the goods remain in the legal possession of the seller, he may be stuck with them in an unfavorable situation. Also, the seller has no legal basis to file claim against the buyer. At this point the seller may have the goods returned or try to sell the goods to another buyer. If no action is taken, the goods will be auctioned or otherwise disposed of by customs.

A seller should only agree to payment by documentary collection if:

1. The seller does not doubt the buyer's ability and willingness to pay for the goods;
2. The buyer's country is politically, economically, and legally stable;
3. There are no foreign exchange restrictions in the buyer's country, or all licenses for foreign exchange have already been obtained; and
4. The shipped goods are easily marketable.

Procedure

Refer to the illustration on the next page for a graphic representation of these steps.

① The seller/exporter ships the goods.

②-③ The seller forwards the agreed upon documents to his (remitting) bank, which in turn forwards them to the buyer's (collecting) bank.

④ The buyer's bank notifies the buyer/importer (drawee) of the conditions under which he may take possession of the title and other documents.

⑤ The buyer makes payment or signs a time draft and takes possession of the documents.

⑥-⑦ If the buyer draws the documents against payment (D/P terms), his bank transfers payment to the seller's bank for credit to the seller's account. If the buyer draws the documents against acceptance (D/A terms), his bank sends the acceptance to the seller's bank or retains it up to maturity. On maturity, the buyer's bank collects the bill and transfers it to the seller's bank for payment to the seller.

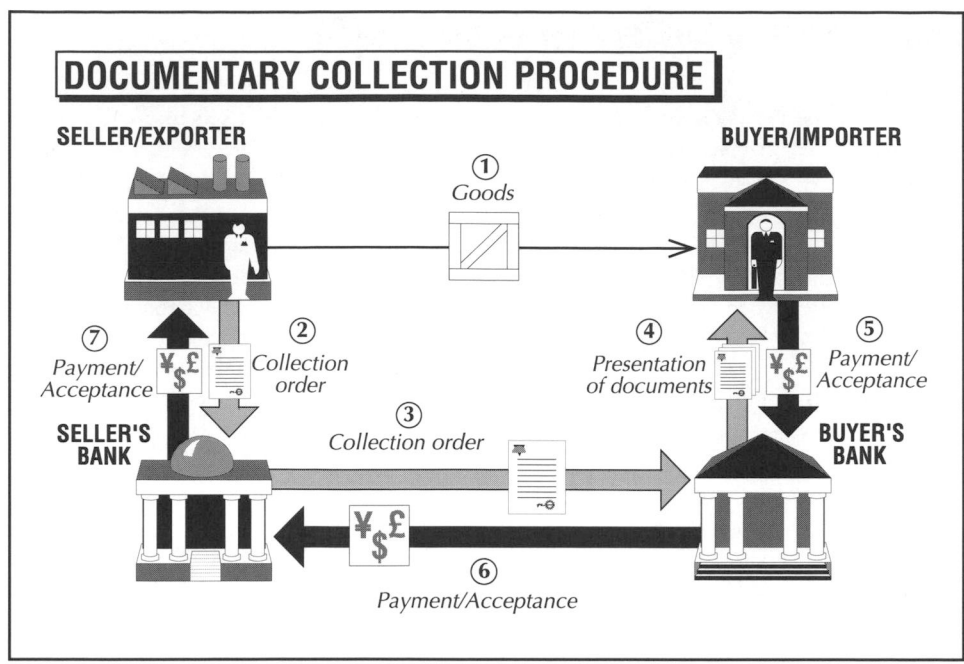

DOCUMENTARY COLLECTION PROCEDURE

Tips for Parties to a Documentary Collection

Tips for Sellers

1. The seller assumes risk because the goods are shipped before receipt of payment. Buyer has no legal obligation to pay for or to accept the goods.
2. Before agreeing to a documentary collection, the seller should check on the buyer's creditworthiness and business reputation.
3. The seller should make sure the buyer's country is politically and financially stable.
4. The seller should find out from the buyer what documents are required for customs clearance in the buyer's country.
5. The seller should assemble the documents carefully and make sure they are in the required form and endorsed as necessary.
6. As a rule, the seller's bank will not review the documents before forwarding them to the buyer's bank. This is the responsibility of the seller.
7. The goods travel and are stored at the risk of the seller until payment or acceptance.
8. If the buyer refuses acceptance or payment for the documents, the seller retains ownership. The seller may have the goods shipped back or try to sell them to another buyer in the region.
9. If the buyer takes no action, customs authorities may seize the goods and auction them off or otherwise dispose of them.
10. Because goods may be refused, the seller should only ship goods which are readily marketable to other sources.

Tips for Buyers

1. The buyer is generally in a secure position because ownership or responsibility for goods do not have to assumed until documents have been paid for or a time draft signed.
2. The buyer may specify a certificate of inspection as part of the required documentation. The buyer may not sample or inspect the goods before accepting and paying for the documents without authorization from the seller.
3. As a special favor, the collecting bank can allow buyers to inspect the documents before payment. The collecting bank assumes responsibility for the documents until redemption.
4. In the above case, the buyer should immediately return the entire set of documents to the collecting bank if the buyer cannot meet the agreed upon payment procedure.
5. The buyer assumes no liability for goods if there is a refusal to take possession of the documents.
6. Partial payment in exchange for the documents is not allowed unless authorized in the collection order.
7. With documents against acceptance, the buyer may receive the goods and resell them for profit before the time draft matures, thereby using the proceeds of the sale to pay for the goods. The buyer is responsible for payment, however, even if the goods cannot be sold.

Documentary collections are not without risk. Both buyer and seller should be careful to understand the process as well as the limitations of this payment method.

Documentary Letters of Credit (L/C)

Buyers and sellers share risk about equally in a letter of credit transaction. Letters of credit are often called documentary letters of credit because the banks handling the transaction deal in documents as opposed to goods.

A letter of credit is a document issued by a bank stating its commitment to pay someone (seller/exporter) a stated amount of money on behalf of a buyer (importer) so long as the seller meets very specific terms and conditions. Letters of credit are the most common method of making international payments because the risks of the transaction are shared by both the buyer and the seller.

Basic L/C Procedure

The letter of credit process has been standardized by a set of rules published by the International Chamber of Commerce (ICC). These rules are called the Uniform Customs and Practice for Documentary Credits (UCP) and are contained in ICC Publication No. 500. The following is the basic set of steps used in a letter of credit transaction. Specific letter of credit transactions follow somewhat different procedures.

1. After the buyer and seller agree on the terms of a sale, the buyer arranges for his bank to open a letter of credit in favor of the seller. Note: The buyer will need to have a line of credit established at the bank or provide cash collateral for the amount of the L/C.

2. The buyer's bank (issuing bank) prepares the letter of credit, including all of the buyer's instructions to the seller concerning shipment and required documentation.

3. The buyer's bank sends the letter of credit to a correspondent bank (advising bank) in the seller's country. The seller may request that a particular bank be the advising bank, or the buyer's bank may select one of its correspondent banks in the seller's country. (Note: For the sake of simplicity in this example we will call this the seller's bank.)

4. The seller's bank forwards the letter of credit to the seller.

5. The seller carefully reviews all conditions the buyer has stipulated in the letter of credit. If the seller cannot comply with one or more of the provisions, the buyer is immediately notified and asked to make an amendment to the letter of credit.

6. After final terms are agreed upon, the seller prepares the goods and arranges for shipment to the appropriate port.

7 The seller ships the goods, and obtains a bill of lading and other documents as required by the buyer in the letter of credit. Some of these documents may need to be obtained prior to shipment.

8. The seller presents the documents to his (seller's) bank, indicating full compliance with the terms of the letter of credit. Required documents usually include a bill of lading, commercial invoice, certificate of origin, and possibly an inspection certificate.

9. The seller's bank reviews the documents. If they are in order, they are forwarded to the buyer's bank. If it is an irrevocable, confirmed letter of credit, the seller is guaranteed payment and may be paid immediately by his bank.

10. Once the buyer's bank receives the documents it notifies the buyer who then reviews them. If they are in order the buyer signs off, makes payment to the bank, and receives the documents which enable the holder to take possession of the shipment.

11. The buyer's bank initiates payment to the seller's bank, which pays the seller.

The transfer of funds from the buyer to the bank, from the buyer's bank to the seller's bank, and from the seller's bank to the seller may be handled at the same time as the exchange of documents, or under terms agreed upon in advance.

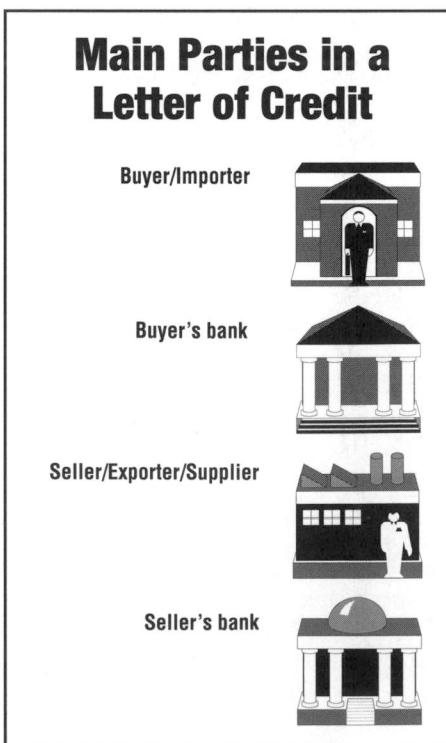

Main Parties in a Letter of Credit

Buyer/Importer

Buyer's bank

Seller/Exporter/Supplier

Seller's bank

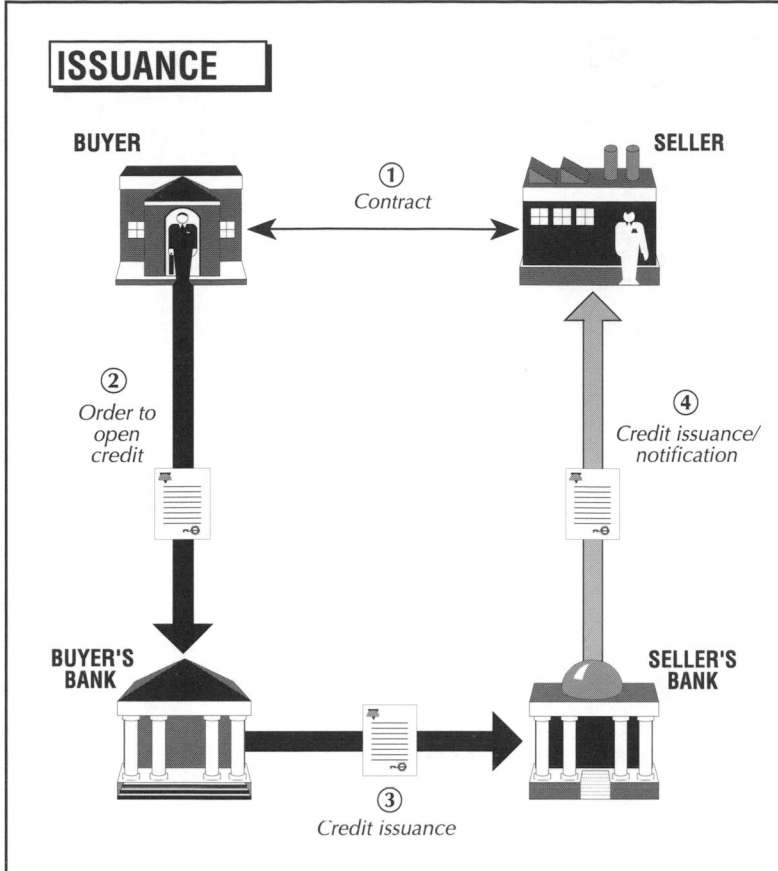

Issuance

Issuance of a letter of credit

① Buyer and seller agree on a purchase contract.

② Buyer applies for and opens a letter of credit with his (issuing) bank.

③ Buyer's bank issues the letter of credit, forwarding it to advising (seller's) bank.

④ Seller's bank notifies seller of the letter of credit.

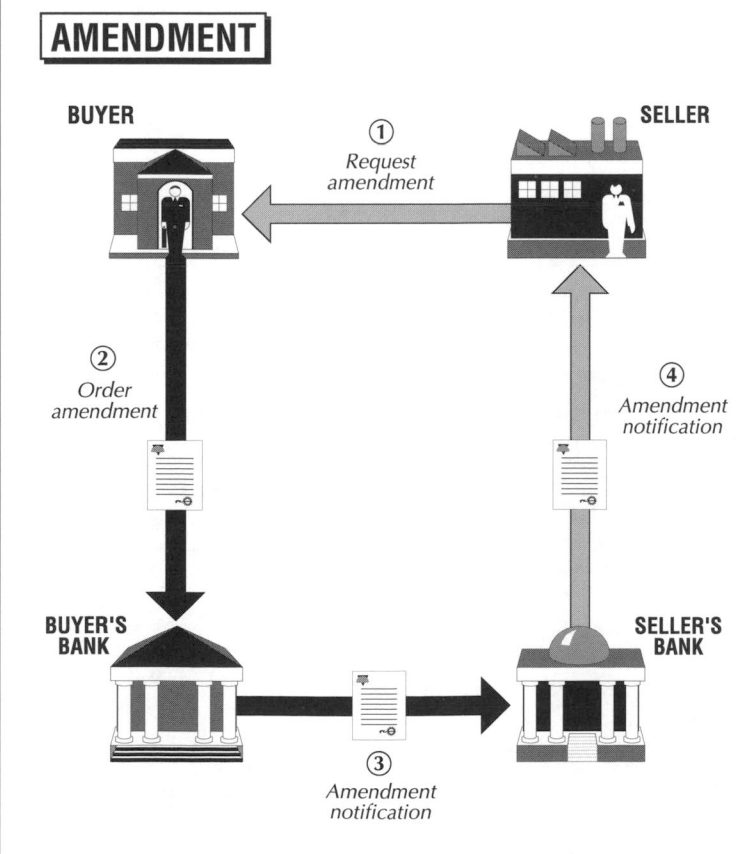

Amendment

Amendment of a letter of credit

① Seller requests a modification or amendment of any questionable terms in the letter of credit. If the terms are agreed upon...

② Buyer issues order to his (buyer's) bank to make an amendment to the terms of the letter of credit.

③ Buyer's bank notifies seller's bank of amendment.

④ Seller's bank notifies seller of amendment.

Utilization

Utilization of a letter of credit (Irrevocable, confirmed)

Once the buyer opens a letter of credit at his bank and the seller receives notification of credit issuance, the following steps take place:

① Seller ships goods to the buyer.

② Seller forwards all documents (as stipulated in the letter of credit) to his bank. Once the documents are reviewed and accepted, buyer's bank pays seller for the goods.

③ Seller's bank forwards documents to buyer's bank. Once the documents are reviewed and accepted, buyer's bank pays seller's bank.

④ Buyer's bank forwards documents to buyer. Buyer makes payment or his account is debited.

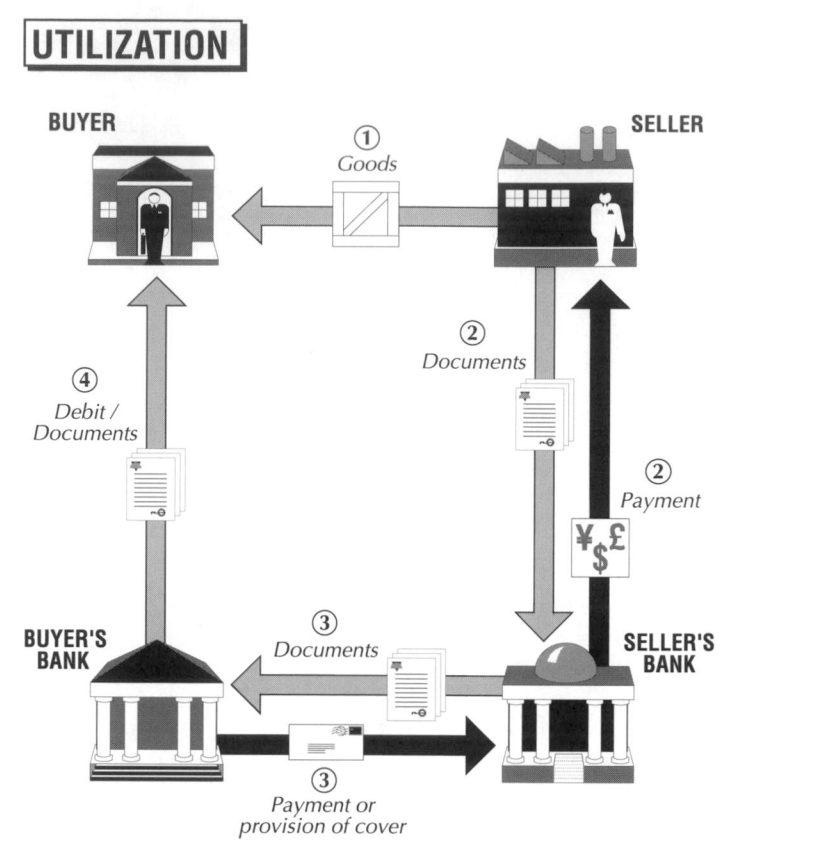

UTILIZATION

As many as half of all letters of credit are amended or renegotiated entirely.

Common Problems in Letter of Credit Transactions

Most problems with letter of credit transactions have to do with the ability of the seller to fulfill obligations the buyer establishes in the original letter of credit. The seller may find the terms of the credit difficult or impossible to fulfill and either tries to fulfill them and fails, or asks the buyer for an amendment to the letter of credit. Since most letters of credit are irrevocable, amendments to the original letter of credit can only be made after further negotiations and agreement between the buyer and the seller. Sellers may have one or more of the following problems:

- Shipment schedule stipulated in the letter of credit cannot be met.
- Stipulations concerning freight costs are deemed unacceptable.
- Price is insufficient due to changes in exchange rates.
- Quantity of product ordered is not the expected amount.
- Description of product to be shipped is either insufficient or too detailed.
- Documents stipulated in the letter of credit are difficult or impossible to obtain.

Even when sellers accept the terms of a letter of credit, problems often arise at the stage in which banks review, or negotiate, the documents provided by the seller against the requirements specified in the letter of credit. If the documents are found not to be in accord with those specified in the letter of credit, the bank's commitment to pay is invalidated. In some cases the seller can correct the documents and present them within the time specified in the letter of credit. Or the advising bank may ask the issuing bank for authorization to accept the documents despite the discrepancies found.

Limits on Legal Obligations of Banks

It is important to note once again that banks deal in documents and not in goods. Only the wording of the credit is binding on the bank. Banks are not responsible for verifying the authenticity of the documents, nor for the quality or quantity of the goods being shipped. As long as the documents comply with the terms specified in the letter of credit, banks may accept them and initiate the payment process as stipulated in the letter of credit. Banks are free from liability for delays in sending messages caused by another party, consequences of Acts of God, or the acts of third parties whom they have instructed to carry out transactions.

Types of Letters of Credit

Basic Letters of Credit

There are two basic forms of letters of credit: the Revocable Credit and the Irrevocable Credit. There are also two types of Irrevocable Credit: the Irrevocable Credit Not Confirmed and the Irrevocable Confirmed Credit. Each type of credit has advantages and disadvantages for the buyer and for the seller. Also note that the more the banks assume risk by guaranteeing payment, the more they will charge for providing the service.

Revocable Credit

Revocable credits may be modified or even canceled by the buyer without notice to the seller. As a result, they are generally unacceptable to the seller.

Irrevocable Credit

Irrevocable credits may not be modified or canceled by the buyer. The buyer's (issuing) bank must follow through with payment to the seller so long as the seller complies with the conditions listed in the credit. Changes in the credit must be approved by both the buyer and the seller. This is the most common form of credit used in international trade. There are two forms of irrevocable credits:

- **Unconfirmed credit (the irrevocable credit not confirmed by the advising bank)** In an unconfirmed credit the buyer's bank issuing the credit is the only party responsible for payment to the seller. The seller's bank is obliged to pay only after the payment from the buyer's bank is received. The seller's bank merely acts on behalf of the issuing bank and therefore incurs no risk.

- **Confirmed credit (the irrevocable, confirmed credit)** In a confirmed credit, the advising bank adds its guarantee to pay the seller to that of the buyer's (issuing) bank. If the buyer's bank fails to make payment, the seller's bank will pay. If a seller is unfamiliar with the buyer's bank issuing the letter of credit, an irrevocable, confirmed credit may be insisted upon. These credits may be used when trade is conducted in a high-risk area where there are fears of war or social, political, or financial instability. Confirmed credits may also be used by the seller to enlist the aid of a local bank to extend financing to help an order be filled. A confirmed credit costs more because the bank has added liability.

Special Letters of Credit (L/C)

The following is a brief description of some special letters of credit.

Back-to-Back Letter of Credit

This is a new credit opened on the basis of an already existing, nontransferable credit. It is used by traders (middlemen) to make payment to the ultimate supplier. A trader receives a letter of credit from the buyer and then opens another letter of credit in favor of the supplier. The first letter of credit is used as collateral for the second credit. The second credit makes price adjustments from which come the trader's profit.

Deferred Payment (Usance) Letter of Credit

In Deferred Payment Letters of Credit, the buyer accepts the documents and agrees to pay the issuing bank after a fixed period of time. This credit gives the buyer a grace period for payment.

Red Clause Letter of Credit

Red Clause Letters of Credit are used to provide the seller with some funds prior to shipment to finance production of the goods. The credit may be advanced in part or in full, and the buyer's bank finances the advance payment. The buyer, in essence, extends financing to the seller and incurs ultimate risk for all advanced credits.

Revolving Letter of Credit

With a Revolving Letter of Credit, the issuing bank commits to restore the credit back to the original amount once it has been used or drawn down. The credit also states the number of times it can be used and the period of validity. The credit can be cumulative, meaning sums can be added to the next installment, or non-cumulative, meaning partial amounts expire if not used in the time stated.

Standby Letter of Credit

This credit is basically a payment or performance guarantee used primarily in the United States. They are often called non-performing letters of credit because they are only used as a back-up payment if the collection on a primary payment method is past due. Standby letters of credit can be used, for example, to guarantee repayment of loans, fulfillment by subcontractors, and securing the payment for goods delivered by third parties. The beneficiary to a standby letter of credit can draw from it on demand, so the buyer assumes added risk.

Transferable Letter of Credit

This type of credit allows the seller to transfer all or part of the proceeds of the original letter of credit to a second beneficiary, usually the ultimate supplier of the goods. This is a common financing tactic for middlemen and is used extensively in East Asia.

There are numerous special letters of credit designed to meet the needs of buyers, sellers, and intermediaries.

Opening a Letter of Credit (guidelines for the buyer)

A letter of credit should be simple, but specific.

Buyers:

be sure to stipulate all documents that are required for customs clearance and other regulatory requirements.

Level of Detail

The wording in a letter of credit should be simple, but specific. The more detailed an L/C is, the more likely the seller will reject it as too difficult to fulfill. At the same time, the buyer will wish to define in detail what is being paid for.

Although the L/C process is designed to ensure the satisfaction of all parties in the transaction, it cannot be considered a substitute for face-to-face agreements to do business in good faith. It should therefore contain only those stipulations required concerning the bank's involvement in the documentary process.

Type of Credit

L/Cs used in trade are usually either irrevocable, unconfirmed credits or irrevocable, confirmed credits. In choosing the type of L/C to open in favor of the seller, the buyer should take into consideration generally accepted payment processes in the seller's country, the value and demand for the goods to be shipped, and the reputation of the seller.

Documents

In specifying documents required of the seller, it is very important to stipulate those that are required for customs clearance and those that reflect the agreement reached between the buyer and the seller. Required documents usually include the bill of lading, a commercial and/or consular invoice, the bill of exchange, the certificate of origin, and the insurance document. Other documents required may be an inspection certificate, copies of a cable sent to the buyer with shipping information, a confirmation from the shipping company of the state of its ship, and a confirmation from the forwarder that the goods are accompanied by a certificate of origin. Prices should be stated in the currency of the L/C, and documents should be supplied in the language of the L/C.

Electronic Applications

It is becoming more and more common to apply for letters of credit electronically. Firms that open five or more letters of credit per month will find this to be a real time saver.

The process is rather simple. Your bank gives you a computer disk containing a software program. You open a new document (application), follow the prompts asking for information, and then send it to the bank via modem. You save courier costs and transit time. The program also saves you from having to reenter repetitive transaction data over and over again.

The Application

The following information should be included on an application form for opening an L/C:

① **Beneficiary** Always write the seller's company name and address completely and correctly. A simple mistake here may translate to inconsistent or improper documentation at the other end.

② **Amount** State the actual amount of the credit. You may state a maximum amount in a situation where actual count or quantity is in question. You also may use the words approximate, circa, or about to indicate an acceptable 10 percent plus or minus from the stated amount. If you use such wording you will need to be consistent and use it also in connection with the quantity.

③ **Validity Period** The exporter will require time to prepare the shipment as well as the necessary documents. Make sure that the validity and period for document presentation following shipment of the goods is sufficiently long.

④ **Beneficiary's Bank** Either name the seller's bank or leave blank to indicate that the issuing bank may freely select the correspondent bank.

⑤ **Type of Payment Availability** Sight drafts, time drafts, or deferred payment may be used, as previously agreed to by the seller and buyer.

⑥ **Desired Documents** The buyer specifies which documents are needed. Buyers can list, for example, a bill of lading, a commercial invoice, a certificate of origin, certificates of analysis, etc.

⑦ **Notify Address** This is the address to notify upon the imminent arrival of goods at the port or airport of destination. Notification can also be used for damage of goods in shipment. An agent representing the buyer may be used.

⑧ **Description of Goods** A short, precise description of the goods is given, along with quantity. Note the comments in #2 above concerning approximate amounts.

⑨ **Confirmation Order** Foreign beneficiaries may insist on confirming the credit with the bank in their country.

Sample Letter of Credit Application

Sender Argentine Trading Company Lavalle 1716, Piso 2 1048 Buenos Aires Argentina Our reference AB/02	**Instructions** **to open a Documentary Credit** Buenos Aires, 30th September 19.. Place / Date

Please open the following [X] irrevocable [ ] revocable documentary credit	**Argentine Bank Corporation** Documentary Credits P.O. Box 1040 Buenos Aires, Argentina

Beneficiary ① American Import-Export Co., Inc. 123 Main Street San Francisco, California USA	Beneficiary's bank (if known) ④ US Domestic Bank 525 Main Street San Francisco, CA 94105 USA
Amount ② US$1,250,000.--	
Date and place of expiry ③ 25th November 19.. in San Francisco	Please advise this bank [ ] by letter [X] by letter, cabling main details in advance [ ] by telex / telegram with full text of credit

Partial shipments	Transhipment	Terms of shipment (FOB, C & F, CIF)
[X] allowed [ ] not allowed	[ ] allowed [X] not allowed	CIF Buenos Aires

Despatch from / Taking in charge at	For transportation to	Latest date of shipment	Documents must be presented not later than
Oakland	Buenos Aires	10th Nov. 19..	③ 15 days after date of despatch

Beneficiary may dispose of the credit amount as follows [X] at sight upon presentation of documents ⑤ [ ] after ....days, calculated from date of	[ ] by a draft due .... drawn on [ ] you [ ] your correspondents which you / your correspondents will please accept

against surrender of the following documents ⑥
 	
[X] invoice   (....3....copies)
 	
Shipping document
[X] sea: bill of lading, to order, endorsed in blank
[ ] rail: dublicate waybill
[ ] air: air consignment note
[ ]
	[X] insurance policy, certificte (............... copies)
	covering the following risks:
	  "all risks" including war up to
	[ ] Additional documents final destination in
	              Argentina
	[X] Confirmation of the carrier that the
	    ship is not more than 15 years old
	[X] packing list (3 copies)

Notify address in bill of lading / goods addressed to ⑦ Argentine Trading Company Lavalle 1716, Piso 2 1048 Buenos Aires Argentina	Goods insured by [ ] us [X] seller

Goods ⑧
1,000 "Computers model 486 as per pro forma invoice
      no. 74/1853 dd 10th September 19.."
 	
     at US$1,250.00 per unit

Your correspondents to advise beneficiary [ ] adding their confirmation [X] without adding their confirmation ⑨ Payments to be debited to our...U.S. Dollars................account no 10-32679150

NB. The applicable text is marked by [X]

E 6801 N 1/2 3.81 5000

Argentine Trading Company

Signature _____

For mailing please see overleaf

Tips for Parties to a Letter of Credit

Seller

Buyer

Buyers and sellers can avoid most problems by understanding the process and adhering to a set of common sense rules.

Tips for Sellers

1. Before signing a contract, the seller should make inquiries about the buyer's creditworthiness and business practices. The seller's bank may be able to assist in this investigation.

2. The seller should confirm the good standing of the buyer's bank if the credit is unconfirmed.

3. For confirmed credit, it should be determined that the seller's local bank is willing to confirm credits from the buyer and the buyer's bank.

4. The seller should carefully review the L/C to make sure its conditions can be met: specified schedules of shipment, type of goods to be sent, packaging, and documentation. All aspects of the L/C must be in conformance with the terms agreed upon, including the seller's address, the amount to be paid, and the prescribed transport route.

5. The seller should ensure that the L/C is irrevocable.

6. The seller must comply with every detail of the L/C specifications; otherwise the security given by the credit is lost.

7. If conditions of the credit have to be modified, the seller should contact the buyer immediately so that the buyer can instruct the issuing bank to make the necessary amendments.

8. The seller should confirm with the insurance company that it can provide the coverage specified in the credit and that insurance charges in the L/C are correct. Typical insurance coverage is for CIF (cost, insurance, freight) often the value of the goods plus about 10 percent.

9. The seller must ensure that the details of goods being sent comply with the description in the L/C and that the description on the invoice matches that on the L/C.

10. The seller should be familiar with foreign exchange limitations in the buyer's country that could hinder payment procedures.

Tips for Buyers

1. Before opening a letter of credit, the buyer should reach agreement with the seller on all particulars of payment procedures, schedules of shipment, type of goods to be sent, and documents to be supplied by the supplier.

2. When choosing the type of L/C to be used, the buyer should take into account standard payment methods in the country of the seller.

3. When opening a letter of credit, the buyer should keep the details of the purchase short and concise.

4. The buyer should be prepared to amend or renegotiate terms of the L/C with the seller. This is a common procedure in international trade. With an irrevocable L/Cs, the most common type, amendments may be made only if all parties involved in the L/C agree.

5. The buyer can eliminate exchange risk involved with import credits in foreign currencies by purchasing foreign exchange on the forward markets.

6. The buyer should use a bank experienced in foreign trade as the L/C issuing bank.

7. The validation time stated on the L/C should give the seller ample time to produce the goods or to pull them out of stock.

8. The buyer should be aware that an L/C is not fail-safe. Banks are only responsible for the documents exchanged and not the goods shipped. Documents in conformity with L/C specifications cannot be rejected on grounds that the goods were not delivered as specified in the contract. The goods shipped may not in fact be the goods ordered and paid for.

9. Purchase contracts and other agreements pertaining to the sale between the buyer and seller are not the concern of the issuing bank. Only the terms of the L/C are binding on the bank.

10. Documents specified in the L/C should include those the buyer requires for customs clearance.

Glossary of Terms
Documents in International Trade

The following is a description of some of the documents used in the course of international trade. For the importer/buyer this serves as a checklist of documents to consider requiring of the seller/exporter in a letter of credit or documentary collections transaction.

bill of lading A document issued by a transportation company (such as a shipping line) to the shipper (consignor) that serves as a receipt for goods shipped and a contract for delivery. A bill of lading may also serve as a title document. A bill of lading, therefore, is both a receipt for merchandise shipped and a contract to deliver it as freight to the consignee.
The major types are:
straight (nonnegotiable) bill of lading Indicates that the shipper will deliver the goods to the consignee. The document itself does not give title to the goods. The consignee need only identify himself to claim the goods. A straight bill of lading is often used when the goods have been paid for in advance.
order (negotiable or "shippers order") bill of lading This is a title document which must be in the possession of the consignee (buyer/ importer) in order for him to take possession of the shipped goods. Because this bill of lading is negotiable, it is usually made out "to the order of" the consignor (seller/exporter).
air waybill A bill of lading issued for air shipment of goods, which is always made out in straight, non-negotiable form. It serves as a receipt for the shipper and needs to be made out to someone who can take possession of the goods upon arrival—without waiting for other documents to arrive.
overland/inland bill of lading Similar to an air waybill, except that it covers ground or water transport.
certificate of origin A document certifying the country of origin of the goods. Because a certificate of origin is often required by customs for entry, a buyer will often stipulate in a letter of credit that a certificate of origin is a required document.
The Certificate of Origin Form A is the official certificate of origin required for imports of products under the GSP (Generalized System of Preferences) and other tariff reduction programs.

certificate of manufacture A document in which the producer of goods certifies that production has been completed and that the goods are at the disposal of the buyer.
consular invoice An invoice prepared on a special form supplied by the consul of an importing country, in the language of the importing country, and certified by a consular official of the foreign country of origin.
dock receipt A document/receipt issued by an ocean carrier when the seller/exporter is not responsible for moving the goods to the final destination, but only to a dock in the exporting country. The document/receipt indicates that the goods were, in fact, delivered and received at the specified dock.
export license A document, issued by a government agency, giving authorization to export certain commodities to specified countries.
import license A document, issued by a government agency, giving authorization to import certain commodities.
inspection certificate An affidavit signed by the seller/exporter or an independent inspection firm (as required by the buyer/ importer), confirming that merchandise meets certain specifications.
insurance document A document certifying that goods are insured for shipment.
invoice/commercial invoice A document identifying the seller and buyer of goods or services, identifying items such as: invoice number, date, shipping date, mode of transport, delivery and payment terms, and a complete listing and description of the goods or services being sold including prices, discounts, and quantities. The commercial invoice is usually used by customs to determine the true cost of goods when assessing duty.
packing list A document listing the merchandise contained in a particular box, crate, or container, plus type, dimensions, and weight of the container.
phytosanitary (plant health) inspection certificate A document certifying that an export shipment has been inspected and is free from pests and plant diseases considered harmful by the importing country.
shipper's export declaration A form prepared by a shipper/exporter indicating the value, weight, destination, and other information about an export shipment.

The key document in most documentary transactions is the bill of lading, especially when it serves as the title document to the goods (negotiable bill of lading).

General Banking Terms

The following is a list of general banking terms used in international transactions.

advice The forwarding of a letter of credit or an amendment to a letter of credit to the seller, or beneficiary of the letter of credit, by the advising bank (seller's bank).

advising bank The bank (usually the seller's bank) receiving a letter of credit from the issuing bank (the buyer's bank) and handling the transaction from the seller's side. This includes validating the letter of credit, reviewing it for internal consistency, forwarding it to the seller, forwarding seller's documentation back to the issuing bank, and, in the case of a confirmed letter of credit, guaranteeing payment to the seller if documents are in order and the terms of the credit are met.

amendment A change in the terms and conditions of a letter of credit, usually to meet the needs of the seller. In the case of irrevocable letters of credit, amendments may only be made with the agreement of all parties to the transaction.

beneficiary The entity to which credits and payments are made, usually the seller/supplier.

bill of exchange A written order from one person to another to pay a specified sum of money to a designated person. *See* draft.

collecting bank (also called the presenting bank) In a documentary collection, the bank (usually the buyer's bank) that collects payment or a time draft from the buyer to be forwarded to the remitting bank (usually the seller's bank) in exchange for shipping and other documents which enable the buyer to take possession of the goods.

confirmed letter of credit A letter of credit containing a guarantee on the part of both the issuing and advising banks of payment to the seller so long as the seller's documentation is in order and terms of the credit are met.

discrepancy The noncompliance with the terms and conditions of a letter of credit. A discrepancy may be as small as a misspelling, an inconsistency in dates or amounts, or a missing document. Some discrepancies can easily be fixed; others may lead to the eventual invalidation of the letter of credit.

documentary collection A method of effecting payment for goods whereby the seller/exporter instructs the bank to collect a certain sum from the buyer/importer in exchange for the transfer of shipping and other documentation enabling the buyer/importer to take possession of the goods.

draft A financial/legal document where one individual (the drawer) instructs another individual (the drawee) to pay a certain amount of money to a named person, usually in payment for the transfer of goods or services. **Sight drafts** are payable when presented. **Time drafts** (also called **usance drafts**) are payable at a future fixed (specific) date or determinable (normally 30, 60, 90 days) date. Time drafts are used as a financing tool (as with documents against acceptance D/A terms) to give the buyer time to pay for a purchase.

drawee The buyer in a documentary collection.

forward foreign exchange An agreement to purchase foreign exchange (currency) at a future date at a predetermined rate of exchange. Forward foreign exchange contracts are often purchased by buyers of merchandise who wish to hedge against foreign exchange fluctuations between the time the contract is negotiated and the time payment is made.

irrevocable credit A letter of credit that cannot be revoked or amended without prior mutual consent of the seller, the buyer, and all intermediaries.

issuance The act of the issuing bank (buyer's bank) establishing a letter of credit based on the buyer's application.

issuing bank The buyer's bank which establishes a letter of credit in favor of the seller, or beneficiary.

letter of credit A document stating commitment on the part of a bank to place an agreed upon sum of money at the disposal of a seller on behalf of a buyer under precisely defined conditions.

negotiation In a letter of credit transaction, the examination of the seller's documentation by the (negotiating) bank to determine if it complies with the terms and conditions of the letter of credit.

remitter In a documentary collection, an alternate name given to the seller who forwards documents to the buyer through intermediary banks.

remitting bank In a documentary collection, a bank acting as an intermediary, forwarding the remitter's documents to and payments from the collecting bank.

revocable letter of credit A letter of credit which may be revoked or amended by the issuer (buyer) without prior notice to other parties in the letter of credit process. It is rarely used.

validity The time period for which a letter of credit is valid. After receiving notice of a letter of credit opened on their behalf, the seller/exporter must meet all the requirements of the letter of credit within the period of validity.

Glossary

Including Incoterms 1990

The following is a representative sampling of commonly used trade terms. For a comprehensive listing we recommend the *Dictionary of International Trade*, also by World Trade Press.

admiralty

(law/shipping) Any civil or criminal issue having to do with maritime law.

ad valorem

Literally: according to value.

(general) Any charge, tax, or duty that is applied as a percentage of value.

(customs/taxation) A tax calculated on the value of the property subject to the tax.

See also duty.

(shipping) A freight rate set at a certain percentage of the declared value of an article.

advice

(banking) The term "advice" connotes several types of forms used on the banking field. Generally speaking, an advice is a form of letter that relates or acknowledges a certain activity or result with regard to a customer's relations with a bank. Examples include credit advice, debit advice, advice of payment and advice of execution. In commercial transactions, information on a business transaction such as shipment of goods.

(banking/letters of credit) The forwarding of a letter of credit, or an amendment to a letter of credit to the seller, or beneficiary of the credit, by the advising bank (seller's bank).

See also issuance; letter of credit; amendment.

advising bank

(banking) The bank (also referred to as the seller's or exporter's bank) which receives a letter of credit or amendment to a letter of credit from the issuing bank (the buyer's bank) and forwards it to the beneficiary (seller/exporter) of the credit. *See also* letter of credit; issuing bank.

air waybill (airbill)

(shipping) A shipping document used by the airlines for air freight. It is a contract for carriage that includes carrier conditions of carriage including such items as limits of liability and claims procedures. The air waybill also contains shipping instructions to airlines, a description of the commodity and applicable transportation charges. Air waybills are used by many truckers as through documents for coordinated air/truck service.

Air waybills are not negotiable. The airline industry has adopted a standard formatted air waybill that accommodates both domestic and international traffic. The standard document was designed to enhance the application of modern computerized systems to air freight processing for both the carrier and the shipper. *See also* bill of lading; negotiable.

amendment

(law/general) An addition, deletion, or change in a legal document.

(banking/letters of credit) A change in the terms and conditions of a letter of credit (e.g., extension of the letter of credit's validity period, shipping deadline, etc.), usually to meet the needs of the seller. The seller requests an amendment of the buyer who, if he agrees, instructs his bank (the issuing bank) to issue the amendment. The issuing bank informs the seller's bank (the advising bank) who then notifies the seller of the amendment. In the case of irrevocable letters of credit, amendments may only be made with the agreement of all parties to the transaction. *See also* letter of credit.

antidumping duties

Duties assessed against a particular class of imports when the imports are being sold (that is dumped) at less than fair market value in the importing country.

ATA Carnet

(customs) ATA stands for the combined French and English words "Admission Temporair/Temporary Admission." An ATA Carnet is an international customs document which may be used for the temporary duty-free admission of certain goods into a country in lieu of the usual customs documents required. The carnet serves as a guarantee against the payment of customs duties which may become due on goods temporarily imported and not re-exported. Quota compliance may be required on certain types of merchandise. ATA textile carnets are subject to quota and visa requirements.

The ATA Convention of 1961 authorized the ATA Carnet to replace the ECS ("Echantillons Commerciaux/Commercial Samples") Carnet that was created by a 1956 convention sponsored by the Customs Cooperation Council.

ATA Carnets are issued by National Chambers of Commerce affiliated with the Paris-based International Chamber of Commerce (ICC). These associations guarantee the payment of duties to local customs authorities should goods imported under cover of a foreign-issued carnet not be re-exported.

beneficiary

(banking/letter of credit) The individual or company in whose favor a letter of credit is opened.

(insurance) The person or legal entity named to receive the proceeds or benefits of an insurance policy.

bill of exchange

(banking) An unconditional order in writing, signed by a person (drawer) such as a buyer, and addressed to another person (drawee), typically a bank, ordering the drawee to pay a stated sum of money to yet another person (payee), often a seller, on demand or at a fixed or determinable future time.

The most common versions of a bill of exchange are:

(a) A **draft**, wherein the drawer instructs the drawee to pay a certain amount to a named person, usually in payment for the transfer of goods or services. **Sight drafts** are payable when presented. **Time drafts** (also called usance drafts) are payable at a future fixed (specific) date or determinable (30, 60, 90 days etc.) date. Time drafts are used as a financing tool (as with Documents against Acceptance, D/A terms) to give the buyer time to pay for his purchase.

(b) A **promissory note**, wherein the issuer promises to pay a certain amount.

bill of lading

(shipping) A document issued by a carrier to a shipper, signed by the captain, agent, or owner of a vessel, furnishing written evidence regarding receipt of the goods (cargo), the conditions on which transportation is made (contract of carriage), and the engagement to deliver goods at the prescribed port of destination to the lawful holder of the bill of lading.

A bill of lading is, therefore, both a receipt for merchandise and a contract to deliver it as freight. There are a number of different types of bills of lading.

(a) A **straight bill of lading** indicates that the shipper will deliver the goods to the consignee. The document itself does not give title to the goods (non-negotiable). The consignee need only identify himself to claim the goods. A straight bill of lading is often used when payment for the goods has been made in advance.

(b) A **shipper's order bill of lading** is a title document to the goods, issued "to the order of" a party, usually the shipper, whose endorsement is required to effect its negotiation. Because it is negotiable, a shipper's order bill of lading can be bought, sold, or traded while goods are in transit and is commonly used for letter-of-credit transactions. The buyer usually needs the original or a copy as proof of ownership to take possession of the goods.

(c) An **air waybill** is a form of bill of lading used for the air transport of goods and is not negotiable. *See* air waybill for a fuller explanation.

(d) A **clean bill of lading** is a bill of lading where the carrier has noted that the merchandise has

ICC No. 460 INCOTERMS 1990, Copyright © 1990 by ICC Publishing S.A. All rights reserved. Reprinted with the permission of the International Chamber of Commerce through ICC Publishing, Inc., in New York.

been received in apparent good condition (no apparent damage, loss, etc.) and which does not bear such notations as "Shipper's Load and Count," etc.

(e) A **claused bill of lading** is a bill of lading which contains notations which specify deficient condition(s) of the goods and/or packaging.

bond

(finance) The obligation to answer for the debt of another person.

(insurance/customs) A contract between a principal and a surety (insurance company or agent) which is obtained to insure performance of an obligation (often imposed by law or regulation). Posting of a bond is commonly required by the customs authority of a country to guarantee payment of duties or performance of a procedural requirement.

bonded

(customs) Goods stored under supervision of customs until the import duties are paid or the goods are exported.

carnet

(customs) A customs document permitting the holder to carry or send merchandise temporarily into certain foreign countries (for display, demonstration, or similar purposes) without paying duties or posting bonds. *See also* ATA Carnet.

certificate of origin

(customs) A document attesting to the country of origin of goods. A certificate of origin is often required by the customs authorities of a country as part of the entry process. Such certificates are usually obtained through an official or quasi official organization in the country of origin such as a consular office or local chamber of commerce. A certificate of origin may be required even though the commercial invoice contains the information.

Certificate of Origin Form A. A document required by the customs authority of many developed countries to prove country of origin eligibility of merchandise under duty-free import programs such as the Generalized System of Preferences and the Caribbean Basin Initiative.

CIP—carriage and insurance paid to (... named place of destination)

(Incoterm) "Carriage and insurance paid to..." means that the seller has the same obligations as under CPT, but with the addition that the seller has to procure cargo insurance against the buyer's risk of loss of or damage to the goods during the carriage. The seller contracts for insurance and pays the insurance premium. The buyer should note that under the CIP term the seller is only required to obtain insurance on minimum coverage. The CIP term requires the seller to clear the goods for export. This term may be used for any mode of transport including multimodal transport.

CFR—cost and freight (... named port of destination)

(Incoterm) "Cost and Freight" means that the seller must pay the costs and freight necessary to bring the goods to the named port of destination but the risk of loss of or damage to the goods, as well as any additional costs due to events occurring after the time the goods have been delivered on board the vessel, is transferred from the seller to the buyer when the goods pass the ship's rail in the port of shipment. The CFR term requires the seller to clear the goods for export.

This term can only by used for sea and inland waterway transport. When the ship's rail serves no practical purpose, such as in the case of roll-on/roll-off or container traffic, the CPT term is more appropriate to use.

classification

(general) The categorization of merchandise.

(shipping) The assignment of a category to a specific cargo for the purpose of applying class rates, together with governing rules and regulations.

(customs) The categorization of merchandise according to the tariff schedule of a country. Classification affects the duty status of imported merchandise.

See also Harmonized System; valuation.

collecting bank

(banking) The bank that acts as agent for the seller and seller's bank in collecting payment or a time draft from the buyer to be forwarded to the remitting bank (usually the seller's bank).

commingling

(customs) The packing or mingling of various articles subject to different rates of duty in such a way that the quantity or value of each class of articles cannot readily be ascertained by customs without the physical segregation of the shipment or the contents of any package thereof. Commingled articles are generally subject to the highest rate of duty applicable to any part of the commingled lot, unless the consignee or his agent segregates the articles under customs supervision.

compound rate of duty

(customs) A combination of both a specific rate of duty and an ad valorem rate of duty. For example: 0.7 cents per pound plus 10 percent ad valorem. *See also* duty; ad valorem.

consular invoice

(customs) An invoice covering a shipment of goods certified (usually in triplicate) by the consul of the country for which the merchandise is destined. This invoice is used by customs officials of the country of entry to verify the value, quantity, and nature of the merchandise imported. *See also* invoice.

consular visa

An official endorsement by a consul of a country, sometimes required for certification of country of origin or compliance with export and import requirements.

CIF—cost, insurance, freight (... named port of destination)

(Incoterm) "Cost, Insurance, Freight" means that the seller has the same obligations as under CFR but with the addition that he has to procure marine insurance against the buyer's risk of loss of or damage to the goods during the carriage. The seller contracts for insurance and pays the insurance premium.

The buyer should note that under the CIF term the seller is only required to obtain insurance on minimum coverage. The CIF term requires the seller to clear the goods for export.

This term can only be used for sea and inland waterway transport. When the ship's rail serves no practical purpose such as in the case of roll-on/roll-off or container traffic, the CIP term is more appropriate to use.

countertrade

An umbrella term for several sorts of trade in which the seller is required to accept goods or other instruments or trade, in partial or whole payment for its products.

Countertrade transactions include barter, buyback or compensation, counterpurchase, offset requirements, swap, switch, or triangular trade, evidence or clearing accounts.

countervailing duties

Special import duties assessed to offset export manufacturing subsidies received by businesses in an exporting country.

country of origin

The country where merchandise was grown, mined, or manufactured.

CPT—carriage paid to (... named place of destination)

(Incoterm) "Carriage paid to..." means that the seller pays the freight for the carriage of the goods to the named destination. The risk of loss of or damage to the goods, as well as any additional costs due to events occurring after the time the goods have been delivered to the carrier, is transferred from the seller to the buyer when the goods have been delivered into the custody of the carrier. "Carrier" means any person who, in contract of carriage, undertakes to perform or to procure the performance of carriage, by rail, road, sea, air, inland waterway or by a combination of such modes. If subsequent carriers are used for the carriage to the agreed destination, the risk passes when the goods have been delivered to the first carrier. The CPT term requires the seller to clear the goods for export. This term may be used for any mode of transport including multimodal transport.

custom house

(customs) The government office where duties, tolls, or taxes placed on imports or exports are paid and vessels entered or cleared.

customs

(a) A government authority designated to regulate flow of goods to/from a country and to collect duties levied by a country on imports and exports. The term also applies to the procedures involved in such collection. (b) Taxes imposed by a government on the import or export of items. *See also* duty, tariff.

customs broker

(customs) An individual or firm licensed by the customs authority of a country to act for importers in handling the sequence of custom formalities and other details critical to the legal and speedy exporting and importing of goods.

customs classification

(customs) The particular category in a tariff nomenclature in which a product is classified for tariff purposes; or, the procedure for determining the appropriate tariff category in a country's nomenclature system used for the classification, coding and description of internationally traded goods. *See also* Harmonized System.

documents against acceptance (D/A)

See documentary collection.

documents against payment (D/P)

See documentary collection.

DAF—delivered at frontier (... named place)

(Incoterm) "Delivered at Frontier" means that the seller fulfils his obligation to deliver when the goods have been made available, cleared for export, at the named point and place at the frontier, but before the customs border of the adjoining country. The term "frontier" may be used for any frontier including that of the country of export. Therefore, it is of vital importance that the frontier in question be defined precisely by always naming the point and place in the term. The term is primarily intended to be used when goods are to be carried by rail or road, but it may be used for any mode of transport.

DDP—delivered duty paid (... named place of destination)

(Incoterm) "Delivered duty paid" means that the seller fulfils his obligation to deliver when the goods have been made available at the named place in the country of importation. The seller has to bear the risks and costs including duties, taxes and other charges of delivering the goods thereto, cleared for importation. While the EXW term represents the minimum obligation for the seller, DDP represents the maximum obligation.

This term should not be used if the seller is unable directly or indirectly to obtain the import licence. If the parties wish the buyer to clear the goods for importation and to pay the duty, the term DDU (delivered duty unpaid) should be used.

If the parties wish to exclude from the seller's obligations some of the costs payable upon importation of the goods (such as value added tax (VAT)), this should be made clear by adding words to this effect: "Delivered duty paid, VAT unpaid (... named place or destination)."

This term may be used irrespective of the mode of transport.

DDU—delivered duty unpaid (... named place of destination)

(Incoterm) "Delivered duty unpaid" means that the seller fulfils his obligation to deliver when the goods have been made available at the named place in the country of importation. The seller has to bear the costs and risks involved in bringing the goods thereto (excluding duties, taxes and other official charges payable upon importation as well as the costs and risks of carrying out customs formalities). The buyer has to pay any addi-

tional costs and to bear any risks caused by his failure to clear the goods for import in time.

If the parties wish the seller to carry out customs formalities and bear the costs and risks resulting therefrom, this has to be made clear by adding words to this effect.

If the parties wish to include in the seller's obligations some of the costs payable upon importation of the goods (such as value added tax (VAT)), this should be made clear by adding words to this effect: "Delivered duty unpaid, VAT paid (... named place or destination)." This term may be used irrespective of the mode of transport.

DEQ—delivered ex quay (duty paid) (... named port of destination)

(Incoterm) "Delivered Ex Quay (duty paid)" means that the seller fulfils his obligation to deliver when he has made the goods available to the buyer on the quay (wharf) at the named port of destination, cleared for importation. The seller has to bear all risks and costs including duties, taxes and other charges of delivering the goods thereto.

This term should not be used if the seller is unable directly or indirectly to obtain the import licence.

If the parties wish the buyer to clear the goods for importation and pay the duty the words "duty unpaid" should be used instead of "duty paid."

If the parties wish to exclude from the seller's obligations some of the costs payable upon importation of the goods (such as value added tax (VAT)), this should be made clear by adding words to this effect: "Delivered ex quay, VAT unpaid (... named port of destination)." This term can only be used for sea or inland waterway transport.

DES—delivered ex ship (... named port of destination)

(Incoterm) "Delivered Ex Ship" means that the seller fulfils his obligation to deliver when the goods have been made available to the buyer on board the ship uncleared for import at the named port of destination. The seller has to bear all the costs and risks involved in bringing the goods to the named port of destination. This term can only be used for sea or inland waterway transport.

demurrage

(shipping) (a) The detention of a freight car or ship by the shipper beyond time permitted (grace period) for loading or unloading, (b) The extra charges a shipper pays for detaining a freight car or ship beyond time permitted for loading or unloading. Used interchangeably with detention. Detention applies to equipment. Demurrage applies to cargo.

discrepancies

(banking/letters of credit) The non-compliance of documents with the terms and conditions of a letter of credit. Information (or missing information or missing documents/papers, etc.) in the documents submitted under a letter of credit, which: (1) is not consistent with its terms and conditions; (2) is inconsistent with other documents submitted; (3) does not meet the requirements of the Uniform

Customs and Practice for Documentary Credits (UCPDC), ICC brochure no. 500, 1993 revision. If the documents show discrepancies of any kind, the issuing bank is no longer obliged to pay and, in the case of a confirmed letter of credit, neither is the confirming bank (strict documentary compliance). *See also* letter of credit.

dock receipt

A document/receipt issued by an ocean carrier when the seller/exporter is not responsible for moving the goods to their final destination, but only to a dock in the exporting country. The document/receipt indicates that the goods were, in fact, delivered and received at the specified dock.

documentary collection

(banking) A method of effecting payment for goods whereby the seller/exporter ships goods to the buyer, but instructs his bank to collect a certain sum from the buyer/importer in exchange for the transfer of title, shipping and other documentation enabling the buyer/importer to take possession of the goods. The two types of documentary collection are:

(a) **Documents against Payment (D/P)** where the bank releases the documents to the buyer/importer only against a cash payment in a prescribed currency; and

(b) **Documents against Acceptance (D/A)** where the bank releases the documents to the buyer/importer against acceptance of a bill of exchange (draft) guaranteeing payment at a later date.

In documentary collections, banks act in a fiduciary capacity and make every effort to ensure that payment is received, but are liable only for the correct execution of the collection instructions, and do not make any commitment to pay the seller/exporter themselves.

Documentary collections are subject to the Uniform Rules of Collections, Brochure No. 322, revised 1978, of the International Chamber of Commerce (ICC) in Paris.

documentation

(general) All or any of the financial and commercial documents relating to a transaction.

Documents in an international trade transaction may include: commercial invoice, consular invoice, customs invoice, certificate of origin, bill of lading, inspection certificates, bills of exchange and others.

draft; draft bill of exchange

See bill of exchange.

drawback—refund of duties

The refund of all or part of customs duties, or domestic tax paid on imported merchandise which was subsequently either manufactured into a different article or reexported.

drawee

(banking) The individual or firm on whom a draft is drawn and who owes the indicated amount. In a documentary collection, the drawee is the buyer. *See also* drawer; bill of exchange.

drawer

(banking) The individual or firm that issues or signs a draft and thus stands to receive payment of the indicated amount from the drawee. In a documentary collection, the drawer is the seller. *See also* drawee; bill of exchange.

dumping

(customs) The sale of a commodity in a foreign market at less than fair value, usually considered to be a price lower than that at which it is sold within the exporting country or to third countries.

duty

(customs) A tax levied by a government on the import, export or consumption of goods. Usually a tax imposed on imports by the customs authority of a country. Duties are generally based on the value of the goods (ad valorem duties), some other factors such as weight or quantity (specific duties), or a combination of value and other factors (compound duties).

Duties are imposed for purposes of protecting domestic industries from more competitive foreign-made products and generating state revenue. Most countries employ a range of duties, allowing a large number of products to pass duty-free while imposing greater duties as the perceived risks rise. Although still prevalent, duties are being reduced and eliminated among certain trading partners with the creation of international agreements, such as GATT and regional free trade agreements. Duties are also known as "tariffs."

See also ad valorem; specific rate of duty; compound rate of duty.

export declaration

A document required by the customs authority of various countries for the export of goods. This form typically requires complete particulars on an individual export shipment.

export license

A document prepared by a government authority, granting the right to export a specified quantity of a commodity to a specified country. This document may be required in some countries for most or all exports and in other countries only under special circumstances.

EXW—ex works (... named place)

(Incoterm) "Ex works" means that the seller fulfills his obligation to deliver when he has made the goods available at his premises (i.e. works, factory, warehouse, etc.) to the buyer. In particular, he is not responsible for loading the goods on the vehicle provided by the buyer or for clearing the goods for export, unless otherwise agreed. The buyer bears all costs and risks involved in taking the goods from the seller's premises to the desired destination. This term thus represents the minimum obligation for the seller. This term should not be used when the buyer cannot carry out directly or indirectly the export formalities. In such circumstances, the FCA term should be used.

foreign trade zone (FTZ)

FTZs (or free zones, free ports, or bonded warehouses) are special commercial and industrial areas in or near ports of entry where foreign and domestic merchandise, including raw materials, components, and finished goods, may be brought in without being subject to payment of customs duties. Merchandise brought into these zones often may be stored, sold, exhibited, repacked, assembled, sorted, graded, cleaned, or otherwise manipulated prior to reexport or entry into the national customs territory.

FAS—free alongside ship (... named port of shipment)

(Incoterm) "Free Alongside Ship" means that the seller fulfills his obligation to deliver when the goods have been placed alongside the vessel on the quay or in lighters at the named port of shipment. This means that the buyer has to bear all costs and risks of loss of or damage to the goods from that moment. The FAS term requires the buyer to clear the goods for export. It should not be used when the buyer cannot carry out directly or indirectly the export formalities. This term can only be used for sea or inland waterway transport.

FCA—free carrier (... named place)

(Incoterm) "Free Carrier" means that the seller fulfills his obligation to deliver when he has handed over the goods, cleared for export, into the charge of the carrier named by the buyer at the named place or point. If no precise point is indicated by the buyer, the seller may choose within the place or range stipulated where the carrier shall take the goods into his charge. When, according to commercial practice, the seller's assistance is required in making the contract with the carrier (such as in rail or air transport) the seller may act at the buyer's risk and expense.

This term may be used for any mode of transport, including multimodal transport.

"Carrier" means any person who, in a contract of carriage, undertakes to perform or to procure the performance of carriage by rail, road, sea, air, inland waterway or by a combination of such modes. If the buyer instructs the seller to deliver the cargo to a person, e.g. a freight forwarder who is not a "carrier," the seller is deemed to have fulfilled his obligation to deliver the goods when they are in the custody of that person.

"Transport terminal" means a railway terminal, a freight station, a container terminal or yard, a multi-purpose cargo terminal or any similar receiving point.

"Container" includes any equipment used to unitise cargo, e.g. all types of containers and/or flats, whether ISO accepted or not, trailers, swap bodies, ro-ro equipment, igloos, and applies to all modes of transport.

FOB—free on board (... named port of shipment)

(Incoterm) "Free On Board" means that the seller fulfills his obligation to deliver when the goods have passed over the ship's rail at the named port of shipment. This means that the buyer has to bear all costs and risks of loss of or damage to the goods from that point. The FOB term requires the seller to clear the goods for export.

This term can only be used for sea or inland waterway transport. When the ship's rail serves no practical purpose, such as in the case of roll-on/roll-off or container traffic, the FCA term is more appropriate to use.

foreign exchange

(banking/foreign exchange) Current or liquid claims payable in foreign currency and in a foreign country (bank balances, checks, bills of exchange). Not to be confused with foreign bank notes and coin, which are not included in this definition. *See also* bank notes.

forward foreign exchange

(foreign exchange) An agreement to purchase foreign exchange (currency) at a future date at a predetermined rate of exchange. Forward foreign exchange contracts are often purchased by international buyers of goods who wish to hedge against foreign exchange fluctuations between the time the contract is negotiated and the time payment is to be made.

freight forwarder

(shipping) A person engaged in the business of assembling, collection, consolidating, shipping and distributing less-than-carload or less-than-truckload freight. Also, a person acting as agent in the trans-shipping of freight to or from foreign countries and the clearing of freight through customs, including full preparation of documents, arranging for shipping, warehousing, delivery and export clearance.

Harmonized System (HS)

A multipurpose international goods classification system designed to be used by manufacturers, transporters, exporters, importers, customs, statisticians, and others in classifying goods moving in international trade under a single commodity code. It divides products into more than 5,000 classifications.

import license

A document, issued by a government agency, giving authorization to import certain commodities.

in bond

A procedure by which an importer can move goods into or through a country before paying duties by posting a bond or other security.

Incoterms

A codification of international rules for the uniform interpretation of common contract clauses in export/import transactions. Developed and issued by the International Chamber of Commerce (ICC) in Paris. The version which is currently valid is publication no. 460 from 1990. The thirteen Incoterms 1990 are:
(1) Ex Works (EXW),
(2) Free Carrier (FCA),
(3) Free Alongside Ship (FAS),
(4) Free On Board FOB),
(5) Cost and Freight CFR),
(6) Cost, Insurance and Freight (CIF),
(7) Carriage Paid To (CPT),
(8) Carriage and Insurance Paid To (CIP),
(9) Delivered At Frontier (DAF),
(10) Delivered Ex Ship (DES),
(11) Delivered Ex Quay (DEQ),
(12) Delivered Duty Unpaid (DDU), and
(13) Delivered Duty Paid (DDP).
See specific listings for each individual Incoterm.

inspection certificate
An affidavit signed by the seller/exporter or an independent inspection firm (as required by the buyer/importer), confirming that merchandise meets certain specifications.

invoice
A document identifying the seller and buyer of goods or services, identifying numbers such as invoice number, date, shipping date, mode of transport, delivery and payment terms, and a complete listing and description of the goods or services being sold including prices, discounts and quantities.

issuance
(banking) The establishment of a letter of credit by the issuing bank (buyer's bank) based on the buyer's application and credit relationship with the bank. *See* letter of credit; advice; amendment.

issuing bank
(banking) The buyer's bank which establishes a letter of credit at the request of the buyer, in favor of the beneficiary (seller/exporter). Also called the buyer's bank or the opening bank. *See also* advising bank.

legal kilo
See legal weight.

legal weight
Total weight of the merchandise and its own packaging, exclusive of any exterior containers or packing materials.

letter of credit (L/C)
(banking) Formal term: Documentary credit or documentary letter of credit.

A letter of credit is a document issued by a bank stating its commitment to pay someone (supplier/exporter/seller) a stated amount of money on behalf of a buyer (importer) so long as the seller meets very specific terms and conditions. Letters of credit are more formally called documentary letters of credit because the banks handling the transaction deal in documents as opposed to goods.

The terms and conditions listed in the credit all involve presentation of specific documents within a stated period of time, hence the formal name—documentary credits.

The documents the buyer requires in the credit may vary, but at a minimum include an invoice and a bill of lading. Other documents the buyer may specify are certificate of origin, consular invoice, insurance certificate, inspection certificate and others.

Letters of credit are the most common method of making international payments, because the risks of the transaction are shared by both the buyer and the supplier.

Documentary letters of credit are subject to the Uniform Customs and Practice for Documentary Credits (UCPDC), Brochure No. 500, of the International Chamber of Commerce (ICC) in Paris.

Basic Letters of Credit
There are two basic forms of a letter of credit: the Revocable Credit and the Irrevocable Credit. There are also two types of irrevocable credit: the Irrevocable Credit not Confirmed, and the Irrevocable Confirmed Credit. Each type of credit has advantages and disadvantages for the buyer and for the seller. Also note that the more the banks assume risk by guaranteeing payment, the more they will charge for providing the service.

(a) **Revocable credit**—This credit can be changed or canceled by the buyer without prior notice to the supplier. Because it offers little security, revocable credits are generally unacceptable to the seller and are rarely used.

(b) **Irrevocable credit**—The irrevocable credit is one which the issuing bank commits itself irrevocably to honor, provided the beneficiary complies with all stipulated conditions. This credit cannot be changed or canceled without the consent of both the buyer and the seller. As a result, this type of credit is the most widely used in international trade. Irrevocable credits are more expensive because of the issuing bank's added liability in guaranteeing the credit. There are two types of irrevocable credits:

(1) **Irrevocable credit not confirmed (Unconfirmed credit)**—This means that the buyer's bank which issues the credit is the only party responsible for payment to the supplier, and the supplier's bank is obliged to pay the supplier only after receiving payment from the buyer's bank. The supplier's bank merely acts on behalf of the issuing bank and therefore incurs no risk.

(2) **Irrevocable, confirmed credit**—In a confirmed credit, the advising bank adds its guarantee to pay the supplier to that of the issuing bank. If the issuing bank fails to make payment, the advising bank will pay. If a supplier is unfamiliar with the buyer's bank which issues the letter of credit, he may insist on an irrevocable confirmed credit. These credits may be used when trade is conducted in a high risk area where there are fears of outbreak of war or social, political, or financial instability. Confirmed credits may also be used by the supplier to enlist the aid of a local bank to extend financing to enable him to fill the order. A confirmed credit costs more because the bank has added liability.

Special Letters of Credit
There are numerous special letters of credit designed to meet specific needs of buyers, suppliers, and intermediaries. Special letters of credit usually involve increased participation by banks, so financing and service charges are higher than those for basic letters of credit. The following is a brief description of some special letters of credit.

(a) **Standby letter of credit**—This credit is primarily a payment or performance guarantee. It is used primarily in the United States because U.S. banks are prevented by law from giving certain guarantees. Standby credits are often called nonperforming letters of credit because they are only used as a backup payment method if the collection on a primary payment method is past due.

Standby letters of credit can be used, for example, to guarantee the following types of payment and performance:
- repayment of loans,
- fulfillment by subcontractors,
- securing the payment for goods delivered by third parties.

The beneficiary to a standby letter of credit can draw from it on demand, so the buyer assumes added risk.

(b) **Revolving letter of credit**—This credit is a commitment on the part of the issuing bank to restore the credit to the original amount after it has been used or drawn down. The number of times it can be utilized and the period of validity is stated in the credit. The credit can be cumulative or noncumulative. Cumulative means that unutilized sums can be added to the next installment, whereas noncumulative means that partial amounts not utilized in time expire.

(c) **Deferred payment letter of credit**—In this credit the buyer takes delivery of the shipped goods by accepting the documents and agreeing to pay the bank after a fixed period of time. This credit gives the buyer a grace period for payment.

(d) **Red clause letter of credit**—This is used to provide the supplier with some funds prior to shipment to finance production of the goods. The credit may be advanced in part or in full, and the buyer's bank finances the advance payment. The buyer, in essence, extends financing to the seller and incurs ultimate risk for all advanced credits.

(e) **Transferable Letter of Credit**—This credit allows the supplier to transfer all or part of the proceeds of the letter of credit to a second beneficiary, usually the ultimate supplier of the goods. This is a common financing tactic for middlemen and is used extensively in the Far East.

(f) **Back-to-Back Letter of Credit**—This is a new credit opened on the basis of an already existing, nontransferable credit. It is used by traders to make payment to the ultimate supplier. A trader receives a letter of credit from the buyer and then opens another letter of credit in favor of the supplier. The first letter of credit is used as collateral for the second credit. The second credit makes price adjustments from which come the trader's profit.

liquidation
(customs) Final customs review, payment of duties, and approval of a shipment for import.

manifest
(shipping) A document giving the description of a ship's cargo or the contents of a car or truck.

Most Favored Nation (MFN)
A non-discriminatory trade policy commitment on the part of one country to extend to another country the lowest tariff rates it applies to any other country.

negotiable
Anything that can be sold or transferred to another for money or as payments of a debt. In international trade, usually refers to the transferability of a title document—such as a negotiable bill of lading.

negotiable bill of lading

(shipping) Bill of lading transferred by endorsement. There are three possibilities: (1) to XY & Co. or their order; (2) to the order of XY & Co.; and (3) to order, without the name of the party. In the latter case the bill remains to the order of the shipper until he endorses it.

These types of bills of lading are usually endorsed on the reverse. The opposite of a negotiable bill of lading is the straight bill of lading *See also* bill of lading.

negotiation

(banking) (a) The action by which a negotiable instrument is circulated (bought and sold) from one holder to another. (b) In letter of credit transactions, the examination of seller's documentation by the bank to determine if they comply with the terms and conditions of the letter of credit. *See also* letter of credit.

ocean bill of lading (B/L)

(shipping) A receipt for the cargo and a contract for transportation between a shipper and the ocean carrier. It may also be used as an instrument of ownership (negotiable bill of lading) which can be bought, sold, or traded while the goods are in transit. To be used in this manner, it must be a negotiable "Order" Bill-of-Lading.

(a) A **clean bill of lading** is issued when the shipment is received in good order. If damaged or a shortage is noted, a clean bill of lading will not be issued.

(b) An **on board bill of lading** certifies that the cargo has been placed aboard the named vessel and is signed by the master of the vessel or his representative. In letter of credit transactions, an on board bill of lading is usually necessary for the shipper to obtain payment from the bank. When all bills of lading are processed, a ship's manifest is prepared by the steamship line. This summarizes all cargo aboard the vessel by port of loading and discharge.

(c) An **inland bill of lading** (a waybill on rail or the "pro forma" bill of lading in trucking) is used to document the transportation of the goods between the port and the point of origin or destination. It should contain information such as marks, numbers, steamship line, and similar information to match with a dock receipt.
See also bill of lading.

packing list

(shipping) A document prepared by the shipper listing the kinds and quantities of merchandise in a particular shipment. A copy is usually sent to the consignee to assist in checking the shipment when received. Also referred to as a bill of parcels.

phytosanitary inspection certificate

A certificate, issued by a government authority to satisfy import regulations of a foreign country, indicating that an export shipment has been inspected and is free from harmful pests and plant diseases.

pro forma invoice

An invoice provided by a supplier prior to a sale or shipment of merchandise, informing the buyer of the kinds and quantities of goods to be sent, their value, and important specifications (weight, size, and similar characteristics). A pro forma invoice is used: (1) as a preliminary invoice together with a quotation; (2) for customs purposes in connection with shipments of samples, advertising material, etc.

quota(s)

(customs) A limitation on the quantity of goods that may be imported into a country from all countries or from specific countries during a set period of time.

(a) **Absolute quotas** permit a limited number of units of specified merchandise to be entered or withdrawn for consumption in a country during specified periods.

(b) **Tariff-rate quotas** permit a specified quantity of merchandise to be entered or withdrawn in a country at a reduced rate during a specified period.

remittance

(banking) Funds forwarded from one person to another as payment for bought items or services.

remitting bank

(banking) In a documentary collection, a bank which acts as an intermediary, forwarding the remitter's documents to, and payments from the collecting bank. *See also* documentary collection.

sight draft

(banking) A financial instrument payable upon presentation or demand. A bill of exchange may be made payable, for example, at sight or after sight, which means it is payable upon presentation or demand, or within a particular period after demand is made. *See also* bill of exchange.

tariff

(general) A comprehensive list or "schedule" of merchandise with applicable rates to be paid or charged for each listed article.

(shipping) A schedule of shipping rates charged, together with governing rules and regulations. A tariff sets forth a contract of carriage for the shipper, the consignee, and the carrier. Individual carriers also publish their own tariffs covering special services.

(customs) A schedule of duties or taxes assessed by a government on goods as they enter (or leave) a country. Tariffs may be imposed to protect domestic industries from imported goods and/or to generate revenue. Types include ad valorem, specific, variable, or compound.
See also duty.

Uruguay Round

(GATT) The eighth round of multilateral trade negotiations concerning the General Agreement on Tariffs and Trade (GATT). The Uruguay Round (so named because meetings began in Punta del Este, Uruguay in 1987) concluded in December, 1993 after seven years of talks with 117 member nations. The major goals of the Uruguay Round were to reduce barriers to trade in goods; to strengthen the role of GATT and improve the multilateral trading system; to increase the responsiveness of GATT to the evolving international economic environment; to encourage cooperation in strengthening the inter-relationship between trade and other economic policies affecting growth and development; and the establishment of a multilateral framework of principles and rules for trade in services, including the elaboration of possible disciplines for individual service sectors.

validity

(banking) The time period for which a letter of credit is valid. After receiving notice of a letter of credit opened in his behalf, the seller/exporter/beneficiary must meet all the requirements of the letter of credit within the period of validity.

valuation

(general) The fixing of value to anything. Synonymous with "appraising."

(customs) The appraisal of the worth of imported goods by customs officials for the purpose of determining the amount of duty payable in the importing country.

The GATT Customs Valuation Code obligates governments that sign it to use the "transaction value" of imported goods—or the price actually paid or payable for them—as the principal basis for valuing the goods for customs purposes.

value-added tax (VAT)

(taxation) An indirect tax on consumption that is assessed on the increased value of goods at each discrete point in the chain of production and distribution, from the raw material stage to final consumption. The tax on processors or merchants is levied on the amount by which they increase the value of items they purchase and resell.

waybill

(shipping) A document prepared by a transportation line at the point of a shipment, showing the point or origin, destination, route, consignor, consignee, description of shipment and amount charged for the transportation service, and forwarded with the shipment, or direct by mail, to the agent at the transfer point or waybill destination. *See also* bill of lading; air waybill; ocean bill of lading.

Algeria

Democratic and Popular Republic of Algeria

Economy

Overview

Algeria offers a low cost labor force, ready access to inexpensive energy resources, and proximity to European markets. However, the transition from a socialist to a market economy has been slow, largely because petroleum revenues have enabled it to delay painful reforms in an effort to avoid political unrest. Further, fundamentalist Islamic terrorist attacks against secular elements and foreigners have hampered development and investment. As an indication of the current situation, several foreign governments have issued advisories recommending against visiting this North African nation because of security concerns. Many Western companies continue operations, but with reduced staff and limited commitments.

Trade

Algeria's principal trading partners include France, Italy, the US, the Netherlands, and Germany, with its largest partner, France, representing nearly 20 percent of all trade. Algeria derives about half of its imports of manufactured goods—such as in telecommunications, computer, mining, and water resource equipment and building materials—from Europe, where dominance in certain sectors, including pharmaceuticals and agricultural machinery, approaches monopolistic proportions. After many years of exercising tight controls over imports, Algeria has dramatically eased restrictions in all but a few areas as it moves toward a market economy. Sale of medicines, as well as certain grains and other foodstuffs, is still regulated to ensure equitable nationwide distribution. Algeria is also trying hard to diversify its exports into products unrelated to oil and gas.

Sectors

Agriculture Agriculture employs nearly one-quarter of the work force and contributes about 13 percent of GDP. Major constraints include limited infrastructure, an undereducated work force, and shortages of necessary materials. Despite efforts to improve productivity, these limitations serve to make Algeria one of the world's largest agricultural import markets.

Industry Industry accounts for nearly 50 percent of Algeria's GDP, while employing about 13 percent of its work force. Production of hydrocarbons accounts for 25 percent of Algeria's GDP (and 97 percent of its exports), and a modernization campaign is expected to boost hydrocarbon exports by nearly one-third. Other industries include food processing and textiles.

Services Although accounting for about 40 percent of GDP and employing nearly 60 percent of the work force, the services sector, which revolves around low-level, local distribution, is poorly developed.

Trends

Algeria's future depends on the success of its efforts to diversify its economy. Its work force of 6.2 million people is less than one-quarter of its population of 27 million, indicating the scale of pending demand from young people who will be entering the work force in the future. Failure to diversify would limit the job growth needed to ease unemployment, currently at approximately 25 percent. Such conditions, in combination with continued terrorist activity and a climate of political unrest, could have a devastating effect on the country's stability and its potential for economic growth.

At a Glance

THE COUNTRY
Location Northern Africa, along the Mediterranean Sea, between Morocco and Tunisia.
Terrain Mostly high plateau and desert, some mountains, narrow discontinuous coastal plain.
Climate Arid to semi-arid, wet winters with hot dry summers.

THE PEOPLE
Population 27,900,000
Ethnic composition Mostly Europeans, with large populations of Arabs and Berbers, and smaller populations of Kabyles, Chaouias, and Mzabs.
Religious composition
Sunni Muslim 99%
Christian and Jewish............................... 1%
Languages spoken Arabic is the sole and official language, although there are pockets of French and Berber dialects spoken as well.
Education and literacy Education in Algeria largely continues to follow the pattern laid down during the French administration, but its scope has been greatly extended. Education is officially compulsory for children between six and 15. However, adult literacy stands at a mere 57.8%.
Labor force...6,200,000
By occupation: government 29.5%, agriculture 22%, construction and public works 16.2%, industry 13.6%, commerce and services 13.5%, transportation and commercial 5.2%.

COUNTRY FACTS
Political and legal Algeria is a socialist country, based on French and Islamic law.
Telephone Algeria offers excellent domestic and international services. International country code: [213].
Transportation Railroads are nationally owned. The system consists principally of a main east-west line linked with the railways of Tunisia and Morocco and of lines serving the mining regions of Bechar and the main port cities. Roads are adequate in some areas (Algiers) and relatively poor in others (mountainous). Algiers is the principal seaport. Extensive air services use 124 airports and airstrips.
Environment Vegetation is sparse and widely scattered. Animal life is varied; camels are abundant. Algeria's principal environmental problem is encroachment of the desert on the fertile northeast section of the country. Water shortages and pollution, endangered species, and plant endangerment are also concerns.
Media The Algerian Press Service has a monopoly over the distribution of news within Algeria. There are over 48 periodicals in print. There are 26 AM radio stations and 18 television stations operating in Algeria. There are over six million radios and 1.9 million television sets in use.
Health The Ministry of Health has overall responsibility for the health sector, although the Ministry of Defense runs some military hospitals. Free medical care is available through the Social Security System, which reimburses 80 percent of private consultations and prescription drugs. Most of the population has access to health care.

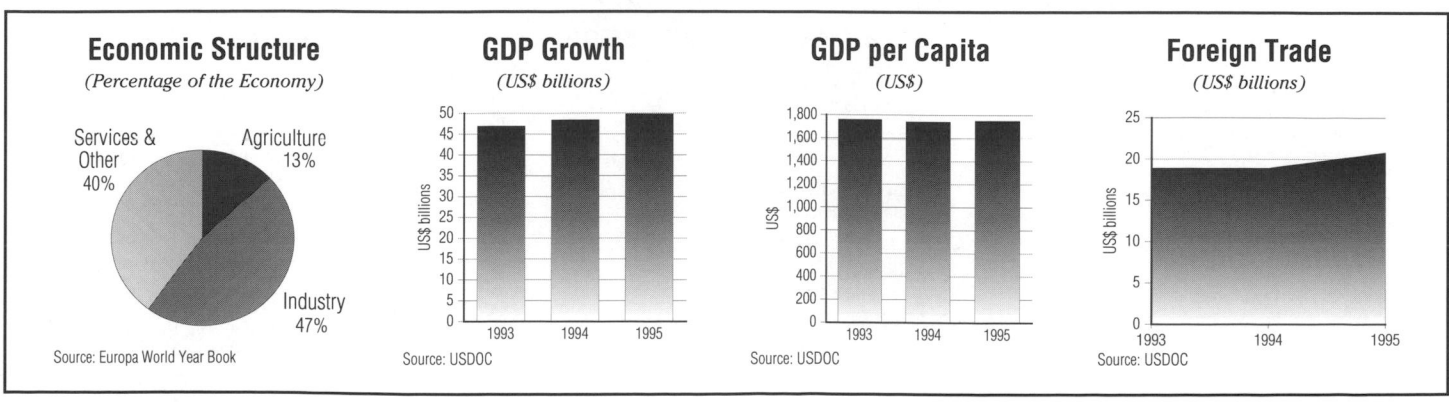

Economic Structure
(Percentage of the Economy)

Services & Other 40%
Agriculture 13%
Industry 47%

Source: Europa World Year Book

GDP Growth
(US$ billions)

US$ billions — 1993, 1994, 1995

Source: USDOC

GDP per Capita
(US$)

US$ — 1993, 1994, 1995

Source: USDOC

Foreign Trade
(US$ billions)

US$ billions — 1993, 1994, 1995

Source: USDOC

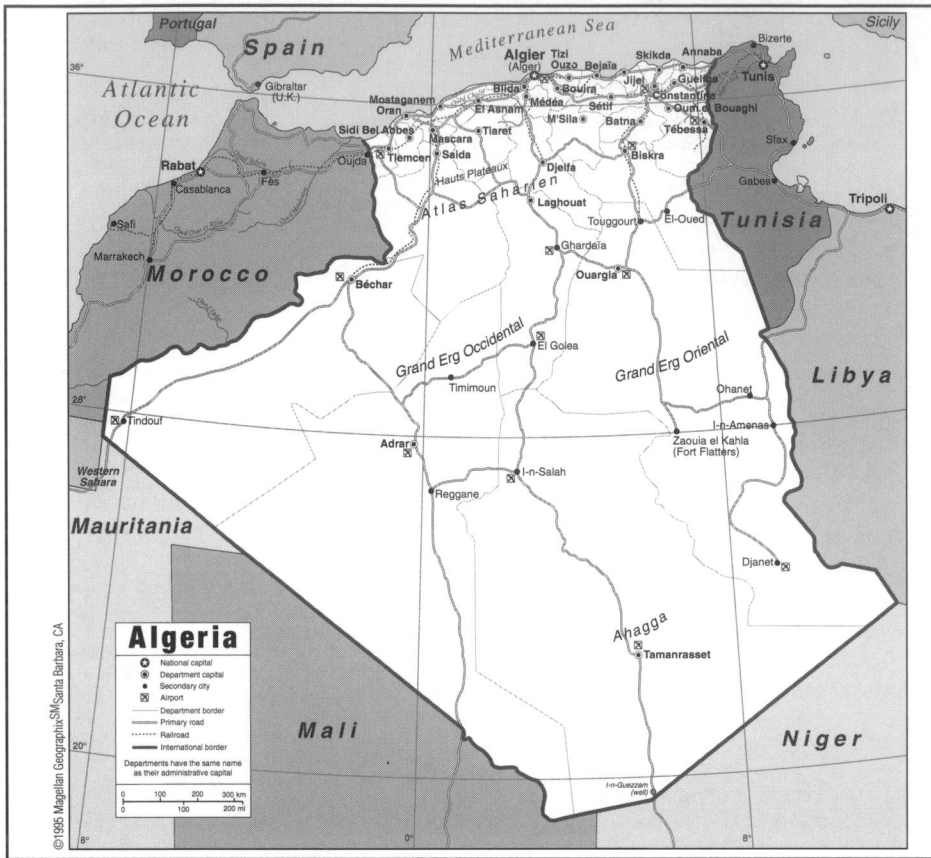

COMMUNICATIONS

Telephones Domestic and international telecommunication services are modern but highly overloaded. Public phones are abundant. Direct dialing international calls from the north is possible, but it will take a number of attempts. In the south, it could take over an hour for a local, internal long-distance, or international connection. Going through an operator at the post office or hotel is easier. All post offices have a telephone office.
Fax This service is available in some of the major hotels, but it is not widespread. Telegram and telex services are available but not efficient.
Post office The mail is slow, but it does eventually get where it is supposed to. Allow at least three weeks for letters to reach their destination. Post mail from a major city or allow an additional week or more for delivery. Post offices can be identified by a yellow-and-red PTT symbol. Service is open 8:00 am to 9:00 pm Saturday-Wednesday, Thursday, 8:00 am to 1:00 pm, and closed Friday.

BEST TRAVEL BOOKS

Morocco, Algeria & Tunisia: A Travel Survival Kit, Lonely Planet Publications. All the information travelers need. 486 pages.
North African Handbook. The ideal practical guide.
The Traveler's Guide to Middle Eastern and North African Customs and Manners. Elizabeth Devine & Nancy Braganti. How to converse, dine, tip, bargain, dress, make friends, and conduct business while in the Middle East and North Africa.
Africa on a Shoestring, Lonely Planet Publications. Filled with useful information.

USEFUL TELEPHONE NUMBERS

If you are calling from outside Algeria you will need to add the country code [213] and any other international dialing requirements from within your country.
- Central Bank 260-1044
- Media News Agency 277-7928
- Railways 277-1150
- Roadways 254-0600
- Chamber of Commerce 273-2881
- Ministry of Transport 274-0699
- National Airline 264-2428
- National Railways 261-1510
- Business Information 280-8649
- Business Information in Algiers 263-7280
Credit Card Information
Lost or stolen credit cards (call collect to the US, regardless of which country the card was issued in).
- Amex .... [1] (919) 333-3211
- Diner's Club .... [1] (303) 799-1504
- MasterCard .... [1] (314) 275-6690
- Visa .... [1] (410) 581-7931

NATIONAL TOURIST OFFICE

National Algerian du Tourisme
National Tourist Office
8 ave. de Pekin
Alger-Gare
Algiers
Tel: 260-5960
Tourism Office (ONAT)
5 blvd Ben Boulaid
Algiers
Tel: 274-3214
Tourism Office
Algiers Airport
Tel: 275-3367

Travelogue

WORKWEEK

Offices Saturday-Wednesday 9:00 am to 3:00 pm; and Thursday mornings.
Banks Saturday-Thursday 9:00 am to 3:00 pm; some banks are closed on Saturdays as well.
Retail Generally shops are open 8:30 am to noon and 2:30 pm to 6:00 pm. They often close all afternoon in summer months.
Business Businesses are closed Thursday afternoons and all day Friday.

HOLIDAYS

Holidays 1996
January 1 New Year's Day
February 21 Aid-El-Fit
April 29 Aid-El-Adha*
May 1 Labor Day
May 19 Awal Mouharrem*
May 28 Achoura*
June 19 Revolutionary Recovery Day
July 5 Independence Day
July 28 El Mouild Ennaboui
November 1 Revolution Day
* The dates for these holidays are tentative, as they are determined by lunar sightings. The definite dates may not be announced until shortly before the holiday itself.

VISA AND PASSPORT

Passports and visas are required for most visitors traveling to Algeria. Visas must be obtained before arriving in the country. Nationals from South Africa and Israel, and persons whose passports indicate travel in these countries, are not permitted entry into Algeria. The Algerian government requires all foreigners entering the country to exchange US$200 into local currency.

DEPARTURE FORMALITIES

Documentary proof of legal exchange of currency is required when departing Algeria. If you are buying a ticket to leave, you will have to exchange money specifically for this purpose, even if you have a receipt to prove you have exchanged other money legally. When exchanging money ask for an Attestation de Cession de Devises, which the bank will fill out in triplicate. Give one copy to the airline when you buy your ticket and keep the other to present when leaving.

IMMUNIZATION

Anyone entering Algeria from the south will need to provide an up-to-date international health certificate with a valid cholera stamp. Visitors arriving from West Africa will need to show a vaccination certificate for yellow fever.

TIPPING

Luggage porters receive about DA5 per bag. Taxi drivers: 10 percent; hotels and restaurants: 10 percent.

CRIME

Foreigners in Algeria are increasingly the targets of politically motivated violence. Murder of foreigners continues and one terrorist group has vowed to intensify these attacks. Those considering traveling to Algeria are strongly urged to contact their embassy in Algeria prior to departure for information regarding appropriate security precautions. Robbery, assault, carjacking, and kidnappings are also increasing. Theft, from car parts to hotel room contents to purse snatching, is common.

INFRASTRUCTURE

Algeria has well-developed air and train networks. Service in the north is more complete and efficient. There was talk at one time of an underground rail system but financial concerns stopped the project. Shared taxis *(louages)* are a transportation option in the north only. The French administration built a good road system, mainly for military purposes; since independence, however, the roads have deteriorated. Only a small number of the roads in Algeria are surfaced. Roads are being worked on and a newly surfaced road now links the Sahara oil fields with the coast. The Trans-Sahara highway is a road project underway. Algiers is the main port but others exist in Annaba, Arzew, Bejaia, Djidjelli, Ghazaouet, Mostaganem, Oran, and Skikda.

Foreign Trade

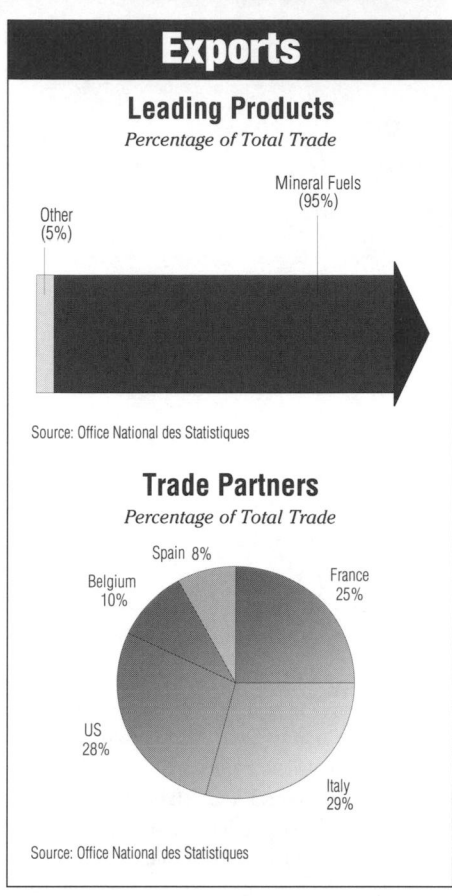

Imports

Leading Products
Percentage of Total Trade

Machinery & Transportation (27%)
Food Live Animals (23%)
Basic Manufacturing (21%)
Other (28%)

Source: Office National des Statistiques

Trade Partners
Percentage of Total Trade

France 23%
Other 36%
Italy 12%
US 12%
Germany 11%
Spain 6%

Source: Office National des Statistiques

Exports

Leading Products
Percentage of Total Trade

Mineral Fuels (95%)
Other (5%)

Source: Office National des Statistiques

Trade Partners
Percentage of Total Trade

Spain 8%
Belgium 10%
France 25%
US 28%
Italy 29%

Source: Office National des Statistiques

Opportunities

FOR IMPORTING TO ALGERIA
- agricultural, oil and gas, and construction machinery
- capital and consumer goods, food and beverages: corn, cereals, dairy, feedgrain, and vegetable oils
- computer products and pharmaceutical goods

FOR EXPORTING FROM ALGERIA
- inorganic chemicals
- natural gas, petroleum products, non-hydrocarbons

GROWTH SECTORS
- agriculture: cereals, milk, oilseeds
- housing
- hydrocarbons
- liquefied petroleum
- natural gas
- oil

Trade News

RULES AND REGULATIONS
- **Regulations** Regulations have been liberalized. Previously all imports valued at more than US$100,000 required approval of an ad hoc committee; related rules are now enforced by five commercial banks.
- **Import restrictions** Prohibited are: firearms, narcotics, and pork. To fairly distribute domestically, regulations exist for wheat, barley, semolina, flour, powdered milk, medicine, coffee, and sugar. In 1995, imports of 69 products manufactured domestically were suspended giving manufacturers a year to adjust to new exchange rates and price regimes before being subjected to international competition. Included: textiles, shoes, bathroom fixtures, and tractors.
- **Shipping ports** Some crude petroleum is exported through the Tunisian port of La Skhirra; petroleum and liquid gas through Arzew, Bejaia and Skikda.

Legal

Legal System
Algeria is a common law system based on Western legal tradition. The courts have recently proved their independence from political interests.

Intellectual Property Rights
Patents Patents, which are administered through the Institut Algerien de Normalisation et de Propriete Industrielle, are effective for 20 years from the filing date. Algerian patent protection law is based upon provisions of the Paris Convention, and adheres in all respects thereto.

Copyrights Copyright protection for literary, dramatic, musical, and visual works, as well as trademarks, are currently under review, and appear subject to change as of this printing. It is likely that protections will be increased from the present levels, to become more consistent with international standards.

Trademarks Trademark protection is available, although the administration of trademark registration and enforcement is currently under review.

Business Registration
All proposed foreign investments must be registered with the Small-and Medium-Sized Industry (PME) Ministry. The assistance of an Algerian lawyer in this matter, which is generally disposed of within one month, is highly advisable. Desirable elements in the document include financial self-sufficiency, relative independence from foreign inputs, extensive technology transfer, and additional employment contributed to the Algerian economy.

Contracts and Dispute Resolution
Algeria's Civil Procedure Code enables full access to international arbitration for companies doing business here, although necessity of such action is extremely rare. Agreements are generally less formal than in Western countries, and many contracts are concluded orally.

Legal Matters

LEGAL BRIEFS
- **Free trade zones** Algeria has stated its intention to establish one or more free trade zones in Algeria but has yet to announce where these will be located. Most likely one will be established on the international fairgrounds of Algiers.
- **International agreements** Third party agreements include the Convention of the International Center for Settlement of Investment Disputes, the New York Convention, and the Multilateral Investment Guarantee Agency (MIGA).
- **State of emergency** The government has broad powers under the state of emergency in effect since 1992.
- **Curfew** There is a late-night curfew in effect in the central region around Algiers.

LEGAL CONTACTS
Law Office of Mourad Hamdi
Immeuble Lafayette
7 rue Lafayette
16000 Algiers
Tel: 263-7052
Fax: 261-3127

Yamina Kebir
BP 298 Hydra
16035 Algiers
Tel: 256-2788

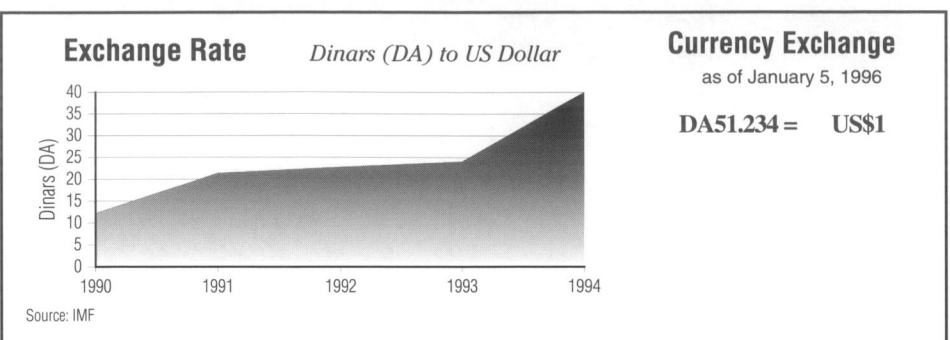

Exchange Rate *Dinars (DA) to US Dollar*

Dinars (DA)

Source: IMF

Currency Exchange
as of January 5, 1996

DA51.234 = US$1

Currency

The currency in use is the Algerian dinar (DA).

Foreign Exchange

The Bank of Algeria sets all exchange rates. It creates legislation and regulates currency, but delegates exchange power to five commercial banks and the Postal Administration.

Algeria recognizes different types of nonresident accounts, depending on the amount and type of currency, and the status of the nonresident. Accounts may be opened, however, with any authorized bank in Algeria, and any foreign currency may be used.

Capital Transfers

Residents are obliged to surrender capital assets (or the sales proceeds thereof) held or acquired outside Algeria. Capital transfers to any destination abroad are subject to individual license. Repatriation in respect of the sale or liquidation proceeds from invested foreign capital is guaranteed. Payments to countries can be made in any currency. All imports or exports with Israel are prohibited. All imports payments are subject to domiciliation at an authorized intermediary bank. Import payments may be made only through the domiciled bank. Banks may also require a deposit in dinars up to the full value of the imports before payments are effected. The Bank of Algeria must approve all payments for invisibles to all countries. When supporting documents are presented, however, approval may be granted by authorized banks or even by the Postal Administration.

Investment Incentives

As part of its effort to diversify and modernize the Algerian economy, the government is placing increasing emphasis on promoting foreign investment. The government does not distinguish between investments made by foreigners and Algerians. It also offers the following incentives; a three-year exemption from the value-added tax on goods and services acquired locally or imported; an exemption on property taxes; a two to five year exemption from corporate income taxes; the right to pay just three percent in customs duties for several products on which the duties range between 40 and 60 percent.

Investment Restrictions

As part of Algeria's efforts to develop an attractive investment promotion regime, foreign investors in Algeria are not subject to any performance requirements or production incentives.

Money Matters

BITS AND PIECES

- **Import divisions** Algeria divides imports into three categories: priority imports, restricted imports, and imports promoting production and investments. Each category carries certain requirements.
- **Salary transfer** Nonresidents working in Algeria can transfer a percentage of their net salaries abroad.
- **Investments** Nonresident investment is permitted without any restrictions, provided all laws and regulations are followed and prior declaration is made to Algerian authorities.
- **Import payments** Before effecting import payments, banks may require a deposit from the importer up to the full value of the imports. Anyone licensed under Algeria's Commercial Register can import goods without prior approval, provided the imports are not prohibited.
- **Exports** All proceeds from some exports, including crude and refined hydrocarbons, by-products from gas, and mineral products, must be surrendered. For other exports, a percentage of the earnings may be retained. These funds can then be used for imports or other business payments.
- **Invisibles** All proceeds from invisibles must be surrendered.
- **Restrictions** There are no restrictions on bank notes, checks, foreign bank notes, letters of credit, or coins (except gold coins), but nonresidents must declare these upon entering Algeria.

BANKS

Al-Baraka Bank of Algeria (ABA)
12 blvd. Col. Amirouche
Algiers
Tel: 274-5627

Banque Centrale d'Algerie
8 Boulevard Zirout Youcef
16000 Algiers
Tel: 264-7000

Banque d'Algerier
38 ave. Franklin Roosevelt
Algiers
Tel: 259-4200

Banque du Maghreb Arabe pour l'Investissement et le Commerce
21 blvd. des Freres Bouaddou Bir Mourad Rais
Algiers
Tel: 256-0446

Banque Exterieure d'Algerie (BEA)
11 blvd Colonel Amirouche
BP 471
Algiers
Tel: 261-1252

Banque Nationale d'Algerie
8 Boulevard Ernesto Che Guevara
Algiers

Banque Nationale de Paris (BNP) (France)
53 rue No 5
Le Paradou-Hydra
1600 Algiers
Tel: 259-1390
Fax: 259-3822
Telex: 66209

Beogradska Banks (Yugoslavia)
12 rue Ali Azil
Algiers
Tel: 263-5619
Fax: 279-6942

Credit Lyonnais (France)
2 blvd Mohamed Khemisti
Algiers
Tel: 263-3075
Fax: 263-3076
Telex: 56160

Societe Generale
53 rue Abri-Arezki
BP 294
Hydra, Algiers
Tel: 259-0293
Fax: 260-0487
Telex: 66569

TAXATION
- **Social security** All firms must pay a contribution to social security of seven percent of salary for each employee.
- **Export enterprises** Enterprises which export 100 percent of their production receive a 100 percent exemption on all taxes, and pay only the seven percent employer contribution to social security. Those exporting 50 percent of their production, receive a 50 percent exemption on all taxes and pay the same seven percent social security contribution. This sliding scale applies to all export enterprises.
- **Foreign technical and supervisory personnel changes** Prior to 1993, most foreign workers paid taxes of up to 70 percent of their salaries. As part of its investment promotion efforts, the government has now reduced the tax rate for foreign personnel working in most industrial sectors, whose monthly salaries are in excess of 80,000 dinars (approximately US$2,200), to a flat rate of 20 percent of salary.
- **Value-added tax** The government continues to impose a VAT on most goods and services.

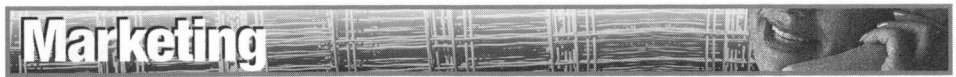

Marketing

Distribution

Successful marketing in Algeria requires creativity. Algeria has a recently privatized distribution system with outlets countrywide to supply its population of 27 million. Most distribution outlets are privately run, but the state still operates all wholesale distributorships for foodstuffs, industrial products, and pharmaceuticals and all retail outlets for hardware and foodstuffs. The primary import channels are large government and private companies that purchase by international tender. Foreign suppliers can use local agents or set up distributorships with approval from the Bank of Algeria's Council on Money and Credit. Policies on earnings repatriation, taxes, and exchange rates are still being adopted, impeding the entry of foreign agencies and distributorships. Franchising is in demand but inhibited because of a lack of hard currency for royalty payments. Foreign suppliers can establish liaison offices to promote products, but sales must be through distributorships. Algeria is actively seeking joint ventures and technology transfer arrangements. Seek tax and legal advice from a local professional before setting up an office.

Selling Techniques

Technical presentations, seminars, and trade fairs are well-attended. When consumer marketing becomes more open, product packaging, quality, and price will mean the difference in breaking into the long-established marketing monopolies. Use of a local representative may be essential in gaining a share of newly opening consumer markets.

Advertising

Direct advertising has little impact on consumers because most imports are brought in by large companies that purchase by tender without regard to brand name.

Customer Service and Support

All suppliers of capital goods must provide after-sales support, referred to as "technical assistance," for one year, usually free. Thereafter, after-sales support depends on the contract between the parties. No such requirements are imposed for consumer goods. Foreign liaison offices can provide services and customer support, but cannot directly import or distribute equipment or spare parts.

Business Culture

Greetings and Courtesies

Algerians enjoy good conversation, but being overly frank and direct is considered bad manners. Shake hands on meeting and departing. Kissing both cheeks or a light slap on the back is common among male and female nationals but rarely extended to foreigners. First impressions are the strongest in this part of the world.

Business Ethic and Framework

No Algerian will conduct business without two elements: refreshments in a congenial setting and endless, polite haggling. Algerians do not understand the desire to offer one's best price first; talks usually begin with inflated expectations which will be pared to an acceptable bone after hours of genteel whittling. Men and women commonly wear Western attire in urban areas. Visitors' dress should be conservatively cut Western clothing in all but sporting circumstances.

Women

Many women continue to dress in chador, traditional Muslim clothing which covers the entire body except for the eyes. In this strongly male-dominant society, gender roles are clearly and rigidly defined. This may seem repressive to visitors with Western values, but Algerians see these attitudes as accepting different roles for which each sex is obviously suited. Recent legislation has given women more rights.

Meetings

Appointments are necessary for meetings with government officials. Punctuality is not a major concern to most Algerian nationals, but being on time will make a good impression even if you may have to wait a while. Algerians prefer to approach business talk in a leisurely fashion; relaxed conversation over snacks and coffee is a customary opening. Tips: Sales approach should be low-key. Be courteous, firm, and politely persistent. Signals interpreted as temper or arrogance will stifle progress. Avoid negative opinions or criticism. Quote CIF prices in Algerian dinars.

Marketing in Algeria

MARKETING TIPS

- **Fast entry** Much importing into Algeria is through international tenders offered by the large importing companies.
- **Go high-tech** The Algerian government has far-reaching goals, supported by tax and financing incentives, for modernizing industries and diversifyng exports. These goals are opening Algerian markets particularly for capital goods, high-tech products, and services.
- **Government markets** Distribution of food, hardware, pharmaceuticals, and industrial products is still government-controlled. Goods are purchased through international tender.
- **Product sensitivity** Algeria's foreign trade has been centered in the Middle East and Europe, particularly France, for many decades. Products, packaging, and promotions should be designed with the traditions of this market in mind.
- **Label language** Product labels and instructions should be in French and Arabic.
- **Sales financing** Plan to offer adequate financing because hard currency and credit lines are difficult to obtain within the country.
- **Free trade agreements** Algeria, Tunisia, Morocco, Mauritania, and Libya agreed to form in 1989 the Arab Maghreb Union (known by its French acronym UMA).

RADIO & TELEVISION

Radiodiffusion Television Algerienne (RTA)
Immeuble RTA
21 blvd des Martyrs
Algiers
Tel: 260-2300

Cultural Cautions

DO'S

- Tip the taxi driver 10 percent.
- Leave a little food on your plate; the host will view this as a sign of his ability to more than adequately provide for his guests.

DON'TS

- In view of the current political unrest, travel here is not recommended. If visits are essential, take all possible security precautions. Stay away from the southern borders with Mali and Niger.
- Refusing coffee or tea is impolite.
- Avoid conversation about politics, industrial problems, members of the opposite sex, or the host's family, unless the host introduces the topic.
- Do not drink tap water; bottled water is widely available.
- Pointing with fingers at objects or people is generally considered impolite.
- Keep the soles of the feet or shoes out of sight; never point the soles at anyone.

CUSTOMS

- When dining with Muslims, never use the left hand in any way; it is considered the "toilet hand" and is never used in anyone's presence.
- Business gifts are a token of friendship and are appropriate after a deal is made or during a second visit. Souvenirs from your country, such as an item with historical significance or with a unique tie-in to your product, are welcome. Avoid bringing religious items and alcohol.
- Business cards should be exchanged at every opportunity. Use your title with a surname and treat your hosts similarly. Have cards printed in English-Arabic, French-Arabic, or English-French.
- Conversation can include inquiries about health and family, as well as increasing industrialization and agrarian reforms.

GOVERNMENT AGENCIES

Chamber of Commerce
CNC
Chambre Nationale de Commerce
Palais Consulaire
Place des Martyrs
Algiers
Tel: 257-4444
Fax: 262-9991

Direction du Port
Seaport Authority
BP 708
Algiers
Tel: 263-0162
Telex: 52295

Direction Generale dos Douanes
Customs Headquarters
19 rue du Docteur Saadane
Service des Douanes de l' Algerie
Algiers
Tel: 261-1616

Ministry of Agriculture
4 Rue des Quatre Canons
Algiers
Tel: 271-1712
Fax: 261-2542

Ministry of Commerce
Palais du Gouvernement
Algiers
Tel: 273-2340
Fax: 273-3091

Ministry of Equipment
Grand Séminaire
Kouba
Algiers
Tel: 268-9503

Ministry of Finance
7 Bd Zighout Youcef
Algiers
Tel: 273-2340
Fax: 273-5472

Ministry of Industry and Energy
Immeuble Le Colisee
Rue Ahmed Bey
Algiers
Tel: 259-2440
Fax: 260-4584

Ministry of Small and Medium Size Industry
Immeuble Le Colisee
Rue Ahmed Bey
Algiers
Tel: 259-2232
Fax: 259-2658

Ministry of Post and Telecommunications
2 Bd Krim Belkacem
Algiers
Tel: 273-1220
Fax: 273-1771

Ministry of Transport
119 Rue Didouche Mourad
Algiers
Tel: 274-7506
Fax: 265-6637

GENERAL TRADE ASSOCIATIONS

ACE
Association des Chefs d'Entreprise
Villa le Minaret
4 rue Isidore Pouget
Les Tagarins
Algiers
Tel: 263-8929
Fax: 263-9188

CAP
Confédération Algérienne du Patronat
Hotel Aurassi, Niveau C, Bureau 7
Algiers
Tel: 264-7020
Fax: 264-1041

CGOEA
Confédération Générale des Opérateurs Economiques Algériens
27 Rue Ferhat AEK
Staouéli
Tipaza, Algiers
Tel: 258-2851
Fax: 281-4353

Entreprise Nationale de Siderurgie
Steel and Metal Products
Complexe Siderurgique d'El-Hadjar
BP 342 El-Hadjar Annaba
Annaba 23000
Tel: (8) 831-999
Fax: (8) 838-957

Entreprise Nationale des Industries de l'Electromenager
Household Equipment Industry
BP 71
Poste Chikhi 15000
Tel: (3) 402-971
Fax: (3) 205-498

Entreprise Nationale des Plastiques et du Caoutchouc
Production and Marketing of Plastic and Rubber
Rue des Freres Moslim
BP 452
Sétif
Tel: (5) 906-499
Fax: (5) 900-565

Société Nationale des Industries Textiles
Industrial Textiles
4-6, rue Patrice Lumumba
Algiers
Tel: 263-4135
Telex: 252929

Société Nationale des Transports Routiers
Goods Transport by Road
27 rue des 3 Frères Bouadou, Birmandreis
Algiers
Tel: 256-2121
Telex: 252962

BUSINESS ORGANIZATIONS

Algiers Chamber of Commerce
6 Boulevard Anatole France
Algiers
Tel: 272-7044

Constantine Chamber of Commerce
6 rue du 26 Novembre 1974
BP 394 RP
Constantine
Tel: (4) 935-923, 935-959

National Chamber of Commerce
87 rue Didouche Mourad
Algiers
Tel: 266-8040

Oran Chamber of Commerce
8 boulevard de la Soumman
Oran
Tel: (6) 391-299, 330-127

DIRECTORIES AND YEARBOOKS

Algerian Export Import Directory
Available from the Embassy of Algeria
2118 Kalorama Road, NW
Washington, DC 20008
Tel: [1] (202) 265-2800
Fax: [1] (202) 667-2174

BUSINESS PERIODICALS

Middle East Business Weekly
MEED–Middle East Economic Digest
MEED House
21 John Street
London WC1N 2BP, UK
Tel: [44] (171) 404-5513

WEEKLIES/NEWSPAPERS

Al-Hadef
Zone Industrielle
BP 388
La Palma
Constantine
Tel: (4) 939-216

Algerie Presse Service (APS)
20 rue Zouieche
Kouba, Algiers
Tel: 271-2462

RADIO & TELEVISION

Radiodiffusion Television Algerienne (RTA)
Immeuble RTA
21 blvd des Martyrs
Algiers
Tel: 260-2300

FREIGHT FORWARDERS

Compagnie Algero-Libyenne de Transports Maritimes CAL-TRAM
21 blvd des Trois Fréres Bouaddou
Bir Mourad Rais
Algiers
Tel: 263-5807

Entreprise Nationale de Consignation et d'Activitiés Annexes aux Transports Maritimes ENCATM
2 rue de Beziers
Algiers
Tel: 264-2782

Entreprise National de Réparations Navales ERENAV
Algiers
Tel: 264-0010

BANKS

Banque Nationale de Paris (BNP) (France)
53 rue No 5
Le Paradou-Hydra
1600 Algiers
Tel: 259-1390
Fax: 259-3822
Telex: 66209

Beogradska Banks (Yugoslavia)
12 rue Ali Azil
Algiers
Tel: 263-5619
Fax: 279-6942

Credit Lyonnais (France)
2 blvd Mohamed Khemisti
Algiers
Tel: 263-3075
Fax: 263-3076
Telex: 56160

INTERNET ADDRESSES

Usenet group
soc.culture.algeria

Argentina
Argentine Republic

Overview

Since the implementation of its Convertibility Law —which fixes the peso at parity with the US dollar—in 1991, Argentina's economy has stabilized. Its GDP growth has been the highest in Latin America and among the highest in the world, while its inflation has fallen from nearly 5,000 percent in 1989 to less than four percent in 1994. However, these improvements mask major social consequences: the unemployment rate has risen higher than 12 percent, the result of restructuring that has improved operations but at the expense of Argentina's well-educated and relatively high-cost work force. Nevertheless, elections in May 1995 seemed to provide popular endorsement for the direction of the reforms.

Trade

Major exports include commodities such as fuels, fats and oils, food byproducts, cereals, oilseeds, and meats. Imports include machinery and electronic equipment, transportation equipment, chemicals, base metals, plastics, and textile products. Brazil is Argentina's main trading partner—accounting for roughly 15 percent of total trade—followed by the US, Germany, Italy, and Chile. The inauguration of Mercosur among Argentina, Brazil, Paraguay, and Uruguay is expected to change the trade picture substantially, focusing Argentina's trade more on this developing regional block.

Sectors

Agriculture Although known for its agriculture, Argentina derives only about 13 percent of its GDP directly from this sector, which provides direct employment for about 20 percent of the work force. Cereals, oilseeds, and beef are the major cash crops.

Industry Industry accounts for about 40 percent of both GDP and employment. Manufacturing appears to be rebounding: the automotive industry is showing renewed strength; the production of nontraditional, higher-value intermediate and end products has been strong and growing; and production of specialized intermediate petrochemical, steel, and aluminum products is up.

Services Nearly 50 percent of GDP comes from the services sector, which employs about 20 percent of the work force. Argentina has been attempting to upgrade its professional and technical services to make them more competitive, and the contribution of the service sector is growing in sophistication and importance.

Trends

For too long, Argentina lacked a development policy; but, in 1989, the Menem Administration put in place a framework based on deregulation, decentralization, privatization, open markets, and policies designed to achieve economic stability. Argentina's policies are designed to make the country's finances more transparent and provide greater confidence to both national and international investors. Other, current policies include reforming the social security system, bankruptcy and employment laws, workers' compensation, and the small business regime. Argentina will have to improve its production of higher value-added nontraditional exports to reverse its trade deficit, create jobs for its large number of unemployed, revamp its archaic provincial government structure, improve tax collection and revenue generation, and eliminate vestiges of special interest dealing and corruption. This it is attempting to do.

At a Glance

THE COUNTRY

Location South America, bordering Chile on the west and the Atlantic Ocean on the east.
Terrain Ranges from the Andes Mountains to long coastal regions; vast, grassy plains cover large parts of the landscape.
Climate Varies, but predominantly temperate.

THE PEOPLE

Population 32,000,000
Ethnic composition 97 percent of the country is of European descent, predominantly Spanish and Italian.
Religious composition
Roman Catholic 92%
Protestant 2%
Jewish.. 2%
Other.. 4%
Languages spoken Spanish is the official language, but English, Italian, German, and French are also widely spoken.
Education and literacy Seven years of schooling is compulsory and the adult literacy rate is 95 percent.
Labor force
Total...12,000,000
By occupation: industry and commerce 36%, services 20%, agriculture 19%, and transport and communications 6%.

COUNTRY FACTS

Political and legal A republic divided by constitution into executive, legislative, and judicial branches at both the national and provincial level. Each province also has its own constitution that roughly mirrors the structure of the national one. The President also selects his cabinet and appoints members of the Supreme Court with the consent of the Senate.
Telephone Over half the telephones in the country are located in or around Buenos Aires. Internal telegraph facilities and some international circuits to nearby countries are wholly government operated. International country code: [54]. City codes: Buenos Aires (1), Cordoba (51), Mendoza (61), Rosario (41).
Transportation A major airport with international service is in Buenos Aires.
Environment Principal environmental responsibilities are vested in the Ministry of Public Health and the Environment. 27 percent of urban residents and 83 percent of rural people do not have drinkable water. Current issues include pollution and loss of agricultural lands, and the lack of pure water for citizens.
Media A large number of Spanish-language daily newspapers are published in Buenos Aires; there are also more than 50 publishing houses, and three news agencies. Community newspapers are published in a number of foreign languages, including English, French, and German. There are 171 AM radio stations and 231 TV stations.
Health Healthcare compares favorably with other Latin American countries. Nutritional requirements are comfortably met. Employers are usually required to provide free medical and pharmaceutical care for workers; 71 percent of the population has access to health services. Life expectancy of males is 68 years; for females, 71 years.

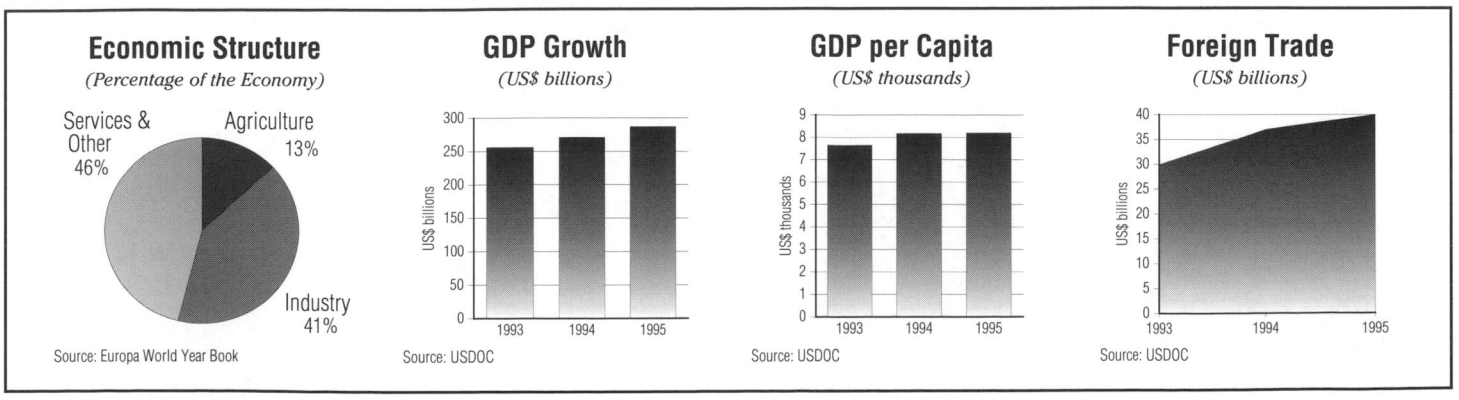

Economic Structure
(Percentage of the Economy)

Services & Other 46%
Agriculture 13%
Industry 41%

Source: Europa World Year Book

GDP Growth
(US$ billions)

Source: USDOC

GDP per Capita
(US$ thousands)

Source: USDOC

Foreign Trade
(US$ billions)

Source: USDOC

Argentina

⊛ National capital
⊙ Provincial capital
● Secondary city
········· Railroad
—— Primary road
—— International border
—— Province border

| 0 | 200 | 400 km |
| 0 | | 300 mi |

Falkland Islands (U. K.)
(Las Malvinas-
claimed by Argentina)

Foreign Trade

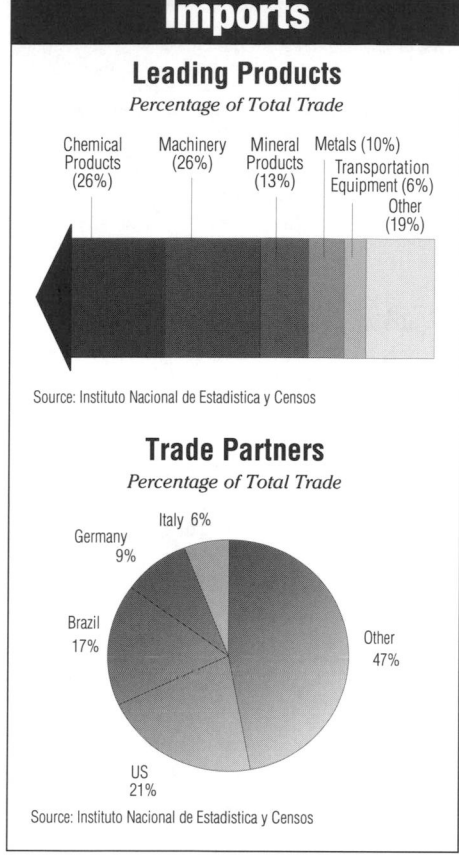

Imports

Leading Products
Percentage of Total Trade

Chemical Products (26%)
Machinery (26%)
Mineral Products (13%)
Metals (10%)
Transportation Equipment (6%)
Other (19%)

Source: Instituto Nacional de Estadistica y Censos

Trade Partners
Percentage of Total Trade

Italy 6%
Germany 9%
Brazil 17%
US 21%
Other 47%

Source: Instituto Nacional de Estadistica y Censos

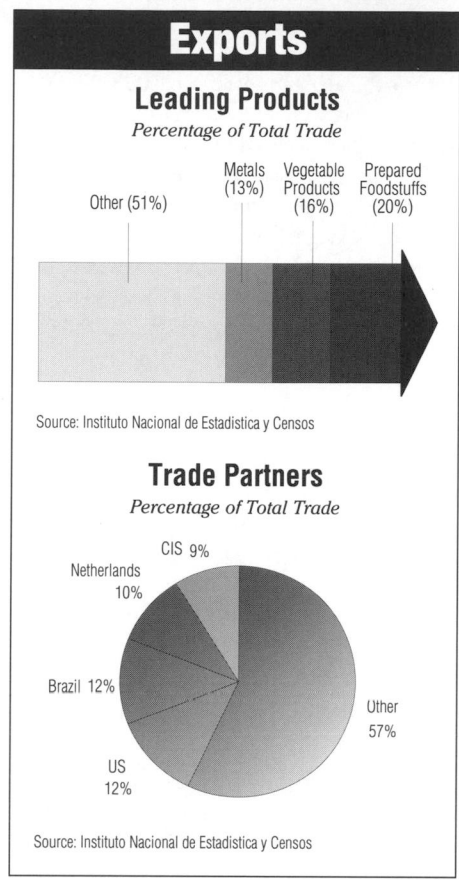

Exports

Leading Products
Percentage of Total Trade

Other (51%)
Metals (13%)
Vegetable Products (16%)
Prepared Foodstuffs (20%)

Source: Instituto Nacional de Estadistica y Censos

Trade Partners
Percentage of Total Trade

CIS 9%
Netherlands 10%
Brazil 12%
US 12%
Other 57%

Source: Instituto Nacional de Estadistica y Censos

Opportunities

FOR IMPORTING TO ARGENTINA
- agricultural machinery
- agricultural products
- chemicals
- computer products
- electric power equipment
- environmental protection goods and services
- food processing equipment
- fuels and lubricants
- housewares
- industrial machinery
- laboratory and scientific instruments
- medical instruments
- metals
- motor vehicles
- oil and gas field machinery
- sporting goods
- telecommunication products

FOR EXPORTING FROM ARGENTINA
- cereals
- corn
- fish
- fruit
- leather
- meat
- minerals (metal): silver, uranium, zinc
- minerals (nonmetal): argil, gypsum, salt
- oil
- oilseeds
- petroleum products
- processed foods
- vegetables
- wheat
- wood products
- wool

GROWTH SECTORS
- agricultural production and manufacturing
- automotive parts
- consumer goods
- franchising
- housing construction
- legal services
- mining
- petroleum and natural gas
- telecommunications
- tourism

GOVERNMENT PROCUREMENT
- computer products
- educational goods and services
- environmental protection goods and services
- health care goods and services
- highway construction goods and services
- railroad construction and expansion goods and services
- telecommunication products
- water and sanitation goods and services

Trade News

RULES AND REGULATIONS

- **Regulations** The office which administers customs rules, regulations, and tariffs is the Dirección Nacional de Impuestos, Ministerio de Economia (The National Office of Duties and Taxes, Ministry of Economy).

- **Import restrictions** One of the key free market reforms of the Menem Administration has been to open the Argentine economy to foreign producers. Only a few import restrictions now remain in effect, most notably for automobiles. Temporary quotas exist on paper, pulp, and a few other items. Other goods such as pharmaceuticals, foodstuffs, and defense materials require the approval of the related government department.

- **Import licenses** The government abolished the import licensing system in 1989.

- **Tariff rates** The Argentine tariff classification–Harmonized System (HS)–was implemented on January 1, 1992, and is aligned with the GATT Customs Classification Code adopted in 1979. Since 1989 the average tariff rate has been reduced from 29 percent to less than 10 percent. Tariffs are as low as 0 percent on capital goods and 0.5 percent on raw materials. In addition to customs duties, however, a 10 percent import statistics fee is applied to the CIF (cost + freight + insurance) value of all goods landed in Argentina.

- **Document requirements** Since 1989, the government has simplified document requirements substantially and opened the trade registry to potential exporters and importers.

- **Export subsidies** Argentina adheres to the GATT Subsidies Code and provides minimal supports to its exporters, such as reimbursement of indirect tax payments.

- **Trade agreements** Beginning on January 1, 1995, an agreement took effect to form a common market among Argentina, Brazil, Paraguay, and Uruguay. The Mercado Comun del Sur (Common Market for the South or MERCOSUR) Agreement brings together 200 million people in a US$600 billion annual market. The agreement offers reduced tariffs and other trade benefits to the participating countries and provides opportunities for additional countries, in particular, Bolivia and Chile, to join the Common Market at a later date.

PORT AUTHORITIES

Administración General de Puertos (Buenos Aires)
Avda Julio A. Roca 734/42
1067 Buenos Aires
Tel: (1) 34-5744
Telex: 21879

Administración General de Puertos (Bahia Blanca)
Calle 1
Muelle de Carga General
Puerto Bahia Blanca
Provincia de Buenos Aires
Tel: (91) 715666
Telex: 81849

Adminsitración General de Puertos (Santa Fé)
Duque 1 Cabacera
Santa Fé
Tel: (42) 41732
Telex: 41732, 48149

Capitania General del Puerto
Avda Julio 732, 2 °
1067 Buenos Aires
Tel: (1) 34-9784

FREIGHT FORWARDERS

Empresa Lineas Maritimas Argentinas, SA (ELMA)
Avda Corrientes 389
1327 Buenos Aires
Tel: (1) 312-9245
Telex: 2231
Fax: (1) 311-7954

Marketing

Overview

Argentina's markets are more open now to foreign imports and direct foreign investment than ever before, but a few drawbacks remain. Many industries are being fundamentally restructured while competition from new foreign and domestic entrants is increasing. Moreover, information as to which markets are open to what extent, and which remain closed is in a fluid state. Many distribution channels have yet to be developed. However, firms willing to brave this uncertainty and continued regulation will find opportunities in Argentina. Market research is readily obtainable through an embassy's commercial service, Argentine trade associations, or on contract from local marketing research firms set up to provide customized research. Companies new to this market should concentrate on urban centers, where more than 80 percent of Argentines live. Note that the recent slowdown in population growth has resulted in a dominant bulge of 20- to 40-year-old consumers who look for quality, variety, and price. Marketers should also be aware of the emerging awareness among Argentines of environmental concerns.

Distribution

Until recently, distribution was fragmented among numerous layers of small operators, but that situation is changing rapidly. Where there were once numerous small participants in the distribution chain and hundreds of small outlets, the system is now being consolidated and concentrated rapidly. This response comes from a desire to fill the needs of a fast-growing consumer constituency which demands cheaper goods of higher quality than the old system could provide. Another major factor is the pressure generated by the new, larger outlets such as supermarkets and discount chains. Consumer goods are usually sold through supermarkets; industrial products are offered primarily through trade fairs and direct calls on buyers. Franchises have experienced some success, but the franchisor's obligations must be clearly defined to avoid legal disputes in case of default or bankruptcy. Joint ventures may be formed by Argentine companies with branches of foreign companies and individuals residing in Argentina; however, this arrangement is not regarded as a legal entity.

Agents, Distributors, and Partners

Agents and Argentine importers have access to already established distribution channels; they know where the markets are, what they require, approaches, and what reasonable prices are. On the other hand, selling through an intermediary cuts into profits and reduces direct knowledge of the territory. Agents provide introductions, arrange for exhibitions at local fairs, and undertake general promotional activities. They aid in negotiations and perform support services. Importers and distributors purchase goods directly for resale, performing more functions and taking more risks than agents. Most distributors expect exclusive rights, even though they usually handle competing product lines. Foreign corporations often operate here through a separately incorporated subsidiary, limiting the foreign corporation's legal financial liability to the assets owned by that subsidiary.

Selling Techniques

Personal contact from a foreign company's representative is regarded as a mark of trust, and measurably increases the local distributor's status among local peers. Any factor which acts as a filter between the producer and the customer is negative. One important technique is to keep costs as low as possible, possibly through direct sales, in order to establish a toehold. Another is to make filling orders and after-sales service a priority.

Advertising

With deregulation and a stable currency, advertising is becoming more dynamic than in the recent past. Available media include radio and television, print, and other outlets such as billboards, posters, and signage. Television accounts for more than half of all advertising expenditures in the Buenos Aires market, where there are 469 stations. Radio is much less expensive and has wider coverage, with 163 AM and 10 shortwave stations. The leading product advertisements in Argentina are foods, household articles, and non-alcoholic beverages. Ads need to be highly persuasive—and somewhat but not too aggressive—to overcome the generally strong initial reluctance to try new products.

Service and Customer Support

Foreign sellers must approach exporting as a commitment, not as something to fall back on when a domestic market falters, and as such must make after-sales support a high priority. This approach can only yield positive results by developing a serious concern for product quality and continued assistance when problems develop. End-users may take as much as a year to win over, but if a company is persistent about providing high quality service they will come to believe in the sincerity of that company.

Marketing in Argentina

MARKETING TIPS

- **Be sophisticated** Argentines are not only well-educated—more than 95 percent are literate—but consider themselves to be highly sophisticated, especially in the major urban markets. They respond well to classy marketing campaigns that provide them with copious amounts of information.

- **Be environmentally aware** Although not at the top of the list of priorities, environmentalism is gaining in public awareness and concern; marketers who can offer environmentally sensitive products and incorporate an environmental message should have an advantage.

- **Quality** Argentines expect high quality, and this should be stressed in any selling campaign.

- **Variety** Argentines like to have a choice and can be convinced to try new products which come in many styles and models, or with multiple features.

- **Availability of consumer credit** For years there was effectively no consumer credit available in Argentina; the new economic boom in the 1990's has made credit available to Argentine consumers once again, although it continues to be restrictively high.

- **Be prepared to overcome conservative buying resistance** Argentines are conservative, suspicious consumers with a high degree of brand loyalty. They require considerable information and coaxing to try a new product.

AD AGENCIES

Ayer Vazquez S.A. De Publicidad
Av. Callao 1046, Piso 3
1023 Buenos Aires
Tel: (1) 815-4850
Fax: (1) 814-0494
Tlx: 23802

Leo Burnett Co., Inc. Sucursal Argentina
Carlos Pellegrini 1363, Piso 12
1011 Buenos Aires
Tel: (1) 394-5062/6, 394-5033
Fax: (1) 112049
Tlx: 24504

McCann-Erickson (Div. De Interpublic S.A. De Publicidad)
Tucuman 512
1049 Buenos Aires
Tel: (1) 322-4361, 322-5922
Fax: (1) 322-4257
Tlx: 24327

J. Walter Thompson Argentina S.A.
Alsina 465
1087 Buenos Aires
Tel: (1) 331-4550/9
Fax: (1) 331-3219
Tlx: 18823

Young & Rubicam Argentina
Paseo Colón 275, Piso 13
1063 Buenos Aires
Tel: (1) 331-8491/5
Fax: (1) 334-2739

MARKET RESEARCH FIRMS

A&C
Salta 1007
1074 Buenos Aires
Tel: (1) 27-9007, 304-6309/8213
Fax: (1) 27-8800

Commercial Network
Dorrego 2648,
Piso 10, "A"
1246 Buenos Aires
Tel: (1) 777-7121

Guillermo Bravo y Asociados
Av. de Mayo 1480 E.P.
Buenos Aires
Tel/Fax: (1) 381-7892/2540/5625

Jorge Fernandex Bussy y Asociados
Leandro N. Alem 1080
Piso 2, "C"
1001 Buenos Aires
Tel: (1) 311-7440

Business Culture

Greetings and Courtesies

Argentines are generally somewhat formal, although relations can involve considerable warmth and banter once a relationship has been established. The appropriate greeting consists of a firm handshake, firmness being taken as a sign of strength and confidence. Men should wait for a woman to initiate the handshake. Titles are generally used. At large gatherings, you usually introduce yourself to others, while at small and more formal gatherings, the host makes the introductions. Considerable social talk precedes any discussion of business. Be prepared to exchange business cards—yours should be in Spanish—at some point during an initial meeting. No formalities are associated with business card exchanges, however. Small gifts may be exchanged between those who are already acquainted, but wait until after the main business has been concluded to present a gift. Always bring a gift—flowers or chocolates—when invited to a home. When departing, say goodbye individually to everyone present.

Business Ethic & Framework

Argentine values emphasize the importance of personal relationships, and Argentines take time and effort to establish a personal relationship as a prerequisite to a business relationship. Individuality and candor are considered important, as are tact and diplomacy. Argentines are generally reserved and avoid calling attention to themselves. Conservative family and religious values are important guides to personal and professional behavior. Argentines also consider it a matter of pride to know the correct response, which can lead to misunderstandings when they do not in fact have a firm answer. They have a stronger work ethic than what is found in many other Latin American societies and are highly competitive. Nevertheless, they view work as a single component of rather than the central focus of life.

Decision Making

Although middle level managers may be responsible for implementing decisions, actual decisions are almost always made at a high level of authority. Argentines will want to know your standing within the hierarchy and will wish to match you with someone of similar rank, although only their senior people will actually be able to approve agreements. Nevertheless, it is important to cultivate personal relationships with employees at all levels, because the quality of these relationships may strongly influence the actual decision maker even when your immediate counterpart is not the one making the decision.

Women

Argentina is a traditional, male-dominated society, and women continue to occupy a secondary position in all aspects, including business. Despite this, Argentine women are generally considered to have more freedom and a greater opportunity than women in many other Latin American societies. Generally restricted to a position in the home, Argentine women nevertheless tend to be well-educated. More women are entering the work force, albeit often in relatively low level positions, and they are becoming more responsible for monetary contributions to the family budget. Foreign businesswomen should experience few difficulties in Argentina, although they may face some rather frank questioning regarding their personal situation, as well as public comments (although these are less aggressive here than elsewhere).

Meetings

Meetings should be scheduled well in advance—preferably with the help of an introduction from a mutual business or social acquaintance—if possible, when meeting for the first time. Meetings usually begin late, although you should generally arrive at the appointed time. Do not expect to conclude your business in a single meeting: business is a process, not an event, and time is usually not of the essence. Business may be conducted over meals or in other social situations, but this is still relatively uncommon in Argentina.

Business Attire

Argentines prefer and expect conservative, formal business attire—suits for men and suits or dresses for women. Understated British style is preferred over US, French, or Italian. Women should wear conservative hemlines and necklines, although a sense of style is appreciated. Accessories, jewelry, and makeup should be understated and of good quality: Argentines often judge people by their dress, paying special attention to the shoes, which should be expensive and well-maintained. Attire in more rural areas and at lower levels of authority is less precise, but remains an important indication of your seriousness, status, and sense of appropriateness.

Cultural Cautions

DO'S

- Listen carefully and respectfully to your Argentine counterpart—this is taken as a mark of your respect for the person's individuality and an indication of your goodwill and relational skills.
- Look the person with whom you are conversing directly in the eye—it is a sign of honesty and sincerity.
- Bring your own toilet paper with you—public bathrooms seldom have any.
- Prepare to be frank, yet tactful and patient, when talking with Argentinians.

DON'TS

- Do not stand with your hands on your hips—it indicates anger or confrontation.
- Do not yawn in public—it is considered rude.
- Do not speak loudly or use extravagant gestures.
- Do not make unfavorable comparisons between Argentina and your own country.

CUSTOMS

- The national beverage is *maté*, a leaf infusion similar to tea. An acquired taste, it is usually served in homes but not in restaurants and is high in caffeine.
- The midday meal is usually the main meal of the day; the evening meal seldom begins much before 9:30 or 10:00 pm.
- Argentines stand much closer in conversation than do members of many other cultures; when conversing with acquaintances, they also touch for emphasis. Do not back away, as it can indicate disagreement or disrespect.

OBSERVATIONS

- Argentine businespeople are generally sophisticated and well-informed regarding international business developments, standards, and techniques; they expect to be treated accordingly.
- Family and friends are the top priorities of Argentine businesspeople—foreign businesspeople should adapt themselves to this fact, being patient and showing interest in their counterpart's relationships.
- The practice of paying a *propina*—tip—or a *coima*—bribe—remains common, although it is less prominent than in the past; a tip implies additional encouragement, while a bribe is an illicit payment.
- The Argentine view of time is more like that of Europeans and North Americans than that of many other Latin Americans—the *mañana* attitude is uncommon in Argentina—although Argentines still have a much more flexible and relaxed view of time than do their northern counterparts. A sense of urgency will be viewed with mistrust or as rudeness, and people are expected to arrive at least 30 minutes late for social occasions unless *hora americano* ("American time") is specified.

NEGOTIATIONS

- An Argentine attorney retained by you may be more useful—and more acceptable to the other side—than an interpreter in helping work through the linguistic and technical details of negotiations.
- To avoid misunderstandings, be sure you know who has the authority to make a decision and the procedures and time frames that must be considered.
- Argentines present a united front during negotiations, deferring to the senior member.
- Allow negotiations to remain open-ended, so that confrontation can be avoided and talks can be allowed to fade away if agreement cannot be reached quickly and easily.

Legal System

Argentina is a Civil Code Country.

Intellectual Property Rights

Patents At present there is a gap in the law arising from the existence of two separate statutes which are contradictory. The first is the statute approving the GATT treaty, and the second is a statute recently passed by Congress. The issue will probably have to be resolved by the Supreme Court which, in previous cases, has held that treaties prevail over local laws. The problem arises over the patentability of pharmaceuticals. In any case, new industrial products, new methods or new applications of known methods are patentable. Patents are granted for five, 10, or 15 years depending on the merits of the invention.

Trademarks Ownership and exclusive use of trademarks is obtained by registration and may be challenged by third parties. The registration is valid for a 10-year period, and may be renewed for successive 10-year periods.

Copyrights Copyrights may be obtained for scientific, literary, and artistic works, films, paintings, maps, software, etc. Privilege pertains to the author until his death, and then to his heirs until 50 years after his death. In the case of corporations the protection extends only for 50 years.

Trade Secrets Trade secrets are not specifically protected by law, but can be protected through contract.

Business Registration

Companies formed abroad and having only occasional dealings in Argentina are governed by the laws of the place where they are legally constituted. They are authorized to do isolated transactions and to sue and be sued in Argentina. Foreign businesses operating in Argentina do not require any approval, except for areas in which local investments also require approval (i.e., broadcasting, mining, etc.). Companies participating as shareholders in Argentine companies must (i) register their articles of incorporation and by-laws in order to evidence their existence, capacity, and good standing in their place of incorporation, (ii) establish a domicile and representative in Argentina, and (iii) justify the business decision to establish the representation.

Contracts and Dispute Resolution

The form and purposes of contracts are governed, in principle, by the Civil Code. However, the Commercial Code and other statutes govern specific contracts. Most contracts do not require a specific formality and may be entered into orally. Form of contract is determined by the place of performance. Penalty clauses in contracts are enforceable. Contracts made in Argentina that violate laws of a foreign country are void. Contracts are shorter and not so detailed as in common law countries, as they always refer to Civil Code contractual rules.

Alternative dispute resolution is permitted and encouraged under Argentine law, but it is not yet mandatory. In principle the parties may agree to a foreign jurisdiction in almost any matter as long as it does not affect *ordre public* principles, and the governing law and forum chosen by the parties bear some reasonable connection with it. Lawsuits are expensive and take a long time; this is one of the reasons why the parties prefer arbitration. The most common arbitration tribunal in commercial matters is the Arbitration Tribunal of the Buenos Aires Stock Exchange. In international matters, it is common to refer cases to the International Chamber of Commerce. Argentina has ratified the Convention on the Recognition and Enforcement of Foreign Arbitral Awards.

Notaries

Notaries authenticate documentary instruments (which must be in the Spanish language), certify signatures, and attest to the capacity of the signatories. Notaries must hold a law degree but cannot practice law. Many contracts, in order to have effect, must be executed before a notary and preserved in his record. Foreign documents must be legalized before being included in the registry of a notary. Notarized documents are deemed public documents and bear a strong presumption of validity.

Labor

Hours of labor are limited to 48 per week. Workers have a constitutional right to associate freely and to bargain collectively. The right to strike is explicitly mentioned in the Argentine Constitution and is exercised freely. Annual paid vacation periods depend on the seniority of the worker, but minimum paid vacations are 14 days. Government grants social security benefits, which are mandatory, and contributions are payable by the employer and the worker. Minors under 14 years of age cannot be employed. In principal, terminations without cause can freely take place, but the worker is entitled to severance payments depending on his seniority. Compensation for labor-related accidents is limited by law.

Source: Negir, Teijeiro & Incera, Buenos Aires

Legal Matters

LEGAL BRIEFS

- **Remedies** In case of breach of contract Argentine law usually does not provide for specific performance, but for monetary damages.
- **Bankruptcy** In bankruptcy procedures, those creditors whose claims must be satisfied from assets located in Argentina will take priority over creditors whose claims must be paid exclusively out of assets located abroad, although the latter do have claim upon any assets of debtor remaining after all domestic claims are paid.
- **Federal and province systems** Argentina has both federal laws, which apply throughout the country, and province laws, which are enacted by each province and can vary significantly in their application.
- **Legal counsel** Argentine lawyers are not just litigators. Argentine businesses routinely solicit their lawyers' opinions and advice during all stages of a transaction, requiring their assistance in structuring, negotiating, and consummating deals.
- **International agreements** Argentina is a member of MERCOSUR (common market comprising Argentina, Brazil, Uruguay and Paraguay), is part of the GATT, has ratified the U.N. Convention on International Sale of Goods, and the Paris Convention for Protection of Industrial Property, among others.

LEGAL CONTACTS

Negri, Teijeiro & Incera
Avenida Corrientes 330
4th Floor
1378 Buenos Aires
Tel: (1) 111-304

Argentine Bar Federation
Av. de Mayo 651
Buenos Aires
Tel: (1) 331-8009

Baker & McKenzie
Piso 13
1001 Buenos Aires
Tel: (1) 311-5427

Brons & Salas
Marcelo T. de Alvear 624, Piso 1
1058 Buenos Aires
Tel: (1) 311-9271/9
Fax: (1) 311-7025

Estudio Beccar Varela
Cerrito 740, Piso 16
1309 Buenos Airews
Tel: (1) 372-5100
Fax: (1) 372-6619, 372-6809

Estudio E.P.
Reconquista 671, Piso 1
1003 Buenos Aires
Tel: (1) 311-7392
Fax: (1) 312-1670

Estudio Marval & O'Farrell
Carlos Pellegrini 885/887
1338 Buenos Aires
Tel: (1) 322-8336
Fax: (1) 322-4122

Estudio Munoz del Toro & Quevedo
25 de Mayo 294
1002 Buenos Aires
Tel: (1) 343-3903
Fax: (1) 334-1718

Estudio O'Farrell
Av. de Mayo 645/51
1084 Buenos Aires
Tel: (1) 342-5740
Fax: (1) 331-1659

Estudio Abeledo Gottheil
Maipú 757
1006 Buenos Aires
Tel: (1) 322-4848, 322-4869
Fax: (1) 322-4848

Estudio Allende Brea
Maipú 1300, Piso 10
1006 Buenos Aires
Tel: (1) 313-9191, 313-9292
Fax: (1) 312-5288, 313-9010

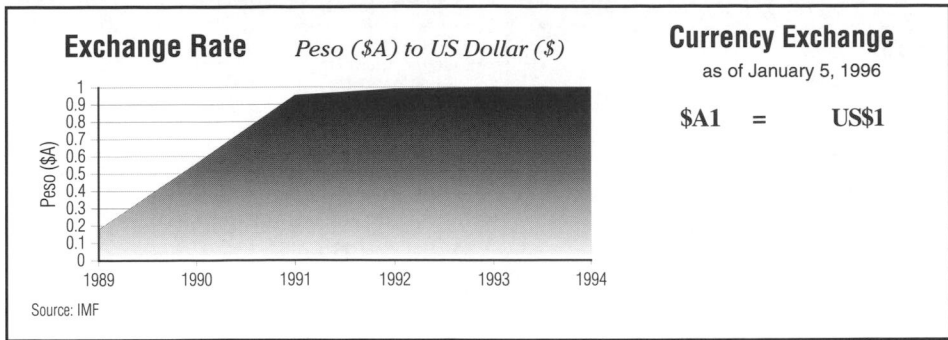

Exchange Rate *Peso ($A) to US Dollar ($)*

Source: IMF

Currency Exchange
as of January 5, 1996

$A1   =   US$1

Money Matters

BITS AND PIECES

- **National treatment** Foreign investors enjoy much the same treatment as do Argentines throughout the system, to the point that they occasionally suffer from the same inconsistent application of laws and regulations and alleged cases of favoritism that Argentine businesses face.
- **Expropriation** Expropriation has virtually disappeared as a policy option since the Argentine government began its far-reaching economic reform program in 1989.
- **Bank accounts** Authorized banks may open accounts in pesos or foreign exchange in the name of residents or nonresidents who have met certain identification requirements that are aimed at preventing money laundering.
- **Checking accounts** The use of checking accounts denominated in US dollars is allowed for domestic transactions.
- **Payments for invisibles** Neither payments for invisibles nor the export of domestic and foreign bank notes is restricted.
- **Loans** All private sector loans may be transacted in the free exchange market without restriction. Local enterprises based on foreign capital may borrow domestically with the same rights and on the same terms as local enterprises based on domestic capital.
- **Gold** Residents may hold gold coins and gold in any other form in Argentina or abroad. The importation of gold coins and gold-delivery bars is not restricted. Gold exports must be paid in convertible currencies.

Currency

The currency of Argentina is the peso, $A, which is divided into 100 centavos.

Foreign Exchange

The external value of the peso is pegged to the US dollar. Exchange rates of other currencies are based on the buying and selling rates for the US dollar in markets abroad. All exchange transactions are carried out through entities authorized expressly for this purpose with no restrictions on the purchase or sale of foreign exchange.

Capital Transfers

Both resident and nonresident holders of demand or time foreign currency accounts may use their credit balances freely in Argentina or abroad. The government does not maintain an explicit policy about Argentine investment abroad. Proceeds from invisible transactions need not be repatriated. There are no restrictions on the movement of capital in or out of Argentina, and there are no effective delays in transmitting funds associated with investment abroad.

Investment Incentives

The government maintains a system of incentives which can be enjoyed by both national and foreign firms. There are performance incentives monitored and approved by the Ministry of Economy, and directed primarily at auto manufacturers; and the Ministry also approves reductions in import duties when they can be directly related to an increase in exports. Foreign entities may establish and own businesses and engage in all forms of economic activity. Foreign investors may also participate in publicly financed research or subsidized research and development programs on a national treatment basis.

Mining activities Mining investment enjoys guaranteed tax stability for the coming 30 years; exemption from taxation on assets; deductions for prospecting and exploration expenses and environmental conservation expenses; accelerated depreciation; and exemptions from certain taxes and duties.

Investment Restrictions

There remain a few sectors where national treatment is denied. Foreigners cannot invest directly in nuclear power generation, and foreigners have been denied broadcasting licenses as well, although their participation is not expressly prohibited by law. Foreigners can only enter the fishing and insurance industries by purchasing control of existing firms; no new licenses are being issued to foreign enterprise.

BANKS

Banco Credito Argentino S.A.
Reconquista 40
1002 Buenos Aires
Tel: (1) 334-5241/4421/6561
Fax: (1) 334-8089

Banco Central de la Republica Argentina
Reconquista 266
1003 Buenos Aires
Tel: (1) 394-8411

Banco de Galicia y Buenos Aires
Tte. Gral. J. D. Peron 407
1038 Buenos Aires
Tel: (1) 394-7080/7291/8151
Fax: (1) 325-8886

Banco de la Ciudad de Buenos Aires
Sarmiento 611
1041 Buenos Aires
Tel: (1) 325-5881

Banco del Buen Ayre
Bartolome Mitre 899
1036 Buenos Aires
Tel: (1) 45-3446

Banco de la Provincia de Buenos Aires
San Martin 137
1004 Buenos Aires
Tel: (1) 331-2561/9/4011/3584

Banco Florencia, S.A.
Reconquista 353
1003 Buenos Aires
Tel: (1) 325-6541

Banco Rio de la Plata S.A.
Bme. Mitre 480
1036 Buenos Aires
Tel: (1) 331-0555/7551/8361

Bank of the Argentine Nation
Bartolome Mitre 326
1036 Buenos Aires
Tel: (1) 343-1011/1021
Fax: (1) 331-8745

FOREIGN INVESTMENT CONTACT

Fundación Invertir
Bartolomé Mitre 326
Edif. Banco Nación, Piso 1, Of. 109
1036 Buenos Aires
Tel: (1) 342-7723
Fax: (1) 342-7370

TAXATION

Taxation requires sophisticated knowledge of complex rules and regulations specific to each country. The information presented here is from the Ernst & Young Corporate Tax Guide and Directory, available from the Ernst & Young accounting office in your country, or from:

Henry Martin, Lisdero y Asociados
Maipú 942 - Ground Floor
1340 Buenos Aires
Argentina
Tel: (1) 313-7006
Fax: (1) 313-1528

At a Glance

Corporate Income Tax Rate (%)	30
Capital Gains Tax Rate (%)	30
Branch Tax Rate (%)	30
Withholding Tax (%)	
Dividends	0
Interest *	12
Royalties from Patents, Know-how, etc. *	24
Branch Remittance Tax	0
Net Operating Losses (Years)	
Carryback	0
Carryforward	5

*Final tax applicable only to payments to nonresidents

Business Travel

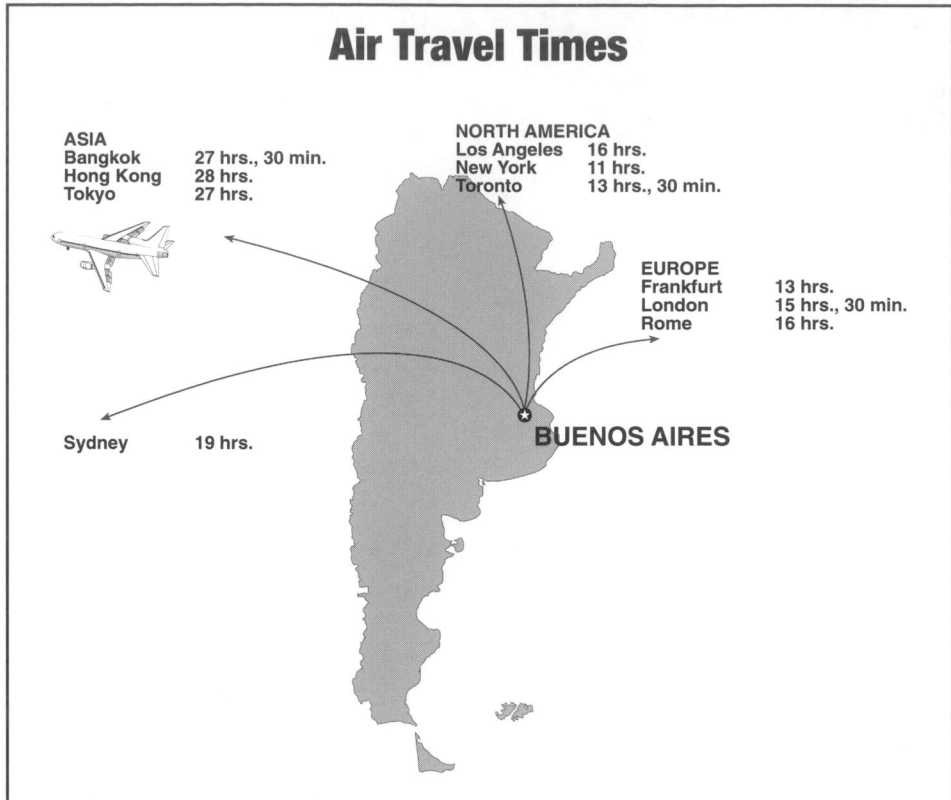

Air Travel Times

ASIA
Bangkok 27 hrs., 30 min.
Hong Kong 28 hrs.
Tokyo 27 hrs.

Sydney 19 hrs.

NORTH AMERICA
Los Angeles 16 hrs.
New York 11 hrs.
Toronto 13 hrs., 30 min.

EUROPE
Frankfurt 13 hrs.
London 15 hrs., 30 min.
Rome 16 hrs.

★ BUENOS AIRES

COMMUNICATIONS

Telephones The telephone system is outmoded and overburdened. Service for international calls is adequate, but domestic calls are hard to connect and of poor quality. Domestic and international long distance calls are very expensive, especially from hotels. Cellular phones are a good alternative and are used by many businesspeople. Public phones use tokens available from street kiosks. It is best to make international calls from major hotels.

Fax Fax machines, while not prevalent, are available at most hotels and businesses, telephone company centers, and photocopying shops.

Post office Mail service is adequate if slow. Outgoing mail is delivered to the US in five days, Europe in a week. Incoming mail takes much longer.

BEST TRAVEL BOOKS

Argentina, Uruguay & Paraguay: A Travel Survival Kit, by Wayne Bernhardson and Marla Massolo. Australia: Lonely Planet Publications. 606 pages. Written for the budget traveler but has good practical information.

South American Handbook, edited by Ben Box. London: Trade & Travel Publications. Tourist oriented but has solid details, especially for cities other than Buenos Aires.

Do's and Taboos Around the World, edited by Roger Axtell. New York: John Wylie & Sons. 196 pages. A humorous compilation of cultural do's and don'ts for business travelers.

The Travelers Guide to Latin America Customs and Manners. Elizabeth Devine & Nancy Braganti. An invaluable guide for people not wanting to put foot in mouth.

BEST BUSINESS BOOK

Argentina Business: The Portable Encyclopedia for Doing Business with Argentina. Available from: World Trade Press, 1505 Fifth Ave., San Rafael, Calif. 94901, USA; Tel: [1] (415) 454-9934. A comprehensive reference covering 25 business topics about doing business with and in Argentina.

USEFUL TELEPHONE NUMBERS

If you are calling from outside Argentina you will need to add the country code [54] and any other international dialing requirements from within your country.

- International direct dial access 00
- DHL Courier Service .... (1) 343-0790

Visitor Information
- Buenos Aires .... (1) 312-2232 or 312-6560
- Cordoba 9510 44-027
- Mendoza .... (61) 24-2800
- Rosario .... (41) 24-8382
- Airport and flight information
- Aeroparque Jorge Newbery .... (1) 771-2071
- Ezeiza Airport .... (1) 620-0271
- Taxi problems and complaints .... (1) 343-5001
- Automovil Club Argentino .... (1) 802-606
- Touring Club Argentino .... (1) 392-6742

Car Rental
- Avis: Maipu 944; (1) 3111000
- Budget .... (1) 313169
- Hertz .... (1) 3121317
- National .... (1) 3124318

Hotels
- Hotel Inter-Continental .... (1) 322-4051
- Buenos Aires Sheraton Hotel .... (1) 318-9346
- Marriott Plaza Buenos Aires Hotel ...... (1) 318-3000
- Crowne Plaza Buenos Aires Hotel ...... (1) 348-5000

Airlines
- Aerolinas Argentinas .... (1) 362-5008
- Austral .... (1) 325-0777

Credit Card Information:
Lost or stolen credit cards (call collect to the US, regardless of which country the card was issued in).
- Amex ....[1] (919) 333-3211
- Diner's Club.............................. [1] (303) 799-1504
- MasterCard .... [1] (314) 275-6690
- Visa ....[1] (410) 581-7931

Travelogue

WORKWEEK

Offices Monday-Friday 8:30 am to 6:00 pm, usually closed noon to 3:00 pm.
Banks Monday-Friday 10:00 am to 3:00 pm.
Government Monday-Friday noon to 7:00 pm during winter and 7:00 am to 2:00 pm in summer.
Retail Monday-Saturday* 9:00 am to 7:00 pm.
*Saturday afternoons and Sundays are considered days of rest and are obligatory. Agreements have been established for shorter work weeks, sometimes providing for a full day of rest on Saturday.

HOLIDAYS

Holidays 1996
January 1 New Year's Day
April 13 Holy Thursday
April 14 Good Friday
May 1 Labor Day
May 25 Revolution Day
June 10 Sovereignty Day*
June 19 Flag Day*
July 9 Independence Day
August 21 Death of General Jose de San Martin*
October 16 Discovery of America*
December 8 Immaculate Conception
December 25 Christmas Day
In addition, there are a few holidays during which government offices, banks, insurance companies, and courts are closed, but closing is optional for business and commerce. These are: April 4-5, Holy Thursday and Good Friday, and December 8, Feast of the Immaculate Conception*.
*Celebrated on Monday, regardless of actual date.

VISA AND PASSPORT

Foreigners with valid passport can stay up to 90 days. Visas are not required for tourists from Canada, the US, and Western Europe. Other nationals must obtain visas from an Argentine embassy or consulate. Business travelers are technically required to obtain visas, but most enter as tourists. Business visas require a letter from employer stating reason, length, and acceptance of financial responsibility for visit.

IMMUNIZATION

No vaccinations are required unless arriving from an area infected with yellow fever.

DEPARTURE FORMALITIES

There are no departure formalities for Argentina.

TIPPING

For restaurant tips, simply round up the bill to the next $A5 to $A10. Taxi drivers expect 15 percent; and ushers 5 percent. Porters get 25 centavos or A$1 for all bags at a hotel.

CRIME

Violent crime is rare, even in Buenos Aires, but pickpockets and pursesnatchings are increasing. Wallets are often dropped in mailboxes after money is removed, so be sure to report any loss to police. There is a chance of recovering passport, credit cards, identification, or other contents of wallet. In general, it is safe to walk in commercial or residential areas day or night.

INFRASTRUCTURE

Argentina has developed hotel, air, rail, bus, car rental, and taxi industries making getting around the country easy. Yellow and black taxis available 24 hours a day, are inexpensive and reliable. Buenos Aires also has an excellent subway. Plan on paying tolls if renting a car as many main roads are owned by private enterprises. The four branches of the Pan-American highway run from Buenos Aires to the borders of Chile, Bolivia, Paraguay, and Brazil.

NATIONAL TOURIST OFFICE

Tourist Office
Av. Sante Fe 833
Buenos Aires
Tel: (1) 312-2232, 312-5550

GOVERNMENT AGENCIES

Ministry of Culture And Education
Pizzurno 935
1020 Buenos Aires
Tel: (1) 42-4551/9

Ministry of Defense
Paseo Colon 255
1063 Buenos Aires
Tel: (1) 343-1561/9

Ministry of Economy
Hipolito Yrigoyen 250
1310 Buenos Aires
Tel: (1) 342-6411, 342-6421/29
Fax: (1) 331-0292

Ministry of Foreign Affairs
Reconquista 1088
1003 Buenos Aires
Tel: (1) 331-0071/9
Fax: (1) 312-3593/3423

Ministry of the Interior
Balcarce 24
1064 Buenos Aires
Tel: (1) 46-9841/9

Ministry of Justice
Gelly Obes 2289
1425 Buenos Aires
Tel: (1) 803-4051/2/3
Fax: (1) 803-3955

Ministry of Labor and Social Security
Av. L.N. Alem 650
1001 Buenos Aires
Tel: (1) 311-3303/2945

Ministry of Public Health and Social Action
Defensa 120
1345 Buenos Aires
Tel: (1) 34-0048
Fax: (1) 953-3223

National Bureau of Water Resources
Paseo Colon 171
1063 Buenos Aires
Tel: (1) 383-1152/5250

Secretariat of Agriculture, Livestock and Fisheries
Av. Paseo Colon 982
1063 Buenos Aires
Tel: (1) 362-2365, 362-5091
Fax: (1) 349-2504

Secretariat of Energy and Hydrocarbons
Av. J. A. Roca 651
1322 Buenos Aires
Tel: (1) 334-5138, 343-0890, 343-7118/7138
Fax: (1) 343-6404

Secretariat of Finance
Hipolito Yrigoyen 250
1310 Buenos Aires
Tel: (1) 331-0731, 342-2937

Secretary of Industry
Av.J.A. Roca 651
1322 Buenos Aires
Tel: (1) 334-5068, 342-7822 Fax: (1) 331-3218

Secretariat of International Economic Relations
Reconquista 1088
1003 Buenos Aires
Tel: (1) 331-7281/407
Fax: (1) 312-0965

Secretariat of Mining
Av. J. A. Roca 651
1322 Buenos Aires
Tel: (1) 331-9954, 343-6314

Secretariat of Public Works and Communications
Sarmiento 151
1041 Buenos Aires
Tel: (1) 49-9481, 312-1283

Secretariat of Trade and Investment
Hipolito Yrigoyen 250
1310 Buenos Aires
Tel: (1) 331-2208

Secretariat of Transportation
Av. 9 de julio 1925
1332 Buenos Aires
Tel: (1) 381-1435/4007

BUSINESS AND TRADE ASSOCIATIONS

Argentine Agricultural Association
Florida 460
1005 Buenos Aires
Tel: (1) 322-3431/2030

Argentine Industry Association
Av. Leandro N. Alem 1067
Pisos 10 y 11
1001 Buenos Aires
Tel: (1) 313-2561/2611, 311-6188/8429

Association of Super Markets
Paraguay 577, Piso 3
1057 Buenos Aires
Tel: (1) 312-3790/5419
Fax: (1) 312-5846

Confederacion de Productores y Exportadores de la Republica Argentina
Bartolome Mitre 2241/43
POB 1013
Buenos Aires
Tel: (1) 48-8145, 48-7286

Chamber of Commerce, Industry and Production of the Argentine Republic
Florida 1, Piso 4
1005 Buenos Aires
Tel: (1) 342-8252, 343-5638, 331-0813
Fax:(1) 331-9116

Chamber of Foreign Trade of Central Argentina
Av. Callao 332, P.B.
1022 Buenos Aires
Tel: (1) 46-6912

Chamber of Foreign Trade of Cordoba
Av. Callao 332, P.B.
1022 Buenos Aires
Tel: (1) 374-6912

Chamber of Importers
Av. Belgrano 427, Piso 7
1092 Buenos Aires
Tel: (1) 342-1101/0523
Fax: (1) 331-9342

American Chamber of Commerce
Av. L. N. Alem 1110, Piso 13
1001 Buenos Aires
Tel: (1) 311-5420/5126
Fax: 311-9076

Asociación de Dirigentes de Empresas
(Association of Company Leaders)
Paraguay 1338, Piso 2
1057 Buenos Aires
Tel: (1) 811-6735

Asociación de Importadores y Exportadores de la República Argentina
(Association of Importers and Exporters)
Av. Belgrano 124, Piso 1
1092 Buenos Aires
Tel: (1) 342-0010/9
Fax: (1) 342-1312
Telex: 25761

Centro de Promoción de Negocios Bolsa de Comercio de Buenos Aires
(Center for Business Promotion Buenos Aires Stock Exchange)
Sarmiento 299, Piso 1
1353 Buenos Aires
Tel: (1) 311-5231/4, 313-4812, 313-4544
Fax: (1) 312-9332

Cámara Argentina de Comercio
(Argentine Chamber of Commerce)
Av. L.N. Alem 36, Piso 8
1003 Buenos Aires
Tel: (1) 331-8051/5, 343-9423, 343-7783
Fax: (1) 331-8055   Telex: 18542

Cámara de Comercio Exterior de Córdoba
(Chamber of Foreign Trade of Córdoba in Buenos Aires)
Av. Callao 332, P.B.
1022 Buenos Aires
Tel: (1) 374-6912

Cámara de Comercio Exterior de la Federación del Comercio e Industria
(Chamber of Foreign Trade of the Federation of Commerce and Industry)
Av. Córdoba 1868
Rosario
Prov. de Santa Fe
Tel: (41) 23896

Cámara de Comercio Exterior del Centro de la República
(Chamber of Foreign Trade of Central Argentina)
Rosario de Santa Fe 231, Piso 4, Of. 9
5000 Córdoba
Tel: (51) 44-804

Cámara de Comercio Exterior del Centro de la República
(Chamber of Foreign Trade of Central Argentina)
Av. Callao 332, P.B.
1022 Buenos Aires
Tel: (1) 46-6912

Cámara de Comercio, Industria y Producción de la República Argentina
(Chamber of Commerce, Industry, and Production)
Florida 1, Piso 4
1005 Buenos Aires
Tel: (1) 342-8252, 331-0813, 343-5638
Fax: (1) 331-9116

Cámara de Consorcios y Cooperativas de Exportación de la República Argentina
(Chamber of Consortiums and Export Cooperative)
Tte. Gral. Perón 2630, Piso 6
1040 Buenos Aires
Tel: (1) 953-8445, 953-8266, 951-3916
Fax: (1) 953-8445
Telex: 21420

Cámara de Exportadores de la República Argentina
(Chamber of Exporters)
Av. Roque Sáenz Peña 740, Piso 1
1035 Buenos Aires
Tel: (1) 320-9583, 320-5944, 320-8556
Fax: (1) 328-1003
Telex: 22910

Cámara de Importadores de la República Argentina
(Chamber of Importers)
Av. Belgrano 427, Piso 7
1092 Buenos Aires
Tel: (1) 342-1101, 342-0523
Fax: (1) 331-9342

Cámara de Sociedades Anónimas
(Corporations)
Florida 1, Piso 3
1005 Buenos Aires
Tel: (1) 342-9013, 342-9225, 342-9272

Consejo Argentino de la Industria
(Argentine Council of Industry)
Piedras 83, Piso 3, Of. E
1070 Buenos Aires
Tel: (1) 343-9977, 208-1032, 208-1398
Fax: (1) 331-2809
Telex: 17155

Coordinadora de Cámaras de Comercio Exterior del Interior del Pais (CICATEX)
(Coordinator of Foreign Trade Chambers of the Provinces)
Callao 332, P.B.
1002 Buenos Aires
Tel/Fax: (1) 46-6912

Foro de Comercio Exterior de la República Argentina
(Forum of Foreign Trade of the Argentine Republic)
Maipú 671, Piso 4
1006 Buenos Aires

Tel: (1) 322-8468
Fax: (1) 322-7813
Telex: 24247
Fundación Invertir
Bartolomé Mitre 326
Edif. Banco Nación, Piso 1, Of. 109
1036 Buenos Aires
Tel: (1) 342-7723
Fax: (1) 342-7370
Unión Industrial Argentina
(Argentine Industry Association)
Av. L.N. Alem 1067, Piso 10
1001 Buenos Aires
Tel: (1) 313-2012, 313-2512, 313-2561
Fax: (1) 313-2413   Telex: 21749
World Trade Center
Moreno 584, Piso 6
1091 Buenos Aires
Tel: (1) 331-3432, 331-2604
Fax: (1) 343-4270

DIRECTORIES AND YEARBOOKS
Directorio de Exportadores Argentinos
America Edita SRL
Defensa 1460 (1143)
Buenos Aires
Fax: (1) 361-6610/8801/886
Fax: (1) 343-7303

CONSULTING FIRMS
Mercados Directos
Lavalle 1515, Piso 1
(1048) Buenos Aires
Tel: (1) 375-0772/0773
Fax: (1) 375-2012
R.G. Asociados
Defensa 649, P. 5 "A"
1265 Buenos Aires
Tel: 342-9355

SHIPPING
Antártida Pesquera Industrial
Moreno 1270, 5°
1091 Buenos Aires
Tel: (1) 38-0167
Telex: 21141
Bottacchi SA de Navegación, SAC
Maipú 509, 2°
1006 Buenos Aires
Tel: (1) 392-7411
Telex: 22639
Maruba S. ec C. por Argentina
Maipú 535, 7 °
1006 Buenos Aires
Tel: (1) 322-7173
Telex: 24147
Dirección Nacional de Construcciones Portuarias y Vias Navegables
Avda Espana 221, 4°
Buenos Aires
Tel: (1) 361-5964
Ferrocarriles Argentinos (FA)
Avda Ramos Mejia 1302
1104 Buenos Aires
Tel: (1) 312-1746
Cámara de Industriales Ferroviarios
Alsina 1607, 1°
1088 Buenos Aires
Tel: (1) 40-5571 Telex: 21355
Fax: (1) 49-0958

DAILY NEWSPAPERS
Buenos Aires Herald
Azopardo 455
1107 Buenos Aires
Tel: (1) 342-8476/9
Fax: (1) 334-7917
Clarín
Piedras 1743
1140 Buenos Aires
Tel: (1) 307-0330, 307-0340
Fax: (1) 307-0311/2
Comercio y Justicia
Mariano Moreno 378
5000 Córdoba

Tel: (51) 3-3788
Crónica
Av. Juan de Garay 124/30
1063 Buenos Aires
Tel: (1) 361-1001, 361-1051
Fax: (1) 361-6668
El Cronista Comercial
Honduras 5673
1414 Buenos Aires
Tel: (1) 777-1234, 775-4476
Fax: (1) 774-1016
La Nación
Bouchard 557
1106 Buenos Aires
Tel: (1) 319-1600, 313-1003
Fax: (1) 319-1611/3
La Prensa
Azopardo 715
1107 Buenos Aires
Tel: (1) 349-1000
Fax: (1) 349-1040
La Voz del Interior
Av. Colón 37/39
5000 Córdoba
Tel: (51) 72-9535
Fax: (51) 72-8550
Página 12
Belgrano 671/7
1067 Buenos Aires
Tel: (1) 334-2334/5
Fax: (1) 334-2330, 313-1299

PERIODICALS
Americas Trade & Finance: Report on the Emerging Common Markets of the Americas
Latin American Information Services, Inc.
159 W. 53rd St., 28th Fl.
New York, NY 10019, USA
Tel: [1] (212) 765-5520
Fax: [1] (212) 765-2927
Argentine Economic Development
Ministerio de Economía y Obras y Servicios Públicos
Hipólito Yrigoyen 250
1310 Buenos Aires
Tel: (1) 342-6411, 342-6421/9, 349-8814, 349-8810/2
Fax: (1) 331-0292, 331-2619, 331-2090
Telex: 21952
Argentine Letter
Ayacucho 1370, P.B., Of. A
1111 Buenos Aires
Fax: (1) 311-4385
(US address: POB 855, Bethesda, MD 20817, USA)
Boletín Estadístico: Banco Central
Banco Central de la República Argentina
Centro de Estudios Monetarios y Bancarios
Reconquista 266-78
1003 Buenos Aires
Tel: (1) 394-8411, 394-8119, 393-0021
Fax: (1) 334-6489, 334-6468, 325-4860
Telex: 1137
Business Trends: Argentine Economic Legislation
Consejo Técnico de Inversiones
Tucumán 834, Piso 1
1049 Buenos Aires
Fax: (1) 322-4887
Chronicle of Latin American Economic Affairs
Latin American Institute
801 Yale NE
Albuquerque, NM 87131-1016, USA
Tel: [1] (505) 277-6839
Fax: [1] (505) 277-5989
Comercio Exterior Argentina
Instituto Nacional de Estadística y Censos (INDEC)
Dirección de Difusión Estadística
Centro de Servicios Estadísticos
Av. Jullo A. Roca 615
1067 Buenos Aires
Tel: (1) 349-9654
AMCHAM Weekly News
American Chamber of Commerce in Argentina
Av. Leandro N. Alem 1110, Piso 13
1001 Buenos Aires,
Tel: (1) 311-5420, 311-5126
Fax: (1) 311-9076

Economía
Viamonte 1582
Buenos Aires
Economic Report: Summary
Ministerio de Economía y Obras y Servicios Públicos
Hipólito Yrigoyen 250
1310 Buenos Aires
Tel: (1) 342-6411, 342-6421/9, 349-8814, 349-8810/2
Fax: (1) 331-0292, 331-2619, 331-2090   Telex: 21952
El Economista
Av. Córdoba 632, Piso 2
Buenos Aires
Tel: (1) 322-7360, 322-8157, 322-8187
Economic magazine
Guía Practica del Exportador e Importador
Lavalle 1125, Piso 3
1048 Buenos Aires
Tel: (1) 35-2829, 35-8533
Fax: (1) 46-1000
Impuestos: Revista Critica Mensual de Jurisprudencia y Legislación
Ediciones la Ley S.A.
1471 Tucumán
Buenos Aires
Covers Argentine taxation
Latin American Finance & Capital Markets
Latin American Law & Business Report
WorldTrade Executive, Inc.
POB 761
Concord, MA 01742
Tel: [1] (508) 287-0301
Fax: [1] (508) 287-0302

RADIO AND TELEVISION
Radio National
Maipu 555
1006 Buenos Aires
Tel: (1) 325-9433
Radio Rivadavia
Arenales 2467
1124 Buenos Aires
Tel: (1) 824-1080
Asociacion Argentina de Television por Cable (ATVC)
Av. de Mayo 749, Piso 2, Of. 10
1084 Buenos Aires
Tel: (1) 342-3382

INTERNET ADDRESSES
Ministry of Economy and Public Works and Services
http://www.mecon.ar/
Ministry of Foreign Affairs and International Trade
http://www.mrec.ar or http://www.ar/
National Institute of Statistics and the Census
http://www.mecon.ar/indec/indecnet.htm
Usenet group
soc.culture.argentina

Australia

Commonwealth of Australia

Economy

Overview

Australia is a well-developed, affluent, well-educated, and industrialized country that supplies its own basic food needs while exporting large quantities of foodstuffs and mineral products. It is also one of the world's most urbanized and technologically advanced societies. It faced a sharp recession in the early 1990s, but has begun a somewhat slow recovery as it refocuses on aligning itself with its Asian neighbors and away from its traditional European and North American markets.

Trade

Until recent years, Australia's exports regularly outnumbered imports, although export performance has deteriorated somewhat. Exports of various mineral products, meat, cereals, and textile fibers dominate, while vehicles, machinery and equipment, and petroleum products are the main imports. Japan is Australia's chief trading partner, accounting for about 22 percent of trade, followed by the US, New Zealand, the UK, and South Korea. Australia has begun to focus its efforts on high value-added trade in high-tech and sophisticated service products.

Sectors

Agriculture Although noted for its agricultural production, Australia derives very little of its GDP from this sector, which employs only about five percent of the work force. Some 90 percent of Australia's arable lands are limited to extensive grazing. Sheep raising has been a mainstay of the economy since the early 1800s—Australia produces more than one-quarter of the world's wool supply—and it also produces meat and dairy products, wheat, oilseeds, a growing range of processed foods, and other specialty products, such as wines.

Industry Australia is one of the world's most industrialized countries. The industrial sector contributes over one-third of Australia's GDP, while employing only about 40 percent of its work force. The manufacturing sector has undergone significant expansion in recent years and turns out goods ranging from automobiles to chemicals and textiles. Rapid growth has been noted in high-tech industries, including aircraft and scientific equipment. Many manufacturing companies are closely connected, both financially and technologically, with foreign firms. Australia produces many mineral products, including coal, which is its major power source and a prime export.

Services Australia has a well-developed domestic service sector which contributes nearly 50 percent of GDP and employs 60 percent of the work force. It is rapidly becoming a significant provider of services regionally. Finance, high-tech and information services, regional operating headquarters, and training are among the growth areas, both domestically and as exports.

Trends

Australia's mineral and agricultural resources should ensure its continued position as one of the world's major economies. It can also look forward to a growing industrial base, driven by high-tech, value-added products, as well as a sophisticated and growing service sector. However, the country continues to suffer from a relatively small, fragmented domestic market, high labor costs, and sluggishness in re-orienting itself toward the competitive Asian markets on which it has pegged future growth.

At a Glance

THE COUNTRY

Location Southwestern Oceania between Indonesia and New Zealand.
Terrain Mostly low plateau with deserts; fertile plain in southeast.
Climate Generally arid to semi-arid; temperate in south and east; tropical in the north. Expect warm summers and mild winters.

THE PEOPLE

Population 18,100,000
Ethnic composition
European 94%
Asian 5%
Aboriginal 1%
Religious composition
Anglican 24%
Roman Catholics 26%
Other 50%
Languages spoken English.
Education and literacy Education is compulsory to age 15 in all states except Tasmania, where it is 16. Literacy rate is 89% of the adult population.
Labor force 8,600,000
By occupation: services 70%, mining, manufacturing and utilities 21%, agriculture 5%, public administration and defense 4%.

COUNTRY FACTS

Political and legal Under the British monarch, Australia has a democratic government with a state system. There are three political parties that dominate the center of the Australian political spectrum: the Liberal Party (LP), nominally representing urban business-related groups; the National Party (NP), nominally representing rural interests: and the Australian Labor Party (ALP), nominally representing the trade unions and liberal groups.
Telephone Telecommunications are sophisticated and reliable. International telephones, telegraph, telex and postal services are widely available with state of the art equipment. International country code: [61]. City codes: Adelaide (8), Brisbane (7), Canberra (6), Melbourne (3), Perth (9), Sydney (2).
Transportation Australia has state of the art transportation infrastructure.
Environment Many distinctive forms of plant and animal life are found, especially in the coastal and tropical areas. The Environment Protection Act established procedures for ensuring that environmental impact is considered in governmental decision making. The government assures water quality and availability, and sets safety standards for uranium mining, and oversees the transport safety of radioactive materials.
Media Australia has a diverse media, and newspapers, radio and television can be received in English and some Asian languages. Australia has over 300 radio stations, 134 television stations, 68 newspapers and many magazines. There are over 22 million radios and 8 million television sets in use.
Health Australia has no unusual health problems or serious endemic diseases, and no special health precautions are necessary for tourists. Hospitals are modern. Australia is one of the healthiest countries in the word. Life expectancy is 80 for females and 74 for males.

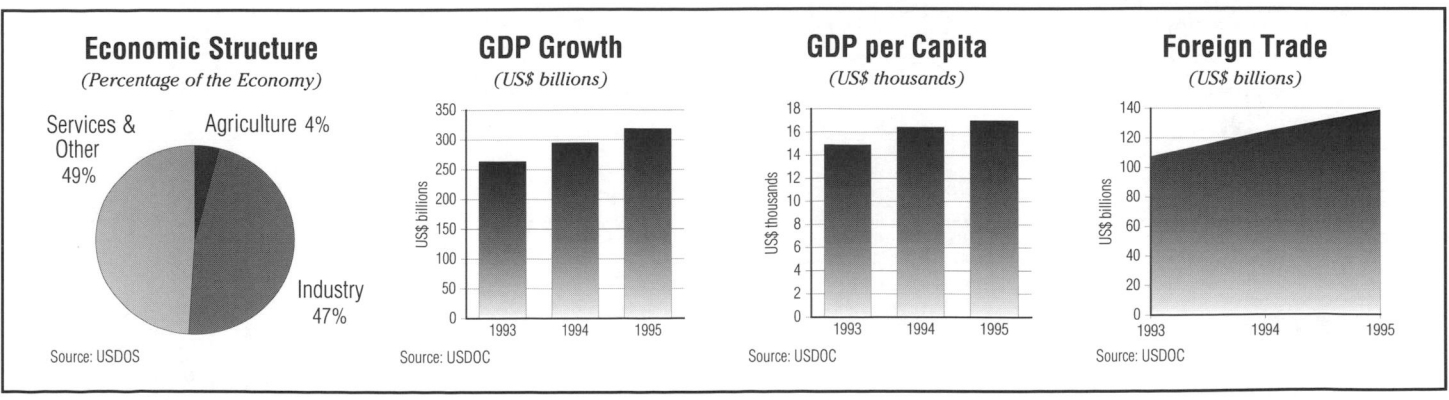

Economic Structure
(Percentage of the Economy)
Services & Other 49%
Agriculture 4%
Industry 47%
Source: USDOS

GDP Growth
(US$ billions)
Source: USDOC

GDP per Capita
(US$ thousands)
Source: USDOC

Foreign Trade
(US$ billions)
Source: USDOC

Foreign Trade

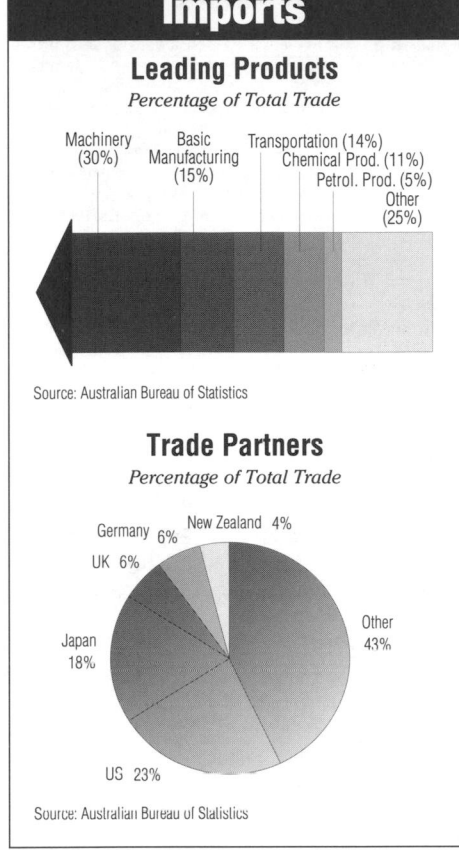

Imports

Leading Products
Percentage of Total Trade

Machinery (30%)
Basic Manufacturing (15%)
Transportation (14%)
Chemical Prod. (11%)
Petrol. Prod. (5%)
Other (25%)

Source: Australian Bureau of Statistics

Trade Partners
Percentage of Total Trade

Germany 6%
New Zealand 4%
UK 6%
Japan 18%
US 23%
Other 43%

Source: Australian Bureau of Statistics

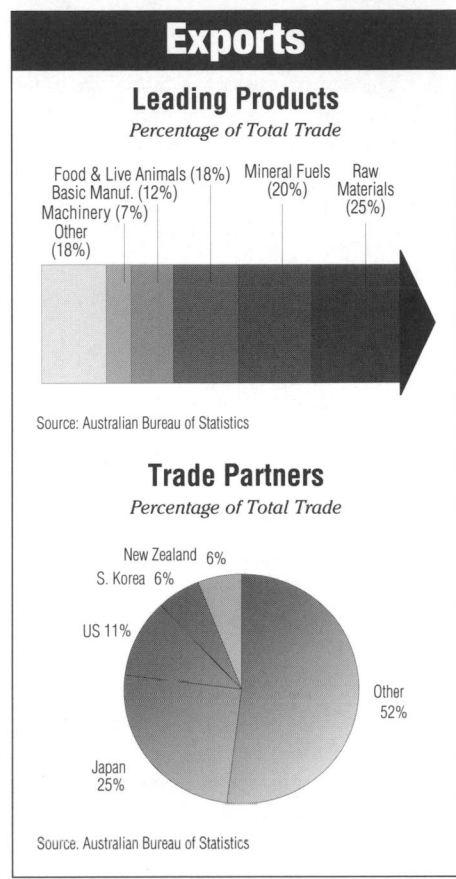

Exports

Leading Products
Percentage of Total Trade

Food & Live Animals (18%)
Basic Manuf. (12%)
Machinery (7%)
Other (18%)
Mineral Fuels (20%)
Raw Materials (25%)

Source: Australian Bureau of Statistics

Trade Partners
Percentage of Total Trade

New Zealand 6%
S. Korea 6%
US 11%
Japan 25%
Other 52%

Source: Australian Bureau of Statistics

Opportunities

FOR IMPORTING TO AUSTRALIA

- agricultural machinery
- agricultural products, consumer-ready foods
- aircraft parts
- clothing
- computer products
- electrical power equipment
- fiber optics
- food processing and packaging equipment
- medical equipment
- mining equipment
- pollution control equipment
- security and safety equipment
- telecommunications products: fax, voice mail
- textiles
- toys and games
- vehicles and parts

FOR EXPORTING FROM AUSTRALIA

- aluminum
- cement and chemical products
- coal
- fish: crustaceans, mollusks, tuna
- gold
- iron ore
- meat
- metal products
- mineral products and oil
- plastic and rubber goods
- petroleum products
- processed foods
- professional services, especially construction and telecommunications
- wheat
- wood products
- wool

GROWTH SECTORS

- agriculture
- computers
- environmental protection goods and services
- franchising
- health services
- manufacturing
- mining and energy
- professional services
- telecommunications
- tourism

GOVERNMENT PROCUREMENT

- defense equipment
- fiber optic networks
- gas pipelines
- health care goods and services
- highway construction goods and services
- hydroelectric power equipment
- rail lines
- water and sewerage systems

Trade News

RULES AND REGULATIONS

- **Regulations** Trade regulations are implemented and enforced by the Australian Customs Service.
- **Tariffs** Tariffs on manufactured goods average about 7 percent, which is slightly higher than the average tariff levels for other industrialized countries. Certain goods - like textiles and automotive products —are now protected by rates as high as 25 and 30 percent, but those rates are scheduled to be steadily reduced by the year 2000.
- **Import taxes** There are no import taxes in Australia but the government will impose a tax on the last wholesale sale for domestic consumption. The general rate of this tax is 21 percent of the sale value, although a large number of goods may be exempt from this tax or may receive a reduced tax.
- **Import licenses and quotas** Australia has phased out its import licensing requirements. Effective March 1993, import quotas were terminated, except for those on cheese and curd.
- **Import restrictions** Australia has prohibitions against products that are considered to be of potential public danger, products of national interest, and agricultural products that are considered to have the potential to introduce contamination or disease. Restricted items include drugs, steroids, weapons and firearms, heritage items, cordless telephones and CB radios (unless they have been approved by Department of Communications), food, plants, animals, and protected wildlife.
- **Temporary entry** Goods may be imported into Australia duty free for a temporary period if they are for display purposes in a trade show certified by the Australian Customs Service. Australia adopts the ATA Carnet, which eliminates value-added taxes, duties, and temporary import bonds.
- **Export controls** 40 percent of Australian exports are subject to some kind of restriction. Controls are applied through permits issued by the Department of Defense and licenses issued by various Government agencies. Mandatory export clearance numbers are issued by Customs based on export data lodged by shippers.
- **Exporting** Goods may not be exported until all necessary export permits, including an export clearance number, are obtained from the relevant permit issuing agency.
- **Anti-dumping** Anti-dumping legislation imposes dumping duties on the importer.
- **Customs valuation** The Australian customs valuation system is a self-assessment system under which it is the responsibility of the importer to value imports correctly.
- **Free trade zones** The only Trade Development Zone in Australia is located in Darwin, and includes a wide range of industries and service providers.

FREIGHT FORWARDERS

Customs Brokers Council of Australia
POB 303
Hamilton, QLD 4007
Tel: (7) 3252-1248

Burns Philip International Forwarding
286 Coward St.
Mascot, NSW 2020
Tel: (2) 9693-5566

D.L.R. Freight Express Pty Ltd.
7 Kent Rd.
Mascot, NSW 2020
Tel: (2) 9667-1261

Hawkair Cargo Pty Ltd.
12 Daniel St.
Botany, NSW 2019
Tel: (2) 9666-9301

International Cargo Control Pty Ltd.
31 Bay St.
Broadway, NSW 2007
Tel: (2) 9660-5999

Overview

Doing business successfully in Australia means first abandoning the stereotype of the sporting, shrimp-barbecuing, frontier country down under. Australia is a modern, prosperous, industrialized nation with a population of more than 18 million. Australians are educated, sophisticated consumers of products from all over the world. They eagerly buy the latest equipment. They make reliable, prosperous partners for companies expanding into the Asia-Pacific region, although they expect foreign suppliers to make long-range commitments, ensuring availability of products, parts, and services. The great physical distance between Australia and its trading partners has little effect on getting any goods to market because the country offers efficient transportation and distribution systems. International companies often choose Australia as a staging area for entry into sales and service in southern Asia. Importing is subject to minimal regulation; no exchange controls and few import restrictions exist.

Distribution

Well-developed distribution channels exist through direct sales, distributors and agents, and partnerships with local enterprises. Mail and telemarketing techniques have proven to be a successful, cost-effective means of entering the Australian consumer market, owing to Australia's highly reliable international and domestic telephone, telegraph, fax, and postal services. Warehouse superstores have become popular outlets for discount consumer goods. Licensing and technology transfer agreements are common, as are franchise arrangements, joint ventures, strategic alliances, and wholly owned subsidiaries or branches. Once foreign goods have arrived in Australia they move remarkably well across this vast continent; both urban centers and outback rural towns are well served.

Agents, Distributors, and Partners

The most common method for marketing foreign products in Australia is to utilize local sales agents, distributors, franchisees, and licensees. Most agents do not negotiate terms or finalize contracts; they generally forward a proposed contract to the principal for approval or rejection. Distributors act as independent contractors, purchasing directly from foreign companies and distributing products to local wholesalers or retailers. Distributors usually ask for exclusive nationwide or statewide geographic rights.

Selling Techniques

Selling in Australia is much like selling in any other Western country. Media, entertainment, and franchising have put foreign programs, fashions, consumer products, and fast food into almost every Australian home. Located in the southern hemisphere, Australia's seasons are polar opposites of the seasons in the northern hemisphere, providing year-round selling advantages for companies that offer seasonal goods. Quality, reliability, and value pricing are the keys to successfully marketing products in Australia. A price list should always be available on request; in addition, any extra costs, including packaging and shipping, should be indicated. Comparison shopping is a fundamental aspect of Australian consumer behavior. Industry-specific, country-specific, and international trade fairs, primarily in Melbourne and Sydney, are held annually. Other opportunities for market entry include establishment of companies for manufacturing exports, participation in major publicly funded projects, and investment in industries that are being privatized.

Advertising

Various well-developed advertising channels are available. The traditional mediums of television, radio, and newspapers hold the greatest percentage of advertising dollars. Nearly all Australian homes have at least one television and radio. Newspaper and magazine advertising expenditures top those for radio. More than 500 newspapers are published in the country, and foreign publications are easily accessible. Billboards and other forms of outdoor advertising are popular, and creative new methods are constantly being developed. Australians are open to them all. Many large firms employ cinema and video trailers, and electronic networks also offer new advertising opportunities.

Service and Customer Support

Australians expect strong customer and after-sales support from foreign suppliers. Timely delivery of goods and prompt response to correspondence is essential. High quality service can often overcome cost differences. Training, advertising, and promotional assistance may be requested from an overseas supplier, along with product warranties for a specified time. Foreign suppliers need to commit to a continuing presence in Australia. Buyers want to be reassured that goods, parts, and servicing will be available for the long-term. Foreign suppliers should ensure that their representatives can service imported equipment. If a company does not stock parts locally, it should have a system to supply spare parts quickly, even though fast delivery from overseas is rarely a problem.

Marketing in Australia

MARKETING TIPS

- **Affluence** With a relatively high per capita GDP, Australians can afford to buy innovative, high quality consumer products.
- **Go high-tech** Cellular telephones, facsimile machines, computers, electronic mail, and electronic appliances and gadgets are all the rage among consumer and business markets. Business can be conducted at a rapid pace in Australia.
- **Franchising** Australia has the highest rate of franchised business per capita in the world, with an estimated 15,000 to 20,000 outlets. Franchising is growing at a rate of about 20 percent per year and accounts for 25 percent of all retailing.
- **Think urban** With 86 percent of the population concentrated in cities, direct marketing can be effectively targeted to a large number within a small area.
- **Personal touch** Customer service and respect are extremely important. Personal contact with important customers is a must. Direct marketing is most successful if it includes personalized offers or requests a response.
- **Government markets** The Australian federal market for government contracts is estimated to be worth at least US$7 billion annually, and the state governments make large purchases as well.

MARKET RESEARCH AND CONSULTING FIRMS

Note: Phone and fax numbers will be effective Summer of 1996.

Market Research Society of Australia Ltd.
Tower Building
Miller Street
North Sydney, NSW 2060
Tel: (2) 9955-4830 Fax: (2) 9955-5746

AC Nielsen
85 Epping Rd
North Ryde, NSW 2113
Tel: (2) 9887-2222 Fax: (2) 9887-4533

BIS Shrapnel Pty Ltd.
168 Miller Street
North Sydney, NSW 2060
Tel: (2) 9959-5924 Fax: (2) 9959-5795

Coopers & Lybrand
580 George Street
Sydney, NSW 2000
Tel: (2) 9285-7777 Fax: (2) 9261-8777

Field Technologies
244 Malvern Road
Prahran, VIC 3181
Tel: (3) 9525-1313 Fax: (3) 9525-1367

Frank Small & Associates (Aust) Pty Ltd.
144 Riley Street
East Sydney, NSW 2000
Tel: (2) 9332-4433 Fax: (2) 9331-7973

Info-Line
Australian Financial Review Research Service
GPO Box 506
Sydney, NSW 2001
Tel: (2) 9282-3052 Fax: (2) 9282-1640

Lenehan Lynton Bloom Blaxland Pty Ltd.
7 West Street
North Sydney, NSW 2060
Tel: (2) 9959-4700 Fax: (2) 9929-7524

Lennon, Walck & Associates
Ste 12, 1051 Pacific Highway
Pymble, NSW 2073
Tel: (2) 9988-3277 Fax: (2) 9988-3395

Mossfield Pty. Limited
17 Quarter Sessions Road
Westleigh, NSW 2120
Tel: (2) 9875-4478 Fax: (2) 9484-2300

Orm Cooper International
33 Harrow Road
St. Peters, SA 5069
Tel/Fax: (8) 8362-0030

Polymex Consultants
4th Floor, 63 York Street
Sydney, NSW 2000
Tel: (2) 9299-5244 Fax: (2) 9290-3468

Business Culture

Greetings and Courtesies

Australians are friendly, outgoing, informal people who move to a first-name basis rather quickly. In general, let your Australian associate set the level of informality, and do not be offended if they become quite friendly immediately. The accepted greeting is smiling, making eye contact, and shaking hands. Handshakes are generally firm and brief, with a rapid, simple up-and-down motion. It is not necessary or appropriate to squeeze the other person's hand. The standard verbal greeting is "Good morning" or "Good afternoon." Avoid "G'day mate," which will be seen as patronizing. Handshakes and greetings will usually be followed by a question such as "How are you doing?" A long, detailed answer is not expected or especially wanted. After this quick, seemingly superficial exchange, the next topic will be business.

Business Ethic and Framework

Originally a country of people rejected by Old World Europe (it began as a penal colony), Australia has a history and tradition of egalitarianism that can make it an easy place to do business. Australians are leery of appearing boastful or arrogant. This extends to their own accomplishments, successes, and expertise, often to the point of withholding information about themselves. This is modesty, not dishonesty. Because a person does not say they have certain experience, doesn't mean they are unqualified in a particular area. A sensitively worded direct question will get an honest answer. Similarly, Australians usually don't praise someone for a job well done. They assume everyone is doing their best. Australians value friendship, feel that being "good mates" is as important as doing business together, and consider mutually respectful relationships extremely important. They are likely to be insulted if a business relationship is deemed more important than a personal relationship. Humor is an essential part of the Australian personality. Their humor is often aimed at themselves or their country, and is often self-deprecating.

Decision Making

Except for situations involving large corporations, Australians are generally results-oriented. They prefer to make quick decisions, and move fast to put their decision into action. In smaller businesses, one person could be the sole decision-maker for the entire company and might make a decision immediately. Australians are fairly conservative, however, and the decision-making process reflects this. If the proposal contains unusual or innovative terms, they will generally need time to consider it before committing to a deal.

Women

Men still hold the vast majority of management positions, but Australian women are being increasingly hired for higher-level jobs. They expect to be treated seriously and with the respect to which their position entitles them. If you are dealing with a woman, do not treat her any differently than you would treat a man. Do not assume that her particular style is based on her gender. Australian companies hire people whose personalities fit the company's style. Whether a woman is friendly or more formal will not be a reflection of her gender, but her company's way of doing business. Foreign women can expect to be treated the same as men, but exactly how a woman is dealt with will depend on the person she is encountering.

Meetings

Meetings start on time. If you are going to be late, let your Australian associates know in advance. Australians are relaxed and informal, and will be on a first name basis very quickly. High level executives may introduce themselves by their first name, and not do or say anything that calls attention to their rank in the company. Lower level employees can have considerable power, and authority well beyond what is usual in other countries. You might get a sense of a person's rank in the company by observing how others treat them.

Business Attire

In the corporate world, conservative suits are standard. Women wear skirted suits or (not as often) suits with pants, ensembles or skirts with blouses, or dresses and jackets. Hemlines vary from just above the knee to a few inches above the ankle. Women executives tend to wear little or no makeup and simple hair styles. There is generally more latitude when dealing with smaller companies or in rural areas, where ties are not as essential or suits may not be expected. Minimal attire is a jacket and tasteful pants, shirt (understated design), and shoes. Avoid extremes in fashion, and excessive jewelry or accessories.

Cultural Cautions

DO'S

- Treat everyone equally and with the same respect. Rank means little to Australians.
- Australians prefer to meet with someone with authority, who can make a decision. If your representative cannot make decisions without permission from the home office, it is better to state this at once rather than to complete negotiations and then reveal that a decision cannot be made.

DON'TS

- Don't take an Australian's jokes about their country as an invitation that you can say the same things. Their frequent jokes about themselves, their countrymen, and their country are not meant to be taken seriously, and they will not appreciate such remarks from foreigners.
- Don't view Australians' easy-going informality or disregard for protocol as a sign of disrespect or lack of seriousness. They are more interested in results than ritualized behavior.
- Don't mistake Australian informality for an indifference to quality.

CUSTOMS

- Australians integrate a chummy informality into all aspects of their lives, both personal and business. Rigid hierarchies have virtually no place in their society.
- Business cards are exchanged casually and informally. They are often placed on the table while people are talking, and kept for future reference. Your card should be well-designed, but clearly convey the important information about your company.

OBSERVATIONS

- Sports are an extremely important part of Australian culture, and will very likely come up in conversation. You may not follow sports, or be familiar with Australian sports, but do be aware of how important they are to Australians. At least be ready to listen to talk about this important topic.
- Australians pride themselves on their honesty, directness, and saying exactly what they mean. They will tend to take you at your word, so it is best to be equally honest and direct.
- Australians are extremely sensitive to environmental issues. This sensitivity–and your own environmental awareness–will affect their receptiveness to a proposed business arrangement.

NEGOTIATIONS

- Australians tend to trust others, until they are given a reason not to. Once this happens, it can be extremely difficult, and sometimes impossible, to regain that broken trust. One of the quickest ways to lose trust is in the area of ethics. Bribery, or any other less-than-honest behavior, is regarded as highly improper and can destroy a business relationship.
- Australians usually negotiate openly and directly, clearly stating what they want. If you are unclear about anything, ask a direct question.
- Business and personal relationships are two different parts of life. Business dealings may get difficult or tense, but once these discussions are over Australians can still be "good mates."
- Australians generally do not haggle over prices. When they hear a price they often accept that figure and might respond immediately if it is too high. Responding by changing the price might raise questions about your honesty and the general good faith of your negotiations.
- For Australians, good personal relationships are important to business relationships. While both sides will be negotiating for the things they want, aggressive tactics that show little regard for fairness and reaching a mutually beneficial arrangement will be viewed negatively.

Legal System

Australia is a common law country, having inherited its legal system from the English. Each State and Territory has its own legislative and court structure, as does the Commonwealth of Australia. Generally, State and Territory legislation is subordinate to Federal legislation. Australia's highest appeal court is the Full Court of the High Court of Australia.

Intellectual Property Rights

Patents Australia has recently updated its Patent Act and recast it in plain English. Both standard patents and petty patents are available, the former having a maximum period of protection of six years. The process of registration can be lengthy, with an application for a standard patent being granted some two to three years after the date the complete application was filed. All applications for the registration of patents are handled by patent attorneys who do not, normally, practice other law.

Trademarks Trademark applications take about 18 months to process though once that mark has been registered the protection dates back to the date that the application was filed. Protection is indefinite provided the application registration fees are paid. It is anticipated that a new Trademarks Act will be implemented in 1996, which will, among other things, broaden the categories of registerable marks.

Registered designs The registration of designs can secure a period of monopoly protection for up to 16 years. The legislation covers mainly industrial designs, which protects the shape or configuration of an article, and provides fairly limited protection.

Copyrights Copyrights are governed by a different set of laws, do not undergo a registration process, and are administered under general civil law rather than through a regulatory agency. The period of copyright protection is generally the life of the author plus 50 years. As there is no registration system for copyright material, protection is secured by law as soon as the material in question is created, provided it satisfies certain threshold tests of originality, substantiality and authorship. The steady wave of new multimedia products resulting from new technologies has raised questions as to whether the present Copyright Act can accommodate the new products, and it is likely that a more technology neutral Copyright Act will be implemented in the not too distant future.

Business Registration

All business entities must be registered. Corporations must comply with the Corporations Law requirements as to preparation and submission of corporate documents. A corporate memorandum and the Articles of Association must be filed with the National Companies and Securities Commission. All other commercial enterprises must register in accordance with the requirements set forth by applicable state law.

Contracts and Dispute Resolution

Australian businesses generally expect formal written agreements to be entered into once the "deal" has been struck. There is a trend toward "plain English" drafting so that the agreements are readily understandable by the parties. Business disputes are generally, in the first instance, settled through negotiation, though legal proceedings can result should the negotiations be unsuccessful. Australian businesses expect the terms of an agreement to be complied with (and not merely used as guidelines) and much litigation arises as a result of differing interpretations of the agreement. There is a steady move toward alternative forms of dispute resolution such as mediation and arbitration, with many agreements containing clauses for the appointment of a mediator or arbitrator should disputes arise.

Notaries

Notaries are licensed by the State and are usually solicitors, or others with specialized knowledge approved by the licensing authority.

Labor

Australia has in the past been strongly unionized, though there has recently been a reduction in union membership accompanied by a proliferation of enterprise agreements and collective bargaining arrangements. Most unions belong to the national body of the Australian Council of Trade Unions (ATCU) which represents their interests at a national level. Australia has an established industrial relations court system. Amendments in 1994 to the Federal Industrial Relations Act dramatically changed the way in which Australian employers are required to handle terminations of employees, providing greater levels of protection to employees and constraining an employer's right to arbitrary and unfair termination. In order for an employee to be terminated for failure to perform, an employer must now first follow certain procedures, including formal counseling, written warnings, and an opportunity to improve performance.

Source: Cowley Hearne, North Sydney

Legal Matters

LEGAL BRIEFS

- **Trade practices** Since the mid-1970s Australian businesses have been subject to Federal legislation, which regulates the way businesses conduct themselves and includes consumer protection provisions as well as anti-competitive rules. Recently, the anti-competitive rules were amended to bring all trade associations, State and Territory government trading enterprises, and the professions within the same trade practices compliance regime as is presently applied to other private sector and Federal government businesses. In addition to the Federal legislation, each State and Territory has its own fair trading legislation principally for the protection of consumers.

- **Environment** Continuous political and social focus on environmental issues throughout Australia is now the norm. Legislation in this area outlaws all forms of pollution and provides hefty fines and in some instances terms of imprisonment for offenders.

- **Property law** Foreign nationals are able to acquire Australian real estate, subject to certain controls affecting urban land. Most urban land is held under a "torrens" system, although other forms of land title are common in rural areas.

- **Shipping** Foreign ships which engage in the coasting trade become subject to Australia's shipping laws, which provide broad environmental and employee protections.

- **Trade agreements** Australia is a member of GATT, the IMF, and the Patent CooperationTreaty, and it has concluded bilateral trade agreements with most of its trading partners.

LEGAL CONTACTS

Cowley Hearne
80 Mount Street
North Sydney NSW 2060
Tel: (2) 9956-2100
Fax: (2) 9959-3614

Madgwicks
535 Bourke Street
Melbourne VIC 3000
Tel: (3) 9242-4744
Fax: (3) 9242-4777

Erlington Boardman
ALLPORT
CML BUILDING
17-21 University Avenue
Canberra ACT 2601
Tel: (6) 247-7122
Fax: (6) 247-7086

Hill & Taylor
1 Eagle Street
Brisbane QLD 4000
Tel: (7) 3361-3333
Fax: (7) 3361-3300

Majteles & Salmon
St Martins Tower
44 St. Georges Terrace
Perth WA 6000
Tel: (9) 325-5811
Fax: (9) 325-6963

Page Seagar
162 Macquarie Street
Hobart TAS 7001
Tel: (02) 355-155
Fax: (02) 310-352

Cowell Clarke
12th Floor, 50 Pirie Street
Adelaide SA 5000
Tel: (8) 8212-3711
Fax: (8) 8231-0259

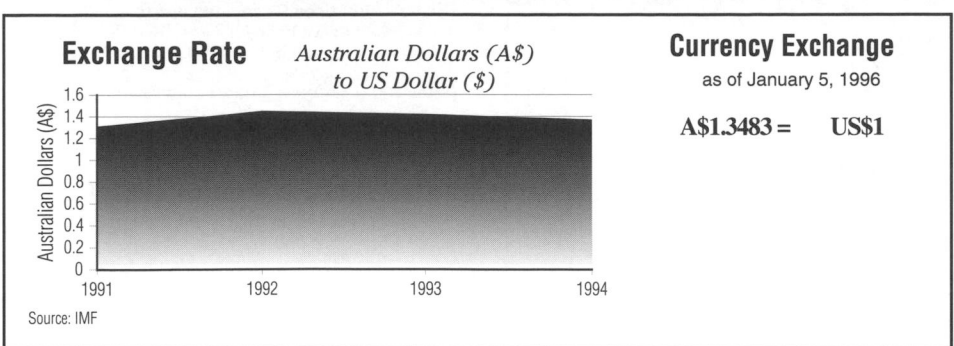

Money

Exchange Rate
Australian Dollars (A$) to US Dollar ($)

	1991	1992	1993	1994
Australian Dollars (A$) — axis: 0, 0.2, 0.4, 0.6, 0.8, 1, 1.2, 1.4, 1.6

Source: IMF

Currency Exchange
as of January 5, 1996

A$1.3483 =   US$1

Currency

The currency of Australia is the Australian dollar.

Foreign Exchange

There is no official exchange rate for the Australian dollar. Spot and foreign exchange rates are determined by the market; the Australian authorities do not maintain margins. The Reserve Bank of Australia does, however, retain the power to intervene in the foreign exchange market if necessary.

Authorized foreign exchange dealers may deal among themselves, with their customers, and with overseas customers at mutually negotiated rates. There is no restriction on the amount of currency which can be taken out of Australia, so long as the foreign currency was purchased from an authorized dealer. Persons leaving Australia with cash in any currency totaling $A5,000 or more must complete a report for the Australian Transaction Reports and Analysis Center; the report forms are available at ports or airports from the Australian customs authorities.

Investment Incentives

Australia does not provide any direct federal tax incentives for investment in the country. Those incentives which are available apply equally to foreign and domestic investors. Incentives include: research and development tax concessions for companies incorporated in Australia; the discretionary grants scheme, which can cover up to 50 percent of research and development tax losses; the national procurement development program, which provides grants to underwrite the development of Australian products required by the public sector which have export potential; the generic technology scheme and the advanced manufacturing technology development program, which provide development grants for selected new technologies; and the investment promotion program, which encourages investment in greenfield resource processing projects and links with global markets. In addition, each state government negotiates investment incentives on a case-by-case basis, and they often offer concessionary packages to attract companies to establish themselves in their state.

Investment Restrictions

Foreign investment in three sectors is limited severely. In the media industry a foreign person may not exercise any control over most operations; foreign investments in mass circulation newspapers is limited; and in the civil aviation area, foreign airlines may only acquire very limited equity in Australian domestic carriers. The purchase of urban real estate by foreigners is also regulated closely.

TAXATION

Taxation requires sophisticated knowledge of complex rules and regulations specific to each country. The information presented here is from the Ernst & Young Corporate Tax Guide and Directory, available from the Ernst & Young accounting office in your country, or from:

Ernst & Young
The Ernst & Young Building
321 Kent Street
Sydney, NSW 2000
Australia
Tel: (2) 9248-55559
Fax: (2) 9262-6565, 9248-5314

At a Glance

Corporate Income Tax Rate (%)	33
Capital Gains Tax Rate (%)	33
Branch Tax Rate (%)	33
Withholding Tax (%)	
Dividends (a)	
Franked	0
Unfranked (b)	30
Interest	10
Royalties	30
Branch Remittance Tax	0
Net Operating Losses (Years)	
Carryback	0
Carryforward	Indefinite

(a) Franking of dividends is explained in Section B
(b) Final tax is imposed on payments to nonresidents only. A reduced rate (15%) applies to residents in treaty countries. An exemption from dividend withholding tax is available for unfranked dividends paid by Australian resident companies to nonresidents on or after July 1, 1994. The exemption applies if the payer of the dividends satisfies certain specified conditions.

Money Matters

BITS AND PIECES

- **Screening of foreign investments** The Foreign Investment Review Board screens investment proposals for conformity with Australian law and policy.
- **Capital markets** Australia has well developed and sophisticated financial markets. Credit is allocated on market terms.
- **Expropriation** Private property can be expropriated for public purposes in accordance with established principles of international law.
- **Performance requirements** There are no performance requirements affecting investment per se. However, occasionally the government will impose some type of export requirement on businesses seeking government contracts.
- **Real estate** Although restrictions apply on proposed acquisitions, approval is normally granted to acquisitions of real estate for development; purchases of vacant residential land; and acquisitions of developed nonresidential commercial real estate.
- **Preferred sectors** Australia has targeted the following sectors to encourage increased foreign investment: food, food processing; information technology; mineral and chemical processing; textile fibers and skins processing; waste and environmental management industries; and advanced business services.
- **Gold** Australia has no restrictions applying to owning, buying, selling, importing, or exporting gold.

BANKS

Bank Australia Limited
POB R221
Royal Exchange, NSW 2000
Tel: (2) 9964-5000 Fax: (2) 9964-5111

Australia and New Zealand Banking Group Limited
GPO Box 537E
Melbourne, VIC 3001
Tel: (3) 9658-2955
Fax: (3) 9658-2909

Commonwealth Bank of Australia
GPO Box 2719
Sydney, NSW 2000
Tel: (2) 9227-7111
Fax: (2) 9227-3317

National Australia Bank Limited
GPO Box 84A
Melbourne, VIC 3001
Tel: (3) 9641-3500
Fax: (3) 9641-4916

Westpac Banking Corporation
GPO Box 1
Sydney, NSW 2001
Tel: (2) 9226-3311
Fax: (2) 9233-1990

Bank of America
Levels 17/18, 135 King Street
Sydney, NSW 2000
Tel: (2) 9221-1588
Fax: (2) 9235-2882

Bankers Trust Company
38th Level, Tower Building
Australia Square
Sydney, NSW 2000
Tel: (2) 9259-3555
Fax: (2) 9235-2882

Chase Manhattan Bank Australia Limited
33-36 Level, World Trade Centre
18 Jamieson Street
Sydney, NSW 2000
Tel: (2) 9250-4111
Fax: (2) 9250-4554

Citibank
1 Margaret Street
Sydney, NSW 2000
Tel: (2) 9239-9100
Fax: (2) 9239-9193

Chemical Australia Limited
14th Fl, State Bank Centre
52 Martin Place
Sydney, NSW 2000
Tel: (2) 9230-1000
Fax: (2) 9221-5090

Business Travel

	LH	1906	MADRID	945	113-3
	LH	1022	STUTTGART HBF.	935	
	AF	1701	LYON	940	683-6
	AY	822	HELSINKI	940	113-3
	AA	071	SFRANCISCO-DALLAS	945	731-7

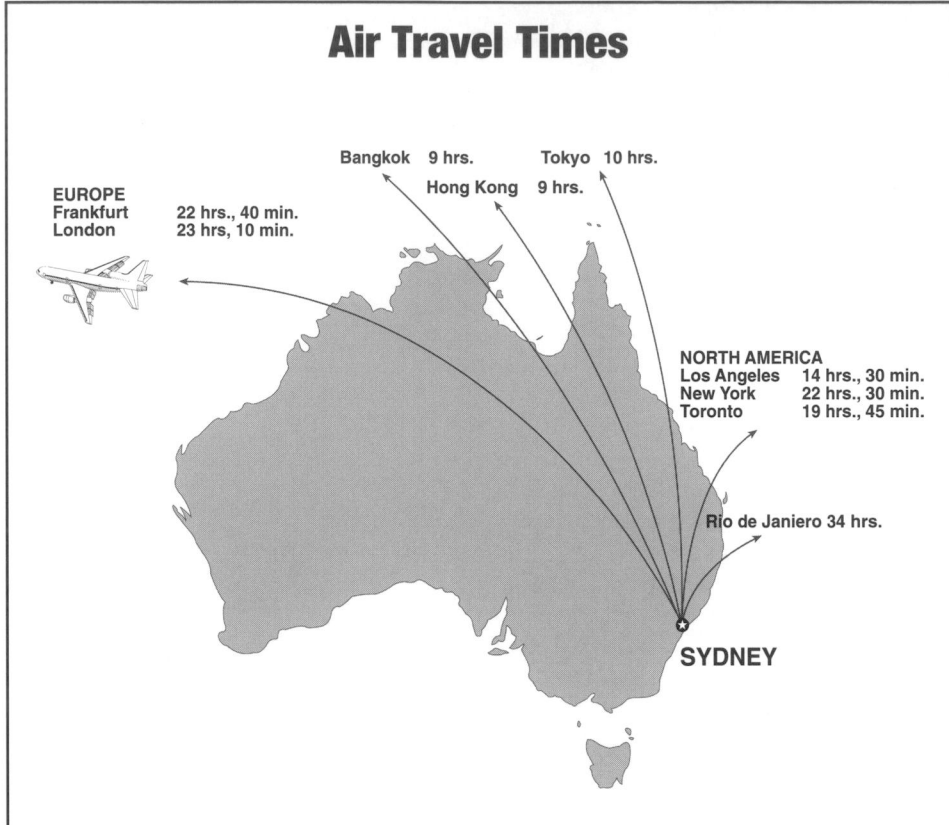

Air Travel Times

Bangkok 9 hrs.   Tokyo 10 hrs.
Hong Kong 9 hrs.

EUROPE
Frankfurt 22 hrs., 40 min.
London 23 hrs, 10 min.

NORTH AMERICA
Los Angeles 14 hrs., 30 min.
New York 22 hrs., 30 min.
Toronto 19 hrs., 45 min.

Rio de Janiero 34 hrs.

SYDNEY

COMMUNICATIONS

Telephones Telephone service is modern and efficient. Phone cards, in amounts from A$2 to A$20, can be purchased at retail outlets to use on silver pay phones. The cards can be used for local calls (unlimited time for 40 cents), long distance calls (STD), or international calls (ISD). ISD and credit card phones can be found at post offices, airports, and hotels. Calls from hotel rooms usually incur substantial service charges. It is easier and less expensive to dial long-distance directly. Telephone directories clearly list rates, dialing instructions, and area codes in the white pages. Cellular telephone services are widely available throughout most of the country.
Fax Fax machines are widely available and can be found in offices, hotels, post offices, pharmacies, and photocopy shops.
Post office Mail service is usually efficient. Stamps can be purchased from post offices and hotels.

BEST TRAVEL BOOKS

Australia: A Lonely Planet Travel Survival Kit, by Hugh Finlay, Mark Armstrong, Michelle Coxall, Jon Murray, and Jeff Williams. 927 pages. Budget-travel oriented, but provides very detailed practical information.
Fodor's Australia & New Zealand, edited by Chelsea Mauldin and Marcy Pritchard. New York: Fodor's Travel Publications. Tourist oriented, an excellent source of city details.
Do's and Taboos Around the World, edited by Roger Axtell. New York: John Wylie & Sons. 196 pages. A humorous compilation of cultural do's and don'ts for business travelers.
The Travelers Guide to Australia Customs and Manners. Elizabeth Devine & Nancy Braganti. An invaluable guide for people not wanting to put foot in mouth.

USEFUL TELEPHONE NUMBERS

When calling the Australian numbers listed below from outside Australia, delete the first digit of the area code. The country code for Australia is [61]. Dial 00 for international access.
Visitor Information
- Australian police, fire, or ambulance 000
- Sydney .... (2) 9231-4444
- Melbourne .... (3) 9726-7777
- Brisbane .... (7) 3221-6111
- Canberra .... (6) 201-6004
- Adelaide .... (8) 8212-1505
- Perth.. (9) 483-1111
In Sydney
- Computer Rentals .... (2) 9736-2066
- Tourist Attractions 00552-0554
- Sydney Nightlife 00552-0551
- National Roads & Motorist Assn .... (2) 6243-8900
- Qantas Airlines .... (2) 2236-3636
- Ansett Airlines .... (2) 3668-1211
- Business Information .... (2) 2281-2266
- Railroad Information .... (2) 3608-0811
In Melbourne
- Computer Rental .... (3) 9696-4189
- Nightlife 00553-4360
Credit Card Information
Lost or stolen credit cards (call collect to the US, regardless of which country the card was issued in.)
- Amex .... [1] (919) 333-3211
- Diner's Club................................. [1] (303) 799-1504
- MasterCard .... [1] (314) 275-6690
- Visa .... [1] (410) 581-7931

Travelogue

WORKWEEK

Offices Monday-Friday 9:00 am to 5:00 pm.
Banks Monday-Thursday 9:30 am to 4:00 pm, Friday 9:30 am to 5:00 pm. Some states offer some bank services on Saturday mornings.
Retail Generally open longer hours, Saturdays, and at least one late evening in large cities.
Government Monday-Friday 8:30 am to 4:30 pm.

HOLIDAYS

Holidays 1996
January 1 New Year's Day
January 26 Australia Day
April 5 Good Friday*
April 8 Easter Monday*
April 25 Anzac Day*
June 10 Queen's Day*
December 25 Christmas
December 26 Boxing Day**
* Date varies in some states.
**Boxing Day is not observed in South Australia.
There are also several regional holidays on which most establishments in the particular state are closed for business. Exact dates should be confirmed before going to these areas.

VISA AND PASSPORT

Foreigners must have a passport, a visa, and a departure ticket and may be required to prove sufficient funds. Your passport must be valid for six months after your departure date. Visas are available at Australian embassies and consulates at no charge for a stay of up to three months. There is a charge for visas for longer stays or extensions. Some airlines also issue visas, usually free to their customers and for a fee to others. New Zealanders do not need a visa.

DEPARTURE FORMALITIES

Visitors must pay a departure tax of A$27 and will receive a tax stamp that must be attached to their ticket. The tax must be paid in Australian dollars. Travelers with multiple departures only pay the tax once. No more than A$5,000 can be exported. There are no other restrictions for departing Australia.

IMMUNIZATION

No proof of vaccination is required unless you have visited an infected area in the past two weeks, such as tropical South America or Africa where yellow fever is endemic.

TIPPING

Tipping is not prevalent, although it is becoming more common in restaurants and pubs; 10 percent of the bill is appropriate. Other services are tipped only for special assistance.

CRIME

Australia's crime rate is low, but foreigners are often targets for pickpockets and petty thieves. Do not carry large amounts of cash, use travelers' checks. Car theft is also a possibility. Most hotels offer safes in the rooms and safety deposit boxes; it is a good idea to use them.

INFRASTRUCTURE

Australia offers an extremely efficient airline network, interstate bus line, railway, rental car, taxi, and telecommunication systems. The cost for these services vary from location to location. Australia has the world's most extensive, high-capacity optical fiber system for video conferencing, high-speed image and file transfer. Modern seaports are frequently used. Australia has long, open expanses of land, making air transportation a quicker mode of transportation than driving across the country.

NATIONAL TOURIST OFFICE

Australian Tourist Commission
80 William Street
Woolloomooloo
Sydney NSW 2011
Tel: (2) 93601111, 96542288

GOVERNMENT AGENCIES

AUSTEL
5 Queens road
Melbourne, VIC 3004
Tel: (3) 9828-7300
Fax: (3) 9820-3021

Australian Customs Service
Customs House
5 Constitution Avenue
Canberra City, ACT 2601
Tel: (6) 275-6666
Fax: (6) 275-6999

Australian Industrial Property Organization
POB 200
Woden, ACT 2606
Tel: (6) 283-2211
Fax: (6) 281-1841

Australian Quarantine & Inspection Service
Broughton Street
Barton, ACT 2600
Tel: (6) 272-5455
Fax: (6) 272-5697

Australian Taxation Office
POB 900
Civic Square, ACT 2608
Tel: (6) 275-2222
Fax: (6) 275-2538

Department of Communications and the Arts
GPO Box 2154
Canberra City, ACT 2601
Tel: (6) 279-1893
Fax: (6) 279-1890

Department of Defense
Russell Offices
Canberra, ACT 2600
Tel: (6) 265-9111
Fax: (6) 265-3000

Department of Health
National Health and Medical Research Council
GPO Box 9848
Canberra, ACT 2601
Tel: (6) 289-7019
Fax: (6) 289-6957

Department of Foreign Affairs and Trade
Administrative Building
Parkes, ACT 2600
Tel: (6) 261-9111
Fax: (6) 261-3111

Department of Immigration and Multicultural Affairs
Benjamin Offices
Chan Street
Belconnen, ACT 2617
Tel: (6) 264-1111
Fax: (6) 264-2672

Department of Industry, Science and Tourism
51 Allara Street
Canberra, ACT 2600
Tel: (6) 276-1000
Fax: (6) 276-1111

Department of Primary Industries and Energy
GPO Box 858
Canberra, ACT 2600
Tel: (6) 272-3933
Fax: (6) 272-5161

Department of Transport
22 Cooyong Street
Canberra City, ACT 2601
Tel: (6) 274-7111
Fax: (6) 257-2505

Department of the Treasury
Parkes Place
Parkes, ACT 2600
Tel: (6) 263-2111
Fax: (6) 273-2614

Foreign Investment Review Board
Parkes Place
Parkes, ACT 2600
Tel: (6) 263-2111
Fax: (6) 263-2940

GENERAL TRADE ASSOCIATIONS

Apparel Importers Association of Australia
POB E326, Queen Victoria Terrace
Canberra, ACT 2600
Tel: (6) 281-0722
Fax: (6) 282-5477

ASEAN-Australia Business Council
POB E14
Queen Victoria Terrace
Canberra, ACT 2600
Tel: (6) 273-2311
Fax: (6) 273-3196

Asia Pacific Business Association
GPO Box 2924
Sydney, NSW 2000
Tel: (2) 9221-2002
Fax: (2) 9221-1767

Australian Bankers' Association
42nd Floor, 55 Collins Street
Melbourne, VIC 3000
Tel: (3) 9654-2203
Fax: (3) 9650-1756

Australian Chamber of Commerce and Industry
POB 18008
Collins Street East
Melbourne, VIC 3001
Tel: (3) 9289-5289
Fax: (3) 9289-5250

Australian Chamber of Manufactures
GPO Box 1469N
Melbourne, VIC 3001
Tel: (3) 9698-4111
Fax: (3) 9699-1729

Australian Computer Society
Ste 1, 200 Riley Street
Darlinghurst, NSW 2010
Tel: (2) 9211-5855
Fax: (2) 9281-1208

Australian Direct Marketing Institute
POB 479
Doncaster, VIC 3108
Tel: (3) 9848-9044
Fax: (3) 9848-6146

Australian Electrical and Electronic Manufacturers Association
POB 1966
Canberra City, ACT 2601
Tel: (6) 247-4655
Fax: (6) 247-9840

Australian Information Industry Association (AIIA)
12 Campion Street
Deakin, ACT 2600
Tel: (6) 282-4700
Fax: (6) 285-1408

Australian Institute of Management
POB 112
St. Kilda, VIC 3182
Tel: (3) 9534-8181
Fax: (3) 9534-5050

Australian Scientific Industry Association
580 Church Street
Richmond, VIC 3121
Tel: (3) 9428-8966
Fax: (3) 9427-9824

Australian Sporting Goods Association
437 St. Kilda Road
Melbourne, VIC 3004
Tel: (3) 9267-8399
Fax: (3) 9267-7141

Australian Telecommunications Users Group (ATUG)
11th Floor, 80 Alfred Street
Milsons Point, NSW 2061
Tel: (2) 9957-1333
Fax: (2) 9925-0880

Business Council of Australia
POB 7225
Melbourne, VIC 3004
Tel: (3) 9274-7777
Fax: (3) 9274-7774

Chamber of Manufactures of NSW
Private Bag No. 938
North Sydney, NSW 2059
Tel: (2) 9957-5792
Fax: (2) 9923-1166

Customs Brokers Council of Australia
Ste 3, Level 6, Eastgardens
Bunnerong Road
Pagewood, NSW 2035
Tel: (2) 9314-1711
Fax: (2) 9314-1711

Fashion Industries of Australia
3rd Floor, 15-17 Park Street
South Melbourne, VIC 3205
Tel: (3) 9698-4470
Fax: (3) 9698-4472

Food and Beverage Importers Association
POB 209
South Melbourne, VIC 3004
Tel: (3) 9690-7600
Fax: (3) 9699-8338

Food Industry Council of Australia (FICA)
POB E14
Queen Victoria Terrace
Canberra, ACT 2600
Tel: (6) 273-2311
Fax: (6) 273-3196

Franchisors Association of Australia and New Zealand
Unit 9, 2-6 Hunter Street
Parramatta, NSW 2150
Tel: (2) 9891-4933
Fax: (2) 9891-4474

Industrial Supplies Office
Level 1, 10 Moore Street
Canberra, ACT 2600
Tel: (6) 257-1881
Fax: (6) 257-1763

Institution of Engineers
Engineering House
11 National Circuit
Barton, ACT 2600
Tel: (6) 270-6555
Fax: (6) 273-1488

Jewellers Association of Australia
POB E446
Queen Victoria Terrace
Canberra, ACT 2600
Tel: (6) 282-3211
Fax: (6) 282-2725

Master Builders Australia Inc.
3rd Floor, 217 Northbourne Avenue
Turner, ACT 2601
Tel: (6) 249-1433
Fax: (6) 249-1373

Retailers Council of Australia
Illoura Plaza, 424 St. Kilda Road
South Melbourne, VIC 3004
Tel: (3) 9820-0466
Fax: (3) 9866-5510

Standards Australia
POB 1055

Strathfield, NSW 2135
Tel: (2) 9746-4700
Fax: (2) 9746-8450
Textile Clothing and Footwear Council of Australia Limited
380 St Kilda Road
Melbourne, VIC 3004
Tel: (3) 9698-4460
Fax: (3) 9698-4459
The Association for Computer Aided Design
16 High Street
Glen Iris, VIC 3146
Tel: (3) 9885-6586
Fax: (3) 9885-5974
The Australian Booksellers Association Inc. (ABA)
P.O. Box 173
North Carlton, VIC 3054
Tel: (3) 9387-5422
Fax: (3) 9380-1913

CHAMBERS OF COMMERCE

International Chamber of Commerce
POB E118, Queen Victoria Terrace
Canberra, ACT 2600
Tel: (6) 295-1961
Fax: (6) 295-0170
Australian Chamber of Commerce
POB E139, Queen Victoria Terrace
Canberra, ACT 2600
Tel: (6) 285-3523
Fax: (6) 285-3590
Australian Chamber of Commerce and Industry
POB E14, Queen Victoria Terrace
Canberra, ACT 2600
Tel: (6) 273-2311
Fax: (6) 273-3196
Chamber of Commerce and Industry SA, Inc.
136 Greenhill Road
Unley, SA 5061
Tel: 8-373-1422
Fax: 8-272-9662
Chamber of Commerce and Industry of Western Australia (CCIWA)
Confederation House
190 Hay St. East Perth
POB 6209
East Perth, WA 6892
Tel: (9) 421-7555
Fax: (9) 481-0980
Telex: 93609
Hobart Chamber of Commerce
POB 969
Hobart, TAS 7001
Tel: (02) 931-1007
Fax: (02) 931-1639
Launceston Chamber of Commerce
POB 1854
Launceston, TAS 7250
Tel: (02) 319-364
Fax: (02) 319-364
NSW State Chamber of Commerce and Industry
93 York St
POB 4280
GPO Sydney, NSW 2001
Tel: (2) 9290-5400
Telex: 127113
Fax: (2) 9290-3278
QLD State Chamber of Commerce and Industry
GPOB 1390
Brisbane, QLD 4001
Tel: (7) 3221-1766
Fax: (7) 3221-6872
Victorian Employers' Chamber of Commerce and Industry
Employers' House
50 Burwood Rd.
Hawthorn, VIC 3122
Tel: (3) 9810-6333
Fax: (3) 9819-3676
American Chamber of Commerce in Australia
Ste 4, Gloucester Walk
88 Cumberland Street
Sydney, NSW 2000
Tel: (2) 9241-1907
Fax: (2) 9251-5220

NEWSPAPERS

The Canberra Times
Federal Capital Press of Australia
9 Pirie Street
Fyshwick, ACT 2609
Fax: (6) 280-4884
The Australian
News Ltd.
2 Holt Street
Surry Hills, NSW 2010
Fax: (2) 9288-2370
The Australian Financial Review
235 Jones Street
Broadway, NSW 2822
Fax: (2) 9282-2484
The Sydney Morning Herald
John Fairfax Group Ltd.
235 Jones Street
Sydney, NSW 2000
Fax: (2) 9282-3121
Northern Territory News
News Ltd.
3 Printers Place
Darwin, NT 0800
Fax: 89-81-8392
The Courier Mail
Queensland Newspapers Ltd.
41 Campbell Street
Bowen Hills, QLD 4006
Fax: (7) 3252-6698
The Adelaide Advertiser
Advertiser Newspaper Ltd.
121 King Street
Adelaide, SA 5000
Fax: 8-231-0679
The Age
250 Spencer Street
Melbourne, VIC 3001
Fax: (3) 9670-7514
The West Australian
WA Newspapers Ltd.
219 St Georges Terrace
Perth, WA 6000
Fax: (9) 481-2130
The Mercury
Davies Brothers Limited
91-93 Macquarie Street
Hobart, TAS 7000
Fax: (02) 30-0766

BUSINESS PERIODICALS

Business Review Weekly
BRW Publications
Level 2/469 La Trobe Street
Melbourne, VIC 3000
Fax: (3) 9670-4328
The Bulletin with Newsweek
ACP Publishing Pty Limited
54 Park Street
Sydney, NSW 2000
Fax: (2) 9282-8200
Business Council Bulletin
Business Council of Australia
15th Fl, 10 Queens Road
Melbourne, VIC 3000
Fax: (3) 9274-7744
The National Business Bulletin
National Business Magazines Pty Ltd.
66 Foveaux Street
Surry Hills, NSW 2010
Fax: (2) 9212-3709
Scitech
Scitech Publications
GPO Box 1915
Canberra, ACT 2601
Fax: (6) 249-6648
The Land Newspaper
159 Bells Line of Road
North Richmond, NSW
Fax: (2) 4570-4650

RADIO AND TELEVISION

Associated Broadcasting Services Ltd.
Walder St.
Ballarat, VIC 3350
Tel: (3) 53 31-3166
Telex: 32011
Fax: (3) 5333-1598
Australian Broadcasting Company Ptl. Ltd.
POB 1107
Neutral Bay, NSW 2089
Tel: (2) 9908-1900
Fax: (2) 9909-3035
Australian Capital Television
Private Bag 10
Dickson, ACT 2602
Tel: (6) 242-2400
Fax: (6) 241-7230
ENT Ltd.
37 Watchorn St.
Launceston, TAS 7250
Tel: (02) 44-0844
Fax: (02) 44-9533
Television and Telecaster Ltd.
GPOB 10
Sydney, NSW 2001
Tel: (2) 9844-1010
Fax: (2) 98441368

INTERNET ADDRESSES

Usenet group(s):
aus.ads.commercia
soc.culture.australia
soc.culture.australian
Yahoo Entry for Australia
http://www.yahoo.com/Regional/Countries/Australia/
Australian Department of Foreign Affairs and Trade
http://www.dpie.gov.au/dfat/home.html
Commonwealth Government Entry Points
http://www.nla.gov.au/oz/gov/federal.html
Bureau of Industry Economics
Department of Industry, Science and Technology
http://www.das.gov.au/~dist/bie/bie-home.html
The Full Index of Australian Web Sites
http://www.sofcom.com.au/cgi-bin/search.cgi
WWW.AUDB/URL.db
Australian Information Services
http://www.bio.mq.edu.au/australian.html
Australia's International Trade
http://www.aust.emb.nw.dc.us/intrade.htm
Australian Diplomatic and Trade Offices
http://www.dpie.gov.au/dfat/director/offices.html

Austria

Republic of Austria

Economy

Overview

Austria's strategic location between Central and Western Europe helps offset the limitations of its small and highly structured, though affluent, industrialized economy. Its economy remains stable, sustaining a highly skilled work force of 3.7 million people, sizable reserves of raw materials, and increasing trade with its neighbors. Organized labor remains a powerful factor in Austria, with unions representing nearly two-thirds of the work force, although the Austrian Trade Union Federation has generally cooperated with government and industry. Austria's major industries were nationalized at the close of World War II to prevent their seizure as Soviet war reparations; now many of these enterprises—including public utilities, banks, and transportation networks—are being fully or partially privatized, which, along with the opening of Central Europe, has the potential to revitalize the economy.

Trade

The export of goods and services is equivalent to more than 40 percent of Austria's GDP. Major exports include electrical machinery, generalized and specialized industrial machinery, paper products, and auto parts. Imports include automobiles, electrical and general industrial machinery, fuels, and apparel. Germany is Austria's main trading partner, accounting for more than 40 percent of total trade, followed by Italy, Hungary, Switzerland, and France.

Sectors

Agriculture Employing seven percent of the work force, but producing only about three percent of GDP, Austria's agricultural industry nevertheless produces nearly enough food to feed the entire nation plus a surplus—primarily of dairy products—for export. Grains and sugar beets are the main products.

Industry This sector employs roughly 40 percent of the work force and contributes about the same percentage of GDP. Production of high value-added specialized machinery and equipment—computers, medical diagnostics, and avionics—shows strong growth potential, especially for the EU market. Other areas include processing metal, wood, paper, chemical, and food products. Business alliances with companies in neighboring Central European countries are expected to stimulate increased international competitiveness through the synergies of low foreign labor costs coupled with high managerial skills.

Services The relatively productive service sector employs about 56 percent of the work force while producing a slightly larger percentage of GDP. Tourism lies at the profitable core of Austria's service industry, and management services for neighboring Central European economies offer export growth potential, although local distribution and personal services account for the bulk of the sector.

Trends

Tax reform, privatization of state-owned industries, and an emphasis on international trade, especially with its European neighbors, are likely to bolster Austria's economy for the foreseeable future. Projected GDP growth of about 3 percent is slightly greater than the 2.2 percent predicted for Europe as a whole. However, its extensive commercial subsidies, an aging population, and the challenge of matching generous welfare benefits with budgetary limitations are expected to have negative effects on the Austrian economy in future years.

At a Glance

THE COUNTRY
Location Central Europe, between Germany and Hungary.
Terrain In the west and south mostly mountains (Alps); along the eastern and northern margins mostly flat or gently sloping.
Climate Temperate; continental, cloudy; cold winters with frequent rain in lowlands and snow in mountains; cool summers with occasional showers.

THE PEOPLE
Population 7,954,974
Ethnic composition
German.. 99.4%
Croatian.. 0.3%
Slovene.. 0.2%
Other.. 0.1%
Religious composition
Roman Catholic 85%
Protestant 6%
Other.. 9%
Languages spoken German
Education and literacy Virtually the entire population age 15 and over can read and write. Austria maintains an excellent and efficient education system.
Labor force
Total:...3,700,000
By occupation: services 56.4%, industry and crafts 35.4%, agriculture and forestry 8.1%.

COUNTRY FACTS
Political and legal Austria is a federative republic. Its legal system is based on civil law, with Roman law origins. The Constitutional Court has judicial review of legislative acts. There are separate administrative and civil/penal supreme courts. Austria has not accepted compulsory ICJ jurisdiction.
Telephone Austria's telecommunications systems are highly developed, modern and comprehensive. Domestic and international calls can be dialed direct, and service is reliable. International country code: [43]. Selected city codes: Salzburg (662), Vienna (1).
Transportation Railways are a very common means of travel, both within Austria and between Austria and neighboring countries. Roads are well paved and traffic moves efficiently. There are major highways connecting large urban centers, although mountainous conditions require narrow, winding passages in some instances. International air service is available to all parts of the globe.
Environment Current issues include some forest degradation caused by air and soil pollution. Soil pollution results from the use of agricultural chemicals; air pollution results from emissions by coal and oil-fired power stations and industrial plants. The government has not yet made significant progress in reducing these pollutants.
Media Austrians are well-informed. There are numerous newspapers, 6 AM, 21 FM broadcast radio stations, and 47 TV stations.
Health High quality medical care is available to virtually the entire population. Life expectancy averages 77 years for both males and females.

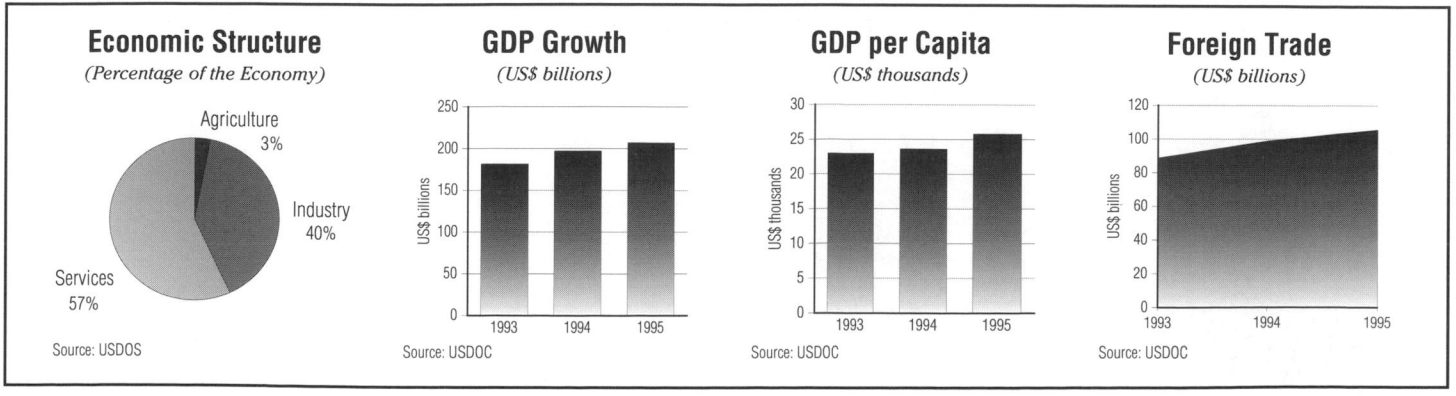

Economic Structure
(Percentage of the Economy)

Agriculture 3%
Industry 40%
Services 57%

Source: USDOS

GDP Growth
(US$ billions)

US$ billions

1993 1994 1995

Source: USDOC

GDP per Capita
(US$ thousands)

US$ thousands

1993 1994 1995

Source: USDOC

Foreign Trade
(US$ billions)

US$ billions

1993 1994 1995

Source: USDOC

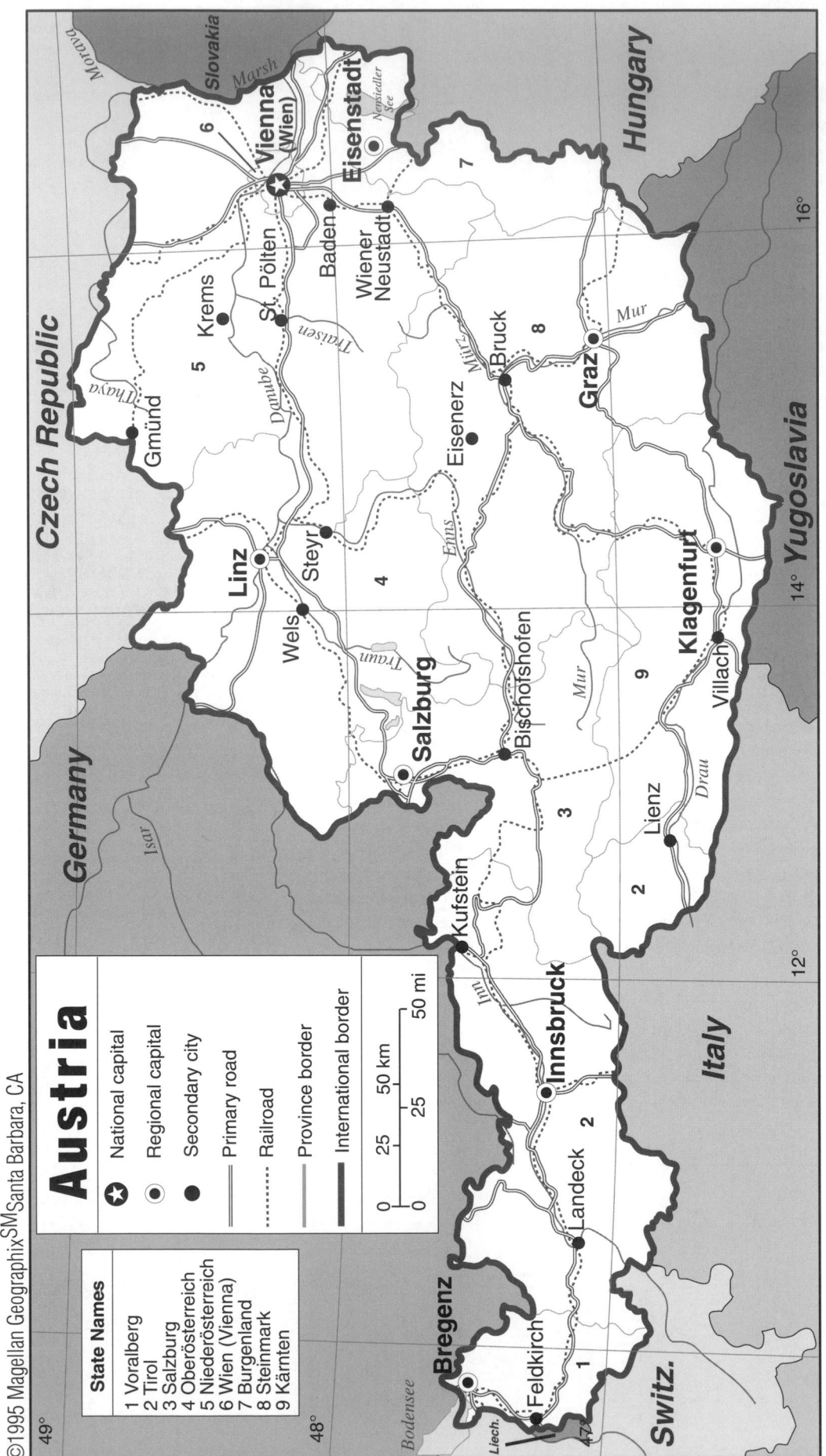

Austria

©1995 Magellan Geographix℠ Santa Barbara, CA

Legend:
- ⭐ National capital
- ⊙ Regional capital
- ● Secondary city
- —— Primary road
- ···· Railroad
- —— Province border
- ▬▬ International border

State Names
1. Voralberg
2. Tirol
3. Salzburg
4. Oberösterreich
5. Niederösterreich
6. Wien (Vienna)
7. Burgenland
8. Steinmark
9. Kärnten

Scale: 0 25 50 km / 0 25 50 mi

Czech Republic

Slovakia

Hungary

Yugoslavia

Italy

Switz.

Germany

Vienna (Wien)

Eisenstadt

St. Pölten

Baden

Wiener Neustadt

Krems

Gmünd

Bruck

Graz

Eisenerz

Linz

Steyr

Wels

Salzburg

Bischofshofen

Klagenfurt

Villach

Lienz

Kufstein

Innsbruck

Landeck

Bregenz

Feldkirch

Bodensee

Liech.

Marsh

Neusiedler See

Mur

Mürz

Danube

Traisen

Thaya

Morava

Enns

Traun

Mur

Drau

Inn

Isar

49° 48° 47°

16° 14° 12°

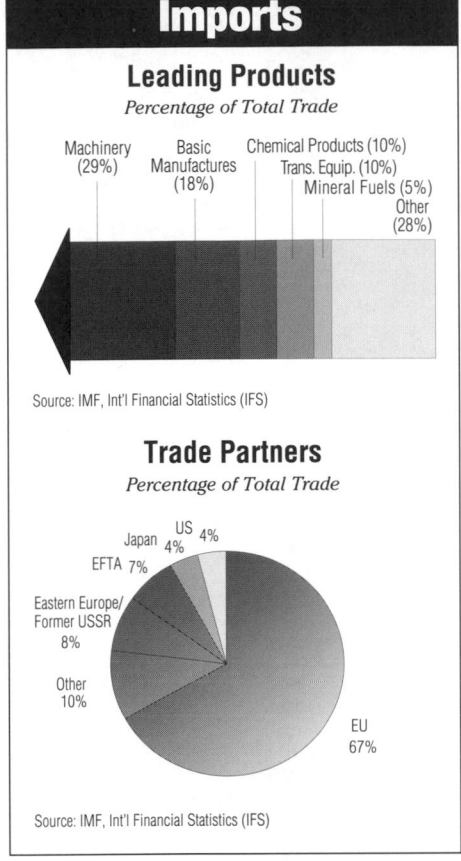

Imports

Leading Products
Percentage of Total Trade

Machinery (29%)
Basic Manufactures (18%)
Chemical Products (10%)
Trans. Equip. (10%)
Mineral Fuels (5%)
Other (28%)

Source: IMF, Int'l Financial Statistics (IFS)

Trade Partners
Percentage of Total Trade

Japan 4%
US 4%
EFTA 7%
Eastern Europe/Former USSR 8%
Other 10%
EU 67%

Source: IMF, Int'l Financial Statistics (IFS)

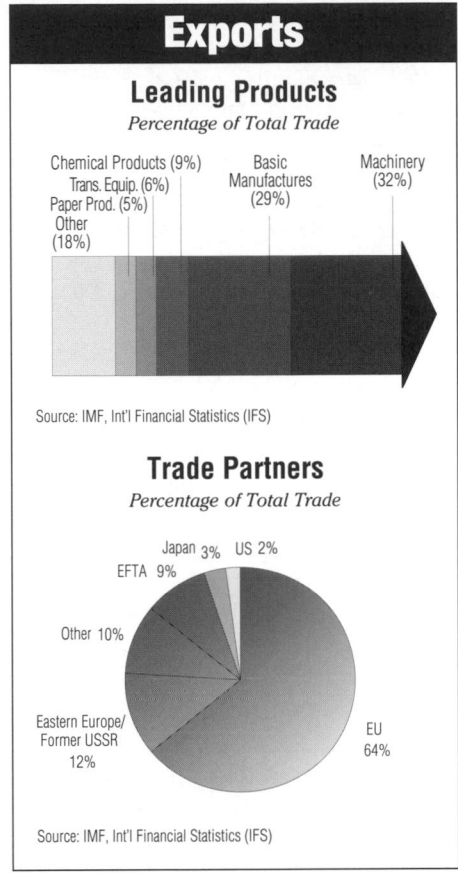

Exports

Leading Products
Percentage of Total Trade

Chemical Products (9%)
Trans. Equip. (6%)
Paper Prod. (5%)
Other (18%)
Basic Manufactures (29%)
Machinery (32%)

Source: IMF, Int'l Financial Statistics (IFS)

Trade Partners
Percentage of Total Trade

Japan 3%
US 2%
EFTA 9%
Other 10%
Eastern Europe/Former USSR 12%
EU 64%

Source: IMF, Int'l Financial Statistics (IFS)

Opportunities

FOR IMPORTING TO AUSTRIA
- agricultural goods: beef, cotton, rice, tobacco
- computer products
- cosmetics
- electronic components
- fuels
- industrial chemicals
- industrial machinery
- industrial process controls
- iron and steel
- medical and scientific equipment
- metal goods
- pharmaceuticals
- pollution control equipment
- raw materials
- telecommunication products
- vehicles and parts

FOR EXPORTING FROM AUSTRIA
- chemical products
- clothing
- construction machinery
- dairy products
- electro-technical machinery
- glass and glassware
- industrial machinery
- iron and steel products
- optical equipment
- paper
- pharmaceuticals
- photographic equipment
- plastics
- textiles
- timber
- vegetables

GROWTH SECTORS
- analytic and scientific instruments
- automotive manufacturing
- electronic components and parts
- information technology
- pharmaceuticals
- service industries
- tourism

GOVERNMENT PROCUREMENT
- civil and military aviation equipment
- civil and military telecommunications products
- electric power equipment
- highway construction goods and services
- industrial machinery

Trade News
RULES AND REGULATIONS

- **Tariffs** General rates are as follows: imported raw materials (zero to 10 percent); semi-finished products (zero to 20 percent); and finished goods (zero to 15 percent). Austria implemented the European Union common external tariff on January 1, 1995. This raised the tariff on some high-technology goods.

- **Import taxes** A 20 percent value-added tax (VAT) is charged on most imports, although the number can fluctuate. For example, a 10 percent VAT is charged on most imported food products.

- **Import restrictions** Except for a few items, such as weapons and pharmaceuticals, Austria has removed restrictions on imports of all industrial items. Imports of some commodities from certain countries are subject to controls, however. Restrictions exist for textiles and agricultural products. Foodstuffs, plant pesticides, pharmaceuticals, and electrical equipment must pass governmental standards to be imported.

- **Import licenses** Import licenses are required for tobacco products, salt, munitions, and poisonous substances. Permission to import controlled goods can be obtained from the Economic Ministry or the Ministry of Agriculture. Certain goods imported from countries other than the country of origin require import licenses, but these are usually granted automatically.

- **Export controls** Controls are placed on sensitive goods such as weapons and materials useful in waging war.

- **Export subsidies** Austria provides export financing for small- and medium-sized companies whose annual exports do not exceed US$9.09 million (AS100 million).

- **Free trade zones (FTZs)** Austria has four foreign trade zones, where products of foreign origin can be stored, displayed, sampled, mixed, sorted, repacked or reexported with the obligation to pay duty then. Their impact has been limited, and investors have shown little interest. Austrian FTZs are considered to be outside Austrian customs territory and exist in Graz, Linz, Solbad Hall near Innsbruck, and Vienna-Freudenau.

- **Screening procedures** Only those foreign exporters with an application for government financial assistance are subject to scrutiny by the government, and then only to ensure compliance with EU regulations restricting such assistance to disadvantaged geographic areas.

- **EU compliance** Austria has eased the majority of importing and exporting rules and regulations in an attempt to comply with EU standards. Much of the governmental red tape that brought complaints a few years ago has been reduced.

- **Expropriations** Expropriation of private property can proceed only on the basis of special legal authorization. It must be exclusively in the public interest and with appropriate compensation.

- **Imports** A license is required by the Federal Ministry for Economic Affairs or the Federal Ministry of Agriculture and Forestry for any industrial or agricultural imports, respectively. Any other imports are free from licenses and restrictions. Except for certain agricultural products, licenses are granted by customs for most goods at the time of clearance. Austria provides special treatment for imports from developing countries and, in particular, countries defined as the least developed by the UN General Assembly.

- **Payments for invisibles** All payments for invisibles may be made without restrictions.

- **Exports** Industrial or agricultural exports require licenses from the same federal boards as imports. For most exports, however, no license is required.

- **Proceeds from invisibles** There are no restrictions for any proceeds from invisibles, and they may be deposited freely.

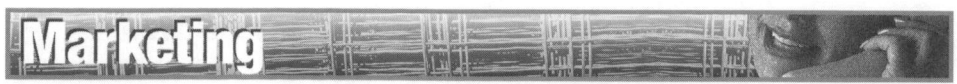

Overview

Importers to Austria will find a diverse and prosperous market of nearly 8 million people, characterized by a love for art and education and a strong work ethic. A high standard of living and a long history of industrialization are reflected in consumer demands for product quality, competitive pricing, and innovative technologies. There are no major political or social barriers to selling foreign products in Austria. A variety of business entities are available to foreign suppliers who want to establish a local presence, and formation procedures are relatively simple. Goods move rapidly to market through Austria's network of airports, roads, railways, and seaports. Immediate and reliable communications are the norm, and many firms have facsimile and electronic capability. Most of the country's largest firms have been wholly or partially privatized. Still, the government operates several utilities and enterprises as state monopolies. Austria's strategic location and political neutrality have made it a gateway to markets in Central and Eastern Europe as well.

Distribution

Several distribution channels are available for foreign goods entering the Austrian marketplace. These include branch offices, franchising, joint ventures, civil law associations, licensing and technology transfer arrangements, and direct wholesaling and retailing. Supermarkets, discount houses, and retail chains are well-established. Many retailers belong to cooperatives that provide central purchasing and marketing for the members. Franchising is growing rapidly, from 30 systems in the early 1990s to more than 200 systems with countrywide outlets. Royalties and license fee payments can be freely transferred from Austria. Direct mail and telephone marketing is subject to substantial legal controls, but companies have had some success with catalog sales. Government procurement contracts are also available to foreign bidders, particularly in the industries which remain under state control.

Agents, Distributors, and Partners

Any foreign supplier—whether individual, partnership, or corporation—may market in Austria through a commission agent located in the country. The agency arrangement is subject to the laws of the country of which the agent is a citizen, which need not be Austria. An Austrian citizen may be employed as either a *handlungsvolimaechtigter* (an agent acting only on specific authority of the principal) or a *handelsagent* (an independent agent authorized to transact most business for the principal). Agencies are often exclusive for a defined geographical area within the country or for designated clients. Most foreign suppliers that choose to operate with Austrian partners prefer to form entities in which liability can be limited, such as a corporation or limited liability company.

Selling Techniques

Price and quality are more important than sophisticated marketing or high-pressure selling. Marketing policies should be aimed at establishing lasting business relationships, not counting up immediate sales. New products are often introduced cautiously, and foreign suppliers may be more successful over the long-term if at first they provide samples and make smaller sales at substantial discount. Shopping hours are regulated by law. Companies that use Sunday sales to promote products will have to change their strategy in Austria: Sunday and round-the-clock shopping are not done. Particular care should be taken with designing attractive, creative, and eye-catching window and in-store displays.

Advertising

Newspapers and magazines take in over 50 percent of advertising outlays, although television and radio advertising are gaining popularity. The radio and television channels are owned by the Austrian state. A long-time advertising tradition in Austria, the poster, is still common along well-traveled public routes and in the more frequented public places—post offices, telephone booths, train stations, streetcar terminals, airports, public conveyances, motor vehicles, and outdoor kiosks sport colorful advertising displays. Poster sites are so popular that they are often hard to obtain because many advertisers retain them year after year. Direct mail and commercial fliers are also commonly utilized, but must be in compliance with government regulations. The Consumer Forum of the Austrian Trade Ministry examines advertising materials for truthfulness, information value, and ethnic sensitivity. Advertisers who make false claims can be held liable.

Service and Customer Support

A company that establishes a reputation for prompt satisfactory service and commitment to after-sales support will have an edge in this high-priced, competitive market. Exporters to Austria are usually required to provide post-sales service. Technical brand names have extensive customer service and support networks in Austria.

Marketing in Austria

MARKETING TIPS

- **Competitive pricing** Everything is probably going to cost at least a little more in Austria. Cost of living is high in Austria, and pricing is affected by subsidies, labor expenses and payrolls, and government controls.

- **Fast entry** Austria's business community is driven by quality and customer support. Small orders for quality products combined with high customer service and personal contact (preferably with a principal) can lead to lucrative contracts. Trade fairs are an integral part of doing business.

- **Networking** Trade organizations are strong on both federal and regional levels and offer many useful services for little money, including directories, trade promotion events, financial support, and advice in setting up local offices. Contacting one should be one of your first steps when planning a marketing campaign.

- **Government markets** Powerful, state-controlled industries still play a major role in Austria and are a source of lucrative procurement contracts. Foreign businesses are treated with fairness; no official policy favors domestic products over foreign ones.

- **Formalities** Austrians are conservative and formal about their business. Austrians like traditions, titles, and courtesy. Appointments are made in advance. Prompt correspondence is essential. Respect is the key.

- **Label language** Trade literature, catalogs, instructions, and labels should be in German, the main language of business and the government. Multi-lingual materials should include French and English as well, for maximum impact.

- **Postal service** Austria's postal service is excellent, but should only be used for correspondence with agents. Austrian businesses prefer a face-to-face approach.

- **Telephone** Telephone service is excellent in Austria. International calls can be made from cities and some rural areas as well. Fax machines are also becoming more prevalent.

- **Credit terms** Favorable credit terms are important to compete against imports from neighboring European countries, which often allow extended terms and discounts for prompt payment.

AD AGENCIES

Conquest Europe
Reisnerstrasse 27
1030 Vienna
Tel: (1) 712476186
Fax: (1) 7124741

DDB Needham Heye & Partner GMBH
Eroicagasse 1
1190 Vienna
Tel: (1) 37-15-46-0
Fax: (1) 37-15-46-20

GGK Wien Werbeagentur GMBH
Linzer Str. 375
1144 Vienna
Tel: (1) 710-10
Fax: (1) 710-1012

Grey Austria
Schonbrunner Str. 80
1050 Vienna
Tel: (1) 54-624
Fax: (1) 545-5531

McCann-Erickson GESMBH
Gregor Mendel-Str. 50
1191 Vienna
Tel: (1) 313-030
Fax: (1) 313-0368

Saatchi & Saatchi Advertising
Kopfgasse 7
1130 Vienna
Tel: (1) 878-870
Fax: (1) 878-877

Business Culture

Greetings and Courtesies

High standards of cordial formality are practiced in Austria's business society where titles and positions are very important. Forms of address are Herr (Mr.), Frau (Mrs.), and Fraulein (Miss), followed by professional titles, followed by professional degrees. For instance, the director of a laboratory with a doctoral degree is addressed "Herr Direktor Dr." It is important to acknowledge all honorifics during first introductions. Titles of royalty (Baron, Duke, Duchess, etc.) are not used in public or business life. However, in private social settings, if a royal title is offered during introductions, it is proper to address the individual by the title—given the social circumstances. Until you are invited to use the first name, refer to both men and women over 20 as *Herr* or *Frau*, regardless of their marital status. Handshaking is a ritual in Austria. When introduced, offer a firm handshake. Men should always wait for a woman to initiate the handshake. Additionally, a younger person should wait for an older person to be the first to extend a hand. Gift giving is not a standard practice in Austrian business situations. If a gift is your favored gesture of appreciation, keep it very simple. A small token of special significance, such as an item bearing your company logo, or representing your city, country, etc. is appropriate. Gifts of substantial value are considered bad form in Austrian business practices; expensive gifts often cause the recipient discomfort while calling into question the motives of the gift-giver. If you're invited to someone's home, a gift of flowers, an assortment of chocolates, or a fine cognac is a thoughtful gesture and will be well received. Though English is widely spoken in business and government, some familiarity with their official German language is appreciated by Austrians. If nothing else, it is helpful to use the German pronunciation of frequently used place and proper names.

Business Ethic and Framework

Again, the emphasis is on cordial formality; third party introductions will be necessary. Appointments should be made by written correspondence well in advance of your arrival. Cold calls are not recommended. Austrians are very fond of joining business organizations. Making contact with such groups may facilitate your entrance into large sectors of the business community. Austrians are industrious people who take their professions very seriously and take pride in a job well done. The Austrian corporate structure involves a hierarchy where relations between corporate levels are formal and rule-bound. It serves the visitor well to respect this hierarchy, and to understand the strong commitment held by Austrian workers, regardless of a worker's rank in the hierarchy. Last but not least, punctuality in meeting engagements and thorough preparedness in presentations signify discipline of character, a personal trait the Austrian business community highly reveres.

Decision Making

Because most of Austria's businesses are small, with fewer than 100 employees, you will likely be talking with the people who have decision-making authority. How rapidly decisions are rendered may depend on how thorough the foreign venturer has been in researching Austria's extensive regulatory environment.

Women

Austrian women represent 50 percent of the work force. While many women can be found in high levels of management they are rarely found as company presidents. A woman representative from a foreign company is accorded respect, and can expect to be addressed as "Mrs." regardless of whether or not she is married or uses her husband's name.

Meetings

Business cards are exchanged at the beginning of a meeting. Generally, Austrians embark with friendly small talk concerning background information. A first meeting may begin with conversation about the history of the company as well as Austrian history. Don't cut this discussion short by zipping to future interests. It would be appropriate to share the history of your own company with your hosts.

Business Attire

In banks and law firms, dress is formal, and European tailored suits are favored. Otherwise, a charcoal gray suit, white shirt and conservative tie will never be incorrect. You may note men wearing metal clips on their shoes as a symbol of status often associated with high rank in the corporation. Women's fashions tend to be classic and elegant. A smart tailored dress will serve, and pantsuits are usually acceptable.

Cultural Cautions

DO'S

- Always arrive promptly to business meetings and social engagements alike.
- Enter a row of seats at a theater or business meeting by facing the people rather than turning your back to them.
- When presenting flowers to your hostess, unwrap them as you hand them to her.

DON'TS

- Do not put your hands in your pockets while talking to an Austrian. It is considered an insult.
- Do not become overly familiar with your Austrian business associates until the business relationship is well underway.
- If dining in the home of an associate, do not present red roses to the hostes, as they impliy romance.
- When in an Austrian home, do not follow your host into the kitchen. This room is considered an inappropriate place for a guest.

CUSTOMS

- Austrians tend to take a somewhat indirect approach when discussing business and small talk often precedes actual business deliberations.
- An exchange of business cards is expected. The lettering should be black and white engraved with no color and include your position in the company as well as any college or advanced degrees you hold—lawyer, doctor, etc.
- Austria has advanced laws regarding maternity leave; a working mother receives a fully paid leave for the last two months of pregnancy through three months after the birth. If desired, she may extend her leave up to two years, receiving a modest salary, and will be guaranteed her same position upon return.
- Austrians take pride in the natural splendor of their country and their grand cultural heritage in literature, science, the arts—and especially their contribution to great music known throughout the world. Some familiarity with the works of Strauss, Mozart, Schubert, and other of its great composers will enhance the foreigner's visit while doing business in Austria.

OBSERVATIONS

- Titles and positions are even more important than in Germany and failure to acknowledge an individual's titles upon first introductions may be deemed an insult.
- Traditions dating back to the days of the Austrian empire are still carried out in many areas of today's Austrian republic. It is remarked that Austrians exercise a "courtly cordiality," and though they enjoy exchanging friendly small talk more than their German counterparts, business is conducted with German-like formality.
- Austrians enjoy mixing business with pleasure and often do business entertaining in restaurants. A popular setting to entertain is the Heurigen, an afterwork restaurant where people go to share Heurigen wine and listen to Viennese music. In these relaxed conditions business may or may not be discussed. You'll want to follow the lead of your counterparts in these situations. When Austrians dine they are polite but relaxed. Expect an enjoyable evening and lively conversation.

NEGOTIATIONS

- Be well studied in your background information concerning the Austrian firms you approach. Also, be thoroughly prepared in your presentations and forthright in responding to questions.
- You will undoubtedly be deliberating with authorized decision-makers and, depending on your preparedness, decisions may be rendered quickly and with relative ease.
- Upon completion of your meeting, as well as during initial introductions, handshaking is done in sequence of importance.

Legal System

Austria is a republic of nine federal states with a codified law system. Austria has been a member of the European Union since 1995.

Intellectual Property Rights

Austria is a member of virtually all the European and most international conventions relating to intellectual property rights. Intellectual property rights are well protected and enforcement is adequate.

Patents After examination by the Patent Office in Vienna as to the patentability of the invention, application is published. Within four months of publication, objections may be filed by third parties. If no objections are filed or if the objections are rejected, patent is granted; patents are valid for 18 years from the date of publication, provided that annual fees are duly paid. Foreign applicants must act through an Austrian patent attorney or attorney at law. Law suits on the grounds of patent infringements are handled by courts. The Vienna Commercial Court has exclusive jurisdiction in civil infringement cases.

Trademarks Trademarks are registered in the trademark register of the Austrian Patent Office in Vienna. The period of protection is 10 years and there is no limit of prolongation. On average, registration requires several weeks to several months.

Copyrights Under Austrian Copyright Law, works of literature, music, fine arts, and cinematography, as well as computer programs, are protected. No registration procedure is required.

Business Registration

Under the Austrian Business and Trade Code (Gewerbeordnung) a business license must be obtained as a prerequisite for doing business. Depending on the nature of the business to be opened, the qualification of the responsible employee or manager has to be proved to the competent administrative authority.

Contracts and Dispute Resolution

Due to the codified law system Austrian contracts are much shorter than those used in common law system. In major commercial matters, the successful party can recover court fees as well as attorney's fees from the defeated party according to an established legal tariff schedule. The International Arbitral Center of the Austrian Federal Economic Chamber, Vienna, is a key arbitration institution. The Austrian Code of Civil Procedure also establishes rules for arbitration, especially for the establishment of 'ad hoc' tribunals. Austria is also a member of the International Center for the Settlement of Investment Disputes. Austria has adhered to many multilateral or bilateral treaties, which grant enforcement of foreign court judgements and especially arbitral awards. No bilateral investment disputes are pending. The legal system provides for effective enforcement of property and contractual rights.

Notaries

Austrian notaries public are appointed by the Federal Minister of Justice; however, the notary is not employed by the state. An important part of the notary public's work is the drafting and execution of notarial deeds, in cases where such notarized form is required, as well as legalization of written documents and official assistance to probate courts in inheritance proceedings. Notaries also attest to the validity of bills of exchange.

Labor

Austria boasts about a labor force that is one of the most educated in the world. Strikes are extremely rare in Austria. The Austrian Labor Union (Österreichischer Gewerkschaftsbund) is the only accredited union of workers and employees entitled to conclude collective bargaining agreements. The Austrian Labor Union consists of some 15 specific trade unions, which are not legal entities, but subordinate bodies; however, they may act on behalf of the federation depending on the matter concerned. Membership of the Austrian Labor Union is not compulsory. Collective bargaining agreements are binding for the individual employer and employee. Individual employment contracts cannot change most provisions of the law or of collective bargaining agreements, if such contract provisions are detrimental to the employee. While demographic trends indicate little growth in the labor force in the next decade or so, productivity gains, industrial restructuring, and measures to increase female employment and raise the retirement age will ensure adequate labor over the next few years. Despite a relatively low unemployment rate, the government is formulating programs to prevent the persistence of unemployment at high levels.

Source: Siemer-Siegl-Fúreder & Partner, Vienna

Legal Matters

LEGAL BRIEFS

- **Corporate legal forms** The limited liability company (Gesellschaft mit beschränkter Haftung) and the stock corporation (Aktiengesellschaft) are the most common types of corporations.
- **Capital** The minimum registered capital of a limited liability company is AS$500,000.00. Articles of association as well as the transfer of shares require the legal form of a notarial deed. The minimum registered capital of an Austrian stock corporation is AS$ 1,000,000. Formation procedures for organization are more complicated.
- **Land transfer** In general, purchase and lease of real property by foreigners as well as transfer of real property in rural areas are subject to approval of a local real property transfer commission.
- **Vacation** Generally, employees are entitled to annual paid vacation of between 30 and 36 working days, depending on seniority. Saturday counts as a working day for this purpose.
- **Employment termination** In general, if an employment contract is terminated by the employer without good cause, employees are entitled to receive severance payment of between two months' salary and 12 months' salary, depending on the length of service with the same employer.
- **Workweek** Standard working hours are up to 8 hours per day and 38 to 40 hours per week.
- **Maternity leave** The employee (either mother or father) is entitled to unpaid maternity leave lasting until the second birthday of the child.
- **Eastern European countries** Austrian entrepreneurs have excellent relationships with Eastern European countries (former East Bloc countries); not only are they most welcome there, but they have also gathered a wealth of business experience in those countries.

LEGAL CONTACTS

Rechtsanwälte Siemer - Siegel - Füreder & Partner
1010 Vienna
Dominikanerbastei 10
Tel: (1) 512 14 45 Fax: (1) 513 79 84

Austrian National Bar Association
Rotenturmstraße 13
1011 Vienna
Tel: (1) 535 12 75 Fax: (1) 535 12 75-13

International Arbitral Centre of the Austrian Federal Economic Chamber
Wiedner Hauptstraße 63, POB 319
1045 Vienna
Tel: (1) 501 05,43 97 Fax:(1) 502 06,216

Austrian Patent Office
Kohlmarkt 8 - 10
1014 Vienna
Tel: (1) 534 24 - 0 Fax: (1) 534 24 535

Austrian National Chamber of Notaries Public
Landesgerichtsstrabe 20
1010 Vienna
Tel: (1) 402 45 09 Fax: (1) 406 34 75

Federal Ministry of Justice
Museumstraße 7
1070 Vienna
Tel: (1) 521 52 - 0
Fax: (1) 521 52 2727

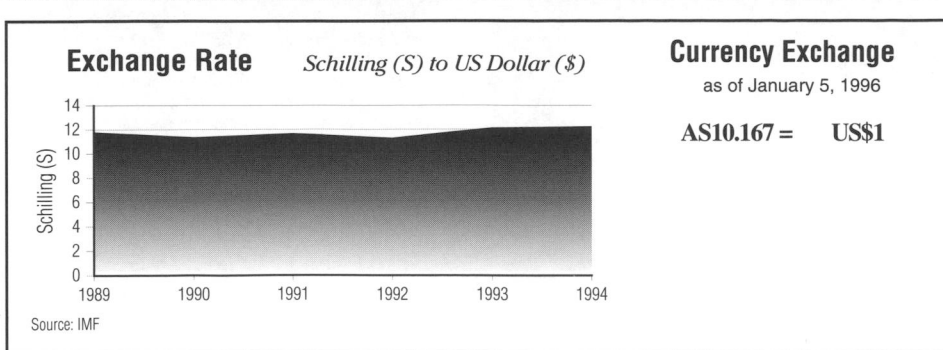

Exchange Rate *Schilling (S) to US Dollar ($)*

Schilling (S)

14 12 11 10 8 6 4 2 0

1989   1990   1991   1992   1993   1994

Source: IMF

Currency Exchange
as of January 5, 1996

AS10.167 =   US$1

Currency

The currency in use is the Austrian schilling, S.

Foreign Exchange

Austria maintains a stable relationship with the currencies involved in the European Monetary System. Most exchange transactions are completed through select Austrian banks authorized by the Austrian National Bank. The Austrian National Bank does not intervene in the forward market or provide cover for the forward positions of commercial banks; premiums and discounts are left to market forces.

Capital Transfers

Settlements with all countries may be made either in foreign currencies or through free schilling accounts (the only type of account nonresidents may hold in schillings). Free schilling account balances may be freely converted into any foreign currency, and transfers between these accounts are free. Persons entering Austria may import Austrian or foreign bank notes and coins without limit. Residents are permitted to conclude transactions with nonresidents involving payments for invisibles without restriction.

Investment Incentives

The Austrian government generally welcomes all foreign direct investment, but particularly investment which creates new jobs in high technology and capital intensive industry, improves productivity, replaces imports and/or increases exports, and does not have a negative impact on the environment. Special investment incentives are accorded to projects in economically depressed areas, districts bordering on Austria's East European neighbors, and specified areas adversely affected by the ailing steel industry or by bankruptcies.

Investment Restrictions

In general, there are no performance requirements imposed as a condition for establishing, maintaining, or expanding an investment to gain access to tax and other investment incentives. Some performance requirements may be imposed when foreign investors seek special financial assistance from the Austrian government. There is no requirement that nationals own shares in foreign investments, that the share of foreign equity be reduced over time, or that technology be transferred. Foreign investments are not generally subject to screening, and there are few reports of discrimination against foreign investors or of any regulations that disadvantage foreign investors.

Money Matters

BITS AND PIECES

- **Corporate income tax** In general, all Austrian companies and foreign companies with a branch in Austria are subject to a corporate income tax.
- **Administration** The Austrian tax year usually corresponds to the calendar year. Annual returns must be filed by March of the following calendar year.
- **Acquisitions** Takeover of domestic enterprises is permitted and not covered by special legislation.
- **Cartels** Cartels are not generally prohibited, but are subject to approval and to the control of the cartel court to prevent the abuse of market power.
- **Resident agents** Nonresidents must appoint a resident to represent them in Austria.
- **Nationalization** Nationalization has not been an issue in Austria, and expropriation of private property may proceed only on the basis of special legal authorization.
- **National ownership** There is no requirement that nationals own shares in foreign investments, that the share of foreign equity be reduced over time, or that technology be transferred.
- **Joint ventures** Specific regulations concerning requirements for joint ventures do not exist.
- **Investment insurance programs** OPIC has a cooperation agreement with Austria's Finance Guarantee Company enabling US firms to secure cover for investments in Central and Eastern Europe through Austrian partners.
- **Mergers** International takeovers of domestic enterprises are permitted. International cartels are allowed in Austria, but are subject to oversight by the cartel court to prevent any abuse of market power. Prior notification is required in the case of mergers and acquisitions with combined sales in excess of AS3.5 billion, or any sale that entails the transfer of production facilities or rights, or which result in the direct or indirect purchase of 25 percent or more of one firm by another.
- **Export incentives** The central bank refinances commercial bank loans for Austrian firms to acquire and participate in firms abroad. There are also available start-up loans for financing Austrian investment and joint ventures in developing countries that serve to promote Austrian exports.
- **Privatization** Foreign and domestic investors are treated equally. In privatization involving banks or basic industries, however, there is a stated policy of "maintaining the Austrian interest." With no specific regulations issued to achieve this goal so far, it is not known what the Austrian government will do.
- **Guarantees** Guarantees to cover the economic risks of foreign investments in all countries are available under a separate program from the Finance Guarantee Company, which operates the East-West Fund.

BANKS

Austrian National Bank
Otto Wagner-Platz 3
1090 Vienna
Tel: (1) 40-42-00 Fax: (1) 404-20-6714

Citibank (Austria) Aktiengesellschaft
Lothringerstrasse 7
1010 Vienna
Tel: (1) 71-71-70 Fax: (1) 713-92-06

Creditanstalt
Schottengasse 6
POB 72
1010 Vienna
Tel: (1) 53131-0 Fax: (1) 531-31-7566

Girozentrale und Bank der Österreichischen
Sparkassen AG
Schubertring 5
POB 255
1010 Vienna
Tel: (1) 71194/0

TAXATION

Taxation requires sophisticated knowledge of complex rules and regulations specific to each country. The information presented here is from the Ernst & Young Corporate Tax Guide and Directory, available from the Ernst & Young accounting office in your country, or from:

Süd-Ost Treuhand AG
Prstergraße 23
1021 Vienna, Austria
Tel: (1) 21170-1071
Telex: 13-29-75
Fax: (1) 216-20-77

At a Glance

Corporate Income Tax Rate (%) (a)	34
Capital Gains Tax Rate (%)	34
Withholding Tax (%)	
Dividends (b)	22
Interest (from Bank Deposits and Securities only) (c)	22
Royalties from Patents, Know-how, etc. (d)	20
Net Operating Losses (Years)	
Carryback	0
Carryforward	7

(a) Applies to distributed or undistributed profits.
(b) In general, applicable to dividends paid to residents and nonresidents. Certain dividends paid to Austrian companies are exempt from tax (See Section B).
(c) For details, see Section B.
(d) Applicable to nonresidents.

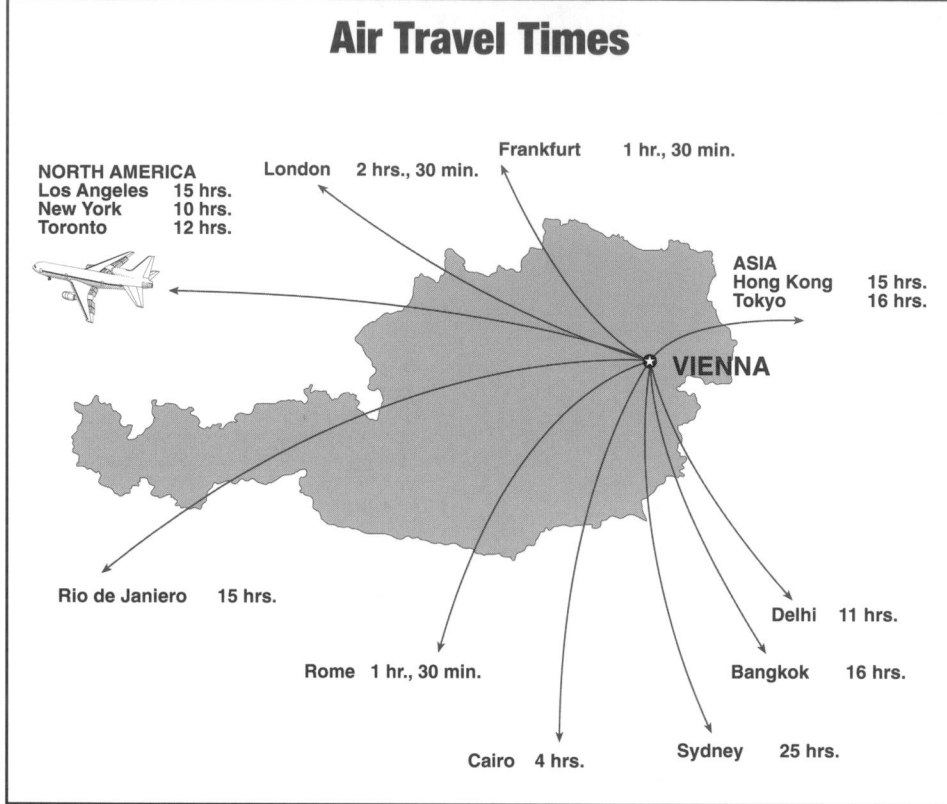

Air Travel Times

NORTH AMERICA
Los Angeles   15 hrs.
New York   10 hrs.
Toronto   12 hrs.

London   2 hrs., 30 min.

Frankfurt   1 hr., 30 min.

ASIA
Hong Kong   15 hrs.
Tokyo   16 hrs.

VIENNA

Rio de Janiero   15 hrs.

Delhi   11 hrs.

Rome   1 hr., 30 min.

Bangkok   16 hrs.

Cairo   4 hrs.

Sydney   25 hrs.

Travelogue

WORKWEEK

Offices Monday-Friday 8:00 am to 5:00 pm.
Banks Monday-Friday 9:00 am to 12:30 pm; and 1:30 pm to 3:00 pm, with late hours on Thursdays.
Retail Shops are generally open Monday-Friday 8:00 am to 6:30 pm and until 1:00 pm, on Saturdays. They usually close for two-hour lunches, except in big cities.
Government Monday-Friday 8:00 am to 4:00 pm.

HOLIDAYS

Holidays 1996
January 1 New Year's Day
January 6 Epiphany
April 7 Easter Sunday*
April 8 Easter Monday*
May 1 Labor Day
May 16 Ascension Day*
May 26 Whit Monday*
June 6 Corpus Christi Day*
August 15 Assumption Day
October 26 National Day
November 1 All Saint's Day
December 8 Immaculate Conception
December 25 Christmas Day
December 26 St. Stephen's Day
*Dates vary; exact dates should be confirmed.

VISA AND PASSPORT

Foreigners must have a valid passport. Visas are not required for EU, US, Australian, Canadian, and New Zealand citizens for a visit of up to 90 days. Many other nationals require a visa. All travelers must hold onward tickets, valid travel documents, and sufficient funds. Passports must be valid for 6 months beyond date of departure.

DEPARTURE FORMALITIES

There are no departure fees to pay when leaving Austria and no other restrictions unless you take out more money than you entered with. Special permits need to be completed upon departure to do so.

IMMUNIZATION

International certificates of vaccination not required unless arriving from infected areas.

TIPPING

It is customary to tip 5 to 10 percent for good service in restaurants. Taxi drivers expect a 10 percent tip. Porters expect 10 schillings per piece. Beauticians, barbers: 10 percent. Other small services expect 10 schillings.

CRIME

Austria has a low crime rate, and violent crime is rare. Theft of personal property has increased in recent years; tourists are the primary targets. Pickpockets and pursesnatchers are most prevalent in areas with many tourists, such as train stations. Do not leave valuables within sight in your car.

INFRASTRUCTURE

Austria has well-organized, reliable, and efficient transportation, telecommunication, and hotel and guest house industries. Air and train travel is speedy, comfortable, and very reliable. Major Austrian cities have efficient public transportation systems, including buses (which are reliable), metros, and street cars, as well as readily available taxis (metered) and car rentals. Trams always have the right of way; do not pass on the right when they are stopped.

NATIONAL TOURIST OFFICE

Austrian National Tourist Office
Margaretenstrl
Vienna
Tel: (1) 58866

COMMUNICATIONS

Telephones Austria has highly developed and efficient telephone services, although they are expensive. Calls within Austria are a third less expensive on weekends and between 6:00 p.m. and 8:00 a.m. on weekdays. International calls can be dialed directly or operator assisted. Public phones are widely available and much less expensive than hotel phones. Public phones can always be found at a post office. You can dial direct to many foreign countries from most phone booths. Public phones are in green and yellow booths. Push the red button when your party answers. To save a little money, and avoid the hassle of change, phone cards are available.
Fax Fax machines are widely used in Austria and telex facilities are also widely available. All major post offices have public fax facilities and there is a public telex in the main telegraph office in Vienna.
Post office Postal service in Austria is very efficient. Post office hours vary but are typically Monday-Friday from 8:00 am to noon and 2:00 pm to 6:00 pm and Saturdays from 8:00 am to 11:00 am. There are 24-hour centers open every day of the week at the main post office and the main telegraph office in Vienna and at some of the larger train stations. Stamps can also be purchased in tobacco shops.

BEST TRAVEL BOOKS

Berlitz Business Travel Guide. Oxford, England, 384 pages. Provides useful, diverse business travel information on several European countries.
Multinational Travel Companion, Executive. Stanford, CT: Strand Publishing. Provides concise information for the international business traveler.
Do's and Taboo's Around the World. The Bestselling Guide to International Behavior. Edited by Roger Axtell, compiled by the Parker Pen Company. The ultimate guide to international behavior, now completely updated and expanded.
Fodor's Travel Guides: Austria. Tourist oriented, excellent source of city details.

USEFUL TELEPHONE NUMBERS

Inside Austria, to dial long distance within the country, first dial city code and number. To dial to Austria from another country first dial country code [43].
- Commerce ....(1) 52-65-65
- Time 1503
- Weather 1566
- Taxi .... (1) 31300
- Limousine .... (1) 6049191
- Railway Information .... (1) 58000
- Airport - Vienna .... (1) 711102233; 77700
- Police 133
- Ambulance 144
- Fire 122
- Operator 09
- Doctor 141
- Duty Pharmacist 1550
- International Information 08
- Domestic Information 16
- American Express .... (1) 51540
- Thomas Cook .... (1) 515330
- Medical Information .... (1) 563511
Credit Card Information
Lost or stolen credit cards (call collect to the US, regardless of which country the card was issued in).
- Amex ....[1] (919) 333-3211
- Diner's Club...............................[1] (303) 799-1504
- MasterCard ....[1] (314) 275-6690
- Visa ....[1] (410) 581-7931

Contacts

GOVERNMENT AGENCIES

Federal Ministry for Agriculture and Forestry
Stubenring 1
1012 Vienna
Tel: (1) 71-10-00
Fax: (1) 713-93-11

Federal Ministry of Economic Affairs
Stubenring 1
1011 Vienna
Tel: (1) 71-10-00
Fax: (1) 713-93-11

Federal Ministry for Education and Culture
Minoritenplatz 5
1014 Vienna
Tel: (1) 53-12-00
Fax: (1) 531-20-2310

Federal Ministry for Environment, Youth and Family Affairs
Radetzkystrasse 2
1030 Vienna
Tel: (1) 71-15-80
Fax: (1) 711-58-4221

Federal Ministry for Finance
Himmelpfortgasse 4, 8&9 und Johannesgasse 5
1011 Vienna
Tel: (1) 51-43-30
Fax: (1) 514-33-1938

Federal Ministry for Foreign Affairs
Ballhausplatz 2
1014 Vienna
Tel: (1) 53-11-50
Fax: (1) 535-45-30

Federal Ministry for Health and Sport
Ballhausplatz 2
1014 Vienna
Tel: (1) 53-11-50

Federal Ministry for Public Economy and Transport
Radetzkystrasse 2
1030 Vienna
Tel: (1) (1) 71-16-20
Fax: (1) (1) 713-78-76

Federal Ministry for Science and Research
Minoritenplatz 5
1014 Vienna
Tel: (1) 53-12-00
Fax: (1) 531-20-4499

Federal Ministry for Social Affairs and Labor
Stubenring 1
1011 Vienna
Tel: (1) 71-10-00
Fax: (1) 713-93-11

Federal Ministry for Women's Affairs
Ballhausplatz 1
1014 Vienna
Tel: (1) 53-11-50

Austrian Federal Railways
Elisabethstrasse 9
1010 Vienna
Tel: (1) 5800-0
Fax: (1) 5800/25001

BUSINESS AND TRADE ORGANIZATIONS

Bundeskammer der gewerblichen Wirtschaft (Federal Economic Chamber)
Wiedner Haupstr. 63
1045 Vienna
Tel: (1) 50105
Telex: 111871
Fax: (1) 50206

Austrian Industries AG
Kantgasse 1
1015 Vienna
Tel: (1) 7111-4
Fax: (1) 7111-42-45

Central Federation of Austrian Industries
Wiedner Hauptstrasse 63
1045 Vienna 1
Tel: (1) 50105
Fax: (1) 50206

Fachverband der Chemischen Industrie (Chemicals)
Wiedner Hauptstrasse 63
1045 Vienna 4
Tel: (1) 50105 Telex: 111871

Fachverband der Elektroindustrie (Electric)
Rathausplatz 8
1010 Vienna
Tel: (1) 42-55-97
Fax: (1) 408-53-13

Fachverband der Glasindustrie (Glass)
Wiedner Haupstrasse 63
1045 Vienna 4
Tel: (1) 50105
Telex: 111871

Fachverband der Eisen/Metallwarenindustrie (Iron and metal goods)
Wiedner Hauptstrasse 63
1045 Vienna 4
Tel: (1) 50105

Bundeskammer der gewerblichen Wirtschaft-Bundessektion Industrie
Wiedner Hauptstr. 63
1045 Vienna I
Tel: (1) 501-05
Fax: (1) 502-06
Telex: 11871

Facjverbamd der Aidopvosopm- und Filmindustrie Osterreichs (Film)
Wiedner Haptstr. 63
1045 Vienna
Postfach 327
Tel: (1) 501-05
Fax: (1) 50206/270
Telex: 111871

Fachverband der Bauindustrie (Building)
Karlsgasse 5
1040 Vienna
Tel: (1) 504-15-51
Fax: (1) 504-15-55
Telex: 135284

Fachverband der Bekleidungsindustrie (Clothing)
Schwarzenbergplatz 4
1030 Vienna III
Tel: (1) 712-12-96
Fax: (1) 713-92-04

Fachverband der Bergweke und Eisenerzeugenden Industrie (Mining and Iron Producing)
Goethegasse 3
1015 Vienna
Postfach 300
Te: (1) 512-46-01-0
Fax: (1) 512-46-01/20

Fachverband der Erdolindustrie (Oil)
Erdbergstr. 72
1031 Vienna
Tel: (1) 713-23-48
Fax: (1) 713-05-10
Telex: 132138

Fachverband der Fahrzeugindustrie (Vehicles)
Wiedner Hauptstr. 63
1045 Vienna 4
Tel: (1) 501-05
Fax: (1) 502-06-289
Telex: 111871

Fachervand der Gas- und Warmeversorgungsunternehmungen (Gas and Heating)
Schubertring 14
1010 Vienna
Tel: (1) 513-15-55
Fax: (1) 513-15-88-25

Fachverband der Giessereiindustrie (Foundries)
Wiedner Hauptstr. 63
1045 Vienna
Postfach 339
Tel: (1) 50105-3463
Fax: (1) 50206-279

Fachverband der Holzerarbeitenden Industrie (Wood Processing)
Schwarzenbergplatz 4
1037 Vienna III
Postfach 123
Tel: (1) 712-26-01
Fax: (1) 713-03-09
Telex: 134891

Fachverband der Ledererzeugenden Industrie (Leather Producing)
Wiedner Hauptstr. 63
Postfach 312
1045 Vienna 4
Tel: (1) 501-05
Fax: (1) 502-06/278
Telex: 111871

BANKS

Adria Bank AG
Tegetthoffstr. 1
1011 Vienna
Tel: (1) 514-09
Fax: (1) 51409-43
Telex: 134892

AVA Bank GmbH
Operngasse 2
1015 Vienna
Tel: (1) 51-5-71
Fax: (1) 515-71-481
Telex: 111173

Banco do Brasil AG
Tegetthoffstr. 4
1010 Vienna
Tel: (1) 512-66-63
Telex: 111997

Bank der Österreichischen Postsparkasse AG
Opernring 3-5
1015 Vienna
Tel: (1) 588-09-0
Fax: (1) 588-09-127
Telex: 112268

Bank fur Arbeit und Wirtschaft AG
Seitzergase 2-4
1010 Vienna
Tel: (1) 53-4-53-0
Fax: (1) 534-53-2840
Telex: 115311

Bank fur Wirtschaft und Freie Berufe AG
Zieglergasse 5
1072 Vienna
Tel: (1) 52107
Fax: (1) 52107-5
Telex: 1323467

Bank Gebrud. Gutmann Nfg AG
Schwarzenbergplatz 16
1011 Vienna
Tel: (1) 50220-0
Fax: (1) 50220-249
Telex: 136506

Bank Winter & Co AG
Singerstr. 10
1011 Vienna
Tel: (1) 515-04-0
Fax: (1) 513-48-44
Telex: 135858

Bankhaus Feichtner & Co AG
Wipplingerstr. 1
1011 Vienna
Tel: (1) 533-16-06
Fax: (1) 533-16-02-222
Telex: 114260

Bankhaus Kathrein & Co AG
Wipplingerstr. 25
1013 Vienna
Tel: (1) 53451
Fax: (1) 53451/384
Telex: 14123

Bankshaus Rossler AG
Karntner Ring 17
1015 Vienna
Tel: (1) 514-68
Fax: (1) 514-68/34
Telex: 131815

Bankhaus Schelhammer & Schattera AG
Goldschmiedgasse 3
1011 Vienna
Tel: (1) 53-4-34
Fax: (1) 53-4-34/65
Telex: 112323

Central Wechsel- und Creditbank AG
Karntner Str. 43
1015 Vienna
Tel: (1) 515-66-0
Fax: (1) 515-66-9
Telex: 112387

STOCK AND COMMODITIES EXCHANGES

Wiener Borsekammer (Vienna Stock Exchange)
Wipplingerstr. 34
1011 Vienna
Tel: (1) 53-4-99
Fax: (1) 535-68-57

Österreichische Termin- und Optionenborse (Austrian Futures and Options Exchange)
Postfach 192
Strauchgasse 1-3
1014 Vienna
Tel: (1) 531-650
Fax: (1) 532-9740

TRADE FAIRS

Contact Fachmessen Salzburg GmbH & Co. KG
Postfach 285
5021 Salzburg
Tel: (662) 4477-0
Fax: (662) 430115
Telex: 633131

Dornbirner Messe GmbH
Messesr. 4
6854 Dornbirn
Postfach 805
Tel: (5572) 25-6-94
Fax: (5572) 25-6-94-11

Grazer Messe International
Postfach 63
8011 Graz
Tel: (315) 8088-0
Fax: (316) 8088-244
Telex: 311511

Innsbrucker Messe GmbH
Falkstr. 2-4
6020 Innsbruck
Tel: (512) 58-59-11
Fax: (512) 58-42-90

Klagenfurter Messe
Postfach 380
99021 Klagenfurt
Valentin-Leitgeb-Str. 11
Tel: (463) 56-800-0
Fax: (463) 56-800-28
Telex: 422268

Praesenta, Werbe- und Ausstellungs GmbH
Praterstr. 12/17
1020 Vienna
Tel: (1) 26-65-26
Fax: (1) 26-65-29-22
Telex: 135205

Rieder Messe
Postfach 61
4910 Ried im Innkreis
Tel: (7752) 4011-0
Fax: (7752) 4011-44
Telex: 027/720

Vienna Fairs and Congress Ltd.
Messeplatz 1
1071 Vienna
Postfach 124
Tel: (1) 52-120-0
Fax: (1) 52-120/290
Telex: 133491

Welser Messe
Messehau
4601 Wels
Tel: (7242) 6-22-22
Fax: (7242) 66-8-40-74

NEWSPAPERS

Neue Zeit
Ankerstr 4
8054 Graz
Tel: (316) 28-08-0
Fax: (316) 28-08-325
Telex: 311703

Tiroler Tageszeitung
Ing.-Etzel-Str. 30
6020 Innsbruck
Tel: (512) 5354-0
Fax: (512) 57-59-24
Telex: 534482

Karntner Tageszeitung
Viktringer Ring 28
9020 Klagenfurt
Tel: (463) 58-660
Fax: (463) 4866-321
Telex: 422415

Kleine Zeitung
Funderstr. 1A
9020 Klagenfurt
Tel: (463) 200-58-00
Fax: (463) 56500
Telex: 422413

Neues Volksblatt
Hafenstr. 1-3
4010 Linz
Tel: (732) 78-19-01
Fax: (732) 77-92-42
Telex: 221235

Oberosterreichische Nachrichten
Promenade 23
4010 Linz
Tel: (732) 780-50
Fax: (732) 78-05-217

Salzburger Nachrichten
Bergstr. 14
5021 Salzburg
Tel: (662) 8880-0
Fax: (662) 8880-348
Telex: 633583

Salzburger Volkszeitung
Elisabethkai 582
5021 Salzburg
Tel: (0662) 879-49
Fax: (0662) 8794-91-13
Telex: 633627

Kurier
Seidengasse 11
1072 Vienna
Tel: (1) 52100
Fax: (1) 52100-2263
Telex: 131006

Neue Kronen-Zeitung
Muthgasse 2
1190 Vienna
Tel: (1) 3601-0
Fax: (1) 36-83-85
Telex: 114327

Die Presse
Parkring 12A
1015 Vienna
Tel: (1) 51-4-14
Fax: (1) 514-14-400
Telex: 114110

Der Standard
Herrengasse 1
1014 Vienna
Tel: (1) 53-1-70
Fax: (1) 53170-13
Telex: 155667

Wiener Zeitung
Rennweg 12A
1037 Vienna
Tel: (1) 79789
Fax: (1) 79789
Telex: 131805

PERIODICALS

Basta
Pezzlg. 66
1170 Vienna
Tel: (1) 49152
Fax: (1) 49152-4091

Profil
Marc-Aurel-Str. 10-12
1010 Vienna
Tel: (1) 53-4-70-0
Fax: (1) 535-32-50
Telex: 136404

Trend
Marc-Aurel-Str. 10-12
1010 Vienna
Tel: (1) 53-4-70
Telex: 136404

Welt der Frau
Lustenauerstr. 2
4020 Linz
Tel: (732) 77-02-91-11

Wiener
Donaustr. 102
3400 Klosterneuburg
Tel: (1) 88-600
Fax: (1) 88600-199

Wirtschaftswoche-Wochenpresse
Seidengasse 11
1072 Vienna
Tel: (1) 52150-0
Fax: (1) 52150-2221
Telex: 135869

Eurocity
Leberstr. 122
1110 Vienna
Tel: (1) 74095-0
Fax: (1) 74095-183
Telex: 132312

Forum
Museumstr. 5
1070 Vienna
Tel: (1) 93-27-33
Fax: (1) 93-83-68

itm praktiker
ZB-Verlag
1125 Vienna
Marochallplatz 23-1-21
Tel: (1) 804-04-74
Fax: (1) 804-44-39

Juristische Blatter (mit Beilage 'Wirtschaftsrechtliche Blatter)
Springer Verlag
1201 Vienna
Sachsenplatz 4
Tel: (1) 330-24-15-0

RADIO AND TELEVISION

Österreichischer Rundfunk (ÖRF) (Austrian Broadcasting Company)
Wurzburggasse 30
1136 Vienna
Tel: (1) 878-78-0
Fax: (1) 878-78/22-50
Telex: 133601

INTERNET ADDRESSES

Information Servers in Austria
University of Vienna, Institute of Applied Computer Science and Information Systems
http://www.ifs.univie.ac.at/austria.html
Austrian Press and Information Service, Washington DC
http://www.globescope.com/web/austria/
Austrian Federal Economic Chamber, Vienna
http://www.wk.or.at/wkoehome.htm
Austrian Business Information
http://www.telecom.at/AustrianBusinessInfo/welcome.html

Bahamas

Commonwealth of the Bahamas

Economy

Overview

The Bahamas offers a stable democratic government with a relatively diversified economy based on tourism, financial services, a few other relatively small but skills-intensive operations, and tax advantages. Efforts to further diversify the economy, especially in the industrial and agricultural sectors, have met with resistance from opponents fearing potential negative effects of foreign competition on local businesses. Personal income, corporate income, capital gains, dividends, interest, royalties, estates, sales, inheritances, and payrolls are all tax-free in the Bahamas, although real estate holdings are taxable and foreign-owned enterprises are expected to make generous contributions to civic projects.

Trade

Petroleum products represent more than half of Bahamian exports, these are followed by chemicals—mostly petrochemicals; other export categories are negligible. Imports include crude petroleum (52 percent), machinery and transportation equipment, basic and miscellaneous manufactured goods, foodstuffs, and chemicals. The US is the country's largest trading partner, representing roughly 32 percent of all Bahamian trade; it is followed by the Japan; Saudi Arabia, Nigeria, Mexico, and Indonesia supply mostly oil. About 60 percent of government revenues come from import tariffs.

Sectors

Agriculture This sector accounts for about six percent of employment and four percent of GDP. Although the Bahamas exports seafood and some specialty vegetable crops, about 80 percent of its food is imported. Agricultural work is generally shunned by the populace, so that a lack of capital and land suitable for exploitation is compounded by an effective labor shortage.

Industry Although industry employs about 14 percent of the work force, it accounts for only about 4 percent of GDP—down from 14 percent in the early 1980s (the drop is largely the result of the closure of an oil refinery). Industrial activities include production of pharmaceuticals, beer, and rum; shipfitting; limestone, chalk, and salt mining; and transshipment of petroleum products.

Services Accounting for about 90 percent of GDP and 80 percent of employment, the service sector includes the most marginal as well as the most highly paid and skilled of Bahamian operations. Tourism employs more than 40 percent of the work force and provides 55 percent of GDP. Increased competition from other Caribbean islands, the worldwide economic slump, relatively high prices in the Bahamas, and an overdependence on US traffic have hampered the industry. The financial sector, accounting for more than 10 percent of GDP, serves the sophisticated and burgeoning offshore tax shelter market. The Bahamas' shipping registry is also a significant contributor to the economy.

Trends

The Bahamas will likely continue to be troubled by high unemployment and underemployment as large numbers of people from its 1970s baby boom enter a marketplace where joblessness already hovers near 25 percent. Offshore financial services are likely to remain strong and current upgrading of tourism infrastructure is expected to bolster related industries over the near term, but agriculture, petroleum, shipping, and other industries are unlikely to improve significantly in the foreseeable future.

At a Glance

THE COUNTRY
Location The Bahamas extends 950 km (590 mi) SE-NW and 298 km (185 mi) NE-SW between southeast Florida and northern Hispaniola.

Terrain The Bahamas were formed as surface outcroppings of two oceanic banks, the Grand Bahama Bank and the Little Bahama Bank. The islands are for the most part low and flat, rising to a peak elevation of about 63 m (206 ft.) on Cat Island. The terrain is broken by lakes and mangrove swamps and the shorelines are marked by coral reefs.

Climate The climate is pleasantly subtropical, with an average winter temperature of 23°C (73°F) and an average summer temperature of 27°C (81°F). Rainfall averages 127 cm (50 in), and there are occasional hurricanes.

THE PEOPLE
Population 269,300
Ethnic composition
Black African 85%
European 12%
Asian and Hispanic 3%
Religious composition
Baptist 35%
Roman Catholic 19%
Anglican 20%
Evangelical Protestants 12%
Methodist 6%
Church of God 6%
Languages spoken English, Creole.

Education and literacy Education is under the jurisdiction of the Ministry of Education and Culture and is free in all government maintained schools. About 96% of the adult population is literate.

Labor force
Total: 136,900
By occupation: government, 30%; hotels and restaurants, 25%; business services, 10 percent; agricultural, 5%.

COUNTRY FACTS
Political and legal The Bahamas is an independent commonwealth. It is a parliamentary democracy and holds regular elections.

Telephone The Bahamian telecommunications system is highly developed and easily accessible. International country code: [1]. The area code is (809) for all points. In October, 1996, it will change to (242).

Transportation There are several airports through which most visitors and commerce pass. There is a road system, though it is neither well developed nor well maintained. There are no railroads. Two ports, Nassau and Freeport, handle virtually all pleasure and business shipping.

Environment Tourists come to the Bahamas for its beautiful waters, beaches, and subtropical weather. Current issues include provision of potable water and regular garbage collection throughout the country, maintenance and beautification of public parks and beaches, and the removal of abandoned vehicles.

Media There are three AM and two FM stations and one television station. An estimated 140,000 radios and 56,000 television sets exist on the island.

Health Overall health is good, with an average life expectancy of 72 years. The country is free from tropical diseases.

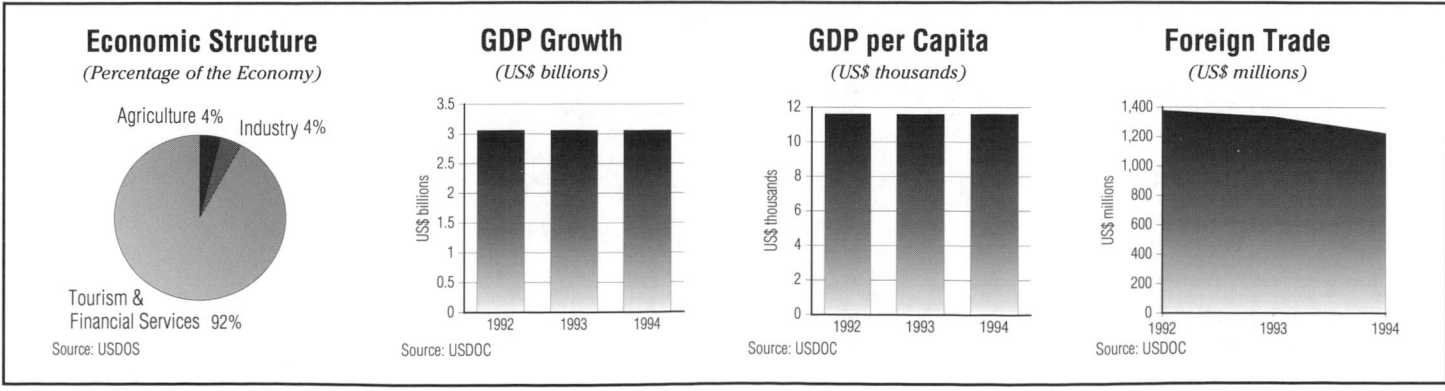

Economic Structure
(Percentage of the Economy)

Agriculture 4%
Industry 4%
Tourism & Financial Services 92%

Source: USDOS

GDP Growth
(US$ billions)

1992, 1993, 1994

Source: USDOC

GDP per Capita
(US$ thousands)

1992, 1993, 1994

Source: USDOC

Foreign Trade
(US$ millions)

1992, 1993, 1994

Source: USDOC

Business Travel

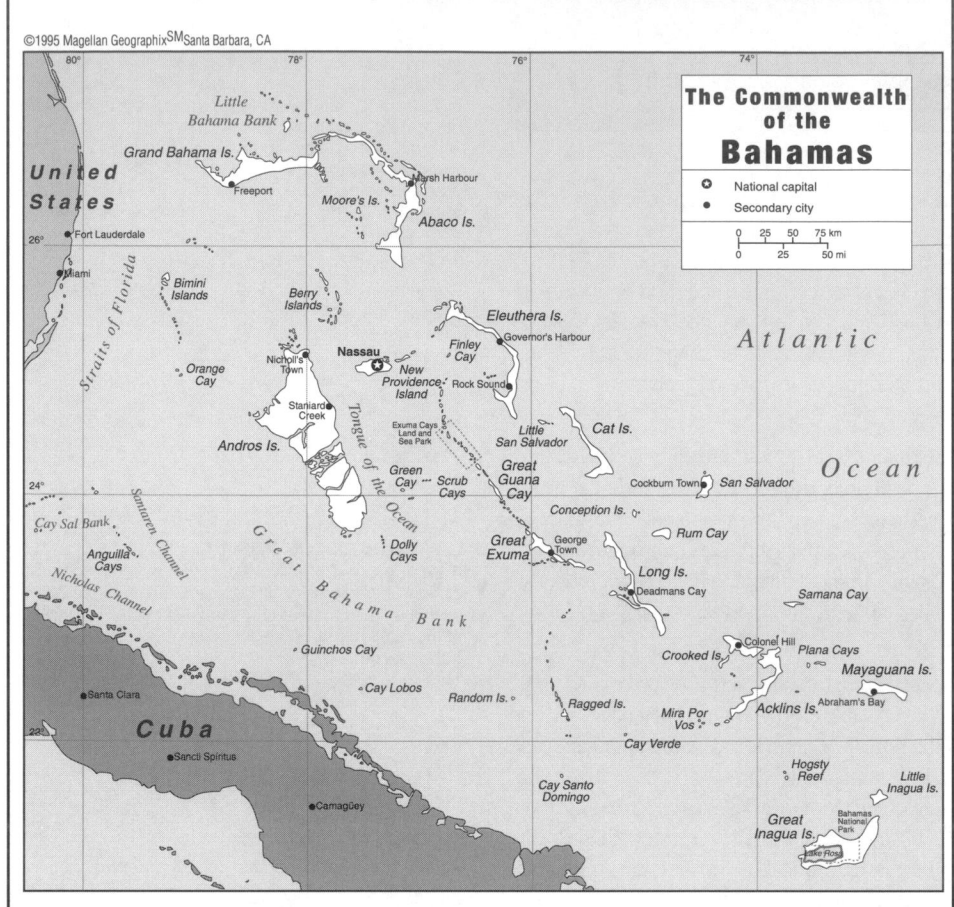

©1995 Magellan Geographix℠ Santa Barbara, CA

The Commonwealth of the Bahamas

⊙ National capital
● Secondary city

0 25 50 75 km
0 25 50 mi

Travelogue

WORKWEEK

Offices Monday-Friday 9:00 am to 5:00 pm. Closed Saturdays.
Banks Monday-Thursday 9:30 am to 3:00 pm, Friday 9:00 am to 5:00 pm, and closed Saturday and Sunday.
Government Monday-Friday 9:00 am to 5:00 pm.
Retail Monday-Saturday 9:00 am to 5:00 pm.

HOLIDAYS

Holidays 1996
January 1 New Year's Day
April 5 Good Friday
April 8 Easter Monday*
May 27 Whit Monday*
June 7 Labour Day*
July 10 Independence Day
August 5 Emancipation Day
October 12 Discovery Day
December 25 Christmas Day
December 26 Boxing Day
Holidays which fall on Saturday or Sunday are usually observed on the following Monday.
*Dates vary each year. Whit Monday is seven weeks after Easter; Labour Day is the first Friday in June; Emancipation Day is the first Monday in August.

VISA AND PASSPORT

Foreigners must have a valid passport, but visas are not required to enter the Bahamas. All travelers must hold onward tickets, valid travel documents, and sufficient funds. United States citizens do not need a passport but need a departure ticket, a birth certificate, and two forms of identification.

DEPARTURE FORMALITIES

When you leave the Bahamas by air, you will have to pay a US$13 departure tax at the airport. There are no other departure formalities for the Bahamas.

IMMUNIZATION

No vaccinations are required to enter the Bahamas unless arriving from an infected area.

TIPPING

A tip of 15 percent is usual for any service rendered, including taxi and food services. Hotels often automatically add this amount to your bill. Maid service tips may also be added to your hotel bill at a rate of around US$2 a day.

CRIME

Crime has become a growing problem in Nassau. Visitors are advised to avoid deserted areas at night, to avoid flashy displays of expensive items, and not to walk by themselves on beaches at night. Be wary of pickpockets in crowded areas. The crime rate is lower outside of Nassau and is practically nonexistent on most of the family islands.

INFRASTRUCTURE

Both Nassau and Freeport boast a wide variety of excellent hotels and resorts, plentiful taxis, and rental cars. While Bahamian hotels are more used to catering to the vacationer, they offer fax and other business services to the business traveler.

NATIONAL TOURIST OFFICE

Note: The area code for the Bahamas changes from (809) to (242) in October, 1996.
Tourist Office
Rawson Square
Nassau
Tel: (809) 3224066

COMMUNICATIONS

Telephones Telephone service in the Bahamas is run by a government agency and is modern and efficient. Calls are slightly less expensive at night than during the daytime hours. Calling cards are accepted. The area code for the Bahamas changes from (809) to (242) in October, 1996.
Fax Services for faxing and telegraph are available at major hotels and post offices.
Post office The postal service is adequate and inexpensive. Airmail letters are 45 cents to United States and 50 cents to Europe per half ounce.

BEST TRAVEL BOOKS

Fodor's Pocket Guide to the Bahamas. Tourist oriented, excellent source of city details.
Caribbean Islands Handbook. Passport Books. Updated annually.

USEFUL TELEPHONE NUMBERS

If you are calling from outside the Bahamas you will need to add the country code [1] and any other international dialing requirements from within your country.
Note: The area code for the Bahamas changes from (809) to (242) in October, 1996.
- Bahamas Fire and Police 919
- Information 916
- Nassau Bahamas Transport (taxi) .... (809) 3235111
- Calypso Taxi .... (809) 3277031
- Freeport Taxi Co. .... (809) 3526666
- Bahamas Air Sea Rescue .... (809) 3522880
- Nassau International Airport.............. (809) 3776833
- Prince George Wharf .... (809) 3259155
  (Cruise ship port at Freeport)
- Freeport International Airport .... (809) 3522052
- Harbour Cruiseship Port.................... (809) 3527888
- Nassau International Airport.............. (809) 3223344
Credit Card Information
Lost or stolen credit cards (call collect to the US, regardless of which country the card was issued in).
- Amex ....[1] (919) 333-3211
- Diner's Club.................................[1] (303) 799-1504
- MasterCard ....[1] (314) 275-6690
- Visa ....[1] (410) 581-7931

Foreign Trade

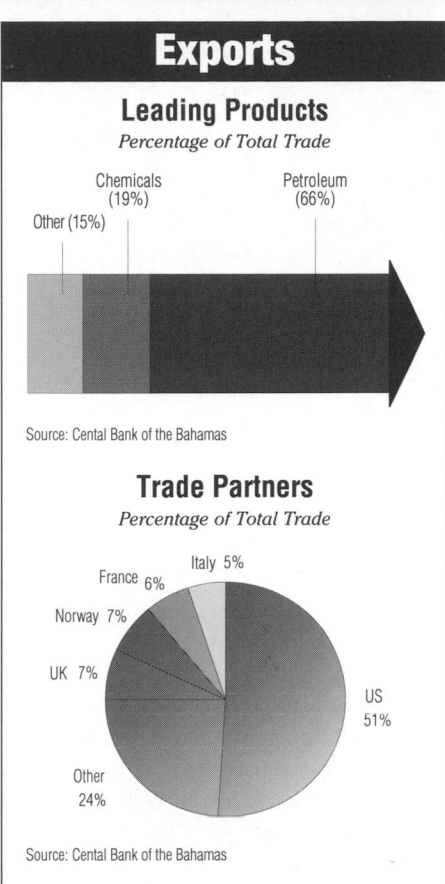

Imports

Leading Products
Percentage of Total Trade

Crude Petroleum (52%)
Machinery & Trans. Equipment (9%)
Food & Live Animals (7%)
Basic Manufacturing (7%)
Chemicals (5%)
Other (20%)

Source: Central Bank of the Bahamas

Trade Partners
Percentage of Total Trade

Norway 6%
Denmark 7%
Nigeria 12%
Japan 17%
Other 26%
US 32%

Source: Cental Bank of the Bahamas

Exports

Leading Products
Percentage of Total Trade

Chemicals (19%)
Petroleum (66%)
Other (15%)

Source: Cental Bank of the Bahamas

Trade Partners
Percentage of Total Trade

Italy 5%
France 6%
Norway 7%
UK 7%
US 51%
Other 24%

Source: Cental Bank of the Bahamas

Opportunities

FOR IMPORTING TO BAHAMAS
- cereal
- clothing
- computer products
- dairy products
- electronic goods
- fuels
- hotel supplies

FOR EXPORTING FROM BAHAMAS
- cement
- crawfish

GROWTH SECTORS
- beer and spirits
- financial services
- fisheries
- manufacturing
- tourism

Trade News

RULES AND REGULATIONS

- **Tariffs** The Bahamian government raises approximately 60 percent of its total revenue from import tariffs, which, as a result, tend to be high.
- **Import restrictions** The Ministry of Agriculture occasionally issues temporary bans on the import of certain agricultural products when it determines that a sufficient supply of locally grown items exist.
- **Export tax** The Bahamian government charges an export stamp tax of four percent on most exports from the country.
- **Export subsidies** The Bahamian government does not provide direct subsidies to industry.

Legal

Legal System

The Bahamas is a parliamentary democracy with regular elections. As a Commonwealth country, its political and legal traditions closely follow those of the UK. A bicameral legislature enacts laws under the 1973 Constitution.

Business Registration

It is relatively simple and very inexpensive to register a business in the Bahamas. The standards are lax, and require only registration. Prior approval is not generally necessary.

Contracts and Dispute Resolution

Contracts are intended as fully as possible to set out the details of the relationship between the parties thereto. Where disputes arise initial attempts are made to settle the same informally; however, many result in actual litigation. Arbitration is not common. Judgments made in the courts in the Bahamas may be enforced in other jurisdictions subject to registration there. In other cases, the judgments may provide the evidence on which legal proceedings may be commenced. The reverse is also true.

Labor

Workers have a constitutional right to associate freely. Generally, staff works a maximum of 40 hours per week or five 8-hour days. In addition to 10 national holidays, employees are entitled to annual paid vacations. There is no automatic right for the employee to work. He or she must, in accordance with the terms of employment, give a good day's work for a good day's pay. The employer has the right to dismiss the employee for cause, and all rights under an employment contract are determined impartially and fairly by the court without bias.

Legal Matters

LEGAL BRIEFS

- **Corporations** International Business Corporations featuring bearer shares, no filing of accounts and shareholder information, freedom from exchange control, ability to conduct business in any non-Bahamian currency anywhere in the world, and protection by secrecy laws are ideal for the conduct of business worldwide from the Bahamas. However, foreign investors carrying on projects in the Bahamas must establish domestic corporations.
- **Legal protection** All persons, whether foreign or local, have access to the Court for the determination of any matters in dispute, and the Court determines all such issues in strict accordance with law, without favoritism.
- **Property** Nonresident aliens may acquire real property.
- **Trade agreements** The Bahamas is an associate member of Caricom, a group of former Commonwealth Caribbean countries, and a part of GATT.

LEGAL CONTACT

Note: The area code for the Bahamas changes from (809) to (242) in October, 1996.
Anthony Thompson & Co.
Marron House
Virginia & Augusta Street
Nassau, Bahamas
POB N-4826
Virginia & Augusta Street
Nassau, Bahamas
Tel: (809) 325-1126, 322-1038, 322-8549
Fax: (809) 322-3919

Source: Anthony Thompson & Company, Nassau

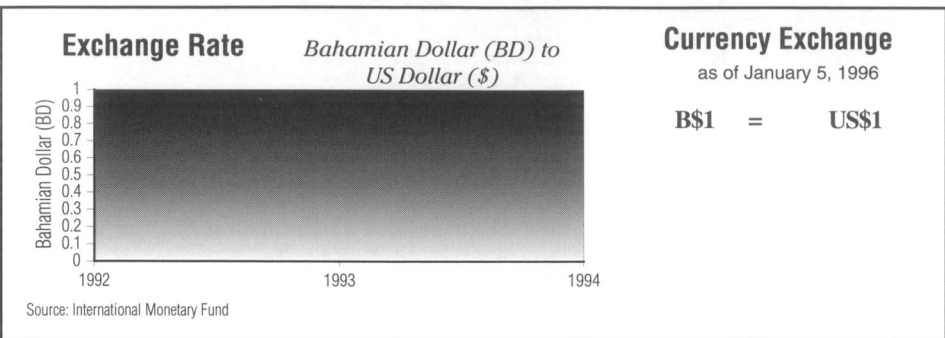

Exchange Rate
Bahamian Dollar (BD) to US Dollar ($)

1
0.9
0.8
0.7
0.6
0.5
0.4
0.3
0.2
0.1
0

Bahamian Dollar (BD)

1992   1993   1994

Source: International Monetary Fund

Currency Exchange
as of January 5, 1996

B$1   =   US$1

Money Matters

BITS AND PIECES

- **Bank notes** Foreign bank notes may be brought into the country without restriction or limit, but domestic bank notes brought into the country may require approval from the Central Bank.
- **Commercial banks** Commercial banks generally charge the public a commission of 0.50 percent buying and 0.75 percent sell per US$1.
- **Investment currency** There is a market in investment currency which can be negotiated between residents through the Central Bank at freely determined rates, usually attracting a premium above the official market rate.
- **Cover** Commercial banks may provide forward cover for residents of the Bahamas when the resident is due to receive or must pay foreign currency under a contractual commitment.
- **Winter residents** Authorized banks may freely open external accounts denominated in Bahamian dollars for winter residents and for persons with residency permits who are not gainfully employed in the Bahamas.
- **Export of notes** Travelers may export Bahamian bank notes not exceeding B$70 in value; Bahamian travelers may not export the bank notes of any other country, except with specific approval from the Central Bank.
- **Stamp tax** A stamp tax of 1.5 percent is applied to all outward remittances.
- **Gold** Residents of the Bahamas, other than authorized dealers, are not permitted to hold or deal in gold bullion. However, residents who are known users of gold for industrial purposes may, with the approval of the Central Bank, meet their current industrial requirements. There is no restriction on residents' acquisition or retention of gold coins.
- **Agricultural Manufactories Act** This law allows any materials necessary for the construction, alteration, or repair of an "agricultural factory," as well as any machinery or supplies used in establishing such a factory, to be imported duty free.
- **Spirits and Beer Manufacture Act** This law provides for the duty-free importation of materials used in the construction, alteration, or repair of approved liquor distilleries or beer breweries and the duty-free importation of raw materials and equipment for liquor or beer production.
- **Hotels Encouragement Act** Hotels and resorts can be exempted from real property taxes for 10 years from the date the new facility opens. In addition, the act allows the duty-free importation of materials used for the construction of new facilities or the substantial renovation of existing facilities acquired by new owners for a set period of time.

Currency

The currency of the Bahamas is the Bahamian dollar (BD), which is pegged to the US dollar at B$1 per US$1. The US dollar circulates concurrently with the Bahamian dollar.

Foreign Exchange

The exchange rates of currencies other than the US dollar are based on the buying and selling rates for the US dollar in markets abroad. All exchange transactions are carried out through entities authorized expressly for this purpose with no restrictions on the purchase or sale of foreign exchange. Exchange control is administered by the Central Bank, which deals only with commercial banks.

Capital Transfers

Settlements with residents of foreign countries may be made in any foreign currency or in Bahamian dollars through an external account. With approval of the Central Bank, authorized banks may open external accounts in Bahamian dollars for nonresident companies that have local expenses in the Bahamas and for nonresident investors. External accounts in Bahamian dollars are normally funded entirely from foreign currency originating outside the Bahamas, but income on registered investments may also be credited to these accounts with the approval of the Central Bank. Balances may be converted freely into foreign currency and transferred abroad. The proceeds of exports must be offered for sale to an authorized dealer as soon as the goods have reached their destination or within six months of shipment; or, export proceeds may be otherwise used in a manner acceptable to the Central Bank. All capital transfers to countries outside the Bahamas require exchange control approval, and outflows of resident-owned capital are restricted. Prior approval from the Central Bank is required to make payments for imports exceeding B$100,000, irrespective of origin.

Investment Incentives

The Bahamian government actively seeks investments aimed at increasing agricultural exports, particularly specialty food items.

Investment Restrictions

Nonresidents acquiring control of or participating in an incorporated company controlled by residents must first obtain permission from the Central Bank. There are also limits on foreign investments in real estate.

BANKS

Note: The area code for the Bahamas changes from (809) to (242) in October, 1996.

Bahamas Development Bank
Bay Street
POB N-3034
Nassau
Tel: (809) 322-8721
Fax: (809) 322-6457
Telex: 20297

Central Bank of the Bahamas
Frederick Street
POB N-4868
Nassau
Tel: (809) 322-2193
Fax: (809) 322-4321
Telex: 20115

National Insurance Board
Farrington Road
POB N-7508
Nassau
Tel: (809) 322-2005
Fax: (809) 322-2923

TAXATION

Taxation requires sophisticated knowledge of complex rules and regulations specific to each country. The information presented here is from the Ernst & Young Corporate Tax Guide and Directory, available from the Ernst & Young accounting office in your country, or from:

Ernst & Young
Mail Address:
POB N-3231
Nassau, Bahamas
Street Address:
Sassoon House
Shirley & Victoria
Nassau, Bahamas
Tel: (809) 322-3805/7/8
Telex: 20240 Ans bk AUDAC
Fax: (809) 326-8180

At a Glance

Corporate Income Tax Rate (%)	0
Capital Gains Tax Rate (%)	0
Branch Tax Rate (%)	0
Withholding Tax (%)	0

- No taxes are levied on corporate income or gains.

Distribution

Goods typically enter Bahamian markets through local wholesalers or commission agents or direct sales from manufacturers. Most foreign retail and wholesale chains are prohibited from opening outlets in the Bahamas, although distributorships and franchises can be negotiated with local partners. Local wholesalers and agents commonly specialize in particular lines. Most wholesalers and some retailers will purchase directly from manufacturers, which can develop into exclusive distributorship arrangements.

Selling Techniques

Selling in the Bahamas is like marketing in Europe and the US. Bahamians are educated consumers and the market is highly competitive. Products must be attractive, high in quality, and priced to sell. Personal contacts go far, and a regular trip to the Bahamas may make the difference in successful market penetration. In any event, foreign sellers should make every effort to establish personal relationships with major customers, rather than relying solely on local distributors.

Advertising

Goods and services are advertised extensively in local news and magazine publications. The country's several major daily newspapers accept ads at reasonable rates, as do a number of weekly tabloids. The single state-owned television station sells advertising, as do the three state-controlled and two independent radio stations. Bold, aggressive advertising works well in this market; a subtle approach is often overlooked.

Service and Customer Support

For products that need after-sales servicing, local representation is essential. To hold an edge in this highly competitive market, local agents must be well-trained and current on the latest product technology. Delivery of spare parts from overseas is relatively fast, but having spare parts and equipment in stock can mean the difference in the competition for business.

Marketing in Bahamas

MARKETING TIPS

- **Go to the beach** Hotel and retail tourist outlets are a major market in the Bahamas. More than 3.5 million tourists visit the Bahamas every year, 81 percent of them from the US. November to May is peak tourist season. The islands are a popular business convention site.
- **Financial heart** Nassau is a major bank, trust, and financial service center, creating significant demand for up-to-the-minute computer and communication technologies and investment, insurance, and banking advisors.
- **Tropical touch** Products should be geared to the hot, humid climate and the cultural tendency toward casual living. Equipment may have to be modified to keep it operational.
- **Credit terms** Short-term credit (30 to 90 days) is commonly extended. Incidence of bad debts is relatively low, but debt collection is expensive.

RADIO & TELEVISION

Note: The area code for the Bahamas changes from (809) to (242) in October, 1996.
Broadcasting Corporation of the Bahamas
3rd Terrace Centerville
POB N-1347
New Providence
Tel: (809) 322-4623
Fax: (809) 322-3915

Business Culture

Greetings and Courtesies

Bahamians are noticeably formal, but perhaps less so than in many other areas of the English-speaking Caribbean. Titles and last names are used, although Bahamians are less addicted to the use of titles than many others in Latin America and the Caribbean. Business cards (in English) are normally exchanged, but without particular formality.

Business Ethic and Framework

The Bahamas is largely a consensus driven society. Confrontation is to be avoided and tailoring the business at hand to meet criteria of broad, general acceptability is often necessary to reach an agreement. Personal contacts are important, but less so than is the case in many cultures in Latin America and elsewhere.

Meetings and Decision Making

Introductions are helpful but not absolutely necessary. Bahamians are often late for appointments, but foreigners are expected to be on time. Business lunch meetings are common—these are low-key events, usually limited to the people involved in the immediate discussions. Dinner meetings are uncommon, as are other outside events which combine business and social elements. Because of the importance of consensus, few individuals have full authority to make binding decisions concerning any but the most mundane matters. Locals may assume that foreign businesspeople are fully aware of this without making it clear to them, leading to disappointments and misunderstandings.

Women

Women in the Bahamas occupy a secondary status, although they often form the backbone of small-scale enterprises and are generally accorded considerable personal freedom and influence. Foreign businesswomen should experience few problems and may even be accorded special treatment by more traditional senior businessmen.

Cultural Cautions

DO'S

- For business wear dark, conservative business suits or jackets with ties and long trousers. Women should wear conservative business suits or dresses.
- Do prepare to spend a great deal of time and effort introducing and promoting new products, as Bahamians tend to be suspicious of new concepts.
- Always accept an invitation to join your Bahamian business associate at church, regardless of your denomination or affiliation. Such an invitation is a sign of personal respect and affection.

DON'TS

- Don't wear shorts for business; they are not acceptable.
- Do not expect to be invited to a business associate's home for a meal. This is considered personal time, usually reserved for the family.
- Do not drink very much at a business lunch, even if your Bahamian counterpart urges you to do so.

OBSERVATIONS

- Due to its proximity and heavy orientation toward the US, Bahamian business customs tend to be similar to those in the US, albeit slightly more formal.
- Bahamians tend not to trust the intentions of foreigners at first (regardless of the foreigner's ethnic background).

NEGOTIATIONS

- Negotiations tend to proceed pleasantly, and Bahamians are often eager to end a meeting even if real differences remain.
- Bahamian businesses tend to operate on a tight margin, often juggling financing from one commitment to another.

Contacts

GOVERNMENT AGENCIES

Investment Authority (BIA)
POB N 7147
Nassau
Tel: (809) 327-5826
Fax: (809) 327-5806

Agricultural and Industrial Corporation (BAIC)
POB N 4940
Nassau
Tel: (809) 322-3740
Fax: (809) 322-2123

Ministry of Tourism
POB N-3701
Nassau
Tel: (809) 322-7500
Fax: (809) 328-0945

Ministry of Employment and Immigration
P. O. Box N-831
Nassau
Tel: (809) 322-7530

Ministry of Agriculture, Trade, and Industry
POB N-3028
Nassau
Tel: (809) 325-7502

Ministry of Finance
POB N-3017
Nassau
Tel: (809) 322-4151
Fax: (809) 328-8294

Ministry of Health
POB N-3730
Nassau
Tel: (809) 322-7425
Fax: (809) 328-7788

Ministry of Transport
POB N-3008
Nassau
Tel: (809) 322-3349
Fax: (809) 328-2220

Controller of Customs
POB N-155
Nassau
Tel: (809) 328-1023
Fax: (809) 322-6223

Telecommunications Corp. (Batelco)
POB N-3048
Nassau
Tel: (809) 323-5200
Fax: (809) 326-7474

Bahamas Electricity Corp. (BEC)
POB N-7509
Nassau
Tel: (809) 328-7700
Fax: (809) 323-6852

Bahamas Water and Sewage Corp. (W&SC)
POB N-3905
Nassau
Tel: (809) 323-3944
Fax: (809) 322-5080

GOVERNMENT CORPORATIONS

Bahamas Agricultural and Industrial Corporation
BAIC Building
East Bay Street
POB N-4940
Nassau
Tel: (809) 322-3740
Fax: (809) 322-2123

Bahamas Electricity Corporation
Blue Hill Road
POB N-7509
Nassau
Tel: (809) 325-4101
Fax: (809) 323-6852

Bahamas Telecommunications Corporation
John F. Kennedy Drive
POB N-3048
Nassau
Tel: (809) 325-8531
Fax: (809) 326-0699

Hotel Corporation
West Bay Street
POB N-9520
Nassau
Tel: (809) 327-8395
Fax: (809) 327-8398

CHAMBERS OF COMMERCE

Chamber of Commerce
POB N-665
Nassau
Tel: (809) 322-2145
Fax: (809) 322-4649

The Grand Chamber of Commerce
POB F-808
Nassau
Tel: (809) 352-8329
Fax: (809) 352-9864

NEWSPAPERS

Freeport News
Cedar St.
POB F-7
Freeport
Tel: (809) 352-8321
Fax: (809) 352-8324

Nassau Daily Tribune
Shirley St.
POB N-3207
Nassau
Tel: (809) 328-1986
Fax: (809) 328-2398

Nassau Guardian
4 Carter St.
Oakes Field
POB N-3011
Nassau
Tel: (809) 323-5654
Telex: 20100
Fax: (809) 325-3379

RADIO AND TELEVISION

Broadcasting Corporation of the Bahamas
POB N-1347
Centreville
New Providence
Tel: (809) 322-4623
Telex: 20253
Fax: (809) 322-3924

BANKS

Bahama Bank Ltd.
POB N-272
Nassau

Bahamas International Trust Co. Ltd. (Bitco)
Bitco Bldg
Bank Lane POB N-7768
Nassau
Tel: (809) 322-1161
Telex: 20143
Fax: (809) 326-5020

Bank of the Bahamas Ltd.
50 Shirley St.
Nassau
Tel: (809) 326-2560
Fax: (809) 325-2762

Bank of New Providence Ltd.
Claughton House
Shirley and Charlotte Sts
POB N-4723
Nassau
Tel: (809) 322-8134
Telex: 20156
Fax: (809) 339-1987

Commonwealth Industrial Bank Ltd.
610 Bay St.
POB SS-5541
Nassau
Tel: (809) 328-1854

Coutts and Co. (Bahamas) Ltd.
West Bay St.

POB N-7788
Nassau
Tel: (809) 326-0404
Fax: (809) 326-6709

Dominion Charter Bank Ltd.
POB SS-5539
Nassau
Tel: (809) 393-8777
Fax: (809) 393-0582

Equator Bank Ltd.
Norfolk House
Frederick St.
POB N-9925
Nassau
Tel: (809) 322-2754
Fax: (809) 326-5706

Euro-Dutch Trust Co. (Bahamas) Ltd.
Charlotte House
POB N-9204
Nassau

Fidenas International Bank Ltd.
Bolam House
George St.
POB N-4816
Nassau
Tel: (809) 325-6052
Telex: 20278
Fax: (809) 325-2592

Finance Corp of the Bahamas Ltd. (FINCO)
Frederick St.
POB N-3038
Nassau
Tel: (809) 322-4822
Fax: (809) 328-8848

First Home Banking Centre Ltd
The Mall, POB F-2644
Freeport
Tel: (809) 352-6676

Leadenhall Trust Co. Ltd.
Cumberland Court
1 Cumberland St.
POB N-1965
Nassau
Tel: (809) 325-1033
Fax: (809) 328-7030

Meridien International Bank Ltd.
Meridien House
East Bay St.
POB N-3209
Nassau
Tel: (809) 393-4857
Fax: (809) 393-4974

Rawson Trust Co. Ltd.
Euro Canadian Centre
POB N-4465
Nassau
Tel: (809) 322-7461
Fax: (809) 326-6177

INTERNET ADDRESSES

Bahamas Online
http://thebahamas.com/

The Bahamas!
http://www.gti.net/bahamas

Bahamas On-Line
http://www.bahamas.net.bs

Usenet group:
soc.culture.caribbean

Bahrain

State of Bahrain

Economy

Overview

Considered one of the best business environments in the Middle East, Bahrain has attempted to move beyond its petroleum-based economy, enhancing it through government-sponsored diversification efforts that support growth of a strong financial services sector in particular. With solid labor-management relations and a relatively well-educated work force of approximately 200,000, this island nation offers a well-developed infrastructure, a fairly high standard of living, a history of political stability, and favorable economic policies. Bahrain was one of the first Arab nations to discover and refine oil, which generates roughly 60 percent of the country's revenues. However, its rapidly depleting domestic reserves—predicted to last only 15 years—provide the incentive for accelerated diversification.

Trade

Bahrain's trade regulations are designed to encourage development of export-oriented industries which must compete based on free market forces. Higher value-added processed petroleum products represent the vast bulk of Bahrain's exports, with metal products (aluminum, iron, and steel) and chemicals representing a relatively small but growing source of exports. Trade in services—particularly financial services—is also a growth sector. Bahrain remains dependent on imports of food, manufactured consumer goods, capital, and intermediate goods. Saudi Arabia is Bahrain's largest trading partner, based primarily on purchases of crude petroleum as refinery stock. The US is Bahrain's next largest trading partner, followed by Japan, the UK, and Australia, which purchase petroleum products and provide capital, intermediate, and consumer goods.

Sectors

Agriculture Bahrain's agricultural sector—which employs less than five percent of the work force and contributes less than five percent of GDP—can neither feed the country nor provide exports. Despite heavy subsidies and underexploitation of fish resources, the sector is unlikely to develop significantly.

Industry Industry employs 35 percent of the work force and produces 40 percent of GDP. Oil and gas—including refining, natural gas liquification, and ammonia and methanol production for export—still dominate the economy. Other industries include aluminum, iron, steel, and chemical production. Since the mid-1980s the government has encouraged development of high value-added light manufacturing.

Service Employing more than 60 percent of the work force, services constitute about 55 percent of GDP. Bahrain's financial services industry is the most sophisticated in the Middle East, retaining a major role in Middle Eastern business despite setbacks in the regional economy.

Trends

Although the US and the UK have long dominated foreign investment and trade, Bahrain's economic relations with other Gulf states, as well as with Asian nations such as Japan and Australia, are increasing; this pattern is likely to continue. Financial services and related industries are especially promising. Further infrastructural development is likely, providing new opportunities for foreign sellers. Projects planned or under discussion include desalination plants, expanded port facilities, new hospitals, and a US$400 million upgrade of Bahraini's aging oil refinery.

At a Glance

THE COUNTRY

Location Situated in the western Persian Gulf, NW of Qatar, the State of Bahrain consists of a group of 33 islands extending 48 km (30 mi) N-S and 19 km (12 mi) E-W.

Terrain A narrow strip of land along the north coast of Bahrain is irrigated by natural springs and artesian wells. South of the cultivable area, the land is barren. The landscape consists of low rolling hills with numerous rocky cliffs and wadis. Most of the lesser islands are flat and sandy, while Nabih Salih is covered with date groves.

Climate Summers in Bahrain are hot and humid, and winters are relatively cool. Rainfall is less than 10 cm (4 in) annually and occurs mostly from December to March. Prevailing southeast winds occasionally raise dust storms.

THE PEOPLE

Population 508,037
Ethnic composition
Arab 73%
Iranian.. 9%
Pakistani 9%
Indian 9%
Religious composition
Shi'a Muslim 70%
Sunni Muslim 30%
Languages spoken Arabic, English, Farsi, and Urdu are all widely spoken. A relatively high percentage of the business population speaks English.
Education and literacy Bahrain introduced a free public education system to the Gulf region in 1919. The government aims to provide free educational opportunities for all children. The adult literacy rate is 77.4%.
Labor force
Total:..197,000
By occupation: agriculture 4%, industry and commerce 35%, services 60%.

COUNTRY FACTS

Political and legal Bahrain operates as a traditional emirate with a cabinet-executive system. There are no political parties.
Telephone Connections are excellent because international calls enter the satellite communications system from Bahrain. International country code: [973].
Transportation Many major airlines serve Bahrain's modern international airport. Taxis and rental cars are available in Manama.
Environment Wildflowers are noticeable after rain. Desert shrubs, grasses, and wild date palms are also found. Birds, mammals, and lizards share the environment. Current issues: Bahrain's principal environmental problems are scarcity of fresh water, desertification, and pollution from oil production.
Media The government operates a radio station and a television station. Radio Bahrain transmits AM and FM broadcasts on two channels. There are over 278,000 radios and 215,000 televisions in Bahrain.
Health Bahrain has a free national health service, available to both foreign and indigenous populations through a system of primary care health centers and modern hospital facilities.

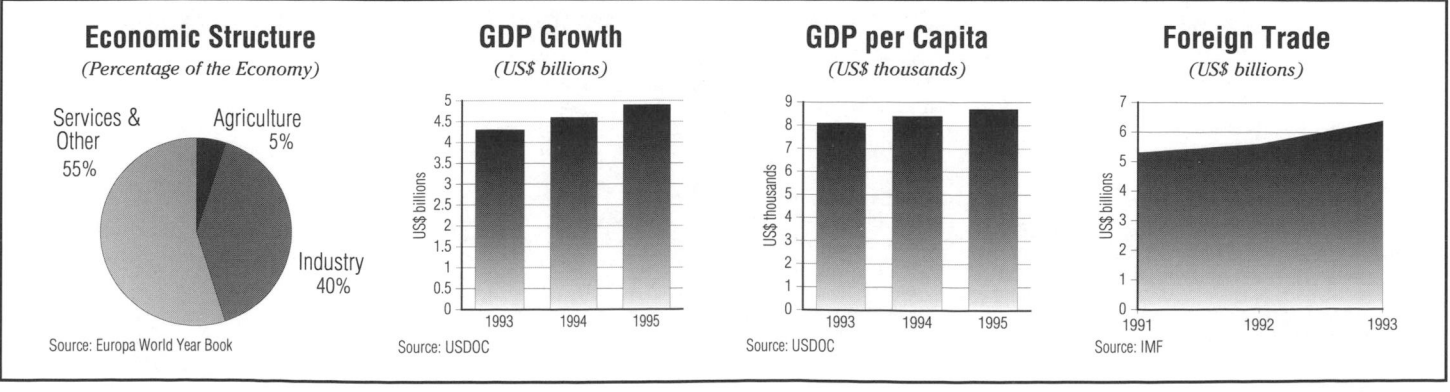

Economic Structure
(Percentage of the Economy)

Services & Other 55%
Agriculture 5%
Industry 40%

Source: Europa World Year Book

GDP Growth
(US$ billions)

Source: USDOC

GDP per Capita
(US$ thousands)

Source: USDOC

Foreign Trade
(US$ billions)

Source: IMF

Business Travel

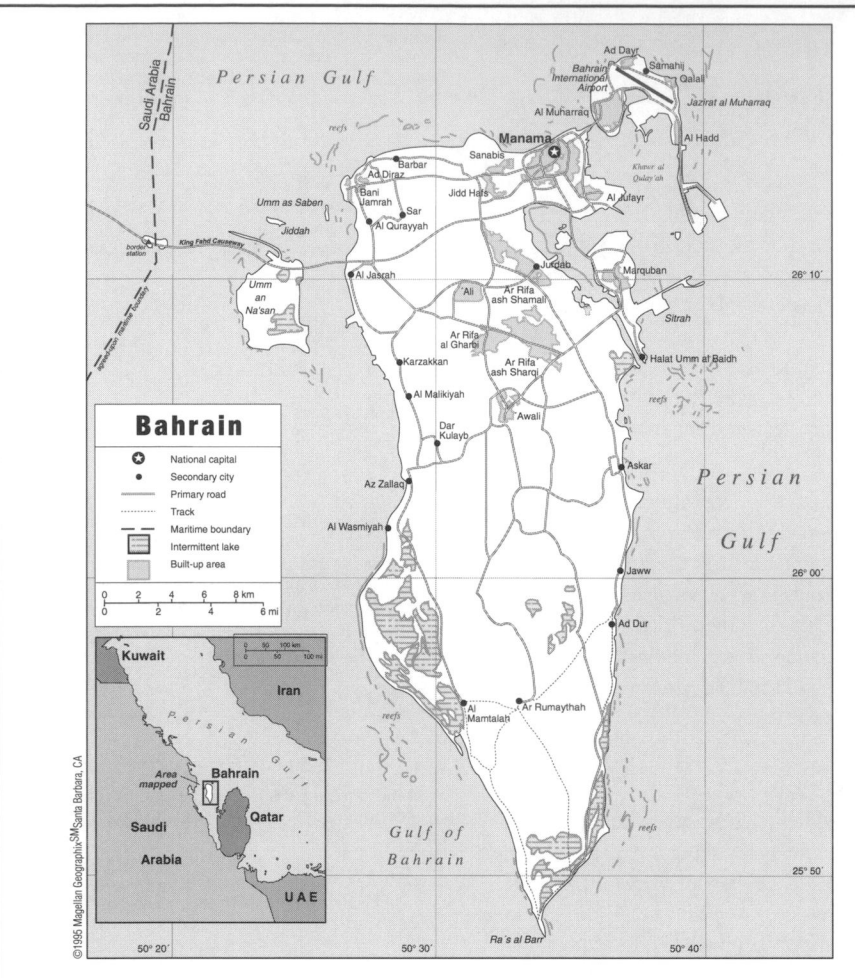

COMMUNICATIONS

Telephones Telephone service is excellent. Direct dialing and local direct calls are available. International calls, fax, telegraph, and telex services are available at the Telecommunications Office located on Government Avenue, open from 6:30 am to 11:30 pm. Public phones can be found in hotels, restaurants, the Telecommunications office and phone booths. Pay phones require deposit of coin or phone card for dial tone. Local calls are charged in increments of 50 fils. Insert a minimum of 100 fils. Phone cards can be purchased at the Telecommunications Office.

Fax Most major hotels have fax facilities.

Post office The main post office is located on Government Avenue and is open from 7:00 am to 7:30 pm.

Radio/TV Bahrain Broadcasting Station: POB 194, Manama. Radio Bahrain: POB 702, Manama. Bahrain Radio and Television Corp: POB 1075, Manama.

BEST TRAVEL BOOKS

The Traveler's Guide to Middle Eastern and North African Customs and Manners. Elizabeth Devine & Nancy Braganti. How to converse, dine, tip, bargain, dress, make friends and conduct business while in the Middle East and North Africa.

Middle East, On a Shoestring. Lonely Planet Details, details, details! 126 maps.

Do's and Taboo's Around the World. The Bestselling Guide to International Behavior. Edited by Roger Axtell, compiled by the Parker Pen Company. The ultimate guide to international behavior, now completely updated and expanded. Helpful, fun to read!

Bahrain, a Travel Guide, by Philip Ward. Oleander Press.

USEFUL TELEPHONE NUMBERS

If you are calling from outside Bahrain you will need to add the country code [973] and any other international dialing requirements from within your country. There are no city codes in Bahrain.

- Directory Assistance 100
- International Information 191
- Fire, Police, Ambulance 999
- Directory Assistance 100
- Directory Inquires 181
- Manama Police 253545
- Muharraq Police 322633
- Mina Sulman Police 243555
- Flight Information 322295
- Airport Information.. 325555
- Gulf Air 531166
- Fax Services 270270
- Secretarial Services 712851
- Translation Services 258283
- Medical Center 252761
- American Hospital 253447
- Manama Taxi 253349
- Airport Taxi.. 320982

Credit Card Information

Lost or stolen credit cards (call collect to the US, regardless of which country the card was issued in).

- Amex...[1] (919) 333-3211
- Diner's Club................................[1] (303) 799-1504
- MasterCard ....[1] (314) 275-6690
- Visa ....[1] (410) 581-7931

Travelogue

WORKWEEK

Offices Saturday-Thursday 7:00 am to noon and 2:30 pm to 5:00 pm.

Banks Saturday-Wednesday 7:30 am to noon and 7:30 am to 11:00 am Thursday.

Government Saturday-Thursday 7:00 am to 1:00 pm.

Retail Saturday-Thursday 7:00 am to noon and 2:30 pm to 5:00 pm.

The standard work week is Saturday-Thursday.

HOLIDAYS

Holidays 1996

January 1 New Year's Day
February 21-26 Eid Al Fitr*
May 19 Islamic New Year*
May 27-28 Ashura*
July 28 Prophet's Birthday
December 16 National Day

*The dates for these holidays are tentative, as they are determined by lunar sightings. The definite dates may not be announced until shortly before the holiday itself.

VISA AND PASSPORT

Most foreign visitors require a valid passport and a visa issued in advance by a Bahrain consulate. In some cases, visas for very short visits may be obtained upon arrival. Visas valid for 72 hours can be obtained in Bahrain. Visas can be extended upon application of a Bahraini sponsor. UK passport holders do not require a visa for stays up to four weeks.

DEPARTURE FORMALITIES

A departure tax of BD 3 will be collected. There are no other departure formalities for Bahrain.

IMMUNIZATION

International certificate of vaccination for yellow fever and cholera required if arriving from infected areas within the last two weeks. Vaccinations for polio, cholera, tetanus, and typhoid advised.

TIPPING

Taxi: 10 percent. Hotels will add 10 to 15 percent service charge. Porters expect 100 fils per bag and hotel attendants expect 100 fils each. In general, tipping is not expected, but the increase in foreigners has begun to ingrain the practice.

CRIME

Crime is not a big problem; however, normal precautions against pickpockets and petty theft should be considered. Political demonstrations in Manama are common and should be avoided.

INFRASTRUCTURE

Bahrain has a well-developed, modern infrastructure with good hotel and transportation systems. Taxis are readily available but do not have meters so fares should be negotiated at the beginning of your trip. The ride from the airport to town should take about 20 minutes, longer during rush hour. Expect to pay BD4 (US$10.65) for the ride, more after midnight. Car rental agencies are located at the airport; major hotels also have facilities. Buses are available, but not commonly used by business travelers. The airport is a modern regional hub and a major transit point for international travelers. Most major hotels provide airport pickup, but this must be reserved in advance.

TOURIST OFFICES

Directorate of Tourism
Manama
Tel: 211199

Tourist Office
Al-Khalifa Ave.
Manama
Tel: 231375

Foreign Trade

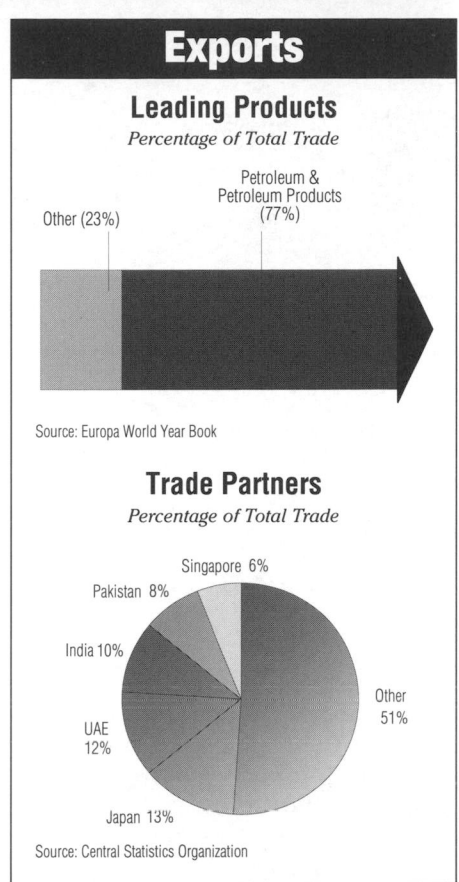

Imports

Leading Products
Percentage of Total Trade

- crude petroleum
- machinery and transporation equipment
(percentages not available)

Source: Europa World Year Book

Trade Partners
Percentage of Total Trade

Japan 5%   Germany 4%
UK 7%
US 14%
Saudi Arabia 42%
Other 20%

Source: Central Statistics Organization

Exports

Leading Products
Percentage of Total Trade

Other (23%)   Petroleum & Petroleum Products (77%)

Source: Europa World Year Book

Trade Partners
Percentage of Total Trade

Singapore 6%
Pakistan 8%
India 10%
UAE 12%
Japan 13%
Other 51%

Source: Central Statistics Organization

Opportunities

FOR IMPORTING TO BAHRAIN
- clothing and textiles
- foodstuffs
- fuels and motor vehicles
- furniture and industrial equipment
- high-end consumer goods

FOR EXPORTING FROM BAHRAIN
- aluminum
- natural gas, oil, petroleum products
- clothing
- fish

GROWTH SECTORS
- aluminum
- financial services
- petroleum products

GOVERNMENT PROCUREMENT
- roadway construction goods
- roadway services
- water treatment facilities

Legal

Legal System

Bahrain's legal system comes from several sources: customary tribal law, Islamic Sharia law, and civil law. All laws in Bahrain are created by the Al Khalifa family, who also controls the government.

Intellectual Property Rights

Patents Once registered, patents are adequately protected by Bahrain's legal system. Without registration, however, patents are not considered valid. The registration process is complex, and can sometimes take several years to complete.

Trademarks Bahrain's laws actively protect registered trademarks. Registration is generally undertaken by a local attorney to ensure adequate protections.

Copyrights Bahrain passed a copyright law recently, but it does not meet the international standards of copyright protection, and copyrights are not considered to be adequately protected in Bahrain.

Business Registration

Bahrain has made registration very easy and quick. Procedures for obtaining licenses have been streamlined, and all the necessary formalities can usually be accomplished within one week.

Contracts and Dispute Resolution

Businesses in Bahrain prefer contracts that are short and general. Most commercial disputes are handled informally, without the courts or formal arbitration. Bahrain is in the process of establishing an international arbitration center.

Labor

Labor management relations are relatively smooth. In general, employers have broad authority over the hiring, firing, and working conditions of employees. Workers in the non-public sector can bargain collectively, and have the right to strike, although unions have not gained widespread acceptance.

Legal Matters

LEGAL BRIEFS
- **Political violence** Bahrain is a peaceful country, with crime rates far below those of other countries.
- **Competition** Bahraini law allows competition, but then limits it in several ways. It sets the prices of key consumer goods by taxing foreign goods.
- **Registration** The government has established offices to help businesses through the registration process.
- **JCCs** In the major state-owned industries, joint labor-management consultative councils (JCCs) have been set up to help workers and management discuss various labor issues, including wages and productivity.
- **Minimum wages** Minimum wage levels for workers are generally lower than those in neighboring countries, but well above third world averages.

LEGAL CONTACTS

Law Offices of Ahmed Zaki Yamani
Manama Center
POB 342
Manama

Law Office of Shaikh Isa Bin Mohammed Al Khalifa
(Associated with Clifford Chance)
POB 20717
Manama, Bahrain
Tel: 53-1535, 53-1073
Fax: 53-6272, 53-0608

Sayadi, Taqi & Mohamed Ahmed
Office 302-304
Yateem Centre 2, 2d floor
Alkhalifa Avenue
POB 1414
Manama, Bahrain
Tel: 210212, 213343
Fax: 213633, 211392

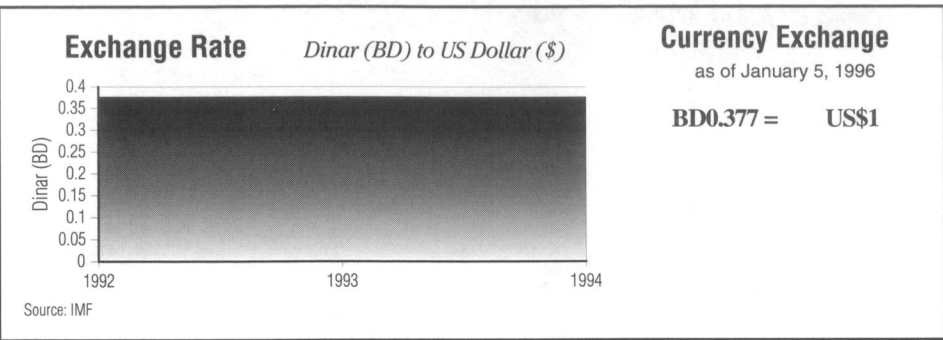

Exchange Rate   *Dinar (BD) to US Dollar ($)*

Dinar (BD): 0.4, 0.35, 0.3, 0.25, 0.2, 0.15, 0.1, 0.05, 0

1992 — 1993 — 1994

Source: IMF

Currency Exchange
as of January 5, 1996

BD0.377 =   US$1

Currency

The currency in use is the Bahrain dinar (BD), which is divided into 1,000 fils.

Foreign Exchange

The Bahrain Monetary Agency (BMA) controls exchange, but there is no legislation to control exchange rates in Bahrain. There are no restrictions on converting or transferring funds, whether or not associated with an investment.

Capital Transfers

There are no restrictions on capital or profit repatriation.

Investment Incentives

Investment incentives offered to foreign firms are equal to those available to Bahraini companies. Companies wishing to qualify for investment incentives must hire 30 percent Bahraini employees in existing industries; and for pioneering industries, there is a requirement of 15 percent Bahraini employees the first year and 25 percent in subsequent years. Factories must also produce a value-added of at least 40 percent, and must export at least 25 percent of their production (15 percent for existing industries) in order to qualify for incentives.

Labor Substantial subsidies are given for each Bahraini employee employed.

Land rental and electricity charges The government rebates 50 percent of electricity and up to 100 percent of land rental charges for the first five years.

Customs and tariffs The government offers rebates and exemptions in many cases.

Investment Restrictions

There are no special performance requirements imposed on foreign investors. The Bahraini government does not license companies wishing to compete with existing government-owned companies, or which would be a danger to public health or other aspects of the general welfare. Foreign-owned companies may not be set up for the exclusive purpose of engaging in commercial sales in Bahrain, except in minority partnership with one or more Bahraini companies. Foreigners may not acquire legal control of a Bahraini company, and expatriate ownership of a publicly listed Bahraini corporation may not exceed 24 percent of total outstanding shares. Foreigners, with a few exceptions, may not own land in Bahrain.

Money Matters

BITS AND PIECES

- **Investment advantages** Bahrain offers many advantages to foreign investors, including: no personal or corporate taxation, no restriction on capital and profit repatriation, a developed infrastructure with excellent transportation and communication facilities, and duty-free access to other Gulf states for products manufactured in Bahrain.
- **Expatriates** Under a law adopted in 1994, individual expatriates who have been living in Bahrain for at least three years may buy up to 1 percent of the shares in any publicly listed Bahraini corporation.
- **Financing** Foreign-owned companies are eligible for partial financing from the state-owned Bahrain Development Bank, if they meet certain criteria such as providing employment to a significant number of Bahrainis.
- **Deposits** Banks do not pay interest on customer deposits.
- **Joint ventures** Joint ventures–up to 49 percent foreign ownership–are permitted with Bahraini companies, but a 100 percent purchase of an existing Bahraini company would probably not be permitted.
- **Competent enterprises** In general, industrial enterprises which would compete with government-owned or parastatal firms are not permitted; this rule applies equally to Bahraini and foreign-owned companies.
- **Expropriation** There have been no expropriations in recent years, and none are anticipated. Denationalization, or partial denationalization, of some government-owned enterprises may take place in the near future.
- **Financial sources** Bahrain's banking policies facilitate the free flow of financial resources, with credit generally being allocated on market terms. Foreign investors are able to borrow on the local market, and the private sector has access to a variety of credit instruments. Legal, regulatory, and accounting systems in the financial sector are transparent and consistent with international norms.
- **Gold** Residents may freely purchase, hold, and sell gold in any form, at home or abroad. Imports and exports of gold in any form are freely permitted and do not require a license. Imports of gold jewelry are subject to a 10 percent customs duty, but gold ingots are exempt.

BANKS

Bahrain Monetary Agency
POB 27
Manama
Tel: 535535
Fax: 533342

National Bank of Bahrain B.S.C.
POB 106
Manama
Tel: 258-800
Fax: 263-876

Citibank, N.A.
POB 548
Manama
Tel: 257-124
Fax: 250-510

Bank of Bahrain and Kuwait B.S.C.
POB 597
Manama
Tel: 253-388
Fax: 275-785

British Bank of the Middle East
POB 57, Bahrain
93 Al Khalifa Avenue
Manama 304
Tel: 242555
Fax: 256822

The Hongkong Shanghai Banking Corp. Ltd.
POB 5497
Manama
Tel: 255828
Fax: 251570

TAXATION	At a Glance	
Taxation requires sophisticated knowledge of complex rules and regulations specific to each country. The information presented here is from the Ernst & Young Corporate Tax Guide and Directory, available from the Ernst & Young accounting office in your country, or from: **Ernst & Young** POB 140 Manama, Bahrain Street Address: 14th Floor, The Tower Sheraton Commercial Complex Manama, Bahrain Tel: 535 455 Telex: 8453 Ans bk ERNST BN Fax: 535405	Corporate Income Tax Rate (%) *	0
	Capital Gains Tax Rate (%)	0
	Branch Tax Rate (%)	0
	Withholding Tax (%)	0
	* Oil companies are subject to a special income tax.	

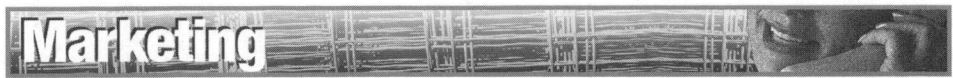

Marketing

Distribution

Bahrain's long history as a regional trading center has brought it into the modern world as a well-developed, highly competitive market where products from all over the world are sold. It has become a transshipment hub to markets in other Middle East countries. Sales within the country tend to be dominated by a few large, local companies, although distribution facilities and services may be 100 percent foreign-owned. A foreign business that seeks to become established in Bahrain must generally have a local sponsor, though many hotels, restaurants, and catering companies purchase food items directly from foreign concerns. No local agent or partner is needed to operate a regional office; however, except for factories or regional offices, commercial sales in Bahrain can be made only through a Bahraini agent or a joint company with at least 51 percent Bahraini ownership.

The Bahrain Promotions and Marketing Board can recommend agents and advise on agency agreements. Foreign sellers must check agency agreements and contracts carefully because seemingly innocuous changes in wording can have big effects on the nature of the agreement.

Selling Techniques

Licensing, joint companies, partnerships, and consortiums are all effective means of selling products in Bahrain. Retail and other franchise opportunities abound, and fast food franchises are highly sought after by local entrepreneurs. Already, almost all major food franchise companies are represented. Prices are generally higher in Bahrain than elsewhere, and consumers expect higher quality commensurate thereto. Thus, selling techniques which focus on quality, exclusivity, or uniqueness work well here.

Advertising

The one English and two Arabic newspapers carry advertising. As religious and cultural norms play a big role in day-to-day life, advice from a local agent is helpful in developing an advertising campaign.

Service and Customer Support

As in any highly competitive market, service and customer support are keys to success. Service can be offered through a regional office, but spare parts should be available through a local distributor.

Marketing in Bahrain

MARKETING TIPS

- **Ethnic complexities** Minor changes in product appearance or labeling can spell success in marketing to this highly diverse society.
- **Local introduction** An in-country agent can provide crucial contacts, insure cultural sensitivity, and advise on pricing and market entry.
- **Fast entry** With assistance from the Bahrain Marketing and Promotion Office, setting up business operations can be accomplished in as little as one week, after registration forms have been completed.
- **Legal advice** Although not technically necessary, retaining a local attorney to draw up agency and sales agreements is generally advisable.
- **Government markets** An agent is generally necessary for sales to government agencies, although in some cases (such as sales to the Bahrain Defense Force) agents are not permitted.
- **Labels** Arabic labels are almost essential to the success of a foreign product, although Arabic can complement foreign language labelling.

CONSULTING FIRMS

Fortune PromoSeven
POB 5989
Manama
Tel: 250-148
Fax: 274-451

Middle East Research and Consultancy (MERAC)
POB 26018
Manama
Tel: 742-024
Fax: 740-061

Nawat
POBo5952
Manama
Tel: 212-555
Fax: 243-555

Business Culture

Greetings and Courtesies

Bahrainis generally shake hands in the Western style upon greeting, but might then just as well continue to hold the other person's hand while talking. They are conscientious about greeting everyone they see, and can be offended if others do not return the courtesy. Business cards are usually exchanged upon first meeting, and it is wise to have yours printed in both Arabic and English.

Business Ethic and Framework

The most modern of the Gulf countries, and long accustomed to dealing with foreigners, Bahrainis are considered more tolerant of Western culture than are many other Arab people. They are very honest in their business dealings, and expect foreigners to be the same. Western-style business attire is more commonly found in Bahrain than in neighboring countries. Still, it is conservative and, for women, modest.

Decision Making and Meetings

There is generally one decision maker in a company. Like other Arabs, Bahrainis are concerned about people issues and they will place emphasis on human factors when they make a decision or analyze a proposal. If they like you, they will try to work out an arrangement or a compromise. Prior appointments should always be made for business meetings, and foreigners should arrive on time. Meetings will be continuously interrupted by family, friends, and business associates, as well as by frequent telephone calls. Once the business discussion has begun, however, it will proceed in a relatively straightforward manner.

Women

Women enjoy relative freedom in Bahrain. Foreign women are treated with courtesy and respect by Bahraini businessmen, and in business contexts at least they are generally treated as equals. They should, however, dress conservatively when doing business. Bahrain is probably one of the easiest Gulf countries for foreign women to conduct business in.

Cultural Cautions

DO'S

- Take the time to establish solid personal relationships.
- Take advantage of "government relations" employees. They can greatly assist you in a positive outcome for your proposal.

DON'TS

- Do not openly refuse a favor. If one is asked and it is unreasonable, illegal, or too difficult, listen carefully and indicate the doubtfulness of the outcome, but assure that you will make an attempt to perform.
- When you plan social events, do not mix people from different social classes at the same occasion or event.

CUSTOMS

- Arabs assume the role of host or hostess. A guest, even an unexpected one, will always be offered something to drink or eat.

OBSERVATIONS

- Arabs do not view their social customs and restrictions as repressive, but as complimentary to the status and nature of both men and women.
- Arabs mistrust people who do not appear to be sincere or who fail to demonstrate an interest in them personally or in their country.

NEGOTIATIONS

- A low-key approach will work well in Bahrain, although you must indicate your willingness and sincerity by establishing solid personal relationships.
- Do not be afraid to display emotion during negotiations.
- If you receive evasive answers, do not press the point further.

GOVERNMENT AGENCIES

Capital Markets & International Financial Services Unit
POB 333
Manama
Tel: 278677
Fax: 210363

Bahrain Marketing and Promotion Office
POB 11299
Manama
Tel: 533-886
Fax: 531-117

Ministry of Development and Industry
Industrial Development Directorate
POB 1435
Manama
Tel: 525-522
Fax: 290-302

National Information Technology Unit
POB 1435
Manama
Tel: 525-514
Fax: 294-188

Ministry of Commerce and Agriculture
Director of Commerce and Companies Affairs
POB 5479
Manama
Tel: 530-335
Fax: 530-455

Bahrain Chamber of Commerce and Industry
Second Assistant Secretary General
POB 248
Manama
Tel: 233-913
Fax: 241-294

WORLD TRADE CENTER

World Trade Center Bahrain
POB 669
Manama
Tel: 725-522, 214-933
Fax: 728-184, 213-808

BANKS

Bahrain Monetary Agency
POB 27
Manama
Tel: 535535
Fax: 533342

National Bank of Bahrain B.S.C.
POB 106
Manama
Tel: 258-800
Fax: 263-876

Citibank, N.A.
POB 548
Manama
Tel: 257-124
Fax: 250-510

Bank of Bahrain and Kuwait B.S.C.
POB 597
Manama
Tel: 253-388
Fax: 275-785

British Bank of the Middle East
POB 57, Bahrain
93 Al Khalifa Avenue
Manama 304
Tel: 242555
Fax 256822

The Hongkong Shanghai Banking Corp. Ltd.
POB 5497, Manama
2/F, Yateem Centre Two
Road 385.304, Al Khalifa Avenue
Manama
Tel: 255828
Fax: 251570

Al-Ahli Commercial Bank BSC
POB 27
Manama
Tel: 244333

Telex: 9130
Fax: 241301

Arlabank International EC
POB 5070
Manama Centre
Manama
Tel: 232124
Telex: 246239

Bahrain Middle East Bank EC
POB 797
Manama
Tel: 532345

CONSULTING FIRMS

Fortune PromoSeven
POB 5989
Manama
Tel: 250-148
Fax: 274-451

Middle East Research and Consultancy (MERAC)
POB 26018
Manama
Tel: 742-024
Fax: 740-061

Nawat
POB 5952
Manama
Tel: 212-555
Fax: 243-555

AD AGENCIES

Fortune Promoseven
POB 5989
609 City Centre Bldg.
Government Ave.
Manama
Tel: 250-148
Fax: 271-451

PUBLIC RELATIONS

Gulf-Hill and Knowlton
POB 1596
Manama
Tel: 533-532
Fax: 533-370

NEWSPAPERS

Gulf News
POB 5300
Manama
Tel: 620111
Telex: 8565

The Days
POB 3232
Manama
Tel: 727111
Fax: 729009

Gulf Daily News
POB 5300
Manama
Tel: 620222
Fax: 622141
Telex: 8565

PERIODICALS

Al-Bahrain
POB 26005
Isa Town
Tel: 683986
Fax: 686355
Telex: 8399

Al-Mawakif (Attitudes)
POB 1083
Manama
Tel: 231231
Fax: 271720

Arab Agriculture
POB 10131
Manama
Tel: 213900
Fax: 211765

Arab World Agribusiness
POB 10131
Manama
Tel: 213900
Fax: 211765

Discover Bahrain
POB 10704
Manama

Gulf Construction
POB 224 Exhibition Ave.
Manama
Tel: 293131
Fax: 293400
Telex: 8981

Al-Hayat at-Tijariya (Commerce Review)
POB 248
Manama
Tel: 233913
Fax: 241294
Telex: 8691

Shipping and Transport New International
POB 224 Exhibition Ave.
Manama
Tel: 293131
Fax: 293400
Telex: 8981

This is Bahrain and What's On
POB 726
Manama Tel: 250014
Telex: 8494
Fax: 230025

RADIO AND TELEVISION

Bahrain Broadcasting Station
POB 194
Manama
Tel: 781888
Telex: 9259

LEGAL CONTACTS

Law Offices of Ahmed Zaki Yamani
Manama Center
POB 342
Manama

Law Office of Shaikh Isa Bin Mohammed Al Khalifa
(Associated with Clifford Chance)
POB 20717
Manama, Bahrain
Tel: 53-1535, 53-1073
Fax: 53-6272, 53-0608

Sayadi, Taqi & Mohamed Ahmed
Office 302-304
Yateem Centre 2, 2d floor
Alkhalifa Avenue
POB 1414
Manama, Bahrain
Tel: 210212,213343
Fax: 213633,211392

Law Offices of Ahmed Zaki Yamani
POB 342
Manama, Bahrain
Tel: 211-433,622
Fax: 210-373
Telex: 8991 YAMANI

INTERNET ADDRESSES

State of Bahrain
http://www.ncl.ac.uk/~n4368939/bahrain.html

Bahrain Information
http://www/copper.ucs/indiana.edu/~hqasem/bahrain/

Al-Ayam Newspaper
http://www.bahrain/com/alayam

Belgium

Kingdom of Belgium

Economy

Overview

Densely populated Belgium is one of the most highly industrialized countries in a heavily industrialized region. With few exploitable natural resources, its industrial sector has become a complex processing machine that imports raw materials and semi-finished goods, and processes them for re-export. Heavily reliant on trade, Belgium's exports are equivalent to about two-thirds of its GDP; it exports twice as much per capita as Germany and five times as much as Japan. Because of its location and excellent transport infrastructure, Belgium boasts a distinct trade advantage. It also prides itself on a highly skilled, multilingual, and productive work force. Although in the past Belgian ethnicity has led to conflict, it has in recent years worked out a model arrangement in which differing groups interact socially, politically, and commercially within semi-autonomous spheres and with a minimum of friction.

Trade

Major exports include vehicles, non-metallic mineral manufactures (including diamonds), iron and steel, textiles, plastics and resins, and petroleum products. Imports include vehicles, non-metallic minerals, petroleum, electrical machinery, organic chemicals, and general industrial machinery. Trading partners include Germany—accounting for nearly one-quarter of total trade—followed by France, the Netherlands, the UK, and the US.

Sectors

Agriculture In this highly industrialized nation, agriculture plays a minor role: it contributes about 2 percent of GDP and employs about 2 percent of the work force. Major cash crops include sugar beets, cereals, potatoes, and meats. Belgium is also noted for such value-added processed food products as chocolates.

Industry Industry accounts for about 30 percent of both GDP and employment. A specialist in processing raw materials into intermediate components, Belgian industry is heavily involved in plastics, chemicals, metals, and such lower-end operations as textile and food processing. High-value products such as diamonds are also important, and specialty and high-tech products are becoming more so.

Services Services provide more than two-thirds of both GDP and employment. Such high skill areas as engineering, financial, and business services are growing, although most service activities are far less specialized. The headquarters for the EU and NATO, Belgium also provides employment for skilled, internationally oriented diplomats, bureaucrats, and support service personnel.

Trends

Unemployment levels greater than 10 percent continue to plague Belgium. A significant portion of this unemployment results from uncompetitively high, union-influenced wage rates and older, low-skilled workers who are essentially unemployable in the newer, fast-moving, high-tech industries. The government's new economic austerity program could help turn things around by reducing its high budget deficit and making more funds available for investment. One of the founding members of the EU, Belgium strongly supports European economic and political integration and hopes to see implementation of the EU's Monetary Union, which it believes will further its trade prospects.

At a Glance

THE COUNTRY

Location Situated in northwestern Europe, surrounded by the Netherlands, Germany, and France.
Terrain Mostly flat, with some gently rolling plains.
Climate In the coastal region, the climate is mild and humid. There are marked temperature changes further inland. The average annual temperature is 8°C (46°F) in Brussels, ranging from 3°C (37°F) in January to 18°C (64°F) in July. Average annual rainfall is 79 cm (28 in).

THE PEOPLE

Population 10,000,000
Ethnic composition Belgium's population consists mainly of Dutch and French ancestry.
Religious composition
Roman Catholic 75%
Languages spoken Dutch 58%, French 32%.
Education and literacy Adult illiteracy is virtually nonexistent. Education is free and compulsory for children between the ages of six and 16; education in secondary schools is also free. Most classes are taught in French, Dutch, or German.
Labor force
Total: 4,300,000
By occupation: services and transportation 44%, industry and construction 34%, public service 20%, agriculture 2%.

COUNTRY FACTS

Political and legal Belgium is a parliamentary democracy under a constitutional monarch, and there are many political parties which actively contest each election.
Telephone Belgium has excellent and up-to-date telephone equipment and services. International country code: [32]. City codes: Antwerp (3), Brussels (2), Liege (4).
Transportation Belgium has an excellent transportation network of ports, railways, and highways.
Environment Belgium's most significant environmental problems are air, land, and water pollution due to the heavy concentration of industrial facilities in the country. Although the government has made a few attempts to address these problems, the industries are critical to its economic health, so progress has been slow.
Media Belgium has four national televisions stations, two in each language. Cable television subscribers can receive up to 23 additional stations, from the UK and Belgium's continental neighbors. There are over 4,500,000 television sets and 7,675,000 radios in use. There are 23 daily newspapers and several others dealing with a variety of matters, including several devoted entirely to economics and financial concerns. About 500 weeklies appear in Belgium, most of them in French or Dutch, and a few in German or English.
Health Every city or town in Belgium has a public assistance committee which is in charge of health and hospital services in its community. These committees organize clinics and visiting nurse services, run public hospitals, and pay for relief patients in private hospitals. There is a national health insurance plan, membership of which covers practically the whole population. A number of private hospitals are run by local communities or mutual aid societies attached to religious organizations.

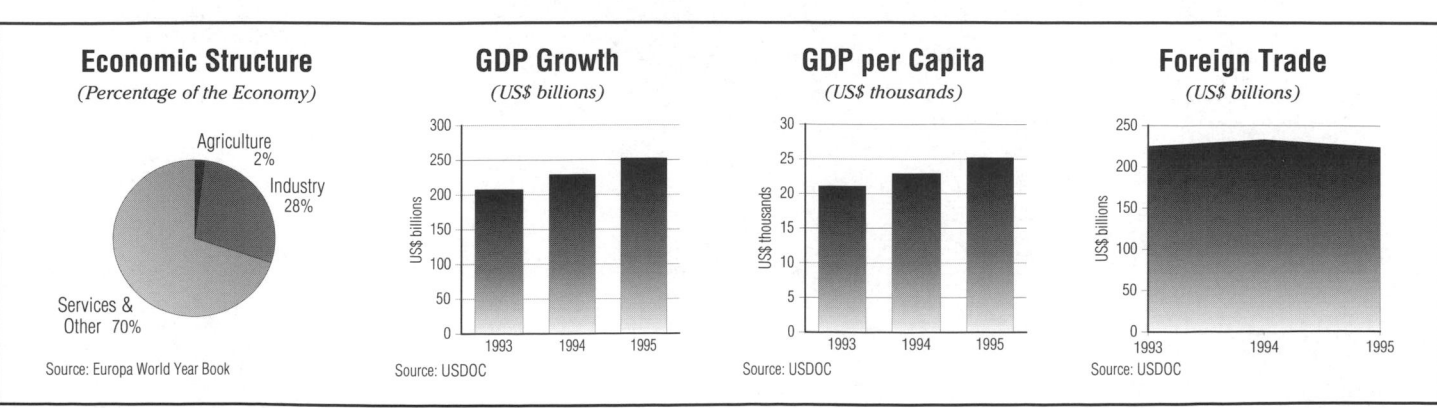

Economic Structure
(Percentage of the Economy)

Agriculture 2%
Industry 28%
Services & Other 70%

Source: Europa World Year Book

GDP Growth
(US$ billions)

Source: USDOC

GDP per Capita
(US$ thousands)

Source: USDOC

Foreign Trade
(US$ billions)

Source: USDOC

North Sea

The Netherlands

Provinces of Belgium
1 West-Flanders
2 East Flanders
3 Brabant
4 Antwerp
5 Limburg
6 Liege
7 Luxembourg
8 Namur
9 Hainaut

Maas

Germany

Baarle-Hertog

Knokke-Heist
Oostende
Turnhout
4
Brugge
2
St.-Niklaas
Antwerp
Herentals
5
Gent
Dendermonde
Mechelen
Hasselt
Roeselare
Aarschot
Kortrijk
Leuven
Leie
Schelde
Tienen
St. Truiden
5
Mouscron
Brussels
9
Rónse
9
Halle
Wavre
6
Liège
Verviers
Lys
Tournai
Ath
3
Soignies
Leuze
Huy
Spa
Meuse
Malmédy
Mons
Namur
Escaut
8
Marche en
Famenne
Philippeville
Dinant
7
Chimay
Bastogne
Oise
Neufchâteau
Bouillon
Luxembourg
France
Arlon
Aisne
Luxembourg
Meuse
Moselle

Belgium

⭐ National capital
⊙ Province capital
● Secondary city
— Primary road
···· Railroad
┼ Canal
···· Administrative border
━━ International border

0 10 20 30 km
0 10 20 30 mi

©1995 Magellan Geographix℠Santa Barbara, CA

51°
50°
3°
4°
5°
6°

Foreign Trade

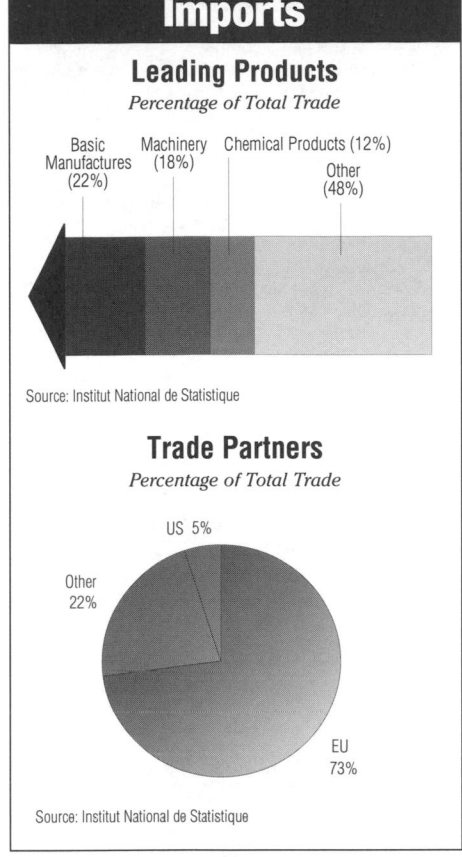

Imports

Leading Products
Percentage of Total Trade

Basic Manufactures (22%)   Machinery (18%)   Chemical Products (12%)   Other (48%)

Source: Institut National de Statistique

Trade Partners
Percentage of Total Trade

US 5%
Other 22%
EU 73%

Source: Institut National de Statistique

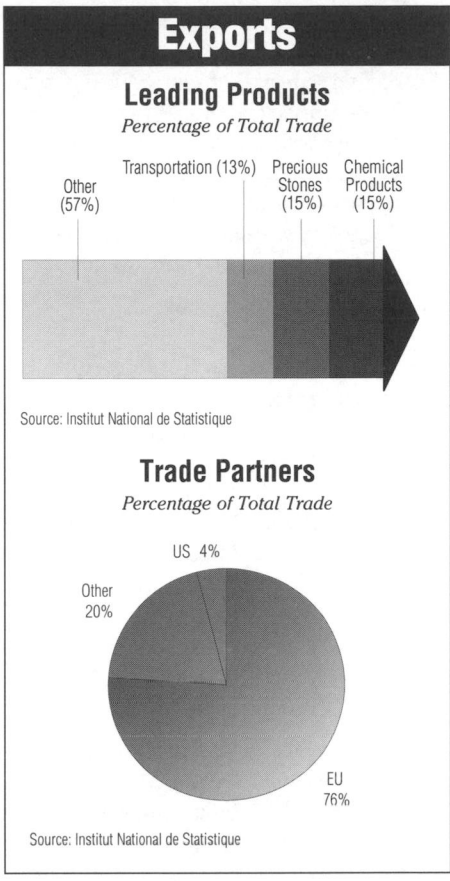

Exports

Leading Products
Percentage of Total Trade

Other (57%)   Transportation (13%)   Precious Stones (15%)   Chemical Products (15%)

Source: Institut National de Statistique

Trade Partners
Percentage of Total Trade

US 4%
Other 20%
EU 76%

Source: Institut National de Statistique

Opportunities

FOR IMPORTING TO BELGIUM
- chemicals
- computer hardware and software
- electrical equipment
- environmental goods and services
- foodstuffs
- fuels
- grains
- laboratory and scientific instruments
- medical equipment
- motor vehicles
- petroleum products
- plastic
- rough diamonds
- telecommunication products

FOR EXPORTING FROM BELGIUM
- cut diamonds
- electrical equipment
- iron and steel
- motor vehicles
- organic chemicals
- pharmaceuticals
- plastic
- refined petroleum
- textiles
- tractors
- transportation equipment
- wood and paper products

GROWTH SECTORS
- aircraft and parts
- building products
- computer hardware and software
- environmental protection goods and services
- laboratory and scientific instruments
- medical equipment
- telecommunication products

GOVERNMENT PROCUREMENT
- electrical energy facilities and equipment
- military supplies
- office equipment
- telecommunication products
- transportation equipment
- water treatment facilities

Trade News

RULES AND REGULATIONS

- **Customs valuation** As a member of the European Union, Belgium applies the EU common external tariff to goods imported from non-EU countries. For goods imported into Belgium from other EU countries, no customs duties apply unless the goods contain components imported from outside the EU upon which customs duties have not been paid in another EU country.
- **Customs documentation** Minimal documentation for EU countries. Complete documentation is required for non-EU countries.
- **Value-added tax** A VAT is added to all goods produced in and imported to Belgium. In practice, the VAT is greater for imported goods since it is added after all customs duties have been imposed. Standard VAT rates are as follows: daily necessities, foodstuffs, six percent; tobacco, fuel, 12 percent; most commercial items, 20.5 percent.
- **Import and export licenses and quotas** Many products may be imported or exported without any prior license, but products from certain countries and certain listed products are subject to an import license. An application for such a license must be made to the Office of Quotas and Licenses. Strategic goods are also subject to an import and/or quota license. A list of products subject to license or quota can be obtained from the Office of Quotas and Licenses.
- **Export controls and subsidies** Belgium applies export controls to weapons. It abides by the common EU export control and tax scheme. There are no direct export subsidies offered by the government to industry, but the government conducts active trade promotion.
- **Samples** Samples having no commercial value may be imported free of duty and without special formalities. Samples having commercial value may be imported against payment of a deposit in lieu of duty and taxes plus a fee. Articles intended for public display may not be imported as samples.

GOVERNMENT AGENCIES

Office Central des Contingents et des Licences-Centrale Dienst
Boulevard Emile Jacqmain
162 - Emile Jacqmainlaan
1210 Brussels
Tel: (2) 219-44-50

FREIGHT FORWARDERS

Beckmann & Jorgensen NV
Ankerrui 13
B-2000
Antwerp
Telex: 31402 BJANTW

Belgian Rhine Transit NV
POB 59
Frankrijklei 53-55
Antwerp
Telex: 31262 NEPTRA B

Deckers & Wirtz Ltd.
Napoleonskaai 3-7
B-2000
Antwerp
Fax: (3) 233-0459
Telex: 31241 DWANT

Kuehne & Nagel NV
Gebouw Rijnpoort
Stijfselfui 44
B-2000 Antwerp
Fax: (3) 233-4252
Telex: 31305 KNANTB

Depaire, Edmond SA
Havenlaan 94
Brussels
Fax: (2) 424-0065
Telex: 221145 DEPA B

Thomas & Ellis SA
Rue Picard 48
Brussels
Telex: 221099

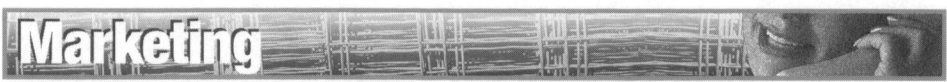

Marketing

Overview

Belgium is Central Europe's second smallest country, but its location makes it an important regional emporium. As a member of the European Union, it is part of a single market of some 340 million customers. Belgium is a cultural microcosm of Europe with three linguistic colonies: French, Dutch, and German. This rich mix makes Belgium an excellent test market and launching pad for foreign enterprises; Brussels and other Belgian cities rank among the top 10 sites for establishing foreign business. Government leaders are generally supportive of open trade, and restrictions on the entry of foreign goods into Belgian markets are minimal. Goods move quickly through its modern seaports, air terminals, railroads, and highways. The market is a sophisticated, competitive environment; those who like "swimming with sharks" should dive into Belgium.

Distribution

A foreign supplier may work through local representatives or establish a branch, subsidiary, or independent company. Sales can be made directly to stores, chains, retail and consumer cooperatives, and other purchasers. Belgium's excellent network of distributorships is often regarded by Europeans as a neutral source of goods. Foreign companies may set up their own distribution or coordination centers in Belgium. A distribution center is permitted to purchase raw materials for a company group; store, manage, and package those materials; sell them to the group members; and handle the processed goods. Through a coordination center, a multinational group may perform certain service and financial activities on behalf of the member companies. Multinationals can derive significant tax and other benefits when operating through distribution or coordination centers. Joint venture and franchising agreements are popular means for entering the market; franchise outlets are widespread throughout the European Community. There are no significant restrictions on opening franchise operations in Belgium.

Agents, Distributors, and Partners

Several thousand foreign companies sell their products on the Belgian market through local distributors and agents. Many distributors operate cross-border, often including Belgium, the other Benelux countries (Netherlands and Luxembourg), and even several other neighboring European countries within their sales territories. Belgium distributors tend to be small and specialized. They do not have ready access to inexpensive capital and thus often take a conservative approach to risk-taking. Agents and distributors are protected by law against sudden or unjustifiable termination of the arrangement.

Selling Techniques

The Belgian importer is looking for the best quality at the best price; a foreign supplier will have to be aggressive and keep a sharp watch on the market to compete successfully. Competition is tough. An advantage to marketing in Belgium is that there is a single standard for marketing in all of the European Union countries, and therefore foreign suppliers can plan to structure their pan-European advertising and marketing campaigns accordingly. However, companies should also take into account the many cultural and linguistic differences among these countries. There are several trade journals in Belgium. Many are sponsored by the professional associations of commercial or industrial interests and offer sufficient coverage to be of interest to foreign manufacturers.

Advertising

Advertising is widely used, although it is somewhat complicated by the language issue. Many advertising firms offer a complete line of services—consulting, planning, art and copy work, media selection, placement, and translation. A large number of firms also offer various marketing research services. The best advertising medium is probably a daily newspaper, of which there are nearly 40 that target various markets including financial, regional, national, and language-specific readers. Total circulation of the Belgian daily press is estimated at nearly 2.5 million. In addition, advertisements can be placed in many of the more than 3,900 monthly and weekly technical and special interest periodicals. Radio and television are state-controlled, and advertising is available on a very limited basis. Other common advertising mediums include direct mailings, billboards, posters, and streetcar placards.

Service and Customer Support

Belgium's sophisticated, relatively wealthy consumers expect prompt, efficient, and skilled technical service and customer support. Competition for market share is keen in nearly all sectors and customers will readily switch to competing brands if satisfactory support and service are not forthcoming. Most foreign firms make it a point to stock adequate parts and supplies and to have sufficiently trained personnel available to respond to customer needs.

Marketing in Belgium

MARKETING TIPS

- **High-tech and motorized** Belgium is a land of automobiles, computers, robotics, and sophisticated industries. Parts, service, upgrades, and security equipment are in high demand.
- **Franchising** Nearly 10% of retail sales are through franchised outlets.
- **From the sea** Belgium is Europe's sixth largest market for seafood. Per capita consumption is 37 pounds annually, most of which is imported.
- **Trade mart** The largest trade center in Europe is located in Brussels. More than 1,000 permanent exhibits serve as a sales base for comparative shopping by buyers from Belgium, and all of Europe.
- **Buying season** The viewing and buying seasons for clothing and other seasonal items are February to May for autumn and winter fashions and September to November for spring and summer fashions. There is no clearly defined buying season for capital goods.
- **Posters** Poster sites are available in railway stations, controlled by the Belgian National Railways. Poster sites in towns, and road hoarding emplacements, are in most cases operated by private concessionaires.
- **Trade fairs** There are many trade fairs and exhibitions in Belgium covering nearly all categories of exhibits.

AD AGENCIES

Leo Burnett Worldwide Inc.
Chaussee de Wavre 1789, Box 16
1160 Brussels
Tel: (2) 675-4900
Fax: (2) 675-2046

Conquest Europe S.A.
Gulledelle 98
1200 Brussels
Tel: (2) 773-1711
Fax: (2) 772-0259

Grey Europe/Brussels
Blvd. de la Woluwe 56
Brussels

McCann-Erickson Co. S.A.
122 Chaussee de La Hulpe
1200 Brussels
Tel: (2) 7674-1311
Fax: (2) 660-8180

Saatchi & Saatchi Advertising
Imperiastraat 16
1930 Zaventern
Tel: (2) 725-6600
Fax: (2) 725-2466

J. Walter Thompson S.A./N.V.
Gulledelle 98
1200 Brussels
Tel: (2) 775-0200
Fax: (2) 772-7276

Wunderman Cato Johnson
Avenue des Pleiades 19
1200 Brussels
Tel: (2) 770-5415
Fax: (2) 772-7276

Young & Rubicam Belgium S.A.
Dieweg 3B
1180 Brussels
Tel: (2) 375-8012
Fax: (2) 375-8843

TRADE FAIRS

Brussels International Fair
Foire Internationale de Bruxelles
Parc des Expositions
Place de Belgique
B-1020 Bruxelles
Tel: (2) 477-0477
Fax: (2) 477-0391

Festival de l'Enfance
Nature, science, music, and books
Festival International de l'Enfance et de la Jeunesse
ASBL
Rue Paul Spaak, 28
B-1050 Bruxelles
Tel: (2) 649-3187

Business Culture

Greetings and Courtesies

The familiar use of first names is not the Belgium custom. Belgians who are Flemish use *Mijnheer* (Mr.), *Mevrouw* (Mrs.) or *Juffrouw* (Miss), followed by the last name only. French speaking Belgians use *Monsieur* (Mr.), *Madame* (Mrs.) and *Mademoiselle* (Miss), again followed by the last name only. First names are confined to family members and close friends. Belgians shake hands with everyone at the beginning and end of every meeting, and the famous Belgian handshake is quick without being too firm. As in other European countries, men should wait until a woman extends her hand in greeting. Likewise, Belgian men will wait for a woman to extend her hand to them. A polite greeting when being introduced is, "Pleased to meet you." Avoid the phrase, "How do you do?" You may be asked to be more specific. The exchange of gifts in business is not a standard Belgian practice. However, remembering someone on a special occasion is appreciated. Keep such gifts simple and practical; a gift representative of your country is acceptable. When visiting someone's home, take a small gift with you as well as flowers for your hostess, avoiding the color red if the flowers are roses. Finally, if you are the seller, it is advised you invite your colleagues to a business lunch. While business may be discussed over lunch, refrain from talking too much shop or presenting serious issues.

Business Ethic and Framework

Both the Flemish and Dutch are reserved and formal in their business conduct. The foreign venturer will want to carefully study regional differences before approaching Belgium trade. Belgians speak several languages. German is a formal language of business in Belgium where German, French, and Flemish are the three official and constitutional languages. The reverse side of your business card should be printed in both Flemish and French. Though not uncommon to conduct meetings in English, it is advised that documents and presentation materials be translated into German as well as French or Flemish depending on the region. Third party introductions will be necessary and foreigners are recommended to take advantage of the hundreds of trade organizations in Brussels that can steer them through the markets. Making the right contacts requires patience and diligence. Being well-organized and remaining flexible to the different regional work environments will further aid your success when doing business in Belgium.

Decision Making

Belgians are tough-minded deliberators and convincing your Belgian counterpart of a deal will be difficult. They are also extremely conservative when deciding on suitable business partners for joint ventures. Much depends on the nature of your business–be it export, manufacturing, or service provider–in determining the most viable route to eliciting agreements. Be thorough when investigating Belgium's markets, and be patient as you forge a path to those who are positioned to render decisions.

Women

Women play a dynamic role in the work force and are found at all levels, including senior management. There are several female ministers in the government. Foreign businesswomen should experience no difficulty in getting business done, and they should find they are treated with respect and courtesy.

Meetings

Belgians are extremely focused; following the exchange of greetings and business cards, they will normally proceed directly to the objectives of the business meeting. Never be condescending in your attitude during business discussions; displaying airs or superiority is bad form. Ask questions instead of giving advice, and listen carefully to answers. Belgian standards and quality are very high and you are expected to be able to perform at the same level. By demonstrating your interest and desire to learn about their business markets you will more successfully win their confidence in your own business practices. It is considered bad form to remove your coat in a meeting or to use first names prematurely. A Belgian's respect is difficult to regain once it has been lost by a casual or overly familiar attitude.

Business Attire

Belgians are inclined to socially rank you by appearance alone, particularly in the French region. A dark suit and white shirt are safe. Wear lace-up shoes as opposed to loafers. Businesswomen dress conservatively, wearing skirts and blouses. Neutral colors are preferred over bright colors. Belgians are in general formal, and their dress reflects this. Casual attire can be seen as an indication that you are not serious.

Cultural Cautions

DO'S

- Study regional differences well.
- Send written thank you notes; never phone an expression of thanks.
- Arrive promptly to scheduled luncheon and dinner engagements or your Belgian hosts will be highly insulted.
- When dining in a private home, or attending a house party, be sure to tip the household help. A tray is often available near the coat room.

DON'TS

- Don't snap your fingers in public. It is considered disrespectful.
- Do not bring or send chrysanthemums. They are a flower for funerals only.
- Don't cross your knife and fork on your plate at the end of a meal. It is considered impolite.
- Avoid switching eating utensils back and forth if possible. Belgians, who eat with their fork in the left hand and knife in the right, consider constant utensil switching bad manners.

CUSTOMS

- Bourse Days, weekly business days designated by local Belgium communities for buying, selling, and exchanging current information over luncheons, are traditional activities. Avoid making appointments on Monday in Antwerp or on Wednesday in Brussels when Bourse Days are in swing. Additionally, business dinners are rare as Belgians usually like to be with their families in the evenings. However, they do enjoy entertaining, so don't be surprised if you're invited home for a social dinner and the delights of Belgian hospitality.
- Well-organized daycare centers for children are available to working mothers. Public schools have a nursery section where pre-schoolers can enroll. For a small fee, children will be cared for from 7:30 am to 6:00 pm.
- Close friends may greet each other with three kisses on the cheek. The correct way is to press the cheek first to one side then the other and then repeat the kiss, taking care to never actually press lips to cheek but to aim the kiss in the air.

OBSERVATIONS

- There are regional sensitivities between the Walloons in the south, who speak French, and the Flemish in the north, who speak Dutch. Remember though, that regardless of the region they are Belgians. It is important to be attentive to regional distinctions and differences when transacting business in Belgium.
- Belgians are formal in their dining customs. Wait until your host or hostess indicates where you are to sit. If you're accompanied by your spouse, you will never be seated together. The female guest of honor will be to the right of the host, and the male guest of honor will be to the right of the hostess.
- Toasting with business associates or friends is an important gesture and as the host of a luncheon, you may be expected to toast your guests. The toast is made before you drink and the proper form is to raise your glass, exchange glances with your guests, raise your glass again and take a sip.

NEGOTIATIONS

- Be prepared to respond to some energetic questioning. Belgian business traders like to know the precise nature of agreements they are entering into with their foreign counterparts.
- Proceed cautiously through negotiations until you are able to determine if there is a receptiveness to you, your company, and your products.
- Belgium's primary market is the EU. Be aware that it is not easy to penetrate this export-oriented market.

Legal System

Belgium is a constitutional monarchy with a civil law system influenced by English constitutional theory.

Intellectual and Industrial Property Rights

Patents Patents can be obtained by the filing of application and adherence to specific procedures related thereto. The time between the filing of the application and the grant of a patent varies depending on the product or procedure involved.

Trademarks Trademarks can be registered, but the registration remains subject, in case of dispute, to the sole interpretation of the Courts. Belgium adheres to Benelux legislation on trademarks, which can be particularly effective for firms operating in this region in that it allows a claim to be lodged in Belgium, with interim injunction that can ultimately lead to a decision enforceable in the whole territory of the Netherlands, Belgium, and Luxembourg (Grand Duchy).

Copyrights A revised legislation on Copyright protection has updated the previous protection exclusively granted by the case law. Computer software is also protected by a very new legal framework, a characteristic of which is a discovery procedure to such evidence of infringement.

Business Registration

Operating a business in Belgium is theoretically and generally speaking free. However, some specific commercial activities are regulated and therefore subject to the fulfillment of certain skill and legal conditions. Operators of businesses must be registered with the Register of Commerce (a specific section of the Commercial Court) before starting their activities. They must also apply to the tax authorities for a VAT (value-added tax) number, and register with the social security authorities both for themselves and for their staff. A foreign citizen of a non-EU country who wants to operate a personal commercial activity or to act as director of a company (either the branch of a foreign company or a Belgian company) is required to get a professional card with the appropriate authorities. Opening a branch of a foreign company is also subject to the previous fulfillment of formalities, which are more restrictive for non-EU foreign companies.

Contracts and Dispute Resolution

The Belgian contract system is based on the Napoleonic civil code. According to article 1134 of the Civil Code, parties are free in deciding the terms of their contracts as long as they comply with the laws of public order and with the compulsory laws directed specifically at business agreements. A contract is considered to dictate the terms of the agreement, rather than merely as a set of guidelines, and it must be performed in good faith. The courts are fully independent and the people are confident in the judges. Alternative dispute resolution is not generally resorted to in Belgium. There are sometimes delays in obtaining a decision due to the heavy caseload of the courts; but for urgent cases–such as infringement of trademarks, unfair commercial practices, or the appointment of special experts–the court will encourage the parties to submit to court-supervised arbitration on that issue.

Notaries

Notaries public are appointed by the King. They authenticate legal documents which must be reported in the official property books, particularly those which relate to real estate, such as mortgages. The bylaws of limited companies must also be authenticated by a notary.

Labor

Workers in Belgium are entitled to associate freely in unions and to bargain collectively. The Constitution does not recognize their right to strike, but this right is exercised freely. Labor laws regulate and limit the employment hours and conditions of women and children, and are strongly protective thereof. Labor laws govern the terms of employment contracts. They strongly support and protect the rights of workers, and proscribe the ability of employers to terminate without cause or arbitrarily. Laws provide for a minimum notice period prior to termination, and for severance payments; in the case of labor contracts for an undefined period, severance payments must be equal to at least three months of salary for every five years of service.

There are minimum wage laws which generally provide a livable wage level for the average family. All workers and employers contribute to the national social security system through a process of direct wage deduction, and a matching amount by employers.

Source: De Caluwe & Dieryck Law Firm, Brussels - Antwerp.

Legal Matters

LEGAL BRIEFS

- **Intellectual property** Most patent work (application and registration) is handled by specialized patent attorneys, with law firms focusing their work on other aspects of intellectual property. Law firms are particularly recommended for patent, trademark, and copyright opinion (e.g. for advertising), and litigation

- **Corporations** Most of the commercial activities in Belgium are operated through corporations. The most commonly used corporations are the *society anonyme* (limited company) with a minimum registered capital of BF 1,250,000 (BF 2,500,000 after July 1, 1996), and the *society privie Ö responsability limitie* (private company) with a minimum registered capital of BF 750,000. The limited company is managed by a board of at least three (two if there are only two shareholders, after July 1, 1996) directors while a private company is managed by one of several managers. Directors and managers are fully liable for their management of the company and for their errors toward third parties.

- **Notarized deed** Incorporating a limited or a private company requires an authentic deed executed before a notary. The formation costs largely depend on the amount of the registered capital.

- **Social matters** Maximum work week: legally 40 hours, but generally 38 through collective labor agreements.

- **Minimum annual holidays** Holidays are calculated on the basis of two days per working month during the previous year (regularly 24 days).

- **Vacation bonus** Vacation bonuses are given at 14.8 percent of the annual salary.

- **Property** Belgium places no restriction on the ownership of property by foreigners.

- **Competition** The EEC rules (mainly art. 85, 86 of the Rome Treaty) apply. Antitrust and monopoly loans are strictly enforced in an effort to insure fair competition. At national level, a law has been enforced since April 5, 1995.

LEGAL CONTACTS

De Caluwe & Dieryck
98, rue Saint-Bernard
1060 Brussels
Tel: (2) 536-58-11
Fax: (2) 536-59-11
Ordre National des Avocats
65 Avenue de la Toison d'Or
1060 Brussels
Tel: (2) 534-67-73
Fax: (2) 539-39-20
Clifford Chance
Avenue Louise 65
Box 2
Brussels 1050
Tel: (2) 533-59-11
Fax: (2) 533-59-59
Stephenson Harwood
Avenue du Diamant 139
Brussels 1040
Tel: (2) 735-91-90
Fax: (2) 932-2237
Taylor Johnson Garrett
14 Rue Montoyer
1040 Brussels
Baker & McKenzie
(Crousse, De Keyser, Hinnekens)
40 Boulevard du Regent
Regentlaan 40
Fifth Floor
1000 Brussels
Tel: (2) 506-3611
Fax: (2) 511-6280

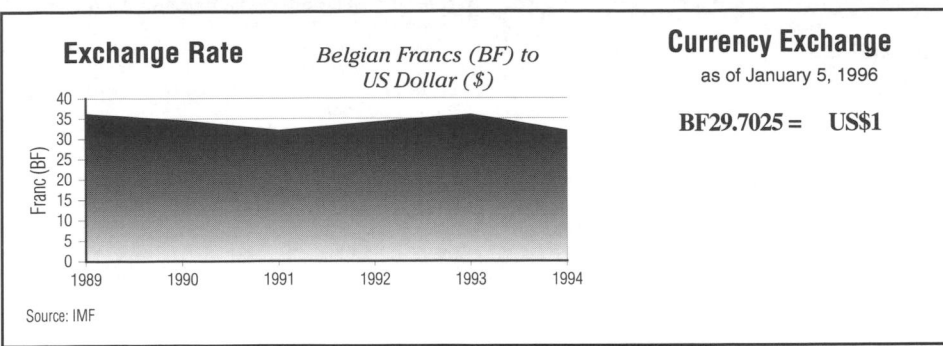

Exchange Rate
Belgian Francs (BF) to US Dollar ($)

Currency Exchange
as of January 5, 1996

BF29.7025 = US$1

Source: IMF

Currency

The currency in use is the Belgian franc (BF).

Foreign Exchange

Belgium is economically linked with Luxembourg and the Belgium franc is on par with the Luxembourg franc. Belgium adjusts its exchange rates through the Exchange Rate and Intervention Mechanism (ERM) of the European Monetary System (EMS). In accordance with this agreement, Belgium maintains spot exchange rates between its currency and the currencies of the other participants within margins of 15 percent above or below specified rates. The National Bank of Belgium stands ready to buy or sell the currencies of the other participating countries in unlimited amounts at specified rates. There are no other exchange controls, and there are no taxes or subsidies on purchases or sales of foreign exchange.

Capital Transfers

Payments may be made freely, in any currency. Domestic and foreign bank notes and coins, and other means of payment, may be exported freely. Foreign exchange proceeds from exports do not have to be surrendered and may be used for all payments. Residents and nonresidents may export capital freely. Banks may freely accept foreign currency deposits from residents or nonresidents.

Investment Incentives

The government actively encourages foreign investment. Any foreign company can set up as a subsidiary or branch. In general, all incentives, regional or national, are available to foreign and domestic investors alike. Belgium has historically been near the top of the EU in providing state aids including investment incentives, although these seem likely to shrink in the near future as pressures from the EU to limit them and from declining budget resources intensify. Currently, the government offers tax deductions for certain types of investments, including new venture capital companies, coordination centers, and distribution centers. Information on other current incentive programs can be obtained from the Ministry of Economic Affairs, Foreign Investors Service, Square de Meeus 23, 1040 Brussels.

Investment Restrictions

All investors, local and foreign alike, must obtain special permission to open department stores, provide transportation, produce and sell certain food items, cut and polish diamonds, and sell firearms and ammunition.

TAXATION

Taxation requires sophisticated knowledge of complex rules and regulations specific to each country. The information presented here is from the Ernst & Young Corporate Tax Guide and Directory, available from the Ernst & Young accounting office in your country, or from:

Ernst & Young Tax Consultants
Avenue Marcel Thirty 204
B-1200 Brussels, Belgium
Tel: (2) 774-91-11
Fax: (2) 774-90-90
Telex: 22125

At a Glance

Corporate Income Tax Rate (%) (a)	40.17
Capital Gains Tax Rate (%) (a) (b)	10.17
Branch Tax Rate (%) (c)	44.29
Withholding Tax (%)	
Dividends (a)	25.75
Interest (a)	13.39
Royalties from Patents, Know-how, etc. (a)	13.39
Branch Remittance Tax	0
Net Operating Losses (Years)	
Carryback	0
Carryforward (d)	Unlimited

(a) This rate includes a 3% surtax (crisis contribution). The expiration date for the surtax has not yet been announced. The rate of withholding tax is reduced to 13.39% (including the 3% surtax) for certain dividends.
(b) Certain capital gains are exempt form tax.
(c) The amount of the deduction is limited.

Money Matters

BITS AND PIECES

- **Performance requirements** There are no performance requirements applicable to foreign investors, and it does not appear likely that the government will establish such requirements.
- **Development zones** High-tech investments in depressed areas of the country are eligible for a 10-year tax holiday and certain exemptions concerning the personal income taxation of their foreign executives.
- **Incentive programs** Emphasis is being placed on investments that promote innovation, research and development, energy savings, environmental cleanliness, exports, and employment.
- **Expropriation** There are no reported instances of expropriation.
- **Credit** Foreign investors have access to the local credit market on the same terms and conditions as domestic investors.
- **Payments** Foreign exchange proceeds from exports do not have to be surrendered and may be used for all payments.
- **Securities** The prior approval of the Ministry of Finance is required for issues of securities on the Belgian capital market by nonresidents and for public bids by nonresidents for the purchase or exchange of shares issued by Belgian companies.
- **Gold** Residents may freely purchase, hold, and sell gold coins and bars, at home or abroad. Imports and exports of gold in these forms by residents and nonresidents are unrestricted and free of license; licenses are required for imports of semi-processed gold. Settlements of gold may be made freely.

BANKS

National Bank of Belgium
Boulevard de Berlaimont 5
1000 Brussels
Tel: (2) 221-2111
Fax: (2) 221-3101

Gewestelijke Investeringsmaatachappij voor Vlaanderen
37 Karol Oomstraat
2018 Antwerp
Tel: (3) 248-2312
Fax: (3) 221-3101
Telex: 34167

Institut de Reescompte et de Garantie (IRG)/ Herdisconteringen Waarborginstituut (HWI)
78 rue de Commerce
1040 Brussels
Tel: (2) 511-7330
Fax: (2) 514-3450

Crédit Communal SA/Gemeentekrediet NV
44 blvd. Pachéco
1000 Brussels
Tel: (2) 222-1111
Fax: (2) 222-5504
Telex: 26245

Institut National de Crédit Agricole/Nationaal Instituut Vodbouwkrediet
56 rue Joseph II
1040 Brussels
Tel: (2) 287-7111
Fax: (2) 230-6649
Telex: 26863

Société Nationale de Crédit á l'Industrie (SNCI)/ Nationale Maatschappij voor Krediet aan de Nijverheid (NMKN)
14 ave de l'Astronomie
1030 Brussels
Tel: (2) 214-1211
Fax: (2) 218-0478
Telex: 25996

ABN AMRO Bank (Belgie) NV
53 Regentlaan
1000 Brussels
Tel: (2) 518-0211
Fax: (2) 513-2765
Telex: 27040

Business Travel

Air Travel Times

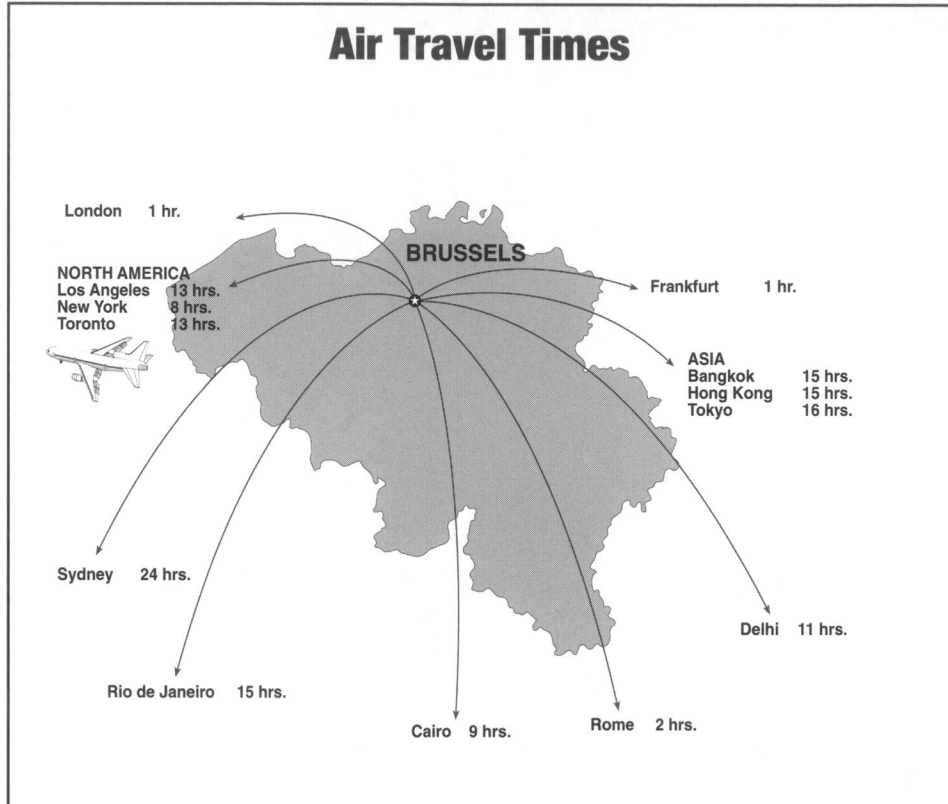

London 1 hr.

NORTH AMERICA
Los Angeles 13 hrs.
New York 8 hrs.
Toronto 13 hrs.

BRUSSELS

Frankfurt 1 hr.

ASIA
Bangkok 15 hrs.
Hong Kong 15 hrs.
Tokyo 16 hrs.

Sydney 24 hrs.

Delhi 11 hrs.

Rio de Janeiro 15 hrs.

Cairo 9 hrs.

Rome 2 hrs.

COMMUNICATIONS

Telephones Telephone service is modern. It is possible to dial direct to most areas in Europe and North America. Public phone booths can be found in cafes, hotels, and restaurants. Telegrams may also be sent by phone by dialing 905.

Fax Most major hotels are equipped with fax machines. International hotel chains also have public telex booths.

Post office Mail service in Belgium is reliable and efficient. Post Offices are open Monday-Saturday from 9:00 am to 5:00 pm. Stamps are also sold at shops and newsstands, and letters can be mailed from the bright red mailboxes on the streets.

BEST TRAVEL BOOKS

Fodor's Travel Guide, The Netherlands, Belgium and Luxembourg. Tourist oriented, excellent source of city details.

Dollarwise Guide to Belgium, Holland and Luxembourg. New York: Prentice-Hall.

Fodor's Europe, Best of 31 Countries. Contains information on historical towns, great culture, scenic coastal countryside.

Do's and Taboos Around the World. The Bestselling Guide to International Behavior. Edited by Roger E. Axtell, compiled by the Parker Pen Company. The ultimate guide to international behavior, now completely updated and expanded. Helpful, fun to read.

Berlitz Business Travel Guide, Europe. Concise economic details, successful trip planning, background information on people and cities, useful facts and addresses.

USEFUL TELEPHONE NUMBERS

If you are calling from outside Belgium, you will need to add the country code [32] and any other international dialing requirements from within your country.

- Belgium Tourist Reservation .... (2) 2305029
- National Railway Information .... (2) 523080
- Train-Ferry Service Information .... (59) 707601
- Tourist Information .... (2) 5181211, 5139090
- Immigration and Foreign Affairs .... (2) 5168111
- Sabena/Belgian World Airways............. (2) 5119060
- Telegrams 905

Telephone Directory Information
- Belgium 1308
- Brussels 1307

Rental Car Agencies
- Avis .... (2) 7240625
- Europcar.. (2) 6409400
- Hertz... (2) 7354050

Credit Card Information
Lost or stolen credit cards (call collect to the US, regardless of which country the card was issued in.)
- Amex ....[1] (919) 333-3211
- Diner's Club...............................[1] (303) 799-1504
- MasterCard ....[1] (314) 275-6690
- Visa ....[1] (410) 581-7931

Travelogue

WORKWEEK

Offices Monday-Friday 9:00 am to 6:00 pm, closed weekends.

Banks Monday-Friday 9:00 am to 3:30 pm, some with Saturday morning hours.

Government Monday-Friday 9:00 am to noon and 2:00 to 5:00 pm.

Retail Monday-Saturday 9:00 am to 6:00 pm.

HOLIDAYS

Holidays 1996
January 1 New Year's Day
April 8 Easter Monday*
May 6 Belgian Labor Day
May 16 Ascension Day
May 26 Whit Monday
July 21 Independence Day
August 15 Assumption Day
November 1 All Saints' Day
November 11 Veterans Day
December 25 Christmas Day
*Date varies each year.

VISA AND PASSPORT

A passport is required for entry to Belgium. A visa is not required for business or tourist stays up to 90 days. All travelers must hold onward or return tickets and sufficient funds. Travelers without valid travel documentation will not be allowed to enter.

DEPARTURE FORMALITIES

There are no restrictions on currency exportation or departure fees in Belgium.

IMMUNIZATION

Proof of smallpox, cholera, and yellow fever vaccinations is required only of travelers arriving from infected areas.

TIPPING

A service charge is included in most restaurant and hotel bills. Taxi fares also include a tip. Barbers and hairdressers should be tipped about 15 percent. Chambermaids and theater attendants are usually tipped BF 20-30, while washroom and service station attendants get BF 10-20.

CRIME

Belgium has a relatively low crime rate in most regions. Foreigners in major cities can be targets for pickpockets and purse snatchers, especially on subways and at tourist attractions. Theft of and from vehicles is the most common crime in Belgium. Assaults and robberies are increasing.

INFRASTRUCTURE

Belgium has advanced and efficient air, rail, taxi, hotel, car rental, and telecommunication networks. The airport is undergoing extensive renovation and expansion. The railway system in Belgium is extensive and dependable. Taxis are available, but must be found in front of hotels or at the airport. Belgians are considered bad drivers with a high accident rate, heavy penalties on traffic infringements are common.

NATIONAL TOURIST OFFICE

Tourist Information
61 rue du Marche-aux-Herbes
B-1000 Brussels
Tel: (2) 513-9090
Fax: (2) 504-0390

GOVERNMENT AGENCIES

Minister President of the Walloon Region
Rue Mazy, 25-27
5100 Namur
Tel: (81) 33-12-11
Fax: (81) 33-12-99

Minister President of the Brussels Region
Rue Ducale, 7-9
1000 Brussels
Tel:(2) 506-32-11
Fax:(2) 514-40-22

Ministry of Communications and Public Enterprises
Rue de la Loi 65
1040 Brussels
Tel: (2) 237-67-11
Fax: (2) 231-19-12

Ministry of Development Cooperation
Avenue Galilée 5
1030 Brussels
Tel: (2) 219-19-11, 210-19-11
Fax: (2) 217-33-28

Ministry of Economic Affairs
Square de Meeus 23
1040 Brussels
Tel: (2) 511-19-30
Fax: (2) 514-03-89

Ministry of Foreign Affairs
Rue des Quatre-Bras 2
1000 Brussels
Tel: (2) 516-81-11
Fax: (2) 511-83-65

Ministry of Foreign Trade and European Affairs
Rue des Quatre-Bras 2
1000 Brussels
Tel: (2) 516-83-11
Fax: (2) 512-72-21

Ministry of the Interior, Civil Service and Immigrant Affairs
Rue Royale 60-62
1000 Brussels
Tel: (2) 504-85-11
Fax: (2) 504-85-00

Ministry of Small- and Medium-Size Business and Agriculture
Rue Marie Thérese 1
1040 Brussels
Tel: (2) 211-06-11
Fax: (2) 219-61-30

Ministry of Social Integration, Public Health, and Environment
Rue de la Loi 66
1040 Brussels
Tel: (2) 238-28-11
Fax: (2) 230-38-62

WORLD TRADE CENTERS

The World Trade Center Association of Antwerp
Korte Sint Annastraat 11
2000 Antwerp
Tel:(3) 231-80-71/2
Fax:(3) 234-31-66

World Trade Center Association Brussels A.S.B.L.
162/52 Boulevard Emile Jacqmain-Boite
B-1210 Brussels
Tel:(2) 219-44-00
Fax:(2) 217-28-20

GENERAL TRADE ASSOCIATIONS

Wallonia Investment Office
Place Joséphine Charlotte, 19, Box 1
5100 Namur
Tel:(81) 32-22-11
Fax:(81) 30-64-24

Flanders Investment Office
Markiesstraat, 1
1000 Brussels
Tel:(2) 507-38-52
Fax:(2) 507-38-51

Office for Foreign Investment (Brussels Region)
Rue du Champ de Mars, 25
1050 Brussels
Tel:(2) 513-97-00
Fax:(2) 511-52-55

Federation of Belgian Enterprises
Rue Ravenstein, 4
1000 Brussels
Tel:(2) 515-08-11
Fax:(2) 515-09-99

Federation of Metalworking Industries
Rue des Drapiers, 21
1050 Brussels
Tel:(2) 510-23-11
Fax:(2) 510-23-01

Federation of Chemical Industries
Square Marie Louise, 49
1040 Brussels
Tel:(2) 238-97-11
Fax:(2) 231-13-01

Federation of Textile Industries
Rue Montoyer, 24
1040 Brussels
Tel:(2) 287-08-11
Fax:(2) 230-65-85

Flemish Economic Union
Brouwersvliet, 5, Box 4
2000 Antwerp
Tel:(3) 231-16-60
Fax:(3) 233-76-60

Wallonian Enterprise Association
Rue Stocquoy, 1
1300 Wavre
Tel:(10) 45-11-41
Fax:(10) 45-33-43

CHAMBERS OF COMMERCE

Chamber of Commerce and Industry
Markgravestraat 12
2000 Antwerp
Tel: (3) 232-22-19
Fax. (3) 233-64-42 Telex: 71536

American Chamber of Commerce in Belgium
Avenue des Arts, 50, Box 5
1040 Brussels
Tel: (2) 513-67-70
Fax: (2) 513-79-28

Brussels Chamber of Commerce
Avenue Louise, 500
1050 Brussels
Tel:(2) 648-50-02
Fax:(2) 640-93-28

NEWSPAPERS

De Antwerpse Morgen
Antwerp
Tel:(3) 216-49-30
Fax:(3) 237-79-73

De Financieel Ekonomische Tijd
5 Brouwersvliet
bus 3
2000 Antwerp
Tel:(3) 231-57-56
Fax:(3) 234-36-41

Gazet van Antwerpen
2 Katwilgweg
2050 Antwerp
Tel:(3) 210-02-10
Fax:(3) 216-41-65

De Nieuwe Gazet
10 Leopoldstraat
2000 Antwerp
Tel:(3) 231-96-80
Fax:(3) 234-16-66

Courrier de la Bourse
131 rue de Birmingham
1070 Brussels
Tel:(2) 526-56-66
Fax:(2) 526-55-26

La Lanterne
134 rue Royale
1000 Brussels
Tel:(2) 218-21-08
Fax:(2) 217-68-56

La Libre Belgique
127 blvd Emile Jacqmain
1000 Brussels
Tel:(2) 211-27-77
Fax:(2) 211-28-32
Telex: 21550

Het Nieuwsblad
28 Gossetlaan
1702 Groot Bijgaarden
Tel:(2) 467-22-11
Fax:(2) 466-30-93
Telex: 23039

Le Soir
21 place de Louvain
1000 Brussels
Tel:(2) 225-55-55
Fax:(2) 225-59-09

Krantengroep De Standard (group combining De Standard Het Nieuwsblad, De Gentenaar)
30 Gossetlaan
1702 Groot Bljgaarden
Tel:(2) 467-22-11
Fax:(2) 466-30-93

De Standaard
28 Gossetlaan
1702 Groot Bijgaarden
Tel:(2) 467-22-11
Fax:(2) 466-30-93
Telex: 23039

La Libre Belgique-Gazette du Liége
26-28 blvd d'Avroy
4000 Liége
Tel:(41) 23-16-33
Fax:(41) 22-41-26
Telex: 41297

La Meuse
8-12 blvd de la Sauveniére
4000 Liége
Tel:(41) 20-08-11
Fax:(41) 20-08-40

La Wallonie
55 rue de la Régence
4000 Liége
Tel:(41) 20-18-11
Fax:(41) 23-21-52

PERIODICALS

La Cité
26 rue St. Laurent
1000 Brussels
Tel:(2) 217-23-90
Fax:(2) 217-69-95

DeBoer en de Tuinder
8 Minderbroedersstraat
3000 Leuven
Tel:(16) 24-21-60
Fax:(16) 24-21-68

De Bond
170 Langestraat
1150 Brussels
Tel:(2) 779-00-00
Fax:(2) 779-16-16

Brugsch Handelsblad
4 Eekhoutstraat
8000 Bruges
Tel: (50) 33-06-61
Fax: (50) 33-46-33

Femmes d'Aujourd'hui
27A ave Brugmann
1060 Brussels
Tel: (2) 534-28-00
Fax: (2) 537-99-04
Telex: 25104

Flair
7 Jan Blockxstrat
2018 Antwerp
Tel:(3) 247-45-11
Fax:(3) 237-95-11
Telex: 32979

RADIO AND TELEVISION

Radio-Television Belge de la Communaute Francaise (RTBF)
52 blvd Auguste Reyers
1040 Brussels
Tel: (2) 737-21-11

Belgische Radio en Televisie Instituut der Nederlandse Uitzendingen
52 August Reyerslaan
1040 Brussels
Tel: (2) 737-31-11
Fax: (2) 735-36-62
Telex: 24216

Belgisches Rundfunk- und Fernsehzentrum der Deutschsprachigen Gemeinschaft (BRF)
82 Herbesthaler Str.
4700 Eupen
Tel: (87) 59-44-11
Fax: (87) 59-44-99
Telex: 49427

Canal Plus Belgique
656 chaussee de Louvain
1030 Brussels
Fax: (2) 732-18-48

Television Independante (TVI)
67 ave Franklin Roosevelt
1050 Brussels
Tel: (2) 640-51-50
Telex: 64430

Vlaamse Televisie Maatschappij
22 Luchthavenlaan
1800 Vilvoorde
Tel: (2) 254-56-11
Fax (2) 252-37-87

BANKS

Antwerpse Diamantbank NV/Banque Diamantaire Anversoise SA
54 Pelikaanstraat
2018 Antwerp
Tel: (3) 233-90-80
Fax: (3) 233-90-95
Telex: 31673

Antwerpse Hypotheekkas/Caisse Hypothécaire Anversoise (AN-HYP)
214 Grotesteenweg
2600 Antwerp
Tel: (3) 218-211
Fax: (3) 218-24-07
Telex: 33100

Asahi Bank (Belgium) SA
27 ave des Arts
BP 4
1040 Brussels
Tel: (2) 230-81-00
Fax: (2) 230-29-52
Telex: 24368

ASLK-CGER Bank
48 Wolvengracht
1000 Brussels
Tel: (2) 213-61-11
Fax: (2) 213-67-99
Telex: 26860

BACOB SC
25 Trierstraat
1040 Brussels
Tel: (2) 237-82-11
Fax: (2) 230-71-78
Telex: 62199

Banco Hispano Americano (Benelux) SA
227 rue de la Loi
1040 Brussels
Tel: (2) 230-61-06
Fax: (2) 230-09-40
Telex: 21219

Banco de Roma (Belgio) SA
24 rue Joseph II
1040 Brussels
Tel: (2) 220-72-11
Fax: (2) 218-83-91
Telex: 21573

Bank J. van Breda & Co. GCV
295 Plantin & Moretuslei
2140 Antwerp
Tel: (3) 217-51-11
Fax: (3) 217-00-18
Telex: 31788

Bank of Yokohama (Europe) SA
287 ave Louise
BP 1
1050 Brussels
Tel: (2) 648-82-85
Fax: (2) 648-31-48
Telex: 21709

Bank van Roeselare NV
38 Noordstraat
8800 Roeselare
Tel: (51) 23-52-11
Fax: (51) 21-00-06
Telex: 81734

Banque Bruxelles Lambert
24 ave Marnix
1050 Brussels
Tel: (2) 517-21-11
Fax: (2) 517-38-44
Telex: 21421

Banque Européenne pour l'Amérique Latine SA
59 rue de l'Association
1000 Brussels
Tel: (2) 219-00-15
Fax: (2) 217-67-57
Telex: 22431

Banque Indosuez Belgique SA
9 Grote Market
2000 Antwerp
Tel: (3) 221-55-11
Fax: (3) 231-98-75
Telex: 23406

Banque Nagelmackers 1747 SA
12 place de Louvain
1000 Brussels
Tel: (2) 211-57-11
Fax: (2) 211-57-63
Telex: 21612

Banque Paribas Belgique SA Paribas Bank Belgie NV
162 blvd E. Jacqmain
BP 2
1210 Brussels
Tel: (2) 220-41-11
Fax: (2) 218-51-42
Telex: 21349

Belgolaise SA
1 Cantersteen
BP 807
1000 Brussels
Tel: (2) 518-72-11
Fax: (2) 518-75-15
Telex: 21375

CC-Banque Belgique SA
32 rue du Fossé-aux-Loups
1000 Brussels
Tel: (2) 211-32-11
Fax: (2) 217-97-99
Telex: 21670

CERA
100 Brusselsesteenweg
3000 Leuven
Tel: (16) 30-31-11
Fax: (16) 30-31-99
Telex: 24166

Crédit Lyonais Belgium SA
17 ave Marnix
1050 Brussels
Tel: (2) 516-05-11
Fax: (2) 511-24-58
Telex: 20227

Generale Bank NV
3 Montagne du Parc
1000 Brussels
Tel: (2) 516-21-55
Fax: (2) 516-32-83
Telex: 21283

Generale de Banque Belge pour l'Etranger
3 Montagne du Parc
1000 Brussels
Tel: (2) 511-26-31

Internationale Nederlanden Bank (Belgium) SA NV
1 rue de Ligne
1000 Brussels
Tel: (2) 217-40-40
Fax: (2) 217-04-91
Telex: 21780

Ippa Bank NV/SA
23 Vorstlaan
1170 Brussels
Tel: (2) 676-12-11
Fax: (2) 676-12-13
Telex: 24806

Kredietbank NV
7 Arenbergstraat
1000 Brussels
Tel: (2) 517-41-11
Fax: (2) 517-42-09
Telex: 21207

Lloyds Bank (Belgium) SA
2 ave de Tervueren
1040 Brussels
Tel: (2) 739-58-11
Fax: (2) 733-11-07
Telex: 64359

The Long-Term Credit Bank of Japan (Europe) SA
blvd du Régent
1000 Brussels
Tel: (2) 513-90-20
Fax: (2) 512-73-20
Telex: 61393

Metropolitan Bank NV
191-197 blvd du Souverain
1160 Brussels
Tel: (2) 673-80-01
Fax: (2) 673-75-19T
elex: 24036

Mitsubishi Bank (Europe)
39 ave des Arts
1040 Brussels
Tel: (2) 513-97-70
Fax: (2) 513-28-51
Telex: 24168

Mitsui Trust Bank (Europe) SA
287 ave Louise
BP 5
1050 Brussels
Tel: (2) 640-88-50
Fax: (2) 640-73-29
Telex: 64720

Takugin International Bank (Europe) SA
40 rue Montoyer
1040 Brussels
Tel: (2) 230-07-14
Fax: (2) 231-18-99
Telex: 23568

INTERNET ADDRESSES
Embassy of Belgium, Washington DC
http://www.belgium-emb.org/usa/index.html
Belgian Federal Government Online
http://giulian.online.be/belgium/
OSTC, Federal Office for Scientific, Technical, and Cultural Affairs
http://www.belspo.be/
EUNet Belgium
http://www.eunet.be/

Bermuda

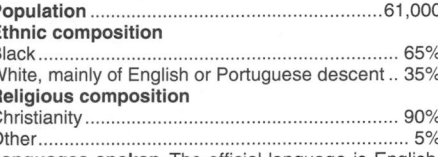

Economy

Overview

Bermuda's economy and livelihood are dependent almost entirely on tourism and international business. Its only appreciable resources are its great scenic beauty and its people. Still, it has made the most of these resources. Thousands of international businesses operate in Bermuda under a variety of organizational structures, and the country maintains active trading relationships with many countries around the world. Its GDP continues to show steady growth; GDP per capita now ranks among the highest in the world.

Trade

Bermuda is almost entirely dependent on imports, has very few commodity exports, and, therefore, consistently records a large visible trade deficit. However, receipts from its huge service industries normally ensure a surplus on the current account of the balance of payments. The US is Bermuda's principal source of imports (providing over 60 percent of total imports), and the principal market for exports (buying nearly 25 percent of Bermuda's product). Other important trading partners include the UK, Canada, and Japan. The main exports are rum, flowers (especially orchids), pharmaceuticals, and the re-export of petroleum products. The principal imports are machinery, transport equipment and other manufactured articles, and food.

Sectors

Agriculture This sector (including forestry and fishing) engages only 0.9 percent of the employed labor force, and the sector makes a minimal contribution to GDP. The principal crops are potatoes, tomatoes, carrots, bananas and cabbages. Flowers are grown for export. Other vegetables and fruit are also grown, but Bermuda remains very dependent upon food imports. There is a small fishing industry, mainly for domestic consumption.

Industry Industry contributes about 10 percent of GDP and engages almost 13 percent of the work force. The main activities include ship repairs, boat-building, and the manufacture of paints, pharmaceuticals, and cosmetics. The principal industrial sector is construction.

Services Bermuda is overwhelmingly a service economy, the traditional principal sector being tourism. Despite the recent growth of financial services, tourism still accounts for nearly two-thirds of foreign exchange earnings, and over one-third of total GDP. The total number of tourists, including cruise ship passengers, is strictly controlled, in order to maintain Bermuda's environment and its market for wealthier visitors.

There is a significant commercial "offshore" financial sector, and Bermuda is one of the world's leading insurance markets. This sector accounts for about 40 percent of foreign exchange earnings and approximately 25 percent of GDP.

Trends

The maintenance of the service economy is fundamental to Bermuda, although the government continues its effort to more strictly control offshore financial operations. If it is able to control this industry and maintain its status as a draw for wealthy tourists, Bermuda's economy should continue to flourish.

At a Glance

THE COUNTRY

Location The Bermuda islands are an isolated archipelago, comprising about 150 islands, in the Atlantic Ocean, about 917 km (570 miles) off the coast of South Carolina, US.
Terrain Mostly flat and rocky, beautiful semitropical vegetation.
Climate Lying in the Gulf Stream, Bermuda is generally mild and humid, with a mean annual temperature of 21°C (70°F) and an average rainfall of 147 cm (58 in).

THE PEOPLE

Population 61,000
Ethnic composition
Black 65%
White, mainly of English or Portuguese descent .. 35%
Religious composition
Christianity 90%
Other 5%
Languages spoken The official language is English, but there is a small community of Portuguese speakers.
Education and literacy Education is free and compulsory for children between the ages of 5 and 16. Most adults can read and write.
Labor Force 32,000

COUNTRY FACTS

Political and legal Bermuda was acquired by the British in 1684. The governor represents the sovereign and is advised by a cabinet of legislators appointed at the recommendation of the prime minister. There is also a legislature consisting of an 11-member Senate and a 40-member House of Assembly (elected by universal suffrage).
Telephone There are 52,000 telephones on the island. International service is excellent in the cities and the major tourist resorts. International country code: [1]; area code (441).
Transportation There is a free port at Ireland Island. Most transportation is adequate to keep up with the heavy tourism sector. Most of the 240 kilometers of roads are surfaced. Public transportation is mostly by bus. Hamilton has a deepwater harbor. Kindley Field, near St. George, is Bermuda's only international airport.
Environment Tourism has hurt the local environment somewhat. The high density of population has given rise to environmental concerns and local disquiet at the cost of property. Since 1972 no new hotels have been built, although the government is now planning to develop a couple of new areas—over fierce objections from the local population.
Media The Bermuda Broadcasting Co., Ltd. runs the two commercial television stations and five of the six radio stations. The only daily newspaper is the Royal Gazette.
Health The Hospital Insurance Act provides hospital insurance for all, and provides for free hospital care for children and subsidized rates for the elderly. All medical services are private. The well-equipped hospitals receive government support.

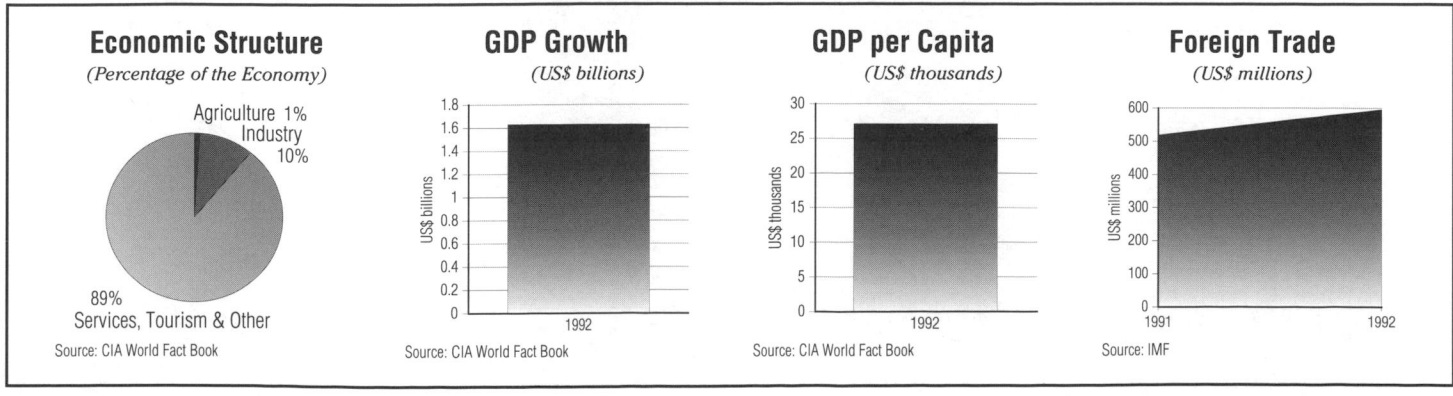

Economic Structure (Percentage of the Economy)	GDP Growth (US$ billions)	GDP per Capita (US$ thousands)	Foreign Trade (US$ millions)
Agriculture 1% Industry 10% 89% Services, Tourism & Other	1992	1992	1991 1992
Source: CIA World Fact Book	Source: CIA World Fact Book	Source: CIA World Fact Book	Source: IMF

Business Travel

LH	1906	MADRID	935	113-3
LH	1022	STUTTGART HBF.	935	-
AF	1701	LYON	940	683-6
AY	822	HELSINKI	940	113-3
AA	071	SFRANCISCO-DALLAS	945	731-7

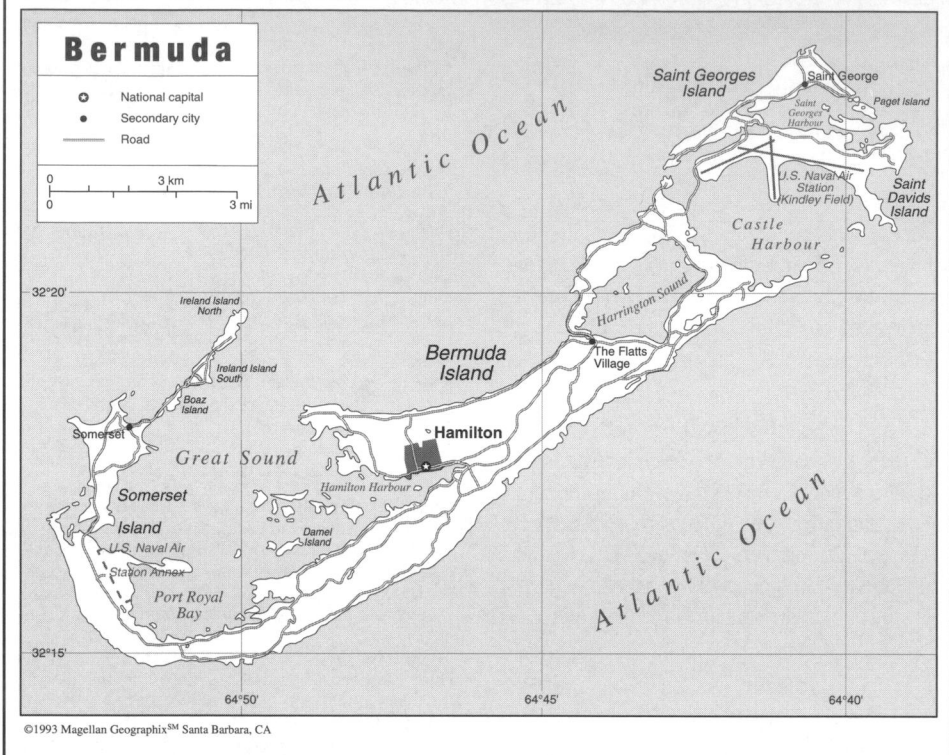

©1993 Magellan Geographix℠ Santa Barbara, CA

COMMUNICATIONS

Telephones Public phones accept coins only. Pay phones take phone deposit cards or cash cards. Hotels can add large surcharges to the cost of long distance calling. To avoid these charges use MCI or AT&T calling services with your long distance carrier.

Fax All hotels are happy to offer faxing services to visitors, but expect to pay a high price for this accommodation.

Post office The postal service is considered excellent in Bermuda. Post office hours are Monday-Friday 8:00 am to 5:00 pm with Saturday hours of 8:00 am to noon. Hotels sells stamps, and stamp vending machines are available throughout Bermuda.

BEST TRAVEL BOOKS

Bermuda AAA Travel Book. Getting away from it all.
Birnbaum's Bermuda. Filled with travel information.
Fodor's Bermuda. A complete guide with the best tourist information including the best beaches, golf, shopping, and dining in Bermuda.

USEFUL TELEPHONE NUMBERS

If you are calling from outside Bermuda, you will need to add the country code [1] and any other international dialing requirements from within your country.

- Cable & Wireless for faxing ....(441) 297-7000
- Taxi ....(441) 292-4476, 295-4141
- Taxi touring ....(441) 297-1001, 236-3040
- Department of Immigration ....(441) 295-5151
- Emergency 911
- Operator 0
- Local information 411

Credit card information:
Lost or stolen credit cards (call collect to the US, regardless of which country the card was issued in).

- Amex ....[1] (919) 333-3211
- Diner's Club...............................[1] (303) 799-1504
- MasterCard ....[1] (314) 275-6690
- Visa ....[1] (410) 581-7931

NATIONAL TOURIST OFFICE

Department of Tourism
43 Church Street
Hamilton, HM12
Tel: (441) 292-0023
Fax: (441) 292-7537

Travelogue

WORKWEEK

Offices Monday-Saturday 9:00 am to 5:00 pm.
Banks Monday-Thursday 9:00 am to 3:00 pm and Fridays from 9:00 am to 4:30 pm.
Government Monday-Friday 9:00 am to 5:00 pm or 6:00 pm.
Retail Monday-Friday 9:00 am to 5:00 pm, Saturdays 9:00 am to 9:00 pm.

HOLIDAYS

Holiday 1996
January 1 New Year's Day
April 5 Good Friday
May 24 Bermuda Day
June 17 Queen's Official Birthday
August 1 & 2 Cup Match and Somer's Day
September 2 Labour Day
November 11 Remembrance Day
December 25 Christmas
December 26 Boxing Day

VISA AND PASSPORT

Proof of citizenship and a passport, birth certificate, or voter's registration is required for entry into Bermuda, along with an official photo ID. Onward tickets, proof of reserved hotel accommodations are also required for stays of less than three months. For longer stays a letter, written in advance, must be sent to the Department of Immigration for approval.

DEPARTURE FORMALITIES

Goods of total dollar amounts ranging from US$300-400 are permitted to be taken out of Bermuda without having to pay duty. Over that dollar amount, a 10 percent duty is applied. Bring all receipts for proof of purchase to avoid delays at customs. There is a US$20 departure tax.

IMMUNIZATION

There are no required immunizations for entry into Bermuda. However, it is advised for people with hay fever or allergies that medications be kept on hand as pollen air conditions are usually high. Bermuda's warm weather and hot sun can be unforgiving; bring sun protection with you and wear it at all times.

TIPPING

Restaurants already add into the bill their desired tip rate of 15 percent. 10 percent is the standard tipping amount for taxis, nighspots, hotels, barbers, and beauticians. Bartenders are usually tipped US$1.00 per drink and porters US$1.00 per bag.

CRIME

Although violent crime is not a significant problem, logical precautions are advised, such as: use traveler's checks instead of carrying large amounts of cash, lock your hotel rooms and rental mopeds. Do not leave valuables or passports in hotel rooms; have them locked in the hotel safe.

INFRASTRUCTURE

The island of Bermuda is a tourist attraction in itself. All sorts of transportation is available, reliable, and affordable. It is also close at hand and can be an adventure! Moped rental is among the most popular, as are horse drawn buggy rides. Buses are pink with a dark blue stripe; they are efficient and available during daytime hours. If traveling by sea, sea ferries are reasonably priced. Taxis are metered; the drivers are considered helpful and friendly. There are no car rentals in Bermuda but taxi renting or taxi touring for the day is not an uncommon mode of transportation.

Foreign Trade

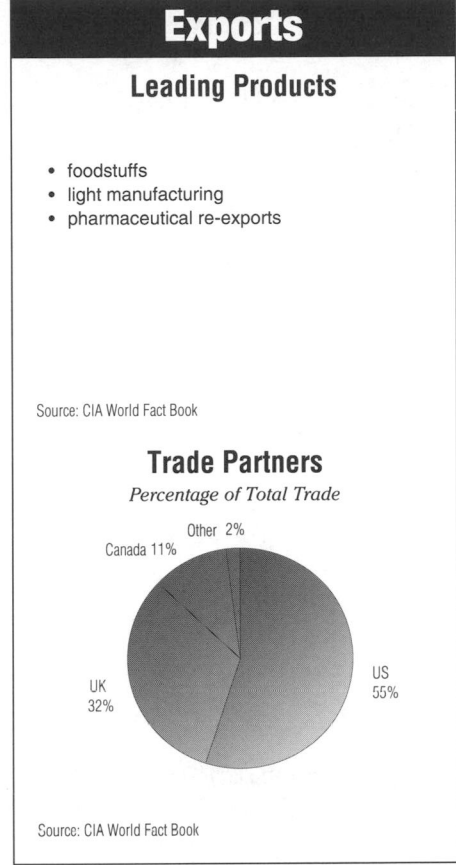

Imports

Leading Products

- fuel
- foodstuffs
- machinery

Source: CIA World Fact Book

Trade Partners
Percentage of Total Trade

- Other 15%
- Japan 5%
- Canada 5%
- Venezuela 7%
- UK 8%
- US 60%

Source: CIA World Fact Book

Exports

Leading Products

- foodstuffs
- light manufacturing
- pharmaceutical re-exports

Source: CIA World Fact Book

Trade Partners
Percentage of Total Trade

- Other 2%
- Canada 11%
- UK 32%
- US 55%

Source: CIA World Fact Book

Opportunities

FOR IMPORTING TO BERMUDA

- machinery and transportation equipment
- beverages and processed food
- clothing
- live animals

FOR EXPORTING FROM BERMUDA

- rum
- flowers (especially orchids)
- pharmaceuticals
- processed petroleum products

GROWTH SECTORS

- professional financial services
- tourism
- telecommunications

Trade News

GOVERNMENT PROCUREMENT

- construction, electrical, communications equipment
- power distribution transformers and equipment

RULES AND REGULATIONS

- **Customs duty** Customs duty is normally calculated on an ad valorem basis, generally the fob value of imported goods. The standard rate is 22.25 percent, although many food items are exempt and lower rates apply to certain essentials and to materials used in local manufacture. Luxury items carry a duty of 33.5 percent.

Legal

Legal System

Bermuda is a dependent territory of Great Britain, and it maintains the British system of justice.

Intellectual Property Rights

Patents Patents are granted for a period of 16 years but may be extended for additional periods of seven years upon consent of the Minister of Labor and Home Affairs. The Court, upon application by an interested party, has the power to order the holder of a patent to license others to use the patent where the invention is not being used in Bermuda by the owner and the patent holder has unreasonably refused to license others to do so.

Trademarks To be eligible for registration in Bermuda the mark must be used in connection with goods or services distributed in, or exported from, Bermuda, or where there is a *bona fide* intention to use a mark at some point in the future. A registration is valid for seven years, and for a minimal cost may be renewed for additional terms of 14 years each. It generally takes between 18 and 24 months for an application to be processed.

Business Registration

The prior consent of the Minister of Finance is required to incorporate an exempted company or partnership. Information on the proposed beneficial owners of the company or partnership, together with a bank reference letter with respect to each, must be submitted to the Minister for review. All information submitted is treated confidentially.

Contracts and Dispute Resolution

Contracts generally follow the British model of being lengthy and quite detailed. The parties and their legal representatives enjoy complete freedom from government and local professional restrictions in the conduct of arbitrations. Because of this, arbitration is increasingly being utilized for dispute resolution in Bermuda.

Source: Cox & Wilkenson, Bermuda

Legal Matters

LEGAL BRIEFS

- **Labor laws** Labor laws are protective of employees, who have the right to join unions and to bargain collectively.
- **Foreign employees** The policy of the Bermuda Government is not to permit the employment of non-Bermudians in Bermuda where there are qualified and experienced Bermudians to perform the job. In order to be entitled to work in Bermuda the non-Bermudian must hold a work permit.
- **Bermudan trusts** A Bermuda trust is a trust established and administered in Bermuda. Bermuda law imposes powers and obligations on the trustee. It limits the life of a trust to a "perpetuity period", which is defined with reference to lives in existence at the creation of the settlement plus up to 21 years. The law does not prevent a trust from accumulating its income and this can continue throughout the life of the trust. A trustee can, if so empowered in the instrument, disburse both principal and income to the full extent of the trust assets (thus terminating the trust) at any time after its creation.

LEGAL CONTACTS

Cox & Wilkerson
Milner House
18 Parliament Street
Hamilton
Tel: (441) 295-4630
Fax: (441) 292-7880

Bermuda Bar Association
Reid House
31 Church Street
Hamilton, HM 12
Tel/Fax: (441) 295-4540

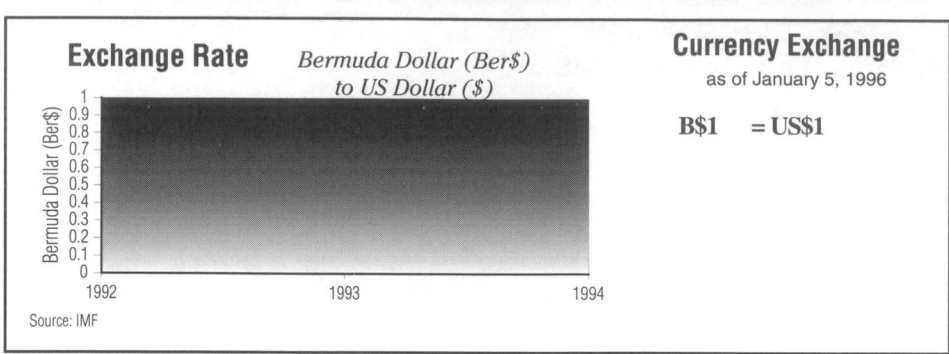

Exchange Rate
Bermuda Dollar (Ber$) to US Dollar ($)

Bermuda Dollar (Ber$): 1, 0.9, 0.8, 0.7, 0.6, 0.5, 0.4, 0.3, 0.2, 0.1, 0
1992   1993   1994

Source: IMF

Currency Exchange
as of January 5, 1996

B$1 = US$1

Currency

The currency in use is the Bermuda dollar (B$), which is divided into 100 cents. The US dollar is used by business visitors, tourists, international companies based in Bermuda and their non-Bermudian employees, who may be paid in US dollars. International companies may open US dollar bank accounts with the local banks.

The US dollar is traded at par with the Bermuda dollar. It is accepted everywhere in Bermuda as the currency of Bermuda's main industries of tourism and international business. US business visitors or tourists in any category do not need to exchange their US dollars for Bermuda money while in Bermuda.

Foreign Exchange

Bermuda does not impose any exchange controls on its currency or on the inflow or outflow of foreign currency.

Capital Transfers

Capital can move freely into or out of the country. Profits need not be repatriated and very few controls are placed on foreign businesses.

Investment Incentives

There is no taxation in Bermuda based on profits, dividends, or income, and neither is there any capital gains tax or gift tax. The only form of tax imposed on an exempted company or partnership is an annual fee of B$1,200; except the annual fee is B$2,250 in the case of companies writing insurance or reinsurance as a principal, mutual fund businesses, or companies engaged in raising money from the public. In addition, an exempted company can apply for an undertaking from the government that, in the event taxation is introduced in the future, it will not be applicable to that exempted company until March 29, 2016. This undertaking is normally sought by exempted companies and is routinely granted by the government. Exempted companies are not required to pay employment tax. Where the tax is applicable, the standard rate is five percent of an employer's total payroll, and applies only to employers with an annual payroll of more than B$50,000.

Investment Restrictions

There are few restrictions generally, although Bermuda has begun to tighten controls on offshore financial services in an attempt to control the laundering of illegal drug and gem smuggling profits.

Money Matters

BITS AND PIECES

- **Exempted companies** Exempted companies are exempt from the 60 percent Bermudian ownership requirement. This type of company is commonly used by international businesses, since it may be owned entirely by non-Bermudians, although up to 20 percent Bermudian ownership is permitted. Exempted companies commonly transact international business from Bermuda, and they may not normally compete with local companies in the Bermuda (as opposed to the international) market. Exempted companies may not own real estate in Bermuda.

- **Permit companies** Permit companies are companies which are incorporated in jurisdictions other than Bermuda but which have a "permit" to transact business from Bermuda. Similar regulations govern the operation of permit and exempt companies. Permits are obtained through a license granted by the Ministry of Finance.

- **Trusts** Bermudan trusts can accumulate income and this can continue throughout the life of the trust. Nevertheless, a trustee can, if so empowered in the instrument, disburse both principal and income to the full extent of trust assets (thus terminating the trust) at any time after its creation.

- **Insurance companies** Bermuda over the years has established itself as the leading offshore base for insurance companies.

- **US Currency** Canadian, European, and other business visitors or tourists should arrive with US dollars.

BANKS

Bermuda Monetary Authority
Sofia Bldg.
48 Church St.
POB HM 2447
Hamilton, HM 12
Tel: (441) 295-5278
Fax: (441) 292-7471
Telex: 3567

Bank of Bermuda Ltd.
6 Front St.
Hamilton, HM 11
Tel: (441) 295-4000
Fax: (441) 295-7093
Telex: 3212

Bank of N.T. Butterfield & Son Ltd.
65 Front St.
POB HM 195
Hamilton, HM AX
Tel: (441) 295-1111
Fax: (441) 292-4365
Telex: 3211

Bermuda Commercial Bank Ltd.
Barclays International Bldg.
44 Church St.
POB HM 1748
Hamilton , HM 12
Tel: (441) 295-5678
Fax: (441) 295-8091
Telex: 3336

TAXATION

Taxation requires sophisticated knowledge of complex rules and regulations specific to each country. The information presented here is from the Ernst & Young Corporate Tax Guide and Directory, available from the Ernst & Young accounting office in your country, or from:

Ernst & Young
Mail Address:
POB HM 463
Hamilton, HMBX Bermuda
Street Address:
Reid Hall
3 Reid Street
Hamilton, Bermuda
Tel: (441) 295-7000
Telex: 3680 Ans bk ERNST BA
Fax: (441) 295-5193

At a Glance

Corporate Income Tax Rate (%)	0
Capital Gains Tax Rate (%)	0
Branch Tax Rate (%)	0
Withholding Tax (%)	0

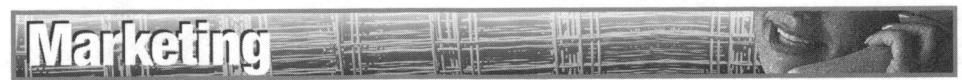

Marketing

Distribution

Goods typically enter Bermuda markets through local wholesalers or commission agents or direct sales from manufacturers. Most foreign retail and wholesale chains are prohibited from opening outlets in Bermuda, although distributorships and franchises can be negotiated with local partners. Local wholesalers and agents commonly specialize in particular lines. Most wholesalers and some retailers will purchase directly from manufacturers, which can develop into exclusive one-to-one distributorship arrangements.

Selling Techniques

Selling in Bermuda is like marketing in Europe and the United States. Bermudians are educated consumers and the market is highly competitive. Products must be attractive, high in quality, and priced to sell. Personal contact goes far, and a regular trip to Bermuda may mean successful market penetration for those willing to take this extra step.

Advertising

Goods and services are advertised extensively in local news and magazine publications. The major daily newspapers accept ads at reasonable rates, as do a number of weekly tabloids. The single state-owned television station sells advertising, as do the state-controlled and independent radio stations. Bold, aggressive advertising works well in this market; a subtle campaign is likely to be overlooked.

Service and Customer Support

For products that need after-sales servicing, local representation is essential. To hold an edge in this highly competitive market, local agents must be well-trained and current on the latest product technology. Delivery of spare parts from overseas is relatively fast, but having them in stock can mean the difference in the competition for business. When selling a product that will require maintenance, be sure to give the additional information up front.

Marketing in Bermuda

MARKETING TIPS

- **Leisure products and services** The large tourism sector provides many opportunities for sales of leisure products and services. The tourist activities offered are relatively high end, so sales of sailing equipment, diving gear, etc. are brisk year round.
- **Affluence** Both tourists and residents are relatively affluent so foreign sellers can push their higher-end lines and find ready markets.
- **Processed foods** Bermudians purchase expensive, high-end processed food products from North America and Europe.
- **Newspapers** Newspapers sell briskly and are full of ads for foreign consumer products. This is a good place to give information that will reach many potential customers.
- **Tropical touch** Products should be geared to the hot, humid climate and the cultural tendency toward casual living. Equipment may have to be modified to keep it operational.
- **Customer service** Good follow through will result in continued business.
- **Quality materials** and workmanship are appreciated. Since the business opportunities are on-going it makes sense to sell only highest quality products, insuring continued sales to the Bermuda people and the many tourists who travel here yearly.
- **Credit terms** Short-term credit (30 to 90 days) is commonly extended. Incidence of bad debts is relatively low, but debt collection is expensive.
- **Mail order** Postal services are excellent in Bermuda; mail order catalogues and brochures reach the people.
- **Competition** To avoid the stiff competition in Bermuda, always use superior products so there is no doubt as to the quality you are offering.

Business Culture

Greetings and Courtesies

 Bermudians are noticeably formal, but perhaps less so than in many other areas. Titles and last names are used, although Bermudians are less addicted to the use of titles than many others in Latin America and the Caribbean. Business cards (in English) are normally exchanged, but without particular formality.

Business Ethic and Framework

 Bermuda is largely a consensus driven society. Confrontation is to be avoided and tailoring the business at hand to meet criteria of broad, general acceptability is often necessary to reach an agreement. Personal contacts are important, but less so than is the case in many cultures in Latin America and elsewhere. Due to its sophisticated financial services sector, most businesspeople are savvy and cosmopolitan in their dealings.

Meetings and Decision Making

 Introductions are helpful but not absolutely necessary. Bermudians are often late for appointments, but foreigners are expected to be on time. Business lunch meetings are common—these are low-key events, usually limited to the people involved in the immediate discussions. Because of the importance of consensus, few individuals have full authority to make binding decisions concerning any but the most mundane matters. Locals may assume that foreign businesspeople are fully aware of this without making it clear to them, leading to disappointments and misunderstandings.

Women

 Women often form the backbone of small-scale enterprises and are generally accorded considerable personal freedom and influence. Foreign businesswomen should experience few problems and may even be accorded special treatment by more traditional senior businessmen. There are many businesswomen from both North America and Europe operating in Bermuda in fairly high management positions.

Cultural Cautions

DO'S

- For business wear dark, conservative business suits or jackets with ties and long trousers. Women should wear conservative business suits or professional looking dresses.
- Do prepare to spend a great deal of time and effort introducing and promoting new products, as competition is still tough and the population small.
- Always accept an invitation to join your Bermudan business associate at church, regardless of your denomination or affiliation. Such an invitation is a sign of personal respect and affection.

DON'TS

- Don't wear Bermuda shorts for business; they are not acceptable.
- Do not expect to be invited to a business associate's home for a meal. This is considered personal time, usually reserved for the family.
- Do not drink very much at a business lunch, even if your Bermudan counterpart urges you to do so.

OBSERVATIONS

- Due to its proximity and heavy orientation toward the US, Bermudan business customs tend to be similar to those in the US, albeit slightly more formal.
- Bermudians tend not to trust the intentions of foreigners at first (regardless of the foreigner's ethnic background).

NEGOTIATIONS

- Negotiations tend to proceed pleasantly, and Bermudians are often eager to end a meeting even if real differences remain.
- Bermudan businesses tend to operate on a tight margin, often juggling financing from one commitment to another.

GOVERNMENT AGENCIES

Ministry of Community and Cultural Affairs
Old Fire Station Bldg.
81 Court St.
Hamilton, HM 12
Tel: (441) 292-1681
Fax: (441) 292-2474

Ministry of Education
POB HM 1185
Hamilton, HM EX
Tel: (441) 236-6904
Fax: (441) 236-4006

Ministry of the Environment
Government Administration Bldg.
30 Parliament St.
Hamilton, HM 12
Tel: (441) 295-5151
Fax: (441) 292-2349

Ministry of Finance
Government Administration Bldg.
30 Parliament St.
Hamilton, HM 12
Tel: (441) 295-5151
Fax: (441) 295-5727

Ministry of Health, Social Services and Housing
Old Hospital Bldg.
7 Point Finger Rd.
Paget, DV 04
Tel: (441) 236-0224
Fax: (441) 236-3971

Ministry of Labour and Home Affairs
Government Administration Bldg.
30 Parliament St.
Hamilton, HM 12
Tel: (441) 295-5151, Telex: 3775
Fax: (441) 295-4115

Ministry of Management and Information Services
Global House
43 Church St.
Hamilton, HM 12
Tel: (441) 292-6384
Fax: (441) 295-5267

Ministry of Telecommunications
Golinsky Bldg.
60 Reid St.
Hamilton, HM 12
Tel: (441) 292-4595
Fax: (441) 295-1462

Ministry of Tourism
Global House
43 Church St.
Hamilton, HM 12
Tel: (441) 292-0023
Fax: (441) 292-7537
Telex: 3243

Ministry of Transport
Global House
43 Church St.
Hamilton, HM 12
Tel: (441) 292-2463
Fax: (441) 295-2858

Ministry of Works and Engineering
Post Office Bldg.
56 Church St., POB 525
Hamilton, HM 12
Tel: (441) 295-5151
Fax: (441) 295-0170

CHAMBERS OF COMMERCE

Bermuda Chamber of Commerce
50 Front St., POB HM 655
Hamilton, HM CX
Tel: (441) 295-4201
Fax: (441) 292-5779

Bermuda Small Business Development Corpn
POB HM 637
Hamilton, HM CX
Tel: (441) 292-5570

BUSINESS AND TRADE ORGANIZATIONS

Construction Association of Bermuda
POB HM 238
Hamilton, HM AX
Tel: (441) 292-5920
Fax: (441) 292-5864

Hotel Employers of Bermuda
c/o Bermuda Hotel Association
'Carmel'
61 King St.
Hamilton, HM 19
Tel: (441) 295-2127
Fax: (441) 292-6671

Bermuda Industrial Union
49 Union Sq.
Hamilton, HM 12
Tel: (441) 292-0044
Fax: (441) 295-7992

Bermuda Public Services Association
POB Hm 763
Hamilton, HM CX
Tel: (441) 292-6985
Fax: (441) 292-1149

Bermuda International Business Association (BIBA)
P. O. Box HM 2452
Hamilton, HM JX
Tel: (441) 292-0632
Fax: (441) 292-1797

Bermuda Association of Securities Dealers
P. O. Box HM 66
Hamilton, HM AX
Tel: (441) 292-4708, 291-1442
Fax: (441) 292-7313

Bermuda Bar Association
Reid House, 31 Church Street
Hamilton, HM 12
Tel/Fax: (441) 295-4540

Bermuda Chamber of Commerce
P. O. Box HM 655
Hamilton, HM CX
Tel: (441) 295-4201
Fax: (441) 292-5779 or 295-2086

Bermuda Employers Council
Suite 304, Mechanics Building
12 Church Street
Hamilton, HM 11
Tel: (441) 295-5070
Fax: (441) 295-1966

Bermuda Insurance Management Association (BIMA)
P. O. Box FL 288
Smiths Parish, FL BX
Tel: (441) 295-2121
Fax: (441) 292-6735

Business & Professional Women's Association of Bermuda
P. O. Box HM 2282
Hamilton, HM HX
Tel: (441) 292-7124

NEWSPAPERS

Bermuda Business
POM HM 2032
Hamilton, HM HX
Tel: (441) 292-7279

The Bermuda Sun
41 Victoria St., POB HM 1241
Hamilton, HM FX
Tel: (441) 295-3902
Fax: (441) 292-5597

The Bermuda Times
9 Burnaby St.
Hamilton
Tel: (441) 292-2596
Fax: (441) 295-8771

The Bermudian
Addendum Lane
POB HM 283
Hamilton, HM AX
Tel: (441) 295-0695
Fax: (441) 295-8616

The Mid-Ocean News
POB HM 1025
Hamilton, HM DX
Tel: (441) 295-5881
Fax: (441) 295-9650

The Royal Gazette
Par-la-Ville Rd.
POB HM 1025
Hamilton, HM DX
Tel: (441) 295-5881
Fax: (441) 295-9667

The Worker's Voice
49 Union Sq.
Hamilton, HM 12
Tel: (441) 292-0044
Fax: (441) 295-7992

RADIO AND TELEVISION

Bermuda Broadcasting Company
POB HM 452
Hamilton, HM BX
Tel: (441) 295-2828
Fax: (441) 295-4882

Defontes Broadcasting Co Ltd-VSB
POB HM 1450
Hamilton, HM FX
Tel: (441) 295-1450
Fax: (441) 295-1658

SHIPPING

Department of Marine and Ports Services
POB Hm 180
Hamilton, HM AX
Tel: (441) 295-6575
Telex: 3505
Fax: (441) 295-3718

Bermuda Registry of Shipping
POB HM 1628
Hamilton, HM GX
Tel: (441) 295-7251, Telex: 3505
Fax: (441) 295-3718

Atlantic Marine Ltd.
Richmond House
12 Par-la-Ville Rd., POB HM 2089
Hamilton, HM HX
Tel: (441) 295-0614, Telex: 3658
Fax: (441) 292-1549

Gotass-Larsen Shipping Corpn
Perry Bldg.
Church St.
Hamilton
Tel: (441) 295-3457, Telex: 3641

World-Wide Shipping Managers Ltd.
Clarendon House
2 Church St.
Hamilton, HM 5

INTERNET ADDRESSES

Bermuda–L (Mailing List)
To subscribe, send mail to: BERMUDA-L-request@ber col.bm. Type "subscribe" on body of message.

Bermuda Pages
http://www.fes.uwaterloo.ca/u/kmayall/Bermuda

Forbes' Bermuda Online!
http://www.clark.net/pub/micros/forbes/

Bolivia

Republic of Bolivia

Economy

Overview

Bolivia, the least developed country in South America, is trying to move beyond its past economic instability. The government initiated a series of reforms to open the economy—allowing the currency to float, decontrolling some financial operations, eliminating import permit restrictions, and entering into an agreement with the IMF to obtain standby financing. The government has also agreed to privatize several larger state-owned firms. As a result, inflation has plummeted and economic growth has been steadily improving. Although Bolivia currently supports an extremely high foreign debt relative to its GDP and on a per capita basis, it has reduced its commercial bank debt to virtually nothing, potentially allowing it future access to international financing. The major barrier to increased development and international involvement remains the role of illicit narcotics trafficking in the Bolivian economy and society.

Trade

Trade surpluses have improved Bolivia's growing foreign reserve position, although the country remains heavily dependent on foreign assistance to finance development projects. Bolivia's major imports include industrial machinery, transportation equipment, and consumer goods. Its main legal exports are metallic minerals, natural gas, soybeans, and wood. According to some estimates, the value of illegal drug exports is roughly equal to that of legal exports, and it will be difficult to replace this stream of foreign exchange. Bolivia's trade with neighboring countries is growing, in part because of preferential trade agreements. The US is Bolivia's largest trade partner, followed by Argentina, Brazil, Japan, and the UK.

Sectors

Agriculture Agriculture accounts for slightly more than 20 percent of GDP, while employing more than 40 percent of the work force. Much agricultural activity is at an essentially subsistence level, although investment is increasing productivity in certain geographic and product areas. Major cash crops include soybeans, sugar, and coffee; beef and hides are also significant export products.

Industry Industry represents roughly 32 percent of GDP, while employing only about 20 percent of the work force. However, industrial production has been shrinking in recent years. Mining—of zinc, tin, lead, silver, gold, and antimony—provides a major source of foreign exchange. Bolivia is self-sufficient in oil and exports natural gas. Other industries include the processing of food, petroleum, leather, and nonmetallic metal products. A lack of infrastructure and investment capital limits industrial development.

Services The service sector employs (often marginally) somewhat less than half of the work force and produces about the same proportion of GDP. Attempts to streamline government procedures have begun to improve operations in the service sector, although activity remains fragmented and inefficient.

Trends

Recent economic reforms have helped rein in Bolivia's inflation, and its economy has begun to achieve steady growth results. Additional adjustments will be required to compensate for increased economic demands and the costs of structural reforms. On balance, these factors should benefit Bolivia's economy in the near future, although the issue of the substantial role played by illicit drugs in the economy will have to be dealt with before structural reforms can bring the desired benefits.

At a Glance

THE COUNTRY

Location Bolivia is located in central South America between Brazil and Chile.
Terrain High plateau (*altiplano*), temperate and semitropical valleys, and tropical lowlands.
Climate Varies with altitude—from humid and tropical to semi-arid and cold.

THE PEOPLE

Population 7,800,000
Ethnic composition
Quechua 30%
Aymara 25%
Cholos 25–30%
European 15–20%
Religious composition Predominantly Roman Catholic.
Languages spoken Spanish, Quechua, Aymara.
Education and literacy Adult literacy is 20%. Primary education, which lasts for eight years, is compulsory and free of charge.
Labor force
Total: 3,600,000
By occupation: agriculture 41%, industry and commerce 20%, services 39%.

COUNTRY FACTS

Political and legal Bolivia maintains a republic government with several major political parties which actively contest elections. The major parties are Nationalist Revolutionary Movement (MNR), Nationalist Democratic Action (AND), Movement of the Revolutionary Left (MIR), Conscience of the Fatherland (CONDEPA), Free Bolivia Movement (MBL), Civic Solidarity Union (UCS).
Telephone Service is very poor for the general population, and for local calls made within the country. International services are somewhat better, although all services tend to be unreliable. International country code: [591]. City codes: La Paz (2), Santa Cruz (3).
Transportation Bolivia's transportation system is undeveloped. Roads are bad or nonexistent; rail service is sporadic, unreliable, and inconvenient; and domestic air services are not really comparable to those of other countries.
Environment Because of the wide range in altitude, Bolivia has plants representative of every climatic zone, from arctic growth high in the sierra to tropical forests in the Amazon basin. Soil erosion resulting from poor cultivation methods plague Bolivia, and the government is making some effort to update methods and equipment to make better use of the land. Inadequate sanitation and solid-waste disposal, as well as effluents from mining activities, contribute to the *altiplano's* declining water quality, which poses a threat both to fish life and to human health.
Media The government supervises all broadcasting and communications. There are 129 AM radio stations and 43 television stations.
Health The general health of the population is notably poor, owing to poor hygiene and an insufficient number of doctors and hospitals, especially in rural areas. Life expectancy is estimated at 61 years.

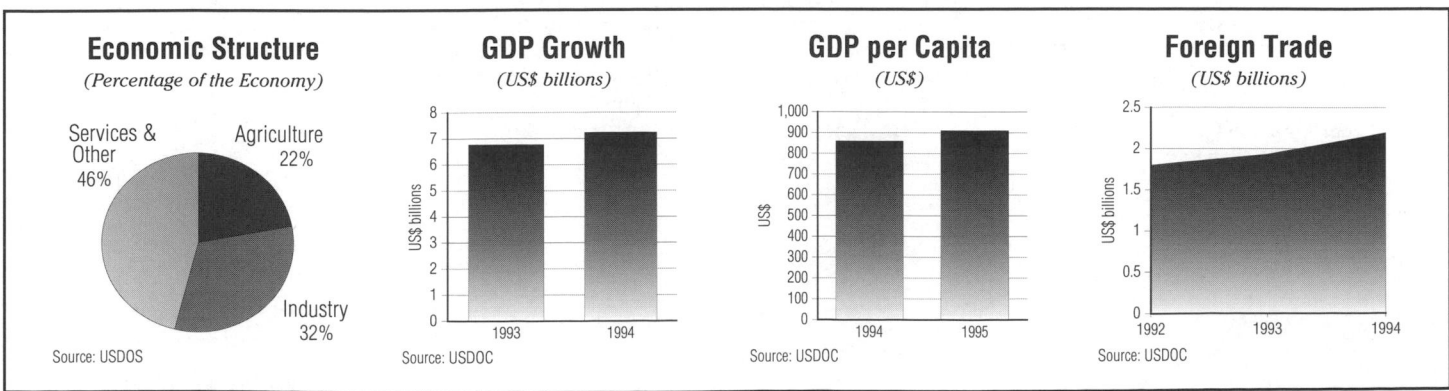

Economic Structure
(Percentage of the Economy)

Services & Other 46%
Agriculture 22%
Industry 32%

Source: USDOS

GDP Growth
(US$ billions)

1993, 1994

Source: USDOC

GDP per Capita
(US$)

1994, 1995

Source: USDOC

Foreign Trade
(US$ billions)

1992, 1993, 1994

Source: USDOC

Business Travel

Travelogue

WORKWEEK

Offices Monday-Friday 9:00 am to noon, 2:00 pm to 6:00 pm.
Banks Monday-Friday 8:30 am to 11:30 am, 2:30 pm to 5:00 pm.
Retail Monday-Friday 9:00 am to noon, 2:00 pm to 6:00 pm, Saturday 9:00 am to noon.
Government Monday-Friday 8:30 am to 12:30 pm, 1:00 pm to 5:00 pm, Wednesday, 8:30 am to 2:30 pm only.

HOLIDAYS

Holidays 1996
January 1 New Year's Day
February 19-20 Carnival
April 5 Good Friday
May 1 Bolivian Labor Day
June 6 Corpus Christi
August 6 Bolivian Independence Day
November 1 All Saints Day
December 25 Christmas
In addition, there are many regional and religious holidays celebrated in different areas.

VISA AND PASSPORT

A valid passport, but not a visa, is required for entry to Bolivia. There is no customs control on hand luggage and it is therefore not necessary to register cameras, business samples, and other personal items. Product samples are admitted duty-free if the intended stay is no longer than 90 days. Obtain a Determined Object Visa to avoid paying travel tax. This allows for a 30-day entry permit and may be extended if necessary. All visitors are required to register with the immigration authorities. For hotel guests, this is done through the hotel; anyone staying at a private residence is required to present their passport to the Ministry of Immigration. This will eliminate any delay when leaving the country.

DEPARTURE FORMALITIES

An airport tax is collected at departure. All visitors must have registered with Immigration. Be prepared to show papers upon departure. There are no other departure formalities for Bolivia.

IMMUNIZATION

No required vaccinations, though they are recommended for typhoid and yellow fever. Gamma globulin is suggested (to help prevent hepatitis) as are anti-malarial medications.

TIPPING

Restaurants and hotels generally expect 10 percent. In addition to a hotel service charge, small tips such as one to two bolivianos for luggage are expected. Waiters and taxi drivers expect the same.

CRIME

Pickpocketing and theft from vehicles is fairly common, but violent crimes involving the use of weapons are rare. Avoid demonstrations in La Paz where tear gas has been used to control crowds. Anyone convicted of drug trafficking will face severe penalties and might wait up to two years in prison for sentencing.

INFRASTRUCTURE

Two international airports, El Alto near La Paz and Viru Viru near Santa Cruz, have direct flights to Brazil and North America. Air travel is the most practical way to reach any destination in Bolivia. The domestic airline, LAB, has flights to all parts of the country. Taxi service is available at the airports and within the major cities. Negotiate the fare before departing. Roads connect to Argentina, Chile, Peru, Paraguay, and Brazil; but road travel is not recommended as roads are rough and there are no service facilities. If you do travel by car, four-wheel drives are recommended but expensive to rent. Railroads run to Chile and Argentina but travel is slow and not recommended for business purposes.

COMMUNICATIONS

Telephone Direct dialing is available for international calls but not in all parts of the country. Microwave circuits and radio telephone services link the major cities. Telex facilities are recommended for urgent messages.
Fax Available in La Paz, but still in development stages.
Post office There is no delivery of letters or packages to street addresses. All mail is collected at post office boxes. Airmail will arrive within five to seven days; surface mail requires a minimum of three months for delivery. Some service is unreliable and all important documents should be sent registered mail.

BEST TRAVEL BOOKS

Bolivia, Lonely Planet. Concise background information as well as detailed travel information.
The Travelers Guide to Latin America Customs and Manners. Elizabeth Devine & Nancy Braganti. An invaluable guide for people not wanting to put foot in mouth.
Do's and Taboo's Around the World. The Bestselling Guide to International Behavior. 3rd edition. Edited by Roger Axtell, compiled by the Parker Pen Company. The ultimate guide to international behavior, now completely updated and expanded. Helpful, fun to read!

TELEPHONE NUMBERS

If you are calling from outside Bolivia you will need to add the country code [591] and any other international dialing requirements from within your country.

- Chamber of Commerce .... (2) 350042
- Emergency Medical Care .... (2) 783371
- Radio/TV 368788

Car Rental
- IMBEX .... (2) 379884
- Hertz Rent-a-Car/La Paz............ (2) 325592/322654
- National .... (2) 376581

Credit Card Information
Lost or stolen credit cards (call collect to the US, regardless of which country the card was issued in).
- Amex ....[1] (919) 333-3211
- Diner's Club................................[1] (303) 799-1504
- MasterCard ....[1] (314) 275-6690
- Visa ....[1] (410) 581-7931

NATIONAL TOURIST OFFICE

Direccion Nacional de Turismo
Calle Mercado 1328
La Paz
Tel: (2) 367441
Magri Turismo
16 de Julio 1490
La Paz
Tel: (2) 341201

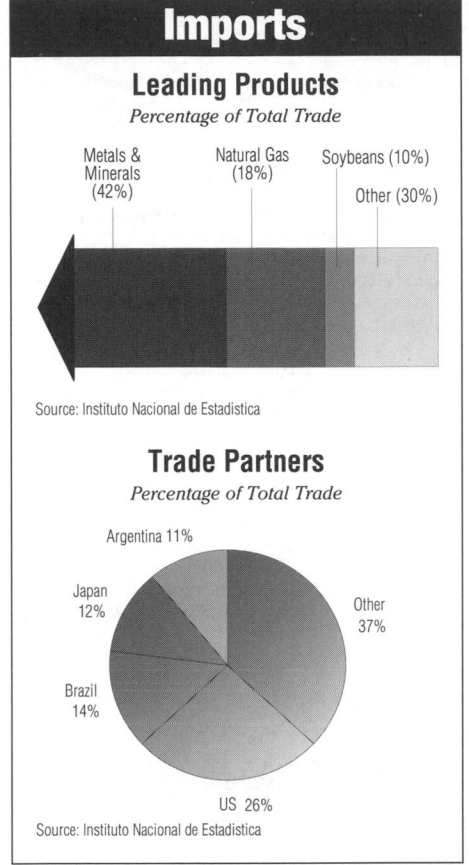

Imports

Leading Products
Percentage of Total Trade

Metals & Minerals (42%)
Natural Gas (18%)
Soybeans (10%)
Other (30%)

Source: Instituto Nacional de Estadistica

Trade Partners
Percentage of Total Trade

Argentina 11%
Japan 12%
Brazil 14%
US 26%
Other 37%

Source: Instituto Nacional de Estadistica

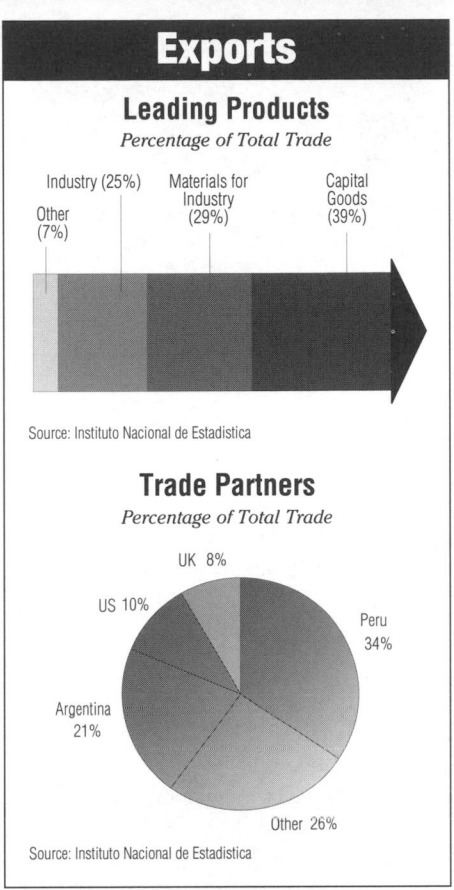

Exports

Leading Products
Percentage of Total Trade

Industry (25%)
Other (7%)
Materials for Industry (29%)
Capital Goods (39%)

Source: Instituto Nacional de Estadistica

Trade Partners
Percentage of Total Trade

UK 8%
US 10%
Argentina 21%
Peru 34%
Other 26%

Source: Instituto Nacional de Estadistica

Opportunities

FOR IMPORTING TO BOLIVIA
- capital goods
- consumer products, food products
- machinery, mining, transport, and construction equipment
- petroleum

FOR EXPORTING FROM BOLIVIA
- coffee, soybeans, and sugar
- cotton
- timber
- natural gas, oil, and petroleum products
- silver, tin, tungsten, and zinc

GROWTH SECTORS
- mining
- oil
- telecommunications

Trade News

RULES AND REGULATIONS
- **Import licenses** Under certain circumstances, import licenses are used to control the importation of goods considered undesirable or dangerous, or to facilitate importation of needed goods.
- **Government procurement** An official qualifying agency will call for bids, which must be presented in Bolivian territory. Qualifying proposals will be submitted to the public entity, along with recommendations. The qualifying agency will sign the purchasing or services agreement in the name of the public entity.

FREIGHT FORWARDERS
SGS (Bolivia) SA
POB 3282
La Paz
Fax: (2) 361190

Legal

Legal System
Bolivia operates under a state political constitution and legal codes.

Intellectual Property Rights
Patents Industrial inventions may be patented for 15 unpostponable years. Patents are attained upon application, and the processing takes approximately two years.

Trademarks Trademark registration is effective from the date of filing for a period of 10 years, which may be indefinitely renewed. The registration process usually takes about two years.

Copyrights Legal dispositions protect moral and patrimonial rights of authors of literary, artistic, and scientific works (logical support or software), in its literary, plastic, or sounding form. No protection is given to ideas enclosed in literary and artistic works, or the ideological or technical content of scientific works. Copyright registration takes 30 days. Author of work protected has patrimonial rights throughout life. Upon death the protection transfers to heirs, legatees, and assignees for a period of 50 years.

Contracts and Dispute Resolution
Commercial and Civil Codes permit named and unnamed contracts. Disputes are solved in Justice Courts or arbitration, which is more common now as local and foreign enterprises enter into agreements.

Notaries
Licensed by government, notaries authenticate private documents that become public, and give a strong presumption of validity. Certain contracts are only recognized when issued by a notary public.

Labor
Workers are unrenounceable, and are protected by the State's Political Constitution and by labor laws. Striking is allowed if union representatives have fulfilled all requirements. Workers are entitled to severance pay. Laws mandate benefits for workers, and regulate child employment.

Legal Matters

LEGAL BRIEFS
- **Property** Foreigners may freely buy and sell chattels and real estate, with one limitation: They are under no circumstances entitled, directly or indirectly, individually or in society, to purchase or own ground or underground within 50 kilometers from country boundaries.
- **Societies** Foreigners may associate or constitute societies for every kind of activity. Any society constituted abroad may have subsidiaries and/or representations in Bolivia if their legal capacity is already recognized. Recognition may be granted after a procedure which takes approximately three months.
- **Guarantee for foreign investments** Foreign investments and remittance of utilities abroad are guaranteed. Remittance to foreign countries of money, when proceeds derive from Bolivian sources, has a retention of 12.5 percent as tax payment on profits.
- **Monopolies** Bolivian law prohibits private monopolies, although many industries are still controlled by the State, and operate under monopoly conditions.
- **Agency** Agents have broad authority to act for their principals and have ability to terminate agreements.
- **Social rights and benefits** Workers are unrenounceable, are protected by the state's political constitution, and by specific labor laws. Striking is allowed if union representatives have fulfilled all legal requirements.
- **Social benefits** Workers are entitled to severance pay (three months per each year of work) and indemnification for years of service in case of termination without due notice or without just cause for dismissal.
- **Labor laws** The law provides benefits for workers and special laws regulate child employment.

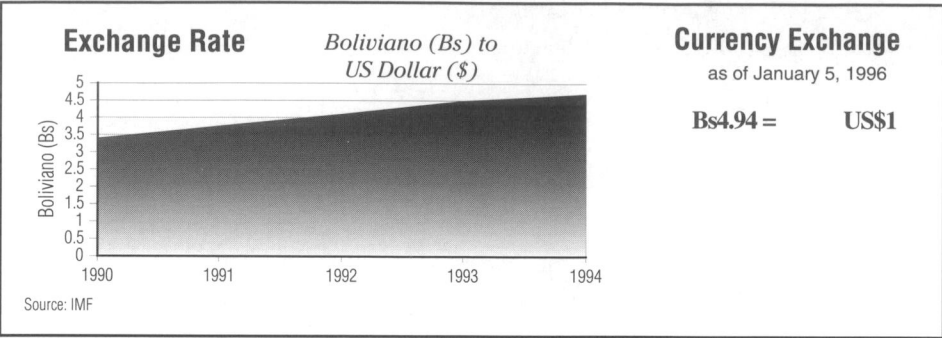

Exchange Rate

Boliviano (Bs) to US Dollar ($)

Source: IMF

Currency Exchange

as of January 5, 1996

Bs4.94 = **US$1**

Money Matters

BITS AND PIECES

- **Petroleum** Private investors can invest in the petroleum industry through the state-owned petroleum company, YPFB, utilizing joint ventures or operation contracts.
- **Mining** Foreign companies can invest in mining projects through COMIBOL, the state-owned mining company.
- **Taxes** Business taxes are based on net worth, rather than on the amount of profit or loss made in any one year.
- **Capital gains** Capital gains are not taxed for either domestic or foreign companies.
- **Commissions** Sales of foreign exchange by the Central Bank to the public are subject to a commission of Bs 0.01 per US$1 over its buying rate.
- **Parallel market** There is a parallel but tolerated foreign exchange market which often offers better exchange rates than the official market.
- **Loans** Financial institutions may make loans in the form of credits denominated in foreign currency for imports of capital goods and inputs for the external sector with resources from international financial institutions, foreign government agencies, or external lines of credit.
- **Banks** Banks are authorized to conduct foreign trade operations, such as letters of credit, bonds and guarantees, advances and acceptances, loans for required financing with their correspondents abroad; and other operations generally accepted in international banking, in favor of the country's importers and exporters.
- **Deposits** Banks may hold deposits and make loans in foreign currencies.

Currency

The currency of Bolivia is the boliviano (Bs), divided into 100 centavos.

Foreign Exchange

The Central Bank of Bolivia regulates foreign exchange. Foreign currencies may be exchanged freely at the Central Bank, commercial banks, and exchange bureaus. The foreign exchange rate is determined at auctions held daily by the Central Bank, and this rate applies to all exchange operations in Bolivia. All banks, exchange houses, companies, and individuals may buy and sell foreign exchange freely; however, the Central Bank and the Ministry of Finance must approve public-sector purchases of foreign exchange for debt-service payments.

Capital Transfers

Settlements are usually made in US dollars or other convertible currencies. There are no restrictions on payments. All proceeds from exports must be sold to the Central Bank at the official exchange rate within three days of receipt, with the exception of reasonable amounts deducted for foreign exchange expenditures undertaken to effect export transactions. Banks, exchange houses, hotels, and travel agencies may retain the proceeds from their foreign exchange transactions, including those from tourism. Foreign exchange for outward capital transfers by residents or nonresidents can be purchased only from the commercial banks or from the Central Bank. Inward capital transfers may be made freely.

Investment Incentives

Bolivia is committed to attracting foreign investment, and offers several incentives.

National treatment Foreign investors receive the same advantages as locals.

Free currency convertibility For the most part, currencies are freely convertible in Bolivia.

Registration Requirements for business registration have been greatly streamlined or eliminated.

Special sectors Hydrocarbons and mining offer special incentives and opportunities for investors.

Investment Restrictions

There are very few restrictions on investment within Bolivia.

BANKS

Central Bank of Bolivia
Calle Ayacucho esq. Mercado
Cajón Postal 3118
La Paz
Tel: (2) 363207, 377124
Fax: (2) 392398

Citibank, NA
Plaza Venezuela 1434
Casilla 260
La Paz
Tel: (2) 321742/3
Fax: (2) 355755, 354645

Santa Cruz de la Fierra Bank
POB 865
Santa Cruz
Tel: (33) 39911, 50500
Fax: (33) 50114

Banko Boliviano Americano
Avenida Camacho y Loayza
La Paz
Tel: (2) 378993
Fax: (2) 353984

Banco de Inversion Boliviano SA
Avenida 16 de Julio 1571
POB 8639
La Paz
Tel: (2) 354233
Telex: 2465

Banco Mercantil SA
Ayachucho y Mercado
POB 423
La Paz
Tel: (2) 356902
Telex: 2270

Banco National de Bolivia
Avenida Camacho esq. Colon
POB 360
La Paz
Fax: (2) 371279

Distribution

Import trade can follow several paths into Bolivia: local commission or independent sales representatives, import houses, foreign firm subsidiaries, and government agencies. Manufacturers can also distribute directly through international trade fairs. The government agencies and large, publicly owned corporations buy most of the heavy machinery and equipment imports. They are legally required to tender for purchases exceeding US$50,000, and only firms legally established under Bolivian laws may bid for government purchases. Therefore, overseas firms must be represented through import houses, commission or independent sales agents, or local subsidiaries. Import houses are usually large; they import for their own use and also represent foreign firms on a commission basis. The largest of these firms have their own subdistributors and sales forces. These firms are the most financially secure channels; they can also sell to the government agencies in response to tenders.

Agents, Distributors, and Partners

The ideal agent for this market is experienced, aggressive, and financially solvent. Periodic visits by foreign firm representatives are essential to provide assistance to the local representative and to establish personal contact with customers. Agents take orders on a direct shipment basis; their commission ranges from five to 10 percent. They usually represent more than one line of merchandise.

Advertising

Television is the most widespread advertising forum; there are 38 stations. Print media comes next, with six national dailies and several regional dailies. Trade, technical, and professional magazines are published monthly or quarterly, and nearly all of them take advertisements. There are 125 AM radio stations, almost all of which are privately owned and outside government control. This is an ideal medium for reaching the rural population. Cinema advertising and outdoor poster sites are also used. The most important advertising agencies are in La Paz, though only a few are accustomed to the needs of international trade.

Marketing in Bolivia

MARKETING TIPS

- **Socioeconomic horizon** Two out of three citizens live in poverty. Yet Bolivia's economic ties through the Andean Pact, and its large legal trade with the United States offers considerable promise.
- **Shipping** Bolivia is landlocked; most heavy equipment, machinery, and general merchandise must enter through seaports in Peru, Chile, Brazil, or Argentina. Bad weather, landslides, port congestion, and other factors can block or slow these channels. Air transport may be the most efficient for heavy items.

RADIO & TELEVISION

Dirección General de Telecomunicaciones
Government-controlled Broadcasting Authority
Edificio Guerrero, Mercado 1115
Casilla 4475
La Paz
Tel: (2) 368788
Telex: 2595

Empresa Nacional de Televisión Boliviana-Canal 7
National Television
Avenida Camacho 1486, Edif. La Urbana, 6 y 7
Casilla 900
La Paz
Tel: (2) 376356
Fax: (2) 359753

Asociacion Boliviana de Radiodifusoras (ASBORA)
Potosi 920
Casilla 7958
La Paz
Tel: (2) 32-8513

Television Universitaria - Canal 13
Av. 6 de Agosto 2170, Edlf. "Hoy", PIsos 12-13
La Paz
Tel: (2) 35-9297
Fax: (2) 35-9491

Greetings and Courtesies

Men and women shake hands at the beginning and end of each encounter. In smaller groups—both business and social—the host will introduce guests individually; in larger groups, you generally introduce yourself. Have business cards printed in Spanish available as a courtesy.

Business Ethic & Framework

Bolivian values are extremely traditional, emphasizing the importance of personal relationships. Bolivians view work as a single and often subsidiary component rather than the central focus of life. Business attire consists of conservative, dark suits for men and suits or dresses for women. Remember the wide climatic differences between cold, high altitude areas and hot, tropical lowland areas.

Meetings and Decision Making

Meetings should be scheduled two to three weeks in advance. Foreigners are expected to be punctual, although locals are often late. Although middle-level managers may be responsible for implementing decisions, actual decisions are almost always made at a high level of authority. While you will want to approach senior people, Bolivians will wish to match you with someone of similar business rank. It is important to cultivate personal relationships with these peers, because the quality of these relationships may strongly influence the actual decision maker, even when your immediate counterpart is not the one making the decision.

Women

Women in Bolivia occupy a secondary status, although they often form the backbone of small-scale enterprises and are generally afforded considerable personal freedom. Bolivian women are becoming more involved in business, and foreign businesswomen should experience few problems.

Cultural Cautions

DO'S

- Learn something about Bolivian history and culture—your interest will be appreciated as will attempts to speak Spanish (relatively few Bolivians speak other languages and Spanish may be critical).
- Bring your own copies of promotional materials and proposals (in Spanish). Graphics impress Bolivian businesspeople.

DON'TS

- Do not whisper in a group—to do so excludes others and implies that you are conspiring or saying something derogatory about them.
- Generally avoid religion and politics as topics of conversation, although these issues are less sensitive here than in some other places. However, references to drugs and drug trafficking are taboo.

CUSTOMS

- Visitors bring small gifts, such as flowers (but not yellow or purple blossoms), for the host or hostess; gifts are opened after the guest has left.

OBSERVATIONS

- Bolivia's high altitude is very debilitating—arrive early and acclimate before attempting to do business.
- Foreign businesspeople gain prestige by frequenting first-class hotels and restaurants.

NEGOTIATIONS

- Bolivians respond poorly to aggressive tactics; be understated while avoiding any hint of pressure.
- Allow negotiations to remain open-ended, so that confrontation can be avoided and talks can be allowed to fade away if agreement cannot be reached.
- Agreements should be written; although historically, contracts have consisted of schematic outlines, Bolivians now expect somewhat more detailed documents.

GOVERNMENT AGENCIES

Ministry of Economy and Housing
Piso 19 del Edif. del Ministerio de Transportes
Avenida Camacho esq. Bueno No. 1113
Tel: (2) 377220, 377234
Fax: (2) 359955

Secretariat of Agro-Industry
Avenida Camacho 1407
La Paz
Tel: (2) 361348, 374262, 361396, 374260
Fax: (2) 357535

Secretariat of Exports and Economic Competitiveness
Avenida Camacho esq. Bueno
Casilla 4430
La Paz
Tel: (2) 372040, 372042/3
Fax: (2) 359875

Secretariat of Transportation and Communications
Edificio La Urbana
Avenida Camacho
La Paz
Tel: (2) 377220/1/2
Telex: 2648

Ministry of Foreign Affairs and Worship
Junin esq. Ingavi
La Paz
Tel: (2) 371150
Fax: (2) 371155

Ministry of Government
Avenida Arce esq. Belisario Salinas
Casilla 3274
La Paz
Tel: (2) 370460, 370474/5/6
Fax: (2) 371334

Ministry of Human Resources
La Paz
Tel: (2) 372060
Fax: (2) 371376

Ministry of Information
Avenida Mariscal Santa Cruz
Edificio La Urbana
La Paz
Tel: (2) 376350, 379920, 376351
Fax: (2) 391607

Ministry of Labor
Calle Yanacocha, esq. Calle Mercado
La Paz
Tel: (2) 374350/1/2, 374369, 374142
Fax: (2) 359998

Ministry of Sustainable Development
La Paz
Tel: (2) 372063
Fax: (2) 392892

Empresa Nacional de Ferrocarriles
National Railway
Estación Central de Ferrocarriles
Plaza Zalles
Casilla 428
La Paz
Tel: (2) 327401

Dirección Nacional de Turismo
Calle Mercado 1328
Casilla 1868
La Paz
Tel: (2) 367463
Fax: (2) 374630

TRADE AND BUSINESS ORGANIZATIONS

National Chamber of Commerce
POB 7
La Paz
Tel: (2) 379941, 351276
Fax: (2) 340916
Telex: 2305

National Chamber of Commerce of La Paz
Ed. Camara Nacional de Comercio P-1
La Paz
Tel: (2) 391004

National Chamber of Exporters of Bolivia
POB 12145
La Paz
Tel: (2) 341230
Fax: (2) 361491

Camara Agropecuaria
del Oriente 3 anillo internao entre Pirai y Roca
Coronado, Casilla 116
Santa Cruz
Tel: (33) 23164
Fax: (33) 22621
Telex: 4438

Camara Agropecuaria
de La Paz Calle Santa Cruz 266
Casilla 6297
La Paz
Tel: (2) 32-6854

Camara Naiconal de Industrias
Edif. Camara Nacional de Comercio 14º
Avda Mariscal Santa Cruz
1392 Casilla 611
La Paz
Tel: (2) 37-4478
Fax: (2) 35-0620
Telex: 3533

Consejo Nacional de Planificacion (CONEPLAN)
Edif. Banco Central de Bolivia 26º
La Paz
Tel: (2) 37-7115

Empresa Metalurgica Vinto (EMV)
Casilla 612
Oruro
Tel: (52) 52857
Fax: (52) 50458
Telex: 2255

Empresa Nacional de Electricidad, SA (ENDE)
Colombia No 655, esq. Falsuri
Casilla 565
Cochabamba
Tel: (42) 46322
Fax: (42) 42700
Telex: 6251

BANKS

Central Bank of Bolivia
Calle Ayacucho esq. Mercado
Cajón Postal 3118
La Paz
Tel: (2) 363207, 377124
Fax: (2) 392398

Citibank, NA
Plaza Venezuela 1434
Casilla 260
La Paz
Tel: (2) 321742/3
Fax: (2) 355755, 354645

Santa Cruz de la Fierra Bank
POB 865
Santa Cruz
Tel: (33) 39911, 50500
Fax: (33) 5011

Banko Boliviano Americano
Avenida Camacho y Loayza
La Paz
Tel: (2) 378993
Fax: (2) 353984

Banco de Inversion Boliviano SA
Avenida 16 de Julio 1571
POB 8639
La Paz
Tel: (2) 354233
Telex: 2465

Banco Mercantil SA
Ayachucho y Mercado
POB 423
La Paz
Tel: (2) 356902
Telex: 2270

> **REMEMBER**
> - When you telephone (or fax) to Bolivia from another country you must always include the country code [591] before the numbers given.
> - When you send mail to Bolivia, be sure to write BOLIVIA in capital letters on its own line below the addresses given.

Banco National de Bolivia
Avenida Camacho esq. Colon
POB 360
La Paz
Fax: (2) 371279

NEWSPAPERS

Los Timpos
Plaza Quintanilla-Norte
Casilla 525
Cochabamba
Tel: (42) 41870

El Diario
Loayza 118
Casilla 5
La Paz
Tel: (2) 35-6835
Telex: 5530

Hoy
Avda 6 de Agosto 2170
Casilla 47
La Paz
Tel: (2) 32-6683
Fax: (2) 37-0564
Telex: 2613

Jornada
Junin 608
Casilla 1628
La Paz
Tel: (2) 35-3844

Presencia
Avda Mariscal Santa Cruz 1295
Casilla 3276
La Paz
Tel: (2) 37-2344
Fax: (2) 39-1040
Telex: 2659

Ultima
Hora Avda Camacho 309
Casilla 5920
La Paz
Tel: (2) 37-0416

El Deber
Suarez Arana 264
Casilla 2144
Santa Cruz
Tel: (33) 23588

El Mundo
Parque Industrial
Casilla 1984
Santa Cruz
Tel: (33) 46-4646
Fax: (33) 46-505
Telex: 4296

INTERNET ADDRESSES

Usenet group
soc.culture.bolivia

Bolivia on the Internet
http://www.latinworld.com/countries/bolivia/

Bolivia
http://www/ntural.com/bolivia/

BolNet
http://www.bolnet.bo/

Brazil

Federative Republic of Brazil

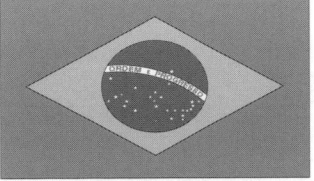

Economy

Overview

Despite Brazil's rich natural resources and numerous other advantages, it has not lived up to its economic potential. Industrial development has been concentrated in the southeastern states around Rio de Janeiro and São Paulo, although expansion is now occurring in the northeast and central west as well. Brazil is a country of dynamic contrasts. It has suffered from high inflation, chronic fiscal indiscipline, protectionism, antiforeign bias, corruption, and political and social instability. Nevertheless, lately it seems to be on the track of greater development, productivity, and integration into the global economy.

Trade

Brazil depends on value-added processing and reexport of imported as well as locally produced raw materials. Major exports include processed foodstuffs, machinery, mineral products, commodity vegetable products, and transportation equipment. Imports include mineral products, machinery, chemicals, processed foodstuffs, metals and metal manufactures, and precision instruments. The US is Brazil's main trading partner—accounting for more than 20 percent of total trade—followed by Japan, Germany, the Netherlands, and Italy. Trade with Argentina and other members of Mercosur is expected to skyrocket.

Sectors

Agriculture Agriculture accounts for somewhat less than 11 percent of GDP but employs nearly 35 percent of the work force. Principal products include coffee, sugarcane, cocoa, rice, beef, corn, oranges, and cotton. About one half of the country is forested, and heavy exploitation of timber, as well as deforestation to create grazing land for cattle, is causing considerable concern over the sustainability of the Brazilian agricultural system.

Industry Industry provides roughly 30 percent of GDP and 35 percent of employment in Brazil. With an increasingly sophisticated and up-to-date industrial base, Brazil produces steel, chemicals, petrochemicals, aircraft, and finished consumer goods. A computer industry is also burgeoning, showing the most growth of all Brazil's industries over the last decade.

Services About 40 percent of Brazilians work in the services sector, which produces nearly 60 percent of GDP. Promising growth has been noted for transportation, communications, insurance, biotechnology, engineering, and franchising. Brazil's increasing need for computers has created greater demand for programmers, consultants, and others in the field.

Trends

Brazil's industrial economy should continue to thrive, albeit at a slower pace than in the recent past. Transportation, electronics, and the communications equipment industries have been registering the highest growth, while the chemicals sector has been shrinking. Stiff competition exists in the import markets, primarily from Europe and Japan, but local manufacturing operations are beginning to become competitive, even without the protectionism that has long characterized Brazilian markets. Brazil must still rein in its inflation and anarchic business and fiscal system, becoming more open, stable, and in tune with international standards, in order to develop over the long term.

At a Glance

THE COUNTRY

Location Eastern South America, bordering the Atlantic Ocean.
Terrain Dense forests in northern regions, including the Amazon Basin; semi-arid along the northeast coast; mountains, hills, and rolling plains in the southwest; plus a narrow coastal strip.
Climate Tropical or semitropical with temperate zone in the south.

THE PEOPLE

Population 155,000,000
Ethnic composition Portuguese, Italian, German, Japanese, African, Indians (principally Tupi and Guarani linguistic stock).
Religious composition
Roman Catholic 80%
Languages spoken Portuguese, Spanish, English, French.
Education and literacy Public education is free at all levels, and the government helps fund private schools. Literacy is estimated at 81 percent of the adult population.
Labor force
Total: 65,000,000
By occupation: services 40%, agriculture 35%, and industry 25%.

COUNTRY FACTS

Political and legal Brazil is a federative republic with broad powers granted to the federal government. The legal system is based on Roman codes.
Telephone An adequate modern system. International country code: [55]. Selected city codes: Brasilia (61), Rio de Janeiro (21), São Paulo (11), Salvador (71).
Transportation Brazil's transportation systems generally have kept pace with development. However, some facilities are inadequate, due to lack of investment and maintenance funds. Efficient air service runs throughout the country. Railroads run throughout the country.
Environment The world's largest rainforest is in the Amazon Basin. Recent migrations into the Amazon and controversial large-scale burning of forest areas placed the international spotlight on Brazil. The government has subsequently reduced incentives for such activity and has begun to implement an ambitious environmental plan. Fears that forests in eastern Brazil and in the southern highlands are being cut down so fast that they are in danger of rapid extinction have led the industry to move north. Major timber supplies now come from the tropical hardwoods of the Amazon. The thorn forests of the northeast interior contain dry, cactus-infested, drought-resistant vegetation, its sparseness due as much to overgrazing and overcultivation as to the unreliability of rainfall. Current issues are deforestation of the Amazon Basin; air and water pollution in Rio de Janeiro, São Paulo, and several other large cities; and land degradation and water pollution caused by improper mining activities.
Media There are 1,223 AM radio stations and 112 television stations. Freedom of the press is constitutionally guaranteed, however some political subjects are censored.
Health A national health care plan is in the works. Health and sanitary conditions vary throughout the country. Life expectancy of males is 57 years; of females, 67 years.

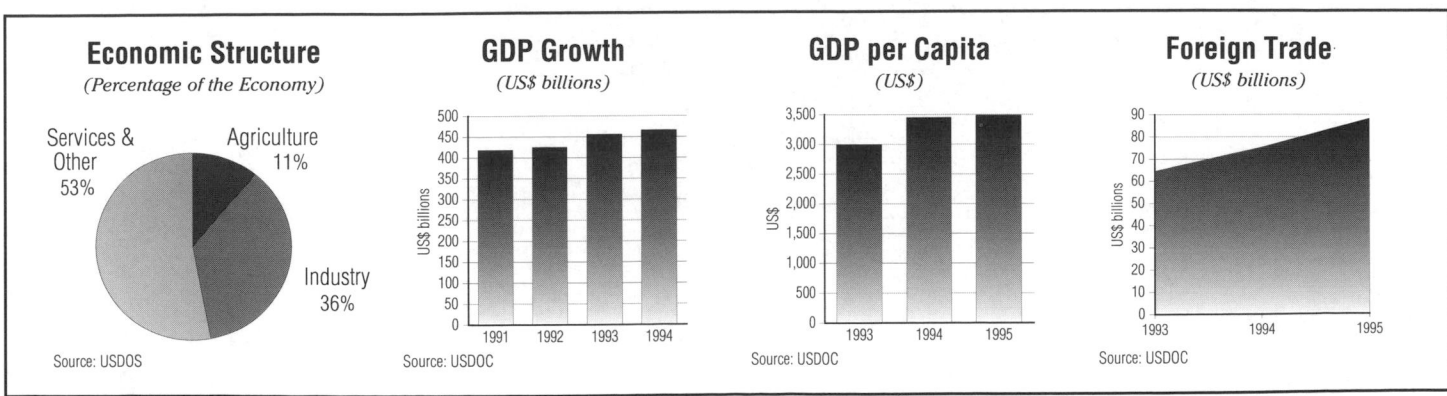

Economic Structure
(Percentage of the Economy)

Services & Other 53%
Agriculture 11%
Industry 36%

Source: USDOS

GDP Growth
(US$ billions)

US$ billions — 1991, 1992, 1993, 1994

Source: USDOC

GDP per Capita
(US$)

US$ — 1993, 1994, 1995

Source: USDOC

Foreign Trade
(US$ billions)

US$ billions — 1993, 1994, 1995

Source: USDOC

States of Brazil

1 Rio Grande do Sul
2 Santa Catarina
3 Paraná
4 Mato Grosso do Sul
5 São Paulo
6 Rio de Janeiro
7 Espírito Santo
8 Minas Gerais
9 Goiás
10 Mato Grosso
11 Rondônia
12 Acre
13 Amazonas
14 Pará
15 Tocantins
16 Bahia
17 Sergipe
18 Alagoas
19 Pernambuco
20 Paraíba
21 Rio Grande do Norte
22 Ceara
23 Piauí
24 Marnahão
25 Amapa
26 Roraima

Note: Brasilia is surrounded by a federal district.

Brazil

⊛ National capital
◉ State capital
● Secondary city
— State border

— Primary road
— Secondary road
‧‧‧ Railroad
━ International border

0   250   500   750 km
0   250   500 mi

Foreign Trade

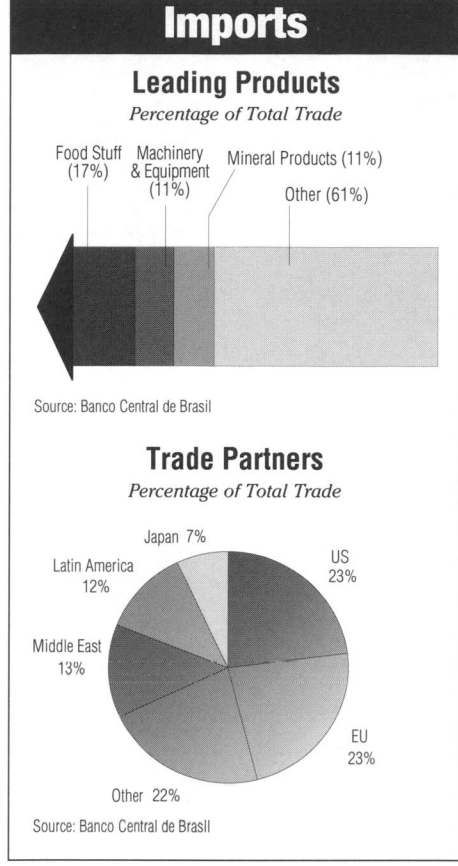

Imports

Leading Products
Percentage of Total Trade

Food Stuff (17%) — Machinery & Equipment (11%) — Mineral Products (11%) — Other (61%)

Source: Banco Central de Brasil

Trade Partners
Percentage of Total Trade

Japan 7%
Latin America 12%
Middle East 13%
US 23%
EU 23%
Other 22%

Source: Banco Central de Brasil

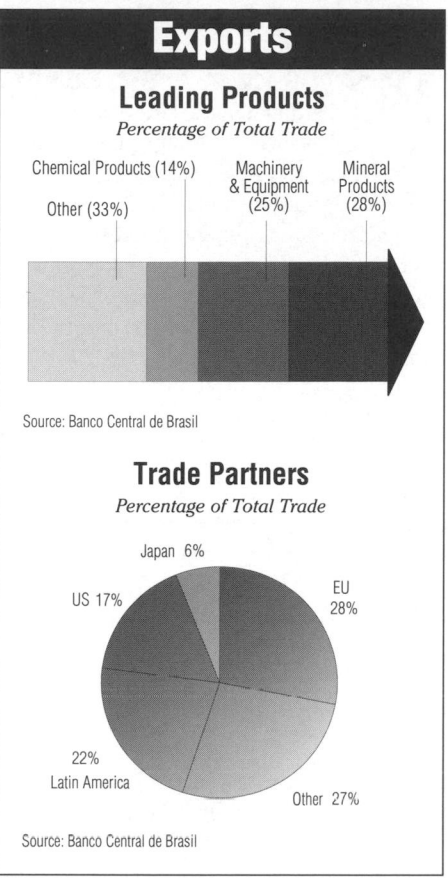

Exports

Leading Products
Percentage of Total Trade

Chemical Products (14%) — Machinery & Equipment (25%) — Mineral Products (28%) — Other (33%)

Source: Banco Central de Brasil

Trade Partners
Percentage of Total Trade

Japan 6%
US 17%
EU 28%
Latin America 22%
Other 27%

Source: Banco Central de Brasil

Opportunities

FOR IMPORTING TO BRAZIL
- chemical products
- coal
- computer products
- electronic components
- food processing equipment
- household consumer goods
- medical equipment and supplies
- oil
- oil and gas field machinery
- plastics
- pollution control equipment
- professional services
- sporting goods
- telecommunication products
- wheat

FOR EXPORTING FROM BRAZIL
- cocoa and coffee
- fish
- footwear
- iron ore
- minerals
- motor vehicle parts
- natural gas
- oil and petroleum products
- orange juice concentrate
- plastics
- rubber
- soybeans
- sugar
- textiles
- tobacco
- wood products

GROWTH AREAS
- electrical energy technology
- environmental protection goods and services
- ethyl alcohol fuel
- information technology
- insurance
- manufacturing
- medical supplies and equipment
- pharmaceuticals
- telecommunications
- soybeans and sugar

GOVERNMENT PROCUREMENT
- environmental protection goods and services
- health care goods and services
- natural gas pipelines
- public transportation links and expansion
- telecommunications
- water treatment facilities

Trade News

RULES AND REGULATIONS

- **Regulations** Directives on foreign trade are issued by the National Council of Foreign Trade (CONCEX). The directives are implemented by the Industry, Commerce, and Tourism Secretariat (SECEX), which is part of the Ministry of Foreign Trade. All importers of goods to Brazil must be registered with SECEX.
- **Tariffs and import taxes** Brazil's import duties range from 0 to 35 percent, with a few items as high as 40 percent. The average duty is 14 percent. Brazil also assesses a number of additional taxes and fees on imports, including syndicate and brokerage fees and a warehouse tax.
- **Import licenses** The import permit is the single most important document required for exporting goods to Brazil. An import permit must be obtained by the importer for all but a very limited list of products.
- **Import restrictions** The Brazilian government has eliminated import prohibitions. However, certain categories of imports are subject to control. They include used materials, computer software, petroleum products, arms and ammunition, soft drinks, flammables, airplanes, dangerous substances, chlorinated pesticides, insecticides, other agricultural chemicals, and animal foodstuffs.
- **Export controls** Normally, there are no restrictions on exports, but export licenses are required. Some commodities, such as coffee and timber, may be subject to export quotas or other controls.
- **Free trade zones/warehouses** There are four free trade zones in Brazil: Manaus, Macapá/Santana, Tabatinga, Guajari. Three others are authorized: Bofim, Pacaraima and Brasilia.
- **Manaus Free Trade Zone** The Manaus Free Trade Zone is the most extensively developed and has a constitutional mandate through the year 2013. Both foreign and domestic firms can operate in Manaus. Fiscal incentives for Manaus include exemption from taxes and from tariffs on imported components, and reduced tariffs on products shipped from Manaus to the rest of Brazil; reduced state tax on products imported from or exported to the rest of Brazil; up to 10 years' exemption from federal income tax; and exemption from import license fees.
- **Export processing zones** In addition to the free trade zones, 14 export processing zones have been authorized. They are administered by the Ministry of Industry, Commerce and Tourism. To date, only four have begun initial infrastructure construction; the remainder are still in the planning stages.
- **Membership in free trade arrangements** Brazil is a member of ALADI, a Latin American organization providing duty rate reductions to its members. Brazil also is a member of the Southern Common Market, composed of Brazil, Argentina, Paraguay, and Uruguay (named MERCOSUL in Portuguese and MERCOSUR in Spanish).

GOVERNMENT AGENCIES

Departamento de Promocao Comercial do Ministerio das Rel a coes Exteriores (Ministry of Industry and Commerce)
Esplanada dos Ministérios, Bloco J, 6 andar
70056-900 Brasília, DF
Tel: (61) 225-8105

Department of Trade Promotion
Palacio Itamarafy
Esplanada dos Ministerios Anexo
Administrativo 1
CEP 70120
Brasília, DF
Tel: (61) 211-6240
Telex: 611319

Instituto Brasileiro de Administracao Municipal (Municipal Administrative Department)
Largo IBAM 1
Botafogo
CEP 22282
Rio de Janeiro SP
Tel: (21) 266-6622

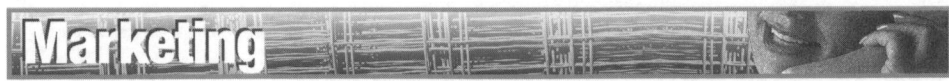

Marketing

Overview

Brazil warrants a close examination by foreign investors, not only because of its richly diverse and sizeable domestic consumer market, but also because of its booming manufacturing export market. With an overall population of more than 155 million—São Paulo alone has 17 million and Rio de Janeiro another 11 million—Brazil is just slightly smaller than the US in geographic size. Telecommunications systems are generally good throughout the country, even in remote areas, and a growing portion of international transactions are conducted via facsimile. Recently liberalized regulations and procedures affecting imported software, business registration, and international franchising have added new and promising markets, although most market segments are already open to foreigners and highly competitive. However, pockets of protectionist regulation remain, and—although friendly—Brazilians tend to distrust foreigners and insist on a high degree of control in mutual dealings. This suspicion must be overcome in marketing campaigns to get the virtues of the product across to the potential buyer.

Distribution

All the usual import channels exist in Brazil including agents, distributors, import houses, trading companies, and foreign subsidiaries. Capital goods and raw materials are in high demand and many companies import these directly from abroad—rather than through intermediaries—to produce for either domestic or export markets. Brazilian import firms do not generally maintain a well-stocked inventory of foreign products, due to a shortage of working capital and legal limitations. However, restrictions on bonded warehouses have been eased, allowing more flexibility for such operations to stock goods within the country, and large-scale distribution agreements have begun to flourish as a result. Joint ventures and license agreements with local partners are permissible under Brazilian law and can be formed freely, although advice from local legal and tax professionals is important when structuring the arrangement. Establishing a separate, locally incorporated entity is favored over setting up a branch office.

Agents, Distributors, and Partners

Agents provide an important means of doing business. Because of Brazil's large size and geographical diversity, a single agent may not be able to cover the entire country. Despite improvements in internal transportation and communications systems, local agents will often demand a larger commission to be split with other agents located elsewhere (or fail to devote sufficient attention to the standard commission business). Foreign sellers should firmly limit the scope of their agency agreements or make the terms applicable to all subagents used by the contracting agent. A foreign supplier may become subject to additional Brazilian income taxes if an agency relationship is deemed to create a presence in Brazil. It is wise to seek advice from Brazilian attorneys on the effects of a proposed agency arrangement. Brazilian agents are protected by law from unilateral termination of the contract without cause (acts that are negligent, in breach of contract, damaging to the principal, or result in a criminal conviction constitute cause).

Selling Techniques

Sales of industrial products are typically price-driven, although quality has become increasingly important, especially for companies that are modernizing their production methods and targeting international markets. After price and quality, selling techniques that focus on delivery and after-sales service are also highly effective. Consumers tend to buy by brand names. Price discounts are a common sales tool. Products often reflect a substantial markup when first offered, allowing for a series of price reductions until they are finally sold. Participation in Brazil's many trade fairs can be crucially important for any foreign company that seeks to enter this huge and lucrative market. São Paulo alone hosts approximately 300 trade fairs each year, most with an international quality and reputation.

Advertising

Advertising in specialized trade and technical publications is an important marketing tool. With a well-established and diversified industrial sector, Brazil has a variety of high-quality periodicals that serve the industrial and business communities. Most of these carry significant amounts of advertising. Brazil's sophisticated advertising agencies are recognized for their creative approaches. Television advertising is highly developed, particularly for promoting consumer goods and food products.

Service and Customer Support

Buyers of industrial goods consider customer service crucial, but small- and medium-sized suppliers often find it impossible to offer after-sales support because of economic instability and rapid market changes. However, more and more firms are implementing tighter quality control systems and good faith customer service programs in order to remain competitive with the larger manufacturers. Toll-free telephone numbers have become a popular connection to after-sales support.

Marketing in Brazil

MARKETING TIPS

- **Price is right** High inflation during the past two decades has made it difficult to establish a reasonable pricing system in Brazil. As the government takes steps to bring inflation under control, reasonable pricing will be a top consideration in keeping products competitive in this market.

- **Industry/consumer market characteristic** A major privatization program has already begun in Brazil with an estimated US$10 billion in public assets up for sale in the next few years. Foreign investors are welcome to bid in some areas.

- **Language** The official language is Portuguese. However, English is widely used in the business community. Other European languages are spoken by the country's diverse population, especially German.

CONSULTING FIRMS

A.C. Nielsen S/C Ltda.
Av. Bernardino de Campos, 98, 9o. andar
04004-040 São Paulo, SP
Tel: (11) 889-7077
Fax: (11) 889-8220

Booz, Allen and Hamilton do Brasil Consultores Ltda.
Rua Gomes de Carvalho 1765, 5 andar
04547-901 São Paulo, SP
Tel: (11) 820-1900
Fax: (11) 820-6750

M & L Magnus Landman Consultores Empresariais
Av. Brig. Faria Lima 1544, 4 andar, cj.41
01452-001 São Paulo, SP
Tel: (11) 816-3144
Fax: (11) 816-7864

Bichuetti Consultoria Empresarial S/C Ltda.
Av. Brig. Faria Lima 1541 - 6B
01451-000 São Paulo, SP
Tel: (11) 813-9744
Fax: (11) 816-0908

Datamark Consultores S/C Ltda.
Av. Brig. Faria Lima 1238, 3 andar, cj.31
01452-000 São Paulo, SP
Tel: (11) 814-7355
Fax: (11) 814-8890

Barros Ribeiro Planejamento, Consultoria e Representac es Ltda.
Rua Dr. Joao Climaco Pereira 46
04532-070 São Paulo, SP
Tel: (11) 820-7422
Fax: (11) 820-0720

Adela Empreendimentos e Consultoria Ltda.
Av. Brig. Faria Lima 1541, 7 andar, cj.7D
01451-000 São Paulo, SP
Tel: (11) 813-7111
Fax: (11) 212-7675

Arthur D. Little S/C Ltda.
Av. Brig. Faria Lima 2003,19/20 andares, cj.1901/2015
01451-001 São Paulo, SP
Tel: (11) 814-8144
Fax: (11) 815-7540

Schlochauer & Associados Consultoria e Representac o Ltda.
Caixa Postal 21151
04698-970 São Paulo, SP
Tel: (11) 247-6631
Fax: (11) 247-6631/829-7556

S. Bekin & Consultores S/C Ltda.
Rua Estela 265, casa 11
04011-001 São Paulo, SP
Telefax: (11) 572-3112

Lindsey Consultores S/C Ltda.
Rua Bela Cintra 1932
01415-002 São Paulo, SP
Tel: (11) 280-8122
Fax: (11) 853-7787

Simonsen Associados S/C Ltda.
Av. 9 de Julho 5017, 12 andar
01407-200 São Paulo, SP
Tel: (11) 853-4733
Fax: (11) 883-4958

Business Culture

Greetings and Courtesies

Portuguese-speaking Brazilians are generally less formal than their Spanish-speaking Latin compatriots. Brazilians of both sexes shake hands upon meeting and when departing. Men's handshakes tend to be prolonged by most standards, especially when first introduced. Women friends touch alternate cheeks in a "kiss" (married women kiss twice, while a single woman receives a third kiss). In business, men are addressed as *Senhor* plus their surname (women as *Senhora* plus the surname). Brazilians often move rapidly to first names, often used with a title or honorific (such as *Douter—Dr.*—Fernando) for professionals. Business cards (printed in your language and Portuguese) are a necessity. Say goodbye to everyone individually when leaving.

Business Ethic and Framework

Brazilians can be quite nationalistic and xenophobic, usually wishing to do business only with foreigners interested in a long-term commitment to operating in Brazil on Brazilian terms. Brazilians emphasize the importance of the personal relationship, taking time and effort to establish such a relationship as a prerequisite to a business relationship. Brazilians view work as a single component of rather than the central focus of life. They usually enjoy bargaining, however, with the social interchange and battle of wits that that entails.

Decision Making

Although middle level managers may be responsible for implementing decisions, actual decisions are almost always made at a high level of authority. While you should approach senior people, Brazilians will want to know your standing within the hierarchy and will wish to match you with someone of similar rank, while only their senior people will actually be able to approve agreements. Nevertheless, it is important to cultivate personal relationships with these peers, because the quality of these relationships may strongly influence the actual decisionmaker even when your immediate counterpart is not the one making the decision.

Women

Women in Brazil occupy a secondary status in this traditionally male-dominated society, although many operate businesses and are generally accorded considerable personal freedom. Brazilian women are becoming more involved and accepted in business, and foreign businesswomen should experience few problems. Foreign female visitors should recognize that Brazilian men are easily encouraged and persistent; and that while physical contact is considered unacceptable, bold comments and exaggerated leering are commonplace. Foreign businesswomen are expected to be highly professional and not aggressive or confrontational.

Meetings

Contacts and introductions are important. If you do not have a mutual business acquaintance to make introductions, consult your embassy for a referral. Make appointments at least two weeks in advance. Do not try to schedule too many meetings: you are almost sure to be kept waiting for anywhere from 15 minutes to more than an hour—although you should be on time. Meetings are often interrupted and do not end abruptly. Business lunches are common, dinners less so, although business-related after-hours entertaining is highly developed.

Business Attire

Brazilian standards of dress are less formal than those in other Latin American countries. Nevertheless, men should wear business suits, although they can wear a more broad range of colors and styles—for example, Italian suits in lighter weights and colors in place of the traditional dark conservative British tailoring favored elsewhere in South America. Executives usually wear three-piece suits. All ranks wear long-sleeved shirts. Foreign businesswomen should wear business suits or dresses, but more stylishness, color, makeup, and accessories are accepted and appreciated, especially in larger, coastal cities (dress is somewhat more traditional in less cosmopolitan inland locations). When invited to a home, men wear a suit, women a dress. For less formal social occasions, men wear shirts and trousers and women dresses or skirts—or pants—and blouses. Ties are seldom required for social events, although jackets may be. Jeans and sandals are for "kids," and are therefore unbusinesslike. Both sexes should wear regular shoes and avoid shorts. Women in general have greater freedom in dress—although local fashions are often brash and provocative and dress that is too informal may invite unwanted attention.

Cultural Cautions

DO'S

- Learn about Brazil's history and culture—your interest will be appreciated, as will your attempts to speak Portuguese.
- Place your silverware horizontally across your plate (but do not cross your silverware) and push it back from you to indicate you have finished.
- If invited out, bring a small gift, such as fruit, candy, wine, or flowers—but not purple flowers, which are associated with death.

DON'TS

- Avoid wearing green or yellow—the colors of the Brazilian flag; you may be ridiculed.
- Do not eat anything with your hands—even sandwiches are eaten with a knife and fork. Rare finger foods are wrapped in a napkin to protect the hands.
- Do not drink from a bottle or can—always use a glass.
- Smoking is common almost everywhere, but do not smoke during a meal.
- Never try to use Spanish or Spanish-language materials; it is insulting, as well as ineffective.
- You may wave to an acquaintance from a distance, but never shout—it is considered rude.

CUSTOMS

- Eating is serious business: conversation is reserved until after the food has been eaten.
- Do not rush off after a meal—this is time for socializing.
- Dinner parties may begin at 10:00 pm, with the meal being served at midnight, and festivities continuing until the next morning.
- Coffee is always served sweetened—if you don't want sugar ask for *sin suco* when ordering. A very strong *cafezinho* is served in a demitasse after dinner.
- A separate fruit course—eaten with a knife and fork—is frequently served.
- You must ask for your check in better restaurants—it will not be brought until you do. Hand the tip directly to the waiter (never leave it on the table), or pay with a larger bill and leave before the change is returned.

OBSERVATIONS

- Brazilians generally distrust the intentions of foreigners, and resist any loss of control over operations.
- Brazilians consider themselves to be South Americans, but not Hispanics. They are proud of their distinct heritage and expect it to be recognized and acknowledged.
- Note that Brazilians alphabetize lists of names by the first name.
- If you interrupt someone at a meal, you will be invited to join. Always decline in case there is not enough.
- Brazilians consider the home to be private and seldom invite outsiders. However, accustomed to living in extended families, they consider the concept of individual privacy and needing time alone to be strange. Always call before visiting someone.
- Retain a *despachante*, or expediter, to handle local issues.
- You may be able to get helpful information and enhance your cause by being attentive to the secretaries of the Brazilian firms with which you are doing business.

NEGOTIATIONS

- Brazilians often accept invitations or proposals as a matter of courtesy; confirm that a particular acceptance indicates an intention to follow through.
- Brazilians are offended by an overly direct approach and consider direct confrontation as a challenge. However, they have few reservations about saying "no."
- Brazilians talk constantly during negotiations.
- Brazilians tend to stand very close and touch a lot during discussions; some such contact is fairly aggressive by many standards.

Legal

Legal System

Brazil is organized as a Federal Republic and its legal system is based on a civil code. All laws are promulgated by the federal government, states, or municipalities, depending in which sphere of authority the matter falls.

Intellectual Property Rights

Patents Brazil is a member of the 1883 Paris Union Convention, and its Industrial Property Code can be found in Law 5772/71. The National Institute of Industrial Property ("INPI") is the governmental entity in charge of industrial property rights. Patents may be granted for the protection of inventions, utility models, industrial designs and models. The protection extends for 15 years for inventions and 10 years for other categories. Proceedings are rather lengthy, and more than a year can pass between filing of the application and the grant of a patent.

Trademarks Brazil has an attributive system for trademark protection. The owner of a trademark is considered to be the individual that first files a specific trademark with the INPI. Trademarks can be registered either as a foreign trademark or as a Brazilian trademark, and may be nominative, symbolic, or mixed in form. The term of validity for a trademark's registration in Brazil is 10 years, which can be extended indefinitely for additional 10-year periods. The holder of the trademark must use the trademark within the first two years from the date of its registration, or risk the possibility of losing rights thereunder. Moreover, if the trademark is not used during any consecutive two-year period, there will also be a risk of losing the rights to the trademark. Use of the trademark can be established by sales invoices, advertising or promotional materials, samples of packaging, etc.

Copyrights Software is governed by a specific law that grants 25 years of protection, beginning from the date such software was launched in any country, provided that the software's country of origin grants software originating from Brazil the same rights. If this is the case, then there is no requirement to register the copyright in Brazil; nevertheless, it is advisable to obtain such registration because copyright piracy is rampant.

Business Registration

The foreign company must submit an application to the Brazilian Government to obtain permission to operate a branch in Brazil. Brazilian law provides several forms of corporate enterprise, with the most widely adopted being the "Sociedade Por Quotas de Responsabilidade Limitada" (limited liability company) and the "Sociedade Anónima" (joint-stock company). These commercial companies must obtain an approval from the Board of Trade as well as other appropriate authorities, depending on the type of business. All foreign operations are handled by the Central Bank of Brazil.

Contracts and Dispute Resolution

Arbitration clauses are not commonly used in Brazil because, under the Brazilian system, arbitration is considered to be an option which may be freely chosen by the parties as a means of reaching a compromise position in the context of an actual dispute. Thus, Brazilian courts recognize arbitration clauses only in connection with specific existing disputes, and only if both parties agree to submission thereto. In addition, general arbitration clauses included in international agreements are often not effective since a Brazilian party to the contract may simply refuse to submit to arbitration, and the courts will not require him to do so.

Notaries

All foreign documents, in order to be admissible in a Brazilian court, must have the foreign participants' signatures notarized in their home country, and then be legalized by the nearest Brazilian Consulate in such country. If the document is in a language other than Portuguese, then this notarized and legalized document must also be translated into Portuguese in Brazil by a certified translator.

Labor

Labor legislation defines an employee as any person who renders services on a regular basis to, and under the direction of, an employer in return for a wage. The rights and duties of employers and employees are set out in the Consolidated Labor Laws and collective labor agreements. Employment contracts may establish either a definite or an indefinite term of employment. Employees are granted certain rights thereunder regarding termination, minimum wage, and holiday and other benefits. Employees may choose either of two regimes under which to recover benefits for employment termination, both of which provide significant termination payments. Brazilian law also provides for vacation, holiday, and overtime pay; as well as significant limitations on the exploitation of child and female labor. Brazil maintains retirement and social security systems to which both employers and employees contribute.

Source: Felsberg e Associados, São Paulo

Legal Matters

LEGAL BRIEFS

- **Constitution** Four constitutional amendments were recently passed prohibiting discrimination between foreign-controlled companies and nationally controlled companies, ending the constitutional restriction that only Brazilian-flag vessels can navigate in coastal waters; and ending the government monopolies over telecommunications and pipeline gas supply services. Some of these, however, require implementing legislation before they can take effect.

- **Corporations** A Limitada must be incorporated by at least two quotaholders, who can be legal or natural persons, and either residents or foreigners. The rules governing limitadas do not require that annual meetings be held, nor that financial statements or minutes of quotaholders' meetings be published.

- **Temporary visas** The laws governing both multiple-entry temporary business and tourist visas were recently changed allowing these visas to have a maximum validity period of five years, subject to a reciprocity test. The holder can only stay in Brazil, however, a maximum of 180 days for each year.

- **Trade agreements** Brazil created a free-trade block (Mercosul, or MERCOSUR) with three neighboring countries, which officially took effect on January 1, 1995. And, Brazil signed an agreement with 34 other countries to establish a Western Hemisphere-wide free-trade union by early next century.

LEGAL CONTACTS

Felsberg e Associados
Avenida Paulista
1776-20o andar
01310 São Paulo, SP
Tel: (11) 285-2422
Fax: (11) 287-1129

Stroeter, Trench e Veirano Advogados
Av. Nilo Pecanha 50 17th Floor
Edificio Rodolpho de Paoli
10041 Rio de Janeiro, RJ
Tel: (21) 262-2833
Fax: (21) 262-4247

Stroeter, Trench e Veirano Advogados
Rua Martiniano de Carvalho 1049
Paraiso, CEP 01321
São Paulo, SP
Tel: (11) 288-7999
Fax: (11) 287-6967

Azevedo Sette Advogados S.C.
Av. Afonso Pena, 3.111 - 7th Floor
30130-008 Belo Horizonte, MG
Tel: (31) 223-2866

Grebler, Pinheiro, Mourao & Raso - Advogados
Av. Afonso Pena, 3.130 - 10 Andar
30130 Belo Horizonte, MG
Tel: (31) 223-6111
Fax: (31) 225-2529

Pinheiro Neto - Advogados
SCS - 1, B ED. Central
70304-900 Brasília, DF
Tel: (61) 223-2347
Fax: (61) 226-0676

Bertao e Couto - Avagados
Av. Rio Branco, No. 50 - 9th Floor
20090 Rio de Janeiro RJ
Tel: (21) 253-9141
Fax: (21) 253-6143

Briger e Associados
Edificio Centro Candido Mendes
Rua Da Assembleia, 10-GR, 2720
20011 Rio de Janeiro 20119-900
Tel: (21) 531-1213
Fax: (21) 531-1447

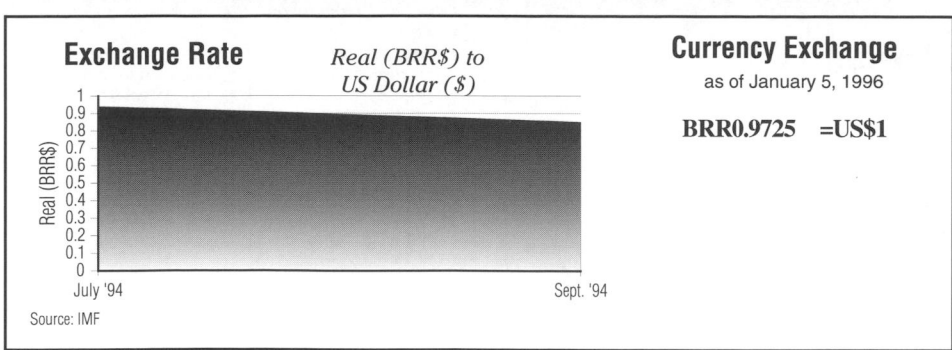

Money

Exchange Rate Real (BRR$) to US Dollar ($)

Source: IMF

Currency Exchange
as of January 5, 1996

BRR0.9725 =US$1

Currency

The currency of Brazil is the real (BRR). The plural is reales.

Foreign Exchange

The National Monetary Council (CMN) is responsible for creating all currency exchange policies. Exchange market transactions are carried out by authorized banks, brokers, and tourist agencies. Tourist agencies deal only with bank notes and traveler's checks. Exchange rates are freely negotiated between the authorized institutions and their clients in all operations. Exchange transactions that amount to more than US$100,000 are subject to brokerage fees.

Capital Transfers

Settlements with countries with which Brazil maintains payments agreements (including its LIAI partners) are made in clearing dollars through the relevant agreement account. Settlements with countries with which Brazil has no payments agreements and no special payments arrangements are made in US dollars or other freely usable currencies. Travelers may take out domestic and foreign bank notes without restriction but must declare to customs any values over US$10,000 or the equivalent in other currencies. Capital inflows in the form of financial loans which originate from abroad require prior approval from the Central Bank. All foreign investment must be registered with the Central Bank; the certificate of registration issued by the Central Bank permits remittances of profits and repatriation of invested capital without additional Central Bank authorization.

Investment Incentives

In general, most investment incentives are offered by state and municipal governments although some federal government incentives exist for export production, capital goods production, investment in certain underdeveloped areas or export processing zones. Many state and local governments provide tax holidays and/or reductions for certain investments and expansions. Performance requirements are not usually tied to incentives.

Investment Restrictions

Discriminatory local production and assembly requirements for government procurement exist in the areas of telecommunications, computers, and digital electronic goods and services. Foreign investment is prohibited in health care services, financial institutions, and print and electronic media.

Money Matters

BITS AND PIECES

- **Corporate income tax** All companies in Brazil need to pay an income tax. A 10 percent Social Contribution Tax is levied on corporate income.
- **Capital gains** Capital gains are usually included in taxable income and are subject to tax at the regular corporate income tax rate.
- **Foreign tax relief** No foreign tax relief is provided, because foreign branches, subsidiaries, and agencies are exempt from a corporate income tax.
- **Gold** Rules for transactions for industrial purposes are decided by federal states. They also establish rates for taxes levied on them. Imports of gold are subject to a certificate by SECEX.
- **Foreign capital** Foreign capital other than that invested in Brazilian securities is classified as direct investments or loans.
- **National treatment** The language of the Constitution effectively denies national treatment to foreign investors.
- **Central Bank** The Central Bank has broad discretionary powers which have often created problems for foreign investors in Brazil.
- **Royalties** Investments involving royalties—including franchises—must be registered with the National Institute of Industrial Property.
- **Unregistered investments** Unregistered investments can and are made using the floating exchange rate rather than the commercial rate, in which case the investor does not have access to the commercial rate for remittances and repatriation of capital and cannot register reinvestment. The floating market is not a legal means for profit and capital remittances, and using it could lead to difficulties.

BANKS

Brazilian Central Bank
70074-900 Brasília, DF
Tel: (61) 214-1020/214-1000
Fax: (61) 224-4119

Bank of Brazil
SBS, Qd.4, Lote 32, Bloco C,Ed. Sede III, 20 andar
70073-900 Brasília, DF
Tel: (61) 212-2211
Fax: (61) 223-0156

Banco do Estado da Bahia, SA
Av. Estados Unidos 26
CP 68
40010 Salvador BA
Tel: (71) 242-1822
Fax: (71) 243-6397

Banco do Estado de Minas Gerais, SA
Rua Rio de Janeiro 471 Salas 15, 20-25
CP 300
30160 Belo Horizonte, MG
Tel: (31) 239-1211
Telex: 2134
Fax: (31) 239-1859

Banco do Estado do Paraná, SA
Rua Máximo Joao Kopp 274
CP 3331
80000 Curitiba, PR
Tel: (41) 253-8311
Telex: 6002
Fax: (41) 253-8383

Banco do Estado de Pernambuco, SA
Cais do Apolo 222
14 andar
50038 Recife, PE
Tel: (81) 224-5276
Telex: 2164
Fax: (81) 224-8814

Banco do Estado do Rio Grande do Sul, SA
Rua Capitao Montanha 177
CP 505
90010 Porto Alegre, RS
Tel: (521) 21-5023
Telex: 474
Fax: (521) 28-6473

TAXATION	At a Glance	
Taxation requires sophisticated knowledge of complex rules and regulations specific to each country. The information presented here is from the Ernst & Young Corporate Tax Guide and Directory, available from the Ernst & Young accounting office in your country, or from: **Ernst & Young** Mail Address: Caixa Postal 4660 20001-970 Rio de Janeiro, RJ Brazil Street Address: Avenida Rio Branco, 128 16th Floor 20042-900 Rio de Janeiro, RJ Brazil Tel: (21) 203-2424 Fax: (21) 232-0196, 224-2751	Corporate Income Tax Rate (%) (a)	25
	Capital Gains Tax Rate (%) (a)	25
	Branch Tax Rate (%) (a)	25
	Withholding Tax (%)(b)	
	Dividends	15
	Interest	25
	Royalties from Patents, Know-how, etc.	25
	Branch Remittance Tax	15
	Net Operating Losses (Years)	
	Carryback	0
	Carryforward	Unlimited
	(a) A significant surtax is also levied.	
	(b) Remittance withholding tax.	

Business Travel

Air Travel Times

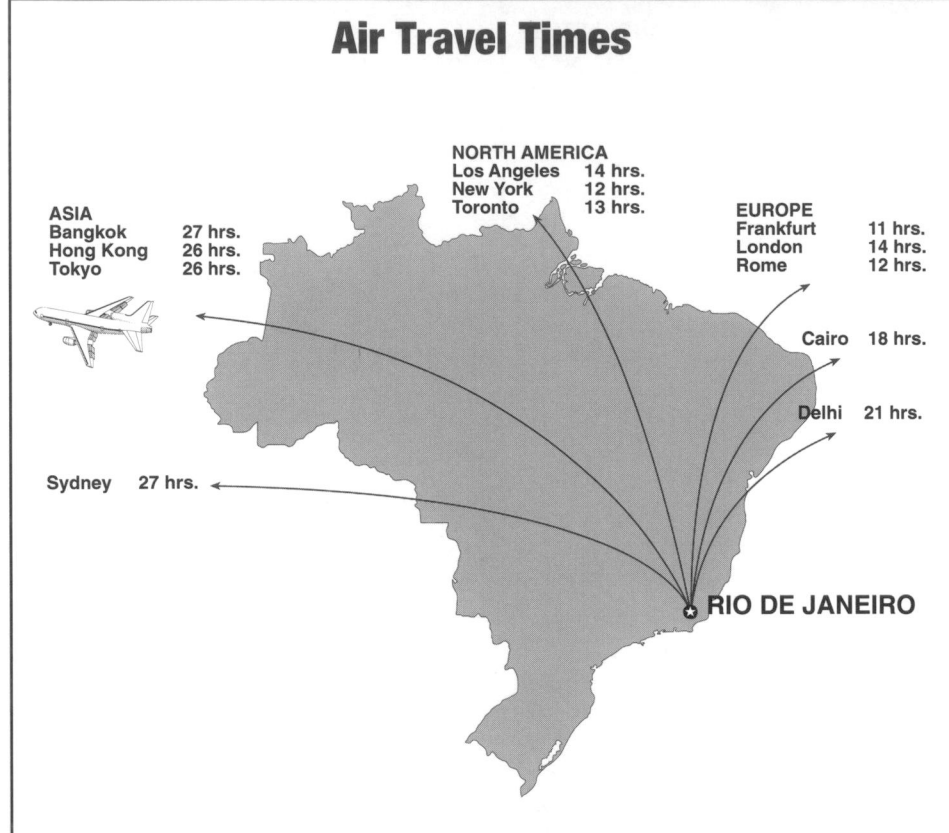

ASIA
Bangkok 27 hrs.
Hong Kong 26 hrs.
Tokyo 26 hrs.

NORTH AMERICA
Los Angeles 14 hrs.
New York 12 hrs.
Toronto 13 hrs.

EUROPE
Frankfurt 11 hrs.
London 14 hrs.
Rome 12 hrs.

Cairo 18 hrs.

Delhi 21 hrs.

Sydney 27 hrs.

RIO DE JANEIRO

COMMUNICATIONS

Telephones Telephone services are good but becoming overburdened. International calls can be dialed directly to Canada, UK, and US locations. Calls within Brazil may take hours to connect and have very poor audibility. All long-distance calls originating from Brazil are subject to a 40 percent tax. Yellow phones are for local, blue phones for long distance calling.

Fax The same crowded lines that can make a telephone call difficult can affect the quality of a fax. Still, fax machines are used in many offices. Fax service is also available in larger post offices.

Post office Mailing letters and buying stamps can only be done at post offices. Airmail takes four to six days to or from the US or UK, two weeks to Canada. Surface mail takes at least four weeks to any destination. Parcel post is subject to customs duties, red tape, and pilfering.

BEST TRAVEL BOOKS

Lonely Planet, Brazil. 'Different, superior...the most thorough travel guide to Brazil...' 632 pages, 16 color pages.

Fodor's Travel Guide: Brazil. Tourist oriented, excellent source of city details.

The Travelers Guide to Latin American Customs and Manners. Elizabeth Devine & Nancy Braganti. 'An invaluable guide for people not wanting to put foot in mouth.'

A Guide to International Behavior, Do's and Taboos Around the World. Edited by Roger E. Axtell, compiled by the Parker Pen Company. Now completely updated and revised, the ultimate guide to international behavior. Helpful and fun to read.

South American Handbook, Passport Books. Updated annually.

USEFUL TELEPHONE NUMBERS

If you are calling from outside Brazil, you will need to add the country code [55] and any other international dialing requirements from within your country.

Emergencies
- Medical Emergencies.. 192
- Rio de Janeiro .... (21) 270-1442
- São Paulo.. (11) 251-1733
- Brasilia .... (61) 224-3330 or 224-7474
- Belo Horizonte.................................... (31) 464-3999

Car Rental Agencies
- Hertz .... (21) 275-4996
- Avis .... (21) 542-4249
- Budget .... (11) 256-4355

Hotels
- Copa d'Or Hotel .... (21) 235-6244
- Sheraton Rio Hotel & Towers .... (21) 274-1122
- Aerolineas Argentinas Airlines .... (21) 221-4255
- American .... (21) 210-3126
- United .... (21) 220-5046

National Airlines
- Varig Brazilian Airlines[Rio].............. (21) 297-5141
- Vasp, Aeroporto Congonhas .... (11) 533-7011
- Transbrasil Rio .... (21) 220-6066
- Transbrasil São Paulo...................... (11) 533-5455

Credit Card Information
Lost or stolen credit cards (call collect to the US, regardless of which country the card was issued in).
- Amex .... [1] (919) 333-3211
- Diner's Club................................ [1] (303) 799-1504
- MasterCard .... [1] (314) 275-6690
- Visa .... [1] (410) 581-7931

Travelogue

WORKWEEK
Offices Monday-Friday 8:00 am to 6:00 pm; closed for lunch midday.
Banks Monday-Friday 10:00 am to 4:00 pm.
Government Monday-Friday 9:30 am to 6:00 pm.
Retail Monday-Friday 9:00 am to 5:00 pm. Some shops have Saturday morning hours.

HOLIDAYS
Holidays 1996
January 1 New Year's Day
February 28-29 Carnival*
April 13 Holy Thursday*
April 14 Good Friday*
April 15 Easter Sunday
April 21 Tiradentes' Day
May 1 Labor Day
June 15 Corpus Christi*
September 7 Independence Day
October 12 Nossa Senhora Aparecida
November 1 All Saints' Day
November 2 All Souls' Day
November 15 Proclamation of the Republic
December 8 Immaculate Conception
December 24 Christmas Eve
December 25 Christmas Day
*Dates vary each year.
In addition there are various state and religious holidays celebrated regionally.

VISA AND PASSPORT
Foreigners must have a passport, valid for at least six months, a return ticket, and a visa for entry into Brazil. Visas must be obtained prior to entry. Business travelers must have a temporary business visa (valid for 90 days) to transact any business such as signing documents, research, or financial transactions. Visas are not required for Canadian or UK citizens. Travelers must hold onward tickets, valid documents, and sufficient funds.

DEPARTURE FORMALITIES
The immigration permit issued to travelers upon entry to Brazil must be retained and produced when exiting. Failure to do so can result in a US$100 fine. Travelers may not take out more money than is brought into Brazil.

IMMUNIZATION
Vaccinations are not required unless the following conditions apply: travelers arriving from the Amazon region or any country bordering it will need a yellow fever vaccination, and those coming from areas infected with cholera must show proof of a recent inoculation.

TIPPING
No tip is necessary for taxi drivers. Porters enjoy BRR1 per piece. Hotels, restaurants: 10 to15 percent included in bill but additional 5 percent to staff is usual. Chambermaids, BRR1 per week; barbers & beauticians: 10 percent.

CRIME
Crime against tourists is the greatest in areas surrounding hotels, discotheques, bars, nightclubs, and similar establishments that cater to visitors, dusk and evening hours being the worst. Rio de Janeiro understandably experiences a proportionately high amount of crime against tourists. Thefts at airports involving carry-on luggage and briefcases have increased.

INFRASTRUCTURE
Brazil has efficient air service between major cities and other parts of the country. Taxis are plentiful in most urban areas, although they can be difficult to find in certain areas or hours of the day; catch them outside your hotel. Taxis are also the safest mode of transportation. Radio taxis are more reliable than meter taxis. Avoid walking or taking the metro.

NATIONAL TOURIST OFFICE
CEBITUR
Rua Mariz E. Barros 13
20270-004 Rio de Janiero
Tel: (21) 2931313

> **REMEMBER**
> - When you telephone (or fax) to Brazil from another country you must always include the country code [55] before the numbers given.
> - When you send mail to Brazil, be sure to write BRAZIL in capital letters on its own line below the addresses given.

GOVERNMENT AGENCIES

Ministry of Agriculture
Secretariat of Agriculture & Livestock Defense
MAARA/SDA Esplanada dos Ministerios
Bloco D, Anexo B, 4o.andar
70043-900 Brasilia, DF
Tel: (61) 226-9771
Fax: (61) 224-3995

National Bank of Economic Social Development
Av. República do Chile 100
20139-900 Rio de Janeiro, RJ
Tel: (21) 277-7447
Fax: (21) 262-8513

Ministry of Science and Technology
Esplanada dos Ministérios
Bloco E, 4 andar
70062-900 Brasília, DF
Tel: (61) 321-8886
Fax: (61) 225-1141

Brazilian Aeronautic Company
Av. Brig. Faria Lima 2170
12227-901 São José dos Campos, SP
Tel: (123) 25-1000
Fax: (123) 21-8466

Brazilian Telecommunications Company
Av. Presidente Vargas 1012
Edifício Sede, 15 andar
20179-900 Rio de Janeiro, RJ
Tel: (21) 216-8182
Fax: (21) 224-1175

Brazilian Industrial Property Institute
Praça Mauá 7, 18 andar -Centro
20081-240 Rio de Janeiro, RJ
Tel: (21) 291-1224
Fax: (21) 263-2539

Ministry of Aeronautics
Esplanada dos Ministérios - Bloco M
70045-900 Brasília, DF
Tel: (61) 313-2345
Fax: (61) 313-2110

Ministry of Finance
Esplanada dos Ministérios - Bloco P
70048-900 Brasília, DF
Tel: (61) 314-2000
Fax: (61) 223-5239

Brazilian Petroleum Company
Av. República do Chile 65, 24 andar
20031-900 Rio de Janeiro, RJ
Tel: (21) 534-4477
Fax: (21) 240-9394

Department of Civil Aviation
Aeroporto Santos Dumont, 4 andar
20021-000 Rio de Janeiro, RJ
Tel: (21) 220-6927
Fax: (21) 220-5177

Ministry of Industry and Commerce
Esplanada dos Ministérios, Bloco J, 6 andar
70056-900 Brasília, DF
Tel: (61) 225-8105

WORLD TRADE CENTERS

World Trade Center Rio de Janeiro
Rua da Candelária, 9-12 andar
20091-020 Rio de Janeiro
Tel: (21) 291-1229, 263-9461
Fax: (21) 263-7613, 253-6236

World Trade Center de São Paulo
Rua Estado Unidos,1093
01427-001
São Paolo
Tel: (11) 851-2811
Fax: (11) 883-7493

TRADE ASSOCIATIONS

Automotive Components Manufacturers
Rua Abilio Soares 1487
04005-005 São Paulo, SP
Tel: (11) 884-4599
Fax: (11) 884-0584

Electric and Electronic Industry
Av. Paulista 1313, 7 andar
01311-923 São Paulo, SP
Tel: (11) 251-1577
Fax: (11) 285-0607

Electric Conductors
Rua Mariana Correa 52
01444-000 São Paulo, SP
Tel: (11) 883-2622
Fax: (11) 883-2814

Food Processing/Dairy Products
Praça Dom José Gaspar 30, 10 andar
01047-901 São Paulo, SP
Tel: (11) 259-3251
Fax: (11) 259-8482

Associaçao Brasileira da Indústria Alimentícia
Av. Brigadeiro Faria Lima, 2003, 11o. andar
01451 São Paulo, SP
Tel: (11) 816-5733
Fax: (11) 814-6688

Franchising
Travessa Meruipe 18
04012-000 São Paulo, SP
Tel: (11) 571-1393
Fax: (11) 575-5590

Food Industry Association
Av. Brig. Faria Lima 2003, 11 andar, cjs. 1104/1116
01451-001 São Paulo, SP
Tel: (11) 816-5733
Fax: (11) 814-6688

Foundries
Av. Eng. Billings 526
05321-010 São Paulo, SP
Tel: (11) 819-2515
Fax: (11) 819-3783

Machines Manufacturers
Av. Jabaquara 2925, 3 andar
04045-902 São Paulo, SP
Tel: (11) 579-5044
Fax: (11) 579-3498

Motor-Vehicles Importers Association
Rua Bento da Andrade 103
04503-010 São Paulo, SP
Fax: (11) 884-1622

Motor-Vehicles Independent Importers Association
Av. Brigadeiro Faria Lima 1885, 4 andar, cj.420
01451-001 São Paulo, SP
Fax: (11) 211-9447

Pharmaceuticals Association
Rua Beira Rio 57, 7 andar
04548-050 São Paulo, SP
Tel: (11) 820-3775
Fax: (11) 822-6628

Plastics
Av. Paulista 2439, 8 andar, cjs.81/82
01311-936 São Paulo, SP
Tel: (11) 282-8288
Fax: (11) 282-8042

Printing Association
Rua Marquês de Itú 70, 12 andar
01270-900 São Paulo, SP
Tel: (11) 231-4733
Fax: (11) 231-4743

Software Association
Av. Brig. Faria Lima 1857, 3 andar, cj.307
01451-001 São Paulo, SP
Tel: (11) 813-2057/9511/9704
Fax: (11) 815-0359

Toiletries
Av. Paulista 1313, 9 andar, cj.901
01311-923 São Paulo, SP
Tel: (11) 251-1999
Fax: (11) 287-9207

Toys
Av. Pedroso de Morais 2219
05419-001 São Paulo, SP
Tel: (11) 816-3644
Fax: (11) 211-0226

CHAMBERS OF COMMERCE

American Chamber of Commerce São Paulo
Rua Alexandre Dumas 1976
04717-004 São Paulo, SP
Tel: (11) 246-9199
Fax: (11) 246-9080

American Chamber of Commerce Rio de Janeiro
Praça Pio X 15, 5 andar
20040-020 Rio de Janeiro, RJ
Tel: (21) 203-2477
Fax: (21) 263-4477

Confederacao das Associacoes Comerciais do Brasil
SCS, Edif. Presidente Dutra, Quadra 11
70327 Brasília
Tel: (61) 2230578

LAW FIRMS

Castro, Barros, Sobral e Xavier Advogados S.C.
Praia De Botafogo, 228 - 15 Andar
22359-900 Rio de Janeiro
Tel: (21) 551-1149
Fax: (21) 552-1796

H.B. Cavalcanti e Mazzillo Advogados
Rua Alvaro Alvim, 31 Grupos 1402-1502
CEP 20.031-010
Rio de Janeiro RJ
Tel: (21) 262 7738
Fax: (21) 240 1474

Franco, Bhering, Barbosa e Novaes
Avenida Rio Branco, 103
20040 Rio de Janeiro
Tel: (21) 252-2060
Fax: (21) 242-4193

NEWSPAPERS

Correio Braziliense
SIG Q2 Lotes 300/340
70610-901 Brasília DF
Tel: (61) 321-1314
Telex: 1727
Fax: (61) 321-2856

Journal Brasília
SIG Trecho 1 Lotes 585/645
70.610-400 Brasília DF
Tel: (61) 225-2515
Telex: 1208

Diário de Pernambuco
Praca da Indpendencia 12, 2 andar
50010-300 Recife PE
Tel: (81) 424-3666
Fax: (81) 424-2527
Telex: 1057

O Dia
Rua Riachuelo 359
20235 Rio de Janeiro RJ
Tel: (21) 272-8000
Fax: (21) 507-1767
Telex: 22385

O Globo
POB 1090
Rua Irineu Marinho 35
20233-900 Rio de Janeiro RJ
Tel: (21) 292-2000
Telex: 22595

Jornal do Brasil
Av. Brasil 500
São Cristovao
20949 Rio de Janeiro RJ
Tel: (21) 585-4422
Telex: 23262

Jornal do Comércio
Rua do Livramento 189
20225 Rio de Janeiro RJ
Tel: (21) 507-6313
Telex: 22193

Jornal dos Sports
Rua Tenente Possolo 15/25
Cruz Vermelha
20230 Rio de Janeiro RJ
Tel: (21) 232-8010
Telex: 39567

Ultima Hora
Rua Equador 702
20220 Rio de Janeiro RJ
Tel: (21) 223-2444
Fax: (21) 223-2444
Telex: 22551

Jornal da Bahia
Rua Peruvia Carneiro 220
41100 Salvador, BA
Tel: (71) 384-2919
Fax: (71) 384-5726
Telex: 1296

Jornal Correio da Bahia
Av. Luis Viana Filho s/n
41100 Salvador, BA
Tel: (71) 371-2811
Fax: (71) 231-3944
Telex: 1594

Jornal Correio da Bahia
Av. Tancredo Neves 1092
41820-020 Salvador BA
Tel: (71) 231-9683
Fax: (71) 231-1064
Telex: 2638

Diário do Grande ABC
Rua Catequese 562
09090-900 Santo André, SP
Tel: (11) 449-5533
Fax: (11) 449-5472
Telex: 44034

PERIODICALS

Amiga
Rua do Russel 766/804
22214 Rio de Janeiro RJ
Tel: (21) 285-0033
Fax: (21) 205-9998
Telex: 21525

Antenna-Eleconica Popular
Av. Marechal FLoiano 143
CP 1131
20080-005 Rio de Janeiro RJ
Tel: (21) 223-2442
Fax: (21) 263-8840

Carinho
Rua do Russel 766/804
22214 Rio de Janeiro RJ
Tel: (21) 285-0033
Fax: (21) 205-9998
Telex: 21525

Conjuntura Economica
Praia de Botafogo 190
22253-900 Rio de Janeiro RJ
Tel: (21) 551-3792

Desfile
Rua do Russel 766/804
22214 Rio de Janeiro RJ
Tel: (21) 285-0033
Fax: (21) 205-9998
Telex: 21525

Ele Ela
Rua do Russel 766/804
22214 Rio de Janeiro RJ
Tel: (21) 285-0033
Fax: (21) 205-9998
Telex: 21525

Manchete
Rua do Russel 766/804
20214 Rio de Janeiro RJ
Tel: (21) 285-0033
Fax: (21) 205-9998
Telex: 22214

RADIO AND TELEVISION

**Departmento Nacional de Servicos Privados
(Secretaria Nacional de Comunicacoes)**
Via N2
Anexo do Ministério da Infraestrutura
Esplanada dos Ministérios
Bloco R
70044 Brasília DF
Tel: (61) 223-3229
Fax: (61) 223-3916
Telex: 1175

**Empresa Brasileira de Comunicacao, SA
(Radiobrás) (Brazilian Communications Company)**
CP 04-0340
70710 Brasília DF
Tel: (61) 321-3949
Fax: (61) 321-7602
Telex: 1682

TV Bandeirantes-Canal 13
Rádio e Telvisao Bandirantes Ltda
Rua Radiantes 13
05699 São Paulo SP
Tel: (11) 842-3011
Fax: (11) 842-3067
Telex: 56375

RBS TV-Canal 12
Rua Radio y TV Gaúcha 189
90650 Porto Alegre RS
Tel: (512) 900-5000
Telex: 4118

TV Globo-Canal 4
Rua Lopes Quintas 303
Jardim Botanico
22463 Rio de Janeiro RJ
Tel: (21) 529-2000
Fax: (21) 294-2042
Telex: 22795

TV Manchete-Canal 6
Rua do Russel 766
20000 Rio de Janeiro RJ
Tel: (21) 265-2012
Telex: 21525

TV Record-Canal 7
Av. Miruna 713
Aeroporto
01000 São Paulo SP
Tel: (11) 542-9000
Fax: (11) 532-0894

TVSBT-Canal 4 de São Paulo, SA
Rua Dona Santa Veloso 535
Vila Guilherme
02050 São Paulo SP
Tel: (11) 292-9044
Fax: (11) 264-6004

**Associacao Brasileira de Emissoras de Rádio e
Televsao (ABERT)**
Mezanino do Hotel Nacional
salas 5 a 8
CP 04280
70322 Brasília DF
Tel: (61) 224-4600
Fax: (61) 321-7583
Telex: 2001

BANKS

Conselho Monetário Nacional
SBS
Edif. Banco do Brail
6 andar
Brasília DF

Banco do Brasil, SA
Sector Bancário Sul
Lote 23, Bloco C
Edif Sédelll
CP 562
Brasilia, DF
Tel: (61) 212-2633
Fax: (61) 223-0156
Telex: 8196

Banco do Estado do Rio Grande do Sul, SA
Rua Capitao Montanha 177
CP 505
90010 Porto Alegre RS
Tel: (521) 21-5023
Fax: (521) 28-6473
Telex: 474

Banco do Estado de Santa Catarina, SA
Rua Padre Miguelinho 80
Florianópolis SC
Tel: (48) 224-7222
Telex: 2501

STOCK EXCHANGES

Comissao de Valores Mobiliário CVM
SAS, Q02
Siderbrás 2 andar
Brasília DF
Tel: (61) 224-0779
Fax: (61) 225-9103

Bolsa de Valores do Rio de Janeiro
Praca XV de Novembro 20
20010 Rio de Janeiro RJ
Tel: (21) 271-1001
Fax: (21) 232-2796
Telex: 35100

Bolsa de Valores de São Paulo (BOVESPA)
Rua XV de Novembro 275
01013-001 São Paulo SP
Tel: (11) 258-7222
Fax: (11) 36-0871
Telex: 21000

INTERNET ADDRESSES

Usenet group
soc.culture.brazil

Brasil Web
http://www.escape.com/~jvgkny/Brasil.Web.html

Brazilian Mall
http://www.deltanet.com/brazil/

Brazilian Business Connection
http://www.embratel.net.br/infoserv/quattro/brbuscon/
brbuscon.htm

Online WWW Index
http://www.embratel.net.br/infoserv/online/windex/

Brazilian Embassy in Washington, DC
http://www.cr-df.rnp.br/hipertextos/usabremb/ht/
embport.html

Brunei

State of Brunei Darussalam

Economy

Overview

Despite certain cultural and historical similarities, Brunei stands substantially apart from neighboring Malaysia and Indonesia. The economy of this nation—constituted as a fully independent monarchy in 1984—is based on petroleum extraction. GDP soars when oil prices increase and plummets when oil prices drop. Recently, revenues have been barely adequate to cover expenditures in this small state in which the government provides numerous services; the disappearance of residual surpluses from prior high price years has made Brunei's undiversified economy even more vulnerable to current petroleum price fluctuations. The statist orientation of much of the economy has inhibited plans to attract private investment.

Trade

Oil and liquefied natural gas (LNG) account for virtually all of Brunei's exports. Because very few items are produced locally, almost everything must be imported. Major imports include basic manufactures, machinery, transportation equipment, chemicals, foodstuffs, and intermediate and consumer goods. Japan has been Brunei's main trading partner, followed by Singapore, the United States, and the United Kingdom. In an effort to develop import substitution and export industries, and promote general economic diversification, the government has attempted to encourage foreign investment. However, high costs, restrictions, the shortage of labor, and the small domestic market have limited investment and kept trade narrowly focused on the exchange of commodity exports for higher value-added imports.

Sectors

Agriculture Employing about five percent of the work force, agriculture (including forestry and fishing) contributes only slightly more than two percent of GDP. Despite government intentions to develop agriculture, little has been done, and Brunei must still import 80 percent of its food requirements.

Industry Accounting for about half of GDP and employing nearly 33 percent of the work force, industry is almost exclusively oriented toward petroleum extraction and processing. Despite plans to start manufacturing operations–ranging from high-tech semiconductor production to less capital, and skill-intensive areas such as food processing, textile production, furniture-making, and building materials (e.g., concrete and bricks)—little movement has occurred, and industrial development is limited by severe shortages of both skilled and unskilled labor.

Services Although it employs almost 60 percent of the work force and contributes nearly half of GDP, Brunei's service sector remains relatively undeveloped. Most service activities involve local distribution.

Trends

Brunei's GDP continues to rise slowly, but at a rate insufficient to cover the growth of its expenditures. The government has made some reforms it hopes will help the citizens and the economy; however, the changes may be too heavily dependent on funding from oil revenues for effective implementation. If oil prices continue to remain flat, prospects for Brunei's economy could stagnate. Although Brunei has sought to limit the number of foreign workers to maintain social homogeneity and control, it may soon have little choice, unless the size and training level of the domestic work force can be increased dramatically.

At a Glance

THE COUNTRY

Location Southeastern Asia, on the northern coast of Borneo, nearly surrounded by Malaysia.
Terrain Flat, eastern coastal plain rises to mountains and hilly lowland in the west.
Climate Equatorial, with high temperatures, humidity, and rainfall.

THE PEOPLE

Population 285,000
Ethnic composition
Malay 70%
Other indigenous 5%
Chinese 18%
Other.. 7%
Religious composition
Muslim 63%
Buddhism... 14%
Christian.. 8%
Indigenous beliefs and other................................ 15%
Languages spoken Malay, English, Chinese, and Iban and other indigenous dialects.
Education and Literacy Education through university training is free. Most college students attend institutions abroad. Literacy among younger people is 95%. For the entire population, literacy is 69% for adult females; 85% for adult males. These rates should equalize in the future as more women complete their education.
Labor force
Total:...89,000
By occupation, government 47.5%, oil, gas, services, and construction 41.9%, agriculture 3.8%.

COUNTRY FACTS

Political and Legal In this constitutional sultanate, the sultan is both head of state and prime minister. The legal system is based on the Indian penal code and English common law.
Telephone Service throughout the country is adequate, and is especially good to adjacent Malaysia. International calls are more reliable than service within the country. International country code: [673]. City codes: Bandar Seri Begawan (2) , Mumong (3).
Transportation Transportation can be difficult. There are two seaports for shipping, but they aren't adequate for all deepwater traffic. Roads are being built, but many are still unpaved. There are bus services, but they are unreliable. The Brunei River is a major throughway.Two airports serve the country.
Environment Oil industry reserves are estimated to last 20 years. Forests are strictly protected by law. The government is primarily concerned with the efficient development of other industries with minimal impact on the environment.
Media Radio is the dominant media. There are four AM/FM stations and one television station. There are only a couple of commercial daily newspapers and a weekly paper published by the government. Papers from Singapore and China circulate widely.
Health The free government-sponsored health care system is one of Asia's finest. Malaria has been eradicated, and cholera is virtually non-existent. The government also subsidizes food and housing. The life expectancy for males is 73 years; for females, 76 years.

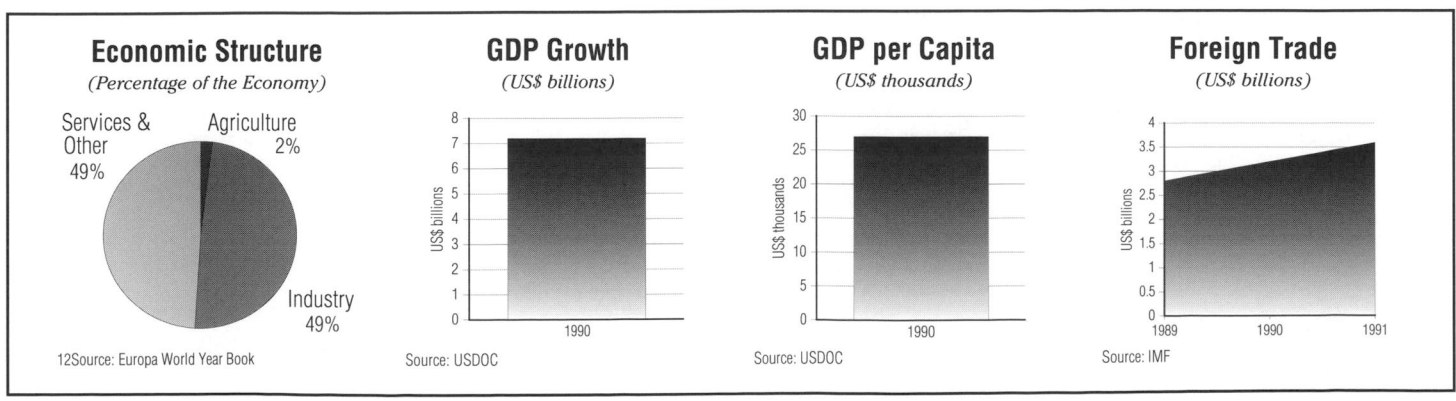

Economic Structure
(Percentage of the Economy)

Services & Other 49%
Agriculture 2%
Industry 49%

12Source: Europa World Year Book

GDP Growth
(US$ billions)

Source: USDOC

GDP per Capita
(US$ thousands)

Source: USDOC

Foreign Trade
(US$ billions)

Source: IMF

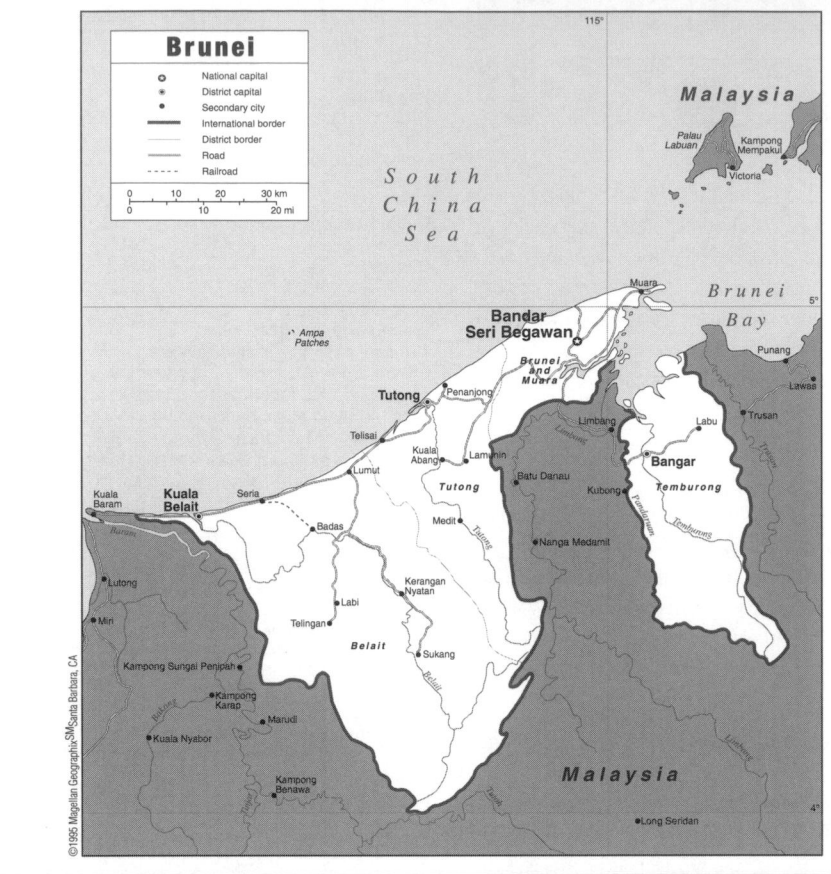

COMMUNICATIONS

Telephone Telephone facilities are modern and reliable, even state-of-the-art in urban areas.
Fax Fax and telex networks are available and easily meet international business needs.
Post office Postal services are available and reliable. Express delivery services are available through DHL and Federal Express.
Media Radio is the dominant media. There are four AM/FM stations and one television station. There are only a couple of commercial daily newspapers and a weekly paper published by the government. Papers from Singapore and China circulate widely.

BEST TRAVEL BOOKS

Lonely Planet, Malaysia, Singapore and Brunei Travel Survival Kit. In a word, excellent. 552 pages with 16 color pages.
All-Asia Travel Guide, Southeast Asia, Volume One. The best guide available for the business traveler.

NATIONAL TOURIST OFFICE

National Tourist Office
Information Bureau
Department of Information
Prime Minister's Office
Bandar Seri Begawan 2041
Tel: (2) 240400

USEFUL TELEPHONE NUMBERS

If you are calling from outside Brunei, you will need to add the country code [673] and any other international dialing requirements from within your country.
• Chamber of Commerce .... (2) 236601
• Chamber of Commerce and Industry ..... (2) 227297
• Chinese Chamber of Commerce .... (2) 224374
• Indian Chamber of Commerce .... (2) 223886
• Borneo Bulletin Newspaper .... (3) 334344
• The Brunei Press .... (3) 334344
• Royal Brunei Airlines Ltd .... (2) 240500
• Brunei Shell Tankers .... (3) 773999
• Capital Trading & Printing .... (2) 244541
• Radio Television Brunei .... (2) 243111
• Ministry of Development .... (2) 241911
• Ministry of Law .... (2) 244872
• Ministry of Foreign Affairs .... (2) 241177
• Ministry of Finance .... (2) 242405
Hotels
• Ang's Hotel .... (2) 243553
• Brunei Hotel .... (2) 242372
• Hotel Sentosa .... (3) 234341
• Seaview Hotel .... (3) 332651
• Sheraton Utama Hotel .... (2) 244272
Credit Card Information
Lost or stolen credit cards (call collect to the US, regardless of which country the card was issued in).
• Amex .... [1] (919) 3333211
• Diner's Club.................................. [1] (303) 7991504
• MasterCard .... [1] (314) 2756690
• Visa .... [1] (410) 5817931

Travelogue

WORKWEEK

Business Eight hours per day, six days a week.
Government Monday-Thursday 7:45 am to 12:15 pm. and 1:30 pm to 5:30 pm. Closed on Fridays and Sundays; shorter working days during Ramadan.
Banks Monday-Friday 9:00 am to 3:00 pm. Saturday 9:00 am to 11:00 am. Closed on Saturday afternoons and Sundays.
Retail Daily 7:30 am to 9:00 pm.

HOLIDAYS

Holidays 1996
January 1 New Year's Day
February * Meraj
February * Chinese New Year
February * National Day
March First day of Ramadan*
March Good Friday*
April 2 Anniversary of the Revelation of the Koran
April Hari Raya Puasa*
June 1 Anniversary of the Royal Brunei Armed Forces
June Hari Raya Haji*
June Banks' half-yearly closing*
July 13 First day of "Hijrah (Muslim New Year)
July15 The Sultan's Birthday
September 21 Maulud
December 25 Christmas Day
December 31 Banks' yearly closing
*Dates change and subject to alterations.

VISA AND PASSPORT

Visits up to 30 days for Malaysians, Singaporeans, and British nationals do not require a visa. Visas are waived for visitors from the following countries up to 14 days: Indonesia, Philippines, Thailand, Belgium, Canada, Germany, France, Japan, South Korea, Luxembourg, the Netherlands, Switzerland, Sweden, and the Republic of Maldives. Visitors must be in possession of a valid passport. Visas can be obtained at Brunei embassies overseas. If there is no embassy in your country, try the nearest British diplomatic mission.

DEPARTURE FORMALITIES

There are no departure formalities for Brunei. There are no currency issues for departure in Brunei.

IMMUNIZATION

If arriving from an infected area, yellow fever inoculations are required above one year of age. Malaria, cholera, and small pox inoculations are not required.

TIPPING

Tipping for good service is appreciated in Brunei. The tip for taxis should be considered on the negotiated dollar amount before taking the ride as taxis are not metered in Brunei.

CRIME

Crime is not a problem in Brunei, but normal precautions should be taken.

INFRASTRUCTURE

Brunei Darussalam is a fast growing country which offers an extensive and stable infrastructure. Helicopter services are available at Anduki, a private airfield. Strategically located airports, seaport facilities, internally sound communications and transports systems reach the most remote areas. Taxis are hard to come by, but can be booked in advance. They are not metered; negotiate a fare before setting out. Very little public transportation is available since most people own their own cars, although buses do run. Cars are not available to rent in this small country. River taxis are the popular mode of transportation for residents of water villages, larger water taxis operate daily to the Temburong district. There are no public railways in Brunei.

Foreign Trade

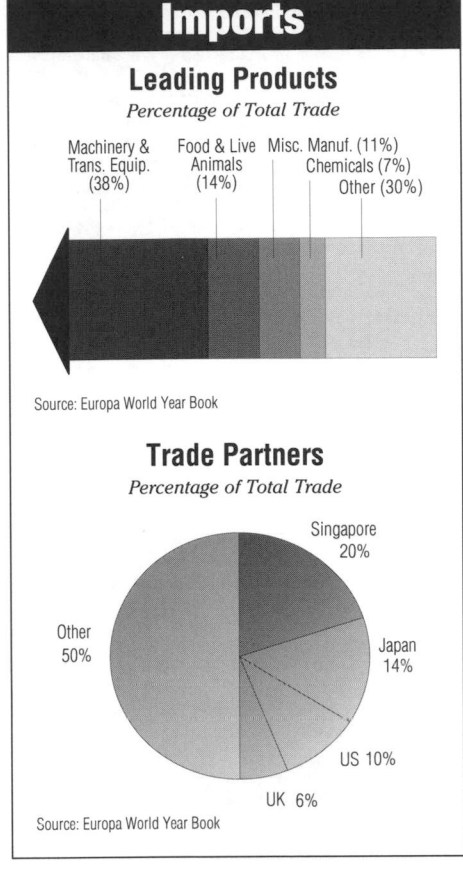

Imports

Leading Products
Percentage of Total Trade

Machinery & Trans. Equip. (38%)
Food & Live Animals (14%)
Misc. Manuf. (11%)
Chemicals (7%)
Other (30%)

Source: Europa World Year Book

Trade Partners
Percentage of Total Trade

Singapore 20%
Japan 14%
Other 50%
US 10%
UK 6%

Source: Europa World Year Book

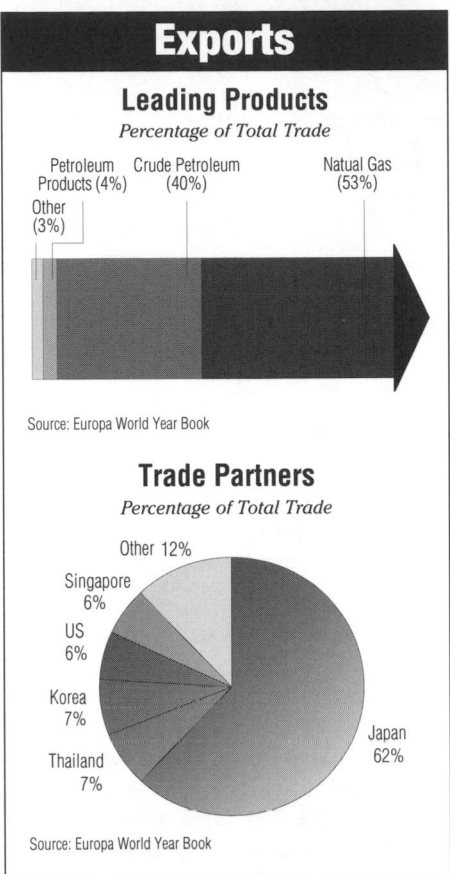

Exports

Leading Products
Percentage of Total Trade

Petroleum Products (4%)
Crude Petroleum (40%)
Natual Gas (53%)
Other (3%)

Source: Europa World Year Book

Trade Partners
Percentage of Total Trade

Other 12%
Singapore 6%
US 6%
Korea 7%
Thailand 7%
Japan 62%

Source: Europa World Year Book

Opportunities

FOR IMPORTING TO BRUNEI
- chemicals
- construction, machine, and transport equipment
- electronic and manufactured goods
- food products, furniture, and household appliances

FOR EXPORTING FROM BRUNEI
- natural gas
- oil and petroleum products

GROWTH SECTORS
- agriculture
- fishing
- industry

Trade News

RULES AND REGULATIONS
- **Alcohol** Non-Muslims over 17 years of age may be allowed to bring a small amount of liquor into the country.
- **Duties** Duties, which may be specific or ad valorem, are waived for all goods except non-development and luxury items. No duty is levied on foodstuffs, building and construction material, industrial machinery, and non-alcoholic beverages.
- **Imports** Most items may be imported under an open general license. However, some goods, including certain drugs and poisons, used vehicles, gaming machines, and converted timber, require special import licenses. Brunei maintains a list of prohibited imports.

Legal

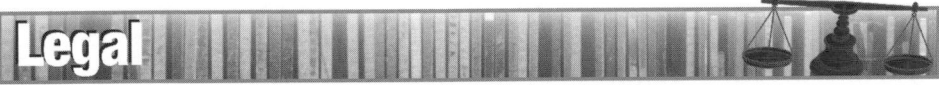

Legal System
Islamic Law and English Common Law, with an independent judiciary. Legislation is by the Sultan.

Intellectual Property Protection
Patents Brunei is not a member of any international patent organization, and foreign patents must be re-registered in Brunei to be protected.

Trademarks No foreign trademarks are considered legal.

Copyrights No international copyright treaties have been signed; it is difficult for foreign copyrights to be protected.

Trade Secrets Few laws regarding trade protection exist, and it is difficult to prove trade secret violations in the courts.

Business Registration
All businesses must be registered with the Registrar. Public companies require a minimum of seven founders, and private businesses require a minimum of two founders. At least half of the board must be Brunei nationals or residents. Business registered documents can be written in English or Malay.

Contracts and Dispute Resolution
All contracts must be written to be considered valid. Most disputes are handled by the local magistrates' courts, although more serious cases go before the High Court that meets for about two weeks every few months.

Labor
The Trade Unions Act of 1962 permits the formation of trade unions, but prohibits any affiliation outside Brunei. There are four registered unions in the oil sector, with total membership of less than 5 percent of the work force. Skilled labor is in short supply, and 33 percent of the work force is foreign.

Legal Matters

LEGAL BRIEFS
- **Levels of courts** There are five levels of courts with final recourse available through the Privy Council in London.
- **The Court of Appeals** Decisions of the High Court can be taken to the Court of Appeals, presided over by the President and two commissioners appointed by the Sultan.
- **Agreement with Hong Kong** Brunei has an arrangement with the government of Hong Kong whereby Hong Kong judges are appointed as the judges for Brunei's High Court and Court of Appeal.
- **Companies** There are few restrictions on the types of business which can be set up in Brunei. Businesses which directly affect the public interest such as banks, finance companies, motor vehicle insurers, money-lenders, and travel agents must obtain special licenses from the appropriate government authority.
- **Land ownership** Non-Bruneians are normally prohibited from owning land, but leases of up to seven years may be registered with the Land Department.

LEGAL CONTACTS
Hilborne, Hawkin & Co.
Ste. 31, 3rd Floor, Britannia House
38 Jalan Cator
Bandar Seri Begawan 2085
Tel: (2) 228382
Fax: (2) 228389

Y.C. Lee & Company
Suites 507-508, 5th Floor
Kompleks Jalan Sultan
Bandar Seri Begawan 2085
Tel: (2) 228725
Fax: (2) 240786

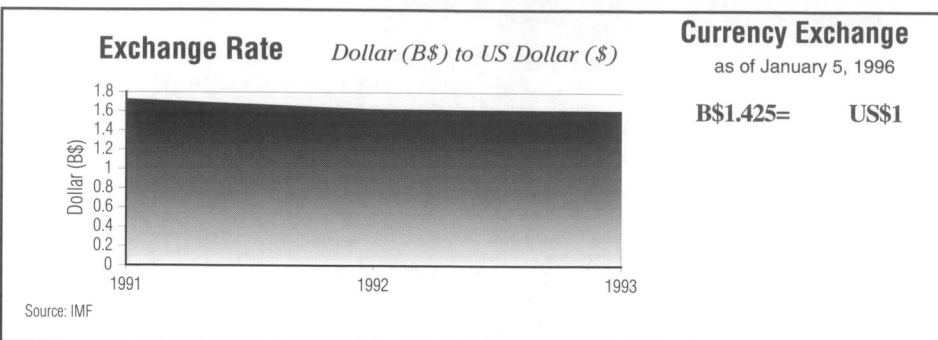

Exchange Rate *Dollar (B$) to US Dollar ($)*

Dollar (B$)

1.8
1.6
1.4
1.2
1
0.8
0.6
0.4
0.2
0

1991   1992   1993

Source: IMF

Currency Exchange

as of January 5, 1996

B$1.425=   US$1

Currency

The currency in use is the Brunei dollar (B$), which is divided in 100 cents.

Foreign Exchange

There are no exchange controls in Brunei, except in the case of capital or profits to be repatriated to a country outside the "Scheduled Territories" of the Sterling area, for which permission must be obtained from the Currency Board. Brunei has no central bank but its functions are undertaken by the Department of Financial Services (Treasury Department), the Brunei Currency Board, and the Brunei Investment Agency.

Investment Incentives

The Brunei government welcomes foreign investment in most sectors of the economy, and it offers incentives to encourage the development of industrial enterprises. An enterprise may qualify for tax incentives if it is awarded pioneer status by the Economic Development Board. Pioneer status will be granted to a firm if 1) it is of a kind not previously operating in Brunei on a commercial scale and is suited to local economic requirements or development, and there are favorable prospects for the industry to develop exports; or 2) there are insufficient local facilities for the industry to operate on a viable commercial scale, and it is expedient and in the public interest to encourage the development or establishment of the industry.

Incentives include tax exemption from the date it commences production on a time scale which varies according to the size of its fixed capital investments. Tax exemption may be extended by up to three additional years in certain circumstances. Pioneer companies are also exempted from customs duty on items to be installed in the pioneer factory, and they are exempted from taxes on imported raw materials if the materials are not available or produced in Brunei for the production of the pioneer products.

Brunei also offers incentives to any established enterprises intending to incur new capital expenditure for purpose of the manufacture or increased manufacture of "approved products."

Investment Restrictions

Generally, there is no restriction on foreign participation in equity except in the case of newly established firms engaging in car dealerships. Joint-venture companies are required to train local staff on managerial and technical levels, and joint-venture companies should have active local participation in both the areas of capital investment and management.

Money Matters

BITS AND PIECES

- **Direct taxation** Brunei does not have any direct taxation. There is no income tax even within partnerships. Individuals do not pay any capital gains tax and profits arising from the sale of capital assets are not taxable.
- **Pioneer industries** Tax exemption is available for a minimum of two years for a fixed capital investment of up to US$350,000, and a maximum of five years of a fixed capital investment of over US$1 million.
- **Capital gains** There is no capital gains tax. However, the Collector of Income Tax can establish that the gains from part of the normal trading activities can become taxable as revenue.
- **Tax scope** A nonresident company is only taxed on its income arising in Brunei Darussalam.
- **Residence** A company, whether incorporated locally or overseas, is considered as resident in Brunei for tax purposes if the control and management of its business is exercised in Brunei. The control and management of a company is normally regarded as resident in Brunei if, among other things, its directors meetings are held in Brunei.
- **Withholding taxes** Interest paid to nonresident companies under a charge, debenture, or in the respect of a loan, is subject to withholding tax of 20 percent. There are no other withholding taxes.
- **Reporting** Companies incorporated in Brunei are not required to file their annual accounts with the Registrar of Companies. However, most business organizations are required to submit accounting data annually to the Economic Planning Unit for statistical purposes.

BANKS

International Bank of Brunei Bhd.
Bangunan IBB, Lott 155
POB 2725
Bandar Seri Begawan
Tel: (2) 220686

Citibank NA (USA)
Darussalam Komplex 12-15
Jalan Sultan Bandar
Bandas Seri Begawan 2085
Tel: (2) 243983
Fax: (2) 225704

The Hongkong and Shanghai Banking Corp (Hong Kong)
cnr Jalan Sultan and Jalan Pemancha
POB 59
Bandar Seri Begawan
Tel: (2) 242305
Fax: (2) 241316
Telex: 2273

Malayan Banking Bhd (Malaysia)
148 Jalan Pemancha
Bandar Seri Begawan 2085
Tel: (2) 242494
Fax: (2) 226101
Telex: 2316

Overseas Union Bank (Singapore)
RBA Plaza Unit G5
Jalan Sultan
Bandar Seri Begawan
Tel: (2) 225477
Fax: (2) 240792
Telex: 2256

Standard Chartered BAnk (UK)
51-55 Jalan Sultan
POB 186
Bandar Seri Begawan 1901
Tel: (2) 242386
Fax: (2) 242390
Telex: 2223

United Malayan Banking Corp Bhd (Malaysia)
141 Jalan Pemancha
POB 435
Bandar Seri Begawan 2085
Tel: (2) 222516
Telex: 2207

TAXATION

Taxation requires sophisticated knowledge of complex rules and regulations specific to each country. For more detailed information we suggest you refer to the Ernst & Young Corporate Tax Guide and Directory, available from the Ernst & Young accounting office in your country, or from:

Ernst & Young
POB 2162
Bandar Seri Begawan 1921
Brunei Darussalam
Tel: (2) 239139
Fax: (2) 239142

- Limited companies, regardless of place of incorporation, must pay corporate income tax on any income derived from Brunei. Some industries may be exempted from tax by the Sultan-in-Council if they are essential to the country's development.

At a Glance

Corporate Income Tax (%)	30
Capital Gains Tax Rate (%)	0
Branch Tax Rate (%)	30
Withholding Tax (%)	
Dividends	0
Interest (a)	20
Royalties	0
Branch Remittance Tax	0
Net Operating Losses (Years)	
Carryback	0
Carryforward (b)	6

(a) This rate is applicable to payments to nonresident companies. A nonresident company is one that is neither incorporated in, nor has a place of business in Brunei.
(b) Continuity of trade or ownership is not required to carry forward losses. A loss in one trade can be set off against other income sources. An unabsorbed capital allowance can be carried forward indefinitely if the company involved continues to carry on the same trade.

Marketing

Overview

Brunei is heavily dependent on international trade to supply many of its needs, especially in the areas of capital, raw, and intermediate goods, as well as consumer and service products unavailable from its small, albeit well-funded, domestic economy. Demand for many foreign supplied goods and services should be strong in affluent Brunei at least through the end of the century. Given its location, Brunei also provides potential access to one of the largest and fastest growing regional markets in the world. The government operates many key portions of the economy and provides a wide range of extensive social services, meaning that it has a large, ongoing need to procure numerous goods and services. It often does this through foreign tender.

Agents, Distributors, and Partners

Distribution is fairly sophisticated and developed in the urban areas of the country, although considerably less so in rural areas. Many overseas firms find choosing an agent to be the simplest way to start trade here. A natural resident in Brunei must be appointed as an agent. Most larger multinational firms form joint ventures with local citizens, qualifying the enterprise for favorable loan rates. To receive such benefits, these companies must make capital investments and train local staff for management and technical levels.

Advertising

Standard advertising is poorly developed: there are few outlets, and while Brunei is fairly international and cosmopolitan, it is also officially Islamic and restricts "improper" advertising. Radio Brunei broadcasts from four AM/FM stations and one television station; both accept some advertising. The English-language *Borneo Bulletin* is the only local daily newspaper and the only print outlet to accept advertising. The government puts out a weekly paper—*Pelita* in Malay and *Brunei Darussalam* in English—as does the Shell Oil Company—*Salam*, in English, Malay, and Chinese—although neither accepts advertising. The *Straits Times* and other English, Malay, and Chinese papers circulate from Singapore, and these accept advertising.

Business Culture

Greetings and Courtesies

The two largest ethnic groups are Malays (about 78 percent) and Chinese (about 18 percent). Their greetings and courtesies are often very different. Malays are generally Muslim, and their accepted greeting is the handshake, which is usually accompanied by a slight bow or nod of the head. In addition, when an older person enters a room people usually stand. Women and elderly people often don't shake hands but will offer a verbal greeting.

Business Ethic and Framework

The government is the country's largest employer, and government workers enjoy subsidized holidays as well as trips to Mecca. This gives people little incentive to work particularly hard or take risks. A businessperson could find a sympathetic ear and willing associates for a venture that promotes this diversification

Meetings and Decision Making

Punctuality is a sign of respect and politeness, so be on time for appointments. However, in this leisured culture people are often late for appointments. Small talk often begins meetings, with business addressed after people feel comfortable with each other. Consensus is important to Malays and they will probably require time for discussion before making a decision. These conversations will be amongst themselves, and never with outsiders present. Chinese try to avoid saying no, for fear of causing embarrassment or losing face. Rather than say no, they might say something is inconvenient or suggest an alternative.

Women

Brunei is primarily a Muslim country and women should be prepared for the restrictions this culture places on them. When meeting Malays, women will be asked personal questions about their age, marital status, and children. (These questions are asked of both men and women.) Commenting on a woman's looks might be regarded as flirting, which is taboo and might cost a woman her job. Women should dress tastefully and conservatively.

Marketing in Brunei

MARKETING TIPS

- **Private industry** Most private businesses are owned by members of the Chinese minority and are staffed by expatriates.
- **Government markets** Government tenders often list a wide variety of seemingly random products which must be bid in the same offering. Tenders are issued weekly in the government newspaper. Local firms specialize in dealing with such offers, and foreigners interested in bidding should consult with these companies.
- **Legal advice** Although not technically required, retaining a local attorney to draw up agency agreements, contracts, and sales agreements is generally advisable.
- **Product sensitivity** Brunei is an Islamic country whose adherents avoid pork and alcohol; local Chinese and Malays may have other cultural preferences and restrictions.

AD AGENCIES

Adison Marketing Services
POB 575
BSB 1905
22 Spg 80-27 Jln Gadong
Bandar Seri Bagawan
Tel: (2) 42 7899
Fax: (2) 44 3900

Ahmad Isa Lee & Lind
Unit 407-A 410A 4th Floor
Bang Wisma Jaya
Bandar Seri Begawan
Tel: (2) 23 9091
Fax: (2) 23-9096

Cultural Cautions

DO'S

- Remember that Brunei is an Islamic country with strict laws governing public behavior.
- When dealing with Chinese, remember the importance of face. Never do or say anything that could cause a Chinese to lose face.

DON'TS

- The head is considered sacred. Do not touch a person's head (not even a child's).
- When entertaining Malays, never offer alcohol, pork, or meat that is not properly prepared.

CUSTOMS

- Do not make a fist with one hand and hit it against the open or cupped palm of the other hand. To Malays, this is an obscene gesture.
- Neat, tasteful pants, shirt, and tie (no jacket) will be appropriate attire for most business situations. If you wear a jacket and no one else does, you may remove yours once the meeting begins.

OBSERVATIONS

- Brunei's cultural center is its capital, Bandar Seri Begawan. Other cities are Seria and Kuala Belait. Inland areas are mainly undeveloped, have little contact with the outside world, and are quite conservative and traditional.

NEGOTIATIONS

- Malays can be both subtle and aggressive.
- A common tactic is delaying major negotiations until you're about to leave the country, then making unreasonable demands.
- Malaysian Chinese sometimes negotiate with several competing companies at the same time and let it be known they are doing so as a way of applying pressure.

GOVERNMENT AGENCIES

Land Transport Department
Km 4, Jalan Gadong
Bandar Seri Begawan
Tel: (2) 224775
Fax: (2) 224775

Ministry of Communication
Old Airport
Berakas
Bandar Seri Begawan 1150
Tel: (2) 242526
Fax: (2) 220127

Ministry of Culture, Youth and Sports
Jalan Residency
Bandar Seri Begawan 1200
Tel: (2) 240585
Fax: (2) 241620

Ministry of Development
Jalan Airport Lama
Berakas 1190
Bandar Seri Begawan
Tel: (2) 241911
Telex: 2722 midev bu

Ministry of Education
Jalan Airport Lama
Berakas
Bandar Seri Begawan 1170
Tel: (2) 244233
Fax: (2) 240250

Ministry of Finance
Bandar Seri Begawan 1130
Tel: (2) 242405
Fax: (2) 241829

Ministry of Foreign Affairs
Jalan Subok
Bandar Seri Begawan 1120
Tel: (2) 241177
Fax: (2) 229904

Ministry of Health
Old Airport
Bandar Seri Begawan, 1210
Tel: (2) 226640
Fax: (2) 240980

Department of Civil Aviation
Brunei International Airport
Bandar Seri Begwan 2015
Tel: (2) 330142
Fax: (2) 331706
Telex: 2267

CHAMBERS OF COMMERCE

Brunei State Chamber of Commerce
POB 2246
Bandar Seri Begawan 1922
Tel: (2) 236601 Telex: 2214
Fax: (2) 228389

Brunei Malay Chamber of Commerce and Industry
Bangunan Guru-Guru
Melayu Brunei
Suite 301, 2nd Floor
Jalan Kianggeh
Bandar Seri Begawan 1910
Tel: (2) 227297
Fax: (2) 227298
Telex: 2445

Chinese Chamber of Commerce
POB 2819
Jalan Pretty
Bandar Seri Begawan
Tel: (2) 224374

Indian Chamber of Commerce
POB 974
Bandar Seri Begawan 1909
Tel: (2) 223886
Fax: (2) 229271

ACCOUNTING FIRMS

Coopers & Lybrand
POB 1628
Bandar Seri Begawan 1916
Tel: (2) 2233341
Fax: (2) 242402

Ernst & Young
POB 2162
Bandar Seri Begawan 1921
Tel: (2) 239139

Goh Tan & Co. (Deloitte Touche)
POB 1966
Bandar Seri Begawan 1919
Tel: (2) 223640
Fax: (2) 223380

Nanafiah Raslan & Mohamad (Arthur Andersen & Co)
POB 2470
Bandar Seri Begawan 1924
Tel: (2) 220564
Fax: (2) 228542

Lee & Raman
POB 502
Bandar Seri Begawan 1905
Tel: (2) 225125
Fax: (2) 22 8426

P L Yap & Co
POB 682
Bandar Seri Begawan 1906
Tel: (2) 42 5194
Fax: (2) 44 0884

Price Waterhouse
POB 2843
Bandar Seri Begawan 1928
Tel: (2) 22 8593
Fax: (2) 22 8594

NEWSPAPERS

Borneo Bulletin
74 Jalan Sungei
POB 69
Kuala Belait 6000
Tel: (3) 334344
Fax: (3) 334400
Telex: 3336

Brunei Darussalam Newsletter
Dept of Information, Prime Minister's Office
Istana Nurul Iman
Bandar Seri Bagawan

Pelita
Brunei Dept of Information Prime Minister's Office
Istana Nurul Iman
Bandar Seri Begawan 2041
Fax: (2) 225942

Salam
c/o Brunei Shell Petroleum Co
Sdn Bhd
Seria 7082
Tel: (3) 78624
Fax: (3) 78494

RADIO & TELEVISION

Radio Television Brunei
Jalan Elizabeth II
Bandar Seri Begawan 2042
Tel: (2) 243111
Fax: (2) 241822

TRANSPORTATION FIRMS

Econopak Forwarding Co
POB 377
Gadong 3103
22nd Floor Bang Hallmatut Saadiah
Bandar Seri Begawan
Tel: (2) 44 6800

International Packing Service
Rm. 4 & 9 1st Floor
Freight Terminal Building
Bandar Seri Begawan
Tel: (2) 33 3297
Fax: (2) 33 3754

ISMACO Forwarders
POB 382
Gadong 3103
Tel: (2) 33 5869

Multimodal Sea and Airfreight Services SND BHD
POB 1054
Bandar Seri Begawan 3110
Tel: (2) 44 5089
Fax: (2) 24 4736

ZAS Co. SDN BHD
POB 464
Kuala Belait 6004
Tel: (3) 33 1751
Fax: (3) 33 1751

Skynet Sunny
145 2nd Floor
Jin Permancha
Bandar Seri Begawan
Tel: (2) 22 2940
Fax: (2) 24 3433

Abdul Saman Freight Forwarding
Block C, No. 10
Beribi Industrial Complex 1
Jalan Gadong
POB 2984
Bandar Seri Begawan
Tel: (2) 44 8278
Fax: (2) (2) 44 7397

Bee Seng Shipping Company
1 Mile, Jalan Tuton
POB 92
Bandar Seri Begawan
Telex: 2219

Brunei Shell Tankers Sdn Bhd
Seria 7082
Tel: (3) 773999
Telex: 3313

Royal Brunei Airlines Ltd
RBA Plaza
POB 737
Bandar Seri Begawan 1907
Tel: (2) 240500
Fax: (2) 244737
Telex: 2737

INTERNET ADDRESSES

About Brunei
http://sunsite.nus.sg/SEAlinks/brunei-info.html
Brunei Backgrounder
http://www.ic.gov/94fact/country/38.html

Bulgaria

Republic of Bulgaria

Economy

Overview

Bulgaria is largely an industrial economy, and the industrial sector employs over a third of the Bulgarian work force. Bulgaria has grown since World War II largely as a result of aid furnished by the Soviet Union, and its seemingly endless demand for heavy industrial products. As such, Bulgaria now finds itself with an abundance of outdated industrial equipment and an economy unprepared to develop other sectors. The government recognizes this problem, and has made preliminary moves to diversify the economic base, but progress has been slow due to the faltering economies of many neighboring Eastern European countries.

Trade

Foreign trade is critical to Bulgaria's prosperity. Roughly US$16.8 billion worth of Bulgarian goods are exported each year; about the same amount is imported, mostly for use as industrial product inputs. Principal trading partners include Russia, Germany, Italy, the US, and developing economies such as the Baltic countries. The Bulgarian tradition of trading manufactures for Russian raw materials (mostly energy) is slowly being replaced by the exportation of agricultural products and light manufactures in exchange for consumer goods.

Sectors

Agriculture Although private agriculture was legalized only in 1990, nearly 25 percent of the country's laborers build their workday around the harvesting of such products as grain, tobacco, fruits, vegetables, and sunflower seeds. Tobacco accounts for nearly 20 percent of the value of all agricultural production. Other agricultural output is in livestock, such as sheep, hogs, and poultry, cheese, and wine. Despite its lower priority, agriculture is an integral piece in Bulgaria's economic puzzle. Only 40 percent of the land is arable, but the nation has one of the highest land ratios proportionate to its population in all of Europe.

Industry Despite industry being the hub of Bulgarian economic activity for over 40 years, the country has only recently stepped into more modernized industrialization. As such, robotics and machine building are becoming part of the nation's plan to overhaul this sector. Mining and quarrying have shown strong growth in the recent past, as the country seeks to diversify its industrial base.

Services Most Bulgarian service jobs continue to be in the government sector. Banking and other financial services have simply not yet had the chance to develop into significant contributors to GDP. Tourism, however, has been especially lucrative for the past several years, and will remain strong throughout the 1990s.

Trends

Bulgaria's current economic plan involves modernizing and reconstructing existing plants and equipment rather than simply initiating new projects. Bulgaria also plans to maintain its strong ties with Russia, while being more active in its relations with West European countries and certain developing countries—especially those of the Middle East and Africa.

At a Glance

THE COUNTRY

Location Southeastern Europe, on the Balkan Peninsula, bordering the Black Sea, between Romania and Turkey.
Terrain About 75 percent mountainous with lowlands in the north and south.
Climate Temperate, with dry, hot summers and damp, cold winters.

THE PEOPLE

Population 8,400,000
Ethnic composition
Bulgarian 85.3%
Turk 8.5%
Gypsy 2.6%
Macedonian 2.5%
Armenian 0.3%
Russian 0.2%
Other 0.6%
Religious composition
Bulgarian Orthodox 85%
Muslims 13%
Jewish 0.8%
Roman Catholic 0.5%
Protestant 0.5%
Other 0.5%
Languages spoken Bulgarian, Turkish, and Gypsy; some English, German, French, and Russian.
Education and literacy Education is free and compulsory to age 15. Scientific, technical, and vocational training is stressed. The government estimates that literacy is 98 percent; Western sources estimate at a much lower rate.
Labor force
Total: 4,000,000
By occupation: agriculture 22%; industry and commerce 43%; construction 8.3%; transport 5.9%; government 1.3%; and other 19.5%.

COUNTRY FACTS

Political and legal An emerging democracy in transition; the legal system is based on Civil law system, with some Soviet law influence.
Telephone An extensive, but antiquated transmission system; communications within and to Bulgaria are difficult, though major programs are underway to modernize the system. Local and long-distance telephone and telegraph services are available. International country code: [359]. Selected city codes: Sofia (2), Varna (52).
Transportation Rail service is government-owned and commonly used for freight traffic. The national road system is generally acceptable. Water transport is significant through three major river ports and two major seaports. There are many airports, and several foreign airlines serve Sofia.
Environment Government concern for the environment has precipitated penalties for automobile pollution, the construction of a waste recycling plant, and a limitation on industrial development around the capital. Pollution of the rivers, deforestation, and soil contamination from metallurgical plants and industrial wastes are current environmental issues.
Media State-owned and controlled, the media generally reports accurately and objectively, including the opposition positions. There are 20 AM and 15 FM radio stations and 29 television stations.
Health Private and government-sponsored health care are both available. Hospital care is inadequate. Life expectancy of males is 69 years; of females, 74 years.

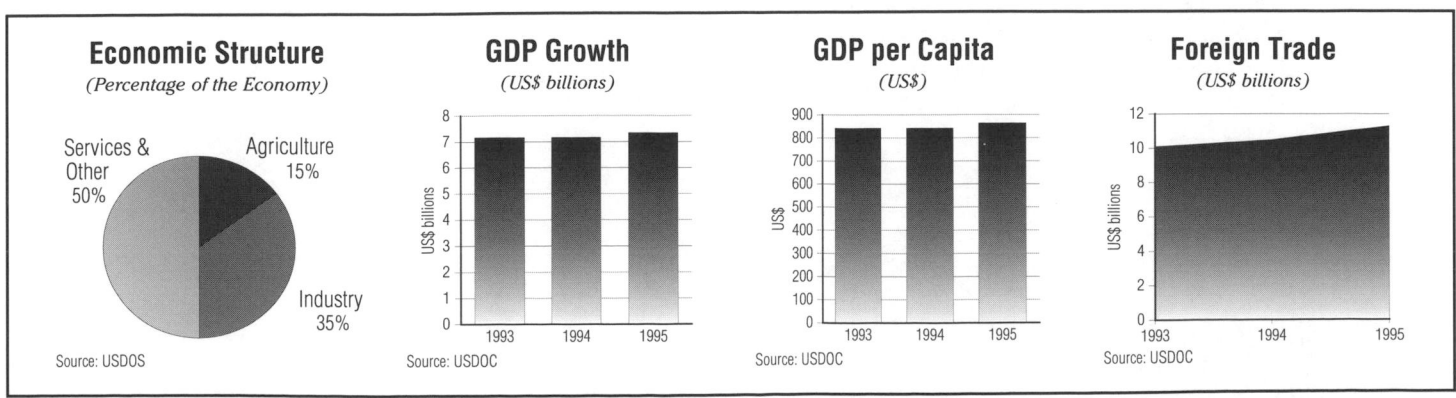

Economic Structure
(Percentage of the Economy)

Services & Other 50%
Agriculture 15%
Industry 35%

Source: USDOS

GDP Growth
(US$ billions)

Source: USDOC

GDP per Capita
(US$)

Source: USDOC

Foreign Trade
(US$ billions)

Source: USDOC

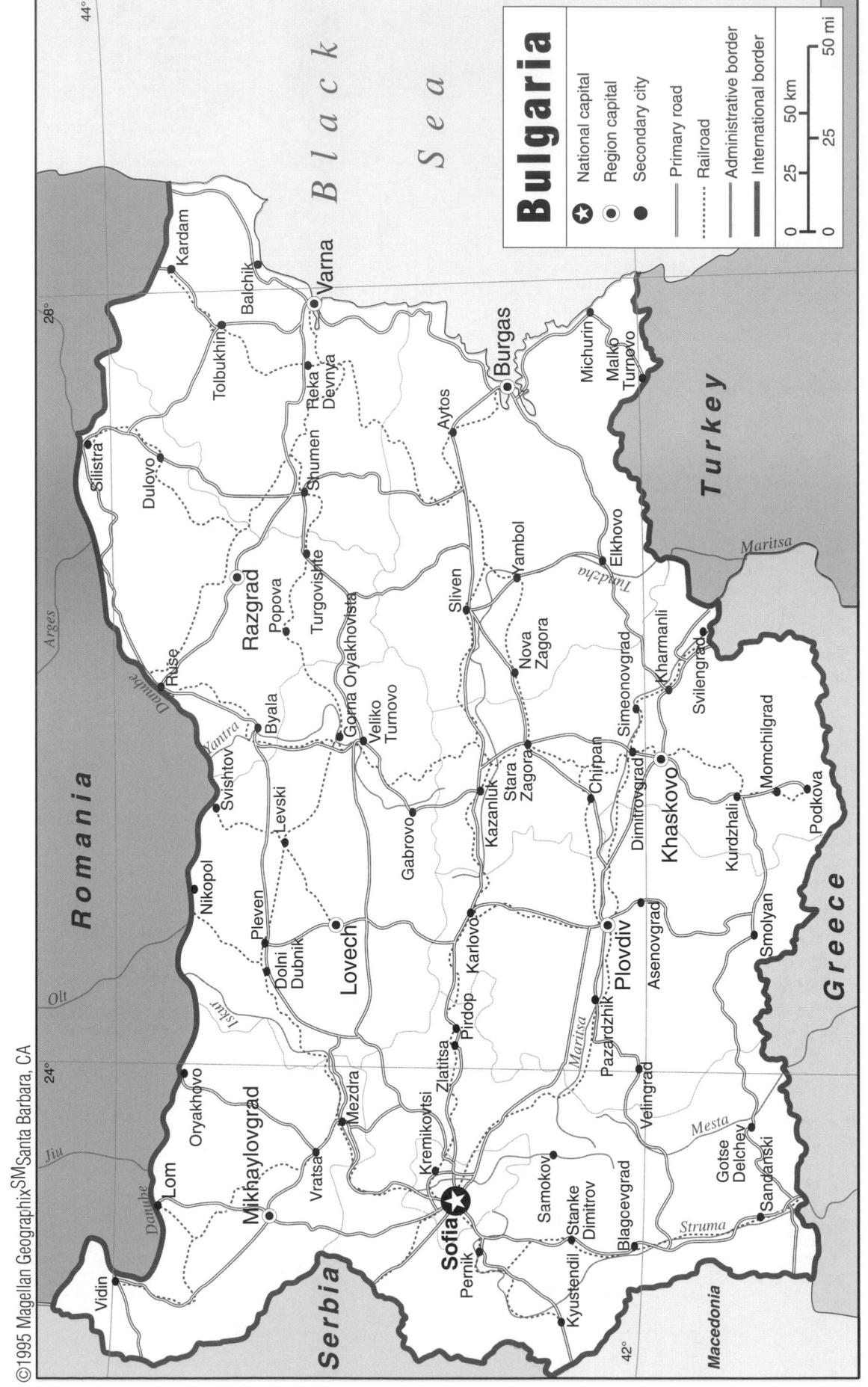

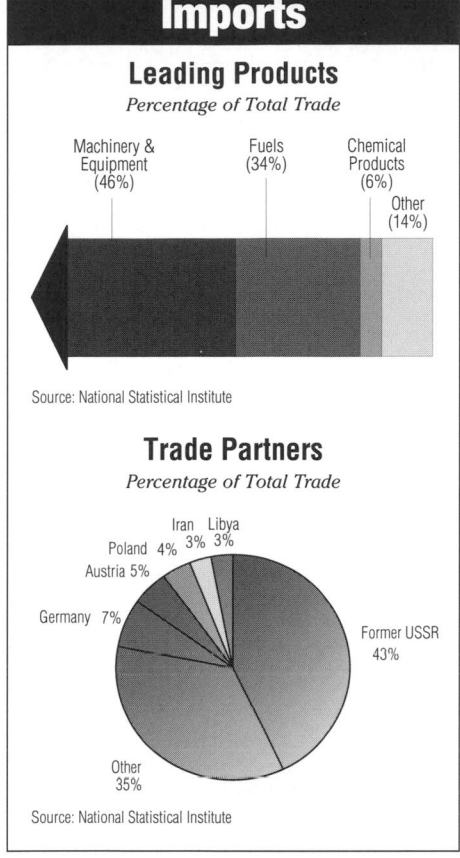

Imports

Leading Products
Percentage of Total Trade

Machinery & Equipment (46%)
Fuels (34%)
Chemical Products (6%)
Other (14%)

Source: National Statistical Institute

Trade Partners
Percentage of Total Trade

Iran 3%
Libya 3%
Poland 4%
Austria 5%
Germany 7%
Former USSR 43%
Other 35%

Source: National Statistical Institute

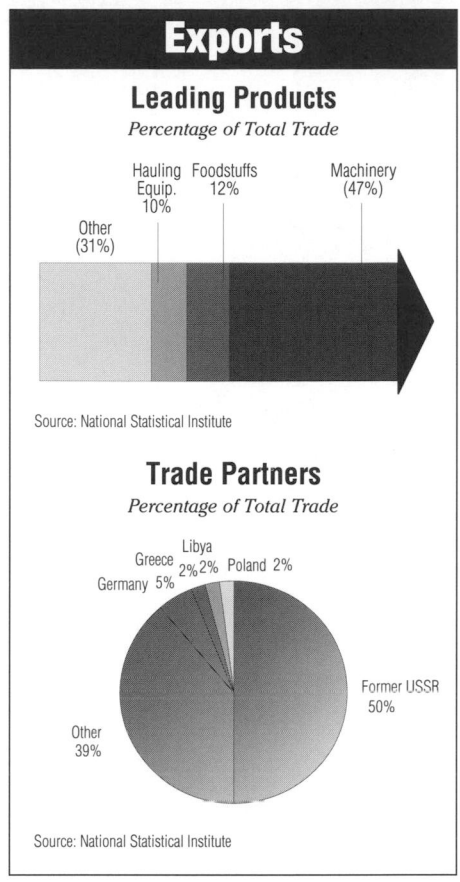

Exports

Leading Products
Percentage of Total Trade

Hauling Equip. 10%
Foodstuffs 12%
Machinery (47%)
Other (31%)

Source: National Statistical Institute

Trade Partners
Percentage of Total Trade

Libya 2%
Greece 2%
Germany 5%
Poland 2%
Former USSR 50%
Other 39%

Source: National Statistical Institute

Opportunities

FOR IMPORTING TO BULGARIA
- agricultural products
- coal
- electrical machinery and equipment
- fuels
- manufactured consumer goods
- minerals
- motor vehicles and parts
- raw materials

FOR EXPORTING FROM BULGARIA
- cheese
- clothing
- fertilizer
- fresh fruits and vegetables
- fuels
- iron and steel
- machinery and equipment
- minerals
- raw materials
- textiles
- tobacco
- wine

GROWTH SECTORS
- agriculture
- chemicals
- metallurgy
- oil
- services
- telecommunications
- tourism

GOVERNMENT PROCUREMENT
- health care goods and services
- highway construction goods and services
- revenue-generating products
- telecommunications products

Trade News

RULES AND REGULATIONS

- **Regulations** The Ministry of Trade issues import licenses and regulates trade.
- **Tariffs and import taxes** Bulgaria's new harmonized tariff schedule recently increased average tariffs, although a 15 percent import tax was eliminated (the import tax remains on 10 agricultural goods). Examples of tariff rates are: 15 to 25 percent for grains; 10 to 15 percent for oilseeds; 10 to 40 percent for processed products. Rates are significantly lower for goods originating in European Union countries, due to Bulgaria's Association Agreement with the EU. All imports are subject to an 18 percent value-added tax (VAT) and a 0.5 percent customs processing fee assessed on the valuation of the goods.
- **Import licenses** Only a limited number of products require import licenses. Products include some agricultural goods, pharmaceuticals, nuclear materials, weapons, and precious metals.
- **Prohibited imports** The European Community's standards may be applied as a general guideline for Bulgaria. Items such as electrical appliances not meeting safety standards and food products not meeting health standards will be prohibited.
- **Free trade zones** Seven free trade zones were established in Bulgaria in 1987. Although functions of FTZs are now limited mostly to storage, handling, and transshipment of goods, interest in FTZs and their possibilities is growing.
- **Trade agreements** Bulgaria has signed an EC Association Agreement, permitting eventual free access of EC origin goods in a phase-out of gradual tariffs depending on product category. It has observer status with GATT and is negotiating for access.
- **Prohibitions** Several sectors are temporarily prohibited from any exports, including crude oil, raw hides of cattle, vegetable oils, motor petrol, gas oil for engine and industrial application, and fuel oil.
- **Prices** The Ministry of Industry and Trade periodically sets threshold export prices for the export of live animals, meat, dairy products, and striped sunflower seeds. These prices are published in the Official Gazette.
- **Export licenses** Companies have to apply for export licenses to the Ministry of Industry and Trade. Applications must be cleared in advance with one of the following competent authorities depending on the specific commodity: the Ministry of Industry and Trade, the Ministry of Agriculture, the Ministry of Environment, the Ministry of Culture, the Ministry of Health, the Government Regulating and Supervising the Production and Trade in Military, and the Committee of the Use of Atomic Energy for Peaceful Purposes.
- **Customs** The customs regime of the Republic of Bulgaria has been revised recently. The "customs regime" means the totality of customs procedures applied to a commodity and established according to the character of the commodity.
- **Control of goods** All goods carried across the Bulgarian border are subject to customs control. Import duty is charged according to the Tariff Schedule, the amount of duty depending on the origin of the goods. A charge at the rate of .05 percent of the customs tax value of imports and exports is collected for customs clearance.
- **Taxes** The rate of tax or duty depends on the type of the commodity. Most goods are taxed at 22 percent. Food products, baby products, medicines, and sanitary materials are usually taxed at 10 percent. Some items are taxed much higher than the usual 22 percent. Alcoholic products are taxed at 70 percent, tobacco products are taxed at 60 percent, leatherwear (excluding work clothes and special-purpose clothes) are taxed at 50 percent, and perfumes and audio video equipment are taxed at 40 percent.

Business Travel

LH 1906	MADRID		935	113-3
LH 1022	STUTTGART HBF.		935	-
AF 1701	LYON		940	683-6
AY 822	HELSINKI		940	113-3
AA 071	SFRANCISCO-DALLAS		945	731-7

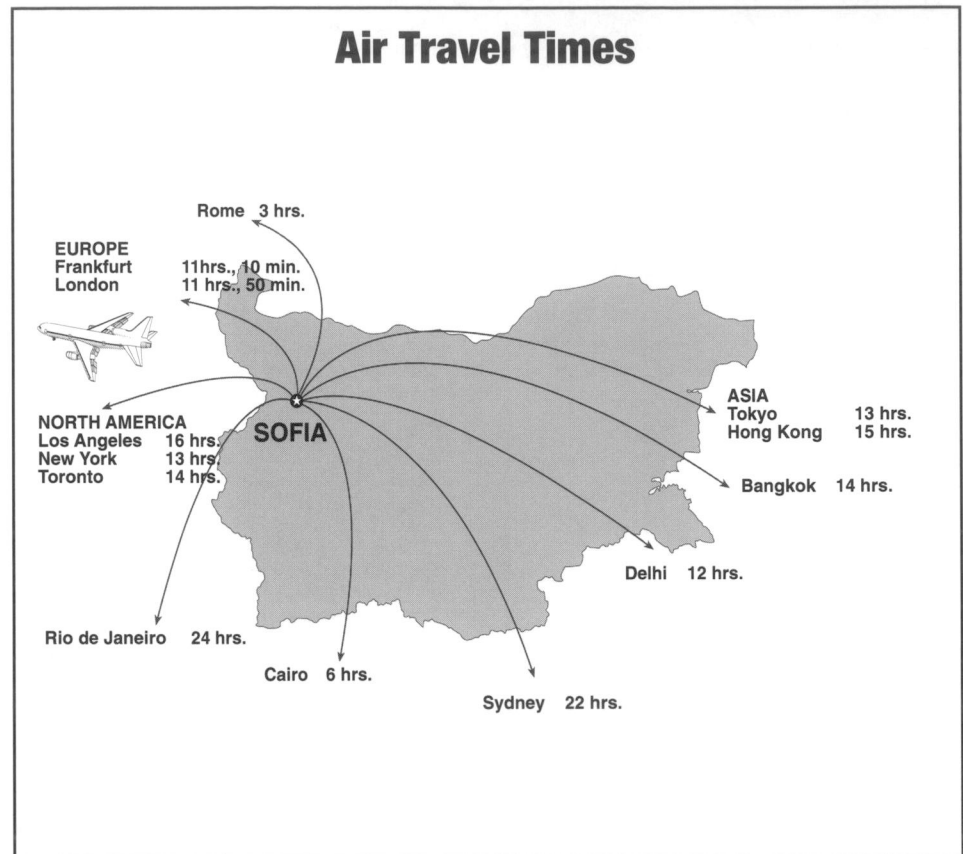

Air Travel Times

Rome 3 hrs.

EUROPE
Frankfurt 11hrs., 10 min.
London 11 hrs., 50 min.

NORTH AMERICA
Los Angeles 16 hrs.
New York 13 hrs.
Toronto 14 hrs.

SOFIA

ASIA
Tokyo 13 hrs.
Hong Kong 15 hrs.

Bangkok 14 hrs.

Delhi 12 hrs.

Rio de Janeiro 24 hrs.

Cairo 6 hrs.

Sydney 22 hrs.

COMMUNICATIONS

Telephones The telephone system in Bulgaria is outdated and unreliable. Connections are often difficult. Direct dialing is available to most major European cities. The telephone office at Stefan Karadzha 6 in Sofia is best for international calls. Use black phone cards with orange phones for domestic calls only. Use the smaller, picture phone cards with silver phones for international calls.

Fax Available in large hotels, but the telephone system is antiquated, so it may take time to send and receive faxes.

Post office The mail in Bulgaria is slow and undependable. It may take more than two weeks for packages to reach their target in Sofia, and about that long for packages in Bulgaria to reach their destinations in other countries. Mail is rarely used as a marketing tool, and is not primarily used for anything more than correspondence.

BEST TRAVEL BOOKS

Fodor's 96 Europe, Best of 31 Countries. Contains information on historical towns, great culture, scenic coastal countryside.

Bulgaria, A Travel Guide. Pelican Publishing Co. An up-to-date travel guide. Philip Ward.

A Guide to International Behavior, Do's and Taboos Around the World. Edited by Roger E. Axtell, compiled by the Parker Pen Company. Now completely updated and revised, the ultimate guide to international behavior. Helpful, easy to read.

Berlitz Business Travel Guide, Europe. Concise economic details, successful trip planning, background information on people and cities, useful facts and addresses.

USEFUL TELEPHONE NUMBERS

If you are calling from outside Bulgaria, you will need to add the country code [359] and any other international dialing requirements from within your country.

- Road Service... 146
- Phone Service... 144
- Long distance.. 121
- International calls 0123
- Clinic for Foreign Citizens .... (2) 75361
- Bulgarian Industrial Association .... (2) 882501
- Chamber of Commerce and Industry ...... (2) 872631
- Dentist .... (2) 75361
- Doctor .... (2) 51531; 720052
- Information 144; 145
- Pharmacy 24 hour 178
- Fire... 160
- Police.. 166
- Ambulance 150

National Airlines
- Balkan Bulgarian Airlines .. (2) 8844-33; (2) 884493
- Sofia International Airport.......................... (2) 71201

Car Rental
- Sofia Airport .... (2) 720157
- Plovdiv .... (32) 5892
- Varna .... (52) 223358
- Burgas .... (56) 432646

Credit Card Information
Lost or stolen credit cards (call collect to the US, regardless of which country the card was issued in).
- Amex .... [1] (919)3333211
- Diner's Club................................. [1] (303) 7991504
- MasterCard .... [1] (314) 2756690
- Visa .... [1] (410) 5817931

Travelogue

WORKWEEKS

Offices Monday-Friday 8:30 am to 5:30 pm.
Banks Monday-Friday 8:00 am to noon and 1:00 to 5:00 pm.
Government Monday-Friday 8:30 am to 5:30 pm.
Retail Monday-Saturday generally 9:00 am to 7:30 pm with lunch from 1:00 to 2:00 pm.

HOLIDAYS

Holidays 1996
January 1 New Year's Day
March 3 Liberation from the Ottoman Yoke Day
April 14 Bulgarian Easter•
April 15 Easter Monday*
May 1 Labor Day
May 24 Cyril and Methodius Day
December 25 Christmas
*The observation date of these holidays can vary from year to year.

VISA AND PASSPORT

Foreigners must have a valid passport and visa for entry into Bulgaria. Visas cost US$23. US citizens do not need visas for stays of less than 30 days. All visitors to Bulgaria must register with the police, a hotel, or a guest house within 48 hours of arrival.

DEPARTURE FORMALITIES

It is illegal to export any amount of Bulgarian currency. No other departure formalities are found in Bulgaria.

IMMUNIZATION

No immunizations are necessary to gain entrance into Bulgaria unless coming from an infected area. When planning to stay for more than one month, an AIDS test may be required. Test results from other countries are not accepted.

TIPPING

Officially discouraged, but privately welcome. Tipping is not prevalent in Bulgaria. Round bills up to tip at restaurants. Tips of 10 to 15 percent are given only in the most expensive restaurants. Taxi drivers are tipped 5 to 10 percent.

CRIME

There has been a recent rise in street crime against foreigners. Pickpocketing, pursesnatching, and theft from automobiles are frequent occurrences. Automobile theft is also on the rise. Security measures are encouraged.

INFRASTRUCTURE

Bulgaria has adequate air and train networks, roadways, intercity public transportation, ferry and cruise boat systems, and tourist facilities. Note that trains are rather slow and uncomfortable. First-class reservations are advised. The bus system is crowded, make advance reservations. Communications within and to Bulgaria are difficult. Taxi drivers from Sofia's airport are notorious for refusing to run their meters. Insist on a prepaid fare, fares are usually reasonable. Roads are good, but narrow. There are few road signs but those available are somewhat confusing. Ferries, cruise boats, and hydrofoils are available on the Danube and Black Sea coast. To rent a car you will need an international driver's license.

NATIONAL TOURIST OFFICE

Pirin Tourist Bureau
B. Alexander Stambolijski 30
Sophia
Tel: (2) 881079

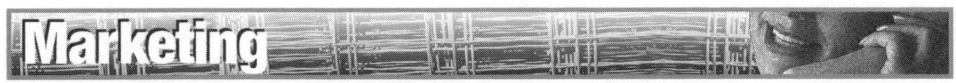

Distribution

A country in transition, Bulgaria offers lucrative markets for suppliers willing to be patient. On the bright side, Bulgarian markets are new and small, with less entrenched competition than in other central European locations. Entry is hampered, however, by unclear government regulation and weak infrastructure. The problems are certainly surmountable, but require time, expense, and ingenuity to overcome.

Local representation is the major means of entry. The distribution system is fairly limited to the major commercial center at Sofia and a few secondary sites, particularly Plovdiv and Varna. Most wholesalers, import firms, and agents specialize in a region because of unreliable transportation. Most retailers run small independent shops; a few chains exist in urban areas. The state distributes basic agricultural commodities. Establishing an office or company is costly and time-consuming; a joint venture or partnership with a local entrepreneur may be the fastest, least expensive means of setting up a business.

Selling Techniques

Market strategy must account for fluctuating market demands, unreliable statistics on disposable income, limited government spending, and minimal consumer education. Focus on quality, price, and before and after sales service is a start, but it must be supported with lenient credit terms, consumer education, and sales training. Industry purchasing is now decentralized, but many firms are still establishing their own purchasing systems, so patient assistance from a foreign supplier may be helpful in closing a sale. Technical sales seminars often attract a broad audience of decisionmakers.

Advertising

Mass promotion ranges from print to broadcast media. Specialized magazines and journals that carry advertising are increasingly available. Major trade shows, single theme shows, and single company presentations enjoy substantial success.

Service and Customer Support

Multinational companies have found high consumer demand for product selection, quality, and service. A system of after-sales support is difficult because of infrastructure problems, but it is still necessary.

Business Culture

Greetings and Courtesies

Bulgarians like to do business on a friendly basis; business meetings in Bulgaria are frequently held at dinner and include food and wine. Because Bulgarians value punctuality so highly, it is socially correct for foreign businesspeople to always arrive on time, or earlier. The proper greeting in Bulgaria is a hand shake and the salutation, "Good day."

Business Ethic and Framework

Because they are naturally hospitable, Bulgarians strive to make their foreign business associates welcome in their country. However, it is customary for foreign businesspeople to host dinners at public restaurants for their Bulgarian associates. Bulgarians do not expect business gifts, but a small souvenir from your country or token of your company is appropriate after an agreement has been signed.

Meetings and Decision Making

Bulgarians prefer to do business in person, not by telephone or fax, and in a social environment. In this setting, Bulgarians are reluctant to turn down a proposal outright, preferring instead to delay a decision or change the topic of discussion. Therefore, it is difficult to assess the Bulgarians' position during a meeting. Decisions are made in Bulgaria through a step-by-step process, in which no further progress is made until affirmation of the previous step. Decisions in Bulgaria are rarely final. A favorable decision could be overturned in a matter of days. Conversely, a rejection may also be turned around just as quickly. Patience in dealing with Bulgarians is often rewarded.

Women

Women in Bulgaria are a presence in all professions but seldom hold the higher paying jobs. Bulgarian women are more flexible than their male colleagues and are generally more receptive to proposals of foreign business associates.

Marketing in Bulgaria
MARKETING TIPS

- **Commit to service** Firms that offer supreme customer service are likely to gain high customer loyalty. Customer service has largely been lacking, but computer, telecommunication, and other high-tech product firms have started to introduce this concept, and it is spreading fast. This is such a relatively small market that word about bad service spreads fast in Bulgaria.
- **Legal advice** Bulgaria's bureaucracy is complex and confusing. To navigate commercial regulations in Bulgaria, local legal counsel is essential. Do not operate without it.
- **Creative touch** Market entry may require exploring creative channels, such as establishing ties with marketing institutes that have been spun off from major state enterprises.
- **Telephone** Phone service in Bulgaria has improved recently, and international calls can now be made from most major cities. Service is still slow in rural areas. Fax machines are very new to the country, and are rarely found anywhere except in government offices. Bulgaria's business culture is very personal anyway, so phone calls and fax machines should not be used for anything except correspondence with your agents.
- **Postal service** Postal service in Bulgaria is slow and unreliable. It may take more than two weeks for packages to reach their target in Bulgaria, and about that long for packages in Bulgaria to reach their destinations in other countries. Mail is rarely used as a marketing tool, and is not primarily used for anything more than correspondence.
- **Experience counts** For information on markets, product adaptability, and advertising media, a local advertising or public relations firm can prove invaluable.

Cultural Cautions
DO'S
- Be patient; things move slowly in Bulgaria.
- When invited to a Bulgarian home, guests should bring flowers, candy, or another small gift.
- Use proper titles when addressing Bulgarians.

DON'TS
- Don't give up. When satisfaction is not forthcoming, often persistence pays off in getting what you want.
- Don't rely on telephones. The system is out-of-date, and connections are often unreliable.

CUSTOMS
- In opposition to Western customs, a nod means "no" in Bulgaria and a shake of the head from side to side means "yes."
- Bulgarians are reluctant to show their feelings.
- Limit your physical contact with Bulgarian businesspeople to a handshake.

OBSERVATIONS
- Bulgarians tend to avoid conflict.
- Most things get done on the basis of personal contacts and favors.
- Documents need stamps, seals, and signatures, which slows business.
- Bulgarians are tolerant of foreigners and easy to work with.

NEGOTIATIONS
- Make business appointments far in advance.
- All proposals in Bulgaria are competitive. None are final until a signed agreement is reached.
- Signed agreements are often reversed. Negotiators may have to start negotiations anew because elections, personnel changes, or new laws caused a reversal of the agreement.

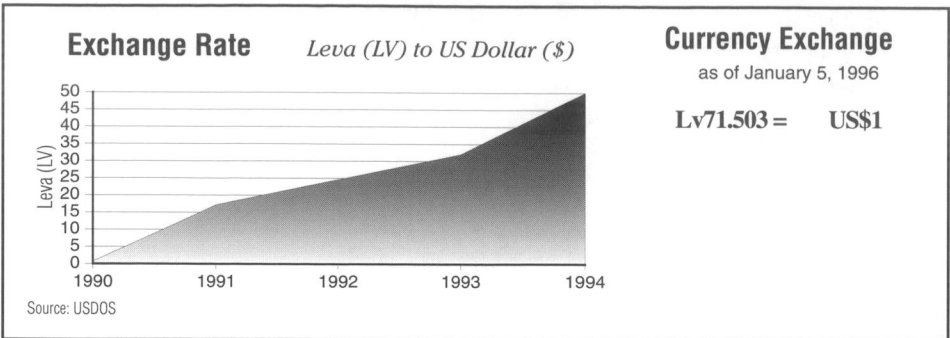

Exchange Rate *Leva (LV) to US Dollar ($)*

Source: USDOS

Currency Exchange
as of January 5, 1996

Lv71.503 =   US$1

Currency

The currency of Bulgaria is the leva (LV).

Foreign Exchange

The Ministry of Finance and the Bulgarian National Bank control all foreign exchange. Transactions are carried out by 17 commercial banks and one financial institution. Nonresidents can maintain accounts in any currency for transactions while in Bulgaria without restriction or authorization. Accounts can be credited without restriction, but any transfers abroad require permission from the Ministry of Finance and the Bulgarian National Bank. There are no taxes on purchases or sales of foreign exchange.

Capital Transfers

Bulgarian bank notes may be imported or exported, but any amount over LV10,000 requires permission from the Bulgarian National Bank. Nonresidents may bring in or take out unlimited amounts of foreign currency without restriction, provided the amount is declared with customs. Documentation is required for most payments for invisibles, including banking commissions, insurance fees, and health care. All proceeds from invisibles must be repatriated but do not need to be surrendered.

Investment Incentives

Bulgaria has taken several steps to open the country up to foreign investment. Bulgarian law doesn't differentiate between foreign and domestic investors, and there is no minimum investment amount for nonresidents. The government has stressed that it will not place any requirements for investment, and in many sectors, 100 percent foreign ownership is possible.

Investment Restrictions

Foreign investment in Bulgaria has been slow. The government rarely supports investments once made and there is some suspicion among residents that foreign businesses will deplete the country of its natural resources. Perhaps the biggest reason for so little foreign investment is the extremely slow privatization rate of state enterprises. There is also a lack of transparency and consistency when dealing with investors, particularly with tax practices. Despite the investment barriers, a number of foreign investors who have thoroughly researched opportunities and pursued them have met with success.

TAXATION

Taxation requires sophisticated knowledge of complex rules and regulations specific to each country. The information presented here is from the Ernst & Young Corporate Tax Guide and Directory, available from the Ernst & Young accounting office in your country, or from:

Ernst & Young
46 Alabin Street
Sofia 1000
Bulgaria
Tel: (2) 543005, 518616
Telex: 24611
Fax: (2) 542908

At a Glance

Corporate Income Tax Rate (%)	40
Capital Gains Tax Rate (%)	40
Branch Tax Rate (%)	40
Withholding Tax (%)	
Dividends (a)	0/10/15
Interest (b)	15
Royalties from Patents, Know-how, etc. (b)	15
Technical Service Fees (b)	15
Rental Income from Leases (b)	15
Branch Remittance Tax	0
Net Operating Losses (Years)	
Carryback (c)	1
Carryforward	5

(a) The 0% rate applies to dividends paid to Bulgarian companies wholly owned by Bulgarians and to resident individuals as well as to dividends used to purchase Bulgarian government stocks and bonds. The 10% rate applies to dividends paid to Bulgarian companies with foreign participation. Dividends paid to foreign companies and nonresident individuals are subject to withholding tax at a rate of 15%.
(b) Applicable to payments to foreign companies and nonresident individuals.
(c) If permission is obtained from the Ministry of Finance.

Money Matters

BITS AND PIECES

- **Corporate income tax** All companies are subject to a profit tax based on their worldwide income.
- **Capital gains** Any capital gains are included in ordinary income and are subject to a profit tax at the regular rates.
- **Taxable income** Taxable income is based on annual accounts prepared in accordance with accounting principles in Bulgaria.
- **Gold** All gold is controlled by the Ministry of Finance. The Bulgarian National Bank is the only institution entitled to hold, import, and export gold. Domestic transactions can only be performed at the national bank. There are limits to the amount of gold that may be brought into the country, and permission is required to buy gold in Bulgaria.
- **Business licenses** Everyone doing business in Bulgaria must buy an annual license. The fee depends on the type and location of the business, and the number of employees.
- **Exports payments** All export proceeds must be repatriated within one month but they don't have to be surrendered. There is an export tax on most items.
- **Imports payments** Most imports are subject to declaration and registration at the Ministry of Foreign Economical Relations for statistical purposes. Certain goods are restricted and others are subject to a quota. There is a tariff system for all imports, with rates ranging from 5 to 55 percent. There is also a surcharge of 2 percent placed on most imports.
- **Trade representation offices** Foreign persons can open their own trade representation offices, but this requires permission. At least half of the employees of such offices must be Bulgarian citizens.
- **Foreign employees** There is no restriction on the number of employees a foreign company can hire.
- **Types of ownership** All types of ownership–state, municipal, cooperative, and private–are accorded equal economic and legal treatment.
- **Credit cards** Major credit cards are accepted at many hotels and restaurants, and traveler's checks are accepted in many shops. Nonresidents of Bulgaria must pay hotel bills in convertible currency.
- **Joint stock companies** As of 1990, joint stock companies with less than 20 percent foreign participation pay a profits tax of 50 percent, and companies with more than 20 percent foreign participation pay a 30 percent profits tax.
- **Tax holidays** Local companies entering in tax holidays are provided to some joint ventures between local and foreign enterprises.
- **Black market** The black market is prevalent throughout Bulgaria. Avoid it at all costs; it is not only illegal, but you can be cheated.
- **Investment banks** A major banking reform was undertaken in 1987 and since then a number of new investment banks have been created. In the fall of 1990 it was announced that the government would facilitate the opening of foreign banks' branches in Bulgaria.
- **Permission** In general, permission is not required for foreigners to invest, nor is there a minimum dollar amount set for foreign investments. Investors are, however, required to obtain a license to own or have controlling interest in firms producing arms, ammunition, and military equipment.
- **Debt** Arrears are maintained with respect to certain external payments.
- **Nonresident accounts** Nonresidents can maintain accounts in foreign currencies and leva without authorization for the purpose of making transaction in Bulgaria.

BANKS

National Bank of Bulgaria
2, Knyaz A. Batemberg Street
1000 Sofia
Tel: (2) 85-51
Fax: (2) 88-05-58

Legal

Legal System

Bulgaria's republic, which was established in 1991, is based upon a new constitution and separation of powers. The president is elected to a single five-year term. Members of Parliament are elected to four year terms. The Council of Ministers, which implements policy, is elected by Parliament. Local governments, established in municipalities, are chosen by direct ballot from the populace. A multi-level judicial system operates autonomously from the other branches of government. The Bankruptcy Law of 1994 and other revisions of the Commercial Code are designed to further develop a market economy, and significantly reflect similar measures passed by Western legislatures.

Intellectual Property Rights

Bulgaria recently enacted a new Patent and Copyright Law that brought, at least on paper, the country's intellectual property right protection up to international standards. Bulgaria's other piece of intellectual property legislation, the Law on Trademarks and Industrial Designs, is in need of updating, but generally considered adequate. The legal system generally protects intellectual property rights, but the processes for legislation, not to mention the judicial bureaucracy, can be very cumbersome.

Patents Protection remains in effect for 20 years from the filing date. The actual granting of a patent can take several years from application date, although this time period is expected to be reduced as the new commercial laws take effect. The semiconductor chip layout design is not specifically covered in Bulgarian legislation.

Trademarks Trademarks are issued by the Institute of Inventions and Innovations for a 10-year term, which is indefinitely renewable. Bulgaria is a signatory of the Madrid Agreement Concerning International Registration of Marks, with local laws enumerated in the Law on Trademarks and Industrial Designs, passed in 1967 and amended in 1975.

Copyrights Copyright law in Bulgaria is substantially enumerated in the Side Letter of the United States-Bulgarian Trade Agreement of 1991 and the European Community Bulgaria Association Agreement of 1993.

Business Registration

All companies and specified details regarding their commerce must be registered with District Courts that issue approvals and maintain the availability of these aforementioned documents for public inspection.

Contracts and Dispute Resolution

Consideration is not necessary to establish the validity of contracts in Bulgaria, unless such is made an express term thereof. Also, unless at the time an offer is made a specific period of time is given for acceptance thereof, the offer is considered withdrawn in the absence of immediate acceptance. This is not the case if the offer is furnished in writing, in which case it is deemed open and subject to acceptance until withdrawn. Terms of the US-Bulgarian Bilateral Investment Treaty specify a graduated dispute settlement procedure, ranging from consultation and negotiation to binding arbitration. However, these agreements have not yet been tested in practice. Most commercial disputes continue to be resolved in the courts.

Notaries

Duties of notaries public include certification of documents and signatures, in addition to the creation of articles of business incorporation, mortgages, real estate transactions, and wills. Fees are set by law on a sliding scale, based on the value of the transaction.

Labor

Bulgaria's Labor Code is weighted somewhat in favor of management, and takes precedent on all issues not specifically enumerated by contract. Collective bargaining was to have been instituted in July 1992, but is not yet in effect. Privatization has slowed, negotiating partners are not always clearly identifiable, and a Government organized commission continues to negotiate wage agreements at the national level. Disputes are heard by regional courts or tribunals. The code mandates the minimum wage (as determined by the Council of Ministers); the minimum notice requirements for employment separation; the maximum number of hours in a workweek; employer liability for occupational hazards and safety; and mandatory insurance and social security, paid by the employer. All workers have a constitutional right to join labor unions, which have gained in popularity since the fall of communism. Bulgaria has two unions, the Confederation of Independent Trade Unions of Bulgaria (CITUB) and Podkrepa. There are few restrictions on trade union activity and both confederations operate freely. Judgment on the new Labor Code is premature but bureaucratic impediments continue to exist at a number of levels.

Legal Matters

LEGAL BRIEFS

- **New laws** It should be noted that extreme bureaucracy and confusion as to legal principles remains an impediment to efficient business.
- **International agreements** Bulgaria is a party to the Berne Convention for the Protection of Literary and Artistic Works, and is considering adherence to the Rome Convention for the Protection of Performers, Producers of Phonograms and Broadcasting Organizations of 1961, as well as the Geneva Phonograms Convention of 1973.
- **Education** Bulgaria offers an educated and highly competent populace with a solid work ethic, despite the fact that experienced managerial talent is in short supply.
- **Land ownership** Agricultural land is to be restituted to owners or their descendants according to ownership rights prior to the Communist era. The process has gone very slowly, and as of April 1994, only 10 to 15 percent of the land was in the hands of owners with legal title.
- **Monopolies** The Bulgarian Parliament has adopted a "Protection of Competition Act," designed to protect against monopolies, restraint of trade, and unfair competition. The act also established the "Commission for the Protection of Competition," and sets penalties. Prosecutions under the Act can be brought either by aggrieved persons or the commission. As a result of over 50 years of central economic planning, significant monopoly power exists in state enterprises. Elimination of this power is the aim of the government's privatization program.
- **Political violence** There have been no incidents in recent years involving politically motivated damage to projects or installations, but the tone of political debate in the country has grown increasingly angry, making the possibility of industrial action, including strikes, somewhat more likely.

LEGAL CONTACTS

Snelling & Snelling
23 V, San Stefano Street, Suite 34
Sofia
Tel: (2) 46-60-57 Fax: (2) 44-34-04

Ivo Baev, Attorney at Law
29 Ferdinandova Street
Burgas 8000
Tel: (56) 47010
Fax: (56) 42491

Dr. Coeler & Partner, Rechtsanwalte
44 Benkorski Str.
BG-1000 Sofia
Tel: (2) 818866
Fax: (2)881727

Frick & Frick
Boulevard Witoscha 25
POB 475
BG-1000 Sogia
Tel: (2) 81.33.88
Fax: (2) 81.33.85

Goleminov & Goleminov
36 A Anri Barbus Street
Sofia 1113
Tel: (2) 700-081
Fax: (2)706-203

Kristian Krastev Law Office
World Trade Center
36 B Dragan Tzankov Blvd., Office 513
1040 Sofia
Tel: (2) 73 15 41
Fax: (2) 738 551

CHAMBERS OF COMMERCE

Bulgarian Chamber of Commerce and Industry
11-a, Al. Stamboliiski Boulevard
Sofia 1000
Tel: (2) 87-25-2
Fax: (2) 87-32-09

GOVERNMENT AGENCIES

Ministry of Agriculture
1000 Sofia
55 Khristo Botev Boulevard
Tel: (2) 88-17-90

Ministry of Environment
1000 Sofia
67 William Gladstone Street
Tel: (2) 88-25-77

Ministry of Finance
1000 Sofia
102 Rakovsky Street
Tel: (2) 86-92-11/87-06-22

Ministry of Foreign Affairs
1000 Sofia
2 Al. Zhendov Street
Tel: (2) 7143-217

Ministry of Health
1000 Sofia
2 Sveta Nedelia Square
Tel: (2) 87-50-51

Ministry of Housing & Construction
1000 Sofia
17 Kiril and Methodius Street
Tel: (2) 80-39-69

Ministry of Industry
1000 Sofia
8 Slavianska Street
Tel: (2) 80-10-06

Ministry of Justice
1000 Sofia
2 Dondukov Street
Tel: (2) 87-55-20, 87-40-58

Ministry of Labor
2 Triaditsa Street
1000 Sofia
Tel: (2) 87-65-08

Ministry of Trade
1000 Sofia
12 Battenberg Street
Tel: (2) 87-03-87

Agency for Economic Programming and Development
1000 Sofia
1,V. Levski Street
Tel: (2) 54-33-86, 867-23-00

Central Archives Administration
1000 Sofia
5, Moskovska Street
Tel: (2) 80-08-97, 887-08-25

Committee on Energy
1000 Sofia
8, Triyaditza Street
Tel: (2) 861-91, 88-59-32
Fax: (2) 87-58-26

Committee on Posts and Telecommunications
1000 Sofia
6, Gurko Street
Tel: (2) 88-20-95, 80-00-00
Fax: (2) 80-38-93

Committee on Tourism
1000 Sofia
1, Sveta Nedelya Square
Tel: (2) 84-131

National Statistics Institute
1000 Sofia
10, Shesti Septemvri Street
Tel: (2) 43-401, 44-31-19

BUSINESS AND TRADE ORGANIZATIONS

Bulgarian Industrial Association
Sofia 1000
16-20 Alabin Street
Tel: (2) 54-50-66 Fax: (2) 87-26-04

Union for Private Economic Enterprise
Sofia 1000
2a Suborna Street
Tel: (2) 65-93-71

MARKET RESEARCH FIRMS

Advertising International Network Ltd.
Sofia
36, Dragan Tzankov Boulevard, Suite 613 B
Tel: (2) 70-33-28
Fax: (2) 70-45-77

Continental Information
Sofia
32 Skobelev Boulevard
Tel: (2) 51-18-4
Fax: (2) 54-12-84

Expocenter
1000 Sofia
37, Ekzarch Jossif
Tel: (2) 80-36-03
Fax: (3) 80-12-01

Institute for Marketing and Research MBMD
Sofia 1111
26 A, Sabi Dimitrov Street
Tel/Fax: (2) 73-99-19

RADIO AND TELEVISION

Bulgarian Committee for Television and Radio
1504 Sofia
San Stefano St 29
Tel: (2) 46-81
Telex: 22581

Bulgarsko Radio
1421 Sofia
Blvd Dragan Tsankov 4
Tel: (2) 85-41
Telex: 22557

Bugarska Televiziya
1504 Sofia
ul. San Stefano 29
Tel: (2) 46-31
Telex: 22581

BANKS

Bank for Economic Projects (Mineralbank)
1000 Sofia, Legué St 17
POB 589
Tel: (2) 80-17-37
Telex: 23390

Biochim (Commercial Bank)
1040 Sofia
Ivan Vazov St 1
Tel: (2) 54-11-21
Telex: 23862
Fax: (2) 54-13-78

Bulgarian Foreign Trade Bank
1040 Sofia
Sofiiska Komuna St 2
Tel: (2) 85-51
Telex: 22031
Fax: (2) 88-56-81

Electronica (Commercial Bank Electronica)
1574 Sofia
Chapaev St 55
Tel: (2) 70-74-47
Telex: 23745
Fax: (2) 88-54-67

Stroybank Ltd.
1202 Sofia
Dunav Str. 46
POB 112
Tel: (2) 8-38-41
Telex: 23887

Transportna Banka (Transport Bank)
9000 Varna
5 Shlpka St.
Tel: (2) 22-30-73
Telex: 77293
Fax: (2) 23-19-64

Zemedelska i kooperativna (Agricultural and Co-operative Bank)
4018 Plovdiv
G. Dimitrov Blvd 37
Tel: (2) 23-18-76 Fax: 22-39-64
Telex: 44324

INSURANCE

Bustrade (Bulgarian Foreign Insurance and Reinsurance Co. Ltd)
1000 Sofia
Dunav St 5
POB 627
Tel: (2) 8-51-91
Telex: 22564

INTERNATIONAL FREE ZONE

Ruse International Free Zone
7000 Ruse
Blagoev St 5
POB 107
Tel: (2) 722-47
Telex: 62285
Fax: (2) 700-84

FOREIGN TRADE ORGANIZATIONS

Bulgarcoop
1000 Sofia
99 Rakovski St.
Tel: (2) 84-41
Telex: 23429

Bulgariafilm
1000 Sofia
Rakovski St 96
Tel: (2) 87-66-11
Telex: 22447
Fax: (2) 88-24-9931

Bulgarplodexport
1040 Sofia
7 Blvd A. Stamboliiski
Tel: (2) 88-59-51
Telex: 23297
Fax: (2) 88-48-77

Bulgartabac
1000 Sofia
Sofiska Komuna St 1
Tel: (2) 88-38-11
Telex: 22521

Koraboimpex Co Ltd.
9000 Varna D.
Blagoev Blvd 128
Tel: (2) 22-81-60
Telex: 77550
Fax: (2) 82-33-86

Lessoimpex
1303 Sofia
Antim 1 St 17
Tel: (2) 88-53-21
Telex: 23425
Fax: (2) 87-56-75

INTERNET ADDRESSES

A Reader's Guide to Bulgaria
http://asudesign.eas.asu.edu/places/Bulgaria/ref/index.html

Information About Bulgaria
http://pisa.rockefeller.edu:8080/Bulgaria/

FAQ About Bulgaria
http://www.cs.columbia.edu/~radev/cgi-bin/bgfaq.cgi

Bulgarian Privatization Agency
http://www.privatization.bg/

Usenet Group
soc.culture.bulgaria

Canada

Economy

Overview

Canada is one of the major industrial economies of the world. The Canadian economy is firmly entrenched in the free enterprise system, although the government has historically retained tight control over many of its major industries. The Canadian economy is healthy, broad based, and diverse; it grew by 4.6 percent in 1994, the best performance in six years. Its industrial base ranges from large multinationals to small businesses, most concentrated in Ontario and Québec. The government is in the process of further reducing its intervention in the economy, which should result in lower taxes, and a reduction of its ever-rising budget deficit.

Trade

Major exports include completed vehicles, newsprint, automotive parts and components, petroleum, lumber, and wood pulp. Imports include finished vehicles, vehicle parts and components, chemicals, hand tools, specialized and general industrial machinery, and petroleum products. Canada's main trading partners include the US—accounting for nearly 70 percent of total trade—followed by Japan, the UK, Germany, and France. However, in an effort to diversify away from its wholesale dependence on the US economy, Canada is developing growing trade relationships with Pacific Rim countries such as Korea, China, and Taiwan, which are now its next three largest trade partners.

Sectors

Agriculture Although it has historically been the backbone of the economy, agriculture now contributes only about three percent of GDP and four percent of employment. Major products include cereals, livestock, timber—Canada is the world's largest exporter of forest products—and fish and seafood.

Industry Employing somewhat less than 25 percent of the work force, industry produces about 40 percent of GDP. Major industries include mining and primary metals processing, transportation equipment, food processing, machinery, wood and paper products, and chemicals.

Services Services provide over 50 percent of Canada's GDP and employ nearly 75 percent of its work force. Canada has one of the world's highest rates of university-educated adults, many of whom hold various skilled technical and professional positions, allowing Canada to offer a variety of sophisticated services. Tourism has grown significantly in recent years, especially from Germany and the fast growing Asia Pacific countries. Canada is actively pursuing continued growth in this area.

Trends

Canada has enjoyed economic growth and prosperity in recent decades. Nevertheless, the country's economy remains less diversified than many would like to see, and heavily dependent on the US economy. The country also will need to reach some long-term accommodation between the demands of its English-speaking majority and the French-speaking minority that periodically threaten to splinter the nation. Also of growing concern is its immense public debt—the legacy of generous government social welfare and investment programs in the past, combined with revenue shortfalls. Although the currency remains weak, inflation is well under control, and unemployment is expected to continue to decrease as the development of a variety of trading relationships provides greater diversity.

At a Glance

THE COUNTRY
Location Northern North America, extending from the Atlantic Ocean to the Pacific Ocean north of the US.
Terrain Mostly plains, with mountains in the west and lowlands in the southeast.
Climate Varies from temperate in the south to subarctic and arctic in the north.

THE PEOPLE
Population 29,000,000
Ethnic composition
British.. 28%
French.. 23%
Other European 15%
Asian/Arab/African 6%
Indigenous Indian and Eskimo........................... 1.5%
Mixed background 26.5%
Religious composition
Roman Catholic 46%
Protestant 41%
Other 23%
Languages spoken English, French.
Education and literacy Of those aged 15 and over literacy is 99%. Primary and secondary education is generally free.
Labor force
Total:...14,800,000
By occupation: services 75%, manufacturing 14%, agriculture 4%, construction 3%.

COUNTRY FACTS
Political and legal Canada is a confederation with a parliamentary democracy. Its legal system is based on English common law, except in Quebec, where the civil law system is based on French law.
Telephone Excellent service from a modern system. International country code: [1]. Selected area codes: British Columbia (604), Alberta (403), Saskatchewan (306), Manitoba (204), Ottawa (613), Quebec (819, 418), Newfoundland (709), New Brunswick (506), Montreal (514), Toronto (416).
Transportation Canada has an advanced transportation system except in some parts of the North. An extensive air network links all major and many minor traffic points. A good highway system exists within 200 miles of the US border and supports extensive truck, bus, and automobile traffic. Canada also has an extensive railway connecting the country from sea to sea.
Environment Acid rain from Canadian and American industry has severely affected lakes and damaged forests. The two nations are working toward a solution. Canada is also working to protect its plant and animal resources. Current issues are acid rain; pollution from metal smelting, coal-burning utilities, and vehicle emissions; and contamination of ocean waters due to agricultural, industrial, mining, and forestry activities.
Media National broadcasting is provided by a publicly owned corporation. In 1991, there were 900 AM and 800 FM radio stations and 2,039 television stations. In the same year, 107 daily newspapers were published, along with many consumer magazines.
Health 40 percent of health care costs are contributed by the government. Life expectancy of males is 75 years; of females, 82 years.

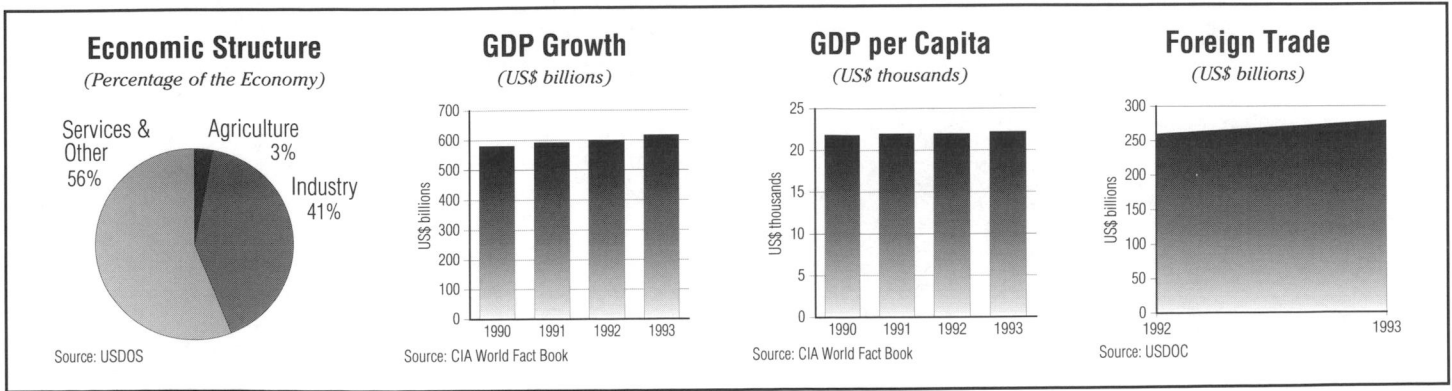

Economic Structure
(Percentage of the Economy)
Services & Other 56%
Agriculture 3%
Industry 41%
Source: USDOS

GDP Growth
(US$ billions)
1990 1991 1992 1993
Source: CIA World Fact Book

GDP per Capita
(US$ thousands)
1990 1991 1992 1993
Source: CIA World Fact Book

Foreign Trade
(US$ billions)
1992 1993
Source: USDOC

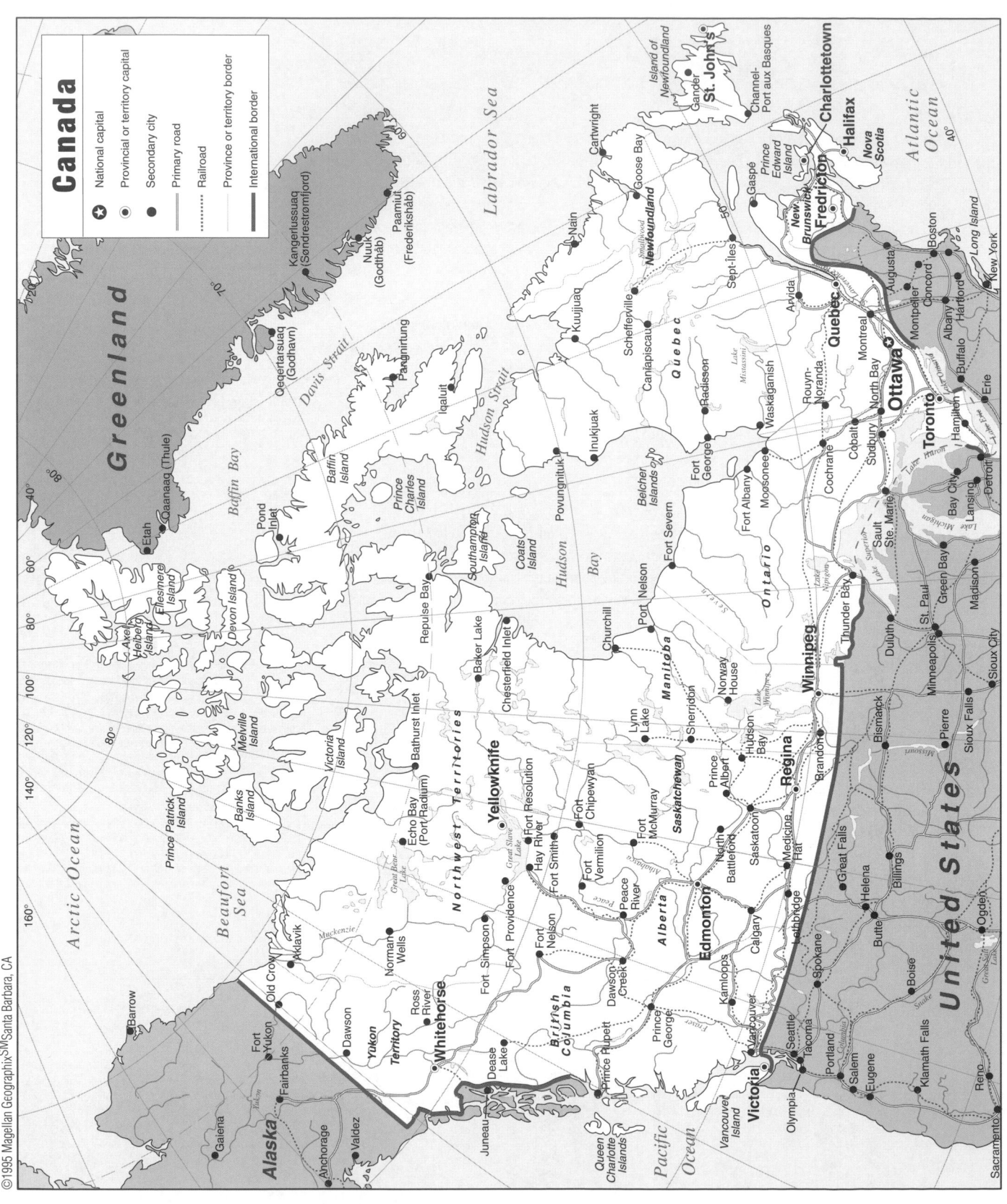

Canada

- ★ National capital
- ◉ Provincial or territory capital
- ● Secondary city
- —— Primary road
- —— Railroad
- ········· Province or territory border
- —— International border

Greenland

Baffin Bay

Davis Strait

Labrador Sea

Atlantic Ocean

Arctic Ocean

Beaufort Sea

Hudson Bay

Hudson Strait

Pacific Ocean

United States

Alaska

Yukon Territory

Northwest Territories

British Columbia

Alberta

Saskatchewan

Manitoba

Ontario

Quebec

Newfoundland

Nova Scotia

New Brunswick

Prince Edward Island

Ottawa

Yellowknife

Whitehorse

Victoria

Edmonton

Calgary

Regina

Winnipeg

Toronto

Quebec

Fredricton

Charlottetown

Halifax

St. John's

Foreign Trade

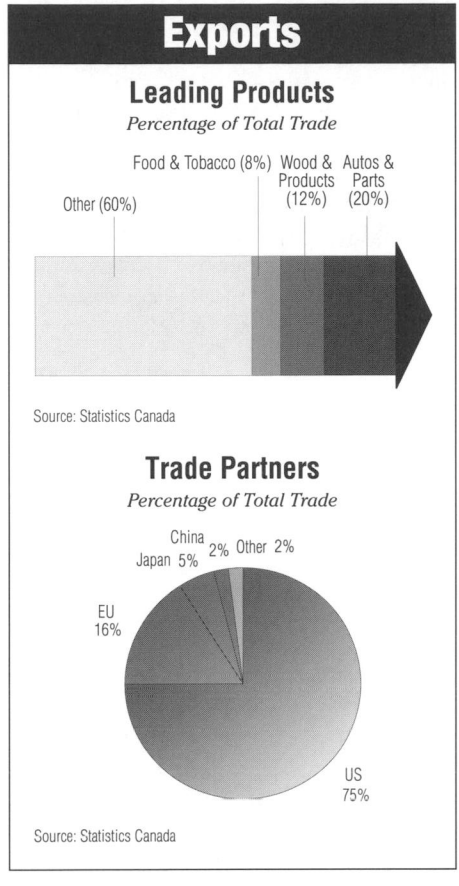

Imports

Leading Products
Percentage of Total Trade

Fabricated Materials (18%)   Autos & Parts (17%)   Machinery (9%)   Other (56%)

Source: Statistics Canada

Trade Partners
Percentage of Total Trade

- Other 18%
- Taiwan 2%
- Japan 7%
- EU 8%
- US 65%

Source: Statistics Canada

Exports

Leading Products
Percentage of Total Trade

Food & Tobacco (8%)   Wood & Products (12%)   Autos & Parts (20%)   Other (60%)

Source: Statistics Canada

Trade Partners
Percentage of Total Trade

- China 2%
- Japan 5%
- Other 2%
- EU 16%
- US 75%

Source: Statistics Canada

Opportunities

FOR IMPORTING TO CANADA

- agricultural machinery
- building products
- chemicals
- computer products
- electronic components
- fresh fruits
- high-value agricultural products
- household consumer goods
- industrial machinery
- livestock products
- medical equipment
- motor vehicles and parts
- petroleum
- plastic materials and resins
- pollution control equipment
- sporting goods and recreational equipment
- telecommunication products
- vegetables

FOR EXPORTING FROM CANADA

- barley
- beverages and spirits
- cereals
- clothing
- crude and fabricated metals
- crude petroleum
- fish
- lumber
- minerals: asbestos, gypsum, nickel, potash, silver, sulfur, titanium, uranium, zinc
- motor vehicles and parts
- natural gas
- newsprint
- paper and paperboard
- textiles
- wheat
- wood pulp

GROWTH SECTORS

- computer products
- environmental protection goods and services
- industrial machinery and equipment
- professional services
- telecommunications
- tourism
- transportation and storage

GOVERNMENT PROCUREMENT

- building materials
- computers and information services
- fiber optics
- hydroelectric power equipment
- local infrastructure development projects
- military communication systems
- motor vehicles
- scientific equipment

Trade News

RULES AND REGULATIONS

- **Regulatory agencies** The agency responsible for inspection of imports is Canada Customs. The agency responsible for collecting all taxes is Revenue Canada. The agency which oversees most import and export matters is the Department of Foreign Affairs and International Trade.

- **Tariffs** Canada has acceded to the GATT customs valuation code, which provides that the customs value of imported goods will be the transaction value—the price actually paid or payable for the goods. There is no tariff on goods imported from Mexico or the US, in accordance with the North American Free Trade Agreement (NAFTA).

- **Import taxes** Revenue Canada collects a 7 percent value-added tax (VAT), known as the Goods and Services tax (GST), on most imported goods. Goods exempted from the GST include basic groceries, prescribed drugs and medical devices, most educational services, most financial services, and health and dental care services.

- **Import licenses and permits** There are no general licenses required for importing goods into Canada. There are, however, provisions related to a variety of prohibited, controlled, and restricted goods. Items regulated under the Export and Import Permits Act require an import permit or certificate to be eligible for importation into Canada.

- **Import restrictions** Certain commodities, such as oleomargarine, reprints of Canadian copyrighted work, and some game birds, cannot be imported. Examples of regulated goods include: alcoholic beverages, food products, clothing, drugs and medical devices, hazardous products, some offensive weapons and firearms, endangered species, and motor vehicles.

- **Export controls** Canada controls exports under authorization of the Export and Import Permits Act (EIPA), the Export Control List (ELC), and the Area Control List (ACL). The EIPA ensures that there is an adequate supply and distribution of any article, particularly wood products and those products produced from other natural resources. The ELC lists particular items under control and the ACL lists countries which require export permits for all goods.

TRANSPORTATION CONTACTS

Canadian Society of Customs Brokers
121 York St.
Ottawa, ON K1N 5T4
Tel: (613) 238-3394
Fax: (613) 238-6313

Canadian International Freight Forwarders' Association
Box 929
Streetsville, ON L5M 2C5
Tel: (416) 567-4633
Fax: (416) 542-2716

Canadian Trucking Association
#300, 130 Albert St.
Ottawa, ON K1P 5G4
Tel: (613) 236-9426
Fax: (613) 563-2701

Transportation Association of Canada
2323 St. Laurent Blvd.
Ottawa, ON K1G 4K6
Tel: (613) 736-1350
Fax: (613) 736-1350

GOVERNMENT AGENCIES

Foreign Affairs and International Trade Canada
Lester B. Pearson Building
125 Sussex Drive
Ottawa, ON K1A 0G2
Tel: (613) 944-4000
Fax: (613) 944-0699

Office of the Minister for International Trade
515S, House of Commons
Ottawa, ON K1A 0A6
Tel: (613) 992-7332

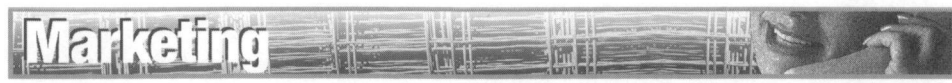

Overview

Canada recently restructured its business environment and government policies to support and encourage international trade. Given its geographical proximity, cultural and historical ties, and recent business developments, including the North America Free Trade Agreement (NAFTA), Canada's strongest trade links are with the United States, though Asian sellers have a strong presence on the West Coast, and European traders are well represented in the East. Nevertheless, regionalism remains a barrier to domestic business traffic, and commerce between Canadian provinces is much more complicated. Many companies deal exclusively within their own province, and there are only a few national chains or distribution networks. Moreover, a component of many government contracts requires a regional benefit clause outlined within the overall bid, and bidders outside a specific province are definitely at a disadvantage. Competition in Canada is generally fair and offers interesting opportunities, especially for products in engineering, steel, and consumer goods.

Distribution

Canada is a large territory, yet sales to Canadian industries use relatively short marketing channels, with an emphasis on producer-to-user distribution. Often, as many as 90 percent or more of the customers for a specific industrial product are located in only two or three cities. The market for consumer goods is more diffuse, however, and many marketing intermediaries spread representation across several commercial centers. Toronto and Montreal are national distribution centers and the logical locations for a single representative. For western Canada, Vancouver and Calgary are strategically more suitable. Distribution throughout the entire country usually means adhering, for the most part, to Canada's regional divisions, or three predominant territories, with an office in Quebec to represent the Atlantic Provinces, a second in Toronto for the Ontario Province, and a third located in Vancouver or Calgary to cover the four western provinces. Franchising is becoming increasingly effective in Canada, primarily because it is almost totally unregulated. Mail order sales are also a preferred buying method of a growing number of Canadians. For many companies, tapping into this market requires no more than placing an advertisement in a magazine.

Agents, Distributors, and Partners

Large, expensive industrial equipment is usually bought directly from manufacturers. Smaller equipment and industrial supplies are imported either by wholesalers, who sometimes act as exclusive distributors, or by manufacturers' sales subsidiaries. Many international firms prefer to appoint agents who regularly call on potential customers. Major distributors work on a two-tier commission system. For contract shipments, agents receive the lower commission; when purchases are made from the local agent's stock, the commission is higher. Many wholesalers, department stores, mail order houses, and purchasing cooperatives buy consumer goods through agents stationed abroad. Agents also help import and distribute consumer goods.

Selling Techniques

First-time sellers in the Canadian market should not treat Canada as a northern extension of the United States, though techniques successful in the United States will often apply effectively to Canada. Market research and cautious initial promotion lay the best groundwork for trading here. Consumers are generally cautious and direct-selling efforts usually work the best.

Advertising

Although most Canadians speak English, there is a substantial French-speaking market concentrated in Quebec, and it should be dealt with separately. More than 97 percent of Canadian households have at least one television, with at least 116 stations, and television accounts for the largest percentage of net advertising revenues. Newspaper advertisements are also important, circulated by more than 124 dailies, about 10 percent of which are in French. There are almost 700 radio stations, and nearly all Canadians own radios. More than 450 advertising agencies operate in Canada; their rates compare favorably with those in the United States. Trade magazines typically carry heavy advertising. Two business weeklies, *The Financial Post* and *The Financial Times*, cover most business and financial news, servicing that community with news and advertisements.

Service and Customer Support

Canadians expect efficient and courteous customer service and after-sales product service and support. Foreign sellers should be prepared to match the high level of service and support offered by Canadian companies and firms located in the United States, and should maintain an adequate inventory of replacement parts and equipment in the country.

Marketing in Canada

MARKETING TIPS

- **Business customs** Most Canadians closely follow Western European and US values in business, but a discrete check for preferences is always in order.
- **Duty** The temporary entry of business-related material for display or demonstration may be subject to the full tax, or a portion thereof, or may enter duty-fee. This status depends on the length of the visit, items ordered, and end-use.
- **Language** Canada's two official languages are English and French, with the former more popular and more common in business.
- **Market size** The population of Canada is approximately 29 million, with a large proportion living in smaller, rural communities.
- **Infrastructure** Telecommunications are modern with satellite services for long distance. With ample supplies of natural gas and several major pipelines, energy supplies are domestically met in several areas.
- **Ad agencies** If you need help finding an advertising agency, call the Canadian Advertising Foundation in Toronto.
- **Direct marketing** Direct marketers have had good success in Canada, although this method of marketing has yet to really take off.
- **Videoconferencing** Videoconferencing is becoming a common way to market new products to long-term customers.
- **French Canadians** Differences in lifestyle between French Canadians and English Canadians sometimes result in surprising differences in consumer behavior. For example, English Canadians make twice as many long distance telephone calls as French Canadians.

CONSULTING AND MARKETING FIRMS

Angus Reid Group, Inc.
160 Bloor Street East, Suite 610
Toronto, ON M4W 1B9
Tel: (416) 324-2900
Fax: (416) 324-2865

The Coopers & Lybrand Consulting Group
145 King Street West, Suite 2300
Toronto, ON M5H 1V8
Tel: (416) 869-1130
Fax: (416) 863-0926

Decima Research
1 Eglinton Avenue East, 7th Floor
Toronto, ON M4P 3A1
Tel: (416) 483-1724
Fax: (416) 483-4441

Deloitte & Touche—Consulting and Market Research
98 Macdonell Street, Suite 400
Guelph, ON N1H 8L1
Tel: (519) 822-1090
Fax: (519) 822-0247

Dun & Bradstreet Canada
Dun's Marketing Services
5770 Hurontario Street
Mississauga, ON L5R 3G5
Tel: (905) 568-6000
Fax: (905) 568-6197

Gallup Canada Inc.
180 Bloor Street West
Toronto, ON M5S 2V6
Tel: (416) 961-2811
Fax: (416) 961-3662

Goldfarb Consultants
4950 Yonge Street, 17th Floor
North York, ON M2N 6K1
Tel: (416) 221-9200
Fax: (416) 221-2214

Southam Marketing Research Services
1450 Don Mills Road
Don Mills, ON M3B 2X7
Tel: (416) 445-6641
Fax: (416) 442-2248

Business Culture

Greetings and Courtesies

Canadian customs are similar to those in the US, but Canadians are generally more formal. They do not move to a first-name basis as quickly, and are more reserved. Behavior tends to be particularly formal in Ontario and eastern Canada, and somewhat more casual in Quebec and the West. However, even reserved Canadians are open, direct, and friendly. The accepted greeting is smiling, making eye contact, and shaking hands. Handshakes are generally firm and brief, with a rapid, simple up-and-down motion. It is not necessary or appropriate to squeeze the other person's hand. In general, Canadians do not welcome body contact, casual touching, or frequent gesturing. Greetings will often be followed by a question about your trip, your health, or the weather. Such questions are a form of politeness. Long, detailed answers are not expected or especially wanted. After this quick, often superficial exchange, the next topic will be business.

Business Ethic

Initiative, independence, and efficiency are highly valued. In the words of one Canadian scholar, Canadians move slowly but with remarkable speed. Canadians admire self-reliance and original thinking. They are hard-working, and believe that diligence and effort will bring success and a better life. As a group, Canadians have a definite sense of national pride; they actively encourage one another to buy Canadian. Still, they are open minded and will not hesitate to explore their options in terms of available goods and services.

Decision Making

Canadians have conservative natures, a respect for formality, and are visibly polite; they do not generally act in haste, but neither is excessive time taken with thinking about moving forward. Once a proposition has been laid out and all its ramifications considered, decisions are made fairly quickly. Large corporations will take longer to come to a final decision, but this is mainly due to the hierarchies and bureaucratic nature of almost any large company. In smaller businesses, where one person might be the sole authority, decisions can be made very quickly.

Women

Men still hold the vast majority of management positions, but more and more women are being found at the higher levels of business. Canadian women expect to be treated seriously and with the respect to which their position entitles them. Failure to do this is considered insulting. A woman may not respond to such behavior at the moment, but she will probably express her displeasure to her colleagues later. Businesswomen are as open and direct as men, but this should not be viewed as anything more than being friendly. Treat women as you would any business associate. Foreign women should expect to be treated the same as their male counterparts, but exactly how a woman is dealt with will depend on the Canadian she is encountering. Sexual discrimination is against the law and not openly practiced, but private biases do exist. If a woman encounters discrimination, remember that this is more a reflection of that person than the company. In general, foreign women who are confident, professional, and self-assured can expect to be treated with respect and taken seriously.

Meetings

Meetings tend to be formal. They start on time and punctuality is expected. There will often be some polite social conversation, but business will be addressed fairly quickly. Canadians value efficiency, and once a meeting begins in earnest they like to proceed in an organized manner, wasting no time and without interruption. It is also important to always be courteous and polite. Canadians appreciate thoroughness, and will expect to be provided with all the information essential to any proposal. Not being prepared or appearing to be evasive will not be viewed positively.

Business Attire

Standard attire is a business suit, especially when dealing with large companies or doing business in cities. There is generally more latitude when dealing with smaller companies, or when doing business in western Canada and rural areas. Minimal attire is a jacket and tasteful pants, shirt, and shoes. Canadian women generally favor business dresses over suits. Women should dress professionally, tastefully, and conservatively when conducting business. Avoid extremes in fashion, including excessive jewelry or accessories.

Cultural Cautions

DO'S

- Although it is commonly heard, French-Canadian is not an entirely correct term to use. French-speaking Canadian is preferred.
- Eskimo is no longer considered a proper term. The preferred word is Inuit.

DON'TS

- Canada is not an extension of the US, and Canadians resent being viewed as such. Do not talk about Canada as if it is part of the US, and do not compare the two countries.
- The political and cultural tensions between English-speaking and French-speaking Canadians are sensitive issues. Do not bring them up in conversation.
- Do not make the 'Thumbs Down' gesture in Quebec. It's considered insulting.
- Do not talk with your hands in your pockets. Canadians will find this rude.

CUSTOMS

- Business cards are exchanged casually and informally. They are usually filed away or pocketed with only a quick glance or not read at all, unless a name, address, or phone number is being verified. In Canada, the person is more important than the card. Your card should be well-designed, but clearly convey the important information about your company. A card that effectively communicates information is ultimately more important than one that looks good but might be hard to read. If you are doing business in Quebec or an area with a large French-speaking Canadian population (New Brunswick, Nova Scotia, Prince Edward Island), you might consider having your card printed in French as well as your own language.
- Direct eye contact is common, and is a sign of openness and honesty. Staring at someone is rude and invasive, but refusing to make eye contact or quickly looking away can be taken as a sign that you're hiding something or are not to be trusted.

OBSERVATIONS

- In Canada, both English and French are spoken, depending on what part of the country a company is in. In Quebec, Quebecois insist on doing business in French. If Quebec is your area of interest and you plan to have your company's promotional material translated, hire a Quebecois to do your translating.
- Canada is the biggest country in North America, and the second largest country in the world. It covers six and one-half time zones, and most of its people identify more strongly with the province in which they live than with the country as a whole. Overall, Canada has a unified culture, but customs vary from region to region. Quebec tends to identify most strongly with its French heritage.
- There are many different ethnic groups in Canada. Some prefer to be treated as you would treat anyone in the larger business world. Others want to be seen as different. Be sensitive to this situation and treat ethnic minorities as you would treat anyone else, unless they indicate that they want to be treated differently.

NEGOTIATIONS

- Canadians generally do not haggle over prices. When they hear a price they often accept that figure. Responding to a negative answer by changing the price might raise questions about your honesty and the general good faith of your negotiations.
- Canadian businesspeople tend to trust others until they are given a reason not to. Once this happens, it can be extremely difficult, and sometimes impossible, to regain that broken trust.
- Tactics depend largely on the personality of the individual with whom you are dealing. Other factors include how big a company is, and how much international experience it has.

Legal System

Legislative and regulatory jurisdiction in Canada is divided and sometimes shared between the federal parliament and the legislatures of the 10 provinces and two territories. All except the Province of Quebec have a British-based common-law system. Quebec has a Civil Code.

Intellectual Property Rights

Patents Patent protection in Canada extends for a period of 20 years from the date of application and can be obtained for new or useful improvements in known products and processes. Canada is a member of the Patent Cooperation Treaty recognizing international patents from many countries.

Trademarks Trademarks are protected at common law, without registration, in trading areas where the trademark is used or has become known. Registration provides many advantages, including a presumption of validity. Trademark registration must be reviewed every 15 years.

Copyrights Copyrights of Canadians and most foreign nationals are recognized without registration, although registration confers additional rights and protections. For most qualifying works, copyright protection lasts for the life of the author and for a period of 50 years from the death of the author or from the death of the surviving author in cases of joint authorship. Legislation has recently been amended to strengthen protection for computer software and to prevent infringement through telecommunications.

Industrial Designs Ornamental design may be protected in Canada by registration. A design may be registered only once for a period of 10 years.

Business Registration

Enterprises, both foreign and domestic, are required to register in each province and territory in which they carry on business. Certain regulated industries have particular federal or provincial licensing requirements. Transfers of control or assets of business in these industries may require reporting or approval on a public interest basis. Certain acquisitions by non-Canadians require notification and some are reviewable, depending on the value of the business and/or industry sector. Businesses must register for a variety of taxes relating to income, sales, employment, and property.

Contracts and Dispute Resolution

Rights and obligations of parties to agreements are determined primarily by written contracts. Without a formal agreement, evidence of intention or customary practice may be considered. For certainty, detailed contracts are preferred. Canadian business documents tend to follow American precedents. Litigation is the usual means of determining commercial disputes which cannot be settled informally. Many contracts now provide for reference of disputes to arbitration. Most commercial litigation is heard in Provincial or Territorial courts, though certain matters must be litigated in the Federal Court of Canada. The litigation process in normal commercial disputes can take several years. Most provinces and territories have simple, quick small claims procedures with limits ranging from US$5,000 to US$15,000. Most arbitrations are under provincial legislations. Procedural rules are generally discretionary, so arbitration may be simple or complex depending on the wishes of the parties or the ruling of the arbitrator(s). Serious efforts are being made to make litigation and dispute resolution more effective and affordable.

Notaries

Notaries are provincially appointed. They authenticate documents as being true copies of originals and notarize sworn statements. Acknowledgments are not generally used. Consular certification is not required for acceptance of foreign notarized documents.

Labor

Provincial and territorial labor codes and legislation govern most employment. Some industries, transportation and communications, for example, may be subject to the Federal Labor Code. Workers have the right to unionize and bargain collectively. The right to strike is generally permitted except for essential services relating to public health and safety. Minimum wages and employment age are set provincially. Employers and employees both contribute to federal unemployment insurance which provides a limited interim income for employees who are terminated or laid off. The trend in employment law is to lessen intervention by the state and encourage freedom to contract and resolve disputes. Recent economic conditions have led to lower dismissal compensation, and a trend towards term contracts rather than permanent employment conditions for many professionals.

Sources: McKercher McKercher & Whitmore, Regina, Saskatchewan
Pitblado & Hoskin, Winnipeg, Manitoba

Legal Matters

LEGAL BRIEFS

- **Language** Canada is constitutionally bilingual—French and English. The federal government and a number of the provinces are required to legislate, regulate and provide services in both official languages. The Province of Quebec provides certain restrictions on use of the English language in commercial matters. Outside of Quebec, business can function effectively in English.

- **Corporations** A corporation may be formed federally or under individual, provincial, or territorial legislation. While most jurisdictions do not restrict foreign shareholding, most require that a majority of directors be Canadian or provincial residents. Federal corporations are able to choose and change the province or territory where the head office is located.

- **Termination of employment** A business has the right to arbitrarily terminate employment subject to legislated minimum notice periods or pay in lieu of such notice. Statutory termination rights tend to be minimal, and are supplemented by common-law right of reasonable notice or pay in lieu.

- **Legal protection** Non-nationals are not subjected to discriminatory treatment by civil courts.

- **American influence** The great volume of trade along with Canada's proximity to the United States have resulted in a strong American influence on Canadian business practices and documents. However, damage awards by Canadian Courts tend to be far more conservative than those of many American states. Class action suits are not common and product liability is based on a standard of reasonable care, not absolute liability.

- **Real property** Most land in developed areas is subject to provincial or territorial title or deed registration systems. Foreign ownership of land may be restricted, but those restrictions generally do not preclude foreign business operations. Security for loans and obligations can be registered against land.

- **Capital markets** Issuance of securities is provincially regulated. Attempted moves towards Canada-wide conformity have not been achieved. There are a number of stock markets which list publicly traded securities.

- **Trade agreements** Canada belongs to NAFTA along with the US and Mexico. The country is a part of GATT and seeks to encourage reciprocal trade opportunities.

LEGAL CONTACTS

Pitblado & Hoskin
1900-360 Main Street
Winnipeg, MB R3C 3Z3
Tel: (204) 942-0391 Fax: (204) 957-1790

McKercher McKercher & Whitmore
374 Third Avenue South
Saskatoon, SK S7K 1M5
Tel: (306) 653-2000 Fax: (306) 244-7335

Canadian Bar Association
902-50 O'Connor Street
Ottawa, ON K1P 6L2
Tel: (613) 237-2925 Fax: (613) 237-0185

Federation of Law Societies
480-445 boul. Saint-Laurent
Montreal, PQ H2Y 2Y7
Tel: (514) 875-6350 Fax: (514) 875-6115

Atkinson Milvain
1990-350-7 Avenue S.W.
Calgary, AB T2P 3N9
Tel: (403) 260-8500 Fax: (403) 264-7084

Boughton Peterson Yang Anderson
2500-1055 Dunsmuir Street
Vancouver, BC V7X 1S8
Tel: (604) 687-6789 Fax: (604) 683-5317

Hanson, Hashey
Suite 400 371 Queen St.
Fredricton, NB E3B 4Y9
Tel: (506) 453-7771 Fax: (506) 453-9600

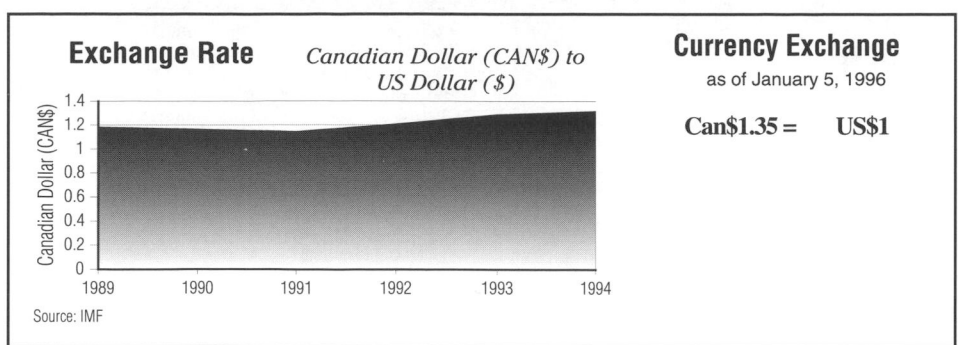

Exchange Rate *Canadian Dollar (CAN$) to US Dollar ($)*

Source: IMF

Currency Exchange
as of January 5, 1996

Can$1.35 = US$1

Currency

The currency of Canada is the Canadian dollar; its international symbol is Can$, and the principal subdivision is 100 cents.

Foreign Exchange

Canada does not impose foreign exchange control restrictions, and the Canadian dollar is fully convertible. The Canadian authorities do not maintain margins in respect of exchange transactions, and exchange rates are determined on the basis of supply and demand conditions. There are no taxes or subsidies on purchases or sales of foreign exchange.

Capital Transfers

The surrender of proceeds from exports is not required and exchange receipts are freely disposable. There are no controls imposed on capital receipts, or payments by residents or nonresidents.

Investment Incentives

With few exceptions, Canada offers foreign investors full national treatment within the context of a developed open market economy. For the vast majority of small acquisitions and the establishment of new businesses, non-Canadian investors need only notify the Canadian government of their investment. Both federal and provincial governments offer a wide array of incentives which are available to any qualified investor, Canadian or foreign, who agrees to use the funds for the stated purpose. Provincial incentives may be restricted to firms established in the province or who agree to establish in the province. Incentives may take the form of grants, loans, loan guarantees, venture capital, or tax credits.

Investment Restrictions

Canada is one of the few major economies that still has a formal investment review process, and foreign investment remains prohibited or restricted in a few sectors of the economy. Most restrictions are confined to the purchase of land and to the financial services industry. There are also restrictions on foreign investment in Canadian cultural industries due to Canada's fear that its own cultural identity will otherwise be overwhelmed by neighboring and powerful US cultural influences. Book publishing, newspapers and periodicals, television and broadcasting all retain significant limits on foreign investment, although it is allowed under certain conditions.

Money Matters

BITS AND PIECES

- **Capital receipts and payments** Capital receipts and payments by either residents or nonresidents may be transacted without restrictions, and Canada does not impose limitations on the transfer of funds into or out of the country.
- **Private ownership** Canadians and foreigners have the right to establish, own, and dispose of business enterprises and engage in all forms of remunerative activity which are not otherwise limited.
- **Currency** Banks, corporations and individuals are able to deal in foreign funds or arrange payments in any currency they choose.
- **Performance requirements** NAFTA prohibits Canada from imposing export or domestic content performance requirements upon US or Mexican products.
- **Capital markets** The Canadian capital market offers foreign investors the same full range of financial services and products that are available to Canadians.
- **Banking** Canada's banking system is dominated by five large banks that operate nationwide and account for 85 percent of total banking system assets.
- **Hostile takeovers** Canadian-controlled firms do not appear to have devised anti-hostile takeover provisions that discriminate against foreigners.
- **Debt-to-equity** Canada imposes a thin capitalization rule restricting nonresidents from withdrawing profits through interest charges. The interest deduction is restricted if interest is paid by a Canadian resident corporation to a specified nonresident on debt exceeding three times the shareholder's equity in the corporation.
- **Capital gains** Nonresidents are generally required to pay Canadian tax on their net taxable capital gains arising from the disposition of taxable Canadian property.
- **Gold** Residents may freely buy, hold, and sell gold in any form, at home or abroad. Gold of US origin requires a permit when re-exported to all countries except the United States.

BANKS

Bank of Canada (Central Bank)
234 Wellington St.
Ottawa, ON K1A 0G9
Tel: (613) 782-8111 Fax: (613) 782-8655

Bank of Montreal
129 rue St-Jacques ouest
Montreal, PQ H2Y 1L6
Tel: (514) 877-7110

Bank of Nova Scotia (Scotiabank)
44 King Street West
Toronto, ON M5H 1H1
Tel: (416) 866-6161 Fax: (416) 866-4988

Canadian Imperial Bank of Commerce (CIBC)
Commerce Court
Toronto, ON M5L 1G9
Tel: (416) 980-2211

Canadian Western Bank
10303 Jasper Ave., Suite 2300
Edmonton, AB T5J 3X6
Tel: (403) 423-8888 Fax: (403) 423-8897

National Bank of Canada
50 O'Connor Street, Suite 1224
Ottawa, ON K1P 6C2
Tel: (613) 238-8385

Royal Bank of Canada
200 Bay Street
Royal Bank Plaza
Toronto, ON M5J 2J5
Tel: (416) 974-5151

Toronto-Dominion Bank
POB 1
Toronto-Dominion Centre
55 King Street
Toronto, ON M5K 1A2
Tel: (416) 982-7730 Fax: (416) 982-5671

TAXATION

Taxation requires sophisticated knowledge of complex rules and regulations specific to each country. The information presented here is from the Ernst & Young Corporate Tax Guide and Directory, available from the Ernst & Young accounting office in your country, or from:

Ernst & Young
Mail Address:
Ernst & Young Tower
POB 251
Toronto-Dominion Centre
Toronto, ON M5K 1J7
Canada
Street Address:
Ernst & Young Tower
222 Bay Street
Toronto, ON M5K 1J7
Canada
Tel: (416) 864-1234
Fax: (416) 864-1174

At a Glance

Corporate Income Tax Rate (%) (a)	28.84
Capital Gains Tax Rate (%) (a)(b)	21.63
Branch Tax Rate (%) (c)	25
Withholding Tax (%)	
Dividends (d)	25
Interest (d)	25
Royalties from Patents, Know-how, etc. (d)	25
Branch Remittance Tax	0
Net Operating Losses (Years)	
Carryback	3
Carryforward	7

(a)The rates reflect budget proposals at December 31, 1994. The rate is applied to income that is not eligible for the manufacturing and processing deduction or the small business deduction. It comprises a basic rate of 38% plus a 3% surtax. Additional tax is levied by the provinces and territories of Canada, and the combined federal and provincial or territorial rates vary from 37.74% to 45.84%.
(b)75% of capital gains is subject to tax.
(c)This tax is imposed in addition to the regular corporate income tax.
(d)Final tax applicable only to nonresidents.

Business Travel

LH 1906	MADRID	935	113-3
LH 1022	STUTTGART HBF.	935	-
AF 1701	LYON	940	683-6
AY 822	HELSINKI	940	113-3
AA 071	SFRANCISCO-DALLAS	945	731-7

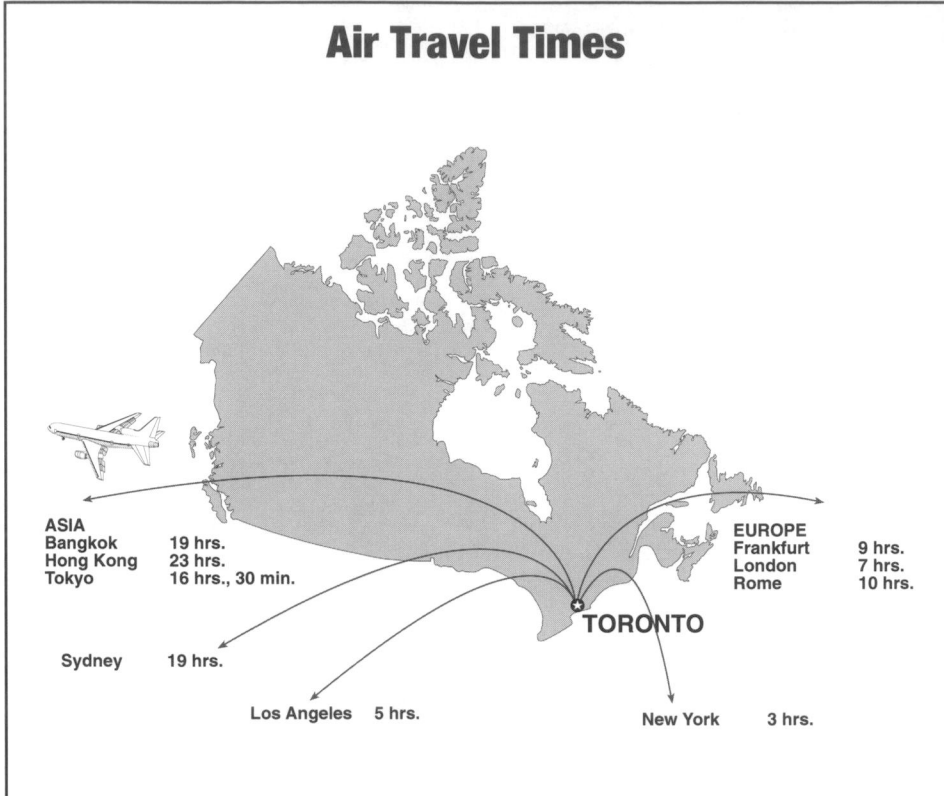

Air Travel Times

ASIA
Bangkok 19 hrs.
Hong Kong 23 hrs.
Tokyo 16 hrs., 30 min.

Sydney 19 hrs.

Los Angeles 5 hrs.

EUROPE
Frankfurt 9 hrs.
London 7 hrs.
Rome 10 hrs.

TORONTO

New York 3 hrs.

COMMUNICATIONS

Telephone Bell Canada provides service in Canada with standards equal to the United States. Pay phones are available in stores, restaurants, and street booths.
Fax Services are widely available, as are telex services. Contact the nearest Canadian National and Canadian Pacific (CN-CP) telegraph office or ask at the hotel desk for assistance.
Post office Service is excellent unless disrupted by labor strikes. Main post offices and smaller branches are listed in the phone book under "Canada Post Corporation." Stamps are available at hotels, convenience stores, pharmacies, vending machines, and post offices. Mailboxes are red. Courier service is available to most major cities worldwide the following business day.
Radio/TV The Canadian Broadcasting Corporation owns two radio networks and two television networks, one in English and one in French. The Canadian Television Network (CTV), privately owned, broadcasts in English nationwide, along with many other privately owned stations.

BEST TRAVEL BOOKS

Canada, Lonely Planet. The most complete guide a potential visitor could hope for. 852 pages, 16 color pages.
Fodor's Travel Guide, Canada. Tourist oriented, excellent source of city details.
Culture Shock, A Guide to Customs and Etiquette, Canada.
A Guide to International Behavior Do's and Taboos Around the World. Edited by Roger E. Axtell, compiled by the Parker Pen Company. Now completely updated and revised, the ultimate guide to international behavior. Helpful, fun to read.

TELEPHONE NUMBERS

If you are calling from outside Canada you will need to add the country code [1] and any other international dialing requirements from within your country. Toll-free (800) numbers may only be available from within Canada and/or the United States.

- Emergency 911
- VAT Refunds .... (800) 668-4748
- Canadian Immigration Division .... (613) 953-5118

Travel and Tourism Services
- Air Canada .... (800) 776-3000
- Canadian Airlines International .... (800) 426-7000
- Canadian Auto Association .... (613) 226-7631
- Avis .... (800) 879-2847
- Hertz .... (800) 263-0600
- Toronto Conv. & Visitors Assoc. ...... (416) 203-2500
- Vancouver Tourist Information .... (604) 683-2000
- Tourism Quebec .... (514) 643-2280
- Ottawa Tourism & Conv. Auth. .... (613) 237-5150

Courier Services
- DHL Courier/Montreal .... (514) 636-8703
- FedEx/Montreal .... (514) 345-0130
- DHL Courier/Toronto .... (416) 244-3278
- FedEx/Toronto .... (416) 897-9322
- DHL Courier/Vancouver .... (604) 278-3984
- FedEx/Vancouver .... (604) 273-1544

Business Associations
- Chamber of Commerce/Ottawa .... (613) 995-5771
- Canadian Economic Council .... (613) 952-1711
- Canadian Importers Association ...... (416) 595-5333

Credit Card Information
Lost or stolen credit cards (call collect to the US, regardless of which country the card was issued in).
- Amex .... [1] (919) 333-3211
- Diner's Club .... [1] (303) 799-1504
- MasterCard .... [1] (314) 275-6690
- Visa .... [1] (410) 581-7931

Travelogue

WORKWEEK

Offices Monday-Friday 9:00 am to 5:00 pm.
Banks Monday-Wednesday, Friday 10:00 am to 3:30 pm; Thursday 10:00 am to 4:30 pm.
Government Monday-Friday 9:00 am to 5:00 pm.
Retail Monday-Wednesday, Saturday 9:30 am to 6:00 pm; Thursday-Friday 9:30 am to 9:00 pm.

HOLIDAYS

Holidays 1996
January 1 New Year's Day
April 5 Good Friday
April 8 Easter Monday*
May 20 Victoria Day
July 1 Canada Day
September 2 Labor Day
October 14 Thanksgiving Day*
November 11 Remembrance Day
December 25 Christmas
December 26 Boxing Day
*Dates vary year to year.
In addition, there are many regional religious and other holidays.

VISA AND PASSPORT

Citizens of the United States and some other countries may not need a passport or visa to enter Canada for short periods of time; however, a passport is always the best form of identification. If you think you may need a visa, be sure to contact the Canadian embassy or high commission in your country before departure as visas must be issued in advance.

DEPARTURE FORMALITIES

There are no departure formalities for Canada.

IMMUNIZATION

A smallpox vaccination certificate is required for anyone in an infected country within the previous two weeks. There are no other required vaccinations, and no special precautions or serious health problems. In the Toronto area the pollen count is high and may require allergy medication.

TIPPING

Taxi: 15 percent. Porters: 75 cents per piece. Hotels: room service, transport of luggage included in bill. Restaurants, nightspots: 15 percent seldom included in bill, but taxes are included. Beauticians, barbers: 15 percent. Doorman, attendants, small services: 50 cents.

CRIME

Canada has a reputation of being safe and clean, but be aware that incidents of robbery and assault occur. Crime is more prevalent in urban areas than rural areas but is generally not common. Severe penalties are imposed on anyone found driving under the influence of alcohol.

INFRASTRUCTURE

All major cities are served by international airlines; most fly through Edmonton. There are few direct flights to Quebec, and most connect through Montreal or Toronto. Air Canada provides excellent domestic service and Canadian Airlines now flies to Europe, Latin America, and the Far East. Air shuttle buses operate regularly between Calgary and Edmonton with additional service to outer parts of the province. Taxi service is available at all airports to downtown areas. Airporter buses are also available to most major hotels. In Montreal, Aerocar is the most efficient way to travel from the airport. Limousine services are also available. All major car rental agencies are available across the country. An international driver's license is required for all drivers except US residents. Bus and rail service is available and efficient within all the major cities. Due to the vast size of Canada, it is most sensible to travel by air between cities. Passenger rail service between cities has been cut nearly 50 percent nationwide.

NATIONAL TOURIST OFFICE

Tourism Canada
Industry, Science and Technology Canada
235 Queen Street, 4th Floor East
Ottawa, ON K1A 0H6
Tel: (613) 954-3851 Fax: (613) 952-7906

GOVERNMENT AGENCIES

Enquiries Canada
(reference office for federal programs and services)
Tel: (613) 941-4823

Provincial Government Contacts
Alberta: (403) 427-2711
British Columbia: (604) 387-6121
Manitoba: (204) 945-3744
New Brunswick: (506) 453-2525
Newfoundland: (709) 729-3610
Northwest Territories: (403) 873-7110
Nova Scotia: (902) 424-5200
Ontario: (416) 326-1234
Prince Edward Island: (902) 368-5050
Quebec: (514) 873-2111
Saskatchewan: (306) 787-0222
Yukon: (403) 667-5811

Agriculture and Agri-Food Canada
Sir John Carling Building
930 Carling Avenue
Ottawa, ON K1A 0C5
Tel: (613) 995-5222
Fax: (613) 996-9564

Environment Canada
Ottawa, ON K1A 0H3
Tel: (819) 997-2800 Fax: (819) 953-2225

Fisheries and Oceans, Dept. of
200 Kent Street
Ottawa, ON K1A 0E6
Tel: (613) 993-0999 Fax: (613) 990-1866

Foreign Affairs and International Trade, Dept. of
Lester B. Pearson Building
125 Sussex Drive
Ottawa, ON K1A 0G2
Tel: (613) 944-4000 Fax: (613) 944-0699

Health Canada
Tunney's Pasture
Ottawa, ON K1A 0K9
Tel: (613) 957-2991

Industry Canada
235 Queen Street
Ottawa, ON K1A 0H5
Tel: (613) 954-2788

Public Works and Government Services Canada
Place du Portage
Phase III, 18A1
11 Laurier Street
Hull, PQ K1A 0S5
Tel: (819) 997-5421

Revenue Canada
Customs, Excise and Taxation
Connaught Building
MacKenzie Avenue
Ottawa, ON K1A 0L5

Transport Canada
330 Sparks Street
Ottawa, ON K1A 0N5
Tel: (613) 990-2309, 996-2358

Finance Canada
L'Esplanade Laurier, East Tower
140 O'Connor Street
Ottawa, ON K1A 0G5
Tel: (613) 986-7861 Fax: (613) 995-5176

Natural Resources Canada
580 Booth Street
Ottawa, ON K1A 0E4
Tel: (613) 995-4269 Fax: (613) 992-8922

Canada Labor Relations Board
4th Floor, C.D. Howe Building
240 Sparks Street
Ottawa, ON K1A 0X8
Tel: (613) 995-7046
Telex: 534426

Immigration and Refugee Board
116 Lisgar Street
Ottawa, ON K1A 0K1
Tel: (613) 995-6486

Department of External Affairs
Lester B. Pearson Buildings
125 Sussex Drive
Ottawa, ON K1A 0G2

Office of the Minister for International Trade
515S, House of Commons
Ottawa, ON K1A 0A6
Tel: (613) 992-7332

WORLD TRADE CENTERS

World Trade Center Edmonton
POB 1480
Edmonton, AB T5J 2N5
Tel: (403) 471-7283 Fax: (403) 477-0128

World Trade Center Halifax
1800 Argyle Street
POB 955
Halifax, NS B3J 2V9
Tel: (902) 428-7233 Fax: (902) 420-8308

World Trade Center Montreal
380 Saint-Antoine Street West, Suite 2100
Montreal, PQ H2Y 3X7
Tel: (514) 849-1999 Fax: (514) 847-8343

World Trade Centre Ottawa
45 O'Connor, Suite 300
Ottawa, ON K1P 1AH
Tel: (613) 230-5223 Fax: (613) 236-7498

World Trade Centre Vancouver
999 Canada Place, Suite 400
Vancouver, B.C. V6C 3C1
Tel: (604) 681-2111 Fax: (604) 681-0437

BUSINESS AND TRADE ORGANIZATIONS

Canadian Chamber of Commerce
55 Metcalfe Street, Suite 1160
Ottawa, ON K1P 6N4
Tel: (613) 238-4000 Fax: (613) 238-7643

Canadian Exporters' Association
99 Bank Street, Suite 250
Ottawa, ON K1P 6B9
Tel: (613) 238-8888 Fax: (613) 563-9218

Canadian Importers' Association Inc.
210 Dundas Street West Suite 700
Toronto, ON M5G 2E8
Tel: (416) 595-5333 Fax: (416) 595-8226

Canadian Manufacturers' Association
75 International Boulevard, 4th Floor
Etobicoke, ON M9W 6L9
Tel: (416) 798-8000 Fax: (416) 798-8050

Aerospace Industries Association of Canada
60 Queen Street, Suite 1200
Ottawa, ON K1P 5Y7
Tel: (613) 232-4297 Fax: (613) 232-1142

Automotive Industries Association of Canada
1272 Wellington Street
Ottawa, ON K1Y 3A7
Tel: (613) 728-5821 Fax: (613) 728-6021

Canadian Advanced Technology Association
388 Albert Street
Ottawa, ON K1R 5B2
Tel: (613) 236-6550 Fax: (613) 236-8189

Canadian Packaging Association
2255 Sheppard Avenue E. Suite E330
Willowdale, ON M2J 4Y1
Tel: (416) 490-7860 Fax: (416) 490-7844

National Arts Center Corporation
POB 1534, Station B
Ottawa, ON K1P 5W1
Tel: (613) 996-5051

Agricultural Institute of Canada
151 Slater Street, Suite 907
Ottawa, ON K1P 5H4
Tel: (613) 232-9459

Canadian Construction Association
85 Albert Street, 10th Floor
Ottawa, ON K1P 6A4
Tel: (613) 236-9455 Fax: (613) 236-9526

Apparel Manufactures-Marketers Association
116 Albert Street, Suite 803
Ottawa, ON K1P 5G3
Tel: (613) 565-3047 Fax: (613) 429-0158

Canadian Association of Fish Exporters
71 Bank Street
Ottawa, ON K1P 5N2
Tel: (613) 232-6325 Fax: (613) 232-7697

Canadian Shipowners Association
350 Sparks Street, Suite 705
Ottawa, ON K1R 7S8
Tel: (613) 232-3539 Fax:(613) 232-6211

Air Transport Association of Canada
99 Bank Street, Suite 747
Ottawa, ON K1P 6B9
Tel: (613) 233-7727 Fax: (613) 230-8648

LEGAL CONTACTS

Federation of Law Societies
480-445 boul, Saint-Laurent
Montreal, PQ H2Y 2Y7
Tel: (514) 875-6350 Fax: (514) 875-6115

Canadian Bar Association
902-50 O'Connor Street
Ottawa, ON K1P 6L2
Tel: (613) 237-2925 Fax: (613) 237-0185

Cox Downie
1100-1959 Upper Water Street
Halifax, NS B3J 3E5
Tel: (902) 421-6262 Fax: (902) 421-3130

Atkinson Milvain
1990-350-7 Avenue S.W.
Calgary, AB T2P 3N9
Tel: (403) 260-8500 Fax: (403) 264-7084

Boughton Peterson Yang Anderson
2500-1055 Dunsmuir Street
Vancouver, BC V7X 1S8
Tel: (604) 687-6789 Fax: (604) 683-5317

Hanson, Hashey
Suite 400-371 Queen Street
Fredericton, NB E3B 4Y9
Tel: (506) 453-7771 Fax: (506) 453-9600

Harrison, Elwood
450 Talbot Street
London, ON N6A 4K3

Minden, Gross, Grafstein & Greenstein
111 Richmond Street West, Suite 600
Toronto M5H 2H5
Tel: (416) 362-3711 Fax: (416) 362-9631

Wilson Walker Hochberg Slopen
443 Ouellette Avenue
Suite 300
Windsor, ON N9A 6R4
Tel: (519) 977-1555 Fax: (519) 977-1566

Lafleur Brown
1 Place Ville Marie, 37th Floor
Montreal, PQ H3B 3P4
Tel: (514) 878-9641 Fax: (514) 878-1450

Baker & McKenzie
112 Adelaide Street East
Toronto, ON M5C 1K9
Tel: (416) 863-1221 Fax: (416) 863-6275

Pitblado & Hoskin
1900-360 Main Street
Winnepeg, Manitoba R3C 3Z3
Tel: (204) 942-0391 Fax: (204) 957-1790

STOCK EXCHANGES

Alberta Stock Exchange
300 Fifth Ave. SW, 21st Floor
Calgary, AB T2P 3CR
Tel: (403) 262-7791 Fax: (403) 237-0450

Montreal Stock Exchange/Bourse de Montreal
#800, Tour de la Bourse
Square Victoria
CP 61
Montreal, PQ H4Z 1A9
Tel: (514) 871-2424 Fax: (514) 871-3553

Toronto Stock Exchange
The Exchange Tower
2 First Canadian Place
Toronto, ON M5X 1J2
Tel: (416) 947-4700 Fax: (416) 947-4585
Telex: 062-177759

Vancouver Stock Exchange
Stock Exchange Tower
609 Granville St.
PO Box 10333
Vancouver, BC V7Y 1H1
Tel: (604) 689-3334 Fax: (604) 688-6051

Winnipeg Stock Exchange
One Lombard Place, Suite 2901
Winnipeg, R3B 0Y2
Tel: (204) 942-8431 Fax: (204) 947-9536

NEWSPAPERS

Calgary Sun
2615 12th St. NE
Calgary, AB T2E 7W9
Tel: (403) 291-4200 Fax: (403) 291-4242

Edmonton Journal
PO Box 2421
Edmonton, AB T5J 2S6
Tel: (403) 429-5400 Fax: (403) 498-5604

Edmonton Sun
4990 92nd Avenue, Suite 250
Edmonton AB T6B 3A1
Tel: (403) 468-0100

Financial Post
777 Bay Street
Toronto, ON M5W 1A7
Tel: (416) 350-6000

The Gazette
250 rue St-Antoine ouest
Montreal, PQ H2Y 3R7
Tel: (514) 987-2222 Fax: (514) 987-2270

The Globe and Mail
444 Front St. West
Toronto, ON M5V 2S9
Tel: (416) 585-5000 Fax: (416) 585-5085

Le Journal de Montreal
4545 rue Frontenac
Montreal, PQ H2H 2R7
Tel: (514) 521-4545 Fax: (514) 525-5442

Ottawa Citizen
1101 Baxter Rd.
PO Box 5020
Ottawa, ON K2C 3M4
Tel: (613) 829-9100 Fax: (613) 596-3755

Ottawa Sun
380 Hunt Club Rd.
Ottawa, ON K1G 3N3
Tel: (613) 739-7000 Fax: (613) 739-8043

La Presse
7 rue St-Jacques
Montreal, PQ H2Y 1K9
Tel: (514) 285-7272 Fax: (514) 285-8943

Toronto Star
One Yonge St.
Toronto, ON M5E 1E6
Tel: (416) 367-2000 Fax: (416) 865-3642

Toronto Sun
333 King St. East
Toronto, ON M5A 3X5
Tel: (416) 947-2222 Fax: (416) 368-0374

Vancouver Sun
2250 Granville St.
Vancouver, BC V6H 3G2
Tel: (604) 732-2111 Fax: (604) 732-2323

Winnipeg Sun
1700 Church Ave.
Winnipeg, MB R2X 3A2
Tel: (204) 694-2022 Fax: (204) 697-0759

PERIODICALS

Affairs Plus
1100 blvd. René-Lévesque ouest, 24e étage
Montreal, PQ H3B 4X9
Tel: (514) 392-9000 Fax: (514) 392-1586

BC Business
4180 Lougheed Hwy., Suite 401
Burnaby, BC V5C 6A7
Tel: (604) 299-7311 Fax: (604) 299-9188

Brunswick Business Journal
599 Main St., Suite 203
Moncton, NB E1C 1C8
Tel: (506) 857-9696 Fax: (506) 859-7395

Canada & The World
PO Box 7004
Oakville, ON L6J 6L5
Tel: (905) 338-3394

Canada Gazette
(Official bulletin of the Canadian government)
45 Sacre Coeur Blvd.
Ottawa, ON K1A 0S9
Tel: (819) 997-1988 Fax: (819) 956-5134

Canadian Banker
Commerce Court West
Toronto, ON M5L 1G2
Tel: (416) 362-6092 Fax: (416) 362-5658

Canadian Bar Review
Canadian Bar Foundation
50 O'Connor St., Suite 902
Ottawa, ON K1P 6L2
Tel: (613) 237-2925 Fax: (613) 237-0185

Canadian Business
70 The Esplanada, 2nd Fl.
Toronto, ON M5E 1R2
Tel: (416) 364-4266 Fax: (416) 364-2783

Financial Times of Canada
440 Front St. West
Toronto, ON M5V 3E6
Tel: (416) 585-5555 Fax: (416) 585-5549

L'Actualité
101 blvd. de Maisonneuve ouest
Montreal, PQ H3A 3E1
Tel: (514) 845-2543 Fax: (514) 845-4393

Maclean's: Canada's Weekly Newsmagazine
Maclean Hunter Ltd.
777 Bay St.
Toronto, ON M5W 1A7
Tel: (416) 596-5955 Fax: (416) 593-3162

Revue Commerce
1100 blvd. René-Lévesque ouest, 24e étage
Montreal, PQ H3B 4X9
Tel: (514) 392-9000 Fax: (514) 392-4726

Toronto Life Magazine
59 Front St. East, 3rd Fl.
Toronto, ON M5E 1B3
Tel: (416) 364-3333 Fax: (416) 861-1169

Trade and Commerce
PO Box 6900
Winnipeg, MB R3C 3B1
Tel: (204) 632-2606

WestWorld Magazine
4180 Lougheed Hwy., Suite 401
Burnaby, BC V5C 6A7
Tel: (604) 299-7311 Fax: (604) 299-9188

RADIO AND TELEVISION

Canadian Broadcasting Corporation
CBC Building, 1500 Bronson Avenue
POB 8478
Ottawa, ON K1G 3J5
Tel: (613) 724-1200, 738-6505 Fax: (613) 738-6843

CTV Television Network
42 Charles Street, East
Toronto, ON M4Y IT5
Tel: (416) 928-6000 Fax: (416) 928-0907

Global Television Network
81 Barber Greene Rd.
Don Mills, ON M3C 2A2
Tel: (416) 446-5311 Fax: (416) 446-5371

Telesat Canada
1601 Telesat court
Gloucester, ON K1B 5PA
Tel: (613) 748-0123

INTERNET ADDRESSES

Usenet group(s):
misc.invest.canada
soc.culture.canada
soc.culture.quebec
can.general

The Department of Foreign Affairs and International Trade (DFAIT)
http://www.dfait-maeci.gc.ca/english/menu.htm

Canadian-based Information Systems
http://www.cs.cmu.edu/Web/Unofficial/Canadiana/CA-gophers.html

Canadian - The Canadian Resource Page
http://www.cs.cmu.edu/Web/Unofficial/Canadiana/

Canadian Government Departments
http://www1.cciw.ca/opengov/departments.html

Canada Business Center
http://csclub.uwaterloo.ca/u/nckwan/html/directory.html

Welcome to Industry Canada
http://info.ic.gc.ca/ic-data/ic-eng.html

Chile

Republic of Chile

Economy

Overview

Chile has a prosperous, essentially free market economy that has experienced a decade of growth by applying free trade policies and vigorously promoting foreign investment. Investment, exports, and consumer spending have grown substantially during this period. This growth may slow due to high domestic interest rates and lower world prices for Chile's copper, fishmeal, and cellulose. Chile's liberal import policies and expanding economy provide an attractive market for a wide range of products and services.

Trade

Chile is working to diversify its products and trade relationships. Main export products include copper, processed foods, fruits and vegetables, other (non-copper) minerals, and chemicals. Imports include machinery, chemicals, consumer goods, miscellaneous manufactures, and metal products. The US is Chile's main trading partner, accounting for nearly 20 percent of total trade. Japan, Germany, Brazil, and Argentina are its next largest trading partners. Chile is attempting to increase trade with its Latin American neighbors, as well as with other countries in Asia and Europe.

Sectors

Agriculture Agriculture contributes less than 10 percent of GDP, but employs nearly 20 percent of the work force. Fruit and vegetables and wood and forest products are the main areas of focus, and fishing is also significant. The government encourages forestry production through subsidies, and foreign investors have targeted this already relatively well-established sector for further growth.

Industry Industry accounts for more than 35 percent of GDP and slightly more than 25 percent of employment. The main activities include food processing (wine is a significant export), mining (Chile is the world's largest producer and exporter of copper, which has accounted for as much as 90 percent of export earnings in some recent years), petroleum refining, paper, and chemicals. Chile has attempted to develop more high value-added manufacturing, such as automotive production, but the small scale and need for the use of imported components has kept this area from developing.

Services More than half of Chile's GDP and a comparable percentage of its employment come from the service sector. Chileans are generally well-educated, and pockets of sophisticated services exist, especially in the areas of financial and business services, although most services are more basic, involving distribution and personal service activities.

Trends

The export boom, principally in copper, fresh fruit, and forest and fisheries products, is slowing but should continue to experience strong moderate growth for the remainder of the decade. Foreign and domestic investment have created jobs and increased wages, and overall dependency on copper is declining. Latin America is joining the US, Asia, and the EU as important purchasers of Chilean products. International reserves have risen, and despite increased total indebtedness, foreign debt remains under control. Chile's reliance on exports and interest in market diversification has led it to seek membership in various trade pacts as well as to sign trade-liberalizing agreements with several Latin American nations.

At a Glance

THE COUNTRY

Location Southern South America, bordering the South Pacific Ocean between Argentina and Peru.
Terrain Desert in north; fertile central valley; volcanoes and lakes toward the south, giving way to a rugged and complex coastline; with the Andes Mountains on the eastern border.
Climate Arid in the north; Mediterranean climate in the center; and cool and damp in the south.

THE PEOPLE

Population 13,900,000
Ethnic composition
European and European-Indian............................ 95%
Indian 3%
Other.. 2%
Religious composition
Roman Catholic 80%
Protestant 16%
Languages spoken Spanish.
Education and literacy State schools provide free, compulsory, primary education. Adult literacy rates have been estimated at 94 percent, although this is primarily for younger adults in urban areas. The literacy rate for the country as a whole is probably much lower.
Labor force
Total:...5,200,000
By occupation: services and government 36%, industry and commerce 34%, agriculture, forestry, and fishing 20%, construction 7%, and mining 2%.

COUNTRY FACTS

Political and legal The legal system of this republic is based on the Code of 1857, derived from Spanish law. Chile is a civil code country, with current codes heavily influenced by French and Austrian law. There is judicial review of legislative acts in the Supreme Court. Chile has not accepted compulsory International Court of Justice jurisdiction.
Telephone Chile boasts the best telecommunications system in Latin America. Fax and phone services are widely available. An extensive telegraph service links larger cities and towns. International country code: [56]. Selected city codes: Santiago (2), Valparaiso (32), Concepcion (41).
Transportation Chile has the fourth largest railway system in Latin America; railroads are the most commonly used means of transport. Air transportation is also important, with over 40 commercially usable airports.
Environment Chile and the US signed in 1993 an environmental framework agreement under which Chilean payments on aid loans are used for domestic environmental projects. Current issues include air pollution from industrial and vehicle emissions; water pollution from untreated sewage; deforestation contributing to loss of biodiversity; soil erosion; and desertification.
Media Television and radio service is available throughout the country and operated by both the state and private sectors. There are 159 AM radio stations and 131 television stations.
Health Chile has made considerable progress in raising health standards, and medical care and facilities exist throughout the country. Life expectancy of males is 71.5 years; of females, 77.6 years.

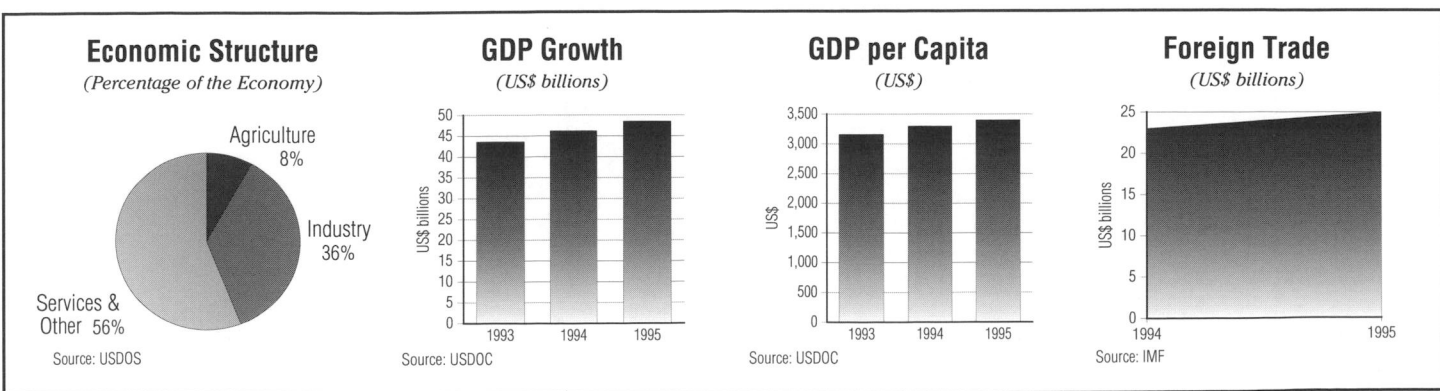

Economic Structure
(Percentage of the Economy)

Agriculture 8%
Industry 36%
Services & Other 56%

Source: USDOS

GDP Growth
(US$ billions)

Source: USDOC

GDP per Capita
(US$)

Source: USDOC

Foreign Trade
(US$ billions)

Source: IMF

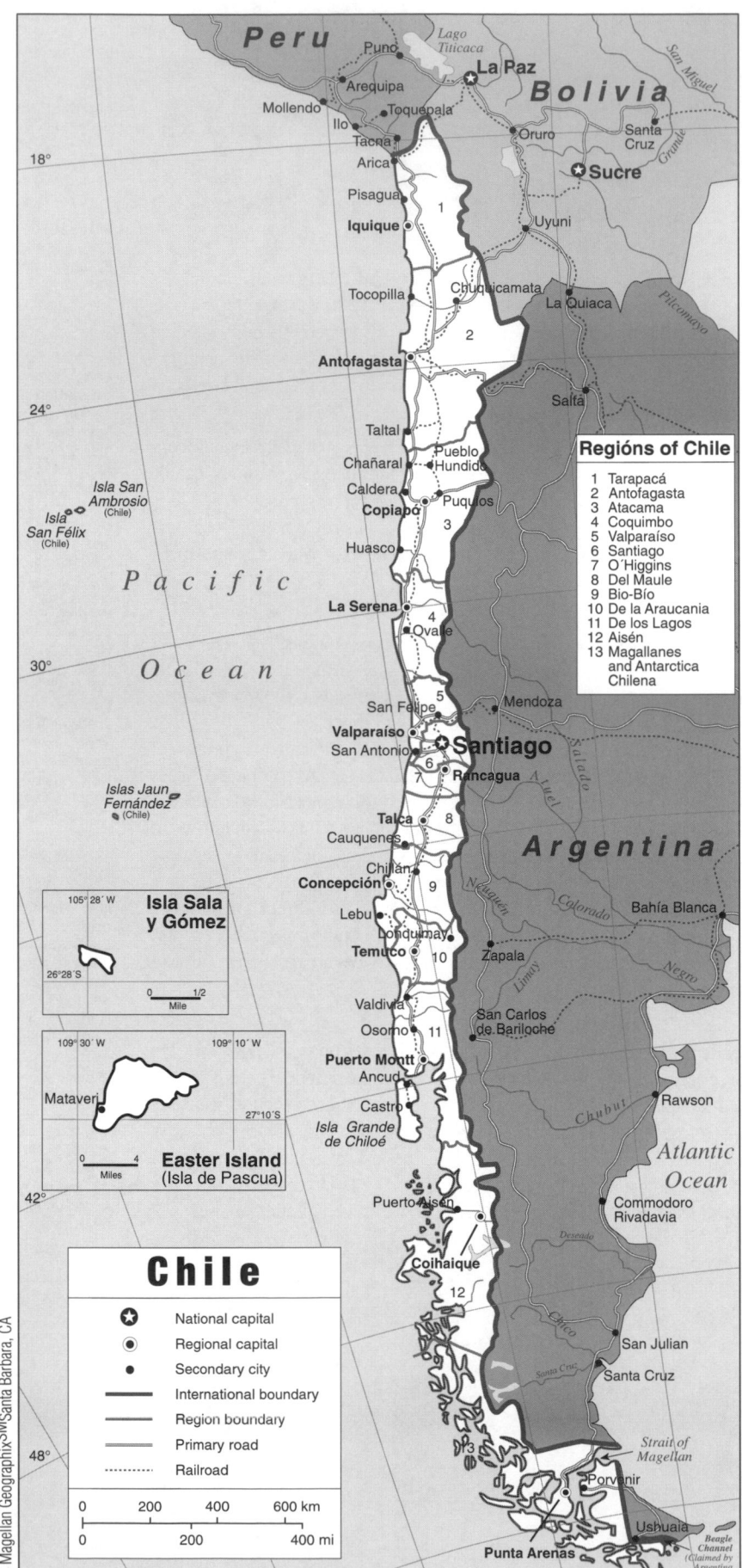

Regións of Chile

1 Tarapacá
2 Antofagasta
3 Atacama
4 Coquimbo
5 Valparaíso
6 Santiago
7 O´Higgins
8 Del Maule
9 Bio-Bío
10 De la Araucania
11 De los Lagos
12 Aisén
13 Magallanes and Antarctica Chilena

Isla Sala y Gómez

105° 28´ W
26°28´S

0   1/2
Mile

109° 30´ W   109° 10´ W

27°10´S

Mataveri

0   4
Miles

Easter Island
(Isla de Pascua)

Chile

⊛ National capital
◉ Regional capital
● Secondary city
── International boundary
── Region boundary
── Primary road
····· Railroad

0   200   400   600 km

0   200   400 mi

Foreign Trade

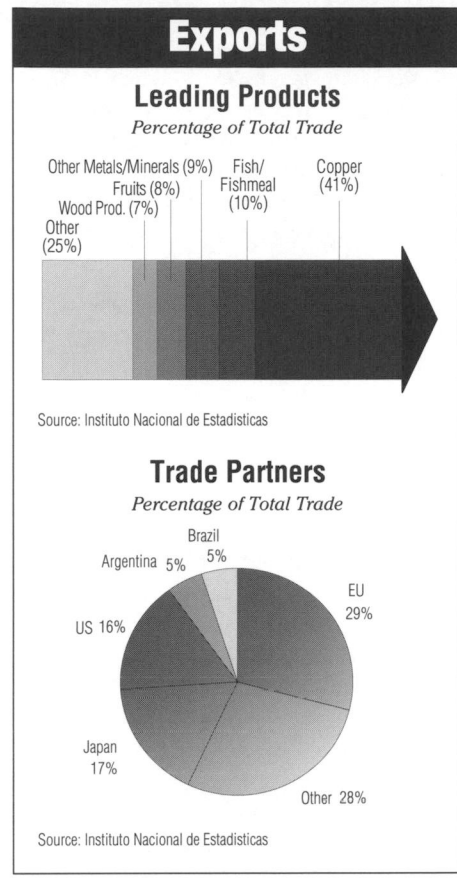

Imports

Leading Products
Percentage of Total Trade

Capital Goods (25%)
Spare Parts (25%)
Raw Materials (15%)
Petroleum (10%)
Foodstuffs (6%)
Other (19%)

Source: Instituto Nacional de Estadisticas

Trade Partners
Percentage of Total Trade

Japan 10%
Brazil 10%
Other 35%
US 21%
EU 24%

Source: Instituto Nacional de Estadisticas

Exports

Leading Products
Percentage of Total Trade

Other Metals/Minerals (9%)
Fruits (8%)
Wood Prod. (7%)
Other (25%)
Fish/Fishmeal (10%)
Copper (41%)

Source: Instituto Nacional de Estadisticas

Trade Partners
Percentage of Total Trade

Brazil 5%
Argentina 5%
US 16%
Japan 17%
EU 29%
Other 28%

Source: Instituto Nacional de Estadisticas

Opportunities

FOR IMPORTING TO CHILE
- aircraft and aircraft parts
- avionics equipment
- beef
- capital goods
- chemical products
- computer products
- consumer durables
- corn
- dry milk
- electronic equipment
- fertilizer
- medical equipment
- petroleum
- pollution control equipment
- telecommunication products
- vegetable oils
- vehicles and parts
- wheat

FOR EXPORTING FROM CHILE
- chemicals
- copper
- fish, especially farmed salmon
- fruits
- gold
- iron ore
- metal products
- paper products
- silver
- textiles
- transportation equipment
- vegetables
- wood products

GROWTH SECTORS
- computers
- construction
- environmental protection goods and services
- financial services
- industrial chemicals
- mining
- telecommunications

GOVERNMENT PROCUREMENT
- avionics and ground support equipment
- highway construction

Trade News

RULES AND REGULATIONS

- **Regulations** The National Customs Service (Servicio Nacional de Aduanas) oversees tariff control.
- **Tariff** An 11 percent tariff applies to more than 95 percent of Chile's imports. One exception is the agricultural price band or surcharge mechanism on wheat, edible oils and derivatives, and raw sugar. The surcharge is designed to maintain domestic prices for these commodities, within a pre-determined band, in order to shield Chilean producers from international price fluctuations.
- **Value-added tax (VAT)** Chile levies a VAT of 18 percent on practically all goods. The VAT is calculated on the basis of the CIF (cost + freight + insurance) value of the goods plus the import duty. Some capital goods are eligible for a postponement or waiver of import duties and exemptions from VAT.
- **Luxury items** In addition to import duties and VAT, luxury items are taxed based on their CIF value at the time of their entry into Chile. Taxes for luxury items range from 50 percent for precious jewels to 30 percent for some liquors and 13 percent for mineral water. Automobiles are subject to additional taxes based on value and engine size.
- **Import restrictions** Firearms can be imported, but they require a special permit from a military authority in Chile. Imported foodstuffs and live animals must be accompanied by phytosanitary or health certificates from the country of origin.
- **Registration certificate** Chile's Central Bank requires that importers obtain a registration certificate, known as the "Informed de Importacion," for all imports valued over US$3,000. The certificate is free and is used for statistical purposes.
- **Import licenses** Import licenses are granted as a routine procedure. Licenses are required for weapons and pharmaceuticals. Licensing requirements are maintained largely as a statistical gathering mechanism, not as a control.
- **Free trade zones** Chile has two free trade zones: Iquique, in the north; and Punta Arenas, in the south.
- **Export control** Chile applies export controls through the requirement of an export license, as well as phytosanitary and quality controls on certain products controlled by the National Health Service, the Agricultural and Livestock Service, and the National Fishing Service. Licenses are generally granted routinely, and are required more as a means of gathering statistics than as a means of control.
- **Temporary entry** Temporary imports of goods are authorized for government-approved exhibitions and for temporary demonstration purposes. For Chilean government-approved exhibitions, no duty or VAT is levied, and goods may remain in the country up to six months, but must be kept in a warehouse.
- **Labeling** Imported products customarily consumed by the public must display the country of origin on them before being sold in Chile. Packaged goods must be marked to show the quality, purity, ingredients or mixtures, as well as the net weight or measure of the contents.
- **Prohibited imports** The importation of used passenger and cargo transportation vehicles is prohibited.

GOVERNMENT AGENCIES

National Customs Service
Plaza Sotomayor 60
Valparaiso
Tel: (32) 217-911
Beaucheff 1525; Santiago
Tel: (2) 683-6807

Ministry of Foreign Relations
Morande 441
Santiago
Tel: (2) 696-2574/4574
Fax: (2) 696-8796

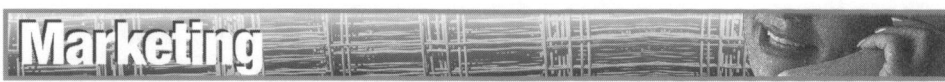

Marketing

Overview

The population of Chile is very centralized within about 100 miles of the capital. Although the Chilean government has for the past 10 years undertaken serious efforts to decentralize the economy, Santiago remains the only real place to do business. Two major nearby ports, Valparaiso and San Antonio, and a large modern airport provide ready access to and from markets the world over. Chileans are proud of their recent economic growth and are eager to be seen as modern, sophisticated consumers of high quality goods. As such, they readily try new products, especially those from Europe and North America. Local wholesalers and retail outlets regularly offer competitively priced foreign goods.

Distribution

A local subsidiary or branch office is relatively easy to establish and provides the best guarantee that a foreign seller will receive efficient service and appropriate promotion of its products. The primary sales outlet, both in number and volume, remains the traditional small store front, but large department and chain stores and shopping malls are growing in number and influence. Foreign suppliers may establish a subsidiary or branch office. Most do so near the manufacturing and commercial center of Santiago, although larger companies often move on to establish smaller regional offices as well.

Agents, Distributors, and Partners

Suppliers often enter the Chilean market by appointing local agents, distributors, or wholesalers. In the relatively small but highly competitive Chilean markets, a local representative must be chosen with care. Almost all representatives have their main offices in Santiago and branch offices throughout the country, including the free trade zones. The norm in Chile calls for exclusive agency relationships, and despite varied individual markets, the small overall market size usually makes this a reasonable arrangement. The representative should be aggressive, know the product, and have connections to end-users. Potential difficulties arise over conflict of interest if an agent handles a competing product, but also has a lock on the connections and expertise in the product area. Chilean agents will usually not work through an intermediary; they deal only with principals.

Selling Techniques

The single most important selling factor in Chile is price, although where dependability is a factor, consumers will more often purchase a higher priced item with a good reputation. Franchising, direct marketing, joint ventures, and licensing are all well-established and effective ways of selling products in Chile. Franchising especially has really taken off in the past few years. While franchises currently remain focused on the fast-food sector, good opportunities exist in other retail and service sectors. Direct marketing is especially well-established in the services sector, although direct retail marketing and catalog sales are not yet common. High-tech companies have made good use of joint ventures and licensing arrangements to penetrate the Chilean market. However, to reach clients located far from the usual distribution points, many of these firms simply employ well-trained traveling salespeople.

Advertising

Television, radio, newspaper, and magazine advertisements heavily reinforce in-store merchandising methods. Private agencies handle most advertising packages. A significant share of advertising revenues are spent on television broadcasting, which reaches nearly all of Chile's outlying communities. Cable television is available in Santiago and other major cities and offers viewers access to stations from North America and Europe. All newspapers accept ads. However, few newspapers are national in scope, circulation, or outlook. The most important are the dominant regional newspapers, and it is most effective to put together a national campaign using these main provincial papers rather than a single, supposedly national newspaper. Specialty consumer, trade, and business weekly and monthly periodicals offer the option of targeting specific audiences. The Chamber of Commerce's *El Informativo* is a good way to publicize products because it is read extensively in the business community.

Service and Customer Support

Chileans expect fast customer service and high quality after sales product support, although this is difficult to deliver reliably outside Santiago. Distance and unreliable or unavailable communications can separate outlying buyers from foreign suppliers. Once acquired, a reputation for disregarding customer needs will be difficult to lose. Firms can build customer loyalty by providing local representatives who look after warranty service and technical support, and foreign sellers should take into account the fact that products sold with extended lifetime warranties or requiring operator training require a longer time horizon and greater commitment from the overseas supplier. The concept of consumer rights is only slowly emerging in Chile, but is nevertheless becoming a more important part of the selling proposition.

Marketing in Chile

MARKETING TIPS

- **Cosmopolitan** Chilean business people are educated professionals who travel internationally and often speak English. They have sophisticated tastes and are savvy purchasers.
- **Go capital and high-tech** Chile has significant projects underway to transform its manufacturing sectors and infrastructure with high-tech systems.
- **Credit terms** The extension of credit terms is particularly important in securing contracts, especially large contracts. When using invoices, payment for major purchases is generally on a net 30-day basis. Over-the-counter purchases are done with cash, check, or credit card. Major department stores and chains issue their own credit cards.
- **Government markets** Those interested in competing for government business in tenders should have a local representative and be prepared to certify the relationship with the local representative, attesting to the representative's ability to deal and respond with service locally.
- **Agency agreements** Agency agreements, especially when the principal is competing for government business, must comply with Chilean law, which provides wide protection for agents.
- **Technical products** Many technical product categories are generally sold by visiting salesmen rather than in showrooms or retail outlets.
- **El Mercurio** This major newspaper has weekly inserts on agriculture and construction, and a monthly insert on computers. It also puts out special inserts on various topics, including vehicles, throughout the year.
- **Commissions** Most specialized products are sold by stocking representatives, or by commissioned agents who generally earn five to 10 percent on their sales.
- **Agency agreements** To comply with Chilean legal requirements regarding termination, wages, benefits, etc., foreign sellers should have a Chilean attorney draw up their agency agreements.

MARKET RESEARCH AND CONSULTING FIRMS

Instituto Profesional de Estudios Bancarios Guillermo Subercaseaux
Agustinas 1476, Piso 10
Santiago
Tel: (2) 698-1972, 696-8920
Fax: (2) 699-3634

Adimark Ltda.
Luis Thayer Ojeda 1106
Santiago
Tel: (2) 231-5061, 232-8618
Fax: (2) 231-0642

C. H. & Associates
Av. Suecia 0119, Edificio Holley, Oficina 501
Santiago
Tel: (2) 232-5485
Fax: (2) 232-5486

Instituto Chileno de Administracion Racional de la Empresa
Huerfanos 801, Piso 6
Santiago
Tel: (2) 639-4202
Fax: (2) 639-3628

Search Marketing
Av. Fsco. Bilbao 2841
Santiago
Tel: (2) 204-5103, 204-9411
Fax: (2) 204-7466

Price Waterhouse
Huerfanos 863, Piso 2
Santiago
Tel: (2) 638-3023
Fax: (2) 633-3329

Langton Clarke (Coopers & Lybrand)
Huerfanos 812, Piso 5
Santiago
Tel: (2) 638-1320/3569
Fax: (2) 638-2850

Business Culture

Greetings and Courtesies

Men shake hands with men; acquaintances also pat each other on the back or hug. Women usually do not shake hands, although more will now initiate a handshake (men should not try to shake hands with a woman unless she offers first). Men are expected to rise when women enter the room. Women may kiss female friends lightly on the right cheek. In small groups, introductions are made individually by the host, while at larger gatherings, a group "Hello" from the person being introduced suffices. Titles are not generally used, except by medical doctors. Business cards may be in English, which is commonly used by internationally oriented Chilean businesspeople (Spanish is more considerate—and practical—for smaller national firms). Write your hotel telephone number on your card to allow Chilean colleagues to reach you.

Business Ethic and Framework

Chilean business and social culture is based on mutual respect and personal dignity, with correct but personal relationships being of paramount importance. Chileans view work as constituting only a part of life, and not necessarily the most important part at that. They have a relatively well-developed work ethic, and executives often work late. Saving face—while not as important as in Asia—remains crucial, and Chileans value tactfulness and sensitivity as much as they dislike overt aggressiveness. Nevertheless, Chileans also value straight talk more than many other South American businesspeople; they will seldom temporize simply to avoid a response they fear will give offense.

Decision Making

Although middle-level managers may be responsible for implementing decisions, actual decisions are almost always made at a high level of authority. Although you should approach senior people, Chileans will want to know your standing within the hierarchy and will wish to match you with someone of similar rank. Nevertheless, it is important to cultivate personal relationships with these peers, because the quality of these relationships may strongly influence the actual decisionmaker even when your immediate counterpart is not the one making the decision.

Women

Women in Chile generally occupy a somewhat secondary status in this traditionally male-dominated society, although many operate businesses and are generally accorded considerable personal freedom. Many Chilean women reach high levels of professional attainment, and foreign businesswomen should experience few problems, although some may feel more comfortable if they are escorted when in public to avoid possible difficulties. Nevertheless, foreign businesswomen are expected to be highly professional, appropriate, and not aggressive or confrontational.

Meetings

Contacts and introductions are important. If you do not have a mutual business acquaintance to make an introduction, consult your embassy for a referral. Appointments should be made at least two weeks in advance, and reconfirmed. Chileans are generally punctual, although either you or your Chilean counterpart may be acceptably late by about 15 minutes. Meetings are also expected to end on time, although not abruptly. Initial meetings are spent largely on introductory and social matters—you must be prepared to discuss yourself and your company to establish your bona fides—and several meetings are usually required to complete an agreement. Eye contact and good posture are necessary and lapses may be noted unfavorably. The atmosphere is usually informally relaxed but correct. Business lunches are common and are restricted to the parties discussing the business at hand. Dinners are likely to be more social, and spouses may be included if the primary purpose is social. Chileans are also generally more likely to invite foreign associates to their homes than are many other South Americans.

Business Attire

Chileans, who are fairly fashion conscious, expect both men and women to dress conservatively and elegantly in dark suits of good quality. Remember that climate varies widely by latitude and altitude. Dark suits and dresses are appropriate for most social occasions, such as dinner, while a dark suit and a cocktail dress constitute appropriate formalwear. Flashy attire, jewelry, makeup, and accessories are inappropriate. Note that Chileans wear only real jewelry and look down on costume jewelry.

Cultural Cautions

DO'S

- Learn about Chilean history and culture; business-people are expected to be familiar with the Chilean economy in general and exports in particular.
- Ask about families, children, and local tourist information and recommendations, but do not probe about work or family economics.
- Stay in the best hotels—it indicates your seriousness and substance.
- If you are hosting a business lunch, ask your Chilean colleagues for a restaurant recommendation; host dinners or other similar events at your hotel.
- Arrive for a dinner invitation about 15 minutes after the stated time; for a party, arrive 30 minutes late.
- If invited out, send flowers in advance (but not yellow roses, which signify contempt) or bring chocolates with you. Call afterward to thank the host and hostess (thank you notes are uncommon and considered excessive).
- Always eat with utensils; finger food is never served at a formal, sit-down meal.

DON'TS

- Avoid the topics of politics, religion, and human rights.
- Watch gestures carefully: many are considered offensive in Chile. Holding the hand palm up with fingers spread is an accusation of stupidity, while slapping the fist into the opposite hand is obscene, as is an extended cupped hand, held palm up.
- Do not pour wine using your left hand—it is an insult.
- Never do anything that can be construed as the offer of a bribe—it is an egregious insult.

CUSTOMS

- You may either be given a plate of food or asked to serve yourself buffet-style at a private dinner; service is never "family style."
- You are expected to eat everything on your plate, although Chileans will understand if you have a medical reason, such as an allergy, for not eating something; they have less understanding of (or sympathy for) dietary preferences.
- The person who issues an invitation is expected to pay, and one person pays for all, even on informal occasions; do not try to repay the host for your share, but do plan to reciprocate later.
- If you have been invited to a Chilean home, bring gifts for the children on a later trip.

OBSERVATIONS

- Many Chileans are sophisticated international travelers. Discussion of mutually familiar foreign locations can establish rapport.
- Businessmen are expected to drink whisky (scotch), which Chileans consider a sign of sophistication. Women may have a single glass of wine with a meal, but otherwise generally do not drink, especially not distilled alcoholic beverages or beer. Soft drinks are standard.
- Better neighborhoods have pubs which may offer food and entertainment as well as drinks. Avoid common bars, which are considered low class.
- Downtown areas close up at the end of the business day; either eat at your hotel or go to a residential neighborhood where restaurants stay open.
- Virtually all businesses are closed on Sundays.

NEGOTIATIONS

- Avoid any hint of confrontation or pressure. Chileans have a very low opinion of the "hard sell" or other aggressive behavior in business or social relations.
- Bargaining is not part of Chilean culture, as it is in most of South America. Chileans negotiate shrewdly, but not with the gusto or the flamboyant tactics common in Latin cultures accustomed to haggling in markets.
- Attorneys do not attend negotiations, but always review agreements.

Legal System

Chile is a civil code country based on Spanish and French legal tradition.

Intellectual Property Rights

Patents An industrial patent may be granted for the exclusive right to exploit a product or procedure for a sole period of 15 years. Patents for inventions already patented abroad are granted only for the equivalent of the term remaining in the country in which they were first patented.

Trademarks The registration of a trademark, national or foreign, grants ownership for 10 years, and is renewable for consecutive 10 year periods. Trademarkable items are classified into groups and trademarks must be registered in each applicable classification.

Copyrights Copyright protection exists for Chilean and foreign authors domiciled in Chile. The protection is granted to authors for the duration of their lives and then extends to their heirs for 50 years thereafter. Chile ratified the Universal Convention on Author's Rights in July 1977.

Business Registration

As a general principle under the Company Law, it is necessary for at least two parties (individuals or companies) to form a company. Single-party ownership of a company is not permitted, although individuals may operate commercial enterprises as sole proprietorships.

Chile has no minimum local participation requirements, so the decision to include a local partner is guided strictly by commercial considerations and is a matter of personal decision for foreign investors. Foreign investors can conduct business in Chile through the following legal arrangements: a limited liability partnership, a corporation, a branch of a foreign corporation, or a general or silent partnership. Each of these options is governed by different tax and legal regulations. In general, there are no restrictions on the type of businesses that can be started by foreigners and no limits to the percentage of ownership that can be held by foreigners in local companies.

Contracts and Dispute Resolution

Chilean and foreign entrepreneurs prefer general contracts that regulate relations between partners and grant rights and privileges. Business disputes normally are resolved through negotiations, but it is possible to act before the Judiciary Power. Arbitration is allowed and utilized, and many businesspeople agree to procedural aspects thereof in the contract. The courts will uphold these provisions. Arbitration has recently become very important with the creation of the Arbitration Centre of the Santiago Commerce Chamber, an entity that provides candidates to act as arbitrators.

Notaries

Notary publics are licensed by the state and act like ministers of faith. They are subject to the control of the judiciary. Documents and deeds subscribed before a notary public must be extended in Spanish.

Labor Issues

Under Chilean Law, the legal minimum age to start working is 18 years, and the age for retirement is 60 for women and 65 for men. The law states that, for companies with more than 25 employees, at least 85 percent of the employees must be Chilean. Chilean law guarantees workers the right to join unions and to bargain collectively. Collective bargaining agreements must exist in writing within 15 consecutive days after the agreement has taken place, otherwise the employer faces a fine. Collective bargaining agreements must have a duration of no less than two years.

The work contract can be terminated for cause, including business necessity of the company. This cause must be communicated to the employee at least 30 days prior to termination, unless the employee receives an amount equal to his latest monthly salary. If the contract has been in effect for more than one year, the employer must pay the equivalent of one month's salary for each year of service and a fraction thereof over six months. However, the parties involved may agree on a different amount of severance payment in the work contract. Foreigners may receive their payment in foreign currency, but it must be authorized by the Central Bank. The law provides for a minimum monthly wage of about US$50.00.

Source: Robles & Compañia, Santiago, Chile.

Legal Matters

LEGAL BRIEFS

- **Corporations** Corporations and Limited Liability Companies are the favored business entities. To establish them requires a public deed, publication of the deed in the corresponding Commercial Registry, and publication of a summary of the deed in the *Official Gazette.*

- **Maximum work week and holidays** The normal working week is limited to 48 hours, which may be divided into eight-hour days from Monday through Saturday. Workers with more than one year tenure have the right to an annual paid vacation of 15 working days. After 10 years, vacations are extended by one working day for every three years of service. Vacations may not exceed 35 days.

- **Legal protection** Chilean Courts provide effective legal protection and the legal tradition of Chilean judges is well known around the world.

- **Companies law** Chilean law provides for two basic types of corporations: open corporations and closed corporations. Open corporations are those whose stock is traded on the stock market, or the shareholders of which number five hundred or more. Closed corporations are all others.

- **Shareholder liability** Shareholders of both open and closed corporations have no financial liability in excess of their stock holdings.

- **Foreign investment law special regime** Foreign investors who enter into a foreign investment contract with the Republic of Chile, and are therefore subject to the Foreign Investment Statute, are entitled to agree in their respective contracts to a fixed overall income tax rate of 49.5 percent for a term of 10 years, instead of the normal tax rates generally applied.

- **Executives and collective bargaining** Executives and high-level officials cannot participate in collective bargaining.

- **Maternity leave** Pregnant women are allowed six weeks paid leave prior to delivery, and 12 weeks paid leave after birth. In both cases the labor contract remains in force during the period of absence.

- **Trade agreements** Chile is a member of WTO and APEC, and is currently negotiating an affiliation with NAFTA. Chile has free trade agreements with Mexico, Columbia, and Venezuela, which provide for duty-free trade in most products by the late 1990s. Chile also has trade liberalization agreements with Argentina and Bolivia and is negotiating an agreement with Ecuador. It seems likely that negotiations on a trade agreement with the US will begin soon.

LEGAL CONTACTS

Robles & Compañia
Ahumada N2312 Of. 508
Santiago
Tel: (2) 698-6476
Fax: (2) 672-5519

Langton Clarke y Cia. Ltda.
Huerfanos N2770 - Piso 52
Santiago
Tel: (2) 638-1320
Fax: (2) 638-2850

Ossandón, Uribe, Hóbner y Cia
Nueva York N225 Of. 62
Santiago
Tel: (2) 695-2719, 696 1372

Arbitration Centre of the Santiago Commerce Chamber
Santa Lucia N2302
Santiago
Tel: (2) 632-1232
Fax: (2) 633-3395

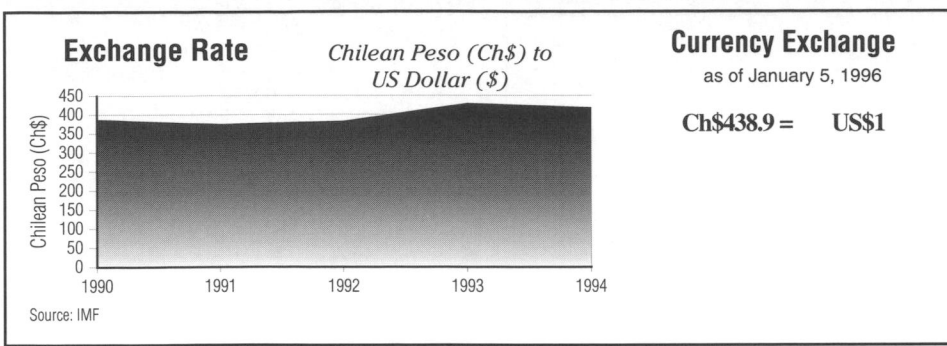

Exchange Rate

Chilean Peso (Ch$) to US Dollar ($)

Source: IMF

Currency Exchange

as of January 5, 1996

Ch$438.9 =   US$1

Currency

The currency of Chile is the Chilean peso (Ch$).

Foreign Exchange

The value of the peso is pegged to a basket of currencies consisting of the US dollar (50.6 percent), the deutsche mark (26.7 percent), and the Japanese yen (22.7 percent). The official foreign exchange market consists of commercial banks, exchange houses, and other entities licensed by the Central Bank. In addition, there is an informal exchange market through which all transactions not required to be channeled through the official foreign exchange market are allowed to take place. In both markets, economic agents are free to negotiate exchange rates. Commercial banks are authorized to purchase all spot foreign exchange proceeds from exporters.

Capital Transfers

The current administration has made it easier to raise funds abroad by placing securities and eliminating the requirement that a set percentage of export earnings must be repatriated to Chile. Foreign investors may use the inter-bank rate of exchange to repatriate capital and earnings. Others must use the parallel exchange market. There are no special provisions for exports of domestic bank notes. All foreign exchange proceeds from exports in excess of US$2,000 must be surrendered through commercial banks, which are required to inform the Central Bank. Exporters are allowed to retain up to 10 percent of export proceeds in special foreign exchange accounts. Export proceeds subject to surrender requirements must be repatriated within 150 days of shipment and surrendered within 11 days.

Investment Incentives

Chile maintains a welcoming attitude toward foreign investment. Although nearly all foreign investments must be approved by the Foreign Investment Committee, approval procedures are expeditious and are not burdensome. Typically, applications are approved within a matter of days. Chile does not subsidize or otherwise offer specific incentives to attract foreign investment.

Investment Restrictions

Although profits may be repatriated immediately, capital may not be repatriated until after one year. Also, 30 percent of borrowed funds and deposits from foreign sources must be placed in a non-interest bearing account (an "*encaje*") at the Central Bank for one year.

TAXATION

Taxation requires sophisticated knowledge of complex rules and regulations specific to each country. The information presented here is from the Ernst & Young Corporate Tax Guide and Directory, available from the Ernst & Young accounting office in your country, or from:

Ernst & Young
Mail Address:
Casillas 50080 and 2186
Santiago, Chile
Street Address:
Paseo Phillips 56
Santiago, Chile
Tel: (2) 6393-043, 6395-081, 6332-998
Cable: Baudit, Santiago, Chile
Telex: 341092 Ans bk BAUDIT CK
Fax: (2) 6383-622

At a Glance

Corporate Income Tax Rate (%)	15
Capital Gains Tax Rate (%)	15
Branch Tax Rate (%)	15
Withholding Tax (%)	
Dividends (a)(b)	20
Interest (c)	15
Royalties from Patents, Know-how, etc. (a)	35
Technical Services (a)	20
Branch Remittance Tax (b)	20
Net Operating Losses (Years) (d)	
Carryback	Unlimited
Carryforward	Unlimited

(a) If paid to nonresidents.
(b) The rate is 35% less a 15% credit for the corporate tax paid.
(c) The tax is generally 35% if interest is paid to nonresidents, but 4% if paid to foreign banks.
(d) See Section C.

Money Matters

BITS AND PIECES

- **Copper** The Chilean Copper Commission is responsible for supervising copper exports and all imports of the copper industry.
- **Gold** Monetary gold can only be traded by authorized banks, but ordinary transactions in gold are permitted. There are three gold coins in Chile, but they are not legal tender. Gold may be imported or exported without restrictions.
- **Corporate income tax** Nonresident corporations must pay taxes based on income from Chilean sources only.
- **State-owned banks** The only state-owned bank in Chile is the Banco del Estado. It accounts for 15 percent of all loans and 19 percent of all deposits.
- **Financial market** The Chilean financial market is sophisticated by developing world standards. Interest rates and financial prices are set by the market.
- **Fisheries** Vessels fishing in Chile's 200-mile exclusive economic zone must have majority Chilean ownership.
- **Border areas** Purchase of land in border areas is limited to Chilean nationals
- **Banks** Foreign-owned banks may operate in Chile, but only as branches or subsidiaries.
- **Tax exemptions** Corporate tax exemptions are available to both foreign and Chilean firms investing in the extreme northern or southern areas of the country.
- **Royalty payments** The Central Bank reserves the right to disallow access to the inter-bank market for royalty payments in excess of five percent of sales, although in such cases, firms would have access to the informal market, which almost always has a rate within one-half of one percent of the inter-bank rate.
- **Expropriation** Chilean law grants the government broad authority to expropriate the property of foreign investors, although this has not been done in the recent past.
- **Performance requirements** There is only one provision for performance requirements, pertaining to automobile assembly.

BANKS

Banco Concepcion
Huerfanos 1072
Santiago
Tel: (2) 698-2741
Fax: (2) 696-0271

Banco de Chile
Ahumada 251
Santiago
Tel: (2) 637-1111
Fax: (2) 698-8288

Banco de Crédito e Inversiones
Huerfanos 1134
Santiago
Tel: (2) 696-6633
Fax: (2) 672-8666

Banco de Santiago
Bandera 172
Santiago
Tel: (2) 692-4000
Fax: (2) 698-7948

Banco del Desarrollo
Av. Lib. Bernardo O'Higgins 949, Piso 3
Santiago
Tel: (2) 698-2901
Fax: (2) 671-5547

Banco Internacional
Moneda 818
Santiago
Tel: (2) 695-3623, 698-1722
Fax: (2) 633-9134

Banco Security
Agustinas 621
Santiago
Tel: (2) 632-5502
Fax: (2) 633-2156

Business Travel

	LH 1906	MADRID	935	113-3
	LH 1022	STUTTGART HBF.	935	-
	AF 1701	LYON	940	683-6
	AY 822	HELSINKI	940	113-3
	AA 071	SFRANCISCO-DALLAS	945	731-7

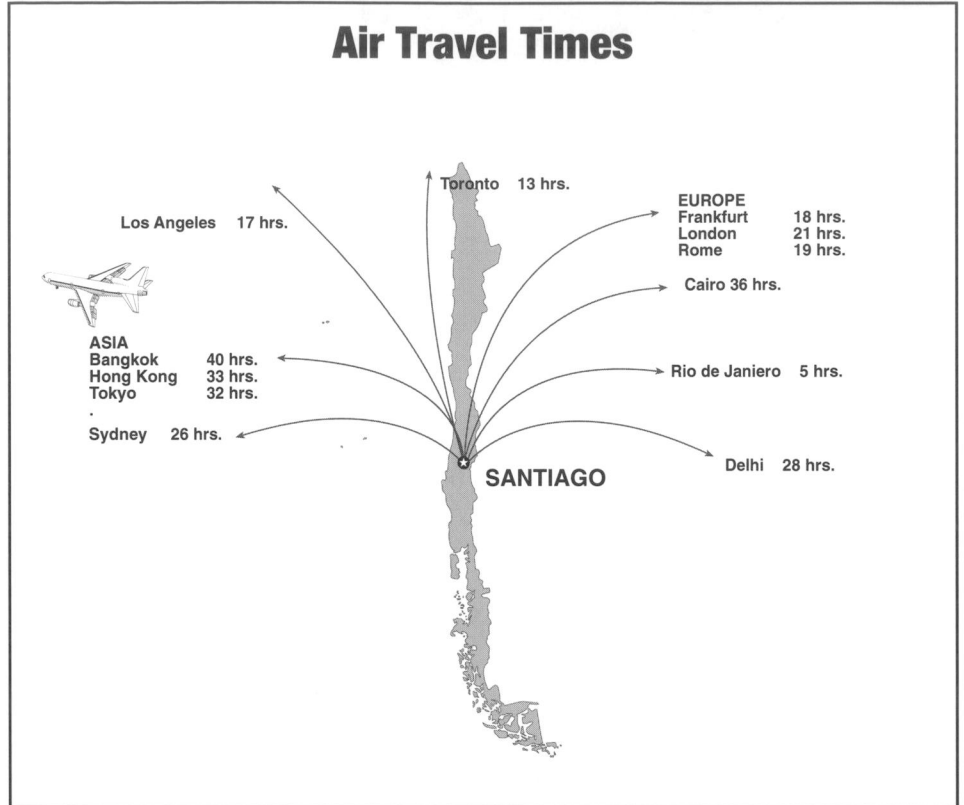

Air Travel Times

Toronto 13 hrs.

Los Angeles 17 hrs.

EUROPE
Frankfurt 18 hrs.
London 21 hrs.
Rome 19 hrs.

Cairo 36 hrs.

ASIA
Bangkok 40 hrs.
Hong Kong 33 hrs.
Tokyo 32 hrs.

Rio de Janiero 5 hrs.

Sydney 26 hrs.

Delhi 28 hrs.

SANTIAGO

COMMUNICATIONS

Telephones Telephone service is good in Santiago but less adequate in other areas. International service is available, but expensive, with reduced rates on weekends and evenings. Local service is fair. Public phones use tokens, fichas, or four one-peso coins. Private phones for a residence are very difficult to obtain; look to rent where one has already been installed.
Fax Facsimile, telex, and telegraph services are offered by Telex Chile, Transradio Chilena, and ITT Comunicaciones Mundiales.
Post office Mail service in Chile is efficient and timely, airmail to Britain or North America can take three to four days.
Radio/TV AM and FM stereo is available, all in Spanish. Three TV channels and a number of dubbed US and European programs are broadcast.

BEST TRAVEL BOOKS

Chile & Easter Island Travel Survival Kit. Lonely Planet. Thoroughly researched, this book is full of down-to-earth advice. 420 pages and 16 color pages.
The Travellers Guide to Latin America Customs and Manners. Elizabeth Devine & Nancy Bagaranti. "An invaluable guide for people not wanting to put foot in mouth."
A Guide to International Behavior, Do's and Taboos Around the World, Edited by Roger E. Axtell, compiled by the Parker Pen Company. Now completely updated and revised, the ultimate guide to international behavior, helpful, fun to read!

NATIONAL TOURIST OFFICE

Servicio Nacional de Turismo (SERNATUR)
1550 Providencia Avenue
Casilla 14082
Santiago
Tel: (2) 698-2151

USEFUL TELEPHONE NUMBERS

If you are calling from outside Chile, you will need to add the country code [56] and any other international dialing requirements from within your country.
- Long Distance Operator 108
- Police/Fire 132
- Ministry of Economy .... (2) 72-5522
- Foreign Investment Committee .... (2) 698-3246
- International Operator Assistance .... 00 or 182
Hotel Information
- Empresa Hotelera Panamericana .... (2) 696-6826
- Asociacion Chilena de Hoteles y Restaurantes .... (2) 698-8765
Automobile and Rail Information
- Automovil Club de Chile .... (2) 212-5702
- Railway Information Center .... (2) 91-682
Chambers of Commerce
- Camara de Comercio de Chile .... (2) 39-7694
- Camara de Comercio de Santiago .... (2) 33-0962
Credit Card Information
Lost or stolen credit cards (call collect to the US, regardless of which country the card was issued in).
- Amex .... [1] (919) 333-3211
- Diner's Club .... [1] (303) 799-1504
- MasterCard .... [1] (314) 275-6690
- Visa .... [1] (410) 581-7931

Travelogue

WORKWEEK

Offices Monday-Friday 8:30 am to 6:00 or 7:00 pm, with lunch from 12:30 to 2:00 pm.
Banks Monday-Friday 9:00 am to 2:00 pm.
Government Monday-Friday 8:30 am to 6:00 pm, with lunch from 12:30 to 2:00 pm.
Retail Monday-Friday 10:30 am to 7:30 pm, Saturdays 9:30 am to 1:30 pm.
Stores and factories commonly close for two weeks between January and March, which is considered vacation season.

HOLIDAYS

Holidays 1996
January 1 New Years Day
April 13 Holy Thursday
April 14 Good Friday
April 16 Easter Sunday*
May 1 Labor Day
May 21 Navy Day
June 6 Corpus Christi*
June 29 Saint Peter and Saint Paul
August 15 Assumption Day
September 11 Official Holiday
September 18 Independence Day
September 19 Day of the Army
October 12 Columbus Day
November 1 All Saints' Day
December 8 Immaculate Conception
December 25 Christmas Day
December 31 Bank Holiday
*Dates vary each year.

VISA AND PASSPORT

Foreigners traveling to Chile need a valid passport and a visa, which is issued at the airport upon arrival. Businesspeople usually travel on a tourist visa, which is valid for 90 days. Those who intend to make sizable business investments should consider a resident visa (valid for one year and renewable for a second year).

DEPARTURE FORMALITIES

Visitors leaving from Santiago's international airport will have to pay a departure tax of US$8 international and US$1 domestic.

IMMUNIZATION

International certificates of vaccination are not required unless arriving from infected areas. Cases of cholera have been reported. Recommended vaccinations: cholera, hepatitis, polio, tetanus, and typhoid.

TIPPING

The standard tip for restaurants, hotels, and hairdressers is 10 percent of the bill, 20 percent in bars and soda fountains. Porters should be tipped 100-200 pesos, and ushers and attendants a similar amount. Taxi drivers expect a small tip.

CRIME

In Santiago and other large cities, thieves thrive in rush hour crowding on the street and aboard public transportation. The display of expensive-looking jewelry, luggage, or cameras increases a visitors' risk of mugging. Downtown areas are particularly risky on weekends and after dark. In general, Chile has fewer safety problems than any other Latin America or third-world countries.

INFRASTRUCTURE

Thanks to a five-year modernization plan, Chile has a modern infrastructure and the best telecommunications system in South America. Air and bus industries are efficient and comfortable. Train service and roadways are fair. Car rentals and taxis are available. In Santiago, public transportation connects the entire metropolis. People renting automobiles should expect toll gates throughout the country.

Contacts

GOVERNMENT AGENCIES

Ministry of Foreign Relations
Morande 441
Santiago
Tel: (2) 696-2574/4574
Fax: (2) 696-8796

Ministry of Finance
Teatinos 120, Piso 12, Oficina 32
Santiago
Tel: (2) 671-0706/6479
Fax: (2) 671-6479

Ministry of Economy
Teatinos 120, Piso 10
Santiago
Tel: (2) 698-3115, 672-5164
Fax: (2) 698-9476

Ministry of Labor and Social Security
Huerfanos 1273, Piso 6
Santiago
Tel: (2) 671-6443, 696-4654
Fax: (2) 671-6539

Ministry of Public Works
Morande 59, Piso 6
Santiago
Tel: (2) 672-4506 ext. 282, 671-4179
Fax: (2) 672-6609

Ministry of Public Health
Mac Iver 541, Piso 3
Santiago
Tel: (2) 639-4084
Fax: (2) 639-4001

Ministry of Housing and Urban Development
Alameda Bdo. O'Higgins 924, Piso 6
Santiago
Tel: (2) 633-1624, 638-2654
Fax: (2) 633-3892

Ministry of Agriculture
Teatinos 40, Piso 9
Santiago
Tel: (2) 696-5896/4496
Fax: (2) 671-6500

Ministry of Mines
Teatinos 120, Piso 9, Oficina 5
Santiago
Tel: (2) 696-1544/5872
Fax: (2) 698-9262

Ministry of Transportation and Telecommunications
Amunategui 139, Piso 3
Santiago
Tel: (2) 672-6503 ext. 338
Fax: (2) 672-4531

Ministry of National Resources
Juan Antonio Rios 6
Santiago
Tel: (2) 222-4669
Fax: (2) 633-6521

National Energy Commission
Teatinos 120, Piso 7
Santiago
Tel: (2) 698-1757, 671-4375
Fax: (2) 698-1757

National Development Corporation
Moneda 921, Piso 8, Oficina 809
Santiago
Tel: (2) 638-0577/0521
Fax: (2) 671-1328

Agency of International Development (AID)
Merced 230, Piso 1
Santiago
Tel: (2) 638-1014, 632-5211, 330-3708
Fax: (2) 638-0931

National Customs Service
Plaza Sotomayor 60
Valparaiso
Tel: (32) 217-911

National Environmental Commission
Alameda Bdo. O'Higgins 949, Piso 13
Santiago
Tel: (2) 699-2476/6127
Fax: (2) 671-8805

National Forestry Commission
Av. Bulnes 285, Piso 5, Oficina 501
Santiago
Tel: (2) 696-2833/3664
Fax: (2) 671-5881

National Fisheries Service
Teatinos 120, Piso 8, Oficina 806
Santiago
Tel: (2) 696-0784, 698-0543
Fax: (2) 696-0784

Port Authority
Morande 59, Piso 5
Santiago
Tel: (2) 696-4629
Fax: (2) 672-6609

Chilean State Railways
Alameda Bdo. O'Higgins 3322, Piso 3
Santiago
Tel: (2) 779-6515
Fax: (2) 776-2609

WORLD TRADE CENTER

World Trade Center
Av. Nva. de Lyon 72, Piso 3
Santiago
Tel: (2) 233-7050
Fax: (2) 233-7034

BUSINESS AND TRADE ASSOCIATIONS

Chilean Quality Control Association
Alsacia 165, Las Condes
Santiago
Tel: (2) 242-9474

Chilean Association of Chilean Tourism Agencies
Moneda 973, Oficina 647
Santiago
Tel: (2) 699-2140, 696-5677
Fax: (2) 699-4245

Food Processing and Agroindustry Chilean Association
Ahumada 254, Oficina 1209
Santiago
Tel: (2) 698-0682, 699-5400
Fax: (2) 696-3506

Chilean Assoc. of Information Technology Companies
Santa Maria 0508, Piso 4
Santiago
Tel: (2) 735-5755
Fax: (2) 735-5754

Rubber Industry Association
Condor 968, Piso 2, Depto. A
Santiago
Tel: (2) 639-3789

Plastics Industry Association
Pedro de Valdivia 1481, Providencia
Santiago
Tel: (2) 274-9312, 205-2231
Fax: (2) 223-4546

Chilean Small and Mid-Size Industry Association
Republica 371
Santiago
Tel: (2) 689-6363/4260
Fax: (2) 689-4260

Small and Mid-size Metallurgic Industry Association
Ejercito 426
Santiago
Tel: (2) 671-0873/4150
Fax: (2) 671-0873

National Assoc. of Commercial Establishment Owners
Santa Lucia 302, Piso 4
Santiago
Tel: (2) 633-1108/9

National Association of Importers
Santa Lucia 302, Piso 5
Santiago
Tel: (2) 639-7859
Fax: (2) 639-7859

Chilean Association of Exporters
Cruz del Sur 133, Piso 2
Santiago
Tel: (2) 206-6604/4163
Fax: (2) 672-7791

Chilean Construction Chamber
Marchant Pereira 10, Piso 3, Providencia
Santiago
Tel: (2) 233-1131
Fax: (2) 232-7600

Textile Institute
Bandera 566, Oficina 101, Piso 10
Santiago
Tel: (2) 696-0210/0768
Fax: (2) 672-5214

Chilean Franchising Association
Huerfanos 1373, Oficina 810
Santiago
Tel: (2) 697-2813, 695-1833
Fax: (2) 633-0521

CHAMBERS OF COMMERCE

National Chamber of Commerce
Santa Lucia 302, Piso 4
Santiago
Tel: (2) 639-7094/0609
Fax: (2) 638-0234

Chilean-American Chamber of Commerce
Americo Vespucio Sur 80, Piso 9
Santiago
Tel: (2) 208-3451/4140
Fax: (2) 206-0911

Santiago Chamber of Commerce
Santa Lucia 302, Pisos 1,2,3
Santiago
Tel: (2) 632-1232
Fax: (2) 632-1232

MARKET RESEARCH AND CONSULTING FIRMS

Adimark Ltda.
Luis Thayer Ojeda 1106
Santiago
Tel: (2) 231-5061, 232-8618
Fax: (2) 231-0642

C. H. & Associates
Av. Suecia 0119, Edificio Holley, Oficina 501
Santiago
Tel: (2) 232-5485
Fax: (2) 232-5486

Centro de Estudios del Cobre y la Mineria
Luis Thayer Ojeda 059, Depto. 43;
Santiago
Tel: (2) 231-7345

Instituto Chileno de Administracion Racional de la Empresa
Huerfanos 801, Piso 6
Santiago
Tel: (2) 639-4202
Fax: (2) 639-3628

Search Marketing
Av. Fsco. Bilbao 2841
Santiago
Tel: (2) 204-5103/9411
Fax: (2) 204-7466

Price Waterhouse
Huerfanos 863, Piso 2
Santiago
Tel: (2) 638-3023
Fax: (2) 633-3329

AD AGENCIES

Chilean Association of Advertising Agencies (ACHAP)
Guardia Vieja 181, Of. 302
Santiago
Tel: (2) 231-0935
Fax: (2) 251-2354

ABM Zegers
Silvina Hurtado 1815
Santiago
Tel: (2) 225-5392
Fax: (2) 204-0686

Baumlis Publicidad Ltda.
Dr. Ernesto Prado Tagle 83
Santiago

Leo Burnett Chile
Eliodoro Yanez 2376
Santiago
Tel: (2) 223-3662
Fax: (2) 204-9436

Grey Chile S.A.
Ernesto Pinto Lagarrique 148
Santiago
Tel: (2) 737-7094
Fax: (2) 737-1989

McCann-Erickson S.A. de Publicidad
Eliodoro Yanez 2290
Santiago
Tel: (2) 235-2620
Fax: (2) 223-0331

J. Walter Thompson Chilena S.A.C.
Casilla 16383, Carreo 9
Santiago
Tel: (2) 251-3303
Fax: (2) 204-3625

BANKS

Banco Security
Agustinas 621
Santiago
Tel: (2) 632-5502
Fax: (2) 633-2156

Citibank
Ahumada 48, Piso 10
Santiago
Tel: (2) 690-8000
Fax: (2) 690-8505, 672-2325

Central Bank of Chile
Agustinas 1180
Santiago
Tel: (2) 670-200
Fax: (2) 698-4847

Banco Concepcion
Huerfanos 1072
Santiago
Tel: (2) 698-2741
Fax: (2) 696-0271

Banco de Chile
Ahumada 251
Santiago
Tel: (2) 637-1111
Fax: (2) 698-8288

Banco de Crédito e Inversiones
Huerfanos 1134
Santiago
Tel: (2) 696-6633
Fax: (2) 672-8666

Banco de Santiago
Bandera 172
Santiago
Tel: (2) 692-4000
Fax: (2) 698-7948

Banco del Desarrollo
Av. Lib. Bernardo O'Higgins 949, Piso 3
Santiago
Tel: (2) 698-2901
Fax: (2) 671-5547

Banco Internacional
Moneda 818
Santiago
Tel: (2) 695-3623, 698-1722
Fax: (2) 633-9134

Banco Osorno
Bandera 140
Santiago
Tel: (2) 696-0414
Fax: (2) 672-1648

STOCK EXCHANGE

Bolsa de Comercio de Santiago
La Bolsa 64, Casilla 123-D
Santiago
Tel: (2) 698-2001
Telex: 340531
Fax: (2) 672-8046

Bolsa de Corredores - Valores de Valparaiso
Prat 798, Casilla 218-V
Valparaiso
Tel: (32) 25-0677
Fax: (32) 21-2764

NEWSPAPERS

Diario Oficial de la Republica de Chile
Agustinas 1269
Santiago
Tel: (2) 698-3969
Fax: (2) 698-2222

La Epoca
Olivares 1229, 5º, 6º y 9º
Santiago
Tel: (2) 699-0067
Telex: 240990

El Mercurio
Avda Santa Maria 5542
Casilla 13-D
Santiago
Tel: (2) 228-4078

La Nacion
Agustinas 1269
Santiago
Tel: (2) 698-2222

La Tercera de la Hora
Vicuna Mackenna 1870
Santiago
Tel: (2) 551-7067
Fax: (2) 556-1017

Las Ultimas Noticias
Avda Santa Maria 5542
Santiago
Tel: (2) 228-7048

El Sur
Casilla 8-C
Calle Freire 799
Concepcion
Tel: (41) 23-5825

La Prensa
Austral Waldo
Seguel 636, Casilla 9-D
Punta Arenas
Tel: (61) 24-3166
Telex: 280336
Fax: (61) 24-7406

La Estrella
Esmeralda 1002, Casilla 57-V
Valparaiso
Tel: (32) 25-8011
Telex: 230531
Fax: (32) 25-0497

El Mercurio
Esmeralda 1002 , Casilla 57-V
Valparaiso
Tel: (32) 25-8011
Telex: 330445
Fax: (32) 25-6438

PERIODICALS

Cauce
Huerfanos 713, Of. 604-60
Santiago
Tel: (2) 38-2304

Cosas
Almirante Pastene 329
Providencia
Santiago
Tel: (2) 235-2705
Telex: 340905
Fax: (2) 235-8331

Creces
Manuel Montt 1922
Santiago
Tel: (2) 223-4337
Telex: 341011

Economia y Sociedad
Maclver 125, 10º
Santiago
Tel: (2) 33-1034
Telex: 340656

Estrategia
Rafael Canas 114
Casilla 16485, Correo 9
Santiago
Tel: (2) 235-6959
Telex: 34036
Fax: (2) 236-1114

Gestion
Rafael Canas 114
Santiago
Tel: (2) 235-6959
Telex: 440001
Fax: (2) 236-1114

Hoy
Mons. Miller 74
Clasificador 654, Correo Central
Santiago
Tel: (2) 204-7771
Fax: (2) 225-2430

Microbyte
Passy 056, Providencia
Santiago
Tel: (2) 222-8556
Telex: 243259
Fax: (2) 222-2699

Vea
Luis Thayer Ojeda 1626
Casilla 3092 Providencia
Santiago
Tel: (2) 74-9421
Telex: 341194

RADIO AND TELEVISION

Asociacion de Radiodifusores de Chile
Paseje matte 956, Of. 801
Casilla 10476
Santiago
Tel: (2) 39-8755

Radio Nacional de Chile
San Antonio 220, 2º
Casilla 244-V, Correo 21
Santiago
Tel: (2) 33-9071

Television Nacional de Chile - Canal 7
Bellavista 0990, Casilla 16104
Santiago
Tel: (2) 777-4552

Universidad de Chile - Canal 11
Ines matte urrejola 0825, Casilla 16457
Correo 0, Providencia
Santiago
Tel: (2) 37-7851
Fax: (2) 37-7923

Universidad del Norte - Red Telenorte de Tele.
Carrera 1625, Casilla 1045
Antofagasta
Tel: (83) 22-6725
Telex: 325142

INTERNET ADDRESSES

CHILNET, Chile's Electronic Yellow Page
http://www.chilnet.cl/

CONICYT (National Commission for Scientific and Technological Research)
http://www.conicyt.com/

Usenet group
soc.culture.chile

China

People's Republic of China

Economy

Overview

China is the fastest growing economy in the world, and the third largest market. This strong growth continues to be accompanied by rampant inflation and social dislocation, however. Although the Chinese government has periodically cracked down with restrictive monetary and credit policies designed to contain inflation, it has recently been forced to loosen up to preserve the growth that has become critical to maintaining its political stability. China has also been walking a tightrope as it tries to strengthen its emerging free market economy while avoiding reforms that might threaten social stability by slowing growth or raising unemployment. At the same time, it has gambled its economic expansion by trying simultaneously to exert international influence while maintaining control over its rapidly changing populace and keeping its fractious provincial authorities under central control.

Trade

Major exports include apparel, textiles, food products, machinery, fuels, metal products, and chemicals. China imports machinery, chemicals, raw materials, textiles, foodstuffs, and iron and steel. Hong Kong has been China's largest trading partner in recent years, serving as an entrepôt, followed by Japan, the US, Taiwan, and Germany. China is currently working to diversify its trade, establishing relations with the new Central Asian states, India, South Korea, Russia, and Vietnam, as well as building ties with other developing economies in Asia, Africa, and Latin America. Central planning rather than market forces often determine the composition and price structure of many exports and imports.

Sectors

Agriculture Agriculture employs over 50 percent of the work force, but produces less than one-third of GDP. Low government-set prices for agricultural products and a lack of adequate distribution and storage facilities, coupled with rising demand, have prevented China from achieving self-sufficiency, much less export capability. Capital investment to promote improved production is needed.

Industry Employing little more than 20 percent of the work force, industry produces more than 50 percent of GDP. China's major industries are iron, steel, coal, machinery, armaments, and textiles and apparel. Government authorities are easing operating restrictions but remain reluctant to allow open competition—most industry continues to be state-run.

Services The service sector employs about 20 percent of the work force and produces about 14 percent of GDP. Despite certain pockets of sophistication, most Chinese services operate on a fairly rudimentary and local level.

Trends

Rapid growth, significant reforms, and massive infrastructure projects, coupled with a huge population that is beginning to attain the economic means to become serious consumers, point to enormous potential in China. The key task of the next decade will be to create a functioning and sustainable version of the "socialist market economy." Continuity in the political system coupled with reform in the economic system are the hallmarks of its plans. China's GDP is projected to continue to grow at close to nine percent annually through the end of the century, a rate which could make it the world's largest economy within 30 years.

At a Glance

THE COUNTRY

Location Eastern Asia, between India, Mongolia, and the East and South China seas.
Terrain Mostly mountains, high plateaus, and deserts in the west; plains, deltas, and hills in the east.
Climate Tropical in the south to subarctic in the north; typhoons and floods cause damage every year.

THE PEOPLE

Population 1,200,000,000
Ethnic composition
Han Chinese 93%
Zhuang, Uygur, Hui, Yi, Tibetan, Miao, Manchu, Mongol, Buyi, Korean, and other nationalities 6.7%
Religious composition
Officially atheist, but some important elements of religion are Confucianism, Taoism, and Buddhism
Muslim 2-3%
Christian... 1%
Languages spoken Standard Chinese (Putonghua), plus many local dialects.
Education and literacy Literacy for males is 84 percent, and for females is 62 percent. About 96 percent of eligible children are enrolled in first grade, but only 65 percent complete primary school. Adult education is free.
Labor force
Total:..650,000,000
By occupation: agriculture and forestry 60%, industry 22%, and services (including commerce) 18%.

COUNTRY FACTS

Political and legal The state is led by the Communist Party. The legal system is a mix of custom and statute, largely addressing criminal laws.
Telephone The telephone system is undergoing rapid development, and service quality varies from state-of-the-art digital exchanges and cellular systems to woefully outdated coaxial cables. Generally, in major cities, there is good local service as well as high quality international phone and fax service. International country code: [86]. City codes: Beijing (1), Guangzhou (20), Shanghai (21), Liaoning (24), Sichuan (28).
Transportation Railroads, highways, and inland waterways are the most important modes of travel. Railways reach even the remote areas of the country. Several major river and sea ports serve the merchant marine fleet. Seven international airports serve the country.
Environment The environmental situation is grim. A harmful by-product of China's rapid industrial development is increased pollution—air pollution from the use of coal as a fuel and water pollution from industrial effluents. These issues seriously threaten to undermine the base of China's economic development. Many people do not have access to safe drinking water; less than 10 percent of sewage receives treatment.
Media The press is carefully controlled by the government. There are nearly 800 national and provincial newspapers and more than 5,750 periodicals. There are 274 radio broadcasting stations and more than 215 million radio receivers. There are 75 million television sets picking up more than 200 stations. The government also operates a wired broadcast network linked to 100 million loudspeakers.
Health The Ministry of Health has focused on preventive medicine and improvement of sanitary conditions.

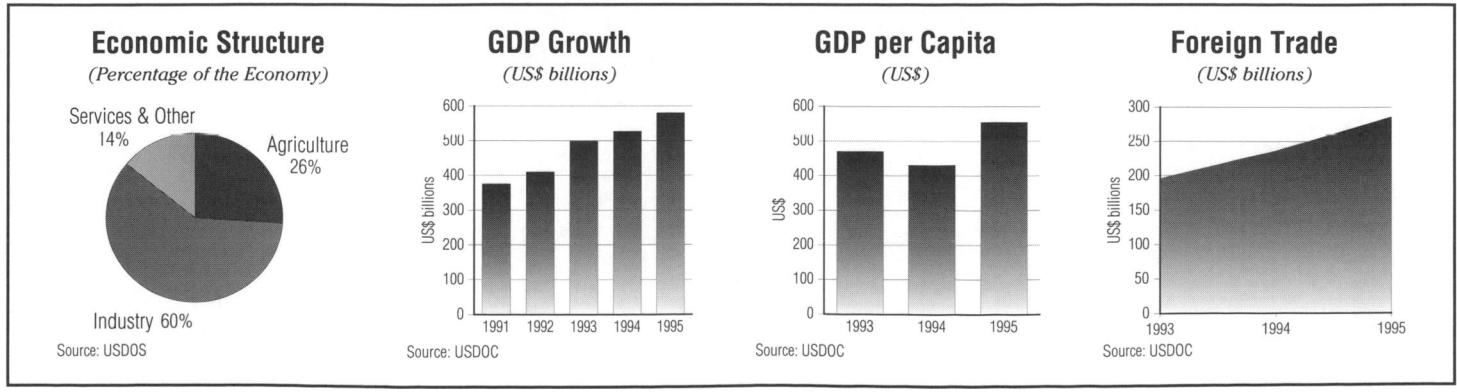

Economic Structure
(Percentage of the Economy)
Services & Other 14%
Agriculture 26%
Industry 60%
Source: USDOS

GDP Growth
(US$ billions)
1991 1992 1993 1994 1995
Source: USDOC

GDP per Capita
(US$)
1993 1994 1995
Source: USDOC

Foreign Trade
(US$ billions)
1993 1994 1995
Source: USDOC

China

- ✪ National capital
- ◉ Province capital
- • City
- ⋯⋯ Province border
- ——— Road
- ━━━ Railroad
- ━━━ International border

0 ————— 500 km
0 ————— 500 mi

Foreign Trade

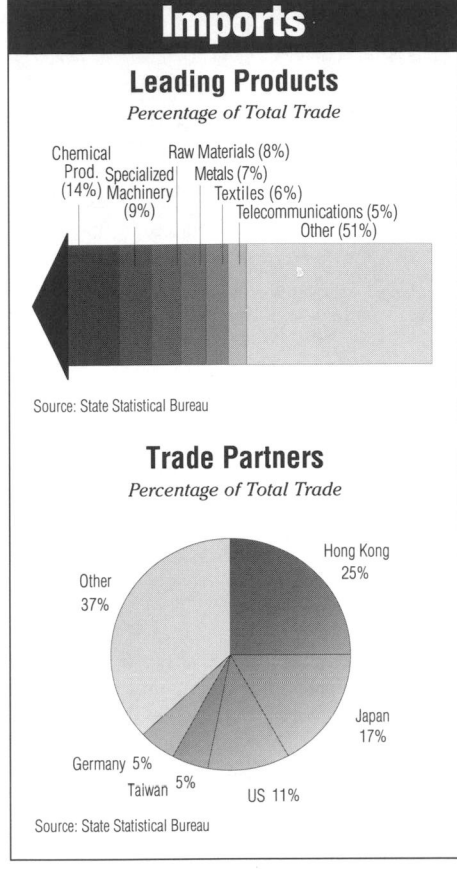

Imports

Leading Products
Percentage of Total Trade

Chemical Prod. (14%)
Specialized Machinery (9%)
Raw Materials (8%)
Metals (7%)
Textiles (6%)
Telecommunications (5%)
Other (51%)

Source: State Statistical Bureau

Trade Partners
Percentage of Total Trade

- Hong Kong 25%
- Japan 17%
- US 11%
- Taiwan 5%
- Germany 5%
- Other 37%

Source: State Statistical Bureau

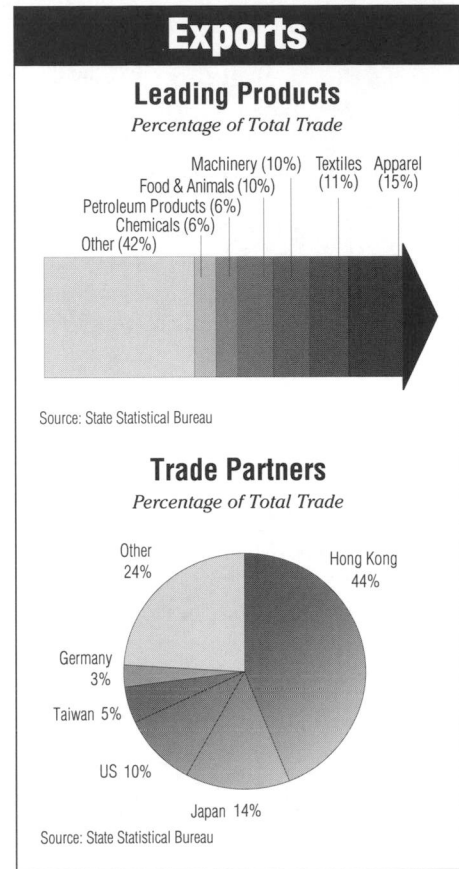

Exports

Leading Products
Percentage of Total Trade

Machinery (10%)
Food & Animals (10%)
Petroleum Products (6%)
Chemicals (6%)
Textiles (11%)
Apparel (15%)
Other (42%)

Source: State Statistical Bureau

Trade Partners
Percentage of Total Trade

- Hong Kong 44%
- Japan 14%
- US 10%
- Taiwan 5%
- Germany 3%
- Other 24%

Source: State Statistical Bureau

Trade News

RULES AND REGULATIONS

- **Regulation** The Ministry of Foreign Trade and Economic Cooperation (MOFTEC) in Beijing formulates and implements China's foreign trade policy. The State Planning Commission, the State Council's Machinery and Electronics Coordination Office, and the State Economic and Trade Commission also administer certain nontariff barriers at central and provincial levels.

- **Trade reforms** In October 1992, China agreed to reduce import tariffs on virtually all commodities, eliminate import licensing requirements on most goods, and end overlapping nontariff barriers. Reforms are being phased in over time.

- **Import approval** Imports are regulated through a complex approval process. Controlled products need approval of both central and local government authorities. As many as 15 clearances from various ministries or bureaus may be required, depending on locality.

- **Import licenses** About 50 product categories, including various consumer goods, raw materials, and production equipment, require import licenses. They account for about 50 percent of China's trade. Elimination of import licenses is being phased in between 1992 and 1997.

- **Tariffs and other duties** Tariff rates can be as low as three percent on imports China wishes to encourage and as high as 250 percent on goods it considers threatening to its domestic economy. Rates of 30 percent are not uncommon. Taxes and duties may also be added on the basis of shipment cost, insurance, and freight (CIF) value and may be appealed by the trader if deemed too high.

- **Export policies** MOFTEC determines national export policy and authorizes exporters and foreign trade corporations (FTCs) in each province to help coordinate actual trade. Export policies in China have been liberalized since the late 1980s. New economic freedom and less government intervention bring both advantages and risk. Traders should be certain to select suppliers that can guarantee delivery of goods.

Opportunities

FOR IMPORTING TO CHINA

- agricultural chemicals
- aircraft, avionics, and support equipment
- clothing
- computers and peripherals
- computer software
- construction equipment and building supplies
- electronic components
- food processing and packaging machinery
- industrial process controls
- laboratory instruments
- medical and dental equipment
- oil and gas field machinery
- pharmaceuticals
- pollution control equipment
- printed circuit board equipment
- printing equipment
- telecommunications equipment
- textile equipment

FOR EXPORTING FROM CHINA

- arts and handicrafts
- bicycles
- canned fruits and vegetables
- clocks and watches
- clothing
- consumer electronic products: radios, tape recorders, television sets
- electronic components
- footwear
- machine parts
- metals and minerals
- musical instruments
- paper products
- pharmaceuticals and medicines
- rubber and plastic products
- sewing machines
- textiles
- toys

GROWTH SECTORS

- cable television
- electronics
- franchises
- manufacturing
- oil exploration and petrochemicals
- professional services, including accounting, advertising, financial, legal, and tourist services
- real estate

GOVERNMENT PROCUREMENT

- agricultural and industrial chemicals
- aircraft and parts
- computers and peripherals
- efficient industrial equipment
- machinery for oil and gas drilling and refining
- mining and construction equipment
- road construction equipment and materials
- telecommunication products

TRANSPORTATION FIRMS

Register of Shipping of the PRC
40 Donghuangchenggen, Nan Jie
Beijing 100006
Tel: (1) 5136633 Fax: (1) 5130550

Beijing Air Cargo Transportation Service Center
Inside Chao Yang Gymnasium
Tuan Jie Hu Liu Litun Xi Kou, Chao Yang Qu
Beijing 100026
Tel: (1) 5011015/9 Fax: (1) 5005765
Telex: 211175 BACT ON

Beijing Friendship Packing and Transportation Corp.
5 Sanlitun, Xi Liujie, Chaoyang Qu
Beijing 100053
Tel: (1) 5324806, 4652303, 4673893
Fax: (1) 5324304 Telex: 210349 BFPTC CN

Beijing Large Goods and Materials Transportation Co.
10 Guangyi Jie, Xuanwu Qu
Beijing 100053
Tel: (1) 338551

Beijing Materials Storage and Transportation Co.
Yangrou Lane, Xisi, Xicheng Qu
Beijing 100034
Tel: (1) 6034143 Fax: (1) 6020728

China Interocean Transport Inc.
Rm. 63614, Beijing Friendship Hotel
3 Baishiqiao Lu
Beijing 100873
Tel: (1) 8498888

China National Chartering Corporation (SINOCHART)
21 Xisanhuan Bei Lu
Beijing 100081
Tel: (1) 8415313/4 Fax: (1) 8415312
Telex: 222508 CHART CN

Overview

Rapid economic growth, bold reform measures, and massive infrastructure plans point to enormous market potential in China. It is becoming a major trading nation, and international firms can continue to ignore it only at the risk of losing a key marketplace, as well as a competitive edge in the global arena. The Chinese government expects to spend at least US$100 billion a year until the end of the century on imports, and what used to be an essentially unified market has become several regional markets, each competing to attract foreign investment and technology. Ties to Hong Kong, Taiwan, Japan, and Korea, as well as trade linkages along the Russian border, are all growing. More foreign investment has gone inland to an area formerly shut off from external development, particularly in natural resource extraction. Some 8,000 Chinese companies now have import and export rights; markets are developing which did not exist as little as three years ago. Recently liberalized trade policies will likely continue to respond to international pressures for freer markets. Meanwhile, companies new to China find the competition fierce for developing long-term relationships.

Distribution

Traditional Chinese trade corporations are no longer the only available distribution channels. International merchants may distribute their products through any number of new foreign trade companies. Factories and manufacturers now have a greater influence in their purchasing decisions and processes, or they may handle distribution through a representative office. While foreign trade companies and manufacturers are generally more flexible and bring the seller closer to the end-user, time and effort must be expended to determine their reliability and financial standing. The first step should be to visit the commercial office of the Chinese embassy in the prospective investor's country; foreign embassies and consultants in China are also good points of contact.

Agents, Distribution, and Partners

China has a long tradition of dealing with Western companies; careful selection and frequent contact are the best ingredients for a profitable relationship. Only those companies authorized by the central government to handle import and export business may sign trade contracts. A domestic agent must arrange both for the importation of a product into China, as well as marketing that product once it is inside the country. Besides trading companies, or *hongs*, China is witnessing an explosion in local sales agents, which are usually representatives from Hong Kong or international trading companies, or Chinese firms with regional or national networks. Given China's size and diversity, exporters may choose to hire several agents to cover different territories. Local accountants and consultants would also make economical additions to a firm new to this market.

Selling Techniques

Chinese prefer to deal with "old friends," and exporters, importers, and investors must adapt their behavior to establish and maintain close relationships with Chinese counterparts and relevant government agencies. Strong ties are the only secure way to develop business here. Various sales approaches are appropriate for the China market, including exhibitions and trade fairs, direct mass mailing to end-users, advertisements in Chinese-language publications, hosting technical seminars in China, and the establishment of a representative office.

Advertising

Whether targeted for a specific industry or a mass audience, advertising can spur product awareness in China. Publications, radio, television, and billboard displays, as well as sports sponsorships and other innovative methods are all available for marketing purposes. Advertising agencies are very accessible, and they can be either Chinese, foreign, or joint ventures. Prices are regulated by the government and are higher for overseas companies, although this discrimination is expected to end soon. Hundreds of international exhibitions are held every year in China. Participation in these shows is costly, but it is an effective way to contact agents, trading companies, and end-users. For firms already present in China, trade shows can be platforms for conducting surveys and introducing new products.

Service and Customer Support

Foreign companies and Chinese-foreign joint ventures generally cannot service products, except products manufactured in China. Most firms contract a local provider to establish centers with spare parts and after-sales service. Some companies are concerned that this gives them little control over service quality and may lower consumer confidence. However, consumer expectations are not particularly high in China, and any level of after-sales service and product support is welcomed. A frequent option is to provide service from bases in Hong Kong, Shanghai, or Taiwan.

Marketing in China

MARKETING TIPS

- **Names** In China the family or surname is placed first; Li Da Ming is addressed as Mr. Li.
- **Meetings** Meetings are conducted formally, and usually in a conference or meeting room. Invitation to an executive's office is a rare favor and connotes special status.
- **Banquets** Food frequently accompanies business in China. It is appropriate, and expected, to introduce business over a meal.
- **Appointments** Most foreign firms will be contacted through a middleman, host organization, or the foreign affairs office of an organization.

AD AGENCIES

Advertising Association for Foreign Economic Relations and Trade [China National]
7 Liufang Beili, Xiangheyuan
Chaoyang Qu
Beijing 100028
Tel: (1) 4081118 Fax: (1) 4082319

BBDO/CNUAC
23rd Fl., Capital Mansion
6 Xin Yuan Nan Road, Chao Yang Qu
Beijing 100004
Tel: (1) 4663318 Fax: (1) 4662311

Beijing Advertising Corp.
10-11th Fl., Office Building, Universe Building
14 Dongzhimen Nan Dajie
Dongcheng Qu
Beijing 100027
Tel: (1) 5001188 Fax: (1) 5019471
Export Advertising Dept. Tel: (1) 5019479

China International Advertising Corp.
5th Fl., 12 Jian Guo Men Wai Dajie
Beijing 100022
Tel: (1) 5061172 Fax: (1) 5061167

Daiko Advertising Inc.
3007, Jing Guang Center
Hijialou, Chaoyang Qu
Beijing
Tel: (1) 5013008

Dentsu Inc. (Beijing)
Suite 1518, Beijing Fortune Building
5 Dong San Huan Bei-Lu, Chao Yang Qu
Beijing 100004
Tel: (1) 5014141 Fax: (1) 5002851

Dentsu Inc. (Shanghai)
Rm. 605, Garden Hotel Shanghai
58 Mao Ming Nan-Lu
Shanghai 200020
Tel: (21) 4333507 Fax: (21) 4335499

Dentsu, Young & Rubicam (Beijing)
10th Fl., Asia-Pacific Building
8 Ya Bao Lu, Chaoyang Qu
Beijing 100020
Tel: (1) 5125559 Fax: (1) 5125988 Telex: 716-211209

Dentsu, Young & Rubicam (Shanghai)
Rm. 1206, Shanghai International Trade Center
2200 Yan An Road West
Shanghai 200335
Tel: (21) 2752949 Fax: (21) 2754202
Telex: 716-30029

Hakuhodo Inc.
Rm. 507, Beijing Fortune Building
5 Dong, Sanhuan Bei-lu, Chaoyang Qu
Beijing
Tel: (1) 5011351 Fax: (1) 5011350
Telex: 85-210011 (CLH CN)

RADIO & TELEVISION

Ministry of Radio, Film, and Television
2 Fu Xing Men Wai Jie
POB 4501
Beijing 100866
Tel: (1) 8012176, 6092141
Fax: (1) 8012174
Telex: 22236

Business Culture

Greetings and Courtesies

Handshaking is the accepted greeting. Chinese usually shake hands very lightly instead of taking the hand firmly and forcefully pumping it, and in China a handshake may last as long as 10 seconds. Upon meeting someone, Chinese lower their eyes slightly as a sign of respect. Staring into the eyes of a Chinese might make them uncomfortable. Face—being respected by one's peers—is very important to the Chinese. They are enormously sensitive to maintaining face in everything they do. Saying or doing anything that causes someone to lose face can instantly destroy a relationship and any business that might result from it. Never insult or openly criticize someone in front of others. Don't make fun of a Chinese, even if only as a joke. Do not treat someone as a person of lowly rank if their position in the company is high. A person's face is also their company's face. The relationship you develop with a person represents your relationship with his entire company. Gifts are important, expressing friendship and symbolizing hopes for success. But expensive gifts can cause personal embarrassment and political or social awkwardness. For wrapped gifts, gold or red are appropriate colors. White and black are colors of mourning.

Business Ethic

Much of China's ethical system is derived from Confucianism. It teaches respect for superiors, duty to family, loyalty to friends, humility, sincerity, and courtesy. In the work arena, age brings with it increased respect and status, and older businesspeople are likely to be treated more seriously than younger ones. Chinese put more emphasis on groups rather than individuals. They become uncomfortable when people speak as individuals, or make statements that are not in harmony with the stated group view. One person, preferably your group's senior member, should be designated as your spokesman. Chinese will assume all major communications come from him, and accept what he says as the position of your company.

Decision Making

Written contracts are secondary in China to personal commitments between associates. Some executives prefer to sign a principal agreement and let their subordinates work out the details at a later time. Chinese usually feel that single contracts are just one component of a larger relationship.

Women

Officially, women are given many of the same rights as men in China. There are still many disciminatory practices taking place, however, and recent legislative changes may lead to women losing ground. Women are usually the first to be laid off from economically hurting businesses, and few business leaders are women. Foreign businesswomen should not experience any discrimination. Women in China for business should act and dress in a formal manner.

Meetings

Meetings are considered very formal in China. It is a good idea to send a list of your representatives before the meeting, and to include their rank in your company. You should also request a  similar list. You will be led into a room in which the Chinese are already present. Your team leader should enter first. Teams sit across a table, leaders opposite each other and others seated in descending order of importance. Small talk will come first. Business is addressed once people feel comfortable with each other. The head of the host team will deliver a short welcome speech, then turn the floor over to the visitors. Your senior team member should speak for your company; avoid conflicting statements from other team members. When talking, your spokesman should address the senior Chinese representative. Chinese prefer to hear a proposal as a broad overview, and then respond to specific issues or questions point by point. Business cards are a common opening to business meetings, and are more impressive if one side is translated into Chinese characters.

Business Attire

Dress styles are changing quickly in today's China. The uniform-like Mao jacket is being replaced  by Western-style suits and, sometimes, ties. Foreigners should dress formally. Women should avoid low necklines and hemlines that rise above the knee. Jewelry will be noticed; modest gold jewelry and a quality watch will count in your favor. However, avoid overly expensive jewelry or showy ornaments.

Cultural Cautions

DO'S
- Be aware of all favors done for you and gifts you are given. Find a way to reciprocate in kind.
- In China, business relationships are personal relationships. To establish a good business relationship, establish a personal relationship that demonstrates your respect and trustworthiness.

DON'TS
- Do not insult or harshly criticize someone in front of others.
- Don't make fun of someone, even as a playful joke.

CUSTOMS
- Humility is valued highly in Confucianism. Chinese are often so polite and humble that they appear to be self-effacing.
- Chinese are extremely courteous to friends. This often includes arranging every detail of a friend's visit, and refusing to let a guest spend any money at all.
- Punctuality is very highly valued in China. Be on time for all meetings and appointments.
- Business cards are important. At first meetings, handshakes are followed by a formal exchange of cards. Always carry plenty of cards, ideally with Chinese text on one side.

OBSERVATIONS
- Business dealings can be made easier by having a Chinese advisor or consultant. They should speak the same language as you, have expertise in your type of business, have experience doing business in China, and be well thought of by their associates.
- The transition to a free market can be difficult. Under Communism, the work unit controlled every aspect of a person's life. Embarking on a new career means leaving one's work unit, which can bring personal and economic hardship. Keep this in mind when seeking Chinese associates for new ventures, and consider helping with this transition.
- China is an enormous bureaucracy. Local bosses have great power, and bureaucrats have been known to sabotage dealings for their own gain or personal satisfaction. Having influential local officials for friends can be a great advantage.

NEGOTIATIONS
- Chinese have a reputation for being tough negotiators. Their tactics are both subtle and aggressive. Often, they will wine and dine potential associates as a way of gaining an advantage.
- Negotiating tactics include getting angry as a means of intimidation, flattery to get you off-guard, and prolonging negotiations to wear you down.
- A common tactic is delaying major negotiations until you're about to leave the country, then making unreasonable demands.
- Extensive entertaining, particularly at night, is sometimes used to make visitors less alert at the negotiating table.
- Chinese sometimes negotiate with several competing companies at the same time and let it be known they are doing so as a way of applying pressure.
- Be prepared to walk away. You will gain more from making it clear that you would rather have no deal at all than a bad deal.
- China is only beginning to enact formal business laws. The idea of a contract being a legal document is accepted in places familiar with foreigners, but may not be common in remote areas.
- Many Chinese tend to take a long-term view, regarding an agreement as a single element of a bigger, ongoing relationship that is, ultimately, more important than any one venture.

Legal System

China is primarily a civil code country, whose legal system also recognizes principles based on custom in specific instances, provided such principles do not conflict with written statutes. China's constitution proclaims that Chinese Communist ideology controls in all matters.

Intellectual Property Rights

Patents Inventions, utility models, and exterior designs may be patented. Authority to examine patent applications and issue patents is held by the Patent Office, which maintains a staff of several hundred persons, including scientists and attorneys. Application for patent registration must be made within six months of first application for a utility model, or 12 months from first application for patent in foreign country. Patent application by nonresident foreigners or foreign businesses without offices in China is to be made either to Patent Agency of China Council for the Promotion of International Affairs, the Hong Kong based China Patent Agent (HK) Ltd., or the Shanghai Patent Office. All applications and proceedings are published in the Patent Gazette 18 months after the date of filing, and information on the status of patent applications can be obtained through any of the above offices. If a patent has not been granted within three years of filing, the applicant must begin paying annual maintenance fees, which is also payable after the patent has been granted. Failure, without justified reason, to exploit patent after three years from its issuance can, upon application by another entity capable of exploiting the product, result in an order to issue a compulsory license.

Trademarks Registered trademarks enjoy the benefit of exclusive use and legal protection. Foreigners applying for trademark registration must submit an application to the State Administration of Industry and Commerce. Application must be in Chinese, and should include a specific power of attorney, which must be notarized. Registration is valid for 10 years from the date of approval, and may be renewed upon application made six months prior to termination of term.

Copyrights Irrespective of whether their works are published or not, Chinese citizens have copyright protection; foreigners enjoy protection if their works were published in China first. Foreigners' books that are published outside of China enjoy copyright protection pursuant to agreements executed between their country and China or international conventions. Copyright protection extends to the life of the individual plus 50 years. Registration of work is not required, and legal protection is afforded by statute.

Business Registration

Business operations of private enterprise may commence only after application for registration is approved by local Administration of Commerce and Industry, and a business license is procured. A private enterprise that successfully registers as a legal person must additionally register commencement of its operations and any amendments or cancellation of registration, according to administrative regulations.

Contracts and Dispute Resolution

Contracts are generally written and are quite detailed. Courts will uphold the provisions of contracts made between individuals if the agreement was freely made and accurately reflects the intentions of the parties. Remedies for breach of contract include payment of penalties, as well as consequential damages. If disputes cannot be settled by consultation, any of the parties may request the government, or its representative in charge of managing contracts, to apply for mediation or arbitration within one year of discovering breach, or may directly commence litigation. Arbitration, after conciliation, is the favored Chinese means of resolving international commercial disputes. In cases of arbitration, either party may appeal a decision by the court arbitrator within 15 days after judgment.

Notaries

Notarization not merely encompasses attestation of signature, but also evidences legality of document. At times, special forms and careful examination of law are required for notary seal to be properly affixed. Notaries public are Chinese citizens with rights to vote and having legal education or training.

Labor

Although communist ideology still prevails, there is some movement toward utilizing labor contracts and a more market-oriented compensation system. Labor contracts generally cover salaries, bonuses, subsidies and the worker's job requirements for a fixed term of anywhere between six months and 10 years. Such contracts normally tie bonuses to job performance, and at the end of their term, both parties or either one are, theoretically, free to discontinue the employment relationship. In practice, however, the traditional Communist system restricting an employee's ability to change jobs, and an employer's ability to terminate workers, has inhibited the full application and greater utilization of labor contracts.

Legal Matters

LEGAL BRIEFS

- **Workweek** There are no regulations governing the hours of operation or maximum employment hours of private enterprise.
- **Employment termination** The only accepted reason for firing a worker in China is flagrant absenteeism without a medical excuse. Poor performance is not generally seen as an accepted ground for dismissal.
- **Minimum wage** There is no legal minimum wage.
- **Bankruptcy** There are two sets of bankruptcy regulations: those dealing strictly with the Shenzhen Special Economic Zone (SEZ), and the Enterprise Bankruptcy Law of China. They are similar in their definitions and application, but are administered differently. The SEZ Bankruptcy Law applies only to enterprises in Shenzhen partially or fully owned by non-Chinese interests.
- **Agency** If the agency agreement is unclear as to the authority and entrustment of the agent, then both principal and agent shall have joint liability to third parties.
- **Statute of limitations** Civil case to enforce civil rights must be brought within two years. Cases for compensation for personal injury must be brought within one year.
- **Damages** The concept of damages for breach of contract is known, understood, and not infrequently explicated in Chinese contracts, including international contracts which often have severe penalty clauses.
- **Fraud** Sales concluded under influence of fraud are generally regarded by Chinese legal authorities as invalid, with the wrongdoer being required to return what was received under contract.
- **Social benefits** Enterprises having foreign investment must pay retirement and pension funds and employment insurance premuims for Chinese employees. Many must also pay housing subsidy funds, which are expenses incurred in building and purchase of housing for employees of said enterprise.
- **Monopolies** Chinese policy and law provide dual, and sometimes contradictory, goals for both combinations and competition. Many industries are still run as monopolies by the state.

LEGAL CONTACTS

Baker & McKenzie China Consultants
Suite 427, China Hotel
Liuhua Lu
Guangzhou 510015
Tel: (20) 6665959, 6666888 x427
Fax: (20) 6665950 Telex: 44888

Beijing Foreign Economic Law Office
Working People's Cultural Palace
Beijing 100006
Tel: (1) 5513167/8 Fax: (1) 6016171

Beijing Lawyers Association
1 Xishiku Dajie
Xiching Qu
Beijing 1000034
Tel: (1) 6016172

Bull, Housser & Tupper
58244 #3 Jin Jiang Office Building
59 Mao Ming nan lu
Shanghai 200020
Tel: (21) 4374897 Fax: (21) 4375066 Telex: 33011

Buxbaum and Choy
60 Xi Chang An Street
West Cheug Qu
Beijing
Tel: (1) 667007 Fax: (1) 3261232

Guangzhou Foreign Economics Law Office
5th Fl., Dongjian Building
503 Dongfeng Zhong Lu
Guangzhou 510030
Tel: (20) 6677846 Fax: (20) 3350001

China Law Society
6 Xizhimen, nan Dajie
Beijing 10035
Tel: (1) 6689719 x5209 Fax: (1) 8317502

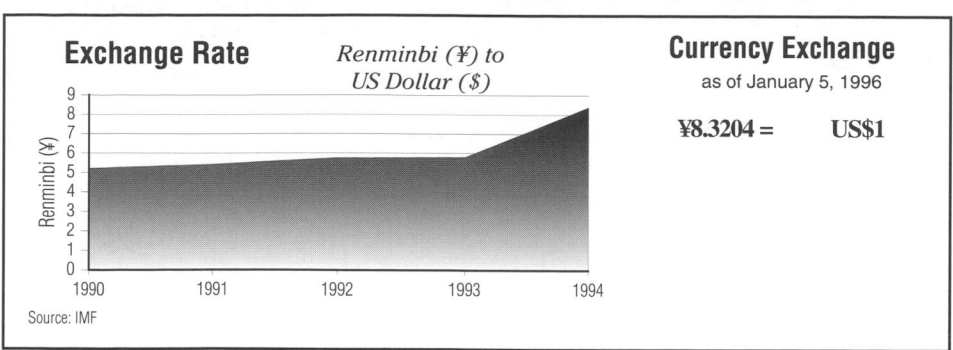

Exchange Rate

Renminbi (¥) to US Dollar ($)

Source: IMF

Currency Exchange

as of January 5, 1996

¥8.3204 =   US$1

Money Mattters

BITS AND PIECES

- **Exchange rates** Rates are reflected against the US dollar and other convertible currencies on the basis of the previous day's rates in the nationwide swap markets.
- **Private ownership** The Chinese government still imposes numerous restrictions on the establishment of business enterprises. For example, foreign audio-visual companies do not have the right to establish wholly owned subsidiaries or joint ventures.
- **Gold and silver** Sales are restricted to pharmaceutical, industrial, and other approved uses. Private persons may hold gold, but are not allowed to trade gold. Gold and silver may be imported without limitations. Exports must accompany the necessary documents from customs or a permit.
- **Import payments** Foreign exchange may be purchased from the Bank of China, as well as other specialized banks, to settle trade and trade-related transactions upon the proper presentation of contracts or payment notices, and do not require the approval of the SAEC. Residents may not transact payments for imports with local currency.
- **Export proceeds** All foreign exchange earnings with certain exceptions must be repatriated and sold to designated banks.

Currency

The currency of the People's Republic of China is the renminbi, and its basic monetary unit is the yuan, symbol Y.

Foreign Exchange

The People's Bank of China, together with the State Administration for Exchange Control (SAEC), set foreign exchange policies. Other banks and financial institutions, including affiliates of nonresident banks, may transact foreign exchange with proper authorization. Foreign institutions and nonresidents may hold foreign exchange in special accounts, but are excluded from the new interbank market. Since foreign-invested enterprises generally may not trade foreign exchange or conduct arbitrage operations, the Chinese government has accordingly retained foreign exchange swap markets, where foreign institutions can trade foreign exchange and renminbi among one another.

Capital Transfers

Repatriation of profits from China can be difficult if they are not generated in foreign exchange. Chinese regulations insist that foreign-invested projects balance foreign exchange receipts with expenditures, and require that foreign-funded enterprises maintain foreign exchange earnings in a special account. Approval for the repatriation of funds from this account must be obtained from the SAEC. Nonresidents may make payments for invisibles after taxes with approval from the relevant authorities. Businesses, except foreign-funded enterprises, must sell all foreign exchange earnings from invisible transactions to the Bank of China or another authorized bank. Foreign exchange from invisibles to Chinese residents may be retained or sold.

Investment Incentives

There is a complex system of investment incentives. Some areas designated as economic zones promote investment with unique packages of tax exemptions, reductions, and incentives. There are also a number of free ports and bonded zones.

Investment Restrictions

Potential investments must go through a thorough screening process. Certain sectors also have their own requirements, in areas like hiring and using foreign products. Investment restrictions arise more from the extreme bureaucracy permeating the economy than from specific prohibitions.

BANKS

Agricultural Bank of China (Beijing)
25 Fuxing Lu
Beijing 100036
Tel: (1) 8413128 Fax: (1) 8416682

Agricultural Bank of China (Guangzhou)
International Business Dept.
Ground Fl., Zhonghua Center
180 Taikang Lu
Guangzhou 510115
Tel: (20) 3327747 Fax: (20) 3350903
Telex: 44285 ABCGZ CN

Bank of China (Beijing)
410 Fuchengmen Nei Dajie
Beijing 100818
Tel: (1) 6016688 Fax: (1) 6016869
Telex: 22254 BCHO CN

Bank of China (Guangzhou)
International Financial Building
197-9 Dongfeng Xi Lu
Guangzhou 510180
Tel: (20) 3338080 Fax: (20) 3344066
Telex: 441042 GZBOC CN

Bank of China (Shanghai)
23 Zhongshan Dong Yi Lu
Shanghai 200002
Tel: (21) 3291979, 3211410 Fax: (21) 3234872
Telex: 33062 BOCSH CN

Bank of Communications (Beijing)
Beijing Branch
12 Tiantan Dongli Beiqu, Chongwen Qu
Beijing 100061
Tel: (1) 7012255 Fax: (1) 7016524, 7016529
Foreign Trade Dept. Tel: (1) 7016524

Bank of Communications (Guangzhou)
4 Guangwei Lu
Guangzhou 501328
Tel: (20) 3341285 Fax: (20) 3340494

Central Bank
People's Bank of China (Beijing)
32 Chengfang Street
Beijing 100800
Tel: (1) 6016491, 6016722 Fax: (1) 6016724

People's Bank of China (Guangzhou)
421 Yanjiang Dong Lu
Guangzhou 510100
Tel: (20) 7789154, 7771874

People's Bank of China (Shanghai)
23 Zhongshan Dong Yi Ku
Shanghai 200002
Tel: (21) 3217466
Tel: (21) 3233898

TAXATION	At a Glance	
Taxation requires sophisticated knowledge of complex rules and regulations specific to each country. The information presented here is from the Ernst & Young Corporate Tax Guide and Directory, available from the Ernst & Young accounting office in your country, or from:	National Corporate Income Tax Rate (%) (a)	30
	Local Corporate Income Tax Rate (%) (a)	3
	Capital Gains Tax Rate (%)	33
	Branch Tax Rate (%)	33
	Withholding Tax (%)	
Ernst & Young	Dividends (b)	20
10/F, Hong Kong Macau Centre	Interest	20
Dong Si Shi Tiao Li Jiao Qiao	Royalties from Patents, Know-how, etc. (c)	20
Beijing 100027	Branch Remittance Tax	0
People's Republic of China	Net Operating Losses (Years)	
Tel: (1) 5011520	Carryback	0
Fax: (1) 5011519	Carryforward	5
	(a) An income tax surcharge of 15% is also levied through the 1994-95 fiscal year.	
	(b) Rates vary depending on holding period.	

Business Travel

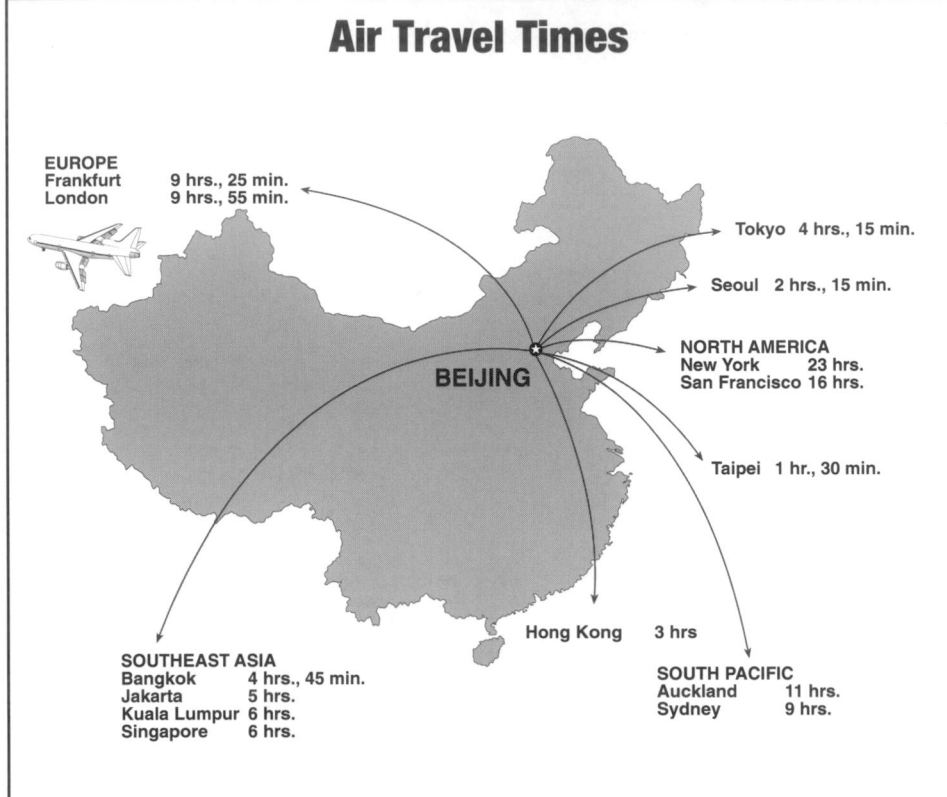

Air Travel Times

EUROPE
Frankfurt   9 hrs., 25 min.
London   9 hrs., 55 min.

Tokyo 4 hrs., 15 min.

Seoul 2 hrs., 15 min.

NORTH AMERICA
New York   23 hrs.
San Francisco 16 hrs.

BEIJING

Taipei 1 hr., 30 min.

Hong Kong 3 hrs

SOUTHEAST ASIA
Bangkok   4 hrs., 45 min.
Jakarta   5 hrs.
Kuala Lumpur 6 hrs.
Singapore   6 hrs.

SOUTH PACIFIC
Auckland   11 hrs.
Sydney   9 hrs.

COMMUNICATIONS

Telephones Telephone service is acceptable though not advanced in urban areas, but it is improving. International service is available 24 hours a day. Private phones are uncommon and pay phones generally do not work well. Local calls are free. For calls placed from a hotel room, it is best to arrange for the call from the hotel desk and wait in your room for the connection. It may require 15 minutes to three hours to make an overseas call. Telegrams are sent from the Post, Telegraph and Telecommunications (PTT) buildings or the FTC head offices. Telex and telegraph are also available and very reliable.

Fax All major hotels offer fax service, and telegrams can be sent from most Post, Telegraph and Telecommunication buildings and offices. Service is fast and dependable.

Post office China's postal system is one of the most efficient in the world with deliveries twice a day, seven days a week. No independent messenger services are available in Beijing. Hotels will arrange for deliveries of correspondence.

Radio/TV The Central Broadcasting Administration of the PRC, controlled by the CCP Central Committee, operates all radio and television stations. Stations broadcast four hours each evening. The news, documentaries, and films primarily concern government ideology.

BEST TRAVEL BOOKS

Lonely Planet, China Travel Survival Kit. Brimming with hard-to-find travel advice and detailed city maps. Essential for the independent traveler. 1100 pages, 16 color pages.

Fodor's Travel Guide, China. Tourist oriented, excellent source of city details.

Culture Shock, China. A Guide to Customs and Etiquette, China.

The Travellers Guide to China Customs and Manners. Elizabeth Devine & Nancy Braganti. An invaluable guide for people not wanting to put foot in mouth.

TELEPHONE NUMBERS

If you are calling from outside China you will need to add the country code [86] and any other international dialing requirements from within your country.

- Police/Beijing 110
- Fire/Beijing 119
- Information 116
- Local information 114
- Capital Hospital/Beijing 553731
- International calls 337431
- Post Office/ Beijing .... (1) 555414
- Vaccinations .... (1) 461857
- Taxi/ Beijing.. (1) 557461
- China Int'l Exhibition Center.................. (1) 4678309
- China World Trade Center .... (1) 5052277
- General Information .... (1) 5130828
- DHL-Sinotrans... (1) 486761
- Federal Express .... (1) 5011017
- TNT Skypak .... (1) 4811894
- Shanghai Exhibition Centre................ (21) 3276060
- Guangzhou Exhibition Center .... (20) 677000

Chamber of Commerces

- Chamber of Commerce/Shanghai....... (21) 4332492
- Chamber of Commerce/Guangzhou ..... (20) 677842
- National Tourism Administration .... (1) 5138866
- Ministry of Communications .... (1) 8642021
- US Embassy/Beijing.............................. (1) 5323831

Credit Card Information

Lost or stolen credit cards (call collect to the US, regardless of which country the card was issued in).

- Amex .... [1] (919) 3333211
- Diner's Club................................. [1] (303) 7991504
- MasterCard .... [1] (314) 2756690
- Visa .... [1] (410) 5817931

Travelogue

WORKWEEK

Offices Monday-Friday 8:00 am to noon, 2:00 pm to 5:00 pm, Saturday 8:00 am to noon.

Banks Monday-Friday 8:00 am to noon, 2:00 pm to 5:00 pm., Saturday 8:00 am to noon.

Government Monday-Friday 8:00 am to noon, 2:00 pm to 5:00 pm, Saturday 8:00 am to noon.

Retail Monday-Sunday 8:00 am to 6:00 pm.

HOLIDAYS

Holidays 1996
February Chinese New Year *
3 days late February or early March Spring Festival *
May 1 International Labor Day
October 3 Chinese National Day
*Dates vary year to year.
Note: Many take the entire week of Spring Festival off. Chinese National Day celebration may be up to 3 days.

VISA AND PASSPORT

All passports and visas must be current and are usually valid for only one entry. Be prepared to show a copy of your itinerary indicating arrival and departure dates. A tourist visa is required to enter the country, a transit visa is required to leave the country. Both are available at any Chinese embassy or consulate. Anyone arriving without a visa will be fined 2,000 renminbi at the point of entry and may not be allowed to enter the country. A transit visa is required for any stopover, even if travelers do not intend to leave the plane. Visas are required when exiting the country and when traveling between hotels within the country. Carry it with you at all times. Any travel to Tibet must be approved prior to arrival.

DEPARTURE FORMALITIES

An airport departure tax of RMB 60 will be collected. You can only take out of China what you brought in. Keep all money exchange receipts. They must verify the amount of foreign currency claimed upon arrival, or the excess will be confiscated.

IMMUNIZATION

Cholera and yellow fever vaccinations are required if arriving from any infected area within five to six days. Vaccinations for hepatitis, typhoid, tetanus, and influenza are suggested for all travelers, as is a polio booster and a TB skin test. If planning to reside over one year, an HIV test is required.

TIPPING

Tipping is prohibited. Hotels and restaurants add a service charge to the bill. Offering a tip is considered offensive.

CRIME

Crime rate is low but has increased recently in large cities. Theft is common, and violent crimes are very unusual.

INFRASTRUCTURE

Travel in China is rugged. Most flights connect through Hong Kong. International and domestic airlines service all large cities, but there is commonly a shortage of available seats. An express train operates frequently each day between Hong Kong and Guangzhou. For travel from the airport, taxis and hotel limousines are recommended. Buses are available, but often crowded with no room for luggage. Domestic flights are the only recommended way to travel throughout the country. Trains are slow and uncomfortable. Buses are available in urban areas, but routes are confusing. It is easier to find a taxi at a hotel than on the street. Have the taxi wait for you between appointments. The subway in Beijing is modern, fast, inexpensive, and clean. Bicycling is very common in China and highly recommended for travel in urban areas. Hotel rooms are abundantly available once you arrive. Service and quality in hotels are improving, but there are often errors in reservations.

NATIONAL TOURIST OFFICE

China National Tourism Office
Beijing
Tel: (1) 5158844, 5662801, 5666843

Contacts

GOVERNMENT AGENCIES

Beijing Foreign Economic Relations and Trade Commission
3 Nan Li Shi Road Tou Tiao
Beijing 100045
Tel: (1) 862015, 866511 Fax: (1) 8010353
Telex: 22476 BJGVT CN

Customs General Administration
Building East
6 Jian Guo Men Wei Dajie
Beijing 100730
Tel: (1) 5194114, 5195013 Fax: (1) 5126020, 5194004

Ministry of Foreign Trade & Economic Cooperation (MOFTEC)
2 Dongchangan Jie, Dongcheng Qu
Beijing 100731
Tel: (1) 5198114, 5198322, 5198804
Fax: (1) 5129568, 5198904
Telex: 22168
American & Oceanian Affairs Dept.
Tel: (1) 5198821 Fax: (1) 5198834
Asian Affairs Dept. Tel: (1) 5198716
European Affairs Dept. Tel: (1) 5198662
Foreign Aid Dept. Tel: (1) 5197558
Foreign Credit Dept. Tel: (1) 5197316
Foreign Economic & Trade Policy Dept.
Tel: (1) 5198529 Fax: (1) 5198912
Foreign Investment Dept. Tel: (1) 5197303
Foreign Trade Dept.
Tel: (1) 5197420, 5198328, 5198504
International Economic Research Institute
Tel: (1) 4211078
International Trade & Economic Affairs Dept.
Tel: (1) 5197973
International Trade Research Institute
Tel: (1) 5129589 Fax: (1) 5128928
Protocol Dept. Tel: (1) 5198203
Science & Technology Dept. Tel: (1) 5196822
Treaty & Law Dept. Tel: (1) 5198723

China Council for Promotion of International Trade (CCPIT)
1 Fu Xing Men Wai Dajie
Beijing 100860
Tel: (1) 8013344, 8013866 Fax: (1) 8011370
Telex: 22315 CCPIT CN
China Trade Promotion Review
Tel: (1) 4664999

China National Light Industry Council
22-B Fuwai Dajie
Beijing 100833
Tel: (1) 8396338 Fax: (1) 8396351

China National Textile Council
12 Dongchangan Jie
Beijing 100742
Tel: (1) 5129303 Fax: (1) 5136020

Ministry of Agriculture
11 Nonzhanguan Nanli, Hepinli
Beijing 100026
Tel: (1) 5003366, 5004606 Fax: (1) 5002448

Ministry of Chemical Industry
Foreign Affairs Dept.
3rd Fl., Second Building, Building 16
Hepingli Qiqu, Dongcheng Qu
Beijing 100013

Ministry of Communications
10 Fuxing Lu, Haidian Qu
Beijing 100845
Tel: (1) 3265544 Fax: (1) 3273943
Telex: 22462

Ministry of Construction
9 San Li He Lu, Haidian Qu
Beijing 100853
Tel: (1) 8394049, 8393833 Fax: (1) 8313669
Telex: 222302

Ministry of Culture
Jia 83, Donganmen Bei Jie
Beijing 100820
Tel: (1) 4012255

Ministry of Electronics Industry
27 Wanshou Road
Beijing 100846
Tel: (1) 8282233 Fax: (1) 8221838

Ministry of Finance
3 Nansanxiang, Sanlihe, Xicheng Qu
Beijing 100820
Tel: (1) 868731 Fax: (1) 8013428 Telex: 222308
Foreign Affairs Bureau
Tel: (1) 8033606 Fax: (1) 8013428

Ministry of Foreign Affairs
225 Chaoyangmennei Dajie, Dongsi
Beijing 100701
Tel: (1) 553831, 5135566, 5555323
Telex: 210070 FMPRC CN

Ministry of Forestry
18 Hepinglidong Jie, Dongchang Qu
Beijing
Tel: (1) 463061 Telex: 22237

Ministry of Labor
12 Hepinglizhong Jie, Dongcheng Qu
Beijing 100708
Tel: (1) 4212454, 4213431 Fax: (1) 4211624

Ministry of Machine-Building Industry
46 San Li He, Xicheng Qu
Beijing 100823
Tel: (1) 3294966 Fax: (1) 8013867

Ministry of Materials and Equipment Supplies
25 Yuetanbei Jie, Xicheng Qu
Beijing 100834
Tel: (1) 8021247, 8391108 Fax: (1) 8391148
Telex: 200155 WUZIJ CN

Ministry of Metallurgical Industry
46 Dongsixi Dajie
Beijing 100071
Tel: (1) 5133322, 5131921 Fax: (1) 5130074

Ministry of Posts and Telecommunications
13 Xichangan Jie
Beijing 100804
Tel: (1) 6016137, 6020540
Foreign Affairs Dept.
Tel: (1) 6011365 Fax: (1) 6011370 Telex: 222187

Ministry of Radio, Film and Television
2 Fu Xing Men Wai Jie
POB 4501
Beijing 100866
Tel: (1) 8012176, 6092141 Fax: (1) 8012174
Telex: 22236

Ministry of Railways
10 Fuxing Lu, Haidian Qu
Beijing 100845
Tel: (1) 8640011 Telex: 22483

Ministry of Transportation
10 Fuxing Road
Beijing 100845
Tel: (1) 3264895, 8643369 Telex: 22462 COMCT CN

Ministry of Urban and Rural Construction and Environmental Protection
Baiwanzhuang
Beijing
Tel: (1) 8992211 Telex: 222302 MURC CN

Ministry of Water Resources
1 Baiguang Lu, Ertiao, Xuanwu Qu
Beijing
Tel: (1) 3273322 Fax: (1) 3260365 Telex: 22466
Foreign Affairs Dept. Tel: (1) 3260192

Press and Publishing Administration
85 Dongsi South Avenue
Beijing 100703
Tel: (1) 5127806 Fax: (1) 5127875

State Administration for Industry and Commerce
8 Sanlihe Dong Lu, Xicheng Qu
Beijing 100820
Tel: (1) 8031133, 8013300 Fax: (1) 4914783, 8013394

State Administration of Building Materials Industry
Baiwanzhuang
Beijing 100831
Tel: (1) 8311144 Fax: (1) 8311497

State Bureau of Foreign Exports
Friendship Hotel
Dongbei Qu
Beijing 100873
Tel: (1) 8323260 Fax: (1) 8315382

State Bureau of Tax
Zhaolin Quan Jie
Beijing
Tel: (1) 3263366 Fax: (1) 3266836

State Council Office for Special Economic Zones
22 Xianmen Dajie
Beijing 100017
Tel: (1) 3099065

State Council Office of Leading Group for Foreign Investment
22 Xianmen Dajie
Beijing 100017
Tel: (1) 3099065

State Council Overseas Chinese Affairs Office
1 Beixinqiao Santiao
Beijing 100710
Tel: (1) 4015671 Fax: (1) 4014639

State Economic and Trade Commission
25 Yuetan North St.
Beijing 100834
Tel: (1) 8392227 Fax: (1) 8392222

State Science and Technology Commission
54 Sanlihe Road
Beijing 100862
Tel: (1) 8012594 Fax: (1) 8012594

WORLD TRADE CENTERS

China World Trade Center (Beijing), Ltd.
China World Tower
1 Jian Guo Men Wai Dajie
Beijing 100004
Tel: (1) 5052288, 5058340 Fax: (1) 5051002
Telex: 210087

World Trade Center Beijing
Rm. 409 4th Fl., 2nd Central Building
Hualong St., Nanheyan
East City District
Beijing 100006
Tel: (1) 5125176/7 Fax: (1) 5125165
Telex: 210333 BCPIT CN

World Trade Center Club Chengdu
17th Fl., Shudu Building
15 Shudu Road
Chengdu 610016
Tel: (28) 673888, 51715,336693 Fax: (28) 334675
Telex: 60131 SFTC CN

World Trade Center Club Guanzhou
Rm. 835-837, Garden Tower, Garden Hotel
368 Huanshi Dong Lu
Guanzhou 510064
Tel: (20) 3338999 x7835/6/7 Fax: (20) 3354241
Telex: 44341 WTCG CN

World Trade Center Shanghai
33 Zhong Shan Dong Yi Lu
Shanghai 20002
Tel: (21) 3232348, 3213850 Fax: (21) 3291442
Telex: 33290 SCPIT CN

World Trade Center Shenzhen
2nd Fl., Area B, International Trade Center Mansion
Renmin South Road
Shenzhen 518014
Tel: (755) 250140/1/2 Fax: (755) 252043, 250140
Telex: 420296 ITC CN

World Trade Center Tianjin
Tianjin Leader (Group) Corp.
3 Xinyuan, Kumming Road
Heping Qu
Tianjin, 300050
Tel: (22) 314882 Fax: (22) 317471
Telex: 23254 TJEDC CN

BUSINESS AND TRADE ORGANIZATIONS

All China Federation of Industry and Commerce
93 Beiheyan Dajie
Beijing 100006
Tel: (1) 5136677 Fax: (1) 5122631, 5131769

Beijing Federation of Industry and Commerce
30 Zhushikou Xi Dajie
Xuanwu Qu
Beijing 100050
Tel: (1) 3033236 Fax: (1) 3014194

CCOIC (China Chamber of International Commerce)
1 Fu Xing Men Wai Dajie
Beijing 100860
Tel: (1) 8011156, 8013344 x1304 Fax: (1) 8011370

CCOIC Commercial Chamber of Commerce
45 Fuxingmennei Dajie
Beijing 100801
Tel: (1) 6016043 Telex: 22547 CCOC CN

CCOIC, Shanghai Chamber of Commerce
14th Fl., New Town Mansion
55 Loushanguan Lu
200335 Shanghai
Tel: (21) 2750700 Fax: (21) 2756364

China International Economic and Trade Arbitration Commission, Shanghai
33 Dongshan Dong Yi Lu
200002 Shanghai
Tel: (21) 3295443 Fax: (21) 3291442

China Society of Int'l Economic Cooperation
28 Donghou Xiang, Andingmenwai
Beijing 100710
Tel: (1) 4216661 Telex: 22559 COMPT CN

Shanghai Federation of Industry and Commerce
893 Huashan Lu
Shanghai 200031
Tel: (21) 4336914, 4745021 Fax: (21) 4335795

Shanghai Industry Foundation
45 Jiujiang Lu
Shanghai 200002
Tel: (21) 3210264 Fax: (21) 3290385

FOREIGN BUSINESS ORGANIZATIONS

American Chamber of Commerce (AmCham)
Great Wall Sheraton Hotel #301
Beijing 100026
Tel: (1) 5005566 x2271, Fax: (1) 5018273
Guangzhou Tel: (20) 6663388 x1293
Shanghai Tel: (21) 2798056

Hong Kong Trade Development Council
Rm. 1004, 10th Fl., Union Building
100 Yan An Dong Lu
Shanghai 200002
Tel: (21) 3264196 Fax: (21) 3287478

Italian Institute for Foreign Trade, Shanghai
Rm. 404, Hotel Equatorial
65 Yan An Xi Lu
Shanghai 200040
Tel: (1) 2568600 Fax: (1) 2562169

Japan Association for Promotion of International Trade, Shanghai Office
Rm. 359 New Building, Jinjiang Club
191 Changle Lu
Shanghai 200020
Tel: (1) 4373033

US-China Business Council
Rm. 22-C, CITIC Building
19 Jian Guo Men Wai Dajie
Beijing 100004
Tel: (1) 5051314, 5051302 Fax: (1) 5052201

DIRECTORIES & YEARBOOKS

China International Book Trading Corp.
POB 399
Chegongzhuang Xilu 21
Beijing
Fax: (1) 8412023

China Importers & Exporters Directory
Han Ying Shan Research
POB 71006
Wuhan, Hubei Province 430071
Tel: (27) 812804 Fax: (27) 711242

China Telephone Directory (Chinese)
China Telephone Directory Company
Ministry of Posts and Telecommunications
13 Xichangan Jie
Beijing 100804
Tel: (1) 6016137
Foreign Affairs Dept.
Tel: (1) 6011365 Fax: (1) 6011370 Telex: 222187

Directory of CCOIC Membership Enterprises
1 Fu Xing Men Wai Dajie
Beijing 100860
Tel: (1) 8011156, 8013344 x1304
Fax: (1) 8011370

Directory of Chinese Foreign Economic Relations and Trade Enterprises
China Foreign Economic Relations & Trade Publishing House
28 Dong Hou Xiang
An Ding Men Wai St.
Beijing 100710

NEWSPAPERS

Asian Wall Street Journal
Dow Jones Publishing Co. (Asia)
2nd Fl. AIA Building
1 Stubbs Road
GPOB 9825
Hong Kong
Tel: [852] 25737121 Fax: [852] 28345291

China Daily
15 Huixin Dongjie, Chaoyang Qu
Beijing
Tel: (1) 4220955 Fax: (1) 4220922

Guangzhou Ribao (Guangzhou Daily)
(Chinese)
10 Dongle Lu
Renmin Zhonglu
Guangzhou

International Commerce (Guoji Shangbao She)
(Chinese)
POB 6115
Building 14, Part 3, Fangxing Yuan
Fangxhuanglu
Beijing 100061
Tel: (1) 7019921

Jingji Ribao (Economic Daily)
(Chinese)
27 Wangfujing Dajie
Beijing
Tel: (1) 5125522 Fax: (1) 5125015

Shenzhen Tequ Bao (Shenzhen Special Zone Daily)
1 Shennan Zhonglu
Shenzhen

BUSINESS PERIODICALS

Beijing Industrial and Commercial Management
(Beijing Gondshang Xingxheng Guangli)
18 Enjizhuang, Haidian Qu
Beijing 100036
Tel: (1) 8311924

Beijing Institute of Finance and Trade Journal
(Beijing Caimao Xueyuan)
68 Nanxiange Jie
Guanganmennei
Beijing 100053

Beijing Review
24 Baiwanzhuang Lu
Beijing 100037
Tel: (1) 8315599 Fax: (1) 8314318 Telex: 222374

China Today
China Welfare Institute
24 Baiwanzhuang Lu
Beijing 100037
Tel: (1) 8326037 Fax: (1) 8328338

China's Foreign Trade CCPIT
1 Fu Xing Men Wai Dajie
Beijing
Tel: (1) 8013344 Fax: (1) 8011370 Telex: 22315 CCPIT

International Market (Guoji Shichang)
Shanghai Guoji Jingji Maugi Yanjiusuo
Shanghai International Economics and Trade Institute
33 Zhongshan Dongyi Lu
Shanghai 200002
Tel: (21) 3212659

International Trade Journal
University of International Business and Economics
Yinghua Dongjie Beikou
Andingmenwai
Beijing 100029
Tel: (1) 4225522 Fax: (1) 4212022

International Trade News MOFTEC
International Trade Research Institute
Donghouxiang 28
Andingmenwai
Beijing 100710
Tel: (1) 5129589 Fax: (1) 5128928

Yazhou Zhoukan
(Weekly; Chinese)
13th Fl., South, Somerset House
28 Tong Chong St.
Quarry Bay, Hong Kong
Tel: [852] 25630232 Fax: [852] 25657730

RADIO AND TELEVISION

Ministry of Radio, Film and Television
Fu Xing Men Wai Jie 2
POB 4501
Beijing
Tel: (01) 862753
Telex: 22236
Fax: (01) 8012174

Central People's Broadcasting Station
Fu Xing Men Wai Jie 2
Beijing

INTERNET ADDRESSES

China Business Corner
http://206.31.83.175/cbc/welcome.htm

ChinaPages
http://wwwchinapages.com

China Business Bulletin Board
http://odin.pat.dcu.ie:8080/cgi-bin/bbs.pl

China Chamber of International Commerce
http://www1.usa1.com/~ibnet/ccpithp.html

China Business and Commerce (China.com)
http://www.worldtel.com/enercana/china.html

China Home Page (Institute of High Energy Physics, Beijing)
http://www.ihep.ac.cn/china.html

NetChina
http://www.netchina.com/

Shanghai Panorama
http://msdisk.wustl.edu/~li_n/shanghai.html

Colombia
Republic of Colombia

Economy

Overview

Colombia has undergone rather dramatic changes over recent years. Aided by a reform program that has opened the economy to greater international trade, investment, and competition, Colombia is experiencing strong growth in many sectors of its economy. It has also assumed a greater leadership role in Latin America, signing free trade agreements with many of its trading partners. The Colombian government has pursued more prudent fiscal, exchange rate, and monetary policies, as well as instituted major changes in the areas of finance and labor. However, Colombia continues to be plagued by the debilitating influence exercised by illegal drug marketers, haunted by drug- and guerilla-related violence, and undercut by the inflation spurred by an influx of large volumes of uncontrolled drug money.

Trade

Colombia's major exports include minerals (one-third of which represent sales of coal), coffee, textiles, bananas, and cut flowers. Imports include electrical and mechanical equipment, chemicals, metals, and transportation equipment. Accounting for nearly 40 percent of total trade, the US is Colombia's principal trading partner, followed by Germany, Venezuela, Japan, and France. As a result of economic reforms, imports have been growing substantially, reversing years of trade surpluses. The situation has been further aggravated by a general decline in coffee prices, one of Colombia's primary legal exports.

Sectors

Agriculture Although only about five percent of Colombia's land is cultivated, its diverse climate and topography allow it to grow a wide variety of crops, accounting for more than 20 percent of its GDP and providing employment for about one-quarter of the work force. Coffee is the predominate agricultural export, followed by bananas, cut flowers, and sugar cane. Timber and beef are also significant cash crops.

Industry Employing less than 25 percent of the work force, industry provides about 20 percent of GDP. Colombia has rich mineral and energy resources, including hydroelectric power, petroleum, the largest coal reserves in Latin America, nickel, gold, and emeralds. Major industries include food and beverage processing, textiles, chemicals, and transportation equipment, although many national industries have suffered because of competition from imports and a revalued peso.

Services The service sector employs nearly 50 percent of the work force, and produces about the same for the GDP. Current reforms—including the privatization of banking systems and telecommunication services—are designed to improve service, productivity, and delivery.

Trends

The ongoing reforms that began in 1991 and the government crackdown on large drug traffickers are expected to continue to spur the economy as Colombia seeks to internationalize its trade patterns. However, the disruptive influence of drug trafficking remains substantial, and there exists no credible plan to replace the earnings lost by eliminating this trade. The government has also failed to make progress in defusing the claims of the long-standing leftist guerilla insurgency, and this continues to inhibit foreign investment in the country. However, Colombia should soon show some positive growth.

At a Glance

THE COUNTRY

Location Northern South America, between Panama and Venezuela.
Terrain Flat coastal areas, central highlands, volcanic mountains, and eastern plains with extensive coastlines on the Pacific Ocean and Caribbean Sea.
Climate Tropical on the coast and eastern plains, and cooler in the highlands.

THE PEOPLE

Population 36,000,000
Ethnic composition An intermingling of indigenous Indians, Spanish colonists, and African slaves. About one percent identified as fully Indian on the basis of language and customs.
Religious composition
Roman Catholic 95%
Languages spoken Spanish.
Education and literacy School is free and compulsory for nine years; for five years in rural areas. Literacy is 93 percent in urban areas and 67 percent in rural areas. Education is of a high standard.
Labor force
Total: 12,000,000
By occupation: services 46%, agriculture 30%, industry 24%.

COUNTRY FACTS

Political and legal Colombia is a republic, with an executive branch which dominates government structure. The legal system is based on Spanish law, with judicial review of executive and legislative acts.
Telephone Telecommunications services are quickly undergoing modernization and privatization. Colombia is linked to other countries via satellite, fiber optics, and undersea cable. Congress has recently approved the operation of cellular telephone networks with private investment, local and foreign. International country code: [57]. Selected city codes: Bogotá (1).
Transportation Although the mountainous topography makes it difficult to construct and maintain roads, main cities are connected by a fairly good road network. The major port cities are joined by modern highways. The railway transport system extends over 3,200 kilometers, although tracks and equipment require substantial improvement. No regular passenger service is provided and there is a very limited and poor freight transport facility. However, the government has plans to privatize this sector in an effort to modernize equipment and services. Five international airports provide direct air connections to many foreign cities. Colombia maintains several well-equipped ports which handle a large quantity and variety of freight traffic.
Environment Soil damage and deforestation have resulted from overdevelopment and the overuse of pesticides. Lack of environmental controls has resulted in air pollution in the major cities, which the government is only now beginning to address.
Media Colombian radio consists of 413 AM, and no FM stations; there are three nation-wide television channels, and four regional channels. Cable TV is available in the main cities. Colombia has 46 daily newspapers, and a variety of periodicals.
Health Health standards have improved significantly, but malaria is still prevalent, as are intestinal parasites. Health services are available to most of the population. Life expectancy is 69 years.

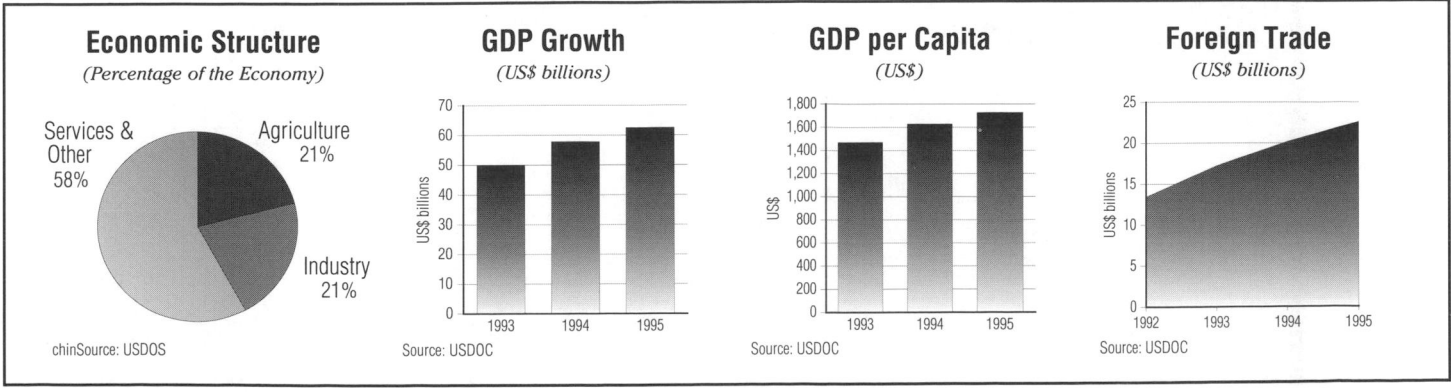

Economic Structure
(Percentage of the Economy)

Services & Other 58%
Agriculture 21%
Industry 21%
chinSource: USDOS

GDP Growth
(US$ billions)
US$ billions
70 60 50 40 30 20 10 0
1993 1994 1995
Source: USDOC

GDP per Capita
(US$)
US$
1,800 1,600 1,400 1,200 1,000 800 600 400 200 0
1993 1994 1995
Source: USDOC

Foreign Trade
(US$ billions)
US$ billions
25 20 15 10 5 0
1992 1993 1994 1995
Source: USDOC

Caribbean Sea

Isla de San Andrés
78°
12° 35'
San Andrés
0 2
Miles
12° 30'
81° 40'

Isla de Providencia
Caribbean Sea
13° 20'
0 2
Miles
81° 22'

Note: Isla de San Andrés , Isla de Providencia and Isla de Malpelo form the administrative unit: San Andrés y Providencia

74° 70° 12°
Willemstad

Guajira
Ríohacha
Santa Marta
Ciénaga
Barranquilla
Atlantico
Cartagena

Maracaibo
Valledupar
La Guaira
Valencia
Caracas

Magdalena
El César

Tolú
Sincelejo
Montería
Sucre
Bolivar
Turbo
Córdoba

Norte de Santander
Cúcuta
Pamplona
Bucaramanga

V e n e z u e l a
8°
Arauca

Panama
Panama City
Pacific Ocean

Chocó
Antioquia
Medellín
Quibdó

Isla de Malpelo
Pacific Ocean
3°58'
0 1
Mile
81° 35'

Atrato
Cauca
Pan
1 2 3
Manizales
Pereira
Armenia
Valle del Cauca
4
Ibagué
5

Magdalena
Santander
Barbosa
Paz del Río
Boyacá
Tunja
Girardot
Bogotá
6
Puerto López
Villavicencio

Arauca
Arauca
Casanare
El Yopal
Vichada
Puerto Carreño

Meta

Buenaventura
Cali
Cauca
Popayán
Neiva
Meta
San José del Guaviare
Guaviare

Guaviare
Puerto Inirida
4°
Puerto Inirida
Guainía
Guainía
San Felipe

Tumaco
Nariño
Pasto
Mocoa
Huíla
Florencia

Quito

Putomayo
Caquetá
Vaupés
Mitú
Vaupés
Vaupés
B r a z i l
0°

E c u a d o r

Central Departments
1 Risaralda
2 Caldas
3 Cundinamarca
4 Quindío
5 Tolima
6 Districto Especial

P e r u

Amazonas
Amazon
Iquitos
Putomayo
Leticia
Javari
Negro

Colombia
⭐ National capital
◉ Department capital
• Secondary city
⊠ Airport
⚓ Port
━━ International border
── Province border
── Road
···· Railroad
0 100 200 km
0 100 mi

©1995 Magellan GeographixSMSanta Barbara, CA

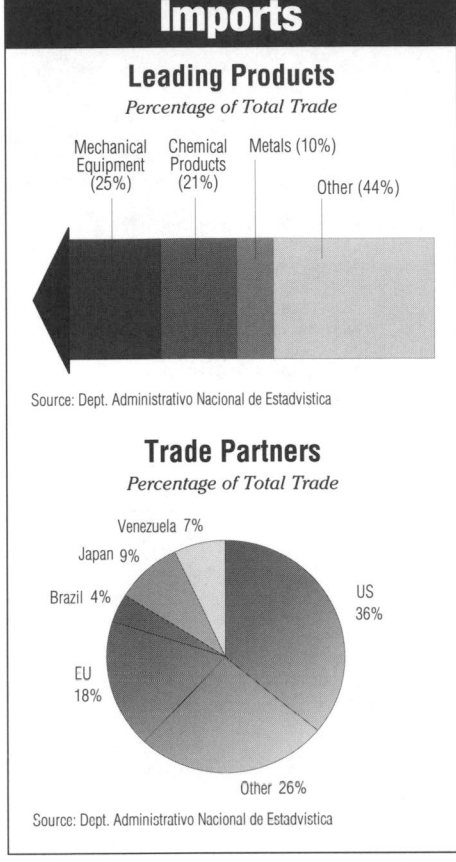

Imports

Leading Products
Percentage of Total Trade

Mechanical Equipment (25%)
Chemical Products (21%)
Metals (10%)
Other (44%)

Source: Dept. Administrativo Nacional de Estadvistica

Trade Partners
Percentage of Total Trade

Venezuela 7%
Japan 9%
Brazil 4%
US 36%
EU 18%
Other 26%

Source: Dept. Administrativo Nacional de Estadvistica

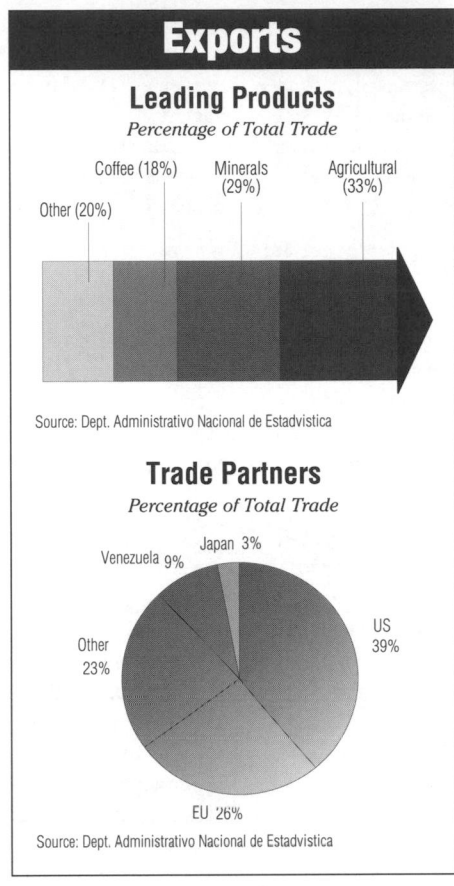

Exports

Leading Products
Percentage of Total Trade

Coffee (18%)
Minerals (29%)
Agricultural (33%)
Other (20%)

Source: Dept. Administrativo Nacional de Estadvistica

Trade Partners
Percentage of Total Trade

Venezuela 9%
Japan 3%
Other 23%
US 39%
EU 26%

Source: Dept. Administrativo Nacional de Estadvistica

Opportunities

FOR IMPORTING TO COLOMBIA
- oil and gas machinery and equipment
- telecommunications equipment, especially fiber optic equipment
- computers and peripherals
- electric power generation equipment
- automotive parts and accessories
- plastics
- medical equipment
- aircraft and parts
- agricultural chemicals
- pollution control equipment
- office products
- mining equipment
- textile machinery
- machine tools

FOR EXPORTING FROM COLOMBIA
- coffee
- vehicles
- boiler machinery
- electrical machinery
- organic chemicals
- exotic flowers

GROWTH SECTORS
- services
- construction
- financial
- manufacture

GOVERNMENT PROCUREMENT
- engineering design
- construction and equipment
- oil and gas pipeline
- airports
- railways
- roads

TRADE NEWS
RULES AND REGULATIONS

- **Import licenses** Import licenses are valid for six months, except those for agricultural and livestock products, which are valid for three months. Capital goods licenses are good for 12 months. Import licenses may be extended for one period only.
- **Imports of crude oil and petroleum products** These are under the control of Empresa Colombiana de Petroleo (ECOPETROL).
- **Prior licensing** Items subject to prior licensing are medicines and chemical products, weapons and munitions.
- **Import registrations** Import registrations are given automatically. Import registrations by some public sector agencies are screened by INCOMEX to determine whether local substitutes are available
- **Freely importable goods** Even goods which can be imported freely require registration with INCOMEX.
- **Export Licenses** Export licenses are not generally required.
- **Exports of coffee** Coffee exports are subject to a minimum surrender price that is fixed on the basis of the international market prices. Exporters pay a coffee contribution, which is determined by the difference between the export value of the coffee surrendered and its estimated cost, taking into account the domestic buying price for export-type coffee. Exporters pay a 6.4% tax on surrendered export proceeds, of which 2.7% goes to the National Federation of Coffee Growers and 3.7% for the National Coffee Fund. Exports must also surrender without payment a certain proportion of the volume of coffee that they wish to export or pay the National Federation of Coffee Growers the peso equivalent. The National Coffee Committee establishes a domestic buying price for export-type coffee, paid pesos per cargo of 125 kilograms.
- **Customs tariffs** Imported goods are subject to customs duties based on the CIF value of the goods. The duties fluctuate from one percent to 200 percent.
- **Import registration** Not only must an import license be obtained, but all imports must be registered with the Institute of Foreign Trade before a firm order is placed abroad.
- **Commercial invoices** Six originals of the commercial invoice are required–copies are no longer acceptable. Facsimile signatures are not acceptable.
- **Special certificates** Special import certificates are required for plants and seeds, unprepared vegetable products, preserved meat and milk, livestock, alcoholic beverages, and used sacks.
- **Storage** Goods arriving in customs may be stored free of charge for up to 12 working days.
- **Marking** The country of origin must be shown on the labels of foodstuffs. There are no special requirements that other goods be marked to show the country of origin.
- **Commercial samples** Samples of no commercial value are admitted free of duty. To qualify they must either be mutilated or be of such a size as to be of no practical value.
- **Customs valuation** Establishing the value of imported merchandise, previously performed only by customs officials, is now done in many cases directly by the importer. Customs clearance, which frequently took months, can now be completed in a few hours.
- **Brokers** Brokers with terminals can complete most clearance procedures in their offices before picking up the merchandise at the port of entry.

GOVERNMENT AGENCY

Instituto Colombiana de Comercio Exterior, INCOMEX
Edificio Centro de Comercio Internacional
Calle 28 No. 13-A-15
Santa Fe de Bogotá, DC
Tel. (1) 281-2200

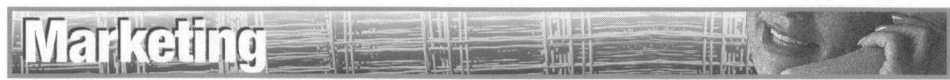

Overview

In the past, government bureaucracy often imposed frustrating detours along the routes of foreign business trade which could only be navigated with patience and perseverance. However, the government is now attempting to remove many of these obstacles and open its markets to foreign firms interested in providing competitive products. Consumer products from countries around the world can now be found on the shelves of many stores in Colombia, although high duty-related markups continue to make it difficult for many foreign products to compete effectively. Thus, many retail products are still coming through contraband channels.

Distribution

Since Colombia began opening its economy to foreign competition, distribution channels and sales of imported products have changed drastically. The marketing of most imported items is still conducted through agents and distributors, although a few large companies directly import a good percentage of the equipment and materials they need— including many consumer products which are imported directly into large chain stores. There are a vast array of retail outlets, ranging from large department stores, specialty shops, and general merchandise stores to public markets, street vendors, and truckers who engage in door-to-door peddling to provide whatever the market demands.

Agents, Distributors, and Partners

Foreign enterprises that export only to the Colombian private sector do not legally need to retain a local agent or representative. Nevertheless, a local agent can provide invaluable help with import procedures and sales promotion, and an agent is required in international public bidding and for contracts with the government. Agents and representatives are legally associated with the principal, and may enter into agreements that result in a legal obligation on the principal. Distributors, however, act independently of their suppliers, and create their own pricing, marketing, and ancillary services. Although agency agreements are contractual in nature, they must be registered and follow the Colombian Commercial Code, which tends to favor the local agent. Now that the economy has begun to open up, more large Colombian firms are beginning to deal directly with overseas suppliers and customers for industrial goods without the use of intermediaries, and retail chains are becoming more experienced at dealing directly with consumer goods.

Selling Techniques

Sales in Colombia depend largely on personal relationships. A well-connected local agent can bring crucial contacts and a local reputation to negotiations, without which the deal may not be concluded or may be delayed indefinitely while the foreign party establishes its good faith and reliability. Direct marketing, however, is becoming popular, and many stores and distributors are starting to publish their own catalogs. Customers may also pick up the phone and order direct; many consumers are eager to utilize this sales method. Direct marketing of imported products is being conducted through a few local companies that specialize in this field, although the delivery of the products in Colombia is usually conducted through a legally established local company which imports the goods and handles the order originated in the local market. Franchising is opening up fairly rapidly, and the parties to any agreement are pretty much free to negotiate the terms thereof. Joint ventures and licensing agreements have been used in Colombia for many years as an important way for transferring technology. In general, Colombians are prudent consumers, often relying on the experience of friends or relatives with regard to a product before making a purchase decision themselves.

Advertising

Introducing new consumer products to the Colombian market usually requires a massive promotion campaign. The average middle-class Colombian family has two or more television sets and they watch them often. Radio is also commonly used. Colombian ad campaigns often involve a massive combination of ads in all media. Another popular technique allows customers to exchange product labels or wrappings for tickets used in raffles for prizes.

Service and Customer Support

After-sales service and customer support are decisive factors to successful marketing efforts in Colombia. Because a low-priced product that cannot be made to work is of little value, purchasers will often opt for a higher-priced product with the same specifications, provided it has an established reputation and facilities in place for follow-up service. In fact, government and private firms often request potential suppliers to provide statements proving client satisfaction with equipment and, especially, with the equipment's after-sales service.

Marketing in Colombia

MARKETING TIPS

- **Marking and labeling** In general, all marking and labeling must be in Spanish and in the metric system; however, the petroleum industry uses US gallons and quarts as a convention, while engineering-related products often are calibrated using the English system.
- **Government markets** Those interested in bidding on tenders must register with the individual agencies, all of which have different procedures. Sales to official agencies require the use of a Colombian agent.
- **Market segmentation** Most purchasing power is concentrated among a few affluent, internationally oriented decision makers who demand up-to-date products. However, Colombian systems may not support all the features available, and sellers should carefully tailor their offerings to provide the maximum usable options without overloading the product with elements that cannot be used or may even interfere with the main function of the product.
- **Advertising channels** Print media are available and inexpensive, but reach relatively few potential consumers (although they may well reach the most affluent and educated); radio reaches almost as many consumers as television but also reaches a broader spectrum of the total population and at a lower cost.
- **TV watchers** A recent market survey revealed that 82 percent of the respondents had watched TV, while only 37.2 percent had read a newspaper, and less than 15 percent had read magazines.
- **Credit cards** The number of Colombians with international credit cards is increasing and they are using this system to order small quantities of consumer goods.
- **Franchising** Because of the rapidly changing laws in this area, legal advice is essential in all steps of a franchising negotiation.
- **Agency agreements** Agency agreements are regulated by the Colombian commercial code which imposes significant limits on the principal with regard to termination, compensation, and indemnification.
- **Pricing** FOB prices for imported products may increase from 60 to 120 percent in the several steps of the sales network in Colombia.
- **Trade fairs** The Bogotá Trade Fair, held every two years in July, is the largest, but there are several smaller trade fairs held from time to time throughout the country.
- **Cinema advertising** High quality slides and filmlets are used for advertising in cinemas.
- **Highway posters** The use of posters on highways for advertising is common.

MARKET RESEARCH FIRMS

A.C. Nielsen De Colombia S.A.
Calle 80 No. 5-81
Santa Fe de Bogotá, DC
Tel: (1) 211-9100 Fax: (1) 211-8894

Optimos Ltda.
Transversal 19A No. 124-59
Santa Fe de Bogotá, DC
Tel: (1) 213-3308/1289 Fax: (1) 215-9576

Market Research de Colombia
Carrera 16A No. 76-31
Santa Fe de Bogotá, DC
Tel: (1) 236-2826/6755 Fax: (1) 257-2949

Analizar Mercade Ltda.
Calle 64 No. 4-88
Santa Fe de Bogotá, DC
Tel: (1) 249-5413 Fax: (1) 210-1127

Data Research de Colombia
Calle 45 No. 21-28
Santa Fe de Bogotá, DC
Tel: (1) 232-1213, 285-0943 Fax: (1) 287-1270

Centro Nacional de Consultoria
Diagonal 34 No. 5-27
Santa Fe de Bogotá, DC
Tel: (1) 288-3100/1811 Fax: (1) 287-2670

Business Culture

Greetings and Courtesies

Men shake hands with each other and with women; women grasp each others' forearms. Men and women friends may kiss each other on the cheek, and men may hug. If meeting lower level workers, shake hands with those closest to you when you are introduced and upon leaving. Business cards in Spanish are not considered necessary, although always be sure that your card contains your title. Status distinctions are very important in Colombia, and people will want to know yours immediately. When presenting a business card, hold it by the end between the index and middle fingers so the print faces the recipient and no print is obscured. At social gatherings, you will be introduced individually by the host or hostess; when leaving, say goodbye individually to anyone to whom you have been introduced.

Business Ethic and Framework

Colombians are reputed to be the most formal and reserved of all South Americans, and Colombian business and social culture is based on strongly hierarchical but personal relationships. To Colombians, work is far from the most important part of life, but they do adhere strictly to the official forms and protocol that govern this nevertheless important sphere.

Decision Making

Actual decisions are almost always made at a high level of authority. Although Colombians will want to know your standing within the hierarchy and will wish to match you with someone of similar rank, always try to approach the most senior person. Not only are senior people likely to be more internationally oriented, but they will also be able to play host while assessing you in order to pair you with the correct Colombian counterpart. It is important to cultivate personal relationships with both superiors and peers, because the quality of these relationships may strongly influence the actual decisionmaker.

Women

Women in Colombia generally occupy a somewhat secondary status in this traditionally male-dominated society, although many operate businesses and are generally accorded considerable personal freedom. Colombian women are becoming more common and accepted in business, and foreign businesswomen should experience few problems. Nevertheless, in Colombia foreign businesswomen are expected to be highly professional, appropriate, and not aggressive or confrontational. They should also avoid any behavior that might be construed as flirtatious, as Colombians can engage in extremely macho behavior. Women should take taxis and go out escorted at night.

Meetings

Introductions are very important. If you do not have a mutual business acquaintance to make an introduction, consult your embassy for a referral. Many foreign businesspeople find it highly useful to have a local contact to serve as a go-between and to handle local arrangements. Make appointments at least one week in advance. Be punctual for appointments, but do not expect Colombians to be on time (although punctuality is becoming more valued in larger cities and internationally oriented firms). Expect to be offered coffee at the beginning of every meeting; always accept graciously, even if you only take a sip. Never attempt to plunge directly into a discussion of business—social topics must always be addressed first to establish the necessary personal connection. In fact, social preliminaries may consume several meetings before business matters can be broached—always allow more time for business in Colombia than you would elsewhere, even in South America. Because the midday meal remains largely a family occasion when many businesspeople return home, business lunches generally have not caught on in Colombia. Dinners with colleagues are more common, but these are essentially social occasions.

Business Attire

Colombians judge people by their appearance and by how well they are dressed—dress impeccably to make a favorable impression. Men's hair should be short and conservatively cut. Men should wear a dark conservatively cut suit and tie; women should wear a dark suit or an elegant business-like dress. Climate varies by altitude, but men should always wear a jacket regardless; if it is hot, they will probably be invited to remove it, but let your Colombian colleague suggest it. A suit or a dress are the appropriate attire for a social occasion, such as a dinner invitation.

Cultural Cautions

DO'S

- Learn about Colombia's history, art, and literature — Colombians will appreciate your interest, especially if you attempt to speak Spanish. Sports—especially football (soccer)—are also a good topic of conversation.
- Expect delays. Do not complain, but practice patience and grace.

DON'TS

- Avoid politics as a subject of discussion; politics are especially tricky for businesspeople.
- Do not plan to jump right into business in Bogotá—take an extra day to become acclimated to the altitude.

CUSTOMS

- If you smoke, always offer cigarettes to all those present.
- Tapping the elbow with the hand implies stinginess; holding the hand flat, palm down while making a sawing motion across it with the other hand indicates the intention of splitting the proceeds of a deal; indicate size by measuring along the right forearm.
- If invited to a home for dinner, you will usually be served several drinks—whisky (scotch), gin, port, or sherry—before the meal. Wine will usually be served with the meal.
- Dinner generally starts around 7:00 pm. After dinner, plan to stay until around 10:00 pm on a weeknight, 11:00 pm on a weekend. Weekend parties can last until the next morning, but may not start until around 11:00 pm.
- If staying with a family, always wear pajamas, robe, and slippers any time you exit your room when not fully dressed for the street. Also bring your own soap, which is considered a very personal item.
- If invited to a meal at a home, send roses in advance or bring imported wine, liquor, or brandy, or chocolates.
- Gifts are not opened in the presence of the presenter and in fact may never be openly acknowledged.

OBSERVATIONS

- Colombians will rarely say "no" to a direct request, even if they have no intention of complying. Never push for a direct, definitive answer—it is considered extremely rude, insensitive, and insulting. You must learn to ask very indirect questions and interpret subtle cues.
- In homes, women often entertain other women in their bedrooms. Formal living rooms are infrequently used.
- Never offer a bribe. Some will be gravely offended, while others will try to get more out of you. Try to let a Colombian contact handle the situation if it comes up.
- Despite their usual decorousness, Colombians generally push and shove rather than form orderly lines.

NEGOTIATIONS

- Avoid confrontation or pressure. Colombians view direct tactics such as the "hard sell" or other aggressive behavior a serious breach of manners that could serve to kill a deal.
- Bargaining does not play as large a role in Colombian culture as it does in other parts of South America. Proper Colombians negotiate shrewdly, but generally without the gusto or flamboyant tactics common in Latin cultures accustomed to haggling in markets.
- Attorneys do not attend negotiations, but always review agreements.
- Allow negotiations to remain open-ended, so that confrontation can be avoided and talks can be allowed to fade away if agreement cannot be reached.
- Try not to respond with a definite "no," to even the most minor of terms.

Legal System

Colombia is a civil code country.

Intellectual Property Rights

Patents Although Colombia continues to improve its protection of intellectual property rights, many of its trading partners harbor concerns over deficiencies in patent and copyright enforcement efforts, arising not only at the police level, but also in the judicial system. The Andean Pact, to which Colombia officially adheres, provides patent protection for most products, and extends patent protection for a 20-year term from the date the application is filed. Enforcement, however, is extremely lax.

Trademarks Colombia's trademark protection laws are predicated on registration and use in Colombia. Trademark registrations have a 10-year term, renewable for successive 10-year periods. Priority rights are granted to the first application for a trademark from another Andean Pact country, or any country that grants reciprocal rights. Overall, trademark enforcement legislation in Colombia is weak, and in any event, trademark owners do not have a cause of action against the importation of products from other Andean Pact countries that bear their trademark without authorization.

Copyrights Colombian copyright law expressly protects software. It also provides copyright protection for the life of the author, plus 80 years. If the holder of a copyright is a legal entity, then the term of protection drops to 30 years from the date of first publication. Weak enforcement remains a serious problem, and video cassette and satellite signal piracy is widespread. Amendments to the copyright law now allow police agencies to seize pirated material and impose other penalties. Nevertheless, enforcement efforts have been sporadic.

Trade Secrets Industrial secrets and other information with commercial value are protected when the person possessing the secret has taken reasonable steps to insure secrecy. Semiconductor design layouts are not currently protected under Colombian law.

Business Registration

Articles of incorporation must provide specific information about the shareholders, the business, and accounting procedures of a corporation. The name of a corporation must be followed by the words *"suicided anónima,"* or "S.A." A copy of the articles of incorporation must be recorded at the Mercantile Register of the Chamber of Commerce in the municipality where the company is located and any other municipality where the company does business. Before a corporation can begin operations, it must also obtain permission from the Superintendent of Corporations, accompanied by a notarized copy of the articles of incorporation, and a certificate from a Colombian bank stating that an account has been opened in the name of the corporation.

Contracts and Dispute Resolution

The nature, form, objects, and obligations of contracts are governed generally by the Colombian Civil Code, but there is a definite class of contracts known as commercial or mercantile contracts which are supplemented by the Commercial Code. Contracts are generally short and to the point, and are used as specific points of reference rather than as said instruments governing all the terms of the agreement.

Notaries

Instruments executed before notaries require that the original instrument is written and signed in a record book, which the notary retains as a permanent record. Notaries issue to parties formal certified copies that have the same effect as the originals and may be presented in court. Notaries keep the originals.

Labor

The right of workers to organize unions, engage in collective bargaining, and to strike is recognized by the Colombian Constitution. The labor code authorizes automatic legal recognition of unions that have obtained 25 signatures from a workplace, and it guarantees the independence of labor organizations to determine internal rules and elect officers. It also protects unions and union activities from governmental interference. Before carrying out a strike, unions must negotiate directly with management and engage in conciliation procedures. Unions have been successful in organizing larger firms and public services, but their membership comprises less than eight percent of Colombia's labor force. Weak union organizations have limited workers' bargaining power in the private sector. Anti-union discrimination or the obstruction of union association is illegal, as is the use of strikebreakers. Forced or compulsory labor is prohibited by the Constitution. Specific laws govern minimum wages and employment benefit levels.

Legal Matters

LEGAL BRIEFS

- **Minimum employment age** The Colombian Constitution prohibits the employment of children under the age of 14. The labor code prohibits children under age 18 from receiving government work permits. While this provision is generally respected by larger private companies, the extensive informal economy, as well as specific economic areas such as cut flowers, coal mining, and leather tanning are effectively outside governmental control and employ significant numbers of underage workers.

- **Conditions of work** Colombia annually sets a national minimum wage that serves as an important benchmark for wage negotiations. However, an estimated one-quarter of the labor force, mainly in the informal sector, earns less than the minimum wage. The labor code also establishes a standard workday of eight hours and a 48-hour workweek. Enforcement of these laws is the responsibility of the Ministry of Labor and the court system.

- **Copyrights** Amendments to the copyright law have significantly increased penalties for infringement, and the police can now seize pirated material and close an establishment where copyright infringement has occurred.

- **IPR enforcement** Enforcement of intellectual property rights remains lax not only at the police level, but in the judicial system as well.

- **Semiconductors** Semiconductor design layouts are not currently protected under Colombian law.

- **Partnerships** Partnerships are considered legal entities. Before a mercantile partnership can do business, the partnership agreement must be drawn up in a public instrument executed before a notary.

- **Trade Agreements** Colombia has a bilateral trade agreement with the United States, as well as agreements with Argentina, Belgium, Bolivia, Brazil, Chile, Czechoslovakia, Denmark, Ecuador, Finland, France, Germany, Great Britain, Italy, Luxembourg, Norway, Peru, Spain, Sweden, and Switzerland.

LEGAL CONTACTS

Gomez Pinzon & Asociados Abogados
Carrere 9 No. 73-24 Pisos 2 y 3
Santa Fe de Bogotá
Tel: (1) 310-7055 Fax: (1) 310-6646

Baker & McKenzie
(Raisbeck, Lara, Rodriquez, Rueda & Gonzalez)
Calle 35 No. 7-25
4th Floor
Santa Fe de Bogotá, DC
Tel: (1) 285-1400 Fax: (1) 285-6908

Araujo Ibarra y Asociados Ltda.
Torre Colpatria
Carrera 7 No. 24-89, Offices 1901-1903
Santa Fe de Bogotá, DC
Tel: (1) 281-1977
Fax: (1) 284-2316

Arenas, Plazas Asociados
Calle 62 No. 5-31
Santa Fe de Bogotá, DC
Tel: (1) 249-8411
Fax: (1) 211-5960

Brigard & Urrutia
Calle 70, N 4-60
Apartado Aero P.O. Box 3692
Santa Fe de Bogotá, DC
Tel: (1) 210-3955
Fax: (1) 310-0586

Gamboa & Gamboa
Carrera 9 No. l70A-35
Piso 7
P.O. Box 075792
Santa Fe de Bogotá, DC
Tel: (1) 211-5338
Fax: (1) 211-4598

Gomez & Diaz
Carrera 7 No. 32-85, Fifth Floor
P.O. Box 19585
Santa Fe de Bogotá, DC
Tel: (1) 285-9058
Fax: (1) 285-9919

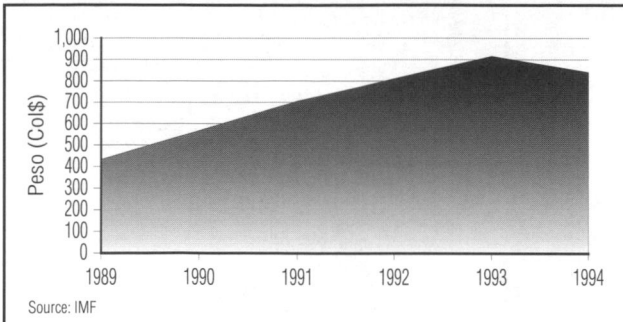

Currency Exchange
as of January 5, 1996

Col$998.16 = US$1

Source: IMF

Currency

The currency of Colombia is the Colombian peso (Col$).

Foreign Exchange

All foreign exchange transactions take place at a market-determined exchange rate. The Banco de la Republica conducts foreign exchange transactions only with the Ministry of Finance and authorized financial intermediaries and does not conduct foreign exchange transactions directly with the private sector. Residents are permitted to buy forward cover against exchange rate risks in respect of foreign exchange debts in inconvertible currencies registered at the Banco de la Republica.

Capital Transfers

No restrictions apply to converting or transferring funds associated with foreign investment. The only condition is that foreign investment must be registered at the Central Bank. All net profits may be remitted or converted, regardless of the type or amount of investment.

Investment Incentives

The government provides several investment incentives which, though numerous, do not actually offer much in the way of benefits.

Tax reimbursement certificates There is a direct allowance to exporters of non-traditional goods.

Duty-free import for exports This offers a remission of customs duties for imports of raw materials, inputs, equipment, and spare parts used in the production of export goods.

Export controls Exporters have access to funds provided by the foreign trade bank (Bancoldex) for working capital, discounting of loans to foreign importers of Colombian goods, equipment used in the production of exported goods, or in the provision of services to exporters, and capital contributions.

Investment Restrictions

Colombia imposes few investment restrictions on foreign investments that it does not impose on national investments.

Legal The provision of legal services is limited to those licensed under Colombian law, and foreign firms are not permitted a commercial presence.

Advertising For public broadcast network programming, at least 50 percent of programmed advertising must have local content.

TAXATION

Taxation requires sophisticated knowledge of complex rules and regulations specific to each country. The information presented here is from the Ernst & Young Corporate Tax Guide and Directory, available from the Ernst & Young accounting office in your country, or from:

Ernst & Young
Mail Address:
Apartado Aéreo 092638
Santa Fe de Bogotá, DC, Colombia
Street Address:
Transversal 22 No. 100-15
Santa Fe de Bogotá, Colombia
Tel: (1) 621-0411
Fax: (1) 610-3060

At a Glance

Corporate Income Tax Rate (%) (a)	30
Capital Gains Tax Rate (%)	30
Branch Tax Rate (%) (a)	30
Withholding Tax (%)	
Dividends (b)(c)	8
Interest (d)	35.6
Royalties from Patents, Know-how, etc. (e)	35.6
Branch Remittance Tax (c)(f)	8
Net Operating Losses (Years)	
Carryback	0
Carryforward	5

(a) Excluding temporary 25% surcharge.
(b) Applicable to dividends paid to nonresidents. Dividends paid to residents are not subject to withholding tax.
(c) This rate applies for the 1995 taxable year. The rate will be reduced to 7% for 1996 and subsequent taxable years.
(d) Effective tax rate of income and remittance taxes imposed on nonresidents. Interest paid to residents is subject to withholding of 7%.
(e) Applicable to royalties in excess of 3% of sales or production. Royalties not exceeding this amount are subject to a 30% withholding tax.
(f) For the hydrocarbon sector.

Money Matters

BITS AND PIECES

- **Corporate income tax** Resident companies are taxed on worldwide income, but foreign businesses are based on Colombian income only.
- **Capital gains** Gains of fixed asset sales are included in ordinary income.
- **Foreign tax relief** A foreign tax credit is allowed for domestic corporations.
- **Privatization** The government is in the process of privatizing 76 key companies, including banks, vacation resorts, and oil/gas distributorships.
- **Commercial presence** Although Colombian law does not discriminate against foreign investors, it does require a commercial presence in the country (registered place of business, a branch, or an agent) in order to participate in many industries.
- **Investment screening** Investment screening has been largely eliminated, and those mechanisms still in place are generally routine and non-discriminatory.
- **Export subsidies** Colombia is phasing out all export subsidies consistent with GATT requirements.
- **Mining and petroleum** Under special regulations, companies in these sectors are required to bring back currency earned from foreign currency sales except what is necessary to cover local operating expenses.
- **Expropriation** Colombia has not expropriated property of foreign investors in the past 50 years, although the Constitution does allow some amount of expropriation without compensation.
- **Performance requirements** Performance requirements still exist in the automotive assembly industry in the form of local content requirements.
- **Gold** Residents are allowed to hold, deal, import, and export gold. The Banco de la República issues commemorative gold coins from time to time, and they are considered legal tender.

BANKS

Banco Cafetero
Calle 28 No. 13-A-15/53
Santa Fe de Bogotá, DC
Tel: (1) 341-1511, 281-3548, 243-1481
Fax: (1) 284-6516

Banco Ganadero
Carrera 9 No. 72-21
Santa Fe de Bogotá, DC
Tel: (1) 217-0100, 310-7766
Fax: (1) 235-1248

Banco de Bogotá
Calle 36 No. 7-47 Piso 15
Santa Fe de Bogotá, DC
Tel: (1) 288-1188/0192
Fax: (1) 245-0520

Banco de Colombia
Calle 30A No. 6-38 Piso 11
Santa Fe de Bogotá, DC
Tel: (1) 285-0300, 232-9817
Fax: (1) 288-7198/7252

Banco de Occidente
Carrera 5 No. 12-42
Cali, Valle
Tel: (23) 823-208
Fax: (23) 834-715

Banco de la Republica
Carrera 7 No. 14-78 Piso 6
Santa Fe de Bogotá, DC
Tel: (1) 342-1111, 281-7445, 283-2492
Fax: (1) 286-1686/1731

Banco Andino
Carrera 7A, No. 14-23
Apdo Aereo 6826
Santa Fe de Bogotá, DC
Tel: (1) 284-8800
Fax: 91) 286-7919

Banco Colpatria
Carrera 7A, No 24-89, 10º
Apdo Aereo 7762
Santa Fe de Bogotá, DC
Tel: (1) 234-0600

Business Travel

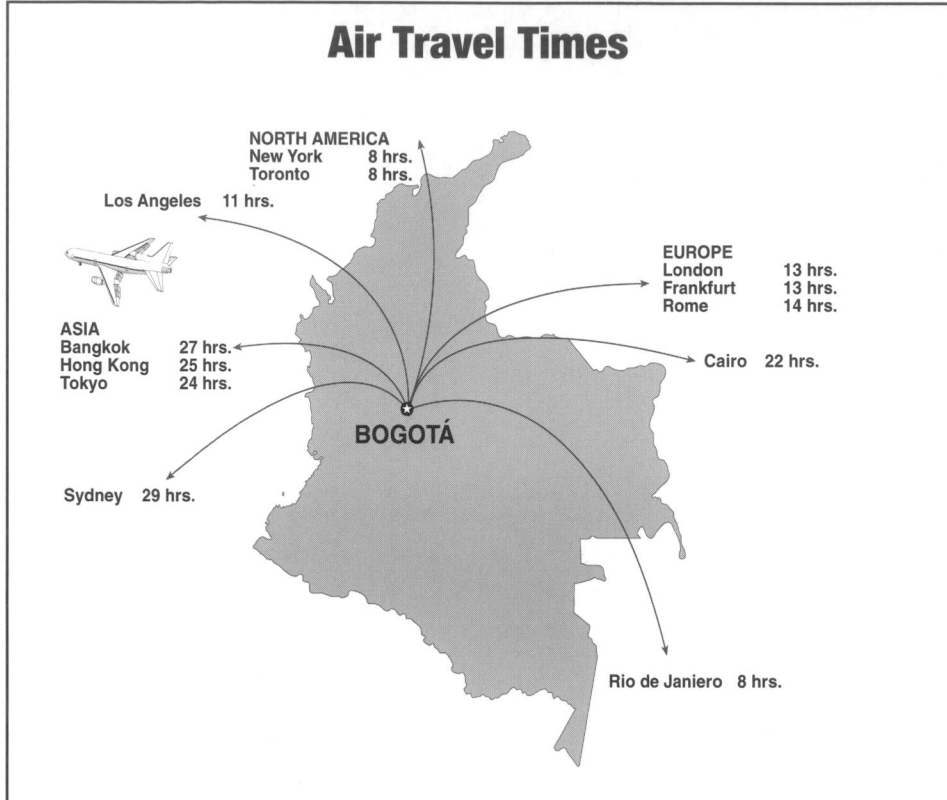

Air Travel Times

NORTH AMERICA
New York   8 hrs.
Toronto   8 hrs.

Los Angeles   11 hrs.

EUROPE
London   13 hrs.
Frankfurt   13 hrs.
Rome   14 hrs.

ASIA
Bangkok   27 hrs.
Hong Kong   25 hrs.
Tokyo   24 hrs.

Cairo   22 hrs.

BOGOTÁ

Sydney   29 hrs.

Rio de Janiero   8 hrs.

COMMUNICATIONS

Telephones Telecom, the state-run system, is modern and reliable. Public phones are plentiful. Long-distance calls must be made on private phones or from long-distance pay phones located outside of most Telecom offices, bus stations, and airports. Most phones are direct-dial capable; if not, callers must go through a long-distance operator. The Empress Telecom office is the best location for international calls, a deposit for the call is required.

Fax Service is widely available and efficient. Internal and International telegraph service is widely available. Public telex facility is available by telephone by dialing 044982.

Post office There are separate post offices for surface and air mail in Colombia. All mail should be mailed air mail, even domestic, as surface mail is unreliable. Air mail is processed by the airline Avianca. Stamps and mailboxes can be found at Avianca offices and travel agencies. Local mail can be mailed at the green local mail boxes found in many stores.

Radio/TV Hundreds of privately owned radio stations broadcast varied programs. Reception is good for government-owned television stations.

BEST TRAVEL BOOKS

Colombia Travel Survival Kit, Lonely Planet. Truly a travel survival kit.'

The Travellers Guide to Latin America Customs and Manners. Elizabeth Devine & Nancy Bragaranti. An invaluable guide for people not wanting to put foot in mouth.

Do's and Taboo's Around the World; A Guide to International Behavior. Edited by Roger E. Axtell, compiled by the Parker Pen Company. Now completely updated and revised, the ultimate guide to international behavior. Helpful, fun to read!

South American Handbook. Chicago: Passport Books. An excellent resource; updated annually.

USEFUL TELEPHONE NUMBERS

If you are calling from outside Colombia, you will need to add the country code [57] and any other international dialing requirements from within your country.

- Long-distance Operator 09
- Operator (Bogotá) .... 13 or 14
- Telex 044982
- Emergency Medical Help (Bogotá) ...... (1) 277-6666
- Accommodations (Bogotá) .... (1) 6692
- Tourist assistance (Bogotá) ....(1) 810-510

Temporary Secretarial Services
- Action Bogotá .... (1) 217-6030
- Manos de Bogotá .... (1) 232-4540
- A-Servil .... (1) 211-5922

Translation & Interpreting
- Berlitz .... (1) 236-0040
- Alyev .... (1) 284-8539

Computer Equipment Rental
- IBM de Colombia .... (1) 257-0111
- Macintosh Dealer .... (1) 218-1151

Courier Services
- DHL .... (1) 413-9565
- Intertrade Courier .... (1) 244-0309
- Sky Courier International .... (1) 236-3122

Airlines
- SAM .... (1) 266-9600
- Iberia .... (1) 610-5066
- American Airlines .... (2) 285-1111

Credit Card Information
Lost or stolen credit cards (call collect to the US, regardless of which country the card was issued in).
- Amex ....[1] (919) 333-3211
- Diner's Club...............................[1] (303) 799-1504
- MasterCard ....[1] (314) 275-6690
- Visa ....[1] (410) 581-7931

Travelogue

WORKWEEK

Offices Monday-Friday 8:00 am to 6:00 pm, with lunch from noon to 2:00 pm.
Banks Monday-Thursday 9:00 am to 3:00 pm, and until 3:30 pm on Fridays (closed at noon on last Friday of the month).
Government Monday-Friday 9:00 am to 3:00 pm.
Retail Generally open Monday-Saturday 9:00 am to 7:00 pm, with lunch from 12:30 pm to 2:30 pm, and a few hours on Sundays.

HOLIDAYS

Holidays 1996
January 1 New Year's Day
January 6 Epiphany
March 19 Saint Joseph's Day
April 4 Holy Thursday
April 5 Good Friday*
April 7 Easter Sunday*
May 1 Labor Day
May 20 Ascension Day
June 10 Corpus Christi*
June 14 Feast of the Sacred Heart
July 4 Saint Peter and Saint Paul
July 20 Colombian Independence Day
August 7 Battle of Boyaca
August 15 Assumption Day
October 12 Columbus Day
November 4 All Saints' Day
November 14 Independence of Cartagena
December 8 Immaculate Conception
December 25 Christmas Day
*Dates vary each year.

VISA AND PASSPORT

A passport and a return ticket are required for stays of up to three months. Colombia requires a business visa, which is available for no charge at any Colombian consulate or embassy. Business visas are valid for up to three years and are renewable.

DEPARTURE FORMALITIES

Travelers leaving from El Dorado International Airport will pay a US$18 departure tax for international flights and US$5.50 for domestic flights.

IMMUNIZATION

There are no vaccinations required for entry to Colombia. Cases of cholera and yellow fever reported. Vaccinations recommended: cholera, hepatitis, malaria, polio, tetanus, typhoid and yellow fever.

TIPPING

Taxi: None. Porters: 500 pesos per piece. Hotels, restaurants: one percent usually included in bill, or add 15 percent. Chambermaids: 200 pesos per day. Barbers, beauticians: 10 to 15 percent. Doorpersons, attendants, small services: 200 pesos.

CRIME

Minor crime is prevalent in the cities of Colombia, especially in the vicinity of hotels and airports. At airports, theft of hand luggage and travel documents is common. Attempted extortion and kidnapping on rural buses is not unusual. Colombia also has a very high murder rate. While narcotics and guerrilla-related violence account for many murders, common criminals are responsible for three-quarters of the murders reported. Due to guerrilla activity, travel by road outside the major cities is considered dangerous. US companies and citizens are targets for violence in Colombia.

INFRASTRUCTURE

Telecommunications are in the process of being modernized. Railways do not provide passenger service, but larger cities are connected by an adequate road network. Major hotels in big cities offer good services and facilities.

NATIONAL TOURIST OFFICE

Corporación Nacional de Turismo
Calle 28, 13A-15
Santa Fe de Bogotá, DC
Tel: (1) 283-9466

GOVERNMENT AGENCIES

National Planning Department
Calle 26 No. 13-19
Santa Fe de Bogotá, DC
Tel: (1) 282-4055/2785
Fax: (1) 281-3348

National Bureau of Statistics
Avenida El Dorado CAN
Santa Fe de Bogotá, DC
Tel: (1) 221-3066
Fax: (1) 222-2305

Foreign Trade Institute
Calle 28 No. 13A-15
Santa Fe de Bogotá, DC
Tel: (1) 281-2200
Fax: (1) 281-2560

Superintendency of Banks
Calle 7 No. 4-49
Santa Fe de Bogotá, DC
Tel: (1) 280-0280/0187
Fax: (1) 280-4759

Colombian Customs
Carrera 7 No.6-45 P6
Santa Fe de Bogotá, DC
Tel: (1) 284-3400
Fax: (1) 286-5789

Institute of Industrial Development
Calle 16 No. 6-66 P15
Santa Fe de Bogotá, DC
Tel: (1) 284-0984
Fax: (1) 286-8116

WORLD TRADE CENTERS

World Trade Center Bogotá
Calle 98 No. 9-03 PH
Santa Fe de Bogotá, DC
Tel: (1) 218-4411
Fax: (1) 218-5848

World Trade Center de Cali
Calle 8a, #3-14 18 Floor
PO Box 7795
Cali
Tel: (23) 899-295, 894-882
Fax: (23) 899-292

GENERAL TRADE ASSOCIATIONS

Association of Flower Growers
Carrera 9A No. 90-53
Santa Fe de Bogotá, DC
Tel: (1) 257-9311
Fax: (1) 218-3693

Apparel Manufacturers Association
Carrera 10 No. 28-49 P5 Torre A
Santa Fe de Bogotá, DC
Tel: (1) 342-3442
Fax: (1) 341-0524

Association of Automotive Parts
Calle 28 No. 16-22 P4
Santa Fe de Bogotá, DC
Tel: (1) 288-3367
Fax: (1) 287-1629

Association of Metal Industries
Calle 35 No. 4-81
Santa Fe de Bogotá, DC
Tel: (1) 232-3600
Fax: (1) 285-7086

Association of National Merchants
Carrera 4 No. 19-85 P7
Santa Fe de Bogotá, DC
Tel: (1) 286-0600
Fax: (1) 282-7573

Banking and Finance Association
Carrera 9 No. 74-08
Santa Fe de Bogotá, DC
Tel: (1) 211-4811
Fax: (1) 211-9915

Colombian Electric Power Institute
Carrera 13 No. 27-00 P3
Santa Fe de Bogotá, DC
Tel: (1) 281-6200

National Industries Association
Carrera 13 No. 26-45 P6
Santa Fe de Bogotá, DC
Tel: (1) 281-0600
Fax: (1) 281-3188

National Association of Exporters
Carrera 10 No. 27-27 Int. 137
Santa Fe de Bogotá, DC
Tel: (1) 342-0788
Fax: (1) 284-6911

Plastic Industry Association
Calle 69 No. 5-33
Santa Fe de Bogotá, DC
Tel: (1) 249-6997 Fax: (1) 255-2317

Colombian Chamber of the Oil Industry
Calle 100 No. 14-26 Of. 301
Santa Fe de Bogotá, DC
Tel: (1) 214-6919
Fax: (1) 226-8876

CHAMBERS OF COMMERCE

Bogotá Chamber of Commerce
Carrera 9 No. 16-21
Santa Fe de Bogotá, DC
Tel: (1) 334-7900
Fax: (1) 284-7735

Colombian-American Chamber of Commerce
Calle 35 No. 6-16
Santa Fe de Bogotá, DC
Tel: (1) 285-7800
Fax: (1) 288-6434

TRADE ORGANIZATIONS

Carbones de Colombia, SA (CARBOCOL)
Carrera 7, No 31-10
Apdo Aereo 29740
Santa Fe de Bogotá, DC
Tel: (1) 287-3100
Fax: (1) 287-3278

Departamento Nacional de Planeacion
Calle 26, No 13-19
Mezanini 17
Santa Fe de Bogotá, DC
Tel: (1) 282-2586
Fax: (1) 281-3348

Empresa Colombiana de Minas-ECOMINAS
Calle 32, No 13-67
Apdo Aereo 17878
Santa Fe de Bogotá, DC
Tel: (1) 287-7136
Fax: (1) 87-4606

Empresa Colombiana de Petroleos(ECOPETROL)
Carrera 13, No 36-24, Apdo Aereo 5938
Santa Fe de Bogotá, DC
Tel: (1) 285-6400

Empresa Colombiana de Uranio(COLURANIO)
Centro Administrativo Nacional (CAN) 4°
Ministerio de Minas y Energia
Santa Fe de Bogotá, DC
Tel: (1) 244-5440

Empresa Nacional de Telecomunicaciones-TELECOM
Calle 23, No 13-49
Santa Fe de Bogotá, DC
Tel: (1) 269-4077
Fax: (1) 284-2171

Fondo de Promocion de Exportaciones-PROEXPO
Calle 28, no 13A-15, 35°-42°
Apdo Aereo 2400092
Santa Fe de Bogotá, DC
Tel: (1) 269-0777
Fax: (1) 282-507

Fondo Nacional de Proyectos de Desarrollo-FONADE
Calle 26, No 13-19, 18°-21°
Apdo Aereo 24110
Santa Fe de Bogotá, DCTel: (1) 282-9400
Telex: 45634
Fax: (1) 282-6018

MARKET RESEARCH FIRMS

A.C. Nielsen de Colombia S.A.
Calle 80 No. 5-81
Santa Fe de Bogotá, DC
Tel: (1) 211-9100
Fax: (1) 211-8894

Analizar Mercade Ltda.
Calle 64 No. 4-88
Santa Fe de Bogotá, DC
Tel: (1) 249-5413
Fax: (1) 210-1127

Centro Nacional de Consultoria
Diagonal 34 No. 5-27
Santa Fe de Bogotá, DC
Tel: (1) 288-3100/1811
Fax: (1) 287-2670

Data Research de Colombia
Calle 45 No. 21-28
Santa Fe de Bogotá, DC
Tel: (1) 232-1213, 285-0943
Fax: (1) 287-1270

Optimos Ltda.
Transversal 19A No. 124-59
Santa Fe de Bogotá, DC
Tel: (1) 213-3308/1289
Fax: (1) 215-9576

Market Research de Colombia
Carrera 16A No. 76-31
Santa Fe de Bogotá, DC
Tel: (1) 236-2826/6755
Fax: (1) 257-2949

TRADE FAIRS

Corporacion de Ferias y Exposiciones, S.A.
Caarrera 40, No 22c-67
Apdo Aereo 6843
Santa Fe de Bogotá, DC
Tel: (1) 244-0100
Telex: 44553
Fax: (1) 268-8469

AD AGENCIES

Leo Burnett Colombia, S.A.
Carrera 13 No. 89-59
Santa Fe de Bogotá, DC
Tel: (1) 218-6900
Fax: (1) 218-9073

Centrum Ogilvy & Mather
Calle 90 No. 9A-32
Santa Fe de Bogotá, DC
Tel: (1) 616-9599
Fax: (1) 611-0476

Demo Bozell
Calle 79A, No. 8-66
Santa Fe de Bogotá, DC
Tel: (1) 217-1455
Fax: (1) 210-0313

McCann-Erickson Corp, S.A.
Calle 93 #12-65
Santa Fe de Bogotá, DC
Tel: (1) 616-6711
Fax: (1) 617-0625

J. Walter Thompson de Colombia
Carrera 17 #93A-02
Pismo 4 & 5, Apdo. 4163
Santa Fe de Bogotá, DC
Tel: (1) 622-5282
Fax: (1) 622-5260

BANKS

Banco Cafetero
Calle 28 No. 13-A-15/53
Santa Fe de Bogotá, DC
Tel: (1) 341-1511, 281-3548, 243-1481
Fax: (1) 284-6516

Banco Ganadero
Carrera 9 No. 72-21
Santa Fe de Bogotá, DC
Tel: (1) 217-0100, 310-7766
Fax: (1) 235-1248

Banco de Bogotá
Calle 36 No. 7-47 Piso 15
Santa Fe de Bogotá, DC
Tel: (1) 288-1188/0192
Fax: (1) 245-0520

Banco de Colombia
Calle 30A No. 6-38 Piso 11
Santa Fe de Bogotá, DC
Tel: (1) 285-0300, 232-9817
Fax: (1) 288-7198/7252

Banco de Occidente
Carrera 5 No. 12-42
Cali, Valle
Tel: (23) 823-208
Fax: (23) 834-715

Banco de la Republica
Carrera 7 No. 14-78 Piso 6
Santa Fe de Bogotá, DC
Tel: (1) 342-1111, 281-7445, 283-2492
Fax: (1) 286-1686/1731

STOCK EXCHANGES

Comision Nacional de Valores
Carrera 7A, No 31-10, 43° Apdo
Aereo, 39600
Santa Fe de Bogotá, DC
Tel: (1) 287-3300

LAW FIRMS

Gomez Pinzon & Asociados Abogados
Carrere 9 No. 73-24 Pisos 2 y 3
Santa Fe de Bogotá, DC
Tel: (1) 3107055 Fax: (1) 3106646

Baker & McKenzie
(Raisbeck, Lara, Rodriquez, Rueda & Gonzalez)
Calle 35 No. 7-25
4th Floor
Santa Fe de Bogotá, DC
Tel: (1) 285-1400 Fax: (1) 285-6908

Araujo Ibarra Y Asociados Ltda.
Torre Colpatria
Carrera 7 No. 24-89, Offices 1901-1903
Santa Fe de Bogotá, DC
Tel: (1) 2811977
Fax: (1) 2842316

Arenas, Plazas Asociados
Calle 62 No. 5-31
Santa Fe de Bogotá, DC
Tel: (1) 249 8411
Fax: (1) 211 5960

Brigard & Urrutia
Calle 70, N 4-60
Apartado Aero (P.O. Box) 3692
Santa Fe de Bogotá, DC
Tel: (1) 2103955
Fax: (1) 3100586

Gamboa & Gamboa
Carrera 9 No. l70A-35
Piso 7
P.O. Box 075792
Santa Fe de Bogotá, DC
Tel: (1) 211-5338
Fax: (1) 211-4598

Gomez & Diaz
Carrera 7 No. 32-85, Fifth Floor
P.O. B ox 19585
Santa Fe de Bogotá, DC
Tel: (1) 285-9058
Fax: (1) 285-9919

Lewin & Wills Abogados
Calle 72 # 4-15
Santa Fe de Bogotá, DC
Tel: (1) 312-5577
Fax: (1) 211-7626

Lleras, Caicedo, Suescun y Asociados
Carrera 9. No. 74-08 Oficina 409
Apartado Aero 56809
Santa Fe de Bogotá, DC
Tel: (1) 210-0700
Fax: (1) 212-2485

Jose Lloreda Camacho & Co.
Calle 72 No. 5-83, 6th Floor
P.O. Box 12304
Santa Fe de Bogotá, DC
Tel: (1) 217-0400
Fax: (1) 212-6426

NEWSPAPERS

El Espacio
Carrera 61, No 45-35
El Dorado
Santa Fe de Bogotá, DC
Tel: (1) 263-6666

El Espectador
Avda 68 No 22-71 Apdo Aereo 3441
Santa Fe de Bogotá, DC
Tel: (1) 260-6044
Telex: 44718

La Prensa
Calle 123 No. 20-80
Santa Fe de Bogotá, DC
Tel: (1) 612-6366
Fax: (1) 215-9467

La Republica
Calle 16 No 4-96
Apdo Aereo 6806
Santa Fe de Bogotá, DC
Tel: (1) 282-1055

El Siglo
Avda El Dorado
No 96-50 Apdo Aereo 5452
Santa Fe de Bogotá, DC
Tel: (1) 298-7328

El Tiempo
Avda El Dorado No 59-70
Apdo Aereo 3633
Santa Fe de Bogotá, DC
Tel: (1) 295-5555
Telex: 44812

Occidente
Calle 12, No 5-22
Cali Valle del Cauca
Tel: (23) 85-1110
Fax: (23) 83-6097

El Pais
Carrera 2A No 24-46
Apdo Aereo 1608
Cali Valle del Cauca
Tel: (23) 89-3011
Fax: (23) 83-5014

El Pueblo
Avda 3A Norte 35-N-10
Cali Valle del Cauca
Tel: (23) 68-8110
Telex: 55669

El Universal
Calle 31, No 3-81
Cartagena, Bolivar
Tel: (53) 40484
Telex: 37788

El Colombiano
Calle 54 No. 41-22
Apdo Aereo 5236
Medellin Antioquia
Tel: (4) 51-0444
Telex: 44727

El Mundo
Calle 53 No 74-50
Apdo Aereo 53874
Medellin Antioquia
Tel: (4) 264-2800
Fax: (4) 264-0342
Telex: 65058

El Liberal
Carrera 3 No 2-60
Apdo Aereo 538
Popayan
Tel: (928) 23-2418
Fax: (928) 23-3888

PERIODICALS

Arco
Carrera 6, No 35-39
Apdo Aereo 8624
Santa Fe de Bogotá, DC
Tel: (1) 285-1500
Telex: 45153

Arteen Colombia
Apdo Aereo 90193
Santa Fe de Bogotá, DC
Tel: (1) 262-5178
Fax: (1) 260-6339
Telex: 44611

El Campesino
Carrera 39A No 15-11
Santa Fe de Bogotá, DC

Coyuntura Economica
Calle 78 No 9-91
Apdo Aereo 75074
Santa Fe de Bogotá, DC
Tel: (1) 211-6714
Fax: (1) 212-6073

Cromos Magazine
Calle 70A, No 7-81
Apdo Aereo 59317
Santa Fe de Bogotá, DC

Economia Colombiana
Edif. de los Ministerios, Of. 126A, No 6-40
Bogotá,

Escala
Calle 30 No 17-70
Santa Fe de Bogotá, DC
Tel: (1) 287-8200

Nueva Frontera
Carrera 7A No 17-01 5º
Santa Fe de Bogotá, DC
Tel: (1) 334-3763

Sintesis Econonomica
Calle 70A 10-52
Santa Fe de Bogotá, DC
Tel: (1) 212-5121
Fax: (1) 212-8365

Tribuna Medica
Calle 8B No 68A-41 and Calle 123 8-20
Santa Fe de Bogotá, DC
Tel: (1) 262-6085

RADIO AND TELEVISION

Ministerio de Comunicaciones, Division de Telecomunicaciones
Edif. Murillo Toro
Apdo Aereo 14515
Santa Fe de Bogotá, DC

Instituto Nacional de Radio y Television (INRAVISION)
Centro Administrativo Nacional
Avda El Dorado
Santa Fe de Bogotá, DC
Tel: (1) 222-0700

Asociacion Nacional de Medeios de Comunicacion
Carrera 22, No 85-72
Santa Fe de Bogotá, DC
Tel: (1) 611-1300
Fax: (1) 236-0896

INTERNET ADDRESSES

Usenet group(s):
soc.culture.colombia

Basic Colombia / Colombia Básica
http://www.univalle.edu.co/~servinfo/colombia.sp.html

Colombia FactBook
http://www.ic.gov/94fact/country/55.html

Colombian Internet Directory
http://ee1.bradley.edu/~mrr2ro/colombia/

Latin America - Colombia
http://lanic.utexas.edu/la/colombia/

Costa Rica

Republic of Costa Rica

Economy

Overview

Although in many ways more democratic and egalitarian than many of its Central American and Caribbean neighbors, Costa Rica is one of the few remaining Latin American countries in which the state participates directly in economic activities in a major way. Following an economic crisis in the 1980s, Costa Rica has aimed for macroeconomic stability and growth through diversification of its exports. However, recent efforts to liberalize the economy through the privatization of state enterprises, as well as attempts to open certain sectors of the economy to market competition have been largely disappointing. An impressive average GDP growth rate of five percent—largely the result of an increase in tourism revenues coupled with a general decrease in unemployment and inflation—has served to mask serious underlying fiscal difficulties, not the least important of which is a near-chronic and substantial public-sector deficit.

Trade

Costa Rica has a relatively open international trade regime, but state monopolies in several areas may limit opportunities for private enterprise. Major exports include bananas and coffee, which together account for 40 percent of all exports. Other exports are of far lesser quantities and importance. Costa Rica relies heavily on imports of a wide range of goods, including raw materials, machinery and equipment, consumer products, and fuels. The US is its major trading partner—accounting for about 40 percent of total trade—followed by Germany, Japan, Venezuela, and Guatemala. Costa Rica has attempted to improve trade relations through participation in bilateral and multilateral trade agreements.

Sectors

Agriculture Despite a growing dependency on imports to fill domestic demand, agriculture remains a focal point of the economy, employing roughly 25 percent of the work force and accounting for nearly 20 percent of GDP. Agricultural products are also the main sources of foreign exchange.

Industry Industry provides slightly more than 30 percent of GDP and employs about the same proportion of the work force. In general, industry is poorly developed and little diversified, relying primarily on food and beverage processing, and the refining of imported crude oil for domestic use.

Services Service businesses related to the country's burgeoning tourist trade are growing considerably, continuing the trend of recent years. Services contribute almost half of GDP and employ roughly 50 percent of the work force. However, aside from tourism, most services are involved in local distribution and personal service activities.

Trends

Costa Rica has come to rely heavily on international aid programs focused on maintaining stability in the country while promoting the liberalization of trade and investment. These programs have had moderate success, and Costa Rica has been promoted to the status of an "advanced developing country." Further liberalization plans designed to increase prosperity, improve trade and investment regimes, and facilitate access to foreign markets by the country's exporters could provide promising opportunities for foreign and local investors in the future, provided Costa Rica is able to meet its foreign debt obligations and rein in public sector spending.

At a Glance

THE COUNTRY

Location Central America, between Nicaragua and Panama.
Terrain A rugged, central range separates eastern and western coastal plains.
Climate Mild in the central highlands, tropical and subtropical in other areas.

THE PEOPLE

Population 3,200,000
Ethnic composition
European and some mestizo 95%
African origin 3%
Indigenous 2%
Religious composition
Roman Catholic 80%
Evangelical Protestant 15%
Other... 5%
Languages spoken Spanish, with Jamaican dialect of English spoken around Puerto Limon.
Education and literacy One of the most literate populations in Latin America, adult literacy is 93%. Primary and secondary education is free.
Labor force
Total:..1,100,000
By occupation: agriculture 19%; community and personal services 22%; industry 30%; commerce 12%; construction 5%; transportation and warehouse 4%; and banking and finance 4%.

COUNTRY FACTS

Political and legal This democratic republic has a legal system based on the Spanish civil law system.
Telephone Reliable domestic telephone service provided by the state. Several US companies offer international services at lower prices. International country code: [506]. No city codes are required.
Transportation Among the best developed transportation systems in the region, there are more than 7,000 kilometers (4,400 miles) of principal highways and roads and some 16,000 kilometers (9,600 miles) of rural roads. Road maintenance varies. Railways are used infrequently and are not well maintained. There are many regional and private air landing fields. The capital's international airport is served by several passenger and cargo airlines.
Environment The government has instituted broad pollution controls, including standards for air and water quality. However, the country lacks trained personnel and equipment to enforce them. Automobile gas emissions are the highest per capita in North and Central America. Costa Rica maintains the most extensive national park system in Latin America. Current issues include deforestation, largely a result of land clearing for cattle ranching, which has caused many problems, including soil erosion and loss of soil fertility. Water contamination by agricultural chemicals is also a problem.
Media Government and privately owned broadcast stations include 71 AM radio stations and 18 television stations. By law, there is no censorship of the press. Four daily newspapers are published in the capital.
Health All workers and their dependents are covered by a public health care system administered by the government. Though there are serious shortages and hospital overcrowding, most medical services are good. Life expectancy of males is 72 years; of females, 76 years.

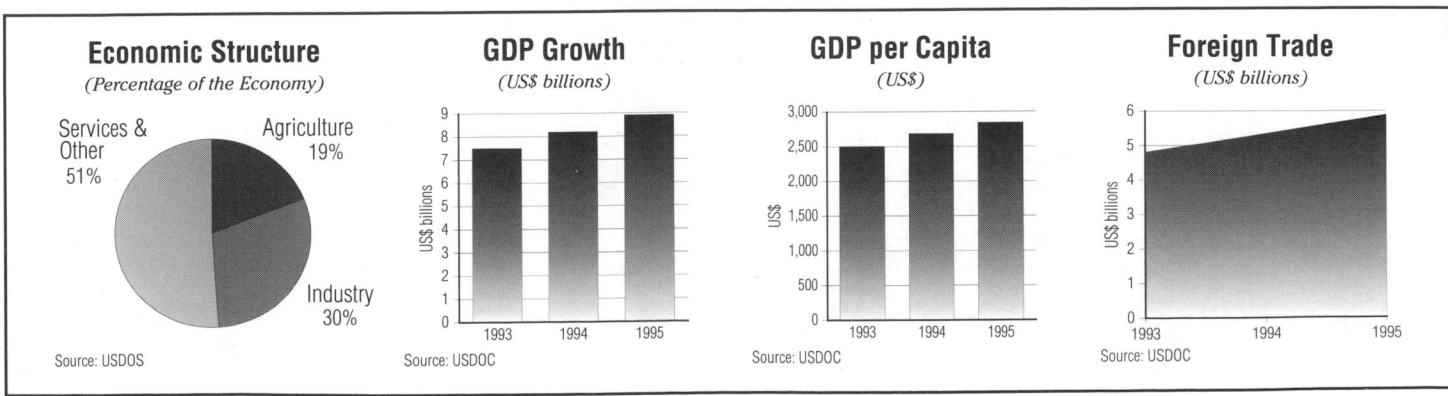

Economic Structure
(Percentage of the Economy)
Services & Other 51%
Agriculture 19%
Industry 30%
Source: USDOS

GDP Growth
(US$ billions)
1993 1994 1995
Source: USDOC

GDP per Capita
(US$)
1993 1994 1995
Source: USDOC

Foreign Trade
(US$ billions)
1993 1994 1995
Source: USDOC

Costa Rica

- ★ National capital
- ◉ Province capital
- ● Secondary city
- ▲ Volcano
- ▬ International border
- — Province border
- ═ Inter-American highway
- ═ Primary road
- ⋯ Railroad

| 0 | 25 | 50 | 75 km |
| 0 | 25 | | 50 mi |

*All Provinces have the same name as their capital, except Guanacaste.

Nicaragua

Lago de Nicaragua

Rivas
San Juan del Sur
Colón
San Carlos
La Cruz
Los Chiles
Caño Negro National Wildlife Refuge
Cuajiniquil
Santa Rosa National Park
Rincon De La Vieja N.P.
San Juan del Norte
Frio
San Carlos
Indio
Barra del Colorado National Wildlife Refuge
Guanacaste
Coco
Liberia
Guardia
Lomas de Barbudal Biological Reserve
Lake Arenal
Arenal
Pital
Tortuguero
Ocotal
Chirripó
Tortuguero National Park
Tamarindo
Palo Verde National Park
Cañas
Puerto Viejo
Caribbean Sea
Tempisque
Peñas Blancas Wildlife Refuge
Santa Cruz
Barra Honda N.P.
Quesada
Poas Volcano N.P.
Braulio Carrillo N.P.
Guacimo
Reventazón
Nicoya
Puerto Jesús
Sarchí
Grecia
Matina
Moín
Ostional National Wildlife Refuge
Puntarenas
Barranca
Heredia
San José
Irazu Volcano N.P.
Siquirrres
Liverpool
Puerto Limón
Alajuela
Cartago
Turrialbe
Naranjo
Santiago
Pandora
Cahuita National Park
San Ignacio
Tapanti National Wildlife Refuge
Hitoy Cerere Bioligical Reserve
Cahuita
Jabilla
Carara Biological Reserve
Pirrís
San Marcos
Uatsi
Puerto Viejo
Gulfo de Nicoya
Jacó
Chirripo National Park
Sixaola
Bratsí
Elena
Cabo Blanco Absolute Natural Reserve
Chirripo Intern'l Friendship Park
Gandoca-Manzanillo National Wildlife Refuge
Puerto Quepos
San Isidro
Panama
Manuel Antonio National Park
Dominical
P a c i f i c
Palmar Norte
General
O c e a n
San Vito
Drake
Golfito National Wildlife Refuge
Rincón
Golfito
Neily
La Concepción
Corcovado N.P.
Jiménez
Gulfo Dulce
Armuelles
Bahía de Charco Azul

Central America

Gulf of Mexico
Cayman Islands (U.K.)
Mexico
Belmopan
Belize
Jamaica
Kingston
Guatemala
Guatemala
Honduras
Tegucigalpa
San Salvador
El Salvador
Caribbean Sea
Nicaragua
Managua
P a c i f i c
O c e a n
San José
Costa Rica
Panamá
Panama
Colombia

©1995 Magellan GeographixSMSanta Barbara, CA

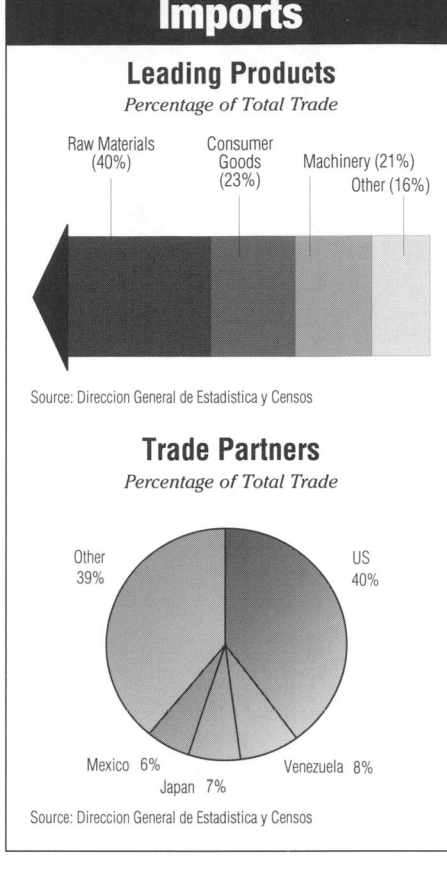

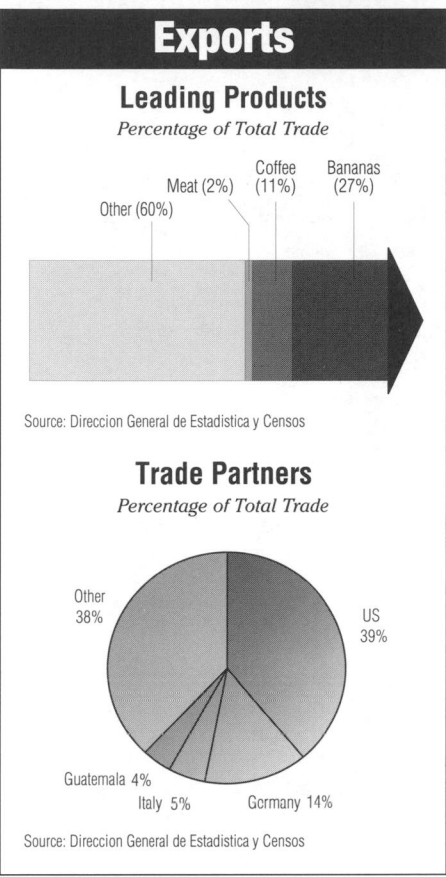

Trade News

RULES AND REGULATIONS

- **Tariff rates** Tariff reductions began in 1992, falling from 40 percent to a maximum 19 percent in 1993 for most consumer items. Costa Rica has reduced customs tariffs in accordance with the open, free market goals of the Central American Common Market (CACM). Some popular import items—vehicles, apparel, arms, munitions, and custom jewelry—are still subject to relatively high tariffs.

- **Import taxes** A number of taxes are levied on imports, including a consumption tax ranging from 5 to 75 percent; a sales tax of 10 percent; and a one percent surcharge imposed on all imports—although medicines are exempt from this tax.

- **Import licenses** Import licenses are not required for most products. However, pharmaceuticals, drugs, cosmetics, chemical products, and processed food and beverage products require an import permit from the Costa Rican Ministry of Health. Arms and munitions require a license from the Costa Rican Ministry of Security.

- **Prohibited imports** Costa Rica prohibits the importation of used tires without wheels, as a means to protect the country from the yellow fever mosquito. There are no restrictions on the importation of other products.

- **Export controls** Exports of livestock, wood, and ornamental plants require a license from the Ministry of Agriculture; metal scrap is subject to an export license from the Ministry of Industry, Energy, and Mines. Coffee and sugar exports are regulated; gold cannot be exported.

- **Pending legislation** Pending legislation would remove most price and all profit margin controls, impose antitrust rules, and protect consumers against product misrepresentation and price fixing.

- **Chemicals and pesticides** Chemicals and pesticides exported to Costa Rica must be legally available in the exporting country.

- **Surgical and dental instruments** Surgical and dental instruments can be sold only to licensed importers and health professionals.

- **Customs procedures** Customs procedures are legendary for their cost and complexity. Most large enterprises are forced to have customs specialists on the payroll, in addition to buying the services of customs brokers. All importers and exporters suffer from defective customs procedures, poor administration, theft, graft, and inadequate facilities.

- **Customs brokers** Customs brokers must be bonded Costa Rican companies, and these enjoy a monopoly on the handling of imports.

- **Trade agreements** Costa Rica gives duty free access to members of the Central American Common Market (CACM): El Salvador, Guatemala, Honduras, and Nicaragua. Costa Rica also has trade agreements with Panama and the Dominican Republic and a free trade agreement with Mexico.

- **Free trade zones (FTZs)** There are several authorized export processing zones in Costa Rica. Most are privately operated. FTZs exist in Alajuela, Cartago, Heredia, Limon, Moin, Puntarenas, San Jose, and Santa Rosa.

GOVERNMENT AGENCY

Ministerio de Obras Publicas y Transportes
Apdo 10.176
1000 San Jose
Tel: 26-7311
Fax: 27-1434
Telex: 2493

TRADE ASSOCIATION

Camara Nacional de Transportes
Calle 20, Avda 7
San Jose
Tel: 22-5394

Opportunities

FOR IMPORTING TO COSTA RICA

- chemicals
- fertilizers
- foodstuffs: corn, fruits, rice, soybeans, vegetables, wheat
- fuels
- hotel and restaurant equipment
- machinery
- manufactured goods
- medical supplies and equipment
- motor vehicles and parts
- telecommunications
- transportation equipment

FOR EXPORTING FROM COSTA RICA

- bananas
- coffee
- flowers and ornamental plants
- fruits
- rubber and plastic products
- sugar
- textiles and clothing

GROWTH SECTORS

- agricultural products
- construction
- hotels and restaurants
- tourism

GOVERNMENT PROCUREMENT

- educational goods and services
- electrical power equipment
- health care goods and services
- telecommunications products
- waste management systems

Business Travel

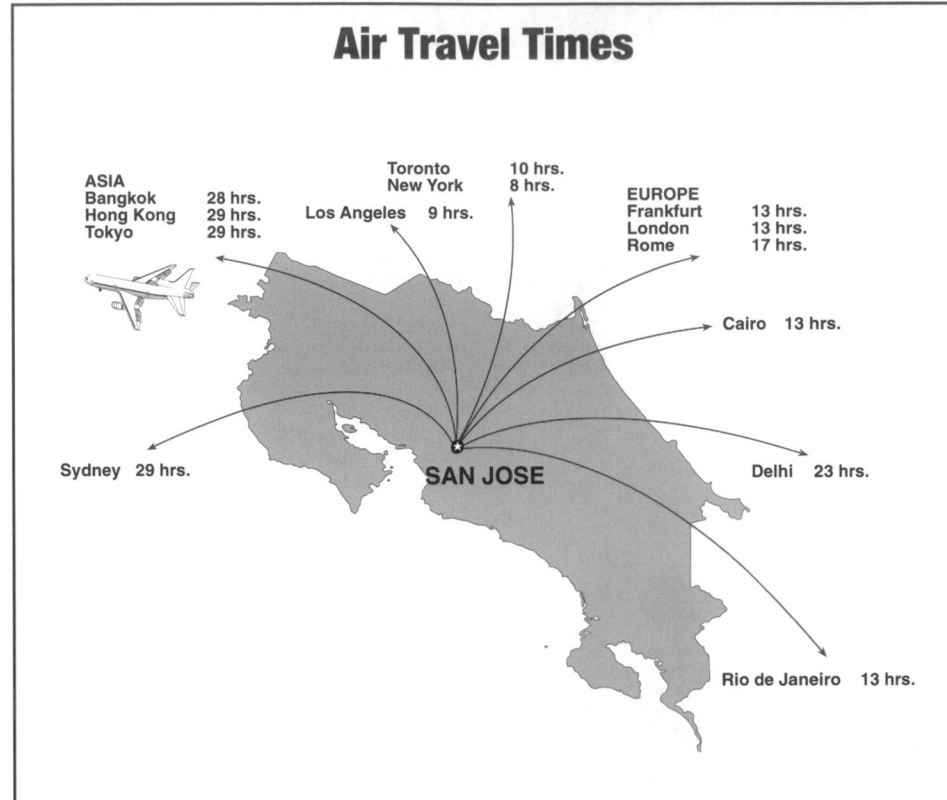

Air Travel Times

ASIA
Bangkok 28 hrs.
Hong Kong 29 hrs.
Tokyo 29 hrs.

Toronto 10 hrs.
New York 8 hrs.

Los Angeles 9 hrs.

EUROPE
Frankfurt 13 hrs.
London 13 hrs.
Rome 17 hrs.

Cairo 13 hrs.

Sydney 29 hrs.

SAN JOSE

Delhi 23 hrs.

Rio de Janeiro 13 hrs.

COMMUNICATION

Telephones Telephone service is modern and reliable. Direct dialing is available from any phone. Radiografica has international telephone services with English-speaking assistance.

Fax Faxes are widely used in Costa Rica and are available in most modern hotels in San Jose. Radiografica also offers fax and telex services in San Jose. They are open 7:00 am to 10:00 pm and will receive and hold faxes. The number to fax is 23-1609. To check if you have received a fax there, call 87-0513 or 87-0511.

Post office Mail service is modern and efficient. When sending mail, do so from a post office and not a mailbox, as they are rarely used. Domestic telegrams can be sent from the post office. The main post office in San Jose is open weekdays 7:00 am to 6:00 pm and Saturdays 7:00 am to noon. Express mail is available but it is not overnight service.

BEST TRAVEL BOOKS

Lonely Planet, Costa Rica Travel Survival Kit. Rainforest lush with information, this guide will flood perspective visitors with inspiration...

Fodor's Travel Guide, Costa Rica, Belize, and Guatemala. Tourist oriented, excellent source of city details.

Inside Central America; The Essential Facts Past and Present on El Salvador, Nicaragua, Honduras, Guatemala, and Costa Rica. P. Berryman. New York: Patheon Books.

Mexico and Central America Handbook. Bath, England: Trade & Travel Publications New York Prentice Hall. Updated annually.

The Travellers Guide to Costa Rica Customs and Manners. Elizabeth Devine & Nancy Braganti. An invaluable guide for people not wanting to put foot in mouth.

The Wall Street Journal Guide to Business Travel, Mexico and Central America. The most electrifying of practical travel guides.

USEFUL TELEPHONE NUMBERS

If you are calling from outside Costa Rica, you will need to add the country code [506] and any other international dialing requirements from within your country.

- English Speaking Operator 116
- International Telephone Information 124
- Train Information 233311
- Pacific Station 26-0011
- Atlantic Station 23-3311
- DHL Courier Service 223-1423
- Corobici Hotel 328-122
- Hotel San Jose Palacio 202-034
- Le Galeria Restaurant 340-850
- Information about Vaccinations 40-4332/4555
- Rental Car Information 33-4406
- Avis Car Rental 232-9922
- Hertz Car Rental 44-10097
- Budget Car Rental 23-3284
- National Car Rental 33-4406
- Juan Santamaria International Airport 44-10744
- Juan Santamaria International Airport......... 42-1820

Chambers Of Commerce
- Camara de Comercio de Costa Rica 21-0005
- Camara de Industrias de Costa Rica 232-411

Airlines
- LACSA 31-0033
- Aviateca 55-4949
- American Airlines 22-5655

Credit Card Information
Lost or stolen credit cards (call collect to the US, regardless of which country the card was issued in).
- Amex ....[1] (919) 333-3211
- Diner's Club...............................[1] (303) 799-1504
- MasterCard ....[1] (314) 275-6690
- Visa ....[1] (410) 581-7931

Travelogue

WORKWEEK

Offices Monday-Friday 8:00 am to noon and 2:00 pm. to 6:00 pm; and Saturday 8:00 am to 11:00 am.
Banks Monday-Friday 9:00 am to 3:00 pm; and 3:30 to 6:00 pm.
Government Monday-Friday 7:30 am to 4:00 pm.
Retail Monday-Saturday 8:00 am to noon and 2:00 to 8:00 pm.

HOLIDAYS

Holidays 1996
January 1 New Year's Day
January 15 US Martin Luther King Jr.'s Birthday
February 19 US Presidents Day
March 19 Saint Joseph's Day
April 11 Juan Santamaria's Day
April 13 Holy Thursday*
April 14 Good Friday*
April 15 Holy Saturday*
April 7 Easter Sunday*
May 1 Labor Day
May 27 US Memorial Day
June 15 Corpus Christi*
June 29 Saint Peter and Saint Paul
July 25 Annexation of Guanacaste
August 2 Our Lady of Los Angeles
August 15 Assumption Day
September 15 Independence Day
October 12 US Columbus Day
November 11 US Veterans' Day
November 24 US Thanksgiving
December 8 Immaculate Conception
December 25 Christmas Day
December 28-31 National Holidays
*Dates vary each year.

VISA AND PASSPORT

A valid passport is required. Citizens of Canada, Japan, US, and most EU countries can stay for up to 30 days without a visa. Nationals from some Latin American, Asian, African, and East European countries must obtain a visa and may have to pay a deposit upon entry. Canadian and US citizens may purchase a tourist card, for a nominal fee, in lieu of a passport as long as they have a birth certificate or driver's license, sufficient funds, and a return ticket. Entry is prohibited to males with long hair and beards, indigenous people, or anyone with insufficient funds or of Gypsy heritage.

DEPARTURE FORMALITIES

Every traveler is required to pay a 980 colones or US$7.25 tax upon departure from Costa Rica. Visitors may exchange no more than the equivalent of US$50 in local currency.

IMMUNIZATION

No inoculations are required for Costa Rica. Vaccinations advised: cholera, hepatitis, malaria, and typhoid.

TIPPING

Taxi: none. Porters: US$1 per piece. Hotels, restaurants, nightspots: 10 to 15 percent generally included in bill, plus 12 percent tax. Barbers, beauticians: 10 percent. Small services: US$.25.

CRIME

Foreigners are frequent victims of pickpocketing, muggings, house and car break-ins. Thefts are common and increasingly violent. Downtown San Jose, banks, beaches, airports, and tourist attractions are troublesome areas. Credit card fraud is a growing problem, as is the theft of US passports.

INFRASTRUCTURE

Costa Rica has highly developed telecommunications, bus, and air industries. In San Jose, hotel, taxi, and bus services are modern and efficient.

NATIONAL TOURIST OFFICE

Instituto Costarricense de Turismo (ICT)
Plaza de las Cultur, Calle 5, Av. ctl./2
San Jose
Mail address: Apartado 777, San Jose
Tel: 231733

Marketing

Overview

Agriculture and industry are key markets in Costa Rica. Exporters should be willing to accept smaller than usual sales here—Costa Rica's population is only 3.1 million—in return for loyalty and future growth in sales as the country develops. Costa Rica has an active, relatively modern infrastructure with several major projects for energy, hotels, and highways underway.

Distribution

Distributorships are restricted to Costa Rica residents, except for foreign firms that actually manufacture the products to be distributed in Costa Rica. Hence, foreign firms should generally plan to work through a local agent unless they contemplate developing a major manufacturing presence.

Agents, Distributors, and Partners

Local agents are essential, and legal counsel is strongly encouraged when negotiating and drafting agency arrangements as a preventive measure against questionable operators. The agreement should include a precise description of the conditions to which an agent may be regarded as unresponsive. Costa Rica's compact size usually requires only a single agent for the entire territory.

Selling Techniques and Advertising

Because business in Costa Rica is usually based on personal relationships, a soft approach is more effective than a hard sell. Newspapers are the best way to advertise products. There are three major Spanish and one English newspaper, as well as magazines produced by the Chamber of Commerce. Price is an important criterion, but quality, features, and service can also be critical.

Service and Customer Support

Consumers expect maintenance contracts, repair shops, and technical support with an emphasis on efficiency and quick service, and exporters should always arrange to supply service for all products. It is best to maintain stocks and spare parts and supplies in the country.

Marketing in Costa Rica

MARKETING TIPS

- **Business customs** Costa Rican business executives expect to meet foreign suppliers at their own facilities rather than in a hotel.
- **Language** Although Costa Rica is a Spanish-speaking country, most businesspeople speak English. Sales materials should be translated into Spanish, however.
- **Trade agreement** The new Free Market Treaty with Mexico will permit Costa Rica to reduce even further the ad valorem tax on Mexican imports, giving sellers located in that country an added edge.
- **Community** Firms new to Costa Rica will find a thriving expatriate community, including large groups from the US, Spain, Germany, Israel, and China.
- **Open-ended negotiations** Allow marketing negotiations to remain open-ended, so that confrontation can be avoided and talks can be allowed to fade away if an agreement cannot be reached.
- **Use of attorneys** Attorneys may not be involved directly in negotiations, but always review agreements—Costa Rica is very legalistic and supports one of the highest per capita populations of lawyers in the world.

CONSULTING FIRMS

CA Consulting
Central America Consulting Inc.
POB 1425-2050
San Jose
Tel/Fax: 253-3235

Conalas, S.A.
Apartado Postal 33881000
San Jose
Tel: 223-1450
Fax: 222-5156

Business Culture

Greetings and Courtesies

Men and women customarily shake hands on meeting and when departing; some women pat each others' left arms. Titles are abundant and important, with people usually being addressed by their title and last name. Business cards in both your language and Spanish are useful, although not indispensible, and translations into Spanish of any literature are appreciated as a courtesy.

Business Ethic and Framework

Initial business encounters are usually quite formal. Although the emphasis on hierarchy is largely lacking in Costa Rica, the country adheres faithfully to the general Latin precept that a business relationship is based on personal relationship. Costa Rica generally has a much less hierarchical culture than most Latin American countries, and many decisions are made by consensus rather than by a single executive. Senior executives will usually go along with group wishes.

Women

Although women in Costa Rica generally occupy a somewhat secondary status in this traditionally male-dominated society, they are becoming more common and more accepted in business in general, and foreign businesswomen should experience few problems. Although women can feel comfortable traveling alone, foreign businesswomen should wear dark-colored, conservatively cut, and tailored suits or dresses.

Meetings

If you do not have a mutual business acquaintance to make an introduction, consult your embassy for a referral. Prior appointments are necessary—make them two weeks in advance. Be punctual—Costa Ricans generally will not keep you waiting. A personal relationship must be established before any agreement can be reached; expect considerable discussion of nonbusiness topics.

Cultural Cautions

DO'S

- Learn something about Costa Rica's history, art, geography, and growing industrialization—interest is appreciated, as are attempts to speak Spanish.
- Families and children, in particular, are good topics of conversation, although you should avoid asking about women's jobs or family economics.

DON'TS

- Avoid religion and any negative aspects of the local economy as topics of conversation.
- Don't make personal criticisms or do anything giving an impression of arrogance. Never lose your temper.

CUSTOMS

- If invited to a home bring flowers and a box of candy for the hostess (such gifts often go unopened or even unacknowledged, but they are appreciated).

OBSERVATIONS

- A tone that is polite and courteous but good natured serves best; foreigners generally do better if they are seen not to take themselves too seriously.
- Gift-giving is more prevalent in Costa Rica than in many other Latin American cultures, although the gifts should not be elaborate. Wait until you have first been offered a gift by a Costa Rican associate before attempting to present one.
- Evening events usually begin and end fairly early because Costa Ricans begin their days early; if invited for a meal, leave shortly after it is over.

NEGOTIATIONS

- Negotiators should be polite, confident, and persistent—Costa Ricans may need persuading; however, avoid overt aggressiveness or pressure.
- Bargaining does not play as large a role as it does in much of Latin America. Negotiate shrewdly, but generally without flamboyant tactics.

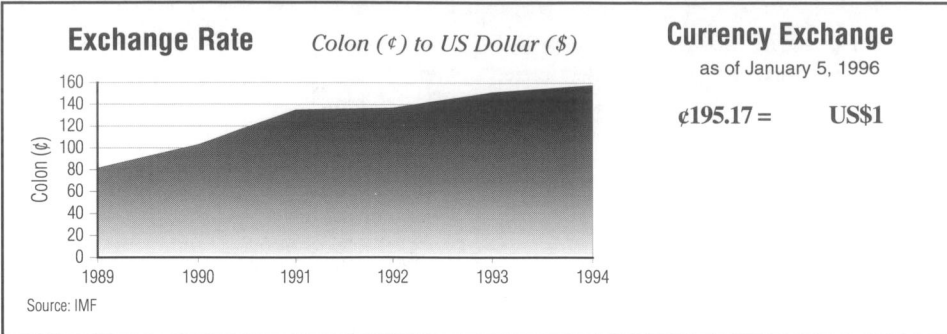

Exchange Rate *Colon (¢) to US Dollar ($)*

Colon (¢): 160, 140, 120, 100, 80, 60, 40, 20, 0
1989 1990 1991 1992 1993 1994

Source: IMF

Currency Exchange
as of January 5, 1996

¢195.17 =   US$1

Currency

The currency in use is the Costa Rican colón (plural colones). It is divided into 100 céntimos.

Foreign Exchange

All regulations are created by the Central Bank. Only the Central Bank, the state commercial banks, private banks, and a few other non-bank financial institutions authorized by the Central Bank may perform exchange transactions. Nonresident participation in some service industries is so regulated it may be impossible. Doctors and lawyers, for example, must prove long-time residence in Costa Rica to practice their crafts.

Capital Transfers

There are no limits or regulations for funds brought in or taken out of Costa Rica. Withholding taxes are placed on remittances of dividends, dividends distributed by stock companies, or remittances of interest abroad. These taxes range from five to 15 percent. There are no restrictions on proceeds from invisibles, but receipts from invisibles can only be exchanged for colones at the Central Bank or other authorized institutions. Nonresidents can legally own any equity in Costa Rica except for a select few reserved for the government.

Investment Incentives

Costa Rica created a number of incentives for foreign investment, including exemption from duties for raw material imports and exemption from sales or consumer taxes. Costa Rica's regulations regarding nonresident investment are identical to those for Costa Rican citizens, and any laws concerning foreign ownership of businesses are fairly transparent. It is illegal for foreign investments to be discriminated against in any way.

Investment Restrictions

Participation in some service industries, including medicine and law, by foreign individuals can be so rigorously controlled that in practical terms it may be impossible. There are no performance requirements imposed on foreign investors. The state has a monopoly in public utilities, insurance, production and distribution of electricity, and other sectors, limiting investment.

Money Matters

BITS AND PIECES

- **Corporate income tax** All businesses in Costa Rica are subject to a corporate income tax, but based only on income derived in Costa Rica.
- **Foreign tax relief** Foreign-source income is not taxable. There are no benefits for foreign taxes paid.
- **Gold** Gold can be held in any form and licenses from the Central Bank are required for gold exportation.
- **The National Budget Authority** The National Budget Authority authorizes the negotiation of new external credits. It is also in charge of decentralizing agencies and state agencies.
- **Capital** There are no restrictions on capital transfers. Any transfer between residents and nonresidents is permitted.
- **Import payments** Most imports must be registered with the Central Bank before clearing customs. Customs tariff rates range from 0 to 20 percent. There are additional taxes that could be placed on imports as well, ranging from one to 75 percent.
- **Export payments** Exporters may keep up to 10 percent of proceeds in foreign currency to care for their own needs, but the remainder must be surrendered to any institution authorized to deal with foreign exchange. Costa Rica has lowered tariffs recently, making it more attractive to exporters. Nontraditional exports to markets outside Central America are eligible for freely negotiable tax credit certificates ranging from 15 to 20 percent.
- **Key investment industries** Industries with the following characteristics are considered to have the best development potential in Costa Rica: those which are labor intensive, have low capital costs, require medium skill complexity, and produce CBI-eligible goods which have high US duties or quotas that impede imports from outside the Caribbean area.
- **Where to invest** Investments can typically be administered freely, although bureaucracy associated with customs, banking, and a wide variety of transactions is often detrimental to the smooth conduct of business.

BANKS

Central Bank of Costa Rica
Avenidas Central y Primera, Calle 4
1000 San José
Tel: 23-9095, 32-5866, 33-4233, 33-4344
Fax: 23-4658

Banco Central de Costa Rica
Avdas Central y Primera
Calles 2-4, Apdo 10.058
San Jose
Tel: 33-4233
Telex: 2163
Fax: 23-4658

Banco Anglo-Costarricense
Avda 2, Calles 1 y 3
Apdo 10.038
San Jose
Tel: 22-3322

Banco de Costa Rica
Avdas Central y Segunda
Calles 4 y 6
Apdo 10.035
1000 San Jose
Tel: 33-1100
Telex: 2103
Fax: 33-3316

Banco Credito Agricola de Cartago
Avda 2, Calles 3 y 5
Apdo 297
Cartago
Tel: 51-3011
Telex: 8006
Fax: 52-0364

Banco Nacional de Costa Rica
Calles y 4
Avda 1A, Apdo 10.015
San Jose
Tel: 23-2166
Telex: 2120

TAXATION

Taxation requires sophisticated knowledge of complex rules and regulations specific to each country. The information presented here is from the Ernst & Young Corporate Tax Guide and Directory, available from the Ernst & Young accounting office in your country, or from:

Marin Mendez & Co.
Mail Address:
Apdo. Postal 3301
1000 San Jose, Costa Rica
Street Address:
Ninth Avenue No. 1155
(Streets 11-13)
San Jose, Costa Rica
Tel: 257-23-27
Fax: 233-53-51

At a Glance

Corporate Income Tax Rate (%) (a)	30
Capital Gains Tax Rate (%)	0
Branch Tax Rate (%)	30
Withholding Tax (%)	
Dividends	15
Interest	15
Transportation and Communications	8.5
Salaries	10
Fees and Commissions	15
Reinsurance	5.5
News Service, Video and Films	20
Royalties from Know-how /Technical Services	25
Other	30
Branch Remittance Tax	15
Net Operating Losses (Years)	
Carryback	0
Carryforward (b)	3

(a) Lower rates (10% or 20%) apply to small businesses.
(b) Three years for industrial activities; five years for agricultural activities.

Legal

Legal System

A Supreme Court of Justice presides over the judicial branch, consisting of superior courts, collegiate tribunals, civil courts, and arbitrators.

Intellectual Property Rights

Patents and Trademarks Patents are available for new products and equipment, subject to a variety of qualifications. Costa Rican patents are typically in effect for 12 years. Trademarks can be registered for a 10-year period with no requirement for actual use by the registration holder.

Copyrights Copyright protections generally resemble those found in the United States. Works must be submitted for the Copyright Register, which makes no practical distinction between foreign works and those of Costa Rican creators.

Business Registration

A wide variety of organizational formats are acceptable, including corporations, partnerships, and joint ventures, which are the most common mode of foreign business in Costa Rica. The registration process requires several documents, and is best undertaken by a local attorney.

Contracts and Dispute Resolution

Contract law is essentially covered by Civil Code sections 1007 through 1044. Additional rules may be applicable, and largely depend on whether the given contract is classified as commercial law, administrative law, labor law, or a contract involving the Costa Rican government. Liability in civil contracts must be expressly defined by the parties.

Labor

The rights and obligations of workers are defined in the Costa Rican Labor Code, which was subject to significant reforms in 1993. Provisions include equitable pay, limited hours, weekly days of rest, and paid holidays. The right to organize labor unions and conduct strikes is also sanctioned by the Constitution. Special protectionary provisions are in effect for women and children. Termination without due cause generally necessitates severance payments based on duration of service.

Legal Matters

LEGAL BRIEFS

- **Foreign claimants** Although it is theoretically possible for foreign claimants to receive redress through Costa Rican courts, results are mixed.
- **Land expropriation** Issues surrounding the government expropriation of land formerly owned by foreign, mainly US, citizens have not yet been resolved with adequate compensation. Some claims are more than 25 years old.
- **Corporations** Corporations must be managed by a council of administration of no less than three members who need not be shareholders.
- **Monopolies** The Constitution prohibits monopolies and any commercial act which is intended or does in fact restrict or hinder free trade.
- **Commission merchant** A commission merchant is a professional agent who normally acts for undisclosed principals and thus becomes personally liable to other contracting parties who have no rights or duties toward principal.
- **Assignment** Costa Rican law contains no specific provision regarding assignment for the benefit of creditors.
- **Notaries** Notaries operate anywhere in the country and remain in office indefinitely, upon authority of the Costa Rican Supreme Court. Their bond is subject to annual renewal. In areas where the services of a notary are not available, local judges or alcaldes may provide identical services in their stead.
- **Trade secrets** Trade secrets are protected through Constitutional law protecting confidentiality. Prison sentences can be imposed, with sentences doubled for violations committed by public servants.
- **Consumer protection** Consumer protection laws in Costa Rica fix prices, regulate profit margins, and prohibit price speculation, although these laws are in the process of being liberalized so businesses will have more freedom to make their economic decisions.

Contacts

GOVERNMENT AGENCIES

National Product Council
Apartado 2205
1000 San Jose
Tel: 223-6033
Fax: 255-4729

Ministry of Agriculture and Livestock
Apartado 10093
1000 San Jose
Tel: 231-2344
Fax: 232-2103

Ministry of Foreign Trade
Apartado 96, Montes de Oca
San Jose
Tel: 222-5855
Fax: 233-9176

Ministry of Public Works and Transport
Apartado 10176
San Jose
Tel: 226-7311
Fax: 227-1434

Ministry of Tourism
Apartado 777
1000 San Jose
Tel: 233-9605
Fax: 223-5107

Ministry of Economy, Industry and Commerce
Apartado 10216
1000 San Jose
Tel: 222-0898, 222-1016 Fax: 222-2305

Ministry of Health
Food Registration & Control Department
Apartado 10123
1000 San Jose
Tel/Fax: 255-4426

Costa Rican Promotion and Export Center
Apartado 5418
1000 San Jose
Tel: 221-7166
Fax: 223-5722

Ministry of Natural Resources, Energy and Mines
Apartado 10104
1000 San Jose
Tel: 233-4533
Fax: 257-0697

Costa Rican Institute of Electricity and Telecommunication
Apartado 10032
1000 San Jose
Tel: 220-7630
Fax: 231-5354

Costa Rican Institute of Aqueducts and Sewage
Apartado 5120
1000 San Jose
Tel: 233-2155
Fax: 255-7334

Costa Rican Customs Office
San Jose
Tel: 255-3011, 233-9525
Fax: 223-7334

WORLD TRADE CENTER

World Trade Center of San Jose
1515 South Federal Highway
Suite 211
Boca Raton, Florida 33432-7404 USA
Tel: [1] (407) 394-9033
Fax: [1] (407) 394-9094

REMEMBER

- When you telephone (or fax) to Costa Rica from another country you must always include the country code [506] before the numbers given.
- When you send mail to Costa Rica, be sure to write COSTA RICA in capital letters on its own line below the addresses given.

GENERAL TRADE ASSOCIATIONS

Centro de Promoción de Exportaciones e Inversiones
(Export Promotion)
Calle 7
Avenidas 1 y 3
Apartado 5.148
San José
Tel: 21-7166
Fax: 23-5722

Costa Rican Association of the Plastic Industry
Apartado 8247
1000 San Jose
Tel: 255-0961
Fax: 255-0961

National Association of Distributors of Electrical Appliances and Furniture
Apartado Postal 7454
1000 San José
Tel: 223-5273
Fax: 223-5273

Costa Rican Association of Importers of Automotive Parts
Apartado 242
1002 Paseo de Estudiantes
San José
Tel/Fax: 222-8168

Costa Rican Association of Importers of Vehicles, Equipment and Machinery
Apartado 413
1000 San Jose
Tel: 222-5513
Fax: 233-5432

Assoc. of Concessionaires of American Vehicles
Apartado 1429
1000 San José
Tel: 220-1582
Fax: 232-2571

Costa Rican Federal Board of Engineers and Architects
1000 San José
Tel: 224-7322
Fax: 224-9774

Costa Rican Investment and Development
Costa Rica Coalition for Development Initiatives
Apartado 7170-1000
San Jose
Tel: 220-0036
Fax: 220-4754

BUSINESS AND TRADE ORGANIZATIONS

Chamber of Commerce
Avenida 10
detràs estatua de San Martín
Apartado 1783-2100 Goicoechea
San José
Tel: 23-2763
Fax: 55-4873

Chamber of Representatives of Foreign Firms
Apartado 3738
1000 San José
Tel: 253-0126
Fax: 234-2557

Costa Rican Chamber of Restaurants and Related Affairs
Apartado 113-2150
San Pedro
San José
Tel: 225-0838
Fax: 253-1879

Chamber of Automotive and Related Topics of Costa Rica
Apartado Postal 790 - 1150 La Uruca
San José
Tel: 233-3331, 223-7343
Fax: 223-7343

National Chamber of Agriculture
Apartado 1671
1000 San José
Tel: 221-6864, 233-8567
Fax: 233-8658

Costa Rican Food Industry Chamber
Apartado 7097
1000 San Jose
Tel: 234-0966
Fax 225-0901

Federation of Chambers of Livestock Breeders
Apartado 6464
1000 San Jose
Tel: 221-9268, 223-1059
Fax: 233-2180, 224-9181

Costa Rican Chamber of Industries
Apartado 10003
1000 San José
Tel: 223-2411
Fax: 222-1007

Costa Rican Chamber of Commerce
Apartado 1114
1000 San José
Tel: 221-0005, 221-0124
Fax: 233-7091

Chamber of Food Industry of Costa Rica
Apartado 7097
1000 San Jose
Tel: 234-0966
Fax: 225-0901

National Chamber of Agriculture and Agro-industry
Apartado 1671
1000 San José
Tel: 221-6864, 233-8567
Fax: 233-8658

Costa Rican-American Chamber of Commerce
Apartado 4946
1000 San José
Tel: 220-2200
Fax: 220-2300

Costa Rican Chamber of Textile and Confection
Apartado 1512 1002 Paseo de Estudiantes
San José
Tel: 225-1254, 253-5936
Fax: 225-1078

Chamber of Highway and Bridge Construction
Apartado 3803
1000 San José
Tel/Fax: 221-9418

Chamber of Architects and Engineers
Apartado 10263
1000 San José
Tel: 224-0244
Fax: 224-2882

NEWSPAPERS

General Directorate of Information and the Press
Presidential House
Apdo 520
Zapote, San Jose
Tel: 25-6205
Telex: 2376

Diario Extra
Calle 4, Avda 4
Apdo 177
1,009 San Jose
Tel: 23-9505
Fax: 23-6101

La Gaceta
La Uruca
Apdo 5,024
San Jose
Tel: 31-5222

AD AGENCIES

Consumer Publicidad SA
150 Sur del Grmnasio Nacional
Sabana Sur
San Jose
Tel: 232-8626
Fax: 231-0380

Jiminez, Blanco & Quiros, SA
Apdo 60, San Pedro
San Jose
Tel: 225-6612
Fax: 225-6261

Publicentro, SA
Apdo. 2930
1000 San Jose
Tel: 253-8182
Fax: 253-5143

RADIO AND TELEVISION

Control Nacional de Radio
Direccion Nacional de Communicaciones
Ministerio de Gobernacion y Policia
Apdo 8.000
1000 San Jose
Tel: 25-7364

Camara Nacional de Medios de Comunicacion Colective (CANAMECC)
Apdo 6.574
1000 San Jose
Tel: 22-4820

Radio Costa Rica
Apdo 365
1009 San Jose
Tel: 27-4693

Radio Monumental
Apdo 800
San Jose
Tel: 22-0000
Fax: 22-8237

Sistema Nacional de Radio y Television Cultural (SINART)
Apdo 7-1.980
San Jose
Tel: 31-0839
Telex: 2374

Commercial Television
Canal 2
Apdo 2.860
San Jose
Tel: 31-2222

Televisora de Costa Rica (Canal 7), SA (Teletica)
Apdo 3.876
San Jose
Tel: 32-2222
Telex 2220
Fax: 31-7545

Televisora Sur y Norte (Canal 11)
Apdo 5.542
San Jose
Tel: 23-7130

BANKS

Banco Popular y de Desarrollo Communal
Calle 1, Avda 2 y 4
Apdo 10.190
San Jose
Tel: 22-8122
Telex: 2844
Fax: 33-2350

Banco Metropolitano, SA
Calle Central, Avda 2a
Apdo 6.714
San Jose
Tel: 33-8111
Telex: 2955
Fax: 55-3826

LAW FIRMS

Carballo Abogados
Calles 29-31, Avenida 5, No. 2949
Barrio Escalante
San Jose
Tel: 221-0317

Bufete Daremblum
Apartado Postal 1756
San Jose
1000
Tel: 233-2233

Juan de Dios Alvarez y Asociados
Barrio Escalante
First Avenue, 29 and 31 Street, Number 3144
POB 5093
1000
San Jose
Tel: 224-9466

Serrano & Soley
Calle 31, Avenida 13
Rotonda "El Farolito", Barrio Escalante
San Jose
Tel: 221-3260

Vargas, Jimenez & Peralta
Apartado 2727QSan Jose
Tel: 222-8622

INTERNET ADDRESSES

Listserv: CENTAM-L
Send mail to: LISTSERV@UBVM.cc.buffalo.edu
Subscribe in the body of the message.

The Costa Rican Investment & Trade Development Board
http://www.cool.co.cr/usr/cinde/ing/cinde_cr.html

The Tico Times Online
http://infoweb.magi.com/calypso/ttimes.html

Complete Costa Rica
http://www.cocori.com/links.html

Latin America - Costa Rica
http://lanic.utexas.edu/la/ca/cr/

Côte d'Ivoire
Ivory Coast

Economy

Overview

The Côte d'Ivoire —or Ivory Coast—is among the world's largest producers and exporters of commodity agricultural products including coffee, cocoa beans, and palm-kernel oil. Consequently, the economy is highly sensitive to fluctuations in international commodity prices, weather, and crop conditions. Despite attempts by the government to encourage diversification, the economy remains heavily dependent on agriculture and related industries for employment and foreign exchange. A collapse of world cocoa and coffee prices in the mid-1980s threw the country into a recession; neither prices nor the country have yet to fully recover. In the wake of a 50 percent devaluation, the annual inflation rate was greater than 30 percent in mid-1995 and unemployment remained high, although the government managed to maintain the economy within the parameters established for it by the World Bank.

Trade

Major export products include cocoa, fuels, coffee, miscellaneous manufactured goods, and wood. Imports include miscellaneous manufactured goods, fuels, machinery and equipment, chemicals, and cereals. France is Côte d'Ivoire's main trading partner, accounting for roughly 20 percent of total trade, followed by the Netherlands, Germany, Italy, and the US. Côte d'Ivoire has also been trying both to diversify its export products and increase trade with neighboring countries to diversify its markets.

Sectors

Agriculture Agriculture employs somewhat more than 50 percent of the work force, while providing somewhat less than 50 percent of GDP. Côte d'Ivoire produces primarily cash crops—including cocoa beans, coffee, bananas, palm kernels, and rubber—and food crops such as corn, rice, and sweet potatoes. The country is not self-sufficient in the production of grain or dairy products, however, and must rely on imports to satisfy domestic demand.

Industry Industry contributes about 25 percent of GDP, but employs only about 10 percent of the work force. Mining holds the greatest potential, although difficulties in developing petroleum and natural gas deposits have limited exploitation; and production of gold, diamonds, and other minerals has also been restricted.

Services Although it employs roughly 40 percent of the work force and contributes more than 25 percent of GDP, the service sector remains poorly developed, consisting almost exclusively of local distribution and personal service activities, and a bloated public sector work force.

Trends

Despite a 50 percent currency devaluation in January 1994 designed to restore international price competitiveness, Côte d'Ivoire has continued to suffer from sluggish economic development. Principal culprits include weak commodity prices for major export products, a bloated public sector wage bill, and a large foreign debt. In an effort to restore economic viability, the Côte d'Ivoire targeted more than 50 state enterprises for privatization. Nearly 50 percent of these firms have been sold, including key companies involved in energy, transportation, and industrial materials processing. The government plans more privatization, which should help opportunities for foreign investment.

At a Glance

THE COUNTRY

Location Western coast of Africa, on the North Atlantic Ocean between Ghana and Liberia.
Terrain A 550-kilometer (340-mi.) coastline on the Gulf of Guinea gives way to mostly flat rolling plains. The mountainous northwest has dense forests that extend to the sea.
Climate Tropical along the coast and semi-arid in the far north. There are three seasons: warm and dry (November to March); hot and dry (March to May); and hot and wet (June to October).

THE PEOPLE

Population 13,200,000
Ethnic composition
Baoule.. 23%
Bete 18%
Senoufou 15%
Malinke 11%
Non-Africans (including French and Lebanese) 9%
Agni, foreign Africans.. 4%.
Religious composition
Animist.. 15-30%
Christian.. 26%
Muslim 38%
Languages spoken French (official), Baoule, Dioula, and more than 65 other ethnic dialects.
Education and literacy Primary education is six years, followed by seven years of secondary education. About 54% of the population over age 15 can read and write.
Labor force
Total:... 5,700,000
Agriculture, forestry, and livestock-raising engage more than 50% of the population. Most of the rest are employed in the public sector.

COUNTRY FACTS

Political and legal The legal system is based on the French civil code system combined with customary law.
Telephone Well-developed by African standards, but local service is only adequate. International calls can be dialed directly and are sometimes easier to make than local or in-country calls. International country code: [225]. City codes not required.
Transportation One of the best-developed and well-maintained transportation systems in Africa, with railroads that reach the major cities. An excellent network of roads links nearly all major towns. There is one international and several domestic airports and two major seaports, plus navigable rivers, canals, and numerous coastal lagoons.
Environment Attempts at reforestation of what once were the largest forests in West Africa have been cursory. Water pollution remains a pressing concern.
Media The one French-language daily, like all news media, radio and television, is owned or controlled by the government. There are an estimated 1.7 million radios and about 700,000 television sets in the country.
Health Despite public medical services, only about 33 percent of the population has access to health care. Most tapwater is not potable. Malaria, yellow fever, and other diseases are a significant health risk. Life expectancy of males is 46 years and of females 51 years.

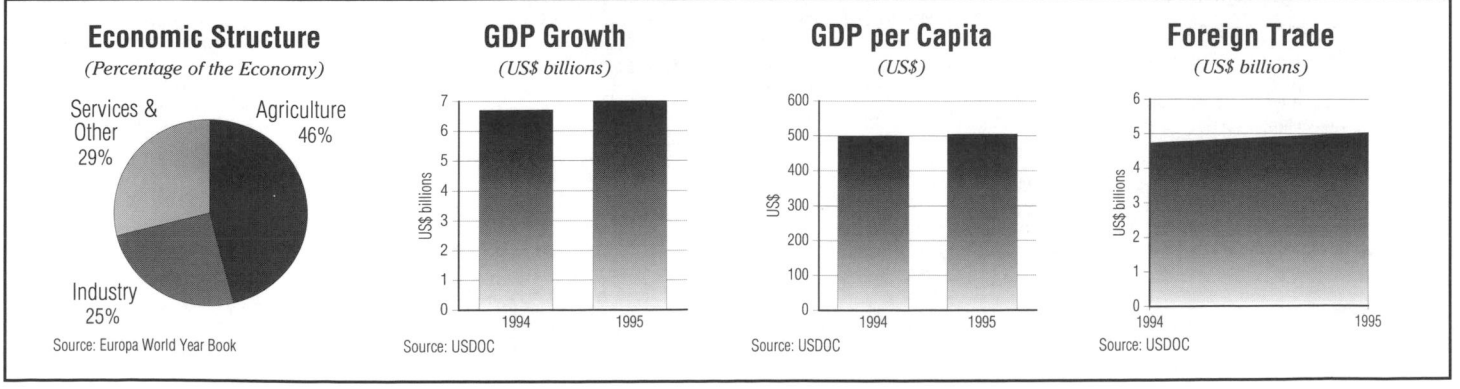

Economic Structure (Percentage of the Economy)
Services & Other 29%
Agriculture 46%
Industry 25%
Source: Europa World Year Book

GDP Growth (US$ billions)
1994, 1995
Source: USDOC

GDP per Capita (US$)
1994, 1995
Source: USDOC

Foreign Trade (US$ billions)
1994, 1995
Source: USDOC

Business Travel

	LH 1906	MADRID	935	113-3
	LH 1022	STUTTGART HBF.	935	-
	AF 1701	LYON	940	683-6
	AY 822	HELSINKI	940	113-3
	AA 071	SFRANCISCO-DALLAS	945	731-7

Travelogue

WORKWEEK

Offices Monday-Friday 8:00 am to noon and 2:30 pm to 6:00 pm.
Banks Monday-Friday 8:00 am to 11:30 am and 2:30 pm to 4:30 pm.
Government Monday-Friday 8:00 am to noon and 2:30 pm to 6:00 pm.
Retail Monday-Friday 8:00 am to noon and 2:30 to 6:30 pm, Saturday 8:00 am to noon and 2:30 pm to 5:30 pm.

HOLIDAYS

Holidays 1996
January 1 New Year's Day
March End of Ramadan
April 5 Good Friday
April 8 Easter Monday
May 1 Labor Day
May 16 Ascension Day
May 27 Pentecost Monday
August 15 Assumption Day
November 1 All Saints' Day
November 15 National Peace Day
December 7 Independence Day
December 25 Christmas Day
In addition, Muslims celebrate other holidays, including Mohammed's Birthday, which are determined by the lunar Islamic calendar

VISA AND PASSPORT

Foreigners must have a valid passport. Visas are not required for visits less than 90 days. Visitors should be sure that their passport is stamped by government officials at the port of entry. A long-term visa is required for business travelers. Visas must be obtained prior to arrival and must be accompanied by a letter of recommendation from the company the businessperson is representing. All Canadian citizens must have visas.

DEPARTURE FORMALITIES

Exportation of Ivorian currency is strictly prohibited. Dollars may be exported only with permission from an authorized Ivorian bank.

IMMUNIZATION

An international health certificate showing current yellow fever and cholera immunizations is required. In addition, advance malaria treatment as well as inoculation against typhoid, tetanus, diphtheria, and typhus are strongly advised.

TIPPING

Restaurants usually include a 10 to 15 percent service charge. Taxi fares are negotiated, so tips are not necessary.

CRIME

Theft is common, from petty street crime to armed robbery. Security guards protect clients at many hotels, restaurants, supermarkets, and nightclubs. In Abidjan, avoid visiting the Treichville or the Plateau business districts after dark, and avoid walking on the DeGaulle and Houphout-Boigney bridges at all times. Political instability in neighboring Liberia makes the Liberia-Côte d'Ivoire border potentially dangerous.

INFRASTRUCTURE

Côte d'Ivoire's developing infrastructure includes an excellent paved roadway system; good telecommunications; rail links; modern developments for commercial, industrial, and retail use; and modern hotels and banks. Bus travel is not advised, but the numerous city taxis are reasonably priced and available at all times. Rates are legally doubled between midnight and 5:00 am.

NATIONAL TOURIST OFFICE

Ministere du Tourisme
B.P. V06
Abidjan
Tel: 22830

COMMUNICATIONS

Telephones Local phone service is automatic and generally adequate, but breakdowns occur. International calls can be dialed direct from hotel phones.
Fax While fax service has been slow to catch on, facilities are available in the major hotels and at the Central Post Office.
Post office Côte d'Ivoire has regular air and sea international postal service, although transit time can be slow. Post office box numbers are preferable to street addresses for mail sent to Côte d'Ivoire.

BEST TRAVEL BOOK

Meet Me in West Africa: The Côte d'Ivoire, Togo and Senegal, by Judith Rothberg. Vantage.
Côte d'Ivoire on a Shoe String, Lonely Planet. Informative, and interesting.
Africa on a Shoestring, Lonely Planet. Filled with useful information.
Do's and Taboo's Around the World. The Bestselling Guide to International Behavior. Edited by Roger Axtell, compiled by the Parker Pen Company. The ultimate guide to international behavior, now completely updated and expanded. Helpful, fun to read!.

USEFUL TELEPHONE NUMBERS

If you are calling from outside Côte d'Ivoire, you will need to add the country code [225] and any other international dialing requirements from within your country.

- Ambulance/Fire 180
- Abidjan Airport Information 278101
- Post Office/Telecommunications 346000
- Telex Service 325230
- Customs Authority 325223
- Ministry of Tourism 228308
- Health Department 294000
- Bouake Tourist Information 632755
- Yamoussoukro Tourist Information 640814
- Federation des Hoteliers 373463
- Railroad information 210245
- Bus information 353368
- Air Ivoire 323429
- Air Afrique 220500
- Train Information 320245

Credit Card Information
Lost or stolen credit cards (call collect to the US, regardless of which country the card was issued in).

- Amex .... [1] (919) 333-3211
- Diner's Club .... [1] (303) 799-1504
- MasterCard .... [1] (314) 275-6690
- Visa .... [1] (410) 581-7931

Foreign Trade

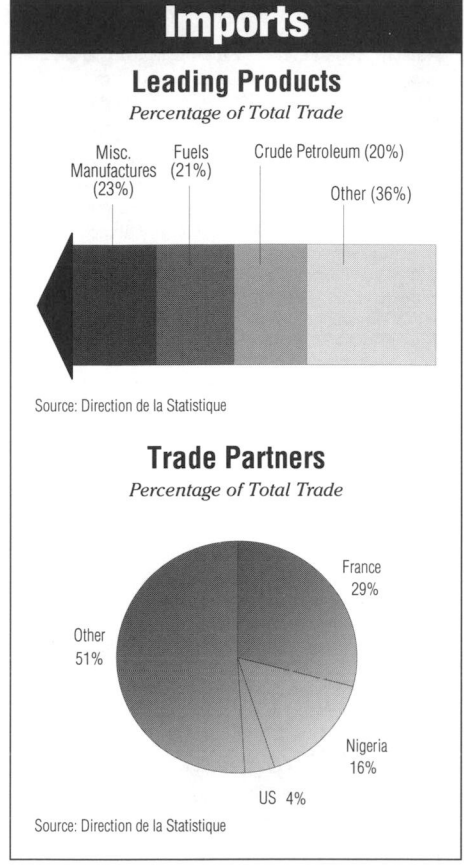

Imports

Leading Products
Percentage of Total Trade

Misc. Manufactures (23%)
Fuels (21%)
Crude Petroleum (20%)
Other (36%)

Source: Direction de la Statistique

Trade Partners
Percentage of Total Trade

France 29%
Other 51%
Nigeria 16%
US 4%

Source: Direction de la Statistique

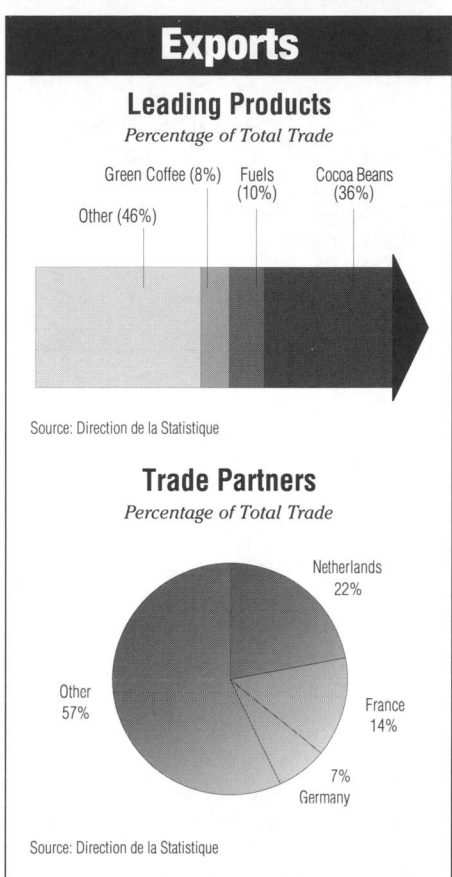

Exports

Leading Products
Percentage of Total Trade

Green Coffee (8%)
Fuels (10%)
Cocoa Beans (36%)
Other (46%)

Source: Direction de la Statistique

Trade Partners
Percentage of Total Trade

Netherlands 22%
Other 57%
France 14%
Germany 7%

Source: Direction de la Statistique

Opportunites

IMPORTING TO CÔTE D'IVOIRE
- agricultural chemicals, foodstuffs
- computers and peripherals, telecommunications equipment, air conditioning and refrigeration, food processing equipment, agricultural machinery
- industrial machinery, iron and steel

EXPORTING FROM CÔTE D'IVOIRE
- bananas, cocoa, coconuts, coffee, pineapples
- cotton, palm oil, rubber
- tropical wood products

GROWTH SECTORS
- agriculture: cotton, rubber, sugar
- construction
- food processing
- mining: gold, natural gas, oil
- telecommunications
- textiles and apparel

Trade News

RULES AND REGULATIONS
- **Quota system** The government regulates foreign trade transactions (particularly imports) through a quota system.
- **Import licenses** All importers are required to obtain either an import license or an approval of intent to import document from the Ministry of Commerce before importing goods into Côte d'Ivoire.

GOVERNMENT AGENCIES
Ministry of Commerce
Immeuble SCIAM
Ave Marchand, BP V163
Abidjan
Tel: 21-05-66

Legal

Legal System
Côte d'Ivoire's laws are derived primarily from the French system. The court is independent, but is hampered by backlogs.

Intellectual Property Rights
Patents and Trademarks Patent validity is 10 years, with two five-year extensions. Trademarks are also valid for 10 years, but can be renewed indefinitely. Neither patents nor trademarks are protected by the government; counterfeit clothing, textiles, footwear, and watches can be found, particularly among street vendors.

Copyrights Copyrights are valid for 50 years following the death of the author (or 50 years if it is printed posthumously). The government rarely enforces the laws, particularly for audio and video tapes.

Trade Secrets Any video tape violation is handled by the civil court system, and may be delayed because of problems in the court system.

Contracts and Dispute Resolution
Enforcement of contract rights can be time consuming and expensive. Cases usually aren't decided quickly, and some do not appear to be judged on their legal or contractual merits. A new Arbitration Tribunal is being established where businesses may settle their commercial disputes. This is designed mainly to avoid the backlogged and inefficient court system. Côte d'Ivoire is a member of the International Center for the Settlement of Investment Disputes.

Labor
Côte d'Ivoire has a highly trained and capable work force, although it is segmented. Unskilled workers are prevalent, professional and technical labor may be more difficult to find. A new labor code in 1995 has introduced greater flexibility into the labor system; fewer restrictions on recruitment, for example. Work permits for expatriates are difficult to get.

Legal Matters

LEGAL BRIEFS
- **Wage costs** The government is eliminating or reducing taxes affecting wage costs to promote employment.
- **Crime** A high crime rate and corrupt court system have created barriers for foreign investors.
- **Wage rates** Wages are relatively high by regional standards. Costs of capital goods, transport, and energy are also high.
- **Political violence** There have been a few instances of political violence in the past, but it is not a common occurrence in Côte d'Ivoire.

LEGAL CONTACTS
Scpa Adje-Assi-Metan
59 Rue des Sambas
(Indenie)
01 B.P. 6568
Abidjan 01
Tel: 21-5343, 22-8256, 22-7248 Fax: 21-5945

Jean Pierre Elisha
10th Floor, Ste 102, Eden
44 Avenue Lamblin 04
B.P 1687
Abidjan, 04
Tel: 21-18-80, 33-18-70 Fax: 21-18-70

N'Goan, Die-Kacou & Associes
Immeuble CCIA (World Trade Center)
01 B.P. 5797
Abidjan
Tel: 21-4424, 21-4108 Fax: 21-6308

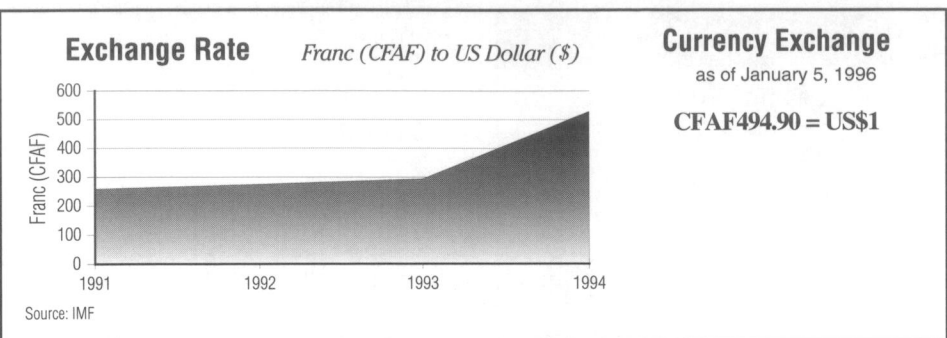

Exchange Rate *Franc (CFAF) to US Dollar ($)*

Franc (CFAF): 0, 100, 200, 300, 400, 500, 600
1991, 1992, 1993, 1994

Source: IMF

Currency Exchange
as of January 5, 1996

CFAF494.90 = US$1

Currency

The currency of Côte d'Ivoire is the CFA franc, or CFAF. It is issued by the Central Bank of West African States (BCEAO), and is fixed with the French franc at a rate of CFAF100 per F1.

Foreign Exchange

Foreign exchange operations are administered by the Directorate of the Treasury of Money and Banking Affairs in the Ministry of Economy, Finance, and Planning. Exchange control regulations apply to financial transfers outside the franc zone, which is a monetary zone that includes France and its former colonies. Exchange control regulations do not apply to France, Monaco, and Operations Account countries: Benin, Burkina Faso, Cameroon, Central African Republic, Chad, Comoros, Congo, Equatorial Guinea, Gabon, Mali, Niger, Senegal, and Togo. All other countries are considered foreign and exchange transactions must be handled by an authorized bank or the Postal Administration.

Capital Transfers

Spot and forward exchange transactions are limited to specific imports and certain time restrictions. There are no taxes or subsidies on purchases or sales of foreign exchange. Nonresident accounts are based on regulations applied in France.

Investment Incentives

There are no general incentives for investments. If a company seeks designation as a priority enterprise eligible for the tax and other benefits provided in the investment code, it may be required to purchase Ivorian products. Designation as a priority enterprise is available to investors in some fields, including agriculture, livestock and fishing, storage and treatment of agricultural and food products, and low-cost housing construction.

Investment Restrictions

There are no specific restrictions or performance requirements for foreign investments. Corruption is prevalent throughout the government, and the country's key export crops are under the control of vested interests. Tax and duty rates have fallen, but they remain relatively high.

Money Matters

BITS AND PIECES

- **Gold** Residents are free to hold and deal in gold in any form. Imports and exports of gold require approval from the Minister of Economy, Finance, and Planning, though authorization is rarely granted.
- **Loans** The World Bank and the African Development Bank offer financing for feasibility studies and loans to finance government-sponsored procurement in Côte d'Ivoire.
- **Performance requirements** Côte d'Ivoire currently has no general performance requirements.
- **Counterfeit material** Although counterfeit material is theoretically prohibited, bootleg clothing, textiles, footwear, watches, and audio and video tapes are readily available, especially among street vendors.
- **Imports and exports** Transactions with foreign countries valued at more than CFAF500,000, or transactions undertaken before customs clearance, must be domiciled with an authorized bank. Payment for exports to foreign countries, including Operations Account countries, must be made within 180 days of the arrival of the goods to their destination. Receipts must be collected and repatriated through authorized intermediary banks within one month of the due date. All export transactions valued at more than CFAF500,000 must be domiciled with an authorized bank.
- **Invisibles** Payments for invisibles to France, Monaco, and the Operations Account countries may be made without restrictions. Payments to other countries must be approved. Proceeds from invisibles within the franc zone may be retained, while all amounts due from residents of other countries for services and all income earned in those countries from foreign assets must be surrendered within two months of the receipt date.

BANKS

African Development Bank
01 BP 1387
Abidjan 01
Tel: 20-44-44

Banque Centrale des Etats de l'Afrique de l'Ouest (BCEAO)
ave. Terrasson de Fougeres
01 BP 1769
Abidjan 01
Tel: 21-04-66
Fax: 22-28-52
Telex: 23474

Banque Paribas Côte d'Ivoire
Immeuble Alliance
17 ave Terrason de Fougeres
17 BP 09
Abidjan 17
Tel: 21-86-86
Fax: 21-88-23
Telex: 23474

B.I.C.I.C.I.
01 BP 1298
Abidjan 01
Tel: 22-03-79

Citibank, NA
28 Avenue de la Fosse
01 BP 3698
Abidjan 01
Tel: 32-46-10 Fax: 32-76-85

S.G.B.C.I.
5-7 Avenue Joseph Anoma
01 BP 1355
Abidjan 01
Tel: 32-03-33

TAXATION

Taxation requires sophisticated knowledge of complex rules and regulations specific to each country. The information presented here is from the Ernst & Young Corporate Tax Guide and Directory, available from the Ernst & Young accounting office in your country, or from:

FFA Ernst & Young
5, Avenue Marchand
B.P. 1222
Abidjan 01, Côte d'Ivoire
Tel: 21-11-15, 21-19-57
Telex: 22446
Fax: 21-12-59

AT A GLANCE

Corporate Income Tax Rate (%)	35
Capital Gains Tax Rate (%) (a)	35
Branch Tax Rate (%)	35
Withholding Tax (%)	
Dividends, Directors' Fees and Nondeductible Expenses (b)	12
Interest (c)	18
Royalties from Patents, Know-how, etc.	20
Other Payments to Nonresidents (d)	20
Branch Remittance Tax (e)	12
Net Operating Losses (Years)	
Carryback	0
Carryforward	3

(a) In certain circumstances, the tax is deferred or reduced.
(b) The rate is 18% in certain situations.
(c) The withholding rate is 9%, 13.5% or 16.5% in certain cases if the income is received through a bank or broker. The withholding rate on "lots" (exceptionally high bond discounts given only for certain specified bonds selected at random) is 25%. The withholding tax is imposed on the amount of the discount.
(d) Applicable to payments by resident companies.
(e) On one-half of the before-tax profit (18% if the profit is exempt from corporate tax).

Marketing

Distribution

Successful distribution in the Côte d'Ivoire starts with research. Many products sold in the Côte d'Ivoire are channeled through wholesale organizations. Most small-scale retail outlets are individually owned "general-store" type operations, and there are as yet no major large outlets. A successful distribution plan must allow for the wide range of goods these outlets carry. The local Lebanese community has largely been responsible for importation and distribution in the Côte d'Ivoire.

Agents, Distributors, and Partners

Although the law does not require foreign firms to engage a local agent, a carefully chosen Ivorian representative can facilitate business dealings in the country. A local representative of foreign business should be thoroughly familiar with the Ivorian economy. Ivorian agents usually represent several businesses simultaneously. The Commercial Service in Côte d'Ivoire is available to help foreign companies through its Agent Distributor Service program.

Selling Techniques

Price is important, but quality, service, and delivery are also critical. Foreign companies in Côte d'Ivoire need to take the time to build local trust in themselves and their products. A high level of contact with local Ivorian business associates will help foreign businesses transcend the cultural and language differences. Ivorians remain suspicious of large foreign businesses—a result of their colonial history—so every effort should be made to personalize sales presentations. Trade fairs offer one of the best places for foreign companies to reach Ivorian customers.

Advertising

One of the best mediums for advertising in the Côte d'Ivoire is the government-controlled *Fraternité Mate*, the Ivorian newspaper with the highest circulation in the country. Television advertising is also available in Côte d'Ivoire; Ivorians own more than three million television sets. Movie theaters in Cote d'Ivoire also carry advertising consisting of short films that are shown during intermission. These traditionally feature automobiles and tobacco products.

Business Culture

Greetings and Courtesies

Greetings are relatively simple in the French-speaking Côte d'Ivoire. A firm handshake is always acceptable between people. When introduced to a group, it is considered polite to wait for the locals to extend their hands. Professional titles—Doctor, Director, or Chief—should always be used. In conversation, Ivorians tend to be somewhat aggressive by Western standards. Allow them to tell you about themselves, limiting your own initial conversation to a brief description of who you are, your company position, and the nature of your business in their country. An inquiry about a person's family is a basic courtesy in the Côte d'Ivoire and should always be extended. Discussions of politics, however, are to be generally avoided.

Business Ethic and Framework

Business in the Côte d'Ivoire is conducted slowly, and standards of punctuality are often very lax. A well-recommended strategy for initiating action in your business trip is to announce to your contacts that you have but a week to spend in the country—regardless of your actual plans. Business is often conducted in a more social context rather than an official one. Lunch is more popular than dinner for business entertaining and can often last for several hours. Similarly, Ivorians interested in cultivating your business will usually wine and dine you in the privacy of their homes.

Meetings and Decision making

Official business meetings invariably start late—often several hours—and appointments are often skipped entirely by Ivorian businessmen. The Ivorian system is heavily bureaucratic and decisions are usually made only by the top members of a company. However, given the strong family ties that abound in the Côte d'Ivoire, a lower-level connection may prove valuable in expediting the usual slow procedures and red tape.

Marketing in Côte d'Ivoire

MARKETING TIPS

- **Pricing** Pricing in French francs, especially for deliveries over a six-to-12-month period will help products penetrate the market.
- **Credit** Local sources of commercial credit are extremely limited, therefore liberal credit terms may be required to close sales. Credit is often granted for 180 days on consumer goods and 24 months for capital equipment.
- **Government** The government of the Côte d'Ivoire periodically advertises for products it needs in local newspapers and sometimes in international journals. Usually there is a charge to purchase the bid documents, which are normally in French.
- **Business style** Ivorians tend to be laid back and patient. They may find more aggressive business styles disturbing, and salespeople should behave accordingly.

RADIO AND TELEVISION

Radiodiffusion Ivoirienne
BP V191
Abidjan 01
Tel: 21-48-00
Telex: 22635

Television Ivoirienne
08 BP 883
Abidjan 08
Tel: 43-90-39
Telex: 22293

NEWSPAPERS

La Chronique du Soir
09 BP 150
Abidjan 09
Tel: 22-15-12

Cultural Cautions

DO'S

- Upon arriving, always reconfirm all of your appointments.
- Always arrive late by 15 minutes or so for a dinner or lunch invitation.
- Prepare to spend time letting your hosts get to know you.

DON'TS

- Don't make appointments during holidays, such as the Muslim period of Ramadan, or the Christmas/ New Year's period.

CUSTOMS

- Use only the right hand when eating.
- Eat heartily when a guest at someone's home; anything less can be very insulting.
- An exchange of gifts is a standard method of building social and business relations.

OBSERVATIONS

- A woman doing business in the Côte d'Ivoire should be experienced and prepared for the decidedly double-standard treatment that women receive in most African countries. She should certainly be married, as marriage is a respected institution. She should also dress in modest attire, and be serious and professional in her deportment.
- Ivorians are very fashion conscious and dress in the French style. For business, men wear a two- or three-piece suit. Women should wear a conservative dress or suit.

NEGOTIATIONS

- Be persistent. Business decisions usually take time.

BUSINESS AND TRADE ASSOCIATIONS

Association of Importers and Exporters of Côte d'Ivoire
01 BP 3792
Abidjan 01

Chamber of Industry of Côte d'Ivoire
11, Avenue Lamblin
01 BP 1758
Abidjan 01
Tel: 22-55-80, 32-65-34

Farmers' Association
Chamber of Agriculture of Côte d'Ivoire
01 BP 1291
Abidjan 01
Tel: 32-16-11, 22-61-57
Fax: 21-46-18

Industrial Association of the Côte d'Ivoire
01 BP 1340
Abidjan 01

Conseil Economique et Social
04 BP 301
Abidjan
Tel: 21-20-60

Caisse Francaise de Dévelopment (France)
01 BP 1814
Abidjan 01
Tel: 44-53-05
Telex: 28113

Mission Francaise de Coopération
01 BP 1839
Abidjan 01
Tel: 21-60-45

Chambre d'Agriculture de la Côte d'ivoire
11 ave Lamblin
01 BP 1291
Abidjan 01
Tel: 21-16-11

Chambre de Commerce et d'Industrie de Côte d'Ivoire
01 BP 1399
Abidjan 01
Tel: 32-46-79
Fax: 32-39-46

American Chamber of Commerce Côte d'Ivoire
5, Rue Jesse Owens
BP 1712 Abidjan 01
Tel: 21-09-79 x348/9
Fax: 22-32-59

Chamber of Commerce of Côte d'Ivoire
01 BP 1399
Abidjan 01
Tel: 32-39-42, 32-47-00

WORLD TRADE CENTER

Centre de Commerce International d'Abidjan (CCI-A)
POB V. 68
Abidjan
Tel: 21-30-92, 21-43-78
Fax: 22-71-12

NEWS AGENCIES

Agence Ivoirienne de Presse (AIP)
04 BP 312
Abidjan 04
Telex: 23781

Agence France-Presse (AFP)
18 ave du Docteur Crozet
01 BP 726
Abidjan 01
Tel: 21-90-17
Telex 22481

Agenzia Nazionale Stampa Associata (ANSA)
01 BP 3570
Abidjan 01
Tel: 35-60-82
Telex: 26118

Associated Press (AP)
01 BP 5842
Abidjan 01
Tel: 41-37-49
Telex: 28129

Xinhua (New China) News Agency
(People's Republic of China)
Cocody Danga Nord Lot 46, 08 BP 1212
Abidjan 08
Tel: 44-01-24

NEWSPAPERS

La Chronique du Soir
09 BP 150
Abidjan 09
Tel: 22-15-12

Fraternité-Matin
Blvd du Général de Gaulle
01 BP 1807
Abidjan 01
Tel: 21-27-27
Telex: 23718

Ivoir Soir
Blvd du Général de Gaulle
01 Bp 1807
Abidjan 01
Tel: 21-27-27
Telex: 23718

La Voie
17 BP 656
Abidjan 17
Tel: 25-85-25

PERIODICALS

Abidjan 7 Jours
01 BP 1965
Abidjan 01
Tel: 35-39-39

Le Démocrate
01 BP 1212
Abidjan 01
Tel: 24-25-61

La Dépeche
05 BP 1924
Abidjan 05

Le Dialogue
01 BP 89
Abidjan 01
Tel: 24-35-77

Djeliba-le journal des jeunes Chrétiens
01 BP 1287
Abidjan 01
Tel: 21-69-79

Eclosion
08 BP 668
Abidjan 08
Tel: 42-42-43

Entente Africaine
Cocody-les-Deux-Plateaux
rue des Jardins
01 BP 8534
Abidjan 01
Tel: 41-04-76
Fax: 41-04-15

L'Essor du Paysan
01 BP 2007
Abidjan 01

L'Eveil des Foyers
01 BP 1287
Abidjan 01
Tel: 22-31-08

Forum Economique
04 BP 488
Abidjan 04
Tel: 24-09-07

Gazelle Africaine
12 BP 577
Abidjan 12
Tel: 32-04-88

Le Guido (Abidjan Jour et Nuit)
01 BP 1807
Abidjan 01
Tel: 37-06-66
Telex: 372545

Ivoire-Dimanche (ID)
01 BP 1807
Abidjan 01

Le Jeune Démocrate
08 BP 1866
Abidjan 08
Tel: 45-69-22

Journal Officiel de la Côte d'Ivoire
Service Autonome des Jounaux Officiels
BP V70
Abidjan
Tel: 22-67-76

La Nouvelle
01 BP 1287
Abidjan 01
Tel: 21-69-79

La Nouvelle Presse
Cocody-les-deux-Plateaux
rue des Jardins
01 BP 8534
Abidjan 01
Tel: 41-04-76
Fax: 41-04-15

L'Observateur du Lundi
BP 1987
Abidjan Cedex 04 - Yopougon
Tel: 45-68-18

Réalités
06 BP 100
Abidjan 06
Tel: 41-41-79

Revue Ivoirienne de Droit
BP 3811
Abidjan

Téré
20 BP 43
Abidjan 20

Tribune du Banco
22 BP 302
Abidjan 22

L'Union
04 BP 2295
Abidjan 04
Tel: 22-49-59

La Voix d'Afrique
Cocody-les-Deux-Plateaux
Rue des Jardins
01 BP 8534
Abidjan 01
Tel: 41-04-76
Fax: 41-04-15

INTERNET ADDRESSES

African Nations - Côte d'Ivoire
http://www.webperfect.com/afrinet/ivory/ivory.html

Côte d'Ivoire Homepage
http://www.sas.upenn.edu/African_Studics/Country_Specific/Cote.html

City Net - Côte d'Ivoire
http://www.city.net/countries/cote_divoire/

Cuba

Republic of Cuba

Economy

Overview

Cuba is a communist, totalitarian state dominated by Fidel Castro, who exercises almost complete control over social and economic life. For nearly 30 years, the results of an economic embargo by the United States were at least partially offset by heavy subsidies from the former Soviet Union and favorable trade relationships with the countries of the former Soviet Bloc. But those supports collapsed with the dismantling of the Soviet Union in 1991. Combined with Cuba's failure to undertake needed reforms, this produced an unprecedented economic crisis, and Cuba's economy is only about half what it was in 1989. It has only recently begun to court limited foreign participation.

Trade

During the 1980s, the former Soviet Bloc accounted for more than 80 percent of Cuba's external trade. The Soviet Union alone bought 80 percent of all Cuban sugar and 40 percent of all its citrus fruit, in addition to subsidizing Cuba's oil imports. Now Cuban trade with Russia represents only a fraction of previous trade levels. Today, major markets for Cuban sugar, nickel, seafood, citrus, tobacco, and rum include Russia, Canada, Ukraine, China, and Spain. Spain, China, France, Venezuela, Mexico, and Canada provide Cuba with the majority of its consumer goods, industrial raw materials, food, and petroleum imports.

Sectors

Agriculture The Cuban economy has traditionally been dominated by sugar production, prospering or suffering with fluctuations in sugar prices. The Castro regime has been unable to break that pattern, and sugar still accounts for more than half of its export earnings. Cuba's famous tobacco provides a second source of export earnings, but it is also subject to market forces. Cuba has never diversified from a basic single-crop economy despite some development of natural resources such as nickel, iron ore, copper, and timber.

Industry The state owns and operates all industrial enterprises. In recent years, many Cuban firms have closed or reduced production because of shortages of foreign exchange and limited access to spare parts and imported components. Light industry, electronics, pharmaceuticals, and biotechnology have all been hit hard, as have sugar and food processing, oil refinement, cement, and consumer products. Cuba's nickel reserves, the fourth-largest in the world, have traditionally accounted for a significant part of its export earnings.

Services Tourism has increased more than 20 percent annually for the last several years and continues to draw many Europeans and Latin Americans.

Trends

The economic prospects are not promising for Cuba, largely because of Castro's decision to maintain highly centralized control over economic decisionmaking. With the loss of trade and aid from the former Soviet Bloc, Cuba has attempted to attract foreign buyers for its sugar and nickel, as well as its biotech products. Except for tourism, it has had limited success primarily because of its dilapidated economy, its unpaid debt to Western countries, and the general lack of clear title to expropriated property.

At a Glance

THE COUNTRY
Location An island in the Atlantic Ocean, off the coast of Florida, US.
Terrain Flat or gently rolling plains, hills, mountains in the southeast.
Climate Tropical, moderated by trade winds; dry season is November to April, and rainy season is May to October.

THE PEOPLE
Population 10,800,000
Ethnic composition
Whites (of Spanish descent).................................. 66%
Blacks 12%
Mixed races 22%
Note: virtually the entire population is native born Cuban.
Religious composition
Roman Catholic 40%
A variety of religions are practiced in Cuba: Santería, a group of cults that meld African and Christian beliefs, several Protestant churches, and a very small Jewish population.
Languages spoken Spanish.
Education and literacy Education has always been a high priority of the government. Almost 95 percent of the population aged 15 years and older can read and write. Education is free and compulsory for five years. Students in urban schools must spend at least seven weeks in rural labor. Cuba has five universities.
Labor force
Total...3,600,000
By occupation: government and services 30%, industry 22%, agriculture 20%, commerce 11%, construction 11%, and transportation and communications 6%.

COUNTRY FACTS
Political and legal A totalitarian state dominated by Fidel Castro, president of the Council of State and the Council of Ministers. There are 10 vice presidents on the Council of Ministers. The PCC is Cuba's only legal political party. Although the constitution calls for an independent judicial system, it is in reality subordinate to the National Assembly, and to the state.
Telephone All telephone service is free. About 95 percent of the phones are automatic. International service is slow. The country code is [53]. City code: Havana (7).
Transportation Only about half the roads are paved. Buses are available throughout the urban areas but are usually crowded and in some state of disrepair. Public transport has been further hindered by a lack of fuel. Bicycles have replaced automobiles. There are 11 major ports, Havana being the most important.
Environment Several agencies have been formed to protect the environment, including the National Parks Service and the National Commission of Environmental Education Program. Current issues include deforestation and the protection of wildlife.
Media The government controls the radio and television stations and the press. Cuba's two major newspapers have a combined circulation of 570,000.
Health Sanitation is generally good. Almost all inhabitants have access to safe water and adequate sanitation. Life expectancy is 76 years for both males and females.

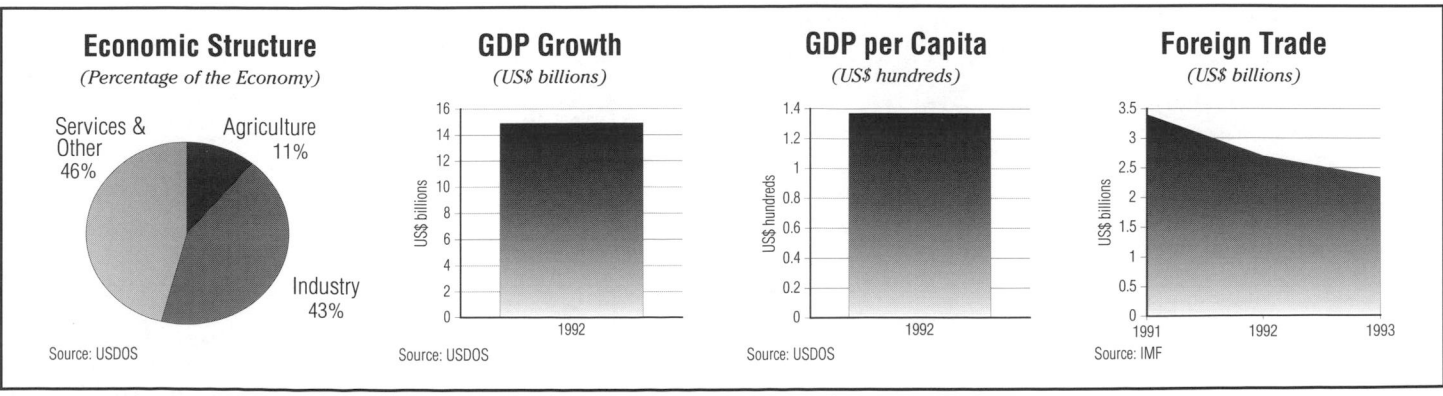

Economic Structure
(Percentage of the Economy)

Services & Other 46%
Agriculture 11%
Industry 43%

Source: USDOS

GDP Growth
(US$ billions)

1992

US$ billions

Source: USDOS

GDP per Capita
(US$ hundreds)

1992

US$ hundreds

Source: USDOS

Foreign Trade
(US$ billions)

1991 1992 1993

US$ billions

Source: IMF

Business Travel

LH 1906	MADRID	930	113-3
LH 1022	STUTTGART HBF.	935	-
AF 1701	LYON	940	683-6
AY 822	HELSINKI	940	113-3
AA 071	SFRANCISCO-DALLAS	945	731-7

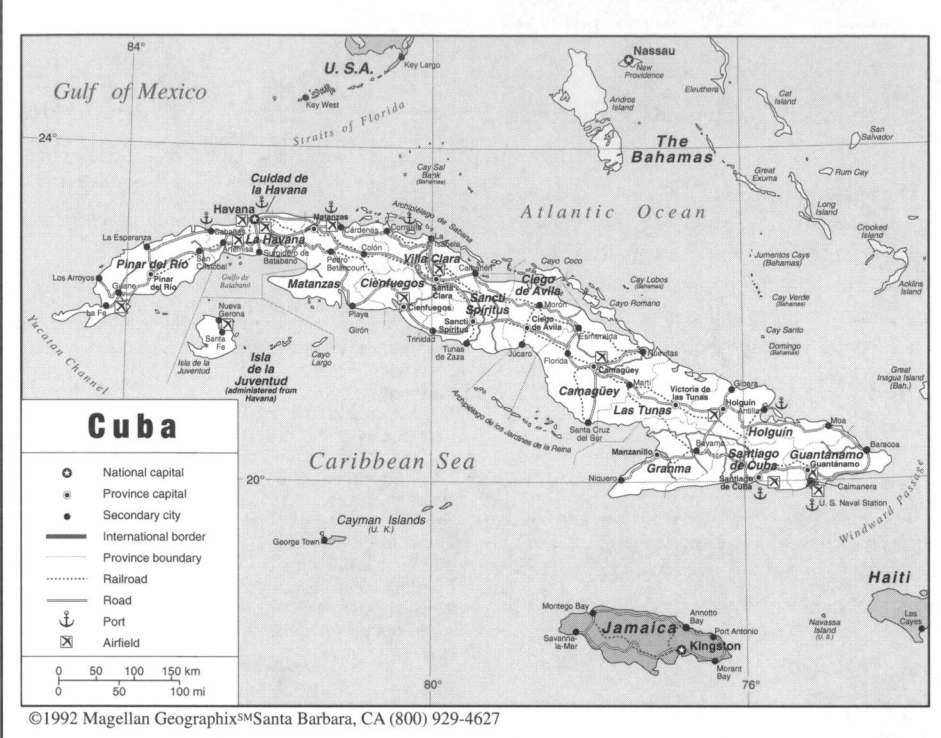

© 1992 Magellan Geographix℠Santa Barbara, CA (800) 929-4627

COMMUNICATIONS

Telephones Long distance calling along with international calling is available. New phone lines installed recently make calls more dependable and service much faster.
Fax Services are available through major hotels and businesses.
Post office There are post and telegraph services in the Hotel Habana Libre. Mail service is considered adequate.

BEST TRAVEL BOOKS

Cuba, Pearl of the Caribbean, Passport Books. Practical information, easy to read maps.
Cuba, Official Guide. Caribbean Guides. A. Gerald Gravette. Comprehensive coverage of the island from "tip to tail." Easy to read, very informative.

USEFUL TELEPHONE NUMBERS

If you are calling from outside Cuba, you will need to add the country code [53] and any other international dialing requirements from within your country.
- Victoria Hotel .... (7) 333510
- Melia Congiba Hotel .... (7) 333636
- Chamber of Commerce .... (7) 303356
- Telex .... (7) 511174
- Telex .... (7) 511175
- Publicitor .... (7) 329881
- Cuban Airlines .... (7) 74911
- Cuban Airlines .... (7) 74916
- Cuba TV & Radio .... (7) 225893
- Cuba TV & Radio .... (7) 321746
- Medical Center .... (7) 709566

Credit card information:
Lost or stolen credit cards (call collect to the US, regardless of which country the card was issued in).
- Amex ....[1] (919) 333-3211
- Diner's Club.................................[1] (303) 799-1504
- MasterCard ....[1] (314) 275-6690
- Visa ....[1] (410) 581-7931

Travelogue

WORKWEEK
Offices Monday-Friday 8:30 am to noon and 1:30 pm to 5:00 pm.
Banks Monday-Friday 8:30 am to noon and 1:30 pm to 5:00 pm.
Government Monday-Friday 8:30 am to 12:30 pm and 1:30 pm to 5:30 pm.
Retail Monday-Friday 12:30 pm to 6:30 pm, some Saturday mornings also.

HOLIDAYS
Holidays 1996
January 1 Liberation Day
January 2 Victory of Armed Forces
May 1 Labour Day
July 26 Revolution Day*
October 10 Beginning of War of Independence
*Dates vary year to year.

VISA AND PASSPORT
Visitors from many countries only need a tourist card to enter Cuba, as long as the visit is for tourism. Visitors traveling on a visa must go in person to Cubatur or the Immigration Office for registration immediately upon arrival during normal business hours. When you register you will be given an exit permit. Note: The US does not maintain diplomatic relations with Cuba. The US Treasury Department requires US visitors to Cuba acquire a license. Call (202) 622-2840 for more information.

DEPARTURE FORMALITIES
You must have your exit permit for departure. There is a departure tax collected at departure. Keep receipts whenever money is changed officially. This will allow pesos to be changed back into foreign currency.

IMMUNIZATION
Travelers coming from or going through infected areas must have certificates of vaccination against cholera and yellow fever.

TIPPING
Tipping customs have changed and are now recommended. Restaurants: 10 percent. Turistaxis are not generally tipped, but drivers appreciate tips anyway. Hotel staff accept leftover pesos, and they are much appreciated.

CRIME
Keep an eye on luggage, leave valuables in hotel safes. Pickpocketing and pursesnatching on buses is common. Street lighting is poor, and care is needed when walking in the city at night.

INFRASTRUCTURE
Buses are available, but reservations must be made in advance. Trains are recommended whenever possible. There is the NB, a major bus and train line, but special arrangements are necessary in advance for tourists. Taxis can be expensive. Car hire is often used to travel though Cuba. Frequencies of flights depend on time of year. Internal air services are advised to pre-book flights; demand can be heavy. No passenger ships call regularly.

NATIONAL TOURIST OFFICE
Cubatur
Calle 23, No 156
La Rampa Vedado
Havana
Tel: (7) 32-4521/3157

Foreign Trade

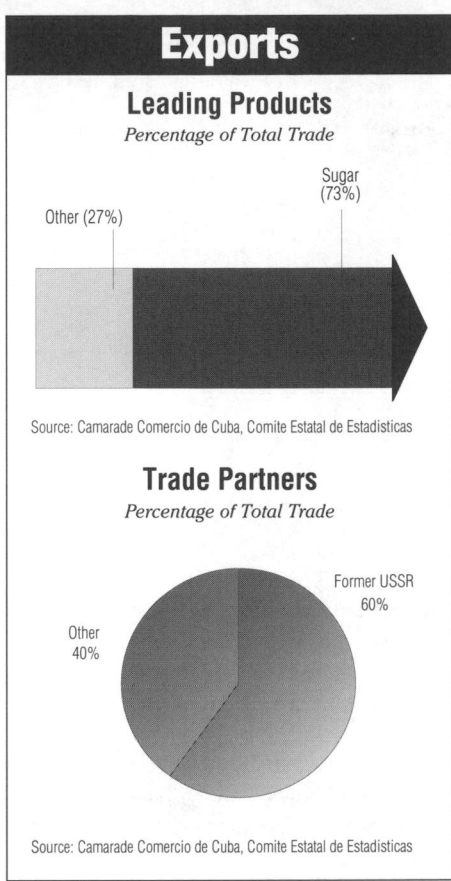

Imports

Leading Products
Percentage of Total Trade

Mineral Fuels (32%)

Machinery & Trans. Equip. (31%)

Other (37%)

Source: Camarade Comercio de Cuba, Comite Estatal de Estadisticas

Trade Partners
Percentage of Total Trade

Former USSR 68%

Other 32%

Source: Camarade Comercio de Cuba, Comite Estatal de Estadisticas

Exports

Leading Products
Percentage of Total Trade

Sugar (73%)

Other (27%)

Source: Camarade Comercio de Cuba, Comite Estatal de Estadisticas

Trade Partners
Percentage of Total Trade

Former USSR 60%

Other 40%

Source: Camarade Comercio de Cuba, Comite Estatal de Estadisticas

Opportunities

FOR IMPORTING TO CUBA
- capital and consumer goods; food
- industrial raw goods
- petroleum

FOR EXPORTING FROM CUBA
- citrus and seafood; sugar by-products
- nickel
- tobacco products

GROWTH SECTORS
- mining
- services
- tourism

Trade News

RULES AND REGULATIONS
- Cuba has liberalized its foreign trade regulations, and is actively seeking to increase trade with European nations—many of which are responding enthusiastically.
- Although the US maintains its 33-year old trade embargo against it, Cuba has trading relations with nearly 140 countries.
- Many Canadian companies are investing heavily in Cuba's tourism, mining, and oil exploration industries.
- Mexico has invested heavily in Cuba's telecommunications industry, as well as in Cuban electronics and chemicals.

Legal

Legal System
Based on Spanish and American law with large elements of Communist legal theory.

Intellectual Property Protection
Patents There are several laws protecting patents. Cuba belongs to the United Nations Paris Union.

Trademarks Several international treaties are signed for the protection of foreign trademarks.

Copyrights Cuba is not a member of any international copyright protection treaties though it recognizes foreign copyrights.

Trade Secrets Trade secret violations are difficult to prove under Cuban law, primarily because of the problems inherent in Cuba's judicial system, including lack of discovery methods.

Business Registration
All businesses must be registered, and include the business name, address, goods produced or distributed, and the date business is expected to start. Foreign businesses must present a document stating they are legally authorized to do business in another country.

Contracts and Dispute Resolution
Cuban companies prefer contracts that are to the letter, and always in writing. Most contracts are in Spanish. Disputes are handled by the courts, although most decisions are time consuming because of backlogs and administrative inefficiencies.

Labor
All Cuban workers belong to a trade union, under the central control of the Confederation of Cuban Workers, affiliated with the World Federation of Trade Unions. Independent unions and strikes are prohibited. There is a shortage of skilled workers, and most positions requiring any technical skill are filled with foreign workers. The government sets a minimum wage, but it isn't enough to support a family.

Legal Matters

LEGAL BRIEFS
- **The National Assembly** All members of the court are elected by the National Assembly, as are the attorney general and deputy attorneys general.
- **Courts of appeal** There are seven regional courts of appeal.
- **Suffrage** All citizens over the age of 16 are able to vote, except for those who have applied for permanent emigration.
- **Information** The government controls all electronic and print media.
- **Freedoms** Cuban residents are not entitled to equal protection under the law; they do not have the right to freely choose government representatives; they do not have freedom of expression; and they do not have the freedom to travel to and from Cuba without restriction.
- **Legal proceedings** The state enjoys many rights and privileges, and defense attorneys face severe disadvantages under the Cuban judicial system.

Exchange Rate

Cuban Peso (C$) to US Dollar ($)

Cuban Peso (C$)

1
0.9
0.8
0.7
0.6
0.5
0.4
0.3
0.2
0.1
0

1992   1993   1994

Source: IMF

Currency Exchange

as of January 5, 1996

C$1 =   US$1

Currency

The currency in use is the Cuban peso (C$ or $MN), which is divided into 100 centavos.

Foreign Exchange

The government sets foreign exchange values, although the Cuban peso is non-convertible. Foreign exchange is strictly limited and there is no market.

Capital Transfers

Curious juxtapositions of socialism and capitalism are becoming less of an anomaly as foreign capital pours into Cuba. Most of the capital has flowed into tourism, mining, agriculture, construction, and manufacturing. Cuba has signed investment-guarantee agreements with the UK, Colombia, Germany, Italy, Russia, and Spain. Although the accords are only as good as Cuba's word of honor, they betoken a profound change in the country's attitude toward foreign investment.

The US embargo robs Cuba of a major market and investment capital; Cuba was once second only to Venezuela in US overseas investment in Latin America. Non-convertible currency is an increasing liability as Russia demands payment for oil in dollars, and Cuba loses the ex-Communist states as trading partners.

Investment Incentives

Cuba is drafting legislation that would ease rules for foreign investors and provide more guarantees against nationalization of property. The government is anxious to draw more foreign investment and is realizing that to do so it must offer some degree of liberalization previously unavailable. It seems prepared to do so. It is not, however, yet in a position to offer financial incentives or to give up its pervasive control over the economy. It has recently begun to offer foreigners the possibility of buying property, rather than renting from the state, though there are still many restrictions and lots of red tape to untangle before any deals are concluded.

Investment Restrictions

Until a few years ago, foreign investment was accepted only if delivered to the government to be used as it saw fit. The enterprises in which the government invested were so-called "national enterprises." However, in recent years, the Cuban government has seen the necessity of opening its declining economy to foreign investment, either via joint ventures or other forms of association. Still, the government maintains rigid control and each investment proposal is reviewed individually on its merits, and approved or denied based on the benefits it can provide to Cuba.

Money Matters

BITS AND PIECES

- **Exchange** Foreign visitors should be careful to retain the receipt every time money is changed officially; this will enable Cuban pesos remaining at the end of a visit to be changed back into foreign currency (but only to a maximum of US$10 equivalent).

- **Foreign currencies** Traveler's checks expressed in US or Canadian dollars or sterling are valid in Cuba, although traveler's checks issued on US bank paper are generally not accepted so it is best to take an international brand.

- **Dinero Cubatur** Also known as Monopoly money or funny money, this will often be given as change when paying a hotel or restaurant bill. Dinero Cubatur can be used at any dollar store, including the Cubatur tiendas. But do not get left with Dinero Cubatur as it cannot be changed into dollars late at night or when the airport bank is closed.

- **Black market** Although there are heavy penalties for exchanging money on the black market, or by other illegal means, foreigners will be constantly approached to do so.

- **Remittances from abroad** The Cuban government has recently legalized the use of foreign currency by Cuban citizens in an attempt to increase remittances of foreign exchange from abroad.

- **Tourism** A large proportion of foreign investment remains in the tourism industry—one of the few sectors which can turn a profit. Also rules and regulations are somewhat more relaxed than in other sectors, as the government has long-term experience with foreign investment in this area.

- **Joint ventures** Since 1992 Cuba has attempted to partially lift its regulations limiting foreign ownership of an enterprise to 49 percent. While some progress has been made, the government has been extremely reluctant to actually let go of any control in most enterprises.

- **US money** Bring US cash with you. It is widely accepted and you may even get a better deal when paying in US cash. Make sure you have small bills, since any change you receive in return will be in Cuban pesos.

BANKS

Comite Estatal del Finanzas
Obispo esq. a Cuba
Havana
Tel: (7) 62-5971

Banco Nacional de Cuba
Cuba y Amargura
No. 402 Esz. Lamparilla
Apartado 736
Havana
Tel: 62-8001
Telex: 511822

Banco Financiero Internacional, SA
Calle Linea, No 1
Vedado
Havana
Tel: (7) 33-3423
Fax: (7) 33-3006
Telex: 512405

Banco Popular del Ahorro
Calle 16, No 306
entre 5a y 3a Avda Playa
Havana
Tel: (7) 22-8240
Telex: 511608

Overview

The Cuban government exercises almost total control over the entire economy, including production, marketing and distribution channels, product specifications and price controls. Cuba does not, therefore, represent a promising market for any but the most optimistic and long-viewed of foreign sellers. Cubans do not generally possess the cash or capital necessary to support a large marketing effort, although opportunities do exist in the tourism industry, which draws large numbers of European and Latin American tourists.

Distribution

Due to Cuba's small size and highly centralized economy, distribution channels are limited. Most foreign goods are purchased by wholesalers or retailers who operate non-competitive enterprises serving the entire country.

Agents and Distributors

As all commercial activities are the responsibility of, and controlled by, the government, agencies and distributorships are tightly controlled, and very limited in both nature and scope.

Advertising and Selling Techniques

Cubans are well educated, and are avid readers of the many Spanish and English language newspapers and periodicals published on the island. Although the government controls the content, advertisements are common, and feature many foreign goods. Radio and television advertising are also common, although, again, the content is controlled by the government. Outside posters and billboards can be found throughout the island. However, bear in mind that Cuban consumers have very little disposable income to spend on foreign goods; therefore, expensive selling techniques will probably not yield profitable results.

Marketing in Cuba

MARKETING TIPS

- **Multinational retailers** Cuba has extended invitations to international retailers to open operations in the country. Some have responded favorably, though most Cuban consumers cannot yet afford brand name items.
- **US embargo** The US embargo has prohibited US companies from selling to Cuba, thereby creating opportunities for sellers from other countries who might otherwise be eclipsed by US businesses.
- **Mexico/Canada** Several sellers from Mexico and Canada continue to ignore US calls for a trade embargo of Cuba and are upping their investment in the island nation.
- **TV Center** A Spanish business group plans to set up a television broadcast center in Cuba to send news, sports and entertainment programs by satellite to Latin America.
- **Media** Radio, television, and press agencies are all owned and controlled by the government. There are several major newspapers and magazines, in both English and Spanish, most of which accept advertising.
- **Tourism** Cuba attracts tourists from South America and Europe, who provide ready and affluent markets for high-priced foreign goods otherwise unavailable on the island.

Greetings and Courtesies

Men usually shake hands with women and each other, although women seldom shake hands with other women. Titles are commonly used, especially "Doctor" and "Professor." Business cards printed in both Spanish and English are the norm, although most business-people do speak English. Cubans love to entertain, and will not hesitate to invite visiting business associates to a meal at their home or in a restaurant.

Business Ethic and Framework

Cubans follow the Latin American tradition of approaching business in a very casual way. Siestas are common in the afternoon, and many businesses close for at least an hour and a half during lunchtime. Personal relationships are not as important in Cuba as they are in other Latin American countries; while people prefer to do business with those they know, they are more concerned with making a good deal. Cuban businesspeople are savvy and adept at making do (and turning a profit) with few resources.

Meetings and Decision Making

Foreign businesspeople are expected to be on time, but Cubans can be more relaxed about scheduling. It is best to have a prior appointment, but many Cuban businesspeople will accept a cold call. Authority is narrowly concentrated and actual decisions are almost always made at a high level—more often than not at a government agency. However, cultivate your Cuban business relationships; they will be invaluable in cutting through the bureaucracy and getting a deal accomplished.

Women

Women are well-educated and respected in the business environment, although most managerial positions are still held by men. Foreign businesswomen should experience few problems in business, generally experiencing greater acceptance than do local women. Women may dress as they please; trousers are acceptable, though shorts are not.

Cultural Cautions

DO'S

- Learn something about Cuba's history, culture, and the coup which brought Castro into power. These are favorite topics of conversation (Remember to use discretion and refrain from making judgments about Castro and his policies.)
- Always use somebody's professional title and their surname when addressing them.
- Be prepared to "sell" your personal belongings or items of clothing when you visit Cuba.

DON'TS

- Do not discuss wealth or possessions with Cubans; you may be considered boastful by emphasizing material achievements which may well be unattainable even to relatively prosperous Cubans.
- If the person you are meeting is late, do not complain.
- Do not complain if goods or services are not readily available; shortages are a way of life here and Cubans needn't be reminded of it.

OBSERVATIONS

- Social position and professional status are important. Dress well, and stay at the best hotel you can afford.
- Tropical weight (the very lightest due to the extreme heat) suits or sports coats and trousers are expected of men for business dealings.
- Cuba is a leisurely society, and Cubans are accustomed to waiting for things. Deadlines are not extremely important.

NEGOTIATIONS

- While posturing and haggling are practiced, they do not play a large role in Cuban negotiations. The emphasis is on reaching agreement and concluding a deal.

GOVERNMENT AGENCIES

Ministry of Agriculture
Avenida de Independencia
Havana
Tel: (7) 70-1434
Telex: 511966

Ministry of Basic Industries
Avenida Salvador Allende No. 666
Havana
Tel: (7) 70-7711
Telex: 511183

Ministry of Communications
Plaza de la Revolución
Havana
Tel: (7) 70-5581
Telex: 51945, 51975, 511657

Ministry of Construction Materials Industry
Calle o Esq. 17, Vedado
Havana
Tel: (7) 32-2541
Telex: 511517

Ministry of Culture
Calle 2 No. 258, entre 11 & 13
Vedado
Havana
Tel: (7) 3-9945
Telex: 511400

Ministry of Domestic Trade
Habana No. 258 el Empedrado
San J. de Dios
Havana
Telex: 511171, 511480

Ministry of Education
Obispo No. 160
Havana
Tel: (7) 61-488
Telex: 511188, 511455

Ministry of the Fishing Industry
Barlovento, Santa Fe
Havana
Tel: (7) 22-7474
Telex: 511189, 511206, 511434, 511444

Ministry of the Food Industry
Calle 41 No. 445 Playa
Havana
Tel: (7) 2-6801
Telex: 511163 ind alimenticia

Ministry of Foreign Trade
No. 16, Vedado
Havana
Tel: (7) 70-9341
Fax: (7) 7-6234

Ministry for Public Health
Calle 23, No. 201
Vedado
Havana
Tel: (7) 32-2561
Telex: 511149

Ministry for Transportation
Avenida Independencia y Tulipán Sotanto
Havana
Tel: (7) 81-2076
Telex: 511135, 511181

State Committee for Material and Technical Supply
44 Monserate No. 261
Mariano
Havana
Tel: (7) 62-9390
Telex: 511757

State Committee for Statistics
Calle 5TA y Paseo
Vedado
Havana
Tel: (7) 31-5171
Telex: 511449, 511257, 511365

State Committee for Prices
Amistad No. 552
Havana
Tel: (7) 62-0888

State Committee for Standardization
Egido No. 610 entre Gloria y Apodaca
Havana
Tel: (7) 61-2068
Fax: (7) 62-7657

BUSINESS AND TRADE ORGANIZATIONS

Chamber of Commerce of the Republic of Cuba
Calle 21 No. 661
Apartado 370, Vedado
Havana
Tel: (7) 30-3356
Telex 511752 camar cu

ALIMPORT-Empresa Cubana Importadora de Alimentos
Import of Foodstuffs
Infata No. 16, 3º
Apartado 7006
Havana
Tel: (7) 70-2437
Fax: (7) 7 33-300679-1274

CONSUMIMPORT-Empresa Cubana Importada de Articulos de Consumo General
Import of General Consumer Goods
Calle 23 No. 55
Apartado 6427, Vedado
Havana
Tel: (7) 70-0302
Telex: 512355

CUBAEXPORT-Empresa Cubana Exportada de Alimentos y Productos Varios
Export of Foodstuffs and Various Products
Calle 23 No. 55
Apartado 6719, Vedado
Havana
Tel: (7) 79-1669
Tel: 511178 cuba export hab

CUBANIQUEL-Empresa Cubana Exportadora de Minerales y Metales
Export of Minerals and Metals
Calle 23 No. 55
Apartado 6128
Havana
Tel: (7) 7-8460
Telex: 511178

CUBATEX-Empresa Cubana Importadora de Fibras, Tejidos, Cueros y sus Productos
Import of Fibers, Fabrics, and Leathers
Calle 23 No. 55
Apartado 7115, Vedado
Havana
Tel: (7) 70-3269
Telex: 512361

Empresa Comercial de Industrias de Materiales, Construcción y Turismo
Import and Export of Construction Materials and Tourism
Calle 1aC entre 152 y 154
Miramar
Havana
Tel: (7) 21-9783
Telex: 511926

Ediciones Cubanas-Empresa de Comercio Exterior de Publicaciones
Import and Export of Books, Cultural and Technical Periodicals
Obispo 527
Apartado 605
Havana
Tel: (7) 6-9174
Telex: 511424

EGREM-Empresada de Grabaciones y Ediciones Musicales
Musical Recording and Publishing Enterprise
Campanario No. 315, entre San Miguel y Neptuno
Apartado 2217
Havana
Tel: (7) 62-2762
Telex: 512171

REMEMBER
- When you telephone (or fax) to Cuba from another country you must always include the country code [53] before the numbers given.
- When you send mail to Cuba, be sure to write CUBA in capital letters on its own line below the addresses given.

MAPRINTER-Empresa Cubana Importadora de Materias Primas y Productos Intermedios
Import of Raw Materials and Intermediate Products
Infanta 16, Apartado 2110
Miramar
Havana
Tel: (7) 7-4981

NOIMPORT-Empresa Cubana Importadora e Exportadora de Productos Técnicos
Import and Export of Technical Products
Infanta No. 16
Apartado 7024
Havana
Tel: (7) 22-3681
Telex: 511572

BANKS

Comite Estatal del Finanzas
Obispo esq. a Cuba
Havana
Tel: (7) 62-5971

Banco Nacional de Cuba
Cuba y Amargura No. 402 Esz. Lamparilla
Apartado 736
Havana
Tel: (7) 62-8001
Telex: 511822

Banco Financiero Internacional, SA
Calle Linea, No 1
Vedado
Havana
Tel: (7) 33-3423
Fax: (7) 33-3006
Telex: 512405

Banco Popular del Ahorro
Calle 16, No 306
entre 5a y 3a Avda Playa
Havana
Tel: (7) 22-8240
Telex: 511608

INTERNET ADDRESSES

Usenet group(s):
soc.culture.cuba

CUBA!
http://ix.urz.uni-heidelberg.de/~pklee/Cuba/

Republic of Cuba W.W.W.
http://www.unipr.it/~davide/cuba/home.html

Latin America - Cuba
http://lanic.utexas.edu/la/ca/cuba/

Cyprus
Republic of Cyprus

At a Glance

THE COUNTRY

Location Located in the extreme northeast corner of the Mediterranean, 71 kilometers south of Turkey and 105 kilometers west of Syria.

Terrain Most of the island is covered in two mountain ranges. There are a few lakes and rivers, and a small cultivable area.

Climate For the most part dry and sunny, although there are occasional rainy periods in the hills.

THE PEOPLE

Population 725,000
Ethnic composition
Greek 80%
Turkish Cypriots.. 18.6%
The rest of the population is predominantly Lebanese Maronites, Armenians, and British.
Religious composition
Greek Orthodox 76.2%
Muslim 18.7%
Various Christian denominations 2.7%
Other.. 2.4%
Languages spoken Greek and Turkish are the official languages; Greek in the north and Turkish in the south. English is also used extensively.
Education and literacy Adult literacy is 92.4%. Education is compulsory for nine years: three years of primary education and six years of secondary. The Greek and Turkish communities are responsible for their own educational systems. There is no college in the Turkish area, and many students study abroad. The Greeks planned to open a university for both Greeks and Turks, but the Turks refused to participate.
Labor force
Total...279,000

COUNTRY FACTS

Political and legal The Constitution calls for a representation in the government from both the Greek and Turkish populations. The legal system derives from the British tradition, including the right to appeal and the presumption of innocence. The judiciary is independent from any political or military control.
Telephone The Cyprus Telecommunications Authority (CTA) operates the internal communications system for the entire country. International service is usually not a major problem. There are over 300,000 telephones. International country code: [357]. City codes: Nicosia (2), Larnaca (4).
Transportation Almost all towns are linked by a road, although some in the more rural areas are not in good condition. There are no inland waterways, but ports Limassol and Larnaca are considered excellent deepwater harbors. There are two international airports.
Environment The government can enact "reservation orders" to protect specific environmental areas. All citizens have access to clean water. Currently, the primary issue is the danger to wildlife due to urban expansion.
Media The Cyprus Broadcasting Corp. maintains regular service. Commercial and program sponsorship are allowed. There are 16 daily newspapers and eight weeklies, published in English, Greek, or Turkish.
Health There is a low incidence of infectious diseases. There are both public and private medical facilities, and about 50 rural health centers.

Economy

Overview

The Cypriot economy has made a substantial recovery following the hostilities that split the island in 1974. Cyprus benefited from the boom in the Middle East during the 1970s, and it grew into a substitute base for firms leaving Lebanon. Cyprus and the EU have recently agreed to phase out tariffs on most trade between them. There remains a pronounced disparity between the Greek and Turkish Cypriot economies, however, with the Greek Cypriot economy roughly three times the Turkish Cypriot economy on a per capita basis. Only Turkey recognizes Turkish Cyprus, which lacks investment capital and is short on skilled labor and experienced management. Turkey has been unable to adequately fund investment or even subsidize operations, and development has lagged in the Turkish sector.

Trade

Major exports include apparel and footwear—accounting for about 33 percent of all exports—potatoes, citrus fruit, tobacco products, pharmaceuticals, and cement. Imports include vehicles, textiles, mineral products, metal products, aerospace equipment, and chemicals. Cyprus' main trading partners include the UK, France, Japan, Germany, Italy, Turkey, and Greece. Other significant trade is carried on with various Middle Eastern nations.

Sectors

Agriculture The government-controlled Greek sector derives only about seven percent of GDP from agriculture, although the sector employs about 12 percent of the work force (it provides employment for nearly 33 percent of the work force in the Turkish Cypriot zone). Citrus fruit, potatoes, cereals, and grapes are the main crops, with fishing being locally significant.

Industry Industry provides somewhat less than 30 percent of both GDP and employment in the Greek Cypriot section (it provides much less in the Turkish zone). Food processing, apparel, pharmaceuticals, and cement are the main industrial activities. Mining is a small but significant activity.

Services Services contribute about 63 percent of GDP and about 60 percent of employment in the Greek sector. Tourism is a particularly important source of revenue in the Turkish sector, while financial services have become a mainstay in the Greek sector, where several offshore banking units have been set up to replace those in Lebanon. Shipping—involving Cypriot flag registry and Mediterranean transshipment—is also an extremely important and growing activity in the Greek sector.

Trends

Over the short term, the already considerable gap between the economies of the two unreconciled sectors of this country will continue to grow. To a large extent, the development of the Turkish sector will depend on the level of Turkish aid. The illicit drug traffic—which uses Cyprus primarily as a transit point—has been ruthlessly pursued by international law enforcement and shows signs of shifting to other routes. As Cyprus enters the EU, ready access to that large and growing market should contribute to further economic prosperity. Long-term, the stability and development of Cyprus will depend on accomodation being reached between the so-far implacable Greek and Turkish interests, although such accomodation could be effected if greater economic parity and prosperity were to come to all parties.

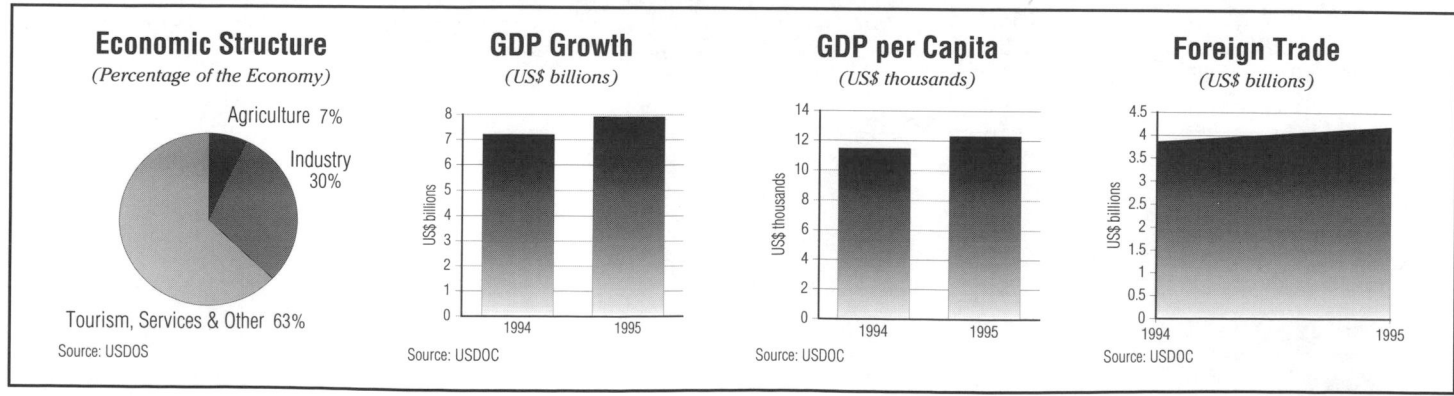

Economic Structure (Percentage of the Economy)
Agriculture 7%
Industry 30%
Tourism, Services & Other 63%
Source: USDOS

GDP Growth (US$ billions)
1994 1995
Source: USDOC

GDP per Capita (US$ thousands)
1994 1995
Source: USDOC

Foreign Trade (US$ billions)
1994 1995
Source: USDOC

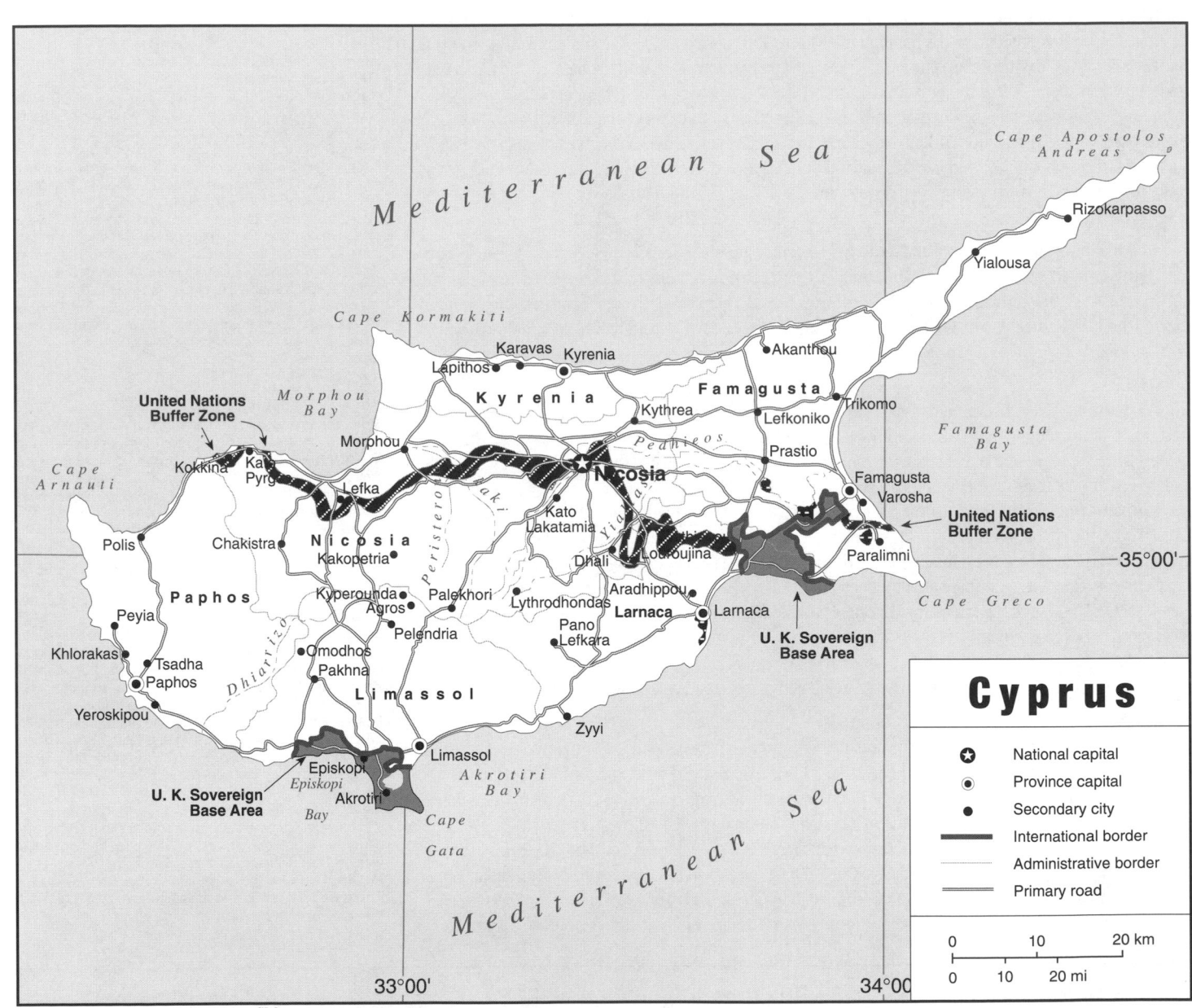

Mediterranean Sea

Cape Apostolos Andreas

Rizokarpasso

Yialousa

Cape Kormakiti

Karavas   Kyrenia

Lapithos

Kyrenia   Akanthou

Morphou Bay

United Nations Buffer Zone

Famagusta

Kythrea   Lefkoniko   Trikomo

Morphou   Prastio

Famagusta Bay

Kokkina   Kato   *Pedhieos*

Pyrgos   Lefka   ☆ **Nicosia**   Famagusta

Varosha

United Nations Buffer Zone

Chakistra   **Nicosia**   Kato   *Peristero*   Lakatamia

Yialias   Louroujina   Paralimni

Polis   Kakopetria   Dhali   35°00'

Paphos   *Dhiarrizo*   Kyperounda   Palekhori   Aradhippou   *Cape Greco*

Peyia   Agros   Lythrodhondas   **Larnaca**

Pelendria   Pano   Larnaca

Khlorakas   Omodhos   Lefkara   **U. K. Sovereign Base Area**

Tsadha   Pakhna

Paphos   **Limassol**

Yeroskipou   Zyyi

Episkopi   Limassol

U. K. Sovereign Base Area   *Episkopi Bay*   *Akrotiri Bay*

Akrotiri   *Cape Gata*

Mediterranean Sea

Mediterranean Sea

Cyprus

- ☆ National capital
- ◉ Province capital
- ● Secondary city
- ▬ International border
- ⋯ Administrative border
- ─ Primary road

| 0 | 10 | 20 km |
| 0 | 10 | 20 mi |

33°00'   34°00'

©1992 Magellan Geographix℠Santa Barbara, CA

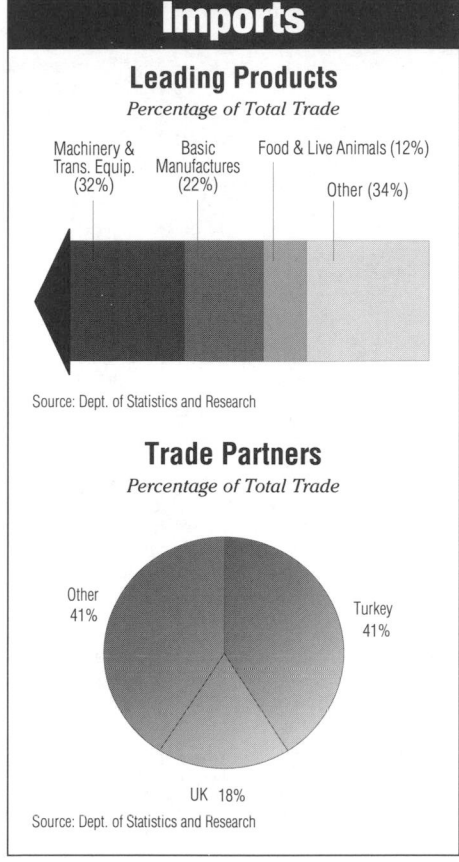

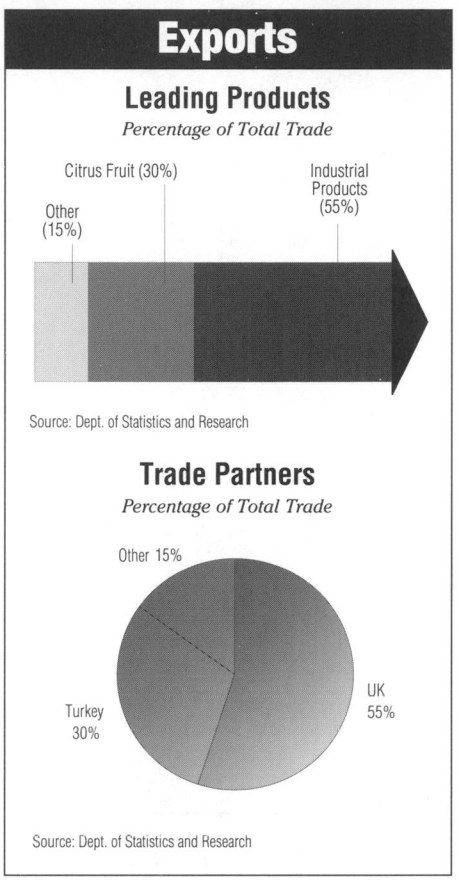

Opportunities

FOR EXPORTING TO CYPRUS
- electrical supply equipment
- medical equipment
- computers, peripherals, and software
- telecommunications equipment
- pumps, valves, and compressors
- security equipment
- safety equipment
- pollution control equipment

FOR IMPORTING FROM CYPRUS
- clothing
- textiles
- footwear
- canvas
- dairy products
- processed food

GROWTH SECTORS
- shipping
- tourism
- golf
- theme parks
- pleasure marinas

GOVERNMENT PROCUREMENT
- airport ground support equipment
- aircraft
- pollution control equipment

Trade News

RULES AND REGULATIONS

- **Import licenses** Although import licenses have traditionally been required for many goods, as Cyprus starts to implement the Uruguay Round GATT agreement, the government has removed most of these.
- **License required** An import license is required for certain commodities such as fresh fruits, fresh vegetables, fresh meat, and other goods produced or manufactured locally.
- **EU imports** Import tariffs on products imported from the EU are lower than on products imported from non-EU countries.
- **Customs duties** Customs duties are regulated by a tariff system based on the harmonized commodity description and coding system. Luxury items carry the highest duties.
- **Customs tariff** The majority of rates of duty are levied ad valorem and may reach up to 180 percent. Essential food items, mineral products, fertilizers, plants, machinery, and computers are either duty-free or exempt from customs duties unless they are available in Cyprus.
- **Government policy** The government's policy is to protect local industries that have prospects of developing into viable concerns but currently require a period of protection before they can compete with foreign producers. The customs tariff is revised periodically with a view to affording such protection to local industries.
- **VAT** In addition to import tariffs, there is an eight percent value-added tax levied on all goods.
- **Free trade zones** There are free trade zones at the ports of Larnaca and Limassol, as well as bonded warehouses where goods are kept for onward transhipment. Foreign participation in the free trade zones is usually granted.
- **Free trade zone taxes** Foreign shareholders of companies in the free zone will pay tax at either the Cypriot rate applicable to the company's profit or at the Cypriot tax rate applicable to that shareholder's dividend, whichever is lower.
- **Special exports** Exports of potatoes and carrots are carried out by the respective marketing boards, and exports of wheat, barley, and maize are carried out by the Cyprus Grain Commission.
- **Ports** The two main ports, Limassol and Larnaca, are administered by the Cyprus Ports Authority. They offer containerized and break-bulk facilities. Turn-around time averages one day for container vessels and two to three days for conventional ships. In addition, there are a number of specialized oil terminals and a deep-water industrial port at Vasilikos, half-way between Larnaca and Limassol.
- **Import payments** Payment for imports is usually made on a collection basis, although documentary credits are also used. Payments for imports that are free from licensing requirements must be effected within 200 days of the date of shipment. Advance payments require the prior approval of the exchange control section of the Central Bank.
- **Classification** Importers or their agents are required to classify goods in accordance with the tariff headings and sub-headings; for this purpose it is essential that in the case of piece goods, for example, the invoice should clearly indicate the percentage content of each material used in the manufacture.

GOVERNMENT AGENCIES

Ministry of Commerce and Industry
6 A. Araouzos Str.
Nicosia
Tel: (2) 403441
Fax: (2) 366120
Telex: 2283

Business Travel

LH 1906	MADRID	935	113-3
LH 1022	STUTTGART HBF.	935	-
AF 1701	LYON	940	683-6
AY 822	HELSINKI	940	113-3
AA 071	SFRANCISCO-DALLAS	945	731-7

Air Travel Times

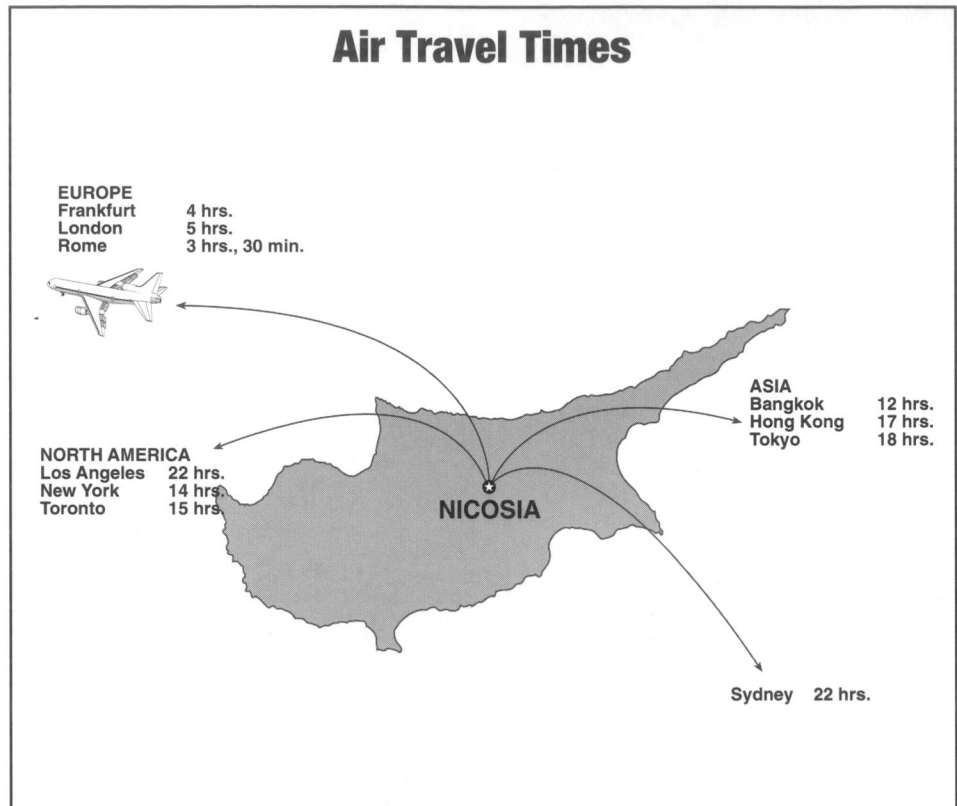

EUROPE
Frankfurt   4 hrs.
London   5 hrs.
Rome   3 hrs., 30 min.

NORTH AMERICA
Los Angeles   22 hrs.
New York   14 hrs.
Toronto   15 hrs.

NICOSIA

ASIA
Bangkok   12 hrs.
Hong Kong   17 hrs.
Tokyo   18 hrs.

Sydney   22 hrs.

COMMUNICATIONS

Telephones Cyprus offers a sophisticated, fully automated telephone system. International direct dial is available from private telephones and public pay phones. International direct dialing connects the island with 120 countries, and all other countries can be reached via the operator on a 24-hour basis. Fully automatic telex facilities are available, with automatic access to 148 countries. No public telex booths exist in Cyprus, but most hotels and all banks will permit their facilities to be used by their guests or clients.

Fax Under the public switched telephone network, facsimile terminals of groups I, II, and III can be connected to any telephone line. International communication is possible with any correspondents equipped with a facsimile terminal of the same group. Public facsimile booths are generally unavailable.

Post office There are post offices in urban and rural areas. The use of post office boxes is widespread, although there are daily deliveries of mail to households. Airmail letters take an average of two to four days to reach continental Europe. An international courier service is also available. In addition, the Department of Postal Services operates the international express mail services and the electronic mail service.

Radio/TV There are two local radio stations in Cyprus, and it is estimated that there are about 175,000 radio sets in use on the island. Most households have at least one television set, and programming is diverse, including educational TV.

BEST TRAVEL BOOKS

Cyprus Travellers Handbook. Available from Cypriot embassies and consulates and on the Internet at http://exp3.wam.umd.edu/%7ECyprus/handbook/

USEFUL TELEPHONE NUMBERS

If you are calling from outside Cyprus, you will need to add the country code [357] and any other international dialing requirements from within your country.

- American Express office .... (2) 443777
- Cyprus Automobile Association .... (2) 313233
- Cyprus Hotel Association .... (4) 643186
- Cyprus Airways .... (2) 443054
- KLM .... (2) 451777
- Olympic Airways .... (2) 462101
- Lufthansa .... (2) 451777
- Ambulance/Fire/Police 99
- DHL .... (2) 490450, 490386
- TNT Express .... (2) 336940, 336941

Credit Card Information
Lost or stolen credit cards (call collect to the US, regardless of which country the card was issued in).

- Amex ....[1] (919) 333-3211
- Diner's Club...............................[1] (303) 799-1504
- MasterCard ....[1] (314) 275-6690
- Visa ....[1] (410) 581-7931

Travelogue

WORKWEEK

Offices Monday-Friday, 8:00 am to 4:00 pm.
Banks Monday-Friday, 8:15 am to 12:30 pm. Hours vary extensively.
Government Monday-Friday, 8:00 am to 4:00 pm.
Retail Monday-Friday, 8:00 am to 1:00 pm and 4:00 pm to 7:00 pm.
Note: from May to October, expect long lunch breaks.

HOLIDAYS

Holiday 1996
January 1 New Year's Day
January 6 Epiphany
April 12-15 Greek Easter*
May 1 May Day
June 3 Pentecost
August 15 Assumption
October 1 Cyprus Independence
October 28 Greek National Day
December 25 & 26 Christmas
*Dates may vary.

VISA AND PASSPORT

There are no visa requirements in Cyprus for visitors from Europe, the US, Canada, Australia, Japan, and some other countries. The ports of Erdjan, Lefkoniko, Famagusta, Kyrenia, and Karavostassi in the Turkish-controlled area have been declared closed ports by the Cyprus government and travelers arriving at them are liable to a fine and deportation on crossing to the Cyprus government-controlled area. Travelers arriving at ports controlled by the Cyprus government (Larnaca or Paphos airports, or Limassol or Larnaca ports) can only enter the Turkish-Cypriot sector through the Ledra Palace checkpoint in Nicosia. However, attitudes are subject to change upon short notice depending on the political environment.

DEPARTURE FORMALITIES

It is prohibited to remove extinct antiques and artifacts from Cyprus. There is a departure tax of US$8.

IMMUNIZATION

No immunizations are necessary for visitors from most countries. However, passengers from areas in which smallpox, cholera, or yellow fever is endemic (including passengers who have merely passed through such areas in transit) must present International Certificates of Vaccination against these diseases. Although it is not compulsory, travelers are advised to be vaccinated against typhoid.

TIPPING

A 10 percent tip is standard in Cyprus for good service. 10 percent is generally added automatically to restaurant bills, but an additional tip (small change) is appreciated. An added eight percent VAT is added to all bills.

CRIME

Cyprus suffers from a fair amount of petty crime. As such, exercise common sense regarding your activities and your possessions. Do not wear excessive jewelry, don't leave your valuables unattended in your hotel room or elsewhere, and do not carry large amounts of cash. Although travel is relatively safe, do not venture out alone late at night to sparsely populated areas.

INFRASTRUCTURE

Taxis and buses are the only forms of local public transportation. In Nicosia, good taxi service is always available at moderate prices. Roadways are well-developed and adequately maintained, although travel between the two areas can be difficult.

NATIONAL TOURIST OFFICE

National Tourist Office
Leoforos Lemesou 19
Nicosia 1390
Tel: (2) 337715

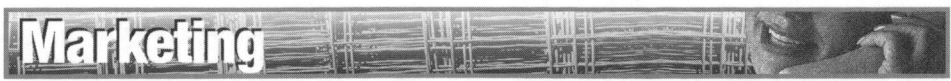

Marketing

Overview

Prosperous Greek Cypriots are concentrated in the urban south, while largely poor and rural Turks are found in the north. Indeed, the Turkish sector port of Famagusta is subject to Greek blockade which, although easy to circumvent, makes commerce more difficult. Most businesses find dealing in the south to be both simpler and more profitable. The government's drive to develop industry and services—especially as an alternative to Lebanon in serving the Middle East—generate many needs that must be filled through imports. Indeed, virtually all consumer needs are filled with foreign products.

Distribution and Agents

There are no restrictions on representation agreements; however, local custom has generally been to grant exclusive distribution rights for an indefinite period, and agents may be owed compensation if the firm chooses to change agents after an agreement has been in place. Franchising is a recent innovation, but shows potential for substantial development. Distributorships or joint ventures are generally viewed as preferable because non-Cypriot citizens and companies may not acquire property here other than by inheritance—even then they may not hold more than a single parcel—and an outside entity interested in establishing a substantial presence would be at a disadvantage if it were to attempt to operate on its own as an independent unit. Generally, only government agencies purchase direct; these purchases are carried out by public tender, some of which are open to foreign bidding.

Advertising

Television—with 29 operating stations based in Nicosia—is the most popular medium. Broadcasts are in Greek, Turkish, and English. Several weekly and daily newspapers are published in those same languages. There is little in the way of either a general interest or specialized trade press or magazine industry. Radio carries ads over 10 AM and 14 FM stations. Cinemas also offer advertising trailers. Signage is used thoughout the country. Trade fairs are limited. There is a specialized market research organization, and local advertising agencies will also handle market research studies. Many of these will also plan and execute advertising campaigns.

Business Culture

Greetings and Courtesies

Cypriots have a tradition of hospitality and courtesy. Business visitors will invariably be offered Turkish coffee or a cold drink. It is impolite to refuse, especially at the first meeting. The custom of shaking hands is widespread; shake everybody's who is present, both on greeting and leaving. The large Muslim population does not eat pork or pork products, or drink alcohol. Food and drink should always be passed to a Muslim with the right hand. Titles are important; if you know somebody has one, use it along with the surname. Both Turkish and Greek Cypriots tend to be generous and hospitable, even toward strangers.

Business Ethic and Framework

There are two very distinct economies in Cyprus, and each operates under the customary and ethical frameworks of their heritage. Greek businesspeople value personal contact, individual responsibility, and collective effort. There is a great deal of importance placed on educational background and financial standing in business. The Turkish business community incorporates long hours with strong family ties; the company is often treated as extended family.

Decision Making

Both Greek and Turkish Cypriots love to haggle before a deal is concluded, and they will rarely make a decision before both terms and price have been endlessly negotiated. Meetings are flexible, and are subject to interruption, delay, and unexpected guests (who sometimes become participants in the negotiations). Most deals are concluded in person, rather than by letter, phone, or fax.

Women

While Greek women are somewhat more outspoken and are found more frequently in the business world than Turkish women, both are still fairly restricted. Few women hold management positions, and men dominate both business and the government. Still, businessmen are becoming more receptive to professional women.

Marketing in Cyprus

MARKETING TIPS

- **Ambiance** Cyprus is generally informal, even in its business community, although outsiders should plan on a more formal approach when marketing to government authorities.
- **Credit** Although Cypriot businesses have had a generally good payment record in recent years, and the island is even operating as an offshore financial center, some buyers may require financing to close a deal. Most Cypriot buyers will request extended payment terms (90 to 180 days); however, sellers are advised to require cash against document payment.
- **Language** Although materials on lower level consumer goods should be in Greek or Turkish, most materials—especially for more sophisticated items—can be in English, which is in general use and is preferred over other languages.
- **Buying seasons** Buying seasons are confined mainly to the clothing trade in ready-made and piece goods. Generally speaking, orders are placed from February to April for delivery in the autumn and winter, and from October to December for delivery in the spring and summer.
- **Trade fairs** The Cyprus International (State) Fair is held annually at the end of May or June in the purpose-built exhibition complex on the outskirts of Nicosia.
- **Two economies** There are essentially two separate economies in Cyprus. Consumer buying patterns (and abilities) vary between the two and marketing strategies will have to be adapted accordingly.

AD AGENCY

Telia & Pavla Advertising
92 Makarios Ave.
Nicosia
Tel: (2) 377745

Cultural Cautions

DO'S

- If you are invited to an associate's home for a meal, take flowers or a cake for the hostess.
- Modest gifts are generally exchanged at the conclusion of a deal, and at the New Year.

DON'TS

- Avoid talking about religion, racial strife, and especially, the Cyprus-Greece incident.
- Waving your whole hand is an insult, so avoid doing so at all costs.

CUSTOMS

- Cypriot hospitality is sincere and sometimes overwhelmingly generous. A host may insist on giving you a certain object if you praise it.
- Cypriots love to entertain foreign business associates with long, lavish lunches in restaurants. Whoever does the inviting, pays.

OBSERVATIONS

- There is a sometimes uncomfortable blending of traditional culture, modern society, and European-Greek-Turkish traditions. As such, almost anything goes, and there are no rigid rules or social obligations.

NEGOTIATIONS

- Contractual provisions are more general than in the West, and much of the final agreement is often simply agreed upon orally.
- Turkish Cypriots will often adhere to Islamic negotiation and business strategies.
- Haggling is endemic, and Cypriots expect it of those they do business with.
- Negotiations are protracted, and will sometimes extend over days, weeks, or months.

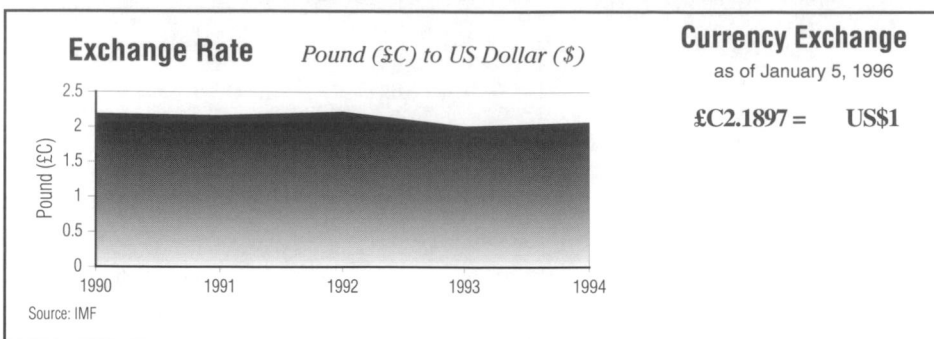

Exchange Rate *Pound (£C) to US Dollar ($)*

Source: IMF

Currency Exchange
as of January 5, 1996

£C2.1897 = US$1

Currency

The currency of Cyprus is the Cyprus pound (£C or CY), which is divided into 100 cents.

Foreign Exchange

Exchange controls are administered by the Central Bank in cooperation with authorized dealers. The external value of the pound is pegged to a basket based on the European Currency Unit (ECU), and the intervention currency is the US dollar. Authorized dealers are allowed to trade in the forward market at rates that may be freely negotiated with their customers.

Capital Transfers

Transfers abroad of capital require authorization from the Central Bank. Direct investment abroad by residents is permitted, provided that the proposed investments will promote exports of goods and services or will benefit the Cypriot economy. Investments in Cyprus by nonresidents require the prior approval of the Central Bank, which, in considering applications, gives regard to the purpose, the extent of possible foreign exchange earnings, and the benefits accruing to the national economy.

Investment Incentives

Attracting foreign investment is among the primary objectives of the development policy of the government of Cyprus. The government therefore offers numerous advantages and incentives to foreign investors, including full protection of property rights and:

Low corporate tax rates Resident companies are taxed at the rate of 20 percent for chargeable income up to £C100,000 and 25 percent for chargeable income in excess of £C100,000.

Allowances Investment and depreciation allowances are given, as well as carry-forward of losses.

Exemptions Exemptions from customs and excise charges for operations are done in the Industrial Free Zone.

Offshore incentives More incentives are offered to offshore companies in the form of tax breaks.

Shipping Customs duties exemptions and tax breaks are given to Cypriot shipping operations.

Investment Restrictions

In "saturated" sectors, such as land development, tourist agencies, and trade within Cyprus, no approvals are granted for nonresident participation by foreign investors. In several other sectors, foreign participation is limited to 49 percent.

Money Matters

BITS AND PIECES

- **Equity capital** Equity capital issued to nonresident investors must be funded from abroad. Total capital must be commensurate with the total cost of the project.
- **Financing** Loan financing must be raised from local and foreign sources in proportion to the equity participation by residents and nonresidents. This requirement is waived if nonresident participation is 24 percent or less.
- **Foreign loans** Terms for foreign loans must be approved by the Central Bank. Interest and other costs must be at market prices.
- **Royalties** Royalties and other payments for the use of patents, know-how, brand names, etc. must be approved in advance, but then may be readily remitted abroad.
- **Professional services** Nonresidents wishing to participate in a Cypriot business enterprise are required to obtain the services of an attorney or accountant practicing in Cyprus who must submit, on their behalf, an application to the Central Bank with the requisite information.
- **Investment evaluation** The Central Bank evaluates each investment proposal on its own merits. Whether the bank grants permission to go ahead with the project and the percentage of foreign participation allowed depends on how desirable the project is from the Cypriot point of view.
- **Exchange control** The exchange control law does not distinguish between Cypriot nationals and aliens but rather between residents and nonresidents. Residents are subject to exchange control restrictions; nonresidents are not. Nonresidents may hold and manage assets and liabilities in any foreign currency, including freely convertible and transferable balances with banks on the island.
- **Expropriation** Private property is only expropriated for public purposes in a non-discriminatory manner and in accordance with established principles of international law.
- **Double taxation** Cyprus has concluded 23 treaties for the avoidance of double taxation.
- **Foreign participation** In industry, foreign ownership of up to 100 percent is allowed in firms manufacturing products new to Cyprus or exclusively for export.

BANKS

Central Bank of Cyprus
POB 5529
36 Metochiou St
Nicosia
Tel: (2) 445281
Fax: (2) 472012
Telex: 2424

Bank of Cyprus Ltd.
POB 1472
86-90 Phaneromenia St
Nicosia
Tel: (2) 464064
Fax: (2) 464096

Co-operative Central Bank Ltd.
POB 4537
Gregoris Afxentiou St
Nicosia
Tel: (2) 442921
Fax: (2) 443088

The Cyprus Popular Bank Ltd.
POB 2032, Popular Bank Bldg.
39 Archbishop Makarios III Ave.
Nicosia
Tel: (2) 450000
Fax: (2) 453355

Hellenic Bank Ltd.
POB 4747
92 Dhigenis Akritas Ave.
Nicosia
Tel: (2) 360000
Fax: (2) 454074

TAXATION	At a Glance	
Taxation requires sophisticated knowledge of complex rules and regulations specific to each country. The information presented here is from the Ernst & Young Corporate Tax Guide and Directory, available from the Ernst & Young accounting office in your country, or from: **Ernst & Young** Nicosia Tower Centre POB 1656 36 Byron Avenue Nicosia 162, Cyprus Tel: (2) 467000 Telex: 2978 Ans bk E&Y CY Fax: (2) 365870	Corporate Income Tax Rate (%) (a)	25
	Capital Gains Tax Rate (%)	20
	Branch Tax Rate (%) (a)	25
	Withholding Tax (%)	
	Dividends (b)	30
	Interest (c)	25
	Royalties from Patents, Know-how, etc.	10
	Branch Remittance Tax	0
	Net Operating Losses (Years)	
	Carryback	0
	Carryforward	to 1995
	(a) 20% on income up to £C100,000.	
	(b) This tax is refunded if the shareholder is a nonresident foreign corporation.	
	(c) 20% on interest income up to £C100,000.	

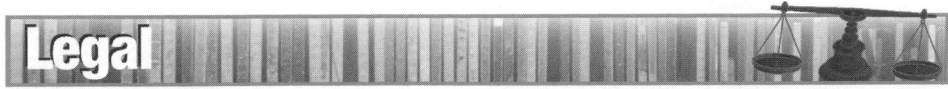

Legal

Legal System

Cyprus is a common law country, which closely follows the Anglo-Saxon legal system.

Intellectual Property Rights

Patents Patents are protected by law and may be registered directly in Cyprus. Holders of patents from the UK, upon compliance with certain procedures, are deemed to have received a patent directly from Cyprus and are entitled to all rights connected thereto.

Trademarks Trademarks may be registered in Cyprus under the Trade Mark Law of 1951. Once registered, trademarks are valid for seven years and are renewable thereafter for periods of 14 years. Trademarks may be assigned or licensed. The licensee may be recorded in the Register upon the application of the registered owner of the mark, as a "registered user." Cyprus is also a signatory to the Paris Convention for the Protection of Industrial Property.

Copyrights An amendment to the Copyright Law in 1993 brought about a major change: It included computer software as one of the categories of works protected by copyright in Cyprus, and also increased and made more severe the penalties in cases of infringement. Copyright subsists and protects rights in scientific, literary, musical, and artistic works, cinematographic films, photographs, recordings, and broadcasts. Copyright is acquired automatically as soon as a work is recorded and there are no registration requirements. Notices on copyright works are not required under Cyprus legislation. Breach of copyright is a criminal offense which carries a stiff fine and/or two years' imprisonment for a first offense, and a stiffer fine and/or three years' imprisonment in the case of a second conviction. The Court can order the confiscation and return or destruction of all infringing copies, irrespective of conviction.

Business Registration

A permit from the Central Bank is required in order to establish an offshore entity, and bank references for prospective shareholders are required from a bank outside Cyprus. Nominees may, and are, widely used and thus secrecy is preserved as to the identity of investors where this is desirable. Expatriate employees of offshore entities which have full fledged offices in Cyprus require work permits from the Immigration Department. A large percentage of Cypriot companies are shipowning companies, which are totally tax exempt.

Contracts and Dispute Resolution

The existence, as well as the contents, of formal contracts varies and depends on many factors such as: whether the parties are natural or legal persons, whether both are Cypriot or one or both are foreign, and the value of the subject matter of the contract. In effect, agreements may be made orally and concluded on gentlemen's terms, or they may be lengthy and complicated written documents. Provision may be made in contracts for disputes to go to arbitration either in Cyprus or in any other country, as well as for the choice of law governing the contract. Under the Arbitration Law of Cyprus, arbitrators are appointed by the parties in dispute. A neutral third party is usually appointed if the dispute cannot be settled by the arbitrators. Cyprus has also ratified the New York Convention on the Recognition and Enforcement of Foreign Arbitral Awards and the Uncitral Model Law. The Chartered Institute of Arbitration of London recently set up a branch in Cyprus.

Certifying Officers

There are no notaries as such in Cyprus. In their stead, there are certifying officers who attest to and authenticate signatures on documents, but may not administer oaths. Certification by apostle, in accordance to the Hague Convention, is recognized and so is the authentication by the consulate or embassy of the country where the specific document is to be used.

Labor

Workers have the constitutional right to associate freely in trade unions and to strike. More than 85 percent of the labor force in the government-controlled area of Cyprus is unionized, and unions have become quite powerful. The minimum wage for blue collar workers varies according to the degree of skill. Holidays are guaranteed and the employer makes contributions to social security, the Redundancy Fund, and the Holiday Fund, for most employees. Employers can lay off employees who have been employed for six months or longer only on one of five specified grounds, which must be proved by the employer. The employee is entitled to compensation in the event of an unfair dismissal. If the reason for the layoff is redundancy, then the employee is allowed compensation from the Redundancy Fund. There have been no incidents of labor-induced violence during the past few years.

Source: George L. Savvides & Co., Limassol

Legal Matters

LEGAL BRIEFS

- **Offshore companies** Cyprus is now an internationally recognized offshore center. It granted 4,238 permits for offshore companies in 1994 and another 13,368 in the first three months of 1995. The net profits of an offshore company are taxed at 4.25 percent, there is no tax on dividends, no estate duty, no capital gains tax, and very substantial tax benefits are offered to expatriate personnel living and working in Cyprus. Internationally, Cyprus has signed and ratified a very impressive network of double taxation treaties which enable the beneficial use of Cyprus in international tax planning. For example, the current treaty with the CIS makes it possible for the Cypriot company to acquire its dividends, interest, and royalties free from any withholding taxes.

- **Shipping** There is no tax in Cyprus on the profits from the operation of a Cypriot-registered vessel or on dividends received from a shipowning company. Again, there is no capital gains tax on the sale or transfer of Cypriot registered vessel or the shares of a shipowning company.

- **International trusts** Relatively recent legislation provides that the income and gains of an international trust derived, or deemed to be derived, from sources outside Cyprus are exempt from all taxes imposed in Cyprus and no estate duty shall be chargeable in respect of assets belonging to such a trust. Such a trust affords protection to the assets of the trust unless it will be proven that the trust was made with the intent to defraud the creditors of the settler at the time of the transfer of the assets. The burden of proof to show such an intent lies with the creditors.

LEGAL CONTACTS

George L. Savvides & Co.
Omega Court
4, Rigas Phereos & Andreas Zakos Corner
1st, 2nd & 4th Floor
POB 4098
3720 Limassol
Tel: (5) 376886
Fax: (5) 374930

Law Offices of Christodoulos G. Pelaghias
Acropolis Bldg., Ste. 14
27, Gregory Afxentiou Ave.
POB 672
Larnaca
Tel: (4) 654900
Fax: (4) 620319

Andreas Neocleous & Co.
Neocleous House
199, Makarios III Avenue
POB 613
Limassol
Tel: (5) 362818
Fax: (5) 359262

Patrikios Pavlou & Co.
Omega Court, 3rd Floor
4, R. Fereos Street
POB 4543
Limassol
Tel: (5) 364738
Fax: (5) 344548

Lellos P. Demetriades Law Office
9th Floor, The Chanteclair House
2 Sophoulis Street
POB 1646
Nicosia 136
Tel: (2) 444391
Fax: (2) 451620

Contacts

TRADE ASSOCIATIONS

Cyprus Employers' and Industrialists' Federation
POB 1657
30 Grivas Dhigenis Ave
Nicosia
Tel: (2) 445102
Fax: (2) 459459

Kibris Turk Isverenler Sendikasi
Turkish Cypriot Employers' Association
PK 674
Lefkosa (Nicosia), Mersin 10
Tel: (520) 76173

CHAMBERS OF COMMERCE

Cyprus Chamber of Commerce and Industry
POB 1455
38 Grivas Dhigenis Ave
Nicosia
Tel: (2) 449500
Fax: (2) 449048
Telex: 2077

Famagusta Chamber of Commerce and Industry
POB 3124
339 St Andrews St.
Andrea Chambers, 2nd Floor, Office No 201-202
Limassol
Tel: (5) 370165
Fax: (5) 370291

Larnaca Chamber of Commerce and Industry
POB 287
12 Gregoris Afxentiou St
Apt 43, 4th Floor, Skouros Bldg
Larnaca
Tel: (4) 655051
Fax: (4) 628281

Limassol Chamber of Commerce and Industry
POB 347
25 Spyrou Araouzou St
Veregaria Bldg. 3rd Floor
Limassol
Tel: (5) 362556
Fax: (5) 371655

Nicosia Chamber of Commerce and Industry
POB 1455
38 Grivas Dhigenis Ave
Nicosia
Tel: (2) 456858
Fax: (2) 367483
Telex: 2077

Paphos Chamber of Commerce and Industry
POB 62
Grivas Dhigenis Ave
Demetra Court, Paphos
Tel: (6) 235115
Fax: (6) 244602
Telex: 2888

Turkish Chamber of Industry
Osman Pasa Cad. 14
PK 563, Koskluciftlik
Lefkosa (Nicosia) Mersin 10
Tel: (520) 74607
Fax: (520) 84595

Turkish Cypriot Chamber of Commerce
Bedrettin Demirel Cad.
PK 718 Lefkosa (Nicosia), Mersin 10
Tel: (520) 81517
Fax: (520) 83089

BANKS

Lombard NatWest Bank Ltd.
POB 1661
Corner of Chilon and Gladstone St
Stylianos Lenas Square Nicosia
Tel: (2) 474333
Fax: (2) 457870

Mortgage Bank of Cyprus Ltd.
POB 1472
86-90 Phaneromenis St
Nicosia
Tel: (2) 464064
Fax: (2) 464096

AS Bank Ltd.
23B Sarayonu Sok
PK 448 Lefkosa (Nicosia), Mersin 10
Tel: (520) 83023
Fax: (520) 81244

Kibris Ticaret Bankasi Ltd (Cyprus Commercial Bank Ltd)
53 Kyrenia Ave
Lefksosa (Nicosia), Mersin 10
Tel: (520) 83180
Fax: (520) 82278

Turk Bankasi Ltd (Turkish Bank Ltd)
92 Kyrenia St
PK 242 Lefkosa (Nicosia), Mersin 10
Tel: (520) 83313
Fax: (520) 82432

The Cyprus Development Bank Ltd
POB 1415
Alpha House
50 Archbishop Makarios III Ave
Nicosia
Tel: (2) 457575
Fax: (2) 464322

Arab Bank PLC
POB 5700
28 Santarosa St
Nicosia
Tel: (2) 457111
Fax: (2) 457890

Barclays Bank PLC
POB 2081, Galaxias Bldg
33 Archbishop Makarios III Ave
Nicosia
Tel: (2) 461861
Fax: (2) 461734

National Bank of Greece SA
POB 1191
36 Archbishop Makarios III Ave.
Nicosia
Tel: (2) 441412
Fax: (2) 447089
Telex: 2445

NEWSPAPERS

Agon
POB 1417
Makarios Ave and Agapinoros St
Nicosia
Tel: (2) 477181

Cyprus Mail
POB 1144
24 Vassilios Voulgaroktonos St
Nicosia
Tel: (2) 462074
Fax: (2) 366385

Simerini Today
POB 1836
31 Archangelos Ave, Strovolos
Nicosia
Tel: (2) 353532
Fax: 352298

Kibris Postasi (Cyprus Post)
M. Ifran Bey Sok. 30
Lefkosa (Nicosia)
Tel: (520) 75242
Telex: 57244

PERIODICALS

Cyprus Weekly
POB 1992
Office 102, Trust House, 1st Floor
Gryparis St
Nicosia
Tel: (2) 441433 Telex: 2260
Fax: (2) 458665

Economiki Kypros
POB 4706
51 Dhigenis Akritas Ave
Nicosia
Tel: (2) 472510
Fax: (2) 461470

Enimerossi Briefing
POB 1417
Makarios Ave and Agrapinoros St
Nicosia
Tel: (2) 477181
Fax: (2) 457887

Epikeri Current Affairs
POB 3786
19 Bouboulinas St
Nicosia
Tel: (2) 455788

Flash
POB 4626
11 Kolokotronis St
Kaimakli, Nicosia
Tel: (2) 437887
Fax: (2) 434197

Middle East Economic Survey
Middle East Petroleum and Economic Publications
POB 4940
Nicosia
Tel: (2) 445431
Fax: (2) 474988
Telex: 2198

Katanalotis Consumer
POB 4874
28 Gladstone St
Nicosia 162
Tel: (2) 451092
Fax: (2) 467080

Nicosia This Month
POB 1015
Nicosia
Tel: (2) 473124
Fax: (2) 463363
Telex: 5374

Cyprus View
POB 3947
Nicosia
Tel: (2) 458413
Telex: 4787
Fax: (2) 442613

Cyprus Today
Nicosia
Tel: (2) 454733
Fax: (2) 366123
Telex: 2526

RADIO AND TELEVISION

Cyprus Broadcasting corporation (CyBC)
POB 4824
Broadcasting House
Nicosia
Tel: (2) 422231
Fax: (2) 314050
Telex: 2333

Bayrak Radio and TV Corp (BRTK)
Dr Fazil Kucuk Ave
Lefkosa (Nicosia), Mersin 10
Tel: (520) 85555
Fax: (520) 81991
Telex: 57264

INTERNET ADDRESSES

Republic of Cyprus HomePage
http://www.ucy.ac.cy/cyprus/cyprus.html

Cyprus Home Page
http://www.wan.unnd.edu/~cyprus/root.html

Czech Republic

Economy

Overview

As a relatively small, but growing and largely industrialized Central European market, the Czech Republic has enacted legislation to stabilize its financial system while privatizing many formerly state-owned enterprises. The government has thus set the foundations for a free market by applying broad economic policy reforms and restructuring its institutions. However, despite this promising outlook, the Czech Republic continues to suffer from a significant lack of capital as well as a shortage of marketing and financial expertise. One of the lingering legacies of the Communist era has been a pervasive distortion of financial relationships, insolvency, and a generally underdeveloped financial sector. The foreign exchange controls which remain have prevented the Czech economy from liberalizing to a greater degree.

Trade

The Czech Republic's highly industrialized economy exports generalized and specialized industrial machinery, iron and steel, non-metallic mineral manufactures, and transportation equipment; imports include petroleum and natural gas, specialized and general industrial machinery, vehicles, and office machines. Fundamental to the Czech Republic's plan for economic recovery has been a trend to diversify its trade away from neighboring markets. Since 1989 total trade with formerly socialist Central European countries has dropped from 60 percent of the total to less than 20 percent. Imports from Western Europe—mostly from Germany, Austria, and Poland—currently outpace Czech exports, translating into a regular trade deficit. However, its current account remains in a surplus position, and foreign debt is low.

Sectors

Agriculture Accounting for somewhat less than 10 percent of GDP and 11 percent of work force employment, agriculture has been in decline since the Czech Republic became independent in the late 1980s. There is little prospect for significant improvement in this sector in the immediate future.

Industry Industry employs somewhat less than half of the work force, while providing somewhat more than half of GDP. In the mid-1990s Czech industry began to register growth for the first time since 1989. Major industries include food processing, heavy machinery, iron and steel, transportation equipment, and oil refining. Czech industry is heavily dependent on coal, nuclear power, and imported petroleum fuels.

Services The service sector employs about 40 percent of the work force and provides about 36 percent of GDP. Tourism and transportation are major contributors to this sector, although the bulk of the sector is involved in distribution and personal service activities.

Trends

Opportunities associated with infrastructure improvements, privatization, and retail ventures are expected to continue to drive economic revitalization in the Czech Republic. Most enterprises are now at least partly privatized, and a burgeoning service sector is emerging. Major upgrades in energy production and distribution, telecommunications, housing and municipal infrastructure, medical services, and environmental protection will continue to consume a major portion of domestic investment resources. Largely foreign-funded new investments in plant and equipment are also expected to continue. Overall, growth in the Czech economy is expected to accelerate by about one percentage point per year over the next several years.

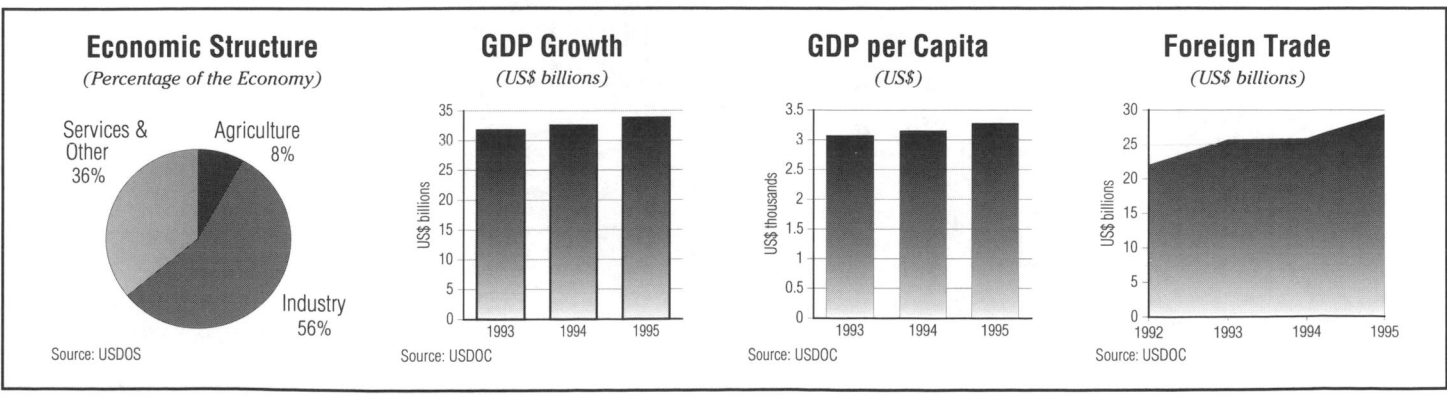

Economic Structure
(Percentage of the Economy)

Services & Other 36%
Agriculture 8%
Industry 56%

Source: USDOS

GDP Growth
(US$ billions)

1993 1994 1995

Source: USDOC

GDP per Capita
(US$)

1993 1994 1995

Source: USDOC

Foreign Trade
(US$ billions)

1992 1993 1994 1995

Source: USDOC

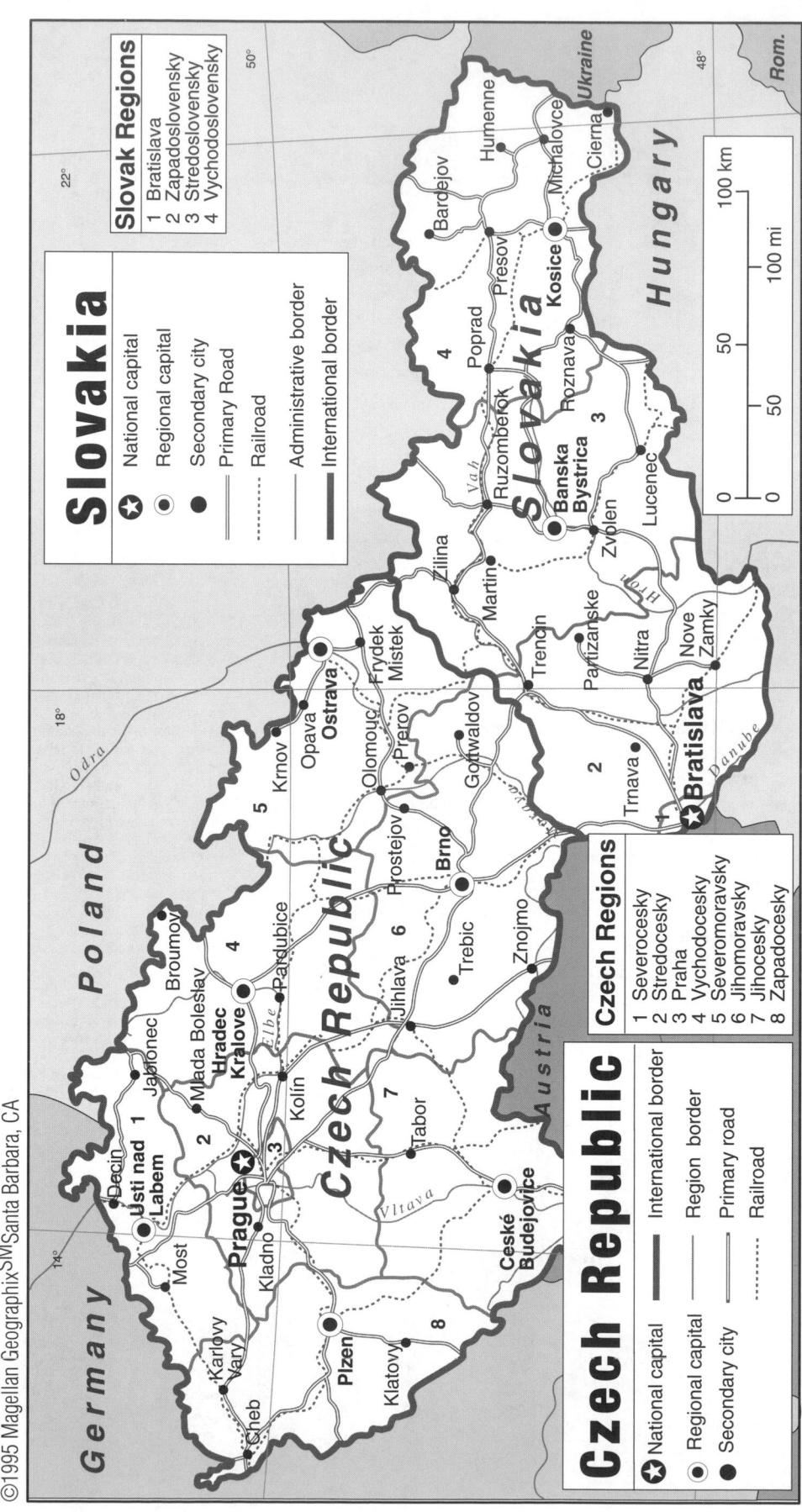

Slovakia

- ⭐ National capital
- ◉ Regional capital
- ● Secondary city
- —— Primary Road
- ---- Railroad
- —— Administrative border
- ▬▬ International border

Slovak Regions
1 Bratislava
2 Zapadoslovensky
3 Stredoslovensky
4 Vychodoslovensky

Czech Regions
1 Severocesky
2 Stredocesky
3 Praha
4 Vychodocesky
5 Severomoravsky
6 Jihomoravsky
7 Jihocesky
8 Zapadocesky

Czech Republic

- ⭐ National capital
- ◉ Regional capital
- ● Secondary city
- ▬▬ International border
- —— Region border
- —— Primary road
- ---- Railroad

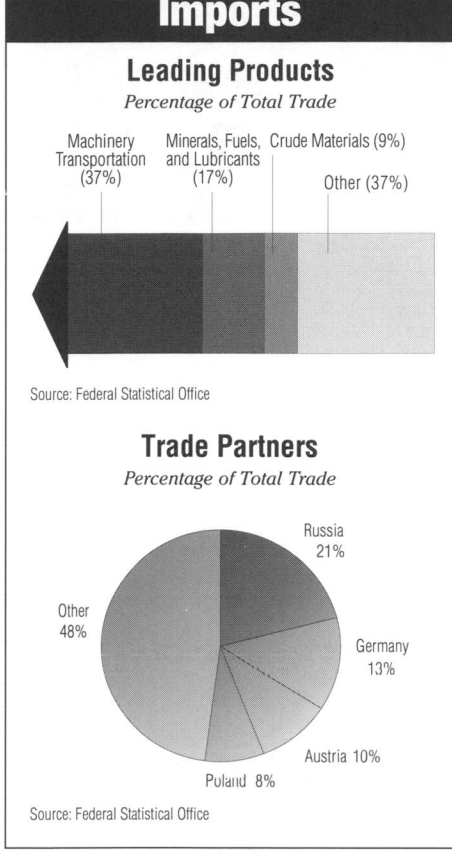

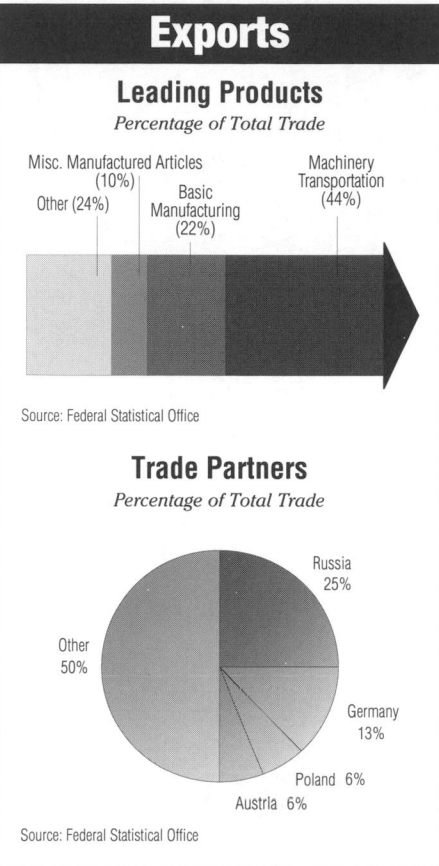

Opportunities

FOR IMPORTING TO THE CZECH REPUBLIC

- agricultural products
- automobiles
- chemicals
- computer products
- consumer goods
- environmental protection technology
- food processing and packaging equipment
- fuels and lubricants
- industrial process controls
- machine tools
- machinery and transport equipment
- manufactured products
- medical equipment
- raw materials
- telecommunication products

FOR EXPORTING FROM THE CZECH REPUBLIC

- building stone
- cement
- chemicals
- fuels
- glass and glassware
- iron and steel
- machinery and transport equipment
- manufactured goods
- metals
- minerals
- textiles and clothing
- timber

GROWTH SECTORS

- energy production
- environmental protection goods and services
- medical services
- telecommunications
- tourism

GOVERNMENT PROCUREMENT

- building supplies
- computer products
- electrical power systems
- electronic goods
- military defense equipment
- water treatment systems

Trade News

RULES AND REGULATIONS

- **Regulations** Foreign trade is regulated by the Ministry of Trade and Industry.
- **Tariffs and import taxes** Czechoslovakia was a founding member of the GATT. The Czech Republic has adopted the GATT tariff code, which has an average tariff of five to six percent.
- **Import licenses** Import licenses are required for certain classes of goods into the Czech Republic. Licenses are automatically granted, after an administrative fee is paid, for certain products, including uranium ore, scrap metals, textile products, and certain agricultural and food products. Other products, including chemicals, minerals, pharmaceuticals, raw hides, poisonous and toxic substances, military equipment, and certain agricultural goods, are granted licenses depending on domestic needs.
- **Prohibited imports** There are few prohibited imports.
- **Special import provisions** Where a foreign firm owns more than 30 percent and not less than US$1.8 million (50 million koruny) of a local joint venture, the firm may import duty free goods which are intended for processing, reprocessing, completion, or assembly into final products. The customs value of the imported goods must not be more than the price of the goods exported by the venture.
- **Export controls** The Czech Republic adheres to former Coordinating Committee on Multilateral Export Controls (COCOM) regulations and implements export controls on certain technologies.
- **Export subsidies** A legal framework is being drafted to enable the Czech export bank to provide export guarantees and credits to Czech exporters. For some commodities, pricing is established at a level which includes a subsidy to local producers.
- **Free trade agreements** The Czech Republic is a member of the Central European Free Trade Area (CEFTA), comprised of Poland, Hungary, Slovakia, and the Czech Republic. It is also an associate member of the European Union.
- **Import payments** All imports are subject to an ad valorem customs duty extending to 80 percent. There is also a value-added tax (VAT) ranging from five to 23 percent.
- **Export payments** All export receipts must be repatriated and sold to commercial banks.
- **Imports** Imports from developing countries are granted preferential treatment under the Generalized System of Preferences (GSP).

FREIGHT FORWARDERS

Cechofracht
International Forwarding and Shipping Corporation
Na Prikope 8
111 83 Prague
Fax: (2) 269295
Telex: 12221 CFT

Ceskoslovenska Namorni Plavba
Czechoslovak Ocean Shipping
Pocernika 168
10099 Prague
Fax: (2) 773962
Telex: 121143 CNP

Cesmad
Perucka 5
12067 Prague 2
Fax: (2) 256273
Telex: 122086 CSMA

GOVERNMENT INFORMATION

Agency for Foreign Investment and Assistance
Slovak Republic
Videsska Cesta 5
85220 Bratislava
Fax: (7) 849804

Agency for Foreign Investment and Assistance
Czech Republic
Trida SNB 65
Prague

Business Travel

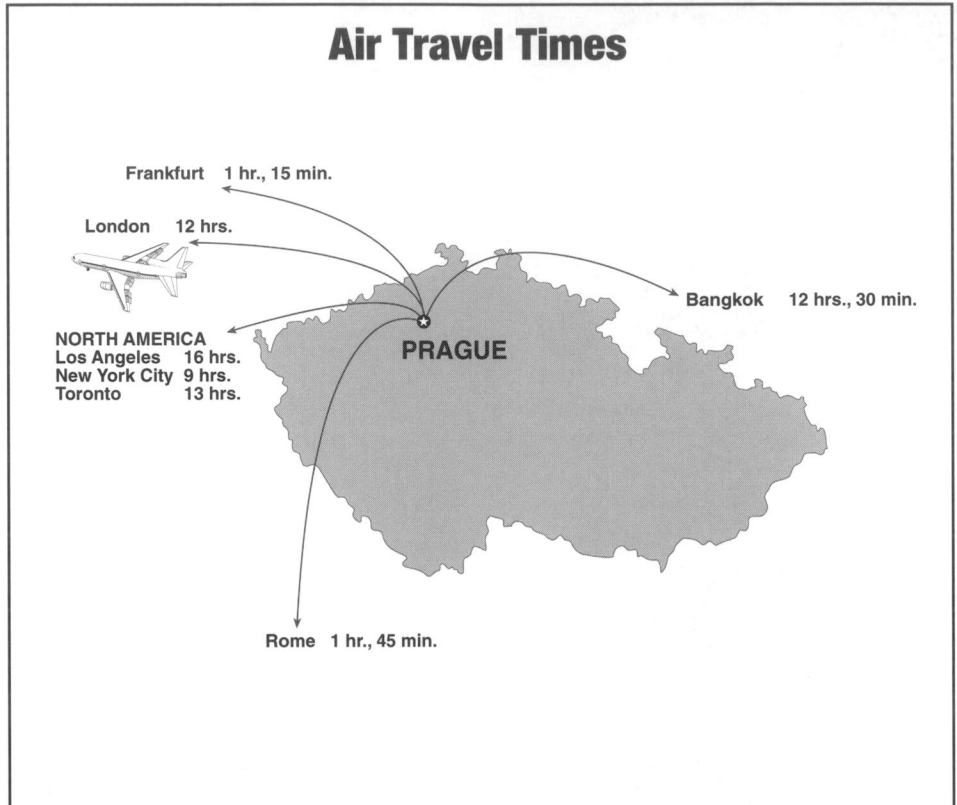

Air Travel Times

Frankfurt 1 hr., 15 min.

London 12 hrs.

Bangkok 12 hrs., 30 min.

NORTH AMERICA
Los Angeles 16 hrs.
New York City 9 hrs.
Toronto 13 hrs.

★ PRAGUE

Rome 1 hr., 45 min.

COMMUNICATIONS

Telephones The Czech telephone system is overburdened and outdated but it is being updated now. Public phones are available at the post office, and these phones are usually more reliable than those on the street. Calls within Europe usually go through without delay. New blue public phones that use phone cards have recently been added throughout the country, but the international lines are not yet sufficient and callers usually have to wait for a connection to go through. Long distance calls: Post office in Prague, Jindrisska Ul. 14.

Fax Fax machines are prevalent and are available at offices, hotels, and some post offices. Telegrams can be sent from any post office or by dialing 127. A telegram sent by phone must be sent in Czech or Slovak. Telex machines are available in most major hotels.

Post office Post offices are usually open from 8:00 am to 7:00 pm. Mail service is reliable, as well as faster and cheaper than in many surrounding countries.

BEST TRAVEL BOOKS

Czech & Slovak Republic Travel Survival Kit, Lonely Planet. Filled with relevant and reliable travel information.

Fodor's Travel Guides, The Czech Republic and Slovakia. An indispensable guide for travelers who know that there's more to these two republics than irresistible Prague..

Do's and Taboo's Around the World. The Bestselling Guide to International Behavior. Edited by Roger Axtell, compiled by the Parker Pen Company. The ultimate guide to international behavior, now completely updated and expanded. Helpful, fun to read!

Berlitz Business Travel Guide, Europe. Concise economic details, successful trip planning, background information on people and cities, useful facts and addresses.

USEFUL TELEPHONE NUMBERS

If you are calling from outside the Czech Rep., you will need to add the country code [42] and any other international dialing requirements from within your country.

- Local Telephone Directory Assistance 120
- Int'l Telephone Directory Assistance 0135
- Telegram service 127
- Emergency 158
- Medical emergency 155
- Fire 150
- Emergency Road Service 154
- Prague Information Service .... (2) 544-444
- Chamber of Commerce .... (2) 2317495
- Czechoslovak Management Center ... (2) 20391441
- Taxi (Prague) .... (2) 20-29-51
- Train Information .... (2) 236-4441
- Bus Information .... (2) 221-445
- Ruzyne Airport .... (2) 367-760
- Airport Information.............................. (2) 33-41-111

Airlines:
- CSA .... (2) 231-460
- British Airways .... (2) 236-0353
- Delta Airlines .... (2) 232 4772
- Finnair .... (2) 223-012
- SAS .... (2) 228-141
- Swissair .... (2) 232-4707

Credit card information:
Lost or stolen credit cards (call collect to the US, regardless of which country the card was issued in).
- Amex .... [1] (919) 333-3211
- Diner's Club .... [1] (303) 799-1504
- MasterCard .... [1] (314) 275-6690
- Visa .... [1] (410) 581-7931

Travelogue

WORKWEEK

Offices Monday-Friday 7:00 or 8:30 am to 4:00 or 5:00 pm.
Banks Monday-Friday 8:00 am to 4:00 pm.
Government Monday-Friday, 8:00 am to 4:00 pm.
Retail Generally open around 8:00 am and close at 6:00 pm Monday through Friday with some Saturday hours.

HOLIDAYS

Holidays 1996
January 1 New Year's Day
April 7 Easter Sunday*
April 8 Easter Monday*
May 1 Labor Day
May 8 Liberation Day
July 5 Cyril and Methodius Day
July 6 Jon Hus Day
October 28 National Day
December 25 Christmas Day
December 26 Saint Stephen's Day
*Dates vary each year.

VISA AND PASSPORT

Foreigners must have a valid passport, but a visa is not required for stays of up to 30 days. All travelers must have onward tickets, valid travel documents, and sufficient funds.

DEPARTURE FORMALITIES

The exportation of Czech currency is forbidden for nonresidents. There are no other restrictions for departure from the Czech Republic.

IMMUNIZATION

No immunizations are necessary for visitors from any country unless arriving from an infected area.

TIPPING

Tipping is optional in the Czech Republic. Rounding up a bill is sufficient for good service. Taxi: 10 percent. Hotels: none. Restaurants: 10 percent. Barbers and beauticians, small services: five to 10 percent.

CRIME

The Czech Republic has a low rate of violent crime. Street crimes have been increasing, especially at night near major tourist sites. Take normal precautions, try to venture out with someone, and you should experience few problems.

INFRASTRUCTURE

The Czech Republic has well-developed air, train, subway, taxi, and bus industries. Tourist facilities are not as developed as those found in Western Europe. Some services are not yet available here. Taxi service is fair; for important engagements, book in advance. Car rentals are expensive, as is the cost of gasoline. When buying a map for driving, make sure the map contains the new street names chosen after the "Velvet Revolution" of November 1989 as dozens of streets have new names. Railway service is extensive, subways modern, streetcars and buses require advance tickets. Domestic flights are inexpensive with frequent trips offered.

NATIONAL TOURIST OFFICE

Cedok
Na príkope 18
Prague 1
Telephone: (2) 2127111

Prague Information Service
Staromestské nám 22
Prague
Tel: (2) 224453

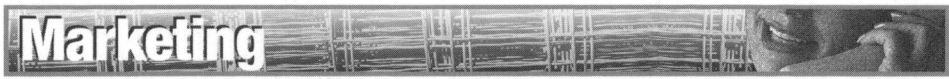

Marketing

Overview

The Czech Republic may be the most economically advanced re-emerging market of the former Eastern Bloc. There is a small but growing market for imported computers and software, medical equipment, and manufacturing and environmental technologies. Although European competition in the Czech market is strong, Czech firms continue to suffer from a lack of capital, marketing, and financial expertise. The key to success for multinational firms will hedge on price, delivery, and service terms that compete with European enterprises.

Distribution

Once an inextricable part of a monopolistic economy, distribution is being broken up into smaller entities. The distribution of most goods is flexible and responsive to consumers, with a combination of public and private networks, each scrambling for its niche in the new economy. Many companies are developing local warehouse systems, and goods are now shipped by truck.

Agents, Distributors, and Partners

Foreign companies usually locate agents and distributors through referrals and newspaper ads, and generally one agent can cover the entire country. Margins for distributors are similar to those in the West.

Selling Techniques and Advertising

Czech consumers pay attention to price, and financing terms are key to any sales transaction. Retail operations and door-to-door sales have became fairly successful. Television, radio, print, trains, buses, and billboards are effective mediums for advertisement. Trade fairs and shows are also a popular way to engage local customer interest.

Service and Customer Support

Almost all foreign products and services sold in the Czech Republic are supported by local sales and service, either through a subsidiary or a local representative. Although price is a foremost consideration, for many consumers support is also important when buying a product or service.

Business Culture

Greetings and Courtesies

Czechs typically greet foreigners warmly. Shake hands with everyone you first meet in the Czech Republic, even children. It is customary to shake hands again on your departure. However, a man usually waits for women and older people to extend their hands first. Czechs also commonly greet others with "How do you do?" It is polite to use titles when greeting Czechs.

Business Ethic and Framework

The usual work day in the Czech Republic begins early in the morning and ends at mid-afternoon. Business is generally conducted in a straightforward manner. Czech businesspeople are punctual and they expect foreign associates to be, also. Czechs generally follow conservative patterns of dress. Conservative suits are usually worn by businessmen. Women's business attire consists of skirts and dresses rather than suits.

Women

Because they are viewed as a novelty, foreign women often have more success in business than Czech women. Women make tremendous contributions to the Czech economy, composing more than 47 percent of the Czech Republic's labor force, although most of their jobs are entry level. There is a significant inequity in wages, favoring men .

Meetings and Decision Making

Business meetings in the Czech Republic need extensive advance planning. Appointments should be scheduled months in advance. Most Czechs take their vacations in July and August; scheduling meetings for those months will be unproductive. A patient demeanor is crucial when doing business in the Czech Republic. Foreign businesspeople should be prepared to make several trips to the country before any decision is finalized.

Marketing in the Czech Republic

MARKETING TIPS

- **Trade** More than half the Czech Republic's trade is conducted with Germany—neighboring Austria, Slovakia, and Poland are the next closest competitors—and potential competitors must match or better the offerings of German suppliers.
- **Trucking** The predominant means of distribution is overland trucking, and there are approximately 2,000 trucking firms in the Czech Republic, assuring delivery.
- **Legal advice** Although not technically necessary, retaining a local attorney to draw up agency, sales, and other contracts is generally advisable.
- **Competing channels** Because of the degree of change experienced in the breakup first of the USSR and second of the Czech and Slovak Republics, business is in a state of flux. Potential sellers should expect to be flexible and entrepreneurial in working to establish their own distribution arrangements and channels. Few established channels exist at present.

MARKET RESEARCH FIRMS

AISA
Lesanska 2a
140 00 Prague 4
Tel: (2) 2424-5521 Fax: (2) 2424-5523
Point, SRO
Frantiska Krizka 4
170 00 Prague 7
Tel: (2) 377-730 Fax: (2) 372-251
Corum Business Services
Legerova 15
120 00 Prague 2
Tel/Fax: (2) 297-134

Cultural Cautions

DO'S

- Double-check everything. Confusion prevails over new rules; situations change constantly.
- Visitors should speak softly, as Czechs usually do.

DON'TS

- Don't discuss politics, religion, socialism, or money.
- Avoid taking photographs in museums or art galleries. Do not photograph military installations.

CUSTOMS

- Czechs do not applaud in a church, whether the occasion is a wedding, concert, or other function.
- It is customary to take off shoes upon entry to a Czech home.
- Compliment the host on the meal.
- Czechs do not put their knife and fork down while eating, except when using a napkin or when involved in lengthy dinner conversation.
- Czechs generally can be expected to be honest.

OBSERVATIONS

- Czechs are not "touchers," especially in business.
- Telephone systems of the Czech Republic are not too reliable; you might not be able to make a call at a prearranged time.

NEGOTIATIONS

- Take proposals with a grain of salt. Czechs may agree to something even if there is only a small possibility of success or when they can't possibly deliver.
- Negotiate, don't dictate. Treat your partners as equals.
- Business contacts should not be limited to senior management in the Czech Republic. The support of middle management and labor will help to advance negotiations.
- It can be difficult to determine where Czechs stand on an issue. Rather than saying "no," they are more likely to say "We shall see."

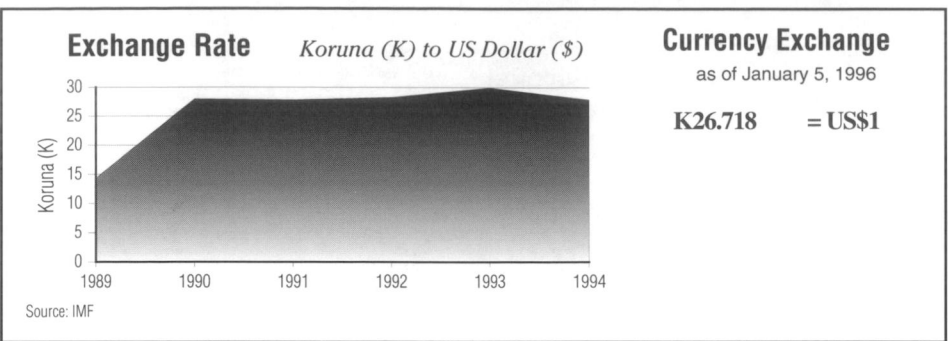

Exchange Rate *Koruna (K) to US Dollar ($)*

Koruna (K): 0, 5, 10, 15, 20, 25, 30
1989, 1990, 1991, 1992, 1993, 1994

Source: IMF

Currency Exchange
as of January 5, 1996

K26.718   = US$1

Money Matters

BITS AND PIECES

- **Corporate income tax** Domestic businesses are subject to a corporate income tax based on their worldwide income. All foreign businesses are taxed based on their Czech-source income only.
- **Capital gains** Capital gains are included with other taxable income and taxed at the regular corporate income tax rate. In general, they are not deductible.
- **Gold** Within 30 days of acquisition, residents are required to sell gold to banks authorized to conduct foreign currency exchange transactions. Gold can be exported by nonresidents, provided they submit a certificate confirming the coins are of no historical value. Any gold imported into the Czech Republic by nonresidents can also be exported.
- **Foreign tax relief** The Czech Republic offers a foreign tax credit for foreign tax paid on income earned abroad.
- **Forward transactions** Forward exchange transactions are permitted.
- **Resident accounts** Natural residents may open interest-bearing foreign exchange accounts at any resident commercial bank authorized to deal in foreign exchange without revealing the source of foreign exchange. Balances on these accounts may be used by the holder without restriction.

Currency

The currency of the Czech Republic is the Czech koruna (K); the plural is koruny. One K equals 100 hallers.

Foreign Exchange

The Ministry of Finance and the Czech National Bank (CNB) are responsible for administration of exchange controls and regulations.

Capital Transfers

Nonresidents may open two types of accounts. Domestic accounts may be made in koruny but most transfers abroad require a permit from the CNB or the Ministry of Finance. Nonresidents can also open accounts in foreign currency without restrictions. There is no limit to the amount of currency that may be brought in or taken out of the Czech Republic by nonresidents. Most transactions abroad, including alimony and inheritances, are permitted on a reciprocal basis. Permits are required for most remittances relating to family maintenance, education, and medical treatment. There are no restrictions to invisible proceeds, but all repatriation of wage savings by nonresident workers must be authorized by the CNB.

Investment Incentives

There is no legal difference between domestic or foreign investment. The government feels special incentives meant to entice foreign investment are ineffective, however, so there are only a few limited tax benefits for foreign investors. All other incentives are available for both foreign and domestic investors. These include a full or partial tax exemption for profits up to two years after the start of operations. Businesses can also request exemption for income taxes for one taxation year.

Investment Restrictions

There have been a number of complaints from foreign investors, including high taxes, bureaucratic red tape, and slow decision-making from the government. These are probably more a result of recent radical changes in the economy, however, than a function of government policy or regulation.

BANKS

Czech State Bank
Na Prikope 28
110 03 Prague
Tel: (2) 2112
Fax: (2) 235-4141
Telex: 121555

Agrobanka Praha a.s.
Rumunska 1
120 00 Prague 2
Tel: (2) 295398
Fax: (2) 6911315

Banka Bohemia a.s.
Husinecka 11A
130 00 Prague 3
Tel: (2) 6912002
Fax: (2) 276614
Telex: 276614

Ceskoslovenska obchodni banka a.s.
Commercial Bank of Czechoslovakia
Na Prikope 14
115 20 Prague 1
Tel: (2) 224444
Fax: (2) 2355105
Telex: 122201

Investicni Banka
Gorkeho nam. 32
113 03 Prague 1
Tel: (2) 2362065
Fax: (2) 2368945
Telex: 122459

Komercni banka a.s., Praha
Na Prikope 33
POB 839
114 07 Prague 1
Tel: (2) 21221111
Fax: (2) 2356158
Telex: 121831

Pragobanka a.s.
Jungmannova 32
112 59 Prague 1
Tel/Fax: (2) 220128

Zivnostenska banka a.s.
Na Prikope 20
113 80 Prague 1
Tel: (2) 21121111
Fax: (2) 21125555
Telex: 122313

Czech State Savings Bank
Vaclavske nam. 42
110 00 Prague 1
Tel: (2) 225237
Fax: (2) 267023

TAXATION

Taxation requires sophisticated knowledge of complex rules and regulations specific to each country. The information presented here is from the Ernst & Young Corporate Tax Guide and Directory, available from the Ernst & Young accounting office in your country, or from:

Ernst & Young Consulting
Vinohradska 184
130 52 Praha 3
Czech Republic
Tel: (2) 6713 3010, 6713 3011
Fax: (2) 6713 3002, 6713 3012, 6713 3013
Telex: 122 241 Stime

At a Glance

Corporate Income Tax Rate (%)	41
Capital Gains Tax Rate (%)	41
Branch Tax Rate (%)	41
Withholding Tax (%) (a)	
Dividends (b)	25
Interest (b)(c)	0/15/20/25
Royalties from Copyrights (d)	25
Income from Media (e)	10
Rental Income Leases (d)(f)	1
Winnings and Prizes (g)	20
Net Operating Losses (Years)	
Carryback	0
Carryforward	7

(a) Rates may be reduced by treaty.
(b) Applies to residents and nonresidents.
(c) Interest on mutual deposits with banks in the interbank market and interest on deposits of insurance companies with banks is exempt from tax. The 15% rate applies to interest from savings accounts of individuals. The 20% rate applies to interest on employees' deposits held by an employer. Employees' deposits are deposits accepted by an employer, including a bank, solely from its employees under conditions that differ from those applying to other individuals. The 25% rate applies to other interest.
(d) Applicable to nonresidents.
(e) Income from media consists of amounts paid to authors for contributions to newspapers, radio and television. A 10% withholding tax applies to income from media of up to K 3,000 a month received by residents. Any income from media received by residents exceeding such amount is included in taxable income and is subject to tax at the regular tax rates. Income from media received by nonresidents is considered a copyright royalty and is subject to a 25% withholding tax.
(g) Winnings and prizes from competitions organized according to a special law are exempt from withholding tax.

Legal

Legal System

The post-Communist Czech Republic was founded in 1993 with a bicameral legislature. The president is elected to a five-year term by both chambers. Members of the House of Representatives serve a four-year term, while senators serve staggered six-year terms. The formation of political parties is permissible, and established political organizations are sometimes partly subsidized by the government.

Intellectual Property Rights

Patents Patents are generally effective for 20 years from the date of issuance. Czech patent law for products may be different from those pertaining to patentable procedures. Pharmaceuticals, food products, theories, and mathematical formulae are not typically covered. Applications must be filed with the National Patent Office, which conducts an investigation into the product or procedure, and generally responds within 18 months.

Copyrights Copyright protections for literary, scientific, and other creative works (including video and software) are effective for the duration of the author's lifetime plus 50 years. Photographic images are protected for lifetime plus 10 years. Video and software piracy remains a major copyright issue. Although enforcement levels have improved in recent years, levels of violation remain high enough to threaten any possible viability of commerce. Investors should be aware that protection may not be fully enforced.

Trademarks Trademark protections are effective from the date of entry to the Registry of Trademarks, which is administered by the Industrial Property Office in Prague. Priority is generally established by consecutive order of registration. Trademark priorities for international trade as established by treaty must be claimed at the time of application, and followed by supporting documents within three months. Trademark protections are issued in 10-year terms, renewable indefinitely. The Czech Republic adheres to the Arrangement of Madrid for Trademarks. Symbols which are commonly in use or which are detrimental to the public interest will not likely be approved.

Business Registration

The Czech government maintains a public register of companies doing business in the country. Documents necessary for entry include a memorandum of association, a certification of capital contribution, signature specimens, any pertinent powers of attorney, valid trade authorization, and other materials relating to the company's past and present circumstances. New ventures require approval from the Federal Ministry of Finance, the Czech or Slovak Ministry of Finance (as appropriate), and, for international concerns, the Federal Ministry of Foreign Trade. Failure to register or advise changes in status may result in disqualification.

Contracts and Dispute Resolution

Contracts may be written, oral, or even implied if sufficient indication of intent is given; although it should be noted that silence does not necessarily convey consent in all cases. Contracts are, for the most part, governed by laws applicable to the location of the seller or work provider. There have been few disputes, but issues have arisen concerning foreign investment in entities being privatized. Alternative dispute resolution has not yet taken hold in the Czech Republic. It is difficult to find qualified arbitrators, and there is no official mechanism for enforcement of arbitration awards.

Labor

Workers may freely unionize, and roughly two-thirds of the work force has elected to do so, despite a relative decline in the popularity of unions during the last four years. With the exception of certain specified occupations, (such as police and other professions related to the public well-being), unions have the right to call strikes. However, there are certain procedures which must be followed beforehand, including specified discussions and negotiations between the workers and management. Unions have been ineffective recently, but there have been no signs of unrest since the economic transition started. The minimum working age is 16, although persons as young as 14 may be activated under certain circumstances, for limited hours and in non-dangerous situations. The standard workweek in the Czech Republic is 42.5 hours; however, collective bargaining has reduced that number to 40 in most cases. Paid rest periods during the work day and paid vacations are also mandated, as are overtime and minimum wage requirements. The Federal Ministry of Labor and Social Affairs sets the minimum wage standards to guarantee a livable salary for a worker and his or her family. Wages are on the rise, but some estimates predict the Republic will still have lower labor costs than neighboring industrialized countries. The same labor standards apply to foreign workers in the Czech Republic, although the process of obtaining the various permits may take a few months, during which time the workers are permitted to take up employment.

Legal Matters

LEGAL BRIEFS

- **Companies** The Czech Commercial Code allows for the establishment of joint stock companies, limited liability companies, general partnerships, limited partnerships, partnerships sponsored by corporate entities, consortia, associations, and sole proprietorships.

- **International agreements** The Czech Republic adheres to the Berne Convention on Protection of Literary and Artistic Works (and subsequent Paris amendments); the Universal Convention on Copyright, (and subsequent Paris amendments); the International Convention for Protection of Producers of Phonograms; the Convention on International Entry of Audio-Visual Works; and the Convention on the Establishment of a World Organization for Intellectual Property (and subsequent Paris amendments).

- **Environmental laws** Laws exist in the Czech Republic that set limits on the commercial use of forests.

- **Bankruptcy** A revised bankruptcy law allows creditors to pursue claims through a forced debt restructuring of debtors and through liquidation. The new law's effectiveness remains unclear. There is a three- to four-year backlog in the Czech Republic's bankruptcy courts, and there is no secondary market for the liquidation of seized assets.

- **Securities law** A securities law was formed, allowing the formation of financial markets in the Republic.

- **Employment laws** The Czech Republic is broadly in line with EU and International Labor Organization practice.

- **Czech companies** Foreign companies have a distinct legal advantage over local companies. Current legislation penalizes Czech companies by denying corporate tax deductibility of bad debt reserves and the possibility of reclaiming value-added tax on bad debts, generally until bankruptcy proceedings are initiated.

- **Labor market** The Czech Republic's current legislation limits wage growth, and inhibits the creation of a free market for labor.

LEGAL CONTACTS

Advokatni Kancelar
V Jame 12
110 00 Prague 1
Tel: (2) 26 02 93
Fax: (2) 26 02 93

Alliance Prague
Jachymova 2
110 00 Prague 1
Tel: (2) 2 232 11 30
Fax: (2) 2 232 63 71

Baker & McKenzie
Celakovskeho Sady, No. 4
110 00 Prague 1
Tel: (2) 24 22 7330
Fax: (2) 24 22 2124

Frick & Frick
Office 422A, 4th Floor
Narodni Trida 10
11319 Prague 1
Tel: (2) 24 91 30 44
Fax: (2) 24 91 34 35

Kocian, Solc, Touska a spol.
Jindrisska 34
110 00 Prague 1
Tel: (2) 24103316
Fax: (2) 24103234

Squire, Sanders & Dempsey
Celetna 4
11000 Prague 1
Tel: (2) 2315661
Fax: (2) 2315482

White and Case
Euro-Invest (CSR), Inc.
Jeruzalemska 13
11000 Prague 1
Tel: (2) 227229

GOVERNMENT AGENCIES

Czech Government Office
Nabr. Dr. E. Benese 4
118 01 Prague 1
Tel: (2) 24-2111
Fax: (2) 2481-0231

Ministry of Agriculture
Tesnov 17, 117 05 Prague 1
Fax: (2) 2481-0478

Ministry of Defense
Nabr. L. Svobody 471
160 00 Prague 6
Tel: (2) 330-51111
Fax: (2) 311-4121

Ministry of Economy
Staromestske nam. 6
110 00 Prague 1
Tel: (2) 2481-3131
Fax: (2) 2481-2894

Ministry of Economic Competition
Jostova 8, 601 56 Brno
Tel: (5) 4216-1111
Fax: (5) 4221-0023

Ministry of Foreign Affairs
Loretanske nam. 5
125 10 Prague 1
Tel: (2) 2414-1111
Fax: (2) 2418-2048

Ministry of Industry and Trade
Na Frantisku 32
110 15 Prague 1
Tel: (2) 285-1111
Fax: (2) 2481-1089

National Property Fund
Rasinovo nabr. 42
128 00 Prague 2
Tel: (2) 2491-1907
Fax: (2) 2491-0290

WORLD TRADE CENTERS

World Trade Center Brno
Vystaviste 1
660 91 Brno
Tel: (5) 4115-2670 Fax: (5) 4115-2929

World Trade Center Prague
Palac KOVO, Jankovcova 2
170 88 Prague
Tel: (2) 6678-3680/1
Fax: (2) 6671-0044

GENERAL TRADE ASSOCIATIONS

Chamber of Trade and Industry
Argentinska 38
170 00 Prague 7
Tel: (2) 6679-4111
Fax: (2) 6671-0805

Czech Trade Inspection
Staromestske nam. 5
110 00 Prague 1
Tel: (2) 268-158
Fax: (2) 2408-3410

Artia, Ltd.
Import and Export of Cultural Commodities
Ve Smeckhach 30
111 27 Prague

CS Trading Company
Export of Capital Goods
Kodanska 46
100 10 Prague 10

Exico
Import and Export of Footwear and Leather Products
Panska ul. 9
111 77 Prague

Ferromet
Import and Export of Metallurgical Products
Opletalova ul. 27
111 81 Prague

Imex
Import and Export of Consumer Goods
Revolucni tr. 25

110 15 Prague
Tel: (2) 231-1054

Inspekta
Quality Control of Imports and Exports
Na Strzi 63
140 62 Prague

Koospol
Import and Export of Foods and Agricultural Products
Ed. Banese 178
160 67 Prague

Ligna
Import and Export of Timber and Wood Products
Vodickova ul. 41
112 09 Prague

Press Agency
Pankrac Kotrska 16
140 00 Prague
Tel: (2) 2147

Unicoop
Import and Export of Folk Art, Food, and Agricultural Products
Revpicmo tr/ 13
110 00 Prague

BUSINESS ORGANIZATIONS

American Chamber of Commerce
Karlovo namesti 24
120 00 Prague 2
Tel: (2) 299-887
Fax: (2) 291-481

Czech Chamber of Commerce and Industry
Argentinska ul. 38
170 00 Prague
Tel: (2) 872-4111

NEWSPAPERS

Moravian Democratic Daily
Moravske nam. 13
658 22 Brno
Tel: (5) 751243
Fax: (5) 743832

Hradec News Daily Torch
Skroupova 695
501 72 Hradec Kralove
Tel: (49) 613511

Karlovy Vary News
Trida TGM 42
360 21 Karlovy Vary
Tel: (17) 29895
Fax: (17) 25115

Moravian and Silesian Citizens' Paper Freedom
Novinarska 3
709 07 Ostrava
Tel: (69) 262280
Fax: (69) 262144

Moravia-Silesia Daily
Havlicko no nabt. 32
700 00 Ostrava 1
Tel: (69) 216282
Fax: (69) 262144

Moravia-Silesia Evening News
Puchmajerova 1
701 00 Ostrava 1
Tel: (69) 231046
Fax: (69) 232091

Czechoslovak Sport
Na porici 30
115 23 Prague 1
Tel: (2) 2322528
Fax: (2) 2327377

Czech Daily
Na Florenci 19
115 43 Prague 1
Tel: (2) 2323249
Fax: (2) 2320925

Economic News
Na Florenci 19
112 86 Prague 1
Tel: (2) 2367487
Fax: (2) 2327236

Labour
Vaclavske nam. 17
112 58 Prague 1
Tel: (2) 2353732
Fax; (2) 2369462

Evening Prague
Na Florenci 19
110 00 Prague 1
Tel: (2) 2367487
Fax: (2) 2327361

PERIODICALS

100 + 1 ZZ
Zirovnicka 2389
106 00 Prague 10
Tel: (2) 7192248

Cinema Review
Klimentska 30
110 15 Prague 1
Tel: (2) 2314605
Fax: (2) 2311351

Respekt
Bolzanova 7
110 00 Prague 1
Tel: (2) 2219960
Fax: (2) 2359983

Radio Weekly
Na florenci 3
112 86 Prague 1
Tel: (2) 2323261
Fax; (2) 2323261

Television Weekly
Na porici 30
110 40 Prague 1
Tel: (2) 2322796
Fax: (2) 2320127

Czechoslovak Foreign Trade
V Jircharich 8
110 00 Prague 1
Tel: (2) 203758
Fax: (2) 203953

Prague Post
Politickych veznu 9
110 00 Prague 1
Tel: (2) 2359455
Fax: (2) 265186

RADIO AND TELEVISION

Cesky Rozhlas (Czech Radio)
Vinohradska 12
120 99 Prague 2
Tel: (2) 2115590
Telex: 121100
Fax: (2) 2321020

Ceska Televize (Czech Television)
Jindrisska 16
111 50 Prague 1
Tel: (2) 221247
Telex: 121800

INTERNET ADDRESSES

Usenet group(s):
soc.culture.czecho-slovak

Czech Info Center
http://turnpike.net/metro/muselik/index.html

Welcome to the Czech Republic
http://www.czech.cz

News from the Czech Republic
http://www.columbia.edu/~js322/czech.html

Denmark

Kingdom of Denmark

Economy

Overview

This modern developed economy features highly productive, high-tech agriculture; state-of-the-art, large- and small-scale industry; extensive government social welfare; a high standard of living; and heavy dependence on foreign trade. Denmark's government is committed to reducing its high unemployment rate and budget deficit and to stabilizing its currency. As a member of the EU, Denmark has weathered the worldwide slump of the early 1990s better than many Western European countries, primarily because of its reasonably well diversified economy and low but dependably steady economic growth. Denmark exports approximately 25 percent more than it imports, and its recent current account surplus remains strong; limitations on wage increases and low inflation are contributing to improved export competitiveness.

Trade

Denmark is a highly industrialized country with a tradition of open and extensive foreign trade, political stability, an efficient banking sector, and free capital movement. Major exports include meat, fish, furniture, specialized industrial machinery, dairy products, and pharmaceuticals. Imports include vehicles, petroleum, office machinery and computers, other transportation equipment (mostly aircraft and ship-related), generalized industrial machinery, and other electrical equipment. Germany—accounting for more than 20 percent of total trade—is Denmark's main trading partner, followed by Sweden, the UK, France, Norway, and the US. EU membership should increase trade with member nations.

Sectors

Agriculture This sector contributes slightly less than five percent of GDP, while employing slightly more than five percent of the work force. Although Denmark is largely self-sufficient in food production, the sector is primarily oriented toward export. Major activities include pig and dairy farming and fishing.

Industry Industry provides somewhat more than 20 percent of both GDP and employment. Food processing, offshore petroleum extraction, steel and metals, chemicals and pharmaceuticals, printing, machinery, electronics, and transportation equipment are the main areas of activity.

Services Services account for nearly 70 percent of GDP and about 65 percent of employment. Government, business, and financial services dominate, although shipping—especially tourist cruise line operations—is also of major significance.

Trends

Denmark cut its hefty income tax rates at the beginning of 1994 and, together with falling interest rates, this encouraged domestic demand for consumer durables—such as automobiles—other imported goods, and investment. These factors, coupled with the lowest inflation rate in Europe, created an increase in disposable income, which should improve competitiveness by increasing Danish industry's market share both at home and abroad. Denmark should continue to run a balance-of-payments surplus sufficient to pay down the country's foreign debt to a level equivalent to a more manageable 25 percent of GDP, allowing funds to be redirected toward investment, as well as reducing the budget deficit.

At a Glance

THE COUNTRY

Location Southern Scandinavia, surrounded by water, except for its southern boundary with Germany. Denmark also includes the Faroe Islands and Greenland.

Terrain Low and flat, or slightly rolling; the highest elevation is 173 meters (568 ft.).

Climate Temperate, though changeable day-to-day. Rainfall is fairly even throughout the year.

THE PEOPLE

Population 5,000,000

Ethnic composition Scandinavian, Eskimo, Faroese, German.

Religious composition

Evangelical Lutheran 97%

Languages spoken Danish, English, Faroese, Greenlandic, German.

Education and literacy Education is a priority, and tuition is free through the university level. Schooling is compulsory for nine years, and attendance is universal. Literacy is 99 percent.

Labor force

Total:...2,500,000

By occupation: private services 37.1%, government services 30.4%, manufacturing and mining 20%, construction 6.3%, agriculture, forestry, and fishing 5.6%, and electricity/gas/water 0.6% (1991).

COUNTRY FACTS

Political and legal This constitutional monarchy has a civil law system, which includes judicial review of legislative acts. The Supreme Court is the highest legal body, and the judiciary is independent from other branches of government.

Telephone Modern and sophisticated equipment provides good telephone and telegraph service throughout the country. International calls can be made easily. Denmark has international electronic mail capabilities. International country code: [45]. No city codes are required. All numbers are eight digits.

Transportation The highway system is 97 percent paved, well-engineered, and well-maintained. Danish State Railways operates both the train and bus lines, which are efficient and reliable. Bridges, trains and autos link the mainland and the islands. The large merchant marine fleet sails out of several excellent harbors. There is one international airport.

Environment Denmark has long had laws forcing polluters to pay the costs of adapting to environmental regulations. However, overused dumping areas for harmful chemicals have endangered land quality. Current issues are air pollution; nitrogen and phosphorus pollution of the North Sea; and drinking and surface water pollution from animal wastes. Much of Denmark's industrial and household waste is recycled.

Media The state does not allow for commercial advertising on radio or television. There are three AM and two FM radio stations and 50 television stations. Freedom of the press is guaranteed. There are nearly 50 daily newspapers and several periodicals in circulation.

Health Medical quality is excellent. Anybody can go to a physician for no fee, and the public health system entitles each Dane to his/her own doctor. Expert medical and surgical aid is available, as well as a qualified nursing staff. Life expectancy of males is 71.5 years; for females, 77.5 years.

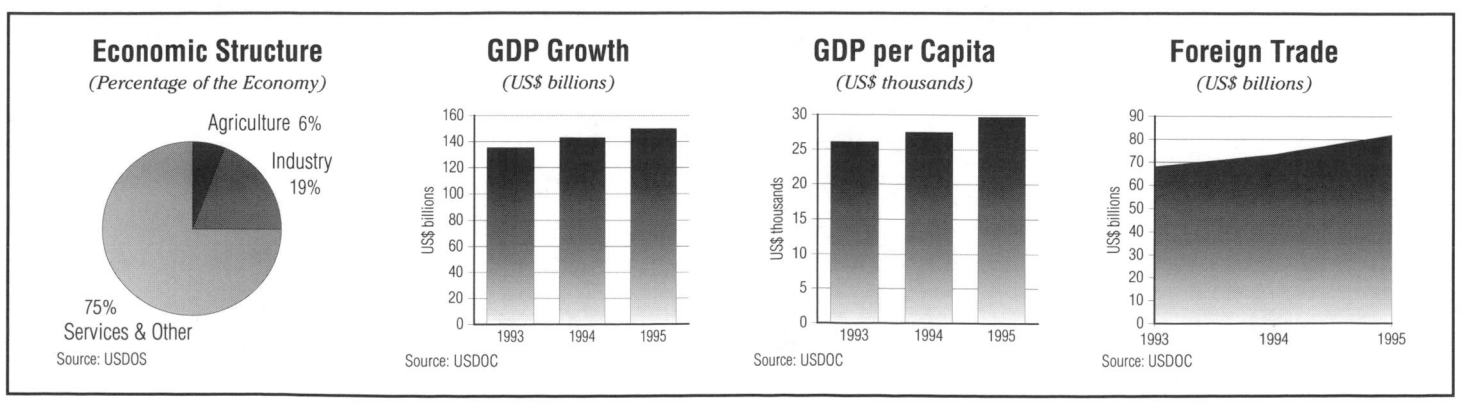

Economic Structure
(Percentage of the Economy)

Agriculture 6%
Industry 19%
75% Services & Other

Source: USDOS

GDP Growth
(US$ billions)

Source: USDOC

GDP per Capita
(US$ thousands)

Source: USDOC

Foreign Trade
(US$ billions)

Source: USDOC

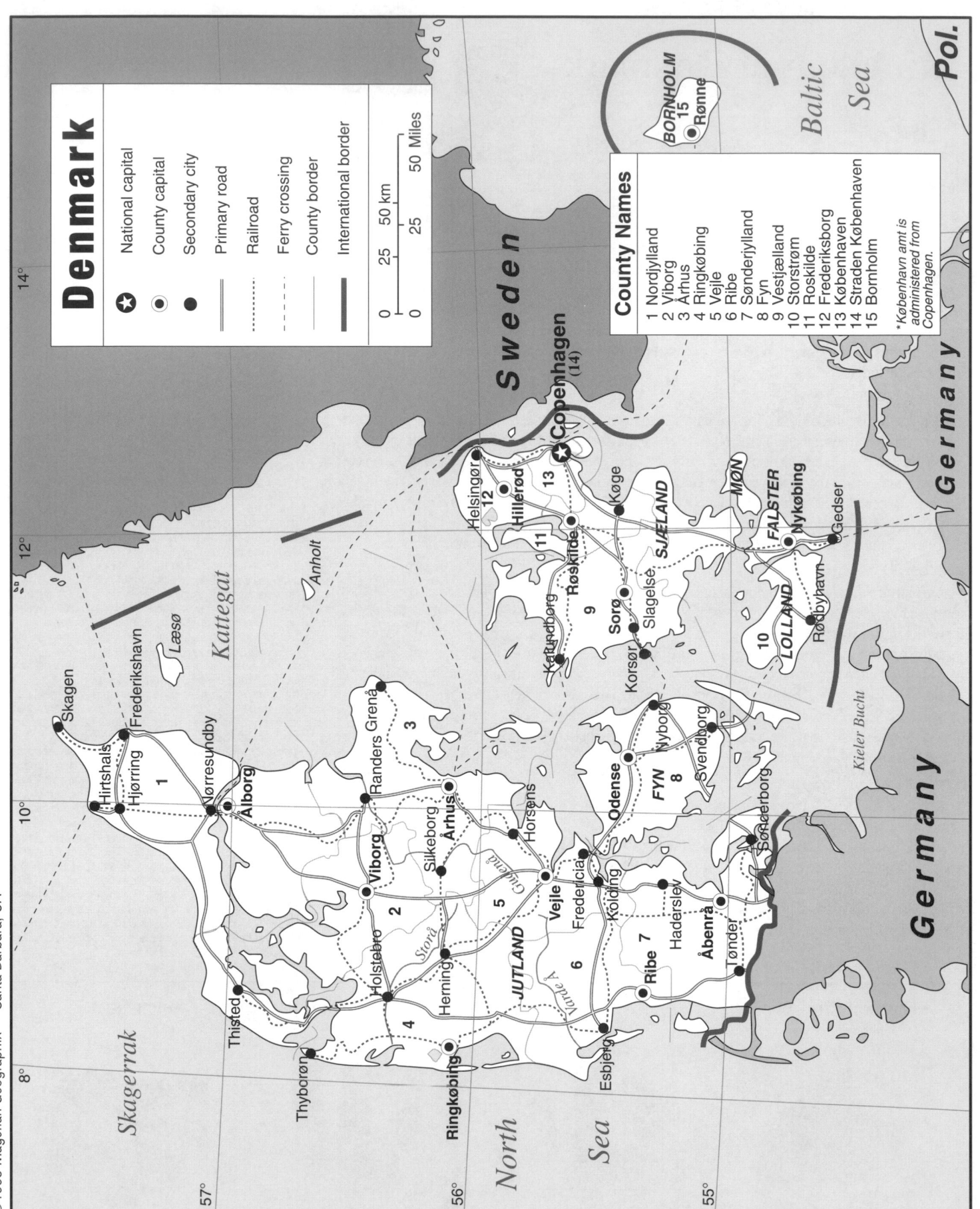

Foreign Trade

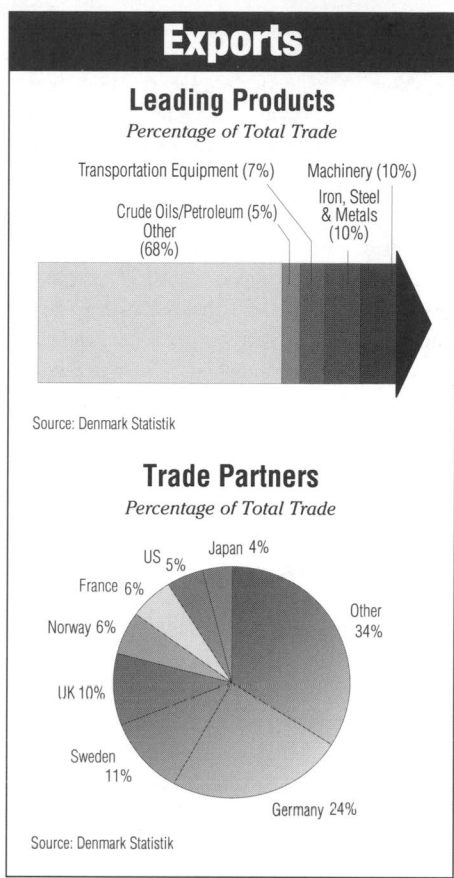

Imports

Leading Products
Percentage of Total Trade

Machinery & Instruments (24%)
Meat&Meat Products (10%)
Chem., Med. & Pharm. Products (10%)
Fish/Fish Products (6%)
Transport Equipment (5%)
Other (45%)

Source: Denmark Statistik

Trade Partners
Percentage of Total Trade

Norway 5%
Japan 4%
France 6%
Other 37%
US 6%
UK 8%
Sweden 11%
Germany 23%

Source: Denmark Statistik

Exports

Leading Products
Percentage of Total Trade

Transportation Equipment (7%)
Machinery (10%)
Crude Oils/Petroleum (5%)
Iron, Steel & Metals (10%)
Other (68%)

Source: Denmark Statistik

Trade Partners
Percentage of Total Trade

US 5%
Japan 4%
France 6%
Other 34%
Norway 6%
UK 10%
Sweden 11%
Germany 24%

Source: Denmark Statistik

Opportunities

FOR IMPORTING TO DENMARK

- agricultural products: cereals, dry nuts, grains, wine
- apparel and textiles
- architectural, construction, and engineering services
- automotive vehicles and parts
- computer products
- crude oil
- fish
- iron, steel, and other metals
- machinery
- medical supplies and equipment
- paper and paperboard
- petroleum products
- pollution control equipment
- sporting goods and recreational equipment
- telecommunications equipment
- transport equipment

FOR EXPORTING FROM DENMARK

- chemicals
- dairy products
- fish
- furniture
- machinery and instruments
- meat and meat products
- medical products
- plastic and rubber products
- pharmaceuticals
- textiles and apparel
- transport equipment

GROWTH SECTORS

- children's clothing
- computer software
- electronics
- fast food franchises
- management consulting
- shipping
- tourism

GOVERNMENT PROCUREMENT

- computer products
- construction goods and services for bridges and tunnels
- educational goods and services for job training
- electrical power transformers and generating equipment
- fiber optic cables
- health care goods and services
- urban light rail construction goods and services

Trade News

RULES AND REGULATION

- **European Union** Denmark is the only Nordic country in the EU, and its role as a bridge between the two regions recently became much more important, particularly with the sharp increase in Nordic business investments in Denmark in order to exploit the opportunities of the EU Single Market Plan.
- **Import licenses** Imports of most products, except for textiles, are free of licensing from all sources.
- **Licensing agencies** Licenses for imports and exports, when required, are issued by the Ministry of Industry, the Ministry of Agriculture, or the Ministry of Fisheries.
- **Textiles** For textiles, a common EU system of export-import licenses has been established for almost all countries exporting low-priced textiles.
- **Certificate of origin** Under Danish regulations, only in very rare cases (such as for imports of certain wines and spirits) are certificates of origin required by the importer, who should normally advise his supplier of this fact.
- **Government procurement** Since the purchasing authority in Denmark is decentralized, an entity could possibly issue specially designated documents with the tender and require each bidder submitting proposals to purchase and incorporate the documents with the bid, but this would not be normal practice. In some cases, a deposit of less than US$100 for documents may be required; but this is primarily earnest money.
- **Export licenses** Except for certain items subject to strategic controls, licenses for exports are required only for the waste and scrap of certain metals.
- **Free ports** The only free port in Denmark is the Copenhagen Free Port. The facilities in the free port are basically used for imports, exports, and transit trade but there are also a few manufacturing firms. The Copenhagen Free Port welcomes foreign companies establishing warehouse and storage facilities. Freight rates to and from Copenhagen Free Port are identical with rates to other ports in northern Europe. It is a key center for shipping to the Baltic region, with direct liner services to most ports there.
- **European integration** Denmark expects to see international markets for goods, services, labor, and capital to become steadily more integrated, with this process being most pronounced in the European Community and among the Nordic countries.

TRANSPORTATION FIRMS

Atlas Spedition A/S
Belvedere Kajen
Elvaerksvej 11
2450 Copenhagen SV
Tel: 31-21-90-00
Fax: 31-21-55-99
Telex: 19993 asas dk

Dantransport A/S
Kornmarksvej 12-20
POB 318
2600 Glostrup
Tel: 33-14-16-88
Fax: 33-48-19-99
Telex: 15000 danhq dk

GOVERNMENT AGENCIES

Trade Department of Ministry of Foreign Affairs
Asiatisk Plads 2
1448 Copenhagen K
Tel: 33-92-00-00

National Agency of Industry and Trade
Tagensvej 137
2200 Copenhagen N
Tel: 31-85-10-66
Fax: 31-81-70-68

FDI Export Contact Service - IREG
H C Andersens Boulevard 18
1790 Copenhagen V
Tel: 33-15-22-33
Fax: 33-32-32-81
Telex: 91-12-217 iraad dk

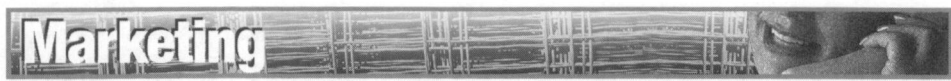

Marketing

Overview

Denmark is a highly industrialized country which has long held preeminent status as a regional sales center and a springboard to Scandinavian, Northern European, and Baltic markets. Denmark was one of the first Scandinavian countries to enter the EU, and has established primacy within that body; even as others follow, Denmark is expected to retain its role as an entry point between the EU and Scandinavian nations.

Distribution

Capital goods, commodities, and industrial raw materials are usually handled by specialized non-stocking sales agents. More specialized and high-technology products are channeled through distributors who operate their own service and maintenance networks. Import agents and distributors deal in consumer goods but, increasingly, such commodities are imported directly by larger department and chain stores. The food sector is dominated by approximately 30 large retail chains supporting in-house wholesale and import divisions. Nearly 25 percent of Danish retail food shops are cooperatives. However, the two largest private chains—FDB and Dansk Supermarked—account for more than 50 percent of this market.

Agents, Distributors, and Partners

Most Danish companies prefer to deal with established local agents or distributors rather than buying from abroad. The agents and distributors form a selective group of businesses. A few powerful, conservative companies have spent decades establishing relationships with their clientele; they now dominate most sectors. Companies entering Denmark or introducing a new product usually find it to be an expensive undertaking. However, there is a growing trend toward direct purchasing from European suppliers. There is also an increasing trend among foreign companies to open branch offices. Franchising is well-known, including not only the ubiquitous fast food outlets, but also shoe repair, car rental, health clubs, and indoor tanning salons. Danes are used to having easy access to retail outlets for most all goods and services. Danish firms are also familiar with licensing and joint ventures; agreements need not be registered and there are no restrictions on remittance of royalties or fees. Joint ventures with foreigners are treated the same as national firms. A local attorney should be used when establishing a corporation or negotiating a partnership arrangement.

Selling Techniques

Price, quality, prompt delivery, and availability of service are key selling factors in Denmark. The market also requires patience and commitment. Danes are generally conservative in business dealings, and relationships with suppliers are typically long-term commitments that may have been developed over decades. Foreign companies seeking to operate in a hit-and-run fashion—rushing in, turning a quick profit, and pulling out—are unlikely to succeed. In general, door-to-door sales are prohibited, but telephone marketing, catalog sales, and television shopping are all fast growing means of selling.

Advertising

Foreign companies seeking to introduce a product in Denmark are generally expected to pay for initial advertising and promotion expenses incurred by the local representative. Successful marketing strategies vary with the territory; some require a serious, conservative approach with a focus on consumer protection, while for other product areas these considerations don't apply. For example, graphic nudity is used in some Danish advertising. Overseas firms should carefully examine the Act on Marketing; compliance is overseen by the Consumer Ombudsman. The Ombudsman will investigate complaints involving misleading statements, unfounded claims, and sexual discrimination. Television commercials cannot interrupt a program. Only TV2, one of the national stations, regularly carries commercials; Denmark's Radio broadcasts only restricted types of sponsored programs. Print media is widespread, including national, regional, daily, morning, evening, weekly, and Sunday newspapers. There are also general and specialty-circulation as well as trade and technical magazines. Cinema and outdoor ads are common. The *Berlingske Tidende* and *Jyllandsposten* have large business sections; *Borsen* is the main Danish business and finance newspaper.

Service and Customer Support

Danish importers demand a high degree of after-sales service. The more technically advanced the product, the higher the quality of support required. Immediate response to consumer requests is mandatory; the supplier should be available by fax or electronic mail for routine communications, and should employ overnight courier service when necessary. Replacement parts should be well stocked and maintained in the country.

Marketing in Denmark

MARKETING TIPS

- **Go high-tech** Danish industry is dependent on trade and has huge incentives to incorporate the latest innovations; the selling proposition should focus on the competitive edge offered by the product, but do not make promises indiscriminately.

- **Government markets** Procurement is decentralized, and most bidders must be pre-qualified, although permanent lists are not required. Bids must usually be received within 30 days of the tender. A Danish agent is not required, but one is usually necessary to demonstrate local service capability.

- **Cooperatives** Although direct chain store purchasing is growing, cooperatives still act as purchasing agents for many retail product distributors.

- **Marking and labeling** All imports are subject to EC as well as special national requirements that vary by specific product and product type.

- **Colors** Red is considered a particularly positive color, and is liberally used in advertising.

CONSULTING FIRMS

Price Waterhouse/Seier-Petersen
Tuborg Boulevard 1
2900 Hellerup
Tel: 39-47-00-00 Fax: 39-47-00-10

AIM Research A/S
Strandboulevarden 89
2100 Copenhagen O
Tel: 35-43-35-43 Fax: 35-43-26-34

Burson-Marsteller A/S
Ostergade 26
1100 Copenhagen K
Tel: 33-32-30-00 Fax: 33-32-30-01

Nielsen Marketing Research A/S
Strandboulevarden 89
2100 Copenhagen O
Tel: 35-43-35-43 Fax: 35-43-13-31

T. I. Sorensen Marketing & Material
Jaegersborg Alle 16
2920 Charlottenlund
Tel: 31-64-32-88 Fax: 31-64-52-88

Vilstrup Research A/S
Rosenvaengets Alle 25
2100 Copenhagen O
Tel: 35-43-66-33 Fax: 35-43-66-16

AD AGENCIES

Leo Burnett Denmark
Vesterbrogade 2B
1620 Copenhagen V
Tel: 33-14-99-66
Fax: 33-14-11-55

Createam
Overgaden neden Vandet 19
1414 Copenhagen K
Tel: 32-96-17-00
Fax: 32-96-44-14

McCann-Erickson A/S
Oster Faelled Torv 5
2100 Copenhagen
Tel: 35-27-01-00
Fax: 35-27-01-01

Ogilvy & Mather Reklamebureau
Martinsvej 7-9
1926 Copenhagen C
Tel: 35-28-88-88
Fax: 35-88-88-00

Wunderman Cato Johnson A/S
Blegdamsvej 104
2100 Copenhagen
Tel: 35-43-77-77
Fax: 35-43-08-04

Young & Rubicam Copenhagen
Enhjorningens Bastion, Langebrogade 6V
1411 Copenhagen K
Tel: 32-96-11-22
Fax: 32-96-10-14

Business Culture

Business and Courtesies

Handshakes are the formal greeting between Danes and with foreign businesspeople. Handshakes are usually firm and brief, and are done upon each meeting and when leaving. Although businesspeople will often deal on a first name basis with those they know, family names and titles are always used for initial introductions. Gifts are rarely exchanged in business, and are not expected as part of the business relationship. If invited into a home, a bouquet of flowers will always be appreciated. Presenting business cards upon introduction is most important. Listing a street address instead of a P.O. box lends credibility and builds confidence in your company.

Business Ethic and Framework

Danes are always receptive to meeting anyone who has a business idea or wishes to make a presentation. It is best to utilize a third-party contact, but the Danes are generally open to companies or individuals who write for an appointment in advance. The Danes are warm and friendly, and are open and accepting of foreigners. The business environment is informal, though not overly casual. It is important to establish the appropriate level and rank of executives with whom you must deal, and executives should be matched not only by title, but also by technical expertise; this should not be difficult in a Danish firm. The Danes are usually straightforward and receptive. You should always consider developing a long-term objective, especially as the small size of the Danish market will limit the quantity of goods ordered each time. Business dinners are unusual and shouldn't be expected. If one is necessary, make it casual and entertaining—and include spouses.

Decision Making

Decisions in Danish firms are normally made by the ranking officer present. Each division has authority to make decisions and capitalize on opportunities that may present themselves. The size of the deal usually has a lot to do with who makes the final decision; larger deals are usually decided upon by senior members. There usually isn't a lot of haggling; Danes prefer well organized and factually informative presentations that are efficient and to the point.

Women

Women are highly accepted and respected in business; they generally receive equal pay and hold high positions within Danish firms. Working mothers are given flexible work hours so they can maintain both career and family. Danish women expect to be treated seriously and with the respect to which their position entitles them. Failure to do this is considered insulting. Businesswomen are as open and direct as men, but this should not be viewed as anything more than being friendly. Foreign women should expect to be treated the same as their male counterparts. It is usually acceptable to shake hands with a woman when being introduced in a business environment.

Meetings

Meetings should be scheduled in advance and you should be prompt for appointments. When you arrive for a meeting and are greeted by the receptionist or secretary you should present your business card and wait until being escorted to the meeting room. Advise your Danish counterparts in advance of who will be attending from your firm and do not bring anyone unannounced. The Danes do not like a lot of paperwork or memos exchanged either during or following a meeting. They prefer to sit down together, and discuss issues and keep everyone informed with short meetings. Documenting all stages of a negotiation is not required or advised.

Business Attire

Proper attire is very important to Danish businesspeople. Suits and ties are always worn; a double breasted jacket or a vested suit is considered proper business attire. Wearing colorful suspenders or bow ties is considered silly or trivial. Women usually wear dresses or skirts and blouses, but the dress code for women is a bit informal. It is, however, always conservative. Men may consider packing a tuxedo because senior businessmen stage more black-tie dinners than in many other countries. Be sure to prepare for the cold climate which prevails most of the year.

Cultural Cautions

DO'S

- Acknowledge that Denmark is known as the "land of fairy tales." The Danes are proud of Hans Christian Andersen.
- When meeting a couple, be sure to shake the woman's hand first. If you are seated, rise before shaking hands.

DON'TS

- Aggressive negotiating tactics do not do well; being aggressive is not part of the national character of the people.
- Don't leave your host's house too soon after dinner. It is considered impolite. Never get up from the dining table until the host or hostess does.
- Avoid any discussion of religion, politics, and taxes.
- Do not criticize Danish culture.
- Never try to barge into the middle of a line of waiting people.
- Do not put your hands in your pockets when talking; it is considered rude.

CUSTOMS

- Toasting with a *skoal* is common—directly to an individual or to the whole crowd. Before sipping, look around at the group or toast person directly, then sip and once again make eye contact.
- Danes are friendly but not very physical. The quiet approach is usually the best.
- Never toast anyone senior to you in rank or age unless they toast you first; don't drink until the host says *skoal*. If you are seated at your hostess's left, you should make a toast to her; if on her right, be prepared to make a short speech of appreciation or thanks.
- Danes constantly use phrases of please and thank you; it is part of the ritual of sharing together.
- Politeness is very important. Women always go through a door first, and men should allow their host to hold the door. Men always go up a flight of stairs first, but women always come down first. In theaters, always face the people who are already seated when you enter the aisle.
- Most business people enjoy a long holiday during the months of July and August. It can be quite difficult to conduct serious business during these months.

OBSERVATIONS

- Danes are very direct, no nonsense, and conservative. They are more concerned with the substance than with the form of a matter, and prefer direct businesspeople who do not beat around the bush.
- Be aware of the potent aquavit Danes love to drink; it is a fiery alcoholic beverage—and powerful to say the least.
- Be aware: Pointing your index finger at your temple and rotating it back and forth is a sign of someone else's contempt.
- Formal dinners are very common in Denmark. A card will be presented to each man with the name of his female dining partner who will be seated on his right. After being introduced to the woman, you should always escort her to the table at the proper time.
- The man usually is in charge of all details at a restaurant. Waiters are signaled by raising the hand and index finger.

NEGOTIATIONS

- Generally, each division with an enterprise has some authority to make decisions and act on opportunities that present themselves.
- Although money is an important consideration, focusing only on money and not on opportunities will be looked on with disfavor. Be prepared to give up some current income for a long-lasting relationship with growth potential.

Legal System

Denmark is a civil law country with the emphasis on written statute law and derivative legislation. As a consequence of its EU membership, much Danish legislation conforms to EU Directives and Regulations.

Intellectual Property Rights

Patents A European patent application can designate Denmark as an included country of coverage, although applications for a "national patent" may still be made directly to the Danish Patent Office. Patents will not be granted for plant or animal varieties, computer programs, or "biological processes". The protection period is 20 years from the date of the application.

Trademarks The Danish Trademark Act corresponds to the EC Directive on trademarks, and protection is available for any graphic symbol which distinctively distinguishes a product or service from others (words, phrases, letters, figures, depictions or shape, get-up or packaging). Trademark rights may be obtained either by express registration or through the mere use of a particular mark. The trademark holder is under a duty to exploit a registered trademark within five years of the date of registration; otherwise the registration and protection will lapse.

Utility Models This form of protection supplements patent protection and is available for technical inventions such as instruments, various forms of apparatuses, tools, chemical components, food stuffs, etc. (plant and animals are specifically excluded) and registration is subject to somewhat less stringent conditions than a "full" patent.

Copyrights Copyright protection does not require any form of registration (and no copyright registration is available). Copyright exists as soon as a particular work is created. Copyright protection may protect specific computer programs (but not the idea or algorithm) and reverse engineering is allowed when necessary to ensure compatibility between programs. Protection is given for a 70-year period.

Trade Secrets Although not defined by statute, trade secrets and information with commercial value are protected by the Marketing Practices Act.

Business Registration

Foreign businesses may operate in Denmark by way of incorporation and registration of a Danish subsidiary. The establishment of a branch office also requires registration with the Corporate Register. With only a few exceptions, representative offices are not subject to any specific restrictions. All business operations must register with the local tax authorities for VAT purposes, social security, etc. Some technology transfer agreements may have to be submitted to the European Commission. Agreements (or concerted practices) which exert a dominant influence on a specific market must be registered with the Danish Competition Board, and failure to register the agreement will make the agreement null and void. On the national level there is no merger control, but the EU Merger Control Regulations also apply to Danish companies.

Contracts and Dispute Resolution

Danish contracts are generally shorter than the extensive contracts known in Anglo-Saxon (common law) countries. In some cases, a foreign business partner may be surprised to see some matters either not mentioned at all, or dealt with in a very short manner. Business disputes which cannot be settled through negotiation can be referred to either the ordinary Danish courts or, in some cases, to a special court with specific commercial experience (the Maritime and Commercial Court in Copenhagen). The parties are also free to agree to submit to arbitration. The Institute of Copenhagen Arbitration is capable of conducting arbitration in foreign languages, principally English, and is widely used for business disputes.

Notaries

Practically no commercial documents are subject to a notarization requirement. In most cases, agreements are simply witnessed. Notaries are available, however, and are part of the local city courts.

Labor

Most Danish employees are members of a trade union and are consequently covered by collective bargaining agreements. Collective bargaining agreements are negotiated for two years at a time and cover wage levels, maximum weekly working hours, benefits, and other terms. There is no statutory minimum wage level but collective bargaining agreements invariably provide for certain minimums. Overtime is typically subject to a 50 percent premium for overtime in excess of one hour and 100 percent premium for overtime during weekends and public holidays. There are no mandatory profit sharing schemes in force. Holiday entitlements are regulated by statute (five weeks per year). Large scale redundancies will in some cases have to be negotiated with local authorities.

Source: Reumert & Partners, Copenhagen

Legal Matters

LEGAL BRIEFS

- **Corporations** Public limited companies must have a minimum paid up share capital of DKK 500,000; private limited companies a minimum paid up share capital of DKK 200,000. Registration fees are nominal.

- **Employment termination** Clerical and salaried staff are protected by statutory minimum notice periods prior to termination. Notice periods increase according to seniority, from a minimum period of one month (after five months of service), to a maximum of six months, after eight years of service. Additional compensation is payable to employees with seniority in excess of 12 years.

- **Property** Property ownership is listed in the official property register which is open for public inspection. Companies having their registered domicile within the EU may acquire commercial property without restrictions. Non-EU companies require prior permission, which will almost certainly be granted if the property is acquired for commercial purposes.

- **Work permits** Working permits are not required for EU citizens. Working permits are required for citizens of non-EU countries and are normally easily obtained.

- **Injunction** Intellectual property rights can be defended not only by ordinary legal action but also by injunction.

- **International agreements** Denmark is a party to the 1970 Patent Co-operation Treaty and the European Patent Convention.

LEGAL CONTACTS

Reumert & Partners
26, Bredgade
1260 Copenhagen K
Tel: 33-93-39-60
Fax: 33-93-39-50

Advodan
Dongens Nytorv 22
1050 Copenhagen K
Tel: 33-14- 32- 36
Fax: 33-32-38-99

Advokatfirmaet Berning Schluter Hald
6 Bredgade
1260 Copenhagen K
Tel: 33-14-33-33
Fax: 33-32-43-33

Dragsted
29, Toldbodgade
1253 Copenhagen K
Tel: 33-33-88-88
Fax: 33-13-40-44

Jarding & Kyed
Q2 Frederiksberggade
P.O. Box 1008
1006 Copenhagen
Tel: 33-145-145
Fax: 33-112-741

Kromann & Munter
Raadhuspladsen 14
1550 Copenhagen V
Tel: 33-11-11-10
Fax: 33-11-80-28

Lett & Co.
Borgergade 111
1300 Copenhagen K
Tel: 33-12-00-66
Fax: 33-12-12-66

Moltke-Leth Advokater
Amaliegade 12
1256 Copenhagen
Tel: 33-11-65-11
Fax: 33-11-49-11

Pedersen & Jantzen
Nyropsgade 45
1602 Copenhagen V
Tel: 33-12-95-12
Fax: 33-12- 95-12

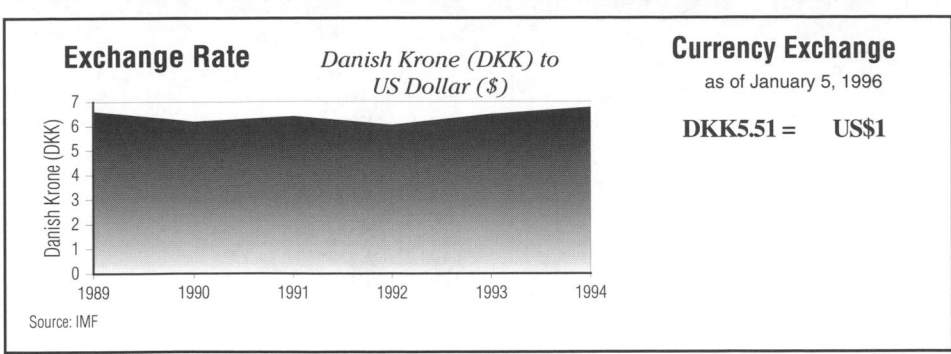

Exchange Rate — Danish Krone (DKK) to US Dollar ($)

Source: IMF

Currency Exchange
as of January 5, 1996

DKK5.51 =   US$1

Currency

The currency of Denmark is the Danish krone (DKK or Dkr), divided into 100 øre.

Foreign Exchange

Denmark participates in the exchange rate and intervention mechanism (ERM) of the European Monetary System. Except for its obligations under this agreement, all other foreign exchange regulations were lifted in 1988. Residents may hold positions in foreign currencies without limitation with respect to the amounts, currencies, or instruments involved. There are no restrictions on foreign exchange dealing, although payments of more than Dkr 60,000 between residents and nonresidents must be reported to the central bank for statistical purposes.

Capital Transfers

No exchange control requirements are imposed on capital receipts or payments by residents or nonresidents. There are no exchange control requirements imposed on payments for imports, on receipts from exports, or on payments for or receipts from invisibles. There are no restrictions on inward or outward capital transfers. There is no prescription of currency requirements. Profits may be freely repatriated, but are subject to Danish taxation.

Investment Incentives

Denmark is heavily dependent on foreign trade in international cooperation, and it follows liberal trade and investment policies aimed at encouraging increased foreign investment. Denmark treats foreign investors on a non-discriminatory, national treatment basis, and offers several incentives of which they may take part. Most incentives are related to environmental protection, although there are some financial incentives connected to investments in special "business zones" and regional development areas, including grants and access to preferential financing.

Investment Restrictions

There is a general requirement that managers and at least half of the Board of Directors of companies located in Denmark must be Danish or EU residents. Other ownership restrictions apply in a few sectors, including hydrocarbon exploration, arms production, aircraft, and shipping.

TAXATION

Taxation requires sophisticated knowledge of complex rules and regulations specific to each country. For more detailed information we suggest you refer to the Ernst & Young Corporate Tax Guide and Directory, available from the Ernst & Young accounting office in your country, or from:

Ernst & Young A/S
Tagensvej 86
2200 Copenhagen N
Denmark
Tel: 35 82 48 48
Telex: 27348 Ans bk ERNST DK (International)
Fax: 35 82 47 10

- Companies registered in Denmark with trading profits from foreign subsidiaries may receive tax relief from the foreign portion of profits. Other tax relief may be granted in accordance with tax treaties; if no tax treaty exists, a tax credit may still be applied according to internal Danish rules.

At a Glance

Corporate Income Tax Rate (%)	34
Capital Gains Tax Rate (%)*	34
Branch Tax Rate (%)	34
Withholding Tax (%)	
Dividends	30
Interest	0
Royalties from Patents, Know-how, etc.	30
Branch Remittance Tax	0
Net Operating Losses (Years)	
Carryback	0
Carryforward	5

*Capital gains are taxed as regular income, although certain capital gains are tax-exempt. Gains from disposal of shares owned for three years or more are exempt from taxation, unless the seller deals in shares. Up to 30% of gains derived from disposal of real property owned for at least nine years is exempt, unless the seller deals in real property.

Money Matters

BITS AND PIECES

- **Credit** Most firms are financed by commercial bank credit lines, usually extended on a revolving basis. Larger corporations may also acquire capital through stock offerings on the Copenhagen Stock Exchange.
- **Export financing** Exports to Denmark are typically financed by the importer or the importer's bank. Although Eximbank financing is available, it is not typically used. A common payment method is an irrevocable letter of credit from a commercial bank.
- **Foreign exchange dealers** Foreign exchange dealers are commercial banks, savings banks, and stockbrokerage companies or other financial institutions, provided that they settle payments between residents and nonresidents on a commercial basis through accounts held in or on behalf of foreign banking institutions.
- **Gold** Residents may freely buy, hold, and sell gold in bars or coins in Denmark; they may also import gold in bars or coins. Imports of gold in bars or coins are generally subject to a value-added tax at the rate of 22 percent. There is no customs duty on imports of gold in bars or coins.
- **Foreign investments** As a general rule, foreign direct investment in Denmark may take place without restrictions or screening.
- **Foreign managers** High-paid foreigners stationed temporarily in Denmark are subject to lenient income taxation.
- **Expropriation** Public expropriation of private property is almost entirely limited to public construction purposes, such as bridge and highway projects, and then only with full compensation.
- **Performance requirements** Performance requirements are applied only in connection with investment in hydrocarbon exploration.
- **Private ownership** As a general rule, any foreign or domestic private entity may freely establish, own, and dispose of a business enterprise in Denmark.

BANKS

Danmarks Nationalbank
Havnegade 5
1092 Copenhagen K
Tel: 33-14-14-11
Fax: 33-13-35-21
Telex: 27051

Citibank N.A. (Subsidiary of Citicorp)
Industriens Hus
Vesterbrogade 1-B
1620 Copenhagen V
Tel: 33-15-50-30
Fax: 33-32-88-73

Den Danske Bank A/S
Holmens Kanal 2-12
1092 Copenhagen K
Tel: 33-44-00-00
Fax: 31-18-58-73

Unibank A/S
Torvegade 2
1786 Copenhagen V
Tel: 33-33-33-33
Fax: 31-54-21-33

A/S Jyske Bank
Vestergade 8-16
8600 Silkeborg
Tel: 89-22-22-22
Fax: 89-22-24-96

Sydbank Sonderjylland A/S
Peberlyk 4
6200 Aabenraa
Tel: 74-63-11-11
Fax: 74-63-13-20

Baltica Bank A/S
Bregade 40
1296 Copenhagen K
Tel: 33-33-99-99
Fax: 33-33-97-97
Telex: 19599

Business Travel

LH 1906	MADRID	935	113-3
LH 1022	STUTTGART HBF.	935	-
AF 1701	LYON	940	683-6
AY 822	HELSINKI	940	113-3
AA 071	SFRANCISCO-DALLAS	945	731-7

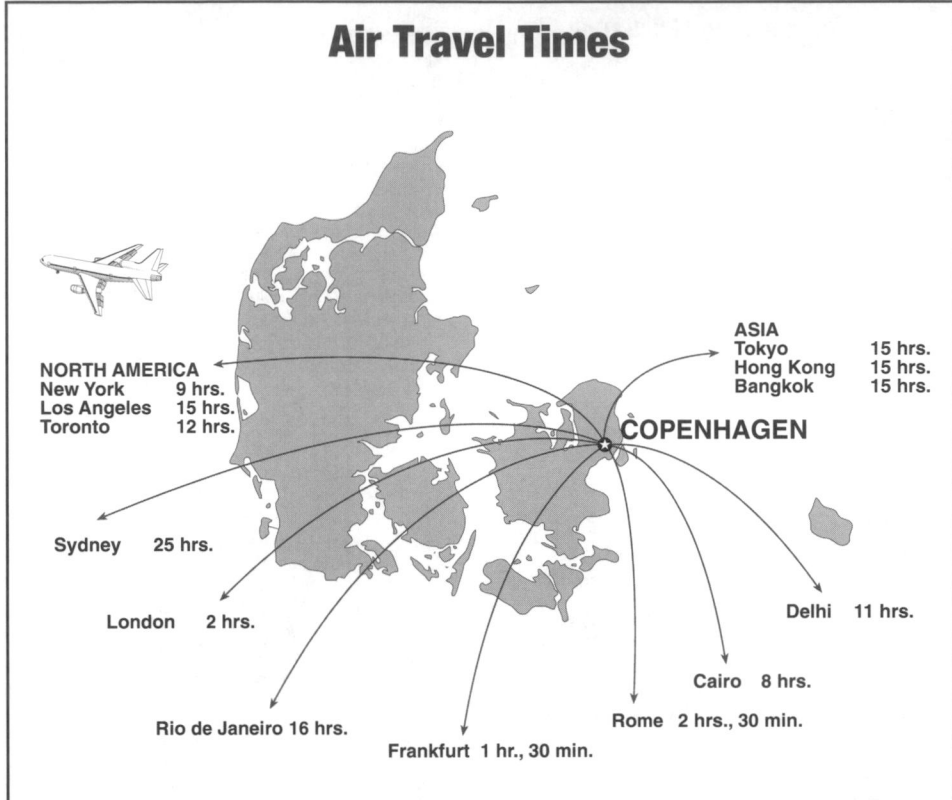

Air Travel Times

NORTH AMERICA
New York 9 hrs.
Los Angeles 15 hrs.
Toronto 12 hrs.

Sydney 25 hrs.

London 2 hrs.

Rio de Janeiro 16 hrs.

Frankfurt 1 hr., 30 min.

Rome 2 hrs., 30 min.

Cairo 8 hrs.

COPENHAGEN

ASIA
Tokyo 15 hrs.
Hong Kong 15 hrs.
Bangkok 15 hrs.

Delhi 11 hrs.

COMMUNICATIONS

Telephones Denmark's telephone service is convenient with good connections and direct dialing; however, avoid old phones which require coins for dial tone. If line is busy, coins are credited to next caller.

Fax Telefax and telegram service is available (Fax widely available) at most post offices or Central Telegraph Offices. Telegrams can be called in by dialing 0022 for inside Denmark and 0024 for overseas. The main telegraph office is in Copenhagen at Kobmagergade 37.

Post office Postal services are modern and efficient. Post offices are generally open from 10:00 am to 5:00 pm on weekdays and until noon on Saturday.

BEST TRAVEL BOOKS

Fodor's Travel Guides, Europe. New York: Fodor Travel Guides. Tourist oriented, excellent source of city details.

Lonely Planet, Insight Pocket Guides, Denmark. I can't think of another book which so effectively captures the essence of a country.

A Guide to International Behavior, Do's and Taboo's Around the World. Edited by Roger E. Axtell, compiled by the Parker Pen Company. Now completely updated and revised, the ultimate guide to international behavior. Helpful, fun to read.

Berlitz Business Travel Guide, Europe. Concise economic details, successful trip planning, background information on people and cities, useful facts and addresses.

USEFUL TELEPHONE NUMBERS

If you are calling from outside Denmark, you will need to add the country code [45] and any other international dialing requirements from within your country. Area codes must be dialed for all calls within Denmark, local as well as long distance.

- International Directory Assistance 0039
- International Operator 0029
- Central Telegraph Office 0022
- Danish Chamber of Commerce 33-91-23-23
- Copenhagen Chamber of Commerce ..33-15-53-20
- Trade Promotion Department................33-44-00-00
- Government Information Service 33-92-92-00
- Cimber Air 74-42-22-23
- Danair 33-52-33-33
- Scandinavian Airline System 31-50-91-11
- Maersk Air 33-52-33-33
- National Railway 33-14-04-00
- Doctor 33-93-63-00
- Taxi 31-35-35-35
- Emergency Police/Fire/Ambulance 112
- Directory Assistance 118
- Operator Assistance 140
- Copenhagen Waterways 33-14-88-80
- Mechanical Services 33-14-22-22
- Copenhagen Tourist Info.....................33-11-13-25

Credit Card Information
Lost or stolen credit cards (call collect to the US, regardless of which country the card was issued in).
- Amex ....[1] (919) 333-3211
- Diner's Club ....[1] (303) 799-1504
- MasterCard ....[1] (314) 275-6690
- Visa ....[1] (410) 581-7931

Travelogue

WORKWEEK

Offices Monday-Friday 8:00 am to 4:00 pm.
Banks Monday-Friday 9:30 am to 4:00 pm, closing at 6:00 pm on Thursdays.
Government Monday-Friday 9:00 am to 5:00 pm or 8:00 am to 4:00 pm.
Retail Generally open Monday-Thursday 9:00 am to 5:00 pm, Friday until 7:00 pm, and Saturday until 1:00 pm.

HOLIDAYS

Holidays 1996
January 1 New Year's Day
April 4 Maundy Thursday
April 5 Good Friday*
April 7 Easter Sunday*
April 8 Easter Monday*
May 1 Labor Day
May 3 Prayer Day
May 16 Ascension Day
May 26 Whit Monday
June 5 Constitution Day**
December 25 Christmas Day
December 26 Second Christmas Day
December 31 New Year's Eve**
*Dates vary each year.
** Half day holidays.

VISA AND PASSPORT

A valid passport is required of visitors to Denmark, but a tourist or business visa is not necessary for stays of up to 90 days. The 90-day period begins upon entering any of the Scandinavian countries. All travelers must have onward tickets, valid travel documents, and sufficient funds.

DEPARTURE FORMALITIES

No more than DKr 40,000 per person may be taken out of Denmark. There are no other restrictions for departure from Denmark.

IMMUNIZATION

No inoculations are required for entry. International certificate of vaccination not required unless arriving from an infected area.

TIPPING

Tipping is the exception rather than the rule in Denmark. Hotels and restaurants add a 15 percent service charge to all bills. It is not necessary to tip taxi drivers.

CRIME

While Denmark has a low crime rate, travelers to major cities can be targets for pickpockets and pursesnatchers by gangs. Contact Lost and Found offices for stolen goods and call police. Hotel lobbies and breakfast rooms, airports, and train stations are favorite arenas for purse and luggage thieves.

INFRASTRUCTURE

Denmark has highly sophisticated air, train, bus, taxi, roadway, ferry, rental car, hotel, and telecommunication networks. Boat connections are time-consuming, the 11 airports and train facilities are the transportation methods of choice. First class intercity trains have business meeting compartments. Regular ferry service is reliable. Taxis can be hailed from the street but are expensive. Bus services are also expensive but easily attainable; bus tickets are purchased from the driver. An international driver's license is needed for car rentals, along with proof of insurance. When driving a car, be aware it is illegal to use the car horn except in cases of danger; blinking car headlights to attract the needed attention is accepted. Heavy fines are payable on the spot for even minor infractions, making Danes well-disciplined drivers.

NATIONAL TOURIST OFFICE

Tourist Office
Vestebrog 6D
Copenhagen
Tel: 33-11-14-15

GOVERNMENT AGENCIES

Ministry of Foreign Affairs
Asiatisk Plads 2
1448 Copenhagen K
Tel: 33-92-00-00
Fax: 31-54-05-33

Ministry of Industry and Coordination
Slotsholmsgade 12
1216 Copenhagen K
Tel: 33-92-33-50
Fax: 33-12-37-78

Ministry of Communications & Tourism
Tietgensgade 37
1530 Copenhagen V
Tel: 33-93-00-98
Fax: 33-11-22-23

Ministry of Transport (Public Works)
Frederiksholms Kanal 27-F
1220 Copenhagen K
Tel: 33-92-33-55
Fax: 33-12-38-93

The Danish Working Environment Services
Landskronagade 33-35
2100 Copenhagen O
Tel: 31-18-00-88
Fax: 31-18-35-60

Danish Bureau of Statistics
Sejerogade 11
2100 Copenhagen O
Tel: 39-17-39-17
Fax: 31-18-48-01

Danish Board for Testing & Approval of Electrical Equipment
Lyskaer 8
2730 Herlev
Tel: 44-94-72-66
Fax: 44-94-72-61

Government Purchasing Office
Suomisvej 2
1927 Frederiksberg C
Tel: 31-35-95-00
Fax: 31-35-95-44

The National Consumer Agency of Denmark
Amagerfaelledvej 56
2300 Copenhagen S
Tel: 31-57-01-00
Fax: 32-96-02-32

Danish State Railways
Solvgade 40
1349 Copenhagen K
Tel: 33-14-04-00
Fax: 33-14-04-40

The National Agency of Environmental Protection
Strandgade 29
1401 Copenhagen K
Tel: 31-57-83-10
Fax: 31-57-24-49

The Patent Agency
Helgeshoj Alle 81
2630 Taastrup
Tel: 43-71-71-71
Fax: 43-71-71-70

National Board of Health
Amaliegade 13
1256 Copenhagen K
Tel: 33-91-16-01
Fax: 33-93-16-36

National Telecom Agency
Holsteinsgade 63
2100 Copenhagen O
Tel: 35-43-03-33
Fax: 35-43-14-34

National Food Agency
The Import Section
Moerkhoej Bygade 19
2860 Soeborg
Tel: 39-69-66-00
Fax: 39-66-01-00

Veterinary Directorate
Rolighedsvej 25
1958 Frederiksberg C
Tel: 31-35-81-00
Fax: 35-36-19-12

Danish Customs
Customs and Tax Region 1
Strandgade 100
1401 Copenhagen K
Tel: 32-88-93-00
Fax: 31-95-10-12

BUSINESS AND TRADE ORGANIZATIONS

Danish Standards Association
Baunegaardsvej 73
2900 Hellerup
Tel: 39-77-01-01
Fax: 39-77-02-02

Confederation of Danish Industries
H.C. Andersens Boulevard 18
1596 Copenhagen V
Tel: 33-77-33-77
Fax: 33-77-33-00

Association of Commercial Agents in Denmark
Borsen
1217 Copenhagen K
Tel: 33-14-49-41
Fax: 33-12-69-81

Landsforeningen Dansk Arbejde (National Association for Danish Enterprise)
Gravene 2
8800 Viborg
Tel: 86-62-42-22
Fax: 86-62-45-88

Det Okonomiske Rad (Economic Council)
Kampmannsgade 1 IV
1604 Copenhagen V
Tel: 33-13-51-28

The Danish Chamber of Commerce
Borsen
1217 Copenhagen K
Tel: 33-95-05-00
Fax: 33-32-52-16

BANKS

Finanstilsynet (Financial Supervisory Authority)
Gammel Kongevej 74A
1850 Frederiksberg C
Tel: 31-23-11-88
Fax: 31-23-04-41

Danmarks Nationalbank
Havnegade 5
10932 Copenhagen K
Tel: 33-14-14-11
Fax: 33-13-35-21
Telex: 27051

Aktivbanken A/S
POB 2350
Ladegardsvej 3
7100 Vejle
Tel: 75-85-71-00
Fax: 75-85-81-55
Telex: 61113

Amagerbanken A/S
Amagerbrogade 25
2300 Copenhagen S
Tel: 31-95-60-90
Fax: 31-54-45-34
Telex: 31262

Amtssparekassen Fyn A/S
Vestre Stationsvej 7
POB 189
5100 Odense C
Tel: 66-14-04-74
Fax: 65-91-01-10
Telex: 5559778

Arbejdernes Landsbank A/S
Vesterbrogade 5
1502 Copenhagen V
Tel: 33-14-88-77
Fax: 33-32-18-73

Telex: 15633

Baltica Bank A/S
Bregade 40
1296 Copenhagen K
Tel: 33-33-99-99
Fax: 33-33-97-97
Telex: 19599

Egnsbank Nord A/S
Jernbanegad 4-6
POB 701
9900 Frederikshavn
Tel: 98-42-04-33
Fax: 98-42-47-92
Telex: 67102

Forstaedernes Bank A/S
Malervangen 1
2600 Glostrup
Tel: 42-96-17-20
Fax: 42-63-32-36
Telex: 33261

NEWSPAPERS

Berlingske Tidende
Pilestraede 34
1147 Copenhagen K
Tel: 33-75-75-75
Fax: 33-75-20-20
Telex: 27143

Berlingske Tidende
Pilestraede 34
1147 Copenhagen K
Tel: 33-32-01-02
Fax: 33-12-24-45
Telex: 22903

B.T.
Kr. Bernikowsgade 6
1147 Copenhagen K
Tel: 33-75-75-33
Fax: 33-75-20-33
Telex: 27115

Ekstra Bladet
Radhuspladsen 37
1785 Copenhagen V
Tel: 33-11-13-13
Fax: 33-14-10-00
Telex: 22300

Det Fri Aktuelt
Radhuspladsen47
1595 Copenhagen V
Tel: 33-32-40-01
Fax: 33-13-00-48
Telex: 19785

Information
Store Kongensgade 40
POB 188
1006 Copenhagen K
Tel: 33-14-14-26
Fax: 33-93-80-83
Telex: 22658

Kristeligt Dagblad
Fanogade 15
2100 Copenhagen 0
Fax: 39-27-08-00
Tel: 39-27-12-35

Politiken
Politikens Hus
Radhuspladsen 37
1585 Copenhagen V
Tel: 33-11-85-11
Fax: 33-15-41-17
Telex: 16885

Fyens Stiftstidende

Blangstedgardsvej 2-6
5220 Edense S0
Tel: 66-11-11-11
Fax: 65-93-25-74
Telex: 59858

Dagbladet
Sogade 4-12
4100 Ringsted
Tel: 53-61-25-00
Fax: 53-61-07-17

Skive Folkeblad
Gemsevej 7
7800 Skive
Tel: 97-51-34-11
Fax: 97-51-28-35

Viborg Stifts Folkeblad
Sct Mathiasgade 7
8800 Viborg
Tel: 86-62-68-00
Fax: 86-62-22-20

Den Bla Avis (East edition)
Generatorves 8D
2730 Herlev
Tel: 44-92-44-44

Den Bla Avis (West edition)
Frederiksgade 45
POB 180
8000 Arhus C
Tel: 86-19-14-11
Fax: 86-20-20-08

Weekendavisn Berlingske
Pilestraede 34
1147 Copenhagen K
Tel: 33-75-75-75
Fax: 33-75-20-50
Telex: 27143

PERIODICALS

Det Bedste fra Reader's Digest A/S
Jagtvej 169B
2100 Copenhagen 0
Tel: 31-18-12-13
Fax: 31-18-12-36
Telex: 27357

Bo Bedre
Strandboulevarden 130
2100 Copenhagen K
Tel: 31-29-55-00
Fax: 31-29-01-99
Telex: 15712

Familie Journalen
Vigerslev Allé 18
2500 Valby
Copenhagen
Tel: 31-30-33-33
Fax: 31-30-24-40
Telex: 22390

Femina
Vigerslev Allé 18
2500 Valby
Copenhagen
Tel: 36-30-33-33
Fax: 36-44-19-79

Gor det selv
Strandboulevarden 130
2100 Copenhagen 0
Tel: 31-29-55-00
Fax: 31-29-01-99
Telex: 15712

Helse-Familiens Laegemagasin
Classensgade 36
2100 Copenhagen 0
Tel: 35-26-79-00
Fax: 35-26-87-60

Hjemmet (The Home)
Vognmagergade 10
1145 Copenhagen K
Tel: 33-15-15-95
Fax: 33-91-15-62

I form
Strandboulevarden 130
2100 Copenhagen 0
Tel: 31-29-55-00
Fax: 31-29-01-99
Telex: 15712

Idé-0nyt
Gl. Klausdalsbrovej 482
2730 Herlev
Tel: 44-53-40-00
Fax: 44-92-11-21

Illusteret Videnskab
Strandboulevarden 130
2100 Copenhagen 0
Tel: 31-29-55-00
Fax: 31-29-01-99

Landsbladet
Vester Farimagsgade 6
1606 Copenhagen V
Tel: 33-11-22-22
Fax: 33-11-31-48

Lexicon
Strandboulevarden 130
2100 Copenhagen 0
Tel: 31-29-55-00
Fax: 31-29-01-99

Manedsmagasinet Bilen
Strandboulevarden 130
2100 Copenhagen 0
Tel: 31-29-55-00
Fax: 31-29-01-99
Telex: 15712

Praxis
Gl. Bjert 22
6092 Varmark
Tel: 75-57-27-00

TIPS-bladet
Alsgarde Centret 2
3140 Alsgarde
Tel: 42-10-93-00
Fax: 42-10-88-30

TV Bladet
Vesterbrogade 16
1506 Copenhagen V
Tel: 31-23-16-11
Fax: 31-24-10-08

Ude og Hjemme
Vigerslev Allé 18
2500 Valby
Copenhagen
Tel: 36-30-33-33
Fax: 36-30-74-44

Ugenmagasinet Sondag
Vesterbrogade 16
POB 424
1505 Copenhagen V
Tel: 31-23-16-11
Fax: 31-24-10-08

Ugens Rapport
Skt Annae Plads 8
1250 Copenhagen K
Tel: 33-13-60-60
Fax: 33-15-64-46

Aktuel Elektronik
Skelbaekgade 4
1780 Copenhagen V
Tel: 31-21-68-01
Fax: 31-21-23-96

Atl om Data
St. Kongensgade 72
1264 Copenhagen K
Tel: 33-91-28-33

Annonce Avisen Erhvery
Farum Gydevej 59
3520 Farum
Tel: 42-95-72-10
Fax: 42-95-57-25

Arbejde og Daginstitution
Paedagogisk Medhjaelper Forbund
Sct Kongensgade 79
1264 Copenhagen K
Tel: 33-11-03-43
Fax: 33-13-27-01

Arbejdsgiveren
Vester Voldgade 113
1790 Copenhagen V
Tel: 33-93-40-00
Telex: 16464
Fax: 33-12-29-76

Arbejdslederen
Vermlandsgade 65
2300 Copenhagen S
Tel: 31-57-56-22
Fax: 31-57-90-22

Automatik
Algade 10
POB 80
4500 Nykobing sj
Tel: 73-41-23-10

Badnyt (Boats)
Strandboulevarden 130
2100 Copenhagen 0
Tel: 31-29-55-00
Fax: 31-29-01-99
Telex: 15712

Bankstanden
Esplanaden 8
1014 Copenhagen K
Tel: 33-15-83-11

Computerworld
Krumtappen 4
2500 Valby
Tel: 36-44-28-00
Fax: 36-44-25-69

Forbrugsforeningsbladet
Knabrostraede 12
1210 Copenhagen K
Tel: 33-15-88-26

Haven
Aby Baekgardsvej 6
8230 Abyhoj
Tel: 86-15-56-88
Fax: 86-15-33-23

RADIO AND TELEVISION

General Directorate of Posts and Telegraphs
Tietgensgade 37
1530 Copenhagen V

Danmarks Radio (Radio Denmark)
Radiohuset
Rosenorns Allé 22
1999 Frederiksberg C
Tel: 35-20-30-40
Fax: 31-67-29-97
Telex: 22695

Danmarks Radio TV
TV-Byen
2860 Soborg
Tel: 35-20-30-40
Fax: 31-67-29-97
Telex: 22695

TV 2
Rugardsvej 25
5100 Odense C
Tel: 65-91-33-22
Fax: 65-91-33-22
Telex: 59660

STOCK EXCHANGE

Kobenhavns Fondsbors
(Copenhagen Stock Exchange)
Nikolaj Plads 6
POB 1040
1007 Copenhagen K
Tel: 33-93-93-66
Fax: 33-12-86-13

INTERNET ADDRESSES

Usenet group(s):
soc.culture.nordic

Denmark Info
http://ai.eecs.umich.edu/people/skyt/DANMARK/
danmark.html

JUBII (Danish equivalent to YAHOO for Denmark)
http://www.jubii.dk/default.htm

Links to scandanavia Denmark Page
http://www.infoserve.net/netquest/nordic/
danmark.html

Dominican Republic

At a Glance

Location In the northern Caribbean Sea, about halfway between Cuba and Puerto Rico.
Terrain Rugged highlands and mountains interspersed with fertile valleys.
Climate Tropical maritime, with little seasonal temperature variation and great variation in rainfall.

THE PEOPLE

Population 7,500,000
Ethnic composition
European 16%
African origin 11%
Mixed 73%
Religious composition
Roman Catholic 95%
Other 5%
Languages spoken Spanish.
Education and literacy The government has focused on enrolling all children between 7 and 14 in school, and in keeping them there. Literacy for the adult population is 83 percent.
Labor force
Total: 2,600,000
By occupation: agriculture 33%, services and industry 67%.

COUNTRY FACTS

Political and legal This republic has a legal system based on French civil codes. It maintains a multiparty political system. The constitution provides that members of the armed forces and the police services cannot vote.
Telephone The domestic system is generally efficient. Modern equipment is utilized and services are fairly reliable; most international calls can be dialed directly. International country code: [1]. Area code for all points is (809).
Transportation The major form of transport is the national highway system, followed by railroad services. Most roads are unpaved, but the government does attempt to keep them well maintained. There are eight major harbors and three international airports.
Environment Extensive deforestation has led to the recent enactment of laws which limit tree cutting. Still, depletion of forests, and soil erosion remain significant problems. Rapid population growth has resulted in a problematic decrease in the supply of water. This problem is exacerbated by water pollution caused by mining, as well as industrial and agricultural chemical effluents. The government is currently focusing its efforts on alleviating water shortages, deforestation, and the chemical damage to surrounding coral reefs.
Media There are 120 AM, no FM radio stations, and 18 television stations. The press is among the freest in Latin America. There are several newspapers, and a variety of international periodicals are available.
Health The government has made a tremendous effort to improve health care and expand coverage. As a result, nearly the entire population now has access to adequate health care services. Life expectancy of males is 66 years; of females, 70 years.

Economy

Overview

The Dominican Republic is one of the larger markets in Latin America. Following the economic turmoil of recent years, when the GDP fell by 5 percent and inflation doubled, the Dominican Republic implemented a series of governmental reforms, eliminating many price controls and subsidy programs, in an attempt to stabilize its economy and put it on a free market basis. As a result, GDP increased 3 percent, and inflation dropped to single-digit rates. However, increased government spending led to renewed inflationary pressures, the consumer price index jumped, and exchange rates fell. Today, the economy has stabilized and most prices are determined by market forces. However, the Dominican Republic has been slow to resolve the question of its foreign debt obligations, and doubts remain that it has effectively eschewed its interventionist practices in manipulating the economy.

Trade

The Dominican Republic is heavily dependent on imports and has maintained a steep and chronic trade deficit equal to roughly one-third of total trade. Major exports include ferro-nickel, sugar, coffee, doré (gold-silver alloy), and cocoa beans. Major imports include petroleum, machinery, vehicles, foodstuffs, and chemicals. The US is the Dominican Republic's main trading partner, accounting for more than 40 percent of total trade. It is followed by Venezuela, Japan, Mexico, and the Netherlands.

Sectors

Agriculture Contributing about 15 percent to GDP, agriculture employs more than 33 percent of the work force. Sugar, coffee, and cocoa are the major cash crops and tobacco, rice, beef, and cut flowers are also economically significant. The sector is heavily dependent on external international commodity prices.

Industry Industry contributes about 30 percent of GDP and employs about 20 percent of the work force. The dominant industries are food and beverage processing—primarily sugar refining—petroleum refining, and chemicals; other developing industries include pharmaceuticals, cement, light manufacturing, and off-shore assembly operations, primarily of apparel. Growth in this sector has come primarily from sugar processing, output from free trade zones, and construction.

Services Employing nearly half of the work force and accounting for somewhat more than half of GDP, services are relatively poorly developed outside of tourism, which is a major foreign exchange earner. Although efforts are being made to upgrade the financial system in hopes of attracting offshore business, it remains weak. Otherwise, most services involve distribution and personal service activities.

Trends

The future of the economy will depend on the maintenance of policies conducive to both continued economic stability and adaptation to the requirements of an open, competitive global marketplace. Issues confronting decisionmakers include proposals for investment reform and a reduction of the government's dependence on levies on international trade as a major source of revenue. New legislation for a financial code, foreign investment law, and export promotion schemes could create a more comfortable climate for foreign investors, while laying a foundation for greater international integration. Prospects for integration have been hampered by high tariffs aimed at protecting domestic industry.

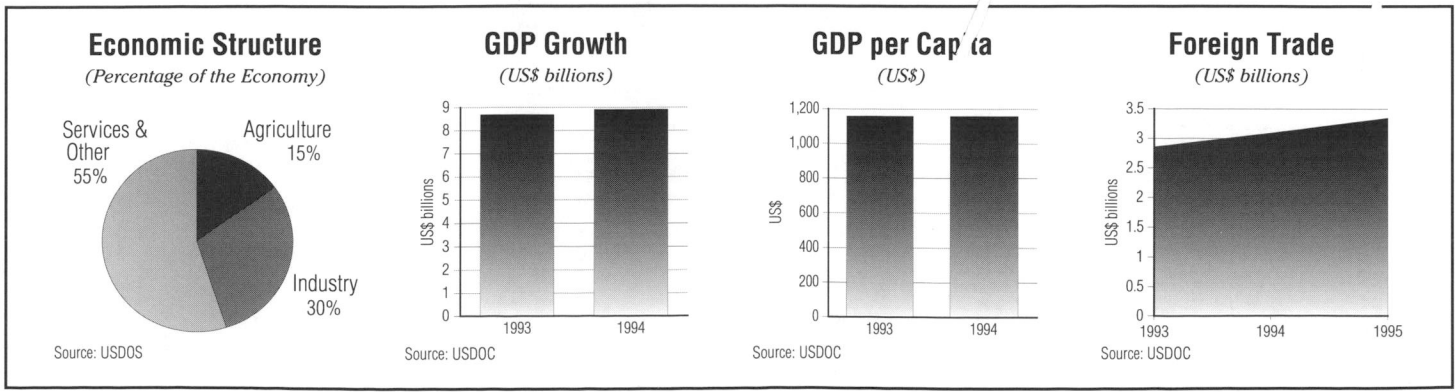

Economic Structure
(Percentage of the Economy)
Services & Other 55%
Agriculture 15%
Industry 30%
Source: USDOS

GDP Growth
(US$ billions)
1993 1994
Source: USDOC

GDP per Capita
(US$)
1993 1994
Source: USDOC

Foreign Trade
(US$ billions)
1993 1994 1995
Source: USDOC

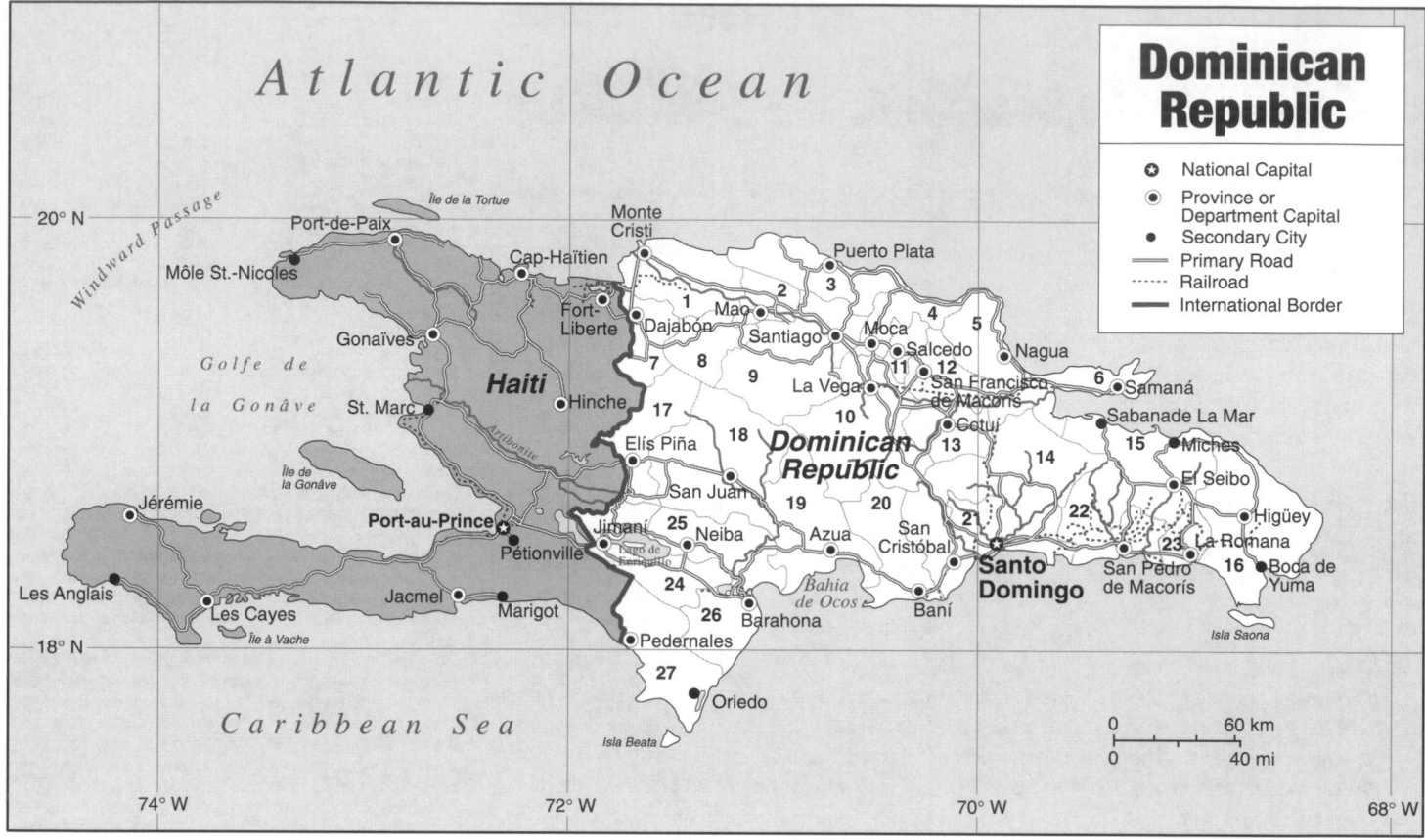

©1992 Magellan Geographix℠ Santa Barbara, CA

Dominican Provinces

1. Monte Cristi
2. Valverde
3. Puerto Plata
4. Espaillat
5. María Trinidad Sánchez
6. Samaná
7. Dajabón
8. Santiago Rodríquez
9. Santiago
10. La Vega
11. Salcedo
12. Duarte
13. Sánchez Ramírez
14. San Cristóbal
15. El Seibo
16. La Atlagracia
17. La Estrelleta
18. San Juan
19. Azua
20. Peravia
21. Distrito Nacional
22. San Pedro de Macorís
23. La Romana
24. Independencia
25. Baoruco
26. Barahona
27. Pedernales

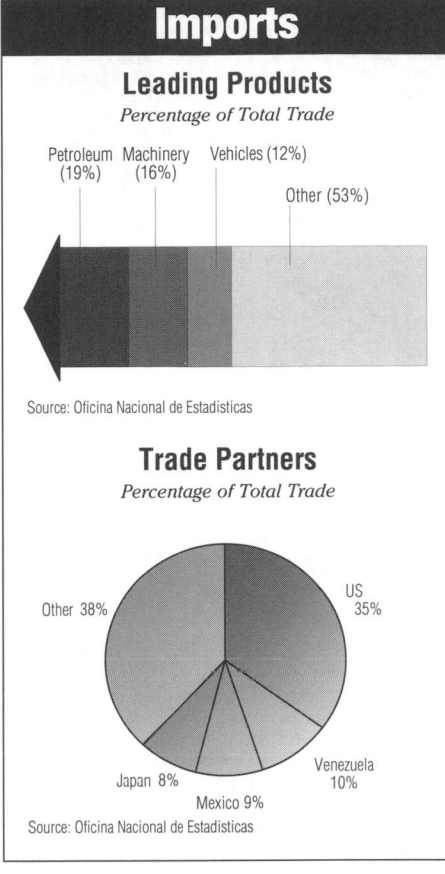

Imports

Leading Products
Percentage of Total Trade

Petroleum (19%) Machinery (16%) Vehicles (12%) Other (53%)

Source: Oficina Nacional de Estadisticas

Trade Partners
Percentage of Total Trade

US 35%
Other 38%
Venezuela 10%
Mexico 9%
Japan 8%

Source: Oficina Nacional de Estadisticas

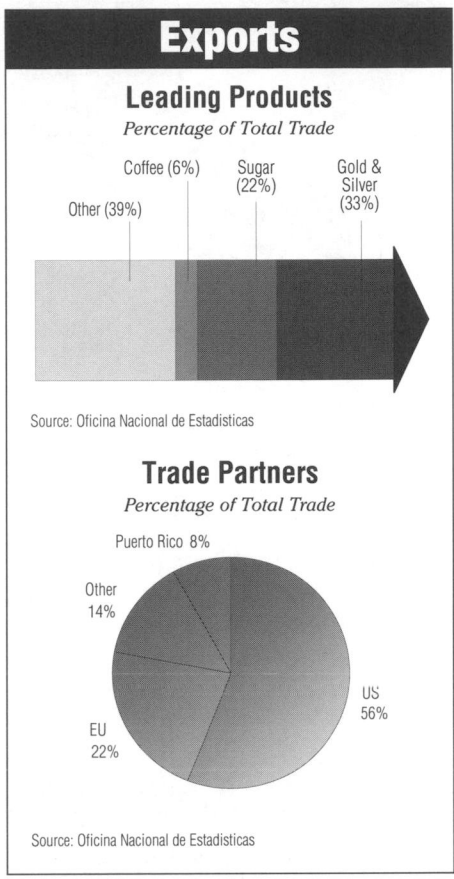

Exports

Leading Products
Percentage of Total Trade

Coffee (6%) Sugar (22%) Gold & Silver (33%) Other (39%)

Source: Oficina Nacional de Estadisticas

Trade Partners
Percentage of Total Trade

Puerto Rico 8%
Other 14%
US 56%
EU 22%

Source: Oficina Nacional de Estadisticas

Opportunities

FOR IMPORTING TO THE DOMINICAN REPUBLIC

- air conditioning and refrigeration equipment
- automobiles and automotive parts
- capital goods
- chemicals
- consumer foods: snacks, meats, dairy products, fruits and vegetables
- cotton and fabrics
- drugs and pharmaceuticals
- electrical power systems
- foodstuffs
- hotel and restaurant equipment
- household appliances
- industrial raw materials
- medical equipment
- petroleum
- soybean meal, wheat
- telecommunications equipment

FOR EXPORTING FROM THE DOMINICAN REPUBLIC

- cocoa
- coffee
- electrical machinery and equipment
- ferronickel
- gold
- leather products
- meats
- plastic products
- silver
- sugar
- textiles and clothing
- tobacco

GROWTH SECTORS

- construction
- hotels, bars, and restaurants
- free trade zones
- sugar processing
- tourism

GOVERNMENT PROCUREMENT

- avionics equipment
- electrical transmission lines, transformers, and switches
- industrial machinery
- medical supplies and equipment
- office supplies and equipment

Trade News

RULES AND REGULATIONS

- **Tariffs and import taxes** There are generally four taxes on imports except for those subject to exemptions provided by law. They are (1) the basic import tax—three to 35 percent; (2) a consumption tax for luxury imports—generally 30 percent for agricultural goods and 15 to 60 percent for nonagricultural, nonessential goods; (3) an eight percent tax on industrialized goods and services for processed agricultural goods and all nonagricultural goods; and (4) a 1.5 percent tax which must be paid to the central bank for the purchase of foreign exchange.

- **Import licenses** Import licenses are not required for most products. However, import licenses are required for pharmaceutical products and agro-chemicals. "No objection" permits are required to import certain agricultural goods, and phytosanitary certificates must accompany live plants and agricultural material used in planting.

- **Prohibited imports** There are no official prohibited goods, but other import permissions are used to effectively bar the importation of certain products, usually for reason of oversupply in the country. Products in which the Dominican Republic is usually self-sufficient, such as garlic, onions, potatoes, pinto beans, whole powdered milk, and rice are often restricted.

- **Prohibited exports** Certain exports are prohibited, including some food products and animal species, unprocessed wood (for environmental protection purposes), and blood. In addition, products imported under some bilateral trade agreements are prohibited from being exported under the terms of such agreements.

- **Government involvement** The government's extreme dependence on taxes on international trade (tariffs and other tariff-like charges) magnifies the government's involvement in productive activities. Productive inputs and finished products must pass through the government's customs apparatus.

- **Non-essential imports tax** The government imposes a five to 80 percent selective consumption tax on "non-essential" imports such as home appliances, alcohol, perfumes, jewelry, automobiles, auto parts, and certain agricultural products.

- **Customs procedures** Many foreign businesspeople complain that bringing goods through the Dominican customs is a slow and arduous procedure. The customs department's often arbitrary interpretations of the regulations provoke many complaints. Certain goods which are supposedly exempted from duties are frequently delayed by customs, and businesspeople must spend large amounts of time and money getting materials through customs. Merchandise can be held up in customs for as long as one year.

- **Free trade zones (FTZs)** In 1993, the number of free trade companies grew from 380 to 462. Free trade zone operators and enterprises are entitled to 100 percent exemptions from most corporate and municipal taxes and import duties, and they can manipulate goods and transfer goods and labor from one FTZ to another.

- **Free trade agreements** Although the Dominican Republic receives the benefits of the Caribbean Basin Initiative and GATT, it does not belong to any free trade association. It is exploring membership in the Caribbean Common Market (where it has observer status), the Central American Common Market, and is a founding member of the newly formed association of Caribbean states.

FREIGHT FORWARDER

Agencia Maritima y Comercial
POB 1125
Santo Domingo
Telex: 0071 Amarlt

GOVERNMENT AGENCY

Center for Promotion of Export
POB 199-2
Santo Domingo
Telex: RCA 4504 CEDPEX

Travelogue

WORKWEEK
Offices Monday-Friday 8:00 am to 5:00 pm with lunch from noon to 1:00 pm or 1:00 to 2:00 pm.
Banks Generally Monday-Friday 8:00 am to 4:00 pm.
Government Monday-Friday 7:30 am to 2:30 pm.
Retail Monday-Friday 8:00 am to noon and 2:00 pm to 5:00 pm, and Saturday 8:00 am to noon.

HOLIDAYS
Holidays 1996
January 1 New Year's Day
January 6 Epiphany
January 21 Our Lady of Grace
January 26 Duarte's Birthday
February 27 Dominican Independence
April 14 Good Friday*
May 1 Labor Day
May 16 Election Day
June 15 Corpus Christi*
August 16 Restoration Day
September 24 Our Lady of the Mercedes*
December 25 Christmas Day
*Dates vary each year.

VISA AND PASSPORT
A passport and a tourist card or visa are required for entry to the Dominican Republic. Tourist Cards are available for US$10 at the airport.

DEPARTURE FORMALITIES
Visitors departing at Las Americas International Airport will have to pay a departure tax of US$10. Black market transactions are illegal for exchange of pesos to hard currency of your country.

IMMUNIZATION
No immunizations are required of Canadian, UK, or US citizens. Other nationals should check with their consulate. For long-term stays, typhoid, tetanus, diphtheria, polio, and gamma globulin immunizations and malaria suppressants are recommended.

TIPPING
While a 10 percent service charge is included in most bills, it is customary to tip an additional 10 percent. Porters, taxi drivers, housekeeping staff, and attendants should be tipped about 10 percent.

CRIME
Petty street crime involving tourists is not common in the Dominican Republic. Theft does occur when valuables are left unattended in parked automobiles, on beaches, and in other public places. Puerto Plata, Sosua, Cabarete, and other resort areas on the north coast have experienced an increase in violent crime. Some incidents have involved foreign residents and tourists. The larger resort complexes rely on private security services and have generally not been affected greatly.

INFRASTRUCTURE
The Dominican Republic has developed air, bus, rental car, taxi, telecommunication, and hotel industries. There is no railroad system. Bus service can be hectic. Advanced telephone reservations are suggested. Few private airports exist in outlying areas. Rental cars are a good option as the country is small enough that all areas can be reached by car within a short time. Taxis are available at hotels and airports; they are unmetered, you'll have to negotiate the fare. When renting a car, maps purchased from companies other than rental car companies are more reliable. Dominican Republic has good road networks, which need frequent maintenance after the rainy season. Highways are poorly lit.

NATIONAL TOURIST OFFICE
National Tourist Offices
Las Americas International Airport
La Union Airport
Puerto Plata
Maledon 20
Santo Domingo
Tel: (809) 5863676

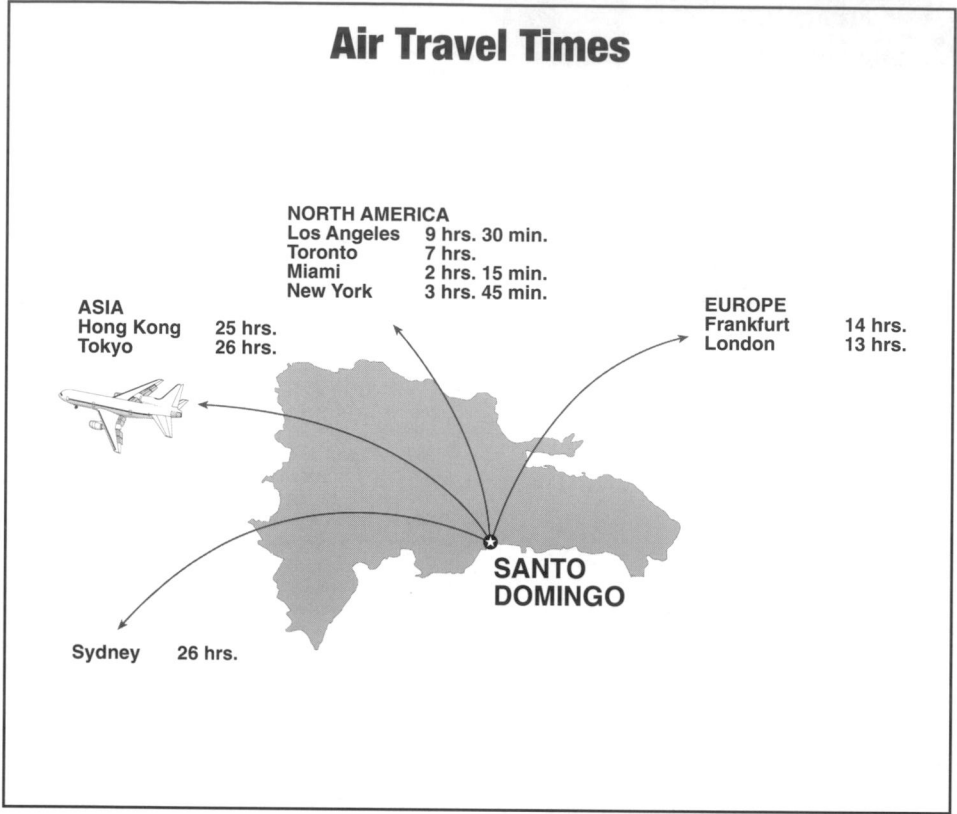

COMMUNICATIONS
Telephones The telephone system is excellent with direct dialing to Canada, Puerto Rico, and the US. Operators are bilingual in Spanish and English. Hotels add a surcharge for calls originating in-house.
Fax Fax communications present no problem.
Post office Postal service in the Dominican Republic is slow and unreliable.
Radio/TV Many television stations broadcast throughout the Dominican Republic, along with foreign-language broadcasts stations. There are over 100 radio stations on the island.

BEST TRAVEL BOOKS
Practical Travel A to Z, Dominican Republic, 1992 Hayt Publishing, Cologne, Germany.

USEFUL TELEPHONE NUMBERS
If you are calling from outside the Dominican Republic, you will need to add the country code and any other international dialing requirements from within your country.
- Courier Service (Island Couriers) .... (809) 567-9547
- All American Cable .... (809) 682-3115
- RCA Global Communications .... (809) 682-3491
- DHL Courier Service .... (809) 534-7888
- Ramada Renaissance Resort Casino .... (809) 221-2222
- Santo Domingo Hotel & Casino ...... (809) 221-6666
- Vesuvio Restaurant .... (809) 221-3333
- Meson de Castilla .... (809) 688-4319
- Centers for Disease Control ...... [01] (404) 332-4559
Flights/Airports
- All America Cables & Radio .... (809) 682-3115
- RCA Global Communications (telegrams) .... (809) 682-3491
- American Airlines .... (809) 542-5151
- Viasa Airlines .... (809) 566-0698
Credit Card Information
Lost or stolen credit cards (call collect to the US, regardless of which country the card was issued in).
- Amex .... [1] (919) 333-3211
- Diner's Club .... [1] (303) 799-1504
- MasterCard .... [1] (314) 275-6690
- Visa .... [1] (410) 581-7931

Marketing

Distribution

Distribution follows a fairly familiar path: from a foreign manufacturer to a distributor/agent to the local importer or wholesaler, to a retailer, and, finally, to the end user. Because there are few large outlets or purchasers, distribution has many layers serving numerous localized networks of traditionally affiliated parties.

Agents, Distributors, and Partners

Agents and distributors are not required; however, unless a foreign firm has a substantial direct local presence, an agent is recommended. Laws regarding agents and distributors favor Dominicans and are strictly enforced. Licensing agreements must be approved by the government. Franchising is developing and offers opportunities in general sectors. Few Dominican entities deal directly with overseas suppliers.

Selling Techniques

Price is generally the main criterion in the purchase decision, although quality, features, and service are becoming more important considerations. Personal relationships often spill over into business, where partners are treated as near-relatives. Because these relationships are cultivated slowly, agents and distributors can hasten the process as well as advise on approaches and selling propositions.

Advertising

Most businesses advertise in major newspapers and on television and radio. There is no trade press as such, but trade associations are active and publish directories and internal newsletters. Trade shows are also useful means of establishing a presence in the market. Because of taxes, posters are infrequently used; leaflets, loudspeaker vans, raffles, and premiums are commonly used.

Service and Customer Support

This concept is relatively new in the Dominican Republic. Although still unlikely to be a major factor in the decision to buy, after-sales support and service can be helpful in building reputation and consumer confidence in a product or a provider.

Marketing in the Dominican Republic

MARKETING TIPS

- **Language** Most Dominican businesspeople speak English, but speaking and providing promotional materials in Spanish shows extra thoughtfulness.
- **Agents** Most business is conducted through local agents and it is difficult to change agents. The selection of an agent is a critical and personal decision, and should be done first-hand through an on-site review, not by correspondence.
- **Government markets** To compete in government tenders, a foreign firm must have a Dominican partner, not merely a Dominican agent.
- **Credit** Transactions among parties with established relationships may be accomplished using standard terms; letters of credit are also common, but many sellers demand cash with an order.

AD AGENCIES

Ecocaribe, S.A.
Av. John F. Kennedy Esq. Lope de Vega
Edif. Scotiabank
Santo Domingo
Tel: (809) 541-1090 Fax: (809) 567-7661

Tecnoamerica, S.A.
Jose Contreras No. 34
Santo Domingo
Tel: (809) 686-6559 Fax: (809) 686-6559

Asesores Asociados, S.A.
Tetelo Vargas No. 23, Ens. Naco
Santo Domingo
Tel: (809) 566-8926 Fax: (800) 567-9843

Centro Dominicano de Estudios de Mercadeo Social
Juan Baron Fajardo No. 7, Ens. Piantini
Santo Domingo
Tel: (809) 567-7138

Business Culture

Greetings and Courtesies

 Handshakes are common for both men and women, both when meeting and upon departing. Friends may embrace, and women friends may hold each other by the shoulders and kiss. Business cards should be printed in Spanish, although most businesspeople speak English. At social events, the host will usually make individual introductions.

Business Ethic and Framework

 Dominicanos are generally considered to be relatively informal, although they are nevertheless concerned with formal dignity, hierarchy, and class. Dominicano values emphasize the importance of the personal relationship, and time and effort is taken to establish a personal relationship as a prerequisite to a business relationship. Men should wear conservative business suits and women should wear conservative suits or dresses.

Meetings and Decision Making

 Make appointments for meetings well in advance, but reconfirm shortly beforehand. Dominicanos are not punctual, although you should be. Business lunches are relatively common, but only as a means to further the development of the social bond. Actual decisions are almost always made at a high level of authority. Although you should approach senior people, Dominicanos will wish to match you with someone of similar rank. It is important to cultivate personal relationships with these peers, because the quality of these relationships may strongly influence the actual decisionmaker.

Women

 Although women in the Dominican Republic generally occupy a somewhat secondary status in this traditionally male-dominated society, many operate businesses and may be accorded considerable personal freedom. Dominicano women are becoming more common and more accepted in business in general, and foreign businesswomen should experience few problems.

Cultural Cautions

DO'S

- Learn something about the Dominican Republic's history and culture—your interest will be appreciated, as will attempts to speak Spanish.

DON'TS

- Race, religion, politics, and the economic situation—other than the tourist economy—are topics best avoided.

CUSTOMS

- People tend to stand quite close together; attempts to increase the space between persons in conversation may be viewed as evasive and even insulting.
- Small gifts are given frequently and are usually unwrapped immediately.
- It is considered polite to refuse anything offered a few times before ultimately accepting.

OBSERVATIONS

- Dominicanos are generally offended by evidence of what they consider aggressiveness and greed.
- Although appointments are generally required, you may be able to schedule them on short notice because of the relative informality that prevails.
- Because of the tropical climate, most business is conducted earlier in the day.

NEGOTIATIONS

- Dominicanos present a united front during negotiations, deferring to the senior member.
- Allow negotiations to remain open-ended, so that confrontation can be avoided and talks can be allowed to fade away if agreement cannot be reached.
- Agreements should be written; although historically, contracts have consisted of schematic outlines, Dominicanos now expect somewhat more detailed documents.

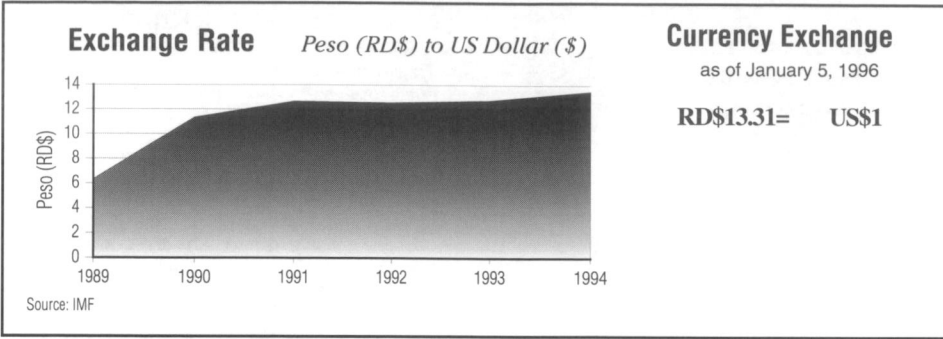

Exchange Rate *Peso (RD$) to US Dollar ($)*

Peso (RD$)

14
12
10
8
6
4
2
0

1989   1990   1991   1992   1993   1994

Source: IMF

Currency Exchange
as of January 5, 1996

RD$13.31=   US$1

Currency

The currency of the Dominican Republic is the Dominican peso (RD$), divided into 100 centavos.

Foreign Exchange

Exchange control policy is determined by the Monetary Board and is administered by the Central Bank. There are about 15 banks operating in the foreign exchange market. The official exchange rate is set daily on the basis of the previous day's rates in the interbank market, where the rates are determined by supply and demand.

Capital Transfers

All payments must be invoiced in US dollars, or else no obligations are imposed on importers, exporters, or other residents regarding the currency to be used for payments to or from nonresidents. All invisibles payments may be made freely through commercial banks, subject to documentation requirements. Foreign exchange proceeds from all invisibles may be sold in the interbank market, except for those originating in transactions with foreigners using international credit cards, which must be sold in the Central Bank. Foreign-owned businesses may exchange pesos for hard currency and remit their profits abroad, provided the remittances do not exceed 25 percent of the value of their registered capital per year. The exportation of domestic bank notes and coins is subject to approval from the Central Bank.

Investment Incentives

The government officially welcomes foreign investment and has enacted legislation to encourage and facilitate investment. Although it does offer some incentives to foreign investment, it has since 1990 undertaken reforms to reduce or eliminate many prior incentive programs. Some foreign goods can still enter the country virtually duty-free, including raw materials and capital equipment. However, there are complaints that the customs authority frequently delays entry of these goods and in some instances requires the payment of duties.

Investment Restrictions

Significant barriers to foreign investment continue to exist. The law permits 100 percent ownership by foreign investors, but imposes significant restrictions on the sectors involved and on the means of acquiring ownership. Weighty bureaucracy and corruption act to further restrict foreign investment.

TAXATION

Taxation requires sophisticated knowledge of complex rules and regulations specific to each country. The information presented here is from the Ernst & Young Corporate Tax Guide and Directory, available from the Ernst & Young accounting office in your country, or from:

Francisco & Asociados
Mail Address:
Apartado No. 140
Santo Domingo
Dominican Republic
Street Address:
Torre BHD, 5to. piso
Plaza BHD
Av. 27 de febrero esq.
Av. Winston Churchill
Santo Domingo
Dominican Republic
Tel: (809) 541-3837, 541-3881
Fax: (809) 541-3883

At a Glance

Corporate Income Tax Rate (%)	25
Capital Gains Tax Rate (%)	25
Branch Tax Rate (%)	25
Withholding Tax (%)	
Dividends (a)	25
Interest (b)	15
Royalties (b)	25
Branch Remittance Tax	
Net Operating Losses (Years)	
Carryback	0
Carryforward	3

(a) The payer of the dividends may immediately use the withholding tax as a credit against its corporate income tax.
(b) Final tax applicable to payments to both residents and nonresidents.

Money Matters

BITS AND PIECES

- **Royalties** Royalties are paid as a percentage of total sales. All contracts that provide royalty payments must first be approved by the foreign investment directorate.
- **Expropriation** Dominican expropriation standards seem to be at variance with international norms, and several foreign investors have outstanding disputes with the Dominican government concerning expropriated property. Even when compensation has been ordered, investors and lenders often have not received prompt or adequate payment.
- **Foreign investment** Foreign investment in the Dominican Republic falls into two main categories: free trade zone investment and non-zone investment. The rules and regulations are significantly more liberal for investments in the free trade zones.
- **Investment applications** All proposed new foreign investment must first be applied for in writing to the Directorate of Foreign Investment. The application must comply with the provisions set forth in the Directorate's internal regulations, and approval takes between 60 and 90 days after the application is submitted.
- **Commission payment** A commission equivalent to 7 percent of the f.o.b. value of imports is collected by the Customs Office, and the proceeds are deposited in the Central Bank for the servicing of external debt.
- **Gold** Residents may purchase, hold, and sell gold coins for numismatic purposes; otherwise residents are not allowed to hold or acquire gold in any form other than jewelry in the Dominican Republic or abroad. Imports and exports of gold in any form other than jewelry constituting the personal effects of a traveler require licenses issued by the Central Bank. However, such licenses are not normally granted.

BANKS

GODR Development Bank
Ave. Independencia
Santo Domingo
Tel: (809) 535-8088
Fax: (809) 532-4645

GODR Central Bank
Leopoldo Navarro
Santo Domingo
Tel: (809) 221-9111
Fax: (809) 686-7488

Central Bank of the Dominican Republic
Calle Pedro Henríquez Ureña esq.
Leopoldo Navarro, Apdo. 1347
Santo Domingo
Tel: (809) 221-9111
Fax: (809) 686-7488

Banco del Comercio Dominicano, SA
Avda 27 de Febrero esq. Winston Churchill
Apdo 1440
Santo Domingo, DN
Tel: (809) 545-5000
Telex: 326-4533
Fax: (809) 566-3694

Banco Espanol
Avda John F. Kennedy
Santo Domingo, DN
Tel: (809) 565-8555
Telex: 346-0260
Fax: (809) 565-2829

Banco Nacional de Credito, SA
Avda Tiradentes
Apdo 1502
Santo Domingo, DN
Tel: (809) 540-4441
Telex: 760-7572
Fax: (809) 567-4954

Bank of Nova Scotia
Avda John F. Kennedy esq. Lope de Bega
Santo Domingo, DN
Tel: (809) 566-5671
Telex: 3460067

Legal

Legal System

The Dominican Republic is a civil law country. Its legal system is based on the Napoleonic Code.

Intellectual Property Rights

Patents The registration procedure for patents is relatively simple. Patents may be obtained for periods of five, 10, or 15 years, depending on the product or procedure involved. After expiration of the patent, the invention enters the public domain. A patent-holder must commercially exploit its invention or lose the patent protection. The Dominican Republic is a signatory of the Buenos Aires Convention of Invention Patents, Drawings and Industrial Models.

Trademarks Like patents, the registration procedure for trademarks is relatively simple. They can be registered for five, 10, 15, or 20 years and renewed for successive and indefinite equal periods.

Copyrights The registration procedure for copyrights is also fairly simple. Copyrights may be obtained for, among other things, literature, cinematic works, art work, computer programs, and electronic data bases.

Trade secrets Trade secrets are not specifically protected by Dominican law. They can, however, be protected by contract, and the courts will uphold such provisions.

Business Registration

Stock companies (*Companias por Acciones* or *Sociedades Anonimas*) are the most widely used corporate vehicles in the country. A minimum of seven shareholders is required to form and operate a stock company and there are no nationality restrictions. The incorporation of stock companies is relatively simple, generally taking four to five weeks. Stock companies must register with the Income Tax Agency and obtain a routine operational permit. Incorporation taxes are levied in proportion to the corporation's authorized capital.

Contracts and Dispute Resolution

Dominican contracts tend to be simple and straightforward. Provisions of the Civil Code govern all matters not explicitly provided for in a contract. Contractual provisions generally are enforceable as long as they are not at variance with "public order" statutes whose provisions take precedence over private agreements. Courts frequently require foreign plaintiffs to post a high bond prior to filing suit. Notification of an action against a foreign defendant without known domicile in the country may be effected by service of such notice upon the office of the District Attorney. The Dominican court system is slow and unpredictable. Dominican law recognizes arbitration as an alternative to civil or commercial litigation. Arbitration can be conducted in any language and there are no restrictions on the nationality of the arbitrators. To be enforceable, arbitrators' decisions must be ratified by a court of law. If, however, the arbitration is conducted through the Chamber of Commerce and Production of Santo Domingo, the decision is enforceable without such ratification. Arbitration conducted outside of the Dominican Republic is enforceable in the country if the decision is ratified by a Dominican court of law.

Notaries

Notary publics are attorneys who prepare and authenticate written documents. The signatures in most private documents need to be legalized by a notary public who attests to their authenticity. If the documents are executed abroad, this legalization requirement is most easily met by executing documents before a Dominican Consulate. The alternative is to have the signatures notarized by a foreign notary; the foreign notary's signature must then be verified by a county clerk or similar official whose signature, in turn, can be legalized by a Dominican consulate.

Labor

The regular workweek is 44 hours. Work contracts can be for a definite or indefinite term, or for the performance of a specific job or service. Employee benefits established by law include: two weeks of paid vacation per year; distribution among employees of up to 10 percent of the company's net yearly profits; double salary for the month of December as a Christmas bonus; statutorily set higher pay schedules for night work and overtime; and three months of paid maternity leave. Dominican workers have the right to unionize, bargain collectively and strike. An employee can be terminated without cause by payment of a severance indemnity, the amount of which is determined by the employee's salary and seniority. The Labor Code specifies 19 justified causes for which an employee can be terminated without being compensated. Terminations are closely scrutinized by the Ministry of Labor, and are the source of frequent court action.

Source: Russin, Vecchi & Heredia, Bonetti; Santo Domingo

Legal Matters

LEGAL BRIEFS

- **Export free zone enterprises** With more than 30 free zone parks operating in the country, these enterprises constitute a large and growing segment of Dominican economic activity. Export Free Zone companies enjoy full exemption from Dominican taxes, including import duties on equipment and raw materials, corporate income taxes, incorporation taxes and property transfer taxes.

- **Trade incentives** The Dominican Republic enjoys privileged access to the US market as the premier beneficiary country of the Caribbean Basin Initiative. The Dominican Republic is a member of the Lome Convention, qualifying for important trade concessions vis-a-vis the European Union.

- **Agents** Dominican Republic law grants extraordinary protection to local agents and distributors of foreign corporations. The terms of the Distributor and Agent Law take precedence over the provisions of private contracts. Under the law, a principal can only terminate a contract with a local distributor or agent by showing just cause, a term that is vaguely defined by the law and narrowly interpreted by the courts. Terminated agents and distributors often sue for damages, claiming absence of just cause. The courts usually find in favor of the local distributor.

- **Residency** It is relatively easy for foreigners to obtain residency and Dominican citizenship. Residency status is generally required for obtaining a work permit.

- **Banking** Over the past few years, restrictions on the banking industry have been lifted. Dollar denominated accounts are now available and the largest banks are allowed to offer a broad range of banking services.

- **Exploitation of natural resources** The Dominican State exercises a monopoly over the exploitation of natural resources and has the power to grant concessions to private companies.

- **Calvo doctrine** Dominican Republic courts follow the Calvo doctrine, which holds that commercial disputes may be settled in the courts of the territory in which they occur.

- **Competition laws** During the last two years, the government has carried out a major reform effort aimed at improving the transparency and effectiveness of the laws affecting competition. However, bureaucratic red tape and differences between law and actual practice remain significant problems.

- **Worker rights** Both Dominican and international labor organizations have charged that the Dominican Republic does not enforce compliance with internationally recognized worker rights. Specifically, there seems to be a tendency of employers to ignore the right of freedom of association by firing union organizers and workers who join unions.

LEGAL CONTACTS

Russin, Vecchi & Heredia Bonetti
Edificio Monte Mirador
Calle El Recodo #2
Santo Domingo
Tel: (809) 535-9511
Fax: (809) 535-6649, 535-751

Rafael F. Bonnelly
Pedro Henriquez Urena 84
Santo Domingo
Tel: (809) 541-0353
Fax: (809) 541-0640

Oficina Marranzini
Cesar Nicolas Penson No. 24
Segunda Planta
Santo Domingo
Tel: (809) 682-3397
Fax: (809) 688-2886

Bufete Ramos Messina
Rosa Duarte #8 (Gascue)
POB 20700
Santo Domingo
Tel: (809) 682-4964
Fax: (809) 686-5962

GOVERNMENT AGENCIES

Secretariat of State for Industry and Commerce
Ave. Mexico
Edificio Gubernamental
Juan Pablo Duarte, Piso 7
Santo Domingo
Tel: (809) 688-2449, (809) 685-5171
Fax: (809) 686-1973

Secretariat of State for Agriculture
Centro de los Heroes
Santo Domingo
Tel: (809) 532-1032
Fax: (809) 535-3894

Price Stabilization Institute
Plaza Independencia
Santo Domingo
Tel: (809) 530-0871, (809) 530-1166
Fax: (809) 530-0343

Corporation of Government-Owned Enterprises
Ave. Antonio Duverge
Santo Domingo
Tel: (809) 535-4291
Fax: (809) 533-5522

National Livestock Patronage
Ciudad Ganadera
Santo Domingo
Tel: (809) 535-7165
Fax: (809) 535-7167

Dominican Agrarian Institute
Ave. 27 De Febrero, Plaza Independencia
Santo Domingo
Tel: (809) 530-5585

Higher Institute for Agriculture
POB 166, La Herradura
Santiago
Tel: (809) 581-6653
Fax: (809) 5812-6626

Interamerican Institute for Agricultural Sciences
Centro de los Heroes
Santo Domingo
Tel: (809) 533-2797
Fax: (809) 532-5312

State Sugar Council
Centro de los Heroes
Santo Domingo
Tel: (809) 533-1161, (809) 533-2575
Fax: (809) 533-7393

BUSINESS AND TRADE ORGANIZATIONS

Dominican Electricity Corporation
Centro de los Heroes
Santo Domingo
Tel: (809) 533-7027
Fax: (809) 535-7472

Dominican Export Promotion Center
POB 199-2
Santo Domingo
Tel: (809) 530-5505
Fax: (809) 530-8208

Dominican Importers' Association
Roberto Pastoriza No. 16
Santo Domingo
Tel: (809) 562-6909
Fax: (809) 541-2574

Dominican Exporters' Association
Winston Churchill No. 5
Santo Domingo
Tel: (809) 532-6779
Fax: (809) 532-1926

Dominican Businessmen Council
Ave. Abraham Lincoln Esq. John F. Kennedy
Santo Domingo
Tel: (809) 562-1666
Fax: (809) 544-1280

Dominican Agribusiness Council
Euclides de Morillo No. 51, Arroyo Hondo
Santo Domingo
Tel: (809) 563-6178
Fax: (809) 563-6181

Association of Industries of the Dominican Republic
Apartado 850
Santo Domingo
Tel: (809) 532-5523
Fax: (809) 533-7520

Dominican Development Foundation
Mercedes No. 4, Zona Colonial
Santo Domingo
Tel: (809) 688-8101
Fax: (809) 686-0430

Agricultural and Livestock Development Foundation
Max Henriquez Urena No. 18-B
Santo Domingo
Tel: (809) 530-2160
Fax: (809) 544-4727

Santo Domingo Chamber of Commerce
Arzobispo Nouel No. 206
Santo Domingo
Tel: (809) 682-2688
Fax: (809) 685-2228

American Chamber of Commerce of the Dominican Republic
Ave. Winston Churchill Esq. Luis F. Thomen
Torre Bhd, 4to. Piso
Santo Domingo
Tel: (809) 544-2222
Fax: (809) 544-0502

MARKET RESEARCH FIRMS

Fundacion Economia y Desarrollo
Ave. Abraham Lincoln Esq. John F. Kennedy
Edif. Nissan, 2nd Floor
Santo Domingo
Tel: (809) 566-7375/6
Fax: (809) 566-7367

Orientacion Economica
Ave. John F. Kennedy
Edif. Chase Manhattan Bank, 4th Floor
Santo Domingo
Tel: (809) 540-4441 x2280, (809) 566-0023
Fax: (809) 541-0221

Orientacion Mercadologica, S.A.
Enrique Henriquez No. 67, 3rd Floor
Santo Domingo
Tel: (809) 682-6887, (809) 686-4252, (809) 686-4243

Proinversion
Ave. Tiradentes with Gustavo Mejia Ricart
Santo Domingo
Tel: (809) 562-7666, (809) 562-6212

Sistemas Mercadologicos, S.A.
Ave. Romulo Betancourt No. 1302
Santo Domingo
Tel: (809) 532-5769
Fax: (809) 532-0723

Read and Associates
San Martin de Porres No. 8-B, Naco
Santo Domingo
Tel: (809) 566-4157
Fax: (809) 566-4157

Market Probe
Av. Abraham Lincoln No. 40, 2nd Floor
Santo Domingo
Tel: (809) 535-0280
Fax: (809) 535-0250

AD AGENCIES

Mercadesa
Winston Churchill Esq. Charles Summer
Edif. Plaza Paraiso, Apt. 201
Santo Domingo
Tel: (809) 567-5321, (809) 567-5323
Fax: (809) 544-2503

Codeinsa
Cayetano Rodriguez No. 257, Gazcue
Santo Domingo
Tel: (809) 689-6175
Fax: (809) 685-4890

NEWSPAPERS

El Caribe
Autopista Duarte, Km 7 1/2
Apdo 416
Santo Domingo
Tel: (809) 566-8161

Diario Las Americas
Avda Tiradentes
Santo Domingo
Tel: (809) 566-4577

Listin Diario
Paseo de los Periodistas 52
Ensanche Miraflores
Santo Domingo
Tel: (809) 686-6688
Fax: (809) 686-6595

El Nacional
San Martin 236
Santo Domingo
Tel: (809) 565-5581

La Noticia
Julio Verne 14
Santo Domingo
Tel: (809) 687-3131

El Sol
Carrera Sanchez
Km 6 1/2
Santo Domingo
Tel: (809) 532-9511

Ultima Hora
Paseo de los Periodistas 52
Ensanche Miraflores
Santo Domingo
Tel: (809) 688-3361
Telex: (809) 346-0206
Fax: (809) 688-3019

PERIODICALS

Agroconocimiento
Apdo 345-2
Santa Domingo

Carta Dominicana
Avda Tiradentes 56
Santa Domingo
Tel: (809) 566-0119

Horizontes de America
Alexander Fleming 2
Santo Domingo
Tel: (809) 565-9717

RADIO & TELEVISION STATIONS

Radio Televisión Dominicana
(Dominican Radio and Television)
Dr. Tejada Florentino 8
Apdo. 969
Santo Domingo
Telephone: (809) 689-2121

INTERNET ADDRESSES

Usenet group(s):
soc.culture.dominican-rep

Latin American - DR HomePage
http://lanic.utexas.edu/la/ca/dr/

Dominican Republic - General
http://www.webspace.com/~pedro/dominica.html

Ecuador

Republic of Ecuador

Economy

Overview

Despite often heavy bureaucratic regulation, subsidies, and state ownership of strategic economic assets, for the most part Ecuador's economy is oriented toward a free market. Nevertheless, the state has historically played a significant economic role, particularly in oil development during the 1970s, which fueled a decade of free public spending. When oil prices fell in the 1980s the government failed to cut back spending before a high level of debt accumulated. The economy stagnated under the weight of this debt, high inflation, and a volatile oil market where prices were generally falling. A program designed to eliminate the budget deficit, reduce inflation, and slow the depreciation of the currency has been moderately successful, but fundamental structural reforms are still needed to improve the investment climate and prepare the foundation for growth; these have been difficult to achieve.

Trade

Ecuador is heavily dependent on imports and is becoming more open to trade. In general, its protectionist tariff system has been replaced by a simplified structure with fewer, lower duties. The country also generally balances its trade accounts, although it is subject to deficits depending on the often volatile prices of its commodity exports. Major exports include petroleum (nearly 40 percent of total exports), bananas (Ecuador is the world's largest exporter of bananas), seafood, coffee, and cocoa, which together represent about 80 percent of all exports. Imports include industrial raw materials, capital goods, transportation equipment, consumer goods, and agricultural raw materials. The US is Ecuador's leading trade partner (accounting for about 40 percent of total trade), followed by Japan, Germany, Italy, and Peru.

Sectors

Agriculture Ecuador is basically an agricultural country; agriculture employs about 35 percent of the work force and produces about 20 percent of GDP. Grains, vegetables, and livestock are raised for domestic consumption, while bananas, coffee, and cocoa are the major cash crops. Other products include tropical fruit, cut flowers, winter vegetables, and shrimp.

Industry Industry employs about 20 percent of the work force and accounts for about 35 percent of GDP. Petroleum extraction and processing is the primary industry, and food processing, textiles, and chemicals also make significant contributions. Domestic producers of import-substitution industrial goods are now becoming competitive with foreign producers.

Services Services employ about 25 percent of the work force, while contributing about 45 percent of GDP. Ecuador is attempting to develop tourism and its financial sector as substantial sources of foreign exchange, but most service activity consists of local distribution and personal services.

Trends

Ecuador recently opened up certain areas to foreign oil and gas exploration, and privatization of some major state enterprises—including telecommunications, electricity, and its new petroleum pipeline—should in turn trigger additional investment and procurement. As part of its application to GATT, the government is addressing remaining trade barriers. It also hopes to reform the social security and education systems; however, there exists substantial political opposition to such modernization programs.

At a Glance

THE COUNTRY

Location Western South America, bordering the Pacific Ocean at the Equator, between Colombia and Peru.

Terrain Ecuador consists of coastal plains, inter-Andean central highlands, and flat-to-rolling eastern jungles.

Climate The climate is tropical along the coast, but becomes cooler inland and in the highlands.

THE PEOPLE

Population 11,200,000
Ethnic composition
Indian 25%
Mestizo (mixed Indian-Caucasian) 65%
Caucasian and others.. 7%
African.. 3%
Religious composition Predominantly Roman Catholic, but religious freedom is practiced.

Languages spoken Spanish is the official language, and there are several Indian languages which are widely spoken, most prominent of which is Quechua.

Education and literacy Education is compulsory for ages 6-14, but enforcement varies from virtually none in remote rural areas to complete in urban centers. Literacy has risen from 56 percent in 1960 to nearly 90 percent today. Advanced education is of good quality. The government has undertaken efforts to teach the older population to read and write.

Labor force
Total:...2,800,000
By occupation: agriculture 35%, manufacturing 21%, commerce 16%, services and other activities 28%.

COUNTRY FACTS

Political and legal Ecuador maintains a republican government, with a legal system based on civil law. There is a multiparty political system, and elections are widely contested. Ecuador has not accepted compulsory ICJ jurisdiction.

Telephone Telephone services are operated by the government. There are radiotelephone links between the main cities and towns. International country code: [593]. Selected city codes: Guayaquil (4), Quito (2).

Transportation Only about 10 percent of the roadways are paved, and only about half of the paved roads are well maintained. Rail services are not widely available and do not reach much of the country. There are several airports which provide local services, but only the main airport handles international traffic. There is an inland waterway system.

Environment Lack of systematic controls during recent economic development has resulted in deforestation, soil erosion, desertification, and water pollution.

Media There are over 300 radio stations with one central government network, Radio Nacional del Ecuador. There are 33 television stations; 910,000 televisions sets are in use. There is no censorship of the media. The government requires all mass periodicals to participate in literacy and adult education.

Health Malnutrition and infant mortality are the country's two main health problems. Life expectancy is 70 years. Heath facilities are largely concentrated in the towns. They are expensive and not closely located to distant highland Amerindian peoples.

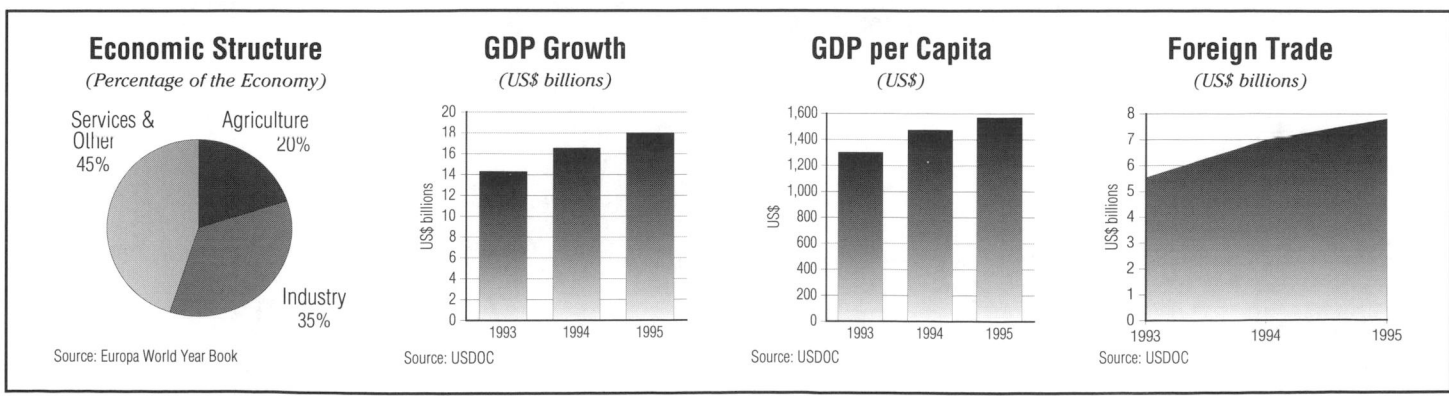

Economic Structure (Percentage of the Economy)
Services & Other 45%
Agriculture 20%
Industry 35%
Source: Europa World Year Book

GDP Growth (US$ billions)
1993, 1994, 1995
Source: USDOC

GDP per Capita (US$)
1993, 1994, 1995
Source: USDOC

Foreign Trade (US$ billions)
1993, 1994, 1995
Source: USDOC

Ecuador

☆ National capital
◉ Provincial capital
● Secondary city
━━━ International border
─── Province border
─── Road
······ Railroad

| 0 | 50 | 100 | 150 km |
| 0 | 50 | 100 mi |

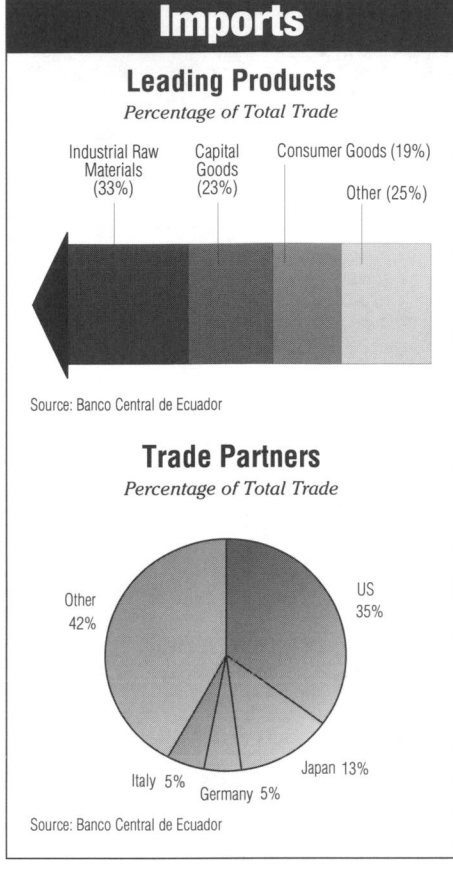

Imports

Leading Products
Percentage of Total Trade

Industrial Raw Materials (33%) Capital Goods (23%) Consumer Goods (19%) Other (25%)

Source: Banco Central de Ecuador

Trade Partners
Percentage of Total Trade

Other 42%
US 35%
Japan 13%
Germany 5%
Italy 5%

Source: Banco Central de Ecuador

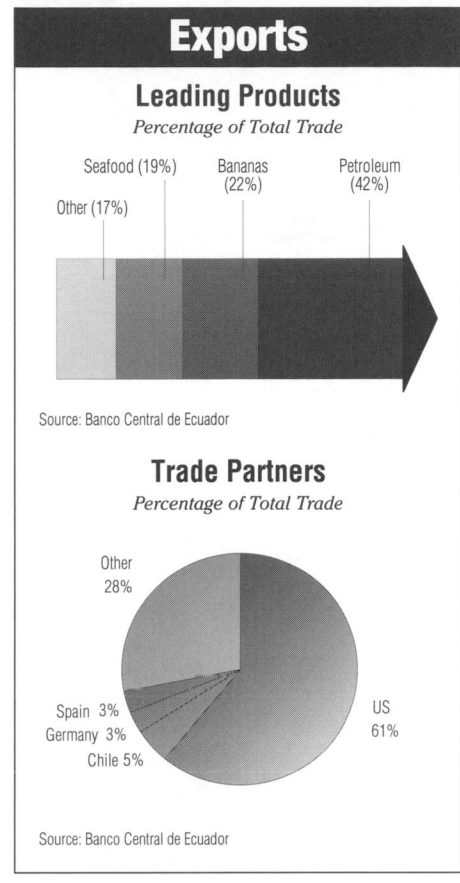

Exports

Leading Products
Percentage of Total Trade

Other (17%) Seafood (19%) Bananas (22%) Petroleum (42%)

Source: Banco Central de Ecuador

Trade Partners
Percentage of Total Trade

Other 28%
US 61%
Chile 5%
Germany 3%
Spain 3%

Source: Banco Central de Ecuador

Opportunities

FOR IMPORTING TO ECUADOR

- agricultural and industrial machinery
- automobiles, trucks, and auto parts
- chemicals and chemical products
- computers and computer products
- construction and drilling equipment
- cotton
- electrical power equipment
- industrial raw materials
- paper and paperboard
- petroleum products
- plastics
- pollution control equipment
- processed foods
- semifinished iron and steel products
- soybean meal
- telecommunications equipment
- transportation equipment
- wheat

FOR EXPORTING FROM ECUADOR

- bananas
- cocoa
- coffee
- flowers
- metal products
- petroleum and petroleum products
- shrimp
- textiles and clothing
- tuna
- winter vegetables
- wood products

GROWTH SECTORS

- automobile assembly
- electrical power systems
- environmental protection goods and services
- financial services
- high-value fruits and vegetables
- mineral exploration
- petroleum refining
- telecommunications

GOVERNMENT PROCUREMENT

- airport construction goods and services
- electrical power equipment
- medical supplies and equipment
- military supplies and equipment
- natural gas pipelines
- petroleum refining equipment
- water treatment goods and services

Trade News

RULES AND REGULATIONS

- **Regulations** Price indexes are set by the Ministries of Industry, Agriculture, and Finance. Import and export licenses are issued by the Central Bank of Ecuador.
- **Tariffs and import taxes** The Ecuadorean tariff schedule is based on the Harmonized System (HS) of Nomenclature. Tariff duties are consistent with the Andean Pact common external tariff. The highest duty, 37 percent, is levied on automobile imports to protect the local assembly industry. Other rates include: 20 percent for most consumer goods; 10 to 15 percent for intermediate goods; and zero to five percent for raw materials and capital goods. All imports are subject to a 1 percent customs fee and the 10 percent value-added tax.
- **Customs procedures** Customs procedures in Ecuador can be difficult, but a new Customs Service Law enacted in March 1994 should facilitate the creation of a modern, computerized system and reduce inefficiencies.
- **Import licenses** Importers must register with the Central Bank of Ecuador and obtain registration numbers. The license is good for 180 days and may be renewed.
- **Prohibited imports** Approximately 30 items cannot be imported to Ecuador, including used clothing, used vehicles older than 1993 (or older than 1990 if more than five tons), used tires, certain pesticides, certain woven fabrics, and certain iron mill plates.
- **Export controls** Ecuador prohibits the export of certain artistic, cultural, archeological, and historical products, as well as endangered species of wildlife and flora. These items may be exported on a temporary basis, however. Certain basic consumption products and raw materials may be subject to export restrictions and quotas.
- **Government procurement** Government procurement practices do not usually discriminate against foreign suppliers. However, bidding for government contracts can be cumbersome and time-consuming. Many bidders object to the requirement for a bank-issued guarantee to insure execution of the contract.
- **Oil production** Annual crude oil production is projected to increase for the next few years as new fields are brought on line by state-owned Petroecuador and foreign contractors.
- **Mining** Ecuador has extensive, but so far undeveloped, mining potential, especially for gold. Though production to date has been limited, it has been growing steadily, and looks set to grow by about three percent each year in the near term.
- **Free trade zones (FTZs)** A free trade zone exists in Esmeraldas Province.
- **Free trade agreements** Ecuador is a member of the Andean Pact along with Colombia, Bolivia, Venezuela, and Peru.

TRANSPORTATION FIRM

Coka Barriga, Mario Cia Ltda
POB 4814
Guayaquil
Telex: 43615 MACOBA ED

GOVERNMENT AGENCIES

Centro de Desarrolo Industrial del Ecuador
POB 2321
Avenida Orellana 1715 y 9 de Octubre
Quito
Telex: 22350 CENDES ED

Centro Nacional de Promocion de la Pequena Industria y Artesania
POB 2083
Piedrahita 359 y Ponce
Quito

FEDEXPOR - QUITO
Avs. Republica y Amazones
Edif. "Las Camaras" 3er. Piso
Quito
Tel: (2) 452769
Telex: 22957 FDXPOR ED

Business Travel

LH 1906	MADRID	935	113-3
LH 1022	STUTTGART HBF.	935	-
AF 1701	LYON	940	683-6
AY 822	HELSINKI	940	113-3
AA 071	SFRANCISCO-DALLAS	945	731-7

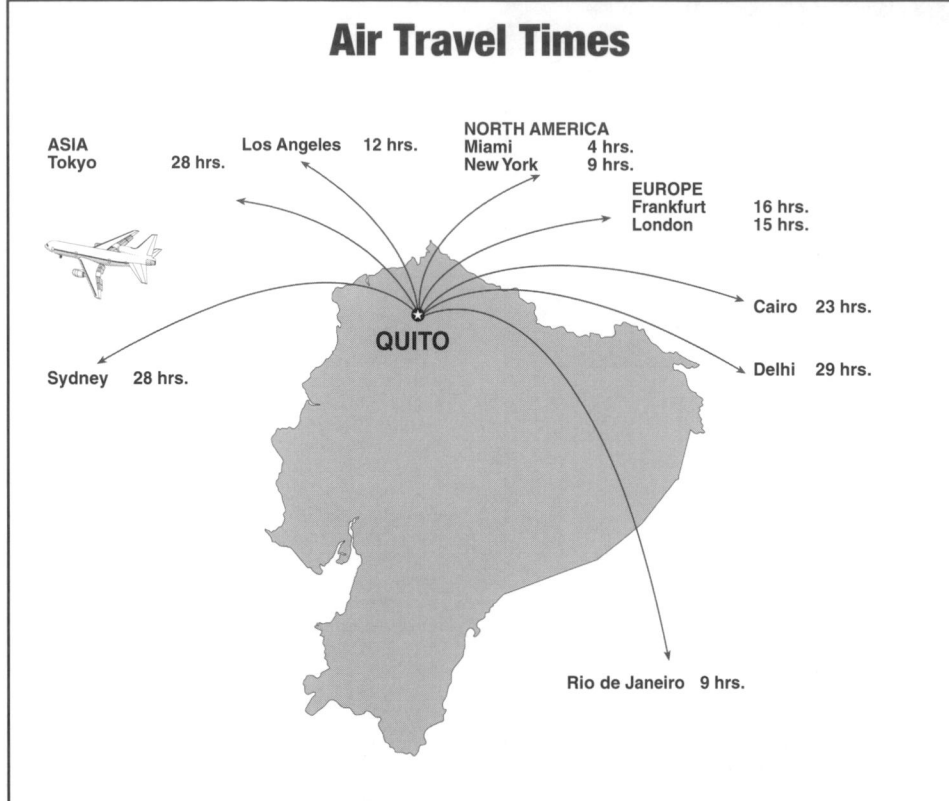

Air Travel Times

ASIA Tokyo 28 hrs.

Los Angeles 12 hrs.

NORTH AMERICA
Miami 4 hrs.
New York 9 hrs.

EUROPE
Frankfurt 16 hrs.
London 15 hrs.

Cairo 23 hrs.

QUITO

Delhi 29 hrs.

Sydney 28 hrs.

Rio de Janeiro 9 hrs.

COMMUNICATIONS

Telephones International service is available in most major hotels. It is more economical to call from a public phone rather than a hotel room phone as hotels will charge a substantial surcharge for all long distance calls. Person-to-person calls will be charged even if the party is not available.

Fax Fax service is common in major hotels and used in many large companies and organizations. Telex service is also available.

Post office The postal service is not reliable and is commonly subject to theft and loss. Be certain to send all correspondence certified mail. When in Ecuador, buy *certificado* stamps so the correspondence will be stamped separately. Airmail requires 10 days for delivery, surface mail two to six weeks, and parcel post requires one month with a standard delay at customs.

Radio/TV Four television stations operate between 1 p.m. and midnight Monday through Friday, with extended hours on the weekend. Several AM and FM stations are available and broadcast from Quito. Short wave reception is excellent.

BEST TRAVEL BOOKS

Ecuador & The Galapagos Islands Travel Survival Kit. Lonely Planet. This is the way travel guides were meant to be written. 480 pages, 16 color.

The Travellers Guide to Latin America Customs and Manners. Elizabeth Devine & Nancy Braganti. 'An invaluable guide for people not wanting to put foot in mouth.'

TELEPHONE NUMBERS

If you are calling from outside Ecuador you will need to add the country code [593] and any other international dialing requirements from within your country.

- Quito Telex .... (2) 210300
- Ecuadorian-Amer. Chamber of Commerce (2) 2432
- Ecuatoriana de Aviacion Guayaquil ..... (2) 4322025
- Ecuatoriana de Aviacion Quito .... (2) 2563003
- Rail Travel Information .... (2) 214545
- Railway Office/Quito............................... (2) 214545
- US Embassy/Quito................................ (2) 562-890
- US Consulate/Guayaquil........................ (2) 323-570
- Police 101
- Fire 102
- Ambulance .... (2) 214966
- Local Operator 104
- Directory 104
- Long Distance Operator 105
- International Operator 116
- Centers for Disease Control........[1] (404) 332-4559

Credit Card Information
Lost or stolen credit cards (call collect to the US, regardless of which country the card was issued in).

- Amex ....[1] (919) 333-3211
- Diner's Club...............................[1] (303) 799-1504
- MasterCard ....[1] (314) 275-6690
- Visa ....[1] (410) 581-7931

NATIONAL TOURIST OFFICE

National Tourist Centur
Calle Reina Victoria 514
Quito
Telephone: (2) 527074

Travelogue

WORKWEEK

Offices Monday-Friday 9:00 am to 1:00 pm; 3:00 pm to 6:00 pm.
Banks Monday-Friday 9:00 am to 1:30 pm.
Government Monday-Friday 8:00 am to 4:30 pm.
Retail Monday-Saturday 9:00 am to 12:30 pm; 3:00 pm to 7:00 pm.

HOLIDAYS

Holidays 1996
January 1 New Year's Day
February 27-28 Carnival*
April 14 Good Friday*
May 1 Labor Day
May 24 Battle of Pichincha*
July 24 Simon Bolivar
August 10 Independence Day
October 12 Columbus Day*
November 2 All Souls' Day
November 3 Independence of Cuenca
December 25 Christmas Day
*Dates may vary, check current calendar.

VISA AND PASSPORT

Passports are required and must be carried at all times. You are subject to arrest if caught without a passport. For stays of 90 days or less, a return or onward travel ticket is required upon entry to Ecuador.

DEPARTURE FORMALITIES

A US$25 airport departure tax is payable in US funds or sucres.

IMMUNIZATION

Preventive measures against cholera are recommended. Malaria and dengue fever are reported in the coastal area of Oriente, diptheria is reported in Quito, and rabies has been reported in Guayaquil. Rabies is widespread in Ecuador.

TIPPING

Taxi: none. Porter: 50 centavos per piece. Hotels, restaurants: 15 to 20 percent generally included in bill. Barber, beauticians: 10 percent. Small services: 50 centavos.

CRIME

If in Guayaquil be extremely cautious on all city streets. In Quito the area surrounding the landmark, the Virgin of Panecillo, is a high-crime area with frequent theft and muggings. Criminals are often armed. Hiking and mountain climbing should be done with a qualified guide only. Avoid the northeastern border with Colombia. Demonstrations are common and can develop into looting and random violence.

INFRASTRUCTURE

Ecuatoriana Airlines and Saeta Airlines have nonstop flights available to and from North America. International connecting flights are available from major cities throughout Europe. Domestic flights are available between Quito and Guayaquil. For transportation from Mariscal Sucre Airport near Quito, taxi service and bus service are available to downtown. The airport buses are labeled Areopuerto. Rental cars are available at all large airports and downtown. Within the urban areas, the bus system is extensive but crowded and not recommended for business travel. If traveling from Guayaquil to Quito use the Viatur buses. Bus travel is not recommended at night as there are frequent accidents and crimes are committed against bus travelers. Use only taxis that are yellow and part of the cooperative. Taxis in Quito have meters, those in Guayaquil do not. Travel by train is slow, but inexpensive.

Distribution

Most trade passes through the main commercial centers of Guayaquil and Quito, and local outlets receive most of their imported inventory through agents operating out of these centers. Although much business is being rationalized, distribution is often still based on fragmented, personalized relationships.

Agents, Distributors, and Partners

Successful selling in Ecuador generally requires a local agent or representative, especially for big ticket, complicated equipment. Distributors cover the entire country and utilize their own sales forces, with branches and warehouses in major cities. These firms maintain inventories. Commission or indent agents may specialize in an area of trade, although many handle a range of unrelated products. They may import goods for resale with their own funds, with their commission paid by the company filling the orders. Large manufacturing companies and government agencies import directly by purchasing equipment or materials for their own use. Franchising, although not widely used, is growing. Direct marketing is most often through television advertising giving contact telephone numbers. Joint ventures, licensing, and locally registered corporations are all used successfully in Ecuador.

Selling Techniques

This is a small market, so sales targets should be set accordingly. Competitive price is the feature most consumers look for first. Firms selling high-tech products need to train and provide maintenance support for their distributors and agents, and in general after-sales service is becoming more of a selling point. However, few products sold in Ecuador come with warranties.

Advertising

Media centers are in Quito, Guayaquil, and Cuenca. All of the major newspapers carry large amounts of advertising, as well as economic and commercial news; *El Comercio* and *El Universo* are favored by the business community. There are five Ecuadorean television networks and two cable networks; an estimated 6.4 million viewers watch more than 1 million sets. Approximately 375 radio stations have 8 million daily listeners. Movie theaters show 15 minutes of advertising before each feature.

Marketing in Ecuador

MARKETING TIPS

- **Language** Business is usually conducted in Spanish and all materials should be translated and made available in that language.
- **Agents** Under Ecuadorean law, agents and representatives are heavily protected; terminating such relationships is costly, so foreign sellers should choose their agents carefully. However, non-exclusive representatives are not covered by agency legislation and so may provide an option for many foreign sellers.
- **Legal advice** The use of a local attorney is imperative when setting up business, collecting outstanding debts, or negotiating sales agreements in Ecuador.

MARKET RESEARCH FIRMS

BDO Stern C. Ltda.
Av. Amazonas 540 y Carrion
Edif. Londres, P. 6
Quito
Tel: (2) 566-917
Fax: (2) 504-477

Deloitte & Touche C. Ltda.
Av. Amazonas 3617 y Juan Pablo Sanz
Edif. Xerox, P. 7
Quito
Tel: (2) 246-095
Fax: (2) 435-807

Price Waterhouse del Ecuador C. Ltda.
Av. 12 de Octubre 394 y Pasaje Jimenez
Quito
Tel: (2) 562-288
Fax: (2) 567-097

Business Culture

Greetings and Courtesies

Handshakes are standard for both men and women when meeting and departing, although handshakes become less common at subsequent meetings. Male friends hug and female friends kiss. Titles are important indicators of status and are used extensively (along with last names). The host will usually introduce each guest individually to others.

Business Ethic and Framework

Ecuadoreans are generally considered relaxed and easygoing by Latin American standards, although they are nevertheless concerned with formal dignity, hierarchy, and class. Ecuadorean values emphasize the importance of the personal relationship, and Ecuadoreans like to establish a personal relationship before a professional one. Conservative, dark business suits are favored for men and suits or conservatively cut dresses with stockings for women. Visitors should dress appropriately for business, but should generally dress down at other times—thieves prey on the well-dressed.

Meetings and Decision Making

Prior appointments are necessary for meetings, especially with larger firms. Be punctual, although your Ecuadorean counterpart may be as much as 20 minutes late. Decisions are almost always made at a high level of authority. It is important to cultivate personal relationships with Ecuadorean employees, because these relationships may strongly influence decisions in the long run.

Women

Although women in Ecuador generally occupy a somewhat secondary status, many operate businesses and are generally accorded considerable personal freedom. Foreign businesswomen should experience few problems, but they are expected to be highly professional. Do not appear flirtatious or available; a friendly but somewhat aloof manner will suit any business occasion.

Cultural Cautions

DO'S

- Visitors to Quito should arrive a day early to acclimate to the altitude.
- Compliment the host and hostess on their home, and thank them for their hospitality when leaving.

DON'TS

- Avoid religion, politics, the economy, or any topic that implies the inferiority of Ecuador.
- Do not make derogatory comments about bullfighting—it is considered an art form.

CUSTOMS

- If invited to a meal in an upper class home, leave some food on the plate as a sign of sufficiency. In a middle or lower class home, eat everything.
- Invitations to a meal are relatively rare, but parties—which start late, last until the early morning hours, and may include breakfast—are popular.

OBSERVATIONS

- Ecuadoreans stand very close to others when conversing and often touch the other as well.
- Quito—the political capital—is very traditional and conservative, while Guayaquil—the economic capital—is much more progressive and fast-moving.
- Relatively few Ecuadoreans speak a language other than Spanish; a knowledge of Spanish is very helpful and an interpreter may be a necessity.

NEGOTIATIONS

- To avoid misunderstandings, be sure you know who has the authority to make a decision and the procedures and time frames that must be considered.
- Ecuadoreans present a united front during negotiations, deferring to the senior member.
- Allow negotiations to remain open-ended, so that confrontation can be avoided and talks can be allowed to fade away if you cannot reach agreement.

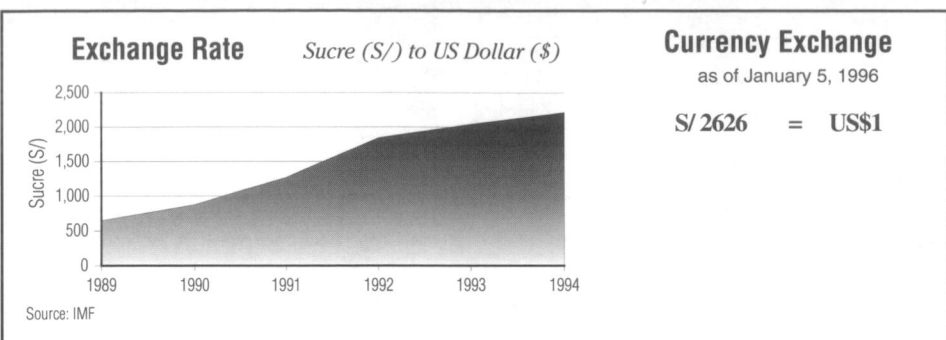

Exchange Rate *Sucre (S/) to US Dollar ($)*

Sucre (S/): 2,500 / 2,000 / 1,500 / 1,000 / 500 / 0

1989 1990 1991 1992 1993 1994

Source: IMF

Currency Exchange

as of January 5, 1996

S/ 2626 = US$1

Currency

The currency of Ecuador is the Ecuadorean sucre, symbol S/, and its principal subdivision is 100 centavos.

Foreign Exchange

Foreign exchange and financial policies are administered by the Monetary Board; the Central Bank of Ecuador issues currency and sets interest and exchange rates.

The foreign exchange system has two exchange rates: the official rate and the free market rate. The official rate, which is fixed by the Central Bank and used primarily for internal accounting purposes, equals the average exchange rate for sales on the interbank free market during the previous week. The free market rate covers only unregulated private-sector transactions, including payments of service fees and royalties, reinsurance payments and receipts, dividends of some foreign investors, currency exchanges separate from the Central Bank, and other activities undertaken by private citizens.

Capital Transfers

Foreign currency is readily available on the free market, and there are no restrictions on the movement of foreign currencies into or out of Ecuador. Capital may freely enter or leave the country through the free market. Capital in the petroleum sector, and loan disbursements to the public sector, must be transacted at the Central Bank rate.

Investment Incentives

Although there are no specific incentives offered to foreign investors, foreigners enjoy the same treatment in most sectors as national investors. All foreign and domestic private entities can own business enterprises and engage in almost all forms of business activity. Private entities can compete freely with the public sector in most areas. Foreign and private firms enjoy equal access in bidding for purchase of state-owned firms or long-term concession contracts.

Investment Restrictions

Ecuador imposes limitations on foreign investment in some sectors, including petroleum, mining, fishing, electricity, telecommunications, and media. Most of these sectors are reserved for domestic investment, and some are reserved for public enterprises.

Money Matters

BITS AND PIECES

- **Foreign investments** Foreign investment is encouraged, and the trend has been toward increased liberalization of investment regulations. While some foreign investors have confronted bureaucratic obstacles in recent years, Ecuador is committed to attracting foreign investment and breaking bureaucratic barriers. Foreign investments are allowed without authorization in most sectors of the economy.
- **Transfer policies** Foreign investors are free to remit 100 percent of net profits, repatriate liquidation proceeds, and convert inward investment flows through the free market.
- **Royalties** There is no limit on the amount of royalties which may be remitted in connection with technology agreements, and the only requirement is that all technology contracts be registered with the Ministry of Industries. It is not necessary to obtain prior authorization.
- **Expropriation** Expropriation is provided for in Ecuadorean law with appropriate compensation. In infrequent cases of expropriations, the individual has the right to petition a judge to establish the appropriate price for expropriated holdings.
- **Performance requirements** There are no performance requirements associated with foreign investment in Ecuador.
- **Investment protection agreements** Ecuador has bilateral investment protection agreements in place with Germany, Switzerland, and the US.
- **Invisibles receipts** All receipts from invisibles must be sold in the free market, except for interest income on exchange reserves of the Central Bank and all invisible receipts of the public sector, which are transacted at the Central Bank rate.
- **Private ownership** All foreign and domestic private entities can own business enterprises and engage in almost all forms of business activity, as well as compete freely with the public sector in most areas.
- **Credit** is generally allocated on market terms, and foreign investors are able to borrow competitively on the local market.
- **Gold** The private sector is authorized to buy and sell gold in the international and domestic markets.

BANKS

Banco Central del Ecuador
Avda 10 de Agosto y Briceno
Plaza Bolivar, Casilla 339
Quito
Tel: (2) 519-384
Telex: 2359
Fax: (2) 570-253

Banco de Desarrollo del Ecuador, SA
Paez 655 y Ramirez Davalos
Casilla 17-01-00373
Quito
Tel: (2) 551-033
Telex: 2655
Fax (2) 563-725

Banco Ecuatoriano de la Vivienda
Avda 10 de Agosto 2270 y Cordero
Casilla 3244
Quito
Tel: (2) 521-311

Banco Nacional de Fomento
Ante 107 y 10 de Agosto
Casilla 685
Quito
Tel: (2) 230-010

Banco Internacional, SA
Avda Patria 640 y 9 de Octubre
Casilla 17-01-2114
Quito
Tel: (2) 565-547

Banco Holandes Unido, SA
Avda Amazonas 4272
Casilla 17-01-42
Quito
Tel: (2) 460-333
Fax: (2) 443-151

TAXATION

Taxation requires sophisticated knowledge of complex rules and regulations specific to each country. The information presented here is from the Ernst & Young Corporate Tax Guide and Directory, available from the Ernst & Young accounting office in your country, or from:

Ernst & Young Romero & Associates
Mail Address:
POB 09-01-9094
Guayaquil, Ecuador
Street Address:
Junin No 114 y Malecon
Edif. Torres Del Rio, Piso 6
Guayaquil, Ecuador
Tel: (4) 560-655, 565-613
Fax: (4) 562-199

At a Glance

Corporate Income Tax Rate (%) (a)	25
Capital Gains Tax Rate (%)	25
Branch Tax Rate (%)	25
Withholding Tax (%) (b)	
Dividends	0
Interest	8
Royalties	33
Branch Remittance Tax	0
Net Operating Losses (Years)	
Carryback	0
Carryforward	

(a) The rate for companies performing oil exploration and exploitation service contracts if 44.4% on profits that are not reinvested. Profits derived from all other types of oil and gas contracts are subject to tax at the general corporate income tax rate of 25%.

Legal

Legal System

Ecuador is a civil code country, with laws based on those of France and Chile.

Intellectual Property Rights

Patents All the necessary credentials and documents must be submitted by the applicant to the Ministry of Industry, Commerce, Integration and Fishing (MICIP). If the application has been accepted it will be published in the *Journal of Industrial Property*. Usually, it takes two to three years to obtain patent registration in Ecuador. In general, a patent expires after 20 years, although in some instances, and for some products, the patent is valid for a shorter time. If a product or procedure is not exploited within two years after a patent is issued, the patent will expire.

Trademarks Andean Pact regulations have caused some changes in Ecuadorean trademark law. On average, the processing of trademark applications takes one year. Applications must be presented to MICIP. Parallel registrations by different owners of identical trade/service marks in Andean Pact member countries are not allowed. Import of a product bearing a mark substantially similar to a trademark registered in Ecuador is prohibited. The registration of a trademark is valid for 10 years from the date of registration. Registration may be renewed thereafter, and proof of use is not required. However, a registration may be cancelled on application, if it has not been used for three years.

Copyrights Copyright applications must be presented to the Ministry of Education. Usually, it takes not more than one week to obtain registration. Ecuadorean copyright protection covers all scientific, literary, artistic, and intellectual property held by any residential person or company. Each registration will be protected until 50 years after the owner's death.

Business Registration

Business operations are regulated by the civil code and by specific laws governing commerce and companies. The incorporation of a company or the arrangement of a representative office first requires approval by the Superintendency of Companies. After that, all documents must be filed with MICIP. There are no limitations or restrictions on foreign investment, and it is possible to operate a business that consists only of foreign investment, knowledge, and employees. Due to recent privatizations, strategic sectors such as the social security administration, which were previously managed exclusively by the government, are now accessible to private companies.

Contracts and Dispute Resolution

Ecuadorean contracts are usually very specific. Every single detail needs to be addressed therein. However, business relationships and prior dealings are also considered very important and will often be considered as dictating some contract terms over and above the contract. Arbitration of business disputes is widely accepted; in fact, the tendency is to submit to arbitration in front of the Cámara de Comercio instead of going through judicial proceedings, which can be quite lengthy. Settling disputes through informal negotiation is not very common, however.

Notaries

Ecuadorean notaries edit and legalize documents, which, to be official, must be written in Spanish. It is not obligatory to have private documents acknowledged by a notary, but if they are, they are generally considered almost as trustworthy as official records or documents.

Labor

Establishing a union in the private sector requires an affirmative vote from thirty associated workers and the election of representatives. The right to strike is constitutionally guaranteed, but has to be exercised in conformity with the labor code, and only after certain prior procedures have been adhered to. Minors are allowed to start working at the age of 14, if they have an authorization of either the parents or the juvenile court. For each category of employees, there exists a legal minimum wage. Also, workers are entitled each year to an additional month's salary payable by December 15th, and to other bonuses according to their length of service and the type of work performed. After a person has worked for a company for two years, social security must be paid, 10 percent contributed by the employee and 10 percent by the employer. In the absence of a collective bargaining agreement which provides otherwise, employers have broad discretion to hire and fire employees.

Source: Romero Arteta Ponce, Quito

Legal Matters

LEGAL BRIEFS

- **Corporations** In Ecuador a corporation is the most common form of business entity. Formation is always done with the help of a lawyer, even though it is not obligatory. Formation costs are usually around US$1,000. After everything is set up, the formation will be announced in a public newspaper, which provides information about the capital of the corporation and the primary associates thereof.

- **Child labor laws** Children under the age of 14 are prohibited by law from working except in special circumstances, such as apprenticeships. Children between the ages of 14 and 18 require the permission of their parent or guardian to work, although many rural children begin working as farm laborers at approximately 10 years old.

- **Maximum workweek** The maximum workweek is restricted to 40 hours, but 12 hours may be added, if overtime is paid. Minors under the age of 16 must be given 20 days of vacation each year; those over age 16 but not yet 18 must be given 18 days per year. All employees are entitled to 15 days of vacation each year, which accrues upon employment. All who have worked for more than five years for the same company get one additional day each year (after six years 16 days, after seven years 17 days and so on) with a maximum of 30 days. In addition, there are nine paid holidays.

- **Statute of limitations** The time period allowed to enforce an obligation varies according to the nature of the duty. Most ordinary actions are limited to 10 years, while actions to rescind contracts for error, fraud, or legal incapacity are four years. Actions for fees due to lawyers, physicians, teachers, and others are three years. Actions involving goods sold, employee salaries, and amounts due for certain services must be commenced within two years.

- **Legal protection** Ecuador has signed various treaties with different countries, for example the US, to protect and increase foreign investment.

- **Property** Property is guaranteed in the constitution. Foreigners may acquire real property the same way and under the same conditions as national citizens, except that they cannot acquire property in border areas.

- **Trade agreements** On the 27th of September,1995, Ecuador became a member of the World Trade Organization.

LEGAL CONTACTS

Romero Arteta Ponce Attorneys at Law
Av. 18 de Septiembre 213 y 6 de Diciembre, 9th Floor
POB 17-03-719
Quito
Tel: (2) 563332, 563334, 563338, 563719, 563720, 563721
Fax: (2) 563718
521394

Colegio de Abogados de Quito
Palacio de Justicia
Av. 6 de Diciembre y Piedrahita
Quito
Tel: (2) 547241, 568567

GOVERNMENT AGENCIES

Ministry of Agriculture and Livestock
Av. Amazonas y Eloy Alfaro
Quito
Tel: (2) 554-122 Fax: (2) 564-972

Ministry of Social Welfare
Robles 850 y Av. Amazonas
Quito
Tel: (2) 540-750 Fax: (2) 563-469

Ministry of National Defense
Exposicion 208
Quito
Tel: (2) 572-583 Fax: (2) 573-210

Ministry of Education
Mejia 322 y Guayaquil
Quito
Tel: (2) 216-224 Fax: (2) 580-178

Ministry of Public Works
Av. 6 de Diciembre 1184
Quito
Tel: (2) 561-180 Fax: (2) 500-880

Ministry of Public Health
Juan Larrea 444
Quito
Tel: (2) 521-411 Fax: (2) 569-786

Ecuadorian Petroleum Company
Alpallana y Av. 6 de Diciembre
Quito
Tel: (2) 563-060 Fax: (2) 569-738

Municipal Potable Water Company
Av. Mariana de Jesus e Italia
Quito
Tel: (2) 501-225

National Railway Authority
Bolivar 433
Quito
Tel: (2) 210-262 Fax: (2) 582-921

Ecuadorian Institute of Sanitary Works
Toledo 684 y Lerida
Quito
Tel: (2) 544-400 Fax: (2) 560-338

Social Security Institute
9 de Octubre y J. Washington esq.
Quito
Tel: (2) 568-846 Fax: (2) 504-572

Ecuadorian Telecommunications Institute
Av. 6 de Diciembre y Colon
Edif. Partenon
Quito
Tel: (2) 560-700 Fax: (2) 568-000

Ecuadorian Water Resources Institute
Juan Larrea 534
Quito
Tel: (2) 545-566

Center for the Economic Development of Azuay, Canar and Morona Santiago
Bolivar 528
Cuenca
Tel: (7) 830-799

Center for the Development of Manabi
18 de Octubre y Sucre
Portoviejo
Tel: (4) 633-497

WORLD TRADE CENTER

World Trade Center Quito
Av. 12 de Octubre 1830 y Cordero
Quito
Tel: (2) 529-340, 238-242, 501-184
Fax: (2) 563-844, 564-419

BUSINESS AND TRADE ORGANIZATIONS

Ecuadorian Exporters Federation
Av. Republica y Amazonas, Piso 3
Quito
Tel: (2) 449-723 Fax: (2) 440-574

Chamber of Construction
Juan Pablo Sanz y Calle Inaquito
Quito
Tel: (2) 432-369, 432-370, 432-773

Chamber of Agriculture
Av. Amazonas 1429 y Colon
Quito
Tel: (2) 230-195

National Association of Entrepreneurs
Avs. Amazonas 1429 y Colon
Edif. Espana, Piso 6, Ofc. 67
Quito
Tel: (2) 238-507, 550-879 Fax: (2) 238-507

Automotive Association
Av. Colon 535 y 6 de Diciembre
Quito
Tel: (2) 232-136

Marketing Association of Ecuador
Casilla 6279
Cdla. Kennedy Calle 4ta 119
Guayaquil
Tel: (4) 399-033 Fax: (4) 280-940

Graphic Industry Association
Acuña 167 entre 10 de Agosto e Inglaterra
Quito
Tel: (2) 525-178

Wood Industry Association
Av. Republica y Amazonas
Edif. Las Camaras, Piso 8
Quito
Tel: (2) 439-560

Textile Industry Association
Av. Republica y Amazonas
Edif. de las Camaras, Piso 8
Quito
Tel: (2) 249-434 Fax: (2) 445-159

Association of Paint, Resins and Chemical Manufacturers of Ecuador
Av. 18 de Septiembre 213, Edif. Lufthansa, Piso 5
Quito
Tel: (2) 529-416

Association of Construction Material Suppliers
Av. 10 de Agosto 5070 y Naciones Unidas
Quito
Tel: (2) 458-395

Pharmaceutical Industry and Suppliers Assoc.
Av. República El Salvador y Portugal
Edif. Gabriela No. 3
POB 17-07-8842
Quito
Tel: (2) 454-212, 243-578 Fax: (2) 243-578

Association of Medical, Hospital, Scientific & Dental Equipment Suppliers
J. Washington 624 y Av. Amazonas
Quito

Electric & Electronic Engineers Association
Av. Amazonas 477 y Robles
Edif. Banco de los Andes
Quito
Tel: (2) 564-332

Businessmen Association of Azuay
Pdte. Córdova 12-15
Cuenca
Tel: (7) 827-040

CHAMBERS OF COMMERCE

Chamber of Commerce of Quito
Av. Republica y Amazonas Edf. de las Camaras, Pisos 5 y 6
Quito
Tel: (2) 443-787, 435-844 Fax: (2) 435-862

Ecuadorian-American Chamber of Commerce
Av. 6 de Diciembre y La Nina,
Edf. Multicentro, Piso 4
Quito
Tel: (2) 507-450/1, 507-459 Fax: (2) 504-571

Chamber of Commerce of Guayaquil
Av. Olmedo 414
Guayaquil
Tel: (4) 323-130 Fax: (4) 323-478

Chamber of Commerce of Cuenca
Av. Federico Malo 1-90 y 12 de Abril
Edif. de las Camaras, Piso 1
Cuenca
Tel: (7) 827-531, 823-008 Fax: (7) 833-891

Chamber of Commerce of Ambato
Montalvo 630
Ambato
Tel: (3) 841-906 Fax: (3) 841-906

Chamber of Commerce of Manta
Av. 2 1047 entre 10 y 11
Manta
Tel: (4) 621-306, 613-553 Telex: 46132

Chamber of Commerce of Machala
Rocafuerte y Buenavista
Machala
Tel: (7) 920-640

Chamber of Industries of Machala
Av. Las Palmeras y 13a. Sur
Machala
Tel: (7) 922-286

CENTRAL BANK

Central Bank of Ecuador
Avenida 10 de Agosto y Briseño
POB 339
Quito
Tel: (2) 571-807, 571-803 Fax: (2) 570-250

CONSULTING FIRMS

BDO Stern C. Ltda.
Av. Amazonas 540 y Carrion
Edif. Londres, P. 6
Quito
Tel: (2) 566-917 Fax: (2) 504-477

Deloitte & Touche C. Ltda.
Av. Amazonas 3617 y Juan Pablo Sanz
Edif. Xerox, P. 7
Quito
Tel: (2) 246-095 Fax: (2) 435-807

Price Waterhouse del Ecuador C. Ltda.
Av. 12 de Octubre 394 y Pasaje Jimenez
Quito
Tel: (2) 562-288 Fax: (2) 567-097

LEGAL CONTACTS

Cámara de Comercio de Quito
Av. Amazonas y De la República
Quito
Tel: (2) 456-364

Cámara de Comercio Ecuatoriano-Americana
Av. 6 de Diciembre y La Niña
Edf. Mulicentro, Of. 404
Quito
Tel: (2) 507-450 Fax: (2) 504-571

Romero Arteta Ponce
Attorneys at Law
Av. 18 de Septiembre 213 y 6 de Diciembre, 9th Floor
POB 17-03-719
Quito
Tel: (2) 563-332
Fax: (2) 563-718, 521-394

INTERNET ADDRESSES

Usenet group(s)
soc.culture.ecuador

Latin America - Ecuador
http://lanic.utexas.edu/la/Ecuador/

Ecuador and the Galapagos
http://www.ecnet.ec/

YAHOO - Ecuador
http://www.yahoo.com/Regional/Countries/Ecuador/

Egypt

Arab Republic of Egypt

Economy

Overview

Although Egypt's business community represents only a small fraction of its total population, which is largely peasant, it is nevertheless larger and more active than that typically found in the Middle East or in markets of comparable size elsewhere in the developing world. In 1991, confronted with debt, declining growth, severe payment imbalances, double-digit inflation, and shrinking foreign reserves, Egypt launched a comprehensive economic reform program that freed interest and exchange rates and sharply reduced the budget deficit, while reining in growth of the money supply. The government also developed a framework for public sector reform and privatization, and it liberalized trade and investment policies as well. The result has been relative improvement in overall economic stability.

Trade

Liberal trade reforms have removed nearly all of Egypt's import bans as well as most tariff preferences and nontariff barriers. With a narrow range of largely low value-added export products, coupled with across-the-board import needs, Egypt consistently runs a huge trade deficit, offset to some extent by tourism revenues and foreign aid. Exports include petroleum, textiles, nonferrous metals, raw cotton, and food products. Imports include foodstuffs, chemicals, iron and steel, and general and specialized industrial machinery. Egypt's largest trading partners are the US, Germany, France, Italy, and Japan.

Sectors

Agriculture As a result of economic reforms, agriculture production has increased steadily in recent years. Nevertheless, it accounts for about 20 percent of GDP and employs about 35 percent of the Egyptian work force. Practically all Egyptian agriculture occurs within the narrow Nile Valley and Delta, where several crops can be grown annually. Cotton is its largest agricultural source of foreign exchange.

Industry Industry accounts for about 30 percent of GDP, while employing about 20 percent of the work force. The Egyptian government still dominates the industrial sector, controlling virtually all heavy manufacturing; overall industrial production, especially in the public sector, has been declining.

Services Although employing only 40 percent of the work force, services contribute slightly less than half of GDP. Egypt's relatively well developed services sector is dominated by tourism and the Suez Canal. Although tourism has declined because of terrorism and general economic conditions, services as a whole remain strong, partially because of steady Suez Canal revenues and the positive impact of debt reduction.

Trends

The pace of economic reform, particularly with regard to trade liberalization and privatization, has slowed significantly. An explicit demonstration of renewed government commitment to the reform program will be necessary to stimulate private sector interest in the Egyptian economy and create a climate encouraging economic growth. Key to the next stage of the government's reform effort will be continued privatization, a further reduction of trade barriers, and the elimination of remaining trade regulations and restrictions. Major proposed structural reforms include the sale of state enterprises, reductions of minimum tariff rates, and the unification of laws regarding investment and commercial activity. Long term, Egypt must develop a more productive internal economy to reduce import dependence.

At a Glance

THE COUNTRY

Location Northern Africa, bordering the Mediterranean Sea and the Red Sea, between Sudan and Libya.
Terrain Desert, except the Nile Valley and Delta.
Climate Dry, hot summers, moderate winters.

THE PEOPLE

Population 60,000,000
Ethnic composition
Egyptian, Debouin Arab, and Nubian.
Religious composition
Sunni Muslim 90%
Coptic Christian 10%
Languages spoken Arabic (official), English, French.
Education and literacy Compulsory for ages 6 to 12. Adult literacy remains relatively low at 48%. Education is free through university level, and the government has undertaken programs to encourage adults to learn to read and write.
Labor force
Total:...15,000,000
By occupation: government, public sector enterprises, and armed forces 36%, agriculture 34%, privately owned service and manufacturing enterprises 30%.

COUNTRY FACTS

Political and legal Egypt's legal system is based on English common law, Islamic law, and Napoleonic codes. The Supreme Court and Council of State have judicial review of legislative acts. Egypt has accepted compulsory ICJ jurisdiction, with reservation.
Telephone The telecommunications system is outdated and wholly inadequate for today's requirements. The government has undertaken an ambitious program to modernize and upgrade the entire system. International country code: [20]. Selected city codes: Alexandria (3), Cairo (2).
Transportation Egypt's transportation system is well developed, although only about 34 percent of its extensive road system is paved. Most systems and facilities are centered in Cairo and follow the Nile. The railway network is not really adequate, but the government is working to expand and improve services. Air services to major cities are available, and there are many ports which handle a large quantity of shipping freight traffic.
Environment Extensive urbanization and recurrent desert sandstorms have resulted in the loss of valuable agricultural lands, which must somehow be reclaimed. Increasing soil salinization below the Aswan High Dam project must be addressed in order to maintain agricultural output from these lands. Also, desertification, oil pollution, and water pollution from pesticides and untreated sewage remain pressing problems.
Media There are three television channels, broadcasting mostly in Arabic, and several radio stations. Radio and television are owned and controlled by the government through the Egyptian Radio and Television Federation. There are two major Arabic and one English language newspaper, all of which are subject to some form of censorship.
Health Malaria and rabies can be prevalent. Health care is improving steadily, and health services are constantly being upgraded and are provided to an increasing proportion of the population. There are many hospitals and rural health units available. Life expectancy is 61 years.

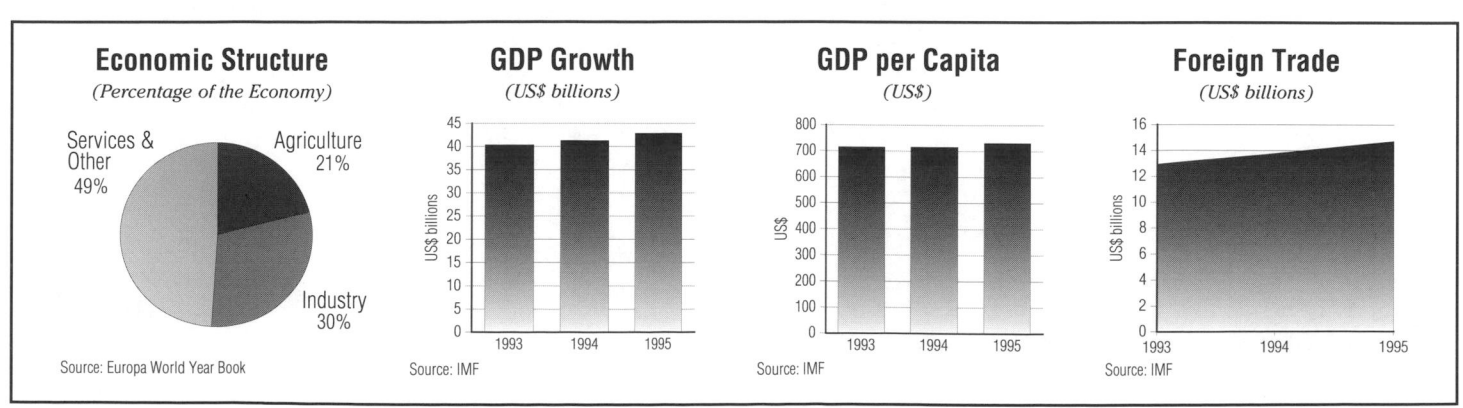

Economic Structure
(*Percentage of the Economy*)

Services & Other 49%
Agriculture 21%
Industry 30%

Source: Europa World Year Book

GDP Growth
(*US$ billions*)

US$ billions

1993 1994 1995

Source: IMF

GDP per Capita
(*US$*)

US$

1993 1994 1995

Source: IMF

Foreign Trade
(*US$ billions*)

US$ billions

1993 1994 1995

Source: IMF

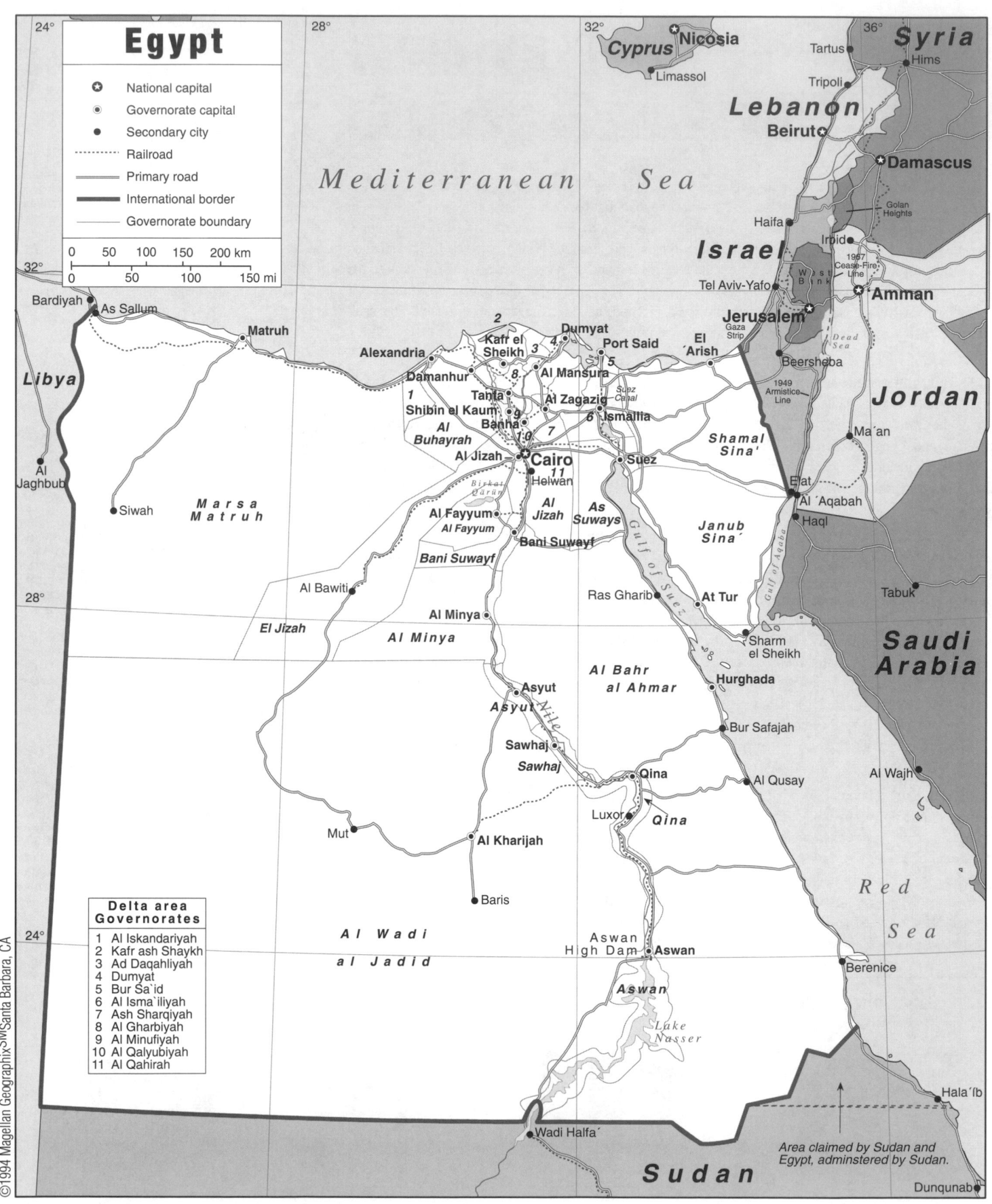

Egypt

- ✪ National capital
- ◉ Governorate capital
- ● Secondary city
- ······ Railroad
- —— Primary road
- ━━ International border
- —— Governorate boundary

0 50 100 150 200 km
0 50 100 150 mi

Delta area Governorates

1. Al Iskandariyah
2. Kafr ash Shaykh
3. Ad Daqahliyah
4. Dumyat
5. Bur Sa`id
6. Al Isma`iliyah
7. Ash Sharqiyah
8. Al Gharbiyah
9. Al Minufiyah
10. Al Qalyubiyah
11. Al Qahirah

Mediterranean Sea

Cyprus
Nicosia
Limassol

Syria
Tartus
Hims
Tripoli

Lebanon
Beirut

Damascus

Haifa
Israel
Irbid
1967 Cease-Fire Line
Tel Aviv-Yafo
West Bank
Golan Heights

Jerusalem
Gaza Strip
Beersheba
1949 Armistice Line

Jordan
Amman
Ma´an

Bardiyah
As Sallum
Matruh

Libya

Al Jaghbub

Siwah

Marsa Matruh

Alexandria
Damanhur
Tanta
Shibin el Kaum
Al Buhayrah
2
Kafr el Sheikh
3
8
9
Banha
10
Al Jizah
Cairo
Helwan
Dumyat
4
Port Said
5
Al Mansura
Al Zagazig
7
6
Ismailia
Suez Canal
Suez

El ´Arish

Shamal Sina´

Eſat
Al ´Aqabah
Haql

Tabuk

Saudi Arabia

Birkat Qarun
Al Fayyum
Al Fayyum
Al Jizah
As Suways
Bani Suwayf
Bani Suwayf

Janub Sina´

Gulf of Suez

Gulf of Aqaba

Al Bawiti

El Jizah

Al Minya
Al Minya

Ras Gharib
At Tur

Sharm el Sheikh

Hurghada

Al Bahr al Ahmar

Asyut
Asyut
Nile

Bur Safajah

Sawhaj
Sawhaj

Qina
Al Qusay
Al Wajh

Luxor
Qina

Red Sea

Mut

Al Kharijah

Baris

Al Wadi al Jadid

Aswan High Dam
Aswan
Aswan

Berenice

Lake Nasser

Hala´ib

Wadi Halfa´

Area claimed by Sudan and Egypt, administered by Sudan.

Sudan

Dunqunab

Foreign Trade

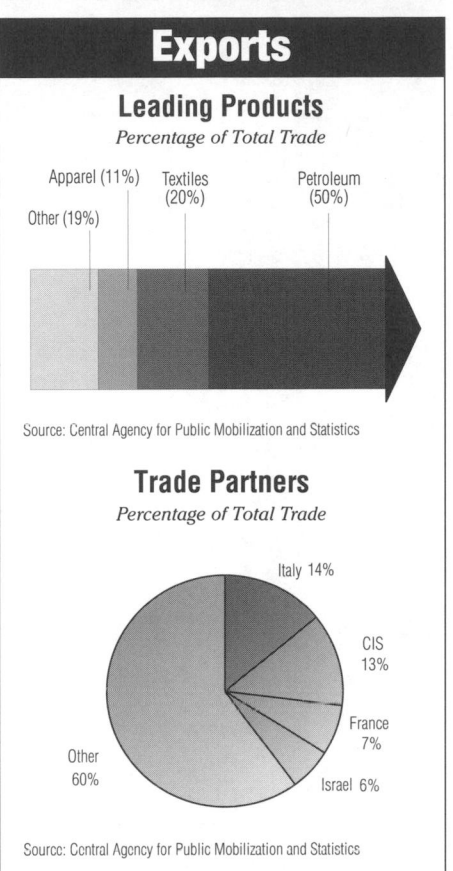

Imports

Leading Products
Percentage of Total Trade

Machinery (24%)
Basic Manufactures (22%)
Chemical (14%)
Other (40%)

Source: Central Agency for Public Mobilization and Statistics

Trade Partners
Percentage of Total Trade

US 18%
Germany 10%
France 9%
Italy 6%
Other 57%

Source: Central Agency for Public Mobilization and Statistics

Exports

Leading Products
Percentage of Total Trade

Apparel (11%)
Textiles (20%)
Petroleum (50%)
Other (19%)

Source: Central Agency for Public Mobilization and Statistics

Trade Partners
Percentage of Total Trade

Italy 14%
CIS 13%
France 7%
Israel 6%
Other 60%

Source: Central Agency for Public Mobilization and Statistics

Opportunities

FOR IMPORTING TO EGYPT

- agricultural products: corn, wheat, and soybean meal
- aircraft and parts
- architectural, construction, and engineering services
- computer products
- food processing and packaging equipment
- furniture
- machinery and transport equipment
- medical equipment
- plastic materials and resins
- sporting goods and recreation equipment
- telecommunications products
- water resources equipment
- wood and paper products

FOR EXPORTING FROM EGYPT

- beans
- clothing
- cotton
- iron and steel
- manufactured goods
- metal products
- onions
- petroleum and petroleum products
- rice
- textiles

GROWTH SECTORS

- agriculture
- clothing and personal care products
- electrical power systems
- environmental protection goods and services
- franchised restaurants
- highway construction
- telecommunications

GOVERNMENT PROCUREMENT

- building materials
- industrial machinery
- medical supplies and equipment
- military defense equipment
- natural gas pipelines
- telecommunication products
- water treatment systems

Trade News

RULES AND REGULATIONS

- **Regulations** Trade regulations are administered by the General Authority for Control of Imports and Exports and by the Customs Authority.
- **Tariff rates** Tariff rates have been steadily reduced since 1991. Nevertheless, Egyptian tariffs are still relatively high compared to other developing countries. The government has currently pledged to reduce the maximum rate from 60 to 50 percent. In February 1994, Egypt implemented the Harmonized System (HS).
- **Import licenses** Egypt no longer requires import licenses. In July 1993, the government canceled the list of items requiring prior approval before importation. All commodities may be freely imported into Egypt except for those specifically banned.
- **Prohibited imports** Certain textile and apparel items cannot be imported.
- **Customs procedures** Customs procedures are complicated and rigid in areas such as duty rates. Customs procedures are subjective when it comes to identifying whether a commodity fits in one tariff category or another.
- **Tariff valuation** Tariff valuation is based on the so-called "Egyptian selling price," based on the commercial invoice that accompanies a product the first time it is imported from any source, although some allowance is given on an ad hoc basis for different sources of supply (such as expensive versus cheap labor source countries). Customs authorities retain information from the original commercial invoice and expect subsequent imports of the same product to have a value no lower than noted on the invoice from the first shipment. As a result of that expectation, and the belief that under-invoicing is widely practiced, customs officials routinely increase invoice values from 10 to 30 percent.
- **Export controls** Controls have been set on scrap metal, hide, and alpaca fibers. An export duty may be imposed on certain metal and agricultural commodities.
- **Free trade zones** There are eight free trade zones in Egypt: Cairo, Alexandria, Port Said, Suez, Ismailia, Damietta, Safaga, and Sohag. Although exempt from taxes and fees stipulated by Egyptian laws, free zone investment companies are subject to an annual fee of one percent of the value of goods entering or leaving the free zone, or on the gross revenues realized by the project if the activity of the project does not require the entry or exit of goods.
- **Export companies** Companies producing largely for export (normally 80 percent or more of total production), may be established in the free zones and may operate in foreign currency.
- **Government procurement** Although Egypt does not employ systematic or discriminatory policies which adversely affect foreign businesses, the government buys from public sector firms whenever possible. Egypt's tender regulations are written by the government, for the government's benefit. Egyptian bidders (both public and private sector) receive a 15 percent price preference.
- **Cotton** The government is in the process of deregulating the cotton sector and reactivating the cotton exchange.
- **Free trade agreements** Egypt is not a member of any free trade agreements.

TRANSPORTATION FIRMS

Cook, Thomas & Son, Ltd.
Four Champollion Street
Cairo
Telex: 92413 TCOOK UN

Favia Transport Internationaux
18 Adly Street
Cairo
Telex: 92589 FAVIA UN

Canal Shipping Agency
POB 262
Port Said
Telex: 63075 AGEN UN

Business Travel

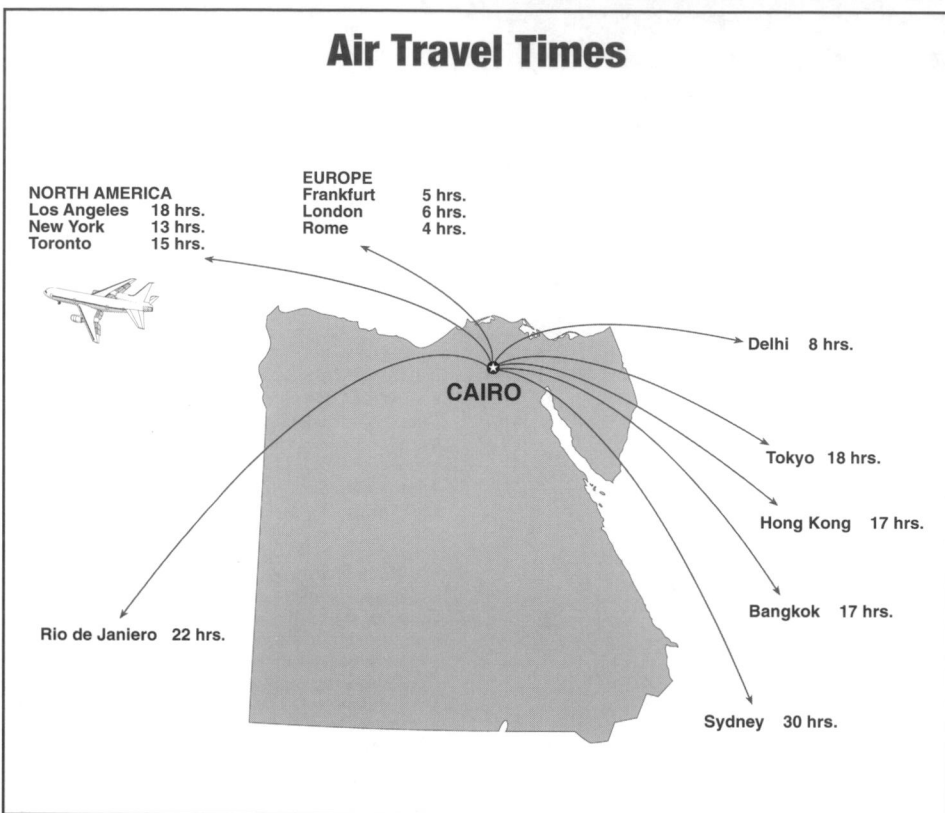

Air Travel Times

NORTH AMERICA
Los Angeles   18 hrs.
New York   13 hrs.
Toronto   15 hrs.

EUROPE
Frankfurt   5 hrs.
London   6 hrs.
Rome   4 hrs.

CAIRO

Delhi   8 hrs.

Tokyo   18 hrs.

Hong Kong   17 hrs.

Bangkok   17 hrs.

Rio de Janiero   22 hrs.

Sydney   30 hrs.

COMMUNICATIONS

Telephones Telephone service is inadequate for its population but international direct dialing is available. Public phones (PTT) can be found at post offices, railroad stations, and main squares in big cities.

Fax Fax machines are common but are hindered by crowded telephone lines. Most luxury hotels have fax service. Telegrams and telex services are also available at larger hotels and post offices.

Post office Main post office branches are generally open Saturday to Thursday from 9:00 am to 7:00 pm and Fridays until noon. Local rumor has it that letters mailed from major hotels are delivered more quickly than those mailed from a post office.

BEST TRAVEL BOOKS

Egypt & Sudan Travel Survival Kit. Lonely Planet. Packed with solid valuable advice. 608 pages.
Fodor's Travel Guide, Egypt.
Do's and Taboos Around the World. Roger E. Axtell. New York: Wiley.
North African Handbook. The ideal practical guide. Updated annually.
The Traveler's Guide to Middle Eastern and North African Customs and Manners. Elizabeth Devine & Nancy Braganti. How to converse, dine, tip, bargain, dress, make friends and conduct business while in the Middle East and North Africa.
Africa on a Shoestring, Lonely Planet. Filled with interesting information.

USEFUL TELEPHONE NUMBERS

If you are calling from outside Egypt, you will need to add the country code [20] and any other international dialing requirements from within your country.

- Emergency Police Service .... 122 or 930900
- Ambulance .... 123 or 770123
- Fire 125
- Tourist Police Cairo .... (2) 3906027
- Tourist Police Pyramids Area .... (2) 850259
- Egyptian Promotion of Tourism .... (2) 2824858
- Ministry of Tourism .... (2) 3552600
- Express Mail Service DHL .... (2) 3557301
- Egyptian National Railways................... (2) 2753555
- Pharmacy 24 hour .... (2) 3402406

Car Rental
- Avis Airport...................................... (2) 2678681
- Budget Airport .... (2) 2914277
- Europecar/Bita Airport .... (2) 2666688
- Hertz Airport .... (2) 2914255

Airlines
- Egypt Air.. (2) 922444
- Air Sinai .... (2) 2744711
- ZAS Airline of Egypt............................. (2) 2843483

Credit Card Information
Lost or stolen credit cards (call collect to the US, regardless of which country the card was issued in).
- Amex ....[1] (919) 333-3211
- Diner's Club..............................[1] (303) 799-1504
- MasterCard ....[1] (314) 275-6690
- Visa ....[1] (410) 581-7931

Travelogue

WORKWEEK

Offices Sunday-Thursday 8:30 am to 3:30 pm.
Banks Monday-Thursday 8:30 am to 1:30 pm, Sunday 10:00 am to noon.
Government Sunday-Thursday 8:00 am to 3:00 pm.
Retail Daily from 9:00 am to 7:00 pm in winter and until 8:00 pm in summer.

HOLIDAYS

Holidays 1996
January 1 New Year's Day
February 20-22 Ramadan Bairam*
April 25 Sinai Liberation Day
April 27-30 Kurban Bairam*
May 1 Labor Day
May 2 Sham El Nessim
May 19 Islamic New Year*
July 23 National Day
July 28 Moulid El-Nabi*
August 19 Prophet's Birthday
October 6 Armed Forces' Day.
*Dates depend on a lunar calendar and vary each year.

VISA AND PASSPORT

A passport and visa are required for foreigners entering Egypt. Citizens of Arab countries do not require visas. Travelers arriving by air can get a renewable 30-day tourist visa at the airport upon arrival. Visitors arriving overland and by sea, or those who have previously experienced difficulty with their visa status in Egypt, must obtain a visa prior to arrival. Military personnel are not exempt from passport and visa requirements. Tourists must register with local authorities (at hotel, local police station, or the central passport office) within seven days of arrival.

DEPARTURE FORMALITIES

A maximum of 100 Egyptian pounds may be exported out of Egypt at any time.

IMMUNIZATION

There are no vaccinations required for entry to Egypt unless you are arriving from an area infected with yellow fever or cholera (Egypt considers most of Africa and Asia infected areas). Travelers arriving without proper health records may be quarantined. Evidence of an AIDS test is required for everyone staying more than 30 days. Anti-malaria pills are recommended from June to October.

TIPPING

Taxi drivers are tipped 10 to 15 percent. Porters: 50 piastres per piece. Hotels, restaurants, nightspots: 10 percent included in bill, but an additional 5 percent is usual. Chambermaid: 50 piastres per day. Barbers and beauticians: 10 percent. Small services: 30 piastres.

CRIME

Egypt's crime rate is low. While street crime and petty theft is not uncommon, violent incidents are rare. Women traveling alone may be subject to sexual harassment and verbal abuse. Do not carry a lot of cash, and do not stay in one spot for too long as pickpockets abound. It is advisable to use traveler's checks. Beggars, peddlers, and self-appointed guides can be aggressive.

INFRASTRUCTURE

Egypt has highly developed airline, railway, hotel, telecommunication, and taxi industries, as well as excellent road and waterway networks. Cairo also has an efficient light rail system for intercity travel. When traveling by taxi, use only from the official stand, which is watched 24 hours by the Tourist Police. The fastest, cleanest, and safest mode of public transportation is the Cairo Metro or subway. Keep your ticket; it is needed to depart the train. There is an express train connecting Cairo, Alexandria, Luxor, and Aswan. Bus services links Cairo and Tel Aviv, Israel.

NATIONAL TOURIST OFFICE

Ministry of Tourism and Civil Aviation
110 Qasr El Aini Street
Tahrir Square
Cairo
Telephone: (2) 355 2600

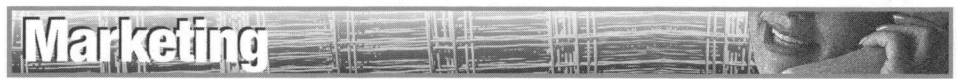

Distribution

Virtually all international, and the vast majority of significant domestic, business activity is conducted by recognized firms in Cairo. Major operators located there may deal directly or through intermediaries with any level of potential supplier or customer. Few markets outside the capital have the resources to attract business, and most receive their merchandise from Cairo-based distributors.

Agents, Distributors, and Partners

Foreign firms must register to sell their products in Egypt. Most foreign—and domestic—companies rely on local representation for wholesale and retail distribution. Several types of agency relationships exist, ranging from large general or specialized distributors to individuals who handle any and every product they can. Most large retailers do their own importing and prefer getting quotes directly from the overseas supplier instead of from a local agent.

Selling Techniques

Egyptian business professionals are typically internationally oriented and sophisticated. They also pride themselves on their ability to negotiate the best price, and price is the primary consideration in purchase decisions. However, quality and features can be close second tier considerations among these cosmopolitan buyers. Although after-sales service and support is seldom a stated concern, poor performance will generally be blamed on the foreign supplier—and sales will suffer—so suppliers should protect themselves by training and supporting distributors and dealers to supply such service. The annual Cairo International Trade Fair is the center for launching any new campaign, and several other fairs take place each month. Consumer goods are often sold door-to-door.

Advertising

More than half of all Egyptians reportedly read one or more newspapers every day, and strategically placed print media ads can produce excellent results. Almost all Egyptians watch television as well. Other advertising media include billboards, neon signs, wall-size posters, and mass mailings. Trade promotion is also becoming more sophisticated.

Business Culture

Greetings and Courtesies

Businesspeople in Egypt are generally friendly and open. They will usually greet people with a firm handshake. Always wait for a woman to extend her hand before shaking; if no hand is offered, simply smile and nod. Social status is very important in Egypt. Family and social connections are also important, perhaps even more so than personal accomplishments. Expect several invitations to have coffee and meals, to the point where you may feel crowded and overwhelmed. Titles are used often; wait to use first names until you are invited.

Business Ethic and Framework

Egyptians clearly define the limits between friends and strangers; this extends both to social occasions and business. Personal relationships can be the most important factor in future business success in Egypt. Egyptians tend to be patient and slow to make decisions, so pressing for a specific deadline will probably do more harm than good.

Meetings and Decision Making

Always make appointments; cold calls are not appreciated. Although you should always be on time for meetings, your Egyptian counterparts will probably be late. Time is not as fixed and segmented as in the West. Meetings will usually go much later than planned; Egyptians enjoy socializing. Businesspeople in Egypt won't usually say "no," but if your question doesn't get an answer you should take it as a negative response. "Yes" also means different things in Egypt; Arabs may say "yes" even when they mean something less.

Women

Egypt is one of the most progressive countries in the Arab world regarding women's rights. Women are very active at all levels of society. Drastic revisions have been made in marriage and divorce laws. An Egyptian woman can sue for divorce if her husband takes a second wife without her permission. Foreign businesswomen should have no problems in Egypt. Women discarded the veil over 50 years ago, but still wear very conservative clothing.

Marketing in Egypt

MARKETING TIPS

- **Agents** Egyptian agency law is the most liberal in the Middle East. Cancelling an agency does not require compensation, and no minimum notification is required. Exclusivity is not required, although most agents try to get it. Most foreign companies have one or two local agents, and territories can be split geographically, by customer type, or on some other basis.
- **Legal counsel** Although not technically necessary, retaining a local attorney to draw up agency, sales, and contract agreements is generally advisable.
- **Government markets** Egyptian commercial agents are required for foreign company bids on most civilian government tenders (foreign concerns cannot bid on military tenders).
- **Sensitive products** Egypt is an Islamic country, and although it is modern and secular by many standards, it continues to experience strife from fundamentalists; sellers should exercise sensitivity in order not to offend Egyptian sensibilities.

MARKETING FIRMS

International Business Associates
1079 Corniche El Ni
Garden City, Cairo
Tel: (2) 355-2803, 355-0427
Fax: (2) 355-7454

Rada Research & Public Relations Co.
1 Mostafa El Wakil Street
Heliopolis, Cairo
Tel: (2) 291-7956
Fax. (2) 291-7563

Fiani & Partners
143 Tahrir Street
Dokki, Cairo
Tel: (2) 348-7353, 348-5204
Fax: (2) 348-5204

Cultural Cautions

DO'S

- Always be hospitable. If you bring food back into the office, be sure to bring enough for everyone.

DON'TS

- You will be asked out repeatedly. While it is okay to decline occasionally, to turn down too many offers is seen as a slight.
- Don't try to speed a meeting along. Egyptians enjoy socializing and taking their time. Trying to hurry a meeting will be considered rude.

CUSTOMS

- A person's dignity, honor, and reputation are of paramount importance.
- The most popular form of entertainment is conversation, and Arabs enjoy long discussions over coffee.
- Egyptians are very expressive and loud. Yelling and screaming during meetings is not uncommon.

OBSERVATIONS

- Supervisors and managers constantly praise their employees, to reassure them that their hard work is noticed.
- Egyptians stand or sit closer to each other than Westerners. Men often hold hands and kiss each other on the cheek, both signs of friendship. It is also common to touch someone repeatedly during a conversation.

NEGOTIATIONS

- Don't press a sensitive issue. If you don't get a direct answer, it is probably best to move on.
- Egyptians usually don't criticize openly. They are more likely to hint that changes may be necessary.
- Beware of false flattery or praise from Egyptians. It is usually just good manners rather than an indication of success in a business relationship.

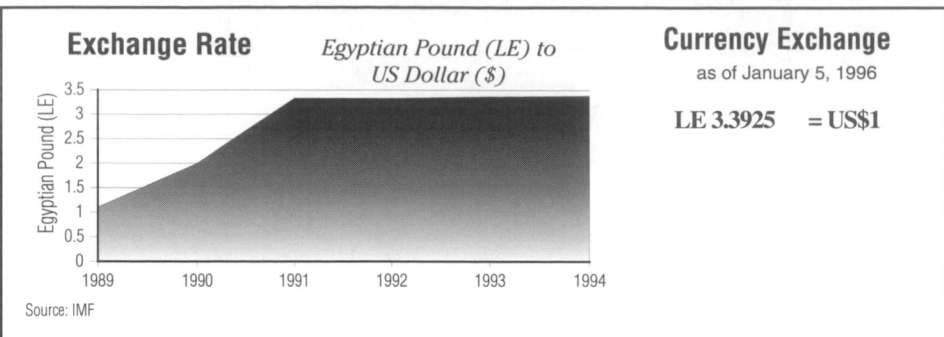

Exchange Rate

Egyptian Pound (LE) to US Dollar ($)

Source: IMF

Currency Exchange

as of January 5, 1996

LE 3.3925   = US$1

Currency

The currency of Egypt is the Egyptian pound (LE), which is divided into five tallaris and 100 piastres.

Foreign Exchange

Authorized commercial banks can conduct foreign exchange operations without prior approval by the Central Bank of Egypt. The banks are free to determine the rates applied for forward transactions. Nonbank foreign exchange dealers can operate in the free market, dealing with domestic and foreign currency (including traveler's checks) on their accounts. Authorized nonbank dealers can broker any foreign exchange operation and transaction, except transfers to and from the country.

Capital Transfers

Transfers of funds by foreign nationals leaving the country permanently are not restricted. Imports and exports of securities and transfers related to their purchases or sales must be effected through authorized banks. Nonresidents arriving in Egypt may import up to LE100 in bank notes and are permitted to bring in, and use locally, unlimited amounts of foreign exchange. Payments may be made in convertible currency, Egyptian pounds, or in any other manner permitted by foreign exchange regulations. Import payments in foreign exchange are effected through the commercial banks or the importer's own foreign exchange resources.

Investment Incentives

The government of Egypt is open to foreign direct investment and generally encourages private sector activity in most sectors of the economy. Many foreign investments, especially those companies registering under the Inland Investment Law 230, receive a five-year exemption from tax payments on profits and dividends. Other exemptions include stamp tax duties; notarization and notification fees; and income tax liability.

Investment Restrictions

Only those foreign investments which are included on the Negative List are restricted. The Negative List currently includes all military products, related industries, and tobacco products, as well as all investments in the Sinai.

Money Matters

BITS AND PIECES

- **Airline Tickets** Only Egyptian nationals, nonresidents who have lived in the country for five years, and nonresidents permitted to reside in Egypt for 10 years can purchase airline tickets in Egyptian pounds. Everyone else must buy tickets with convertible currencies or Egyptian pounds converted at the commercial bank exchange rate.
- **Gold** Banks can not deal or speculate in any precious materials. The importation and exportation of gold is regulated by the government.
- **Corporate income tax** Resident companies are subject to taxes based on all income, foreign and domestic. Nonresident companies are taxed on Egyptian income only.
- **Export payments** Proceeds from any published materials (books, magazines, etc.) must be repatriated immediately after receipt and proceeds from a few exports, including cotton and rice, must be repatriated within three months. Any other export proceeds must be repatriated within two years of the date of shipment.
- **Payments for invisibles** Banks are authorized to provide foreign exchange for all invisible payments by the government.
- **Personal exports** Anyone leaving Egypt carrying items valued at more than LE250 needs to show evidence that they exchanged foreign exchange equivalent to the excess value of the purchase in the free markets.
- **Nonresident accounts** Egypt recognizes three types of nonresident accounts, but most nonresidents are eligible for free accounts. They may be opened by any entity other than governments, public authorities, and public sector entities. They can be credited with any currency and any amount.
- **Investment screening** The General Authority for Investment and Free Zones (GAFI) decides on a request to establish a project within two days. If the request is rejected, an appeal may be lodged within 15 days. After approval of the investment request, the investor must submit a four-page application for incentives giving detailed information on the project's objective, location, capital, investment costs, sources of finance, labor, and wages. The GAFI Board then makes a final decision.
- **Inland Investment Law 230** This is the primary law governing foreign investments, allowing 100 percent foreign ownership of ventures. It provides a secure basis for a foreign investor to operate in Egypt by guaranteeing the right to remit income earned in Egypt and to repatriate capital.
- **Companies Law 159** Foreigners may also choose to invest under provisions of this law provided that at least 49 percent of the shares are offered to Egyptians upon formation.

BANKS

National Bank of Egypt
24 Sharia Sherif
Cairo
Tel: (2) 392-4143

Arab International Bank
35 Abdel Khalek Tharwat St.
Cairo
Tel: (2) 390-5765
Fax: (2) 391-6233

Commercial International Bank
Nile Tower Bldg., 4th Fl.
21/23 Giza St.
Giza
Tel: (2) 348-1797, 570-3043, 570-3022
Fax: (2) 570-1945

Egyptian British Bank
Ex-Hong Kong Bank
3 Aboul Feda St.
Zamalek, Cairo
Tel: (2) 340-4687
Fax: (2) 341-4010

TAXATION

Taxation requires sophisticated knowledge of complex rules and regulations specific to each country. The information presented here is from the Ernst & Young Corporate Tax Guide and Directory, available from the Ernst & Young accounting office in your country, or from:

Zarrouk, Khaled & Co.
Mail Address:
POB 110/12655
Mohandessin
Cairo, Egypt
Street Address:
1, Wadi El Nil Street
Mohandessin
Giza Cairo 12411
Egypt
Tel: (2) 303 9779, 303 2229
     (2) 303 0701
Telex: 94245 Ans bk ZAROK UN
Fax: (2) 303 2228

At a Glance

Corporate Income Tax Rate (%)	40
Capital Gains Tax Rate (%)	40
Branch Tax Rate (%)	40
Withholding Tax (%)	
Dividends	0
Interest*	32
Royalties from Patents, Know-how, etc.*	32
Branch Remittance Tax	0
Net Operating Losses (Years)	
Carryback	0
Carryforward	5

* Final tax applicable to payments to corporations. The rate may be reduced under a tax treaty.

Legal System

Egypt's legal system is currently derived from the French, although Muslim activists are trying to advance the impact of Islamic law.

Intellectual Property Protection

Patents Patents are valid for 15 years and may be renewed for an additional 15 years. In general, enforcement is adequate, although it is difficult to pursue a private cause of action against a local enterprise which may be infringing foreign patent rights.

Trademarks Egypt has trademark laws which adequately protect identifiable trade or service marks in use by a commercial enterprise. All trademarks are issued for 10 years and may be renewed indefinitely in 10-year increments.

Copyrights Egyptian laws conform to, and enforcement adheres to, most international conventions.

Trade Secrets Although trade secrets have not traditionally been protected by Egyptian law, several recent laws have been passed which address these and other commercial protections.

Business Registration

The Egyptian government has made it a priority to encourage private investment into the country, and has streamlined registration priorities to make it simple and quick for foreign businesses and investors to engage in commercial enterprises in the country. Branch offices and agencies are also allowed, and registration procedures are much simpler for these.

Contracts and Dispute Resolution

All contracts must be in writing to be valid in Egypt. The civil code does provide for arbitration of business disputes and it is encouraged by the government as an alternative to submitting disputes to the judicial system. Arbitration awards rendered abroad will generally be enforced in Egypt.

Labor

Egypt has several labor-related laws regarding maximum hours, minimum wage, and child and female labor. Labor unions are allowed in Egypt, although they generally work closely with management.

Legal Matters

LEGAL BRIEFS

- **Judiciary** Most cases are tried by tribunals. The judiciary is independent of other state powers and the judges are not subject to enforced retirement.
- **Labor arbitration** Labor disputes are generally submitted to arbitration, and strikes are prohibited while these proceedings are being conducted.
- **Due process** Political violence has led to detention without due process for many persons.
- **Religious courts** Islamic Shari'ah courts dealing with matters of personal status, including marriage and divorce, were abolished in 1956, although there has recently been a move to renew their authority.
- **Appointees** The president appoints all civilian judges.
- **Freedom of information** The freedom of the press has increased dramatically in Egypt, though it is still restrictive by Western standards.
- **Court freedoms** The courts have demonstrated increased independence recently. The legal code comes mostly from the Napoleonic Code.
- **Trademarks** The new trademarks law provides for registration not only of visual marks but also of sound and smell marks.
- **Commercial laws** The Egyptian Constitution of 1980 states that Islamic Law is the source of all laws passed subsequent thereto. The civil code and most commercial laws predate this mandate.

LEGAL CONTACT

Sherif Saad
Maadi Palace Tower
Maadi Station Square, 5th Floor
Arab African International Bank Building
POB 90
Maadi, Cairo
Tel: (2) 3786201
Fax: (2) 3786204

Contacts

GOVERNMENT AGENCIES

Cabinet of Ministers
Magles El Shaab St., Kasr El Aini St.
Cairo
Tel: (2) 391-0008, 390-9749
Fax: (2) 390-8159

Ministry of Agriculture, Animal & Fish Wealth, and Land Reclamation
Nadi El Seid St., Dokki
Giza
Tel: (2) 702-677, 702-596, 702-758
Fax: (2) 703-889, 704-660

Ministry of Transport, Communication and Civil Aviation
105 Kasr El Aini St.
Cairo
Tel: (2) 354-3623
Fax: (2) 355-5564
Telex: 92137 UN, 92802 UN

Ministry of Electricity and Energy
Abbassia, Nasr City
Cairo
Tel: (2) 261-6299, 261-6514, 261-6317
Fax: (2) 261-6302

Ministry of Information
Maspero, Corniche El Nil
Cairo
Tel: (2) 747-193, 749-394, 747-416
Fax: (2) 757-144

Ministry of Foreign Affairs
Maspero
Cairo
Tel: (2) 354-1414, 354-2215 Fax: (2) 354-6285

Ministry of Supply & Home Trade
99 Kasr El Aini St.
Cairo
Tel: (2) 355-0360
Fax: (2) 354-4973

Ministry of Finance
Lazoughly Square, Justice & Finance Bldg.
Cairo
Tel: (2) 355-7027, 354-1055, 355-7136, 354-0601

Ministry of Education
4 Ibrahim Naguib St., Garden City
Cairo
Tel: (2) 354-3454, 356-4065, 354-5479
Fax: (2) 356-2952, 354-2163

Ministry of Housing & Utilities
1 Ismail Abaza St., off Kasr El Aini
Cairo
Tel: (2) 355-7013, 355-3468, 355-7978
Fax: (2) 354-5666

Ministry of Tourism
Abassia Square, Borg Misr Travel
Cairo
Tel: (2) 282-8457/6, 282-9778
Fax: (2) 282-8771

Ministry of Economy & Foreign Trade
8 Adly St.
Cairo
Tel: (2) 390-6796, 390-6804, 391-9661, 391-9278
Fax: (2) 390-3029

Ministry of Public Works & Water Resources
El Nil St., Embaba
Cairo
Tel: (2) 354-5884, 354-1478
Fax: (2) 355-8008

Ministry of Health
Magles El Shaab St.
Cairo
Tel: (2) 354-1076, 354-3462, 354-0426
Fax: (2) 355-3966

REMEMBER

- When you telephone (or fax) to Egypt you must always include the country code [20] before the numbers given.
- When you send mail to Egypt, be sure to write EGYPT in capital letters on its own line below the addresses given.

Ministry of Industry & Mineral Wealth
2 Latin America St., Garden City
Cairo
Tel: (2) 354-3600, 355-7034, 355-4826
Fax: (2) 354-8362

Ministry of Transport, Communications & Aviation
Ramses St.
Cairo
Tel: (2) 744-909, 777-551, 777-676
Fax: (2) 771-306

Customs Authority
4 El Tayaran St., Nasr City
Cairo
Tel: (2) 260-5710, 604-402, 608-683
Fax: (2) 261-5557

Taxation Authority
5 Hussein Hegazi Street
Cairo
Tel: (2) 355-7784

Radio & TV Union
TV Bldg., Corniche El Nil
Cairo
Tel: (2) 749-508, 760-454
Fax: (2) 574-6989

State Information Service
22 Talaat Harb St.
Cairo
Tel: (2) 762-766, 758-511
Fax: (2) 752-187

WORLD TRADE CENTER

World Trade Center Co., Cairo
1191 Corniche El Nil
POB 2007
Cairo
Tel: (2) 764-424, 764-425, 764-494
Fax: (2) 774-233

BUSINESS AND TRADE ORGANIZATIONS

Commercial Representation Division Economy and Foreign Trade
96 Ahmed Orabi St., Mohandessin
Cairo
Tel: (2) 347-1892/3/4/5
Fax: (2) 345-1840

Social Fund for Development
Hussein Hegazy and Kasr El Nil Sts.
Cairo
Tel: (2) 354-8339
Fax: (2) 355-0628

Information & Decision Support Center
Cabinet Bldg., Magles El Shaab St.
Cairo
Tel: (2) 356-1600
Fax: (2) 354-1222

General Authority for Supply Commodities
99 Kasr El Aini St.
Cairo

Egyptian Export Promotion Center
106 Gameat El Dowal El Arabia St., 5th Fl.
Mohandessin, Giza
Tel: (2) 349-3919, 349-3921
Fax: (2) 348-4142

General Authority for Control of Imports & Exports
Atlas Bldg., El Sheikh Maarouf & Ramses Sts.
Cairo
Tel: (2) 574-2830, 575-6095, 575-6031
Fax: (2) 766-971

General Authority of Int'l Fairs & Exhibitions (GOIEF)
Fair Grounds, Nasr City
Cairo
Tel: (2) 260-7811, 260-7815
Fax: (2) 260-7845

Federation of Egyptian Industries
Immobilia Building, 26A Sherif St.
Cairo
Tel: (2) 392-8238
Fax: (2) 392-8075

Egyptian Businessmen Association
21 Giza St., Nile Tower
Giza
Tel: (2) 736-030
Fax: (2) 737-258

Alexandria Business Association
Ragab Exp. & Imp. Co.
18 Avenue El Horria St.
Alexandria
Tel: (3) 482-5518
Fax: (3) 482-9576

American Chamber of Commerce in Egypt
Cairo Marriott Hotel, Suite 1541
Zamalek
Cairo
Tel: (2) 340-8888
Fax: (2) 340-9482

Federation of Egyptian Chambers of Commerce
4 Falaky Square
Cairo
Tel: (2) 355-1136, 355-1164, 355-1813
Fax: (2) 355-7940

MARKETING AND ADVERTISING

Intermarkets Advertising
42 Abdel Moneim Riad Street, Dokki
Cairo
Tel: (2) 360-3017
Fax: (2) 360-3019

Research & Advertising Consultants
30 Gameat Al Dowal Al Arabia St., Mohandessin
Cairo
Tel: (2) 360-8439
Fax: (2) 360-4815

Americana Advertising Agency
32H Radwan Ibn Tabib St.
Giza
Tel: (2) 730-855
Fax: (2) 733-550

BANKS

National Bank of Egypt
24 Sherif St.
Cairo
Tel: (2) 574-6858
Fax: (2) 574-6000

Arab International Bank
35 Abdel Khalek Tharwat St.
Cairo
Tel: (2) 390-5765
Fax: (2) 391-6233

Commercial International Bank
Nile Tower Bldg., 4th Fl.
21/23 Giza St., Giza
Tel: (2) 348-1797, 570-3043, 570-3022
Fax: (2) 570-1945

Egyptian British Bank (Ex-HongKong Bank)
3 Aboul Feda St., Zamalek
Cairo
Tel: (2) 340-4687
Fax: (2) 341-4010

Delta International Bank
1113 Corniche El Nil
Cairo
Tel: (2) 574-0831
Fax: (2) 750-904

Misr International Bank
54 El Batal Ahmed Abdel Aziz St., Mohandessin
Cairo
Tel: (2) 349-4424, 349-7091, 349-0164
Fax: (2) 349-8072

Misr Exterior Bank
Cairo Plaza Bldg., Corniche El Nil
Cairo
Tel: (2) 778-021
Fax: (2) 762-806

Misr Iran Development Bank
Nile Tower Bldg., Giza St.
Giza
Tel: (2) 572-7311, 572-7004, 572-7890
Fax: (2) 570-1185

Central Bank of Egypt
31 Kasr El Nil St.
Cairo
Tel: (2) 392-3679, 392-6211, 393-1514
Fax: (2) 392-5045
4 Ahmed Pacha St., Garden City
Cairo
Tel: (2) 355-1501, 355-1161, 355-1873/7
Fax: (2) 355-8056

Bank of Alexandria
49 Kasr El Nil St.
Cairo
Tel: (2) 391-9686
Fax: (2) 390-7793

Cairo Bank
22 Adly St.
Cairo
Tel: (2) 390-9575
Fax: (2) 390-1735

Bank Misr
151 Mohamed Farid St.
Cairo
Tel: (2) 391-4239, 391-1159
Fax: (2) 393-5381

LEGAL CONTACTS

Eidib & Partners
32 Boulevard Saad Zaghloul
POB 152
Alexandria
Tel: (3) 482-0111/5, 482-0161, 482-0178, 482-0216
Fax: (3) 4821900
Telex: 54046 ELDIB UN/54696 ELDIB UN
Cairo office:
78 Al Goumhouria Street
Tel: (2) 912983
Fax: (2) 924564

Baker & McKenzie
20th Floor
56 Gamyat El Dowal
El Arabeya Street
Mohandessin, Giza, Cairo

Elghatit Law Firm
36, Mansour Muhammad Street, Zamalek
Cairo
Tel: (2) 340-6015, 340-7367
Fax: (2) 341-0706
Telex: 21439 GHLF UN

Fox & Gibbons
126 Hohei el Din Abul Ezz Street
9th Floor
Mohandessin, Giza, Cairo
Tel: (2) 348-5955
Fax: (2) 349-2210

Hashem, Ibrahim & Tawfik
23, Kasr El-Nil Street
Cairo
Tel: (2) 393-3376, 393-3827, 393-3948, 393-3974
Fax: (2) 393-3585

Kamel Law Office
4 El Shaheed Ahmed Yehia Irbrahim Street
Mohandesseen, Giza, Cairo
Tel: (2) 347-4102, 347-9453, 347-3597, 347-7179
Fax: (2) 345-2009

NEWSPAPERS

Al-Ahram (The Pyramids)
Sharia al-Galaa
Cairo
Tel: (2) 5747011
Telex: 92544

Al-Akhbar (The News)
Dar Akhbar al-Yawm
Sharia as-Sahafa
Cairo
Tel: (2) 5748100
Telex: 20321

Arev
3 Sharia Soliman Halaby
Cairo
Tel: 754703

Egyptian Gazette
24-26 Sharia Zakaria Ahmad
Cairo
Tel: (2) 751511
Telex: 92475

Al-Gomhouriya (The Republic)
24 Sharia Zakaria Ahmad
Cairo
Tel: (2) 751511
Telex: 92475

Le Progres Egyptien
24 Sharia Zakaria AHmad
Cairo
Tel: (2) 741611
Telex: 92475

Le Journal d'Alexandrie
1 Sharia Rolo
Alexandria

INTERNET ADDRESSES

Usenet group(s):
soc.culture.arabic
soc.culture.egyptian

Technology Development Program
http://163.121.10.41/tdp/doc/main.htm

Index to Egyptian Information on the Internet
http://santos.doc.ic.ac.uk/~mmg/EgyptianInfo.html

Egypt Interactive
http://apps.channel1.com/users/m ansoorm/index.html

Egypt–Net
ftp://ftp.cs.sunysb.edu/pub/EN/www/home.html

Egyptian WWW Index
http://pharos.bu.edu/Egypt

El Salvador

Republic of El Salvador

Economy

Overview

The economy of El Salvador continues to reap benefits from sound economic programs, a commitment to a free economy, and careful fiscal management, with the recent result that economic growth has approached six percent while inflation has held at 10 percent. Overall economic reforms include the elimination of price controls and tariff barriers; the removal of government and government-sanctioned monopolies in coffee, sugar, and cotton exports; a reduction of import duties; the adoption of a free-market system; and deficit reduction. The government has also formulated a plan to privatize the banking system.

Trade

As a predictable consequence of free market economic reforms, El Salvador's import market has exploded in recent years. The open trade and straightforward tariff regime that untangled a web of high import duties and nontariff barriers increased imports rapidly during the first years of trade liberalization, spinning healthy levels of economic growth. Several factors combine to make the commercial environment in El Salvador highly attractive, such as its location in Central America. Major competitors in the El Salvador market include Central America, Japan, Brazil and Germany. Presently the highest areas of growth are in the manufacturing and transportation sectors.

Sectors

Agriculture Although it employs 40 percent of the work force, agriculture accounts for only about 10 percent of GDP. Recognizing the need to diversify the agricultural economy—coffee production still accounts for one-third of El Salvador's agricultural output, while sugar is its second most important agricultural product—planners have focused on nontraditional agricultural specialty export products. Despite the social benefits to be conferred by agrarian reform, it is expected to disrupt production.

Industry Industry accounts for about 25 percent of GDP while employing somewhat less than this proportion of the work force. Expanded regional sales and increased factory utilization are key factors behind the growth of the manufacturing sector, located around San Salvador. With the dismantling of protectionist policies that allowed inefficient import substitution industries to prosper, El Salvador's industrial sector—nearly half of which is involved in food processing—has been facing competition.

Services Although relatively poorly developed, services account for about 65 percent of GDP while employing about 40 percent of the work force. The government has sold the remainder of its stake in state-owned banks, and is considering the future privatization of services now provided by government including telephone and electric companies, various port facilities, and sugar mills.

Trends

El Salvador has secured major loans from international donor agencies to repair war damage and years of infrastructure neglect, presenting major opportunities for infrastructure projects. A productive labor force, liberal foreign investment regulations, free trade zone laws, and the near absence of quotas have drawn heavy investments in apparel assembly from Asian and US investors. However, post-war economic recovery remains fragile and heavily dependent on a favorable balance of payments.

At a Glance

THE COUNTRY
Location Central America, bordering the North Pacific Ocean between Guatemala and Honduras.
Terrain Mostly mountainous with a narrow coastal belt and central plateau.
Climate Located in the tropical zone, El Salvador has two distinct seasons: the dry season, from November to April, and the wet season, from May to November. The coastal plain receives the heaviest rainfall.

THE PEOPLE
Population 5,800,000
Ethnic composition
Mestizo 94%
Indian 5%
White... 1%
Religious composition
Roman Catholic 75%
Other 25%
Languages spoken Spanish, Nahua (Indians).
Education and literacy 73 percent of the population age 15 and older can read and write.
Labor force
Total:...1,700,000
By occupation: agriculture 40%, commerce 16%, manufacturing 15%, government 13%, financial services 9%, transportation 6%, other 1%.

COUNTRY FACTS
Political and legal The Republican government operates under a constitution and a legal system based on civil and Roman law, with traces of common law. The Supreme Court has judicial review of legislative acts. El Salvador accepts compulsory ICJ jurisdiction, with reservations.
Telephone The telecommunications system consists of a nationwide trunk microwave radio relay system, connected into the Central American microwave system. It can efficiently and reliably handle both domestic and international calls. However, much of the population do not have telephones. International country code: [503]. No city codes required.
Transportation Although there is an extensive network of roads, only about 10 percent are paved. The Pan American Highway links El Salvador with Guatemala and Honduras. There are rail connections to Puerto Barrios, Guatemala, which provides El Salvador with a port on the Caribbean. International air services are available from the main airport near San Salvador.
Environment Deforestation has resulted from heavy and mostly unregulated cutting; 45 percent of the wood taken from the forests, however, is used for fuel. Also, excessive burning of foliage to clear the land for planting has resulted in soil erosion. Water and air pollution is widespread and waste disposal is lax. Still, there is no comprehensive national law addressing environmental protection. The government has not undertaken this as a priority.
Media There are several daily newspapers, mostly available in the capital, and some smaller regional dailies. There are many commercial radio stations, and a government owned station, and 6 commercial television stations.
Health Health standards have improved considerably in the past decade. Still, less than two-thirds of the population have access to adequate health care. Life expectancy is 67 years.

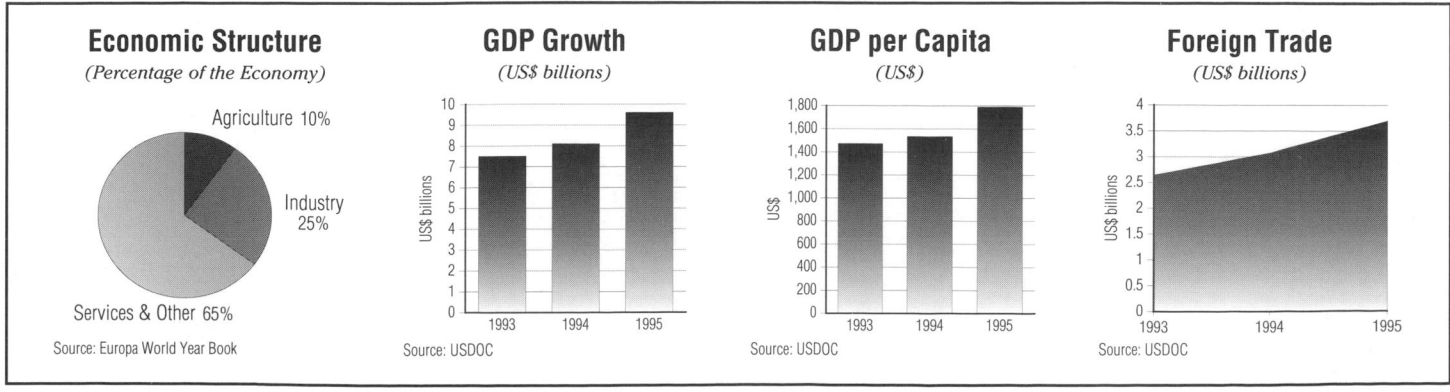

Economic Structure
(Percentage of the Economy)

Agriculture 10%
Industry 25%
Services & Other 65%

Source: Europa World Year Book

GDP Growth
(US$ billions)

US$ billions

1993 1994 1995

Source: USDOC

GDP per Capita
(US$)

US$

1993 1994 1995

Source: USDOC

Foreign Trade
(US$ billions)

US$ billions

1993 1994 1995

Source: USDOC

Business Travel

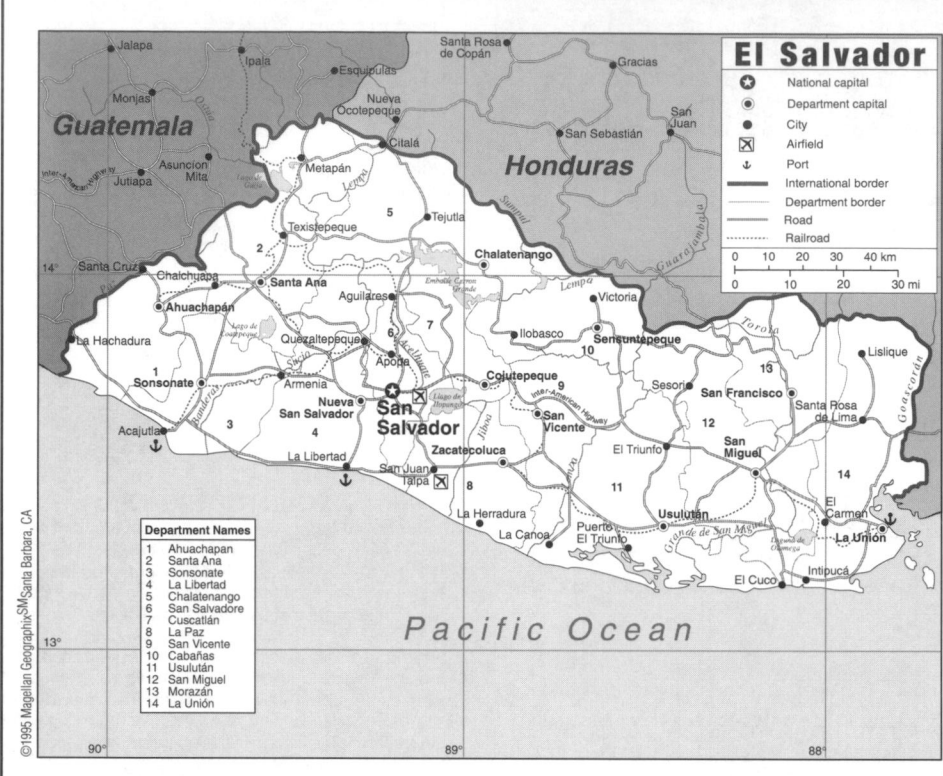

Department Names

1 Ahuachapan
2 Santa Ana
3 Sonsonate
4 La Libertad
5 Chalatenango
6 San Salvadore
7 Cuscatlán
8 La Paz
9 San Vicente
10 Cabañas
11 Usulután
12 San Miguel
13 Morazán
14 La Unión

© 1995 Magellan Geographix℠ Santa Barbara, CA

COMMUNICATIONS

Telephones The telecommunications network in El Salvador is connected to a satellite system that serves the other countries of Latin America, the US, Europe, Asia, and Africa and is considered one of the most advanced in Latin America. Direct dialing is available to most countries, though heavy surcharges are charged when calling from hotels.

Fax Fax and telex facilities are available and can connect to most countries. Fax services are also available at most major hotels.

Post Office Mail service is adequate. Private courier services are also available.

BEST TRAVEL BOOKS

The Wall Street Journal Guide to Business Travel, Mexico and Central America. The most electrifying of all practical travel guides.

Do's and Taboo's Around the World. The Bestselling Guide to International Behavior. Edited by Roger Axtell, compiled by the Parker Pen Company. The ultimate guide to international behavior, now completely updated and expanded. Helpful, fun to read!

Mexico & Central American Handbook. Passport Books. Annually updated, regionally organized travel handbook for all travelers.

USEFUL TELEPHONE NUMBERS

If you are calling from outside El Salvador, you will need to add the country code [503] and any other international dialing requirements from within your country.

- American Airlines 298-0777
- Aviateca Airlines.. 50-3240
- Copa Airlines.. 23-9129
- Lacsa Airlines 98-1322
- Taca Airlines 98-5066
- United Airlines 298-5462

Deluxe Hotels in San Salvador

- Hotel Camino Real 79-3888
- Hotel El Salvador 79-0777
- Hotel Presidente El Salvador 79-4444

Car Rental Agencies

- Avis 24-2623
- Hertz Rent-a-Car... 26-8099
- Budget... 23-1668
- Sure Rent 25-1810
- Dollar... 24-4385

Credit Card Information

Lost or stolen credit cards (call collect to the US, regardless of which country the card was issued in).

- Amex ....[1] (919) 333-3211
- Diner's Club...............................[1] (303) 799-1504
- MasterCard ....[1] (314) 275-6690
- Visa ....[1] (410) 581-7931

Travelogue

WORKWEEK

Offices Monday-Friday 8:00 am to noon and 2:00 pm to 5:30 pm, Saturday 8:00 am to noon.
Banks Monday-Friday 9:00 am to 1:00 pm.
Government Monday-Friday 8:00 am to 4:00 pm.
Retail Monday-Saturday 9:00 am to 8:00 pm.

HOLIDAYS

Holidays 1996
January 1 New Year's Day
January 16 Salvadoran Peace Day
April 13 Holy Thursday*
April 14 Good Friday*
April 7 Easter Sunday*
May 1 Labor Day
June 30 Bank Holiday*
August 3-6 San Salvador Feasts
September 15 Independence Day
October 12 Columbus Day
November 2 All Souls' Day
November 5 Day of First Cry of Independence
December 25 Christmas Day
December 30 Bank Holiday*
*Dates vary each year.

VISA AND PASSPORT

Visitors to El Salvador require a valid passport and either a visa or a tourist card. Visas are available at Salvadoran consulates for free and can be issued for multiple entry over a 10-year period. Tourist cards are issued from Salvadoran consulates, major airlines servicing El Salvador, and at El Salvador International Airport after arrival. Tourist cards cost US$10, are valid for one entry, and for up to a 90-day stay. There are no airport visas or tourist cards available for last-minute entry.

DEPARTURE FORMALITIES

There are no departure formalities in El Salvador but searches through luggage and belongings are common.

IMMUNIZATION

Medication against malaria should be taken when spending time on the coast. Otherwise an international certificate of vaccine is not required unless arriving from an infected area.

TIPPING

Hotels and restaurants: 10 percent, Taxi drivers: none, except when hired for the day. Porters: US$1.00 per bag.

CRIME

Violent as well as petty crimes are prevalent throughout El Salvador. Visitors should avoid carrying valuables in public places. Criminals often become violent quickly and may even shoot their victims if they do not immediately surrender valuables. Armed assaults and car-jackings are especially frequent on the roads outside San Salvador, where police patrols are infrequent; in areas that had been restricted during the war, especially unpaved roads; and during evening and early morning hours.

INFRASTRUCTURE

Despite the long period of war in El Salvador, transportation and communications systems throughout the country have remained adequate. There is a developed highway system that provides access to major Salvadoran cities, good taxi service, rental cars, and a range of accommodations. Public transportation (including buses) is not adequate. Taxis are old but remain the best mode of transportation over walking or venturing on public transit systems.

NATIONAL TOURIST OFFICE

Instituto Salvadoreno de Turismo (ISTU)
Calle Ruben Dario 619
San Salvador

Foreign Trade

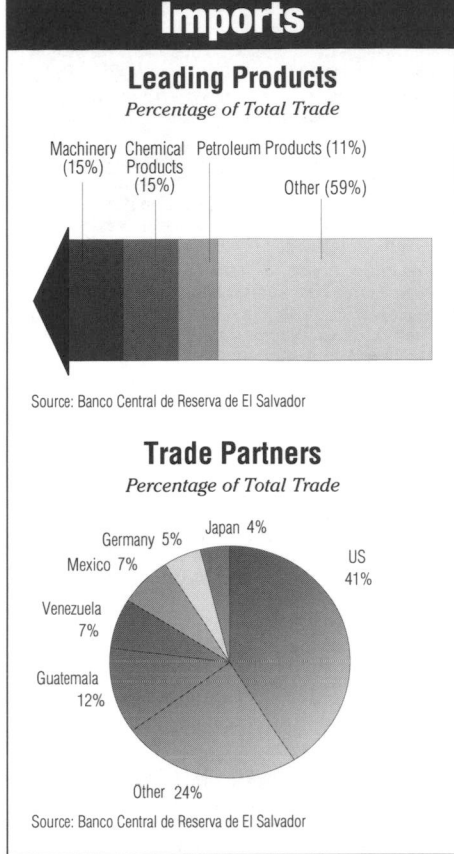

Imports

Leading Products
Percentage of Total Trade

Machinery (15%)
Chemical Products (15%)
Petroleum Products (11%)
Other (59%)

Source: Banco Central de Reserva de El Salvador

Trade Partners
Percentage of Total Trade

Germany 5%
Japan 4%
Mexico 7%
US 41%
Venezuela 7%
Guatemala 12%
Other 24%

Source: Banco Central de Reserva de El Salvador

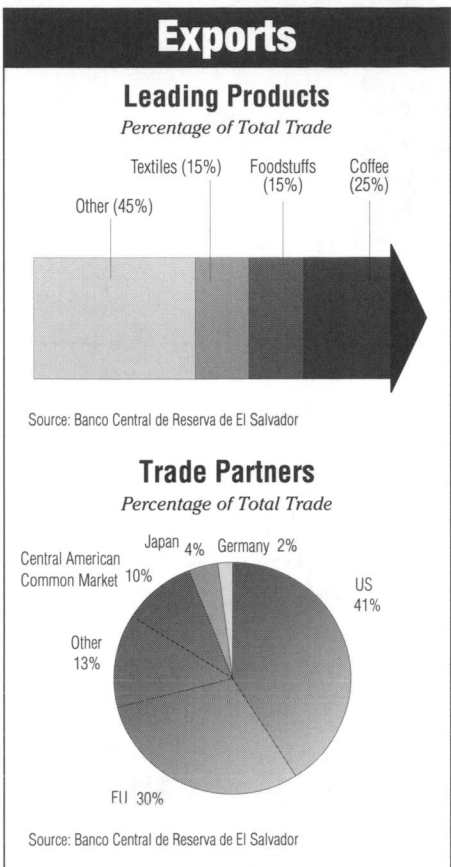

Exports

Leading Products
Percentage of Total Trade

Textiles (15%)
Foodstuffs (15%)
Coffee (25%)
Other (45%)

Source: Banco Central de Reserva de El Salvador

Trade Partners
Percentage of Total Trade

Central American Common Market 10%
Japan 4%
Germany 2%
US 41%
Other 13%
EU 30%

Source: Banco Central de Reserva de El Salvador

Opportunities

FOR IMPORTING TO EL SALVADOR
- automobiles, buses, heavy trucks, and machinery
- consumer goods, foodstuff
- electrical power generation and equipment

FOR EXPORTING FROM EL SALVADOR
- beverages, spirits and coffee, sugar, shrimp
- clothing, cotton
- electrical machinery and equipment

GROWTH SECTORS
- apparel
- construction
- electricity
- financial services
- mining
- water supply facilities

Trade News

RULES AND REGULATIONS
- **Import licenses** Generally, import licenses are not needed. However, a license must be obtained from the Ministry of Agriculture for imports of vegetables and animals, and from the Ministry of Defense for imports of firearms.
- **Import restrictions** El Salvador restricts or prohibits the import of a number of products. They include books or information of a subversive nature, obscene material, movies contrary to ethical behavior, gambling products, coffee trees, and coffee seeds. The Customs Bureau is now recommending that laws be revised so that fewer items are restricted.

Legal

Legal System
El Salvador's legal system is based on civil and Roman law, with traces of common law.

Intellectual Property Rights
Patents Invention patents are good for 20 years, industrial designs five years, patents on redesigns 10 years. Rights are transferable and revert to the government in case of emergency.

Copyrights Works are protected for the life of the creator plus 50 years, including adaptations. Corporations and consortiums are protected for 50 years from January 1st of the year following issuance.

Trademarks Trademarks may be registered for a 10-year term with an optional 10-year extension.

Trade secrets These are protected as confidential information, even if not presented in writing.

Business Registration
Business registration is necessary for individual enterprises holding assets in excess of 10,000 colones (about US$1,142) and companies holding assets in excess of 20,000 colones (about US$2,285).

Contracts and Dispute Resolution
Contract terms specify the parameters of business agreements, but do not define conditions. The relationship of the parties and intervening events are also taken into consideration. Alternative dispute resolution has not yet taken hold; parties are free to submit to arbitration in lieu of judicial proceedings.

Notaries
Notaries are lawyers or naturalized Central Americans with two years' local residence. Judges and diplomatic personnel also act as notaries. Documents must be in Spanish; notary keeps original.

Labor
Laws establish wages, hours, vacations, social security program, and workers' compensation system. Ninety percent of employees must be Salvadorans. Work by women and minors is regulated.

Legal Matters

LEGAL BRIEFS
- **Bankruptcy** Bankruptcy of a company also causes bankruptcy of members with unlimited liability, but bankruptcy of members does not produce bankruptcy of company.
- **Promissory notes** A promissory note must contain the words "promissory note", and, if it does not mention when it is due, it shall be considered payable at sight.
- **Monopolies** El Salvador's law proscribes all types of monopolies, and forbids any practices or financial transactions on production, commercial, or pricing practices aimed at elimination of free competition.
- **Real property** Rural real property may not be acquired by foreigners in whose countries of origin El Salvadorans do not have this right, except in case of land acquired for industrial establishments.

LEGAL CONTACTS
Francisco Jose Barrientos
73 Av. Norte #239
Col. Escalon
San Salvador
Tel: 223-8123
Fax: 223-8490

Romero Pineda & Asociados
Compania de Abogados
Final 67 Avenida Sur
Sasaje "A" 11-C
Colonia Roma
San Salvador
Tel: 223-1622

Jaime, Medina, Minero & Associates
Colonia y Calle Roma No. 23
San Salvador
Tel: 279-3678
Fax: 273-4977

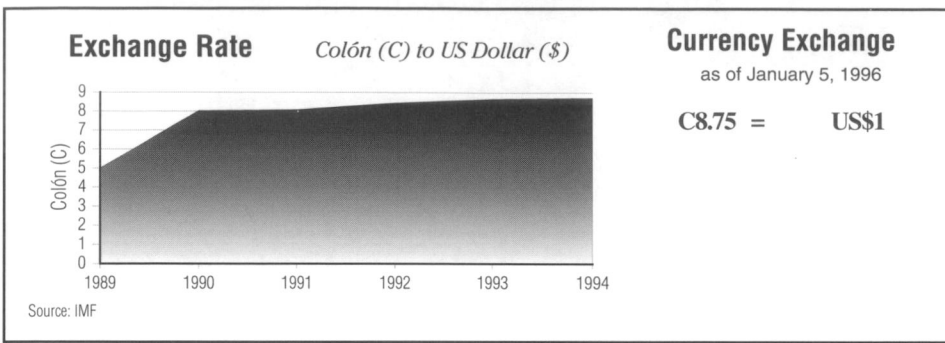

Exchange Rate *Colón (C) to US Dollar ($)*

Colón (C): 0–9 scale, years 1989, 1990, 1991, 1992, 1993, 1994

Source: IMF

Currency Exchange
as of January 5, 1996

C8.75 = US$1

Currency

The currency in use is the colón (the plural is colones), divided into 100 centavos.

Foreign Exchange

El Salvador adopted a free market exchange rate system in 1989. Exchange regulations are administered by the Central Reserve Bank. All private sector imports and payments for invisibles are delegated to the commercial banks and exchange houses. The external value of the colón is determined by commercial banks and exchange houses at rates determined by supply and demand conditions.

Capital Transfers

Foreign direct investments and inflows of capital with a maturity of more than one year must be registered with the Ministry of Economy but are not restricted. Outward remittance of interest and amortization on external loans may be made without restriction. There are no prescription of currency requirements. Settlements are usually made in US dollars or other convertible currencies. All exchange receipts from invisibles must be surrendered to an authorized commercial bank or exchange house.

Foreign Currency Deposit Accounts

Both residents and nonresidents may maintain deposit accounts in foreign currencies with authorized banks. Balances on these accounts may be sold to the commercial banks or used to make payments abroad without restriction.

Investment Incentives

El Salvador maintains an open investment climate built on the commitment of the government to a free market. While foreign investment is generally welcomed, investors operating in El Salvador's export promotion and free zones enjoy special incentives, including:

Up to 20 years income tax exemption; duty free importation of machinery, equipment, tools, spare parts, furniture, and other products necessary for the operation; duty free importation of raw materials, semi-manufactured, and intermediate products; duty free importation of fuels and lubricants.

Investment Restrictions

There are very few regulatory restrictions to foreign investment in El Salvador. However, many local companies complain that loan interest rates are too high, especially given the current inflation outlook.

TAXATION

- On September 1, 1992, the GOES implemented a 10 percent value-added tax (VAT) to replace the decades-old five percent stamp tax. The VAT has increased tax revenue, broadened the tax base, and provided about 42 percent of El Salvador's tax revenue in 1993. Exports are exempt from the VAT.
- According to the 1991 income tax law, published on December 21, 1991, in the "Diario Official," resident corporations as well as non-resident corporations pay income tax on taxable income above 75,000 colones (about US$8,720), unless otherwise exempt, for instance, those in an export zone. The tax rate is fixed at 25 percent on amounts above 75,000 colónes.
- On taxable income above 75,000 colones, but less than 200,000 colones, the tax rate is 20 percent on the excess of 80,001 colones plus 6,300 colones.
- On taxable income between 200,001 and 594,000 colones, the tax rate is 30 percent on the excess of 200,001 colones plus 30,000 colones.
- On taxable income above 594,001 colones, the tax rate is 25 percent on the excess of 594,001 colones plus 148,500 colones.

Money Matters

BITS AND PIECES

- **Banking system** After the 1979 revolution, the banks were nationalized by the ruling civilian-military junta. Recent free market initiatives undertaken by the Cristiani government include the privatization of the banking system.
- **Inflation** The economy maintained positive growth in 1991 and 1992, although inflation reached 20 percent in 1992.
- **Trade with Honduras** El Salvador had a border dispute with Honduras in 1969, although the two countries have since settled the dispute before the International Court of Justice, and there are now good trade relations between the two countries.
- **Free market policy** The economy has been improved since free market policy initiatives have been initiated since 1989. Price controls have been eliminated on several consumer products, and government export monopolies have been broken up. Import duties have been reduced, non-tariff barriers have been eliminated, and a free-market exchange rate system has been adopted.
- **Credit** Banks allocate credit on commercial terms and are conservative in their lending practices, whether the prospective borrower is foreign or local.
- **Expropriation** There are no current expropriation claims against the El Salvador government, and it appears that El Salvador adheres to international standards regarding compensation for property taken for public purposes.
- **Performance incentives** There are no requirements regarding performance incentives, and no requirement that national citizens own shares in companies.

BANKS

Central Reserve Bank
Calle Ruben Dario y 17 Avenida Norte
San Salvador
Tel: 22-5502
Fax: 71-0381
Telex: 20088 bacen

Banco Cuscatlan, S.A.
Alameda Roosevelt y 41
Avenida Sur
San Salvador
Tel: 23-2076
Fax: 23-2016

Banco Salvadoreno
Calle Ruben Dario y 21
Avenida Norte No. 1236
San Salvador
Tel: 22-9881
Fax: 21-3778

Banco de Comercio de El Salvador
43 Avenida Norte y Alameda
Roosevelt
Edificio Grane
San Salvador
Tel: 98-1958
Fax: 24-3238

Banco Agricola Comercial
Boulevard del Hipodromo No. 803
Colonia San Benito
San Salvador
Tel: 71-6126

Banco de Desarrollo e Inversion
67 Avenida Norte, Plaza Las Americas
San Salvador
Tel: 23-7888

Banco Hipotecario
4a. Calle Oriente No. 124
San Salvador
Tel: 22-2122

Citibank, N.A.
Alameda Dr. Manuel Enrique Araujo
3530 Edificio SISA, 2 piso
San Salvador
Tel: 24-3011

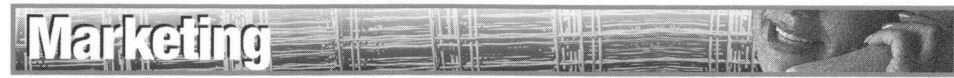

Distribution

Most foreign products are imported by large distributors who pass the goods on to small local retailers. Distributors serve networks of retailers, many of whom may have exclusive relationships with specific distributors, at least for certain products. Large department stores import directly from manufacturers or exporters. Some small retailers also make buying trips to bring back small quantities of goods—often used goods which are in demand, but difficult to import in volume. Many unlicensed goods also find their way into El Salvador in this fashion.

Agents, Distributors, and Partners

Foreign firms interested in selling products in El Salvador usually appoint an agent or distributor. Such local entities may be quite capable and maintain large, efficient networks. However, many represent so many accounts and products that they cannot give adequate attention to any given client. Licensing and joint ventures are encouraged, but must be formally executed and registered.

Selling Techniques

Price is usually the primary buying criterion, although quality and features are important, and availability of service and support can be the deciding factor, especially for technical equipment. Name recognition and brand loyalty are often quite strong, and some international consumer products have become well known even prior to their introduction. Franchising has been introduced and is growing in a few product areas. Direct marketing is limited by poor telephone and mail service. Existing products often sponsor contests, raffles, premium giveaways, and other promotions to remind customers that they are there, attract attention, and enhance sales.

Advertising

Television, radio, newspapers, billboards, and leaflets advertise new products here. Trade association newsletters also accept ads. The country's four major newspapers reach about 80 percent of the literate population. Door-to-door sales and direct television campaigns (with a call-in number) are also common.

Marketing in El Salvador

MARKETING TIPS

- **Agents** Agents are not required, nor do agreements have to be exclusive or written. However, laws generally favor local agents, requiring compensation for termination of an agreement other than for cause.
- **Government markets** Government agencies buy direct for small orders. Larger purchases are made by tender, which requires the use of a local agent. Some projects are subject to local preferences, but many must consider international bids. Availability of product servicing is critical for government sales.
- **New product introduction** New product introductions often involve a reception for dignitaries, coupled with an extensive billboard and print media campaign.
- **Franchising** As franchising becomes more common, many opportunities will open up in international retail and service franchise operations.

MARKET RESEARCH FIRMS

RIMO, S.A. DE C.V.
Edificio A, Local 31
Avenida Revolucion y Calle
Circunvalacion San Benito
San Salvador
Tel: 79-0679
Fax: 79-0725

PROCISA DE C.V.
Residencial Altos de Montebello
Calle Paracutin, Grupo 2 No. 22
San Salvador
Tel: 74-1976

CCM
Calle El Progreso, Pasaje El
Rosal No. 23
POB 2790 (CG)
San Salvador
Tel: 24-4374

Business Culture

Greetings and Courtesies

Handshakes are common among both men and women, when meeting and upon departing, although some people will limit greetings to a nod. Male friends may hug, and women friends may kiss briefly and lightly on the cheek. Titles are commonly used—with last names—and only very close friends use first names or surnames without a title. Business cards in Spanish are a valuable courtesy.

Meetings and Decision Making

Prior appointments are necessary —make them two weeks in advance. A personal relationship is considered a prerequisite to a business relationship, and must be established before any agreements can be reached. Salvadorans will want to know your standing within the hierarchy and will wish to match you with someone of similar rank, although only their senior people will actually be able to approve agreements. Nevertheless, it is important to cultivate personal relationships with these peers, because the quality of these relationships may strongly influence the actual decisionmaker even when your counterpart is not the one making the decision.

Women

Salvadoran women are becoming more common and more accepted in business in general, and foreign businesswomen should experience few problems. Nevertheless, foreign businesswomen are expected to be highly professional, appropriate, and not aggressive or confrontational. Women may generally go on the streets and dine alone, but may feel more comfortable if escorted.

Business Attire

Dark, conservative business suits are worn by men. Conservative business suits or elegant dresses—with stockings and heels—are worn by women. A business suit or a dress is appropriate if you are invited to a meal or other social occasion.

Cultural Cautions

DO'S

- Learn something about El Salvador's history and culture—your interest will be appreciated.
- Maintain good eye contact during conversation and business—it is considered a sign of respect and sincerity.

DON'TS

- Do not refer to people from the US as "Americans"—this is offensive to Salvadorans; use US or North American to refer to the country and its citizens.
- Do not yawn in public or in a business or social situation—it is considered highly impolite.
- Avoid pointing your finger—or your feet—at a person; this is impolite behavior.

CUSTOMS

- Men rise when a woman enters the room; polite respect is also accorded to the elderly.
- Small gifts are exchanged frequently; lavish gifts are considered inappropriate.
- If invited to a home for a meal, compliment the hostess and the person who prepared the food.

OBSERVATIONS

- Handshakes are prolonged, and may involve touching of the arms; likewise Salvadorans may put their arms around others as a mark of friendship.
- Salvadorans use a wealth of gestures and facial expressions to convey meaning; watch carefully for cues besides the usual verbal ones.

NEGOTIATIONS

- To avoid misunderstandings, be sure you know who has the authority to make a decision and the procedures and time frames that must be considered.
- Salvadorans present a united front during negotiations, deferring to the senior member.

GOVERNMENT AGENCIES

Ministry of Economy
Paseo General Escalon 4122
San Salvador
Tel: 24-3536
Fax: 98-6356

Ministry of Finance
Condominio Las Tres, Torre 2
Avenida Alvarado, Diagonal
San Salvador
Tel: 71-0250
Fax: 71-0591

Ministry of Agriculture and Livestock
83 Avenida Norte 704
Colonia Escalon
San Salvador
Tel: 24-4898
Fax: 79-1941

Minister of Public Works
1a. Avenida Sur 630
San Salvador
Tel: 71-5873
Fax: 71-0163

Direction General of Air Transportation
Aeropuerto de Ilopango
San Salvador
Tel: 95-0265
Fax: 95-0345

BUSINESS AND TRADE ORGANIZATIONS

Salvadoran National Association of Private Enterprise
1a. Calle Poniente y 71
Avenida Norte 204
San Salvador
Tel: 23-3893
Fax: 23-8932

Salvadoran Association of Industrialists
Calles Roma y Liverpool
Colonia Roma
San Salvador
Tel: 79-2488
Fax: 79-2070

Salvadoran Exporters Corporation
Condominios del Mediterraneo
Edificio A-23, Jardines de Guadalupe
San Salvador
Tel: 24-4019, 23-1388
Fax: 98-0951

Superindentencia de Empresas Sociedades y Mercantiles
1a. Calle Poniente y 45
Avenida Norte
San Salvador
Tel: 79-2152, 98-0284

Direccion General de Impuestos Internos
Avenida Alvarado y Diagonal
Condominio Las Tres Torres, No. 2
San Salvador
Tel: 25-1022
Fax: 26-7170

Registro de Comercio
Calle Ruben Dario 924
San Salvador
Tel: 71-0017, 71-0021

Alcaldia Municipal de San Salvador
9a. Calle Oriente No. 320
San Salvador
Tel: 22-1788, 21-1579
Fax: 22-8670

Direccion General de Estadistica y Censos
1a. Calle Poniente y 43
Avenida Norte
San Salvador
Tel: 24-1603

Consejo Superior de Salud Publica
Avenida Espana No. 736
San Salvador
Tel: 21-0497, 21-0151

Fondo de Financiamiento y Garantía para la Pequeña Empresa
(Assistance to Small Industries)
Diagonal Principal y la diagonal
Urbanización La Esperanza
Apartado 1990
San Salvador
Tel: 25-9466

BUSINESS ORGANIZATIONS

Salvadoran Chamber of Commerce and Industry
9a. Avenida Norte y 5a. Calle
Poniente
San Salvador
Tel: 71-2055
Fax: 71-4461

American Chamber of Commerce of El Salvador
87 Avenida Norte No. 720
Apto. A, Colonia Escalon
San Salvador
Tel: 23-3292
Fax: 24-6856

BANKS

Central Reserve Bank
Calle Ruben Dario y 17 Avenida Norte
San Salvador
Tel: 22-5502
Fax: 71-0381
Telex: 20088 bacen

Banco de Construccion y Ahorro S.A.
75 Avenida Sur No. 209
Colonia Escalon
San Salvador
Tel: 98-0122

BANFIDEX
1a. Calle Poniente 3649
Colonia Escalon
San Salvador
Tel: 98-5777
Fax: 98-0772

Financiera Credisa S.A.
Edificio Credisa
Alameda Juan Pablo II Pte.
San Salvador
Tel: 98-5633

Financiera Atlacatl S.A.
Alameda Roosevelt y 55
Avenida Sur
Centro Comercial Roosevelt
San Salvador
Tel: 79-0033

Financiera Ahorromet S.A.
Inicio Paseo General Escalçn
Edificio Ahorromet
San Salvador
Tel: 71-0888

Banco Hipotecario
4a. Calle Oriente No. 124
San Salvador
Tel: 22-2122

STOCK EXCHANGE

Bolsa de El Salvador
San Salvador
Tel: 23-8342

NEWSPAPERS

El Diario de Hoy
11A Calle Oriente y Avda Cuscatencingo 271
Apdo 495
San Salvador
Tel: 71-0100
Fax: 22-9441

Diario Latino
23a Avda Sur 225
Apdo 96
San Salvador
Tel: 21-3240

Diario Oficial
4a Calle Poniente 829
San Salvador
Tel: 21-9101

El Mundo
2a Avda Norte 211
Apdo 368
San Salvador
Tel: 71-4400

La Noticia
Edif. Espana
Avda Espana 321
San Salvador
Tel: 22-7906
Fax: 71-1650

La Prensa Grafica
3a Calle Poniente 130
San Salvador
Tel: 71-3333

RADIO AND TELEVISION

Asociacion Salvadorena de Radiodifusores - ASDER
4a Calle Oriente 528
Apdo 210
San Salvador
Tel: 22-0872

YSS Radio El Salvador
Direccion General de Medios
3a Avda Norte y 11 Calle Poniente
San Salvador
Tel: 21-4376
Telex: 20145

Canal 2, SA
Alameda Dr. Manuel Enrique Araujo
Apdo 720
San Salvador
Tel: 23-6744
Telex: 20443

Canal 4, SA
Carretera de San Salvador a Santa Tecla
Apdo 444
San Salvador
Tel: 24-4555

Canal 6, SA
Km. 6, Alameda Dr. Manuel E. Araujo
Apdo 06-1801
San Salvador
Tel: 23-5122

Canal 12
5a Avda las Acacias 130
Col. San Benito
San Salvador
Tel: 24-6171

Canal 19
Pasaje YSI 2021
entre 37 y 39 C.O.,
Col. La Rabida
San Salvador
Tel: 26-9759
Fax: 26-2087

INTERNET ADDRESSES

Listserv: CENTAM-L
Send mail to: LISTSERV@UBVM.cc.buffalo.edu
Subscribe in the body of the message.

Latin America - El Salvador
http://lanic.utexas.edu/la/ca/salvador/

The Latino Connection
http://www.webspace.com/~pedro/elsalvad.html

Estonia
Republic of Estonia

Economy

Overview

Although Estonia's incorporation into the USSR allowed the rebuilding of an economy largely destroyed during World War II, the rebuilding was done within the context of a centrally planned command economy. However, as a model for economic experiments, especially in industrial management techniques, Estonia enjoyed greater success, prosperity, and industrialization than did many other regions under Soviet domination. Since 1992, following the collapse of the USSR, Estonia has aligned itself with Western capitalist countries, freed most prices, and encouraged privatization and foreign investment in advance of other Soviet bloc countries. Now fully independent, the government of Estonia has positioned the country as the gateway between East and West, while aggressively pursuing trade reform and economic integration to attract foreign businesses and joint ventures.

Trade

Estonia's system for imports and exports is one of the most liberal in the world. Exports include textiles, electrical machinery, chemicals, animal products, miscellaneous manufactured products, and minerals. Imports include textile materials, machinery, minerals, vegetables, and chemicals. The country supplies 60 percent of its own energy, but depends heavily on imports of Russian refined petroleum products. Its major trading partners include Finland, Russia, Sweden, Germany, Latvia, Lithuania, the Netherlands, and the United States.

Sectors

Agriculture The agricultural sector as a whole is small but largely self-sufficient, contributing about 15 percent of GDP and employing about 20 percent of the work force. However, productivity declined substantially during the early 1990s. Products include dairy products, meat, fish, cereals, potatoes, and vegetables. Forestry is also important.

Industry Industry supplies nearly half of GDP while employing somewhat more than 40 percent of the work force. Heavy machinery, electrical and electrical engineering products, textiles, fish and food processing, and consumer products are the primary contributors. Although Estonia has a generally well developed and efficient industrialized economy, industrial production nevertheless plummeted during the early 1990s, the result of political disruption and economic structural reorganization.

Services Services provide nearly 40 percent of GDP and employ about 40 percent of the work force. Because of continued disputes with Russia over assets, many services remain in disarray.

Trends

Fear of massive unemployment among the urban ethnic Russian work force delayed efforts to privatize many inefficient factories, and the issue of compensation or restitution to pre-1940 property owners remains contentious. Nonetheless, Estonia is dedicated to economic reform and privatization. After having balanced its budget in recent years, the government has so far refused to relax its stringent fiscal standards, instead allowing some bankruptcies and a temporary decline in economic indicators. As part of its campaign to internationalize, Estonia recently ratified several trade agreements and is now a member of GATT.

At a Glance
THE COUNTRY
Location Estonia is located in northeastern Europe, bordering the Baltic Sea, between Sweden and Russia.
Terrain The topography of Estonia consists mainly of marshy lowlands.
Climate The proximity of the Baltic Sea influences the coastal climate. Rainfall averages 50 cm (20 in) on the coast. Inland, rainfall averages 70 cm (28 in). Rainfall is heaviest during the summer and lightest in the spring.

THE PEOPLE
Population 1,600,000
Ethnic composition
Estonians 64%
Russians 30%
Ukrainians 3%
Belorussians 2%
Finns 1%
Religious composition Primary religions are Lutheran, Russian Orthodox, and Baptist.
Languages spoken Estonian is the official language and is spoken by most of the population. Russian is also widely spoken.
Education and literacy The country's adult literacy rate is 99%. Estonian-language schools have 12 years of schooling and Russian-language schools have 11 years of schooling.
Labor force
Total: 785,500
By occupation: industry and construction, 42%; agriculture and forestry, 20%; other 38%.

COUNTRY FACTS
Political and legal Estonia is a parliamentary democracy, with multiple political parties.
Telephone Estonia's telephone system is antiquated but is being upgraded and expanded. International calls are carried by the former USSR republics by land line or microwave. International country code: [372]; city codes: Tallinn (2), (6), or (5).
Transportation Estonia's transportation system is well developed and provides readily available services through airlines, trains, buses, taxis, ferries, and rental cars. Gasoline prices are moderate.
Environment Calcareous soil and a relatively mild climate permit growth of rich flora and fauna in western Estonia. Current issues include air, water, and land pollution, which rank among Estonia's most significant environmental challenges.
Media Estonian radio was the first in the former Soviet Union to carry advertising. It broadcasts in Estonian, Russian, Finnish, and several other languages. Estonian television broadcasts on four channels in Estonian and Russian. There are 111 official newspapers. All media is lively and diverse.
Health Estonia immunizes children up to one year old against tuberculosis, diphtheria, pertussis and tetanus, polio, and measles. In general, most of the population have access to adequate healthcare. Life expectancy in 1992 averaged 71 years.

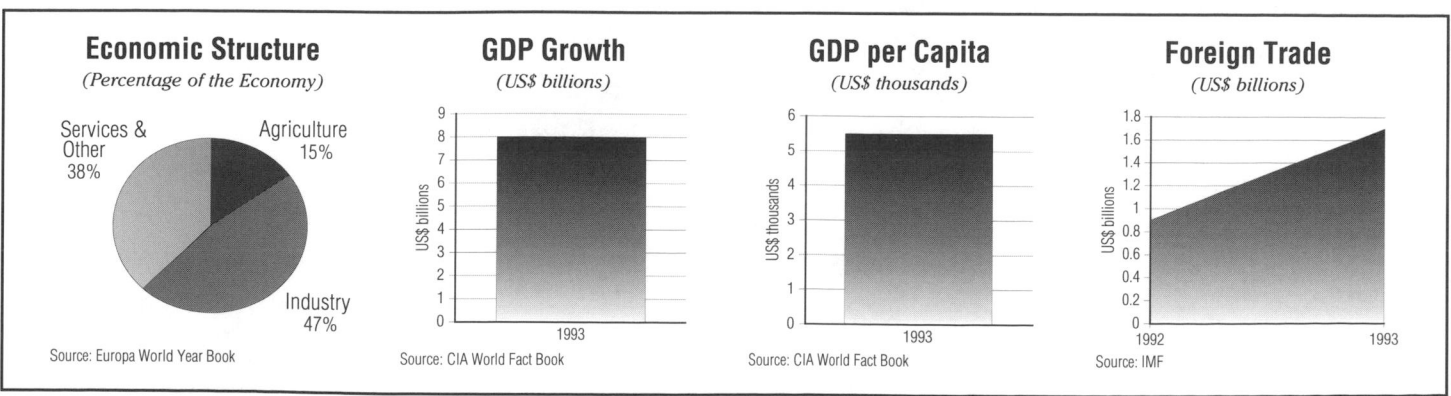

Economic Structure
(Percentage of the Economy)

Services & Other 38%
Agriculture 15%
Industry 47%

Source: Europa World Year Book

GDP Growth
(US$ billions)

US$ billions

1993

Source: CIA World Fact Book

GDP per Capita
(US$ thousands)

US$ thousands

1993

Source: CIA World Fact Book

Foreign Trade
(US$ billions)

US$ billions

1992   1993

Source: IMF

Business Travel

COMMUNICATIONS

Telephones The telephone system in Estonia is adequate and is being upgraded and expanded. Most international calls must be placed through an international operator. Public phones are available. The most expensive time to call is from 1:00 pm to 2:00 am. Public telephones are free. Phone numbers change frequently.

Fax Fax machines are available at most businesses and hotels and at the central post office. Telex services are available where fax services are found.

Post office Mail service is reliable but slow. To speed things along, address mail in the local language or at least the familiar format (country, city with index number, street, house number, and then name). Major hotels have postal facilities for posting mail and buying stamps. Mailboxes are rare.

BEST TRAVEL BOOKS

Hayit's Budget Travel, the Baltic States (Estonia, Latvia, Lithuania). Affordable, practical, up-to-date, covering topics such as travel preparations, background information, practical information, and budget travel.

Berlitz Business Travel Guide, Europe. Concise economic details, successful trip planning, background information on people and cities, useful facts and addresses.

USEFUL TELEPHONE NUMBERS

If you are calling from outside Estonia, you will need to add the country code [372] and any other international dialing requirements from within your country.

- Police 02
- Emergency 03
- International Operator 007
- Taxi .... (2) 603044, 430330
- Tallinn Train Station .... (2) 446-756
- Emergency Police .... (2) 445266
- Doctor/Dentist .... (2) 605761

Airlines
- Estonia Air .... (2) 212-836
- SAS .... (2) 212-553

Credit Card Information
Lost or stolen credit cards (call collect to the US, regardless of which country the card was issued in).
- Amex ....[1] (919) 333-3211
- Diner's Club ....[1] (303) 799-1504
- MasterCard ....[1] (314) 275-6690
- Visa ....[1] (410) 581-7931

Travelogue

WORKWEEK

Offices Monday-Friday 9:00 am to 6:00 pm.
Banks Monday-Friday 9:00 am to 1:00 pm.
Government Monday-Friday 9:00 am to 6:00 pm.
Retail Monday-Saturday 10:00 am to 8:00 pm with lunch from noon to 1:00 pm. Larger department stores may open at 8:00 am and remain open until 9:00 pm.

HOLIDAYS

Holidays 1996
January 1 New Year's Day
February 24 Independence Day
April 5 Good Friday*
April 7 Easter Sunday*
May 1 May Day
June 23-24 Midsummer Festival
December 25-26 Christmas
*Dates vary each year.
By custom, the Monday preceding a public holiday on a Tuesday is taken as an additional public holiday in which case the preceding Saturday is a working day.

VISA AND PASSPORT

Travelers to Estonia will need a valid passport and a visa. Visas are available from Estonian embassies. A visa to Latvia or Lithuania will also be accepted for entry into Estonia.

DEPARTURE FORMALITIES

Registration with local police within 24 hours of arrival is not mandatory in cities like Tallinn or Tartu; but it is advisable to register if traveling along the Gulf of Finland and Russian borders. Customs declaration forms may be required on arrival.

IMMUNIZATION

International certificate of vaccine not required unless arriving from an infected area.

TIPPING

Tipping is officially discouraged but appreciated by small services. Taxi: 10 to 15 percent. Hotels: none. Restaurants: 10 to 15 percent. Beauticians & barbers: 10 percent. Small services: 5 to 10 percent.

CRIME

Crime is an increasing problem in Estonia, and violent crime is on the rise. Street muggings, car vandalism, and car thefts are not uncommon. Foreigners traveling the streets of Tallinn after dark are particularly targeted, especially if they have been drinking. Robberies occur in high trafficked areas such as trains, train stations, hotels, bars, restaurants, and on the street even during the day.

INFRASTRUCTURE

Estonia is connected to surrounding areas by a network of air, train, and bus services. Bus, taxi, and rental car services are available within the capital. Renting a car requires an International Driving Permit or Foreign Driver's License. Seat belts are mandatory. Drinking while driving is illegal and expensive. Walking and cycling are popular modes of transportation.

TOURIST OFFICES

Estonia Tourist Board
Pikk 71
Tallinn
Tel: (2) 601700

Tourist Office
Raekoja Plats 8
Tallinn
Tel: (2) 666959

Foreign Trade

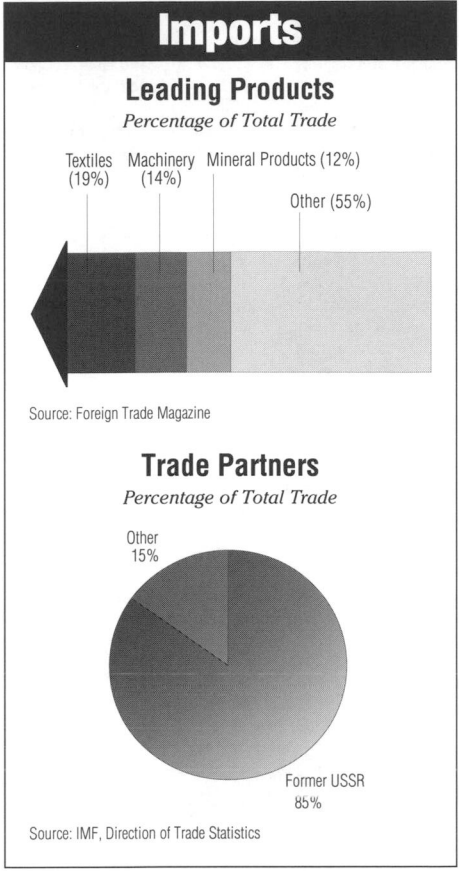

Imports

Leading Products
Percentage of Total Trade

Textiles (19%)
Machinery (14%)
Mineral Products (12%)
Other (55%)

Source: Foreign Trade Magazine

Trade Partners
Percentage of Total Trade

Other 15%
Former USSR 85%

Source: IMF, Direction of Trade Statistics

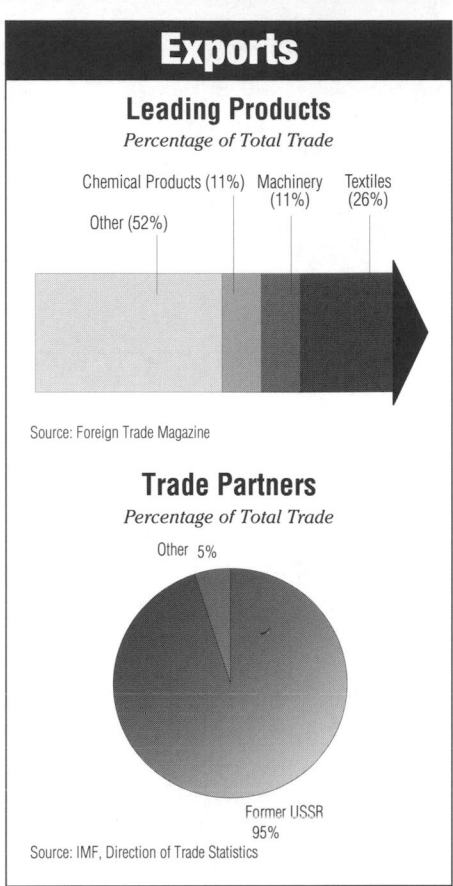

Exports

Leading Products
Percentage of Total Trade

Chemical Products (11%)
Machinery (11%)
Textiles (26%)
Other (52%)

Source: Foreign Trade Magazine

Trade Partners
Percentage of Total Trade

Other 5%
Former USSR 95%

Source: IMF, Direction of Trade Statistics

Opportunities

FOR IMPORTING TO ESTONIA
- automobiles, machinery
- consumer foods, wheat, textiles
- fuels, petroleum
- raw materials

FOR EXPORTING FROM ESTONIA
- food products
- glassware
- footwear
- textiles
- wood and wood products

GROWTH SECTORS
- labor-intensive light industry
- retail trade
- services

Trade News

RULES AND REGULATIONS
- **Regulatory policy** There are no major domestic hardships to imports, but minor ones exist due to infrastructure deficiencies and undeveloped financial institutions.
- **Import duties** Import duties exist for fur at 16 percent; 10 percent for cars, bicycles, and yachts.
- **Export duties** Export duties exist on a few items, such as grapeseed oil, some automobiles, and some metals.
- **Trade licenses** The trading of alcohol, metals, pharmaceuticals, tobacco products, and weapons requires licensing. Any legal entity can apply for an operational license.

Legal

Legal System
Estonia is now in the process of drafting new criminal and civil procedural codes.

Intellectual Property Protection
Patents Estonia has passed a Patent Law, regulating the legal protection of patents in the Republic. Most provisions are in accordance with World Intellectual Property Organization mandates, although several products and procedures are exempt from patent.

Trademarks Trademarks are registerable and protected from unauthorized use. Counterfeiting is not a significant problem at this time as enforcement is considered adequate.

Copyrights Estonia recently passed the Copyright Law, providing protection for all sorts of literary and artistic creations, as well as for computer software. Enforcement to date has been sporadic, but this is considered to be more a result of lack of experience than from a lack of attention.

Business Registration
Under Estonia's Foreign Investment Act, all foreign companies are treated the same as domestic companies. Foreign businesses must have a permit from the State Foreign Economic Board of the Republic of Estonia before they can open a business or branch in Estonia.

Contracts and Dispute Resolution
Contracts tend to be detailed (perhaps overly so) in Estonia. Disputes are handled in the courts, but there are severe delays due to a lack of funds and untrained staff. Arbitration is not yet fully accepted, although the parties are free to agree to submit any disputes to arbitration in lieu of the courts.

Labor
Workers have the right to organize and bargain collectively, but due to the weak economy unions do not have much clout when it comes to the negotiation of wage rates and termination policies.

Legal Matters

LEGAL BRIEFS
- **Price controls** The only prices still controlled directly by the government are electricity, precious stones and metals, and energy outputs such as oil and shale. Some goods and services are subject to indirect price regulation, such as subsidies.
- **Licenses** Any legal entity registered in Estonia can apply for an operational license.
- **Reform** The Judicial Reform Law of 1993 will not be implemented until all vacant judicial seats are filled.
- **EAKL** The Central Organization of Estonian Trade Unions was founded to replace the Estonian branch of the Soviet labor confederation.
- **Trade secrets** Trade secrets are not currently protected under Estonian law, although some remedies may be available through breach of contract actions. The government is considering legislation specifically directed to the protection of trade secrets.
- **International agreements** Estonia is a member of the World Intellectual Property Organization (WIPO).
- **Employment termination** Employers are required to give two months notice to any employee prior to layoff.
- **Minimum wage** Estonia has a minimum wage, which is rising, and is expected to rise again to correspond with rising inflation rates throughout the Russian Federation.
- **Child labor** The statutory minimum employment age is 16.
- **Workweek** The standard workweek is legally set at 41 hours, and any hours worked in excess of that are required to be paid at overtime rates.

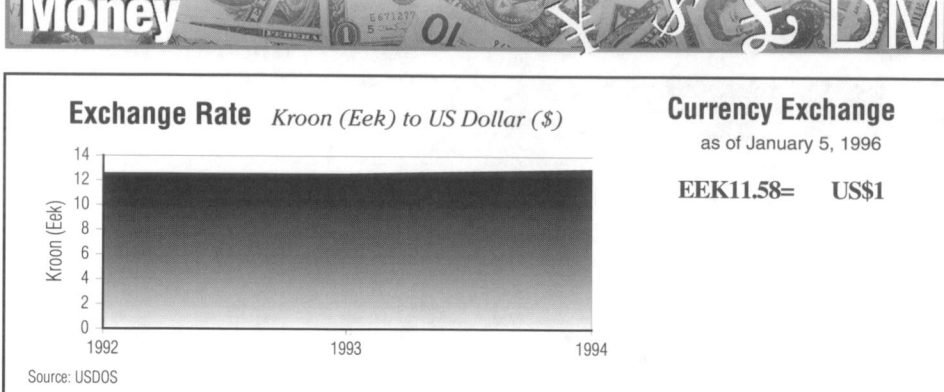

Money

Exchange Rate *Kroon (Eek) to US Dollar ($)*

Source: USDOS

Currency Exchange
as of January 5, 1996

EEK11.58=   US$1

Money Matters

BITS AND PIECES

- **Capital gains** Capital gains are included in taxable income and taxed at the regular rates.
- **Tax incentives** Enterprises with foreign participation of at least 30% and US$50,000 are exempt from income tax for two years, beginning with the first year the company earns a profit.
- **Worldwide operations** Resident companies are taxed on worldwide income; nonresident companies are taxed on income derived from Estonia. Foreign tax credits are granted for foreign tax credits paid on income earned abroad.
- **Foreign property** All property brought into Estonia by foreign investors as an initial capital investment is exempt from customs duties, but is subject to VAT.
- **Profits** A foreign investor has the right to repatriate profits after paying income tax on proceeds which it has received after the liquidation of the enterprise.
- **Export subsidies** The government provides no subsidies to Estonian exports.
- **Banks** Performance of Estonian banks is uneven, although several have begun to offer services roughly comparable to Western banks.
- **Taxes** The general trend with Estonian tax legislation has been to decrease taxes associated with production of goods and increase taxes associated with consumption.
- **Privatization** Estonia's privatization program has made commendable progress in the past couple of years, with approximately 50 percent of larger state enterprises now in private hands. Small and medium scale privatization is virtually complete. Estonia has also made headway in introducing vouchers into its privatization scheme and in creating mutual funds markets for voucher holders.
- **Export fees** All exports are subject to an ad valorem fee of 0.5 percent to cover the cost of administrative processing.
- **Gold** International and domestic trade in gold is subject to licensing requirements administered by the Ministry of Finance.
- **Correspondent accounts** Commercial banks in Estonia are permitted and encouraged to open their own correspondent accounts with counterpart commercial banks in the former USSR to effect payments associated with trade with these states.

Currency

The currency in use is the kroon (Eek) or crown, which is divided into 100 sents.

Foreign Exchange

The convertibility of the kroon is guaranteed by the Bank of Estonia (BOE). The kroon is fully convertible for all international transactions. Commercial banks may handle transactions in convertible currencies, and commercial banks may quote their own exchange rates. Settlements with the former states of the USSR are made through a system of correspondent accounts. Balances in these accounts may be used by the holders to purchase goods or services in the country involved without restriction.

Estonia has very few foreign exchange controls. Registered enterprises with bank accounts abroad are required to submit a monthly report to the Bank of Estonia to report account activity.

Capital Transfers

There are no restrictions on the import or export of domestic bank notes or traveler's checks, and there are no controls over the inward or outward transfer of capital. There are no restrictions on import payments. A license is not needed to operate a foreign currency account in a domestic bank.

Companies operating in Estonia must acquire a license to operate a foreign exchange account with a foreign bank, although the licensing process is for statistical purposes only and is granted freely. A license is not needed for an enterprise to operate a foreign currency account in a domestic bank. Individuals may not open a foreign currency account in a domestic bank. Residents may open a foreign currency account with a foreign bank abroad with a license. Monthly reports must be submitted to the BOE to report the turnover on the foreign account.

Investment Incentives

Estonia operates under open and liberal investment policies, aimed at encouraging foreign investment in all sectors. While there are no set investment incentives, individual concessions and incentives may be offered which are specifically tailored to draw certain investments or investors. In general, foreign investment is treated equally to local investments in all regards.

Investment Restrictions

Although there are no regulatory restrictions, except those limiting foreign investment in a few key sectors, some aspects of Estonian life and law serve to deter foreign investment. Telephone service remains uneven, and service in areas outside the capital is greatly inferior even to that. In addition, trade financing is difficult to obtain (particularly for new enterprises without a track record) and high interest rates present some obstacles. Some local banks have limited experience with trade financing options, such as letters of credit, and this can deter foreign operations.

BANKS

Bank of Estonia
Kentmanni 13
Tallinn EE0100
Tel: (6) 310-800
Fax: (6) 310-954

Estonian Commercial Bank of Industry
Suur-Karja 7
Tallinn EE0001
Tel: (2) 442-410
Fax: (2) 440-495

Estonian Provincial Bank
Estonia pst. 11
Tallinn 200105
Tel/Fax: (2) 441-797

Estonian Savings Bank
Kinga 1
Tallinn EE0100
Tel: (2) 441-758
Fax: (2) 442-840

Tartu Commercial Bank
Munga 18
Tartu EE2400
Tel: (34) 33197
Fax: (34) 33593

TAXATION

Taxation requires sophisticated knowledge of complex rules and regulations specific to each country. For more detailed information we suggest you refer to the Ernst & Young Corporate Tax Guide and Directory, available from the Ernst & Young accounting office in your country, or from:

Ernst & Young Eesti AS
Tallinn Business Center
Harjustrat 6, Suite 510
Tallinn EE0001
Tel: (6) 310612
Fax: (6) 310611

At a Glance

Corporate Income Tax Rate (%)*	29
Capital Gains Tax Rate (%)*	29
Branch Tax Rate (%)*	29
Withholding Tax (%)	0
Net Operating Losses (Years)	
Carryback	0
Carryforward	0

* Taxable profit that is retained for investment in capital assets is taxed at a rate of 10%. A 10% rate also applies to companies producing agricultural products and to specialized enterprises rendering services to agriculture.

- Note: New tax laws revising corporate taxation may be in effect as of January 1, 1995.

Marketing

Overview

Since the breaking away of the Baltic Republics and the subsequent collapse of the Soviet Union in the early 1990s, the situation in Estonia has been in flux. Estonia has a wide variety of needs, but few established mechanisms for filling them, and little foreign exchange with which to pay for them. Nevertheless, it is a relatively highly industrialized country with a potential for developing sophisticated engineering design service and other high value-added exports. Foreign traders must be extremely self-reliant in constructing their own arrangements in an environment in which virtually nothing is set.

Distribution

The Estonian economy operated as part of the Soviet centrally planned economy, and distribution and marketing were rigid but poorly developed. Many existing distribution systems are the remnants of that era and are totally oriented toward Russia. Externally oriented networks are growing as local groups and individuals make contacts and undertake specific transactions. In general, distribution is wide open, and local sellers are open to new options.

Agents, Distributors, and Partners

There is currently little in the way of organized intermediaries; most are individuals operating on their own, and foreigners interested in selling their goods must evaluate the capabilities of such contacts as they are able to make on their own.

Selling Techniques

Given the lack of foreign exchange, price is a major selling point, although Estonians are fairly sophisticated when it comes to quality and features. Service is becoming a more important decision factor.

Advertising

There are more than 150 registered newspapers and about 325 other periodicals, about three-quarters of which publish in Estonian. State-run radio and television broadcast over four channels each; these outlets are adapting themselves to a free market regime involving advertising.

Marketing in Estonia

MARKETING TIPS

- **Language** Languages in use are, in order of local preference: Estonian, Finnish, and English. Avoid using Russian.
- **Government markets** Government agencies may buy direct for small orders. Larger purchases are made by tender. Most projects are subject to local preferences, but some solicit international bids. Availability of quality service is critical for government sales.
- **Legal counsel** Although not technically necessary, retaining a local attorney to consult with and to draw up agency, sales, and contract agreements is generally advisable.
- **Financing** Because of a chronic lack of foreign exchange, sales may be heavily dependent on the willingness of the seller to provide financing and deal in small quantities. Those interested in this market should consider current operations primarily in the light of developing long-term relationships.

RADIO AND TELEVISION

Eesti Raadio
(Estonian Broadcasting Co)
Gonsiori 21
Tallinn EE0100
Tel: (2) 343-115
Fax: (2) 434-457
Telex: 173271

Eesti Televisioon
(Estonian Television)
Faehlmanni 12
Tallinn EE0100
Tel: (2) 434-113
Fax: (2) 434-155
Telex: 173271

Business Culture

Greetings and Courtesies

Estonians pride themselves on their politeness; in turn they expect to be treated courteously. It is customary in Estonia to shake hands before and after a meeting, but this gesture should always be initiated by the Estonian associate. It is proper to address Estonians using their professional titles.

Business Ethic and Framework

Estonians are eager to enter business with foreign companies although they appear reticent at first. They are methodical in their work, and do not put their jobs above all else in their lives. The intensely patriotic Estonians prefer to do business with foreigners in their own language. Dark, conservative clothing is proper. Shoes and hats in winter should reflect the high status they are afforded in Estonia. Estonians are extremely clean and neat in their attire; they notice quickly if foreign representatives are attired in the same manner.

Decision Making

Setting up meetings can be difficult. Telecommunications there are still primitive, and can be a problem. Successful meetings in Estonia are best arranged in writing and confirmed in writing. Estonians are fond of following rules and procedures; they distrust any variation from these standards. Estonians take care to not offend those with whom they disagree. Honesty is important to Estonians, who take great pride in keeping their word in business.

Women

Estonian women have always considered themselves equal partners with men. Women in Estonia occupy almost every profession in the work force, and they are represented in the government as well. Most physicians are women and it is principally women who teach at the primary and secondary levels in Estonia. Increasingly, women are found in higher management positions in the business world, and foreign businesswomen should experience few difficulties in conducting business in Estonia.

Cultural Cautions

DO'S

- Give a small gift when meeting with an Estonian associate, possibly something with your company logo.
- Use formal titles of address such as "Doctor" and "Professor."
- Always make appointments for meetings.

DON'TS

- It is not politically correct for visitors to speak Russian on the street.
- It is considered rude in Estonia to ask someone to refrain from smoking.

CUSTOMS

- Deliveries, payments, and other commitments should be assured wisely; Estonians will not tolerate reneging on promises, or "shimming."
- It is routine in Estonia for foreign business people to ask permission before smoking. If you smoke, you will be expected to share your cigarettes generously.

OBSERVATIONS

- Estonians are quiet and unassuming.
- In public lavatories, "M" stands for men and "N" for women.

NEGOTIATIONS

- Estonians prefer to do business in their own language.
- Estonians want foreign business associates to use bilingual business cards, in English and Estonian.
- Negotiations by Estonians are careful and thorough. They favor a direct approach and will not tolerate insincerity in concluding a deal.
- Beware of prospective business partners who do not display the customary Estonian reserve.

GOVERNMENT AGENCIES

Ministry of Agriculture
Lai 39/41
Tallinn EE0100
Tel: (2) 441-166
Fax: (2) 440-601

Ministry of Economy
Gonsiori 29
Tallinn EE0104
Tel: (2) 683-444
Fax: (2) 682-097

Ministry of Education and Culture
Pronksi 3
Tallinn EE0001
Tel: (2) 437-760
Fax: (2) 437-892

Ministry of the Environment
Toompuiestee 24
Tallinn EE0100
Tel: (2) 452-507
Fax: (2) 453-310

Ministry of Finance
Kohtu 8
Tallinn EE0100
Tel: (2) 452-801
Fax: (2) 452-992

Ministry of Foreign Affairs
Rävala 9
Tallinn EE0100
Tel: (2) 443-266
Fax: (2) 771-677

Port of Tallinn
Sadama 25
Tallinn EE0102
Tel: (2) 427-070, 428-301
Fax: (2) 422-950

Statistics Board
Endla 15
Tallinn EE0105
Tel: (2) 452-812
Fax: (2) 453-923

Patent Office
Toompuiestee 7
Tallinn EE0100
Tel: (2) 451-342

Ministry of the Interior
Pikk 61
Tallinn EE0102
Tel: (2) 663-262
Fax: (2) 441-112

Ministry of Social Affairs
Lossi Platx 1a
Tallinn EE0100
Tel: (2) 666-930
Fax: (2) 449-565

Ministry of Trade
Kiriku 2/4
Tallinn EE0100
Tel: (2) 421-597
Fax: (2) 450-540

Ministry of Transportation and Communications
Viru 9
Tallinn EE0100
Tel: (2) 443-842
Fax: (2) 449-206

Customs Department
Kohtu 8
Tallinn EE0100
Tel: (2) 452-767

Department of Employment
Lomonossovi 29
Tallinn EE0104
Tel: (2) 422-945

Department of Housing and Municipal Services
Harju 11
Tallinn EE0001
Tel: (2) 445-173

Department of Statistics
Endla 15
Tallinn EE0106
Tel: (2) 453-889
Fax: (2) 453-923

Department of Technical Inspection
Lossi plats 4
Tallinn EE0103
Tel: (2) 606-715

Estonian State Department for Foreign Relations
Komsomoli 1
Tallinn 200100
Tel: (2) 683-559
Fax: (2) 683-622

Immigration Department
Vana-Viru 12
Tallinn EE0001
Tel: (2) 444-473

National Maritime Board
Viru 9
Tallinn EE0100
Tel: (2) 442-725, 443-003
Fax: (2) 449-206

National Tourist Board
Saur-Karja 23
Tallinn EE0101
Tel: (2) 441-239
Fax: (2) 440-963

Pricing Department
Toompea 1
Tallinn EE0001
Tel: (2) 443-733

Taxation Department
Kohtu 8
Tallinn EE0100
Tel: (2) 452-329

Estonian Chamber of Commerce and Industry
Toom-Kooli 17
Tallinn EE0106
Tel: (2) 446-726,443-482
Fax: (2) 443-656

BUSINESS AND TRADE ORGANIZATIONS

Estonian Association of International Companies
Olevima gi 12
Tallinn EE0101
Tel: (2) 601-980

Estonian Small Business Association
Gonsiori 29
Tallinn EE0104
Tel: (2) 426-637, 421-484
Fax: (2) 422-279

Foreign Trade Association "ESTIMPEX"
UUS 32-34
Tallinn
Tel: (2) 601-462
Fax: (2) 602184

Agricultural Trading Company "POVEL"
Lai 38-41
Tallinn
Tel: (2) 601-210
Fax: (2) 602-160

Trading Center "INREKO"
Adala 4 A
Tallinn
Tel: (2) 493-091
Fax: (2) 493-000

Estonian Trade Exchange Organization
Punane 30
Tallinn
Tel: (2) 328-081
Fax: (2) 211-964

BANKS

Estonian Forexbank
Rävala pst. 8
Tallinn EE0090
Phone: (6) 313 020
Fax: (6) 313 021

Estonian Innovation Bank
Kentmanni 13
Tallinn EE0100
Phone: (2) 441-264
Fax: (2) 441-537

NEWSPAPERS

Daily Business
Raua 1A
Tallinn EE0010
Tel: (2) 431-201
Fax: (2) 426-700

The Baltic Independent
Parnu mnt. 67A
Tallinn EE0090
Tel: (2) 683-074
Telex: 173193
Fax: (2) 682-331

Estonian Express
Tatari 25
Tallinn EE0001
Tel: (2) 683-057
Fax: (2) 681-488

Estonia
Parnu mnt. 67A
Tallinn EE0090
Tel: (2) 440-580

Evening Gazette
Paunu mnt. 67A
Tallinn EE0090
Tel: (2) 681-154
Fax: (2) 441-924

RADIO AND TELEVISION

Eesti Raadio (Estonian Broadcasting Co)
Gonsiori 21
Tallinn EE0100
Tel: (2) 343-115
Fax: (2) 434-457
Telex: 173271

Eesti Televisioon (Estonian Television)
Faehlmanni 12
Tallinn EE0100
Tel: (2) 434-113
Fax: (2) 434-155
Telex: 173271

INTERNET ADDRESSES

Usenet group(s):
soc.culture.baltics
soc.culture.estonia

BALT-L, a moderated list covering the republics of Lithuania, Latvia, and Estonia, is accessed through the address balt-l@ubvm.cc.buffalo.edu. This group contains news items from the wire services, discussions on cultural, political and academic issues.

About Estonia
http://www.eenet.ee/english/intro.html

Estonia Country Guide
http://www.nlib.ee/ESTCG/

Estonia Network Resources
http://www.nlib.ee/ESTONIA/

YAHOO - Estonia
http://www.yahoo.com/Regional/Countries/Estonia/

EENet
http://www.eenet.ee

Finland

Republic of Finland

Economy

Overview

Finland's open market economy is currently in a growth mode built on brisk international trade, a solid manufacturing base, a highly skilled labor force, and a well-developed infrastructure. However, the recession of the early 1990s has had negative effects on domestic consumer demand, while boosting social expenditures and increasing the national deficit. Although the number of Finns in debt is decreasing, many of those in debt are sinking deeper. Privatization of government-owned companies is scheduled for completion by the end of the 1990s. Investment, which was down sharply in 1993, has improved, largely due to liberalized trade restrictions, rising capacity utilization, increased export orders, lower interest rates, and decreased corporate debt. Tax changes have also encouraged the growth of small to medium-sized businesses.

Trade

Major exports include paper, and wood, wood products—accounting for nearly 40 percent of export earnings—industrial and electrical machinery, chemicals, and transportation equipment. Imports include petroleum and fuels, industrial and electrical machinery, chemicals, and transportation equipment. Germany is Finland's largest trading partner, followed by Sweden, the UK, the US, and the countries of the former USSR. Imports have lagged, due to the depressed domestic marketplace, but exports comprise roughly 35 percent of the GDP. Commerce with Finland is also a useful prelude to trade with Russia and other Baltic states of the former Soviet Union, which, historically, have purchased as much as 25 percent of Finnish exports.

Sectors

Agriculture This sector employs about 10 percent of the work force but contributes only about five percent of GDP. Forestry is the dominant activity, but animal products is a growing sector and is becoming more significant. Imports are an important factor; Finland is far from self-sufficient in food production.

Industry Industry provides somewhat less than 30 percent of both GDP and employment. Export-oriented manufacturing is on a firm footing, and increased growth is projected. Paper, industrial machinery, ship-building, chemicals, and electronics—particularly telecommunications—are strong. The relative weakness of the Finnish currency, increased cutbacks, and high labor productivity—despite generally high labor costs—support strength in the sector.

Services Services contribute nearly 65 percent of GDP and employ well over 40 percent of the work force. Domestic services are plagued by the soft domestic economy, although tourism shows strong growth. Banking and retail sales have been especially hard hit, and reduced construction demand will likely lead to additional restructuring before conditions improve.

Trends

Additional strengthening of the Finnish economy should primarily benefit the manufacturing sector. Consumer confidence should improve, provided high unemployment and the decline in real wages can be addressed and reversed. Finland has taken a leadership position in environmental protection, becoming involved in cleanup projects in Russia and the Baltic states. Further development of this growth industry could become a major economic stimulus.

At a Glance

THE COUNTRY

Location Finland borders the former USSR to the east, the Gulf of Finland to the southeast, the Baltic Sea to the southwest, the Gulf of Bosnia and Sweden to the west, and Norway to the north and northwest.

Terrain Mostly coastal plains with a severely indented coastline and thousands of small islands. Central Finland is an extensive lake plateau containing a majority of the country's 60,000 lakes. Northern Finland is densely forested upland.

Climate Because of the warming influence of the Gulf Stream and the prevailing wind patterns, Finland's climate is comparatively mild for its high latitude. There is some snow in the highlands in winter, and average rainfall ranges from 40 cm (16 in) in the north to 70 cm (28 in) in the south.

THE PEOPLE

Population 5,113,000

Ethnic composition Mostly of Germanic stock, intermingled with the tribes that originally inhabited west-central Russia. There are also Laps and Gypsies in small numbers.

Religious composition

Lutheran Church 87.8%
Orthodox Church 1.1%
Not affiliated 9.7%

Languages spoken Finnish is the official language and is spoken by virtually the entire population.

Education and literacy Compulsory schooling is a nine-year program. Virtually all adults are literate.

Labor force

Total: 2,559,000

By occupation: agriculture 8.7%, industry, commerce, and finance 53.3%, services (public and personal) 24.7%, government 5.4%, transport (storage and communication) 7.1%.

COUNTRY FACTS

Political and legal Finland operates under a constitutional republic government, with an active, multiparty political system.

Telephone Telecommunications systems are efficient and available throughout most parts of Finland and the world. Helsinki is seven time zones ahead of eastern standard time. International country code: [358]. City code: Helsinki (0).

Transportation Finland's transportation system is well developed and consists of numerous roads, an extensive rail network, a shipping system with modern and well-developed sea and inland waterway ports, and a well-run and comprehensive air transportation system.

Environment Care is taken to protect the flora and fauna of the forest, which are of recreational as well as economic importance. Current issues include air and water pollution, and the preservation of wildlife.

Media Freedom of the press is guaranteed by the constitution. There are 66 daily newspapers. Broadcasting is run by Yleisradio. There are an estimated 4.9 million radios and 2.7 million televisions.

Health The local authorities are responsible for the majority of health services. The entire population is covered by health insurance, and life expectance is 76 years.

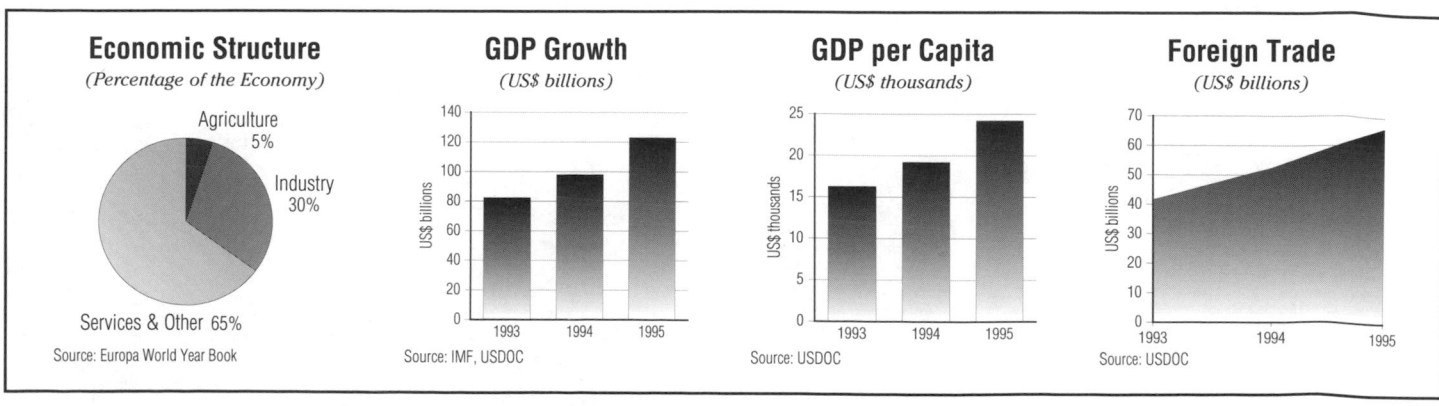

Economic Structure
(Percentage of the Economy)

Agriculture 5%
Industry 30%
Services & Other 65%

Source: Europa World Year Book

GDP Growth
(US$ billions)

Source: IMF, USDOC

GDP per Capita
(US$ thousands)

Source: USDOC

Foreign Trade
(US$ billions)

Source: USDOC

Finland

- ★ National capital
- ◉ Provincial capital
- ● Secondary city
- —— Primary road
- ---- Railroad
- — Province border
- ▬▬ International border

| 0 | 50 | 100 km |
| 0 | 50 | 100 mi |

Province (lääni) Name
1 *Lappi*
2 *Oulu*
3 *Vaasa*
4 *Keski Suomi*
5 *Kuopio*
6 *Pohjois-Karjala*
7 *Turku Ja Pori*
8 *Häme*
9 *Mikkeli*
10 *Kymi*
11 *Uusimaa*
12 *Ahvenanmaa*

Norway

Sweden

Russia

Barents Sea

Estonia

Baltic Sea

Gulf of Finland

Gulf of Bosnia

Arctic Circle

Helsinki

Mariehamn

Turku
Hangö
Salo
Hyvinkää
Forssa
Uusikaupunki
Rauma
Pori
Parkano
Kaskö
Vaasa
Seinäjoki
Virrat
Tampere
Hämeenlinna
Lahti
Porvoo
Kotka
Vaalimaa
Kouvola
Lappeenranta
Imatra
Mikkeli
Jämsä
Jyväskylä
Pieksämäki
Varkaus
Savonlinna
Joensuu
Ilomantsi
Lieksa
Kuopio
Iisalmi
Äänekoski
Kajaani
Ylivieska
Kokkola
Jakobstad
Raahe
Oulu
Taivalkoski
Kemi
Tornionjoki
Rovaniemi
Kemijärvi
Kelloselkä
Kolari
Muonio
Ivalo

Inarijärvi
Pielinen
Saimaa
Päijänne
Näsijärvi
Oulujärvi
Ladozhskoye Ozero
Ozero Imandra
Pyaozero
Topozero

Könkämäälven
Torneälven
Muoniojoki
Luleälv
Tornionjoki
Ounasjoki
Inarijoki
Tenojoki
Lurio
Kemijoki
Kemijoki
Oulujoki
Iijoki

18°   24°   30°
68°
64°
60°

Foreign Trade

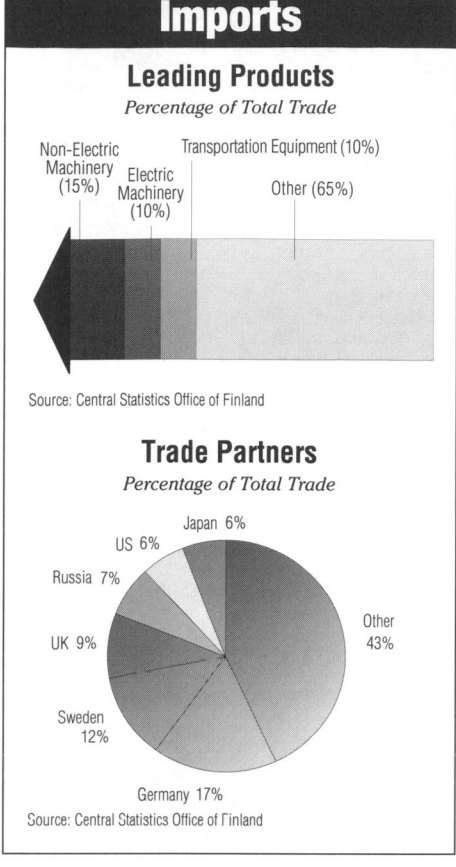

Imports

Leading Products
Percentage of Total Trade

Non-Electric Machinery (15%)
Electric Machinery (10%)
Transportation Equipment (10%)
Other (65%)

Source: Central Statistics Office of Finland

Trade Partners
Percentage of Total Trade

Japan 6%
US 6%
Russia 7%
UK 9%
Sweden 12%
Germany 17%
Other 43%

Source: Central Statistics Office of Finland

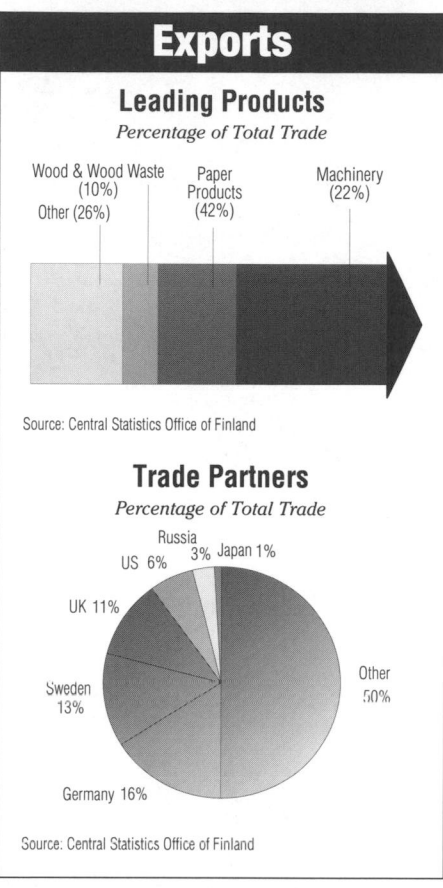

Exports

Leading Products
Percentage of Total Trade

Wood & Wood Waste (10%)
Other (26%)
Paper Products (42%)
Machinery (22%)

Source: Central Statistics Office of Finland

Trade Partners
Percentage of Total Trade

Russia 3%
Japan 1%
US 6%
UK 11%
Sweden 13%
Germany 16%
Other 50%

Source: Central Statistics Office of Finland

Opportunities

FOR IMPORTING TO FINLAND

- aircraft and parts
- automotive vehicles and parts
- beverages: wine, spirits, beer
- coffee
- computer software
- consumer-ready foods
- electronic components
- fodder grains
- forestry products
- fresh fruits and vegetables
- industrial chemicals and machinery
- laboratory scientific instruments
- medical equipment
- petroleum and petroleum products
- pollution control equipment
- sea food, snack foods, soybeans
- telecommunications equipment
- textiles
- tobacco

FOR EXPORTING FROM FINLAND

- analytic instruments
- cereals
- clothing and footwear
- dairy products
- electro-technical products
- glassware
- iron and steel
- machinery
- mobile phones
- paper and pulp products
- porcelain
- textiles
- timber

GROWTH SECTORS

- chemicals
- electronics
- fast-food franchises
- industrial machinery
- metal goods
- paper goods
- shipbuilding
- telecommunications
- tourism

GOVERNMENT PROCUREMENT

- construction goods and services
- health care goods and services
- industrial machinery
- telecommunications
- water treatment systems

Trade News

RULES AND REGULATIONS

- **Regulations** The Ministry of Trade and Industry is in charge of licensing, policy, and information sharing for industries and authorities. The National Board of Customs administers all import procedures.
- **Tariff rates** The Finnish customs tariff system is based on the Harmonized Commodity Description and Coding System (HS). About 35 percent of Finnish imports enter duty free. The average industrial tariff is about nine percent. Goods exempt from duty are also exempt from other import taxes.
- **Import taxes** Various tax levels apply to adjust the prices of imported goods to domestic goods; this is especially true for agricultural goods. Cars and motorcycles are subject to a special tax. Excise duties exist for certain products, including tobacco, candy, beer and other alcoholic beverages, sugar, and fertilizers. A value-added tax of 22 percent also applies.
- **Import restrictions** A permit is required for the import of live animals and most animal products, as well as meat and meat products.
- **Import prohibitions** Prohibitions in Finland exist for the import of the following products: PCB and PCT chemicals used in transformers and condensers causing problem wastes; alcoholic beverages which contain 60 percent or more alcohol; home wine manufacturer kits; whale meat; halogenated derivatives of acylic hydrocarbons containing two or more different halogens.
- **Import licenses** There are only a few significant licensing requirements for industrial imports. Countries that have most-favored nation (MFN) status with Finland generally do not need import licenses. Import licenses are needed for imports from Taiwan and North Korea.
- **Export controls** Finland aims to align its export control system with the European Union export control policy. Currently a license is required for the export of certain high technology goods and scrap metal.
- **Free trade zones** A free trade port exists in Hanko, located at the southern-most tip of the country.
- **Free trade agreements** In addition to having trade agreements with the European Free Trade Association and the European Union, Finland also has trade agreements with Turkey, Israel, the Czech Republic, Slovakia, Bulgaria, Hungary, Poland, Estonia, Latvia, and Lithuania. Imports of industrial goods from these countries is duty free.

FREIGHT FORWARDERS

Etein-Suomen Laiva OY
Suolakivenkatu 10
00810 Helsinki
Tel: (0) 759-5777
Fax: (0) 787315

FG Shipping Oy Ab
Lönnrotinkatu 21
POB 406
00121 Helsinki
Tel: (0) 16221
Fax: (0) 693-1873

Finncarriers Oy Ab
Porkkalankatu 7
00180 Helsinki
Tel: (0) 134311
Telex: 124462

The Nielsen Group
Lönnrotinkatu 18
00121 Helsinki
Tel: (0) 17291
Fax: (0) 1729256

GOVERNMENT AGENCIES

The Board of Customs
Ratakatu 1b A
00120 Helsinki
Tel: (0) 1641
Fax: (0) 614-2256

Ministry of Trade and Industry
Aleksanterinkatu 10
00170 Helsinki

Air Travel Times

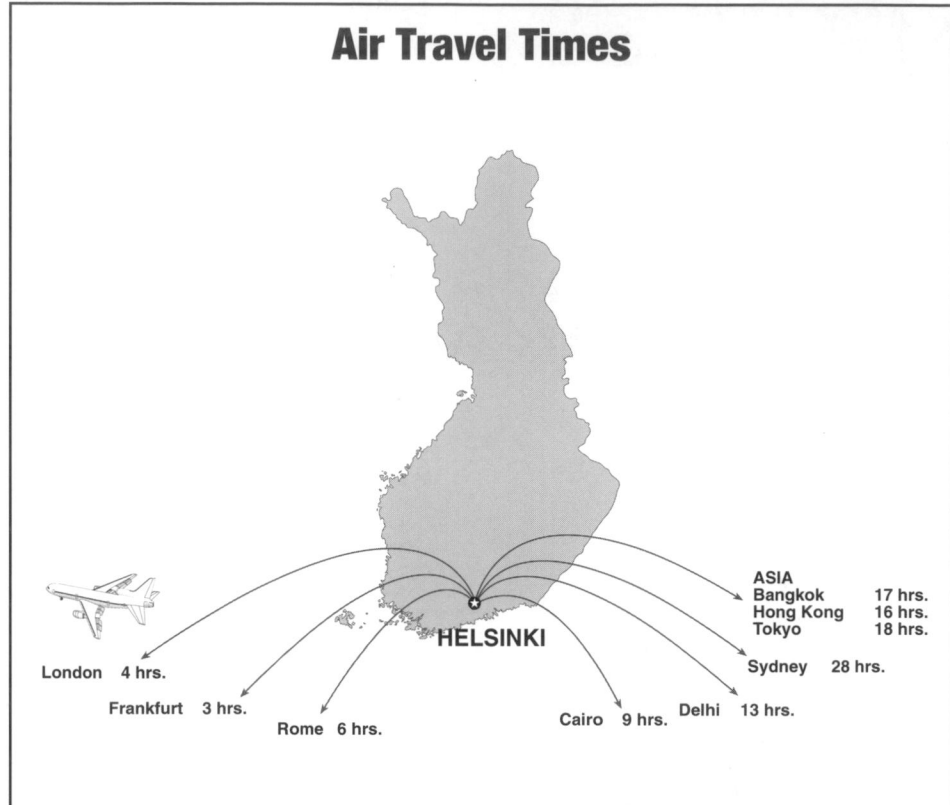

ASIA
Bangkok   17 hrs.
Hong Kong 16 hrs.
Tokyo   18 hrs.

HELSINKI

Sydney   28 hrs.

London   4 hrs.

Frankfurt   3 hrs.

Rome   6 hrs.

Cairo   9 hrs.

Delhi   13 hrs.

COMMUNICATIONS

Telephones Finland is a forerunner in the development and usage of telecommunications. Telephone and telegraph services are efficient and available to most parts of Finland and the world—almost 200 countries. Finland also has one of the most extensive mobile phone networks in the world.

Fax Faxes are prevalent and widely available.

Post office Post offices are marked Posti and are generally open weekdays from 9:00 am to 5:00 pm. Stamps can be purchased at hotels, newsstands, and tobacco shops. Mailboxes are yellow and are usually affixed to a wall.

BEST TRAVEL BOOKS

Lonely Planet, Finland. Firsthand travel information from two natives. Contains money-saving tips for all budgets. 382 pages with 16 color pages.

Fodor's Europe, Best of 31 Countries. Contains information on historical towns, great culture, scenic coastal countryside.

Do's and Taboo's Around the World. The Bestselling Guide to International Behavior. Edited by Roger Axtell, compiled by the Parker Pen Company. The ultimate guide to international behavior, now completely updated and expanded. Helpful, fun to read!

Berlitz Business Travel Guide, Europe. Concise economic details, successful trip planning, background information on people and cities, useful facts and addresses.

USEFUL TELEPHONE NUMBERS

If you are calling from outside Finland, you will need to add the country code [358] and any other international dialing requirements from within your country.

- Police/Emergency Services 112
- General Emergency Helsinki............................. 000
- Medical Emergency Helsinki 008
- Events, Entertainment 058
- Telegrams 24 hours 021
- Finnish Customs Dept. .... (0) 6142255
- Finnair .... (0) 81881
- Automobile Association Helsinki .... (0) 124839
- Dental Emergency Helsinki .... (0) 736-1666

Chambers of Commerce

- Central Fabianinkatu .... (0) 650133
- Helsinki Chamber of Commerce .... (0) 644601

Credit Card Information

Lost or stolen credit cards (call collect to the US, regardless of which country the card was issued in).

- Amex ....[1] (919) 333-3211
- Diner's Club................................[1] (303) 799-1504
- MasterCard ....[1] (314) 275-6690
- Visa ....[1] (410) 581-7931

Travelogue

WORKWEEK

Offices Monday-Friday 8:30 am to 4:30 pm.
Banks Monday-Friday 9:00 am to 4:00 pm.
Government Monday-Friday 8:00 am to 4:15 pm in winter, until 5:15 pm in summer.
Retail Monday-Friday 9:00 am to 6:00 pm and Saturday until 4:00 pm. Shops may close an hour earlier in summer.

HOLIDAYS

Holidays 1996
January 1 New Year's Day
January 6 Epiphany
April 5 Good Friday*
April 7 Easter Sunday*
April 8 Easter Monday*
May 1 May Day
Mid May-June Whitsun Eve*
May 16 Ascension Day
June 21 Midsummer's Eve
November 3 All Saints' Day
December 6 Independence Day
December 24-25 Christmas
*Dates vary each year.

VISA AND PASSPORT

Visitors to Finland need only a valid passport. Visas are not required for stays of up to three months (the 90-day period begins when a traveler enters any of the Scandinavian countries). Transit visas are required by all travelers except those continuing their journey within 24 hours and who do not leave the airport.

DEPARTURE FORMALITIES

No more than US$1500 may be taken out of Finland by foreigners. There are no other restrictions for departure in Finland.

IMMUNIZATION

There are no inoculation requirements for entry to Finland unless you are arriving from an infected area.

TIPPING

The bill in hotels, restaurants, and bars always includes a 15 percent service charge. It is customary to round a bill up to an even amount. Ushers, attendants, and barbers are not tipped. Tip porters FMk 5 and reception clerks FMk 5 to 10 for extra service. Taxi drivers do not expect tips but add FIM4 to fare after 6:00 pm.

CRIME

Finland has a low crime rate but normal precautions should be taken.

INFRASTRUCTURE

Finland has an efficient network of telecommunication, air, train, and long-distance bus services. Roads are well maintained and most cities have abundant and efficient public transportation, taxis, and tourist facilities. Helsinki also has tram and subway services. Train services are popular and reliable modes of transportation.

NATIONAL TOURIST OFFICES

Tourist Association
Lonnrutinkatiu 7B
Helsinki
Tel:(0) 645225

Tourist Board
Etelaesplanadi 4
Helsinki
Tel: (0) 174631

Marketing

Overview

The most important challenges to overcome when entering the Finnish import market are the current state of the economy and the traditional, cartel-like behavior of local companies. But as Finland moves toward EU membership, Finnish decision-makers will have to play by different rules. Overseas firms can gain indirect entry through Finland, to many Central European and former Soviet countries by linking up with Finnish firms developing business in Russia and the Baltic region. Finns like doing business with the rest of the world, especially when offered products and services that are on the cutting edge of technology.

Distribution

Goods may be sold through an agent, distributor, wholesaler, or directly to retailers. The four largest trading houses account for as much as 90 percent of all imports of certain categories of product. Wholesalers control distribution for most goods and have strong contacts with the trading houses. Firms marketing capital goods, industrial raw materials, and similar commodities should work through Finnish commission agents; companies involved in electronics, precious metals, and chemicals should hire Finnish private wholesalers or trading houses. Generally, an exclusive agent or distributor covers the entire country, and most importers represent several product lines. Trade fairs are important, and many Finnish importers attend trade fairs in the US and Europe.

Selling Techniques

Quality and features are generally more important than price. Strong promotion is important when introducing new products to this market. Sales offices are well supported by dealers here who usually take responsibility for training. Most Finnish importers maintain low stock levels, so swift deliveries are important. A responsible distributor makes full service, maintenance, and training facilities and after-sales service available to the customer. Most advertising and sales promotion is through the mass media. Newspapers account for 60 percent of all media advertising, television 20 percent, magazines 10 percent, and radio and other media about 10 percent.

Business Culture

Greetings and Courtesies

Mr., Mrs., and Miss are rarely used in Finland. Upon first meeting a businessperson of high rank, speak the person's first name and last name followed by their title or position. From then on, address the person by title alone. Persons without senior position are greeted by first and last names; from then on, first name alone. The standard greeting is a handshake followed by "hello" or "good day."

Business Ethic and Framework

Though casual and relaxed at work, Finns are formal and well structured in conducting business. You may approach Finland's business community without introductions, but cold calls are not appreciated. A letter initiating contact will serve best. The letter should include your background and detailed company information. Business cards as well as presentation materials may be in Finnish, Swedish, or English. Be well prepared with substantial information and facts concerning the business at hand, as Finns are not given to small talk.

Meetings and Decision Making

Following greetings, few pleasantries will be exchanged as Finns like to get right down to business. Promptly after the meeting, a follow-up letter outlining what was discussed should be sent to reduce the possibility of a misunderstanding. Decisions are rendered by ranking personnel depending on the size of the deal you are promoting. Finns do not like to haggle. Well organized, straight-forward, and factually informed presentations are most likely to speed a business relationship.

Women

Almost all women work outside the home and can be found in all levels of the business world, including top management, top levels of government including prime minister, in education, and within the Finnish Interpol. Foreign businesswomen should therefore experience few, if any, difficulties conducting business in Finland.

Marketing in Finland

MARKETING TIPS

- **Legal advice** Companies planning to enter into contracts with Finnish corporations are advised to consult an experienced Finnish attorney.
- **Language** Suppliers should provide the local distributor with product literature and documentation in Finnish, although English is also a popular choice.
- **Advertising** Because advertisements are subject to content standards, outsiders should work closely with Finnish ad firms; more than 60 advertising agencies are located in Finland.
- **Agents** There are approximately 300 commission agents in Finland, most of whom belong to the Finnish Foreign Trade Agents' Federation.

AD AGENCY

AT + Grey
Tukhoimankatu 2
00250 Helsinki
Tel: (0) 477-1122
Fax: (0) 477-1130

MARKETING FIRMS

Finnish Direct Marketing Association
Vuorikatu 4 A 6
00100 Helsinki
Tel: (0) 663-744
Fax: (0) 663-772

Finnpap - Marketing Association
Eteläesplandi 2
00130 Helsinki
Tel: (0) 132-41
Fax: (0) 658-949

Cultural Cautions

DO'S

- Speak clearly, remain composed. Avoid loudness or large physical gestures.
- Maintain reserve with Finnish colleagues; friendships are long in developing.
- Show interest in the Finnish language; ask how to speak a few common expressions and your hosts will be charmed.

DON'TS

- Don't stand too close to the Finns or you'll be perceived as overbearing.
- Don't give a gift of alcohol until sure of your colleague's health habits.
- It is never proper to eat with fingers, even if you're eating fruit.

CUSTOMS

- The sauna is an important part of Finnish life and Finns do a great deal of business entertaining in the sauna (rarely in restaurants or their homes). The business sauna is usually used by one gender only, and saunas are separated by sex. The Finns take their sauna naked, but you may wear a towel or bathing suit.
- A simple gift bearing your company logo is appreciated, but avoid expensive gifts as they may be interpreted as an effort to gain favor.

OBSERVATIONS

- Not given to emotional expression, Finns appear reserved and distant. Don't be offended. The Finnish are friendly and hospitable. Do know that you are welcomed.
- In banking circles, dark suits, white shirts and a tie are standard. Other industries are less formal. Finns tend to wear suits in winter only. In the summer, sports jackets, trousers, a tie, or short sleeve shirts and no tie. Women dress in relatively informal dresses or skirt and blouse combinations.

NEGOTIATIONS

- Again, emphasis on preparedness, organization, information, and clarity; exercise these skills from the beginning and your Finnish counterparts will be well inclined to do business with you.

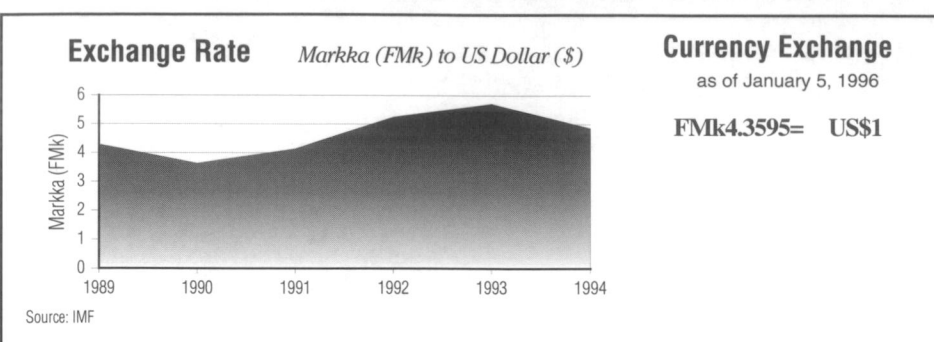

Exchange Rate   *Markka (FMk) to US Dollar ($)*

Markka (FMk)

1989 1990 1991 1992 1993 1994

Source: IMF

Currency Exchange

as of January 5, 1996

FMk4.3595=   US$1

Currency

The currency in use is the Finnish markka (FMk), divided into 100 pennia.

Foreign Exchange

Exchange controls have been gradually phased out since 1991; currently there are no more exchange controls in place. There are no regulations on Finnish banks with respect to international banking, although they must comply with some supervisory reporting requirements. Authorized banks may deal between themselves, with residents, and with nonresident banks in US dollars and other convertible currencies. Capital transactions, except for the acquisition of real estate by foreigners, are permitted without restriction. Although there are no foreign exchange controls, the Bank of Finland does compile balance of payments data.

Capital Transfers

There are no restrictions on repatriating earnings, interest, and royalties, although the commercial bank involved in the transfer must notify the Bank of Finland (Suomen Pankki) for statistical purposes. There are no limits on repatriation of capital or profits abroad, and no limit on dividend distributions. The distributions, however, must correspond with the company's official earnings records.

Investment Incentives

There are no specific investment incentives, although all registered companies have equal access to government assistance under special development programs. The government provides aid and loans for the development of technology, and for new products to improve competitiveness.

Investment Restrictions

There are few restrictions for foreign investors, although anyone investing in the largest Finnish firms must be screened for a three-year transition period. To date, the government has not turned down any requests for investment.

TAXATION

Taxation requires sophisticated knowledge of complex rules and regulations specific to each country. For more detailed information we suggest you refer to the Ernst & Young Corporate Tax Guide and Directory, available from the Ernst & Young accounting office in your country, or from:

Tilintarkastajien Oy
Ernst & Young
Kaivokatu 8
00100 Helsinki, Finland
Tel: (0) 172-771
Fax: (0) 622-1323

At a Glance

Corporate Income Tax Rate (%)	25
Capital Gains Tax Rate (%)(a)	25
Branch Tax Rate (%)	25
Withholding Tax (%)(b)	
Dividends (c)	25
Interest (d)	0
Royalties (e)	25
Branch Remittance Tax	0
Net Operating Losses (Years)	
Carryback	0
Carryforward	10

If there are no tax treaties in force, relief for foreign tax paid is granted.

(a) Capital gains are treated as ordinary business income.
(b) This rate is applicable only to payments to nonresidents.
(c) No withholding tax is imposed on dividends paid to a parent company resident in another European Union (EU) country if, at the time of the distribution, the recipient has owned at least 25% of the share capital of the distributing company and if the receiving company is not entitled to an imputation credit on the dividend.
(d) In general, interest paid to resident individuals is subject to a final withholding tax of 25% if it is paid on bonds, debentures, and certain bank deposits. Interest paid to nonresidents is generally exempt from tax.
(e) Royalties paid to resident individuals are normally subject to salary withholding.

Money Matters

BITS AND PIECES

- **Banking system** The Finnish banking system consists of six banking groups: Kansallis-Osake-Pankki, the Union Bank of Finland, Okobank, Postipankki, the Savings Bank of Finland, and Skopbank. The banking sector has undergone a great deal of consolidation after an expansion of credit and questionable lending practices that were widespread in the 1980s.

- **Credit** All major banks have export financing units, and there are several government financing options. Credit is available on market terms, and foreigners can get credit on the local market.

- **Incentives and free ports** There are no specific incentives for foreign investment, but companies have equal access to government assistance under special development programs. Enterprises located in developing areas may receive assistance or subsidies from the Regional Development Fund (KERA). The only free port is Hanko; Hanko Harbor is the only port in Finland that is consistently free of ice. There are several free storage areas in other locations, and these are available to all domestic and foreign corporations. Warehousing, assembly, and manufacturing are permitted, with government permission.

- **Foreign ownership** Foreign investors are permitted to have 100 percent ownership in all sectors, except for certain areas that are restricted because of national security.

- **Nonresident accounts** Nonresidents may hold accounts in an authorized bank denominated in any convertible currency or the Finnish markka. Nonresidents may credit and debit their accounts without restriction; foreign and domestic currency may be brought into the country without limit. No taxes exist for buying or sale of foreign exchange.

BANKS

Citibank Ltd.
Aleksanterinkatu 48A
00100 Helsinki
Tel: (0) 173381 Fax: (0) 651194

Interbank Osakepankki
Unioninkatu 12
00130 Helsinki
Tel: (0) 166-721 Fax: (0) 632-705

Kansallis-Osake-Pankki
Aleksanterinkatu 42
00100 Helsinki
Tel: (0) 1631 Fax: (0) 163-3595

Mordbanken Finland Oy
Kaivokatu 10A
00100 Helsinki
Tel: (0) 170411 Fax: (0) 653316

Osuuspankkien Keskuspankki (Okobank)
Arkadiankatu 23
00100 Helsinki
Tel: (0) 4041 Fax: (0) 404-2652

Postipankki
Unioninkatu 22
00007 Helsinki
Tel: (0) 1641 Fax: (0) 164-2608

Skopbank (Snnstîpankkien Keskus-Osake-Pankki)
(Central Bank of the Finnish Savings Banks)
Mikonkatu 4
POB 400
00101 Helsinki
Tel: (0) 13341 Fax: (0) 1334896

STS-Bank Ltd.
POB 53
00531 Helsinki
Tel: (0) 73181 Fax: (0)73182540

Suomen Pankki/Finlands Bank
Snellmaninaukio
POB 160
00101 Helsinki
Tel: (0) 1831 Fax: (0) 174872

Union Bank of Finland
Aleksanterinkatu 30
00100 Helsinki
Tel: (0) 1651 Fax: (0) 165-2838

Legal System

Finland is a civil code country. A great deal of statutes are influenced by Nordic co-operation and harmonization with EC legislation.

Intellectual Property Rights

Patents It usually takes from two to four years to obtain patent registration. In most cases, the application becomes public after 18 months of filing date. There is no discovery procedure as known in the US to seek evidence of infringement. The number of patent infringement cases is limited and the courts adjudicate cases slowly. Finland is a member of Patent Cooperation Treaty.

Trademarks On average it takes at least 10 months to obtain trademark registration. Registration can be obtained also for service marks. Only widely known trademarks enjoy protection through established use, without registration. The trademark protection covers unusually similar goods or services.

Copyrights No registration is needed or possible for protection of copyrights. Computer programs are considered literary works. The copyright of a computer program created by an employee in the course of employment is vested directly to the employer.

Trade Secrets The Unfair Business Practice Act protects against use of trade secrets in some cases. Illegal use of trade secrets in certain cases is criminalized. A special court, the Market Court, has jurisdiction in matters based on the Unfair Business Practice Act.

Business Registration

The limited liability company is the most common form of business in Finland. The minimum capital required is FMk 15,000 (approximately US$3,750). However, an amendment to the Companies Act is expected in 1996, and this will increase the minimum capital required and introduce a distinction between public and private companies. Registration with the Trade Register and the local tax authorities is required for limited liability companies and for branch offices. For certain businesses licenses are required. Usually the same rules apply both for EU citizens and Finnish citizens. Companies shall have at least one appointed representative in Finland to receive legal notices. Acquisitions by foreigners leading to one third or more of the voting power in Finnish businesses with more than 1,000 employees and turnover more than FMk 1 billion are subject to approval by the Ministry of Trade and Industry.

Contract and Dispute Resolution

Finnish companies prefer short contracts, but the American style of drafting has become more and more popular in larger transactions. Arbitration, though expensive, is widely used, especially in disputes of considerable interest. Arbitration awards are secret and there is no appeal, except on formal grounds. The Finnish Arbitration Act or the rules of the Finnish Chamber of Commerce are usually chosen to be applicable to arbitration. The judicial litigation procedure has been subject to a comprehensive reform. Litigation may still be lengthy, especially in business disputes, and in bigger cities it may take 6 to 12 months before the first preparatory hearing will take place. Appellate proceedings are conducted in most cases by exchange of briefs instead of oral hearings.

Notaries

Transfer of real property shall take place in the presence of a notary public. Acknowledgment of a notary is not otherwise necessary to the validity of a document.

Labor

Employees enjoy broad protections. In addition to employment statutes, labor market organizations have collective bargaining agreements which generally provide better working conditions and higher salaries than those provided by statute. Collective bargaining agreements may be generally binding even if an employer is not a member of the labor organization. The collective bargaining agreements set forth minimum wage rates and minimum benefits applicable to the enterprise. Minors under the age of fifteen cannot be employed. There are limited possibilities for an employer to dismiss an employee, and certain procedures must be followed prior thereto. In case of an illegal dismissal the employer may be liable to pay considerable damages. Employers' costs of employees is high. Employers must pay social security, unemployment insurance, pension contributions, collective life insurance, and accident insurance. The cost of these payments may amount to as much as 45 percent of the gross salary. In addition, there are legal paid holidays and overtime pay requirements.

Source: Bützow & Co. Ltd., Helsinki

Legal Matters

LEGAL BRIEFS

- **IPR applications** For applications to protect intellectual property rights a foreign applicant needs to authorize a Finnish agent to receive notices.
- **Maximum work week** The statutory maximum work week for all employees is 40 hours or five 8-hour days. Employees are given two days paid vacation per month of employment and after one year of continuous employment two and a half days paid vacation per month. An additional holiday bonus of 50 percent of the monthly salary is common. Worker co-operation is required for enterprises with 30 or more regular employees.
- **Employee participation** In many cases of transfer or restructuring of a business employees must be consulted.
- **Property** Foreigners residing outside of Finland may acquire real property, although in some cases prior permission is required. A stamp duty between four and six percent of the sales price is payable on the purchase of real estate. The ownership of real property is to be entered into the appropriate register within a certain time period, at the risk of increased stamp duties.
- **Disputes** The losing party of a dispute in court is usually obligated to pay the legal costs of the winning party, in full, with overdue interest rate.
- **Sole proprietorships** County governments issue permits to foreign nationals willing to do business under their own name. A foreign executive must designate a Finnish citizen to handle all relevant legal matters in the foreigner's absence.
- **Agency agreements** When formulating an agency agreement, parties are free to designate both choice of law and choice of forum clauses, but such clauses should not be in violation of the Commercial Representatives Act.
- **Branch offices** Branch offices are not legal entities under Finnish law and the use of such is rare.
- **Partnerships** Local county governments issue business permits to foreigners forming or joining partnerships, but the foreigners must also apply to the national Ministry of Trade and Industry.
- **Residency** Foreigners are considered residents of Finland if they have been in the country for a continuous period of more than six months.
- **Eduskunta** The 200 member legislative body is the supreme authority in Finland. It may alter the constitution, bring about the resignation of the Council of State, and override presidential vetoes; its acts are not subject to judicial review.
- **Trade agreements** Finland is a member of the EU as of 1 January 1995.

LEGAL CONTACTS

Bützow & Co. Ltd.
Pohjoisesplanadi 21A
POB 121
00101 Helsinki
Tel: (0) 651-744
Fax: (0) 665-417

Ahola, Pentzin, Rantasila & Sokka
Italahdenkatu 15-17
00210 Helsinki
Tel: (0) 682-2399

Attorneys' House ANPR Stenback Street
Stenbackinkatu 26
00250 Helsinki
Tel: (0) 47421

Castren & Snellman
Erottajankatu 5AQ
00130 Helsinki
Tel: (0) 228-581
Fax: (0) 655-919

Heikki Haapaniemi
Mannerheimintie 14B
00100 Helsinki
Tel: (0) 177-613

Peltonen, Orndahl, Ruokonen & Itainen
Fredrikinkatu 48 A
00100 Helsinki
Tel: (0) 694-4966

Contacts

GOVERNMENT AGENCIES

Statistics Finland
Työpajankatu 13
00580 Helsinki
Tel: (0) 173-41 Fax: (0) 1734-2279
National Board of Patents and Registration
Albertinkatu 25 A
00180 Helsinki
Tel: (0) 6939-500 Fax: (0) 6939-5601
National Consumer Administration
POB 5
00531 Helsinki
Tel: (0) 77-261 Fax: (0) 7726-7557
Ministry of Trade and Industry
Export Control Unit
Lastenkodinkatu 5
00180 Helsinki
Tel: (0) 160-5850 Fax: (0) 160-5866
Ministry of Agriculture and Forestry
Hallituskatu 3 A
00170 Helsinki
Tel: (0) 1601 Fax: (0) 1605044
Ministry of Culture
Meritullinkatu 10
00170 Helsinki
Tel: (0) 134171 Fax: (0) 1359335
Ministry of Environment
Ratakatu 3
00120 Helsinki
Tel: (0) 19911 Fax: (0) 1991499
Ministry of Finance
Snellmaninkatu 1 A
00170 Helsinki
Tel: (0) 1601 Fax: (0) 1604755
Ministry of Transport, Communications and Nordic Cooperation
Eteläesplanadi 16
00130 Helsinki
Tel: (0) 17361 Fax: (0) 1736340

WORLD TRADE CENTER

World Trade Center Turku
Puolalankatu 1
20100 Turku
Tel: (21) 2501-440 Fax: (21) 2514-860

BUSINESS AND TRADE ASSOCIATIONS

Finnish Standardization Association
Maistraatinportti 2
00241 Helsinki
Tel: (0) 149-9331 Fax: (0) 146-4914
Federation of Finnish Commerce and Trade
Mannerheimintie 76 A
00250 Helsinki
Tel: (0) 441-651 Fax: (0) 496-142
Finnish Foreign Trade Agents' Federation
Museokatu 9 B 21
00100 Helsinki
Tel: (0) 446-768 Fax: (0) 408-807
Association of Finnish Advertisers
Meritullinkatu 17
00170 Helsinki
Tel: (0) 662-622 Fax: (0) 665-030
Confederation of Finnish Industry and Employers
Eteläranta 10
00130 Helsinki
Tel: (0) 686-81 Fax: (0) 6868-2316
Finnish Foreign Trade Association
Arkadiankatu 2
00100 Helsinki
Tel: (0) 695-91 Fax: (0) 694-0028
Invest in Finland Bureau
Arkadiankatu 2
00100 Helsinki
Tel: (0) 695-91 Fax: (0) 694-7934

CHAMBERS OF COMMERCE

Central Chamber of Commerce
Fabianinkatu 14 B
00100 Helsinki
Tel: (0) 650-133 Fax: (0) 650-303

Finnish Section of the Int'l Chamber of Commerce
Fabianinkatu 14
00100 Helsinki
Tel: (0) 650-133 Fax: (0) 650-303
Helsinki Chamber of Commerce
Kalevankatu 12
00100 Helsinki
Tel: (0) 644-601 Fax: (0) 604-228
Central Finland Chamber of Commerce
Sepankatu 4
40100 Jyvaskyla
Tel: (41) 652-400 Fax: (41) 652-411
Finnish-American Chamber of Commerce
Arkadiankatu 2
00100 Helsinki
Tel: (0) 695-91 Fax: (0) 694-0028

NEWSPAPERS AND PERIODICALS

Helsingin Sanomat
Ludviginkatu 2-10
POB 975
00101 Helsinki
Tel: (0) 1221 Telex: 122772
Iltalehti
POB 372
00101 Helsinki
Tel: (0) 507721 Fax: (0) 533512
Ilta-Sanomat
Korkeavuorenkatu 34
POB 375
00101 Helsinki
Tel: (0) 1221 Fax: (0) 1223419
Kauppalehti
(The Commercial Daily)
POB 189
00101 Helsinki
Tel: (0) 50781 Telex: 125827
Akava
Rautatieläisenkatu 6
00520 Helsinki
Tel: (0) 141822 Fax: (0) 142595
Kymppi
Korkeavuorenkatu 45
POB 42
00131 Helsinki
Tel: (0) 13341 Fax: (0) 1334870

RADIO & TELEVISION STATIONS

OI Yleisradio Ab
(Finnish Broadcasting Company)
POB 10
00241 Helsinki
Tel: (0) 14801 Fax: (0) 14803390
Oy Kolmostelevisio Ab (Channel 3)
Ilmalankatu 2c
00240 Helsinki
Tel: (0) 15001 Fax: (0) 150-0

INDUSTRY SPECIFIC ORGANIZATIONS

Enigheten Centrallaget
(Cheese Export)
Päiväläisentie 2
00390 Helsinki
Tel: (0) 5624188 Fax: (0) 5622630
Kalatalouden Keskusliitto
(Federation of Fisheries Associations)
Kïydenpunojankatu 7B 23
00180 Helsinki
Tel: (0) 648212 Fax: (0)642597
Suomen Betoniteollisuuden Keskusjärjestî
(Association of the Concrete Industry of Finland)
Iso Roobertinkatu 30
00120 Helsinki
Tel: (0) 648212 Fax: (0)642597
Converta
(Finnish Paper and Board Converters' Association)
Fabianinkatu 9
POB 35
00131 Helsinki
Tel: (0) 131711 Fax: (0) 650152

Finncell
(Finnish Pulp Exporters' Association)
Eteläesplanadi 2
POB 60
00101 Helsinki
Tel: (0) 18051 Fax: (0) 1805372
Finnpap
(Finnish Paper Marketing Association)
Eteläesplanadi 2
POB 380
00101 Helsinki
Tel: (0) 13241
Suomen Taknillinen Kauppaliitto
(Finnish Technical Traders Association)
Mannerheimintie 76A
00250 Helsinki
Tel: (0) 440391 Fax: (0) 407643
Central Association of Finnish Clothing Industries
Fredrikinkatu 41c
00120 Helsinki 12
Finnish Federation of Food Industries
Unioninkatu 14
00130 Helsinki 13
Finnish Association of Furniture Exporters
POB 908
Arkadiankatu 4-6b
00101 Helsinki 12
Association of Finnish Textile Industries
Etelaranta 10
00130 Helsinki 13

AD AGENCIES

Bates Saatchi & Saatchi
Mikonkatu 8 A
00100 Helsinki
Tel: (0) 134431
Fax: (0) 626566
Lowe Brindfors OY
Tehtaankatu 27-29a
00150 Helsinki
Tel: (0) 177711
Fax: (0) 170600
Ogilvy & Mather OY
Mikonkatu 19
00100 Helsinki
Tel: (0) 177626
Fax: (0) 659137
J. Walter Thompson-Finland OY
Bulevardi 42
00120 Helsinki
Tel: (0) 6188345
Fax: (0) 61883499
Wunderman Cato Johnson
Munkkisaarenkatu 2
00150 Helsinki
Tel: (0) 6220350
Fax: (0) 61883499

INTERNET ADDRESSES

Usenet group(s):
soc.culture.nordic
Embassy of Finland in Washington, D.C.
http://www.finnemb.nw.dc.us/web/finland/index.html
Finnish WWW Servers
http://www.cs.hut.fi/finland.html
Finland - Basic Facts
http://www.mofile.fi/finland.htm
YAHOO - Finland
http://www.yahoo.com/text/Regional/Countries/Finland/
FINFO—Finland Information Pages
http://www.vn.fi/vn/um/findeng.html

France

French Republic

Economy

Overview

France is a heavily industrialized, highly competitive, and extremely sophisticated economy, one in which establishing a commercial foothold can be quite challenging. France has a substantial demand for high-tech electronic goods, on both consumer and business-to-business levels. However, many raw and intermediate materials are scarce, and unemployment remains high—running at around 10 percent despite lower labor costs than some of its European neighbors. France's sophisticated industrial plants and equipment are formidable and its extensive infrastructure network is among the most modern in the world. Preference for local products is strong; this serves to discourage a large import market.

Trade

The French economy is heavily oriented towards trade, but nevertheless maintains stringent product standards, procedures, subsidies, and tariff and nontariff barriers that are periodically assailed as protectionist distortions of trade. Major exports include chemicals, transportation equipment, food products, electrical machinery, and iron and steel. Imports include chemicals, fuels, transportation equipment, food products, and electrical machinery. Germany is its largest trading partner, followed by Italy, Spain, Belgium, Luxembourg, the UK, and the United States.

Sectors

Agriculture Despite its traditionally revered status in France, agriculture contributes less than five percent of GDP and employs little more than five percent of the work force. France is experiencing rapid growth in the food processing industry, but remains vulnerable to growing international competition, especially as it reduces subsidies under the terms of EU and GATT agreements.

Industry Industry employs about 30 percent of the work force and accounts for about the same percentage of GDP. The 1993 recession affected manufacturing, especially businesses with a heavy export component, such as the automotive industry; however, most are expected to recover as the domestic economy improves. Although highly sophisticated, much of French industry remains tightly regulated.

Services Services employ somewhat less than 65 percent of the work force and provide slightly more than 60 percent of GDP. Transportation, financial services, and telecommunications all look particularly healthy for the 1990s as France's economic recovery continues. Retail sales have lagged somewhat, however, pending the rebuilding of consumer confidence.

Trends

Government regulation in business is more common in France than in many other highly developed countries. During the past 10 years, there has been a trend to decrease government control, including the privatization of more than 20 state-owned enterprises, with transformation of additional businesses either planned or under way. Traditional subsidies for important industries will likely be reduced or eliminated, pursuant to terms of the EU agreement. But debate continues as to whether France will still protect its transportation and agricultural sectors. The French government maintains that continued subsidies are essential, despite international pressure in this regard.

At a Glance

THE COUNTRY

Location Western Europe, bordering the North Atlantic Ocean between Spain and Germany.
Terrain Mostly flat plains or gently rolling hills in north and west; remainder is mountainous.
Climate Temperate, cool in winter, mild in summer.

THE PEOPLE

Population 58,000,000
Ethnic composition Celtic and Latin with Teutonic, Slavic, North African, Indochinese, and Basque minorities.
Religious composition
Roman Catholic 90%
Languages spoken French. A large percentage of the population speaks English, although they prefer not to.
Education and literacy Education is free and mandatory between the ages of six and 16. The public education system is highly centralized. Private education is primarily Roman Catholic. Ninety-nine percent of the population 15 years and older can read and write.
Labor force
Total:...24,000,000
By occupation: services 61.5%, industry 31.3%, agriculture 7.2%.

COUNTRY FACTS

Political and legal France operates as a democratic republic. Its legal system is based on civil law, with indigenous concepts. There is judicial review of administrative but not legislative acts.
Telephone France has a sophisticated and extensive telecommunications system, consisting of far-reaching cable and microwave radio relay networks. International calls can be dialed directly, and local calls are efficient and reliable. International country code: [33] Effective October 1995, France has phased out city codes. All telephone numbers are now nine digits.
Transportation France has one of the most highly developed transportation systems in Europe. It is highly centralized at Paris, offering easy access which radiates from the city in all directions, including navigable rivers with broad valleys which converge on Paris from all sides. Most of the roadways are paved. The French National Railway System serves the entire country with efficient and reliable service. International air service is available to and from Paris and from some locations directly to and from the southern coast. Flights leave often.
Environment Current issues center around forest damage as a result of acid rain from industrial and vehicle emissions. Air pollution is beginning to be addressed by the government in consignment with other European countries. Water pollution from urban wastes and agricultural run-off is also a problem that the French are starting to address.
Media A lively, diverse, and free media provides newspaper, periodical, radio, and television services to the entire country.
Health A national health care system which operates through centralized funding provides excellent health care. Patients have the option of seeing a private doctor on a fee basis, where their fees are reimbursed in part, or going to a state-operated facility. Life expectancy is 78 years for males and females.

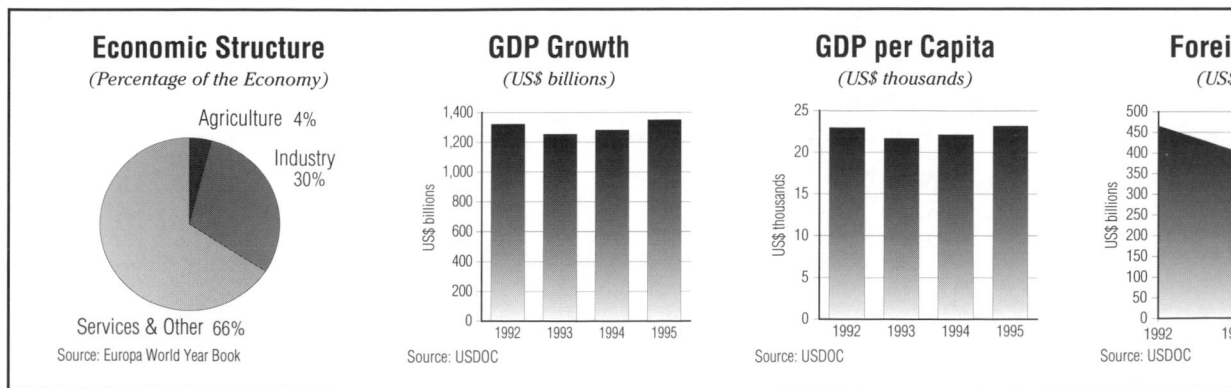

Economic Structure
(Percentage of the Economy)
Agriculture 4%
Industry 30%
Services & Other 66%
Source: Europa World Year Book

GDP Growth
(US$ billions)
Source: USDOC

GDP per Capita
(US$ thousands)
Source: USDOC

Foreign Trade
(US$ billions)
Source: USDOC

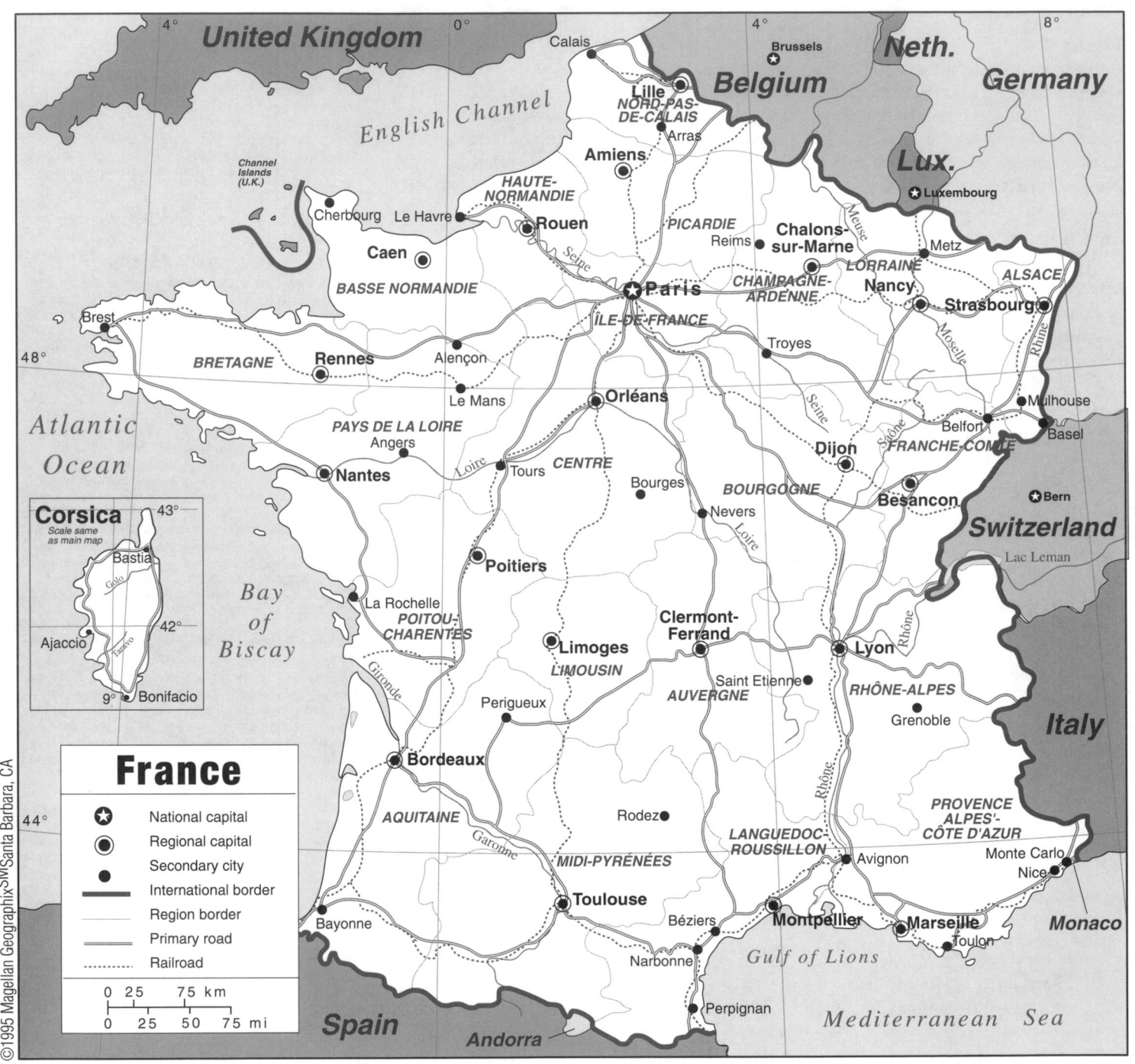

France

- ★ National capital
- ◉ Regional capital
- ● Secondary city
- ▬ International border
- ── Region border
- ── Primary road
- ··· Railroad

0 25   75 km
0 25 50 75 mi

Foreign Trade

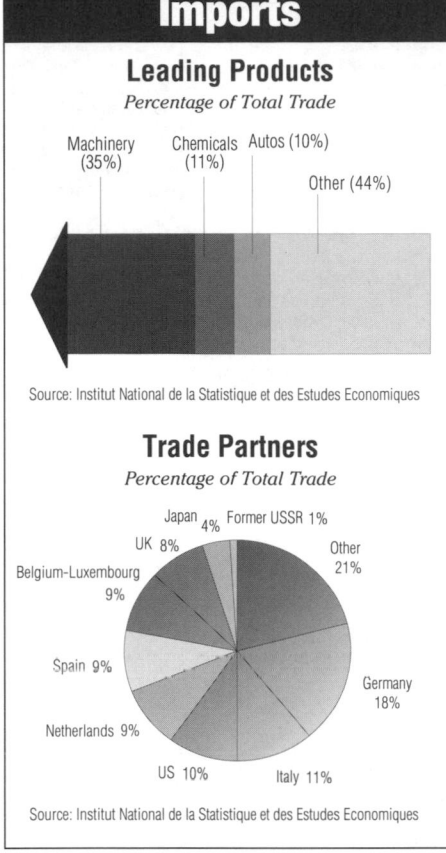

Imports

Leading Products
Percentage of Total Trade

Machinery (35%)   Chemicals (11%)   Autos (10%)   Other (44%)

Source: Institut National de la Statistique et des Estudes Economiques

Trade Partners
Percentage of Total Trade

Japan 4%   Former USSR 1%
UK 8%
Belgium-Luxembourg 9%
Spain 9%
Netherlands 9%
US 10%
Italy 11%
Germany 18%
Other 21%

Source: Institut National de la Statistique et des Estudes Economiques

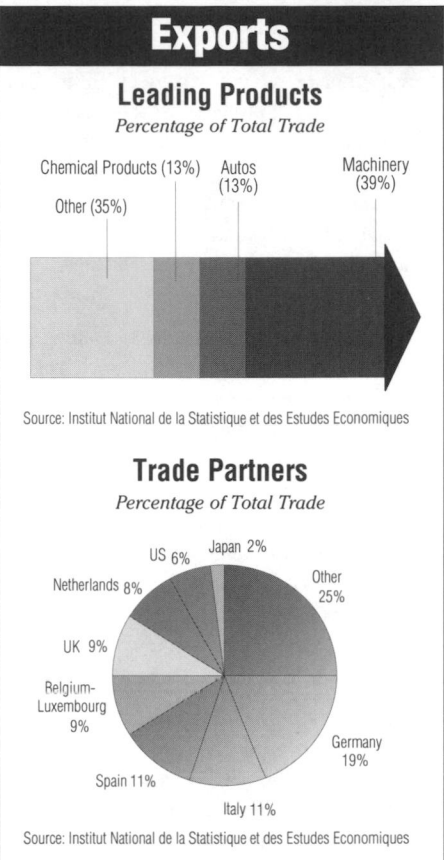

Exports

Leading Products
Percentage of Total Trade

Chemical Products (13%)   Autos (13%)   Machinery (39%)   Other (35%)

Source: Institut National de la Statistique et des Estudes Economiques

Trade Partners
Percentage of Total Trade

US 6%   Japan 2%
Netherlands 8%
UK 9%
Belgium-Luxembourg 9%
Spain 11%
Italy 11%
Germany 19%
Other 25%

Source: Institut National de la Statistique et des Estudes Economiques

Opportunities

FOR IMPORTING TO FRANCE
- aircraft, automobiles, and automobile parts
- beverages and seafood
- building products
- chemicals
- computer products and electronics
- consumer-ready foods
- crude petroleum
- electronics industry production and testing equipment
- films, videos, and recordings
- jewelry
- medical equipment
- pollution control and equipment
- pumps, valves, and compressors
- security and safety equipment
- telecommunication products
- textiles and clothing
- wood and wood products

FOR EXPORTING FROM FRANCE
- art and antiques
- aircraft and aircraft parts
- automobiles and automobile parts
- beverages: wine and spirits
- chemicals
- cosmetics
- dairy products
- electrical equipment
- electronics
- foodstuffs
- iron and steel
- machinery
- textiles and clothing
- wheat

GROWTH SECTORS
- building materials
- computer products
- energy
- food processing
- laboratory and scientific instruments
- plastics and resins
- pollution control equipment
- services
- telecommunications

GOVERNMENT PROCUREMENT
- airport expansion goods and services
- computer products
- environmental protection technologies
- fiber optic cables
- transportation goods and services
- medical supplies and equipment
- military equipment
- multimedia products
- water treatment facilities

Trade News

RULES AND REGULATIONS

- **Regulations** Customs procedures are administered by Centre de Renseignements des Dounas (French Customs).
- **Tariffs** France abides by the tariff rates of the European Union (EU). The duties levied on imports from non-EU countries are moderate. Most raw materials enter duty-free or at low rates, while most manufactured goods are subject to rates of between five and 17 percent. Rates on agricultural goods may vary to equalize the prices of imported and domestic goods, and to not affect domestic productions. Tariff preferences are extended to over 100 developing countries under the Generalized System of Preferences (GSP).
- **Internal taxes** In addition to tariff duties, a value-added tax (VAT) is levied on many imported goods. The standard VAT is 18.6 percent. A reduced rate of 5.5 percent applies mostly to agricultural products, original artworks, and certain medicines.
- **Import restrictions** Products subject to restrictive regulations at this time include poultry, meat; enriched flour, genetic material, "exotic meats" such as buffalo or alligator, crayfish, several fruits, and many vegetables.
- **Export controls** Export controls are applied to strategic products and antiques.

FREIGHT FORWARDERS

Consortium Europeen de Transports Maritimes Cetramar
87, ave de la Grande Armee
75782 Paris Cedex 16
Tel: 1-40-66-11-11
Fax: 1-45-00-23-97
Telex: 611234

Danzas Satem
15, rue de Nancy
75010 Paris
Tel: 1-42-03-99-60
Fax: 1-42-03-98-26

Kuhne & Nagel
Gare Routiere Sogaris 169
94564 Rungis Cedex
Tel: 1-49-79-87-87
Fax: 1-46-86-84-78

Mory-Overseas
21, quai de la Citadelle
BP 4190
59378 Dunkerque Cedex 1
Tel: 3-28-63-19-00
Fax: 3-28-66-02-55

Compagnie Générale Maritime et Financiare
22, quai Galliéni
92158 Suresnes Cedex
Tel: 1-46-25-70-00
Telex: 630387

Compagnie Nationale de Navigation
50, blvd Haussmann
75009 Paris
Tel: 1-42-85-19-00
Fax: 1-42-81-20-37

Navale Delmas International
Tour Delmas-Vieljeux
31-32, quai de Dion-Bouton
92811 Puteaux Cedex
Tel: 1-46-96-44-33
Fax: 1-46-96-40-74

Sealink Voyages
23, rue Louis le Grand
75002 Paris
Tel: 1-47-42-86-87
Fax: 1-42-65-10-17
Telex: 281710

Total Transport Maritime
Tour Aurore
18, place des Reflets
92080 Paris La Defense
Tel: 1-47-78-52-00
Fax: 1-47-78-59-99
Telex: 616258

Overview

France is heavily oriented toward, and dependent on, international trade. The French market is highly sophisticated. Restrictions on doing business in France are minimal, centering on broadcast restrictions of non-European films and programs, and limitations on the provision of professional services by non-French practitioners. Intense competition is a characteristic of virtually every area of the coveted French market. Not only can it be lucrative in and of itself, but it also can confer an imprimatur on products accepted by the French, who are often international taste-setters and among the most demanding of consumers. Despite the predatory nature of business here, foreign suppliers can prosper by focusing on innovative products, new design, outstanding service, and a keen eye for comparative advantage.

Distribution

Many distribution options are available to the importer. France's distribution network increasingly resembles that of other developed Western nations, ranging from behemoth department store chains to small individual proprietorships. Previously, the majority of transactions were handled through small outlets; however, the trend has been toward bigger, more specialized operations. An extensive network of transportation and distribution channels assures consumers they will receive products in good condition and in a timely fashion. Frequent strikes by dockworkers, truck drivers, or other segments of the labor force occasionally disrupt this process, but alternative channels are readily available, and the days of labor being able to hamstring distribution in order to achieve its demands are largely past. Hypermarkets, a recent development, are self-service retail stores carrying tens of thousands of food and non-food articles at competitive prices. They are generally located in huge warehouses in the suburbs. The number of such outlets is now approaching 1,000, and their number and influence continues to grow.

Agents, Distributors, and Partners

French buyers prefer to purchase through a local distributor, agent, or salaried representative, and direct sales arrangements are infrequent. A distributor—or concessionaire—purchases goods for resale directly from a producer. The distributor operates independently and is bound only by the specific terms of the distribution agreement. An agent brings buyers and sellers together for a commission. Agents are free to act on behalf of any firm, although they need the principal's consent to represent a direct competitor. Agents exercise their sales activity in an independent manner and their principals usually are exempt from payment of incidental costs. Agents with a written contract have the status of commercial agents if they exercise their activity as a continuing independent profession. A salaried representative acts as an employee. Establishing a business presence in France requires considerable advance planning; an attorney versed in French business practice should be involved in the decision making as well as in the drafting of all agreements.

Selling Techniques

A wide variety of techniques are used for marketing goods in France. Expensive, technically sophisticated goods are frequently sold directly to the end-user, although most French buyers prefer to purchase through a local intermediary. Capital equipment is generally sold by commission agents. Specialty goods, consumer goods, and engineering products are principally sold through importers and distributors who purchase on their own account. Consumer products may be sold to department and chain stores through their own buying offices, some of which are maintained in overseas production locales. Selling this way is an excellent means of introducing items to the French market, especially because smaller retailers often follow their lead and add the same items to their stocks. On rare occasions, sales may be made directly to some specialty stores.

Advertising

Judicious use of the media is an important part of any promotional program. The French are voracious readers and avid television viewers, and efforts should usually be concentrated on print and broadcast media. France has numerous newspapers, magazines, and technical journals. Locating a reputable advertising agency, many of which are experienced in handling the needs of foreign firms, will help foreign sellers navigate the bewildering maze of possibilities and achieve the optimal exposure at the most reasonable cost.

Service and Customer Support

Trends change rapidly, making many items quickly obsolete, and France is becoming a "throwaway" society. French buyers nevertheless continue to rely on after-sales service and support as a major factor in deciding which products to purchase. Because of this, a well-developed local support system is critical in selling a wide variety of products.

Marketing in France
MARKETING TIPS

Retail outlets Paris has the most department stores of any French city, with nine of the 10 top-selling stores being located there.

Language Not only are foreign businesspeople expected to use French, legislation is under consideration that would require French as the exclusive language for all marketing and product information materials.

Price quotations Prices should be quoted in francs.

Terms of payment Most business is accomplished in Bills of Exchange. Delivery of shipping documents is normally given against acceptance of 30-, 60-, or 90-day bills.

Delivery dates French buyers expect a delivery date given by a supplier of goods to be honored.

Debt collection One or two reputable agencies undertake the collection of debts, but only on behalf of their subscribers. It is more usual to entrust this kind of work to a lawyer qualified to practice in France.

AD AGENCIES

McCann-Erickson France
48, rue de Villers
92309 Levallois-Perret Cedex
Tel: 1-47-59-34-56
Fax: 1-47480757

J. Walter Thompson S.A.
35, rue Baudin
92593 Levallois-Perret Cedex
Tel: 1-41-05-80-00
Fax: 1-41-05-80-01

MARKET RESEARCH AND CONSULTING FIRMS

A.C. Nielsen
44, boulevard de Grenelle
75732 Paris Cedex 15
Tel: 1-40-58-40-00
Fax: 1-45-79-13-31

Adege
45, boulevard Brotteaux
69006 Lyon
Tel: 4-72-74-44-57
Fax: 4-72-74-23-57

Arthur D. Little France
230, rue du Faubourg Saint Honoré
75008 Paris
Tel: 1-45-63-14-59
Fax: 1-42-89-03-02

Aviso Conseil
11, quai Rambaud
69002 Lyon
Tel: 4-78-37-52-71
Fax: 4-78-42-16-10

Burke Marketing Research
Tour Gallieni 1
7880, avenue Gallieni
93174 Bagnolet Cedex
Tel: 1-43-60-20-40
Fax: 1-43-60-72-93

Brulé Ville Associates
191, avenue du General Leclerc
78200 Viroflay
Tel: 1-30-84-88-00
Fax: 1-30-84-88-01

Catherine Delannoy & Associates
21, rue de Miromesnil
75008 Paris
Tel: 1-42-65-27-42
Fax: 1-47-42-25-89

CEGOS
Tour Chenonceaux
204, Rond Point de pont de Sèvres
92516 Boulogne Billancourt Cedex
Tel: 1-46-20-63-03
Fax: 1-46-20-88-60

E.S.O.P.
92, avenue d'Ivry
75013 Paris
Tel: 1-45-80-50-60
Fax: 1-45-85-24-93

Business Culture

Greetings and Courtesies

As well as demonstrating high levels of pride in their culture, heritage, and country, the French take a special pride in their language. It is a boon to the foreign businessperson to be fluent in French. However, an apology for not being familiar with their language will smooth the path to a relationship with your French associates. The customary greeting includes *Monsieur* (Mr.), *Madame* (Mrs.), or *Mademoiselle* (Miss), followed by the last name. Do not use first names unless invited to do so. Appropriate titles such as Doctor and Professor should be honored. Common salutations are "*Bonjour*" (Hello), and "*Comment allez-vous*?" (How are you?). Always use the *vous* form, not the *tu* form, in addressing business colleagues. Shake hands with everyone during introductions and again when taking leave. Normally, one waits for the woman to extend her hand. However, in large groups where several introductions are going on, it is not a fall from grace should a man first extend his hand to a woman. The French handshake is a light grip and one shake; avoid arm-pumping firmness as it is considered an uncultured gesture in France. Though the exchange of business gifts is not a general practice, gifts that appeal to the intellect or the aesthetics are well-received. Avoid gifts with large, prominent stamps of your company name. The French tend to exercise formality; they are very private people who adhere to tradition and revere a bit of ceremony. While an invitation into a French colleague's home is rare, the visitor who wants to demonstrate French "etiquette" will appreciate the following: send flowers in advance; bring chocolates or a gift to the hostess; and send a thank you note the very next day.

Business Ethic and Framework

Generally speaking, the business community is one of conservative formality. Cold calls are useless and appointments are necessary. Third party introductions are most helpful but a letter of self-introduction can initiate an eventual meeting, provided the business you propose is worthy of French time and attention. An important ingredient of self-introductions is offering substantial amounts of information regarding you, your firm, and the business you propose. Proper use of the language and good grammar are essential. Business cards and documents should be provided in French. Meetings are best scheduled between 10 am and noon, or after 3 pm. If a meeting extends into the lunch hour, use this time to get acquainted and delay business talk until dessert is served. French traditions of formality do not necessarily mean business without pleasurable conversation.

Decision Making

Patience is required here. There is a hierarchy in place often involving a cumbersome bureaucracy, and few managing executives are inclined to cross boundaries or speed up the process. Extensive labor laws and a complex system of social benefits and protections encourage French caution and impede the decision-making process. Additionally, the French have an inordinate amount of interest in details and foreign venturors should be prepared to linger over details with their French colleagues.

Women

French women have yet to realize their numbers in the higher levels of corporate management where age-old patriarchal customs still reign. However, women's presence is substantial in traditional occupations from secretarial to mid-management work. Additionally, they are highly regarded for their entrepreneurial achievements as well as their contributions in academics, education, and the arts.

Meetings

As in many European countries, punctuality is very important. The French tend to be very diplomatic, reserved, sober, and discreet. A foreign representative's program should be well-presented, formal, logical, comprehensive, and intelligent; and, speakers will want to be well-prepared to field detailed questions. It is important to know in advance if French is the only language of the firm. To assume that English or your native language will be spoken is a grave mistake when dealing with the French business community.

Business Attire

Dress is conservative: dark suits and ties. Sports jackets and ties are not uncommon in the South. Women also dress conservatively in suits, or classic coordinates of subdued colors. Slacks are never worn by women in the French business arena; business suits are considered the norm.

Cultural Cautions

DO'S

- Always use a handkerchief or tissue when sneezing, and be as discreet as possible when you blow your nose in public.
- Anticipate lively debates, arguments, criticism, and controversy over subjects such as California wine vs. French, why soccer is superior to football, etc. The French love a good conversation, and more so if you conduct yourself intelligently.
- Find ways to yield in these debates if there is any suggestion that the conversation has turned hostile to avoid being in a potentially difficult situation.
- Keep your hands above the table at all times when dining.
- Share in appreciation for the French educational system.

DON'TS

- When sending flowers for a social occasion, avoid roses and chrysanthemums.
- Slapping an open palm over a closed fist is considered vulgar. Avoid the gesture.
- Do not take wine to your host or hostess unless you're sure of its quality. Many French people are wine connoisseurs and are excessively proud of their French vintages.
- Never cut your salad. Fold lettuce into bite size pieces with your fork.
- Avoid personal questions, politics, and money in conversations. Good topics of discussion are culture, food, and sports.

CUSTOMS

- The French are class conscious. They tend to measure success by level of education achieved, school attended, family name and reputation, and financial status. Manners, dress, and all modes of social behavior count in their assessment of an individual. Excellence in the French language is a mark of achievement and the French are as quick to judge their own countrymen as they are foreigners who fail to manage the language adequately.
- In France, workers believe that there is more to life than their jobs. People work hard but there is no appreciation for those who are all work and no play. Weekends are for family, culture, and relaxation. Vacations are a sacred part of working conditions and are commonly four weeks long in summer—usually during August; some shops close down for the month. Another week is taken off during the Christmas season and New Year.
- France is a world leader in fashion and Paris often sets the pace for European fashion tastes. It is important to be clean and well-dressed in public, and to avoid casual attire when going into town or out to public establishments.
- A large portion of family income is spent on food, for the French consider cooking an art. French cuisine is popular all over the world.

OBSERVATIONS

- The French are patriotic and extremely proud of their culture, heritage, and nation. They are very private people and even a casual inquiry of a personal nature may be felt as inappropriate and intrusive. "Secrecy in business" is a common French sentiment and, again, even casual inquiries during dinner conversation may foster suspicion in your French colleagues.
- Paris, having traditionally dominated French attitudes, is not known for its congeniality to foreigners. However, people outside of Paris are likely to be more hospitable.

NEGOTIATIONS

- Prepare for a bit of a process. The French do not like to be rushed and are known to deliberate matters long and hard. Their fascination for details is likely to impede progress. However, they are not ambiguous in the final outcome and whether negotiations conclude favorably or not, you will clearly understand what happened and why.

Legal

Legal System

France is a civil code country, with laws substantially influenced by European regulations.

Intellectual Property Rights

Since 1994, France has increased protection against infringements of intellectual property rights by applying stricter criminal penalties, by increasing civil damages, and by extending the power of customs.

Patents Prior to any application, the applicant must justify the novelty of his invention, and show that his invention stems from his inventive activities and that it has an industrial application. Patent applications must be filed with the INPI (Institut National de la Propriété Industrielle) which delivers (usually after an 18-month period) a patent registration. The holder of such a patent is entitled to an exclusive right of exploitation of his invention for a 20-year period. Under French law, once the patent has been issued, the patent holder rights are protected against any infringement, known as counterfeit. A person found guilty of counterfeit may be liable to pay financial damages as well as be subject to criminal penalties.

As a party to the Paris Union Convention, France must guarantee to any citizen of a signatory state the following rights: priority to register patents within a 12-month period from the first date of application; and application under the same conditions laid down for French nationals.

Copyrights Copyrights are governed by a 1957 law which provides a 50-year protection for a registered author. Under articles 1 and 3 of the 1957 law, an intellectual creation consists in an original expression of thought, expression, or feeling. French law distinguishes two categories of rights: moral rights which are perpetual, unlimited, and not transferable; and commercial rights which are protected during the authors' lives and 50 years after their death. Such rights may be sold through a license. In 1994, France enacted a specific law to protect software infringements in accordance with EU regulations.

Trademarks To benefit from protection under French law, the trademark must be registered with the National Register of Trademarks and published in the official journal of Industrial Property. To file an application, foreigners must be domiciled in France. Once the trademark is registered, the holder has the right to an exclusive use of the mark for 10 years.

Business Registration

Foreign business in France has been encouraged by the government authorities since the 1990s. Direct investments over Fr 50 million which do not originate from EU member states and are made in companies whose annual turnover is over Fr500 million require prior authorization from the Treasury Department. Direct investments, less than Fr 50 million which do not originate from EU member states and are made in companies whose annual turnover is less than Fr500 million require only a declaration to the Treasury Department. Direct investments which originate from EU member states require only a declaration to the Treasury Department. Foreigners may purchase shares in a French company, establish a branch in France, or establish a subsidiary in France.

Contracts and Dispute Resolution

French commercial contracts and disputes are determined by the Commercial Court, whose judges are merchants and not professional judges. Articles 1442 to 1507 of the French Civil Procedure Code deal specifically with arbitration proceedings, and French law distinguishes domestic arbitration from international arbitration, though both are recognized and accepted.

Notaries

French notaries are specialized legal professionals with a state-granted monopoly over the drafting of certain documents and deeds, especially concerning real estate. These documents bear strong legal presumption of validity as opposed to the *"actes sous seing privé"* which are established privately, without any formality between the parties concerned.

Labor

The right to associate fully in unions and the right to strike are constitutional rights. French labor law is extremely detailed and is very protective of the labor force. The dismissal of an employee is difficult and is subject to many regulations. In general, an employer cannot dismiss an employee without a good and justified reason, and without compensating him or her. There is also a special jurisdiction, the "Conseil de Prud'homme," handling disputes arising from execution of a labor contract between employers and employees. This court consists of non-professional judges.

In 1950, France established a minimum wage below which no labor contract may be concluded. Minimum wage levels in recent years have generally been sufficient to support a family of four.

Source: Rambaud Martel, Paris

Legal Matters

LEGAL BRIEFS

- **Corporations** The two most popular entities in France are: limited liability companies known as "Société à Responsbilité Limitée (SARL)" and "Sociétés Anonymes."
- **Workweek** The legal number of work hours is 39 per week.
- **Legal protection** Legal protection is well-covered in France. Any person within a minimum income range may benefit from special "free judicial help" performed by lawyers.
- **Acquisition of property** An alien may easily acquire real estate property in France and many foreigners have taken advantage of this opportunity for business and pleasure.
- **Trade agreements** France is a member of the European Union, formerly known as the EEC. France has been a member of GATT since 1945, and is now a full member of the World Trade Organization.

LEGAL CONTACTS

Rambaud Martel
25 Boulevard de l'Amiral Bruix
75116 Paris
Tel: 1-40-67-17-00
Fax: 1-45-01-26-73

Clifford Chance
112, avenue Kléber
BP 163 Trocadéro
75770 Paris Cedex 16
Tel: 1-44-05-52-52
Fax: 1-44-05-52-00

Barreau de Paris
Rue Pierre l'Escot
75001 Paris

Baker & McKenzie
67-69, avenue Victor Hugo
75783 Paris Cedex 16
Tel: 1-45-01-57-70
Fax: 1-45-00-82-67

Adler Jolibois & Associes
26, boulevard Raspail
75007 Paris
Tel: 1-45-44-10-33
Fax: 1-45-48-80-27

Baker & McKenzie
32, avenue Kleber
75116 Paris
Tel: 1-44-17-53-00
Fax: 1-44-17-45-75

Casanova & Associes
250 BIS, Boulevard St. Germain
75341 Paris Cedex 07
Tel: 1-44-39-89-89

Freshfields
69, boulevard Haussmann
75008 Paris
Tel: 1-44-56-44-56
Fax: 1-44-56-44-00

Gide Loyrette Nouel
26, Cours Albert 1er
75008 Paris
Tel: 1-40-75-60-00

HSD Ernst & Young
Tour Manhattan, 6, Place de l'Iris
92095 Paris La Defense 2
Tel: 1-46-93-70-00
Fax: 1-47-67-01-06

Michel Normand, Francois Sarda et Associes
37, rue Galilee
75116 Paris
Tel: 1-47-20-30-01
Fax: 1-47-20-06-01

Shubert & Dusausoy
190, boulevard Haussmann
75008 Paris
Tel: 1-40-76-01-43

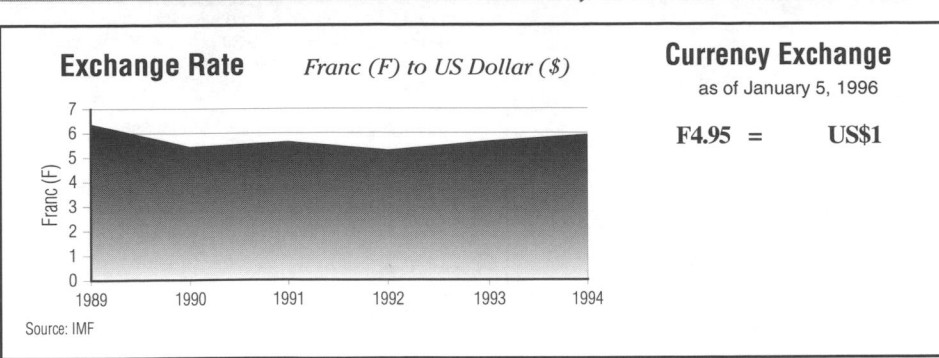

Exchange Rate — *Franc (F) to US Dollar ($)*

Franc (F)

1989 1990 1991 1992 1993 1994

Source: IMF

Currency Exchange

as of January 5, 1996

F4.95 = US$1

Currency

The currency in use is the franc (F or Fr), which is divided into 100 centimes.

Foreign Exchange

French exchange control regulations have been relaxed since 1990. Both French and foreign citizens are subject to the same foreign exchange rules, and may open foreign currency accounts in France and abroad. France maintains spot exchange rates between the franc and currencies of other countries participating in the European Monetary System. The Bank of France will buy or sell currencies of the participating countries in unlimited amounts at specified intervention rates. France and other EMS countries do not maintain exchange rates for other currencies within fixed limits, but may intervene occasionally to smooth out erratic fluctuations.

There are no taxes on purchases or sales of foreign exchange. Registered banks in France and Monaco may deal spot or forward in the French exchange market. Nonbank residents may purchase foreign exchange forward in respect of specified transactions. Any resident may purchase or sell foreign exchange forward without restriction, regardless of whether it is for hedging purposes.

Capital Transfers

Capital may be repatriated without restriction, but must be reported to the Ministry of Economy within 20 days of its occurrence.

Investment Incentives

France's investment promotion agency, DATAR, provides assistance to investors in France and through various agencies around the world. The government also grants investors full or partial holidays on local taxes.

Investment Restrictions

Despite the government's pro-investment rhetoric, many foreign investors have faced interference from government officials. The French system historically has maintained some level of control over the private sector. Resident enterprises may hold foreign currency accounts in France or abroad. Any resident may hold an ECU-denominated account in France, a foreign currency account in France or abroad, and franc accounts abroad.

Money Matters

BITS AND PIECES

Economic stability The government of France works to maintain the stability and strength of the franc within the European Monetary System through policy, monetary discipline, and regulatory control.

Banking system The French banking system underwent fundamental restructuring in 1984. Some French commercial banks are the largest banks in the world, and offer all classic financing instruments. France also has more than 170 foreign banks, some with large branch networks. The Bank of France is both a central bank and an issuing bank.

Repatriation There are no restrictions on repatriation of capital, although it must be executed through an authorized bank. There are also no restrictions on transfer of profits, interest, royalties, or service fees.

Stock market The Paris stock exchange is the center of the French stock market. There are also six provincial exchanges. An options exchange, the "Marche des Options Negociables de Paris" also trades a limited number shares of larger companies.

Resident and nonresident accounts Resident enterprises may hold foreign currency accounts in France or abroad, and may also hold franc accounts abroad. Any resident may hold an ECU-denominated account in France, a foreign currency account in France or abroad, and franc accounts abroad. Nonresident franc accounts may be opened and operated freely, and nonresidents may also hold foreign currency accounts in a French bank.

BANKS

Banque Francaise du Commerce Exterieur
21, boulevard Haussman BP 265-09
75427 Paris Cedex 09
Tel: 1-48-00-48-00
Fax: 1-45-23-10-56

Banque Nationale de Paris
16, boulevard des Italiens
75450 Paris Cedex 09
Tel: 1-40-14-45-46
Fax: 1-40-14-69-73

Banque Paribas
5, rue d'Antin
75002 Paris
Tel: 1-42-98-12-34
Fax: 1-42-98-11-42

Compagnie Bancaire
5, avenue Kléber
75116 Paris
Tel: 1-45-25-25-25
Fax: 1-45-01-78-05

Credit Commercial de France
103, avenue des Champs-Elysées
75008 Paris
Tel: 1-40-70-70-40
Fax: 1-47-23-71-04

Banque de France
39, rue Croix-des-Petits-Champs
75001 Paris
Tel: 1-42-92-42-92
Fax: 1-42-96-04-23

Société Générale
29, Boulevard Haussmann
75009 Paris
Tel: 1-40-98-20-00
Fax: 1-40-98-27-01

Banque de France
39, rue Croix-des-Petits-Champs
75001 Paris
Tel: 1-42-92-42-92
Fax: 1-42-96-04-23

STOCK EXCHANGE

Bourse de Paris
4, place de La Bourse
75080 Paris Cedex 02

TAXATION

Taxation requires sophisticated knowledge of complex rules and regulations specific to each country. For more detailed information we suggest you refer to the Ernst & Young Corporate Tax Guide and Directory, available from the Ernst & Young accounting office in your country, or from:

HSD Ernst & Young
Societe d'Avocats
Tour Manhattan
Cedex 21
92095 Paris La Defense 2
France
Tel: 1-46 93 70 00
Fax: 1-47 67 01 06

- French law generally does not allow foreign tax credits; income subject to foreign tax is taxable net of the foreign tax paid. However, most treaties provide a tax credit that corresponds to withholding taxes on passive income.

At a Glance

Corporate Income Tax Rate (%)	33.3
Capital Gains Tax Rate (%)(a)	19 or 33.3
Branch Tax Rate (%)	33.3
Withholding Tax (%)(b)	
Dividends	25
Interest (c)	15
Royalties from Patents, Know-how, etc.	33.3
Branch Remittance Tax	25
Net Operating Losses (Years)	
Carryback	3
Carryforward	5

(a) Long-term capital gains, those held for two years or more, are taxed at 19%, except that capital gains from the sale of bonds, equity loans, mutual fund shares, and equities are taxed at 33.3%. Short-term capital gains are taxed at the regular 33.3% rate.
(b) Taxes are calculated before application of international tax treaties.
(c) In general, withholding tax is not imposed on interest paid to nonresidents on certain loans. However, this exemption does not apply to loans from shareholders.

Business Travel

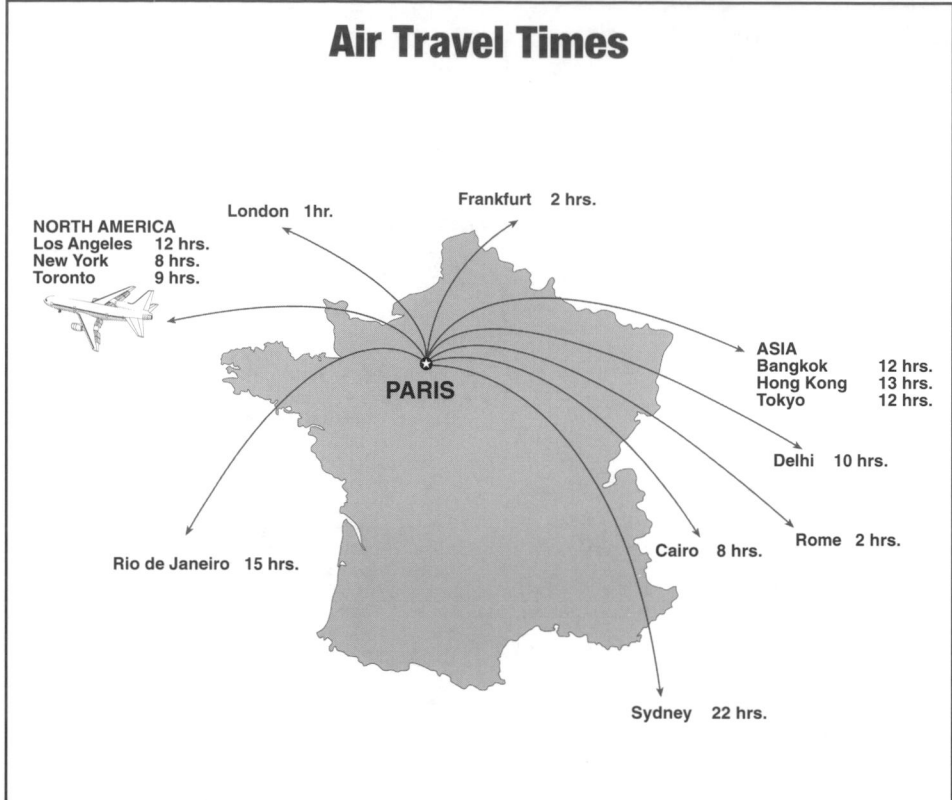

Air Travel Times

NORTH AMERICA
Los Angeles 12 hrs.
New York 8 hrs.
Toronto 9 hrs.

London 1hr.

Frankfurt 2 hrs.

PARIS

ASIA
Bangkok 12 hrs.
Hong Kong 13 hrs.
Tokyo 12 hrs.

Delhi 10 hrs.

Rome 2 hrs.

Cairo 8 hrs.

Rio de Janeiro 15 hrs.

Sydney 22 hrs.

COMMUNICATIONS

Telephones Telephone service in France is modern and efficient. Most countries can be dialed directly. A phone card *(telecarte)* can be purchased at tobacco shops, post offices, and subway stations for use on most public phones.

Fax Fax machines are available at central post offices and most major hotels.

Post office Once notoriously slow, French postal service is efficient and timely. Post offices are generally open weekdays from 8:00 am to 7:00 pm and until noon on Saturdays. In addition, one post office in each district stays open until 11:00 am on Sundays and holidays. Stamps can also be purchased from tobacco stores and hotels. Post offices are marked Postes et Telecommunications and display a stylized blue bird.

BEST TRAVEL BOOKS

Fodor's Travel Guide, France.

Fodor's Exploring Guide, France. Tourist oriented, excellent source of city details.

Culture Shock, A Guide to Customs and Etiquette, France.

France, Travel Survival Kit, Lonely Planet. To give travelers expert, in depth, off the beaten track coverage of this marvelous country.

Fodor's Europe, Best of 31 Countries. Contains information on historical towns, great culture, scenic coastal countryside.

Do's and Taboo's Around the World. The Bestselling Guide to International Behavior. Edited by Roger Axtell, compiled by the Parker Pen Company. The ultimate guide to international behavior, now completely updated and expanded. Helpful, fun to read!

Berlitz Business Travel Guide, Europe. Concise economic details, successful trip planning, background information on people and cities, useful facts and addresses.

USEFUL TELEPHONE NUMBERS

If you are calling from outside France, you will need to add the country code [33] and any other international dialing requirements from within your country.

- Medical Team and Ambulance (SAMU) 15
- Police 17
- Fire Department 18
- Local Telephone Directory Assistance 12
- Computer Rentals 1-42-00-70-01
- Secretarial Services 1-46-22-98-98
- Avis De Gaulle 1-48-62-34-34
- Europcar Orly 1-49-75-47-47
- Hertz De Gaulle................................1-48-62-29-00
- Hertz Orly 1-49-75-37-52
- Thrifty De Gaulle 1-34-29-90-50

Airlines
- Air France Paris 1-42-27-98-01
- Air France Lyon 4-78-52-80-45
- Air UK..1-49-27-98-01
- American Airlines 1-42-89-05-22
- British Airways.................................1-47-78-14-14
- British Midland.................................1-47-42-30-62
- Continental Airlines 1-42-25-31-81
- Delta Airlines 1-47-68-92-92
- Northwest Airlines 1-42-66-90-00
- TWA 1-47-20-62-11

Credit Card Information
Lost or stolen credit cards (call collect to the US, regardless of which country the card was issued in).
- Amex ....[1] (919) 333-3211
- Diner's Club................................[1] (303) 799-1504
- MasterCard ....[1] (314) 275-6690
- Visa ....[1] (410) 581-7931

Travelogue

WORKWEEK

Offices Monday-Friday 9:00 am to 6:00 pm.
Banks Monday-Friday 9:00 am to 4:30 pm, closed at noon on days before a legal holiday.
Government Monday-Friday 9:00 am to noon and 2:00 pm to 6:00 pm.
Retail Stores are generally open Monday-Saturday by 9:00 am and closed by 6:30 pm.

Many businesses are closed during the month of August, when most French workers take vacation time. All public offices are closed on holidays.

HOLIDAYS

Holidays 1996
January 1 New Year's Day
April 8 Easter Monday*
May 1 Labor Day
May 8 Veterans' Day/WWII
May 16 Ascension Day
May 27 Pentecost
July 14 Bastille Day
August 15 Assumption Day
November 1 All Saints' Day
November 11 Armistice Day/WWI
December 25 Christmas
*Dates vary each year.

VISA AND PASSPORT

Visitors to France must have a valid passport, but a visa is not required for tourist or business stays of up to three months.

DEPARTURE FORMALITIES

Personal effects in luggage are normally not subject to customs duties or the 18 percent VAT. There are no restrictions on bringing in or taking out French or foreign currency, but amounts exceeding Fr50,000 or the equivalent must be declared.

IMMUNIZATION

No vaccinations are required of visitors from North America or Europe. Current immunizations against typhoid, paratyphoid, smallpox, tetanus, and polio are recommended. Influenza immunizations are suggested also.

TIPPING

Tips are included in the service charge normally added to restaurant bills. Small additional tips are sometimes left for particularly good service. Taxi drivers may be tipped 10 percent, but tipping is not obligatory.

CRIME

France has a relatively low rate of violent crime. Pickpocketing, theft of unattended baggage, and theft from rental cars or vehicles with out-of-town or foreign license plates is common. Criminals often operate around popular tourist attractions such as museums, monuments, restaurants, hotels, beaches, and on trains and subways. Muggings and purse snatching are common in tourist locations; many of these thieves are children. Keep an eye on personal belongings; valuables should be stored in hotel safes. Keep packages out of sight in automobiles.

INFRASTRUCTURE

France has excellent telecommunication, hotel, airline, bus, and rental car services. The French railway system is among the best in the world, and it ties in conveniently with public transportation in most cities. Taxis are inexpensive, but difficult to catch. Ordering one though your hotel porter is advisable. The Metro is clean, maps are easy to follow. There are thirteen subway lines and one commuter rail system, the Reseau Express Regional (RER), that crisscross the capital and suburbs.

NATIONAL TOURIST OFFICE

National Tourist Offices
127 av. des Champs-Elysees
75008 Paris
Tel: 1-47-23-61-72

GOVERNMENT AGENCIES

Premier ministre
57, rue de Varenne
75700 Paris
Tel: 1-42-75-80-00

Ministre de la Justice
13, place Vendôme
75042 Paris
Tel: 1-44-77-60-60

Ministre de l'économie, des finances et du plan
139, rue de Bercy
75572 Paris Cedex 12
Tel: 1-40-04-04-04

Ministre de l'éducation nationale, de l'enseignement supérieur, de la recherche et de l'insertion professionnelle
110, rue de Grenelle
75700 Paris
Tel: 1-49-55-10-10

Ministre de l'aménagement du territoire, de l'équipement et des transports
69, rue de Varenne
75700 Paris
Tel: 1-40-81-21-22

Ministre des affaires étrangères
37, quai d'Orsay
75351 Paris Cedex 07
Tel: 1-43-17-53-53

Ministre de la défense
14, rue Saint-Dominique
75700 Paris
Tel: 1-42-19-30-11

Ministre de l'intérieur
Place Beauvau
75800 Paris
Tel: 1-49-27-49-27

Ministre des relations avec le Parlement
246, bd Saint-Germain
75700 Paris
Tel: 1-40-81-21-22

Ministre du travail, du dialogue social et de la participation
127, rue de Grenelle
75700 Paris
Tel: 1-40-56-60-00

Ministre de la culture
3, rue de Valois
75044 Paris Cedex 01
Tel: 1-40-15-80-00

Ministre de la réforme de l'Etat, de la décentralisation et de la citoyenneté
1 bis, place des Saussaies
75800 Paris
Tel: 1-49-27-49-27

Ministre de la fonction publique
32, rue de Babylone
75700 Paris
Tel: 1-42-75-80-00

Ministre de la santé publique et de l'assurance maladie
8, avenue de Ségur
75700 Paris
Tel: 1-40-56-60-00

Ministre de l'agriculture, de la pêche et de l'alimentation
78, rue de Varenne
75700 Paris
Tel: 1-49-55-49-55

Ministre de l'Industrie
101, rue de Grenelle
75700 Paris
Tel: 1-43-19-36-36

Ministre du logement
Grande Arche - La Défense
40, passage de l'Arche - Plot H
92055 Paris - La Défense Cedex 04
Tel: 1-40-81-21-22

Ministre des petites et moyennes entreprises, du commerce et de l'artisanat
80, rue de Lille
75700 Paris
Tel: 1-43-19-24-24

Ministre des technologies de l'information et de la Poste
20, avenue de Ségur
75700 Paris
Tel: 1-43-19-20-20

Ministre de l'outre-mer
27, rue Oudinot
75358 Paris 07 SP
Tel: 1-47-83-01-23

Ministre de l'environnement
20, avenue de Ségur
75302 Paris 07 SP
Tel: 1-42-19-20-21

Ministre de la jeunesse et des sports
78, rue Olivier de Serres
75015 Paris
Tel: 1-40-45-90-00

Ministre du tourisme
3, place de Fontenoy
75007 Paris
Tel: 1-44-49-80-00

Ministre délégué aux affaires européennes
37, quai d'Orsay
75351 Paris Cedex 07
Tel: 1-43-17-53-53

Secrétaire d'Etat pour l'emploi
40, rue du Bac
75700 Paris
Tel: 1-44-39-24-40

Secrétaire d'Etat aux transports
Arche de La Défense, Pilot sud
92055 Paris La Defense Cedex
Tel: 1-40-80-21-22

Secrétaire d'Etat aux quartiers en difficulté
8, avenue de Ségur
75700 Paris
Tel: 1-40-56-60-00

Secrétaire d'Etat au commerce extérieur
101, rue de Grenelle
75700 Paris
Tel: 1-43-19-36-36

WORLD TRADE CENTERS

Le Havre World Trade Center
BP 1000
76061 Le Havre Cedex
Tel: 2-35-21-43-41
Fax: 2-35-21-06-81

Mediterranean World Trade Center, Marseille/CMCI
CMCI-2 rue Henri Barbusse
13241 Marseille Cedex 01
Tel: 4-91-39-33-50
Fax: 4-91-39-33-60

World Trade Center Lyon/Lyon Commerce International
16, rue de la Republique
69289 Lyon Cedex 02
Tel: 4-72-40-57-52
Fax: 4-72-40-57-61

World Trade Center Grenoble
Place Robert Schuman - Europole
POB 1509
38025 Grenoble Cedex 1
Tel: 4-76-28-28-40
Fax: 4-76-28-28-35

World Trade Center Nantes
16, quai Ernest Renaud. BP 718
44027 Nantes Cedex 04
Tel: 4-40-44-60-91
Fax: 4-40-44-61-28, 44-63-80

World Trade Center Paris
Paris Chamber of Commerce Industry
2, place de la Defense

CNIT-BP 460
92053 Paris-La Defense
Tel: 1-46-92-25-80
Fax: 1-47-73-60-04

World Trade Center Strasbourg
MCIS-4, quai Kleber
67080 Strasbourg Cedex
Tel: 4-88-76-42-24
Fax: 4-88-76-42-00

BUSINESS AND TRADE ORGANIZATIONS

Appliance Manufacturers' Association
39, avenue d'Iéna
75783 Paris
Tel: 1-47-20-32-20
Fax: 1-47-20-20-73

Association of French Banks
18, rue Lafayette
75440 Paris Cedex 08
Tel: 1-48-00-52-52
Fax: 1-42-46-76-40

Automotive Equipment Industry Association
79, rue J.J. Rousseau
92150 Suresnes
Tel: 1-46-97-00-56
Fax: 1-46-97-00-80

Bakery Equipment Industry Association
13, rue Saint-Lazare
75009 Paris
Tel: 1-42-80-44-41
Fax: 1-42-85-29-00

Building Material, Components and Equipment Association
11, rue Hamelin
75783 Paris Cedex 16
Tel: 1-45-05-71-28

Business Gifts Professionals Union
34, boulevard Haussmann
75009 Paris
Tel: 1-48-01-48-01
Fax: 1-45-23-18-30

Cycle Manufacturers Association
79, rue J.J. Rousseau
92150 Suresnes
Tel: 1-46-97-00-56
Fax: 1-46-97-00-80

French Federation of Jewelry, Goldsmithing, Gifts, Diamonds, Gems, Pearls and Related Activities
58, rue du Louvre
75002 Paris
Tel: 1-42-33-61-33
Fax: 1-40-26-29-51

French Federation of Toy Industries
47, boulevard Berthier
BP 518
75825 Paris Cedex 17
Tel: 1-43-80-60-75
Fax: 1-42-27-82-72

French Fishing Equipment Industry Association
17, rue Arnoux
92340 Bourg-la-Reine
Tel: 1-40-91-03-24

French International Trade Association
31, avenue Pierre-1er-de-Serbie
75784 Paris Cedex 16
Tel: 1-40-69-44-43/5 04
Fax: 1-47-23-47-32

Food Product Industry Association
52, rue du Faubourg Saint-Honoré
75008 Paris
Tel: 1-42-66-40-14
Fax: 1-47-42-22-45

Importers' Association for Mechanics and
Electronics
25-27, rue d'Astorg
75008 Paris
Tel: 1-44-51-14-60
Fax: 1-42-65-39-49

National Union of Product Advertising
15, rue de Chateaudun
75009 Paris
Tel: 1-48-78-75-98
Fax: 1-45-26-25-39

National Association of Home Repair and Related
Hobbies
14, rue du 8 Mai 1945
75010 Paris
Tel: 1-40-35-34-30
Fax: 1-40-35-59-52

National Union of French Furniture Industries
28 bis, avenue Daumesnil
75012 Paris
Tel: 1-46-28-68-61
Fax: 1-43-45-04-04

National Wood Federation
1, place André Malaraux
75001 Paris
Tel: 1-42-60-58-94
Fax: 1-42-60-58-94

Nautical Industry Federation
Port de Javel-haut
75015 Paris
Tel: 1-45-77-79-79
Fax: 1-45-77-61-88

Optical Industry Association
39-41, rue Louis Blanc
Cedex 72
92038 Paris La Défense
Tel: 1-47-17-64-00
Fax: 1-47-17-63-98

Paints & Inks Industry Association
42, avenue Marceau
75008 Paris
Tel: 1-47-23-36-12
Fax: 1-47-20-90-30

Paper, Cardboard, Cellulose Industry Association
154, boulevard Haussmann
75008 Paris
Tel: 1-42-62-87-07
Fax: 1-45-62-82-47

Perfume Industry Association
57, avenue de Villiers
75017 Paris
Tel: 1-44-15-83-83
Fax: 1-42-12-01-37

Pharmaceutical Industry Association
88, rue de la Faisanderie
75782 Paris Cedex 16
Tel: 1-45-03-88-70
Fax: 1-45-03-34-25

Photographic and Video Equipment Industry
Association
5 bis, rue Jacquemont
75017 Paris
Tel: 1-46-27-47-29
Fax: 1-42-29-02-22

Printing and Graphic Arts Federation
115, boulevard Saint-Germain
75006 Paris
Tel: 1-46-34-21-15
Fax: 1-46-33-73-34

Sporting Good Industry Association
3/5, rue Jules Guesde
92305 Levallois-Perret
Tel: 1-47-31-56-23
Fax: 1-47-31-56-32

Stationery and Office Products Association
9 ter, rue Auguste-Barbier
75011 Paris
Tel: 1-43-57-63-13
Fax: 1-43-57-81-41

Telecommunication Industry Union
64, rue de Monceau
75008 Paris
Tel: 1-45-63-96-44
Fax: 1-45-62-05-14

Textile Industry Union
37-39, rue de Neuilly
92110 Clichy
Tel: 1-47-56-31-21
Fax: 1-47-30-25-28

Union of Plastic and Rubber Industry Distributors
1, square La Bruyère
75009 Paris
Tel: 1-42-82-10-22
Fax: 1-42-80-55-45

Veterinarian Drug Industry Association
6, rue de la Trémoille
75008 Paris
Tel: 1-47-23-94-20
Fax: 1-40-70-00-13

CHAMBERS OF COMMERCE

American Chamber of Commerce
21, avenue Georges V
75008 Paris
Tel: 1-47-23-80-26
Fax: 1-47-20-18-62

French Chamber of Commerce
7, rue Jean Goujon
75008 Paris
Tel: 1-42-56-05-00
Fax: 1-43-59-50-15

Chamber of Commerce and Industry of Paris
2, rue de Viarmes
75001 Paris
Tel: (1) 45-08-36-0
Fax: (1) 45-08-35-80

Assemblee des Chambres Francaises de
Commerce et d'Industrie
45, avenue d'Iéna
BP 448 16
75769 Paris Cedex 16
Tel: 1 40 69 37 00
Fax: 1 47 20 61 28

BUSINESS PERIODICALS

Annales-Economies, sociétés, civilisations (Every
2 months)
54, boulevard Raspail
75006 Paris
Tel: 1-49-54-23-75

L'Expansion (Every 2 weeks)
25, rue Leblanc
75015 Paris
Tel: 1-47-63-12-11
Telex: 650242

Revue Economique (Every 2 months)
54, Boulevard Raspail
75006 Paris
Tel: 1-49-54-25-65

Science et Vie Economie (Monthly)
1 rue du Colonel Pierre Avia
75015 Paris
Tel: 1-46-48-48-48
Fax: 1-46-48-48-09

Valeurs Actuelles (Weekly)
54, rue Martre
92586 Clichy Cedex
Tel: 1-49-68-18-18
Fax: 1-47-37-85-00

RADIO & TELEVISION STATIONS

Société France Media International
78, avenue Raymond Poincare
75116 Paris
Tel: 1-45-01-55-90
Fax: 1-45-01-28-39

Société Nationale de Radiodiffusion (Radio France)
116, avenue Président Kennedy
75786 Paris Cedex 16
Tel: 1-42-30-22-22
Fax: 1-42-30-14-88

Société Nationale de Télévision en Couleur--
France-2
22, avenue Montaigne
75387 Paris Cedex 08
Tel: 1-44-21-44-22
Telex: 642313

Société Nationale de Programmes--France-3
116, avenue du Président Kennedy
75790 Paris Cedex 16
Tel: 1-42-30-22-22
Telex: 630720

Télédiffusion de France, SA
21-27, rue Barbäs
92542 Montrouge Cedex
Tel: 1-46-57-11-15
Fax: 1-45-55-35-35

NEWSPAPERS

French Official Gazette - J.O.
26, rue Desaix
75727 Paris Cedex 15
Tel: 1-40-58-75-00
Fax: 1-40-58-77-80

Le Figaro
25, avenue Matignon
75398 Paris Cedex 08
Tel: 1-42-56-80-80
Fax: 1-42-21-64-05

International Herald Tribune
181, avenue Charles de Gaulle
92521 Neuilly-sur-Seine Cedex
Tel: 1-46-37-93-00
Fax: 1-46-37-21-33

Le Monde
7, rue des Italiens
75427 Paris Cedex
Tel: 1-42-47-97-27
Fax: 1-45-23-06-81

La Tribune de l'Economie
12, rue Béranger
75003 Paris
Tel: 1-48-04-99-99
Telex: 230735

L'Indépendent
4, rue Emmanuel Brousse
66844 Perpignan
Tel: 68-35-51-51
Fax: 68-34-10-46

INTERNET ADDRESSES

Usenet group(s):
clari.world.europe.france
soc.culture.french
fr.biz.produits
France - AdminNet
http://www.ensmp.fr/~scherer/adminet/
Lyon Capitale - Newspaper from Lyon, France
(French)
http://www.dtr.fr/lyoncap/
Webfoot's Guide to France
http://www.webfoot.com/travel/guides/france/
france.html
MINITEL in France
http://www.minitel.fr/English/Minitel/presentation.html
Paris Pages
http://www.paris.org/
FranceNet (French)
http://www.francenet.fr/franceweb/
FWCarnetRoute.html
Liste des serveurs W3 en France
http://web.urec.fr/docs/www_list-fr.html

Gabon

Gabonese Republic

Economy

Overview

With only a rudimentary industrial base and limited transportation infrastructure, Gabon is highly dependent on narrowly concentrated but substantial French interests dating back to its colonial period. Gabon's economy underwent an enormous shock during 1993 when this sub-Saharan nation devalued its currency by half in response to a combination of massive foreign debt and deceases in petroleum export revenues. This move doubled import prices, hurt domestic sales, and temporarily shifted the market away from its traditional suppliers and toward lower-priced goods from Spain, North Africa, and Asia. Despite the havoc of 1993—from which the economy is only slowly recovering—and the resulting unemployment levels in the 20 percent range, Gabon has one of the highest per capita incomes in Africa, even though this is based largely on the number of French expatriates within its borders.

Trade

Like many other developing countries, Gabon is currently in the midst of antiprotectionist reform efforts. Nonetheless, domestic companies still receive preferential treatment, especially in Gabon's limited manufacturing and agricultural sectors. The petroleum sector is largely unimpeded, however, given the country's dependence upon foreign partners to drive the industry. Exports include petroleum, manganese, timber, and uranium, which together account for more than 95 percent of all exports. Gabon imports virtually all its needs, including machinery, food, metals, and transportation equipment. France is still, by far, Gabon's most dominant trade partner, followed by the US, the UK, and the Netherlands.

Sectors

Agriculture The agricultural sector employs 66 percent of the work force, but produces less than 10 percent of GDP. Forestry is Gabon's third-largest industry and is expected to become increasingly profitable, due to internal administrative changes, a decrease in Southeast Asian competition, and continued price advantages associated with the currency devaluation of 1993. Most agriculture is subsistence based.

Industry By contrast, industry, employing only about 30 percent of the work force, contributes nearly half of GDP. Oil and related industries provide roughly 33 percent of GDP, 66 percent of government revenues, and nearly all exports. Most international petroleum trade is conducted with France and other European partners. Gabon has large reserves of manganese and uranium.

Services Although providing 40 percent of GDP, the service sector employs only about five percent of the work force. Most of this service sector is involved in trade support and personal services for the wealthy expatriate community. The rest of the service economy is poorly developed.

Trends

Despite one of the best telecommunications networks in Africa, limited transportation infrastructure will continue to pose a major obstacle. Gabon has fewer than 800 kms of paved roads, mostly located in its two primary cities. Growth is further hampered by comparatively high labor costs. Privately funded infrastructure projects, however, along with petroleum, mining, and telecommunications investments, offer solid opportunities and viable entry points to Gabonese commerce. The prognosis for forestry-related industry is also strong.

At a Glance

THE COUNTRY

Location Western Africa, bordering the Atlantic Ocean at the Equator between the Congo and Equatorial Guinea.
Terrain Narrow coastal plain; hilly interior; savannah in east and south.
Climate Tropical, always hot, usually very humid.

THE PEOPLE

Population 1,200,000
Ethnic composition Fang, Myene, Bapounou, Eschira, Bandjabi, Bateke/Obamba.
Religious composition Christian, Muslim, indigenous.
Languages spoken French (official), Fang, Meyene, Bateke, Bapounou/Eschira, Bandjabi.
Education and literacy Education is compulsory to age 16. Adult literacy rate is 70%.
Labor force
Total: 122,000
By occupation: agriculture 65%, industry and commerce 30%, services and government 5%.

COUNTRY FACTS

Political and legal Gabon operates as a republic, with a multiparty presidential regime. Its legal system is based primarily on the French civil law system and on customary law. The Constitutional Chamber of the Supreme Court has judicial review of legislative acts. The judiciary is predominantly independent of other branches of the government. Gabon has not accepted compulsory International Court of Justice jurisdiction.
Telephone Local and long-distance telephone service is available 24 hours a day and is moderately reliable. International telephone rates are expensive, and not available in most rural areas. International country code: [241]. City codes are not required, and all numbers are six digits.
Transportation Roadways connect virtually all major communities, but maintenance work is difficult because of heavy rainfall. The railway system is new and not yet fully developed, although the government continues work on it at a steady pace. There are three ports handling both freight and passengers. River transportation is used extensively, mostly to float logs. There are three international airports, and another 56 airports provide domestic service.
Environment Gabon's environmental problems include deforestation, pollution, and wildlife preservation. The forests that cover 85 percent of the country are threatened by excessive logging activities and business interests.
Media Gabon has just recently begun to receive color television broadcasts, although they are still limited to the major cities. The national press service for Gabon is the Gabonese Press Agency, which publishes a daily bulletin.
Health Most of Gabon's health services are public, but there are some private institutions as well. Gabon's medical structure is considered one of the best in West Africa. Over 90 percent of the population has access to medical care, and the vast majority of children have been immunized for a number of diseases. However, life expectancy remains at just 52 years for both males and females.

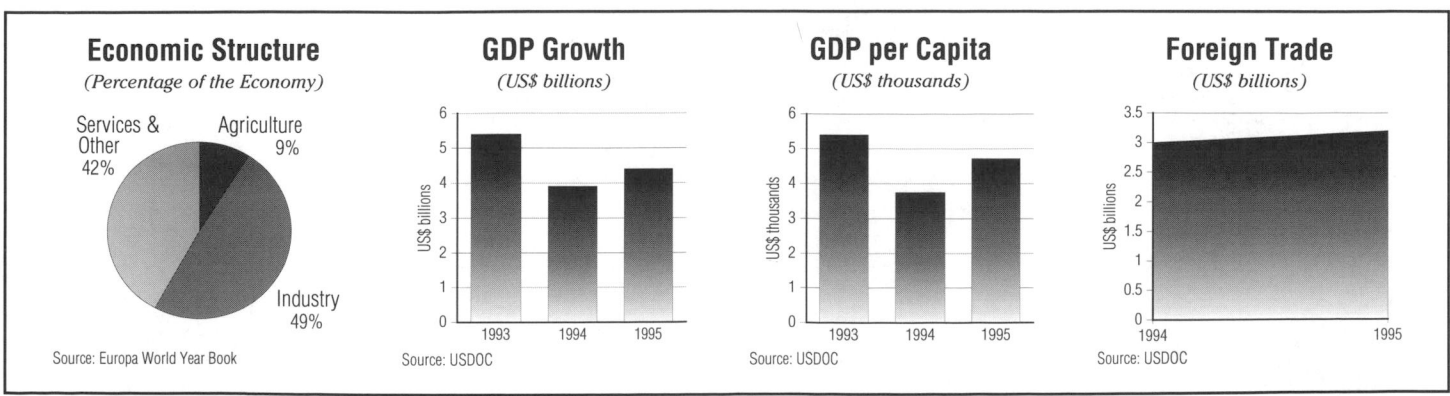

Economic Structure
(Percentage of the Economy)

Services & Other 42%
Agriculture 9%
Industry 49%

Source: Europa World Year Book

GDP Growth
(US$ billions)

1993, 1994, 1995

Source: USDOC

GDP per Capita
(US$ thousands)

1993, 1994, 1995

Source: USDOC

Foreign Trade
(US$ billions)

1994, 1995

Source: USDOC

Business Travel

••	LH 1906	MADRID	935	113-3
••	LH 1022	STUTTGART HBF.	935	-
••	AF 1701	LYON	940	683-6
••	AY 822	HELSINKI	940	113-3
••	AA 071	SFRANCISCO-DALLAS	945	731-7

Travelogue

WORKWEEK

Offices Monday-Saturday 8:00 am to noon and 3:00 pm to 6:00 pm.
Banks Monday-Friday 9:00 am to 3:00 pm.
Government Monday-Friday 9:30 am to noon and 3:30 pm to 5:30 pm.
Retail Monday-Saturday, 8:00 am to noon and 3:30 pm to 7:00 pm.

HOLIDAYS

Holidays 1996
January 1 New Year's Day
March The Last Day Of Ramadan**
April 7 Easter Sunday*
April 8 Easter Monday*
May 1 Labor Day
May 27 Pentecost Monday
July * Id-al-Adha**
August 15 Assumption
August 17 Independence Day
November 1 All Saints' Day
December 25 Christmas
*Dates vary each year.
**Dates are based on a lunar calendar and vary each year. The actual dates are sometimes not announced until shortly before the holiday itself.

VISA AND PASSPORT

Visitors to Gabon need a valid passport and a visa. Most visas can be acquired at Gabonese embassies.

DEPARTURE FORMALITIES

There are no departure formalities for Gabon.

IMMUNIZATION

Proof of yellow fever inoculations are required for entry into Gabon. Immunization certificates must be more than 10 days old but not older than 10 years. Malaria is endemic in Gabon.

TIPPING

It is not necessary to tip taxi drivers.

CRIME

Petty crime is common in urban areas. Violent crime is not rampant but is on the rise.

INFRASTRUCTURE

Gabon has modern telephone, air, and taxi industries. Most major cities are linked by air travel. There is no bus service in Libreville, but taxis are readily available. Tourism facilities outside of Libreville are limited.

NATIONAL TOURIST OFFICE

Airports provide tourist information for Gabon.

COMMUNICATIONS

Telephones Telephone service is available for local and long distance calls 24 hours a day; however rates are very expensive. Service is moderately reliable in the cities, but international calling is unavailable from many rural exchanges.
Fax Fax machines are not widely used or available in Gabon. Most major hotels will have fax services, but not many businesses will.
Post office Postal service is adequate. Post offices often close a little earlier than posted hours. When addressing mail to Gabon, use post office box numbers rather than street addresses.

USEFUL TELEPHONE NUMBERS

If you are calling from outside Gabon, you will need to add the country code [241] and any other international dialing requirements from within your country. There are no city codes in Gabon.
- Hotel Information 732820
- Air Gabon 762358
Credit Card Information
Lost or stolen credit cards (call collect to the US, regardless of which country the card was issued in).
- Amex ....[1] (919) 333-3211
- Diner's Club ....[1] (303) 799-1504
- MasterCard ....[1] (314) 275-6690
- Visa ....[1] (410) 581-7931

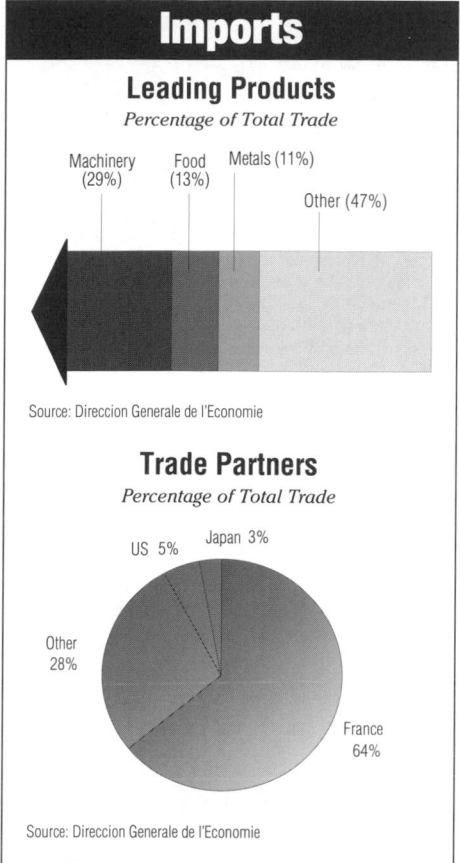

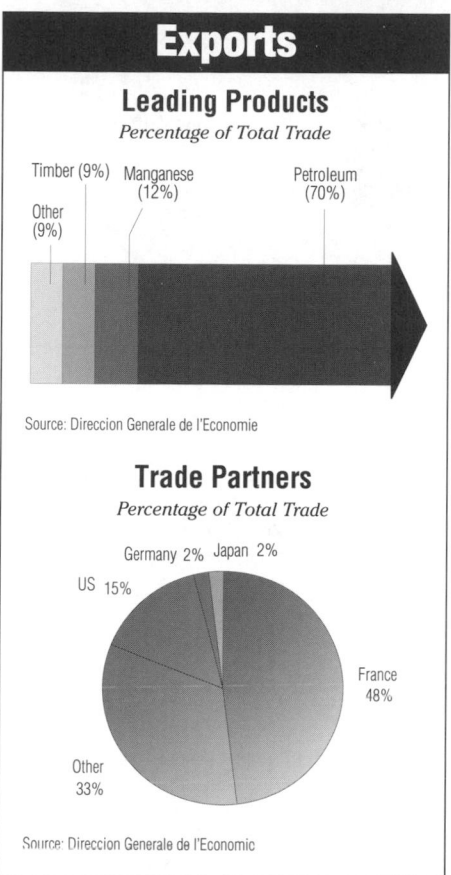

Opportunities

FOR IMPORTING TO GABON

- food products, clothing, cosmetics
- construction materials, machinery
- telecommunications equipment

FOR EXPORTING FROM GABON

- cocoa, coffee
- iron, manganese, uranium
- petroleum and wood

GROWTH SECTORS

- consumer goods
- forestry products
- mining
- petroleum production
- telecommunications

Trade News

RULES AND REGULATIONS

- **Tariff and import taxes** There is a five percent tax on medicines, rice, and wheat; a 10 percent tax on raw materials; a 20 percent tax on intermediate goods; and a 30 percent tax on consumer goods.
- **Licenses and documentation** Documentation is required for all imports exceeding US$845 (500,000 CFA francs). An export license is also required. All goods entering Gabon must be accompanied by a bill or lading.
- **Prohibited imports** Prohibited imports include sugar, oil, some soaps, cement, mineral waters having the same quality as the Gabonese mineral water Andza, and firearms and munitions.

Legal

Legal System

Gabon's legal system is pervasive, heavily bureaucratic, and leans toward protectionism, with cumbersome customs requirements.

Intellectual Property Rights

Copyrights The African Intellectual Property Office (OAPI) establishes copyrights valid in all nations participating in the Central African Customs and Economic Union (UDEAC). Enforcement is sporadic, however, and foreigners cannot expect to adequately protect their copyrights from infringement by members of the UDEAC.

Patents and trademarks Invention patents remain in effect for 20 years past the application date. Gabon's legal system does not mandate novelty examinations or opposition provisions. Applications, once filed, are generally approved eventually. Trademarks and service marks may be registered and, once approved by the OAPI, are in effect for 20 years.

Contracts and Dispute Resolution

Gabon's capacity to resolve business disputes remains largely untested, with few precedents and little case law from which to draw conclusions. Contract law is largely determined by the circumstances of each case, and is more dependent on surrounding facts and circumstances than on the terms of any agreement. Gabon does not pursue mediation through any international organizations, but parties are free to agree to submit to such in the event of business disputes, and the arbitration may be upheld in the courts.

Labor

Gabon's population includes a pool of skilled white-collar workers. Despite high unemployment levels, blue-collar jobs remain largely unpopular with the citizenry. Workers have few rights; employers are fairly free to hire, pay, and terminate at will, subject to minimal requirements.

Legal Matters

LEGAL BRIEFS

- **Local preference** Although Gabon's legal system is more equitable than that of many other African nations, some level of local preference is arguably present.
- **Doing business** By law, all physical or legal persons wishing to do business in Gabon must first request preliminary approval from the Ministry of Commerce. Specifically, the Ministry of Commerce requires a substantial business authorization levy (the levy is changeable; check with the Ministry for current rate); and the establishment of a business card with stamp tax. The Ministry also requires six copies of the firm's articles of incorporation and the minutes of the meeting of the board of directors in which the firm decided on the founding of a corporation or branch in Gabon.
- **Letters of approval** It is customary for companies not engaged in purely commercial activities to seek a letter of approval from the ministry in charge of the activity concerned.
- **Business entities** The most common business entities are the corporation (Societe Anonyme, or SA) and the limited liability company (Societe a Responsabilite Limitee, or SARL). The SA must have at least seven shareholders, as well as a chairperson, a board of directors, and a president. The law does not require that the chairman be a physical person.
- **Registration** Foreign companies may operate a branch in Gabon for up to two years without registering.
- **International agreements** Gabon is a member of the World Intellectual Property Organization (WIPO), the Berne Convention for Protection of Literary and Artistic Works, the Paris Convention for the Protection of Industrial Property, and the Patent Cooperation Treaty.

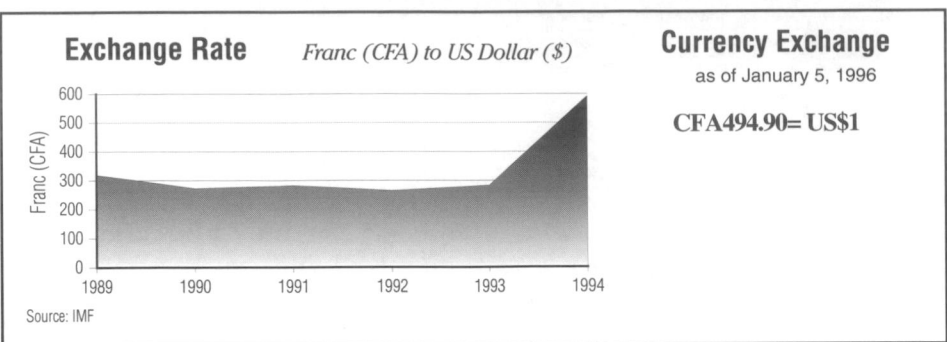

Exchange Rate *Franc (CFA) to US Dollar ($)*

Franc (CFA): 600, 500, 400, 300, 200, 100, 0

1989 1990 1991 1992 1993 1994

Source: IMF

Currency Exchange

as of January 5, 1996

CFA494.90= US$1

Currency

The currency in use is the CFA franc (F or CFA).

Foreign Exchange

The CFA franc is pegged to the French franc at a fixed rate. Exchange control regulations apply only to financial transfers outside of the franc zone (a monetary zone that includes France and its former overseas colonies). Exchange transactions in French francs between the Bank of Central African States (BEAC) and commercial banks take place at the same rate. Buy and sell rates for other foreign currencies are also officially posted, with quotations based on the fixed rate of the French franc and the currency rates posted by the Paris exchange market. Rates include a 25 percent commission. Exchange transactions with foreign countries must be effected through the Postal Administration or an authorized bank.

Capital Transfers

The Ministry of Economy must approve all capital repatriation; funds must come from documented salary, wages, or profits.

Investment Incentives

Gabonese law allows foreign firms to operate as branches, and most enterprises may be wholly owned by foreign investors.

Investment Restrictions

The government often does not formally recognize equal national treatment and often favors Gabonese firms.

TAXATION

Taxation requires sophisticated knowledge of complex rules and regulations specific to each country. For more detailed information we suggest you refer to the Ernst & Young Corporate Tax Guide and Directory, available from the Ernst & Young accounting office in your country, or from:

Ernst & Young
Immeuble Sonagar
Avenue du Colonel Parant
B.P. 1013
Libreville, Gabon
Tel: 74-32-17, 74-21-68
Fax: 72-64-94

• Gabonese companies carrying out business outside Gabon are not taxed in Gabon on the related profits. A Gabonese company is one that is registered in Gabon, regardless of the shareholders' nationality, or where the company is managed or controlled.

At a Glance

Corporate Income Tax Rate (%)(a)	40
Capital Gains Tax Rate (%)(b)	40
Branch Tax Rate (%)(a)(c)	40
Withholding Tax (%)	
Dividends (d)(e)(f)	20
Interest (d)(g)	20
Royalties from Patents, Know-how, etc. (d)	10
Payments for Services (h)	10
Branch Remittance Tax (i)	20
Net Operating Losses (Years)	
Carryback	0
Carryforward (j)	3

(a) The maximum tax is 1.1% of turnover, but not less than CFA 600. There are several categories of priority status and exemptions.
(b) In certain circumstances, the tax may be deferred or reduced, if the proceeds are used to acquire new fixed assets in Gabon within three years.
(c) If an election is made, the tax for CIE Petroleum Contractors (foreign companies without a permanent establishment in Gabon that have contracted with petroleum companies established in Gabon) is a specified percentage of taxable turnover. For 1994, 1995 and 1996, the percentage is 7.444%.
(d) This rate is applicable to payments to residents and nonresidents.
(e) This rate also applies to directors' fees, nondeductible expenses and adjustments of profits following a tax examination.
(f) The rate is 22% for directors' fees.
(g) This tax applies to interest on bonds and debentures. A 10% withholding tax is imposed on interest paid on debt claims, bank deposits and guarantees to corporations that do not have their seat in Gabon or to nonresident individuals. A 30% withholding tax is imposed on "lots," which are exceptionally high bond discounts given only for certain specified bonds selected at random. The withholding tax is imposed on the amount of the discount.
(h) Applicable to payments by resident companies to nonresidents for services, including professional services, rendered in Gabon.
(i) This tax applies if profits are remitted to the head office.
(j) Losses attributable to depreciation may be carried forward indefinitely.

Money Matters

BITS AND PIECES

• **Banking system** There are seven commercial banks in Gabon, and four specialized financial institutions. The local banking system is comprised mostly of French and foreign banks, is fairly sophisticated, and offers most standard banking services.

• **Credit** Local credit is available to both foreign and local investors in equal terms.

• **Common currency** All states in the Central African Monetary Zone use a single currency, the CFA franc, which is issued by the BEAC.

• **Operations account countries** Operations Account countries include Benin, Burkina Faso, Cameroon, Central African Republic, Chad, Comoros, Congo, Cote d'Ivoire, Equatorial Guinea, Mali, Niger, Senegal, and Togo. Payments between any of these countries may be made freely.

• **Exportation of bank notes** Residents may take out BEAC bank notes up to CFA two million if traveling to other countries in the franc zone. For amounts more than 2 million, funds may be taken out in other means of payment. Travel to other countries carries a limit of CFA 100,000 per day for tourism, or CFA 250,000 per day for business travel.

• **Capital movement** There are no controls for capital movement between Gabon and France, Monaco, and other Operations Account countries. Capital transfers to other countries require approval, but capital receipts are freely allowed. Foreign currency held in Gabon by residents or nonresidents must be deposited with an authorized bank.

BANKS

Bank of Central African States
BP 112
Libreville
Tel: 76-13-52, 76-13-73
Fax: 74-45-63

Banque Gabonaise de Développement
Rue Alfred Marche
BP 5
Libreville
Tel: 76-24-89
Fax: 74-26-99

Banque Internationale pour le Commerce & l'Industrie du Gabon
Ave. Colonel Parant
BP 2241
Libreville
Tel: 76-26-13

Banque Meridien BIAO Gabon, SA
Immeuble Concorde
Boulevard de l'Indépendance
BP 106
Libreville
Tel: 76-26-27 Fax: 76-20-63

Banque Nationale de Crédit Rural
Avenue Bouet
BP 1120
Libreville
Tel: 72-47-42
Telex: 5830

Banque Paribas Gabon
Boulevard de l'Independence
BP 2253
Libreville
Telex: 5265

Citibank, NA
Boulevard Quaben & Rue Kringer
BP 3940
Libreville
Tel: 73-30-00, 73-19-16
Fax: 5429 GO

Société Nationale d'Investissements du Gabon
BP 479
Libreville
Tel: 72-09-22 Fax: 74-81-70

Union Gabonaise de Banque
BP 315
Libreville
Tel: 76-15-14
Telex: 5232

Marketing

Distribution

Gabon's consumers are relatively affluent and eager to buy quality imported items. At one end, imports are handled by large, vertically integrated trading houses that import and retail products. At the other end, there are several layers of intermediaries. Most foreign products are marketed through Gabonese who serve as agents for international firms. Smaller accounts are handled through small local firms, most of which have a single outlet in Libreville. Distribution channels are limited by poor infrastructure and unreliable delivery systems.

Agents, Distributors, and Partners

The main avenues for foreign firms include agents, distributors or dealers, and branches or subsidiaries. Some foreign firms offering complementary products band together to fund a local subsidiary to achieve economies of scale rather than operate through a local agent. Joint ventures and licensing arrangements exist, but only in limited form and for major international consumer products. Direct marketing is most successful for firms who can send motivated, French-speaking representatives on frequent visits to establish the kind of close contact essential to doing business in Gabon.

Selling Methods

Price is less of a consideration in Gabon than might seem likely, with quality, features, and brand occupying more prominence. Service has been a minor consideration; however, high-quality service and adequate inventories are rare and confer a significant competitive advantage.

Advertising

Choices are limited to three agencies in Libreville. The broadcasting system is government-owned and does not accept commercial advertising. Commercial radio operates in neighboring Cameroon and the Congo. The press consists of one daily and two weekly newspapers, all of which carry advertisements. Handbills and posters are frequently used forms of local advertising, and these and other local advertising are becoming both more common and sophisticated.

Marketing in Gabon

MARKETING TIPS

- **Cost of operations** Foreign firms considering operating in Gabon should note that Libreville is ranked as more expensive than New York and just slightly less expensive than Tokyo.
- **Credit** Because many consumer goods are distributed through appointed wholesalers who buy stock for their own account, suppliers may wish to establish a credit policy that allows these distributors to maintain an adequate inventory.
- **Government markets** Government agencies seldom buy via formal tender, usually taking the first acceptable bid.

MARKETING ASSOCIATIONS

Centre Gabonais de Commerce Extérieur
BP 3906
Libreville
Tel: 76-11-67

Commerce et Développement
BP 2142
Libreville
Tel: 76-06-73
Telex: 5214

NEWSPAPERS

Gabon-Matin (Daily)
BP 168
Libreville

L'Union (Daily)
BP 3849
Libreville
Tel: 73-21-84
Fax: 73-83-26

Business Culture

Greetings and Courtesies

Greetings are relatively simple in Gabon. A firm handshake is always acceptable between people. When introduced to a group, it is considered polite to wait for the locals to extend their hands. Allow them to tell you about themselves, limiting your own initial conversation to a brief description of who you are, your company position, and the nature of your business in their country. An inquiry about a person's family is a basic courtesy in Gabon and should always be extended. Discussions of politics, however, are to be generally avoided.

Business Ethic and Framework

Business in Gabon is conducted slowly, and standards of punctuality are often very lax. A well-recommended strategy for initiating action in your business trip is to announce to your contacts that you have but a week to spend in the country—regardless of your actual plans. Business is often conducted in a more social context rather than an official one. Lunch is more popular than dinner for business entertaining and can often last for several hours.

Meetings and Decision Making

Official business meetings invariably start late—often several hours late—and appointments are often skipped entirely by businesspeople in Gabon. Gabon's system is heavily bureaucratic and decisions are usually made only by the top members of a company. However, given the strong family ties that abound in Gabon, a lower-level family connection may prove valuable in expediting the usual slow procedures and red tape.

Business Attire

Formal attire is the norm. Most businesspeople in Gabon dress in the French style. Loose pants are an appropriate casual style for women. To keep from looking too much like a tourist, men should avoid wearing shorts.

Cultural Cautions

DO'S

- Titles are important. Use them whenever possible, even without the person's name.
- Always inquire about a person's family.

DON'TS

- Try not to ask too many questions initially.
- Don't ask too many questions about politics, Gabon's economic problems, or the high unemployment.

CUSTOMS

- Most business is conducted in French; the majority of businesspeople and government officials cannot speak or write English, and the majority of letters in English rarely receive a reply.
- Drink only boiled and filtered or bottled water. Malaria is a problem in the country, so be sure to take proper medication.
- Women planning to do business in Gabon may face discrimination.

OBSERVATIONS

- It is common to leave a small tip, about five percent, in restaurants, hotels, and bars. In some restaurants, service is included on the bill.
- Women should never wear shorts. If they are necessary, bring a wraparound skirt to wear over them.
- Don't make appointments during Ramadan, or the Christmas/New Year's holidays.
- Lunches, sometimes lasting longer than two or three hours, are popular for conducting business.

GOVERNMENT AGENCIES

Ministry of Agriculture, Livestock, and Rural Economy
BP 551
Libreville
Tel: 76-29-43
Telex: 5587

Ministry of Commerce, Industry, and Scientific Research
BP 3906
Libreville
Tel: 76-30-55
Telex: 5347

Ministry of Finance, Budget, and Participation
BP 165
Libreville
Tel: 72-12-10
Telex: 5238

Ministry of Foreign Affairs, Cooperation, and Francophone Affairs
BP 2245
Libreville
Tel: 76-22-70
Telex: 5255

Ministry of Labor, Human Resources, and Professional Training
BP 4577
Libreville
Tel: 74-32-18

Ministry of Mines, Hydrocarbons, Energy, and Hydraulic Resources
BP 576
Libreville
Tel: 72-31-96
Telex: 5629

Ministry of Public Health and Population
BP 13116
Libreville
Tel: 76-35-90 Telex: 5385

Ministry of Tourism, Environment, and National Parks
BP 403
Libreville

Ministry of Transport
BP 3974
Libreville
Tel: 72-11-62
Fax: 77-33-31

Ministry of Water and Forests
BP 403
Libreville
Tel: 72-16-09

Ministry of Youth, Sports, and Women
Libreville
Tel: 76-35-76
Telex: 5642

BUSINESS AND TRADE ORGANIZATIONS

Agence Nationale de Promotion de la Petite et Moyenne Enterprise (PROMO-GABON)
Promotion of Small- and Medium-Size Industry
BP 3939
Libreville
Tel: 74-31-16
Telex: 000576

Société de Développement de l'Agriculture au Gabon
Agricultural Development
BP 2248
Libreville
Tel: 76-40-82
Telex: 5468

Confederatioin Patronale Gabonaise
BP 410
Libreville
Tel: 76-02-43
Fax: 74-86-52

Syndicat des Entreprises Minieres du Gabon (SYNDIMINES)
BP 260
Libreville
Telex: 5388

Syndicat des Importateurs Exportateurs du Gabon (SIMPEX)
BP 1743
Libreville

Syndicat des Producteurs et Industriels du Bois du Gabon
BP 84
Libreville
Tel: 72-26-11

Syndicat Professionnel des Usines de Sciages et Placages du Gabon
BP 417
Port-Gentil

Union des Representations Automobiles et Industrielles (URAI)
BP 1743
Libreville

Union Nationale du Patronat Syndicat des Transports Urbains, Routiers et Fluviaux du Gabon (UNAPASYFTUROGA)
BP 1025
Libreville

Caise Francaise de Developpement
BP 63
Libreville
Tel: 72-23-89
Telex: 5362

Commerce et Developpement (CODEV)
BP 2142
Libreville
Tel: 76-06-73
Telex: 5214

Mission Francaise de Cooperation
BP 2105
Libreville
Tel: 76-10-56
Fax: 74-55-33
Telex: 5249

Societe Gabonaise de Recherches Petrolieres (GABOREP)
BP 564
Libreville
Tel: 75-06-40

Chamber of Commerce, Industry and Mines
BP 2234
Libreville
Tel: 722-064, 72-07-53, 76-15-80
Telex: 5554

Office Gabonais d'Amélioration et de Procution de Viande
BP 245
Moanda
Tel: 66-12-67

Palmiers et Hévéas du Gabon
BP 75
Libreville

Société de Développement de l'Hévéaculture
BP 316
Libreville
Tel: 70-03-43
Fax: 70-19-89

Société Gabonaise de Recherches et d'Exploitations Miniäres
boulevard de Nice
Libreville

Société Nationale de Développement des Cultures Industrielles
BP 256
Libreville
Tel: 76-33-97
Telex: 5362

NEWSPAPERS AND PERIODICALS

Bulletin Mensuel de la Chambre de Commerce, d'Agriculture, d'Industrie et des Mines (Monthly)
BP 2234
Libreville
Tel: 72-20-64
Telex: 5554

L'Economiste Gabonais (Quarterly)
BP 3906
Libreville

Gabon d'Aujourd'hui
BP 750
Libreville

Gabon Libre
BP 6439
Libreville
Tel: 74-42-22

La Griffe
BP 4928
Libreville
Tel: 74-73-45

Ngondo
BP 168
Libreville

Le Progressiste
blvd Léon-M'ba
BP 7000
Libreville
Tel: 74-54-01

La Relance
BP 268
Libreville
Tel: 70-31-66

RADIO & TELEVISION

Africa No. 1
BP 1
Libreville
Tel: 76-00-01
Fax: 74-21-33

Radiodiffusion-Télévision Gabonaise
BP 150
Libreville
Tel: 73-20-25
Fax: 73-21-53
Telex: 5342

TRANSPORTATION FIRMS

Société Nationale d'Acconage et de Transit
BP 3897
Libreville
Tel: 70-04-04
Fax: 70-13-11

Société Nationale de Transports Maritimes
BP 3841
Libreville
Tel: 74-06-32
Fax: 74-59-67

INTERNET ADDRESSES

Eye on Africa Page
http://www.webperfect.com/afrinet/news.html

AdminNet - Africa - Gabon
http://www.ensmp.fr/~scherer/adminet/world/ga/

Georgia

Republic of Georgia

Economy

Overview

Georgia, along with the other republics of the former Soviet Union, has suffered a major economic depression since the break-up of the USSR in the late 1980s. Georgia initially attempted to reach out directly to Western and other non-Soviet block countries, refusing to join the Russian-dominated CIS. Internal problems caused by ethnic strife, political infighting, and corruption, however, have led it to accept an uncomfortable degree of Russian leadership, although stability has yet to be reestablished. Nevertheless, Georgia enjoys some advantages, including fertile agricultural land, that could suggest an optimistic future if it can rise above its immediate economic constraints. The government has vowed to lower inflation and unemployment, but recent attempts have largely failed to halt the economic slide. The government continues to have a hand in almost all business operations, and state-owned enterprises account for almost 75 percent of all industrial output. Only about 25 percent of the companies approved for privatization by the government in 1994 were actually privatized, and to date the most successful enterprises have been those trading on company-to-company relationships established when all were part of the USSR.

Trade

Georgia is strategically located between Armenia and Azerbaijan, and is committed to improving its infrastructural contacts with its neighbors. Georgia occupies the most convenient location in the Transcaucasus, not only because of its Black Sea ports and geographic location, but also because of the fact that political difficulties in adjoining Armenia and Azerbaijan are in an even worse state than in Georgia. Exports include food products, various miscellaneous manufactures, machinery, fuels, and metals. Imports include machinery, miscellaneous manufactures, foodstuffs, fuels, and metal products.

Sectors

Agriculture Agriculture—accounting for about 40 percent of GDP—has declined a great deal recently, although a significant part of this is due to disruption caused by privatization of farming operations. The main agricultural products are tea, grapes, fruit and vegetables, and tobacco.

Industry Georgia produces light industrial goods and is highly dependent on imported raw materials, intermediate goods, and energy products. Mining includes marble, granite, and copper ore. Manufacturing output has declined by more than 20 percent in the past few years. However, Georgia does have a labor force that is technically experienced, and is heir to a number of advanced scientific and production facilities formerly used by the USSR.

Services Tourism is the most important industry in the as yet undeveloped service sector. Recent conflicts and hostilities in the country have nearly destroyed this incipient tourist trade, however, and some tourist facilities are occupied by internally displaced persons. Most other services involve ideal distribution and personal service activities.

Trends

Georgia's immediate task is to quell current political strife and establish the minimal stability necessary to pursue its economic goals. It will have to renew its efforts to attract foreign interest and investment in order to develop not only its infrastructure but also its local industry.

At a Glance

THE COUNTRY

Location Southeastern Europe, bordering the Black Sea, between Turkey and Russia.
Terrain Mostly mountainous, with the great Caucasus Mountains in the north and lesser Caucasus Mountains in the south. Good soil is found in the river valley flood plains.
Climate Along the Black Sea, the climate is Mediterranean. Further inland the climate is continental, with warm summers and cold winters.

THE PEOPLE

Population 5,500,000
Ethnic composition
Georgian 78%
Armenian 8%
Russian 6%
Ossetian 3%
Greek 2%
Abkhazian 2%
Ukrainian 1%
Religious composition
Christian 65%
Most Christians are members of the Georgian Orthodox Church. Significant Muslim populations are found in select areas.
Languages spoken Georgian is the major language; others spoken include Abkhaz, Ossetian, Armenian, Russian, and Greek.
Education and literacy Adult literacy is estimated at 99 percent. Georgian schools were based on the Soviet model until the late 1980s, but now emphasize Georgian history. Georgian students are taught in a variety of languages, including Georgian, Russian, and Ossetian. Several universities are located in Georgia.

COUNTRY FACTS

Political and legal Legislation is created by a 234-member parliament. The current legal system combines laws from the pre-Soviet and Soviet system.
Telephone Georgia has international communications links via landline to other former Soviet republics and Turkey. As of 1992, 339,000 telephone applications were left unfilled. International country code: [995]. City codes: Tbilisi (32), Batumi (88200).
Transportation Highways stretch throughout the country, but many are in disrepair. Most forms of transportation are in poor condition due to neglect.
Environment Nearly 70 percent of the water remains unsafe to drink. Pesticides from agricultural areas have contaminated much of the soil. Current issues are land and water pollution.
Media There are 149 newspapers, 128 published in Georgian, with a combined circulation of 3.2 million.
Health Medical facilities are in poor condition throughout the country. Little information can be found since the dissolution of the Soviet Union. The birth rate is projected at 18 per 1,000 citizens. There are almost 6 physicians per 1,000 inhabitants. Immunization rates are very low; only 63 percent of the children up to one year old were vaccinated against tuberculosis, and only 45 percent were given medication to prevent polio. Life expectancy is an average of 72 years. The overall mortality rate is 9 per 1,000 citizens, and the infant mortality rate is especially high, at 25 per 1,000 live births.

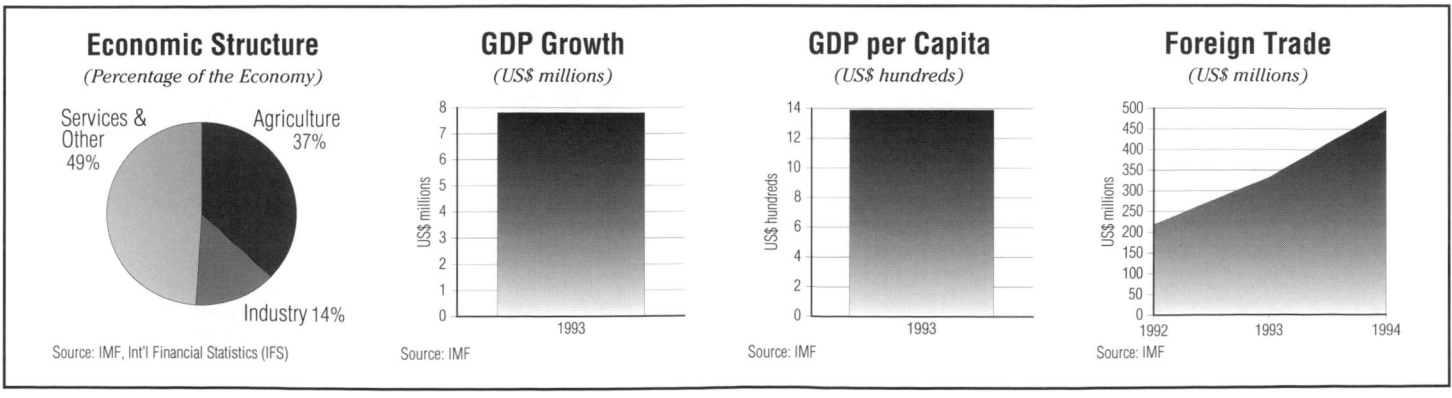

Economic Structure
(Percentage of the Economy)

Services & Other 49%
Agriculture 37%
Industry 14%

Source: IMF, Int'l Financial Statistics (IFS)

GDP Growth
(US$ millions)

1993

Source: IMF

GDP per Capita
(US$ hundreds)

1993

Source: IMF

Foreign Trade
(US$ millions)

1992   1993   1994

Source: IMF

Business Travel

	LH 1906	MADRID	935	113-3
	LH 1022	STUTTGART HBF.	935	-
	AF 1701	LYON	940	683-6
	AY 822	HELSINKI	940	113-3
	AA 071	SFRANCISCO-DALLAS	945	731-7

Georgia

- ⊚ Republic capital
- ⊛ Autonomous republic center
- ⊛ Autonomous oblast center
- • City
- ━━ International border
- ─── Province boundary
- ········ Railroad
- ─── Primary road

0   25   50   75 km
0   25   50 mi

©1994 Magellan Geographix℠ Santa Barbara, CA

COMMUNICATIONS

Telephones Georgia's telephone system is antiquated and in short supply. International calls are difficult to make, even in the cities.

Fax Facsimile technology is relatively new to Georgia and is pretty much unknown outside of government offices. Faxes are rarely used.

Post office There have been a number of complaints regarding Georgian postal delivery. Some packages take months to arrive, if at all.

BEST TRAVEL BOOKS

From Da to Yes, Understanding the East Europeans. An informative overview of the Eastern European countries.

USEFUL TELEPHONE NUMBERS

If you are calling from outside Georgia, you will need to add the country code [995] and any other international dialing requirements from within your country.

- Georgian Ministry of Foreign Affairs:
  (Visas) .... (32) 98-94-25, 98-94-22
- Georgian Committee of Foreign Economic Relations
  .... (32) 22-37-64, 22-51-86
- Georgian Customs Dept.... (32) 96-96-38, 96-96-27
- Small Business Dev. Center in Tbilisi .(32) 98-73-67

Credit Card Information

Lost or stolen credit cards (call collect to the US, regardless of which country the card was issued in).

- Amex ....[1] (919) 333-3211
- Diners Club ....[1] (303) 799-1504
- MasterCard ....[1] (314) 275-6690
- Visa ....[1] (410) 581-7931

Travelogue

WORKWEEK

Banks Monday-Friday 9:00 am to 1:00 pm.
Government Monday-Friday 9:00 am to 6:00 pm.
Retail Monday-Saturday 10:00 am to 8:00 pm with lunch from noon to 1:00 pm. Larger department stores may open at 8:00 am and remain open until 9:00 pm.

HOLIDAYS

Holidays 1996
January 1 New Year's Day
January 7 Christmas
January 19 Baptism Day
March 3 Mother's Day
April 9 Memorial Day
May 2 Recollection of the Deceased
May 26 Independence Day
August 28 August Day of the Virgin
October 14 Svetitskhovloba
November 23 St. George's Day

VISA AND PASSPORT

Travelers to Georgia must be in possession of a valid passport. Foreigners will receive a temporary stamp in their passport and will be instructed to obtain a tourist or business visa from the Consular section of the Georgian Ministry of Foreign Affairs upon arrival. Multiple-use visas cost US$90, and single-use visas are US$30. Visas usually take five days to process. Travelers with valid multiple-entry visas from Armenia or Azerbaijan are not required to obtain a Georgian visa.

DEPARTURE FORMALITIES

Visitors arriving from or departing to other countries, including other former Soviet states, must obtain a Georgian visa in order to leave the country.

IMMUNIZATION

International certificate of vaccine not required unless you are arriving from an infected area.

TIPPING

Tipping is officially discouraged but is much appreciated by small services. Taxi: 10 to 15 percent. Hotels: none. Restaurants: 10 to 15 percent. Beauticians and barbers: 10 percent. Small services, five to 10 percent.

CRIME

Georgia has a high crime rate. Petty thefts and pickpocketing are particularly common in crowded open-air markets and Tbilisi's metro system. Violent crimes occur most frequently at night. Security of overland travel within Georgia is minimal. Train and vehicular traffic is vulnerable to robbery. Unescorted travel in South Ossetia is particularly risky. Trains destined for Armenia have occasionally been targeted by terrorists.

INFRASTRUCTURE

Tourist facilities outside of the capital are not highly developed, and many goods and services are not yet available. Travel, especially by air, may be disrupted by fuel shortages and other problems.

NATIONAL TOURIST OFFICE

State Department of Tourism
80 Chavchavadze Avenue
380074 Tbilisi
Tel: (32) 22-61-25, 29-40-61
Fax: (32) 29-40-52
Telex: 212257 TOUR SU

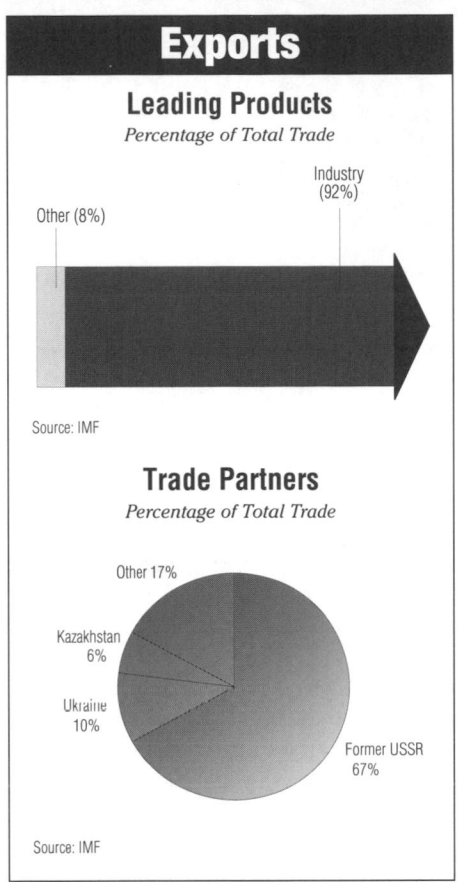

Foreign Trade

Imports

Leading Products
Percentage of Total Trade

Industry (91%)

Other (9%)

Source: IMF

Trade Partners
Percentage of Total Trade

Other 13%
Azerbaijan 7%
Ukraine 20%
Former USSR 60%

Source: IMF

Exports

Leading Products
Percentage of Total Trade

Other (8%)

Industry (92%)

Source: IMF

Trade Partners
Percentage of Total Trade

Other 17%
Kazakhstan 6%
Ukraine 10%
Former USSR 67%

Source: IMF

Opportunities

FOR IMPORTING TO GEORGIA
- candies
- clothing
- coffee
- dairy products
- flour

FOR EXPORTING FROM GEORGIA
- chemicals
- citrus fruits
- copper ore
- fuel

GROWTH SECTORS
- agribusiness (wine and citrus fruits)
- energy management
- mining
- port development
- telecommunications

Trade News

RULES AND REGULATIONS
- **Regulations** The Ministry of Trade regulates all exports and imports.
- **Tariff and import taxes** Customs tariffs in Georgia include import taxes, customs fees, and other payments including excise taxes and value-added taxes.
- **Prohibited imports** There are no prohibited imports.
- **Import licenses** Georgia requires import licenses for: medicines, medical equipment, plant protection chemicals, industrial by-products, drugs, weapons, and ammunition. Licenses are obtained through the Committee of Foreign Economic Relations after preliminary permission from the appropriate ministry.

Legal

Legal System

Georgia's current legal system retains traces of the Soviet era, and adds elements of new, market oriented legislation as well. The judiciary remains subject to political pressures and other influences. The government supervises the courts, and sometimes asks the Supreme Court to reconsider its own decisions.

Intellectual Property Protection

Patents and trademarks Georgia is a member of the Patent Cooperation Treaty and the World Intellectual Property Organization. A patent office under the Committee of Science and New Technologies approves all patents. Patents are valid for 20 years. Georgia is a member of the Madrid Agreement on Trademarks, and it recognizes the validity of most foreign trademarks. Registration of a trademark lasts for five years, and can be renewed for indefinite five-year periods upon payment of the registration fee, currently about US$520.

Labor

Although the legislation favors workers, the government has few resources available to enforce laws or even investigate complaints of employer abuse. The labor code grants to workers the right to organize and to bargain collectively. Workers are allowed to form unions, but they must be registered with the Ministry of Justice. Workers can strike after certain minimum attempts to otherwise resolve disputes have failed. There were a number of strikes as late as 1992, but very few recently as labor and management begin to work more closely together. The minimum wage has recently been raised by the government, and is set to rise monthly to keep pace with inflation. Forced labor is prohibited under the labor code, and instances of this practice are rare. The minimum age for employment of children is 14. Children between 14 and 16 are allowed to work a maximum of 30 hours a week. Acceptable conditions of work generally follow the old Soviet pattern.

Legal Matters

LEGAL BRIEFS
- **Government interest** Government investments are still high, contributing 67 percent of total investments, though reliable information on private investments is not available.
- **New laws** The current laws on foreign investment do not specifically hinder investment from most countries.
- **Watch lists** Georgia is not on any special trade lists for copyright and patent protection violations.
- **Supreme Court** The highest court in Georgia is the Supreme Court of the Republic.
- **Business registration** Georgia has streamlined registration for businesses and investors, making it relatively simple and quick. Certain documents must be submitted to the authorities.
- **Contracts and dispute resolution** Enterprises in Georgia operate under a wide variety of agreements, but the final contracts are usually very detailed, and should always be in writing. Any disputes are usually handled in the courts, although they are very unpredictable and time consuming. Some foreign businesses do agree to submit any disputes to arbitration, although it is unclear whether arbitration awards are binding and enforceable.
- **Copyrights** There are no copyright laws in Georgia. The government is considering some, but they are not expected to be passed in the near future. There is some piracy, although it has so far been limited to individual or small dealers.
- **Trade secrets** There is very little legislation on trade secret violations, a concern with many foreign businesses and investors. There is currently no indication that Georgia is even considering laws to protect trade secrets.

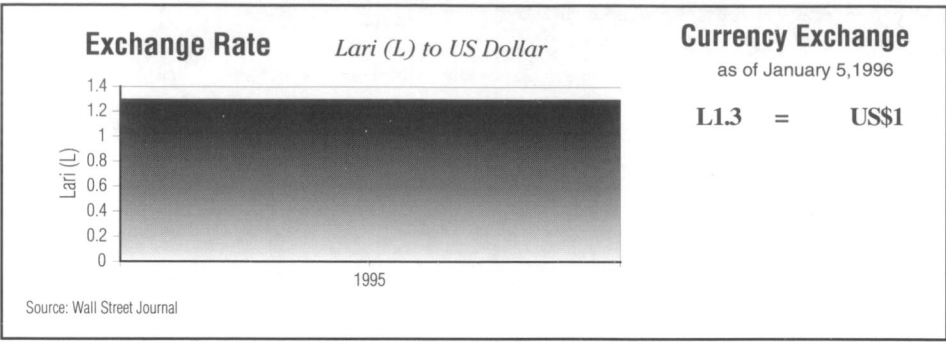

Exchange Rate
Lari (L) to US Dollar

Lari (L): 1.4, 1.2, 1, 0.8, 0.6, 0.4, 0.2, 0

1995

Source: Wall Street Journal

Currency Exchange
as of January 5, 1996

L1.3 = US$1

Currency

In late 1995, the Lari (L) replaced the Georgian coupon. It is set at one value and not currently convertible.

Foreign Exchange

The National Bank of Georgia (NBG) and 15 commercial banks participate in foreign exchange transactions. The exchange rates are freely negotiated between banks and foreign exchange bureaus and their customers. There are no taxes on the purchase or sale of foreign exchange, and no arrangement for forward cover against exchange rate risk. All residents may acquire and hold foreign currency, and all residents may open a foreign exchange account at an authorized bank. Commercial banks may be authorized by the NBG to engage in foreign exchange transactions with residents and nonresidents, and to open correspondent accounts with banks outside of Georgia. The NBG can also issue licenses to exchange bureaus for the purpose of buying and selling foreign currency and engaging in other routine cash transactions.

Capital Transfers

Individuals can import foreign currency without restriction, as long as the amount is declared on arrival. Exportation of foreign currency by nonresidents is permitted, up to the amount originally imported. Residents can freely export foreign currency, so long as income taxes have been paid on the funds used to purchase the foreign currency. Inward and outward capital transactions are not restricted, but may be monitored.

Investment Incentives

Any equipment or material imported for industrial maintenance is exempt from import duties and customs taxes. Tax benefits are also available to companies within specific areas designated by the government. Foreign investor companies have an Enterprise Property Tax holiday for the first year of operations, and a 50 percent reduced tax period for the next two years.

Investment Restrictions

Georgia's unstable government could cause problems for foreign investors. There are as yet no foreign trade zones and free ports in Georgia.

TAXATION

The tax system is composed primarily of four taxes:
- A 14 percent value-added tax (VAT).
- A corporate profits (income) tax, with a 20 percent rate for enterprises, a 10 percent rate for construction enterprises, and a 35 percent rate for banks.
- Excise taxes of up to 90 percent on the price of goods.

- Personal income tax, progressive in nature but with lots of loopholes and not strictly enforced.
Other sources of government income are customs duties, or import tax of two percent, an export tax of eight percent, a 20 percent tax for bartered goods, and a fixed tax levied on the foreign exchange kiosks.

Money Matters

BITS AND PIECES

- **Banking system** Twenty-nine banks are permitted to participate in currency exchange, but not all of them are actually involved in international transactions.
- **General payments** Payments may be made in any convertible currency. Settlements with other former states of the USSR may be made through correspondent accounts or convertible currency.
- **Electronic transfers** Two banks, the NBG and the Iberiabanki, have the ability to carry out electronic transfers.
- **Payments** Generally, payments can be made in any convertible currency. Settlements with other former states of the USSR may be made through correspondent accounts or convertible currency.
- **Import payments** There are no quantitative restrictions on imports. Foreign exchange for import payments may be purchased from authorized banks at market rates.
- **Export payments** Exporters must surrender 32 percent of their proceeds in convertible currencies.
- **Invisibles** Payments for invisibles may be made without restriction. Residents may either purchase foreign exchange for the invisibles transactions, or use foreign exchange balances in their foreign exchange bank accounts. Proceeds from invisibles are subject to the same regulations as proceeds from any export.
- **Banking regulation** Georgia's banking regulation of July 1993 allows foreign companies to open interest-bearing accounts by depositing dividends and income through the sale of foreign currency to the national or authorized banks.
- **Foreign property and import duties** Property contributed by foreign investors in accordance with the firm's articles of incorporation, as well as foreign investors' personal-use property, are exempt from import duties and customs taxes. Also, material brought in for industrial maintenance is exempt from any duties and customs taxes.
- **Tax benefits** Tax benefits are available to foreign companies within specific areas of activity designated by the government of Georgia.
- **Value-added tax (VAT)** The VAT does not apply to several goods and services, including: foreign companies' transshipment of goods, public health care equipment, goods exported by a manufacturer, any services related to the above goods, goods and services intended for foreign diplomatic organizations, agricultural raw materials and products, and financial operations related to credits.

BANKS

Georgian Central Bank
Leonide ul. 3/5
380027 Tbilisi
Tel: (32) 99-98-85
Fax: (32) 99-07-38
Hard Currency Department
Tel: (32) 93-21-03, 98-19-38
Fax: (32) 99-98-85

Eximbank
Chorokhi 5
380002 Tbilisi
Tel: (32) 99-72-04
Fax: (32) 99-93-94

COMMODITY EXCHANGE

Caucasian Commodity Exchange
Vazha Pshavela Ave. 72
380086 Tbilisi
Tel: (32) 38-09-46

Overview

During Soviet rule, Georgian consumers enjoyed one of the highest standards of living in the USSR; however, the population has experienced a drastic drop in purchasing power recently. A scarcity of capital and foreign exchange has hindered local businesses and consumers from acquiring needed materials. Official economic policy has attempted to create favorable conditions for developing business and foreign investment. However, the pre-existing bureaucratic structure hampers business more than usual and a poorly functioning infrastructure constitutes additional roadblocks to developing trade.

Distribution and Agents/Distributors

Several ministries and organizations, including the Ministry of Trade, Ministry of Agriculture and Food Industry, and Tourism Department, have commodity distribution and sales functions. The leading trade organization is the Georgian Cooperative Union. Although private entities are developing to distribute goods, usually at a lower level, these remain unofficial and there is no easy way to access information regarding such local distributors and sellers.

Establishing an Office

Foreign companies looking to establish an office must first apply for registration with the Gamgeoba, the local district government. The type of documentation required depends on the type of entity to be established. After all required documents are in, the Gamgeoba special commission schedules a meeting, to which the applicant is invited, to consider the application. If approved, a temporary registration certificate is issued which allows preparation of a firm's seal and letterhead, the opening of a bank account, and initial investment.

Advertising

The most effective advertising channels in Georgia are television and newspapers. There are two television channels and three daily Russian language newspapers. Exhibition, marketing, and sales facilities—such as "universal shops"—are located in major cities. Foreign companies usually organize their trade promotion events through the Georgian Chamber of Commerce and Industry.

Marketing in Georgia

MARKETING TIPS

- **Language** Although the official language is Georgian, most business executives are fluent in Russian as well.
- **Credit** Because of the lack of foreign exchange, creative financing may be required to close a sale. Sellers should carefully assess the level of exposure that they want and view transactions in terms of a long-term developing relationship, rather than for near-term returns.
- **Telephone** Georgia's telephone system is slow and international calls can only be made from cities; sometimes not even from there. Faxes are very new to the country and not used much. Personal contact works best.
- **Government markets** Government agencies may buy direct for small orders. Larger purchases are usually made by tender. Most projects are subject only to local preferences, but some solicit international bids. Availability of service is critical for government sales.

RADIO AND TELEVISION

TV and Radio Broadcasting Corporation
68 Kostava Street
380071 Tbilisi
Tel: (32) 36-81-66, 36-83-31
Fax: (32) 36-25-54, 36-86-65
Telex: 212106 RADIO SU

Greetings and Courtesies

Georgians are hospitable and welcoming toward foreign businesspeople. They consider it an honor and a pleasure to entertain foreign guests. An invitation to a Georgian home is an invitation to a feast, and your host will be offended if you do not partake generously. Georgian hosts propose endless rounds of toasts at dinner, usually with the local wines. In business settings, greet others with their professional title and surname; first name greetings are appropriate only for friends and relatives.

Business Ethic and Framework

As a country located in a geographic crossroads, Georgia has always been a trading nation. Georgian as well as Russian is spoken by nearly everyone in Georgia. Conservative dark suits are appropriate attire in Georgia. Women should wear understated, conservative suits or dresses. Rather than formal wear, conservative suits are worn to formal evening functions.

Meetings and Decision Making

Arrange business meetings in Georgia far in advance. It is important to arrive on time. It may take weeks, or even months, to arrange visas and travel details. Georgians are benefiting from a modern economy, but are new to capitalist business procedures. Georgian businesspeople have difficulty with the decision-making process. They have a reputation for saying "yes" to everything and continuing to do as they please.

Women

Women are treated traditionally in Georgia, and professional women must work hard to prove themselves before they are treated equally. Despite the difficulties, women there hold a wide variety of positions in government and business. In addition to their careers, most Georgian working women also have full responsibility for their homes and children.

Cultural Cautions

DO'S

- Before shaking hands with women and older people, wait for them to extend their hands.
- It is common practice to take flowers or a small gift when invited to a Georgian home, perhaps a book or item with your company name.
- Take the time to learn a little about Georgia's history and culture. It will be very appreciated.
- Become familiar with the nationality map of Georgia.

DON'TS

- Avoid discussing Georgia's turbulent history, especially Bloody Sunday.
- Never cut into a line of people. Long and orderly lines are part of Georgian daily life.
- Avoid going out after dark. Armed gangs rule the streets at night.

CUSTOMS

- Most Georgians are very friendly toward foreign businesspeople.
- Business attire is usually quite conservative. A suit and tie should be worn for all meetings. Women should usually wear conservative clothing as well. Avoid excessive jewelry, it won't get you any additional sales and may attract thieves.

OBSERVATIONS

- Georgians often shake hands and state their name when meeting someone for the first time. Greetings among friends may include hugging and kisses on the cheek.

NEGOTIATIONS

- Negotiations can be rather lengthy and usually involve socializing.

Contacts

GOVERNMENT AGENCIES

Ministry of Agricultural and Food Industry
41 Kostava Avenue
380023 Tbilisi
Tel: (32) 99-62-61, 93-23-34
Fax: (32) 98-57-78
Telex: 212910 SU

Ministry of Communication
2 Nine April Street
380008 Tbilisi
Tel: (32) 95-08-15, 99-96-66
Fax: +43-1-602-96-90 x 148
Telex: 212911 PTB SU

Ministry of Culture
4 Rustaveli Avenue
380008 Tbilisi
Tel: (32) 98-74-33, 93-22-55
Fax: (32) 98-74-26
Telex: 212102 ARGO SU

Ministry of Economy
170 Barnov Street
380062 Tbilisi
Tel: (32) 23-09-25, 23-53-82
Fax: (32) 29-00-63

Ministry of Education
52 Uznadze
380002 Tbilisi
Tel: (32) 95-88-86
Fax: (32) 96-21-63

Ministry of Environmental Protection
68 A, Kostava St
Tbilisi 380015
Tel: (32) 23-06-64
Fax: (32) 98-34-25
Telex: 212314 IREMI SU

Ministry of Finance
170 Barnov Street
380062 Tbilisi
Tel: (32) 23-09-25, 22-68-05
Fax: (32) 29-23-68
Telex: 212348 MOFIN SU

Ministry of Foreign Affairs
4 Nine April Street
380018 Tbilisi
Tel: (32) 98-93-77, 98-93-54
Fax: (32) 98-94-56
Telex: 212184 SLAVA SU

Ministry of Industry
28 Gamsakhurdia Avenue
380060 Tbilisi
Tel: (32) 38-50-28
Fax: +49-5-151-130-57 ext 149
Telex: 212107 GORDA

Ministry of Justice
19 Griboedov Street
380046 Tbilisi
Tel: (32) 93-27-21, 98-92-52
Fax: (32) 99-02-25

Ministry of Public Health Protection
30 Gamsakhurdia Avenue
380060 Tbilisi
Tel: (32) 38-70-71, 38-98-29
Fax: (32) 38-88-02
Telex: 212223

Ministry of Social Security and Labor
2 Leonodze
38007 Tbilisi
Tel: (32) 93-62--36, 98-69-74
Fax: (32) 93-61-51

Ministry of State Property
64, Chavchavadze ave
380062 Tbilisi
Tel: (32) 29-48-75, 98-99-67, 98-99-68 , 98-23-93

Ministry of Trade and Supply
42 Kazbegi Street
380077 Tbilisi
Tel: (32) 38-96-52, 38-96-67
Fax: (32) 38-07-23
Telex: 212146 FOTON SU

State Committee on Foreign Economic Relations
12 Kazbegi Street
380060 Tbilisi
Tel: (32) 22-37-64, 22-51-86, 22-52-33
Telex: 212343 SFMV SU

State Committee on Patent, Licensing, and Scientific Technical Information
12 Georgiashvili
380004 Tbilisi
Tel: (32) 98-94-37
Telex: 212148 HALLO SU

State Department of Air Transport
28 Rustaveli Avenue
380008 Tbilisi
Tel: (32) 93-30-92, 93-53-59, 93-30-90
Fax: (32) 98-96-39
Telex: 212186 ZENA SU

State Department of Customs
24 Akhvlediani Street
380003 Tbilisi
Tel: (32) 96-96-38, 96-96-27
Fax: (32) 96-96-21

State Department of Forest Industry
9 Mindeli
380086 Tbilisi
Tel: (32) 30-43-77, 30-43-79

State Department of Land Resources and Land Cadastre
15 A Tamarashvili Street
380077 Tbilisi
Tel: (32) 39-28-52, 39-65-74

State Department of Railway Transport
15 Tamar Mepe Avenue
380012 Tbilisi
Tel: (32) 95-25-27, 95-51-84

State Department of Tourism
80 Chavchavadze Avenue
380074 Tbilisi
Tel: (32) 22-61-25, 29-40-61
Fax: (32) 29-40-52
Telex: 212257 TOUR SU

STATE CORPORATIONS

Georgian Shipping Company
60 Gogebashvili Street
384517 Batumi
Tel: (88200) 25595, (88200) 36404
Fax: (88200) 25001
Telex: 412617 GESC
Satellite Phone: +873-1402312

Sakenergo (Georgian Energy Company)
1 Vekua Street
380026 Tbilisi
Tel: (32) 99-75-67, 98-03-01, 99-95-46
Fax: (32) 98-98-14

Sakgazi (Georgian Gas Comapny)
10 Lermontov Street
Tbilisi, Georgia
Tel: (32) 99-72-33, 93-55-80
Fax: (32) 98-23-05

Saknaftobi (Georgian Oil Company)
65 Kostava
380015 Tbilisi
Tel: (32) 36-16-42
Fax: (32) 36-54-85
Telex: 212330 METRA SU

Saknavtobproductebi (Georgian Oil Products)
142 Akaki Tsereteli Avenue
380019 Tbilisi
Tel: (32) 34-37-75, 34-35-54
Fax: (32) 34-28-59

BUSINESS AND TRADE ORGANIZATIONS

Business Development Center, USAID
5 Zandukeli
380008 Tbilisi
Tel: (32) 982-456
Fax: (32) 987-367

Commercial Center Service at the Georgian Food and Agribusiness Ministry
21 Kostava
380023 Tbilisi
Tel/Fax: (32) 999-821

Fund of Small Business and New Technology Development
Mayor of Tbilisi
4 Tabidze Street
380008 Tbilisi
Tel: (32) 934-925
Fax: (32) 932-594
Telex: 212185 MIR

Georgian Chamber of Commerce and Industry
11 Chavchavadze Prospect 1
380079 Tbilisi, Georgia
Tel: (32) 122-554, 230-045, 220-709
Fax: (32) 235-760
Telex: 212183 Inter SU

Georgian Fund, Medical Industry Development
123 David Agmashenebeli Avenue
380002 Tbilisi
Tel: (32) 999-200, 968-679, 237-012
Fax: (32) 965-837
Telex: 212110 TAG SU

Georgian Republic Cooperative Union (Tzekavshiri)
7 Freedom Square
380007 Tbilisi
Tel: (32) 988-729, 934-143, 934-831
Fax: (32) 999-077
Telex: 212101 FENIX SU

Georgian Small Business Development Fund
Georgian Ministry of Economy
170 Barnov Street
380062 Tbilisi
Tel: (32) 291-523
Fax: (32) 290-063

Gruzimpex (Foreign Trade Organization)
12 Georgiashvili Street
380008 Tbilisi
Tel: (32) 997-090
Fax: (32) 997-313
Telex: 212191 Daisi SU

Mayor of Tbilisi, Department of Foreign Relations
2 Liberty Plazza
Tbilisi 380008
Tel: (32) 93-36-16, 99-05-36
Satellite fax: +43-1-6029690
Telex: 212185 MIR

Union of Georgian Independent Manufacturers
123 Tsinamdzgvrishvili Street
380012 Tbilisi
Tel: (32) 963-650

RADIO AND TELEVISION

TV and Radio Broadcasting Corporation
68 Kostava Street
380071 Tbilisi
Tel: (32) 36-81-66, 36-83-31
Fax: (32) 36-25-54, 36-86-65
Telex: 212106 RADIO SU

INTERNET ADDRESSES

Usenet group:
soc.culture.rep-of-georgia

Asian Studies - Georgia
http://coombs.anu.edu.au/WWWLAsian/Georgia.html

Parliament of Georgia
http://www.parliament.ge/

Sa*NET
http://www.sanet.ge/

Germany

Federal Republic of Germany

Economy

Overview

The third-largest economy in the world, Germany accounts for roughly 25 percent of the EU's combined GDP and boasts one of the world's highest standards of living. Its infrastructure, skilled work force, overall stability, and geographical location at the crossroads of Western and Central Europe have transformed Germany into an economic stronghold, despite restrictive regulation, reunification issues, high taxes, high and rising wages, and the world's shortest work week. The reunification of Germany has been far more challenging and costly than had been projected. Although most Germans support full integration of the former East Germany, there have been bitter disputes regarding assistance to eastern regions at the expense of other priorities. Rapid wage rate increases during the early 1990s, combined with extensive business regulation and the high costs of Germany's expansive social welfare system, have further stalled the economy. Moderately high levels of bankruptcies and unemployment, however, have been reversed by an economic stimulus package which includes low-interest loans and tax breaks.

Trade

Germany is heavily oriented towards international trade, concentrating on high value-added manufactured goods. Major exports include chemicals, specialized machinery, miscellaneous transportation equipment, food products, and general industrial machinery, followed by iron and steel and electrical machinery. Imports include fuels—petroleum and natural gas accounting for nearly 40 percent of imports—chemicals, specialized industrial machinery, vehicles, and non-fuel raw materials. Trade is heavily weighted toward the nations of Central and Eastern Europe, and Germany's main trading partners are Poland and the Czech Republic, followed by the Netherlands, France, and Italy.

Sectors

Agriculture Although it employs nearly four percent of the work force, agriculture contributes only slightly more than one percent of GDP. Major cash crops include sugar beets, wheat, barley, and wine.

Industry German industry produces 35 percent of GDP and employs 40 percent of the work force. Major industries include transportation equipment—Germany is the world's third-largest producer of automobiles—machinery, metals and metal manufacturing, chemicals, and electrical machinery. Manufacturing continues to grow, while mining shrinks.

Services Services account for over 60 percent of GDP and only a slightly smaller proportion of employment. The sector is well-developed, especially in financial services, telecommunications, and business services. Franchising and direct marketing are on the rise in the commercial sector.

Trends

Germany's economic strength continues to gather momentum and may be able to establish preeminence in the EU. Western markets are strong and regions formerly aligned with the East Bloc constitute the fastest-growing economies in Europe, a trend some experts predict will last 20 years. German producers are focused on the Single European Market concept, compounding the challenges faced by companies outside the Continent. Germany's high cost structure could limit its long-term prospects, however.

At a Glance

THE COUNTRY
Location Central Europe, bordering the North Sea between France and Poland.
Terrain Low plain in the north; high plains, hills, and basins in the center and east; mountainous alpine region in the south.
Climate Temperate.

THE PEOPLE
Population 81,000,000
Ethnic composition Primarily German; Danish minority in the north, Sorbian (Slavic) minority in the east, seven million foreigners.
Religious composition Protestants slightly outnumber Roman Catholics.
Languages spoken German.
Education and literacy Education is compulsory for 10 years. Literacy rate is 99 percent of adults.
Labor force
Total..39,000,000

COUNTRY FACTS
Political and legal The government is led by a president and a chancellor. Legislative decisions are made by a bicameral chamber (no official name for the two chambers as a whole). Legal system: Civil law system with indigenous concepts; judicial review of legislative acts in the Federal Constitutional Court; has not accepted compulsory International Court of Justice jurisdiction.
Telephone Highly developed in the west, with modern telecommunication services. Telephone systems in the east need improvement and modernization. There are 40,300,000 telephones. International country code: [49]. Selected city codes: Berlin (30), Frankfurt (69), Hamburg (40), Munich (89).
Transportation Railroads cover more than 31,000 kilometers; roads are in good condition and most of the 625,000 kilometers of highway are paved. A number of usable ports and major airports are available with international capabilities.
Environment A strategic location on the North European Plain and along the entrance to the Baltic Sea. Raw sewage and industrial effluents from rivers in eastern Germany have polluted the Baltic Sea; air pollution rates are climbing because of vehicle exhausts. Current issues include emission from coal-burning utilities and industries in the southeast, and lead emissions from vehicle exhausts, air pollution, acid rain.
Media Germany has a large number of newspapers and total circulation is almost 30 million. There are hundreds of small press agencies and services. Much of the national and international news is furnished by the German Press Agency. There are 70 million radios and 44.4 million television sets; and 80 AM, 470 FM, and 225 TV stations.
Health Good medical facilities throughout the country, with health insurance available to everyone. Benefits are broad, including free choice of doctors, unlimited physician visits, and comprehensive dental benefits. Water is drinkable and safe. The birth rate is 11.4 per 1,000; the death rate is 11.4 per 1,000 citizens. The vast majority of children are immunized for a variety of illnesses, including tuberculosis and polio. Life expectancy is 76 years.

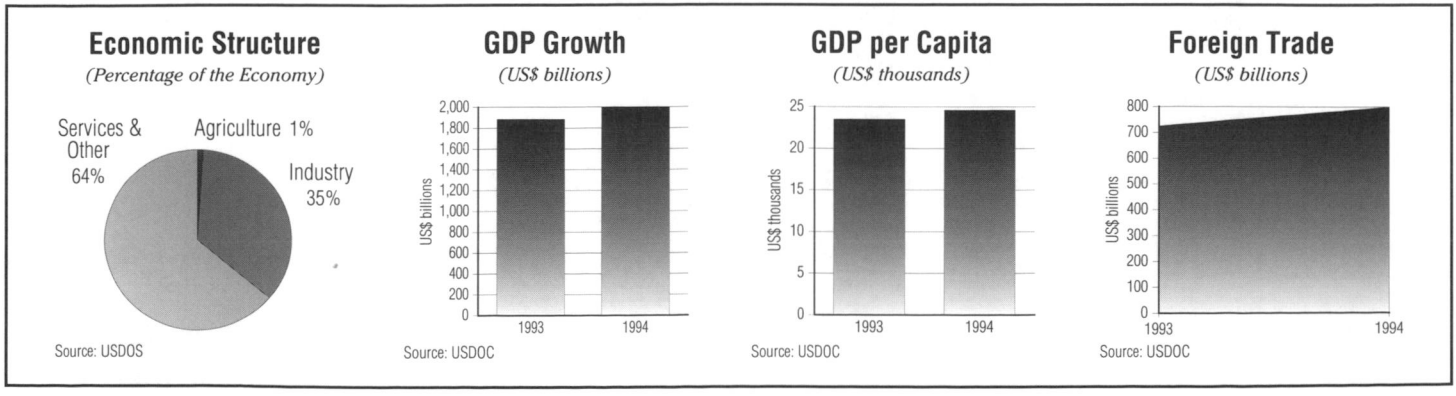

Economic Structure
(Percentage of the Economy)

Services & Other 64%
Agriculture 1%
Industry 35%

Source: USDOS

GDP Growth
(US$ billions)

1993   1994

Source: USDOC

GDP per Capita
(US$ thousands)

1993   1994

Source: USDOC

Foreign Trade
(US$ billions)

1993   1994

Source: USDOC

Germany

- ★ National capital
- ⊙ State capital
- ● Secondary city
- ── Primary road
- ── Secondary road
- ······ Railroad
- ── State border
- ━━ International border

0   50   100 km
0   50   100 mi

*The seat of the unified German government is being relocated from Bonn to Berlin over the next 10-12 years.

North Sea

Denmark

Baltic Sea

Flensburg
Puttgarden
Kiel
Schleswig-Holstein
Lübeck
Stralsund
Rostock
Schwerin
Mecklenburg-Vorpommern

Bremerhaven
Hamburg
Bremen
Boizenburg
Hamburg
Schwedt
Poland

Oldenburg
Niedersachsen (Lower Saxony)
Wittenberge
Brandenburg

Netherlands

Osnabrück
Hannover
Wolfsburg
Helmstedt
Potsdam
★ Berlin
Berlin

Münster
Braunschweig
Magdeburg
52°

Bielefeld
Nordrhein-Westfalen (North Rhine Westphalia)
Paderborn
Sachsen-Anhalt (Saxony Anhalt)
Dessau
Leipzig
Sachsen (Saxony)

Essen
Dortmund
Kassel
Dresden

Düsseldorf
Cologne
Erfurt
Weimar
Karl-Marx-Stadt

Belgium

Aachen
★ Bonn
Hesse
Bad Hersfeld
Rudolstadt
Thüringen (Thuringia)
Hof

Koblenz
Frankfurt
Czech Republic

Wiesbaden
Rhineland-Pfalz
Mainz
Bamberg

Luxembourg

Saarland
Mannheim
Würzburg
Nürnberg

Saarbrücken
Heidelberg
Heilbronn
Regensburg

Karlsruhe
Bayern (Bavaria)
Passau

Stuttgart

France

Baden-Württemburg
Ulm
Augsburg
Munich
48°

Freiburg

Konstanz
Austria

Switzerland
Liechtenstein
Italy

Foreign Trade

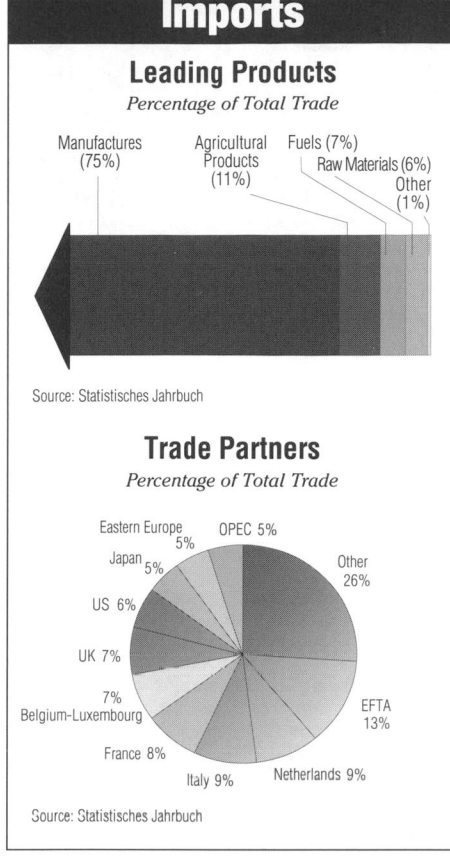

Imports

Leading Products
Percentage of Total Trade

Manufactures (75%)
Agricultural Products (11%)
Fuels (7%)
Raw Materials (6%)
Other (1%)

Source: Statistisches Jahrbuch

Trade Partners
Percentage of Total Trade

Eastern Europe 5%
OPEC 5%
Japan 5%
US 6%
UK 7%
Belgium-Luxembourg 7%
France 8%
Italy 9%
Netherlands 9%
EFTA 13%
Other 26%

Source: Statistisches Jahrbuch

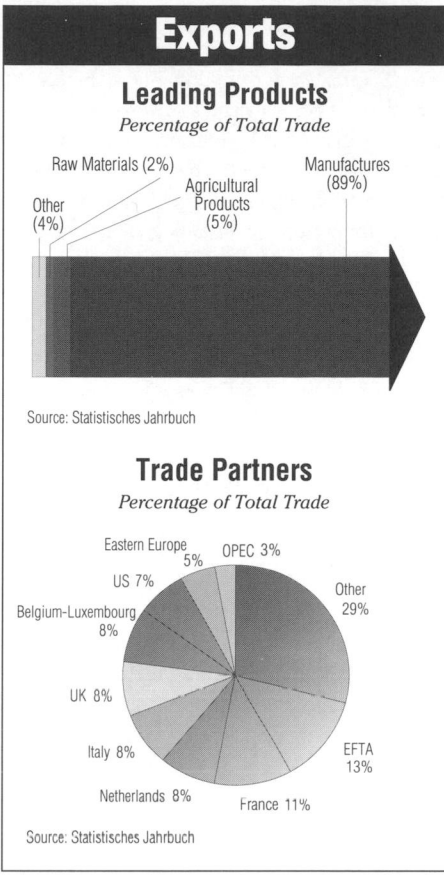

Exports

Leading Products
Percentage of Total Trade

Raw Materials (2%)
Other (4%)
Agricultural Products (5%)
Manufactures (89%)

Source: Statistisches Jahrbuch

Trade Partners
Percentage of Total Trade

Eastern Europe 5%
OPEC 3%
US 7%
Belgium-Luxembourg 8%
UK 8%
Italy 8%
Netherlands 8%
France 11%
EFTA 13%
Other 29%

Source: Statistisches Jahrbuch

Opportunities

FOR IMPORTING TO GERMANY

- air conditioning and refrigeration equipment
- aircrafts and parts
- analytic and scientific instruments
- automobiles and automobile parts
- clothing
- computers and computer software and peripherals
- consumer foods
- electrical power generating equipment
- electronic components
- environmental protection goods and services
- fiber optic cables, telecommunication products
- fish, beer, and wine
- industrial chemicals
- industrial process controls
- lumber products
- medical equipment and supplies
- metalworking equipment
- sporting goods and recreational equipment
- synthetics

FOR EXPORTING FROM GERMANY

- agricultural products
- automobiles and automobile parts
- cement
- chemicals
- coal
- cutlery
- electrical equipment
- electronic products
- fuel
- glass and ceramic products
- household tools
- iron and steel products
- machine tools
- machinery
- military goods and equipment
- optical and photographic goods
- textiles
- toys, games, and sporting goods

GROWTH SECTORS

- audio-visual and multimedia equipment
- computer software and services
- convenience foods
- electrical power generating equipment
- franchises
- pollution control equipment
- sporting goods
- telecommunication products

GOVERNMENT PROCUREMENT

- educational goods and services
- electrical power equipment
- environmental protection technology
- health care goods and services
- infrastructure development goods and services
- telecommunication products

Trade News

RULES AND REGULATIONS

- **Tariffs and import taxes** In Germany, a variable levy system exists for a wide range of products. The variable system will be replaced by a fixed tariff under the GATT Uruguay Round agreement.
- **Standards** Safety standards are zealously applied in the German market and can complicate the process of importing goods. Even if an import product does not require modification, it will often require testing and certification. Two important certificates are (1) the Gepruefte Sicherheit (GS) certificate, for mechanical goods, and (2) the Verband Deutscher Electrotechniker (VDE) certificate for electrical components. These certificates are not always legally required—a common exception is for insurance purposes—but they do enhance marketing opportunities. German standards will probably form the basis for the European Union (EU) standards that are being developed.
- **Import licenses** No import licenses are needed in Germany at this time except for those imposed by the EU.
- **Customs procedures** The customs procedures in Germany are relatively streamlined and efficient; things move swiftly.

FREIGHT FORWARDERS

Argo Reederei Richard Adler & Söhne
Argo-Haus
Postfach 107529
2800 Bremen
Tel: (421) 3630725
Fax: (421) 321575
Telex: 245206

Aug. Bolten, Wm. Miller's Nachfolger GmbH & Co.
Mattentwiete 8
2000 Hamburg 11
Tel: (40) 3601-1
Telex: 211431

Bugsier-Reederei-und Bergungs-Gesellschaft mbH
Johannisbollwerk 10
Postfach 112273
2000 Hamburg 11
Tel: (40) 311110
Fax: (40) 313693
Telex: 211228

Christian F. Ahrenkiel GmbH & Co. KG
Ander Alster 45
Postfach 100220
2000 Hamburg 1
Tel: (40) 248380
Fax: (40) 24838346
Telex: 2195560

DAL Deutsche Afrika-LinienGmbH & Co.
Palmaille 45
2000 Hamburg
Tel: (40) 308160
Fax: (40) 38016-663
Telex: 212897-0

DSR-Lines, Deutsche Seereederei Rostock GmbH
Haus der Schiffahrt
POB 2188
2500 Rostock 1
Tel: (81) 458-0
Fax: (81) 36-62-18-31

Deutsche ShellTanker GmbH
Ueberseering 35
Postfach 600 440
2000 Hamburg 60
Tel: (40) 6324
Fax: (40) 6319446
Telex: 2163091

F. Laeisz Schiffahrts GmbH & Co.
Trostbräcke 1
Postfach 111111
2000 Hamburg 11
Tel: (40) 36880
Fax: (40) 403143

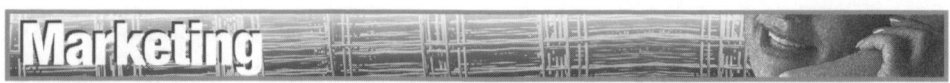

Overview

At the center of the new Europe, Germany's developed infrastructure, stability, and highly qualified work force is attractive to international trading firms. Intense competition from domestic suppliers and EU producers make it imperative that foreign companies compete vigorously and follow sound business practices. The German market can be approached through various channels, some entailing little or no participation by the exporter and others requiring direct and active involvement. The choice of an appropriate channel depends upon the product itself, financial considerations, and such other factors as the size of the targeted market, long-term sales potential, and the need for promoting, installing, or servicing the products. For suppliers of manufactured goods, the principal marketing area in Germany is a great urban-industrial complex running north to south along the Rhine and Main River systems. Richly endowed, densely populated, and heavily industrialized, this area is among the most productive in the world. Outside this major area, a number of specialized market centers also exist, such as Bremen, Berlin, Hamburg, Munich, Nuremberg, and Stuttgart, and particular industries have tended to congregate there.

Distribution

A number of foreign firms import or produce and sell their products through their own branch offices or subsidiaries. This clearly offers the most effective means of reaching the market since the branch office can devote its full attention and resources to the parent firm's product, and also give an added sense of permanency—Germans fear that foreigners may not be committed to a long-term presence in their markets. Distribution through franchises can also be an effective means of operating, but without the expenses of overhead, payrolls, and direct management. Franchising, as a vertically structured, strict form of cooperation has developed into a well-accepted business practice in Germany over the last decade and is expected to gain even greater importance in the years to come. But by far the greatest portion of Germany's imports move through import houses, wholesalers, and other general importer-distributors. These firms handle all kinds of consumer and industrial supplies, as well as smaller types of equipment.

Agents, Distributors, and Partners

It is not always possible to appoint a single agent to cover all of Germany, which is large, diverse, and has no single acknowledged commercial center serving the entire country. Most firms willing to take on agency business are medium-sized and are usually unable to cover the entire territory. Exporters contemplating sales to the German market may find it advisable to concentrate in one or two areas. For example, the southern German areas of Bavaria and Baden-Wurttemberg represent dynamic growth areas which have been largely overlooked by many companies. The most popular form of an agency is a commission agency. German law favors the agent over the principal; the legal implications of concluding an agency agreement should be carefully considered and German legal counsel consulted.

Selling Techniques

Historically, Germany has long been the world leader in trade fairs, which are the most important sales tool in the German market and offer ideal forums for introducing new firms and products. German fairs also serve as meeting places for manufacturers to inspect competitive products, for licensors to negotiate arrangements, and for technicians to exchange ideas. With regard to certain restricted products, an exhibition in a trade fair is a precondition for obtaining a quota allocation.

Advertising

Under the impact of the EU, advertising is expected to continue to adjust to the subtleties of a multinational market. German advertising is regulated partly by judicial rules and partly by voluntary guidelines developed by major industry associations. Legal regulations allow competitors to bring suit if advertising violates "good manners." It should be noted that use of comparisons and superlatives in advertising in Germany is strictly regulated. The offer of premiums—common in many markets—is prohibited in Germany. Any proposed campaign needs to be carefully discussed with local business partners or a German advertising agency. Many technical and specialized periodicals deal with all aspects of technology and business in Germany, and most of these carry advertising. There are also many newspapers and magazines that accept advertising and provide guidelines to appropriate style. Television and radio are also extremely important for mass market products.

Service and Customer Support

The German commercial customer expects quick and easy access to product information, replacement parts, and service and repairs. Firms without a branch or agency presence capable of providing such attention will find it difficult to do business in Germany.

Marketing in Germany

MARKETING TIPS

- **Language** It is essential that correspondence be in German.
- **Metric system** Weights and measures should be in the metric system.
- **Price quotations** When first approaching the market, and especially when using the official services, please note that prices must be quoted in Deutsche marks.
- **Buying seasons** With regard to consumer goods, the dates of important specialized trade fairs and exhibitions are a useful guide to buying seasons. Contact the Trade Fair Association for current date information.
- **Long-term commitment** The main complaint cited by Germans with regard to foreign suppliers is a lack of commitment to their market; foreigners should plan to be in the market for an extended period and to provide backup service commensurate with such intentions.
- **Consumer guarantee** Guarantees for goods purchased is a confidence-building effort to show good faith in the product.
- **Government markets** Although Germany currently subscribes to GATT and EU conventions requiring open competition for procurement, it in fact has many specific requirements, established relationships, and effective national and EU preferences in place.
- **Legal counsel** Complying with Germany's restrictions on advertising content may require the advice of local legal counsel.
- **Trade shows** Trade shows are considered to be one of the best resources of gathering and giving information in Germany. These highly attended functions are held often and are known for their resource availability throughout the world. Trade shows in Germany are well-publicized throughout the world.

AD AGENCIES

Bates Frankfurt
Hanauer Landstrasse 287-289
60314 Frankfurt/Main
Tel: (69) 40572-00
Fax: (69) 40572-359

Conquest Europe
Bockenheimer Landstrasse 104
60323 Frankfurt/Main
Tel: (69) 130-900
Fax: (69) 131-507

D'Arcy Masius Benton & Bowles GmbH
Schaumainkai 87
60598 Frankfurt/Main
Tel: (69) 63-00-70
Fax: (69) 63-07-355

McCann-Erickson Deutschland GmbH
Grosser Hasenpfad 44
60598 Frankfurt/Main
Tel: (69) 60507-0
Fax: (69) 60507-666

Saatchi & Saatchi Advertising
Wiesenau 38-40
60599 Frankfurt/Main
Tel: (69) 96225-0
Fax: (69) 96225-555

J. Walter Thompson GmbH
Bockenheimer Landstr. 104
60313 Frankfurt/Main
Tel: (69) 2192-0
Fax: (69) 2192-430

MARKET RESEARCH CONTACTS

Federal Association of German Consultants
Friedrich-Wilhelm-Strasse 2
53133 Bonn
Tel: (228) 23-80-55
Fax: (228) 23-06-25

Federation of German Market Research Institutes
Marktplatz 9
63065 Offenbach
Tel: (69) 81-43-25
Fax: (69) 81-43-88

Business Culture

Greetings and Courtesies

High standards of impersonal formality are practiced in Germany's business society where titles and positions are very important. Use professional titles, followed by professional degrees. For instance, the director of a laboratory with a doctoral degree is addressed "Herr Direktor Dr." Normally, you will be introduced to persons of high rank by a junior member. If many introductions are taking place, you need only shake hands with the senior colleague. A firm handshake and direct eye contact leaves a good impression. When meeting a German couple, shake hands with the wife first. Though English is spoken with familiarity, German is the language of business. Do not assume English will be spoken, as this assumption offends Germans. Ask, prior to meetings, if English is acceptable, and prepare accordingly—bringing a translator if necessary. Gift-giving is not a business practice. In fact, the exchange of business gifts is subject to German laws. A small gift representing your country or company is allowable (less than US $60), and all goods given or exchanged must be marked by your company name and logo. The Germans are avid card senders, and remembering someone's birthday or a special occasion in the form of a card is greatly appreciated. In business as well as social situations, always be punctual. Germans gauge a good amount of your character on punctuality; sometimes, even a traffic jam won't exonerate you from tardiness.

Business Ethic and Framework

Germans are disciplined, hardworking people who generally keep their personal lives very private and their business lives in the office. Third-party introductions are imperative and a letter of introduction is very important. Cold calls are not advised. Germans work with foreign firms primarily when they have something that can't be purchased locally and providing the product or service will not interfere with existing German commercial strengths. Further, Germans disfavor any potential relationship that does not clearly define the advantages to their own side in the business proposition. Hierarchy abounds in German business and it is important to familiarize yourself to such nuances. Be respectful of secretaries and receptionists for they will convey their impressions of you to those executives behind the door. Do not try to go over the head of the authorized manager dealing with you. Again, expect to encounter impersonal formality in your initial relations.

Decision Making

Within German corporations, many departments will make a decision by consensus. Decisions involving new projects or large amounts of money must be made by a top level management board. Individuals do not make independent decisions but can make strong recommendations. Otherwise, Germans don't like to be pushed for a decision and too much pressure could jeopardize your success. There are normally at least two signatures appended to agreements, and you'll want to take care to note precisely who is allowed to authorize or decide upon what specific matters. Some executives have "binding power," while some have authority to commit the firm in specific areas only.

Women

Over 40 percent of the German work force are women, but only a few are found in the hierarchy of top corporate management. While scrupulously polite to foreign businesswomen, German men usually do not take them as seriously as they do male representatives. However, a conscientious, well-prepared presentation will receive the attention and respect it deserves.

Meetings

Few pleasantries will precede the business at hand. After greetings, cards will be exchanged and your card should note your title, degrees, and the founding date of your firm. Do not sit until you are invited to do so. Be thoroughly prepared with facts and information regarding your product, business, and industry, and be well informed about competitors in your field, for it's guaranteed your German counterparts will be highly knowledgeable and will use their information to question you.

Business Attire

Dress conservatively; a dark or gray suit, white shirt, and subdued tie serve best. Good posture and a physically fit appearance are a reflection of the discipline Germans so admire. Well-tailored suits and dresses—not too tight or too short—are worn by businesswomen. Avoid flashy costume jewelry.

Cultural Cautions

DO'S

- Appointments are essential and should be scheduled well in advance, avoiding late afternoon hours as Germans like to leave work promptly at the end of the day.
- If invited to a German home for a meal, take flowers to the hostess (in odd numbers except 13, and no roses). Unwrap them before you hand them to her.
- Always maintain a polite, formal reserve until your German colleague indicates a more relaxed and casual relationship is in order.

DON'TS

- Handshaking is a national ritual in Germany. When meeting several people at once, don't cross over a handshake to extend your hand to another. Bad form.
- Do not be offended by what appears to be a terse greeting or an abrupt farewell as Germans are efficiently adept at the business of doing business.
- Don't point your finger to your head and make a screwing motion. It's interpreted as "You're crazy" and is a major form of insult in German society.

CUSTOMS

- Gentlemen walk and sit to the left of ladies and men of senior business rank. But on busy streets, men always walk on the side where traffic is passing.
- Most Germans are well-educated, practical, sophisticated, and hardworking business practitioners who prefer a clear separation between work life and private life. They do not generally entertain foreigners around business matters (though a younger generation appears to be breaking with this tradition). Meetings are usually conducted on the business premise, and it's not uncommon for visitors to be left to fend for themselves if a meeting intrudes on the lunch hour. Similarly, their well-focused work efforts stop promptly at the end of a workday, and a visitor's attempt to extend business beyond the day is not appreciated. German social codes can be as demanding as business codes.
- As a dinner guest, you should wait to drink from your wine glass until your host has made a toast or taken the first sip. You'll find your fork on your left and knife on your right, and the fork remains in your left hand—no switching utensils. Keep both hands above the table at all times; avoid resting your hands in your lap. Sometimes, the guest to the hostess' left is expected to say a few words of appreciation, on behalf of all the guests, at the end of a meal. Wait until others have gotten up from the table before rising yourself.

OBSERVATIONS

- Regardless of their distinct formality in both business and social practices, Germans are generally very tolerant and will go to extremes to make a guest feel at ease.
- Germans have a well-deserved and long-standing sense of pride for their national heritage in the arts, sciences, and education. Theirs is a status-conscious society where manners, intelligence, charm, and physical appearance count in the evaluation of character. Likewise, clothes, cars, and other material symbols of success have a bearing on the assessments of their own countrymen, as well as foreigners.

NEGOTIATIONS

- Germans are very firm negotiators and particularly shrewd bargainers with the ability to garner concessions out of a deal right up to the moment of signing a contract.
- Negotiators will often pressure you on price and regularly mention your competition. Be realistic in your expectations; allow room to negotiate prices if necessary. Be assured, your German colleagues will be well-briefed before a meeting and may know your market, competitors, and your product better than you do. You'll want to be prepared for such an eventuality.

Legal

Legal System

Germany is a civil law country with a legal system that is very similar to that of other Western European countries.

Intellectual Property Rights

Patents Patent protection is strong and litigation over patent infringement is not unusual in Germany. The time between patent application and the official approval may extend from a few years to several years. In addition to the national patent registration procedure, the European Patent Convention allows for parallel patent protection in the EU member states. Patent protection is 20 years from the date of the application, not from the date the application was approved. The government has acceded to the World Intellectual Property Organization (WIPO).

Trademarks On average, it takes six months to obtain trademark registration; however, it can take longer. Protection for the layout design of semiconductor chips is provided through topology registration. This entails copyrighting a blueprint of the chip. The 10-year protection period begins with application, not the date the registration was initially approved, and registration is renewable at its protection period.

Copyrights Copyright protection extends 70 years after the author's death. To register copyrights, authors need only attach a small "c" to their work and are thus copyrighted. To contest the authorship of the work, someone must prove that they are the originators of the work. Due to recent amendments to the German Copyrights Act, computer software will now as a rule be copyright protected. In practice, product piracy concerning software does remain a problem.

Trade secrets Although often there is no formal statutory protection, trade secrets will be protected under general contract laws, and infringement will give rise to claims for substantial damages if pursued. Infringement often may also justify an injunction against the transferee of the protected trade secret information.

Business Registration

Generally, the same rules apply to a business registration regardless of whether the owner of the business is German or not. A business must be registered with tax and social security authorities, as well as with the local Chamber of Commerce and the local trade supervisory authorities, and usually (always if a company or partnership) it must be entered into the Commercial Register. In addition, specific licenses from the appropriate authorities may be required, often depending on the type of business in question.

Contracts and Dispute Resolution

German contracts are traditionally short as compared to Western contracts. They often only show those details in which the parties wish to deviate from the statutory provisions. General terms and conditions are widely used but subject to close scrutiny by the courts as to the fairness of their content and application. Remedies for breach of contract normally include specific performance as well as damages or rescission. In international contracts, a choice of law and competent court is usual. Arbitration clauses are common practice in contracts and are given with substantial weight. There is no discovery procedure either in litigation or arbitration, and it is advisable to evidence important agreements in writing and obtain the other party's signature.

Notaries

Certain documents, including the Articles of Private and Public Companies, the transfer of shares in private companies, and the sale or encumbrance of real property, cannot be set up validly except before a notary. Notaries will also certify signatures and are specialized legal professionals certified with the State. The notarial authentication of a document will bear a strong presumption of validity similar to official records of documents.

Labor

Employees have constitutional rights to associate in unions and to strike if desired. The collective bargaining power of the unions—organized by lines of business rather than by company—is considerable. Although there is no legal minimum wage, de facto minimum wages are quite substantial, and related costs to be borne by the employer (such as half of mandated social security costs) are rather high. The average work week is 38.5 hours, depending on the collective agreement made with the unions in a particular line of business, and 30 days' paid vacation per year is usual. An employer may find it extremely difficult to give notice of dismissal to some employees because of the strong statutory protection available.

Source: Hasche & Eschenlohr

Legal Matters

LEGAL BRIEFS

- **Corporations** A private limited company which can be set up by a sole shareholder must have a legal minimum capital of DM50,000. Formation costs are reasonably low. The shareholders have a large degree of autonomy as to the content of the company's by-laws.

- **LImited partnership** A limited partnership is formed by having a private limited company as its sole general partner.

- **Employee participation** German law provides for employee participation in certain business decisions, the extent of which varies with the number of employees and the type of business involved.

- **Antitrust** German antitrust laws are strongly influenced by European and American rules and laws. Mergers are often structured to allow the European antitrust authorities, which focus more on industrial policy, rather than the more competition-oriented German authorities, to look into the antitrust impact of a transaction.

- **Unfair competition** German rules tend to be much stricter than those in many other European countries. It goes without saying that this fact does not help in unifying European unfair competition rules.

- **Foreign ownership** Foreign ownership of real estate and companies is permitted and needs no approval. The transfer of profits back to a foreign owner's regular place of residence is allowed. Foreigners may act as general managers, CEOs, presidents, and board members of German companies.

LEGAL CONTACTS

Hasche & Eschenlohr
Meinkestraße 13
10719 Berlin
Tel: (30) 881-9783
Fax: (30) 882-3479

Baker & McKenzie
Döser, Amereller, Noack
Rankestrasse 9
1000 Berlin 30
Tel: (30) 882-3100, 882-7397
Fax: (30) 882-5796

Hasche & Eschenlohr
Valentinskamp 88
20355 Hamburg
Tel: (40) 35-0020
Fax: (40) 35-002-152

Haarmann, Hemmelrath & Partner
Budapester Strasse 40a
1000 Berlin

Albert Flad & Schlosshan
Cronstettenstrasse 66
60322 Frankfurt/Main
Tel: (69) 55 02 26

Doser Amereller Noack
Bethmannstrasse 50-54
60311 Frankfurt/Main
Tel: (69) 299080
Fax: (69) 29908108

Heuking Kuhn Kunz Wojtek
Lindenstrasse 37
60325 Frankfurt/Main
Tel: (69) 975610
Fax: (69) 97561200

Leipnitz & Partner
Feuerbachstrabe 8
60325 Frankfurt/Main
Tel: (69) 17000017

Norr, Stiefenhofer & Lutz
Freiherr-Vom-Stein-Strabe 11
60323 Frankfurt/Main
Tel: (69) 172917

Punder, Nolhard, Weber & Axster
Mainzer Landstrasse 46
60325 Frankfurt/Main
Tel: (69) 71 99-01
Fax: (69) 71 99-4000

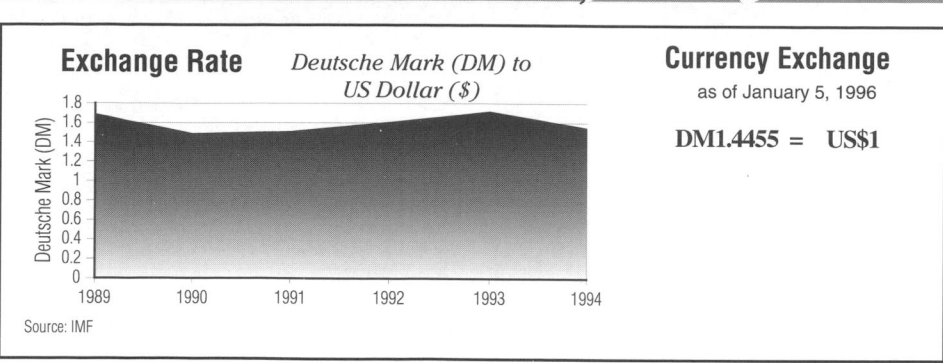

Exchange Rate — Deutsche Mark (DM) to US Dollar ($)

Source: IMF

Currency Exchange
as of January 5, 1996

DM1.4455 = US$1

Currency

The currency in use is the Deutsche Mark (DM).

Foreign Exchange

Official buy and sell rates are quoted by the central bank, the Deutsche Bundesbank, for 17 foreign currencies. The Bundesbank will buy and sell currencies of other states participating in the European Monetary System in unlimited amounts at specified intervention rates. Germany and other participating countries do not maintain exchange rates within fixed limits, but countries may intervene occasionally to smooth out erratic fluctuations. There is no official fixed rate in the forward exchange market, and all transactions are negotiated at a free market rate. Restrictions have been imposed for transfers with the Federal Republic of Yugoslavia, Haiti, and Libya.

Capital Transfers

There are no restrictions on the movement or repatriation of capital, foreign exchange earnings, or dividends. There are no restrictions on currency convertibility at the market rate, and no queuing for foreign exchange. Residents do not have to repatriate or surrender foreign exchange earnings. Domestic and foreign securities may be freely imported or exported.

Investment Incentives

A comprehensive package of incentives was created to accelerate the pace of investment in Germany. Some particular incentives include tax-based investment allowances, research investment grants, and Federal Guarantee programs for investment credits.

Investment Restrictions

There are no restrictions for acquisition, takeovers, or reinvestment by foreigners that are at variance with regulations for nationals.

Money Matters

BITS AND PIECES

- **Infrastructure** Germany's financial infrastructure is highly developed and modern. There are over 45,000 bank offices capable of taking deposits, making loans, and trading in securities. Private banks, publicly-owned banks, and cooperatives all offer a full range of services to customers.
- **Credit** Credit is available at market rates to both foreign and domestic investors. Several types of credit instruments are available.
- **Free trade zones** Free trade import zones exist, with the major ones in Hamburg, Bremen, and Bremerhaven.
- **Gold** There is a free gold market in Frankfurt. Residents may hold gold in any form and may negotiate with residents or nonresidents.
- **Investment restrictions** Although private direct investment in either direction can be restricted for policy reasons, no such restrictions have been imposed to date.

BANKS

Bankhaus Gebrüder Bethmann
Bethmannstr. 7-9
Postfach 100349
6000 Frankfurt/Main
Tel: (69) 2177-0
Fax: (69) 2177-283

BfG-Bank AG
Theaterplatz 2
6000 Frankfurt/Main
Tel: (69) 2580
Fax: (69) 2587578

Citibank N.A.
Neue Mainzer Strasse 75
60311 Frankfurt/Main
Tel: (69) 136-60
Fax: (69) 13-66-11-13

Commerzbank AG
Neue Mainzer Strasse 32-36
60261 Frankfurt/Main
Tel: (69) 136-20
Fax: (69) 12-62-40-21

Deutsche Bank AG
Taunusanlage 12
60262 Frankfurt/Main
Tel: (69) 910-30
Fax: (69) 91-03-42-27

Deutsche Bundesbank
(Bank of the Federal Republic of Germany)
Wilhelm-Epstein-Str. 14
60431 Frankfurt/Main
Tel: (69) 1581
Fax: (09) 5601071

Dresdner Bank AG
Juergen-Ponto-Platz 1
60631 Frankfurt/Main
Tel: (69) 263-0
Fax: (69) 263-40-04

J.P. Morgan GmbH
Mainzer Landstrasse 46
60325 Frankfurt/Main
Tel: (69) 712-40
Fax: (69) 712-43-06

Salomon Brothers AG
Wiesinhuettenstrasse 10
60329 Frankfurt/Main
Tel: (69) 260-70
Fax: (69) 23-25-70

Merill Lynch Bank AG
Neue Mainzer Strasse 75
60311 Frankfurt/Main
Tel: (69) 299-40
Fax: (69) 97-11-72-47

Westdeutsche Landesbank
Herzogstrasse 15
40199 Dusseldorf/Main
Tel: (211) 862-01
Fax: (211) 826-61-20

TAXATION

Taxation requires sophisticated knowledge of complex rules and regulations specific to each country. For more detailed information, we suggest you refer to the Ernst & Young Corporate Tax Guide and Directory, available from the Ernst & Young accounting office in your country, or from:

Ernst & Young GmbH
Fraunhoferstrasse 33-36
10587 Berlin
Federal Republic of Germany
Tel: (30) 34 78 6-600
Fax: (30) 34 78 6-603

At a Glance

Corporate Income Tax Rate (%)(a) (c)	45
Trade Income Tax Rate (Average Rate) (%) (b)	16
Capital Gains Tax Rate (%)(c)	45
Branch Tax Rate (%)(c)	42
Withholding Tax (%)(c) (d)	
Dividends (e)	25
Interest (f)	0
Royalties from Patents, Know-how, etc. (g)	25
Branch Remittance Tax	0
Net Operating Losses (Years)	
Carryback (h)	2
Carryforward (i)	Unlimited

(a) A 30% rate applies to distributed profits.
(b) This is a local income tax imposed by municipalities. The rate varies from 13% to 20.5%, depending on the municipality.
(c) Effective January 1, 1995, a 7.5% tax surcharge is imposed. Prepayments of corporate income tax and withholding tax payments due after December 31, 1994, are subject to the surcharge.
(d) These rates may be reduced by tax treaties.
(e) This rate is applicable to dividends paid to residents and nonresidents. Special rules apply to distributions to EU parent companies. A reduced 5% withholding tax is applied to dividends paid to a company in an EU country, if at the time of distribution, the recipient has owned at least 25% of the capital of the distributing company for an uninterrupted period of 12 months.
(f) A 30% interest withholding tax is imposed if a bank is the paying entity. For over-the-counter business, the rate is 35%. Over-the-counter business refers to bank transactions carried out over the bank counter, without the securities being on deposit at the bank. The interest withholding tax is not imposed on intercompany loans and interbank loans. Interest paid to nonresidents is not subject to the withholding tax, except for the 35% withholding on over-the-counter business. However, nonresidents may apply for a refund of the 35% withholding tax if a treaty exemption applies. A 25% withholding tax is imposed on certain types of debt instruments.
(g) Applicable to payments to nonresidents.
(h) The loss carryback, which is optional, is available for corporate income tax purposes, but not for trade income tax purposes. The maximum carryback is DM 10 million.
(i) Unlimited carryforward is applicable for both corporate income tax and trade income tax purposes.

- **Note:** Foreign source income is usually taxable, with a credit for foreign income taxes paid.

Business Travel

LH 1906	MADRID	935	113-3
LH 1022	STUTTGART HBF.	935	-
AF 1701	LYON	940	683-6
AY 822	HELSINKI	940	113-3
AA 071	SFRANCISCO-DALLAS	945	731-7

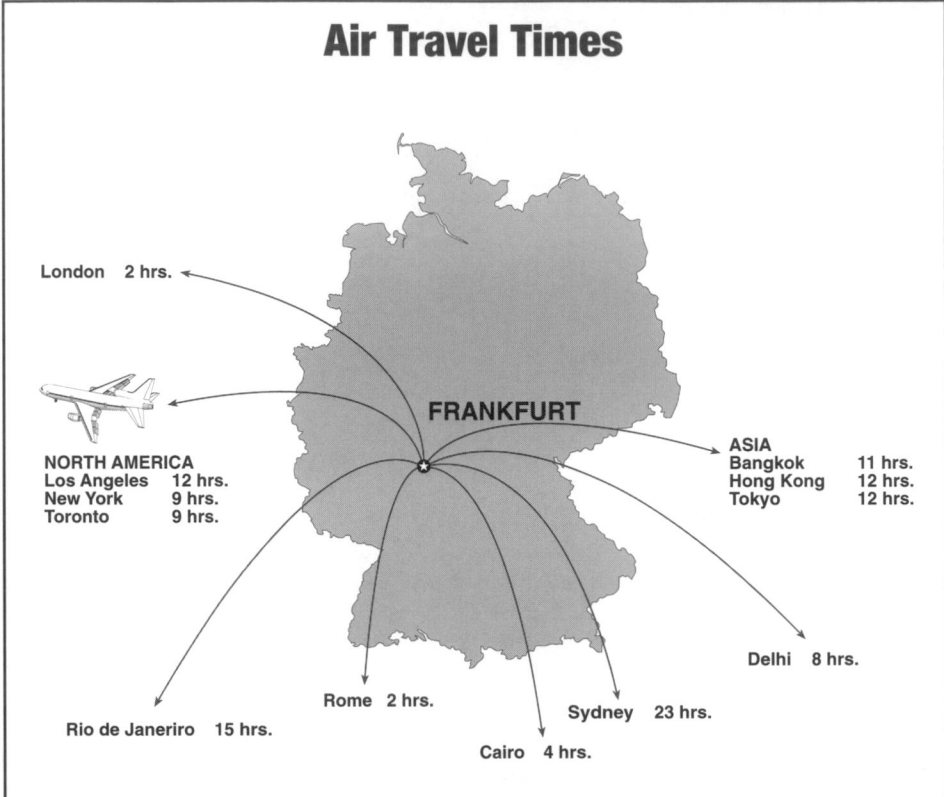

Air Travel Times

London   2 hrs.

FRANKFURT

NORTH AMERICA
Los Angeles   12 hrs.
New York   9 hrs.
Toronto   9 hrs.

ASIA
Bangkok   11 hrs.
Hong Kong   12 hrs.
Tokyo   12 hrs.

Delhi   8 hrs.

Sydney   23 hrs.

Rome   2 hrs.

Cairo   4 hrs.

Rio de Janeriro   15 hrs.

COMMUNICATION

Telephones Telecommunications are excellent in Germany. Public phones are available on streets and in post offices. There are phones for domestic calls only, and phones marked with green signs for international calls. Many public phones require phone cards that can be purchased from post offices, banks, and some newsstands. Callers should have no problem calling directly to just about anywhere in the world.

Fax Fax and telegram services are also available at post offices but are expensive. Some shops and businesses offer slightly cheaper service.

Post office Postal service in Germany is excellent. Post offices are generally open on weekdays from 8:00 am until 6:00 pm. The main post office in each city is usually open Saturdays until noon as well.

BEST TRAVEL BOOKS

Fodor's Travel Guide, Germany. Tourist oriented, excellent source of city details. Good for business traveling and tourist information.

Fodor's Exploring Guide, Germany. Tourist oriented, excellent source of city details.

Fodor's Europe, Best of 31 Countries. Contains information on historical towns, great culture, scenic coastal countryside.

Berlitz Business Travel Guide, Europe. Concise economic details, successful trip planning, background information on people and cities, useful facts and addresses.

Culture Shock, A Guide to Customs and Etiquette, Germany.

Do's and Taboo's Around the World. The Bestselling Guide to International Behavior. Edited by Roger Axtell, compiled by the Parker Pen Company. The ultimate guide to international behavior, now completely updated and expanded. Helpful, fun to read!

Multinational Travel Companion Executive. Strand Publishing.

USEFUL TELEPHONE NUMBERS

If you are calling from outside Germany, you will need to add the country code [49] and any other international dialing requirements from within your country.

Services in Berlin
- Audiovisual .... (30) 21370808
- Computer Rental .... (30) 2190070
- Messenger .... (30) 344011
- Office Space .... (30) 811108, 7923098
- Photocopying ..... (30) 7846058, 8617448, 8025006
- Secretarial .... (30) 241097
- Translation .... (30) 3926567, 3239047
- DHL .... (30) 8815026
- Chamber of Commerce Berlin .... (30) 3031801

Services in Munich
- Computer Rentals .... (89) 4482480, 7551013
- Messenger .... (89) 555444, 3103301
- Secretarial .... (89) 4707071, 4488496
- Translation .... (89) 29015158
- DHL .... (89) 3208111
- Chamber of Commerce Munich .... (89) 8951160
- Telegram .... (89) 1131

Taxis
- Berlin .... (30) 6902 or 240202
- Köln .... (221) 555555
- Bonn .... (228) 555555
- Dusseldorf .... (211) 19410 or 772670
- Frankfurt .... (69) 250001
- Munich .... (89) 21611

Credit Card Information
Lost or stolen credit cards (call collect to the US, regardless of which country the card was issued in.)
- Amex .... [1] (919) 333-3211
- Diner's Club .... [1] (303) 799-1504
- MasterCard .... [1] (314) 275-6690
- Visa .... [1] (410) 581-7931

Travelogue

WORKWEEK

Offices Monday-Friday generally 8:00 am to 5:00 pm.
Banks Monday-Friday 8:30 am to 1:00 pm and 2:30 to 4:00 pm, plus one late evening a week—usually Thursday.
Government Monday-Friday 8:00 am to 12:30 pm and 2:00 to 5:00 pm, Saturday 8:30 am to noon.
Retail Monday-Friday 8:00 am to 6:30 pm, with some shops open until noon on Saturdays. Businesses are open until 10:30 pm on Thursdays. More and more stores are staying open on Sundays.

HOLIDAYS

Holidays 1996
January 1 New Year's Day
April 5 Good Friday*
April 7 Easter Sunday*
April 8 Easter Monday*
May 1 May Day
May 16 Ascension Day
May 27 Whit Monday*
June 17 National Unity Day
November 20 Prayer and Repentance*
December 24 Christmas Eve**
December 25-26 Christmas
*Dates vary each year
**Half day

VISA AND PASSPORT

Foreigners must have a valid passport; however, no business or tourist visa is required for stays of up to 90 days. Citizens of EU countries may enter Germany on an official identity card.

DEPARTURE FORMALITIES

Any amount of German or foreign currency may be brought into or taken out of the country without formality. No other restrictions apply to Germany.

IMMUNIZATION

Immunizations are not necessary for visitors unless they are arriving from an area infected with yellow fever or other communicable disease.

TIPPING

Tipping is not widespread in Germany. Service is included on most bills (*Bedienung*), but it is usual to round up to the nearest whole number if satisfied with service. Taxi drivers and other service providers appreciate a slight tip, but it is not necessary.

CRIME

While Germany has a low rate of violent crime, street crime is not uncommon. Pickpocketing and purse snatching occur in crowded areas, such as public transportation, department stores, train stations, and tourist attractions. Keep an eye on valuables, and be sure to lock and keep belongings out-of-sight in automobiles. Crimes such as burglary, petty theft, and narcotics trafficking seem to be on the rise.

INFRASTRUCTURE

Germany has highly developed and extensive air, train, highway, hotel, and telecommunications networks. Some areas in eastern Germany have less developed but adequate facilities. The primary gateway to Germany is the Frankfurt/Mainz Rhein-Main Airport. It is also the busiest airport in Europe. Express trains leave often to major cities and local areas. Subways, underground railway, and efficient tram and bus networks are excellent everywhere except eastern Germany, and that is being updated. Taxis are usually beige or white Mercedes and are hired at stands labeled "Taxi" or "*Droschke.*" Car rental services are available at the airports; make advance reservations. Speeds are fast on the motorways; drive with caution.

NATIONAL TOURIST OFFICE

Deutsche Zentrale fur Tourismus (DZT)
Beethovenstrasse 69
60325 Frankfurt/Main
Tel: (69) 75720

GOVERNMENT AGENCIES

Bundesministerium fuer Wirtschaft
Villemombler Strasse 76
53123 Bonn
Tel: (228) 6-15-44-14
Fax: (228) 6-15-44-31

Federal Bureau for Foreign Trade Information
Agrippastrasse 87-93
50676 Köln
Tel: (221) 2-05-72-49
Fax: (221) 2-05-72-12

Federal Ministry of Economics
Villemombler Strasse 76
53123 Bonn
Tel: (228) 6-15-21-58
Fax: (228) 6-15-26-52

Federal Ministry of Finance
Graurheindorfer Strasse 108
53117 Bonn
Tel: (228) 682-0
Fax: (228) 682-44-20

Federal Ministry of Food, Agriculture and Forestry
Rochusstr. 1
53123 Bonn
Tel: (228) 5291
Fax: (228) 5294262

Federal Ministry of Posts and Telecommunications Information Office of the Federal Government
Welckerstr. 11
53113 Bonn
Tel: (228) 2080
Fax: (228) 2082555

Ministry of Education and Science
Heinemannstr. 2
POB 200108
5300 Bonn 2
Tel: (228) 570
Fax: (228) 57-2096

Ministry of the Environment
Kennedyallee 5
5300 Bonn 2
Tel: (228) 305-0
Fax: (228) 3053225

Ministry of Foreign Affairs
Adenauerallee 99-103
5300 Bonn 1
Tel: (228) 170
Fax: (228) 17-3402

Ministry of Health
Deutschherrenstr. 87
5300 Bonn 2
Tel: (228) 9300
Fax: (228) 9304078

Ministry of Labour and Social Affairs
Rochusstr. 1
Postfach 140280
5300 Bonn 1
Tel: (228) 5271
Fax: (228) 527-2965

Ministry of Research and Technology
Heinemannstr. 2
5300 Bonn 2
Tel: (228) 59-0
Fax: (228) 593601

Ministry of Transport
Kennedyallee 72, POB 200100
5300 Bonn 2
Tel: (228) 300-0
Fax: (228) 300-3428

WORLD TRADE CENTERS

World Trade Center Bremen
Birkenstrasse 15
28195 Bremen
Tel: (421) 174-660
Fax: (421) 174-66-22

World Trade Center Hamburg
Neuer Wall 50
20354 Hamburg
Tel: (40) 37-26-30
Fax: (40) 36-48-82

World Trade Center Hannover GmbH
Aegidientorplatz 1
30159 Hannover
Tel: (511) 302-90-50
Fax: (511) 302-90-55

World Trade Center Leipzig
Grassistrasse 12
04107 Leipzig
Tel: (341) 211-40-75
Fax: (341) 717-03-88

World Trade Center Rostock
Parkstrasse 51
18119 Rostock
Tel: (381) 5-13-95
Fax: (381) 5-22-55

World Trade Center Ruhr Valley
Sparkassenstrasse 1
45879 Gelsenkirchen
Tel: (209) 179-710
Fax: (209) 179-7159

BUSINESS AND TRADE ORGANIZATIONS

Federation of German Industries
Gustav-Heinemann-Ufer 84-88
50968 Köln
Tel: (221) 37-08-00
Fax: (221) 3-70-87-30

Federation of German Wholesale and Foreign Trade
Kaiser-Friedrich Strasse 12
53133 Bonn
Tel: (228) 26-00-40
Fax: (228) 260-04-55

German Electrical and Electronic Manufacturers Association
Stresemannallee 19
60596 Frankfurt/Main
Tel: (69) 630-20
Fax: (69) 630-23-17

German Association of Machinery and Plant Manufacturers
Lyoner Strasse 18
60528 Frankfurt/Main
Tel: (69) 660-30
Fax: (69) 660-35-11

General Association of Commercial Agents and Brokers
Geleniusstrasse 1
50931 Köln
Tel: (221) 51-40-43-44
Fax: (221) 52-57-67

Federation of German Chambers of Industry and Commerce
Adenauerallee 148
53113 Bonn
Tel: (228) 10-40
Fax: (228) 10-41-58

INDUSTRY-SPECIFIC ORGANIZATIONS

Association of Ceramics Industry
Am Hauptbahnhof 12
6000 Frankfurt/Main
Tel: (69) 271050
Fax: (69) 232799

Association of the German Building and Construction Industry
Abraham-Lincoln-Str. 30
Postfach 29 66
6200 Wiesbaden
Tel: (611) 7720
Fax: (611) 7722 0

Association of Jewelry and Silver Industry
Industriehaus
Postfach 470
7530 Pforzheim
Tel: (7231) 33041

Association of German Wood and Synthetics Industry
An den Quellen 10
6200 Wiesbaden
Tel: (611) 17090
Fax: (611) 378908

Federal Association of the Clothing Industry
Mevissenstr. 15
5000 Köln
Tel: (221) 77440
Fax: (221) 7744128

Federal Association of the German Food Industry
Rheinallee 18
5300 Bonn 2
Tel: (228) 351051
Fax: (228) 351992

Federal Association of Glass and Mineral Fibre Industry
Stresemannstr. 26
Postfach 8340
4000 Dusseldorf 1
Tel: (211) 168940
Fax: (211) 1689427

General Association of the Paper, Cardboard and Plastics Processing Industry
Arndstr. 47
6000 Frankfurt/Main
Tel: (69) 740311
Fax: (69) 747714

Federal Printing Association
Biebricher Allee 79
Postfach 1869
6200 Wiesbaden
Tel: (611) 8030
Fax: (611) 803113

General Association of the German Shoe Industry
Waldsts. 44
Postfach 100761
6050 Offenbach/M
Tel: (69) 816272/3

General Association of the Textile Industry in the FRG
Frankfurter Str. 10-14
6326 Eschborn
Tel: (6196) 9660
Fax: (6196) 42170

NEWSPAPERS

Aachener Nachrichten
Dresdner Str. 3
Postfach 110
5100 Aachen
Tel: (241) 5101-0
Telex: 832365

Berliner Morgenpost
Kochstr. 50
Postfach 110303
1000 Berlin 61
Tel: (30) 25910
Fax: (30) 2510928

Berliner Zeitung
Karl-Liebknecht-Str. 29
1026 Berlin
Tel: (30) 2327
Fax: (30) 2125203

Bild-Zeitung
Axel-Springer-Platz 1
2000 Hamburg 36
Tel: (40) 3471
Fax: (40) 345811

Frankfurter Allgemeine Zeitung
6000 Frankfurt/Main
Hellerhofstr. 2-4
Postfach 100808
Tel: (69) 75910
Fax: (69) 75911743

Frankfurter Neue Presse
Frankenallee 71-81
Postfach 100808
6000 Frankfurt/Main
Tel: (69) 75010
Fax: (69) 7306965

Hannoversche Allgemeine Zeitung
Bemeroder Str. 58
Postfach 209
3000 Hannover 71
Tel: (511) 5180
Fax: (511) 513175
Telex: 923911-15

Magdeburgische Zeitung Volksstimme
Bahnhofstr. 17-21
3010 Magdeburg
Tel: (91) 3980
Fax: (91) 38840
Telex: 8462

Main-Post
Berner Str. 2
8700 Würzburg
Tel: (931) 60010
Fax: (931) 6001-242
Telex: 68845

Neues Deutschland
Franz-Mehring-Platz 1
1017 Berlin
Tel: (30) 58310
Fax: (30) 5831-2625
Telex: 112051

Sáddeutsche Zeitung
Sendlingerstr. 80
Postfach 202220
8000 München 2
Tel: (89) 21830
Telex: 523426

Südkurier
Südkurierhaus
Postfach 4300
7750 Konstanz
Tel: (7531) 2820
Telex: 733231

Welt am Sonntag
Axel-Springer-Platz 1
2000 Hamburg 36
Tel: (40) 3471
Telex: 2170010
Fax: (40) 34724912

Westfalenpost
Mittelstr. 22
5800 Hagen
Tel: (2331) 2040
Telex: 823861

BUSINESS PERIODICALS

Absatzwirtschaft (Monthly)
Kasernenstr. 67
Postfach 101102
4000 Düsseldorf 1
Tel: (211) 887-1422
Fax: (211) 887-1420

Capital (Monthly)
Postfach 110001
2000 Hamburg 11
Tel: (40) 3703-2480
Fax: (40) 3703-5607

Finanzwirtschaft (Monthly)
Am Friedrichshain 22
1055 Berlin
Tel: (30) 4287237
Fax: (30) 426124

RADIO & TELEVISION

Berliner Rundfunk
Nalepastr. 10-50
1160 Berlin
Tel: (30) 6360
Fax: (30) 5589119

Deutsche Welle
Raderberggürtel 50
Postfach 100444
5000 Köln 1
Tel: (221) 3890
Fax: (221) 389-3000

Zweites Deutsches Fernsehen
Postfach 4040
6500 Mainz 1
Tel: (6131) 701
Telex: 4187930

Radio Free Europe/Radio Liberty Inc.
Oettingenstr. 67
8000 München 22
Tel: (89) 21020
Fax: (89) 2285188

TRADE FAIRS

AMK Berlin Ausstellungs-Messe-Kongress-GmbH
Messdamm 22
1000 Berlin 19
Tel: (30) 30380
Telex: 182908
Fax: (30) 3038-2325

Dusseldorfer Messegesellschaft/mbH-NOWEA
Stockhumer Kirchstr. 61
Postfach 320203
4000 Düsseldorf 30
Tel: (211) 456001
Telex: 8584853
Fax: (211) 4560668

Messe Essen GmbH
Postfach 100165
Norbertstr.
4300 Essen 1
Tel: (201) 7244-0 /
Telex: 8579647
Fax: (201) 7244-248

Messe Frankfurt GmbH
Ludwig-Erhard-Anlage 1
6000 Frankfurt a.M. 1
Tel: (69) 7575-0
Telex: 411558
Fax: (69) 7575-6433

Internationale Bodensee-Messe GmbH
Messegelände
7990 Friedrichshafen
Tel: (7541) 708-0
Telex: 734315
Fax: (7541) 708-10

Hamburg Messe und Congress GmbH
Jungiusstr. 13
2000 Hamburg 36
Tel: (40) 3569-0
Telex: 212609
Fax: (40) 3569-2180

Deutsche Messe, AG
Messegelände
3000 Hannover 82
Tel: (511) 8910
Telex: 922728
Fax: (511) 89-32626

Karlsruher Kongress- und Ausstellungs-GmbH
7500 Karlsruhe1
Postfach 1208
Tel: (721) 37200
Fax: (721) 3720348
Telex: 7826240

Messe-und Ausstellungs GmbH
Messeplatz 1
Postfach 210760
5000 Köln 21
Tel: (221) 821-0
Fax: (221) 8212574
Telex:8873426

Leipziger Messe GmbH
Markt 11-15
Postfach 720
7010 Leipzig
Tel: (341) 223-0
Fax: (341) 2234575
Telex: 512294

Münchener Messe-und Ausstellungs GmbH
8000 München 12
Messegelände
Postfach 121009
Tel: (89) 51070
Fax: (89) 5107506
Telex: 5212086

Nürnberg Messe GmbH
Messezentrum
8500 Nürnberg 50
Tel: (911) 8606-o
Fax: (911) 8606-228
Telex: 623613

Offenbacher Messe GmbH
6050 Offenbach/M. 1
Kaiserstr. 108-112
Postfach 101423
Tel: (69) 228155-0
Fax: (69) 22815560

Saarmesse GmbH
Messegelände
6600 Saarbrücken
Tel: (681) 53056
Fax: (681) 53052

Stuttgarter Messe- und Kongress-GmbH
7000 Stuttgart 1
Am Kochenhof 16
Postfach 103252
Tel: (711) 25890
Fax: (711) 2589-440
Telex: 722584

Blenheim Heckmann GmbH
Kapellenstr. 47
6200 Wiesbaden
Tel: (611) 58040
Fax: (611) 580417
Telex: 4186518

INTERNET ADDRESSES

Usenet group(s):
soc.culture.german
clari.world.europe.germany

YAHOO - Germany
http://www.yahoo.com/Regional/Countries/Germany/

German Resources
http://www.rz.uni-karlsruhe.de/Outerspace/
VirtualLibrary/

City-Net - Germany
http://www.city.net/countries/germany/

Webfoot's Guide to Germany
http://www.webfoot.com/travel/guides/germany/
germany.htm

Greece

Hellenic Republic

Economy

Overview

Greece is heavily dependent upon imports; among its other economic problems it maintains a substantial trade deficit. Despite major restructuring, Greece remains troubled by high national debt, weak economic growth, and a narrowing industrial base. However, tax increases, a broadening of the tax base, a crackdown on evasion, and the sale of government stakes in key industries are either in progress or under discussion and may soon be implemented. The government controls more than 50 public enterprises, including the most prominent social insurance funds and nearly three-quarters of the banking industry. Inflation has stabilized somewhat because of higher interest rates. A change in accounting methodology during 1994 yielded a 20 percent "increase" in GDP, but this artificial increase has had little real impact. To its credit, Greece has made great strides in infrastructure development, particularly in transportation and communications.

Trade

Greek exports include apparel, fruit and vegetables, refined petroleum products, textiles, tobacco products, and beverages. Imports include vehicles, foodstuffs, miscellaneous manufactures, petroleum, and transportation equipment. Goods and services from other members of the EU account for nearly two-thirds of Greek trade. Major trading partners—in descending order of importance—include Germany, Italy, France, the UK, and the Netherlands. Greece is actively expanding its commercial relationships with various Balkan countries in an effort to increase its export markets.

Sectors

Agriculture This sector accounts for about 16 percent of GDP but provides employment for about 29 percent of the work force. The main cash crops include fruit, vegetables, grain, and tobacco; fishing is also an important activity. The Greek agricultural sector has begun to serve export markets in the Balkans.

Industry Industry provides about 30 percent of GDP and employs a comparable proportion of the work force. Food processing, textiles, oil refining, metals, and electrical machinery are major industries. High-technology activities—particularly telecommunications—building materials, and electrical appliances are also showing indications of long-term growth.

Services The strongest and fastest-growing sector of the Greek economy, services accounts for nearly 55 percent of GDP while providing employment for nearly half the work force. Much of this productivity is due to a highly developed tourist industry along with its related services. The construction industry is posting moderate to heavy gains, due to the recent emphasis upon infrastructure expansion.

Trends

Greece is in a position to become an integral force within the EU, provided current and anticipated measures to overhaul its economy meet with success. The government has often been criticized, however, for being overly optimistic in its projections and an underachiever in its reform programs. Greece will also have to overcome its heavily regulated, socialist-oriented economic structure to operate competitively in an international free market environment.

At a Glance

THE COUNTRY

Location Balkan State, southern Europe, bordering the Mediterranean Sea between Turkey and Bulgaria.
Terrain Largely mountainous interior, with coastal plains and many islands.
Climate Temperate.

THE PEOPLE

Population 10,500,000
Ethnic composition
Greek... 98%
Other.. 2%
Religious composition
Greek Orthodox 97%
Muslim 2%
Other.. 1%
Languages spoken Greek.
Education and literacy Education is compulsory for nine years, and is highly esteemed in Greece. Current literacy rates are 96 percent for men and 89 percent for women.
Labor force
Total:..4,600,000
By occupation: agriculture 29%, industry 27%, and services 43%.

COUNTRY FACTS

Political and legal Presidential parliamentary republic, which has precise guarantees of civil liberties and vests the powers of the head of state in a president elected by parliament and advised by the council of the Republic. Legal system is based on codified Roman law; with a judiciary divided into civil, criminal, and administrative courts.
Telephone The Greek Telecommunications Authority operates domestic telegraph and telephone communications. Telecommunications are adequate; modern networks reach all areas. There are over four million telephones in the country. International country code: [30]. Selected city codes: Athens (1), Iraklion (Crete) (81), Thessaloniki (31).
Transportation Streets and highways in Greece are hard-surfaced; smaller roads can be rough and ungraded. Less than half of the almost 39,000 kilometers of highway are paved. International driver's licenses are required. Intercity and local public transportation is available, inexpensive, and crowded at rush hours. Taxis are easily attainable in Athens.
Environment Current issues include air and water pollution.
Media All media and communications are owned and controlled by the government. The principal newspapers and magazines have nationwide circulation. The Constitution guarantees freedom of the press. Daily newspapers are read by 307 million. The Hellenic National Radio and Television Institute operates radio stations. Some stations are operated by the armed forces. There are 29 AM and 17 FM broadcast stations, and 361 television stations.
Health Over 95 percent of the population has access to safe, drinkable water. No special inoculations are required, but health requirements change from time to time. Travelers should check for current requirements before arriving in Greece. Life expectancy averages 77 years for both males and females.

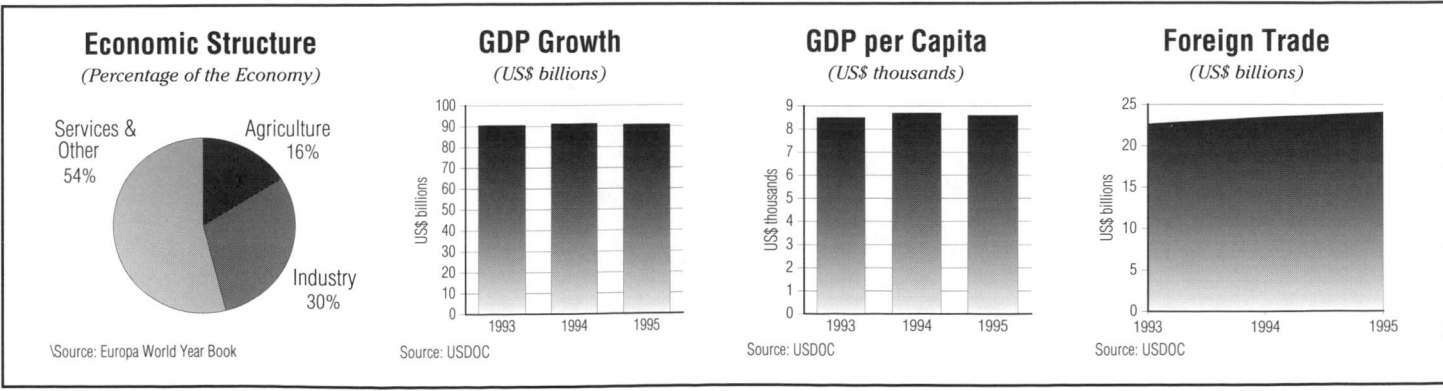

Economic Structure
(Percentage of the Economy)
Services & Other 54%
Agriculture 16%
Industry 30%
\Source: Europa World Year Book

GDP Growth
(US$ billions)
Source: USDOC

GDP per Capita
(US$ thousands)
Source: USDOC

Foreign Trade
(US$ billions)
Source: USDOC

Lake Scutari

Macedonia
(The Former Yugoslav Republic of Macedonia)

Black Sea

Bulgaria

Maritsa

Néstos

Orestiás

Turkey

Dm. L.

Lake Ohrid

Lake Prespa

Vardar

1

5 Sérrai Dhráma

4 3 Xánthi 2 Komotiní

Bosporus

Albania

7

6 Kilkís

14

Thrace

Sea of Marmara

8 Flórina

Édhessa

13

Struma

Kaváta

Alexandroúpolis

Samothráki

Dardanelles

Kastoria

12

Veróia

Macedonia

Thásos

9

11

15 Polîyros

Mt. Athos

Límnos

51

Lésvos

10

Kozáni

16 Kateríni

Grevená

40°

17

21

Kalabáka

22 Lárisa

Northern

24 *Sporades*

Aegean Sea

Mitilíni

Ioánnina

Epirus

18 Igoumenítsa

Corfu

Kérkira

Tríkala 23 **Thessaly**

Kardhítsa Vólos

Skíros

25

19 Árta

30

Prévéza

Ionian Islands

26

Levkás

Levkás

31

Karpenísion

Lamía

Évvoia

Agrínion

29

Ámfissa

Levádhia

32

33

Central Greece And Eurboea

Khalkís

34

50 Khíos

Khíos

Aegean Islands

Kefallinía

27

Argostólion

Mesolóngion

Pátrai

38 37

Mégara

35

Piraíevs ★ Athens

Sámos Váthí

48

Ándros

Síros

Kórinthos

36

39

Pírgos

28

Zákinthos

Zákinthos

Trípolis

Návplion

41

Peloponnisos

40

Kalámata

Spárti

42

Yíthion

Ionian Sea

Tínos

Ermoúpolis

Cyclades

Náxos

49

Ikaría

Dodecanese

Kos

47

Ródhos

36°

Kíthira

Thíra

Rhodes

Meyísti

Kárpathos

Sea of Crete

Crete

Khaniá

Kissamos 43

Réthimnon Iráklion

44 *Crete* Áyios Nikólaos

45

Sitía

46

Mediterranean   Sea

20°

24°

28°

Region Names

1	Évros	27	Kefallinía
2	Rodhópi	28	Zákinthos
3	Xánthi	29	Fthiótis
4	Dráma	30	Evritanía
5	Sérrai	31	Aitolía Kai
6	Kilkís		Akarnanía
7	Pélla	32	Fokís
8	Flórina	33	Voiotía
9	Kastoría	34	Évvoia
10	Grevená	35	Attikí
11	Kozáni	36	Argolís
12	Imathía	37	Korinthía
13	Thessaloníki	38	Akhaïa
14	Kavála	39	Ilía
15	Khalkidhikí	40	Messinía
16	Piería	41	Arkadhía
17	Ioánnina	42	Lakonía
18	Thesprotía	43	Khaniá
19	Préveza	44	Rethímni
20	Árta	45	Iráklion
21	Lárisa	46	Lasíthi
22	Tríkala	47	Dhodhekánisos
23	Kardhítsa	48	Sámos
24	Magnisía	49	Kikládhes
25	Kérkira	50	Khíos
26	Levkás	51	Lésvos

Greece

★ National capital

◉ Regional capital

● Secondary city

—— Primary road

········ Railroad

—— Region border

━━ International border

| 0 | 50 | 100 km |
| 0 | 50 | 100 mi |

©1995 Magellan GeographixSMSanta Barbara, CA

Foreign Trade

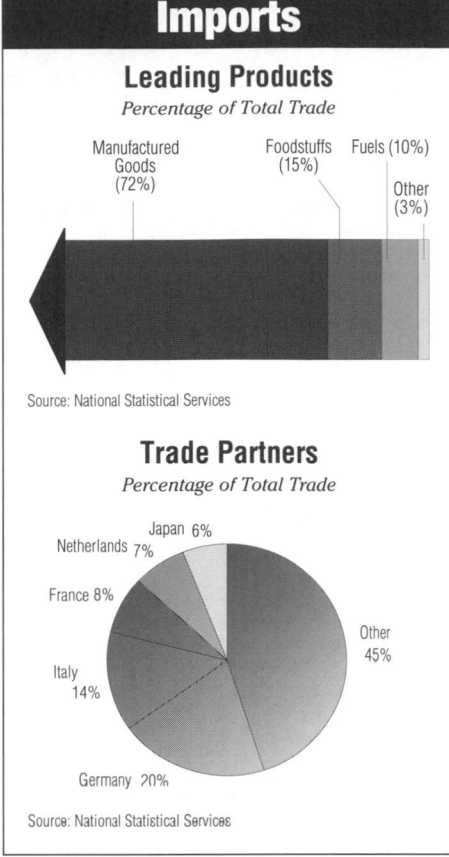

Imports

Leading Products
Percentage of Total Trade

Manufactured Goods (72%)
Foodstuffs (15%)
Fuels (10%)
Other (3%)

Source: National Statistical Services

Trade Partners
Percentage of Total Trade

Japan 6%
Netherlands 7%
France 8%
Italy 14%
Germany 20%
Other 45%

Source: National Statistical Services

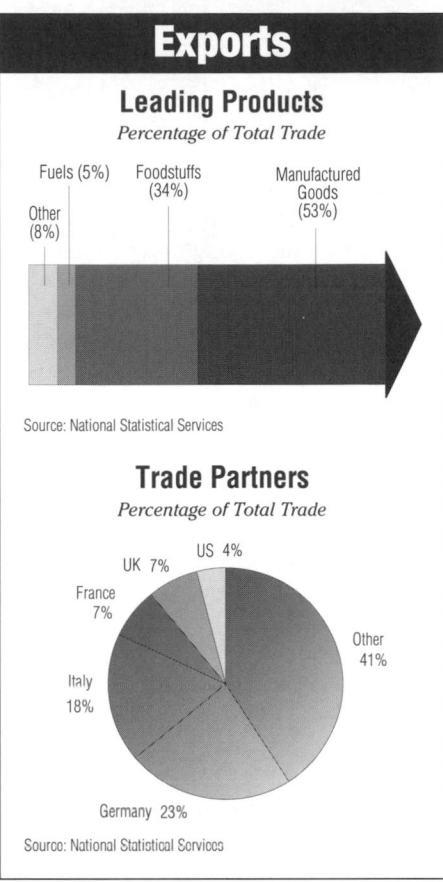

Exports

Leading Products
Percentage of Total Trade

Fuels (5%)
Other (8%)
Foodstuffs (34%)
Manufactured Goods (53%)

Source: National Statistical Services

Trade Partners
Percentage of Total Trade

US 4%
UK 7%
France 7%
Italy 18%
Germany 23%
Other 41%

Source: National Statistical Services

Opportunities

FOR IMPORTING TO GREECE

- agricultural goods: cotton, soybeans, grains
- air conditioning and refrigeration equipment
- automotive parts and service equipment
- chemicals
- clothing and textiles
- computers and peripherals
- construction equipment
- drugs and pharmaceuticals
- household consumer goods
- machinery
- management consulting services
- meat products
- medical equipment and supplies
- paper and paper products
- petroleum
- pollution control equipment
- processed foods

FOR EXPORTING FROM GREECE

- art and antiques
- cement
- chemicals
- clothing
- fruits: olives, olive oil, raisins
- furskins and artificial fur
- metal products
- pharmaceuticals
- processed foods
- shoes
- textiles
- vegetables
- wine and other beverages

GROWTH SECTORS

- construction
- food industry
- pollution control equipment
- services
- telecommunications
- tourism

GOVERNMENT PROCUREMENT

- electrical power equipment
- environmental protection goods and services
- hospital construction and renovation projects
- medical supplies and equipment
- oil refining equipment
- telecommunication products
- transportation development goods and services (airport, bridge, highway, railway, seaport, subway, and tunnel development projects)

Trade News

RULES AND REGULATIONS

- **Tariffs and import taxes** Greece subscribes to the European Union (EU) common external tariff. Trade between EU countries is duty free. Import duties applied to products from non-EU countries average between five and seven percent for most manufactured products. Duties are lower for most raw materials and higher for some other products, including textiles. Agricultural products from non-EU countries are subject to additional surcharges.
- **Import restrictions** The EU applies certain quota restrictions to products from low-cost countries. Pharmaceutical imports require special approval that is granted by the National Pharmaceutical Organization. Firearms, weapons, illegal drugs, and narcotics are prohibited at all times.
- **Export subsidies** The Greek government allows exporters to pay tax-deductible commissions and expenses to support exports. Some agricultural products receive subsidies from the EU. As a member of the EU, Greece is a member of the GATT Subsidies Code.
- **Free trade zones (FTZs)** Greece has free trade zones in the cities of Piraeus, Thessaloniki, and Heraklion.

SHIPPING FIRMS

Anangel Shipping Enterprises, SA
Akti Miaouli 25
185 10 Piraeus
Tel: (1) 4112511
Telex: 213037

Bilinder Marine Corp, SA
Odos Diligianni 59
Kifissias
145 62 Athens
Tel: (1) 8080211
Telex: 215394

Ceres Hellenic Shipping Enterprises, Ltd.
Akti Miaouli 69
185 37 Piraeus
Tel: (1) 4591000
Fax: (1) 4180549
Telex: 2122257

Chandris (Hellas) Inc.
Akti Miaouli 95
185 36 Piraeus
Tel: (1) 4120932
Fax: (1) 4110891
Telex: 212218

Costamare Shipping Co, SA
Akti Miaouli 59
185 36 Piraeus
Tel: (1) 4293140
Fax: (1) 4292037
Telex: 211399

European Navigation Inc.
Odos Artemissiu 2 and Fleming Sq.
166 75 Athens
Tel: (1) 8981581
Fax: (1) 8946777
Telex: 216428

Tsakos Shipping and Trading, SA
Akti Miaouli 85
185 38 Piraeus
Tel: (1) 418-2111
Fax: (1) 418-3116

United Shipping and Trading Co. of Greece, SA
Odos Iassonos 6
185 37 Piraeus
Tel: (1) 452-2511
Fax: (1) 452-2564

Varnima Corporation International, SA
Marine Enterprises Bldg.
Akti Miaouli 53-55
185 36 Piraeus
Tel: (1) 4522911
Fax: (1) 4537888
Telex: 212461

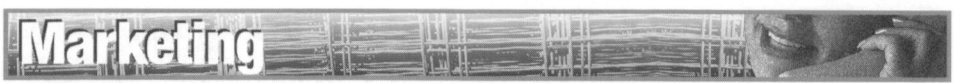

Overview

Any foreign firm willing to comply with EC standards and certifications can enter all EU markets through the Greek market. Proximity to the Balkans and the traditional trade ties of Greek businesspeople with these and Central European countries offer a variety of opportunities for multinational firms.

Distribution

Importers usually operate out of offices in Athens, Piraeus, or Thessaloniki; they may also have branch offices, subagents, and traveling sales staff covering the rest of the country, although coverage usually deteriorates rapidly outside the major urban markets. In a recent trend, small importers have been joining to form cooperatives to strengthen their positions. Most wholesale and retail trade is characterized by small, family-owned operations, each handling a narrow range of goods. There are few larger outlets—such as department stores and supermarkets, although European operators have acquired and upgraded many of these to make them competitive—and most retail sales are still made in small specialized shops dealing through a lengthy network of suppliers and intermediaries. The franchising concept is becoming somewhat more familiar, but remains restricted largely to fast food; no special laws govern it, suggesting both potential opportunity and danger for foreign operators. Purchases of capital equipment and supplies by the Greek government play an important role in the country's economic climate. The government and its quasi-governmental agencies are required by law to purchase through international tenders. Bidders must post a bond for all tenders. Bonds are returned to unsuccessful bidders within five business days after the contract is awarded. When the contract is signed, the winning firm must post a performance bond, usually 10 percent of the bid value. Construction bids are normally reserved for national firms; however, international bids are accepted when projects require specific technical expertise. Foreign as well as local bidders must quote and accept payment in Greek *drachmas*.

Agents, Distributors, and Partners

Approximately 80 percent of Greece's import trade is handled by sales agents or distributors. It is imperative that foreigners seeking to enter the Greek market retain an experienced agent with an already-established network of sales and service personnel who can offer extensive support, replacement parts, and service and support to purchasers. Joint ventures with local partners are also quite popular. Because the Greek government still controls a substantial portion of the economy, official agencies account for a large portion of major purchases. Local agents or joint-venture partners are critical in obtaining and fulfilling government tenders on behalf of foreign suppliers. Generally, agents do not buy for their own accounts. Non-exclusive agency agreements are allowed, although many established agents require exclusivity. Agency contracts are nonstandard, relatively open to negotiation of specific terms, and can run for any period of time. Distributors generally operate as wholesalers with exclusive sales rights either for certain territories or for the entire country. Foreign sales agents must obtain an operating license from a special committee of the Athens Chamber of Commerce; foreign licensing is contingent on Greek nationals being accorded reciprocal treatment in the applicant's home country. Prior to licensing, applicants are screened for reputation, experience in the specific business area, and financial standing.

Selling Techniques

Selling factors that work in Western Europe and North America generally work as well in Greece, especially in more internationalized, urban markets. Less developed markets may require more locally tailored approaches. Business tends to be more personalized than in industrialized countries, and the intervention of a local agent can be essential in making approaches and closing deals. Direct marketing has been limited, largely because payment mechanisms remain poorly developed—most Greeks still do not operate using checking accounts, much less credit cards or other non-cash mechanisms. Pricing is critical, but payment terms may become even more important to closing a sale.

Advertising

Sales promotion is usually handled by a Greek advertising firm, which generally utilizes a campaign involving all available media to reach the target group. Media employed may include some of the four state-owned and over 50 privately owned television channels, or any of the roughly 500 radio stations throughout Greece. There are also eight large daily newspapers and many specialized magazines.

Service and Customer Support

The Greek commercial customer expects a fairly high degree of access to product information, replacement parts, and service and repairs. Firms without a distributor or agency presence capable of providing such attention will find it difficult to do business in Greece.

Marketing in Greece

MARKETING TIPS

- **Price controls** Except for pharmaceuticals and agricultural products, Greece has recently liberalized its price controls.
- **Guarantees** Letters of credit and drafts are very expensive in Greece. Banks require the cash equivalent to be deposited before issuing any guarantees, which can influence orders.
- **Bad debts** There are no bill collection agencies in Greece. If a case is troublesome, debts can be collected only through a long, expensive court process.
- **Calling services** Greek telecommunications are being upgraded. Digital service and cellular telephones are available and are becoming popular.
- **Government markets** The main criteria in selling to government agencies are price and technical specifications; while private buyers may be willing to compromise on specifications for an attractive price break, failure to meet the specifications exactly will disqualify a bid on a government tender.

MARKET RESEARCH AND CONSULTING FIRMS

A.C. Nielsen Hellas Ltd.
2 Charokopou Street - 196 Syngrou Avenue
176 71 Kallithea, Athens
Tel: (1) 958-8771 x4 Fax: (1) 937-2450

Deloitte & Touche S.A.
252-254 Kifissias Avenue
152 31 Halandri
Tel: (1) 687-6230 Fax: (1) 687-6221

Delos S.A.
3 Alexandrou Soutsou Street
106 71 Athens
Tel: (1) 362-8457 Fax: (1) 364-6144

Ernst & Young (Hellas) S.A.
2 Mesogion Avenue, Athens Tower
115 27 Athens
Tel: (1) 775-9780 Fax: (1) 775-9790

ICAP Hellas S.A.
64 Vas. Sophias Avenue
115 28 Athens
Tel: (1) 724-7884 x8 Fax: (1) 722-0255

Industrial Development & Planning Consultants
26-28 Asklipiou Street
106 80 Athens
Tel: (1) 361-7165 Fax: (1) 645-0322

Kantor S.A.
4 Vasilissis Sophias Avenue
106 71 Athens
Tel: (1) 724-8294 Fax: (1) 724-9528

KPMG Peat Marwick Kyriacou
15 Mesogion Avenue
115 26 Athens
Tel: (1) 775-2001 Fax: (1) 770-4182

LDK S.A.
7 Spyron Triantafyllon Street
113 61 Athens
Tel: (1) 862-9660 Fax: (1) 861-7681

Marketing Research Center Hellas Ltd.
24 Ippodamou Street
116 35 Athens
Tel: (1) 701-8082, 701-6965 Fax: (1) 701-7837

MRB Hellas
17 Valaouritou Street
106 71 Athens
Tel: (1) 362-5801 Fax: (1) 362-9141

Price Waterhouse
330 Thisseos Avenue
176 75 Kallithea, Athens
Tel: (1) 930-8180 Fax: (1) 930-8182

Research International Hellas S.A.
8-12 Halkidonos Street
115 27 Athens
Tel: (1) 775-3001 Fax: (1) 779-5886

Business Culture

Greetings and Courtesies

There are no strict rules for greeting people. In general, Greeks shake hands, usually making direct eye contact, both on meeting and departing. Slapping a friend's arm at shoulder level is common among men. An embrace and kiss is customary among family and friends. Use titles whenever applicable; Greeks are proud of their professional standing. Formality is soon dispensed with, however, and Greeks may ask you to use their first name. Pretentiousness isn't appreciated. If invited into a Greek home, always bring the hostess a wrapped gift. Praise your host's children and, with parental approval, give them a small gift. Favorite topics of conversation for Greeks include sports (especially the Olympics), food, wine, and Greece's contributions to history. Avoid speaking about Cyprus, Turkey, and other aspects of international politics which have affected Greece. Greek is the main language of politics and business. English and French are also widely spoken in the cities; a knowledge of German is also useful.

Business Ethic

All commercial life is concentrated in Athens, and most business can be completed without leaving the capital. If agents are necessary outside the capital, placing one in Crete to handle business in southern Greece, and Salonica for business in the north, should suffice. Put all terms in writing, no matter how insignificant they may seem; Greek businessmen have a highly developed, often ironic sense of humor and don't mind trapping the unwary. Greeks value personal contact, individual responsibility, and collective effort. The family is very important in Greek life, more so than business. Extended families generally live together, and there is some concern that an individual may bring shame to his family's name. There is a great deal of importance placed on educational background and financial standing in business. Friendly behavior among business associates is common, but this is a separate quality from trust, which is not lightly given and must be slowly earned. Greeks are usually very hospitable and generous to foreigners.

Meetings and Decision Making

Prior appointments are not usually necessary unless visiting a factory or government office, but phoning ahead is appreciated. Punctuality is a flexible concept in Greece; if you are going to be late, a phone call is appreciated. Avoid making appointments on Wednesday afternoons; many businesses are closed. Also keep in mind most business vacations are taken in July and August. Never predict when a meeting should end. Patience and courtesy will develop the trust vital to Greek business transactions, and trying to hurry a meeting along may be considered rude. Also prepare for a number of interruptions during meetings. Specific agendas and memos are usually regarded as impolite. Introduce written documents as the very last item. Most successful deals here are made in person, not over the telephone. Greeks tend to be verbally and physically expressive; if your host becomes quiet and withdrawn, something is probably wrong. Be prepared for leisurely discussions over strong coffee and *ouzo*, the national liqueur; refusing such an invitation is considered an insult. Greeks usually take an extended afternoon break, then work late into the evening. Greeks would rather work in an existing market than create a new one, and it is very difficult to find a firm willing to work with goods that aren't already in demand. Greeks love to haggle in all aspects of business and may consider it an insult if you do not haggle back.

Women

Women gained greater prominence and rights in the 1980s, but Greek society is still mainly male dominated. Greek women do hold many jobs, but most powerful positions are still held by men. Cooking, running the home, and taking care of children is widely regarded as "women's work." Greek women speak their minds freely, but not in front of strangers. Women wear dresses more often than their Western counterparts and are fond of traditional costumes at folk festivals and other special occasions.

Business Attire

Wear a conservative, lightweight suit for most of the year. Winters can be wet and chilly, so bring a raincoat and umbrella, especially if you are staying in northern Greece. Women should bring woolen clothing and a heavy coat if they plan on staying in Greece in the winter. In the spring and autumn, a light raincoat may be needed. White and light-colored suits are not worn often. Business attire remains conservative, even during the heat of summer.

Cultural Cautions

DO'S

- If the visitor is invited to dance, accepting the invitation is taken as a gesture of appreciation.
- Learn to read street and direction signs in Greek.

DON'TS

- Do not use either the US "OK" sign or the fig gesture (a clenched fist with the index finger over a protruding thumb); they are considered obscene. Also, waving your whole hand is an insult, so avoid doing so at all costs.
- Never complain about the high pollution rates in the cities and near the beaches. It is a touchy subject for most Greeks.

CUSTOMS

- Greek hospitality is sincere and sometimes overwhelmingly generous. A host may insist on giving you a certain object if you praise it. Refusing a generous invitation for anything is regarded as a personal insult.
- It is not necessary to tip, but you should leave the waiter a little extra, perhaps five percent. It is also customary to tip hairdressers and barbers 10 percent, and to round off the fare as a tip for taxi cab drivers.
- If you are invited to a Greek home, take flowers or a cake for the hostess.
- "No" is a slight upward nod; tilting the head to one side is "yes." A cheek stroke means the person is considered "attractive." Smiles can mean either happiness or intense anger, so pay attention to the words as well.
- The main meal of the day is lunch, served between noon and 2:00 pm. Eating alone is unheard of in Greece.

OBSERVATIONS

- The elderly are greatly respected in Greece and always come first in Greek culture. They are always addressed by courteous titles, they are served first, their opinions are given great weight, and they are highly trusted by younger generations.
- The Greek Orthodox Easter holiday usually falls on a different date as observed so check before you go.
- Upon arriving, it is usually helpful to register your presence in the country with the consular section of your embassy in Greece. You will be able to access information ranging from crime rates to currency regulations. It also offers the most objective and reliable source for last minute information and answers to any questions you may have once you are in the country.
- Many persons here finger "worry beads" to promote personal peace, a common practice throughout the Mediterranean.
- Telecommunications can be reliable, but the mail is generally slow. Greece's telephone system has direct dialing facilities to international locations, but during peak times there may be a two-hour wait.
- Drinking water is safe in Athens and resorts, but avoid well water.
- An international driving permit is needed to operate a car in Greece, except for those with EU licenses. Parking regulations are strictly enforced.
- Toll-motorways are well-surfaced, but other roads, even in the city, may be rough. In the country, beware of wandering livestock. Right of way is usually a matter of who gets there first. Greek drivers tend to be impatient.
- Keep in mind that there are no official restrictions on any items bought duty-free, provided they are for personal use only.
- Athens is one of the most polluted cities in western Europe, mainly because of the heavy industry and traffic in the area.
- Hiring a local lawyer to represent your local interests would be a good idea.

Legal System

Greece operates under a codified civil law system which is influenced by German law.

Intellectual Property Rights

Patents It takes no more than two years to obtain patent registration in Greece. Patent applications and documentation are made available to the public on the date of the grant of the patent and in any case after 18 months from the date of the application. The Munich Convention of October 1973 on the grant of European patents, the Paris Convention of 1883 on the Protection of Industrial Property, and the Multilateral International Treaty signed in Paris on September 21, 1960, are in force in Greece.

Trademarks Trademark applications are examined by a special committee and a decision is rendered after about seven months from the date of the application. Decisions approving trademarks are published in the *Commercial and Industrial Property Bulletin* with considerable delay (about one year after the decision is rendered). Third parties may file objections within a four-month period from said publication. After their final approval, trademarks are protected in accordance with the "Law on Trademarks" (Law 2239/1994). Prior to such approval they are protected in accordance with the "Law on Unfair Competition" (Law 146/1914). Trademark infringements are also subject to penalties.

Copyrights A new copyright law is in force and grants civil and criminal protection to intellectual property, the concept of which has been considerably enlarged. The protection lasts not only during the life of the original beneficiary but also for a period of 70 years after his or her death.

Trade Secrets An employee who discloses business secrets to third parties and the third parties to whom he discloses are liable to pay damages, and are also subject to criminal prosecution under the "Law on Unfair Competition."

Business Registration

Foreign companies may operate branch offices or establish affiliates in Greece. Registration is necessary. However, Greek law encourages foreign participation in the economy, and registration procedures are not burdensome. Special liberalized provisions apply to off-shore companies.

Contracts and Dispute Resolution

Freedom of contract is a long-established principle of Greek law. Commercial and civil disputes are dealt with by the civil courts (First Instance Courts, Courts of Appeal, and Supreme Court). Arbitration is also possible, but it is less common than litigation in court. Proceedings in court are time-consuming, especially if the court decides that witnesses must be heard. Appeal to a court of appeal and further appeal to the Supreme Court are possible. Administrative matters (taxation, social security, responsibility of the state, etc.) are dealt with by the special administrative courts.

Notaries

Notaries public draw up and record contracts, powers of attorney, and affidavits. Certain contracts (e.g., transfer of real estate, establishment of a corporation) must be drawn up and recorded by a notary public. All documents must be drawn up in Greek.

Labor

The right of employees and workers to associate freely in unions and to bargain collectively is guaranteed by the Constitution and the international conventions ratified by Greece. Employment laws protect women; collective agreements and firm regulations must provide for equal pay for work of equal value. The minimum starting salary amounts to about 130,000 drachmas per month. Employment of minors under the age of 18 is subject to restrictions. The Constitution recognizes the right to strike, although abuse of this right will make the strike illegal. Employee lock-outs are prohibited.

Maximum Work The current regulation provides for 40 working hours per week. Extended working hours are permitted in exceptional cases under certain conditions and must be paid at higher rates. Employees with a minimum continuous employment of 12 months by the same firm are entitled to paid annual leave of 24-26 working days (or 20-22 working days for some employees). During the leave the employee receives regular wages plus an extra half-month's salary. There are 14 paid holidays and also special leaves for certain persons (e.g., students, teachers, parents, etc.).

Termination of the Contract of Employment Contracts for a definite period of time can be prematurely terminated only for important reasons. Contracts for an indefinite period of time can be terminated at any time on certain conditions, including prior written notice, offer of compensation, and fair use of right.

Source: Law Office P. Sotiropoulos, Athens, Greece

Legal Matters

LEGAL BRIEFS

- **Minimum stock capital** The minimum stock capital for corporations is 10,000,000 drachmas and for companies with limited liability 3,000,000 drachmas. No minimum capital is prescribed for partnerships.
- **Greek corporations** Corporations are subject to a flat income tax rate of 40 percent (or 35 percent if their stock is quoted on the Greek Stock Exchange or is registered). This taxation is deemed to cover also the tax liability of the shareholder. Dividends are not taxed.
- **Employees** Employees are entitled to two extra months' salaries every year (one month's salary in December and half month's salary in April and at the time of the annual leave).
- **Legal protection** Foreigners enjoy the same legal protection as Greek citizens.
- **Fairness** Greece has an independent court system and effective means for enforcing property and contract rights. However, foreign companies sometimes do not feel that they are treated fairly in the courts.
- **Accepting foreign judgments** Foreign judgments are accepted by the local courts but the legality of the procedures followed and the compatibility of foreign and Greek laws are currently being investigated. The enforcement of foreign court decisions remains to be tested. European Court judgments also supersede local court decisions.
- **Bankruptcy laws** Commercial and bankruptcy laws in Greece are in accordance with international norms. Under Greece's bankruptcy laws, creditors are compensated after state and insurance funds are satisfied.
- **Judgments** Monetary judgments are usually made in local currency unless otherwise stipulated.
- **Security interests** Greece has a reliable system of recording security interests in property.
- **International dispute agreements** Greece is a member of the International Center for the Settlement of Investment Disputes, but there have been no cases forwarded to the Center for settlement since 1982. Greece is also a member of the New York Convention on the Recognition and Enforcement of Foreign Arbitral Awards.
- **Property rights** As a member of the EU, Greece is changing all legislation regarding intellectual property rights to EC rules and regulations.
- **Piracy** Copyright protection has been a problem in Greece. The country took a step toward addressing the problem by enacting the new copyright law, offering a higher standard of protection for all copyrighted works. The copyright law now relies heavily on a new Intellectual Property Office (OPI) to supervise implementation, an office that has not yet been established. How effective this new law is will probably depend directly upon how well OPI functions.
- **Technological trademarks** Violation of protection for the semiconductor chip layout designs is not a major problem in Greece.
- **Regulations** Most business laws and regulations are not transparent and their complexity is often regarded as the greatest impediment to operating in Greece.
- **Political violence** There are several terrorist groups whose declarations regularly denounce capitalism. There have been several terrorist attacks against foreign property, and most foreign businesses keep a low profile in Greece compared to those of other EU countries.
- **Workers' rights** ILO Conventions protecting workers' rights have been ratified by the Greek government.

LEGAL CONTACT

Law Office P. Sotiropoulos
Lykavittou 4
106 71 Athens
Tel: (1) 3630017, 3604676
Fax: (1) 3646674
Telex: 218253 JURA

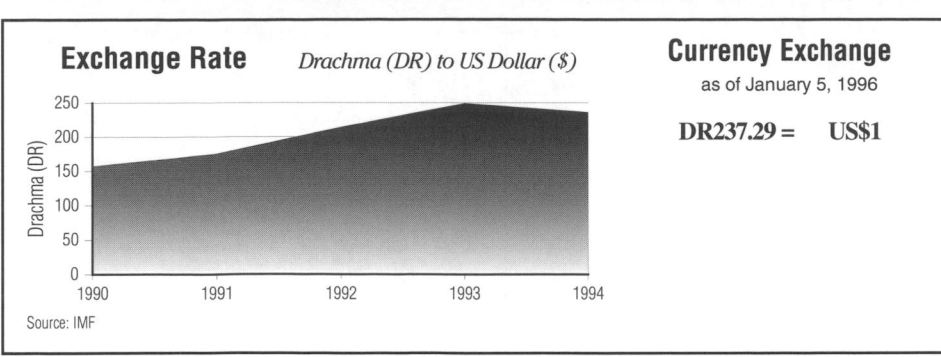

Exchange Rate *Drachma (DR) to US Dollar ($)*

Source: IMF

Currency Exchange
as of January 5, 1996

DR237.29 =   US$1

Currency

The currency in use is the Greek drachma(DR).

Foreign Exchange

The Bank of Greece and authorized commercial banks set the exchange rate in a daily fixed position. The commercial banks quote their own rates on the domestic spot exchange market. Commercial banks may charge a commission for foreign exchange transactions on both the domestic spot and forward exchange markets.

Capital Transfers

Residents may bring in any amount of foreign exchange, but it must be declared on entry in order to retain the right to take it back out of the country. Nonresident travelers may import any amount of undeclared foreign currency, but cannot take out more than the equivalent of US$1,000. There is no limit for taking out traveler's checks and other means of payment.

Investment Incentives

Incentives are available for foreign and domestic investments, and are provided on a rising scale based on the level of development in a particular area. More generous incentives are offered in the less-developed regions. Incentives can include investment grants, interest rate subsidies, tax allowance, reduced tax rates, and accelerated depreciation.

Investment Restrictions

Restrictions exist for non-EU investors in select sectors, such as land purchasing and banking. There are also performance requirements when an investor wants to take advantage of tax and investment incentives. Also, Greece's complex laws and its sometimes comprehensive bureaucracy can serve to inhibit foreign investment.

Money Matters

BITS AND PIECES

- **Free trade zones** Greece has three free trade zones in Piraeus, Thessaloniki, and Heraklion. Goods brought into these areas are exempt from customs duties and other taxes.
- **Banking system** The Greek banking system includes the central bank, 42 commercial banks, three investment banks, three specialized banks, the postal savings bank, and the Consignments and Loans Bank. The National Bank of Greece is the largest Greek commercial bank. The banking sector has been liberalized and is now generally free from state interference. Banks provide the primary source of financing, since the bond and equity markets are underdeveloped.
- **Checks and credit cards** Checks are used for commercial transactions only on a limited basis. Credit cards are widely available.
- **Repatriation** Investment proceeds may be repatriated at market exchange rates. Although Greece has had strict currency controls in the past, these restrictions, for investment purposes, have been lifted over the past two years. Both principal and interest is freely transferable abroad.
- **Inflation** The value of the drachma is determined by a crawling-peg system. Because of the country's high inflation rate, the Bank of Greece permits the drachma to gradually depreciate against the currencies of other members of the EU.

BANKS

Agricultural Bank of Greece
23 Eleftheriou Venizelou Street
102 21 Athens
Tel: (1) 323-2777
Fax: (1) 325-5079

American Express Bank Ltd
31 Panepistimiou Street
102 26 Athens
Tel: (1) 323-4781
Fax: (1) 322-4919

Bank of America
39 Panepistimiou Street
102 27 Athens
Tel: (1) 325-1901
Fax: (1) 323-1376

Citibank N.A.
8 Othonos St.
105 57 Athens
Tel: (1) 322-7471
Fax: (1) 324-0829

Commercial Bank of Greece
11 Sofokleous Street
102 35 Athens
Tel: (1) 321-0911
Fax: (1) 323-4333

Credit Bank
40 Stadiou Street
102 52 Athens
Tel.: (1) 326-0000
Fax: (1) 326-5488

Ergobank
3-5 Kolokotroni & Voulis Streets
105 62 Athens
Tel: (1) 322-1345
Fax: (1) 322-8906

General Hellenic Bank
9 Eleftheriou Venizelou Street
102 29 Athens
Tel: (1) 325-0301
Fax: (1) 322-2271

Ionian Bank
45 Eleftheriou Venizelou Street
102 43 Athens
Tel: (1) 322-5501
Fax: (1) 323-4488

The Chase Manhattan Bank
3 Korai Street
102 10 Athens
Tel: (1) 323-7711
Fax: (1) 324-2511

TAXATION

Taxation requires sophisticated knowledge of complex rules and regulations specific to each country. For more detailed information, we suggest you refer to the Ernst & Young Corporate Tax Guide and Directory, available from the Ernst & Young accounting office in your country, or from:

Ernst & Young
3-5 Ilisson St.
115 28 Athens
Tel: (1) 748 8610/20
Fax: (1) 778-2044

At a Glance

Corporate Income Tax Rate (%)(a)	35/40
Capital Gains Tax Rate (%)(a)	35/40
Branch Tax Rate (%)	40
Withholding Tax (%)	
Dividends (b)	0
Interest	
Bank Interest (c)	15
Other Interest	
Paid to Legal Persons (d)	20/40
Paid to Individuals	20
Royalties from Patents, Know-how, etc.	20
Branch Remittance Tax	0
Net Operating Losses (Years)	
Carryback	0
Carryforward	5

(a) All Greek legal entities are taxed on worldwide income. Branches of foreign companies are taxed only on income derived from Greek establishments.
(b) Corporate profits are taxed at 35% or 40%, and dividends are paid out of net profits after taxes. No further tax is payable on dividends by the corporation or its shareholders.
(c) The difference between the tax withheld on the interest and tax at the corporate income tax rate must be paid if such interest is distributed to shareholders or the head office.
(d) The 40% rate applies to interest paid to foreign legal entities that do not have a permanent establishment in Greece. The 40% tax is final withholding tax; the 20% tax is considered to be a prepayment of corporate income tax.

Air Travel Times

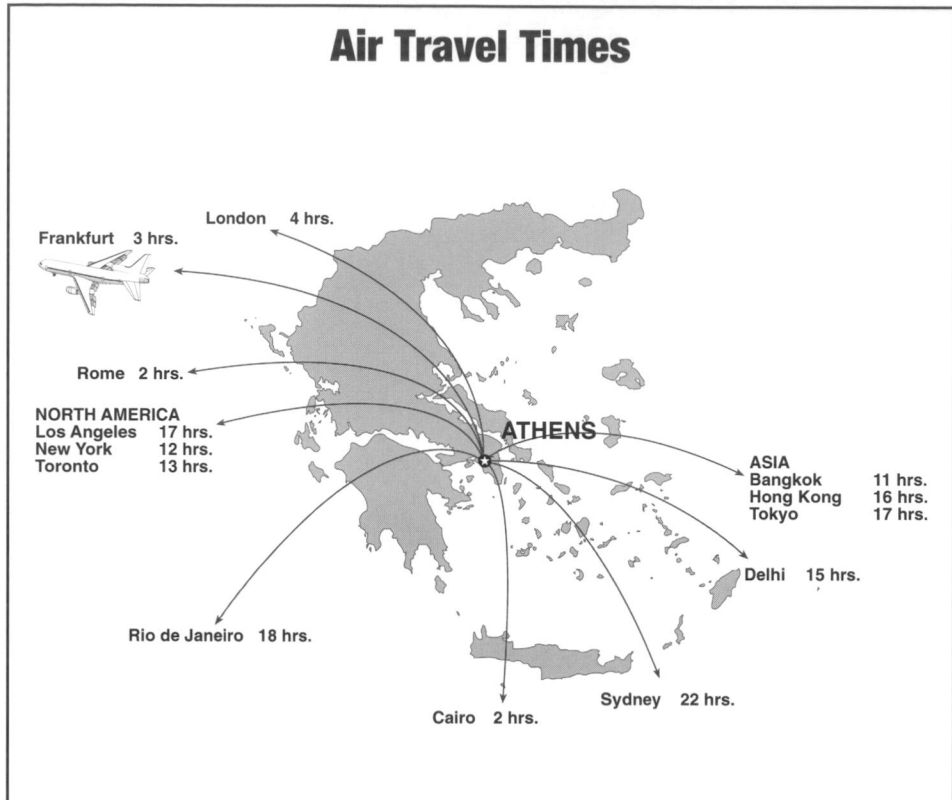

Frankfurt 3 hrs.
London 4 hrs.
Rome 2 hrs.

NORTH AMERICA
Los Angeles 17 hrs.
New York 12 hrs.
Toronto 13 hrs.

ATHENS

ASIA
Bangkok 11 hrs.
Hong Kong 16 hrs.
Tokyo 17 hrs.

Delhi 15 hrs.

Rio de Janeiro 18 hrs.

Sydney 22 hrs.

Cairo 2 hrs.

COMMUNICATIONS

Telephones Telephone service within Greece is satisfactory with service to 88 countries, 22 of which can be dialed direct. International calls can take an hour or more to get through during peak times. Public phones are available at newsstands and hotels. Domestic long-distance calls are cheaper from 9:00 pm to 5:00 am. Hotels often charge exorbitant fees on long-distance calls charged to rooms.

Fax Fax machines are common business tools in Greece and are available in major hotels in Athens. Telegraph services are available at OTE offices in each city, and Telex is available at post offices and larger hotels.

Post office Mail service in Greece can be unreliable. Post offices are identified by a yellow sign reading E.A.T.A. and are usually open weekdays 8:00 am to 7:00 pm with shorter hours on Saturdays. Mail boxes on the street are also bright yellow. Stamps can also be purchased at newsstands and hotels.

BEST TRAVEL BOOKS

Greece Travel Survival Kit, Lonely Planet. From the mountains to the islands, this is the one guide you'll need to find information on all aspects of travel in Greece.

Fodor's Travel Guide, Greece. Tourist oriented, excellent source of city details.

Berlitz Business Travel Guide, Europe. Concise economic details, successful trip planning, background information on people and cities, useful facts and addresses.

Deck With A View, On the Water Vacations in Greece and Turkey. A wealth of information.

USEFUL TELEPHONE NUMBERS

If you are calling from outside Greece, you will need to add the country code [30] and any other international dialing requirements from within your country.

- Local Operator 131
- Overseas Operator 161
- Executive Services .... (1) 17783698
- International Business Services .... (1) 17245541
- Audiovisual equipment .... (1) 18618724
- Rotary Club .... (1) 3623150
- Athens Cosmopolitan Lions Club .... (1) 3601311
- Athens Business & Prof'l Women's Club
  .... (1) 8613522
- Athens Chamber of Commerce .... (1) 3604815
- Federation of Greek Industries .... (1) 3237325
- Ministry Chamber of Commerce .... (1)3160879

Airlines in Athens

- Olympic Airways.................................(1) 961-6161
- Air Canada ....(1) 322-3206
- British Airways....................................(1) 325-0602
- Delta...(1) 323-5242
- TWA..(1) 322-6451
- United...(1) 922-9826

Credit Card Information

Lost or stolen credit cards (call collect to the US, regardless of which country the card was issued in).

- Amex ....[1] (919) 333-3211
- Diner's Club...............................[1] (303) 799-1504
- MasterCard ....[1] (314) 275-6690
- Visa ....[1] (410) 581-7931

Travelogue

WORKWEEK

Offices Monday-Friday 8:00 am to 5:00 pm, with a one hour lunch and Saturday 8:00 am to 1:30 pm.
Banks Monday-Friday 8:30 am to 2:00 pm.
Government Monday-Friday 7:30 am to 3:00 pm from October to May, and 7:00 am to 2:30 pm May to October.
Retail Monday-Saturday 8:00 am to 1:30 pm, with many shops open again from 5:30 pm to 8:30 pm Tuesdays, Thursdays, and Fridays. Many offices close Wednesday afternoons.

HOLIDAYS

Holidays 1996
January 1 New Year's Day
January 6 Epiphany
February 26 Clean Monday
March 25 Greek Independence Day
April 12 Good Friday
April 14 Easter Sunday
April 15 Easter Monday
May 1 May Day
August 15 Assumption Day
October 28 OXI Day
December 24 Christmas Eve**
December 25 Christmas Day
December 26 Boxing Day
There are also several regional holidays: February 20, Liberation of Ioannina observed in Ioannina only; March 7, Dodecanese Accession Day observed in Dodecanese Islands only; October 4, Liberation of Xanthi observed in Xanthi only; October 26, Saint Demetrios Day observed in Thessaloniki only; and November 30, Saint Andrea's Day observed in Patras only.
**Half-day holiday, only shops open all day.

VISA AND PASSPORT

Foreigners need a valid passport and may stay for up to three months without a visa. To extend beyond that time, visitors must submit an application to the immigration authorities at least 20 days before expiration of the initial three-month stay. Travelers must declare funds exceeding the equivalent of US$12,500 on entry.

DEPARTURE FORMALITIES

All travelers must declare any amount exceeding the equivalent of US$2,500 upon departure. Artifacts taken out of Greece without appropriate authorization can result in prosecution, fines, and a possible jail sentence.

IMMUNIZATION

No inoculations are required for entry to Greece unless visitors are arriving within six days of leaving areas where yellow fever is endemic.

TIPPING

Taxi: not expected, but 10-15 percent is appreciated. Porters: 60 drachma per piece. Restaurant, hotels, nightspots: 15 percent included in bill but add 5-10 percent. Barbers, beauticians: 10 percent. Stewards: 400 drachma per day.

CRIME

Greece has a low rate of crime. Some pickpocketing, purse-snatching, and luggage theft does occur at popular tourist areas.

INFRASTRUCTURE

There are extensive airline and port networks connecting points within Greece and the rest of Europe. Hotel facilities, roadway and rail networks are adequate to excellent and are expanding. Intercity and local public transportation is adequate. Taxis are inexpensive and widely available. Major expansion to the subway is occurring now. Buses are frequent and reasonably priced. Long-distance buses are slow and uncomfortable. Domestic air travel is regular and dependable except during tourist season.

NATIONAL TOURIST OFFICE

Ellinikos Organismos Tourismou (EOT)
Odos Amerikis 2B
105 64 Athens
Tel: (1) 3223111

GOVERNMENT AGENCIES

Greek Standards Organization
313 Aharnon Street
111 45 Athens
Tel: (1) 201-5025
Fax: (1) 202-0776

Hellenic Industrial Development Bank
87 Syngrou Avenue
117 45 Athens
Tel: (1) 929-4000
Fax: (1) 924-1513

Hellenic Radio-Television
432 Mesogion Avenue
153 42 Aghia Paraskevi, Athens
Tel: (1) 639-5970
Fax: (1) 639-6012

Hellenic Railways Organization
1 Karolou Street
104 37 Athens
Tel: (1) 524-1510
Fax: (1) 524-3290

Hellenic Telecommunications Organization
OTE Building
99 Kifissias Avenue
151 24 Amaroussion, Athens
Tel: (1) 123-1
Fax: (1) 611-745

Ministry of Commerce
20 Kaningos Street
101 81 Athens
Tel: (1) 361-6240 x54
Fax: (1) 364-2642

Ministry of Defense
Pentagono, Holargos
151 61 Athens
Tel: (1) 646-5201, 646-5301
Fax: (1) 644-3788, 653-2713

Ministry of Industry, Energy, & Technology
80 Michalakopoulou Street
101 92 Athens
Tel: (1) 648-2762
Fax: (1) 777-2485, 778-8279

Ministry of National Economy
Syntagma Square
106 71 Athens
Tel: (1) 333-2000
Fax: (1) 323-0801

Ministry of Public Works
182 Charilaou Trikoupi Street
101 78 Athens
Tel: (1) 644-9113, 644-7324
Fax: (1) 642-6836, 642-7520

Ministry of Transportation & Communications
13 Xenofontos Street
105 57 Athens
Tel: (1) 325-1211 - 9
Fax: (1) 324-7400, 325-3947

Piraeus Port Authority
2 Defteras Merarchias Street
185 35 Piraeus
Tel: (1) 452-0910 x19
Fax: (1) 452-0852

Thessaloniki Port Authority
POB 10467
541 10 Thessaloniki
Tel: (31) 593-217, 530-721
Fax: (31) 530-729, 510-500

The National Pharmaceutical Organization
284 Mesogion Avenue
155 62 Halandri
Tel: (1) 654-5193, 654-5525
Fax: (1) 654-5535

BUSINESS AND TRADE ORGANIZATIONS

Athens Association of Commercial Agents
15 Voulis Street
105 63 Athens
Tel: (1) 323-2622
Fax: (1) 323-8378

Association of Pharmaceutical Companies of Greece
15-17 Tsoha Street
115 21 Athens
Tel: (1) 644-7271
Fax: (1) 641-1463

Federation of Greek Food Industries
69 Ethnikis Antistaseos Street
152 31 Halandri
Tel: (1) 671-1177
Fax: (1) 671-1080

Federation of Greek Industries
5 Xenofontos Street
105 58 Athens
Tel: 323-7325 x9
Fax: 322-2929, 322-7245

Machinery Importers and Representatives Association
111 Orfeos Street
118 55 Athens
Tel: (1) 345-0511
Fax: (1) 342-1126

Technical Chamber of Greece
4 Karagiorgi Servias Street
102 48 Athens
Tel: (1) 325-4590
Fax: (1) 322-1772

Pharmaceutical Research and Manufacturers of American Pharmaceuticals
290 Mesogion Avenue
155 62 Holargos
Tel: (1) 654-4962
Fax: (1) 654-4964

Union of Greek Shipowners
85 Akti Miaouli Street
185 38 Pireaus
Tel: (1) 429-1159
Fax: (1) 429-1166

American-Hellenic Chamber of Commerce
16 Kanari Street
106 74 Athens
Tel: (1) 362-3231 x3, 363-0707
Fax: (1) 361-0170

American Hellenic Chamber of Commerce
20 Venizelou Street
546 24 Thessaloniki
Tel: (31) 225-162
Fax: (31) 286-453

Athens Chamber of Commerce and Industry
7 Academias Street
106 71 Athens
Tel: (1) 360-2411, 360-4815
Fax: (1) 360-7897

Hellenic Central Union of Chambers of Commerce and Industry
7 Academias Street
106 71 Athens
Tel: (1) 363-2702
Fax: (1) 361-6464

Piraeus Chamber of Commerce and Industry
1 Loudovikou Street, Rousvelt Square
185 31 Piraeus
Tel: (1) 417-7241
Fax: (1) 417-8680

Thessaloniki Chamber of Commerce and Industry
29 Tsimiski Street
546 24 Thessaloniki
Tel: (31) 275-341, 276-016
Fax: (31) 230-237

Association of Industries of Northern Greece
1 Morihovou Square
546 35 Thessaloniki
Tel: (31) 539817
Fax: (31) 546244

Athens Chamber of Small and Medium-Sized Industries
Odos Akademias 18
106 71 Athens
Tel: (1) 363-5313
Fax: (1) 361-4726

Handicraft Chamber of Piraeus
Odos Karaiscou 111
185 32 Piraeus
Tel: (1) 417-4152

Hellenic Organization of Small- and Medium-Size Industries and Handicrafts
Odos Xenia 16
115 28 Athens
Tel: (1) 771-5002
Telex: (1) 218819

Hellenic Cotton Board
Leoforos Syngrou 150
176 71 Athens
Tel: (1) 922-5011
Fax: (1) 324-8416

NEWSPAPERS

Imerisia (Daily)
Odos Geraniou 7A,
105 52 Athens
Tel: (1) 5231195
Fax: (1) 5245839

Kathimerini (Daily)
Odos Geraniou 7A
105 62 Athens
Tel: (1) 5231001
Fax: (1) 5247685
Telex: 226692

Athens Daily Post
Odos Stadiou 57
Athens
Tel: (1) 324-9504

Athens News
Odos Lekka 23-25
105 62 Athens
Tel: (1) 322-4253
Fax: (1) 323-1384

Eleftheros Typos Free Press
Odos Mitropoleos 1
105 57 Athens
Tel: (1) 323-7671
Fax: (1) 323-3142

Naftemboriki Daily Journal
Odos Lenorman 205
104 42 Athens
Tel: (1) 513-0605
Fax: (1) 514-6013

Ta Nea News
Odos Christou Lada 3
102 37 Athens
Tel: (1) 325-0811
Fax: (1) 322-8797

BUSINESS PERIODICALS

Agora
Market
Leoforos Kifissias 178
Halandri
151 31 Athens
Tel: (1) 647-3384
Fax: (1) 647-7893

Aktines
Odos Karytsi 14
105 61 Athens
Tel: (1) 3235023

The Athenian
Odos Peta 4
105 61 Sthens
Tel: (1) 3222802
Fax: (1) 3223052

Deltion Diikiseos Epichiriseon
Business Administration Bulletin
Odos Rhigillis 26
106 74 Athens
Tel: (1) 7235736
Telex: 29006

Demosiografiki
Journalism
Procopiou 7-9
171 24 Athens
Tel: (1) 9731338

Ekonomicos Tachydromos Financial Courier
Odos Christou Lada 3
102 37 Athens
Tel: (1) 324-3515
Fax: (1) 323-8740

Eleftherotypia
Press Freedom
Odos Kolokotroni 8
105 61 Athens
Tel: (1) 324207
 Fax: (1) 3242418

Estia Vesta
Odos Anthimou Gazi 7
105 61 Athens
Tel: (1) 3230650
Fax: (1) 3220631

Ethnos Nation
Odos Benaki 152
Metamorfosi Chalandriou
152 35 Athens
Tel: (1) 6580640
Fax: (1) 6396515
Telex: 2104415

Express
Odos Halandrious 39
Paradissou Amaroussiou
151 25 Athens
Tel: (1) 6850200
Fax: (1) 6852202
Telex: 219746

Filathlos
Odos Dimitros 11
777 78 Athens
Tel: (1) 3424090
Telex: 218440

Kerdos
Profit
Leoforos Kifissias 178
Halandri
152 31 Athens
Tel: (1) 6474241
Tax: (1) 6472003

Epiloghi
Odos Stadiou 4
105 64 Athens
Tel: (1) 323-8427
Fax: (1) 323-5160

Greece's Weekly for Business and Finance
Odos Fokiodos 10
115 26 Athens
Tel: (1) 770-7280
Telex: 210899

Mesimvrini
Odos Stadiou 5
105 62 Athens
Tel: (1) 3646010
Fax: (1) 3636125
Telex: 216497

Nikii
Victory
Odos Sina 14
106 72 Athens
Tel: (1) 3638642
Fax: (1) 3627270

Vradyni
Evening Press
Odos Piraeus 9-11
105 52 Athens
Tel: (1) 3250811
Fax: (1) 3228797
Telex: 210608

Peloponnesos
Odos Alex
Ypsilantou 177
262 25 Patras
Tel: (61) 272452

Ellinikos Vorras
Greek North
Odos Grammou-Vitsi 19
551 34 Thessaloniki
Tel: (31) 416621
Telex: 412213

Thessaloniki
Odos Monastiriou 85
546 27 Thessaloniki
Tel: (31) 521621

Technika Chronika
Technical Times (Monthly)
Odos Karageorgi Servias 4
105 62 Athens
Tel: (1) 323-4751

Viomichaniki Epitheorissis (Monthly)
Industrial Review
Odos Valaoritou 7
106 71 Athens
Tel: (1) 362-5666
Fax: (1) 362-3879

Hellenews Halandriou 39
Paradissos Amaroussiou
151 25 Athens
Tel: (1) 6850200
Fax: (1) 6825858
Telex: 219746

Makedoniki Zoi
Macedonian Life
Odos Mitropoleos 70
546 22 Thessaloniki
Tel: (031) 277700

48 Ores
48 Hours
Leoforos Alexandras 19
114 73 Athens
Tel: (1) 6430313
Fax: (1) 6461361

Pantheon
Odos Christou Lada 3
102 37 Athens
Tel: (1) 3230221
 Fax: (1) 3228797

Politika Themata
Odos Ypsilantou 25
106 75 Athens
Tel: (1) 7218421

Pontiki
Mouse
Odos Massalias 10
106 81 Athens
Tel: (1) 3609531

Radiotileorash
Radio-TV
Odos Mourouzi 16
106 74 Athens
Tel: (1) 3609531

RADIO & TELEVISION

Elliniki Radiophonia Tileorassi
Greek Radio-Television
Odos Mourouzi 16
106 74 Athens
Tel: (1) 639-5970
Fax: (1) 639-0652

Elliniki Tileorassi 1 (Television)
Fax: (1) 639-2263

Elliniki Tiliorassi 2
Tel: (1) 770-1911
Fax: (1) 779-7776

Elliniki Tiliorassi 3
Aggelaki 2
546 21 Thessaloniki
Tel: (31) 278784
Fax: (31) 236466

Elliniki Radiophonia (Radio)
Fax: (1) 639-0583

AD AGENCIES

Bates Hellas
11b Konitsis St.
15125 Athens
Tel: (1) 6125520
Fax: (1) 8053064

Leo Burnett S.A.
Sygrou Ave. 371
17564 Athens
Tel: (1) 9412365
Fax: (1) 9430432

Conquest Europe
Kifissias Ave. 38
15125 Athens
Tel: (1) 6840812
Fax: (1) 6840856

Geo-Young & Rubicam
49 Vas Sofias Ave.
16076 Athens
Tel: (1) 7243511
Fax: (1) 723-1490

Grafis Advertising
198 Kifissias Ave.
11524 Athens
Tel: (1) 6710353
Fax: (1) 6476307

McCann-Erickson Advertising SA
7 Ventiri St.
11528 Athens
Tel: (1) 7250801
Fax: (1) 7244942

Proad Ogilvy & Mather Direct
3 Gravias St.
Athens

Spot/Thompson Adv., Ltd.
10-12 Kifissias Ave.
15125 Athens
Tel: (1) 684-7302/3
Fax: (1) 684-5636

BANKS

National Bank of Greece
86 Eolou Street
105 69 Athens
Tel: (1) 321-8954
Fax: (1) 321-1491

Agricultural Bank of Greece
23 Eleftheriou Venizelou Street
102 21 Athens
Tel: (1) 323-2777
Fax: (1) 325-5079

Commercial Bank of Greece
11 Sofokleous Street
102 35 Athens
Tel: (1) 321-0911
Fax: (1) 323-4333

Credit Bank
40 Stadiou Street
102 52 Athens
Tel.: (1) 326-0000
Fax: (1) 326-5488

General Hellenic Bank
9 Eleftheriou Venizelou Street
102 29 Athens
Tel: (1) 325-0301
Fax: (1) 322-2271

Ionian Bank
45 Eleftheriou Venizelou Street
102 43 Athens
Tel: (1) 322-5501
Fax: (1) 323-4488

INTERNET ADDRESSES

Usenet group(s):
soc.culture.greek
YAHOO - Greece
http://www.yahoo.com/Regional/Countries/Greece/
Greek WWW Servers around the world
http://www.softlab.ntua.gr/greekWWW.html
City-Net - Greece
http://www.city.net/countries/greece/
Hellas On Line
http://www.hol.gr/greece

Guatemala

Republic of Guatemala

Economy

Overview

Lying on the southern flank of Mexico and the market created by NAFTA, Guatemala is strategically located to serve as a conduit between North, Central, and South America. A member of the Central American Common Market, it enjoys duty-free access to neighboring countries. However, Guatemala has a relatively undeveloped industrial economy and will have to modernize its often rudimentary infrastructure to stimulate sustained economic growth, which is currently about four percent per year. Power is scarce and the obsolete telecommunications system remains state-owned, despite calls for privatization. Better roads and rail service would help Guatemala capitalize on its north-south access as well as on its access to both oceans. The Guatemalan work force is generally poorly trained; although costs are low, so are quality and productivity.

Trade

Despite a relatively high level of basic industrialization, exports remain almost exclusively agricultural. Guatemala depends heavily on trade to fuel its import substitution-based industrial activity. Major exports include coffee, sugar, bananas, cardamom, and meat; together these products account for about half of all exports. Major imports include intermediate products, industrial raw materials, consumer non-durable products, industrial capital goods, and fuels. The US is Guatemala's main trading partner, accounting for more than one-third of trade—followed by El Salvador, Germany, Mexico, and Japan.

Sectors

Agriculture Agriculture accounts for over 22 percent of GDP but employs about 50 percent of the work force. Cash crops include coffee, sugar, bananas, spices, and cotton, although most activity is of a subsistence nature. Meat, seafood, and timber are also growing in significance.

Industry Industry provides about 20 percent of GDP, and employment for a similar proportion of the work force. The most industrialized country in Central America, Guatemala has nonetheless focused on import substitution. It produces processed food products, textiles, chemicals, and pharmaceuticals.

Services Although poorly developed, services account for about 50 percent of GDP and employ—albeit often marginally—about 22 percent of the work force. Attempts are being made to develop specialized business services, but most services involve local distribution or personal service activity.

Trends

The construction industry and financial services sectors, among others, have begun growing rapidly in recent years. The long-term viability of these and other activities hinges, however, on much-needed infrastructure improvements, and the attraction of foreign capital in amounts adequate to convert expansion plans into reality. Guatemala has insufficient funds to accomplish this task on its own. Further privatization of government-held industries is anticipated, however, and could become an important element in the campaign for infrastructure capital. Export and investment opportunities have already risen in cellular communications and road construction, as well as the generation and distribution of electricity. Overall, Guatemala has the potential to really compete in world markets; but it will have to zealously commit to significant structural reforms in order to do so.

At a Glance

THE COUNTRY

Location Middle Central America, between Honduras and Mexico.
Terrain Mountainous, with fertile coastal plains.
Climate Temperate in highlands; semitropical on coasts.

THE PEOPLE

Population 10,700,000
Ethnic composition Mestizo (mixed Spanish-Indian), indigenous.
Religious composition Roman Catholic, Protestant, traditional Mayan.
Languages spoken Spanish, 21 Indian languages (including Quiche, Cakchiquel, Kekchi).
Education and literacy Education is compulsory six years. The literacy rate is 52%.
Labor force
Total: 2,500,000
By occupation: agriculture 50%, industry 18%, services 22%.

COUNTRY FACTS

Political and legal Constitutional democratic republic. Civil law system; judicial review of legislative acts; has not accepted compulsory International Court of Justice jurisdiction.
Telephone The government owns all telephone and telegraph services. There are over 200,000 telephones in the country, and most services are automatic (1990). A fairly modern network is centered in the city of Guatemala. International country code: [502]. City codes: Guatemala City (2), all other cities (9).
Transportation Guatemala has a basic lack of infrastructure, which affects transportation options. Less than 15 percent of the highways are paved, and most are in poor condition. The government owns most of the railroads. Major ports include Puerto Barrios, Puerto Quetzal, and Santo Tomas de Castilla. There are no natural harbors on the west coast. Only 11 of the 523 airports have permanent-surface runways, and most service only domestic flights.
Environment Only 12 percent of the land is arable; 780 square miles have been irrigated. Current issues include deforestation, soil erosion, and water pollution. The land is subject to several natural disasters. Volcanoes are numerous in the mountains, with frequent violent earthquakes, and the Caribbean coast is subject to hurricanes and other tropical storms.
Media There are an estimated 625,000 radios and 490,000 television sets serving 91 AM and 25 television stations. Four newspapers are published in Guatemala City, with a combined circulation of 157,000, and range from moderately liberal to moderately conservative. The government publishes the *Diario de Centro America*.
Health Malnutrition, alcoholism, and inadequate sanitation and housing pose serious health problems. Only 62 percent of the population has access to safe water, and only 60 percent has adequate sanitation. Thirty-four percent of the population has access to health care services. Life expectancy is 60 years.

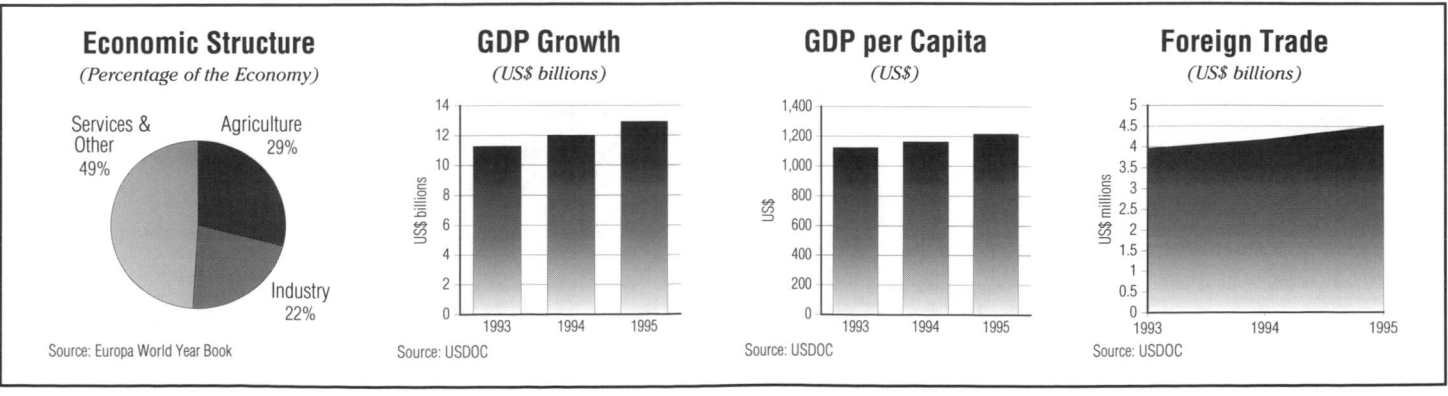

Economic Structure
(Percentage of the Economy)

Services & Other 49%
Agriculture 29%
Industry 22%

Source: Europa World Year Book

GDP Growth
(US$ billions)

Source: USDOC

GDP per Capita
(US$)

Source: USDOC

Foreign Trade
(US$ billions)

Source: USDOC

Guatemala

- ⊛ National capital
- ⊙ Departmento capital
- ● Secondary city
- —— International border
- —— Departmento border
- —— Primary road
- ······ Railroad

0   70 km
0   50 mi

NOTES: Departmentos that are not labeled have the same name as their Capitals.

Guatemala asserts historical claims to Belize and shows it as a Departmento on its official government maps.

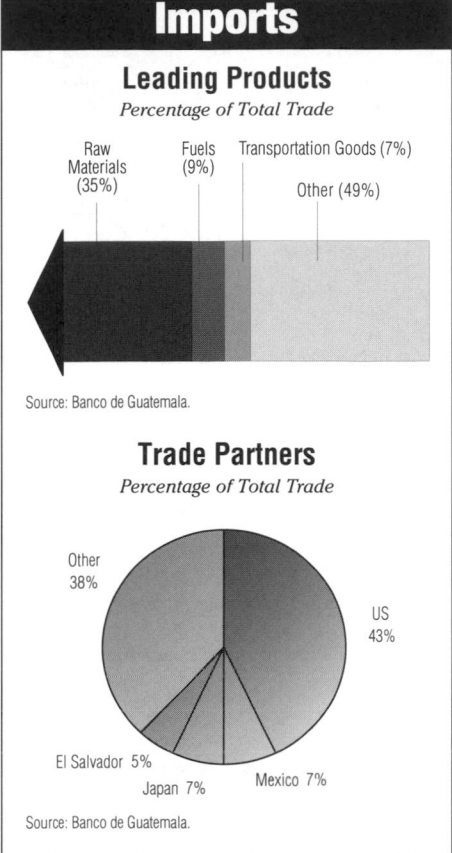

Imports

Leading Products
Percentage of Total Trade

Raw Materials (35%)
Fuels (9%)
Transportation Goods (7%)
Other (49%)

Source: Banco de Guatemala.

Trade Partners
Percentage of Total Trade

- Other 38%
- US 43%
- El Salvador 5%
- Japan 7%
- Mexico 7%

Source: Banco de Guatemala.

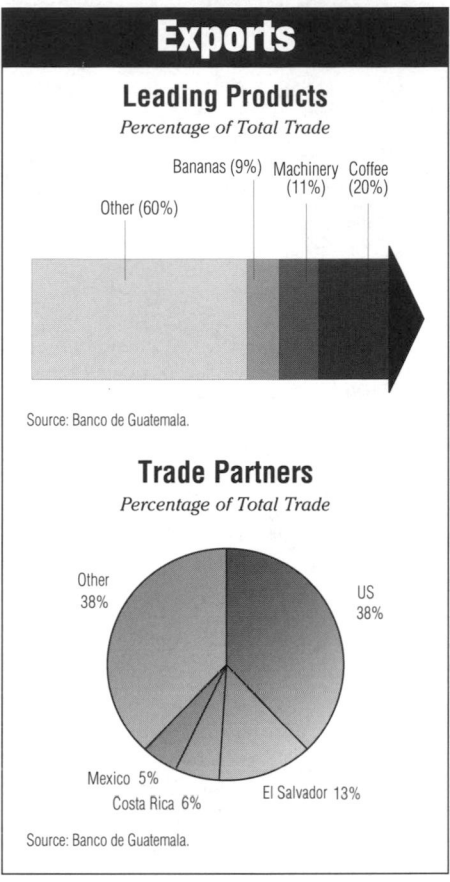

Exports

Leading Products
Percentage of Total Trade

Bananas (9%)
Machinery (11%)
Coffee (20%)
Other (60%)

Source: Banco de Guatemala.

Trade Partners
Percentage of Total Trade

- Other 38%
- US 38%
- Mexico 5%
- Costa Rica 6%
- El Salvador 13%

Source: Banco de Guatemala.

Opportunities

FOR IMPORTING TO GUATEMALA
- agricultural machinery
- air conditioning and refrigeration equipment
- computers and peripherals
- consumer-ready food products
- electrical power equipment: transformers and transmission lines
- food processing and packaging equipment
- fuels and lubricants
- hotel and restaurant equipment
- industrial machinery
- iron and steel
- medical instruments
- motor vehicles and parts
- paper and paper products
- telecommunication products
- wheat

FOR EXPORTING FROM GUATEMALA
- apparel
- bananas
- cardamom
- ceramics and glassware
- coffee
- fruits and vegetables
- meat
- petroleum
- sugar
- textiles

GROWTH SECTORS
- agriculture
- apparel and textiles
- construction
- financial services
- tourism

GOVERNMENT PROCUREMENT
- airport maintenance goods and services
- environmental protection goods and services
- oil exploration goods and services
- telecommunications products

Trade News

RULES AND REGULATIONS

- **Tariffs and import taxes** Guatemala applies the Common External Tariff schedule of the Central American Common Market (CACM) to almost all agricultural and industrial goods. These tariffs range from five to 20 percent for most goods. A seven percent value-added tax applies to most imported goods at the point of sale.

- **Import licenses** Guatemala allows the import of wheat flour by permit only. There are no other significant import licensing requirements.

- **Prohibited imports** The import of offensive weapons—a category encompassing automatic weapons and a range of military weapons and hardware—is prohibited.

- **Export controls** Guatemala operates a one-stop office for the granting of export permits. The average exporter is able to receive authorization within four to five hours.

- **Export subsidies** Significant tax exemptions are granted to both foreign and domestic enterprises producing for export. Guatemala is not a member of the GATT Subsidies Code.

- **Free trade zones (FTZs)** Although two private and one public free trade zones exist in Guatemala, many domestic companies enjoy tax benefits similar to those offered by the FTZs.

- **Free trade arrangements** The Central American countries reestablished a uniform tariff range (five to 20 percent) as of April 1, 1993, and are working to establish a common external tariff system. Internally, they are striving to establish a true free trade zone, with duties eventually to be eliminated on all but four designated products.

FREIGHT FORWARDERS

Aerovias
Avda Hincapíe y 18a Calle
Lado Sur Aeropuerto 'La Aurora'
Zona 13
Guatemala City
Tel: (2) 34-7935 Telex: 5010
Fax: (2) 522-32568

Armadora Maritima Guatemalteca, SA
14a Calle 8-14
Zona 1
Apdo 1008
Guatemala City
Tel: (2) 53-7243 Telex: 5214
Fax: (2) 53-7464

Empresa Portuaria 'Quentzal'
Edif. 74, 6°
7a Avda y 4a Calle
Zona 9
Guatemala City
Tel: (2) 31-4824
Telex: 6134

Ferrocarriles de Guatemala- FEGUA
9a Avda 18-03
Zona 1
Guatemala City
Tel: (2) 83030
Telex: 5342
Fax: (2) 83807

Flota Mercante Gran Centroamericana, SA
Edit. Canella, 5 la Calle 7-21
Zona 9
Guatemala City
Tel: (2) 31-6666
Telex: 5211

Líneas Marítimas de Guatemala, SA
6a Avda 20-25
Edificio Plaza Marítima, 8°
Zona 10
Guatemala City
Tel: (2) 37-0166
Telex: 5174

Schenker Panamericana SA, Ltda.
POB 1159
Guatemala City
Telex: 5292 SCHE GU

Business Travel

LH 1906	MADRID	935	113-3
LH 1022	STUTTGART HBF.	935	-
AF 1701	LYON	940	683-6
AY 822	HELSINKI	940	113-3
AA 071	SFRANCISCO-DALLAS	945	731-7

Air Travel Times

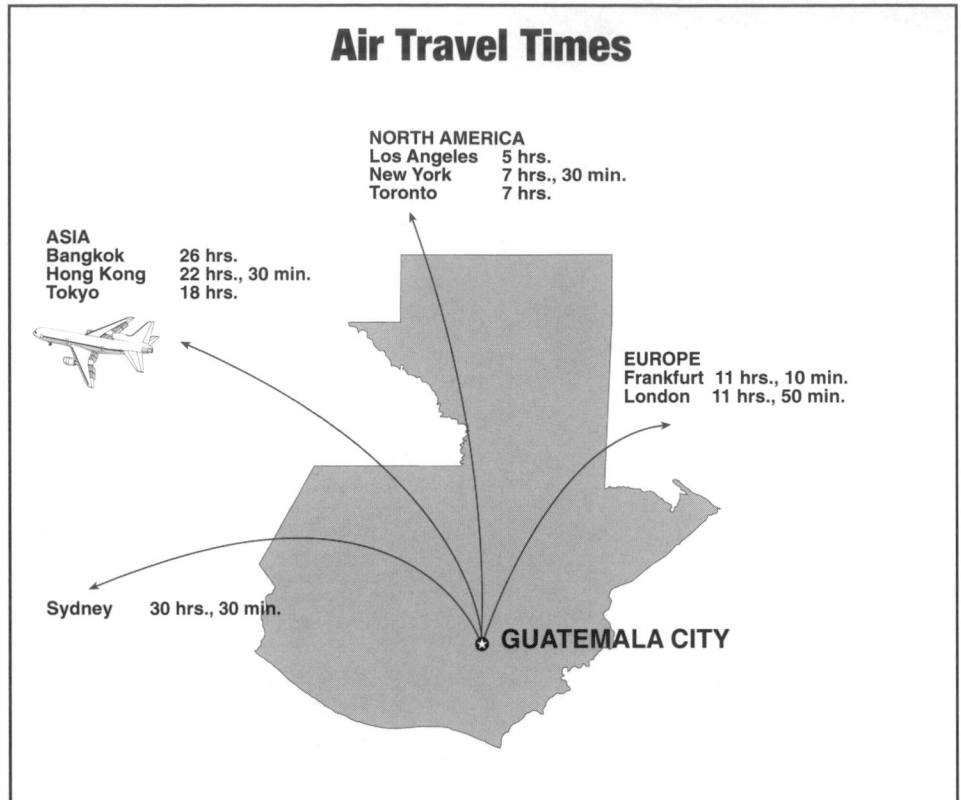

NORTH AMERICA
Los Angeles 5 hrs.
New York 7 hrs., 30 min.
Toronto 7 hrs.

ASIA
Bangkok 26 hrs.
Hong Kong 22 hrs., 30 min.
Tokyo 18 hrs.

EUROPE
Frankfurt 11 hrs., 10 min.
London 11 hrs., 50 min.

Sydney 30 hrs., 30 min.

GUATEMALA CITY

COMMUNICATIONS

Telephones Telephone communications are readily available in Guatemala City. Calls can generally be placed without any problem. Calls can be placed through the hotel operator, directly with calling cards, or collect. Never rent a house or apartment that does not come with a telephone; demand is high for this service.

Fax Increasingly popular, fax services are becoming more readily available. Because of the shortage of telephone lines, many offices do not have a dedicated fax line although they do have a fax machine. Call first and let them know you are sending a fax.

Post office Domestic and international mail service is adequate by Latin American standards. Express mail costs double normal rates; it is not overnight delivery but is a reasonably efficient service.

BEST TRAVEL BOOKS

Lonely Planet, Guatemala, Yucatan and Belize Travel Survival Kit. 552 pages.
Fodor's Travel Guide, Costa Rica, Belize, Guatemala. Tourist oriented, excellent source of city details.
The Travellers Guide to Latin America Customs and Manners. Elizabeth Devine & Nancy Bragaranti. An invaluable guide for people not wanting to put foot in mouth.
The Wall Street Journal Guide to Business Travel, Mexico and Central America. The most electrifying of all practical travel guides.

USEFUL TELEPHONE NUMBERS

If you are calling from outside Guatemala, you will need to add the country code [502] and any other international dialing requirements from within your country.
- Advisor for Exportation .... (2) 346872
- Chamber of Commerce .... (2) 82681
- Camino Real Hotel .... (2) 334-633
- Hotel Guatemala Fiesta .... (2) 322-555
- Hotel Princess Reforma .... (2) 344-545
- DHL Courier Service .... (2) 32-3023

Airlines
- Aviateca .... (2) 81372
- Continental .... (2) 312051
- KLM Royal Dutch Airlines .... (2) 370222
- Iberia .... (2) 373914
- Avenida .... (2) 373905
- Mexicana .... (2) 62084
- TACA International Airlines .... (2) 80061

Car Rental
- Avis .... (2) 316990
- Hertz .... (2) 322242
- Budget .... (2) 316546
- National .... (2) 68017

Credit Cards Information
Lost or stolen credit cards (call collect to the US, regardless of which country the card was issued in).
- Amex ....[1] (919) 333-3211
- Diner's Club................................[1] (303) 799-1504
- MasterCard ....[1] (314) 275-6690
- Visa ....[1] (410) 581-7931

NATIONAL TOURIST OFFICE

Instituto Guatemalteco de Turismo (Inguat)
7 Av 1-17, Zona 4
Guatemala City
Telephone: 800-742-4529

Travelogue

WORKWEEK

Offices Monday-Friday from 9:00 am to 6:00 pm, often closed from 12:30 pm to 2:30 pm or from 1:00 pm to 3:00 pm for lunch.
Banks Monday-Friday 9:00 am to 3:00 pm (with many differences in banks.)
Government Monday-Friday 8:00 am to 5:30 pm.
Retail Monday-Saturday 8:00 am to 8:00 pm.

HOLIDAYS

Holidays 1996
January 1 New Year's Day
January Early Epiphany*
April 13 Holy Thursday **
April 14 Good Friday*
April 15 Holy Saturday*
May 10 Mother's Day
May 1 Labor Day
June 30 Army Day
August 15 Feast of the Assumption
September 15 Independence Day
October 20 Revolution Day
November 1 All Saints' Day
December 24 Christmas Eve**
December 25 Christmas Day
December 31 New Year's Eve**
The banking sector also celebrates July 1, Bank Workers' Holiday, and October 12, Columbus Day.
*Dates vary each year.
**Businesses are closed for the afternoon only.

VISA AND PASSPORT

A passport and a tourist card are required for travel into Guatemala. Tourist cards are available at the point of entry for US$5 (US currency only) and are valid for 30 days. Visas are required for longer stays or if a traveler has an official or diplomatic passport. Visas are available from Guatemalan embassies.

DEPARTURE FORMALITIES

There are no departure formalities for Guatemala.

IMMUNIZATION

No immunizations are necessary unless you are coming from an infected area; however, be advised that cholera is found in Guatemala, so precautions are suggested. Malaria prophylaxis is advised for those traveling in the lowlands.

TIPPING

Taxi: tipping is not necessary as the fare is negotiated beforehand and included in the charge. In restaurants, 15 percent is considered normal.

CRIME

Street crime is the main threat to visitors in Guatemala. Most larger hotels have safes for storage of cash and valuables; it is suggested that you utilize them. Common sense rules of not publicly displaying valuables, not resisting would-be muggers, and not traveling alone outside of touristed areas or at night apply in Guatemala. Unfounded rumors that foreigners are stealing Guatemalan children to harvest their organs have led to threats and incidents of mob violence in several parts of the country. These incidents have not occurred in the traditional tourist destinations or the tourist/business sections of Guatemala City.

INFRASTRUCTURE

Telephone, hotel, and taxi services are modern and available. Intercity public bus systems are somewhat primitive but this is the primary mode of public transportation within and between Guatemalan cities. Taxis are available around the clock, but must be reserved. Negotiate all fares; taxis are not metered. Train service is slow, not adequate, and uncomfortable. The International Airport is 10 minutes from Guatemala City and boasts modern facilities. The lines at immigration counters are long during peak tourist season (November through May). Immigration and customs procedures are standard.

Marketing

Distribution

One of the key decisions a foreign company must make in Guatemala is the selection of a qualified, competent sales representative or distributor. More so than in many foreign markets, successful sales are tied to a local presence. A distributor with well-positioned sales outlets in major commercial locations will increase a seller's opportunity to capture a significant share of its product market.

Agents, Distributors, and Partners

Most business conducted in Guatemala is based on personal relationships. Sales are generally made by local or freelance representatives with price lists and promotional material, but without current inventories. It is generally recommended that foreign firms use representatives, in which the appointed distributor collects orders from wholesalers or retailers. However, once a local company receives exclusive representation, it cannot easily be taken away, so use caution in your choice of local representatives.

Advertising

Advertising media include newspapers, magazines, radio, and television. Highway billboards have proliferated in recent years. Consultation with the local media association before launching a campaign is usually a good idea. Guatemala has six television channels, six radio stations, and five major magazines. Trade associations can also provide assistance, coordination, and logistics support for trade promotion events especially for demonstrations, seminars, and conferences.

Service and Customer Support

Although after-sale service is not required by the commercial code, most wholesalers and retailers provide customer service as a matter of practical business sense. Although Guatemalan law does not require guarantees, electro-domestic appliances and consumer equipment, telephone equipment and sets, and sound equipment generally have 60- to 90-day guarantees provided by the retailer. Auto sales usually include the first three services free of charge. Foreign firms should encourage their local representatives to keep sufficient supplies of parts for after-sale service.

Marketing in Guatemala

MARKETING TIPS

- **Language** Written material should be in Spanish.
- **Holidays** Avoid business on holidays, as transportation and other services are unreliable; more so during Easter week, when businesses shut down.
- **Suppliers** Overseas suppliers should have a local distributor or representative and be prepared to travel to Guatemala personally. Local buyers are much more open and decisionmakers more accessible when dealing with a recognized local person.
- **Representatives** Because terminating an exclusive contract within two years can require payment of substantial compensation to the Guatemalan agent; foreign companies must be absolutely certain that they have chosen the right person before undertaking this powerful relationship.

CONSULTING FIRMS

Arevalo Pérez, Aranky y Asociados
Centro Generencial Las Margaritas
Diagonal 6, 10-65, Zona 10
01010 Guatemala City
Tel: (2) 327939
Fax: (2) 316914, 316916

Coopers & Lybrand
Edif. El Triángulo, Nivel 17
7 Ave. 6-53, Zona 4
01004 Guatemala City
Tel: (2) 321867
Fax: (2) 347059

Tuncho Granados y Asociados
(Deloitte & Touche)
Edif. Plaza del Sol, Of. 413
12 Calle 2-04, Zona 9
01009 Guatemala City
Tel: (2) 319744, 319725, 324061
Fax: (2) 314217

Business Culture

Greetings and Courtesies

Handshakes are the common greeting among both men and women; handshakes are gentle—almost limp—and somewhat prolonged. Women may pat each others' right forearm or shoulder instead of shaking hands. Male friends often hug and may kiss on the cheek; female friends may also hug and lightly kiss each other on the cheek. Business cards in Spanish are a courtesy rather than a necessity (although other materials should be translated).

Business Ethic and Framework

Guatemalans are among the most formal of Latin Americans, and Guatemalan business and social culture is based on correct but personal relationships. To Guatemalans, work is far from the most important part of life, but they do adhere strictly to the forms that govern this nevertheless important sphere. Conservative business suits are the preferred attire for men; women should wear conservative dresses or a skirt and blouse—never pants.

Meetings and Decision Making

Appointments should be made two weeks in advance. Punctuality is generally observed by Guatemalans. Actual decisions are almost always made at a high level of authority. Guatemalans will want to know your standing within the hierarchy and will wish to match you with someone of similar rank.

Women

Although women in Guatemala generally occupy a somewhat secondary status in this traditionally male-dominated society, many operate businesses and may be accorded considerable personal freedom. In general, foreign businesswomen should experience few problems. Women can generally go on the streets and dine alone, but may feel more comfortable escorted.

Cultural Cautions

DO'S

- Learn something about Guatemala's history and culture—it will be appreciated, as will attempts to speak Spanish. Family, children, and jobs are also good topics of conversation.
- Express your admiration for colleagues and superiors and their positive personal traits for goodwill.

DON'TS

- Avoid race, politics, religion, any sexual topic (especially in mixed company), *la violencia*—the local term for the longstanding and ongoing political unrest—and human rights issues as conversational topics.
- Do not directly criticize individuals, who may feel obligated to defend their honor, sometimes physically.

CUSTOMS

- Bring business associates a bottle of imported cognac, whisky (scotch), or wine as a gift.
- Maintain good eye contact—to do otherwise is considered a sign of evasiveness or disrespect.
- To wave goodbye, raise the hand, moving it from side to side with the palm facing you.
- If invited to a meal, plan to stay until about 11:00 pm on a weeknight, midnight on a weekend.
- Call the waiter to bring the check; at better restaurants it will not be brought until requested.

OBSERVATIONS

- Guatemalans speak in a soft voice; loud voices are disliked and considered rude and disrespectful.
- Business is usually discussed only in a narrowly defined business context and never at a social event.
- Men usually answer questions put to both men and women, especially in more rural areas; if you wish to talk individually to a woman, do so away from a man.
- Bargaining is expected everywhere except in large stores.

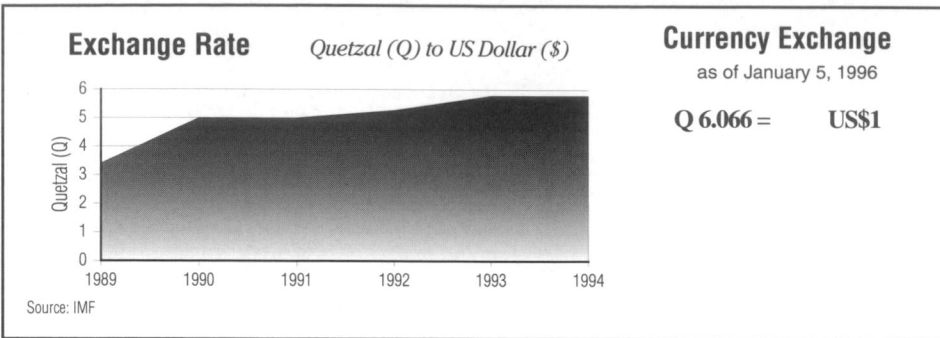

Exchange Rate *Quetzal (Q) to US Dollar ($)*

Source: IMF

Currency Exchange
as of January 5, 1996

Q 6.066 =   US$1

Currency

The currency in use is the Guatemalan quetzal (Q), divided into 100 centavos.

Foreign Exchange

The exchange rate is set in daily auction by the Bank of Guatemala. Access for the private sector is unrestricted. The Bank of Guatemala may control the amount of foreign exchange supplied to the auction and may restrict bidding to within Q.05 of the exchange base rate. The Bank of Guatemala intervenes only to smooth fluctuations. The exchange rates are largely determined by market forces. Exporters must sell their foreign exchange proceeds to an authorized institution. Financial institutions may purchase foreign exchange from the public and charge a one percent commission. Foreign exchange houses may also offer foreign exchange services on the same basis as commercial banks. The Bank of Guatemala may also sell foreign exchange to producers who require it to pay for imports. There are no exchange rate guarantees and no arrangements for forward cover against risk. The capital market is developing, but still remains thin. There are 27 private commercial banks, 11 investment firms, 12 bonded warehouses, and five exchange houses.

Capital Transfer

There is no general requirement for local participation. Guatemala's exchange system is very open, and there are no constraints on remittance quantities or capital flows. Capital may be repatriated without restriction.

Investment Incentives

Incentives are available for forestry, mining, tourism, and petroleum investments. Firms developing projects in designated tourist zones receive real estate tax exemptions. Investors in tourism are also exempt from all import duties on goods not produced in Central America.

Investment Restrictions

Guatemala has few investment restrictions and requirements directed at foreigners. There is no general requirement for local participation. Foreign companies face many more registration procedures than domestic firms, however. These additional requirements are lengthy, but they are not used to screen or discriminate against foreign companies.

TAXATION

Taxation requires sophisticated knowledge of complex rules and regulations specific to each country. For more detailed information we suggest you refer to the Ernst & Young Corporate Tax Guide and Directory, available from the Ernst & Young accounting office in your country, or from:

Lizarralde, Ayestas, Asturias y Ramos Ernst & Young
13 Calle 1-51, Zona 10
Guatemala City, Guatemala
Tel: (2) 321-249, 315-662
Fax: (2) 315-687

- Both resident and nonresident corporations are taxed only on Guatemalan-source income; foreign income is not taxable. Interest received from abroad is considered to be Guatemalan-source income.

At a Glance

Corporate Income Tax Rate (%)	30
Capital Gains Tax Rate (%)	15
Branch Tax Rate (%)	30
Withholding Tax (%)(a)	
Dividends	12.5
Interest (b)	20
Royalties from Patents, Know-how, etc.	30
Branch Remittance Tax	0
Net Operating Losses (Years)	
Carryback	0
Carryforward	4

(a) These rates are applicable to nonresidents. Income subject to these taxes are not included in taxable income.
(b) A 10% final withholding tax is imposed on interest paid to residents that is derived from savings accounts and from investments.

Money Matters

BITS AND PIECES

- **Availability of foreign exchange** Although the Bank of Guatemala may occasionally intervene in the foreign exchange market, there are no delays in the acquisition of foreign exchange.
- **Stock exchange** There are two small stock exchanges, but the exchanges trade primarily in government bonds and local corporate paper. Trading in currency futures also has recently begun.
- **Credit** Domestic credit tends to be expensive, so many businesses seek project financing abroad. The government's Financial Modernization Program is an attempt to lower interest rates and make credit more widely available, standardize accounting practices, and require external audits of financial institutions. Larger importers typically have their own source of capital abroad for financing imports.
- **Banking services** The government seeks to increase the number of financial instruments available, and permit banks and other financial institutions to offer a wider range of services.

BANKS

Banco Agricola Mercantil, SA
7a Avda 9-11
Zona 1
Guatemala City
Tel: (2) 21601
Telex: 5347
Fax: (2) 51-0780

Banco de Guatemala
7 Ave. 22-01, Zona 1
01001 Guatemala City
Tel: (2) 534053 Fax: (2) 534035

Banco de Occidente
7 Ave. 11-15, Zona 1
01001 Guatemala
Tel: (2) 531333, 535831, 535882
Fax: (2) 514348

Banco del Agro
9 Calle 5-39, Zona 1
01001 Guatemala City
Tel: (2) 514026 Fax: (2) 300322

Banco del Café, S.A.
Ave. La Reforma 9-00, Zona 9
01009 Guatemala City
Tel: (2) 311311 Fax: (2) 311418

Banco del Quetzal, S.A.
Plaza El Robel
7 Ave. 6-26, Zona 9
01009 Guatemala City
Tel: (2) 318333 Fax: (2) 326937

Banco Granai & Townson, S.A.
7 Ave. 1-86, Zona 4
01004 Guatemala City
Tel: (2) 312333/7 Fax: (2) 323532

Banco Industrial, S.A.
7 Ave. 5-10, Zona 4
01004 Guatemala City
Tel: (2) 312323 Fax: (2) 319437

Banco Nacional de Desarrollo Agricola
9 Calle 9-47, Zona 1
01001 Guatemala City
Tel: (2) 535222/9 Fax: (2) 537927

Banco Nacional de la Vivienda
6 Ave. 1-22, Zona 4
01004 Guatemala City
Tel: (2) 325777, 325786

Citibank
Ave. La Reforma 15-45, Zona 10
01010 Guatemala City
Tel: (2) 336574
Fax: (2) 336860

Crédito Hipotecario Nacional
7 Ave. 22-77, Zona 1
01001 Guatemala City
Tel: (2) 500112

Lloyds Bank International
6 Ave. 9-51, Zona 9
01009 Guatemala City
Tel: (2) 327580/9 Fax: (2) 327641

Legal System

Guatemala is a civil code country.

Intellectual Property Rights

Patents Any invention considered new with potential industrial applications is eligible for a patent. Inventions may be products or methods. Patents are not granted for plants, animals, beverages and food products, commercial and financial systems, methods for therapeutic and surgical treatment, and generally all discoveries of natural products without any human intervention. Patents are granted, however, for methods for processing chemicals. Patents are granted for 15 years from filing date. Methods involving the process of chemical compounds are only granted patents for 10 years. Patents may expire if the invention is not used locally within six years after the date it is granted or if its industrial exploitation is interrupted for more than two consecutive years. Infringement upon a patent is a punishable crime, and the patent owner may also file civil proceedings to recover damages.

Trademarks Trademarks are classified as industrial or manufacturers' marks, commercial marks, and service marks. In general, the use or registration of the following as trademarks is prohibited: (1) national flags, coats-of-arms, insignia, or the distinguishing marks of foreign nations, states, municipalities, and other public bodies; (2) names, emblems, and devices of the Red Cross, or religious or charitable institutions; (3) designs of coins or notes that are legal tender, reproductions of securities and other commercial documents, or stamps in general; (4) signs, words, or expressions that ridicule other persons, ideas, religions, or national symbols; (5) names, signatures, and portraits of persons without consent; (6) technical or common names of products, goods, or services; and (7) terms, signs, or locations that have passed into general use.

Copyrights A copyright may be granted for literary, scientific, or artistic works, whether published or not. The right is inherent by the mere creation of a work without the need of deposit, registry, or other formality; however, the work may not be utilized publicly or for profit without registration with the Guatemalan Association of Authors and Composers. The right terminates 50 years after the death of the author. The law applies only to nationals and resident aliens. Protection for other aliens is governed by the international treaties and conventions ratified by Guatemala.

Trade Secrets Guatemala does not currently have laws directed at the protection of trade secrets.

Business Registration

Foreign corporations constituted abroad, but whose businesses are administered or principally maintained in Guatemala, are governed by the Guatemala Commercial Code; however, the specific form of incorporation is governed by the laws of the country of origin. Corporations legally incorporated abroad that wish to establish or operate in any way in Guatemala must comply with the provisions of the Commercial Code and must have at least one agent permanently residing in the country. To operate in Guatemala, foreign corporations must prove that they have been constituted in accordance with laws of their country of incorporation; they must submit certified copies of their articles of incorporation and by-laws, and appoint in Guatemala a representative agent with broad powers to conduct business and legally represent the corporation before the courts.

Contracts and Dispute Resolution

Civil contracts involving more than 300 quetzals (about US$50) must be in written form. All contracts which must be registered or recorded in public registries have to be executed as public deeds, regardless of amount. Generally, commercial contracts are less formally executed than are civil contracts. Clauses concerning arbitration are valid even when contracts are not executed as public instruments. Guatemalan courts will uphold binding arbitration agreements and awards issued pursuant thereto.

Notaries

Instruments executed before a notary must state the date, names of the parties, their ages, domiciles, professions, and marital status. The notary must declare that he or she knows the parties or that they were identified by witnesses. The notary retains the original document in a protocol and furnishes the parties with copies, which have the same legal effect as originals in court.

Labor

Collective contracts must be in written form and include three copies. If an employer terminates a contract without reason, the employee is entitled to indemnification for an amount related to the time the employee has worked for the employer, as well as damages equivalent to two months' salary.

Legal Matters

LEGAL BRIEFS

- **Limited liability companies** The name of a limited liability company, with no more than 20 members, must reflect the partnership and include the word *"Limitada,"* abbreviated *"Ltda.,"* or *"Cía. Ltda.,"* or else the company is regarded as a general partnership. Limited Partnership or *"Sociedad en Comandita,"* consists of one or more partners who are jointly and unlimitedly liable and one or more partners with limited liability. The company name can consist of the name of one or two of the unlimited partners followed by the obligatory inclusion of *"y Compañía, Sociedad en Comandita,"* abbreviated as *"y Cía. S. en C."*

- **Foreign judgments** In the absence of a specific treaty, foreign judgments are given the same effect as Guatemalan judgments in the foreign country. If the foreign country does not execute Guatemalan judgments, the foreign judgment will not be executed in Guatemala.

- **Monopolies** Any kind of monopoly is prohibited. An enterprise must contract with any other enterprise that requests its products or services, observing equal treatment among diverse categories of consumers. An act contrary to bona fide commerce or to normal and honest development of mercantile activities is considered unfair competition and, therefore, unjust and prohibited.

- **Sale of enterprises** The seller of an enterprise must abstain for five years following the date of sale from opening a new enterprise that might divert customers from the sold enterprise, thereby constituting unfair competition.

- **Pledges** A pledge contract must be in writing and any pledged objects must normally be delivered to a creditor or third person designated by parties.

- **Shipping** Guatemalan vessels must touch at Guatemalan ports at least once or twice a year for their license to remain valid.

- **Public contracts** Special rules apply to contracts executed with government, state agencies and state enterprises.

LEGAL CONTACTS

Quezada Urruela & Asociados
13 Calle 2-60, Zona 10
Edif. Topacio Azul
Nivel 12, Of. 1202
Guatemala City
Tel: (2) 390397
Fax: (2) 631688

Asenio, Flores & Andrade
Centro Financiero
7A. Avenida 5-10 Zona 4
Torre 1 - 10. Nivel, Oficina 3
Gautemala City
Tel: (2) 2 318168

Carillo y Asciados
1A Avenida 8-24
Zona 10
Guatemala City
Tel: (2) 315441-311091
Fax: (2) 346135

Mayora & Mayora
Edificio Camara De Industria
Ruta 6, 9-21
Zona 4, Nivel
Guatemala City
Tel: (2) 347921
Fax: (2) 323523

Saravia y Munoz
14 Calle 4-32
Zona 10, Cuarto Nivel
Guatemala City
Tel: (2) 233-6576
Tel: (2) 233-6577

Jorge Skinner-Klee
9A Calle 3-72
Zona 1
Guatemala City
Tel: (2) 516235
Fax: (2) 538811

GOVERNMENT AGENCIES

Aduana Central
10 Calle 13-92, Zona 1
01001 Guatemala City
Tel: (2) 516262, 513024

Empresa Electrica
6 Ave. 8-14, Zona 1
01001 Guatemala City
Tel: (2) 3090662, 300659, 300671

Guatel
7 Ave. 12-39, Zona 1
01001 Guatemala City
Tel: (2) 83380, 531042, 532398

INDE
7 Ave. 2-29, Zona 9
01009 Guatemala City
Tel: (2) 345775/6, 345711

Ministerio de Trabajo y Prevision Social
14 Calle 5-49, Zona 1
01001 Guatemala City
Tel: (2) 82522, 515644, 301366

Ministry of Agriculture
Palacio Nacional, Zona 1
01001 Guatemala City
Tel: (2) 393333, 536816, 517560

Ministry of Communications
Palacio Nacional, Zona 1
01001 Guatemala City
Tel: (2) 512769, 393333, 82975

Ministry of Economy
8 Ave. 10-43, Zona 1
01001 Guatemala City
Tel: (2) 518606, 515086, 530903

Ministry of Energy and Mines
Diagonal 17, 29-78, Zona 11
01011 Guatemala City
Tel: (2) 762459, 760682, 762044

Ministry of Exterior Relations
Palacio Nacional, Zona 1
01001 Guatemala City
Tel: (2) 26748, 393333, 516509, 534788

Ministry of the Interior
Palacio Nacional, Zona 1
01001 Guatemala City
Tel: (2) 393333

Ministry of Tourism
7 Ave. 1-17, Zona 4
01004 Guatemala City
Tel: (2) 311333, 311342, 311334

Ministry of Public Finances
8 Ave. y 21 Calle, Zona 1
01001 Guatemala City
Tel: (2) 537484, 533284, 513542

Registrol Mercantil
9 Calle 3-39, Zona 1
01001 Guatemala City
Tel: (2) 20719, 20481, 20151

Registro Propiedad Industrial
6 Ave. 11-43, Zona 1
01001 Guatemala City
Tel: (2) 23541, 23618

Ventanilla Unica de Inversiones
8 Ave. 10-43, Zona 1
01001 Guatemala City
Tel: (2) 83331/4

GENERAL TRADE ASSOCIATIONS

Asociación de Agricultores de Guatemala
9 Calle 3-43, Zona 1
01001 Guatemala City
Tel: (2) 21468, 80336

Asociación de Azucareros de Guatemala
Edif. Tívoli Plaza, 6 Ave. 11-08, Zona 9
01009 Guatemala City
Tel: (2) 318197, 313087, 340628

Asociación de Comerciantes de Guatemala
18 Calle 2-75, Zona 1
01001 Guatemala City
Tel: (2) 82614, 84492

Asociación de Gerentes de Guatemala
6 Ave. 1-36, Zona 14
01014 Guatemala City
Tel: (2) 682744, 683289

Asociación Expen Gasol
6 Ave. 0-60, Zona 4
01004 Guatemala City
Tel: (2) 322352, 352227

Asociación Nacional del Cafe
5 Calle 0-50, Zona 14
01014 Guatemala City
Tel: (2) 370075, 337535

Gremial EPNT
Edif. Cámara de Industria
Ruta 6, 9-21, Zona 4
01004 Guatemala City
Tel: (2) 346872, 323590, 315947

Guatemalan Bankers Association
12 Calle 4-74, Zona 9, Nivel 2
01009 Guatemala City
Tel: (2) 318211, 321448

CONSULTING FIRMS

Bocanegra Cruz y Asociados
(Horwath & Horwath International)
Edif. El Reformador, Nivel 4
Avenida La Reforma 1-50, Zona 9
01009 Guatemala City
Tel: (2) 345345, 351738 Fax: (2) 345362, 352333

Klynveld Peat Marwick Goerdeler
Edif. Centro Financiero
Torre I, Nivel 16
7 Ave. 5-10, Zona 4
01004 Guatemala City
Tel: (2) 311701

Lizarralde, Ayestas, Asturias y Ramos
(Ernst & Young International)
13 Calle 1-51, Zona 10
Oficina 204
01010 Guatemala City
Tel: (2) 315662, 321856 Fax: (2) 315687

Price Waterhouse
Edif. Tívoli Plaza, Nivel 4
6 Calle 6-38, Zona 9
01009 Guatemala City
Tel: (2) 345080

NEWSPAPERS

Diario de Centroamérica
18a Calle 6-72
Zona 1
Guatemala City
Tel: (2) 24418

El Gráfico
14a Avenida 9-18
Zona 1
Guatemala City
Tel: (2) 51-0021

Prensa Libre
13a Calle 9-13
Zona 1
Guatemala City
Tel: (2) 51-1838

BUSINESS PERIODICALS

Industria
3a Avenida 12-21
Zona 1
Guatemala City

El Industrial
Ruta 6, No. 9-21
Zona 4
Guatemala City

Inforpress Centroamericana
9a Calle 'A' 3056
Zona 1
Guatemala City
Tel: (2) 29432 Fax: (2) 83859

Panorama
12a Calle 6-40
Guatemala City

RADIO & TELEVISION STATIONS

Canal 3-Radio-Televisión Guatemala, SA
30a Avenida 3-40
Zona 11
Apartado 1367
01901 Guatemala City
Tel: (2) 94-7491 Fax: (2) 94-7492

Dirección General de Radiodifusión y Televisión Nacional
Edificio Tipografía Nacional, 3°
18 de Septiembre 6-72, Zona 1
Guatemala City
Tel: (2) 53-2539

La Voz de Guatemala
18a Calle 6-72, Zona 1
Guatemala City
Tel: (2) 71-4378

Tele Once
20a Calle 5-02, Zona 2
Guatemala City
Tel: (2) 68-2165

AD AGENCIES

APCU Thompson Asociados, S.A.
12 Calle 1-25, Zona 10
Edif. Geminis 10, Nivel 17
Torre Norte
Guatemala City
Tel: (2) 35-3346

BBDO Guatemala
13 Calle 2-60, Zona 10
Edif. Topacio Azul, Nivel 11
Guatemala City 01010
Tel: (2) 390-385
Fax: (2) 390-396

Comunica Leo Burnett
5TA Avenida 6-39, Zona 14
Col. El Campo
Guatemala City
Tel: (2) 37-3144
Fax: (2) 37-3150

Foote, Cone & Belding
Av. La Reforma 8-60, Zona 9
Edif. Galerias Reforma
Torre I, Nvel 9
Guatemala City
Tel: (2) 32-0921
Fax: (2) 34-0509

Publicidad McCann-Erickson Centroamericana
Av. La Reforma 8-60, Zona 4
Centro Financiero - Torre 11, 502 Nivel
Guatemala City
Tel: (2) 31-8037
Fax: (2) 34-7270

INTERNET ADDRESSES

City-Net - Guatemala
http://www.city.net/countries/guatemala/

YAHOO - Guatemala
http://www.yahoo.com/Regional/Countries/Guatemala/

Latin America - Guatemala
http://lanic.utexas.edu/la/ca/guatemala/

Listserv: CENTAM-L
Send mail to: LISTSERV@UBVM.cc.buffalo.edu
Subscribe in the body of the message.

Honduras

Republic of Honduras

Economy

Overview

Economic reforms over the last five years have improved conditions somewhat, but Honduras is still one of the poorest countries in the western hemisphere. Its problems range from heavy public debt to inadequate health, education, and other social systems. In an effort to attract investment capital to the country, the Honduran government has reduced certain trade and other barriers, particularly in the areas of exchange and interest rates. While these measures have had some success, high inflation and substantial protectionism remains firmly entrenched. The Honduran legal system is poorly developed, especially in the area of commercial law, and the financial services sector has suffered from excessive restrictions and thus a lack of investment capital. However, port facilities are reasonably well-developed, the road network is adequate, and extensive air transportation links provide relatively straightforward access. The potential to develop Honduran natural resources is reasonably high, and the expansion of infrastructure and energy should boost opportunities for new development.

Trade

Trade remains generally protectionist with high tariffs and other costs, and Honduras has suffered from a growing trade deficit in recent years. Honduras' major exports are all agricultural or extractive products: bananas, coffee, shellfish, meat, and wood; lead and zinc are also exported. Major imports include machinery, chemicals, basic manufactures, fuels, and foodstuffs. The US is the country's largest trading partner, accounting for roughly half of all trade; it is followed by Japan, Germany, the Netherlands, and Italy, although trade with Central American neighbors Guatemala and Mexico, as well as with Caribbean venues, is increasing.

Sectors

Agriculture This sector supplies less than 25 percent of GDP but employs more than half of the work force, although many of them are underemployed and involved in subsistence activities. Cash crops include coffee, bananas, sugar, seafood, and timber.

Industry Industry provides about 15 percent of GDP, while employing about 19 percent of the work force. The major industries are food processing, textiles and apparel, chemicals, machinery, and transportation equipment.

Service Services account for somewhat more than 50 percent of GDP, but employ only about 30 percent of the work force. The service sector is relatively undeveloped, involving mostly distribution and personal service activities.

Trends

Economic growth is closely tied to the success of efforts to increase the domestic energy production, which is necessary to sustain growth in the manufacturing and services sectors. Construction is expected to grow as demand for new public and private building and infrastructure projects takes off. Also, increased telecommunications investment and favorable trends in the commodities market should further counter-balance downturns in other areas. These developments will be necessary to replace the loss of foreign military funds that largely sustained the country during the 1980s.

At a Glance

THE COUNTRY

Location Middle America, between Guatemala and Nicaragua.
Terrain Mountainous, narrow coastal plains.
Climate Tropical to subtropical, depending on elevation.

THE PEOPLE

Population 5,500,000
Ethnic composition
Mestizo 90%
Other ethnicities include European, Arab, African, Asian descent, and indigenous Indians.
Religious composition Roman Catholic is the predominant religion, although there is a fast-growing Protestant minority.
Languages spoken Spanish.
Education and literacy Six years is compulsory. Literacy rate is 68% of those 15 years and older.
Labor force
Total: 1,300,000
By occupation: agriculture 62%, services 20%, manufactures 9%, construction/housing 10%.

COUNTRY FACTS

Political and legal Democratic constitutional republic. Rooted in Roman and Spanish civil law; some influence of English common law; accepts International Court of Justice jurisdiction, with reservations.
Telephone telecommunications The government owns and operates all telephone and telegraph services. It is an inadequate and antiquated system with only seven telephones per 1,000 persons. International country code: [504]. No city codes are in use.
Transportation Only about 19 percent of the nearly 9,000 kilometers of highway are paved. Rail service exists in the north, connecting the coastal zone with the principal ports and cities. Four principal ports, Puerto Cortés, Tela, La Ceiba, and Puerto Castilla, serve the country on the Caribbean side. There are more than 30 landing fields in Honduras, including three major airports with international service.
Environment Smoke from slash-and-burn foresting methods causes air pollution. Slash-and-burn agricultural methods continue to destroy the Honduran forests, though there is growing awareness to confront this problem. The armed forces have become involved with issues ranging from reforestation projects to forest fire-fighting. Current issues include urban population escalation; deforestation resulting from logging and land clearing for agricultural purposes; improper land use causing soil erosion and land degradation; and mining activities causing pollution in rivers and streams.
Media There is no press censorship. The major newspapers are *La Tribuna*, *El Tiempo*, and *El Heraldo*, with a combined circulation of 111,000. There are 176 AM, six FM, and 28 television stations.
Health Water must be boiled and filtered. It is often in short supply during the dry season. Fruits and vegetables must be cleaned carefully and meats fully cooked. Rabies and various intestinal diseases are the main health concerns. Cholera is also found here. Malaria suppressants are advised when traveling outside Tegucigalpa.

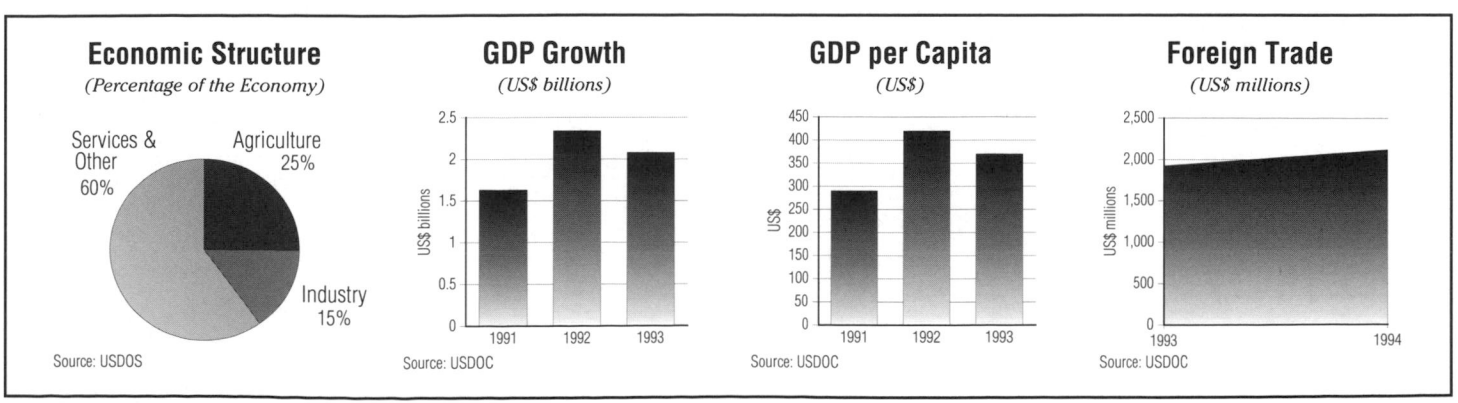

Economic Structure
(Percentage of the Economy)

Services & Other 60%
Agriculture 25%
Industry 15%

Source: USDOS

GDP Growth
(US$ billions)

US$ billions — 1991, 1992, 1993

Source: USDOC

GDP per Capita
(US$)

US$ — 1991, 1992, 1993

Source: USDOC

Foreign Trade
(US$ millions)

US$ millions — 1993, 1994

Source: USDOC

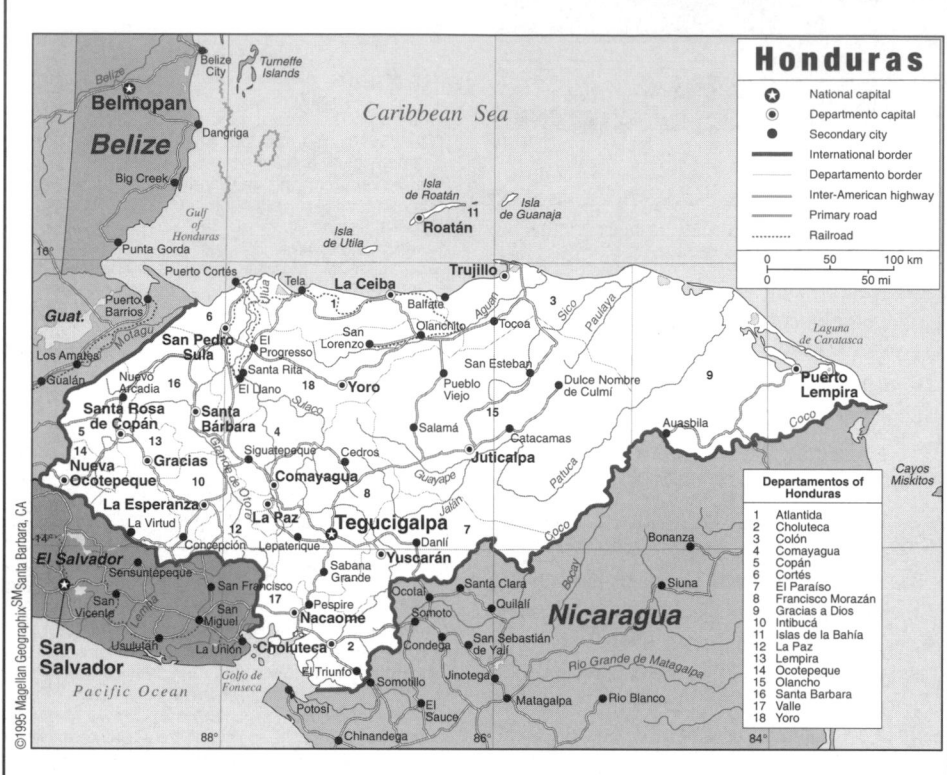

Travelogue

WORKWEEK

Offices Monday-Friday 9:00 am to noon and 2:00 pm to 6:00 pm, Saturdays 8:00 am to noon.
Banks Monday-Friday 9:00 am to 3:00 pm.
Government Monday-Friday 9:00 am to 4:00 pm.
Retail Monday-Friday 9:00 am to noon and 2:00 pm to 6:00 pm, Saturdays 8:00 am to noon.

HOLIDAYS

Holidays 1996
January 1 New Year's Day
January 2 New Year's Holiday
April 13 Holy Thursday*
April 14 Good Friday*
May 1 Labor Day
September 15 Independence of Central America
October 3 Francisco Morazan's Birthday
October 12 Columbus Day
October 21 Dia de las Fuerzas Armadas de Honduras
December 25 Christmas
*Dates vary each year.

VISA AND PASSPORT

Visitors to Honduras need a valid passport for stays of less than 60 days. No visas or tourist cards are required for people traveling from the US, Canada, Australia, New Zealand, or Japan. Citizens of other countries need a tourist card which can be purchased from Honduran consulates for US$2-3. Officials at land borders and airports allow only 30 days for visitors, even when prior arrangements are made. Although it is possible to obtain extensions, make sure all papers are completed properly by border officials. Visitors must show proof of departure arrangements upon arrival.

DEPARTURE FORMALITIES

There are no departure formalities for Honduras or any entry or exit taxes at land borders; however, almost always, travelers are charged about US$2 on entry and exit.

IMMUNIZATION

No immunizations are required for entry to Honduras unless you are arriving from an infected area. Dysentery and stomach parasites are common and malaria is endemic in coastal regions. Prophylactics against these should be taken and mosquito nets brought along for a good night's sleep. It is advised to inoculate against typhoid and tetanus. Only drink bottled water or boil to sterilize other water.

TIPPING

Ten percent of the bill is the normal tipping protocol in Honduras; however for exceptional service, 15 percent is considered appropriate.

CRIME

The level of street crime in Honduras, such as robberies and assaults, continues to rise in urban areas. Rural crime is also high. Tourists are often targeted by criminals in some areas of San Pedro Sula and Tegucigalpa. There have been reports of armed bandits in rural areas and the border regions near Guatemala, El Salvador, and Nicaragua.

INFRASTRUCTURE

Tourist facilities are generally adequate but vary in quality. Road travel can be hazardous near the Nicaragua-Honduras border due to extensive minefields. Only about 20 percent of the roads are paved and many that are paved are routes to access coffee plantations and forestry development areas. Railroads are networked in the northern part of the country but most lines are used for fruit cargo and not passenger travel. Tourists can arrange travel to the Mayan ruins by calling the Instituto Hondureno de Turismo for transportation information.

NATIONAL TOURIST OFFICE

Instituto Hondureno de Turismo
Barrio Guancaste
Edif. Centro Guanacaste
Apdo 3261
Tegucigalpa
Tel: 38-3975 Fax: 38-2102

COMMUNICATIONS

Telephones Telephone services are adequate. Direct dial and long-distance calling are available to several countries. Hondutel is the international long distance carrier.
Fax Faxing is available at Tegucigalpa, San Pedro Sula, Puerto Cortes, Tela, La Ceiba, Comayagua, Siguatepeque, Santa Rosa de Copan, Danli, Choluteca, Juticalpa, La Paz, La Lima, El Progreseo, Valle de Angeles, El Paraiso, Catacamas, and Marcals. Telegraph service is good to all parts of the world.
Post office Mail service is adequate. It takes between four and seven days for delivery. There is no air mail for packages weighing over 2 kg; sea mail is the best but can take from six to 10 months.

BEST TRAVEL BOOKS

The Wall Street Journal Guide to Business Travel, Mexico and Central America. The most electrifying of all practical travel guides.
Do's and Taboo's Around the World. The Bestselling Guide to International Behavior. Edited by Roger Axtell, compiled by the Parker Pen Company. The ultimate guide to international behavior, now completely updated and expanded. Helpful, fun to read!
Mexico & Central American Handbook. Passport Books. Passport's Handbooks of the World, are annually updated, regionally organized travel handbooks for all independent travelers, whatever their age or budget. Based on the legendary South American Handbook, they are essential for practical, dependable travel information.

USEFUL TELEPHONE NUMBERS

If you are calling from outside Honduras, you will need to add the country code [504] and any other international dialing requirements from within your country. There are no city codes in Honduras.
- DHL Courier Service 534-238
- Hotel & Club Copanti 530-900
- Hotel Suites Los Andes 534-425
- La Galeria Restaurant 530-900
- Sim Kon Restaurant 576-370
- Setco Charter Company 33-70-25
- Isle Charter Company 41-01-79/43-23-54
- La Moskitia Ecoaventuras tours 37-93-98
- Tuk-tuks canoes 32-64-74
- Dentist 72-00-54
- Car Repair San Pedro Sula...................... 52-70-83
- Cultural Institutions 53-39-11
- Travel agent San Pedro Sula 45-11-60

Car Rental Agencies
- Budget Car Rental 522-295
- Amigo Car Rental.................................... 72-03-71

Airlines
- American 580-518
- Taca 522-646
- Lacsa 525-893
- Copa 520-628

Credit card information
Lost or stolen credit cards (call collect to the US, regardless of which country the card was issued in).
- Amex...[1] (919) 333-3211
- Diner's Club...............................[1] (303) 799-1504
- MasterCard ....[1] (314) 275-6690
- Visa ....[1] (410) 581-7931

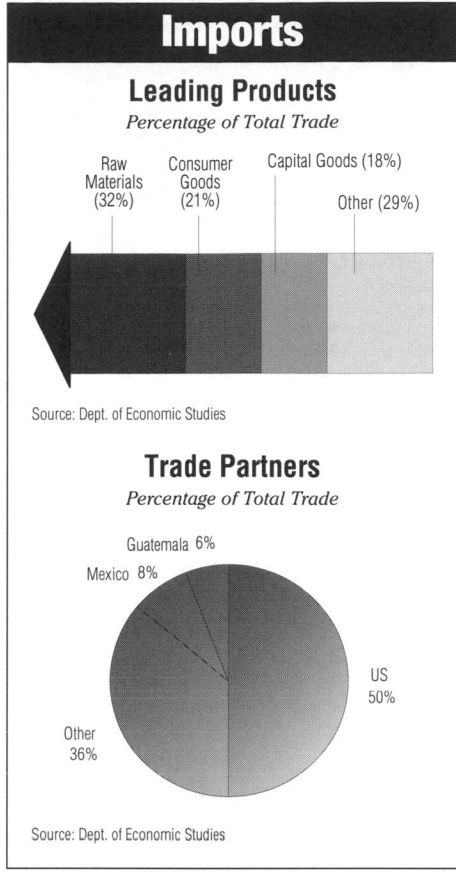

Imports

Leading Products
Percentage of Total Trade

Raw Materials (32%)
Consumer Goods (21%)
Capital Goods (18%)
Other (29%)

Source: Dept. of Economic Studies

Trade Partners
Percentage of Total Trade

Guatemala 6%
Mexico 8%
US 50%
Other 36%

Source: Dept. of Economic Studies

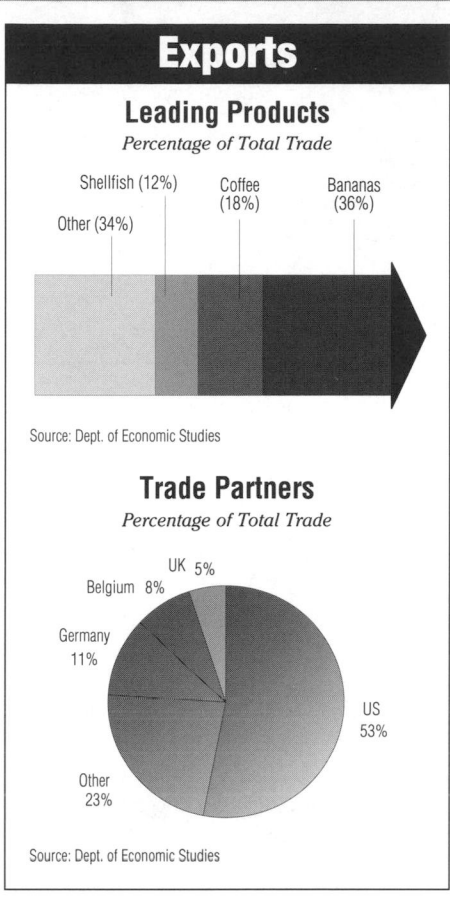

Exports

Leading Products
Percentage of Total Trade

Shellfish (12%)
Coffee (18%)
Bananas (36%)
Other (34%)

Source: Dept. of Economic Studies

Trade Partners
Percentage of Total Trade

UK 5%
Belgium 8%
Germany 11%
US 53%
Other 23%

Source: Dept. of Economic Studies

Opportunities

FOR IMPORTING TO HONDURAS
- agricultural machinery, tools, petroleum products
- construction, food processing-packaging equipment
- computers and computer products

FOR EXPORTING FROM HONDURAS
- bananas, citrus fruits, coffee, shrimp, sugar, beef
- clothing
- lead, zinc, lumber

GROWTH SECTORS
- construction
- mining
- services
- tourism

Trade News

RULES AND REGULATIONS
- **Customs procedures** Honduras' customs administrative procedures are complicated. There are extensive documentary requirements involving the payment of numerous import duties, customs surcharges, selective consumption taxes, consular fees, and warehouse levies.
- **Tariffs and import taxes** A five to 20 percent tariff exists for most products. Certain items, however, including grains, poultry, leather, and textiles, have tariffs of up to 100 percent. A 10 percent surtax was recently eliminated on 20,000 products, but high surtaxes remain on a number of others. A consumption tax exists for luxury items.
- **Prohibited imports** Import of items that compete with certain domestic industries is prohibited. Protected industries include footwear and basic grains.

Legal Matters

LEGAL BRIEFS
- **Shipping** The Code of Commerce contains provisions regarding the rights and duties of captains and crews, as well as the rules relating to admiralty matters. These provisions are similar to those in other Latin American countries.
- **Statutes** The more important legal provisions are codified; the principal codifications are the Civil Code, Code of Civil Procedure, Code of Family, Code of Commerce, Penal Code, Law of Criminal Procedure, Law of Organization and Powers of the Courts, Mining Code, Code of Public Instruction, and Notarial Law. Copies of other laws are often difficult to obtain. Current laws appear in the official newspaper called *La Gaceta*.
- **Trade agreements** Honduras maintains multilateral agreements with most Central American countries, as well as a bilateral treaty with the United States.
- **Notaries** A notary must be a lawyer or hold a notary's diploma. Notaries keep a registry containing the originals of all documents executed before them and issue only certified copies, which have the same legal force as the originals.

LEGAL CONTACTS

Ortez Sequeira, Colindres y Asociados
Edificio Ortez Sequeira
2DO Piso Una Cuadra
Al Este del Instituto San Miguel
PO Box 3861
Teguicilgapa
Tel: 39-1800/7
Fax: 39-1808/9

Bufete Pena y Asociados
14 Avenue 10 Calle S.O. #78
San Pedro Sula
Tel: (504) 52-7079
Fax: (504) 57-9038

Legal

Legal System
Honduras is a civil code country.

Intellectual Property Rights
Patents and Trademarks New discoveries or inventions may be patented for 10, 15, or 20 years. Foreign patents can be registered in Honduras, but only for the time remaining on the original patent. Trademarks can be registered for 10 years, subject to renewals for subsequent 10-year periods.

Copyrights Copyrights are granted for 10, 15, or 20 years for literary works, including musical compositions, pictures, and films. A copyright already registered in a foreign country may also be registered in Honduras for the remaining time that the original copyright is still in effect.

Business Registration
A petition must be made to the Department of Finance prior to conducting business in Honduras. Foreign corporations must (1) prove that they are legally constituted under the laws of their country; (2) prove that they have the right to establish branches; (3) maintain a permanent residence in Honduras; (4) assign a fund for their activities in Honduras; (5) show that their objects are legal; and (6) agree to adhere to the courts and laws of Honduras.

Contracts and Dispute Resolution
Civil contracts involving more than 200 Lempira (about US$21) must be in writing. Arbitration and other alternative methods of resolution are accepted in Honduras, although most disputes are settled through the court system. There is no specific legislation directed at the protection of trade secrets.

Labor
Honduras has only recently enacted major labor laws, and they are rarely enforced. In general, workers have few rights, and employers have broad authority to set wages and terminate employment.

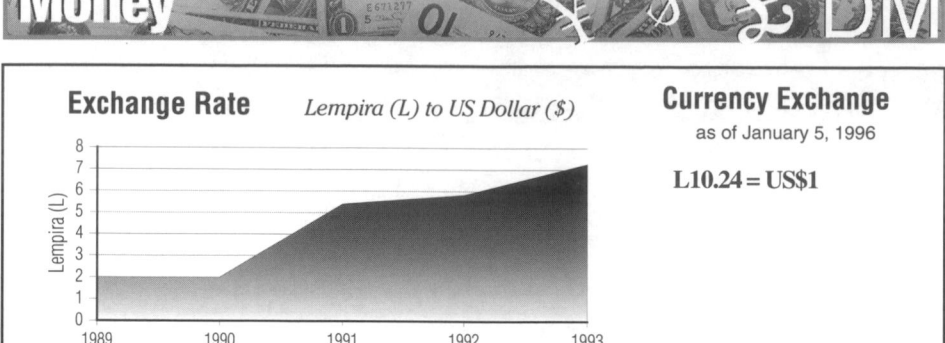

Exchange Rate

Lempira (L) to US Dollar ($)

Source: IMF

Currency Exchange

as of January 5, 1996

L10.24 = US$1

Money Matters

BITS AND PIECES

- **Worldwide income** Resident corporations are only taxed on worldwide income; nonresident corporations are taxed based only on Honduras-source income. There are no provisions for avoiding double taxation.

- **Stability** Honduras has a long history of an unstable economy, although the situation has been slowly stabilizing since a new constitution was approved in 1982. The government has addressed the over-valued exchange rate and unfavorable trade terms, and it has introduced reforms to lessen the high rate of inflation.

- **Exemptions** Honduran duty-free zones in Puerto Cortes, industrial processing zones, and firms registered in the regime of temporary imports are exempt from customs duties.

- **Foreign investments** Direct foreign investments and purchases of shares in existing domestic firms are permitted and unrestricted, except for defense industries, hazardous industries, and small-scale industry and commerce. Foreign investments must be registered with the Secretary of Economy and Trade.

Currency

The currency in use is the Honduran lempira (L).

Foreign Exchange

Exchange regulations are administered by the Central Bank of Honduras. All exchange transactions except for debt-equity conversion are carried out by the interbank market, and the exchange rate is determined exclusively through supply and demand. There are no taxes on the purchase or sale of foreign exchange, and no arrangement for forward cover against risk. Travelers may bring in foreign bank notes without restriction.

Capital Transfers

Transactions with other Central American countries may be executed in local currencies or US dollar proceeds from exports. There are no restrictions on foreign currency bank accounts opened in domestic banks. Receipt and transfer of foreign exchange for mutual fund investments, housing developments, or real estate is unrestricted. Repatriation of registered capital, and transfers of dividends and profits earned on registered capital, is not restricted.

Investment Incentives

There are very few investment requirements for foreign companies. The 1992 Investment Law guarantees equal treatment to all private firms, foreign and domestic. Imports of machinery, equipment, fixtures, parts, raw material, and supplies can be imported duty-free. Many foreign companies are exonerated from income, export, sales, or consumer taxes. Many countries, including Japan and the US, provide insurance and guarantees for their companies doing business in Honduras. Honduras is also a party to the Multilateral Investment Guarantee Agency (MIGA).

Investment Restrictions

Although the Investment Law guarantees freedoms to all foreign investors, they are in actuality discriminated against by the government. Companies must have at least 51 percent Honduran ownership.

BANKS

Banco Atlantida, S.A.
POB 3164
Tegucigalpa, D.C.
Tel: 32-1742 Fax: 32-1273

Banco Continental, S.A.
POB 390
San Pedro Sula, Cortes
Tel: 53-1310 Fax: 52-2750

Banco de El Ahorro Hondureño, S.A.
POB 3185
Tegucigalpa, D.C.
Tel: 37-5161 Fax: 37-4638

Banco Financiera Centroamericana, S.A.
POB 1432
Tegucigalpa, D.C.
Tel: 38-1661 Fax: 38-1630

Banco Hondureno del Cafe
POB 583
Tegucigalpa, D.C.
Tel: 32-8370 Fax: 32-8332

Banco La Capitalizadora Hondureña, S.A.
POB 344
Tegucigalpa, D.C.
Tel: 37-1171 Fax: 37-2775

Banco de La Exportacion, S.A.
POB 3988
Tegucigalpa, D.C.
Tel: 39-4256 Fax: 39-4265

Banco de Las Fuerzas Armadas, S.A.
POB 877
Tegucigalpa, D.C.
Tel: 31-2051 Fax: 31-3832

Banco de Los Trabajadores, S.A.
POB 3246
Tegucigalpa, D.C.
Tel: 37-9501 Fax: 37-8422

Banco de Occidente, S.A.
POB 3284
Tegucigalpa, D.C.
Tel: 37-0310 Fax: 37-0486

Banco del Comercio, S.A.
POB 160
San Pedro Sula, Cortes
Tel: 53-3600 Fax: 53-3128

Banco del Pais, S.A.
POB 314
San Pedro Sula, Cortes
Tel: 52-5202 Fax: 52-5229

Banco SOGERIN, S.A.
POB 440
San Pedro Sula, Cortes
Tel: 53-3888 Fax: 57-2001

Central Bank of Honduras
6a-7a Avenida, 1a La Calle, Apartado 58-C
Tegucigalpa
Tel: 22-2270 Telex: 1121

TAXATION

Taxation requires sophisticated knowledge of complex rules and regulations specific to each country. For more detailed information, we suggest you refer to the Ernst & Young Corporate Tax Guide and Directory, available from the Ernst & Young accounting office in your country, or from:

Morales Palao William y Asociados
Apdo. Postal 2232
San Pedro Sula, Honduras
Tel: 313712
Fax: 313709

At a Glance

Corporate Income Tax Rate (%)(a)	40.25
Capital Gains Tax Rate (%)(a)	40.25
Branch Tax Rate (%)(a)	40.25
Withholding Tax (%)(b)	
Dividends (c)	15
Interest	5
Royalties	35
Branch Remittance Tax	35
Other Payments	20
Net Operating Losses (Years)	
Carryback	0
Carryforward (d)	3

(a) This is a maximum rate that includes surcharges. Nonresident corporations are taxed at special rates.
(b) This rate is applicable to nonresidents.
(c) This amount represents the final tax. A 10% final withholding tax is imposed on dividends paid to residents.
(d) A deduction is permitted under certain circumstances.
Other significant taxes include a social security tax of 7% paid by the employer and 3.5% by the employee on monthly salaries up to L 600, a social fund tax of 1.5% paid equally by employer and employee, and various municipal taxes on production and sales.

Marketing

Overview

Several factors combine to make Honduras attractive to experienced overseas exporters. The country has a history of social stability, and most business and political leaders speak English. Geographically, Honduras is an excellent location from which to penetrate Central American markets. There are drawbacks, however. The legal system ignores precedent and commercial cases are settled in the civil courts, which only occasionally provide clear and timely adjudication. In addition, the Honduran market is small, most citizens have little purchasing power, and local financing is constricted.

Distribution

The Honduran Agent/Distributor Law provides penalties for wrongful termination that discourage exclusive distribution agreements. Representatives and distributors usually carry broad lines on a non-exclusive basis, and only a few local distributors carry large inventories of parts and equipment. Most local buyers contact suppliers directly at the factory or warehouse level, since this reduces costs. Store owners usually buy goods in small lots from stores and export brokers. Firms carrying automobiles, computers and electric power generation equipment often stock products from several overseas competitors.

Agents, Distributors, and Partners

Foreigners exporting to Honduras are required to sell through a registered agent or distributor. Only Honduran nationals or legal entities registered with a local chamber of commerce and the Ministry of Economy and Commerce may represent foreign firms.

Selling Techniques and Customer Support

Honduras has been split into the North Coast, which includes San Pedro Sula, the commercial and industrial capital, and the Central region, where Tegucigalpa, the political capital, is located. As in most Latin American countries, establishing positive personal relationships is the best way to penetrate the market. This long-term strategy usually produces mutually profitable alliances. Service availability usually makes the difference in the purchasing choice, especially when selling to the government.

Business Culture

Greetings and Courtesies

Handshakes are the common greeting among both men and women; handshakes are gentle—almost limp—and somewhat prolonged, except among Hondurans already involved in and familiar with international business standards. Titles are important, and foreign visitors should call their business counterparts by their title and last name unless requested to do otherwise.

Business Ethic and Framework

Respect and personal dignity lie at the core of Honduran business and social culture. Hondurans are rather formal, and business and social culture is based on correct, often strongly hierarchical, yet personal relationships. Conservative, dark business suits are the preferred attire for men; women should wear conservative dresses or a skirt and blouse— never pants. A suit or a dress are appropriate for relatively formal social event.

Meetings and Decision Making

Appointments are necessary and should be made two weeks in advance. It is important to first establish a personal relationship, possibly through several meetings, before a business deal can be concluded. It is important to cultivate relationships with Honduran peers, because the quality of these relationships may strongly influence the actual decisionmaker even when your immediate counterpart is not the one making the decision.

Women

Although women generally occupy a secondary status in heavily male-dominated and *macho*-influenced Honduras, many operate businesses and may be accorded considerable personal freedom. Foreign businesswomen are expected to be highly professional, appropriate, and not aggressive or confrontational. Women may generally go on the streets and dine alone, but may feel more comfortable if escorted.

Marketing in Honduras

MARKETING TIPS

- **Negotiations** Do not expect an appointment if you only have one day to spare, nor expect terms to be quickly finalized. This is less a sign of disinterest than a cultural difference. Hondurans will not be rushed.
- **Language** Although many professionals were educated in English-speaking countries, foreigners should prepare materials in Spanish.
- **Advertising** There are five local television stations, six Spanish newspapers, and one English daily in Honduras. Local agencies focus their efforts on these media.

AD AGENCIES

FCB
POB 574
San Pedro Sula
Tel: 57-5851
Fax: 52-9706

McCann-Erickson Centroamericana S. De R.L.
POB 1161
San Pedro Sula
Tel: 53-1633
Fax: 52-2748

CONSULTING FIRMS

Morales Palao Williams y Asociados
POB 5878
Tegucigalpa, D.C.
Tel: 32-0799
Fax: 31-3709

Peat Marwick Mitchell & Co.
POB 841
Tegucigalpa, D.C.
Tel: 32-2806
Fax: 32-5925

Price Waterhouse
POB 20541
Tegucigalpa, D.C.
Tel: 31-1911 Fax: 31-1906

Cultural Cautions

DO'S

- Learn something about Honduras' history and culture—it will be appreciated, as will attempts to speak Spanish. Family and children are also good topics of conversation.

DON'TS

- Avoid race, politics, religion, any sexual topic (especially in mixed company), human rights issues, and drugs and drug trafficking as conversational topics.
- Do not directly criticize individuals, who may feel obligated to defend their honor, sometimes physically.

CUSTOMS

- Hondurans are highly hospitable and frequently invite foreign colleagues to a meal at their homes. No gifts are necessary, but effusive and respectful thanks are necessary.
- Hondurans stand close to each other during conversation; to attempt to increase the distance between yourself and a Honduran by moving backward is considered rude.

OBSERVATIONS

- Shaking the index finger back and forth in front of the face means "no." Pulling the outside corner of the eye down with the index finger means "watch out."

NEGOTIATIONS

- Although they like to bargain, Hondurans do not respond well to aggressive tactics; particularly avoid raising your voice or showing impatience.
- Hondurans present a united front during negotiations, deferring to the senior member.
- Allow negotiations to remain open-ended at all times. This way confrontation can be avoided and talks can be allowed to fade away if agreement cannot be reached.

GOVERNMENT AGENCIES

Central Bank of Honduras
Edif. Banco Central
Tegucigalpa, D.C.
Tel: 37-1668, 37-1677
Fax: 37-6261

Ministry of Communications, Telecommunications and Public Works
Bo. La Bolsa
Comayaguela, D.C.
Tel: 33-6768
Fax: 34-2223

Ministry of Economy and Commerce
Edif. Salamé, 2o. Piso
Calle Peatonal
Tegucigalpa, D.C.
Tel: 38-2025, 22-1850, 22-3251
Fax: 38-1336

Ministry of the Environment
Cll. La Fuente
Fte. Centro Cultural Alemán
Tegucigalpa, D.C.
Tel: 39-0241, 32-6721
Fax: 32-5375

Ministry of Finance and Public Credit
Palacio de Hacienda
3a. Calle
Tegucigalpa, D.C.
Tel: 22-0111-0119
Fax: 38-2309

Ministry of Foreign Affairs
Palacio José Cecilio del Valle
Blvd. Juan Pablo II
Tegucigalpa, D.C.
Tel: 31-4200
Fax: 31-0097

Ministry of Natural Resources
Col. Loma Linda Norte
Blvd. Centro America
Tegucigalpa, D.C.
Tel: 32-8613
Fax: 32-5375

Presidential House
Tegucigalpa, D.C.
Tel: 34-4921-22-23
Fax: 37-8521

BUSINESS AND TRADE ORGANIZATIONS

Federation of Agricultural Producers and Exporters
POB 1442
San Pedro Sula, Cortes
Tel: 52-6794
Fax: 52-7852

Foundation for Industrial Development and Export Promotion
POB 2029
Tegucigalpa, D.C.
Tel: 32-0937, 32-9345
Fax: 31-1808

Honduran Chamber of the Construction Industry
Edif. Simon
Boulevard Suyapa
Tegucigalpa, D.C.
Tel: 32-1756
Fax: 39-0973

National Association of Exporters of Honduras
Edif. Banco Atlantida, 6to. Piso
San Pedro Sula, Cortes
Tel/Fax: 53-3626

Private Enterprise Council of Honduras
POB 3240
Teguciglapa, D.C.
Tel: 37-4371
Fax: 37-4339

Chamber of Commerce and Industry of Cortes
POB 14
San Pedro Sula, Cortes
Tel: 53-0761
Fax: 53-7777

Federation of Chambers of Commerce and Industry of Honduras
c/o Tegucigalpa Chamber of Commerce
POB 3444
Tegucigalpa, D.C.
Tel: 32-8110 Fax: 31-2049

Honduran-American Chamber of Commerce
POB 1838
Tegucigalpa, D.C.
Tel: 32-7043
Fax: 32-2031

Honduran-American Chamber of Commerce
POB 1209
San Pedro Sula, Cortes
Tel: 58-0165
Fax: 52-2401

Chamber of Commerce and Industry of Tegucigalpa
POB 3444
Tegucigalpa, D.C.
Tel: 32-8110
Fax: 31-2049

NEWSPAPERS

Cambo Empresarial
Apdo 111
Tegucigalpa
Tel: 37-2853
Fax: 37-0480

El Herealdo
Avenida los Próceres
Frente Instituto de Tórax
Tegucigalpa

El Tiempo
7a Avenida No. 6
Calle SO 55
Apartado 450
San Pedro Sula

La Tribuna
Apartado 1501
Tegucigalpa

La Prensa
3a Avenida No. 34
Apartado 143
San Pedro Sula

BUSINESS PERIODICALS

Cambio Empresarial
Apartado 1111
Tegucigalpa
Tel: 37-2853
Fax: 37-0480

El Comercio
Cámara de Comercio e Industrias de Tegucigalpa
Bulevar Centroamérca
Apartado 3444
Tegucigalpa
Tel: 32-8210
Fax: 31-2049

RADIO & TELEVISION STATIONS

Compañía Televisora Hondureña, SA
Blvd Suyapa
Apartado 734
Tegucigalpa
Tel: 32-7835
Fax: 32-0097

La Voz de Honduras
Apartado 642
Tegucigalpa

Radio América
Apartado 259
Tegucigalpa
Tel: 32-7028
Fax: 31-2923

Radio Nacional de Honduras
Apartado 403
Tegucigalpa
Tel: 38-5478
Telex: 1147

Telesistema Hondureño, SA
Apartado 642
Tegucigalpa
Tel: 32-0710
Telex: 1126

LEGAL CONTACTS

Bufete Batres y Asociados
Avenida Juan Lindo
Sendero Guyana N.E. No 2429
Colonia Palmire
Tegucigalpa, M.D.C.
Tel: (504) 36-9200
Fax: (504) 36-6872

Bufete Ortez Colindres y Asociados
Edificio El Centro
POB 850
Tegucigalpa
Tel: (504) 37-5687
Fax: (504) 37-2572

AD AGENCY

FCB
POB 574
San Pedro Sula
Tel: 57-5851
Fax: 52-9706

McCann-Erickson Centroamericana S. De R.L.
POB 1161
San Pedro Sula
Tel: 53-1633
Fax: 52-2748

Zeus/BBDO
4A Avenida 1222
Col. Alameda
Tegucigalpa, D.C.
Tel: 32-7742
Fax: 32-9379

TRANSPORTATION

Empresa Nacional Portuaria
(National Port Authority)
Apdo 18
Pier Cortes
Tel: 55-0987
Fax: 55-1402

Ferrocarril Nacional de Honduras
(National Railway of Honduras)
1a Avda entre la y 2a Calle
Apdo 496
San Pedro Sula
Tel: 53-1879
Fax: 52-8001

INTERNET ADDRESSES

Listserv: CENTAM-L
Send mail to: LISTSERV@UBVM.cc.buffalo.edu
Subscribe in the body of the message.

Latin America - Honduras
http://lanic.utexas.edu/la/ca/honduras/

YAHOO - Honduras
http://www.yahoo.com/Regional/Countries/Honduras/

CityNet - Honduras
http://www.city.net/countries/honduras/

Hong Kong

Economy

Overview

Despite its tiny area, Hong Kong is the world's eighth-largest economy and the critical staging area for international transactions with China. The territory has highly developed business, communications, and transportation infrastructures, and one of the best ports in East Asia. Port facilities are currently beyond capacity, however, and improvements will not be ready for several years. Hong Kong has lost much of its traditional manufacturing business to lower-cost Chinese plants, but remains paramount in management and trading with China. Nevertheless, despite Chinese protestations that it will allow Hong Kong to continue to operate freely following its takeover of the territory from Britain in 1997, worries persist that the control-oriented Chinese will place insurmountable limits on Hong Kong's laissez faire business dealings.

Trade

Trade is Hong Kong's reason for existing, and total trade revenues are roughly 2.5 times greater than GDP. Major exports include textiles and apparel; toys, games, and sporting goods; watches and clocks; footwear; and telecommunications equipment. Imports include textiles, electrical machinery, apparel, telecommunications equipment, and foodstuffs. Hong Kong's trade is heavily distorted by its role as a re-export center for China, with many products merely passing through rather than originating or being processed there. China is Hong Kong's largest trading partner, followed by Japan, the US, Taiwan, and Singapore.

Sectors

Agriculture Although it continues to employ almost three percent of the work force, agriculture and related activities contribute less than one percent of GDP. Seafood and vegetables are the main crops.

Industry Industry contributes about 25 percent of GDP but employs nearly 30 percent of the work force. Both levels are falling because Hong Kong is redefining itself as a re-exporter rather than a manufacturer. Traditional areas of specialization include textiles and apparel, watches and clocks, appliances, jewelry, and plastics and metal fabrication.

Services The services sector represents 75 percent of GDP and almost 60 percent of the work force. An increased emphasis on tourism has further strengthened the services sector, although the greatest contributors are business and financial services.

Trends

Continued infrastructure development will continue to fuel the red-hot Hong Kong economy for the next several years. Growth levels have caused labor shortages in key industries, although some increases in unemployment have been noted in certain areas. General low unemployment has fostered job-hopping, as employees sell their services to the highest bidder with little risk of prolonged unemployment if the latest opportunity fails. Large numbers of skilled workers are leaving the territory as the 1997 lease expiration date draws near, but immigrants seeking to capitalize on Hong Kong's towering economy have so far flowed in rapidly enough to replace them. Nevertheless, there is considerable uneasiness concerning the practical effects of the power transfer. Although business remains strong, many firms are hedging their bets, especially as China makes increasingly autocratic noises regarding the status of social and political autonomy in its proposed post-transfer state.

At a Glance

THE COUNTRY

Location Eastern Asia, on the southeast coast of China bordering the South.
Terrain Hilly to mountainous with steep slopes; lowlands in north.
Climate Tropical monsoon; cool and humid in winter, hot and rainy from spring through summer, warm and sunny in fall.

THE PEOPLE

Population 5,550,000
Ethnic composition
Chinese... 95%
Other... 5%
Religious composition
Eclectic mixture of local religions........................ 90%
Christian... 10%
Languages spoken Chinese (Cantonese), English.
Education and literacy All children are required by law to be in full-time education between the ages of 6 and 15. Pre-school education for most children begins at age three. Primary school begins normally at the age of six and lasts for six years. Most stay in school and continue into senior secondary courses; others join full-time vocational training.
Labor force
Total:...2,800,000
By occupation: manufacturing 28.5%, wholesale and retail trade, restaurants, and hotels 27.9%, services 17.7%, financing, insurance, and real estate 9.2%, transport and communications 4.5%, construction 2.5%.

COUNTRY FACTS

Political and legal A direct territory of the United Kingdom, Hong Kong will return to Chinese rule on July 1, 1997. China has promised to respect Hong Kong's existing social and economic systems and life-style. The constitution is unwritten; the legal system is based on English common law, combined with statutes. The Supreme Court is the highest legal body and is independent of the other branches of government. Citizens must be at least 21 years of age to vote.
Telephone Modern facilities provide excellent domestic and international services. There are over three million telephones. Hong Kong has international electronic mail capabilities. International country code: [852]. There are no city codes; all telephone numbers are now eight digits.
Transportation Most highways and roads are in relatively good condition.
Environment Rapid urbanization has caused air and water pollution. Overpopulation in some areas continues to be a problem.
Media Hong Kong maintains excellent broadcast media capabilities. There are a number of newspapers and magazines published in both Chinese and English. There are six AM and six FM broadcasting stations with four TV stations.
Health Medical care is readily available and most care facilities are good. The birth rate is 12.16 births per 1,000 live births, and the death rate is 5.85 deaths per 1,000. Life expectancy of males is 77 years; of females, 84 years.

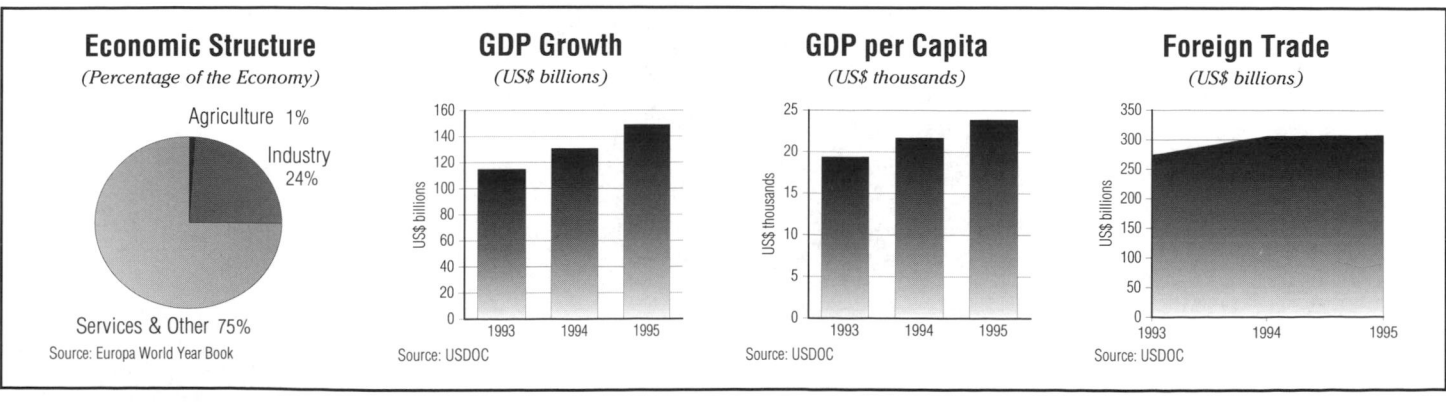

Economic Structure
(Percentage of the Economy)

Agriculture 1%
Industry 24%
Services & Other 75%
Source: Europa World Year Book

GDP Growth
(US$ billions)
Source: USDOC

GDP per Capita
(US$ thousands)
Source: USDOC

Foreign Trade
(US$ billions)
Source: USDOC

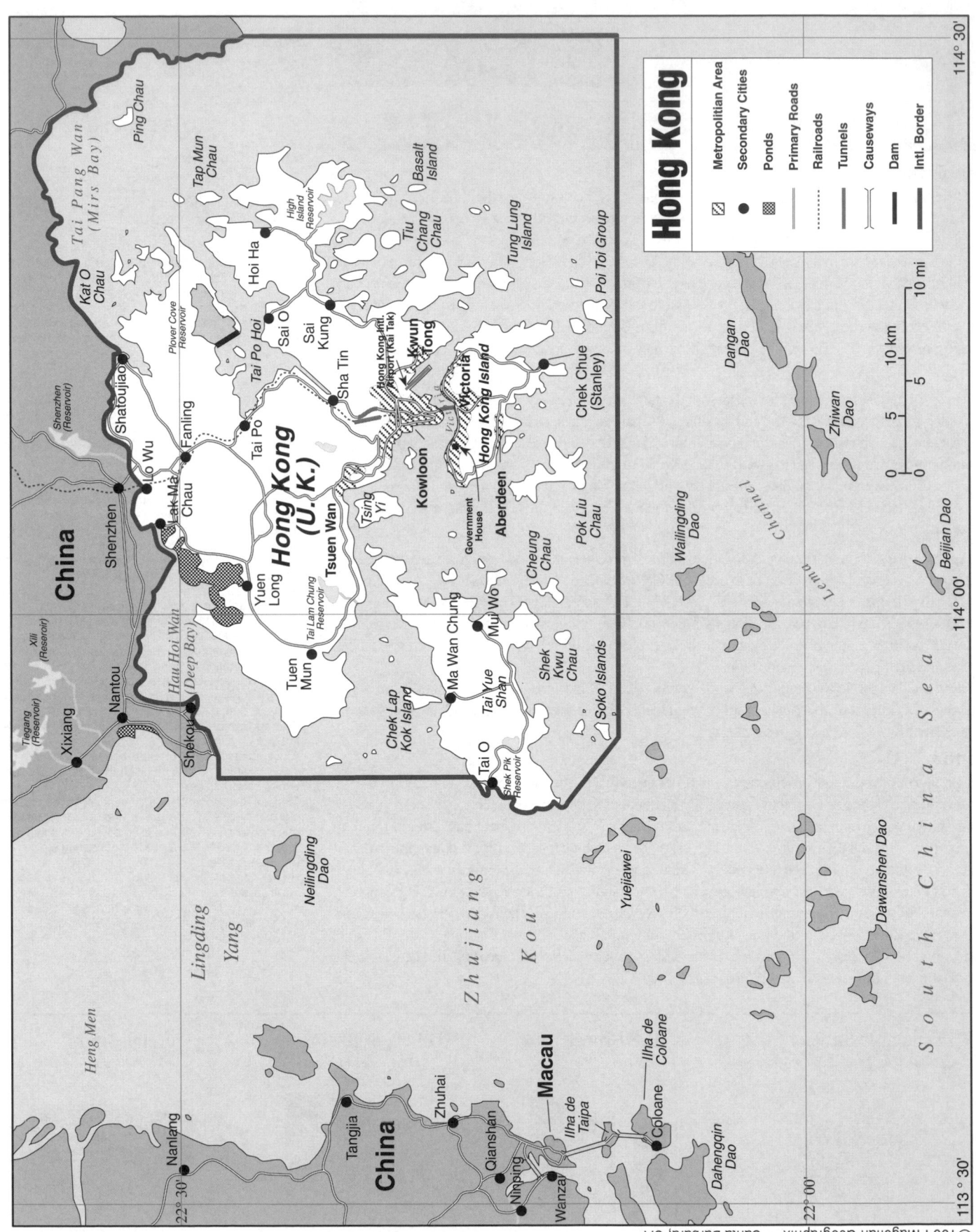

Hong Kong

	Metropolitian Area
•	Secondary Cities
	Ponds
	Primary Roads
	Railroads
	Tunnels
	Causeways
	Dam
	Intl. Border

China

Shenzhen

Tai Pang Wan (Mirs Bay)

Ping Chau

Tap Mun Chau

Basalt Island

High Island Reservoir

Hoi Ha

Tiu Chang Chau

Tung Lung Island

Poi Toi Group

Kat O Chau

Plover Cove Reservoir

Shatoujiao

Sai O

Sai Kung

Tai Po Hoi

Hong Kong Intl. Airport (Kai Tak)

Kwun Tong

Lo Wu

Fanling

Sha Tin

Victoria

Chek Chue (Stanley)

Tai Po

Hong Kong (U.K.)

Kowloon

Hong Kong Island

Lak Ma Chau

Shenzhen (Reservoir)

Tsing Yi

Tsuen Wan

Government House

Aberdeen

Yuen Long

Tai Lam Chung Reservoir

Cheung Chau

Pok Liu Chau

Nantou

Xili (Reservoir)

Tiegang (Reservoir)

Xixiang

Hau Hoi Wan (Deep Bay)

Shekou

Tuen Mun

Chek Lap Kok Island

Ma Wan Chung

Mui Wo

Tai Yue Shan

Shek Kwu Chau

Soko Islands

Tai O

Shek Pik Reservoir

Wailingding Dao

Dangan Dao

Zhiwan Dao

Lema Channel

Beijian Dao

Nanlang

Lingding Yang

Heng Men

Neilingding Dao

Zhujiang Kou

Yuejiawei

Dawanshen Dao

South China Sea

Tangjia

Zhuhai

Qianshan

Macau

Ilha de Taipa

Ilha de Coloane

Coloane

Dahengqin Dao

Nanping

Wanzai

China

10 mi

10 km

5

5

22° 30'

114° 00'

114° 30'

113° 30'

22° 00'

Foreign Trade

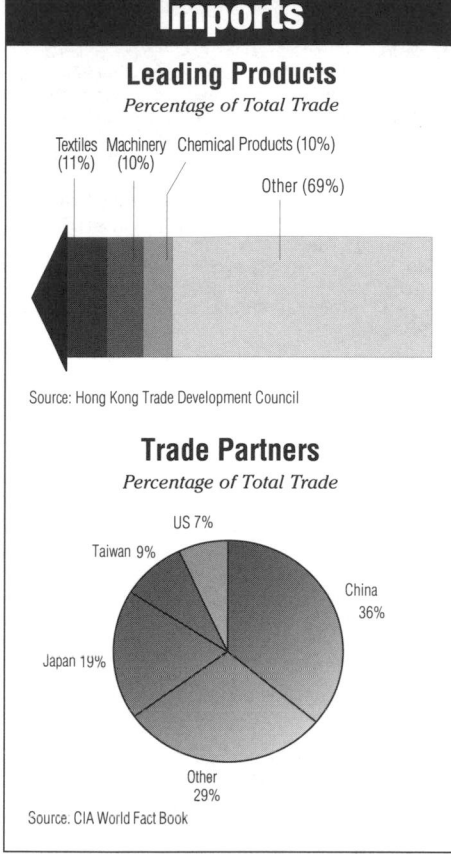

Imports

Leading Products
Percentage of Total Trade

Textiles (11%) Machinery (10%) Chemical Products (10%)
Other (69%)

Source: Hong Kong Trade Development Council

Trade Partners
Percentage of Total Trade

US 7%
Taiwan 9%
Japan 19%
China 36%
Other 29%

Source: CIA World Fact Book

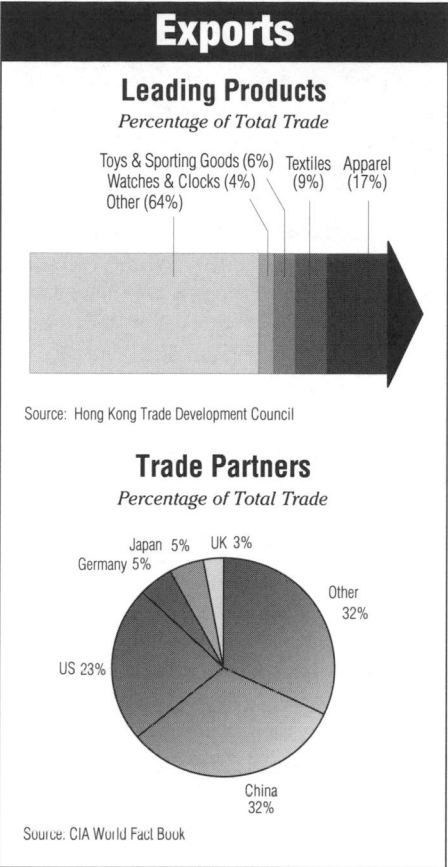

Exports

Leading Products
Percentage of Total Trade

Toys & Sporting Goods (6%)
Watches & Clocks (4%)
Other (64%)
Textiles (9%)
Apparel (17%)

Source: Hong Kong Trade Development Council

Trade Partners
Percentage of Total Trade

Japan 5%   UK 3%
Germany 5%
US 23%
Other 32%
China 32%

Source: CIA World Fact Book

Opportunities

FOR IMPORTING TO HONG KONG

- air conditioning equipment
- airborne avionics equipment
- cargo handling equipment
- clothing
- computers and peripherals
- consumer electronics
- cosmetics and toiletries
- drugs and pharmaceuticals
- electrical machinery and appliances
- electronic parts and components
- food and beverages
- hotel and restaurant equipment
- industrial process controls
- medical diagnostic equipment
- paper and paperboard
- plastic material and resins
- textile yarns and fabrics
- telecommunication products

FOR EXPORTING FROM HONG KONG

- apparel and textiles
- cameras and photography equipment
- computers and peripherals
- consumer electronics
- electrical machinery
- footwear
- housewares
- jewelry
- office machines and supplies
- plastic products
- printed materials
- radios
- semiconductors
- sporting goods
- telecommunication products
- travel goods and handbags
- watches and clocks

GROWTH SECTORS

- banking and financial services
- consumer retail
- franchising
- home health care
- insurance
- real estate
- telecommunications
- travel and tourism

GOVERNMENT PROCUREMENT

- airport facilities
- building construction
- electrical power systems
- road and railway building and expansion
- seaport facilities
- telecommunication products
- water supply equipment

Trade News

RULES AND REGULATIONS

- **Regulations** Import documentation is filed through the Customs and Excise Department of the Trade Department.

- **Trade climate** Hong Kong must import virtually everything it consumes, including half of its water, all of its energy, and essentially all of its raw materials and goods. To pay for this, it must export vast quantities of value-added items and process large volumes of third-party trade for which it gets paid as an intermediary.

- **Import restrictions** Hong Kong is a free port with few import restrictions. Restrictions exist primarily for health, safety, and security reasons, and to fulfill international trade obligations. It has no foreign exchange controls and allows a wide range of financial transactions with minimal oversight and a high level of confidentiality. Licensing formalities are kept to a minimum.

- **Tariffs, duties, and excise taxes** Hong Kong has no general tariff. Excise duties (also called taxes) are levied on certain commodities such as motor vehicles, tobacco, and alcohol.

- **Export licenses and inspection** Export licenses are required for most commodities. Hong Kong does not require pre-export inspection, except for consignments for which certificates of origin are being requested. Foreign buyers needing inspection certificates should stipulate requirements in the purchase contract and letter of credit.

TRANSPORTATION CONTACTS

Air Sea Worldwide Logistics Ltd.
1102 Kan Chung Building
52 Jaffe Road
Hong Kong
Tel: 28656868 Fax: 25296928 Telex: 67851

American President Lines Ltd.
16/F., World Shipping Centre
7 Canton Road
Kowloon, Hong Kong
Tel: 27353630 Fax: 27225870 Telex: 54953

Barwil Agencies Ltd.
10/F., Stanhope House
738 King's Road
Hong Kong
Tel: 28801688 Fax: 28805048

Crown Pacific Ltd.
Crown Pacific Building
9 Yuen On Street
Siu Lek Yuen, Hong Kong
Tel: 26368388 Fax: 26371677 Telex: 33894

Danzas Freight (HK) Ltd.
P-05 Hunghom Commercial Centre
Tower A 37 Ma Tau Wai Road
Kowloon, Hong Kong
Tel: 23330211 Fax: 27656379

Hong Kong Association of Freight Forwarding Agents Ltd.
M/F., AHAFA Cargo Centre
12 Kai Shun Road
Kowloon, Hong Kong
Tel: 27963121 Fax: 27963719

Hong Kong International Courier Association
c/o DHL International Ltd.
13 Mok Cheong Street, Tokwawan
Kowloon, Hong Kong
Tel: 27747298 Fax: 23339668

Hong Kong Liner Shipping Association
2111 Wing On Centre
111 Connaught Road
Central, Hong Kong
Tel: 25445077 Fax: 28151350

Hong Kong Shippers' Council
Rm. 2707A, Convention Plaza
1 Harbour Road
Wanchai, Hong Kong
Tel: 28241228 Fax: 28240394

Marketing

Overview

A local presence, whether through a branch office or an agent or distributor, is important to getting established in Hong Kong's fast-paced market, and all business relationships in this venue depend on maintaining a full-time presence. For more than 150 years Hong Kong's primary function has been to act as an entrepôt between China and the West. That purpose not only remains unchanged but expands when Chinese sovereignty returns to the British colony in 1997. With an economy heavily dependent on international commerce, Hong Kong has consistently provided an open, multilateral trading system as it has increasingly become a transit and shipping point for goods manufactured or consumed in rapidly growing southern China. Geographic proximity, cultural and linguistic ties with the rest of Asia, an excellent infrastructure, and a well developed services sector have strengthened Hong Kong's importance to China. Chinese companies view Hong Kong's highly developed financial, transportation, and marketing capabilities as their best route to Western markets. Its open economy and sophisticated bilingual consumer population present outstanding opportunities for foreign businesses to sell everything from food products to airport equipment. Firms new to Hong Kong must be prepared to deal with a combination of near-monopolistic local dominance in some sectors and a strong preference for dealing with "old friends" in nearly all sectors. This can be overcome by persistence and value-pricing practices. Hong Kong may be one of the last places where entrepreneurship not only survives but thrives, and the many sophisticated high-fliers in the region ensure a tough competitive environment with lots of opportunities.

Distribution

Concentrated efforts on establishing a strong distributor or agent relationship, combined with a carefully managed market penetration program, offer the best possibilities for results. The Hong Kong market itself is small and compact, but it serves as a springboard to the Chinese market. Agents and distributors for China can be found in Hong Kong, and most foreigners will initially find it easier to operate through Hong Kong intermediaries familiar with Western business standards. Hong Kong companies are always interested in potential exporters, whatever their product and destination.

Agents, Distributors, and Partners

Hong Kong has no special legislation regarding agents and distributors; virtually any such contractual arrangement is acceptable and enforceable. Obviously, the more complex a contract, the more helpful legal counsel can be in drafting the terms. Most contracts include provisions for exclusivity and sales territories, handling and protection of proprietary information, expected and minimum levels of sales activity, duration, payment terms, and quality control. Agents and distributors range from those who stock retail stores with standard items, to those providing sales, engineering, and technical support for complex systems. A single company often handles all aspects of a sale from inventory to marketing and after-sale service. Hundreds of companies specializing in high-tech consumer goods prefer to open their own showrooms, qualifying local personnel through a rigorous training program.

Selling Techniques

Virtually all selling techniques work in some form in Hong Kong. Aggressive campaigns that focus on price breaks are especially effective. Initial sales require considerable face-to-face contact, which Asians tend to view as essential to developing reliable connections. Suppliers should provide technical catalogs in English; other information, such as company brochures, should be provided in Chinese. English-Chinese business cards are essential; cards are exchanged much more formally and frequently than in the West. There are numerous trade fairs, exhibitions, and seminars, all of which welcome foreign sellers, as well as frequent in-store promotions and joint promotions with wholesale outlets.

Advertising

Broadcast media include two Cantonese and two English television stations—watched by 90 percent of the population—and several radio stations in both languages. Print media is abundant, with 600 publications, including 51 Chinese newspapers and three English dailies. Most advertising agencies in Hong Kong are sophisticated and up-to-date, have international connections, and provide a full range of services, often on an international basis.

Service and Customer Support

Prompt after-sales service is crucial to success, and virtually all successful companies make a special effort to provide such service. Foreign companies should maintain a well-trained staff and adequate spare parts in Hong Kong to ensure the prompt and reliable service that local consumers expect. Hong Kong can also serve as a regional center for after sales service, although depending on the product involved, some firms may be able to subcontract out to lower-cost local service providers.

Marketing in Hong Kong

MARKETING TIPS

- **Discounts** During the third or fourth weeks of August and February, most large retailers drastically reduce prices, often by as much as 50 percent.
- **Language** English and Chinese, the two official languages of Hong Kong, are widely spoken—the former in commercial and financial circles, and the latter by the local Chinese community. Cantonese is the most commonly spoken Chinese dialect, but more and more people are learning to speak Putonghua or Mandarin.
- **Population** The total population of Hong Kong is estimated to be 5.8 million, about 97 percent of which is Chinese. The foreign community, estimated at about three percent of the total population, has been growing, especially in recent years, owing to an increase in the number of foreign companies operating in Hong Kong.

AD AGENCIES

Asatsu International (HK), Ltd.
9/F., 11 Leighton Road
Causeway Bay, Hong Kong
Tel: 28952805 Fax: 25764762

Association of Accredited Advertising Agents of Hong Kong
504-505 Dominion Centre
43-59 Queen's Road East
Wanchai, Hong Kong
Tel: 25299656 Fax: 28610375

Backer Spielvogel Bates
10/F., Malaysia Building
50 Gloucester Road
Hong Kong
Tel: 28230111 Fax: 28613935 Telex: 65321 BATES

Ball Partnership
12/F., Vicwood Plaza
199 Des Voeux Road
Central, Hong Kong
Tel: 25443800 Fax: 28455411 Telex: 62517 BALL

BBDO
30/F, Bank of China Tower
1 Garden Road
Central, Hong Kong
Tel: 28201888 Fax: 28772164

Bozell
1101 Citicorp Centre
18 Whitfield Road
Causeway Bay, Hong Kong
Tel: 28075678 Fax: 28073503, 28063846
Telex: 74383

BSB Graffix Limited
1201 Lam Chung Building
52-54 Jaffee Road
Wanchai, Hong Kong
Tel: 25272766 Fax: 28611216

BSB Hong Kong
2/F., Asian House
1 Hennessy Road
Hong Kong
Tel: 28230111 Fax: 28613935 Telex: 65321 BATES

Chuo Senko Advertising (HK) Ltd.
Rm. 503, Silvercord, Tower 1
30 Canton Road
Kowloon, Hong Kong
Tel: 27211194 Fax: 27210574 Telex: 45615 CSAD

Daiko Communications Asia Co., Ltd.
Rm. 513-516, Sun Hung Kai Centre
30 Harbour Road
Hong Kong
Tel: 28919688 Fax: 28384896

Saatchi & Saatchi
22/F, Shui On Centre
6-8 Harbour Road
Wanchai, Hong Kong
Tel: 28643333 Fax: 28651213

Triangle Pacific
2/F, Mount Parker House
1111 King's Road
Hong Kong
Tel: 28865128 Fax: 28865470

Business Culture

Greetings and Courtesies

A handshake is the accepted greeting. Chinese usually shake hands very lightly instead of taking the hand firmly, and forcefully pumping it, and in Hong Kong a handshake may last as long as 10 seconds. Upon meeting someone, Chinese lower their eyes slightly as a sign of respect. Staring into the eyes of a Chinese might make them uncomfortable. The Chinese deem it crucial to show sincerity and respect, as failure to do so will make a Chinese very uncomfortable. The concept of face is also important in Hong Kong, and foreigners should be aware of this factor in all aspects of their Hong Kong business dealings. Saying or doing anything that causes someone to lose face can instantly destroy a relationship, perhaps forever.

Business Ethic and Framework

Although Hong Kong has experienced a great deal of Western influence, local behavior is still largely determined by Confucianism, which teaches respect for superiors, duty to family, loyalty to friends, humility, sincerity, and courtesy. In business, the boss is in charge of those who work for him, and employees work hard to help the company flourish. Among coworkers, people of higher status and age are respected by those beneath them and deferred to in speech and action. Business friends trust and respect each other and help each other succeed. Hong Kong Chinese work hard and are efficient and highly productive. Management styles are a combination of Confucianism and Western behavior, depending on an individual's background. Business is conducted formally, with great value placed on punctuality, efficiency, and thriftiness.

Decision Making

Hong Kong Chinese try to avoid a direct negative response, for fear of causing embarrassment or losing face. Instead of directly saying no, they are likely to say something is inconvenient or is under consideration. They might also say, "Yes, but it will be difficult," which is often their way of saying no. If there is bad news, they might convey it through an intermediary or hint at it rather than saying it directly. After a deal has been negotiated, some executives prefer to sign a short general agreement and allow others to work out the details. Avoid this if possible, as it can lead to misunderstandings and result in strained relationships.

Women

Women are treated better than in many other business arenas, but are still not regarded as equal to men. Most executives are men, with women being relegated to the role of secretary. Chinese women with high social standing can achieve higher positions. Most travel agents, public relations executives, and sales staff are women. Women traveling to Hong Kong will find little if any open discrimination; however, they should behave professionally and dress formally. A self-confident, poised woman might accomplish more, and do it faster, than a male colleague because Chinese may feel that if she has been chosen to represent her company, she must be someone with great ability.

Meetings

Before a meeting, it is customary to provide as much detail as possible about the issues under discussion. Also include a list of your representatives who will attend the meeting, with the team leader's name first. Others should be listed in order of seniority or importance at the meeting. Your team will be led into a room in which the Hong Kong team is already present. Your team leader should enter first. Teams sit across a table, leaders opposite each other and others seated in descending order of importance. Small talk will come first. Business is addressed after people feel comfortable with each other. The head of the host group will deliver a short welcome speech, then turn the floor over to the visitors. Your senior team member should speak for your company; always avoid conflicting statements from other team members. When speaking, your spokesman should address the Hong Kong senior representative. Hong Kong Chinese prefer to hear a proposal as a broad overview; they will then respond to specific issues or questions point by point.

Business Attire

Business attire is Western in style and relatively formal. Summers are extremely hot and humid; lightweight clothing is more comfortable, but it should remain formal. Winters can be chilly, but extremely heavy clothing is not needed. In monsoon season, raincoats and umbrellas should be kept handy.

Cultural Cautions

DO'S

- Be aware of all favors done for you and gifts you are given. Find a way to reciprocate in kind.
- In Hong Kong, business relationships are personal relationships. To establish a good business relationship, first establish a personal relationship that demonstrates your respect and trustworthiness.

DON'TS

- Never do or say anything that could cause someone to lose face.

CUSTOMS

- Hong Kong Chinese are extremely courteous to friends. This often includes arranging every detail of a friend's visit and refusing to let a guest spend any money at all.
- When dealing with strangers, people in Hong Kong are often indifferent and rude. In this crowded city, pushing and shoving are common, and no apologies are given or expected.
- Business cards are important. At first meetings, handshakes are followed by a formal exchange of cards. Always carry plenty of cards, ideally with Chinese text on one side. If possible, get expert advice on the specific Chinese characters, as some ideograms are considered more favorable than others.
- Gifts are important to express friendship, symbolize hopes for success, and show appreciation. In a business situation, business-related gifts (pens, paperweights) are appropriate.

OBSERVATIONS

- Though often viewed as a Western city, Hong Kong remains definitely Chinese in culture and tradition. Understanding Chinese culture has always been crucial to doing business here; now more than ever as Hong Kong returns to mainland Chinese control in 1997.
- Business dealings can be made easier by having a Chinese advisor or consultant.
- Chinese prefer to deal with the same person, and thus the same person should always represent your company. If this is not possible, the initial contact should personally introduce his replacement to all Hong Kong associates.
- In contrast to Japan and Korea, Hong Kong companies tend to be small and entrepreneurial, and competition is fierce.

NEGOTIATIONS

- Hong Kong Chinese have a reputation for being tough negotiators, and every aspect of a venture is open to negotiation. Their tactics are both subtle and aggressive. Often, they will wine and dine potential business associates as a way of gaining an advantage.
- Negotiating tactics include getting angry as a means of intimidation, flattery to get you off-guard, and prolonging negotiations to wear you down.
- A common tactic is delaying major negotiations until you are about to leave the country, then making unreasonable demands.
- Extensive entertaining, particularly at night, is sometimes used to make visitors less alert at the negotiating table.
- Hong Kong Chinese sometimes negotiate with several competing companies at the same time and let it be known they are doing so as a way of applying pressure.
- Be prepared to walk away. You will gain more from making it clear that you would rather have no deal at all than a bad deal.
- Under Hong Kong law, contracts are legally binding. But Hong Kong Chinese tend to take a long-term view, regarding an agreement as a single element of a bigger, ongoing relationship that is, ultimately, more important than any one venture.

Legal System

Hong Kong is a common law country. Its courts rely on judicial precedent as set by court decision in earlier cases.

Intellectual Property Rights

Patents To acquire protection under the Registration of Patents Ordinance, the grantee must apply for its registration in Hong Kong within five years of the grant. Applications must be accompanied by several required documents, including a certified copy of the English translation. Upon payment of prescribed fees and after application is advertised in the Hong Kong Government Gazette, a Certificate of Registration will be granted. Registration in Hong Kong conveys the same protection as for UK or European patentees and remains in force for as long as the patent is maintained. Assignment or license of patent or patent application should be recorded in order to be effective against third parties. The remedies for infringement include injunction, damages, seizure of goods, and discovery.

Trademarks A trademark can only be registered if it is adapted to distinguish or is capable of distinguishing goods or services of the owner from those of another person. The register is divided into two parts. To be registrable in Part A, the mark must contain or consist of at least one of several specified particular and distinguishable traits. In cases in which the mark does not appear, on the face of it, to be inherently distinctive, it can nevertheless be registered in Part B. Registration is initially valid for seven years and can thereafter be renewed indefinitely for successive periods of 14 years each. Civil remedies of damages, injunction, and seizure of goods apply. In addition, the common law action in tort of "passing off" is available upon sufficient proof.

Copyrights No registration is required to receive legal copyright protection. In most cases, copyright protection extends from the date of publication until 50 years after the death of the creator. Civil remedies for infringement include injunction, seizure of goods, recovery of damages (including, where appropriate, damages on conversion basis), taking of accounts, and discovery. Criminal penalties apply.

Business Registration

Foreign firms doing business in Hong Kong must register to operate in the colony. Companies must register a Memorandum of Association setting out the name, address, registered office, objects of business, statement of liability of members, and the amount of company's authorized share capital, with number and value of shares into which such capital is divided.

Contracts and Dispute Resolution

The Hong Kong Law of Contract essentially follows that of England and in many respects English common law and equity applies. For the most part, the parties choose which law will govern the contract; the law expressly stipulated will be the proper law of the contract provided the selection is bona fide and there is no objection on grounds of public policy—even where the law has no real connection with the contract. The parties are free to agree to submit to arbitration, binding or otherwise, and the courts will uphold these provisions. Courts will also uphold arbitration awards made pursuant to such agreements. Hong Kong businesspeople prefer to negotiate informally to resolve contract or other disagreements. If negotiations fail, firms will usually mediate before resorting to litigation.

Notaries

Notaries are governed by the Legal Practitioners Ordinance. Notaries are usually solicitors or others with significant legal training; they generally attest to the validity of an agreement or the authenticity of a signature.

Labor

There are no restrictions on the number or capacity of foreign employees that a company in Hong Kong may recruit, but foreign personnel must obtain an employment visa issued by the Immigration Department before they arrive in Hong Kong. Hong Kong's labor law provides some protections for workers. Employees are entitled to regular holidays and to one day of rest during each seven-day period. There are no legal restrictions on the number of hours that men can work per week; children between the ages of 15 and 17 years of age and women employed in industry may work a maximum of eight hours per day and six days per week, and children are prohibited from working overtime. No child under the age of 15 may be employed in industry. There are legal holidays and minimum vacation days stipulated in the law. Employers may dismiss an employee at any time and for any reason unless the employee is a pregnant woman who has requested maternity leave. Unless the employer can justify otherwise, however, workers are entitled to one month's advance notice prior to dismissal, or to one month's salary.

Legal Matters

LEGAL BRIEFS

- **Social benefits** There is no contributory social security system in Hong Kong for the provision of health care or retirement pensions. The government provides such benefits in limited amounts.

- **Employment benefits** In addition to their regular wage or salary, workers typically receive fringe benefits. These can include subsidized meals or food allowances, bonuses for high attendance, free medical treatment, and a Chinese New Year's bonus equal to at least one month's pay.

- **Attorneys** A foreign business owner may retain a foreign attorney in Hong Kong, but foreign firms are permitted to practice only foreign law; a local attorney must be employed for legal advice and transactions involving Hong Kong law.

- **Monopolies** There is no anti-monopoly law; companies are free to dominate the Hong Kong market and, in certain industries, government-authorized franchises are given. However, actual monopolies are few because competition is so fierce.

- **Lawsuits** Actions on foreign contracts or course of dealings can be brought in Hong Kong if any party to the action is in Hong Kong, if the contract was made or was to be performed in Hong Kong, or if there is sufficient connection with Hong Kong. The unsuccessful party will pay the costs of the successful party. In practice, only a portion of recoverable costs are actually recovered.

- **Bankruptcy** Hong Kong has a bankruptcy law similar to the English law. As a general rule, bankruptcy does not affect the rights of secured creditors.

- **Prohibition orders** If the court is satisfied that a person owing money or subject to monetary judgment or order will leave Hong Kong, thereby obstructing or delaying satisfaction of judgment, it may make an order prohibiting that person from leaving Hong Kong.

- **Interest** Interest on a debt may be charged only if it is specifically agreed between the parties. It is an offense to lend or offer to lend money at an effective rate of interest exceeding 60 percent per annum.

- **Limitations** Actions in contract or tort or to enforce a judicial award must be brought within six years from the date on which cause of action accrued.

LEGAL CONTACTS

Baker & McKenzie
14th Floor, Hutchison House
Hong Kong
Tel: 28461888 Fax: 28450490

Clifford Chance
30th Floor, Jardine House
One Connaught Place
Hong Kong
Tel: 28100229 Fax: 28104708, 28104858

Clyde & Co.
Admiralty Centre Tower II, 19/F
Harcourt Road
Hong Kong
Tel: 25290017 Fax: 28654259

Fairbairn, Cately, Low & Kong
11-12/F, Wheelock House
20 Pedder Street
Hong Kong
Tel: 25222041 Fax: 28452928

Vincent T.K. Cheung, Yap & Company
17/F, Worldwide House
19 Des Voeux Road
Hong Kong
Tel: 25235011 Fax: 28612944

Johnson, Stokes & Master
17/F, Prince's Building
10 Charter Road
Hong Kong
Tel: 28432211 Fax: 28451735

Stephenson Harwood & Lo
18th Floor, Edinburgh Tower
The Landmark
15 Queen's Road
Central Hong Kong
Tel: 28680789 Fax: 28681504

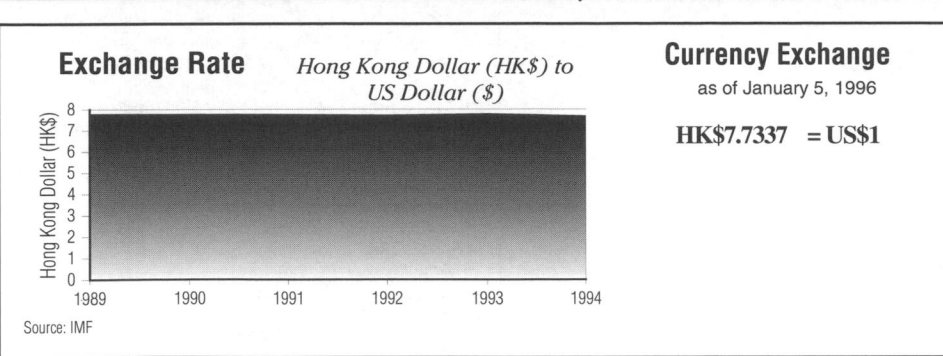

Exchange Rate — *Hong Kong Dollar (HK$) to US Dollar ($)*

Hong Kong Dollar (HK$): 8, 7, 6, 5, 4, 3, 2, 1, 0

1989   1990   1991   1992   1993   1994

Source: IMF

Currency Exchange

as of January 5, 1996

HK$7.7337   = US$1

Currency

The currency in use is the Hong Kong dollar (HK$), divided into 100 cents.

Foreign Exchange

There are no foreign exchange controls in Hong Kong, and the Hong Kong dollar is freely convertible. The Hong Kong dollar is linked to the US dollar, which is the intervention currency. Under this agreement, the two note-issuing banks deliver to the Exchange Fund an amount equal to the local currency issued at the linked exchange rate, as backing for the Hong Kong dollar note issues. Other licensed banks wishing to exchange local currency may buy or sell them against an equivalent amount of US dollars at the linked exchange rate with one of the note-issuing banks. For other transactions, the exchange rate of the Hong Kong dollar is freely negotiated. The free market rate is generally in line with the linked rate, however. There are no taxes on the purchase or sale of foreign exchange. The forward exchange market is run by the private sector; the government has no role in this area. Residents and nonresidents may bring in or take out any amount of domestic or foreign currency, traveler's checks, and other means of payment.

Capital Transfers

Hong Kong's financial system is very open, with no controls over currency movements. The banking system is very efficient and highly developed. As a world financial center, there are 172 licensed banks offering the full range of banking facilities and services. In addition, there are many other restricted license banks and deposit-taking companies, as well as local offices of foreign banks. There is no distinction between resident and nonresident bank accounts.

Investment Incentives

There are no special or direct incentives for foreign investors. All matters are left to the market. There is no capital gains tax nor are there withholding taxes on dividends.

Investment Restrictions

There are no special or direct foreign requirements or restrictions. Residents do not need to own any shares of capital and need not participate in any capacity in a foreign enterprise. All matters are left to the market.

TAXATION

Taxation requires sophisticated knowledge of complex rules and regulations specific to each country. For more detailed information, we suggest you refer to the Ernst & Young Corporate Tax Guide and Directory, available from the Ernst & Young accounting office in your country, or from:

Ernst & Young
17/F Hutchison House
10 Harcourt Road
Central, Hong Kong
Tel: 28469888, 25265371
Fax: 28770578

- The basis of taxation in Hong Kong is territorial. Determination of locality of the source of profits can be very complicated and must be considered on a case-by-case basis.
- Earnings from foreign investments are not taxed, and interest earned on individuals' bank deposits are not taxed.

At a Glance

Corporate Income Tax Rate (%)	16.5
Capital Gains Tax Rate (%)	0
Branch Tax Rate (%)	16.5
Withholding Tax (%)	
Dividends	0
Interest	0
Royalties from Patents, Know-how, etc.	
Paid to Corporations	1.65/16.5*
Paid to Individuals	1.5/15*
Branch Remittance Tax	0
Net Operating Losses (Years)	
Carryback	0
Carryforward	Unlimited

*Final tax applicable to persons not carrying on business in Hong Kong. The rates of 16.5% and 15% apply to royalties paid to associates in certain circumstances.

Money Matters

BITS AND PIECES

- **Double taxation** The only foreign tax relief agreement in effect concerning taxation of shipping income is with the United States. No such agreements exist with any other country. Although there is some relief due to some British Commonwealth countries, this is usually not granted in practice. Otherwise, no credit is given for foreign taxation, although under some circumstances, deductions may be granted for foreign taxes paid.
- **Capital transfers** There are no controls over capital receipts or payments by either residents or nonresidents.
- **Gold** The gold market is unrestricted, and gold futures are open to residents and nonresidents.
- **Credit** Commercial trade financing is readily available. Licensed banks can provide loans to residents and nonresidents in any currency. Letters of credit and other instruments are widely used, and asking for a letter of credit will not be seen as a sign of mistrust.
- **Chinese rule** When Hong Kong reverts to Chinese rule in 1997, it will retain its status as an international financial center, and the Hong Kong dollar will continue to be freely convertible.
- **Stock exchange** The Stock Exchange of Hong Kong is the sixth largest in the world. Between 1990 and 1993, the number of firms listed grew from 299 to 477. The SEHK has a regulatory framework consistent with international standards.

BANKS

Bank of East Asia Ltd.
10 Des Voeux Road
Central, Hong Kong
Tel: 28423200 Fax: 28459333

Hong Kong and Shanghai Banking Corp.
1 Queen's Road
Central, Hong Kong
Tel: 28221111 Fax: 28101112

Bank of America
12 Harcourt Road
Central, Hong Kong
Tel: 28475333

Bank of Tokyo
Far East Finance Center, 1/F
16 Harcourt Road
Central, Hong Kong
Tel: 28627888 Fax: 28652006

Korea Exchange Bank
Far East Finance Center, 32/F
16 Harcourt Road
Hong Kong
Tel: 25201221 Fax: 28612379

National Westminster Bank PLC
One Exchange Square, 23/F
8 Connaught Place
Central, Hong Kong
Tel: 25247071 Fax: 28459025

Royal Bank of Canada
Gloucester Tower, 18/F
11 Pedder Street
Central, Hong Kong
Tel: 28430888 Fax: 28585802

STOCK EXCHANGES

Hong Kong Securities and Futures Commission
Exchange Square, 38/F, Tower II
Hong Kong
Tel: 28409222 Fax: 28459553

Chinese Gold & Silver Exchange Society
Gold & Silver Exchange Building
1/F, 12-18 Mercer Street
Hong Kong
Tel: 25441945 Fax: 28540869

Hong Kong Stock Exchange
Exchange Square, Towers I & II
Hong Kong
Tel: 25221122 Fax: 28104475

Business Travel

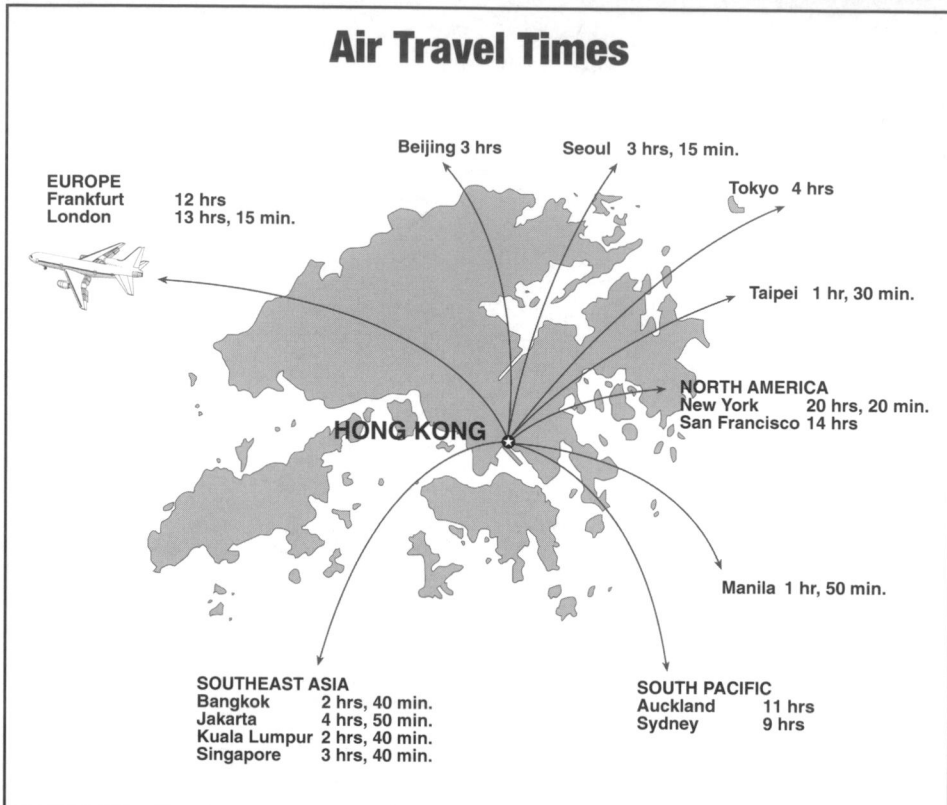

Air Travel Times

Beijing 3 hrs

Seoul 3 hrs, 15 min.

EUROPE
Frankfurt   12 hrs
London   13 hrs, 15 min.

Tokyo 4 hrs

Taipei 1 hr, 30 min.

NORTH AMERICA
New York   20 hrs, 20 min.
San Francisco 14 hrs

HONG KONG

Manila 1 hr, 50 min.

SOUTHEAST ASIA
Bangkok   2 hrs, 40 min.
Jakarta   4 hrs, 50 min.
Kuala Lumpur   2 hrs, 40 min.
Singapore   3 hrs, 40 min.

SOUTH PACIFIC
Auckland   11 hrs
Sydney   9 hrs

COMMUNICATIONS

Telephones All telecommunications are highly advanced and reliable. Local phone calls are free, though there is a charge if using a public phone. Not many public phones are found on the street and most are in lobbies, post offices, airports, ferry terminals and Telecom offices. Hotel rooms commonly have international direct dial service.

Fax This type of communication transmission dominates business in Hong Kong. With free local calls, fax machines are now available in most businesses and hotels.

Post office Mail service is fast and efficient, with delivery twice a day, six days a week. Overnight delivery to the main business areas is standard. Postfax is now offered through the post office with the assistance of the Cable and Wireless company. All major international couriers operate in Hong Kong.

BEST TRAVEL BOOKS

Lonely Planet Hong Kong, Macau and Canton Travel Survival Kit. 'Proves that there is far more to Hong Kong than just duty-free shopping.'
Fodor's Foreign Guide, Hong Kong.
Culture Shock, A Guide to Customs and Etiquette, Hong Kong.
The Travellers Guide to Hong Kong Customs and Manners. Elizabeth Devine & Nancy Braganti. An invaluable guide for people not wanting to put foot in mouth.
Wall Street Journal Guide to Business Travel, Hong Kong and Singapore.
Far Eastern Economic Review, All Asia Travel Guide Volume 2. The best guide available for the business traveller.

TELEPHONE NUMBERS

If you are calling from outside Hong Kong you will need to add the country code [852] and any other international dialing requirements from within your country.

- International Direct Dial Assistance 001
- International Calling Assistance 013
- Operator-assisted International Calls 010
- Local Directory Service 1081
- Fire/Police/Ambulance 999
- Police Visitor Hot Line 25277177
- Information Services Department............. 28428777
- General Post Office.................................. 25231071
- Federal Express 23661889
- UPS 27353535
- Princess Margaret Hospital 27427111
- International Information Service 27391818
- Asia Business Centre 25448773
- US Embassy/Hong Kong 25239011
- Customs & Excise Department 28521411

Airline Information
- Cathay Pacific 27471888
- United Airlines 28104888
- Air China 28610322
- China Airlines 28439800
- Japan Airlines.. 27484600
- Dragonair 25901328

Credit Card Information
Lost or stolen credit cards (call collect to the US, regardless of which country the card was issued in).
- Amex ....[1] (919) 333-3211
- Diner's Club...............................[1] (303) 799-1504
- MasterCard ....[1] (314) 275-6690
- Visa ....[1] (410) 581-7931

Travelogue

WORKWEEK

Offices Monday-Friday 9:00 am to 1:00 pm, 2:00 pm to 5:00 pm, Saturday 9:00 am to 1:00 pm
Banks Monday-Friday 9:00 am to 4:30 pm, Saturday 9:30 am to 12:30 pm
Government Monday-Friday 9:00 am to 4:30 pm
Retail Monday-Sunday 10:00 am to 6:00 pm or 10:00 pm.

HOLIDAYS

Holidays 1996
January 1 New Year's Day
Lunar New Year's*
April 5 Good Friday
April 5 Ching Ming Festival
April 8 East Monday
June 12 Queen's Birthday
Dragon Boat Festival*
Liberation Day*
September 21 Day following Mid-Autumn Festival*
Mid October Chung Yeung Festival*
December 25 Christmas
December 26 Boxing Day
*These holidays are based on a lunar calendar and shift from year to year.

VISA AND PASSPORT

A valid passport is required for entry to Hong Kong. The visa policy is fairly liberal: British citizens are allowed a 12-month stay without a visa; US citizens are allowed a one-month stay; others are allowed a three-month stay. It is required by law to have a return ticket when entering Hong Kong, but it is seldom requested. Carry a letter of intent when traveling on business. To obtain a work visa, submit a letter of employment and a visa application to Hong Kong Immigration. The process generally takes eight weeks to complete.

DEPARTURE FORMALITIES

No requirements other than a ticket to another destination are needed for departure.

IMMUNIZATION

No vaccinations are required unless traveling recently from an area infected with cholera or yellow fever.

TIPPING

The tipping custom now has become Westernized and tips are expected in restaurants and hotels. A 10 percent surcharge is added to the restaurant bill, and you are expected to leave another 10 percent at the table. Taxi drivers and hotel attendants also expect 10 percent gratuity.

CRIME

Organized gangs exist in Hong Kong as they do in Western cities. They run drugs, gambling operations, prostitution, weapons, and loan sharking, but due to the heavy police presence, travelers are relatively safe. Pickpocketing is common. Do not carry large amounts of cash or wear expensive jewelry.

INFRASTRUCTURE

All major airlines fly to Kai Tak International Airport from all cities worldwide. For transportation to and from the airport, the airbus is most efficient; they are comfortable and stop at all the large hotels. Taxis are more convenient but the waiting lines are usually quite long. All taxis are red and should have meters. Limousine service can be arranged through the hotel. The traffic congestion is ranked among the world's worst. The city buses and minibuses are not recommended for non-Chinese speaking travelers. The Star Ferry is the most scenic way to travel between Hong Kong and Kowloon. The subway system (MTR) is fast and clean, also connecting Hong Kong and Kowloon. The Kowloon-Canton Railway is recommended for travel between Sha Tin and the New Territories.

NATIONAL TOURIST OFFICE

Convention & Travel Bureau
Jardin House
Connaught Pl
Hong Kong
Tel: 21171128

GOVERNMENT AGENCIES

Agriculture & Fisheries Department
12/F., Canton Road Government Offices
393 Canton Road
Kowloon, Hong Kong
Tel: 27332235, 27332211 Fax: 23113731

Building & Lands Department
Mezzanine F., Murray Building
Garden Road
Hong Kong
Tel: 28482198 Fax: 28684707

Civil Engineering Services Department
9/F., Empire Centre
68 Mody Road
Kowloon, Hong Kong
Tel: 27212527, 28481111 Fax: 23110725

Companies Registry
13/F., Queensway Government Offices
66 Queensway
Wanchai, Hong Kong
Tel: 28672600 Fax: 28690423

Customs & Excise Department
8/F., Harbour Building
38 Pier Road
Central, Hong Kong
Tel: 28521411, 28523324 Fax: 25423334

Department of Health
Sunning Plaza
4-13/F., 10 Hysan Avenue
Causeway Bay, Hong Kong
Tel: 28900770 Fax: 25765166

Economic Services Branch
Government Secretariat
2/F., Main and East Wings
Lower Albert Road
Hong Kong
Tel: 28102717 Fax: 28101530

Environmental Protection Department
28/F., Southorn Centre
130 Hennessy Road
Wanchai, Hong Kong
Tel: 28351349 Fax: 25910636

Intellectual Property Department
15/F., Ocean Centre Curved Block
5 Canton Road
Kowloon, Hong Kong
Tel: 27372633

Hong Kong Export Credit Insurance Corporation
South Seas Centre, Tower I
75 Mody Road, 2/F.
Tsimshatsui East
Kowloon, Hong Kong
Tel: 27233883 Fax: 27226277

Hong Kong Productivity Council
World Commerce Centre, 12-13/F.
Harbour City, 11 Canton Road
Kowloon, Hong Kong
Tel: 27351656 Fax: 27357229

Hong Kong Securities and Futures Commission (SEC)
Exchange Square, 38/F., Tower II
Hong Kong
Tel: 28409222 Fax: 28459553

Immigration Department
2/F., Wanchai Tower II
7 Gloucester Road
Wanchai, Hong Kong
Tel: 28293456, 28246111
Fax: 28241133 Telex: 269996

Industry Department
14/F., Ocean Centre
5 Canton Road
Kowloon, Hong Kong
Tel: 27372573, 27372208 Fax: 27304633

Information Services Department
Beaconsfield House
4 Queen's Road
Central, Hong Kong
Tel: 28428777

Inland Revenue Department
Business Registration Office
Wanchai Tower
5 Gloucester Road
Wanchai, Hong Kong
Tel: 25490888

Labour Department
16/F., Harbour Building
38 Pier Road
Hong Kong
Tel: 28524118, 28155066 Fax: 25443271

Legal Department
1-8/F., Highblock
Queensway Government Offices
66 Queensway
Hong Kong
Tel: 28672123 Fax: 28690720

Monetary Affairs Branch
Government Secretariat
Admiralty Centre, Tower II
Hong Kong
Tel: 25290003 Fax: 28656146

Office of the Commissioner of Banking
28/F., Queensway Government Office
66 Queensway
Central, Hong Kong
Tel: 28672671 Fax: 28690462 Telex: 264282

Radio Television Hong Kong
Broadcasting House
30 Broadcast Drive
Kowloon, Hong Kong
Tel: 23396441 Fax: 23380279

Registrar General's Department
10-21/F., Queensway Government Offices
66 Queensway
Central, Hong Kong
Tel: 28672811

Registry of Trade Unions
11/F., Harbour Building
38 Pier Road
Hong Kong
Tel: 28523456

Television and Entertainment Licensing Authority
National Mutual Centre, 9/F.
151 Gloucester Road
Wanchai, Hong Kong
Tel: 25743130 Fax: 28382219

Trade and Industry Branch
Government Secretariat
2/F., East Wing, Central Government Offices
Lower Albert Road
Hong Kong
Tel: 28102717 Fax: 28401621

Trade Department
Trade Department Tower
700 Nathan Road
Kowloon, Hong Kong
Tel: 27897555 Fax: 27892491
Telex: 245126 CNDI

Transport Department
2-6/F., East Wing, Central Government Offices
Lower Albert Road
Hong Kong
Tel: 28102717 Fax: 28684643

GENERAL TRADE ASSOCIATIONS

Chinese Manufacturers' Association
3-4/F., CMA Building
64-66 Connaught Road
Central, Hong Kong
Tel: 25456166 Fax: 25414541

Federation of Hong Kong Industries
Hankow Centre, 4/F.
5-15 Hankow Road, Tsimshatsui
Kowloon, Hong Kong
Tel: 27230818 Fax: 27213494

Hong Kong Chinese Importers & Exporters Association
7-8/F., Champion Building
287-291 Des Voeux Road

Central, Hong Kong
Tel: 25448474 Fax: 25444677

Hong Kong Exporters' Association
Rm. 825, Star House
3 Salisbury Road, Tsimshatsui
Kowloon, Hong Kong
Tel: 27309851 Fax: 27301869

Hong Kong General Chamber of Commerce
22/F., United Square
95 Queensway
Hong Kong
Tel: 25299229 Fax: 25279843

Hong Kong Junior Chamber of Commerce
1/F., 60 Bonham Strand East
Sheung Wan, Hong Kong
Tel: 25438913 Fax: 25436271

Kowloon Chamber of Commerce
3/F., KCC Building
2 Liberty Avenue
Kowloon, Hong Kong
Tel: 27600393 Fax: 27610166 Telex: 232624

New Territories General Chamber of Commerce
25/F., 11 Nelson Street
Kowloon, Hong Kong
Tel: 23961845

Po Yick General Chinese & Foreign Goods Import & Export Commercial Society of Hong Kong
2/F., 17-19 Hillier Street
Hong Kong
Tel: 25439524, 25457490

Wah On Exporters & Importers Association
1/F., 46 Bonham Strand East
Sheung Wan, Hong Kong
Tel: 25433111

Hong Kong Trade DevelopmentCouncil (HKTDC) Offices
Head Office
38/F., Convention Plaza
1 Harbour Road
Wanchai, Hong Kong
Tel: 25844333 Fax: 28240249

DIRECTORIES & BUSINESS YEARBOOKS

Asia Pacific Leather Directory (Annual)
Asia Pacific Leather Yearbook (Annual)
Asia Pacific Directories, Ltd.
6/F., Wah Hen Commercial Centre
381 Hennessy Road
Hong Kong
Tel: 28936377 Fax: 28935752

Asia Yearbook (Annual)
POB 160
Hong Kong
Tel: 28328300 Telex: 266452 REVCD

Asian Computer Directory (Monthly)
Washington Plaza
1/F., 230 Wanchai Road
Wanchai, Hong Kong
Tel: 28327123 Fax: 28329208

Asian Printing Directory (Annual; English, Chinese)
Travel & Trade Publishing (Asia)
16/F., Capitol Centre
5-19 Jardines Bazaar
Causeway Bay, Hong Kong
Tel: 28903067 Fax: 28952378

Bankers Handbook For Asia (Annual)
Asian Finance Publications
Suite 9D, Hyde Centre
223 Gloucester Road
Hong Kong

Computer-Asia Software Guide (Annual)
Syme Media Enterprises
6-12 Wing Kut Street
Central, Hong Kong

Directory of Hong Kong Industries (Annual)
Hong Kong Productivity Council
HKPC Building
78 Tat Chee Avenue, Yau Yat Chuen
Kowloon, Hong Kong
Tel: 27885964 Fax: 27885900

Government Publications Directory (Annual;
English, Chinese)
HK Information Services Department
Beaconsfield House
4 Queen's Road
Central
Hong Kong
Tel: 28428777

Hong Kong Builder Directory (Annual)
Far East Trade Press Ltd.
2/F., Kai Tak Commercial Building
317 Des Voeux Road
Central, Hong Kong
Tel: 25453028 Fax: 25446979

Hong Kong Review of Overseas Trade (Annual)
HK Information Services Department
Beaconsfield House
4 Queen's Road
Central
Hong Kong
Tel: 28428777

International Tax and Duty Free Buyers Index
(Annual)
Pearl & Dean Publishing, Ltd.
9/F., Chung Nam Building
1 Lockhart Road
Hong Kong
Tel: 28660395 Fax: 22999810

Textile Asia Index (Annual)
Business Press Ltd.
Tak Yan Commercial Building
11/F.30-32 d'Aguilar Street
GPO Box 185
Central Hong Kong
Tel: 25247441 Telex: 260275 TEXIA

World Jewelogue (Annual)
Headway International Publications Co.
907 Great Eagle Centre
23 Harbour Road
Hong Kong
Tel: 28275121 Fax: 28277064

NEWSPAPERS

Asian Wall Street Journal
Dow Jones Publishing Co. (Asia)
2/F., AIA Building, 1 Stubbs Road
GPO Box 9825, Hong Kong
Tel: 25737121 Fax: 28345291

Hong Kong Standard
Sing Tao Building, 4/F.
1 Wang Kwong Road
Kowloon Bay, Hong Kong
Tel: 27982798 Fax: 27957330

International Herald Tribune
7/F., Malaysia Building
50 Gloucester Road
Wanchai, Hong Kong
Tel: 28610616 Fax: 28613073

Oriental Daily News
(Chinese)
Oriental Press Centre
Wang Tai Road
Kowloon Bay, Hong Kong
Tel: 27953333 Fax: 27953322

Sing Pao Daily News (Chinese)
Sing Pao Building
101 King's Road
North Point, Hong Kong
Tel: 25702201 Fax: 28072013

South China Morning Post
Tong Chong Street, POB 47
Hong Kong
Tel: 25652222 Fax: 28111278

PERIODICALS

Asia Labour Monitor (Bimonthly)
Asia Monitor Resource Centre
444-446 Nathan Road, 8/F., Flat B
Kowloon, Hong Kong
Tel: 23321346

Asian Business (Monthly)
Far East Trade Press, Ltd.
2/F., Kai Tak Commercial Building
317 Des Voeux Road
Central, Hong Kong
Tel: 25457200 Fax: 25446979

Asian Finance (Monthly)
3/F., Hollywood Centre
233 Hollywood Road
Hong Kong
Tel: 28155221 Fax: 28504437

Asian Monetary Monitor (Bimonthly)
Asian Monetary Monitor
GPOB 12964
Hong Kong
Tel: 28427200

Asiaweek (Weekly)
Asiaweek Ltd.
199 Des Voeux Road
Central, Hong Kong
Tel: 28155662 Fax: 28155903

Business Week, Asia Edition (Weekly)
2405 Dominion Centre
43-59 Queen's Road East
Hong Kong
Tel: 23361160 Fax: 25294046

The Economist, Asia Edition (Weekly)
The Economist Newspaper, Ltd.
1329 Chater Road
Hong Kong
Tel: 28681425

The Executive (Monthly)
Asian Finance Publications
Suite 9D, Hyde Centre
223 Gloucester Road
Hong Kong
Tel: 27244221 Telex: 283013

CHAMBERS OF COMMERCE

American Chamber of Commerce
10/F, 1030 Swire House
7 Charter Rd.
Central, Hong Kong
GPO Box 355, Hong Kong
Tel: 2526 0165
Fax: 2810 1289

Australian Chamber of Commerce
701A, 7/F, Euro Trade Centre
13-14 Connaught Rd.
Central, Hong Kong
Tel: 2522 5054

Canadian Chamber of Commerce
13/F, One Exchange Square Connaught Place
Central, Hong Kong
Tel: 2526 3207
Fax: 2845 1654

Chinese General Chamber of Commerce
7/F, 24-25 Connaught Rd.
Central, Hong Kong
Tel: 2525 6385
Fax: 2845 2610
Telex: 89854 CGCC HX

British Chamber of Commerce in Hong Kong
1712 Shui On Center
8 Harbour Rd.
Central, Hong Kong
Tel: 2824 2211
Fax: 2824 1333

French Business Association of Hong Kong
18/F, Tower 2
Admiralty Center
18 Harcourt Rd.
Central, Hong Kong
Tel: 2866 1007, 2523 6818
Fax: 2861 0806
Telex: 76715 UAPHK HX

German Business Association of Hong Kong
Room 701, Euro-Trade Centre
13-14 Connaught Rd.
Central, Hong Kong
Tel: 2526 5481
Fax: 2810 6093

Indian Chamber of Commerce
2/F, Hoseinee House
69 Wyndham St.
Hong Kong
Tel: 2523 3877
Fax: 2845 0300
Telex: 64993 INCHA HX

Korean Society of Commerce
Rm 503, Korea Centre Bldg.
119-121 Connaught Rd.
Central, Hong Kong
Tel: 2544 9282
Fax: 2815 8779

Swedish Chamber of Commerce
7B Shun Ho Tower
24-30 Ice House St.
Central, Hong Kong
Tel: 2525 0349
Fax: 2868 5344 , 2537 1843
Telex: 68350 KAMVI HX

Swiss Business Council
GPO Box 9501
Hong Kong
Tel: 2524 0590 Fax: 2877 2504

TELEVISION AND RADIO

Asia Television Ltd.
81 Broadcast Drive
Kowloon, Hong Kong
Tel: 23387123 Fax: 23384347

Hong Kong Commercial Broadcasting Co.
GPO 30
Hong Kong
Tel: 23365111

Radio Television Hong Kong
Broadcasting House
30 Broadcast Drive
Kowloon, Hong Kong
Tel: 23396441 Fax: 23380279

Television Broadcasts Ltd.
TV City, Clearwater Bay Road
Kowloon, Hong Kong
Tel: 27194828 Fax: 23581337

INTERNET ADDRESSES

Usenet group(s):
soc.culture.hongkong

Hong Kong Starting Points
http://csclub.uwaterloo.ca/u/nckwan/hk/hongkong.html

**Hong Kong - Hong Kong Government's Economic
and Trade Office**
http://www.hongkong.org/

Doing Business in Hong Kong
http://www.hk.super.net/~rlowe/bizhk/bhhome.html

Hungary

Republic of Hungary

Economy

Overview

Hungary has made a largely successful transition to free enterprise as a result of laws enacted during the 1980s that have helped attract the tremendous amount of foreign investment flowing into the region. The country's well-educated work force has adapted well to changes in the economic environment, despite rising unemployment levels and inexperienced management. Hungarian demand for imported goods—particularly those from neighboring European nations and the US—is sizeable. Economic growth has been slow, but is expected to gain momentum in the next few years unless it is derailed by inflation, unfavorable tax and exchange rates, or rising gasoline prices—all of which remain distinct possibilities. Although Hungary has an acceptable road network and an extensive railway system, its limited air facilities and a poor telecommunications system are in dire need of upgrading and this serves to limit economic growth in the short term.

Trade

Hungary has continued to liberalize its trade regime, although import quotas on consumer goods, a few excessive tariff rates, infrastructure limitations, and a substantial bureaucracy remain formidable obstacles. Major exports include meat, apparel, electrical machinery, non-fuel raw materials, and fruits and vegetables. Germany is Hungary's largest trade partner, followed by the countries of the former USSR, Austria, Italy, and the US.

Sectors

Agriculture Agriculture contributes about 12 percent of GDP and employs about 14 percent of the work force. Economic conditions are improving in Hungary's agricultural sector, but farmers remain plagued by low prices, high costs, and slow reform from the previous collective structure. Grains, sugar beets, potatoes, and wine are the dominant cash crops.

Industry Industry provides about 40 percent of GDP and a slightly smaller proportion of employment. Because use existing facilities require substantial upgrading, current manufacturing output remains low and high-cost, low-quality products are for the most part uncompetitive. Textiles, coal, metals, and chemicals are among Hungary's major industries.

Services The services sector accounts for roughly 45 percent of both GDP and employment. Hungary's services are relatively well-developed, especially when compared to those in neighboring Central European countries, and observers expect rapid development in future years.

Trends

Despite its former membership in the Soviet Bloc, Hungary has historically had close ties with Western Europe, thus laying a promising foundation for future growth and potential membership in the EU (some limited agreements are already in place). Anticipate further growth in the services sector, the food processing industry, and a domestic automotive industry, which has generated support from foreign producers who plan to participate. Investment in infrastructure, new domestic construction, and potential opportunities for the sale of goods and services to neighboring Central European and Balkan countries bode well for future development.

At a Glance

THE COUNTRY
Location Central Europe, between Slovakia and Romania.
Terrain Much of Hungary is flat with low mountains in the north and northeast and north of Lake Balaton.
Climate Temperate.

THE PEOPLE
Population 10,000,000
Ethnic composition
Magyar.. 92%
Romany 3%
German, Slovak, Jews, Southern Slav, other 1%
Religious composition
Roman Catholic 68%
Calvinist 20%
Lutheran.. 5%
Jewish, Baptist, Adventist, Pentecostal, Unitarian.. 5%
Languages spoken Magyar 98% (official), other 2%.
Education and literacy Education is compulsory and free until age 16. Literacy is high: 99 percent for both men and women.
Labor force
Total:...5,000,000
By occupation: agriculture 14%, industry and commerce 37%, government 5%, services 44%.

COUNTRY FACTS
Political and legal Parliamentary democracy. Principal political parties: Socialists (MSZP, reform Communists) 32 percent, Alliance of Free Democrats (SZDSZ center-left) 19 percent, Hungarian Democratic Forum (MDF center) 12 percent, Independent Smallholder's Party (FKGP center right) 9 percent, Federation of Young Democrats (FIDESZ center-left) 7 percent, Christian Democratic People's Party (KDNP center-right) 7 percent. Legal system is in the process of revision, moving toward rule of law based on Western model.
Telephone The Ministry of Transport and Communications controls all telephone and telegraph systems. International calls are readily available at standard international rates. There is currently a 12- to 15-year wait for a telephone. International country code: [36]. Selected city codes: Budapest (1), Derberecen (52).
Transportation All railroads are government owned. Half of the highways are paved.
Environment There are many protected national parks. Flooding occurs almost every year in many parts of Hungary. Current issues include air pollution and industrial and municipal pollution of Lake Balaton.
Media All means of communication are considered government property. There are 28 daily newspapers with a combined circulation of 2.9 million. Most newspapers lean toward a socialist ideology. Several magazines are published in Budapest, the center for Hungarian publishing. There are 32 AM, 15 FM, and 41 television broadcast stations.
Health Medical services and medications are available and adequate. Hungary has a declining population which is aging rapidly. About 99 percent of the children are immunized for diseases such as tuberculosis and tetanus. Tapwater is safe and drinkable. Avoid unpasteurized milk. Life expectancy is 67 years for men and 75 years for women.

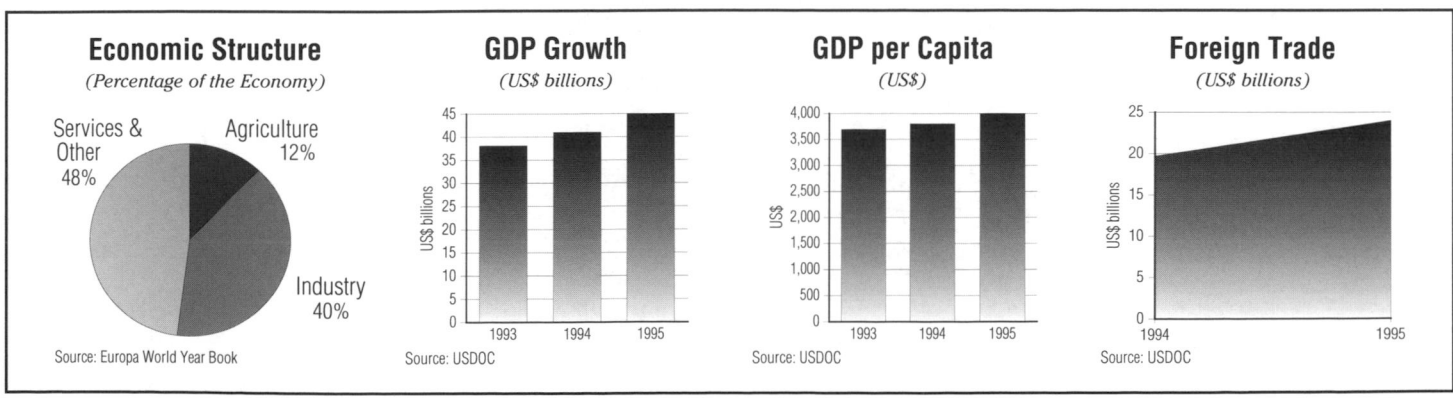

Economic Structure
(Percentage of the Economy)

Services & Other 48%
Agriculture 12%
Industry 40%

Source: Europa World Year Book

GDP Growth
(US$ billions)

Source: USDOC

GDP per Capita
(US$)

Source: USDOC

Foreign Trade
(US$ billions)

Source: USDOC

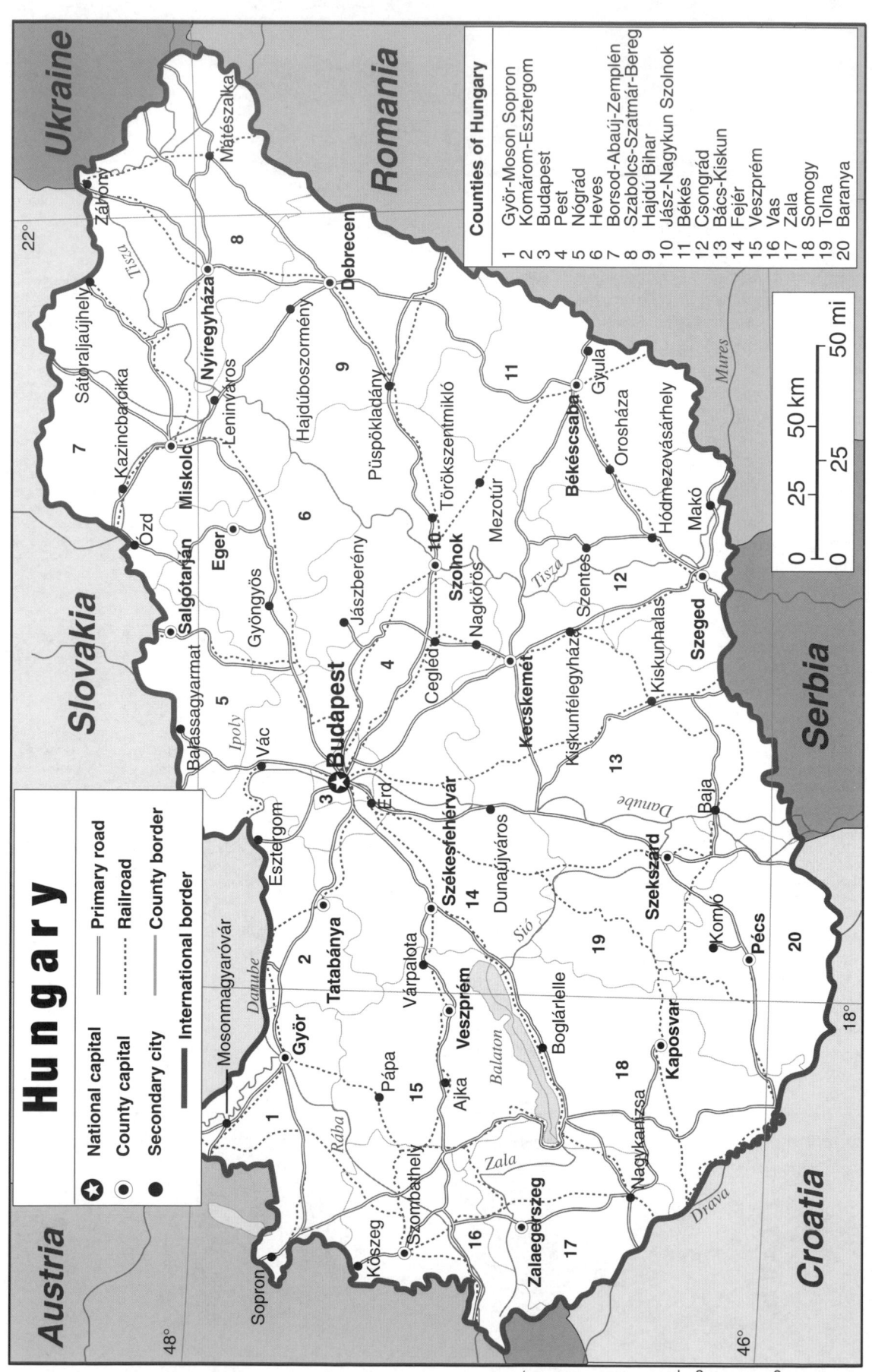

Hungary

Legend:
- ★ National capital
- ◉ County capital
- ● Secondary city
- —— Primary road
- ········ Railroad
- County border
- —— International border

Counties of Hungary

1. Győr-Moson Sopron
2. Komárom-Esztergom
3. Budapest
4. Pest
5. Nógrád
6. Heves
7. Borsod-Abaúj-Zemplén
8. Szabolcs-Szatmár-Bereg
9. Hajdú Bihar
10. Jász-Nagykun Szolnok
11. Békés
12. Csongrád
13. Bács-Kiskun
14. Fejér
15. Veszprém
16. Vas
17. Zala
18. Somogy
19. Tolna
20. Baranya

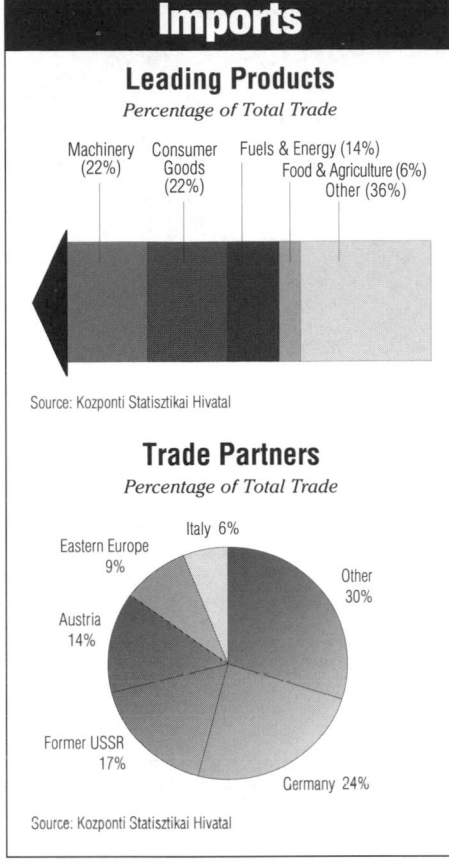

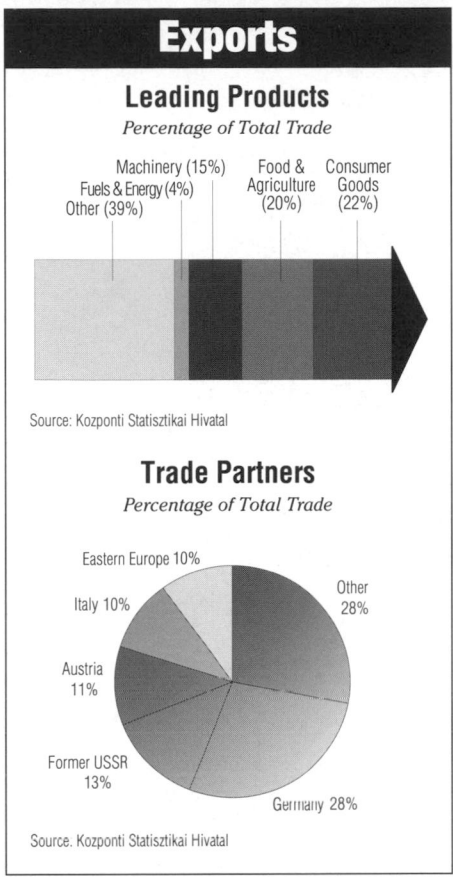

Opportunities

FOR IMPORTING TO HUNGARY

- automotive parts and equipment
- clothing
- computers and computer products
- cosmetics
- cotton
- energy products
- industrial chemicals
- medical equipment and supplies
- oil and gas field machinery
- pharmaceuticals
- processed foods
- raw materials
- telecommunication products

FOR EXPORTING FROM HUNGARY

- automotive parts and vehicles
- ceramics and glassware
- clothing and footwear
- household consumer products
- meat products
- medical instruments
- organic chemicals
- pharmaceuticals
- vegetables

GROWTH SECTORS

- advertising
- automotive vehicle and parts production
- capital goods
- construction
- financial services
- food processing
- telecommunications

GOVERNMENT PROCUREMENT

- electrical power generating equipment
- motorway construction goods and services
- railway construction goods and services
- telecommunication products
- water treatment facilities

Trade News

RULES AND REGULATIONS

- **Regulations** Hungary's trade regulations are administered by the Ministry of Industry and Trade.
- **Tariffs and import taxes** Average import duties have been cut from 50 to 13 percent and should fall to eight percent with the implementation of the GATT Uruguay Round Agreement. Nearly 90 percent of Hungary's tariffs are bound by the GATT tariff schedule. In addition to tariff duties, a two percent customs clearance fee and a three percent statistical fee is applied. If the product requires an import license, a one percent licensing fee is often assessed depending on the product.
- **Prohibited imports** Hungary does not prohibit the import of any goods.
- **Import licenses** Nearly 90 percent of goods need no import license. Import licenses are necessary for goods subject to quota and controlled products such as arms and ammunition and hazardous materials.
- **Special import provisions** Equipment and other goods which are deemed capital in kind for joint ventures may enter duty-free. Hungary maintains tariff preferences for developing countries and some former communist countries.
- **Free trade arrangements** Hungary has signed an Association Agreement with the European Union. Full membership is expected in 2000. Hungary, the Czech Republic, and Poland have created a Central European Free Trade Area. Hungary also has a free trade agreement with the European Free Trade Association.

TRANSPORTATION FIRMS

Gyor-Sopron-Ebenfurti-Vasut-Gysev-Roeee
(Railway of Eyor-Sopron-Ebenburt)
9400 Sopron
Matyas Kiraly u. 19
Hungarian-Austrian-owned railway.

Hungarian Shipping Co.
Budapest
Magyar Hajozasi Rt.
PO Box 58
Tel: (1) 118-1880

Hungarocamion
1442 Budapest
POB 108
Tel: (1) 157-3811
Telex: 22-5455

MAHART-Magyar Hajózási Rt.
(Hungarian Shipping Company)
1366 Budapest
PO Box 58
Tel: (1) 118-1880
Fax: (1) 118-0733

MAFRACHT
1364 Budapest 4
PO Box 105
Tel: (1) 118-5276
Fax: (1) 118-4170

Masped Hungarian General Forwarding Co Ltd.
1052 Budapest
Kristof ter 2
Tel: (1) 118-2922
Telex: 22-4471
Fax: (1) 118-8343

Volán Vállalatok Központja
1391 Budapest
Erzsebet krt 96
POB 221
Tel: (1) 112-4290
Telex: 22-5177

Business Travel

	LH 1906	MADRID	935	113-3
	LH 1022	STUTTGART HBF.	935	-
	AF 1701	LYON	940	683-6
	AY 822	HELSINKI	940	113-3
	AA 071	SFRANCISCO-DALLAS	945	731-7

Air Travel Times

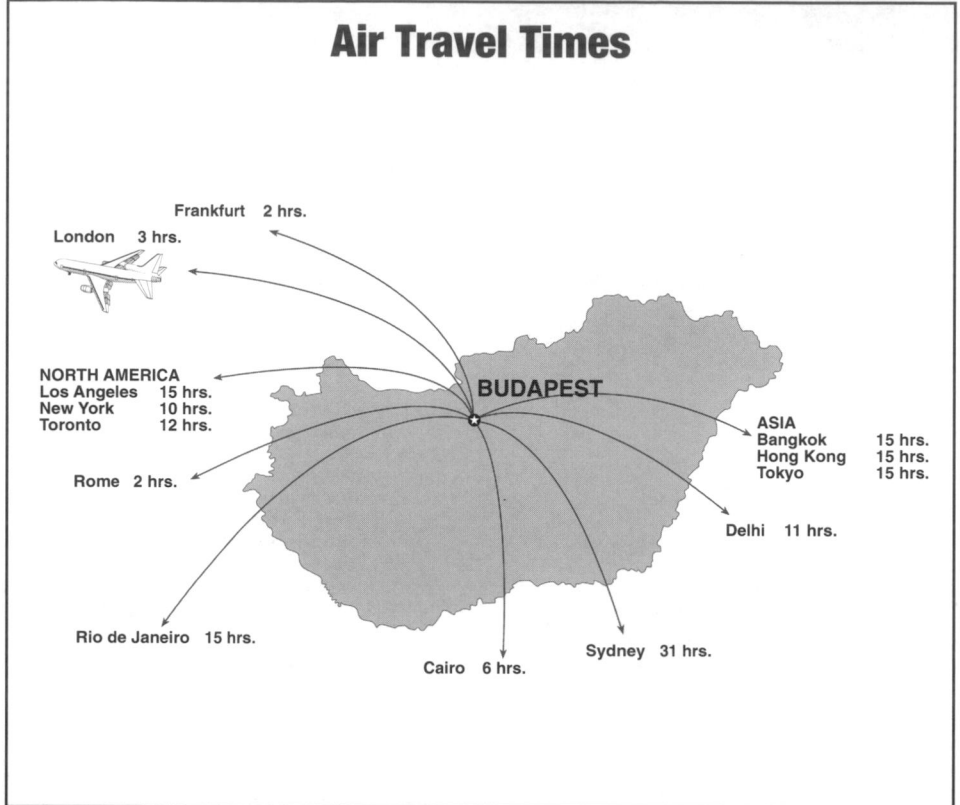

Frankfurt 2 hrs.
London 3 hrs.

NORTH AMERICA
Los Angeles 15 hrs.
New York 10 hrs.
Toronto 12 hrs.

Rome 2 hrs.

Rio de Janeiro 15 hrs.

BUDAPEST

ASIA
Bangkok 15 hrs.
Hong Kong 15 hrs.
Tokyo 15 hrs.

Delhi 11 hrs.

Cairo 6 hrs.

Sydney 31 hrs.

COMMUNICATIONS

Telephones Telephone service in Hungary is poor. Getting a line can be very difficult and call completion is only 40 percent. The service is more reliable in Budapest, where many hotels and businesses are hooked into digital switches. Most hotels can accommodate calling card services. Outside Budapest, telephone calls can be difficult since many rural towns have older systems. The public phone system is being updated, but slowly. Old phones are unreliable, and rate signs on phones are probably not accurate due to outmoded phone devices. Long distance and international service is available at Telefon Centers.

Fax Receiving international facsimiles is fairly reliable; sending them can be problematic due to line interference.

Post office Main branches of the post office are usually open until 8:00 pm, with some branches open all night. For postal information in English, French, German, or Russian, call 117-2200. Stamps can be purchased at post offices and major hotels.

BEST TRAVEL BOOKS

Lonely Planet, Hungary Travel Survival Kit. This guide leads to the enchantment of Hungary. Only a short hop from Vienna, this gateway to Eastern Europe welcomes visitors. 480 pages.

Do's and Taboo's Around the World. The Bestselling Guide to International Behavior. Edited by Roger Axtell, compiled by the Parker Pen Company. The ultimate guide to international behavior, now completely updated and expanded. Helpful, fun to read!

Berlitz Business Travel Guide, Europe. Concise economic details, successful trip planning, background information on people and cities, useful facts and addresses.

Multinational Travel Companion Executive. Strand Publishing Company, Inc. Travel tips world-wide. Updated annually.

USEFUL TELEPHONE NUMBERS

If you are calling from outside Hungary, you will need to add the country code [36] and any other international dialing requirements from within your country.

- Ambulance 04
- Police 07
- Time 08
- Telegrams 02
- Pharmacy 41
- Operator Assistance........ (1) 117-0000 or 157-3333
- International Information ....(1) 118-6977
- MALEV Hungarian Airlines.................(1) 118-4333
- Train ....(1) 122-8405, 142-9150
- Bus Information ....(1) 117-2369
- Taxi .... (1) 122-2222, 166-6666, 129-4000
- Autoclub ....(1) 166-6404
- Avis Car Rental ....(1) 118-4240
- Budget Car Rental Airport ....(1) 149-0684
- Hertz Car Rental Airport ....(1) 157-8629
- Europcar Airport ....(1) 134-2540
- Chamber of Commerce ....(1) 175-6764
- Astora Hotel ....(1) 117-3411
- Dentist ....(1) 142-4257
- Tourist Infomation ....(1) 180-860
- General Clinic ....(1) 133-0360
- TourInform..(1)117-9800

Credit Card Information
Lost or stolen credit cards (call collect to the US, regardless of which country the card was issued in).
- Amex ....[1] (919) 333-3211
- Diner's Club.................................[1] (303) 799-1504
- MasterCard ....[1] (314) 275-6690
- Visa ....[1] (410) 581-7931

Travelogue

WORKWEEK

Offices Monday-Friday 8:00 am to 4:00 pm. During the summer months businesses often close by mid-afternoon.

Banks Monday-Friday 8:30 am to 4:30 pm.

Government Monday-Friday 8:00 am to 4:00 pm.

Retail Monday-Friday 10:00 am to 6:00 pm, and Saturday 10:00 am to 1:00 pm.

Most business vacations are taken between June and August. Also, many businesses are closed the week before Easter and the two weeks before and after Christmas.

HOLIDAYS

Holidays 1996
January 1 New Year's Day
March 15 Revolution Day
April 7 Easter Sunday*
April 8 Easter Monday*
May 1 Labor Day
May 26 Whit Monday*
August 20 National Day
October 23 Republic Day
December 25 Christmas
December 26 Boxing Day
*Dates vary each year.

VISA AND PASSPORT

Foreigners need only a valid passport and no visas are required for visits up to 90 days for visitors from many countries. Carry two additional passport photographs for unexpected document requirements. All passengers must hold onward tickets, valid travel documents, and sufficient funds. Travelers are required to declare any foreign funds in their possession upon entry to facilitate re-export of the funds upon departure. It is advised to keep your embassy informed of your plans.

DEPARTURE FORMALITIES

There is no departure tax for visitors leaving from Ferihegy Airport in Budapest. Special permits are required to export many items, such as food, medicine, tools, textiles, art work, and items of precious metal. Stamps and protected works of art cannot be exported. For more information call (1) 175-7533 or (1) 116-0170, extension 460.

IMMUNIZATION

There are no inoculations necessary to gain admittance into Hungary, however tetanus and typhoid shots are recommended. Drinking water is safe in major cities and resorts; boil water in other areas before drinking.

TIPPING

Just about everyone in the service industries gets tipped in Hungary; however, it is officially discouraged. A tip of 10 to15 percent is customary even when service charges are added to a bill; porters should receive F30 per piece; small services, F20.

CRIME

Hungary has a low rate of violent crime. Street crime has increased, especially at night near major hotels and restaurants and on public transportation. Vehicle theft, particularly of high value automobiles, is a major problem. Avoid traveling alone at night and stick to the main roads.

INFRASTRUCTURE

Hungary's infrastructure is still in a developing stage. Air, train, taxi, and rental car services are efficient and readily available. Budapest has well-developed hotel, metro, bus, tram, and trolley systems. Long, extensive roads for buses are available. Tourist facilities outside Budapest are not as developed as those found in most of Western Europe.

NATIONAL TOURIST OFFICE

Orszagos Idegenforgalmi Hivatal (OIH)
Hungarian Tourist Board
1024 Budapest
Margit Krt. 85, 6th Fl.
Tel: (1) 156-5566
Fax: (1) 175-3646

Marketing

Overview

Consumer segments of Hungary's market are experiencing a release of pent-up demand for many previously unavailable items. Hungary's Western European neighbors provide most of the competition for new enterprises; company representatives visit frequently to advise on business strategy or provide prompt equipment servicing. Firms entering this environment must keep these factors firmly in mind and plan accordingly before entering this market.

Distribution

Hungary's consumer products wholesale sector is controlled by 11 major state-owned companies with geographic territories. These wholesalers once distributed exclusively through small shops, but they are increasingly opening retail and discount stores. Smaller companies are filling market niches by offering more integrated services.

Agents, Distributors, and Partners

Choosing agents and distributors is becoming ever simpler as distribution channels broaden and local distributors obtain international experience. Several Hungarian companies have established exclusive representational agency or distributor relationships with foreign companies. Representative offices do not provide legal protection to foreign companies; investors should secure a local attorney's services before undertaking any sales activities in Hungary.

Selling Techniques and Advertising

Brand awareness is low among Hungarian consumers, making price the most significant factor in a consumer's buying decision. There is also a high demand for products that symbolize Western culture; goods promoted as trend-setting will sell better. Exhibitions and printed material are the most popular forms of advertising. Advertising is regulated by the Domestic Trade Law, which prohibits all ads (except point-of-sale) for tobacco products, alcoholic beverages, and pharmaceuticals. Advertisers who mislead consumers or endanger their competitors' reputations are subject to various consequences. Trade fairs are held in several outdoor facilities.

Business Culture

Greetings and Courtesies

The customary greeting in Hungary is a handshake, and a man waits for a woman to extend her hand first. When greeting a Hungarian, use the person's proper title, along with the surname. Bring a good supply of business cards to Hungary. They should be printed in your language as well as in Hungarian. Businesspeople are accustomed to having letters and accounts translated into Hungarian. Hand out your business cards at business, as well as social, meetings. A polite gesture in Hungary is to bring a gift to your hosts. Because Hungarians typically begin work early in the morning, evening visits usually end before 11:00 pm.

Business Ethic and Framework

Hungarians have a strong work ethic. Many have had to take on extra part-time jobs to keep up with the rising cost of living of Hungary and they expect foreigners to approach their business with the same no-nonsense can-do zeal. Dark, conservative business attire is befitting for all functions; women normally wear suits or conservative dresses.

Meetings and Decision Making

Make all the essential arrangements weeks ahead of time, especially for governmental meetings. Hungarians are greatly legalistic in their approach to negotiations. They will want to review the terms of an agreement many times, seeking clarification of each item and asking numerous questions. The decision-making process is long and complicated, but once a decision is made it will usually remain in place.

Women

Although women are found in a wide variety of business and government positions, they must usually still prove themselves capable to their male counterparts before they are accepted as equals. Nonetheless, foreign businesswomen should experience few difficulties in conducting their business, and they will generally be accorded respect by Hungarian businessmen.

Marketing in Hungary

MARKETING TIPS

- **Retail Markets** Most of the retail market is dominated by small-scale shops whose owners are unaware of modern marketing methods and sales promotion. There are several department store chains.
- **Media** Some of the most prominent newspapers are *Figyelo, Magyar Hirlap, Nepszabadsag, Nepszava,* and *Heti Volaggazdassag.* Cinema, television and radio ads are less significant than point-of-sale advertisements.

AD AGENCIES

DDB Needham Worldwide Budapest
1117 Budapest
Budafokl u. 79
Tel: (1) 182-0772
Fax: (1) 182-0506

Euro RSCG Havasl
1370 Budapest
POB 319
Tel: (1) 163-7852
Fax: (1) 164-3206

CONSULTING FIRMS

Arthur Andersen & Co.
1088 Budapest
East West Business Center
Rakoczi ut 1-3.
Tel: (1) 251-9744
Fax: (1) 251-9661

Coopers & Lybrand Consulting Group
1024 Budapest
Lov haz u 30.
Tel: (1) 212-4720
ax: (1) 156-4895

Deloitte and Touche
1052 Budapest
Varmegye u. 3-5.
Tel: (1) 267-2062
Fax: (1)267-4182

Cultural Cautions

DO'S

- Make appointments well in advance. Be on time to the meeting.
- Maintain a reserved disposition.
- Shake hands upon meeting and when departing from Hungarians.

DON'TS

- Don't photograph soldiers or military installations.
- Do not discuss politics or religion.
- Confusing the Hungarian capital with Bucharest is a social error.

CUSTOMS

- Good conversation topics are food, wine, history, and Hungary itself.
- Hungarians like their personal space and usually stand about two feet apart when conversing.
- If you compliment Hungarians, expect them to disparage themselves, rather than to thank you.
- The official language is Magyar, referred to as Hungarian in other countries. Magyar is part of the Finno-Ugrian group of languages.
- Hungarians enjoy the company of foreign visitors and are skilled in the art of hospitality.

OBSERVATIONS

- Hungarians are known to be pessimistic, even when things are going well. Don't be frightened away by sorrowful attitudes; it's part of their character.
- Hungarians tend to be highly educated, technically accomplished, and very patriotic.
- Personal security and safety in Hungary is high, on or near the level of Japan.
- Cameras are now permitted in Hungary, but ask permission to photograph even ordinary parades. At outside urban locations, it is still possible for cameras and film to be confiscated.

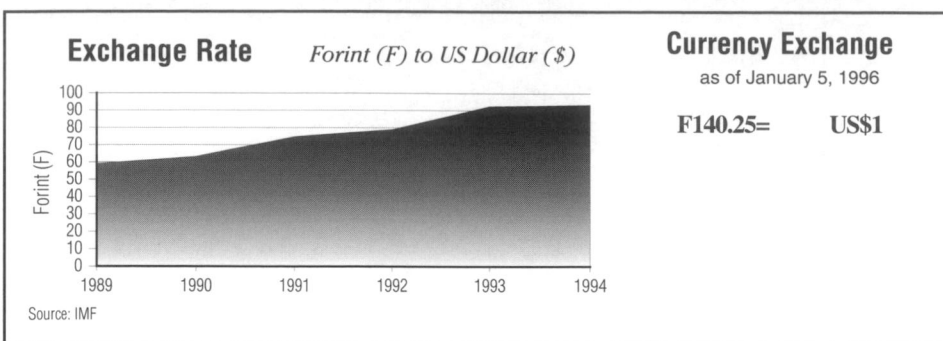

Exchange Rate   *Forint (F) to US Dollar ($)*

Forint (F): 0, 10, 20, 30, 40, 50, 60, 70, 80, 90, 100
Years: 1989, 1990, 1991, 1992, 1993, 1994

Source: IMF

Currency Exchange
as of January 5, 1996

F140.25=   US$1

Currency

The currency in use is the Hungarian forint (F or HUF).

Foreign Exchange

The exchange rate is periodically determined by a currency basket of US dollars and European Currency Units. Banks may freely set exchange rates for currency and traveler's checks. Forward exchange rates may be freely negotiated between commercial banks and their customers, but there are few banks which actually provide this service. Any economic entity or private person in Hungary may carry out a foreign trade activity in convertible currencies or Hungarian forint upon registering with the National Bank of Hungary (NBH). Transactions with the Federal Republic of Yugoslavia are restricted.

Capital Transfers

Nonresident travelers have no minimum spending or conversion requirements, but a specified amount of money must be at a traveler's disposal to cover anticipated expenditures. There is no limit on the amount of hard currency that may be brought into the country, but travelers must declare foreign funds upon entry. Nonresidents may take foreign exchange out of the country without a license. Residents may bring in or take out domestic currency up to F 10,000 per person; nonresidents are limited to F 1,000.

Investment Incentives

Foreign investments are given the same privileges as domestic ones. Parliament introduced a new general tax reduction, effective January 1, 1994, which is available based on a percentage of future taxes to be paid. Individual incentives for specific projects may be negotiated as well.

Investment Restrictions

Specific restrictions on foreign investment are few, although the bureaucratic procedures, investment procedures in general, and the overall business climate do not favor foreign investment. Only Hungarian companies can own land, and foreigners must make all payments in hard currency.

TAXATION

Taxation requires sophisticated knowledge of complex rules and regulations specific to each country. For more detailed information we suggest you refer to the Ernst & Young Corporate Tax Guide and Directory, available from the Ernst & Young accounting office in your country, or from:

Ernst & Young Kft
1146 Budapest
Hermina ut 17
Hungary
Tel: (1) 252-8333
Fax: (1) 251-8778

- The Hungarian economic situation is rapidly changing. Readers should ensure that information is still current before engaging in any transactions.

At a Glance

Corporate Income Tax Rate (%)(a)	18
Capital Gains Tax Rate (%)(a)	18
Branch Tax Rate (%)(a)	18
Withholding Tax (%)(b)	
Dividends	

Paid Out of Profits Earned Before January 1, 1995 (c)	0/10/20
Paid Out of Profits Earned on or After January 1, 1995	23
Interest (d)(e)	18
Royalties (d)	18
Branch Remittance Tax	0
Net Operating Losses (Years)	
Carryback	0
Carryforward (f)	5

(a) Foreign companies are subject to special rules for calculating these taxes, based on their Hungarian net profits and Hungarian turnover.
(b) These rates may be reduced by tax treaties.
(c) Dividends paid to nonresident corporations out of profits earned before January 1, 1995 are exempt from Hungarian tax. For dividends paid to individuals, a 10% withholding tax is imposed if the payer is subject to the normal corporate income tax rate; the withholding tax rate is 20% if the payer is subject to corporate income tax at a reduced rate.
(d) Final tax imposed on payments to foreign companies without a permanent establishment in Hungary.
(e) Bank interest and interest on Hungarian treasury notes are not subject to withholding tax.
(f) For companies established after January 1, 1992, losses incurred during the first three years of the company's existence may be carried forward indefinitely. Effective January 1, 1993, a successor company may not carry forward losses of the predecessor company.

Money Matters

BITS AND PIECES

- **Overvaluation** Many exporters criticize the Hungarian government's exchange rate policy, stating that its overvaluation of the *forint* has priced them out of foreign markets.
- **Convertibility** Although the *forint* is not fully convertible, for business purposes it is nearly so. Foreigners may repatriate profits and dividends in hard currency, and there has been progress in liberalizing foreign exchange controls.
- **Stock exchange** The Budapest Stock Exchange was formally reestablished in 1990. As of May 1994, 86 securities were listed on the exchange. There are some limitations on foreign participation in certain investment funds.
- **Duty-free zones** Foreign investors may set up or acquire an interest in companies in a duty-free zone. All firms in these zones are considered for legal purposes to be foreign companies.
- **Banking system** A two-tier banking system was created in 1987, when the former Hungarian National Bank's portfolio was divided between three new commercial banks. Banking has developed rapidly, and now consists of the National Bank of Hungary, 37 commercial banks, six specialized financial institutions, one off-shore bank, and 260 savings cooperatives. The banking system is still considered difficult to deal with, and many branches are not electronically connected. Bank transfers are time-consuming and there is a high degree of human error. It is not possible to cash checks other than at the branch at which they are drawn.
- **Transfer of assets** Transfer of economic assets abroad by residents is subject to licensing by the government. Outward capital transfers by residents is usually not approved.

BANKS

ABN-Amro Bank
1022 Budapest
Arvacska u 6
Tel: (1) 135-0969 Fax: (1) 115-1267

Banque Indo-Suez
1088 Budapest
Rakoczi ut 1-3
Tel: (1) 266-2713 Fax: (1) 266-5231

Central European International Bank
1052 Budapest
Vaci u 16/B
Tel: (1) 118-8377 Fax: (1) 118-9415, 118-8541

Citibank Budapest
Vaci utca 19-21
1052 Budapest
Tel: (1) 138-2666 Fax: (1) 118-9694

Commercial and Credit (K&H) Bank
1051 Budapest
Arany Janos u. 24
Tel: (1) 112-5200 Fax: (1) 111-1825

Credit Lyonnais
1051 Budapest
Jozsef nador ter 7
Tel: (1) 266-1578, 266-9000 Fax: (1) 266-9950

Creditanstalt
1054 Budapest
Akademia utca 17
Tel: (1) 269-0812 Fax: (1) 153-4959

Hungarian Credit Bank (Magyar Hitel Bank)
1054 Budapest
Szabadsag ter 5-6
Tel: (1) 269-2122 Fax: (1) 269-2245, 252-1220

Hungarian Foreign Trade Bank
1051 Budapest
Szent Istvan ter 11
Tel: (1) 269-0922, 153-4211 Fax: (1) 269-0959

Internationale Nederlanden (ING) Bank
1075 Budapest
Karoly krt. 11
Tel: (1) 269-7800 Fax: (1) 269-7814

Leumi Credit Bank
1053 Budapest
Barczy Istvan utca 3-5

Legal

Legal System

Hungary is a civil code country with laws strongly influenced by German and Swiss law.

Intellectual Property Rights

The Hungarian legal system protects and facilitates the acquisition and disposition of property rights.

Business Registration

Companies are established by creating and filing Articles of Association according to the Company Law, and all companies must be registered by the Court of Registration. The Company Law divides companies into two major groups, those with no legal entity and the others which are legal entities. An offshore company must be 100 percent foreign owned and may only be engaged in business activities between third-world countries, with the exception of financial services, which may be performed in Hungary as well.

Contracts and Dispute Resolution

Commercial claims may be determined by arbitration if at least one of the parties involved performs business activities and if the claim is in connection with such activity, or if the parties freely designate that they will submit to arbitration over the subject of the claim, and if they have determined in writing the exclusive competency of an arbitration. The parties may freely determine the number of arbitrators; generally each party designates one, and they together elect a president of the tribunal.

Labor

Hungary's labor force is highly educated and skilled. Many foreign investors have praised the productivity, motivation, and adaptability of Hungarian workers, although there have been complaints about the general lax attitude regarding sick leave and absenteeism. Approximately 50 percent of the work force is unionized, but unions are relatively weak and divided. The minimum employment age is 16, although some apprentice programs may begin at age 15. The unemployment level is about 10 percent, although in the Northeastern area, it may exceed 20 percent.

Source: Dr. Bán György Ügyvédi Iroda, Budapest

Legal Matters

LEGAL BRIEFS

- **Constitutional Court** Since 1990, Hungary has had a Constitutional Court which is responsible for protecting the constitutional order and protecting the rights provided in the Constitution. The Constitutional Court performs prior and post control of legal regulations and has the right to annul them if found to be infringing the Constitution.

- **Economic laws** On May 30, 1995, the Parliament enacted numerous amendments to the laws providing economic stability. This package of amendments affects virtually every economic law, mainly amending the tax laws, duty law, and social security provisions.

- **Taxation** The corporate tax was changed in 1995, introducing a new tax structure for businesses. Gross corporate income is taxed by 18 percent and an additional 23 percent tax is payable on dividends.

- **Competition law** Hungary has a competition law prohibiting any unfair business activity, including the performance of business activities which are against the interests of the consumer or which breach the principals of fair business.

LEGAL CONTACTS

Dr. Bán György Ügyvédi Iroda
International Trade Center
1052 Budapest
Váci u. 19-21, Suite 607
Tel: (1) 266-9168 Fax: (1) 251-4237

Baker & McKenzie
1062 Budapest
Andrássy-út 125
(1) 142-0560 Fax: (1) 142-0513

Arent Fox Kintner Plotkin & Kahn
Nagymezo Utca 44
1065 Budapest
Tel: (1) 269 0596
Fax: (1) 269 0599

Contacts

GOVERNMENT AGENCIES

Ministry of Industry & Trade
1024 Budapest
Margit krt. 85
Tel: (1) 156-5566 Fax: (1) 175-0219

Ministry of Finance
1051 Budapest
Jozsef nador ter 2/4
Tel: (1) 118-3111 Fax: (1) 118-2570

Ministry of Environment and Regional Policy
1011 Budapest
Fu. 44-50
Tel: (1) 201-4133 Fax: (1) 201-2846

National Bank of Hungary
1054 Budapest
Szabadsag ter 8-9
Tel: (1) 153-2600 Fax: (1) 132-3913

State Property Agency
1133 Budapest
Pozsonyi utca 56
Tel: (1) 269-8860 Fax: (1) 140-2723

WORLD TRADE CENTER

World Trade Center Budapest
c/o WTC Club Hotel Korona
1053 Budapest
Kecskemeti utca 14
Tel: (1) 117-5122, 138-2416 Fax: (1) 118-3731

BUSINESS AND TRADE ASSOCIATIONS

Hungexpo
(Advertising, Public Relations, Fairs and Exhibitions)
1101 Budapest
PO Box 44
Tel: (1) 122-5008 Fax: (1) 157-2647

Foreign Trade Company for Industrial Cooperation
1367 Budapest
PO Box 111
Tel: (1) 142-4950 Fax: (1) 132-6371

National Association of Entrepreneurs
1087 Budapest
Konyves Kalman krt. 44.
Tel: (1) 185-3377 Fax: (1) 115-8453

Hungarian Banking Association
Budapest
Roosevelt ter 7-8
Tel: (1) 112-5826 Fax: (1) 111-6037

Association of Computer Software and Organizational Enterprises
1138 Budapest
Vaci ut 168/A
Tel: (1) 269-7323 Fax: (1) 269-7166

Hungarian Chamber of Database Suppliers
1012 Budapest
Kuny Domokos u. 13
Tel: (1) 202-2998, 175-9722 Fax: (1) 202-2894

Association of Hungarian Building Materials Industry
1027 Budapest
Futca 68.
Tel: (1) 201-2011 x479, 201-6682 Fax: (1) 156-1215

Association of the Hungarian Chemical Industries
1406 Budapest
POB 4O
Tel: (1) 142-8920 Fax: (1) 142-0980

Association of the Hungarian Electronic and Informatics Industries
1525 Budapest
POB 33
Tel: (1) 131-8986, 111-6271 Fax: (1) 131-6320

National Professional Association of the Environment Protection Industry
1063 Budapest
Sziv u. 15.
Tel: (1) 122-4896 Fax: (1) 122-5111

Association of Hungarian Foreign Trading Companies
1012 Budapest
Kuny D. u. 13-15.
Tel: (1) 175-9722, 155-4858 Fax: (1) 155-8219

Hungarian Franchise Association
1015 Budapest
POB 446
Tel: (1) 115-4619 Fax: (1) 135-9349

Association of Hungarian Insurance Companies
Deak F. u. 10.
1052 Budapest
Tel: (1) 118-3473 Fax: (1) 137-5394

Association of the Hungarian Light Industries
POB 329
1390 Budapest
Tel: (1) 144-4793 Fax: (1) 141-4790

Association of the Plastics Industry
Erzsebet kiralyne u. 1/c.
1146 Budapest
Tel: (1) 142-0759
Fax: (1) 142-0980

Chamber of Public Road Transport Companies
1066 Budapest
Terez krt. 38., II. 228.
Tel: (1) 132-9939
Fax: (1) 132-993

Chamber of Small and Medium Enterprises
1016 Budapest
Krisztina krt. 99.
Tel: (1) 156-8281
Fax: (1) 175-0401

Hungarian Chamber of Customs Agents
c/o METCOSPED Kft.
1393 Budapest 62
POB 330
Tel: (1) 142-8306
Fax: (1) 142-8908

Hungarian Chamber of Real-Estate Dealers
1052 Budapest
POB 688
Tel/Fax: (1) 118-9857
Tel: (1) 266-2076

Hungexpo Publicity Co Ltd
1441 Budapest
POB 44
Tel: (1) 157-3555
Telex: 22-4188
Fax: (1) 183-6502

Joint Venture Association
1012 Budapest
Kuny D. u. 13-15.
Tel: (1) 156-0040
Fax: (1) 156-0728

Konsumex
1446 Budapest
Hungaria krt 162
Tel: (1) 153-0511
Telex: 22-5151
Fax: (1) 141-4747

National Association of Building Contractors
1012 Budapest
Kuny D. u. 13-15, 2nd floor
Tel: (1) 155-8203

National Association of Packaging and Material Handling
1085 Budapest
Rigo u. 3. 1st floor
Tel: (1) 113-7460
Fax: (1) 113-8170

American Chamber of Commerce in Hungary
1068 Budapest
Dozsa Gyorgy ut 84/A, Room 405
Tel: (1) 269-6016
Fax: (1) 122-8890

Hungarian Chamber of Commerce
1055 Budapest
Kossuth Lajos tér 6-8
Tel: (1) 153-0835, 153-3333
Fax: (1) 153-1285

Licencia
1368 Budapest
POB 207
Tel: (1) 118-1111
Fax: (1) 138-2304
Telex: 22-5872

Lignitrade Co Ltd
1393 Budapest
POB 323
Tel: (1) 112-9850
Fax: (1) 132-2181
Telex: 22-4251

Masped Hungarian General Forwarding Co Ltd
1052 Budapest
Kristof ter 2
Tel: (1) 118-2922
Fax: (1) 118-8343
Telex: 22-4471

Monimpex Trading House
1392 Budapest
POB 268
Tel: (1) 153-1222
Fax: (1) 112-1072
Telex: 22-53771

Pharmatrade Hungarian Trading Co
1367 Budapest
POB 126
Tel: (1) 118-5966
Telex: 22-6650
Fax: (1) 118-5346

Tannimpex
1395 Budapest
POB 406
Tel (1) 112-3400
Telex: 22-4557
Fax: (1) 153-2170

BANKS

Budapest Bank
1054 Budapest
Honved utca 10
Tel: (1) 269-2397, 269-2358
Fax: (1) 269-2400

National Bank of Hungary
1850 Budapest
Szabadság tér 8-9
Tel: (1) 153-2600
Fax: (1) 153-0288

CONSULTING FIRMS

Ernst & Young Ltd
1146 Budapest
Hermina ut 17.
Tel: (1) 252-8333, 252-8231
Fax: (1) 251-8778

Price Waterhouse
1075 Budapest
Rumbach S. u. 21.
Tel: (1) 269-6910
Fax: (1) 269-69

NEWSPAPERS

Daily News
1016 Budapest
Naphegy tér 8
Tel: (1) 175-6928
Fax: (1) 118-8384

Esti Hirlap (Evening Journal)
1962 Budapest
Blaha Lujza tér 3
Tel: (1) 138-2399
Fax: (1) 138-4550

Magyar Hirlap (Hungarian Journal)
1087 Budapest
Kerepesi út 29b
Tel: (1) 134-3330
Telex: 22-4268

Magyar Nemzet (Hungarian Nation)
1073 Budapest
Erzsébet krt 9-11
Tel: (1) 141-4320
Telex: 22-4269

Mai Nap (Today)
1087 Budapest
Könyves Kálmán Bldg. 76
Tel: (1) 113-0284
Fax: (1) 133-9153

NAPI Gazdaság (World Economy)
1034 Budapest
Bécsi út 126-128
Tel: (1) 168-2002
Fax: (1) 188-9504

BUSINESS PERIODICALS

Business Partner Hungary (Quarterly)
1051 Budapest
Dorottya u. 6
Tel: (1) 117-0850
Fax: (1) 118-6483

Tózsde Kurir (Hungarian Stock Market Courier)
(Weekly)
1074 Budapest
Rákóczi út 54
Tel: (1) 122-3273
Fax: (1) 142-8356

RADI O & TELEVISION

Magyar Radio
1800 Budapest
Brody Sandor u. 5-7
Tel: (1) 138-8388
Fax: (1) 138-7004

Magyar Televizio
1810 Budapest
Szabadsag ter. 17
Tel: (1) 153-3200
Fax: (1) 153-4568

LEGAL CONTACTS

Baker & McKenzie
1062 Budapest
Andrassy-Ut 125
Tel: (1) 251-5777
Fax: (1) 342-0513

Eorsi and Partners
1056 Budapest
Belgrad Rakpart 13-15
Tel: (1) 266-5570
Fax: (1) 266-1444

McDowell, Rice & Smith
1027 Budapest
Kapas Utca 11-15
Tel: (1) 361-202-6044
Fax: (1) 361-202-6790

Nagy Es Trocsanyi
1012 Budapest
Palya Utca 9
Tel: (1) 1-212-0444
Fax: (1) 1-212-0443

AD AGENCIES

Magyar Media Advertising Agency
1392 Budapest
POB 279
Tel: (1) 141-4749
Telex: 22-3040

HUNGOEXPO Advertising Agency Co Ltd
1425 Budaapest
POB 801
Tel: (1) 1225-008
Telex: 22-4525
Fax: (1) 122-1021

McCann-Erickson Budapest
1068 Budapest
Benczur utca 29
Tel: (1) 322-5258
Fax: (1) 322-4077

Saatchi & Saatchi Advertising
1022 Budapest
Alvinci ut. 16
Tel: (1) 212-4039
Fax: (1) 212-5506

Topreklam/BBDO
1204 Budapest
Torok Floris u. 72
Tel: (1) 283-0313
Fax: (1) 283-0626

Young & Rubicam Hungary
1055 Budapest
Falk Miksa U.B.
Tel: (1) 112-3229
Fax: (1) 131-5345

INTERNET ADDRESSES

Usenet group
soc.culture.magyar

Hungarian Homepage
http://www.fsz.bme.hu/hungary/homepage.html

Hungarian Prime Ministers Homepage
http://www.meh.hu/

Hungary Online Directory
http://www.hungary.com/hudir/

Iceland

Republic of Iceland

Economy

Overview

Although basically capitalistic, Iceland's economy follows the Scandinavian model and supports an extensive welfare system. The fishing industry has historically dominated the country's economy, and Iceland produces very few other items for trading purposes. The worldwide recession of the early 1990s led to falling international commodities prices, and its effects have continued to plague Iceland which has experienced major disruptions in its economy, as well as the highest unemployment levels since World War II. The government is currently working to return the economy to its former growth. Some of its goals include: reducing the budget and current account deficits, limiting foreign borrowing, and containing inflation. Inflation, a serious problem a few years ago, has been largely tamed, falling to only 3.7 percent in recent years.

Trade

Iceland is heavily dependent on imports of virtually all capital and consumer goods, and raw and intermediate materials. The island's main export is seafood products—which account for about 80 percent of export revenues and foreign exchange—followed by aluminum, ferro-silicates, and dairy products, all of which are relatively insignificant contributors. Imports include machinery and transportation equipment, chemicals, fuels, foodstuffs, basic manufactures—including consumer goods—and industrial raw materials. Iceland's main trading partners include the UK, the US, Germany, Japan, France, and Denmark. Located between North America and Europe, Iceland is used largely as an intermediate stopover port for traders from other countries.

Sectors

Agriculture This sector—dominated by the important but relatively small fishing industry—contributes about 12 percent of GDP and employs somewhat less than 20 percent of the work force. In addition to fish products, dairy, stock-raising, and root crops are the main activities in terms of cash value.

Industry Employing fewer than 20 percent of the work force, industry provides less than 33 percent of GDP. Most industrial activity centers around fish processing. Other main industries include aluminum smelting and production of ferrosilicon, diatomite, fertilizers, and geothermal power. Dependence on largely low-value-added commodity products has made the economy vulnerable to fluctuations in world markets.

Services The service sector employs about 60 percent of the work force and accounts for about the same proportion of GDP. The sector primarily involves local distribution and personal service activities.

Trends

Iceland's reliance on fishing has resulted in prolonged economic problems as world competition in the industry rose while overall demand for the country's specific products fell. In order to make itself more attractive to foreign interests, Iceland needs to reduce its government intervention, expand its industrial base, and improve its transportation infrastructure. Attempts are being made to attract foreign investment to set up high-value-added processing facilities to take advantage of Iceland's highly educated work force. However, its relative isolation and high cost structure have so far hampered much development in the area.

At a Glance

THE COUNTRY

Location Nordic State, northern Europe, in the North Atlantic Ocean, between Greenland and Norway.
Terrain Mostly plateau interspersed with mountain peaks, icefields; coast deeply indented by bays and fiords.
Climate Temperate; moderated by North Atlantic Current; mild, windy winters; damp, cool summers.

THE PEOPLE

Population 264,000
Ethnic composition Homogeneous mixture of descendants of Norwegians and Celts.
Religious composition
Evangelical Lutheran 93%
Other Lutheran denominations 3.7%
Roman Catholic 1%
Languages spoken Icelandic.
Education and literacy 100% of the people over 15 can read and write. Tuition to universities is free; only nominal registration and examination fees must be paid.
Labor force
Total:...127,900
By occupation: commerce, transportation, and services 60%, manufacturing 12.5%, fishing and fish processing 11.8%, construction 10.8%, agriculture 4.0%.

COUNTRY FACTS

Political and legal Republic, headed by a president and a unicameral legislature. Legal system: civil law system based on Danish law; the Supreme Court is the highest legal body. Iceland does not accept compulsory International Court of Justice jurisdiction.
Telephone There are almost 125,000 telephones. Radio and radiotelephone communications are maintained with Europe and America. All telephone and telegraph systems are publicly owned and administered, with adequate domestic services. International country code: [354]. City codes are no longer in use.
Transportation The lack of waterways and railways hamper services. Most roads are in poor condition, and few are paved. Domestic and international air service is good.
Environment Only one percent of the land is arable. The country is frequently subject to earthquakes and volcanic activity. Current issues are water pollution from fertilizer runoff and inadequate wastewater treatment.
Media Three daily newspapers are published in Reykjavík and distributed throughout the country; they are: *Morgunblaoid, Timinn,* and *Pjóoviljinn.* They are predominantly progressive publications. Nondaily newspapers are published throughout the country. Various popular and scholarly periodicals are published in Reykjavík. Iceland radio broadcasts primarily in FM, and two television stations broadcast seven days a week.
Health The Director of Public Health is responsible for all health matters. The threat of tuberculosis, once a major problem, has been virtually eliminated. Life expectancy of males is 76 years; of females, 80 years.

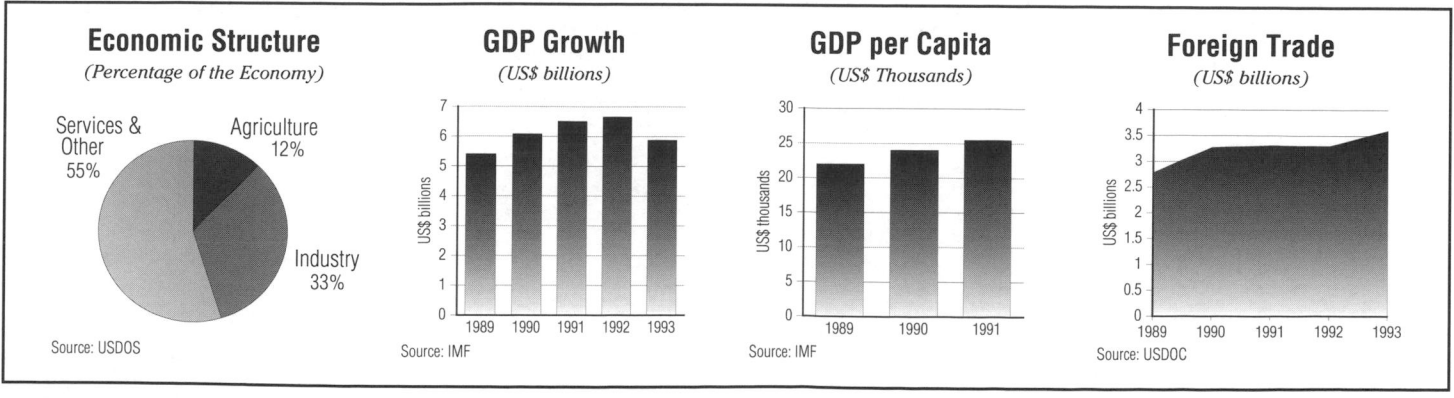

Economic Structure
(Percentage of the Economy)
Services & Other 55%
Agriculture 12%
Industry 33%
Source: USDOS

GDP Growth
(US$ billions)
1989 1990 1991 1992 1993
Source: IMF

GDP per Capita
(US$ Thousands)
1989 1990 1991
Source: IMF

Foreign Trade
(US$ billions)
1989 1990 1991 1992 1993
Source: USDOC

Business Travel

	LH 1906	MADRID	935	113-3
	LH 1022	STUTTGART HBF.	935	-
	AF 1701	LYON	940	683-6
	AY 822	HELSINKI	940	113-3
	AA 071	SFRANCISCO-DALLAS	945	731-7

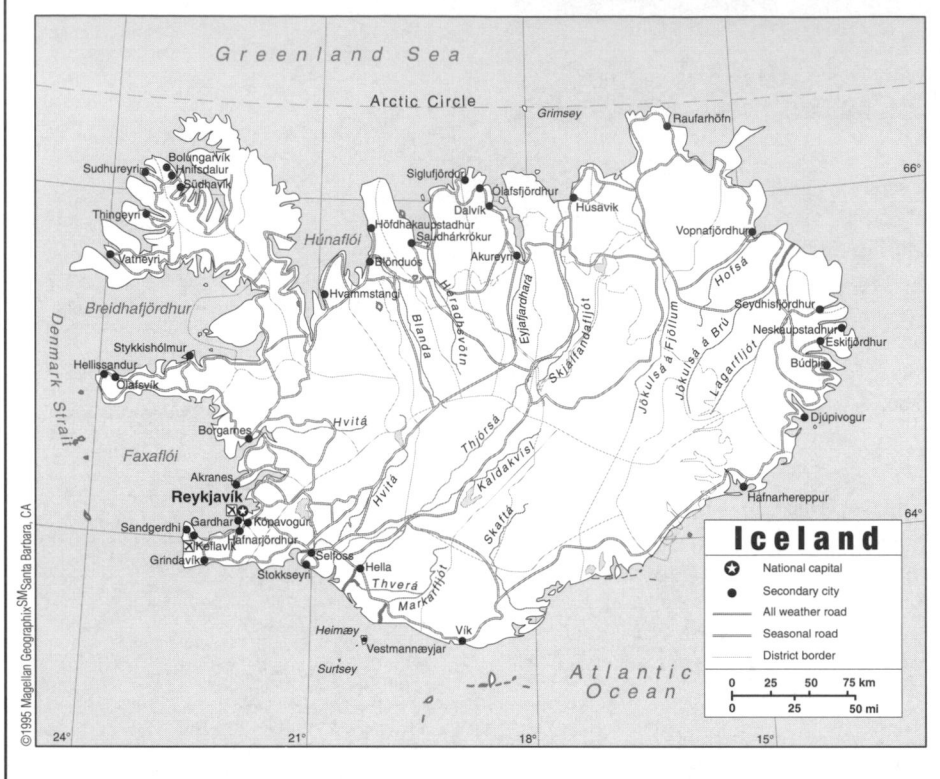

COMMUNICATIONS

Telephones Phone service operates 24 hours a day. Direct dial for domestic and international connections are available and are usually reliable.

Fax Telex and fax services are available at larger hotels and the main telephone headquarters in Austurvoll Square in Reykjavík. For urgent correspondence, telex is recommended.

Post office The postal service sends all letters and printed literature by airmail. Packages intended for airmail must be marked with airmail labels.

BEST TRAVEL BOOKS

Iceland, Greenland & the Faroe Islands Travel Survival Kit, Lonely Planet. Offers more practical advice than I thought possible... 642 pages.

Do's and Taboo's Around the World. The Bestselling Guide to International Behavior. 3rd edition. Edited by Roger Axtell, compiled by the Parker Pen Company. The ultimate guide to international behavior, now completely updated and expanded. Helpful, fun to read!

Berlitz Business Travel Guide, Europe. Concise economic details, successful trip planning, background information on people and cities, useful facts and addresses.

Essential Iceland. All sights to visit with star ratings, superb maps, shopping locations, nightlife, and tips on how to save money in Iceland.

Iceland. Insight Guides.

USEFUL TELEPHONE NUMBERS

If you are calling from outside Iceland you will need to add the country code [354] and any other international dialing requirements from within your country.

- Emergencies 112
- Operator 08
- Telegrams day 06
- Telegrams night 5516411
- US Embassy/Reykjavík............................. 5629100
- Ambulance 5511100
- Dentist 5522411
- Doctor 5686811
- Pharmacy 5518888
- Police 5511166
- Travel Guides Association 5888670
- Iceland Air 5690200
- Bus Terminal, Reykjavík 5876000
- Avis 5624433
- Hertz.. 5690500
- Hotel and Restaurant Association 5527410

Credit Card Information

Lost or stolen credit cards (call collect to the US, regardless of which country the card was issued in).

- Amex ....[1] (919) 333-3211
- Diner's Club................................[1] (303) 799-1504
- MasterCard ....[1] (314) 275-6690
- Visa ....[1] (410) 581-7931

Travelogue

WORKWEEK

Offices Monday-Friday 9:00 am to noon,1:00 pm to 5:00 pm.

Banks Monday-Friday 9:15 am to 4:00 pm, Thursday 5:00 pm to 6:00 pm.

Government Monday-Friday 9:00 am to noon, 1:00 pm to 5:00 pm.

Retail Monday-Thursday 9:00 am to 6:00 pm, Friday 9:00 am to 10:00 pm, Saturday 9:00 am to 4:00 pm.

HOLIDAYS

Holidays 1996
January 1 New Year's Day
April 4 Maundy Thursday*
April 5 Good Friday*
April 8 Easter Monday*
April 21 First day of summer*
May 16 Ascension Day*
May 26 Whit Monday*
June 17 Icelandic National Day
August 5 Bank Holiday
December 25 Christmas
December 26 Boxing Day
*Dates vary every year.

VISA AND PASSPORT

Passports are required. For stays less than 90 days, visas are not required for visitors from most countries. For any stay exceeding 90 days, a business or tourist visa is required. The time period for a traveler's stay begins when entering any Nordic area.

DEPARTURE FORMALITIES

A departure tax will be collected when leaving from the Keflavík airport. To avoid delays, pay the exit tax at the time you reserve your airline ticket.

IMMUNIZATION

No vaccinations are required unless you are arriving from an infected area.

TIPPING

Tipping is not customary and not expected. Service is included in restaurant prices.

CRIME

The crime rate is very low in Iceland, though pickpockets and purse snatchings do occur. Downtown Reykjavík can become disorderly on weekend evenings and should be avoided. Driving under the influence of alcohol is considered a serious crime and penalties are severe.

INFRASTRUCTURE

The International airport is located at Keflavik, near Reykjavik. Iceland Air offers domestic flights to all parts of the country and flights to Heathrow and Glasgow. Small aircraft are available for charter. For transportation from the airport to Reykjavík, the airporter bus is recommended. Taxis are available in all towns but much more expensive than the bus service. One ferry does operate between Britain and Iceland and provides a weekly car ferry service during the summer between Lerwick, Seydisfjordur, and Thorshavn. Roads connect the urban areas but are generally unpaved. In winter months, some routes are impassable. There is no train system in Iceland.

NATIONAL TOURIST OFFICE

Iceland Tourist Board
Laekjargata 3
Gimli
101 Reykjavik
Tel: 5527488
Fax: 5624749

Foreign Trade

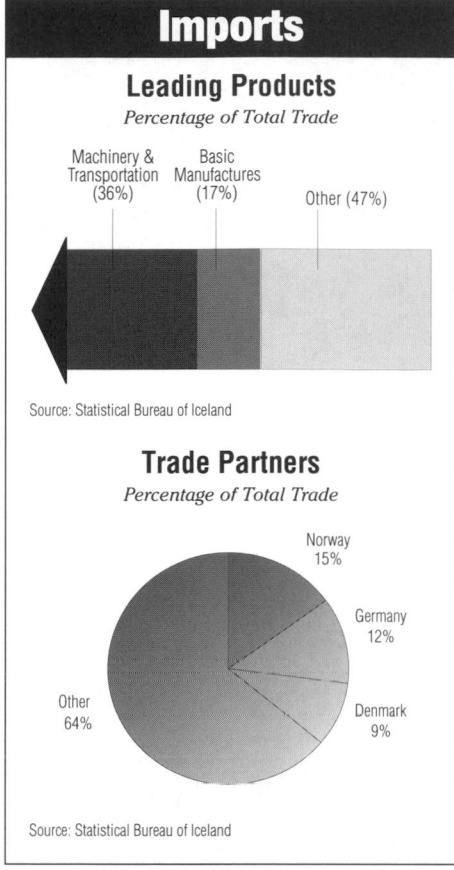

Imports

Leading Products
Percentage of Total Trade

Machinery & Transportation (36%)
Basic Manufactures (17%)
Other (47%)

Source: Statistical Bureau of Iceland

Trade Partners
Percentage of Total Trade

Norway 15%
Germany 12%
Denmark 9%
Other 64%

Source: Statistical Bureau of Iceland

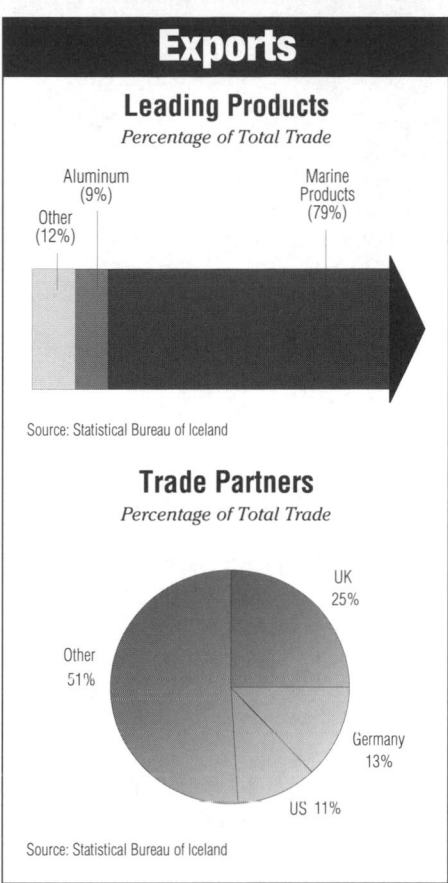

Exports

Leading Products
Percentage of Total Trade

Aluminum (9%)
Other (12%)
Marine Products (79%)

Source: Statistical Bureau of Iceland

Trade Partners
Percentage of Total Trade

UK 25%
Other 51%
Germany 13%
US 11%

Source: Statistical Bureau of Iceland

Opportunities

FOR IMPORTING TO ICELAND
- automobiles and automobile parts
- clothing, food, paper, and paper products
- machinery and transportation equipment

FOR EXPORTING FROM ICELAND
- aluminum, diatomite, ferrosilicon
- fish: cod, flounder, haddock, lobster, perch, salmon
- iron and steel

GROWTH SECTORS
- fish processing
- geothermal energy production

Trade News

RULES AND REGULATIONS
- **Import license** Most imports are free except live animals and certain agricultural products.
- **Trade arrangements** Fertilizers, tobacco, and alcoholic beverages are admitted only under state trading arrangements.
- **Periodic import control** Some fresh vegetables, potatoes, and flowers are subject to import controls.
- **Foreign exchange permits** Foreign exchange permits are required for goods not requiring licenses before shipment from abroad. The permit must be shown to domestic banks to obtain foreign exchange.
- **Special import tax** A special import tax is applied to automobiles, buses, heavy trucks, ambulances, and public services. The fees are based on the weight of the vehicle and engine capacity.

Legal

Legal System
Iceland's legal system is administered and controlled by the Supreme Court. The courts are free from political control.

Intellectual Property Protection
Patents and Trademarks Patents are valid for 15 years, but must be made open to licensing. Most foreign patents are recognized in Iceland.

Copyrights Iceland's copyright protections are very similar to those of other Nordic countries. The Copyright Statute of 1972 provides copyright protection for 50 years after the death of the author.

Trade Secrets There are no laws specifically directed to the protection of trade secrets. The courts can uphold prior agreements between parties, however, thereby offering some protection to trade secrets.

Business Registration
To register in Iceland, a company must file copies of its bylaws, articles of incorporation or Memorandum of Association, and copies of state or national charter. In addition, a notarized document attesting to the proper legal standing and existence of the company in its home country must be submitted to the Limited Liabilities Registration Office.

Contracts and Dispute Resolution
Contracts are generally detailed, and used to define the terms of the business relationship, rather than as mere guidelines thereto. Parties may choose the laws they will agree to follow and are free to decide the venue for conflict mediation. Arbitration is available, though it is not yet widely used.

Labor
Workers have the right to join unions and to bargain collectively. Labor disputes are settled by direct negotiations or by special courts.

Legal Matters

LEGAL BRIEFS
- **Company accounts** Copies of company accounts must be submitted to the Registrar within 90 days after the end of the fiscal year.
- **Power of attorney** Power of attorney must be executed in favor of the representative the company is required to appoint for purposes of conducting business in Iceland.
- **Agents and distributors** The legal difference between agents and distributors under Icelandic law is that the agent acts in the name of the principal while the distributor acts on his own accord and buys goods for resale from the principal.
- **Special courts** There are special courts for maritime cases, labor disputes, and other types of cases.
- **LLCs** The Limited Liability Company (LLC) is the most common organization for foreign businesses and investors. Foreign LLCs must be registered with the Limited Liabilities Registration Office in Iceland if the corporation has been legally formed and has obtained the appropriate licenses from its home country.
- **Unemployment** Unemployment is very low by international standards, averaging less than two percent in 1991.

LEGAL CONTACTS
Adalsteinsson & Partners
Borgartun 24
P.O. Box 399
121 Reykjavik
Tel: 562-76-11 Fax: 562-71-86

Logmannastofan
Armula 26
108 Reykjavik
Tel: 5658122 Fax: 5686503

Law Office of Gudjon Styrakarsson
Adalstreet 9, 101 Reykjavik
Tel: 5518354 Fax: 5628370

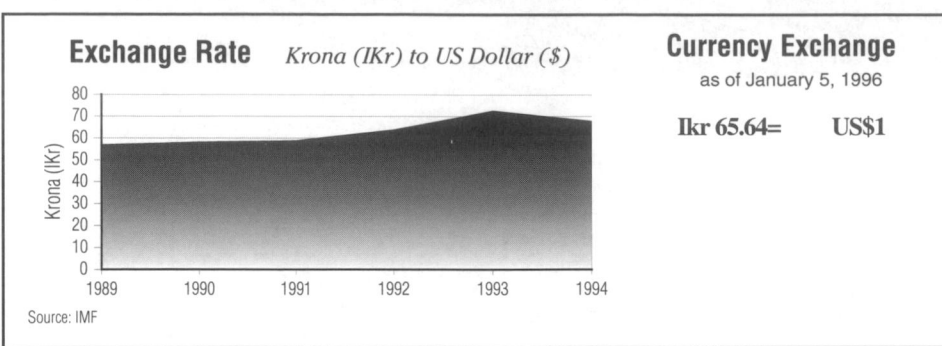

Exchange Rate *Krona (IKr) to US Dollar ($)*

Krona (IKr): 80, 70, 60, 50, 40, 30, 20, 10, 0
1989 1990 1991 1992 1993 1994

Source: IMF

Currency Exchange

as of January 5, 1996

Ikr 65.64=   US$1

Currency

The currency in use is the Icelandic krona (Ikr).

Foreign Exchange

Proceeds from sales of investments and profits may be freely transferred. Foreign exchange transactions and capital movements are free of restrictions, unless explicitly prohibited by the foreign exchange act enacted November 17, 1992. There are no limits on foreign exchange for travel abroad, and no limits on outward investments. The tax on bank fees for transfers of foreign currency was abolished effective January 1996. The external value of the krona is pegged to a currency basket of the Japanese yen, US dollar, and European currency unit. The daily rate is set by the interbank foreign exchange market. The market is comprised of the Central Bank, the three commercial banks, and Icebank (the savings banks' loan institution). Banks may carry out exchange transactions between themselves and may engage in arbitrage in the foreign exchange market.

Capital Transfers

Nonresidents may acquire Icelandic securities without restriction and may transfer abroad the interest and any proceeds from the sale of said securities. Nonresidents may open krona accounts in domestic banks and may freely transfer balances abroad. Nonresidents may also open foreign currency accounts. Residents with legitimately acquired foreign exchange may maintain accounts with nonresident institutions. Residents and nonresident travelers may bring in or take out Icelandic bank notes in any amount, so long as it has been legally acquired.

Investment Incentives

Foreign investment in Iceland has been minimal, but the government is creating some incentives to lure investment. The new regulations will be phased in over the next few years. There are no specific incentives or guidelines for foreign investment.

Investment Restrictions

The majority of the founders of a company must have had residency in Iceland for the past two years. The new regulations to attract foreign investment will not apply to the fishing industry.

TAXATION

Taxation requires sophisticated knowledge of complex rules and regulations specific to each country. For more detailed information, we suggest you refer to the Ernst & Young Corporate Tax Guide and Directory, available from the Ernst & Young accounting office in your country, or from:

Endurskodun & Radgjöf HF
Ernst & Young International
Skeifan 11 A
POB 8693
108 Reykjavík, Iceland
Tel: 568-55-11
Fax: 568-95-85

At a Glance

Corporate Income Tax Rate (%)(a)	33
Capital Gains Tax Rate (%)(b)	33
Branch Tax Rate (%)	33
Withholding Tax (%)	
Dividends (c)	27
Interest	0
Royalties from Patents, Know-how, etc., and Lease and Rent Payments (d)	33/40
Branch Remittance Tax	33
Net Operating Losses (Years)	
Carryback	0
Carryforward	5

(a) Special tax deductions are allowed. Corporations may deduct dividends distributed throughout the year, to a maximum of 10% of the shares' stated value. Corporations may also deduct 5% of accounts receivable.
(b) Capital gains is taxed as ordinary income.
(c) This rate is applicable to payments to nonresidents.
(d) The 33% rate applies to payments to nonresident corporations; the 40% rate applies to payments to nonresident individuals.

Money Matters

BITS AND PIECES

- **Joint stock companies** The majority of founders of a joint stock company must reside in Iceland one year prior to establishing company.
- **Credit** Residents may obtain long-term credits for general financing, and may provide long-term credit to nonresidents.
- **Investments** Nonresidents may invest in most industries, but must first notify the Central Bank. Portfolio investments in long-term securities are not restricted. Residents trading in foreign securities must do so through a licensed broker. Foreign securities may be invested in up to Ikr 1 million for resident individuals, and up to Ikr 175 million for resident mutual funds. Investments in short-term domestic securities by nonresidents may be made up to Ikr 75 million.
- **Real estate** For joint stock companies to own real estate, they must be registered in Iceland, at least 80 percent must be owned by Icelandic citizens, and all of the members of the board of directors must be Icelandic citizens or have resided in Iceland for at least five years. Icelandic citizens must control the majority of the voting power at annual meetings. The same conditions apply if real estate is to be leased for more than three years or if the lease agreement cannot be terminated with less than one year's notice.
- **Gold** A commemorative gold coin with a face value of Ikr100 is legal tender but does not circulate. Residents may hold and acquire gold in Iceland.
- **Debts** Considering the amount of business done, bad debts are few, and are fairly easily collected through the judicial process.
- **Automobile tax** A special car tax of between 16 percent and 66 percent is levied on certain motor vehicles. Motorcycles carry a 70 percent tax, and public service vehicles are taxed at 30 percent.
- **Equalization tax** An equalization tax of five percent of the CIF value is levied on many goods imported from all sources, if the import duty has been reduced or removed under the terms of the Iceland/EFTA/EU agreements.

BANKS

Búnadarbanki Íslands
Agricultural Bank of Iceland
Austurstraeti 5
155 Reykjavík
Tel: 5525600
Fax: 5621340

Central Bank of Iceland
Kalkofnsuegi 1
150 Reykjavík
Tel: 5699600
Fax: 5621802

Icebank Ltd.
Lzeanastofnun sparisjódanna hf
Raudarárstígur 27
105 Reykjavík
Tel/Fax: 5623400

Íslandsbanki hg
Kringlunni 7
155 Reykjavík
Tel: 5681175
Fax: 5687784

Landsbanki Íslands
National Bank of Iceland
Austurstraeti 11
101 Reykjavík
Tel: 5606600
Fax: 5529882

Overview

Iceland's population is accustomed to prosperity, generous welfare programs, and evenly distributed income; these attitudes make them avid customers for a wide range of high-tech consumer goods, apparel, and telecommunications equipment—particularly cellular car phones, and automobiles, parts, and accessories. Businesses should be transacted through established representatives in Iceland, rather than merely using agents in Europe.

Distribution

Over half the country's population lives in the capital city, Reykjavík. Consumer goods are distributed most efficiently through an importer who maintains his own inventory. Commission agents handle industrial goods. Exporters should supply their agents with literature, samples, and other promotional materials. Large orders, rare in this small market, should be backed up by a company representative. Generally, a single agent can cover the entire country. Payments are usually salary, commission, or a combination. There are more than 300 wholesalers and importers in Iceland, most of whom belong to business associations based in Reykjavík.

Advertising

There are no billboards except for those in sports stadiums and little outdoor advertising of any kind. Wine and alcohol, pharmaceuticals and medicines, margarine, and tobacco products cannot be advertised at all. Many Icelandic advertising firms are small and do not have the resources necessary to cover the whole country. It is essential for foreign sellers to give their agents as much advice and assistance as possible in advertising and trade promotion. The small population makes word-of-mouth advertising particularly important. Short television films are effective and relatively cheap. Commercial radio and television stations recently started accepting advertising, and most programs reach about 90 percent of the total population.

Marketing in Iceland

MARKETING TIPS

- **Mailing** Direct mail is used, but not extensively. The agent's advice should be sought for issues including the form of approach and mailing lists.
- **Cinemas** There are 12 cinemas in Iceland, with a total seating capacity of about 8,000. Six of them are in Reykjavík and the surrounding district, and few accept advertising.
- **Foreign publications** Some foreign newspapers, magazines, and periodicals are on sale at book shops, often on the day after publication.
- **Trade organizations** Several Icelandic trade organizations exist, helping exporters, importers, and domestic businesses.

AD AGENCY

YDDA Advertising Agency
Grjotagata 7
PO Box 927
121 Reykjavík
Tel: 5622992
Fax: 5517829

NEWSPAPERS

DV-Dagbladid-Visir
Thverholt 11
PO Box 5380
Reykjavik
Tel: 5527022
Fax: 5527079

Morgunbladid
(Morning News)
Adalstraeti 6
PO Box 1555
Reykjavik
Tel: 5691100
Fax: 5691181

Business Culture

Greetings and Courtesies

In Iceland, only first names are used while Mr. and Mrs. are deemed honorific titles to address someone of rank, such as the nation's president or bishop. You are welcome to introduce yourself using Mr. *(Herra)*, Mrs. *(Fru)* and Miss *(Froken),* and Icelanders will honor that courtesy title, for they enjoy making foreigners feel comfortable. When being introduced to either men or women, a handshake and a pleasant greeting is the standard greeting. Gifts that represent your company or country are considered thoughtful. Things are very expensive in Iceland and even the smallest gift is well-received. You will never insult an Icelander with a bottle of Scotch or a fine liquor.

Business Ethic and Framework

Icelanders like to combine business and pleasure, and the business environment is relatively informal. Third-party introductions aren't necessary, and you are welcome to make "drop in" calls. It will be to your advantage, however, to phone ahead and make sure the person you wish to see is in. A scheduled appointment is a good idea.

Meetings and Decision Making

Business meetings are not formal. However, your Icelandic colleagues appreciate getting straight down to business. Icelanders are friendly and receptive during meetings and exercise reserve when making presentations. They will appreciate your preparedness. Because Icelandic corporations are small, you'll likely be in the company of an authorized decision maker.

Women

The fact that Iceland has had the first woman president in the world tells the visitor much about women's contribution to the Icelandic business culture. Women are included in practically every aspect of commerce in the country and have, for centuries, worked along side the men to develop their land and business communities.

Cultural Cautions

DO'S

- Be prepared with good walking shoes and pack your swimsuit. Icelanders are avid walkers and enjoy year-round swimming in the many warm natural springs.
- As a dinner guest, it is appropriate to bring a basket of cheese to the hostess and send flowers in appreciation the day following your visit.

DON'TS

- Don't stand too close to another person. Keep your distance, and wait for them to react by stepping in closer.

OBSERVATIONS

- Icelanders are among the most literate and informed people in the world. Though identified as Europeans, they feel removed from the continent and a bit separated from their Scandinavian neighbors. Be sensitive to the pride they take in their own Icelandic culture.
- Following introductions in meetings, business cards will be exchanged. Cards in English need not be translated.
- In meetings, be thorough in your programs and proposals, and decisions may be rendered with relative ease.
- Icelanders are fashion conscious and casual attire will never mean jeans. Dark suits are worn in banking circles; jackets and ties are the business norm. Women should dress conservatively in light woolens of natural colors, avoiding too much make-up.

NEGOTIATIONS

- Discussions might focus on making certain concessions, but haggling is not an Icelandic business practice. After you have given a price, you should not deviate from it too much.

GOVERNMENT AGENCIES

Ministry of Agriculture
Raudararstig 25
150 Reykjavik
Tel: 5560300
Fax: 5521160

Ministry of Commerce
Arnarhváli
v/Lindargötu
150 Reykjavík
Tel: 5609070
Fax: 5621289

Ministry of Communications
Hafnarhúsinu
v/Tryggvagötu
150 Reykjavík
Tel: 5621700
Fax: 5621702

Ministry of Education and Culture
Huerfisgötu
6150 Reykjavík
Tel: 52500

Ministry of the Environment
Sölvkólsgötu 4
150 Reykjavík
Tel: 5609600
Fax: 5624566

Ministry of Finance
Arnarhváli
v/Lindargötu
150 Reykjavík
Tel: 5609200
Fax: 5528280

Ministry of Fisheries
Sölvkólsgötu 4
150 Reykjavík
Tel: 5609670
Fax: 5621853

Ministry for Foreign Affairs
Hverfisgätu 115
150 Reykjavík
Tel: 5623000
Telex: 2225

Ministry of Health and Social Security
Laugavegi 116
105 Lindargötu
150 Reykjavík
Tel: 5609000
Fax: 5519165

Ministry of Industries and Energy
Arnarhváli
v/Lindargötu
150 Reykjavík
Tel: 5525000

Ministry of Social Affairs
Hafnarsúsinu vid Tryggvagötu
150 Reykjavík
Tel: 5525000
Telex: 3000

National Energy Authority
Grensásvegi 9
108 Reykjavík
Tel: 583600

National Power Company
Háleitisbraut 68
101 Reykjavík
Tel: 5686400

TRADE AND BUSINESS ORGANIZATIONS

Iceland Chamber of Commerce
Húsverslunarinnar
103 Reykjavik
Tel: 5676666
Fax: 5686564

Industrial Development Fund
Kalkofnsvegur 1
150 Reykjaviík
Tel: 5699990
Fax: 5629992

Trade Council of Iceland
POB 8020
128 Reykjavík
Tel: 5517-272
Fax: 5517-222

Union of Icelandic Fish Producers
Adalstraeti 6
P Box 835
121 Reykjavík
Tel: 5511480
Fax: 5623623

PERIODICALS

Economic Statistics
Central Bank of Iceland
Kalkofnsvegur 1
150 Reykjavík
Tel: 5699600
Fax: 5621802

Frjáls verzlun
Free Trade
Ármúla 18
108 Reykjavík
Tel: 5812300
Fax: 5689982

Islendingur-Isafold Icelander-Icecountry
Kaupangi v/Myrarveg
600 Akureyri
Tel: 5521500

ABC
Armula 18
108 Reykjavík
Tel: 5812300
Fax: 5689982

Atlantica
Hofdabakki 9
POB 8576
112 Reykjavík
Tel: 5675700
Fax: 5674066

Billinn
Bildshoefda 18
112 Reykjavík
Tel: 5685830
Fax: 5689982

Eidfaxi
Armula 38
108 Reykjavík
Tel: 5685316
Fax: 5686318

Farvis-Afangar Travelwise
Bolholti 4
105 Reykjavík
Tel: 5680699
Fax: 576390

Gestgjafinn
Arumula 18
108 Reykjavík
Tel: 519200
Fax: 5623058

Hagtidindi
Statistical Bureau of Iceland
Skuggasund 3
150 Reykjavík
Tel: 55609800
Fax: 5628865

Hagtolur Manadarins
Kalkofnsvegur 1
150 Reykjavík
Tel: 5699600

Hus og Hibyli
Armula 20-22
Reykjavík
Tel: 5813122

Iceland Review
Hofdabakki 9
POB 8576
112 Reykjavík
Tel: 5675700
Fax: 5674066

News from Iceland
Hofdabakki 9
POB 8576
112 Reykjavík
Tel: 5675700

Mannlif
Armula 18
108 Reykjavík
Tel: 5812300
Fax: 5689982

Samuel
Armula 20-22
105 Reykjavík
Tel: 5813122
Fax: 5680102

Urval
Thverholti 11
Reykjavik
Tel: 5527022

RADIO & TELEVISION

Radio Bylgjan
Snorrabraut 54
105 Reykjavík

Ríkisútvarpid
Icelandic National Broadcasting Service
Radio Division
Efstaleiti 1
150 Reykjavík
Tel: 5693000 Fax: 5693010

Ríkisútvarpid-Sjónvarp
Icelandic National Broadcasting Service-Television
Laugavegur 176
105 Reykjavík
Tel: 5693900 Fax: 5693988

NEWSPAPERS

Althydubladid The Labor Journal
Armuli 36
Reykjavik
Tel: 55681866
Fax: 5582019

Dagur The Day
Strnadgata 31
POB 58
600 Akurieyri
Tel: (6) 5524222

Timinn The Times
Lynghalsi 9
Box 370
Reykjavík
Tel: 5686300

INTERNET ADDRESSES

Usenet group
soc.culture.nordic

Icelandic Business Web
http://www.mmedia.is/ibw/

Icelandic Embassy in Washington, DC
http://www.icelandemb.nw.dc.us/web/iceland/index.html

Islania - A Guide to Iceland
http://rvik.ismennt.is/~gummih/islandia.html

Icelandic Webpages (alphabetical)
http://iceweb.ismennt.is/inn/stafr_uk.html

Trade Council of Iceland
http://www.arctic.is/FedAndOrg/BisFed/Trade/Trade.html

The Iceland Connection
http://www.arctic.is/

India

Republic of India

Economy

Overview

In 1991 the Indian economy was near default, the result of high inflation, deficit spending, and the fall of the USSR, a crucial Indian market. Protectionist policies and a nationalistic state-planning system assured the survival of firms producing low-quality goods at high prices. Recent policy changes, including devaluation of the rupee, reduction of import duties, and efforts to adjust traditional approaches to commerce to operate more in tune with international business norms, have helped to stabilize the situation. Foreign capital has begun to return, lured by liberalized trade policies replacing strict government controls. The energy, transportation, financial services, and telecommunications sectors are specifically targeted for development. The Indian economy is evolving into a hybrid with both central planning and slow, yet steady movement toward open markets. Disturbing instances of nationalism, anti-foreign bias, and the failure of due process protections have recurred of late, however.

Trade

India's attempts to liberalize investment and trade began paying dividends, although significant barriers remain. India's principle exports include gems and jewelry, apparel, engineering products, leather goods, chemicals, and cotton fabric. Imports include fuels, machinery, gems and jewelry, iron and steel, and electrical machinery. The US is India's largest trading partner, followed by the countries of the former USSR, Japan, Germany, and the UK, although trade is growing with other European, Asian, and Middle Eastern countries.

Sectors

Agriculture India remains largely agrarian, with agriculture producing about 32 percent of GDP but employing about 66 percent of the work force. Important cash crops include cotton, tea, rice, spices, nuts, coffee, and jute, although much agriculture remains on a subsistence basis.

Industry Industry contributes less than 30 percent of GDP, but employs only about 12 percent of the work force. Machinery, transportation equipment, textiles, apparel, and chemicals are the main industries, although high-tech opportunities are growing. India has huge pockets of highly trained and skilled but low-cost labor, making it a potential competitor for the development of a wide range of specialized industries.

Services Services account for about 40 percent of GDP, but employ only about 20 percent of the work force, indicating that at least some segments are highly productive. Although many areas are still government controlled, there is growing awareness that the services sector could be a major contributor to growth and stability.

Trends

Government efforts to encourage economic liberalization continue, but the staying power of these policies is uncertain. At this point, a reversion to previous ways of doing business would not only reverse India's growth trend, but would make it that much harder to restart it in the future. In order to succeed with its current reforms, India will have to demonstrate that it is serious about entering the global community on international rather than strictly Indian terms, and that it is actually going to adequately protect foreign interests.

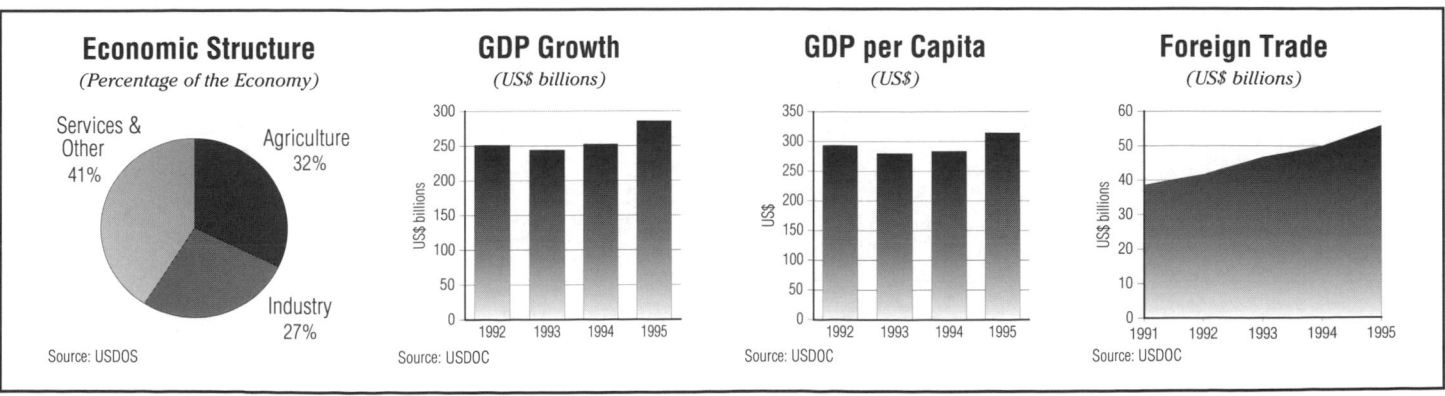

Economic Structure (Percentage of the Economy)
Services & Other 41%
Agriculture 32%
Industry 27%
Source: USDOS

GDP Growth (US$ billions)
Source: USDOC

GDP per Capita (US$)
Source: USDOC

Foreign Trade (US$ billions)
Source: USDOC

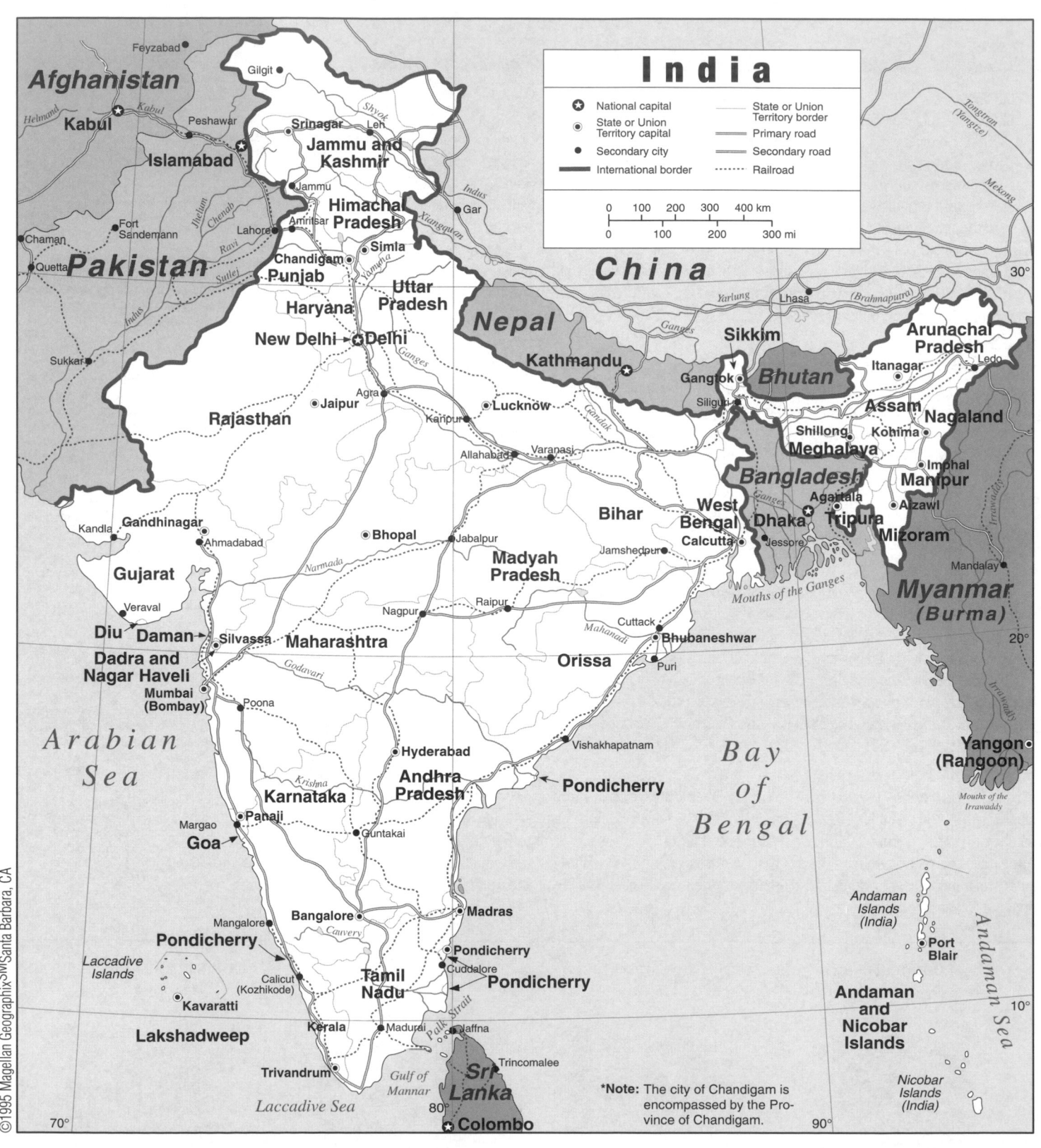

India

- ⊛ National capital
- ⊙ State or Union Territory capital
- • Secondary city
- ▬ International border
- ─── State or Union Territory border
- ─── Primary road
- ═══ Secondary road
- ···· Railroad

0 100 200 300 400 km
0 100 200 300 mi

Note: The city of Chandigam is encompassed by the Province of Chandigam.

Foreign Trade

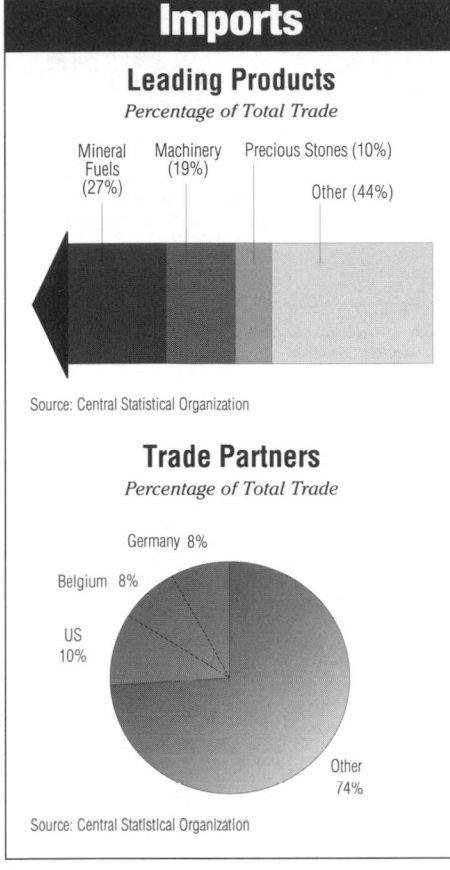

Imports

Leading Products
Percentage of Total Trade

Mineral Fuels (27%)
Machinery (19%)
Precious Stones (10%)
Other (44%)

Source: Central Statistical Organization

Trade Partners
Percentage of Total Trade

Germany 8%
Belgium 8%
US 10%
Other 74%

Source: Central Statistical Organization

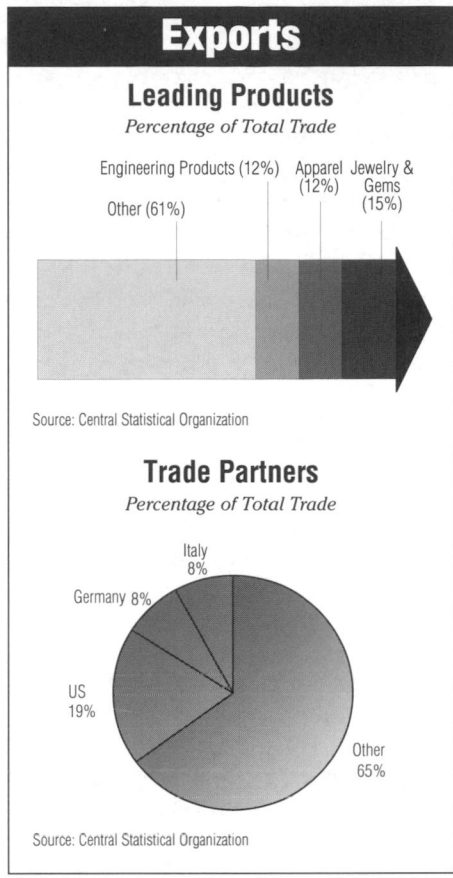

Exports

Leading Products
Percentage of Total Trade

Engineering Products (12%)
Apparel (12%)
Jewelry & Gems (15%)
Other (61%)

Source: Central Statistical Organization

Trade Partners
Percentage of Total Trade

Italy 8%
Germany 8%
US 19%
Other 65%

Source: Central Statistical Organization

Opportunities

FOR IMPORTING TO INDIA

- aircrafts and parts
- computer and computer products
- computer software
- drugs and pharmaceuticals
- edible oils
- electronic and scientific equipment
- fertilizer
- fruits and nuts
- gems
- jewelry
- iron and steel
- machine tools and metalworking equipment
- machinery and transportation equipment
- medical equipment
- oil and gas field machinery
- petroleum
- telecommunications equipment

FOR EXPORTING FROM INDIA

- carpets and other textile products
- cotton apparel and fabrics
- crude oil
- diamonds, jewelry, and precious stones
- engineering goods
- fish
- fruits and vegetables
- handicrafts
- jute
- leather
- tea
- tobacco
- wood and wood products

GROWTH SECTORS

- air, land, sea transportation
- electrical power generation
- financial services
- petroleum exploration
- telecommunications

GOVERNMENT PROCUREMENT

- educational goods and services
- electrical power equipment
- health care goods and services
- rural development projects
- telecommunications products
- transportation goods and services

Trade News

RULES AND REGULATIONS

- **Regulations** India controls the import of goods into its market through the Import Trade Control Organization, part of the Ministry of Commerce.
- **Tariffs and import taxes** India is committed to tariff reform but tariffs remain high. In the 1994-95 budget, tariffs were reduced to 65 percent on most goods. Favored capital goods for export industries have 25 percent tariffs. Excise taxes on imports are comparable to levels charged to domestic producers of such goods and may be as high as 40 percent.
- **Import prohibitions** Addictive drugs, weapons and explosives, and a number of other products including ivory, animal fats, and many apparel and fabric items are prohibited.
- **Import licenses and restrictions** Import licenses are needed for restricted items, which include many consumer goods, seeds, plants, animals, insecticides, pesticides, electronics, chemicals, and pharmaceuticals.
- **Export policies** Private firms are facing fewer restrictions and less administrative control on their international trade transactions. India promotes exports by simplifying procedures and reducing duties on imports needed by exporters. India has established classes of exporters based on cumulative value of goods exported. From lowest to highest value, the classes are export houses, trading houses, and star trading houses.
- **Import/export documentation** Firms seeking to move goods in and out of India are advised to obtain the advice of an experienced international freight forwarder. The administrative discretion of customs officers is wide and the procedures at each port of entry vary.
- **Free trade zones** Seven free trade zones exist in India: Cochin (in the state of Kerala), Falta (in the state of West Bengal, near Calcutta), Kandla (in the state of Gujarat), Madras (in the state of Tamil Nadu), Noida (in the state of Haryana, near Delhi), Santa Cruz (in the state of Maharashtra, near Mumbai, formerly Bombay), and Visakhapatnam (in the state of Andrha Pradesh).
- **Free trade arrangements** India is a member of the South Asia Association for Regional Cooperation. India was a founding member of GATT.
- **Tariffs** The government recently imposed a 110 percent ceiling on basic tariff rates. The government of India has kept most additional duties in place, raising effective tariff rates above the ceiling for some products.
- **Import licensing** India's licensing system was recently liberalized but still places severe limits on a wide range of foreign goods that would be competitive in a more open trading environment.
- **Commodity imports** Some commodity imports must be channeled through public sector companies although many 'canalized' items have been decontrolled recently. The main canalized items are petroleum products, bulk agricultural products, and some pharmaceutical products.
- **Export subsidies** Export measures include exemptions or concessional tariffs on raw materials and access to special import licenses for restricted inputs.

TRANSPORTATION FIRMS

Cox and Kings Ltd.
POB 398
Mumbai
Telex: 112865 COX IN

Mackinnon Mackenzie & Company Ltd.
Bank of Baroda Building
16 Parliament Street
Telex: 3174178 MACK IN

Shipping Corporation of India
245 Madame Cama Road
Mumbai 40002
Telex: 112304

United Liner Agencies of India
17 Brabourne Road
Calcutta
Telex: 212535 ULA IN

Overview

Indian markets can be difficult to operate in. There is residual anti-foreign suspicion and bias, as well as extreme internal diversity and disharmony. Indian bureaucrats may insist on setting basic goods prices, regulating industry entry and expansion, and often deciding what consumers, farmers, and manufacturers want. These roadblocks can sometimes be avoided through careful analysis of consumer preferences, existing sales channels, and an eye to changing conditions. India is highly fragmented; each region has a unique character, and consumer and business preferences vary considerably, requiring a multiplicity of adaptations to specific situations by those interested in penetrating this huge potential market.

Distribution

The center of the Indian consumer purchasing is each city's major market district. Shopping centers are unknown and there are no national department store chains. Retail outlets are usually locally owned. Most goods are distributed through the largest cities: Mumbai (formerly known as Bombay) in the west, Delhi in the north, Calcutta in the east, and Madras in the south, and to a lesser extent through secondary cities. Outside major metropolitan areas, India is a collection of villages loosely tied together by poor roads and cable television, but which are really small, separate venues often having little connection to each other.

Agents, Distributors, and Partners

Finding the right agent here is as crucial as it is problematic. Old-line firms may not be aggressive enough to introduce a new foreign product or provider, while aggressive new outfits may be inadequately experienced, capitalized, or connected to carry the necessary weight in Indian markets. Foreign firms are now allowed to set up Indian branches and subsidiaries, and many Indian buyers now prefer to deal directly with third-party suppliers rather than through an intermediary, but most foreign sellers nevertheless continue to operate through local firms. Sellers of capital goods are required to maintain substantial service capabilities in India, which usually means a relationship with an Indian firm. Foreign exchange controls can also effectively require that an Indian firm be employed as an agent. Family-owned businesses have grown, sometimes over centuries, to dominate certain businesses and sectors. Three paths to locating an effective distributor are advertising in business journals; attending trade fairs or exhibitions; and requesting a contact list from an embassy's business office. Licensing arrangements and joint ventures are possible, but usually require the foreign partner to provide virtually all technology, components, and financing, while the Indian partner provides labor and distribution capabilities. There are limits on royalty payments, effective periods of patent protection, and basic enforcement issues. Franchising is almost unknown. Direct marketing is essentially door-to-door, although more innovative methods are being explored as infrastructure develops.

Selling Techniques

Given high protective tariffs, Indian firms have tended to produce high-cost, low-quality products, and most Indian consumers have had no other choices. As import duties have dropped, the idea of consumer choice has begun to be introduced. For example, Coca-Cola and Pepsi have waged "cola wars" with lower prices and increasing bottle sizes playing a major role. India's growing middle class is pioneering markets for products formerly regarded as luxuries and carefully targeted appeals to this audience could yield substantial rewards. In this largely unsophisticated, unaffluent market, the primary selling proposition will continue to be price, although more affluent market segments are already beginning to distinguish among products based on specific features and after-sales support.

Advertising

The press is by far the most popular advertising platform. Some 12,000 periodicals are published, including more than 800 daily newspapers and 3,000 weeklies; however, there is no national press, and campaigns must be designed around regional outlets. Cinema trailers are the next largest advertising medium, followed by radio, and nascent direct marketing and mail efforts. Television programs can be sponsored using commercials, but programs cannot be interrupted by them. Most foreign firms retain an advertising agency in Mumbai (formerly Bombay), the center of the advertising and publicity industry. Nearly all agencies conduct market research and can arrange for promotional campaigns. International industrial trade fairs are a popular means for entering this market or promoting a new product.

Service and Customer Support

The basic requirements of an Indian customer are quality, price, availability, delivery, and after-sales service. Businesses especially insist on the highest quality of maintenance and prompt response. The government and private firms require engineering support for manufacturing technologies, medical equipment, and any high-technology products.

Marketing in India

MARKETING TIPS

- **Family-owned businesses** Some of the major family-owned businesses and their areas include Ambani—textiles, petrochemicals and refining; Tata—iron and steel, hotels, automobiles, finance, engineering; Goenka—telecommunications, power, electronics; Baja—the world's largest manufacturer of two wheelers; and Shiram—fertilizers, fibers, real estate, sugar.

- **Sensitive products** The cow is generally considered sacred in India; many Indians are vegetarians, and Muslim Indians avoid pork products. Care must therefore be taken in product development to avoid unacceptable ramifications and in marketing to observe local, culturally-based sensitivities.

- **Regional markets** Mumbai (formerly Bombay), Calcutta, Madras, and Delhi dominate commerce in India—work through import firms in these metropolitan areas.

- **Government markets** Still the dominant buyers in many geographic and product areas, official agencies require careful cultivation and guarantees of follow-up service, as well as price considerations.

- **Telephone** Telephone service is fair at best; very little business is done over the phones. Faxes are not new to India but the vast majority of businesses do not use them. Face-to-face meetings are still the best way to market your materials.

- **Postal service** The postal service in India is reliable but not very fast. It may take a week or more for packages from other countries to arrive at their destination in India.

- **Newspaper advertising** India does not have a national press and advertisements must be placed in newspapers throughout the country to achieve national exposure.

AD AGENCIES

Note: The city of Mumbai was formerly known as Bombay.

Madison Advertising
Zoroastrian Bldg. Third Fl.
16 Horniman Circle
Mumbai 400 023
Tel: (22) 266-2376
Fax: (22) 266-3997

Chaitra Leo Burnett Private Ltd.
9/11, N.S. Patkar Marg.
Mumbai 400 036
Chiatra
Tel: (22) 363-0373
Fax: (22) 364-9090

Hindustan Thompson Associates Ltd.
131 Residency Rd.
Bangalore 560 025
Tel: (80) 221-5606
Fax: (80) 221-4067

Newfields Advertising Private Ltd.
3/4-A, Asaf Ali Rd.
New Delhi

Ogilvy & Mather Ltd.
Dinja Wacha Rd
Mumbai 400 020
Tel: (22) 287-3877
Fax: (22) 204-6988

Trikaya Grey Direct/Mumbai
Phoenix Estate Block 2-D
462 Tulsi Pipe Rd.
Mumbai 400 013
Tel: (22) 493-9336
Fax: (22) 493-2619

McCann-Erickson India
20 Altamount Rd.
Mumbai 400 026
Tel: (22) 387-5478
Fax: (22) 387-2575

Business Culture

Greetings and Courtesies

Indians greet each other (and say good-bye) with the *namaste*, which is formed by pressing the palms together (fingers up) below the chin and nodding the head. When greeting superiors or to show respect, a slight bow is added. When meeting foreigners, Indian men will shake hands. Indian men do not generally shake hands with or otherwise touch women (as a gesture of respect for a woman's dignity and privacy). Indian women who are educated or familiar with international customs may offer their hands to foreigners as a courtesy. When meeting a woman, a man should wait for her to initiate a handshake. If she does not, smile and nod slightly. When in public, men should not initiate a conversation with an Indian woman who is alone. Indians value titles; if someone has a title, use it when greeting them. The suffix *"ji"* after a last name is a general term of respect. Indians generally ask permission before leaving other people. Showing respect for others (especially those who are older) is very important. In a group, greet the eldest person first.

Business Ethic and Framework

Indians are religious, philosophical, and family-oriented in all aspects of their lives, including business. Spiritual accomplishments are ultimately more important than material success; humility and self-denial are highly respected—if not always practiced—virtues. Fate is also an important element of Indian culture, and it is widely believed that once a person does the best they can the outcome is in the hands of the divine. The most important social unit is the family, which is placed ahead of individual or business concerns.

Decision Making

Decisions are made slowly. Indians require time to discuss every aspect of a deal, and then usually take more time before giving a final answer. Be patient and plan other activities while waiting. Impatience is viewed as rude, and high-pressure attempts to get things done faster will be resisted and resented. Decisions are made at the top of the hierarchy, so whenever possible cultivate and maintain good relationships with the highest-ranking executives.

Women

India is a male-dominated society. Foreign businesswomen should experience few problems but, in general, women are not accorded the same level of respect as men. Indians who have had more exposure to international dealings will be more used to dealing with women; older men will usually be more traditional and less open. Behaving in a professional, confident, and poised manner will help overcome some of this resistance. Women should be particularly aware of any behavior that might be considered flirtatious. Women who wish to entertain a male associate should do so during the day (business lunches are more popular than dinners anyway). An Indian man will probably offer to pay the bill, but will not push the point if you politely insist on paying. Women should be prepared for personal questions about their age, marital status, and whether they have children. (These are common topics of conversation and are asked of both men and women.)

Meetings

Indians value punctuality in others, but will often be late themselves. Also traffic is extremely heavy in Indian cities and sometimes prevents people from getting to an appointment at all. This can require rescheduling, so if possible build a few extra days into your travel plans. Indian executives generally prefer to meet in the late morning or early afternoon. Schedule appointments well in advance (30 days ahead is suggested) and reconfirm appointments when you arrive in India. Most meetings will begin with pleasant small talk over a cup of tea and perhaps food. Do not refuse any food or drink offered. Always accept; if you do not like it, leave it in front of you.

Business Attire

Business clothing is casual but neat. Standard attire for men is pants and short-sleeved shirts; however, a jacket should be worn to initial meetings or when seeing government officials. For more formal meetings (and during the cooler season) a lightweight suit will suffice. Do not wear leather clothing or any accessories made from animals. If you are traveling to New Delhi in northern India during the winter months, bring warmer clothes. Women should wear casual dresses or pants ensembles. It is acceptable for foreign women to wear the traditional sari (Indian women in particular admire foreigners who do so), but wear a sari only if you feel comfortable in one. Women should always dress conservatively. Do not wear skirts that rise above the knee, and never wear a sleeveless dress or blouse. Men should not wear Indian caps (they are generally worn by villagers and lower-class people).

Cultural Cautions

DO'S
- If a garland of flowers is placed around your neck, it is a gesture of affection and respect. Accept it in this spirit, but also remove it as quickly as is politely possible, to show your own humility.

DON'TS
- Do not use your left hand to gesture toward someone, give or receive anything, eat with, or touch people. The left hand is considered unclean.
- The head is considered sacred. Do not touch a person's head (not even a child's).
- Do not touch another person with your feet or shoes. If this happens accidentally, apologize.
- Do not point at or beckon to someone with a single finger; always use the entire hand.
- Cows are sacred. Do not do or say anything that shows disrespect toward a cow, and refrain from conversations about eating cows or beef.
- Whistling is considered very impolite in India.
- Women should avoid winking, which is considered improper.
- Do not directly refuse an offer of hospitality. If you cannot accept an invitation or do not want to accept it, respond with something polite but noncommittal like, "Thank you, I will try."
- Muslims are forbidden contact with dogs; even pictures of dogs are considered improper. Do not give a Muslim child a toy dog or anything printed with images of dogs.

CUSTOMS
- Many Hindus do not eat meat or drink alcohol.
- Orthodox Sikhs wear turbans and do not smoke tobacco, cut their hair, or eat beef. Parsees are also forbidden to smoke tobacco.
- Muslims do not eat any form of pork, and many do not drink alcohol.
- Grasping one's ears is a sign of sincerity or apology.
- Business cards are exchanged when people are introduced. Ideally, offer your card with both hands, with the inscription facing your associate. English is the customary language for business, but if you are doing business in the rural north, consider having one side of your card translated into Hindi.
- Gifts are common; they are usually given after a first meeting, after a relationship has been established. Avoid very expensive, personal, or religious gifts. Appropriate gifts include candy, flowers, crystal, something that represents your country, or an office accessory with your company logo. If a gift is wrapped, appropriate colors include green, red, or yellow (but not black or white).

OBSERVATIONS
- India is the second most populous nation in the world. The broad cultural pattern is similar throughout the country, but customs and beliefs vary in different regions and among different religious or ethnic groups. Hindus are the largest group, comprising about 82 percent of the population. The other two major groups are Muslims (about 12 percent) and Sikhs (9 percent).
- The best time for business travel to India is December through March. June through August is monsoon season. During Dussehra-Diwali (October/November), it is extremely hard to travel via public transportation. In addition, there are numerous regional holidays during which businesses close.
- Some Indian states prohibit the sale of alcohol, and some have days on which no alcohol may be sold. Foreigners can obtain a tourist introduction card and an All India Liquor Permit at an Indian consulate or tourist office allowing them to buy alcoholic drinks in many states.

NEGOTIATIONS
- Shaking the head does not necessarily mean no. Indians move their heads left to right to show agreement.
- It will take some time to negotiate any agreement. Negotiations are a leisurely process conducted with great politeness, respect, and extended discussion.

Legal System

India's current legal system is very similar to the system of British India, with only slight modifications. Islamic law covers many noncriminal matters involving Muslims, including family law and inheritance. The Supreme Court interprets the Constitution, handles all disputes between the federal government and the states, and decides appeals from lower courts.

Intellectual Property Protection

Patents All patents must be registered to be considered legal in India. The government is currently drafting new legislation meant to make the licensing of patents easier and make the patents valid for longer periods of time. Enforcement of patent infringement laws is not consistent or reliable, although the government is taking steps to better protect these important rights.

Trademarks Trademarks must be registered with the Registrar of Trade Marks. After acceptance, the trademark is advertised in the Trade Marks Journal. Any person interested may oppose registration of any mark. If there are no oppositions, the registration holds for seven years and is renewable every seven years on application. If there is sufficient opposition with proof, or if use of the mark lapses, the registration will not be renewed.

Copyrights Copyright registration is not necessary, but the creator can register the work with the Registrar, who has powers to prevent the importation of any works constituting infringement of an Indian copyright. Any accusation of breach of copyright is settled by the Copyright Board, which has powers similar to civil courts when determining infringement cases. The civil courts can also grant any remedies required or set damages. India is a signatory member of the Berne and Geneva conventions.

Trade Secrets India has several laws to protect businesses against trade secret violation, but case backlogs often lead to delays in the adjudication of these disputes.

Business Registration

Corporations and partnerships must register with the Registrar of Companies and with the Ministry of Finance. Businessmen need not register individually. Founders should deliver a memorandum with the name of the company and the state in which they wish to do business, along with other pieces of information as requested by the Registrar. The registered office of a company may not be moved from one state to another in India without special resolution and confirmation of Company Law Board.

Contracts and Dispute Resolution

Indian businesses consider just about any agreement to be a contract, including verbal agreements. Concepts of proposal, promise, consideration, voidable and void agreements, free consent, undue influence, fraud, and misrepresentation are similar to those under Western laws. Disputes filed with the court are usually delayed because of case backlogs. Arbitration is not often resorted to and, in any case, arbitration decisions can be appealed to the courts. However, India will enforce foreign arbitration awards if based on sufficient evidence. The government is currently considering reforms in its judicial system to permit arbitration panels in cases involving large foreign investment projects.

Notaries

All notaries must enter their names in registry, and be either a legal practitioner or have other qualifications as prescribed by the appointing authority (either the State or Federal government). They are certified for three years. All notaries have wide-reaching powers, and they are necessary as witnesses for several legal proceedings and transactions.

Labor

Workers have the right to join unions, bargain collectively, and to strike. However, there are certain dispute resolution procedures which must be followed prior to striking. Unions are quite powerful in India, and in industrial establishments with 100 or more workers Works Committees are usually established to promote and maintain good relations between workers and management.

Indian laws provide for the health and safety of the workers, and make provisions for hours of work, holidays, meal-time, and overtime. Employers are prohibited from terminating workers without cause unless they comply with certain notice and payment provisions. Children under the age of 14 years cannot work in factories. India has a workers compensation law which provides benefits to workers injured in the course of their employment. Workers are entitled to disability and social security payments under a state-administered system to which both employers and employees contribute. Minimum wages, including required bonuses and holiday pay, are set by the state, although most collective bargaining agreements provide for amounts in excess of the minimums. Factories operate on a 48-hour week, while office employees usually work 35-40 hours a week.

Legal Briefs

- **Supreme Court** The Supreme Court consists of a chief justice and up to 17 judges, appointed by the president. They hold office until age 65.
- **Shari'a law** Islamic law governs many noncriminal laws, including family law, inheritance, and divorce.
- **Judicial independence** There are strong constitutional safeguards assuring the independence of the judiciary in India.
- **Suffrage** Anyone over 21 can vote.
- **Limitation of action** In most civil cases the statute of limitations for commencing an action is three years from the date the cause of action arises.
- **Foreign judgments** Foreign judicial decrees and judgments will be enforced by Indian courts if a certified copy of the judgment or decree is presented.
- **Women** In some locations, such as Pudah, women are not compelled to appear before the courts.
- **Property** The right to property is not a fundamental one and property may be acquired by competent authorities in exercise of powers statutorily conferred.
- **Hindu divorce** Any Hindu marriage may be dissolved by petition presented by either spouse on any of several grounds.
- **Muslim divorce** Muslim customary law governs divorce among Muslims, which may be had by any husband at his will without intervention of the court, or by judicial decree upon suit of either spouse.
- **Monopolies** Indian law ensures that the operation of the economic system does not result in concentration of economic power to the detriment of industry as a whole.
- **Agency** Agents cannot personally enforce contracts or be bound by contracts on behalf of principal.
- **Dearness allowance** In addition to a basic wage, employees can also earn a cost of living compensation called a "dearness allowance," based on the consumer price index for industrial workers.

LEGAL CONTACTS

Note: The city of Bombay was formerly known as Bombay.

Khaitan & Company
9 Old Post Office Street
7th and 8th Floor
Calcutta 700 001
Tel: (33) 248-8590, 248-1249
Fax: (33) 248-7656, 220-7857

Surana & Surana
National Insurance Building
3rd Floor
No. 224 Bose Road
Madras 600 001
Tel: (44) 580-387   Fax: (44) 583-339

Desai & Diwanji
Lentin Chambers, Dialal Street, Fort
Mumbai 400 023
Tel: (22) 2651729   Fax: (22) 2658245

Gagrat & Co.
Alli Chambers
Nagindas Master Road, Fort
Mumbai 400 001
Tel: (22) 2650057   Fax: (22) 2657876

Mulla & Mulla & Craigie Blunt & Caroe
Jehangir Wadia Building
51 Mahatma Gandhi Road
Mumbai 400 001
Tel: (22) 204 4960   Fax: (22) 2040246

Ashok C. Pratap & Co.
Cooks Building
Dr. D. N. Road
Mumbai 400 001
Tel: (22) 2048090   Fax: (22) 2871901

J.B. Dadachanji and Co.
Jeevan Vihar Building
3 Parliament Street
New Delhi 110 001
Tel: (11) 311013   Fax: (11) 3732505

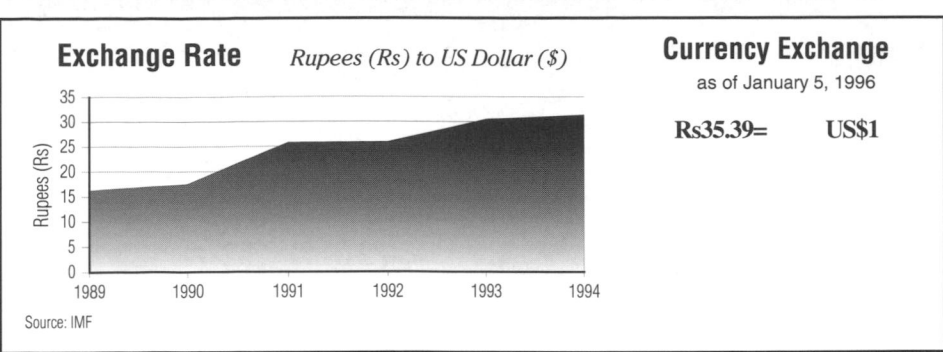

Exchange Rate *Rupees (Rs) to US Dollar ($)*

Source: IMF

Currency Exchange
as of January 5, 1996

Rs35.39=   US$1

Money Matters

BITS AND PIECES

- **Double taxation** Tax relief to avoid double taxation is governed by tax treaties with several countries. In the absence of a treaty, resident corporations enjoy foreign tax credits for the amount of foreign taxes paid.
- **Foreign investments** Foreign equity investments of up to 51 percent are automatically permitted for a list of 34 high priority industries. Burdensome constraints on foreign investors were lifted in 1991.
- **Export exemptions** The Indian Income Tax Act exempts export earnings from corporate income tax for both Indian and foreign firms.
- **Foreign brokers** The Securities and Exchange Board of India (SEBI) has issued guidelines for foreign brokers operating in India on behalf of registered Foreign Institutional Investors (FII's). Brokers are now permitted to open foreign currency or rupee accounts, which can be credited with inward remittances, commissions, and brokerage fees.
- **Property ownership** The Foreign Exchange Regulation Act permits foreigners to own property in India only for residential purposes.
- **Stock market** Foreign individuals and corporations may not directly invest in the stock market. The National Stock Exchange of India permits dealing in scriptless and floorless trading; futures trading is unavailable. There are few safeguards against manipulation, and there can be significant delays in delivery of certificates.

Currency

The currency in use is the Indian rupee (R, plural is Rs).

Foreign Exchange

Transactions with nonresidents are subject to foreign exchange controls. However, the rupee is fully convertible for trade and current account purposes. Foreign currency is readily available, and can be freely purchased for trade and account purposes at the market rate. The exchange value of the rupee is determined by supply and demand conditions and there is an active market in dealing against other major currencies. Authorized dealers are permitted to keep balances and positions in permitted currencies, and may maintain balances abroad as well as positions in European currency units.

Capital Transfers

Exchange control regulations pertaining to foreign companies have been amended in order to curtail discriminatory bias against foreign firms. Foreign institutional investors may open foreign currency accounts and nonresident rupee accounts.

Investment Incentives

Reforms to lure foreign investors include the deregulation of most domestic industries, removing licensing requirements, and permitting foreign and domestic firms a great deal of investment independence. A 15-year tax holiday is available for companies engaged in the development of infrastructural facilities.

Investment Restrictions

There are no requirements to employ Indian nationals, and previous restrictions on the employment of foreign technicians and managers have been eliminated, although companies still complain that hiring expatriate employees is extremely time-consuming. Foreign investors still complain that India's cumbersome bureaucracy and pervasive rules and regulations stifle investment, although much of the permit process has recently been liberalized.

BANKS

Note: The city of Mumbai was formerly known as Bombay.

Allahabad Bank
2 Netaji Subhas Road
Calcutta 700 001
Tel: (33) 209258 Telex: 217547

Bank of India
Express Towers
Nariman Point
POB 234
Mumbai 400 021
Tel: (22) 202-3020 Telex: 112281

Barclays Bank PLC
21-23 Maker Chambers VI, 2nd Floor
Nariman Point
Mumbai 400 021
Tel: (22) 2044353 Fax: (22) 2043238

Central Bank of India
Chandermukhi
Nariman Point
Mumbai 400 021
Tel: (22) 202-6428 Telex: 112909

Indian Bank
31 Rajaji Salai, POB 1866
Madras 600 001
Tel: (44) 514151 Fax: (44) 513211

Indian Overseas Bank
151 Anna Salai
POB 3765
Madras 600 002
Tel: (44) 868141 Fax: (44) 825-3395

New Bank of India
1 Tolstoy Marg
New Delhi 110 001
Tel: (11) 331-6472 Fax: (11) 332-0889

Oriental Bank of Commerce
Harsha Bhavan, E Block
Connaught Place
POB 329
New Delhi 110 001
Tel: (11) 332-1459 Telex: 3165462

Reserve Bank of India
Central Office, Shahid Bhagat Singh Road
POB 406
Mumbai 400 023
Tel: (22) 295000, 295602 Telex: 2318, 2455, 4222

State Bank of India
Madame Cama Road
POB 10121
Mumbai 400 021

TAXATION

Taxation requires sophisticated knowledge of complex rules and regulations specific to each country. For more detailed information we suggest you refer to the Ernst & Young Corporate Tax Guide and Directory, available from the Ernst & Young accounting office in your country, or from:

S.R. Batliboi & Co.
Himalaya House, 7th Floor
23, Kasturba Gandhi Marg
New Delhi 110 001, India
Tel: (11) 331-0528, 331-0186, 371-4447, 332-6734, 371-4387
Telex: 3166718 SRB IN
Fax: (11) 331-4802

At a Glance

Resident Corporation Income Tax Rate (%)(a)	40
Capital Gains Tax Rate (%)(b)	
On Equity Shares in a Venture Capital Company Held by Another Venture Capital Company (a)(c)	20
On Other Assets (a)	30
Branch Tax Rate (%)(d)	55
Branch Capital Gains Tax Rate (%)(b)	20
Withholding Tax (%)(e)	
Dividends Paid to Resident Companies	24.725
Dividends Paid to Foreign Companies	20
Interest Paid to Resident Companies	23
Interest Paid to Foreign Companies (f)	20
Royalties from Patents, Know-how, etc. (g)	30
Branch Remittance Tax	0
Net Operating Losses (Years)	
Carryback	0
Carryforward (h)	8

(a) Excluding temporary surcharge of 15% levied on tax payable if income exceeds Rs 75,000.
(b) Applicable to long-term capital gains.
(c) Applicable to resident corporations and to nonresident corporations that are approved by the central government for the purposes of this reduced rate.
(d) There are exceptions to this basic rate. Foreign institutional investors meeting certain conditions may be taxed at 20% for gross interest and dividends, 10% for long-term capital gains, and 30% for short-term capital gains.
(e) Withholding taxes imposed on resident and nonresident individuals are subject to withholding taxes on dividends, interest, commissions, and gambling winnings. Nonresidents are subject to a 20% withholding tax on investment income and long-term capital gains from assets acquired with convertible foreign currency.
(f) Applicable only to interest from foreign currency loans. Other interest is subject to tax at a rate of 55%.
(g) Applicable to nonresident corporations.
(h) Applicable to losses other than losses resulting form unabsorbed depreciation, which may be carried forward indefinitely.

Business Travel

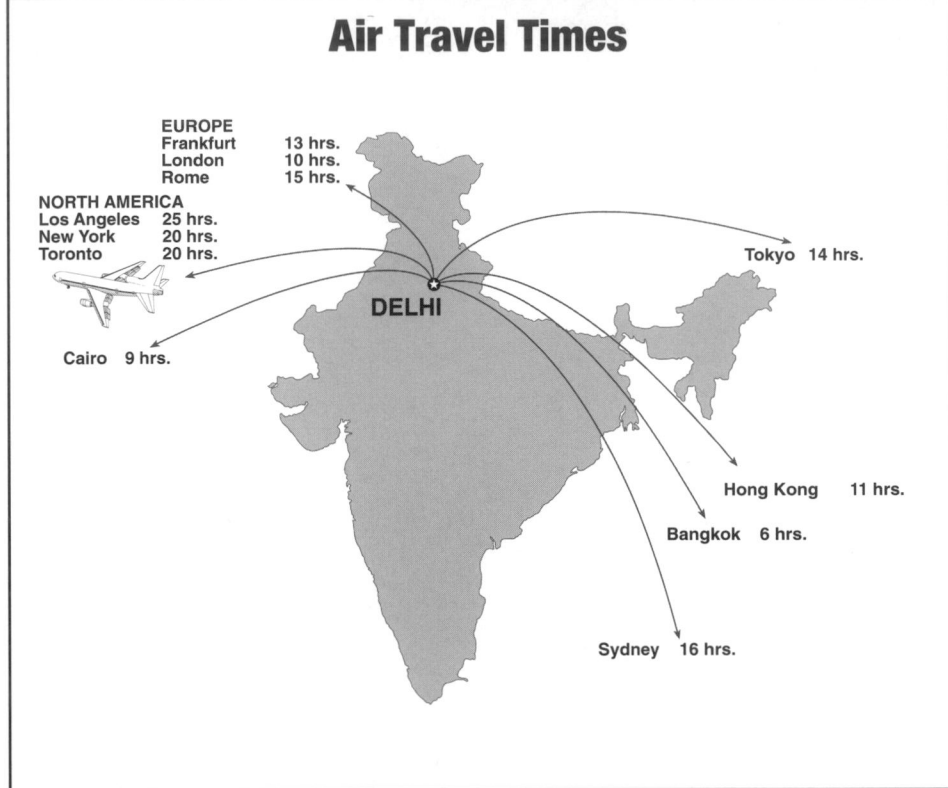

Air Travel Times

EUROPE
Frankfurt 13 hrs.
London 10 hrs.
Rome 15 hrs.

NORTH AMERICA
Los Angeles 25 hrs.
New York 20 hrs.
Toronto 20 hrs.

Cairo 9 hrs.

DELHI

Tokyo 14 hrs.

Hong Kong 11 hrs.

Bangkok 6 hrs.

Sydney 16 hrs.

COMMUNICATIONS

Telephones Indian telephone service is irregular and slow both within India and internationally. Telephone offices are located in the four major cities: Mumbai (formerly known as Bombay), Calcutta, Madras, and New Delhi. There are separate offices for domestic and international calls.

Fax Services are available at larger hotels, but due to crowded lines, it can be difficult to get through. Telegram service is available at telephone offices but tends to be unreliable. Telexes can be sent from telex offices, large hotels, and Central Telegraph Offices.

Post office Postal service in India is reliable and inexpensive. International surface mail is very slow, but airmail is timely. Post offices are generally open weekdays 10:00 a.m. to 5:00 p.m. and Saturday until noon.

BEST TRAVEL BOOKS

Lonely Planet, India Travel Survival Kit. One of the best guidebooks to India. 1104 pages.
Fodor's Travel Guide, India. Tourist oriented, excellent source of city details.
Trade and Investment Guide, India.
The Travellers Guide to India Customs and Manners. Elizabeth Devine & Nancy Bragaranti. 'An invaluable guide for people not wanting to put foot in mouth.'
Far Eastern Economic Review, All Asia Travel Guide Volume 3. The best guide available for the business traveller.

USEFUL TELEPHONE NUMBERS

If you are calling from outside India, you will need to add the country code [91] and any other international dialing requirements from within your country.

- Police 100
- Fire 101
- First Aid 102
- Information 183
- Time 174
- Weather 175
- Operator 199, 197
- Local International Operator 186, 187
- Tourist Information Mumbai 293144
- Tourist Information Dehli 320005
- India Car Hire Agra 64771/2
- New Dehli Car Hire 3715657/8
- Railway Information Office .... (11) 331-3535
- Air India .... (22) 400021
- National Airlines .... (11) 331-0085

Credit Card Information
Lost or stolen credit cards (call collect to the US, regardless of which country the card was issued in.)
- Amex .... [1] (919) 333-3211
- Diner's Club .... [1] (303) 799-1504
- MasterCard .... [1] (314) 275-6690
- Visa .... [1] (410) 581-7931

Travelogue

WORKWEEK

Offices Monday-Friday 10:00 am to 5:00 pm with an hour lunch from 1:00 to 2:00 pm.
Banks Monday-Friday 10:00 am to 2:00 pm and Saturday until noon.
Government Monday-Friday 9:00 am to 5:30 pm with an hour lunch from 1:00 to 2:00 pm.
Retail Monday-Friday 10:00 am to 7:00 pm.

HOLIDAYS

Holidays 1996
January 1 New Year's Day
January 26 Republic Day
February 21 Idu'l Fitr*
March Holi* Hindu death of Holika*
April Ramanavami* Hindu birth of Rama*
April Mahavira Jayanti* Hindu birth of Mahavira
April 5 Good Friday*
April 7 Easter Sunday*
May Buddha Pumima* Hindu birth of Buddha*
May 18 Muharram**
Aug 15 Independence Day
August Januarymashtami**
October 2 Mahatma Gandhi's Birth Day
November Dussehra* Hindu 10 day festival*
November Diwali-Opavali* Hindu festival*
November 18 Guru Nanak's Birth Day
*Dates vary each year.
**Determined by lunar sightings so exact date is uncertain.

VISA AND PASSPORT

Travelers must have a valid passport and a visa to enter India for tourism or business. Visas must be obtained prior to arrival. Foreign currency exceeding US$10,000 (including traveler's checks) must be declared to customs on arrival. Importing Indian currency is prohibited.

DEPARTURE FORMALITIES

A departure tax of US$2 for flights to neighboring countries and US$10.50 to other international destinations must be paid at international airports. It is strictly prohibited to export any amount of Indian currency.

IMMUNIZATION

Travelers must provide evidence of yellow fever immunization if they arrive from an infected area (such as tropical Africa or South America). The World Health Organization considers cholera endemic in India, and a vaccination may be required if traveling on to other countries.

TIPPING

Taxi drivers are tipped 10 percent and porters US$.50. Hotels, restaurants, nightspots: 10 to 15 percent. Small businesses, barbers, and beauticians: 10 percent or Rs5.

CRIME

Petty crime involving theft of personal property is common. There are areas of disturbances and terrorist activity within India. Travelers should check with their consulate or embassy for updated information.

INFRASTRUCTURE

India has extensive air, rail, and roadway networks connecting the interior of the country. There can be long waits for trains and buses. Hiring a car is the safest mode of travel. Major cities have hotel, taxi, and a vast variety of transportation industries, although buses can be unreliable. Telecommunication is only mediocre.

NATIONAL TOURIST OFFICE

Department of Tourism of the Government of India
Ministry of Tourism
Transport Bhavan
Parliament Street
New Delhi 100 001
Telephone: (11) 360233

GOVERNMENT AGENCIES

Ministry of Agriculture and Rural Development
Krishi Bhawan
Dr. Rajendra Prasad Road
New Delhi 110 001
Tel: (11) 382651
Telex: 3165423

Ministry of Commerce
Udyog Bhawan
New Delhi 110 011
Tel: (11) 3016664
Fax: (11) 3013583

Ministry of Communications
Sanchar Bhawan
20 Ashoka Road
New Delhi 110 001
Tel: (11) 3710448
Telex: 314422

Ministry of Electronics
Lok Nayak Bhawan
3rd Floor
Khan Market-3
New Delhi 110 003
Tel: (11) 372312, 374560, 698713

Ministry of Energy
Shastri Bhawan
New Delhi 110 001
Tel: (11) 382966

Ministry of Environment and Forests
Paryavaran Bhawan
CGO Complex Phase II
Lodi Road
New Delhi 110 003
Tel: (11) 4628633

Ministry of External Affairs
South Block-11
New Delhi 110 111
Tel: (11) 3012318
Telex: 3161880

Ministry of Finance
North Block
New Delhi 110 001
Tel: (11) 3012611
Telex: 3166562

Ministry of Food Processing Industries
Krishi Bhawan
New Delhi 110 001
Tel: (11) 382349

Ministry of Health and Family Welfare
Mirman Bhawan
New Delhi 110 001
Tel: (11) 3018863, 373619

Ministry of Human Resource Development
Shastri Bhawan
New Delhi 110 001
Tel: (11) 386451, 385315
Telex: 3161336

Ministry of Industry
Udyog Bhawan
Maulana Azad Marg
New Delhi 110 011
Tel: (11) 3010221
Telex: 3166294

Ministry of Information and Broadcasting
Shastri Bhawan
New Delhi 110 001
Tel: (11) 382639
Telex: 3166349

Ministry of Labor
Shram Shakhti Bhawan
Rafi Marg
New Delhi 110 001
Tel: (11) 382945, 3717515, 3710240
Telex: 3161131

Ministry of Railways
Rail Bhaven
Raisina Road
Rail Bhawan
New Delhi 110 001
Tel: (11) 384010

Ministry of Science and Technology
CSIR Building
Rafi Marg
New Delhi 110 001
Tel: (11) 3710472

Ministry of Surface Transport
1 Transport Bhawan, Sansad Marg
Parliament Street
New Delhi 110 001
Tel: (11) 384938
Telex: 3161159

Ministry of Textiles
Udyog Bhawan
New Delhi 110 011
Tel: (11) 3011769

Ministry of Urban Development
Nirman Bhawan, Rafi Marg
New Delhi 110 001
Tel: (11) 3019377

Ministry of Water Resources
Shram Shakti Bhawan, Rafi Marg
New Delhi 110 001
Tel: (11) 383098
Telex: 3166568

Ministry of Welfare
Shastri Bhawan
New Delhi 110 001
Tel: (11) 382683
Telex: 3166256

WORLD TRADE CENTER

World Trade Center Mumbai
M. Visvesvaraya Industrial
Research & Development Centre
Centre 1, 31st Floor, Cuffe Parade
Mumbai 400 005
Tel: (22) 2184434
Fax: (22) 2188175

TRADE ASSOCIATIONS

India Trade Promotion Organization
Pragati Bhawan, Pragati Maidan
Lal Bahadur Shastri Marg
New Delhi 110 00
Tel: (11) 3318374, 3313292
Fax: (11) 3318142, 3320855

Bharat Electronics Ltd.
Trade Centre
116/2, Race Course Road
Bangalore 560 001

Food Corporation of India
16-20 Barakhamba Lane
New Delhi 110 001
Tel: (11) 3316871
Telex: 3162797

Handicrafts and Handloom Export Corporation of India Ltd.
Lok Kalyan Bhawan, 11-A Rouse Ave Lane
New Delhi 110 002
Tel: (11) 3311086
Fax: (11) 3315351

Hindustan Paper Corporation
Ruby Building
75-C Park Street
Calcuta 700 016
Tel: (11) 298802, 294243, 294996

Hotel Corporation of India
Centur Hotel
5th Floor, Mumbai Airport
Mumbai 400 057
Tel: (11) 6126670

Indian Institute of Foreign Trade
B-21, Meharauli Industrial Area
New Delhi 110 016
Tel: (11) 6824320020

Indian Tourism Development Corporation
Scope Complex, Core VIII
7 Lodi Road
Jeevan Vihar, 3 Sansed Marg
New Delhi 110 003
Tel: (11) 36030

Industrial Finance Corporation of India
Bank of Baroda Building
16 Sansad Marg, POB 363
New Delhi 110 001
Tel: (11) 3322052
Fax: (11) 3320245

Minerals and Metals Trading Corporation of India Ltd.
Scope Complex, Core 1
7 Lodi Road
New Delhi 110 003
Tel: (11) 3319448
Fax: (11) 362077

National Small Industries Corporation Ltd.
NSIC Bhawan
Okhla Industrial Estate
New Delhi 110 020
Tel: (11) 6837071, 632864
Fax: (11) 6837669

Shipping Corporation of India Ltd.
Shipping House
245 Madame Came Road
Mumbai 400 021
Tel: (22) 2026666
Fax: (22) 2026905

State Trading Corporation of India Ltd.
Jawahar Byapar Bhawan
Tolstoy Marg
New Delhi 110 001
Tel: (11) 353164
Fax: (11) 3326741

Trade Development Authority
Bank of Boroda Building
16 Sansad Marg
POB 767
New Delhi 110 001
Tel: (11) 3320214
Fax: (11) 3320855

EXPORT PROMOTION AGENCIES

Federation of Indian Export Organizations
PHD House
Opp: Asian Games Village
New Delhi 110 016
Tel: (11) 666582
Telex: 031-73194
Cable: APEXLINK

Apparel Export Promotion Council
Sahyog Building
58 Nehru Place
New Delhi 110 019
Tel: (11) 6416709
Telex: 031-66431
Cable: APEXCIL

Basic Chemicals, Pharmaceuticals and Cosmetics Export Promotion Council
Jhansi Castle, 4/F
7 Cooperage Road
Mumbai 400 039
Tel: (11) 2021330
Telex: 01-4047
Cable: CHEMEXCIL

Cashew Export Promotion Council of India
P.B. No. 1709, Chittur Road
Ernakulam South
Cochin 682 016
Tel: (11) 351973
Telex: 0885-667
Cable: PROMOTION

Chemicals and Allied Products Export Promotion Council
World Trade Centre
14/1-B Ezra St. 2/F
Calcutta 700 001
Tel: (33) 267735
Telex: 021-4386
Cable: CAPEXIL

Council for Leather Exports
Leather Centre
3-4/F
53 Sydenhams Road
Periamet
Madras 600 003
Tel: (44) 33498
Telex: 041-7354
Cable: LEXPOCIL

Indian Silk E.P. Council
No. 62, Mittal Chambers
Nariman Point
Mumbai 400 021
Tel: (22) 2027662
Telex: 011-3190
Cable: INSILKEXPO

Overseas Construction Council of India
Flat No. H-118
Himalaya House, 11/F
K.C. Marg
New Delhi 110 001
Tel: (11) 3312936
Telex: 031-65588
Cable: OVERSECONS

Synthetic and Rayon Textiles Export Promotion Council
Resham Bhavan
78 Veer Nariman Rd.
Mumbai 400 020
Tel: (22) 2048797
Telex: 011-3703
Cable: SILKRAYON

Wool and Woollens E.P. Council
612/714, Ashoka Estate
24 Barakhamba Road
New Delhi 110 001
Tel: (11) 3315512
Telex: 031-66673
Cable: WARMTH

Electronics and Computer Software Export Promotion Council
Vandhna, 4th Floor
11 Tolstoy Marg
New Delhi 110 001
Tel: (11) 3314560
Telex: 031-61669

Indian Institute of Foreign Trade
B-21 Institutional Area, South of IIT
New Delhi 110 018
Tel: (11) 655124
Telex: 031-73185
Cable: INDIFT

Trade Development Authority
Head Office
Bank of Baroda Bldg
16 Parliament Street
New Delhi 110 001
Tel: (11) 3320214
Telex: 031-65155
Cable: ADEPT

Trade Fair Authority of India
Pragati Maidan
L.B. Shastri Marg
New Delhi 110 001
Tel: (11) 804320
Telex: 031-2751
Cable: COMEXH

Consultancy Development Centre
Apartment E-1
Qutab Hotel
New Mehroli Road
New Delhi 110 016
Tel: (11) 6862196
Telex: 031-73119
Cable: COUNSELINK

CHAMBERS OF COMMERCE

Associated Chambers of Commerce and Industry of India
Allahabad Bank Building, 2nd Floor
17 Parliament Street
New Delhi 110 001
Tel: (11) 310704
Fax: (11) 312193

Mumbai Chamber of Commerce and Industry
Mackinnon Mackenzie Building
Ballard Estate
Mumbai 400038
Telex: 011-73571

Federation of Indian Chambers of Commerce and Industry
Federation House
Tansen Marg
New Delhi 110 001
Tel: (11) 3319251
Telex: 3162521

Indian Chamber of Commerce
India Exchange Buildiing
Calcutta 700001
Telex: 021-7432

BANKS

Citibank, NA
Sakhar Bhavan
230 Backbay Reclamation
Nariaman Point
Mumbai 400 021
Tel: (22) 286-0871
Telex: 1185379

United Bank of India
16 Old Court House Street
Calcutta 700 001
Tel: (33) 237471
Telex: 217387

NEWSPAPERS

Financial Express
Bahadur Shah Zafar Marg
New Delhi 110 002
Tel: (11) 331-1111

Navbharat Times
7 Bahadur Shah Zafar Marg
New Delhi 110 002
Tel: (11) 331-2277
Fax: (11) 332-3346

The Economic Times
7 Bahadur Shah Zafar Marg
New Delhi 110 002l
Tel: (11) 331-2277
Fax: (11)332-3346

The Times of India
7 Bahadur Shah Zafar Marg
Delhi 110 002
Tel: (11) 331-2277
Fax: (11) 332-3346

BUSINESS PERIODICALS

Business India
Nirmal, 14th Floor
Nariman Point
Mumbai 400 021
Tel: (22) 202-4422
Fax: (22) 202-6164

Capital
1/2 Old Court House Corner
POB 14
Calcutta 700 001
Tel: (33) 200099

Economic and Political Weekly
Hitkari House
284 Shahid Bhagatsingh Road
Mumbai 400 038
Tel: (22) 261-6072

Journal of Industry and Trade
Ministry of Commerce and Supply
Delhi 110 011
Tel: (11) 301-6664

RADIO & TELEVISION

All India Radio
Akashvani Bhawan
Parliament Street
New Delhi 110 001
Tel: (11) 310704
Telex: 313225

Doordarshan India (Television)
Mandi House
Doordarshan Bhavan
Copernicus Marg
New Delhi 110 001
Tel: (11) 387786 Telex: 316-6143

LEGAL CONTACTS

Intel Advocare
C-27, Greater Kailash Enclave1
New Delhi 110048
Tel: (11) 6470971
Fax: (11) 6464000

Indian Council of Arbitration
Federation House
Tansen Marg
New Delhi 110 001
Tel: 3319251
Telex: 031-245
Cable: ARBITRATOR

New Delhi Law Offices
Rajendra Bhawan (5th Floor)
210 Deen Dayal Upadhyay Marg.
New Delhi 110 001
Tel: (11) 332 7081
Fax: (11) 332 7101

Rajinder Narain & Co.
14-F Connaught Place
New Delhi 110 001
Tel: (11) 331 32 32
Fax: (11) 332 83 19, 372 33 92

INTERNET ADDRESSES

Usenet group(s):
soc.culture.india
soc.culture.indian
soc.culture.indian.delhi

India Online
http://IndiaOnline.com/

Embassy of India, Washington, DC
gopher://india.bgsu.edu/11/
Embassy%20of%20India,%20Washington,%20DC

India - Economic and Business Overview
http://sunsite.sut.ac.jp/asia/india/jitnet/india/mea/

India
http://spiderman.bu.edu/misc/india/

Information about India
http://SunSITE.sut.ac.jp/asia/india/

Indonesia

Republic of Indonesia

Economy

Overview

Formerly a totally agricultural society, Indonesia has now become a commodity producer and is adding a significant high-growth manufacturing community. While the government continues to control prices, operate state-owned firms, and impose comprehensive restrictions, Indonesia is largely a free market economy with a strong private sector. There are barriers to continued economic development, however, including lack of investment capital, an inadequate and slowly developing infrastructure, rising foreign debt and inflation, an undereducated work force, human rights problems, and rampant and endemic corruption.

Trade

Indonesia's main export is petroleum—crude petroleum and liquefied natural gas account for about 40 percent of all exports—but it is trying to diversify into other, higher-value-added products. Nevertheless, major exports remain largely confined to commodity and intermediate goods, such as wood products and plywood veneers, rubber, and apparel and footwear. Imports are dominated by capital goods, including general and specialized industrial machinery, electrical machinery, intermediate inputs, such as iron, steel, and fuels, and some consumer products, such as foodstuffs.

Sectors

Agriculture Although it contributes less than 20 percent of GDP, agriculture employs nearly 55 percent of the work force, a legacy of Indonesia's traditional agricultural background. Timber (despite concern over deforestation, which led to a ban on timber exports in the early 1990s), rubber, coffee, tea, sugar, tobacco, and rice are major crops, although agriculture continues to decline in overall importance.

Industry Industry employs less than 17 percent of the work force, and produces nearly 20 percent of GDP. Until recently, petroleum products dominated the economy, although government efforts to diversify are beginning to show results. Textiles, tin mining, chemicals, and wood products are also becoming major industries as Indonesia tries to encourage development of high value-added industries.

Services Services provide a large proportion of GDP. Tourism is a growth industry and an increasing source of foreign exchange, although most services involve shipping, distribution, and personal service activities.

Trends

The biggest deterrent to continued economic growth in Indonesia is poor infrastructure, which has not kept up with growing demand. Recognizing this, the government is investing funds in new roads, airports, and telecommunication services. The government has also created policies aimed at containing inflation and limiting the amount of foreign commercial borrowing, while also promoting foreign investment. For long-term success, Indonesia must open up its economy, reduce corruption, and address the human rights issues that have kept Western nations from deepening commercial relationships. It must also better educate its burgeoning work force if it is to attract the necessary outside capital to construct a stable base.

At a Glance

THE COUNTRY

Location Southeastern Asia, between Malaysia and Australia.
Terrain Mostly coastal lowlands; larger islands have interior mountains.
Climate Tropical; hot and humid; more moderate in highlands.

THE PEOPLE

Population 200,000,000
Ethnic composition
Javanese 45%
Sundanese.. 14%
Madurese 7.5%
Coastal Malays 7.5%
Other.. 25%
Religious composition
Muslim 87%
Protestant 6%
Roman Catholic 3%
Hindu 2%
Buddhist.. 1%
Other... 1%
Languages spoken Bahas Indonesia (a modified form of Malay; official), English, Dutch, local dialects, the most widely spoken of which is Javanese.
Labor force
Total:..67,000,000
By occupation: agriculture 55%, manufacturing 10%, construction 4%, transport and communications 3%.

COUNTRY FACTS

Political and legal Indonesia is a republic, with a Roman-Dutch legal system, substantially modified by indigenous concepts and by a new criminal procedures code. It has not accepted ICJ jurisdiction.
Telephone Local telephone service is irregular. International country code: [62]. Selected city codes: Jakarta (21), Medan (61), Surabaya (31).
Transportation Metered taxis are available, bus service is crowded, and pedicabs and motorized pedicabs can be dangerous. Many thefts have been reported on public transport, especially in Jakarta and Bali. Inter-urban rail service is available inter-urban on Java. Garuda Indonesia Airways and local airlines provide domestic service between cities.
Environment Current issues include deforestation, water pollution from industrial wastes, sewage, and water shortages in urban areas.
Media The government owns or controls all telecommunications facilities. There are limits placed on the press by the government. Most newspapers are published in Bahasa Indonesian, with a small number appearing in English, Chinese, and local dialects.
Health The general level of sanitation and health is relatively low. Tuberculosis, malaria, dengue fever, hepatitis A and B, typhoid fever, cholera, parasitic and sexually transmitted diseases are prevalent. AIDS is also a growing problem. Take care in eating and drinking; preventive measures (immunizations) are suggested. Sanitary standards in Indonesia international-class hotels range from adequate to excellent. Adequate medical care is available in all major cities. Emergency services are inadequate outside major cities. Life expectancy is 61 years.

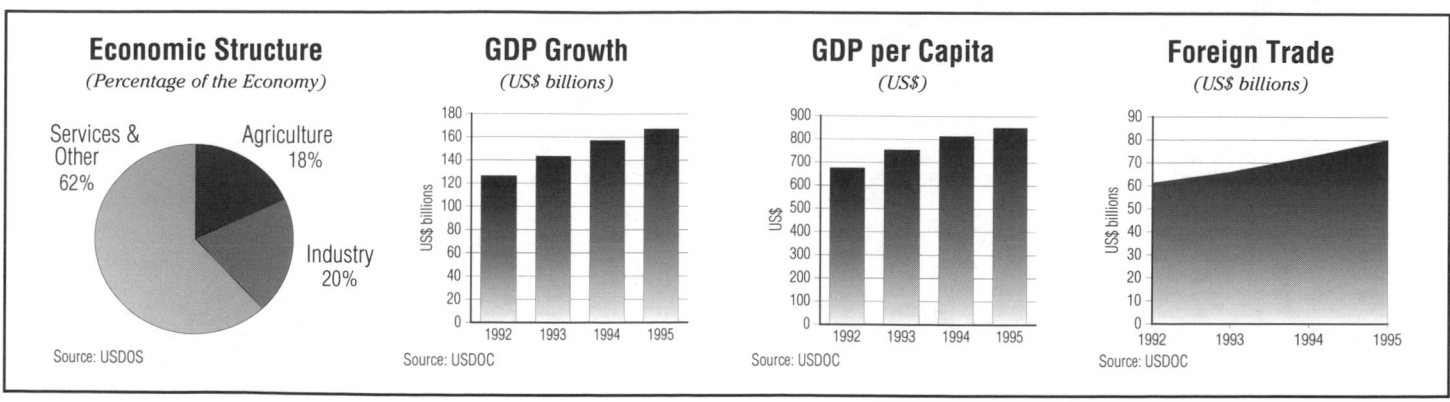

Economic Structure (Percentage of the Economy) — Services & Other 62%, Agriculture 18%, Industry 20%. Source: USDOS

GDP Growth (US$ billions) — 1992, 1993, 1994, 1995. Source: USDOC

GDP per Capita (US$) — 1992, 1993, 1994, 1995. Source: USDOC

Foreign Trade (US$ billions) — 1992, 1993, 1994, 1995. Source: USDOC

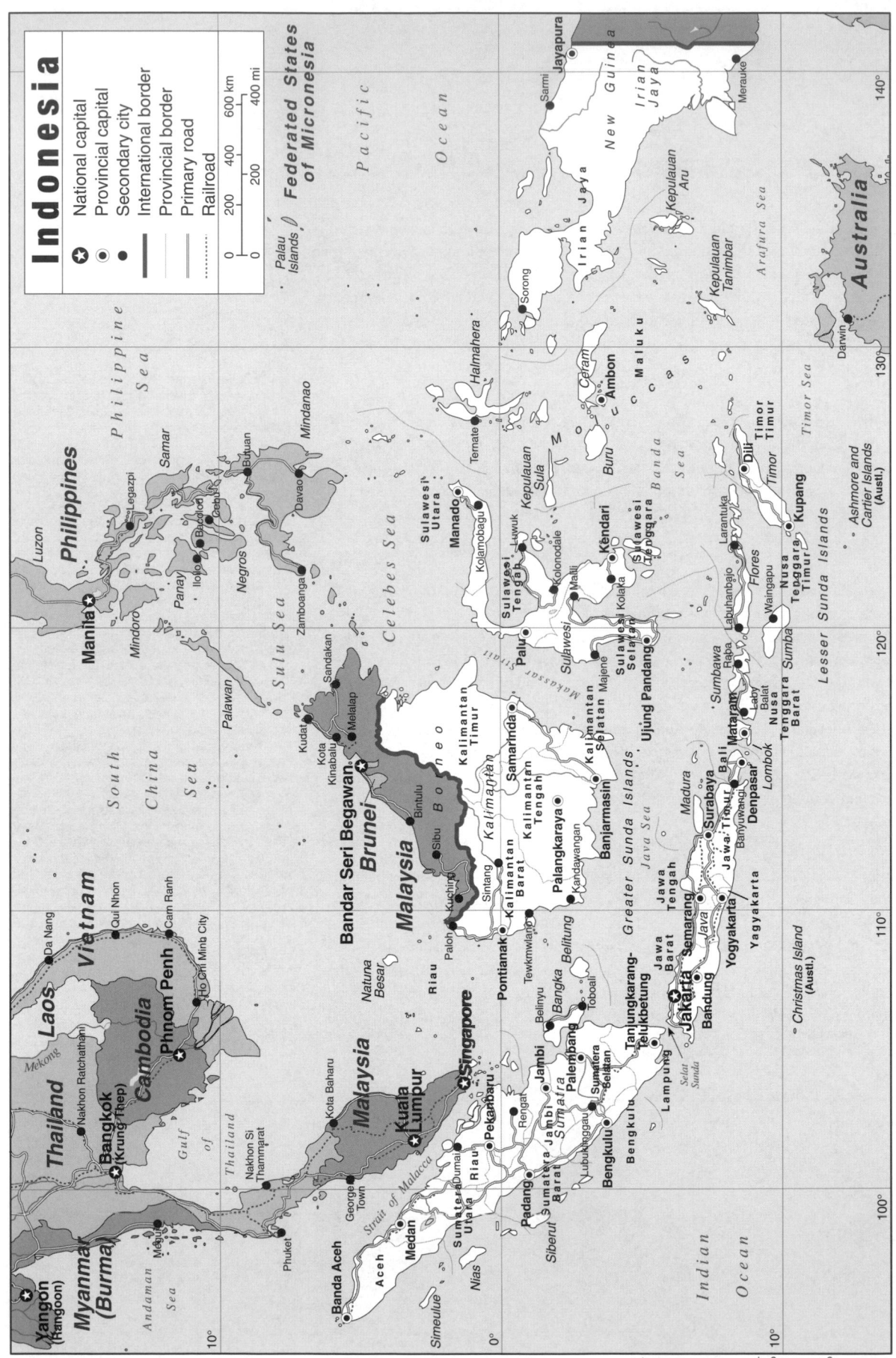

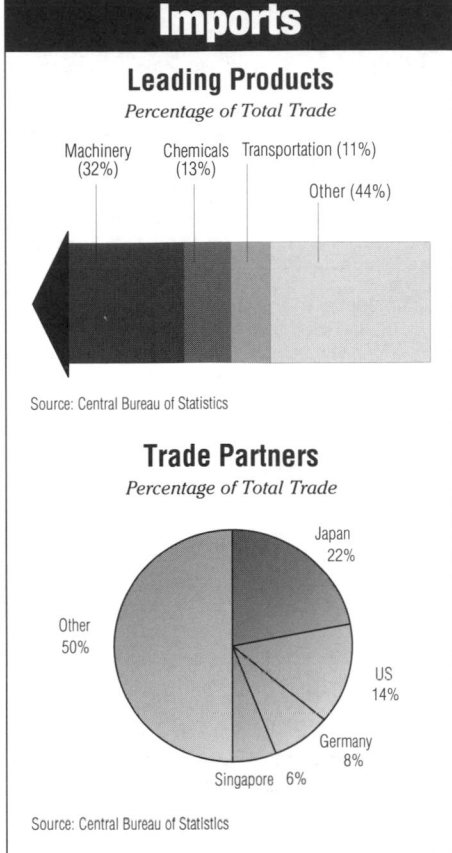

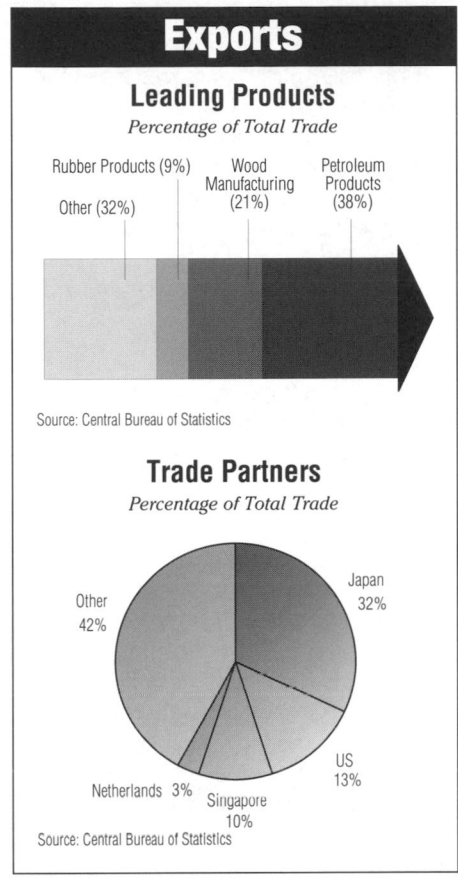

Opportunities

FOR IMPORTING TO INDONESIA

- capital goods
- chemicals
- computers and software
- construction equipment
- consumer goods
- food processing equipment
- food products
- industrial pumps, valves, and equipment
- laboratory and scientific equipment
- meat products
- medical and hospital equipment
- mineral and chemical refining equipment
- pulp and paper machines
- railroad equipment
- textile production equipment
- wood and wood products

FOR EXPORTING FROM INDONESIA

- chemicals
- coffee
- electronic goods
- fish
- footwear
- furniture
- minerals: bauxite, coal, copper, gold, nickel, silver, tin
- natural gas
- oil
- paper and paper products
- petroleum products
- rubber
- spices
- textiles and garments
- wood and wood products

GROWTH SECTORS

- aviation
- chemicals
- electronics
- infrastructure development projects
- pulp and paper
- textiles
- tourism
- wood products

GOVERNMENT PROCUREMENT

- airport and sea port construction goods and services
- electrical power generating equipment
- environmental protection technologies
- fiber optic cables
- road construction goods and services
- telecommunication products

Trade News

RULES AND REGULATIONS

- **Regulations** The Department of Trade administers import and export regulations. In 1986, the Indonesian government began reforming its trade policy to increase competition in the economy, open up domestic companies to foreign involvement (although there are still a number of restrictions), and increase opportunities for international trade.

- **Tariffs** Import tariffs range from five to 200 percent, with the majority falling between five and 40 percent. The simple average import tariff is approximately 20 percent. The average effective tariff is lower, however, due to many exemptions. Approximately 50 percent of potential duties and taxes are exempted, including capital goods for approved investments, imports used to produce exported goods, and imports exempted by the Ministry of Finance.

- **Import surcharges** Import surcharges, or supplemental import duties, apply to 200 customs tariff lines. The surcharges range from five to 100 percent (the highest figure is applied to motor vehicles). The government also levies a 10 percent value-added tax on all domestic and imported goods.

- **Import licenses** There are four types of import licenses, ranging from the least restrictive Import Producer (IP) licenses—available to domestic producers who use IP items as inputs into their production process—to Producer Importer (PI) licenses, which restrict PI items to domestic producers of the same product or to a designated sole importer. Affected products include milk, garlic, wheat, rice, soybeans, flour, sugar, beer, wine and spirits, petroleum products, iron and steel, steel products, aluminum, machinery and heavy equipment, engines, motor vehicles, and explosives.

- **Prohibited imports** The government currently bans the import of printed material in Bahasa Indonesian, Chinese languages, or other Indonesian languages. Video tapes pass the censor review. There is also an import ban on plastic waste and scrap.

- **Export controls** Export regulations apply to rattan, sawn timber, processed wood, and sandalwood. Export taxes on forestry products account for the bulk of Indonesia's export restrictions. Cement production and prices are also tightly controlled.

- **Free trade zones** There are a number of export processing zones in Indonesia, including one on Batam Island, located 20 kilometers south of Singapore, and a facility near Tanjung Priok in north Jakarta.

- **Import payments** A preshipment inspection must be done by the exporting country, but at the expense of the Indonesian government. The inspecting agency must submit a survey report directly to the bank holding the corresponding letter of credit, or to a bank designated by the importer. Indonesian buyers prefer that the supplier provide the necessary financing for a commercial transaction.

- **Export payments** There are no restrictions on which types of financial arrangements may be used by the exporter. Proceeds do not have to be surrendered or repatriated. For those goods subject to export taxes or surcharges, payment is due when the export is registered with a foreign exchange bank.

- **Service barriers** There are a number of service barriers, although the restrictions have been loosening in recent years, particularly in the financial sector. Foreign banks are permitted to form joint ventures with domestic companies.

- **Video quotas** There is a quota imposed on the number of foreign films that can be shown every year.

FREIGHT FORWARDERS

Gesuri Lloyd
Jalan Tiang Bendera 45
Jakarta
Fax: (21) 67 48 47 Telex: 42043 GESURI

Schenker Delegate
Jalan Hayam Wuruk 8
Room 445
Jakarta
Telex: 46641 SHENK IA

Overview

Foreign investors face serious challenges, but the rewards include high rates of return and the establishment of connections that may reap even greater profits in the future. Bali is focused on tourism, as it has been for decades, and Surabaya remains a trade capital; however, the focus on agriculture in most of the rest of the country is no longer dominant. Obstacles include labyrinthine trade regulations, monopolistic and protectionist distribution arrangements, and Indonesian firms' dependence on supplier-arranged financing. Although daunting, these drawbacks do not eliminate foreign firms from the action, but do require planning, maneuvering, and commitment. Companies that take the time to learn about the market, adapt their products and services to suit local circumstances, and make long-term plans to build relationships will find that Indonesians will welcome the opportunity to do business with them.

Distribution

The government has reserved all distribution channels for Indonesian national companies. Although foreigners may participate in such firms, joint entities must have at least 51 percent local ownership and a board of directors consisting mostly of Indonesian nationals. Foreigners can own all the local operations engaged in production or manufacturing, and may manage export and offsetting import activity, but may not handle domestic market sales.

Agents, Distributors, and Partners

Foreign investors may not distribute their products directly in local markets, and must arrange for a separate company owned by a local trading partner to handle distribution. The representative may be an Indonesian company or individual, or a foreign national, but only one trade office is permitted. Representatives may not sell directly, but may do sales promotion and marketing or provide market research and technical advice. Over time, representative offices have become so closely tied to Indonesian importers that the two companies nearly always operate in concert. Sole distributorships have been established for heavy equipment and vehicles. Indonesian importers tend to stock competing product lines, and many specialize in a given sector. An aggressive agent with several offices who can handle the entire range of necessary trade activities provides the primary path to achieving market penetration and expanding sales. Agent contracts are exclusive and tend to run for periods of three to five years. Although franchising is relatively new here and is so far limited to fast food, it is rapidly gaining popularity as a concept with substantial future potential in other areas. All joint ventures require that an Indonesian resident be majority partner. Because joint venture arrangements are unusually difficult to dissolve, foreigners must be exceedingly careful in choosing their Indonesian venture partner.

Selling Techniques

Price, quality, and delivery are the most important criteria for Indonesian buyers, and marketers should tailor their selling propositions accordingly. Low-interest financing can often be the deciding factor in making a sale. Indonesians are fond of dealing with "old friends"—that is, companies that demonstrate a long-term commitment will make more sales than those that appear to be interested only in a quick or one-time deal. Indonesians are also relatively brand loyal. Willingness to establish a joint venture production operation is another favorable factor, especially in cases in which the new operation is designed to expand production to serve the rest of Asia.

Advertising

Newspapers and magazines are the most popular media, especially in more urbanized Jakarta and West Java. A newspaper may not carry advertising consisting of more than 35 percent of its content, so rates are high; a full-page ad in *Kompas*, the main national circulation newspaper, can cost more than US$50,000. New television stations are cropping up, replacing the old single, government-operated channel; most Indonesians do watch television, making it a good means of conveying a product message. There are more than 600 radio stations. Outdoor advertising on signs and billboards is also important. Direct mail is low-cost and effective in certain cases. Jakarta advertising agencies are accustomed to dealing with international clients and to introducing and producing foreign products. Existing trade shows provide the opportunity to display new products to specialized buyers.

Service and Customer Support

Companies must not forget that customers need to be comfortable with the ability of a supplier to provide rapid service, high-quality replacement parts, and technology upgrades. Although the local distribution partner will usually be responsible for providing such support, overseas firms should not try to economize by limiting their investment in making theirs a first-class support and service provider.

Marketing in Indonesia

MARKETING TIPS

- **Government markets** Many government contracts not only have a "buy Indonesian" bias built in to them, but also specify low maximum percentages of the total contract for which foreign bidders are eligible to participate. They will also often stipulate a high minimum markup (15 percent) for such bid pricing.

- **Packaging** Often the best advertising for the product is the product itself; therefore the design of the product, its packaging, and associated promotional copy should be specifically tailored to the Indonesian market.

- **Sensitive products** The local population is overwhelmingly Muslim, and does not eat pork products or drink alcohol; thus care must be taken in product development to avoid unacceptable ramifications, and in marketing to observe local, culturally based sensitivities.

- **Ethnic politics** Ethnic Chinese have traditionally run Indonesian big business, and tensions exist between old-line Chinese and up-and-coming Indonesian businesspeople. Marketers must be careful how they align themselves with local interests.

AD AGENCIES

Adforce, Inc.
Jalan Proklamasi
No. 46
Jakarta
Tel: (21) 310-0367
Fax: (21) 314-4292

Wisma Slejahtera, 3rd Fl.
Fl. S. Parman Kav. 75
Slipi, Jakarta 11410
Tel: (21) 548-5105
Fax: (21) 548-0242

MARKETING CONTACTS

Association of Indonesian Consultants
Jalan Bendungan Hilir Raya, No. 29
Jakarta Pusat
Indonesia
Tel: (21) 573-8577/8
Fax: (21) 573-3474

Business Advisory Indonesia
Kuningan Plaza, Suite 304 North
Jalan H.R. Rasuna Said CII- 14
Jakarta 12941
Tel: (21) 520-7696, 520-7689
Fax: (21) 525-0604, 520-2557

Harvest International Inc.
Wisma Metropolitan I, l0th Floor
Jalan Jendral Sudirman, KAV 29
Jakarta Pusat, 12920
Tel: (21) 525-1641
Fax: (21) 520-7789

Importers Association of Indonesia
CTC Building, 4th Fl.
Jalan Kramat Raya 94-96
POB 2744
Jakarta 10027
Tel: (21) 390-1559, 390-8480/1
Fax: (21) 390-8479

Indonesian Exporters Association
Jalan Kramat Raya 4-6
Jakarta Pusat
Tel: (21) 356-099

National Agency for Export Development
Jalan Gajah Mada No. 8
Jakarta 10130
Tel: (21) 362-666, 384-5096, 385-7184
Fax: (21) 384-4588, 384-8380, 385-3135

P.T. Data Consult Inc.
Jalan Kramat Raya No. 5- L
Jakarta 10450
Tel: (21) 390-4711, 471-4752
Fax: (21) 390-1878, 489-5196

P.T. SRI International
Wisma Bank Dharmala, 15th Fl.
Jalan Jend Sudirman Kav 28
Jakarta 12920
Tel: (21) 521-2200
Fax: (21) 521-2203

Business Culture

Greetings and Courtesies

It is important to show respect for status, position, and age. Indonesians are quiet, discrete, and polite almost to the point of shyness. They neither disagree in public nor express anger in public. The accepted greeting (for both meeting and saying good-bye) is the handshake, which is gentle. First introductions are usually accompanied by a slight bow of the head. At subsequent meetings, the handshake is omitted and a simple nod or slight bow is standard. When greeting older people, the bow takes on more significance. Titles are important. If a person has a title, it should be used in greetings as well as general conversation. A man may shake a woman's hand, but this should be the only public physical contact between men and women.

Business Ethic and Framework

The family is the main social unit. Indonesians place loyalty to family and friends above the concerns of any business relationship, and will always find time for personal issues, no matter how pressing their business. Establishing a truly successful business relationship means taking the time to establish a personal relationship that includes trust, honor, and respect. It is well worth the effort, especially if you want to succeed in Indonesia. Business relationships are personal relationships; always try to inject a personal element into business dealings. When possible, do things face-to-face and take the time to do them "properly," which means not placing business matters ahead of your concern for your associate as an individual.

Decision Making

Decisions are made slowly. Indonesians avoid saying no, and might instead say *belum* ("not yet"). Because harmony is so highly valued, they will go to great lengths to avoid disagreeing for fear of disappointing someone. They might also agree with something simply to be polite, agree to do something that cannot be done, or may not admit to mistakes. Impatience will be viewed as rude, and high-pressure attempts to speed up any process will be resisted and resented.

Women

Women hold positions of responsibility in Indonesian businesses, and foreign women are accepted and respected. The family is important, and women should be prepared for personal questions about their age, marital status, and whether they have children. (These are common topics of conversation and are asked of both men and women.) Women should be very careful about their handbags on the street (purse-snatchers often use motorcycles). Foreign businesswomen will probably not face discrimination, but they may encounter some conservative thinking from businesspeople in Indonesia. Women who take male associates to a business dinner should arrange payment beforehand (with the restaurant maitre d'), or the man might insist on paying for the meal. On Java, women who invite a man to a business dinner should include his wife in the invitation.

Meetings

A simple rule for business in Indonesia is to be patient and be prepared. Indonesians value punctuality in others, but will often be late themselves. Expect meetings to start late, and do not express impatience about this. If you are late to an appointment, traffic will be readily accepted as a reason (and, in Jakarta at least, will probably be the truth). Business is not as important as individual relationships, and meetings can easily be interrupted by personal matters. Do not show annoyance at this. At group meetings, never publicly criticize anyone or anything. All criticism is given in private. It is difficult to get around Jakarta, and all meetings tend to last longer than expected. As such, do not schedule too many appointments for one day (ideally, no more than three or four), and leave adequate time between meetings so you won't be progressively later as the day goes on.

Business Attire

The climate is tropical. There is a dry season (June to September) and a wet season (December to March), but whenever you go expect it to be hot and humid. A lightweight jacket and tie are required when calling on government officials, and suits are standard for most business situations. Outside Jakarta, business is conducted less formally, especially with smaller companies. A jacket is not always required in such situations, but men should at least wear a shirt and tie. Women should dress tastefully and conservatively. Fashionable short skirts are accepted in Jakarta and other large cities, but women should never wear a sleeveless dress or blouse. Except at beaches and sports facilities, shorts should not be worn by men or women.

Cultural Cautions

DO'S

- Always treat people with the respect to which their position entitles them.
- In Indonesia, business relationships are personal relationships.

DON'TS

- Never do or say anything that will embarrass an Indonesian.
- The head is considered sacred. Do not touch a person's head (not even a child's).
- Don't use gestures when calling to an Indonesian (except for cab drivers), and don't point at or beckon to someone with a single finger.
- Do not use your left hand to gesture toward someone, give or receive anything, eat with, or touch people. The left hand is considered unclean.
- Never point the soles of your feet at someone. The feet are the lowliest part of the body. Also, do not point to or gesture at someone with your feet.
- It is considered impolite to cross your legs. If you do, cross one knee over the other. Do not rest your ankle on your knee.
- Indonesians have conservative attitudes regarding physical contact, especially among members of the opposite sex. Never kiss or hug someone of the opposite sex in a business situation.
- When entertaining Muslims, never offer alcohol, pork, or meat not properly prepared.
- Muslims are forbidden contact with dogs, and consider pictures of dogs improper. Do not give a Muslim child a toy dog or anything printed with images of dogs.

CUSTOMS

- Business cards are important and are exchanged when saying hello. The exchange of cards is not as ritualistic as in many other Asian countries, but do not be too casual. When you receive a card, take the time to read it, and put it away respectfully. Do not write or make notes on it. It is not necessary to have your card translated into Indonesian. It will be helpful if your card indicates any degrees you have.
- Gifts are common when dealing with both businesspeople and government officials, but avoid overly expensive presents. Appropriate gifts are calculators, quality pens, a book with pictures of your country, or items that somehow represent your country or region.

OBSERVATIONS

- September through June is the best time for business travel to Indonesia. Don't plan to conduct business during the holiday of Lebaran, which marks the end of Ramadan (the holy month of fasting). Also be aware that many businesspeople vacation during July and August.
- The Indonesian bureaucracy can slow any project. Sometimes money is solicited to help speed things up. People unsure about how to handle such matters might consider hiring an Indonesian consultant. If you do, be sure you work with someone who is honest and respected.

NEGOTIATIONS

- It can take as long as a week to negotiate the simplest agreement. Negotiations are slow, complex, and must be done with the proper mutual respect, politeness, and harmony.
- Indonesians are usually very passive when it comes to business. Avoid anger, shouting, or any kind of aggression. Indonesians find this extremely distasteful, and will only react to it negatively.
- Disagreement will not be openly expressed, and criticism of anyone or anything will be voiced only in private.
- Be patient. Impatience will be seen as rude; high pressure tactics will be resisted and resented.
- Many Asians view foreigners as always being in a hurry, and will encourage them to sign an agreement without proper time to study the details.

Legal

Legal System

Indonesia is a civil law jurisdiction with most laws based on the pre-1945 Dutch Civil and Commercial Codes. Today new, purely Indonesian laws are being promulgated in the spirit of economic reform.

Intellectual Property Rights

Trademarks Indonesia's new Trademark Law of 1992 affords protection based on registration, rather than first use. It applies the standard International Classifications of Goods and Services. Applications are posted in the trademark office and if no objection is lodged within six months the final registration certificate will be issued, although this may take up to a further six months. Registration lasts 10 years and is renewable. Infringement and counterfeiting may be subject to both civil action and criminal penalties. Injunctive relief may also be available.

Copyrights Indonesia's copyright law follows the civil law tradition and protects creations in the fields of science, art and literature, and now also computer programs. Creations by Indonesian interests are automatically protected if created in Indonesia. Registration is not necessary, but it creates a presumption of ownership. Duration of copyright varies from 25 years to life of creator plus 50 years, depending on the type of creation.

Patents Patents are granted for 14 years from date of application and may be renewed for only two years. The Patent Office has two years to carry out its examination and grant or reject a patent application. Both civil and criminal actions are available for infringement.

Trade Secrets There is no legal provision for protection of trade secrets or other types of confidential information, and thus these may be protected only by contract.

Business Registration

Foreign companies may not freely operate as such in Indonesia. A foreign company may open a trade representative office for purchasing and demonstration purposes, but no sales may be effected directly by such representative office without use of a local agent. A license from the Ministry of Trade is required for a representative office.

Foreign investment regulations promulgated at the end of 1994 now permit foreign interests to own up to 100 percent of the equity of Indonesian companies in most fields and up to 35 percent in many others. Very few fields are still completely closed to foreign investment. Formulation of any foreign investment company requires prior approval of the government, which should be issued within two months of application. Application is made through the Investment Coordinating Board (BKPM). Legal assistance is strongly recommended as the requirements are continually changing.

Contracts and Dispute Resolution

There is little restriction on freedom of contract provided the contract is neither illegal nor against public policy. A contract has the force of law as between the contracting parties. The parties may contractually choose any dispute resolution body and, for the most part, governing law they wish. However, resolution by the courts is uncertain and, although Indonesia is a signatory to the New York Convention on enforcement of arbitration awards, in practice few, if any, foreign arbitration awards have been enforced by the Indonesian courts. Many commercial disputes are resolved through conciliation, which is consistent with Indonesian cultural philosophy. KANI, the national arbitration body, covers primarily domestic disputes, but a new international arbitration law is in process and an international arbitration institution is also expected to emerge in the near future.

Notaries

Notaries act as representatives of the government and as such are authorized to prepare and authenticate certain official deeds, such as transfers of land and company shares, formation of companies, creation of security interests, and acknowledgments of debt. For the most part these must be in the Indonesian language. Notaries may also simply legalize documents and perform lesser functions. Notarial charges are usually based on a percentage of the transaction.

Labor

Workers are free to establish in-house unions, but these must be members of the single recognized national labor union. Rights of and benefits due to workers are strictly protected by law, and employees may not be dismissed without consent of the local manpower office. Minimum wage requirements vary geographically and are quite low relative to other jurisdictions —and are even low with respect to the cost of living in Indonesia. The minimum wage is not sufficient to provide a subsistence living for a family of four.

Source: Albert Hasibuan & Rekan, Jakarta

Legal Matters

LEGAL BRIEFS

- **Foreign investment** The Investment Coordinating Board (BKPM) has streamlined processing procedures for foreign investment and it serves as a single source of advice and guidance for prospective investors.
- **Land ownership** The acquisition of land by foreigners is prohibited, but exceptions may be made. Land may be bought under joint ventures approved by the BKPM.
- **Property leases** Legal advice should definitely be sought for any transaction involving a long-term lease on land.
- **Management** Expatriates can only hold positions which cannot be filled by Indonesian nationals and then only if regular training is provided to allow the gradual replacement of expatriates by Indonesians for managerial and technical positions at all levels.
- **Indonesian-US cooperation** Indonesia and the US participate in a reciprocal copyright law which provides American copyright holders with the same copyright protection given to Indonesian copyright holders.
- **Nationalization** Indonesian law forbids the government from initiating nationalization of foreign investments except pursuant to valid law and only when such action is necessary in the interests of the state. Even then, the foreign owner shall be compensated in accordance with international law.
- **Civil service employees** Civil servants are not allowed to strike. They are not allowed to join unions and must belong to KORPRI, a non-union association led by the Minister of Home Affairs.
- **Pre-strike ceremonies** Before a strike can occur in the private sector, the law requires intense mediation by the Department of Manpower and prior notice of the intent to strike. No approval is necessary.
- **Union registration** In order to bargain on behalf of employees, a union must register with the Department of Manpower.
- **Minimum age** Child labor exists in both industrial and agricultural sectors. Children must have prior consent to work and cannot engage in dangerous or difficult work. Their workday is limited to a maximum of four hours. Enforcement, however, has been criticized and called weak, and employers often do not report when they employ children. Employment of children and child labor concerns are not considered problems in the petroleum sector.
- **Petroleum employees** Employees of foreign companies operating in the petroleum sector are organized in the labor group KORPRI. They enjoy most of the protection of Indonesian labor laws but cannot strike, join labor organizations, or negotiate agreements.
- **Union membership** The major Indonesian union is the All Indonesia Workers Union (Serikat Pekerja Seluruh Indonesia, SPSI). Its membership is approximately 1.4 percent of the total work force.
- **Technological device protection** Biotechnology and integrated circuits are not protected under Indonesia's intellectual property laws.
- **Copyright protection** The government has stated that it would like to stop copyright piracy and that it is willing to work with copyright holders. Piracy has slowed recently but not stopped.

LEGAL CONTACTS

Albert Hasibuan & Rekan
Jalan Mangunsarkoro No. 85
Menteng, Jakarta 10320
Tel: (21) 310-2656 Fax: (21) 310-1586

Hanafish Soeharto Ponggawa
BNI Building, Suite 2702
Jalan Jenderal
Sudirman I
Jakarta

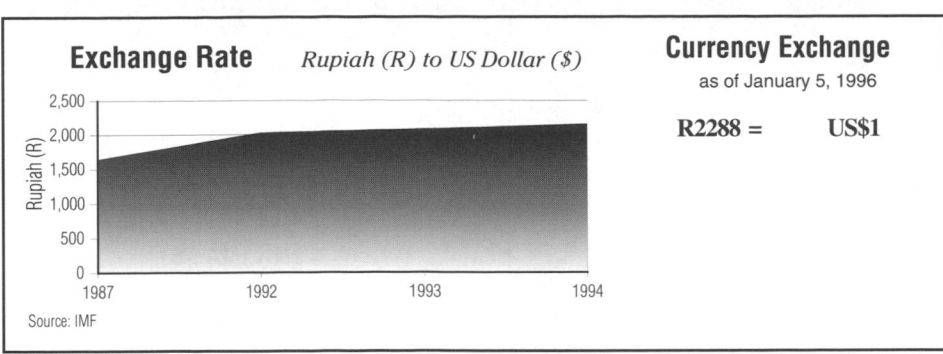

Exchange Rate
Rupiah (R) to US Dollar ($)

Rupiah (R): 0 – 2,500 scale (1987–1994)

Source: IMF

Currency Exchange
as of January 5, 1996

R2288 =   US$1

Money Matters

BITS AND PIECES

- **Foreign investment** The procedure for obtaining approval for foreign investment has been simplified, and incentives have been created to attract foreign investment. Since 1994, there are no initial equity requirements for most types of foreign investment.
- **Banking system** Indonesia's banking system is one of the most deregulated, market-based systems in the world. Since 1988, the expansion of the banking system has been dominated by private domestic banks. This rapid growth has led to a deterioration in the quality of many banks' assets. New capital regulations were introduced by the government to stabilize the banking system. Most banks have been able to meet the requirements; most of the remaining problems are concentrated in the five state-owned banks.
- **Credit** Credit is available to foreign investors on the local market, where rates are determined by individual banks. All types of financing are available, although most imports are financed with letters of credit.
- **Stock market** Volume on the Jakarta Stock Exchange has grown from 27,000 shares in 1988 to 15 million shares in 1993. There is a developing market for bonds and commercial paper, but little trading in the secondary market.
- **Negative investment** The Indonesian government has reduced the number of sectors closed to new investment. In 1991, the number of closed sectors shrank from 75 to 60. Some sectors which remain absolutely closed to invesments include casinos and gambling, and some chemical production and distribution.
- **Land use** The basic Agrarian Law of 1960 states that any land, including agricultural land, can only be owned by an Indonesian.
- **Investment procedures** In order to streamline investments, the Badan Koordinasi Penanaman Modal (BKPM) was created as the government's investment board. It coordinates licenses and approvals from other departments.

Currency

The currency in use is the Indonesian Rupiah (R).

Foreign Exchange

There are no exchange controls over repayment of loans or remittance of dividends, interest and royalties. Travelers may bring in or take out any amount of foreign bank notes, but only up to R 50,000 in Indonesian bank notes. The value of the rupiah is determined by the Bank of Indonesia through a system of managed float, and the rupiah is freely convertible and traded in the interbank market in Jakarta. There are no capital controls, and foreign exchange is permitted to flow freely into and out of the country. There is no tax on the purchase or sale of foreign exchange, and banks may set their own exchange rates. Foreign exchange transactions may be carried out by authorized foreign exchange banks, nonbank financial institutions, and licensed money changers. There are no limits on residents or foreign nationals opening rupiah or foreign currency accounts in a foreign exchange bank.

Capital Transfers

Citizens and residents may freely transfer securities denominated in either rupiah or foreign currency. Foreign investors may repatriate capital and profits at prevailing exchange rates. Permits are not required to transfer foreign exchange, and there are no restrictions on outward direct investment.

Investment Incentives

The government has removed most regulatory obstacles to investment, including bank credit ceilings and controls on state banks' interest rates. In addition, licensing procedures have been greatly simplified, import monopolies reduced, and stock market rules simplified. The government also eliminated any local equity requirements for foreign investment.

Investment Restrictions

While there are few official restrictions, Indonesia must create more than two million jobs every year to keep up with the growing population entering the work force. However, most of the labor force has little or no training in technical or managerial positions, and this has impeded foreign investment, particularly in high-technology manufacturing industries.

BANKS

Bank Ekspor Impor Indonesia
Jalan Lapangan Setasiun
POB 1032
Jakarta 11110
Tel:(21) 673122
Fax: (21) 674734

Bank Rakyat Indonesia
Jalan Jenderal Sudirman
Kav. 44-46
POB 94
Jakarta 10210
Tel: (21) 570-4313
Fax: (21) 570-1182

Bank of America NT and SA
Wisma Antara
1st Floor
Jalan Medan Merdeka Selatan 17
POB 1195
Jakarta
Tel: (21) 384-8031
Fax: (21) 384-9872

Bank of Tokyo Ltd.
Midplaza Building, 1st-3rd Floors
Jalan Jenderal Sudirman
Kav. 10-11
POB 2711
Jakarta
Tel: (21) 570-6185
Fax: (21) 581927

Citibank, NA
Jalan Jenderal Sudirman 1
Jakarta 12930
Tel: (21) 578-2007

Deutsche Bank
Jalan Imam Bonjol 80
POB 135
Jakarta 10001
Tel: (21) 331092

TAXATION

Taxation requires sophisticated knowledge of complex rules and regulations specific to each country. For more detailed information we suggest you refer to the Ernst & Young Corporate Tax Guide and Directory, available from the Ernst & Young accounting office in your country, or from:

Kantor Akuntan
Drs. Santoso Harsokusumo & Rekan
P.O. Box 2333
Jakarta 10001, Indonesia
Tel: (21) 5220358, 5220314

At a Glance

Corporate Income Tax Rate (%)(a)	30
Capital Gains Tax Rate (%)(b)	0.1/5/30
Branch Tax Rate (%)(a)	30
Withholding Tax (%)(c)	
Dividends (d)	15/20
Interest (d)	15/20
Royalties from Patents, Know-how, etc. (d)	15/20
Fees for Services (d)	15/20
Branch Remittance Tax	20
Net Operating Losses (Years)	
Carryback	0

(a) Lower rates apply to profits up to R 50 million.
(b) Capital gains are taxed at the same rates as other profits. Transferred value of the right to use land or buildings is subject to a 5% withholding tax. A 0.1% final withholding tax applies to gross proceeds from sales of shares on the stock market.
(c) Rates may be reduced by tax treaties.
(d) The 20% tax is a final tax applicable to payments to nonresidents. The 15% tax, which may be credited against the recipient's income tax, is imposed on payments to residents. Certain dividends and interest paid to residents are exempt from tax

Business Travel

Air Travel Times

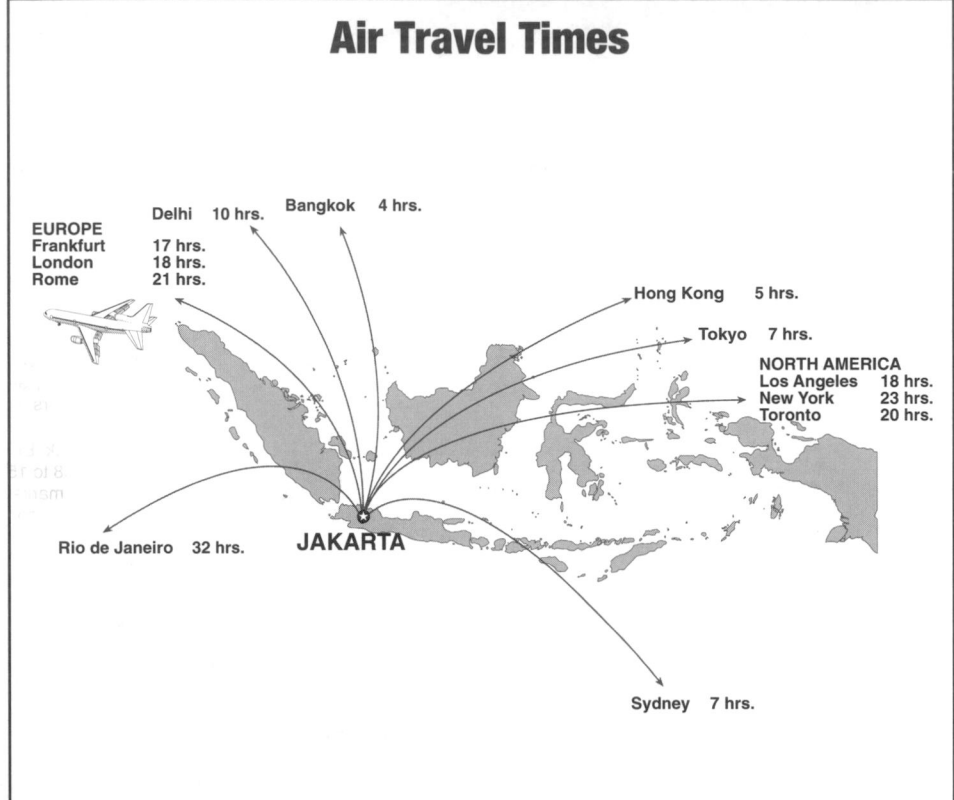

Delhi 10 hrs. Bangkok 4 hrs.

EUROPE
Frankfurt 17 hrs.
London 18 hrs.
Rome 21 hrs.

Hong Kong 5 hrs.

Tokyo 7 hrs.

NORTH AMERICA
Los Angeles 18 hrs.
New York 23 hrs.
Toronto 20 hrs.

Rio de Janeiro 32 hrs.

JAKARTA

Sydney 7 hrs.

COMMUNICATIONS

Telephones Although phone lines have been known to go out, occasionally making service somewhat undependable, telephone service is generally adequate. There is a 10% VAT tax on all phone calls.

Fax Telexes, cables, and faxes are sent easily by hotels. Allow 36 hours for cables. Faxing is being used often, but the shortage of telephone lines has inhibited its growth. Faxes can be sent and received at Permutel and Wartel offices.

Post office Mailboxes are large and round and found in many areas. Postal service is adequate in the capital, slow in the provinces. Courier services are used mainly in these areas. Express service for international mail takes about five days. There are many post offices, but some branches do not accept parcels. Customs require that all parcels be opened for international mailing. Register any important mail.

BEST TRAVEL BOOKS

Lonely Planet, Indonesia Travel Survival Kit. Lively, often funny and packed with details.

All-Asia Travel Guide, Southeast Asia, Volume One.

Do's and Taboo's Around the World. The Bestselling Guide to International Behavior. 3rd edition. Edited by Roger Axtell, compiled by the Parker Pen Company. The ultimate guide to international behavior, now completely updated and expanded. Helpful, fun to read!

The Travelers Guide to Indonesia Customs and Manners. Elizabeth Devine & Nancy Braganti. An invaluable guide for people not wanting to put foot in mouth.

USEFUL TELEPHONE NUMBERS

If you are calling from outside Indonesia, you will need to add the country code [62] and any other international dialing requirements from within your country.

- Jakarta Fire 113
- Jakarta Ambulance 113
- Jakarta Accident 118
- Operator 101
- International Calls 104, 194
- Jakarta Police 110, (21) 587771
- Computer Rentals .... (21) 7201671
- Courier Services .... (21) 517989, 333432, 735613
- Interpreters and Translators ... (21) 344485, 656021
- Secretarial Services .... (21) 510073, 5700279
- Chamber of Commerce Jakarta .... (21) 365609
- Dewan Perniagaan dan Perusahaan Chamber of Commerce .... (21) 377459
- Flight information .... (21) 5501884
- Garuda Indonesian Airways Jakarta .... (21) 380059
- Merpati Nusantara Airlines .... (21) 413608
- Indonesia Railways ....(21) 20275; (21) 20279
- Indonesia Hotels and Restaurant Association .... (21) 548-2335

Car Rental

- Avis .... (21) 332900, 5507088
- Hertz .... (21) 332610, 332739

Credit Card Information

Lost or stolen credit cards (call collect to the US, regardless of which country the card was issued in).

- Amex ....[1] (919) 333-3211
- Diner's Club...............................[1] (303) 799-1504
- MasterCard ....[1] (314) 275-6690
- Visa ....[1] (410) 581-7931

Travelogue

WORKWEEK

Offices Monday-Friday 8:00 am to 4:00 pm, Saturday until 1:00 pm.
Banks Monday-Friday 8:00 am to 4:00 pm, Saturday until 1:00 pm.
Government Monday-Friday 8:00 am to 3:00 pm, Saturday until 2:00 pm.
Retail Monday-Saturday 9:00 am to 6:00 pm.
It is not uncommon for businesses to start at 6:30 am to avoid the heat and humidity factors. During the fasting month of Ramadan and the two weeks following, businesses generally are not operational.

HOLIDAYS

Holidays 1996
January 1-2 New Year's Day
January 1 Ascension of Mohammad**
February 21-22 Idulfitri 1415H, 1416H**
March 13 Saka New Year
April 5 Good Friday *
May 12 Ascension of Christ*
May 29 Idul Adha 1415H, 1416H-Haj New Year**
May 20 Moslem New Year 1416H and 1417H
July 28 Mohammad's Birthday**
August 17 Independence Day
December 25 Christmas Day
December 30 Ascension Day
*Dates vary each year.
**Dates based on lunar calendar and vary each year.

VISA AND PASSPORT

Foreigners entering Indonesia from an international airport or other recognized entry point need only a passport valid for six months and a return ticket. These visitors can stay for up to 60 days without a visa. Those who enter from other points will need to obtain a visa from the Indonesian embassy. Business travelers who will be concluding commercial transactions or performing professional or technical services will need to get a regular business visa. A visa is required for a visit to Indonesia of any duration. Tourists and business visitors from the United States may obtain free visas upon arrival if they have a return ticket, and the period of stay does not exceed two months.

DEPARTURE FORMALITIES

There is a departure tax of US$6 for international flights and US$1.25 for domestic flights. Currency exchange can be accomplished at most airports.

IMMUNIZATION

No immunizations are required for entry to Indonesia.

TIPPING

Taxi: 15 percent. Porters: R 500 per piece. Hotels, restaurants: 10 percent included in bill with an additional 10 to 11 percent government tax. Small services: R 400.

CRIME

The crime rate in Jakarta is moderate. Minor street crimes occur at popular tourist sites and on public transportation. Incidents of car-jackings and robbery have also occurred.

INFRASTRUCTURE

Indonesia has developed but somewhat unpredictable air, train, and ferry service between major cities and islands. Jakarta and other major cities do have public transportation, but it is not considered reliable. There are established hotel, taxi, and private car industries in Indonesia. There are 13 international gateways into Indonesia. Taxis are available but add an additional surcharge and toll fee to the cost. Regular buses to and from the airport are not recommended to the business traveler. Rail service is limited to Java and local trains in parts of Sumatra. Pelni is a main seaport and is modern. Rickshaws are available in a few provincial towns. There are many inter-island domestic flights.

NATIONAL TOURIST OFFICE

Indonesia Tourist Promotion Board
Bank Pacific Bldg., 4th Floor
Jalan Jenderal Sudirman
Jakarta

GOVERNMENT AGENCIES

Department of Agriculture
Jl. Harsono, Room 3
Ragunan, Pasar Minggu
Jakarta Selatan
Tel: (21) 783-006, 780-406, 780-4265/6

Department of Communications and Transportation
Jl. Medan Merdeka Barat 8
Jakarta Pusat 10110
Tel: (21) 366-332
Telex: 44310, 46117

Department of Cooperatives and Small Business
Jl. Hr. Rasuna Said
Blok X-7 Kav 3-5
POB 177
Jakarta Selatan
Tel: (21) 520-4375/6/7
Fax: (21) 520-4383

Department of Education and Culture
Jl. Jen. Sudirman
Senayan
Jakarta Pusat
Tel: (21) 581-618, 581-665

Department of Finance
Jl. Lapangan Banteng Timur 2-4
Jakarta Pusat
Tel: (21) 348-938, 373-309, 365-364

Department of Forestry
Gedung Manggala Wanabakti
Jl. Jend. Gatot Subroto, Senayan
Jakarta 10270
Tel: (21) 581-820, 580-3181, 570-450 4, 570-4506
Fax: (21) 570-0226, 588-732, 570-0226

Department of Health
Jl. H.R. Rasuna Said
Blok X-5 Kav. No. 49/2nd Floor
Jakarta Pusat
Tel: (21) 520-1595, 520-1587, 520-1591, 520-4395

Department of Public Works
Jl. Pattimura 20
Kebayoran Baru
Jakarta Selatan 12110
Tel: (21) 717-564 Telex: 47247

Department of Tourism, Post and Telecommunications
Jl. Kebon Sirih 36
Jakarta 10110
Tel: (21) 346-855, 372-305, 373-862
Fax: (21) 315-409

Department of Trade
Jl. Moh. Ikhwan Ridwan Rais 5
Kotak Pos 229
Jakarta 10110
Tel: (21) 341-961, 341-187, 341-403

Perusahaan Jawatan Kereta Api
(Indonesian State Railways)
Jalan Perintis Kermedekaan 1
Bandung 40113
Java
Tel: (22) 430031
Telex: 28263
Fax: (22) 50342

Directorate General of Highways
Ministry of Public Works
Jalan Pattimura 20
Kebayoran Baru Jakarta
Tel: (21) 7203165

Directorate General of Sea Communications
Ministry of Communications
Jalan Medan Merdeka Timur 5
Jakarta
Tel: (21) 363009
Telex: 46117

WORLD TRADE CENTERS

World Trade Center Jakarta
World Trade Center Building, 2nd Floor
Jl. Jend. Sudirman Kav. 29-31
Jakarta 12920
Tel: (21) 521-1125/6, 251-0644
Fax: (21) 252-2135, 571-1673

World Trade Center Surabaya
Jalan Pemuda 27-31
Surabaya 60275
Tel: (31) 519-310/1/2
Fax: (31) 519-287

BUSINESS AND TRADE ORGANIZATIONS

Gabungan Perusahaan Ekspor Indonesia
(Indonesian Exporters' Federation)
Jalan Kramat Raya 4-6
Jakarta

GINSI
(Importers' Association of Indonesia)
CTC Building, 4th Floor
Jalan Kramat Raya 94-96
Jakarta 10420
Tel: (21) 390-1559
Fax: (21) 390-847

Kamar Dagang dan Industri Indonesia
(Indonesian Chamber of Commerce and Industry)
Chandra Building, 3rd-5th Floors
Jalan J.G. Thamrin 20
Jakarta 10350
Tel: (21) 324000
Fax: (21) 310-6098

Asosiasi Perusahaan Perindustrian Pesticida Indonesia
(Association of Indonesian Pesticide Factories)
Jl. Sisingamangaraja No. 14
Ebayoran Baru, Jakarta Selatan
Tel: (21) 714-845

Asosiasi Produsen Pupuk Indonesia (APPI)
(Indonesian Fertilizer Producers Association)
Unawar Centre
Jl. Kapten Tendean 28
Jakarta 12710
Tel: (21) 520-4234
Fax: (21) 520-435
Telex: 42297 APPI IA

Asosiasi Pulp Dan Kerta Indonesia
(Indonesian Pulp and Paper Association)
Jl. Cimandiri No. 6, Flat 1/2
Jakarta Pusat
Tel: (21) 326-084
Fax: (21) 320-168
Telex: 61830 KI IA

Asosiasi Indusri Mesin Perkakas Indonesia - ASIMPI
(Indonesian Machine Tools Industry Association)
Jl. Kramat Raya 172
Jakarta Pusat
Tel: (21) 323-080
Fax: (21) 326-018

Asosiasi Pabrik Besi Beton Seluruh Indonesia - APBESI
(Association of Indonesian Concrete Bars Producers)
Wisma Argo Manunggal, 9th Fl.
Jl. Jend. Gatot Subroto Kav. 22
Jakarta 12930
Tel: (21) 514-756, 514-778
Fax: (21) 514-829

Asosiasi Pabrik Ingot dan billet Baja Indonesia - ASPIBI
(Association of Indonesian Steel Ingot and Billet Manufactures)
Wisma Argo Manunggal, 9th Fl.
Jl. Jend. Gatot Subroto Kave. 22
Fax: (21) 514-829

Gabungan Industri Kendaraan Bermotor Indonesia - Gaikindo
(Association of Indonesian Automotive Industry)
Jl. Hos Cokroaminoto No. 6
Jakarta Pusat
Tel: (21) 332-100
Fax: (21) 332-100

Gabungan Industra Alat-Alat Mobil Dan Motor - GIAMM
(Association of Automotive Components Parts Manufacturers)
Artamas Bldg., GOVI, 1st Fl., Room 7/8
Jl. Jend. A. Yani No. 2
Jakarta Timur
Tel: (21) 489-8979

Gabungan Industri Pengerjaan Logam Dan Mesin Indonesia/GAMMA
(Federation of Indonesia Metalworks and Machinery Industry)
Pavilion GAMMA
Arena Pekan Raya Jakarta
Jakarta 10110
Tel: (21) 377-008 ext. 239
Fax: (21) 359-224 att. gamma

Himpunan Pengusaha Perikanan Negara - HPPN
(Association of State-Owned Fisheries Companies)
c/o P.T. Usaha Mina Persero
Jl. Salemba Raya 16
Jakarta Pusat
Tel: (21) 312-102685
Telex: 61458 USAHAM IA

HimpunanPengusaha Pertambakan Indonesia - HIPERINDO
(Union of Indonesian Fish Breeders)
Hanurata Bldg., 6th Fl.
Jl. Kebon Sirih 67-69
Jakarta Pusat
Tel: (21) 327-8110 ext. 409
Fax: (21) 334-926

Indonesian Textile Association
Panin Bank Centre
3rd Floor
Jalan Jenderal Sudirman 1
Jakarta Pusat 10270
Tel: (21) 739-6094
Fax: (21) 739-6341

Indonesian Tobacco Association
Jalan H. Agus Salim 85
Jakarta 10350
Tel: (21) 3206627
Fax: (21) 325181

American Chamber of Commerce Indonesia
(Amcham Indonesia)
Landmark Center
22nd Floor, Suite 2204
Jl. Jendral Sudirman 1
Jakarta, Indonesia
Tel: (21) 5780650
Fax: (21) 5780656

Indonesian Chamber of Commerce and Industry
(Kadin Indonesia)
Jl. M.H. Thamrin No. 20
Tel: (21) 324000, 324064
Fax: (21) 3106098

Jakarta Chamber of Commerce and Industry
(Kadin Jaya)
Majapahit Permai, Blok B21-23
J. Majapahit No. 18-20
Jakarta Pusat
Tel: (21) 3808089, 3808091

IMPORT/EXPORT FIRMS

PT Dharma Niaga Ltd.
(Import and Export)
Jl. Abdul Muis 6/10
POB 2028
Jakarta 10160
Tel: (21) 384-9978
Fax: (21) 381-0434

PT Indosat
(Telecommunications)
Jl. Merdeka Barat 21
Jakarta 10110
Tel: (21) 380-2614
Telex: 44383

PT Tjipta Niaga
(Import and Distribution of Basic Goods and Export of Produce)
Jl. Kalibesar Timur IV/1
POB 1314/JAK
Jakarta
Tel: (21) 691-2823
Fax: (21) 691-2471

BANKS

Perhimpunan Bank-Bank Nasional Swasta - PERBANAS
Indonesian National Private Banks Association
Jalan Perbanas
Karet Kuningan
Setiabudi
Jakarta 12940
Tel: (21) 515731
Fax: (21) 513887
Telex: 41467

Bank Indonesia
Jl. M.H. Thamrin No. 2
Jakarta 10310
Tel: (21) 372-408, 341-081 through 9
Telex: 44164

American Express Bank
Arthaloka Building
Jl. Jend. Subirman
Jakarta
Tel: (21)587401

Bank of America
Wisma Antara
Jl. Merdeka Selatan
17 Jakarta Pusat
Tel: (21) 347031
Fax: (21) 3806484

Chase Manhattan
Chase Plaza, 5th Floor
Jl. Jend. Sudirman
Jakarta
Tel: (21) 578-80088

Pan Indonesia Bank
Pain Bank Centre
Jl. Sudirman
Jakarta
Tel: (21) 739-4545
Fax: (21) 720-0340

Standard Charter Bank
Wisma Kosgoro
Jalan M.H. Thamrin 53, POB 57/JKWK
Jakarta 10350
Tel: (21) 325008
Fax: (21) 323619
Telex: 44160

Westpac Banking Corp
17th Floor
BNI Bldg
Jalan Jenderal Sudirman
Jakarta
Tel: (21) 5705137
Fax: (21) 5705138
Telex: 44277

NEWSPAPERS

Berita Buana
Gedung Puri Mandiri
Jalan Warung Buncit Raya 37
Jakarta 12510
Tel: (21) 780-041
Telex: 46472

Berita Yudha
Jalan Bangka II/2, 2nd Floor
Kebayoran Baru
Jakarta
Tel: (21) 75286

Bisnis Indonesia
Jalan Kramat V/8
Jakarta 10430
Tel: (21) 342191

Indonesian Observer
Jalan A.M. Sangaji 11
POB 2211
10001
Jakarta
Tel: (21) 352664

Jakarta Post
Jalan Palmerah Selatan 15B/C
Jakarta 10270
Tel: (21) 548-3948
Fax: (21) 549-2685

The Indonesia Times
Jalan Letjenderal S. Parman
Kav. 72
POB 1224
Slipi
Jakarta 10012
Tel: (21) 592403
Fax: (21) 375012

BUSINESS PERIODICALS

Business News
Jalan H. Abdul Muis 70
Jakarta 10160
Tel: (21) 384-8207
Fax: (21) 354820

Economic Review
c/o BNI 1946
Jalan Jenderal Sudirman
Kav. 1
POB 2955
Jakarta 10001
Tel: (21) 570-1001
Fax: (21) 570-0926

Ekonomi Indonesia
Jalan Merdeka
Timur 11-12
Jakarta
Tel: (21) 494458

Intisari
Jalan Kebahagiaan 4-14
Jakarta 11140
Tel: (21) 629-7809
Fax: (21) 639-0080

Majalah Ekonomis
Jakarta

MARKET RESEARCH FIRMS

SGV Utomo Management Consultants
Chase Plaza
Jl. Jend. Sudirman Kav. 21
Jakarta Pusat, Indonesia
Tel: (21) 588-175, 588-366

P.T. Sri International
c/o Sumarno Pabotinggi
Jl. Kamboja 9
Tomang Raya, Jakarta 11440
Indonesia
Tel: (21) 560-0361
Fax: (21) 310-6488

Plansearch Associates
Jl. Limau 1/28A
Jakarta Selatan, Indonesia
Tel: (21) 739-5017
Fax: (21) 739-5018

RADIO & TELEVISION

Radio Republik Indonesia
Jalan Merdeka Barat 4-5
POB 157
Jakarta 10110

Rajawali Citra Televisi Indonesia
Jalan Raya Pejuangan Kebon Jeruk
Jakarta 11063
Tel: (21) 530-3540
Fax: (21) 549-3852

Televisi Pendidikan Indonesia
Jakarta
Tel: (21) 384-9091
Fax: (21) 367132

Voice of Indonesia
Medan Merdeka Barat 4-5
Jakarta
Tel: (21) 366811

Yayasan Televisi Republik Indonesia
TVRI Senayan
Jalan Gerbang Pemuda
Senayan
Jakarta
Tel: (21) 582328
Fax: (21) 583122

ACCOUNTING FIRMS

Kantor Akuntan Public Prasetion, Utomo & Rekan
Jualan Sulanjania No. 4
Bandung
Tel: (22) 420-4464
Fax: (22) 420-4604

P.T. Byrnindo Setiatama
Kopo Plaza Blok A-14
Jalan Peta
Bandung 40233
Tel: (22) 636-433
Fax: (22) 636-443

AAJ Associates
JL Letjen S. Parman Kav. 35
Jakarta11480
Tel: (21) 568-2703
Fax: (21) 566-3569

Drs. Hertanto & Co.
JL. H.R. Rasuna Said Kav. C-1 #605
Jakarta 12950
Tel: (22) 512-590
Fax: (22) 520-5154

INTERNET ADDRESSES

Usenet group:
soc.culture.indonesia

Central Bureau of Statistics - Indonesia
http://www.bps.go.id/

The Republic of Indonesia Homepage
http://www.prica.org/indonesia.html

Indonesian Information
http://sunsite.nus.sg/SEAlinks/indonesia-info.html

Indonesian Homepage
http://www.umanitoba.ca/indonesian

Indonesian Homepage (Jakarta)
http://www.inn.bppt.go.id/

Iran

Islamic Republic of Iran

Economy

Overview

Traditionally an agricultural society, Iran had achieved significant industrialization and modernization by the 1970s. However, its economy was seriously hurt by a series of distortions—beginning with the Islamic revolution in 1979, and including a prolonged war with Iraq and falling oil prices in the 1980s—from which it has yet to recover. The government recently imposed austerity measures, adding to the hardships faced by Iranian citizens. Economic reforms have been hindered by government infighting, continued high military spending, and fundamentalist Islamic precepts that do not mesh well with contemporary international business practices. Unemployment is a major problem, stemming from rapid population growth and shortages of raw materials. Despite oil revenues, Iran has borrowed heavily, and its foreign debt is estimated as high as US$30 billion, which limits its ability to invest in infrastructure development. Although several European nations are beginning to increase business ties with Iran, in early 1995 the US declared a boycott of the country.

Trade

One of Iran's major goals is to exclude foreign influences while building trade ties. Exports include petroleum (accounting for about 66 percent of export revenues), foodstuffs, leather products, carpets, and textiles. Imports include machinery, chemicals, intermediate industrial components, foodstuffs, and fuels. Major trade partners include Germany, the UK, Italy, and the United Arab Emirates.

Sectors

Agriculture Agriculture produces about 20 percent of GDP, while employing more than 30 percent of the work force. Much activity is on a subsistence basis, although major cash crops include fruit and nuts, cereal crops, sugar, and sheep and poultry. Along with other sectors, agriculture suffers from a lack of investment necessary to boost productivity.

Industry Dominated by oil, industry contributes somewhat more than 20 percent of GDP while employing roughly 21 percent of the work force. In addition to oil, industrial products include food processing (particularly sugar and vegetable oils), textiles, and transportation equipment. Iran's manufacturing sectors suffer from low labor productivity, lack of foreign exchange, and shortages of raw materials and spare parts. Many industries are also heavily dependent on imports of raw materials.

Services Services provide about 60 percent of GDP while employing about half of the work force. Tourism—a former source of foreign exchange—has been pretty much basically eliminated. Services are government operated, and the remainder include local distribution and personal service activities.

Trends

Iran's five-year plan for economic development was cut short because of mismanagement and inefficient bureaucracy, as well as political and ideological infighting. The government has pulled back from its only attempt at modernization—the unification of exchange rates—and as a result, the Iranian rial plunged. Parliament opposed most of the liberalizing reforms included in the five-year plan, and this political infighting and the continued studied exclusion of all foreign influences, combined with continued low oil prices, will continue to slow economic development overall.

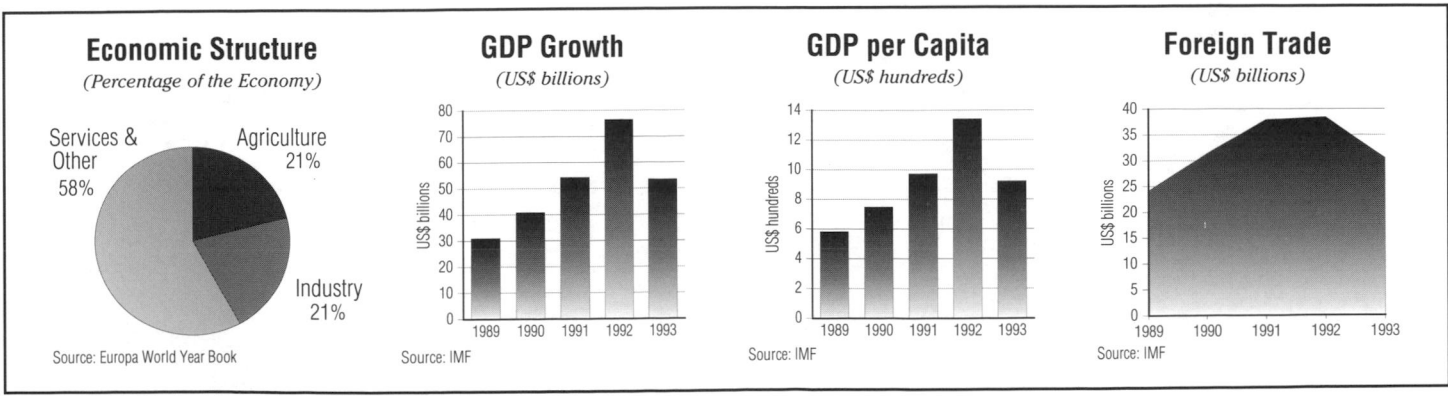

Economic Structure
(Percentage of the Economy)

Services & Other 58%
Agriculture 21%
Industry 21%

Source: Europa World Year Book

GDP Growth
(US$ billions)

Source: IMF

GDP per Capita
(US$ hundreds)

Source: IMF

Foreign Trade
(US$ billions)

Source: IMF

Business Travel

LH 1906	MADRID	935	113-3
LH 1022	STUTTGART HBF.	935	
AF 1701	LYON	940	683-6
AY 822	HELSINKI	940	113-3
AA 071	SFRANCISCO-DALLAS	945	731-7

Iran

- National capital
- Province capital
- Secondary city
- Interntional border
- Province border
- Primary road
- Railroad

0   100   200 km
0   150 mi

©1995 Magellan Geographix℠Santa Barbara, CA

COMMUNICATIONS

Telephone Telephone service is very good, although limited in some remote areas. Use hotels for international and long distance calls. It may take a couple of hours to make long distance calls at the telephone office. Public telephones are in hotels and telephone offices.

Fax Telex, fax, and telegram services are available, though expensive and time consuming to send. It can take up to a couple of hours for connections; major hotels and post offices may be faster.

Post office Stamps can be purchased at post offices and major hotels. Mail service is adequate, if slow.

BEST TRAVEL BOOKS

Iran, Travel Survival Kit, Lonely Planet. Crammed full of practical information to budget travelers traveling independently. 352 pages.

Middle East on a Shoestring, Lonely Planet. Details, details, details! 126 maps.

Do's and Taboo's Around the World. The Bestselling Guide to International Behavior. Edited by Roger Axtell, compiled by the Parker Pen Company. The ultimate guide to international behavior, now completely updated and expanded. Helpful, fun to read!

USEFUL TELEPHONE NUMBERS
Credit Card Information
Lost or stolen credit cards (call collect to the US, regardless of which country the card was issued in).
- Amex ....[1] (919) 333-3211
- Diner's Club ....[1] (303) 799-1504
- MasterCard ....[1] (314) 275-6690
- Visa ....[1] (410) 581-7931

TOURIST OFFICE
Tourist offices are under the control of the Tourism and Exploration Office or the Press & Information Officer at Iranian embassies.

Travelogue

WORKWEEK

Offices Saturday-Wednesday, 8:30 am to 12:30 pm and 2:00 pm to 7:30 pm.

Banks Saturday-Wednesday, 8:30 am to noon and 5:00 pm to 7:00 pm; Thursday, 8:30 am to 11:30 am.

Government Saturday-Wednesday, 7:30 am to 2:30 pm.

Retail Friday is the Muslim Sabbath and Thursday is a weekly holiday for most offices. Hours are limited during Ramadan and the Haj (pilgrimage) period.

HOLIDAYS

Holidays 1996
February Id-Al-Fitr/Ramadan
February/March Petroleum Day
February/March Now Rooz (lasts four days)
February/March Martyrdom of Imam Jaffar Sadeq
June/July Ashoura
July/August Demise of the Prophet Mohammed and Martyrdom of Iman Hassan Majtaba
July/August Arbin
November/December Birthday of Imam Ali
November/December Prophet's Mission
Not all religious days are public holidays. Businesses customarily close for seven days for observance of the end of Ramadan. Religious days are based on the lunar calendar, and exact dates are announced by the royal palace upon the sighting of the moon or at the beginning of the month. Check with an Iranian embassy or consulate for precise information on holidays when making travel plans.

VISA AND PASSPORT

Visas can be tricky. Those who want to go badly enough can usually obtain one, while telephone inquiries usually get the runaround. Regulations can change with little or no warning. A number of forms must be filled out and then sent by the Ministry of Tourism. These forms can take a number of months to return or may never come at all. A transit visa is necessary for a stay of up to two weeks, and a tourist visa is necessary for a stay of up to one month.

DEPARTURE FORMALITIES

There is an airport tax of 1500 rials, payable by foreigners on all international departures. It is not included in the price of the ticket and must be paid in cash at the airport.

IMMUNIZATION

Vaccinations for malaria, typhoid, polio, yellow fever, cholera, rabies, viral hepatitis, tetanus, tuberculosis, and dysentery are recommended, though not required.

TIPPING

Unless a service charge is already added, it is customary to include a 10 percent tip for restaurant bills.

CRIME

Most of the crimes against Westerners in Iran have toned down compared to the fanaticism of the early 1980s. Nevertheless, it is best to be cautious at all times. It is advisable for tourists not to carry any valuables but to store them in a hotel safety box. Beware of individuals who may impersonate police or hotel employees. Beware that some areas of Iran, especially the north near Turkey, can be extremely dangerous to travelers.

INFRASTRUCTURE

Iran's infrastructure has improved greatly recently, especially with air travel. Airlines from all over the world land in Iran's airports. Several new roads have been opened that run through Iran. There are no longer any Iranian buses going further west than Istanbul, and the decorations on the sides of buses advertising such faraway destinations as Munich and London are for decoration only.

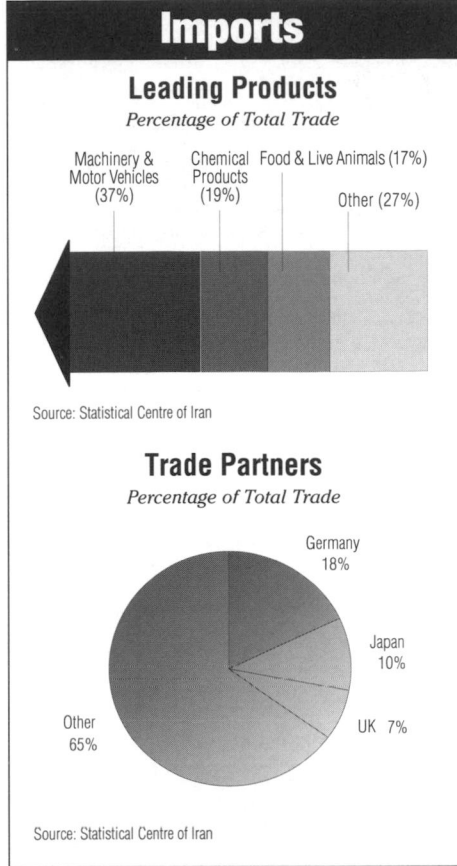

Imports

Leading Products
Percentage of Total Trade

Machinery & Motor Vehicles (37%)
Chemical Products (19%)
Food & Live Animals (17%)
Other (27%)

Source: Statistical Centre of Iran

Trade Partners
Percentage of Total Trade

Germany 18%
Japan 10%
UK 7%
Other 65%

Source: Statistical Centre of Iran

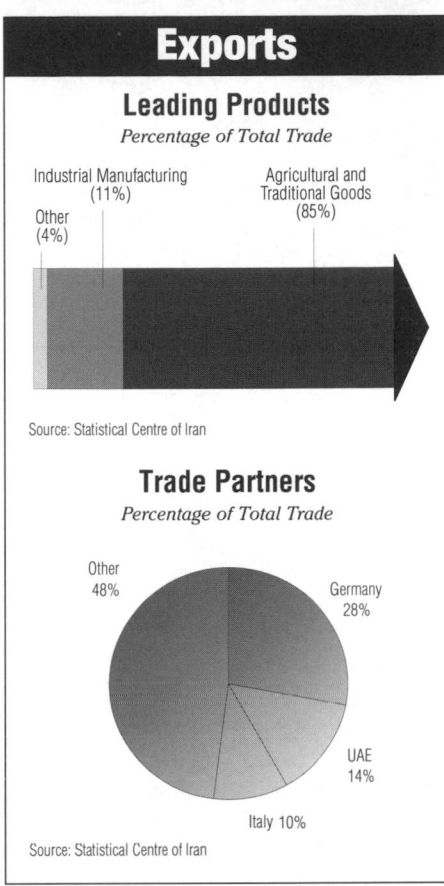

Exports

Leading Products
Percentage of Total Trade

Industrial Manufacturing (11%)
Other (4%)
Agricultural and Traditional Goods (85%)

Source: Statistical Centre of Iran

Trade Partners
Percentage of Total Trade

Other 48%
Germany 28%
UAE 14%
Italy 10%

Source: Statistical Centre of Iran

Opportunities

FOR IMPORTING TO IRAN
- cereals, corn, rice, fruits, fats, oils, and vegetables
- medical supplies and equipment, pharmaceuticals
- plastic, rubber, refined oil, wood, and wood products

FOR EXPORTING FROM IRAN
- carpets, textiles
- fruits and nuts
- metal and petroleum products

GROWTH SECTORS
- food processing
- metal fabrication
- petroleum products
- textiles

Trade News

RULES AND REGULATIONS
- **Barriers** Trading could face several barriers from intense government bureaucracy. There are many limits placed upon the types of products and amounts that can be imported into the country. A great deal of prior knowledge about Iran's trading restrictions is more than a suggestion, it should be taken as a rule.
- **Oil** Revenues from oil have been affected by the decline of oil prices. Oil accounts for about 90 percent of Iran's exports. Because of reduced revenues, the government has imposed austerity measures, adding to the hardships of the Iranian people.
- **Export problems** Iran's exports, especially in the agricultural sector, have suffered from shortages of capital, raw materials, and equipment, as well as from the war with Iraq.

Legal Matters

LEGAL BRIEFS
- **Maximum workweek** The statutory maximum work-week for employees is 44 hours. In addition to paid national holidays, employees are given special leave, as well as annual paid vacations. The work-week starts on Saturday and terminates on Thursday, noon. Thursday and Friday are weekend holidays.
- **Foreign documents** After being certified by the local consulates of the Islamic Republic of Iran, foreign investments should be officially translated to Farsi in order to be valid for use in the country.
- **Property** Resident aliens may acquire real property under certain terms and conditions.
- **Arbitration** For public sector contracts, referral to international arbitration is subject to the approval of the Islamic Assembly (parliament), but acceptance of the UNICITRAL arbitration model is under examination by the relevant authorities.
- **Foreign investment laws** Foreigners are able to participate in the joint ownership of companies, up to a share of 49 percent. Joint ownership requires prior approval and the amount of foreign participation allowed is determined on the merits of each project. Foreign investors in Economic Free Zones face fewer restrictions and enjoy less government interference.
- **Trade agreements** Iran is not a member of GATT, although its application to join is under examination.

LEGAL CONTACT
Pars Associates
POB 11365-6665
Tehran
Tel: (21) 651169
Fax: (21) 657197
Telex: 212107 MATN IR

Legal System

The country's traditional law is entirely Western, but its civil and penal codes are inspired more by Islamic laws and traditions.

Intellectual Property Rights

Patents and Trademarks Iran has not joined the Bern convention on the protection of intellectual property, but intellectual property rights are protected by law, and enforcement is adequate and consistent. Trademark registration procedures take about two or three months.

Trade Secrets Trade secrets are not specifically protected by law, and there is little enforcement of provisions attempting to address the wrongful dissemination of valuable commercial information.

Business Registration, Contracts, and Dispute Resolution

The operation of an incorporated company, a joint venture, or a branch office or a representative office requires registration with the Company Registration Bureau. Foreign Businesses operating in Iran require investment approval by the Ministerial authorities. Private business and trade contracts should be drawn in detail, and the method of dispute resolution and governing law should be specifically addressed.

Notaries

Notaries prepare and authenticate documentary instruments, which must be written in the Farsi language.

Labor

The association and syndication of labor unions exist according to the law, and the right to strike has also been recognized. However, Iran's labor laws, and concepts of unionization, are different from those in the West, and the syndications do not operate on Western models.

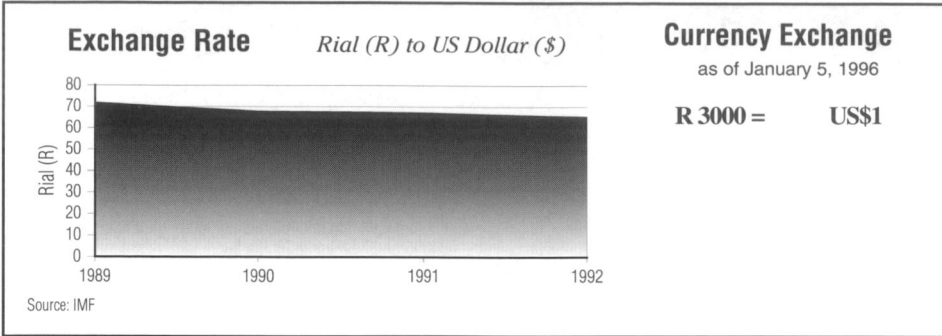

Source: IMF

Currency

The currency in use is the Iranian rial (R), divided into 100 dinars.

Foreign Exchange

The Bank Markazi Jomhouri Islami Iran (central bank) sets a daily exchange rate based on supply and demand conditions. There are no taxes on the purchase or sale of foreign exchange, and no arrangement for forward cover against exchange rate risk. An open market rate of exchange also exists, and is operated by authorized exchange shops.

Capital Transfers

Iranian and foreign resident individuals and corporations may open external foreign exchange bank accounts. Currencies from external sources may be repatriated through the banking system. Travelers arriving in or leaving Iran may take out up to R200,000; foreign exchange may be brought into the country in unlimited amounts. Travelers may import or export any amount of Iranian bank notes through foreign branches of Iranian banks. Foreign nationals may open a rial account and a foreign currency account, but funds in the rial account may be used only in Iran. Foreign nationals and Iranian nonresidents may open rial or foreign exchange accounts with branches of Iranian banks, in the Persian Gulf region.

Investment Incentives

Foreign investors are welcome to participate in the private sector and there are joint ventures in operation from all countries except Israel. Investors can enjoy tax exemptions and their products will not be subject to price controls. Other incentives include favorable tariffs and 15-year tax breaks.

Investment Restrictions

The government imposes strict restrictions on the type of investments made in Iran. Some products cannot be produced or imported into the country. The political instability and economic woes hurt any successful investment potential. Shortages of goods have led to government rationing and inflation increases.

TAXATION

Taxation requires sophisticated knowledge of complex rules and regulations specific to each country. For more detailed information we suggest you refer to the Ernst & Young Corporate Tax Guide and Directory, available from the Ernst & Young accounting office in your country, or from:

Tadvin Co.
POB 19395/3149
Tehran 19177, Iran
Tel: (21) 888680310, 8886535, 8884661
Fax: (21) 8886150
Telex: 212589 ans bk EWTC

At a Glance

Corporate Income Tax Rate (%)(a)	10
Capital Gains Tax Rate (%)(a)(c)	10
Branch Tax Rate (%)(b)	54
Withholding Tax (%)	
Payments to:	
Contractors (d)	5
Registered Branches (d)	5
Unregistered Foreign Contractors (b)(e)	54
Fees and Commissions (d)	5
Dividends and Undistributed Profits, including Capital Gains (b)	54
Interest (f)	0
Royalties from Know-how, Technical Services (b)(g)	54
Net Operating Losses (Years)	
Carryback	0
Carryforward (h)	Unlimited

(a) The 10% tax is not applicable to branches of foreign companies. An additional progressive tax is levied on shares.
(b) This is the maximum rate. Branches of foreign companies are taxed on a progressive basis on their Iranian-source income.
(c) A transfer tax is also imposed on sales of land and buildings.
(d) This amount is deducted from gross receipts and deductible in full from final assessments.
(e) This withholding tax is computed on taxable income at progressive rates.
(f) Interest is included in taxable income and subject to tax at the regular corporate income tax rates. In general, interest received from Iranian banks is exempt from tax.
(g) This rate is applied to deemed profit.
(h) The maximum offset is one-third of the profit for the year.

Money Matters

BITS AND PIECES

- **Accounting books** All registered entities must have accounting books bearing the seal of the Registrar of Companies before the beginning of the entity's accounting year. Books must be maintained in the Persian language.
- **Tax credits** Foreign tax credits are available to resident companies for foreign taxes paid on income earned abroad.
- **Exchange rates** There are two official exchange rates for the rial: the floating rate and the export rate. The floating rate applies to imports of essential goods, the export rate applies to other imports and nongovernmental foreign currency disbursements.
- **Repatriation** Capital may be repatriated with the approval of the central bank, and the Organization for Investment and Economic and Technical Assistance of the Ministry of Economic Affairs and Finance.
- **Gold** Residents may hold, sell, and purchase gold, platinum, and silver in the domestic market without a license.
- **General payments** Settlements with member countries of the Asian Clearing Union (ACU) may be executed in Asian Monetary Units (AMUs). There are no bilateral payment agreements in effect.
- **Import payments** Payments for imports are made through the official local banking system. Advance import payments, ranging between 15 and 100 percent, are required in lieu of a registration deposit. Payments for imports with foreign currency must be accompanied by evidence that the currency was obtained by an Iranian bank.
- **Payments for invisibles** There are no restrictions on transfer of profits and dividends on foreign direct investments. Iranian insurance companies may issue insurance contracts in foreign currencies for imports, but only the Iran Insurance Company may issue war risk insurance in foreign currency.
- **Export payments** Exporters may sell foreign exchange proceeds to commercial banks without restriction at the official exchange rate.
- **Proceeds from invisibles** Iranian nationals are permitted to retain foreign exchange earnings in foreign currency accounts at an authorized bank.

BANKS

Central Bank of the Islamic Republic of Iran
Ferdwso Avenue
POB 3362
Tehran
Tel: (21) 310101 through 19

Bank Keshavarzi
Agricultural Bank
POB 14155-6395
129 Patrice Lumumba Avenue
Jalal al-Ahmad Expressway
Tehran
Tel: (21) 9121 Telex: 212058

Bank Mellat
Nation's Bank
POB 11365-5964
Park Shahr, Varzesh Avenue
Tehran
Tel: (21) 32491 Fax: (21) 892868

Bank Melli Iran
Ferdowsi Avenue
Tehran
Tel: (21) 3231

Bank Saderat Iran
The Export Bank of Iran
Bank Saderat Tower
Somayeh St.
Tehran
Tel: (21) 836091 Fax: (21) 836095

Bank Tejarat
Commercial Bank
POB 11365-5416
130 Taleghani Avenue
Tehran 15994
Tel: (21) 890130 Fax: (21) 828215

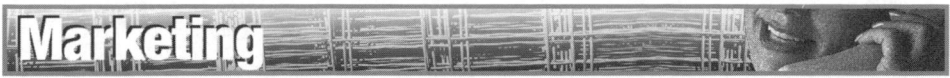

Overview

Iran is beginning to open its doors to foreign markets, but the country is known for its system of myriad, medieval regulations. Japan took its usual lead in opening trade here, at least partly due to Iran's chronic energy shortage, and it now successfully markets consumer goods. Several European nations are also testing these quick-to-boil waters. Domestic demand for goods has fallen, however, due to elevated costs of living and a significant drop in wages.

Distribution

The ports of Abadan, Bandar, and Khorranmshahr are where most goods arrive; Tehran, the capital, has the country's only major airport. Distribution chains and large wholesalers do not exist. There are thousands of small independent dealers, and this is the dominant distribution pattern.

Agents

Haggling in this part of the world approaches high art, and local agents are the best hagglers. Only Iranian nationals may be agents, and foreign firms must appoint representatives to handle their product lines. Agents may not intervene in sales to the military, though overseas companies must have registered representation when dealing with the government.

Advertising

Iran plans to implement a ban on cigarette advertising. Voice and Vision of the Islamic Republic of Iran runs the radio, the two television stations, and the news agency. This group must review and rule on all proposed media promotion. No ads may feature any human figure or its representation, in accordance with Muslim law. All marketing and advertising materials must be sensitive to the extremely strong Muslim doctrine which influences every aspect of life here.

Marketing in Iran

MARKETING TIPS

- **Education** Iranians tend to be well-educated, but they are for the most part unfamiliar with Western technology.
- **Economy** Most of Iran's public has very little spending money, and cannot afford a number of products.
- **Language** Most advertising should be in Farsi.
- **Postal service** The postal service in Iran is moderate, although still a bit slow. Mail should be used, at best, only for correspondence with local agents.
- **Telephone** International service is possible from the cities, but the telephone service in rural areas is poor and not up to international standards.

RADIO & TELEVISION

Islamic Republic of Iran Broadcasting
Mossadegh Avenue, Jame Jam Street
POB 19395-333
Tehran
Tel: (21) 21961 Telex: 212431

NEWSPAPERS

Kayhan
Ferdowsi Avenue
Tehran
Tel: (21) 310251
Telex: 212467

Tehran Times
Nejatullahi Avenue
32-Kouche Bimeh
Tehran
Tel: (21) 839900
Fax: (21) 822951

Greetings and Courtesies

The standard greeting is the handshake. The addition of a slight nod or bow when shaking hands is a sign of respect. A man should not shake a woman's hand unless she initiates the handshake. If she does not, smile and nod slightly. Greetings are often accompanied by questions about one's health and family. Titles are used to show respect, and are important. Iranians usually stand when someone first enters or leaves a room. Iranians require less personal space than those in Western cultures, so don't be surprised if Iranian associates stand close.

Business Ethic and Framework

People, family ties, and personal relationships are placed above business. Fate is an important part of Iranian culture. One does the best one can; but the outcome is ultimately in the hands of God. Class distinctions often determine a person's opportunities and influence their attitude toward getting ahead in life.

Meetings and Decision Making

Punctuality will be respected, although your Iranian associates may be late. Social amenities are important; generally business will not be addressed until there are inquiries about one's health and family, as well as other small talk. Personal relationships are more important than schedules. People's feelings are considered, and a person's needs can influence how a decision is made and what it will be. Iranians avoid direct criticism. Instead, they might hint they'd like to see changes, or suggest an alternative that leaves room for compromise. Decisions are made slowly. If you push for faster action or impose a deadline, you could do more harm than good.

Women

Iran is a conservative Islamic culture that puts many restrictions on women. During the 1980s, Iranian women had to be completely covered (and veiled) when in public. Women are no longer required to wear veils, but only their hands and face may be visible in public. Foreign women should be prepared for such attitudes, and behave with discretion at all times. Do not make prolonged, direct eye-contact with Iranian men. Being professional, poised, and self-confident will help in business, but male colleagues may nonetheless be taken more seriously and given more respect.

Cultural Cautions

DO'S

- Eat food with the right hand only. Use the right hand or both hands to give and receive things. Using the left hand is offensive.
- Accept all simple gestures of hospitality. If you must reject such a gesture, be sure to give an explanation.

DON'TS

- Avoid conversation about local or national politics, Israel, or anti-US feelings.
- Do not give a Muslim child a stuffed toy dog or anything printed with images of dogs.

CUSTOMS

- To keep distance between genders, men and women do not maintain eye contact when talking.
- Public displays of affection between men and women (even if married) are forbidden.
- Standard attire is a conservative suit. Women should wear tasteful, very conservative clothing. Women should never wear a sleeveless dress or blouse.

OBSERVATIONS

- Iran is an extremely conservative, fundamentalist Islamic society. To avoid difficult or awkward situations, or inadvertently offending Iranian associates, become somewhat familiar with Islamic customs and be aware of current political events or issues before you visit the country.
- In Iran, business relationships are personal relationships. To establish a good business relationship, establish a personal relationship that demonstrates your good faith and honor.

NEGOTIATIONS

- Iranians have a tradition of negotiating and genuinely enjoy it. Long, enthusiastic discussions are typical, and are an occasion for demonstrating one's wit and intelligence.
- "Yes" is generally indicated by tilting the head down, sometimes with a slight twist. "No" is indicated by quickly tilting the head up.

Contents

GOVERNMENT AGENCIES

Ministry of Agriculture and Rural Development
Keshavarz Boulevard
Tehran
Tel: (21) 927831, 927832

Ministry of Commerce
Vali-e-Asr Avenue
Tehran
Tel: (21) 310041 through 9

Ministry of Economic Affairs and Finance
Central Building, Bab-Homayoun Avenue
Tehran
Tel: (21) 301161

Ministry of Education and Training
1, Ekbatan Avenue
Tehran

Ministry of Energy
North Palestine Avenue
Tehran
Tel: (21) 822017

Ministry of Foreign Affairs
Sheikh Abdul Majid Avenue
Koushke Mesri
Tehran
Tel: (21) 303916, 321514

Ministry of Heavy Industries
18 Sepahbod Gharani Avenue
Tehran

Ministry of Labor and Social Affairs
Azadi Avenue
Tehran
Tel: (21) 930051

Ministry of Post, Telegraph and Telephones
Dr. Shariati Avenue
Tehran
Tel: (21) 763004, 84075

Ministry of Roads and Transport
Taleghani Avenue 49
Tehran
Tel: (21) 531191/2/3, 6665012

Islamic Republic News Agency
Vali Asr Avenue 873
POB 764
Tehran
Tel: (21) 892050

BUSINESS AND TRADE ORGANIZATIONS

National Iranian Industries Organization
POB 14155-3579
133 Dr. Fatemi Avenue
Tehran
Tel: (21) 656031
Fax: (21) 658070

National Iranian Industries Organization Export Company
No. 8
Second Alley
Bucharest Avenue
Tehran 15944
Tel: (21) 4162384
Telex: 212429

National Iranian Oil Co.
POB 1863
Taleghani Avenue
Tehran
Tel: (21) 6151
Telex: 212514

Iran Chamber of Commerce, Industries and Mines
254 Taleghani Avenue
Tehran
Tel: (21) 836031
Fax: (21) 825111

Iranian Offshore Oil Co
POB 15875-4546
339 Dr. Beheshti Avenue
Tehran
Tel: (21) 624102
Fax: (21) 627420

National Iranian Steel Co.
POB 15875-4469
Tehran
Tel: (21) 816-2243
Fax: (21) 893715

National Petrochemical Co. of Iran
POB 7484
Karimkhan Zand Blvd.
Tehran
Tel: (21) 839060-74
Fax: (21) 822087

NEWS AGENCY

Islamic Republic News Agency
Vali Asr Avenue 873
POB 764
Tehran
Tel: (21) 892050

NEWSPAPERS

Abrar Rightly Guided
Apadan Ave. 198
Abbasabad
Tehran
Tel: (21) 859971

Alik
POB 11365-953
Jomhoori Islami Ave.
Alik Alley
Tehran 11357
Tel: (21) 676671

Ettel'at Information
Khayyam St., Tehran
Tel: (21) 3281
Telex: 212336
Fax: (21) 315530

Khorassan
Khorassan Daily Newspapers
14 Zohre St.
Mobarezan Ave.
Tehran

Tehran Times
Nejatullahi Ave.
32-Kouche Bimeh
Tehran
Tel: (21) 839900
Fax: (21) 822951
Telex: 213662

PERIODICALS

Acta Medica Iranica
Faculty of Medicine
Enghelab Ave.
Tehran Medical Sciences University
Tehran 14-174
Tel: (21) 6112743

Auditor (Quarterly)
77 Ferdowsi Avenue Noartsh
Tehran

Iran Press Digest (Weekly)
POB 11365-5551
Hafiz Avenue
4 Kucheh Hurtab
Tehran
Tel: (21) 668114

Iran Trade and Industry (Monthly)
POB 1228
Hafiz Avenue
Tehran

Al-Akha
Khayyam Ave.
Tehran
Telex: 212336

Akhbar-e-Pezeshki
86 Ghaem Magham Farahani Ave.
Tehran

Daneshkadeh Qezeshki
Faculy of Medicine
Tehran Medical Sciences University
Tel: (21) 6112743

Daneshmand
POB 15875-3649
Tehran
Tel: (21) 854969

Dokhtaran and Pesaran
Khayyam Ave.
Ettel'at Bldg.
Tehran
Tel: (21) 3281
Fax: (21) 315530
Telex: 212336

Majda
POB 14155-3695
94 West Pirouzi St.
Kooye Nasr
Tehran
Tel: (21) 639591
Fax: (21) 639592
Telex: 212918

Soroush
POB 15875-1163 Motahhari Ave.
Corner Mofatteh St.
Tehran
Tel: (21) 830771

TRANSPORTATION FIRMS

Irano-Hind Shipping Co
No. 3, 13th Street
Miremad Avenue
Dr. Beheshti Avenue
Tehran
Tel: (21) 50213 Telex: 215233

Islamic Republic of Iran International Transport
Ortad Morahari Avenue
Tehran
Telex: 214209 IRIT IR

Ports and Shipping Organization
751 Enghetab Avenue
Tehran
Telex: 212271 BNDRIR

INTERNET ADDRESSES

Usenet group(s):
soc.culture.iranian
clari.world.mideast.iran

CityNet - Iran
http://www.city.net/countries/iran/

IRAN
http://grad.csee.usf.edu/suds/docs/farhad-iran.html

Iran Business Journal
http://simorgh.gpg.com/ibd/

Iran/Persia Home Page
http://www.ed.ac.uk/~bhm/persia.html

IRANET
http://www.nic.ir

Ireland

Eire

Economy

Overview

Ireland's economy is small and heavily dependent on trade. Agriculture, once the most important sector, is now overshadowed by industry, which accounts for about 80 percent of its export revenues and most of the growth in its economy. Inflation has fallen sharply since 1987 and chronic trade deficits have been transformed into annual surpluses. Unemployment among Ireland's generally highly educated work force remains a serious problem and job creation is the main focus of government policy. The tense political situation between largely Catholic Ireland and largely Protestant, UK-affiliated Northern Ireland remains to be resolved, although a cease-fire and ongoing negotiations offer new hope for permanent resolution. This would help considerably to promote stability and growth in the economy.

Trade

Ireland has a small, open economy. Exports have recently given Ireland a trade surplus, while its import business serves as a key base for the entire European market. Major exports include office and data processing machinery—an indication of the success of high-tech assembly industries—organic chemicals, electrical machinery, meat products, and dairy products. Imports include office and data processing machinery and components, electrical machinery, vehicles, petroleum products, and apparel. Ireland's main trading partner is the UK, accounting for about 33 percent of total trade, followed by the US, Germany, France, and the Netherlands, Ireland is currently trying to diversify its trade and investment base beyond these traditional partners.

Sectors

Agriculture Formerly an almost exclusively agricultural country, Ireland now derives less than 10 percent of the GDP and only about 15 percent of its employment from the sector. Major cash crops include beef and dairy cattle, with cereals, sugar beets, and potatoes representing the main domestic crops.

Industry Industry employs somewhat more than 29 percent of the work force while contributing more than 33 percent to the GDP. High-technology assembly operations—predominantly foreign-owned and accounting for more than 50 percent of net output—have been growing more rapidly than traditional sectors, and now represent about 75 percent of overall manufacturing growth. Primary industries for the 1990s include pharmaceuticals, office and data processing machinery, and food processing.

Services About 60 percent of the work force is involved in services, accounting for about 55 percent of GDP. Government incentives designed to encourage investment in Ireland as a regional base for off-shore financial and business services are expected to increase the service sector tremendously.

Trends

Overall, export volume exceeds import volume, reflecting the relatively weak growth in domestic demand. The Irish economy is expected to keep growing, however, although the agricultural sector is not expected to generate further growth. High-tech exports are likely to continue growing, though at a slower pace than in previous years—reflecting slower overall export growth. New car and machinery sales are expected to pick up. Overall, a healthy trade surplus is anticipated, bringing new prosperity and many opportunities for foreign business.

At a Glance

THE COUNTRY

Location Western Europe, the island is in the eastern North Atlantic Ocean, across the Irish Sea from Great Britain.
Terrain Mostly level, to rolling interior plains surrounded by rugged hills and low mountains, with sea cliffs on the west coast.
Climate Temperate, with mild winters and cool summers. Consistently humid, the weather is overcast about half the time.

THE PEOPLE

Population 3,500,000
Ethnic composition Celtic, with an English minority.
Religious composition
Roman Catholic 95%
Church of Ireland 4%
Protestant 1%
Languages spoken English and Irish (Gaelic), which is spoken mainly in the western coastal areas.
Education and literacy Education is compulsory for nine years, much of it free. Adult literacy is 99 percent.
Labor force
Total: 1,370,000
By occupation: agriculture 15%, industry 29%, services 51%, and government 5%.

COUNTRY FACTS

Political and legal Ireland is a sovereign, independent, democratic state with a parliamentary system of government.
Telephone Government-operated telephone and other telecommunications services are good. International country code: [353]. Selected city codes: Dublin (1), Cork (21).
Transportation A good, state-sponsored road and rail system connects towns and cities. There are three major airports, run by the Ministry for Transport and Power. Several boat services carry passengers and freight to Great Britain and France.
Environment About 40 percent of the population lives in rural areas. Industry Is the major source of solid and hazardous waste pollution. Air pollution is usually dispersed by strong winds. Pollution control is the responsibility of both federal departments and local authorities. Current issues are water pollution, especially of lakes, from agricultural runoff.
Media Radio Telefis Éireann, a statutory corporation, is Ireland's national broadcasting organization. There are two state-run television stations, both also run by Radio Telefis Éireann. The four daily newspapers and three Sunday papers published in Dublin are distributed throughout the country. Smaller cities have their own papers as well. In 1991, there were more than two million radios and eight million television sets in Ireland.
Health Ireland has competent specialists in all fields of medicine and dentistry. Comprehensive health services are free for low-income groups, and the middle classes are entitled to some free services. The birth rate is 18.8 per 1,000; the death rate is 9.2 per 1,000. Life expectancy of males is 70 years; of females, 76 years.

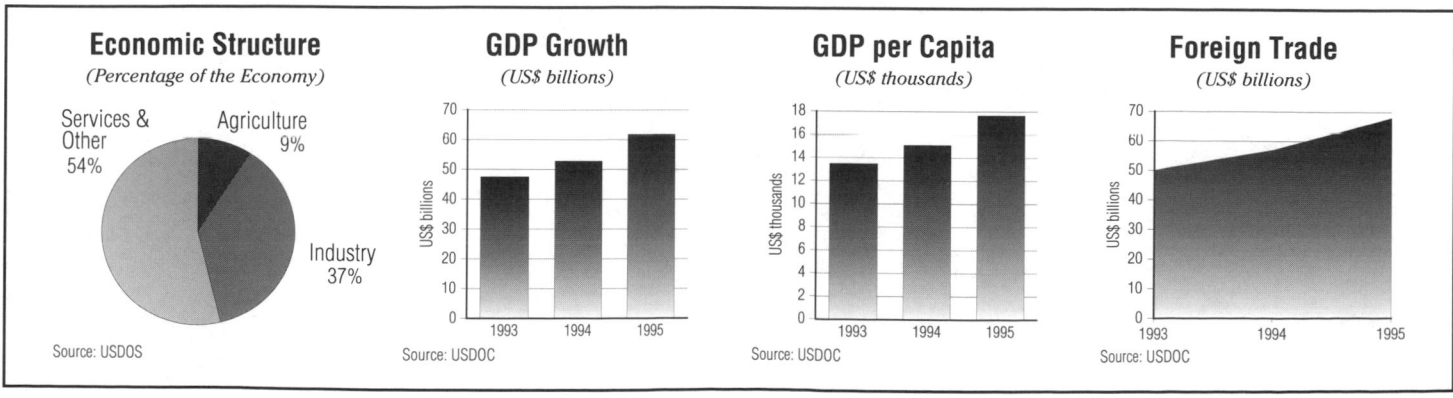

Economic Structure
(Percentage of the Economy)

Services & Other 54%
Agriculture 9%
Industry 37%

Source: USDOS

GDP Growth
(US$ billions)

1993 1994 1995

Source: USDOC

GDP per Capita
(US$ thousands)

1993 1994 1995

Source: USDOC

Foreign Trade
(US$ billions)

1993 1994 1995

Source: USDOC

Ireland

- ⭐ National capital
- ◉ County capital
- ● Secondary city
- —— Primary road
- ‑‑‑‑ Railroad
- —— Administrative border
- ▬▬ International border

0 25 50 km
0 25 50 mi

Counties of Ireland

1	Donegal
2	Mayo
3	Sligo
4	Leitrim
5	Cavan
6	Monaghan
7	Louth
8	Galway
9	Roscommon
10	Longford
11	Westmeath
12	Meath
13	Dublin
14	Clare
15	Tipperary
16	Offaly
17	Kildare
18	Wicklow
19	Kerry
20	Limerick
21	Laois
22	Kilkenny
23	Carlow
24	Wexford
25	Cork
26	Waterford

Scotland (U.K.)

Northern Ireland (U.K.)

NORTH ATLANTIC OCEAN

Irish Sea

St. George's Channel

Foreign Trade

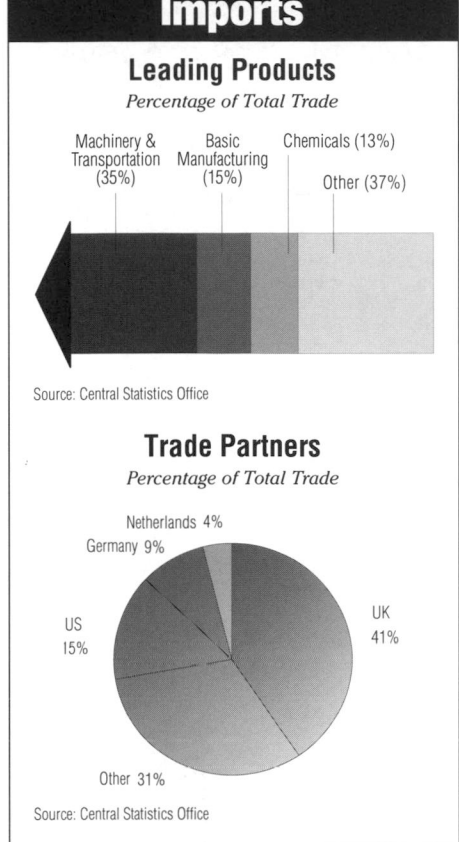

Imports

Leading Products
Percentage of Total Trade

Machinery & Transportation (35%)
Basic Manufacturing (15%)
Chemicals (13%)
Other (37%)

Source: Central Statistics Office

Trade Partners
Percentage of Total Trade

Netherlands 4%
Germany 9%
US 15%
UK 41%
Other 31%

Source: Central Statistics Office

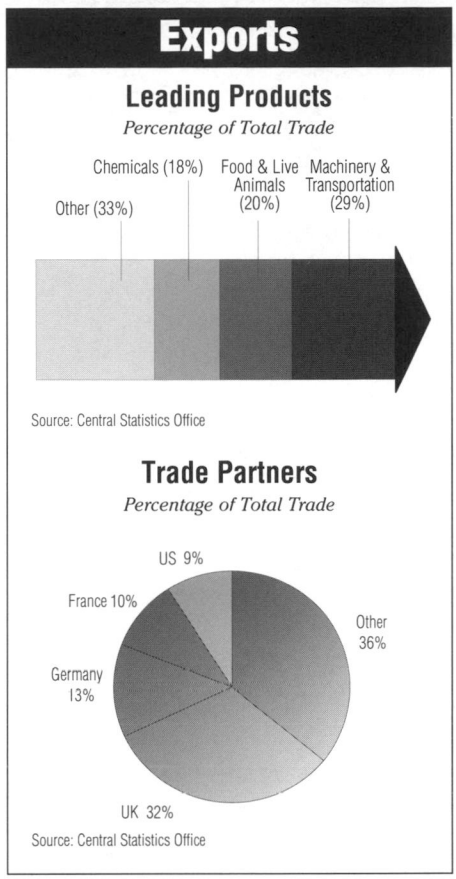

Exports

Leading Products
Percentage of Total Trade

Chemicals (18%)
Food & Live Animals (20%)
Machinery & Transportation (29%)
Other (33%)

Source: Central Statistics Office

Trade Partners
Percentage of Total Trade

US 9%
France 10%
Germany 13%
Other 36%
UK 32%

Source: Central Statistics Office

Opportunities

FOR IMPORTING TO IRELAND

- building products
- chemicals
- computer software
- computers and computer products
- construction equipment
- drugs and pharmaceuticals
- electronic components
- food products
- household consumer goods
- industrial chemicals
- laboratory instruments
- machinery
- medical equipment
- petroleum products
- telecommunications equipment
- textiles and clothing
- transport equipment

FOR EXPORTING FROM IRELAND

- alcoholic beverages
- chemicals
- computer equipment
- dairy products
- glassware
- machinery
- meat products
- natural and cultured pearls
- pharmaceuticals
- textiles and clothing

GROWTH SECTORS

- biotechnology
- building construction
- clothing
- furniture
- pharmaceuticals
- telecommunications
- tourism

GOVERNMENT PROCUREMENT

- electricity transmission and distribution equipment
- environmental protection technologies
- medical supplies and equipment
- telecommunication products

Trade News

RULES AND REGULATIONS

- **Regulations** Decisions regarding customs classification, duties, and taxes are made by the Office of the Revenue Commissioners.
- **Tariffs** Ireland applies the European Union (EU) tariffs, which are based on the International Harmonized System (HS) of product classification. Agricultural and food items are often subject to import levies that vary depending on world market prices.
- **Customs rulings** Before signing a long-term contract or sending a shipment of considerable value, foreign sellers should consider first obtaining an official ruling on the customs classification, duty rate, and taxes of the proposed shipment. Requests can be made to the Revenue Commissioners.
- **Import taxes** For imports into Ireland, the value-added tax (VAT) is levied at the same rate as for domestic products. The standard VAT is 21 percent. Excise taxes are also levied on a small number of products such as gasoline and diesel fuel, spirits, beer, wine, bottled water, cider, tobacco, motor vehicles, and liquid petroleum gas. The excise rates vary, depending on the products.
- **Import licenses** Products subject to import licensing include agricultural and food items, coal and lignite fuel, certain chemical products, specified iron and steel products, various textiles and textile products, natural and synthetic precious and semi-precious stones, zinc products, and controlled items such as arms and munitions.
- **Transferability** Import licenses are not transferable.
- **Inwards and outwards processing** Merchandise imported for additional processing and eventual re-export out of the EU is eligible for customs-free treatment. In outwards processing, an Irish firm may export goods for further manufacture or processing from the EU customs area and then re-import the final product. Duties and taxes are levied on the increased value added by the expatriate manufacturing or processing when the goods are returned to Ireland, not on the total value of the product.
- **Marking and labeling** With only minor exceptions, there are no general requirements for marking imported goods with the county of origin. There are no regulations for the marking of shipping packages.
- **Free trade zones** The Shannon Free Trade Zone, located at the Shannon International Airport, is the world's oldest free zone and was established in 1947. It offers a reduced 10 percent corporate tax rate and can be used as an international distribution and warehouse center serving Western Europe.

GOVERNMENT AGENCIES

An Bord Trachtala (Irish Trade Board)
Merrion Hall, Strand Road
Sandymount
Dublin 4
Tel: (1) 2695011 Fax: (1) 2695820

Industrial Development Authoirity
Wilton Park House
Wilton Place
Dublin 2
Fax: (1) 603703
Telex: 24525 IDA EI

Irish Export Board
Merion Hall
Strand Road, Sandymount
Dublin 4
Fax: (1) 695820
Telex: 93678 CTT EI

TRANSPORTATION FIRMS

Containers Transporters Ltd.
Airways Industrial Estate
Swords Road
Dublin 9
Telex: 30153 CAS EI

Cargo Superintendents
10 Burgh Quay
Dublin 2

Business Travel

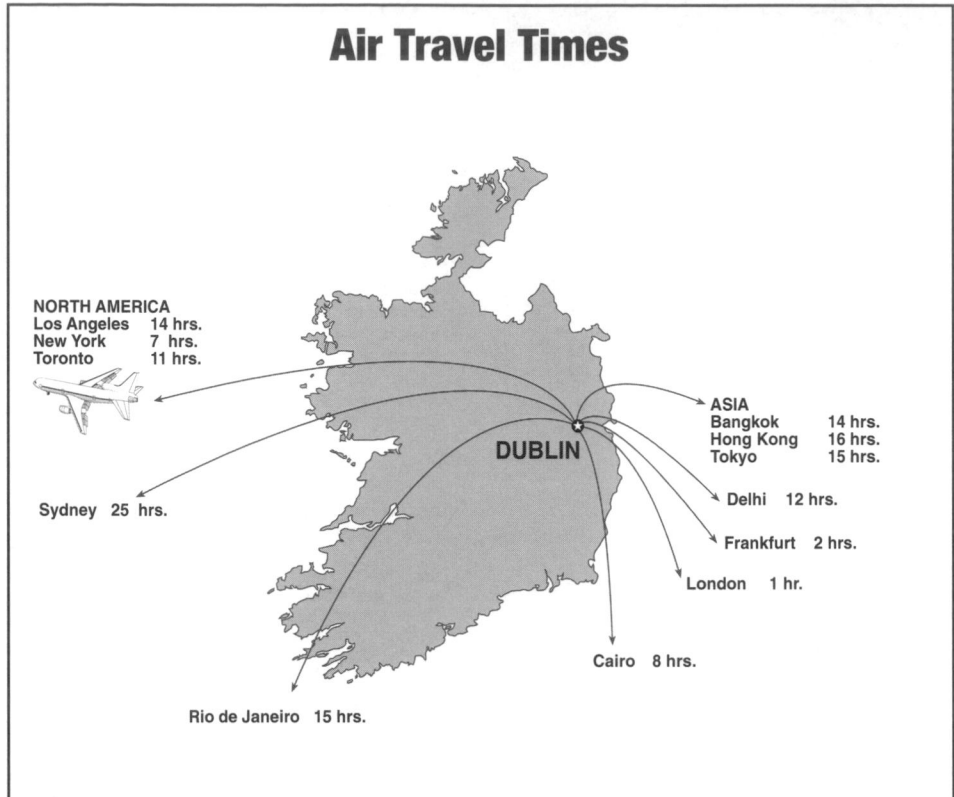

Air Travel Times

NORTH AMERICA
Los Angeles   14 hrs.
New York   7 hrs.
Toronto   11 hrs.

Sydney   25 hrs.

Rio de Janeiro   15 hrs.

DUBLIN

ASIA
Bangkok   14 hrs.
Hong Kong   16 hrs.
Tokyo   15 hrs.

Delhi   12 hrs.

Frankfurt   2 hrs.

London   1 hr.

Cairo   8 hrs.

COMMUNICATIONS

Telephone Ireland's telephone system is among the most sophisticated in Europe, with direct dialing service connecting all of Ireland to more than 90 percent of the world.
Fax Ireland's telecommunications utility offers a wide range of business services including fax, telex, and video communications.
Post office Ireland's mail service is generally good, with delivery from Monday to Friday. In small towns, the post office is often in a shop. Irish mailboxes are painted green.

BEST TRAVEL BOOKS

Birnbaum's Ireland, by Alexandra Birnbaum, Birnbaum Travel Guides Series. 608 pages, illustrated.
Berlitz Editors Ireland Travellers Guide, Travellers Guides Series. 320 pages, illustrated.
Lonely Planet, Ireland Travel Survival Kit. The rugged West Coast, the gentle greenfields of the interior, the remote Aran Islands, convivial pubs—this book shows it to you. 652 pages.
Fodor's Travel Guide, Ireland.
Do's and Taboo's Around the World. The Bestselling Guide to International Behavior. Edited by Roger Axtell, compiled by the Parker Pen Company. The ultimate guide to international behavior, now completely updated and expanded. Helpful, fun to read!
Insight Pocket Guides, Ireland. I can't think of another book which so effectively captures the essence of a country.
Berlitz Business Travel Guide, Europe. Concise economic details, successful trip planning, background information on people and cities, useful facts and addresses.

USEFUL TELEPHONE NUMBERS

If you are calling from outside Ireland, you will need to add the country code [353] and any other international dialing requirements from within your country.
- Fire, Police, Ambulance 999
- Operator Assistance... 10
- Directory Assistance 190
- Telemessage 196
- Irish Visiting Motorist's Bureau .... (1) 774569
- Dublin Taxi .... (1) 507777
- CIE (train and bus information) .... (1) 300777
- Association Chambers of Commerce...... (1) 764291
- Confederation of Irish Industry .... (1) 779801
- Irish Tourist Board.................................. (1) 765871
- Irish Tourist Board Central Res. Hotels... (1) 747733
- Department of Tourism and Transport .... (1) 789522
- Ministry of Foreign Affairs .... (1) 780822

Car rental:
- Avis .... (1) 6776971
- AutoEurope .... (1) 6772723
- Europcar Baggot St.............................. (1) 6681177
- Europcar Airport .... (1) 8444179
- Hertz .... (1) 676559

Credit card information:
Lost or stolen credit cards (call collect to the US, regardless of which country the card was issued in).
- Amex... [1] (919) 3333211
- Diner's Club................................. [1] (303) 7991504
- MasterCard .... [1] (314) 2756690
- Visa .... [1] (410) 5817931

Travelogue

WORKWEEK

Offices Monday-Friday 9:00 am to 1:00 pm and 2:00 pm to 5:30 pm.
Banks Monday-Friday 10:00 am to 4:00 pm, some evenings.
Government Monday-Friday 9:00 am to 5:30 pm.
Retail Monday-Saturday 9:00 am to 6:00 pm, some evenings.

HOLIDAYS

Holidays 1996
January 1 New Year's Day
March 17 Saint Patrick's Day
April 5 Good Friday*
April 8 Easter Monday*
June 3 Bank Holiday
October 28 Bank Holiday
December 25 Christmas Day
December 26 Saint Stephen's Day
In addition, the first Monday of May, June, August, and October is a public holiday. Most businesses close for the Christmas festive period from December 24 through January 2 and many business executives take vacations in July and August.
*Dates vary each year.

VISA AND PASSPORT

Foreigners must have a valid passport. Visas are not required for stays under 90 days, but foreigners may be asked to show return or onward tickets.

DEPARTURE FORMALITIES

You can take up to £IR100 in Irish currency and US$786 in foreign currency out of the country.

IMMUNIZATION

Foreigners do not need vaccination certificates, but they can be useful in the event of temporary restrictions.

TIPPING PERCENT

Taxi drivers and waiters generally receive 15 percent. A service charge is often included in a hotel or restaurant bill; tip extra only for extraordinary service. For porters and bellhops, 50 pence (US$1.50) per bag is standard.

CRIME

Ireland has a low crime rate, but petty theft is on the rise in tourist areas, drugs and violent crime are increasing in Dublin. Heightened security is in place along Ireland's northern border, where terrorist violence can spill over from the political unrest of Northern Ireland.

INFRASTRUCTURE

Ireland has highly developed hotel and telecommunications industries. Paved roads abound, but the highway system is inefficient and slated for modernization with EU structural funds. Meanwhile, clean, modern trains and reliable, comfortable buses serve Ireland's cities, towns, and villages. Taxis are expensive, hard to snare, and the easiest way to get around. Rental cars are widely available; drive on the left and watch for oncoming cars. Trains with first and second class accommodations are available.

NATIONAL TOURIST OFFICE

Irish Tourist Information
114 Upper O'Connell St.
Dublin
Tel: (1) 747733

Overview

Foreign companies doing business with Ireland will find their efforts helped on every level by the Irish. Their economy depends on foreign trade. Businesses seeking to introduce new products in Ireland will find the process uncomplicated. Success, however, is not guaranteed. Foreign businesses must be highly motivated and offer high quality products in order to achieve their goals in reaching Irish customers. Ireland's proximity to the European market influences associates' business methods.

Distribution and Agents

Distribution in Ireland flows through standard channels, although the distribution system is composed almost entirely of small outlets. The best distribution process for foreign businesses is to establish a local sales office. A presence in Ireland is vital, as Ireland offers the advantage of being the gateway for distribution in Western Europe. A personal visit to Ireland is the ideal first step for outside business people seeking an Irish associate, as it gives foreigners an opportunity to develop personal working relationships.

Selling Techniques and Customer Support

Often Irish distributors will request that foreign business partners adjust their products to sophisticated European tastes of the Irish. Packaging and presentation must appeal to the preferences of Irish customers who are accustomed to refined selling methods. Irish business associates expect after-sales service to be an integral part of any sales campaign. Irish companies often purchase from nearby international sources and are accustomed to receiving prompt service from them. Therefore, foreign companies must be willing to provide excellent service and customer support in order to succeed in the highly competitive Irish market.

Advertising

Ireland has two national radio stations and two national television stations. These are part of Radio-Telefis Eireann (RTE), a state-owned corporation. All advertisers must adhere to RTE's code of standard; and all advertising must be approved before airing.

Marketing in Ireland

MARKETING TIPS

- **Quality** Irish businesspeople buy from international sources and expect well-designed, quality goods.
- **Food products** The Irish retail trade is receptive to new food ideas and constantly monitors developments in the international marketplace.
- **Market research** Market research firms are all headquartered in Dublin. These firms provide all necessary services, including consumer surveys and product field testing.
- **Advertising** Advertising that works in other markets may not be effective in Ireland. Ads need to be adapted to the unique Irish market by first obtaining and analyzing local opinion.
- **Government** Foreign companies with operations in Ireland will be able to easily sell to the Irish government.

ADVERTISING AND MARKETING CONTACTS

The Institute of Advertising Practitioners in Ireland
35 Upper Fitzwilliam Street
Dublin 2
Telex: 93381 IAPI EI

Marketing Institute of Ireland Ltd.
12 Fitzwilliams Place
Dublin 2

Marketing Research Services
8 Leeson Street Lower
Dublin 2

Market Research Bureau of Ireland Ltd.
43 Northumberland Avenue
Dun Laoghaire
Co. Dublin
Tel: (1) 2804661 Fax: (1) 2809848

Business Culture

Greetings and Courtesies

Ireland standards of business and etiquette are less formal than most European countries, and the Irish have a reputation for friendliness and sociability. While the country is bilingual—English and Gaelic—English is the language of business. Proper greetings include the forms Mr., Mrs., or Miss before you are invited to use first names, an invitation the Irish quickly extend. A handshake and a few words such as "How do you do" or "Pleased to meet you" are common greetings. A handshake following meetings is considered good manners. In all cases, men should wait for a woman to extend her hand first.

Business Ethic and Framework

Though Ireland's is a relaxed and informal business environment, the Irish are reserved when meeting with foreigners with whom they have not dealt before. Further, they are reluctant to do business with someone to whom they have not been properly introduced so third party introductions are helpful. Cold calls are not advised. A letter introducing your company and requesting an appointment is acceptable.

Meetings and Decision Making

While punctuality is always good practice, the Irish tend to be on the late side when keeping appointments. Cards may be exchanged before the meeting begins or after formal introductions have taken place. Spend some time in the initial meeting stages developing rapport with your Irish counterparts before launching into highly technical or serious presentations. There is a very democratic system of hierarchy within the corporate or work environment. Joint consultation between management and employees is an important activity towards the rendering of decisions. This interactive process between management and employees is highly meaningful to Irish workers and it serves foreign ventures to respect the process. While senior management is involved in the majority of decisions, lower levels are consulted and heard from before final decisions are made.

Cultural Cautions

DO'S

- When at a pub, it is considered good manners to buy a round for everyone at the table.
- If invited home for dinner, candy or flowers are appropriate gifts of appreciation for the hostess.

DON'TS

- Don't introduce the topics of Northern Ireland, the IRA, Britain's treatment of Ireland over the years, or religion into your discussions.

CUSTOMS

- The Irish are a gregarious and hospitable people— informal at both business lunches and dinners—dinners being more for social activities than business activities.
- While toasting is informal, it is a ritual in which everyone at the table should participate.

OBSERVATIONS

- While gift-giving is not a common business practice in Ireland, inexpensive souvenirs from your country or company may be viewed as a token of friendship.
- Sending your agenda or an outline of your discussion points well in advance of the meeting is advised. The Irish like to know early on what is expected from them in the proposed business arrangement.
- Business attire should be informal and comfortable. However, ties are always worn to a business meeting. Women should wear suits or wool blazers with a skirt. Men and women alike are advised to remember their raincoats and umbrellas.

NEGOTIATIONS

- Because the Irish tend to minimize difficulties, the words "don't worry" are indicative of potential problems in forthcoming negotiations. The best way to avoid the "don't worry" signal is to avoid last minute surprises in your program of mutual business.

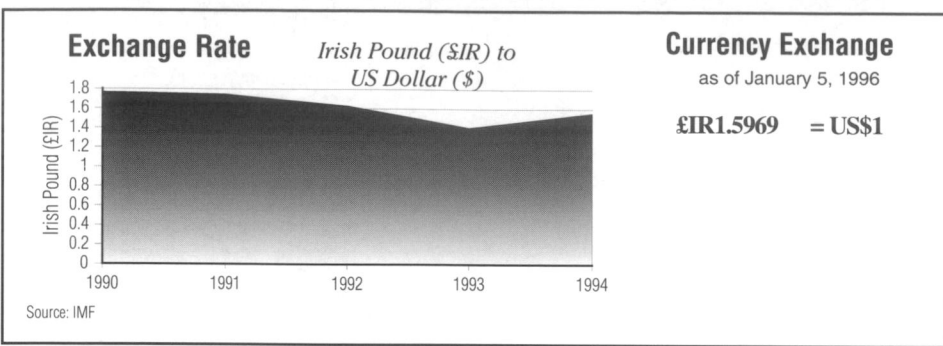

Exchange Rate

Irish Pound (£IR) to US Dollar ($)

Source: IMF

Currency Exchange

as of January 5, 1996

£IR1.5969 = US$1

Currency

Ireland's currency is the Irish pound or punt. The symbol is £IR, and the principal subdivision is 100 pence; singular, penny.

Foreign Exchange

Ireland participates with Belgium, Denmark, France, Germany, Luxembourg, the Netherlands, Portugal, and Spain in the exchange rate and intervention mechanism of the European Monetary System (EMS). Under this arrangement, Ireland maintains spot exchange rates between the Irish pound and the currencies of the other participants within margins of 15 percent above or below the cross rates based on the central rates expressed in European currency units. This agreement requires the Central Bank of Ireland to buy or sell the currencies of other participating countries in unlimited amounts at specified intervention rates. No foreign exchange controls are in effect in Ireland, except in very limited circumstances at the discretion of the Minister for Finance, and there are no taxes or subsidies on purchases or sales of foreign currency.

Capital Transfers

Residents and nonresidents may transfer capital without restrictions, and nonresidents may maintain unlimited deposits in Irish pounds. Visitors may import or export any amount of domestic and foreign bank notes or any other means of payment.

Investment Incentives

Manufacturing companies, firms engaged in international financial services, data processing, research and development, and other priority industries are eligible for a corporate tax rate of 10 percent compared to the standard 38 percent. Grants are administered to investors for capital equipment, land, buildings, training, research and development, etc.

Investment Restrictions

Requirements are few, but foreign ownership of agricultural land is prohibited. There are employment creation targets established between the state investment agencies and foreign investors, which can sometimes serve as deterrants, but are more often easily negotiated.

TAXATION

Taxation requires sophisticated knowledge of complex rules and regulations specific to each country. The information presented here is from the Ernst & Young Corporate Tax Guide and Directory, available from the Ernst & Young accounting office in your country, or from:

Ernst & Young
Ernst & Young Building
Harcourt Centre
Harcourt Street
Dublin 2, Republic of Ireland
Tel: (1) 4750555
Cable: Ernstaudit, Dublin
Fax: (1) 4750599

At a Glance

Corporate Income Tax Rate (%) (a)	40
Capital Gains Tax Rate (%)	40
Branch Tax Rate (%)	40
Withholding Tax	(%)
Dividends	0
Interest (b)(c)	27
Royalties from Patents, Know-how, etc. (b)	27
Branch Remittance Tax	0
Net Operating Losses (Years)	
Carryback	1
Carryforward	Unlimited

(a) Profits from the sale of goods manufactured in Ireland and from certain other activities are taxed at an effective rate of 10%. For details concerning special rates of income tax.
(b) Applicable to both residents and nonresidents.
(c) Bank interest paid to nonresidents is exempt from withholding tax. Irish resident companies and pension funds are exempt from withholding tax on interest derived from bank accounts, subject to certain conditions.

Money Matters

BITS AND PIECES

- **Repatriation** No restrictions are imposed on the repatriation of profits, provided initial exchange control approval is obtained from the Central Bank of Ireland.
- **Banking** The banking system of Ireland operates on a basis similar to that of the UK. Sources of finance are available directly from banks, building societies, other financial institutions, and through financial markets such as the Stock Exchange.
- **Capital markets** Capital markets and portfolio investments operate freely, subject to common Central Bank of Ireland exchange control regulations. Foreign investors are afforded full access to Irish credit markets. In some instances, development authorities and banks are able to facilitate loan packages to foreign firms with favorable credit terms. Irish legal, regulatory, and accounting systems are consistent with international practices.
- **Gold** Residents may freely hold, buy, borrow, sell, or lend gold coins in Ireland. However, Ireland does not permit the free circulation of gold coins minted after 1960, originating in the Republic of South Africa.

BANKS

A.I.B. Group
Bankcentre
Ballsbridge
Dublin 4
Tel: (1) 6600311 Fax: (1) 6682508

ACC Bank PLC
ACC House
Upper Hatch Street
Dublin 2
Tel: (1) 780644 Fax: (1) 780723

Algemene Bank Nederland Ltd.
121-122 St Stephen's Green
Dublin
Tel: (1) 6717333 Fax: (1) 6717689
Telex: 93217 ALGM EI

Anglo Irish Bank Corporation PLC
Stephen Court
18-21 St. Stephen's Green
Dublin 2
Tel: (1) 6763225 Fax: (1) 6611981

Bank of America
Russell Court
St. Stephen's Green
Dublin 2
Tel: (1) 4781222 Fax: (1) 755906
Telex: 93817 BKAM EI

Bank of Ireland
Lower Baggot Street
Dublin 2
Tel: (1) 6615933 Fax: (1) 6615675

Banque Nationale de Paris Ltd.
111 St. Stephen's Green, West
Dublin 2
Tel: (1) 6712811 Fax: (1) 6713884
Telex: 90641 BNPI EI

Barclays Bank International Ltd.
47/48 St. Stephen's Green
Dublin 2
Tel: (1) 6611777 Fax: (1) 6600139
Telex: 30427 BARD EI

Central Bank of Ireland
POB 559
Dame Street
Dublin 2
Tel: (1) 6716666 Fax: (1) 6716561

Chase Bank Ltd.
Stephen Court
POB A51
18-21 St. Stephen's Green
Dublin 2
Fax: (1) 780727 Telex: 93644 CHAS EI

Legal

Legal System

Ireland is a civil code country based on common law.

Intellectual Property Rights

Patents Ireland is a signatory member of the European Patent Convention (EPC), which has simplified the process for obtaining patent protection in European countries. Only a single application filed at the European Patent Office is required for protection in all EPC member states. Inventions may now be patented for 20 years.

Trademarks Trademark protection is valid for seven years following the application filing date, and it is renewable for successive 14-year periods, subject to cancellation if not used for five consecutive years. The examination process takes one month. A five-year coverage is offered for industrial designs and models. Present trademark legislation does not specifically cover the service industry, although some court cases have recently extended protection to trademarks for these businesses.

Copyrights Ireland's entire copyright system is under review and new copyright legislation should be introduced soon, including new EU directives. In the meantime, Ireland is a signatory member of both the Berne Convention for the Protection of Literary and Artistic Works and the Universal Copyright Convention. The Berne Convention provides protection to an author's work for the author's life, plus an additional 50 years. Ireland also provides protection under its own Copyright Act of 1963.

Business Registration

Any seven or more persons may form a public company, and any two or more persons may form a private company, providing the company restricts the right to transfer its shares, limits the number of its members to fifty, and does not solicit its shares or debentures to the public. A foreign incorporated company establishing a business in Ireland must file with the Registrar of Companies within one month of commencing business: (1) a certified copy of its charter, or memorandum and articles, or by-laws written in English; (2) a list of the directors and secretaries, the name of at least one resident individual in Ireland, and the company's principal place of business; and (3) a balance sheet, profit and loss accounts, and group accounts if the company is a holding company.

Contracts and Dispute Resolution

Irish contract law derives from common law. A contract's validity and its enforceability are determined by the law of the country where the contract was written. With regard to actions brought on foreign contracts partially or wholly executed in Ireland, proof of the contract, as well as matters of procedure, are regulated by Irish law. Irish law will also determine the rights and obligations of the parties as specified in the contract. A statute of limitations provides that actions for breach of contract cannot be brought after six years. There are no special requirements or conditions for government contracts.

Notaries

Affidavits intended to be used in foreign courts of law are notarized by public officers of the Supreme Court of Justice.

Labor

Workers have the right to associate freely. The right to join a union is guaranteed by law, as is the right to refrain from joining. The right to strike is freely exercised in both public and private sectors. Forced or compulsory labor is prohibited by law. It does not exist in Ireland. The minimum age for employment of children is 15 years; however, children over 14 years are permitted to perform light, non-industrial work during school holidays with the written permission of their parents. There is no general minimum wage legislation in Ireland, although some workers are covered by minimum wage laws applicable only to specific industrial sectors, mainly those where wage levels tend to be below average.

Legal Matters

LEGAL BRIEFS

- **Company names** In the case of private companies, the last word of a company name with limited liabilities must be "limited," which is usually shortened to "Ltd." The last words of the name of a public company with limited liabilities must be "public limited company," or simply "p.l.c."
- **Agency agreements** Agency agreements are subject to a minimum termination notice of 1 month for the first year of service, 2 months for the second year, and 3 months for the third and subsequent years.
- **Safety, health and welfare at work** The Safety, Health and Welfare at Work Act establishes a national authority to supervise occupational safety and health in the workplace. The act sets down some general responsibilities of employers and employees. It also covers the design and construction of workplace buildings, as well as criminal prosecution for failure to comply.
- **Licenses** Professions and certain types of businesses are licensed and controlled under separate statutes. These include moneylenders, pawnbrokers, betting shops, chemist shops, and liquor sales.
- **Women** Under the Anti-Discrimination Act it is an implied term of employment contracts that women must be paid the same rate as men for equal work. The Employment Equality Act makes it further unlawful to discriminate on the grounds of sex or marital status. The Maternity Protection of Employees Act entitles women to 14 weeks of paid maternity leave, with an extended option for an additional four weeks of unpaid leave.
- **Holidays** Employers are required to give employees at least three weeks paid leave, in addition to public holidays.
- **Termination** Legislation regulates the terms of dismissal of employees. The law requires a minimum notice of one week after 13 weeks of service and up to eight weeks after 15 years of service. However, it is permissible to terminate an employee without notice for misconduct or inefficiency.
- **Worker councils** The appointment of workers on the corporate board or establishment of joint employer/worker councils, as found in some other European countries, is not common in Ireland.
- **Limitations** The limitations period for commencing legal actions is three years where a claim arises for personal injuries or defamation.

LEGAL CONTACT

The Incorporated Law Society of Ireland
Solicitors' Buildings
Blackhall Place
Dublin 2

REMEMBER
- When you telephone (or fax) to Ireland from another country you must always include the country code [353] before the numbers given.
- When you send mail to Ireland, be sure to write IRELAND in capital letters on its own line below the addresses given.

GOVERNMENT AGENCIES

Department of Agriculture, Forestry, and Food
Kildare Street
Dublin 2
Tel: (1) 6789011 Fax: (1) 6789211

Department of Enterprise and Employment
Kildare Street
Dublin 2
Tel: (1) 6614444 Fax: (1) 6762654

Department of the Environment
Custom House
Dublin 1
Tel: (1) 6793377 Fax: (1) 8742710

Department of Finance
Government Buildings
Upper Merrion Street
Dublin 2
Tel: (1) 6767571 Fax: (1) 6789936

Department of Health
Hawkins House
Dublin 2
Tel: (1) 6714711 Fax: (1) 6711947

Department of the Marine
Leeson Lane
Dublin 2
Tel: (1) 6785444 Fax: (1) 6618214

Department of Tourism and Trade
Kildare Street
Dublin 2
Tel: (1) 6621444 Fax: (1) 6766154

Department of Transport, Energy & Communications
Clare Street
Dublin 2
Tel: (1) 6715233 Fax: (1) 6773169

Irish Patents Office
45 Merrion Square
Dublin 2
Tel: (1) 6614144

Office of the Revenue Commissioners
Dublin Castle
Dublin 2
Tel: (1) 6715233 Fax: (1) 6773169

Bord Iascaigh Mhara (The Irish Sea Fisheries Board)
Crofton Road
Dun Laoghaire
Co. Dublin
Tel: (1) 2841544 Fax: (1) 2841123

Electricity Supply Board
Lower Fitzwilliam Street
Dublin 2
Tel: (1) 6765831 Fax: (1) 6615376

Environmental Protection Agency
St. Stephens Green House
Dublin 2
Tel: (1) 6785933 Fax: (1) 6761170

An Post (The Irish Postal Service)
General Post Office
Dublin 1
Tel: (1) 8728888 Fax: (1) 8723553

Telecom Eireann (Irish Telecommunications Organization)
St. Stephens Green
Dublin 2
Tel: (1) 6714444 Fax: (1) 6716916

BUSINESS AND TRADE ORGANIZATIONS

Electro-Technical Council of Ireland
Parnell Avenue
Harolds Cross
Dublin 12
Tel: (1) 4545819 Fax: (1) 4545821

Federation of Jewelery Manufacturers of Ireland
Temple Hall
Blackrock
Co. Dublin
Tel: (1) 2831021 Fax: (1) 2889483

Goldsmiths of Dublin
Assay Office
Dublin Castle
Dublin 2
Tel: (1) 4751286 Fax: (1) 4783838

Irish Business and Employers Confederation
84-86 Lower Baggot Street
Dublin 2
Tel: (1) 6601011 Fax: (1) 6601717

Irish Business Equipment and Technology Association
59 Merrion Square South
Dublin 2
Tel: (1) 6761679 Fax: (1) 6610758

Irish Direct Marketing Association
The Powerhouse
Pigeon House Road
Dublin 4
Tel: (1) 6687155 Fax: (1) 6687945

Irish Farmers' Association
Irish Farm Centre
Bluebell
Dublin 12
Tel: (1) 4500266 Fax: (1) 4551043

Irish Franchise Association
13 Frankfield Terrace
Summerhill South
Cork
Tel: (21) 270859 Fax: (21) 271856

Irish Medical Organization
10 Fitzwilliam Place
Dublin 2
Tel: (1) 6767273 Fax: (1) 6682168

Irish Printing Federation
Baggot Bridge House
84-86 Lower Baggot Street
Dublin 2
Tel: (1) 6601011 Fax: (1) 6601717

Irish Security Industry Association
Huband House, 16 Upper Mount Street
Dublin 2
Tel: (1) 6610595 Fax: (1) 6614769

Irish Travel Agents Association
3rd Floor, Heaton House
32 South William Street
Dublin 2
Tel: (1) 6719622 Fax: (1) 6719897

Retail, Grocery, Dairy & Allied Trades Association
Rock House
Main Street, Blackrock
Dublin 2
Tel: (1) 2888313
Fax: (1) 2832206

The Building Information Centre
College of Technology
Bolton Street
Dublin 1
Tel: (1) 8732329 Fax: (1) 8732329

The Construction Industry Federation
Federation House, Canal Road
Dublin 6
Tel: (1) 4977487 Fax: (1) 4966953

The Society of the Irish Motor Industry
5 Upper Pembroke Street
Dublin 2
Tel: (1) 6761690 Fax: (1) 6619213

The Chambers of Commerce of Ireland
22 Merrion Square
Dublin 2
Tel: (1) 6612888 Fax: (1) 6612811

US Chamber of Commerce in Ireland
20 College Green
Dublin 2
Tel: (1) 6793733 Fax: (1) 6793402

DIRECTORIES & YEARBOOKS

American Business Directory
US Chamber of Commerce in Ireland
20 College Green
Dublin 2

Tel: (1) 6793733 Fax: (1) 6793402

Kompass (Register of Industry & Commerce)
Kompass Ireland
Parnell Court
Granby Row
Dublin 1
Tel: (1) 8728800 Fax: (1) 8733711

Million Dollar Directory (Marketing Guide to Ireland)
Dun & Bradstreet
Holbrook House
Holles Street
Dublin 2
Tel: (1) 6764239 Fax: (1) 6789301

MARKET RESEARCH FIRMS

AGB International
15 Adelaide Street
Dun Laoghaire
Co. Dublin
Tel: (1) 2803351 Fax: (1) 2801008

Behaviour and Attitudes Ltd.
26 Burlington Road
Dublin 4
Tel: (1) 6682299 Fax: (1) 6682820

Dale Parry Market Research Ltd.
59A Belgrave Square
Dublin 6
Telex: 90148 DPMR EI

Irish Marketing Surveys
20-21 Upper Pembroke Street
Dublin 2
Tel: (1) 6761196 Fax: (1) 6760877

Lansdowne Market Research Ltd.
12 Lower Hatch Street
Dublin 2
Tel: (1) 6613483 Fax: (1) 6613479

Marketing Research Society of Ireland
c/o Irish Distillers Ltd.
Bow Street
Dublin 7

Quaestus Ltd.
11 Clanwilliam Square
Dublin 2
Tel: (1) 6760922 Fax: (1) 6760840

NEWSPAPERS

Evening Herald
Independent Newspapers Ltd.
Middle Abbey Street
Dublin 1
Tel: (1) 8731666 Fax: (1) 8731787

Evening Press
Parnell House
13-15 Parnell Square
Dublin 1
Tel: (1) 6713333 Fax: (1) 6713097S

INTERNET ADDRESSES

Usenet group(s):
soc.culture.celtic

Irish Businesses on the Web
http://iol.ie/~aidanh/business/categor.htm

Industrial Development Agency - Ireland
http://www.ireland.net/marketplace/ida/

Irish Information Services
http://www.ieunet.ie/ieunet/launch/irish/

Irish On-Line Home Page
http://www.iolie/resources/home/testindex.html

Israel

State of Israel

At a Glance

THE COUNTRY
Location The Middle East, bordering the eastern Mediterranean Sea, between Egypt and Lebanon.
Terrain Negev Desert in the south; low coastal plain; central mountains; Jordan Rift Valley.
Climate Temperate, except in desert areas.

THE PEOPLE
Population 5,400,000
Ethnic composition
Jewish.. 83%
Non-Jewish (mostly Arab)..................................... 17%
Religious composition
Judaism 82%
Islam (mostly Sunni Muslim)................................. 14%
Christian.. 2%
Druze and other 2%
Languages spoken Hebrew (official), Arabic, English.
Education and literacy Free, compulsory education in religious and secular schools is 11 years. Adult literacy is 97 percent for males and 93 percent for females.
Labor force
Total:...1,900,000
By occupation: public services 29.3%, industry 22.1%, commerce 13.9%, finance and business 10.4%, personal and other services 7.4%, construction 6.5%, transport, storage, and communications 6.3%, agriculture, forestry, and fishing 4.1%.

COUNTRY FACTS
Political and legal A Parliamentary democracy with a legal system that is a mixture of English common law, British Mandate regulations, and, in personal matters, Jewish, Christian, and Muslim legal systems.
Telephone The state-owned and operated telecommunications system is the most highly developed in the Middle East. Israel also has international electronic mail capabilities. International country code: [972]. Selected city codes: Jerusalem (2), Tel Aviv (3), Haifa (4).
Transportation Thanks to an excellent highway system, private automobiles are the most used system of transport. There are also a state-owned rail system and three seaports. Along with one international airport, there are several domestic airports.
Environment Water pollution and an adequate water supply are the greatest concerns, along with air pollution from industry, oil facilities and vehicles. Reforestation has helped in conserving water resources and preventing soil erosion. Current issues include limited arable land and freshwater resources that limit development capabilities; deforestation; air pollution from industrial and vehicle emissions; and groundwater pollution from industrial and domestic waste, chemical fertilizers, and pesticides.
Media There are several state-owned radio stations, including one aimed at the Jewish population in Europe and the US. The country has more than 2.2 million radios and 1.3 million television sets. There are nearly 50 daily newspapers and several monthly and weekly periodicals, published in Hebrew, English, and other languages. There is no censorship, but restrictions are placed on the coverage of national security issues.
Health The health care system is a combination of private- and government-sponsored care. The Ministry of Health regulates all health matters. Life expectancy of males and females is 76 years.

Economy

Overview

Israel's overall economy depends heavily on government participation. Despite limited natural resources, Israel has intensively developed its agricultural, industrial, and service sectors over the past 20 years. The government has, however, incurred a massive foreign debt —half of which is owed to the US, a major source of economic and military aid. To earn needed foreign exchange, Israel has targeted high-technology development designed to serve international markets. The economy has recently been hurt by the burden placed on it by the influx of immigrants from the former USSR between 1990 and 1993. Although the peace process involving the Palestinians has shown signs of progress recently, the political, social, and economic ramifications of this ongoing dilemma will continue to add to both instability and costs.

Trade

Major exports include diamonds, machinery, chemicals, fruit and vegetables, and electrical machinery. Imports include diamonds, machinery, chemicals, petroleum, and vehicles. The US continues to be Israel's largest single trading partner, followed by Belgium, Germany, the UK, and Switzerland. While opening its own market to third country trade, Israel has aggressively diversified, pursuing exports to nontraditional markets primarily in Asia and Central Europe. Israel has a chronic problem with trade deficits, however, and one of its major policy goals is to generate export earnings and foreign exchange.

Sectors

Agriculture Only about 4 percent of the work force is employed in agriculture, while agricultural production accounts for almost 3 percent of GDP. Israel is largely self-sufficient in food production, except for grains. Principal products include citrus and other fruit, vegetables, and cotton, as well as beef, dairy products, and poultry.

Industry Industry accounts for somewhat less than 30 percent of GDP, while employing somewhat more than 20 percent of the work force. In this country that relies heavily on industry, top businesses include: food processing; diamond cutting and polishing; textiles and apparel; chemicals; metal products; military, transport, and electrical equipment; high-tech electronics; and potash mining.

Services Services account for almost 70 percent of GDP, while employing over half of the work force. The Israeli work force includes a very high proportion of scientific, technical, and professional, as well as other skilled, workers. The country lacks an adequate pool of unskilled labor, relying heavily on Palestinian workers from Israeli-occupied territories to fill manual labor jobs in agriculture and construction. Tourism and high-tech design and consulting are important service activities.

Trends

Given Israel's economic expansion and major government investment in infrastructure, opportunities should continue to present themselves in virtually every sector of the Israeli economy. However, much depends on how an accommodation is reached first between the Israelis and the Palestinians, then among various factions within Israel, and finally within the remainder of the Arab world and the rest of the international community.

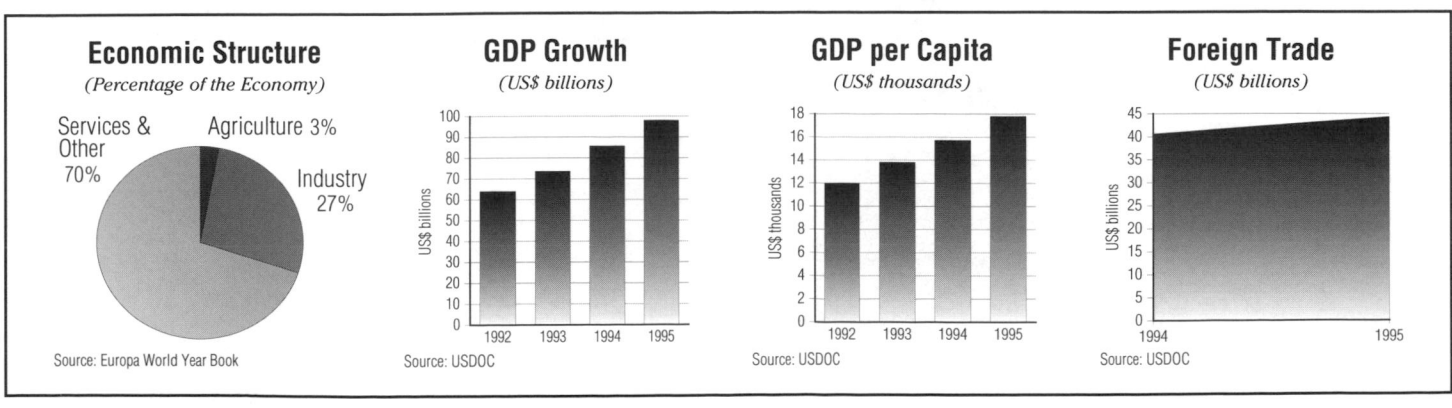

Economic Structure
(Percentage of the Economy)

Services & Other 70%
Agriculture 3%
Industry 27%

Source: Europa World Year Book

GDP Growth
(US$ billions)

Source: USDOC

GDP per Capita
(US$ thousands)

Source: USDOC

Foreign Trade
(US$ billions)

Source: USDOC

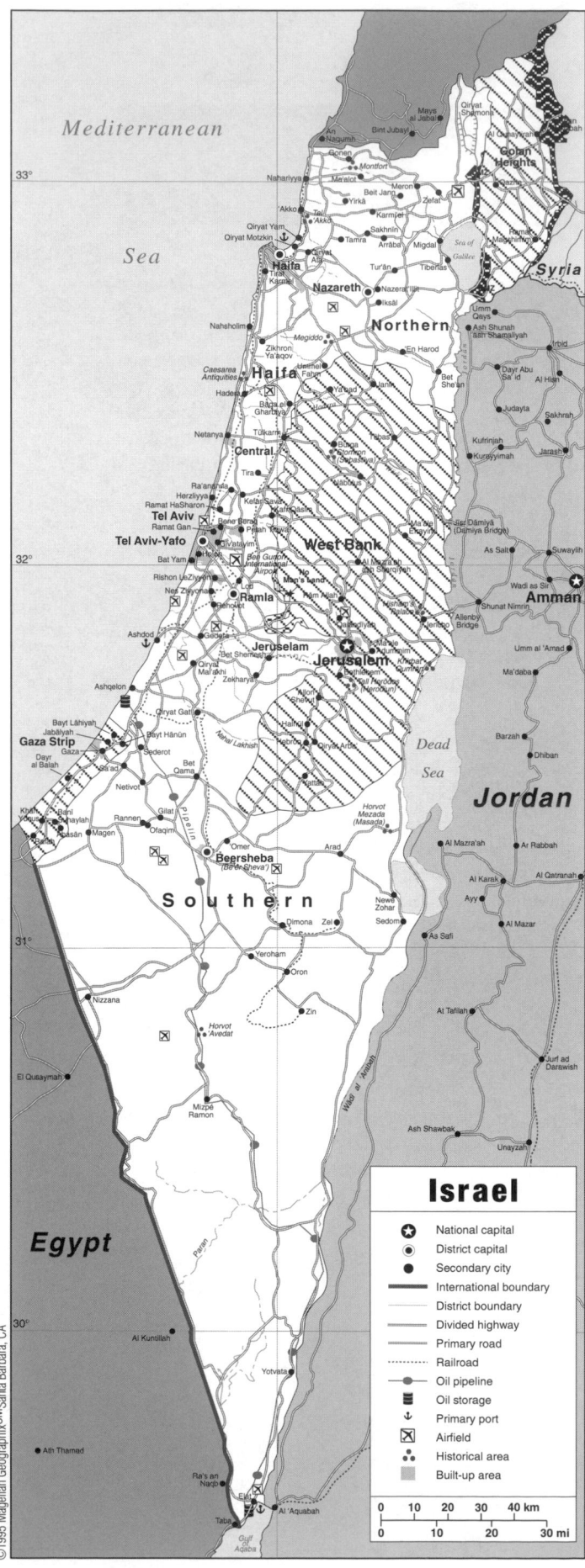

Mediterranean

Sea

Syria

Golan
Heights

Mays
al Jabal

An
Naqura
Qiryat
Shemona
Al Qusayrah

Qonen

Bint Jubayl

33°

Montfort

Nahariyya

Ma'alot
Beit Jann
Meron

'Akko
Tel
'Akko

Karmi'el
Zefat

Ash Shunah
ash Shamaliyah

Irbid

Qiryat Yam
Qiryat Motzkin

Sakhnin

Umm
Qays

Haifa

Tirat
Karmel

Arraba
Tamra
Migdal

Tur'an
Tiberias

Sea of
Galilee

Hamat
Gader

Nazareth

Nazar 'Illit
Iksal

Judayta

Sakhrah

Northern

Nahsholim

Megiddo

En Harod

Bet
She'an

Dayr Abu
Sa'id
Al Hisn

Zikhron
Ya'aqov

Umm el
Fahm

Kufrinjah
Kurayyimah

Haifa

Caesarea
Antiquities

Hadera

Jenin

Ya'bad

Jarash

Baqa el
Gharbiya

Tulkarm

Tubas

Netanya

Nablus
(Shekhem)

Central

Tira

Ra'anana

Mekhola

Herzliyya

Kefar Sava

Jisr Damiya
(Damiya Bridge)

Ramat HaSharon

Kafr Qasim

Tel Aviv

Bene Beraq
Petah Tiqwa

Ma'ale
Efrayim

As Salt

Suwaylih

Ramat Gan

Wadi as Sir

Amman

Tel Aviv-Yafo

Holon

Bat Yam

Ben Gurion
International
Airport

Al Mazra'ah
ash Sharqiyah

Hishmat
Nimrin
Allenby
Bridge

Shunat
Nimrin

West Bank

No
Man's Land

Rishon LeZiyyon

Jericho

Nes Ziyyona

Lod

Umm al 'Amad

Ashdod

Gedera

Ramla

Ramallah

Ma'daba

Bet Shemesh

Jeruselam

Qiryat
Mal'akhi

Zekharya

Jerusalem

Bethlehem
(Bet Lehem)

Khirbat
Qumran

Barzah

Dhiban

Ashqelon

Gilo

Herodium
(Herodyon)

Bayt Lahiya

Qiryat Gat

Jaballya

Bayt Hanun

Halhul

Gaza Strip

Gaza

Dayr
al Balah

Sederot

Bet
Qama

Nahal Lakhish

Hebron

Qiryat Arba

Dead
Sea

Jordan

Khan
Yunus

Bani
Suhaylah

Rannen

Gilat

Ofaqim

Netivot

Yuttah

Al Mazra'ah

Ar Rabbah

Qasan

Magen

Pipeline

Omer

Horvat
Mezada
(Masada)

Al Karak

Al Qatranah

Beersheba
(Be'er Sheva')

Arad

Ayy

Al Mazar

Southern

Newe
Zohar

Sedom

As Safi

Dimona

Zel

At Tafilah

Yeroham

Oron

31°

Nizzana

Zin

Jurf ad
Darewish

Horvot
'Avedat

El Qusaymah

Mizpe
Ramon

Ash Shawbak

Unayzah

Egypt

30°

Al Kuntillah

Yotvata

© 1995 Magellan Geographix℠ Santa Barbara, CA

Ath Thamad

Ra's an
Naqb

Elat

Al 'Aquabah

Tabu

Gulf
of
Aqaba

Israel

- ✪ National capital
- ⦿ District capital
- ● Secondary city
- ▬▬▬ International boundary
- ──── District boundary
- ═══ Divided highway
- ──── Primary road
- ┈┈┈ Railroad
- ●─● Oil pipeline
- ▤ Oil storage
- ↓ Primary port
- ⊠ Airfield
- ⁚⁚⁚ Historical area
- ▦ Built-up area

| 0 | 10 | 20 | 30 | 40 km |
| 0 | 10 | 20 | 30 mi |

Foreign Trade

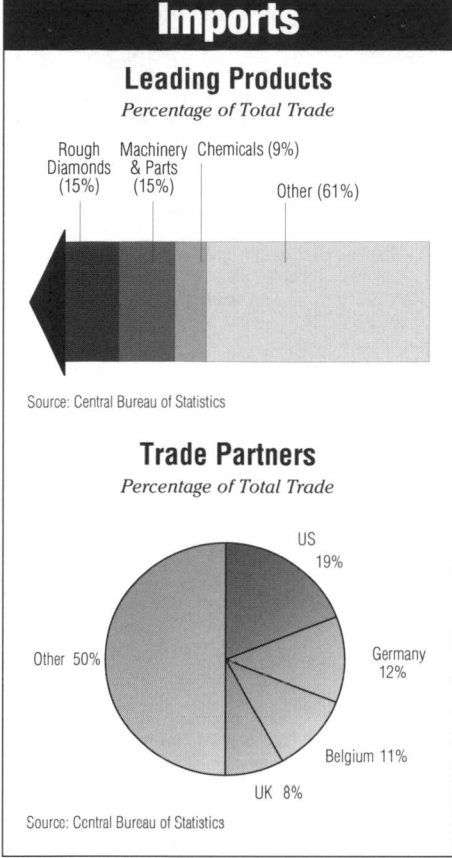

Imports

Leading Products
Percentage of Total Trade

Rough Diamonds (15%)
Machinery & Parts (15%)
Chemicals (9%)
Other (61%)

Source: Central Bureau of Statistics

Trade Partners
Percentage of Total Trade

US 19%
Germany 12%
Belgium 11%
UK 8%
Other 50%

Source: Central Bureau of Statistics

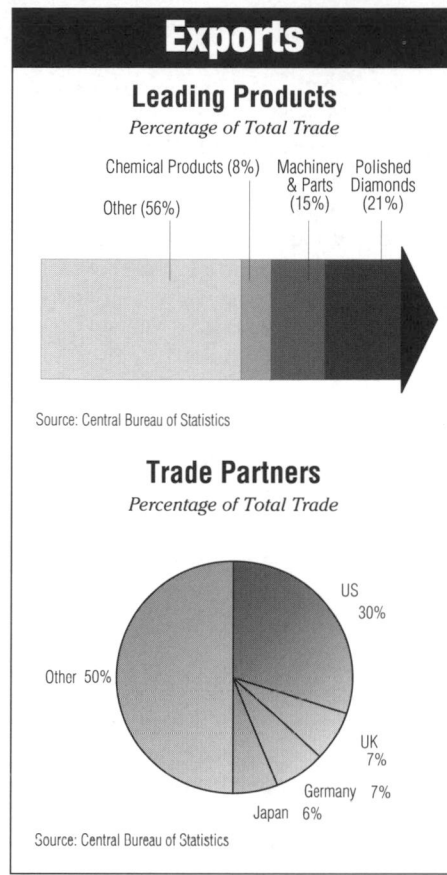

Exports

Leading Products
Percentage of Total Trade

Chemical Products (8%)
Other (56%)
Machinery & Parts (15%)
Polished Diamonds (21%)

Source: Central Bureau of Statistics

Trade Partners
Percentage of Total Trade

US 30%
UK 7%
Germany 7%
Japan 6%
Other 50%

Source: Central Bureau of Statistics

Opportunities

FOR IMPORTING TO ISRAEL

- aircraft and aircraft parts
- automobiles and automobile parts
- beef
- building products and machinery
- chemicals
- computer software
- construction equipment
- cosmetics and toiletries
- dried fruits and nuts
- iron and steel
- laboratory and scientific instruments
- medical equipment and pharmaceuticals
- oil
- pollution control equipment
- rough diamonds
- ships
- telecommunication products
- textiles
- vehicles

FOR EXPORTING FROM ISRAEL

- chemical and oil products
- citrus and other fruits
- dairy products
- electrical and electronic products
- high-technology equipment
- medical scanning equipment
- metals
- natural and cultured pearls
- polished diamonds
- processed foods
- textiles and clothing
- vegetables
- machinery and equipment

GROWTH SECTORS

- chemical and oil products
- construction
- electronics products
- food processing
- hotels and restaurants
- metal products
- rubber and plastic products
- tourism
- transportation equipment

GOVERNMENT PROCUREMENT

- airport and seaport facilities
- electrical power systems
- environmental protection technologies
- housing construction goods and services
- medical supplies and equipment
- military equipment
- telecommunication products
- transportation infrastructure goods and services: highway construction equipment and materials, light rail lines

Trade News

RULES AND REGULATIONS

- **Regulations** Procedures for importing to and exporting from Israel are authorized by Israeli Customs.
- **Tariffs and import taxes** Under GATT, a number of Israel's traditional non-tariff barriers will be replaced by tariffs. Israel maintains free trade agreements with the US, the EU, and the European Free Trade Area (EFTA). Products from the US, EU, and EFTA that are not subject to import duties will still be subject to a value-added tax (17 percent for virtually all products) and a purchase tax (25 to 95 percent) on luxury goods such as automobiles, consumer electronics, wine and other alcoholic beverages.
- **Import licenses** Licensing requirements and quantitative restrictions exist for a wide range of food and agricultural products.
- **Prohibited imports** Israel maintains prohibitions on certain agricultural products and on other substances in order to protect public morals, human, animal, or plant health, or national security.
- **Export financing** Export financing is available through commercial sources.
- **Export licenses** Israel maintains very few export controls; those that do exist are primarily targeted against internationally controlled substances and/or designed to protect national security.
- **Export proceeds** All proceeds in foreign currencies must be received within one year of the export date. They can be held in a special PAMAH account or sold to authorized banks.
- **Value-added taxes** A value-added tax of 17 percent is levied on most imported and domestically produced goods, other than fresh fruit and vegetables.
- **Exporter turnover** Exporters can retain up to 10 percent of their turnover in the previous year in a bank deposit, and use the funds to pay for imports and make other authorized payments abroad.
- **Agents** Most firms exporting to Israel find it convenient to use a local representative. Most distributors import on their own accounts.
- **Export certification** For all exports requiring special certificates of origin, a declaration is needed with all the details of production of the articles.
- **Free trade zones (FTZs)** Israel has one free trade zone, the Red Sea port city of Eilat. In addition to the Eilat FTZ, there are three free ports: Haifa Port, the Port of Ashdod, and the Port of Eilat.

TRANSPORTATION FIRMS

Baumer & Model
POB 663
29 Yevneh Street
Tel Aviv
Telex: 342623 BAMODIL

Cargotrans Foreign Transport Center Ltd.
POB 4554
21 Lilienblum Street
Tel Aviv

International Forwarding Company of Israel Ltd.
POB 20099
88 Hahashmonaim Street
Tel Aviv 67011
Fax: (3) 561-3568 Telex: 33576 INFIS IL

Tashgir Ltd.
POB 958
Ten Harutzim Street
Tel Aviv
Telex: 33761 EXPED IL

ZIM
(International Shipping)
9 Pal-Yam Street
POB 1723
Haifa 31016
Tel: (4) 652-111 Fax: (4) 652-869

Marketing

Overview

Success for foreign companies in the Israeli market means energetically pursuing business opportunities. It also means making sure your presence in Israel is widely recognized. Most businesses in Israel are concentrated in the cities of Tel Aviv and Haifa; approximately 25 percent of Israel's 5.4 million population live in the Tel Aviv area. Any products imported into Israel pass through either Haifa in the north or Ashdod in the south. Both of these cities are important transportation connections to the rest of Israel and beyond. Israelis are highly price conscious, so foreign products in Israel need to be priced competitively. There are no clearly defined buying seasons, but the peak retail selling periods for consumer goods usually are at New Year (September/October) and Passover (March/April). Buying for these periods can take place two to three months beforehand. Although Hebrew is the official language of Israel, the population is multilingual, and English is frequently used in the business community.

Distribution

As an overnight retail success, consumer malls are the most popular form of retail distribution in Israel, with many more in the planning stages, and Israeli consumers are growing increasingly familiar with the trendy, specialized chain stores therein. The greater variety of goods and services has spurred the popularity of these new outlets. Although some consumer goods in Israel are marketed through wholesalers, many products are not wholesaled at all. To save money, chain stores and department stores prefer to buy directly from foreign suppliers. Most foreign companies select agents and distributors to market their products in Israel, and these representatives maintain their own distribution networks.

Agents, Distributors, and Partners

The key to success for foreign businesses in Israel is effective local representation. For the most part, importers in Israel buy through local commission agents. Some agencies also trade as importers on their own account and, in a few instances, have retail and wholesale businesses. A few specialize only in one type of commodity, while some experienced and capable firms deal in a wide range of goods. In some cases, for the sake of convenience, importers have grouped together to buy certain commodities, such as iron, steel, and timber. Foreign exporters are well advised to conduct their business through a local agent instead of attempting to sell direct to importers. Israeli agents and distributors usually request exclusive representation of their foreign business associates. Since the country is small and communications adequate, the particular location of an agent's office is not of great importance, as the whole market can be covered from any one of its commercial centers.

Selling Techniques

Direct marketing is a relatively new approach to selling in Israel, introduced only a few years ago by major credit card companies. Cable television has been primarily responsible for expanding its scope. Six Israeli marketing companies provide direct marketing services, including telemarketing. Franchising has also only recently been employed in Israel, especially in the fast food industry, but it has not yet entered other industries to the same extent.

Advertising

Assertive product advertising is indispensable in Israel, especially for foreign products that face competition from European and domestic goods. Cable television is the most effective means of advertising, and it is available throughout all of Israel. Foreign companies can also promote their products through the privately owned Israeli channel or major international cable networks. Advertising in major Hebrew language newspapers, especially weekend editions, is also very effective; circulations for major papers range from 6,000 to 150,000. Advertising in trade magazines has also proven successful, including the bi-monthly *Journal of the Association of Engineers and Architects* and the agriculture journal *Hassadeh*. Slide advertising is available for Israel's cinemas; there are 190 throughout the country. Poster advertising is limited, mostly to films, although illuminated signs are becoming more popular and widespread. The Israel Trade Fair Authority sponsors several major trade fairs each year, and these are an excellent method for introducing new products and services. Consult with an advertising agency before embarking on any campaign.

Service and Customer Support

The ability to provide proper after-sales service and customer support is key to remaining competitive in the Israeli market, especially in sophisticated, high-tech areas. Foreign companies need to make sure their local representatives receive adequate, ongoing training and technical support. Prompt after-sales service is a major factor affecting purchasing decisions by Israeli companies and government-owned businesses.

Marketing in Israel

MARKETING TIPS

- **Promotions** Promotions in supermarkets, drug-stores, and malls are very effective in Israel, especially when free samples are available.
- **Pricing** Price is a key factor affecting purchasing decisions by Israeli companies and consumers. Companies reduce their prices significantly during the introduction of a new product, followed by a price increase once the product is established.
- **Government** Government-owned companies purchase many goods. Proposals are published in the local press and are often open to foreign concerns.
- **Direct sales** Chain and department stores sometimes prefer to deal directly with overseas suppliers in order to cut costs.
- **Correspondence and trade literature** Documents should be in English with weights and measures in the metric system.
- **Price quotations** Prices should be quoted in US dollars.
- **Terms of payment** In the past, the standard terms of payment have been by letter of credit or cash against documents, but since foreign exchange controls were lifted, importers may seek extended terms of payment.
- **Debt collection** The matter of debt collection is one which should be placed in the hands of a good lawyer once the question of litigation arises.

AD AGENCIES

Mimsar & Shifrin
114 Ygal Alon St.
Tel Aviv 67443
Tel: (3) 696-8090
Fax: (3) 696-0905

Fogel Levin Advertising Agency Ltd.
40 Nemal
Tel Aviv 63506
Tel: (3) 544-2110
Fax: (3) 544-4617

May-Tal Advertising Services Ltd.
POB 23333
Tel Aviv 64335
Tel: (3) 528-1188
Fax: (3) 620-4617

Warshavsky Freilich Dover Advertising
POB 3309
Tel Aviv 61032
Tel: (3) 516-4560
Fax: (3) 516-2875

CONSULTING FIRMS

Dun and Bradstreet (Israel) Ltd.
27 Hamered Street
Tel Aviv 68125
Tel: (3) 510-3355

H K Associates
Marketing & Strategy Consultants
13 Hasadna Street
Raanana 43650
Tel: (9) 913-140
Fax: (9) 913-240

Marketing Systems Development Co. Ltd.
13 Namir Road
Tel Aviv 64929
Tel: (3) 695-2967
Fax: (3) 696-8020

MS&P
88 Gordon Street
Tel Aviv 64389
Tel: (3) 522-1058
Fax: (3) 522-2774

Teldan Information Systems Ltd.
7 Derech Hashalom Street
Tel Aviv 67892
Tel: (3) 695-0073
Fax: (3) 695-6359

Ziegelman Market Research
27 Shabadia Street
Haifa 34980
Tel: (4) 257-966

Business Culture

Greetings and Courtesies

A warm handshake is the customary greeting, and good friends will sometimes accompany the handshake with a friendly pat on the back or shoulder. In general, Israelis do not embrace or hug upon greeting. Israelis stand quite close to one another when speaking, and they will often touch each other lightly on the arm as they talk. Many Israelis retain their reserve while in public, though many others are very expressive with their hands and bodies. Israel is so full of settlers from various backgrounds and countries that nearly anything goes—you will see all types of greetings and behaviors on the streets of any Israeli city. All are acceptable; it is one of the easiest countries in the world in which to be a stranger. A variety of languages are heard, and Israelis are accustomed to making do with hand gestures and other pantomimes to make themselves understood—and to understand others.

Business Ethic and Framework

The workweek begins Sunday morning and runs straight through until sundown on Friday. The business environment is fast-paced, hectic, and can be stressful to businesspeople accustomed to a more relaxed approach. It is, however, friendly and direct–there are no hidden agendas or secret deals that foreigners must be aware of. Hardworking and honest may be the best way to describe most Israelis. Most businesspeople are very educated and have achieved their positions by virtue of hard work and talent. They generally work six long days each week; the business day usually starting by about 7:30 in the morning. Most executives do not mind being called at home in the evening to discuss business. Israelis do, however, maintain a strong sense of family; and most of them spend each evening at home with their own.

Decision Making

Like much else in Israel, decision making is loose and flexible. In general there is little emphasis on status, rank, or title. Most managers and executives are accessible, and often have authority to make decisions on the spot. Business success will probably take time, and patience is a must. Every bureaucrat seems to have the power to change, amend, and even ignore rules and regulations which would otherwise seem to be spelled out quite clearly.

Women

Women are well represented and highly visible in the work force and in government, many of them holding positions of significant authority. They serve in the military, where their role is being continuously expanded, and overall discrimination seems to be less evident than in many other countries where they supposedly enjoy equality. Foreign businesswomen should experience few difficulties conducting business as Israelis are quite accustomed to dealing with women. Israeli society remains, however, male-dominated; the Hebrew word for 'woman' is exactly the same as the word for 'wife'.

Meetings

There are no hard and fast rules, although foreign businesspeople should generally make prior appointments for meetings, and should make every attempt to be on time. Be aware, however, that the frenzied and harried pace of business will sometimes require that your appointments run late, or that other distractions will dictate the actual time of appointments. In general, business discussions proceed slowly, often interrupted by coffee and small talk; and it is unwise to attempt to speed this process along. However, meetings do not drag on needlessly—and almost never over long lunches. Instead, they are conducted at the place of business, in a frank and straightforward manner. Terms and potential problems are openly discussed before reaching agreement. Despite the otherwise fast pace of business, most Israelis do not like to conduct meetings by telephone, preferring instead a face to face meeting. They will be well prepared and ready to do business, and foreign businesspeople should also be well prepared and knowledgeable about the discussions.

Business Attire

Israeli business attire tends toward the informal, although Israelis are very fashion conscious and always try to wear what is in style. Use your best judgment. Formal attire is almost never required. Many Israeli businessmen wear slacks and open-collared shirts to the office, but business suits are becoming more common. Women generally wear conservative suits or dresses. In synagogues, women should wear long sleeves and skirts or dresses that cover the knees.

Cultural Cautions

DO'S

- Take the time to get to know all potential business contacts, and chat them up over coffee.
- Allow extra time for errands and tasks; there are long waits and bureaucratic hang-ups at every turn.
- Be punctual, even if your Israeli counterparts are not.
- You can make your presentation in English (most businesspeople speak it) but you should have written documents translated into Hebrew.
- Be sure you have a signed contract once you think you have made a deal.
- Observe religious beliefs and customs while in Israel, even if you do not agree with them.

DON'TS

- Do not attempt to conduct any business from sundown Friday to sundown Saturday, as virtually everything shuts down for the Sabbath.
- Do not even attempt to make a business call during the Sabbath as many people will not answer the telephone.
- It is not advisable to drive in Israel. Traffic is heavy and fast-moving, and rental cars can be obtained with a driver for a reasonable charge. If you do rent a car, it may not be driven over the border into Egypt.
- Do not discuss political issues unless you know the person very well and are familiar with their views. Israelis are passionately involved with politics, and feel deeply about their beliefs.
- Don't bother to queue if there is a wait; people push and shove to get ahead in any line, and they give no quarter to foreigners.

CUSTOMS

- Israelis throw a fit when negotiations don't go their way, or when they are made to wait in line, or for any other reason—or for no reason at all. Do not be alarmed; It is usually merely a performance.
- Older people are treated with respect, regardless of their social or business status.
- The Israeli new year begins in September, with Rosh Hashana.
- Israelis use the term *shalom* for both hello and goodbye.

OBSERVATIONS

- All observations and customs have many exceptions in the diverse and varied country of Israel—where anything goes. Israel is a land of immigrants from all over the world, and each group has its own style and customs.
- Israelis are among the most avid readers in the world, and they love to discuss what they have read.
- Israeli bureaucrats have been known to 'change the procedure' after a deal has seemingly been concluded and the former requirements complied with.
- Labor strikes are an almost daily occurrence in Israel; even in the medical and security professions.
- Israelis treat customers in exactly the same way they themselves are treated; if you are rude, they are rude; if you are pleasant and courteous so too are they.
- The concept of service is much less developed than in other countries due to the small market and relative lack of competition.

NEGOTIATIONS

- The hard sell works in Israel; use it. Softer, subtler approaches will often be ignored.
- Israeli negotiators will often start out with an extreme position that is completely untenable. Don't be afraid to do the same. They are willing to work gradually toward a compromise, and expect you to do the same.
- Don't be offended at the hysterics—including yelling, table pounding and threats—displayed by Israeli negotiators. It is all part of their customary release of tension. It will pass and the negotiator is likely to go on as if nothing untoward has happened.
- Presentations should be well-prepared and thorough; the Israelis will be knowledgeable and ready to ask tough questions.

Legal

Legal System

Israel has a modern legal system based on government mandate and British case law. Courts are independent; there is no government interference in the court system. Israeli civil procedures provide that judgments of foreign courts may be accepted and enforced by the local courts.

Intellectual Property Rights

Patents Israel is a member of the Paris Convention for the Protection of Industrial Property. Patent protection is available comprehensively, and Israel only employs compulsory licensing in limited circumstances, such as for medicines. Patent protection is provided for 20 years from the filing date. To be eligible for a patent, inventions must be unique, and not published or used previously anywhere in the world. Inventions that are not applicable in industry or agriculture are not patentable. Approved applications are published for three months to allow opposition thereto to be filed. Generally it takes two or three years to obtain a patent.

Trademarks Trademark registrations are valid for seven years after the initial filing date and may be renewed for 14-year periods. Approved applications are published for opposition for three months, and after five years, a trademark becomes incontestable. A trademark not employed for two consecutive years can result in cancellation. Trademarks found to be against public order or morality, as well as non-distinctive marks, are not eligible for registration. Appellation of origins are protected under the Appellations of Origins Law.

Copyrights Israel's present copyright law is based on the United Kingdom Copyright Act of 1911, with subsequent amendments. Protection includes the exclusive right to (1) copy or reproduce the work; (2) translate or otherwise adapt the work; (3) distribute copies of the work; and (4) publicly communicate the work. There is no explicit protection for derivative works, but protection could be granted if the derivative work includes sufficient elements of originality. At present, there is no separate statutory protection for computer software, which is protected under the general copyright law as 'literary works'.

Trade Secrets There is no protection for trade secrets under intellectual property law in Israel; however, trade secrets are classified as privileged information under the Evidence and Civil Procedure Law, and the Penal Law provides that an employee with express knowledge of a trade secret who wrongfully reveals it may be imprisoned for up to six months. In addition, a tort action may be brought against an individual who divulges a trade secret. At present, there is no protection for semiconductor chip design.

Business Registration

A foreign company that establishes a place of business in Israel must within one month register as a foreign company. Registration is accompanied by the following documents: (1) a certified copy and Hebrew translation of the company's charter, statutes or memorandum, and articles of incorporation; (2) a list of directors; (3) the names and addresses of residents in Israel authorized to conduct business and accept any notices served on the company; and (4) a certified copy of the power of attorney naming a resident of Israel to act for the company in Israel.

Contracts and Dispute Resolution

All disputes may be submitted to arbitration, and no particular form of submission is required, except that a submission must be in writing. A foreign award is enforceable as a local award and may be relied upon in any legal proceeding. In order for a foreign award to be enforceable, however, it must have been (1) made pursuant to a valid agreement for arbitration; (2) made by the tribunal provided for in the agreement or constituted in a manner agreed upon by the parties; and (3) made in conformity with the law governing arbitration procedure in the country in which it was made.

Notaries

Any deed, power of attorney, or other instrument in writing made outside Israel may be proved in a civil case in Israel if it was authenticated by an ambassador, minister, chargé d'affaires, secretary of an embassy, any consular agent of Israel, or notary.

Labor

Most Israeli workers are organized by the national labor federation, Histadrut. In the private sector, most collective bargaining negotiations take place at the factory or industry level, while most public sector negotiations are conducted on a national level between the Ministry of Finance and Histadrut. The Government and Histadrut cooperate to insure the protection of worker rights as defined by the International Labor Organization (ILO). Strikes and workers' sanctions in the private sector are relatively rare, but occur more frequently in government-owned enterprises, including the defense industry.

Legal Matters

LEGAL BRIEFS

- **Judgments** Foreign judgments are enforceable if they were made by a court having jurisdiction to act, are final, are not subject to appeal, and their contents are not in contradiction to laws in Israel or public policy.
- **Wage protection** Wages must be paid in cash. Other payment is allowed under collective agreement; a small portion can be paid in food and lodging.
- **Women** Employment of women is strictly governed by the Employment of Women Law, which restricts employment and working hours, and makes provisions for the protection of women in the workplace. Maternity leave is extended to adoptive mothers, and vacation without pay is granted to natural mothers and their husbands.
- **Equal employment opportunity** It is unlawful to discriminate against those requesting work because of their sex, marital status, or status as parents, with regard to the actual receipt of employment, conditions of employment, promotion, education or vocational training, dismissal, and severance pay.
- **Sabbath** Israel strictly observes Friday afternoon to Saturday afternoon as Sabbath, and special permits must be obtained from the government authorizing Sabbath employment. Generally, firms have been able to obtain the permits without difficulty.
- **Military service** At the age of 18, most Israelis perform two to three years of national service. Until the age of 50, Israeli males are required to perform 30 to 50 days of military reserve duty annually, compensated by the National Insurance Institute.
- **Medical patents** A revised law is in the works which will eliminate compulsory licenses of patented processes or products for medical purposes.
- **International agreements** Israel belongs to both the Universal Copyright Convention and the Berne Convention for the Protection of Literary and Artistic Works. It is also a member of the World Trade Organization.

LEGAL CONTACTS

Amihud Ben-Porath Law Offices
Century Tower
124, Ibn Gvirol Street
Tel Aviv 62038
Tel: (3) 5222147 Fax: (3) 5222451

Dr. Reinhold Cohn and Partners
9-11 Yavne Street
P.O. Box 4060
Tel Aviv 65791
Tel: (3) 566-4455 Fax: (3) 560-6405, 566-3782
Telex: 341137 COPT IL

Dr. Shlomo Cohen & Co. Law Offices
Century Tower
124, Ibn Gvirol Street
Tel Aviv 62038
Tel: (3) 527-1919 Fax: (3) 527-2666

Goldfarb, Levy, Eran & Co.
Eliahu House
2 Ibn Gvirol
Tel Aviv 64077
Tel: (3) 695-4343 Fax: (3) 695-4344

Lesham, Brandwein & Shlank
Top Tower, 50 Dizengoff Street
Floor 23
Tel Aviv 64332
Tel: (3) 525-5544 Fax: (3) 525-5123

Shraga F. Biran & Co.
City Tower, 34 Ben Yehuda Street
Jerusalem 94583
Tel: (2) 258161 Fax: (2) 259284

Yaacov Salomon, Lipschutz & Co.
Yoel House
64 Hameginim Ave.
P.O. Box 303
Haifa
Tel: (4) 53523115
Fax: (4) 557038

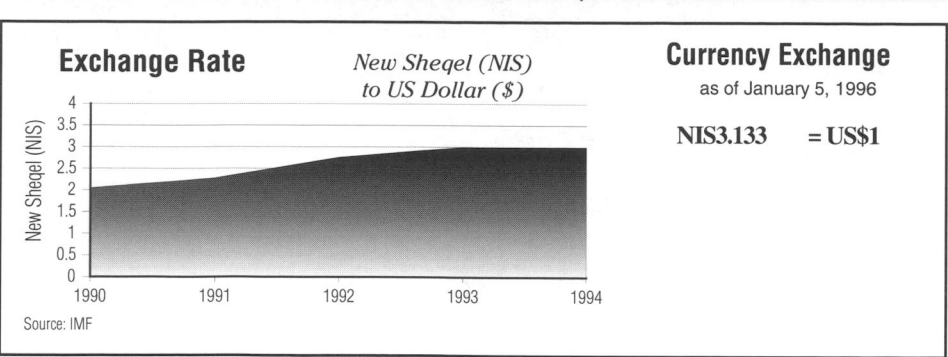

Exchange Rate — *New Sheqel (NIS) to US Dollar ($)*

New Sheqel (NIS)

Source: IMF

Currency Exchange
as of January 5, 1996

NIS3.133 = US$1

Currency

Israel's currency is the New Sheqel, symbol NIS. Its principal subdivision is 100 agorot.

Foreign Exchange

Exchange control is the responsibility of the Comptroller of Foreign Exchange, administered by the Bank of Israel in cooperation with other government agencies and carried out through authorized banks. The exchange rate is defined in relation to a currency basket consisting of the Deutsche Mark, the French franc, the Japanese yen, the pound sterling, and the US dollar. The actual market exchange rate fluctuates within a range of 5 percent above and below the midpoint rate in response to market forces and intervention policy.

Capital Transfers

Israel maintains foreign currency controls; however, the trend is toward increased liberalization. Residents, including companies that conduct business in Israel, may purchase foreign currency for routine trade transactions, but may not transfer capital abroad or hold foreign assets without a permit from the Bank of Israel. Nonresidents may maintain unrestricted, freely transferable accounts with Israel commercial banks.

Investment Incentives

There are generally no restrictions to doing business in Israel. No government approval is needed for investment, but investors must apply for status as an approved enterprise to obtain any incentives; applications must be submitted to the Investment Center. There are incentives for investment in specified regions of the country. There are also reduced tax rates. If the investor pays local corporate taxes, there is no limit on the investment.

Investment Restrictions

There are no universal requirements for investors, but there may be performance requirements included in contracts with the government. Conditions may be imposed if foreign nationals are brought in to work on an enterprise.h

Money Matters

BITS AND PIECES

- **Repatriation** Dividends may be remitted abroad in foreign currency after settling any applicable Israeli taxes. After-tax sales proceeds may be repatriated. Branches of foreign companies must obtain a special permit from the Bank of Israel to repatriate surplus funds. Funds from the sale of real estate and other investments may be transferred abroad in their entirety if made through an authorized foreign currency dealer.
- **Remittance of earnings** Foreign workers are not restricted. Remittances of profits and dividends from foreign direct investment are permitted after local taxes are paid.
- **Foreign investment** There are generally no restrictions for foreign investors doing business in Israel, nor any restrictions on foreign investment in the private sector. Investments in regulated industries require prior approval. There are no regulations regarding acquisitions, mergers, and takeovers that discriminate against foreign investors.
- **Private ownership** The Israeli legal system protects the right of both foreign and domestic entities to establish and own business enterprises. Legal, regulatory, and accounting systems conform with international practices.
- **Capital markets** There are no significant obstacles to the free flow of financial resources. Credit in Israel is allocated on market terms. Various credit instruments are available to the private sector, and foreign investors can receive credit on the local market.
- **Research funding** Research funding is available for some projects in Israel.

BANKS

Bank Hapoalim B.M.
50 Rothschild Boulevard
Tel Aviv 66883
Tel: (3) 567-3333
Fax: (3) 562-2028

Bank Leumi Le-Israel B.M.
POB 2
Tel Aviv 61000
Tel: (3) 514-8111
Fax: (3) 613-573

Bank of Israel
Kiryat Ben Gurion
1 Kaplan Street
Jerusalem 91007
Tel: (2) 552-501
Fax: (2) 535-516

Barclays Discount Bank Ltd.
POB 1292
103 Allenby Road
Tel Aviv 65134
Tel: (3) 514-3422
Fax: (3) 514-3444

The First International Bank of Israel Ltd.
9 Ahad Ha'am St.
Tel Aviv 65251
Tel: (3) 519-6111
Fax: (3) 510-0316

Industrial Development Bank of Israel
2 Dafna Street
Tel Aviv 64928
Tel: (3) 691-6412
Fax: (3) 265-956

Israel Bank of Agriculture Ltd.
POB 2440
83 Hahashmonaim Street
Tel Aviv 61024
Tel: (3) 285141
Telex: 35739

Israel Discount Bank Ltd.
27 Yehuda Halevi Street
Tel Aviv 65546
Tel: (3) 514-5555
Fax: (3) 514-5346

United Mizrahi Bank
13 Rothschild Blvd.
Tel Aviv 66881
Tel: (3) 567-9211 Fax: (3) 560-4780

TAXATION

Taxation requires sophisticated knowledge of complex rules and regulations specific to each country. The information presented here is from the Ernst & Young Corporate Tax Guide and Directory, available from the Ernst & Young accounting office in your country, or from:

Kost Levary and Forer
Certified Public Accountants
29 Ben Yehuda Street
Tel Aviv 63807
P.O. Box 3124
Israel
Tel: (3) 5164561
Fax: (3) 5164565

At a Glance

Corporate Income Tax Rate (%) (a)	37
Capital Gains Tax Rate (%) (a) (b)	37
Branch Tax Rate (%) (a)	37
Withholding Tax (%)	
Dividends (b)(c)(d)	25
Interest (b)(c)(e)(f)(g)	25
Royalties from Patents, Know-how, etc. (b)(c)(d)	25

Branch Remittance Tax (i)	0
Net Operating Losses (Years)	
Carryback	0
Carryforward	Unlimited

(a) This is the regular company tax rate for profits and real capital gains earned in 1995. The rate is scheduled to decrease to 36% for 1996 and subsequent years. Company tax rates ranging from 0% to 25% are available for approved enterprises or properties and in other cases.
(b) This rate is subject to applicable tax treaties.
(c) Applicable to nonresident companies and individuals.
(d) This is a final tax. Dividends paid out of the profits of an approved enterprise or property are subject to a final 15% withholding tax.
(e) In principle, the withholding taxes on interest and royalties are not final taxes, but nonresidents without an Israel presence generally do not take any further action.
(f) Alternatively, nonresident lenders may apply to pay regular company tax on their lending profit margin after deducting proven lending expenses.
(g) At the discretion of the tax authorities, interest paid to recognized foreign financial institutions that lend funds to projects benefiting Israel's economy may be subject to a reduced rate of 15% of the amount by which the loan interest exceeds the London interbank offer rate (LIBOR).
(h) A 15% tax is imposed on the approved enterprise profits and approved property profits of a branch after deducting company tax. In principle, this tax is payable together with the company tax, but the Tax Commissioner may allow payment of this tax on approved enterprise profits and approved property profits to be deferred until the relevant branch profits are withdrawn from Israel business operations. This tax may be overridden by a tax treaty.

Business Travel

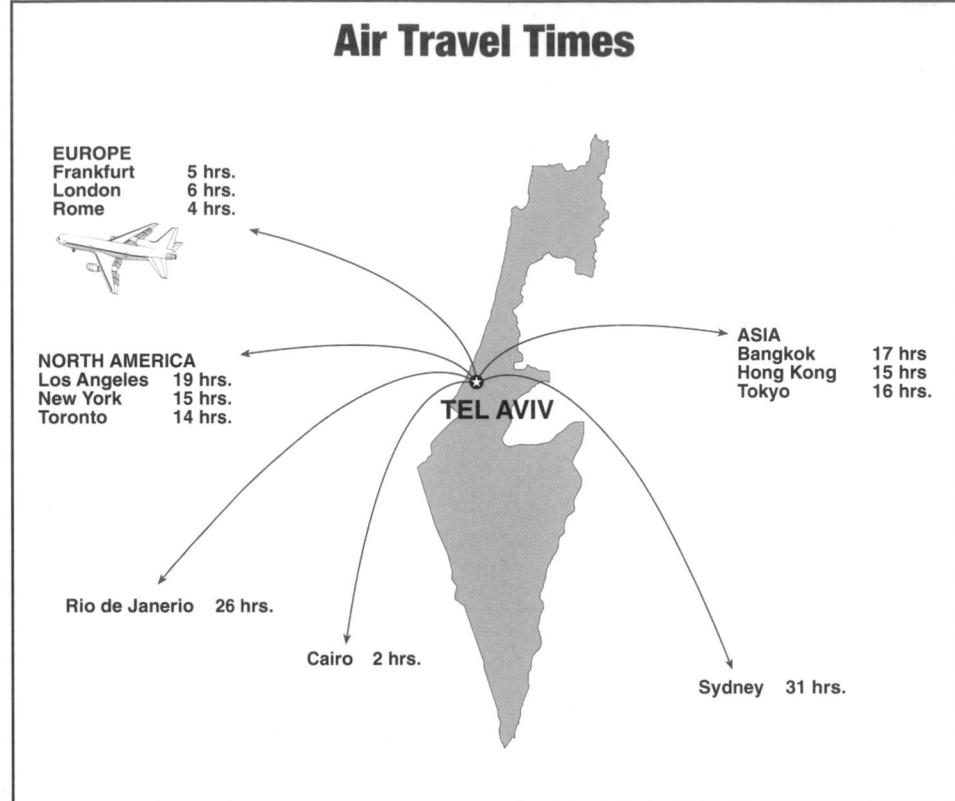

Air Travel Times

EUROPE
Frankfurt 5 hrs.
London 6 hrs.
Rome 4 hrs.

NORTH AMERICA
Los Angeles 19 hrs.
New York 15 hrs.
Toronto 14 hrs.

Rio de Janerio 26 hrs.

Cairo 2 hrs.

TEL AVIV

ASIA
Bangkok 17 hrs
Hong Kong 15 hrs
Tokyo 16 hrs.

Sydney 31 hrs.

COMMUNICATIONS

Telephone Israel's advanced national and international telecommunications systems are continually being upgraded to meet increasing demand. Widespread computerization expedites both domestic and international links.

Fax Machines are found in hotels, business establishments, post offices, and government offices and are replacing telex service as a means of communication.

Post office Israel's internal and international mail services are fairly slow, but the International Express Mail service offered at post offices in Tel Aviv, Jerusalem, and Haifa is faster. Post offices, marked with a blue shield bearing a white deer, are open weekdays from 8:00 a.m. to 12:30 p.m. and from 2:30 p.m. to 6:00 p.m., except Wednesday and Friday afternoons. Stamps are also sold at shops and hotels displaying the deer emblem. Mailboxes are red. Telegrams and cables can be sent from post offices and telegraph offices.

BEST TRAVEL BOOKS

Bazak Guide to Israel, Bazak Guidebook Publishers Staff, 1993. 548 pages, illustrated.
Israel: A Travel Survival Kit by Neil Tilbury. Lonely Planet, 1993, 480 pages.
Fodor's Travel Guide, Israel. Tourist oriented, excellent source of city details.
Culture Shock, A Guide to Customs and Etiquette, Israel.
The Traveler's Guide to Middle Eastern and North African Customs and Manners. Elizabeth Devine & Nancy Braganti. How to converse, dine, tip, bargain, dress, make friends and conduct business while in the Middle East and North Africa.

USEFUL TELEPHONE NUMBERS

If you are calling from outside Israel, you will need to add the country code [972] and any other international dialing requirements from within your country.

- Chamber of Commerce Tel Aviv .... (3) 5612444
- Chamber of Commerce Haifa .... (4) 663471
- Chamber of Commerce Jerusalem .... (2) 224333
- Flight Information Tel Aviv .... (3) 344285
- Flight Information Jerusalem .... (2) 225888
- Flight Information Haifa .... (4) 643371
- Medical, First Aid................................... 101
- Dental... 49
- Police 100
- Fire 102
- Israel Railways Office............................. (4) 531211
- Egged Bus Line....................................... (3) 242271
- Ben Gurion Airport Information Desk ... (3) 971-1485
- Jerusalem Tourist Office .... (2) 241-2812
- Tel Aviv Tourist Office .... (3) 223-26617
- Haifa Tourist Office .... (4) 645359
- International Operator 188
- Information/Directory 144
- Telegrams 24 hours 171
- Time 155
- Toll Free Numbers 177
- Fed. of Israeli Chambers of Commerce (3) 5612444

Credit Card Information
Lost or stolen credit cards (call collect to the US, regardless of which country the card was issued in).
- Amex...[1] (919) 333-3211
- Diner's Club..................................[1] (303) 799-1504
- MasterCard ....[1] (314) 275-6690
- Visa ....[1] (410) 581-7931

Travelogue

WORKWEEK

Offices Sunday-Thursday 8:00 am to 4:00 pm.
Banks Monday-Thursday 8:30 am to 12:30 pm and 4:00 pm to 5:30 pm, closed Wednesday and Friday afternoons.
Government Sunday-Thursday 8:00 am to 3:00 pm.
Retail Sunday-Thursday 8:00 am to 1:00 pm and 2:00 pm to 7:00 pm and Friday 8:00 am to 2:00 pm.
Normal workweek is 5.5 days, from Sunday morning to Friday noon, but becoming increasingly popular is the five-day workweek.

HOLIDAYS

Holidays 1996
April 4 First Day of Passover
April 10 Last Day of Passover
April 24 Independence Day
May 24 Shavuot
September 14-15 Rosh Hashana, Jewish New Year
September 23 Yom Kippur
September 28 Sukkot
October 5 Simhat Tora
Additional Jewish holy days and Muslim, Christian, and Druze feast days are observed, but with shops and offices normally open. Jewish and Muslim holidays, determined by the lunar calendar, vary every year.

VISA AND PASSPORT

Foreigners must have a valid passport, an onward or return ticket, and proof of sufficient funds. A three-month visa may be issued to some foreigners, without charge, upon arrival. Entry requirements are subject to change due to political changes in East Jerusalem and the Gaza Strip, West Bank, and Golan Heights.

DEPARTURE FORMALITIES

Up to US$100 in Israeli currency may be exchanged upon departure without proof of foreign exchange transaction, but keep all exchange receipts anyway.

IMMUNIZATION

Foreigners do not currently need vaccination certificates to enter Israel. Sun, heat, sand, and dust are constant problems for travelers to Israel; take along ointments, eye drops, and sun screens to help these weather conditions.

TIPPING

Tipping is common practice in most tourist areas. Many restaurants include a service charge of 10 to 15 percent; if service was good, add a little extra. If the service charge was not included, add 10 to 15 percent. Hotel rates include a service charge. Taxi drivers do not expect a tip but are happy to get one. Hairdressers and barbers expect 10 percent of the bill.

CRIME

Israel's crime rate is moderate, but terrorist violence can erupt at any time and place. Call police for unattended packages or bags. Avoid bus and train stations late at night. Stick to crowded, well-lit streets. Stay on major tourist routes in the West Bank. Don't pick up hitchhikers, or people dressed as soldiers.

INFRASTRUCTURE

Israel has advanced telecommunications systems. Modern transportation facilities are available internally and internationally, including bus, taxi, rail and air services. Four- and five-star hotels provide all tourist amenities. Taxis are metered and government-regulated. Trains, buses, and domestic air services are available. There are no flights Friday evenings or Saturdays. Ground transportation is considered the best mode of getting around the small country.

TOURIST OFFICES

Ministry of Tourism
POB 101
24 King George St.
Jerusalem 91000
Tel: (2) 754811

Haifa Tourist Office
Haifa
Tel: (4) 645359

GOVERNMENT AGENCIES

Central Bureau of Statistics
Kiryat Romema
Jerusalem, 91130
Tel: (2) 553-553
Fax: (2) 553-325

Government Press Office
Beit Agron, 37 Hillel Street
Jerusalem 94581
Tel: (2) 233-380
Fax: (2) 257-886

Government Tourism Corporation
38 Keren Hayesod Street
Jerusalem 92149
Tel: (2) 663-154
Fax: (2) 663-159

Ministry of Industry & Trade
30 Agron Road
Jerusalem 94190
Tel: (2) 243-981
Fax: (2) 259-274

Ministry of Agriculture
Post Office Box 7011
Hakirya
Tel Aviv 61070
Tel: (3) 697-1704
Fax: (3) 697-1681

Ministry of Construction and Housing
Post Office Box 19110
Jerusalem 91180
Tel: (2) 847-106
Fax: (2) 847-668

Ministry of Defense
Hakirya
Tel Aviv 61909
Tel: (3) 697-6923
Fax: (3) 697-5628

Ministry of Finance
Treasury Building, Room 741
1 Kaplan Street
Jerusalem 91007
Tel: (2) 618-065, 638-330
Fax: (2) 617-028

Ministry of Transportation
95 Jaffa Rd.
Jerusalem 91000
Tel: (2) 319-692
Fax: (2) 319-206, 319-693

Ports and Railways Authority
Post Office Box 20121
Tel Aviv 61201
Tel: (3) 561-6488
Fax: (3) 561-7142

The Israel Electric Corp. Ltd.
Post Office Box 8810
Haifa 31086
Tel: (4) 548-200
Fax: (4) 548-203

Ministry of Economy and Planning
3 Kaplan Street
Jerusalem 91008
Tel: (2) 535178
Fax: (2) 789424

The Investment Center
30 Agron Street, POB 299
Jerusalem 94190
Tel: (2) 210111
Fax: (2) 245110

Office of the Chief Scientist
4 Mevo Hamatmid, POB 2197
Jerusalem 91020
Tel: (2) 226368
Fax: (2) 248159

Income Tax Commission Ministry of Finance
1 Kaplan Street
Jerusalem 91008
Tel: (2) 558111
Fax: (2) 780964

Customs Authority Ministry of Finance
32 Agron Street, POB 320
Jerusalem 91002
Tel: (2) 245951

Israel Securities Authority
24 Lincoln Street
POB 7450 Jerusalem
Tel: (2) 245288
Fax: (2) 2403553

Israel Export Institute
Industry House
29 Hemered Street, Tel Aviv
Tel: (3) 630830
Fax: (3) 630920

Industrial Cooperation Authority
35 Shederot Shaul Hamelech
POB 33231
Tel Aviv 612321
Tel: (3) 262172-4
Telex: 032139

Economic Warfare Authority
3 Kaplan St., POB 883
Jerusalem 91008
Tel: (2) 522194, 668241

WORLD TRADE CENTER

World Trade Center Israel, Tel Aviv
Industry House
29 Hamered Street
POB 50022
Tel Aviv 61500
Tel: (3) 512-8815
Fax: (3) 662-026

BUSINESS AND TRADE ASSOCIATIONS

Association of Contractors and Builders in Israel
18 Mikve Israel Street
Tel Aviv 65115
Tel: (3) 560-4701
Fax: (3) 560-8091

Agricultural Export Co.
POB 7163
121 Hashmonaim Street
Tel Aviv 67011
Tel: (3) 563-0903, 563-0888
Fax: (3) 563-0814

Israel Center for Packaging and Industrial Design
2 Carlebach Street
Tel Aviv 67132
Tel: (3) 561-4431
Fax: (3) 561-1451

Central Union of Artisans and Small Manufacturers
POB 4041
Tel Aviv 61040

Israel Diamond Exchange Ltd.
POB 3222
Ramat-Gan
Tel Aviv
Tel: (3) 576-0211
Fax: (3) 575-0652

Israel Fruit Production Board
119 Rehov Hahashmonaim
Tel Aviv 61070
Tel: (3) 561-0811
Fax: (3) 561-4672

Kibbutz Industries Association
8 Rehov Shaul Hamelech
Tel Aviv 64733
Tel: (3) 695-5413
Fax: (3) 695-1464

Israel Consumer Council
28 Albert Mendler Street
Tel Aviv 67676
Tel: (3) 266-138, 695-9759
Fax: (3) 216-560

Israel Export Institute
Industry House
29 Hamered Street
POB 50084
Tel Aviv 68125
Tel: (3) 514-2830
Fax: (3) 514-2902

Israel Standards Institute
(Product Testing Laboratory)
42 Haim Levanon
Ramat Aviv 69977
Tel: (3) 646-5154
Fax: (3) 646-5043

MALAM
(Software and Data Processing)
208 Jaffa Road
Jerusalem 91130
Tel: (2) 707-611
Fax: (2) 383-547

Manufacturers' Association of Israel
Industry House 29
Hamered Street
Tel Aviv 68125
Tel: (3) 512-8832
Fax: (3) 510-3154

CHAMBERS OF COMMERCE

Federation of Israeli Chambers of Commerce
Post Office Box 20027
Tel Aviv 61200
Tel: (3) 561-1010
Fax: (3) 561-9027

Israel-America Chamber of Commerce & Industry
Post Office Box 33174
Tel Aviv 61333
Tel: (3) 695-2341
Fax: (3) 695-1272

MARKETING BOARDS

Citrus Marketing Board
POB 80
Beit Dagan 50350
Tel: (3) 968-3811
Fax: (3) 968-3838

Cotton Production and Marketing Board
POB 384
Hezlia B'
Tel: (3) 509491
Fax: (3) 509159

RADIO & TELEVISION

Cable Television Council
23 Jaffa Road
Jerusalem 94229
Tel: (2) 706-359
Fax: (2) 242-203

Educational Television Authority
14 Klausner Street
Ramat Aviv 69011
Tel: (3) 543-4343
Fax: (3) 642-7091

Israel Broadcasting Authority
Clal Building, 97 Jaffa Road
Jerusalem 91063
Tel: (2) 291-888
Fax: (2) 242-944

Second Channel TV and Radio Administration
3 Kamfe Nesharim
Jerusalem 95464
Tel: (2) 511-221
Fax: (2) 536-285

NEWSPAPERS

Al-Quds
POB 19788
Jerusalem
Tel: (2) 272663
Fax: (2) 272657

Globes
127 Igal Alon Street
Tel Aviv 67443
Tel: (3) 695-3535
Fax: (3) 210333

Letzte Nyess (Late News)
POB 28034
52 Harakevet Street
Tel Aviv

The Jerusalem Post
POB 81
Romema 91000
Jerusalem
Tel: (2) 315666
Fax: (2) 389527
Internet URL: http://www.jpost.co.il/

Viata Noastra
52 Harakevet Street
Tel Aviv

Yedioth Ahronoth (The Latest News)
2 Yehuda and Noah Mozes Street
Tel Aviv 61000
Tel: (3) 697-2222
Fax: (3) 695-3950

Davar (The Word)
POB 199
45 Sheinkin St.
Tel Aviv
Tel: (3) 286141
Fax: (3) 294783
Telex: 33807

Al-Fajr (The Dawn)
POB 19315
Jerusalem
Tel: (2) 289175
Telex: 26467
Fax: (2) 283336

Ha'aretz (The Land)
POB 233
21 Salman Schocken St.
Tel Aviv 61001
Tel: (3) 5121212
Fax: (3) 810012

Al-Hamishmar (The Guardian)
POB 61999
2 Rehov Choma U'Migdal
Tel Aviv 67771
Tel: (3) 378833
Telex: 341652
Fax: (3) 5370037

Hamodia (The Informer)
POB 1306
Yehuda Hamackabbi 3
Jerusalem
Fax: (2) 539108

Hatzofeh (The Watchman)
66 Hamasger St.
Tel Aviv
Tel: (3) 5622951
Fax: (3) 5621502

Israel Nachrichten (News of Israel)
52 Harakevet St.
Tel Aviv
Tel: (3) 370011

Israelski Far Tribuna
113 Givat Herzl St.
Tel Aviv
Tel: (3) 3700

Al-Ittihad (Unity)
POB 104
Haifa
Tel: (4) 511296
Fax: 511297

Le Journal d'Israel
POB 28330
26 Agra St.
Tel Aviv

Ma'ariv (Evening Prayer)
2 Carlebach St.
Tel Aviv 61200
Tel: (3) 5632111
Telex: 33735
Fax: (3) 5610614

Mabat
8 Toshia St.
Tel Aviv 67218
Tel: (3) 5627711
Fax: (3) 5627719

BUSINESS PERIODICALS

Ariel
POB 2160
Jerusalem 91021
Tel: (2) 248897
Fax: (2) 254896

Business Diary (Weekly)
37 Hanamal Street
Haifa

Etgar (The Challenge)
POB 14338
Tel Aviv 61142
Tel: (3) 225382
Fax: (3) 251614

Frei Israel
POB 8512
Tel Aviv

Gazit
POB 4190
8 Zvi Brook St
Tel Aviv

Al-Hamishmar (The Guardian)
4 Ben Avigdor St.
Tel Aviv

Hapraklit
POB 14152
8 Wilson St.
Tel Aviv 61141
Tel: (3) 5614695
Fax: (3) 561476

Hassdeh
POB 40044
8 Shaul Hamelech Blvd.
Tel Aviv
61141
Tel: (3) 5429024
Fax: (3) 252045

Hed Hahinukh
8 Ben Saruk St.
Tel Aviv 62969
Tel: (3) 5432911
Fax: (3) 5432928

Innovation
POB 7422
Haifa 31070
Tel: (4) 255104

Israel Economist (Monthly)
POB 7052
6 Hazanowitz Street
Jerusalem 91070
Tel: (2) 234131
Fax: (2) 246569

Israel Environmental Bulletin
MInistry of the Environment
POB 6234
Jerusalem 91061
Tel: (2) 701606
Telex: 25629
Fax: (2) 513945

Israel Export and Trade Journal (Monthly)
POB 11586
Tel Aviv

Israel Scene
POB 92
Jerusalem 91920
Tel: (2) 527156
Telex: 26436
Fax: (2) 513542

Kalkala Ubamishar (Economics and Trade)
(Monthly)
POB 20027
Tel Aviv 61200
Tel: (3) 561-2444
Fax: (3) 561-2614

Kalkalan
POB 7052
8 Akiva St.
Jerusalem

Kibbutz Trends
¥ad Tabenkin Ramat
Efal 52960
Tel: (3) 343311
Fax: (3) 346376

Leshonenu La'am
Academy of the Hebrew Language
POB 3449
Jerusalem 91034
Tel: (2) 632242
Fax: (2) 666804

Melaha Vetaassiya (Trade and Industry)(Bi-Monthly)
POB 11587
Tel Aviv

Molad
POB 1165
Jerusalem 91010

Monthly Bulletin of Statistics
Israel Central bureau of Statistics
POB 13015
Jerusalem 91130
Tel: (2) 553400
Fax: (2) 553325

Moznaim (Balance)
POB 7098
Tel Aviv
Tel: (3) 253256

Na'amat-Urim Lahorim
93 Arlozorov St.
Tel Aviv 62098
Tel: (3) 449420
Fax: (3) 5462570

Shivuk (Marketing) (Monthly)
POB 20027
Tel Aviv 61200
Tel: (3) 561-2444
Fax: (3) 561-2614

The Easy Way to do Business with Israel
Federation of Israeli Chambers of Commerce
POB 20027
Tel Aviv

INTERNET ADDRESSES

Usenet group(s):
soc.culture.israel

The Jerusalem Post
http://www.jpost.co.il/

Israel Federation of Chambers of Commerce
http://www1.usa1.com/~ibnet/ficchp.html

City Net - Israel
http://www.city.net/countries/israel/
http://www.israel.org/

Italy

Italian Republic

Economy

Overview

Since World War II, Italy has pulled itself from a largely agricultural economy to become a ranking industrial nation, matching France and UK levels of production and per capita productivity. However, high levels of governmental spending on social services and state industries produce a hugh public-sector deficit. This, coupled with political corruption scandals, currency instability leading to a 30 percent devaluation, and a spiraling inflation rate, forced the government to undertake major structural reforms. The reforms seem to be working—inflation has been reduced to about 4.1 percent, and the lira is steadily increasing in value. The government continues to work toward reducing both unemployment and its public sector debt.

Trade

Italy's economy is relatively dependent on trade to sustain the country's high standard of living. Major exports include transportation equipment, apparel, footwear, nonmetalic mineral products, and iron and steel. Imports include machinery, transportation equipment, petroleum products, iron and steel, and chemicals. Germany is Italy's main trade partner, accounting for about 20 percent of total trade. It is followed by France, the US, the UK, and the Netherlands, as well as other members of the EU. Italy is attempting to diversify its trade, both in terms of products (focusing on nontraditional manufactures) and partners (particularly in Central Europe and Asia).

Sectors

Agriculture Although agriculture accounts for only about four percent of GDP, it engages about 7 percent of the work force. Italy boasts a wide range of crops, including grapes, potatoes, sugar beets, soybeans, grain, and olives. Fishing is also important.

Industry Industry accounts for approximately one-third of the economy and employs a similar percentage of the labor force. Principal industries include: machinery, iron and steel, chemicals, food processing, textiles, motor vehicles, and apparel and footwear. In 1993 industrial production fell noticeably, suffering a disproportionate decline in construction and public works because of government cutbacks.

Services Nearly 60 percent of the Italian work force is employed in services, which produces slightly more than 60 percent of GDP. Italy is noted for a broad range of services, including: banking, telecommunications, insurance, energy, television, and film.

Trends

Italy's privatization program, begun in 1992, covers a large number of industrial and service sectors, although the government has retained major shareholdings in companies in the defense, communications, energy, utility, financial, and insurance industries. Still, the privatization program, coupled with Italy's new, more open public procurement process, should create good opportunities for foreign investment. However, in order to maintain its recovery, Italy will have to address long-term structural problems, principally the underdevelopment of the southern part of the country, a low level of agricultural productivity, and heavy dependence on imported energy supplies.

At a Glance

THE COUNTRY

Location Southern Europe, east of France and south of Switzerland and Austria. The peninsula extends into the central Mediterranean Sea.
Terrain Mostly rugged and mountainous with some plains and coastal lowlands.
Climate Mostly Mediterranean, with cold northern winters. Alpine in the far north, and hot and dry in the south.

THE PEOPLE

Population 58,000,000
Ethnic composition Italian (includes small clusters of German, French, and Slovene-Italians in the north and Albanian-Italians and Greek-Italians in the south), Sicilian, and Sardinian.
Religious composition
Roman Catholic 98%
Languages spoken Italian (official), with German, French, and Slovene in some regions.
Education and literacy Education is free and compulsory between the ages of six and 14. The adult literacy rate is 98 percent.
Labor force
Total:...24,000,000
By occupation: services 60%, industry and commerce 33%, unemployment 11%, and agriculture 7%.

COUNTRY FACTS

Political and legal A parliamentary democracy with a legal system based on a civil law system, influenced by Roman Catholic ecclesiastical law.
Telephone Supervised or owned by the government, telecommunications in Italy are relatively advanced and efficient. International country code: [39]. Selected city codes: Rome (6), Milan (2), Florence (55), Genoa (10), Naples (81), Turin (80), Venice (41).
Transportation Italy has one of the best highway systems in the world, as well as a large, mostly government-owned, railway system. Several major and minor airports serve the peninsula. Many large seaports handle the extensive merchant marine fleet and ocean freight traffic. A network of inland waterways in the north is used for limited shipping.
Environment Slow to confront its environmental problems, Italy now has several government ministries and regional authorities responsible for environmental protection. Current issues include air pollution from industrial emissions such as sulfur dioxide; disposal of organic and chemical waste; coastal and inland rivers polluted from industrial and agricultural effluents; and acid rain that is damaging lakes.
Media Italy's internationally respected free press engages in vigorous, opinionated debate of the issues of the day. It has more than 70 dailies, with the highest readership in Northern and Central Italy. Many newspapers and periodicals are owned by political parties, the Roman Catholic Church, and various economic groups. There are more than 45 million radios and 24 million television sets in Italy.
Health A universal health care system gives all Italians ready access to medical treatment, though these benefits are being scaled back along with other social welfare programs. Life expectancy of males is 74 years; of females, 81 years.

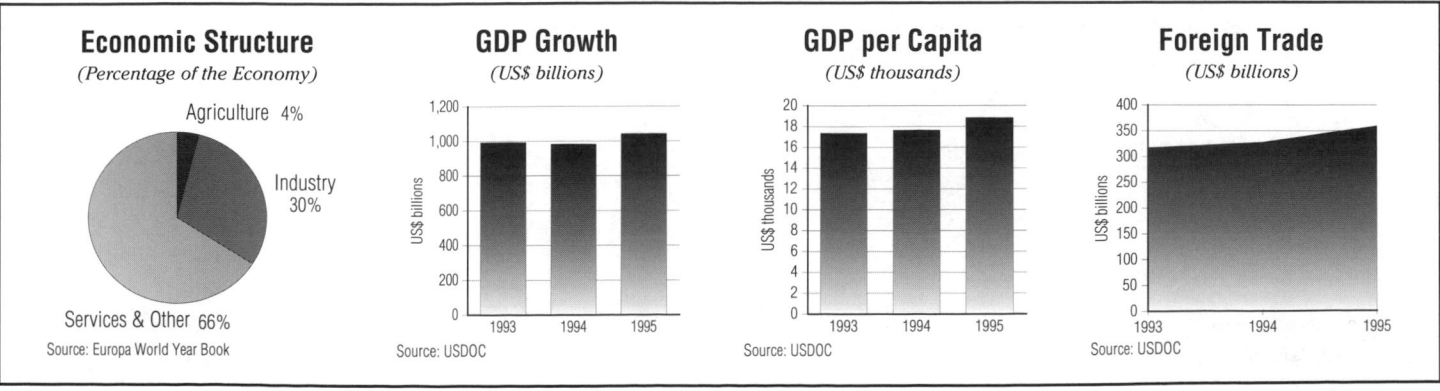

Economic Structure
(Percentage of the Economy)
Agriculture 4%
Industry 30%
Services & Other 66%
Source: Europa World Year Book

GDP Growth
(US$ billions)
1993 1994 1995
Source: USDOC

GDP per Capita
(US$ thousands)
1993 1994 1995
Source: USDOC

Foreign Trade
(US$ billions)
1993 1994 1995
Source: USDOC

Italy

- ⊛ National capital
- ◉ Regional capital
- ○ Provincial capital
- ● Secondary city
- ——— Primary road
- ┈┈┈ Railroad
- ——— Administrative border
- ▬▬▬ International border

| 0 | 50 | 100 km |
| 0 | 50 | 100 mi |

Regions of Italy

1 Valle D'Aosta
2 Piemonte
3 Lombardia
4 Trentino-Alto Adige
5 Veneto
6 Friuli-Venezia Guilia
7 Liguria
8 Emilia-Romagna
9 Toscana
10 Umbria
11 Marche
12 Lazio
13 Abruzzi
14 Molise
15 Campania
16 Puglia
17 Basilicata
18 Calabria
19 Sicilia
20 Sardegna

*Provinces have the same name as their capitals.

Foreign Trade

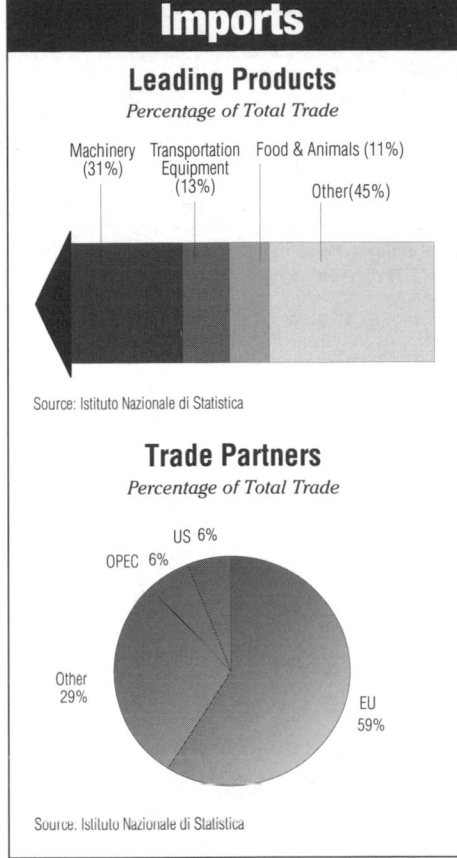

Imports

Leading Products
Percentage of Total Trade

Machinery (31%)
Transportation Equipment (13%)
Food & Animals (11%)
Other (45%)

Source: Istituto Nazionale di Statistica

Trade Partners
Percentage of Total Trade

US 6%
OPEC 6%
Other 29%
EU 59%

Source: Istituto Nazionale di Statistica

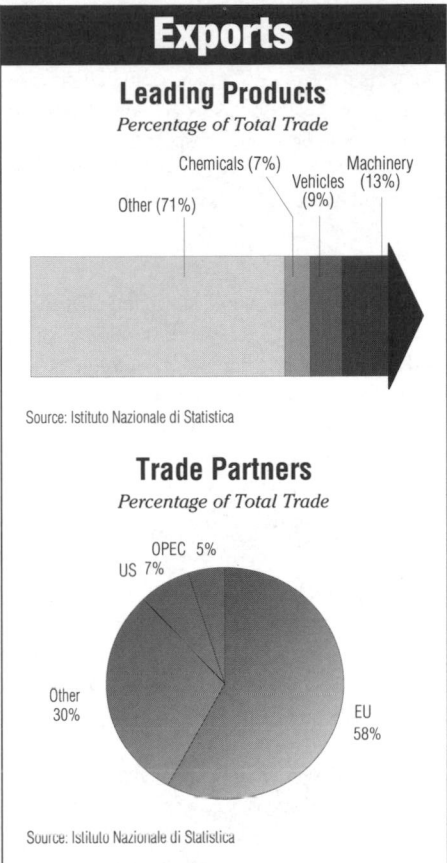

Exports

Leading Products
Percentage of Total Trade

Chemicals (7%)
Vehicles (9%)
Machinery (13%)
Other (71%)

Source: Istituto Nazionale di Statistica

Trade Partners
Percentage of Total Trade

OPEC 5%
US 7%
Other 30%
EU 58%

Source: Istituto Nazionale di Statistica

Opportunities

FOR IMPORTING TO ITALY

- automobiles and automobile parts
- bottled drinks: iced tea, beer
- chemicals
- computers and peripherals
- cotton and wool
- electronic components
- ethnic and health foods
- ferrous and nonferrous metals
- fresh and frozen food
- high-value food products
- industrial machinery
- industrial process controls
- laboratory and scientific equipment
- medical supplies and equipment
- petroleum products
- pulp and paper goods
- telecommunications equipment
- wood and wood products

FOR EXPORTING FROM ITALY

- beverages
- ceramic goods
- cereals
- chemical products
- dairy products and vegetables
- food and agricultural products
- furniture
- glassware
- iron and steel
- leather
- mechanical products
- motor vehicles
- olive oil
- pearls and semi-precious and precious stones
- production machinery
- textiles and apparel
- transportation equipment
- vegetables

GROWTH SECTORS
- advanced factory automatic equipment
- electronic components
- laboratory and scientific instruments
- services
- telecommunications

GOVERNMENT PROCUREMENT
- computer services
- electrical power systems
- environmental protection technologies
- medical supplies and equipment
- military equipment and supplies
- specialty and industrial chemicals
- urban waste management products and services

Trade News

RULES AND REGULATIONS

- **Tariffs and import taxes** Italy applies the European Union (EU) tariffs. Duty rates on manufactured goods generally range from five to eight percent. Most raw materials enter duty free or at low rates while agricultural products face higher rates and special levies. On entry, some stamp or administrative taxes may be levied.
- **Import licenses** With the exception of a small group of largely agricultural items, practically all goods can be imported without import licenses and free of quantitative restrictions. Various apparel and textile products, and controlled items such as arms and munitions, however, are also regulated.
- **Temporary imports** Material may be temporarily imported into Italy without payment of duties and tax only if such materials are to be used in the production, manufacture, or distribution of a product that is to be exported.
- **Import payments** Payments for imports are not regulated.
- **Export liberalization** Italy eased its export regulations to other EU countries, with the exception of high-technology products. Export of gas products is also subject to ministerial authorization and regulation.
- **Prohibited imports** A number of Italian regulations and EC directives prohibit the importation of certain items, including: foodstuffs, food colorings, drugs and narcotics, animal products, plants, seed grains, alcohol, and cosmetics and toiletries.
- **Free trade zones (FTZs)** There are two FTZs in Italy: one in Trieste and the other in Venice. There are also numerous general warehouses, located throughout Italy in all port areas and cities, that enjoy some of the privileges of FTZs. Benefits of a free trade zone include customs duties deferred for 180 days from the date the goods leave the FTZ to enter another EU country. Companies can also employ workers of the same nationality, under that country's labor laws and social security.
- **Free trade arrangements** Italy has been a member of the (EU) since its inception in 1958. Free trade agreements have also been developed with the European Free Trade Association (EFTA).
- **Export prospects** Some of the best export prospects include software and services, cosmetics, pollution control, computers, telecommunications, aircraft and parts, and products for the energy sector.
- **Import duties** Italy uses the EC standard of tariffs for the majority of goods brought into the country, based on the International Harmonized System (HS) of product classification.
- **Export controls** Most exports are shipped under general licenses not requiring formal approval, and carrying no regulations.

GOVERNMENT AGENCY

Istituto Nazionale per il Commercio Estero (ICE)
(National Institute for Foreign Trade)
Via Liszt 21
EUR
00100 Rome
Tel: (6) 59921
Fax: (6) 5910508

TRANSPORTATION FIRMS

Costa Armatori SpA (Linea C)
Via Gabriele D'Annunzio 2
16100 Genova
Tel: (10) 54831 Telex: 270068

Navigazione Alta Italia SpA
Via Corsica 19
16128 Genova
Tel: (10) 56331 Telex: 270181

D'Amico Fratelli, Armatori, SpA
Via Liguria 36
00187 Rome
Tel: (6) 4671 Telex: 614545

Marketing

Overview

Italy is composed of an industrial north and a largely agricultural south, and the market conditions between the two are often worlds apart. Northern Italy accounts for about 65 percent of total Italian imports and is close to important European industrialized areas. This area also has twice the per capita income rate of southern Italy. Rome, Milan, and Naples all have regions for marketing purposes that stretch far beyond their borders. Turin, Italy's automobile capital, is one of the country's leading market areas. Italy offers foreign businesspeople a situation in which they can expect a high volume of sales and, in many cases, a lack of effective local competition.

Distribution

Although foreign business representatives will find that Italy offers many distribution challenges, none are overwhelming. The Italian distribution system is heavily weighted toward serving the small, family-operated stores that make up the bulk of its retail outlets. Along with family-owned stores, the Italian distribution system includes such varied outlets as street vendors, modern shopping malls, specialty stores, and discount stores. Successful and popular new shopping malls are springing up all over Italy and are rapidly becoming valuable outlets for foreign goods. The Italian retail distribution system is in the process of refurbishing its marketing strategies so that foreign business can expect to compete effectively with the more streamlined large chain stores found in other European nations.

Agents, Distributors, and Partners

Foreign companies most often use representatives to sell industrial products in Italy, while well-established distributors sell the bulk of consumer goods. Although foreigners can technically handle their own distribution, the fragmentation of most distribution channels makes the use of an Italian firm that knows the local system and has the requisite established contacts more effective and cost-efficient. An Italian agent for foreign companies is generally regarded to be authorized to act on behalf of the foreign firm. Frequently, agreements in Italy grant exclusive sales rights. Foreign firms that rely on local Italian agents who have contacts and understand the market can generally expect to develop healthy sales.

Selling Techniques

Direct marketing—through mail order and catalog sales—can be among the most effective methods for marketing in Italy. Italian wholesalers and large retailers generally buy directly from the manufacturer and seek the lowest prices. Italian representatives of products with high sales volume and low profit margins also often buy directly from the manufacturer. Foreign concerns may find that sales of appropriate products to large department or chain stores in Italy yield the best results, but these stores often use major promotion campaigns and expect the foreign seller to contribute to the cost. Foreign companies introducing new products into the Italian market should conduct substantial market research in order to accurately assess potential and plan a strategy for their products to reach and attract Italian consumers. Foreign companies need to diligently apply new techniques, management, research, media promotion, and equipment in order to reach sophisticated Italian consumers, regardless of an often archaic distribution system.

Advertising

Advertising in Italy is growing quickly with an increase in the number, size, and sophistication of advertising agencies and services. The chief means of advertising is through one of the many daily newspapers. Italian newspapers do not have their own advertising departments, but use commissioned agencies serving several different clients. Italy has three television networks operated by *Radiotelevisione Italiana* (RAI), a government-regulated company that programs and carries commercials 24 hours a day. The nearly 10,000 motion picture theaters regularly run advertising film clips that foreign businesses can utilize to reach a large, economically diverse audience. Foreign firms find that direct advertising is a successful technique to lure Italian consumers. Show windows are a beautiful method of advertising in Italy, and have become almost an art form. Trade shows are another good way for outside firms to attract Italian customers. *Fiera Milano*, the large trade fair site in Milan, organizes many trade shows each year.

Sales and Customer Support

In developing a distribution network in Italy, foreign companies should be sure to include service by knowledgeable personnel among their top requirements. Foreign firms become successful by aggressively marketing their products and services and by showing a long-term commitment to their products and the Italian market. A key factor in showing commitment is the stocking of parts and the capability to provide immediate, high-quality service to Italian customers. Italians expect personalized service, and repeat sales often depend on their perception of the caliber of initial and after-sales service they receive. Sales and maintenance manuals should all be written in Italian.

Marketing in Italy

MARKETING TIPS

- **Promotion** Promotion of foreign business is best handled by a resident representative. Local agents are familiar with the needs of Italian customers and are in a good position to solve problems either in advance or as they arise.
- **Quality** Department stores in Italy have begun reorganizing to attract more affluent, quality-oriented consumers.
- **European contacts** Italian distributors have excellent contacts with countries in Central Europe and the Circum-Mediterranean area.
- **Commuter advertising** Poster advertisement on walls; along streets; and in and on street cars, buses, and other transportation can be used successfully to reach consumers.
- **Regional markets** Milan is the leading market for most industrial and consumer goods, and it is generally necessary to make a successful entry there in order to be successful nationally.

AD AGENCIES

Bates Italia
Via Paleocapa 7
20121 Milan
Tel: (2) 72223-1
Fax: (2) 867469

Conquest Europe S.P.A.
Via Cino del Duca, 5
20122 Milan
Tel: (2) 76007708
Fax: (2) 782126

Grey Direct S.R.L./Milan
Corso Sempione, 10
20154 Milan
Tel: (2) 3313122
Fax: (2) 311049

J. Walter Thompson Italia S.P.A.
Via Dunini 28
20122 Milan
Tel: (2) 77981
Fax: (2) 782507

Leo Burnett Co., S.R.L.
Via Fatebenefratelli 14
20121 Milan
Tel: (2) 63541
Fax: (2) 29005229

MARKET RESEARCH FIRMS

Addressvitt Montaldi
Via Anna Kuliscioff, 38
20152 Milan
Tel: (2) 483-01334 Fax: (2) 483-01300

Centro Internazionale Ricerche di Mercato
Via Lodovico Mancini 1
Milan 20129

Commark - Communicazione e Marketing S.R.L.
Via Isonzo, 25
00198 Rome
Tel: (6) 8558748 Fax: (6) 8416677

Databank
Corso Italia, 8
20122 Milan
Tel: (2) 866641 Fax: (2) 865579

Demoskopea S.R.L
Instituto per le Ricerche di Pubblicita e Marketing
Via Nino Bixio 4
Milan 20129
Fax: (2) 204-3992 Telex: 313103 DEMOS I

Directa S.R.L.
Via Solari, 8
20144 Milan
Tel: (2) 481-93581 Fax: (2) 481-02277

Etas Kompass
Via S Rita da Cascia 33
Milan 20143
Fax: (2) 891-0454

Loverso Dr. Alfredo
Via Morosini, 39
20135 Milan
Tel: (2) 550-11554 Fax: (2) 720-02889

Business Culture

Greetings and Courtesies

Italians usually greet each other with a handshake, an elbow grasp and *ciao* (hello or good-bye). Male friends also embrace and pat backs. Persons of the same gender often walk arm in arm in public. Good friends often greet each other with kisses on both cheeks. Invitations to meet family are a mark of special favor, not extended until the third or fourth visit, and should always be accepted. All university graduates have a title and expect to be addressed as *dottore* (liberal arts), *avvocato* (law), *ingengnere* (technical field), or *professore* (academics and most medical doctors). Exchange cards only in business situations when introduced; hand a card to everyone present. To show respect, look at a card after receiving one. Have one side of your card printed in Italian. and include your title. Titles should appear on business cards. When invited into a home, bringing a gift is not expected, although the host will accept chocolates or flowers. If you are bringing flowers, take an odd number and avoid chrysanthemums (which are used to decorate graves). Also avoid red flowers that signify secrecy and passion, and yellow flowers, symbolizing jealousy.

Business Ethic and Framework

Most successful organizations in Italy are owned by a family or modeled on a family structure; business relationships are based on the kind of interdependence and mutual obligation which tie families together. Once the partners in a venture see how everyone can benefit, cooperation and commitment follow. Never confuse polite attentiveness for interest in a presentation or product. Facts are treated as closely guarded secrets and are traded only for those of equal or greater value. Italians like people who present their ideas rationally and can demonstrate expertise. Rules in business are usually regarded only as guidelines, so written policies and procedures are rarely followed. Since Italians tend to obey only those provisions they find just and useful, the letter of the contract is usually less significant than its spirit.

Decision Making

The decisionmaker can be hard to find, partly because she or he may not be part of the organizational structure. Most organizations base their power in one person, usually a man, who builds alliances on personal relationships. Power structures here, like those in much of the world, are multi-layered; but in Italy, the most important layers are those farthest from the public eye and are usually centered on an autocratic ruler. Negotiations should be conducted between executives of equivalent rank; though middle-level employees usually begin business relationships. Important decisions are usually not decided upon in meetings because participants may feel forced to agree in order to get along. Arguments are often a test of strength, and visitors who are not prepared for this style can easily get off track. Interruptions are frequent and haggling is common. Italians may display great disappointment when desired concessions are not made; they can readily become loud and emotional.

Women

Women have always been the supreme authority at home. Although they have made recent significant inroads in business, much of the country is still run by men. For a woman to openly contradict her husband in front of strangers is the paramount insult. Older women usually wear dresses and head scarves, though the younger generation is often extremely fashion conscious.

Meetings

Written agendas are made and distributed, but few take them seriously. Allow extra meeting time; up to 20 minutes late is still considered on time, and stopping a meeting that is longer than anticipated may be viewed as rude. Italian businesspeople prefer presentations that are informal but polished, with facts and graphs whenever relevant. They also like presenters who seem confident in themselves and their product. Business hours are usually from 9:00 am to 1:00 pm and 3:00 to 7:00 pm. It is best to make appointments for business and governmental visits.

Business Attire

Italians dress as well as they can at all times, and are proud of their position as world-class fashion-setters. Demand is often for trendy apparel, with a distinctive "American" look and a high content of natural fiber. Wear medium weight clothing with a light topcoat or raincoat in winter and light business clothing for summer. Conservative business suits are best for meetings. Dark glasses are usually removed when entering a building.

Cultural Cautions

DO'S

- Italians enjoy talking about world and local events, soccer, and family.
- Lunch often lasts two to three hours, and a persistent invitation should be accepted.
- Men should remove their hats when entering buildings.
- Cover the mouth when yawning.
- Some dining tips: stay at the table until everyone finishes eating, and always keep both hands above the table.

DON'TS

- Italians are proud of titles. Do not use first names until after a long acquaintance.
- You needn't look for a bread plate; Italians break rolls and loaves and leave them next to the plate. Do not cut salad or bread, or butter bread.
- Avoid talking about business at a social event. At all times, do not mention the Mafia or other organized groups, politics, religion, and taxes.
- Don't remove your shoes in public.
- Never use a spoon to roll pasta; put the fork against the side of the plate to twist.

CUSTOMS

- Italians prefer to haggle over prices, and some may consider it an insult if you don't haggle back.
- Italians love to smoke and drink espresso coffee throughout the day.
- Gestures have extensive, traditional meanings. A nose tap is a friendly warning. Flicking the chin means "not interested" or "get out of here." Rubbing the thumb rapidly against the fingers signals money. Nodding the head up and down with closed eyes means "no." A shoulder shrug indicates ignorance or apathy. A finger pushing down under the eye suggests recognizing cleverness. A raised fist with index and little fingers extended signifies a wife's unfaithfulness. When the left hand clasps the right elbow while the right forearm is jerked up, hand closed in a fist, the signal is obscene.
- Italians are usually very close to their families, and many generations often live in the same house, especially in towns in the south.
- All deliveries should be prompt. Late delivery is one of the biggest complaints Italians have about foreign products. Every delivery should meet any promised deadline.
- Another often heard Italian complaint is poorly prepared paperwork.

OBSERVATIONS

- Italian gestures and voice tones often strike persons from other cultures as violently exaggerated and emotional.
- Tolerance for inefficiency and mistakes is high, but it is low for arrogance and rudeness.
- Southern Italians take a leisurely approach to life and the pace of business, while Northern attitudes are less relaxed.
- Telephone service here is often unreliable; messengers and personal meetings are the best ways to communicate.

NEGOTIATIONS

- A sense of urgency is considered an indication of weakness.
- Consider taking an attorney along for the negotiating process. Italians can be vague or may say things to be polite rather than to be honest. Attorneys may be able to help with the details of the contract.
- The Italian love of wit and humor will not always be apparent during negotiations.
- A soft sell, confidently and concisely presented, is the most successful. Demonstrate patience and flexibility.
- Italians try not to be rude during tense business meetings. When refusing a proposal, Italians can be charming in order to soften the blow.

Legal

Legal System

Italy has a civil law legal system, which also provides for EC Regulations and Directives to be implemented in Italy.

Intellectual Property Rights

Patents A patent may be obtained in Italy provided it refers to a new invention or process. Applications are filed with the Italian Patent Office. A patent is protected for a term of 20 years, after which it becomes public property.

Trademarks A trademark is protected by filing a registration with the Italian Patent Office or by the priority of its use. The registration ensures protection for 10 years and, at the end of the term, the trademark owner may apply for an extension of protection for a further 10 years. The registration of a trademark in Italy may be extended to the other countries which have signed the OMPI Agreement.

Copyrights A copyright protects the author of an original work for life and for a further period of 50 years after death. A special protection is provided for computer software in compliance with EC legislation. Industrial designs are protected for 15 years after their registration.

Trade Secrets Employees are under a general obligation of loyalty. The disclosure of trade secrets or confidential commercial information or know-how is considered a tort if it is in violation of a contract or confidentiality clause, or if it violates good faith and fairness in the execution of a contract.

Business Registration

Except for specially regulated activities, no authorization is required for starting a business in Italy. A foreign company can conduct business in Italy directly a) through a branch which is registered with the competent Court and Chamber of Commerce, and which has appointed a legal representative in Italy; b) through a subsidiary; c) by incorporating a company in Italy; or d) through a joint-venture, whose partner may or may not be Italian. All companies must be registered with the competent Court and Chamber of Commerce, whereas only the deed of incorporation and the Articles of Association of a corporation must be executed before a notary public.

Contracts and Dispute Resolution

In general, contracts are regulated by the will of the parties. Parties are free to include any provisions in their contracts so long as they are worthy for protection, even if they are not specifically provided for by the law. It is usually preferable to settle business disputes through informal negotiations or arbitration proceedings, which may also be conducted before international arbitration bodies, since lawsuits tend to be very lengthy. The Italian civil procedure code provides two different degrees of the proceedings, and a third degree before the Supreme Court exclusively for breach of civil law.

Notaries

Some deeds and agreements must be under seal to be valid or offered into evidence. Notaries prepare and authenticate deeds and documents, which must be in the Italian language or a sworn translation. Italian diplomatic representatives in foreign countries can, in some cases, act as notaries.

Labor

Italian law provides strong protections for workers. Workers can be divided into full-time employees (whose contract has an indefinite term), part-time employees, employees with a fixed term contract, apprentices, and self-employed workers. Specific provisions deal with under-age workers, sick employees, women employees and maternity leave, protected categories (handicapped people, refugees, etc.), and other special situations, providing for special guarantees and additional benefits. Most employment relationships are governed by collective bargaining agreements, but the employer is entitled to execute a specific employment agreement with each employee if necessary. Social security contributions are mandatory and must be paid by both the employer—in an average amount of between 20 and 40 percent of gross pay—and the employee. Upon termination of employment for any reason, including employee's breach or for other cause, the employer must pay to the employee a severance indemnity, allocated in advance in the company accounts each year for each employee. The Italian Social Security office contributes in-whole or in-part benefits for employees of companies operating in particular fields of activity, with certain numbers of employees, and which are undergoing business difficulties. The dismissal of the employee is admitted only for cause or for objective reasons (e.g., difficulties of the companies, shutdown, etc.) and, often, the control of public agencies is requested. The workers have the constitutionally guaranteed right to strike, but certain limitations apply to particular fields (transport, public services, etc).

Source: Studio Legale Tonucci, Rome

Legal Matters

LEGAL BRIEFS

- **Procedure reform** The Italian Civil Procedure Code is undergoing a thorough review. The result should be quicker resolution of lawsuits and more rapidly enforceable decisions.

- **Arbitration** Italian legislation provides for two arbitration procedures: *"Arbitrato Rituale,"* which follows the rules set by the Civil Procedure Code and can be compared to international arbitrations, and *"Arbitrato Irritualle,"* in which the arbitrators act as independent informal negotiators appointed by the parties. In the latter case, the arbitrators themselves set the rules of the procedure, which are usually more flexible.

- **"Automatic termination" of contracts** Most contracts in Italy contain an "automatic termination" clause which provides for the immediate termination of the agreement should one of the parties fail to comply with certain contractual obligations.

- **Good faith** The Civil Code contains general provisions which oblige the contractual parties to act according to good faith and fairness in the execution of contracts. Reference to said provisions can always be made, notwithstanding the text of the agreement.

- **Intellectual property rights** The Italian legal system provides for special legislation concerning intellectual property protection. Registration procedures, however, are usually very slow, even though they do not imply a preliminary discovery procedure. All intellectual property rights can be assigned to third parties. The violation of intellectual property rights entitles the injured party to sue for damages of unfair competition. Courts may enter preliminary injunctions in order to prevent the third party from continuing the illegal use of the intellectual property right.

LEGAL CONTACTS

Studio Legale Tonucci
Via Principessa Clotilde N. 7
00196 Rome
Tel: (6) 321-2215 Fax: (6) 323-5161

Studio Legale Grimaldi e Clifford Chance
Viale G. Rossini 7
Rome 00198
Tel: (6) 807-2251
Fax: (6) 807-8201

Baker & McKenzie
Via Venti Settembre 1
00187 Rome
Tel: (6) 460-374
Fax: (6) 494-0635

Graham & James
Via Visconti di Modrone, 2
Milan

Antonelli & Cocuzza
Via Fregugulia, 8
20122 Milan
Tel: (2) 55 19 04 09

Studio Legale Albisinni
Via Zenale 3
20123 Milan
Tel: (2) 480.21655
Fax: (2) 481.6725

Baker & McKenzie
3 Plazza Meda
20121 Milan
Tel: (2) 76 01 39 21
Fax: (2) 76 00 83 22

Studio Legale Bisconti
Via Santo Spirito, 14
20121 Milan
Tel: (2) 781188
Fax: (2) 781188

Capurro, Marchini, Michetti, Roj & Thomassini
1, Piazza Cavour
20121 Milan
Tel: (2) 65 92 741
Fax: (2) 65 95 822

Conte-Maienza-Vasile
Via Freguglia 8/AQ
20122 Milan
Tel: (2) 55011592
Fax: (2) 5513884

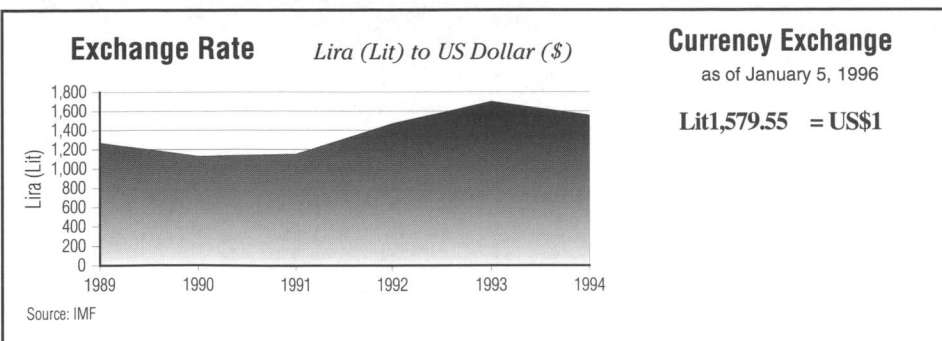

Exchange Rate *Lira (Lit) to US Dollar ($)*

Source: IMF

Currency Exchange
as of January 5, 1996

Lit1,579.55 = US$1

Money Matter

BITS AND PIECES

- **Investments** Foreign investments of any kind in Italy, including portfolio investments and the purchase of real estate, are unrestricted, and no restrictions apply to their repatriation. In general, there is resistance to foreign investment in some sectors and significant bureaucratic obstacles exist to investing in Italy; however, these apply equally to both Italian and foreign investors.
- **Private ownership** There is no specific limitation to the right of private ownership and establishment in the Italian Constitution or Italian civil law.
- **Gold** Purchases and sales of gold are legally reserved for monetary authorities. Exports of unrefined gold are subject to licensing by the Ministry of Foreign Trade. Imports and exports of gold coins are unlimited.
- **New changes** New retail outlets, including chain stores, department stores, supermarkets, hypermarkets, and franchises are restricted by local practice and national legislation, subjecting applications for large retail units to a long authorization process.
- **Banking** The Amato Law of 1990 allows banks and other saving institutions already established in accordance with Italian "public law" to transform themselves into private, joint stock companies and sell up to 49 percent of their assets to private investors.

Currency

Italy's currency is the Italian lira (plural, lire). The symbol is Lit or L, and the principal subdivision is 100 centisimo.

Foreign Exchange

Foreign exchange may be bought or sold from the Bank of Italy or any of its authorized banks. Authorized banks may engage in spot and forward exchange transactions, and rates are determined on the basis of supply and demand. Generally the government does not intervene in the exchange market. There are no taxes or subsidies on purchases or sales of foreign exchange.

Capital Transfers

Residents are permitted to make foreign exchange transactions without restrictions through the Bank of Italy, authorized banks, and the postal administration. Nonresidents may maintain accounts with authorized banks in lire or foreign exchange without restrictions. Italy has no restrictions on the amount of foreign exchange instruments, currency, or checks that are brought into the country. Normally, one million lire may be taken out of the country, but any amount declared on entry may be re-exported.

Investment Incentives

There are a number of incentives available to foreign investors, including subsidized loans, cash grants, labor cost incentives, other non-tax incentives (such as reduction of electric utility costs), and tax incentives. A number of incentives are targeted at southern Italy, primarily the Mezzogiorno region. Investors there receive a 10-year corporate income tax exemption and an exemption from local income tax on any profits earned anywhere in Italy that are reinvested in the south. Some businesses have complained about the substantial information required to earn investment incentives and the delays in receiving them, but the incentives are freely available and widely used.

Investment Restrictions

There are bureaucratic obstacles to investing in Italy, but they apply to domestic as well as foreign investors. There are no screening procedures directed solely at foreign investment, but the 1990 anti-trust law requires notification and possible screening of all acquisitions in which the takeover target has total sales of over 50 billion lire.

BANKS

Banca d'Italia
Via Nazionale 91
00184 Rome
Tel: (6) 47921 Fax: (6) 474-7820

Banca d'America e D'Italia SpA
Via Borgogna 8
20122 Milan
Tel: (2) 77951 Fax: (2) 77952439

Banca Commerciale Italiana SpA-COMIT
Piazza della Scala 6
20121 Milan
Tel: (2) 88501 Fax: (2) 88503026

Banca Popolare Commercio e Industria Srl
Via della Moscova 33
20121 Milan
Tel: (2) 62751 Fax: (2) 659-9072

Banco de Napoli
Via Toledo 177-178
80132 Naples
Naples
Tel: (81) 7911111

Banco di Roma
Via Marco Minghetti 17
00187 Rome

Banco di Sardegna
Viale Umberto 36
07100 Sassari
Tel: (79) 226000 Fax: (79) 226015

Banco San Geminiano e San Prospero SpA
Via Mondatora 14
41100 Modena
Tel: (59) 200111

Cassa di Risparmio delle Provincie Lombarde (CARIPLO)
Via Monte di Pieta 8
20121 Milan
Tel: (2) 88661 Fax: (2) 88662356

Cassa di Risparmio di Verona, Vicenza, Belluno e Ancona
Via G. Garibaldi 1
37121 Verona
Tel: (45) 936111 Fax: (45) 591516

Credito Emiliano
Via Emilia S. Pietro 4
42100 Reggio
Tel: (522) 4501 Fax: (522) 433969

Credito Romagnolo SpA
POB 775
Via Zamboni 20
40126 Bologna
Tel: (51) 338111 Fax: (51) 338377

TAXATION	At a Glance	
Taxation requires sophisticated knowledge of complex rules and regulations specific to each country. The information presented here is from the Ernst & Young Corporate Tax Guide and Directory, available from the Ernst & Young accounting office in your country, or from: **Adonnino Ascoli** Studio Legale Tributario e Amministrativo Via Principessa Clotilde, 7 00196 Rome, Italy Tel: (6) 3220585 Fax: (56) 3219128	Corporate Income Tax Rate (%) (a)	36
	Capital Gains Tax Rate (%) (a)	36
	Branch Tax Rate (%) (a)	36
	Withholding Tax (%)	
	Dividends (b)	32.4
	Interest (c)	12.5/15/30
	Royalties from Patents, Know-how, etc. (d)	21
	Branch Remittance Tax	0
	Net Operating Losses (Years)	
	Carryback	0
	Carryforward (e)	5

(a) Local income tax at a rate of 16.2% is also imposed.
(b) Applicable to nonresidents. A 10% withholding tax is imposed on dividends paid to residents.
(c) The 12.5% rate applies to interest on government bonds issued after 1986 and on bonds issued by listed companies. The 15% rate applies to interest on all types of loans not represented by bonds. The 30% rate applies to interest on other bonds and interest paid by banks. These rates apply to payments to both residents and nonresidents.
(d) Applicable to residents and nonresidents. For payments to nonresident companies and individuals, the rate may be reduced under tax treaties.
(e) Loss carryforwards are not allowed for local income tax purposes.

Business Travel

	LH 1906	MADRID	935	113-3
	LH 1022	STUTTGART HBF.	935	-
	AF 1701	LYON	940	683-6
	AY 822	HELSINKI	940	113-3
	AA 071	SFRANCISCO-DALLAS	945	731-7

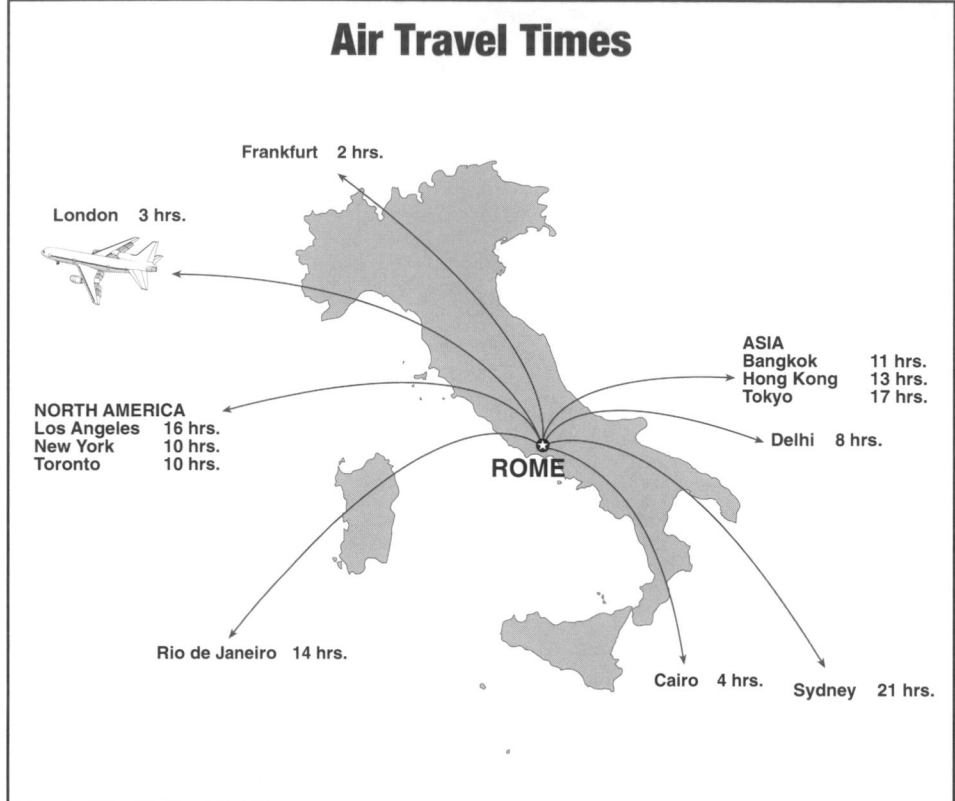

Air Travel Times

Frankfurt 2 hrs.

London 3 hrs.

NORTH AMERICA
Los Angeles 16 hrs.
New York 10 hrs.
Toronto 10 hrs.

ASIA
Bangkok 11 hrs.
Hong Kong 13 hrs.
Tokyo 17 hrs.

Delhi 8 hrs.

ROME

Rio de Janeiro 14 hrs.

Cairo 4 hrs.

Sydney 21 hrs.

COMMUNICATIONS

Telephone Italy's telecommunications systems are not up to date, and telephones are used only when necessary. Usually they are only used to make appointments, and rarely to conduct business. Magnetic cards are phasing out copper tokens for public phones and are sold in various denominations at telephone company (SIP) offices and outlets.

Fax All of the major hotels and most businesses and business centers have fax machines.

Post office Italy's mail service is improving but still poor, with the exception of the more efficient Vatican City post office. Post offices are open Monday-Friday 8:30 am to 7:15 pm (except Wednesday mornings) and Saturday 8:30 am to 6:00 pm. Many companies use private couriers instead of relying on the unreliable telephone and postal services.

BEST TRAVEL BOOKS

Frommer's Italy, by Arthur Frommer. General reference and travel.

Birnbaum's Italy, by Alexandra Birnbaum, Birnbaum Travel Guides Series.

Fodor's Travel Guide, Italy. Tourist oriented, excellent source of city details.

Culture Shock, A Guide to Customs and Etiquette, Italy.

Berlitz Business Travel Guide, Europe. Features include: concise economic details for each country, succesful trip planning, useful facts and addresses, essential words and phrases.

USEFUL TELEPHONE NUMBERS

If you are calling from outside Italy, you will need to add the country code [39] and any other international dialing requirements from within your country.

- Local Operator 1811
- Overseas Operator... 170
- Europe Operator 15
- Directory Assistance 12
- International Telegrams 186
- Time 161
- Weather (Milan) .... (2) 7390
- Weather (Rome) .... (6) 59061
- Police 113
- Carabinca 112
- Highway Police 116
- Ambulance/First Aid 115
- Rome First Aid .... (6) 5100
- Milan First Aid .... (2) 7733
- Taxi Rome .... (6) 3570
- Taxi Milan .... (2) 8388
- Taxi Florence .... (55) 4390
- Taxi Naples ....(81) 324-444
- Weather Rome .... (6) 5906
- Weather Milan .... (2) 7390
- Italy Long Distance Operator 14
- Italian Union of Chambers of Commerce (6) 749961
- World Trade Center Italy .... (2) 8244086
- Ministry of Tourism...................................... (6) 7732
- National Tourist Board (ENIT).................. (6) 49711

Credit Card Information
Lost or stolen credit cards (call collect to the US, regardless of which country the card was issued in).
- Amex ....[1] (919) 333-3211
- Diner's Club...............................[1] (303) 799-1504
- MasterCard ....[1] (314) 275-6690
- Visa ....[1] (410) 581-7931

Travelogue

WORKWEEK

Offices Monday-Friday 9:00 am to 1:00 pm and 2:00 pm to 6:00 pm.
Banks Monday-Friday 8:30 am to 1:30 pm, plus one hour in the afternoon.
Government Monday-Saturday 8:00 am to 2:00 pm.
Retail Monday-Saturday 9:00 am to 1:00 pm and 3:30 pm to 7:30 pm.

HOLIDAYS

Holidays 1996
January 1 New Year's Day
January 6 Epiphany
April 8 Easter Monday
April 25 Liberation Day
May 1 Labor Day
August 15 Assumption
November 1 All Saints' Day
December 8 Immaculate Conception
December 25 Christmas Day
December 26 St. Stephen's Day
In addition to the above public holidays, most business firms are closed for vacation during July and August and during the Christmas festive period from December 24 to January 2. Certain other holidays, such as Patron Saint's Day, are observed in local jurisdictions.

VISA AND PASSPORT

Foreigners must have a valid passport. Foreigners visiting Italy for tourism or business do not need visas for stays less than 90 days.

DEPARTURE FORMALITIES

You must declare in advance if you plan to export the equivalent of L20million (US$15,540) by filling out a V2 declaration form.

IMMUNIZATION

Foreigners do not need proof of vaccination unless arriving from an infected area. Food in Italy can be very rich, as can the wines. Take plenty of stomach remedies.

TIPPING

Tax and tips are usually included in the bill for hotels and restaurants. For excellent service in restaurants that already include a 15 percent service charge, tip the waiter up to 10 percent, the wine steward 10 percent of the cost of the wine, and a few hundred lire to the washroom attendant and checkroom. No taxi tip is necessary, but round off the total.

CRIME

Italy has a very low rate of violent crime directed toward tourists. However, petty crime is a serious problem, particularly in large cities at crowded areas. Thieves often work in groups or pairs.

INFRASTRUCTURE

Italian buses are clean, modern and inexpensive, although crowded during rush hours. Buses do not accept cash; purchase tickets at bus stops or magazine kiosks before boarding. Taxis (the yellow ones charge standard, official rates; avoid the others) are available at taxi stands or by telephone. Taxis are available and can be flagged down but it is advisable to order one in advance. Rail travel is popular but often delayed; the intercity (IC) train will be much faster than the *diretto* train. The Express train is the faster way to get around Rome. Hotels are categorized by the government as deluxe, 1st, 2nd, 3rd, and 4th class. Rental cars are widely used. Rome's Leonardo Da Vinci Airport handles most international flights. Money is saved by arranging for a car rental prior to arriving. A VAT charge of 19 percent is charged on car rentals depending on the type of car, and insurance costs extra.

NATIONAL TOURIST OFFICE

Ministero del Turismo e dello Spettacolo
Via delle Ferratella in Laterno 51
100184 Rome
Tel: (6) 7732

GOVERNMENT AGENCIES

Ministero delle Risorse Agricole Alimentari e Forestali
(Ministry of Agriculture)
Via XX Settembre 20
00187 Rome
Tel: (6) 4884293
Fax: (6) 4819580

Ministero della Sanita'
(Ministry of Health)
Piazzale Marconi 25
Palazzo Italia
00144 Rome
Tel: (6) 5926780
Fax: (6) 59943217

Dipartimento della Dogana
(Department of Customs)
Viale delle Province, 103
00162 Roma
Tel: (6) 4271043

Istituto Nazionale per Il Commercio Estero
Viale Liszt, 21
00144 Rome
Tel: (6) 59921

Ufficio Italiano dei Cambi
(Italian Exchange Office)
Via Quattro Fontane, 123
00184 Rome

Ministero dell'Industria e Commercio
Ufficio Centrale Brevetti per Invenzioni
(Patent and trademark applications and inquiries)
Modelli e Marchi
Via Molise, 19
00187 Rome
Tel: (6) 4884450

Presidenza del Consiglio dei Ministri
Ufficio del Proprietà Letteraria, Artistica e Scientificia
(Applications and inquires concerning copyrights)
Via Boncompagni, 15
00187 Rome

WORLD TRADE CENTERS

World Trade Center Genoa S.p.A.
Torre WTC - 19th Floor
16149 Genoa
Tel: (10) 242-30-01
Fax: (10) 645-68-02

World Trade Center Italy S.R.L., Milan
Palazzo WTC
Centro Direzionale Milanofiori
20090 Assago (Milan)
Tel: (2) 824-40-86
Fax: (2) 824-16-05

BUSINESS AND TRADE ORGANIZATIONS

Italian Trade Commission
Via Liszt, 21
00144 Rome
Tel: (6) 59921
Fax: (6) 5910508

Ente Nazionale Italiano di Unificazione
(Italian National Bureau of Standards)
Piazza Armando Diaz, 2
20123 Milan
Tel: (2) 876914

Comitato Elettrotecnico Italiano
(Electrical standards and certification)
Viale Manza, 259
20126 Milan
Tel: (2) 2550641

Confederazione Generale dell'Industria
Viale dell'Astronomia, 30
00144 Rome
Tel: (6) 59031

Confederazione Generale Italiana del Commercio e del Turismo
Piazza G. G. Belli, 2
00153 Rome
Tel: (6) 58661

Associazione Bancaria Italiana
(Association of Italian Banks)
Piazza del Gesu, 49
00186 Rome
Tel: (6) 67671

Associazione Nazionale fra le Imprese Assicuratrici
(National Association of Business Insurance)
Via della Frezza, 70
00186 Rome
Tel: (6) 3227141

Confederazione Generale dell'Agricoltura Italiana
Corso Vittorio Emanuele II, 101
00186 Rome
Tel: (6) 65121

Lega Nazionale Cooperative e Mutue
(National Cooperative and Mutual League)
Via Guattani, 9/13
00161 Rome
Tel: (6) 8841371

Unione Italiana delle Camere di Commercio Industria Artigianato e Agricoltura
Piazza Sallustio, 21
00187 Roma
Tel: (6) 47041

Associazione Nazionale del Commercio con l'Estero
(National Association for Foreign Trade)
Corso Venezia, 47/49
20121 Milan
Tel: (2) 7750

Azienda Tabacchi Italiani S.p.A.
(Tobacco Association)
Via C. Pascarella, 7
00153 Rome
Tel: (6) 58691
Fax: (6) 5869288

ANEIOA
(National Import/Export Horticulture Association)
Via Sabotino, 46
00195 Rome
Tel: (6) 37515147
Fax: (6) 3723569

FEDECOMLEGNO
(Wood Trade Federation)
Via Guido d'Arezzo, 16
00198 Rome
Tel: (6) 8417195 Fax: (6) 85301785

FEDERVINI
(Wine Trade Association)
Via Mentana, 2B
00185 Rome
Tel: (6) 4469621
Fax: (6) 4941566

UNAPROL
Via Ostiense, 131L
00154 Rome
Tel: (6) 5745032
Fax: (6) 5745039

Pasta Traders Association
UNIPI
Via Po, 101
00198 Rome
Tel: (6) 8543262
Fax: (6) 8415132

Western Wood Products Association
Via Leonida Rech
00156 Rome
Tel: (6) 8293614 Fax: (6) 821977

Confederazione Generale Italiana dell'Artigianato
(General Confederation of Handicrafts Associations)
Piazza Venezia, 11
00187 Rome
Tel: (6) 6791420

Italy-America Chamber of Commerce
Via Rava' 106
00142 Rome
Tel: (6) 5032066
Fax: (6) 5433365

> ### REMEMBER
> - When you telephone (or fax) to Italy from another country you must always include the country code [39] before the numbers given.
> - When you send mail to Italy, be sure to write ITALY in capital letters on its own line below the addresses given.

American Chamber of Commerce in Italy
Via Cesare Cantu', 1
20123 Milan
Tel: (2) 8690661
Fax: (2) 8057737

BANKS

Banca Agricola Mantovana SpA
Corso Vittorio Emanuele 30
46100 Mantova
Tel: (376) 3311
Fax: (376) 331261
Telex: 304265

Banca Agricola Milanese SpA
Via Mazzini 9-11
20123 Milan
Tel: (2) 88091
Fax: (2) 8693745
Telex: 310608

Banca d'America e d'Italia SpA (BAI)
Via Borgogna 8
20122 Milan
Tel: (2) 77951
Fax: (2) 77952439
Telex: 311350

Banca Antoniana
Via 8 Febbraio 5
35100 Padova
Tel: (49) 839111
Fax: (49) 839658
Telex: 430252

Banca Cassa di Risparmio di Torino SpA
Via XX Settembre 31
10121 Turin
Tel: (11) 6621
Fax: (11) 6624377
Telex: 221278

Banca Carige SpA Cassa di Risparmio di Genova e Imperia
Via Cassa di Risparmio 15
15123 Genova
Tel: (10) 20911
Fax: (10) 280013
Telex: 270089

Banca Credito Agrario Bresciano SpA
Via Trieste 8
25175 Brescia
Tel: (30) 22931
Fax: (30) 2293802
Telex: 301558

Banca Nazionale dell'Agricoltura SpA
Via Salaria 231
00199 Rome
Tel: (6) 85881
Fax: (6) 85883396
Telex: 625330

Banca Nazionale delle Comunicazioni
Via S. Martino della Battaglia 4
00185 Rome
Tel: (6) 44761
Fax: (6) 44763555
Telex: 625593

Banca Nazionale del Lavoro SpA
Via Vittorio Veneto 119
00187, Rome
Tel: (6) 47021
Fax: (6) 47025263
Telex: 621030

Banca Popolare dell' Emilia Romagna Scrl
Via San Carlo 8/20
41100 Modena
Tel: (59) 202111
Fax: (59) 220537
Telex: 511392

Banca Popolare di Bergamo-Credito Varesino
Piazza Vittorio Veneto 8
24100 Bergamo
Tel: (35) 392111
Fax: (35) 221417
Telex: 300410

Banca Popolare di Cremona Scarl
Via Cesare Battisti 14
26100 Cremona
Tel: (372) 4041
Fax: (372) 404362
Telex: 321099

Banca Popolare di Lecco SpA
Piazza Garibaldi 12
22053 Lecco
Tel: (341) 480111
Fax: (341) 480279
Telex: 380003

Banca Popolare di Milano Scarl
Piazza F. Meda 4
20121 Milan
Tel: (2) 77001
Fax: (2) 77002993
Telex: 310202

Banca Popolare di Novara Scarl
Via Carlo Negroni 12
28100 Novara
Tel: (321) 4451
Fax: (321) 29012
Telex: 200371

Banca Popolare Veneta Scarl
Piazza Nogara 2
35131 Padova
Tel: (49) 8296111
Fax: (49) 843225
Telex: 430664

Banca Popolare di Verona Scarl
Piazza Nogara 2
37100 Verona
Tel: (45) 930111
Fax: (45) 930474
Telex: 480009

Banca Provinciale Lombarda SpA
Via Gennaro Sora 4
24100 Bergamo
Tel: (35) 394111
Fax: (35) 394292
Telex: 300140

Banca San Paolo di Brescia SpA
POB 346
Corso Martiri della Libertá 13
25100 Brescia
Tel: (30) 29921
Fax: (30) 2992734
Telex: 300010

Banca Toscana SpA
Via Leone Pancaldo 4
50127 Florence
Tel: (55) 43911
Telex: 570507

NEWSPAPERS

La Nazione
Via Ferdinanco Paolieri 2
50121 Florence
Tel: (55) 24851

Corriere Adriatico
Via Berti 20
60100 Ancona
Tel: (71) 42985

Corriere della Sera
Via Solferino 28
20121 Milan
Tel: (2) 6339
Fax: (2) 29002847

Giorno
Piazza Cavour 2
20121 Milan
Tel: (2) 77681

Sole/24 Ore
Via Paolo Lomazzo 52
20154 Milan
Tel: (2) 31031
Fax: (2) 312055

Messaggero
Via del Tritone 152
00187 Rome
Tel: (6) 47201
Telex: 624644

Ore 12
Via Alfana 39
00198 Rome
Tel: (6) 3965473

La Repubblica
Piazza Indipendenza 11b
00185 Rome
Tel: (6) 49821
Fax: (6) 49822923

I Tempo
Piazza Colonna 366
00187 Rome
Tel: (6) 65041
Telex: 614087

La Stampa
Stampa Sera
Via Marenco 32
10126 Turin
Tel: (11) 65681
Telex: 221121

RADIO & TELEVISION

Radiotelevisione Italiana (RAI-TV)
Viale Mazzini 14
00195 Rome
Tel: (6) 3878
Fax: (6) 3725680

Canale 5
Palazzo dei Cigni
Milano 2
20090 Segrate, Milan
Tel: (2) 21621
Telex: 316197

Italia Uno
Via F. testi 7
20090 Milan
Tel: (2) 6073881

Rete Quattro
Via Marconi 27
20090 Segrate, Milan
Tel: (2) 216001

LEGAL CONTACTS

Studio Legale Avv. Prof. Mario Casella E Associati
Via Guastalla 15
20122 Milan
Tel: (2) 5512066
Fax: (2) 5400304

Gianni, Origoni & Partners
Piazza Belgioioso, 2
20121 Milan
Tel: (2) 76009756
Fax: (2) 76009628

MARKETING AGENCIES

Marketing Italia
Via Michelandelo Buonarroti 14
Milan 20145
Fax: (2) 439-5553

Nielson
Via G. di Vittorio, 10
20094 Milan
Tel: (2) 451971
Fax: (2) 45101068

Palandri Horwath S.r.l.
Piazza Navona, 49
00186 Rome
Tel: (6) 6867841
Fax: (6) 6896075

Reseau
Ricerche e Studi su Elettronica & Automazione
Via S. Vittore, 39
20123 Milan
Tel: (2) 481983800
Fax: (2) 4390535

AD AGENCIES

McCann-Erickson Italiana S.p.A.
Via Albricci, 10
20122 Milan
Tel: (2) 85291
Fax: (2) 801207

Ogilvy & Mather S.p.A.
Via Torino, 61
20123 Milan
Tel: (2) 85031
Fax: (2) 72002821

Saatchi & Saatchi Advertising
Corso Monforte 52
20122 Milan
Tel: (2) 760521
Fax: (2) 76005233

Wunderman Cato Johnson Italia SPA
Viale Majno 21
20122 Milan
Tel: (2) 760521
Fax: (2) 76005233

Young & Rubicam Italiana S.P.A.
Piazza Eleonora Duse 2
20122 Milan
Tel: (2) 77321
Fax: (2) 76000904

INTERNET ADDRESSES

Usenet group(s):
soc.culture.italian

Webfoot's Guide to Italy
http://www.webfoot.com/travel/guides/italy/italy.html

Newspapers in Italy
http://www.yahoo.com/Regional/Countries/Italy/
Media/Newspapers/

Italian WWW Servers
http://www.pi.cnr.it/NIR-IT

Jamaica

Economy

Overview

Jamaica's economy is narrowly based on bauxite, sugar, and tourism. It is particularly vulnerable to world commodity price fluctuations and weather. Jamaica also has a high debt position and a shortage of investment capital. Although labor is generally available at a low cost, there is a shortage of skilled labor requiring firms to look abroad for technical and managerial personnel and making it even harder to attract outside investment capital. Jamaica also suffers from occasional foreign exchange shortages, a poor internal transport infrastructure, and declining real income for the majority of the population, which limits the country's purchasing power. Drug trafficking plays a significant role in Jamaica's underground economy, although to a lesser degree than in some other Caribbean countries, and drug related activity has had a deleterious effect on the general social, political, and business climate in the country.

Trade

Jamaica's main exports include industrial raw materials—mostly bauxite—which account for about 60 percent of total exports. These are followed by foodstuffs, miscellaneous manufactured items, beverages and tobacco, and chemicals. Imports include machinery and transportation equipment, basic manufactures, fuels, foodstuffs, and chemicals. Jamaica's main trading partner is the US—which accounts for nearly half of total trade—followed by the UK, Canada, Norway, and Japan.

Sectors

Agriculture Accounting for about five percent of GDP, 25 percent of employment, and 24 percent of exports, commercial crops include sugarcane, bananas, coffee, citrus, potatoes, and vegetables. Livestock and livestock products include poultry, goats, and milk. Fishing is also significant domestically.

Industry Although it provides nearly 50 percent of GDP, industry employs only about 20 percent of the work force. Primary industries include bauxite mining, textiles, food processing, and various light manufacturing and assembly operations. Lower-technology operations such as garment assembly and data entry have been attracted by the availability of low-cost, semi-skilled labor. Although such higher-value-added operations are becoming more important, more than 66 percent of industrial production remains in food, beverage, and tobacco processing, mostly for the domestic market.

Services More than 50 percent of the work force is employed in the services sector, which produces about half of GDP. Although attempts are being made to attract low- to mid-range offshore service operations to Jamaica, the main cash generating service activity is tourism, while the remainder of the sector involves local distribution and personal service activities.

Trends

The increasing average age of sugar workers is generating concern that producers will soon be forced to invest in mechanized operations which will slow growth in this important industry, at least in the short term. Employees in the bauxite industry will continue to be among the best-trained and best-compensated in Jamaica, although a soft world market for aluminum could adversely affect this industry, as could development of alternate ore sources elsewhere in the world. Tourism should remain strong, dominating Jamaica's other industries as an earner of foreign exchange.

At a Glance

THE COUNTRY
Location An island in the northern Caribbean Sea, about 160 km south of Cuba.
Terrain Mostly mountains with a narrow plain in most coastal areas.
Climate Tropical, and more temperate in the island's interior.

THE PEOPLE
Population 2,500,000
Ethnic composition
African.. 76.3%
Afro-European 15.1%
East Indian and Afro-East Indian 3%
White... 3.2%
Chinese and Afro-Chinese.............................. 1.2%
Other.. 1.2%
Religious composition
Protestant 42.9%
Church of God 18.4%
Baptist... 10%
Anglican 7.1%
Seventh-Day Adventist 6.9%
Pentecostal 5.2%
Methodist 3.1%
United Church.. 2.7%
Other.. 2.5%
Roman Catholic 5%
Other, including some spiritual cults 1%
Languages spoken English, Creole.
Education and literacy The government devotes a large part of its budget to education. Literacy above the age of 15 is 98 percent.
Labor force
Total:...1,300,000
By occupation: industry 19%, agriculture 24%, services 57%.

COUNTRY FACTS
Political and legal A parliamentary democracy, the legal system is based on English common law. The Supreme Court is the highest legal body.
Telephone Fully automatic domestic telephone network. Country code: [1]. Area code for all points: (809).
Transportation An extensive system of roads and a government-owned railway provide ground transportation. There are two airports and one major seaport.
Environment There is concern that continuing environmental degradation will hurt tourism, as well as food production, fisheries, and the prospects for sustained development. Water pollution comes partly from bauxite mining. 86 percent of the water used for agriculture is impure. Current issues are land erosion, deforestation, waste disposal, and water pollution.
Media The government and private companies control the television stations. There were about one million television sets and 300,000 radios in 1992. Newspapers are published daily. In addition, there are several weekly and monthly periodicals, some owned by religious groups.
Health The government provides a broad public health program with nearly universal access to medical services. Life expectancy of males is 72 years; of females, 76 years.

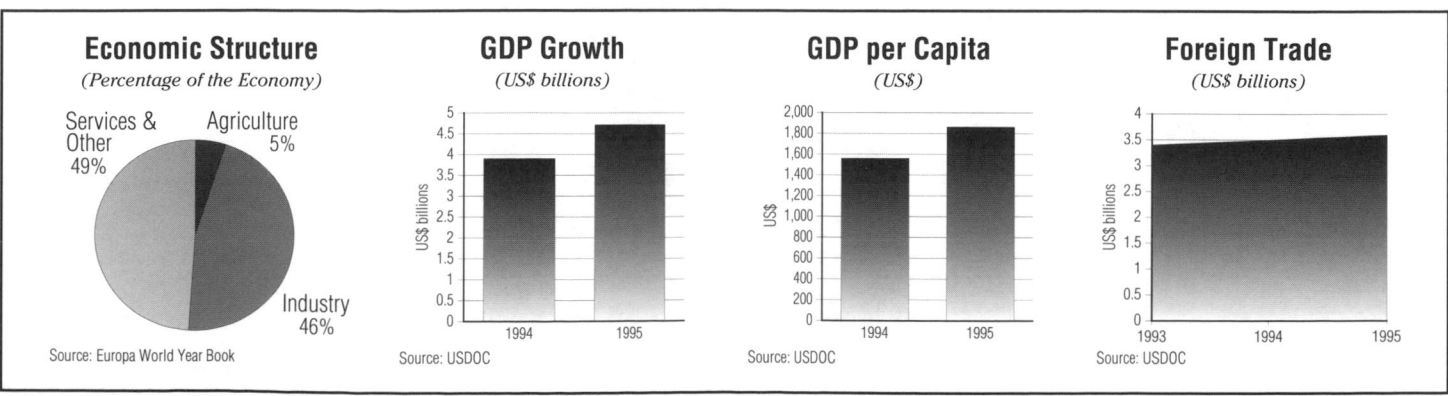

Economic Structure
(Percentage of the Economy)

Services & Other 49%
Agriculture 5%
Industry 46%

Source: Europa World Year Book

GDP Growth
(US$ billions)

Source: USDOC

GDP per Capita
(US$)

Source: USDOC

Foreign Trade
(US$ billions)

Source: USDOC

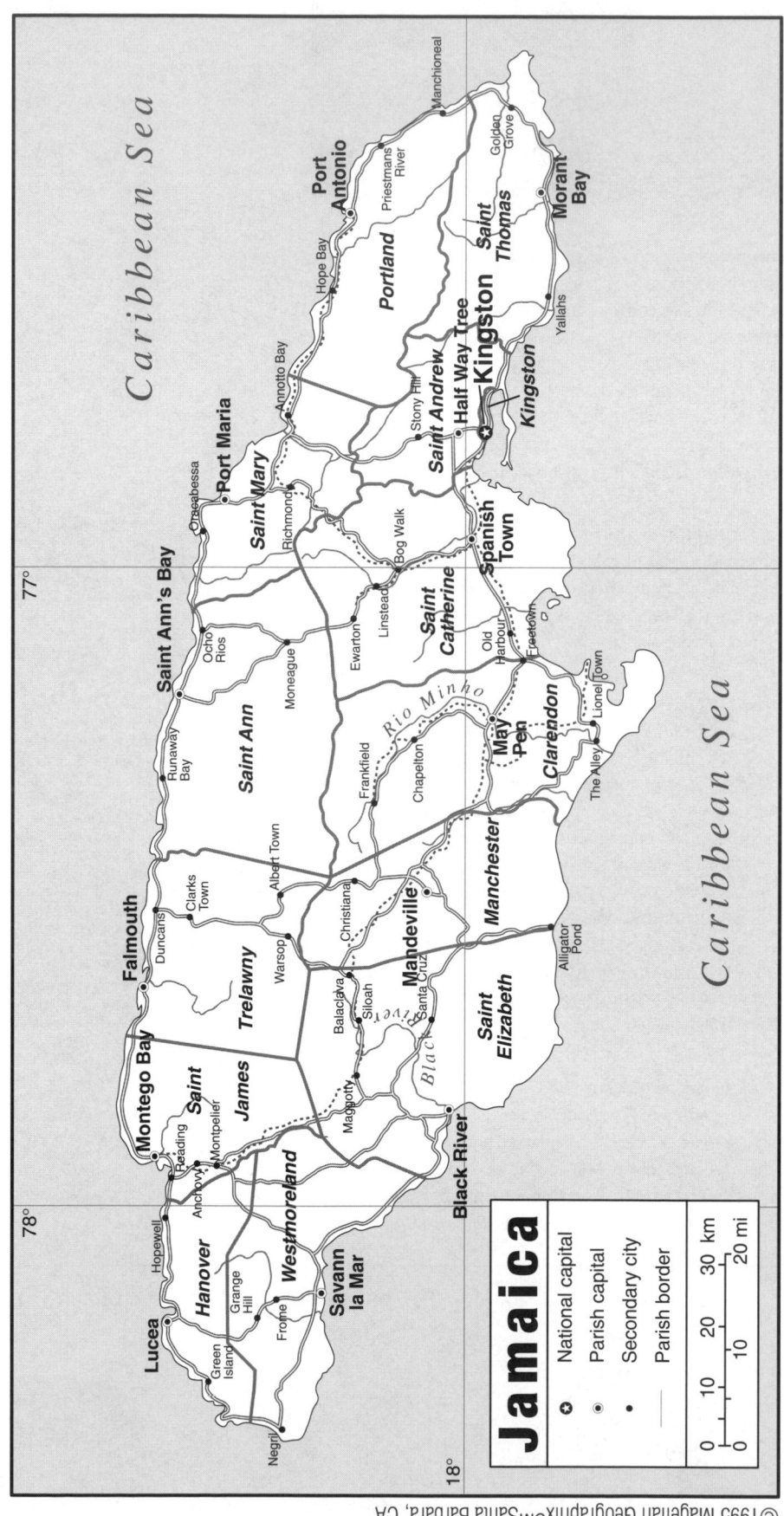

Caribbean Sea

Caribbean Sea

Caribbean Sea

JAMAICA

- ⊕ National capital
- ⊙ Parish capital
- • Secondary city
- —— Parish border

0 10 20 30 km
0   10   20 mi

Manchioneal

Port Antonio

Priestmans River

Golden Grove

Morant Bay

Portland

Saint Thomas

Hope Bay

Kingston

Kingston

Saint Andrew

Annotto Bay

Half Way Tree

Yallahs

Stony Hill

Port Maria

Saint Mary

Oracabessa

Richmond

Bog Walk

Spanish Town

Saint Catherine

Saint Ann's Bay

Linstead

Ewarton

Old Harbour

Freetown

Ocho Rios

Moneague

Saint Ann

Rio Minho

Lionel Town

Runaway Bay

Frankfield

Chapelton

May Pen

Clarendon

The Alley

Falmouth

Duncans

Clarks Town

Albert Town

Christiana

Mandeville

Manchester

Alligator Pond

Trelawny

Warsop

Balaclava

Siloah

Santa Cruz

Saint Elizabeth

Black River

Montego Bay

Saint James

Reading

Anchovy

Montpelier

Maggotty

Black River

Westmoreland

Lucea

Hanover

Hopewell

Green Island

Grange Hill

Frome

Savanna la Mar

Negril

78°

77°

18°

Foreign Trade

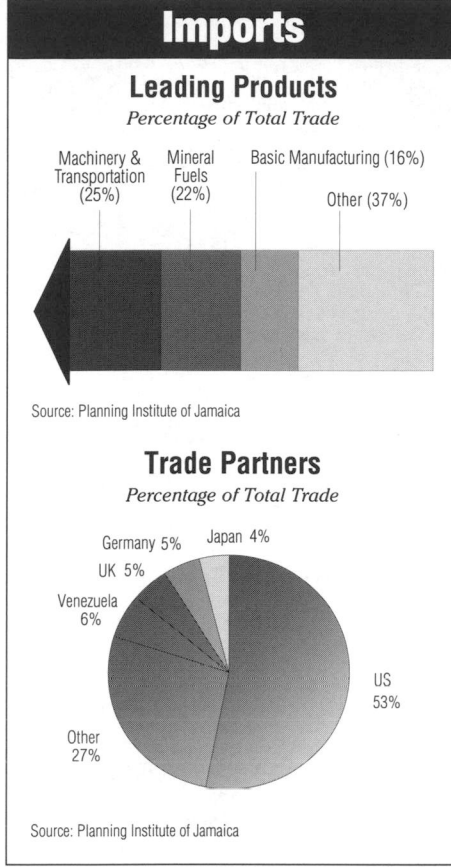

Imports

Leading Products
Percentage of Total Trade

Machinery & Transportation (25%)
Mineral Fuels (22%)
Basic Manufacturing (16%)
Other (37%)

Source: Planning Institute of Jamaica

Trade Partners
Percentage of Total Trade

Germany 5%
Japan 4%
UK 5%
Venezuela 6%
Other 27%
US 53%

Source: Planning Institute of Jamaica

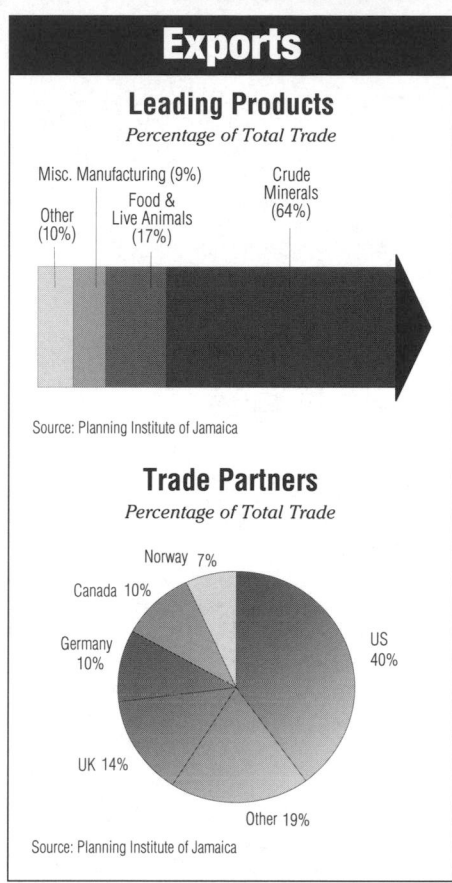

Exports

Leading Products
Percentage of Total Trade

Misc. Manufacturing (9%)
Other (10%)
Food & Live Animals (17%)
Crude Minerals (64%)

Source: Planning Institute of Jamaica

Trade Partners
Percentage of Total Trade

Norway 7%
Canada 10%
Germany 10%
UK 14%
Other 19%
US 40%

Source: Planning Institute of Jamaica

Opportunities

FOR IMPORTING TO JAMAICA
- fabric
- fertilizer
- food products
- fuels
- furnishings
- grains
- industrial machinery
- iron and steel
- low-cost housing materials
- medical supplies and equipment
- mining equipment
- paper and paper products
- pharmaceuticals
- petroleum
- poultry
- transportation equipment

FOR EXPORTING FROM JAMAICA
- alumina
- bananas
- bauxite
- citrus fruits
- cocoa
- garments
- rum
- spices
- sugar

GROWTH SECTORS
- construction
- garment assembly
- light manufacturing
- services
- telecommunications
- tourism

GOVERNMENT PROCUREMENT
- electrical power equipment
- environmental protection technologies
- food items and fertilizers
- medicines and medical supplies
- office supplies
- road construction goods and services
- water and sewage treatment facilities

Trade News

RULES AND REGULATIONS

- **Regulations** Trade regulations are administered by the Trade Board under the Ministry of Industry, Tourism, and Commerce.
- **Tariffs and import taxes** In February 1991, Jamaica implemented the new Caribbean Common Market (CARICOM) Common External Tariff (CET). Goods originating in CARICOM member states are not subject to the CET, which presently ranges between 5 and 35 percent, with an additional 5 percent for agricultural products. Non-basic, finished goods and goods competing with those produced in the CARICOM states carry high duty rates. In addition to the CET, all items carry a 12.5 percent general consumption tax. Alcoholic beverages and tobacco carry an additional stamp duty of 25 to 50 percent and a special consumption tax of 5 to 38.2 percent.
- **Import licenses** There are about 96 items that require an import license. These items include milk powder, plants and parts of plants for perfume or pharmaceutical purposes, gum-resins, vegetable saps and extracts, certain chemicals, motor vehicles and parts, arms and ammunition, certain toys, and gaming machines.
- **Prohibited imports** The following items are prohibited for import into Jamaica: certain gambling machines, racing dogs and dog racing equipment, products from Haiti, arms and ammunition (except with governmental permission), certain animals, dangerous drugs, indecent or obscene printed matter or films, and sugar (except under license).
- **Export controls** Export controls are placed on a number of items, including ammunition, crocodiles, eggs, antique furniture, certain minerals, sugar, petroleum products, motor vehicles, and vehicle parts.
- **Free trade zones (FTZs)** Jamaica has three active industrial park/free trade zones: the Kingston Export Free Zone, the Montego Bay Export Free Zone, and Garmex in Kingston.
- **Free trade arrangements** Jamaica has preferential tariff arrangements with the US under the Caribbean Basin Initiative (CBI), with the countries of the European Union under the Lome Convention, with Canada under CARIBCAN, and with other English-speaking Caribbean states under CARICOM.

FREIGHT FORWARDERS

Air Jamaica Ltd.
72-76 Harbour Street
Kingston
Tel: (809) 922-3460
Fax: (809) 922-0107
Telex: 2389

Jamaica Freight and Shipping Co Ltd. (JFS)
80-82 Second Street
Port Bustamante
POB 167
Kingston 13
Tel: (809) 923-9371
Fax: (809) 923-4091
Telex: 2260

Jamaica Merchant Marine (JMM)
Kingston
Tel: (809) 927-3354

Jamaica Railway Corporation (JRC)
142 Barry Street
POB 489
Kingston
Tel: (809) 922-6620
Fax: (809) 922-4539
Telex: 2190

Shipping Association of Jamaica
5-7 King Street
POB 40
Kingston 15
Tel: (809) 922-8220
Fax: (809) 922-6621
Telex: 2431

Business Travel

LH 1906	MADRID	935	113-3
LH 1022	STUTTGART HBF.	935	-
AF 1701	LYON	940	683-6
AY 822	HELSINKI	940	113-3
AA 071	SFRANCISCO-DALLAS	945	731-7

Air Travel Times

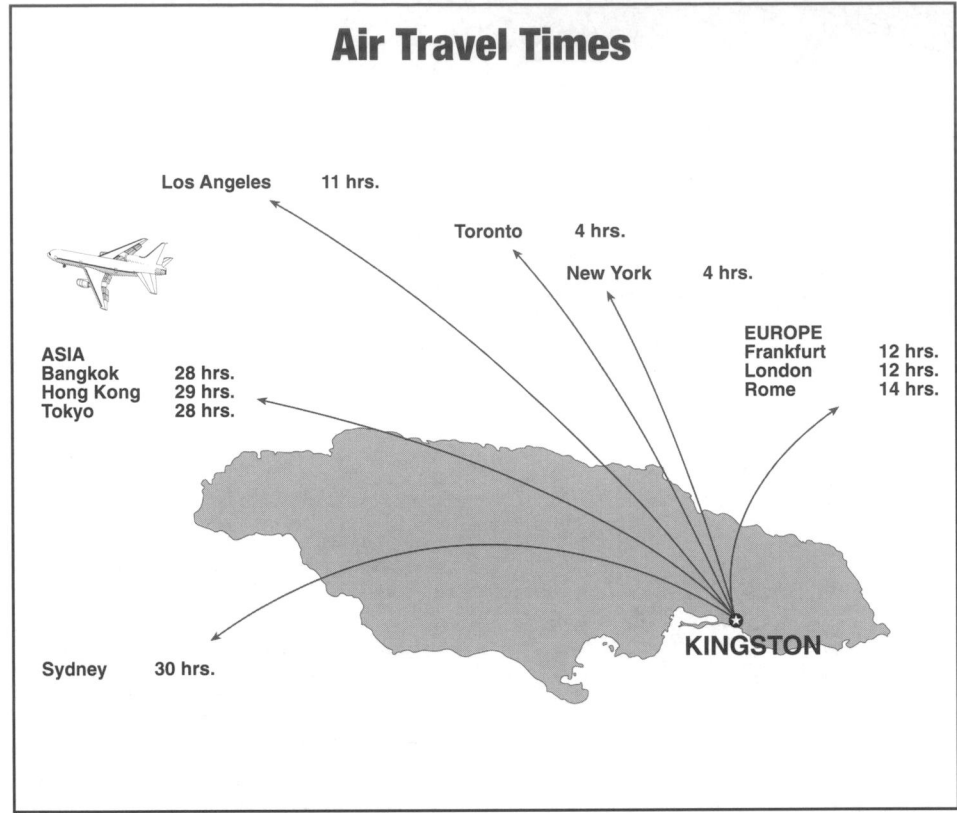

Los Angeles   11 hrs.

Toronto   4 hrs.

New York   4 hrs.

ASIA
Bangkok   28 hrs.
Hong Kong   29 hrs.
Tokyo   28 hrs.

EUROPE
Frankfurt   12 hrs.
London   12 hrs.
Rome   14 hrs.

★ KINGSTON

Sydney   30 hrs.

COMMUNICATIONS

Telephone Local telephone service is adequate, and direct-dial service is available throughout the island. International service is better than local service. Overseas calls made from hotels are subject to a 10 percent tax and a J$2 service charge. Many Jamaican homes do not yet have a telephone, although more will be available as the system is upgraded and digitalized.

Fax Faxes are widely used by business, and their quality depends largely on the telephone connection. Telegrams are posted via JAMINTEL through the postal services. Telexes are not used in business, but are found in government offices.

Post office Jamaica's postal service is undependable, whether local or overseas. First class mail stands a better chance for delivery than parcel post or international surface mail.

BEST TRAVEL BOOKS

Frommer's Jamaica & Barbados Frommer's Comprehensive Travel Guide Series. General reference and travel, 252 pages, illustrated.
Jamaica Handbook, by Karl Luntta. Moon Publications, 220 pages, illustrated.
Fodor's Pocket Jamaica: The Best of the Island. Tourist oriented, excellent source of city details.
Fodor's Travel Publications. Tourist oriented, excellent source of city details.
Do's and Taboo's Around the World. The Bestselling Guide to International Behavior. Edited by Roger Axtell, compiled by the Parker Pen Company. The ultimate guide to international behavior, now completely updated and expanded. Helpful, fun to read!
Berlitz Business Travel Guide. Berlitz Publishing Company. Features include: concise economic details for each country, how to plan a successful trip, background information on people and cities, useful facts and addresses on arrival, essential words and phrases, entertainment, leisure and shopping.

USEFUL TELEPHONE NUMBERS

If you are calling from outside Jamaica, you will need to dial the area code [1].

- Ambulance 110
- Air-Sea Rescue 119
- "Diesel" Train.................................... (809) 922-6620
- Chamber of Commerce.................... (809) 922-0150
- Jamaica Information Service............ (809) 926-3740
- Jamaican Exporters Association ...... (809) 929-1292
- Federal Express .... (809) 926-1456
- Coffee Industry Board .... (809) 923-7211
- Coffee Industry Development Co .... (809) 923-7211
- Sugar Industry Authority .... (809) 926-5930
- Manufacturers' Association .... (809) 922-8880

Airlines
- Air Canada .... (809) 926-2031
- British Airways .... (809) 929-9020
- Trans-Jamaica Airlines .... (809) 923-8680

Car Rental
- Avis .... (809) 926-1560
- Dollar .... (809) 925-1492
- Hertz .... (809) 924-8028
- National .... (809) 929-7204

Credit Card Information
Lost or stolen credit cards (call collect to the US, regardless of which country the card was issued in).
- Amex... (919) 333-3211
- Diner's Club..................................... (303) 799-1504
- MasterCard .... (314) 275-6690
- Visa .... (410) 581-7931

Travelogue

WORKWEEK

Offices Monday-Friday 8:30 am to 4:30 pm. The general work week is 40 hours.
Banks Monday-Thursday 9:00 am to 2:00 pm and Friday 9:00 am to noon and 2:30 pm to 5:00 pm.
Government Monday-Friday 8:30 am to 4:30 pm.
Retail Monday-Saturday, 9:30 am to 5:30 pm, with many seasonal variations.

HOLIDAYS

Holidays 1996
January 1 New Year's Day
February 21 Ash Wednesday
April 5 Good Friday
April 8 Easter Monday
May 23 National Labor Day
August Independence Day *
October National Heroes' Day *
December 25 Christmas Day
December 26 Boxing Day
* Dates vary each year.

VISA AND PASSPORT

Foreigners must have a valid passport and most must also have an onward ticket. Most foreigners do not need visas for visits less than 90 days, but foreigners from some countries will need visas for stays exceeding 30 days.

DEPARTURE FORMALITIES

Foreigners are forbidden to take Jamaican currency exceeding J$20 out of the country and are subject to heavy penalties for violations.

IMMUNIZATION

Foreigners arriving from infected areas must have vaccination certificates for yellow fever and cholera. Polio and typhoid vaccinations are recommended. Drinking water is safe to drink, but in rural areas boiling water to be on the safe side is advisable.

TIPPING

Tipping is appreciated in all service of businesses in Jamaica. Tip taxi drivers 10 to 15 percent, restaurants 10 to 15 percent. Porters get US$0.50 per bag, other small services get 10 percent.

CRIME

Kingston has a serious crime problem. Foreigners should avoid buses for safety reasons, take only licensed taxis, and avoid downtown areas. Pickpocketing and purse snatchings are common on buses. When renting automobiles, keep valuables locked and out of sight as break-ins are common. Tourist areas and airports are prime areas for crime; keep a close eye on personal belongings and valuables at all times.

INFRASTRUCTURE

Between cities, bus service is fast and reliable; although crowded, buses offer services over all parts of the island. Buses are not safe after nightfall. Trains travel between Kingston and Montego Bay daily. Taxis, bearing red PPV license plates, are readily available by telephone or on the street; if the taxi has no meter, negotiate the fare before departing. Most roads are paved and dozens of car rental companies operate in Jamaica. Traffic moves on the left side of the road. Kingston offers excellent hotels for business travellers. Hurricanes can wreak havoc on this island and affect roads in the areas heavily hit; avoid these areas in emergencies.

NATIONAL TOURIST OFFICE

Jamaica Tourist Board
The Tourism Centre
21 Dominica Drive
POB 360
Kingston 5

Marketing

Overview

The most successful method for conducting business in Jamaica is up close and personal. That is how Jamaicans prefer to do business. Although business people in the island country are quite hospitable, business relationships develop best after first forming friendships with Jamaican business associates. Jamaica has sought to warm its business climate to foreigners in the last two years by releasing exchange and price controls and by reforming past licensing laws.

Distribution and Agents

The distribution system in Jamaica flows through typical currents such as importers, distributors, and agent representatives. Close contact with customers during the distribution process is essential. Foreign businesses need to attentively select their Jamaican business partners. Business associates writing agreements in Jamaica frame their own terms and conditions; no Jamaican law restricts agents and distributors. All agents and distributors, however, are required to abide by the Fair Competition Act (FCA), which is aimed at halting practices that would hinder competition at any level.

Selling Techniques and Customer Support

The Jamaican market is small. One of the best methods for increasing sales is by selling to the government. Setting up local representative offices of foreign firms for government purchases of a particular product line could increase business opportunities. Personal contacts are important in initial and continued sales in Jamaica, and in maintaining a close working relationship between Jamaican sales representatives and exporters. The most important part of a sale in Jamaica is after-sales service. Support given in a friendly manner gives foreign businesses a competitive edge in Jamaica. Foreign companies ideally should possess their own distribution system.

Advertising

Customers in Jamaica are best reached by its largest form of mass communication: radio. With seven authorized stations serving the country, radio's impact is exceptional and more far-reaching than other mediums. It offers the best opportunities for advertisers.

Marketing in Jamaica

MARKETING TIPS

- **Accounts** Several advertising agencies in Jamaica handle accounts for the entire country. Foreign businesses can also take advantage of advertising on the two Jamaican television networks: government-owned JBC and privately held CVM. Although cable television is currently unavailable in Jamaica, the country is exploring the feasibility of hooking up to that medium. The disparate Jamaican customers are effectively reached by two daily morning newspapers and one afternoon tabloid, as well as several weekly and bi-weekly periodicals.
- **Franchising** Successful franchising enterprises include service industries such as hotels and fast food.
- **Pricing** Prices are determined by the usual market forces of demand and supply and most are fairly competitive.
- **Government** Government purchasing includes a large range of goods from electricity and water to food and medicine.
- **Local attorney** Local professional advice at the beginning of a business venture ensures smooth start-ups and adherence to Jamaican laws.
- **Timely service** Jamaican customers expect after-sales service to be handled quickly.
- **Billboards** Billboards are an effective advertising tool in both the urban and rural areas of Jamaica.

MARKET RESEARCH FIRMS

Business Research and Agricultural Consultants
14B Cargill Avenue
Kingston 10
Tel: (809) 929-5736

Market Research Services Ltd.
75 Knutsford Boulevard
Kingston 5
Tel: (809) 929-6311

Business Culture

Greetings and Courtesies

Men usually shake hands with women and each other, although women seldom shake hands with other women. Titles are commonly used, especially "Doctor" and "Professor." Business cards printed in English are expected. The host will usually make introductions. Jamaicans like to entertain and are likely to invite foreign businesspeople to their homes for a meal or other event. A small gift is expected and it is appropriate to bring flowers or a bottle of wine.

Business Ethic and Framework

Jamaicans have a fairly strong work ethic, but they are accustomed to their efforts failing to produce results and often allow family and other considerations to take precedence. Because of proximity, experience, and media influence, Jamaicans are shifting toward North American business norms and away from traditional standards.

Meetings and Decision Making

Foreign businesspeople are expected to be on time, but Jamaicans can be more relaxed about schedules. Authority is narrowly concentrated and actual decisions are almost always made at a high level. Foreigners should cultivate peer relationships, because the quality of these relationships may strongly influence the actual decisionmaker even when your immediate counterpart is not the one making the decision.

Women

Although women in Jamaica generally occupy a somewhat secondary status in this traditional, male-dominated society, many operate businesses and are accorded considerable personal freedom. In general, foreign businesswomen should have few problems in business, generally experiencing greater acceptance than do local women. Note that women may be verbally harassed on the street; they can ignore such behavior, but may feel more comfortable if they are escorted or use taxis.

Cultural Cautions

DO'S

- Learn something about Jamaican history, culture, and its distinctive art and music—your interest will be appreciated.

DON'TS

- Race, religion, politics, drugs, and the economy are sensitive and complex topics that should be avoided by outsiders.

CUSTOMS

- Tropical weight suits or sports coats and trousers are expected of men for business dealings. Foreign businesswomen should wear conservative suits or dresses, but may generally dispense with stockings. Styles are somewhat less fashionable and daring than those worn elsewhere.

OBSERVATIONS

- Remember that except as spoken at the highest, best educated levels of the hierarchy, Jamaican English may be quite different from standard English.
- Gift-giving is not common and may be misinterpreted as an improper attempt to influence the other party.

NEGOTIATIONS

- To avoid misunderstandings, be sure you know who has the authority to make a decision and the procedures and time frames that must be considered.
- Although Jamaicans generally have a preference for unambiguous results, such as that found in Europe and North America, allow negotiations to remain open-ended, so that confrontation can be avoided and talks can be allowed to fade away if agreement cannot be reached.
- Agreements should be carefully written with legal help; Jamaicans generally expect detailed documents.

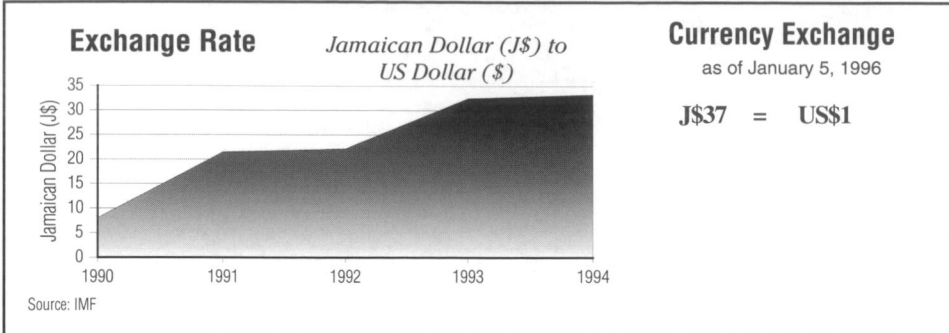

Exchange Rate — *Jamaican Dollar (J$) to US Dollar ($)*

Jamaican Dollar (J$) — 1990, 1991, 1992, 1993, 1994

Source: IMF

Currency Exchange

as of January 5, 1996

J$37 = US$1

Currency

The currency of Jamaica is the Jamaica dollar, or J$, and its principal subdivision is 100 cents.

Foreign Exchange

The foreign exchange market is operated by commercial banks, authorized dealers, and the Bank of Jamaica. Jamaica does not impose foreign exchange controls, nor maintain margins in exchange transactions. Spot and forward exchange rates are determined by supply and demand. While there are no restrictions on transactions in any currency, the principal foreign currencies accepted in the exchange market are the Canadian dollar, the Deutsche mark, the pound sterling, and the US dollar. There are no taxes or subsidies on purchases or sales of foreign exchange. Residents and nonresidents can open foreign currency accounts through authorized dealers, and funds in these accounts may be transferred without restrictions.

Capital Transfers

There is no limitation on the inflow or outflow of funds for any transaction including remittances of profits or returns on intellectual property licenses.

Investment Incentives

Investments bringing in foreign exchange and expanding employment are favorably considered in granting incentives. There are several incentives for foreign investors, including exemption from import duties on raw materials and machinery, income and dividends tax relief, and duty-free importation of articles required for the cottage construction, and duty relief on imported goods and equipment for use in motion picture production.

Investment Restrictions

There are no specific performance requirements imposed as a condition for investing in Jamaica. Foreign ownership is usually limited to 49 percent of a company, although the government is currently considering lifting this rule for the insurance sector. Telecommunications of Jamaica, a subsidiary of the British firm Cable and Wireless, enjoys monopoly rights.

Money Matters

BITS AND PIECES

- **Foreign exchange** Although foreign exchange is freely available, there is generally a waiting period of two to six weeks depending on the sum demanded, as demand usually exceeds availability. During the tourist winter season from December to April, the inflow of foreign exchange and its availability is generally greater than during the rest of the year.
- **Gold** Coins in denominations of J$20, J$100, and J$250 are legal tender but do not circulate. Residents may hold and acquire gold coins, but they are not allowed to hold and acquire gold in any form other than jewelry. Imports and exports of gold in any form other than jewelry require a license from the Ministry of Finance.
- **Credit** Credit is generally allocated on market terms with equal access to both local and foreign companies, but high rates of interest, ranging between 45 to 70 percent, limit actual borrowing.

BANKS

Bank of Jamaica
Nethersole Place
Kingston
Jamaica
Tel: (809) 922-0750

Bank of Nova Scotia Jamaica Ltd.
Scotia Centre
Port Royal Street
Kingston
Tel: (809) 922-1000

Century National Bank Ltd.
14-16 Port Royal Street
Kingston
Tel: (809) 922-3105/6/8/10

CIBC Jamaica Ltd.
23-27 Knutsford Boulevard
Kingston 5
Tel: (809) 929-9310-6

Citibank N.A.
63-67 Knutsford Boulevard
Kingston 5
Tel: (809) 926-3270, 926-3285

Citizens Bank Ltd.
4 King Street
Kingston
Tel: (809) 922-5950

Eagle Commercial Bank Ltd.
6 Grenada Way
Kingston 5
Tel: (809) 929-9355

Island Victoria Bank Ltd.
6 St. Lucia Avenue
Kingston 5
Tel: (809) 968-5800/5

Mutual Security Bank Ltd.
18 Trafalgar Road
Kingston 10
Tel: (809) 929-8950

National Commercial Bank Jamaica Ltd.
The Atrium
32 Trafalgar Road
Kingston 10
Tel: (809) 929-9050/89

National Investment Bank of Jamaica
Duke and Port Royal Streets
Kingston
Tel: (809) 922-0915/9

Trafalgar Commercial Bank Ltd.
60 Knutsford Boulevard
Kingston 5
Tel: (809) 929-3383/6

Workers Savings & Loan Bank
76 Knutsford Boulevard
Kingston 5
Tel: (809) 968-5119

TAXATION

Taxation requires sophisticated knowledge of complex rules and regulations specific to each country. The information presented here is from the Ernst & Young Corporate Tax Guide and Directory, available from the Ernst & Young accounting office in your country, or from:

Ernst & Young
28 Beechwood Avenue
POB 351
Kingston 5
Jamaica
Tel: (809) 926-1616, 926-1617/4421, 926-2373, 926-6489
Fax: (809) 926-7580

At a Glance

Corporate Income Tax Rate (%)	33
Capital Gains Tax Rate (%)	0
Branch Tax Rate (%)	0
Withholding Tax (%)	
Dividends (a)	33
Interest (a)	33
Royalties (a)	33
Management Fees (a)	33
Branch Remittance Tax	33
Net Operating Losses (Years)	
Carryback	0
Carryforward	Unlimited

(a) Final tax imposed on payments to both residents and nonresidents.

Legal

Legal System

Jamaican law follows that of the British, with some variations.

Intellectual Property Protection

Patents and Trademarks Foreign patents must be re-registered in Jamaica to be considered valid there. Patents, once registered, are adequately protected from infringement; however government resources are too limited to undertake complex and lengthy investigations. Foreign trademarks are not considered valid in Jamaica. Trademark applications usually take quite a long time to be processed.

Copyrights Jamaica is a member of the World Intellectual Property Organization and the Berne Union, and considers foreign copyrights equal to those registered in Jamaica.

Trade Secrets Jamaica has laws regarding trade secret violations, but it is very difficult to bring up an injunction for stolen secrets.

Business Registration

All businesses must be registered before they are considered legally valid. All new companies, whether foreign or domestic, must deliver a memorandum to the Registrar, stating information such as the name of the company and the names of the directors.

Contracts and Dispute Resolution

Verbal contracts are usually not upheld by law. The majority of disputes in Jamaica are handled in the court system, in the first instance by a lay magistrate, a magistrate, or a judge in the Supreme Court, depending on the seriousness of the dispute. Arbitration of disputes is allowed, but not many parties will agree to submit to the binding authority of an arbitrator, so it is not much utilized.

Labor

Workers have the right to join unions and to bargain collectively. Striking is allowed after certain alternative dispute resolution measures have been attempted and failed. Labor legislation covers several employment issues, including maximum hours of work, minimum wages, and the employment of women and youths.

Legal Matters

LEGAL BRIEFS

- **Gun court** A special 'gun court' considers only cases involving the illegal use of firearms or ammunition.
- **Recent changes** Jamaica's government has tried to improve its court system recently with increases in salaries, training programs for personnel, and improvements in court facilities.
- **The attorney general** The attorney general does not need to be a member of parliament, and is appointed by the governor general.
- **Suffrage** Anyone over the age of 18 can vote.
- **Strikes** There was a significant increase in strikes and other work stoppages recently, primarily due to the layoff of 8,000 government employees.
- **Workweek** The workweek is generally 40 hours, spread over eight hours a day, five days a week.

LEGAL CONTACTS

Dunn, Cox and Orrett
48 Duke Street, POB 365
Kingston
Tel: (809) 922-1500/8 Fax: (809) 922-9002
Leny, Hanna & Co.
Duke Street
Kingston
Tel: (809) 922-3373 Fax: (809) 924-9354
Livingston, Alexander & Levy
72 Harbour Street, POB 142
Kingston
Tel: (809) 922-6310/9 Fax: (809) 922-0713
Myers, Fletcher and Gordan
Park Place, 21 East Street, POB 162
Kingston
Tel: (809) 922-5860 Fax: (809) 922-4811
Nunes, Scholefield, DeLeon & Co.
4 Duke Street, POB 208
Kingston
Tel: (809) 922-8290/9 Fax: (809) 922-3354

Contacts

GOVERNMENT AGENCIES

Ministry of Defense
Devon Road
POB 272
Kingston 10
Tel: (809) 927-9941
Fax: (809) 929-0005
Ministry of Agriculture
Hope Gardens
Kingston 6
Tel: (809) 927-1731/3
Ministry of Construction
2 Hagley Park Road
Kingston 10
Tel: (809) 926-1590
Commissioner of Customs
Newport East
Kingston 15
Tel: (809) 922-5140
Fax: (809) 967-1140
Ministry of Education and Culture
2 National Heroes Circle
Kingston 4
Tel: (809) 922-1400
Ministry of Finance
30 National Heroes Circle
Kingston 4
Tel: (809) 922-9600
Ministry of Foreign Affairs and Foreign Trade
85 Knutsford Boulevard
Kingston 5
Tel: (809) 926-4220
Fax: (809) 929-6733
Ministry of Health
10 Caldeonia Avenue
Kingston 5
Tel: (809) 926-9191

Ministry of Health
Health Care Corporation
78 Marcus Garvey Drive
Kingston
Tel: (809) 923-6926
Ministry of Labour and Welfare
14 National Heroes Circle, POB 10
Kingston 5
Tel: (809) 922-8000
Ministry of Legal Affairs
12 Ocean Boulevard
Kingston
Tel: (809) 922-5460
Fax: (809) 922-6028
Ministry of Local Government, Youth and Community Development
12 Ocean Boulevard
POB 635
Kingston Mall
Kingston
Tel: (809) 922-1670 Fax: (809) 924-9191
Ministry of National Security and Justice
12 Ocean Boulevard
Kingston Mall
Kingston
Tel: (809) 922-0080
Ministry of Public Service and Environment
Citibank Building
63-67 Knutsford Boulevard
Kingston 5
Tel: (809) 926-3235
Fax: (809) 929-6616
Ministry of Public Utilities, Mining and Energy
POB 9000
2 St. Lucia Avenue
Kingston 5
Tel: (809) 926-8130 Fax: (809) 929-3375

Ministry of Industry, Tourism, and Commerce
Petrojam Building
36 Travalgar Road
Kingston 10
Tel: (809) 926-9170
Ministry of Water and Transport
4 Winchester Road
Kingston 10
Tel: (809) 929-1540
National Water Commission
4 Marescaux Road
Kingston 5
Tel: (809) 929-3530
Jamaica Public Service Company
6 Knutsford Boulevard
Kingston 5
Tel: (809) 926-3190
Jamaica International Telecommunications Ltd.
15 North Street
Kingston
Tel: (809) 922-6031, 922-6041, 922-9644
Fax: (809) 921-5329
Post and Telecommunications Department
Central Sorting Office
South Camp Road
POB 7000
Kingston
Tel: (809) 922-9430 Fax: (809) 92-29449

BUSINESS AND TRADE ORGANIZATIONS

Jamaica Commodity Trading Corporation
8 Ocean Boulevard
Kingston
Tel: (809) 922-0971

Jamaica Exporters Association
13 Dominica Drive
Kingston 5
Tel: (809) 929-1292, 926-0586, 926-7158

Jamaica Hotel & Tourist Association
2 Ardenne Rd
Kingston 10
Tel: (809) 926-3635/6, 926-2796

Jamaica Manufacturers Association Ltd.
85a Duke St
Kingston
Tel: (809) 922-8880/1, 922-0787, 922-2365

Private Sector Organization of Jamaica
39 Hope Road
Kingston 10
Tel: (809) 927-6238, 927-6958, 927-6957, 927-6786

Jamaica Promotions Corporation
35 Trafalgar Road
Kingston 10
Tel: (809) 929-7190/9
Fax: (809) 924-9650

Jamaica Commodity Trading Company Limited
8 Ocean Boulevard
POB 1021
Kingston
Tel: (809) 922-0971 through 9
Telex: 2318 januhold ja

Jamaica Export Trading Co. Ltd.
6 Waterloo Road
POB 645
Kingston 10
Tel: (809) 929-4390
Telex: 2233

Jamaica Information Service
58A Halfway Tree Road
POB 2222
Kingston 10
Tel: (809) 926-3740
Fax: (809) 926-6715

Trade Board Limited
4 Winchester Road
Kingston 10
Tel: (809) 926-3130, 926-1540

American Chamber of Commerce of Jamaica
77 Knutsford Boulevard
Kingston 5
Tel: (809) 929-7866/7
Fax: (809) 92-98597

Jamaica Chamber of Commerce
7E Parade
Kingston
Tel: (809) 922-0150/1

MARKET RESEARCH FIRMS

Caricom Consultants (Ja) Ltd.
30 Grenada Crescent
Kingston 5
Tel: (809) 926-2731

Chen-Young Roache and Associates Ltd.
7 Trinidad Terrace
Kingston 5
Tel: (809) 968-8501

Hamilton Trevor and Associates
10 Kensington Crescent
Kingston 5
Tel: (809) 926-8596

Peat Marwick
6 Duke St
Kingston
Tel: (809) 922-6640

Project Development Services and Associates Ltd.
11 1/2 Ardenne Road
Kingston 10
Tel: (809) 927-8907

NEWSPAPERS

Daily Gleaner
7 North St.
POB 40
Kingston
Tel: (809) 922-3400
Telex: 2319
Fax: (809) 923-5197

Daily Star
7 North St.
POB 40
Kingston
Tel: (809) 922-3400

The Jamaica Herald
29 Molynes Rd.
Kingston 10
Tel: (809) 968-3400

The Jamaica Record
7-11 West St.
Kingston
Tel: (809) 922-3952
Fax: (809) 922-1055

PERIODICALS

Caribbean Shipping
Creative Communications Inc.
29 Munroe Rd.
POB 105
Kingston 6
Tel: (809) 927-4271
Fax: (809) 927-4996

Government Gazette
POB 487
Kingston

Jamaica Chamber of Commerce Journal
7-8 East Parade
Kingston
Tel: (809) 922-0150/1

Jamaica Journal
2A Suthermere Rd.
Kingston

Jamaica Manufacturer
85A Duke St.
Kingston

Jamaica Weekly Gleaner
7 North St.
POB 40
Kingston
Tel: (809) 922-3400

New Kingston Times
1-3 Worthington Terace
Kingston 5
Tel: (809) 929-4595

The Siren
1 River Bay Rd.
POB 614
Montego Bay
Tel: (809) 952-0997

The Western Mirror
Westgate Plaza
POB 1258
Montego Bay
Tel: (809) 952-5253
Fax: (809) 952-6513

RADIO & TELEVISION STATIONS

Grove Street Broadcasting
16A Worthington Terrace
POB 282
Kingston
Tel: (809) 968-5023

Independent Radio
6 Bradley Ave.
Kingston 10
Tel: (809) 968-4891

Island Broadcasting Services, Ltd.
19 Caledonia Rd
Mandeville
Tel: (809) 962-2215
Fax: (809) 962-2004

Jamaica Broadcasting Corporation
5 South Odeon Avenue
POB 100
Kingston 10
Tel: (809) 926-5620
Fax: (809) 929-1029

Radio Jamaica, Ltd.
Broadcasting House
32 Lyndhurst Road
POB 23
Kingston 5
Tel: (809) 926-1100
Fax: (809) 929-7467

AD AGENCIES

CGR Communications
20 W. Kings House Rd.
Kingston 10
Tel: (809) 926-2416

McCann-Erickson (Jamaica) Ltd.
6 Belmond Rd.
Kingston 5
Tel: (809) 926-1410
Fax: (809) 929-1942

Grimax Advertising
15 Haining Rd.
Kingston 5
Tel: (809) 929-8874/5
Fax: (809) 929-6437

BANKS

First Jamaica National Bank Ltd.
88 Harbour St.
POB 115
Kingston
Tel: (809) 922-0110
Telex: 3515

Jamaica Citizens Bank Ltd.
4 King St.
POB 483
Kingston 1
Tel: (809) 922-5850
Telex: 2129
Fax: (809) 922-7625

INTERNET ADDRESSES

Jamaica Tourist Board
http://www.jamaicatravel.com

Latin America - Jamaica
http://lanic.utexas.edu/la/ca/jamaica/

Japan
Nihon

Economy

Overview

A high level of cooperation between government and industry, a strong work ethic, and mastery of high technology, have helped Japan advance with extraordinary rapidity to the rank of second most powerful economy in the world. As a country of few natural resources, it has focused on imports of raw materials and exports of high-value-added products to secure and maintain its preeminent place in the world. After achieving one of the highest economic growth rates in the world Japan's economy has now slowed significantly, although its long-term prospects are positive.

Trade

Japan is surpassed by only the US and Germany in terms of total value of foreign trade. Developed countries are the primary markets for its exports, and it buys almost half of its imports from developing countries. The US is the largest destination for its exports, followed by Germany. Japan's continuing trade surpluses result more from official and unofficial limits on import volumes than from its aggressive mercantilism—exports account for less than 10 percent of its GDP. A strong yen and slower growth overall are containing export growth, although it continues to run a huge trade surplus.

Sectors

Manufacturing and Industry These have driven Japan's postwar economic miracle. Although this sector is perhaps the best in the world in terms of equipment and process, it faces some severe problems, including substantial overcapacity, lack of price competitiveness, and contraction of domestic and international demand due to worldwide recession. Heavy industries predominate, but Japan is shifting more towards high-technology, high-value-added industries, such as semiconductors, office and telecommunications equipment, computers, and biotechnology.

Services Japan is primarily a service nation, and growth in this sector should accelerate in the future as production moves offshore and the economy strengthens. Finance is the largest subsector of the country. Banking and retail businesses continue to operate in a closed, hierarchical style.

Agriculture and Aquaculture Japan has traditionally been an agricultural country, although its contribution to the economy is diminishing due to high input costs, inefficient allocation of farmlands, and stringent government regulations. This means that agricultural imports should flourish, especially imports of high-value, consumer-oriented food products such as dairy goods, produce, and confectionery items. Japan is the leading fishing nation in the world. Depletion of fish stocks and exclusion from other nations' maritime economic zones will cause this industry to shrink in future years, however.

Trends

Japan continues to run a huge trade surplus, which supports its extensive investment in foreign assets. The government has reiterated its previous vows of administrative and economic reforms, including reduction of the trade surplus. It has agreed to open its agricultural markets further, including partial liberalization of the rice market. The strong yen should lead to some downward adjustment in Japan's external trade imbalance as import volumes rise and export volumes fall; opportunities to sell to the huge Japanese domestic market should grow as a result.

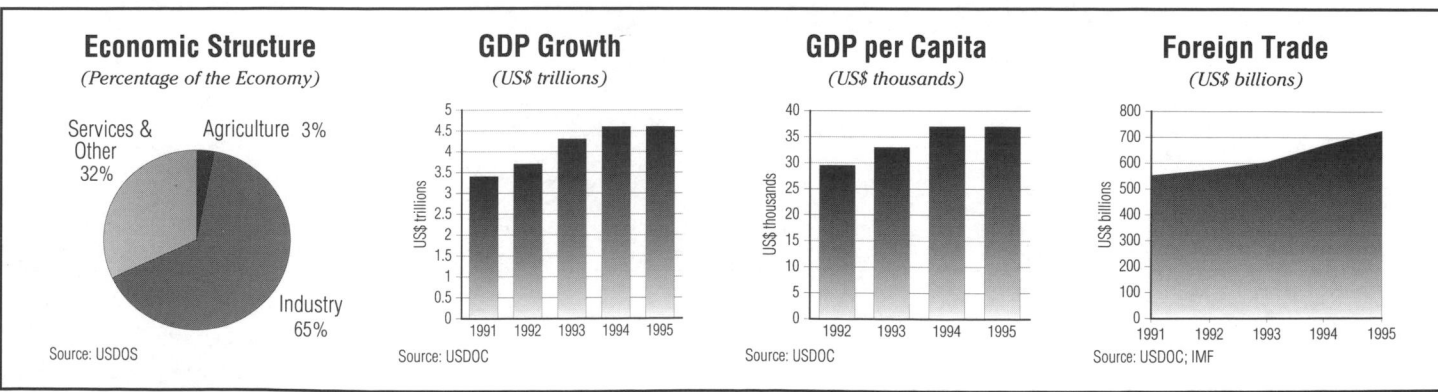

Economic Structure
(Percentage of the Economy)
Services & Other 32%
Agriculture 3%
Industry 65%
Source: USDOS

GDP Growth
(US$ trillions)
US$ trillions — 1991, 1992, 1993, 1994, 1995
Source: USDOC

GDP per Capita
(US$ thousands)
US$ thousands — 1992, 1993, 1994, 1995
Source: USDOC

Foreign Trade
(US$ billions)
US$ billions — 1991, 1992, 1993, 1994, 1995
Source: USDOC; IMF

Japan

- ★ National capital
- ⊙ Prefecture capital
- ● Secondary city
- Prefecture border
- Primary road
- ···· Railroad

| 0 | 100 | 200 | 300 km |
| 0 | | 100 | 200 mi |

China

Russia

Mudanjiang

Lake Khanka

Vladivostok

Nakhodka

Ch'ongjin

Anshan

North Korea

Sinujiu

Hamhung

Wonsan

P'yongyang

Seoul

Inch'on

South Korea

Taejon

Taegu

Kwangju

Mokp'o

Pusan

Yellow Sea

Cheju Do

Korea Strait

Tsushima

East China Sea

Ullung Do

Tok Do (Liancourt Rocks)

Oki-Gunto

Sea of Japan

Ostrov Sakhalin

Wakkanai

La Perouse Strait

Kuril Islands (occupied by Russian Federation, claimed by Japan)

Kunashir

Iturup (Etorofu)

Shikotan To

Habomai Islands

Asahikawa

Sapporo

Hokkaido

Kushiro

Hakodate

Tsugaru-kaikyo

Aomori

3

2

Akita

Honshu

Morioka

16

24

Yamagata

Sado

45

29

Niigata

8

Sendai

Fukushima

Iwaki

Kanazawa

Fukui

43

15

Nagano

10

Maebashi

39

Utsunomiya

Mito

Urawa

35

14

41

Tokyo

Otsu

Kyoto

6

9

47

26

Kofu

19

4

Chiba

Matsue

Tottori

42

13

22

36

Gifu

Shizuoka

1

Yokohama

Hiroshima

37

31

Okayama

11

Kobe

33

Nagoya

38

Hamamatsu

Yamaguchi

46

Osaka

17

28

23

Tsu

Kochi

40

44

Nara

Fukuoka

7

Oita

5

Shikoku

Wakayama

Sasebo

Saga

30

20

Takamatsu

Tokushima

34

Matsuyama

Fukue Jima

27

Nagasaki

21

Uwajima

Kumamoto

25

18

Miyazaki

Kagoshima

Kyushu

Osumi-Shoto

Tokara-Retto

Izu Islands

Nampo Islands

Sumisu

Tori-shima

Bonin Islands (Ogasawara-Gunto)

Philippine Sea

Amami Gunto

Okinawa Gunto

Naha

32

Senkaku-Shoto

Sakishima-Shoto

Ryukyu Islands

Kita Daito Jima

Okino Daito Jima

Volcano Islands (Kazan-Retto)

Iwo Jima

Prefectures of Japan

1 Aichi
2 Akita
3 Aomori
4 Chiba
5 Ehime
6 Fukui
7 Fukuoka
8 Fukushima
9 Gifu
10 Gumma
11 Hiroshima
12 Hokkaido
13 Hyogo
14 Ibaraki
15 Ishikawa
16 Iwate
17 Kagawa
18 Kagoshima
19 Kanagawa
20 Kochi
21 Kumamoto
22 Kyoto
23 Mie
24 Miyagi
25 Miyazaki
26 Nagano
27 Nagasaki
28 Nara
29 Niigata
30 Oita
31 Okayama
32 Okinawa
33 Osaka
34 Saga
35 Saitama
36 Shiga
37 Shimane
38 Shizuoka
39 Tochigi
40 Tokushima
41 Tokyo
42 Tottori
43 Toyama
44 Wakayama
45 Yamagata
46 Yamaguchi
47 Yamanashi

©1995 Magellan GeographixSMSanta Barbara, CA

130°

140°

40°

30°

Foreign Trade

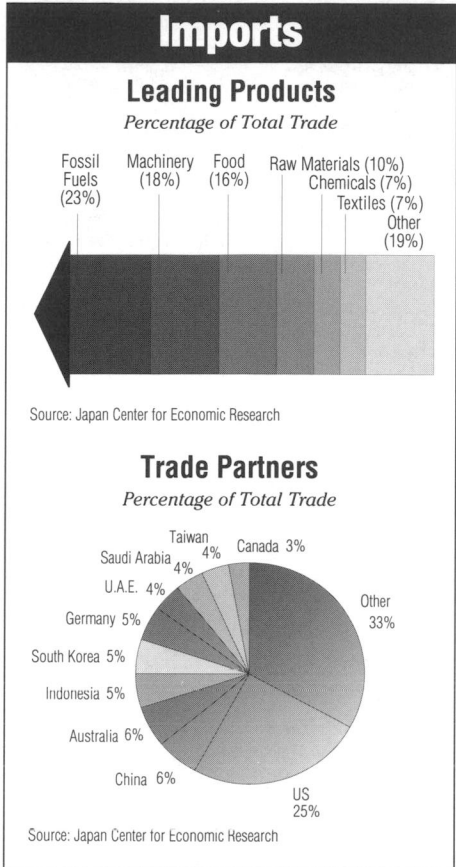

Imports

Leading Products
Percentage of Total Trade

- Fossil Fuels (23%)
- Machinery (18%)
- Food (16%)
- Raw Materials (10%)
- Chemicals (7%)
- Textiles (7%)
- Other (19%)

Source: Japan Center for Economic Research

Trade Partners
Percentage of Total Trade

- Taiwan 4%
- Canada 3%
- Saudi Arabia 4%
- U.A.E. 4%
- Germany 5%
- South Korea 5%
- Indonesia 5%
- Australia 6%
- China 6%
- US 25%
- Other 33%

Source: Japan Center for Economic Research

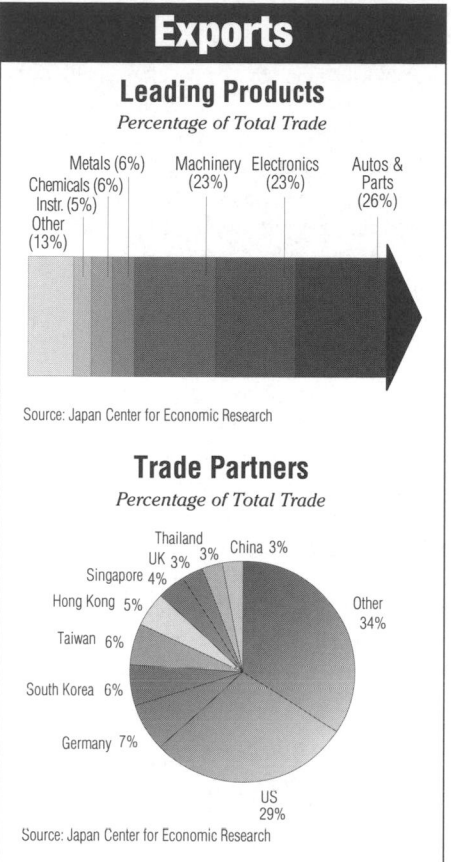

Exports

Leading Products
Percentage of Total Trade

- Metals (6%)
- Chemicals (6%)
- Instr. (5%)
- Machinery (23%)
- Electronics (23%)
- Autos & Parts (26%)
- Other (13%)

Source: Japan Center for Economic Research

Trade Partners
Percentage of Total Trade

- Thailand 3%
- UK 3%
- China 3%
- Singapore 4%
- Hong Kong 5%
- Taiwan 6%
- South Korea 6%
- Germany 7%
- US 29%
- Other 34%

Source: Japan Center for Economic Research

Opportunities

FOR IMPORTING TO JAPAN

- advanced ceramics components
- air conditioning parts
- aircraft and automotive vehicle parts
- apparel and accessories
- cereals
- computer equipment
- cosmetics and toiletries
- diamonds and diamond jewelry
- drugs and pharmaceuticals
- electric and electronic appliances and components
- giftware
- laboratory equipment and precision instruments
- nursing home equipment
- office and institutional furniture
- pollution control equipment
- scientific and medical instruments
- sporting goods
- tobacco products

FOR EXPORTING FROM JAPAN

- motor vehicles and parts and accessories
- consumer electronics
- computer hardware
- cameras
- office machines and printing presses
- radio receivers
- consumer electronics
- musical instruments
- specialty foods
- machine tools
- optical goods
- precision machinery
- photographic equipment
- sporting goods, toys, games
- watches & clocks
- fashion apparel, fashion accessories
- cultured pearls
- Japanese craft products, antiques

GROWTH SECTORS

- construction materials
- furniture, household items, and amenities
- electric machinery
- health care products, especially for the elderly
- information services equipment
- pharmaceuticals
- mail-order catalog shopping
- leisure-related facilities and equipment

GOVERNMENT PROCUREMENT

- generators and turbines
- high voltage power transmissions line equipment
- high voltage transformers
- power distribution transformers, lines and equipment
- military, civil, and general aviation aircraft
- urban development planning, and building construction goods and services
- health care products for elderly diseases

Trade News

RULES AND REGULATIONS

- **Regulation** Foreign trade is regulated primarily by MITI, MOF, and BOJ. MITI handles most import and export reporting requirements, and it issues export licenses. MOF has jurisdiction over customs and tariff control and regulation. (Addresses below)
- **Trading companies** The majority of imports and exports are handled by large trading companies which act as liaisons between buyer and seller, and also provide trade consulting services. Trading companies have extensive worldwide organizations. The names and addresses of major trading companies can be obtained from the Japan External Trade Office (JETRO).
- **Import restrictions** In principle, imports are for the most part unrestricted. In all, Japan's import restrictions cover only 81 items, although other non-tariff barriers are significant.
- **Import licenses** Most goods entering Japan now qualify as "freely importable" and do not require an import license. For restricted items, the importer must obtain authorization and an import quota certificate from the MITI, and then apply for an import license from an authorized foreign exchange bank.
- **Tariff rates** Except for agricultural products, Japan maintains one of the lowest average tariff rates in the world. Most duties are levied ad valorem, assessed on CIF value (cost + freight + insurance).
- **Quotas** Japan applies quota limits to certain imports, most of which are agricultural commodities.
- **Export restrictions** Most export restrictions are the result of voluntary export controls adopted in response to pressure from trading partners seeking to address balance of payments problems with Japan.

GOVERNMENT AGENCIES

Ministry of International Trade and Industry (MITI)
3-1, Kasumigaseki 1-chome, Chiyoda-ku
Tokyo 100
Tel: (3) 3501-1511

Ministry of Finance (MOF)
1-1, Kasumigaseki 3-chome, Chiyoda-ku
Tokyo 100
Tel: (3) 3581-4111
Fax: (3) 3508-7324

Bank of Japan (BOJ)
1-1, Hongoku-cho 2-chome
Nihonbashi, Chuo-ku
Tokyo 103
Tel: (3) 3279-1111
Fax: (3) 3245-0358

FREIGHT FORWARDERS

JAS Forwarding Co. Ltd.
Kayabacho K1 Building
3-14, Nihonbashi, Koami-cho, Chuo-ku
Tokyo 103
Tel: (3) 3661-5856
Fax: (3) 3667-3137

Mitsubishi Warehouse & Transportation Co. Ltd.
19-1, Nihonbashi 1-chome, Chuo-ku
Tokyo 103
Tel: (3) 3278-6611
Fax: (3) 3278-6694

Mitsui-Soko Co. Ltd.
13-12, Nihonbashi Kayaba-cho 1-chome
Chuo-ku
Tokyo 103
Tel: (3) 3667-5333
Fax: (3) 3699-5051

Nippon Express Co. Ltd.
12-9, Sotokanda 3-chome, Chiyoda-ku
Tokyo 101
Tel: (3) 5294-5801
Fax: (3) 5294-5809

Nissin Corp.
Keihin building
84, Onoe-cho 6-chome, Naka-ku
Yokohama 231
Tel: (45) 671-6112
Fax: (45) 671-6118

Marketing

Overview

To be successful in Japan, a foreign company must take a long-term approach to entering the market. First and foremost, a foreign company must have a presence in Japan in order to develop relationships that will show its Japanese business partners that it is a sincere member of the business community. Japanese companies compete in a tough, sophisticated market where customers are highly brand conscious and are still willing to pay a high price for quality. Even for Japanese businesspeople, this huge market is a challenging and expensive place to do business; for a non-Japanese businessperson, the task is formidable, but not impossible. A new generation of individualistic consumers is emerging, centering on the 8.1 million Japanese between ages 18 and 21, who have an estimated $33 million in disposable income and are more price conscious than devoted to specific brands. Establishing a physical presence in the country remains costly: Office space in the major cities is among the most expensive in the world, and the salaries for Japanese nationals are high.

Distribution

Distribution is critical to success. Entering Japan's distribution system, however, is difficult. Many Japanese wholesalers and retailers are hesitant to disrupt their long-standing relationships with Japanese suppliers even when a foreign supplier can offer a superior product at a lower price; they fear that foreign suppliers will not make timely shipments or have adequate systems to handle after-sales service. It is therefore essential to find reliable distributors, and sometimes an agent as well, even with a sales office in the country. Distributors generally cover a specific territory or industry, while import agents are usually appointed as sole agents for the entire country. Imported consumer goods distribution channels are characterized by close, personal relationships between importers, multiple layers of wholesalers, and retailers. Direct sales are the norm for expensive, high-tech equipment. Imported consumer goods are most often sold at larger department stores or discount houses; small, local establishments rarely carry these goods.

Agents, Distributors, and Partners

Choosing a Japanese business associate takes time. The Japanese party's willingness and ability to abide by contract terms is crucial, as is his or her ability and willingness to compete directly with established Japanese products. A foreign company should avoid representatives who target limited, high-price niches, whether in industrial or consumer products, or who are compromised by strong ties to a Japanese manufacturer. Communication by fax or phone is crucial and regular visits are a must to build a personal relationship with a Japanese import agent or distributor.

Selling Techniques

Personal contact with customers is very important, and representatives from foreign companies should accompany their Japanese agents on sales visits as much as possible. Product presentations to retailers and end users should never be left to the sole responsibility of local agents, as the foreign seller will often miss valuable market feedback from buyers. It is key to get into the Japanese trade event circuit; these events are being attended more and more by regulatory officials and decisionmakers from all throughout the Asia region. Direct marketing, including door-to-door sales, mail order, and telemarketing, is increasingly becoming accepted as an alternative sales channel for suppliers.

Advertising

Most broadcast and print media do not deal with advertisers directly, but instead with Japan's top five advertising agencies who reserve and resell time and space slots. Advertising costs are negotiable and interested advertisers should check with several agencies to compare services and costs. The most cost effective method of advertising by small- to medium-size foreign companies is in one of Japan's many weekly or monthly popular magazines, which cover many interest groups, or in one of the many industrial daily, weekly, or monthly newspapers and trade journals. In general, "mood" or "image" advertising sells better in Japan; hard-sell messages and comparative or combative advertising are considered bad taste and do not work well.

Service and Customer Support

Service and customer support (before, during, and after the sale) are critical elements in doing business in Japan and should be considered part of the product package. Every effort should be made to answer technical questions and make sure that shipments are made on time and handled with the greatest of care. If there is a problem, it should be rectified as soon as possible and sincere apologies offered, regardless of who is to blame. Strict arrangements for quality control should be made by the exporter.

Marketing in Japan

MARKETING TIPS

- **Quality** Offer products and services that meet high standards of quality and that appeal to the unique tastes and needs of the Japanese.
- **Adapt your products and services to the market.** Agree to "conform to the system" rather than try to change it.
- **Introductions** Before conducting business be sure you are properly introduced by someone who knows you and is known to the Japanese person or firm you wish to meet.
- **Product modification** Foreign sellers should seriously consider suggestions for product modification or improvement suggested by their Japanese agents.
- **Public promotions** Large flyers, framed posters and stickers located inside commuter railcars and buses or in stations are highly effective advertising.
- **Honesty** It is important to be honest and direct, but avoid being overbearing or boastful.
- **Pricing** The acceptance of a foreign product is based primarily on its quality and after sales service, not its price, although this is changing.
- **Government** Government entities have become large purchasers of a wide range of goods.

AD AGENCIES

Asatsu/BBDO
1-9-6, Shimbashi, Minato-ku
Tokyo 105
Tel: (3) 3575-3171

Daiko Advertising, Inc. (Main office)
3-39 Miyahara 4-chome, Yodogawa-ku
Osaka 532
Tel: (6) 3928111 Fax: (6) 3928004

Dentsu, Young & Rubicam
Kyobashi K-1 Building
2-7-12, Yaesu, Chuo-ku
Tokyo 104
Tel: (3) 3278-4811 Fax: (3) 3278-4809

Hakuhodo Lintas
Tokyo Building
7-3 Marunouchi, 2-chome, Chiyoda-ku
Tokyo 100
Tel: (3) 3240-7640 Fax: (3) 3240-7697

Saatchi & Saatchi Advertising
Akasaka Nine Park Building
9-2-16, Akasaka, Minato-ku
Tokyo 107
Tel: (3) 5410-8600 Fax: (3) 5410-8610

MARKETING ASSOCIATIONS

Japan Direct Marketing Association (JDMA)
Mori Building, No. 32
3-4-30 Shibakoen, Minato-ku
Tokyo 105
Tel: (3) 3434-4700 Fax: (3) 3434-4518

Association for Promotion of International Trade
Nihon Building
6-2, Ohtemachi 2-chome, Chiyoda-ku
Tokyo 100
Tel: (3) 3245-1561

Japan External Trade Organization (JETRO)
2-5, Toranomon 2-chome, Minato-ku
Tokyo 105
Tel: (3) 3582-5511 Fax: (3) 3587-0219

BEST BOOKS

JAPAN Business: The Portable Encyclopedia for Doing Business With Japan, San Rafael, California, USA: World Trade Press, 1994. US$24.95, 374 pages.
Doing Business In Asia: A Small Business Guide to Success In the World's Most Dynamic Market, Cincinnati, Ohio, USA: Betterway Books, 1993. US$18.95, 192 pages.
Japanese Etiquette & Ethics in Business, Chicago, Illinois, USA: NTC Business Books, 1991. US$14.95, 182 pages.

Business Culture

Greetings and Courtesies

Courtesy and etiquette are extremely important in Japanese society. The emphasis on etiquette is so strong that what someone does may be less important than how he does it. When meeting Japanese businesspeople, foreigners should display sincerity and respect. Although the accepted form of salutation between Japanese is the bow, most Japanese with international experience will not expect a bow from a foreigner. If the situation is unclear, you should wait for the Japanese either to offer a hand or to bow, and you should reciprocate accordingly. Business cards are always presented upon first meeting. Failure to do so can indicate to the Japanese that you are unaware of proper business etiquette or lack of interest. Business gifts are often given at first meeting, but they are generally not opened in front of the giver.

Bowing Between Japanese, subordinates will bow deeply and their superiors do not. Businessmen in Japan are so concerned about status that they cannot be sure of how to behave at their first meeting until their relative status has been properly established. They often bow only after they have exchanged business cards and determined who is the superior. The junior person bows lower. Afterward, they continue to behave as superior and subordinate, and the junior person is exceptionally polite.

Business Ethic and Framework

Japanese values emphasize the maintenance of harmonious relations with others, as well as membership in a family and a community. The Japanese take great care to maintain an outward appearance of peace and unity in social and business situations, even when true feelings are otherwise. The Japanese consider it a mark of personal strength for an individual to conform to society as closely as he can and not let his selfish desires get out of hand. The emphasis on harmony leads to a habit of telling a person what they believe he or she wants to hear, whether or not it is true. For these reasons, it is best in situations of uncertainty to use gentle questions and prolonged discussion in order not to upset the harmonious atmosphere that the Japanese prize so much.

Decision Making

Decision making in a Japanese business is a time-consuming process that includes almost every employee involved in the endeavor under discussion. In many companies, ideas and suggestions are often initiated by lower level employees and then passed on via formal and informal channels to higher-ranking managers for review. Middle-level managers are usually the prime source for decisions on company policy. Their importance means that foreign businesspeople must work to establish close relations with many different company employees. They cannot simply meet the top management and assume a solid relationship has been formed. Support from middle-level managers can have decisive importance for the success of a foreign concern.

Women

Although women have recently become more accepted in production and service industries, traditional notions of male supremacy persist in most business circles. Women earn only about 60 percent as much as their male counterparts, and very few women hold senior management positions. While women of exceptional skill or talent may achieve some success in business, they are usually relegated to subservient positions, such as secretaries. This gender inequality carries over into family life, where women are primarily responsible for the family budget and the education and careers of family members, but shoulder the blame for family failures.

Meetings

Any business meeting, especially one with a larger company, needs to be scheduled weeks in advance. Business meetings are conducted formally, and foreigners should always prepare thoroughly. Before the meeting you should mail or fax a detailed document outlining the matter to be discussed. The Japanese do not like surprises. Your first meeting may be with young managers; this is not necessarily a bad sign as business relationships are usually initiated by junior executives. When you enter the Japanese building for the meeting, the members of your delegation should remove their coats immediately on entry and put them back on only when they leave.

Business Attire

Conservative, formal business attire is the norm. British style is favored over American and definitely over Italian. Dark suits of fine tailoring and expensive but understated accessories are recommended for both men and women. Women should wear conservative necklines, hemlines, sleeves, and makeup. Employees of many small, local concerns dress like their fellow workers—often in a company uniform.

Cultural Cautions

DO'S
- Cover your mouth when you yawn, cough, or use a toothpick.
- Carry toilet paper with you as public toilets rarely have any.
- Listen and pay attention in conversations as the Japanese highly admire a good listener.

DON'TS
- Do not point at another person as it is considered accusatory, hostile, or rude.
- Do not blow your nose in public as it is considered very rude.
- Do not stand with your hand or hands in your pockets, especially when greeting someone or when addressing a group of people.
- Do not point your feet at another person; it is impolite. Japanese sit upright in chairs with both feet on the floor.
- Avoid direct eye contact; it can be seen as intruding on another person's personal space.
- Never slouch in public; good posture is important to the Japanese.

CUSTOMS
- Business cards are crucial. Carry plenty of them, always. When you meet a business contact for the first time, shake hands (not too firmly) or bow (be observant; if a bow is offered instead of a handshake, reciprocate). Then exchange cards immediately. Present and receive cards with both hands, and put the card you receive in a pocket above the waist—but only after reading it carefully and respectfully. Your card should have a Japanese translation on the reverse.
- When Japanese are embarrassed they cover their face with their hands.
- Japanese smile when they are nervous or embarrassed, or when responding to an inconvenient request or a sensitive issue, or when another person nearby has committed a faux pas.
- In Japanese homes, shoes are removed at the entrance. Be sure to wear clean socks!
- Personal relationships are more important to the Japanese than are paper contracts.

OBSERVATIONS
- Japanese will rarely say no. If a request cannot be met, Japanese may say that it is inconvenient or under consideration. This generally means no.
- Contrary to popular belief, Japanese respect personal space and do not like to be crowded by other people, though they know it sometimes can't be avoided.
- Forget about personal space in crowds or subways; everybody loses it in all the pushing and shoving. It's all among strangers, who, after all, are not part of the family and thus undeserving of face.
- Lightly touching another person's arm when speaking is a sign of close familiarity. Men and women rarely hold hands in public.
- You will need formal introductions to get your foot in the door of this tightly knit business community.

NEGOTIATIONS
- When Japanese become quiet it could mean they are thinking very hard, but it can also mean that something has been done to displease them.
- Business negotiations may seem to proceed slowly, as the Japanese will usually prefer no agreement over being criticized later for making a mistake.
- The team leader should enter the negotiation room first; he or she will then be seated directly opposite the Japanese team leader. At the end of the meeting, shake the hand of the Japanese team leader. Only then is it appropriate to shake hands with or nod to the other members of the Japanese team.

Legal System

Japan is a civil code country using a blend of Asian and Western legal traditions.

Intellectual Property Rights

Patents On average it takes more than five years to obtain patent registration in Japan, allowing public access to the application. Foreign filers often find that their Japanese rights are closely circumscribed by prior filing of applications for a very similar invention or process. Moreover, patent examiners and Japanese courts interpret patent applications narrowly and the courts adjudicate cases slowly. Japanese patent law lacks a doctrine of equivalence and there is no discovery procedure to seek evidence of infringement.

Trademarks Trademark applications are also processed slowly, averaging more than two years for processing. Infringement carries no penalty until an application is approved. In April 1992, Japan amended the trademark law to protect service marks explicitly.

Copyrights Japan is considering weakening copyright protections on computer software to allow Japanese companies to dissect foreign software and use creative elements that are currently protected under Japanese law. Pirated video sales remain a problem, although the Japanese police have cracked down on video pirates. A revised copyright law took effect in 1992, under which copyright protection was extended from 30 to 50 years.

Trade Secrets Japan's Trade Protection Law provides more protection than ordinary contract law, though it is still very difficult to get an injunction against a third party transferee of purloined trade secrets.

Business Registration

Foreign businesses operating in Japan require foreign investment approval and business licenses from the appropriate authorities. The operation of an incorporated company, a joint venture, or a branch office requires registration with the Ministry of Finance as well as any other ministries governing the specific industry. Joint ventures and licensing and technology transfer agreements must also be reported to the Japan Fair Trade Committee, which can void agreements after the fact. Representative offices do not require approval except for those involved in financial services. All foreign operations must register with Legal Affairs Bureau and local tax authorities. If the new enterprise has any employees, it must also register with the appropriate social security authorities.

Contracts and Dispute Resolution

Japanese companies prefer short, general contracts, and a contract should be viewed as part of a greater effort to create a business relationship rather than as the sum total of the relationship itself. Business disputes are usually settled through informal negotiation rather than by lawsuit, and actual litigation of business disputes is rare. However, some Japanese firms may be less reserved about suing foreign firms than they would be about suing another Japanese firm. Japanese courts often require litigants to compromise, and judicial awards usually decree performance instead of monetary damages. Arbitration is more common than litigation, although less common than informal negotiation, and is usually conducted before the Japan Commercial Arbitration Association (JCAA). Since these proceedings may be as lengthy and expensive as a lawsuit, the arbitrators are Japanese, and all proceedings and decisions are in Japanese, foreign businesspersons should try to insist on another international arbitration body.

Notaries

Notaries prepare and authenticate documentary instruments, which must be in the Japanese language. While acknowledgment is not essential to the validity of a document, authenticated private documents do bear a strong presumption of validity similar to that of official records or documents. Acknowledgments for use in foreign countries may be taken before diplomatic representatives of the country in which the document will be used.

Labor

Workers have a constitutional right to associate freely in unions and to bargain collectively. The right to strike is implicit in the constitution and is exercised freely. Minors under the age of 15 cannot be employed as workers, and the child labor laws are rigorously enforced. The legal minimum wage rate is sufficient to provide workers and their families a decent living. Although it is changing somewhat in response to tighter economic conditions, there is still a strong implied social contract which effectively prevents large companies from terminating or laying off workers except for cause.

Legal Matters

LEGAL BRIEFS

- **Corporations** A corporation is the favored business entity. Formation may be done through a promoters' incorporation or a subscribers' incorporation. Formation costs, including lawyers' fees, registration taxes, and related fees, are generally between ¥1 million and ¥1.5 million.

- **Maximum work week** The statutory maximum work week for all employees is 48 hours, or six 8-hour days. In addition to 12 paid national holidays, employees are given special leave, as well as annual paid vacations. All employees who have worked for one year must receive six days of paid vacation.

- **Employee right to work** An employee's right to work is supported by the courts, and it is often difficult to dismiss an employee, except when there is a violation of the company's employment regulations.

- **Legal protection** Don't expect the same legal protections from Japanese courts as you get from the courts in Western countries—especially with regard to enforcement of contract rights and obligations.

- **Property** Nonresident aliens may acquire real property, although advance notifications must be filed with several government agencies.

- **Trade Agreements** Japan is not a member of any regional trade blocks, although it is a part of GATT and the emerging APEC group.

LEGAL CONTACTS

Japan Commercial Arbitration Association
6th Fl., Tokyo Kotsu Kaikan
10-1, Yuraku-cho, Chiyoda-ku
Tokyo 100
Tel: (3) 3214-0641/3 Fax: (3) 3201-1336

Japan Federation of Bar Associations
1-1-1 Kasumigaseki, Chiyoda-ku
Tokyo 100
Tel: (3) 3580-9841 Fax: (3) 3580-2866

Adachi, Henderson, Miyatake & Fujita (US)
10th Fl., Time & Life Building
3-6, Otemachi 2-chome, Chiyoda-ku
Tokyo 100
Tel: (3) 3270-7461/5 Fax: (3) 3245-1534

White & Case
American International Building
20-5, Ichibancho, Chiyoda-ku
Tokyo 102
Tel: (3) 3239-2350 Fax: (3) 3239-2385

Clifford Chance
6th Fl., South Hill Nagatacho Building
11-30, Nagatacho 1-chome, Chiyoda-ku
Tokyo 100
Tel: (3) 3581-4311 Fax: (3) 3593-0651

McKenna & Co. (UK)
Toyo Kaiji Building, No. 3, 7th Fl.
2-23-1, Nishi-shinbashi, Minato-ku
Tokyo 105
Tel: (3) 3578-0955 Fax: (3) 3578-0958

Blakemore & Mitsuki
912 Lino Building
1-1, Uchisaiwaicho 2-chome, Chiyoda-ku
Tokyo 100
Tel: (3) 3503-5571 Fax: (3) 3503-4707

Oh-Ebasi Law Office
Suite 803, Umedashinmichi Building
1-5, Dojima 1-chome, Kita-ku
Osaka 530
Tel: (6) 341-0461 Fax: (6) 347-0688

Ohara & Kano
#902 City Coop
2-7, Minami-Morimachi, 2-chome, Kita-ku
Osaka 530
Tel: (6) 313-1208 Fax: (6) 313-1209

**Tokyo Aoyama Law Office
(Baker & McKenzie)**
410 Aoyama Building
2-3, Kita Aoyama 1-chome
Tokyo 107
Tel: (3) 3403-5281 Fax: (3) 3470-3152

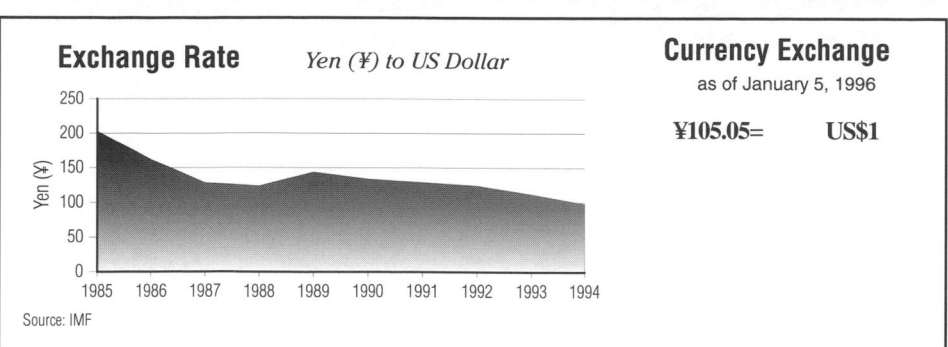

Exchange Rate *Yen (¥) to US Dollar*

Source: IMF

Currency Exchange
as of January 5, 1996

¥105.05=   US$1

Money Matters

BITS AND PIECES

- **Repatriation** Dividends, interest, and other revenue items, as well as capital, may be freely repatriated provided that the original investment was properly introduced.
- **Exchange rates** are generally uniform between the different foreign exchange operators and throughout the country. Businesses will almost always conduct their exchange operations through a bank and may be able to negotiate slight wholesale rates.
- **Stock, commodity, and currency exchanges** Japan has several stock and commodity exchanges, as well as a sophisticated currency market.
- **Nonbank private institutions** Insurance companies, trading houses, and leasing agencies provide businesses with a wide variety of financing, and play a large role in Japan's complex lending and investment system. Leasing agencies are among the best sources of long-term financing for capital equipment and other fixed assets.
- **Automated teller machines (ATMs)** Foreigners can get money from home country accounts by using automated teller machines (ATMs), most of which provide cash advances on major credit cards and some of which will take foreign ATM or debit cards.

BANKS

Bank of Japan (Nihon Gingko)
1-1, Hongoku-cho 2-chome, Nihonbashi
Chuo-ku
Tokyo 103
Tel (3) 3279-1111
Fax (3) 3245-0358

Bank of Tokyo Ltd.
3-2, Nihonbashi, Hongoku-cho 1-chome, Chuo-ku
Tokyo 103
Tel: (3) 3245-1111
Fax: (3) 3279-3926

The Sumitomo Bank Ltd.
1-3-2 Marunouchi, Chiyoda-ku
Tokyo
Tel: (3) 3282-5111
Fax (3) 3282-8330

The Sanwa Bank
3-5-6 Fushimi-machi, Chuo-ku
Osaka
Tel: (6) 202-2281
Fax: (6) 229-1064

The Dai-Ichi Kangyo Bank
1-5 Uchisaiwai-cho 1-chome, Chiyoda-ku
Tokyo 100
Tel: (3) 3596-1111
Fax: (3) 3596-5138

The Fuji Bank
1-5-5 Otemachi, Chiyoda-ku
Tokyo
Tel: (3) 3216-2211
Fax: (3) 3214-4150

Export-Import Bank of Japan
4-1, Otemachi 1-chome, Chiyoda-ku
Tokyo 100
Tel: (3) 3287-1221
Fax: (3) 3287-9540

Japan Development Bank
9-1, Otemachi 1-chome, Chiyoda-ku
Tokyo 100
Tel: (3) 3244-1770
Fax: (3) 3245-1938

Overseas Economic Cooperation Fund
Takebashi Godo Building
4-1, Otemachi 1-chome, Chiyoda-ku
Tokyo 100
Tel: (3) 3215-1311
Fax: (3) 3215-2897

Citibank, N.A.
13F AIU Bldg.
1-1-3, Marunouchi, Chiyoda-ku
C.P.O. Box 108
Tokyo 100-91
Tel: (3) 3214-6600
Fax: (3) 3214-6618

Currency

The currency in use is the yen (¥).

Foreign Exchange

Foreign exchange operations are carried out by authorized banks, including city and local banks, and foreign branch banks. Japanese laws prohibit most direct foreign exchange transactions between individuals and businesses. There are no taxes or subsidies on purchases or sales of foreign exchange. Unlimited amounts of currency can be brought into the country as long as it is declared to customs on entry. Visitors can reconvert yen into foreign exchange when leaving the country up to any amount they have converted while in the country as demonstrated by receipts. No black market in currency exists.

Capital Transfers

Nonresident accounts in yen may be opened with any authorized bank in Japan and there are no restrictions on credits to or payments from these accounts. Payments to all countries may be made in any currency, including yen, and receipts may be obtained in any currency. For transactions that involve payments from Japan to residents of certain countries, or by residents of these countries to foreign countries through Japan, permission from the Minister of Finance is required.

Investment Incentives

Law on Extraordinary Measures for the Facilitation of Imports and Foreign Direct Investment in Japan The government provides eligible foreign firms a preferential tax treatment of 10-year extensions of carry-over periods for losses, exemption from special land-holding taxes, and exemption from stamp duties, as well as various other assistance programs to encourage foreign investment.

Foreign Investment in Japan Development Corporation (FIND) FIND helps foreign affiliates in Japan cope with difficulties such as Japan's unique business practices and hiring qualified workers.

Japan Development Bank JDB maintains loan programs under which foreign-owned companies are eligible for long-term loans for capital investment.

Technopolis MITI provides various assistance to companies locating in areas which have been designated for development as a technology-intensive zone or technopolis.

Investment Restrictions

Legal restrictions are few and narrowly and specifically drawn. However, the close-knit and complicated business environment in Japan does serve to restrict much foreign investment.

TAXATION

Taxation requires sophisticated knowledge of complex rules and regulations specific to each country. The information presented here is from the Ernst & Young Corporate Tax Guide and Directory, available from the Ernst & Young accounting office in your country, or from:

Showa Ota Ernst & Young Co., Ltd.
Hitotsubashi Building
2-6-3 Hitotsubashi
Chiyoda-ku
Tokyo 101, Japan
Tel: (3) 3288-2811

- Nonresident companies pay taxes only on Japanese source income.
- Capital gains are not taxed separately, but are treated as ordinary income, and normal tax rates apply.

At a Glance

Corporate Income Tax Rate (%)	37.5
Capital Gains Tax Rate (%)	37.5
Branch Tax Rate (%)	37.5
Withholding Tax (%) (a)	
Dividends	20
Interest (b)	20
Royalties from Patents, Know-how, etc.	20
Branch Remittance Tax	0
Net Operating Losses (Years)	
Carryback (c)	1
Carryforward	5

(a) Except for the withholding tax on royalties, these withholding taxes are imposed on both residents and nonresidents. For nonresidents, these are final taxes, unless the income is effectively connected with a permanent establishment in Japan. Royalties paid to residents are not subject to withholding.
(b) For residents, this tax consists of a national tax of 15% and a local tax of 5%.
(c) The loss carryback is temporarily suspended.

Business Travel

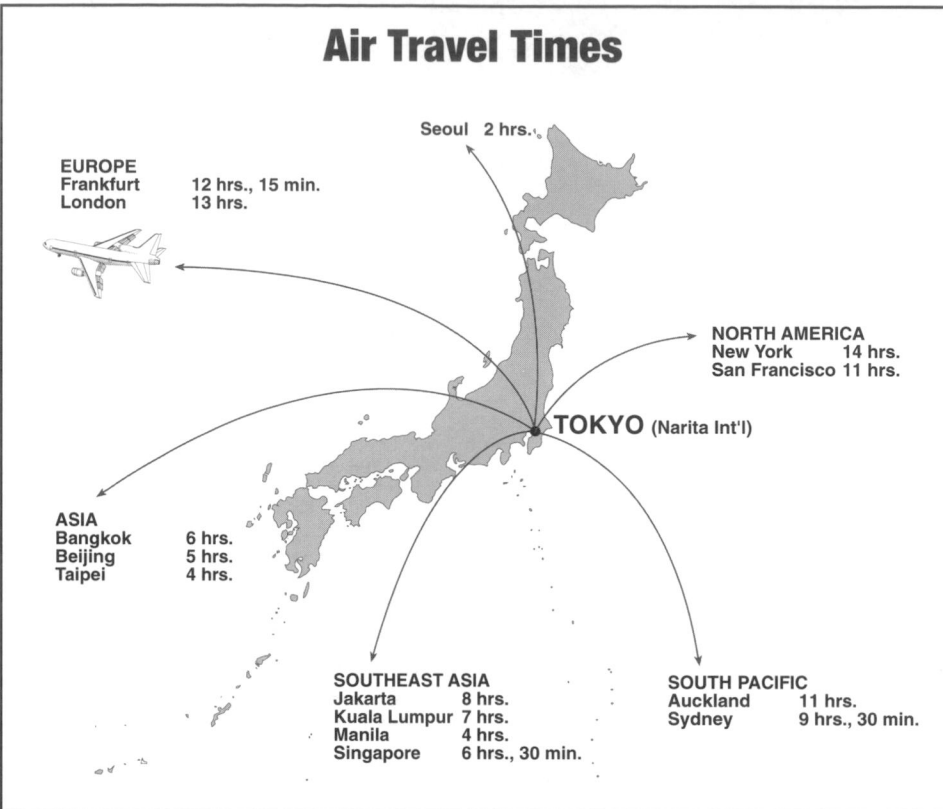

Air Travel Times

Seoul 2 hrs.

EUROPE
Frankfurt 12 hrs., 15 min.
London 13 hrs.

NORTH AMERICA
New York 14 hrs.
San Francisco 11 hrs.

TOKYO (Narita Int'l)

ASIA
Bangkok 6 hrs.
Beijing 5 hrs.
Taipei 4 hrs.

SOUTHEAST ASIA
Jakarta 8 hrs.
Kuala Lumpur 7 hrs.
Manila 4 hrs.
Singapore 6 hrs., 30 min.

SOUTH PACIFIC
Auckland 11 hrs.
Sydney 9 hrs., 30 min.

COMMUNICATIONS

Telephones Telephone service is first-rate and you can call virtually anywhere from nearly any location. Public telephones are everywhere, color-coded in a wide variety of colors and service offerings. Calling cards won't save you any money, but they are very convenient and they can be purchased in stores, souvenir stands, hotels, and vending machines; a ¥1,000 card buys 105 3-minute calls. The green-and-gold phones take as many cards as you can feed them. When you call long-distance within Japan, include the 0 with the area code. When you call to Japan from overseas, omit the 0. Long-distance calls are 40 percent cheaper between 11 pm and 8 am; international rates very according to carrier. Japan has three international call carriers and each has its own international access number.

Fax Fax machines are everywhere - in almost every hotel, most businesses, many homes, even in 24-hour convenience stores.

Post office Japan's mail service is very efficient, and international branches are open until 7 or 8 pm. Post offices are marked with a bright red T with a line above it, while mailboxes are brilliant orange-red. Major post offices can also send telegrams.

BEST TRAVEL BOOKS

Fodor's Japan, New York: Fodor's Travel Publications. 652 pages. Tourist-oriented, strong on hotels, shopping, dining, and nightspots. Includes dozens of excellent maps.

Frommer's Japan, by Beth Reiber. New York: Prentice Hall. 585 pages. More traveler than tourist oriented; written in the first-person by an experienced Japanhand. Dozens of good maps; good hotel and dining sections. Helpful "Fast Facts" and traveler's tips sections.

Japan: A Travel Survival Kit, by Robert Strauss, Chris Taylor and Tony Wheeler. Hawthorn, Victoria, Australia: Lonely Planet Publications. 730 pages. For the independent traveler.

USEFUL TELEPHONE NUMBERS

If you are calling from outside Japan, you will need to add the country code [81] and any other international dialling requirements from within your country.

- International Phone Communications Services (Kokusai Denshin Denwa Co.) 0057
- International Operator 0051
- Tokyo Police...................................... (3) 3814-4151
- Tokyo Taxi...................................... (3) 3648-0300
- JR Trains (Tokyo Station) .... (3) 3231-1880
  (Ueno Station) .... (3) 3841-8069
- Tokyo Subways................................. (3) 3834-5577
- Japan Helpline .... (0120) 461-997
- Subway Information (Tokyo) .... (3) 3837-7111

Telegrams
- Domestic 115
- Overseas... (3) 3344-5151
- Bullet train 107
- Information Corner (Multilingual)........ (45) 671-7209
- Japan Hotline .... (3) 3586-0110

JNTO Tourist Information Centers
  Tokyo .... (3) 3502-1461
  Kyoto .... (75) 371-5649
  Narita.. (476) 32-8711

Japan Travel-Phone
  Eastern Japan 0088-22-2800
  Western Japan 0088-22-7111

Flight Information
  Narita Airport.................................... (476) 32-2800
  Haneda Airport................................. (3) 3747-8010

Credit Card Information
Lost or stolen credit cards (international collect calls only to US regardless of which country your card was issued in).

- Amex.. [1] (919) 333-3211
- Diner's Club............................... [1] (303) 799-1504
- Mastercard .... [1] (314) 275-6690
- Visa .... [1] (410) 581-7931

Travelogue

WORKWEEK

Offices Monday-Friday, 9:00 am to 5:00 pm, and Saturday from 9:00 am to noon.

Banks Monday-Friday, 9:00 am to 3:00 pm, closed Saturday.

Government Monday-Friday, 9:00 am to 5:00 pm, closed Saturday, except local offices are open the first and third Saturdays of the month until noon.

Retail Generally open on weekends and closed one day during the week.

HOLIDAYS

Holidays 1996
January1 New Year's
January 15 Adult's Day
February 11 National Foundation Day
March 21 Vernal Equinox Day*
April 29 Greenery Day
May 3 Constitution Day
May 4 Declared official holiday
May 5 Children's Day
September 15 Respect for the Aged Day
September 23 Autumnal Equinox Day*
October 10 Sports Day
November 3 Culture Day
November 23 Labor Thanksgiving Day
December 23 Emperor's Birthday

In addition to the above public holidays; many Japanese companies and government offices traditionally close for several days during the New Year's holiday season (December 28-January 3). Although it depends on the company, many are closed during "Golden Week" (April 29-May 5) and the traditional "O-Bon" (Festival of Souls) period for several days in mid-August (usually about August 12-15).

* Approximate date. Actual date varies each year.

VISA AND PASSPORT

Foreigners must have a valid passport, but most foreigners visiting Japan for tourism or business don't need visas if they're staying 90 days or less. You do need proof of sufficient funds and your onward ticket out of Japan. If you stay more than 90 days, you can get an extension for tourism or business, but you'll need to get an Alien Registration Card and carry it with you at all times.

DEPARTURE FORMALITIES

You can take up to ¥5 million or any amount of foreign cash out of the country without special permission.
If you leave Japan through Narita Airport, you will have to pay a ¥2,000 "Passenger Facility Service Charge."

IMMUNIZATION

Foreigners need proof of vaccination only if they arrive from an infected area, such as South America, which is experiencing an epidemic of cholera, or tropical Africa or South America, where yellow fever is endemic.

TIPPING

As a general rule, the Japanese neither ask for nor expect tips, and rarely accept them—and even then only with considerable embarrassment.

CRIME

Japan has one of the lowest crime rates in the world, the major crimes being fraud and other white-collar offenses. There are police kiosks at frequent intervals on street corners.

INFRASTRUCTURE

Japan has highly developed hotel, rail, bus, rental car, cellular telephone, telecommunications (except Internet) and taxi industries. Bicycling is the favored mode of transportation.

NATIONAL TOURIST OFFICE

Japan National Tourist Organization
Kotani Building
6-6, Yurakucho 1-chome
Chiyoda-ku
Tokyo 100
Tel: (3) 3502-1461

GOVERNMENT AGENCIES

Center for Development of Power Supply Regions
107 Ark Mori Building1-12-32 Akasaka
Minato-ku Tokyo
Tel: (3) 5562-9711 Fax: (3) 5562-9802

Defense Agency
7-45, Akasaka 9-chome, Minato-ku
Tokyo 107
Tel: (3) 3408-5211

Economic Planning Agency
1-1, Kasumigaseki 3-chome, Chiyoda-ku
Tokyo 100
Tel: (3) 3581-0261

Environmental Agency
1-2-2, Kasumigaseki, Chiyoda-ku
Tokyo 100
Tel: (3) 3581-3351

Hokkaido Development Agency
1-1, Kasumigaseki 3-chome, Chiyoda-ku
Tokyo 100
Tel: (3) 3581-9111

Japan Fair Trade Commission
International Affairs Division
2-2-1 Kasumigaseki, Chiyoda-ku
Tokyo 100
Tel: (3) 3581-5481 x574/5

Kobe Port and Harbor Bureau
5-1, Kano-cho, 6-chome
Kobe
Tel: (78) 331-8181 Telex: 78548

Ministry of Agriculture, Forestry and Fisheries
1-2-1, Kasumigaseki 1-chome, Chiyoda-ku
Tokyo 100
Tel: (3) 3502-8111

Ministry of Construction
1-3, Kasumigaseki 2-chome, Chiyoda-ku
Tokyo 100
Tel: (3) 3580-4311

Ministry of Finance
Customs & Tariff Bureau
1-1 Kasumigaseki 3-chome, Chiyoda-ku
Tokyo 100
Tel: (3) 3581-2852 Fax: (3) 3593-1223, 3581-0460
Telex: 24980 MOFJ

Ministry of Health & Welfare
2-1, Kasumigaseki 1-chome, Chiyoda-ku
Tokyo 100
Tel: (3) 3502-7111, 3503-1711, 3508-7527
Water Supply and Environmental Sanitation Department
Tel: (3) 3501-0040 Fax: (3) 3502-6879

Ministry of International Trade & Industry
3-1, Kasumigaseki 1-chome, Chiyoda-ku
Tokyo 100
Tel: (3) 3501-1511
Industrial Location Guidance
Tel: (3) 3501-0645
IInternational Business Affairs Division
Tel: (3) 3501-6623
Industrial Location & Environmental Protection Bureau
Tel: (3) 3501-1679 Fax: (3) 3580-6379

Ministry of Justice, Immigration Office
1-1, Kasumigaseki 1-chome, Chiyoda-ku
Tokyo 100
Tel: (3) 3213-8111

Ministry of Labor
1-2-2 Kasumigaseki, 1-chome, Chiyoda-ku
Tokyo 100
Tel: (3) 3593-1211, 3508-7505

Ministry of Posts & Telecommunications
3-2, Kasumigaseki 1-chome, Chiyoda-ku
Tokyo 100
Tel: (3) 3504-4411 Fax: (3) 3592-9157

Ministry of Transport
1-3, Kasumigaseki 2-chome, Chiyoda-ku
Tokyo 100
Tel: (3) 3580-3111

WORLD TRADE CENTERS

World Trade Center of Japan
37th Fl., World Trade Center Building
4-1, Hammamatsu-cho 2-chome, Minato-ku
Tokyo 105
Tel: (3) 3435-5651/7 Fax: (3) 3436-4368

World Trade Center Osaka
1-3-20, Nakanoshima, Kita-ku
Osaka 530
Tel: (6) 208-8960 Fax: (6) 202-6966

GENERAL TRADE ASSOCIATIONS

Center for Small Business Development in Asia
58-7, Uchihommachi Hashizzumecho
Higashi-ku
Osaka 540
Tel: (6) 944-6215

Federation of Japan Wholesalers' Association
Zenra Kaikan
6-1, Yushima 3-chome, Bunkyo-ku
Tokyo 113
Tel: (3) 3832-4291

Industry Club of Japan
4-6, Marunouchi 1-chome, Chiyoda-ku
Tokyo 100
Tel: (3) 3281-1711 Fax: (3) 3281-1797

International Management Association of Japan
No. 10 Mori Building
18-1, Toranomon 1-chome, Minato-ku
Tokyo 105
Tel: (3) 3502-3051

Japan Association of Corporate Executives
Kogyo Club Building
1-4-6, Marunouchi, Chiyoda-ku
Tokyo 100
Tel: (3) 3211-1271 Fax: (3) 3213-2946

Japan Committee for Economic Development
4-6, Marunouchi 1-chome, Chiyoda-ku
Tokyo 100
Tel: (3) 3211-1271

Japanese BIAC to the OECD
Keidanren Kaikan
9-4, Otemachi 1-chome, Chiyoda-ku
Tokyo 100
Tel: (3) 3279-1411

Japan Industrial Location Center
Operation Division
1-4-2, Toranomon, Minato-ku
Tokyo 105
Tel: (3) 3502-2361

Japan Regional Development Corporation
3-8-1, Kasumigaseki, Chiyoda-ku
Tokyo 100
Tel: (3) 3501-5211

Japan Small Business Corporation
No. 37, Mori Building
5-1, Toranomon 3-chome, Minato-ku
Tokyo 105
Tel: (3) 3433-8811 Fax: (3) 5470-1506

Japanese Standards Association
1-24, Akasaka 4-chome, Minato-ku
Tokyo 107
Tel: (3) 3583-8001/3 Fax: (3) 3586-2029

Japan Technomart Foundation
3rd Fl., Ringo Building
2-13, Gobancho, Chiyoda-ku
Tokyo 102
Tel: (3) 3288-6901

Nat'l Federation of Small Business Associations
Jitensha Kaikan
9-3, Akasaka 1-chome, Minato-ku
Tokyo 107
Tel: (3) 3586-5071 x2628

Small Business Promotion Corp.
Sankaido Building
9-13, Akasaka 1-chome, Minato-ku
Tokyo 107
Tel: (3) 3584-0351

FOREIGN BUSINESS ORGANIZATIONS IN JAPAN

American Chamber of Commerce
No. 2 Fukide Building
1-21, Toranomon 4-chome, Minato-ku
Tokyo 105
Tel: (3) 3433-5381 Fax: (3) 3436-1446

ASEAN Promotion Center on Trade, Investment and Tourism
Central Building
10-3, Ginza 4-chome, Chuo-ku
Tokyo 104
Tel: (3) 3546-1221 Fax: (3) 3546-9050

Australian Chamber of Commerce
PO Box 1096
Chuo Post Office, Chiyoda-ku
Tokyo 100-91
Tel: (3) 3212-8787

Belgium-Luxembourg Chamber of Commerce
Rm. 802, Ichiban-cho Central Building
22-1, Ichiban-cho, Chiyoda-ku
Tokyo 102
Tel: (3) 3237-9281 Fax: (3) 3237-9282

British Chamber of Commerce
No. 16, Kowa Building
9-20, Akasaka 1-chome, Minato-ku
Tokyo 107
Tel: (3) 3505-1734 Fax: (3) 3505-2680

Canadian Chamber of Commerce
PO Box 79, Akasaka, 107-91
Tokyo
Tel: (3) 3408-4311 Fax: (3) 3408-4190

Far East Trade Service Center (Taiwan)
12-19, Shibuya 2-chome, Shibuya-ku
Tokyo 150
Tel: (3) 3407-9711 Fax: (3) 3407-9715

French Chamber of Commerce
Hanzomon MK Building
8-1, Koji-machi 1-chome, Chiyoda-ku
Tokyo 102
Tel: (3) 3288-9621, 3590-6415
Fax: (3) 3288-9558

German Chamber of Commerce & Industry
7th Fl., Akasaka Tokyu Building
14-3, Nagata-cho 2-chome, Chiyoda-ku
Tokyo 100
Tel: (3) 3581-9881 Fax: (2) 3593-1350

Hong Kong Trade Development Council
4th Fl., Toho Twin Tower Building
5-2, Yuraku-cho 1-chome, Chiyoda-ku
Tokyo 100
Tel: (3) 3502-3251 Fax: (3) 3591-6484

Italian Chamber of Commerce
c/o Montecatini K.K.
21st Fl., 25 Mori Building
4-30, Roppongi 1-chome, Minato-ku
Tokyo 106
Tel: (3) 3224-7238 Fax: (3) 3588-8524

Japan-China Association on Economy and Trade
Aoyama Building
2-3, Kita-Aoyama 1-chome, Minato-ku
Tokyo 107
Tel: (3) 3402-1981 Fax: (3) 3423-2938

Korea Trade Center, Tokyo
2nd Fl., Yurakucho Building
10-1, Yuraku-cho 1-chome, Chiyoda-ku
Tokyo 100
Tel: (3) 3214-6951 Fax: (3) 3214-6950

Korean Chamber of Commerce
Kankoku Chuo Kaikan
7-32, Minami Azabu 1-chome, Minato-ku
Tokyo 106
Tel: (3) 3456-1190 Fax: (3) 3456-3176

Swiss Chamber of Commerce & Industry
CS Tower
11-30, Akasaka 1-chome, Minato-ku
Tokyo 107
Tel: (3) 3587-1122 Fax: (3) 3587-2266

US Trade Center
7th Fl., World Import Mart
103, Higashi-Ikebukuro 3-chome, Toshima-ku
Tokyo 170
Tel: (3) 3987-2441 Fax: (3) 3987-2447

DIRECTORIES & YEARBOOKS

Asia Pacific Directories Ltd.
6th Fl., Wah Hen Commercial Centre
381 Hennessy Rd.
Hong Kong
Tel: [852] 28936377 Fax: [852] 28935752

Asian Computer Directory
(Monthly)
Washington Plaza
1st Fl., 230 Wanchai Rd.
Wanchai, Hong Kong
Tel: [852] 28327123 Fax: [852] 28329208

Asian Printing Directory
(Annual)
Travel & Trade Publishing (Asia)
16th Fl., Capitol Centre
5-19 Jardines Bazaar
Causeway Bay, Hong Kong
Tel: [852] 28903067 Fax: [852] 28952378

Guide to the Motor Industry of Japan
(Annual)
Japan Motor Industrial Federation Inc.
Otemachi Building
6-1 Otemachi, Chiyoda-ku
Tokyo 100
Tel: (3) 3216-5771

Japan Directory: Business & Society
(Annual)
Japan Press Ltd.
CPO Box 6
Tokyo 100-91
Tel: (3) 3404-5161 Fax: (3) 3423-2358

Intercontinental Marketing Corp.
PO Box 5056
Tokyo 100-31
Tel: (3) 3661-7458 Fax: (3) 3667-9646

Japan Trade Directory (Nihon Boeki Shinkokai)
(Annual)
JETRO Publication Department
2-5, Toranomon 2-chome, Minato-ku
Tokyo 105
Fax: (3) 3587-2485
Tel: (3) 3492-2942

NEWSPAPERS

Asahi Evening News
8-5, Tsukiji 7-chome, Chuo-ku
Tokyo 104
Tel: (3) 3546-7181 Fax: (3) 3543-1660

Asahi Shimbun
(Japanese)
3-2, Tsukiji 5-chome, Chuo-ku
Tokyo 104-11
Tel: (3) 3545-0131 Fax: (3) 3545-0358

Asian Wall Street Journal
2nd Fl. AIA Building
1 Stubbs Rd.
GPO Box 9825
Hong Kong
Tel: [852] 25737121 Fax: [852] 28345291

Daily Summary of Japanese Press
US Embassy Tokyo
Office of Translation Services
10-1, Akasaka 1-chome, Minato-ku
Tokyo 107
Tel: (3) 3224-5000 Fax: (3) 3581-0496
Telex: 22118

International Herald Tribune
7th Fl. Malaysia Building
50 Gloucester Rd.
Wanchai, Hong Kong
Tel: [852] 28610616 Fax: [852] 28613073

Japan Times
4-5-4, Shibaura, Minato-ku
Tokyo 108
Tel: (3) 3453-5312

Mainichi Daily News
1-1-1, Hitotsubashi, Chiyoda-ku
Tokyo 100
Tel: (3) 3212-0321

Shipping and Trade News
Tokyo News Service Ltd.
Tsukiji Hamarikyu Building
3-3, Tsukiji 5-chome, Chuo-ku
Tokyo 104
Tel: (3) 3542-8521 Fax: (3) 3542-5086

BUSINESS PERIODICALS

Japan 21st (Monthly)
Nihon Kogyo Shimbun
1-7-2, Ohtemachi, Chiyoda-ku
Tokyo 100
Tel: (3) 3231-7111 Fax: (3) 3295-3991

Japan Quarterly
Shimbun Publishing Co.
5-3-2, Tsukiji, Chuo-ku
Tokyo 103
Tel: (3) 3245-0131 Fax: (3) 3544-1428

Journal of Japanese Trade & Industry (Bimonthly)
Maruzen Company Ltd.
3-10, Nihombashi, 2-chome, Chuo-ku
Tokyo 103
Tel: (3) 3272-7211 Fax: (3) 3274-3238

Journal of the American Chamber of Commerce in Japan (Monthly)
American Chamber of Commerce
No. 2 Fukide Building
1-21, Toranomon 4-chome, Minato-ku
Tokyo 105
Tel: (3) 3433-5381 Fax: (3) 3436-1446

Management Japan (Semiannual)
International Management Association of Japan
No. 10 Mori Building
18-1, Toranomon 1-chome, Minato-ku
Tokyo 105
Tel: (3) 3502-3051

Japan Labor Bulletin
7-6, Shibakoen 1-chome, Minato-ku
Tokyo

Money Japan (Monthly)
S.S. Communications, Inc.
Cosmo Hirakawacho Building
3-14, Hirakawa-cho 1-chome, Chiyoda-ku
Tokyo 102
Tel: (3) 5276-2140 Fax: (3) 5276-2149

Nikkei Business (Weekly; Japanese)
Nikkei Business Publications, Inc.
2-7-6, Hirakawa-cho, Chiyoda-ku
Tokyo 101
Tel: (3) 5210-8502 Fax: (3) 5210-8119

Time, Asia Edition (Weekly)
Time, Inc.
31st Fl., East Tower, Bond Centre
89 Queensway
Hong Kong
Tel: [852] 28446660 Fax: [852] 25108799

Far East Trade Press Ltd.
2nd Fl., Kai Tak Commercial Building
317 Des Voeux Rd.
Central, Hong Kong
Tel: [852] 25457200 Fax: [852] 25446979

Asian Finance (Monthly)
3rd Fl., Hollywood Center
233 Hollywood Rd.
Hong Kong
Tel: [852] 28155221 Fax: [852] 28504437

Asian Monetary Monitor (Bimonthly)
GPO Box 12964
Hong Kong
Tel: [852] 28427200

Asiaweek (Weekly)
Asiaweek Ltd.
199 Des Voeux Rd.
Central, Hong Kong
Tel: [852] 28155662 Fax: [852] 28155903

Business Week, Asia Edition (Weekly)
2405 Dominion Centre
43-59 Queens Rd. East
Hong Kong
Tel: [852] 23361160 Fax: [852] 25294046

The Economist, Asia Edition (Weekly)
The Economist Newspaper Ltd.
1329 Chater Rd.
Hong Kong
Tel: [852] 28681425

Far Eastern Economic Review (Weekly)
Review Publishing Company Ltd.
6-7th Fl., 181-185 Gloucester Rd.
Hong Kong
Tel: [852] 28328381 Fax: [852] 28345571

Tokyo Business Today (Monthly)
Toyo Kezai, Inc.
1-2-1 Nihonbashi Hongokucho, Chuo-ku
Tokyo 103
Tel: (3) 3246-5740 Fax: (3) 3241-5543

RADIO & TELEVISION STATIONS

Asahi National Broadcasting Co. Ltd.
1-1, Roppongi 1-chome, Minato-ku
Tokyo 106
Tel: (3) 3587-5111 Fax: (3) 3505-3539

Fuji Television Network
3-1, Kawada-cho, Shinjuku-ku
Tokyo 162-88
Tel: (3) 3353-1111 Fax: (3) 3358-8038

Japan Broadcasting Corp. (NHK)
2-1, Jinnan 2-chome, Shibuya-ku
Tokyo 150
Tel: (3) 3465-1111 Fax: (3) 3481-1576

National Association of Commercial Broadcasters
3-23, Kioi-cho, Chiyoda-ku
Tokyo 102
Tel: (3) 3265-7481 Fax: (3) 3261-2860

Yomuri Telecasting Corp.
2-33, Shiromi 2-chome, Chuo-ku
Osaka 540-10
Tel: (6) 947-2298

INTERNET SITES

Japan Information Resource Center
http://futures.wharton.upenn.edu/~hernb108/jp.html

Japanese Sources of Information
http://pclsp2.kuicr.kyoto-u.ac.jp/4.html

JETRO (Japan External Trade Organization)
http://www.jetro.go.jp/index.html

Keidanren (Japan Federation of Economic Orgs.)
http://www.keidanren.or.jp

World Wide Web Sites in Japan
http://wisteria.jms.ac.jp/www-in-JP.html

Kenya
Republic of Kenya

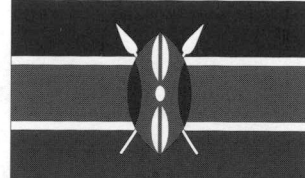

Economy

Overview

Kenya's economy is primarily focused on agriculture. Its rapid rate of population growth led to a decline in per capita output from 1991–1993. However, its current policy framework has begun to emphasize the role of a free market, and the economy has turned to market-based pricing incentives in place of price controls. A liberalized investment code and a newly liberalized foreign exchange system have also been put in place. But, while the government has made some progress in removing impediments to the development of a free market, reform remains far from complete. Divestiture has been slow, with few firms actually moving into private hands. Clashes among ethnic groups, centralized, single-party political control, and corruption and cumbersome bureaucratic procedures that delay and dissipate international donor aid have inhibited growth and continue to scare off investors. Still in process are major government programs to privatize state-run firms and reduce the size of the civil service.

Trade

Kenya is dependent on trade for virtually all of its raw and intermediate materials, as well as its capital and consumer goods. Because it exports low value-added commodity products, it runs a huge chronic trade deficit. Major exports include coffee—which accounts for 25 percent of total exports—tea, petroleum products, leather, pineapple, and soda ash. Imports include industrial machinery, crude oil, vehicles, and fertilizers. Kenya's major trading partner is the UK—accounting for about 20 percent of total trade—followed by Germany, Japan, the United Arab Emirates, the Netherlands, and the US.

Sectors

Agriculture This sector produces about 27 percent of GDP, while employing about 75 percent of the work force. Coffee and tea are the primary export crops, while pyrethrum, sisal, sugar cane, and cotton are also important cash crops. Corn (maize) and dairy farming are important domestically.

Industry Industry (including manufacturing) provides about 30 percent of GDP. Production is mostly on a small-scale, involving activities such as food processing, petroleum refining, chemicals, cement, paper, tobacco, textiles and apparel, leather, rubber, metals, ceramics, and electrical equipment.

Services Producing about 40 percent of Kenya's GDP, services are largely undeveloped, although tourism is a major and critical contributor of foreign exchange. Services employ about 60 percent of the work force, although there is considerable overlap among those who work part-time in agriculture.

Trends

In order to grow significantly, Kenya must begin to reduce its population growth, adopt business practices that are more in line with internationally accepted standards, and diminish its dependence on agricultural commodities. These changes require fundamental shifts in thinking and practice, and could take decades and billions of dollars to accomplish—as well as the backing of a strong, progressive political authority. So far, much of this has been lacking, and Kenya has had difficulties in attracting investment, primarily because it has so far been unwilling to comply with IMF guidelines. From an international perspective, ethnic strife and personalized politics have led to a deteriorating rather than an improving situation.

At a Glance

THE COUNTRY

Location Eastern Africa, bordering the northwestern Indian Ocean between Tanzania and Somalia.
Terrain Kenya rises from a low coastal plain on the Indian Ocean to central mountain ridges and plateaus above 3,000 meters (9,000 ft.).
Climate Varies from the tropical south, west, and central regions, to arid and semi-arid wasteland in the north and the northeast.

THE PEOPLE

Population 28,000,000
Ethnic composition
African
Kikuyu 22%
Luhya 14%
Luo 13%
Kalenjin 12%
Kamba 11%
Kisii 6%
Meru 6%
Other 16%
Religious composition
Indigenous beliefs 24%
Protestant 40%
Roman Catholic 30%
Muslim 6%
Languages spoken English, Swahili, and many local ethnic languages.
Education and literacy The government finances eight years of primary school. Adult literacy averages 69 percent of the population, with literate males outnumbering females. The four state universities enroll only 40 percent of the Kenyan students who qualify for admission.
Labor force
Total: 9,200,000
By occupation: agriculture 75-80%, non-agriculture 20-25%.

COUNTRY FACTS

Political and legal A parliamentary republic, Kenya's legal system is based on English common law, tribal law, and Islamic law.
Telephone The telecommunications system rates among the top of African systems. International country code: [254]. City codes: Mombasa (11), Nairobi (2).
Transportation Many international airlines serve Nairobi, and most major towns are linked by domestic flights. Passenger train services and inter-city bus services are good.
Environment Drought threatens agricultural lands. To preserve wildlife, the government has created national parks and game reserves. Current issues are deforestation, soil erosion, desertification, and poaching. Water pollution and degradation problems stem from urban and industrial waste and the increased use of pesticides and fertilizers.
Media More Kenyans tune into the 16 AM and 4 FM radio stations than the 6 television channels. There are five daily newspapers.
Health About 77 percent of Kenyans have access to health care services. The government is attempting to reduce malnutrition and diseases such as tuberculosis by improving existing health care facilities and opening new ones. Life expectancy of males is 51 years; of females, 55 years.

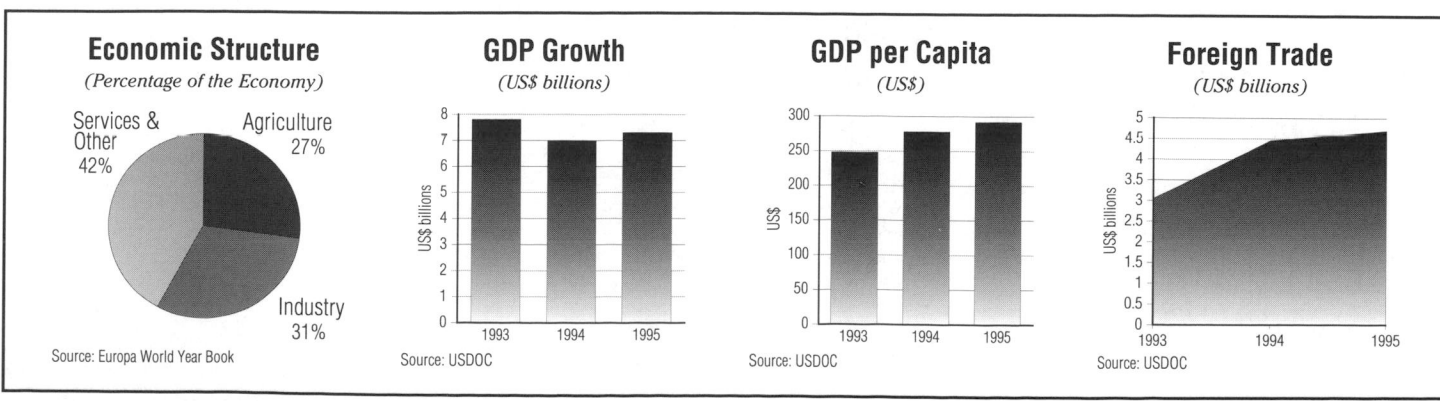

Economic Structure
(Percentage of the Economy)
Services & Other 42%
Agriculture 27%
Industry 31%
Source: Europa World Year Book

GDP Growth
(US$ billions)
1993 1994 1995
Source: USDOC

GDP per Capita
(US$)
1993 1994 1995
Source: USDOC

Foreign Trade
(US$ billions)
1993 1994 1995
Source: USDOC

Business Travel

LH 1906	MADRID		935	113-3
LH 1022	STUTTGART HBF.		935	-
AF 1701	LYON		940	683-6
AY 822	HELSINKI		940	113-3
AA 071	SFRANCISCO-DALLAS		945	731-7

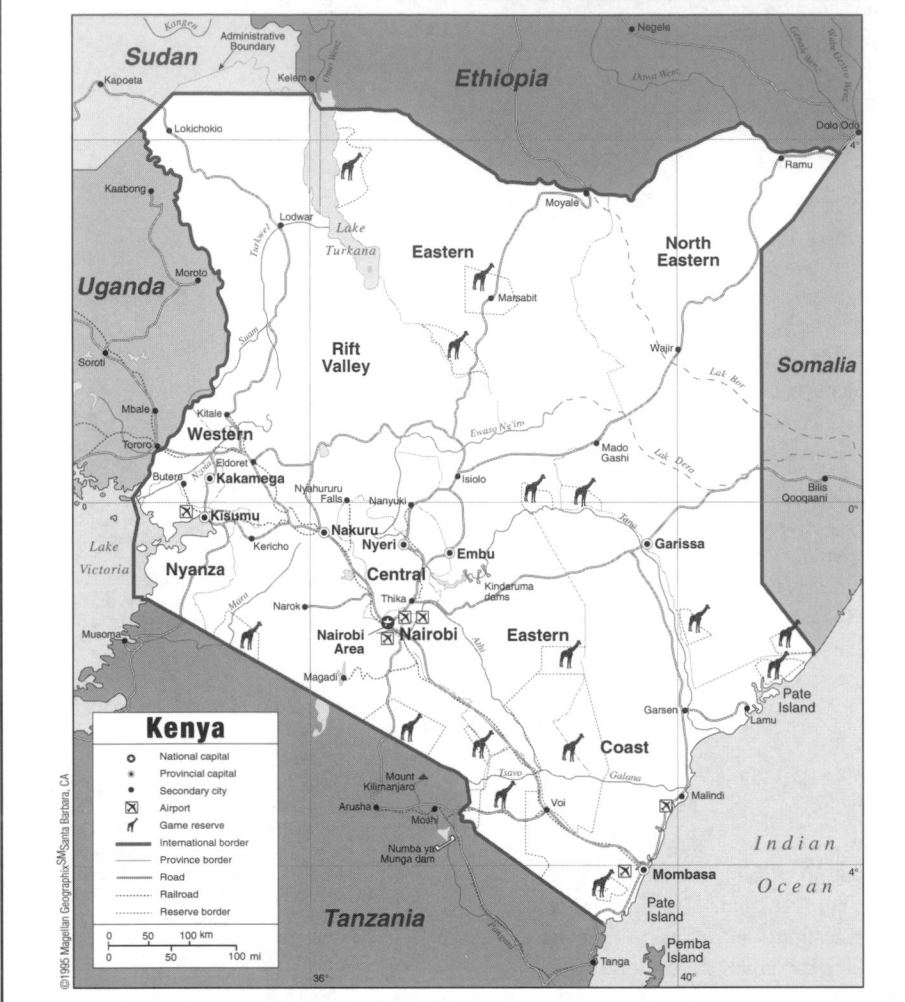

Travelogue

WORKWEEK

Offices Monday-Friday 8:00 am to 1:00 pm, 2:00 pm to 5:00 pm, Saturday 8:30 am to noon.
Banks Monday-Friday, 9:00 am to 2:00 pm, 1st and last Saturday 9:00 am to 11:00 am.
Government Monday-Friday 8:00 am to 1:00 pm, 2:00 pm to 5:00 pm.
Retail Monday-Saturday 8:00 am to 1:00 pm, 2:00 pm to 6:00 pm.

HOLIDAYS

Holidays 1996
January 1 New Year's Day
February 20-21 Id-Ul-Fitr*
April 5 Good Friday
April 8 Easter Monday
May 1 Labor Day
June 1 Madaraka Day
October 10 Moi Day
October 20 Kenyatta Day
December 12 Independence Day
December 25 Christmas Day
December 26 Boxing Day
*Actual date may vary.

VISA AND PASSPORT

For entry to Kenya, travelers must have a valid passport and a visitor's pass, which is issued at the port of entry with proof of adequate funds for the stay and an onward ticket. Visitors' passes are valid for three months and are renewable for up to one year. For any stay exceeding one year, visitors must obtain a visa from immigration authorities.

DEPARTURE FORMALITIES

An airport tax, payable in foreign currency only, will be charged at departure.

IMMUNIZATION

Vaccinations for yellow fever, tetanus, cholera, typhoid, and polio are recommended, though not required, for travelers unless arriving from other African countries. In this circumstance, proof of inoculation for yellow fever and cholera is required.

TIPPING PERCENT

Unless a service charge is already added, it is customary to include 10 percent for restaurant bills. Head porters will expect a tip and taxi drivers should receive no more than 10 percent.

CRIME

There are many incidents of street crime against tourists in downtown Nairobi, Mambosa, and at beach resorts. Assailants are often armed and not alone. It is advisable for tourists to not carry any valuables but to store them in hotel safety boxes. Carjackings and theft through open car windows are also frequent. Beware of individuals who may impersonate police or hotel employees.

INFRASTRUCTURE

Jomo Kenyatta Airport is located near Nairobi and provides all modern facilities and a 24-hour information center. Kenya Airways has many domestic flights connecting Nairobi to Mombasa, Malindi, and Kisumu. Sunbird has flights to Masai Mara and Lamu. Bus service provided by Kenya Airways is available to downtown Nairobi. Rail service is available to many business centers with first and second class overnight accommodations. Service is comfortable but may be unsafe during the rainy season due to lack of maintenance and safety checks. Roads are generally well built and maintained and service stations are located frequently along the highways. Remember to drive on the left side. Taxis are abundant in the major towns and are metered. Older, privately owned yellow-band taxis do not have meters and fares should be negotiated in advance. Cars can be rented by drivers who have had their driver's license for a minimum of two years.

COMMUNICATIONS

Telephones Direct dial service is available to major towns in Kenya and international service is acceptable.
Fax Use of facsimile machines is fairly uncommon but is increasing rapidly.
Post office The General Post Office in Nairobi is open 24 hours. All common postal services are available though are known to be unreliable. Air mail is delivered daily or weekly depending on the destination. Mailboxes are red and stamps are available at hotels and stores. Telex facilities are available at the Nairobi Post Office. Telegrams can be sent from the Post and Telegraph Office.
Radio/TV Kenya Broadcasting Services operates the radio and television service. Limited international news is broadcast.

BEST TRAVEL BOOKS

Lonely Planet, Kenya. A hand-sized, thorough guide with lots of information. 368 pages.
Insight Pocket Guides, Kenya. I can't think of another book which so effectively captures the essence of a country.
Do's and Taboo's Around the World. The Bestselling Guide to International Behavior. Edited by Roger Axtell, compiled by the Parker Pen Company. The ultimate guide to international behavior, now completely updated and expanded. Helpful, fun to read!
Africa on A Shoestring, Lonely Planet. Filled with useful information.

TELEPHONE NUMBERS

If you are calling from outside Kenya you will need to add the country code [254] and any other international dialing requirements from within your country.

- Operator 900
- Directory Assistance 991
- Emergency 999
- International Operator 196
- International Information 191; 991
- Kenya Railways...................................... (2) 221211
- Automobile Association........................... (2) 720382
- Police .... (2) 222222
- Taxi .... (2) 221666 or 225123
- Telegrams 990

Credit Card Information
Lost or stolen credit cards (call collect to the US, regardless of which country the card was issued in).
- Amex...[1] (919) 333-3211
- Diner's Club................................[1] (303) 799-1504
- MasterCard ....[1] (314) 275-6690
- Visa ....[1] (410) 581-7931

NATIONAL TOURIST OFFICE

Kenya Tourist Development Corp.
Uhuru Highway
Nairobi
Tel: (2) 330820

Foreign Trade

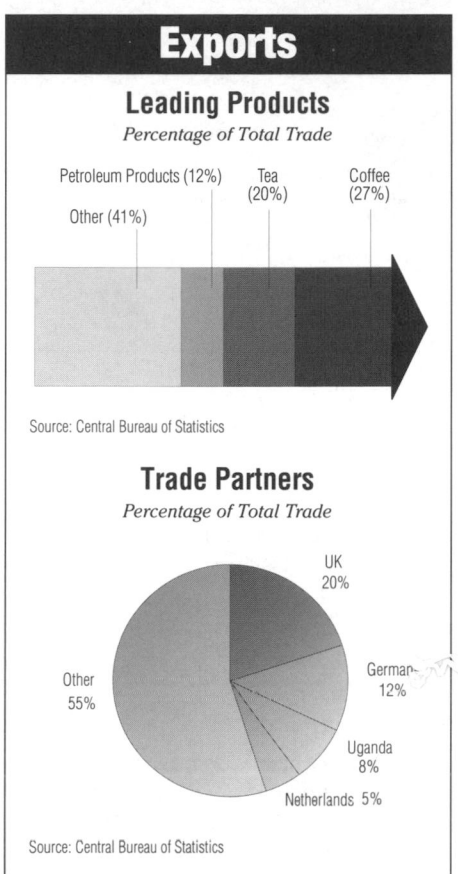

Imports

Leading Products
Percentage of Total Trade

Industrial Machinery (22%)
Crude Petroleum (12%)
Vehicles (8%)
Other (58%)

Source: Central Bureau of Statistics

Trade Partners
Percentage of Total Trade

- UK 20%
- UAE 11%
- Japan 12%
- Germany 9%
- Other 48%

Source: Central Bureau of Statistics

Exports

Leading Products
Percentage of Total Trade

Petroleum Products (12%)
Tea (20%)
Coffee (27%)
Other (41%)

Source: Central Bureau of Statistics

Trade Partners
Percentage of Total Trade

- UK 20%
- Germany 12%
- Uganda 8%
- Netherlands 5%
- Other 55%

Source: Central Bureau of Statistics

Opportunities

FOR IMPORTING TO KENYA
- crude petroleum
- machinery
- vehicles

FOR EXPORTING FROM KENYA
- coffee
- petroleum products
- textiles

GROWTH SECTORS
- petroleum products
- cement
- light manufacturing goods
- industrial products

Trade News

RULES AND REGULATIONS

- **Insurance** Kenyan importers must use local insurance companies for imports. Insurance companies must reinsure part of their business with a government of Kenya parastatal reinsurance company.
- **Commodity inspections** All commodities imported into Kenya are subject to pre-shipment inspection, including price comparison, by an inspection firm appointed by the Government of Kenya.
- **Tariffs** Kenya applies tariffs which are based on the international harmonized system (HS) of product classification.
- **Tariff reductions** Duties on a number of manufactured items have been reduced. Combined duty and value-added tax on automobiles ranges from 65 to 131 percent, as compared to over 200 percent previously.

Legal

Legal System

Kenya's legal system is based on a constitution, the Judicature Act of 1967, and common law court precedent. Although the judicial system is supposed to be independent of the government, the president has considerable authority over the courts.

Intellectual Property Rights

Patents and Trademarks Kenya's government has signed a unified system for the registration of patents from Anglophone Africa. It is a member of several international patent protection treaties, but the laws are rarely enforced. Trademarks are protected by statute and are registrable. However, Kenya's laws regarding trademarks and violations of them are frequently violated.

Copyrights There are few laws regarding copyright protection. There is a great deal of piracy, especially in the home video market, and penalties are insufficient to deter this practice.

Trade Secrets Kenya is a member of the World Intellectual Property Organization, but its laws regarding trade secret violations are rarely enforced.

Business Registration and Labor

All businesses must be registered with the Registrar, which must be provided with the following information: name and address of the company, the products and goods to be produced and /or distributed in Kenya, and the names and addresses of all board members. There is a severe shortage of technically skilled workers in Kenya. The trade union movement is strong and continues to pressure the government for better wages and living conditions. Complex rules severely limit any strikes.

Contracts and Dispute Resolution

Companies in Kenya prefer contracts to be in writing and signed by the parties involved. Disputes are usually settled in court, but resolution is usually lengthy because of backlogs. There is provision for enforcement in Kenya of certain foreign judgments and arbitration awards.

Legal Matters

LEGAL BRIEFS

- **Government control** The president can dismiss judges, the Attorney General, and other officials upon recommendation of a tribunal appointed by the president.
- **The High Court** The High Court consists of a chief justice and 24 associate judges, all appointed by the president.
- **Court of Appeal** Cases can be reviewed by the Court of Appeal, which has final appellate jurisdiction.
- **Miscellaneous courts** Questions of Islamic law are decided by qadis' courts. Military courts handle court martials of military personnel.
- **Membership of International and Regional Organizations** Kenya belongs to the Preferential Trade Area (PTA), Organization of African Unity, United Nations Organization, and the British Commonwealth.
- **Arbitration** Arbitration is not a popular method of dispute resolution and qualified arbitrators are difficult to find. Kenya is a signatory and has adopted the 1923 Protocol on Arbitration Clauses of the League of Nations and the 1958 New York Convention on the Recognition and Enforcement of Foreign Arbitral Awards.

LEGAL CONTACT

Ndungu Njoroge & Kwach
12th Floor, Bruce House
Standard Streeet
POB 41546
Nairobi
Tel: (2) 229281
Fax: (2) 215544

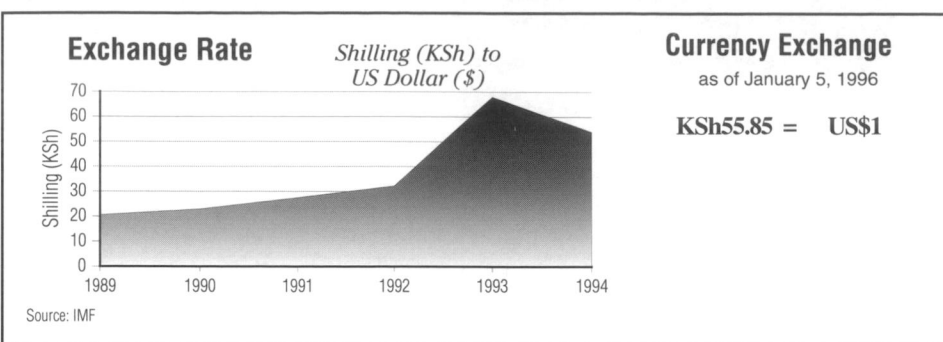

Exchange Rate

Shilling (KSh) to US Dollar ($)

Shilling (KSh)

70
60
50
40
30
20
10
0

1989 1990 1991 1992 1993 1994

Source: IMF

Currency Exchange

as of January 5, 1996

KSh55.85 =   US$1

Currency

The currency of Kenya is the shilling, represented by the symbol KSh. Its principal subdivision is 100 cents.

Foreign Exchange

The Central Bank of Kenya administers foreign exchange regulations through authorized commercial banks. These banks may transact forward exchanges in any currency, without limits or time restrictions.

Residents with foreign exchange earnings may open foreign currency accounts. Nonresidents with work permits in Kenya may also open foreign currency accounts and may credit their local earnings to these accounts. The use of funds in foreign currency accounts is not restricted.

Capital Transfers

Income for foreign investments earned after February 1994 can be remitted without approval from the Central Bank of Kenya, assuming all taxes have been paid. Non-Kenyans with a permit are allowed to operate foreign accounts and remit after-tax earnings without approval. Foreign investors are allowed limited participation in the local stock market. Exporters can retain all their foreign earnings in export retention accounts.

Investment Incentives

There is a one-time, 35 percent investment allowance tax deduction for the cost of investment for industrial plants and machinery in Nairobi and Mombasa, and 85 percent for those located outside these cities. A new investment code is expected to set clear guidelines for processing investment applications through the Investment Promotion Center (IPC).

Investment Restrictions

Until recently, Kenya required foreign investment to include local contact and employment targets. This requirement was waived by the government to encourage more foreign investment. Obtaining work permits for expatriates is still difficult, however. Foreigners also must meet certain total investment requirements.

Money Matters

BITS AND PIECES

- **Exchange** Exchange and market rates are unified. The market rate is determined on the basis of supply and demand in the interbank market, and the official exchange rate reflects the previous day's average market rate.
- **Capital** Transfers to all countries are regulated, and all imports and exports of securities require approval.
- **Investment** Investment of foreign funds in Kenya is generally not restricted, but to ensure future repatriation it is necessary to obtain official documentation for the investment.
- **Gold** Residents may hold and acquire gold coins in Kenya for collection purposes only. They are not allowed to hold or acquire gold in any form other than jewelry. Exports of gold other than personal jewelry require approval. Import licenses for gold are issued with restrictions.
- **Investment restrictions** Despite some easing of investment restrictions, some negative factors do exist. Foreign investors have limited access to domestic credit markets and are excluded from some government tenders.
- **Tax agreements** Kenya's eight tax treaties normally follow the Organization for Economic Cooperation and Development model for the prevention of double taxation of income.
- **Preferential treatment** In approving new investments, the government gives preference to foreign equity capital which brings with it management skill, technical know-how, risk bearing, and profitability.
- **Investment expectations** Foreign investors are expected to be domestic resource-use intensive and base their operations outside the congested centers of Nairobi and Mombasa.

BANKS

Barclays Bank of Kenya Ltd.
Bank House
Moi Ave.
POB 30120
Nairobi
Tel: (2) 332230
Fax: (2) 335219
Telex: 22210

Biahara Bank of Kenya Ltd.
Investment House
Muindi Mbingu St.
POB 30831
Nairobi
Tel: (2) 221064
Telex: 25161

Central Bank of Kenya
Haile Selassie Avenue
POB 60000
Nairobi
Tel: (2) 226431

Commercial Bank of Africa Ltd.
Commercial Bank Bldg
corner Wabera and Standard Sts
POB 30437
Nairobi
Tel: (2) 228881
Fax: (2) 335827
Telex: 23205

National Bank of Kenya Ltd.
National Bank Bldg.
Harambee Ave.
POB 72866
Nairobi
Tel: (2) 226471
Fax: (2) 330784
Telex: 22619

Trade Bank Ltd.
Trustforte Bldg
Moi Ave
POB 46342
Nairobi
Tel: (2) 226413
Fax: (2) 334995
Telex: 25143

TAXATION	At a Glance	
Taxation requires sophisticated knowledge of complex rules and regulations specific to each country. The information presented here is from the Ernst & Young Corporate Tax Guide and Directory, available from the Ernst & Young accounting office in your country, or from: **Ernst & Young** Mail Address: POB 44286 Nairobi Tel: (2) 727640 Fax: (2) 716271	Corporate Income Tax Rate (%)(a)	35
	Capital Gains Tax Rate (%)	0
	Branch Tax Rate (%)	42.5
	Withholding Tax (%)	
	Dividends (2)	10
	Interest (b)	5
	Royalties (b)	20
	Insurance Commissions (b)	5
	Management and Professional fees (b)	20
	Branch Remittance Tax (c)	0
	Net Operating Losses (Years)	
	Carryback	0
	Carryforward	Unlimited
	(b) Applicable to payments to nonresidents. A 10% withholding tax is imposed on payments to residents.	
	(c) Applicable only to payments to nonresidents.	
	(d) Applicable only to payments to residents. The rate is 5% for brokers and 10% for all others.	

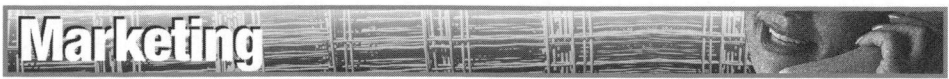

Marketing

Overview

Although much of Kenyan industry is state-owned and losing money, its markets are some of the most open on the African continent.

Distribution

Major cash crops are marketed through cooperatives and marketing boards; minor cash crops are handled by traders who are also wholesale distributors. Nairobi, the capital, is also the commercial hub of East Africa. Most regional firms have offices here. The city also serves as a retail center for much of the surrounding area; most marketing services are available. Mombasa is the leading port and major distribution center for the country; goods pass through here on their way to Uganda, Rwanda, Burundi, and eastern Zaire. Several large import/export firms, and many smaller ones, are based here. Other significant trading centers are in Nakuru, Eldoret, and Kisumu.

Agents, Distributors, and Partners

Agents usually distribute consumer goods and raw materials. Always visit the country to choose an agent; firsthand knowledge is the best way to assess the relative merits of agents or distributors. The large, well-established import houses are often overburdened with agencies and rarely choose to properly promote new product lines. Though smaller agents may lack capital and high-level contacts, they usually devote considerable energy to their goods. Local produce trading and wholesale distribution may be closely linked, particularly in rural districts.

Advertising

Several agencies headquartered in Nairobi offer a full range of promotion services. Most distributors look to their suppliers to provide promotional support, particularly with a new product. The Voice of Kenya, the government-owned broadcasting company, offers advertising on both its radio and television stations. Short films are also a common means for advertising consumer articles. Billboards are prohibited in urban areas but can be used in rural locations. Neon signs are used sparingly, most often in railway stations.

Business Culture

Greeting and Courtesies

Shaking hands is the customary greeting in Kenya, and there are many different types of shakes for different relationships. For example, a long, extended clasp for well-known acquaintances and a brief, standard handshake for someone you've just met. When greeting a person of elder status, grasp your right wrist with your left hand while shaking hands. Kenyans tend to be conservative and formal in business situations. Titles, such as Doctor and Professor, should always be used when applicable. Expect to know someone a while before using their first name. Initial greeting periods in Kenya are always marked by a rather lengthy period of basic questions about your family, country, etc. Politics is an acceptable area of conversation in Kenya, but subjects such as sex and local rituals are considered taboo. Women do not look men in the eye upon greeting.

Business Ethic and Framework

The Kenyan business community functions through a wide network of tightly interconnected personal relationships, often based on family or tribal affiliations. Local personal references are crucial for a foreigner seeking to do business in Kenya. English is the primary language of Kenyan business, and business cards in English, which are essential, should be prepared before your arrival. Standards of punctuality are somewhat loose, and delays and general tardiness should always be expected and tolerated. A general climate of formality does prevail in Kenyan business, however, and a conservative, patient demeanor is always recommended.

Decision Making

As in most highly bureaucratic systems, decisions in Kenyan business almost invariably come from the few people at the top of a particular company or organization. Further, expect progress in your business venture to come very slowly and only after extensive personal interaction between you and your contacts, as Kenyans like to feel they truly know you before reaching any agreements. Don't try to rush any business decision, or you may destroy the entire relationship.

Marketing in Kenya

MARKETING TIPS

- **Publications** Two daily and two Sunday newspapers are published in English; a daily and various weeklies in Swahili; and several trade and professional magazines in English.
- **Trade fairs** Several international trade fairs are held annually; the Nairobi Show, usually held the last week of September, is the best known.
- **After sales support** Kenyan businesspeople prefer to buy from international sources with an established after sales service. An effective servicing and after sale system is recommended in this market to be competitive.
- **Retailers** The distribution system, especially at the retail level, consists of outlets small by international standards. Wholesalers are also retailers. They purchase goods from manufacturers and then distribute them through retail outlets to their customers.
- **Selling techniques** Common methods of selling are through retail outlets, agents or distributors, established wholesalers or dealers, or selling directly to the end-users who include government agencies and other private local organizations.
- **Franchising** In general, franchising has not been successful in Kenya. The main impediments have been infringement of the franchise agreement by the franchisees coupled with incompetent management.
- **Selling to the government** All major government of Kenya procurements are done through a tendering (bidding) system.

AD AGENCIES

Ayton Young & Rubicam
5th Fl., Longonot Place
Kijabe St.
Nairobi
Tel: (2) 334-356, 334-357

MCL
MCL HouseMulthithi Rd.
Museum HIll
Nairobi
Tel: (2) 748-070
Fax: (2) 748-148

Cultural Cautions

DO'S

- Always obtain a written contract for any agreements you may reach.
- Always make appointments at least two weeks in advance, then reconfirm shortly before the date.
- Always ask permission before photographing the locals; don't take a picture of anything bearing the Kenyan flag.

DON'TS

- Don't wear formal attire; that is reserved for members of the diplomatic corps.
- Avoid making appointments around the holiday periods of Christmas/New Year's, Ramadan, Easter, or, for that matter, the rainy season—April through June—as many Kenyans are on vacation during those times.

OBSERVATIONS

- Kenyan businessmen dress in the British fashion. A two- or three-piece suit is standard in Nairobi. In the coastal regions, however, a more casual style is acceptable, including wearing open-necked shirts and shorts to meetings. When dining at a restaurant, a jacket and tie is standard. Women should wear dresses or skirts. The wearing of traditional Kenyan clothes by a foreigner is appreciated, provided they are worn correctly.
- Women in the Kenyan business community are still relatively rare. A foreign woman sent to do business in Kenya should dress very conservatively, conduct herself with the utmost tact and seriousness, and preferably be accompanied by her spouse.

Contacts

GOVERNMENT AGENCIES

Ministry of Agriculture, Livestock, Development and Marketing
Kilimo House
Cathedral Road
POB 30028
Nairobi
Tel: (2) 728370
Fax: (2) 720586

Ministry of Commerce and Industry
Cooperative House
Haile Selassie Avenue
POB 30430
Nairobi
Tel: (2) 340010

Ministry of Culture and Social Services
Reinsurance Plaza
Taifa Road
POB 45958
Nairobi
Tel: (2) 339650

Ministry of Education
New Jogoo House
Harambee Avenue
POB 30040
Nairobi
Tel: (2) 228411
Fax: (2) 214287

Ministry of Environment and Natural Resources
Kencom House
POB 30126
Nairobi
Tel: (2) 229261

Ministry of Finance
Treasury Building
Harambee Avenue
POB 3000
Nairobi
Tel: (2) 338111
Fax: (2) 330426

Ministry of Foreign Affairs and International Cooperation
Harambee House
POB 30551
Harambee Avenue
Nairobi
Tel: (2) 334433
Fax: (2) 335494

Ministry of Information and Broadcasting
Jogoo House "A"
Harambee Avenue
POB 30025
Nairobi
Tel: (2) 228411
Fax: (2) 332797

Ministry of Labor and Manpower Development
National Social Security House
Bishops Road
POB 40326
Nairobi
Tel: (2) 729800

Ministry of Research, Technical Training and Technology
Utalii House
Uhuru Highway
POB 30568
Nairobi
Tel: (2) 336173
Fax: (2) 219420

Ministry of Transportation and Communication
Transcom House
Ngong Road
POB 52692
Nairobi
Tel: (2) 729200

Industrial and Commercial Development Corporation
Uchumi House
POB 45519
Nairobi

Tel: (2) 29213
Fax: (2) 333880

Kenya Industrial Research and Development Institute
POB 30650
Nairobi
Tel: (2) 557762

BUSINESS AND TRADE ORGANIZATIONS

Industrial and Commercial Development Corp.
Aga Khan Walk
Nairobi
Tel: (2) 229213

Kenya Association of Manufacturers
PO Box 30225
Nairobi
Tel: (2) 736005

Kenya External Trade Authority
PO Box 43137
Nairobi
Tel: (2) 333555

Kenya National Trading Corp.
Nkrumah Ave.
Nairobi
Tel: (2) 29141

Investment Promotion Centre
(Advises Local and Foreign Prospective Investors)
National Bank Building, 8th Floor
Harambee Avenue
POB 55704
Nairobi
Tel: (2) 221401

NEWSPAPERS

Daily Nation
POB 49010
Nairobi
Tel: (2) 337691

Kenrail
POB 30121
Nairobi
Tel: (2) 221211
Telex: 22254

Kenya Gazette
POB 30746
Nairobi
Tel: (2) 334075

Kenya Leo
POB 30958
Nairobi
Tel: (2) 337798

Kenya Times
POB 30958
Nairobi
Tel: (2) 24251
Telex: 25008

Sunday Times
POB 30958
Nairobi
Tel: (2) 337798
Telex: 25008

The Standard
POB 30080
Nairobi
Tel: (2) 540280,

Taifa Weekly
POB 49010
Nairobi
Tel: (2) 337691
Fax: 553939
Telex: 24032

STOCK EXCHANGE

Nairobi Stock Exchange
Kimathi St.
Nairobi
Tel: (2) 230692

PERIODICALS

Afya
POB 30125
Nairobi
Tel: 501301
Telex: 23254
Fax: 22244

Busara
POB 30022
Nairobi

East African Agricultural and Forestry Journal
POB 30148
Nairobi

Eastern African Economic Review
Economic Review of Agriculture
POB 30028
Nairobi
Tel: (2) 728370
Telex: 33042

Education in Eastern Africa
POB 5869
Nairobi

Inside Kenya Today
POB 8053
Nairobi
Tel: (2) 223201
Telex: 22244

RADIO & TELEVISION

Kenya Broadcasting Corporation
Broadcasting House
POB 30456
Nairobi
Tel: (2) 334567
Telex: 25361

LEGAL CONTACTS

Hamiltion Harrison & Matthews
I.C.E.A. Building
Kenyatta Ave
POB 30333
Nairobi
Tel: (2) 330870
Fax: (2) 222318

Kaplan & Stratton
Queensway House
Kaunda Street
POB 40111
Nairobi
Tel: (2) 335333
Fax: (2) 340827

Ndungu Njoroge & Kwach
12th Floor, Bruce House
Standard Street
POB 41546
Nairobi
Tel: (2) 229281
Fax: (2) 215544

INTERNET ADDRESSES

Usenet group(s):
soc.culture.african

Africa - Kenya
http://www.sas.upenn.edu/African_Studies/Country_Specific/Kenya.html

City Net - Kenya
http://www.city.net/countries/kenya/

Kenya Homepage
http://www.ms.uky.edu/~rbowen/index.html

Kuwait

State of Kuwait

Economy

Overview

The Kuwaiti economy is driven by oil production and related industries. Since the Iraqi occupation and the Persian Gulf War in 1990-91, Kuwait has expended large sums to reconstruct its infrastructure. Although demand for oil has been strong and the country's wells and refineries have rebounded, the non-oil economy has been more sluggish, due in large part to the changing demographics after the war. Kuwait's population has dropped by more than 20 percent from pre-war levels. Further, many of the Palestinians who previously lived in Kuwait with their families were expelled following the war and have been replaced by single guest workers who tend to send more of their earnings home rather than spend them in the local economy. Despite the continuation of a substantial trade surplus, reconstruction expenditures have significantly reduced Kuwaiti assets and are forcing a reassessment of the existing economic system. Calls are also heard for a reassessment of Kuwait's archaic social and political systems, but to date no changes have been seen in this arena.

Trade

Major exports include petroleum—accounting for more than 85 percent of all exports—machinery, natural gas, basic manufactures, and chemicals. Kuwait must import most of its needs, including foodstuffs, transportation equipment, chemicals, electrical and nonelectrical machinery, and apparel. Following the war, Kuwait has increased its imports of military technology and construction equipment and materials. Major trade partners include Japan, Italy, the Netherlands, the US, Taiwan, and the UK.

Sectors

Agriculture This sector is of minimal importance to the economy, providing only about one percent of both GDP and employment. Production is almost surely for local consumption; fishing satisfies 25 percent of local demand and horticultural crops such as melons, dates, tomatoes, and onions are grown.

Industry The industrial sector contributes nearly 60 percent of GDP and 25 percent of employment. Petroleum extraction and processing is the main activity; food processing plays a minor role.

Services Services produce about 40 percent of GDP but employ over 50 percent of the work force. Much of the high-value-added service area consists of management of overseas financial investments. The government is beginning to privatize many service areas that were formerly state-run, including tourism and health care. Many lower level service occupations are filled by guest workers.

Trends

The Kuwaiti government is currently in the process of implementing plans to privatize telecommunications, housing, power generation, and health care operations. The government is also attempting to alleviate its demographic mix problem by allowing expatriate guest workers to bring their families into the country, which should help strengthen the economy as more wages are spent in Kuwait. Investments are also being made with outsiders to develop secondary industries, such as petrochemicals and plastics, although to date the focus remains almost exclusively on petroleum-based products. There is also a growing dissatisfaction with the autocratic political structure, which will need to be addressed to attract long-term, outside investment.

At a Glance

THE COUNTRY
Location Middle East, at the head of the Persian Gulf, between Iraq and Saudi Arabia.
Terrain Flat to slightly undulating desert plain.
Climate Intensely hot and dry in summers, plus short, cool winters with limited rain.

THE PEOPLE
Population 1,800,000
Ethnic composition
Kuwaiti 45%
Other Arab 35%
South Asian 9%
Iranian... 4%
Other.. 7%
Religious composition
Muslim (Shi'a 30%, Sunni 45%, other 10%) 85%
Christian, Hindu, Parsi, and other........................ 15%
Languages spoken Arabic (official), English.
Education and literacy The 74 percent literacy rate is one of the Arab world's highest. The government provides free public school education, including living expenses, from the primary grades through adult education. It also sends many students abroad for degrees not offered at Kuwait University.
Labor force
Total:...566,000
By occupation: services 45%, construction 20%, trade 12%, manufacturing 9%, finance and real estate 2.6%, agriculture 2%, power and water 2%, and mining and quarrying 1%.

COUNTRY FACTS
Political and legal This nominal constitutional monarchy is ruled by an Amir in conjunction with a freely elected parliament. The civil law system includes rule by Islamic law in personal matters. Kuwait has not accepted International Court of Justice jurisdiction.
Telephone One of the best telecommunication systems in the Middle East. A variety of locations can provide international service. The government controls telephone services, which are fully automatic. International country code: [965]. City codes are not required.
Transportation A modern network of roads and all-weather highways provide most land transport; almost all highways are paved. There are no railways. There are five seaports with significant shipping traffic. One major airport offers good international air transportation with modern facilities.
Environment There is no arable land. The Persian Gulf War caused severe environmental problems for the nation's water supply; large quantities of oil were released into the environment. All Kuwait's water comes from wells and sea water processed in some of the world's largest and most sophisticated desalination facilities. Current issues are air and water pollution and desertification.
Media There are two government-controlled TV stations. Radio Kuwait broadcasts in several languages. Several daily newspapers and monthly magazines are published in Kuwait.
Health Free, government-sponsored medical services are highly advanced. Birth rate is 29.4 births per 1,000; death rate is 2.37 deaths per 1,000. Life expectancy of males is 72.8 years; of females, 77 years.

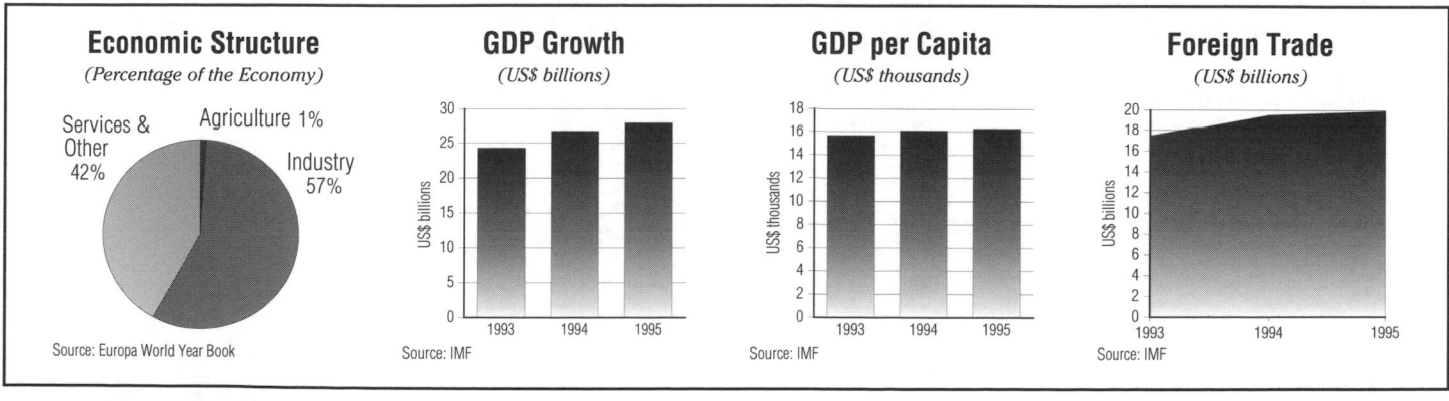

Economic Structure (Percentage of the Economy)
Services & Other 42%
Agriculture 1%
Industry 57%
Source: Europa World Year Book

GDP Growth (US$ billions)
Source: IMF

GDP per Capita (US$ thousands)
Source: IMF

Foreign Trade (US$ billions)
Source: IMF

Business Travel

LH 1906	MADRID	935	113-3
LH 1022	STUTTGART HBF.	935	
AF 1701	LYON	940	583-6
AY 822	HELSINKI	940	113-3
AA 071	SFRANCISCO-DALLAS	945	731-7

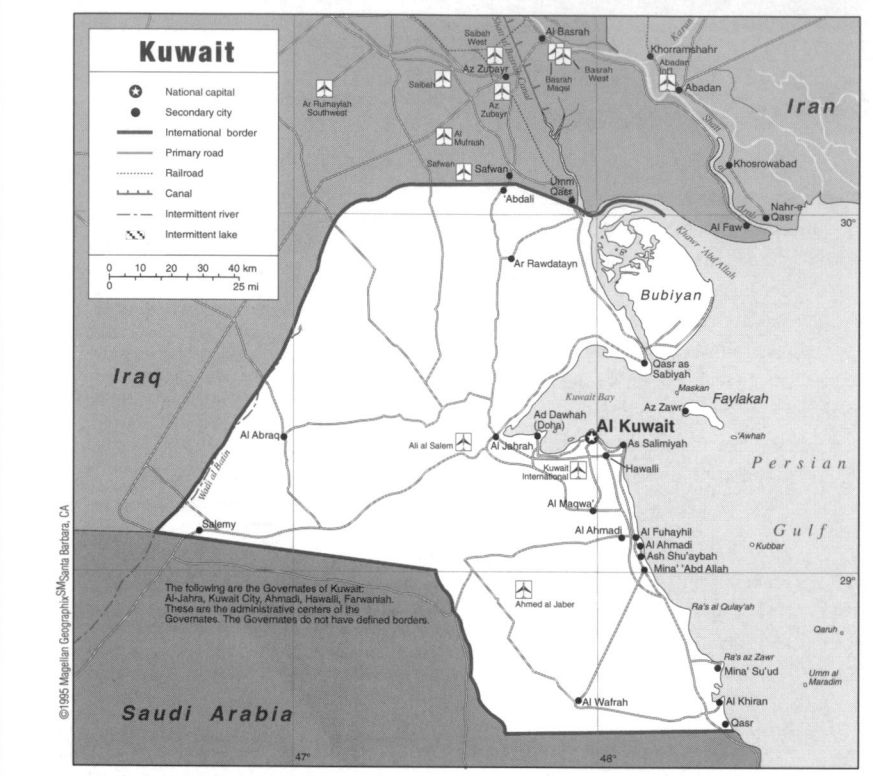

COMMUNICATIONS

Telephones Telephone service in Kuwait is good but has been somewhat inconsistent in the past. International calls can be made from most phones and direct dialing is possible to many destinations. Public phones can be found in shops and hotels.

Fax Services are available in larger hotel business centers and Abdulla Al-Salim is open 24-hours providing international calling, fax, and telex services.

Post office Postal service is adequate. Surface mail is painfully slow and should be avoided. Private couriers are widely used for mail within Kuwait. When addressing mail, use post office addresses, not street numbers.

BEST TRAVEL BOOKS

The Traveler's Guide to Middle Eastern and North African Customs and Manners. Elizabeth Devine & Nancy Braganti. How to converse, dine, tip, bargain, dress, make friends, and conduct business while in the Middle East and North Africa. A must read book.
Middle East, Lonely Planet On a Shoestring. Easy to read, filled with details! 126 maps.
Do's and Taboo's Around the World. The Bestselling Guide to International Behavior. 3rd edition. Edited by Roger Axtell, compiled by the Parker Pen Company. The ultimate guide to international behavior, now completely updated and expanded. Helpful, fun to read!
The Multinational Travel Companion Executive, Twenty-third edition. Strand Publishing Company, Inc., Travel tips world-wide.

USEFUL TELEPHONE NUMBERS

If you are calling from outside Kuwait, you will need to add the country code [965] and any other international dialing requirements from within your country.

- Information 101
- International Operator 104
- Police 102
- Fire 105
- Emergency 109
- Kuwait Airways 4345555, 4346666
- Directory 2444777
- Taxi 2446720
- Business Government Information 2449200
- Bank of Kuwait 2459771
- Industrial Investment 2429073
- Foreign Bureau 2412044
- Stock Exchange 2423130
- Chamber of Commerce 2433864
- Ministry of Communication 4819033
- Ministry of Finance 2468200

Car Rental
- Avis 2453828
- Rent-Al-Mullah 2530000

Hotels
- Carlton Tower: Al-Hilali St 2452740
- Meridien: Al-Hilali St 2455550
- Hunt Room: Sheraton Hilton 2422055
- Mais Alghanim, Arabian Gulf St. 245550

Credit Card Information
Lost or stolen credit cards (call collect to the US, regardless of which country the card was issued in).
- Amex .... [1] (919) 3333211
- Diner's Club .... [1] (303) 7991504
- MasterCard .... [1] (314) 2756690
- Visa .... [1] (410) 5817931

Travelogue

WORKWEEK

Offices Saturday-Wednesday, generally 8:00 am to 5:00 pm, although some close from 12:30 to 4:30 pm and remain open until 8:30 pm, and Thursdays 8:00 am to 1:00 pm.
Banks Saturday-Thursday, 8:00 am to noon.
Government Saturday-Wednesday, 7:30 am to 1:30 pm and Thursday 7:30 to 11:00 am.
Retail Saturday-Wednesday, 8:30 am to 12:30 pm and 4:30 to 9:00 pm.
Friday is a day of rest in Kuwait. When a holiday occurs on Friday, the following day is also a holiday. Hours are shorter during Ramadan.

HOLIDAYS

Holidays 1996
January 1 New Year's Day
January 1 Ascension Day
February 25 National Day
February 26-27 Liberation Day
February 2-21 Eid-Al-Fitr*
April 28-Mar 1 Eid-Al-Adha*
May 20-21 Islamic New Year*
July 28 Birth of the Prophet*
December 25 Christmas
*Dates are based on a lunar calendar and vary each year.

VISA AND PASSPORT

Passports and visas are required for foreigners traveling to Kuwait and must be valid for six months beyond departure date. Two photographs are needed. Visas must be acquired prior to entry. Business visas need letters of guarantee from your company, and must be sponsored by the visiting Kuwaiti company. Large hotels will arrange for and sponsor your visa, which must be collected from a Kuwait Embassy. Entry is prohibited to holders of Israeli passports. Travelers must hold onward tickets, valid travel documents, and sufficient funds.

DEPARTURE FORMALITIES

A departure tax of KD2 must be paid, children under 12 and transit passengers are exempt.

IMMUNIZATION

No vaccinations are necessary unless visitors are arriving from an area infected with yellow fever. Cholera and typhoid vaccinations are advised.

TIPPING

Tipping is not expected but is appreciated. Hotels: None. Restaurants, barbers, and beauticians: 10 percent. Baggage carriers at the airports are tipped 250 fils per piece. Taxi drivers are tipped only for long journeys.

CRIME

The crime rate in Kuwait is moderate. Physical and verbal harassment of women has become an increasing problem. Avoid travel near the demilitarized zone; if required, notify your embassy.

INFRASTRUCTURE

Kuwait has well-developed road and telecommunication networks and hotel, taxi, and car rental industries. Public transportation is available but is not considered reliable. The Kuwait International Airport is fully functioning. Buses are not available. Roads are paved and motorways link Kuwait City to Ahmadi, Mina al-Ahmadi, and other centers of population in Kuwait, and to the Iraqi and Saudi Arabian borders.

NATIONAL TOURIST OFFICE

Touristic Enterprises Co
POB 2331, 13094 Safat
Kuwait City
Tel: 5652775
Telex: 22801
Fax: 5657594

Foreign Trade

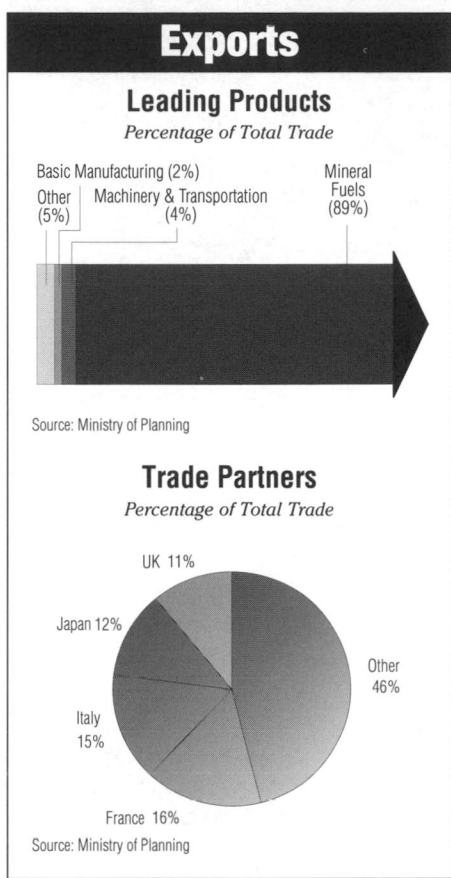

Imports

Leading Products
Percentage of Total Trade

Machinery & Transportation (58%)
Basic Manufacturing (11%)
Misc. Articles Manufacturing (15%)
Other (16%)

Source: Ministry of Planning

Trade Partners
Percentage of Total Trade

Canada 9%
UK 9%
Japan 12%
US 35%
Other 35%

Source: Ministry of Planning

Exports

Leading Products
Percentage of Total Trade

Basic Manufacturing (2%)
Other (5%)
Machinery & Transportation (4%)
Mineral Fuels (89%)

Source: Ministry of Planning

Trade Partners
Percentage of Total Trade

UK 11%
Japan 12%
Italy 15%
France 16%
Other 46%

Source: Ministry of Planning

Opportunities

FOR IMPORTING TO KUWAIT

- construction equipment
- foods, materials, clothing
- industrial, military, consumer products
- vehicles and parts

FOR EXPORTING FROM KUWAIT

- oil

GROWTH SECTORS
- high-tech industry
- agriculture
- petroleum processing

Trade News

RULES AND REGULATIONS

- **Trade news** Kuwait has one of the most competitive markets in the Arab world. It has massive oil reserves and almost no import duties.
- **Import licenses** Importers have to obtain an annual import license from the Ministry of Commerce and Industry which authorizes them to import, on a multiple-entry basis during the one-year term. To obtain this license, importing companies must be registered in the commercial register at the Ministry of Commerce and Industry, as well as the Kuwait Chamber of Commerce and Industry (KCCI). The Kuwait shareholding in the capital of the company must be at least 51 percent.

Legal

Legal System

Kuwait is a politically stable emirate; it operates as a constitutional monarchy.

Intellectual Property Rights

Patents and trademarks Kuwait does have patent and trademark protection laws though they are not actively enforced, except for some individual customs checks for imitation goods and/or trademarks. Penalties for infringement are light. Patented products and processes are protected for only 15 years.

Copyrights Kuwait has no copyright law though one as been proposed. Presently, all published material, including audio and videotapes, are treated as public property. This has led to a thriving market in pirated computer software, videotapes, audiotapes, and unauthorized Arabic translations of books.

Business Registration

Businesses wishing to operate in the country must do so through approved joint ventures with Kuwaiti firms or through registered agreements with Kuwaiti government agencies.

Contracts and Dispute Resolution

Parties can either directly appoint an arbitrator by agreement, or can apply to the court to appoint an arbitrator. An additional advantage to arbitration of business disputes involving foreigners is that all court proceedings in Kuwait are in Arabic, but arbitrations are not required to be so.

Labor

All workers have the right to establish and join unions but the government restricts this right by limiting the number of unions that may be established. The right to strike is limited by laws which stipulate compulsory negotiation and arbitration. There are no laws to prohibit retribution against strikers. In the public sector, Kuwaiti employees receive higher wages than foreign workers. No minimum wage laws exist in the private sector.

Legal Matters

LEGAL BRIEFS

- **Work conditions** The maximum work week in the public sector is 48 hours, with one full day of rest per week. Civil service law provides for a minimum 14-day leave annually. Practices are different in the private sector.
- **Employee right to work** It is difficult to terminate employees without complying with certain notice and compensation requirements.
- **Property** Foreign nationals may not own real property and government regulations have made it difficult for expatriates to sponsor their families in the country. There are exceptions for Gulf Cooperation Council members.
- **Trade agreements** Kuwait has adopted some import regulations to conform with the Gulf Cooperation Council to which it belongs.
- **Foreign workers** Foreign laborers frequently face contractual disputes and poor working conditions.
- **Labor laws** Compliance and enforcement of health, safety, medical care, and compensation laws are poor.
- **Foreign investor discrimination** Foreign corporations and foreign interests are taxed and foreign investors are prohibited from having majority ownership in Kuwaiti businesses.
- **Investment limits** The government discourages joint ventures in the oil, insurance, banking, and finance sectors.
- **International property rights groups** Kuwait is not party to any worldwide conventions for intellectual property right protection and there are no adequate deterrents to piracy.

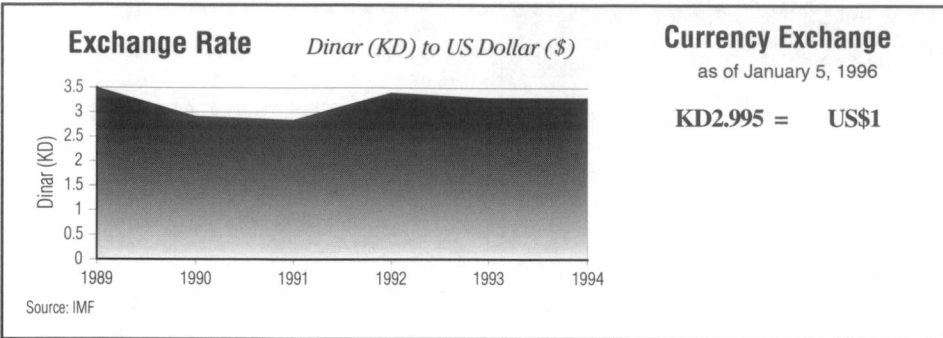

Exchange Rate *Dinar (KD) to US Dollar ($)*

Dinar (KD): 0, 0.5, 1, 1.5, 2, 2.5, 3, 3.5

1989 1990 1991 1992 1993 1994

Source: IMF

Currency Exchange
as of January 5, 1996

KD2.995 =   US$1

Currency

The currency of Kuwait is the Kuwaiti dinar; its symbol is KD. It is divided into 10 dirhams and 1,000 fils.

Foreign Exchange

The Central Bank of Kuwait does not impose foreign exchange restrictions. The only requirement for capital account transactions in Kuwait is that all foreign exchange purchases be made through a bank or licensed foreign exchange dealer. The Kuwaiti dinar is freely convertible, and both residents and non-residents may buy and sell most foreign currencies in Kuwait. Nonresidents may open accounts in dinars and foreign currencies.

Capital Transfers

Capital from loans, interest, dividends, profits, fees, and personal savings can be transferred in or out of Kuwait freely. On capital transfers out of Kuwait, however, a large portion of Kuwait's foreign investment is mediated by public agencies and corporations. There are no taxes or subsidies on purchases or sales of foreign exchange. The forward market for dinar trading has been suspended since the war with Iraq.

Investment Incentives

The Kuwaiti government is currently developing more incentives to attract foreign investment. Some current investments include exemptions from import duties and corporate income taxes for a period of up to 10 years. They are available only for industrial projects approved by the Council of Ministers and in which Kuwaiti citizens hold a majority share.

Investment Restrictions

Kuwait has several foreign investment restrictions. No matter what a foreign firm sells, it should never underestimate the skill and patience with which its Kuwaiti counterpart will bargain. The licensing authority of the Ministry of Commerce and Industry screens all proposals for direct foreign investment. In the past, this has been used to encourage investments in higher technology industries. The primary restriction on foreign investment is that foreigners cannot invest in the most profitable industries—oil, insurance, and banking. In other industries, foreign enterprises are often taxed while their Kuwaiti competitors are not.

Money Matters

BITS AND PIECES

- **Exchange rates** Exchange rates for the Kuwaiti dinar are determined on the basis of a fixed relationship between the Kuwaiti dinar and a weighted basket of currencies, reflecting the relative importance of each currency in Kuwait's trade and financial relations.
- **Capital** Capital may be transferred without restrictions into or out of Kuwait in any currency by either residents or nonresidents. Transactions on the Kuwait Stock Exchange are subject to the approval of the Exchange Committee.
- **Gold** Monetary authorities and merchants registered with the Ministry of Commerce and Industry may import and export gold in any form, provided that such gold is not less than 18-karat fine. Gold jewelry may not be imported or sold unless it is properly hallmarked. Residents may buy, hold, and sell gold in any form without restrictions or license, and nonresidents may hold gold in any form without restrictions or license.
- **Private ownership** Private ownership is respected in Kuwait, but foreigners face special restrictions. Licenses from the Ministry of Commerce and Industry are required for all new companies, and some sectors of the economy are dominated by state-owned monopolies.
- **Investments** Investment by foreigners is restricted in several ways: There is a bar on majority ownership, Kuwaiti nationals must own 51 percent of a company's stock; there is also a bar on investment in prohibited sectors such as oil and financial services; and there is a different corporate tax structure where foreign investors pay to the extent of their ownership, while Kuwaiti firms do not pay at all.

BANKS

Al Ahli Bank of Kuwait
POB 1387
Safat 13014
Tel: 2400900
Fax: 2424557

Bank of Bahrain and Kuwait
POB 24396
Safat 13104
Tel: 2417140
Fax: 2440937

Bank of Kuwait and the Middle East
POB 71
Safat 13001
Tel: 2459771
Fax: 2461430

Burgan Bank
POB 5389
Safat 13054
Tel: 2439000
Fax: 2462516

Central Bank of Kuwait
POB 526
Safat 13006
Tel: 2449200
Fax: 2464887

Commercial Bank of Kuwait
POB 2861
Safat 13029
Tel: 2411001
Fax: 2450150

Industrial Bank of Kuwait
POB 3146
Safat 13032
Tel: 2457661
Fax: 2462057

Kuwait Finance House
POB 24989
Safat 13110
Tel: 2445050

National Bank of Kuwait
POB 95
Safat 13001
Tel: 2422011
Fax: 2459032

TAXATION

Taxation requires sophisticated knowledge of complex rules and regulations specific to each country. The information presented here is from the Ernst & Young Corporate Tax Guide and Directory, available from the Ernst & Young accounting office in your country, or from:

Ernst & Young
(Al Aiban, Al Osaimi & Partners)
Mail Address:
POB 74 Safat
13001 Safat, Kuwait
Tel: 2452880/7
Fax: 2456419

At a Glance

Corporate Income Tax Rate (%) (a)	55
Capital Gains Tax Rate (%) (a)	55
Branch Tax Rate (%) (a)	55
Withholding Tax (%)	
Dividends	0
Interest	0
Royalties	0
Branch Remittance Tax	0
Net Operating Losses (Years)	
Carryback	0
Carryforward	unlimited (b)

(a) Maximum rate.
(b) If presence in Kuwait is continuous.

Marketing

Overview

Post-liberation Kuwait is one of the most competitive markets in the world, but increased trade does not mean Kuwaitis blindly accept whatever importers have to offer. Kuwaitis will buy when products match their interest and are competitive in price and quality. No matter what a foreign firm sells, that company's executive should never underestimate the skill and patience with which his or her Kuwaiti counterpart will bargain. Kuwait's reputation as a trading nation has developed over several centuries, and its people are as fond of a bargain as a proud parent is of a child.

Distribution

Kuwait has wholesale as well as retail outlets; either may be in a company's headquarters or in separate warehouses and shops. Consumer goods are mainly distributed through neighborhood cooperative markets, but larger foodstuffs and spare auto parts also have distribution teams selling and delivering to retail customers. Cooperative-owned stores account for nearly 80 percent of retail food sales, so a handful of large local companies tend to dominate.

Agents, Distributors, and Partners

Selecting an agent is one of the most important decisions an exporter can make after considering the agent's management, financial resources, commitment to marketing the product, and technical support qualifications carefully. Kuwaiti merchants prefer to deal directly with the foreign manufacturer or its sole exporting agent.

Selling Techniques

Reasonable price, good quality, attractive packaging and effective after-sale service are significant factors here. Customers are commonly offered installment purchase plans and discounts for large purchases. Sales techniques include: discount percentages, with especially big discounts twice a year; free service for equipment purchased during a limited period; promotional sales including reduced prices or giveaways; and trade-ins. Stress the quality of food products if the company is well-known.

Marketing in Kuwait
MARKETING TIPS

- **Language** Although English is a second language, it is widely spoken; many Kuwaitis have been educated abroad.
- **Forbidden** No alcohol, pork products or pornographic materials may be imported into or used in Kuwait; travelers with such items are subject to arrest and prosecution.
- **Taxation** Foreign companies have to pay as much as 55 percent of profits earned from doing business in Kuwait.
- **Patent protection** Kuwait does not permit the patenting of food, pharmaceuticals and medicines, so many Western companies are reluctant to market these items.
- **Advertising** Newspapers are the most effective medium here, with two major newspapers each in Arabic and English.
- **Service and customer support** Sales contracts must have a follow-up maintenance clause. Warranties ranging from 90 days to five years normally apply to electrical appliances, vehicles and watches. Independent service centers repair and maintain most consumer products and goods, though a foreign firm would do well to establish its own factory service center.
- **Processors** Packers are especially interested in corn oil, tree nuts, fruit juices and snack foods. Most beef products are purchased by hotels, restaurants, and catering companies.
- **Advertising agencies** Several advertising agencies serve foreign and local companies' needs, some having special US or European ties.

Business Culture

Greetings and Courtesies

As in other Arab countries, greetings are warm and effusive. A brief, firm handshake is acceptable when greeting males; do not offer your hand to a woman unless she initiates a handshake. Traditional Kuwaitis with certain status will sometimes greet each other by bowing and kissing the other's hand, but foreigners need not feel obliged to imitate this greeting. Prepare to spend some time on greetings and pleasantries; Arabs will linger over these things in an effort to gain your acquaintance.

Business Ethic and Framework

Kuwaitis are open to foreigners and are accustomed to doing business with people from all over the world. The Islamic religion influences every aspect of social and business life. It is essential that foreigners adhere to basic Islamic customs and laws if they expect to effectively conduct business. The business community is small and if a foreigner behaves badly with one businessman, there is a good chance that he has cut off many other contacts as well.

Meetings and Decision Making

Prior appointments are always required and visitors are expected to arrive on time; tardiness is considered an insult in the tiny country. Meetings generally progress slowly, with personal discussions and many cups of coffee preceding any talk of business. Decisions are made quickly and seemingly spontaneously. The foreign businessperson in Kuwait must be ready able to conclude a deal.

Women

Kuwait is probably the only country in the Gulf States where women hold any significant positions in business and government. As in the other Arab countries, however, men and women still lead restricted and segregated social lives. In general, it is not wise to send a woman to conduct business, even in Kuwait. She will probably not be effective.

Cultural Cautions
DO'S

- It will be noticed and appreciated if you learn a few Arabic phrases before your trip.
- Send your top people to Kuwait to conduct business. Kuwaitis admire titles, and they resent middlemen. They want to deal with the boss.

DON'TS

- Do not display intimate areas of your body, including bare shoulders, stomach, and calves and thighs. This applies to both men and women, but especially to women.
- Do not put on airs or affect mannerisms. Kuwaitis are very direct and honest and they will not appreciate the subterfuge.

CUSTOMS

- Conservative business suits are worn by businessmen. Women should wear conservative business attire with long sleeves. Short skirts and low necklines should definitely be avoided. Virtually no occasion requires formal attire.

OBSERVATIONS

- Kuwaitis are well-educated, well-read and well-traveled, and they enjoy discussing these topics.
- Kuwaitis are extremely polite and gracious, and they will go out of their way to not to offend an acquaintance.

NEGOTIATIONS

- Be firm, but politely persistent. Show confidence and make your points several times lest you be seen to lack conviction.
- Kuwaitis do not respond well to arrogance or temper. They are low-key and quiet, and they expect negotiations to proceed in this manner.
- Negotiations will generally be formal, will follow ritual guidelines and many people will be involved.

GOVERNMENT AGENCIES

Customs Public Authority
POB 16
Safat
Tel: 812522
Telex: 23135, 23143

Fish Resources
POB 21422
Safat 13075
Tel: 4761116/7
Fax: 4765551

Kuwait Fund for Arab Economic Development (KFAED)
POB 2921
Safat 13030
Tel: 2468800
Telex: 22025
Fax: 2419091

Kuwait Investment Authority (KIA)
POB 64
Safat 13001
Kuwait City
Tel: 2439592
Telex: 46079
Fax: 2454059

Kuwait News Agency
POB 24063
Safat 13101
Tel: 2412040 through 3
Telex: 22758 kt

Ministry of Awkaf & Islamic Affairs
POB 13
Safat 13001
Tel: 2458268
Fax: 2423705

Ministry of Commerce and Industry
POB 2944
Safat 13030
Tel: 2469131
Fax: 2421826

Ministry of Communications
Tel: 4840606
Fax: 4837610

Ministry of Defense
POB 1170
Safat 13012
Tel: 4831570
Fax: 4837601

Ministry of Education
POB 7
Safat 13001
Tel: 4837890
Fax: 4837601

Ministry of Electricity & Water
POB 12
Safat 13001
Tel: 4882991
Fax: 4885710

Ministry of Finance
POB 9
Safat 13001
Tel: 2410513
Fax: 2434862

Ministry of Foreign Affairs
POB 3
Safat 13001
Tel: 2448098/6
Fax: 2430559

Ministry of Higher Education
POB 27130
Safat 13132
Tel: 2463999
Fax: 2465000

Ministry of Housing
POB 8
Safat 13001
Tel: 2457335

Ministry of Information
POB 193
Safat 13002
Tel: 2451566
Fax: 2459530

Ministry of Interior
POB 11
Safat 13001
Tel: 2424007
Fax: 2435771

Ministry of Planning
POB 15
Safat 13001
Tel: 2426077
Fax: 2406984

Ministry of Public Health
POB 5
Safat 13001
Tel: 2422131
Fax: 2419678

Minister of Public Works
POB 8
Safat 13001
Tel: 2449300
Fax: 2424335

Ministry of Social Affairs & Labor
POB 563
Safat 13006
Tel: 2445554
Fax: 2407465

National Council for Culture, Arts and Literature
POB 22235
Safat
Tel: 2423130
Telex: 44554

Petrochemical Industries Co KSC (PIC)
POB 1084
Safat 13011
Tel: 2422141
Telex: 22024

Ports Public Authority
POB 3874
Safat 13039
Tel: 4812625
Telex: 22740 hmshp

Public Authority for Agriculture and Fishing
POB 21422
Safat 13075
Tel: 4711155
Telex: 30072

The Public Authority for Agricultural Affairs and Kuwait Institute for Scientific Research
POB 24885
Safat 13109
Tel: 4830776
Telex: 22299 kisr

CHAMBER OF COMMERCE

The Kuwaiti Chamber of Commerce and Industry
POB 775
Safat 13008
Tel: 2435801
Fax: 2404110

CONSULTING FIRMS

Al-Shall Economic Consultants
POB 5935
Safat 13060
Tel: 2451535
Fax: 2422619

Amar Consulting
POB 711
Safat 13008
Tel: 2463506
Fax: 2463507

Focus Marketing Consultancy Ltd.
POB 29359
Safat
Tel: 4817707
Fax: 4817797

TRANSPORTATION FIRMS

Arab Maritime Petroleum Transport Co (AMPTC)
POB 22525
13086 Safat
Tel: 2411815
Telex: 22180
Fax: 2437468

Kuwait Airways Corporation (KAC)
POB 394
13004 Safat
Tel: 4740166
Telex: 23036
Fax: 4314726

Kuwait Maritime Transport Co (KSC)
POB 22595
13086 Safat
Tel: 2420519
Telex: 30967
Fax: 2420513

Kuwait Oil Tanker Co SAK (KOTC)
POB 810
13009 Safat
Tel: 2455455
Telex: 22013
Fax: 2445907

United Arab Shipping Co SAG (UASC)
POB 3636
13037 Safat
Tel: 4843150
Telex: 22176
Fax: 4845388

LEGAL CONTACTS

Al-Ayoub & Partners
Al-Khatrash & Al-Mishary Building
10th Floor, Fahd Al-Salem Street
POB 1714
Safat 13018
Tel: 2464321
Fax: 2466591

Al-Sarraf, Al-Ruwayeh & Stephenson Harwood
Salhiya Complex, Gate, 3rd Floor
POB 1448
Safat
Tel: 2400061
Fax: 2400064

Law Offices of Mishare M. Al-Ghazali & Partners
POB 4970 Safat
13050 Kuwait
Tel: 2439690
Fax: 2422895

INTERNET ADDRESSES

soc.culture.arabic
soc.culture.kuwait

The State of Kuwait
http://www.cs.cmu.edu/Web/People/anwar/kuwait.html

City Net - Kuwait
http://www.city.net/countries/kuwait/

Latvia

Republic of Latvia

Economy

Overview

Latvia's eastern Baltic location has always made it an important center and connection point for east-west commercial trading. During the years of Soviet domination, however, Latvia's economy exclusively served the internal industrial needs of the centrally planned economy. With the breakup of the USSR, these markets were thrown into turmoil, and the Latvian economy nearly collapsed. Inflation reached 1,000 percent in 1992, although it has since fallen to about 35 percent. Its financial situation has begun to stabilize but its economy remains fragile and its standard of living has fallen considerably. Latvia still relies heavily on its former Soviet bloc neighbors for much of its energy needs and other resources. Unfortunately, most of these economies are themselves struggling and do not offer much in the way of markets for Latvian goods.

Trade

Major exports include machinery, foodstuffs, textiles, chemicals, and wood products. Imports include machinery, textiles, chemicals, foodstuffs, and fuels. Latvia's main trading partner continues to be Russia, which accounts for about half of its total trade. Most remaining trade is with other republics of the former USSR—Lithuania, Belarus, Estonia, Kazakhstan, and the Ukraine—although Latvia is working to diversify its products and trading partners to include other countries, especially its more prosperous Northern European neighbors.

Sectors

Agriculture Agriculture (and forestry and fishing) account for about 25 percent of GDP and 16 percent of employment. Traditionally, Latvia has focused on pig and dairy farming, with cereals, sugar beets, and potatoes as cash crops. Privatization has severely disrupted agricultural production, however. Poor livestock production has made Latvia a net importer of meat and dairy products in the mid-1990s.

Industry Industry produces about half of GDP, employing somewhat more than 35 percent of the work force. Machinery, metalworking, chemicals, and wood processing have been the main areas, although electrical equipment, textiles and footwear, precision instruments, construction materials, and food processing are becoming more important in this sector.

Services Services provide about 25 percent of GDP in this heavily industrialized country, but employ nearly half the work force. Latvia is attempting to develop a financial and business services industry, but most services still consist of local distribution and personal service activities.

Trends

Latvia has made steady progress in replacing the socialist system imposed during Soviet rule with a structure based on free market principles. Latvia's rapidly growing private sector is now estimated to be producing half the country's GDP. The government has managed to lower inflation to more manageable levels and now even boasts a balanced budget, with a cumulative deficit equal to slightly less than two percent of GDP. Led by recovery in light industry and a boom in the newly unleashed commercial and financial services areas, the economy is expected to expand five to six percent annually for the remainder of the decade as the system continues to stabilize.

At a Glance

THE COUNTRY

Location Northeastern Europe, bordering on the Baltic Sea, between Sweden and Russia.
Terrain Mostly fertile low-lying plains, with highlands in the east and hills in the west.
Climate Temperate, with four seasons of almost equal length. Eastern Latvia has warm summers and harsh winters.

THE PEOPLE

Population 2,600,000
Ethnic composition
Latvian 53%
Russians 35%
Belorussians 6%
Ukrainians 4%
Poles 2%
Religious composition Lutheran, Roman Catholic, Russian Orthodox, and Jewish.
Languages spoken Lettish (also called Latvian), Lithuanian, and Russian.
Education and literacy Many Latvians have similar educations, values, and aspirations to those of middle-class inhabitants of Northern and Western Europe. Society places strong emphasis upon education, which is free and compulsory until age 16, and adult literacy approaches 100 percent.
Labor force
Total: 1,400,000
By occupation: industry 30%, agriculture/forestry 16%, trade/mining 9%, transport/communication 7%, construction 10%, and financial services/other 27%.

COUNTRY FACTS

Political and legal In 1993, the newly elected parliament restored the 1933 democratic constitution. The legal system is based on a civil law system.
Telephone Telecommunications are being modernized. Improved telephone and telegraph services are easily available at standard international rates. International country code: [371]. Selected city code: Riga (2).
Transportation Latvia's capital, Riga, is one of the transportation hubs for the northwest Russia/Baltic region. Several international airlines provide service from Riga airport. Domestic train and bus services are also available. Bus and taxi services within the capital and its environs are good. There are three major shipping ports.
Environment Air and water pollution caused by agricultural chemicals and industrial waste are severe problems. Because of a lack of waste-conversion equipment, approximately 70 percent of the nation's sewage isn't treated properly. About half the water supply has dangerous bacteria levels. Current issues include air and water pollution; acid rain; and contamination of soil and groundwater with chemicals and petroleum products at military bases.
Media There are more than one million television sets. Latvian radio broadcasts domestic and international programming. Many newspapers, periodicals, and books are published.
Health Medical care doesn't meet Western standards. Medical facilities face severe shortages of basic medical supplies. Life expectancy of males is 65 years; of females, 75 years.

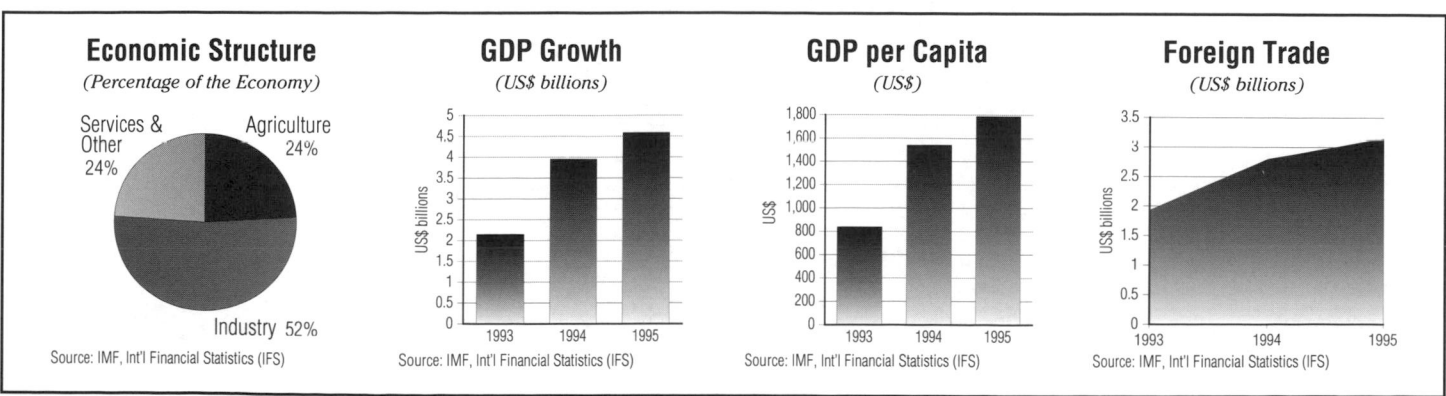

Economic Structure
(Percentage of the Economy)

Services & Other 24%
Agriculture 24%
Industry 52%

Source: IMF, Int'l Financial Statistics (IFS)

GDP Growth
(US$ billions)

Source: IMF, Int'l Financial Statistics (IFS)

GDP per Capita
(US$)

Source: IMF, Int'l Financial Statistics (IFS)

Foreign Trade
(US$ billions)

Source: IMF, Int'l Financial Statistics (IFS)

Business Travel

COMMUNICATIONS

Telephones The telephone system in Latvia is adequate. Most international calls must be placed through an international operator. Public phones are available. The most expensive time to call is from 1:00 p.m. to 2:00 a.m.

Fax Fax machines are available at most businesses and hotels and at the Central Post Office. Telex services are available where fax services are found.

Post office Mail service is reliable but slow. To speed things along, address mail in the local language or at least the familiar format (country, city with index number, street, house number, and then name). Major hotels have postal facilities for posting mail and buying stamps. Mailboxes are rare.

BEST TRAVEL BOOKS

Hayit's Budget Travel, The Baltic States (Estonia, Latvia, Lithuania). Affordable, practical, up-to-date covering topics such as travel preparations, background information, practical information, and travel sections.

Berlitz Business Travel Guide, Europe. Concise economic details, successful trip planning, background information on people and cities, useful facts and addresses.

USEFUL TELEPHONE NUMBERS

If you are calling from outside Latvia, you will need to add the country code [371] and any other international dialing requirements from within your country.

- Fire 01
- Police 02
- Ambulance 03
- Telegram 06
- Directory Assistance 09
- International Operator 812
- Time 004
- Riga Train Station .... (2) 232134
- Riga's Main Bus Terminal .... (2) 213-358
- International Express Mail Service .... (2) 602810
- Chamber of Commerce .... (2) 444929
- Baltlink Car Rental .... (2) 421003
- Operator 8194/5
- DHL .... (2) 210973
- UPS .... (2) 212185
- Latvian Hotel Association .... (2) 212845

Airlines
- SAS .... (2) 207055
- Lufthansa .... (2) 207183
- Finnair .... (2) 207010
- Hamburg Airlines .... (2) 227638

Credit Card Information
Lost or stolen credit cards (call collect to the US, regardless of which country the card was issued in).
- Amex .... [1] (919) 3333211
- Diner's Club .... [1] (303) 7991504
- MasterCard .... [1] (314) 2756690
- Visa .... [1] (410) 5817931

Travelogue

WORKWEEK

Offices Monday-Friday 9:00 am to 6:00 pm.
Banks Monday-Friday 9:00 am to 1:00 pm.
Government Monday-Friday 9:00 am to 6:00 pm.
Retail Monday-Saturday 10:00 am to 8:00 pm with lunch from noon to 1:00 pm. Larger department stores may open at 8:00 am and remain open until 9:00 pm.

HOLIDAYS

Holidays 1996
January 1 New Year's Day
January 7 Orthodox Christmas
May 1 Constitution Day
June 23-24 Midsummers
November 18 Proclamation Day
December 25-26 Christmas
December 31 New Year's Eve
Check exact date for Good Friday, as this date varies each year. By custom, the Monday preceding a public holiday on a Tuesday is taken as an additional public holiday in which case the preceding Saturday is a working day.

VISA AND PASSPORT

All travelers to Latvia will need a valid passport and most also need a visa. Visas are available from a Latvian embassy. A visa to Estonia or Lithuania will also be accepted for entry into Latvia. It is possible to obtain a visa from Riga Airport upon arrival, but these visas are only valid for 10 days.

DEPARTURE FORMALITIES

There are no departure taxes for visitors leaving Latvia from Riga Airport.

TIPPING

Tipping is usually expected, but keep in mind that the value of US$1 is reasonably high in comparison to salaries. In restaurants the bill often includes a service charge.

IMMUNIZATION

No international certificates of vaccination are required unless you are arriving from an infected area.

CRIME

Latvia has a relatively high rate of crime. Street crime is increasing in Riga, especially at night. Robberies on trains and in train stations, apartments, and houses are common.

INFRASTRUCTURE

Latvia is connected to surrounding areas by a network of air, train, and bus services. Bus, taxi, and rental car services are available within the capital. Telecommunication services are modern and well-developed.

NATIONAL TOURIST OFFICE

Latvian Tourist
Pils lauk
Riga
Tel: (2) 4229945

Foreign Trade

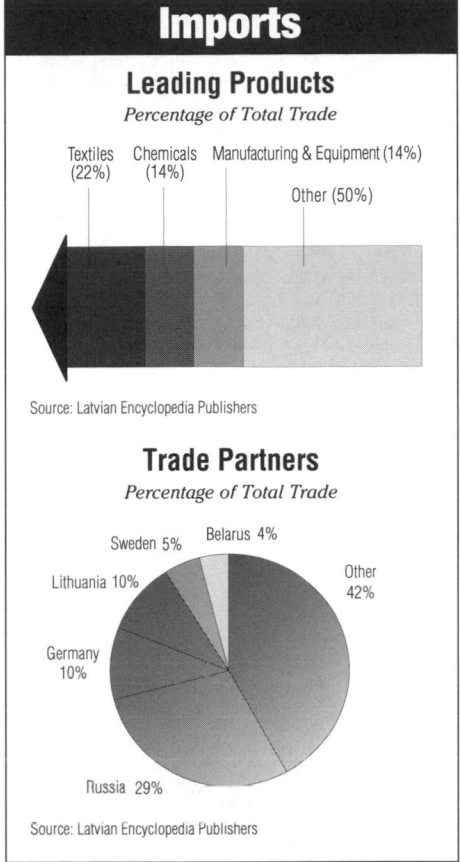

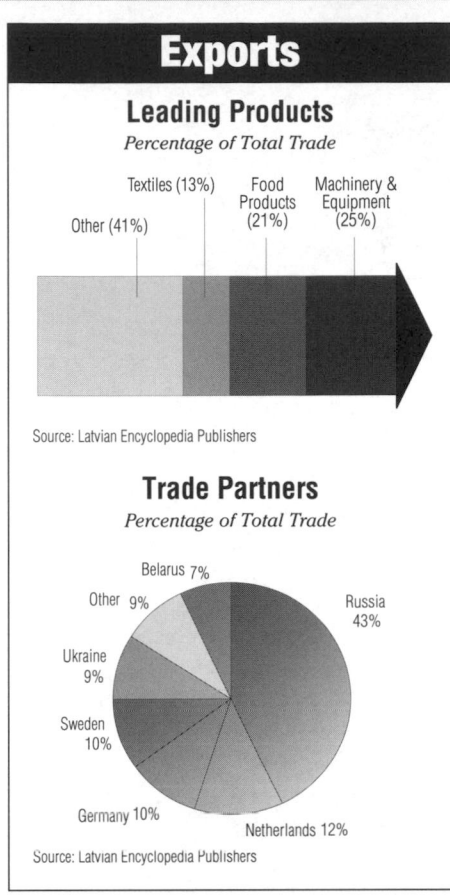

Opportunities

FOR IMPORTING TO LATVIA
- fuels, cars, ferrous metals
- chemicals
- office equipment, computers
- building products
- capital machinery equipment

FOR EXPORTING FROM LATVIA
- oil products, timber, ferrous metals
- dairy products
- furniture, textiles

GROWTH SECTORS
- private sector
- manufacturing
- retail
- agribusiness

Trade News

RULES AND REGULATIONS
- **Barriers to imports** There are no specific barriers to importing to Latvia. While considerable improvement has been made over the last year, Latvia's business, banking, and legal infrastructures have not attained acceptable business standards. While Latvians do not have the income to match their aspirations, there is every reason to believe that they will not be long in attaining it.
- **Tariffs and import duties** According to the new law on customs tariffs, import duties on some agricultural products are as high as 55 percent (for countries without MFN status). Duties on industrial products do not exist. Latvia collects an import duty on timber, metals, leather, paper, and a few other products.
- **Tariff classifications** Tariffs are based on the harmonized commodity description and coding system (HCDC).

Legal Matters

LEGAL BRIEFS
- **Monopolies** Latvia does not allow monopolies. Businesses are prohibited from manipulating prices or quantities of goods offered for sale and may not create artificial shortages in order to boost prices.
- **Capital outflow** Latvia does not have any policies on the outflow of capital. Large amounts of funds flow freely through Latvia to the West from former Soviet countries.
- **Film and video industry** Film and video piracy remains a problem. Most films and videos shown in Latvia are pirated.
- **Commercial markets** The credit and equities markets are seriously hampered by legal and judicial weaknesses.
- **Unions** Labor unions are free from any governmental influence, but weak. Many citizens see the current unions as leftovers from the Soviet era.
- **Strikes and work stoppages** Latvia has not seen any major industrial strikes since achieving independence.
- **Labor laws** The Latvian government appears to be attempting to uphold international labor standards, but its ability to enforce them is weak. Many workers have little protection or financial security against termination.The employment of young children is common, as are long working hours.

LEGAL CONTACT
Blukis & Elksne
Brivibas Street 40-24
Riga 1050
Tel: (2) 288264
Fax: (2) 348185

Legal

Legal System

Latvia's legal system is in a state of transition, following independence from the Soviet Union. It appears Latvia will tend toward adopting the laws of several Western countries.

Intellectual Property Rights

Patents and trademarks Patent registration and protection is currently being restored in Latvia, and the government is committed to attaining a level of patent protection at least comparable to that provided under international conventions. Current trademark laws in Latvia are transparent, though vague, and the government is trying to draft more descriptive laws. Infringement is common and the government is now helpless to do much about it.

Copyrights Similar to patent protection, Latvia is trying to provide the same copyright protections that international conventions require. To halt the use of films imported from Russia by private Latvian television stations, the Latvian radio and television board adopted a rule threatening to revoke the license of any domestic station if it cannot prove that it legally acquired the rights to the films it broadcasts.

Trade secrets There are no laws which specifically protect trade secrets. It is possible to pursue a cause through a civil breach of contract claim, but this is likely to be a lengthy proceeding, and will probably not yield satisfactory redress.

Business Registration

The law on entrepreneurial activities and business operations serves as the legal framework for establishing, registering, operating and closing a business in Latvia. Generally, all companies, and virtually all foreign commercial enterprises, must register with the Ministry prior to doing business in Latvia.

Contracts and Dispute Resolution

Latvian contracts are changing to meet the needs of western businesses. Business disputes are decided by local courts which are composed of three judges, only one of whom is a professional jurist.

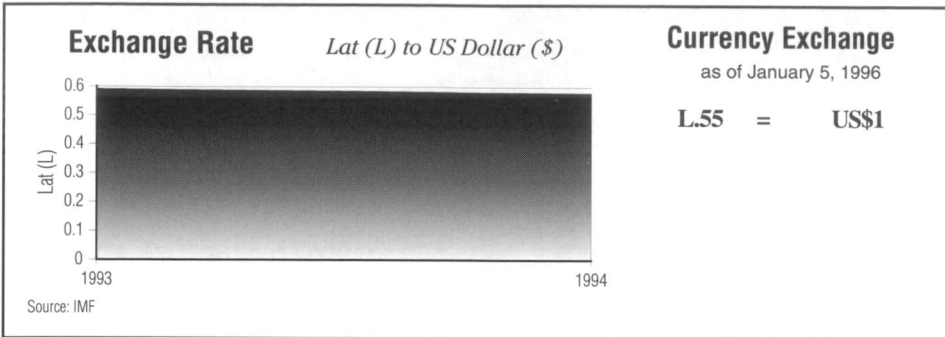

Source: IMF

Currency

The currency of Latvia is the lat (L), which is divided into 100 santims.

Foreign Exchange

Parliament has ultimate control over foreign exchange and trade matters in Latvia, but authority to regulate governing foreign exchange transactions has been delegated to the Bank of Latvia. All foreign exchange transactions must be effected through its authorized banks and licensed agents. No controls are maintained over the exchange of foreign currencies. This laissez-faire currency policy has drawn substantial amounts of foreign currency into the country, making it a mini-Switzerland of the Baltic and Russian region. Residents are allowed to hold foreign currencies in domestic or foreign bank accounts, and to use these funds for domestic payments. Nonresidents are permitted to hold bank accounts in either foreign or domestic currency. The Bank of Latvia quotes weekly the accounting rates of the lats for the currencies of those states of the former USSR that are participating in the system of correspondent accounts.

Capital Transfers

Latvia does not restrict the repatriation or transfer of profits or other capital.

Investment Incentives

There are no incentives offered to foreign investors. Under the 1991 investment law, the laws of the republic of Latvia apply equally to domestic and foreign investors.

Investment Restrictions

The investment law applies some limits to foreign investment. Acquisition of controlling shares in a Latvian enterprise with assets exceeding 530,000 lat (US$ one million) must be approved by the cabinet of ministers. Some factors carry more weight when deciding, including the creation of new jobs, the use of local resources and services, the export potential of goods manufactured in Latvia, and the competitive position of Latvian products in the international market. Except for the restrictions laid down in the Investment Law, there are no restrictions or regulations aimed at restricting foreign participation in the Latvian private sector. There are no performance requirements for a foreign investor to establish, maintain or expand an investment in Latvia. There are, however, some limitations on the types of business organizations in which foreigners may participate. These limitations are primarily to ensure that foreign capital is truly investment-related rather than merely speculative.

Money Matters

BITS AND PIECES

- **Exchange rates** Exchange rates for the lat are determined by supply and demand in the market. The Bank of Latvia's policy is to ensure orderly conditions in the exchange market and limit short-term fluctuations in the exchange rate against convertible currencies.

- **Capital** There are no exchange control regulations governing capital transactions. Government policies do not interfere with the free flow of capital, financial resources or the allocation of credit.

- **USSR settlements** Settlements with the states of the former USSR can be made through any means, including a system of correspondent accounts.

- **Export proceeds** Export proceeds are not subject to repatriation or other surrender requirements.

- **Foreign exchange tax** Licensed foreign exchange dealers must pay a tax of 1.5 percent on purchases of foreign exchange.

- **Export taxes** Latvia imposes a stiff tax on the export of raw materials.

- **Gold** There are no regulations governing international trade in gold; however, a license is required to deal in gold on the domestic market.

- **Land ownership** For business or investment purposes, foreigners may only lease land in Latvia.

- **Investment law** Investment laws in Latvia apply some limits to foreign investment. Foreign investors may engage in, but not control, specific sectors of the national economy. They may also lease but not own land. Under Latvian law, foreigners may conduct business only as limited liability companies, joint stock companies, or as representative branch offices of foreign companies. All other full liability business organizations are closed to foreigners, such as sole proprietorships, partnerships, religious enterprises, and private farms.

BANKS

Baltic Bank (Baltija Banka)
Brivibas Bulvaris 49/53
Riga LV-1050
Tel: (2) 292680
Fax: (2) 225024
Fax: (2) 8828066

Bank of Latvia
Kr. Valdemara Street 2a
Riga
Tel: (2) 323863

Latvian Deposit Bank (Latvija Depositu Banka)
Valnu Street 28
Riga LV-1579
Tel: (2) 222532
Fax: (2) 211465

Parex Bank (Parekss Banka)
Maksim Ter-Oganesov, Kr. Valdemara Street 8
Riga LV-1010
Tel: (2) 325305
Fax: (2) 8820032

Riga Commercial Bank (Rigas Kommerzbanka)
Smilsu Street 6
Riga LV-1050
Tel: (2) 323892
Fax: (2) 323449

Universal Bank (Latvijas Universalu Banka)
Riga LV-1050
Tel: (2) 215650
Fax: (2) 8820332

Baltic Transit Bank
13 Janvara iela 3
Riga LV-1050
Tel: (2) 224261

Latvian Savings Bank
Palasta iela 1
Riga LV-1954
Tel: (2) 222871
Fax: (2) 212083

TAXATION

Taxation requires sophisticated knowledge of complex rules and regulations specific to each country. The information presented here is from the Ernst & Young Corporate Tax Guide and Directory, available from the Ernst & Young accounting office in your country, or from:
For Services in Latvia, please contact
Kari Bjĭrk,
Tallinn, Estonia [372] (6) 310612
Satellite telephone [358] 49-124-525.
Mailing address in Latvia is:
11, Kalku Iela
LV-1050 Riga
Latvia

At a Glance

Corporate Income Tax Rate (%)	25*
Capital Gains Tax Rate (%)	25
Branch Tax Rate (%)	25
Withholding Tax (%)	0
Net Operating Losses (Years)	
Carryback	0
Carryforward	2

* This rate applies to private enterprises. Enterprises that are wholly or partially owned by the state are subject to profit tax at a rate of 35%. Banks, insurance companies, and enterprises engaged in trading and selling currency are subject to profit tax at a rate of 45%.

Marketing

Overview

With a population of less than three million, this is a relatively small market, but it offers opportunities for firms dealing in consumer products, computers and office equipment, building products, and capital machinery and equipment. Riga, the capital, has emerged along with Moscow and St. Petersburg as a commercial, financial, and transportation hub for the northwest Russian/Baltic region. Historical trade relations have encouraged companies from Sweden, Germany, and Finland to enter this market; Polish and Finnish firms tend to dominate the imported food sector. The primary obstacles to business come from government bureaucracy, corruption, and organized crime; though multinational investors are usually sophisticated enough to find paths through these distractions. Many firms regard the Latvian commercial environment as among the best to be found in Eastern Europe. Many Latvians are educated, with aspirations and values similar to Western middle-class citizens. Although their income may not currently match their aspirations, there is every reason to believe it will not take long until they are formidable consumers.

Agents, Distributors, and Partners

Foreign investors enter the Latvian market by any of three paths: a limited liability agreement, joint stock venture, or through a representative office. The first two are formed by registering with the Latvian enterprise register. The chief distinction here is size: a limited liability company may have up to 50 shareholders; the joint stock company has more, but structural and legal requirements for this type of enterprise are unusually complex. Representative offices are established initially for five years, by authority of the ministry of justice, which oversees almost all foreign sales arrangements.

Service and Customer Support

Although customer service and after sale product service and support are not yet well established, Latvian consumers are savvy and will come to expect more of each as their consumer markets grow. Foreign sellers who are willing and able to provide adequate service and support will be well served in the long run by doing so. Latvian consumers are willing to pay a premium for these amenities.

Business Culture

Greetings and Courtesies

Shaking hands during introductions is customary, as is using professional titles. Latvian business people feel an obligation to entertain foreign business guests after normal working hours. Invitations to their homes are rare, however, so obtaining one is considered an honor. Latvian businesspeople shun discussing business in social settings; however, if a host initiates the subject, it is proper to join in.

Business Ethic and Framework

Latvians are fond of insignificant rules, procedures, and legalisms, which can often hamper business transactions. Once these obstacles are surmounted, however, Latvian businesspeople are found to be productive and efficient. Latvians are succinct in business and they waste no words. Seven hundred years of Germanic rule have left them with an earnest work ethic and a partiality for punctualness.

Meetings and Decision Making

Latvians generally come to meetings well prepared, and they expect foreign associates to be organized as well. Details of agreements need to be spelled out clearly before agreement. Many Latvians are new to private business and may not strictly adhere to the terms of a signed agreement; not many laws pertaining to business transactions are yet in place. Before signing agreements in Latvia, you should always verify if your prospective business associates actually have legal rights to the holdings or firm they claim to represent.

Women

The feminist movement has been slow to develop in Latvia. Although they hold a majority of jobs in Latvia, women are paid less than men. Women work in almost all professions, but are usually placed in office jobs. An appreciation for working women is growing, however, and assistance programs for women have been instituted that include child care. Many women in Latvia have the dual responsibilities of their jobs and homes.

Marketing in Latvia

MARKETING TIPS

- **Language** Latvian is the official language and most Latvians speak Russian as well. Many businesspersons speak English, and German is especially common in establishments catering to the tourist trade.
- **Low rates** Office space is cheap and plentiful, from US$7 to 15 dollars per square meter per month, US$30 top rates.
- **Distribution** Marketing consumer products is challenged by the lack of large distributors or wholesalers. Food products are generally imported by a few powerful wholesalers, and retail operations are managed by private food companies, most of which must rely on the wholesalers for their inventories. All major food wholesalers also maintain their own networks of small food stores through which most Latvians buy. Meat-processing enterprises import meat or livestock directly. Seasonal agriculture is primarily sold at public farmers' markets in the largest cities.
- **Advertising** There is no restriction on advertising in either print or electronic media. The leading daily newspaper is *Diena* (Day), published in both Latvian and Russian. The leading business papers are *Dienas Biznes* (Business of the Day) published in Latvian, and *Biznes I Baltiya* (Business and the Baltics) published in Russian. Both carry advertising.
- **Privatization** The privatization of many industries has created new marketing opportunities as managers look for more cost effective and competitive services and supplies.

CHAMBER OF COMMERCE

Latvian Chamber of Commerce and Industry
Brivibas Bulvaris 21
Riga LV-1849
Tel: (2) 225558 Fax: (2) 332276

Cultural Cautions

DO'S

- Be able to discuss Latvia's history.
- Talk trees. Latvians love to go on about the forests that cover more than half their country.
- A good topic for conversation is sports; Latvians are very sports-oriented.
- Ask those around you before you smoke, then share cigarettes lavishly.

DON'TS

- Don't give advice. Latvians are reluctant to accept it from foreigners.
- Avoid questions about age, personal life, family, and military experience.

CUSTOMS

- "V" in public lavatories is for men, "S" is for women.
- Gift giving on meeting with Latvian colleagues is expected. Bring something small that perhaps displays your company's logo.
- Latvians practice formal European etiquette.
- Conservative clothing in dark colors is the rule in Latvia. Don't dress down for business, since you will be expected to live up to Latvians' image of foreign business. Business attire is proper for most occasions, including formal.

OBSERVATIONS

- Latvians are quiet, thoughtful, disciplined, and reserved.
- Hand out your business cards, printed in your language and Latvian, to all participants of meetings.
- Latvians are intensely interested in preserving their environment.

NEGOTIATIONS

- Make sure you know in advance what special licenses, registration numbers and signatures are needed for your proposed business arrangement.
- Negotiations can be rather lengthy and customarily involve socializing.
- Be patient; many Latvians are unfamiliar with negotiating procedures.

Contacts

GOVERNMENT AGENCIES

Latvian Banking Association
Stabu Street 18
Riga LV-1001
Tel: (2) 215650
 Fax: (2) 8828170

Latvian Development Agency
Perses Street 2
Riga LV-1442
Tel: (2) 288842
Fax: (2) 282524

Latvian Food Safety Inspection
Republic Square 2
Riga LV-1981
Tel: (2) 323833, 327311
Fax: (2) 8830272

Ministry of Agriculture
Republic Square 2
Riga LV-1981
Tel: (2) 320162, 327894
Fax: (2) 8830272

Ministry of Economics
Brivibas Bulv. 36
Riga LV-1070
Tel: (2) 288444

Ministry of Education, Culture, and Science
Leona Paegles St. 2
Riga
Tel: (2) 224772

Ministry of Finance
1 Smilu St.
Riga
Tel: (2) 226672

Ministry of Transportation
Brivibas Bulv. 38
Riga LV-1070
Tel: (2) 226922

State Committee for Statistics
Lacplesa 1
Riga
Tel: (2) 270126

Latvian Academy of Sciences
19 Turgeneva iela
Riga
Tel: (2) 223922
Fax: (2) 228784

Government Information Agency
36 Brivibas blvd.
Riga LV-1070
Tel: (2) 282828
Fax: (2) 381781

Ministry of Foreign Affairs
36 Brivibas blvd.
Riga LV-1395
Tel: (2) 222694, 223307
Fax: (2) 227755

Department of Citizenship and Immigration
6 Raina blvd.
Riga LV-1181
Tel: (2) 219406, 219181
Fax: (2) 332154

Department of Customs
1a Valdemara St.
Riga LV-1050
Tel: (2) 323858
Fax: (2) 322440

Ministry of Interior Affairs
Raina blvd. 6
Riga LV-1033

WORLD TRADE CENTER

World Trade Center Riga
2 Elizabetes Street
Riga LV-1340
Tel: (2) 320619
Fax: (8) 830035

CHAMBERS OF COMMERCE

American Chamber of Commerce in Latvia
Jauniela 24
Riga LV-1050
Tel: (2) 215205
Fax: (2) 8820090

LEGAL CONTACTS

Maija Sibilla Blauberga, Zverinatu Advokatu Birojs
Kr. Baona Iela 31
Riga LV-1011
Tel: (2) 348670
Fax: (2) 348670

Peteris Jurjans
Raina Blvd. NR 25 Suite 409
Riga LV-1050
Tel: (2) 210971
Fax: (2) 342568

NEWSPAPERS

The Baltic Observer
Balasta dambis 3
Riga LV-1081
Tel: (2) 462119
Fax: (2) 463387

Dienas Biznes (Daily Business)
Balasta dambis 3
Riga LV-1081
Tel: (2) 464690
Fax: (2) 464719

Latvijas Vestnesis (Latvian Herald)
Palasta iela 10
Riga LV-1502

PERIODICALS

Daugava
Balasta dambis 3
Riga LV-1081
Tel: (2) 465993

Dzentlmenis (Gentleman)
Basteja bulv. 12
Riga LV-1050
Tel: (2) 212223
Fax: (2) 213578

Karos (Banner)
Balasta dambis 3
Riga LV-1081
Tel: (2) 465696

RADIO & TELEVISION

Committee for Television and Radio Broadcasting
Doma Lauk 8
Riga
Tel: (2) 226304, 200016

Latvian Radio and Television
Smilsu iela 1-3
Riga LV-1939
Tel: (2) 206509

Latvijas Radio
Doma lauk 8
Riga LV-1505
Tel: (2) 226304
Fax: (2) 206709

Latvia Televizija
Zakusalas krastmala 3
Riga LV-1509
Tel: (2) 200830
Fax: (2) 200025

NTV-5 (Independent Television-5)
Maskavas iela 40-42
Riga LV-1018
Tel: (2) 225758

INTERNET ADDRESSES

BALT-L, a moderated list covering the republics of Lithuania, Latvia and Estonia, is accessed through the address balt-l@ubvm.cc.buffalo.edu. This group contains news items from the wire services, discussions on cultural, political and academic issues.

Latvia OnLine
http://latvia.vernet.lv/

Latvian Academic Network
http://www.lanet.lv/

City Net - Latvia
http://www.city.net/countries/latvia/

Latvia Network Resources
http://www.nlib.ee/LATVIA/

Lebanon

Republic of Lebanon

Economy

Overview

With the mid-1990s rebirth of the Beirut stock market, Lebanon aims to regain its role as a regional financial and business center. The nation has embarked on an economic recovery plan which calls for reducing its budget deficit, reconstructing its infrastructure, and stabilizing its currency. Since the end of the Lebanese civil war that began in 1975, the country has sought the kind of economic stability that only now appears to begin to become possible, if perhaps not yet fully likely. Positive signs include the rapprochement between neighboring Israel and many of its Arab neighbors, which would allow Lebanon to be removed as a proxy battlefield in the Arab-Israeli conflict, as well as a general easing of tensions among Arab countries in the Middle East. The Lebanese have always displayed an acute entrepreneurial spirit which should serve them well in rebuilding their economy.

Trade

Lebanon has traditionally been an importing country, helping to offset its merchandise trade deficit with revenues derived from its trade surplus in services. Major exports include apparel, metal products, machinery, pharmaceuticals, food products, and paper. Imports have included a wide range of products: raw and intermediate materials, and capital and consumer goods. Most imports come from industrialized nations in Europe, while nearly 90 percent of exports have been purchased by Middle Eastern and Arab countries. Main trade partners include Italy, Saudi Arabia, France, the US, and Germany.

Sectors

Agriculture Agriculture contributes less than 10 percent of GDP and employment. Major cash crops include citrus fruit, cereals, vegetables, cotton, and wine grapes. Livestock raising, fishing, and forestry have all been minor contributors. Lebanon has recently become a net importer of foodstuffs.

Industry Industry produces nearly 25 percent of GDP, while employing about 20 percent of the work force. The industrial sector is still reeling from Lebanon's 17-year civil war. The lack of an adequate infrastructure, rising costs of services, and scarce bank credits are slowing recovery, although industrial activity is beginning to pick up.

Services The Lebanese have specialized in trade and finance, and many foreign interests used Lebanon as their Middle Eastern regional headquarters. Efforts were made to retain this business even during the height of the civil war. As a result of the civil war, heavy immigration led to shortages in all segments of the labor force. Today, Lebanese professionals are returning from abroad to apply their expertise to the nation's businesses, and the country is beginning to see a tentative revival in its high value-added financial service sector.

Trends

The economic and commercial outlook is more promising than it has been in a long time. The government expects robust growth in income, consumption, and investment. Inflation should be moderate in the coming years; and capital inflows induced by pent up and growing demand as the political and social situations stabilize are expected to offset Lebanon's trade deficit. Both domestic production and increasing exports will contribute to economic growth through the remainder of the 1990s.

At a Glance

THE COUNTRY

Location The Middle East, in the eastern Mediterranean Sea, between Israel and Syria.

Terrain A narrow coastal plain meets mountains, followed by a fertile central valley, then more mountains, extending to the Syrian border.

Climate Typically Mediterranean with mild to cool, wet winters and hot, dry summers; the mountains have heavy winter snows.

THE PEOPLE

Population 3,600,000

Ethnic composition

Arab 93%

Armenian 6%

Religious composition Christian (Maronite, Greek Orthodox, Greek Catholic, Roman Catholic, Protestant, Armenian Apostolic, other); Muslim (Sunni, Shi'a, other); Druze.

Education and literacy For the five years of compulsory education, students attend private or free public schools. The adult literacy rate is 75 percent, high for the Middle East.

Labor force

Total: 750,000

There are no current reliable statistics on labor. The civil war and heavy immigration have created shortages in all segments of the labor force. By occupation: industry, commerce, services 79%, agriculture 11%, and government 10%.

COUNTRY FACTS

Political and legal This parliamentary republic has both secular and religious courts, using a combination of Ottoman, civil, and canon law.

Telephone Rebuilding the telecommunications system, which was severely damaged by civil war, is underway. Domestic calls are carried primarily by microwave radio relay and a small amount of cable. Rehabilitation and modernization of telecommunications are a top government priority. International country code: [961]. Selected city codes: Beirut (1).

Transportation The development and rehabilitation of Beirut International Airport and the Beirut Port and Free Zone area have begun. There are eight other airports and eight major shipping ports. Rebuilding Beirut public transport and national highways is under study. The railroad system is considered inoperable.

Environment The effects of political fragmentation and warfare have rendered environmental control efforts non-existent or ineffective. Government efforts are being made to rehabilitate water and sewage treatment plants. The nation's forests and water supplies are still recovering from war damage. Current issues are deforestation; soil erosion; desertification; and air and water pollution.

Media In the Arab world, Lebanon's press has been the least censored. There are several daily newspapers and numerous magazines. There are five AM and three FM regular radio stations; however, several other stations are operated sporadically by various factions. There are 13 television stations.

Health 95 percent of the population have access to health care services. Life expectancy of males is 65 years; of females, 70 years.

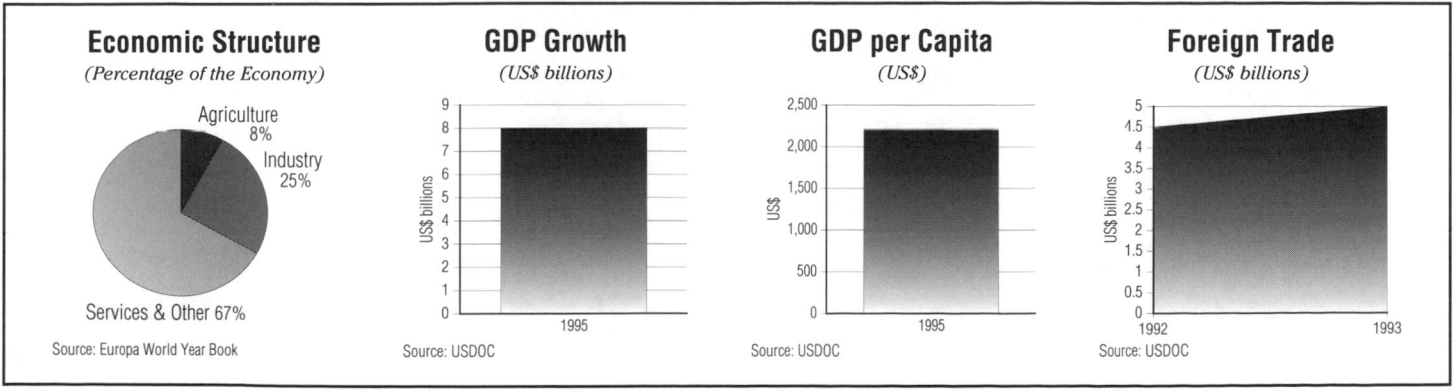

Economic Structure
(Percentage of the Economy)

Agriculture 8%
Industry 25%
Services & Other 67%

Source: Europa World Year Book

GDP Growth
(US$ billions)

1995

Source: USDOC

GDP per Capita
(US$)

1995

Source: USDOC

Foreign Trade
(US$ billions)

1992   1993

Source: USDOC

Business Travel

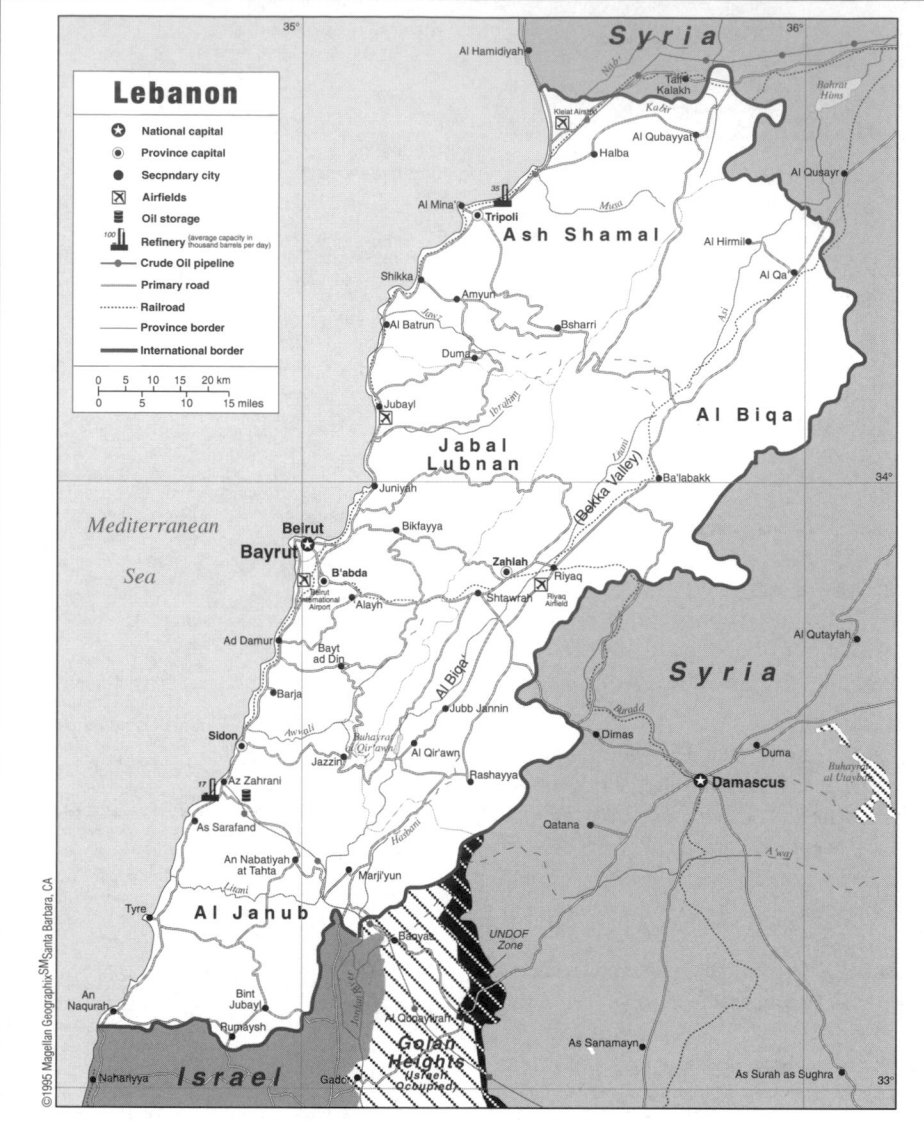

©1995 Magellan Geographix℠Santa Barbara, CA

Lebanon

- ⊛ National capital
- ⊙ Province capital
- ● Secondary city
- ☒ Airfields
- ▤ Oil storage
- ▥ Refinery (average capacity in thousand barrels per day)
- ⊶ Crude Oil pipeline
- — Primary road
- ···· Railroad
- — Province border
- — International border

0 5 10 15 20 km
0 5   10   15 miles

Travelogue

WORKWEEK
Offices Monday - Friday 8:00 am to 5:00 pm.
Banks Monday - Friday 8:00 am to 12:30 pm, Saturday 8:00 am to noon.
Government Monday - Friday 8:00 am to 5:00 pm.
Retail Monday - Friday 9:00 am to 5:00 pm.

HOLIDAYS
Holidays 1996
January 1 New Year's Day
February 9 St. Maron's Day
Feast of Ramadan**
April 5 Good Friday Western Rite*
May 1 Labor Day
Eastern Orthodox Good Friday*
May 6 Martyrs' Day
Feast of Al-Adha**
Ashura**
Moslem New Year**
August 15 Assumption
Prophet's Birthday**
November 1 All Saints' Day
November 22 Independence Day
December 25 Christmas Day
*Dates vary each year.
**Dates are based on a lunar calendar and vary each year.

VISA AND PASSPORT
Passports and visas are required for travel to Lebanon; passports must be valid for at least three months beyond the estimated duration of stay. All foreigners except nationals of the Gulf Cooperation Council must obtain visas from a Lebanese consulate or embassy in advance of arrival. The government of Lebanon refuses entry and transit to holders of Israeli passports and to holders of passports containing a visa for Israel. Nationals of India may be required to present a return or onward ticket. United States passports are not valid for travel to or through Lebanon unless a special validation has been obtained from the US Department of State.

DEPARTURE FORMALITIES
There is a US$15 departure tax for visitors leaving the country by boat or economy class air ticket. First class airline passengers must pay US$30.

TIPPING
Tipping is not expected but is usually given for good service. Most restaurants include a service charge, but it is customary to leave an extra tip of 5–10%.

CRIME
The crime rate in Lebanon is moderate. Car thefts and house break-ins are increasing. US citizens are considered targets for the armed terrorist organizations that continue to operate within the country. Political situations are chaotic and the threat of terrorism remains great.

INFRASTRUCTURE
Railroads are considered inoperable. The absence of a functioning infrastructure affects all sectors, including tourism, greatly. Major projects have started to be rebuilt including airports, highways, and harbors, along with an updated telecommunications system. Roads are good by Middle Eastern standards. Ports are held by militia units but have reopened despite severe damage.

NATIONAL TOURIST OFFICE
National Council of Tourism in Lebanon
550 Central Bank St.
POB 11-5344
Beirut
Tel: (1) 340940
Fax: (1) 343279

COMMUNICATIONS
Telephones Telephone services are available but unreliable due to the damage done to the telephone network during the civil war. The damage is being repaired, and international calls are possible. Various private cellular telephone facilities exist.
Fax Fax facilities are available.
Post office Postal services are available, but unreliable due to the unstable atmosphere in Lebanon.

BEST TRAVEL BOOKS
Middle East, On a Shoestring, Lonely Planet. Details, details, details! 126 maps.
Fieldings, The World's Most Dangerous Places. The hard-core adventurer's guide to getting in, getting around, and getting out. Robert Young and Coskin Aral.
Do's and Taboo's Around the World. The Bestselling Guide to International Behavior. Edited by Roger Axtell, compiled by the Parker Pen Company. The ultimate guide to international behavior, now completely updated and expanded. Helpful, fun to read!

USEFUL TELEPHONE NUMBERS
If you are calling from outside Lebanon, you will need to add the country code [961] and any other international dialing requirements from within your country.
- Tourist police..(1) 343209
- Beirut International Airport ....(1) 629065
- Air France...(1) 200700
- British Airways...(1) 351499
- Japan Airlines (JAL) ....(1) 801859
- KLM ....(1) 601021
- Lufthansa ....(1) 346595
- Tarom ....(1) 342776
- TMA...(1) 820486

Credit Card Information
Lost or stolen credit cards (call collect to the US, regardless of which country the card was issued in).
- Amex ....[1] (919) 333-3211
- Diner's Club................................[1] (303) 799-1504
- MasterCard ....[1] (314) 275-6690
- Visa ....[1] (410) 581-7931

Foreign Trade

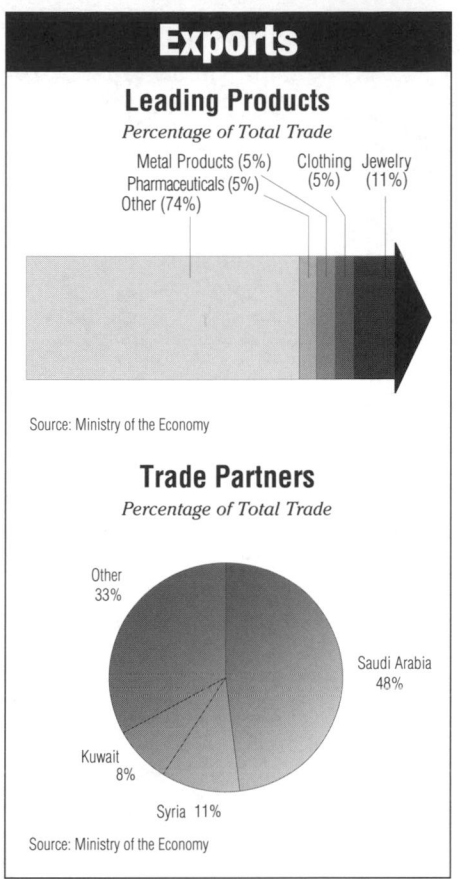

Imports

Leading Products

- consumer goods

- machinery and transport

- petroleum products

Source: CIA World Fact Book

Trade Partners
Percentage of Total Trade

Italy 15%

France 10%

Germany 7%

US 9%

Other 59%

Source: Ministry of the Economy

Exports

Leading Products
Percentage of Total Trade

Metal Products (5%)
Pharmaceuticals (5%)
Other (74%)
Clothing (5%)
Jewelry (11%)

Source: Ministry of the Economy

Trade Partners
Percentage of Total Trade

Other 33%

Saudi Arabia 48%

Kuwait 8%

Syria 11%

Source: Ministry of the Economy

Opportunities

FOR IMPORTING TO LEBANON

- consumer goods
- machinery and transport equipment
- petroleum

FOR EXPORTING FROM LEBANON

- agriculture, chemicals, metal and metal products
- textiles
- precious and semi-precious metals and jewelry

GROWTH SECTORS
- agriculture sector
- construction/real estate
- electric power sector
- industry sector
- trade and services

Trade News

RULES AND REGULATIONS

- **Trade news** Drug trafficking has increased due to lack of government authority.
- **Tariffs and trade** Lebanon is not a member of the General Agreement of Tariffs and Trade (GATT).
- **Licenses** Some goods such as firearms and munitions need an import license from the appropriate government authorities. Non-military weapons and ammunition for hunting are subject to license as well.
- **Exports** Exports of certain goods (arms and ammunition, narcotics, and similar products) to any destination and all exports to Israel and South Africa are prohibited.
- **Export licenses** Export licenses are required for wheat and wheat derivatives to any country. All exports of the Democratic People's Republic of Korea require a license.

Legal

Legal System

The legal system in Lebanon is developed and inspired essentially from the French system, and new laws tend to follow recognized international patterns.

Intellectual Property Rights

Patents and trademarks All petitions for patents must be addressed by inventors or their agents to the Director, Office of Protection of Commercial, Industrial, Literary, and Artistic Property. If the petition is made by an agent, it also must include a valid power of attorney, duly executed and authenticated by the Lebanese Council. Trademarks may be registered, and the period of protection lasts for 15 years. Petitions for trademark registration should include the full name, the nature of trade or business, and four copies of a model, specifying color and dimensions.

Copyrights Petitions to register a copyright should include the following information: full name and nature of the work, name of local agent in Lebanon if necessary, and three copies of the publication.

Business Registration

Except for a small number of businesses where authorization of the government is still required by special laws (banking and insurance, for example), corporations can be formed and business commenced without any special approval. By-laws must be deposited and registered with a notary public.

Contracts and Dispute Resolutions

Court cases are not settled rapidly because of shortage of judges and inadequate support structure. However, most business disputes are still resolved through the court system, and arbitration is not commonly resorted to.

Legal Matters

LEGAL BRIEFS

- **Bankruptcy** Under Lebanese bankruptcy law, a secured creditor has the right to share in the assets of a bankrupt party.
- **Notaries** Notaries draw up and verify all documents that the parties desire to make in authentic form, and they preserve the originals on file as a record. Certified copies of the originals have the same force and effect as the original. Notaries also have additional responsibilities, including receipt of deposits for escrow.
- **Competition** To encourage market-based competition, Lebanese firms can no longer act as exclusive representatives of foreign firms for basic commodities.
- **Wages** Lebanese wages are relatively low, and many businesses tend to be labor intensive.
- **Foreign investment** Foreign-owned firms have the same investment opportunities as local firms. The Beirut Port Management committee is presently reviewing laws related to duty-free import zones.
- **Labor contracts** All labor relations are governed by two forms of contracts: individual contracts between employer and employee, and collective contracts, binding agreements negotiated and entered between employers and labor unions.
- **Labor disputes** Any disputes are settled by the Arbitration Labor Council, composed of a judge, a representative of the workers, and a representative of the employer. Judgments from the ALC are final and are not open to any appeal.
- **Worker benefits** Workers are entitled to certain benefits, which are generally determined by the terms of the collective bargaining agreement.

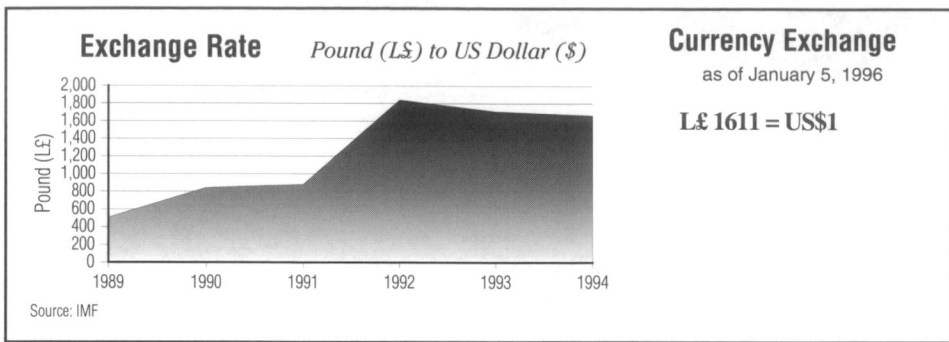

Source: IMF

Currency

The currency of Lebanon is the Lebanese pound, also known locally as the lira. Its symbol is L£ or LL, and the principal subdivision is 100 piasters.

Foreign Exchange

Lebanon has the most liberal banking system in the Middle East. Bank secrecy is strictly enforced, and foreign exchange is widely available from commercial banks or money dealers at market rates. There are no taxes or subsidies on purchases or sales of foreign exchange. Commercial banks are allowed to engage in spot transactions in any currency except the Israeli new shekel, but are prohibited from transacting forward exchanges that exceed L£ 500,000, unless the transactions are related to foreign trade. Banks may not provide loans to nonresidents in Lebanese pounds. They are also prohibited from extending loans secured by guarantees from nonresident banks, unless the transactions are for commercial or investment purposes in Lebanon. Furthermore, banks cannot receive deposits or open accounts in Lebanese pounds for nonresident banks or other foreign financial institutions. Bank credit in Lebanese pounds to residents for the purchase of foreign exchange other than for foreign trade transactions is subject to a special reserve requirement.

Capital Transfers

There are no regulations or restrictions to the transfer of capital into or out of Lebanon. Expropriation of investments is a violation of Lebanese laws and regulations. Land expropriation in Lebanon is rare; the government expropriates property only for public utility projects—mainly for enlarging highways and streets. Compensation is paid at the time of expropriation.

Investment Incentives

Industries located outside Beirut enjoy tax incentives. Investors are not required to disclose proprietary information as part of the regulatory approval process, except for banks.

Investment Restrictions

The government does not discriminate against any foreign investment, company, or representative. There are no performance requirements imposed as a condition for establishing, maintaining, or expanding an investment.

TAXATION

Taxation requires sophisticated knowledge of complex rules and regulations specific to each country. The information presented here is from the Ernst & Young Corporate Tax Guide and Directory, available from the Ernst & Young accounting office in your country, or from:

Ernst & Young S.A.R.L.
Mail Address:
POB 11-1639
Beirut, Lebanon
Street Address:
Sabbagh Center
Hamra Street
Beirut, Lebanon
Tel: (1) 353420, 353421, 346202
Telex: 22845
Fax: (1) 346203

At a Glance

Corporate Income Tax Rate (%)	10
Capital Gains Tax Rate (%)	6
Branch Tax Rate (%	10
Withholding Tax (%) (a)	
Dividends	5
Interest (b)	5
Royalties from Patents, Know-how, etc.	5
Payments for Services	5
Branch Remittance Tax (c)	5
Net Operating Losses (Years)	
Carryback	0
Carryforward (d)	3

(a) Applicable to both residents and nonresidents.
(b) Bank interest is not subject to withholding tax. However, bank interest received by companies is included in taxable income.
(c) Profits derived by branches operating in Lebanon are presumed to be distributed and consequently are subject to dividend withholding tax.
(d) Losses incurred in years of political unrest may be carried forward for eight years.

Money Matters

BITS AND PIECES

- **Investments** The Lebanese constitution emphasizes a free economy with a liberal investment atmosphere. With very few exceptions there is no discrimination between national and foreign investment. A foreigner wishing to conduct business in Lebanon must have both work and resident permits, as well as register with the commercial register.
- **Capital** There are no restrictions on the movement of capital, capital gains, remittances, or dividends. Credit is allocated on market terms and foreign investors can get credit on the local market.
- **Private ownership** Private ownership is a sacred right in Lebanon. Foreigners can freely establish, acquire, and dispose of interests in business enterprises.
- **Gold** Residents may freely hold gold in any form at home or abroad, and may freely negotiate gold in any form with residents and nonresidents. Gold imports and exports in any form are permitted and do not require a license, but must be officially recorded. The importation, exportation, and domestic sale of foreign gold coins must be represented by a certificate issued by the Office for the Protection of the Consumer, indicating their content and weight.

BANKS

Bank of Lebanon
Masraf Loubnane Street
POB 11-5544
Beirut
Tel: (1) 341230 through 40

Adcom Bank SAL
PO Box 866
Jounieh
Tel: (9) 936414, 936855
Fax: (9) 936902

Allied Business Bank
POB 113-7165
Diab Bldg
Makdessi St.
7165 Beirut
Tel: (1) 370994/5, 346934, 349169
Fax: (1) 864551
Telex: 21708

Bank of Beirut SAL
POB 11-7354
Gefinor Centre
Rue Clemenceau
Beirut
Tel: (1) 350723

Bank of Beirut and the Arab Countries SAL
POB 11-1536
Bank Bldg.
250 rue Clemenceau
Beirut
Tel: (1) 867142
Telex: 20761

Bank of Lebanon and Kuwait SAL
Hamra
Pavillon St.
Ghannoum & Sabbagh Bldg.
Beirut
Tel: (1) 866860

Al Moughtareb Bank SAL
POB 11-5508
Sehnaoui Bldg.
Banque du Liban St.
Beirut
Tel: (1) 35006015
Fax: (1) 602009
Tel: 21406

Banque Libanaise pour le Commerce S.A.L
PO Box 11-1126
Tel: (1) 445450, 338736
Fax: (1) 581927

Societe Generale Libano-Europeenne de Banque SAL
PO Box 11-2955
Beirut
Tel: (1) 499813/7, 483001/9, 483151/8
Fax: (1) 495460/2

Overview

Lebanon has had an active, open market for centuries and currently has the most liberal banking regime in the Middle East. It's population is one of the most diverse in the Middle East. The people are relatively well-educated and well-read, especially compared to neighboring countries. Most of the people live in rural areas and work in agriculture, so marketing campaigns shouldn't concentrate on the cities alone. Because the population is so spread out, don't expect a quick turn-around; profits can take months or even years.

Distribution

Many international firms maintain offices in Lebanon, and they are usually staffed with Lebanese. Competition for this slowly reorganizing market is strong, with almost all European countries being represented. Distribution is still plagued by social and political unrest, however, and channels can be distributed and altered with little notice.

Agents, Distributors, and Partners

Most distribution flows either through public bazaars or numerous small dealerships, usually family-owned. Multinational firms usually open offices with a local staff in one or more of the five commercial harbors. One way to enter this market is to form joint ventures with other companies to bid on major projects.

Advertising

There are four major Arabic newspapers, one French, and one English daily. There are also a major business journal in French (*Le Commerce du Levant*), two in Arabic (*Mal-wa-a'mal and Al-Bayan*), and *Arab Ad* in English.

Marketing in Lebanon

MARKETING TIPS

- **Language** Arabic is Lebanon's official language, English and French the next most common. Promotional literature should be prepared in at least two of these three. There are a number of other languages spoken as well, and some prior research is needed for any kind of mass marketing campaign.
- **Open markets** Markets with the greatest current potential include fast food franchises, cosmetics, sportswear, and fashion design franchises.
- **Variety of religions** A variety of religions are represented in Lebanon, including Maronite, Greek Orthodox, Greek Catholic, Armenian Apostolic, Roman Catholic, and Protestant. No matter the belief, Lebanon is still very conservative and religious. These factors should be very important when planning a marketing campaign.

AD AGENCIES

Bates Adco Lebanon
PO Box 113-5273
Beirut
Tel: (1) 352056
Fax: (1) 353306

Fortune Promoseven
PO Box 116-5288
Beirut
Tel: (1) 3783813

Intermarkets Lebanon
PO Box 55434
Sin El Fil
Beirut
Tel: (1) 480477

TMI
PO Box 113-6164
Beirut
Tel: (1) 342573
Fax: (1) 602174

Business Culture

Greetings and Courtesies

Greetings are important, and will often be accompanied by questions about one's health or family. The standard greeting is the handshake, which is acceptable when meeting both men and women. A man should wait for a woman to initiate a handshake, however. If she doesn't, he should smile and nod slightly. Titles are important; if a person has one, be sure to use it. Personal space is less than in many other cultures, so don't be surprised if Lebanese associates stand close.

Business Ethic and Framework

People, family ties, and personal relationships are placed above business. Fate is an important part of Lebanese culture. Most feel that no matter how hard they try the outcome is ultimately in the hands of God. Class distinctions often determine a person's opportunities and influence their attitudes toward getting ahead in life.

Meetings and Decision Making

Arrive on time, but expect your Lebanese associates to be late. Personal relationships are more important than schedules. People's feelings are often taken into account, and an individual's needs can influence how a decision is made or what it will be. Lebanese do not like to directly criticize something. Instead, they might hint they'd like to see changes, or suggest an alternative that leaves room for compromise. Decisions are made slowly. If you push for faster action or impose a deadline, you could do more harm than good. Ultimately, your personal relationship with your Lebanese colleagues will be crucial to how things go.

Women

Women (especially Christians) can be found in many aspects of business. Middle Eastern culture puts many restrictions on women, but foreign women will generally be accepted and treated with respect in business. Being professional, poised, and self-confident will help. Do not make prolonged, direct eye contact with Lebanese men.

Cultural Cautions

DO'S

- Use the right hand or both hands to give and receive things. Using the left hand can be offensive.
- Lebanese pride themselves on their hospitality. If offered tea or coffee, accept it. If you must reject such an offer of hospitality, be sure to give a polite explanation.

DON'TS

- Avoid conversation about local or national politics, and do not bring up the subject of Israel.
- It is considered impolite to discuss business over a meal. If you are eating with Lebanese colleagues, do not talk about business unless they do. This will probably be when the meal is over.

CUSTOMS

- Public displays of affection between men and women (even if married) are highly offensive.
- Standard attire is a conservative suit. Women should wear tasteful, conservative clothing.

OBSERVATIONS

- Lebanese are generally Christian or Muslim. The behavior and attitude of these groups vary, and you should know something about your associate's religious beliefs before you go.

NEGOTIATIONS

- Lebanese have a tradition of negotiating and genuinely enjoy it. Long, enthusiastic discussions are typical, and are an occasion for demonstrating one's wit and intelligence.
- Honor is extremely important. If honor is at stake, it might be difficult for someone to admit they've made a mistake or back down from a position.
- Arguments based on personal need can be more persuasive than "mere" logic.

Contacts

GOVERNMENT AGENCIES

Central Inspection Office
Al-Ghanem Building
Bordeaux Street
Beirut
Tel: (1) 340040

Government Railways and Transports
Souk el-Arwan
POB 109
Beirut

Ministry of Agriculture
Rue Sami Solh
Beirut
Tel: (1) 380460

Ministry of Education and the Fine Arts
Unesco Street
Beirut
Tel: (1) 30511

Ministry of Finance
Rue de l'Etoile (parallele a Riad Solh)
Beirut
Tel: (1) 251600, 642720

Ministry of Foreign Affairs
Rue Sursock
Achrafieh
Beirut
Tel: (1) 333100, 334400, 326905, 427528

Ministry of National Economy, Trade and Industry
Rue Artois
Beirut
Tel: (1) 345051, 340178, 344476

Ministry of Posts and Telecommunications
Rue Sami Solh
Beirut
Tel: (1) 240100, 250100, 382415, 331300,

Ministry of Public Works and Transportation
Shiah
Beirut
Tel: (1) 270225, 384475

Office des Chemins de Fer de l'Etat Libanais et du Transport en Commun de Beyrouth et de sa Banlieue
POB 109
Souk el-Arwan
Beirut
Tel: (1) 443619
Telex: 43088

CHAMBERS OF COMMERCE

Beirut Chamber of Commerce and Industry
POB 11-1801
Sanayeh
Beirut
Tel: (1) 349530, 860750, 353390
Fax: (1) 865802
Telex: 22269

Tripoli Chamber of Commerce and Industry
POB 27
Blvd. Tripoli
Tripoli
Tel: (6) 622790, 432790
Telex: 46024

Chamber of Commerce and Industry in Sidon and South Lebanon
POB 41
Maarouf Saad St.
Sidon
Tel: (7) 720123, 722948
Fax: (7) 722986
Telex: 720123

Zahleh Chamber of Commerce and Industry
POB 100
Zahleh
Tel: (8) 822077, 800050
Telex: 48034

LEGAL CONTACTS

Alem & Associates
Cornishe Mazraa, Gondole Building
5th Floor, Suite 10
Beirut
Tel: (1) 818191, 318615
Fax: (1) 818191

Raphaâl, Ziadé, Abirached et Associés
Immeuble Kassis-Antelias
POB Boite Postale 70-868
Beirut
Tel: (1) 405-401
Fax: (1) 601-908

Zaba K. Zreik Law Offices
Associated with Fox & Gibbons
Autostrade Dora
Cite Dora 3 Building, 10th Floor
POB 90-710
Beirut
Tel: (1) 881322
Fax: (1) 881387

NEWSPAPERS

Aztag
POB 11-587
Rue Selim Boustani
Beirut
Tel: (1) 366607

Al-Jarida The News Paper
POB 220
Place Tabaris
Beirut

Al-Khatib The Speaker
POB 365
Rue Georges Picot
Beirut

Al-Liwa The Standard
POB 2402
Beirut
Tel: (1) 865080
Telex: 43409

An-Nahar The Day
POB 11-226
Rue Banque du Liban-Hamra
Press Co-operative Bldg.
Beirut
Tel: (1) 353699
Telex: 22322

L'Orient-Le Jour
POB 166495
Rue Banque du Liban
Beirut
Tel: (1) 340560

Raqib al-Ahwal The Observer
POB 467
Rue Patriarche Hoyek
Beirut

Le Reveil
POB 8383
Blvd Sin el-Fil
Beirut

As-Safeer The Ambassador
POB 113-5015
Beirut
Tel: (1) 350080
Telex: 21484

Sawt al-Uruba The Voice of Europe
POB 3537
Beirut

Le Soir
POB 1470
Rue de Syrie
Beirut

At-Tayyar The Current
POB 1038
Beirut

Telegraf-Bairut
POB 1061
Rue Bechara el-Khoury
Beirut

REMEMBER
- When you telephone (or fax) to Lebanon from another country you must always include the country code [961] before the numbers given.
- When you send mail to Lebanon, be sure to write LEBANON in capital letters on its own line below the addresses given.

PERIODICALS

Al-Alam al-Lubnani The Lebanese World
POB 462
Imm. Ministry of Foreign Affairs
Beirut

Achabaka Network
POB 1038
Dar Assayad
Beirut

Al-Ahad Sunday
POB 1462
Quartier Chourah
rue Andalous
Beirut

Argus
Bureau of Lebanese and Arab Documentation
POB 16-5403
Beirut
Tel: (1) 219113

Le Commerce du Levant
POB 687
Kantari St.
Commerce and Finance Bldg.
Beirut
Tel: (1) 297770

Al-Liwa' The Standard
POB 4823
Ramel az-Zarif
Independence St.
Saradar Bldg.
Beirut
Tel: (1) 221480
Telex: 43409

Al-Ousbou' al-Arabi Arab Week
Quartier Sursock
Achrafieh
POB 1404
Beirut
Tel: (1) 331200
Telex: 41362

Revue du Liban
POB 165612
Rue Issa Maalouf
Beirut
Tel: (1) 339960 Telex: 20303

Alam at-Tijarat Business World
Strand Bldg., Hamra St.
Beirut

INTERNET ADDRESSES

Usenet group(s):
soc.culture.arabic
soc.culture.lebanon

Lebanon Online Resources
http://www.lebanon.com/

City Net - Lebanon
http://www.city.net/countries/lebanon/

Arab.net
http://www.arab.net/welcome.html

Libya

Socialist People's Libyan Arab Jamahiriya

Economy

Overview

Libya has isolated itself politically from much of the rest of the international community, and its quasi-socialist economic system with a strong central authority heavily dependent on petroleum revenues has further prevented it from developing an open market in the international environment. Since 1981, fiscal problems associated with declining oil revenues, combined with the effects of various socialist welfare schemes, have hurt the economy. Although Libyans have experienced a dramatic rise in their standard of living during the past 20 years, more recent economic austerity measures coupled with tighter internal security controls, have led to the deterioration in the overall quality of life in Libya. Even so, distribution of wealth is more equitable in Libya than in many other developing countries in the world or in many of the partially developed countries in the region.

Trade

Libya is dependent on trade for virtually all of its needs. Exports include crude and refined petroleum and some chemicals. Imports include machinery and transportation equipment, basic manufactures, miscellaneous manufactures, foodstuffs, and chemicals. Major trading partners have included Italy, Germany, France, Japan, and the UK, although most of these have at one time or another imposed trading sanctions in response to Libyan terrorist activities. Beginning in the early 1980s, the US banned the import of Libyan oil, and has since strengthened the ban and attempted to recruit its allies to join in the ban.

Sectors

Agriculture Only somewhat more than five percent of Libya's GDP is derived from agriculture, which employs about 18 percent of the work force. Primary crops include wheat, barley, olives, citrus fruits, vegetables, dates, and peanuts, although livestock raising is the main activity in the sector. Although virtually all production is for domestic consumption, most foodstuffs must be imported.

Industry Industry produces half of GDP, while employing 30 percent of the work force. Petroleum extraction and refining is the main industry, followed by food processing, textiles, cement, and some handicrafts production.

Services Libya gets somewhat less than half of its GDP from services, which employ nearly 60 percent of the work force; about 25 percent of all workers fill government posts, while the rest operate primarily in local distribution and personal service activities.

Trends

Higher incomes and a growing population have caused food consumption to skyrocket, leading to an ever greater need for imported foodstuffs. One of Libya's current goals is to become self-sufficient in food production, though scarcity of water in this desert land is a serious obstacle. Libya is undertaking a multi-billion dollar project to tap water resources deep under the Sahara to meet coastal population water needs in the 1990s, although technical and administrative problems are hampering progress. Official pronouncements and limited actions support the privatization of selected public enterprises and the lifting of restrictions on private wholesale trade; however, the belligerence of the current regime will likely make significant development difficult well into the future.

At a Glance

THE COUNTRY

Location Northern Africa, on the southern coast of the Mediterranean Sea, between Egypt and Tunisia.
Terrain Desert and semi-desert; mostly barren, flat to undulating plains, plateaus, and depressions.
Climate Mediterranean along coast; dry, with extreme desert in the interior. The hot, dry, dust-laden *ghibli* is a southern wind lasting one to four days in spring and fall.

THE PEOPLE

Population 4,900,000
Ethnic composition
Berber and Arab 97%
Some Greeks, Maltese, Italians, Egyptians, Pakistanis, Turks, Indians, and Tunisians.
Religious composition
Sunni Muslim 97%
Languages spoken Arabic, Italian, and English.
Education and literacy The government has invested heavily in education, funding free schooling at all levels. Seven years are compulsory. Adult literacy of males is 75 percent; of females, 50 percent.
Labor force
Total: 1,300,000
500,000 are resident foreign workers.
By occupation: industry 31%, services 27%, government 24%, and agriculture 18%.

COUNTRY FACTS

Political and legal Libya is an Islamic Arabic socialist "Jamahiriya" or "state of masses." The system is based on the ideas of ruler Maj. Gen. Mu'ammar al-Qadhafi, although he holds no formal office. The system is made up of popular assemblies (people's congresses) with executive institutions (people's committees) guided by political cadres (revolutionary committees). Since 1969, civil laws must conform to Shari'a, or Islamic law, which combines previous systems of civil and religious law. Military courts and special "revolutionary courts" operate outside the judicial system.
Telephone Libya's government owns and operates the modern telephone and telecommunications system. International country code: [218]. Selected city codes: Tripoli (21), Gharian (41), Benghazi (61).
Transportation No railroad has been in operation since 1965, and previous systems have been dismantled. Progress on construction plans is unknown. There are seven major seaports to handle shipping. There are two international and several domestic airports.
Environment Underground water resources are scarce due to overuse in agricultural developments. The government has funded a significant project to tap water resources deep under the Sahara. Despite major irrigation projects, climatic conditions and poor soils severely limit farm output, which meets only about 25 percent of the demand. Pollution from sewage and industrial waste threatens the Mediterranean Sea. Current issues are sparse, natural, surface-water resources; water pollution; and desertification.
Media There is one broadcasting corporation, which runs 17 AM and 3 FM radio stations and 12 television stations. The government owns the major newspaper; others are published by the revolutionary committees.
Health One hundred percent of the population has access to health care. Life expectancy of males is 66 years; of females, 71 years.

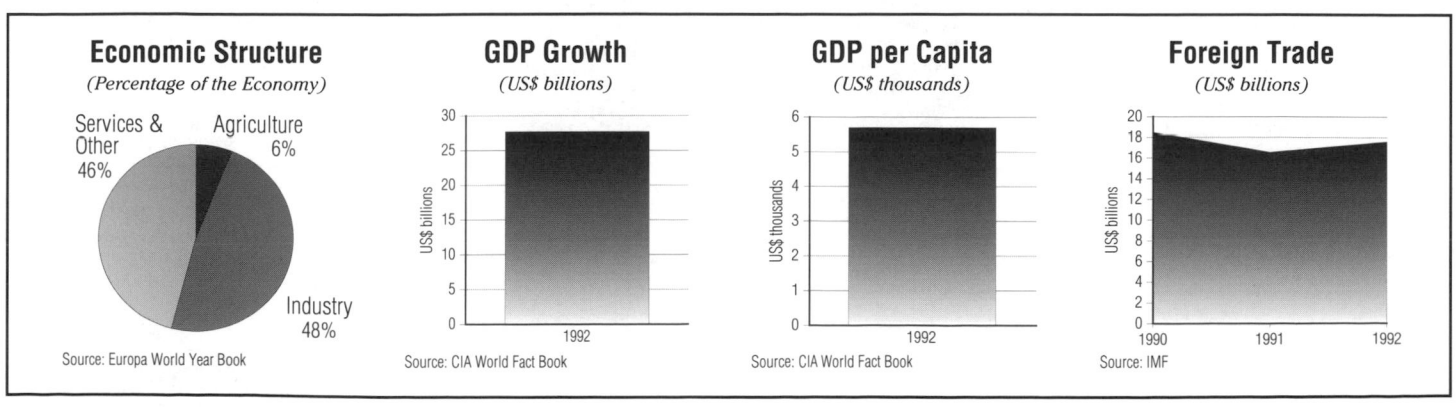

Economic Structure
(Percentage of the Economy)

Services & Other 46%
Agriculture 6%
Industry 48%

Source: Europa World Year Book

GDP Growth
(US$ billions)

1992

Source: CIA World Fact Book

GDP per Capita
(US$ thousands)

1992

Source: CIA World Fact Book

Foreign Trade
(US$ billions)

1990   1991   1992

Source: IMF

Business Travel

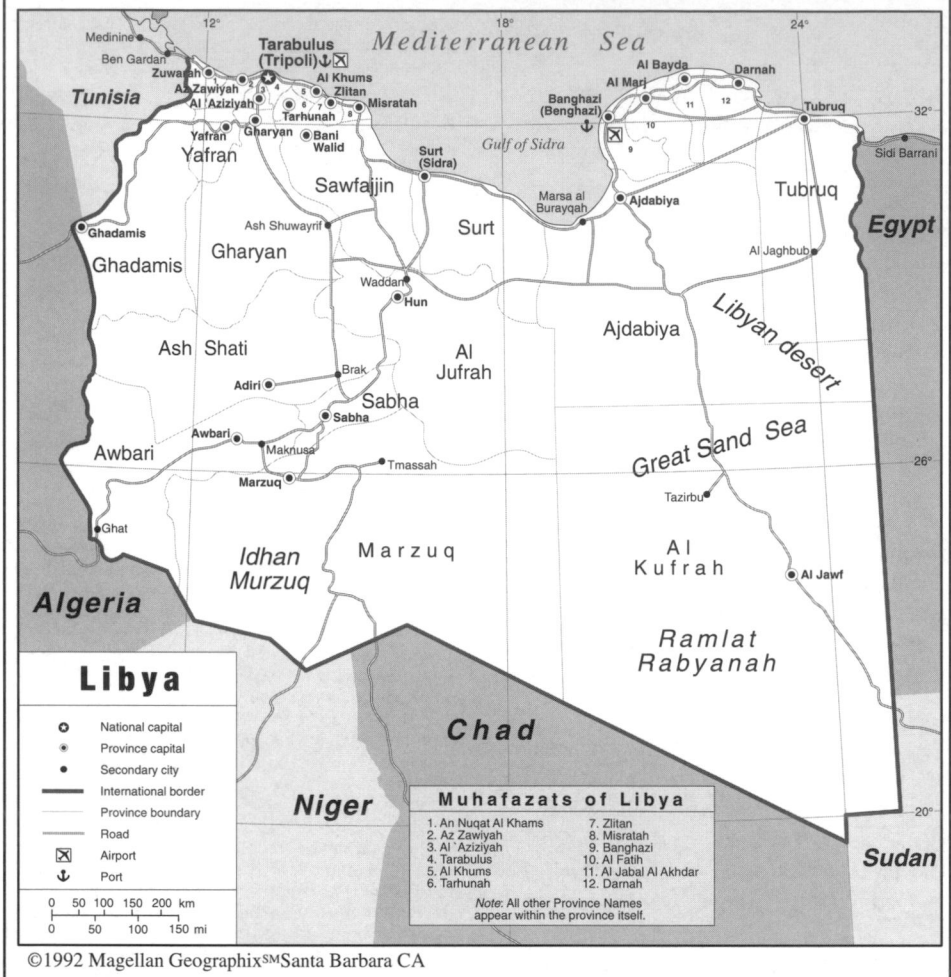

	LH 1906	MADRID	935	113-3
	LH 1022	STUTTGART HBF.	935	-
	AF 1701	LYON	940	683-6
	AY 822	HELSINKI	940	113-3
	AA 071	SFRANCISCO-DALLAS	945	731-7

©1992 Magellan Geographix℠ Santa Barbara CA

COMMUNICATIONS

Telephones Libya has a modern telephone system.
Fax Luxury hotels have available facsimile facilities but suffer from few telephone lines. Late night automatic fax facilities in private offices are a best bet.
Post office Libya has a good postal system. Facilities are available in the main cities.

BEST TRAVEL BOOKS

North African Handbook. The ideal practical guide. Updated annually.
Do's and Taboo's Around the World. The Bestselling Guide to International Behavior. Edited by Roger Axtell, compiled by the Parker Pen Company. The ultimate guide to international behavior, now completely updated and expanded. Helpful, fun to read!
Lonely Planet Travel Survival Kit to Libya.

USEFUL TELEPHONE NUMBERS

If you are calling from outside Libya, you will need to add the country code [218] and any other international dialing requirements from within your country.

- Grand Hotel, Tripoli .... (21) 34940
- General Maritime Transport .... (21) 33155

Credit Card Information

Lost or stolen credit cards (call collect to the US, regardless of which country the card was issued in).

- Amex .... [1] (919) 333-3211
- Diner's Club .... [1] (303) 799-1504
- MasterCard .... [1] (314) 275-6690
- Visa .... [1] (410) 581-7931

NATIONAL TOURIST OFFICE

Libyan Travel and Tourist Company
Sharah Mizran
Tripoli
Tel: (21) 36222

Travelogue

WORK WEEK

Offices Monday-Friday 7:00 am to 1:00 pm summer, 8:00 am to 1:00 pm winter; and 3:00 pm to 7:30 pm in private offices.
Banks Monday-Friday 8:00 am to 2:00 pm.
Government 9:00 am to 1:00 pm and 2:00 pm to 5:00 pm.
Retail Monday-Friday 9:00 am to 2:00 pm and 4:30 pm to 8:30 pm.
Working hours vary from summer to winter. Shops vary depending on area and trade.

HOLIDAYS

Holidays 1996
February 1 Beginning of Ramadan
March 2 Declaration of the People's Authority
March 4 Aid al-Fitr
May 10 Aid al-Aladah
May 31 Islamic New Year 1416
June 11 Evacuation of foreign military bases
August 9 Prophet's Birthday
September 1 Anniversary of the 1969 Revolution
* Dates vary from year to year. Also, Libya, as a Muslim country, observes all the main Islamic festivals as holidays. Fridays are days of rest.

VISA AND PASSPORT

A valid passport and visa are required for travel to Libya. For extension beyond the normal one-month visa period, the immigration police should be informed and the fact noted in the passport. It is necessary to register with the police when arriving at your destination. Visas may be difficult to obtain and may require an invitation from an official agency or business.

DEPARTURE FORMALITIES

Notifying police upon arrival is necessary. If this is not done, departure will be delayed, regardless of your flight time, if officials think that malpractice rather than ignorance is the cause of violating this law. Keeping a copy of the forms given is important since it will be requested upon departure. You must buy an exit stamp upon arrival.

IMMUNIZATION

Although malaria has been eradicated in Libya, inoculation is advisable against other endemic diseases such as typhoid, tuberculosis, and infectious hepatitis, as well as yellow fever. Anti-rabies protection is advised for walkers and cyclists.

NOTE

At press time US passports were not valid for travel to, in, or through Libya without a special validation from the US State Department. In addition, the US Treasury Department had prohibited all travel-related transactions by US persons visiting Libya, except those specifically licensed by the Office of Foreign Assets Control. Current UN Security Council sanctions against Libya include an air and selective export embargo and an assets freeze, making it difficult for nationals of many other countries to enter or leave Libya or to receive funds when in Libya.

TIPPING

Tipping is not widespread in Libya, and is only expected by those giving personalized service. Hotel and restaurants: 10 percent. Small services in hotels: quarter or half dinar notes. Porters: half a dinar per heavy bag. Taxis: appreciated. Drivers: appreciated and expected.

CRIME

Crime is an increasing problem in Libya. Travelers are subject to terrorist activity stemming from political instability. Bribing officials is illegal, but expect the possibility of being approached, which will cause delays.

INFRASTRUCTURE

Libya is a still developing country where facilities to promote visits from foreigners are intentionally not widely available. There is an extensive road network but no rail system.

Foreign Trade

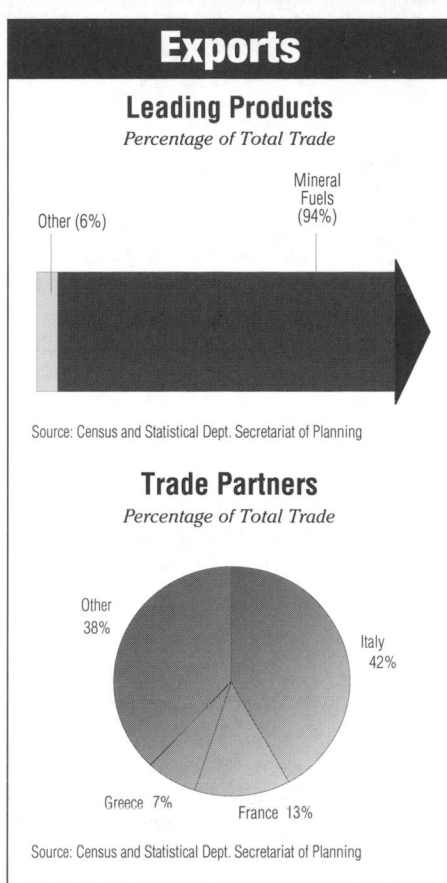

Imports

Leading Products
Percentage of Total Trade

Machinery, Trans. & Equip. (39%)
Basic Manufactures (18%)
Misc. Manufactured Articles (17%)
Other (26%)

Source: Census and Statistical Dept. Secretariat of Planning

Trade Partners
Percentage of Total Trade

Italy 22%
Japan 12%
Germany 12%
Other 54%

Source: Census and Statistical Dept. Secretariat of Planning

Exports

Leading Products
Percentage of Total Trade

Other (6%)
Mineral Fuels (94%)

Source: Census and Statistical Dept. Secretariat of Planning

Trade Partners
Percentage of Total Trade

Other 38%
Italy 42%
France 13%
Greece 7%

Source: Census and Statistical Dept. Secretariat of Planning

Opportunities

FOR IMPORTING TO LIBYA
- water and foodstuffs
- machinery and transport equipment
- manufactured goods

FOR EXPORTING FROM LIBYA
- crude oil
- refined petroleum products
- natural gas

GROWTH SECTORS
- oil sector
- manufacturing
- construction sector
- agricultural sector

Trade News

RULES AND REGULATIONS
- **Trade news** A multilayered, pervasive system of surveillance and control of individual activities exists in Libya. Due to terrorist situations, information is not easily obtained or accurate.
- **Restrictions** Prohibited imports include mostly consumer and luxury goods.
- **Government agencies** Only government agencies are allowed to act as commercial or import agents.
- **Custom duties and custom surcharges** Custom surcharges consist of 10 percent of the applicable customs duty. All products originating in Arab countries are exempt from customs duties, if their domestic value added exceeds 43 percent.
- **Prohibited imports** All imports from Israel and South Africa are prohibited.

Legal

Legal System

The Libyan legal system largely follows Egyptian codes and precedents. Some cases are dealt with according to Muslim law. The private practice of law is abolished, and all lawyers are employees of the secretariat of justice.

Intellectual Property Protection

Although Libya has laws which officially discourage or prohibit the violation of intellectual property rights, virtually none of the laws are enforced, at least as respects foreign intellectual property rights holders.

Patents and trademarks Libya is a member of the World Intellectual Property Organization and foreign patents should be given the same protection as domestic ones. The laws are rarely enforced, however, and infringement is common and largely uncontrolled. Libya is a member of a number of international organizations devoted to trademark protection, but the courts do little to stop violators.

Copyrights Libya signed the Berne agreement in 1994, promoting literary and artistic protection. Few actions are taken against the copyright violators, however, and piracy is widespread.

Trade secrets It is very difficult to prove violation of a foreign company's trade secrets in the Libyan courts.

Contracts and Dispute Resolution

Businesses in Libya prefer a wide variety of contract types, but it is best to get the agreement in writing due to the uncertainty of the courts. As such, the trend has been toward long, detailed contracts, which takes pains to address every contingency. Disputes are common. Although arbitration is allowed and some parties will agree to submit to such in their agreement, it is rarely resorted to, despite the fact that it is very difficult to resolve disputes in Libya due to backlogs in the courts. Domestic businesses are often given precedence over foreign ones.

Legal Matters

LEGAL BRIEFS
- **Revolutionary committees** Since 1981, revolutionary committees have been encouraged to conduct public trials without legal safeguards.
- **Special courts** There are special people's and military courts that try purported crimes against the state.
- **Muslim law** All cases relating to personal status are dealt with according to Muslim law.
- **Minor cases** Minor cases are heard by a sitting judge in each village or town.
- **Labor** Most technical and blue-collar work is done by foreign workers because of a lack of skilled domestic labor. The government provides for a 48-hour work week, pension rights, and minimum rest periods. It also allows unions, one for each trade, but only under strict regulations. Strikes are prohibited.
- **Business registration** All businesses must register with the Traders Registration Office in the Ministry of the Economy. All documents must be printed in the Arabic language. There are no fees except for the cost of publication of the business registration in the official Gazette.

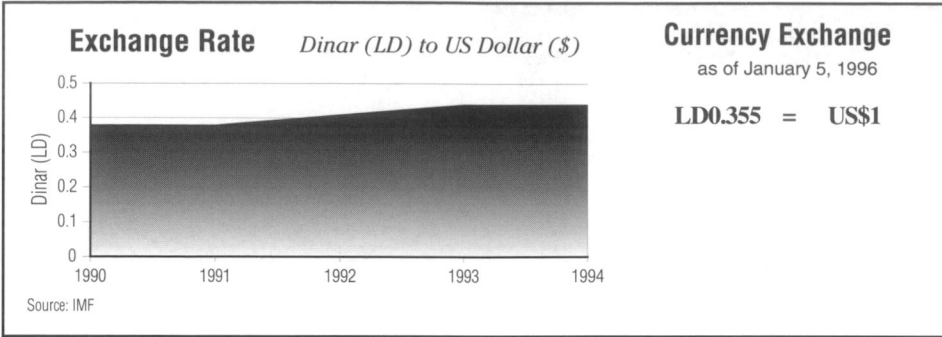

Exchange Rate *Dinar (LD) to US Dollar ($)*

Dinar (LD)

0.5
0.4
0.3
0.2
0.1
0

1990   1991   1992   1993   1994

Source: IMF

Currency Exchange

as of January 5, 1996

LD0.355 = US$1

Money Matters

BITS AND PIECES

- **Exchange rates** Exchange rates for the Libyan dinar are pegged to the SDR based on the market rates of 16 other foreign currencies.
- **Travelers** Travellers leaving Libya may not take out Libyan currency. Traveler's checks or foreign currency notes may be cashed only at an authorized bank, an exchange office, or a hotel licensed by the Central Bank. Travelers entering the country may bring with them traveler's checks, letters of credit, securities, coupons, and other negotiable instruments in unlimited amounts; however, they must be declared at customs.
- **Capital** Capital invested in Libyan projects contributing to its economic development may be transferred freely to the country of origin, provided it is not less than LD 200,000, and at least 51 percent of the project's shares are held by Libyan nationals.
- **Real estate** Only Libyans may own real estate.
- **Gold** Residents may buy, hold, and sell gold in any form other than gold bars without restrictions.
- **Capital gains** Capital gains are taxed as normal business income.
- **Foreign tax relief** Because only Libyan-source income is subject to tax, no foreign tax relief is provided.

Currency

The currency of Libya is the Libyan dinar (LD), and its principal subdivision is 100 dirhams.

Foreign Exchange

The Central Bank of Libya enforces strict exchange controls and delegates some of its regulatory power to authorized banks. Commercial banks may only deal in foreign currencies through foreign correspondents. Authorized banks, importers, and exporters are not allowed to transact forward exchanges in foreign currencies. Other than a fee for outward foreign exchange transfers, there are no taxes or subsidies on purchases or sales of foreign exchange.

Capital Transfers

Nonresidents employed in Libya are permitted to open and maintain nonresident accounts in Libyan dinars with any authorized bank. Such nonresidents may credit their employment earnings to these accounts, but all other credits require the prior approval of the Central Bank. Residents are allowed to hold foreign currencies in domestic bank accounts and transfer balances abroad without restriction. Payments for invisibles related to authorized imports are not restricted. Remittances from nonresident accounts may be approved by authorized banks up to specified limits. All other payments for invisibles, including payments in excess of the limits, require the prior approval of the Central Bank. All foreign exchange receipts must be surrendered.

Investment Incentives

The Libyan government offers no specific investment incentives.

Investment Restrictions

Although "privatization" of public sector activities has been officially encouraged for nearly a decade, there have been few signs of any substantial shift of emphasis in the economy. Foreign investment has been discouraged by Libya's political volatility, and the economic sanctions to which it has been subjected. New infrastructural and industrial projects have been suspended, and foreign exchange reserves have been utilized to purchase food, medicine, and other necessities.

BANKS

Central Bank of Libya
Sharia Al Malik Seoud
POB 1103
Tripoli
Tel: (21) 33591 through 9

Central Bank of Libya
POB 1103
Sharia al-Malik Seoud
Tripoli
Tel: (21) 33591
Fax: (21) 41488
Telex: 20661

Agricultural Bank
POB 1100
52 Sharia Omar Mukhtar
Tripoli
Tel: (21) 38666

Jamahiriya Bank
POB 65155
Gharian
Tel: (41) 31964
Fax: (41) 33763
Telex: 30524

Libyan Arab Foreign Bank
POB 254
That al-Imad Administrative Complex
Tripoli
Tel: (21) 41428
Fax: (21) 42970
Telex: 20200

National Commercial Bank SAL
POB 4647
Shuhada Sq.
Tripoli
Tel: (21) 37191
Telex: 20169

TAXATION

Taxation requires sophisticated knowledge of complex rules and regulations specific to each country. The information presented here is from the Ernst & Young Corporate Tax Guide and Directory, available from the Ernst & Young accounting office in your country, or from:

Ernst & Young
Mail Address:
P.O. Box 91873
That El Emad Towers
Tripoli, Libya
Street Address:
That El Emad Towers
Tower 1, Level 13
Tripoli, Libya
Tel: (21) 75889
Telex: 20945 Ans bk ERNST LY
Fax: (21) 444-8344

At a Glance

Corporate Income Tax Rate (%)(a)(b)	60
Capital Gains Tax Rate (%)(a)	60
Withholding Tax (%)	
Dividends	0
Interest (c)	5
Royalties from Patents, Know-how, etc.	0
Branch Remittance Tax	0
Net Operating Losses (Years)	
Carryback	0
Carryforward	5

(a) This is the maximum rate.
(b) The tax rate for petroleum companies is 65%.
(c) Final tax applicable to residents and nonresidents.

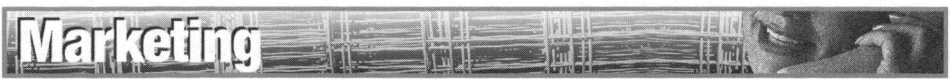

Marketing

Overview

Libya has a number of barriers, both political and cultural, that make any marketing campaign difficult. A good deal of the population is poor and education levels are low. Only about 50 percent of the population is literate. Add to this the incredibly massive bureaucracy, and then realize that any marketing plan takes a great deal of planning. Don't expect an immediate profit; any successful marketing campaign in Libya takes a lot of time. About 95 percent of the people are found in the northern coastal strip, and about 70 percent live in urban areas. Most of the people registered as rural actually commute to towns, so the urban population may be even higher. The country is also very diverse, with a number of different tribes and cultures mixed together, making it difficult to define and target any particular niche.

Distribution

Benghazi, Misratah, and Tripoli have ports; Tripoli has the country's only airport. Goods are typically warehoused in transit sheds and must pass through Tripoli within 15 days and delivered within 24 hours after that.

Agents

Only government agencies may act as commercial agents, including import agents, for foreign companies.

Advertising

Advertising is tightly controlled by the State Advertising Agency. There is no commercial radio or television. Press and cinema advertising are permitted.

Business Culture

Greetings and Courtesies

The standard greeting is the handshake. The addition of a slight nod or bow when shaking hands is a sign of respect. A man should not shake a woman's hand unless she initiates the handshake. If she does not, smile and nod slightly, but do not make prolonged eye contact with her. Greetings are often accompanied by questions about one's health and family. Titles are used to show respect, and are important. Personal space is less than in many other cultures, so don't be surprised if Libyan associates stand close.

Business Ethic and Framework

Libya is a welfare state, and all of its people benefit from the country's significant oil wealth. Officially, social classes have been abolished by the government. The real wealth and power are concentrated in the hands of a small elite upper-class and there is a lack of trained and skilled Libyan workers. People, family ties, and personal relationships are nearly always placed above business.

Meetings and Decision Making

Be on time, but expect your Libyan associates to be late. Social amenities are important, and business will not be addressed before the proper time is taken to inquire about one's health and family, or with other small talk. Relationships are more important than schedules. Decisions are made slowly. If you push for faster action or impose a deadline, you could do more harm than good.

Women

Libya is a very conservative Islamic culture that puts many restrictions on its women. Libyan women marry young, generally do not work outside the home, and when they do are relegated to teaching, secretarial work, and social services. Foreign women should be prepared for such attitudes and behave with discretion at all times. Being professional, poised, and self-confident will help in business, but male colleagues may be taken more seriously and given more respect.

Business Attire

Standard attire is a conservative suit. Women should wear tasteful, very conservative clothing. Women should never wear a sleeveless dress or blouse.

Marketing in Libya

MARKETING TIPS

- **Conservative** Libya is very conservative, and most Western type ads would not be accepted.
- **Tribal traditions** The country is very heterogeneous. Most people are more likely to relate to their tribes than country affiliation.
- **Age differences** More than 45 percent of the population is under the age of 15, and only a little less than four percent is over 60. Libya has a profoundly youthful population even by Third World standards.

MARKETING CONTACTS

Brega Petroleum Marketing Company
POB 402
Sharia Bashir es-Saidawi
Tripoli
Tel: (21) 40830
Telex: 20090

General Publication, Distribution and Advertising Company
POB 959
Tripoli
Telex: 20235

Cultural Cautions

DO'S

- Eat food with the right hand only. Use the right hand or both hands to give and receive things. Using the left hand only is offensive.
- Accept all simple gestures of hospitality. If you must reject such a gesture, be sure to give a polite explanation.

DON'TS

- Avoid conversation about local or national politics, Israel, or the US.
- Muslims are forbidden contact with dogs, and consider pictures of dogs improper. Do not give a Muslim child a toy dog or anything printed with images of dogs.

CUSTOMS

- To keep distance between genders, men and women do not constantly maintain eye contact when talking.
- Public displays of affection between men and women (even if married) are forbidden.
- Interruptions during a conversation are common. Don't be offended by this or take it personally.

OBSERVATIONS

- Libya is an extremely conservative, fundamentalist Islamic society.

NEGOTIATIONS

- Libyans enjoy negotiating. Long, enthusiastic discussions are typical, and are an occasion for demonstrating one's wit and intelligence.
- In Middle Eastern culture, it is common to gesture freely and openly express emotion.
- Honor is extremely important. If honor is at stake, it might be difficult for someone to admit they've made a mistake or back down from a position.
- Arguments based on personal need can be more persuasive than "mere" logic.

Contacts

GOVERNMENT ORGANIZATIONS

Arabian Gulf Oil Company
POB 263
Benghazi
Telex: 40033

National Company for Light Agricultural Equipment
Khafifa
POB 8707
Tripoli
Tel: (21) 830848/9
Fax: (21) 833421

National Oil Corporation
POB 2655
Tripoli
Tel: (21) 46181, 46190
Telex: 61508

General National Organization for Industrialization
POB 4388
Sharia San'a
Tripoli
Tel: (21) 34995
Telex: 200990

General Federation of Producers' Trade Unions
POB 734
2 Sharia Istanbul
Tripoli
Tel: (21) 46011

CHAMBERS OF COMMERCE

Chamber of Commerce, Trade, Industry and Agriculture for the Eastern Province
POB 208
Benghazi
Tel: (61) 94526
Telex: 40077

Tripoli Chamber of Commerce, Industry and Agriculture
POB 2321
Sharia al-Fatah September
Tripoli
Tel: (21) 33755
Telex: 20181

NEWSPAPERS

Ad-Daawa al-Islamia (Islamic Call)
POB 2682
Tanta St.
Tripoli
Tel: (21) 32055
Fax: (21) 38125
Telex: 20480

Economic Bulletin
POB 2303
Tripoli

Al-Jamahiriya
POB 4814
Tripoli
Tel: (21) 49294

Scientific Bulletin
POB 2303
Tripoli

Ath-Thaqafa al-Arabiya (Arab Culture)
POB 4587
Tripoli

Jamahiriya New Agency (JANA)
POB 2303
Sharia al-Fatch
Tripoli
Tel: (21) 37106
Telex: 20841

Informatsuinnoye Trelegrafnoye Agentstvo Rossii-Telegrafnoye Agentstvo Suverennykh (ITAR-TASS)
Sharia Mustapha Kamel 10
Tripoli

BANKS

Central Bank of Libya
POB 1103
Sharia al-Malik Seoud
Tripoli
Tel: (21) 33591
Fax: (21) 41488
Telex: 20661

Agricultural Bank
POB 1100
52 Sharia Omar Mukhtar
Tripoli
Tel: (21) 38666

Jamahiriya Bank
POB 65155
Gharian
Tel: (41) 31964
Fax: (41) 33763
Telex: 30524

Libyan Arab Foreign Bank
POB 254
That al-Imad Administrative Complex
Tripoli
Tel: (21) 41428
Fax: (21) 42970
Telex: 20200

National Commercial Bank SAL
POB 4647
Shuhada Sq.
Tripoli
Tel: (21) 37191
Telex: 20169

Sahara Bank
POB 270
10 Sharia 1 September
Tripoli
Tel: (21) 32771
Telex: 20009

Savings and Real Estate Investment Bank
POB 2297
Sharia Haite
Tripoli
Tel: (21) 49306, 20309

Umma Bank SAL
POB 685
1 Giaddat Omar Mukhtar
Tripoli
Tel: (21) 34031
Fax: (21) 32505
Telex: 20256

Wahda Bank
POB 452
Fadiel Abu Omar Sq.
El-Berkha
Benghazi
Tel: (21) 24709
Telex: 40011

RADIO AND TELEVISION

Great Socialist People's Libyan Arab Jamahiriya Broadcasting Corporation
POB 3731
Tripoli
Tel: (21) 32451

SHIPPING

General National Maritime Transport Company
POB 80173
2 Sharia Ahmad Sharif
Tripoli
Tel: (21) 33155
Telex: 20208

INTERNET ADDRESSES

Usenet group(s):
soc.culture.arabic

The Libya Page
http://www.sas.upenn.edu/African_Studies/Country_Specific/Libya.html

Libya
http://menic.utexas.edu/menic/countries/libya.html

Libya's WWW Sites
http://www.liii.com/~hajeri/libya.html

Lithuania

Republic of Lithuania

Economy

Overview

Industry is Lithuania's main economic sector, a result of Soviet-era central economic planning that decreed Lithuania would serve as an industrial node within the USSR. The disruption brought on by Lithuania's dramatic break with—and the subsequent collapse of—the USSR, and the dismantling of the socialist system, led to sharp drops in productivity, high rates of inflation, and near anarchy on the social and political fronts. Inflation reached nearly 1,000 percent in 1992, but now has fallen to more manageable levels, and some stability has been achieved in all areas, making for a cautiously optimistic outlook.

Trade

Since World War II, when Lithuania was incorporated into the USSR, it has been largely restricted to trading with other Soviet entities. One of its major current goals is to develop new trading relationships beyond the members of the former Soviet Bloc, although the disruption caused by the breakup of the USSR and the weak global economy in the early 1990s has retarded the country's efforts to date. Nevertheless, prospects are good, as Lithuania begins to open new contacts with Europe and other countries. Major exports include refined petroleum products, chemicals, machinery, timber, wood and paper products, and food products. Imports include light industrial manufactures, agricultural products, chemicals, metal-working machinery and products, and food industry equipment. Major trading partners include Russia—accounting for nearly half of total trade—followed by Belarus and the Ukraine.

Sectors

Agriculture Employment in agriculture, forestry, and fishing engages less than 18 percent of the work force, but the sector produces somewhat more than 25 percent of GDP. Livestock raising represents more than 66 percent of production, with cereals, flax, sugar beets, potatoes, and vegetables as the main crops. Privatization has resulted in major disruptions that have temporarily reduced productivity. Forestry and fishing are relatively minor activities and confined to the domestic market.

Industry Industry provides slightly more than 40 percent of GDP, while employing somewhat less than half the work force. Food processing, energy generation, chemicals, and light industry, including precision instruments, textiles and footwear, machinery and spare parts, and metal-working are becoming more significant. The industrial sector is currently being privatized, and most small firms are now under private ownership, although large industries remain under state control.

Services Nearly one-third of GDP comes from the services sector, although only about 30 percent of the work force is employed in it. Lithuania's high value-added services are undeveloped, but the country is trying to capitalize on its cadre of relatively well-trained engineers and other technical personnel.

Trends

The government is focusing on stabilizing the Lithuanian economy, taking measures to secure supplies of energy and other vital inputs, as well as dealing with social problems. Rampant crime—one of the consequences of economic, social, and political disruption—also needs to be dealt with effectively. On a brighter note, the spread of private sector activity is rapidly creating jobs and disposable income, which is boosting consumer spending.

At a Glance

THE COUNTRY

Location Eastern Europe, bordering the Baltic Sea, between Sweden and Russia.
Terrain Lowland with many scattered small lakes and fertile soil.
Climate Often wet, with moderate summers and winters.

THE PEOPLE

Population 3,900,000
Ethnic composition
Lithuanian 80.1%
Russian 8.6%
Polish 7.7%
Byelorussian 1.5%
Other 2.1%
Religious composition Roman Catholic is the main religion, although Lutheranism is widely practiced as well.
Languages Lithuanian is the official language. Polish and Russian are widely spoken as well.
Education and literacy Education is compulsory and free for all children between the ages of six and 16 years old. There are four major universities. The adult literacy rate is extremely high: almost 99 percent. Lithuanian is the most common language, although classes are also taught in Polish, Russian, and Yiddish.
Labor force
Total 1,800,000
By occupation: industry and construction 42%, agriculture and forestry 18%, other 40%

COUNTRY FACTS

Political and legal Lithuania's legal system is based on a civil law system. No judicial body reviews legislative acts. Suffrage begins at age 18.
Telephone Lithuania's telecommunication system ranks among the highest of the former Soviet republics. The country no longer depends on the Soviet Union's assistance for international calls. Several foreign cities are linked to urban areas in Lithuania by satellites. International country code: [370]. City codes: Kaunas (7), Klaipeda (61), Vilnius (2).
Transportation Lithuania's highway system is fairly modern. Of the 44,200 kilometers of highway, over 35,000 are paved. There are 600 kilometers of inland waterways that are perennially navigable. Only 12 of the 96 airports have permanent-surface runways.
Environment Chemical spills around former Soviet military bases have contaminated the soil, and some areas have been heavily polluted from petroleum products.
Media International electronic mail is available. There are 13 AM and 26 FM radio stations, and three television stations. More than 450 newspapers and 104 periodicals are published.
Health Life expectancy is 68 years for males and 76 years for females. There is one physician for every 220 people. Immunization is common for children; though there were recently some minor cases of tuberculosis.

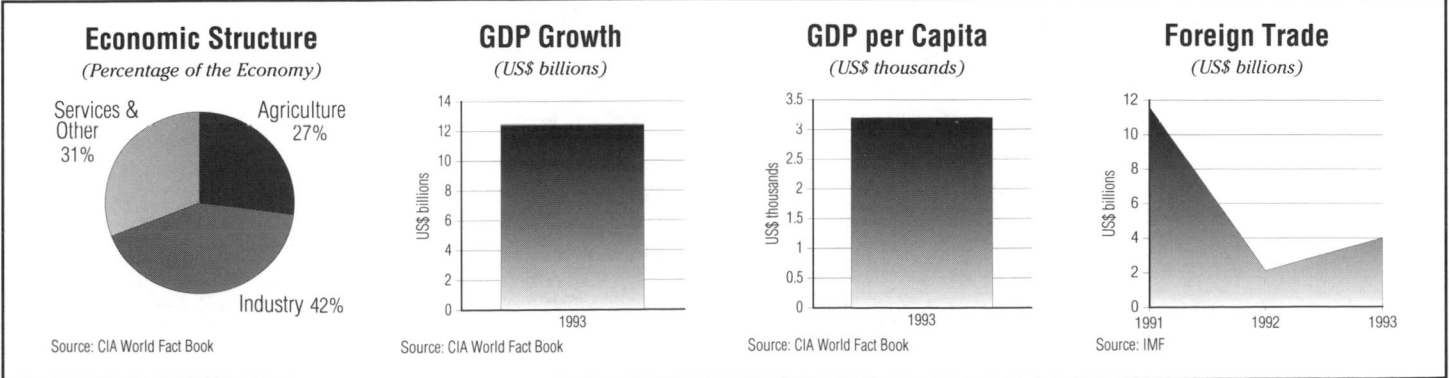

Economic Structure
(Percentage of the Economy)

Services & Other 31%
Agriculture 27%
Industry 42%

Source: CIA World Fact Book

GDP Growth
(US$ billions)

US$ billions
1993

Source: CIA World Fact Book

GDP per Capita
(US$ thousands)

US$ thousands
1993

Source: CIA World Fact Book

Foreign Trade
(US$ billions)

US$ billions
1991 1992 1993

Source: IMF

Business Travel

Lithuania

- ✪ National capital
- ● Secondary city
- Primary road
- Railroad
- International border

0   50 km
0   30 mi

© 1995 Magellan Geographix℠Santa Barbara, CA

Travelogue

WORKWEEK
Offices Monday-Friday 9:00 am to 6:00 pm.
Banks Monday-Friday 9:00 am to 1:00 pm.
Government Monday-Friday 9:00 am to 6:00 pm.
Retail Monday-Saturday 10:00 am to 8:00 pm with lunch from noon to 1:00 pm. Larger department stores may open at 8:00 am and remain open until 9:00 pm.

HOLIDAYS
Holidays 1996
January 1 New Year's Day
February 16 Lithuanian Independence
July 6 Coronation Grand Duke Mindaugas of Lithuania
November 1 National Day of Hope and Mourning
December 25 -26 Christmas
Dates vary each year for Easter Monday and Mother's Day.
By custom, the Monday preceding a public holiday on a Tuesday is taken as an additional public holiday in which case the preceding Saturday is a working day.

VISA AND PASSPORT
Visitors to Lithuania need a valid passport and a visa. Visas are available at Lithuanian embassies. A visa to Estonia or Latvia will also be accepted for entry into Lithuania.

DEPARTURE FORMALITIES
Visitors leaving from Vilnius Airport are not subject to any departure taxes.

IMMUNIZATION
No international certificates of vaccination are required unless you are arriving from infected area.

TIPPING
Taxi: 10-15 percent. Hotels: none. Restaurants: 10-15 percent. Barbers, beauticians: 10 percent. Small services: five to 10 percent.

CRIME
Street crime is not uncommon, especially at night near major tourist hotels and restaurants. Auto theft and vandalism is common, as are robberies on trains, in train stations, and in hotel rooms.

INFRASTRUCTURE
Lithuania is connected to surrounding areas by a network of air, train, and bus services. Bus, taxi, and rental car services are available within the capital.

NATIONAL TOURIST OFFICE
State Tourism Department
Gedimino 30/1
Vilnius
Tel: (2) 226706

COMMUNICATIONS
Telephones The telephone system in Lithuania is adequate. Most international calls must be placed through an international operator. Public phones are available. The most expensive time to call is from 1:00 pm to 2:00 am.
Fax Fax machines are available at most businesses and hotels and at the central post office. Telex services are available where fax services are found.
Post office Mail service is reliable but slow. To speed things along, address mail in the local language or at least the familiar format (country, city with index number, street, house number, and then name). Major hotels have postal facilities for posting mail and buying stamps. Mailboxes are rare.

BEST TRAVEL BOOKS
Berlitz Business Travel Guide, Europe. Concise economic details, successful trip planning, background information on people and cities, useful facts and addresses.
Hayit's Budget Travel, The Baltic States (Estonia, Latvia, Lithuania). Affordable, practical, up-to-date; covering topics such as travel preparations, background information, practical information, and travel sections.
Vilnius In Your Pocket. Available from In Your Pocket Publications, POB 52, 2000 Vilnius. Send four international reply coupons.

USEFUL TELEPHONE NUMBERS
If you are calling from outside Lithuania, you will need to add the country code [370] and any other international dialing requirements from within your country.

- Police 02
- Emergency/Ambulance 03
- Fire 01
- International Operator 8194
- Translator .... (2) 226063; 451510
- Vilnuis Airport .... (2) 630-201
- Vilnius Train Station .... (2) 630-086
- Bus Schedule Information .... (2) 262-482
- Dentist .... (2) 468583
- Doctor .... (2) 616258
- Taxi .... (2) 228888
- DHL .... (2) 725444
- FedEx.. (2) 614654
- Avis .... (2) 733226
- Europcar...................................... (2) 222739

Airlines
- Lithuanian Airlines................... (2) 752-585, 750-082
- SAS ....(2) 662-000
- Air Lithuania .... (2) 227013
- Lufthansa .... (2) 262222

Credit Card Information
Lost or stolen credit cards (call collect to the US, regardless of which country the card was issued in).
- Amex ....[1] (919) 333-3211
- Diner's Club..............................[1] (303) 799-1504
- MasterCard ....[1] (314) 275-6690
- Visa ....[1] (410) 581-7931

Foreign Trade

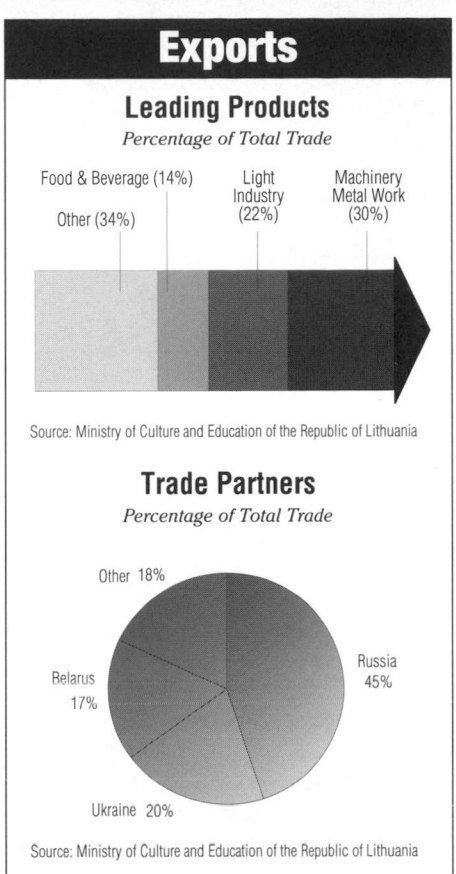

Imports

Leading Products
Percentage of Total Trade

Petroleum & Gas (49%)
Machinery Metal Work (13%)
Other (38%)

Source: Ministry of Culture and Education of the Republic of Lithuania

Trade Partners
Percentage of Total Trade

Other 14%
Ukraine 9%
Belarus 7%
Former USSR 70%

Source: Ministry of Culture and Education of the Republic of Lithuania

Exports

Leading Products
Percentage of Total Trade

Food & Beverage (14%)
Other (34%)
Light Industry (22%)
Machinery Metal Work (30%)

Source: Ministry of Culture and Education of the Republic of Lithuania

Trade Partners
Percentage of Total Trade

Other 18%
Belarus 17%
Russia 45%
Ukraine 20%

Source: Ministry of Culture and Education of the Republic of Lithuania

Opportunities

FOR IMPORTING TO LITHUANIA
- chemicals, fuels, minerals, metals
- food products
- heavy machinery

EXPORTING FROM LITHUANIA
- building materials, vehicles
- cattle, hogs, poultry
- chemicals, energy sources

GROWTH SECTORS
- industry
- food processing
- light industry

Trade News

RULES AND REGULATIONS
- **Transport infrastructure** Facilities are adequate but poor telecommunications and banking facilities make it difficult for trading.
- **Quantitative restrictions** There are no requirements on imports except for health and national security reasons.
- **Statistical information** A tax of 0.01% is imposed on imports and exports for collecting statistical information on trade.
- **Licensing requirements** There are no licensing requirements for importing in Lithuania.
- **Export proceeds** Export proceeds are not required to be repatriated to Lithuania.
- **Export duties** are levied on certain raw materials and selected products.

Legal

Legal System

The legal system is being transformed from that of the Soviet regime to a more democratic model. Lithuania is currently enacting new civil and criminal procedure codes.

Intellectual Property Protection

Patents and trademarks Lithuania is a member of the World Intellectual Property Organization, and it plans to sign the Paris Convention for the protection of industrial property. Lithuania's policy regarding trademarks has been to observe international standards and to consider subscribing to international conventions. Most foreign patents are recognized by the Lithuanian courts, although enforcement of rights against infringement is lax due to lack of resources.

Copyrights The Lithuanian parliament is considering laws for copyright enforcement, including amendments to the criminal and civil codes. There are very few such laws, and piracy is rampant.

Trade secrets Lithuania's government is currently drafting legislation concerning trade secret violations. It remains to be seen how effective this legislation will be.

Contracts and Dispute Resolution

Businesses in Lithuania prefer very detailed contracts. Disputes are generally handled in the courts, but are delayed because of a lack of funds and trained staff. Arbitration is allowed, and is even encouraged, though few people make use of it as a means of alternative dispute resolution.

Labor

The 1991 law on trade unions and the constitution recognizes the right of workers and employees to form and join trade unions and, with certain limitations, to strike. Workers are allowed to organize and to bargain collectively under the Lithuanian collective agreements law. Trade unions usually engage in direct bargaining at the workplace. The Lithuanian constitution prohibits forced labor, a prohibition observed in practice.

Legal Matters

LEGAL BRIEFS
- **Land ownership** Lithuanian law gives foreign businesses and investors the right to lease land for 99 years, but bars foreigners from outright ownership of land.
- **Investment prohibition** Foreign investment is prohibited in state enterprises holding a monopoly in the Lithuanian market, and in areas of defense and security.
- **Hierarchy** The prosecutor general exercises oversight responsibility through a network of local prosecutors.
- **Business registration** There are no performance requirements imposed by law as a condition for foreign businesses or investment. However, foreign companies are often required to offer employment technology when doing business with state companies.
- **New court** A newly created Constitution Court began deliberations in 1993.
- **Minimum wage** Lithuania also has a minimum wage that is adjusted periodically by the parliament, but enforcement of the wage is almost nonexistent, and it is in any event insufficient to support a family of four.
- **Safety and health regulations** There are some minimum legal health and safety standards, but worker complaints indicate that these standards are sometimes ignored.
- **Minimum age** The minimum age for employment of children is 16, and age requirements are enforced through a system of inspections.

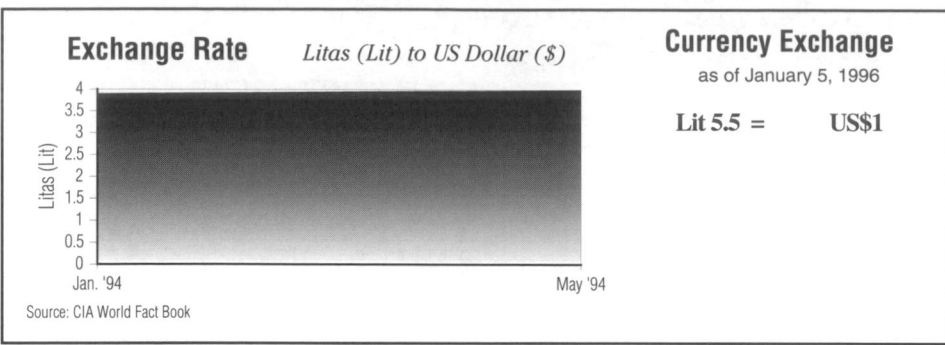

Exchange Rate
Litas (Lit) to US Dollar ($)

Jan. '94 — May '94

Source: CIA World Fact Book

Currency Exchange
as of January 5, 1996

Lit 5.5 =   US$1

Currency

The currency in use is the litas (Lit). It is divided into 100 cents.

Foreign Exchange

The external value of the litas is determined in the interbank foreign exchange market. The exchange rate is determined by supply and demand conditions, and authorized banks quote exchange rates for other convertible currencies based on their cross-relationships for the currencies concerned. Authorized banks may quote buy and sell rates for the Russian ruble at varying rates. Effective October 1, 1992, the Russian ruble was declared a foreign currency, and a general-purpose coupon (talonas) was introduced as a temporary measure. The talonas was phased out when the litas was introduced in 1993. Rates for convertible currencies and currencies of the former states of the USSR are calculated daily by the Central Bank (Bank of Lithuania). There are no taxes on the purchase or sale of foreign exchange, and no arrangement for forward cover against exchange rate risk. Foreign exchange transactions must be effected through authorized banks. Eighteen banks are authorized to deal in foreign exchange between themselves, and with residents and nonresidents of Lithuania. The banks may hold one of four types of licenses for foreign exchange, the simplest being a license to buy and sell foreign exchange. Eight banks have a general license for offering the full range of banking services.

Capital Transfers

Residents, nonresidents and representative offices of foreign enterprises may open foreign exchange accounts at authorized banks. The accounts may be debited and credited without limit. After-tax profits may be repatriated freely, with no limit on timing or amount. Resident firms may borrow foreign exchange from an authorized bank, or borrow directly from banks abroad with the approval of the Bank of Lithuania. There are no regulations for payments for or proceeds from invisibles.

Investment Incentives

Lithuania is creating new incentives for foreign investment, although currently very little is offered. There is a two-year tax holiday for profits on joint ventures.

Investment Restrictions

The Lithuanian government is trying to ease restrictions that have historically scared foreign investors away. Following the two-year tax holiday, however, joint ventures profits are currently usually taxed heavily.

Money Matters

BITS AND PIECES

- **Tax incentives** Enterprises with foreign participation may receive incentives under the Law on Foreign Investments. Starting in the first year the enterprise earns a profit, the enterprise enjoys a reduction in profits taxes for six years.

- **Former states of the USSR** Correspondent accounts exist between the Bank of Lithuania and the central banks of the former states of the USSR, except for Armenia and Georgia. These accounts do not have to be used for payments originating after October 1992. All previous ruble-denominated correspondent accounts have been closed.

- **Privatization** The Law of Foreign Investments permits the state to sell shares of companies to nonresidents. Purchase of state-owned enterprises must be authorized by the Central Privatization Committee, although the registration is usually quick and easy. Firms with 100 percent foreign capital ownership are allowed to operate, but the government retains the right to establish limits on foreign investment.

- **Economic reform** Lithuania's economic reform system has overall been a success. By mid-1993, 92 percent of housing and 60 percent of businesses slated for privatization had been privatized.

- **Gold** There are no imposed restrictions place upon gold. Residents may hold, buy, or sell gold in any form without limit.

FINANCIAL CONTACTS

Bank of Lithuania
Totoriu 4
Vilnius 2629
Tel: (2) 224-008
Telex: 261090
Fax: (2) 221-501

State Commercial Bank of Lithuania
Jogailos 14
Vilnius 2631
Tel: (2) 226-333
Fax: (2) 227-571

Agriculture Bank of Lithuania
Totoriu 4
Vilnius 2600
Tel: (2) 628-842
Fax: (2) 226-047

Baltic Bank
Gedimino 15
Vilnius 2000
Tel: (2) 623-151
Telex: 261163
Fax: (2) 623-583

Lithuanian Joint-Stock Innovation Bank
Sv. Stepono 27
Vilnius 2006
Tel: (2) 260-336
Telex: 261982

Ukio Bankas
J. Gruodzio 9
Kaunas 3000
Tel: (7) 203-651
Telex: 269897

Vilniaus Bankas
Gedimino 12
Vilnius 2600
Tel: (2) 610-723 Telex: 261101

Lithuanian Savings Bank
Vilniaus 16
Vilnius 2736
Tel: (2) 623-173
Telex: 261977
Fax: (2) 221-263

Association of Lithuanian Exchanges
Savanoriu 124A
Vilnius 2600
Tel: (2) 261-919
Fax: (2) 620-726

Vilnius Exchange
Gedimino 14
Vilnius 2001
Tel: (2) 628-804
Fax: (2) 454-866

TAXATION

Taxation requires sophisticated knowledge of complex rules and regulations specific to each country. The information presented here is from the Ernst & Young Corporate Tax Guide and Directory, available from the Ernst & Young accounting office in your country, or for services in Lithuania, please contact:

Kari Bjïrk
Tallinn
Estonia
[372] (6) 310612
satellite telephone [358] 49-124-525.

At a Glance

Corporate Income Tax Rate (%)	29*
Capital Gains Tax Rate (%)	29*
Branch Tax Rate (%)	0
Withholding Tax (%)	0
Net Operating Losses (Years):	
Carryback	0
Carryforward	0

* Taxable profit that is retained for investment in capital assets is taxed at a rate of 10%. A 10% rate also applies to companies producing agricultural products and to specialized enterprises rendering services to agriculture.

Marketing

Overview

Consumer demand is low, due mostly to frozen salaries, rationed gasoline, and shortages of heating oil and gas. The average Lithuanian regards price liberalization as a measure to line the pockets of officials and black marketers. Lithuanians tend to be resistant to any change or marketing campaign that differs wildly from the norm. Perhaps the most important factor when considering a marketing campaign is to consider the long-term. Successful business ventures have taken years.

Agents, Distributors, and Partners

Agents are necessities in modern day Lithuania, in order to navigate through the intense bureaucracy.

Selling Techniques

Don't deviate from what Lithuanians normally consider standard advertising; it probably won't be accepted.

Service and Customer Support

After-sales service is essential in Lithuania; it is one of the factors Lithuanians look at when considering a product. Having an agent available in the country for customer support is helpful, although Lithuania's telephone system is advanced enough to provide telephone service overseas.

Marketing in Lithuania

MARKETING TIPS

- **Language** Lithuanian is the oldest living language in the Western world, Lithuanians are proud of it. Any advertising should be done in Lithuanian.
- **Education** Lithuanians are generally well-educated, especially compared to other countries in Eastern Europe.
- **Expanding markets** Privatizations and a generally expanding economy have created many new opportunities for foreign sellers.
- **Open markets** Many markets in Lithuania are still wide open due to its relatively recent liberalizations and growing prosperity. Foreign sellers who are willing to press forward will be able to find a solid niche for themselves.

RADIO AND TELEVISION

Lithuania Radio and Television
Konarskio 49
Vilnius 2674
Tel: (2) 660-637

Business Culture

Greetings and Courtesies

It is customary to shake hands upon meeting and again on your departure in Lithuania. Always address businesspeople by using their professional titles with their surnames. Lithuanians discourage discussing business at social functions; however it is proper if your hosts bring up the topic first. Lithuanians love to communicate and they especially like to talk about their country.

Business Ethic and Framework

Lithuania is the most productive of the former Soviet republics and Lithuanian businesspeople represent the energy and work ethic of their country. They are ready to learn new, reliable ways of doing business, however; Lithuanians want to leave the problems of the past far behind them.

Meetings and Decision Making

Planning for meetings in Lithuania needs to be done far ahead of time. To avert any misunderstandings, it is best for all participants at a business meeting in Lithuania to sit down and write out what was discussed. Many Lithuanian businesspeople are novices to private business; they make decisions only after cautious consideration. The details of an agreement need to be explicitly written and carefully explained before a Lithuanian will make a final decision. Because of their inexperience, they may not understand the finality of a signed agreement. In addition, before entering an agreement in Lithuania, your prospective associates should be thoroughly examined to verify who and what they represent.

Women

Traditionally, women worked in the house or on the land. They rarely ventured into the business world. However, businesswomen in Lithuania are becoming more common, and are beginning to command respect for their business abilities. The country has approved programs that assist working women with children. While holding full-time jobs, many Lithuanian women also maintain full responsibility for their homes.

Business Attire

Dark, conservative clothing is typical in Lithuania. Lithuanians expect foreign businesspeople to be well dressed, so casual dressing for business functions would be a mistake. Business dress is proper for nearly all occasions, including formal events.

Cultural Cautions

DO'S

- Your opinions on any subject are welcome.
- Try to become familiar with the history, politics, and culture of Lithuania. Lithuanians will appreciate it; they are extremely nationalistic.

DON'TS

- It is rude to ask someone to stop smoking in Lithuania. If you smoke, ask those close by before you light up, then share your cigarettes generously.
- Avoid discussing politics.

CUSTOMS

- Lithuanians give homage to those they believe to be in authority.
- It is correct to hand your business cards, printed in Lithuanian and your language, to everyone you meet.
- Lithuanians like to entertain business guests after usual business hours. Bringing gifts to your host is a standard practice in Lithuania. An appropriate gift might be a small item with your company's logo.
- Lithuanians display formal manners.

OBSERVATIONS

- The Lithuanian language is similar to Latvian.
- Speaking Russian is not improper in Lithuania as it is in other Baltic countries.

NEGOTIATIONS

- Negotiations can be time consuming, and usually involve socializing.
- Avoid impatience and an aggressive approach.
- Agree on an agenda before the meeting gets started.

Contacts

GOVERNMENT AGENCIES

Department of Customs
Jaksto 1/25
Vilnius
Tel: (2) 22 64 15
Fax: (2) 22 49 48

Lithuanian Information Institute
Kalvariju 3
2659 Vilnius
Tel: (2) 75 35 90, 35 19 29
Fax: (2) 35 30 17

Ministry of Economics
Gedimino pr 38/2
Vilnius
Tel: (2) 62 24 16

Ministry of Energy
Vienuolio 8
Vilnius
Tel: (2) 61 51 40

Ministry of Finance
Sermuksniu 6
Vilnius
Tel: (2) 62 51 72

Ministry of Foreign Affairs
Tumo-Vaizganto 2
Vilnius
Tel: (2) 61 85 37
Fax: (2) 62 07 52

Ministry of Industry and Trade
Tuno-Vaizganto 8A/2
Vilnius
Tel: (2) 62 88 30

Ministry of Interior
Sventaragio 2
Vilnius
Tel: (2) 626752

Ministry of Transport
Gedimino 17
Vilnius
Tel: (2) 621445

Press Bureau
Gedimino 11 (42 A-1)
2039 Vilnius
Tel: (2) 62 11 95
Fax 61 34 64

Prime Minister
Gedimino 11 (42 A-1)
2039 Vilnius
Tel: (2) 62 21 01

BUSINESS AND TRADE ORGANIZATIONS

Association of Chambers of Commerce and Industry
Kudirkos 18
Vilnius
Tel: (2) 222630

American Chamber of Commerce
Gedimino pr. 38-2, Room 617
Vilnius
Tel: (2) 62 35 06
Fax: (2) 62 86 04

British Council
Vilniaus 39-6
Vilnius
Tel: (2) 61 23 37
Fax: (2) 22 16 02

French Trade Mission
Didzioji 1
Vilnius
Tel: (2) 22 29 88, 22 37 86
Fax: (2) 22 38 98

Lithuanian Euro Info Correspondence Centre
Pilies 24
2600 Vilnius
Tel: (2) 22 36 13, 22 03 73
Fax: (2) 22 05 80

LEGAL CONTACTS

Ballard Spahr Andrews & Ingersoll
Donelaicio 71-2
3000 Kaunas
Tel: (7) 20 56 66
Fax: (7) 20 56 91

Lideika, Petrauskas, Valiunas & Partners
Vilnius 25
2001 Vilnius
Tel: (2) 6706382
Fax: (2) 6706381

Scheele, Schwartz, Zielcke & Partner
Architektu 194/22
2049 Vilnius
Tel: (2) 443720
Fax: (2) 443720

NEWSPAPERS

Ekho Litvy
(Echo of Lithuania)
Laisves 60
Vilnius 2056
Tel: (2) 428-463
Fax: (2) 428-636

Kurier Wilenski
(Vilnius Express)
Laisves 60
Vilnius 2019
Tel: (2) 427-901
Fax: (2) 427-265

Lietuvos aidas
(Echo of Lithuania)
Maironio 1
Vilnius 2710
Tel: (2) 615-208
Fax: (2) 224-876

Lietuvos rytas
(Lithuania's Morning)
Gedimino 12A
Vilnius 2001
Tel: (2) 622-680
Fax: (2) 227-656

Respublika
(Republic)
Sventaragio 4
Vilnius 2600
Tel: (2) 223-112
Fax: (2) 223-538

Tiesa
(Truth)
Laisves 60
Vilnius 2019
Tel: (2) 429-933
Fax: (2) 421-790

PERIODICALS

Caritas
Vilniaus 29
Kaunas 3000
Tel: (7) 209-683
Fax: (7) 205-549

Gimtasis krastas
(Native Land)
Z. Liauksmino 8/2
Vilnius 2600
Tel: (2) 623-881
Fax: (2) 628-171

Kalba Vilnius
(Vilnius Calling)
Konarskio 49
Vilnius 2674
Tel: (2) 661-022

Krantai
(Banks)
K. Sirvydo 3/8
Vilnius 2001
Tel: (2) 224-844

Kulturos barai
(Domains of Culture)
Universiteto 6
Vilnius 2600
Tel: (2) 616-696

Lietuvos Komersantas
(Lithuania Businessman)
Algirdo 9A, Vilnius 2009
Tel: (2) 652-387
Fax: (2) 267-540

Magazyn Wilenski
(Vilnius Journal)
a/d 1630
Vilnius 2010
Tel: (2) 474-007

Mazofi Lietuva
(Lithuania Minor)
H. Manto 2
Klaipeda 5800
Tel: (61) 18-074
Fax: (61) 13-684

Metai
(Year)
Gedimino 37
Vilnius 2600
Tel: (2) 617-344

Nemunas
Gedimino 45
Kaunas 3000
Tel: (7) 226-067

Politika
(Politics)
Laisves 60
Vilnius 2056
Tel: (2) 428-803

Sluota
(Broom)
Bernardinu 8/8
Vilnius 2722
Tel: (2) 613-171

Svyturys
(Beacon)
Maironio 1
Vilnius 2600
Tel: (2) 627-488

RADIO AND TELEVISION

Lithuanian Radio-Television
Konarskio 49
Vilnius
Tel: (2) 633383

INTERNET ADDRESSES

BALT-L, a moderated list covering the republics of Lithuania, Latvia and Estonia, is accessed through the address balt-l@ubvm.cc.buffalo.edu. This group contains news items from the wire services, discussions on cultural, political, and academic issues.

Lithuania Homepage
http://neris.mii.lt/

The Baltics Online
http://www.viabalt.ee/

Mirror of Lithuania
http://www.mcs.com/~thomas/www/lt/

Lithuanian Index
http://www.nlib.ee/LITHUANIA/

Luxembourg

Grand Duchy of Luxembourg

Economy

Overview

Luxembourg's stable, prosperous economy features moderate growth, low inflation, and negligible unemployment. The industrial sector, until recently dominated by steel, has become increasingly more diversified, particularly as high-tech businesses more firmly establish themselves. During the past decade, growth in the financial services sector has more than compensated for the decline in steel. Services, especially banking, account for an ever-growing portion of the economy. Agriculture remains a small but stable sector and is based on highly productive, family-owned farms.

Trade

Luxembourg enjoys the advantages of the open European market, exporting a variety of industrial products and importing minerals and high-quality consumer goods. Luxembourg has close economic ties to both Belgium and the Netherlands. Its leading trading partners are members of the EU, both for imports and for exports.

Sectors

Agriculture Agriculture's contribution to the economy is diminishing, primarily due to the availability of cheaper goods from other EU markets. Livestock and livestock products are increasingly consumed by those who raise them, and most fruits and vegetables are grown only for the domestic market.

Industry Luxembourg has a worldwide reputation for high-quality industrial products, and the government is seeking to diversify the economy by pursuing continued industrial development. Significant branches of manufacturing are metal and machinery products, paper and printing, and food products.

Services Favorable laws governing banking secrecy and taxation have encouraged the development of Luxembourg as a major international banking center. In 1990, banking, finance, and insurance employed nearly 13 percent of the work force. Stock exchange activities, notably the Eurobond market and investment portfolio management, are also prominent. Many major industrial companies base their reinsurance firms here. The prominence of financial service industries has promoted the development and growth of related service industries. International data processing services, in particular, have begun to locate their operations in Luxembourg. Tourism is still a significant contributor to GDP, although it has declined in relative importance over the past few years.

Trends

The development of Luxembourg as an international financial center coincided with the decline in the importance of the country's iron and steel sector. Although the country's largest industrial employer achieved steady profits during the 1980s, recent drops in international steel prices have placed limitations on the future of this sector. Luxembourg's annual trade deficit is offset by gains in the financial services sector to provide an overall surplus. Prospects for continued growth are largely dependent on the ability of Luxembourg to diversify its economy, however, and attempts by the EU to promote abolition of restrictions on capital could undermine Luxembourg's attractiveness for private and corporate investors.

At a Glance

THE COUNTRY

Location Western Europe, bounded on the east by Germany, on the south by France, and on the west and north by Belgium.

Terrain Rugged uplands cover the north, with fertile lowlands in the south and a floodplain in the southeast.

Climate Temperate and mild, with plentiful rainfall in the extreme southwest. The winters are mild and the summers are cool.

THE PEOPLE

Population 402,000

Ethnic composition Celtic base (with French and German blend), Portuguese, Italian, and European (guest and worker residents.)

Religious composition

Roman Catholic 97%

Protestant and Jewish 3%

Languages spoken Luxembourgish is the predominant language, followed by German, French, and English.

Education and literacy Adult literacy is 100 percent, and school attendance is compulsory between ages six and 15.

Labor force

Total: 177,000

By occupation: services 65%, industry 31.6%, and agriculture 3.4%. One-third of labor force are foreign workers, mostly from Portugal, Italy, France, Belgium, and Germany.

COUNTRY FACTS

Political and legal This constitutional monarchy's legal system is based primarily on Western civil law systems. Suffrage is universal for anyone 18 or older.

Telephone The government-owned telephone system is highly developed, completely automated, and efficient. It includes a nationwide mobile phone system. The telecommunications system is very advanced, with one direct-broadcast satellite earth station and nationwide mobile phone system. International country code: [352]. City codes are not required.

Transportation Facilities are excellent, offering both domestic and international railway services and a well-maintained highway system with almost 5,000 kilometers of paved roads. There are two airports, but only one with permanent-surface runways. The inland waterway on the Moselle River has one port serving industrial transport barges and a merchant marine fleet with 50 ships.

Environment Government efforts have improved pollution controls. Forest reserves are severely depleted. The primary current issue is deforestation.

Media Two AM and three FM radio stations, plus three television stations, reach the domestic audience and surrounding countries. The literacy rate is extremely high, but the five daily newspapers have a small circulation and depend on foreign news agencies for information.

Health An advanced national health service is supervised by the government. Life expectancy of males is 73 years; of females, 80 years.

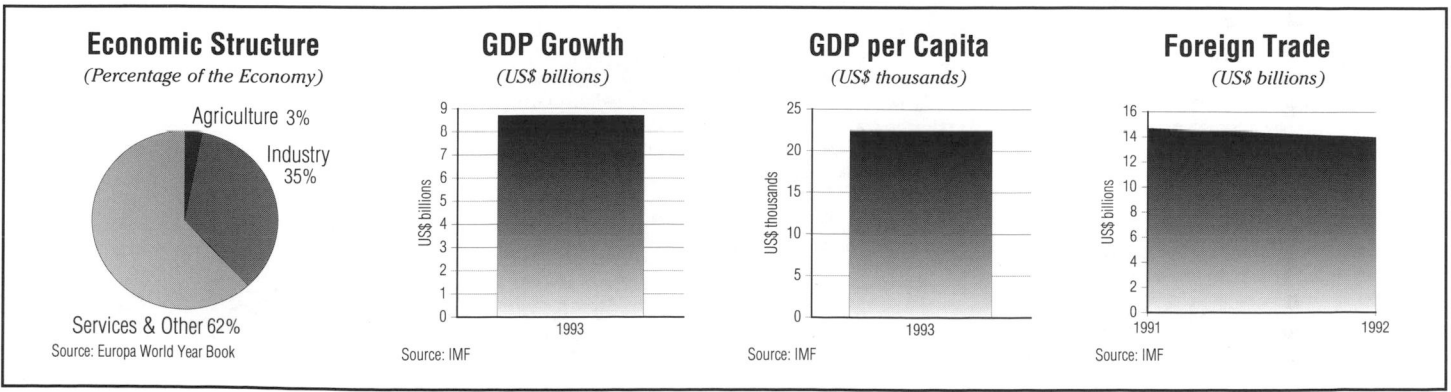

Economic Structure
(Percentage of the Economy)
- Agriculture 3%
- Industry 35%
- Services & Other 62%
Source: Europa World Year Book

GDP Growth
(US$ billions)
1993
Source: IMF

GDP per Capita
(US$ thousands)
1993
Source: IMF

Foreign Trade
(US$ billions)
1991 — 1992
Source: IMF

Business Travel

LH	1906	MADRID	935	113-3
LH	1022	STUTTGART HBF.	935	-
AF	1701	LYON	940	683-6
AY	822	HELSINKI	940	113-3
AA	071	SFRANCISCO-DALLAS	945	731-7

COMMUNICATIONS

Telephones Direct dial is available to most countries in Europe and North America. Installation of international service is in great demand and growing rapidly. Pay phones displaying international flags can accept operator-assisted international calls.

Fax This service is available at large hotels and business centers, as is telex service.

Post office Mail service is efficient. The main post offices in Luxembourg City and at the airport are open until 10:00 pm. Packages will not be accepted after 5:00 pm.

BEST TRAVEL BOOKS

Fodor's Travel Guide, The Netherlands, Belgium and Luxembourg.

Dollarwise Guide to Belgium, Holland and Luxembourg. New York: Prentice-Hall.

Fodor's Europe, Best of 31 Countries. Contains information on historical towns, great culture, scenic coastal countryside.

Berlitz Business Travel Guide, Europe. Concise economic details, successful trip planning, background information on people and cities, useful facts and addresses.

Do's and Taboo's Around the World. The Bestselling Guide to International Behavior. Edited by Roger Axtell, compiled by the Parker Pen Company. The ultimate guide to international behavior, now completely updated and expanded. Helpful, fun to read!

USEFUL TELEPHONE NUMBERS

If you are calling from outside Luxembourg you will need to add the country code [352] and any other international dialing requirements from within your country.

- British Airways.. 2-00-57
- Luxair SA 43-61-61
- Luxembourg Chamber of Commerce.. 435853
- Luxembourg Trade Confederation 473125
- Luxembourg Railways.................................. 492424
- Automobile Club... 450045
- Lodging Information 487165
- Ministry of Tourism...................................... 4794567
- US Embassy 4123
- British Embassy 29864
- Emergencies 012
- Directory Assistance 017
- Telex Inquiries 0016
- Luxembourg Visitor and Conv. Bureau 222809
- Directory Assistance (International) 016
- Operator (International).................................... 0010

Credit Card Information

Lost or stolen credit cards (call collect to the US, regardless of which country the card was issued in).

- Amex...[1] (919) 333-3211
- Diner's Club.................................[1] (303) 799-1504
- MasterCard ....[1] (314) 275-6690
- Visa ....[1] (410) 581-7931

Travelogue

WORKWEEK

Offices Monday-Friday 8:00 am to noon and 2:00 pm to 6:00 pm.

Banks Monday-Friday 9:00 am to noon and 1:30 pm to 4:30 pm.

Government Monday-Friday 9:00 am to noon and 2:00 pm to 5:00 pm.

Retail Monday 2:00 pm to 6:00 pm, Tuesday-Saturday, 8:00 am to noon and 2:00 pm to 6:00 pm.

HOLIDAYS

Holidays 1996

January 1 New Year's Day
February 19 Shrove Monday
April 8 Easter Monday
May 1 Luxembourg Labor Day
May 16 Ascension
May 27 Whit Monday
June 24 Grand Duke's Birthday
August 15 Assumption
November 1 All Saints' Day
December 25-26 Christmas

VISA AND PASSPORT

A valid passport is required for entry to Luxembourg. A visa is not required for a stay of up to three months.

DEPARTURE FORMALITIES

There are no departure formalities for Luxembourg.

IMMUNIZATION

No vaccinations are required unless you are arriving from an infected area.

TIPPING

Restaurants will add a 10 percent service charge to the bill, and it is customary to then round up the total bill for payment. Taxi drivers expect a 10-15 percent gratuity.

CRIME

Crime is minimal, yet it is advisable to take precautions when out at night by not carrying large amounts of cash or displaying valuable jewelry.

INFRASTRUCTURE

Findel Airport is located near Luxembourg City. Taxis and buses are available for airport service and transportation throughout the city. Taxis are metered and can carry up to four passengers. The rail system offers daily express trains to Brussels and Basel, and connecting trains to Paris. Rental cars are available and highly recommended, as the roads are excellent and connect to all major towns. The rail system is extensive with local bus connections and offers first-class and second-class fares.

NATIONAL TOURIST OFFICE

Office National du Tourisme
77 rue d'Anvers
BP 1001
1010 Luxembourg
Tel: 40-08-08
Fax: 40-47-48
Telex: 2715

Foreign Trade

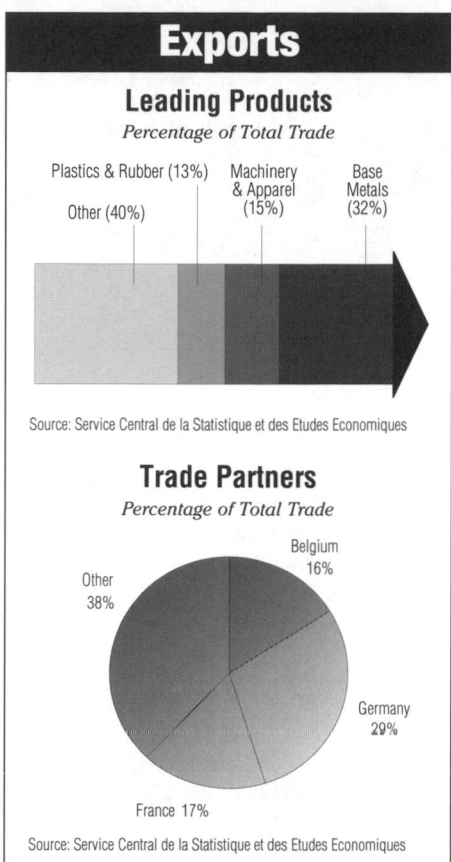

Imports

Leading Products
Percentage of Total Trade

Machinery Transportation (18%)
Base Metals (15%)
Transportation Equipment (12%)
Other (55%)

Source: Service Central de la Statistique et des Etudes Economiques

Trade Partners
Percentage of Total Trade

- Other 19%
- Belgium 39%
- France 11%
- Germany 31%

Source: Service Central de la Statistique et des Etudes Economiques

Exports

Leading Products
Percentage of Total Trade

Plastics & Rubber (13%)
Machinery & Apparel (15%)
Base Metals (32%)
Other (40%)

Source: Service Central de la Statistique et des Etudes Economiques

Trade Partners
Percentage of Total Trade

- Belgium 16%
- Other 38%
- Germany 29%
- France 17%

Source: Service Central de la Statistique et des Etudes Economiques

Opportunities

FOR IMPORTING TO LUXEMBOURG

- foodstuff
- metals and minerals
- quality consumer goods

FOR EXPORTING FROM LUXEMBOURG

- aluminum, chemicals
- finished steel products
- rubber and glass products

GROWTH SECTORS
- industrial products
- financial services

Trade News

RULES AND REGULATIONS

- **Export licenses** are required for a few products such as agricultural, iron, and steel products.
- **Licenses** are required for all imports from Albania, Bulgaria, China, the Democratic People's Republic of Korea, Mongolia, the states of the former USSR and Viet Nam, and specified imports from all other countries including many textile, certain agricultural products and foodstuffs. Coal, petroleum products, diamonds, semi-processed gold, and weapons require licensing also.
- **Import levies** Import duties are levied on non-EU countries for most products covered by the Common Agricultural Policy.

Legal

Legal System

Luxembourg is a civil law country that has been considerably influenced by Belgian and French legislation and jurisdiction.

Intellectual Property Rights

Patents and trademarks On the average, it may take up to seven years to obtain patent registration in Luxembourg, which allows public access to the application. The protection lasts for 20 years, after which the patent falls into the public domain. Trademark applications are processed slowly, averaging between six months and one year for registration.

Copyrights Copyright legislation applies to all creations, without imposing a condition of originality. Infringements carry not only civil but also criminal sanctions. Software programs are also protected under a new law implemented in May, 1995.

Contracts and Dispute Resolution

Unless the deal amounts to less than LuxF 100,000 (approximately US$3,400), the existence and content of a contract may only be evidenced through written documents. Litigation on contracts is very frequent. Arbitration is less common, although the court may provide it upon agreement of the parties.

Labor

Workers have a constitutional right to associate freely in trade unions. Luxembourg's tradition of consensus politics integrates unions in periodic meetings together with employers and government. This has proven very successful in preventing labor disputes. Employment is mainly of unlimited duration and must be evidenced in writing. In the absence of a written contract, both existence and content of the labor contract may be evidenced by any means.

Source: Dupong & Associes, Luxembourg

Legal Matters

LEGAL BRIEFS

- **Workweek** The normal working time is 40 hours per week. 12 official holidays are paid each year and each worker is allowed to take 25 working days off for holiday purposes. Sickness and pension insurances are paid equally by both employer and employee.
- **Notaries** Notaries prepare and authenticate documentary instruments which may be in either the German, French, or English language. Authenticated documents bear a strong presumption of validity similar to that of official documents, unless proven otherwise. Acknowledgments in foreign countries may be taken before representatives of the country in which the document will be used.
- **Business registration** Every commercial and industrial enterprise must be granted a government license to trade.
- **Captive reinsurance company** Fiscal and legal regulations in Luxembourg provide incentives to groups wishing to set up a captive reinsurance company, notably that the latter may set up tax deductible catastrophe provisions within certain limits and under certain conditions.
- **International agreements** Luxembourg is a member state of the Strasbourg Convention of November 27, 1963, on the unification of certain elements of patents, and the 1971 Strasbourg Agreement.

LEGAL CONTACT

Dupong & Associes
14A, rue des Bains
POB 472
2014 Luxembourg
Tel: 461-838
Fax: 461-909

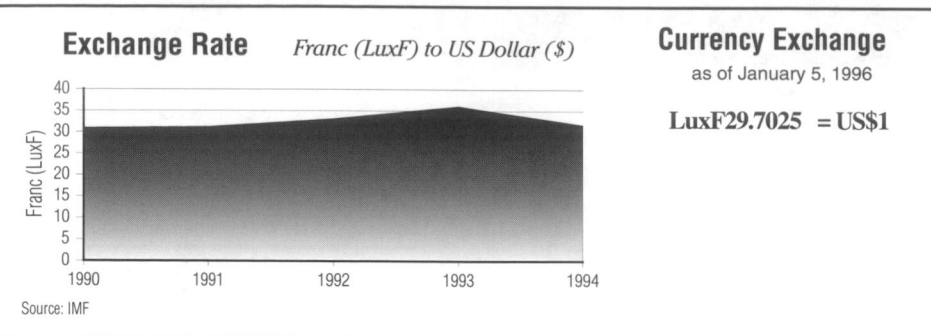

Exchange Rate *Franc (LuxF) to US Dollar ($)*

Franc (LuxF): 40, 35, 30, 25, 20, 15, 10, 5, 0

1990 1991 1992 1993 1994

Source: IMF

Currency Exchange

as of January 5, 1996

LuxF29.7025 = US$1

Currency

The currency of Luxembourg is the Luxembourg franc (LuxF or F). The Belgian franc is also in wide circulation at parity.

Foreign Exchange

The Institut Belgo-Luxembourgeois du Change (IBLC) controls the monetary flow into and out of Luxembourg. Transfers of funds over a specified amount, whether entering or leaving the country, must be accompanied by appropriate documentation. However, documentation is considered a necessary formality, and the controls do not impact the free circulation of currency.

Capital Transfers

There are no restrictions on the flow of foreign capital into Belgium or Luxembourg. Direct capital investment in companies is permitted without authorization. At the time of the original investment, foreign investors can obtain a guarantee that authorization for the repatriation of capital and of income derived from its investment will be granted at any time. Such guarantees are not usually granted, however, if the funds are to be repatriated within a three-year period. Repatriation of funds without a guarantee is normally made through the free market.

Investment Incentives

Luxembourg actively encourages foreign investment. All incentives are applied impartially. The government can award grants for some projects, depending on the job creation potential, degree of local sourcing, and the export potential of the investment. The government especially seeks investments in research and development, high technology operations, and manufacturing with a high value-added process.

Investment Restrictions

There are restrictions for certain sectors only. Some industrial activities require specific approval, including any establishment that may be considered hazardous or injurious to health. Licenses are required for the production, processing, or trading of certain commodities, including food products, fertilizers, and alcoholic beverages.

TAXATION

Taxation requires sophisticated knowledge of complex rules and regulations specific to each country. For more detailed information we suggest you refer to the Ernst & Young Corporate Tax Guide and Directory, available from the Ernst & Young accounting office in your country, or from:

Compagnie Fiduciaire
POB 351
2013 Luxembourg
Tel: 45 12 31
Telex: 2598 Ans bk FINEXB LU
2304 Ans bk FINEX LUX
Fax: 45 12 32 03

At a Glance

Corporate Income Tax Rate (%)(a)	33
Capital Gains Tax Rate (%)(a)	33
Branch Tax Rate (%)(a)	33
Withholding Tax (%)	
Dividends (b)	25
Interest	0
Royalties (b)	12
Branch Remittance Tax	0
Net Operating Losses (Years)	
Carryback	0
Carryforward	Unlimited

(a) Excluding municipal business tax. The local municipal business taxes are levied by different municipalities, and are deductible for corporate income tax purposes. The municipal taxes vary, but average about 9.1%.
(b) This rate is applicable to payments to both residents and nonresidents. For nonresidents, this is a final tax. The rate may be reduced by a tax treaty.

Money Matters

BITS AND PIECES

- **Financial holding companies** Companies qualifying as financial holding companies are not subject to corporate income tax. Dividends from these companies are not subject to withholding taxes, but nonresident beneficiaries are subject to income tax on the dividend income.

- **Capital gains** Capital gains are considered ordinary business income, and are taxed at the normal rate. Capital gains on the sale of shares may be tax-exempt if certain conditions apply.

- **Foreign tax relief** Tax credits are available to resident companies for foreign source income that is subject to foreign taxation. The amount of credit may not exceed the Luxembourg income tax that is chargeable on the foreign income.

- **Groups of companies** A Luxembourg company and its wholly owned Luxembourg subsidiaries may form a "fiscal unity," which is taxed as if it were one single company.

- **Government incentives** Investors wishing to take advantage of government incentives should obtain the necessary information from an office of the Belgian or Luxembourg Government.

- **Corporate tax** Companies whose principal place of management is in Luxembourg are subject to corporate tax on worldwide income, unless otherwise specified by tax treaties. Nonresident corporations are subject to corporate tax only on income derived from Luxembourg sources.

BANKS

Luxembourg Monetary Institute
63, avenue de la Liberté
2983 Luxembourg
Tel: 47-88-88-6
Fax: 49-21-80

Banco di Napoli International SA
10-12 Ave. Pasteur
BP 1301
1301 Luxembourg
Tel: 47-59-59-1
Fax: 47-41-17
Telex: 1533

Banco di Roma International SA
26 Blvd Royal
2449 Luxembourg
Tel: 47-08-51
Fax: 47-79-06-228
Telex: 2436

Banque et Caisse d'Epargne de l'Etat Luxembourg
1 & 2 place de Metz
BP 2105
2954 Luxembourg
Tel: 40-15-1
Fax: 22-76-87
Telex: 3417

Banque Continentale du Luxembourg SA
2 blvd Emmanuel Servais
2535 Luxembourg
Tel: 47-44-91
Fax: 47-76-88-33-3
Telex: 2301

Banque Generale du Luxembourg SA
27 ave. Monterey
2951 Luxembourg
Tel: 47-99-1
Fax: 47-99-25-79
Telex: 2301

Banque Internationale a Luxembourg SA
69 Route d'Esch
2953 Luxembourg
Tel: 45-90-1
Fax: 45-90-20-10
Telex: 3626

Banque Leu (Luxembourg) SA
16 rue Jean-Pierre Brasseur
BP 718, 2017 Luxembourg
Tel: 45-32-22-1
Fax: 45-31-77
Telex: 2492

Marketing

Overview

Luxembourg's markets are part of the EU. Moderate growth, low inflation, and nearly nonexistent unemployment make consumers here sophisticated purchasers of all Western products. The government is justifiably promoting the country as a media and communications specialist, so there is an especially strong market for equipment for all phases of media production as general high-tech companies relocate here.

Agents and Distributors

Most industrial and consumer imports enter in small quantities. Overseas investors looking for prospective agents or distributors should seriously consider quality standards among their evaluation criteria. Businesses have historically been more successful if they appointed a separate agent to cover Luxembourg, instead of one agent handling all of the Benelux countries.

Advertising

Print media has a broad circulation. There are five daily newspapers and many magazines, mainly trade or technical in content. Television carries advertising. About 20 cinemas accept ads. Outdoor advertising facilities are available on building sites and transportation vehicles. Agencies can provide direct mail and some market research and public relations services. Luxembourg hosts two major consumer fairs each year, the Spring Fair in late May emphasizing tourism and food, and the larger Fall Fair in early October. Participants include regional retailers and distributors of a wide range of household goods who sell directly to consumers.

Business Culture

Greetings and Courtesies

Formality and standards of etiquette are well-etched into Luxembourg's business and social communities. While most of its executives speak three languages—French, German, and Luxembourgish—French is the language of commerce. Forms of address will vary depending on whom you meet. The German form is Herr (Mr.), Frau (Mrs. or Ms.), and Fraulein (Miss), followed by the person's title or surname. French forms are Monsieur (Mr.), Madame (Mrs. or Ms.), and Mademoiselle (Miss), also followed by the title or surname.

Business Ethic and Framework

Luxembourg's business environment is friendly and formal, influenced by German/French traditions and international institutions. A letter of introduction should be properly translated into the language of the person receiving it, and all materials translated in French will demonstrate the foreign venture's sincere intent to establish sound business relationships. Luxembourg is very selective as to what type of business it wishes to attract and acceptance into its business community is deemed par with acceptance into an elite club.

Meetings and Decision Making

Phone in advance if you're running late. If you're fluent in the language of your audience, you will be well looked upon. A relationship with Luxembourg business requires a sincere interest in the country, the people, and the desire to improve working conditions. Reply promptly to requests for information, price quotes, deliveries, and terms.

Women

While most women prefer raising families to working outside the home, many women have integrated into the work force. Typically, women are found in traditional positions as secretaries, legal assistants, and translators. Foreign businesswomen shouldn't face discrimination, however, as most businesspeople are well accustomed to dealing with women in high, managerial positions.

Business Attire

Three-piece dark suits are appropriate; as are shirts and ties of somber tones. Women should always wear sweaters, wool skirts, or business suits—never pants—when conducting business.

Marketing in Luxembourg

MARKETING TIPS

- **Standard of living** Luxembourg has a high standard of living. Its relatively affluent consumers are avid purchasers of high-end consumer goods.
- **Telephone** The telephone services in Luxembourg are good, and international calls can be made from most areas. Fax machines are available in the cities, but shouldn't be used for marketing.
- **Postal service** Luxembourg's postal service is excellent. Because businesses in the country prefer face to face meetings, the mail should only be used for correspondence.
- **Subsidiaries** As an alternative to appointing agents, some firms have found it advantageous to set up selling subsidiaries in Luxembourg.

CHAMBER OF COMMERCE

Chamber of Commerce
7, rue Alcide de Gasperi
2981 Luxembourg-Kirchberg
Tel: 43-58-53
Fax: 43-83-26

Cultural Cautions

DO'S

- Know the protocols of European etiquette. Good manners are a prerequisite for successfully blending into this elite and distinguished society.
- Send handwritten thank-you notes following visits to private homes.
- Be as formal as possible with businesspeople from Luxembourg.

DON'TS

- Do not assume, even vaguely, that your Luxembourg colleague "is French" or "is German." Nationals from Luxembourg are proud of their cultural heritage and consider themselves Luxembourgish first.
- Do not bring up any controversial subject as a topic of conversation.

CUSTOMS

- Luxembourg's elegant dining style is representative of its overall sophistication. Dinners tend to be formal. Following dinner, a liquor will usually be served, and gentlemen will light cigars. When the cigar is finished it's time to go home.

OBSERVATIONS

- Business cards are exchanged discreetly, if at all, because formal, third party introductions are generally necessary.
- Meetings are usually scheduled in offices beginning at 10:00 am. Offices close for lunch from noon to 2:00 pm, and afternoon meetings are scheduled after 2:30 pm.
- Shaking hands is the most accepted form of greeting; shake hands with everyone including the secretary.

NEGOTIATIONS

- Negotiations seem to carry diplomatic overtones. Harsh, aggressive sale tactics or haggling about price is not considered good business practice.
- Don't try to rush negotiations.

GOVERNMENT AGENCIES

Ministry of Agriculture, Viticulture and Rural Development
1, rue de la Congrégation
2913 Luxembourg
Tel: 47-81
Fax: 46-40-27

Ministry of Budget
3, rue de la Congrégation
2931 Luxembourg
Tel: 47-81
Fax: 47-52-41

Ministry of Energy
19-21, boulevard Royal
2914 Luxembourg
Tel: 47-81
Fax: 46-04-48

Ministry of Environment
18, montée de la Pétrusse
2918 Luxembourg
Tel: 47-81
Fax: 40-04-10

Ministry of Finance
3, rue de la Congrégation
2931 Luxembourg
Tel: 47-81, 47-82-15
Fax: 47-52-41

Ministry of Foreign Affairs, Foreign Trade and Cooperation
BP 1602
2911 Luxembourg
Tel: 47-82-382
Fax: 22-31-44

Ministry of Labor
26, rue Zithe
2939 Luxembourg
Tel: 47-81
Fax: 47-86-325

Ministry of National Economy
19-21, boulevard Royal
L-2914 Luxembourg
Tel: 47-81

Ministry of Transportation
19-21, boulevard Royal
L-2938 Luxembourg
Tel: 47-81
Fax: 46-43-15

Ministry of Communications
18, montée de la Pétrusse
L-2945 Luxembourg
Tel: 47-81
Fax: 40-89-40

WORLD TRADE CENTER

World Trade Center Luxembourg
6-10, place de la Gare, 4th Floor
1616 Luxembourg
Tel: 40-86-54
Fax: 40-86-08

TRADE ORGANIZATION

Association des Banques et Banquiers Luxembourg
(Bankers' Association)
14, boulevard F.D. Roosevelt
BP 13
2010 Luxembourg
Tel: 46-36-60/1
Fax: 46-0921

LEGAL CONTACTS

Brucher & Tabery
Rue Pierre D'Aspelt 10
POB 619
Luxembourg 2016
Tel: 45 62 62
Fax: 45 4 65

Dupong & Associes
14A, rue Des Bains
POB 472
2014 Luxembourg
Tel: 46 18 38
Fax: 46 19 09

Loesch & Wolter
11, rue Goethe
1637 Luxembourg
Tel: 48 11 48-1
Fax: 49 49 44

BUSINESS AND TRADE ORGANIZATIONS

Confederation of Commerce Luxembourgeois
BP 482
2014 Luxembourg
Tel: 473125
Fax: 220059

Fédération des Industriels Luxembourgeois
BP 1304
1013 Luxembourg
Tel: 435366
Fax: 432328

LUXEMBOURG LAW FIRMS

Arendt & Medernach
8-10, rue Mathias Hardt
PO Box 39
2010 Luxembourg
Tel: 407878
Fax: 407804

Marc Baden
24 rue Marie-Adelaide
2128 Luxembourg
Tel: 444141
Fax: 444166

Bonn & Schmitt
62, avenue Guillaume
1650 Luxembourg
Tel: 455858
Fax: 455859, 450182

Dennemeyer & Associates
55, rue Des Bruyeres
Howald/Luxembourg
1274, Luxembourg
Tel: 499841
Fax: 499841

J. Dennemeyer
Elvinger, Hoss & Prussen
15, Cote d'Eich
BP425
1450 Luxembourg
Tel: 471591
Fax: 223402

Faltz & Associes
6, rue Heine
1720 Luxembourg
Tel: 485050
Fax: 481385

Heldenstein
29, avenue Monterey
2163 Luxembourg
Tel: 220582
Fax: 220583

Thielen & Krieger
10, rue Willy Goergen
PO Box 679
2016 Luxembourg
Tel: 222969
Fax: 222975

Zeyen Beghin Feider
67, rue Ermesinde
PO Box 5017
1050 Luxembourg
Tel: 468946
Fax: 468947

REMEMBER

- When you telephone (or fax) to Luxembourg from another country you must always include the country code [352] before the numbers given.
- When you send mail to Luxembourg, be sure to write LUXEMBOURG in capital letters on its own line below the addresses given.

STOCK EXCHANGE

Societe de la Bourse de Luxembourg
11, ave de la Porte-Neuve
BP 165
2011 Luxembourg
Tel: 4779361
Fax: 473298

RADIO AND TELEVISION

RTL–CLT Multi Media
45, blvd Pierre Frieden
1543 Luxembourg
Tel: 42-14-21
Telex: 3266
Fax: 42-142-27-60

Societe Europeenne des Satellites (SES)
Chateau de Betzdorf
6815 Betzdorf
Tel: 71-72-51
Telex: 60625
Fax: 71-72-52-27

PERIODICALS

Echo de l'Industrie
7, rue Alcide de Gasperi
BP 1013 Luxembourg
Tel: 43-53-66
Telex: 60174
Fax: 43-23-28

Grenge Spoun
BP 684
2016 Luxembourg
Tel: 49-00-49
Fax: 49-29-70

Handelsblad/Le Journal du Commerce
23, allee Scheffer
2520 Luxembourg
Tel: 47-31-25

Horesca–Informations
9, rue des Trevires
BP 2524
1025 Luxembourg
Tel: 48-71-65
Fax: 48-71-56

De Konsument
55, rue des Bruyeres
1274 Howald
Tel: 49-60-22
Fax: 40-03-75
Telex: 2966

De Letzeburger Bauer
16, blvd d'Avranches
2980 Luxembourg
Tel: 48-81-61
Fax: 40-03-75

D'Letzeburger Land
62, rue de Strasbourg
2560 Luxembourg
Tel: 48-57-57
Fax: 40-03-75

INTERNET ADDRESSES

Luxembourg WWW Servers
http://www.restena.lu/other/luxservers.html
Grand Duchy of Luxembourg
http://www.restena.lu/luxembourg/gdlux.html

Macau

Economy

Overview

Macau has historically been a center for trading; it was used by the Portuguese as a staging port for trade and exploration in Asia during the sixteenth century. The oldest European settlement in the Far East, it is currently considered a Chinese territory under Portuguese administration. Although Portugal and China have clashed over ownership of Macau in the past, they recently established diplomatic relations, and Macau is scheduled to revert to China on December 20, 1999. The vast majority of Macau's economy stems from tourism and gambling. Other industries include textiles, manufacturing, and construction, and it serves as a secondary entrepôt for China's trade, after nearby Hong Kong.

Trade

In contrast to Hong Kong, trade accounts for very little of Macau's GDP: nominally less than 10 percent. However, in recent years Macau has been accused of lending its name to manufacturers from China eager to evade quotas on textile products destined for markets that limit imports from China. Because the majority of Macau's relatively small economy comes from tourism and gambling, it must import the majority of its foodstuffs, consumer and capital goods, and raw and intermediate materials; even all of Macau's water comes from China. Most of Macau's trade originates in or is channeled through Hong Kong. The US is Macau's leading export market.

Sectors

Agriculture Very little is grown in Macau—only small quantities of rice and vegetables—and few fisheries exist because silt has largely clogged the port and ruined adjacent fishing grounds.

Industry Most of Macau's industry is involved in improving its infrastructure. A new international airport is being completed, and a bridge linking Macau and Taipa was finished in 1994. Macau has begun construction of a deep-water port and storage facility to revitalize its transportation industry. Light manufacturing and assembly are small, secondary industries, and its manufacturers generally cannot compete with Hong Kong and Guangzhou.

Services Macau has historically been a trading center and was extremely prosperous during World War II, when it was the only neutral port open in South China. However, postwar growth was stifled because of clashes between Portugal and Communist China. Since the establishment of diplomatic relations between the two countries, Macau has become a major tourism center, including gambling as an attraction for day trippers from Hong Kong.

Trends

With its newly upgraded tourist infrastructure and easy accessibility, Macau should remain a tourist center into the intermediate future, especially if Hong Kong becomes a less attractive venue for tourism and entertaining after its takeover by the Chinese in 1997. However, questions remain as to the degree to which Macau will be allowed to retain its open tourist economy following its reversion to China in 1999. Despite protestations that it will allow Macau to retain its autonomy and character, China could balk at the nature of its activities. Macau is less critical than Hong Kong for maintaining China's links to the rest of the world, and its secondary and less competitive position could allow it to fade in the future.

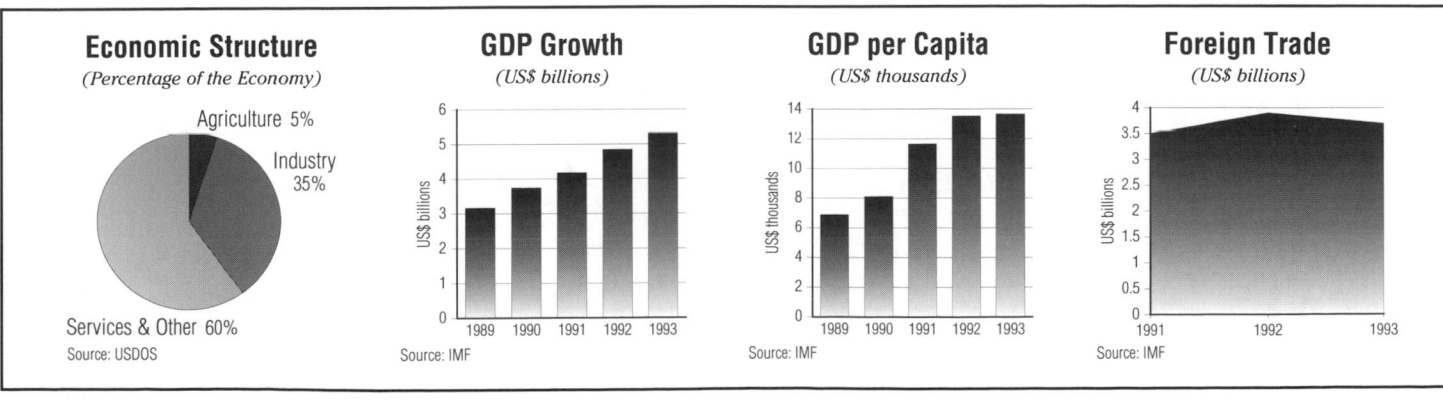

Economic Structure (Percentage of the Economy)
Agriculture 5%
Industry 35%
Services & Other 60%
Source: USDOS

GDP Growth (US$ billions)
1989 1990 1991 1992 1993
Source: IMF

GDP per Capita (US$ thousands)
1989 1990 1991 1992 1993
Source: IMF

Foreign Trade (US$ billions)
1991 1992 1993
Source: IMF

Business Travel

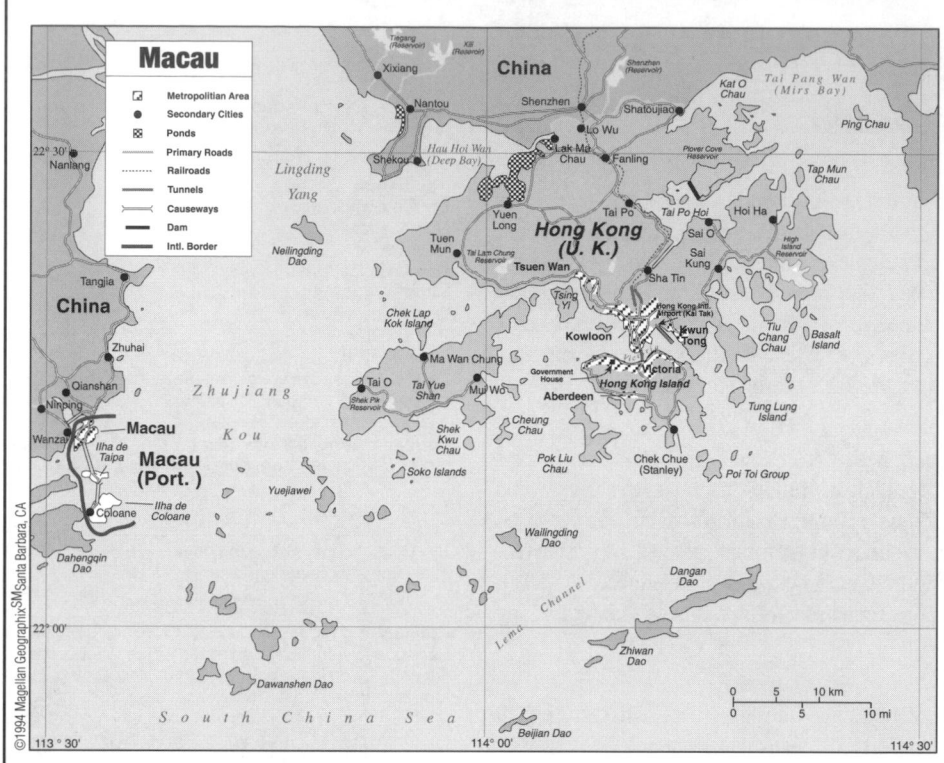

Travelogue

WORKWEEK

Offices Monday-Friday 9:00 am to 1:00 pm and 2:30 pm to 5:30 pm; Saturday, 9:00 am to 1:00 pm.
Government Monday-Friday 9:30 am to 5:00 pm.
Banks Monday-Friday 9:30 am to 5:00 pm; Saturday 9:30 am.to noon.
Retail Monday to Saturday 9:00 am to 5:30 pm.

HOLIDAYS

Holidays 1996
April 2 Liberty Day
June 10 Day of Portugal
October 5 Proclamation of the Republic
November 1 All Saints' Day
December 8 Immaculate Conception
December 24 Christmas Eve
December 25 Christmas
In addition, the Chinese residents of Macao observe Buddhist holidays that vary with the lunar calendar.

VISA AND PASSPORT

Visitors are required to have a valid passport. A visa is not necessary for most travelers on visits of less than 60 days.

DEPARTURE FORMALITIES

There are no departure formalities for Macau.

IMMUNIZATION

No inoculations are commonly required unless you are arriving from an infected area. Check for latest information.

TIPPING

Most hotels and restaurants add a 10 percent service charge, but it is customary to leave a small additional tip.

CRIME

Petty street crime and residential burglaries are a problem, particularly in and around casinos. With reasonable caution, tourists are generally safe.

INFRASTRUCTURE

Macao has well-developed facilities for tourism. Available transportation includes metered taxis, reasonable and convenient buses, hired jeeps, and two-seat carriages pulled by tricycles.

TOURIST OFFICES

Macau Department of Tourism
Leal Senado Square
Macau
Tel: 315566

Direcção dos Serviços de Turismo
9 Largo do Leal Sengo
Edificio Ritz
Macau
Tel: 315566 Telex: 88338 turis om

COMMUNICATION

Telephone Service is good, but pay phones can be hard to find. Most large hotels have pay phones, but you may have to wait in line to use them. Radio telephone calls may be made to Hong Kong and to most parts of the world.
Fax Fax facilities are now available in Macau. The easiest way to send a fax or receive a fax is at the GPO on Leal Senado.
Post office The postal services are efficient. There are many mini-post offices throughout Macau. Post offices are open Monday-Friday 9:00 am to 8:00 pm.

BEST TRAVEL BOOKS

Macau: City of Commerce and Culture, R.D. Cremer. Illustrated, 214 pages, University of Washington Press.
Hong Kong, Macau and Canton: A Travel Survival Kit, by Robert Storey. Illustrated, 360 pages, Lonely Planet Publications.
Far Eastern Economic Review, All Asia Travel Guide Volume 2. The best guide available for the business traveller.
Insight Pocket Guides, Macau. I can't think of another book which so effectively captures the essence of a country.

USEFUL TELEPHONE NUMBERS

If you are calling from outside Macau, you will need to add the country code [853] and any other international dialing requirements from within your country.
- Taxi 519519
- Film/Photo 555959
- Avis Car Rental 336789
- Central Hotel 937761
- Emergency 999
- Government Hospital 514455, 313731
- Kiang Vu Hospital 371333

Credit Card Information
Lost or stolen credit cards (call collect to the US, regardless of which country the card was issued in).
- Amex ....[1] (919) 333-3211
- Diner's Club................................[1] (303) 799-1504
- MasterCard ....[1] (314) 275-6690
- Visa ....[1] (410) 581-7931

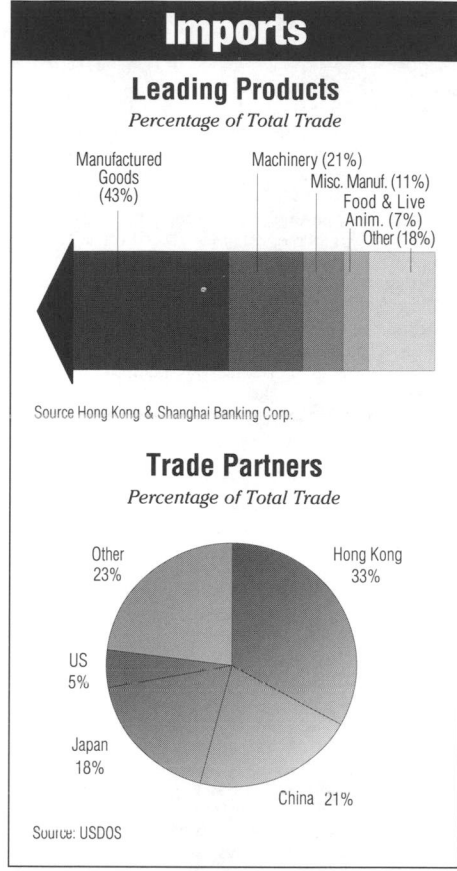

Imports

Leading Products
Percentage of Total Trade

Manufactured Goods (43%)
Machinery (21%)
Misc. Manuf. (11%)
Food & Live Anim. (7%)
Other (18%)

Source Hong Kong & Shanghai Banking Corp.

Trade Partners
Percentage of Total Trade

Other 23%
Hong Kong 33%
US 5%
Japan 18%
China 21%

Source: USDOS

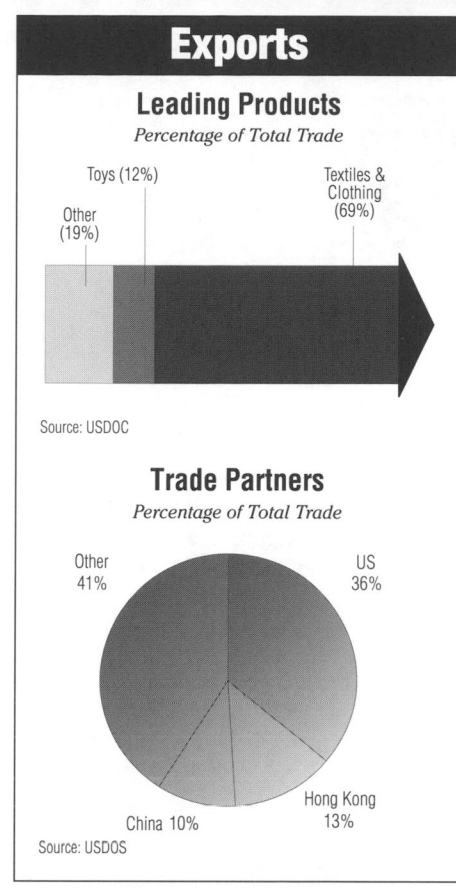

Exports

Leading Products
Percentage of Total Trade

Toys (12%)
Textiles & Clothing (69%)
Other (19%)

Source: USDOC

Trade Partners
Percentage of Total Trade

Other 41%
US 36%
China 10%
Hong Kong 13%

Source: USDOS

Opportunities

FOR IMPORTING TO MACAU
- consumer goods, food, foodstuffs
- fresh water
- energy

FOR EXPORTING FROM MACAU
- clothing
- textiles
- manufactured goods

GROWTH SECTORS
- tourism
- textiles
- construction
- real estate development
- manufacturing

Trade News

RULES AND REGULATIONS
- **Trade news** Macau depends mostly on imports for its food.
- **Import restrictions** Government approval is required to import telephone and telegraph equipment, arms and ammunition, motor vehicles, fuels, electrical equipment, livestock, acids, corrosives, and medicines.
- **Import licenses** Import licenses are issued freely from the Services de Economia de Macau. From the date of issue, licenses are good for three months. Extensions are not given.
- **Stamp tax** There is a three percent stamp tax applied to all shipping documents.

Legal

Legal System

Macau is a Special Territory of Portugal, with executive power vested in the Governor, who is appointed by the President of Portugal after consultation with the Legislative Assembly of Macau. The Macau Basic Law, written in 1988, will come into effect when Macau reverts back to China in 1999.

Intellectual Property Rights

Copyrights, trade names, and trademarks may be registered in Portugal, with an extension of the protection to Macau. After a patent has been registered in Portugal, the certificate of extension must be published in Macau's official gazette before it can be entered in the Registry of Records, after which it will have full legal effect in the territory.

Business Registration

To establish a branch of a foreign company, an application must be made to the Registry of Macau and several documents submitted therewith, including: a certificate issued by a Portuguese consulate declaring that the company is carrying out its business in accordance with the legislation of its country of origin; and a certified Portuguese translation of the company's memorandum and articles of association which has been published in Macau's official gazette. These documents must be registered with the Finance Department and Commercial Registry. All legal documents and government forms must be completed in Portuguese and, in most cases, certified by a notary public in Macau.

Labor

Employment of expatriates is not subject to restrictions other than ensuring that employment papers are in order and the necessary formalities regarding entry into Macau have been completed. However, employers are required to submit a list of all expatriate staff to the police each month for record purposes. The government allows employers to import labor from mainland China on contract to ease the current labor shortage. Permission to import additional manpower is, however, granted on a case-by-case basis.

Legal Matters

LEGAL BRIEFS
- **Business organization** The main types of business organization are sole proprietorship or partnership; company limited by shares or quotas; and branch of a company located outside Macau.
- **Attorneys** Once the form of the business organization has been decided, the services of a Macau lawyer should be employed to ensure compliance with the necessary procedures and requirements. All legal documents and government forms must be completed in Portuguese and, in most cases, be certified by a notary public in Macau.
- **Garment factories** Garment factories are not eligible for free export quotas for the first three years of their establishment.
- **Insurance** An insurance company with its head office in Macau must be established as a joint-stock company with limited liability. Insurance companies are restricted to the insurance business and do not qualify to carry on other forms of trade.
- **Agents** The law on general agents stipulates that only individuals will be granted the authority to act within Macau.
- **Social employment benefits** Employees' compensation insurance and contributions to the social security fund by both employers and employees are compulsory.
- **Residency** A person intending to establish residence in Macau must submit an application to the Immigration Services, including personal details of all members of his family over 14 years of age, such as occupation and the income they will receive.
- **Contracts** Contract practices in Macau are a unique blend of Portuguese and Asian influences.

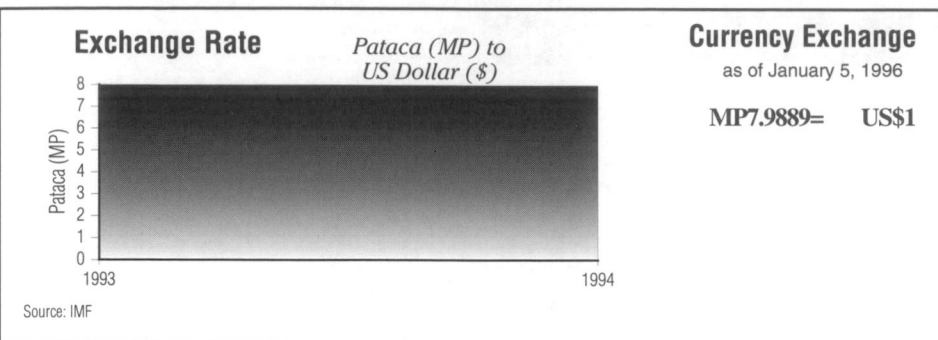

Exchange Rate — Pataca (MP) to US Dollar ($)

Currency Exchange
as of January 5, 1996

MP7.9889=   US$1

Source: IMF

Currency

Macau's currency is the pataca (symbol MP). It has been officially tied to the US–Hong Kong exchange rate since 1977. It is divided into 100 avos.

Foreign Exchange

There are no exchange controls. The state-owned Instituto Emissor de Macau regulates the money, finance, and foreign exchange markets. Banks are allowed to exchange foreign currency with themselves and with residents and nonresidents at free market rates of exchange. The degree of foreign exchange risk banks can take must fall within the limits established by the Instituto Emissor de Macau.

Capital Transfers

There is no difference in Macau between resident and nonresident accounts. Nonresidents can open accounts in any currency. Issuing of securities by nonresidents in a foreign capital market requires prior authorization from the Minister of Finance. Foreign currency can be freely transferred into and out of Macau.

Investment Incentives

The investment code targets the following sectors for investment: agriculture, forestry, industry, transportation, communications, services, and tourism. In addition, the code establishes that the capital and other assets of foreign investors will not be nationalized or otherwise requisitioned by administrative procedure. Incentives provided for foreign investment include tax holidays of up to four years, and allowance for tax-free investment for certain reinvested profits. In the tourist and hotel industry, specific incentives include a 50 percent reduction in the urban housing tax during the 15 years following the expiration of the initial 10-year exemption period, and exemption from the property tax.

Investment Restrictions

There are very few government-imposed restrictions to investments, but restrictions exist nonetheless. The labor force is predominantly unskilled and there are very few natural resources available to foreign investors. There are also some performance requirements that investors must adhere to, varying according to sector. Be sure to study the area in which you wish to invest. Some sectors, like gambling and telecommunications, are owned by the government and are off-limits to any type of private investment.

Money Matters

BITS AND PIECES

- **Manufacturing incentives** All equipment and auxiliary machines for setting up, modifying, and expanding industries, along with raw materials used for industrial production, are exempt from direct import duty and other taxes.

- **Company em comandita** In a company em comandita, the liability of one or more of its members is unlimited as stated by the memorandum of association, and the liability of the remaining members is limited to the value of shares held by them.

- **A company limited by quotas** This is the most common type of organization in Macau. The company must have capital of at least MP 10,000 and the liability of its members is limited by the amount of quotas (shares) held by them.

- **Industrial licenses** Under decree No. 1767 of 1968, a licence is required to set up an industrial enterprise. Licence applications should be completed in Portuguese, certified by a Macau notary public and submitted to the Directorate of Economic Services.

- **Insurance** The insurance sector is regulated by the newly established Monetary Authority of Macau (AMCM). An insurance company with its head office in Macau must be established as a joint stock company with limited liability. Restricted firms are restricted to the insurance business and do not qualify for other forms of trade. There are 20 authorized insurance companies in Macau, three of which are of local origin.

- **Other taxes** There is no inheritance or donations tax on sums of less than MP1,000; for bequests over this amount, the tax rates range from 4 to 35 percent, depending on the relationship to the recipient.

- **Business advantages** Some advantages to investing in Macau: it is strategically located on the western rim of the fast-growing Asia-Pacific region, it has a stable government, it has a low standard rate of taxation and offers certain tax exemptions or reductions, its wages are comparatively low, it has an ample supply of industrial sites and industrial premises can be purchased or leased at a reasonable cost, and it is near the Zhuhai Special Economic Zone, allowing Macau to tap the market and ensure the supply of raw materials at favorable prices.

BANKS

Banco Comercial de Macau, SA
Rua da Praia Grande 22
Macau
Tel: 569622
Fax: 580967
Telex: 88463

Banco Hang Sang, SARL
Av. Conselheiro Ferreira de Almeida 79
Macau
Tel: 559898
Fax: 570068
Telex: 88243

Banco Nacional Ultramarino, SA
Av. Almeida Ribeiro 2
CP 465
Macau
Tel: 376644
Fax: 589191
Telex: 88202

Banco Seng Heng, SARL
Rua da Praia Grande 57
Macau
Tel: 555222
Fax: 570758
Telex: 88210

Banco Tai Fung, SARL
Av. Almeida Ribeiro 32
Macau
Tel: 322323
Fax: 570737
Telex: 88212

TAXATION

Taxation requires sophisticated knowledge of complex rules and regulations specific to each country. Some of the more notable taxes in Macau include:

- An annual business tax that ranges from a few hundred to a few thousand patacas, depending not just on profitability but also on the type of business concerned. All companies, foreign and domestic, are subject.

- A property tax, assessed at 16 percent of the premises' annual rental value regardless of whether it is in the city of Macau or on the islands, is payable by the owner of the property. The rate is reduced to 10 percent for properties completed after July 1, 1988.

- A real estate purchase tax, where the purchaser is obliged to pay six percent of the purchase price of a property in Macau city, or four percent if the property is on Taipa or Coloane. For purchases and transfers within the first four years of the issuance of occupation permits, the applicable tax is reduced by two percent.

- A profits tax, payable by self-employed individuals and companies on total income generated in Macau, irrespective of where the company's registered office is located. For self-employed people, profits tax is based on total income, excluding specified allowances. Profits tax for companies is based on operating profit, excluding profits or dividends distributed to shareholders.

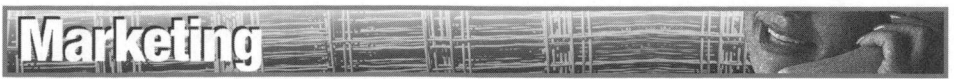

Marketing

Overview

Tourism, primarily keyed to gambling, looks to grow through expanded hotel construction and new facilities, such as the airport between Taipa and Coloane Islands and the horse trotting course on Taipa.

Distribution

Like Hong Kong, Macau is a free port without quota restrictions or customs duties. Distributors and agents generally have ties to firms based in Hong Kong and operate under mutually agreeable terms. The colony is readily accessible by sea and air; there are paved roads throughout and bridges connect Macau to its outlying islands.

Advertising

There are four AM and three FM radio stations. The government-owned television station, Teledifusao de Macau, broadcasts in Portuguese and Cantonese. Two Hong Kong television stations also broadcast to Macau, in English on two channels and in Cantonese on two other channels. Most newspapers read in Macau are printed in Hong Kong or China. Portuguese, Chinese, and English language publications are available. Commercial samples and advertising matter are duty-free.

Business Culture

Greetings and Courtesies

Macau's population is about 95 percent Chinese. Handshaking is the accepted greeting. Chinese usually shake hands very lightly. Upon meeting someone, Chinese lower their eyes slightly as a sign of respect. Staring into the eyes of a Chinese might make them uncomfortable. Face, a measure of one's dignity, is crucial to the Chinese. Saying or doing anything that causes someone to lose face can instantly destroy a relationship. Never insult or openly criticize someone in front of others. Do not treat someone as a person of lowly rank if their position in their company is high. A person's face is also their company's face. The relationship you develop with a person represents your relationship with his entire company.

Business Ethic and Framework

Chinese behavior is largely determined by Confucianism, which teaches respect for superiors, duty to family, loyalty to friends, humility, sincerity, and courtesy. Employees work hard to help their company flourish. People of higher status and age are deferred to in speech and action. Business cards are important. At first meetings, handshakes are followed by a formal exchange of cards. Always carry plenty of cards, ideally with Cantonese Chinese text on one side. If possible, get expert advice on the specific Chinese characters, as some ideograms are considered more favorable than others. When receiving a card, do not just put it in your pocket. Business attire is Western in style, and formal. Summers are hot and humid; winters can be chilly, but extremely heavy clothing is not needed.

Decision Making

Chinese try to avoid saying no, for fear of causing embarrassment or losing face. Instead of directly saying no, they are likely to say something is inconvenient or is under consideration. If there is bad news, they might convey it though an intermediary or hint at it rather than say it directly.

Women

Women will probably not find open discrimination; however they should behave professionally and dress formally. A self-confident, poised woman could achieve a great deal because Chinese may feel that if she has been chosen to represent her company, she is someone with great ability.

Meetings

Meetings will begin with small talk. Business is addressed only after people feel comfortable with each other. One person, preferably your group's senior member, should be designated as your spokesperson, and this person should lead discussions throughout the negotiation process. Ensure that other team members do not openly contradict the designated spokesperson. If there is debate to be had, do it when your hosts are not present.

Marketing Tips

MARKETING TIPS

- **Telephone** The phone system is very advanced in Macau, especially compared to the neighboring countries. Fax machines are also quite prevalent throughout the country.
- **Postal system** The postal system is quite advanced and efficient in Macau.

RADIO AND TELEVISION

Radio Commercial Vila Verde
Rua Francisco Xavier Pereira 133H, 13
Macau
Tel: 573355
Fax: 311668

Teledifusao de Macau, SARL (TDM)
Rua Francisco Xavier Pereira 157-A
CP 446
Macau
Tel: 520204
Fax: 520208
Tolox: 88300

Mun Tin To
Tel: 562528
Fax: 567938

Cultural Cautions

DO'S

- Be aware of the importance of face in all your dealings with Chinese.
- Always treat people with the respect to which their position entitles them.

DON'TS

- Do not insult or harshly criticize someone in front of others.
- Don't make fun of someone, even as a playful joke.

CUSTOMS

- While most people in Macau are Chinese, a small percentage of the population is Portuguese. These are two distinctly different groups that maintain their own cultures and customs.
- Gifts express friendship and symbolize hopes for success. Appropriate gifts include business-related items (pens, paperweights). If you give one gift, present it to the senior person. If you give several, be sure all are of equal value. Don't omit anyone with whom you have a relationship.
- For wrapped gifts, gold or red are appropriate colors. White and black are colors of mourning.

OBSERVATIONS

- Macau has been under Portuguese rule since 1557, but is essentially Chinese. Understanding Chinese culture is crucial to doing business here, now more than ever as Macau returns to mainland Chinese control in 1999.
- The same individual should always represent your company. If they leave their job, they should personally introduce their replacement to all Chinese business associates.

NEGOTIATIONS

- A common tactic is delaying major negotiations until you are about to leave the country, then making unreasonable demands.
- Chinese sometimes negotiate with several competing companies at the same time and let it be known they are doing so as a way of applying pressure.
- Chinese tend to take a long-term view, regarding an agreement as a single element of a bigger, ongoing relationship that is, ultimately, more important than any one venture.

GOVERNMENT AGENCIES

Economic Affairs
Direcçao dos Serviços de Economica
Edificio Luso Internacional
Rua Dr. Pedro José Lobo
Macau
Tel: 562622

Finance
Direcçao dos Serviços de Finanças
69 Rua da Praia Grande
Macau
Tel: 571600

Home Affairs
Administração e Função Pública
Edificio Nam Yut, 11th /15th Floors
37A Calçada de St. Agostinho
Macau
Tel: 323623

Monetary Authority of Macau
Autorida de Monetária e Cambial de Macau
45 Rua Pedro Nolasco da Silva
Macau
Tel: 325435/7, 325416

Public Works and Transport
Direcção dos Serviçao de Solos
Obras Públicas e Transportes
32-36 Est D Maria II
Edificio CEM
Macau
Tel: 722488

Statistics
Direcção dos Serviços de Estatística
4-6D Rua do Inácio Baptista
Sea View Gardens
Macau
Tel: 550935

Tourism
Direcção dos Serviços de Turismo
9 Largo do Leal Sengo
Edificio Ritz
Macau
Tel: 315566
Telex: 88338 turis om

Departamento de Promoção de Exportações
Edificio Luso Internacional, 7th Floor
1-3 Rua Dr. Pedro José Lobo
Macau
Tel: 378221
Telex: 88413 dpe om

GENERAL TRADE ASSOCIATIONS

General Association of Macau Workers
2 Rua Ribeira do Patane, 1st Floor
Macau
Tel: 565469

Hotel Association
8-10 Trav Caldeira, 2nd Floor
Macau
Tel: 317358

Macau Association of Building Contractors
9-11 Rua do Campo, 6th Floor A
Macau
Tel: 573226

Macau Commercial Association
Edificio ACM, 5th Floor, Rua de Xangai
Macau
Tel: 576833

Macau Exporters Association
Centro Comercial, 3rd Floor
A do Infante D Henrique
Macau
Tel: 375859

Macau Industrial Association
Edificio AIM, 17th Floor
34-36 Rua Dr. Pedro José Lobo
Macau
Tel: 574125

Macau Travel Agents Association
c/o Hotel Lisboa, Av da Amizade
Macau
Tel: 377666

Weaving and Spinning of Wool Manufacturers Association
Edificio Kam Wa Kok, 6th Floor A
271 Av de Amizade
Macau
Tel: 553378

BANKS

Associacao de Bancos de Macau (The Macau Association of Banks)
Rua da Praia Grande 69A
Edif. Financas, 15/F
Macau
Tel: 511921
Fax: 346049

Banco Portugues do Atlantico (Portugal)
Rua da Praia Grande 26, 6th Floor
Macau
Tel: 84999
Fax: 595817
Telex: 88532

Banco Totta e Acores, SA (Portugal)
57 Rua da Praia Grande
21st Floor
POB 912
Macau
Tel: 573299
Fax: 56832
Telex: 88517

Banque Indosuez (France)
Rua da Praia Grande 99-D
Macau
Tel: 378366
Fax: 563577
Telex: 88456

Banque Nationale de Paris (France)
Rua da Praia Grande 2B
Macau
Tel: 562777
Fax: 560626
Telex: 88299

Citibank NA (USA)
Rua da Praia Grande 31B-C
Macau
Tel: 378188
Fax: 578451
Telex: 88384

Deutsche Bank AG (Germany)
7/F Nam Wah Commercial Bldg
1L-1LB
Av. Almeida Ribeiro
Macau
Tel: 378440
Fax: 304939
Telex: 88550

Hongkong and Shanghai Banking Corporation (Hong Kong)
Rua da Praia Grande 73-75
CP 476
Macau
Tel: 553669
Fax: 315421
Telex: 88205

Overseas Trust Bank Limited (Hong Kong)
Av. do Infante D. Henrique 51-53
Macau
Tel: 710112
Fax: 382112

Standard Chartered Bank (UK)
16F-17F Edif. Centro Comercial Central
60-64 Av. Infante D. Henrique
Macau
Tel: 378271
Fax: 594134

INSURANCE

Asia Insurance Co. Ltd.
Rm. 1103
Luso International Bank Bldg.
Av. da Amizade 11
Macau
Tel: 563166
Fax: 5700438

China Insurance Co. Ltd.
Centro Comercial de Praia Grande, 10/F
Macau
Tel: 373604
Fax: 373607

Companhia de Seguros de Macau, SARL
Centro Comercial de Praia Grande 57, 18/F
Macau
Tel: 555078
Telex: 88373
Fax: 551074

Crown Life Insurance Co.
37 Rua da Praia Grande, 8/F, Block B
Nam Yue Commercial Centre
Macau
Tel: 570828
Fax: 570844

Forex Insurance Co. Ltd.
Av. Almeida Ribeiro 56
Macau
Tel: 921478
Telex: 88243
Fax: 922976

Min Xin Insurance Co. Ltd.
Luso International Bank Bldg, 27/F, Rm. 2704
Av. da Amizade 11
Macau
Tel: 305684
Fax: 305600

Sumitomo Marine and Fire Insurance Co., Ltd.
Rm. 802, Tai Fung Bank Bldg.
Av. Almeida Ribeiro 32
Macau
Tel: 385917
Fax: 596667

The Wing On Fire & Marine Insurance Co. Ltd.
Centro Comercial de Praia Grande, 11/F
Macau
Tel: 550233
Fax: 333710

INTERNET ADDRESSES

Macau Home Page
http://www.hk.super.net/~ainacio/MC/Main/macauhome_e.html

Asian Studies - Macau
http://coombs.anu.edu.au/WWWVLAsian/Macau.html

Malaysia

Economy

Overview

After four consecutive years of annual growth hovering around nine percent, Malaysia's economy began to decelerate in the second half of 1992, providing much-needed relief from spiraling inflation, high interest rates, and a tight labor market. The government's efforts since then have largely succeeded in slowing growth to a more sustainable pace. Government policy currently emphasizes growth in the private sector, and diversification of production toward manufacturing and export-oriented industries. It is particularly focusing on the development and growth of high-tech, capital intensive industries. Its overall goals for the near term are to transform Malaysia into a fully industrialized country by speeding up the expansion of the manufacturing sector and promoting the efficient use of natural resources. The Malaysian economy has enjoyed significant growth in recent years, averaging between five and 10 percent per annum. Malaysia is now poised to realize even more success; it is, for example, the world's third largest producer and exporter of semiconductors.

Trade

Malaysia is the world's largest exporter of tropical hardwood, and most of the raw timber exported from Malaysia comes from Sabah and Sarawak. Timber and timber products account for almost 20 percent of all exports. The country exports close to 75 billion ringgits (US$30 billion) worth of goods annually, drawing from electronic components, petroleum, palm oil, natural rubber, textiles, and timber and logs. Imports run at 67.5 billion ringgits (US$27 billion) each year, and are comprised of intermediate goods, machinery, metal products, food products, consumer durables, and transport equipment. Japan is Malaysia's primary supplier, followed by the US, Singapore, and Taiwan.

Sectors

Agriculture About 18 percent of the Malaysian labor force hold jobs in agriculture. Products of this tropical nation include palm oil, rubber, timber, cocoa, rice, pepper, and pineapples. As the world's largest supplier of natural rubber, Malaysia provides one quarter of the planet's rubber needs.

Industry Malaysia's sound infrastructure, work force, and stable political climate make it an ideal backdrop for increased industrial growth. Principal businesses are electronics, electrical products, rubber products, automobile assembly, and textiles.

Services Malaysia does not have a particularly strong service economy, but a thriving tourism business engages about 11 percent of the work force, and transportation and communication provide jobs for another seven percent. Tourism looks set to grow in the near future.

Trends

Malaysia's prospects for continued prosperity are excellent, with growth rates in the six percent to eight percent range through 1995. Strong domestic savings provide adequate funds for investment and Malaysia remains attractive to foreign investors. The economy, though, is still vulnerable to external turbulence. A recession in the industrial industries could have severe repercussions for the country. Still, with its strong export markets (exports account for about 70 percent of GDP), Malaysia's economy should be able to weather the storm.

At a Glance

THE COUNTRY

Location Southeastern Asia, bordering the South China Sea, between Vietnam and Indonesia.
Terrain Coastal plains and jungle-covered mountains in the interior. Peninsular Malaysia is separated from East Malaysia in Borneo by the South China Sea.
Climate Tropical, with average temperatures of 27 degrees C (80 degrees F) year-round with high humidity. Annual southwest (April to October) and northeast (October to February) monsoons.

THE PEOPLE

Population 19,300,000
Ethnic composition
Malay and other indigenous.................................. 61%
Chinese 30%
Indian 8%
Others.. 1%
Religious composition Muslim (Malays), Buddhist (Chinese), Hindu (Indians), Christian, and tribal religions.
Languages spoken Malay, Chinese dialects, English, Tamil, and other indigenous languages.
Education and literacy Religious and secular schools train students. Compulsory education lasts nine years. Adult literacy is 80% in Peninsular Malaysia, and 60% in Sabah and Sarawak.
Labor force
Total:...7,200,000
By occupation: manufacturing 28%, agriculture 18%, government 10%, mining and petroleum 9%, local trade and tourism 11%, transportation and communications 7%, and finance 10%.

COUNTRY FACTS

Political and legal This parliamentary democracy is patterned after the Westminster model with a constitutional monarch. The legal system is based on English common law.
Telephone The government-owned telecommunications system is well-developed and well-equipped. There is good intercity and international service on Peninsular Malaysia. International country code: [60]. Selected city codes: Ipoh (5), Kuala Lumpur (3).
Transportation Train service is government-owned on Peninsular Malaysia and Sabah. Sarawak has none. There are three major shipping ports and three international airports that also provide domestic air travel. Malaysia has a good highway system.
Environment Government efforts have not stopped the severe water pollution problem. More than 40 percent of Malaysia's rivers are polluted, and the coasts are damaged by petroleum and sewage. The 59 percent of Malaysia that is tropical rainforest is owned by commercial interests. Current issues are air and water pollution, and deforestation.
Media Radio and television broadcasts offer good coverage by a generally free press. There are about 80 daily and weekly newspapers.
Health Long-established health and medical services provide good care. The government pays for most health care expenses. Life expectancy of males is 66 years; of females, 72 years.

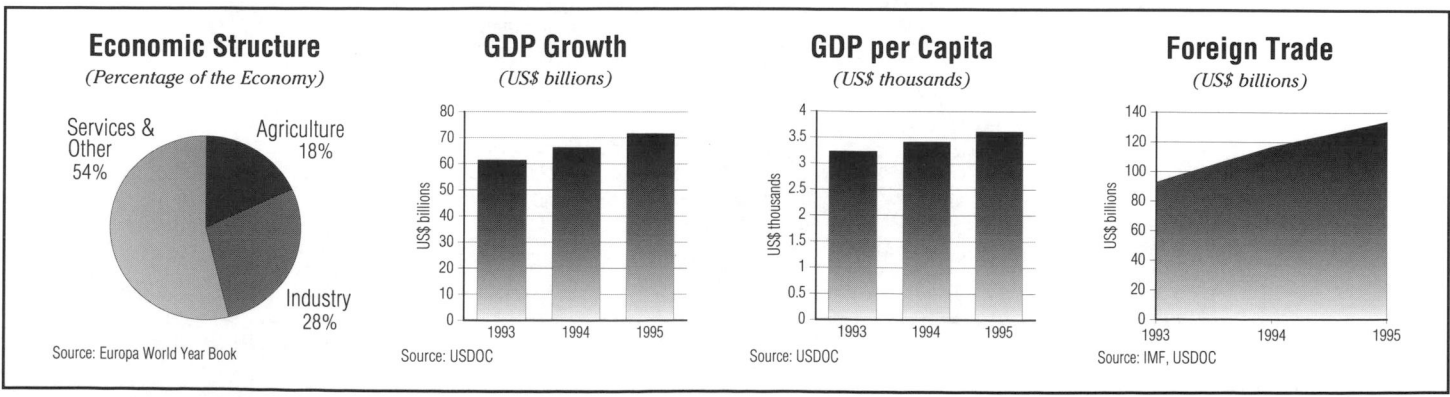

Economic Structure
(Percentage of the Economy)

Services & Other 54%
Agriculture 18%
Industry 28%

Source: Europa World Year Book

GDP Growth
(US$ billions)

Source: USDOC

GDP per Capita
(US$ thousands)

Source: USDOC

Foreign Trade
(US$ billions)

Source: IMF, USDOC

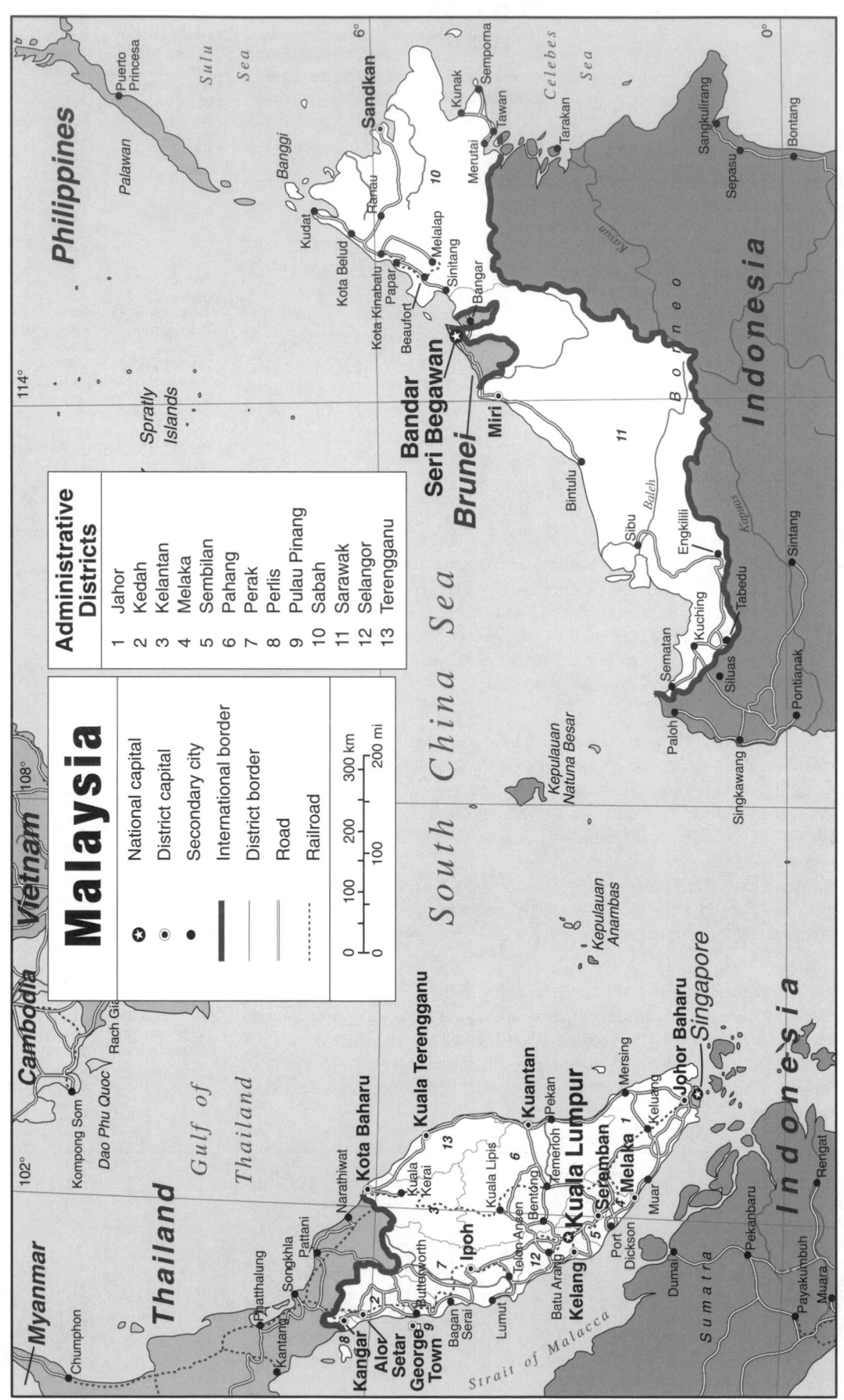

Malaysia

Administrative Districts

1 Jahor
2 Kedah
3 Kelantan
4 Melaka
5 Sembilan
6 Pahang
7 Perak
8 Perlis
9 Pulau Pinang
10 Sabah
11 Sarawak
12 Selangor
13 Terengganu

National capital
District capital
Secondary city
International border
District border
Road
Railroad

300 km
200 mi

©1995 Magellan GeographixSMSanta Barbara, CA

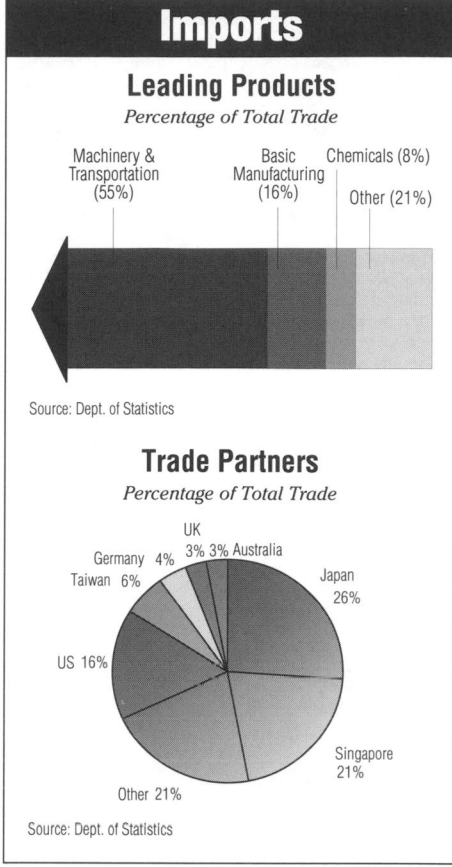

Imports

Leading Products
Percentage of Total Trade

Machinery & Transportation (55%)
Basic Manufacturing (16%)
Chemicals (8%)
Other (21%)

Source: Dept. of Statistics

Trade Partners
Percentage of Total Trade

UK 3%
Australia 3%
Germany 4%
Taiwan 6%
US 16%
Japan 26%
Singapore 21%
Other 21%

Source: Dept. of Statistics

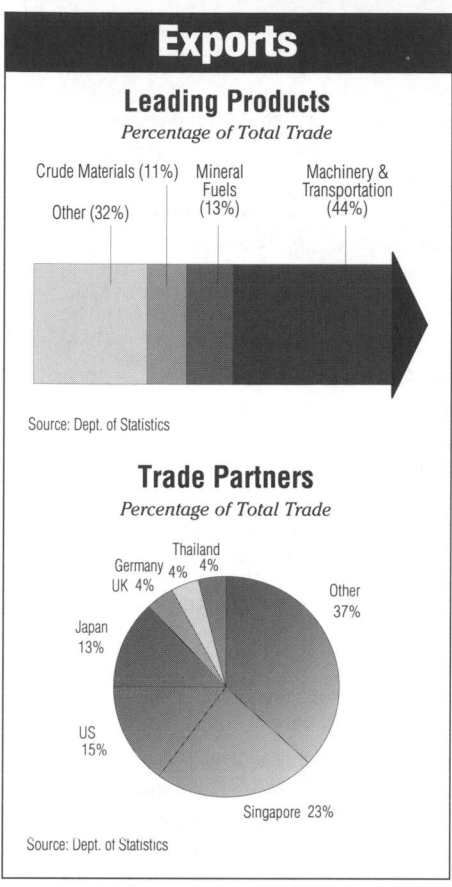

Exports

Leading Products
Percentage of Total Trade

Crude Materials (11%)
Mineral Fuels (13%)
Machinery & Transportation (44%)
Other (32%)

Source: Dept. of Statistics

Trade Partners
Percentage of Total Trade

Thailand 4%
Germany 4%
UK 4%
Japan 13%
US 15%
Other 37%
Singapore 23%

Source: Dept. of Statistics

Opportunities

FOR IMPORTING TO MALAYSIA
- intermediate goods
- machinery
- metal products
- food products
- transportation equipment
- telecommunications
- pollution control equipment
- consumer durables

FOR EXPORTING FROM MALAYSIA
- electronic components
- cocoa
- pepper
- petroleum
- timber and logs
- palm oil
- natural rubber
- semiconductor devices
- chicken

GROWTH SECTORS
- petroleum sector
- manufacturing sectors
- agriculture sectors
- telecommunications

GOVERNMENT PROCUREMENT
- second national airline
- aircraft fire fighting systems
- medical design/construction
- hotel development
- express freight terminal
- equipment and supplies for terminal
- additional airports
- telecommunications
- national sewage system
- national hazardous waste site
- air pollution control

Trade News

RULES AND REGULATIONS

- **Trade news** Malaysia has become one of the most successful economies in the Asian region. It continues to be an excellent market for all products.
- **Agents** It is critically important to develop a close relationship with one's local agent and his customers.
- **Import permits** Permits are required for arms and explosives, motor vehicles, dangerous drugs and chemicals, plants, soil, tin ore, slag or concentrates, and certain essential foodstuffs. Malaysia follows the Harmonized Commodity Description and Coding System of classification of goods.
- **Import duties** Import duties range from zero to 300 percent with the average rate being less than 10 percent. The higher rates apply to luxury goods, including knocked down and assembled automobiles. In addition to import duties, a sales tax of 10 percent is levied on most imported goods. This sales tax is not applied to raw materials or machinery used in export production.
- **Quantitative import restrictions** These restrictions are seldom imposed except on a limited range of products for protection of local industries or for reasons of security. A quantitative license has been instituted for the import of certain plastic resins, for the purpose of protecting a domestic petrochemical operation.
- **Tariffs and import taxes** The agriculture sector does contain some restrictive tariffs and non-tariff barriers which distort trade (e.g. tobacco and rice to boost their own production).
- **Barriers** Malaysia is a member of the ASEAN Free Trade Area (AFTA), which aims to reduce trade barriers between the member countries. Progress to date has been slow.
- **Import licenses** Some technical licenses exist but they are administered fairly and do not appear to constitute a non-tariff barrier. In the few sectors subject to license, exports have not been significantly impaired.
- **Export controls** Raw materials used directly for the manufacture of goods for export are exempted from import duties if such materials are not produced locally or if the local materials are not of acceptable quality and price. Exemptions from duties are also available for machinery and equipment used directly in the manufacturing process or not available locally.
- **Export licensing** In some cases, such as textiles, the system of export licensing is used to ensure compliance with bilateral export restraint agreements. In cases such as rubber exports, special permission from government agencies is required. Export duties are imposed on the principal commodities: petroleum, rubber, pepper, palm oil, and tin. Petroleum faces a flat rate duty of 25 percent.
- **Free trade zones** Malaysia has ten facilities. Raw material and equipment may be imported duty-free into these zones with minimum customs formalities. To be eligible, a firm must export all production (although the government will consider companies exporting at least 80 percent of their goods). No restrictions are placed on a company's choice of suppliers.
- **Trading restrictions** Some barriers to imports and exports include: an import tariff on tobacco to encourage greater use of local tobacco in cigarettes and to maintain high leaf prices, a duty on high value food products that ranges to between 20 and 30 percent, an increased tariff on plastic resin, and a higher tariff on imported craftpaper.
- **Service barrier** Most service sectors are protected in Malaysia, and foreign lawyers, architects, and medical practitioners are generally not allowed to practice. Television advertisements must be largely produced in Malaysia with Malaysian performers unless an exception is obtained.
- **Export subsidies** The largest export allowance is the export credit refinancing (ECR) scheme operated by the Central Bank. Under the ECR, commercial banks and other lenders provide financing to exporters at an interest rate of seven percent for pre- and post-shipment credit.

Marketing

Overview

Malaysia's market is expanding as the economy is retooled and modernized. There has been a concerted effort on the part of the government to promote the development of a local Malay (*bumiputra*) business community—businesses have traditionally been run largely by European expatriates and ethnic Chinese—and preferences have been given to such local operations. Although largely secular, Malaysia is officially Muslim and has in place laws curbing behaviors considered offensive to Islam. These elements add a local twist to marketing in what is a rapidly developing economy whose burgeoning productivity and demand are opening opportunities for the sale of a wide variety of goods.

Distribution

Exports to Malaysia move through a variety of sales and distribution channels. Software is handled by many retail outlets as well as local and international consulting companies. Food and other consumer goods are usually sold by wholesalers to Malaysian general import houses which handle distribution to supermarkets and other retail outlets. Many consumer products—especially food—are distributed at the retail level through a complex network of mostly Chinese small neighborhood shops; the large number of extremely small outlets and the ethnic specificity means that few outsiders will be able to deal effectively with such distributors. Franchises involving local partners have proliferated in recent years, largely a reflection of Malaysia's rising per capita income.

Agents, Distributors, and Partners

Agents range from small commission agents to large trading companies with multiple branches located nationwide. Some specialize in categories of goods, but the larger ones are general importers. Many agents buy and sell for their own accounts, often carrying inventories of standard goods. Most exporters designate an existing Malaysian-based trading company as their local agent. These companies provide a whole range of services, usually including clearing goods through customs, dealing with local wholesalers and retailers, direct marketing, and handling of after-sales support and service. Many firms appoint separate agents in Peninsular Malaysia and Sabah to handle their business, because the two areas constitute sufficiently different markets. Sales to the government require a local agent, as do major equipment sales to both public and private corporations. On occasion, foreign businesses with a large and long-term presence in the markets have preferred to establish their own subsidiary companies in Malaysia to handle sales, distribution, and service, although the government generally discourages outsiders from trying to handle their own distribution. Some foreign subsidiaries also act as local agents for related products of other manufacturers. Government policy encourages foreign firms to work with local firms, transferring know-how and equity to them over time as they become familiar with the business. A foreign operation should consider the long-term potential of its Malaysian agent to become a participant in a range of activities as the relationship progresses. Large firms may also have overseas agents that buy direct and import.

Selling Techniques

Overseas food and consumer goods are primarily marketed to the rapidly growing urban middle class; these are generally sold based on features and quality and tend to be priced higher than their local competitors. Electronics sales depend heavily on specialized trade fairs, publications, and personal visits by company representatives.

Advertising

Many local advertising, accounting, and consulting firms in Kuala Lumpur have international connections. They can provide market survey services and advice on potential agents or partners for interested exporters. A full range of television, press, and outdoor and other advertising approaches is available. There are three television channels—two government-operated and one private—all of which accept advertising, although all such advertising must be locally produced according to local guidelines. The two most important English newspapers are the *New Straits Times* and the *Star*. The primary business-oriented paper is the *Business Times*, and business-oriented magazines include *Malaysian Business*, *Malaysian Industry*, and the *Malaysian Investor*. The main local newspapers include *Utusan Malaysia* and *Berita Harian* (in Bahasa Maleysu) and *Nanyang Siang Pau* and *Sin Chew Jit Poh* (in Chinese). Circulation is generally on the upswing. There is also an active trade press. Cinema trailers, outdoor posters and signs, and direct mail and door-to-door marketing may also be used.

Service and Customer Support

After-sales support is considered to be important for capital and specialty goods, but is less important for commodity products—for which there is a correspondingly lower markup.

Marketing in Malaysia

MARKETING TIPS

- **Government markets** Local Malay firms receive preferential treatment in government business. Local agents are required to bid on such business, and foreign firms should be sure that the agent they choose can obtain contracts.
- **Credit** Most large buyers and agencies operating for their own account are able to buy using standard terms, such as letters of credit or documents against acceptance; many must extend credit to the small retail outlets they serve, however, and may request either financing or a discount from the seller to cover this expense.
- **Sensitive products and ethnicity** More than half of Malaysians are Muslims who avoid pork products and alcohol and consider the left hand unclean. Indians and Chinese constitute significant minorities. Care must therefore be taken in product development to avoid unacceptable ramifications, and in marketing to observe local, culturally based sensitivities.

AD AGENCIES

Bates Malaysia
11th Fl., Pernas International
Jalan Sultan Ismail
50250 Kuala Lumpur
Tel: (3) 261-0290
Fax: (3) 261-0327

Grey Malaysia
37th Fl., Empire Tower
182 Jalan Tun Razak
50400 Kuala Lumpur
Tel: (3) 262-6868
Fax: (3) 262-6363

McCann-Erickson (Malaysia) Sdn. Bhd.
Menara Aik Hua
Changkat Raja Chulan, 18th Fl.
50200 Kuala Lumpur
Tel: (3) 230-5677
Fax: (3) 230-5598

Ogilvy & Mather Sdn. Bhd.
PO Box 180
Jalan Sultan
46720 Petaling Jaya
Tel: (3) 756-9066
Fax: (3) 756-2821

Saatchi & Saatchi Advertising
1th Fl., Block B, Bangunan SPPK
46 Jalan Dungun
Damansara Heights
50490 Kuala Lumpur
Tel: (3) 255-4333
Fax: (3) 255-8105

J. Walter Thompson Sdn. Bhd.
21st Floor, Wisma Sime Darby
Jalan Raja Laut
50350 Kuala Lumpur
Tel: (3) 291-7788 Fax: (3) 293-9363

Burson-Marsteller (M) Sdn. Bhd.
11th Floor, Bangunan Getah Asli
148 Jalan Ampang
50450 Kuala Lumpur
Tel: (3) 261-7900
Fax: (3) 261-3828

Leo Burnett Advertising Sdn. Bhd.
10th Floor, MCB Plaza
6 Changkat Raja Chulan
50200 Kuala Lumpur
Tel: (3) 201-0998
Fax: (3) 201-0972

Lintas Worldwide (M) Sdn. Bhd.
Wisma Perdana, Jalan Dungun
Damansara Heights
50490 Kuala Lumpur
Tel: (3) 254-5122
Fax: (3) 255-9985

Bozell Sdn. Bhd.
18A Jalan SS 22/25
47400 Petaling Jaya
Tel: (3) 719-2332
Fax: (3) 717-1841

Business Culture

Greetings and Courtesies

Malaysia is home to Malays, Chinese, and Indians, and Malaysian behavior is shaped largely by their specific cultural background. Among Malays, the accepted greeting is a handshake, which is usually accompanied by a slight bow or nod of the head, especially when greeting someone older. In addition, when an older person enters a room, people usually stand. Women and elderly people often don't shake hands but will offer a verbal greeting. Chinese lower their eyes slightly as a sign of respect upon meeting someone. Chinese usually shake hands very lightly, and a handshake may last as long as ten seconds. Face, a measure of one's dignity, is crucial to Chinese. Saying or doing anything that causes someone to lose face can instantly destroy a relationship. Indians are the third largest ethnic group in Malaysia.

Business Ethic and Framework

A majority of Malays are Muslims and live by the teachings of the Koran. Their moral code is based on courtesy, respect (especially for elders and parents), and existing in harmony with others. Malaysians will make every effort to do a good job. If they fail, or things do not go as expected, to some extent this will be attributed to fate or the will of God. Among Chinese, behavior is largely determined by Confucianism, which teaches respect for superiors, duty to family, loyalty to friends, humility, sincerity, and courtesy. People of higher status and age are respected by those beneath them, and older, foreign businesspeople are likely to be taken more seriously than younger ones.

Decision Making

Consensus is important to Malays, and they will probably require time for discussion before making a decision. These conversations will be amongst themselves, and never with outsiders present. Decisions will therefore rarely be made quickly. It is best not to press for a response. Chinese try to avoid saying no, for fear of causing embarrassment. Rather than say no, they might say something is inconvenient or suggest an alternative. They may also tell you what they think you want to hear, as a way of being polite.

Women

Women hold positions of leadership in Malaysian businesses, and foreign women can expect to be accepted and respected. The family is important, and women should be prepared for personal questions about their age, marital status, and whether they have children. (These questions are asked of both men and women.) Any compliments a man pays a Malay woman should concern her work, not her looks. Commenting on a woman's looks might be regarded as flirting, which is taboo and might cost a woman her job. Most public physical contact between men and women is taboo. When foreign women deal with Malay men, they should behave formally, avoid touching men (even foreign men), and keep a proper distance. Do not make prolonged eye contact with Malaysian men, as this will probably be looked upon as flirtatious.

Meetings

Punctuality is a sign of respect and politeness, so be on time for appointments. Malays consider people more important than schedules, however, and they are often late for appointments. Asians are more at ease as a group than as individuals. Nevertheless, they prefer to work with one individual from a company for the duration of the relationship. Designate one person, preferably your group's senior member, as your spokesperson. Avoid conflicting statements from other team members in the presence of your Malaysian associates. Your team leader should enter the room first. Group leaders sit opposite each other, with others in descending order of importance. Small talk will usually come first; all business is addressed as people feel comfortable with each other.

Business Attire

Malaysia is hot and humid all year, so wear natural fibers that breathe (cotton, linen); you will be more comfortable. Neat, tasteful pants, shirt, and tie (no jacket) will be appropriate for most business situations. If you wear a jacket and no one else does, you may remove yours once the meeting begins. Women should always dress tastefully and conservatively. A skirt and blouse or shirt and trousers are usually appropriate. Hemlines should never be above the knee, and women should avoid wearing a sleeveless dress or blouse. Both men and women should avoid bright or loud colors. Yellow is the color of royalty; don't wear yellow to a formal event or while visiting the palace.

Cultural Cautions

DO'S

- When dealing with Chinese, remember the importance of face. Never do or say anything that could cause a Chinese to lose face.
- Remember that many Indians do not approve of alcohol and tobacco.

DON'TS

- The head is considered sacred. Do not touch a person's head (not even a child's).
- Do not use your left hand to gesture toward someone, give or receive anything, eat with, or touch people. The left hand is considered unclean.
- Never point the soles of your feet at someone. The feet are the lowliest part of the body. Also, do not point to or gesture at someone with your feet.
- When entertaining Malays, never offer alcohol, pork, or meat not properly prepared.
- Never kiss or hug someone of the opposite sex in a business situation.

CUSTOMS

- Don't use gestures when beckoning to a Malay (except for cab drivers), and don't point at or beckon to someone with a single finger.
- Do not make a fist with one hand and hit it against the open or cupped palm of the other hand.
- Muslims are forbidden contact with dogs, and consider pictures of dogs improper. Do not give a Muslim child a toy dog or anything printed with images of dogs.

OBSERVATIONS

- In Malaysia you will encounter Malays (59 percent of the population), Chinese (32 percent) and Indians (9 percent). To relate best to people, learn about their specific cultures.
- Malaysian culture is relatively the same throughout the country, but customs and beliefs vary among different ethnic groups. Malays are virtually all Muslims; Chinese adhere to Buddhist, Taoist, and Confucian beliefs; Indians are generally Muslims or Hindus.
- Malays do not use family names. Their first name is their name, and their second name is the name of their father. Call a Malay by the first name you hear when you're introduced to them, or you may inadvertently call them by their father's name. The person introducing you to others will probably explain the Malay form of address. Pay attention when they do.
- If you are meeting with government officials, you will probably be dealing with Malays. If you are negotiating with businesspeople, you will probably be dealing with Chinese.
- Business dealings can be made easier by having a local Malaysian advisor or consultant. Your advisor or consultant should speak the same language as you, have expertise in your type of business, and have a reputation for honesty. It may not be easy for the same consultant to effectively deal with both Peninsula Malaysia and Sabah and Sarawak, so if you're doing business in different areas consider hiring separate advisors. Also, the use of Singaporean companies as consultants or agents is not recommended when dealing with Malaysian businesses.

NEGOTIATIONS

- Malays can be both subtle and aggressive.
- A common tactic is delaying major negotiations until you are about to leave the country, then making unreasonable demands.
- Malaysian Chinese sometimes negotiate with several competing companies at the same time and let it be known they are doing so as a way of applying pressure.
- Be prepared to walk away. You will gain more from making it clear that you would rather have no deal at all than a bad deal.
- Be patient. Many Asians view foreigners as always being in a hurry, and will encourage them to sign an agreement without proper time to study the details.

Legal System

Malaysia inherited its common law system from its British colonial past. Much commercial legislation is still transposed from common law countries. Coextensive with the common law are two legal systems of limited ambit: the Islamic law system applicable to Muslims and administered by individual states, and the native law system of Sabah and Sarawak applicable to the native populace of those states.

Intellectual Property Rights

Patents On average patent registration takes two or three years; limited public access to the application is allowed. Foreign filers must apply through a patent agent. A citizen of a country that has acceded to the Paris Convention may rely on an earlier foreign application to claim priority if the Malaysian application is filed within 12 months of the foreign date of filing. Patent examiners and Malaysian courts interpret patent applications strictly. Innovations that cannot be patented may be protected as utility models. Infringement is construed narrowly to include only industrial and commercial exploitation, not scientific research. Malaysian discovery procedures allow parties to actively seek evidence of infringement.

Trademarks Trademarks are registrable only with respect to goods, not services. By late 1996, servicemarks will be protected. Applications take an average of five years to process. Parallel import of trademarked goods is not infringement. For an unregistered trademark, an action for passing-off is the only remedy against infringement. As of late 1995, foreigners may have to file through a trademark agent. In Penninsular Malaysia, industrial designs are protected if registered in the UK. Pending laws will create a Malaysian registry. In Sabah and Sarawak, local ordinances allow registration.

Copyrights No formal registration is required for copyright. Protection extends to computer software, although a specific exemption allows owners to preserve backup copies, unless expressly forbidden by the copyright. Despite increasing statutory protection, piracy of audio and visual material and unauthorized performances of copyright material is still widespread, but the authorities are committed to strong enforcement. A copyright owner may request the border authorities to exclude infringing copies from importation. Criminal penalties may be imposed for violations of the law.

Business Registration

A foreign corporation often conducts commercial activities through an incorporated company or as a registered business. Except for companies engaged in banking, foreign corporations can establish a nonbusiness presence through representative and regional offices without obtaining registration, but they are urged to seek approval from the Ministry of International Trade and Industry. A separate legal regime exists for offshore companies centered in Labuan. Under both regimes, every foreign corporation must appoint a local agent for service.

Contracts and Dispute Resolution

Standard form contracts are used extensively, and commercial legal documents tend to be comprehensive. Negotiation and settlement are the prevailing modes of dispute resolution in a business context. Arbitral contract clauses are increasingly common. Proceedings and decisions are in English, minimizing evidentiary and communication difficulties for foreign entities. Legal and equitable remedies are readily available, although specific performance is rarely awarded if damages are sufficient.

Notaries and Commissioners for Oaths

Notaries and commissioners for oaths prepare and authenticate documentary instruments, which may be in either Bahasa Malaysian or English. Only a commissioner for oaths may take or attest any affidavit or statutory declaration intended to be used in any court or place in Malaysia. Authenticated private documents carry a strong presumption of validity. Acknowledgments for use in foreign countries may be taken before diplomatic representatives of the country of destination, who will then certify to the authenticity of the notary or commissioner for oaths.

Labor

Employees have the right to associate freely in unions. Collective bargaining is voluntary and limited to economic issues unrelated to managerial prerogatives, such as promotions, transfers, and redundancy terminations. Strikes and lockouts are limited to genuine labor disputes and cannot be exercised in altercations between employers and unions or in disputes referred to arbitration. Industrial disputes are often resolved by negotiation and conciliation. Children under the age of 15 cannot be legally employed. Minimum overtime rates and maximum working hours are prescribed for certain employees, but most wages are not fixed by law. An employer must pay the amount agreed, or in the absence of agreement, a reasonable sum for services performed. Termination other than by mutual consent requires due notice and just cause.

Source: Zain & Co., Kuala Lumpur

Legal Matters

LEGAL BRIEFS

- **Business entities** Foreign businesses favor the corporation, whether formed independently or by acquiring a Malaysian company. The incorporation costs inclusive of legal and registration fees average between RM2,000 and RM10,000, depending on such factors as the amount of paid-up share capital and needs special to the particular entity.

- **Joint ventures** A number of fiscal, export, and other incentives are offered to promote joint ventures. There is no specific legislation governing the establishment of joint ventures. The approval of the Foreign Investment Committee is required if the foreign corporation will hold substantial equity in or possess actual control other than through a joint venture entity. The extent of foreign ownership restrictions depends on whether the company is a manufacturer, whether most of the manufactured products are to be exported, and whether the activity relates to tourism and hotel industries.

- **Employment** Malaysia is at or near full employment. The official unemployment rate is three percent, but unlike employment statistics from other countries, Malaysia's figure includes workers no longer actively seeking employment. If the figure were to exclude these workers, the number would fall to well below three percent.

- **Maximum workweek** Employees who earn less than RM 1,250 can only be required to work a maximum of 12 hours (Peninsular Malaysia) or eight hours (East Malaysia) in any one day. In Peninsular Malaysia they are limited to 104 hours maximum of overtime during one month. They are permitted 10 paid public holidays, plus eight to 16 days of paid annual leave depending on their period of continuous service.

- **Employee restrictions** Expatriate personnel may be employed, but only in the absence of qualified Malaysians. Foreign corporations are required to employ and train local personnel and to reflect Malaysia's ethnic composition in their employment policies.

- **Legal process** Malaysian courts maintain high standards and will enforce contractual rights and obligations. The usage of Bahasa Malaysian was declared mandatory in court in the 1990s, but English is still utilized with the court's permission if circumstances so warrant. A foreign lawyer may in certain restricted circumstances be granted the right of audience in Malaysian courts on an ad hoc basis.

- **Skilled workers** Local and foreign firms report difficulty in obtaining workers at all skill levels. There is a particular shortage of workers with technological skills.

- **Labor settlements** Strikes are discouraged through a system promoting settlement through negotiation or arbitration by the Industrial Court.

- **Unions** The government prohibits the formation of a national union in the electronics industry, but allows in-house unions.

- **Arbitration** A Regional Centre for Arbitration has been established in Kuala Lumpur under the auspices of the Asian-African Legal Consultative Committee. It is a recognized international commercial arbitration center that conducts arbitration under the UNCITRAL rules.

- **International agreements** Malaysia is a member of ASEAN; GATT/WTO; Convention on Settlement of Investment Disputes Between States and Nationals of Other States; New York Convention on the Recognition and Enforcement of Foreign Arbitral Awards; Reciprocal Enforcement of Judgments Act; Paris Convention; and Berne Convention.

LEGAL CONTACT

Zain & Co.
6th & 7th Floors
Dato Zainal Building
23 Melaka Street
50100 Kuala Lumpur
Tel: (3) 2986255 Fax: (3) 2986969

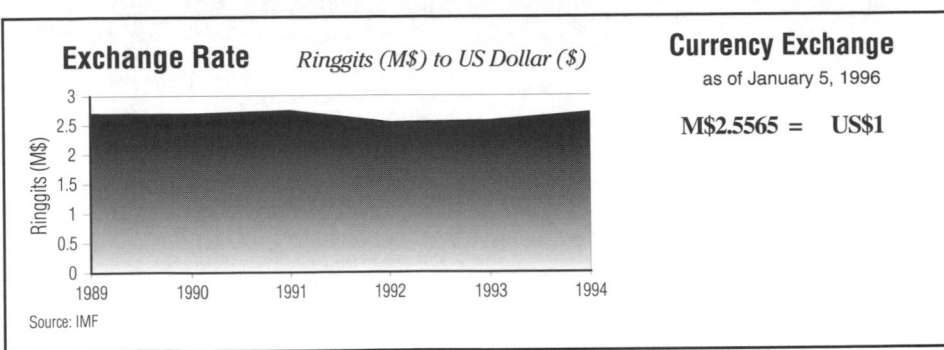

Exchange Rate *Ringgits (M$) to US Dollar ($)*

Ringgits (M$): 3, 2.5, 2, 1.5, 1, 0.5, 0 — 1989, 1990, 1991, 1992, 1993, 1994

Source: IMF

Currency Exchange
as of January 5, 1996

M$2.5565 = US$1

Currency

The currency of Malaysia is the ringgit(M$ or RM), and the principal subdivision is 100 sen.

Foreign Exchange

Relatively free of restrictions, Malaysia has an open foreign exchange system that applies uniformly to all countries except Israel, and the regions of ex-Yugoslavia. Special restrictions apply to these countries. The central bank administers most foreign exchange regulations, and commercial banks are free to quote exchange rates and make forward transactions in all currencies. There are no taxes or subsidies on purchases or sales of foreign exchange.

Capital Transfers

Nonresident accounts in ringgits are designated as external accounts. Debits and credits to these accounts are permitted without restrictions, subject only to the proper completion of exchange control documents for amounts exceeding RM 50,000. Balances may be transferred to any other resident or nonresident account or converted into any currency.

Investment Incentives

The Malaysian government welcomes manufacturing investment, especially in high-tech areas. The government of Malaysia offers a number of fiscal incentives to foreign manufacturing investors. The principal incentives for the manufacturing sector are contained in the Promotion of Investments Act of 1986 and the Income Tax Act of 1967. Some incentives include a partial tax exemption for payment of income tax and a write-off of up to 60 percent of capital expenditures.

Investment Restrictions

The Malaysian government does not generally impose performance requirements on foreign investors. Quite often, however, performance requirements are written into the manufacturing licenses of both local and foreign investors who are granted fiscal incentives. Proposals for a manufacturing license are screened by the Malaysian Industrial Development Authority (MIDA) to determine whether or not they are consistent with the Industrial Master Plan (IMP) and government social policy.

Money Matters

BITS AND PIECES

- **Exchange rates** Exchange rates are determined by supply and demand conditions in the foreign exchange market. The Central Bank of Malaysia intervenes only to maintain orderly market conditions and to avoid excessive fluctuations in the value of the ringgit against a basket of currencies weighted in terms of Malaysia's major trading partners.
- **Investments** Investments in Malaysia impose no regulatory obstacles. In general, credit is allocated on the basis of market conditions. However, foreign investors are required to finance at least 60 percent of their local borrowings with a domestically incorporated bank. As of 1995, all major banks operating in Malaysia were domestically incorporated. Nonresidents are free to make direct and portfolio investments and make remittances abroad, including the repatriation of capital and profits.
- **Gold** Residents of Malaysia are free to buy, sell, import, export, and borrow gold in any form with any person, except residents of Israel, South Africa, and the countries of ex-Yugoslavia.
- **Capital outflow** Malaysia is relatively free of foreign exchange restriction, but Malaysians are currently not permitted to borrow funds on the domestic capital market for investment abroad.
- **Outward investment** The Malaysian government recently announced plans to implement incentives for outward investment for industries where Malaysia has a comparative advantage, such as rubber estate management and palm oil processing.

BANKS

Bank of America
Kompleks Antarabangsa Kuala Lumpur
Post Office Box 10950, Jalan Sultan Ismail
Kuala Lumpur
Tel: (3) 242-2755 Fax: (3) 248-0301

Bank Bumiputra Malaysia Berhad
Menara Bumiputra, Jalan Melaka
50100 Kuala Lumpur
Tel: (3) 298-8011

Bank of Commerce
6 Jalan Tun Perak
50050 Kuala Lumpur
Tel: (3) 292-1722 Fax: (3) 298-6628

Bank Negara Malaysia
Jalan Dato-onn
PO Box 10922
Jalan Kuching
50480 Kuala Lumpur
Tel: (3) 298-8044, 298-9044 Fax: (3) 291-2990

Chase Manhattan Bank
Banganun Pernas International
Kuala Lumpur
Tel: (3) 262-0011

Citibank
Citibank Building
28 Medan Pasar
POB 10112
50904 Kuala Lumpur
Tel: (3) 232-8585 Fax: (3) 232-8763

Malayan Banking Berhad (Maybank)
Menara Maybank
Kuala Lumpur
Tel: (3) 230-8833

MBF Finance Berhad
Plaza MBF
POB 10027
50901 Kuala Lumpur
Tel: (3) 261-1177 Fax: (3) 261-8124

Public Bank Berhad
Banganun Public Bank
6 Jalan Sultan Sulaiman
50000 Kuala Lumpur
Tel: (3) 274-1788 Fax: (3) 274-2179

United Malayan Banking Corporation Berhad
Bangunan UMBC, Jalan Sultan Ismail
Kuala Lumpur
Tel: (3) 230-5833 Fax: (3) 232-2627

TAXATION

Taxation requires sophisticated knowledge of complex rules and regulations specific to each country. The information presented here is from the Ernst & Young Corporate Tax Guide and Directory, available from the Ernst & Young accounting office in your country, or from:

Ernst & Young
Mail Address:
P.O. Box 10068
50704 Kuala Lumpur, Malaysia
Street Address:
First Floor
Kompleks Antarabangsa
Jalan Sultan Ismail
50250 Kuala Lumpur
Malaysia
Tel: (3) 244-2333
Cable: Ernstaudit, Kuala Lumpur
Fax: (3) 244-3492 (Tax)

At a Glance

Corporate Income Tax Rate (%) (a)	30
Capital Gains Tax Rate (%) (b)	0
Branch Tax Rate (%)	30
Withholding Tax (%)	
Dividends (c)	0
Interest (d)	15
Royalties from Patents, Know-how, etc.	10
Payments for Specified Services and for Use of Movable Property (c)	10
Payments to Nonresident Contractors (e)	20
Branch Remittance Tax	0
Net Operating Losses (Years)	
Carryback	0
Carryforward	Unlimited

(a) Petroleum companies are taxed at a 40% rate.
(b) There is a tax on gains realized on the disposal of real property or shares in a real property company.
(d) Final tax applicable only to payments to nonresidents.
(e) Interest on approved loans is exempt from tax. Bank interest paid to nonresidents without a place of business in Malaysia is exempt from tax. Such interest paid to resident individuals is subject to a final 5% withholding tax.
(f) Prepayment of tax on account of final tax liability.

Business Travel

Travelogue

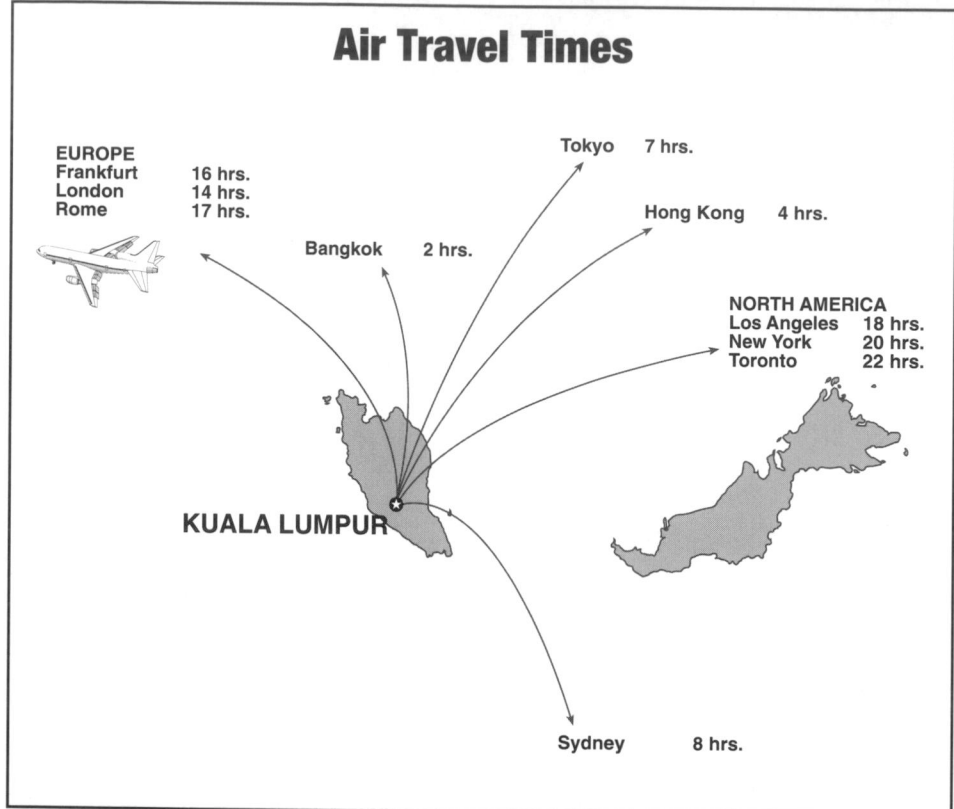

Air Travel Times

EUROPE
Frankfurt   16 hrs.
London   14 hrs.
Rome   17 hrs.

Tokyo   7 hrs.

Hong Kong   4 hrs.

Bangkok   2 hrs.

NORTH AMERICA
Los Angeles 18 hrs.
New York   20 hrs.
Toronto   22 hrs.

KUALA LUMPUR

Sydney   8 hrs.

COMMUNICATIONS

Telephones International telephone service from Malaysia is adequate. While public phones are for local calls only, direct-dial international calls can be made from hotels and post offices. Calls made during off-peak hours and from 6 pm Saturday until 6 am Monday are 30 percent cheaper, except from most hotels.

Fax Services are available at Kedai Telekom and Telegraph offices. Telegrams can be sent to most major cities from hotels, post offices, telegraph offices, and private lines (dial 104).

Post office Postal service in Malaysia is generally efficient.

BEST TRAVEL BOOKS

Malaysia, Singapore & Brunei Lonely Planet Travel Survival Kit. Over 400 pages, 16 color.

Insight Guides Malaysia, 378 colorful pages.

Fielding Worldwide, The adventurer's guide to the wonders of Malaysia and Singapore. 300 pages of in depth information.

All-Asia Travel Guide, Southeast Asia, Volume One. Culture Shock, A Guide to Customs and Etiquette, Malaysia.

The Travellers Guide to Malaysia Customs and Manners. Elizabeth Devine & Nancy Braganti. An invaluable guide for people not wanting to put foot in mouth.'

Do's and Taboo's Around the World. The Bestselling Guide to International Behavior. 3rd edition. Edited by Roger Axtell, compiled by the Parker Pen Company. The ultimate guide to international behavior, now completely updated and expanded. Helpful, fun to read!

USEFUL TELEPHONE NUMBERS

If you are calling from outside Malaysia, you will need to add the country code [60] and any other international dialing requirements from within your country.

- Police/Fire/Emergency 999
- Operator 101
- Operator Information 103
- International Operator 108
- Telegrams 104
- Audiovisual Rentals .... (3) 2980293, 9584911
- Secretarial, Interpreters .... (3) 2747988
- Convention & Exhibition Centers .... (3) 4422999
- Enesty Limo Service .... (3) 2431355
- SMAS Limo Service .... (3) 2307788
- Photocopying/Printing .... (3) 2487989; 7190061
- Chamber of Commerce .... (3) 2924943
- Railway ....(3) 274-3377, 274-9422

Courier Services
- City-Link .... (3) 7032900
- Nationwide Express .... (3) 7928566
- DHL .... (3) 2212044
- Overseas Courier Service .... (3) 2434222
- TNT Skypak .... (3) 7557744

Credit Card Information
Lost or stolen credit cards (call collect to the US, regardless of which country the card was issued in).
- Amex ....[1] (919) 333-3211
- Diner's Club................................[1] (303) 799-1504
- MasterCard ....[1] (314) 275-6690
- Visa ....[1] (410) 581-7931

WORKWEEK

Offices Monday-Thursday, 8:30 am to 12:45 pm and 2:00 to 4:15 pm; Friday, offices open at 8:00 am and lunch begins at 12:15; Saturday 8:00 am to 2:25 pm.

Banks Monday-Friday, 10:00 am to 3:00 pm and Saturday 9:30 to 11:30 am.

Government Same hours as businesses except government offices close at noon on Friday.

Retail Monday-Saturday, 9:00 am until 6:30 or 8:00 pm. On Friday, the Islamic day of prayer, government offices close at noon, but shops generally stay open.

HOLIDAYS

Holidays 1996
January Chinese New Year *
February 1 Kuala Lumpur City Day
February 21-22 Hari Raya Puasa *
May 1 Labor Day
May 21 *Hari Raya Haji
May Wesak Day*
August Prophet Mohammad's Birthday *
August 31 National Day
October or November Deepavali *
December 25 Christmas
*Dates vary each year

VISA AND PASSPORT

Travelers to Malaysia need a valid passport, but visas are not required for visits of up to three months. Business visitors are issued passes upon arrival for attending business meetings and conducting business negotiations in Malaysia. Those visitors who plan to engage in any kind of work (consulting or overseeing of installations) must apply for a business or professional pass prior to arrival in Malaysia.

DEPARTURE FORMALITIES

Visitors leaving from Kuala Lumpur International Airport will have to pay departure tax of M$15 for international flights, M$5 to Singapore, and M$3 for domestic flights.

IMMUNIZATION

No vaccination certificates are required of visitors to Malaysia unless visitors are arriving from an area infected with cholera or yellow fever; countries include Central America and Central Africa. Entering without a valid certificate brings a quarantine period of up to six days.

TIPPING

Taxi: optional. Porters: 1 ringgit per piece. Hotels, restaurants, nightspots: 10 percent included in bill plus 5 percent government tax. Small services: 1 ringgit.

CRIME

While petty crimes such as pickpocketing and purse-snatching are common in tourist areas, major crimes against tourists are uncommon. Credit card fraud is the major crime in Malaysia. A special unit of police, the tourist police, protect visitors from abuses, though it is suggested that visitors not wear expensive jewelry or gold watches. Hotel rooms are occasionally ransacked, so deposit valuables in hotel safes.

INFRASTRUCTURE

Malaysia has highly developed air, train, highway, and hotel industries. The international airport is in Kuala Lumpur and is modern. Taxis are the common transportation mode from the airport, but are known for overcharging by forgetting to put their meters on, or saying their meter is broken. Refuse to ride in a taxi which does not have its meter on and report any abuses to the road transport Office or tourist police. Purchase a taxi voucher at a terminal concourse booth. The Malayan Railway is available, along with fine roads, and ports which allow for travel with a lovely view of Malaysia.

NATIONAL TOURIST OFFICE

Tourism Board
Jalan Tun
Ismail
Kuala Lumpur
Tel: (3) 2935188

GOVERNMENT AGENCIES

Malaysian Industrial Development Agency (MIDA)
Wisma Damansara, Jalan Semantan
Post Office Box 10618
50720 Kuala Lumpur
Tel: (3) 255-3633
Fax: (3) 255-7970

Malayan Railway Administration
Jalan Sultan Hishmuddin
PO Box 10001
50621 Kuala Lumpur
Tel: (3) 274-9422
Fax: (3) 274-9424

Ministry of Agriculture
Wisma Tahi
Jalan Sultan Salahuddin
50624 Kuala Lumpur
Tel: (3) 298-2011
Fax: (3) 291-3758

Ministry of Culture Arts and Tourism
Menara Dato onn,
34th-36th Floors
PO Box 5-7
Putra World Trade Center
45 Jalan Tan Ismail
50694 Kuala Lumpur
Tel: (3) 293-7111
Fax: (3) 291-0951

Ministry of Energy, Telecommunications and Posts
1st Floor, Wisma Damansara
Jalan Semantan
59668 Kuala Lumpur
Tel: (3) 256-2222
Fax: (3) 255-7901

Ministry of Finance
Block 9, Khazanah Malaysia, Jalan Duta
50592 Kuala Lumpur
Tel: (3) 254-0011, 254-8111, 254-6066
Fax: (3) 255-6264

Ministry of Health
Jalan Cenderawashih
50590 Kuala Lumpur
Tel: (3) 298-5077, 298-5176
Fax: (3) 298-5965

Ministry of Information
Angkasapuri
Bukit Putra
50610 Kuala Lumpur
Tel: (3) 274-5333
Fax: (3) 282-1255

Ministry of International Trade and Industry
Blk. 10, Government Offices Complex
Jalan Duta
50622 Kuala Lumpur
Tel: (3) 254-0033
Fax: (3) 255-0827

Ministry of Primary Industries
Menara Dayabumi, 6-8th Floors
Jalan Sultan Hishamuddin
50654 Kuala Lumpur
Tel: (3) 274-7511
Fax: (3) 227-5014

Ministry of Public Enterprises
24th Floor, Medran Mara
Jalan Raja Laut
50652 Kuala Lumpur
Tel: (3) 298-5022
Fax: (3) 291-7623

Ministry of Science, Technology & Environment
14th Floor, Wisma Sime Darby
Jalan Raja Laut, Kuala Lumpur
Tel: (3) 293-8955
Fax: (3) 392-6006

Ministry of Transport
Wisma Perdana, 5th-7th Floors
Jalan Dungun, Damansara Heights
50616 Kuala Lumpur
Tel: (3) 254-8122
Fax: (3) 255-7041

Ministry of Works
Jalan Sultan Salahuddin
50580 Kuala Lumpur
Tel: (3) 291-9011
Fax: (3) 292-1202

WORLD TRADE CENTER

Putra World Trade Centre
Level 3, Convention Complex
41 Jalan Tun Ismail
50480 Kuala Lumpur
Tel: (3) 443-3999
Fax: (3) 443-3777

BUSINESS AND TRADE ORGANIZATIONS

Federation of Malaysian Manufacturers
17th Floor, Wisma Sime Darby
Jalan Raja Laut
50359 Kuala Lumpur
Tel: (3) 293-1244
Fax: (3) 293-5105

Federal Agricultural Marketing Authority (FAMA)
Bangunan KUWASA
5th-8th Floors, Jalan Raja Laut
50350 Kuala Lumpur
Tel: (3) 2932622
Fax: (3) 2910494
Telex: 31669

Federal Land Development Authority (FELDA)
Jalan Maktab
54000 Kuala Lumpur
Tel: (3) 2935066
Fax: (3) 2920087
Telex: 31669

Fisheries Development Authority (MAJUIKAN)
Bengunan PKNS
7th Floor, Jalan Raja Laut
50350 Kuala Lumpur
Tel: (3) 2924044
Telex: 31560

Malaysian Industrial Development Authority
3rd-6th Floors
Wisma Damansara
Jalan Semantan
PO Box 10618
50720 Kuala Lumpur
Tel: (3) 255-3633
Fax: (3) 255-7970

Pergadanan Nasional Bhd
(Trade, Property, Development, Construction, Mineral Exploration, Industrial Development)
Kompleks Antarabangsa, 2nd Floor
Jalan Sultan Ismail
50250 Kuala Lumpur
Tel: (3) 293-5177
Telex: 30399

PITO Malaysia (Private Investment and Trade Opportunities)
Yee Seng Building, 7th floor
15 Jalan Raja Chulan
50200 Kuala Lumpur
Tel: (3) 238-9491
Fax: (3) 238-9493

CHAMBERS OF COMMERCE

American - Malaysian Chamber of Commerce
11.03 AMODA, 22, Jalan Imbi
55100 Kuala Lumpur
Tel: (3) 248-2540
Fax: (3) 242-8540

Associated Chinese Chambers of Commerce and Industry of Malaysia
Office Tower Plaza Berjaya (Kompleks Nagaria)
8th Floor, 12 Jalan Imbi
55100 Kuala Lumpur
Tel: (3) 2452503
Fax: (3) 2452562

Malaysian International Chamber of Commerce and Industry (MICCI)
Wisma Damansara
10th Floor, Jalan Semantan
POB 12921
50792 Kuala Lumpur
Tel: (3) 2542677
Fax: (3) 2554946

Malaysian International Chamber of Commerce & Industry
Wisma Damansara
Post Office Box 10192
50706 Kuala Lumpur
Tel: (3) 254-2205
Fax: (3) 255-4946

National Chamber of Commerce and Industry of Malaysia
37 Jalan Kia Peng
50450 Kuala Lumpur
Tel: (3) 2419600
Fax: (3) 2413775
Telex: 33642

NEWSPAPERS

Business Times
31 Jalan Riong
59100 Kuala Lampur
Tel: (3) 2745444
Fax: (3) 2749434
Telex: 30259

Malay Mail
31 Jalan Riong
59100 Kuala Lumpur
Tel: (3) 2745444
Fax: (3) 2749434

New Straits Times
31 Jalan Riong
59100 Kuala Lumpur
Tel: (3) 2745444
Fax: (3) 2749434

The Star
13 Jalan 13/6
46200 Petaling Jaya
POB 12474
Selangor
Tel: (3) 7578811
Fax: (3) 7554039
Telex: 37373

Kwung Wah Yit Poh
2-4 Chulia St.
Ghaut, Penang
Tel: (4) 612312
Fax: (4) 615407

Nanyang Siang Pau (Malaysia)
80 Jalan Riong
59100 Kuala Lumpur
Tel: (3) 2745133
Fax: (3) 2748991
Telex: 30338

Shin Min Daily News
31 Jalan Riong
Bangsar
59100 Kuala Lumpur
Tel: (3) 2745133
Fax: (3) 2821812

Shin Chew Jit Poh (Malaysia)
19 Jalan Semangat
POB 367
Jalan Sultan
Petaling Jaya
Selangor
Tel: (3) 2821812

Berita Harian
31 Jalan Riong
59100 Kuala Lumpur
Tel: (3) 2745444
Fax: (3) 2749434

Utusan Malaysia
46M Jalan Lima
POB 671
Kuala Lumpur
Tel: (3) 2787055
Fax: (3) 2227876

Tamil Nesan
37 Jalan Ampang
POB 299
Kuala Lumpur
Tel: (3) 284439

Tamil Osai
19 Jalan Murai Dua
Batu Kompleks
Jalan Iph
Kuala Lumpur
Tel: (3) 671644

Tamil Thinamani
9 Jalan Murai Dua
Batu Kompleks
Jalan Ipoh
Kuala Lumpur
Tel: (3) 66719

New Sunday Times
31 Jalan Riong
59100 Kuala Lumpur
Tel: (3) 2745444
Fax: (3) 2749434

Sunday Mail
31 Jalan Riong
59100 Kuala Lumpur
Tel: (3) 2822829
Fax: (3) 2821434
Telex: 30259

Sunday Star
13 Jalan 13/6
46200 Petaling Jaya
POB 12474
Selangor
Tel: (3) 7578811
Fax: (3) 7554039
Telex: 37373

Shin Min Sunday
31 Jalan Riong
59100 Kuala Lumpur
Tel: (3) 2826363
Fax: (3) 2821812

Berita Minggu
31 Jalan Riong
59100 Kuala Lumpur
Tel: (3) 2826363
Fax: (3) 2749434

Mingguan Malaysia
46M Jalan Lima
POB 671
Kuala Lumpur
Tel: (3) 2787055
Fax: (3) 2227876

Utusan Zaman
46M Jalan Lima
POB 671
Kuala Lumpur
Tel: (3) 2787055
Fax: (3) 2227876

BANKS

Bank Utama (Malaysia) Bhd
18B Jalan Haji Taha
93400 Kuching
Tel: (82) 419291
Telex: 70556
Fax: (82) 424954

Ban Hin Lee Bank Bhd
43 Lebuh Pantai
10300 Penang
POB 232
10720 Penang
Tel: (4) 623434
Telex: 40087
Fax: (4) 623601

Bank Buruh (Malaysia) Bhd
Bangunan Kuwasa
24th Floor
5 Jalan Raja Laut
50350 Kuala Lumpur
Tel: (3) 29374566
Fax: (3) 2936308
Telex: 31269

Bank Islam Malaysia Bhd
Menara Tun Razak
9th and 20th Floors
Jalan Raja Laut
POB 11080
50734 Kuala Lumpur
Tel: (3) 2935566
Telex: 31783
Fax: (3) 2922153

Bank Pembangunan Malaysia Bhd
Menara Bank Pembangunan
POB 12352
Jalan Sultan Ismail
50774 Kuala Lumpur
Tel: (3) 2913399
Fax: (3) 2928520
Telex: 30058

Development and Commercial Bank Bhd
Wisma On-Tai, 161B
Jalan Ampang
50450 Kuala Lumpur
POB 10145
50907 Kuala Lumpur
Tel: (3) 2619077
Fax: (3) 2619541
Telex: 31032

Hock Hua Bank Bhd
3 Central Rd
96000 Sibu
Tel: (84) 335677
Fax: (84) 337888

Kwong Yid Bank Bhd
75 Jalan Tun H.S. Lee
50000 Kuala Lumpur
Tel: (3) 2308833
Fax: (3) 2304027

MUI Bank Bhd
MFB Bldg
11A Jalan Raja Chulan
POB 10069
50704 Kuala Lumpur
Tel: (3) 2301322
Fax: (3) 2416306
Telex: 32590

Oriental Bank Bhd
Menara Promet
14th Floor
Jalan Sultan Ismail
50250 Kuala Lumpur
Tel: (3) 2437088
Fax: (3) 2430906
Telex: 30778

Perwira Habib Bank Malaysia Bhd
Wisma SPK 3rd Floor
Jalan Sultan Ismail
POB 10459
50915 Kuala Lumpur
Tel: (3) 2410000
Fax: (3) 2428197
Telex: 30448

Southern Bank Bhd
Wisma Genting
28 Jalan Sultan Ismail
50250 Kuala Lumpur
POB 12281
50772 Kuala Lumpur
Tel: (3) 2309866
Fax: (3) 2322627
Telex: 30484

Wah Tat Bank Bhd
15 Bank Rd.
POB 87
96007 Sibu
Tel: (84) 336733
Fax: (84) 332803
Telex: 72024

STOCK AND COMMODITY EXCHANGES

Kuala Lumpur Commodity Exchange
Citypoint
Dayabumi Complex
4th Floor, Jalan Sultan Hishamuddin
POB 11260
50740 Kuala Lumpur
Tel: (3) 2936822
Fax: (3) 2742215
Telex: 31472

Kuala Lumpur Stock Exchange (KLSE)
Exchange Sq.
4th Floor, off Jalan Semantan
Damansara Heights
50490 Kuala Lumpur
Tel: (3) 2546433
Fax: (3) 2557463
Telex: 30241

INTERNET ADDRESSES

Usenet group(s):
soc.culture.malaysia

Malaysian Internet Business Pages
http://www.beta.com.my/biz/

Prime Minister's Office
http://smpke.jpm.my:1025/

Malaysia Information Services
http://st-www.cs.uiuc.edu/users/chai/malaysia.html

Malaysia Oh Malaysia
http://emporium.turnpike.net/N/nexus/malohmal.html

Malta

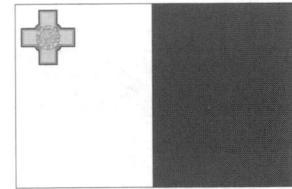

At a Glance

THE COUNTRY
Location Southern Europe, an archipelago in the central Mediterranean Sea, south of Sicily (Italy) and north of Libya.
Terrain Generally low, rocky, flat with dissected plains and coastal cliffs.
Climate Mediterranean, with mild, rainy winters and hot, dry summers.

THE PEOPLE
Population 370,000
Ethnic composition Arab, Sicilian, Norman, Spanish, Italian, and English.
Religious composition
Roman Catholic 98%
Languages spoken Both Maltese and English are official languages.
Education and literacy Compulsory, free primary education lasts between ages 6 and 16. Adult literacy is 84%.
Labor force
Total:..127,200
By occupation: government 37%, services 26%, manufacturing 22%, training programs 9%, construction 4%, and agriculture 2%.

COUNTRY FACTS
Political and legal This parliamentary democracy, led by a president and prime minister, has a legal system based on English common law and Roman civil law. The Constitutional Court reviews can review the legislature. Suffrage is universal for those 18 years of age or older.
Telephone The automatic system is satisfactory; and international calls can easily be made from a number of cities in Malta. There are 153,000 telephones in the country. International country code: [356]. City codes are not required.
Transportation Malta has no railways, but nearly 1,300 kilometers of highway connect the main cities. The majority of major roads are paved and in relatively good condition. There is only one major airport. Several ports and numerous bays provide good harbors for shipping, with ferry and hydrofoil service for passenger travel.
Environment Only a third of the land is arable. The country is actually an archipelago, with only the three largest islands inhabited. There are a number of bays that provide good harbors and ports. The government has made significant legal efforts to control environmental damage. Much of Malta's animal and plant life are in danger of extinction. Fresh water is becoming scarce, so the country relies increasingly on desalination. Current issues include inadequate water supply, deforestation, and wildlife preservation.
Media Broadcast service is excellent, with eight AM and four FM radio stations, and two television stations. Television programs are broadcast from a local service and from Italy. Both local and British daily newspapers are readily available.
Health There are eight hospitals. Medical equipment and treatment are satisfactory. Life expectancy of males is 74.5 years; of females, 79 years.

Economy

Overview

Malta has a higher standard of living than surrounding Mediterranean countries, but this economic well-being has required artificial stimulation. Historically, Malta's significance has stemmed from its strategic location, commanding the narrow stretch of the Mediterranean Sea between Sicily and Tunisia. A British colony until 1964, it served as an important naval base. The majority of its economy stemmed from the military until Britain removed most of its naval forces from the islands. Currently, the bulk of Malta's internally generated revenues come from foreign-owned industry and tourism. However, Malta continues to depend heavily on foreign aid for much of its economy, a situation that is unlikely to be sustainable over the long term. After the British navy left, the government paid considerable attention to social measures such as public housing, welfare payments, and medical facilities. The Emergency Labor Corps has provided work for Malta's relatively well-educated work force, which nonetheless suffers from high unemployment. Industrial growth continues to be rapid, albeit from a small base, especially in textiles and electronics.

Trade

A resource-poor island nation, Malta imports considerably more than it exports, and depends on foreign countries for the vast majority of its needs. Major exports include machinery and transportation equipment, apparel, miscellaneous manufactured goods, basic manufactures, and tobacco products. Imports include machinery and transportation equipment, basic manufactures, miscellaneous intermediate manufactures, foodstuffs, and chemicals. Principal trading partners include Italy—which accounts for about 33 percent of total trade—followed by Germany, the UK, the US, and France.

Sectors

Agriculture Agriculture accounts for much less than even five percent of GDP and an even smaller percentage of employment. Malta is arid and has little arable land. Farming is limited, as is fishing; both are small scale, generally unproductive, and primarily for local consumption.

Industry Industry provides about 40 percent of GDP and employs about 25 percent of the work force. Malta's main industries are apparel, food processing, electronics and electrical machinery, tobacco processing, shipbuilding, printing, metal products, and quarrying. Virtually all raw and intermediate materials must be imported, limiting the development of competitive industry.

Services The service sector employs more than 66 percent of the work force, while producing about 60 percent of GDP. Tourism has become a major industry in recent years—alone it accounts for 25 percent of GDP and employs 35 percent of the work force. A concerted effort has been made to develop Malta as an offshore financial services hub, but this effort has yet to bear fruit.

Trends

To date, tourism has provided the only consistent bright spot in the economy. A number of industries could take advantage of Malta's available labor and be beneficial to its economy, but development would require substantial capital investment, and most such industries would be only marginally competitive. Now that Malta no longer fulfills a strategic role, it will be difficult for it to develop self-sufficiency.

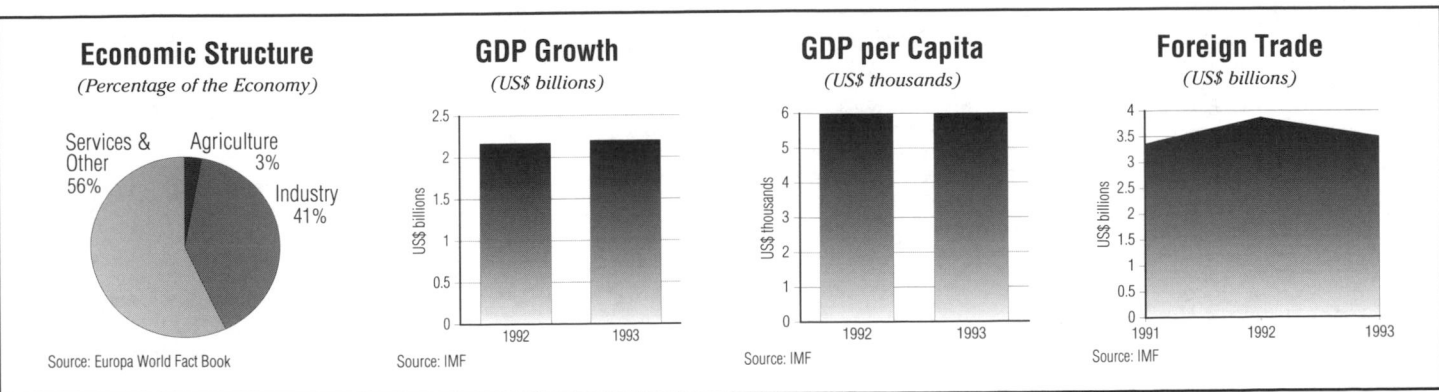

Economic Structure
(Percentage of the Economy)

Services & Other 56%
Agriculture 3%
Industry 41%

Source: Europa World Fact Book

GDP Growth
(US$ billions)

Source: IMF

GDP per Capita
(US$ thousands)

Source: IMF

Foreign Trade
(US$ billions)

Source: IMF

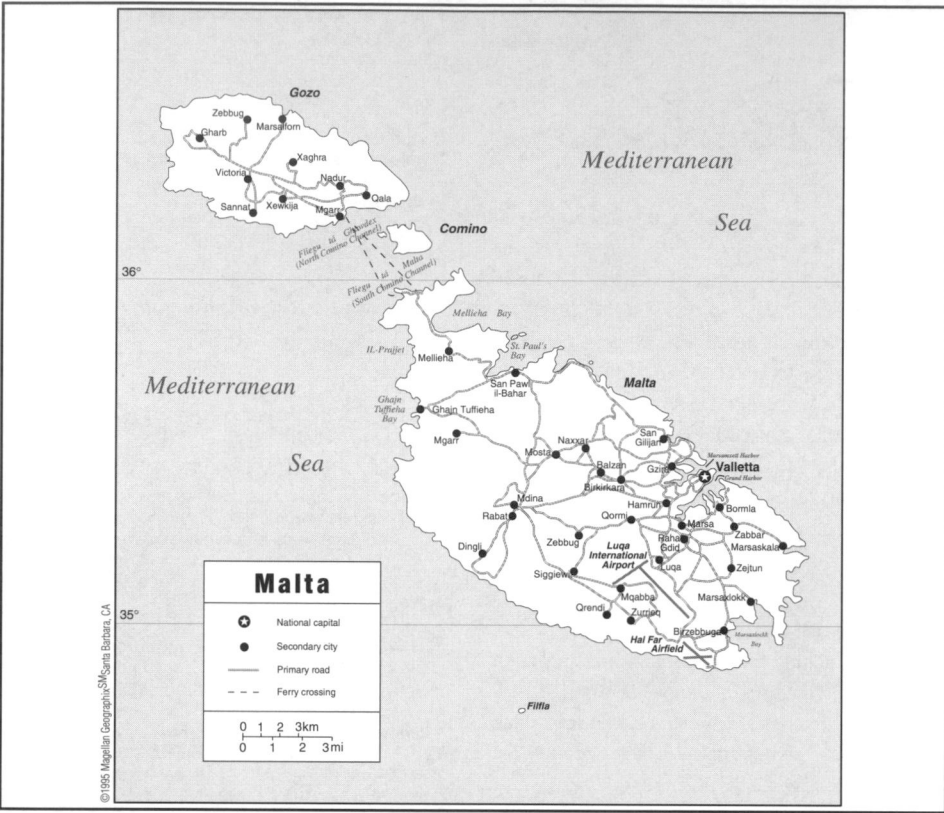

COMMUNICATIONS

Telephone Telephone services in Malta for local, long distance, and international calls are generally reliable and can be made from major hotels and locations throughout Malta. Public telephones are not readily available away from homes or offices. The main telegraph office is on St. George Road, St. Julian's, and is open 24 hours a day; Valletta is open 8 am to 6:30 pm weekdays and the Luqa Airport post office is open 7:00 am to 7:00 pm daily. This location also has a telex booth for public use. Overseas calls can be dialed direct with international dialing codes. Telephone booths are painted red or are made of limestone. Information found in telephone directories are in Maltese and English.

Fax Telegrams, telex, and fax services can be sent from the main telegraph office on South Street in Valletta or from the Luqa Airport post office.

Post office The main post office is located at Auberge d'Italie, Merchants Street, Valletta and is open from 7:30 am to 6:00 pm Monday-Saturday. Luqa Airport post office is open 7:00 am to 7:00 pm. Stamps can also be purchased at hotels also.

BEST TRAVEL BOOKS

Berlitz Business Travel Guide, Europe. Berlitz Publishing Company. Features include: Concise economic details, how to plan a successful trip, background information of people and cities, useful facts and addresses on arrival, entertainment, leisure, shopping, essential words and phrases.

Practical Travel A to Z, Malta (including Gozo and Comino). Hayit Publishing. Comprehensive, compact and convenient. How to get there by air, by car, and by sea, what to take, how to get around, what to see, and how to get the most out of your travel. The Practical Travel A to Z series gives you the answers within the local context. An ideal companion, these titles are comprehensive yet focused; an abundance of tailored information always at your fingertips-condensed into a user-friendly, handy, take-along reference guide.

USEFUL TELEPHONE NUMBERS

If you are calling from outside Malta, you will need to add the country code [356] and any other international dialing requirements from within your country.

- Ambulance 196
- Fire 199
- Police 191
- Traffic Accidents 191
- Inquiries Malta 190
- Inquiries International 194
- Time 195
- Photocopying services 627233
- Chamber of Commerce 627233
- Malta Chamber of Commerce 247233
- Malta Drydocks 822451
- Department of Industry 446250
- Department of Trade 224411
- Maltese Stock Exchange 244051
- A. Vassallo and Sons Publishers (guides) ... 556609
- Mediterranean Trading Shipping Co Ltd 224664
- Mifsud Brothers (Shipping) 232157
- Air Malta Co 824330
- SMS Car-Ferry service 232211

Car Rental
- Avis 225986
- Budget Rent-a-car 231077
- Hertz Unitel Garage 314635/6/7
- John's Garage Europcar 228745

Credit Card Information
Lost or stolen credit cards (call collect to the US, regardless of which country the card was issued in).
- Amex .... [1] (919) 333-3211
- Diner's Club .... [1] (303) 799-1504
- MasterCard .... [1] (314) 275-6690
- Visa .... [1] (410) 581-7931

Travelogue

WORKWEEK
Offices Commercial office: 9:00 am to 1:00 pm and 2:30 to 7:00 pm Monday-Friday (Oct 1-June 15); 8:00 am to 1:00 pm in the summer.
Banks Monday-Friday 8:00 am to 11:30 am (winter) and 8:30 am to 12:30 pm, Saturdays 8:30 to noon.
Government Monday-Friday 7:45 am to 12:30 pm and 1:15 pm to 5:15 pm (Oct 1-June 15) 7:30 am to 1:30 pm in summer.
Retail Monday-Saturday 9:00 am to 5:00 pm, with many shops open later.

HOLIDAYS
January 1 New Year's Day
February 10 St. Paul's Shipwreck
March 19 St. Joseph
March 31 Freedom Day
April 5 Good Friday*
May 1 May Day
June 7 Sette Giugno
June 29 St. Peter and St. Paul
August 15 Assumption
September 8 Our Lady of Victories
September 21 Independence Day
December 8 Immaculate Conception
December 13 Republic Day
December 25 Christmas
*Dates vary from year to year.

VISA AND PASSPORT
Visitors from the EU require only a passport, unless they plan to stay longer than a month, in which case they will need a visa. All other visitors need a visa.

DEPARTURE FORMALITIES
Not more than £M25 in local currency may be exported from Malta. Nonresidents may take out with them the balance of unspent foreign currencies brought in by them.

IMMUNIZATION
No vaccinations are necessary unless visitors are arriving from an area infected with yellow fever. Drinking water is safe to drink.

TIPPING
Tip taxi drivers 10 percent on the fare. Restaurants and hotels include tip in the bill. Tip porters 25 cents per bag; waiters and hairdressers, 10 percent.

CRIME
As this is a popular tourist location, crime is more prominent in tourist areas; watch personal belongings and avoid wearing expensive jewelry. Purse snatching and automobile theft are on the rise; keep valuables out of sight and cars locked at all times.

INFRASTRUCTURE
A few direct flights to Malta from London and Rome exist, but in general connections have to be made. Low-cost buses travel from Valletta to all towns and villages; fare is paid to the driver. International and local car rental agencies are available by telephone and at the airport; tourism is heavy between April and October, so make reservations in advance. Be sure to read and keep the copy of every car rental contract. Larger firms are open 24 hours a day and handle accidents and breakdowns. Be sure to drive on the left wearing your seat belt. Country roads are not adequate and city roads are not the best. There are no toll roads and parking in the larger cities can be difficult. Taxis are the recommended mode of transportation. All taxis are white with red license plates and are metered. Car-ferry transportation between Malta and Gozo makes several trips each day, depending on weather; there can be rough seas.

NATIONAL TOURIST OFFICES
Tourist Information Office
1, City Gate Arcade
Valletta
Tel: 237747
National Tourist Organization of Malta
280 Republic Street
Valletta
Tel: 224444

Foreign Trade

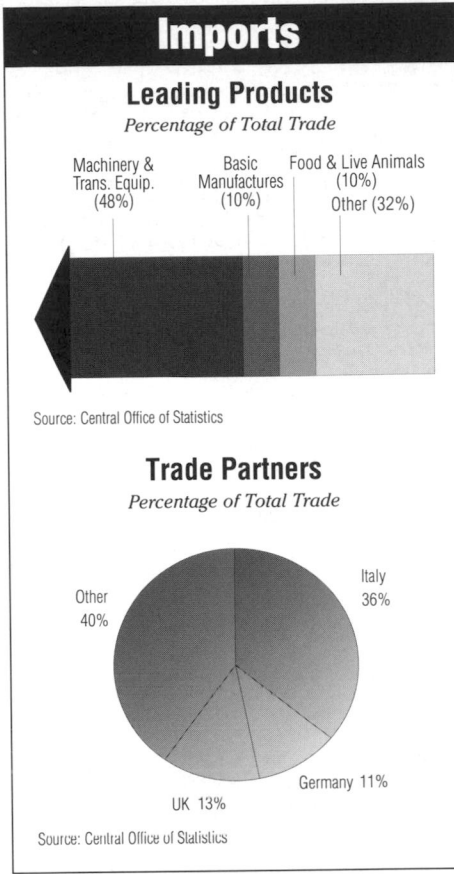

Imports

Leading Products
Percentage of Total Trade

Machinery & Trans. Equip. (48%)
Basic Manufactures (10%)
Food & Live Animals (10%)
Other (32%)

Source: Central Office of Statistics

Trade Partners
Percentage of Total Trade

- Italy 36%
- Other 40%
- UK 13%
- Germany 11%

Source: Central Office of Statistics

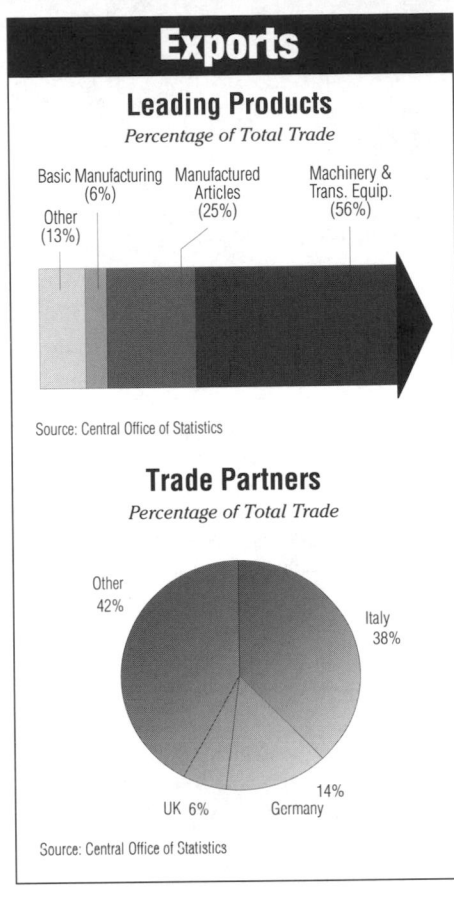

Exports

Leading Products
Percentage of Total Trade

Basic Manufacturing (6%)
Other (13%)
Manufactured Articles (25%)
Machinery & Trans. Equip. (56%)

Source: Central Office of Statistics

Trade Partners
Percentage of Total Trade

- Italy 38%
- Other 42%
- UK 6%
- Germany 14%

Source: Central Office of Statistics

Opportunities

FOR IMPORTING TO MALTA
- food, semi-manufactured goods
- petroleum
- machinery

FOR EXPORTING FROM MALTA
- limestone
- machinery and transport equipment
- clothing and footwear

GROWTH SECTORS
- manufacturing
- tourism
- electronics industry
- textile industry

Trade News

RULES AND REGULATIONS
- **Trade news** Malta is highly dependent on foreign trade and service.
- **Tariff and import taxes** Malta has a very high excise duty on cigarettes.
- **VAT** Value-added tax will be charged at a general rate of 15%. A special rate of 10 percent will apply to the tourist-catering sector.
- **Customs and excise duties** VAT will totally replace customs tariffs on imports from EU countries. Tariffs from non-EU countries will be lowered substantially when this happens.

Legal

Legal System

Malta is a civil law country following mostly European legal traditions. Its judiciary is independent of the executive and legislative branches.

Intellectual Property Protection

Patents After a patent is registered, the Registrar advertises the application three times in the *Government Gazette* and another newspaper. If no opposition is made after two months, the patent is approved. Protection runs for 14 years from the application date and is renewable for seven-year periods. Trademarks must be registered with the Comptroller of Industrial Property. Registration of a trademark is valid for 14 years from the date of registration, and can be renewed for 14 years at a time.

Copyrights Copyrights last for the lifetime of the creator plus 25 years. The Maltese courts have historically upheld laws concerning copyright protection.

Trade secrets The process for obtaining an injunction against trade secret violations tends to be lengthy; in some instances, it can take up to five years.

Business Registration

All companies must register with the Registrar of Partnerships. The application must include the company's name and a list of officers. All companies must have at least two members or shareholders.

Contracts and Dispute Resolution

Most contracts are only considered valid if they are written, executed in the presence of witnesses, or acknowledged by a notary public. Most contract dispute cases are handled in a relatively short time.

Labor

Workers are not required to join trade unions, although they may do so. Collective agreements are common between unions and individual companies, normally drawn for three-year terms.

Legal Matters

LEGAL BRIEFS
- **Business entities** One of the more popular entities for foreign companies in Malta is the limited liability company. Such companies may adopt any name not already in use, but it must end with the word "limited."
- **Copyright infringement** Damages from copyright infringement cannot exceed £M500 (US$180) in addition to restitution of all profits derived from the infringement.
- **Notaries** Notary publics in Malta certify to the authenticity of documents and instruments. Notaries are appointed as in the European tradition.
- **Labor laws** The Malta Employment Act governs basic employment conditions, including maximum work hours, minimum wages, and sick leave.

LEGAL CONTACTS

Busuttil & Busuttil
12 Tagliaferro Mansions
Princess Margaret Street
Ta'xbiex
Tel: 371640
Fax: 345450

Advocates Micallef & Co.
191 Merchants Street, Suite 2
Valletta VLT 10
Tel: 246034
Fax: 244652

Professor J.M. Ganado & Associates
171 Old Bakery Street
Valletta VLT 09
Tel: 242096
Fax: 225908

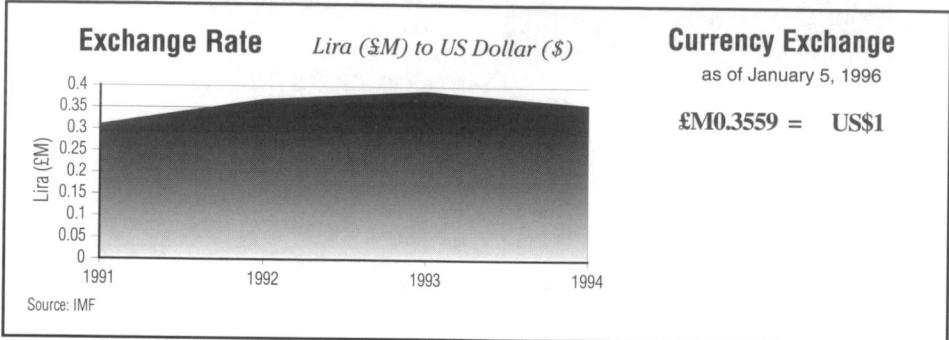

Exchange Rate — *Lira (£M) to US Dollar ($)*

Source: IMF

Currency Exchange

as of January 5, 1996

£M0.3559 =   US$1

Money Matters

BITS AND PIECES

- **Exchange rates** Exchange rates are determined on the basis of a weighted basket consisting of the pound sterling, the US dollar, and the ECU.
- **Investment** Foreign investments in Malta must be approved in advance by the Central Bank. Exchange control approval is also required for residents to issue or transfer securities to nonresidents. However, nonresidents may buy financial instruments listed on the Malta Stock Exchange without approval.
- **Capital receipts** Capital receipts repatriated by residents must be surrendered to an authorized bank for conversion into domestic currency or held in an interest-earning foreign currency account with an authorized bank.
- **Gold** Malta residents are allowed to hold coins and acquire jewelry, but must obtain permission from the Central Bank to buy and sell any gold coin that is not legal tender. A specific import license is required for the importation of gold coins, gold bullion, and manufactured and semi-manufactured articles of gold. The exportation of gold by residents other than monetary authorities also requires exchange control permission.

Currency

The currency of Malta is the Maltese lira, represented as the symbol £M. Its principal subdivision is 100 cents.

Foreign Exchange

The Central Bank of Malta administers foreign exchange operations through authorized banks, which have the authority to oversee most exchange transactions, such as the power to approve and renew payment guarantees and indemnities. Authority to approve foreign exchange payments for travel purposes has been delegated to a limited number of foreign exchange bureaus licensed by the Central Bank. There are no taxes or subsidies on purchases or sales of foreign exchange. Together with the Central Bank, commercial banks cover forward transactions in Belgian francs, Deutsche marks, French francs, Italian lire, Netherlands guilders, Japanese yen, pounds sterling, Swiss francs, US dollars, and European Currency Units (ECU). Any forward contract between a bank and a customer must be accompanied by a similar contract between that bank and the Central Bank. Nonresidents may hold foreign currencies or Maltese lira in external accounts with authorized banks. These accounts may be credited and debited freely.

Capital Transfers

Payments for invisibles require the approval of the Central Bank when amounts exceed authorized limits. Receipts from invisibles must be offered for sale to an authorized bank. Profits of foreign-owned companies may be transferred to any country in any currency with the approval of the Central Bank.

Investment Incentives

Malta's government promotes foreign investment. The Malta Development Corporation (MDC) provides information to prospective investors and serves as a liaison between investors and other government entities. The Industrial Development Act of 1988 authorizes the government to build factories, and give fiscal incentives and customs exemptions.

Investment Restrictions

The Income Tax Act of 1948 established a single tax rate of 35 percent for limited liability companies. The Exchange Control Act of 1972 specifies that the Central Bank of Malta must approve applications for investment and the subsequent repatriation of profits and capital. Some sectors, such as food production, have specific regulations and restrictions.

BANKS

APS Bank Ltd
275 St. Paul St.
Valletta
Tel: 247547
Fax: 238698
Telex: 1226

Bank of Valletta Ltd
58 Zachary St.
Valletta VLT 04
Tel: 243261
Fax: 230894
Telex: 1235

Central Bank of Malta
Castille Place
Valletta
Tel: 247480
Fax: 243051

Investment Finance Bank Ltd
168 Strait St.
Valletta VLT 08
Tel: 232017
Fax: 242014
Telex: 1744

Lohombus Corporation Ltd
Development House
Floriana VLT 01
Tel: 234124
Fax: 242669

Lombard Bank (Malta) Ltd
Lombard House
67 Republic St.
POB 584
Valletta CMR 01
Tel: 248411
Fax: 246600
Telex: 1379

Melita Bank International Ltd
Cavalier House
158 Old Mint St.
POB 30
Valletta CMR 01
Tel: 242031
Fax: 234465
Telex: 1901

Mid-Med Bank Ltd
233 Republic St.
POB 428
Valletta VLT 05
Tel: 245281
Fax: 230406
Telex: 1370

TAXATION

Taxation requires sophisticated knowledge of complex rules and regulations specific to each country. The information presented here is from the Ernst & Young Corporate Tax Guide and Directory, available from the Ernst & Young accounting office in your country, or from:

Ernst & Young
54 St. Dominic Street
Valletta VLT 03
Malta
Tel: 230633
Fax: 230631

At a Glance

Corporate Income Tax Rate (%) (a)	35
Capital Gains Tax Rate (%) (a)	35
Branch Tax Rate (%) (a)	35
Withholding Tax	
Dividends	0
Interest	0
Royalties from Patents, Know-how, etc.	0
Branch Remittance Tax	0
Net Operating Losses (Years)	
Carryback	0
Carryforward	Unlimited

(a) The tax rate for petroleum companies is 50%.

Marketing

Overview

Malta offers several opportunities for foreign sellers, although the small population and limited economy create some investment barriers. Radios, newspapers, and televisions are the main sources of information and Malta receives some broadcasts from Italy. The Maltese are predominately well-educated, literate, and intelligent, and they are receptive to new products and ideas.

Distribution

Marsaxlokk and Valletta are the ports; Valletta is the capital and also has an airport. Prior to distribution, all goods must be off-loaded into customs sheds within six working days of the ship's arrival. Importers may store goods in government-bonded warehouses, usually without being required to pay import duties or any applicable taxes until the goods are entered for consumption. Distribution channels are primarily through retailers and wholesalers.

Agents

No special protective legislation governing agency agreements is in force. A local agent who understands the market is usually an efficient way to begin business here. Due to the population's small size, a single agent can cover the entire country.

Advertising

Almost all printed matter is admitted duty free. The BPC International Ltd. and Crown Advertising Agency, both in Valletta, are familiar with multinational firms' needs. Radio and television stations were nationalized in 1975 but now some private stations are also permitted. Television broadcasts on a cable station; this and 10 radio stations accept commercial ads. All of the eight daily newspapers use advertising; some of those and other publications are in English. The Malta International Trade Fair, held every year at Naxxar, usually during the first two weeks of July, is a primary contact point for this market.

Business Culture

Greetings and Courtesies

Despite their well-deserved reputation for friendliness and a helpful disposition, the Maltese are often reserved with first-time visitors. When this is the case, take the first approach. Even a phrase or two in their complex language will be greatly appreciated. Close male friends will hug briefly. Nearly everyone in Maltese business deals in the English language, although Arabic and Maltese, a challenging Semitic derivative, are also used in many different areas.

Business Ethic and Framework

Malta is saturated with history, so firms or families which can trace their lines back the farthest have the most prestige and power, and tend to stand more on ceremony. When dealing with such firms, concluding a deal approaches a great deal of ritual and ceremony. The younger, more vigorous companies take a more relaxed approach. The country looks to rebuild its ties to Western businesses, so many practices which apply there—such as the importance of a detailed contract—are honored. Being able to judge a person's character in Malta is sometimes more important than price.

Meetings

Malta has been called a rock combining history and romance, lying halfway between Europe and Africa and therefore subject to cultural ambivalence. Maltese generally have a relaxed attitude toward business protocol, but the longer-established firms tend to retain some of the reserve British culture is noted for. The only thing foreign businesspeople can expect is variety; there is no one sure method for dealing with Maltese businesses. Err on the side of caution. Punctuality is always appreciated, however.

Business Attire

Light clothing is adequate in summer as the weather can become quite warm. Layering is appropriate in winter as it can get somewhat cool. Dress conservatively for business meetings and official occasions.

Marketing in Malta

MARKETING TIPS

- **Way of life** Maltese tend to be relaxed and easy-going. Strong, forceful advertising will probably not be successful.
- **Doing business with the government** Most foreign business ventures are with private companies rather than with the government in Malta.
- **Tourism** Malta is a tourist center, and the people are exposed to a number of cultures. Consider a number of different marketing strategies versus only one.
- **Rate of return** Don't expect an immediate profit from any marketing ventures. Malta is not a country where you can look for an instant profit, but once a niche is found, the rate of return can be promising.
- **Italy** Malta is very close to Italy, geographically and culturally. Nevertheless, all marketing campaigns directed to Malta should be tailored specifically for Malta. Many Maltese speak different languages and will take offense to any ties to Italy. Using forethought will help reduce the risk of insulting the Maltese people.
- **People** The people of Malta are charming, dress well, and are polite. English is spoken throughout the country and remnants of the Arab culture abound. The Maltese are prudent businesspeople; using charm and intelligence can be rewarded.
- **Population** Malta has a very dense population, making business possibilities very good.
- **Business hours** Varying from summer to winter, plan your visit around seasonal business-hour changes due to the very warm weather conditions.

Cultural Cautions

DO'S

- Since car thefts are on the rise, empty the car of valuables and keep it locked.
- Sports are favorite topics of conversation and can add to lively discussions.
- Tap water is safe to drink at resorts; you may want to boil the water in more rural areas.

DON'TS

- Politics is a passionate subject with most Maltese; avoid it, especially the recent political tumult.

CUSTOMS

- Malta's mixed influences are often revealed in everyday speech: when ordering milk for coffee, a national asks for *halib*, as an Arabic-speaking person would. When he offers a casual good-bye, he uses the Italian *ciao*. A new visitor needs to listen carefully for these small indicators of the culture's flavor and personal customs.
- Homes are often given names rather than numbered addresses.

OBSERVATIONS

- Telecommunications and postal services are generally reliable. Public telephone boxes, painted red or made from the local limestone, are in short supply. Rely on telegrams or faxes for international business.

NEGOTIATIONS

- Part of Maltese heritage is the full-blooded passion of the Mediterranean, and part is the flexibility to survive the historical and political changes which have swamped many more powerful nations. The result creates a delicately balanced climate for dealing. The most successful traders here are excellent judges of character, which is a more crucial quality to prospective partners than price.

GOVERNMENT AGENCIES

Malta Development Corporation
POB 571
Valletta
Tel: 448944 through 55

Malta Maritime Authority
Maritime House
Lascaris Wharf
Valletta
Tel: 250360 through 4, 243741,239732
Fax: 250365

Ministry for Economic Services
Auberge d'Aragon
Independence Square
Valleta
Tel: 245391 through 5
Fax: 233081

Ministry of Education and Development of Human Resources
Floriana
Tel: 231385
Fax: 221634

Ministry of Finance
St. Calcedonius Square
Floriana
Tel: 232646, 246309
Fax: 224667

Ministry of Food, Agriculture, and Fisheries
Barriera Wharf
Valletta
Tel: 225236, 231629, 232306
Fax: 231294

Ministry of Foreign Affairs
Palazzo Parisio, Merchants Street
Valletta
Tel: 242191
Fax: 237822

Ministry of Transport and Communications
Lascaris
Valletta
Tel: 243880, 239941, 240901
Fax: 243306

National Tourism Organization
280, Republic Street
Valletta
Tel: 238282, 224444, 224445
Fax: 220401

BUSINESS AND TRADE ORGANIZATIONS

Malta Counter Trade Company Ltd.
Block A/31, "Il-Piazzetta"
Tower Road
Sliema
Tel: 342281 Fax: 345338

Malta Export Trade Corporation Ltd.
San Gwann Industrial Estate
POB 44
Gzira
Tel: 446186
Fax: 496687

Malta International Business Authority
Palazzo Spinola
POB 29
St. Julians
Tel: 344230 through 3
Fax: 336851, 344334

NEWSPAPERS

In-Nazzjon Taghna
Stamperija Indipendenza
Herbert Ganado St.
Pieta
POB 37
Hamrun
Tel: 243641
Fax: 242886
Telex: 1941

L-Orizzont
Union Press
Workers' Memorial Bldg.
South St.
Valletta
Tel: 244451
Fax: 243454
Telex: 1307

The Times
Allied Newspapers Ltd
Strickland House
341 St. Paul St.
POB 328
Valletta
Tel: 241464
Fax: 247901
Telex: 1341

WEEKLIES

Il-Gens
Media Centre
National Rd.
Blata I-Bajda
Tel: 249005
Fax: 234057

Il-Helsien
Marsa Press
Industrial Estate
Marsa
Tel: 235313
Fax: 240717

Il-Mument
Stamperija Indipendenza
Herbert Ganado St.
Pieta HMR 08
POB 37
Hamrun HMR 01
Tel: 243641
Fax: 242886
Telex: 1941

Il-Torca (The Torch)
Union Press
Workers' Memorial Bldg.
South St.
Valletta
Tel: 244451
Fax: 242995
Telex: 244451

The Sunday TImes
Allied Newspaper Ltd
Strickland House
341 St. Paul St.
Valletta
POB 328
Valletta CMR 01
Tel: 241464
Fax: 247901
Telex: 1341

PERIODICALS

Commercial Courier (Monthly)
Malta Chamber of Commerce
Exchange Bldgs.
Republic St.
Valletta VLT 05
Tel: 247233
Fax: 245223

Industry Today (Quarterly)
Development House
St. Anne St.
Floriana VLT 01
Tel: 234428
Fax: 240702

Kultura
J.P. Publications
POB 9 Old Bakery St.
Valletta
Tel: 344794
Fax: 344797

Malta
Department of Information
Auberge de Castille
Valletta CMR 02
Tel: 224901
Fax: 237170
Telex: 1448

Malta Economic Update (Monthly)
J.P. Publications
.POB 9
Old Bakery St.
Valletta
Tel: 344794
Fax: 344797

Malta Government Gazette
Department of Information
Auberge de Castille
Valletta CMR 02
Tel: 224901
Fax: 237170
Telex: 1448

Pajjizna
Department of Information
Auberge de Castille
Valletta CMR 02
Tel: 224901
Fax: 237170
Telex: 1448

RADIO AND TELEVISION

Malta Broadcasting Authority
National Rd.
Blata I-Bajda
Tel: 247908
Telex: 1100
Fax: 240855

Publishing Broadcasting Services Ltd
St. Luke's Rd.
POB 82
Gwardamangia
Tel: 225051

Public Broadcasting Service, Ltd.
POB 82
Valletta
Tel: 249060, 225051 Fax: 244601

INTERNET ADDRESSES

Malta Export Trade Corp.
http://www.u-net.com/metcowww/

Malta Homepage
http://www.fred.net/malta/

City Net - Malta
http://www.city.net/countries/malta/

Mauritius

Republic of Mauritius

Economy

Overview

The Mauritian economy is based on export-oriented manufacturing, sugar, and tourism. It has a strong private sector as well as many state-owned enterprises. Currently, there is a shortage of skilled labor, especially evident in industry. A small percentage of labor is imported. Unemployment, which is less than three percent, remains low, due to the rapid expansion of what is called the "export processing zone (EPZ)" over the last 10 years, as well as to successful efforts to curb population growth.

Trade

Mauritius exports goods worth 23 billion rupee (US$1.3 billion) annually, mainly to the US and Europe. Primary products include sugar, textiles, clothing, tea, molasses, jewelry, leather goods, canned tuna, and anthuriums. Mauritians import slightly more—about 28.5 billion rupee (US$1.6 billion) in foodstuffs, refined petroleum products, machinery and transport equipment, construction materials, manufactured goods, and raw textile materials. Major suppliers are Europe, South Africa, Kuwait, Japan, China, Bahrain, Hong Kong, Australia, India, Taiwan, New Zealand, and Southeast Asian countries.

Sectors

Agriculture Agriculture contributes 12 percent of GDP. Production is spread over a diversity of crops, including sugar and sugar derivatives, tea, flowers, tobacco, vegetables, fruits, and flowers.

Industry The success of the EPZ has contributed to strong performance in the manufacturing sector. 32 percent of the work force hold manufacturing jobs, which also accounts for about 31 percent of GDP. Mauritius manufactures large quantities of labor-intensive goods for export, including textiles and clothing, pearls, cut and polished diamonds, semi-precious stones, leather products, and electronic goods. During the second half of the 1980s manufacturing emerged as the most significant sector of the Mauritian economy.

Services Tourism is the most important segment of the services sector. In recent years, the industry has seen impressive growth, both in terms of gross earnings and tourist arrivals. From 1983 to 1990, the number of tourists increased from 124,000 to 292,000, and gross earnings increased from 606 million rupee (US$34 million) to four billion rupee (US$233 million). Tourism accounts for about 11 percent of the GDP, with most visitors arriving from France, South Africa, the French island of Reunion, and Western European countries.

Trends

The Mauritian economy has in the past been too vulnerable to climatic conditions and export price fluctuations, which influence the country's top agricultural exports. The government is now seeking to offset this vulnerability by promoting investment in electronics, light engineering, computer software, pharmaceuticals, plastics, leather, jewelry, and printing and publishing operations, while at the same time consolidating the textile sector. Mauritius is also being developed to include a regional financial center; in 1989, the government set up both an offshore banking center and the Port Louis stock exchange. Mauritius' near-term outlook is very favorable, and, if present policies continue, Mauritius' medium term prospects look extremely promising as well.

At a Glance

THE COUNTRY

Location Southern Africa, in the western Indian Ocean, east of Madagascar.
Terrain A volcanic island surrounded by coral reefs. The small coastal plain rises to mountains encircling the central plateau.
Climate Tropical; warm, dry winters (May to November); hot, wet, humid summers (November to May); and a cyclone season mid-December to April.

THE PEOPLE

Population 1,000,000
Ethnic composition
Indo-Mauritians 68%
Creoles 27%
Sino-Mauritians 3%
Franco-Mauritians 2%
Religious composition
Hindu 52%
Roman Catholic 26%
Protestant 2.3%
Muslim 16.6%
Other.. 3.1%
Languages spoken English, Creole, French, Hindi, Urdu, Hakka, and Bhojpuri.
Education and literacy Education is free up to the college level, but is only compulsory for six years. Attendance is virtually universal. Adult literacy is 80 percent.
Labor force
Total: 410,000

COUNTRY FACTS

Political and legal This parliamentary democracy has a legal system that is primarily derived from French civil law, although there are elements of English common law. The Supreme Court is the highest judicial authority, and there are various lower courts and village councils as well.
Telephone Mauritius' small system offers good service, linking all parts of the island with reliable international and domestic telephone, fax, and telegraph services. International country code: [230]. City codes are not required.
Transportation Rental cars and taxis are readily available throughout the country. Bus service is regular and inexpensive. Most roads are paved, but are narrow, twisting, and poorly lit at night. There is one major port and four usable airports.
Environment Degradation of the environment is considered a pressing socioeconomic problem. Water pollution is caused by sewage and agricultural chemicals. The country ranks third in the world of nations with the most endangered wildlife species. Current issues are water pollution, soil erosion, and preservation of animal and plant species.
Media There are two AM radio stations and four television stations. Several daily newspapers are published in French and English.
Health Virtually the entire population has access to health care. Hospitals, local clinics and pharmacies provide adequate services. Life expectancy of males is 66 years; of females, 74 years.

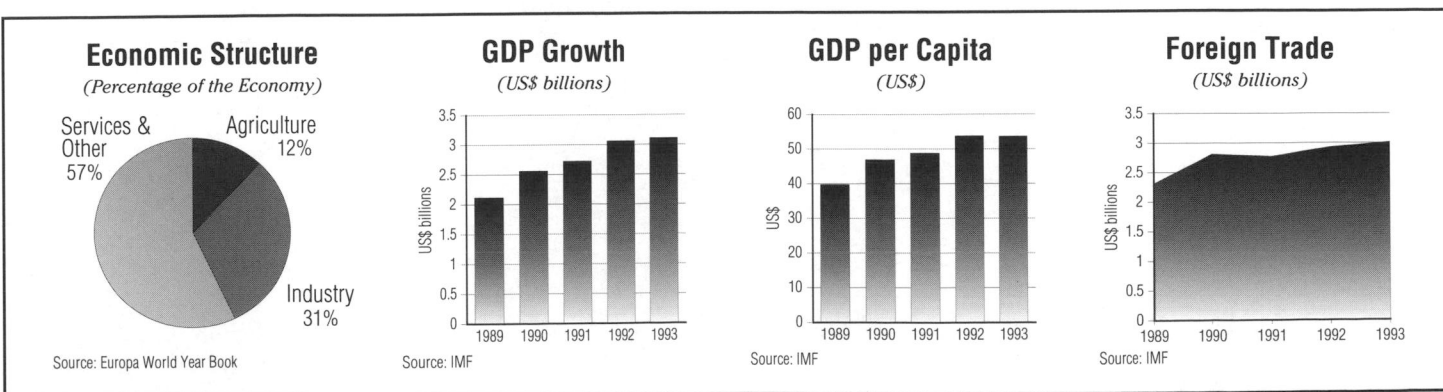

Economic Structure
(Percentage of the Economy)

Services & Other 57%
Agriculture 12%
Industry 31%

Source: Europa World Year Book

GDP Growth
(US$ billions)

Source: IMF

GDP per Capita
(US$)

Source: IMF

Foreign Trade
(US$ billions)

Source: IMF

Business Travel

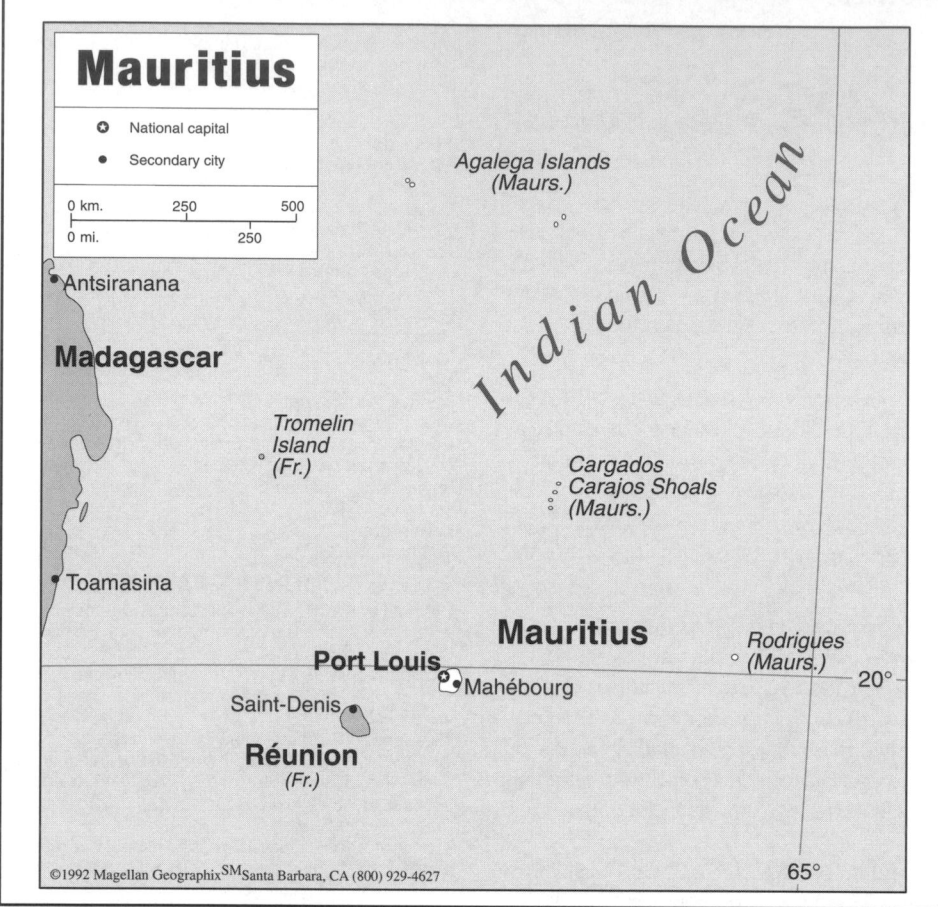

Mauritius

- ✪ National capital
- ● Secondary city

0 km. 250 500
0 mi. 250

Antsiranana
Madagascar
Tromelin Island (Fr.)
Indian Ocean
Agalega Islands (Maurs.)
Cargados Carajos Shoals (Maurs.)
Toamasina
Mauritius
Port Louis
Mahébourg
Rodrigues (Maurs.)
20°
Saint-Denis
Réunion (Fr.)
65°

©1992 Magellan Geographix℠ Santa Barbara, CA (800) 929-4627

COMMUNICATIONS

Telephone The internal telephone service is automatic in all areas. There are public phone booths in Plaisance airport and at some hotels.
Fax Telex and faxing are available through hotels and post offices.
Post office There are numerous post offices and postal agencies throughout the island. Air mail connections are maintained with all parts of the world. Sea mail is extremely slow; all mail should be sent by air.

BEST TRAVEL BOOKS

Mauritius. Visitors Guides Series, 1992, Hunter Publishing, Inc.
Mauritius, Reunion and Seychelles: A Travel Survival Kit, 402 pages. Lonely Planet Publications.
Africa on a Shoestring, Lonely Planet. Filled with useful information.

USEFUL TELEPHONE NUMBERS

If you are calling from outside Mauritius, you will need to add the country code [230] and any other international dialing requirements from within your country.
- Police 17
- Air Afrique 252084
- Air Algerie 252059
- Hospital 252135
- Avis 51713
- Europcar 51136

Credit Card Information
Lost or stolen credit cards (call collect to the US, regardless of which country the card was issued in).
- Amex ....[1] (919) 333-3211
- Diner's Club................................[1] (303) 799-1504
- MasterCard ....[1] (314) 275-6690
- Visa ....[1] (410) 581-7931

Travelogue

WORKWEEK

Office hours Monday-Friday 8:30 am to 5:00 pm.
Banks Monday-Friday 10:00 am to 2:00 pm; Saturday 9:30 am to 11:30 am.
Government Monday-Friday 8:30 am to 4:00 pm.
Retail Monday-Saturday 8:00 am to 6:00 pm or 7:00 pm.

HOLIDAYS

Holidays 1996
January 1-2 New Year's Day
March 12 Independence Day
May 1 Labor Day
August 15 Assumption Day
November 1 All Saints' Day
December 25 Christmas Day
In addition, Hindu and Moslem holidays are observed on varying dates depending on the lunar calendar.

VISA AND PASSPORT

A valid passport is required by all visitors entering Mauritius. Travelers holding return tickets do not require visas. Entry requirements are subject to change, and travelers should check with a Mauritian embassy or conulate before making their trip.

DEPARTURE FORMALITIES

Visitors may take out the unspent balance of currencies they took into Mauritius. Foreign currencies are issued by local banks. Retain all receipts for transactions as they may be requested at departure.

IMMUNIZATION

International certificates of current vaccination against smallpox are required of all visitors; visitors from infected countries must also have certificates of vaccination for yellow fever and cholera, as well as other diseases prevailing in the country they have come from. A yellow fever certificate may be required if the traveler is coming from Africa or an affected area.

TIPPING

It is not customary to tip taxi drivers. A 10 percent tip is generally left in hotels and restaurants.

CRIME

Petty crime is common. Normal precaution should be taken in Mauritius.

INFRASTRUCTURE

Mauritius has no internal air or rail services, but a good network of paved roads with bus service links all parts of the island. The cities and larger villages offer taxi service, and rental cars are available. The Sir Seewoosagur Ramgoolam International Airport at Plaisance offers all the facilities of a modern airport. Mauritius' only port, Port Louis, has 672 meters of aligned, deep-water quays for containerized and conventional vessels. There are also buoy berths for lighter operations, a cement berth, and a bulk sugar terminal.

Foreign Trade

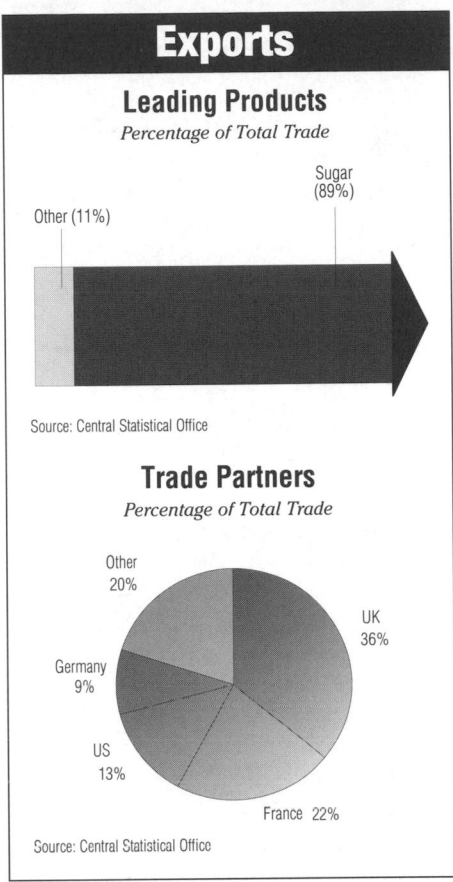

Imports

Leading Products
Percentage of Total Trade

Textiles Fabrication (13%)
Petroleum Products (7%)
Textile Yarn (6%)
Machinery Industries (5%)
Other (69%)

Source: Central Statistical Office

Trade Partners
Percentage of Total Trade

- France 15%
- South Africa 9%
- UK 7%
- Germany 7%
- Other 62%

Source: Central Statistical Office

Exports

Leading Products
Percentage of Total Trade

Sugar (89%)
Other (11%)

Source: Central Statistical Office

Trade Partners
Percentage of Total Trade

- Other 20%
- UK 36%
- Germany 9%
- US 13%
- France 22%

Source: Central Statistical Office

Opportunities

FOR IMPORTING TO MAURITIUS
- foodstuffs, textiles, and manufactured goods
- refined petroleum products
- machinery and transportation equipment

FOR EXPORTING FROM MAURITIUS
- clothing, textiles
- molasses, sugar, tea, canned tuna, anthuriums
- jewelry and leather products

GROWTH SECTORS
- manufacturing
- tourism
- construction
- electricity and water
- retail/restaurants/hotels

Trade News

RULES AND REGULATIONS
- **Tariffs and import taxes** The maximum rates of duties on the bulk of imports covering 4,400 products have been reduced. The duty rates have been reduced to 0-80 percent for countries benefiting from preferential tariff arrangements. Imports from countries currently under general tariffs (i.e. non-preferential tariffs) will pay an additional duty of 20 percent over the preferential rates.

SHIPPING

Islands Service Ltd.
c/o Rogers and Co. Ltd.
5 President John F. Kennedy St.
POB 60
Port Louis
Tel: 208601

Legal

Legal System

Statutes in Mauritius are based mainly on the French civil code, with recent adaptations of some English laws. The judicial system is primarily free from executive and legislative interference, but the president nominates the Chief Justice and the associate judges.

Intellectual Property Protection

Patents Mauritius is a member of several international patent protection conventions. Foreign patents are given the same rights and privileges as domestic ones. Patents are granted for 14 years and may be renewed for one additional 14-year period.

Trademarks Foreign trademarks are considered valid in Mauritius. Trademarks are granted initially for seven years, and registration may be renewed for successive periods of 14 years.

Copyrights Foreign copyrights are considered valid, and carry the same rights as domestic ones.

Trade secrets Mauritius grants greater trade protection than most African countries, but it is difficult to prove trade-secret violations in the courts.

Business Registration

All companies must be registered with the Registrar. Information that must be provided includes the name of the company and a list of employees. A business must also pay a registration fee.

Contracts and Dispute Resolution

Businesses in Mauritius prefer contracts to be written. All disputes are settled in local courts.

Labor

Minimum wages are set by the government, and cost-of-living allowances are mandatory. Labor unions and collective bargaining procedures are permitted, but few workers are unionized. Workers can work a maximum of 45 hours a week.

Legal Matters

LEGAL BRIEFS
- **High courts** The Supreme Court is composed of a chief justice and five other judges, and is the highest judicial authority. There is an additional right of appeal to the Queen's Privy Council. Local government has nine administrative divisions, with municipal and town councils in urban areas and district and village councils in rural areas.
- **Additional labor costs** Basic wages are not high, but employers are often required by law to shoulder various indirect costs, adding about 40 percent to the basic wage bill.
- **Representation** Trade unions often play an important role in business life. In many companies, employees are represented by a workers' council, which holds regular meetings with management to discuss working conditions and problems.
- **Wage increases** Any increases are determined after negotiations between trade union representatives of major market segments, the Mauritius Employers' Federation, and the government.
- **Strikes** The Industrial Relations Act of 1974 governs the conduct of strikes and lock outs.
- **International agreements** Mauritius is a member of the Berne Convention, WIPO, Enforcement of Foreign Arbitral Awards, Convention Abolishing the Requirement of Legalization for Foreign Public Documents, and ATA Carnet Convention.

LEGAL CONTACT

Chambers of Marc Hein
Cathedral Square
Port Louis
Tel: 2085526, 2126976
Fax: 2085586, 2126030

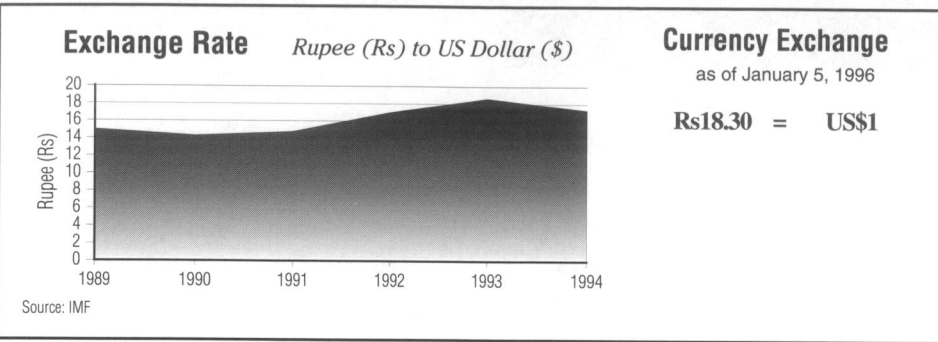

Exchange Rate *Rupee (Rs) to US Dollar ($)*

Source: IMF

Currency Exchange
as of January 5, 1996

Rs18.30 = US$1

Currency

The currency of Mauritius is the Mauritian rupee, represented as the symbol Rs. Its principal subdivision is 100 cents.

Foreign Exchange

Exchange control used to be administered by the Bank of Mauritius, under powers delegated by the financial secretary. As agents of the Central Bank, commercial banks were authorized to approve transactions involving foreign exchange. However, since the Exchange Control Act has been suspended, approval from the Bank of Mauritius is no longer required. Companies operating in the export processing zone (EPZ), as well as other Mauritian exporters and traders dealing in priority imports, may hold accounts in foreign currencies at local commercial banks and transact forward exchanges in foreign markets. Residents and foreign companies may open external accounts to credit or debit authorized payments, transfers, and proceeds or purchases of convertible currencies. Nonresidents may open blocked accounts to credit or debit authorized investments and payments.

Capital Transfers

Payments for invisibles related to imports and purchases of foreign exchange for travel are not restricted. Receipts from invisibles must be repatriated and offered for sale to an authorized dealer. There are no restrictions on the amount of foreign currency notes and coins that may be imported. Capital may be freely repatriated.

Investment Incentives

Most incentives are geared toward the manufacturing, hotel development, and export-oriented sectors. The three major fiscal incentives are: a lower corporate profits tax during the life of the company (15 percent as opposed to the normal 35 percent); exemption from payment of income tax on dividends for the first 10 years; and free repatriation of capital, profits, and dividends.

Investment Restrictions

Although technically any investment proposal is encouraged, prime consideration will be given to more technologically advanced manufacturing with significant inputs of manual skills.

Money Matters

BITS AND PIECES

- **Exchange rates** are pegged to a weighted basket of currencies, representing the major trading partners of Mauritius.
- **Capital** A five percent transfer tax applies to most authorized outward transfers of capital other than balance transfers of bank funds by companies operating in Mauritius, repatriation of approved foreign investments, and inclusive capital appreciation. Under certain conditions a duty of five percent applies to purchases of gold coins. Inward transfers of capital are not restricted.
- **Stock exchange** The development of Mauritius' financial services sector was boosted by the establishment in 1989 of a stock exchange in Port Louis, called La Bourse des Valeurs. The stock exchange, replacing an informal bourse, is regarded as vital for strengthening savings and developing a capital market for Mauritius. Regulations for the new market were drafted by the Stock Exchange Commission with French technical assistance.
- **Stock market incentives** Incentives are offered to encourage participation in the stock market. An individual investor is entitled to a personal income tax deduction of up to Rs40,000 for the interest and dividends he receives. Investors also receive, tax-free, 35 percent of the dividends paid out by a quoted company, and listed companies pay a lower rate of profits tax. Quoted companies do not need to pay stamp duty on new issues of shares and other securities, or registration dues on share transfers. Capital gains and profits of up to US$7,000 from share dealings in any one year are exempt from sales tax.
- **General taxation** Mauritius has a low overall tax structure. Companies and individuals pay tax for the current financial year on the basis of profits or income received in the preceding year. The financial year runs from July 1 to June 30.
- **Corporation tax** All companies, both resident and nonresident, are taxed on net profits earned in Mauritius. All enterprises given approval for any of the investment incentive schemes pay tax at a uniform rate of 15 percent during the life of the company. The normal depreciation allowance for plants and machinery, except for motor vehicles, is an initial rate of 50 percent in the year the expenditure was incurred, followed by a straight line annual allowance ranging from 10 to 20 percent.
- **Personal tax** All residents, defined as those having their domicile in Mauritius or who have been in the country for more than 183 days in the income year, are taxed on a graduated scale.
- **Sales tax** A sales tax of five percent is levied on most items, but certain commodities are exempt.

BANKS

Bank of Mauritius
Sir William Newton Street
PO Box 29
Port Louis
Tel: 208-4164
Fax: 208-9204

Banque Nationale de Paris Intercontinentale
1 Sir William Newton St.
POB 494
Port Louis
Tel: 2084147
Fax: 2088143

Barclays Bank PLC, Mauritius
Sir William Newton St.
POB 284
Port Louis
Tel: 2121816
Fax: 208720
Telex: 4215

Delphis Bank Ltd.
16 Sir William Newton St.
POB 485
Port Louis
Tel: 2085061
Fax: 2085388
Telex: 4366

TAXATION

Taxation requires sophisticated knowledge of complex rules and regulations specific to each country. The information presented here is from the Ernst & Young Corporate Tax Guide and Directory, available from the Ernst & Young accounting office in your country, or from:

Ernst & Young
Louis Leconte Street
Curepipe, Mauritius
Tel: 675-4777, 675-4692/6, 675-4398, 675-4688
Fax: 676-3921

At a Glance

Corporate Income Tax Rate (%)	35
Capital Gains Tax Rate (%)	0
Branch Tax Rate (%)	35
Withholding Tax (%) (a)	0
Net Operating Losses (Years)	
Carryback	0
Carryforward	Unlimited

(a) Withholding taxes technically do not exist in Mauritius. However, before income is transferred abroad to nonresidents, tax on such income must be paid.

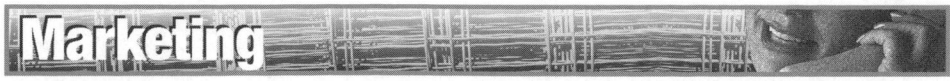

Marketing

Overview

Mauritius is a Third World success story. Tourism is the largest sector, expanding so rapidly that environmental protection is becoming an issue. The government is most interested in ventures which use high-tech manufacturing, with significant input of manual skills based on local raw materials and produce, such as electronic, plastic, and agro-based industries. Residents, however, are eager to buy high-quality foreign consumer goods.

Agents, Distributors, and Partners

There are no laws requiring an agent or distributor, nor is there any special legislation in operation affecting agency agreements; such agreements are covered by the regular laws of contract. Overseas firms should consider appointing a local agent or entering into joint ventures with their local counterparts. Nearly all major projects are won by firms whose proposals are accompanied by attractive financing. Most of the import trade is conducted through local agents and import merchants, and appointing an agent will bring the most success. Rates of commission vary with the type of goods, but generally they are similar to those to which foreign exporters are accustomed in other overseas markets.

Advertising

Newspapers are the most important advertising medium, with several dailies and weeklies published in English, French, Chinese, or Hindi. The four television and two AM radio stations carry advertising, as do outdoor facilities, including billboards and bus panels. There are no government controlled poster sites. A few commercial posters are placed on the sides of main roads, and painted posters are displayed on buses. There are 38 cinemas in the country, 22 of which can project advertising slides. Public relations services, some market research, and limited direct mail services are available through local agencies. Advertising material of a non-marketable kind (show-cards, posters, signs, calendars, etc.) is not subject to import duty. Any goods of a kind which might be used in lieu of similar dutiable articles (matches, clocks, glassware, porcelain items, etc.) are subject to a duty. Correspondence is often done in English, but trade literature should be in both French and English.

Business Culture

Greetings and Courtesies

The standard greeting is a handshake. Business in Mauritius is relatively informal, but professional titles should be used at first. English is the primary language of business and the government, but French, Hindi, and Creole (a patois derived from the French) are universally used in everyday life. Business cards are often exchanged, and most should be in English on one side and French on the other. There are no special social customs apart from handshaking on almost every occasion.

Business Ethic and Framework

Businesspeople usually take a while to make a decision, and do not enjoy being rushed. Standards of punctuality are often relaxed. Business is often conducted in a more social context rather than an official one; business entertaining can often last for several hours.

Meetings and Decision Making

Arrive on time, although you can expect your Mauritian counterpart to be somewhat late. Your meeting will probably be interrupted a number of times, but impatience is not appreciated. Meetings can often take place in social settings, but don't assume that if you're invited to lunch or dinner that it will be a business meal. Follow your host's lead. Final decisions are usually made only at the top, but cultivate any business relationship, because they may pay off in the long run. In any event, even mid-level employees do have some input in the decision and their support can be invaluable.

Business Attire

Conservative clothing is worn for business. Tropical clothing can be worn for informal affairs. Lightweight lounge suits can be worn in the evenings and during the colder months. Women will need cotton or linen dresses, with lightweight woolens for the winter in the highlands. Evening dresses are worn for formal occasions.

Marketing in Mauritius

MARKETING TIPS

- **Buying seasons** There is no seasonal trade for imports, although there is a small decline between January and March when work is scarce and weather is improbable.
- **Posters** There are no government controlled poster sites. A few commercial posters are placed on the sides of main roads, and painted posters are displayed on buses.
- **Trade literature** Display cards, calendars, and other advertising gifts are acceptable in Mauritius. Agents should be well supplied with trade literature.
- **Marketing methods** Orders for new sugar machinery and replacement parts are usually placed so that the equipment reaches Mauritius during the non-harvest season between mid-December and June.
- **Specialized exporters** Most importers in Mauritius prefer dealing direct with manufacturers or with exporters specializing in the goods in which they are interested, rather than with general merchants.
- **Commercial samples** All commercial samples, where the assessed duty does not exceed Rs 1,000, can be imported duty-free. Other samples can be imported on a temporary basis, subject to the deposit of an amount equal to the amount of duty payable.
- **Shipping marks** There are no regulations about packaging but experience has shown that markings should always be stencilled or painted directly on the package. The gross and net weights should preferably be indicated in kilograms.
- **Agent licenses** A traveling agent is required to take out a licence, costing Rs 120 quarterly. A traveling agent is defined as a person taking orders for merchandise, which is to be imported from outside firms.

Cultural Cautions

DO'S

- Arrive on time, although the person you're meeting may be late.
- Prepare to spend a little time socializing and letting your hosts get to know you before getting down to business.

DON'TS

- Try to make appointments at least a month in advance of a meeting, and don't make appointments during Christmas, New Year's, or the Muslim holy month Ramadan.
- Never try to rush a meeting, no matter how long it may take.

CUSTOMS

- Exchanging gifts is acceptable as long as they are not too expensive. A small gift with your company's logo is appreciated.
- Drink only bottled water.

OBSERVATIONS

- Women should not face discrimination while in Mauritius, but it is always possible. Be prepared for questions about your marriage and family (both men and women are generally asked these questions). Be professional at all times.
- Avoid wearing shorts; it looks touristy and unprofessional.
- The metric system is in general use but certain French measures are still used in connection with measurements of land.

NEGOTIATIONS

- Be patient. Good business deals probably will not come quickly.

GOVERNMENT AGENCIES

Ministry of Agriculture, Fisheries and Natural Resources
Government Centre
Port Louis
Tel: 201-1403
Fax: 212-3836

Ministry of Arts, Culture, Leisure and Reform Institutions
Government Centre
Port Louis
Tel: 201-2032

Ministry of Cooperatives, Handicrafts and Small Industries
M.H.C. Building, 4th Floor
Rev. Jean Lebrun Street
Port Louis
Tel: 208-4812
Fax: 208-9265

Ministry of Economic Planning and Development
Emmanuel Anquetil Building
Port Louis
Tel: 201-1576
Fax: 212-4124

Ministry of Education and Science
Sun Trust Building
Edith Cavell Street
Tel: 212-8411
Fax: 212-3783

Ministry of Energy, Water Resources and Postal Services
Government Centre
Port Louis
Tel: 201-1087
Fax: 208-6497

Ministry of Environment and Quality of Life
Barracks Street
Port Louis
Tel: 208-2831
Fax: 208-6579

Ministry of Finance
Government Centre
Port Louis
Tel: 201-1145
Fax: 208-8622

Ministry of Health
Emmanuel Anquetil Building
Port Louis
Tel: 201-1910
Fax: 208-0376

Ministry of Industry and Technology
New Government Centre
Port Louis
Tel: 201-1221
Fax: 212-8201

Ministry of Information
Government Centre
Port Louis
Tel: 201-1278
Fax: 208-8243

Ministry of Labor and Industrial Relations
Government House
Port Louis
Tel: 201-1195
Fax: 208-9265

Ministry of Trade and Shipping
Government Centre
Port Louis
Tel: 201-1067
Fax: 212-6368

Ministry of Works
Treasury Building
Port Louis
Tel: 208-0821
Fax: 212-8373

BUSINESS AND TRADE ORGANIZATIONS

State Trading Corporation
Fon Sing Building
Edith Cavell Street
Port Louis
Tel: 208-5440
Fax: 208-8359

Mauritius Chamber of Commerce and Industry
3 Royal Street
Port Louis
Tel: 208-3301
Fax: 208-0076

BANKS

Bank of Mauritius
Sir William Newton Street
PO Box 29
Port Louis
Tel: 208-4164 Fax: 208-9204

Habib Bank Ltd.
26 Sir William Newton St.
POB 800
Port Louis
Tel: 226273
Fax: 2088062
Telex: 4366

Hongkong and Shanghai Banking Corporation Ltd.
Place d'Armes
POB 50
Port Louis
Tel: 2080121
Fax: 2088449
Telex: 4390

Indian Ocean International Bank, Ltd.
34 Sir William Newton St.
POB 863
Port Louis
Tel: 2080121
Fax: 2080127
Telex: 4390

Mauritius Commercial Bank Ltd.
9-15 Sir William Newton St.
POB 52
Port Louis
Tel: 2082801
Fax: 2087054
Telex: 4218

Mauritius Co-operative Central Bank
Co-operation House
3 Dumas St.
POB 572
Port Louis
Tel: 2081059
Fax: 2087698

South East Asian Bank Ltd.
26 Bourbon St.
POB 13
Port Louis
Tel: 2088826
Fax: 2088825
Telex: 5328

The State Commercial Bank Ltd.
Chancery House
Lislet Geoffrey St.
Port Louis
Tel: 2088909
Fax: 2088209
Telex: 4910

REMEMBER
- When you telephone (or fax) to Mauritius from another country you must always include the country code [230] before the numbers given.
- When you send mail to Mauritius, be sure to write MAURITIUS in capital letters on its own line below the addresses given.

Union International Bank Ltd.
Sir William Newton St.
POB 1076
Port Louis
Tel: 2088080
Fax: 2088085

Development Bank of Mauritius
La Chaussee
POB 157
Port Louis
Tel: 2080241
Fax: 2088498
Telex: 4248

Bank of Baroda
Sir William Newton St.
POB 553
Port Louis
Tel: 2081504
Fax: 2083892
Telex: 4237

Banque Privee Edmond de Rothschild (Ocean Indien) Ltd.
Chancery House, third floor
Lislet Geoffrey St.
POB 1070
Port Louis
Tel: 2122784
Fax: 2084561
Telex: 4547

RADIO AND TELEVISION

Mauritius Broadcasting Corporation
Broadcasting House
Louis Pasteur St. Forest Side
Tel: 6865001
Fax: 6757332
Telex: 4230

INTERNET ADDRESSES

City Net - Mauritius
http://www.city.net/countries/mauritius/

Africa - Mauritius
http://www.sas.upenn.edu/African_Studies/Country_Specific/Mauritius.html

Mexico

United Mexican States

Economy

Overview

Mexico, an aspirant to first-world status, is the most populous Spanish-speaking country in the world. Many people have emigrated from rural areas to the industrialized urban centers and the developing areas along the US-Mexico border. In addition, a large but still poorly educated work force creates unemployment problems that are proving difficult to overcome. The government has begun to privatize and deregulate state-owned companies, eliminate subsidies to inefficient industries, and reduce tariff rates. The North American Free Trade Agreement (NAFTA) is expected to further boost growth, although Mexico's currency devaluation in late 1994 served to derail growth for most of 1995.

Trade

Mexico expects its membership in NAFTA to significantly change its trade, and has provisionally extended comparable treatment to non-NAFTA countries on a country-by-country bilateral basis. However, it remains somewhat protectionist. Major exports include vehicles, vehicle parts, automobile engines, machinery, and vegetables. Imports include automotive components, electrical components, vehicle parts, radio and television receivers, and telecommunications equipment. Mexico's main trading partner is the US—accounting for about two-thirds of total trade—followed by Japan, Spain, Germany, and France.

Sectors

Agriculture Although agriculture remains important—employing more than 20 percent of the work force—it contributes less than 10 percent of GDP. Most agriculture represents subsistence activity. Coffee, sugar cane, fruit, and vegetables are grown as cash crops, and livestock and fishing are also important.

Industry Industry provides about 30 percent of GDP, employing somewhat more than 25 percent of the work force. The automotive, food processing, iron and steel, chemical, and electrical machinery industries are the most important, and petroleum refining and mining are also significant. Although most industry remains on a low to medium technological level, Mexico is increasing the sophistication of its high-tech, value-added operations. Manufacturing sectors have been hurt in the past few years by increased international competition, stagnant domestic demand, and negative growth in the public sector.

Service Services account for about 60 percent of GDP, while employing about half of the work force. Tourism is the main cash-generating activity, although Mexico has been making efforts to improve the level of openness and sophistication of its transportation, communications, and other service areas.

Trends

Mexico's economy is expected to renew its growth over the next few years. In addition to increased trade with the US and Canada, Mexico should also benefit from increased trade with other South American, European, and Asian countries. A number of internal problems, including environmental problems, population growth, and a changing political system, may become even larger as trade increases. Mexico must figure out a way to reorganize its internal relations and adapt itself to international business standards, while becoming more competitive. Over the long term, it must defuse the power of drug traffickers, entrenched politicians, and political interests, and reduce corruption in order to adequately attract stable foreign participation.

At a Glance

THE COUNTRY

Location North America, between Guatemala and the US.
Terrain Coastal lowlands, central high plateaus, desert, and high, rugged mountains up to 5,400 m. (18,000 ft.).
Climate Varies from tropical to desert.

THE PEOPLE

Population 90,000,000
Ethnic composition
Indian-Spanish (Mestizo) 60%
Indian 30%
Caucasian 9%
Other 1%
Religious composition
Roman Catholic 90%
Protestant 5%
Other 5%
Languages spoken Spanish.
Education and literacy Education spending has risen dramatically, from 2.6% of GDP in 1988 to 4% in 1994. School enrollments at all levels have risen accordingly. Schooling is free and compulsory between ages six and 18.
Labor force
Total:..33,000,000
By occupation: services 29%; agriculture, forestry, hunting, fishing 27%; manufacturing 16%; construction 6%; merchandising 5%; mining and quarrying 5%, transportation and communication 4%; and other 8%.

COUNTRY FACTS

Political and legal The judiciary in this federal republic is divided into federal and state court systems.
Telephone The telecommunications system includes cellular telephone services. International country code: [52]. Selected city codes: Acapulco (72), Mexico City (5), Tijuana (66), Monterrey (8), Veracruz (29), Ensenada (617).
Transportation Mexico's land transportation network is one of the most extensive in Latin America, with more than 4,000 km (2,400 miles) of four-lane highways. The 36,000 kilometers (22,000 miles) of railroads are government-owned. There are 79 ports, with two primary seaports. A number of international airlines serve Mexico.
Environment The governments of the United States and Mexico have pledged to improve the environment and conserve natural resources in both countries. As a result of the environmental agreement negotiated as part of the NAFTA package, the US, Mexico, and Canada will strengthen environmental laws and address common environmental concerns. Current issues include the pollution of scarce natural water resources in the north; untreated sewage and industrial effluents polluting rivers in urban areas; deforestation; widespread erosion; desertification; and serious air pollution in the capital and urban centers along the US-Mexico border.
Media There are 126 television stations and 868 radio stations. Freedom of the press is guaranteed by law, however the government exerts censorship indirectly. There are nearly 300 daily newspapers.
Health Progress in public health has been slow. Life expectancy of males is 69 years; of females, 76 years.

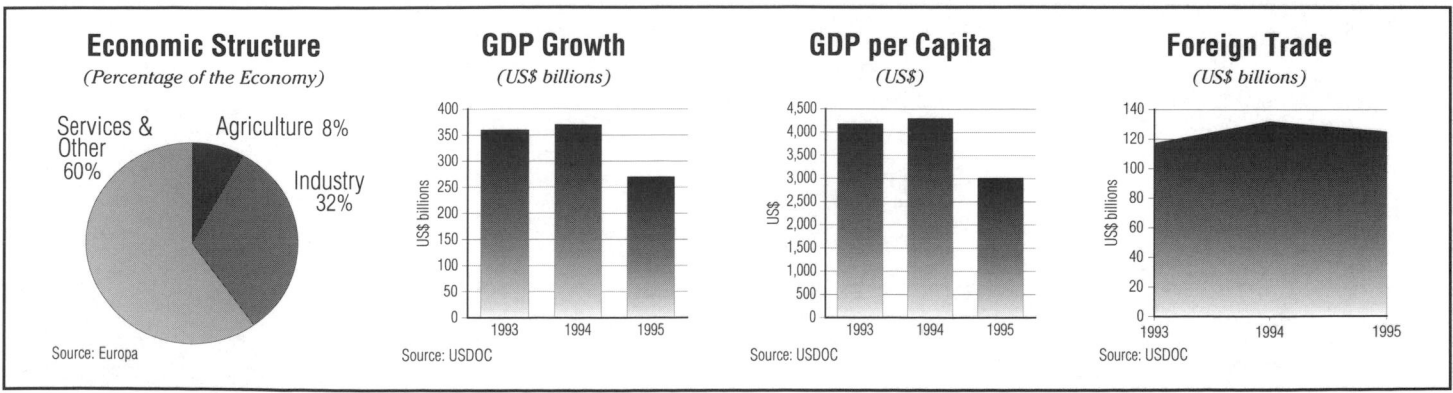

Economic Structure
(Percentage of the Economy)

Services & Other 60%
Agriculture 8%
Industry 32%

Source: Europa

GDP Growth
(US$ billions)

Source: USDOC

GDP per Capita
(US$)

Source: USDOC

Foreign Trade
(US$ billions)

Source: USDOC

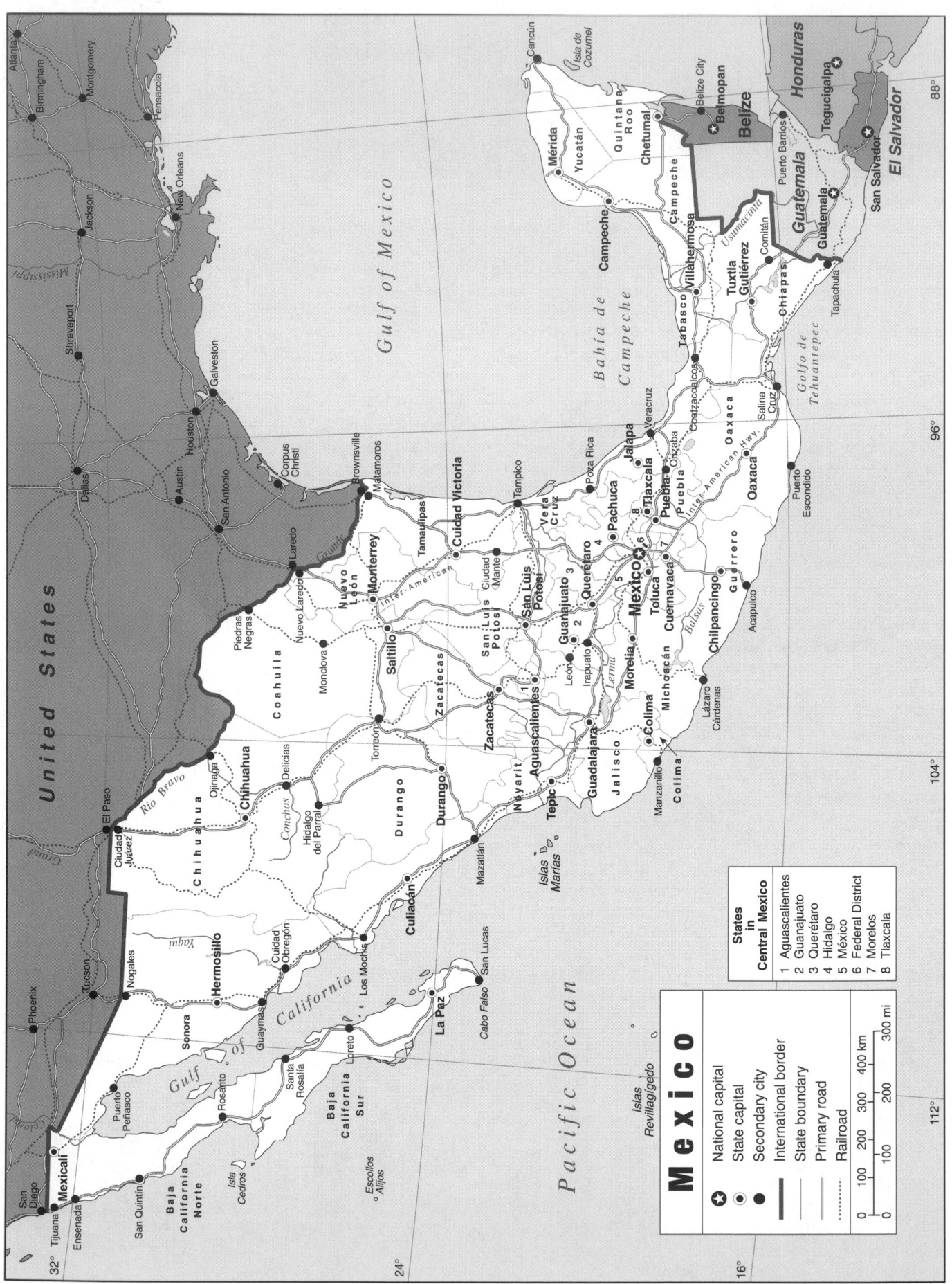

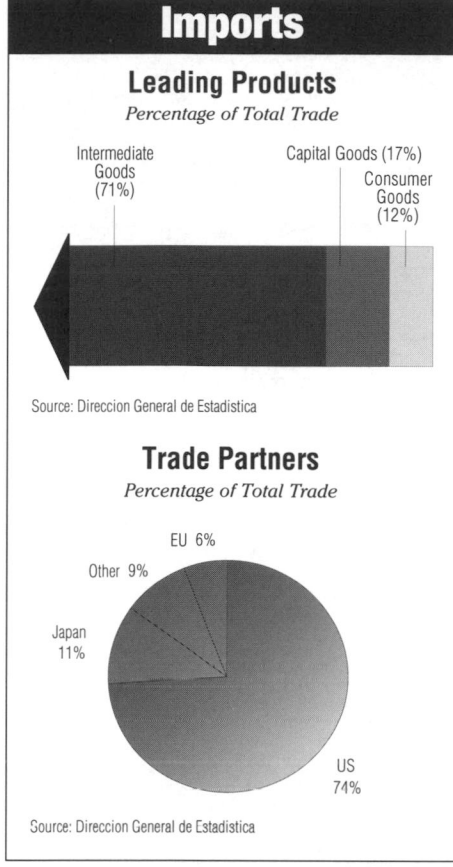

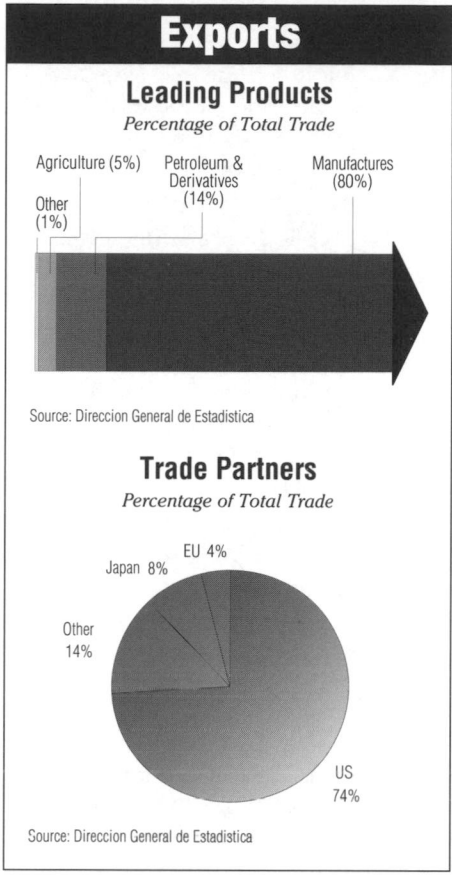

Opportunities

FOR IMPORTING TO MEXICO
- agricultural products
- computers and peripherals
- consumer electronic products
- electrical power systems
- gasoline station equipment and products
- health and cosmetic products
- household consumer goods
- industrial machinery and materials
- lumber
- office supplies and equipment
- telecommunications equipment
- textiles and apparel
- toys, games, and sporting goods
- vehicles and vehicle parts

FOR EXPORTING FROM MEXICO
- agricultural products, especially cattle, coffee, and fresh vegetables
- arts and handicrafts
- audio equipment
- computer products
- electrical switching apparatus
- furniture and wood products
- household products
- minerals
- office machines and parts
- television sets
- textiles and apparel
- vehicles and parts
- videocassette recorders

GROWTH SECTORS
- architectural, construction, and engineering services
- environmental consulting and services
- entertainment industry
- franchises: food, clothing, entertainment, and business
- manufacturing
- media
- mining
- professional services: accounting, financial, insurance, legal, and real estate
- retailing services

GOVERNMENT PROCUREMENT
- airport facility construction equipment and materials
- electrical generation plants
- marine port equipment
- laboratory equipment for medical and scientific research
- oil and gas boring, drilling, and production equipment
- railway and road construction equipment
- vehicles for public transportation and government services
- waste water treatment equipment

Trade News

RULES AND REGULATIONS

- **Regulation** Foreign trade in Mexico is primarily administered by the Secretaría de Comercio y Fomento Industrial (SECOFI), although many other agencies dealing with finances and specific commodities may be involved in the importing process. The Mexican government is taking steps to modernize, streamline, and cut corruption in a process that can now be cumbersome. Professionals should still be hired to facilitate the process.

- **Tariffs** Tariffs range from five to 20 percent, although most effective tariffs are between 10 and 20 percent. Of the 11,951 tariff categories, according to the Harmonized Commodity Description and Coding System (HS), duties are imposed on about 83 percent, 16 percent are duty-free, less than one percent are prohibited, and nearly three percent can be imported only with an advance permit.

- **Other fees and taxes** A Customs Processing Fee (CPF) (0.8 percent of FOB value) and a 10 percent value-added tax are added to most imported goods.

- **Import restrictions** Fewer than 200 products are controlled by import quota and permit requirements in Mexico. These products are in trade sensitive areas such as agriculture, petrochemicals, footwear, vehicles, and electronic equipment.

- **Technical standards** More than 80 classes of products are subject to government-imposed standards of quality and safety, including household appliances, medical instruments, and electronic products.

- **Export permits** Of the more than 5,200 categories of goods on the export tariff schedule, only about 360 require prior export permits. Permits are normally used for goods that must meet safety standards, comply with international conventions, or are important to state security.

FREIGHT FORWARDERS

Aero Despachos Iturbide
Plaza de la Repúblic No. 48, P.B.
06030 México, DF
Tel: (5) 566-2343, 566-6379 Fax: (5) 535-9391

Agencia de Buques Internacional
Barranca del Muerto 525
01600 México, DF
Tel: (5) 664-2242

Air Carga de México
Aeropuerto Internacional
Sec. Agentes Aduanales Loc.
México, DF
Tel: (5) 571-7019, 762-8211

Carga Aerotransportada de México
Río Panuco No. 55-702
Cuauhtémoc
06500 México, DF
Tel: (5) 703-2411, 535-0111 Fax: (5) 703-3994

Central de Aduanas de México
Sinaloa 14 Peñon de los Baños
15520 México, DF
Tel: (5) 785-4755, 571-3400, 571-7080

Central de Aerocarga Internacional
Avda. Insurgentes Centro No. 86, Loc. C, D y E
San Rafael Revolución
06030 México, DF
Tel: (5) 566-4388, 566-7539, 566-7540

Despachos Aduanales
Blvd. Aeropuerto No. 81
Industrial Puerto Aéreo
15700 México, DF
Tel: (5) 784-4188, 762-2640
Fax: (5) 571-9924 Telex: 1777446

Despachos del Centro
Oaxaca No. 96-C
Col. Roma
06700 México, DF
Tel: (5) 533-5864, 207-9106
Fax: (5) 514-0507 Telex: 1774318

Hercel, Oficinas Generales
Paseo de la Reforma No. 383, Piso 10
Col. Cuauhtémoc
06500 México, DF
Tel: (5) 533-4874/6, 514-6767

Overview

Despite the traumas of the collapse of the peso in late 1994, the long-term outlook for Mexico remains positive. Sustained economic growth in recent years has increased demand and competition in newly privatized sectors, public tenders, and major projects. Nearly all sectors offer a chance for judicious growth in sales of capital and intermediate goods, consumer products, and services.

Distribution

Most foreign companies sell into Mexico through a local agent or distributor. Most distribution is through a complex network of intermediaries and small retail sellers, which are limited by practice and infrastructure. As more large retailers establish direct outlets in Mexico, and Mexican businesspeople and consumers become more accustomed to the practice, goods distribution should become easier. Telemarketing and other forms of direct sales are still in their infancy here. While some large retailers purchase goods directly from manufacturers, small shops usually buy from a distributor or wholesaler. Retailers prefer to place small orders frequently and receive rapid delivery. Since the recent economic adjustments, many enterprises which formerly concentrated on manufacturing local goods have begun to show interest in representing or distributing imported goods. Another way to enter this market is to appoint companies based in smaller cities to act as regional distributors; this can give more effective coverage than working through a large, centrally based exclusive distributor.

Agents, Distributors, and Partners

The main channels of international trade in Mexico are private Mexican traders (direct importers, distributors, and sales agents), public and private Mexican-owned end users (manufacturers and institutional buyers), and foreign-owned firms operating in Mexico (making or distributing their own products in the Mexican market). Hundreds of exhibitions are held in Mexico each year, and such events are excellent places to look for local representatives. Selecting an appropriate agent or distributor takes time, effort, and money. The prospective importer should clearly define corporate expectations. Factors should include product and industry contacts, past performance, enthusiasm, and commitment; familiarity with the English language should also be considered. Most potential distributors request exclusivity, but this issue should be carefully weighed. If the product is new to the market or if the market is highly competitive, define the level of advertising and other promotional support that the Mexican entity will be required to provide. Attorneys can be of considerable help with registration, intellectual property issues, labor law consulting, and important settling trade disputes.

Selling Techniques

The Mexican buyer is usually interested in service and price; however, the personal touch, which can take several forms, is just as important. Close relationships between buyer and seller help establish credibility and customer loyalty. The firm looking for success needs to be sensitive to linguistic and cultural considerations. Plan carefully to provide replacement parts and technical support for complex systems. Exporters may want help from one of the full-service advertising agencies in Mexico City; many are familiar with multinational company needs. A representative or office is not absolutely necessary, but may be useful in collecting the information needed to prepare bid documents and provide after-sales support.

Advertising

More than 335 newspapers are published in Mexico, although print advertising is considered a relatively minor means of advertising. Trade papers and magazines are more important for reaching opinion shapers and business leaders. Seven television networks and one cable network operate in Mexico, and Mexicans also receive broadcasts from the US to the north. Radio—with more than 900 stations—reaches a broader spectrum of Mexicans, at a more affordable cost than television. Direct marketing through catalog and other techniques, such as premiums or rebates, have also become popular. Many foreign firms interested in introducing products into Mexico have bypassed traditional advertising agencies that place conventional advertising in standard media outlets, in favor of using public relations firms that market in less conventional ways, such as through sponsorships of public events.

Service and Customer Support

Traditionally, the Mexican market has been seen as one that is driven solely by price. However, that is no longer the case, and after-sales support is increasingly viewed as a key selling point, along with quality and delivery. In fact, many Mexican businesspeople now view an inadequate service program as a warning sign that could kill a deal.

Marketing in Mexico

MARKETING TIPS

- **Deal at the top** Mexicans are very hierarchical and only senior personnel can make decisions. Thus, marketing approaches and campaigns should focus on selling the decisionmakers.
- **Look at second tier partners** The top tier marketing firms may be complacent, while up-and-coming firms may be hungrier, more flexible, and more amenable to working with you rather than insisting on doing things their own way. But remember that local partners can be difficult to leave behind if things go wrong.
- **Government markets** Each agency operates its own qualification and bid procedures. Most require preregistration and prequalification, as well as a local representative, and many recommend setting up a joint venture with a local firm to enhance the firm's ability to compete in a system which continues to favor national providers.
- **Credit** Many smaller Mexican firms operate with few financial resources and require seller financing in order to complete transactions.

AD AGENCIES

Arellano/BSB Publicidad
Goldsmith No. 225
11550 México, DF
Tel: (5) 250-1000, 255-2424 Fax: (5) 203-1511

BBDO México, S.A. de C.V.
Bosques de Ciruelos, Piso 5
Bosques de las Lomas
11700 México, DF
Tel: (5) 251-0175 Fax: (5) 596-5957 Telex: 1773839

BMB Publicidad
Bosque de Duraznos 65-6
Bosques de las Lomas
11700 México, DF
Tel: (5) 596-7979 Fax: (5) 596-8353

Bozell, S.A. de C.V.
Paseo de la Reforma 106
Col. Lomas de Chapultepec
11000 México, DF
Tel: (5) 724-3500 Fax: (5) 202-7260 Telex: 1761371

FCB México
Presidente Masaryk 61
Col. Polanco
11560 México, DF
Tel: (5) 250-1600 Fax: (5) 250-9510

Grey México
Horacio No. 1844, Pisos 2 y 6, esq. Con Periférico
Col. Polanco Reforma
11550 México, DF
Tel: (5) 202-0108 Fax: (5) 202-2360

Griffin Bacal Publicidad
Reyna No. 6
Col. San Angel
01000 México, DF
Tel: (5) 550-7007, 550-4874, 548-0232

Marketing Mercadeo International Co., Inc.
Puebla 151
Col. Roma
06700 México, DF
Tel: (5) 208-8068

McCann Universal
Londres 259, esq. Sevilla
Col. Juárez
06600 México, DF
Tel: (5) 511-8767 Fax: (5) 533-0957

Saatchi & Saatchi Advertising
Bosque de Ciruelos 194, Piso 3
Col. Bosques de las Lomas
11700 México, DF
Tel: (5) 596-8596, 596-2615 Fax: (5) 596-8450

Scali, McCabe, Sloves de México, S.A. de C.V.
Lafayette 88
Col. Anzures
11590 México, DF
Tel: (5) 628-0201 Fax: (5) 255-3326

Young & Rubicam, S.A. de C.V.
Leibnitz No. 13
Col. Anzures
11590 México, DF
Tel: (5) 250-3200 Fax: (5) 250-0862

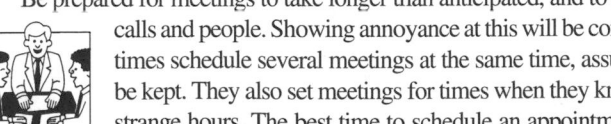

Business Culture

Greetings and Courtesies

It is the norm to shake hands when introduced to someone of the same sex. A man being introduced to a woman will bow slightly, and shake hands only if the woman initiates this interaction. Foreign men should do the same when meeting Mexican women. It is polite to greet (and say good-bye to) every member of a group individually. Direct eye contact between equals can go on for some time. Avoiding eye contact might be interpreted as a sign that a person is hiding something or is not to be trusted.

Business Ethic and Framework

Traditionally, Mexicans believe in working to live, rather than living to work. Work is only a means to an end—the end being the enjoyment of what is truly important in life: family, friends, and the various things that make a person happy. The general attitude is, whatever does not get accomplished today can always be done tomorrow. Foreign businesspeople who are accustomed to a hard-driving government will need to back off somewhat when dealing with Mexican businesspeople.

Decision Making

Mexicans are extremely polite, to the point of avoiding an awkward truth by telling someone what they want to hear instead. They will rarely say something can't be done, and also may agree to do something that is in fact not possible. They have great respect for authority. Power resides in the hands of the few (or one) at the top of the company hierarchy. The head of a company has the final word, and it is not often questioned by employees. Mid-level managers do not make decisions, and are trained to not disturb the status quo.

Women

Latin cultures are known for their male chauvinism and women should be prepared to deal with this. It's very rare for women to hold top management positions in Mexican companies, and a woman simply may not be given the same respect as a man, or be taken as seriously. To counter this, women should be well-poised, behave in a completely professional manner, and dress conservatively. Complementing women is part of Mexican culture, but in some situations such remarks might also be a way to judge a woman's availability. A quick acknowledgment will suffice if the remark is polite. Remaining coolly professional will usually discourage unwanted attention. However, women should be aware that a bruised male ego could destroy a business relationship. Business breakfasts, lunches, and dinners are common, but women traveling alone should not arrange a dinner with a man. Lunches should be in the woman's hotel restaurant so the check can be put on the room bill. If it is presented at the table, a man will not allow a woman to pay. After business hours, women should have an escort if they go out at night. In general, women should not go to a bar alone.

Meetings

Be prepared for meetings to take longer than anticipated, and to be frequently interrupted by phone calls and people. Showing annoyance at this will be considered impolite. Mexicans sometimes schedule several meetings at the same time, assuming some appointments will not be kept. They also set meetings for times when they know they will not be available, or at strange hours. The best time to schedule an appointment is between 10:00 am and 1:00 pm, or 4:00 pm and 6:00 pm. The people you meet with will probably not have the power to enter into an agreement, so determine which of them will be reporting to company superiors. Negotiation meetings will usually take place in a hotel, conference center, or other comfortable surroundings. Subordinates will arrive first; an executive with higher status will arrive later. There will initially be relaxed small talk and pleasantries. Getting right to business will be viewed as rude and perhaps suspicious. When the time is right, the senior Mexican representative will give a welcoming speech and turn the meeting over to the visitors. After your position has been stated, the Mexican team leader will answer, item by item, suggesting any changes.

Business Attire

Your attire will be viewed as a sign of your respect for your associates, and your attitude toward the business in general. In urban areas, especially Mexico City, suits and European fashions are preferred for men. Don't remove your jacket or loosen your tie unless your host makes this suggestion. Women should wear conservative dresses or suits. Jewelry, makeup, and heels are standard, but this a matter of personal taste. In smaller towns and rural areas, suits or expensive clothing are viewed as showing off.

Cultural Cautions

DO'S

- Personal dignity and honor are of the utmost importance to Mexicans. Always be polite and treat people with respect.
- If someone has a title, such as doctor, professor, or engineer *(Ingeniero)*, always use their title when addressing them.
- Be on time for appointments, but it's quite possible that the person you're meeting will be late by as much as 30 minutes to an hour.

DON'TS

- Never do or say anything that belittles someone, especially in front of their peers or in public.
- Do not refer to the United States as America. Mexico is part of the American continent, too.
- If the person you are meeting with is late, do not complain about it.
- Do not travel to Mexico for business between December 15 and January 6.

CUSTOMS

- Business cards are important and are exchanged when greeting someone. Carry plenty of cards, and if possible have your card printed in Spanish on one side.
- "Lic." after a person's name stands for Licenciado. This technically means the person has a university degree.
- Gifts are not as important as in Asian cultures, but may be given as signs of politeness and good will.

OBSERVATIONS

- Business dealings can be made easier by having a Mexican advisor or consultant.
- Virtually all of Mexico's major companies have offices in Mexico City, so there is a good chance this will be your destination.
- Dignity and politeness are very important to Mexicans. Always remember to say good-bye, and never say anything that even suggests someone's morals are not perfect.
- Hospitality is extremely important, and business meals should be reciprocated if possible.
- Social position and professional status are important. Dress well, and stay at the best hotel you can afford.
- Make business appointments at least two weeks in advance. When you arrive, call to reconfirm your meeting.

NEGOTIATIONS

- Mexicans rarely say something can't be done. They are more likely to agree to do something that isn't possible to do.
- Direct questions will be more likely to bring a polite response rather than an accurate one. Try to ask a question two or three times, differently each time, to get an accurate idea of what can and can't, and will or won't be done.
- Mexico is a leisured society. Deadlines usually don't mean much, and will often not be met. Take this into account when agreeing to work or delivery schedules.
- Mexicans are a leisured people. Adjust to this rhythm. If they sense you are in a hurry to complete your business and get on with other things, they will use this to their advantage.
- Don't agree to things too quickly. Mexicans tend to frown on hasty decisions.
- Mexican businessmen usually prefer quick profits to long-term planning. They generally will not be enthusiastic about proposals that take years to show results.
- Contract law is relatively new to Mexico. Many Mexican businesspeople may still consider a written contract to be less binding than a personal commitment between trusted associates. In general, Mexicans tend to regard specific deals as simply part of a larger ongoing relationship.

Legal System

Mexico is a civil law country. Its legal system is based on Roman law and French Napoleonic code.

Intellectual Property Rights

Recent legislation has brought Mexico up to international standards for the granting, protecting, and enforcing of intellectual property rights.

Patents Patents are valid for a nonrenewable term of 20 years from the application date. Patents for which an application has already been submitted in another country are given priority in Mexico if the application is filed according to international treaties. Under normal circumstances it takes approximately three years to obtain a patent, which provides the holder with exclusive use and exploitation of the patent. Litigation of patent rights and infringements is usually slow.

Trademarks Trademark rights are granted for a renewable 10-year term. Rights to use a trademark are granted to the first person to apply for registration. A trademark can be registered for different classes of products. The law protects internationally recognized trademarks. Approximately three months may lapse between the application and grant of a trademark.

Copyrights Copyright protection is generally granted for a term of 50 years. The sale of pirated products remains a problem, although the authorities are taking strict measures to stop copyright infringement.

Trade secrets Trade secrets in Mexico are narrowly defined to encompass information with industrial or commercial application, which information is kept confidential and provides the owner with a competitive advantage.

Business Registration

Foreign investors are treated as nationals. Mexican corporations can be 100 percent foreign-owned, except for corporations involved in a few activities that are reserved to Mexicans or the state. Foreign investors and Mexican companies with foreign ownership must register with the National Registry of Foreign Investment, the tax authorities, and the chambers of commerce of the corresponding industry. A foreign company with employees in Mexico must also register with social security authorities. Foreign companies or branches of foreign companies must register with the Public Registry of Commerce and must obtain approval from the Ministry of Commerce to operate in Mexico.

Contracts and Dispute Resolution

There are minimal legal restrictions on contracts. Most types of contracts are considered valid and are governed by the provisions of specific legislation, but parties can vary the statutory requirements by agreement. Mexican companies view contracts as instruments to be referred to in the case of serious controversies only, preferring to resolve minor problems through negotiations and turning to litigation as a last resort. However, litigation may arise if a contract term or the business relationship is not clear. The parties may contractually agree on the terms and conditions that will apply for dispute resolution. Parties may choose Mexican courts, foreign courts, or arbitration. If a contract applies the law of a foreign jurisdiction, Mexican firms may be reluctant to sue foreign entities, due to the cost and time involved and the difficulty of enforcing a foreign judgment or settlement. Damage awards are minimal. The parties may also select the law that will govern the agreement. Arbitration is normally used in international agreements. Arbitration awards are more easily enforced in Mexico than foreign judgments. Although arbitration is a relatively new method of dispute resolution in Mexico, it is fast becoming popular. Many parties are beginning to submit disputes to the recently created Mexican Association of Commercial Arbitration.

Notaries

Real estate transactions must be registered before a public notary. Other documents of a commercial nature need not be registered. For documents to affect the interests of third parties, however, they must be notarized and registered with the Public Registry of Property and Commerce. There are a limited number of notaries in each jurisdiction, and the documents that are registered with them must be in the Spanish language.

Labor

Among the main constitutional rights granted to workers are the right to associate freely in unions, to bargain collectively, to strike, and to share in profits. A Minimum Wage Commission sets the minimum wages; however, employers usually pay salaries that are higher than the low minimum wage. Federal labor law is extremely protective of workers' rights, and employment may only be terminated for cause. The employment of minors under the age of 14 is forbidden.

Source: Cuesta Campos y Asociados, Guadalajara, Mexico.

Legal Matters

LEGAL BRIEFS

- **Corporations** The most commonly used business entity in Mexico is the *Sociedad Anonima,* which is similar to a US corporation. Incorporation fees and expenses depend on the amount of capital stock.

- **Unique intellectual property rights** Mexican law protects utility models and industrial designs. A utility model is an object, device, or tool that, as a result of a modification of use, configuration, structure, or form, performs a different function than its parts, and provides an additional advantage with respect to its use. Industrial drawings include the plans for industrial products and models used for the manufacture of a product. Rights in these properties are protected for 15 years.

- **Corredores publicos** Corredores have the same powers as notaries, but only in the area of commercial transactions. A *corredor* may register documents so that they become public records and are valid with respect to third parties.

- **International agreements** Mexico is a member of GATT/WTO; NAFTA; OAS; OECD; CISG; New York Convention on the Recognition and Enforcement of Foreign Arbitral Awards; Convention on the Taking of Evidence Abroad in Civil or Commercial Matters; and Inter-American Convention on International Commercial Arbitration, and maintains free trade agreements with Chile, Venezuela, Colombia, Costa Rica, and Bolivia.

LEGAL CONTACTS

Lic. Hugo G. Cuesta Leaso
Cuesta Campos y Asociados S.C.
192 Bismark Planta Baja
44900 Guadalajara Jal.
Tel: (3) 630-05-80, 630-21-29, 616-92-15
Fax: (3) 616-10-05

Baker & McKenzie
Blvd. Agua Caliente No. 4558-1005
22420 Tijuana, BC
Tel: (66) 81-7740 Fax: (66) 81-7745

Brennan Winum John W.
Placeres No. 1220
Col. Chapalita
Guadalajara, Jal.
Tel: (3) 647-7522 Fax: (3) 647-7523

Carlsmith Ball García Cacho y Asociados
Campos Elíseos 385, Torre "B", Piso 6
Col. Chapultepec Polanco
11560 México, DF
Tel: (5) 281-2553 Fax: (5) 281-2196

Hardin Hess Santons Galindo & Hanhausen
Jorge Elliot No. 12, Piso 7
Col. Polanco
11560 México, DF
Tel: (5) 250-9977 Fax: (5) 250-7748

Jaurigui Navarette y Nader
Paseo de la Reforma 199, Pisos 15 y 16
06500 México, DF
Tel: (5) 591-1655

Lopez Molilar, Gayou, Bustamante, Gutierrez y Salvatori, SC
Avenida Hermanos Escobar 6755-Despacho 1
Ciudad Juarez, Chih.
Tel: (16) 18-3030 Fax: (16) 18-3001

Laffan, Mues y Garay
San Jeronimo 500
Jardines del Pedregal
01900 Mexico, D.F.
Tel: (5) 683-3522 Fax: (5) 683-2840

Thompson & Knight
Edificio Losoles TD-4
Avda. Lázaro Cárdenas No. 2400
66220 Garza García, NL
Tel: (83) 63-0096 Fax: (83) 63-3067

White & Case
Paseo de la Reforma 390, Piso 17
Col. Juárez
06600 México, DF
Tel: (5) 207-9717 Fax: (5) 208-3628

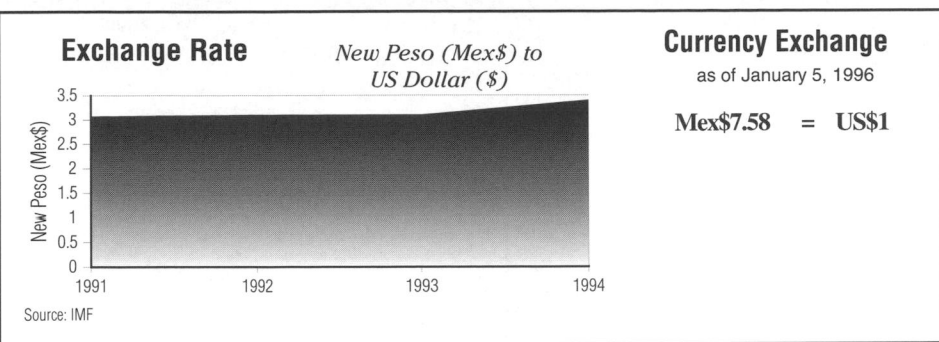

Exchange Rate

New Peso (Mex$) to US Dollar ($)

Source: IMF

Currency Exchange

as of January 5, 1996

Mex$7.58 = US$1

Currency

The currency in use is the new peso (Mex$ or NP), which is divided into 100 centavos.

Foreign Exchange

Mexico abolished foreign exchange controls in 1991; there are no limits on access to, ownership of, or transfer of foreign exchange. The external value of the peso is adjusted daily by the Central Bank, within a range of preestablished values known as the foreign exchange band. Most transactions are handled at a free market exchange rate that floats within the foreign exchange band. Foreign exchange coverage is available in maturities of up to 180 days. Mexico's commercial banks are allowed to offer a full range of services including deposit accounts, lending, corporate finance, the operation of trusts and mutual funds, foreign exchange, and money market trading.

Capital Transfers

Expropriations are governed by international law, and require rapid, fair market value compensation, including accrued interest. Payments for invisibles may be made freely. There are no restrictions on proceeds from invisibles. Foreign direct investments are generally allowed up to 100 percent of equity without prior authorization.

Investment Incentives

Special incentives are available to companies which set up manufacturing plants within 13 miles of the northern or southern border and the free zones, which include both states on the Baja California peninsula, Quintana Roo, and the northern part of Sonora bordering on the United States. To qualify, companies must manufacture products not produced elsewhere in Mexico. Mexico also has two free ports: Puerto Mexico (Coatzacoalcos) and Salina Cruz.

Investment Restrictions

The foreign investment law eliminates such restrictions as export requirements, capital controls, and domestic content percentages, prohibited under the NAFTA. Foreign investors already in Mexico may apply for cancellation of prior commitments. Failure to apply for revocation of performance requirements will result in their staying in effect.

TAXATION

Taxation requires sophisticated knowledge of complex rules and regulations specific to each country. For more detailed information we suggest you refer to the Ernst & Young Corporate Tax Guide and Directory, available from the Ernst & Young accounting office in your country, or from:

Mancera, S.C.
Plaza Polanco
Jaime Balmes No. 11, Torre "D"
Floors 4, 5 and 6
Col. Los Morales-Polanco
11510 Mexico City, Mexico
Tel: (5) 557-5555, 557-9322
Fax: (5) 255-0719, 255-0999 4th Floor
          (5) 255-1199 5th Floor

At a Glance

Corporate Income Tax Rate (%)	34
Capital Gains Tax Rate (%)	34
Branch Tax Rate (%)	34
Withholding Tax (%)	

Dividends (a)	0
Interest	
Paid to Banks (b)	4.9
Paid to Machinery Suppliers (c)	10
Paid to Others (c)	35
Royalties	
From Patents and Trademarks (c)	35
From Know-how and Technical	
Assistance (c)	15
Branch Remittance Tax (a)	0
Net Operating Losses (Years)	
Carryback	0
Carryforward (d)	5

(a) Dividends received by resident and nonresident shareholders from a Mexican corporation are not subject to tax if earnings were already subject to corporate income tax, and if the distributing corporation has sufficient accumulation in its net tax profit ("basket") account to cover the dividend. If the accumulated amount is insufficient, dividends are taxed at a 34% rate. Similar rules apply to remittances abroad by branches of foreign corporations.
(b) Final tax applicable to nonresident banks registered with the Mexican tax authorities.
(c) Final tax applicable to nonresidents.
(d) If also incurred for accounting purposes, the loss may be carried forward for an additional five years.

Money Matters

BITS AND PIECES

- **The new peso** The new peso was introduced January 1, 1993, when it replaced the old Mexican peso at the rate of 1:1,000. By the end of the decade, when all old pesos are taken out of circulation, the new peso will again be known as the peso.
- **Capital** There are no restrictions on capital transactions. Foreign direct investments are generally permitted for up to 100 percent equity without authorization, except for certain critical industries.
- **NAFTA** As is required under NAFTA, Mexico's new foreign investment law eliminates restrictions including export requirements, capital controls, and domestic percentages requirements. Foreign investors already in Mexico may apply to have restrictions cancelled; if no application for revocation is filed, the performance requirements stay in effect.
- **Credit** Credit is limited and expensive in Mexico. Peso-denominated credit is primarily short-term with high interest rates, due to the need to cover the cost of a large non-performing loan portfolio. Competition from new banks and foreign subsidiaries is forcing the interest rates to decrease, however, and the availability of credit to increase.
- **Repatriation** There are no controls over the transfer of currency into or out of Mexico. Profits can be freely repatriated.
- **Trade financing** Exporters are generally unwilling to purchase through advance payment. Most Mexican companies will not provide letters of credit. Some alternative means of financing include documentary collections, or open accounts. Some companies also may export under a standby letter of credit, although these too, may be expensive and hard to acquire for many Mexican companies.

BANKS

Banco del Centro (Bancén)
Paseo de la Reforma 195, Piso 1
06500 México, DF
Tel: (5) 566-7259, 703-3455 Fax: (5) 703-3502

Banco de Oriente (Banorie)
Paseo de la Reforma 506, Piso 20
México, DF
Tel: (5) 286-86-25, 286-8176 Fax: (5) 286-8354

Banco de Oriente (Banorie)
Avda. Dos Oriente 10
Puebla, Pue.
Tel: (22) 41-6752, 41-4251 Fax: (22) 42-0413

Banco Internacional S.A.
Paseo de la Reforma 156
06600 México, DF
Tel: (5) 721-2222, 721-2630/2 Fax: (5) 566-2404

Banco Mercantil del Norte (Banorte)
Madero 22, Mezzanine
06000 México, DF
Tel: (5) 510-1877, 512-7440 Fax: (5) 512-3685

Banco Nacional de México (Banamex)
Isabel la Católica 40
Col. Centro
06089 México, DF
Tel: (5) 225-5178 Fax: (5) 709-9446

Banco Unión
Paseo de la Reforma 364
06694 México, DF
Tel: (5) 625-6000 Fax: (5) 207-0214

Banco
Avda. Universidad 1200
Col. Xoco, Deleg. Benito Juárez
03339 México, DF
Tel: (5) 621-5727 Fax: (5) 621-3265

Bankers Trust
Blvd. Manuel Avila Camacho 1
Desp. 806, Piso 8
Col. Chapultepec
01560 México, DF
Tel: (5) 540-4855 Fax: (5) 520-5740

Credit Suisse
Campos Elíseos 345, Piso 9
11560 México, DF
Tel: (5) 202-3923, 202-4223

Business Travel

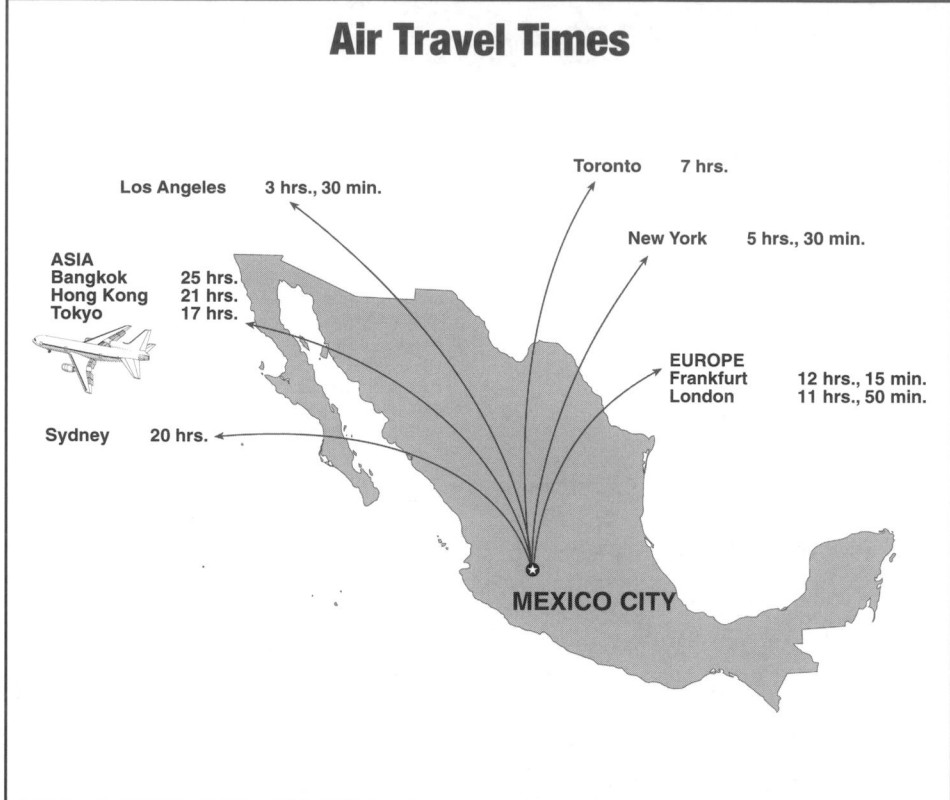

Air Travel Times

Toronto   7 hrs.

Los Angeles   3 hrs., 30 min.

New York   5 hrs., 30 min.

ASIA
Bangkok   25 hrs.
Hong Kong   21 hrs.
Tokyo   17 hrs.

EUROPE
Frankfurt   12 hrs., 15 min.
London   11 hrs., 50 min.

Sydney   20 hrs.

MEXICO CITY

COMMUNICATIONS

Telephones The telephone system in Mexico is over-worked, outdated, and expensive. Connections can be noisy, numbers confusing, and operators of little help. International calls are especially expensive. Due to the numerous public phones that are out of order, calls from hotels are easier, although expensive. Long distance calls within Mexico can be made at long-distance phones in phone offices, bus and train stations, and hotels.

Fax Fax machines are available at larger hotels' front desks (in rooms in some luxury hotels) and at major post offices.

Post office Postal service in Mexico is slow and unreliable. Fax and courier services are more trustworthy.

BEST TRAVEL BOOKS

Fodor's Mexico, edited by Paula Consolo. New York: Fodor's Travel Publications. 572 pages. Tourist oriented, excellent information on transportation, hotels, and restaurants.

Mexico on $45 a Day: Frommer's Budget Travel Guide, by Marita Adair. New York: Prentice Hall Travel. 778 pages. Huge amounts of information on budget hotels and restaurants. Good background, transportation, and communication material.

Mexico: A Travel Survival Kit, by Tom Brosnahan, John Noble, Nancy Keller, Mark Balla, and Scott Wayne. Hawthorn, Victoria, Australia: Lonely Planet Publications. 924 pages. For backpackers, but still the best travel book on Mexico. 174 very good maps.

The Travellers Guide to Latin America Customs and Manners. E. Devine & N. Braganti. An invaluable guide for people not wanting to put foot in mouth.

The Wall Street Journal Guide to Business Travel, Mexico and Central America. The most electrifying of all practical travel guides.

USEFUL TELEPHONE NUMBERS

If you are calling from outside Mexico, you will need to add the country code [52] and any other international dialing requirements from within your country.

- Emergency 06
- Police (Non-Emergency) 08
- International Operator 09
- Long-Distance Operator 02
- Local Directory Assistance 04
- Long-Distance Directory Assistance 01
- Mexican National Railways .... (5) 547-1084
- Central de Autobuses........................... (5) 533-2047
- Hotel /Motel Association....................... (5) 286-5455
- Mexico City Tourist Info... (5) 525-9380 or 525-9383
- Tourist 24-hour Legal Advice.............. (5) 625-8618, ...250-0151, 250-0493, 250-0493, 250-0123
- Taxis (Mexico City)..............(5) 516-6020, 566-0077
- Green Angels Emg. Road Service .... (5) 250-4817
- Highway Patrol .... (5) 684-2142 or 684-9512
- Red Cross .... (5) 557-5757
- Guadalajara Police.............................. (3) 617-5838
- Highway Patrol .... (3) 612-7194

Credit card information
Lost or stolen credit cards (call collect to the US, regardless of which country the card was issued in).

- Amex ....[1] (919) 333-3211
- Diner's Club.................................[1] (303) 799-1504
- MasterCard ....[1] (314) 275-6690
- Visa ....[1] (410) 581-7931

Travelogue

WORKWEEK
Offices Monday-Friday 9:00 am to 2:00 pm and 4:00 to 7:00 pm But vary upon region, check first.
Banks Monday-Friday 9:00 am to 1:30 pm, Saturday and Sunday, 10:00 am to 1:30 pm. Large cities, banks reopen from 4:00 to 6:00 pm daily (not Sunday).
Government Monday-Friday 8:00 am to 3:00 pm.
Retail Generally open weekdays 9:00 am to 2:00 pm and 4:00 to 7:00 pm.

HOLIDAYS
Holidays 1996
January 1 New Year's Day
February 5 Constitution Day
March 21 Benito Juarez's Birthday
April 3 Holy Week Begins
April4 Holy Thursday*
April 5 Good Friday*
April 7 Easter Sunday
May 1 Labor Day
May 5 Anniversary of the Battle of Puebla
October 12 Columbus Day
September 16 Independence Day
October 12 Dia de la Raza
November 1 All Saints' Day
November 2 All Souls' Day
November 20 Anniversary of the Mexican Revolution
Decmeber 24 Christmas Eve
December 25 Christmas Day
December 29 End of the Year Balance
December 31 New Year's Eve (banks only)
*Dates vary each year.

VISA AND PASSPORT
A tourist card, which is provided by flight attendants on airplanes, travel agents, or consulates, is required of all visitors to Mexico. Proof of citizenship is necessary to validate the card. Canadian and US citizens need only the tourist card for entry (original birth certificate and photo ID can be used for proof of citizenship). Citizens of the UK will also need a passport; other nationals need a passport as well as a visa. There are business visas *(visitante)* available from the consulate.

DEPARTURE FORMALITIES
Upon departure, tourist cards must be returned. Missing cards can cause lengthy delays and hassles. There is a departure tax of US$12 at the airport, but it is usually included in the price of your ticket.

IMMUNIZATION
No proof of vaccinations are required unless travelers are arriving from areas where cholera is endemic.

TIPPING
Some restaurants add a 10 to 15 percent service charge to bills. Those that do not should be tipped that amount. Taxi drivers are also tipped 10 percent. Porters, bellboys, maids, and room service waiters should be tipped a small amount (US$.50 per bag or day).

CRIME
Street crime is common in larger cities, especially Mexico City. Tourists are targets for pickpockets and the like in heavily touristed areas, including airports. Mexican poverty has added to the problems associated with thievery, which is rather prevalent.

INFRASTRUCTURE
Mexico has well-developed air, bus, taxi, and hotel industries. Train systems are available but antiquated. Taxis are not metered, settle a price before leaving the airport. Buses are very crowded. Car rental agencies are available, a permit and insurance is required. Mexico is undergoing major reconstruction; therefore traffic often is congested, allow time for city to city travel.

NATIONAL TOURIST OFFICE
Secretaría de Turismo (SECTOR)
Avda. Presidente Masaryk 172
Col. Polanco
11587 México, DF
Tel: (5) 250-8204/6, 250-8228
Fax: (5) 254-0014

GOVERNMENT AGENCIES

Banco de México (BANXICO)
Bank of Mexico
Avda. 5 de Mayo 2, Apdo. 98 bis
Col. Centro
06059 México, DF
Tel: (5) 237-2000, 709-0140, 709-0440
Fax: (5) 510-9337, 512-4813

Comisión Nacional Bancaria
National Banking Commission
República del Salvador 47
Col. Centro
06080 México, DF
Tel: (5) 709-7311
Fax: (5) 709-7327

Comisión Nacional de Valores
National Securities Commission
Barranca del Muerto 275
Col. San José Insurgentes
03900 México, DF
Tel: (5) 651-0129

Departamento del Distrito Federal
Department of the Federal District
Plaza de la Constitución y Pino Suárez, Piso 1
Col. Centro
06068 México, DF
Tel: (5) 585-0187, 510-0349
Fax: (5) 518-2998

Dirección General de Aduanas
Directorate General of Customs
20 de Noviembre 195, Piso 6
Col. Centro
06090 México, DF
Tel: (5) 709-6365, 709-2900, 709-2185, 709-6287
Fax: (5) 709-6038, 709-6360 Telex: 1774303

Dirección General de Aeronáutica Civil
Directorate General of Civil Aviation
Providencia 807, Piso 6
Col. del Valle
03100 México, DF
Tel: (5) 687-7814, 687-7660

Dirección General de Control de Insumos Para la Salud, SS
Directorate General of Control of Medical Products
Insurgentes Sur 1397, Piso 3
Col. Guadalupe Inn
01020 México, DF
Tel: (5) 598-9029

Dirección General de Desarrollo Tecnológico, SECOFI
Technology Development General Directorate
Azafran No. 18, Piso 3
Granjas México
08400 México, DF
Tel: (5) 654-0781, 650-1333
Fax: (5) 654-0771

Dirección General de Normas (DGN)
Departamento de Información Comercial
Department of Commercial Information
Avda. Puente de Tecamachalco 6, Piso 3
Lomas de Tecamachalco
53950 Naucalpan, Edo. de Méx.
Tel: (5) 589-9592
Fax: (5) 540-5153

Dirección General de Prevención y Control de la Contaminación Ambiental
Directorate General of Environmental Contamination, Prevention and Control
Río Elba 20
Col. Cuauhtémoc
06500 México, DF
Tel: (5) 553-2977, 553-9481
Fax: (5) 658-6059, 286-8559

Dirección General de Radio, Televisión y Cine (RTC)
Directorate General of Radio, Television, and Film
Atletas 2
Col. Country Club
04220 México, DF
Tel: (5) 544-9692, 544-3768

Dirección General de Sanidad Vegetal
Directorate General of Plant Protection
Guillermo Pérez Valenzuela No. 127
México, DF
Tel: (5) 554-0512, 658-1671
Fax: (5) 554-0529

Instituto Mexicano de Televisión (IMEVISION)
Mexican Television Institute
Avda. Periférico Sur 4121
Col. Fuentes del Pedregal
14141 México, DF
Tel: (5) 568-5684, 568-1313

Secretaría de Agricultura y Recursos Hidráulicos (SARH)
Secretariat of Agriculture and Water Resources
Avda. Insurgentes Sur No. 476, Piso 13
Col. Roma Sur
06038 México, DF
Tel: (5) 584-0066, 584-0096, 584-0271

Secretaría de Agricultura y Recursos Hidraulicos (SARH)
Departamento de Autorizaciones Zoosanitarias
Department of Animal Health Authorization
Recreo 51
México, DF
Tel: (5) 534-1131/8
Fax: (5) 534-3985

Secretaría de Agricultura y Recursos Hidráulicos (SARH)
Department of Science and Technology
Av. Nuevo León 210, 18
Hipódromo Condesa
06100 México, DF
Tel: (5) 584-7980, 564-9859
Fax: (5) 574-3160

Secretaría de Comercio y Fomento Industrial (SECOFI)
Secretaría de Comunicaciones y Transportes
Secretariat of Communications and Transport
Avda. Universidad y Xola
Col. Navarte
03028 México, DF
Tel: (5) 519-7456, 519-1319, 530-9203, 530-1074
Fax: (5) 519-9748, 530-1074

TRADE ASSOCIATIONS

Asociación Nacional de la Micro, Pequeña y Mediana Industria
National Association of Micro, Small, and Medium Industry
Bajío No. 107
Col. Roma Sur
México, DF
Tel: (5) 584-0494, 564-0694
Fax: (5) 564-5398

Asociación Nacional de Importadores y Exportadores de la República Mexicana (ANIERM)
National Association of Importers and Exporters
Monterrey 130
Col. Roma
México, DF
Tel: (5) 564-9379, 584-9522
Fax: (5) 584-5137

ANIERM Guadalajara
Avda. de la Paz No. 2530
Sector Juárez
Guadalajara, Jal.
Tel: (3) 615-0295

ANIERM Hermosillo
Avda. Serdán No. 20-1
Edif. Seguros del Pacífico
Hermosillo, Son.
Tel: (62) 13-3839, 14-3671

ANIERM Mérida
Calle 21 No. 151-6
Buenavista
Mérida, Yuc.
Tel: (99) 64-656, 60-589

ANIERM Monterrey
San Patricio No. 102
San Francisco
Garza García, NL
Tel: (83) 38-1010

ANIERM Oaxaca
José M. Bocanegra No. 111
Alemán
Oaxaca, Oax.
Tel: (951) 62-622, 63-738

ANIERM Querétaro
Acueducto No. 113
Caleza
Querétaro, Qro.
Tel: (42) 32-0225

ANIERM San Luis Potosí
Avda. Carranza No. 707-2021
San Luis Potosí, SLP
Tel: (48) 143-363, 146-371

ANIERM Toluca
Avda. Juárez Sur No. 204-305
Toluca, Edo. de Méx.
Tel: (72) 14-6744, 15-9088

ANIERM Veracruz
Constitución No. 288
Veracruz, Ver.
Tel: (29) 34-1641, 34-1574

ANIERM Zacatecas
Tacuba No. 123
Zacatecas, Zac.
Tel: (492) 20-032

Comité Empresarial Mexicano para Asuntos Internacionales (CEMAI)
Mexican Business Committee for International Affairs
Homero 527, Piso 7
Col. Polanco
México, DF
Tel: (5) 531-7319, 531-7036

CHAMBERS OF COMMERCE

Confederación de Cámaras Nacionales de Comercio (CONCANACO)
Confederation of National Chambers of Commerce
Balderas No. 144, Piso 3
Col. Centro
06078 México, DF
Tel: (5) 709-1146, 709-1132/8
Fax: (5) 709-1152

Ciudad Juárez Chamber of Commerce
Abraham González y Pino Suárez #311
32000 Cuidad Juárez, Chih.
Tel: (16) 14-1904
Fax: (16) 14-9887

Ciudad Victoria Chamber of Commerce
Juárez 14 y 15 N. 324
87000 Ciudad Victoria, Tamps.
Tel: (131) 20-031, 25-131
Fax: (131) 23-747

Cuernavaca Chamber of Commerce
Morelos Sur 609
62050 Cuernavaca, Mor.
Tel: (73) 12-0031, 18-5701
Fax: (73) 18-5005

Guadalajara Chamber of Commerce
Avda. Vallarta No. 4095
44490 Guadalajara, Jal.
Tel: (3) 647-8331, 647-8081
Fax: (3) 647-9131

Hermosillo Chamber of Commerce
Gastón Madrid 31
83000 Hermosillo, Son.
Tel: (62) 17-3673

León Chamber of Commerce
Edif. Ciel, Piso 3
Blvd. López Mateos y Iguel
37000 León, Gto.
Tel: (417) 42-800, 32-728, 41-467
Fax: (417) 40-397

Mexicali Chamber of Commerce
Calle del Comercio No. 254
21100 Mexicali, BC
Tel: (65) 53-4660
Fax: (65) 54-0372

México, Distrito Federal Chamber of Commerce
Paseo de la Reforma No. 42
06048 México, DF
Tel: (5) 592-2677
Fax: (5) 592-3403

Monterrey Chamber of Commerce
Pte. 250-1P
Edif. de Las Instituciones
64000 Monterrey, NL
Tel: (83) 42-2166, 44-3769, 44-0333
Fax: (83) 45-6700

Puebla Chamber of Commerce
Diag. Def. de la Rep. y Avda. Reforma, Piso 7
72160 Puebla, Pue.
Tel: (22) 48-6435, 48-0998
Fax: (22) 48-3723

San Luis Potosí Chamber of Commerce
Avda. Venustiano Carranza No. 1325
78250 San Luis Potosí, SLP
Tel: (481) 34-966, 34-968
Fax: (481) 34-228

Tijuana Chamber of Commerce
Javier Urrutia entre Villa Juventud y Paseo Tijuana
20200 Tijuana, BC
Tel: (66) 82-8488
Fax: (66) 82-8486

Tlaxcala Chamber of Commerce
Calle Uno Lado Sur
Central Camionera
90000 Tlaxcala, Tlax.
Tel: (246) 21-234, 22-226
Fax: (246) 24-860

NEWSPAPERS

ABC
Editorial Monterrey
Platón Sánchez 411 Sur
64000 Monterrey, NL
Tel: (83) 44-2510, 44-4480, 44-5990

El Día
Avda. Insurgentes Norete 1210
Capukiklan
070370 México, DF
Tel: (5) 546-0456
Fax: (5) 537-6629

El Diario de Guadalajara
Editorial Hispano Mexicana
Calle 14, No. 2550
Zona Industrial
44940 Guadalajara, Jal.
Tel: (3) 612-0043
Fax: (3) 612-0818
Telex: 1774579

El Diario de Monterrey
Periódico El Diario de Monterrey
Eugenio Garza Sada 2245
Col. Roma Sur
64700 Monterrey, NL
Tel: (83) 59-2525, 58-2519
Fax: (83) 59-7380

El Economista
Publicaciones Mercalba
Avda. Coyoacán No. 515
Col. del Valle
03100 México, DF
Tel: (5) 669-1742
Fax: 687-3821, 523-6500

El Financiero
Grupo Editorial SEFI
Lago Bolsena 176
11320 México, DF
Tel: (5) 254-6299
Fax: (5) 255-1881

El Financiero
Lago Bolsena 176
Col. Anahuac
11320 México, DF
Tel: (5) 227-7600 Fax: (5) 227-7634
US subscription address: 2300 S. Broadway, Los Angeles, CA 90007
Tel: [1] (213) 747-7547
Fax: [1] (213) 747-2489

El Heraldo
(Daily; Spanish)
Grupo Editorial SEFI
Lago Bolsena 176
11320 México, DF
Tel: (5) 578-3632
Fax: (5) 578-9824
Telex: 1771219

El Informador
Unión Editorial
Calle Independencia 300
Apdo. 3 bis
44100 Guadalajara, Jal.
Tel: (3) 614-6340
Fax: (3) 614-4653
Telex: 683241

El Nacional
Ignacio Mariscal 25, Piso 3
Col. Tabacalera
Apdo. 446
06030 México, DF
Tel: (5) 535-3074
Fax: (5) 705-5615

RADIO AND TELEVISION

Cablevisión
Dr. Río de la Loza 182
06720 México, DF
Tel: (5) 588-1481 Fax: (5) 588-1546

Cadena Crystal Radio y TV
Montecito 59
Col. Nápoles
03810 México, DF
Tel: (5) 687-8495, 687-8445
Fax: (5) 543-3242

Cámara Nacional de la Industria de Radio y Televisión (CIRT)
Avda. Horacio 1013
Col. Polanco
11550 México, DF
Tel: (5) 545-4165, 726-9909
Fax: (5) 545-6767
Telex: 1777272

Corporación Mexicana de Radiodifusión
Paseo de la Reforma 403, Piso 20
06500 México, DF
Tel: (5) 528-6532, 525-2466
Fax: (5) 207-6503

Dirección de Normas de Radiodifusión
Eugenia 197, Piso 1
Col. Vértiz Narvarte
03020 México, DF
Tel: (5) 590-4372

Dirección General de Radio, Televisión y Cine (RTC)
Atletas 2
Col. Country Club
04220 México, DF
Tel: (5) 544-9692, 544-3768

FM Globo Stereo—Stereorey
Frecuencia Modulada Mexicana
Mariano Escobedo No. 532
Col. Anzures
11590 México, DF
Tel: (5) 203-4120, 203-4520
Fax: (5) 203-4574

AD AGENCIES

Bozell S.A. de C.V.
Paseo de la Reforma 106, C.V.
Lomas de Chapultepec
11000 Mexico, DF
Tel: (5) 724-3500
Fax: (5) 202-7260, 540-5724

Grey Mexico
Horacio No. 1844
2nd & 6th Fls.
Esq. Periferico
Col Polanco Reforma
11550 Mexico, DF

J. Walter Thompson de Mexico S.A. Ejercito Ejercito Nacional No. 519
Colonia Granada
Mexico, DF
11520 Mexico
Tel: (5) 729-4000
Fax: (5) 5454048
Telex: 72681

Latin Ad, Inc.
Vasquez de Mella 421-11
Mexico, D.F. 5
Tel: (5) 280-1283

Leo Burnett S.A. De C.V.
Bosque de Duraznos 65-8P
Bosques de las Lomas
11700 Mexico
Tel: (5) 596-6188
Fax: (5) 596-6248
Telex: 01774278

Lowe & Partners/SMS DE Mexico, S.A. DE C.V.
Lafayette 88
11590 Mexico
Tel: (5) 628-0200
Fax: (5) 255-3755

Nazca S&S
Bosque de Ciruelos 194
Bosque de las Lomas
DF 11700 Mexico, DF
Tel: (5) 245-1133
Fax: (5) 596-2615

Young & Rubicam, S.A. DE C.V.
Leibnitz #13
Colonia Polanco
5 Mexico DF
Tel: (5) 2503200
Fax: (5) 2500862

INTERNET ADDRESSES

Usenet group(s):
bit.listserv.mexico-l
soc.culture.mexican
soc.culture.mexico

Documents on Mexican Politics
http://daisy.uwaterloo.ca/~alopez-o/polind.html

Mexico's Index
http://www.trace-sc.com/

Welcome to Mexico
http://lanic.utexas.edu/la/Mexico/

NAFTA Agreement Online
http://the-tech.mit.edu/Bulletins/nafta.html

Frequently Asked Questions from soc.culture.mexican
http://www.public.iastate.edu/~rjsalvad/scmfaq/faqindex.html

Morocco

Kingdom of Morocco

Economy

Overview

The Moroccan economy is becoming increasingly diversified. Morocco has the largest phosphate reserves in the world, as well as significant amounts of copper, fluorine, lead, barite, iron, and anthracite. It has a varied agricultural sector (including fishing), a thriving tourist industry, a growing manufacturing sector (especially in clothing), and considerable inflows of funds from Moroccans overseas. The clothing sector, in particular, has shown consistently strong growth over the last few years as foreign companies establish large-scale operations for exporting to Europe. The government has reduced its role in the economy, and nearly all sectors have grown rapidly as a result.

Trade

Morocco exports 39.6 billion dirham (US$4.7 billion) annually in food and beverages, semi-processed goods, consumer goods, and phosphates. Major markets include the countries of the European Union, India, Japan, and the United States. Together, these countries import about 64 billion dirham (US$7.6 billion) in goods from Morocco. The European Union, the US, Canada, and Japan are Morocco's major suppliers. Foreign trade continues to increase as Morocco expands its industrial base, produces more competitive products, and continues to develop and maintain good relations with many of its trading partners.

Sectors

Agriculture Agriculture is a dominant part of the Moroccan economy. It generates between 15 and 20 percent of GDP (depending on the harvest), and employs about 50 percent of the work force. Morocco's chief crops include barley, wheat, citrus, fruits, olives, and vegetables, as well as wine and livestock. Fishing also plays a critical role in the country's economy. The government has undertaken a major restructuring of this industry, which has already resulted in significantly raised output.

Industry The industrial sector contributes 34 percent of the GDP. Industries are broad based and diverse. They include phosphate mining, manufacturing and handicrafts, construction and public works, and energy. Roughly 15 percent of the work force hold industrial positions.

Services Tourism has dropped in recent years, largely due to a 25 percent decrease in the number of Algerian visitors. About 26 percent of the work force hold jobs in the clothing industry. Clothing is likely to remain particularly strong due to its low labor costs, generally free access to nearby European markets, and a temporary admission system that allows the duty-free import of necessary inputs. Other services are limited primarily to local distribution and personal services.

Trends

Principal growth sectors for the near term include fishing, agriculture, clothing, and mining. The industrial sluggishness of the early 1990s has already begun to turn around as favorable rainfall spurs agroindustry, both domestically and overseas. Electricity generation is also expected to rise sharply in the near future as new thermal generating capacity comes on line. Last year's heavy rainfall will allow increased hydroelectric production and also substantially help agricultural output, 90 percent of which is rain-fed.

At a Glance

THE COUNTRY

Location Northern Africa, bordering the Atlantic Ocean and the Mediterranean Sea, between Algeria and the Western Sahara Terrain.
Terrain Mostly mountains with rich coastal plains and some desert. The northern mountains are subject to earthquakes.
Climate Mediterranean, becoming more extreme in the interior.

THE PEOPLE

Population 28,000,000
Ethnic composition
Arab-Berber 99%
Religious composition
Muslim 98.7%
Christian... 1.1%
Jewish.. 0.2%
Languages spoken Arabic, several Berber dialects, French, Spanish. French is often the language of business and government.
Education and literacy Education now surpasses national defense as the largest item in the government's budget. Schooling is free and compulsory through primary school. Females leave school younger than males. About 61 percent of males are literate, as are only 38 percent of females. Most university students benefit from government stipends.
Labor force
Total:...7,400,000
By occupation: agriculture 50%, services 26%, industry 15%, and other 9%.

COUNTRY FACTS

Political and legal This constitutional monarchy has an independent judicial structure. Supreme court judges are appointed by the king.
Telephone Local and international telephone and telegraph service is available and operated by the government. Knowledge of French or Arabic is essential. International country code: [212]. Selected city codes: Rabat (7), Casablanca (2), Fes (5), Tangier (99).
Transportation Adequate public transportation by air, rail, and bus is available between major cities. The highway system is good, and directions are clearly marked. There are eight international airports. Several large ports handle shipping and passenger traffic.
Environment Overgrazing, timber cutting, and poor soil conservation practices have caused erosion and desertification. Pollution is due to dumping of sewage and industrial wastes into the ocean, inland water sources, and land. Wildlife destruction is widespread, despite strict laws regulating hunting and fishing. Morocco has pledged to enforce its environmental laws more, and has signed several international environmental agreements. Current issues include land degradation/desertification; contamination of water supplies from untreated sewage; siltation of reservoirs; and oil pollution of coastal waters.
Media There are more than five million radios and almost two million televisions. Many daily newspapers are published. Criticizing the monarchy is illegal.
Health Government-supervised public health services are improving, though standards are still low. Life expectancy of males is 66 years; of females, 69 years.

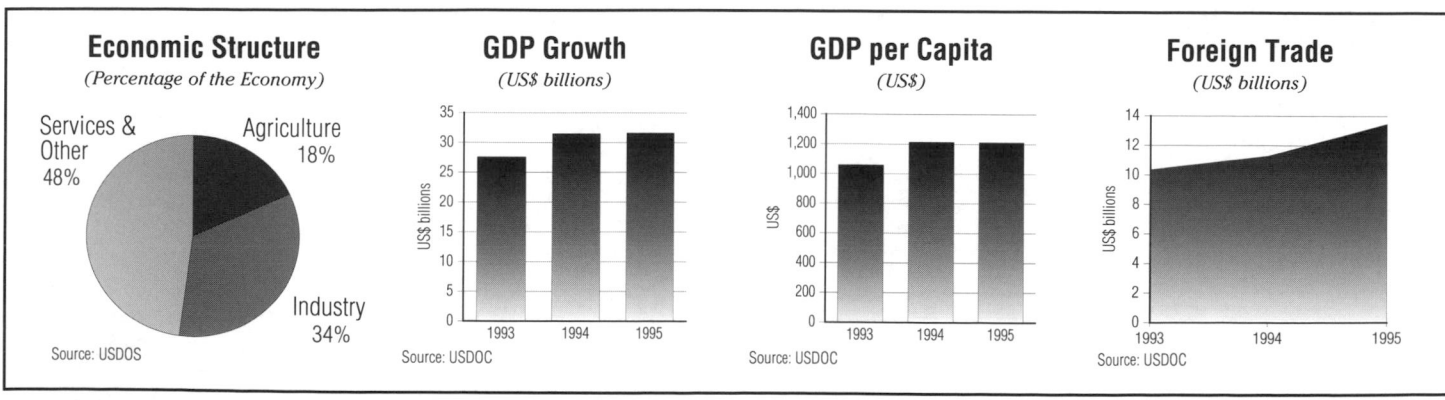

Economic Structure
(Percentage of the Economy)
Services & Other 48%
Agriculture 18%
Industry 34%
Source: USDOS

GDP Growth
(US$ billions)
Source: USDOC

GDP per Capita
(US$)
Source: USDOC

Foreign Trade
(US$ billions)
Source: USDOC

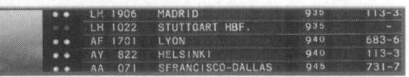

Travelogue

WORKWEEK

Offices Monday-Friday 8:00 am to noon and 2:00 pm to 6:00 pm.

Banks Monday-Friday 8:30 am to 11:30 am and 2:30 pm to 4:30 pm. Friday break lasts from 11:15 am to 3:00 pm for prayers.

Government Monday-Friday 8:30 am to noon and 2:00 pm to 6:30 pm with Friday's break from 11:30 am to 3:00 pm.

Retail Generally open Monday-Friday 8:00 am to 6:00 pm with many shops closed on Fridays. All business hours are shortened in the month of Ramadan, usually 9:00 am to 3:00 pm, and during summer months.

HOLIDAYS

Holidays 1996
January 1 New Year's Day
January 11 Independence Proclamation
March 3 Throne Day
February 21-22 Aid El Fitr*
May 1 Labor Day
May 23 National Holiday
April 29-30 Aid El Adha*
May 19 Muslim New Year*
July 9 King's Birthday
July 28 Prophet's Birthday
August 14 Oued Eddahab Day
November 6 Green March Day
November 18 Independence Day.
*Dates are based on a lunar calendar and vary each year.

VISA AND PASSPORT

Foreigners visiting Morocco need a valid passport. Visas are not required of foreigners for visits of up to three months except for nationals of Benelux countries and South Africa. All currency or traveler's checks must be declared upon entry.

DEPARTURE FORMALITIES

It is illegal to export Moroccan dirhams.

IMMUNIZATION

There are no immunization requirements for visitors to Morocco.

TIPPING

Restaurant waiters in Morocco generally expect to be tipped. Tips vary from 10 percent in more expensive restaurants to a few dirham in cafes, depending on the amount of the bill. Porters, guides, and the like may perform unsolicited services to obtain a tip; for some it is a way to make a living. Taxi drivers should not be tipped.

CRIME

Morocco's crime rate is moderately high in urban areas. Tourists are often targets for assaults, muggings, thefts, pickpocketings, and scams of all sorts. Common scams include falsifying credit-card vouchers and substituting inferior rugs for the rugs purchased by a traveler. It is common for unemployed Moroccans to approach tourists offering service as guides. Traveling alone in the Rif mountain area is risky.

INFRASTRUCTURE

Morocco has well-developed and adequate air, rail, bus, highway, hotel, and telecommunication networks.

NATIONAL TOURIST OFFICE

Office National Marocain du Tourisme
22 Ave d' Alger
Rabat
Tel: (7) 730562

COMMUNICATIONS

Telephones Telephone service in Morocco is improving. Direct dialing to many foreign countries is available but can be expensive. Local calls can be difficult due to noisy connections. There are phone offices in most cities and public phone booths in larger cities. Phone cards are becoming more popular and are available at phone offices, tobacco shops, and newsstands. Phone directories are in French.

Fax Telex facilities are available for communication to most parts of the world. Main post office branches have telex and telegraph services, few have fax capability. Many larger hotels offer fax service at a substantial markup.

Post office The postal system is slow but fairly reliable. Post offices are marked by new colorful La Poste signs (al-barid in Arabic). Stamps can also be purchased at tobacco shops and newsstands.

BEST TRAVEL BOOKS

Fodor's Foreign Guides, Morocco.
Culture Shock, A Guide to Customs and Etiquette, Morocco.
Morocco, Algeria & Tunisia: A Travel Survival Kit, Lonely Planet Publications All the information travelers need. 486 pages.
Morocco, Insight Pocket Guides, Packed full of information and color photographs.
North African Handbook. The ideal practical guide. Updated annually.

USEFUL TELEPHONE NUMBERS

If you are calling from outside Morocco you will need to add the country code [212] and any other international dialing requirements from within your country.

- Operator 10
- International Operator 12
- Directory Assistance 16
- Ambulance, Fire 15
- Police 19

Casablanca
- Tourist Information .... (2) 324199
- Royal Air Maroc .... (2) 912000
- Train Station .... (2) 223011
- Avis .... (2) 312424
- Hertz .... (2) 312223
- Taxi .... (2) 255030
- Holiday Inn .... (2) 294949

Rabat
- Tourist Information .... (7) 730562
- Train Station .... (7) 767353
- Avis .... (7) 767503
- Hertz .... (7) 709227
- Rabat Hyatt Regency .... (7) 712347
- La Tour Hassan .... (7) 721401

Credit Card Services
Lost or stolen credit cards (call collect to the US, regardless of which country the card was issued in).
- Amex .... [1] (919) 333-3211
- Diner's Club .... [1] (303) 799-1504
- MasterCard .... [1] (314) 275-6690
- Visa .... [1] (410) 581-7931

Foreign Trade

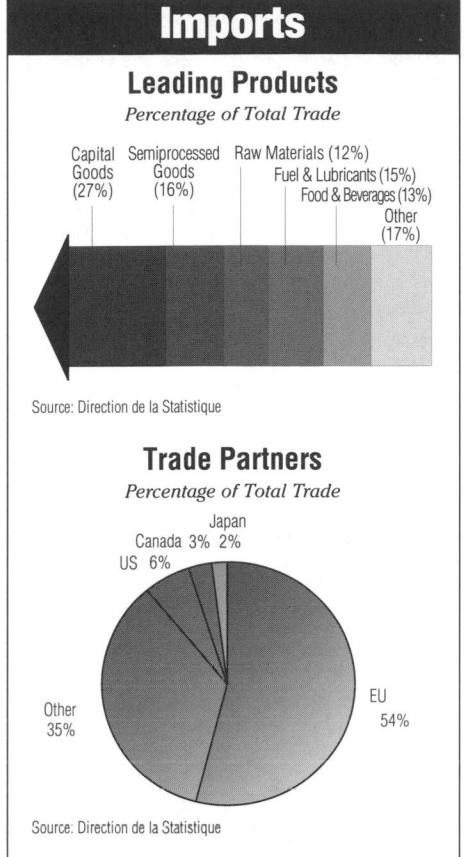

Imports

Leading Products
Percentage of Total Trade

Capital Goods (27%)
Semiprocessed Goods (16%)
Raw Materials (12%)
Fuel & Lubricants (15%)
Food & Beverages (13%)
Other (17%)

Source: Direction de la Statistique

Trade Partners
Percentage of Total Trade

Japan 2%
Canada 3%
US 6%
Other 35%
EU 54%

Source: Direction de la Statistique

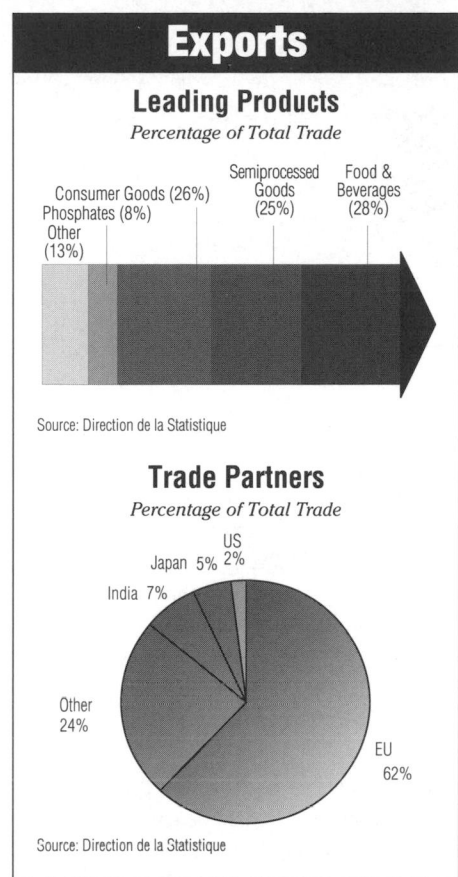

Exports

Leading Products
Percentage of Total Trade

Consumer Goods (26%)
Phosphates (8%)
Other (13%)
Semiprocessed Goods (25%)
Food & Beverages (28%)

Source: Direction de la Statistique

Trade Partners
Percentage of Total Trade

US 2%
Japan 5%
India 7%
Other 24%
EU 62%

Source: Direction de la Statistique

Opportunities

FOR IMPORTING TO MOROCCO
- capital and consumer goods
- fuel and lubricants
- raw materials, semiprocessed goods

FOR EXPORTING FROM MOROCCO
- beverages, fruits, vegetables and other food
- phosphate acid, fertilizers
- semiprocessed foods

GROWTH SECTORS
- agriculture
- clothing
- manufacturing
- tourist

Trade News

RULES AND REGULATIONS
- **Import licenses** The granting of an import license is a lengthy process, requiring approval from each concerned sector, though this process continues to be liberalized.
- **Tariffs and import taxes** Customs formalities have been relaxed so most products can now be imported. Most imports are subject to customs duties at rates up to a maximum of 35 percent of the value of the items imported. In addition, a surcharge of 12.5 percent is also payable.
- **Customs duties** For food and agricultural products, customs duties normally range between zero and 35 percent, an exception is meat and selected dairy products, whose tariffs were recently increased significantly to replace a licensing requirement.

Legal

Legal System
Morocco has a code and statute system based on French law favoring, for the most part, trade and investment.

Intellectual Property Rights
Patents and trademarks Morocco has a relatively complete regulatory and legislative system for patent protection. Patents must be filed in both Casablanca and Tangier and may be issued from the Moroccan patent office or the European patent office in Munich. Trademarks must be filed in both Casablanca and Tangier for complete protection.

Copyrights Protection for copyright lasts the life of the author plus 50 years. No registration is needed to invoke these rights. Computer software is not specifically covered and software piracy is widespread.

Business Registration
Corporations and limited liability companies must register with the Commerce Registry, Moroccan taxation authority, and the exchange control office. The registration will be published in a daily newspaper. Branch offices, which are not considered separate legal entities, are appropriate for temporary business and need not be registered.

Labor
Labor laws tend to be restrictive of employees. Workers are free to form and join unions. The right to bargain collectively exists but the laws governing this right are not highly developed and are poorly enforced. The right to strike is believed to exist, although the government has called this right into question. Minimum wage laws are not enforced in the informal sector. Child labor laws are strictly enforced; children may not legally be employed before age 12. From age 12 to 16 special regulations govern their employment. Laws set minimums for health and safety conditions in the workplace.

Legal Matters

LEGAL BRIEFS
- **Business entities** Corporations, limited liability companies, and branch offices are all widely used. Partnerships and joint ventures are also alternatives for investors.
- **Maximum workweek** The law provides a maximum 48-hour workweek at no more than 10 hours per day. Paid public and annual holidays are provided as well as premium overtime pay. These laws are observed unevenly in the informal sector.
- **Employee right to work** Prior notice is required for dismissal of employees in all cases.
- **Legal environment** Morocco has a poor regulatory environment. The legal system is slow and inefficient and believed to be biased against foreign investors. Corruption is considered widespread.
- **International agreements** Morocco is a member of: WIPO, New York Convention on the Recognition and Enforcement of Foreign Arbitral Awards, Berne Convention, and Paris Convention.
- **Notaries** Notaries prepare and authenticate documents. Notarized documentation is required for establishing corporations but not limited liability ventures.

LEGAL CONTACTS
Mohamed Mehdi Salmouni-Zerhouni
Residence Ibn Batouta-Tour D
Place Prince Sidi Mohamed
(Ex P. Semard)
20300 Casablanca
Tel: (2) 24-24-48, 24-96-42
Fax: (2) 24-20-83

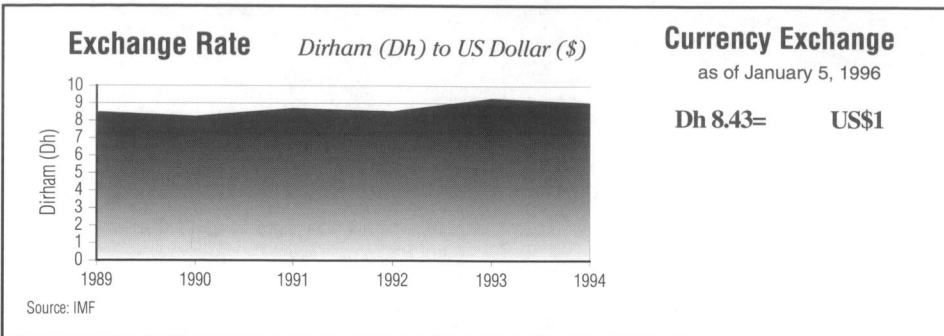

Exchange Rate *Dirham (Dh) to US Dollar ($)*

Source: IMF

Currency Exchange
as of January 5, 1996

Dh 8.43=   US$1

Currency

The currency of Morocco is the Moroccan dirham, represented by the international symbol Dh, and its principal subdivision is 100 centimes.

Foreign Exchange

Exchange control is administered by the exchange office, under the Ministry of Finance. All purchases and sales of foreign currency are centralized in the Bank of Al-Maghrib; however, authority to buy and sell foreign exchange has been delegated to the banking system, which carries out transactions upon the presentation of appropriate documentation, such as an invoice to pay for imports. Forward exchanges for imports and exports may be transacted in any foreign currency for maturity periods ranging from a minimum of one month to a maximum of 12 months.

Capital Transfers

Nonresidents may open accounts in foreign currency or convertible dirhams with certain restrictions outlined by the exchange office. Authorized banks are allowed to settle payments related to commercial transactions accompanied by the relevant documents without the authorization of the Exchange Office. Residents must repatriate foreign exchange receipts accrued from all non-commercial claims and surrender them to an authorized bank.

Investment Incentives

Direct incentives are not readily available, although investors may receive individually negotiated incentives from the government to pursue policies deemed desirable. Companies that export or locate in less developed regions of the country may receive tax breaks and customs exemptions.

Investment Restrictions

There are no foreign investor performance requirements. There are no requirements or incentives regarding local value-added, local equity, substitution of imports, or employment of Moroccan workers, although the government may take these factors into account in deciding whether to approve investments under the various sectoral codes.

TAXATION

Taxation requires sophisticated knowledge of complex rules and regulations specific to each country. The information presented here is from the Ernst & Young Corporate Tax Guide and Directory, available from the Ernst & Young accounting office in your country, or from:

Ernst & Young
44, rue Mohamed Smiha
Casablanca
Morocco
Tel: (2) 30-25-42, 30-37-86
Fax: (2) 31-76-88

At a Glance

Corporate Income Tax Rate (%) (a)	36
Capital Gains Tax Rate (%) (a)(b)	36
Branch Tax Rate (%) (a)	36
Withholding Tax (%)	
Dividends (c)	15
Interest (d)(e)	20/30

Royalties, Scientific Know-how Payments, and Technical Assistance Fees (f)	10
Wages and Indemnities Paid to Nonpermanent Employees (g)	45
Rent on Equipment Used in Morocco (f)	10
Branch Remittance Tax	15
Net Operating Losses (Years)	
Carryback	0
Carryforward	4

(a) A national solidarity tax is also imposed.
(b) Rate decreases depending on the length of time the asset was held.
(c) Final Tax. Certain dividends may be exempt from withholding.
(d) Applies to interest paid to residents on term deposits, certificates of deposit, and loans made through credit or banking institutions. The rate is 20% for individuals who are identified and 30% for unidentified individuals and for societies (corporations, building societies, cooperatives and limited liability companies). The amount of the tax may be credited by a recipient that is identified against its corporate income tax.
(e) A 10% final tax is imposed on interest payments to nonresidents on loans or other fixed interest claims.
(f) Final tax applicable only to nonresidents.
(g) Applies only to payments to persons who are not salaried employees and do not hold a special function in the company paying the indemnities. The rate is 17% for teachers.

Money Matters

BITS AND PIECES

- **Exchange rates** Exchange rates for the dirham are tied to a basket of hard currencies weighted according to Moroccan foreign trade.
- **Private ownership** Private ownership is permitted in most sectors, except public utilities, rail and air transportation, and phosphate mining. Apart from these few sectors reserved for the state, private entities, both domestic and foreign, may freely establish, acquire, and dispose of interests in business enterprises.
- **Payments** Payments between Morocco and the rest of the world may be made in any currency quoted by Bank Al-Maghrib or through foreign accounts in convertible dirhams or foreign currency accounts opened in Moroccan banks in the name of foreign correspondents.
- **Foreign exchange markets** Clearing operations between banks are not permitted; thus, no foreign exchange market exists in Morocco.
- **Foreign currency accounts in the name of foreign nationals** These accounts may be maintained by natural or juridical persons of foreign nationality, either residents or nonresidents, as well as by Moroccan nationals residing abroad. These accounts are freely credited with transfers from abroad, with foreign bank notes or other means of payments, and with foreign currency withdrawn from Bank Al-Maghrib.
- **Gold** Residents may buy, hold, and sell gold coins in Morocco for collection or investment purposes. Imports of gold are subject to authorization from the Directorate of Customs and Indirect Taxes Administration. Exports of gold are prohibited.

BANKS

Bank of Morocco
277, Avenue Mohammed V
POB 445
Rabat
Tel: (7) 76-30-09 Telex: 31006

Banque Centrale Populaire
101 Boulevard Mohammed Zerktouni
Casablanca
Tel: (2) 20-25-33 Fax: (2) 22-26-99

Banque Commerciale du Maroc
2, Boulevard Moulay Youssef
Casablanca
Tel: (2) 22-41-69 Fax: (2) 22-38-25

Banque Marocaine du Commerce Exterieur
140, Boulevard Hassan II
Casablanca
Tel: (2) 20-00-60 Fax: (2) 20-04-90

Banque Marocaine pour le Commerce et l'Industrie
26, Place Mohammed V
Casablanca
Tel: (2) 22-41-61 Fax: (2) 26-57-57

Citibank-Maghreb
52, Avenue Hassan II
Casablanca
Tel: (2) 22-41-68 Fax: (2) 27-54-34

Credit du Maroc
48-58 Boulevard Mohammed V
Casablanca
Tel: (2) 22-41-42 Fax: (2) 27-71-27

Societe Generale Marocaine de Banques
55 Boulevard Abdelmoumen
Casablanca
Tel: (2) 27-92-69 Fax: (2) 26-28-51

Wafabank
163, Avenue Hassan II
Casablanca
Tel: (2) 22-41-05 Fax: (2) 26-62-02

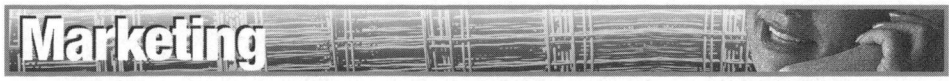

Overview

While General George S. Patton was reviewing Moroccan troops, he was asked what he thought of the country. Reportedly he replied, "It's wonderful; a combination of Hollywood and the Bible." Current firms with business in Morocco take a slightly more pragmatic view. Morocco enjoys a healthy commercial environment, applying a growing spirit of entrepreneurship to a generally pragmatic monarchy and population. There is a growing middle class anxious for consumer goods. New mini-shopping malls are spreading, satellite dishes are sprouting on rooftops, and consumer market turnover is encouraging.

Distribution and Agents

Morocco's market has ample room for overseas branch office operations, joint venture manufacturers, and franchises. Foreign goods are generally imported through Casablanca by companies that distribute either directly to the public or to other wholesalers, distributors, or retailers. Expect a substantial markup in price. Commission agents may also import goods; add at least five percent to the price for this service. Local manufacturers send products directly to retailers, wholesalers and distributors, which helps maintain competitive pricing. Most wholesale and retail enterprises are family-run, with ties reaching back for generations. Wise investors will attempt to utilize these unshakable connections by establishing connections with a local agent or partner. All foreign manufacturers are represented either through a branch office or agent/distributors who import, install, and service equipment. Registered agents tend to form long-term relationships with overseas manufacturers, making contracts with their principals so local importers provide in-bond warehousing.

Advertising

Most advertising agencies in Morocco do not provide all the services a sophisticated investor expects, although media advertising is well-developed. Commercial time is available on the government and private television channels but prohibited on the government-owned radio, though other radio frequencies from Tangier reach the entire Maghreb. Direct mail is also becoming more common; one new firm offers aerial-banner advertising.

Marketing in Morocco

MARKETING TIPS

- **Selling techniques** Most local distributors expect their foreign suppliers to provide advertising and promotional support, especially when the line is new. Promotional material and technical documentation should be in clearly written French. Simple instructions, product-use displays, sample handouts, and personal visits are vital to sales success here. Prices are a key selling factor.
- **Growing industry** The number of fast food franchises is expected to triple over the next three years.
- **Publications** French newspapers and magazines have the largest readership and contain the most advertisements. In addition, *La Vie Economique* and *l'Economiste* are widely read business weeklies. Other trade and industry journals are published by local industry groups.
- **Service and customer support** Agents and distributors are accustomed to receiving the following: back-up service through manufacturer-trained local technicians and engineers; user-oriented products suited for local conditions; partnership agreements which provide expertise on local trading conditions; product information published in French; and shared costs for local and factory technical training programs.

MARKET RESEARCH CONTACTS

Creargie Maroc
106, Rue Abderrahmane Sahraoui
Casablanca
Tel: (2) 27-96-57 Fax: (2) 29-36-66

Kilmer Investments
205, Rue Beni Garfati-Les Ambassadeurs
Rabat
Tel: (7) 73-09-88 Fax: (7) 73-09-88

Multitech Morocco
12, Place des Alaouites
Rabat
Tel: (7) 70-68-68 Fax: (7) 70-40-86

Business Culture

Greetings and Courtesies

Arabic is the preferred language here, though French is also widely spoken. English is gaining in popularity, but the first two languages lend a certain formality to Moroccan greetings and local businesspeople prefer to use them. International sophisticates of both genders brush cheeks or kiss; close friends may exchange several kisses on both cheeks. Most rural Moroccans will shake hands (always the right, or both). Greetings usually include asking about each other's health and that of their families.

Business Ethic and Framework

Muslims view a gradual approach and lengthy discussion as a path to ensure fairness to all concerned. Though this view can try a visitor's patience, once all terms are settled and the contracts drawn, they will be honored as a matter of near-sacred trust. Appointments are a mark of respect. Avoid setting appointments on Friday, the Muslim holy day.

Women

A woman's place in the world of Islam depends almost solely on the dictates of her husband at home; in public, she is all but hidden in robes. The traditional veil has largely disappeared in the cities, though some rural women maintain the custom. These restrictions are less prevalent in Morocco. In urban areas women usually receive more education than their rural counterparts, and may work outside the home.

Meetings

Meetings tend to be slow-paced, beginning with lengthy amenities and only gradually approaching the stated purpose. Any urgency is regarded as indicating uncertainty and therefore identifies an undesirable partner. Those familiar with the game will find chess a reasonable comparison, with one exception: the chess player only cares for winning, while Moroccans will be content with coming out slightly ahead of their visitor.

Cultural Cautions

DO'S

- The tap water is generally good, but there is a risk of illness. Bottled water is readily available.
- At a host's home, eat with the fingers of the right hand; in a restaurant, eat from the section of the dish directly in front of you.

DON'TS

- Compliments about a specific object in a host's home or office may result in being presented with the object.
- Pointing at people, especially with the sole of the foot, is rude here.
- Traditional Moroccans do not cross their legs.
- Consult a calendar before scheduling a visit; the ninth lunar month, Ramadan, means little or no business during the whole month.

CUSTOMS

- Social visits usually last several hours, and meals consist of several courses consumed slowly.
- Have one side of your business cards translated into Arabic or French; present them at the end of formal introductions.
- Morocco's business attire is more relaxed than many Muslim countries, especially in the cities. Conservative Western business dress is becoming more common. Covering the head to limit water loss is always a good idea in this climate.

NEGOTIATIONS

- Visitors with Western senses of time will characterize Moroccan negotiations as endless. Moroccans are extraordinarily fond of haggling at a leisurely pace, partly a ploy to wear down their opponent's resistance.
- A cash-basis policy is preferable until trust is established on both sides.

GOVERNMENT AGENCIES

Customs and Indirect Taxes Administration
Place Mohammed V
Casablanca
Tel: (2) 22-41-16
Fax: (2) 26-07-06

Exchange Office
Place Moulay Hassan
Rabat
Tel: (7) 73-19-12
Fax: (7) 72-20-74

Ministry of External Trade, External Investment & Handicrafts
63, Avenue Moulay Youssef
10 000 Rabat
Tel: (7) 70-33-63
Fax: (7) 73-50-23

Ministry of Finance
Ancien Quartier Administratif
Rabat
Tel: (7) 76-09-43
Fax: (7) 76-40-81

Ministry of Health
335, Avenue Mohommad V
BP 812, Mechanar
Rabat
Tel: (7) 76-11-21
Fax: (7) 76-49-55

Ministry of Interior and Information
Quartier Administratif
Rabat
Tel: (7) 76-47-18
Fax: (7) 76-20-56, 76-87-55

Ministry of Trade and Industry
Quartier des Ministeres
Rabat-Chellah
Tel: (7) 76-18-78
Fax: (7) 76-01-92

Ministry of Trade and Industry
Avenue Tadla Aviation
Mabella, Rabat
Tel: (7) 75-15-32
Fax: (7) 75-17-39

Ministry of Transportation
Rue Maa al Ainaine
Casier Officiel
Rabat-Chellah
Tel: (7) 77-34-86
Fax: (7) 77-95-25

Office Cherifien des Phosphates
Route d'El Jadida
Casablanca
Tel: (2) 23-01-25
Fax: (2) 23-06-35

Office National de l'Eau Potable
6, Bis Rue Patrice Lumumba
Rabat-Chellah, Casablanca
Tel: (7) 72-65-15
Fax: (7) 73-13-55

Office National de l'Electricite
65, Rue Othman Ben Affane
Casablanca
Tel: (2) 22-41-65 Fax: (2) 22-00-38

Office National des Chemins de Fer
8, Zankat El Ghafiki
Rabat
Tel: (7) 77-45-75
Fax: (7) 77-43-76

Office National des Postes & Telecommunications
6, Rue Oqbah
Rabat
Tel: (7) 70-64-64 Fax: (7) 702022

Statistics Direction
Boulevard Maa El Aynain
Agdal-Rabat
Tel: (7) 77-36-06
Fax: (7) 77-30-42

WORLD TRADE CENTER

World Trade Center
c/o Sheraton Casablanca Hotel
100, Avenue de l'Armee Royale
Casablanca
Tel: (2) 31-78-78
Fax: (2) 31-51-36

BUSINESS AND TRADE ORGANIZATIONS

American Chamber of Commerce
18, Rue Colbert
Casablanca
Tel: (2) 31-14-48 Fax: (2) 31-66-07

Chambre de Commerce et d'Industrie de Casablanca
98, Boulevard Mohammed V
Casablanca
Tel: (2) 26-84-36
Fax: (2) 26-43-27

Association des Fabricants d'Aliments Composes
Feed Manufacturers Association, Grain & Feed Imports
c/o INAM
149/151 Route de Ouled Ziane
Casablanca (05)
Tel: (2) 24-28-08, 24-81-88
Fax: (2) 40-35-36

Complexe Textile de Fès
(Textile Complex of Fez)
Quartier Sidi Brahim, Route de Sefrou
BP 2267
Fes
Tel: (6) 413-09
Telex: 51606

Confederation Generale Economique Marocaine
23, Rue Mohamed Abdouh
Casablanca
Tel: (2) 25-26-96 Fax: (2) 25-38-39

Groupement Professionnel des Banques
71, Avenue de l'Armee Royale
Casablanca
Tel: (2) 31-16-24
Fax: (2) 31-49-03

Moroccan Trade and Industry Chamber Federation
6, Rue Arfoud Hassan
Rabat
Tel: (7) 76-70-51
Fax: (7) 76-70-76

Office National de l'Electricité
(National Electricity Bureau)
65 Rue Aspirant Lafuente
BP 13498
Casablanca 201 40
Tel: (2) 22-41-65
Fax: (2) 22-00-38

Office National Interprofessionel des Cereales & Legumineuses
(Grains, Pulses, Rice, Tenders, Government)
3, Avenue Moulay El Hassan
Rabat
Tel: (7) 70-13-66
Fax: (7) 70-13-93

Societe d'Exploitation des Produits Oleagineux
2, Rue Caporal Corbi
Casablanca (05)
Tel: (2) 35-43-29
Fax: (2) 35-40-97

MARKET RESEARCH FIRMS

M.T.D.S.
43, Rue Oukaimeden, No. 2
Rabat-Agdal
Tel: (7) 67-48-61
Fax: (7) 67-48-62

O.T.I. Maghreb
95, Boulevard El Massira Khadra
Casablanca
Tel: (2) 23-37-22
Fax: (2) 25-40-11

> ### REMEMBER
> • When you telephone (or fax) to Morocco from another country you must always include the country code [212] before the numbers given.
> • When you send mail to Morocco, be sure to write MOROCCO in capital letters on its own line below the address given.

AD AGENCY

Klem Euro RSCG
25 Blvd Mohamed Abdouh
Casablanca2
Tel: (2) 25-46-17/18
Fax: (2) 23-14-22

NEWSPAPERS

Al-Bayane (The Manifesto)
62 Blvd de la Gironde
BP 13152
Casablanca
Tel: (2) 30-76-66

Le Matin du Sahara
88 Blvd Muhammad V
Casablanca
Tel: (2) 26-88-60
Fax: (2) 26-29-69

PERIODICALS

Bulletin Immensely de la Chambre de Commerce et d'Industrie de la Waylay du Grand Casablanca
98 Blvd. Muhammad V
BP 423
Casablanca
Tel: (2) 26-43-27

Le Courrier Economique
28 Ave des Forces Armees Royales
Casablanca
Tel: (2) 27-10-94

La Vie Economique
5 Blvd ben Yaciner
Casablanca
Tel: (2) 30-73-32
Fax: (2) 30-45-42

La Vie Industrielle et Agricole
142 Blvd Muhammad V
Casablanca
Tel: (2) 27-44-07

Al-Maghribi
113 Ave Allal ben Abdallah
Rabat
Tel: (7) 68139

Le Journal de Tanger
11 Ave Moulay abd ad-Aziz
BP 420
Tangier
Tel: (9) 40090

RADIO AND TELEVISION

Radiodiffusion Television Marocaine
1 Zenkat el-Brihi
BP 1042
Rabat
Tel: (7) 64951
Telex: 31010

Radio Mediterranee Internationale
3 et 5 rue Emsallah
BP 2055
Tangier
Tel/Fax: (9) 3636

INTERNET ADDRESSES

Usenet group(s):
soc.culture.arabic

Morocco Page
http://www.sas.upenn.edu/African_Studies/Country_Specific/Morocco.html

City Net - Morocco
http://www.city.net/countries/morocco/

Nepal

Kingdom of Nepal

Economy

Overview

Although Nepal ranks as an economically poor country, rich resources such as hydroelectric power, limited but fertile agricultural land, and a bounty of crops advance its overall international viability. Already, it has shown strong growth patterns in the past few years. Growth has been broad-based with strong performances in small industries, construction, transportation, and financial services. Inflation is rising, but remains below 10 percent. Much of this growth is due to the government's decreasing role in the economy. In particular, subsidies have been reduced or eliminated for a number of key products, tax rates have been reduced, and the privatization of industries has been ongoing at a steady pace. If the government continues its present course, Nepal's economy should continue its strong growth pattern.

Trade

Nepal's commercial life is dominated by its southern neighbor, India. Cotton fabrics, medicines, and vehicles and spare parts are the top three imports from India. Nepal does not yet export a large percentage of its product; exports are only about 20 percent of its imports. However, as privatization continues, and its products become more competitive, exports should increase accordingly.

Sectors

Agriculture The rise in agricultural output has led Nepal's economic growth over the past couple of years. Nepal has seen record food, cash crop, and fruit harvests in the past year, at an increase of almost eight percent. Agriculture remains the largest single sector but accounts for about 60 percent of GDP, compared to 66 percent in 1980.

Industry Industry only accounts for about 15 percent of GDP, with products including cigarettes, garments, soap, matches, bricks, sugar, lumber, jute, hydroelectric power, and cement. A great deal of progress has been made in exploiting Nepal's major resources—namely its hydroelectric potential. Several hydroelectric projects have been completed and further development is underway around the rivers flowing south through the Himalayas to the plains. Nepal and India have joint irrigation-hydroelectric projects on the Kosi, Trisuli, and Gandaki Rivers.

Services While the formation of joint ventures in the banking and financial services sectors has been greatly liberalized, foreign banks are still effectively prohibited from establishing branch operations in the country. This is having a chilling effect on the development of many other financial service industries. The tourism industry is strong, however, and wholesale and retail operations have shown tremendous growth in recent years.

Trends

Foreign trade, hotels, and restaurants have had the most growth over the past few years. Together, these new sectors comprise 11 percent of the GDP, up from four percent just three years ago. Manufacturing and construction are also showing healthy gains. If the government's current policies continue, virtually all of Nepal's economy should show strong growth in the near term.

At a Glance

THE COUNTRY

Location Central Asia on the southern slopes of the Himalayan Mountains, bordered by India and the Tibetan region of China.
Terrain Flat and fertile in the south; the lower Himalayas form the hill country in the center; and the high Himalayas form the border with Tibet in the north. Nepal has eight of the world's 10 highest peaks.
Climate Ranges from subtropical in the south to cool summers and severe winters in the northern mountains.

THE PEOPLE

Population 19,000,000
Ethnic composition Brahmans, Chetris, Gurungs, Magars, Tamangs, Newars, Bhotias, Rais, Limbus, Sherpas.
Religious composition
Hindu 89.5%
Buddhist... 5.3%
Islamic.. 2.6%
Others.. 2.6%
Languages spoken Nepali and more than 12 others, plus 30 major dialects.
Education and literacy A free countrywide primary education system is under development. Five years of schooling are compulsory. Literacy is estimated at 37.6 percent for males; 13.2 percent for females.
Labor force
Total:...8,500,000
By occupation: agriculture 91.1%, industry 2%, services 5%, and other 1.9%.

COUNTRY FACTS

Political and legal In this monarchy, the judiciary is legally independent of the executive and legislative branches, but it generally doesn't challenge the executive. Nepal's legal system is based on Hindu legal concepts and English common law. Nepal has not accepted compulsory International Court of Justice jurisdiction.
Telephone The government-operated telephone service is adequate. International country code: [977]. Selected city codes: Kathmandu (1)
Transportation The highway network is expanding, currently there are over 7,000 kilometers of highways. There are 37 airports.
Environment Overpopulation is already straining the resources of the middle hill areas. Forest reserves have been depleted for crop land, fuel, and fodder, contributing to land erosion and flooding. The government has created a policy for forestation and forestry management reform. Current issues include deforestation and soil erosion, and air and water pollution.
Media There are hundreds of small, privately owned newspapers. All press restrictions have been eliminated. Television broadcasts are 23 hours a week. There are 670,000 radios and 40,000 television sets.
Health Most health services are in the Katmandu Valley, and in short supply elsewhere. Epidemics are frequent. Infant mortality rates are high at 90 deaths per 1,000 births. Life expectancy of males is 54.4 years; of females, 51.6 years.

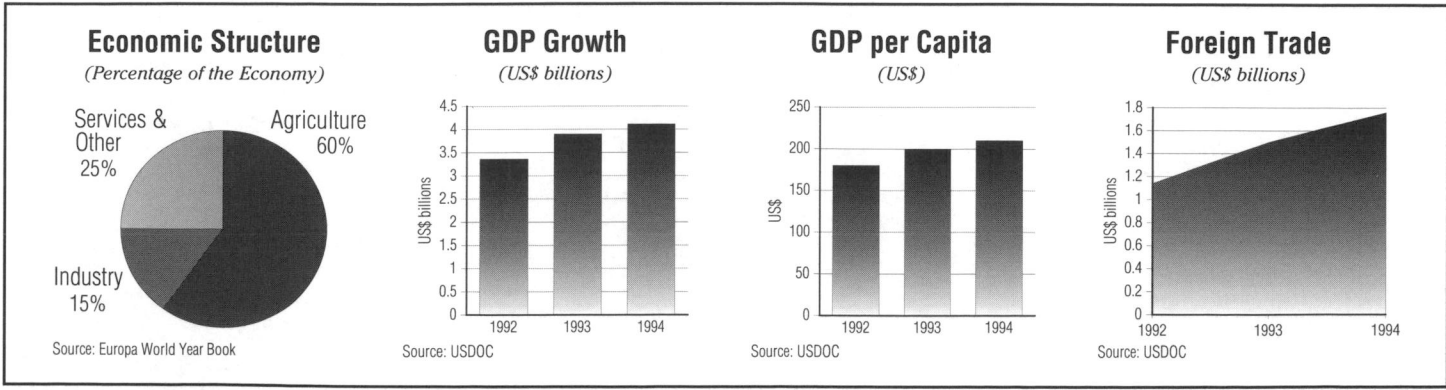

Economic Structure
(Percentage of the Economy)

Services & Other 25%
Agriculture 60%
Industry 15%

Source: Europa World Year Book

GDP Growth
(US$ billions)

Source: USDOC

GDP per Capita
(US$)

Source: USDOC

Foreign Trade
(US$ billions)

Source: USDOC

Business Travel

LH 1906	MADRID	935	113-3
LH 1022	STUTTGART HBF.	935	-
AF 1701	LYON	940	683-6
AY 822	HELSINKI	940	113-3
AA 071	SFRANCISCO-DALLAS	945	731-7

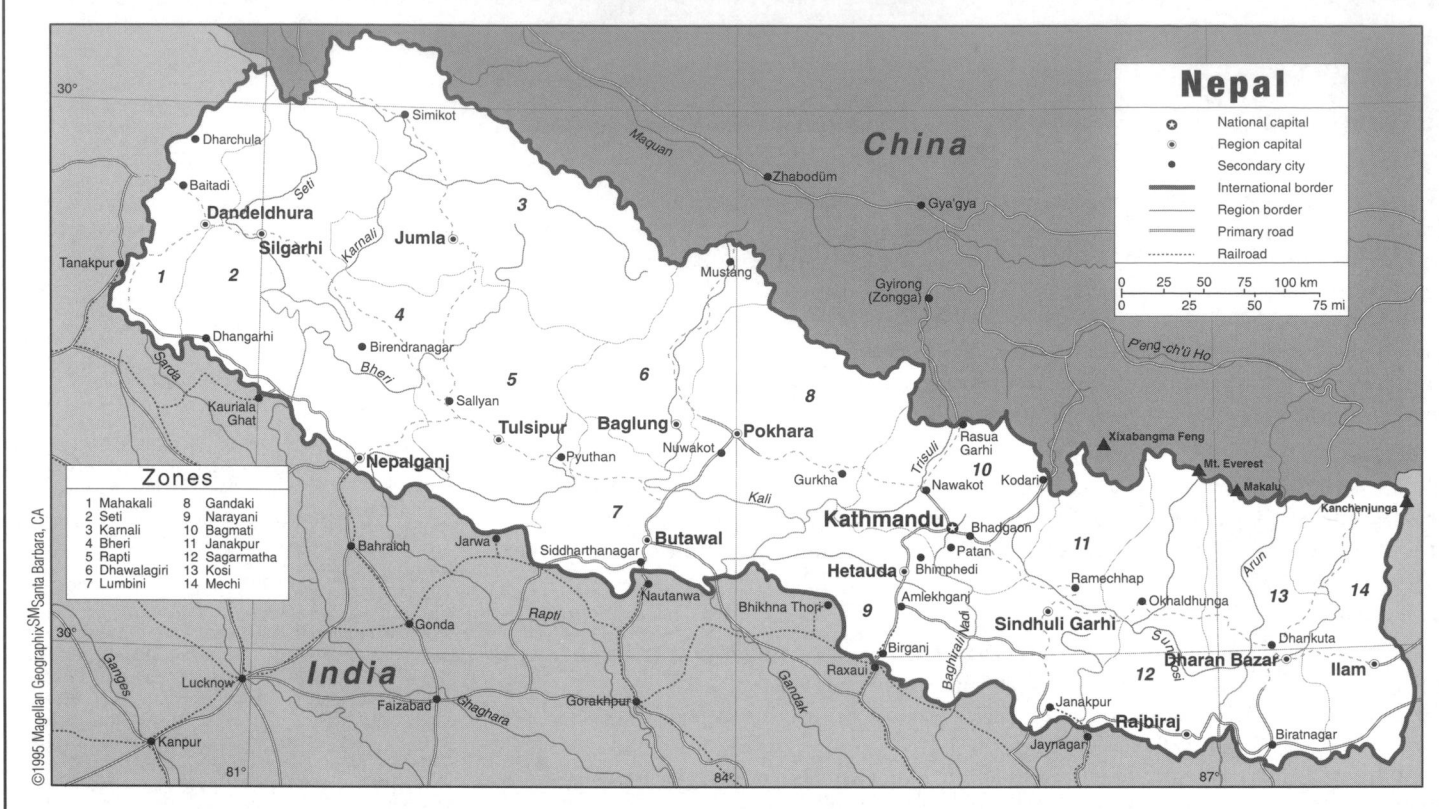

COMMUNICATIONS

Telephones Poor telephone and telegraph services are found in Nepal.

Fax Available in major hotels.

Post office Post offices are found in most towns throughout Nepal; postal services are adequate.

BEST TRAVEL BOOKS

Lonely Planet Travel Survival Kit Nepal. Easily surpasses the competition. 380 pages.

Far Eastern Economic Review, All Asia Travel Guide Volume 3. The best guide available for the business traveler.

Insight Pocket Guides, Nepal. I can't think of another book which so effectively captures the essence of a country.

NATIONAL TOURIST OFFICE

Department of Tourism
HM Government of Nepal
Tripureshor
Kathmandu
Tel: (1) 221306
Fax: (1) 227758
Telex: 2693

TIPPING

Tipping in Nepal averages around 10 percent for all services.

CRIME

While petty crime, especially theft of personal property, is common in Nepal, acts of violent crime are rare.

USEFUL TELEPHONE NUMBERS

If you are calling from outside Nepal, you will need to add the country code [977] and any other international dialing requirements from within your country.

- Kathmandu Airport Facilitation Service ... (1) 470981
- Royal Nepal Airlines .... (1) 214640
- Yeti Travel Service .... (1) 223596
- Tribhuvam International Airport .... (1) 472256
- Lufthansa Airlines .... (1) 223052
- Indian Airlines .... (1) 419649
- Ambulance .... (1) 211959
- Fire .... (1) 221177
- Police .... (1) 226998
- Directory Assistance 197
- Centers for Disease Control .... [1] (404) 3324559

Credit Card Information

Lost or stolen credit cards (call collect to the US, regardless of which country the card was issued in.)

- Amex .... [1] (919) 3333211
- Diner's Club .... [1] (303) 7991504
- MasterCard .... [1] (314) 2756690
- Visa .... [1] (410) 5817931

IMMUNIZATION

Malaria is found in Nepal, so premedication is advised. No other inoculations are required unless you are arriving from an infected area.

INFRASTRUCTURE

The 1993 floods adversely effected Nepal's infrastructure but plans are underway to redevelop it. Tourist related services are usually available, but business related services are harder to come by. Larger hotels in Kathmandu can arrange taxi and other transportation services.

Travelogue

WORKWEEK

Offices Monday-Friday 8:00 am to noon and 1:00 pm to 4:00 pm.

Banks Monday-Friday 8:00 am to 2:00 pm.

Government Monday-Friday 8:00 am to 4:00 pm.

Retail Hours vary in different locations.

HOLIDAYS

Holidays 1996
January 11 National Unity Day
January 29 Martyrs' Day
January-February Basant Panchami *
February 19 National Democracy Day
March 8 Women's Day - for women only
February-March Shivaratri *
April New Year's Day *
March-April Chaitra Ashtami
August Januaryai Purnima *
August Krishnashtami
September 8 TIJ - for women only
October Dasain Festival *
November Tihar Festival *
November 8 Constitution Day
December 29 King Birendra's Birthday
*Dates vary each year.

VISA AND PASSPORT

Foreigners must have a passport and visa to visit Nepal. Tourist visas good for 60 days are issued at ports of entry upon arrival. The fee for a visa varies with the number of entries and duration of stay requested.

DEPARTURE FORMALITIES

Penalties for overstay may include fines and imprisonment.

Foreign Trade

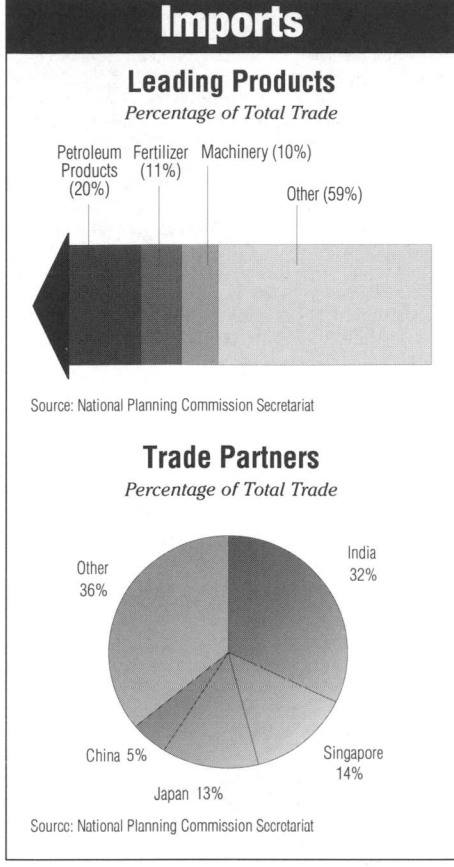

Imports

Leading Products
Percentage of Total Trade

Petroleum Products (20%)
Fertilizer (11%)
Machinery (10%)
Other (59%)

Source: National Planning Commission Secretariat

Trade Partners
Percentage of Total Trade

- India 32%
- Singapore 14%
- Japan 13%
- China 5%
- Other 36%

Source: National Planning Commission Secretariat

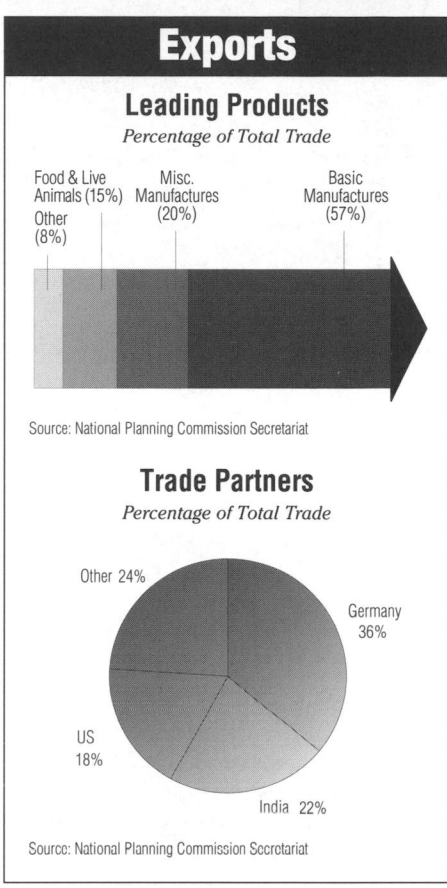

Exports

Leading Products
Percentage of Total Trade

Food & Live Animals (15%)
Other (8%)
Misc. Manufactures (20%)
Basic Manufactures (57%)

Source: National Planning Commission Secretariat

Trade Partners
Percentage of Total Trade

- Germany 36%
- India 22%
- US 18%
- Other 24%

Source: National Planning Commission Secretariat

Opportunities

FOR IMPORTING TO NEPAL
- cotton fabric, textiles, manufactured goods
- medicines
- vehicles and spare parts
- computer hardware, telecommunications equipment

FOR EXPORTING FROM NEPAL
- agricultural products
- Indian textiles and garments

GROWTH SECTORS
- agriculture
- aviation
- construction and cottage industries
- hotels and restaurants
- hydropower
- trade

Trade News

RULES AND REGULATIONS
- **Trade news** Nepal is a landlocked economy with per capita income levels which are among the world's lowest. Corruption and bureaucratic delay still present problems for importers, although regulatory and licensing requirements have been reduced.
- **Import licenses** All imports may be brought in without a license except for banned or quantitatively restricted items such as products injurious to health.
- **Tariffs and import taxes** Tariffs and taxes are generally assessed on an ad valorem basis by using HTS for classification purposes. Import duty rates are 5, 10, 20, 30, 40, and 110 percent. The 5 percent rate is levied on basic necessities, industrial raw materials, and machineries. The 40 percent rate is levied on luxury items. The 110 percent rate is levied on products such as cigarettes, alcoholic beverages, etc.

Legal

Legal System

Nepal's legal system is not yet fully transparent and is generally inconsistent with international norms. The government is taking steps through regulations to improve transparency and to implement laws that will allow more freedom for private enterprise and foster competition.

Intellectual Property Rights

Patents and trademarks Patent protection is valid for seven years and can be extended for an additional seven years. Original formulas can be patented. Trademarks can be registered initially for seven years, and are then renewable. Trademark infringement is not considered a widespread problem.

Copyrights Copyright laws are antiquated and don't include modern forms of intellectual property, such as computer software. The country is not a party to any of the major international agreements on copyright protection, so foreign works are not protected unless registered in Nepal.

Trade secrets Protection of trade secrets is informal at best.

Business Registration

Foreign businesses must meet certain conditions when registering, after which they are treated the same as domestic ones. A business must be within the "industry category," meaning the goods produced must be environmentally sound and must not fall under certain restricted categories (hazardous to health or defense).

Contracts and Dispute Resolution

Most business transactions are based on contract. There have been three recorded disputes relating to foreign companies. In the event of a dispute with a foreign investor or business, the concerned parties are encouraged to settle through consultation in the presence of an official from the Department of Industry. If the dispute still cannot be settled, it is usually referred to arbitration according to the arbitration rules of the United Nations Commission for International Trade Law (UNCITRAL).

Legal Matters

LEGAL BRIEFS
- **Legal environment** Half of the current backlog in Nepal's court system consists of property disputes, which usually take years to settle.
- **Arbitration** All arbitration must be carried out in accordance with UNCITRAL rules. Nepal does not accept international arbitrators.
- **Hostile takeovers** No legal provisions prevent the hostile takeover of private firms.
- **Labor laws** The Labor Act regulates employment, including health and safety conditions, but such laws are not well-enforced.
- **Judiciary** Nepal's judiciary is legally independent of the executive and legislative branches but is generally not assertive in challenging the executive.
- **Courts** All lower court decisions, including acquittals, are subject to appeal, and the Supreme Court is the court of last appeal.
- **Freedom of press** The press is sometimes strictly constrained by laws forbidding criticism of the government, and regulations requiring registration and fixed publication schedules.

LEGAL CONTACTS

Sinha-Verma Law Concern
"Sinha Sadan", Cha 2/207, Gairidham
Kathmandu
Tel: (1) 415773
Fax: (1) 415774

Dhruba Bar Singh Thapi & Associates
Balaju Ring Road
P.O. Box 828
Kathmandu
Tel: (1) 272534
Fax: (1) 272866

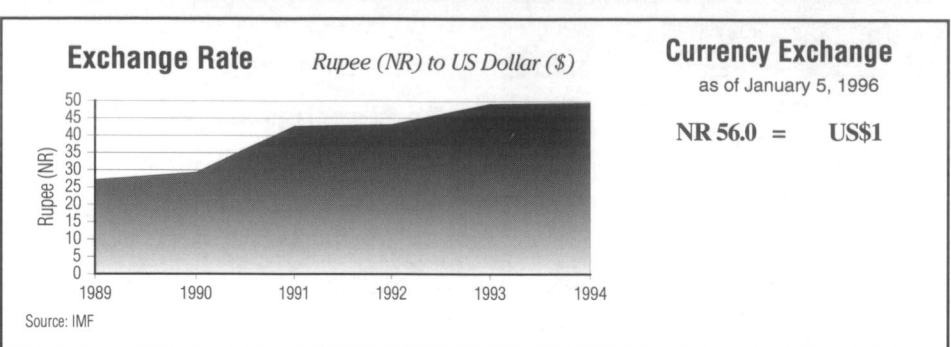

Exchange Rate *Rupee (NR) to US Dollar ($)*

Rupee (NR): 50, 45, 40, 35, 30, 25, 20, 15, 10, 5, 0

1989 1990 1991 1992 1993 1994

Source: IMF

Currency Exchange

as of January 5, 1996

NR 56.0 = US$1

Currency

The currency of Nepal is the Nepalese rupee (NR), and its principal subdivision is 100 paisa.

Foreign Exchange

All exchange transactions must be settled through authorized dealers. Forward exchange cover for trade transactions is only provided by authorized banks. Non-bank authorized dealers are licensed to accept foreign currencies only for services provided to foreign nationals. Nonresidents, foreign diplomats, and foreign nationals working on projects financed by foreign funds under bilateral or multilateral agreements with the government may open foreign currency accounts with Nepalese banks without restrictions. Foreign currency accounts may be held in all specified convertible currencies and balances may be freely transferred abroad.

Capital Transfers

Government clearance is needed for repatriation of any capital. To obtain this clearance, the investor must show a balance sheet, proof of investment, and declaration of dividend in accordance with approved clauses. If all required documents are presented, the application is normally approved within 15 days, after which local commercial banks can make provision for the exchange.

Investment Incentives

The government of Nepal does not give special treatment to foreign investors. There are a number of incentives available, but they are available to both foreign and domestic investors. Incentives include: reimbursements for customs, sales tax, and excise duties within 60 days on raw materials used in the production of export items, and exemptions from income tax for five years for manufacturing industries. An additional two-year income tax exemption is granted when industries fall under the national priority list.

Investment Restrictions

No performance requirements are imposed on foreign investments in Nepal. In particular, there is no local content or export performance requirement. In the case of foreign investments, there is no requirement that nationals own shares, that the share of foreign equity be reduced over time, or that technology be transferred on certain terms.

TAXATION
Indirect Taxes

There are several types of indirect taxes. These are imposed on goods manufactured in or imported into Nepal. The rate of tax varies depending on the nature of goods manufactured or imported.

- **Customs duty** A customs duty is imposed on any goods imported. The duty varies from five to 110 percent. Machinery or goods related to basic needs are charged five percent duty. For products hazardous to health such as cigarettes and liquor, duty is 110 percent.
- **Sales tax** There are two levels for sales tax— 10 percent and 20 percent. The tax is 10 percent on basic needs products like tea and cooking oil, and 20 percent on products like cigarettes, tv's, watches, vehicles, liquor, etc.

- **Countervailing tax** Goods imported are charged a countervailing tax, whereas goods manufactured in Nepal are charged an excise duty only. The rate of tax varies depending on the nature of the goods. For example: cigarettes are taxed on the number of sticks, and televisions are taxed based on total price.
- **Value-added tax (VAT)** Although a VAT has been called for and is included in the current five-year plan and budget, the government has called for further study before implementing any such tax.
- **OCTROI** This is a tax charged by municipalities on the transportation of goods from one municipality to another. The normal charge is one percent of the total value of goods.

Money Matters

BITS AND PIECES

- **Exchange rates** Exchange rates for the Nepalese rupee are tied to the Indian rupee which, in turn, has a managed float against the US dollar. The currencies may be freely converted for all transactions.
- **Investments** With respect to minimum capital requirements, there is a slight discrimination against foreign investors at the time of an initial investment. There are no further restrictions on the amount of future investments, except for limits on cottage industry investments, small businesses, and the agricultural sector. No rules exist on acquisitions, mergers, and takeovers; however, foreign investors must pass a general screening process before a proposal is approved by the Industrial Promotion Board of the Minister of Industry.
- **Repatriation** Repatriation of approved investments is permitted for 100 percent of profits. An investor must first submit a balance sheet, proof of investment, and declaration of dividends to obtain government clearance.
- **Ownership** Entities have the right to freely acquire and dispose of interests in business enterprises.
- **Credit** is allocated on market terms, and foreign companies can obtain loans on the local market.
- **Gold** may be bought, held, and sold freely in any form by residents in Nepal. Imports of gold are banned, except under very limited circumstances.

BANKS

Himalayan Bank Limited
Tridevi Marg, Thamel
Kathmandu
Tel: (1) 418665
Fax: (1) 222800

Nepal Arab Bank Limited
Kanti Path
Kathmandu
Tel: (1) 228549
Fax: (1) 226905

Nepal Bank Limited
Nepal Bank Building
Dharma Path
Kathmandu
Tel: (1) 223790
Fax: (1) 222383

Nepal Grindlays Bank Limited
New Baneshwor
Kathmandu
Tel: (1) 228474, 229333
Fax: (1) 228692

Nepal Indo-Suez Bank Limited
Durbar Marg
Kathmandu
Tel: (1) 227228, 228299
Fax: (1) 226349

Nepal Rashtra Bank
Lalita Niwas
Baluwatar
Kathmandu
Tel: (1) 411250, 213710
Fax: (1) 414553

Nepal SBI Bank Limited
Durbar Marg
Kathmandu
Tel: (1) 226537

Rastriya Banijya Bank
Tangal
Kathmandu
Tel: (1) 413422

Nepal Arab Bank Limited
Kanti Path
Kathmandu
Tel: (1) 228549
Fax: (1) 226905

STOCK EXCHANGE

Securities Exchange Centre Ltd.
Dillibazar
POB 1550
Kathmandu
Tel: (1) 411031

Marketing

Overview

Nepal is relatively small and offers an excellent testing ground for new products; success here could become a strong selling point for market promotion in other South Asian markets. Alternative power generation is an interesting growth area, in which several foreign concerns have shown interest.

Distribution

There are three main sales channels: the foreign producer directly selling to the customer; the foreign producer selling to the customer through an export management or trading company; and the foreign producer working through a Nepalese agent or distributor. The last two are the most common choices for foreign firms.

Agents, Distributors, and Partners

Local agents act as export representatives on a commission basis. Specific responsibilities are subject to contractual agreement. The agent normally receives 5 to 15 percent commission. Distributors sell on commissions, ranging from 15 to 30 percent, and also buy and store goods in stock for resale, engage in local marketing, and handle after-sales service. The commission agent is best used for development-oriented goods such as construction services or heavy equipment; also when selling to government departments and competing for international tenders. The local distributor is more effective when selling durable and nondurable consumer goods.

Advertising

Foreign products are promoted through newspaper, radio, and television advertising. Television reaches only a small number of urban middle- and upper-class consumers; newspapers and radio enjoy country-wide distribution and are most appropriate for basic consumer products. Advertising costs are lower for radio and newspapers than for television. Newspapers in Nepal include two English dailies; radio and television have one channel each and have limited hours of operation.

Marketing in Nepal

MARKETING TIPS

- **Franchises** Franchising is new to Nepal, though it shows some potential for success.
- **Unsuccessful ventures** Direct marketing experiments have not proven cost-effective, due to the small population.
- **Selling techniques** Market promotion campaigns use telemarketing, cataloguing, trade shows and missions, and advertising media. These are best accomplished by a local agent or distributor. Participating in trade shows is probably the best method to introduce new products and to promote brand recognition.
- **Service and customer support** Customers expect after-sales service and product guarantees as primary factors when buying durable products. Shipping times are available for most countries, so availability of spare parts affects product choice. Importers should arrange guarantees with local agents and distributors.

MARKETING CONTACTS

S.R. Shrestha & Co. (P) Ltd.
Jawalakhel, Lalitpur
Tel: (1) 522641
Fax: (1) 522641

Group Three (P) Ltd.
Research and Marketing Division
G.P.O. Box 6227
Kailash Kuli, Kalkasthan
Kathmandu
Tel/Fax: (1) 221594

Himalayan International Marketing Associates (P)
Tripureswor
Kathmandu
Tel: (1) 212409
Tel: (1) 415006

Business Culture

Greetings and Courtesies

The traditional greeting is the *namaste*, formed by placing the palms together in front of the chin or chest and saying *namaste*. Nepalese do not usually shake hands, but some men might shake hands with foreigners. Nepalese generally ask permission before leaving someone. Titles are important. If a person has a title be sure to use it.

Business Ethic and Framework

Nepalese are family-oriented, religious, and spiritual people. Spirituality and humility are ultimately more important than material success. Fate is a central idea; a person does the best they can, but the outcome is ultimately in the hands of God. Another important concept is karma (the consequences, good or bad, of past deeds). Events in this life are often due to a person's karma from a past life. The family is the most important social unit and takes precedence over business matters.

Meetings and Decision Making

Appointments are necessary. Punctuality is important, and being on time will be viewed as an indication of your seriousness about your business. Many government officials will initially meet at a restaurant for a business dinner, but after one or two meetings many extend an invitation to their home. This is generally a sign that things are going well. Decisions are made slowly. Impatience will be viewed as rude, and high-pressure attempts to get things done faster will be resisted and resented.

Business Attire

Standard attire for men is slacks and a short-sleeved shirt. A jacket should be worn to first meetings or when seeing government officials. Avoid leather or any accessories made from animals. Women should wear casual dresses or pants outfits, but never wear a sleeveless dress or blouse. April-September is warm. November-February can be quite cold. The monsoon season is mid-June to mid-September.

Cultural Cautions

DO'S

- Always be polite and respectful of others. Humility is also highly valued.
- Be aware that class and caste are important in Nepal. If someone refuses or is reluctant to do something, do not push the matter. They might be reacting to a situation based on their class or caste.

DON'TS

- Don't touch someone's head or shoulders, not even a child's. It is considered rude.
- Do not touch another person with your feet or shoes. If this happens accidentally, apologize.

CUSTOMS

- Business cards are important. They are exchanged at first meetings and at receptions.
- Women are treated as complete equals to men. Foreign women can expect to be treated with respect and taken seriously.

OBSERVATIONS

- In the south, people remain within their own gender group at social events. In the north, this is not as common.
- Nepalese are very class and caste conscious, and this can affect their social behavior. Though the caste system has been officially abolished, it is still practiced, particularly in rural areas.

NEGOTIATIONS

- Avoid anger, shouting, or any kind of aggression. Nepalese will react to it negatively.
- Always be polite, even when taking a firm position.
- Be patient. Impatience will be seen as rude; high-pressure tactics will be resisted and resented.

GOVERNMENT AGENCIES

Department of Commerce
Naya Baneshwor
Kathmandu
Tel: (1) 227364

Department of Customs
Tripureswor
Kathmandu
Tel: (1) 226662, 220363

Department of Immigration
Tridevi Marg, Thamel
Kathmandu
Tel: (1) 412787, 418573

Department of Industry
Tripureswor
Kathmandu
Tel: (1) 226112

Department of Taxation
Lazimpat
Kathmandu
Tel: (1) 415969, 415970

Ministry of Agriculture
Singha Durbar
Kathmandu
Tel: (1) 223441, 213442, 225108/9

Ministry of Commerce
Babar Mahal
Kathmandu
Tel: (1) 223489
Fax: (1) 225594

Ministry of Communications
Singha Durbar
Kathmandu
Tel: (1) 227525, 229472
Fax: (1) 227310

Ministry of Education, Culture and Social Welfare
Kaiser Mahal
Kanti Path
Kathmandu
Tel: (1) 414054, 411704
Fax: (1) 414887

Ministry of Finance
Bari Bhawan, Bagh Durbar
Kathmandu
Tel: (1) 227367, 215099
Fax: (1) 227529

Ministry of Foreign Affairs
Shital Niwas
Maharajganj
Kathmandu
Tel: (1) 416011
Fax: (1) 416016

Ministry of Health
Teku
Kathmandu
Tel: (1) 215097, 214076, 219820, 211752

Ministry of Industry
Singha Durbar
Kathmandu
Tel: (1) 226686
Fax: (1) 220319

Ministry of Law, Justice and Parliamentary Affairs
Babar Mahal
Kathmandu
Tel: (1) 220621

Ministry of Tourism
Tripureswor
Kathmandu
Tel: (1) 225870, 228840
Fax: (1) 227758

Ministry of Water Resources
Singha Durbar
Kathmandu
Tel: (1) 215046, 216047, 228046, 226788
Fax: (1) 227185

National News Agency
Prithivi Path
POB 220
Kathmandu
Tel: (1) 227912
Fax: (1) 227698

Nepal Bureau of Standards
Balaju
Kathmandu
Tel: (1) 272689

Trade Promotion Center
Kopundole, Lalitpur
Tel: (1) 524771

BUSINESS AND TRADE ORGANIZATIONS

Federation of Nepalese Chambers of Commerce and Industry
Tinkune, Koteshwor
Kathmandu
Tel: (1) 475032, 215920
Fax: (1) 474051

Nepal Chamber of Commerce
Chamber Bhawan, Kantipath
Kathmandu
Tel: (1) 213535, 222890, 229998
Fax: (1) 228324

Nepal-America Chamber of Commerce
TNT Building
Tinkune, Koteshwor
Kathmandu
Tel: (1) 474990, 474991

Nepal-German Chamber of Commerce and Industry
Meera Home
Khichapokhari
Kathmandu
Tel: (1) 228788
Fax: (1) 227424

Central Carpet Industries Association
Kamal Pokhari
Kathmandu
Tel: (1) 413135

Garment Association of Nepal
Kopundole, Lalitpur
Tel: (1) 523372

Hotel Association of Nepal
GAA Building, Thamel
Kathmandu
Tel: (1) 412705
Fax: (1) 415984

Trekking Agents Association of Nepal
Gairidhara
Kathmandu
Tel: (1) 419245

Nepal Association of Travel Agents
Gairidhara
Kathmandu
Tel: (1) 411764

National Trading Limited
POB 128
Teku
Kathmandu
Tel: (1) 211962
Fax: (1) 225151

Nepal Industrial Development Corporation
NIDC Building
Durbar Marga
POB 10
Kathmandu
Tel: (1) 228322
Telex: 2369

Trade Promotion Center Ltd.
Lal Durbar
Kathmandu
Tel: (1) 412771

NEWSPAPERS

The Commoner
Naradevi
POB 203
Kathmandu
Tel: (1) 228236

Daily News
7/358 Hohity Bahal
POB 171
Kathmandu
Tel: (1) 223131
Fax: (1) 225544

Nepal Times
Mruhiti
Nepali Hindi Daily
POB 49
Kathmandu
Tel: (1) 411374

PERIODICALS

Commerce
7/358 Kohity Bahal
POB 171
Kathmandu
Tel: (1) 216636
Fax: (1) 225544

Current
Kamalpokhari
POB 191
Kathmandu
Tel: (1) 413554

Nepal Trade Bulletin
Trade Promotion Centre
Pulchowk, Lalitpur
POB 825
Kathmandu
Tel: (1) 524771
Fax: (1) 521637

Foreign Affairs Journal
5/287 Lagon
Kathmandu

Agricultural Credit
Agricultural Development Bank
Ramshah Path, Panchayat Plaza
Kathmandu
Tel: (1) 216075

RADIO & TELEVISION STATIONS

Nepalese Television Corporation
Singha Durbar
POB 3826
Kathmandu
Tel: (1) 228447
Fax: (1) 228312

Radio Nepal
Department of Broadcasting
HM Government of Nepal
Singha Durbar
POB 634
Kathmandu
Tel: (1) 215773
Telex: 2590

INTERNET ADDRESSES

Usenet group(s):
soc.culture.nepal

City Net - Nepal
http://www.city.net/countries/nepal/

Unofficial Nepal Homepage
http://www.cen.uiuc.edu/~rshresth/nepal.html

The Chanakya Page
http://www.math.grin.edu/~pradhan/chandankya.html

The Netherlands

Kingdom of the Netherlands

Economy

Overview

The Netherlands economy as a whole is showing strong growth; the Dutch guilder has appreciated in the past few years, from two per US$1 to 1.57 per US$1 as of August 1995. The economy is characterized by strong, export-led growth, a positive balance-of-payments situation, a low rate of inflation, and a high level of business investment. Dutch firms are internationally competitive, and are likely to benefit from the govenment's efforts to develop the Netherlands into a center for international trade and finance. These efforts are directed at reducing the country's reliance on revenues from the sale of natural gas, which are subject to wide fluctuations depending on the status of world markets.

Trade

The Netherlands exports over 158 billion guilder (US$100 billion) annually in the areas of mineral fuels, chemical products, machinery and transport equipment, and foodstuffs. Due to its geographic proximity and logistical connections, as well as long established traditional trading ties, Germany is the number one exporter to the Netherlands, followed by Belgium/Luxembourg, and the United Kingdom. The US, France, and Japan also provide large amounts of goods and services.

Sectors

Agriculture Agriculture and fishing, although both high profile Dutch activities, account for only about four percent of GDP, and employ only about four percent of the work force. The Netherlands grows and exports such products as flower bulbs, cut flowers, vegetables and fruits, sugar beets, wheat, potatoes, barley, oats, meat, poultry, and dairy products.

Industry Industry contributes about 33 percent of GDP, and employs 30 percent of the work force. The industrial sector is growing steadily, though not as fast as the economy as a whole. Primary businesses in this country include steel, metal products, electronics, bulk chemicals, natural gas, petroleum products, and transport equipment.

Services This sector accounts for nearly half of the national income and draws primarily from transport and financial areas, such as banking and insurance.

Trends

The Netherlands economy looks set to register positive growth in the medium term. There are, however, a few negatives to consider: unemployment is still rising, deficits are not falling quickly enough, and public debt is increasing. Customers are cautious and corporate investment is forecast to slow sharply in the near future. None of these are critical, and even together, real GDP is expected to continue to grow, and unemployment should soon begin to fall. Overall foreign trade is expected to grow steadily as Eastern European countries develop their economies; Dutch exports should fare well in these new markets. If the government continues its efforts to develop and promote the Netherlands as a business and financial center, it should be able to reduce its dependence on sales of natural gas. Overall, prospects for doing business in the Netherlands look positive.

At a Glance

THE COUNTRY

Location Western Europe, bordering the North Sea, between Belgium and Germany.
Terrain Coastal lowland and dunes to higher sections in the east.
Climate Northern maritime, with cool summers and mild winters.

THE PEOPLE

Population 15,000,000
Ethnic composition
Dutch 96%
Moroccans, Turks, and other 4%
Religious composition
Unaffiliated.. 36%
Roman Catholic 34%
Protestant 20%
Muslim 3%
None 2%
Languages spoken Dutch, English, French, German, Frisian.
Education and literacy The government allocates 17 percent of its national budget to education. The government funds eight universities and five professional institutes. Ten years of schooling are compulsory. Literacy is 98%.
Labor force
Total:..6,700,000
By occupation: agriculture 4%, trade 17%, industry 30%, services 45%. Of the above total, government jobs occupy 23% of the work force.

COUNTRY FACTS

Political and legal The Netherlands is a parliamentary democracy under a constitutional monarch. The civil law system incorporates French penal theory.
Telephone Facilities are highly developed and well-maintained for local and long distance use. There is a nationwide mobile phone system. International country code: [599]. Selected city codes: Amsterdam (20), Rotterdam (10), The Hague (70).
Transportation Good public transportation is available by bus and streetcar. Most Dutch cities are connected by rail, and almost all regions are accessible by good public transportation. Excellent transportation to other principal European cities also is available. There are three major airports.
Environment Awareness of the environment plays a major role in Dutch life. New laws will soon require industry to double its spending on environmental protection, including stricter pollution control guidelines. A CO_2 emissions levy has been introduced, which will be spent on anti-acidification measures, energy conservation, and promotion of public transport. Current issues are water pollution by heavy metals, organic compounds, and nutrients such as nitrates and phosphates; air pollution from vehicles and refining activities; and acid rain.
Media There are three AM and 12 FM radio stations and eight television stations. Complete freedom of the press is guaranteed. Many newspapers are published six days a week.
Health The population's general health has been excellent for many years. Medical facilities and care are good. The social insurance system covers two-thirds of workers; the rest have private medical insurance. Life expectancy averages 76 years.

Economic Structure
(Percentage of the Economy)

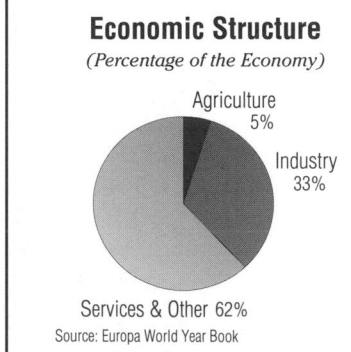

Agriculture 5%
Industry 33%
Services & Other 62%
Source: Europa World Year Book

GDP Growth
(US$ billions)

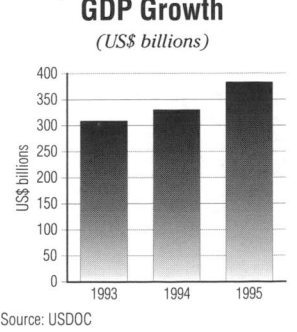

Source: USDOC

GDP per Capita
(US$ thousands)

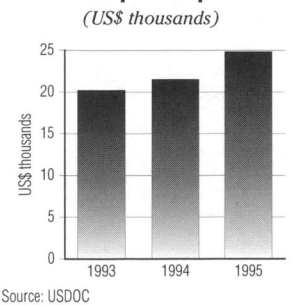

Source: USDOC

Foreign Trade
(US$ billions)

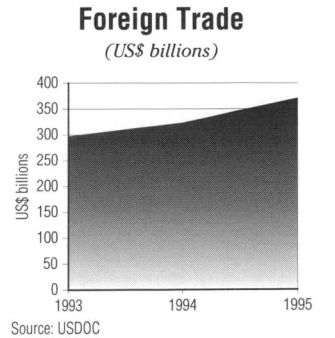

Source: USDOC

Netherlands

- ⊛ National capital
- ⊙ Regional capital
- ● Secondary city
- Primary road
- Railroad
- Administrative border
- International border

0 10 20 30km
0 10 20 30mi

Frisian Islands
Schiermonnikoog
Nes
Ameland
Terschelling
West
Vlieland
Waddenzee
Texel
Den Burg
Den Helder

Friesland
Leeuwarden
Harlingen
Sneek
Heerenveen
Van Kanaal
Margrietkanaal

Groningen
Delfzijl
Groningen
Eemskanaal
Ems

Drenthe
Assen
Emmen
Hoogeveen
Coevorden
Meppel

IJsselmeer

Noord-Holland
Hoorn
Alkmaar
Purmerend
Beverwijk
Zaandam
Noordzeekanaal
Haarlem

Emmeloord
Dronten
Zwolle
Lelystad
Flevoland
Raalte
Overijssel
Almelo
Hengelo
Enschede

North
Sea

⊛ **Amsterdam**
Hilversum
Amstel
Amstel
Ringvaart
Leiden
The Hague
Hoek van Holland
Europoort (International Seaport)
Nieuwe Waterwep
Vlaardingen
Haringvliet
Delft
Gouda
Zuid-Holland
Rotterdam
Dordrecht
Lek

Utrecht
Utrecht
Zeist
Nederrijn
Ede
Amersfoort
Apeldoorn
Deventer
Ijssel
Gelderland
Arnhem
Doetinchem
Nijmegen
Waal
Maas

G e r m a n y
Rhine
Ruhr

Grevelingen
Oosterschelde
Mark
Volkerak
Zeeland
Middleburg
Vlissingen
Westerschelde
Terneuzen
Bergen op Zoom
Roosendaal
Breda
Waalwijk
Tilburg
's-Hertogenbosch
Oss
Zuid-Willemsvaart
Noord-Brabant
Helmond
Wilhelminakanaal
Eindhoven
Velno

Baarle-Hertog (Belgium)

B e l g i u m
Leie
Schelde
Meuse

Weert
Roermond
Limburg
Sittard
Heerlen
Maastricht
Rhine

⊛ **Brussels**

©1995 Magellan Geographix℠Santa Barbara, CA

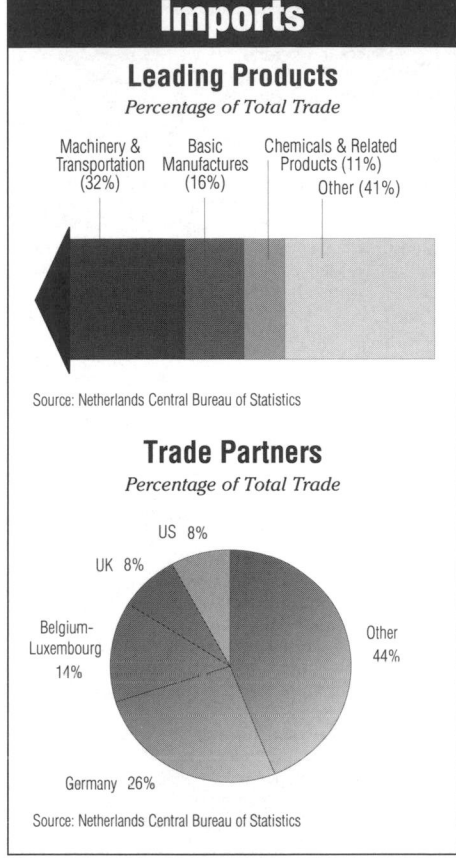

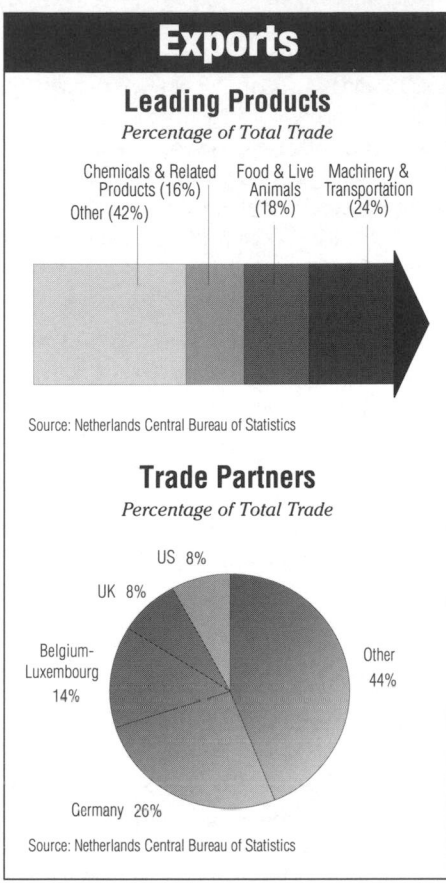

Opportunities

FOR IMPORTING TO THE NETHERLANDS

- data processing
- business equipment
- telecommunications
- medical instrumentation equipment
- scientific instrumentation equipment
- pollution control equipment
- raw materials
- semifinished products
- consumer goods
- transportation equipment
- crude oil
- food products

FOR EXPORTING FROM THE NETHERLANDS

- food
- live animals
- beer
- chemicals
- office machines
- petroleum products
- metal products
- processed food
- tobacco
- agricultural products

GROWTH SECTORS

- financial services
- agriculture
- construction
- tourism

GOVERNMENT PROCUREMENT

- new all-freight rail line between Rotterdam and Germany (The "Betuwelign")
- high speed passenger rail line to Germany and France using the French TGV
- upgrade and expand the Port of Rotterdam ("Havenplan 2010")
- Amsterdam Schiphol International Airport, ("Masterplan 2003")

Trade News

RULES AND REGULATIONS

- **Prohibited imports** Certain imports into the Netherlands and the EU are either prohibited or require an import license. These products fall under the categories of strategic goods or environmentally unfriendly items.

- **Import licenses** Except for agricultural products and minerals, few items are subject to import licensing (coal, lignite fuel, a few specified base metal products, various apparel and textile products, arms and munitions). Licenses are not transferable.

- **Carnets** Carnets are for temporary importation of commercial samples and professional equipment. A carnet is a special customs document that facilitates customs clearance for temporary imports of samples or equipment. With the carnet, goods may be imported without the payment of duty, tax, or additional security. The carnet also usually saves time, since formalities are all arranged beforehand.

- **Tariffs and taxes** The Netherlands applies the EU tariffs (customs duties) which are based on the international Harmonized System (HS) of product classification. Duty rates on manufactured goods range from five to eight percent and are usually based on the CIF value of the goods at the port of entry. Most raw materials enter duty-free or at low rates while agricultural products face higher rates and special levies.

- **Excise taxes** Excise taxes are levied on a small number of products such as soft drinks, wine, beer, spirits, tobacco, sugar, and petroleum products.

- **Industrial products** Industrial products from the European Union (EU) and the European Free Trade Association (EFTA) countries enter the Netherlands duty-free. A 17.5 percent value-added tax (VAT) is applied to most imported and domestic goods.

- **Value-added tax (VAT)** VAT is charged on the sale of goods and services within the country. Unlike the customs duty, which is the same for all EU member countries, the VAT is established by the tax authorities of each country and differs from country to country. At each stage of the manufacturing and distribution chain the seller adds the appropriate amount of VAT to the sales price. The tax is always quoted separately on the invoice. The firm periodically subtracts the VAT paid on its purchases of goods and services from the VAT collected on sales and remits the balance to the government.

- **Barriers** There are no significant trade or investment barriers in the Netherlands.

- **Export importance** Foreign trade heavily influences the open Dutch economy, with exports accounting for 66 percent of the gross national product.

- **Import duties** Most raw materials enter duty-free or at lower rates while agricultural products face higher rates and special levies. A VAT is charged on the sale of goods and services within the country.

- **Free trade zones (FTZs)** There are several free trade zones in the Netherlands, although there are also numerous private and commercial warehouses with the same functions and low costs, so in reality the entire country is a free trade zone. Products can also be transshipped to other countries without technically entering the Dutch customs area.

- **Warehousing** Warehousing is available in all major Dutch cities.

- **Technical standards** The metric system is the key measurement system in international trade. As a member of the EU, the Netherlands applies the product standards and certification approval process developed by the community. For more information about European standard, consult *The Global Approach to Certification and Testing*.

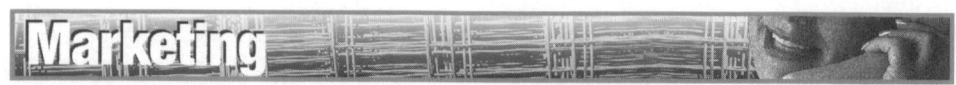

Overview

The Dutch are among the most trade-oriented and multilingual people in the world. It is only recently that industrial production (mostly for export) has surpassed trading as a generator of foreign exchange. This surge in industry has opened even more opportunities to market in the Netherlands because the Dutch now require an even broader range of capital, raw, and intermediate goods to support their own industry, as well as the sophisticated consumer and service products demanded by an affluent, internationally oriented population with access to and knowledge of products from all over the world. The Netherlands also serves as an important entrepôt for commerce with other EU nations. Any company with high quality products and competitive prices should do well in the Netherlands.

Distribution

The trend in the Netherlands is toward streamlined distribution systems, and greater size and specificity of outlets. They are trending away from the small, high overhead local stores that used to dominate the market. There are several ways to introduce products into the Dutch market. Some firms establish a sales office to serve the entire country and provide a base for expansion into Western Europe. Agents and distributors can utilize territorial boundaries to establish specific regional areas, over the entire Benelux group, or sell to all of Europe. Wholesalers or dealers tend to specialize in related product lines. Department stores, specialty chains, retail or consumer cooperatives, and other purchasing organizations also buy directly from foreign suppliers.

Agents, Distributors, and Partners

The Netherlands has a variety of experienced importers, agents, and distributors accustomed to international trade. Most Dutch agents insist on working directly with manufacturers and will refuse to deal with intermediaries. Many importers purchase for their own account and distribute through networks they have established; therefore, they will often also expect exclusive distributorship arrangements. Agency agreements generally assume exclusive authority to deal with the specified products, territories, and customers, so all such agreements must be detailed and carefully drawn; foreigners should consult experienced local attorneys when setting up such arrangements. Wholesalers are the primary source of supplies for small- and medium-sized retail outlets, who are less experienced at dealing with international suppliers and are usually unable to handle large orders on their own. A Dutch commission agent or broker can often provide entry for sales to all of Europe. If a product has a high sales volume and a low profit margin, the Dutch prefer to deal directly with the manufacturer to avoid the extra intermediary fees. Direct selling to a department store, chain store, or other larger end-user can often provide good business, but in turn requires considerable promotional effort. Direct mail and catalog sales are less well-developed, but they do show potential.

Selling Techniques

The Dutch are not generally impressed by clever packaging or elaborate theme or mood advertising; a straightforward, informative, and honest approach is best. However, coupons, samples, premiums, and prizes are commonly used as promotional techniques to accompany the somewhat direct copy and presentation.

Advertising

A full range of media is available in the Netherlands, which supports many radio and television stations and a wide variety of print outlets. There are few national daily newspapers, but competing chains with several local papers can offer advertising deals that provide nationwide coverage. The trade press is well-developed and active, as is the general consumer press. Most advertising agencies offer a wide range of services; the most reliable are usually members of the Institute of Advertising Practitioners. Any firm planning to advertise in the Netherlands should obtain local advice regarding legal provisions and consumer receptivity to a marketing approach, either of which may vary substantially from common practice in the seller's home venue.

Service and Customer Support

Although the Dutch business or household consumer may be attracted by low price, the maintenance of a strong, local after-sales presence in the market is essential in most industry sectors. An effective service provision system must be part of any distribution plan. Too many foreign exporters are satisfied to appoint a representative firm, provide product literature and samples, and sit back to watch profits roll in. However, this market requires regular communication with and visits to the local representative by seasoned sales personnel. If delivery dates are not going to be regarded as firm commitments, plan to bypass the Netherlands. Regular sales reports can identify a potential problem before it becomes serious.

Marketing in the Netherlands

MARKETING TIPS

- **Check promotions and ads carefully** Laws covering gaming and lotteries as well as restrictive trade practices are strictly enforced; review proposed promotions with local advertising specialists.

- **Buying seasons** Apparel is sold largely through trade fairs from July through October for summer fashions and December through April for winter fashions; fabrics are sold May through June (summer) and October through November (winter). Otherwise, there are no established buying seasons.

- **Literature** The Dutch are multilingual, and almost all are functional, if not fluent, in English, as well as other European languages. Nevertheless, materials should be provided in Dutch; if this is not possible, English is preferable to German or French.

- **Downsize but do not downgrade** Homes and other spaces tend to be small and will not hold as much; ostentation is also considered to be in poor taste. However, if redesigning for the Dutch market, remember that the Dutch are highly sophisticated and savvy, and will resent any attempt to eliminate features other than size and glitz.

- **Advertising agencies** Just about every medium is open to advertisers. A local agency should always be consulted before any advertising campaign is launched.

- **Gaming advertisements** Laws covering gaming and lotteries, and those prohibiting restrictive trade practices, are strictly enforced by the government.

- **Location, location, location** Because of the Netherlands' central location and extensive transportation and distribution network, trade fairs tend to attract an interested and active international audience from France, Germany, and other countries.

- **Agent legislation** Under EU legislation, a commercial agent is self-employed and has the continuing authority to negotiate the sale or purchase of goods on behalf of the principal.

- **Agent relationship** A close working relationship is essential between an agent in the Netherlands and the business abroad.

AD AGENCIES

Bates Nederland
President Kennedylaan 1
1079 MB
Amsterdam
Tel: (20) 644-8933
Fax: (20) 642-2545

DDB Needham Worldwide Amsterdam
Jozef Israelskade 46
1072 SB Amsterdam
Tel: (20) 664-6601
Fax: (20) 664-8556

Grey Advertising
Parnassusweg 103
1077 DE Amsterdam
Tel: (20) 664-6641
Fax: (20) 664-2948

Lowe Kuiper & Schouten
Koningslaan 42
1075 AE Amsterdam
Tel: (20) 6642737
Fax: (20) 6643230

Ogilvy & Mather Direct B.V.
Keizersgracht 632
1015 CJ Amsterdam
Tel: (20) 6266061
Fax: (20) 6260790

MARKET RESEARCH CONTACT

The Netherlands Association of Market Research Firms
Hogehilweg 8
1101 CC Amsterdam-Zuidoost
Tel: (20) 697-6951
Fax: (20) 691-0433

Business Culture

Greetings and Courtesies

The Dutch are quite formal, and expect the same from visitors. First names are not used in either business or social settings. The acceptable form of address, *Deheer* (Mr.) and *Mevrouw* (Mrs. or Miss), along with a firm handshake with both men and women is proper. Eye contact is extremely important. When being introduced, use only your last name prefaced by Mr., Mrs., Miss, Dr., etc. The Dutch are disciplined, conservative, polite, and attentive to the smallest detail. Punctuality is essential, and a sense of decorum will serve you well. In business dealings, gifts are only exchanged after a relationship has been well established or a successful transaction completed. Avoid logo trinkets; quality counts and a well-thought-out gift will go much further with your Dutch counterparts than a cheap present with your company's logo. Gifts from your own country, or native to your area of the world, are favorably received. If visiting your colleague's home, a bottle of fine wine is always appreciated.

Business Ethic and Framework

English is the language of business in the Netherlands. The Dutch are a very hard working people, deserving of the familiar saying, "In Rotterdam, shirts are sold with the sleeves rolled up!" Additionally, they are known to "size you up" by how you are introduced into their business community. An introduction from a large banking concern, investment house, or accounting firm will easily gain you access to the top-ranking officer of many Dutch businesses. Should you initiate your own letter of introduction, clearly state your intentions, current credentials, and annual report or background material on the senior management of your company. Conducting business over lunch is not unusual. Business dinners are uncommon, however. If you do find yourself at dinner with your colleague, use the time to develop your relationship; avoid business discussions, and absolutely do not discuss money during the meal.

Decision Making

In The Netherlands the corporate hierarchy often includes a chief executive of the firm and several managing directors who are each responsible for separate departments or divisions in the corporation. The process for making decisions will be very analytical and will require time enough for your Dutch colleagues to consider all aspects of the deal and its consequences. Depending both on the amount of money and business involved in a transaction, a managing director usually has authority to render decisions without consent from the board.

Women

Women still face opposition in achieving senior management positions, and women in the work force must constantly overcome resistance from their male Dutch counterparts. While many of Netherlands' women do choose to work, most feel their duties in life are to family and home. Women traveling to the Netherlands may encounter questions regarding their marital status and their career choices. Respond with humor and patience; be brief in your explanations and get on to business.

Meetings

Formality is essential when doing business in the Netherlands. After being led to the meeting room, your host will direct you to your seat. Business cards are exchanged with everyone at the beginning of meetings and your card should include your title, professional degrees, and the founding date of your company. The meeting will begin with few preliminaries as the Dutch like to get down to business straightaway. Be organized and specific, factual, and to the point. It is advisable to provide an outline of your proposal so that your Dutch colleagues can identify discussion points. Visual aids representing statistical data (graphs, charts, etc.) are considered valuable tools. Make certain these peripherals are relevant. Show-biz techniques and high- pressure sales tactics may bring the meeting to a premature close. Be careful when making promises; oral agreements and statements of intent can be legally binding. Follow up your meeting with a letter outlining the points discussed and future expectations.

Business Attire

Dress conservatively in dark suits of natural fiber, reflecting good quality. Ties should be somber to avoid drawing special attention. The idea is to blend into the Netherlands' business community, not stand out in it. Women should also dress in subdued colors; suits and dresses are appropriate.

Cultural Cautions

DO'S

- Eye contact is an especially important practice during meetings.
- Always be punctual; it speaks for your discipline and organization, qualities revered in the Netherlands. Being late, even once, can wreak havoc on any business negotiations.
- Always identify yourself when initiating or answering a phone call.
- Keep your hands above the table at all times while dining by resting your wrists at the table's edge. Never rest your elbows on the table.
- When eating, try to eat everything on your plate, not doing so may be considered rude; take small portions of food, and at least try to taste every item.
- Getting up during a meal, even for a trip to the bathroom, is impolite.
- Some good topics for conversation include Dutch politics, travel, and sports.

DON'TS

- Don't be offended if your Dutch colleague points a finger to his ear and makes a circular motion. It does not mean you're crazy, as in most European countries. It means you have a phone call.
- Don't offer compliments that aren't genuine. You probably won't fool anyone. The Dutch are skeptical, and trying to make points with insincere compliments will loose you favor.
- During social occasions, never eat before the hostess. She will traditionally serve herself first, and begin eating before anyone.
- Similar to other European countries, chewing gum in front of others is considered impolite.
- Standing with your hands in your pockets is a rude gesture.

CUSTOMS

- The Dutch are well-informed about the changing landscape of international politics and economic affairs, and they always enjoy discussing world events with foreign visitors. While it is best to join in on the conversation and maintain a neutral attitude in discussions of political position or issues of state, it will serve visitors to do a little homework on world affairs.
- Be sure to wipe your feet before entering a house. When a woman enters a room, the men rise.
- "God created the universe, but the Dutch made Holland." This old saying sums up centuries of hard work, tenacity, strength, and determination applied by the Dutch people to forge a leading position in world trade and international affairs. Theirs is a well-deserved pride in their cultural heritage, and the country boasts a skilled, highly educated work force with a flair for languages.

OBSERVATIONS

- Both homes and offices regularly display arrangements of beautiful Dutch flowers. Dutch flowers are exported all over the world.
- The Dutch communicate several messages with hand motions. Some of the more common: sucking the thumb signals that someone is lying; someone tapping their thumbnails together signals that they were offended by what recently took place, such as a joke or comment.
- Physical contact in public is not common unless between close friends, who may embrace or even kiss each other lightly on the cheek.

NEGOTIATIONS

- Be clear from the outset what it is you want from your Dutch associates. Last minute surprises at the bargaining table will impede, if not doom, success.
- The Dutch are not likely to enter into any short-term or risky situations.

Legal

Legal System

The Netherlands is a parliamentary democracy. Most essential private and commercial laws and civil procedures have been codified in the Civil Code, Commercial Code, and the Code of Civil Procedure. These codes are primarily based on French codes.

Intellectual Property Protection

Patents All applications for patents must be in the Dutch language. Patents are usually decided 18 months after the application is filed. Nonresidents applying for a patent must give a representative address in the Netherlands. Most patents last for 20 years. The Dutch government is currently drafting legislation for the granting of national patents without examination. All European patents are automatically granted under the European Patent Act. Any item that was publicly accessible in any manner before registration cannot be registered for patent protection.

Trademarks Only registered trademarks that are recorded in the Trademark Register are considered valid. Unregistered trademarks are not protected. Assignments and licenses of trademarks must be in writing. Trademark protection begins as of the date of filing, rather than the date of registration.

Copyrights The Netherlands belongs to several international copyright organizations. For all practical purposes, works made or published in most countries will also be protected under The Netherlands Copyright Law. No notice, registration, or any other formality is necessary for protection of a copyright. The right continues for 50 years after the creator's death. The Netherlands recently extended its copyright laws to include computer software.

Trade secrets The Netherlands has several laws protecting trade secrets. Disputes are usually handled by local courts.

Business Registration

All companies must be registered in the Netherlands. Information must include the company name, the goods produced or distributed, and a list of officers. Companies are incorporated when the founders create a deed of incorporation and sign it in the presence of a notary public. Prior approval by the Minister of Justice is necessary to incorporate. In addition, chambers of commerce operate trade registers, and every enterprise, branch, or agent must be registered with the relevant chamber.

Contracts and Dispute Resolution

Businesses in the Netherlands prefer informal contracts. No special formalities are required for a contract to be binding on the parties. Almost all disputes are settled through arbitration.

Notaries

Notaries in the Netherlands are lawyers appointed by the Crown. Each notary serves as a public official for a specified district. They have more than document certification duties. Some notaries are permitted to offer legal counsel to clients on request, but they do not litigate. A notary's approval is needed for several legal transactions. Documentation can be in another language, provided the notary can understand the language.

Labor

Workers can be found through government-operated labor exchange programs, a rapidly growing number of private employment firms, or directly through newspaper ads. Employment contracts do not need to be written, but some obligations are legal only if accepted in writing. Relations between labor and management are generally good and days lost to strikes are relatively low. Full-time employees must be at least age 16. The minimum wage for workers under age 23 is lower than that for older workers; the precise amount is dependent on the age of the person. Laws also provide for minimum vacation pay. Unions are allowed in the Netherlands, and various Dutch unions hold strong positions in the communities. Approximately 80 percent of the Dutch working force is covered by collective bargaining agreements, and 65 percent of all private sector workers are covered by union contracts negotiated on a sectorial basis with employers associations and, if accepted by the government, extended by law to the entire sector. Union contracts have resulted in an average work week of 38 hours. Firms of at least 100 employees are required by law to institute works councils with which management must consult on a number of issues, including investment decisions. Smaller firms are also required to consult employees, though not on such a formal basis. Although wage bargaining is increasingly decentralized there still exists a central bargaining system where labor contract guidelines are sought. Workers can legally strike, but there have been no work stoppages in recent years. After a probationary period, firing of noncontract personnel can be extremely difficult and expensive. Investors should be aware of the legal requirements for hiring, firing, and the general conduct of labor relations in the Netherlands.

Legal Matters

LEGAL BRIEFS

- **International agreements** The Netherlands is a signatory to the International Convention on Investment Disputes, and a member of the International Center for the Settlement of Investment Disputes (ICSID).
- **Private ownership** There are full rights of private ownership and establishment of business enterprises available in the Netherlands, except in certain monopoly sectors. Licenses are granted on the basis of competitive equality.
- **Laws and regulations** All laws and regulations affecting investment, such as environmental rules, health and safety regulations, etc., are non-discriminatory and apply equally to foreign and domestic companies.
- **International agreements** The Netherlands is a member of GATT/WTO; EU; BENELUX; CISG; New York Convention on the Recognition and Enforcement of Foreign Arbitral Awards; Convention on the Service Abroad of Judicial and Extrajudicial Documents in Civil or Commercial Matters; Convention on the Taking of Evidence Abroad in Civil or Commercial Matters; Convention Abolishing the Requirement of Legalization for Foreign Public Documents; Universal Copyright Convention; Berne Convention; Paris Convention; and ATA Carnet Convention.

LEGAL CONTACTS

Koster, Claassen & Smallegange
Boompjes 550
3011 XZ Rotterdam
Tel: (10) 413-2180
Fax: (10) 412-2125

Clifford Chance
PO Box 7301
1007 JH Amsterdam
Tel: (20) 577-7111
Fax: (20) 676-9326

Baker & McKenzie
(Caron & Stevens)
Leidseplein 29
1017 PS Amsterdam
Tel: (20) 551-7555

Bos, Oosterbaan & Van Eeghen
Koningslaan 35
1075 AB Amsterdam
Tel: (20) 671-6756
Fax: (20) 671-8669

Dolk-Verburg-Diamand
Cronenburg 75
1081 GM Amsterdam
Tel: (20) 646-4146
Fax: (20) 646-4716

Goudsmit & Branbergen
Advocaten
J.J. Viottastraat 46
1071 JT Amsterdam
Tel: (20) 662 -30 31
Fax: (20) 673 -65 58

Houthoff, Advocaten
Parnassusweg 126
1076 AT Amsterdam
Tel: (20) 57 0-0 200
Fax: (20) 57 0-0 280

Kennedy Van Der Laan
Herengracht 466
PO Box 15744
1001 NE Amsterdam
Tel: (20) 550-6666
Fax: (20) 550-6777

Nauta Dutilh
Prinses Irenestraat 59
NL-1077 WV Amsterdam
Tel: (20) 541-4646
Fax: (20) 661-2827

Parramore Advocaten Amsterdam
Burg. Stramanweg 102
1101 AA Amsterdam
Tel: (20) 696-3211
Fax: (20) 696-8581

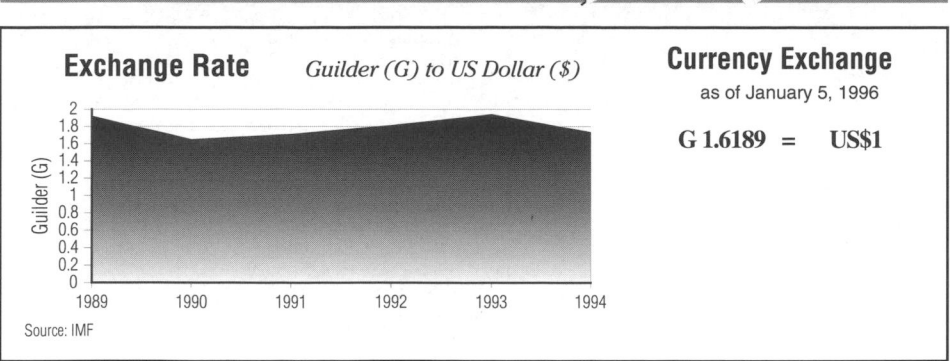

Exchange Rate *Guilder (G) to US Dollar ($)*

Source: IMF

Currency Exchange
as of January 5, 1996

G 1.6189 = US$1

Currency

The currency of the Netherlands is the guilder (G, *f*, or fl). The principal subdivision is 100 cents.

Foreign Exchange

The Netherlands maintains spot exchange rates between the guilder and the European Monetary System (EMS). There are no foreign exchange controls, and no taxes or subsidies on purchases or sales of foreign exchange. Residents and nonresidents are freely permitted to buy and sell convertible and non-convertible currencies, both spot and forward, at market rates.

Capital Transfers

Forward exchange contracts are not limited to a delivery period. Residents and nonresidents are free to hold Netherlands guilder and foreign currency accounts in the Netherlands and abroad. Residents are usually required to settle payments to and receipts from nonresidents through agents authorized by The Netherlands Bank. Payments for invisibles are unrestricted. Residents may take out any amount in foreign and domestic bank notes, coins, and documents of value. Payments for interest, dividends, and contractual amortization are also unrestricted. There are no requirements attached to receipts by residents from invisibles.

Investment Incentives

Investment incentives are a well-publicized tool of Dutch economic policy and are used to facilitate economic restructuring and to promote energy conservation, regional development, environmental protection, and other national socio-economic goals. The Netherlands actively encourages foreign investment. Subsidies and incentives are available to foreign and domestic firms alike. Subsidies are in the form of tax credits which are usually disbursed through corporate tax rebates, or direct cash payments in the event there is no tax liability.

Investment Restrictions

General requirements to qualify for investment subsidy schemes apply equally to domestic and foreign investors. There are no requirements for employment of local capital or managerial personnel, but almost all chief executives are Dutch, and Dutch nationals must be employed unless firms can demonstrate that the job in question cannot be performed by a Dutch national.

Money Matters

BITS AND PIECES

- **Investment** The Dutch government maintains liberal policies toward foreign direct investment, with the exception of military operations, aviation, shipping, electric, gas and water utilities, railways, and radio and television broadcasting.
- **Repatriation** Repatriation or conversion of capital and earnings is not restricted.
- **Private ownership** There are full rights of private ownership and establishment of business enterprises in the Netherlands, and licenses are granted on the basis of competitive equality.
- **Capital** Capital markets facilitate the free flow of financial resources and operate at market rates. Government policy is essentially neutral with regard to inward and outward capital transfers. Both companies and individuals are free to invest abroad.
- **Gold** Banks and residents may freely buy, hold, and sell gold in the Netherlands or abroad. Imports and exports do not require licenses.
- **Tax law** Dutch tax law does not affect the feasibility of attracting non-Dutch personnel to live and work in the Netherlands.
- **Corporate taxes** The Dutch corporate tax rate (40 percent on taxable profits up to 100,000 guilders and 35 percent on profits in excess) is among the lowest in the EU; only the UK is lower.
- **General tariff** Effective January 1, 1996, the corporate tax rate will be reduced in steps to one general tariff of 35 percent by 1999.
- **Corporate taxes** Dutch corporate taxation generally allows for the exemption of dividends and capital gains derived from a foreign subsidiary (participation exemption). Furthermore, the Netherlands maintains an extensive network of tax treaties with a large number of countries.
- **Financial markets** Dutch financial markets facilitate the free flow of financial resources, are fully developed, and operate at market rates.
- **Financial treaties** The Netherlands has signed bilateral investment agreements with a number of countries including: Argentina, Bolivia, China, the Czech Republic, Egypt, Hong Kong, Hungary, Indonesia, the Ivory Coast, Nigeria, Singapore, Sri Lanka, Venezuela, Vietnam, and Slovakia.
- **Single market** The Netherlands is a part of the EU.
- **Investment insurance** The Netherlands has no investment insurance programs, but Dutch companies investing in developing countries through the establishment of subsidiaries or joint ventures can insure their investment against risks with The Netherlands Credit Insurance Company.
- **Liberal laws** There are no general prohibitions against the acquisition of majority holdings by foreign interests in Dutch companies or against foreign ownership, of either business entities or real property. There are also no nationality requirements for directors or shareholders in Dutch commercial entities.
- **Individual taxation** The Dutch apply taxes on resident and nonresident individuals. Income tax rates are fixed annually.

BANKS

The Netherlands Bankers' Association
POB 19780
1000 GW Amsterdam
Tel: (20) 550-2888
Fax: (20) 623-9748

De Nederlandsche Bank, N.V.
Westeinde 1
PO Box 98
1000 AB Amsterdam
Tel: (20) 524-9111
Fax: (20) 620-3426

ABN AMRO Bank NV
POB 600
1000 AP Amsterdam
Tel: (20) 6289898
Fax: (20) 6287740

TAXATION

Taxation requires sophisticated knowledge of complex rules and regulations specific to each country. The information presented here is from the Ernst & Young Corporate Tax Guide and Directory, available from the Ernst & Young accounting office in your country, or from:

Moret Ernst & Young
Mail Address:
P.O. Box 7883
1008 AB Amsterdam
Netherlands
Street Address:
Drentestraat 20
1083 HK Amsterdam
Netherlands
Tel: (20) 5497 222
Telex: 14376
Fax: (20) 6462 553

At a Glance

Corporate Income Tax Rate (%) (a)	35
Capital Gains Tax Rate (%) (a)	35
Branch Tax Rate (%) (a)	35
Withholding Tax (%)	
Dividends (b)	25
Interest	0
Royalties from Patents, Know-how, etc.	0
Branch Remittance Tax	0
Net Operating Losses (Years)	
Carryback	3
Carryforward	Unlimited

(a) The first fl 100,000 of taxable income is taxed at 40%.
(b) This rate may be reduced to 0% if the recipient is a parent company established in a European Union (EU) member state.

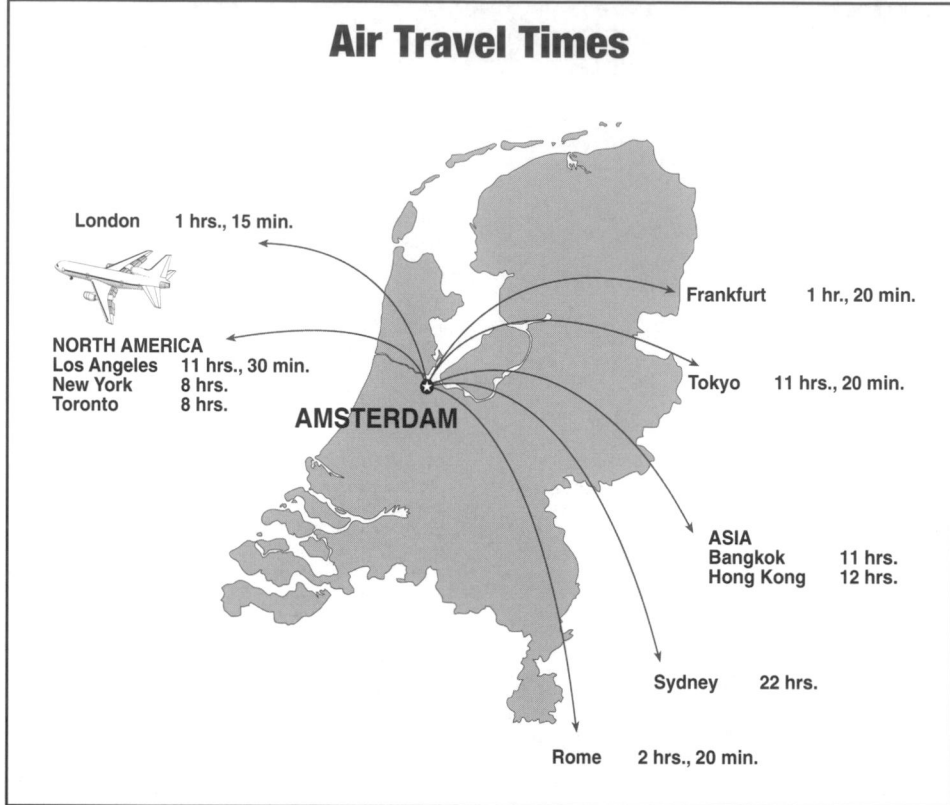

Air Travel Times

London — 1 hrs., 15 min.

Frankfurt — 1 hr., 20 min.

NORTH AMERICA
Los Angeles — 11 hrs., 30 min.
New York — 8 hrs.
Toronto — 8 hrs.

AMSTERDAM

Tokyo — 11 hrs., 20 min.

ASIA
Bangkok — 11 hrs.
Hong Kong — 12 hrs.

Sydney — 22 hrs.

Rome — 2 hrs., 20 min.

Travelogue

WORKWEEK

Government Monday-Friday 8:30 am to 5:00 pm.
Business Monday-Friday 8:30 am to 5:00 pm.
Banks Monday-Friday 9:00 am to 4:00 pm.
Retail Monday-Friday 8:30 am to 6:00 pm.
Hours vary, some shops are open on Saturday, some close for lunch, some open late one evening and close one morning each week.

HOLIDAYS

Holidays 1996
January 1 New Year's Day
April 8 Easter Monday*
April 30 Queen's Birthday
May 5 Liberation Day
May 16 Ascension Day
May 26 Whit Monday*
December 25 Christmas
December 26 Boxing Day
* Dates vary year to year.

VISA AND PASSPORT

All travelers must have a valid passport; visas are not required for any stay less than three months. Anyone entering the country for permanent residence must register as soon as possible after arrival. A work permit is required for employment and must be presented to immigration authorities.

DEPARTURE FORMALITIES

All flower bulbs to be sent or taken out of the country must be inspected by the Plant Disease Service. Dutch flower-bulb dealers will know all the legal provisions and can arrange for shipment. Proof must be shown for taking large quantities of items out of the Netherlands; they must be for personal use only. There are no other departure formalities.

IMMUNIZATION

No vaccinations are required for entry to the Netherlands unless one has been infected within two weeks prior to arrival.

TIPPING

For waiters and cab drivers: 15 percent is the customary gratuity. Hotels, nightspots: 15 percent. Restaurants: included in bill but an additional 10 to 15 percent is usual.

CRIME

The crime rate is low in the Netherlands and rarely directed at tourists. Theft and pickpocketing is most likely to occur on public transportation. Theft of car stereos from automobiles is also common.

INFRASTRUCTURE

Numerous airlines fly into the Netherlands daily, many are with non-stop flights. There are two major airports, Schiphol Airport near Amsterdam and Rotterdam Airport. For transportation from the airport there is direct rail service to downtown Amsterdam and taxi service and bus service is available to Rotterdam. Road maintenance is excellent. Car rentals are widely available at airports, railway stations, and many other places. Public transportation is excellent with railways, buses, streetcars, and subways. Taxis are always available but expensive. It is difficult to hail a cab from the street. It is best to arrange for pick up by telephone. International rail service connects the Netherlands with Brussels, Paris, and other European cities. There are two train services. Railcars are for comfort and speed, diesel trains are for a slower scenic ride.

TOURIST OFFICES

VVV Information Office
Stationsplein 10
Amsterdam
Tel: (20) 6266444

VVV Information Office
Coolsingel 67
3012 AC Rotterdam
Tel: (10) 413-6000

COMMUNICATIONS

Telephones The Dutch telecommunications system is superior. The monopoly has been privatized and has expanded its services. Direct dial is available to countries worldwide.
Fax Services are commonly used in businesses and hotels and are readily available.
Post office The Dutch postal system is very reliable. Mail is delivered once a day and picked up four times a day. Monday-Friday 8:30 am to 6:00 pm. Thursday 8:30 am to 10:30 pm. Saturday 9:00 am to 1:00 pm.
Radio/TV Dutch television is broadcast on two channels from 7:00 pm to 11:30 pm each evening.

BEST TRAVEL BOOKS

Fodor's Travel Guide, The Netherlands, Belgium and Luxembourg.
Do's and Taboo's Around the World. The Bestselling Guide to International Behavior. Edited by Roger Axtell, compiled by the Parker Pen Company. The ultimate guide to international behavior, now completely updated and expanded. Helpful, fun to read!
Berlitz Business Travel Guide, Europe. Berlitz Publishing Company. Concise economic details, successful trip planning, background information on people and cities, useful facts and addresses, major sights and excursions, essential words and phrases.
Multinational Travel Companion Executive. Travel tips worldwide. Strand Publishing Company, Inc.

USEFUL TELEPHONE NUMBERS

If you are calling from outside the Netherlands you will need to add the country code [599] and any other international dialing requirements from within your country.
* Emergency 0611
* International Operator 0010
* Directory Assistance 008
* Telegrams 009
* Time 002
* Weather 003
* DHL International/Amsterdam .... (20) 60552
* Swift Koeriers .... (20) 6421855
* Translation Service .... (20) 7265889
* Amsterdam Chamber of Commerce ... (20) 6172882
* Netherlands Chamber of Commerce .. (70) 3469392
* Rotterdam Chamber of Commerce ..... (10) 4117450
* Amsterdam Post Office .... (20) 558911
* The Hague Post Office .... (70) 3653843
* Rotterdam Post Office .... (10) 4542221
* KLM Airlines .... (20) 491372
* British Airways .... (20) 6015413
* NLM Airways (Domestic) .... (20) 492227
* Delta Airlines .... (20) 6041204
* Avis Car Rental .... (20) 6041301
* Budget Car Rental .... (20) 6041349
* Hertz Car Rental .... (20) 6015416
* Amsterdam Taxi Central .... (20) 777777
* The Hague Taxi Service .... (70) 3907722
* Rotterdam Taxi Central .... (10) 4626060

Credit Card Information
Lost or stolen credit cards (call collect to the US, regardless of which country the card was issued in).
* Amex ....[1] (919) 333-3211
* Diner's Club................................[1] (303) 799-1504
* MasterCard ....[1] (314) 275-6690
* Visa ....[1] (410) 581-7931

GOVERNMENT AGENCIES

Ministry of Agriculture and Fisheries
Bezuidenhoutseweg 73
POB 20401
2500 EK The Hague
Tel: (70) 379-3911
Fax: (70) 381-5153

Ministry of Development Cooperation
Bezuidenhoutseweg 67
POB 20061
2500 EB The Hague
Tel: (70) 348-6486
Fax: (70) 348-4848

Ministry of Economic Affairs
POB 20101
2500 EC The Hague
Tel: (70) 379-8911
Fax: (70) 347-4081

Ministry of Education and Science
Europaweg 4
POB 25000
2700 LZ Zoetermeer
Tel: (70) 531-911
Fax: (70) 531-953

Ministry of Finance
POB 20201
2500 EB The Hague
Tel: (70) 342-8000
Fax: (70) 342-7905

Ministry of Foreign Trade
POB 20101
2500 EC The Hague
Tel: (70) 347-3081

Ministry of Transport and Public Works
Plesmanweg 1
POB 20901
2500 EX The Hague
Tel: (70) 351-6171
Fax: (70) 351-7895

Ministry of Welfare, Health and Culture
Sir Winston Churchillaan 370
POB 5406
2280 JN Rijswijk
Tel: (70) 340-7911
Fax: (70) 340-7834

WORLD TRADE CENTERS

World Trade Center Amsterdam
Strawinskylaan 1
1077 XX Amsterdam
Tel: (20) 575-9111
Fax: (20) 662-7255

World Trade Center Eindhoven N.V.
Bogert 1
POB 2085
5600 CB Eindhoven
Tel: (40) 653-653
Fax: (40) 449-041

World Trade Center Rotterdam N.V.
Beursplein 37
POB 30055
3001 DB Rotterdam
Tel: (10) 405-4444
Fax: (10) 405-5016

BUSINESS ORGANIZATIONS

The American Chamber of Commerce
Carnegieplein 5
2517 KJ The Hague
Tel: (70) 365-9808
Fax: (70) 379-6322

NEWPAPERS

Noordhollands Dagblad
POB 2
1800 AA Alkmaar
Tel: (72) 196196
Fax: (72) 126183

Rijn en Gouwe
POB 1
2400 AA Alphen aan den Rijn
Tel: (1720) 87444
Fax: (1720) 87408

Amersfoortse Courant
Stadsring 2
POB 43
3800 AA Amersfoort
Tel: (33) 647911
Fax: (33) 647334

De Courant Nieuws van de Dag
POB 376
1000 EB Amsterdam
Tel: (20) 5859111
Fax: (20) 5854130

Het Financieele Dagblad
POB 216
1000 AE Amsterdam
Tel: (20) 5574511
Fax: (20) 5574400
Telex: 18326

Apeldoornse Courant
POB 833
7301 BB Apeldoorn
Tel: (55) 766911
Fax: (55) 224282
Telex: 36434

Arnhemse Courant
POB 9008
6800 DK Arnhem
Tel: (85) 693311
Fax: (85) 649460

Drentse Courant
POB 36
9400 AA Assen
Tel: (5920) 29500
Fax: (5920) 14890

Barneveldse Krant
POB 67
3770 AB Barneveld
Tel: (3420) 94911
Fax: (3420) 13141

Nederlands Dagblad/Gereformeerd Gezinsblad
POB 111
3770 AC Barneveld
Tel: (3420) 10720
Fax: (3420) 92619
Telex: 40230

De Stem
POB 3229
4800 MB Breda
Tel: (76) 236911
Fax: (76) 236309
Telex: 54176

De Dordtenaar
POB 54
3300 AB Dordrecht
Tel: (78) 135844
Fax: (78) 147208

Eindhobens Dagblad
POB 534
5600 AM Eindhoven
Tel: (40) 336336
Fax: (40) 436954

Dagblad Tubantia
POB 28
7500 AA Enschede
Tel: (53) 842842
Fax: (53) 842200
Telex: (72112

Nieuwsblad van het Noorden
POB 60
9700 MC Groningen
Tel: (50) 652222
Fax: (50) 130997
Telex: (77296

Haarlems Dagblad
POB 507
2003 PA Haarlem
Tel: (23) 150150
Fax: (23) 311790
Telex: 41866

Dagblad voor Noord-Limburg
POB 65
5900 AB Benlo
Tel: (77) 551234
Fax: (77) 519533

Provinciale Zeeuwse Courant
POB 18
4380 AA Vlissingen
Tel: (1184) 84000
Fax: (1184) 72404
Telex: 37828

Zwolse Courant
POB 67
8000 AAB Zwolle
Tel: (38) 275275
Fax: (38) 213648

PERIODICALS

Libelle
POB 1
2000 MA Haarlem-Schalkwijk
Tel: (23) 304304
Fax: (23) 367904

Margriet
POB 497
1000 AL Amsterdam
Tel: (20) 5734811
Fax: (20) 5734406
Telex: 16597

Mikro-Gids
POB 10050
1201 DB Hilversum
Tel: (35) 713911
Fax: (35) 219058

NCRV-Gids
POB 121
1200 JE Hilversum
Tel: (35) 719911
Fax: (35) 719661

Nederlands Tijdschrift voor Geneeskunde
Dutch Medical Journal
POB 246
3990 GA Houten
Tel: (3403) 95711
Fax: (3403) 50903

Nieuwe Revu
POB 497
1000 AL Amsterdam
Tel: (20) 5734509
Fax: (20) 5734534
Telex: 16597

NRC-Handelsblad
PO Box 824
3000 DL Rotterdam

Panorama
POB 1
2000 MA Haarlem-Schalkwijk
Tel: (23) 304304
Fax: (23) 350382
Telex: 41371

Popfoto
Ceylonpoort 5-25
2037 AA Haarlem-Schalkwijk
Tel: (23) 304304
Fax: (23) 304704

Prive
POB 127
1000 AC Amsterdam
Tel: (20) 5853340
Fax: (20) 5854111
Telex: 10449

Story
POB 1
2000 MA Haarlem-Schalkwijk
Tel: (23) 304304
Fax: (23) 367904
Telex: 41371

Studio
POB 10050
1201 DB Hilversum
Tel: (35) 714911
Fax: (35) 714655

TeleVizier
POB 5000
1200 EW Hilversum
Tel: (35) 717911
Fax: (35) 717443
Telex: 43012

Tina
Ceylonpoort 5-25
2037 AA Haarlem-Schalkwijk
Tel: (23) 304304
Fax: (23) 352554
Telex: 41371

Vara TV Magazine
POB 175
1200 AD Hilversum
Tel: (35) 711911
Fax: (35) 711445

Viva
POB 497
1000 AL Amsterdam
Tel: (20) 5734811
Fax: (20) 5734406
Telex: 16597

Voetbal International
POB 1050
1000 BB Amsterdam
Tel: (20) 5518711
Fax: (20) 6229141
Telex: 16307

VPRO-Gids
POB 11
1200 JC Hilversum
Tel: (35) 712911
Fax: (35) 41291
Telex: 43014

Vrij Nederland
POB 1254
1000 BG Amsterdam
Tel: (20) 5518711
Fax: (20) 6229141
Telex: 16307

Yes
Ceylonpoort 5-25
2037 AA Haarlem
Tel: (23) 304304
Fax: (23) 361624

Bedrijfsdocumentaire
Hettenheuvelweg 41-43
POB 1198
1000 BD Amsterdam
Tel: (20) 916666
Fax: (20) 960396

Computable
POB 9194
1006 CC Amsterdam
Tel: (20) 5102911
Fax: (20) 6175137
Telex: 14407

Elektronica/Databus
POB 23
7400 GA Deventer
Tel: (5700) 48777
Fax: (5700) 43015

Export Channel (Import/Export)
Stolbergstraat 14
2012 EP Haarlem
Tel: (23) 319022
Fax: (23) 317974

Informatie Management
POB 235
2280 AE Rijswijk
Tel: (70) 3988100
Fax: (70) 3988276
Telex: (33702

Intermediair
POB 9194
1006 CC Amsterdam
Tele: (20) 5102911
Fax: (20) 6175137
Telex: 14407

Management Team
POB 397
3900 AJ Veenendaal
Tel: (8385) 21422
Telex: 30485
Fax: (8385) 23136

PC Magazine
POB 9194
1006 CC Amsterdam
Tel: (20) 5102911
Fax: (20) 175137
Telex: 14407

RADIO AND TELEVISION

Algemene Omroepvereniging AVRO
POB 2
1200 JA Hilversum
Tel: (35) 717911
Fax: (35) 717461
Telex: 43012

Evangelische Omroep (EO)
Oude Amersfoortseweg 79A
POB 565 1200
AN Hilversum
Tel: (35) 882411
Fax: (35) 882685
Telex: 43325

Katholieke Radio Omroep (KRO)
Emmastraat 52
POB 9000
1201 DH Hilversum
Tel: (35) 713911
Fax: (35) 217158

Nederlandse Christelijke Radio Bereniging (NCRV)
Bergweg 30
POB 121
1200 JE Hilversum
Tel: (35) 719911
Telex: 43249

BANKS

ABN AMRO Bank NV
POB 600
1000 AP Amsterdam
Tel: (20) 6289898
Fax: (20) 6287740

The Bank of Tokyo (Holland) NV
POB 792
1000 AT Amsterdam
Tel: (20) 5737737
Fax: (20) 6791016
Telex: 14497

Banque Paribas Nederland NV
POB 274
Herengracht 539-543
1000 AG Amsterdam
Tel: (20) 6204911
Fax: (20) 6247502
Telex: 11488

H. Albert de Bary & Co. NV
Herengracht 448-458
1017 CA Amsterdam
Tel: (20) 5554911
Fax: (20) 5554428
Telex: 12029

Cooperatieve Centrale Raiffeisen-Boerenleenbank BA (Rabobank Nederland)
Croeselaan 18
POB 17100
3500 HG Utrecht
Tel: (30) 909111
Fax: (30) 902898
Telex: 40200

Credit Lyonnais Bank Nederland NV
POB 1045
63 Coolsingel
Rotterdam
Tel: (10) 4695911
Fax: (10) 4148391
Telex: 21366

Dai-Ichi Kangyo Bank Nederland NV
Apollolaan 171
1077 AS Amsterdam
Tel: (20) 5740200
Fax: (20) 6760301
Telex: 15717

Friesland Bank
Zuiderstraat 1
Leeuwarden
Tel: (58) 994499
Fax: (58)994591
Telex: 46120

Indonesische Overzeese Bank NV
Stadhouderskade 84
1073 AT Amsterdam
Tel: (20) 5700700
Fax: (20) 6626119
Telex: 11327

ING Bank Internationale Nederlanden Bank NV
POB 1800
1000 BV Amsterdam
Tel: (20) 5639111
Fax: (20) 5635700
Telex: 11402

F. van Lanschot Bankiers NV
POB 1021
5200 HC's Hertogenbosch
Tel: (73) 153911
Fax: (73) 153066
Telex: 50641

Mees Pierson NV
POB 293
1000 AG Amsterdam
Tel: (20) 5279111
Fax: (20) 5274592
Telex: 11424

Nomura Bank Nederland NV
Boelelaan 7
1083 HJ Amsterdam
Tel: (20) 5496969
Fax: (20) 6461642
Telex: 16406

Yamaichi Bank Nederland NV
Strawinskylaan 1057
1077 XX Amsterdam
Tel: (20) 6649966
Fax: (20) 6628415
Telex: 15772

STOCK EXCHANGES

European Options Exchange
POB 19164
1000 GD Amsterdam
Tel: (20) 5504550
Fax: (20) 230012
Telex: 10955

Vereniging voort de Effectenhandel
Amsterdam Stock Exchange
Beursplein 5
1012 JW Amsterdam
Tel: (20) 5234567
Fax: (20) 6248062
Telex: 12302

INTERNET ADDRESSES

Usenet group(s):
soc.culture.netherlands
The Dutch Homepage
http://www.eeb.ele.tue.nl/map/netherlands.html
Statistics Netherlands
http://www.cbs.nl/eng/yifs/index.htm
The Dutch Yellow Pages
http://www.markt.nl/dyp/index-en.html
Netherlands Board of Tourism
http://www.nbt.nl/holland/home.htm
Rabobank - Biweekly Review of Economy
http://rabobank.info.nl/engels/default.htm

New Zealand

Economy

Overview

New Zealand has a very healthy, modern economy with a heavy reliance on foreign trade. Recent growth is strong, inflation is under control, unemployment has fallen in the past few years, and the government is running budget surpluses for the first time in 17 years. This growth is expected to continue, and New Zealand is beginning to repay its large foreign and domestic public debt. The government has refinanced its debt and manages all cash flow through periodic issuance of government stock and treasury bills held by both domestic and foreign investors. There is almost no regulation of the economy, and industry thrives with almost no influence from the government. The only economic powers the government retains are spending and taxing. The Reserve Bank Act of 1989 makes the Reserve Bank's primary function achieving and maintaining price stability.

Trade

The majority of imports come from Australia, followed by the United States. New Zealand welcomes foreign investment without discrimination. Countries wishing to trade should be aware that some preference is given to Australia; any Australian goods can enter New Zealand without tariffs in accordance with the Closer Economic Relationship (CER) agreement between the two countries. Canada also receives preferential tariff treatment on some items. Any barriers to trade will be further diminished as New Zealand implements the GATT Uruguay Round Agreement. Over 90 percent of exports and imports are carried by sea. Foreign goods and investors are welcome, particularly those operating in sectors that can contribute to foreign-exchange earnings and employment.

Sectors

Agriculture Agriculture is one of the largest sectors of New Zealand's economy, accounting for about 27 percent of GDP. The principal food crops are barley, wheat, and maize. Other major agricultural sectors include forestry and logging, and wood manufacturing.

Industry New Zealand industries operate in one of the least regulated markets in the world. Companies frequently make requests for foreign manufacturing and industry contracts. Its manufacturing sectors are still significantly based on a large and mostly efficient agricultural sector. The majority of growth industries include agricultural production items and niche markets, such as cellular phones and videos.

Services Tourism has become the most important foreign exchange earner, surpassing meat products and enjoying an annual growth rate of over 10 percent. This has helped fuel rapid growth in related industries, including construction, gambling, and transportation. Communications and business/personal service industries, however, are showing the strongest growth over the last few years.

Trends

New Zealand boasts an almost completely free market, and the economy shows several signs indicating continued growth in the intermediate term. The government has a net trade surplus and expects to eliminate net foreign currency. The government is very open to foreign investment and to companies opening branches in New Zealand. These factors, combined with a growing tourism market, should give New Zealand a great deal of optimism for the future.

At a Glance

THE COUNTRY
Location Southwestern Oceania, southeast of Australia in the Pacific Ocean. Includes several groups of islands, including the Antipodes Islands and the Auckland Islands.
Terrain Predominately mountainous with some large coastal plains.
Climate Temperate with some sharp regional contrasts.

THE PEOPLE
Population 3,500,000
Ethnic composition
European 88%
Maori 9%
Pacific Islander 3%
Religious composition
Anglican 22%
Presbyterian 16%
Roman Catholic 15%
Other 40%
Languages spoken English, Maori.
Education and literacy Ten years of schooling are compulsory. Literacy is 99 percent.
Labor force
Total: 1,600,000
By occupation: services 67.4%, manufacturing 19.8%, and primary production 9.3%

COUNTRY FACTS
Political and legal This parliamentary democracy has a legal system based on English law, with special land legislation and land courts for Maoris. The Court of Appeals is the highest court, although further appeal is possible with the Privy Council in London. There is no formal, written constitution.
Telephone International and domestic telephone systems are excellent. Submarine cables extend to Australia and Fiji, and there are two Pacific Ocean INTELSAT earth stations. International country code: [64]. Selected city codes: Auckland (9), Christchurch (3), Wellington (4).
Transportation New Zealand has five major ports and 108 airports. The railroad system is government-owned. The highway is extensive, with over 92,000 kilometers of highway, almost 50,000 of which are paved. Inland waterways are extensive, but of little importance to transportation. About 80 percent of the population lives in cities.
Environment Relatively few major problems, though vehicles cause some air pollution, and industrial pollutants and sewage adversely effect water quality. Two-thirds of the forests have been eliminated. There is very little arable land. Current issues are deforestation; soil erosion; and the effect non-native species have had on native flora and fauna.
Media A unified service operates 64 AM and two FM radio stations, plus 14 television stations. Libel laws follow British limitations. There are 35 daily major newspapers.
Health Publicly financed comprehensive health services are supported by the state. Private health insurance is also available. New Zealand has one of the highest incidences of skin cancer in the world. Life expectancy of males is 73 years; of females, 80 years.

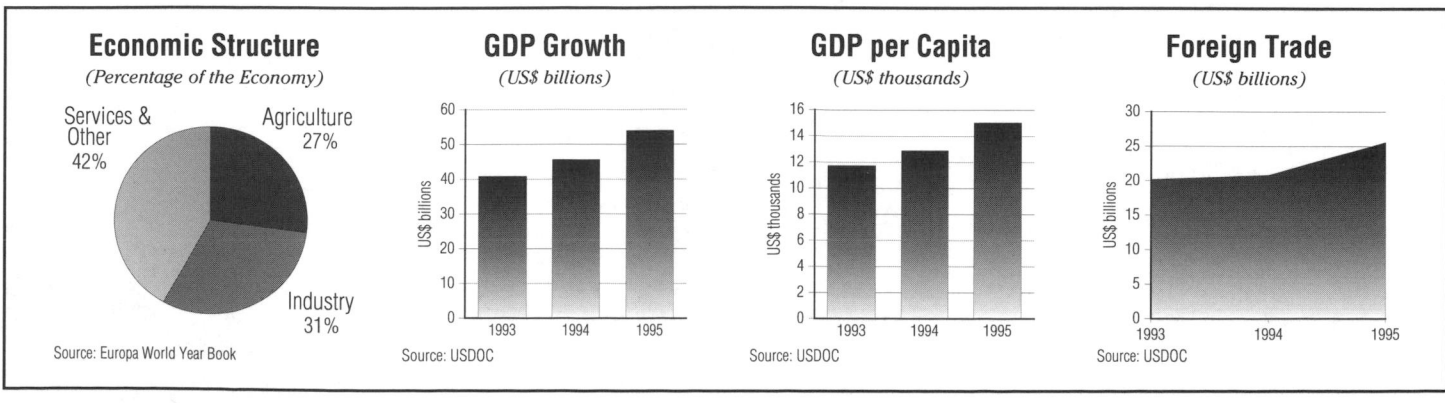

Economic Structure
(Percentage of the Economy)
Services & Other 42%
Agriculture 27%
Industry 31%
Source: Europa World Year Book

GDP Growth
(US$ billions)
Source: USDOC

GDP per Capita
(US$ thousands)
Source: USDOC

Foreign Trade
(US$ billions)
Source: USDOC

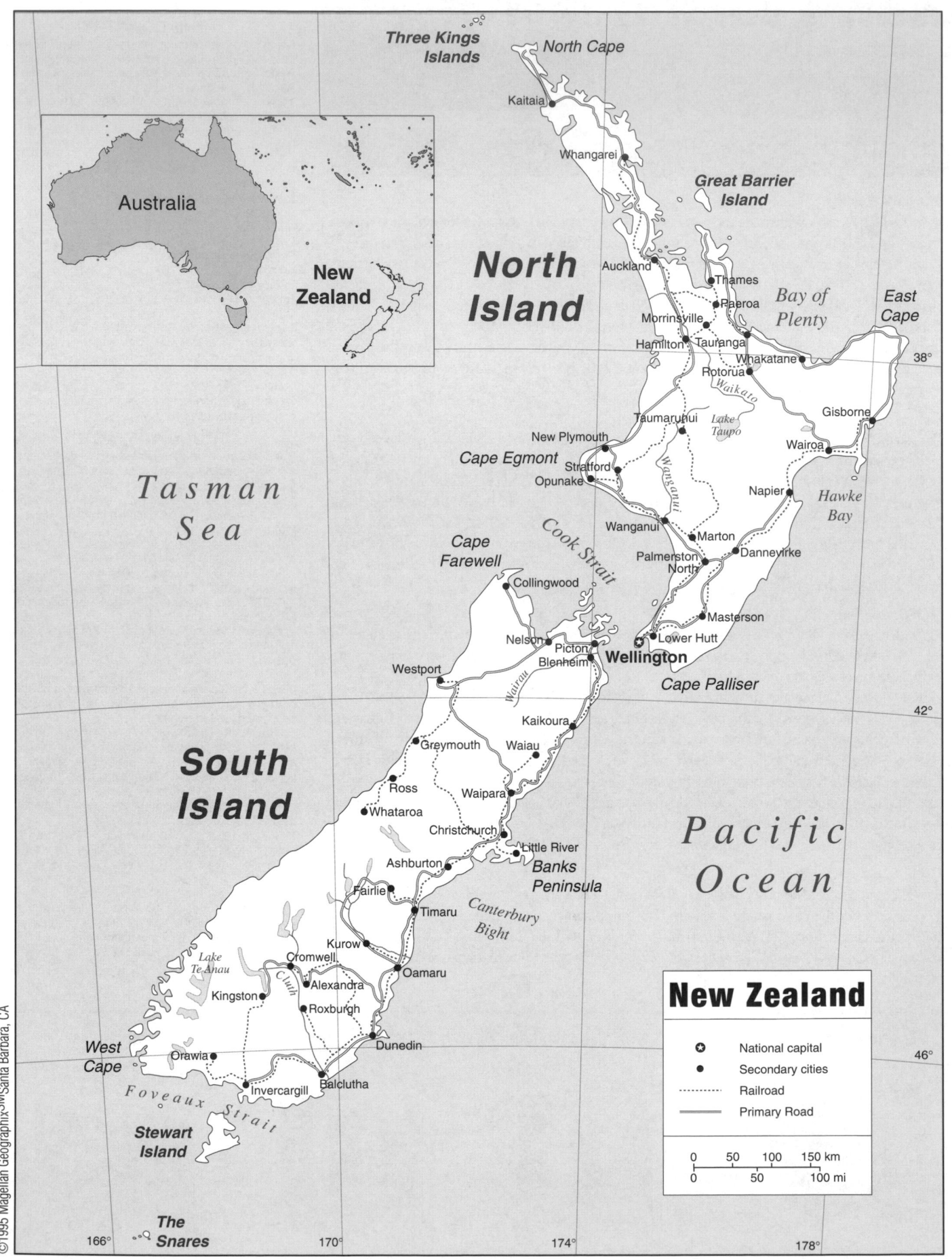

Three Kings Islands

North Cape

Kaitaia

Whangarei

Great Barrier Island

Australia

New Zealand

North Island

Auckland
Thames
Paeroa
Bay of Plenty
East Cape
Morrinsville
Hamilton
Tauranga
Whakatane
Rotorua
38°
Waikato
Taumarunui
Lake Taupo
Gisborne
New Plymouth
Wairoa
Cape Egmont
Stratford
Opunake
Wanganui
Napier
Hawke Bay
Wanganui
Marton
Danneyirke
Palmerston North

Tasman Sea

Cape Farewell

Collingwood

Cook Strait

Masterson
Lower Hutt
Wellington
Cape Palliser

Nelson
Picton
Blenheim

Westport

Wairau

42°

Kaikoura

South Island

Greymouth
Waiau

Ross
Waipara

Whataroa

Christchurch

Little River
Banks Peninsula

Pacific Ocean

Ashburton

Fairlie

Canterbury Bight

Timaru

Kurow
Cromwell
Oamaru

Lake Te Anau

Clutha

Alexandra
Roxburgh

Kingston

West Cape

Orawia

Dunedin

46°

New Zealand

⊛ National capital
● Secondary cities
···· Railroad
— Primary Road

0 50 100 150 km
0   50   100 mi

Invercargill
Balclutha

Foveaux Strait

Stewart Island

The Snares

166°   170°   174°   178°

©1995 Magellan Geographix℠Santa Barbara, CA

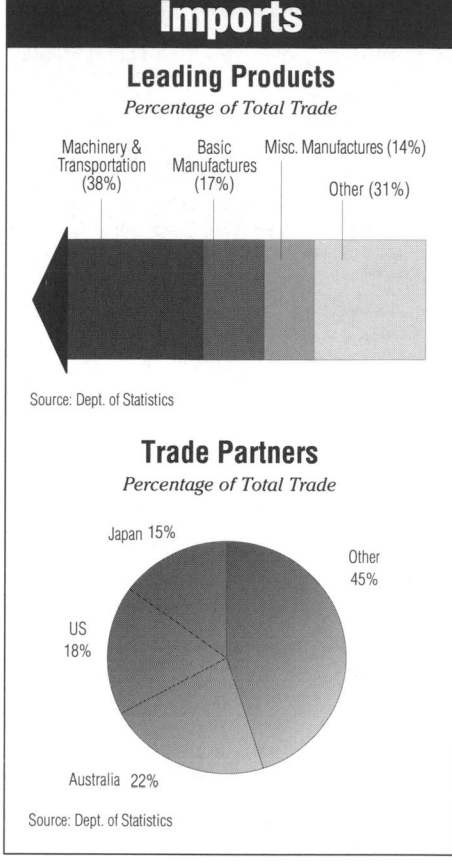

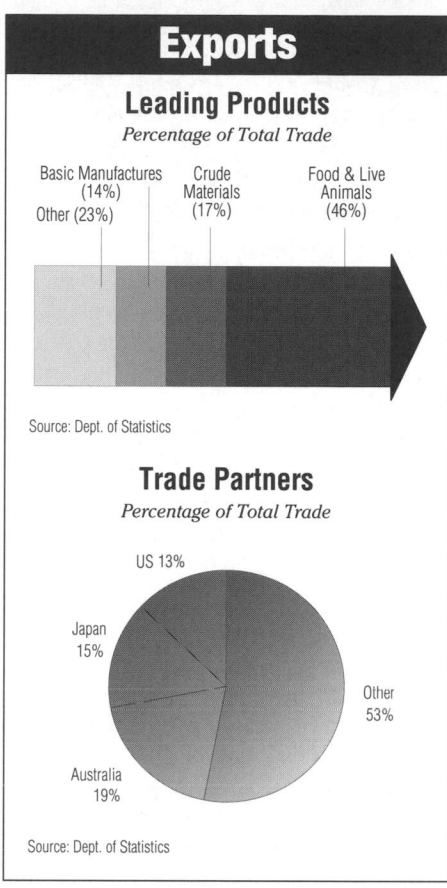

Opportunities

FOR IMPORTING TO NEW ZEALAND

- machinery
- mechanical appliances
- electrical machinery
- electrical equipment
- optical, photographic equipment
- surgical equipment
- plastics
- vehicles, parts, and accessories
- helicopters and parts
- paper
- paperback book products

FOR EXPORTING FROM NEW ZEALAND

- meat
- fish/fisheries
- forestry resources
- albuminoidal substances
- aircraft and parts

GROWTH SECTORS

- public sectors
- niche markets (specialty food, cellular telephones, paperback books, film and video)
- hospital supplies—health care/emergency services
- paper and paperboard
- food processing
- forestry/logging
- tourism
- agricultural production items

GOVERNMENT PROCUREMENT

- expansion of several airports including Auckland International Airport
- several bridge widening projects
- traffic control metering
- oceanic air traffic control
- road expansion

Trade News

RULES AND REGULATIONS

- **Trade news** New Zealand companies and foreign importers operate in one of the least regulated markets in the world. New Zealand continues to deregulate its economy, following a pattern of the recent past. Through sharp reductions in interest and inflation rates, combined with political stability, New Zealand seeks to achieve economic prosperity.

- **Regulations** Principal import channels are sales agents, importer-distributors, direct importers, and users.

- **Prohibited imports** Some agricultural goods are restricted on phytosanitary grounds, with the main commodities affected being pork, poultry, and egg products. Only cooked products in these categories are allowed entry.

- **Standards** Standards cover a wide variety of subjects, including design, safety, specifications of performance, and quality of products. Adoption of these standards is generally voluntary, but can be made compulsory through a statutory reference. Compliance may be an important factor in sales promotion.

- **Import licenses** Import licenses were abolished on July 1, 1992.

- **Tariff concessions** Although some tariffs exist, provision exits for concessions to be granted by the New Zealand Ministry of Commerce for goods not available from New Zealand manufacturers.

- **Tariffs** Tariffs range about 14 percent; rates are higher for motor vehicles, tires, textiles/clothing/carpet, and footwear. Alcoholic beverages (including beer, wine, and spirits), tobacco products, and some petroleum products are subject to additional excise duty. Excise duty is also paid on similar items that are domestically produced. Products from certain South Pacific countries enter duty-free. Canadian imports have a separate tariff rate that is somewhat reduced from the standard rate.

- **Other taxes** With very few exceptions, goods imported into New Zealand are liable for a goods and service tax (GST). This tax, currently set at 12.5 percent, is payable on the sum of the customs value of the goods, plus any customs duty payable thereon, plus freight and insurance costs incurred in transporting the goods.

- **Customs valuation** Duties on goods imported into New Zealand are usually calculated as a percentage of the cost of goods f.o.b. (free on board). In some cases, they are calculated on the basis of a charge on a specific unit of weight, volume, or other measurement (specific rate) and occasionally on the basis of a combination of ad valorem and specific rates. Ad valorem duty is assessed on the f.o.b. value of the goods. The rate of duty payable is determined by the classification of the goods in the New Zealand tariff which is based on the harmonized commodity description and coding system.

- **Barriers** The only major roadblock to doing business in New Zealand would be a determination that one's product or service is inappropriate for the market. Australian goods are imported into New Zealand without tariffs due to the Closer Economic Relationship with Australia (CER); therefore competition can be stiff.

- **Export controls** The only controls on exports (manufacturing, service, and agricultural) have been the commodity marketing boards, who have, through statute monopoly, sole marketing rights on exports of dairy products, apples, and kiwi fruit. Other boards maintain licensing systems, but these tend to be unrestrictive.

GOVERNMENT AGENCY

Customs Department
POB 2218
Wellington
Tel: (4) 473-6099 Fax: (4) 473-7370

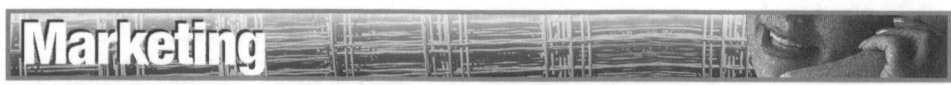

Overview

Despite its relatively small size and isolation, affluent New Zealand offers many attractive niche markets. Historically, it has worked successfully to develop import substitution industries, but it still needs a wide variety of imported capital, raw and intermediate goods, as well as a variety of consumer and other specialized products. Since the 1980s, the government has been attempting to deregulate industry and make it more competitive in international markets. Although this has resulted in hardship for domestic business, it has opened new markets for foreign enterprises to sell in New Zealand.

Distribution

New Zealand is a very small nation, although local distribution can become a problem because of the island geography. Traditionally, most distribution has been through small, specialty retail outlets, with larger, general outlets being relatively unimportant. However, the international trend toward chain store operations, larger outlets, and flatter, more direct distribution networks, is also being seen in New Zealand. Small buyers are also banding together in cooperatives to achieve buying power. Many larger retailers buy direct from manufacturers. There is a reliable network of agencies specializing in refrigerated and frozen foodstuffs with distribution networks operating throughout the country. Many New Zealand importers are also manufacturers, who may also produce or partially produce certain products under license from their overseas suppliers. Distribution through a New Zealand branch or subsidiary is also common when the volume is substantial and the foreign firm wishes to retain control of distribution.

Agents, Distributors, and Partners

The compact size of the New Zealand market usually permits a single or a very few specialized distributors to serve a foreign entity. Most goods pass through sales agents, importer-distributors (who import certain stock lines as well as take orders for direct shipment), and direct importers and users. Sales agents sell a variety of products, from production materials to consumer goods. New Zealand agents and distributors both attend and exhibit at trade fairs all over the world as they look for new opportunities. There is no specific body of law governing agency relationships. Franchises are a recent addition to New Zealand's economy; already they are doing very well in the larger towns and will probably soon expand from fast-food outlets to franchised service providers. Direct marketing has become the fastest-growing distribution channel in the last five years, especially for clothing. Trade fairs remain of lesser importance except for specialized agricultural machinery and related products.

Selling Techniques

New Zealanders are very brand loyal and slow to switch products. The primary criteria for selling in New Zealand are: design and features, quality, price, terms of payment and delivery, and selling propositions that stress special features and quality are especially likely to succeed. Capital intensive or service products are usually sold through one-on-one discussions with potential buyers. When retailers need to introduce consumers to new products or purchasing opportunities, most use telemarketing and mass media advertising.

Advertising

Nearly 100 agencies, most of them New Zealand-owned, are available to foreign sellers; consulting with them is wise, for the media opportunities here are many. By far the largest share of ads run in the 28 daily newspapers. Most major papers are owned by two companies: Independent Newspapers Limited and Wilson and Horton Limited. Together, these firms account for 80 percent of the country's one million daily circulation. The leading business journal is *The National Business Review*, published weekly in Auckland. More than 2,300 magazines are available in New Zealand. There are three television stations and a pay-for-view vendor offers three additional program choices, claiming to cover nearly the entire country. There are more than 33 commercial and community radio stations available. Advertising is self-regulated by the Advertising Standards Authority, which deals with radio and television, and the Advertising Standards Complaint Board.

Service and Customer Support

Service and customer support is a growing area of focus for New Zealand manufacturers and retailers. Prior to the removal of import and export licensing, there was little consumer choice. A buyer's market now exists, however. As the population becomes more well-traveled, it develops higher standards for product quality and service, and this puts pressure on the entire marketing chain. Companies entering this market must take into account New Zealand's location and challenging terrain in order to maintain a steady flow of spare parts and technical support, or they will not be able to remain competitive.

Marketing in New Zealand

MARKETING TIPS

- **Business immigration** BIP policy requires that applicants must demonstrate they have the background, ability, skills, and investment capital for their proposed venture.
- **Keep it separate** Although some foreign businesses try to serve the New Zealand market through Australian organizations, this seldom works. Despite close ties, the markets are different, and New Zealanders resent being subordinated to Australia.
- **Stock and station agents** These agents often act as exclusive intermediaries and often as business managers.

MARKETING CONTACTS

A Winwood & Associates
19 Richmond Avenue
Nelson 7001
Tel: (3) 546-6973 Fax: (3) 546-6973

A C Nielsen (NZ)
POB 17-211
Greenlane
Auckland
Tel: (9) 523-3165 Fax: (9) 524-9030

AGB McNair
POB 33-819
Takapuna
Auckland 1332
Tel: (9) 486-2144 Fax: (9) 486-3836

Applied Support Services
Unit 2, 48 Lemnos Place
Titirangi
Auckland 1007
Tel: (9) 817-7460

Business Information Service
POB 4138
Auckland 1015
Tel: (9) 307-7790 Fax: (9) 307-7791

Business Research Centre
POB 10-617, The Terrace
Wellington 6036
Tel: (4) 499-3088 Fax: (4) 499-3414

Business Research Centre
POB 36-417
Northcote
Auckland
Tel: (9) 480-2715 Fax: (9) 480-5719

Colmar Brunton Research
POB 33-690
Takapuna
Auckland 1332
Tel: (9) 486-1671 Fax: (9) 486-3483

Consumer Link
POB 33-679
Takapuna
Auckland 1332
Tel: (9) 486-1654 Fax: (9) 486-7476

Customer Focus
POB 17-361
Karori
Wellington 6033
Tel: (4) 476-6378 Fax: (4) 476-6178

Startel Communications
Private Bag 92090
Auckland Mail Centre 1030
Tel: (9) 525-3432 Fax: (9) 525-3939

Thinking Cap (NZ)
POB 1299
Palmerston North 5330
Tel: (6) 355-5599 Fax: (6) 355-5598

United Fresh
POB 13-343
Johnsonville
Wellington 6032
Tel: (4) 477-4411 Fax: (4) 477-4466

XPO Exhibitions
POB 4347
Christchurch 8015
Tel: (3) 379-0653 Fax: (3) 379-7931

Business Culture

Greetings and Courtesies

 New Zealanders are generally friendly, outgoing, social people, but are also always polite and can be quite formal. After people get to know each other, behavior becomes more casual, but follow the lead of your host or associate before moving to a more relaxed attitude. Most New Zealanders are of English descent, and their behavior reflects this heritage. They appreciate people who are open, direct, honest, and have a sense of humor. Talking loudly, being physically demonstrative, and any other behavior that calls attention to oneself is frowned upon. The accepted greeting (both for meeting someone and saying good-bye) is smiling, making eye contact, and shaking hands. Handshakes are generally firm and brief, with a rapid, simple up-and-down motion. It is not necessary or appropriate to shake especially hard or squeeze the other person's hand. When meeting a woman, wait for her to extend her hand. If she doesn't, smile and nod slightly.

Business Ethic and Framework

 New Zealanders are practical, hard-working people, and pride themselves on their traditional ability to make something out of nothing. Fundamentally conservative and thrifty, they do not like to see anything go to waste or be casually discarded. It has been said that a New Zealander can fix an entire machine with a piece of wire. New Zealanders tend to trust others, until they are given a reason not to. Once this happens, it can be extremely difficult, and sometimes impossible, to regain that broken trust. Two of the quickest ways to lose trust are acting dishonestly and showing bad faith in your business dealings.

Decision Making

 New Zealanders tend to be very honest and direct. Their inherent thriftiness sometimes becomes evident in an avoidance of unnecessary expenses (such as overseas phone calls or faxes) or unneeded progress reports. It can also delay a final decision or slow down negotiations. If you need a response to a question or issue by a specific time, make this clear to your associates—but do so politely, and never aggressively. If they understand you really do need an answer by a certain time they will do their best to respond. However, this urgency must be real. If you impose a deadline as a negotiating tactic, you will risk being viewed as dishonest, faith will be broken, and you could permanently damage—or destroy—a business relationship.

Women

 Women are found in all levels of business, including management positions, and expect to be treated seriously and with the respect to which their position entitles them. In New Zealand, a certain formality is the norm all the time, and if you are dealing with a woman be sure not to treat her any differently than you would treat a man in the same position. Also, do not assume that the way she responds to you is based on her gender. New Zealand businesswomen are as open and direct as the men; if a woman is friendly, do not attach special importance to this. Treat women as business associates instead of as women. Foreign women can expect to be treated the same as men, but exactly how a woman is treated will depend on the person she is encountering. Women who are professional and self-assured can expect to be treated with respect and taken seriously.

Meetings

 Meetings should be set up in advance, especially when dealing with government officials. Punctuality is important. You might even consider arriving at a meeting or appointment a little early. Before business, there will usually be pleasant small talk, which will probably be about the culture, sports, and sights of New Zealand. If you make a presentation to a New Zealand company, it should be detailed and complete. Agreements and proposals should state everything clearly, and all terms and conditions should be explained in detail.

Business Attire

 Standard attire is a conservative suit (especially when meeting with government officials). Women should wear tasteful, conservative clothing appropriate for business. The climate ranges from subtropical in the north, to temperate in the south (where there can be rain throughout the year). December to March is summer, and warmer temperatures prevail. June to September is winter, with mild weather in the north and cold temperatures (and snow) in the south.

Cultural Cautions

DO'S

- If possible, learn a few things about New Zealand's culture before you arrive. New Zealanders respond warmly to foreigners who have taken the time to understand their country.
- Always ask permission before taking someone's picture. This is especially important when photographing the Maori.
- If English is your native language, always speak and write it correctly. New Zealanders take great pride in their English heritage and are very exact about their language. They will easily make allowances for people from non-English speaking countries, but can be quite unforgiving about mistakes made by people who claim English as their native language.

DON'TS

- New Zealand is not an extension of Australia, and New Zealanders resent being viewed as such. Do not talk about New Zealand as if it is part of Australia, and do not compare the two countries.
- Race is a sensitive issue. Do not bring it up as a topic of conversation. If someone does talk about it, your safest course will be to listen politely without taking a specific position.
- Don't make the "V" for victory gesture with your palm facing inward. In New Zealand, this is extremely insulting.

CUSTOMS

- Business cards are exchanged casually. Your card should be well-designed, but clearly convey the important information about your company. A card that effectively communicates information is ultimately more important than one that looks good but might be hard to read.
- Gifts are not required, or a particularly important element of doing business in New Zealand. If all your contact with an associate is at an office or restaurant (business is often conducted over drinks), gifts can be dispensed with.

OBSERVATIONS

- The original inhabitants of New Zealand were the Polynesian Maori, and their culture is still very much alive and evident today. The traditional greeting among Maori is rubbing noses.
- Sports are a big part of New Zealand's culture, and will very likely come up in conversation. You may not follow sports or be familiar with New Zealand's sports, but do be aware of how important they are to New Zealanders. At least be ready to listen to and talk about this important topic. Water sports, as well as rugby, cricket, and tennis are followed with particular interest.
- The best time for business travel to New Zealand is February through October. December, January, July, and August are popular vacation periods among businesspeople. Don't expect to conduct business the week before or the week after Easter. You should also avoid nationally celebrated holidays or events.

NEGOTIATIONS

- Always be polite and good-natured, even when things aren't going the way you want.
- Being confident in addition to well-mannered will earn you respect and serve you well.
- New Zealanders usually negotiate openly and directly, clearly stating what they want. If you are unclear about anything, ask a direct question.
- Agreements are sometimes reached with a handshake, but always get a written contract so you'll know the deal is legally binding.

Legal System

New Zealand, as an independent nation, retains a "Westminster" system of government. Its legal system is based on the British common law. The Governor-General is the nominal head of state, while the single House of Representatives has full power and authority to make law. District Court judges and High Court judges are appointed from the legal profession only, and appointments are not political. The judiciary is independent of the state.

Intellectual Property

Patents Patents are protected for 20 years. Application can be made through an agent in New Zealand or the United Kingdom.

Trademarks Protection for trademarks runs for seven years and may be renewed for subsequent 14-year terms. Trademark protection has been extended to include the shape of goods and packaging. Registration can be made by an agent in New Zealand or the United Kingdom.

Copyrights To bring New Zealand into line with the GATT Uruguay Round Agreement, new copyright legislation and legislation relating to computer layout designs has been enacted to improve protection for computer hardware and software. New measures also make it easier to prevent the importation of material that infringes copyrights. Copyright protection is generally valid for 50 years.

Industrial Designs Industrial designs continue to receive protection under copyright and registered designs legislation. Proposed legislation will create rights in designs upon creation without regard to registration.

Business Registration

Common business investment structures for nonresidents in New Zealand include branches, subsidiaries, partnerships, and joint ventures. An overseas company must become registered under the Companies Act within 10 working days of commencing business in New Zealand and must have an address for service of process in New Zealand. A New Zealand subsidiary of an overseas company must also be registered under the Companies Act. Both a branch and the subsidiary are required to file annual returns and financial statements. A subsidiary does not need to have a director resident in New Zealand unless it is listed on the NZ Stock Exchange. The NZ Stock Exchange is a private and self-regulating body with detailed compliance rules. Partnerships and joint ventures have no registration requirements (except in the case of a joint venture between companies), but these entities do not offer limited liability to the owners.

Contracts and Dispute Resolution

New Zealand contract law is derived from a mix of case law and statute. Although the law recognizes that most contracts may be concluded by oral agreement, preparation of a written agreement is advisable in all but the simplest cases. Guarantee and land sale contracts must be evidenced in writing to be enforceable. For complex matters significant legal input in both negotiation and the preparation of the transaction documents is the norm. The majority of disputes are resolved by litigation through the courts, although alternative dispute resolution such as arbitration and mediation is common.

Labor

All employees are covered by the Employment Contracts Act. The Act provides for freedom of association, allowing employees to decide who should best represent their interests and whether they will contract with their employer collectively or individually. A number of statutes imply certain terms into employment contracts, notably provisions for holidays, leave benefits, minimum wages, health and safety conditions, wage protection, equal pay, and human rights. In addition, certain terms are implied into employment contracts under the common law, such as the duty of an employer to treat employees fairly and reasonably and the duty of the employee to deal with the employer in good faith. All employees have a statutory right to bring proceedings for unjustified dismissal, disadvantage, discrimination, or sexual harassment. The Employment Tribunal and Employment Court have exclusive jurisdiction to deal with all cases founded on employment contracts. Most New Zealanders work a 40-hour week over five days, Monday to Friday. There is free bargaining between employers and employees over hours of work and days worked. Each employee is entitled to three weeks' paid holiday each year in addition to the 11 statutory holidays.

Source: Martelli McKegg Wells & Cormack

Legal Matters

LEGAL BRIEFS

- **Business entities** A company is the most common business organization. A company is an independent entity apart from its shareholders, and the shareholders can have limited liability. Most commercial law firms have shelf companies that can be purchased or used to form new companies at short notice. Legal fees, including registration fees, can be under NZ$1,000 (US$660) for a basic company.

- **Lawyers** New Zealand has a "fused" legal profession, and most lawyers are both barristers and solicitors. Barristers may practice as barristers only, but they may not practice in partnership and must act only on the instructions of solicitors. Most commercial legal work is carried out by firms of both barristers and solicitors in partnership. Lawyers advise on most substantial business and financial transactions.

- **Free competition** Monopolies and anti-competitive business practices are strictly regulated by law, as enforced by the Commerce Commission, Ministry of Commerce. It is unlawful to acquire the assets or shares of a business if the acquisition would result in dominance or strengthening of dominance in a market, unless advance clearance is obtained from the Commerce Commission.

- **Securities commission** Offers of securities to the public and trading in securities are regulated by the Securities Commission. The Securities Act contains insider trading restrictions.

- **International agreements** New Zealand is a member of GATT/WTO; CISG; New York Convention on the Recognition and Enforcement of Foreign Arbitral Awards; New Zealand-Australia Free Trade Agreement; Paris Convention; and ATA Carnet Convention.

LEGAL CONTACTS

Martelli McKegg Wells & Cormack
Barristers & Solicitors
P.O. Box 5745
Auckland
Tel: (9) 379 7333
Fax: (9) 309 4112

Justice Department
Charles Fergusson Building
Bowen Street
Wellington
Tel: (4) 472 5980
Fax: (4) 499 2295

New Zealand Law Society
P.O. Box 5041
Wellington
Tel: (4) 472 7837
Fax: (4) 473 7909

Auckland District Law Society
P.O. Box 58
Auckland
Tel: (9) 303 1036
Fax: (9) 309 3726

Rudd Watts & Stone
POB 3798
Auckland 1
Tel: (9) 309-4863
Fax: (9) 379-3326

Baldwin Son & Carey
POB 5999
Auckland
Tel: (9) 373-3137
Fax: (9) 373-2123

Russell McVeagh McKenzie Bartlet & Company
POB 8
Auckland 1
Tel: (9) 309-8839
Fax: (9) 377-1849

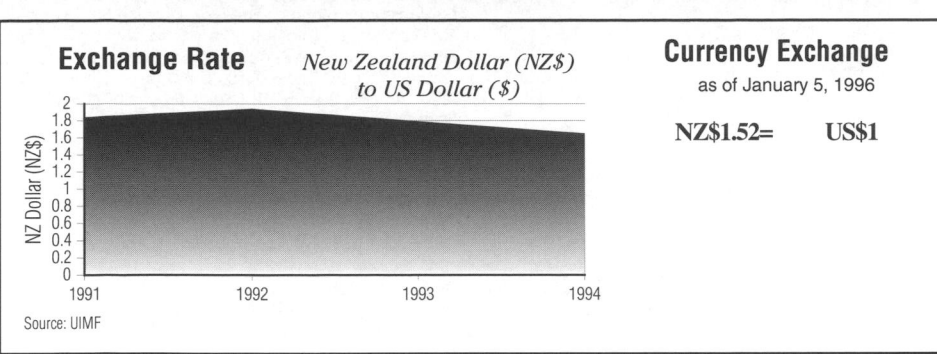

Exchange Rate *New Zealand Dollar (NZ$) to US Dollar ($)*

NZ Dollar (NZ$): 2, 1.8, 1.6, 1.4, 1.2, 1, 0.8, 0.6, 0.4, 0.2, 0
Years: 1991, 1992, 1993, 1994

Source: UIMF

Currency Exchange
as of January 5, 1996

NZ$1.52= US$1

Money Matters

BITS AND PIECES

- **Major investments** Investments more than NZ$ 10 million, or large investments in commercial fishing or rural land, require the approval of the Overseas Investment Commission. Virtually all applications are approved.

- **Money market** Since the removal of controls over the financial sector, money market activity has grown rapidly, particularly with regard to foreign exchange trading; including the development of a secondary market in government securities; the use of hedging devices to handle interest and exchange rate risks; and the introduction of new financial instruments.

- **Stock market** Stock exchanges are located in five cities and engage in the trading of domestic and certain foreign securities.

- **Financing** The main sources of financing for imports or new development are undistributed profits, the share market, merchant banks, insurance companies, savings banks, finance companies, private sources, the investment by overseas companies in New Zealand branches and subsidiaries, and joint venture companies.

- **Capital sources** There are several capital suppliers in the country, but resources remain scarce for start-ups and high-risk ventures. Standard financial products are available for import and export opportunities. Local banks offer secured bank credit and trade finance vehicles, and open account purchase agreements are common between long-time trading partners.

- **Depositor risks** Banks operate on an "at your own risk" policy for both management and depositors. Federal deposit insurance and regulatory functions are not administered by the Reserve Bank of New Zealand.

- **Securities commission** Offers of securities to the public and public trading of securities are regulated by the Securities Commission. The Securities Act contains insider trading restrictions.

- **Nonresident bank accounts** Overseas banks' accounts in New Zealand may be used to settle transactions with other countries.

- **Gold** Residents may hold and acquire gold coins in New Zealand without restriction. There are no restrictions or licensing requirements on the importation and exportation of gold.

Currency

The currency in use is the New Zealand dollar (NZ$), which is divided into 100 cents.

Foreign Exchange

The external value of the New Zealand dollar is determined by supply and demand conditions, although the Reserve Bank of New Zealand may intervene at its discretion. Foreign exchange dealers may adjust their rates in response to market conditions. There are no taxes on the purchase or sale of foreign exchange. Financial institutions may conclude forward exchange contracts to buy or sell foreign currencies against New Zealand dollars at market rates, regardless of the source of funds. There are no controls over the receipt or remittance of foreign exchange.

Capital Transfers

There are no restrictions on the inflow or outflow of capital, and currency is freely convertible. Residents may dispose of foreign income overseas; travelers may bring unlimited amounts of foreign and domestic bank notes into the country.

Investment Incentives

The government offers no incentives to foreign investors. A stable, free, competitive, low-inflation environment is viewed as the strongest incentive for investment that the government can provide. There is no capital gains tax. New Zealand has double taxation agreements with 24 countries, including the United States.

Investment Restrictions

There are very few restrictions on foreign investment. However, resident companies are taxed at a rate of 33 percent of income, while non-resident companies are taxed at a higher 38 percent of income derived from New Zealand.

BANKS

Reserve Bank of New Zealand
POB 2498
Wellington
Tel: (4) 472-2029
Fax: (4) 473-8554

ANZ Banking Group (New Zealand) Limited
NZ Headquarters
POB 1492
Wellington
Tel: (4) 496-7000
Fax: (4) 473-6919

Bank of New Zealand
BNZ Center
1 Willis Street
Wellington
Tel: (4) 474-6999
Fax: (4) 474-9048

National Bank of NZ Ltd.
Corporate Headquarters
170-186 Featherston Street
Wellington
Tel: (4) 494-4000
Fax: (4) 494-4021

Westpac Banking Corporation
General Manager's Office and Administration
318-324 Lambton Quay
Wellington
Tel: (4) 498-1000
Fax: (4) 498-1350

TAXATION

Taxation requires sophisticated knowledge of complex rules and regulations specific to each country. For more detailed information we suggest you refer to the Ernst & Young Corporate Tax Guide and Directory, available from the Ernst & Young accounting office in your country, or from:

Ernst & Young
P.O. Box 2146
Auckland, New Zealand
Tel: (9) 377-4790
Fax: (9) 377-8137

- Resident companies pay income tax on worldwide assessable income. Nonresident companies doing business through a branch pay tax only on New Zealand source income. Taxes paid outside New Zealand by a New Zealand taxpayer can be used as a credit against New Zealand taxes.

At a Glance

Corporate Income Tax Rate (%)	33
Capital Gains Tax Rate (%)	0
Branch Tax Rate (%)	38
Withholding Tax (%)	
Nonresidents	
Dividends (a)	30
Interest (b)	15
Royalties from Patents, Know-how, etc. (c)	15
Payments to Contractors	15
Branch Remittance Tax	0
Residents	
Dividends (d)	33
Interest (e)	24
Net Operating Losses (Years)	
Carryback	0
Carryforward	Unlimited

(a) Final tax.
(b) Final tax if the recipient is not associated with the payer. For an associated person, this is a minimum tax (the recipient must report the income on its annual tax return, but it may not obtain a refund if the tax withheld exceeds the tax that would otherwise be payable on its taxable income). Under the Income Tax Act, associated persons include the following: any two companies in which the same persons have a voting interest of at least 50% and, in certain circumstances, a market value interest of at least 50% in each of the companies; two companies that are under the control of the same persons; and any company and any other person (other than a company) that has a voting interest of at least 25% and, in certain circumstances, a market value interest of at least 25% in the company. Interest paid by an approved issuer on a registered security to a nonassociated person is subject only to an approved issuer levy of 2% of the interest payable.
(c) Final tax on royalties relating to literary, dramatic, musical, or artistic works. For other royalties, this is a minimum tax.
(d) Dividends received by a resident company from a nonresident are subject to a 33% withholding. The withholding is reduced by any foreign withholding tax paid on the dividend.
(e) Tax on interest is increased to 33% if the recipient's tax file number is not supplied.

Air Travel Times

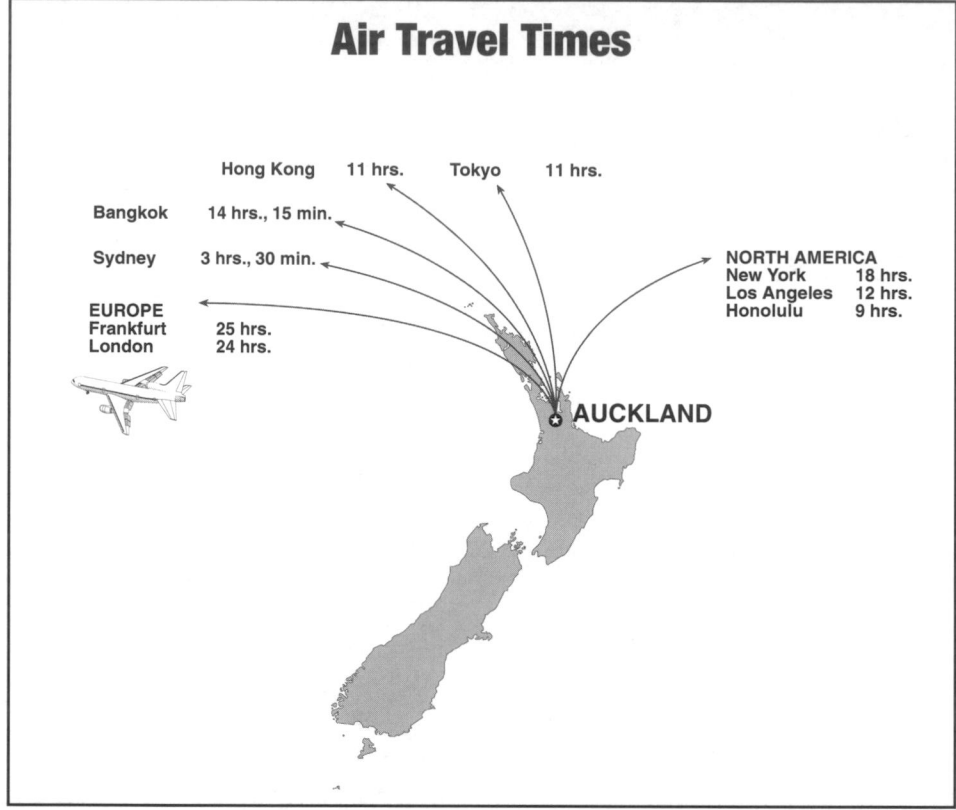

Hong Kong   11 hrs.   Tokyo   11 hrs.

Bangkok   14 hrs., 15 min.

Sydney   3 hrs., 30 min.

NORTH AMERICA
New York   18 hrs.
Los Angeles   12 hrs.
Honolulu   9 hrs.

EUROPE
Frankfurt   25 hrs.
London   24 hrs.

AUCKLAND

COMMUNICATIONS

Telephones New Zealand telephone service is top quality. Long distance services are available for rental to visitors.

Fax International telex facilities are available at main post offices and some hotels. Telegrams may be sent from the post offices and by telephone (although expensive). Inquire at hotels for available local faxing services, which are plentiful in larger towns.

Post office Airmail to most cities worldwide takes four to eight days. Post offices are open Monday-Thursday 8:30 am to 5:00 pm. Friday 8:30 am to 8:00 pm.

TV/Radio New Zealand has two national commercial free television stations, many private commercial stations, and broadcasts on AM and FM NZBC (AM 756).

BEST TRAVEL BOOKS

Fodor's Travel Guides, New Zealand. Tourist oriented, excellent source of city details.

Lonely Planet Travel Survival Kit, New Zealand. The best guide I've found. 776 pages, 24 color.

Fodor's Exploring New Zealand. Stylish and attractive as any guide ever published.

Do's and Taboo's Around the World. The Bestselling Guide to International Behavior. Edited by Roger Axtell, compiled by the Parker Pen Company. The ultimate guide to international behavior, now completely updated and expanded. Helpful, fun to read!

USEFUL TELEPHONE NUMBERS

If you are calling from outside New Zealand, you will need to add the country code [64] and any other international dialing requirements from within your country.

- Emergency 111
- Domestic Operator 010
- International Operator 0170
- International Directory 0172
- Directory Assistance 100
- Audio/Visual rental, Auckland ....(9) 303-4574
- Computer rental, Auckland..................(9) 366-0246
- Auckland Language Center.................(9) 303-1962
- UniService Translation Center ....(9) 302-3378
- Air New Zealand..................................(9) 379-3510
- Ansett New Zealand............................(9) 302-2146
- Qantas Airways ....(9) 379-0306
- United Airlines ....(9) 379-3800
- InterCity (rail and bus).........................(9) 358-4085
- InterIsland Ferry Service ....(4) 498-3999
- Auckland Coop. Taxi Service ....(9) 300-3000
- Airport Limousine Service ....(9) 528-9198
- Auckland Visitor Centre.......................(9) 366-6888
- Wellington Visitor Centre.....................(4) 801-4000

Credit Card Information

Lost or stolen credit cards (call collect to the US, regardless of which country the card was issued in).

- Amex ....[1] (919) 333-3211
- Diner's Club...............................[1] (303) 799-1504
- MasterCard ....[1] (314) 275-6690
- Visa ....[1] (410) 581-7931

Travelogue

WORKWEEK

Government Monday-Friday 9:00 am to 5:00 pm.
Banks Monday-Friday 9:00 am to 4:30 pm.
Business Monday-Friday 8:30 am to 5:00 pm.
Retail Monday-Thursday 9:00 am to 5:30 pm. Friday 9:00 am to 9:30 pm. Saturday 9:00 am to 1:00 pm. Some shopping malls and tourist area shops are also open on Sundays.

HOLIDAYS

Holidays 1996
January 1-2 New Year's
April 5 Good Friday
April 8 Easter Monday
April 25 Anzac Day
June 10 Queen's Birthday
October 4 Labor Day
December 25 Christmas
December 26 Boxing Day

VISA AND PASSPORT

Travel to New Zealand without a visa is allowed for stays up to 90 days. Possession of a return ticket is required. Extensions of stay up to 12 months are available. A valid passport is required and must be valid three months beyond date of departure. This allows one to work but not receive income during visit. Immigration is concerned with appropriate individuals, not business proposals. Contact the New Zealand Embassy or Consulate for permanent residency permits.

DEPARTURE FORMALITIES

All visitors are required to pay a departure tax of NZ$20.

IMMUNIZATION

No vaccinations are required for entry to New Zealand unless one has been infected within two weeks prior to arrival.

TIPPING

Tipping is not necessary in New Zealand as a GST (goods and service tax) is added to all bills; however, many visitors tip anyway.

CRIME

Incidents of crime are infrequent and foreign visitors are seldom victims.

INFRASTRUCTURE

Travel arrangements to New Zealand are available through commercial travel agencies. Travel is simple and car transportation, taxi or rental, is efficient and up-to-date. Remember to drive on the left-hand side of the road. Accommodations are economical and abundant. Sports lodges, bed & breakfast inns, and farmstay inns are available. Quantas and British Airways fly direct to New Zealand. Other airlines include: Japan Airlines, Australian Airlines, Singapore Airlines, Thai International, and Cathay Pacific. Hourly flights operate between Wellington and Auckland. Free or low-cost stopovers are often offered as "circle fares" and create a reasonable way to visit several spots in the Pacific. Taxis, shuttle buses, and airport bus services are available for transportation to and from the airport. Taxis are available only at taxi stands or by telephone. Car rentals are available in all cities and most towns. A current domestic or international driver's license is required and insurance must be purchased for a rented vehicle. If planning to travel between islands with a rented car it is most economical to rent a separate car on each island. If you will be touring the country extensively, camper vans are also available for rental. They are provided with all necessary items, including dishes and bedding.

NATIONAL TOURIST OFFICE

New Zealand Tourism Board
POB 95
Wellington
Tel: (4) 472-8860 Fax: (4) 478-1736

Contacts

GOVERNMENT AGENCIES

Department of Conservation
POB 10420
Wellington
Tel: (4) 471-0726
Fax: (4) 471-1082

Department of Labour
POB 3705
Wellington
Tel: (4) 473-7800
Fax: (4) 471-1906

Department of Survey and Land Information
Private POB 170
Wellington
Tel: (4) 473-5022
Fax: (4) 472-2244

Ministry of Agriculture and Fisheries
POB 2526
Wellington
Tel: (4) 472-0367
Fax: (4) 472-9071, 474-4244

Ministry of Commerce
POB 1473
Wellington
Tel: (4) 472-0030
Fax: (4) 473-4638

Ministry of Consumer Affairs
c/o Ministry of Commerce
POB 1473
Wellington
Tel: (4) 474-2750
Fax: (4) 473-9400

Ministry for the Environment
POB 10362
Wellington
Tel: (4) 473-4090
Fax: (4) 471-0195

Ministry of Foreign Affairs and Trade
Pvt Bag 18-901
Wellington
Tel: (4) 472-8877
Fax: (4) 472-9596

Ministry of Forestry
POB 1610
Wellington
Tel: (4) 472-1569
Fax: (4) 472-2314

Ministry of Health
POB 5013
Wellington
Tel: (4) 496-2000
Fax: (4) 496-2340

Ministry of Research, Science and Technology
POB 5336
Wellington
Tel: (4) 472-6400
Fax: (4) 471-1284

Ministry of Transport
POB 3175
Wellington
Tel: (4) 472-1253
Fax: (4) 473-3697

New Zealand Tourist and Publicity Department
POB 95
Wellington
Tel: (4) 472-8860
Fax: (4) 478-1736

Statistics New Zealand
POB 2922
Wellington
Tel: (4) 495-4600
Fax: (4) 472-9135

CHAMBERS OF COMMERCE

New Zealand Chamber of Commerce
POB 11-043, Manners Street
Wellington
Tel: (4) 472-3376
Fax: (4) 471-7161

Auckland Regional Chamber of Commerce and Industry
POB 47
Auckland
Tel: (9) 309-6100
Fax: (9) 309-0081

Chamber of Commerce and International Trade (Canterbury)
POB 13-157
Christchurch
Tel: (3) 664-992
Fax: (3) 798-658

New Zealand Chambers of Commerce and Industry
POB 1590
Wellington
Tel: (4) 472-3376
Fax: (4) 471-1767

Otago Chamber of Commerce and Industry
POB 5713
Dunedin
Tel: (3) 479-0181
Fax: (3) 477-0341

Overseas Investment Commission
2 The Terrace
Wellington
Tel: (4) 472 2029
Fax: (4) 471 3655

Commerce Commission
P.O. Box 105222
Auckland Central
Tel: (9) 377 3094
Fax: (9) 377 3561

Securities Commission
P.O. Box 1179, Wellington
Tel: (4) 472 9830
Fax: (4) 472 8076

Wellington Chamber of Commerce
9th Floor
109 Featherston St.
POB 1590
Wellington
Tel: (4) 472-2725
Fax: (4) 471-1767

TRADE ASSOCIATIONS

New Zealand Manufacturers' Federation Inc.
Enterprise House
3-9 Church St.
POB 11-543
Wellington
Tel: (4) 473-3000
Fax: (4) 473-3004

Federated Farmers of New Zealand Inc.
6th Floor, Agriculture House
12 Johnston St.
Wellington 1
POB 715
Wellington
Tel: (4) 473-7269
Fax: (4) 473-1081
Telex: 31525

Fruitfed Ltd.
Bldg. 4, 666 Great South Rd.
POB 2116
Auckland
Tel: (9) 525-042
Telex: 60335

New Zealand Council of Wool Exporters Inc.
POB 536
Christchurch
Tel: (3) 379-7484
Fax: (3) 366-6061

New Zealand Dairy Board
Pastoral House
Lambton Quay
POB 417
Wellington 1
Tel: (4) 471-8300
Fax: (4) 471-8600
Telex: 3348

New Zealand Fishing Industry Board
Private Bag 24-901
Wellington
Tel: (4) 385-4005
Fax: (4) 384-2727

New Zealand Meat Marketing Corpn Ltd.
POB 9440
Wellington
Tel: (4) 385-2368
Fax: (4) 385-2387

New Zealand Meat Producers' Board
Seabridge House
110 Featherston St.
POB 121
Wellington
Tel: (4) 473-9150
Fax: (4) 472-3172
Telex: 3525

New Zealand Pork Industry Board
Level 4
Walsh Wrightson Tower
94 Dixon St.
POB 4048
Wellington
Tel: (4) 385-4229
Fax: (4) 385-8522

New Zealand Vegetable and Potato Growers' Federation Inc.
Agriculture House
Johnston St.
POB 10232
Wellington 1
Tel: (4) 472-3795
Fax: (4) 471-2861

New Zealand Wool Board
10 Brandon St.
Box 3225
Wellington
Tel: (4) 472-6888
Fax: (4) 473-7872
Telex: 3472

MARKET RESEARCH FIRMS

Critchlow Associates
POB 4103
Wellington 6015
Tel: (4) 472-8244
Fax: (4) 472-6695

Fact Finders
POB 26254
Epsom
Auckland 1030
Tel: (9) 525-2181
Fax: (9) 525-0876

Forsyte Research
POB 33-498
Takapuna
Auckland 1332
Tel: (9) 486-6526
Fax: (9) 486-3850

IMS (NZ)
POB 3397
Auckland 1015
Tel: (9) 489-7240
Fax: (9) 489-7278

Market Focus
POB 331468
Takapuna
Auckland 1332
Tel: (9) 486-8899
Fax: (9) 486-8890

Market Research Society
POB 7011, Wellesley Street
Auckland 1036
Tel: (9) 410-9569
Fax: (9) 410-9569

Marketing Projects
POB 17-129
Greenlane
Auckland 1130
Tel: (9) 524-9091
Fax: (9) 524-0362

McIntosh Associates
POB 817
Hamilton 2015
Tel: (7) 834-0465
Fax: (7) 834-0465

MDD Corporate Surveys
POB 8506, Symonds Street
Auckland 1035
Tel: (9) 303-4726
Fax: (9) 303-4724

MRL Research Group
POB 33-931
Takapuna
Auckland 1332
Tel: (9) 486-6414
Fax: (9) 486-6417

National Research Bureau
POB 10-118, Dominion Road
Auckland 1030
Tel: (9) 630-0655
Fax: (9) 638-7849

Research International NZ
POB 99-069
Newmarket
Auckland 1031
Tel: (9) 524-8555
Fax: (9) 524-8580

Research Solutions
POB 82-081
Highland Park
Auckland 1730
Tel: (9) 535-5525

RADIO & TELEVISION

Radio New Zealand Limited
Aurora House
The Terrace
PO Box 2092
Wellington
Tel: (4) 474-1555
Fax: (4) 474-1340

Television New Zealand Limited
Television Centre
100 Victoria Street West
PO Box 3819
Auckland
Tel: (9) 377-0630
Fax: (9) 375-0979

AD AGENCIES

Grey New Zealand
Level 5
126 Vincent St.
Auckland 1
Tel: (9) 377-4279
Fax: (9) 307-0741

J. Walter Thompson International (NZ) Ltd.
POB 2566
Auckland
Tel: (9) 379-9625
Fax: (9) 302-2470, 303-1370

McCann-Erickson Ltd.
POB 830
Auckland
Tel: (9) 638-8075
Fax: (9) 6315-744

Ogilvy & Mather Advertising
Symonds St.
POB 8735
Auckland
Tel: (9) 367-9200
Fax: (9) 367-7247

Saatchi & Saatchi Advertising
123-125 The Strand
POB 801
Parnell, Auckland
Tel: (9) 3799403
Fax: (9) 3796149

NEWSPAPERS

The Dominion
84 Willis St.
POB 3740
Wellington
Tel: (4) 474-0000
Fax: (4) 474-0350

Evening Post
Press House
40 Boulcott St.
POB 3740
Wellington
Tel: (4) 47400444
Fax: (4) 474-0237

The National Business Review
Level 26
Bank of New Zealand Tower
125 Queen St.
POB 1734
Auckland
Tel: (9) 307-1629
Fax: (9) 307-9060

New Zealand Herald
46 Albert St.
POB 32
Auckland
Tel: (9) 379-5050
Fax: (9) 366-0146

Otago Daily Times
Lower Stuart St.
POB 517
Dunedin
Tel: (3) 477-4760
Fax: (3) 477-1313
Telex: 5692

Mercantile Gazette
POB 37-424
Parnell
Auckland
Tel: (9) 302-4892
Fax: (9) 302-5292

New Zealand Gazette
Dept. of Internal Affairs
POB 805
Wellington
Tel: (4) 495-7200
Fax: (4) 499-1865

The Star
293 Tuam St.
POB 1467
Christchurch
Tel: (3) 797-100
Fax: (3) 660-180

PERIODICALS

Friday Flash
POB 1034
Wellington
Tel: (4) 676-068
Telex: 3811

Management
POB 5544
Wellesley St.
Auckland
Tel: (9) 358-5455
Fax: (9) 358-5462

New Zealand Dairy Exporter
POB 38-272
Petone
Wellington
Tel: (4) 568-3475
Fax: (4) 568-3474

New Zealand Forest Industries
POB 5544
Auckland
Tel: (9) 358-5455
Fax: (9) 358-5462

New Zealand Horse & Pony
POB 1327
Auckland
Tel: (9) 307-7161
Fax: (9) 309-2279

New Zealand Official Yearbook
Dept. of Statistics
POB 2922
Wellington
Tel: (4) 495-4600
Fax: (4) 472-9135

New Zealand Science Review
POB 1874
Wellington
Fax: (4) 505-623

New Zealandia
POB 845
Auckland
Tel: (9) 784-380
Fax: (9) 360-3065

NZ Business
22 Heather St.
Private Bag 93218
Parnell
Auckland
Tel: (9) 379-4233
Fax: (9) 309-3575

Pacific Way Magazine
Private Bag 92512
Wellesley St.
Auckland
Tel: (9) 373-5408
Fax: (9) 309-8718

World Affairs
UN Asscn. of NZ
POB 11-750
Wellington
Tel: (4) 382-8783

INTERNET ADDRESSES

Usenet group(s):
soc.culture.new-zealand

New Zealand Business Directory
http://webworkshop.co.nz/webworks/nzbd/nzbd.html

New Zealand Government Web Pages
http://www.govt.nz/

New Zealand Press
http://www.icair.iac.org.nz/nz/news/index.html

WWW Sites in New Zealand
http://archpropplan.auckland.ac.nz/misc/sources9.html

Tourism & Travel in New Zealand
http://nz.com/nz/TourTravel/

Nicaragua

Republic of Nicaragua

Economy

Overview

Currently, Nicaragua is one of poorest countries in the Western hemisphere, due in part to poor government decisions made over the past decade. Both overall GDP and GDP per capita have fallen significantly from their early 1980s levels. The government has, however, recently attempted to reform the economy, primarily by stabilizing the currency and implementing basic structural adjustment measures. These reforms have been successful to some extent, but there has been very little economic growth. Unemployment still exceeds 50 percent in some areas, and the country still has a chronic gap in its balance of payments.

Trade

Nicaragua has improved relations with many of its trading partners, and foreign trade has increased accordingly. Its largest trading partner is the US, which accounts for 25 percent of Nicaragua's imports and nearly 40 percent of exports. Other major trading partners include Spain and the UK. The government has reduced tariffs, eliminated most non-tariff trade barriers, and greatly relaxed foreign exchange controls, all in an effort to expand its trading base. Exports have continued to climb, primarily due to high coffee prices and the strong performance of non-traditional agricultural exports.

Sectors

Agriculture Agriculture is the major bright spot on Nicaragua's gloomy economic horizon. Production in agricultural sectors has increased 16 percent in the past couple of years. Agricultural production accounts for approximately 22 percent of GDP, and continues to grow. The aquaculture industry could grow even more with adequate government support, which seems possible in the near future.

Industry Nicaragua's manufacturing sectors have been slow to rise, but the government is trying to improve the industrial base by encouraging development of manufacturing and textile companies. A non-technical labor force and poor infrastructure are just a couple of the barriers the government will have to overcome, however. Nicaragua's mining industry, once a major source of income, has fallen significantly, although the mines have recently been privatized and several companies have sought concessions for new exploration.

Services Most service industries were privatized recently in an attempt to reform the economy. More than 40 percent of telephone operations are now privately operated, and 5 foreign companies have expressed interest in expanding this sector. Eight of Nicaragua's banks are privately owned, and the country has become more open to foreign investors and exchange.

Trends

Nicaragua has made large strides recently to move away from the problems that have plagued it throughout the past decade. In particular, inflation dropped significantly after the currency was stabilized, allowing the government to move forward with more structural reorganization. The real test may be just beginning, however, as Nicaragua tries to move into competitive manufacturing industries and seeks help from foreign investors. An unskilled work force and the overall lack of modern technology will hinder growth somewhat in the near term, until infrastructural developments are put into place.

At a Glance

THE COUNTRY

Location Middle America, between Costa Rica and Honduras.

Terrain Extensive Atlantic coastal plains rising to central interior mountains, with a narrow Pacific coastal plain interrupted by volcanoes. The terrain is subject to earthquakes and landslides.

Climate Tropical in the lowlands and cooler in the highlands.

THE PEOPLE

Population 4,300,000
Ethnic composition
Mestizo (mixed European and Indian) 69%
Caucasian 17%
Black (Jamaican origin) 9%
Indigenous 5%
Religious composition
Roman Catholic 95%
Protestant 5%
Languages spoken Spanish (official), English, indigenous languages.
Education and literacy While schooling is free and compulsory between the ages of six and 13, the completion rate of primary school is only 20 percent. Adult literacy is 77 percent.
Labor force
Total: 1,500,000
By occupation: services 45%, agriculture 37%, and industry 18%. Unemployment is 23%.

COUNTRY FACTS

Political and legal This constitutional democracy has a civil law system. The Supreme Court can review administrative acts. The military has divided the country into different regions for its administrative purposes.

Telephone Telecommunications facilities are government-owned. Basically inadequate outside Managua, the system is currently being expanded. International country code: [505]. Selected city codes: Leon (311), Managua (2).

Transportation The many airports are important because of limited road and railway facilities. The government-owned railway links Corinto to Granada. However, the majority of this system is inoperable. The network of highways includes the Pan-American highway. There are almost 26,000 kilometers of highway, but only 4,000 are paved. The inland waterway system includes two large lakes and five ports. There are 208 airports, but only 149 are usable, and only 11 have permanent-surface runways.

Environment Cultivation on steep slopes and depletion of forests has caused severe soil erosion. Pesticides, sewage dumping, and industrial waste have polluted some lakes and rivers, including Lake Managua. Current issues include deforestation, soil erosion, and water pollution.

Media There is no official state censorship in Nicaragua. The constitution provides for freedom of speech and the press, although there are some constitutional provisions pertaining to an obligation to provide accurate information. There are 45 AM, and no FM, radio stations and 7 television stations.

Health Progress in improving health care is slow. Life expectancy averages 63 years.

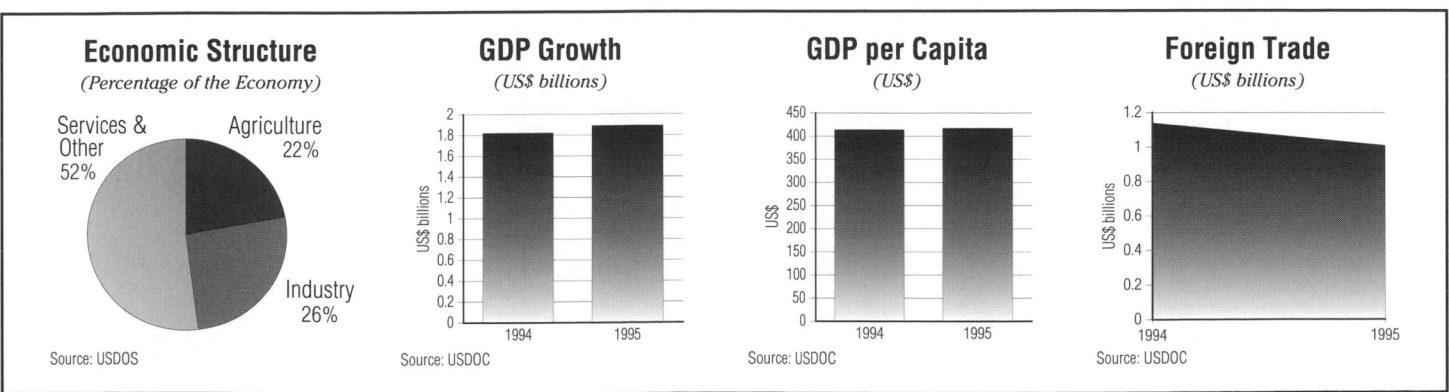

Economic Structure
(Percentage of the Economy)

Services & Other 52%
Agriculture 22%
Industry 26%

Source: USDOS

GDP Growth
(US$ billions)

Source: USDOC

GDP per Capita
(US$)

Source: USDOC

Foreign Trade
(US$ billions)

Source: USDOC

Business Travel

LH	1906	MADRID	935	113-3
LH	1022	STUTTGART HBF.	935	-
AF	1701	LYON	940	683-6
AY	822	HELSINKI	940	113-3
AA	071	SFRANCISCO-DALLAS	945	731-7

Travelogue

WORKWEEK

Offices Monday-Friday 8:00 am to noon and 2:30 pm to 5:30 or 6:00 pm.
Banks Monday-Thursday 8:30 am to noon and 2:00 pm to 4:00 pm.
Government Monday-Friday 8:30 am to noon and 1:00 pm to 4:30 pm.
Retail Monday-Friday 8:30 am to 5:00 pm.

HOLIDAYS

Holidays 1996
January 1 New Year's Day
April 13 Holy Thursday*
April 5 Good Friday*
May 1 Labor Day
July 19 Sandinista Revolution Anniversary
August 1 Festival of Santo Domingo
September 14 Battle of San Jacinto
September 15 Independence Day
November 2 All Souls' Day
December 8 Immaculate Conception
December 25 Christmas
December 26 Boxing Day
*Dates vary year to year.

VISA AND PASSPORT

A passport, a return ticket, and adequate funds for the duration of the stay are required for entry to Nicaragua. All passports must be valid for six months beyond the expected departure date. Visas are not required for stays of less than 30 days. Tourist cards are required and available when entering Nicaragua. For any visit that will exceed 30 days a visa must be requested from the Office of Immigration.

DEPARTURE FORMALITIES

A departure tax is collected at customs in Nicaragua.

IMMUNIZATION

Typhoid, polio, diphtheria, and gamma globulin vaccinations are recommended for all travelers.

TIPPING

Customary tips are 10 percent of the bill for hotels and restaurants; US$.50 per bag for porters; no tip for taxi drivers.

CRIME

Crime incidents have increased in recent years. Theft often occurs on crowded buses. When traveling on roads between Nicaragua and Honduras be particularly cautious. Land mines do exist in rural areas, off main roads. Any road travel after dark is hazardous as many vehicles do not operate with headlights.

INFRASTRUCTURE

Roads and highways are well developed. Six seaports are operated by the government-run Port Authority (ENAP). The Port of Corinto, on the Pacific Coast 110 miles northwest of Managua, is the most suitable for commercial shipping. It has an annual capacity of 1.5 million tons. The airport, Caesar Augusto Sandino International Airport, is seven miles from Managua and handles all passenger and cargo air traffic in and out of Nicaragua. Home or apartment rentals are abundant, but rental rates are high and first class apartment buildings are not available. The large hotels in Managua will exchange currency, including traveler's checks, and will accept some credit cards. Most other businesses accept cash only. It is best to hire taxis for the whole day as they are hard to come by away from the large hotels. Renting cars in not an efficient way to get around Nicaragua.

NATIONAL TOURIST OFFICE

Instituto Nicaraguense de Turismo (INTURISMO)
Avda Bolivar Sur
Apdo 122
Managua, JR
Tel: (2) 25436
Fax: (2) 25314

COMMUNICATIONS

Telephones Fiber optic cables are currently being installed. Approximately one percent of the population has a phone in the home. Cellular phones operate with coverage reaching the entire Pacific Coast. Most telecommunications are currently controlled by the state monopoly, Telcor. The ongoing privatization of this utility is considered an excellent opportunity for investors.
Fax While telegraph services are being updated, fax service is available in Managua.
Post office Services are available in major hotels and available countrywide.

BEST TRAVEL BOOKS

The Wall Street Journal Guide to Business Travel, Mexico and Central America. The most electrifying of all practical travel guides.
Do's and Taboo's Around the World. The Bestselling Guide to International Behavior. Edited by Roger Axtell, compiled by the Parker Pen Company. The ultimate guide to international behavior, now completely updated and expanded. Helpful, fun to read!
Mexico & Central American Handbook. Chicago: Passport Books. Indispensable—updated annually.

USEFUL TELEPHONE NUMBERS

If you are calling from outside Nicaragua, you will need to add the country code [505] and any other international dialing requirements from within your country.

- Information 112
- Operator(Domestic).. 110
- Operator (International)...................................... 116
- Hotel Camino Real/ Managua .... (2) 631410
- Hotel Intercontinental/Managua .... (2) 286991
- Hotel Las Mercedes .... (2) 631715
- US Embassy .... (2) 666010
- American Airlines .... (2) 663-900
- Copa Airlines .... (2) 670-045
- Lacsa Airlines .... (2) 668-268
- Budget Rental Car .... (2) 623-531
- DHL Courier Service .... (2) 284-081
- Hertz... (2) 668-400
- International Bonded Couriers .... (2) 631-411
- TNT Express .... (2) 666-493
- UPS .... (2) 664-289
- Police .... (2) 225-118
- Airport... (2) 316-24

Credit Card Information
Lost or stolen credit cards (call collect to the US, regardless of which country the card was issued in).

- Amex..[1] (919) 333-3211
- Diner's Club.................................[1] (303) 799-1504
- MasterCard ....[1] (314) 275-6690
- Visa ....[1] (410) 581-7931

Foreign Trade

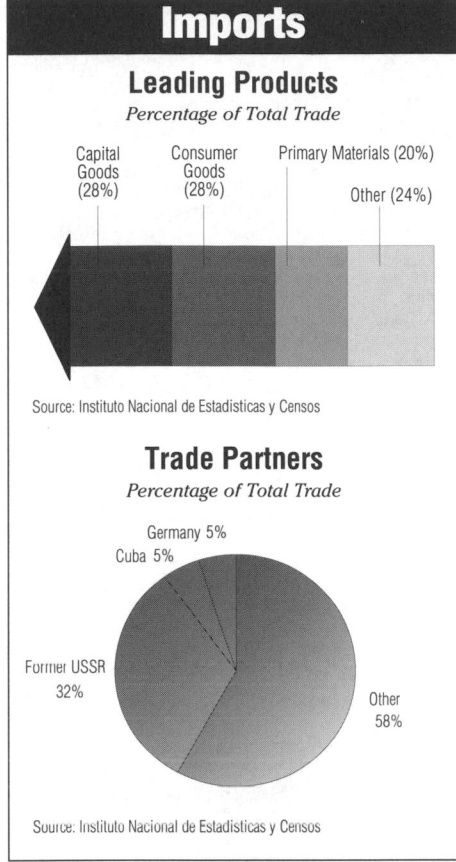

Imports

Leading Products
Percentage of Total Trade

Capital Goods (28%)
Consumer Goods (28%)
Primary Materials (20%)
Other (24%)

Source: Instituto Nacional de Estadisticas y Censos

Trade Partners
Percentage of Total Trade

Germany 5%
Cuba 5%
Former USSR 32%
Other 58%

Source: Instituto Nacional de Estadisticas y Censos

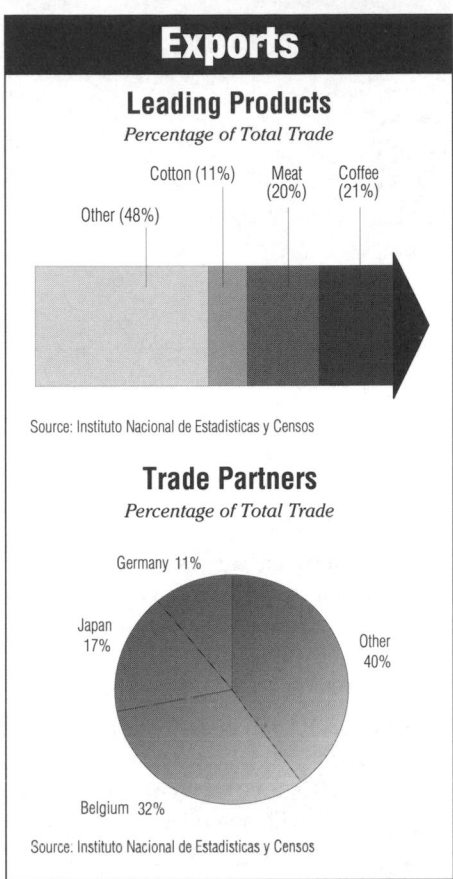

Exports

Leading Products
Percentage of Total Trade

Other (48%)
Cotton (11%)
Meat (20%)
Coffee (21%)

Source: Instituto Nacional de Estadisticas y Censos

Trade Partners
Percentage of Total Trade

Germany 11%
Japan 17%
Other 40%
Belgium 32%

Source: Instituto Nacional de Estadisticas y Censos

Opportunities

FOR IMPORTING TO NICARAGUA
- agricultural, food processing, packaging machinery
- electrical equipment
- fertilizer, petroleum
- franchising

FOR EXPORTING FROM NICARAGUA
- foodstuffs, coffee, cotton
- chemicals

GROWTH SECTORS
- agriculture
- fisheries
- livestock
- mining
- telecommunications

Trade News

RULES AND REGULATIONS
- **Trade news** Import tariffs and taxes are high on many items and often not assessed on CIF/bill of lading value, but on a price determined by Customs officials.
- **Import licenses** In most cases, the issuance of import licenses is only a formality.
- **Percent tariff rates** A maximum tariff level of 20 percent of CIF value is imposed on virtually all imports. A Temporary Protection Tariff of five to 15 percent of CIF value is levied on some 900 imported items. Some 750 other products are assessed a Specific Consumption Tax, generally limited to 15 percent of CIF value. A stamp tax of 5 percent is levied on all imports. The country's 15 percent sales tax is charged on entry of all imported goods that are not categorized as basic food basket items.

Legal

Legal System

Nicaragua is a civil code country. The justices of the Supreme Court, which sits in Managua, are appointed by the National Assembly for six-year terms.

Intellectual Property Rights

Patents and trademarks Patents are granted for periods of five to 10 years. There is an annual payment for registered patents. A patent is lost if not put into use within one year or if the annual tax is not paid. All trademarks must be registered to be considered valid in Nicaragua. Registration terms span 10 years, renewable for equal periods. Licenses must be registered.

Copyrights A copyright may be obtained on literary, musical, and artistic productions. Generally, copyright protection lasts for 30 years after the creator's death. The right may be lost by prescription in 10 years or, with respect to the dramatic works, in four years.

Trade secrets Few laws protect trade secrets in Nicaragua, and injunctions against violators are difficult to obtain.

Business Registration

Foreign corporations must record articles of incorporation, by-laws, and all appointments of agents in the mercantile registry. They must have a representative in Nicaragua with full company authority and must annually publish in the official newspaper the business balance sheet and the names of management. If a corporation's principal business is in Nicaragua and most of its capital is derived from Nicaragua or the shareholders' meetings are held in Nicaragua, it is considered a national company.

Contracts and Dispute Resolution

Nicaraguan businesses prefer contracts in writing. Disputes are handled by the courts, and are usually lengthy and expensive. Distributorship agreements are defined by law, which also provides for contract termination, indemnification, and recovery proceedings.

Legal Matters

LEGAL BRIEFS
- **Partnership names** Company names usually include the names of all the partners or the names of one or more of them, plus the words "y Compañía." The firm name of a company must be followed by the word "Limitada."
- **Common law trusts** Trusts, as they exist in the common law, are unknown in Nicaragua, but the freedom to contract often makes it possible to create relationships similar to trusts.
- **Liquidation** A company must be liquidated if it loses over 66 percent of its capital or becomes bankrupt.
- **Trademarks exceptions** Flags, coats-of-arms, insignia, devices, or denominations of any religion on any label or manufacturer's mark cannot be protected as trademarks.
- **International agreements** Nicaragua is a member of the Central American Convention for the Protection of Industrial Property.
- **Labor** Nicaragua's Labor Code was patterned after Mexican labor legislation. Laws emphasize the rights of workers, rather than collective bargaining. Unions are allowed, but the government imposes strict limits on them.
- **Notary publics** Notaries retain original documents in their file and issue certified copies. Instruments executed before a notary must be in Spanish.

LEGAL CONTACT
Bufete Castillo Ramirez
Cine Altamira 2c. Abajo
Casa No. 435
PO Box 2845
Managua
Tel: (2) 74514 Fax: (2) 75811

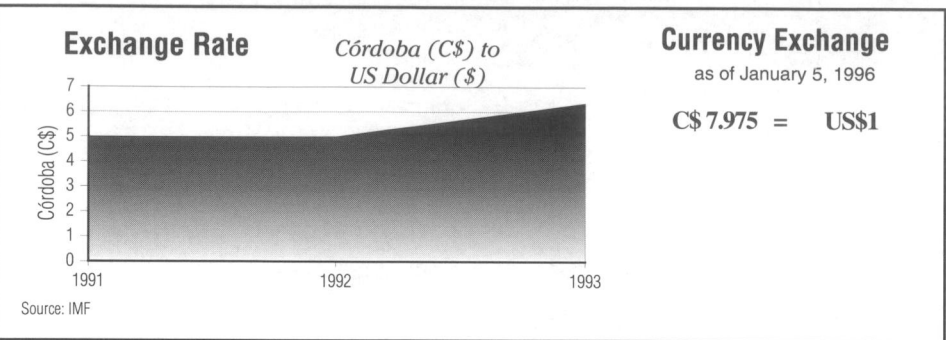

Exchange Rate *Córdoba (C$) to US Dollar ($)*

Córdoba (C$): 0–7 scale, years 1991, 1992, 1993

Source: IMF

Currency Exchange as of January 5, 1996

C$ 7.975 = US$1

Currency

The currency in use is the gold córdoba (C$), which is divided into 100 centavos. It is also called the córdoba oro.

Foreign Exchange

All foreign exchange is controlled by the Central Bank. It has authorized exchange transaction power to commercial banks and exchange houses. All transactions are approved on the basis of priority criteria established in accordance with sources of foreign exchange. Some transactions are not accepted, but they may be approved through an authorized foreign currency deposit account or with currencies from exchange houses.

Capital Transfers

Nicaragua law guarantees nonresident investors the right to remit 100 percent of profits through the official exchange market and repatriation of original capital. Foreign investors can also own 100 percent of Nicaraguan companies in most sectors. All foreign investments must be approved by a Foreign Investment Committee of the Ministry of Economy and Development to benefit from any incentives. Some industries have performance requirements for investors. Nicaragua plans to open even more sectors up to private investment, including telecommunications, water, and sewage. There is no limit to the amount of foreign currency that can be brought in to or taken out of Nicaragua. Any payment related to authorized imports are effected in the official markets.

Investment Incentives

There are very few investment requirements for foreign companies. Some imports can be imported duty-free, and others can be imported with a reduced tariff. Many foreign companies are exonerated from income, export, sales, or consumer taxes.

Investment Restrictions

Increased crime and political unrest are barriers to any successful investment. Despite the government's protests that it is opening investment for foreign companies, the red tape and bureaucracy can significantly slow down any investment. Certain sectors are owned by the government and are not expected to become privatized anytime soon. Foreign investors have complained of favoritism towards domestic investors.

TAXATION

Taxation requires sophisticated knowledge of complex rules and regulations specific to each country. Some of the more important taxes include:

- **Tax on real property** This is paid to municipalities where properties are located. For all acts involving real property originally acquired from the government or its institutions or municipalities with construction over 100 square meters. The tax rate is 100 percent tax on its recorded value. This tax is paid in advance, and notaries public must indicate payment of tax in all notarial deeds related to any of the above mentioned properties.
- **Tax on ownership and use of vehicles** The exact amount of the tax is determined according to the specific type of vehicle.

- **Value tax** A tax is imposed on goods circulated within the country, importation of goods into the country, transfer of real property, works, leasing, and rendering of subjects. The tax is levied on the net price obtained by deducting from the amount of invoice discounts or other reductions made according to commercial usage.
- **Consumers tax** Sale of many items is subject to a tax of five to 50 percent, payable on the price at the time of sale.
- **Stamp tax** Contracts, public documents, promissory notes, and other documents and instruments specified by law, executed, or issued within the country and executed or issued abroad to take effect in Nicaragua are subject to a stamp tax.

Money Matters

BITS AND PIECES

- **Gold** The Central Bank controls all gold sales. All prices are primarily based on international gold markets.
- **Capital** All capital transactions require authorization from the Central Bank.
- **External debt** Authorization for servicing external private debt depends on the availability of foreign exchange.
- **International aid** Nicaragua concluded an agreement with the International Monetary Fund in 1994, on an Enhanced Structural Adjustment Facility (ESAF) for the country. Also in 1994, during the consultative group (CG) meeting of donors in Paris, Nicaragua received high marks on the progress made on political issues over the last year, though the donors said the country could encourage a great deal more investment if it established a more secure property rights regime.
- **Inflation** Inflation has been rising in Nicaragua again lately after an incredible downturn over the past few years. The rise is primarily due to a large currency devaluation.
- **Exchange** Foreign exchange is available, partly because of the existence of a parallel exchange market that offers rates only slightly different from the official exchange rate.
- **Property rights** Definition of property rights has been a problem in Nicaragua, and remains part of the reason the country's economy hasn't improved. Ownership disputes over large tracts of land, businesses, and homes confiscated by the previous government have yet to be resolved.
- **Reform** The government announced sweeping government reform in 1991, and has been successful in reducing inflation and obtaining substantial economic aid from abroad.

BANKS

Central Bank of Nicaragua
Carretera Sur, KM 7
Apartado No. 2252 y 2253
Managua
Tel: (2) 50500 through 04
Fax: (2) 52272

Banco de America (BAMER)
Avda Sandino y 4a Calle Sur Este
Apdo 285
Managua, JR
Tel: (2) 26100
Telex: 1040

Banco Inmobilario (BIN)
Calle Principal Colonia Centroamerica
Apdo 1162
Managua, JR

Banco Nacional de Desarrollo (BND)
Km 31/2
Carretera a Masaya
Apdo 328
Managua, JR
Tel: (2) 67-1771
Fax: (2) 67-4222
Telex: 2078

Banco Nicaraguense (BANIC)
Centro Financiero Oscar Perez Cassar
Km 5.5
Carretera a Masaya
Apdo 549
Managua, JR
Tel: (2) 67-2730
Fax: (2) 67-1356
Telex: 2456

Banco Popular
Estatua Montoya
2 c. arriba
1/2 c. al sur
Apdo 3904
Managua, JR
Tel: (2) 666614
Telex: 22238

Marketing

Overview

Nicaragua is still a burgeoning market, and profits are a long-term prospect at best. There are several barriers, culturally and politically, slowing down any potential sales and inhibiting the entry of many foreign sellers into the Nicaraguan market.

Distribution and Agents

Imported products are handled by distributors and agents. The retail market has no large department stores or other retail operations. Foreign companies are safe when marketing their goods through a local agent or distributor; potential investors should consider taking on a Nicaraguan partner. There is no clearinghouse of information for finding a partner; foreign companies should contact the trade sections of their embassy for advice. Franchises and direct marketing are not regulated, but neither have they been enormously successful.

Advertising

Most advertising takes place on the radio, in newspapers, and on billboards. Major promotional activities are rare. Most business advertising and trade promotion occurs through print media. *La Tribuna*, *La Prensa*, *Barricada*, and *El Nuevo Diario* are the major newspapers; *Cable Centroamericano*, *El Observador Economio*, *Vistazo Economico,* and *Mundo Financiero* are the most important business journals. All the above are published in Managua. Trade shows are not regularly scheduled; when they are held, they take place at the Olof Palme Convention Center in Managua.

Service and Customer Support

Most Nicaraguan businesses place a low priority on service and consumers do not expect too much in this regard. After-market service is not yet an important selling point for imported goods and services.

Marketing in Nicaragua

MARKETING TIPS

- **Communication** Approximately one in 110 households has a telephone line. Public phones are slowly being introduced, and cellular service is available along the country's entire Pacific coast.
- **Selling techniques** The Sandinista years discouraged commercial activity, so sales techniques are currently at a developmental stage. As the economy grows, modern techniques including television and direct marketing are slowly encountering success.
- **Trade news** Import tariffs and taxes are high on many items and often not assessed on CIF/bill of lading value, but on a reference price determined by Customs officials, at times much higher than the actual price paid by importers.
- **Postal service** The postal service is rarely used for marketing goods, primarily because Nicaraguan businesspeople prefer face to face meetings. Mail does get into and out of Nicaragua rapidly and is regularly used for correspondence.
- **Transportation** Port and highway infrastructure is substandard.

AD AGENCIES

APCU de Nicaragua
Colonia Mantica No. 605
Dela Estatua
Montoya 1 Cuadra al
Nortey 1 Cuadra al Oeste
Managua
Tel: (2) 665157
Fax: (2) 665158

Business Culture

Greetings and Courtesies

Handshakes are appropriate for both men and women. Male friends may hug and female friends may hug each other briefly and brush their cheeks while making a kissing motion. Considerable deference is usually shown to the elderly.

Business Ethic and Framework

Respect and personal dignity lie at the core of Nicaraguan business and social culture. Although Nicaraguans are generally informal, their business and social culture is based on correct, often strongly hierarchical, but personal relationships. To Nicaraguans, work is far from the most important part of life, but it is an increasingly important sphere, and they do adhere to the forms and protocols that govern it.

Meetings and Decision Making

Appointments are necessary and should be made at least two weeks in advance. Punctuality is observed by Nicaraguans. Business deals may require several meetings and repeated trips to the country. Despite recent experience with communal forms of decision making, actual decisions are nevertheless almost always made at a high level of authority. It is important to cultivate personal relationships with all peers, however, because the quality of these relationships may strongly influence the actual decision maker even when your immediate counterpart is not the one making the decision.

Women

Although women generally occupy a secondary status in heavily male-dominated and *macho*-influenced Nicaragua, many operate businesses and may be accorded considerable personal freedom. Nicaraguan women are becoming more common and more accepted in business in general, although their presence remains rare in the upper levels of business. In general, foreign businesswomen should experience few problems.

Business Attire

Businessmen are expected to wear suits, but standards are generally informal and businessmen often dispense with jackets and ties. In general, it is somewhat inappropriate to dress too elegantly in Nicaragua. Avoid flashy attire, accessories, jewelry, or makeup.

Cultural Cautions

DO'S

- Learn something about Nicaragua's history and culture—your interest and any attempts to speak Spanish will be appreciated.
- Ask—politely—about people's health and family.

DON'TS

- Avoid race, religion, politics, and the economy as topics of conversation.

CUSTOMS

- Younger persons rise when seated if an older person enters the room.
- It is considered appropriate to bring a small present—such as candy or flowers—if invited to a home for a meal or other event.

OBSERVATIONS

- Nicaraguans smile a lot and maintain eye contact during exchanges; they expect you to do the same.
- Personal spacing is quite close in Nicaragua; persons attempting to increase the amount of space between themselves and others may be considered aloof or evasive.
- Compliments made regarding personal traits will generally be more welcome—and will earn greater respect—than compliments on possessions.
- Note that baseball is significantly more important in Nicaragua than football (soccer).

NEGOTIATIONS

- Although they like to bargain, Nicaraguans do not respond well to aggressive tactics. Avoid raising your voice or showing impatience, which is not only considered rude but can also be taken as a challenge.
- Nicaraguans present a united front during negotiations, deferring to the senior member. To avoid misunderstandings, be sure you know who has the authority to make a decision and the procedures and time frames that must be considered.

GOVERNMENT AGENCIES

Ministry of Agriculture and Livestock
Km 8 1/2 Carretera a Masaya
Managua JR
Tel: (2) 97211
Fax: (2) 678344

Ministry of Construction and Transportation
Km 5 1/2 Carretera Norte
Managua JR
Tel: (2) 43104

Ministry of Economy and Development
Km 6 Carretera a Masaya
Apartado 2412
Managua JR
Tel: (2) 70116, 70176
Fax: (2) 70095

Ministry of Finance
Palacio de Héroes y Mártires de la Revolución
Apartado Postal 78
Managua JR
Tel: (2) 625043, 27061
Fax: 27714

Ministry of Foreign Affairs
Détras de Los Ranchos
Managua JR
Tel: (2) 96563
Fax: (2) 663971

Ministry of Health
Complejo Civico Cmbtel Camilo Ortega Saavedra
Managua JR
Tel: (2) 50039, 97441, 97552
Fax: (2) 97483

Ministry of Labor
Frente donde fue la Cruz Roja
Managua JR
Tel: (2) 25729

Ministry of Natural Resources
Km 12 1/2, Carreta Norte
Apartado 5123
Managua, JR
Tel: (2) 31110
Fax: (2) 31274

Nicaraguan Institute of Energy
Apartado 55
Managua, JR
Tel: (2) 74103
Fax: (2) 72686

Nicaraguan Institute of Tourism
Avenida Bolívar Sur,
Apartado 122
Managua, JR
Tel: (2) 25436
Fax: (2) 25314

Nicaraguan Telecommunications and Postal Service Institute
Apartado 2264
Managua, JR

CHAMBER OF COMMERCE

Chamber of Commerce
Frente a Lotería Popular
Apartado 135
Managua JR
Tel: (2) 70718

RADIO

Radio Nicaragua
Detrás de Telcor Villa Fontana
Managua, JR
Tel: (2) 67-3620
Fax: (2) 67-1448

AD AGENCIES

BBDO Nicaragua
DeCanal 2
Tres Cuadras, Abajo, Casa Esquinera
Managua
Tel: (2) 22-2112
Fax: (2) 22-2039

CCC Publicidad S.A.
Altamira D'Este
Casa #400
Aptdo. 5572
Managua
Tel: (2) 72286
Fax: (2) 780564

NEWSPAPERS AND PERIODICALS

Avance
Ciudad Jardín 0-30
Apdo 4231
Managua, JR
Tel: (2) 23750

Barricada
Camino del Oriente
del Bolerama
Apdo 576
Managua JR
Tel: (2) 24291

El Centramericano
4a Calle Norte
POB 52
León

Diario El Pueblo
Apdo 2346
Managua JR
Tel: (2) 23480

La Gaceta Diario Oficial
Avda Central Sur 604
Managua, JR

Novedades
Pista P. Joaquin Chamorro
Km 4
Carretera Norte Apdo 4591
Managua, JE

Paso a Paso
Managua, JR

La Prensa
Km 4 1/2
Carretera Norte
Apdo 192
Managua, JR

La Semana Comica
C.C. Bello Horizonte Módulos 7 y 9
Apdo SV-3
Managua, JR

Unión de Periodistas de Nicaragua (UPN)
Apdo 4006
Managua JR

Editorial San Jose
Calle Central Este 607
Managua, JR

Editorial Union
Avda Central Norte
Managua, JR

Editorial Universitaria Centroamerica
Col. Centroamerica K-752
Managua, JR

Editorial Vilma Morales M.
Academia Militar David Tejada 2 c. abajo
1/2 c. al Lago
Bello Horizonte K-1-19.

INTERNET ADDRESSES

Usenet
soc.culture.nicaragua

Nicaraguan Economic URLs
http://sashimi.wwa.com/~roustan/econdata.html

Latin American - Nicaragua
http://lanic.utexas.edu/la/ca/nicaragua/

City Net - Nicaragua
http://www.city.net/countries/nicaragua/

Nicaragua On-Line
http://www.deltanet.com/users/drx/nic.htm

Nigeria

Federal Republic of Nigeria

Overview

Nigeria is Africa's most populous nation and one of the world's top oil producers. It offers investors a low-cost labor pool, abundant natural resources, and the second largest market in sub-Saharan Africa. However, it has suffered in recent years from declining rates of GDP growth, resulting from its official abandonment of the 1986 Structural Adjustment Reform Program. Arbitrary pricing, a burgeoning bureaucracy, and the economic drag of a number of loss-making state-owned companies have emerged since abandonment. The country's new economic policy created by these measures is beginning to show what are likely to be far-reaching and largely negative effects on the Nigerian economy.

Trade

Nigeria's current economic regime discourages foreign trade through adherence to intrusive state intervention, tightly regulated and inefficient labor markets, and state-controlled production policies. Official overall foreign trade has fallen as a result, although there is still significant commerce in the underground market. Nigeria continues to rely on foreign sales of petroleum, which provide over 95 percent of official foreign exchange earnings, and about 75 percent of total official revenues.

Sectors

Agriculture Agriculture accounts for nearly 40 percent of GDP and employs about 50 percent of the labor force. It is dominated by small-scale subsistence farming.

Industry Nigeria's non-petroleum manufacturing sector, typically accounting for seven to eight percent of the country's GDP, is concentrated in textiles and food and beverage processing, but also includes some automotive parts manufacturing and vehicle assembly operations. Since 1991, manufacturing companies have suffered from government-induced problems resulting in a number of companies either closing or reducing their operations, and more are expected to follow. By the end of 1993, manufacturing capacity utilization was reported at 36 percent and falling.

Services The banking sector, already under considerable strain, faces additional instability due to the government's setting of deposit and lending rates in early 1994. It, like many other service industries, seems likely to either close down altogether or move underground into informal and hence, nonregulated, nontaxable market transactions.

Trends

The outlook is not promising. The government's new economic policy regime has already had far reaching and damaging effects on the Nigerian economy. Not only have these measures discouraged investment in Nigeria, but companies already present find it increasingly difficult to operate profitably. Nearly all non-oil exports have fallen sharply. The government does not seem to care, and appears determined to pursue its present policies. Sectors having the most potential for economic activity are oil and gas exploration and production, computers, and telecommunications. Potential foreign investors should be aware of the rampant corruption throughout the government, and the potential nationalization of any assets which might be physically present in Nigeria.

At a Glance

THE COUNTRY

Location Western Africa, bordering the North Atlantic Ocean between Benin and Cameroon.
Terrain The southern lowlands merge into central hills and plateaus, followed by mountains in the southeast and plains in the north.
Climate Equatorial in the south, tropical in the center, and arid in the north.

THE PEOPLE

Population 98,000,000
Ethnic composition
Hausa, Fulani, Yoruba, and Ibo 65%
Other.. 35%
Religious composition
Muslim 50%
Christian.. 40%
Indigenous beliefs... 10%
Languages spoken English, Hausa, Yoruba, Ibo, Fulani.
Education and literacy Six years of primary education are compulsory. Education in the southern states is more advanced than in the northern states. Literacy of males is 62%; of females, 40%.
Labor force
Total:...42,000,000
By occupation: agriculture 54%, industry, commerce, and services 19%, and government 15%.

COUNTRY FACTS

Political and legal Nigeria has a military government, and a legal system nominally based on English common law, Islamic law, and tribal law.
Telephone The above-average infrastructure is limited by poor maintenance. International country code: [234]. Selected city codes: Lagos (1), Abuja (9).
Transportation Nigeria has the fifth largest railroad system in Africa. The extensive inland waterway system consists of the Niger and Benue rivers, plus smaller rivers and creeks. There are several ports to handle shipping traffic. There are many airports.
Environment One percent of the nation's budget is allocated for environmental protection and conservation. Over-cultivation has lessened soil fertility and increased erosion. Replanting cannot keep up with timber cutting in forests. Oil spills, the incineration of toxic waste, and air pollution affects urban areas. Improper handling of sewage has polluted water resources. Current issues are soil degradation, rapid deforestation, desertification, and recent droughts in the north that have severely affected already marginal agricultural activities.
Media Military leaders have attempted to limit the freedom of the highly developed press. There are about 31 daily newspapers, some published by the government. There is no private radio or television service in the country. The federal and state governments broadcast on 35 AM and 17 FM radio stations and 28 television stations.
Health Privately owned hospitals outnumber public facilities, but medical supplies and equipment don't meet the need. Several diseases, including malaria and pulmonary tuberculosis, are widespread. Children are especially vulnerable. Life expectancy for men averages 54 years; for women, 57 years.

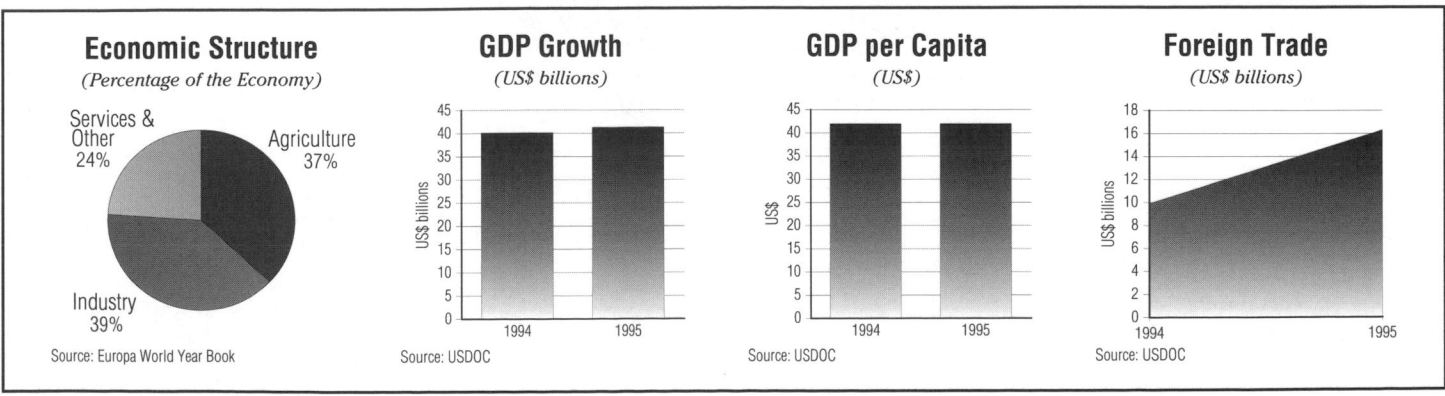

Economic Structure
(Percentage of the Economy)
Services & Other 24%
Agriculture 37%
Industry 39%
Source: Europa World Year Book

GDP Growth
(US$ billions)
Source: USDOC

GDP per Capita
(US$)
Source: USDOC

Foreign Trade
(US$ billions)
Source: USDOC

Business Travel

Travelogue

WORKWEEK

Government Monday-Friday 7:30 am to 3:30 pm.
Banks Monday-Friday 8:00 am to 1:30 pm.
Commerce Monday-Friday 8:00 am to 12:30 pm, 2:00 pm to 4:30 pm; Saturday 8:00 am to 12:30 pm.
Retail Monday-Friday 8:00 am to 4:30 pm, Saturday, 8:00 am to 4:30 pm. Monday and Friday mornings are reserved for staff meetings. Executives and officials are not available for appointments during these times.
Business Lunch hour is 1:00 pm to 2:00 pm.
In the north, Muslim businesses close at noon on Friday. Otherwise, the weekly holiday is Sunday.

HOLIDAYS

Holidays 1996
January 1 New Year's Day
April 5 Good Friday
April 8 Easter Monday
May 1 Labor Day
October 1 National Day
December 24 Christmas Eve
December 26 Boxing Day

VISA AND PASSPORT

All visitors entering Nigeria must have a valid passport and valid visa obtained from Nigerian authorities. Apply for a tourist or business visa at the nearest Nigerian embassy. To obtain a business visa you must present a letter from your Nigerian business contact. Apply well in advance of travel dates. A business visa allows a maximum stay of 90 days. Any attempt to enter Nigeria without a valid visa is considered an illegal activity. Airport visas are not available. All non-commonwealth expatriate residents must immediately apply for the Alien Registration Card at the Alien Office in Lagos or other major cities. *Dash* is the general term used in Nigeria for gift, favor, tip, or bribe. *Dash* is usually paid in advance and is helpful with clearing customs or obtaining visas.

DEPARTURE FORMALITIES

Departing legally: visitors must present an entry visa for proof of legal entry. Exporting more than N20 of Nigerian currency is illegal. A departure tax of N50 for international flight, N5 for domestic flights is charged.

IMMUNIZATION

Yellow fever and cholera vaccinations are required. Anti-malarial medication is recommended. Other immunizations are required only if you are coming from an infected area.

TIPPING

Tipping in hotels in optional as most hotels add a 10 percent service charge. Restaurants and nightspots are generally tipped in the 15 percent range.

CRIME

Violent crime in Nigeria is serious and often committed by criminals wearing police or military uniforms. Armed robberies at roadblocks and car jackings are frequent. Law enforcement response is slow if it occurs at all. The week of June 12 is dangerous due to demonstrations during the anniversary of the annulled presidential election. Fraudulent business schemes targeting foreigners are a potential danger. Do not respond to unsolicited business offers and beware of sophisticated forged documents using government letterhead.

INFRASTRUCTURE

Taxi service is available in downtown areas but should be avoided at night and it is advisable to have exact fare. Taxis are not allowed to pick up passengers at the airport, but are available at the "hire car" parking area. Drivers for hire are available through hotels or car rental agencies, or have a Nigerian colleague arrange for a driver to meet you at the airport. Rental cars are available, the road system is well developed. The airport in Lagos is crowded with frequent delays. Two main train lines exist that run from Lagos to Kano via Kaduna and from Lagos or Port Harcourt to Kafanchan. Trains are slow and crowded.

COMMUNICATIONS

Telephone Above average telecommunications exist in Nigeria but the system is plagued by poor maintenance. A major expansion is in progress.
Fax Faxes may be received and sent at major hotels and businesses.
Post office Postal services are available at post offices and many of the major hotels.
TV/Radio All television stations in the country are run by Nigerian Television. The Nigerian Television Authority manages services and provides a color network for programming that remains mostly black and white. Programs are primarily in English.

BEST TRAVEL BOOKS

Africa on a Shoestring, Lonely Planet. Filled with useful information.
Do's and Taboo's Around the World. The Bestselling Guide to International Behavior. Edited by Roger Axtell, compiled by the Parker Pen Company. The ultimate guide to international behavior, now completely updated and expanded. Helpful, fun to read!

USEFUL TELEPHONE NUMBERS

If you are calling from outside Nigeria, you will need to add the country code [234] and any other international dialing requirements from within your country.

- Emergency 999
- US Embassy .... (1) 2610078
- Abiola Bookshop Ltd./Lagos .... (1) 800450
- Nigeria Airways .... (1) 900476
- Nigerian Railway Corp .... (1) 834302
- Nigeria Hotels Ltd................................. (1) 863295

Chambers of Commerce
- Lagos Chamber of Commerce .... (1) 664202
- Abuja Chamber of Commerce .... (9) 8821555
- Ibadan Chamber of Commerce .... (22) 710021
- Kaduna Chamber of Commerce .... (62) 211216

Credit Card Information
Lost or stolen credit cards (call collect to the US, regardless of which country the card was issued in).
- Amex ....[1] (919) 333-3211
- Diner's Club...............................[1] (303) 799-1504
- MasterCard ....[1] (314) 275-6690
- Visa ....[1] (410) 581-7931

NATIONAL TOURIST OFFICE

The Nigeria Tourist Board
47 Marina, POB 2944
Lagos
Tel: (1) 630247

Foreign Trade

Imports

Leading Products
Percentage of Total Trade

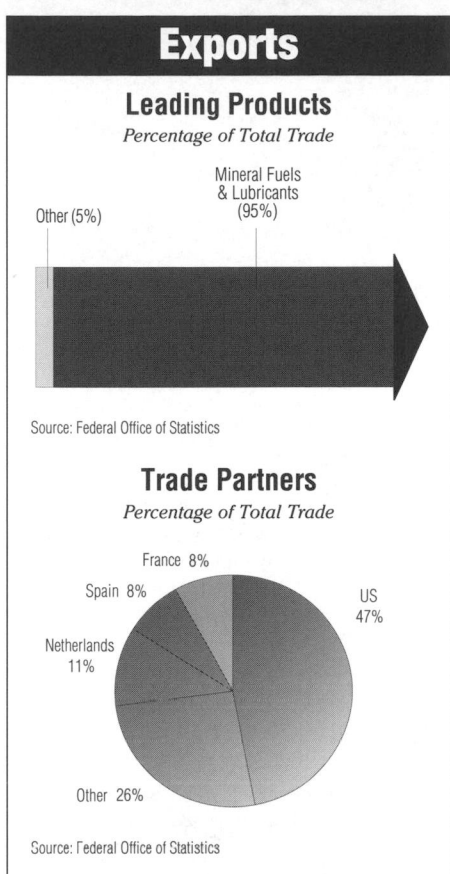

Machinery & Transportation (38%)
Basic Manufactures (25%)
Chemicals (17%)
Other (20%)

Source: Federal Office of Statistics

Trade Partners
Percentage of Total Trade

Japan 8%
France 9%
Germany 12%
UK 15%
Other 56%

Source: Federal Office of Statistics

Exports

Leading Products
Percentage of Total Trade

Other (5%)
Mineral Fuels & Lubricants (95%)

Source: Federal Office of Statistics

Trade Partners
Percentage of Total Trade

France 8%
Spain 8%
Netherlands 11%
US 47%
Other 26%

Source: Federal Office of Statistics

Opportunities

FOR IMPORTING TO NIGERIA
- computers and peripherals
- dairy products, wheat, wine
- drilling equipment, spare parts and accessories

FOR EXPORTING FROM NIGERIA
- cocoa
- oil
- rubber

GROWTH SECTORS
- computers
- telecommunications
- oil and gas exploration and production

Trade News

RULES AND REGULATIONS
- **Special duty** A special duty may be imposed on imported goods if they are being dumped or are being unfairly subsidized by a foreign government with potential to injure the market or Nigeria's domestic industry.
- **Import licenses** Licenses for all imports are necessary primarily to comply with foreign exchange controls. Import bans for an increasing number of goods have steep tariffs and duties to discourage and protect domestic industries from stiff competition.
- **Import levy** Three minor import duty surcharges (totaling six percent) are in place. The tariff structures have been reformed so import duties and the level of effective protection accorded to Nigerian industries have been reduced.

Legal

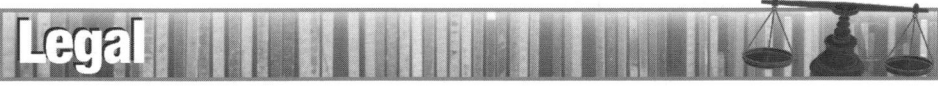

Legal System

The legal system of Nigeria is based mainly on English common law.

Intellectual Property Rights

Patents and trademarks Patent registration is simple. The examination of patent applications is cursory, primarily involving a determination of whether the application is complete. A patent is granted at the risk of the patentee. Trademark applications are processed slowly, sometimes taking four or more years to complete. Applications must be filed directly in Nigeria, since the country is not a member of an international registration system.

Copyrights A 1988 copyright law was introduced based on the WIPO model. The duration of copyright is 70 years from the death of the author for literary, musical, or artistic works. Piracy remains a problem, but enforcement remedies have improved for owners as officials have been given more enforcement powers.

Business Registration

Business permits and investment approvals must be obtained from the appropriate authorities, and other approvals may be required depending on the nature of the business. Licensing and technology transfer agreements must be registered with the National Office for Technology Acquisition and Promotion, which has the power to regulate the fees payable under such agreements.

Contracts and Dispute Resolution

Commercial disputes may be resolved in the courts or through arbitration. The High Court is generally the court of first instance, followed by the Court of Appeal and then the Supreme Court. The arbitration law is based on the UNCITRAL model law. Foreign judgments and arbitral awards are recognized and enforced on the basis of reciprocity.

Source: Anga & Emuwa, Lagos, Nigeria

Legal Matters

LEGAL BRIEFS
- **Business entities** A limited liability company is the preferred business vehicle. A joint venture by itself is not a recognized legal entity, therefore a joint venture needs to be incorporated or operated as a partnership.
- **Labor** Labor disputes are usually resolved through collective bargaining and sometimes through social legislation. All unions are affiliated with the Nigerian Labor Congress.
- **Business fraud** Fraud is a major problem. Foreigners should beware of invitations to make available business stationery, banking details, or signatures.
- **Maximum workweek** The workweek is five eight-hour days.
- **Environmental issues** Awareness of environmental issues is on the rise, and the agency in charge of regulating this area is becoming more active.
- **International agreements** Nigeria is a member of: New York Convention on the Recognition and Enforcement of Foreign Arbitral Awards, and the Berne Convention.

LEGAL CONTACT
**Anga & Emuwa
(Barristers, Solicitors & Notaries)
14, Alhaji Kanike Close
P.O. Box 52901
Ikoyi, Lagos
Tel: (1) 681773, 684042
Fax: (1) 2692072
8 Kaiama Street
P.O. Box 12636
Port Harcourt
Tel: (84) 239873
Fax: (84) 239592**

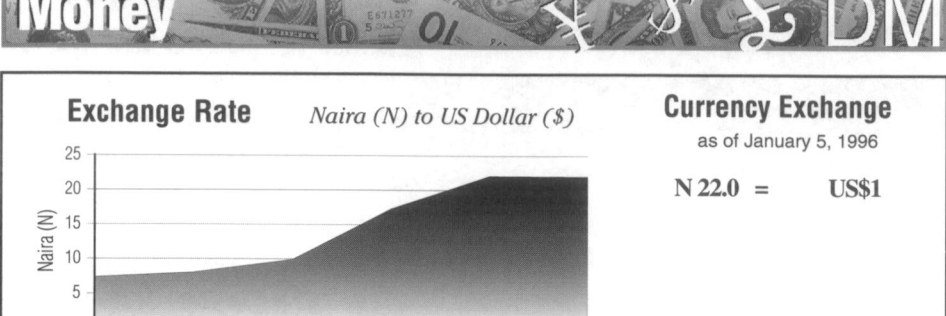

Exchange Rate

Naira (N) to US Dollar ($)

Naira (N) — 1989, 1990, 1991, 1992, 1993, 1994 (0, 5, 10, 15, 20, 25)

Source: US Federal Reserve System

Currency Exchange

as of January 5, 1996

N 22.0 = US$1

Money Matters

BITS AND PIECES

- **Gold** Only monetary authorities and industrial users can hold gold in any form except as jewelry and coins. Importing any gold coins requires a license.
- **Dealing currency** Residents cannot deal foreign currency securities or any security payable in naira without permission from the Ministry of Finance.
- **Corporate income tax** All companies are subject to income tax in Nigeria. Resident companies are taxed based on their worldwide profits, but nonresident companies are taxed based on their operations in Nigeria only.
- **Dividends** All dividends are generally subject to a 10 percent withholding tax.
- **Foreign tax relief** Foreign tax on the profits of Nigerian companies can be credited against income or capital gains tax on the same profit or gains.
- **Import payments** The Central Bank sells foreign currency to importers based on the type of industry and product. Any import payment covered by confirmed letters of credit is made by the overseas correspondents on behalf of Nigerian banks. Bills of entry must be submitted to the authorized dealer within 90 days of negotiation.
- **Export payments** All exports, by both private and public sectors, must be surrendered to the Central Bank. Nigeria is currently developing export processing zones in certain areas of the country, allowing investors duty-free importation of raw materials.

Currency

The currency of Nigeria is the Nigerian naira (N), which is divided into 100 kobo.

Foreign Exchange

All exchange control policy is controlled by the Federal Ministry of Finance. It also, in principle, approves applications for transfers of capital abroad though these are rarely granted. Most exchange regulations are administrated by the Central Bank. Licensed commercial banks and merchant banks are authorized by the Ministry of Finance to deal in foreign currencies and approve applications following guidelines set by the Central Bank.

Capital Transfers

The overwhelming majority of money invested in Nigeria goes to the petroleum sector. All nonresident investments must be approved by the Industrial Development Coordination Committee (IDCC), part of the Ministry of Finance. Approval can take as long as six to 18 months, and in some cases it has taken years. Nonresidents can own no more than 40 percent of a company in Nigeria, and several industries are exclusively reserved for 100 percent Nigerian ownership. Export proceeds are retained in domiciliary accounts maintained by the beneficiary banks in Nigeria.

Investment Incentives

Nigeria offers several incentives to prospective investors. Tax relief is possible, if the company is involved in a so-called pioneer business. Certain companies can be granted capital allowances. Oil companies operating in Nigeria under joint venture agreements with the Nigerian National Petroleum Corporation (NNPC) receive guaranteed after-tax profit margins.

Investment Restrictions

Nigeria's infrastructure could be a major problem. It is extensive, but grossly inadequate for the demands of a large country with a population of nearly 100 million. Political uncertainty, a deteriorating economy, and widespread corruption detract from the Nigerian government's professed interest in attracting foreign investment.

BANKS

Central Bank of Nigeria
Tinubu Square
PMB 12194
Lagos
Tel (1) 660-100 Telex: 21350 cebank ng

Afribank Nigeria Ltd.
94 Broad St.
PMB 12021
Lagos
Tel: (1) 663608 Fax: (1) 662793

African International Bank Ltd.
42-44 Warehouse Rd.
PMB 1040
Apapa, Lagos
Tel: (1) 803820 Fax: (1) 877174

Owena Bank (Nigeria) Ltd.
30-32 Creek Rd.
PMB 1122
Apapa, Lagos
Tel: (1) 877907

Pan African Bank Ltd.
3 Azikiwe Rd.
PMB 5239
Port Harcourt
Tel: (84) 300300 Fax: (84) 330616

Tropical Commercial Bank Ltd.
72B Murtala Mohammed Way
POB 4636
Kano
Tel: (64) 631991 Fax: (64) 644506

Union Bank of Nigeria Ltd.
40 Marina St.
PMB 2027
Lagos
Tel: (1) 2665439 Fax: (1) 2663822

Indo-Nigerian Merchant Bank Ltd.
42 Adeola Hopewell St.
Victoria Island
PMB 12656
Lagos
Tel: (1) 610051

Nigeria-Arab Bank Ltd.
96-102 Broad St.
POB 12807
Lagos
Tel: (1) 2661955

Federal Mortgage Bank of Nigeria
23 Marina St.
POB 2078
Lagos
Tel: (1) 2647372

TAXATION

Taxation requires sophisticated knowledge of complex rules and regulations specific to each country. The information presented here is from the Ernst & Young Corporate Tax Guide and Directory, available from the Ernst & Young accounting office in your country, or from:

Ernst & Young Osindero Oni
Osindero, Oni & Lasebikan
Ebani House (Marina Side)
P.O. Box 2442
62 Marina
Lagos, Nigeria
Tel: (1) 2661462, 2662833
(1) 2665534, 2662881
Cable: OLAUDIT, LAGOS
Telex: 28430 Onila NG
Fax: (1) 2662709

At a Glance

Corporate Income Tax Rate (%)	35
Capital Gains Tax Rate (%)	20
Withholding Tax (%) (a)	
Investment Income (b)	
Dividends (c)	10
Interest (d)	10
Rental Income	10
Royalties	15
Earned Income	
Building, Construction, and Related Activities	2.5
Contracts (Other than on the Sale and Purchase of Goods and Property)	2.5
Consulting, Management, and Technical Services	10
Commissions	10
Branch Remittance Tax	0
Net Operating Losses (Years)	
Carryback	0
Carryforward	4

(a) Applicable to residents and nonresidents.
(b) For nonresidents, these are final taxes. For resident companies, only the withholding tax on dividends is a final tax.
(c) Certain dividends are exempt .
(d) Certain interest is exempt.

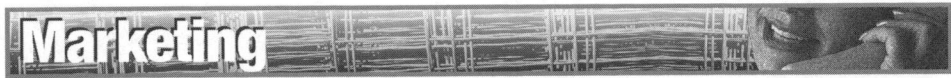

Marketing

Overview

Nigeria's market is controlled by several factors, most of them less than promising. A host of new policy measures announced in 1994 appear to reverse many market reforms introduced in the late 1980s. The currency is unstable and diminishing due to inconsistent government policy, and deficits are driving inflation upward; the situation is far from encouraging to foreign sellers. Many firms trade here, however, and have found some success. Since the Nigerian market is extremely price sensitive, suppliers from Asian countries have made inroads with low-priced, basic equipment and strong, long-term market strategies. As the most heavily populated country in Africa, located in the heart of the continent, and with immense natural resources, Nigeria represents tremendous market potential for the far sighted.

Agents, Distributors, and Partners

Affiliation with a qualified agent or distributor is essential for overseas firms exporting to Nigeria. The agent must be chosen with an eye toward providing adequate market promotion, installation service, and spare parts delivery. Due to the size and ethnic complexity of Nigeria, many firms choose more than one agent or distributor. Principles governing agency and distribution agreements are virtually unregulated and must be thoughtfully defined. Doing effective business in Nigeria depends on creating close, long-term contacts with local agents. Local agents also allow firms to adequately survey the market and determine the best approach to take with reduced investment; commercial opportunities are many, including trade leads and joint ventures, and agents will ease the processing of such transactions.

Advertising

Although advertising is not as widely used as in most Western countries, Nigeria has one of the most highly developed media systems in developing Africa. The intensity varies from area to area and is generally adequate only in urban centers. Generally, information is spread by word of mouth in marketplaces and by itinerant traders. Brand consciousness and loyalty, especially to UK products, are still important factors among the urban African population, though consumers are becoming extremely quality conscious.

Business Culture

Greetings and Courtesies

A simple handshake is the common greeting in Nigeria. Men who are close friends, however, often do not shake hands. Women often hug other women friends. Titles such as doctor, chief, and director should always be used when applicable.

Business Ethic and Framework

Of all African nations, Nigeria is the most populous as well as the most culturally diverse. Over 250 ethnic groups, each with its own language, comprise the extraordinary cultural tapestry that is Nigeria. However, the three largest of these groups, the Ibo in the east, the Yoruba in the west, and the Housa-Fulani in the north, basically dominate both the country and its business community, thus simplifying an otherwise overly complex situation. Entrenched bureaucracy and governmental red tape, unfortunately, remain the basic characteristics of Nigeria's business culture. Nigerians are accustomed to this system, and move easily through it, so follow their lead and do not try to impose different standards in an effort to more quickly get things done.

Meetings and Decision Making

Standards of punctuality are relatively high in Nigeria. Foreigners are expected to be prompt, and meetings usually start on time. "Formally informal" might best describe the standard procedure for meetings. A lengthy period of greetings and personal conversation always precedes any actual talk of business. To show haste during this formality would be very insulting. When attempting to reach an important decision with a Nigerian firm, it is imperative that you deal with the top people in the company. To rely on lower-level people is to risk serious delays and complications. A good inside contact is invaluable in getting through to the necessary decision makers. Further, once you've gained an inside connection to the decision making echelon in a Nigerian firm, you may rest assured that the company will deal with the formidable and imposing governmental regulations affecting all foreign business transactions.

Marketing in Nigeria

MARKETING TIPS

- **News** Nigeria is the most heavily populated country in Africa, located in the heart of the continent and with immense natural resources. This represents tremendous market potential. However, policies and regulations limiting the availability of foreign exchange and prohibiting a variety of imports have caused setbacks to market development. Nigeria has a very underdeveloped infrastructure, which results in higher costs, especially for distribution.
- **Nigerian import market** Nigerians are extremely price sensitive. This oil-rich economy continues to be hobbled by poor macroeconomic management that has resulted in an exceptionally high average annual inflation rate, a growing foreign debt, and unfavorable balance of payment.

AD AGENCIES

Insight Communications
POB 2588
Surulere, Lagos
Tel: (1) 830209
Fax: (1) 832985

Sunrise Marketing Communications
Ebun House, 4th Fl.
104 Obaformi Awolowo Way
Ikeja, Lagos
Tel: (1) 967-717
Fax: (1) 966-197

Cultural Cautions

DO'S

- Make your appointments at least a month in advance of your arrival in Nigeria; reconfirm when you arrive.
- If possible, send an older representative of your company, as Nigerians have a deep tradition of respect for elders.
- Bring a lot of business cards, in English and with the title by which you wish to be addressed.
- Always praise the food.
- Acceptable topics of conversation include Nigeria's rich cultural diversity.

DON'TS

- Avoid discussing politics and religion.
- Nigerians tend to stand very close when talking. Don't pull away, this might appear rude.
- Don't photograph anyone without asking permission.

CUSTOMS

- It is considered rude to ask a man about his children, although it is polite to ask a woman about her children.

OBSERVATIONS

- Nigerians tend to be very fashion conscious and those in the business community are always well-dressed. There is, however, no "dress code," except for formal business events. For important business meetings, however, men should wear a suit and tie, women a dress.
- Women in most of the regions of Nigeria maintain a significant degree of prestigious and powerful positions in the business community. A foreign businesswoman can thus expect to be well-received, though a restrained and unaggressive demeanor is recommended.

NEGOTIATIONS

- The first meeting as a whole will be somewhat formal, conducted in the office. Once the all-important personal rapport is achieved, however, subsequent—and more substantive—meetings will be conducted over long lunches at restaurants, as well as at your Nigerian counterpart's home.

GOVERNMENT AGENCIES

Ministry of Agriculture
Garki, Area 2
Abuja
Federal Capital Territory
Tel: (9) 681-896, 682-732
Telex: 22605 fmard ng

Ministry of Communications
Garki, Area 2
Abuja
Federal Capital Territory
Tel: (9) 633-970
Telex: 21535 links ng

Ministry of Education
Garki, Area 2
Abuja
Federal Capital Territory
Tel: (9) 616-943, 660-944

Ministry of Finance
Garki, Area 2
Abuja
Federal Capital Territory
Tel: (9) 619-577, 613-804, 682-527

Ministry of Health and Human Services
Garki, Area 2
Abuja
Federal Capital Territory

Ministry of Industries
Garki, Area 2
Abuja
Federal Capital Territory
Tel: (9) 682-607, 680-396

Ministry of Information and Culture
Garki, Area 2
Abuja
Federal Capital Territory
Tel: (9) 680-358

Ministry of Labor and Productivity
Garki, Area 2
Abuja
Federal Capital Territory
Tel: (9) 681-463, 612-688

Ministry of Science and Technology
Garki, Area 2
Abuja
Federal Capital Territory
Tel: (9) 617-843, 613-605

Ministry of States and Local Government Affairs
Garki, Area 2
Abuja
Federal Capital Territory

Ministry of Works and Housing
Garki, Area 2
Abuja
Federal Capital Territory
Tel: (9) 631-926, 636-401

National Electric Power Authority
24/25 Marina
Lagos
Tel: (1) 630-563

Nigerian Railway Corporation
Railway Compound
Ebute-Metta, Lagos
Tel: (1) 844-302, 844-235, 834-302
Telex: 26584

Nigerian Telecommunications Ltd.
NITEL Headquarters
2nd Floor, Room 9
Marina, Lagos
Tel: (1) 634-200

Nigerian Ports Authority
26/28 Marina
PMB 12588
Lagos
Tel: (1) 633-979, 655-020

WORLD TRADE CENTER

World Trade Center of Nigeria
Western House (9th Floor)
8-10 Broad Street
Post Office Box 4466
Lagos
Tel: (1) 263-5276
Fax: (1) 683-981

BUSINESS ORGANIZATIONS

Nigerian-American Chamber of Commerce
Marble House, 1 Kingsway Road
Ikoyi, Lagos
Tel: (1) 269-2088 Fax: (1) 269-3041

Lagos Chamber of Commerce & Industry
Post Office Box 109
Lagos
Tel: (1) 613-898, 613-911, 610-533
Telex: 21368 CHACOMNG

MEDIA

Daily Times of Nigeria
New Isheri Rd.
Agidingbi
POB 21340
Ikeja, Lagos
Tel: (1) 900850

Daily Express
30 Glover St.
Lagos

Marketing in Nigeria
POB 1163
Surulere, Lagos

Management in Nigeria
Plot 22, Idowu Taylor St.
Victoria Island
POB 2557
Lagos
Tel: (1) 615105

RADIO & TELEVISION

Federal Radio Corporation of Nigeria
Broadcasting House, Ikoyi Road
PMD 12504
Ikoyi, Lagos
Tel: (1) 681-885, 682-717, 603-010

Nigerian Television Authority
Television House, Ahmadu Bello Way
PMB 12036
Victoria Island, Lagos
Tel: (1) 616-240, 614-893, 615-949
Telex: 21245

LEGAL CONTACTS

F.O Akinrele & Co.
188, Awolowo Road
W.W. Ikoyi, Lagos
Tel: (1) 2693998/9, 686212/3

Babalakin & Co.
PO Box 80320
Lafiaji, Lagos
Tel: (1) 2632559, 2635644
Fax: (1) 263-0594, 2637136

Banwo & Ighodalo
PO Box 53756
Falomo, Ikoyi
Lagos
Tel: (1) 2694576, 2684724
Fax: (1) 2694576, 2690294

George Etomi & Partners
16 Alhaji Kanike Close S.W.
Ikoyi, Lagos
Tel: (1) 2693644, 2693645
Fax: (1) 2691188

AD AGENCIES

Insight Communications Ltd.
PO Box 2588
Surulere, Lagos
Tel: (1) 830-209
Fax: (1) 832-985

Liintas Lagos
PO Box 551
Lagos
Tel: (1) 497-1851
Fax: (1) 497-1857

Sunrise Marketing Communications Ltd.
Ebun House, 4th Fl.
104 Obafemi Awolowo Way
Ikeja, Lagos
Tel: (1) 967-717
Fax: (1) 497-0689

BANKS

Ecobank Nigeria Ltd.
2 Ajose Adeogun St.
Victoria Island
POB 72688
Lagos
Tel: (1) 612953
Fax: (1) 616568

First Bank of Nigeria Ltd.
35 Marina St.
POB 5216
Lagos
Tel: (1) 2665900
Fax: (1) 2669703

Investment Banking and Trust Co. Ltd.
Wesley House
21-22 Marina St.
PMB 12557
Lagos
Tel: (1) 2600200
Fax: (1) 2634146

Nigeria Universal Bank Ltd.
Hospital Road
POB 1066
Lagos
Tel: (1) 213928
Fax: (1) 215024

Nigeria International Bank Ltd.
Commerce House
1 Idowu Taylor St.
Victoria Island
POB (1) 6391
Lagos
Tel: (1) 2690166
Fax: (1) 618916

STOCK EXCHANGE

Securities and Exchange Commission
Mandilas House
96-102 Broad St.
POB 12638
Lagos

Nigerian Stock Exchange
Stock Exchange house
2-4 Customs St.
POB 2457
Lagos
Tel: (1) 2660287

INTERNET ADDRESSES

Usenet group(s):
soc.culture.nigeria

AfricaNet - Nigeria
http://www.webperfect.com/afrinet/nigeria/profile.html

Nigeria Page
http://www.sas.upenn.edu/African_Studies/Country_Specific/Nigeria.html

Norway

Kingdom of Norway

Economy

Overview

Norway is one of the world's richest countries. Its emergence as a major oil and gas producer in the mid-1970s transformed the economy, which is now dominated by energy and energy-based production of crude oil, natural gas, and metals. Norway remains a mixed economy; state-owned or controlled enterprises dominate its key oil and gas industries, telecommunications, and commercial banking, while the private sector remains dominant in shipping, non-bank services, and small- to medium-scale manufacturing. Given the volatility of the oil and gas markets, Norway is seeking to restructure its non-oil economy to reduce subsidies, increase efficiency, and stimulate growth of nontraditional industries.

Trade

The Norwegian economy remains highly dependent on foreign trade. Oil and gas products dominate Norway's exports, representing more than 40 percent of the total. Aluminum, chemicals, and pulp and paper products are substantial, but of significantly lesser importance. Primary imports are manufactured products such as machinery and equipment. Norway's principal trading partners are the UK, Sweden, Germany, and the US. Norway's exports continue every year to grow faster than its imports, resulting in a favorable balance of payments.

Sectors

Agriculture Norway's farm sector remains inefficient and the most heavily subsidized in the OECD. Norwegian subsidies and nontariff barriers, including quotas and state monopolies in alcohol and grain, restrict foreign farm exports. With Norway's approval of the GATT agreement, these agricultural restrictions are subject to predetermined tariffs, which will be gradually reduced.

Industry In addition to the oil and gas industries, metals, pulp and paper products, chemicals, ship-building, and fishing are the most significant traditional industries; energy-intensive manufacturing industries such as metals and fertilizers dominate. Several inefficient sectors survive largely through generous subsidies and state protection from international competition.

Services Norway has taken some steps to deregulate the service sector and is in the process of privatizing its telecommunications industry, although large parts of these markets remain subject to restrictive regulations, including statutory barriers to entry. Recent deregulation of financial markets appears to have eliminated many of the barriers facing foreign financial institutions which seek to operate in the Norwegian market.

Trends

With exports becoming stronger, Norway's balance of payments is expected to remain positive despite prospects for increased imports. Inflation, in the 1.5 percent range during 1994, has been declining steadily since 1987 and is expected to remain low. Should Norway join the EU, its economy and foreign trading patterns will change dramatically to conform with EU standards and regulations, and foreign suppliers will face increased competition from other EU members in the Norwegian market. On the other hand, the government's policy to reduce dependency on the oil and gas industry has forced it to welcome foreign investment in many manufacturing or production industries.

At a Glance

THE COUNTRY

Location Nordic state in Northern Europe, bordering the North Atlantic Ocean, west of Sweden.
Terrain Glaciated; mostly rugged with high plateaus, steep fjords, mountains, and fertile valleys, with arctic tundra in the north and about 50,000 islands off the coastline.
Climate Temperate along the coast; colder in the interior; and rainy year-round on the west coast.

THE PEOPLE

Population 4,300,000
Ethnic composition Norwegian (Nordic, Alpine, Baltic); Lapp (or Sami, a racial-cultural minority of 20,000); foreign nationals (148,000 from Denmark, UK, Sweden, US, Pakistan, Vietnam, Germany, Turkey).
Religious composition
Evangelical Lutheran 94%
Other 6%
Languages spoken Norwegian, Lapp, Finnish.
Education and literacy Education is free through the university level and is compulsory from ages seven to 16. Literacy is 100 percent.
Labor force
Total:..2,000,000
By occupation: government, social, personal services 37%, wholesale and retail trade, hotels, restaurants 18%, manufacturing 15%, transport and communications 8%, financing, insurance, real estate, business services 8%, agriculture, forestry, fishing 8%, construction 6%, and oil extraction 1%.

COUNTRY FACTS

Political and legal This constitutional monarchy has a legal system that is a mixture of customary law, civil law, and common law traditions.
Telephone The government-owned telecommunications service is efficient and high-quality. International country code: [47]. No city codes.
Transportation There are three major and 14 minor airports. Public transportation is efficient. The well-engineered highways cover 88,800 km. Several inland waterways and six major ports serve one of the world's largest merchant fleets.
Environment The growing population and urbanization have adversely affected the environment. Industry and airborne industrial pollution from other countries have polluted forests and waterways. The government has put some limitations on business because of environmental concerns, particularly to prevent oil spills from wells and tankers. It also offers loans and grants for the purchase of pollution control equipment. Current issues are water pollution, acid rain which damages forests and lakes, and threatens fish stocks, and air pollution from vehicle emissions.
Media One public corporation operates 46 AM and 350 FM radio stations, while the government operates 143 FM radio stations. There are 54 television stations, and most households own at least one television set. More than 80 small newspapers appear six days a week; it is illegal to publish on Sundays and holidays.
Health Norway's government-sponsored health system includes free hospital care, physician's compensation, cash benefits during illness and pregnancy, and other medical and dental plans. Life expectancy of males is 74 years; of females, 80 years.

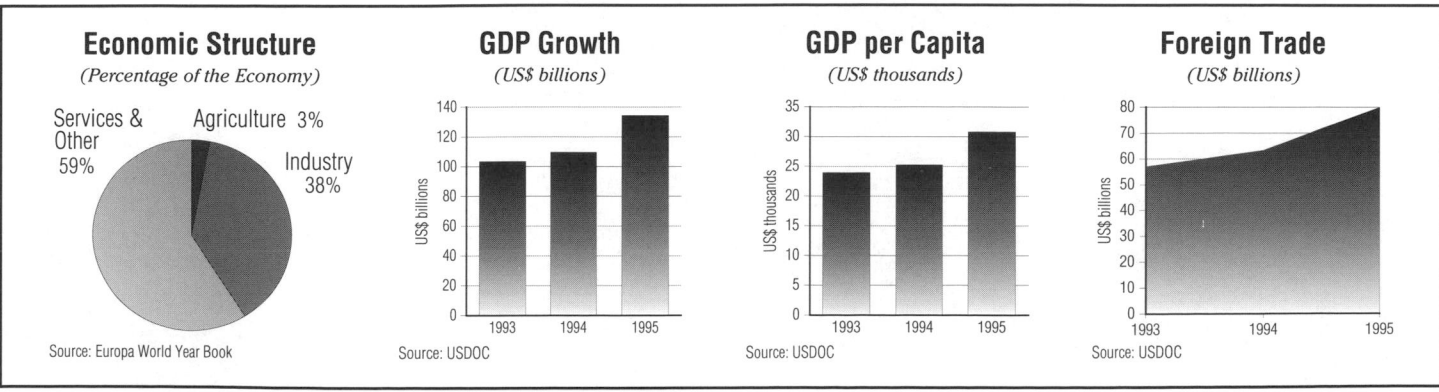

Economic Structure
(Percentage of the Economy)

Services & Other 59%
Agriculture 3%
Industry 38%

Source: Europa World Year Book

GDP Growth
(US$ billions)

Source: USDOC

GDP per Capita
(US$ thousands)

Source: USDOC

Foreign Trade
(US$ billions)

Source: USDOC

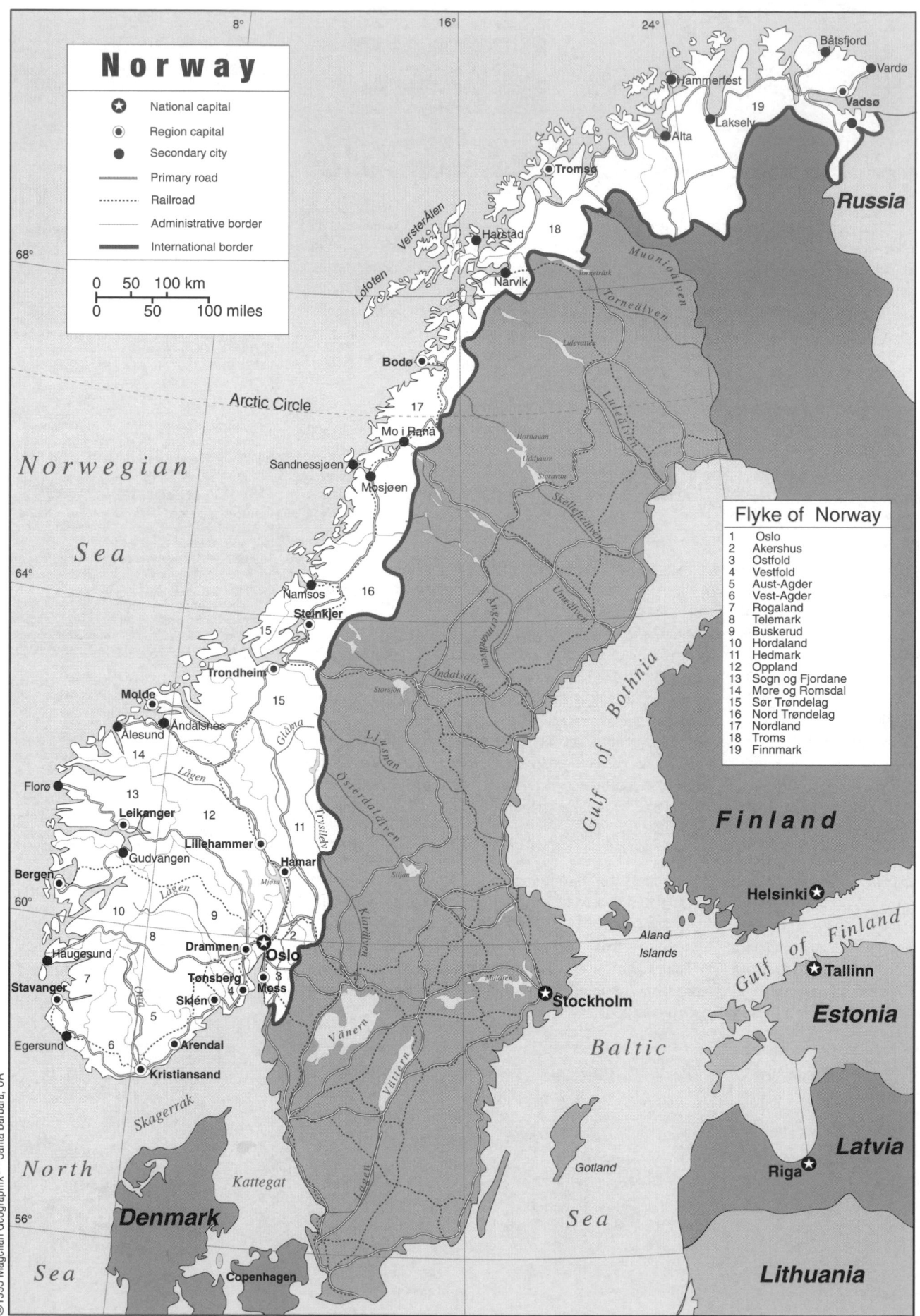

Norway

★ National capital
◉ Region capital
● Secondary city
— Primary road
⋯ Railroad
— Administrative border
━ International border

0   50   100 km
0   50   100 miles

Flyke of Norway

1   Oslo
2   Akershus
3   Ostfold
4   Vestfold
5   Aust-Agder
6   Vest-Agder
7   Rogaland
8   Telemark
9   Buskerud
10   Hordaland
11   Hedmark
12   Oppland
13   Sogn og Fjordane
14   More og Romsdal
15   Sør Trøndelag
16   Nord Trøndelag
17   Nordland
18   Troms
19   Finnmark

Foreign Trade

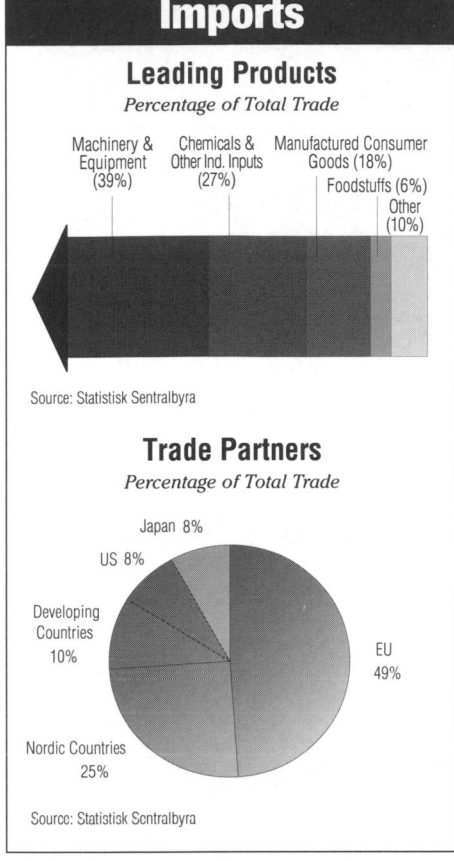

Imports

Leading Products
Percentage of Total Trade

Machinery & Equipment (39%)
Chemicals & Other Ind. Inputs (27%)
Manufactured Consumer Goods (18%)
Foodstuffs (6%)
Other (10%)

Source: Statistisk Sentralbyra

Trade Partners
Percentage of Total Trade

Japan 8%
US 8%
Developing Countries 10%
EU 49%
Nordic Countries 25%

Source: Statistisk Sentralbyra

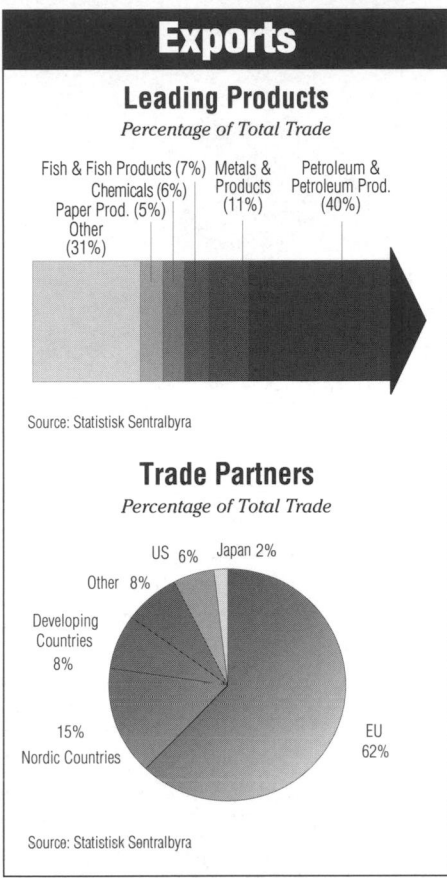

Exports

Leading Products
Percentage of Total Trade

Fish & Fish Products (7%)
Chemicals (6%)
Paper Prod. (5%)
Other (31%)
Metals & Products (11%)
Petroleum & Petroleum Prod. (40%)

Source: Statistisk Sentralbyra

Trade Partners
Percentage of Total Trade

US 6%
Japan 2%
Other 8%
Developing Countries 8%
Nordic Countries 15%
EU 62%

Source: Statistisk Sentralbyra

Opportunities

FOR IMPORTING TO NORWAY

- machinery and equipment
- manufactured consumer goods
- chemicals
- manufactured industrial inputs
- food and drinks
- aircraft
- cheese
- paper products

FOR EXPORTING FROM NORWAY

- crude oil
- natural gas
- petroleum products
- electricity
- metals and metal products
- fish and fish products
- chemicals

GROWTH SECTORS

- agriculture/forestry/fishing
- petroleum production
- export-oriented industry
- services industry
- energy/shipping
- manufacturing/mining
- construction
- financial

GOVERNMENT PROCUREMENT

- industrial equipment
- heavy construction equipment
- engineering services

Trade News

RULES AND REGULATIONS

- **Trade news** Norway is very dependent on foreign trade, and its trade policy is generally aimed at expanding its trade and shipping services. Norway, as an EFTA/EEA member, currently enjoys an industrial free trade agreement with all EU member countries. Norway is using the Harmonized System (HS) for commodity classification, and import duties are relatively low on products imported from third country suppliers.
- **Regulations** There are stringent import regulations on agricultural commodities, approval requirements for telecommunications equipment, and comprehensive labeling requirements for toxic chemicals. A host of new rules and regulations were introduced in 1995 that will liberalize trading activities.
- **Trading agents** Trading agents are useful to navigate the changing and confusing shoals of new EEA regulations.
- **Import restrictions** Electrical and electronic equipment must have an approval from MEMKO. Toxic chemicals must have a composition declaration.
- **Export controls** Exported items require a license.
- **Export proceeds** Export proceeds do not have to be repatriated to Norway.
- **Export payments** Any exports valued at less than Nkr 2,000 are exempt from declaration or export license.
- **Import payments** There are a few quotas for agricultural products. There are no restraints on imports from developing countries. Direct trade credits may be extended for import financing without a license from the Bank of Norway.
- **Government procurement** Norway is a signatory to the GATT Government Procurement Code. Most government procurement opportunities are open to competitive bidding between foreign and domestic parties. Bid invitations are made through public advertisements and circular letters to known suppliers and contractors.
- **National treatment** Norway does not grant non-discriminatory treatment to procurement in petroleum exploration and drilling sectors.
- **Agricultural products** Agricultural products are highly protected from international competition. Imports of milk, meat, berries, fruit, and vegetables are controlled through quantity restrictions, trading by state-owned companies, licensing, health and sanitary regulations, and a price support system.
- **Grain corporation** The Norwegian Grain Corporation controls the importation of grains and feed concentrates, and issues import licenses for fruits and vegetables.
- **Wine monopoly** The Norwegian Wine Monopoly controls the importation of most alcoholic beverages.
- **Tariff schedule** Norway maintains a single-column tariff list. Tariffs on most manufactured goods, and industrial raw materials are low. Clothes and other finished textiles are assessed tariffs normally falling between 15 and 25 percent.
- **VAT** Virtually all imports are subject to a 20 percent value-added tax.

GOVERNMENT AGENCIES

Ministry of Industry and Energy
Pløensat. 8
POB 8011, Dep.
0300 Oslo
Ministry of Petroleum and Energy
POB 8148, Dep.
0033 Oslo 1
Fax: 22-34-95-65
Telex: 21486
Norwegian Export Council
Drammensveien 40
0243 Oslo
Tel: 22-92-63-00

Air Travel Times

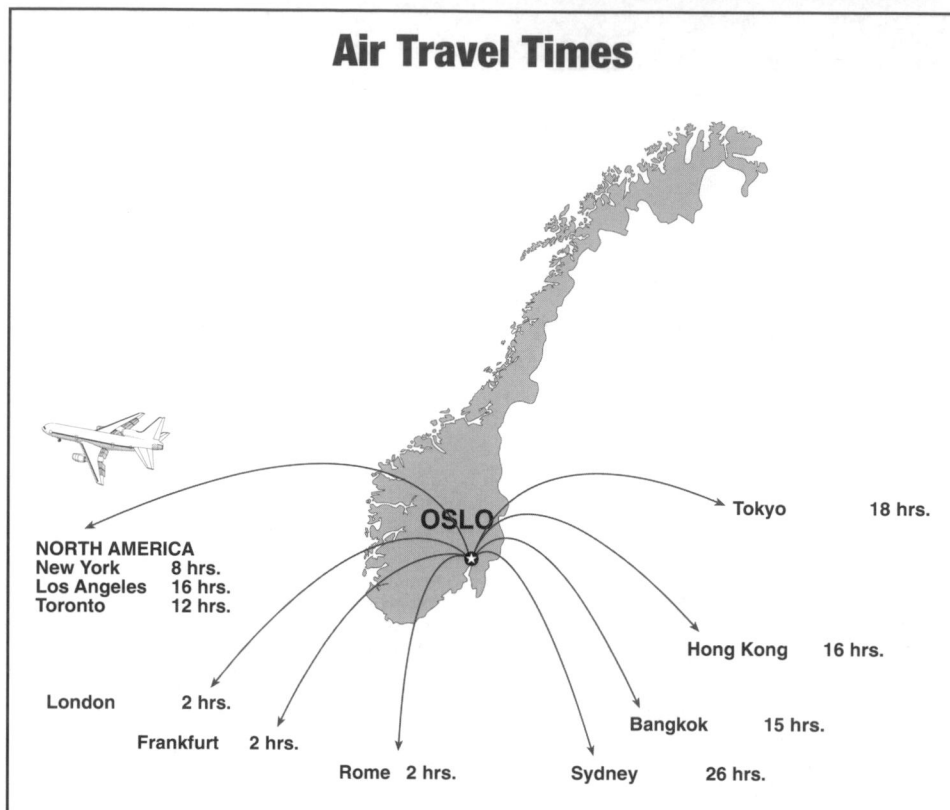

NORTH AMERICA
New York　　8 hrs.
Los Angeles　16 hrs.
Toronto　　　12 hrs.

London　　2 hrs.

Frankfurt　2 hrs.

Rome　2 hrs.

Tokyo　　18 hrs.

Hong Kong　16 hrs.

Bangkok　　15 hrs.

Sydney　　26 hrs.

OSLO

Travelogue

WORKWEEK

Offices Monday-Friday 9:00 am to 6:00 pm.
Banks Monday-Friday, 8:15 am to 5:30 pm.
Government Monday-Friday 9:00 am to 6:00 pm.
Retail Monday-Friday 9:00 am to 6:00 pm.

HOLIDAYS

Holidays 1996
January 1 New Year's Day
April 4 Holy Thursday*
April 5 Good Friday*
April 8 Easter Monday*
May 1 Norwegian Labor Day
May 16 Ascension Day
May 17 Constitution Day
May 26 Whit Monday*
December 25 First Christmas Day
December 26 Second Christmas Day
*Dates vary from year to year.

VISA AND PASSPORT

A passport is required but there are no visa requirements for visitors to Norway. For any stay that will exceed 90 days you must receive authorization from Norwegian authorities. The 90-day period begins when you enter any Nordic area including Sweden, Norway, Finland, Denmark, and Iceland.

DEPARTURE FORMALITIES

There are no departure formalities for Norway.

IMMUNIZATION

There are no requirements for travelers unless you are arriving from an infected area.

TIPPING

Taxi: none although 5 to 10 percent is appreciated. Porters: Nkr 10 per piece. Hotels, restaurant: 10 to 15 percent included in bill. Nightspots: 10 to 15 percent. Barbers, beauticians: 5 to 10 percent.

CRIME

Incidents of crime are comparatively low in Norway. Burglary, pickpockets, and pursesnatchings are reported, yet criminals rarely carry weapons. Always keep valuables out of sight in automobiles.

INFRASTRUCTURE

All airline services primarily use Fornebu Airport, 10 km west of Oslo. Other international airports are near Bergen and Stavanger. Taxis are available for service to and from the airport; fares are high but service is excellent. There will be extra charges for luggage, more than two people, or any fare after 10:00 pm. For arriving passengers, an airline bus is available to meet your flight for transportation to the major hotels or the bus terminal in downtown Oslo. Major car rental companies are located at Fornebu Airport and in most towns. A valid driver's license, issued for at least a year, is required for car rentals and seat belts are mandatory. Drive on the right side. Night driving requires using low beams at all times. Hazardous weather conditions warrant renting four-wheel drive vehicles. Do not drink and drive in Norway as laws are strict. In Oslo there is an underground electrical rail system with frequent departures, along with streetcars and buses for public transportation abilities.

NATIONAL TOURIST OFFICE

Norwegian Tourist Board
Langkaial
POB 499 Sentrum
0105 Oslo
Tel: 22-42-70-44
Fax: 22-33-69-98

COMMUNICATIONS

Telephones All telecommunication services are available and reliable. Televerket is the government-operated telegraph and telephone company, with offices in every city. Direct dialing is available throughout the country. To send a telegram from a residence or a public phone, dial 0138. Rotary pay phones will accept only Nkr1 coins and you must insert two before the call is connected. In Norway, notice the number pad and rotary dial for all phones are in reverse of the usual order. The top row of the number pad is 7,8,9 and on the rotary dial, 9 is at the top descending to zero.
Fax Faxing and telegraph services are readily available.
Post office Airmail is reliable and efficient with international delivery averaging four to seven days. Any surface route shipments require four to six weeks for transit. Post office hours are Monday-Friday 8:00 am to 5:30 pm, Saturday 9:00 am to 1:00 pm.
TV/Radio One national television station, numerous local stations, and many radio channels are operated by the national television service.

BEST TRAVEL BOOKS

Fodor's Travel Guide, Norway. Tourist oriented, excellent source of city details.
Culture Shock, A Guide to Customs and Etiquette, Norway.
Fodor's Europe, Best of 31 Countries. Contains information on historical towns, great culture, scenic coastal countryside.
Do's and Taboo's Around the World. The Bestselling Guide to International Behavior. Edited by Roger Axtell, compiled by the Parker Pen Company. The ultimate guide to international behavior, now completely updated and expanded. Helpful, fun to read!
Berlitz Business Travel Guide, Europe. Concise economic details, successful trip planning, background information on people and cities, useful facts and addresses.

USEFUL TELEPHONE NUMBERS

If you are calling from outside Norway, you will need to add the country code [47] and any other international dialing requirements from within your country.

- Police 002
- Accident/Ambulance 003
- Fire 001
- Operator 093
- International Operator 0115
- Long Distance Operator 011
- Local Information 180
- International Information 181
- Pharmacy 24 hour 22-41-24-82
- Oslo Main Post Office 22-40-73-17
- Oslo Bus Schedule Information.......... 22-59-68-14
- Oslo Taxi 22-38-80-90
- Advance Reservations 22-38-80-80
- US Embassy/Oslo 22-44-85-50
- Medical Center 22-41-24-40
- Dental 22-67-48-41

Airlines
- British Airways....................... 22-59-70-30
- Delta Airlines 22-41-52-20
- Wideroe Airlines 22-83-78-00

Car Rentals
- Avis 22-53-05-57
- Budget.................................... 22-53-79-24

Credit Cards Information
Lost or stolen credit cards (call collect to the US, regardless of which country the card was issued in).
- Amex .... [1] (919) 333-3211
- Diner's Club................. [1] (303) 799-1504
- MasterCard .... [1] (314) 275-6690
- Visa .... [1] (410) 581-7931

Marketing

Overview

Norway's relatively small population of 4.25 million is highly educated and represents an affluent and largely centralized market for foreign companies. Although developed and largely industrialized, Norway depends heavily on commodity products—particularly oil—for revenues, and fluctuations in world commodity prices can have sharp effects on its economy—and thus the purchasing preferences of its consumers. Although self-sufficient in many areas—due in large part to protection and government subsidies of certain key activities—it is also heavily dependent on trade to supply many of its needs.

Agents and Distribution

Distribution for most foreign companies is handled by local agencies in the Oslo area where the bulk of business takes place. To reach the distant and dispersed northern cities, sub-agents and secondary distribution arrangements are common. Most foreign sellers have an agent located in Oslo, who in turn may have sub-agents or traveling salespeople who serve provincial and outlying markets. Despite the small size of the country and market, some firms retain several specialized agents to handle geographic or product market niches. Agents vary in size, experience, and capitalization, and in some cases a smaller firm may be more effective because it has fewer competing interests. Agents may also demand compensation for goodwill when long-term relationships are terminated, and no Norwegian agent will negotiate with a foreign firm while it has another agency agreement in force, even if the agreement is being terminated.

Advertising

Radio ads placed during morning and evening commute times are recommended, but restrictions on radio advertising limit its usefulness. Newspaper readership is extremely large in highly literate Norway, and extensive demographic information concerning readership is available. The main Oslo newspapers are the *Aftenposten*, *Dagbladet*, *Verdens Gang*, and *Dagens Naeringsliv* (the main business paper). Because there is no true national press, regional papers should be used as well; these include the *Bergens Tidende* (Bergen), *Addresseavisen* (Trondheim), and *Aftenblad* (Stavanger); but there are many others throughout the country.

Business Culture

Greetings and Courtesies

Be prepared for a tight grip when shaking hands with your Norwegian associates, both men and women. Upon initially meeting, use titles followed by the family name. In most cases, you'll quickly be asked to use first names, perhaps even nick-names, as formal address is not the custom in either the business or social communities. Titles are seldom used, but be attentive to how Norwegian co-workers address one another and follow the lead. Be sure to stand when being introduced.

Business Ethic and Framework

The business environment is both reserved and relaxed, and while Norwegians are pleasant to do business with, they keep business and personal relationships separate. If sending a letter of self-introduction, provide plenty of background information regarding your firm, and clearly state your purpose and intentions. In Norway, punctuality counts in establishing confidence and trust, so be on time.

Meetings and Decision Making

Meetings will have been scheduled in advance, and be assured your audience has done its homework on your firm, products, competitors, etc. Your presentation should be straightforward and sufficiently backed with essential points, supporting data, and pertinent substance regarding your proposition. Decisions are made by consensus; they take time and require patience. It is advised that foreign ventures highlight the national advantages to Norway in their propositions for business relations.

Women

Norwegian women are found working in every aspect of the business community, holding high positions in government agencies and other organizations. There are even a few women top executives in shipping, rail transport, and banking. Women in business are treated with respect, and they are not openly discriminated against.

Marketing in Norway

MARKETING TIPS

- **Local partner** An astute local business partner will help make the already receptive Norwegian market very practical and efficient for a foreign business.
- **Look ahead** Norway is likely to become a full member of the European Union, and foreign companies can parlay subsidiaries and branch operations into excellent entries into the larger upscale markets of Scandinavia.
- **Sales subsidiaries** Although not as common as distribution agency agreements, sales subsidiaries and branch operations work well for foreign companies in Norway. Such entities may have majority foreign ownership but must have majority Norwegian control. Licensing has been fairly common, although arrangements must be individually approved by the government. Franchising is growing. Trade fairs remain relatively minor despite attempts to encourage growth in this marketing venue. Some larger Norwegian firms maintain overseas agents who buy direct from suppliers abroad.
- **Doubling up** Because Scandinavian countries are small, geographically close, and culturally similar, many firms attempt to have a single agent serve more than one. This ignores subtle market differences, as well as nationalism, and can result in lower sales then would otherwise be attained.
- **Agent support** Because Norway is such a demanding market, foreign sellers should plan to visit frequently and offer substantial support to their local agents. Support can be in the form of travel and promotional allowances, as well as customer visits made with the agent.
- **Materials** Materials should be in Norwegian, but English materials are almost as acceptable. Those prepared or presented in other languages are less acceptable.

Cultural Cautions

DO'S

- Speak clearly as you introduce yourself. Norwegians are conscientious about the pronunciation of foreign names and they want to speak your name correctly.
- Send thank-you notes in appreciation for favors and hospitality. Your Norwegian associates also find it thoughtful to be remembered with cards during the holidays.

DON'TS

- Do not make a number of gestures or speak too loudly while presenting. Norwegians prefer a calm and quiet decorum both in business and social settings.

CUSTOMS

- Norwegians are especially uncomfortable about the number thirteen. Take care that your last-minute cancellation to a Norwegian dinner party doesn't leave your host or hostess with thirteen guests.
- Conservative, casual dress is customary. Light–weight attire is appropriate in summer months. Business suits are more commonly seen in winter months. In many offices, however, men wear sweaters instead of jackets and ties. Women also dress informally, in dresses or coordinated outfits.

OBSERVATIONS

- The exchange of business gifts is not a common business practice, and there are laws that define the monetary value of a gift. Gifts from your country or native town are well-received.

NEGOTIATIONS

- Some knowledge of the hierarchical corporate structure will serve you well. Consensus-driven decisions involve a collective of negotiating representatives and it will be necessary to eke out who is authorized to bargain what points in your proposition.

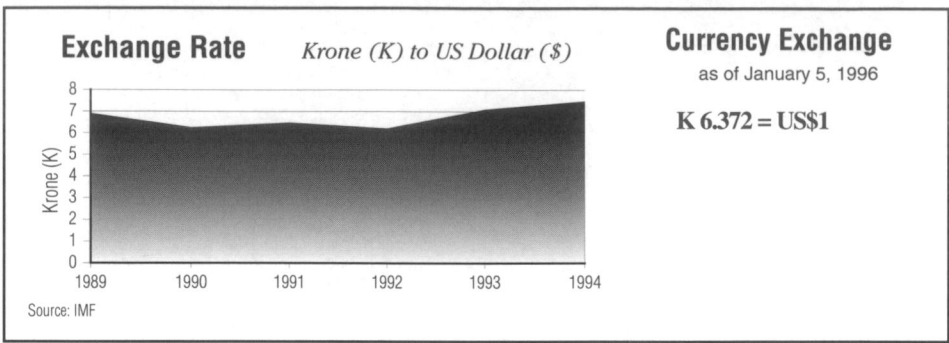

Source: IMF

Currency

The currency in use in Norway is the Norwegian krone (K or Nkr). Norway's economy is tied to the European Currency Unit, the ECU, through the European Monetary System.

Foreign Exchange

All exchange is controlled by the Bank of Norway in cooperation with the Ministry of Finance and Customs. Most currency transactions can be made through commercial banks. There are no currency exchange requirements, except a reporting requirement for any international payments and financial transactions. This is primarily for statistical purposes. The main type of financial account for nonresidents is the convertible krone account. These may be credited with payments from any country, transfers from other convertible krone accounts, and proceeds from the sale in Norway of convertible currencies. There is no limit to the amount of currency that can be imported into or exported from Norway, but any amount over the equivalent of Nkr 25,000 must be reported to the customs authorities. Nonresidents can purchase domestic bonds and certificates without restriction.

Capital Transfers

There are no restrictions for invisible payments. There are no limits applied to proceeds from invisibles. Export proceeds need not be repatriated to Norway.

Investment Incentives

Norway offers no significant tax incentives for either domestic or foreign investors. One exception is investments in Northern Norway, where a reduced payroll tax schedule applies. There are no free trade zones, although taxes are minimal on Svalbard. A state industry and regional development fund provides support (e.g., investment grants, financial assistance) for industrial development in areas with special employment difficulties or with low levels of economic activity.

Investment Restrictions

There are a number of limits to foreign investors in Norway. For example, foreign companies must obtain concessions to acquire rights to own or use various kinds of property such as forests or mines. No specific performance requirements exist in Norway, but in the offshore petroleum sector, Norwegian authorities encourage the use of Norwegian goods and services. Norway discriminates in favor of national companies in procurements including oil exploration and drilling.

Money Matters

BITS AND PIECES

- **Corporate income tax** Resident companies are subject to income tax based on worldwide income. Nonresidents are subject to the same taxes, but only on income from Norway.
- **Sharehold tax** Shareholders owning more than 66 percent of a company and actively participating in the company's business are subject to a personal income tax of up to 24.4 percent.
- **Foreign tax relief** Any foreign taxes paid abroad can be considered a deductible expense. Under special circumstances, it can also be credited against Norwegian tax.

BANKS

Bank of Norway
Bankplassen 2
POB 1179
0107 Oslo 1
Tel: 22-31-60-00
Fax: 22-41-31-05

Chemical Bank Norge
Karl Johansgate 41 B
0162 Oslo
Tel: 22-941-919
Fax: 22-425-861

Norges Bank
(Central Bank)
Bankplassen 2
POB 1179
Sentrum
0107 Oslo
Tel: 22-31-60-00
Fax: 22-41-31-05
Telex: 71369

Citibank
Tordenskiolodsgate 8-10
0116 Oslo
Tel: 22-426-720
Fax: 22-436-796

Den norske Bank
POB 1171 Sentrum
0107 Oslo
Tel: 22-48-10-50

Kreditkassen
Middelthunsgate 17
0368 Oslo
Tel: 22-48-50-00

Landsbanken A/S
Youngsgt. 11
Oslo 1
Tel: 22-40-10-00
Fax: 22-40-19-55
Telex: 76034

Oslobanken AS
POB 1368 Vika
0114 Oslo
Tel: 22-94-16-00
Fax: 22-42-40-04
Telex: 79102

Sparebanken Hedmark
POB 203
2301 Hamar
Tel: 62-51-20-00
Fax: 62-53-29-75
Telex: 19423

Sparebanken Midt-Norge
Kongensgt. 4
POB 701
7000 Trondheim
Tel: 73-58-51-11
Fax: 73-58-64-50
Telex: 55177

Sparebanken NOR
(Union Bank of Norway)
Kirkrgt. 14-18
POB 1172 Sentrum
0107 Oslo
Tel: 22-31-90-50
Fax: 22-42-13-61
Telex: 19470

TAXATION

Taxation requires sophisticated knowledge of complex rules and regulations specific to each country. The information presented here is from the Ernst & Young Corporate Tax Guide and Directory, available from the Ernst & Young accounting office in your country, or from:

Ernst & Young
Tullins gate 2
POB 6834 St. Olavs plass
N-0130 Oslo, Norway
Tel: 22-03-60-00
Fax: 22-03-63-70

At a Glance

Corporate Income Tax Rate (%)	28
Capital Gains Tax Rate (%)	28
Branch Tax Rate (%)	28
Withholding Tax (%)	
Dividends (a)	25
Interest	0
Royalties from Patents, Know-how, etc.	0
Branch Remittance Tax	0
Net Operating Losses (Years)	
Carryback	0
Carryforward	10

(a) Applicable to nonresident shareholders.

Legal System

A hereditary democratic kingdom, Norway built its government on the principle of separation of powers: the king and 19 ministers exercise executive power, Parliament enacts the laws, and the courts operate independently, although the judges are appointed for life by the king.

Intellectual Property Protection

Patents Protection is available for new inventions capable of being industrially utilized. An application to the Patent Office in Oslo is reviewed for novelty and formality and then made accessible to public review. A patent is approved only after inspection and a three-month period for public comment. Protection is for a 20-year term from the date of filing. A foreign applicant must be represented by a Norwegian resident in order to obtain patent protection.

Trademarks Broad protection is available, covering trademarks, servicemarks, slogans, and packaging. A mark is protected by use or registration in Norway. Domestic and foreign owners have the same rights, except that a foreign owner may register a mark only if it is already properly registered in the owner's home country or is protected under an international convention to which Norway is a party. To register in Norway, a foreign owner must secure the assistance of a Norwegian agent.

Copyrights Creators of nearly all intellectual productions can acquire protection in Norway. Protection extends to literature, music, cinema, art, handcrafts, and data software. No registration is needed, and there are no formal requirements for assigning or licensing. Norwegian copyright protection expires at the end of the fiftieth year after the author's death. This protection is available only to Norwegian citizens, foreign works first made public in Norway, or rights accorded under reciprocal agreements.

Business Registration

Most commercial companies must register with the central *Foretaksregisteret*. The application for registration must be signed by the company's board members and witnessed. The registration must be amended if the company's charter changes. Advice from Norwegian counsel may be essential to insure compliance with legal requirements for setting up a business entity. Some activities are licensed, such as banking and stockbrokering. Land purchases are listed in a central public record.

Contracts and Dispute Resolution

Written and oral contracts are considered binding and enforceable, unless performance is contrary to public order. Strong court enforcement is available, and parties can take advantage of a fair and well-developed conciliation or arbitration system. Court judgments, arbitral awards, and conciliation orders can all be enforced by a process of execution against property.

Notaries

There is no notarial system. Judges of the courts of first instance (town or county courts) and sheriffs perform the duties of a notary.

Labor

Unions are strong. Pay and conditions of employment are determined by agreements between the Employer's Association and the union. An employee may be discharged only for cause.

Legal Matters

LEGAL BRIEFS

- **Business entities** Nearly all forms of business entities can be established. Most popular are those that offer limited liability, such as joint stock companies. Procedures are fairly simple and can be accomplished in a relatively short time.
- **Monopolies** Some government-controlled monopolies still exist, primarily in the wine, railway, and telecommunications industries.
- **Expropriation** Private industries are subject to expropriation by the state. The constitution protects the rights of owners to be fully compensated for property taken.
- **Foreign copyrights** If a work is not first published in Norway, it must be published within 30 days after publication abroad. For all other foreign works, copyright protection extends only 10 years.
- **International agreements** Norway is a member of CISG, New York Convention on the Recognition and Enforcement of Foreign Arbitral Awards; Enforcement of Foreign Arbitral Awards; Paris Convention; Berne Convention; ATA Carnet Convention; Convention on the Service Abroad of Judicial and Extrajudicial Documents in Civil or Commercial Matters; Convention on the Taking of Evidence Abroad in Civil or Commercial Matters; and the Convention Abolishing the Requirement of Legalization for Foreign Public Documents.

LEGAL CONTACTS

Wikborg, Rein & Co.
Kronprinsesse Märthas Plass 1
POB 1513 Vika
0117 Oslo
Tel: 22-82-75-00 Fax: 22-82-75-01

Thommessen Krefting Greve Lund
Valkindorfsgate 1A
POB 349
5000 Bergen
Tel: 55-31-13-50 Fax: 55-31-74-75

Wikborg, Rein & Co.
Handelens Og Sjofartens Hus
Olav Kyrresgate 11
5014 Bergen
Tel: 55-31-81-16 Fax: 55-31-00-15

Braekhus & Co.
Tordenskioldsgt. 6
N-0160 Oslo 1
Tel: 22-42-06-15 Fax: 22-33-61-23

Raeder, Wisloff, Aasland & Co.
Drammensveien 30
POB 2843 Solli
0230 Oslo 2
Tel: 22-44-68-33 Fax: 22-43-44-28

Contacts

GOVERNMENT AGENCIES

Ministry of Agriculture
Akersgaten 42
POB 8007 Dep
0030 Oslo 1
Tel: 22-34-90-90 Fax: 22-34-95-55

Ministry of Consumer and Family Affairs
Pløensgate 8
POB 8036 Dep
0030 Oslo 1
Tel: 22-34-90-90 Fax: 22-34-95-15

Ministry of Education and Research
Akersgaten 42
POB 8119 Dep
0032 Oslo 1
Tel: 22-34-90-90 Fax: 22-34-95-40

Ministry of the Environment
Myntgaten 2
POB 8013 Dep
0030 Oslo 1
Tel: 22-34-90-90
Fax: 22-34-95-60

Norwegian State Railways
Prinsensgt. 7-9
0107 Oslo
Tel: 22-36-80-00

Ministry of Finance
Akersgaten 42
POB 8008 Dep
0030 Oslo 1
Tel: 22-34-90-90
Fax: 22-34-95-05

REMEMBER
- When you telephone (or fax) to Norway from another country you must always include the country code [47] before the numbers given.
- When you send mail to Norway, be sure to write NORWAY in capital letters on its own line below the addresses given.

Ministry of Fisheries
Øvre Slottsgate 2
POB 8118 dep
0032 Oslo
Tel: 22-34-90-90

Ministry of Foreign Affairs
7, Juniplass 1
POB 8114 Dep
0032 Oslo 1
Tel: 22-34-36-00
Fax: 22-34-95-80

Ministry of Industry and Energy
Pløensgate 8
POB 8014 Dep
0030 Oslo 1
Tel: 22-34-90-90
Fax: 22-34-95-25

Ministry of Labor and Municipal Affairs
Akersgaten 42
POB 8004 Dep
0030 Oslo 1
Tel: 22-34-90-90 Fax: 22-34-95-15

Ministry of Transport and Communications
Møllergaten 1-3
POB 8010 Dep
0030 Oslo 1
Tel: 22-34-90-90
Fax: 22-34-95-70

WORLD TRADE CENTER

World Trade Center Oslo
Pilestredet 17
0164 Oslo
Tel: 22-48-60-50
Fax: 22-36-19-20

BUSINESS AND TRADE ORGANIZATIONS

Confederation of Norwegian Business and Industry
Middelthunsgt. 27
POB 5250
Majorstna
0303 Oslo
Tel: 22-96-50-00
Fax: 22-69-55-93

Oslo Chamber of Commerce
Drammensveien 30
0225
Oslo
Tel: 22-55-74-00
Fax: 22-55-89-53

Norwegian Trade Council
Drammensvn 40
0243 Oslo
Tel: 22-92-63-00
Fax: 22-92-64-00
Telex: 78532

Bergens Handelskammer
Olav Kyrresgt. 11
5000 Begen
Tel: 55-32-30-50

Trondheim Handelskammer
Dronningensgt. 12
7011 Trondheim
Tel: 73-50-15-75
Fax: 73-52-02-46

AD AGENCIES

Bates Advertising
POB 2464
Solli
0202 Oslo
Tel: 22-87-97-00
Fax: 22-87-97-70

JBR/McCann Norway
Parkveien 39
0258 Oslo
Tel: 22-43-18-00
Fax: 22-43-15-55

Ogilvy & Mather
Sorkedalsveien 10A
0369 Oslo
Tel: 22-56-85-90
Fax: 22-46-10-35

SHIPPING

Bergesm d.y. A/S
Drammensvn 106
POB 7600
Skillebekk
0205 Oslo 2
Tel: 22-55-56-00
Telex: 71172

Sigval Bergesen
POB 44
4001 Stavanger
Tel: (4) 52-75-00
Telex: 33007

A/S Billabong
C. Sundtsgt. 17-19
Grieg Gaarden
POB 781
5002 Bergen
Tel: (5) 57-69-50
Fax: (5) 57-69-10
Telex: 40576

A/S Thor Dahl
POB 2010
3201 Sandefjord
Tel: (34) 65-200
Telex: 21777

A/S Kristain Jebsens Rederi
POB 4145Dreggen
5015 Bergen
Tel: (5) 31-03-20
Telex: 42686

STOCK EXCHANGE

Oslo Børs
Tollbugt. 2
POB 460 Sentram
0105 Oslo
Tel: 22-34-17-00
Fax: 22-41-65-90

NEWSPAPERS

Sunnmorsposten
POB 123
6001 Alesund
Tel: (71) 24-570
Fax: (71) 29-977

Agderposten
POB 8
4801 Arendal
Tel: (41) 27-000
Fax: (41) 27-040

Hamar Arbeiderblad
POB 263
2301 Hamar
Tel: (65) 27-540
Fax: (65) 23-324

Finnmark Dagblad
POB 360
9601 Hammerfest
Tel: (84) 11-422
Fax: (84) 13-436

Aftenposten
Akersgt. 51
POB 1178
Sentrum
0107 Oslo 1
Tel: 22-86-30-00
Fax: 22-42-63-25
Telex: 71230

Akers Avis/Groruddalen Budstikke
POB 100 Grorudhagen
0905 Oslo 9
Tel: 22-25-01-89
Fax: 22-16-01-05

Dagbladet
POB 1184 Sentrum
0107 Oslo 1
Tel: 22-31-06-00
Fax: 22-42-95-48
Telex: 71020

PERIODICALS

Bank
POB 9234 Gronland
0134 Oslo
Tel: 22-17-01-40
Fax: 22-17-06-90

Datatid
POB 293 Okern
0511 Oslo
Tel: 22-63-60-00
Fax: 22-63-60-50

Kontor
A/S Kobo
POB 2883 Toyen
0608 Oslo
Tel: 22-68-63-60
Fax: 22-67-61-55

RADIO AND TELEVISION

Broadcasting Authority
POB 6701 St. Olavs pl.
0130 Oslo 1
Tel: 22-48-89-90

INTERNET ADDRESSES

Usenet group(s):
soc.culture.nordic

Norway Online Information Service
http://www.norway.org/web/norway/

Official Documentation and Information from Norway
http://odin.dep.no/html/english/

Norwegian News Sources
http://www.yahoo.com/News/International/Norway/

City Net - Norway
http://www.city.net/countries/norway/

Oman

Sultanate of Oman

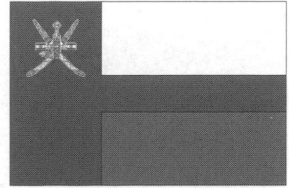

Economy

Overview

The Sultanate of Oman is a small nation of just over two million people and 537,000 expatriate laborers in the southeastern Arabian Peninsula. Oman operates a free-market economy, but the government is the most important economic sector, both in terms of employment and as a purchaser of goods and services. Oil production is the foundation of the economy. The most significant sources of income in addition to oil revenues are tariffs levied on imports, revenues from utilities, and revenues from the 100 percent tariff on tobacco, liquor, and pork. Twenty years of oil revenues have enabled Oman to build a modern infrastructure. Being a one-industry country, Oman's economy moves in lockstep with the world price of oil; when the price of oil falls, Oman's total revenues as well as government spending swiftly follow.

Trade

Apart from oil-related exports and imports, trade is limited to supplies and equipment for government construction projects and small amounts of consumer goods and foodstuffs. Oman's customs procedures are complex, and processing shipments in and out of the port can add significantly to the amount of time that it takes to get goods to their destination. The government is trying to develop the light industry, fisheries, and agriculture sectors to make them more competitive internationally; it has consequently given investors in those areas a full range of tax exemptions and special allowances.

Sectors

Agriculture Fishing and agriculture are the traditional way of life in Oman. Much of farming is still practiced at the subsistence level. Dates and limes, grown extensively in the Batinah coastal plain and the highlands, make up most of the country's agricultural production and exports.

Industry Oman's entire industrial base is currently built around the oil industry. The government is, however, developing a huge liquefied natural gas (LNG) project. The government hopes to begin construction of this facility soon, and aims to have the first LNG exports by the year 2000.

Trends

The economic outlook for the remainder of the 1990s is good, although falling oil prices will require budget cutbacks. A recent development in Oman is an increasing emphasis on privatization; companies currently owned by the government are being partially or completely privatized. The government is also undertaking many developmental projects, employing a significant private sector component, to modernize the economy. This has opened the country to foreign participation, particularly in the form of joint ventures, where Oman is actively seeking foreign investors in the industrial sector. In addition to continued growth in the oil and gas sectors, the areas with the greatest commercial opportunities include water-saving technologies for agriculture, equipment for the treatment of wastewater, medical equipment, telecommunications, joint ventures in light industry, training and vocational education, and the development of an infrastructure for increasing tourism to the Sultanate.

At a Glance

THE COUNTRY

Location Middle East, along the Arabian Sea, between Yemen in the southwest, Saudi Arabia in the northwest, and the United Arab Emirates in the north
Terrain The vast central desert plain is bounded by rugged mountains in the north and south; the coastline stretches for 2,092 km.
Climate Hot and humid along the coast, with strong southwest summer monsoon (May to September) in the far south. Summer winds often raise large sand and dust storms in the hot, dry interior.

THE PEOPLE

Population 2,000,000
Ethnic composition Arab, Baluchi, East African (Zanzabari), South Asian (Indian, Pakistani, Bangladeshi).
Religious composition
Ibadhi and Sunni Muslim 95%
Shia Muslim and Hindu... 5%
Languages spoken Arabic, English, Baluchi, Urdu, Hindi, and Indian dialects.
Education and literacy Since 1970, the government has made education a high priority in order to enhance the domestic work force. In 1986, Oman's first university opened. Students are awarded yearly government scholarships for study abroad. Literacy is estimated at 41 percent.
Labor force
Total:..430,000
By occupation: agriculture and fishing 39%.

COUNTRY FACTS

Political and legal Oman is a monarchy with a legal system based on English common law and Islamic law, with ultimate appeal to the sultan. Civil courts handle criminal cases, while Shari'a (Islamic law) courts oversee family law. In the less-populated areas and among the nomadic Bedouin, tribal custom often is the law.
Telephone Modern telephone service is available in the capital area and several other towns. Telegraphic, mobile telephone, and telex service are also available. International country code: [968]. City codes are not required. All numbers are six digits.
Transportation The capital area has both an international airport and a deep-water port. A national road network includes a highway linking the northern and southern regions.
Environment Maintaining an adequate agricultural and domestic water supply is the most pressing environmental problem. Drought, limited rainfall, and contamination by sea water are problems. Oil tanker spills have caused beach and coastal pollution. Endangered species are protected by law. Current issues are rising soil salinity and sparse natural freshwater resources.
Media The government runs the two AM, three FM radio, and seven television stations. There are several newspapers and journals published. Criticism of the sultan is illegal.
Health Some of the largest funding outlays are in health services. Modern care and most medicines are available. Life expectancy averages 67 years.

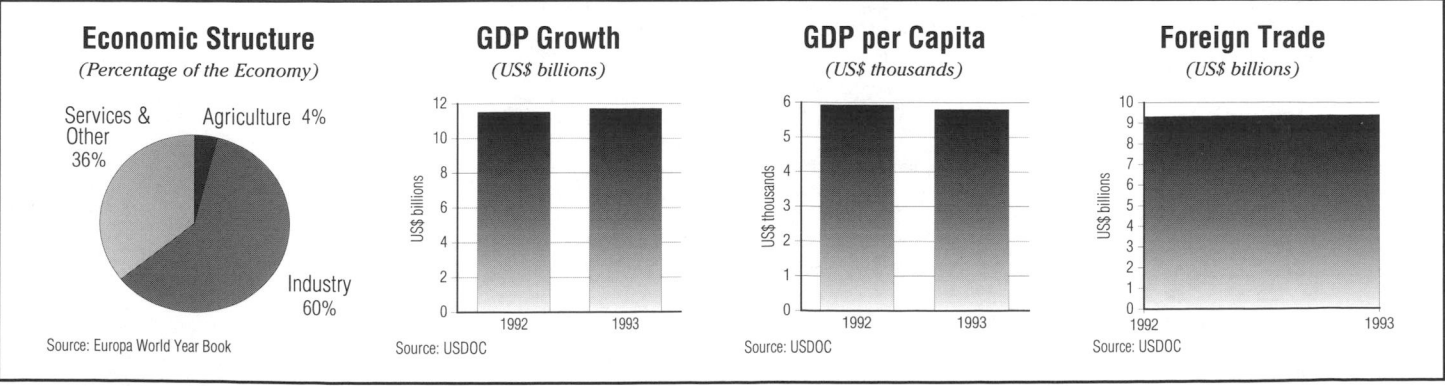

Economic Structure
(Percentage of the Economy)

Services & Other 36%
Agriculture 4%
Industry 60%

Source: Europa World Year Book

GDP Growth
(US$ billions)

1992, 1993

Source: USDOC

GDP per Capita
(US$ thousands)

1992, 1993

Source: USDOC

Foreign Trade
(US$ billions)

1992, 1993

Source: USDOC

Business Travel

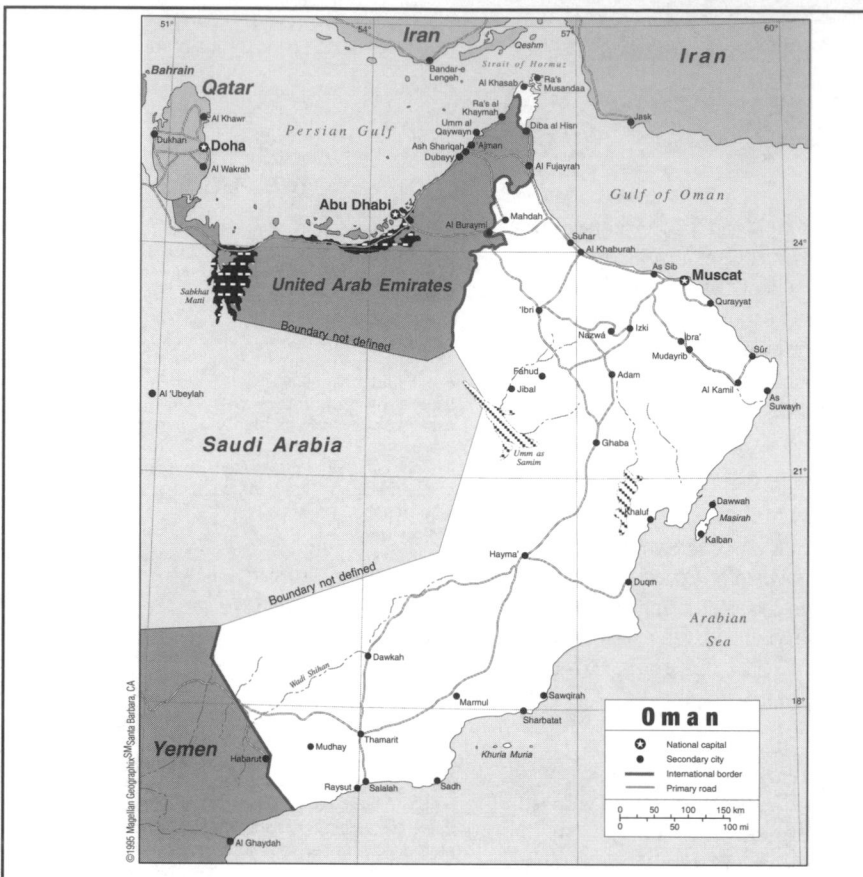

Oman

⊗	National capital
●	Secondary city
—	International border
—	Primary road

0   50   100   150 km
0   50   100 mi

COMMUNICATIONS

Telephones Telephone service is excellent within the Muscat area. Direct dial is available to North America and Europe. Service is not as advanced in rural parts of Oman. Fiber optic cable and digital technology installation began in 1993.
Fax The international hotels have secretarial and translation services, computers, fax machines, and meeting rooms available for business guests.
Post office Fax communication is now more reliable and efficient than the postal service. Mail service is good within Muscat.

BEST TRAVEL BOOKS

Hippocrene Companion Guide to Saudi Arabia. Gene Lindsay.
The Traveler's Guide to Middle Eastern and North African Customs and Manners. Elizabeth Devine & Nancy Braganti. How to converse, dine, tip, bargain, dress, make friends, and conduct business while in the Middle East and North Africa.
Middle East, Lonely Planet On a Shoestring. Details, details, details! 126 maps.

NATIONAL TOURIST OFFICE

ONAT
Muscat
Tel: 590046

USEFUL TELEPHONE NUMBERS

If you are calling from outside Oman, you will need to add the country code [968] and any other international dialing requirements from within your country.
- Police/Ambulance/Fire 999
- International Operator 15, 195
- Local Operator 190, 198
- Oman International Trade and Exhibitions ... 564268
- Oman Chamber of Commerce 707674
- Development Council 698900
- Ministry of Information/Muscat 603222
- US Embassy/Muscat 698989
- Greater Muttrah Post Office 708584
- Muscat Post Office 738547
- Seeb Post Office 510634
- Oman Chamber of Commerce Library 707674
- Department of Immigration/Muscat 602244
- Budget Car Rentals 7977201
- Europcar 700190
- Bus Information 590046
Airlines
- Gulf Air/Muscat... 702613
- Gulf Air/Salalah 461963
- Oman Aviation Services............................... 519211
Credit Card Information
Lost or stolen credit cards (call collect to the US, regardless of which country the card was issued in).
- Amex ....[1] (919) 333-3211
- Diner's Club...............................[1] (303) 799-1504
- MasterCard ....[1] (314) 275-6690
- Visa ....[1] (410) 581-7931

Travelogue

WORKWEEK
Business hours Vary from summer to winter and during Ramadan.
Government Saturday-Wednesday 7:30 am to 2:00 pm, Thursday 7:30 am to 1 pm.
Business Saturday-Wednesday 8:00 am to noon, 4:00 pm to 6:00 pm, Thursday 8:00 am to 1:00 pm.
Banks Saturday-Wednesday 8:00 am to noon, Thursday, 8:00 am to 11:30 pm.
Retail Saturday-Thursday 8:00 am to 1:00 pm, 4:00 pm to 7:00 pm.
Friday is the day of rest.

HOLIDAYS
Holidays 1996
January 1 New Year's Day
January 1 Ascension*
February 20-21 Eid Al-Fitr
April 29-30 Eid Al-Adha*
May 18 Islamic New Year*
July 27 Birth of the Prophet*
November 17-18 National Day
December 25 Christmas
*Dates are tentative, determined by lunar sightings.

VISA AND PASSPORT
All visitors must obtain a visa from an Oman embassy or arrange for a No Objection Certificate (NOC) through a business sponsor in Oman before arriving in Oman. Entry into the country is strictly controlled. Baggage is frequently searched and video tapes may be confiscated to determine if they are pornographic. Anyone attempting entry without prior permission will be deported on the next exiting flight.

DEPARTURE FORMALITIES
An airport departure tax of RO3 is charged to all international travelers.

IMMUNIZATION
Vaccinations against cholera and yellow fever are required of anyone arriving from an infected area. Antimalaria precautions are strongly recommended. Typhoid, gamma globulin, tetanus, and polio shots are also recommended. Importing any pet requires a permit from the Ministry of Agriculture and Fisheries/Department of Animal Health before travel. Owners must submit a rabies vaccination record and a health certificate. Pets may be subjected to a six-month quarantine which may not be necessary if the pet is from a rabies-free area.

TIPPING
Not expected in general. Taxi: 5 to 10 percent; Porters: 200 baiza per piece; hotels, restaurants: 10 percent usually included in tips, which does not go to waiting personnel; barbers, beauticians: 5 to 10 percent. Small services: 100 baiza.

CRIME
Street crimes are infrequent in Oman and violent crimes are very rare. Report the loss of a visa immediately to the nearest embassy or local police.

INFRASTRUCTURE
Seeb International Airport, 40km from Muscat, handles international and domestic flights. There are no direct flights to Oman, but connecting service is available through many airlines. Most major hotels have airport pickup service that should be arranged for in advance. Always determine the taxi fare with the driver before departing for any destination and if you do not speak Arabic have a colleague or hotel clerk write down your destinations in Arabic to show the driver. Car rentals are available at the airport and major hotels. Drivers are required to present a valid driver's license. Be sure you purchase insurance if it is required. A daily bus travels between Muscat and Salalah. The ride takes 12 hours and the bus is air conditioned. It is necessary to make a reservation for this trip.

Foreign Trade

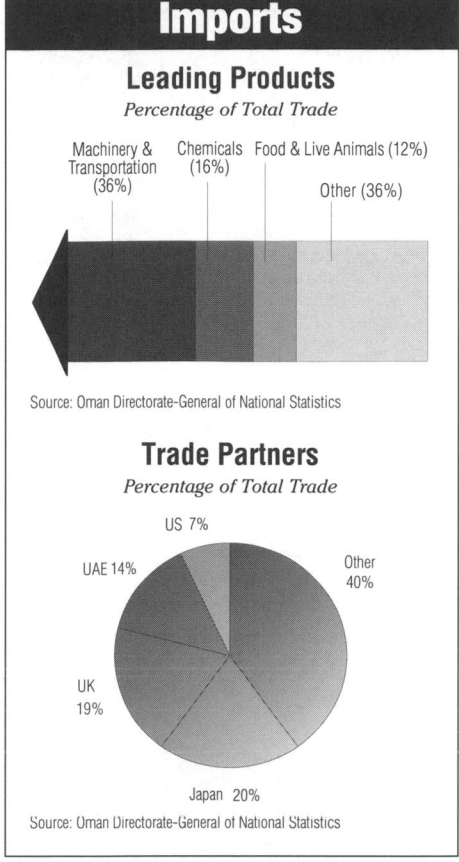

Imports

Leading Products
Percentage of Total Trade

Machinery & Transportation (36%)
Chemicals (16%)
Food & Live Animals (12%)
Other (36%)

Source: Oman Directorate-General of National Statistics

Trade Partners
Percentage of Total Trade

US 7%
UAE 14%
UK 19%
Japan 20%
Other 40%

Source: Oman Directorate-General of National Statistics

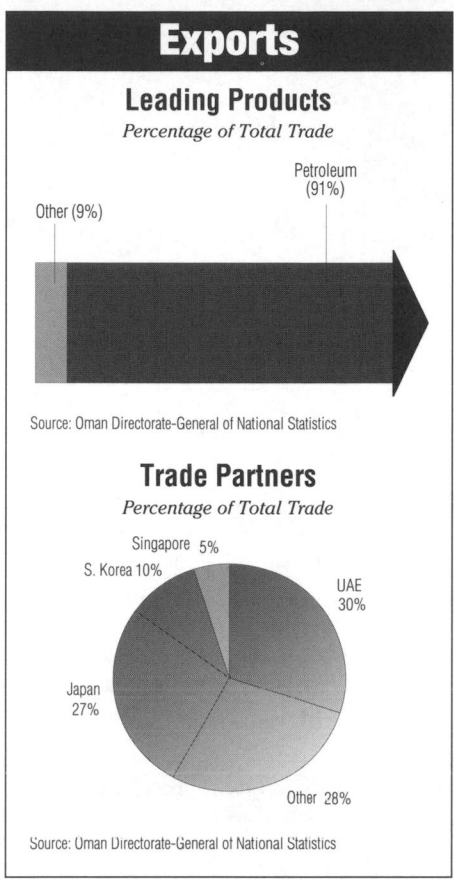

Exports

Leading Products
Percentage of Total Trade

Other (9%)
Petroleum (91%)

Source: Oman Directorate-General of National Statistics

Trade Partners
Percentage of Total Trade

Singapore 5%
S. Korea 10%
Japan 27%
UAE 30%
Other 28%

Source: Oman Directorate-General of National Statistics

Opportunities

FOR IMPORTING TO OMAN
- consumer, electrical, and manufactured goods
- food, cigarettes, and health care products
- machinery and transportation equipment

FOR EXPORTING FROM OMAN
- petroleum products, processed copper
- foodstuffs
- textiles

GROWTH SECTORS
- civilian sectors
- LNG plants
- development of interior for services & employment
- water saving technology and waste water

Trade News

RULES AND REGULATIONS
- **Trade regulations and standards** Companies importing goods or acting as commercial agents in Oman must fulfill the following principal conditions: they must be registered with the Ministry of Commerce and Industry and Oman Chamber of Commerce and Industry, Omani shareholding in the capital of the company must be at least 51 percent, and the company's main purposes should include import trade and commercial agency business.
- **Special license** Certain classes of goods require a special license. Certain essential consumer goods are exempted from customs duty. Examples include currency (gold/silver bullion), agricultural implements, books, refined petroleum products, and foodstuffs. Duties of 10-50 percent exist on some items in order to protect nascent domestic industries.

Legal

Legal System

Oman's legal system is derived from British traditions, but some laws, including health, safety, and environmental standards, are enforced inconsistently.

Intellectual Property Rights

Patents There is no patent protection. Legislation is being drafted.

Trademarks Oman actively enforces its trademark law, and the registration of a trademark is published in the Official Gazette. However, the application process is subject to some delay, which may be less if the company has a local agent.

Copyrights No laws afford copyright protection, but proposed laws are in process. Oman's audio and video cassette markets are comprised almost exclusively of pirated copies. Computer software is also pirated. In terms of computer software, major companies and government agencies buy only legitimate products.

Business Registration

Oman is eager to receive foreign businesses and investors and has dropped nearly all registration requirements.

Labor

There are no provisions for collective bargaining, for wages, and for working conditions in Oman. The Labor Law imposes a statutory obligation on employers with over 50 employees to create a group of representatives from management and workers. This group is responsible for proposing a labor constitution and submitting it to the Ministry of Social Affairs and Labor. The Labor Law applies to foreign workers, who constitute 50 percent of Oman's work force. Any employee may file a grievance with the Labor Welfare Board, which operates impartially and generally gives workers the benefit of the doubt in grievance hearings.

Legal Matters

LEGAL BRIEFS
- **Child labor** Children younger than age 13 are prohibited from working. Children age 13 to 15 are prohibited from performing evening or night work and strenuous labor.
- **Competition** Government policies on development of light industry, fisheries, and agriculture are geared to making those sectors competitive internationally and investors in those areas receive a full range of tax exemptions, utility discounts, and in some cases, tariff protection.
- **Government decisions** There is no complete body of regulations to codify labor laws, and many government decisions are made on an ad hoc basis.
- **Tax laws** Recent changes in the tax laws have, for the first time, required Omani companies to pay taxes on profits.
- **Dispute resolution** Oman is not a member of the International Center for the Settlement of Investment Disputes. The Authority for Settlement of Commercial Disputes, an independent judicial body, makes all decisions regarding contract disputes. Minor disputes are also handled by local authorities, such as *walis,* the district governors appointed by the central government.
- **Arabic** All litigation and hearings must be conducted in Arabic.

LEGAL CONTACT

Fox & Gibbons
PO Box 3552112
Ruwi 112
Tel: 564346
Fax: 564395

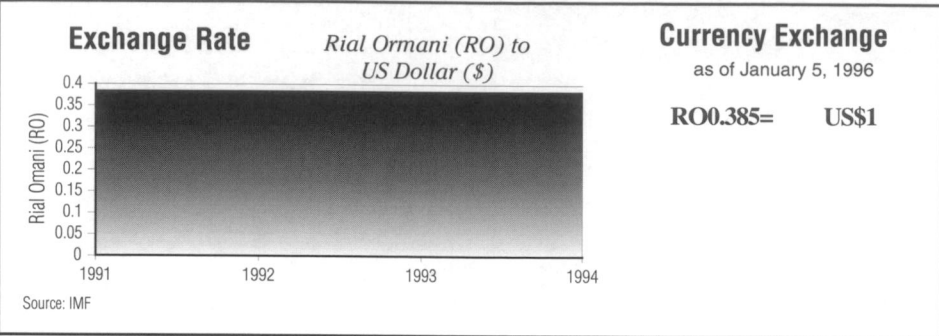

Exchange Rate

Rial Ormani (RO) to US Dollar ($)

Rial Omani (RO): 0.4, 0.35, 0.3, 0.25, 0.2, 0.15, 0.1, 0.05, 0

1991 — 1992 — 1993 — 1994

Source: IMF

Currency Exchange

as of January 5, 1996

RO0.385=   US$1

Currency

The currency of Oman is the rial omani (RO), which is divided into 1,000 baiza.

Foreign Exchange

The Central Bank controls foreign exchange, although there is no exchange control legislation in Oman. There is no distinction between resident and nonresident accounts. Foreign investment is allowed only through joint stock companies or joint ventures. In most cases, majority ownership must be held by residents, and foreign firms interested in starting a company in Oman need approval from government agencies. In addition, foreign workers must have work permits and residency permits. Anyone considering investing in Oman should consider engaging local counsel, because there is no complete body of regulations codifying labor and tax laws and several government decisions are made on a case-by-case basis. Taxes for foreign companies are much higher than for local businesses.

Capital Transfers

Travelers can bring in or take out any amount of currency, including rial omani. There are no requirements placed on invisible payments or proceeds.

Investment Incentives

Under the Industry Organization and Encouragement Law of 1978, incentives are available to licensed industrial installations on the recommendation of the Industrial Development Committee. Companies selling locally produced goods are given priority for government purchases, provided the local products meet standard quality specifications. This incentive is available to all enterprises, foreign and domestic. The government also offers subsidies to offset the cost of feasibility and similar studies if the proposed project is considered sufficiently important to the national economy.

Investment Restrictions

All enterprises in Oman are expected to comply with Omani laws, applying equally to all business representatives. Only companies with a minimum 35 percent Omani ownership can qualify for incentives.

TAXATION

Taxation requires sophisticated knowledge of complex rules and regulations specific to each country. The information presented here is from the Ernst & Young Corporate Tax Guide and Directory, available from the Ernst & Young accounting office in your country, or from:

Ernst & Young
Mail Address:
P.O. Box 1750
Ruwi 112
Sultanate of Oman
Street Address:
Getco Tower, 1st Floor
Muttrah Business District
Muscat
Sultanate of Oman
Tel: 703 105
Cable: Ernstaudit, Muscat
Telex: 3174 Ans bk ERNST OM ON
Fax: 702 734

At a Glance

Corporate Income Tax Rate (%) (a)	50
Capital Gains Tax Rate (%) (a)	50
Branch Tax Rate (%) (b)	50
Withholding Tax (%)	0
Net Operating Losses (Years)	
Carryback	0
Carryforward	5

(a) The tax rate varies according to the level of Omani participation and taxable profit.
(b) The tax rate increases according to the level of taxable profit.

Money Matters

BITS AND PIECES

- **Corporate income tax** All companies in Oman, resident and nonresident, are subject to income tax based on Omani-source income.
- **Capital gains tax** All capital gains are taxed as part of regular income at a rate determined by the level of local participation and taxable profit.
- **Foreign tax relief** Relief is available but allowed on a case-by-case basis only.
- **Capital transfer** There are no requirements for either inward or outward transfers of capital.
- **Gold** Only monetary authorities, authorized banks, and nonresident banks can hold, buy, and sell gold.
- **Import payments** Companies operating in Oman and trading in oil products are prohibited from importing some products as long as domestic production can meet the demand of the public. Foreign payments for payments abroad for imports can be obtained without restriction.
- **Export payments** Export proceeds do not need to be surrendered, and may be disposed of freely, regardless of the currency or amount, without requirement.

BANKS

ANZ Gridlays Bank PLC
POB 500
Ruwi 112
Tel: 706-008, 703-013 Fax: 706-911

Bank Dhofar Al Omani Al Fransi
POB 1507
Ruwi 112
Tel: 790-466/8 Fax: 797-246

Bank Melli Iran
POB 2643
Ruwi 112
Tel: 708-125, 701-579 Fax: 793-017

Bank Muscat Al-Ahli Al-Omani
POB 134
Ruwi 112
Tel: 703-044 Fax: 793-536

Bank of Baroda
POB 231
Mutrah 114
Tel: 714-549, 714-559 Fax: 714-560

Bank of Oman, Bahrain and Kuwait
POB 1708
Ruwi 112
Tel: 701-528, 700-186 Fax: 705-607

Commercial Bank of Oman
POB 1694
Ruwi 112
Tel: 793-224 through 228 Fax: 793-229

National Bank of Oman
POB 751
Ruwi 112
Tel: 708-894 Fax: 704-522, 707-781

Oman Arab Bank
POB 2010
Ruwi 112
Tel: 700-161/2/3 Fax: 797-736

Omani European Bank
POB 1565
Ruwi 112
Tel: 797-410 Fax: 797-410

Oman International Bank
POB 1727
CPO Seeb 111
Tel: 693-200 Fax: 693-199

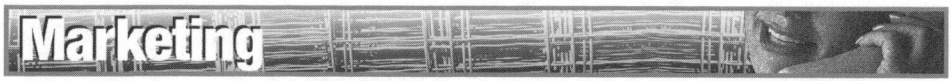

Marketing

Overview

The domestic market in Oman is small and there is almost no modern, high-value consumer market outside the capital of Muscat. While Oman welcomes business from abroad, its laws require a foreign company entering its market to choose and deal exclusively with an approved local agent. Short deadlines and quick market developments are the norm in Omani business, and a local agent's inside knowledge is crucial in both monitoring the shifting situations and maneuvering.

Agents and Distributors

Foreign companies wishing to distribute products in Oman must find a local distributor. Only Omani-controlled firms, duly registered and within the Sultanate, may operate as representatives or agents. Personal visits to agents are the best ways to keep in contact. Although agency agreements are exclusive and allow only the appointed local agency to distribute or sell a foreign company's products, separate agencies are sometimes allowed for the northern and southern regions of the country. Other exceptions exist as well amid the web of Omani regulations, and careful legal counsel is essential in establishing an agency agreement. All agency agreements must be approved and registered with the Ministry of Commerce and Industry and other bureaus, giving the government direct and substantial influence on foreign trade and distribution.

Advertising

While advertising is available on Omani television and radio, the use of newspapers and promotional fliers is most common. Most marketing is subject to the discretion of the local agent, who will order only what he feels he can sell. Two English language newspapers, the *Oman Daily Observer* and the *Times of Oman* are available for advertising, as well as two Arabic dailies, *Al Watan* and *Oman,* which reach a much broader local audience. International reputation and word-of-mouth recommendations weigh heavily here. For mass market consumer goods, billboards and filmed cinema ads may be more effective, since illiteracy is high. Television advertising began in 1987 and continues on 11 stations. Radio ads are permitted on all three AM and three FM stations.

Business Culture

Greetings and Courtesies

English is the primary business language, although Arabic is the official language of the country. Omanis hold titles in high regard. Always use professional titles like doctor or professor. If you are a PhD., be sure to have it printed on your business card; it may help sway your Omani counterparts. Omanis weren't allowed higher education until recently, and in many cases degrees are respected more than an individual's competence.

Business Ethic and Framework

One of the most modern of the Gulf countries, Oman is considered more tolerant of Western culture than are many other Arab countries. Omanis are very honest in their business dealings, and expect foreigners to be the same. Western style business attire is more commonly found in Oman than in neighboring countries.

Meetings and Decision Making

There is generally one decisionmaker in a company. Prior appointments should always be made for business meetings, and foreigners should arrive on time. Meetings will be continuously interrupted by family, friends, and business associates, as well as by frequent telephone calls. Once the business discussion has begun, however, it will proceed in a relatively straightforward manner.

Women

Women have more freedoms in Oman than most other Middle Eastern countries. Many Omani women are educated and hold management positions in companies. Many foreign women who are doctors work in Oman. They can order at restaurants and drink alcohol. Foreign businesswomen are generally treated with respect and are not discriminated against, but they should remember to act professional at all times. There may be some resistance to a woman being sent to close some deals.

Marketing in Oman

MARKETING TIPS

- **Cultural awareness** Sexually suggestive or titillating advertisements are considered unacceptable in Oman's Islamic culture; similarly, avoid any humorous advertisements which might in any way be construed as irreverent or disrespectful to the Islamic creed.
- **Shortage** Exports or re-exports of live animals and foodstuffs may be prohibited in times of shortage in Oman.
- **Trade news** Oman has a small population and a small domestic market.
- **Office space** Office space in the capital area is readily available and will remain so over the next few years. Rental costs are quite reasonable. Furnishings are generally not provided, and rents do not include air conditioning or utility costs.
- **Employees** European (mostly British) managers and South Asian and Philippine laborers and clerical staff comprise almost half of the nonagricultural work force. Expatriates are especially prominent in the construction, petroleum, finance, and transportation industries. There are also large expatriate markets for expensive foreign goods.
- **Terms of payment** Payment in Oman is typically by letter of credit. Japanese sellers, and some European firms, are well-known for their willingness to offer attractive time draft terms that other foreign firms are unable to match.

AD AGENCY

Advertising International (Adinc)
POB 407
118 Muscat
E-mail: adinc@omzest.co.ac

Cultural Cautions

DO'S

- Take the time to establish solid personal relationships.

DON'TS

- Do not openly refuse a favor. If one is asked and it is unreasonable, illegal, or too difficult, listen carefully and indicate the doubtfulness of the outcome, but assure that you will make an attempt to perform.
- It is best not to bring up religion as a topic of conversation in Oman.

CUSTOMS

- Arabs assume the role of host or hostess. A guest, even an unexpected one will always be offered something to drink or eat.

OBSERVATIONS

- Alcohol is a touchy subject. If your host doesn't drink, it is probably a good idea that you abstain as well.
- Women are allowed to wear bathing suits, providing they are one piece.
- Arabs do not view their social customs and restrictions as repressive, but as complimentary to the status and nature of both men and women.
- Arabs mistrust people who do not appear to be sincere or who fail to demonstrate an interest in them personally or in their country.

NEGOTIATIONS

- A low-key approach will work well in Oman, although you must indicate your willingness and sincerity by establishing solid personal relationships.
- If you receive evasive answers, do not press the point further.

GOVERNMENT AGENCIES

Ministry of Defense
POB 113
Muscat 113
Tel: 312-605
Fax: 702-521

Ministry of Development
POB 881
Muscat 113
Tel: 698-900
Fax: 696-285

Ministry of Electricity and Water
POB 1491
Ruwi 112
Tel: 603-597, 603-906
Fax: 699-180, 699-185

Ministry of Communications
POB 684
Muscat 113
Tel: 702-233
Fax: 701-409, 795-266

Ministry of Finance and Economy
POB 506
Muscat 113
Tel: 738-201 through 210, 739-764 through 772
Fax: 737-068

Ministry of Health
POB 393
Muscat 113
Tel: 602-177
Fax: 602-647

Ministry of Petroleum and Minerals
POB 551
Muscat 113
Tel: 603-333, 603-341, 603-563
Fax: 696-972

Ministry of Posts, Telegraphs and Telephones
POB 338
Ruwi 112
Tel: 697-888, 698-931
Fax: 696-817, 696-670

Ministry of Regional Municipalities and Environment
POB 461
Muscat 113
Tel: 696-444, 696-446 through 449
Fax: 602-320

Ministry of Water Resources
POB 2575
Ruwi 112
Tel: 703-552/3
Fax: 799-953, 799-563, 706-782

Public Establishment for Industrial Estates
POB 2
Rusayl 124
Tel: 626-080, 626-094
Fax: 626-053

Muscat Securities Market
POB 3265
Ruwi 112
Tel: 702-607/9, 702-617, 702-621
Fax: 702-691

Ministry of Agriculture and Fisheries
PO Box 467
Muscat
Tel: 696-300
Fax: 696-271

Ministry of Information
PO Box 600
Muscat
Tel: 603-888
Fax: 601-393

Ministry of Social Affairs and Labor
PO Box 560
Muscat
Tel: 602-444
Fax: 701515

Oman National Electric Company
PO Box 4393
Ruwi
Tel: 796-353
Fax: 704-420

BUSINESS AND TRADE ORGANIZATIONS

Development Council
PO Box 881
Muscat
Tel: 698-900
Fax: 696-285

Public Authority for Marketing of Agricultural Produce
PO Box 6510
Ruwi
Tel: 591-540 through 6
Telex: 5676 taswiq on

Oman Chamber of Commerce and Industry
POB 1400
Ruwi 112
Tel: 707-674, 707-684, 707-694
Fax: 708-497

NEWSPAPERS

Oman Newspaper House
PO Box 6002
Ruwi
Tel: 701-555, 707-705
Telex: 3638 onh on

Al Watan
POB 463
Muscat
Tel: 591919

Oman Daily Newspaper
POB 6002
Ruwi
Tel: 701555

Oman Daily Observer
POB 3002
Ruwi
Tel: 701953

Times of Oman
POB 3770
Ruwi
Tel: 701953

PERIODICALS

Al-Ghorfa (Oman Commerce)
POB 4400
Ruwi
Tel: 707674
Fax: 708497

The Commercial
POB 5002
Muscat
Tel: 705972

BANKS

Banque Banorabe
POB 1608
Ruwi 112
Tel: 704-274, 703-850
Fax: 707-782

Bank Saderat Iran
POB 1269
Ruwi 112
Tel: 793-923
Fax: 796-478

British Bank of the Middle East
POB 240
Ruwi 112
Tel: 799-920, 700-020
Fax: 704-241

Central Bank of Oman
POB 1161
Ruwi 112
Tel: 702-222
Fax: 707-913, 702-253

Citibank N.A.
POB 1994
Mutrah 114
Tel: 795-705
Fax: 795-724

Habib Bank A.B. Zurich
POB 2717
Ruwi 112
Tel: 799-865, 799-876
Fax: 703-613

Habib Bank Ltd.
POB 1326
Ruwi 112
Tel: 705-276, 795-282
Fax: 794-386

National Bank of Abu Dhabi
POB 303
Muscat 113
Tel: 798-842
Fax: 794-386

Oman Development Bank SAO
POB 309
Muscat 113
Tel: 738-021 through 024
Fax: 738-026

Oman Housing Bank
POB 2555
Ruwi 112
Tel: 704-444
Fax: 704-071

Oman Bank for Agriculture & Fisheries
POB 3077
Ruwi 112
Tel: 701-761/2/3
Fax: 706-473

Standard Chartered Bank
POB 2353
Ruwi 112
Tel: 703-999
Fax: 796-864

TRANSPORTATION FIRMS

Bhacker Haji Abdul Latiff Fazul
POB 51
Muscat
Telex: 5220 BAKR ON

Transport Services
POB 268
Muscat
Telex: 3301 TRANOMAN ON

Gulf Agency Company (Oman) Ltd.
POB 3740
Ruwi
Fax: 703609
Telex: 3664 GACSHIP ON

INTERNET ADDRESSES

City Net - Oman
http://www.city.net/countries/oman/

Oman Page (Model League of Arab States)
http://192.203.180.62/mlas/Oman.html

Asian Studies - Oman
http://coombs.anu.edu.au/WWWVLAsian/Oman.html

Sultanate of Oman Home Page
http://holly.colostate.edu/~oman/oman.html

Oman's WWW sites
http://www.liii.com/~hajeri/oman.html

Pakistan

Islamic Republic of Pakistan

Economy

Overview

A succession of governments in Pakistan over the past six years have implemented structural reform policies to free the economy and make it more market-oriented. Because the two principal political parties basically agree on the direction of economic policy, the shifts in government have created remarkably little impediment to the liberalizing trend. Early signs of the success of these efforts are seen in the renewed vitality of the private sector, increased investment, and the diversification of output.

Trade

Although Pakistan has traditionally maintained a complex system of indirect taxes in the trade sector, a principal element of structural reform over the past few years has been some significant trade liberalization. The government is now engaged in a sweeping tariff reduction program to force domestic firms to improve their competitiveness and take advantage of Uruguay Round benefits; chief among these from the Pakistani perspective is the integration of textile trade into the GATT. Cotton textile products collectively accounted for over 53 percent of Pakistan's exports in 1992–93. Pakistan is a net exporter of agricultural commodities despite annual imports of more than 31 billion rupees (US$ one billion) of wheat and edible oils.

Sectors

Agriculture Despite some recent diversification, agriculture remains the dominant sector of Pakistan's economy, accounting for just over 25 percent of GDP. Cotton is one of its most important crops, though it remains highly subject to adverse climactic and international trade conditions.

Industry The performance of the manufacturing sector improved marginally in 1993–94, despite power blackouts and a troubled year for the textile industry. Pakistan has a fairly broad industrial base and manufacturing accounts for about 18 percent of GDP. Cotton textile production is the single most important industry, accounting for about 20 percent of large-scale industrial employment. Expansion of the manufacturing sector waits on the development of the electric power sector which is the government's highest priority project for the near term.

Services Service industries account for about 50 percent of GDP, with wholesale and retail trade as the largest component. Finance and insurance show the strongest growth rates of any other activity in the economy. Banks and most of the non-trade services remain nationalized.

Trends

Government's role in the economy continues to shrink. In 1990 the public sector accounted for about 30 percent of value-added in manufacturing. The government has since sold about 80 percent of its industrial concerns and continues to reduce its holdings. Agricultural production continues to decline, although textile production (based on cotton) dominates the manufacturing sector. Pakistan's critical need for electricity generating equipment and for infrastructure improvements offer opportunities for knowledgeable foreign traders to sell to the government. If political stability can be maintained, Pakistan should post healthy growth rates, develop many newly privatized industries, and increase their openness to foreign trade.

At a Glance

THE COUNTRY
Location Southern Asia, along the Arabian Sea, between India and Afghanistan.
Terrain Flat plain in the east; mountains in north and northwest; and the Balochistan plateau in the west.
Climate Generally hot, dry desert, though temperate in the northwest and frigid in the mountainous north.

THE PEOPLE
Population 128,000,000
Ethnic composition Punjabi, Sindhi, Pathan, Baluch, Muhajirs (i.e. Urdu-speaking immigrants from India and their descendents).
Religious composition
Muslim (Sunni 77%, Shi'a 20%) 97%
Christian, Hindu, and other 3%
Languages spoken Urdu, English, Punjabi, Sindhi, Pushtu, Baluchi.
Education and literacy Relatively little funding is devoted to education programs. Literacy for males is 47%; for females, 21%.
Labor force
Total: 28,900,000
By occupation: agriculture 54%, mining and manufacturing 13%, services 33%, extensive export of labor.

COUNTRY FACTS
Political and legal Parliamentary democracy in a federal setting based on English common law, but Sharia (Islamic law) is supreme. Accepts International Court of Justice rulings, with some reservations. The Supreme Court and the Federal Islamic (Sharía) Courts are the highest legal bodies.
Telephone The domestic telephone system is poor, and is primarily used for businesses and the government. There are only about seven telephones per 1,000 persons. The international system is somewhat better. International country code: [92]. Selected city codes: Karachi (21), Lahore (42), Islamabad (51).
Transportation There are more than 100,000 km of highways; some require four-wheel drive vehicles. The government owns and operates the railways. There are three major ports and many airports.
Environment High population growth has contributed to the loss of forestland, causing soil erosion, declining soil fertility, and increased flooding in many areas. Untreated sewage threatens the water supply, and the vast majority of the population does not have safe drinking water. The government is currently considering laws to set air and water quality standards and prevent pollution. Hunting or capturing wild animals has been banned. Current issues are water pollution from untreated sewage, industrial wastes, and agricultural runoff, water scarcity, deforestation, soil erosion, and desertification.
Media The government operates most of the 19 AM, eight FM radio stations, and the 29 television stations. While the press is legally uncensored, the government continues to influence coverage in the more than 180 daily newspapers.
Health Few resources go toward health care programs. Infant mortality reaches 101.9 deaths for every 1,000 live births. Life expectancy for the total population averages 57 years.

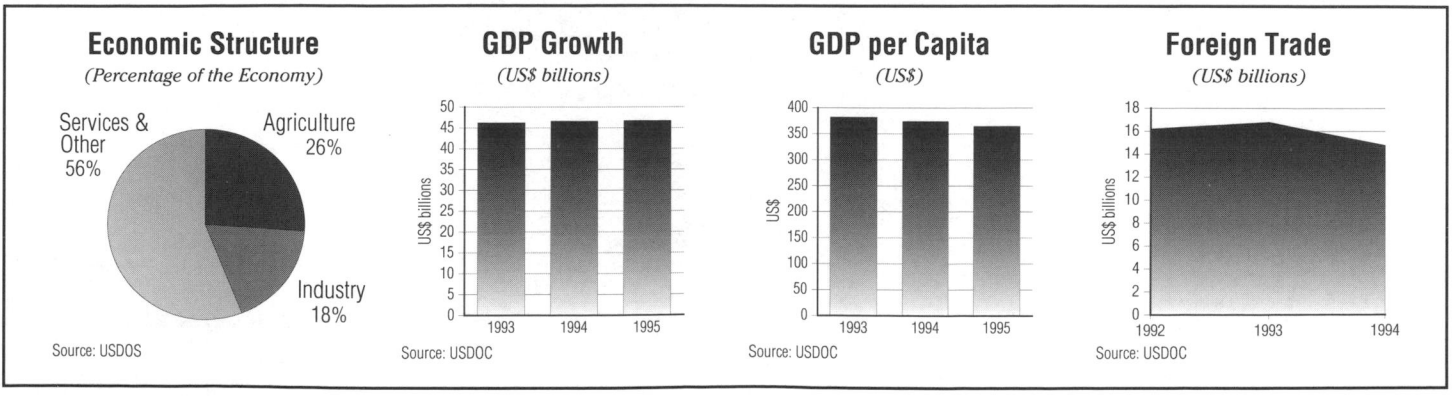

Economic Structure
(Percentage of the Economy)

Services & Other 56%
Agriculture 26%
Industry 18%

Source: USDOS

GDP Growth
(US$ billions)

1993 1994 1995

Source: USDOC

GDP per Capita
(US$)

1993 1994 1995

Source: USDOC

Foreign Trade
(US$ billions)

1992 1993 1994

Source: USDOC

*Note:
The City of Islamabad is encompassed by the Province called Islamabad Captial Territory. Federally Administered Tribal Areas is designated a territory. The Pakistani-administered portion of the disputed Jammu and Kashmir region includes Azad Kashmir and the Northern Areas.

Pakistan

- ☆ National capital
- ⊙ Provincial capital
- ● Secondary city
- ☒ Airport
- ▬▬ International border
- ─── Province border
- ─── Road
- ········ Railroad
- - - - - Trail

| 0 | 100 | 200 | 300 km |
| 0 | 100 | 200 mi |

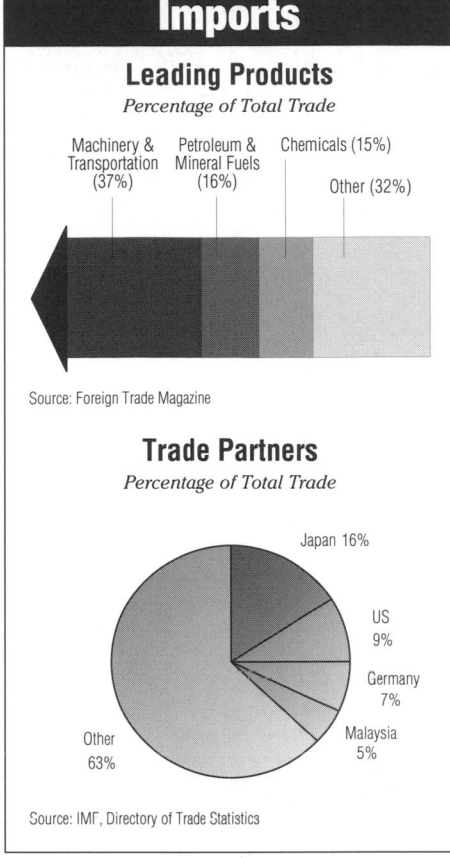

Imports

Leading Products
Percentage of Total Trade

Machinery & Transportation (37%)
Petroleum & Mineral Fuels (16%)
Chemicals (15%)
Other (32%)

Source: Foreign Trade Magazine

Trade Partners
Percentage of Total Trade

Japan 16%
US 9%
Germany 7%
Malaysia 5%
Other 63%

Source: IMF, Directory of Trade Statistics

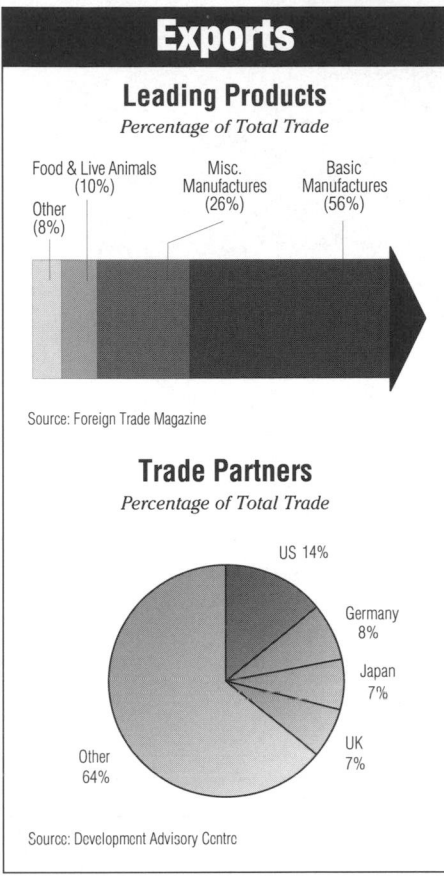

Exports

Leading Products
Percentage of Total Trade

Food & Live Animals (10%)
Other (8%)
Misc. Manufactures (26%)
Basic Manufactures (56%)

Source: Foreign Trade Magazine

Trade Partners
Percentage of Total Trade

US 14%
Germany 8%
Japan 7%
UK 7%
Other 64%

Source: Development Advisory Centre

Opportunities

FOR IMPORTING TO PAKISTAN
- edible oils
- wheat
- electrical generating equipment
- sophisticated machinery for textile production
- machinery imports
- chemicals
- petroleum products
- motor vehicles

FOR EXPORTING FROM PAKISTAN
- cotton
- sugar
- molasses
- marble

GROWTH SECTORS
- agriculture
- industry
- energy
- minerals/mining sector
- coal/mineral development

GOVERNMENT PROCUREMENT
- coal generating power plants
- energy sector
- hydrogeneration
- ports
- highways/roads
- freight and passenger traffic programs
- construction of inter city and farm-to-market roads
- air transport

Trade News

RULES AND REGULATIONS

- **Generally** Pakistan is the world's ninth most populous country, and is well into a successful program of market-oriented reform, offering more new promising markets. There are over 20 languages spoken in Pakistan.
- **Tariffs and import taxes** Pakistan uses the Harmonized System to classify and describe goods. Customs duties are levied on an ad valorem basis. The government of Pakistan continues to rationalize its custom tariff regime.
- **Import taxes** Importers are required to pay an import fee at a rate of six percent ad valorem when applying for a letter of credit. In addition to the customs duty, the government collects a five percent education tax *(iqra)* on all imports, plus a one percent flood relief tax. The government also levies a sales tax of 15 percent on the duty-paid value of a wide variety of goods.
- **Barriers** Pakistan has maintained a complex system of indirect taxes in the trade sector. High basic tariffs, additional surcharges, a variety of excise taxes, and a sales tax with different applicability on domestic and foreign goods combined to distort prices in domestic markets. Tariff rates have been reduced from 90 percent to 70 percent recently. Many tariff rates are too high and stimulate smuggling and corruption.
- **Quotas** Quotas apply to export of items such as wheat flour, bran, soda, and dry red chilies.
- **Special procedures** Special procedures are stipulated for exporting rice, cotton, surgical instruments, cinematographic film, exotic captive birds, and horses.
- **Export goods** Export of most goods generally allowed; however, export of some items banned/restricted or subject to certain conditions because of short supply.
- **Import payments** Any payments can be made against letters of credit. Imports on consignment are allowed by the State Bank of Pakistan.
- **Export payments** Financing is provided for most exports. Some exports are subject to quotas, quality controls, or minimum export prices. Exporters must surrender proceeds within four months of shipment, although the State Bank can extend the period in some cases.
- **Import liberalization** Pakistan eased several of its import regulations in 1991.
- **Telecommunications exports** The government of Pakistan recently privatized the Pakistan Telecommunications Corporation, creating several opportunities for foreign exporters.

GOVERNMENT AGENCIES

Customs Department
Central Board of Revenue
CDA Block No. 111
Khayaban-e-Suhrawardy
Islamabad

Chief Controller of Exports and Imports
5, Civic Center
Islamabad

Trading Corporation of Pakistan
1-1 Chundrigar Road
Karachi

TRANSPORTATION FIRMS

Eastern Shipping Co., Ltd
POB 5174
828 Muhammadi House
I.I. Chundrigar Road
Karachi
Telex: 2620 EAST PK

Oriental Shipping Co., Ltd.
201 Muhammadi House
I.I. Chundrigar Road
Karachi
Telex: 2637 OKING PK

Business Travel

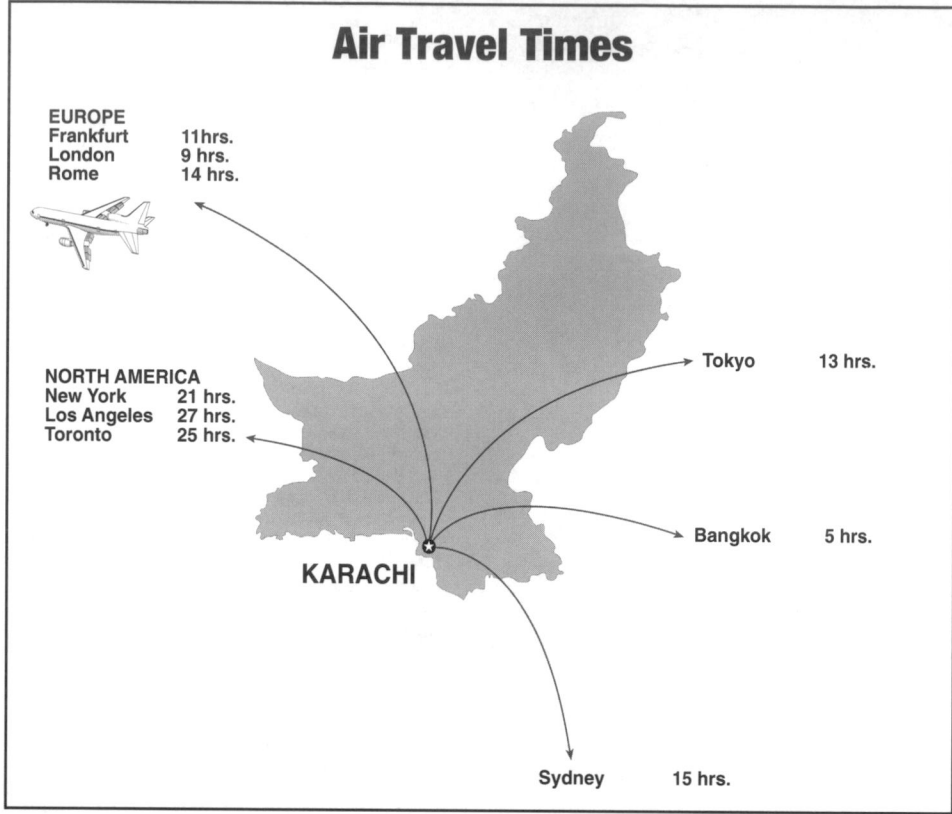

Air Travel Times

EUROPE
Frankfurt   11 hrs.
London   9 hrs.
Rome   14 hrs.

NORTH AMERICA
New York   21 hrs.
Los Angeles 27 hrs.
Toronto   25 hrs.

Tokyo   13 hrs.

Bangkok   5 hrs.

KARACHI

Sydney   15 hrs.

COMMUNICATIONS

Telephones Cellular phones are now more reliable than local conventional phones and there are no public pay phones.

Fax Telex and fax, along with telegram services are available 24 hours a day at the major hotels and post offices.

Post office Domestic mail service is inexpensive and reasonably reliable. Airmail takes approximately six to eight days for delivery. Packages sent by private courier service will be delayed two to three days at customs.

TV/Radio There are five television stations and 15 radio stations, all run by the government.

BEST TRAVEL BOOKS

Culture Shock, A Guide to Customs and Etiquette, Pakistan.

Lonely Planet, Travel Survival Kit, Pakistan. Moves through almost every topic of interest to descriptions of places and attractions detailed enough to help a traveler go places.

Do's and Taboo's Around the World. The Bestselling Guide to International Behavior. Edited by Roger Axtell, compiled by the Parker Pen Company. The ultimate guide to international behavior, now completely updated and expanded. Helpful, fun to read!

The Travelers Guide to Pakistan Customs and Manners. Elizabeth Devine & Nancy Braganti. An invaluable guide for people not wanting to put foot in mouth.

Far Eastern Economic Review, All Asia Travel Guide. The best guide available for the business traveler.

USEFUL TELEPHONE NUMBERS

If you are calling from outside Pakistan, you will need to add the country code [92] and any other international dialing requirements from within your country.

* Police 15
* Operator 17
* International Operator 0102
* Pakistan Chamber of Commerce ....(21) 536-421
* Karachi Chamber of Commerce...........(21) 226-091
* Ministry of Culture and Tourism ....(51) 827-024
* Investment Corp. of Pakistan ....(51) 225-861
* Trading Corp. of Pakistan ....(51) 210-515
* Ministry of Industries ....(51) 824-838
* Economic Affairs Division....................(51) 815-881
* US Embassy ....(51) 82-5-864

Credit Card Information

Lost or stolen credit cards (call collect to the US, regardless of which country the card was issued in).

* Amex ....[1] (919) 333-3211
* Diner's Club................................[1] (303) 799-1504
* MasterCard ....[1] (314) 275-6690
* Visa ....[1] (410) 581-7931

NATIONAL TOURIST OFFICE

Pakistan Tourism Development Corpn
House No.2
St 61 F-7/4
Islamabad 44000
Tel: (51) 811001 Fax: (51) 824173

Travelogue

WORKWEEK

Government Saturday-Thursday 8:00 am to 2:30 pm (summer), 8:30 am to 3:00 pm (winter).
Banks Saturday-Thursday 9:00 am to 1:00 pm.
Business Saturday-Thursday 9:00 am to 6:00 pm.
Retail Saturday-Thursday 8:00 am to 9:00 pm.
Friday is a religious holiday and all businesses and offices are closed. During Ramadan, business and retail hours are shorter.

HOLIDAYS

Holidays 1996
March 23 Pakistani Day
April 5 Eid-Ul-Fitr
June 1 May Day
June 19 Eid-Ul-Azha
August 11 Death of Quaid-I-Azan
August 14 Independence Day
September 9 Iqbal Day
December 25 & 26 Christmas

VISA AND PASSPORT

A valid passport and a Pakistani visa are required for entry to Pakistan. Visas are not available at airports in Pakistan and must be obtained before arrival. Visas are available at any embassy or consulate of Pakistan. To qualify for a visa you must submit a completed application, a valid passport and photo, and documentation for return or further travel plans. For business visas, submit a company letter.

DEPARTURE FORMALITIES

An airport departure tax of R200 and a foreign travel tax of R20 will be collected.

IMMUNIZATION

Vaccinations for cholera, small pox, and yellow fever are required for visitors from infected areas. For anyone intending to stay in Pakistan more than one year an AIDS/HIV-free certificate is required. Anti-malaria medication is suggested.

TIPPING

For restaurant bills add 10 to 15 percent, add 10 percent for taxi drivers, give R5 per bag to porters and hotel clerks.

CRIME

Avoid demonstrations or rallies in urban areas. Local situations change quickly and all travelers should read one of the local papers for the current situation. Sectarian rivalry and violence tend to increase during Ramadan and Moharram. Avoid travel into tribal areas as this can be dangerous without the presence of law enforcement. Travel to Khyber Pass is particularly dangerous. In Karachi there is a high level of crime and an ineffective police force. Car jackings, armed robbery, arson, and kidnapping happen frequently. Criminals are armed and theft of personal property is very common. For personal security, change daily routines, vary times and routes of travel, and avoid demonstrations.

INFRASTRUCTURE

The largest airport in Pakistan is Quaid-i-Azam International Airport in Karachi. Pakistan International Airlines (PIA) is the only Pakistani carrier for international routes. Three domestic airlines serve 36 destinations within Pakistan. PIA offers a bus service from the airport to Karachi. The highway system varies in quality, making it preferable to hire drivers or fly between cities. If you do rent a car, remember to drive on the left. Taxi service is metered and regulated by the government. It is best to hire a driver as traffic is congested and not all drivers obey traffic signals. The rail system is extensive. First-class, air-conditioned coaches are available with prior reservations. Do not leave valuables in your compartment or on your seat.

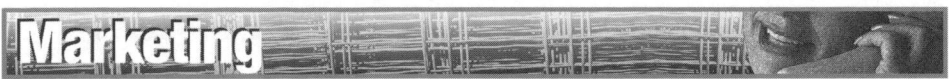

Marketing

Overview

To be successful in Pakistan, a foreign company must be prepared to deal with complicated business regulations and tax structures in addition to a market which is fundamentally archaic. Large chain stores and supermarkets still do not exist in Pakistan. About 75 percent of the country's 100,000 retail outlets are located outside the major cities and require extensive networks of distribution. Often several hundred distributors are required by a single company for nationwide coverage. Almost all business–from distributors to wholesalers to retailers—is conducted on a strictly cash basis with virtually no credit provided.

Distributors and Agents

Karachi is the primary distribution center for the country. In urban areas a mutually exclusive agency agreement is the most common arrangement used by foreign companies, with the agent often assuming responsibility for after-sales service and administrative support. A variety of commission structures is utilized for agency agreements.

Franchises

Franchising is slowly emerging in Pakistan, allowing foreign companies quick access to the market without major capital investment. Several foreign hotel chains as well as auto rental companies have established footholds in Pakistan through franchises, though not without risk. Quality control is often inconsistent and possibilities of conflict of interest on the part of the franchisee can arise as franchise agreements expire. Other potential problems include vague and quickly changing import regulations, especially concerning food items.

Advertising

A variety of advertising venues is available, including radio, television, billboards, periodicals, and trade journals. The most widely used medium, however, is newspapers, with over 115 dailies published nationwide. There are few English language papers, but they are influential in political, business, and academic circles. Trade shows are valuable for gaining insight to the Pakistani market as well as locating potential new distributors and contacts.

Business Culture

Greetings and Courtesies

Pakistanis are a friendly, hospitable people who respect their elders. A handshake is the standard greeting, and should be gentle. Many Pakistanis will extend their wrist rather than their hand. A man should not initiate a handshake with a woman or touch a woman in public. Foreign women may offer a handshake when meeting a Pakistani man, unless there are indications that this will be offensive. Pakistanis should be addressed with their title if they have one.

Business Ethic and Framework

Pakistan is a devoutly Muslim country. The family is the most important social unit, and Pakistanis tend to be loyal to their specific ethnic groups rather than to the country as a whole. Pakistanis work hard, but will often put family or kinship considerations above groups business. Fate is also an important element of Pakistani culture (particularly in rural areas). They truly believe that once people do the best they can, the outcome is in the hands of God.

Meetings and Decision Making

Appointments are necessary. You will very likely be dealing with the Pakistani government or one of its many companies. Pakistanis are not especially concerned about time, but they expect foreigners (Westerners in particular) to arrive punctually. Pakistanis like to socialize before conducting business, so expect meetings to begin with pleasant small talk. You will probably be offered something to drink; always accept, or you might insult your associate. Decisions are made slowly; be patient.

Women

Pakistan is a male-dominated society and women are not accorded the same respect as men. Foreign women should always be professional, confident, and poised. Women should be prepared for questions about their age, marital status, and whether they have children (such questions are asked of both men and women). Women should not go out alone at night; if going to a bazaar, they should be in a group or with a man.

Marketing in Pakistan

MARKETING TIPS

- **Plan ahead** The entrenched bureaucracy of Pakistan's import policies can be expedited by requesting, in advance, detailed instructions for processing your shipments.
- **Cultural awareness** A local partner is all but essential for a foreign company to acclimate its image and products to the Islamic culture of Pakistan.
- **Direct marketing** Potentially cost-effective, the emergence of direct marketing in Pakistan is slowed by a lack of basic market research. The lack of readily available mailing lists and consumer preference reports, for example, limit the use of direct mailing and telemarketing to the two major cities of Karachi and Lahore. Similarly, local customs and cultural mores complicate attempts at direct marketing. The use of one of Pakistan's dozen or so major local advertising agencies is recommended.

AD AGENCY

Asiatic Advertising (Private) Limited
Finlay House, I.I. Chundrigar Rd.
74000 Karachi
Tel: (21) 2417923/4
Fax: (21) 2419886

MARKET RESEARCH FIRMS

Business Research Bureau
A-4 Shaheen Chambers
Block 7 & 8 Commercial Area
K.C.H.S., Karachi
Fax: (21) 445423

Market Research Link
403 Faiyaz Center
3-A S.M.C.H.S.
Shahrah-e-Faisal
Karachi 74400
Tel: (21) 4540502 Fax: (21) 4554120

Cultural Cautions

DO'S

- Avoid talking about economic conditions, disputes with India, or the Afghanistan War.
- Give people who are praying in public the proper respect and privacy.

DON'TS

- Do not use your left hand to gesture toward someone, to give or receive anything, to eat with, or to touch people. The left hand is considered unclean.

CUSTOMS

- In Pakistani culture, it is permitted to gaze or stare at people. Don't be offended if this happens.
- Business cards are exchanged, but no elaborate response is expected. Nevertheless, make the effort to respond politely, at least thank people for giving you their cards.

OBSERVATIONS

- Pakistan has many ethnic groups. The four major groups are the Punjabi (about 65 percent of the population), the Sindhi (12 percent), the Baluchi (nine percent), and the Pashtuns (eight percent). To relate best to people, know which group they belong to and familiarize yourself with its customs.
- In winter, standard attire is a conservative suit (especially when meeting government officials). In warmer weather (and when meeting with private business-people), a white shirt, tie, and pants (no jacket) are acceptable.

NEGOTIATIONS

- Pakistanis tend to be formal and slow-moving. Be firm, persistent, and confident, but also be polite, courteous, and friendly.
- A smile and a "thank you" at the appropriate times are important.

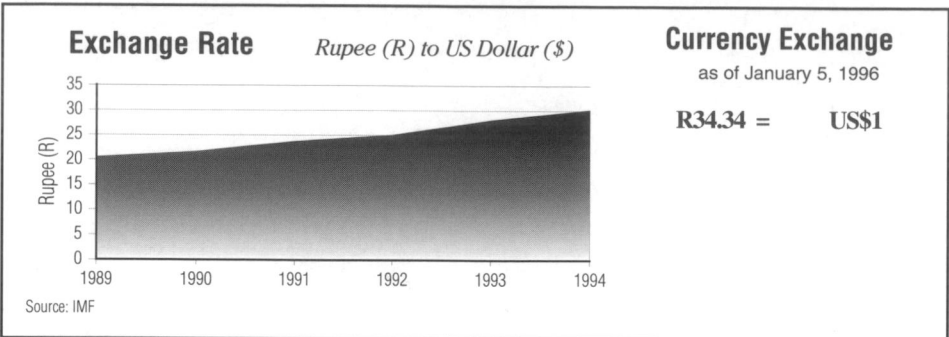

Exchange Rate
Rupee (R) to US Dollar ($)

Currency Exchange
as of January 5, 1996

R34.34 = US$1

Source: IMF

Currency

The currency in use is the Pakistan rupee (R), which is divided into 100 paisa. The US dollar is the intervention currency in Pakistan.

Foreign Exchange

The State Bank has control over all currency exchange regulations, and has delegated exchange authority to a number of banks and financial institutions. Nonresidents can open accounts in any currency, and deposits or withdrawals can be made in any amount. Accounts of residents of India, other than those of the Indian Embassy and its personnel, are blocked.

Capital Transfers

Nonresidents can bring in or take out any amount of currency, both domestic and foreign, without restriction. All invisibles payments are controlled by the State Bank and in most cases require prior approval. Commissions paid to foreign importers by Pakistani exporters are usually limited to a maximum of five percent, and on some items the commission limit is only one percent. Except for Afghan currency, all foreign exchange earned from invisibles must be surrendered within three months.

Investment Incentives

Government policy requires that all incentives and concessions available to domestic investors also be made available to nonresident investors without discrimination. Pakistan also introduced a number of concessions recently to speed up industrial development of the country, including sales tax concessions and exemptions from customs duties. Pakistan has recently relaxed a number of regulations concerning foreign investment, including permitting foreign investors to participate in Pakistani ventures on a 100 percent equity basis. In addition, the average delay period for remitting investment returns such as lease payments and interest on private foreign debt is only a week to ten days.

Investment Restrictions

There are few governmental restrictions concerning foreign investment, but investment has been relatively modest. Possible reasons for this include inadequate infrastructure, perceptions of political instability, and concerns about corruption.

TAXATION

Taxation requires sophisticated knowledge of complex rules and regulations specific to each country. The information presented here is from the Ernst & Young Corporate Tax Guide and Directory, available from the Ernst & Young accounting office in your country, or from:

Ford, Rhodes, Robson, Morrow
Mail Address:
POB 2388
Islamabad, Pakistan
Street Address:
2nd Floor, Khyber Plaza
96 West, Fazluk Haq Road
Blue Area
Islamabad, Pakistan
Tel: (51) 217890
Cable: Raprof (Islamabad)
Fax: (51) 217889

At a Glance

Corporate Income Tax Rate (%) (a)	46
Capital Gains Tax Rate (%) (a)	46
Branch Tax Rate (%) (a)	46
Withholding Tax (%)	
Dividends (b)	15
Interest (a)	46
Royalties from Patents, Know-how, etc. (c)	46
Net Operating Losses (Years)	
Carryback	0
Carryforward	6

(a) 60% for a banking company and 36% for a company quoted on a stock exchange in Pakistan.
(b) Final tax applicable to nonresident corporations. A 10% final withholding tax is imposed on dividends paid to individuals.
(c) On gross income.

Money Matters

BITS AND PIECES

- **Corporate income tax** All companies in Pakistan are subject to a corporate income tax. Resident companies may be taxed on all income, but nonresident companies are taxed on their income from Pakistan only.
- **Technical service fees** For nonresidents, the gross amount of fees for technical services is subject to a 15 percent withholding, not included in taxable income.
- **Foreign-owned companies** Any companies controlled by nonresidents and branches of foreign companies are generally restricted to certain specified percentages of the entities' paid-up capital, reserves, or head-office investment.
- **Gold** Exporting gold is usually prohibited without authorization from the State Bank. Permission is rarely given.
- **Capital transfers** Transfers of capital by resident nationals are generally not permitted.

BANKS

Bank of Oman Ltd.
1st Floor, Bahria Complex
M.T. Khan Road
Karachi
Tel: (21) 551179, 551149
Fax: (21) 552369

Allied Bank of Pakistan Ltd.
14th Floor, NIC Building
Abbasi Shaheed Road
Off Shahra-e-Faisal
Karachi
Tel: (21) 519273, 519436
Fax: (21) 5682568

ANZ Grindlays Bank
Grindlays Bank Building
I.I. Chundrigar Road
Karachi 74000
Tel: (21) 2412671
Fax: (21) 2414914

First Women's Bank
7th Floor, Mehdi Towers
S.M.C.H.S.
Shara-e-Faisal
Karachi
Tel: (21) 4553110, 4556093, 4553149
Fax: (21) 4556983

Habib Bank Ltd.
Habib Bank Plaza
I.I. Chundrigar Road
Karachi
Tel: (21) 219112, 219111-50
Fax: (21) 241566

Jubilee Insurance House
I.I. Chundrigar Road
Karachi
Tel: (21) 2412528, 2412520
Fax: (21) 2415371

Muslim Commercial Bank
Adamjee House
I.I. Chundrigar Road
Post Office Box 4976
Karachi
Tel: (21) 2414099, 2414090, 2415354
Fax: (21) 2416982

National Bank of Pakistan
NBP Building
I.I. Chundrigar Road
Post Office Box 4937
Karachi
Tel: (21) 2416789, 2416780, 2416612
Fax: (21) 2410202

State Bank of Pakistan
Central Directorate
State Bank Building
I.I. Chundrigar Road
Karachi
Tel: (21) 2417864
Fax: (21) 2417865

Legal

Legal System

Pakistan is primarily a civil code country. Its legal system is derived from several Western traditions. The majority of laws related to contracts are adapted from the common law of England.

Intellectual Property Protection

Patents Any inventor or the inventor's assignee can register a patent in Pakistan. A patent is granted for 16 years but can be extended for an additional period of five years if the applicant can satisfy the Controller that the invention has not been sufficiently lucrative.

Trademarks Trademarks are initially registered for seven years, but the protection term can be renewed. Applications rejected by the Registrar can be appealed in court. Infringements against registered and unregistered trademarks are actionable under the provisions of the Trademarks Act, but only registered trademark infringements are punishable under the Penal Code.

Copyrights An owner can register the copyright with the Copyright Office, although copyrights are binding without registration. Copyrights run for 50 years following the creator's death. An assignment of a copyright is valid, provided it is in writing. Disputes concerning copyrights are decided by the Copyright Board, which has all the powers of a civil court.

Trade secrets Injunctions against trade secret violations are difficult to obtain.

Business Registration

Registration is not compulsory, but businesses that aren't registered may not be able to sue in some cases. A fee is paid to the Registrar based on the amount of the authorized capital.

Notaries

There are two types of notaries public. One type is empowered to perform all the usual duties of a notary, such as legalizing documents and entering protests from ships' masters. Other notaries public have powers limited by the Negotiable Instruments Act.

Legal Matters

LEGAL BRIEFS

- **Price control** A few items are subject to price controls. The government still has the power to regulate price and will do so if it believes that prices are being inflated.
- **Government contracts** No special requirements apply to contracts with the government as opposed to private firms.
- **Directors** Every private company must have at least two directors and every public company must have at least seven directors. Directors are elected by members of the company in a general meeting.
- **Labor associations** Employees are legally able to establish and join associations of their own choice. They may elect shop stewards to act as links between them and their employer. Pakistan law prohibits factory management from making any decision without written advice from representatives of the workers, especially in matters that concern employees, such as health and safety conditions and promotion and discipline policies.
- **Labor practices** The government prohibits unfair labor practices by employers and appoints inspectors who are empowered to require factory owners to fulfill health and safety requirements.
- **Contracts and dispute resolutions** Contracts do not necessarily have to be written to be considered valid. Most disputes are settled by lawsuit. Pakistan's legal system is usually lengthy and costly, for both plaintiffs and defendants.

LEGAL CONTACTS

Aziz A. Shaikh & Co. Advocates & Solicitors
A & K Chambers
14 West Wharf Road
Karachi 74000
Tel: (21) 204-047 Fax: (21) 2310-907

Contacts

GOVERNMENT AGENCIES

Export Promotion Bureau
Finance and Trade Center
Shara-e-Faisal
Karachi
Tel: (21) 516285 Fax: (21) 516205

Ministry of Commerce
Investment Promotion Bureau
Block A, Pakistan Secretariat
Islamabad
Tel: (51) 210852

Ministry of Commerce
Registrar Trademark Registry
68-E, Market Block, P.E.C.H.S.
Karachi
Tel: (21) 411227

Ministry of Communications
Controller Patents and Designs
223 Sommerset House, E.I. Lines
Raja Ghazanfar Ali Khan Road
Karachi 75530
Tel: (21) 521656, 511270, 513396 Fax: (21) 521331

Ministry of Finance
Q Block, Secretariat
Islamabad
Tel: (51) 211518

Ministry of Food, Agriculture & Cooperatives
Pakistan Agricultural Research Council
Islamabad
Tel: (51) 823966 Fax: (51) 812968

Ministry of Industries
Asad Chamber, 146 A.M.
Shambunath Street, Saddar
Karachi
Tel: (21) 5685985

Ministry of Industries
Kandawala Building
M.A. Jinnah Road
Karachi
Tel: (21) 7216149 Fax: (21) 7224261

Ministry of Industries
Block A, Pakistan Secretariat
Islamabad
Tel: (51) 211709

Pakistan Customs
Custom House
Karachi
Tel: (21) 201431 Fax: (21) 201288
Ports & Shipping Wing
Tel: (51) 826327 Fax: (51) 824173

Pakistan Environmental Protection Agency
44-E Office Tower, Ali Plaza, Blue Area
Islamabad
Tel: (51) 217882, 826817

Pakistan Railways
Allama Iqbal Road
Lahore
Tel: (42) 6365460 Fax: (42) 6367673

Pakistan Telecommunication Corporation
Head Quarters, Sector G-8/4
Islamabad
Tel: (51) 251939, 844463 Fax: (51) 843991

Pakistan Tourism Development Corporation
House No.2, Street 61, F-7/4
Islamabad

Water & Power Development Authority
WAPDA House, The Mall
Lahore
Tel: (42) 6361230, 6365432
Fax: (42) 6279163, 6369349

REMEMBER

- When you telephone (or fax) to Pakistan from another country you must always include the country code [92] before the numbers given.
- When you send mail to Pakistan, be sure to write PAKISTAN in capital letters on its own line below the addresses given.

WORLD TRADE CENTER

World Trade Center Karachi
10 Khayaban-E-Roomi
Block-5, KDA Scheme No. 5
Clifton, Karachi
Tel: (21) 5681678, 520361-68 Fax: (21) 5684594

BUSINESS AND TRADE ORGANIZATIONS

All Pakistan Textile Mills Association
H.O. 213 Main Soosan Road
near M.C.B.
Ibrahim Plaza, Madina Town
Faisalabad
Tel: (411) 48894, 49013 Fax: (411) 47711

Pakistan Carpet Manufacturers & Exporters Association
40-A, Panorama Center, Fitima
Jinnah Road
Karachi
Tel: (21) 512189 Fax: (21) 528649

Pakistan Readymade Garments Manufacturers Association
53, Idrees Chambers, 4th Floor
Talpur Road
Karachi
Tel: (21) 2416469 Fax: (21) 4550699

Pakistan Sports Goods Manufacturers & Exporters Association
Abbot Road
Sialkot

Pakistan Vanaspati Manufacturer's Association
Suite No. 13, (2nd floor)
Auriga Complex
Main Boulevard
Gulberg, Lahore
Tel: (432) 87962, 65502
Fax: (432) 55441/2

The Pakistan Yarn Merchants' Association
802-803, Business Center (8th Floor)
Dunolly Road
Karachi
Tel: (21) 2410320, 2424896
Fax: (21) 2425578, 437843

Pakistan Woollen Mills Association
Republic Motor Building (2nd Floor)
87, Shahrah-e-Quaid-e-Azam
Lahore
Tel: (42) 306879
Fax: (42) 254704

Pakistan Tanners Association
Plot ST 7, Sector 7A
Korangi Industrial Area
Karachi
Tel: (21) 317409
Fax: (21) 310323

The Surgical Instruments Manufacturers Association of Pakistan
Kutchery Road
Sialkot
Tel: (432) 556240, 563016
Fax: (432) 85978

Trading Corporation of Pakistan
Press Trust House
I.I. Chundrigar Road
Karachi
Tel: (21) 511016
Fax: (21) 515389

CHAMBERS OF COMMERCE

Faisalabad Chamber of Commerce & Industry
2nd Floor, N.B.P. Building, Jail Road
Faisalabad
Tel: (411) 615085

Federation of Pakistan Chambers of Commerce & Industry
Federation House, Main Clifton
POB 13875
Karachi
Tel: (21) 5873691/2/3/4, 5873640/1 Fax: (21) 5874332

Gujranwala Chamber of Commerce & Industry
Aiwan-e-Tijarat Road
Gujranwala
Tel: (431) 256701/2/3/4 Fax: (431) 254440

Gujrat Chamber of Commerce & Industry
Post Office Box 169, 26-A, S.I.E.
G.T. Road
Gujrat
Tel: (4331) 523012/3 Fax: (4331) 523011

Islamabad Chamber of Commerce and Industry
Aiwan-e-Sanat-o-Tijarat Road,
Mauve Area, Sector G-8/1
Islamabad
Tel: (51) 250526, 253145 Fax: (51) 252950

Karachi Chamber of Commerce and Industry
ST-4/2, Sector 23
Korangi Industrial Area
Karachi
Tel: (21) 5061211/2/3/4 Fax: (21) 5061215

Lahore Chamber of Commerce and Industry
Post Office Box 597, 11-Race Course Road
Lahore
Tel: (42) 305538 Fax: (42) 304639

Multan Chamber of Commerce & Industry
Kutchery Road
Multan
Tel: (61) 43530, 40087

Overseas Investors Chambers of Commerce and Industry
Chamber of Commerce Building
Talpur Road, Post Office Box 4833

Karachi 74000
Tel: (21) 2426076, 222557/8 Fax: (21) 2427315

Rawalpindi Chamber of Commerce and Industry
Chamber House, 108-Adamjee Road
Rawalpindi
Tel: (51) 584397, 566238
Fax: (51) 586849

Sialkot Chamber of Commerce & Industry
Shara-e-Aiwan-e-Sanat-o- Tijarat
Sialkot 51310,
Tel: (432) 561881/2/3
Fax: (432) 558835, 557919

Quetta Chamber of Commerce & Industry
P. O. Box 117, Zarghoon Road
Quetta (Baluchistan),
Tel: (81) 821943
Fax: (81) 821948

Sarhard Chamber of Commerce & Industry
Sarhad Chamber House
G.T. Road
Peshawar
Tel: (521) 215459, 216398
Fax: (521) 217412

CONSULTING FIRMS

Aftab Associates (Pvt.) Ltd.
5-E/1 Commercial, Gulberg-III
Lahore 54660
Tel: (42) 875910, 876196, 5710987
Fax: (42) 5711020, 85139

Economic Consultants Group
87 Darul Aman Housing Society
Karachi
Tel: (21) 443885, 434693
Fax: (21) 443885

BANKS

Bank of Oman Ltd.
1st Floor, Bahria Complex
M.T. Khan Road
Karachi
Tel: (21) 551179, 551149 Fax: (21) 552369

Banque Indosuez
Mohammadi House
I.I. Chudrigar Road
Karachi 74000
Tel: (21) 2417146, 2417155 Fax: (21) 2417503

Chartered Bank
I.I. Chundrigar Road
Post Office Box 4896
Karachi
Tel: (21) 2433545, 2428541

Citibank
State Life Building 1
I.I. Chundrigar Road
Karachi 74000
Tel: (21) 2412882/3 Fax: (21) 2424474

Deutsche Bank AG
Unitowers
I.I. Chundrigar Road
Karachi
Tel: (21) 2419619 Fax: (21) 2416970

Doha Bank Ltd.
36/A-2, Lalazar Drive
Off: M.T. Khan Road
Karachi
Tel: (21) 551854, 551851 Fax: (21) 5687105

Emirates Bank International Ltd.
Emirates Bank House
I.I. Chundrigar Road
Post Office Box 831
Karachi
Tel: (21) 2414002/3

First International Investment
Bank Ltd.
7th Floor, Shaheen Complex
Dr. Ziauddin Ahmed Road
Karachi
Tel: (21) 2639046, 2639042 Fax: (21) 2630678

Hong Kong and Shanghai Bank
Shaheen Commercial Complex
M.R. Kayani Road
Karachi
Tel: (21) 2630386/7 Fax: (21) 2635126

Societe Generale The French & International Bank
3rd Floor, PNSC Building
M.T. Khan Road
Karachi
Tel: (21) 551846, 551134 Fax: (21) 551672

United Bank Ltd.
State Life Building No. 1
I.I. Chundrigar Road
Karachi
Tel: (21) 2417021/2 Fax: (21) 2413492

American Express Bank Ltd.
Shaheen Commercial Complex
Dr. Ziauddin Ahmad Road
Karachi
Tel: (21) 2630349, 2630343 Fax: (21) 2631803

The Bank of Tokyo Ltd.
Shaheen Complex, 1st Floor
M.R. Kayani Road
Karachi 74200
Tel: (21) 2630171, 2630175 Fax: (21) 2631368

The Chase Manhattan Bank, N.A.
Shaheen Commercial Complex
M.R. Kayani Road
Karachi 74200
Tel: (21) 2633073, 2633079 Fax: (21) 2631393

AD AGENCIES

Interflow Communications (Pvt.) Ltd.
2 Delhi Mercantile Housing Society
Block 7/8, Tipu Sultan Rd.
POB 11544
Karachi
Tel: (21) 440298
Fax: (21) 4549221

Lintas Karachi
POB 143
Karachi 1
Tel: (21) 453-9901
Fax: (21) 454-9167

Manhattan/BBDO
Manhattan House
127-3/B-II, P.E.C.H.S.
Karachi 75400
Tel: (21) 434310
Fax: (21) 454-6742

NEWSPAPERS

The Muslim
9 Hameed Chambers
Aabpara
Islamabad
Tel: (51) 810296

Pakistan Observer
Ali Akbar House
Markaz G-8
Islamabad
Tel: (51) 25606 Fax: (51) 254501

Aghaz
11 Japan Mansion
Preedy Street
Saddar
Karachi 74400
Tel: (21) 722125

Business Recorder
Recorder House
Business Recorder Rd.
Karachi 74550
Tel: (21) 7210311 Fax: (21) 7228644

INTERNET ADDRESSES

Mailing lists
bit.listserv.pakistan
soc.culture.pakistan

The Voice of Pakistani People from the Heart of United States
http://www2.dtc.net/~aawaz/

Galaxy - Pakistan
http://www.einet.net/galaxy/Community/World-Communities/Asia/Pakistan.html

Asia Resources by Country - Pakistan
http://silkroute.com/silkroute/asia/rsrc/country/pakistan.html

Panama

Republic of Panama

Economy

Overview

Panama has been a country of traders since the 1600s, and the inauguration of the Panama Canal in 1914 ensured Panama's position as a major trading nation for the twentieth century. However, Panama's economy remains one of the most heavily protected ones in Latin America. The government has made some feeble attempts to liberalize trade and modernize government services and operations, but has never gained much support for these programs and actual achievements remain few. Panama has a relatively well-developed infrastructure which can easily accommodate growth, and official policies, if implemented, would indicate continued industrial and foreign trade growth.

Trade

Panama is not a free trade country; imports are subject to the highest tariff rates in Central America, and the agricultural sector is further protected by significant nontariff barriers, including quotas and permits. Export subsidies benefit both local foreign-owned and domestic export industries. Panama's most important trade partner is the US, and its single most important export is bananas, accounting for 35 percent of total merchandise exports. It has one free trade zone, which has been extensively utilized, and which should continue to grow, both in importance and in actual volume.

Sectors

Agriculture Agriculture, forestry, and fisheries account for about 11 percent of GDP. Principal primary products include bananas, shrimp, sugar, coffee, meat, dairy products, tropical fruits, rice, corn, and beans. The Panamanian agricultural sector is protected by high tariffs and significant nontariff barriers.

Industry Manufacturing, mining, utilities, and construction together account for about 20 percent of GDP. Manufacturing is principally geared to the production of items such as processed foods, clothing, chemical products, and construction materials for the domestic market. Mining is expected to increase as a result of official government encouragement.

Services Panama's economy is primarily based on a well-developed services sector accounting for about 70 percent of GDP. Services include the various industries servicing the Panama Canal, banking, insurance, government, the trans-isthmian oil pipeline, and the Colón Free Trade Zone.

Trends

Although a comprehensive national economic plan has been announced incorporating measures to reduce government control, liberalize trade, reduce the public sector payroll, and foster job creation through labor code reform, there has as yet been no specific implementation of proposed structural reforms. Likewise, the 1991 privatization law has resulted in very few actual privatizations. It is likely that any of the privatizations being considered by the new government will require fresh legislation. For these reasons, medium-term prospects for strong economic growth and job creation are uncertain. The prospects are brighter for mining, tourism, and maritime services for which the government is actively seeking foreign participation.

At a Glance

THE COUNTRY

Location Middle America, between Colombia and Costa Rica.

Terrain Interior is mostly steep, rugged mountains and dissected, upland plains; coastal areas are largely plains and rolling hills.

Climate Tropical; hot, humid, cloudy; prolonged rainy season (May to January), short dry season (January to May).

THE PEOPLE

Population 2,600,000

Ethnic composition
Mestizo (mixed Indian and European ancestry) ... 70%
West Indian.. 14%
White.. 10%
Indian.. 6%

Religious composition
Roman Catholic 85%
Protestant 15%

Languages spoken Spanish (official), English.

Education and literacy Education is free and compulsory for children aged seven through 15. Fees may be charged for higher education. Nearly 90 percent of the population can read and write.

Labor force
Total:..921,000
By occupation: government and community services 32%, agriculture, hunting, and fishing 27%, commerce, restaurants, and hotels 16%, manufacturing and mining 9%, construction 3%, transportation and communications 6%, finance, insurance, and real estate 4%.

COUNTRY FACTS

Political and legal Constitutional democracy. Legal system is based on a civil law system and judicial review of legislative acts in the Supreme Court of Justice.

Telephones All telephone and telegraph services are controlled by the Instituto Nacional de Telecomunicaciones (INTEL). Domestic and international facilities are well developed with connections into the Central America Microwave System. There are over 220,000 telephones. International country code: [507].

Transportation The two main cities, Panama City and Colón, are an hour apart by road or rail. There are over 8,500 kilometers of highway, but most of the roads are in disrepair, and only about 2,700 kilometers are paved. The main ports are: Cristobal, Balboa, and Colón. There are a number of major airports with permanent surface runways.

Environment Current issues include water pollution from agricultural runoff threatening fishery resources, deforestation of tropical rain forest, and land degradation.

Media 91 AM and no FM broadcast stations; 23 TV stations and eight major daily newspapers read by more than 100,000 citizens, including the English-language *Star* and *Herald*.

Health Public health services are directed by the government. Free health examinations and medical care are given to citizens. Some other services provided include health education and nutrition services. About 80 percent of the population has access to health care services. Most children are immunized for a number of diseases.

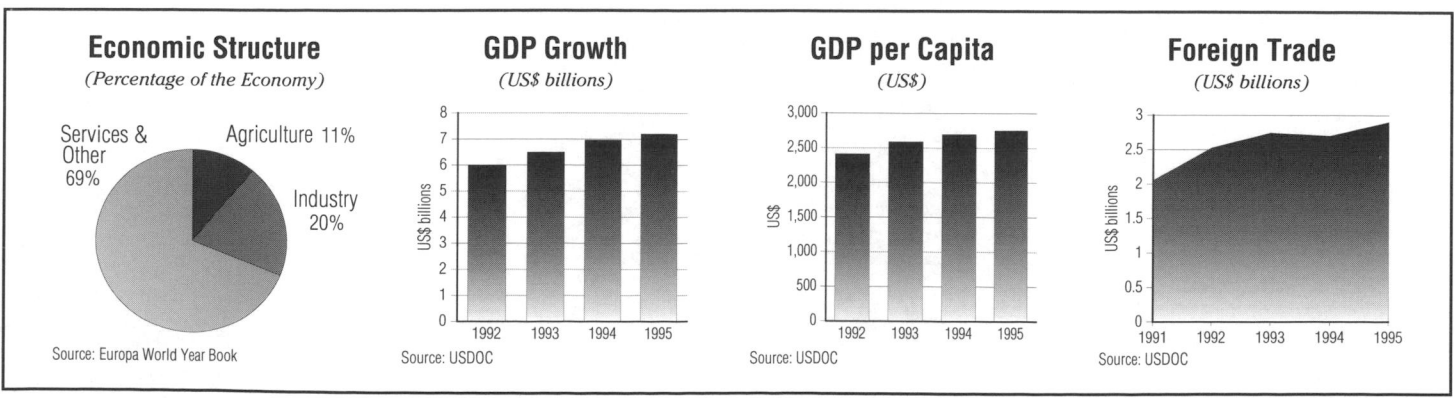

Economic Structure (Percentage of the Economy)
Services & Other 69%
Agriculture 11%
Industry 20%
Source: Europa World Year Book

GDP Growth (US$ billions)
Source: USDOC

GDP per Capita (US$)
Source: USDOC

Foreign Trade (US$ billions)
Source: USDOC

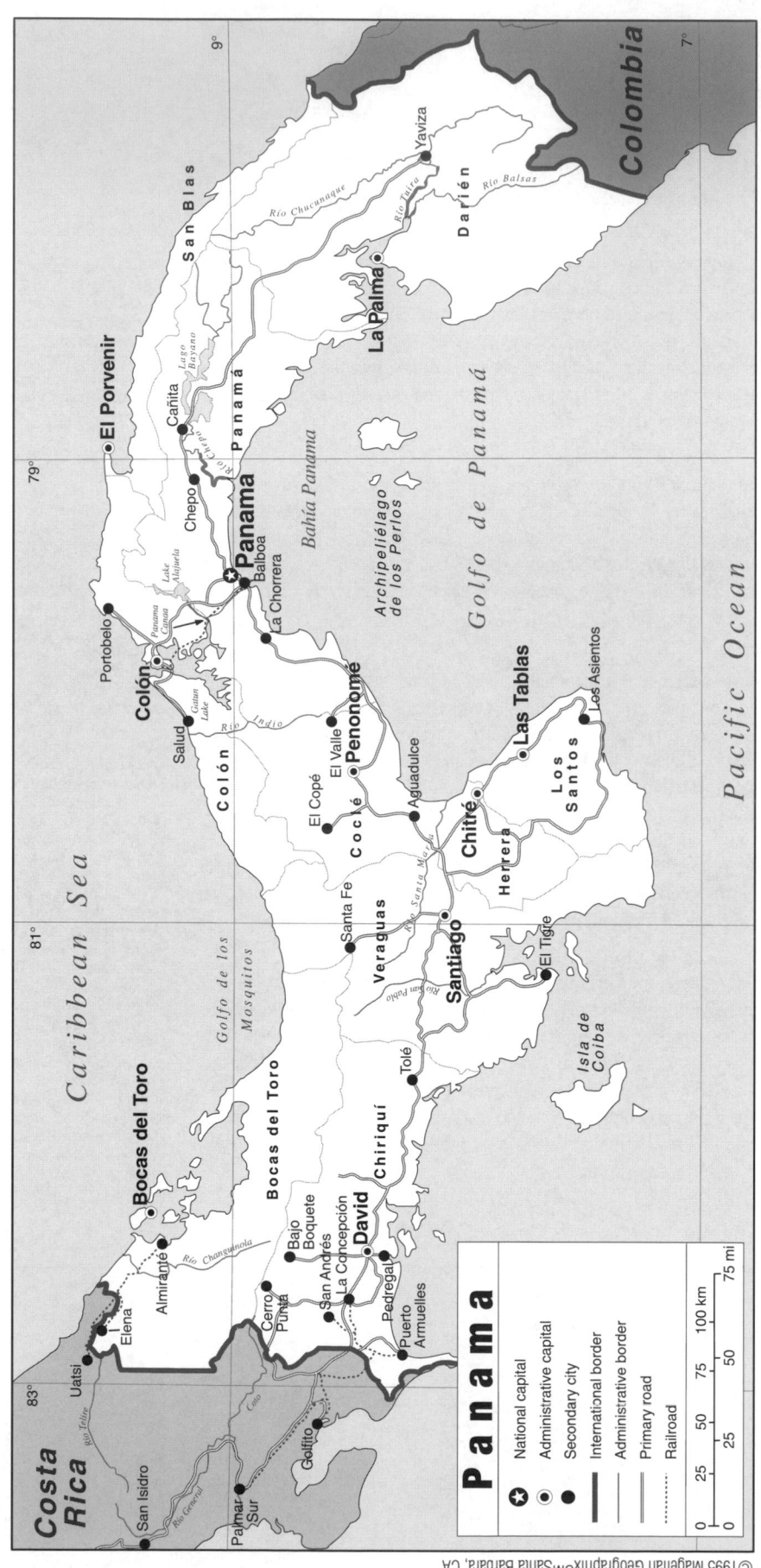

Foreign Trade

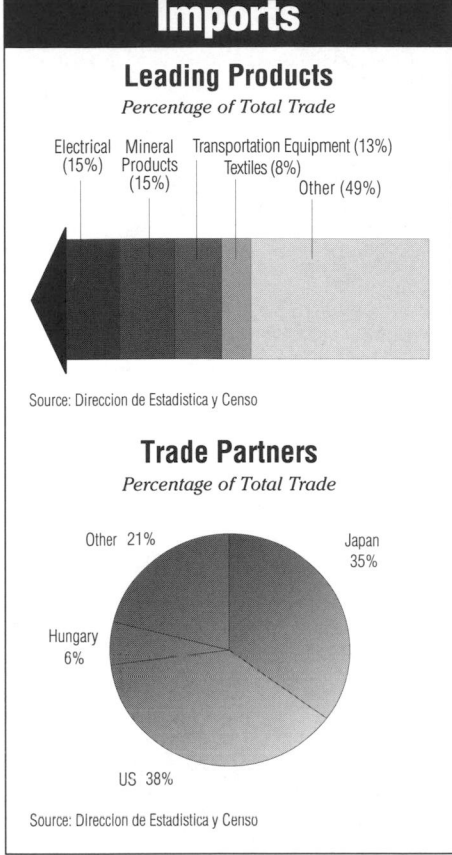

Imports

Leading Products
Percentage of Total Trade

Electrical (15%)
Mineral Products (15%)
Transportation Equipment (13%)
Textiles (8%)
Other (49%)

Source: Direccion de Estadistica y Censo

Trade Partners
Percentage of Total Trade

Other 21%
Japan 35%
Hungary 6%
US 38%

Source: Direccion de Estadistica y Censo

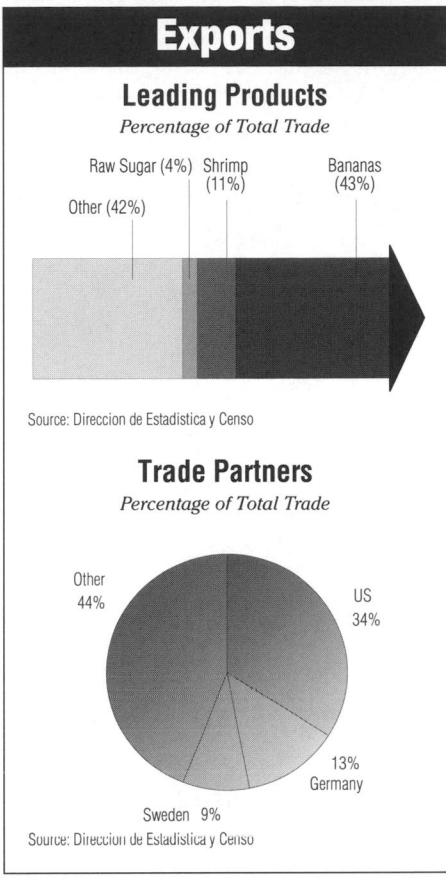

Exports

Leading Products
Percentage of Total Trade

Raw Sugar (4%)
Shrimp (11%)
Bananas (43%)
Other (42%)

Source: Direccion de Estadistica y Censo

Trade Partners
Percentage of Total Trade

Other 44%
US 34%
13% Germany
Sweden 9%

Source: Direccion de Estadistica y Censo

Opportunities

FOR IMPORTING TO PANAMA
- crude oil
- foodstuffs
- consumer goods
- intermediate goods
- telecommunications

FOR EXPORTING FROM PANAMA
- industrial chemicals
- agricultural chemicals
- paper
- carbon
- bananas
- shrimp
- sugar
- computers
- soybean cake

GROWTH SECTORS
- services - banking, insurance, government
- commerce and tourism
- construction
- manufacturing - mining, utilities, processed foods, clothing, chemical products
- agriculture - forestry and fisheries
- mining

GOVERNMENT PROCUREMENT
- transportation - Northern Corridor highway
- telecommunications
- reverted areas - tourism, industry environmental areas
- ports - construction of a container port in the Bay of Manzanillo
- oil terminal port environment - cleanup of Panama Bay - sewage treatment plants

Trade News

RULES AND REGULATIONS

- **Trade news** Panama has always been a country of traders. Panama has the two largest undeveloped copper deposits in the world.

- **Import restrictions** Special import permits are required for all types of firearms and munitions. Import permits can be obtained from the Ministry of Government and Justice. Also, certain agricultural and agroindustrial products are subject to import authorization by the Ministry of Agricultural Development (MIDA). Examples are: wheat, flour, animal fats, vegetable and animal oils, soybean protein, and frozen corn.

- **Prohibited imports** Counterfeit coins or printed material that imitates monetary currencies. Equipment or instruments for manufacturing coins, liquors, wines, beers, or medicines with labels that describe false or deceiving contents, or of any kind of harmful preparation. Certain firearms or war materials, etc. Also, insubstantial products based on phytosanitary concerns.

- **Import licenses** Generally, import licenses are not required in Panama to engage in import activities. Any company holding a commercial license can freely import goods into Panama. A commercial or industrial license is issued to individuals or companies engaged in commercial or industrial activities.

- **Tariffs and import taxes** Panama's nominal tariff duties remain the highest in the region. Panama averages 40 percent in tariff rates, whereas its Central American neighbors average 20 percent. The country has made significant strides to lower its duties and restrictions. However, there are still some basic products subject to tariffs, including processed tomato products, beer, and cigarettes. The long-term view is that, as Panama accedes to GATT, tariff duties will continue to decline and nontariff barriers will be eliminated.

- **Customs valuation** Panama is assessing the majority of its import duties on an ad valorem basis, except for a number of products that are still using a dual ad valorem and specific system.

- **Barriers** The Government of Panama has declared its policy commitment to trade liberation, but liberalization has proceeded slowly.

- **Export controls** The fiscal code regulates all matters concerning the country's exports. The code establishes that all national products may be exported except: drugs, with the exception of those having pharmaceutical or scientific purposes, and staple products determined by the government on a temporary basis due to scarcity in the country. In addition, the government prohibits export of products for reasons of convenience or in the economic interest of the country.

- **Export taxes** Exports subject to the payment of export taxes require an export authorization, which is issued by the Ministry of the Treasury (Hacienda y Tesoro) through the Direccion Nacional de Aduanas. Exports subject to taxes are: bananas, metals, raw sugar, natural resources, and foreign currencies. Exports of textiles are also subject to an export authorization.

- **Import payments** The MICI and the Agricultural Marketing Institute (IMA) impose some quotas on agricultural imports. There may be special requirements for imports by the public sector. The tariff schedule for imports is based on the Customs Cooperation Council Nomenclature (CCCN) and the current range is between 30 and 100 percent. For products with a specific tax, there is an additional 7.5 percent of the value of the import charged.

- **Export credits** Some nontraditional exports are eligible for tax credit certificates up to 20 percent of the value-added.

Business Travel

LH	1906	MADRID	935	113-3
LH	1022	STUTTGART HBF.	935	—
AF	1701	LYON	940	683-6
AY	822	HELSINKI	940	113-3
AA	071	SFRANCISCO-DALLAS	945	731-7

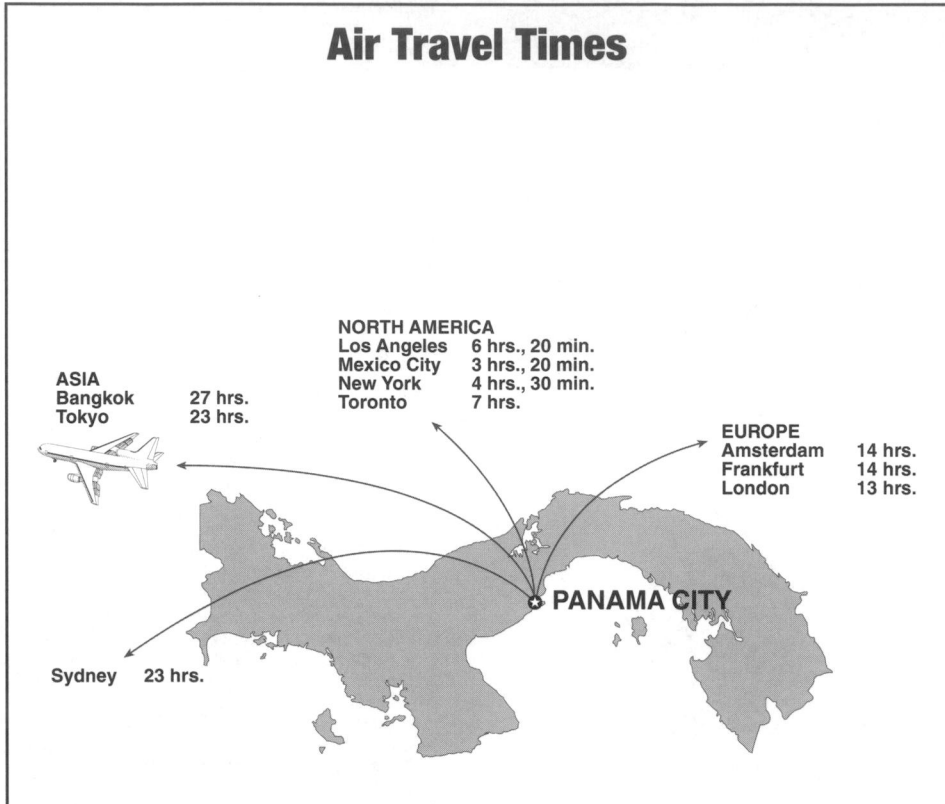

Air Travel Times

ASIA
Bangkok   27 hrs.
Tokyo   23 hrs.

NORTH AMERICA
Los Angeles   6 hrs., 20 min.
Mexico City   3 hrs., 20 min.
New York   4 hrs., 30 min.
Toronto   7 hrs.

EUROPE
Amsterdam   14 hrs.
Frankfurt   14 hrs.
London   13 hrs.

PANAMA CITY

Sydney   23 hrs.

COMMUNICATIONS

Telephones The telephone systems in Panama City and Colón both have automatic exchanges. The Pan-American Earth Satellite provides worldwide long distance service for most parts of the country.
Fax Telex and fax services are available at major hotels and the airport.
Post office Any items mailed to Panama must be addressed "Republic of Panama." All parcels shipped from Panama must be sent through the main post office in Panama City.
Radio/Television All radio and TV broadcasts are in Spanish, although some cable programs are in English.

BEST TRAVEL BOOKS

The Travelers Guide to Panama Customs and Manners. Elizabeth Devine & Nancy Braganti. An invaluable guide for people not wanting to put foot in mouth.
Mexico & Central American Handbook. Passport Books. The most electrifying of all practical travel guides.
Do's and Taboo's Around the World. The Bestselling Guide to International Behavior. Edited by Roger Axtell, compiled by the Parker Pen Company. The ultimate guide to international behavior, now completely updated and expanded. Helpful, fun to read!
Mexico and Central American Handbook. Chicago: Passport Books. Updated annually.

USEFUL TELEPHONE NUMBERS

If you are calling from outside Panama, you will need to add the country code [507] and any other international dialing requirements from within your country.
- Operator/Directory 102
- International Operator 106
- Fire 103
- Police 104
- Ambulance 282187
- Office Equipment Services...................... 30-0621
- Temporary Office Space 63-7555
- Secretarial/Office Support 64-9034
- Translators 25-1354
- DHL Courier 63-8818
- UPS 64-1122
- TransExpress 25-5189
- Chamber of Commerce.............................. 69-2111
- National Investments Council..................... 64-2255
- Banco Nacional de Panama....................... 69-2111
- US Embassy 27-1777

Credit Card Information
Lost or stolen credit cards (call collect to the US, regardless of which country the card was issued in).
- Amex ....[1] (919) 333-3211
- Diner's Club................................[1] (303) 799-1504
- MasterCard ....[1] (314) 275-6690
- Visa ....[1] (410) 581-7931

Travelogue

WORKWEEK

Businesses Monday-Friday 8:00 am to noon, 2:00 pm to 5:00 pm, Saturday 8:00 am to noon.
Government Monday-Friday 9:00 am to 5:00 pm.
Banks Monday-Saturday 8:00 am to 1:00 pm.
Retail Monday-Saturday 8:00 am to noon, 2:00 pm to 6:00 pm.

HOLIDAYS

Holidays 1996
January 1 New Year's Day
January 9 Mourning Day*
February 27-28 Carnival*
April 3 Ash Wednesday*
April 4 Holy Thursday*
April 5 Good Friday*
May 1 Labor Day
August 15 Assumption
November 3 Independence Day from Colombia
November 4 Flag Day
November 10 The Uprising of Los Santos
November 28 Independence Day
December 8 Mother's Day*
December 25 Christmas
*Dates may vary from year to year.

VISA AND PASSPORT

A passport is required for entry to Panama. Also required is an official picture I.D., such as a driver's license, and a Tourist Card that can be purchased on any airline serving Panama. This is valid for 30 days and may be extended for two additional 30-day periods. Three types of visas for stays over 90 days are available: Investor visa, Temporary Visitor's visa, or a Working Permit. These are valid for one year and are renewable.

DEPARTURE FORMALITIES

Any traveler with a visa is required to obtain an exit permit if they have been in the country more than 30 days. The Treasury Ministry will provide a Paz y Salvo form. Take this to Immigration where they will attach the form to your passport and issue an exit stamp valid for one week. All travelers must pay an exit tax.

IMMUNIZATION

For protection against hepatitis, a gamma gobulin shot is recommended. It is also advisable to get vaccinations for typhoid, tetanus, diphtheria, and polio.

TIPPING

Taxi: none. Porter: 50 cents per piece. Hotel, restaurants, nightspots: 10 percent, generally included in bill. Barbers, beauticians: 10 percent. Small services: 25 cents.

CRIME

Travel to the Darien jungle area along the Colombian border can be dangerous if confronted by Colombian guerrillas. There are no police in this area. Some armed robberies occur in urban areas of Panama but not frequently.

INFRASTRUCTURE

Omar Torrijos International Airport is one of the most modern in Latin America. Paitilla Airport is in central Panama City and handles domestic and private flights. Car rentals are available at airports and hotels and through offices in major cities. Buses are available but the schedules are irregular. Fares are paid as you exit the bus. There is no bus service to the airport, only taxi service. Taxis are always available and preferred by business members. In Panama City, taxis do not have meters and charge by zones. Negotiate the fare before the ride begins. A railway line does connect Panama City and Colón but it is unsafe and poorly maintained.

NATIONAL TOURIST OFFICE

Tourist Office
Instituto Panameno de Turismo (IPAT)
Centro de Convenciones ATLAPA
Via Israel, Apdo 4421
Panama 5
Tel: 26-7000

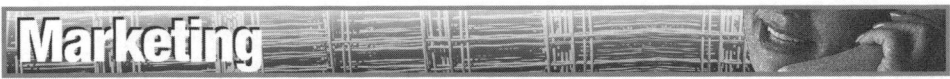

Overview

Enjoying a relatively high per capita income in Central America, Panamanian consumers appreciate and are prepared to pay for high-quality products and services. The marketing structure tends to be simple and straightforward with little government regulatory interference.

Distribution and Agents

Panama's marketing is very centralized, with Panama City accounting for 65 percent of all consumer sales, and the remaining 35 percent distributed between the country's other principal cities of David, Santiago, Colón and Chitre. Many of Panama's major importers are located in the Colón Free Zone (on the Atlantic side of the Canal Zone) and usually act as wholesalers—and often as retailers as well—in marketing automotive parts, apparel and hardware products. Consumer goods, food and medicines are usually handled by separate wholesale and retail operations, while industrial goods are generally marketed through exclusive local agents or distributors.

Advertising

Panama's advertising market is competitive and of good quality. Newspaper promotion and television campaigns are the most common medium for advertisers, while trade shows and exhibitions have also proven effective in promoting and marketing new products. A high-profile, aggressive campaign is recommended for developing and maintaining brand-name recognition in Panama, including the use of large billboards, radio spots, and, in the case of large foreign manufacturers, the sponsoring of sporting events.

Customer Service and Support

Distributors should be prepared to provide after-sales support, counseling, and technical assistance to customers.

Greetings and Courtesies

 Handshakes are considered appropriate among businesspeople, both men and women—when arriving and leaving—although casual acquaintances generally nod when meeting while good friends hug. Panamanian women may embrace lightly or brush cheeks in a kiss; they seldom shake hands with each other, although they may do so in a business situation.

Business Ethic and Framework

 Panamanians are generally considered relaxed, easygoing, and informal by Latin American standards, although they nevertheless have a regard for formal dignity and hierarchical and class distinctions. Although they have become more accustomed to North American business norms, their values continue to emphasize the importance of personal relationships, and they still take time and effort to establish a personal relationship before a business relationship.

Meetings and Decision Making

 Prior appointments are necessary and should generally be made two weeks in advance. Punctuality is generally considered unimportant. Most meetings are held informally. Authority is rather narrowly concentrated and actual decisions are almost always made at a high level. Cultivate relationships at all levels, however, because the quality of these relationships may strongly influence the actual decision maker even when your immediate counterpart is not the one making the decision.

Women

 Although women generally occupy a secondary status in heavily male-dominated and *macho*-influenced Panama, they are accorded considerable personal freedom and many operate businesses. Foreign businesswomen should experience few problems. Although women may generally go out on the streets and dine alone, most will feel more comfortable if escorted.

Marketing in Panama

MARKETING TIPS

- **High quality** Panamanian consumers of both the upper middle class and the majority lower middle class are accustomed to high-quality products and are willing to pay for them.
- **Brand-name recognition** Panamanians are very trend-conscious and respond well to high-profile brand names and services.
- **Attractive packaging** This is a key factor for success in Panama's competitive market.
- **Franchises** Panama's lack of regulatory controls on royalty payments or transfers makes for an attractive franchising market. .

AD AGENCIES

APCU Panama
Edif. Torre Blanco Aliado, Nivel 16
Calle Recardo Arias
Campo Alegre
Panama 5
Tel: 69-9288
Fax: 69-9698

Publicidad Interamericana, SA
Apdo 8434
Calle 64, No. 2
San Francisco
Panama 7
Tel: 26-6077
Fax: 225-7854

Cultural Cautions

DO'S

- Learn something about Panama's history and culture—your interest and any attempts to speak Spanish will be appreciated.
- Family, mutual acquaintances or interests, hobbies, and sports are good topics for conversation.

DON'TS

- Avoid race, religion, politics, drug trafficking, former military and political leaders, and the Canal Zone as topics of conversation.
- Do not discuss possessions with Panamanians, who are generally more impressed with personal qualities and attainments; you may be considered boastful by emphasizing the material over the personal.

CUSTOMS

- Gifts of food are considered appropriate in more rural inland areas to acknowledge an invitation to a meal or a social event or to thank someone for a favor.
- If invited to a home for a meal or a party, plan to stay until well after midnight. For a party, you can arrive as much as two hours after the stated time.
- Business dinners given by foreign businesspeople are usually hosted at a hotel.

OBSERVATIONS

- Foreign businesspeople who fail to make an effort to meet and interact with Panamanians are generally considered aloof, unfriendly, cold, and unworthy of receiving consideration in business or personal dealings.
- Dark, conservative tropical weight suits are appropriate for businessmen. Any shift to more informal attire should be at the suggestion of a Panamanian colleague. Shorts should be avoided at all costs.
- Business gifts may be presented after a relationship has been developed or to commemorate the completion of a deal.

NEGOTIATIONS

- Negotiators should be polite, confident, and persistent—Panamanians may need persuading; however, avoid overt aggressiveness or pressure.
- Bargaining does not play the role in Panamanian culture that it does in some other Latin American countries.

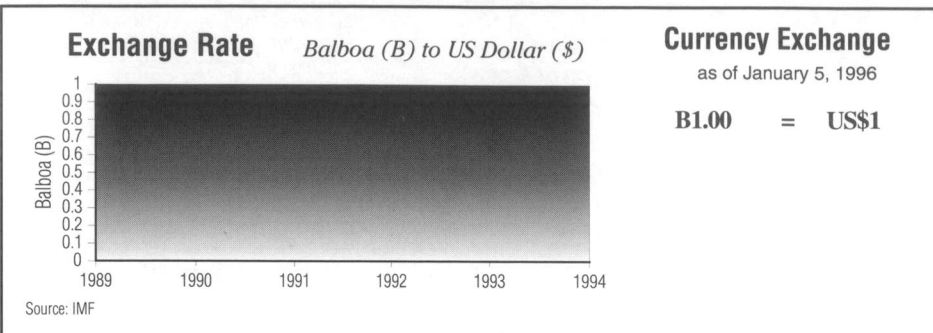

Exchange Rate *Balboa (B) to US Dollar ($)*

Currency Exchange
as of January 5, 1996

B1.00   =   US$1

Source: IMF

Currency

The main currency in use is the Panamanian balboa (B), but the US dollar is considered legal tender and is circulated freely in Panama.

Foreign Exchange

Commercial banks quote all buying and selling rates for currency exchanges. There is very little non-resident investment in Panama, primarily due to poor infrastructure and a negative international image. There have been changes made recently, however. The government is currently attempting to privatize certain sectors, and is open to private investment in high-tech and telecommunication services. The area most open to foreign investment is the Colón Free Zone (CFZ). The CFZ offers special tax incentives and companies there pay a corporate income tax rate of 8.5 percent on income from export sales.

Capital Transfers

There are no restrictions on any payments for invisibles, but a four percent travel tax is placed on air and sea tickets bought in Panama or tickets purchased for travel starting in Panama. There are no restrictions or regulations for proceeds from invisibles.

Investment Incentives

There are special tax and other incentives for manufacturers to locate in an Export Processing Zone (EPZ), the only active one of which currently is at Isla Margarita, outside Colón (nominal but inactive EPZ's exist at Ojo de Agua and Telepuerto). Tax incentives are available to manufacturers, wherever located in Panama, who produce wholly or partially for export, in proportion to the percentage of product exported. There may, as a matter of administrative practice, be an official preference for local procurement of certain types of business insurance. Tax incentives are also available to small businesses (fewer than 10 employees) and to certain types of agricultural production and investment, especially where production is for export.

Investment Restrictions

There are no performance requirements, minimum export percentages, or significant local procurement rules. Very little attention has been paid to infrastructure and public services, however, and these can be problematic for new investors.

Money Matters

BITS AND PIECES

- **Corporate income tax** All companies in Panama, resident and nonresident, are subject to corporate tax based only on income and profits from Panama.
- **Relief for losses** Companies showing a loss in a fiscal year can deduct 20 percent of the loss in each of the five subsequent fiscal years.
- **Service fees** Payments for professional services rendered in Panama are subject to a withholding tax of 15 percent.
- **Capital transfers** There are no exchange controls for capital transfers.
- **Gold** Residents can hold gold in any form and can negotiate gold in any form without restrictions.

BANKS

Banco del Itsmo
POB 6
3823, El Dorado
Panama 6A
Tel: 695555
Fax: 635869

Banco General, Casa Matriz
POB 4592
Panama 5
Tel: 270150
Fax: 273427

Banco Comercial de Panama
POB 7659
Panama 5
Tel: 636800
Tel: 634433
Fax: 638033

Banco Nacional de Panama
POB 5220
Panama 5
Tel: 692966
Fax: 647155

Citibank, N.A.
POB 555
Panama 9A
Tel: 364044
Fax: 361025

PRIBANCO, Primer Banco de Ahorros
POB 7322
Panama 5
Tel: 272225
Fax: 274037

The Chase Manhattan Bank, N.A.
POB 76
Panama 9A
Tel: 635855, 635877
Fax: 636009

The First National Bank of Boston
POB 5368
Panama 5
Tel: 642244, 642146
Fax: 234089

Banco Anco Santnader Panama (Spain)
Via Espana y Calle 55
Apdo 484
Panama 9A
Tel: 63-6262
Fax: 63-7553

Banco Union, CA (Venezuela)
Torre Banco Union
Calle Samuel Lewis
Apdo "A"
Panama 5
Tel: 64-9091

Bank of America National Trust and Savings Association (US)
Calle 50 esq. con Calle 53
Apdo 7282
Panama 5
Tel: 63-5500

TAXATION

Taxation requires sophisticated knowledge of complex rules and regulations specific to each country. The information presented here is from the Ernst & Young Corporate Tax Guide and Directory, available from the Ernst & Young accounting office in your country, or from:

Ernst & Young
Mail Address:
PTY 018
POB 025275
Miami, FL 33102-5275
USA
Street Address:
Calle 51 Bella Vista, No. 26
Panama
Tel: 64-2633, 64-2828, 64-2129, 64-2310
Fax: 63-7719, 64-8984

At a Glance

Corporate Income Tax Rate (% (a)	34
Capital Gains Tax Rate (%) (a)	34
Branch Tax Rate (%) (a)	34
Withholding Tax (%) (b)	
Dividends (c)	
On Nominative Shares	10
On Bearer Shares	20
Interest (d)	6
Royalties from Patents, Know-how, etc. (a)	17
Payments on Leases (a)	17
Payments for Professional Services	
Rendered in Panama	15
Branch Remittance Tax	0
Net Operating Losses (Years)	
Carryback	0
Carryforward	5

(a) Maximum rate.
(b) Applicable only to nonresidents. Nonresident corporations are corporations not incorporated in Panama.
(c) Capitalized dividends are exempt from tax.
(d) Certain interest is exempt from tax.

Legal System

Panama is a civil code country, having derived its law from Colombian and Spanish heritage. The Panama judicial system is independent from the other government branches. Some recent commercial legislation has been influenced by US laws.

Intellectual Property Protection

Patents Patents are granted to domestic and foreign inventors. The protection term is from five to 20 years for domestic inventors, but foreign patents cannot exceed 15 years.

Trademarks Trademarks must be registered to be considered valid. Protection extends to both domestic and foreign owners. All registration documents must be in the Spanish language.

Copyrights Copyrights are run for 80 years after the creator's death. Inscription of the copyright is subject to a stamp tax. Any transfers must be properly recorded with the Ministry of Education.

Trade Secrets Panama's laws regarding trade secrets are transparent though incredibly weak. It is difficult to get an injunction for trade secret violations.

Business Registration

All companies must be registered in the Mercantile Persons Section of the Public Register. If a company resulting from a merger is foreign, its registration must remain on record for at least five years after the merger.

Contracts and Dispute Resolution

Most contracts are governed by the general principles of the civil code, but for certain types of mercantile contracts the principles of the civil code are supplemented by commercial code provisions. Most contracts are written through a broker. Disputes are commonly handled through lawsuits, although the court process tends to be lengthy. A foreign judgment or ruling entered in a country where Panamanian rulings cannot be enforced and may not be valid in Panama. Panamanian courts will otherwise enforce a foreign judicial award.

Legal Matters

LEGAL BRIEFS

- **Bankruptcy** Bankruptcy declared in a foreign country has no effect in Panama until the judgment has been held enforceable by a local court.
- **Contract nonperformance** Delay or nonperformance of a contract is excused only if prevented by "unforeseen events," or "acts of god."
- **Labor** The Panama government sets the minimum wage. All employee and employer relations are regulated by a labor code, which includes a very detailed set of rules on such topics as collective bargaining, strikes, and health and safety requirements.
- **Notaries** Notaries are public officials with important functions in the legal system. They must be attorneys and are appointed by the president for determined circuits.
- **Foreign patents** All documents covering a foreign patent application must be legalized by the Panamanian consul in the country where the patent was issued.
- **Limitations periods** Debts originating on bills of exchange are normally proscribed after two years and ordinary commercial debts originating from the sale of goods are proscribed after three years.

LEGAL CONTACTS

Colegio Nacional de Abogados de Panama
POB 8643
Avenida Mexico y Calle 38 E
Panama 5
Tel: 256371

Aleman, Cordero, Galindo & Lee
POB 6-1014 El Dorado
2nd Floor, Swiss Bank Building
East 53rd Street, Marbella
Panama City
Tel: 264-3111, 269-2620
Fax: 264-3133, 263-5895

Contacts

GOVERNMENT AGENCIES

Ministerio de Comercio e Industrias
(Ministry of Commerce and Industry)
POB 9658
Panama 4
Tel: 274222
Fax: 274134

Ministerio de Comercio e Industrias
Direccion Nacional de Hidrocarburos
POB 9658
Panama 4
Tel: 275674
Fax: 273927

Ministerio de Comercio e Industrias
Direccion General de Registro de la Propiedad Industrial
POB 9658
Panama 4
Tel: 273987
Fax: 272139

Ministerio de Comercio e Industrias
Oficina de Comercio Interior
POB 9658
Panama
Tel: 272161
Fax: 272139

Ministerio de Desarrollo Agropecuario
(Ministry of Agricultural Development)
POB 5390
Panama 5
Tel: 325043
Fax: 325044

Ministerio de Gobierno y Justicia
(Ministry of Government and Justice)
Direccion de Seguridad Publica
POB 1628

Panama 1
Tel: 622929
Fax: 623511

Ministerio de Hacienda y Tesoro
(Ministry of Treasury)
POB 7304
Panama 5
Tel: 274998
Fax: 272357

Ministerio de Hacienda y Tesoro
Direccion Nacional de Aduanas
POB 1671 Balboa, Ancon
Panama
Tel: 325355
Fax: 326494

Ministerio de Salud
(Ministry of Health)
Direccion de Control de Alimentos y Vigilancia Veterinaria
POB 2048
Panama 1
Tel: 621619
Fax: 625443

Ministerio de Obras Publicas
(Ministry of Public Works)
POB 1632
Panama 1
Tel: 325572
Fax: 325776

Autoridad de la Region Interoceanica
POB 2097, Balboa
Panama
Tel: 325517
Fax: 325286

Instituto Panameno de Turismo
(Tourism Institute of Panama)
POB 4421

Panama 5
Tel: 267414, 263751
Fax: 263483

Instituto Panameno de Comercio Exterior
(Panama Trade Development Institute)
POB 61897
Panama 6
Tel: 257244
Fax: 252193

Instituto de Recursos Hidraulicos y Electrificacion
(National Power and Light Company)
POB 5285
Panama 5
Tel: 272240
Fax: 629294

Instituto Nacional de Telecomunicaciones
(National Telephone Company)
POB 659
Panama 9A
Tel: 238620
Fax: 645743

Instituto de Acueductos y Alcantarillados Nacionales
(National Water Works Company)
POB 5234
Panama 5
Tel: 238640
Fax: 640034

WORLD TRADE CENTER

World Trade Center of Panama
POB 6
Panama 6
Tel: 696124
Fax: 696126

BUSINESS AND TRADE ORGANIZATIONS

Asociacion de Comerciantes y Distribuidores de Viveres y Similares de Panama
(Food Retailers and Distributors Association of Panama)
POB 6
3594
Tel: 614304
Fax: 612346

Asociacion de Distribuidores de Automoviles de Panama
(Automobile Distributors Association)
POB 476
Panama 9A
Tel: 611264
Fax: 610906

Asociacion Nacional de Desarrollo Economico
(National Association of Economic Development)
POB 6
3390, El Dorado
Panama
Tel: 277979
Fax: 649280

Asociacion Nacional de la Industria Pesquera Panamena
(National Fisheries Association)
POB 5062
Panama 5
Tel: 510317
Fax: 511995

Asociacion Panamena de Ejecutivos de Empresa
(Panamanian Association of Business Executives)
POB 1331
Panama 1
Tel: 273511, 274085
Fax: 271872

Asociacion Panamena de Exportadores
(Exporters Association of Panama)
POB 6
6527
Panama 6
Tel: 300284, 300169
Fax: 300805

Asociacion Bancaria de Panama
(Banking Association of Panama)
POB 4554
Panama 5
Tel: 637044
Fax: 637783

Camara Panamena de la Construccion
(Construction Chamber of Panama)
Apartado 6793
Panama 5
Tel: 642255
Fax: 642384

Sindicato de Industriales de Panama
(Industrialists Association of Panama)
POB 6
4798
Panama 6
Tel: 300284, 300169
Fax: 300805

American Chamber of Commerce and Industry
POB 168, Balboa
Panama
Tel: 693881 Fax: 233508

Camara de Comercio, Industria y Agricultura de Panama
(Chamber of Commerce, Industry and Agriculture of Panama)
POB 74
Panama 1
Tel: 271285, 271445
Fax: 274186, 253653

MARKET RESEARCH FIRMS

Ditcher & Neira - Marketing Consultant
POB 6
7373, El Dorado
Panama
Tel: 643466
Fax: 231174

Marketing Consultant
POB 6
86, El Dorado
Panama
Tel: 233974
Fax: 233936

AD AGENCIES

APCU de Panama
Associated with J. Walter Thompson
POB 6
7291, El Dorado
Panama
Tel: 639288
Fax: 639698

Boyd, Barcenas, S.A.
Associated with LINTA
POB 11373
Panama 6
Tel: 639300
Fax: 639692

FERGO
Associated with Saatchi & Saatchi Advertising
POB 6
6249, El Dorado
Panama
Tel: 638811
Fax: 638892

BANKS

Banco Nacional de Panama
Cond. Plaza Internacional
Torre Banconal, Via Espana
Apdo 5220
Panama 5
Tel: 63-5151
Fax: 69-0091

Banco de Desarrollo Agropecuario
Avda de los MArtires
Apdo 5282
Panama 5
Tel: 62-0266
Fax: 62-1713

Banco General, SA
Calle 34 Este y Avda Cuba
Apdo 4592
Panama 5
Tel: 27-3200
Fax: 27-3227

Banco Hipotecario Nacional
Edif. Pena Prieta
Avda Balboa y Calle 40 Bella Vista
Apdo 222
Panama 1
Tel: 27-0055
Fax: 25-4190

Banco Panameno de la Vivienda
Avda Chile y Calle 41
Apdo 8639
Panama 5
Tel: 27-4020

NEWSPAPERS

El Panama America
Via Fernandez de Cordoba
Apdo B-4
Panama 9A
Tel: 61-2300

PERIODICALS

Estadistica Panamena
Apdo 5213
Panama 5
Tel: 64-3734
Fax: 69-0094

FOB Colón Free Zone
Apdo 6-3287
El Dorado
Panama
Tel: 25-6638
Fax: 25-0466

Focus on Panama
Apdo 6-3287
Panama
Tel: 25-6638
Fax: 25-0466

RADIO AND TELEVISION

Asociacion Panamena de Radiodifusion
Apdo 7387
Estafeta de Paitilla
Panama
Tel: 63-5252 Fax: 26-4396

Corporacion Panamena de Radiodifusion, SA (Canal 4)
Edif. Chesterfield
Avda 11 y Calle 28
Apdo 1795
Panama1
Tel: 25-0160

Panavision del Istmo, SA (Canal 5)
Torre Plaza Regency
Via Espana
Apdo 6-2605
El Dorado
Panama 8
Tel: 69-6816

RPC Television
Apdo 1795
Panama 1

Sistema de Television Educativa (Canal 11)
Universidad de Panama
Estafeta Universitaria
Calle jose de Fabrega
Panama
Tel: 69-3755

Southern Command Network -SCN (Canal 8)
Edif. 209, Fuerte Clayton
Apdo 919
Panama
Tel: 87-5567

Televisora nacional, SA
Apdo 6-3092
El Dorado
Panama
Tel: 36-3333
Fax: 36-2987

INTERNET ADDRESSES

Latin America - Panama
http://lanic.utexas.edu/la/ca/panama/

City Net - Panama
http://www.city.net/countries/panama/

Panama: A WWW InfoGuide
http://holly.colostate.edu/~panama/panama.html

Republic of Panama
http://leviathan.tama.edu/panama/html

Papua New Guinea

Independent State of Papua New Guinea

Economy

Overview

Papua New Guinea has a free-market economy dominated by the private sector. Although it has historically been an agricultural country, there has been significant urbanization in recent years because of the growth of industrial businesses. The government created the National Development Strategy (NDS) to direct and control the rapid population growth and mass migration to the cities. Economic growth has slowed significantly as the government turns its attention to more pressing concerns, such as the substantial health concerns of the nation, not the least of which is the fact that only 20 percent of the population have access to safe water.

Trade

Papua New Guinea has established strong relations and trading links with other South Pacific nations. It works through the South Pacific Commission to develop and further free trade in the region, although is does not currently have any plans to develop any specific export industries. Although barriers are few, its small population and relative poverty work to limit the overall growth of foreign trade. Its largest trading partner is Australia, from which it receives significant economic and technical assistance.

Sectors

Agriculture Papua New Guinea uses only six percent of its land for agriculture, although much more is potentially arable. The government is currently trying to reform agricultural policy and return expatriate-owned land to native hands. Forests cover a great deal of the country, and half of it is estimated to be commercially viable, although it remains largely undeveloped. Fishing industries could also be economically successful in Papua New Guinea, particularly tuna and prawns. Commercial fishing is mostly concentrated along the coast, conducted from motorized canoes.

Industry Papua New Guinea cannot compete in international industrial markets because its wage scales are relatively high. Oil and gas exploration has been actively conducted by US firms for a number of years, but few discoveries have been made. Industry professionals, however, believe there is a potential for oil deposits, and drilling presently continues in the Gulf of Papua.

Services Tourism is a major industry, with the most current growth potential. Expenditures by tourists total almost 25 million kina (US$19 million) each year. Most travelers come from Australia, the United States, and the United Kingdom.

Trends

Internationally viable industries are only now beginning to emerge in Papua New Guinea, and the country currently remains heavily dependent on foreign aid. There is a great deal of arable land that is economically viable, but there is no technology or infrastructure to utilize it. Papua New Guinea also lacks a technically trained work force, but the government is preoccupied with national environmental and health problems and has not yet adequately addressed many of the underlying factors that would work to build the economy in the long term. The country does have good relations with a number of foreign countries, especially Australia, and it remains very open to foreign trade. There may well be many untapped opportunities for savvy foreigners looking to establish a base in the Pacific Rim.

At a Glance

THE COUNTRY

Location Situated to the north of Australia in the deep ocean basin of the Pacific.

Terrain The largest section is the eastern half of the island, dominated by a massive system of mountain ranges. Active and recently active volcanoes are prominent features of Papua New Guinea. In the lowlands are swamps and floodplains.

Climate The climate of Papua New Guinea is chiefly influenced by altitude and monsoons. Relative humidity is uniformly high in the lowlands at about 80%.

THE PEOPLE

Population 4,200,000

Ethnic composition Indigenous Papua New Guineans vary considerably in ethnic origins, physical appearance and spoken languages. The indigenous people are Melanesians. Of the nonindigenous population, the largest group is Australian, followed by others of European origin and Chinese.

Religious composition

Indigenous beliefs	34%
Roman Catholic	22%
Lutheran	16%
Presbyterian/Methodist	8%
Anglican	5%
Evangelical Alliance	4%
Other Protestant sects	10%

Languages spoken English, Pidgin (a Melanesian lingua franca with roots primarily in English and German), and Hiri Motu (lingua franca of Papuan derivation) are the primary languages.

Education and literacy Education in Papua New Guinea is not compulsory. Only 33 percent of the population is literate. The present government aims at upgrading and improving the system and quality of education.

COUNTRY FACTS

Political and legal Papua New Guinea has a Parliamentary democracy. Its legal system is based on English common law.

Telephone Telephone, telegraph, and telex services are available. International country code: [675]. There are no city codes.

Transportation Transportation is a major problem in Papua New Guinea because of the difficult terrain. Air and sea are the best bets although road construction has increased recently.

Environment Papua New Guinea's environment is rich and varied. Most of the country is covered by tropical and savannah rain forest, with valuable trees such as kwila and cedar found. Current issues include pollution and the loss of the nation's forests.

Media A coastal radio service provides communication between land-based stations and ships at sea. The National Broadcasting Commission operates three radio networks and one national television station.

Health Government policy is to distribute health services widely and provide comprehensive medical care. Pneumonia and related respiratory infections are a major risk. Only 20 percent of the population have access to safe water and bacteria-related diseases are commonplace.

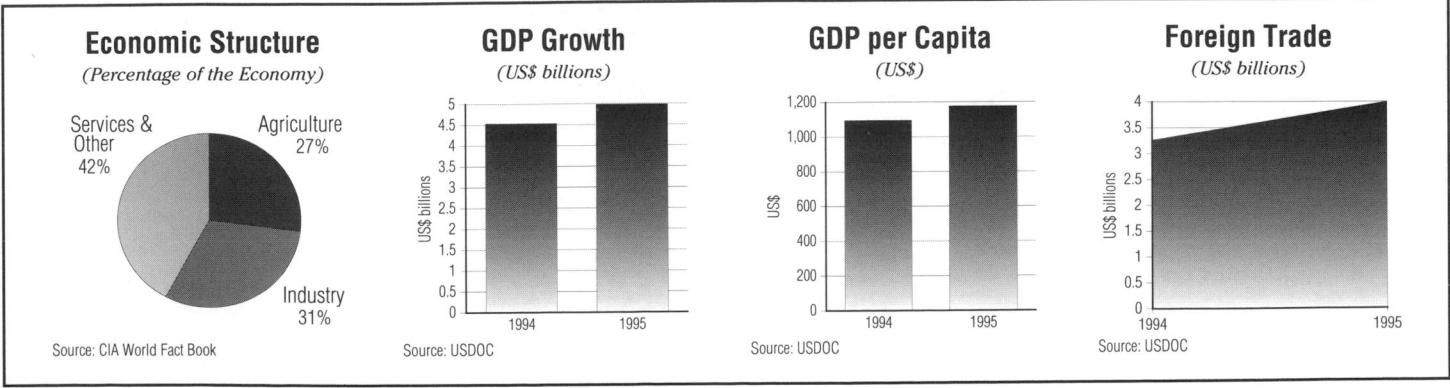

Economic Structure (Percentage of the Economy)
- Services & Other 42%
- Agriculture 27%
- Industry 31%
Source: CIA World Fact Book

GDP Growth (US$ billions) — 1994, 1995
Source: USDOC

GDP per Capita (US$) — 1994, 1995
Source: USDOC

Foreign Trade (US$ billions) — 1994, 1995
Source: USDOC

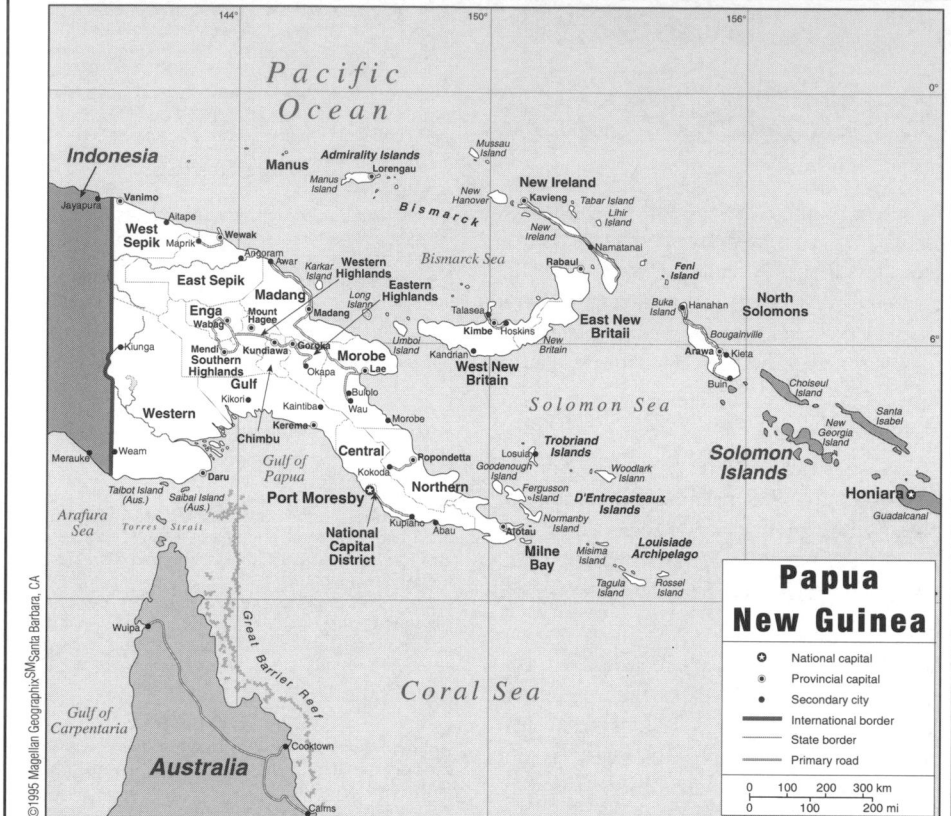

COMMUNICATIONS

Telephones International direct dialing is available in Port Moresby and up-country. Mobile phone services are newly available in major areas.

Fax Services are widely available for faxing internationally.

Post office Postal services are available, along with courier services through DHL, Fastapak and Express Mail Services.

TV/Radio Papua New Guinea has three radio networks and one national television station, run by The National Broadcasting Commission.

BEST TRAVEL BOOKS

All-Asia Travel Guide, Southeast Asia, Volume One.

Papua New Guinea, A Travel Survival Kit. Tony Wheeler. Lonely Planet Guides. A helpful and down-to-earth guide. No serious traveler would set foot in Papua New Guinea without it.

USEFUL TELEPHONE NUMBERS

If you are calling from outside Papua New Guinea, you will need to add the country code [675] and any other international dialing requirements from within your country.

Courier Services
- DHL 25-9866
- Fastpak 25-9788
- Express Mail Service 27-4937

Car Rental
- Avis 25-8429
- Budget 25-4111

Airlines
- Air Niugini 27-3200
- Talair 72-1613
- Island Aviation 92-2900
- Nationair 25-4179
- Micronesia 25-7588

Credit Card Information
Lost or stolen credit cards (call collect to the US, regardless of which country the card was issued in).
- Amex ....[1] (919) 333-3211
- Diner's Club...............................[1] (303) 799-1504
- MasterCard ....[1] (314) 275-6690
- Visa ....[1] (410) 581-7931

Travelogue

WORKWEEK

Offices Monday-Friday 8:00 am to 5:00 pm with one hour for lunch.

Banks Monday-Thursday 9:00 am to 2:00 pm, Friday 9:00 am to 5:00 pm.

Government Monday-Friday 7:45 am to 4:00 pm.

Retail Monday-Friday, 8:30 am to 5:00 pm. Saturdays, 8:00 am to noon. Markets opening hours are 7:00 am to 6:00 pm.

HOLIDAYS

Holiday 1996
January 1 New Year's Day
April 5 *Good Friday
June 18 Queen Elizabeth's birthday
July 23 Remembrance Day
September 16 Independence Day
December 25 Christmas Day
December 26 Boxing Day
* Dates vary from year to year.

VISA AND PASSPORT

All visitors are required to have valid passports and visas. Travelers must obtain a tourist visa before traveling in the country. Visas are usually granted for up to two months. Visitors must have return or onward tickets and sufficient funds to maintain themselves. Visitors must not engage in any form of employment.

DEPARTURE FORMALITIES

Stringent controls on the export of artifacts considered of national, historical, or cultural significance require permits from the National Museum. Taking bird of paradise plumes is illegal.

IMMUNIZATION

Visitors entering from cholera and yellow fever infected areas require inoculation certificates. Anti-malarial pills for two weeks before arrival, during the entire stay, and for four weeks after departure are recommended since the malaria-carrying anopheles mosquito is found in this country.

TIPPING

Tipping is appreciated. Taxis: 10 percent. Hotels, restaurants, nightspots: 15 percent.

CRIME

Crime has been exaggerated in Papua New Guinea but travelers should take precautions. Walking at night is risky in most urban areas. Drivers should stick to main roads. Corruption in official government is found; watch for 'deals' by an official or politician.

INFRASTRUCTURE

Papua New Guinea has a very hilly terrain, making travel by air almost the only viable mode of transport. Port Moresby is often used for travel to and from this country; boat services are available. Many intercountry roads do not link, making travel impossible by automobile. Taxis are available, but expensive and unmaintained. Buses are not recommended for business travelers; a car-for-hire is suggested instead.

NATIONAL TOURIST OFFICES

National Tourist Office
Tel: 25-1269
or
Tourist Association of Papua New Guinea
c/o The Manager
Islander Hotel
P.O. Box 1981
Boroko

Foreign Trade

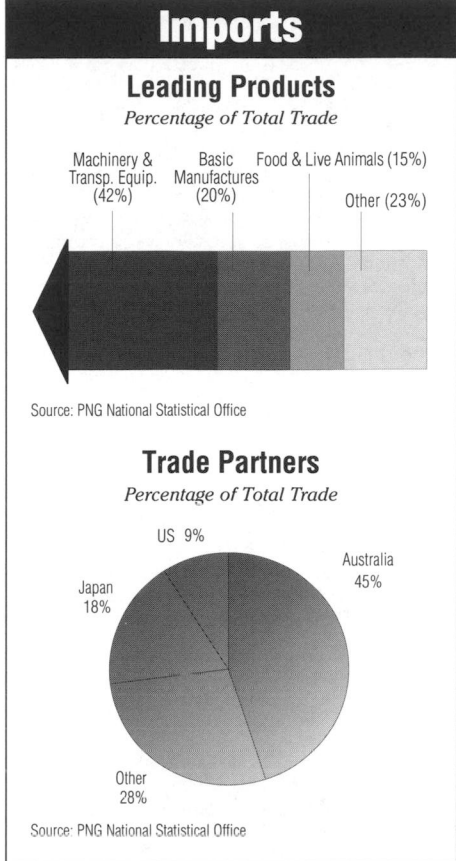

Imports

Leading Products
Percentage of Total Trade

Machinery & Transp. Equip. (42%)
Basic Manufactures (20%)
Food & Live Animals (15%)
Other (23%)

Source: PNG National Statistical Office

Trade Partners
Percentage of Total Trade

US 9%
Japan 18%
Australia 45%
Other 28%

Source: PNG National Statistical Office

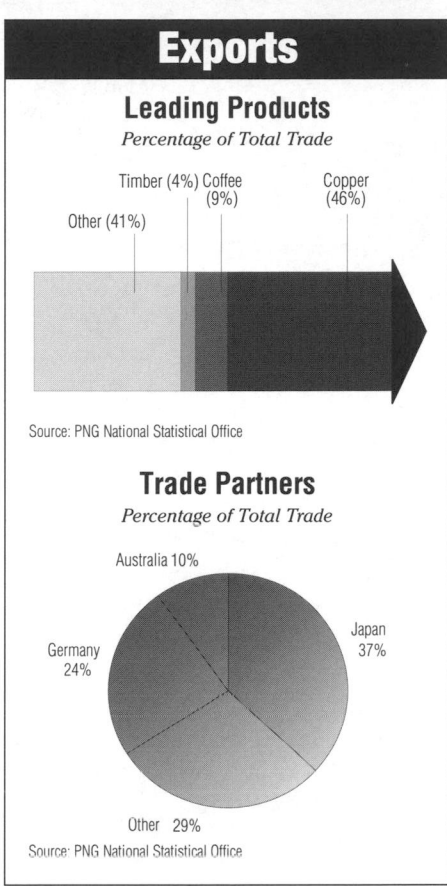

Exports

Leading Products
Percentage of Total Trade

Timber (4%)
Coffee (9%)
Copper (46%)
Other (41%)

Source: PNG National Statistical Office

Trade Partners
Percentage of Total Trade

Australia 10%
Germany 24%
Japan 37%
Other 29%

Source: PNG National Statistical Office

Opportunities

FOR IMPORTING TO PAPUA NEW GUINEA
- chemicals, fuels
- food and manufactured goods
- machinery and transport equipment

FOR EXPORTING FROM PAPUA NEW GUINEA
- cocoa, coffee, lobster, palm oil
- gold, copper, ore, timber, tropical timber, logs, oil

GROWTH SECTORS
- agriculture
- construction
- fishing and forestry
- manufacturing
- mining
- petroleum

Trade News

RULES AND REGULATIONS
- **Import certification** Certification is required for some agricultural products. Quarantine regulations apply to the import of live plants. Import restrictions or quotas apply to laundry soap and plywood. Imports of canned meat, eggs, honey, sugar, chicken, pork, small goods, and several fruits and vegetables are banned.
- **Tariff rates** There are provisions to allow for exemptions/reductions to import duties if investigation warrants. Exempt products are rice, tinned fish, medical goods, books, magazines, vessels, aircraft, and parts for vessels and aircraft. Basic tariff rates apply to fisheries, agriculture, horticulture, textiles, construction, paper, chemicals, plastics, etc. An additional luxury tax applies to certain timber products and other items readily available in the country.

Legal

Legal System
A parliamentary democracy with British and Australian colonial heritage, the head of the independent state of Papua New Guinea continues to be the British crown, locally represented by a Governor General. The Supreme Court is the most powerful judicial body in Papua New Guinea. Most civil cases are tried in lower courts.

Intellectual Property Protection
Patents and trademarks Papua New Guinea is not a signatory to any of the major international agreements on patent protection, and foreign patents are not valid in the country. The Trademark Protection Act provides only minimal protection for foreign trademarks.

Copyrights Foreign copyrights are not protected in Papua New Guinea, and piracy is a problem throughout the country. Papua New Guinea is not a member of any international copyright protection conventions.

Trade secrets Papua New Guinea has laws concerning trade secrets, but rarely enforces them.

Business Registration
All businesses must be registered with the Companies Registry in Waigani. A memorandum and a Statutory Declaration of Compliance are needed, and all articles must be stamped with the proper stamp duty and accompanied by the prescribed registration fee. In addition, foreign businesses must typically apply with the Investment Promotion Authority (IPA) to obtain registration as a legal business entity in Papua New Guinea.

Dispute Settlement
Most disputes are settled through the lower courts, though confusion in the court system has led to severe delays for dispute settlements. The government formed the Law Reform Commission to make the courts more efficient, and they have had some progress, but still have quite a ways to go.

Legal Matters

LEGAL BRIEFS
- **Business entities** Most foreign companies operate in the form of subsidiaries or branches. A company may choose to set up a subsidiary because of the lower tax rate despite higher formation and administration costs. The government favors joint ventures and it may actually purchase up to 30 percent equity in a major foreign investment project.
- **Agents and distributors** Papua New Guinea law does not require a foreign company to hire an agent or distributor. However, an agent may ease the clearance of goods through customs.
- **Workers** Skilled workers are in short supply; 72 percent of professional and semiprofessional positions are held by foreigners.
- **Labor laws** The Employment Act of 1978 regulates major labor concerns, including holidays and work hour limitations. Minimum wages are established by the Minimum Wages Board. Children under age 11 cannot be employed outside of a family business. Children between the ages 11 and 16 can work with parental permission, a medical clearance, and a work permit from a labor office. Except for agriculture, such employment is very rare according to the Department of Labor.
- **Unions** There are over 15 unions, and the majority of them are affiliated with the Papua New Guinea Trade Union Congress.
- **Contracts** Contracts do not need to be written and may be implied by conduct.
- **International agreements** Papua New Guinea is a member of GATT/WTO and is the beneficiary of aid policies or agreements of Australia, Japan, and the US.

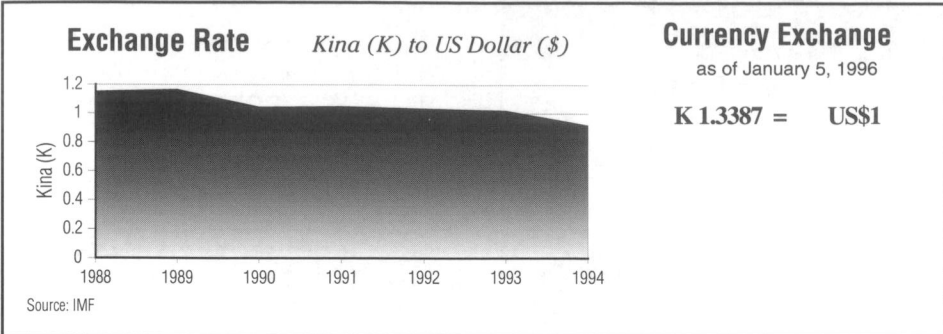

Exchange Rate *Kina (K) to US Dollar ($)*

Kina (K)

1988 1989 1990 1991 1992 1993 1994

Source: IMF

Currency Exchange
as of January 5, 1996

K 1.3387 = US$1

Currency

The currency in use is the Papua New Guinea kina (K), which is divided into 100 toea.

Foreign Exchange

All exchange policy is controlled by the Bank of Papua New Guinea under the Central Banking (Foreign Exchange and Gold) Regulations. Policy is administered by the government with the advice of the Bank of Papua New Guinea and the Ministry of Finance. A considerable amount of exchange control has been delegated to commercial banks. Nonresidents can open accounts at any authorized foreign exchange dealer (at present, the five commercial banks) with any amount of currency, foreign or domestic.

Capital Transfers

Any amount of foreign currency can be brought in or taken out, but no more than US$120 in notes can be transferred. In most cases, invisible payments are approved as long as supporting documents are produced. Payments for foreign debt servicing can be approved without a fixed limit set by authorized dealers. Approval is required for foreign currency proceeds, except for their retention, or for their sale to an authorized dealer in Papua New Guinea.

Investment Incentives

Some incentives include an export-income incentive; a pioneer-industries scheme; a rural-development incentive; a wage subsidy; tax relief for staff training costs; and import-duty exemptions and drawbacks. All of these incentives are subject to certain conditions, and a local law or accountancy firm should be consulted.

Investment Restrictions

There have been several reports charging corruption on the part of the decision makers. Some companies have reported delays in receiving investment incentives and/or approvals. Taxable income is usually much higher for nonresident companies, particularly outside of the mining or petroleum sectors.

TAXATION

Taxation requires sophisticated knowledge of complex rules and regulations specific to each country. The information presented here is from the Ernst & Young Corporate Tax Guide and Directory, available from the Ernst & Young accounting office in your country, or from:

Ernst & Young
Mail Address:
P.O. Box 112
Port Moresby
Papua New Guinea

At a Glance

Corporate Income Tax Rate (%) (a)	25
Capital Gains Tax Rate (%)	0
Branch Tax Rate (%)	48
Withholding Tax (%)	
Dividends	17
Interest (b)	48
Management and Administrative Fees	17
Royalties Various (c)	
Contract Payments to Nonresidents (d)	12
Branch Remittance Tax	0
Net Operating Losses (Years)	
Carryback	0
Carryforward (e)	7

(a) Mining companies and petroleum and gas companies are taxed at higher rates. An additional profits tax is imposed on certain large mining, petroleum and gas projects.
(b) Applicable to payments to nonresidents. With tax planning, this tax can be bypassed. Certain interest is exempt from tax.
(c) The lesser of 10% of the gross royalty or 48% of taxable income; related parties taxed at 30% of the gross payment.
(d) Effective rate.
(e) Certain companies may carry forward losses indefinitely.

Money Matters

BITS AND PIECES

- **Corporate income tax** Resident companies are subject to income tax based on worldwide income. Nonresident companies are subject to a tax based only on their income and profits from Papua New Guinea.
- **Capital gains tax** Capital gains are not subject to tax in Papua New Guinea.
- **Foreign tax relief** A credit for foreign taxes paid is permitted up to the amount of Papua New Guinea tax payable on the foreign income.
- **Capital transfers** All outward transfers of capital are allowed, as long as tax clearance certificates are produced.
- **Gold** There are no regulations for dealings of gold.
- **Import payments** Authorized dealers can approve applications for imports that don't have quotas or licensing regulation imposed. Import tariffs can range from zero to 50 percent, depending on the necessity of the item. In the event of shortages on the domestic market, all imports are subject to a 50 percent tariff.
- **Export payments** Proceeds from exports can be received in any foreign currency. All payments for exports must be received within six months and all proceeds must be sold to the Bank of Papua New Guinea or an authorized dealer in Papua New Guinea. Most export duties have been waived, except for exports of forestry products and fish. Export taxes for forestry products range from 13 to 33 percent, and any exports of fish are subject to a 10 percent tax.

BANKS

Bank of Papua New Guinea
Douglas Street
PO Box 121
Port Moresby
Tel: 212999
Fax: 211617

Australia and New Zealand Banking Group Ltd.
2nd Floor, Defens Haus
Cnr of Champion Parade and Hunter St.
POB 1152
Port Moresby
Tel: 217544
Fax: 211462

Bank of South Pacific Ltd.
Douglas St.
POB 173
Port Moresby
Tel: 212444
Fax: 217302

Indosuez Niugini Bank Ltd.
Burns House
Champion Parade
POB 1390
Port Moresby
Tel: 213533
Fax: 213115

Niugini-Lloyds International Bank Ltd.
POB 336
Port Moresby
Tel: 213111
Fax: 213141

Papua New Guinea Banking Corporation
Cnr of Douglas and Musgrave Sts.
POB 78
Port Moresby
Tel: 211999
Fax: 211683

Westpac Bank - PNG - Ltd.
5th Floor, Mogoru Motu Bldg.
Champion Parade
POB 706
Port Moresby
Tel: 220800
Fax: 213367

Agricultural Bank of Papua New Guinea
POB 6310
Boroko
Tel: 247500
Fax: 259817

Overview

Papua New Guinea is a small market, with little spending capital. Only 15 percent of the population live in the cities, but it is best to center any marketing campaigns in the cities nonetheless. That is where most of the country's consumers are found. In addition, the vast majority of business takes place there, and it is difficult to reach the inland areas of the country.

Distribution and Agents

All the major population centers—Lae, Madang, Rabaul, and Port Moresby (the capital)—are ports of entry. There are few reliable roads or navigable waterways into the interior, so local retailers and wholesalers dominate distribution from each city. Papua New Guinea law does not require a foreign company to hire an agent or distributor. However, a local agent is greatly helpful in clearing goods through customs. Another consideration is the requirement that foreign enterprises must submit a training strategy showing which positions nationals would take over from expatriates within the first three years; well-connected agents can provide advice on this process. Incorporated companies, partnerships, sole proprietors, joint ventures, and branch offices are all familiar forms in PNG, though the government favors joint ventures.

Advertising

The Post and Telecommunications Company of Papua New Guinea operates air and surface mail within Papua New Guinea and outside the country to the rest of the world. It also maintains a telecommunications system. Newspaper and radio broadcasting facilities are available, although newspaper circulation is low and radio set ownership is undetermined. It is best to acquire a local advertising agent for help navigating through Papua New Guinea's bureaucracy. There are two daily newspapers: the *Niugini Nius* and *Papua New Guinea Post Courier*, both published in English. Distribution is slow and some towns receive papers two to three days after the original publication date but both papers do accept advertising. There is one general trade publication, *Papua New Guinea Trade Monthly*, distributed free to all businesses who request it.

Greetings and Courtesies

PNG is a young country (granted independence from Australia only in 1975) and its friendly, open people have a positive attitude. The standard greeting is shaking hands. Papua New Guineans are polite but generally informal, and move to a first-name basis rather quickly.

Business Ethic and Framework

PNG is a leisured society. Its people are by no means lazy, but they believe that there are more important things in life than work and they are generally happy with what they have. Papua New Guineans expect visitors to be punctual, but will themselves be late for appointments. This is especially true of government officials. Many Papua New Guineans have a very casual attitude about time, and will often speak in terms of "PNG time." If operating on PNG time, expect meetings to start later than scheduled. Once started, they will proceed at a relaxed pace.

Meetings and Decision Making

Things do not happen quickly here. Accept this easy rhythm and adjust to it. There is no stock exchange in PNG and if a venture requires financing from a bank, additional time will be required while the necessary approvals are obtained. In addition, this small country has a rather complex political structure, and a bureaucracy that can slow down what appears to be the simplest project.

Women

Foreign women will be dealt with as they are in other Pacific cultures. They can expect to be treated with respect and taken seriously. They are not yet prevalent in the upper echelons of either business or government. Foreign businesswomen may actually have some advantage here; South Pacific males tend to be somewhat intimidated by executive women and might negotiate their preferences vigorously.

Marketing in Papua New Guinea

MARKETING TIPS

- **Trade news** 1995 revealed improved import and export monitoring. Tax collection was also emphasized.
- **Mail and facsimile machines** The post office is reliable but slow. Fax machines are becoming more popular throughout the country and are used regularly for marketing.
- **Trade stores** One kind of retail organization peculiar to the South Pacific, and especially popular in Papua New Guinea, is the trade store. Some trade stores buy as well as sell goods; others are simply retail outlets, selling the kind of goods most sought by villagers.
- **Market segmentation** Because of the wide dispersion of the centers of population and the difficulty of overland communication, it may be convenient to consider PNG as a number of separate markets.

Cultural Cautions

DO'S

- Papua New Guinea is an informal society, but do not take this as a given. In social and business situations, follow your host's lead in determining the level of formality—or lack of it.
- Papua New Guineans are polite people and value this quality in others. Always be polite and show people the respect to which they are entitled.

DON'TS

- Don't be in a hurry to conduct your business and go home. Papua New Guineans are a relaxed people and do not appreciate being rushed by foreigners.
- Do not travel with any material that might be considered erotic (even if it is not viewed as erotic by the standards of your country). Such material is frowned upon and will be confiscated if discovered.

CUSTOMS

- Business cards are exchanged when first meeting someone. There are no special rituals involved with this exchange, but when presented with a card do not just put it in your pocket. Take a moment to give the card a polite response.
- If invited to an associate's home, a gift is in order. Appropriate gifts include flowers, a box of chocolates, or a bottle of wine.

OBSERVATIONS

- Alcohol is common, but many Papua New Guineans are Seventh Day Adventists who do not drink alcohol. Be aware of this at occasions where alcohol is present.
- Taxis are generally poorly maintained and expensive, and walking in urban areas at night can involve risk.
- Business attire is generally casual but neat. For men, pants and a short sleeved shirt will suffice. Women should wear a dress or blouse and skirt.

NEGOTIATIONS

- If you are dealing with government agencies, it is advisable to make your initial contacts through the Investment Promotion Authority (Tel: 25-8777; Fax: 25-8770).
- Sometimes politicians or government officials offer deals that seem too good to be true. They generally are. Do not take such promises seriously, as they seldom become reality.
- Papua New Guineans are a leisured people. Adjust to this rhythm. If they sense you are in a hurry to complete your business and get on with other things, they might use this to their advantage.

GOVERNMENT AGENCIES

Ministry for Administrative Services
PO Box 1207
Boroko
Tel: 272525
Telex: 22144

Ministry for Agriculture and Livestock
PO Box 417
Konedobu
Tel: 213002, 277512
Fax: 211337, 211387

Ministry for Education
P.S.A. Haus, Waigani
Independence Drive
Private Mail Bag
Boroko
Tel: 272342, 276111
Fax: 254648, 257965

Ministry for Environment and Conservation
Central Government Offices
Post Office, Wards Strip
Waigani
Tel: 271788, 271682, 271692
Fax: 271900, 271077

Ministry of Finance and Planning
Central government Offices
Post Office, Wards Strip
Waigani
Tel: 252372
Fax: 213826

Ministry for Fisheries and Marine Resources
PO Box 165
Konedobu
Tel: 211792, 271799
Fax: 214369, 213696

Ministry for Foreign Affairs
Central Government Offices
Post Office, Wards Strip
Waigani
Tel: 271311
Fax: 254467

Ministry of Forests
PO Box 5055
Boroko
Tel: 277800
Fax: 254433

Ministry for Health
PO Box 3991
Boroko
Tel: 248600/1, 248666
Fax: 213821

Ministry for Labor and Employment
PO Box 5644
Boroko
Tel: 277529, 277591, 272200
Fax: 257092

Ministry for Public Services
Central Government Offices
3rd Floor, Morauta House
PO Box 6969
Waigani
Boroko
Tel: 271799, 276758
Telex: 22144

Ministry for Trade and Industry
Central Government Offices
Post Office, Wards Strip
Waigani
Tel: 271115, 271094
Fax: 271750

Ministry for Transport
PO Box 457
Konedobu
Tel: 222524
Fax: 21730

Ministry for Works
PO Box 1108
Boroko
Tel: 241124
Fax: 241182

INVESTMENT AND TRADE PROMOTION

Investment Promotion Authority
PO Box 5053
Boroko
Tel: 217311
Fax: 212819

Bougainville Copper Ltd.
Panguna
Tel: 972800
Fax: 972988

Cocoa Board of Papua New Guinea
POB 532
Rabaul
Tel: 921354
Fax: 921794

Commonwealth Development Corp.
Office of the Representative for PNG and the Pacific Islands
POB 907
Port Moresby
Tel: 212944
Fax: 212867

Copra Marketing Board of Papua New Guinea
Port Moresby
Telex: 22135

Investment Corporation of Papua New Guinea
Hunter St.
POB 155
Port Moresby
Tel: 212855
Fax: 211240

Niugini Produce Marketing Pty. Ltd.
POB 1811
Lae
Telex: 42409

CHAMBERS OF COMMERCE

Papua New Guinea Chamber of Commerce and Industry
POB 1621
Port Moresby
Tel: 213057
Fax: 214203

Port Moresby Chamber of Commerce and Industry
POB 1764
Port Moresby
Tel: 213077
Fax 214203

FREIGHT COMPANIES

Century Group of Companies
Champion Parade
POB 1403
Port Moresby
Tel: 229234
Fax: 229251

Morehead Shipping Proprietary Ltd.
POB 1908
Lae
Tel: 423602

LEGAL CONTACTS

Allens Arthur Robinson
Level 11
Pacific Place
CNR Musgrave Street & Champion Parade
Port Moresby
Tel: 202 000
Fax: 200 588

Blake Dawson Waldron
Mogoru Moto Building
Champion Parade
P.O. Box 850
Port Moresby
Tel: 21 1977
Fax: 21 2630

Gadens Ridgeway
Pacific Place
CNR Musgrave Street & Champion Parade
P.O. Box 1042
Port Moresby
Tel: 21-1033
Fax: 21-1885

NEWSPAPERS AND PERIODICALS

Post Courier
PO Box 85
Port Moresby

Niugini Nius
PO Box 3019
Boroko, NCD

The Times of Papua New Guinea
PO Box 1982
Boroko, NCD

Papua New Guinea Trade Monthly
PO Box 1982
Boroko, NCD

Arawa Bulletin
POB 86
Arawa
North Solomons Province
Tel: 951028
Fax: 952402

Foreign Affairs Review
Dept. of Foreign Affairs, Central Govt. Offices
Kumul Ave
Post Office, Wards Strip
Waigani
Tel: 271260
Telex: 22136
Fax: 254886

Wantok
POB 1982
Boroko
Tel: 252500
Tax: 252579

Ailans Nius
POB 1239
Rabaul

Education Gazette
Dept. of Education
PSA Haus
Boroko
Tel: 272413
Telex: 22193
Fax: 254648

RADIO AND TELEVISION

Media Niugini Pty. Ltd.
POB 443
Boroko
Tel: 257322
Fax: 254450

National Broadcasting Commission of PNG
PO Box 1359
Boroko, NCD

EM-TV
PO Box 443
Boroko, NCD

INTERNET ADDRESSES

City Net - Papua New Guinea
http://www.city.net/countries/papua_new_guinea/

Paraguay

Republic of Paraguay

Economy

Overview

Paraguay has a predominantly agricultural economy with a thriving commercial sector. Although the country has vast hydroelectric potential (including the world's largest hydroelectric generation facility at the Itaipu dam), it lacks significant mineral or petroleum resources. Paraguay has a relatively open market economy; the government allows the free importation of most goods and services but it also plays a major role in the economy—the total public sector budget represents close to 50 percent of GDP. The government has recently reduced its expenditures in an effort to curb inflation, and this has already had a positive impact on economic growth.

Trade

The importation of most goods and services is relatively free, which has encouraged the development of a huge commercial sector based on the importation of goods from the Far East and the US for re-export to neighboring countries. Paraguay's import market is larger than appears in the official records, and includes significant informal and underground commercial activities. Its largest trading partners are Brazil and Argentina, upon whom it is heavily reliant, and its foreign trade is subject to some extent on economic conditions and exchange rate movements in these countries.

Sectors

Agriculture Agriculture, concentrated largely in soybeans, cotton, cattle, and timber, represents 27 percent of GDP. Production is vulnerable to the vagaries of weather and the fortunes and misfortunes of the Argentine and Brazilian economies. Over 200,000 families depend on subsistence farming.

Industry Industry is not a fast-growing sector in Paraguay. Most industries concentrate on production of light consumer goods for the domestic market.

Services Official service industries represent about one third of GDP and adequately serve the domestic market. The lack of modern technology and sophisticated financial services, however, is currently limiting growth of this sector.

The underground economy The underground economy, which is not included in the national accounts, is concentrated in the unregistered sale of imported goods, including computers, sound equipment, cameras, liquor, and cigarettes across the border to Argentina and Brazil. These transactions are estimated to generate between 6,000 billion and 14,000 billion guarani (US$ three to seven billion) per year, or over 50 percent of the official GDP.

Trends

The current government has pledged to continue and strengthen the market-based economic reforms initiated in 1989. Despite high-level support within the government, opposition from many parts of society long accustomed to a large public sector still work to stall further privatization. Paraguay's economy, with its established export industries of soybeans, cotton, cattle, timber, electricity, and the lucrative business of re-exporting products, remains vulnerable to the fortunes and misfortunes of the Argentine and Brazilian economies. It will have to overcome this heavy reliance by broadening its base of export markets in order to maintain steady economic growth over the long term.

At a Glance

THE COUNTRY

Location Central South America, between Argentina and Brazil.
Terrain Grassy plains and wooded hills east of Rio Paraguay; Gran Chaco region west of Rio Paraguay mostly low, marshy plain near the river, and dry forest and thorny scrub elsewhere.
Climate Varies from temperate in east to semiarid in far west.

THE PEOPLE

Population 5,200,000
Ethnic composition
Mestizo (Spanish and Indian) 95%
White and Indian 5%
Religious composition
Roman Catholic 90%
There are also several Mennonite and other Protestant denominations.
Languages spoken Spanish (official), Guarani.
Education and literacy Paraguay maintains a well developed educational system, with the result that its literacy rate is high by South American standards.
Labor force
Total..1,700,000

COUNTRY FACTS

Political and legal system Paraguay is divided into 17 regions, each headed by a popularly elected governor. Its legal system is based on Argentine codes, Roman law, and French codes; the Supreme Court of Justice is the highest legal body and is independent from other branches of government, although members of the Supreme Courts are selected by the Senate and the president. Paraguay does not accept compulsory ICJ jurisdiction.
Telephones Meager telephone service hampers business. The principal switching center is in Asunción. International country code: [595] Selected city codes: Asunción (21), Concepcion (31).
Transportation Inadequate transportation facilities have been a major problem to Paraguay's development. There are more than 28,000 kilometers of highway, but only 2,600 are paved. Waterways are the chief means of transportation, but the cost is high; most riverboats are owned by the Paraguayan government. Often drought conditions affect navigation.
Environment Deforestation is a major problem, creating a loss of soil through erosion. Water pollution is also a problem; 49 percent of the city dwellers and 91 percent of the rural people do not have pure water. Current issues include deforestation, water pollution, and inadequate means for waste disposal, which present some health hazards for many urban residents.
Media There are 79,000 telephones (16 telephones per 1,000 persons), 40 AM, no FM, and seven short-wave radio broadcast stations. Paraguay has five TV stations.
Health Hospital and medical facilities are generally located in the larger towns. Approximately 60 percent of Paraguayans get medical care. Average life expectancy is 67 years.

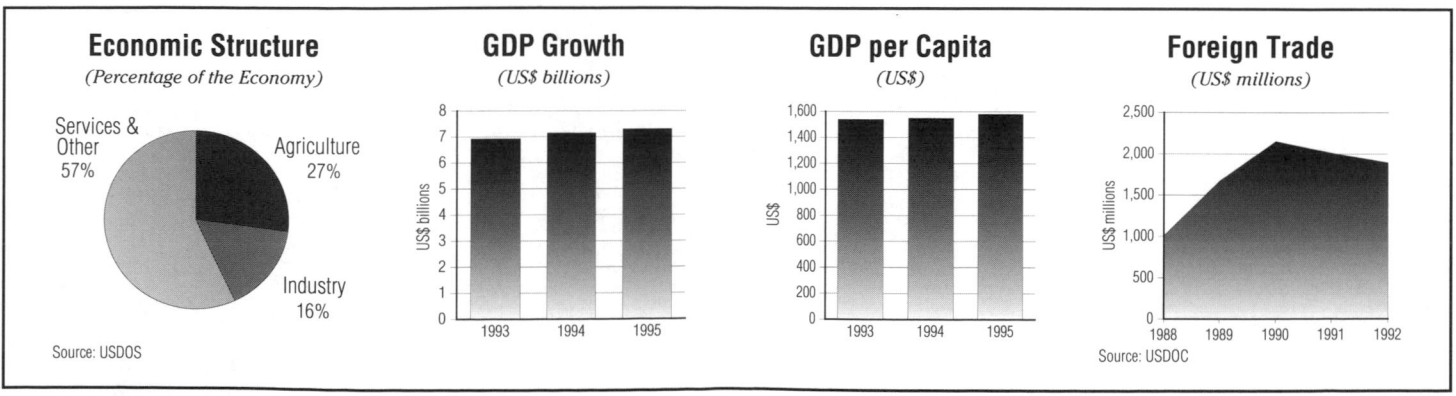

Economic Structure
(Percentage of the Economy)

Services & Other 57%
Agriculture 27%
Industry 16%

Source: USDOS

GDP Growth
(US$ billions)

1993, 1994, 1995

GDP per Capita
(US$)

1993, 1994, 1995

Foreign Trade
(US$ millions)

1988 1989 1990 1991 1992

Source: USDOC

Business Travel

LH 1906	MADRID	945	113-3	
LH 1022	STUTTGART HBF.	935		
AF 1701	LYON	940	683-6	
AY 822	HELSINKI	940	113-3	
AA 071	SFRANCISCO-DALLAS	945	731-7	

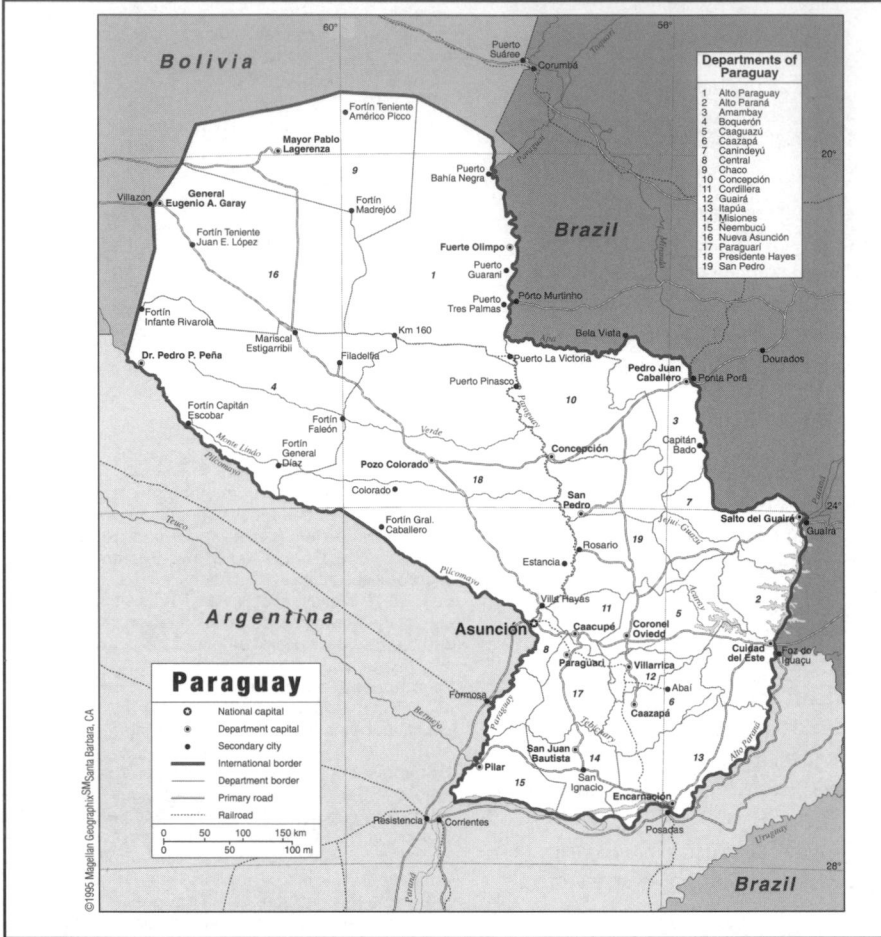

Departments of Paraguay
1 Alto Paraguay
2 Alto Paraná
3 Amambay
4 Boquerón
5 Caaguazú
6 Caazapá
7 Canindeyú
8 Central
9 Chaco
10 Concepción
11 Cordillera
12 Guairá
13 Itapúa
14 Misiones
15 Neembucú
16 Nueva Asunción
17 Paraguarí
18 Presidente Hayes
19 San Pedro

COMMUNICATIONS

Telephones For telecommunications, a good direct dial system does exist with adequate international and national service. Fiber optic cables link connections to operators in the US and Japan. Overseas credit card calls are less expensive than paying through hotels or locally. Public phones can be difficult to come across; major hotels are more apt to these accommodations. Cellular phones are used often in Paraguay.
Fax Services for faxing are available at major hotels.
Post office Register all important mail. Although regular mail is inexpensive to send, it is unreliable.

BEST TRAVEL BOOKS

Argentina, Uruguay and Paraguay, including the Falkland Islands. Lonely Planet Travel Survival Kit. Background on politics and culture. Thousands of places to stay and eat for all budgets. Full travel details including health, visas, and transport. Spanish language sections.
Multinational Travel Companion Executive. Twenty third edition. Travel tips world-wide. Strand Publishing Company, Inc.
South American Handbook. Chicago: Passport Books. Updated annually.

NATIONAL TOURIST OFFICE

Dirección General de Turismo
Ministerio de Obras Publicas y Comunicaciones
Palma 468, Asunción
Tel: (21) 44-1530
Fax: (21) 49-1230
Telex: 162

TELEPHONE NUMBERS

If you are calling from outside Paraguay, you will need to add the country code [595] and any other international dialing requirements from within your country.
- US Embassy/Asunción..........................(21) 213-715
- Automóvil Club ....(21) 24366
- Fundación Moisés Bertoni ....(21) 2386
- Ministry of Agriculture ....(21) 44-5214
- Camara de Exportodores ....(21) 490291
- Centro de Importadores ....(21) 490291
- Ministerio de Industria ....(21) 204833

Credit Card Information
Lost or stolen credit cards (call collect to the US, regardless of which country the card was issued in).
- Amex..[1] (919) 333-3211
- Diner's Club...............................[1] (303) 799-1504
- MasterCard ....[1] (314) 275-6690
- Visa ....[1] (410) 581-7931

Travelogue

WORKWEEK

Offices Monday-Friday 8:00 am to noon and 1:00 pm to 5:00 pm.
Banks Monday-Friday 9:00 am to 3:00 pm.
Government Monday-Friday 9:00 am to 5:00 pm.
Retail Monday-Friday 7:00 am to noon, closed between noon and 3:00 pm and opened again from 3:00 pm until 7:00 or 8:00 pm. Saturday hours are usually 7:00 am until noon.
During the summer, business hours often open and close earlier due to the extreme heat in the afternoons.

HOLIDAYS

Holidays 1996
January 1 New Years
March 1 Heroes' Day
April 4 Holy Thursday
May 1 Labor Day
May 15 Independence Day
June 12 Chaco Armistice
August 15 Founding of Asunción
December 8 Virgin of Caacupe Day
December 25 Christmas Day

VISA AND PASSPORT

Passports are required for entry into the country. Visas are not required for stays up to three months. A renewable temporary residence document is valid for one year. Identity documents issued in Paraguay are based on temporary residence. Travelers under 20 years of age with one parent or a third party must have written authorization from absent parent(s) for travel. This document must be notarized, authenticated by the Paraguayan embassy or consulate, and translated into Spanish. A passport is required. US citizens do not need visas for a three-month stay. A temporary residence visa can be obtained in Paraguay. The temporary residence document is valid for one year and is renewable. The Paraguayan identity document can be obtained based on the temporary residence. Passports are needed for cashing traveler's checks, at military and police checkpoints and for checking into hotels; carry yours with you at all times.

DEPARTURE FORMALITIES

Personal effects such as alcohol and tobacco are allowed to be taken out of Paraguay in limited quantities. Customs officials process papers and check cars sporadically at overland crossings.

IMMUNIZATION

Preventive measures against cholera are recommended. Malaria and diptheria is reported in some areas.

TIPPING

Tipping is sometimes included on the tab, but be sure to check. If it is not included, something extra is expected. Taxi cab drivers usually are not tipped.

CRIME

Street crimes of pickpocketing and mugging do occur in urban areas at night near hotels and airports. There are reported incidents of theft from checked airline baggage. Travelers are advised to keep valuables in carry-on luggage. Immediately report the loss or theft of a passport to local police or the nearest consulate or embassy. Woman should avoid eye contact with men.

INFRASTRUCTURE

In Asunción, taxis are common and recommended for business use. The bus system is available but generally inadequate. Hotels are comfortable and reasonable. Tap water is not acceptable outside of Asunción. Tourist facilities are generally unacceptable in other cities and remote areas. Telecommunications for national and international services are adequate, with a direct dial system available, fax services and cellular telephone are also available.

Foreign Trade

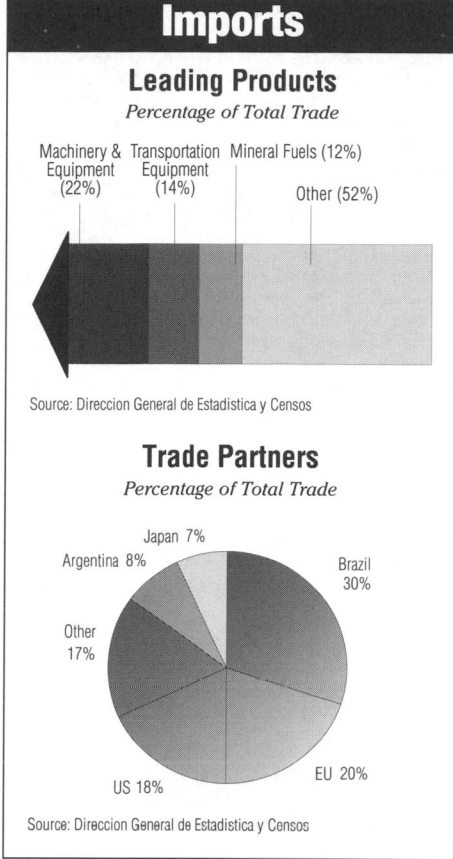

Imports

Leading Products
Percentage of Total Trade

Machinery & Equipment (22%)
Transportation Equipment (14%)
Mineral Fuels (12%)
Other (52%)

Source: Direccion General de Estadistica y Censos

Trade Partners
Percentage of Total Trade

Japan 7%
Argentina 8%
Other 17%
US 18%
EU 20%
Brazil 30%

Source: Direccion General de Estadistica y Censos

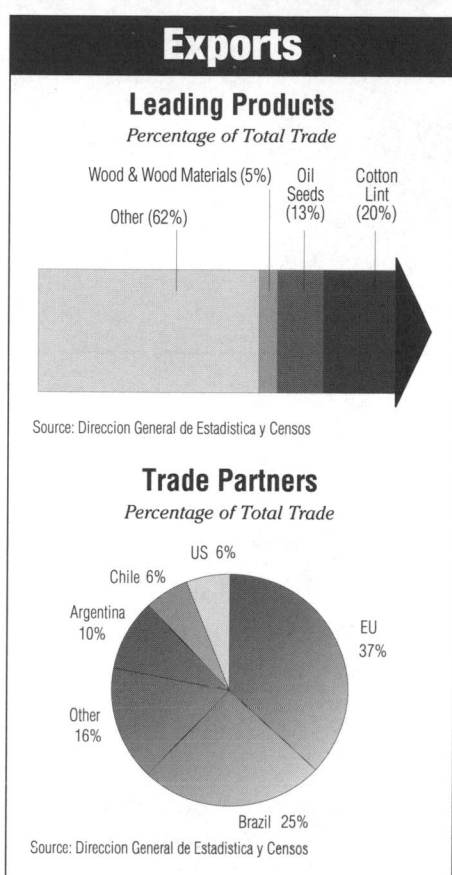

Exports

Leading Products
Percentage of Total Trade

Wood & Wood Materials (5%)
Other (62%)
Oil Seeds (13%)
Cotton Lint (20%)

Source: Direccion General de Estadistica y Censos

Trade Partners
Percentage of Total Trade

US 6%
Chile 6%
Argentina 10%
Other 16%
EU 37%
Brazil 25%

Source: Direccion General de Estadistica y Censos

Opportunities

FOR IMPORTING TO PARAGUAY
- automobiles and machinery
- electronics and consumer goods
- fuels & lubricants

FOR EXPORTING FROM PARAGUAY
- cotton
- lumber
- soybeans, meat and meat products, vegetable oil

GROWTH SECTORS
- transportation/communication
- construction
- commerce and finance
- commercial sector
- underground re-export sector

Trade News

RULES AND REGULATIONS

- **Trade news** The relatively low import tariffs traditionally maintained by Paraguay have encouraged the development of a huge commercial sector based on the importation of goods from the Far East and the US for re-export to neighboring countries. Paraguay enjoys a lucrative business of re-exporting products made elsewhere such as computers, sound equipment, cameras, liquor, and cigarettes; much of it unregistered. Paraguayans prefer Imported goods, and local industry relies on imported capital goods.
- **Import taxes and tariffs** Raw material: zero percent; capital goods: five percent; cigarettes and alcoholic beverages: 10 percent. Fifteen to 20 percent tariff rates are applied to cars depending on their customs assessment value. Automobiles valued above US$20,000 pay the highest rate.

Legal

Legal System

Paraguay is a civil code country, with a judicial system independent from the other government branches.

Intellectual Property Protection

Patents and Trademarks Patents last for 15 years and are subject to an annual tax. All patent transfers must be recorded in the Patent Office with a notary public's stamp of approval. Trademark protection is for 10 years but can be renewed indefinitely on payment of proper fees. Foreign trademarks must be recorded.

Copyrights All copyrights must be registered in Paraguay to be considered valid. The registry publishes each registration for five days in local newspapers. Certificates for registration are available in local newspapers or from the Ministry of Registry.

Business Registration

Shareholders must create and sign a notary public-approved contract. They also have to register with the Public Registry of Commerce, which requires prior governmental authorization.

Contracts and Dispute Resolution

The form and nature of contracts in Paraguay is governed by civil code. Verbal contracts are legally binding. Parties may freely determine their rights in contracts subject to compliance with mandatory laws. Contracts must be interpreted and performed in good faith. Disputes are handled by Paraguayan courts or by arbitration if the parties have agreed.

Labor

Wages may be freely set but cannot be less than the legal minimum wage, set by the Labor Department and based on cost of living studies. By law, work weeks are limited to a fixed number of hours.

Legal Matters

LEGAL BRIEFS

- **Public copyrights** Any works made by public officials or private sector employees related to their employment belong to the state or employer.
- **Corporation prospectus** A corporation prospectus must be rendered as a public instrument, registered, and published three times in an important local newspaper.
- **Corporate directors** Directors do not need to be shareholders. They are elected at a shareholders' general meeting for a term of one fiscal year, unless the corporation's bylaws state otherwise.
- **Workers' bonuses** Employees who have worked for at least one full year with the same employer are entitled to receive additional annual pay in an amount equivalent to one month's salary.
- **Import/export documentation** Operations must be processed through authorized banks and supervised by the Central Bank of Paraguay. Documents required for imports are: import statement issued by the bank; commercial invoice issued by the seller of merchandise; certificate of origin of the merchandise; Paraguayan consular invoice; and bill of lading.
- **Minimum age requirements** The right to work is acquired at age 18. Children between ages 12 and 18 may be able to work, but legal limits are set on the type of work they are permitted to do and the hours they are allowed to work.
- **Trade secrets** Paraguay's laws on trade secrets and penalties for violations are rarely enforced.
- **International agreements** Paraguay is a member of OAS and Inter-American Convention on International Commercial Arbitration.

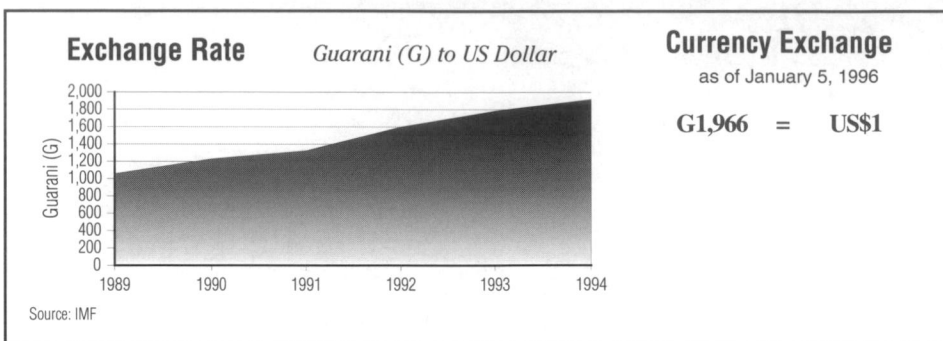

Exchange Rate *Guarani (G) to US Dollar*

Guarani (G): 2,000 / 1,800 / 1,600 / 1,400 / 1,200 / 1,000 / 800 / 600 / 400 / 200 / 0

1989 1990 1991 1992 1993 1994

Source: IMF

Currency Exchange
as of January 5, 1996

G1,966 = US$1

Currency

The currency of Paraguay is the Paraguayan guaraní (G).

Foreign Exchange

The Central Bank of Paraguay has the authority to determine foreign currency exchange policy, with help from other technical agencies within the Government. Most policies are created by the Economic Cabinet on the advice of the Central Bank.

Capital Currencies

Any amount of currency can be brought in or taken out of Paraguay. All invisibles payments are carried out by authorized commercial banks or exchange houses without restriction. A 2.5 percent value-added tax is levied on international transport tickets issued in the country. There are no requirements for invisibles proceeds, except foreign exchange inflows that have to be transferred to the Central Bank.

Investment Incentives

Paraguay is very open to foreign investment. There are no restrictions on foreign investment, except in some areas reserved for government monopolies. These sectors are closed to both foreign and domestic investors. The government also maintains price controls on some items it feels are necessary to public welfare. There is no legal difference between resident and nonresident investors. All corporate incomes are subject to a 30 percent tax rate, but as a further incentive to investment, the income tax on reinvestment profits has been reduced to 10 percent. There are currently no performance requirements for investors in Paraguay. Transfers must be channeled through the commercial banks or exchange houses.

Investment Restrictions

Paraguay's registration procedure is very bureaucratic and can take months to complete. Voting board members of companies incorporated in Paraguay are required to have local residency, which sometimes acts as an impediment to foreign investment.

TAXATION

Taxation requires sophisticated knowledge of complex rules and regulations specific to each country. The information presented here is from the Ernst & Young Corporate Tax Guide and Directory, available from the Ernst & Young accounting office in your country, or from:

Ernst & Young - Paraguay
Mail Address:
Casilla de Correos 2295
Asunción, Paraguay
Street Address:
Edificio Interexpress
Luis Alberto de Herrera 195
Piso 17, Office 1701
Asunción, Paraguay
Tel: (21) 495-581, 447-529
Fax: (21) 447-529

At a Glance

Corporate Income Tax Rate (%)	30
Capital Gains Tax Rate (%)	30
Branch Tax Rate (%)	35
Withholding Tax (%)*	
Dividends	5

Interest	17.5
Royalties from Patents, Know-how, etc.	17.5
Gross Income from Production and Distribution of Films and TV Programs	14
Gross Revenue of International News Agencies	5.25
Gross Income from a Concession on the use of Containers	5.25
Gross Proceeds from Sales of Tickets, Radiograms, etc.	3.5
Insurance or Reinsurance Premiums	3.5
Gross Revenue from International Shipping	3.5
Other Income on Which no Specific Withholding Tax is Imposed	35
Net Operating Losses (Years)	
Carryback	0
Carryforward	3

* The rates shown are the effective rates. These effective rates are calculated by applying a 35% income tax rate to an assured net profit. For example, the assumed net profit on interest payments is 50%, and consequently, the effective withholding rate on such payments is 17.5% (35% x 50%). The withholding taxes are final taxes imposed on payments out of Paraguay to nonresidents. Nonresident corporations are corporations not incorporated in Paraguay.

Money Matters

BITS AND PIECES

- **Corporate income tax** Companies are subject to corporate tax based on the income earned in Paraguay only. The corporate income tax rate is 30 percent for resident companies and 35 percent for nonresident companies (including a five percent tax on remittances by branches to their head office).
- **Income** Taxable income is based on profits from the financial statements after tax adjustments.
- **Export payments** Exporters must be registered at the Central Bank, and all proceeds must be collected within 120 days and sold to authorized banks.
- **Import payments** There is a five percent tariff imposed on capital goods and a ten percent tariff imposed on consumer goods. Automobiles are taxed between 15 and 20 percent. Restrictions can from time to time be imposed on any import to protect domestic businesses from unfair competition.
- **Foreign investment treatment** National treatment of foreign investors is guaranteed by law, as is full repatriation of capital and profits.
- **Tax burden** Paraguay's tax burden is among the lowest in South America, with no personal income tax, limited business taxes, and a 10-percent value-added tax.
- **Transfers policies** In addition to there being no restrictions on conversion or transfer of foreign currency, the government also permits foreign currency contracts and business transactions in foreign currencies.

BANKS

Bapsa
(Banco AlemanParaguayo S.A.)
Casilla Postal 1426
Calle Estrella 505
Asunción
Tel: (21) 490166/7 Fax: (21) 447645

Bancopar
(Banco Comercial Paraguayo)
Casilla Postal 2350
Avenida Mariscal Lopez 780
Asunción
Tel: (21) 606450, 607364 Fax: (21) 6066690

Banco de Asunción S.A.
Casilla Postal 623
Calle Palma y 14 de Mayo
Asunción
Tel: (21) 493191/2 Fax: (21) 493190

Banco General S.A.
Casilla Postal 325
Calle Chile y Haedo
Asunción
Tel: (21) 496815/6 Fax: (21) 496822

Banco Nacional de Trabajadores
Casilla Postal 1822
Calle 15 de Agosto 629
Asunción
Tel: (21) 492214 Fax: (21) 448327

Banco Sudameris Paraguay S.A.
Casilla Postal 1043
Calle Independencia Nacional y Cerro Cora
Asunción
Tel: (21) 444172/3, 494542 Fax: (21) 498187

Banco Union S.A.
Casilla Postal 726
Avenida Mariscal Lopez 3333
Asunción
Tel: (21) 606450, 607364 Fax: (21) 606669

Citibank, N.A.
Casilla Postal 1174
Calle Estrella y Chile
Asunción
Tel: (21) 494951/2 Fax: (21) 444820

Lloyd's Bank
Casilla Postal 696
Calle Palma y O'Leary
Asunción
Tel: (21) 491090/1 Fax: (21) 443569

Marketing

Overview

Paraguay is a net importer for it has no industry, virtually no minerals, and is landlocked and remote. Therefore, sellers of nearly any product may find a market in Paraguay. However, the population is small and incomes are low. Foreign sellers should therefore approach Paraguay as a developing market with future potential, rather than as an end market in itself. Foreign manufacturers or suppliers wishing to participate in government tenders must do so through their registered local representatives or attorneys. The "buy Paraguay" policy requires that all government agencies give preference to Paraguayan firms when contracting for the construction of public works or purchasing services for the public sector. Such preference in the award of bids and tenders allows a price differential of up to 15 percent.

Agents, Distributors, and Partners

Foreign firms interested in establishing operations in Paraguay should hire experienced local attorneys and private sector expertise to assist them in operating in this complex and as yet undeveloped business environment. The selection of an appropriate agent or distributor will be an important determining factor of the success of the enterprise. Many local companies, both large and small, offer specialized marketing skills to foreign companies interested in the local market.

Selling Techniques

Franchising operators are beginning to penetrate the Paraguayan market. Several foreign companies have recently granted franchising rights to local firms, mostly in the areas of fast foods and laundry services. In the past, direct marketing was a rarity but recently a few Paraguayan companies have started to use this method of reaching potential customers. Licensing agreements are widely used for the local production of international brands, especially in the production of apparel, toiletries and cosmetics, pharmaceuticals, processed foods, and audio and video recordings.

Marketing in Paraguay

MARKETING TIPS

- **Financing and credit** Offering attractive financing is important when selling to Paraguayan importers and distributors.
- **Special competitive factors** The government's "buy Paraguay" policy allows domestic firms a price differential of 15 percent on public sector contracts.
- **Special support required** Exporters to Paraguay should expect to provide substantial start-up, marketing, and service support to their agents and distributors.
- **Advertising** The development of Paraguayan advertising has progressed substantially in recent years. The greater Asunción area is by far the principal advertising center, having over one-third of the total population. The principal media for mass advertising are television and newspapers. Other widely used media include radio, billboards, signs, and direct mail. Most advertisers prefer television and newspapers for their promotional campaigns.
- **Customer service and support** The importance of customer service and product support that foreign sellers should provide to their local representatives cannot be overstated. This will initially include expenditures for Spanish language advertising and promotional materials. Even after the products have gained acceptance in the market, foreign suppliers should maintain close contact with their local representatives to keep abreast of problems, and to assess the market—periodic visits by the foreign seller will help to reinforce ties with customers in Paraguay.
- **Distribution** Paraguay does not have preferred or special marketing channels. Imported merchandise may be marketed through importers, distributors, individual dealers, or a subsidiary of the exporting company.

Business Culture

Greetings and Courtesies

Handshakes are customary among both men and women both when arriving and leaving, although there is a range of variations including nods to other men and slight bows to women. Male friends may hug; female friends may kiss each other's cheek. Business cards in Spanish are considered important, and it is a courtesy to translate other materials as well. At social events be sure to shake hands and say good-bye to everyone individually.

Business Ethic and Framework

Paraguayans are punctiliously courteous and genuinely friendly. Respect and personal dignity lie at the core of Paraguayan business and social culture, both of which are based on correct, often strongly hierarchical, but personal relationships. To Paraguayans, work is far from the most important part of life, but they do adhere strictly to the forms that govern this nevertheless important sphere. They will not hesitate, however, to break a business appointment to help out a friend or family member, and foreigners should not be irritated by this type of disruption in plans.

Meetings and Decision Making

Prior appointments are very important, and should be made two to four weeks in advance. Paraguayans are generally punctual. Authority is rather narrowly concentrated and actual decisions are almost always made at a high level. Cultivate all relationships, however. They may strongly influence the actual decision maker even when your immediate counterpart is not the one making the decision.

Women

Paraguayan women are becoming more common and more accepted in business in general, although their presence remains rare in the upper levels of business. In general, foreign businesswomen should experience few problems; some even consider it an advantage that Paraguayans dislike contradicting or offending women and may defer to them.

Cultural Cautions

DO'S

- Learn about Paraguayan history and culture—your interest will be appreciated.
- Other suitable topics of conversation include family, food, and sports.

DON'TS

- Avoid religion, race, politics, and the Paraguayan economic situation as topics of conversation.

CUSTOMS

- Foreign businesspeople hosting a business meal or other event should do so at a top hotel or restaurant.
- Foreign businessmen are expected to wear dark, conservative suits. Foreign businesswomen should wear suits or dresses. Conservative resort-type clothing is accessible for less formal social occasions.

OBSERVATIONS

- Relatively few people speak another language, and a knowledge of Spanish is quite helpful.
- Personal spacing is quite close between Paraguayans; outsiders should avoid trying to increase the space between them because this is interpreted as aloofness, disinterest, and rudeness.

NEGOTIATIONS

- Bargaining does not play the role in Paraguayan culture it does in some other Latin American countries. Paraguayans negotiate shrewdly, but generally without the gusto or flamboyance common elsewhere.
- Allow negotiations to remain open-ended, so that confrontation can be avoided and talks can be allowed to fade away if agreement cannot be reached.
- Attorneys generally review agreements—Paraguayans have historically preferred general contracts but are becoming accustomed to more detailed documents.

GOVERNMENT AGENCIES

Instituto Nacional de Tecnologia y Normalizacion
Casilla Postal 967
Avenida General Artigas y General Roa
Asunción
Tel: (21) 290266
Fax: (21) 290873

Ministerio de Agricultura y Ganaderia
Edificio Ayfra, Piso 1 & 2
Calle Presidente Franco y Ayolas
Asunción
Tel: (21) 493698, 491192

Ministerio de Industria y Comercio
Avenida Espana 323
Asunción
Tel: (21) 204833
Fax: (21) 206130

Ministerio de Obras Publicas y Comunicaciones
Calle General Diaz y Alberdi
Asunción
Tel: (21) 443473, 449785
Fax: (21) 448956

Ministerio de Salud Publica y Bienestar Social
Avenida Pettirossi y Brasil
Asunción
Tel: (21) 204601/3
Fax: (21) 207328

Proparaguay--Direccion de Promocion de Las Exportaciones e Inversiones
Casilla Postal 1772
Calle Padre Cardozo 469
Asunción
Tel: (21) 208276/7
Fax: (21) 200425

BUSINESS AND TRADE ORGANIZATIONS

Centro de Importadores
Calle Montevideo 671
Asunción
Tel: (21) 490291
Fax: (21) 441295

Feprinco
(Federacion de la Produccion, La Industria y el Comercio)
Calle Palma 751, Piso 3
Asunción
Tel/Fax: (21) 446638

UIP
(Union Industrial Paraguaya)
Casilla Postal 782
Calle Cerro Cora 1038
Asunción
Tel: (21) 212556, 212558
Fax: (21) 213360

Camara de Comercio Paraguayo-Americana
Edificio Internacional el Faro, Piso 4
Calle General Diaz 521
Asunción
Tel/Fax: (21) 442135, 442136

Camara de Exportadores
Calle Eligio Ayala 1834
Asunción
Tel: (21) 205740
Fax: (21) 25369

Camara y Bolsa de Comercio
Calle Estrella 540
Asunción
Tel: (21) 493321/2
Fax: (21) 440817

MARKET RESEARCH FIRMS

Benitez-Codas y Asociados
Edificio Inter-Express, Piso 14, Oficina 1401
Calle Herrera 195
Asunción
Tel: (21) 498120
Fax: (21) 442504

Fretes-Ventre y Asociados
Casilla Postal 843
Calle Humaita 994
Asunción
Tel: (21) 491461, 448730 Fax: (21) 493517

Monitor S.A. Consultora
Calle Mariscal Estigarribia 1731
Asunción
Tel: (21) 207391/4
Fax: (21) 207395

LEGAL CONTACTS

Fiorio & Alvarado
Mariscal Lopez Espuina Saravi
Edificio Finansud, 1st Floor
Asunción
Tel: (21) 610229
Fax: (21) 610240

Berkemeyer & Salomoni
780 Palma Street
P.O. Box 285
Asunción
Tel: (21) 443213
Fax: (21) 496179

Estudio Juridico Gross Brown
1st Floor, Benjamin Constant 624
P.O. Box 730
Asunción
Tel: (21) 494 644

Peroni, Sosa & Altamirano
Espana 2012
P.O. Box 114
Asunción
Tel: (21) 208 791

The Supreme Court
Palacio de Justicia
Asunción
Tel: (21) 84383
Telex: 290

NEWSPAPERS

ABC Color
Yegros 745
Asunción
Tel: (21) 49-1160
Telex 44076
Fax: (21) 49-3059

El Diario Noticias
Avda Artigas y Avda Brasilla Casilla
3017
Asunción
Tel: (21) 27-2721
Telex: 22922
Fax: (21) 29-2840

Hoy
Avda Meal López
2948 Asunción
Tel: (21) 60-3401
Telex: 46013
Fax: (21) 66-0385

Patria Tacuari 443 Asunción
Tel: (21) 92011

Ultima Hora
Benjamin Constant
658 Asunción
Tel: (21) 48400

INDUSTRIAL AND DEVELOPMENT GROUPS

Secretaría Técnica de Planificación de la Presidencia de la República
Iturbe 175 esp. Eligio Ayala
Asunción
Tel: (21) 44-8074
Fax: (21) 44-6493

Administración Nacional de Electricidad (ANDA)
Avda Espana 1268
Asunción
Tel: (21) 22713
Telex 142

Consejo Nacional de Coordinación Económica
Presidencia de la República
Paraguayo Independiente y Juan E. O'Leary
Asunción
Tel: (21) 29-0939

Corporación de Obras Sanitarias
José Berges 516 e/Brasil y San José
Asunción
Tel: (21) 25001
Telex: 172
Fax: (21) 21-2624

Federación de la Producción, Industria y Comercio (FEP-RINCO)
Palma 751 y 15 de Agosto
Asunción
Tel: (21) 46638

Instituto Nacional del Indígena (INDI)
Asunción
Tel: (21) 93802

Instituto de Bienestar Rural (IBR)
Tacuary 276
Asunción
Tel: (21) 43930

INTERNET ADDRESSES

Latin America - Paraguay
http://lanic.utexas.edu/la/sa/paraguay/

City Net - Paraguay
http://www.city.net/countries/paraguay/

Peru

Republic of Peru

Economy

Overview

Peru is considered an upper-middle income country. Its free market economy is dominated by the public sector, but has recently shown signs of leaning toward privatization. Peru's economy has been hurt in recent years by declining export volumes, increasing import volumes, and poor foreign relations. The main drawback to its economic development has been its heavy reliance on foreign aid, rather than the development of adequate infrastructure, to sustain its standard of living. Still, Peru has one of the largest fishing industries in the world, and its manufacturing industries are growing at a rapid pace.

Trade

Decreasing exports and increasing imports have seriously hurt the economy in recent years. In response, Peru has lowered tariffs, causing an even greater influx of cheap imported goods. Peru's trading opportunities have been seriously hindered by bad relations with many of its foreign partners; at one time or another it has had problems and conflicts with each of its neighbors. Most of Peru's exports are from its fishing industries. Peru trades mainly with the countries of Mercosur, and with the US, Germany, and Italy.

Sectors

Agriculture Agriculture makes up a good portion of Peru's economy. Almost 25 percent of its land is classified as agricultural, but only about two percent is under actual cultivation. This is mostly due to poor climate. The major portion of coastal farmland is devoted to export crops. Most farmers continue to use technology from hundreds of years ago—such as ox-drawn plows and digging sticks.

Peru ranks second only to Brazil in South America in forest resources. In addition to raw lumber, it also produces a wide range of forest products, such as rosewood oil, achiote seeds, and leche caspi, used in making chewing gum.

Peru is one of the largest fishing nations in the world, with 18 fishing ports, which are known mostly for trout.

Industry Peru's manufacturing sector—especially those industries which require little or no advanced technology, and only a minimum of skilled labor—has shown the largest gains in recent years. Particularly strong industries include textiles, food processing (primarily fish meal), paper, and cement production. Most industrial sectors, including petroleum, mining, and steel and iron production, are controlled by the state.

Services Aside from small, local commerce, service industries are not well-developed in Peru.

Trends

The sector with the most potential is the fishing industry, but this and all of Peru's industries are terribly outdated and need to become more technology driven in order to compete with other Third World powers. Peru's foreign and domestic relations have improved recently but the country continues from time to time to engage in trade disputes with its neighbors and partners. As is the case with other growing countries, Peru must develop its infrastructure and train its workers for more technically skilled labor before it can begin to move ahead in the world market.

At a Glance

THE COUNTRY

Location Western South America, bordering the South Pacific Ocean between Chile and Ecuador.
Terrain Varies; coastal plains to rugged mountains to tropical jungle forests.
Climate Coastal areas arid and mild. Temperate to frigid in mountains. Tropical in lowlands.

THE PEOPLE

Population 23,700,000
Ethnic composition
Indian 45%
Mestizo 37%
Caucasian 15%
Black, Asian, and Other 3%
Religious composition Primarily Roman Catholic.
Languages spoken Spanish is primarily used by the media, the government, and businesses, but Quechua and Aymara are also widely spoken by Indians in the Andean highlands.
Education and literacy Education is nominally free and compulsory; an estimated 82 percent of the urban population can read and write compared with 30 percent of the population living in the isolated mountainous areas. There is a national university in almost every major city but only a fraction of applicants are accepted each year.
Labor force
Total:...8,400,000
By occupation: agriculture 35%, commerce 16%, mining 12%, industry 10%, other services 27%.

COUNTRY FACTS

Political and legal Peru is a constitutional republic with a civil law system. The country is divided into 24 administrative departments and one constitutional province. Universal suffrage at age 18 and mandatory voting until age 70 (excluding military who may not vote).
Telephone Fairly adequate telephone system. There are almost 750,000 telephones in Peru, more than two-thirds of them in Lima. Telecommunications are fairly adequate for most requirements. International country code: [51]. Selected city codes: Lima (14), Callao (14), Arequipa (54).
Transportation Only about 7,500 kilometers of the almost 70,000 kilometers of roadways are paved. Inland waterways provide a great deal of transportation; the main ports are in Callao, Ilo, Iquitos, Matarani, and Talara. There are 252 airports, but only 37 have permanent-surface runways.
Environment Air and water pollution are serious problems, as are soil erosion and deforestation. While numerous measures have been enacted to protect the environment, enforcement is lax. Current issues include deforestation, overgrazing, soil erosion and desertification, and air pollution in Lima.
Media Over 140 television broadcast stations, 273 AM and no FM radio stations for 2.1 million TV sets and 5.6 million radio receivers respectively. The press is somewhat restricted in Peru.
Health Peru continues to have a high maternal mortality rate of 300 per 100,000 live births. Average life expectancy is 65 years. While the health system has made significant improvements, epidemic disease and sanitation remain serious problems.

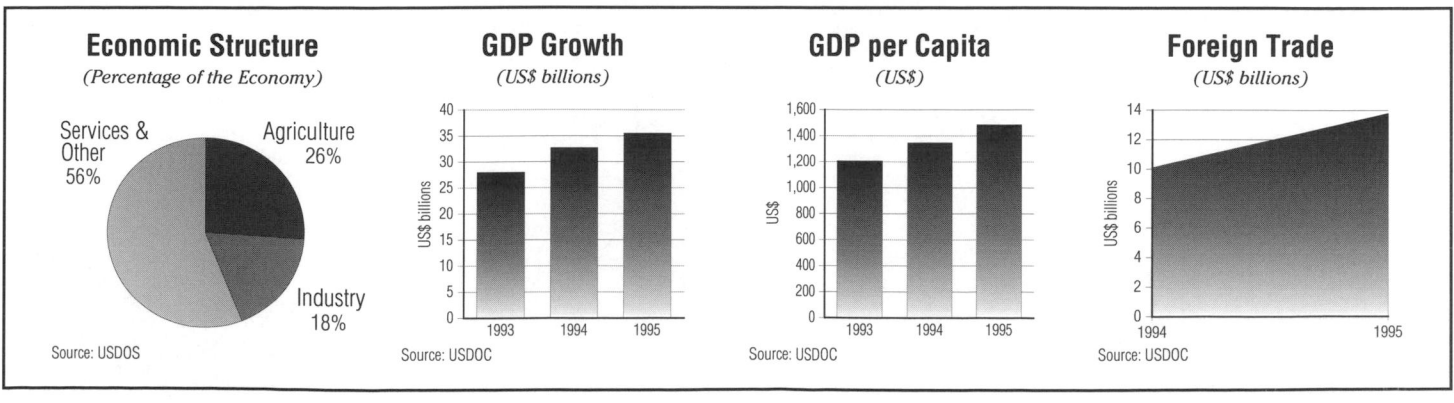

Economic Structure
(Percentage of the Economy)

Services & Other 56%
Agriculture 26%
Industry 18%

Source: USDOS

GDP Growth
(US$ billions)

Source: USDOC

GDP per Capita
(US$)

Source: USDOC

Foreign Trade
(US$ billions)

Source: USDOC

Manta

★ Quito

Ecuador

Colombia

Ambato

Guayaquil

Cuenca

Tumbes

Tumbes

Loja

Amazonas

Loreto

Iquitos

Leticia
Benjamin Constant

Talara

Sullana

Piura

Piura

Paita

Chachapoyas

Yurimaguas

Moyobamba

Tarapoto

Lambayeque

Cajamarca

San
Martin

Brazil

Chiclayo

Cajamarca

La Libertad

Trujillo Salaverry

Cruzeiro

Pucallpa

Chimbote

Ancash

Tingo
María

Huaráz

Huánuco

Ucayali

Huánuco

Goyllarisquizga

Pasco

Cerro de Pasco

Cobija

South

Pacific

Ocean

Lima

Huacho

Junín

Madre de
Dios

Lima

Huancayo

Puerto
Maldonado

Callao

Cusco

Huancavelica

Quillabamba
Machu Picchu
(ruins)

Huancavelica

Ayacucho

Cusco

Abancay

Puno

Pisco

Apurímac

Ica

Ica

Bolivia

Nazca

Ayacucho

Juliaca

Lago
Titicaca

Puno

Arequipa

La
Paz

Arequipa

Desaguadero

Guaquí

Moquegua

Matarani

Moquegua

Ilo

Tacna

Tacna

Arica

Chile

Peru

- ★ National capital
- ◉ Department capital
- ● Secondary city
- —— Department border
- —— Primary road
- —— Secondary road
- ······ Railroad
- ▬▬ International border

| 0 | 100 | 200 | 300 km |

| 0 | 100 | 200 mi |

0°

6°

12°

18°

78° 72°

Foreign Trade

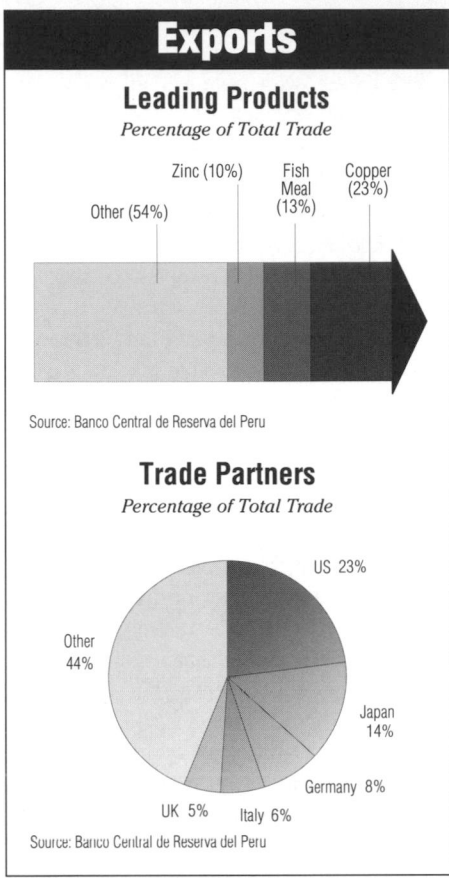

Imports

Leading Products
Percentage of Total Trade

Capital Goods (28%)
Consumer Goods (21%)
Wheat (3%)
Other (48%)

Source: Banco Central de Reserva del Peru

Trade Partners
Percentage of Total Trade

US 29%
Other 47%
Argentina 7%
Brazil 6%
Germany 6%
Switzerland 5%

Source: Banco Central de Reserva del Peru

Exports

Leading Products
Percentage of Total Trade

Zinc (10%)
Fish Meal (13%)
Copper (23%)
Other (54%)

Source: Banco Central de Reserva del Peru

Trade Partners
Percentage of Total Trade

US 23%
Other 44%
Japan 14%
Germany 8%
Italy 6%
UK 5%

Source: Banco Central de Reserva del Peru

Opportunities

FOR IMPORTING TO PERU
- agricultural machinery
- industrial machinery
- cereals
- chemicals
- pharmaceuticals
- petroleum
- mining equipment
- electronics
- telecommunications and telecommunications equipment
- electrical materials

FOR EXPORTING FROM PERU
- petroleum
- copper
- silver
- gold
- zinc
- lead
- fishmeal
- coffee
- sugar
- cotton
- canned and frozen fish

GROWTH SECTORS
- fisheries and agriculture
- construction
- manufacturing
- mining and petroleum

GOVERNMENT PROCUREMENT
- highway rehabilitation
- water, sewage, and rural electrification
- housing
- development of gas reserves
- transport facilities
- construction
- bridges

Trade News

RULES AND REGULATIONS

- **Trade news** Trade, investment, and foreign exchange policies have been liberalized, as have laws on labor and land. Peru's economic restructuring program continues to gain momentum, offering improved trade investment opportunities. Bureaucratic procedures have been streamlined, price controls terminated, the tax systems restructured, and labor laws liberalized. Exchange controls have even been lifted and there are no restrictions on remittance of profits, dividends, royalties, and capital. As an emerging market economy, Peru represents vast business opportunities.

- **Port fees** Port fees remain one of Peru's export problems. All fees have been reduced but are still relatively high for Latin America.

- **Import restrictions** There are no quantitative import restrictions other than for firearms, munitions, and explosives imported by private persons or groups of people. The import of chemical precursors (used in cocaine production) and ammonium nitrate fertilizer, which has been used as a blast enhancer for terrorist car bombs, is prohibited.

- **Import licenses** Import licenses have been abolished or weakened for practically all products, and nontariff barriers have been eliminated. Eighty-seven percent of Peru's tariff categories now have a rate of 15 percent.

- **Tariff rates** Peru has a single ad valorem tariff of 15 percent on practically all items in its tariff schedule and 25 percent on the remainder. The average tariff is about 16 percent, down from 80 percent in mid-1990.

- **Barriers** The Peruvian government maintains a variable import surcharge on wheat and some other agricultural imports, believing they are needed to offset subsidies by exporting countries.

- **Export licenses** Export licenses are required for cultural relics and items of antiquity. Also, end-user certificates and other documents are required for any kind of export or re-export of items on the international munitions list, the international chemical/biological warfare list, and the missile control technology regime list.

- **Prohibited imports** Because of problems with the black market, imports of used clothing and shoes have become prohibited, although donated imports of used clothing and shoes are exempt from the prohibition and may be sold in Peru. The import of plagicides (insecticides against insect plagues) and toxic waste is also prohibited.

- **Exchange from exports and imports** Exporters and importers are not required to channel any of their foreign exchange transactions through the Central Bank and can conduct their transactions freely on the open market.

- **Export competition** The government of Peru has adopted a new, transparent policy and effective laws in order to promote any competition between exporters.

- **Foreign trade zones** There are four types of free trade zones, or FTZs, in Peru: export processing zones, special commercial treatment zones, special development zones, and tourist zones. Any activities in export processing zones are free from customs duties and any taxes except social security for 15 years. Companies can also hire workers under temporary contracts and keep their accounting in foreign currency. Tourist zones receive all the same benefits as export processing zones to promote national or foreign tourist development. Companies in special commercial treatment zones in frontier and jungle areas pay only 10 percent customs duties (normal rates are 15 or 25 percent) and are exempt from sales taxes and may keep all their accounting in foreign currency. Special development zones may be established by the government to encourage investment in designated areas.

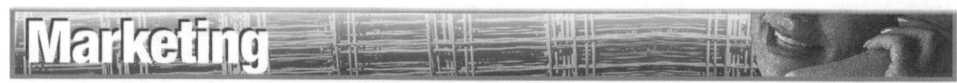

Marketing

Overview

Wealth and most economic activity in Peru is largely confined to the larger cities of the coastal plain; the inhabitants of the interior uplands are mostly subsistence farmers who live a life largely detached from the modern market economy. Foreign sellers should therefore concentrate their business and the majority of their sales campaigns to these large cities along the coast.Overall, the rapidly changing free market economy is providing opportunities for those interested in marketing a wide variety of goods.

Distribution

Distribution channels vary according to product category, industry, target market, and geographic region. It is important that foreign sellers adequately research and utilize the most appropriate channels for their products and circumstances in order to avoid wasting resources. Much business activity is highly personalized, and operations are often conducted through a maze of small intermediaries and end-user or retail outlets. New entrants to the market should establish as many contacts as possible and participate in trade shows, an ideal means of obtaining knowledge of the distribution and marketing opportunities available.

Agents, Distributors, and Partners

Peruvian law does not require the use of local distributors for commercial sales or even for sales to the government. Nevertheless, it is generally necessary to have a distributor who will assist in communicating between purchasers and foreign sellers, as well as with officials, intermediaries, and other interested parties. Most businesspeople in Peru speak only Spanish. The use of agents or distributors is an excellent means of doing business in Peru, because these locals know the market and usually have access to established distribution channels that cover the main markets throughout the country. Currently there is no requirement that a foreign supplier give exclusive representation or distribution rights, although Peruvian intermediaries invariably demand such exclusivity. Because most Peruvian agency firms have rather limited resources, sellers may need to retain more than one agent to cover the entire country effectively. Many observers suggest that the seller establish a temporary trial arrangement with a prospective agent before signing a full agreement; such a contract should be the reward for a successful relationship. Some large companies import directly from overseas, but this is still unusual.

Selling Techniques

Agent distributors, joint ventures, and franchising are becoming favorite ways of doing business in Peru. The advantage is that in all three instances, local expertise is available. Price may well be the number one factor in making or breaking a deal—most Peruvians have extremely limited incomes and little access to foreign exchange—but many also respond to the features and quality offered by foreign products. However, Peruvian consumers are rapidly becoming more sophisticated in their evaluation of such foreign products, which used to be accepted without criticism. Promotions, premiums, and other product tie-ins are common and often bring favorable results. Credit and financing can also become critical in closing a sale, and outside firms willing to extend terms (carefully and selectively) can expect greater sales.

Advertising

It is important for companies doing business in Peru to advertise their products and services in the major newspapers and business journals. *El Comercio* is the main national daily, favored by the business community, although others—*Hoy*, *El Nacional*, *La Crónica*, *Expreso*, and *La República*—are also available, as are magazines and a nascent trade press. Trade events and catalog shows are also excellent ways of promoting products. For consumer goods, radio and television advertising can also be productive—albeit expensive—and posters and similar advertising are also heavily used. Direct marketing remains largely undeveloped in Peru. Many Peruvian and internationally affiliated advertising agencies, market research firms, and public relations consultants can help design effective local messages and campaigns.

Service and Customer Support

Peruvians consider service and support a critical factor in making the final purchasing decision, especially for products that require periodic servicing. The buyer must feel comfortable that service has been guaranteed. It is important for the product to be sold through a reliable distributor who has the reputation for offering the level of quality and service that the client requires.

Marketing in Peru

MARKETING TIPS

- **Product promotions** Trade shows and catalog shows are important and effective in Peru, perhaps the best marketing tools in the country. They draw brokers and businesses from around the world.
- **Product pricing** Pricing will determine the viability of product sales, and must reflect the tariffs and VAT of 18 percent.
- **Quality** Japanese firms have established high standards for product, sales support, and after-sales support and service.
- **Special competitive factors** Peruvians consider service and support a critical factor, especially for products that require periodic servicing.
- **Agent support and handling** Look for an aggressive agent, and support the agent with liberal allowances for advertising and other promotions. Because many agents take on more accounts than they can handle, this helps keep up their interest in your account and is generally seen as a necessary cost of business in this market.
- **Telephone** Peru's telephone system was recently privatized, so some improvement in service is being observed. There are still several problems and delays, however. It is not possible to directly access credit card numbers for several international calling companies.
- **Agent appointment** There are two main classes of commission agents. The specialized salesperson may carry five or six first-class representations of allied goods and devote themselves almost entirely to this line of trade. The other class are the commission agents who deal with a number of various agencies having little or no connection with one another. These are usually not as satisfactory as the specialized agent. There are also commission agents, entirely on their own, holding several agencies at once. Some of them are quite successful, but there are many agents who have set up an office without capital or ability.
- **Postal services** Postal services have improved recently, but still are quite slow. It could take more than two weeks for mail to reach your contact in Peru, and about the same time for any mail from Peru to reach other countries.

AD AGENCIES

BBDO Peru
Ar. Angamos Oeste 1269
Lima 18
Tel: (14) 422-634
Fax: (14) 414-502

Grey Peru S.A.
Las Camelias 891
San Isidro
Lima 27
Peru
Tel: (14) 409-889

Interandina Publicidad S.A.
Av. Grau 273
Lima 18
Tel: (14) 815-8466
Fax: (14) 815-8493

Mig Nazca S&S
Santa Luisa No. 265
San Isidro
Lima 27
Tel: (14) 14-409176, 426305
Fax: (14) 428673

McCann-Erickson (Peru) Publicidad S.A.
Calle Tripoli 102
Miraflores
Apartado 180368
Lima 18
Tel: (14) 470425
Fax: (14) 478035
Telex: 21404

Business Culture

Greetings and Courtesies

Handshakes are customary among both men and women, both when arriving and leaving. Male friends may hug and female friends may kiss each other's cheek; men may also lightly kiss the cheek of women friends. Note that friends of the same sex may walk arm in arm. Titles are important, and business associates are addressed by their title and surname until they request otherwise; Doctor is commonly used as a title of respect as well as a professional title. Business cards in Spanish are expected, and it is a courtesy to translate other materials as well. At social events be sure to shake hands and say good-bye to everyone individually.

Business Ethic and Framework

Peruvians are among the most formal and reserved of all South Americans. To Peruvians, work is far from the most important part of life, but they do adhere strictly to the forms that govern this nevertheless important sphere. Appropriateness is critical, and Peruvians value diplomacy, tactfulness, and sensitivity as much as they dislike overt aggressiveness and bluntness.

Decision Making

Peruvians generally work in a structured environment, and the lines of authority are clearly drawn. Authority is rather narrowly concentrated and actual decisions are almost always made at a high level. Cultivate all employee relationships, because their quality may strongly influence the actual decision maker even when your immediate counterpart is not the one making the decision.

Women

Many women operate businesses, especially small-scale businesses, have considerable personal freedom, and are becoming more common and accepted in general; but their presence remains rare in the top levels of large companies. In general, foreign businesswomen may experience problems gaining acceptance in conservative Peru; some traditional Peruvian businessmen have refused to do business with foreign businesswomen and have considered the assignment of a woman as an insult by the sponsoring firm. Nevertheless, foreign businesswomen are making some progress, but must be careful to be highly professional, appropriate, and neither aggressive nor confrontational. Although women may generally go on the streets and dine alone, many will feel more comfortable if escorted.

Meetings

Contacts and introductions are extremely important. If you do not have a mutual business acquaintance to introduce you, consult your embassy for a referral. Prior appointments are important, should be made two to four weeks in advance, and should be reconfirmed. It is very difficult to see most Peruvians on short notice without a personal introduction. Peruvians are seldom punctual, although you are expected to be on time. Because business relationships are founded on personal relationships, several meetings and more than one trip may be required to conclude an agreement. Business entertaining is fairly common, and the business lunch is rapidly becoming an institution; however, a business dinner is usually a much more social occasion. Business is seldom discussed directly at business lunches and almost never at dinners. During negotiations, only those directly involved are invited out, although following completion of a deal, a more general celebratory invitation may be issued.

Business Attire

Foreign businessmen are expected to wear light- to medium-weight, dark, conservative suits—depending on the season. (Heavier weight fabric is needed in the Andes.) Foreign businesswomen should wear dresses or skirts and blouses, with or without jackets. Formal wear is seldom needed, although it may be for government or top-level private affairs, in which case a tuxedo or cocktail dress is needed. A suit or a dress would be appropriate for social occasions, such as an invitation to dinner (parties are slightly more formal than dinners). For less formal social occasions, conservative resort-type attire is suitable, although jeans may also be worn by both sexes. Neither men nor women should wear shorts, and women should avoid anything revealing. Do not wear Indian clothing; you can lose face or even offend some people. Visitors are advised not to dress too well outside of business situations because this can provoke hostility and attract thieves. Flashy or excessive attire, accessories, or jewelry, and excessive makeup should be avoided.

Cultural Cautions

DO'S

- Learn something about Peru's history and culture—your interest will be appreciated.
- Other appropriate topics include family and work.
- If traveling to the highlands, allow an extra day to acclimate to the altitude.

DON'TS

- Avoid race, religion, politics, salaries, drug trafficking, and the guerilla situation as topics of discussion.
- Peruvians complain vehemently about the government and conditions, but do not join in.

CUSTOMS

- Personal spacing in Peru tends to be closer than in many other cultures; it is considered a sign of aloofness, disinterest, evasion, or rudeness to back away.
- If you smoke, drink, or eat, offer to share with others in your party.
- If invited to a meal, arrive about 30 minutes late, unless the invitation specifies *hora inglesa* (English—or exact—time). In Lima, the invitation will usually be for 9:00 pm, but service will usually not begin until 10:30 pm. Delays are common, but meals usually begin somewhat earlier in the provinces. You are not expected to bring anything when invited to a dinner; however, most people will appreciate a small gift such as flowers.
- Guests usually depart about 30 minutes after the meal is over; you will be asked to remain out of politeness, but should express thanks and depart.
- The person who makes the invitation is always expected to pay. You will be expected to reciprocate later.
- Gifts may be presented on a return visit; they should be small, because an elaborate or expensive gift may imply an improper attempt to gain favor.
- Spouses may be invited to a business dinner (but not a lunch); however, if women are invited, make sure that more than one will be present because men will generally talk only among themselves.

OBSERVATIONS

- Peruvians are generally conservative and quite formal, with social as well as business issues. They also tend to be proud of their country's Indian heritage, in contrast to many other Latin American societies which look down on Indians while glorifying European forebears. However, this pride may be general rather than specific, and it may be insulting to attribute Indian ancestry to individuals unless they make a point of claiming it (which is rare).
- Spanish is the official language and relatively few people speak other languages, especially outside the upper classes and outside Lima. The Indian language Quechua is also an official language; it is spoken exclusively by many people in the Andes.
- Peruvians consider it a point of honor to know the answer to any business question, and will give one whether they have the information or not. Try to get independent confirmation.
- Before-dinner drinks are served on social occasions; local drinks are usually served, but imported whisky (Scotch) is considered especially sophisticated. You are usually expected to have only one drink. Wine or beer may be served with meals. Coffee is served afterward—it is often coffee essence accompanied by hot water which you mix to taste.
- A personal letter of introduction is extremely helpful; a general official letter of introduction is better than none, but will not have the same impact.

NEGOTIATIONS

- Peruvians are formal and subtle negotiators who pride themselves on diplomacy. They also frequently say what they think the other person wishes to hear, and it is necessary to make discussions open-ended to feel them out. Peruvians are offended by pressure and aggressive tactics.

Legal System

Peru is a civil code country. Its law is based on the Roman-Germanic and French traditions. The Constitution currently in effect was adopted in 1993.

Intellectual Property Rights

As of 1995, Peru became a full active member of the Paris Convention for the Protection of Industrial Property. Consequently, Peru will grant the same protection to industrial property rights held by nationals of the other Convention members as are granted to rights held by domestic registrants. Additionally, Peru will guarantee nationals of those member countries priority with regard to protected rights.

Patents Protection is acquired on registration and is granted for 20 years from the date registration is requested. Registration typically takes no more than eight months to complete.

Trademarks Registration is required to protect trademarks in Peru. Ownership protection is granted initially for 10 years and is renewable for consecutive 10-year terms. The registration process takes from three to four months.

Copyrights Once a copyright is registered, it is protected during the owner's life and during the lives of the owner's surviving spouse, sons, and parents. Other heirs can become entitled to the same rights for 50 years. Registration is available for software and videos as well as the traditional copyrightable materials. Although pirated videos and software is a problem, the Peruvian government is tightening its regulations and enforcement procedures.

Trade secrets Legislation protects trade secrets, provided they have commercial value and remain undisclosed to the general public or competitors.

Business Registration

In general, there are no special requirements for foreign businesses operating in Peru. Foreign investments may be registered with the National Commission for Foreign Investment and Technology (CONITE) for statistical purposes and to guarantee the remittance of profits abroad. Special licenses or authorizations are required for any person who desires to develop certain activities, regardless of the national origin of the investors or investments. According to the Peruvian Constitution, foreigners and locals are subject to the same laws and regulations.

Contracts and Dispute Resolution

Litigation in Peru is a long and usually expensive process. Arbitration is becoming popular, although it is less common even than litigation. Most parties prefer to resolve their business differences through negotiation. However, parties are allowed to designate that any disputes will be submitted to arbitration, and the courts will uphold these provisions in a contract. Parties may choose any arbitrator they wish to resolve their dispute. A few private entities now offer arbitration services. The arbitration process may be conducted according to Peruvian law or any foreign legislation chosen by the parties and, if not contrary to public order, the courts will honor the application of that law.

Notaries

The incorporating documents for entities, powers of attorneys, purchase instruments for immovables, and major contracts must be executed through notaries in order to register them with the Public Record registry. Documents prepared in Peru for use in foreign countries must be acknowledged by a notary, the Notaries Association, the Ministry of Foreign Affairs, or a diplomatic representative of the country where the document will be used. Documents issued outside the country require a certification by the correspondent Peruvian Consulate to be valid in Peru.

Labor

For each full year worked, an employee is entitled compensation for 14 months of pay and 30 days of paid vacation. Individual dismissal and collective lay-offs have been liberalized, subject to certain payment requirements. Employees unlawfully dismissed are entitled to an indemnity of from one to 12 months of salary, depending on seniority. Reinstatement and payment of back wages are available remedies only in cases based on discrimination. The rights to unionize, bargain collectively, and to strike are protected by the Constitution; however, the presence of organized labor in the Peruvian economy continues to decline. Probably less than six percent of the labor force is currently unionized. Productivity provisions must be included in any collective bargaining agreement. Strikes may be called only after approval by a majority of all workers (including non-union workers) voting by secret ballot. Official minimum wage is US$60 a month; however, the average minimum wage according to public and private surveys is about US$160 a month.

Source: Estudio Aurelio Garcia Sayin-Abogados, Lima, Peru.

Legal Matters

LEGAL BRIEFS

- **Privatization** Privatization of state–owned companies has continued successfully. In 1995, more than 10 state-owned companies were transferred to the private sector. A significant number of state-owned companies remain to be privatized in 1996 in the mining, power generation, oil, fishing, and hotel industries.

- **Environmental regulations** Environmental regulations for oil, mining, power generation, fishing, and agriculture are in effect. These activities are under the specific authority of each ministry in charge of the related economic activity.

- **Property** Foreigners may freely acquire property except within 50 kilometers (about 30 miles) of the country borders.

- **Arbitration** Peru accepts binding international arbitration of investment disputes between foreign investors and the state, in accordance with national legislation or international treaties signed by the government.

- **Bankruptcy** Peru has a bankruptcy law recognizing creditor rights in a specified hierarchy. In general, secured interests in real and personal property are recognized.

- **Royalties** Parties may freely negotiate contractual conditions related to licensing arrangements and other aspects of technology transfer without prior authorization. Registry of a technology transfer agreement is required for a payment of royalties. Such registration is automatic upon submission to the appropriate government authority.

- **Monopolies** The current administration has dismantled almost all monopolies in all sectors of the economy, including the provision of public services.

- **Benefits** Union benefits, vacations, and other available employment benefits are often readily sacrificed in exchange for regular employment.

- **Business registration** Several agencies oversee the establishment of foreign entities in Peru, including The Bureau of Industry, the Institute for Industries, and the Research Institute for Industrial Technology and Technical Standards.

- **Political violence** Political violence continues to decline in Peru, due in large part to the government's anti-insurgency efforts.

- **Expatriates** The rules regarding hiring of foreigners have been liberalized, although legislation still limits foreigners to no more than a maximum of 20 percent of total employees in a local company, whether owned by foreign or national interests, and their combined salaries to no more than 30 percent of total company salaries.

- **International agreements** Peru is a member of GATT/WTO; OAS; and the Convention on the Recognition and Enforcement of Foreign Arbitral Awards. In 1992 Peru withdrew partially from the Andean Pact.

LEGAL CONTACTS

Estudio Aurelio Garcia Sayin-Abogados
Av. El Rosario 380
Lima 27
Tel: (14) 440-7341, 440-5157
Fax: (14) 440-6393, 440-5618
Colegio de Abogados de Lima (Lima's Bar Association)
Av. Santa Cruz 255
Lima 18
Tel: (14) 441-8360
Fax: (14) 470-7000
Centro Peruano de Arbitraje y Conciliacion (CEARCO)
Arbitration Institution
Av. Paseo de La Republica 6295
Lima 18
Tel: (14) 442-2206, 447-2981
Fax: (14) 442-8118

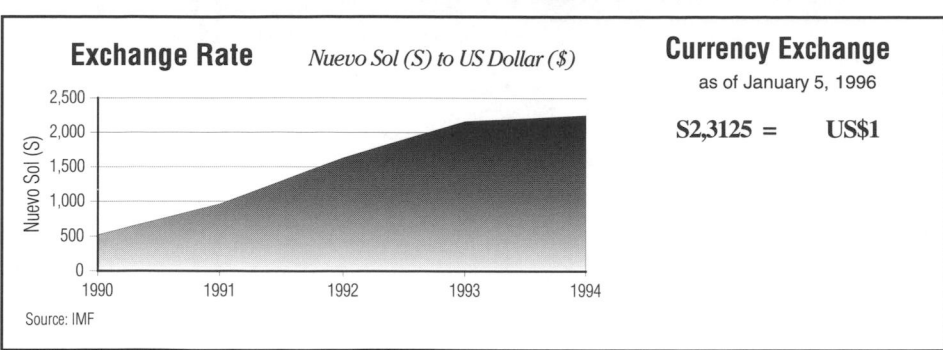

Exchange Rate *Nuevo Sol (S) to US Dollar ($)*

Nuevo Sol (S): 2,500 / 2,000 / 1,500 / 1,000 / 500 / 0

1990 1991 1992 1993 1994

Source: IMF

Currency Exchange
as of January 5, 1996

S2,3125 =   US$1

Currency

The currency in use is the nuevo sol (S), the plural is soles.

Foreign Exchange

Exchange houses can exchange foreign currency and sell foreign currency for repurchases. Anyone in the private sector, foreign or domestic, needs approval by Supreme Decree, on the recommendation of the External Debt Committee, to borrow abroad. New nonresident investments must be registered with the National Commission on Foreign Investment and Technology. Any foreign companies invested in Peru may benefit from the duty-free program of the Cartagena Agreement under the same conditions as domestic enterprises. Arrears are maintained with respect to any external payments of suppliers' credits of commercial banks and loans from Eastern European countries.

Capital Transfers

There are no restrictions or requirements for most payments for invisibles, but remittances of net profits require a prior tax clearance. Public debt services are the only invisible payment subject to payments authorization. There are no requirements for invisibles proceeds. All restrictions on remittances of profits, dividends, royalties, and capital have been eliminated, although foreign investors are required to register their investments (an automatic process) to insure these guarantees.

Investment Incentives

Under the Private Sector Investment Guarantee Regime, the government guarantees nondiscriminatory treatment for foreign investors and private enterprises, protection of property rights, the development of any economic activities, and export incentives. Rules regarding hiring of foreigners have been liberalized. Legislation still limits foreigners to no more than 20 percent of total employees in a local company, whether owned by foreign or national interests, and their combined salaries to no more than 30 percent of total company salaries, but Legislative Decree 689 of November 4, 1991, provided a variety of exceptions to these limits which effectively negate their impact in most cases.

Investment Restrictions

Most restrictions pertaining to foreign investment have been liberalized to the point where they are almost transparent. Almost every sector is open to foreign investors, and there are very few restrictions of consequence directed at foreigners.

Money Matters

BITS AND PIECES

- **Corporate income tax** Resident companies are taxed on their worldwide income. Nonresident companies are taxed on income from Peru only.
- **Capital gains** All capital gains are treated as regular income, but capital gains derived from transactions on a stock exchange are exempt from income tax.
- **Foreign tax relief** In most cases, tax credits are permitted for taxes paid abroad on income earned in most countries.
- **Gold** There are no restrictions or requirements for importing or exporting gold.
- **Payments** Generally payments for other countries tied to Peru by the Latin American Integration Association can be made in special accounts maintained by the Central Reserve Bank of Peru.
- **Import payments** Most imports are subject to a uniform value-added tax of 18 percent. Some agricultural products and items for personal use are exempt from any value-added tax. Tariffs rates range between 15 and 25 percent, excluding any imports subject to trade agreements. Advance import payments are allowed without restriction. Legislation has been created requiring pre-inspection at the port of embarkation by international firms for some imports.
- **National treatment** Foreign investment is now subject to national treatment and is permitted in all economic activities.
- **Registration** Foreign investment is required to be registered with the National Commission on Foreign Investment and Technology (CONITE). All investors need prior approval to invest in industries that manufacture weapons.
- **Export payments** Proceed from exports do not need to be repatriated or surrendered. Sixty-five exports are prohibited in Peru.
- **Exchange controls** There are no exchange controls in Peru. All restrictions on remittances of profits, dividends, royalties, and capital have been eliminated, although foreign investors are required to register their investments to insure any guarantees.
- **Export channeling** Exporters and importers are not required to channel their foreign exchange transactions through the Central Bank and can conduct their transactions freely on the open market.
- **Expropriation** The government's power to expropriate private property is legally limited to when it is required by the public interest and then only through a specific act of congress. Public interest reasons are defined as those required to carry out public works.
- **Additional investment incentives** Companies receiving new investment may also enjoy legal stability with regard to the income tax, provided the new funds amount to more than 50 percent of the equity capital and retained earnings and will enhance productivity or technology. Investors are also offered protection from liability for acquiring state-owned enterprises.
- **Private ownership** Foreign companies are permitted to invest in any legal economic activity and to freely establish, acquire, and dispose of their interests. This includes any kind of direct foreign investment, portfolio investments, and investment in real property.

BANKS

Banco de la Nación
Avenida Nicolás de Piénola 1065
Lima 100
Tel: (14) 330520
Fax: (14) 318949

GOVERNMENT OFFICES

Ministry of Economy and Finance
Jr. Junin 319
Lima 1
Tel (14) 289989, 289550
Fax: (14) 278583

TAXATION

Taxation requires sophisticated knowledge of complex rules and regulations specific to each country. The information presented here is from the Ernst & Young Corporate Tax Guide and Directory, available from the Ernst & Young accounting office in your country, or from:

Alonso y Asociados
Mail Address:
Apartado 3601
Lima 100, Peru
Street Address:
Parque Quinones 198
Jesus Maria
Lima 11, Peru
Tel: (14) 631818
Telex: 25970 PE Ans bk ALCAASOC
Fax: (14) 634523

At a Glance

Corporate Income Tax Rate (%)	30
Capital Gains Tax Rate (%)	30
Branch Tax Rate (%)	30
Withholding Tax (%)	
Dividends	0
Interest (a)	30
Royalties (b)	10
Branch Remittance Tax	0
Net Operating Losses (Years)	
Carryback	0
Carryforward (c)	4

(a) Applicable to payments to nonresidents. A reduced rate of 1% applies to certain interest payments.
(b) Applicable to payments to nonresidents.
(c) Carryforward period begins in the first subsequent profitable year.

Business Travel

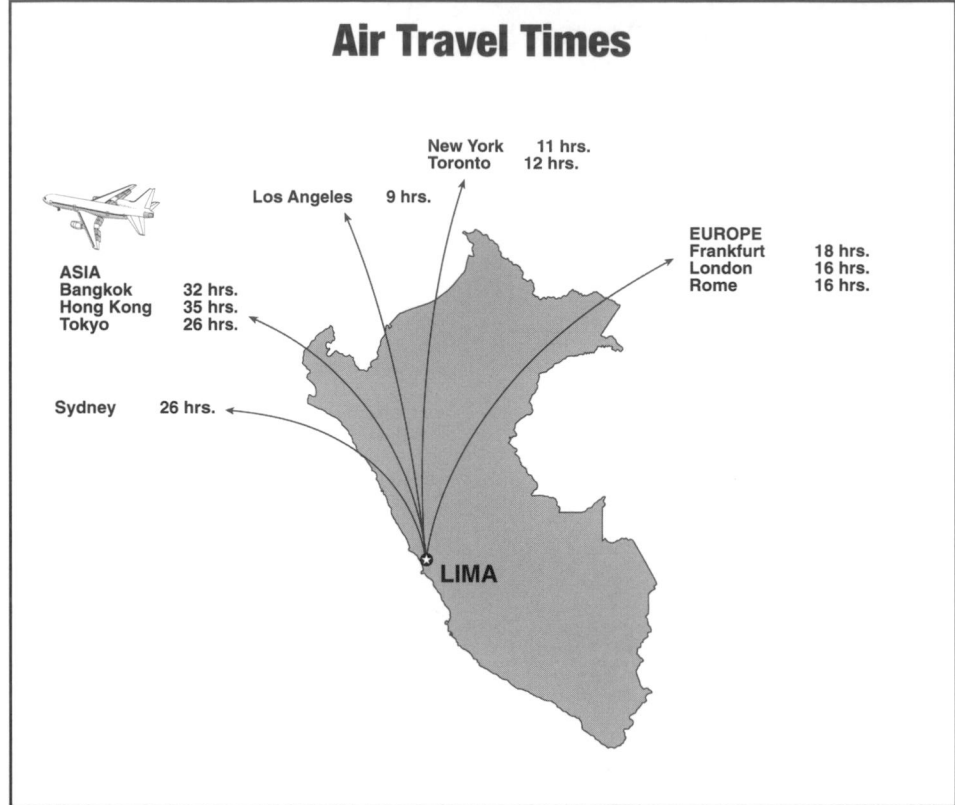

Air Travel Times

New York	11 hrs.
Toronto	12 hrs.
Los Angeles	9 hrs.

EUROPE
Frankfurt	18 hrs.
London	16 hrs.
Rome	16 hrs.

ASIA
Bangkok	32 hrs.
Hong Kong	35 hrs.
Tokyo	26 hrs.

Sydney	26 hrs.

LIMA

COMMUNICATIONS

Telephones Telephone service is adequate, with no delays in placing international calls. The public booths found in hotels and restaurants require tokens called *rin*, which can be purchased from stores, newsstands, or street vendors.

Fax Fax use is on the rise in Peru and services are available in major hotels.

Post office Postal service is erratic; sending mail *con certificado* for a small fee or by express mail through a private company is recommended for important documents.

BEST TRAVEL BOOKS

Peru. Insight Guides Series. Houghton Mifflin.

Do's and Taboo's Around the World. The Bestselling Guide to International Behavior. Edited by Roger Axtell, compiled by the Parker Pen Company. The ultimate guide to international behavior, now completely updated and expanded. Helpful, fun to read!

Peru. Visitors Guides Series. Illustrated, 256 pages. Hunter Publications, Inc.

Peru Lonely Planet Travel Survival Kit. Outstanding, this is the best...

The Travelers Guide to Latin America Customs and Manners. Elizabeth Devine & Nancy Braganti. An invaluable guide for people not wanting to put foot in mouth.

NATIONAL TOURIST OFFICE

Direccion General de Turismo
Avenida Corpac s/n, Calle 1, Oseste Urb.
San Isidro - Lima 27
Tel: (14) 402129

USEFUL TELEPHONE NUMBERS

If you are calling from outside Peru, you will need to add the country code [51] and any other international dialing requirements from within your country.

- Emergency 105
- Operator 108; 107
- Directory 103
- International Operator 104
- Tourist Office.....................................(14) 40-6119
- Giant Express .... (14) 408148
- DHL .... (14) 418686
- Emery Airfreight .... (14) 523643
- Tourist Police .... (14) 714579, 714313
- National Travel Agency ....(14) 72-1928
- Peruvian Tour and Auto Club...............(14) 40-3270
- Clinical Lima Emg Medical Clinic ....(14) 28-8060
- National Railway ....(14) 28-9440
- Central Bank .... (14) 276350

Car Rental Information
- Avis: Airport .... (14) 524774
- Budget: Airport .... (14) 528706
- Hertz: Airport .... (14) 518189

Credit Card Information
Lost or stolen credit cards (call collect to the US, regardless of which country the card was issued in).
- Amex...[1] (919) 333-3211
- Diner's Club...............................[1] (303) 799-1504
- MasterCard ....[1] (314) 275-6690
- Visa ....[1] (410) 581-7931

Travelogue

WORKWEEK

Offices Monday-Friday 8:30 am to 5:00 pm.

Banks Monday-Friday 8:30 am to 11:30 am, January-March; 8:30 am to noon, April-December.

Government January-March: Monday-Friday 9:30 am to 11:30 am, Saturday 9:00 am to 11:30 am. April-December: Monday-Friday 9:30 am to 11:00 am and 3:00 pm to 5:00 pm, Saturday 9:30 am to 11:30 am.

Retail January-March: Monday-Saturday 9:00 am to 12:30 pm and 4:00 pm to 7:00 pm. April-December: Monday-Saturday 9:00 am to 12:30 pm and 3:30 pm to 7:00 pm.

HOLIDAYS

Holidays 1996
January 1 New Year's Day
April 4 Holy Thursday
April 5 Good Friday
May 1 Labor Day
June 28-29 St. Peter and St. Paul
July 28 Independence Day
August 30 St. Rosa de Lima
October 8 Battle of Angamos
November 1 All Saints' Day
December 8 Immaculate Conception
December 25 Christmas
In addition, the summer vacation months of January, February, and March and the weeks before and after Easter and Christmas are not good times for business. Avoid travel in Peru on June 19, the often violent anniversary of a prison massacre in 1986.

VISA AND PASSPORT

Foreigners must have a valid passport, and onward tickets are advised. A visa is not necessary for tourist visits up to 90 days, but visitors for other purposes must have a visa.

DEPARTURE FORMALITIES

The tourist card you have filled in on arrival will be required for departing. Visitors on business visas must have certification from the Ministry of Economy and Finance that Peruvian income taxes were paid.

IMMUNIZATION

Consult a physician on the advisability of gamma globulin shots against hepatitis, malaria suppressants, and yellow fever vaccination for visitors to certain areas.

TIPPING

Hotels: add 10 percent to the 10 percent service charge on the bill. Restaurants: tip five percent if the 15 percent service charge was added, or 15 percent if it was not. Hairdressers and coatcheck attendants: tip only in very expensive establishments. Railway porters get about US$.15 per bag, airport porters US$.50 to US$1 depending on the number of bags. Taxi drivers do not expect tips, but car watchers get about US$.10.

CRIME

Terrorism and common crime are serious throughout Peru. Travelers on group tours are relatively safe. Street crime in downtown Lima is common and petty theft occurs in most other urban areas. Cuzco's tourism police have tightened security in tourist areas. When criminal activity is immediately reported to the nearest police station or tourism police office, stolen property is often recovered. Visitors should not walk alone or resist violent criminals.

INFRASTRUCTURE

Peru has an adequate rail system and a hydrofoil across Lake Titicaca. Taxis are not metered, so negotiate fares before starting. Rental cars are available, but overland road travel by car or bus is unsafe because of terrorism, banditry, and poor road conditions. Two domestic airlines serve Peru with inexpensive, unlimited travel within the country.

GOVERNMENT AGENCIES

Ministerio de Agricultura
Av. Salaverry s/n
Jesús María, Lima
Tel: (14) 320712, 329098
Fax: (14) 320990

Instituto Nacional de Recursos Naturales, Ministerio de Agricultura
Calle 17, No. 355
Urb. El Palomar
San Isidro, Lima
Tel: (14) 414606, 410425
Fax: (14) 414606

Servicio Nacional de Sanidad Agraria, Ministerio de Agricultura
Av. Salaverry s/n
Jesús María, Lima
Tel/Fax: (14) 337802

Ministry of Education
Parque Universitario s/n
Lima 1
Tel: (14) 288425, 313254
Fax: (14) 330230

Ministry of Fisheries
Avenida Javier Prado Este 2465
San Luis, Lima
Tel: (14) 704737, 704149
Fax: (14) 704101

Ministry of Foreign Affairs
Jr. Ucayali 363
Lima 1
Tel: (14) 273860, 271992
Fax: (14) 323266

Ministry of Industry, Tourism, Integration and International Trade Negotiations
Calle 1, Oeste
Corpac, Lima
Tel: (14) 400436, 223588
Fax: (14) 415388

Ministry of Labor and Social Promotion
Avenida Salaverry s/n
Jesús María, Lima
Tel: (14) 243680, 332002

Ministry of Public Health
Avenida Salaverry Cuadra 8
Jesús María, Lima
Tel: (14) 326242, 240285
Fax: (14) 708191

Ministry of Transportation and Communication
Avenida 28 de Julio 800
Lima 1
Tel: (14) 330427, 333430
Fax: (14) 708191

Vice Ministry of Commerce
Centro Civico, 1er nivel
Lima 1
Tel: (14) 318088, 317945
Telex: 25607 pe mincom

WORLD TRADE CENTER

World Trade Center Lima
Av. La Marina 2355
Lima 32
Tel: (14) 528140, 517200
Fax: (14) 523907

BUSINESS AND TRADE ORGANIZATIONS

Asociacion de Industriales Lacteos
Los Ibis 120
Urb. El Palomar-Corpac
San Isidro
Tel: (14) 409758

Asociacion Peruana de Porcicultores
Pomalca 327
Urb. Centro Comercial Monterrico
Lima 33
Tel: (14) 363729, 364168
Fax: (14) 363729

Asociacion Peruana de Avicultura
Esmeralda 255
Chacarilla del Estanque
San Borja
Tel: (14) 379282
Fax: (14) 372555

Central de Cooperativas Agrarias Azucareras de Comercializacion
Jr. A. Miro Quesada 327
5to Piso, Of. 501-503
Lima
Tel/Fax: (14) 338989

Foreign Trade Institute
Avenida José Pardo 275
Miraflores, Lima 18
Tel: (14) 479984, 473641
Telex: 25301 pe fopex

National Development Council
Avenida Garcilaso de la Vega 1456
Lima
Tel: (14) 477273

Empresa Nacional de Comercialización de Insumos
National Commodities Marketing Corporation
Galerías San Felipe 111
Cuadra 7
Gregorio Escobedo, Apdo 1834
Lima 11
Tel: (14) 632122
Fax: (14) 626242

Fondo para El Desarrollo de La Ganaderia Intensiva de Carne de Vacuno
Miguel de Unamuno 277
Urb. Santa Florencia
San Miguel, Lima
Tel: (14) 660124 x20

Asociacion de Fongales
Pumacahua No. 877, Of. 306
Jesús María, Lima
Tel/Fax: (14) 234642

Comite de Fabricantes de Aceites y Derivados
Los Laureles 365
San Isidro, Lima
Tel: (14) 408700
Fax: (14) 424351

Comite de Alimentos Balanceados y Productos Pecuarios
Los Laureles 365
San Isidro, Lima
Tel: (14) 408700
Fax: (14) 424351

Comite de Molinos de Trigo
Los Laureles 365
San Isidro, Lima
Tel: (14) 408700
Fax: (14) 424351

Camara de Comercio de Lima (Lima's Chamber of Commerce)
Gregorio Escobedo 398
Lima 11
Tel: (14) 463-3434/463-8080
Fax: (14) 463-2820

American Chamber of Commerce
Ricardo Palma 836
Lima 18
Tel: (14) 447-9394
Fax: (14) 447-9362

Lima's Chamber of Commerce
Gregorio Escobedo 398
Lima 11
Tel: (14) 463-3434, 463-8080
Fax: (14) 463-2820

American Chamber of Commerce
Ricardo Palma 836
Lima 18
Tel: (14) 447-9394
Fax: (14) 447-9362

> ### REMEMBER
> - When you telephone (or fax) to Peru from another country you must always include the country code [51] before the numbers given.
> - When you send mail to Peru, be sure to write PERU in capital letters on its own line below the addresses given.

NEWSPAPERS

El Comercio
Empresa Editora 'El COmercio'SA
Jirón Antonio Miró Quesada 300
Lima
Tel: (14) 287620
Fax: (14) 310810
Telex: 20115

Expreso
Ica 646
Lima
Tel: (14) 287470
Telex: 25307
Fax: (14) 318314

Extra
Ica 646
Lima
Tel: (14) 287470
Telex: 25307

El Peruano (Diario Oficial)
Quilca 556
Apdo 303
Lima

La República
Jirón Camaná 320
Lima

La Tercera
Jirón Andahuaylas 1472
Apdo 928
Lima

Correo
Call Bolívar
Arequipa
Tel: (54) 235150
Telex: 51229

El Pueblo
Sucre 208
Apdo 35
Arequipa

El Comercio
Apdo 70
Cuzco

El Sol
Mesón de la Estrella 172
Cuzco

El Imparcial
Avda Grau 203
Huacho
Tel: (34) 324410

La Opinión Popular
Huancas 251
Huancayo
Tel: (64) 231149

La Opinión
Callao 176
Apdo 19
Ica

La Voz de Ica
Castrovirreyna 193
Ica

El Eco
Jirón Lima 100-108
Apdo 170
Iquitos

El Oriente
Morona 153
Apdo 161
Iquitos

Ultimas Noticias
2 de Mayo 27-29
Pacasmayo

Correo
Jirón Ica 782
Piura

Ecos y Noticias
Libertad 902 y Ayacucho 307
Apdo 110
Piura

El Tiempo
Ayacucho 751
Piura
Tel: (74) 323671

PERIODICALS

Alerta Agrario
Avda Salaverry 818
Lima 11
Tel: (14) 336610
Fax: (14) 331744

Amatúa
Jirón Lampa 11115
Of. 605
Lima

The Andean Report
Pasaje Los Pinos 156
Of. B6
Miraflores
Apdo 531
Lima
Tel: (14) 472552
Fax: (14) 467888

Caretas
Camaná 615
Of. 308
Lima
Tel: (14) 287520

Debate
Apdo 671
Lima 100
Tel: (14) 467070
Fax: (14) 455946

Debate Agrario
Avda Salaverry 818
Lima 11
Tel: (14) 336610
Fax: (14) 331744

Hora del Hombre
Apdo 2378
Lima 1
Tel: (14) 220208

Industria Peruana
Los Laureles 365
San Isidro
Apdo 632
Lima 27

Lima Times
Pasaje Los Pinos 156
Of. B6
Miraflores
Apdo 531
Lima 100
Tel: (14) 469120
Fax: (14) 467888

Monos y Monadas
Camaná 615
Of. 104, Lima

Oiga
Pedro Venturo 353
Urb. Aurora
Miraflores, Lima
Tel: (14) 475851

Orbita
Avda Pershing 290
Of. 301
Magdalena Nueva, Lima

Perú Económico
Apdo 671
Lima 100
Tel: (14) 467070
Fax: (14) 455946

Quehacer
León de la Fuente 110
Magdalena del Mar
Lima 14
Tel: (14) 617309
Fax: (14) 617309

Runa
Apdo 5247
Lima

Semana Económica
Apdo 671
Lima 100
Tel: (14) 455237
Fax: (14) 455946

RADIO AND TELEVISION

Asociación de Radiodifusoras del Perú (ARP)
Manuel Corpancho 208
Lima 1

Dirección General de Telecomunicaciones
Avda 28 de Julio 800, 2
Lima 1
Tel: (14) 330752
Telex: 25584

Empresa de Cine, Radio y Televisión Peruana, SA (RTP)
Avda José Gálvez 1040
Santa Beatriz
Lima
Tel: (14) 715570
Telex: 25029

Instituto Nacional de Comunicación Social
Jirón de la Unión 264
Lima

Radio Nacional del Perú
Avda Petit Thouars 447
Santa Beatriz
Lima

Radio América
León Velarde 1140
Apdo 1192
Lima 14

Radio El Sol
Avda Uruguay 355, 7
Lima
Tel: (14) 246107

Radio Panamericana
Mariano Carranza 126
Santa Beatriz
Lima 1
Tel: (14) 710040

Andina de Televisión
Avda Arequipa 3570
San Isidro
Lima
Tel: (14) 426666

Compania Latinoamericana de Radiofusión-Canal 2 TV
Avda san Felipe 968
Jesús María
Lima 11

Compania Peruana de Radiofusión, SA (América Televisión-Canal 4)
Montero Rosas 1099
Santa Beatriz
Lima
Tel: (14) 728989
Fax: (14) 719582
Telex: 20217

Panamericana de Televisión, SA-Canal 5
Avda Arequipa 1110, 5
Lima 1
Tel: (14) 718920
Telex: 25670

Unitel-Difusora Universal de Televisión
Roma 160
Miraflores
Lima 18
Tel: (14) 471169

STOCK EXCHANGES

Bolsa de Valores de Lima
Pasaje Acuna 191
Lima 1
Tel: (14) 286280
Fax: (14) 337650
Telex: 25856

STATE COPORATIONS

Centromín SA (Empresa Minera del Centro del Perú)
Edif. Solgas
Avda Javier Prado Este 2175
San Borja
Apdo 2412
Lima 34
Tel: (14) 365924
Fax: (14) 358782

Corpac (Corporation Peruana de Aeropuertos y Aviación Commercial, SA)
Aeropuerto Internacional Jorge Chávez
Avda Elmer Faucett
Lima
Tel: (14) 529570

Electroperú
Centro Cívico
Paseo de la República 144
Lima 1
Tel: (14) 310664
Telex: 25680

Enci (Empresa Nacional de Comercialización de Insumos)
Galerías San Felipe 111
Cuadra 7
Gregorio Escobedo
Apdo 1834
Lima 11
Tel: (14) 632122
Fax: (14) 626242

ENTEL PERU (Empresa Nacional de Telecomunicaciones del Perú, SA)
Avda Javier Prado Este 1980
Apdo 2600
Lima 41
Tel: (14) 752380
Telex: 20442
Fax: (14) 750156

Epsep (Empresa Peruana de Servicios Pesqueros)
Lima
Tel: (14) 362630
Telex: 25498

Minero Perú (Empresa Minera del Perú)
Bernardo Monteagudo 222
Apdo 4332
Lima 17
Tel: (14) 620740
Fax: (14) 627049
Telex: 25598

Minpeco, SA (Empresa Comercializadora de Productos Mineros)
Jirón Scipión Llona 350
Apdo 0274
Miraflores
Lima 18
Tel: (14) 473561
Fax: (14) 402840
Telex: 20360

Pesca Peru (Empresa Nacional Pesquera SA)
Avda Petit Thoars 119-115
Apdo 4682
Lima 1
Tel: (14) 320454
Telex: 25601

INTERNET ADDRESSES

Usenet group(s):
soc.culture.peru

City Net - Peru
http://www.city.net/countries/peru/

The Internet Network in Peru
http://www.rcp.net.pe/rcp_ingles.html

Ministry of Foreign Affairs of Peru
http://www.minrext.gob.pe/i-Defaul.htm

Philippines

Republic of Philippines

Economy

Overview

The Philippines' economy has historically been characterized by boom and bust cycles, based on import substitution rather than export promotion. The current regime, however, has put into place aggressive policies to reform and modernize the economic system to make the Philippines more international and market oriented. Coupled with a reduced fiscal deficit, single-digit inflation, and a moderation of interest rates, the economy has shown real signs of growth in the past few years. Serious market liberalization continues, complemented by significant tariff reductions. The Philippine Government is relying heavily on private sector investments, both domestic and foreign, to achieve and sustain a higher economic growth path. The economy is poised to make a leap into the rapidly emerging Asian markets.

Trade

The Philippine government has made significant progress toward opening its markets to international competition. Already, foreign trade is growing at a much faster pace than GDP. Still, much remains to be done. Agricultural markets, especially, remain protected by high tariffs and import quotas, although the government has committed to continued reductions. Merchandise imports have risen sharply, spurred mainly by strong demand for infrastructure-related capital goods. Exports are dominated by garments and electronics items processed and assembled by local labor, accounting for 40 percent of total receipts. The Philippines' biggest trading partners are the US, Japan, and Taiwan.

Sectors

Agriculture Although the Philippines is rich in agricultural potential, inadequate infrastructure, lack of financing, and past governmental policies have limited productivity gains. The sector employs 47 percent of the work force but contributes only 22 percent of GDP. Good prospects for the aquaculture subsector notwithstanding, the fishing industry continues to face a bleak future due to destructive fishing methods, lack of funds, and absence of government support.

Industry The industrial sector is concentrated in the urban areas, especially the Manila region, and contributes 33 percent of GDP. Manufacturing production consists largely of processing and assembling consumer goods. Indadequate infrastructure and continued severe shortages of electrical power have prohibited industrial growth. Although the country is well-endowed with minerals and resources, having some of the largest chromite, nickel, and copper deposits in the world, mining has been in steady decline since 1989 due to low metal prices, high production costs, and lack of adequate infrastructure.

Services Services account for 45 percent of GDP. Banking restrictions have recently been relaxed, and the government has also improved foreign access to other important service industries such as telecommunications and insurance.

Trends

If the government can maintain its momentum in carrying out structural reforms and policies which will help the economy break free from its traditional 'boom-and-bust' growth patterns, accelerating long-term economic growth is certainly possible. Infrastructure development, especially ensuring an adequate power supply, is one of the highest priorities of the Philippine government's current development plans.

At a Glance

THE COUNTRY

Location Southeastern Asia between Indonesia and China.
Terrain Islands, 65 percent mountainous with narrow coastal lowlands.
Climate Tropical, astride typhoon belt.

THE PEOPLE

Population 68,000,000
Ethnic composition
Christian Malay 91.5%
Muslim Malay... 4%
Chinese... 1.5%
Other... 3%
Religious composition
Roman Catholic 83%
Protestant 9%
Muslim 5%
Buddhist and Other................................ 3%
Languages spoken Filipino (based on Tagalog), English, native dialects, and Spanish.
Education and literacy One of the highest literacy rates in East Asia and Pacific Area. About 90 percent of the population 10 years of age and older are literate, despite the multiplicity of languages.
Labor force
Total:.. 27 million
By occupation: agriculture 47%, government and services 37%, industry and commerce 16%.

COUNTRY FACTS

Political and legal A republic headed by a presidential system of government with a bicameral legislature and an independent judiciary. The legal system is based on Spanish and Anglo-American law. Voting is compulsory for men and women at 15 years of age and older.
Telephone With over one million telephones, local and long-distance service is readily available but not always reliable. Country code: [63].
Transportation Taxis, Jeepneys, motorized tricycles, and long-distance buses serve all parts of the Philippines. Populated areas can be reached by automobile, but roads are often overcrowded and poorly maintained. Philippine Airlines has connections to many of the islands from Manila, as well as international service.
Environment Uncontrolled deforestation with consequential soil erosion and silt build-up constituted a major environmental problem in the 1980s. Combined with urban air and water pollution, natural disasters such as earthquakes, volcanic activity, typhoons, and floods can have devastating effects. Current issues include deforestation, soil erosion, water pollution, and severe air pollution in Manila.
Media There are nearly 40 daily newspapers, 8.8 million radios, and 2.8 million television sets. Radio and television broadcasting are both government and private concerns. There are five major TV networks and 33 broadcasting stations.
Health Increased attention and expenditures on health care have resulted in 75 percent of the population having access to health care services. The infant mortality rate has been lowered to 50 per 1,000 live births. The water supply in Manilla is generally safe, but untreated water should not be drunk outside the city. Average life expectancy is 65 years.

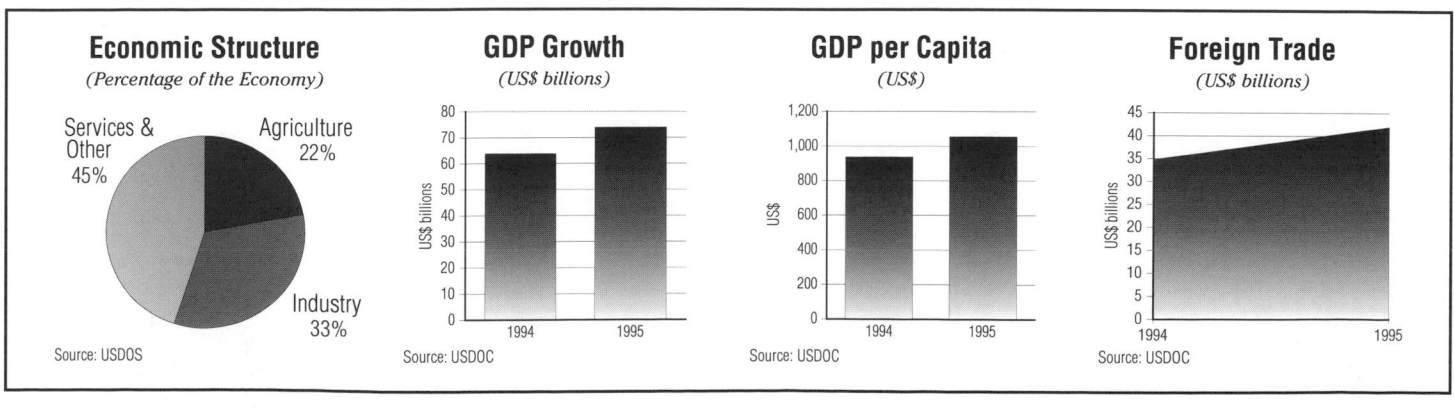

Economic Structure
(Percentage of the Economy)

Services & Other 45%
Agriculture 22%
Industry 33%

Source: USDOS

GDP Growth
(US$ billions)

1994   1995

Source: USDOC

GDP per Capita
(US$)

1994   1995

Source: USDOC

Foreign Trade
(US$ billions)

1994   1995

Source: USDOC

Regions

1. Batanes
2. Cagayan
3. Ilocos Norte
4. Ilocos Sur
5. Abra
6. Kalinga-Apayao
7. Mountain
8. La Union
9. Benguet
10. Ifugao
11. Isabela
12. Nueva Vizcaya
13. Quirino
14. Pangasinan
15. Nueva Ecija
16. Aurora
17. Quezon
18. Zambales
18. Tarlac
20. Bataan
21. Pampanga
22. Bulacan
23. Rizal
24. Cavite
25. Laguna
26. Batangas
27. Camirines Norte
28. Camirines Sur
29. Catanduanes
30. Mindoro Occidental
31. Mindoro Oriental
32. Marinduque
33. Albay
34. Sorsogon
35. Romblon
36. Masbate
37. Northern Samar
38. Samar
39. Eastern Samar
40. Aklan
41. Capiz
42. Antique
43. Iloilo
44. Negros Occidental
45. Negros Oriental
46. Siquijor
47. Cebu
48. Leyte
49. Southern Leyte
50. Bohol
51. Camiguin
52. Surigao del Norte
53. Surigao del Sur
54. Zamboaga del Norte
55. Zamboaga del Sur
56. Misamis Occidental
57. Misamis Oriental
58. Agusan del Norte
59. Agusan del Sur
60. Lanao del Norte
61. Lanao del Sur
62. Burkidnon
63. North Cotabato
64. Maguindanao
65. Sultan Kudarat
66. South Cotabato
67. Davao
68. Davao del Sur
69. Basilian
70. Davao Oriental
71. Sulu
72. Tawi Tawi
73. Palawan

Philippines

- National capital
- Regional capital
- Secondary cities
- Regional boundary
- Railroad
- Primary road
- International border

0 50 100 150 200 km
0 50 100 150 mi

Foreign Trade

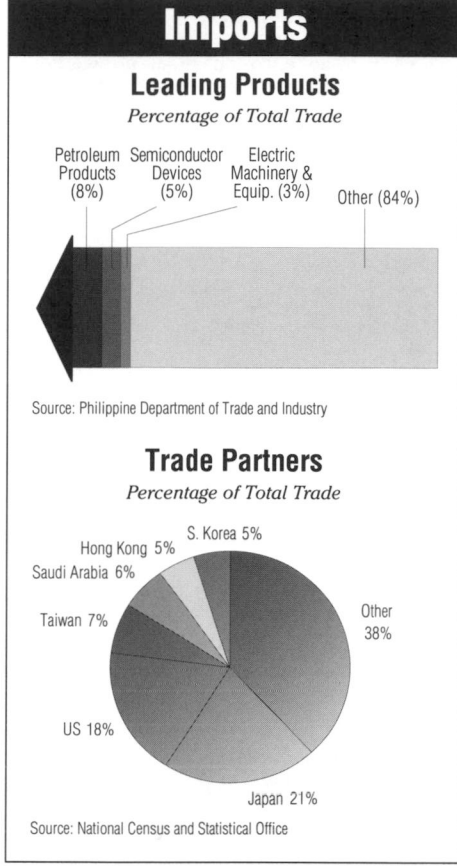

Imports

Leading Products
Percentage of Total Trade

Petroleum Products (8%)
Semiconductor Devices (5%)
Electric Machinery & Equip. (3%)
Other (84%)

Source: Philippine Department of Trade and Industry

Trade Partners
Percentage of Total Trade

Hong Kong 5%
S. Korea 5%
Saudi Arabia 6%
Taiwan 7%
Other 38%
US 18%
Japan 21%

Source: National Census and Statistical Office

Exports

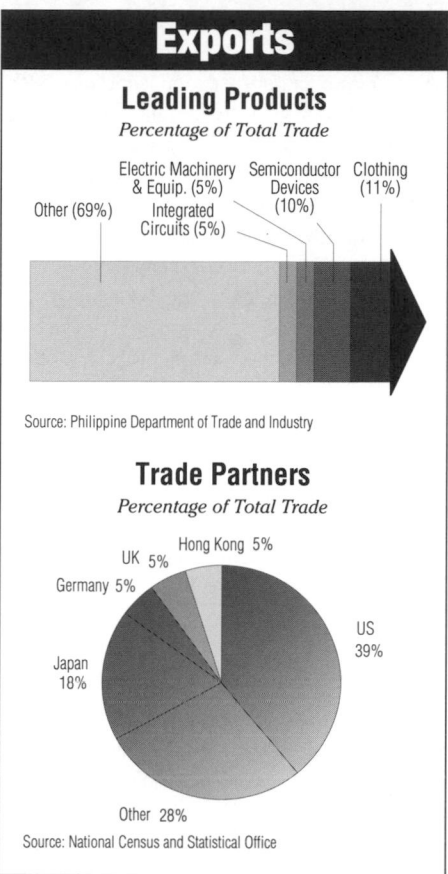

Leading Products
Percentage of Total Trade

Electric Machinery & Equip. (5%)
Semiconductor Devices (10%)
Clothing (11%)
Integrated Circuits (5%)
Other (69%)

Source: Philippine Department of Trade and Industry

Trade Partners
Percentage of Total Trade

Hong Kong 5%
UK 5%
Germany 5%
Japan 18%
US 39%
Other 28%

Source: National Census and Statistical Office

Opportunities

FOR IMPORTING TO THE PHILIPPINES

- cement
- ceramics
- stonework
- vegetables
- processed foods
- minerals
- agriculture
- transportation equipment
- telecommunications
- power generating equipment

FOR EXPORTING FROM THE PHILIPPINES

- raw materials
- textiles
- vehicles
- food
- finished electronic/electrical equipment
- mineral products
- garments
- coconut products
- agro-based products

GROWTH SECTORS

- rural industrialization
- agrarian reform
- rehabilitation and sustainable use of the country's natural resources
- technological upgrading
- textiles
- telecommunications
- basic services
- industry

GOVERNMENT PROCUREMENT

- transportation equipment
- engineering services
- power generating equipment
- highway construction equipment

Trade News

RULES AND REGULATIONS

- **Import restrictions** An ongoing import liberalization program has significantly reduced the items subject to import licensing requirements. For most products, quantitative restrictions are imposed for reasons of public health, morals, and national security. Corn, corn substitutes, poultry and poultry products, hogs, pork products, meat and meat products are prevented from importation in order to protect local producers.

- **Prohibited imports** Prohibited items include: dynamite, gunpowder, ammunition and other explosives, firearms, and weapons of war; written or printed articles in any form containing any matter advocating or inciting treason, or rebellion, insurrection, deception or subversion against the government; obscene or immoral articles; negatives or film, articles, instruments, drugs, and substances designed for producing unlawful abortion, or information on abortion; gambling items, lottery and sweepstakes tickets; gold, silver, or other precious metals; misbranded articles of food, narcotics, marijuana, and opium.

- **Tariffs and import taxes** Restructuring programs have brought average tariffs down to about 20 percent, grouped into four tiers of 3, 10, 20, and 30 percent. About 208 products are totally exempt from the tariff reduction program and remain subject to a 50 percent tariff. Included in this group are rice, coconut oil, sugar, fruits, and luxury consumer-oriented goods such as liquor, wines, processed fruits and vegetables, snack foods, tobacco, candy, and leather goods.

- **VAT** A value-added tax (VAT) of 10 percent is imposed on imports for resale or reuse. The VAT is based on the total value as assessed by the Bureau of Customs when determining tariff and customs duties, plus import duties, excise duties, and other charges. Other charges are imposed on the imports prior to release from customs custody, including postage, insurance, commissions, and similar charges. If duties are determined on the basis of volume or quantity, the base is the landed cost (duties, freight, insurance, and other charges). Some firms located in export processing zones are exempted from VAT.

- **Export controls** Exporters have a variety of incentives to entice them to produce goods for export. Simplified export procedures, exemption from the payment of excise taxes on exports, refunds or value-added taxes paid on imports for re-export, foreign exchange assistance, and the use of low-cost facilities in the country's Export Processing Zones administered by the Export Processing Zone Authority are some of the benefits offered by the government.

FREIGHT FORWARDERS

Dimerco Express
170 Quirino Ave., Tambo
Parañaque, Metro Manila
Tel: (2) 831-0041/5
Fax: (2) 832-5693

Hecny Forwarders, Inc.
30 San Luis St.
Pasay City, Metro Manila
Tel: (2) 833-2561
Fax: (2) 831-0084

Sea-Land Service, Inc.
2nd–3rd Fl., Dynavision Bldg.
108 Rada St.
Legaspi Village
Makati, Metro Manila
Tel: (2) 866-931/4

Associated Freight Consolidators, Inc.
Cargo Center, Nayong Pilipino Complex
Mia Rd.
Pasay City, Metro Manila
Tel: (2) 832-2701
Fax: (2) 833-3779

Overview

Marketing in the Philippines presents the usual challenges found in developing countries, plus a number of local issues. The island's geography poses difficulties with transportation, communication, and overall interaction. The population, about 68 million (projected to grow to 75 million by 2000), is divided equally between rural and urban, with most of the urban population concentrated around Manila, the country's capital, commercial, and national center. Manila provides the entire country with a variety of services and also serves as an inter-regional center for all the northern provinces and remote areas. The industrial sector represents a strong market for foreign sellers, and the retail trade has become quite dynamic, increasing demand for imports. Although price is usually the primary consideration of buyers, Filipinos look favorably on imported goods in general and tend to be extremely brand-conscious; they will often purchase brand goods, even at a premium when budgets allow. The government is itself a large direct importer of construction equipment and supplies. Telephone marketing is a relatively new development, and is rarely used; Filipinos prefer to deal face to face.

Distribution

The nation is composed of a series of small, unconnected islands, with infrastructure still developing, which serves to inhibit the efficient distribution of goods. Philippine agents and distributors have shown creativity and innovation in dealing with these problems, and have established vast networks of workable systems. They are, however, fairly complex and best navigated by a local agent familiar with the route. It is difficult for foreign sellers to sell directly to retailers, as these relationships are usually determined by family or political connections.

Agents, Distributors, and Partners

There is no typical profile of a Philippine agent or distributor. Firms can range in size from small enterprises with fewer than 25 employees handling only a few specialized products on behalf of a limited number of manufacturers, to large trading companies handling a wide range of products and suppliers. Some Philippine firms focus only on the metropolitan Manila area, whereas others also service provincial commercial centers such as Cebu, Davao, Iloilo, and Baguio. Philippine agents and distributors perform a full-range of functions, including negotiating sales transactions, pending storage and shipment arranging and delivery. Foreign sellers should maintain a steady flow of contact with their Philippine agents, and stock them with advertisements and brochures.

Selling Techniques

The trend toward supermarkets, shopping malls, and discount superstores was unheard of just a few years ago, but is on the rise today. Franchising, joint ventures, and direct marketing are becoming popular selling methods. The majority of franchises operating in the Philippines are in the fast food and restaurant business and typically operate under a master license agreement. Excellent opportunities for future franchises are business aids and services, food and beverages, printing, and automotive parts and services.

Advertising

As the Philippines is a brand-conscious market, advertising plays a significant part in promoting the sale of most goods, particularly consumer goods. Most advertising agencies have patterned their organization after US advertising agencies. Radio is the unrivaled mode of communication in the Philippines—it is the least expensive way to reach a large part of the population, and almost two-thirds of all families have one or more radios. While television has grown rapidly in the last decade, it is concentrated mostly in Manila and a few other urban centers; rural areas should not be targeted with television advertising. Television accounts for 60 percent of advertising spending, but is disproportionately expensive and represents a much lower percentage of actual advertisements. Radio, with 17 percent of the spending, is probably the most effective medium since print advertising, while cheaper than broadcast, is concentrated in the larger urban areas, and therefore does not reach the bulk of the population. Poster advertisements are prevalent in the urban areas.

Service and Customer Support

Suppliers must provide full support to their local representatives. Periodic visits to the Philippines should be conducted by suppliers to keep abreast of developments, to touch base with their local representatives, and to visit customers. There should be a strong emphasis on regular customer calls by local representatives in order for them to identify sales targets or opportunities, and to learn about problems with their products. It is imperative for foreign sellers to provide after-sales service and support during and after the warranty period in order to satisfy Philippine customers.

Marketing in the Philippines

MARKETING TIPS

- **Legal concerns** With market and financial controls in a state of flux, a thorough review of the status of the law is essential before transacting business.
- **•Special opportunities** Multi-level marketing has become a popular mode of selling.
- **Government purchasing** The Philippine government is a large direct importer of essential materials and equipment for government construction projects.
- **Postal service** The postal service in the Philippines is quick and reliable compared to neighboring countries, but many businesses may find it slow. Most packages or letters take about a week to reach their destination, either entering or leaving the Philippines.
- **Language** Tagalog, also known by its official name, Filipino, is the national language and is spoken by more than 40 percent of the population. English is widely used, and is the language of business and government. Some Spanish is still spoken, but its use is declining. The Philippines has eight major languages and over a hundred dialects.

AD AGENCIES

AB Communications
20th Fl., Pacific Star Bldg.
Sen. Gil J. Puyat Ave., cor. Makati Ave.
Makati, Metro Manila
Tel: (2) 815-8466/8 Fax: (2) 815-8493

Ace/Saatchi & Saatchi Advertising
9th Fl., Feliza Bldg.
108 Herrera St.
Legaspi Village
Makati, Metro Manila
Tel: (2) 810-1901 to 20
Fax: (2) 812-5035

Andersen Consulting
SGV Development Center
105 de la Rosa St.
Legaspi Village
Makati, Metro Manila
Tel: (2) 817-0301   Fax: (2) 817-2397

Asia Pacific Center for Research
Suite 321, Secretariat Bldg.
PICC, Roxas Blvd.
Pasay City, Metro Manila
Tel/Fax: (2) 831-3524

Campaigns & Grey
12th Fl., Velero Towers
Velero St.
Salcedo Village
Makati, Metro Manila
Tel: (2) 81-83861/3   Fax: (2) 810-3854

Core Alliance
7th Fl., SEDCCO Bldg.
Rada St., cor. Legazpi St.
Makati, Metro Manila
Tel: (2) 816-3766   Fax: (2) 815-9034

Dentsu, Young & Rubicam, Alcantara/Manila
704 Pablo Ocampo Sr. St.
Manila 1072
Tel: (2) 574-681/9   Fax: (2) 521-8129

J. Walter Thompson Co.
(Philippines)
Ramon Magsaysay Center
Manila Central Post Office
POB 1399
Ermita, Metro Manila 1099
Tel: (2) 599-831/9   Fax: (2) 521-1024

Jimenez/DMB&B
23rd Fl., Pacific Star Bldg.
Sen. Gil J. Puyat Ave., cor. Makati Ave.
Makati, Metro Manila
Tel: (2) 815-8318   Fax: (2) 815-8333

Lintas Manila
POB MCC 1081
Makati, Metro Manila
Tel: (2) 811-1111   Fax: (2) 811-0130

Business Culture

Greetings and Courtesies

Filipinos greet each other by establishing direct eye contact, raising their eyebrows slightly, and letting them fall as eye contact is made. This will usually include a friendly smile and, between men, a casual handshake. A man should not initiate a handshake with a woman; wait for her to hold out her hand. Handshakes are not firm; they are light and don't last long. Filipinos should be addressed as Mr., Ms., or Dr., or with another title if they have one. It is important to defer to people of rank, status, age, and seniority. Be formal when first meeting someone whose position entitles them to respect. This includes older members of an associate's family or kinship group. Senior government officials are particularly sensitive to being treated with respectful formality.

Hiya Filipinos are extremely sensitive about individual public image and self-esteem. Their culture combines the Asian idea of face (personal dignity and respect by one's peers) with the Spanish idea of love-of-self (amor propio). The result is an easily-offended sense of dignity, and Filipinos are careful that their words, actions, or thoughts are never insulting. Social behavior is determined by the Philippine concept of *hiya* (translated literally as shame). To be publicly ridiculed or criticized, or to not live up to expectations, results in *hiya* and a loss of self-esteem.

Business Ethic and Framework

Filipinos believe in family loyalty, reverence for religious beliefs, respect for one's self-image, social harmony, and avoiding direct confrontation or conflict. The family is the major social, and often business, unit. It extends to distant relatives, and may include godparents, sponsors, or old friends. Personal favors, granted and owed, are also extremely important. When one is done a favor, it is expected to be returned "with interest," and on request. The dynamic of owed favors ties Philippine groups together, and people will avoid being in the debt of someone from a rival group. In the Philippine business world, someone who has a large accumulation of unreturned favors can be extremely effective in getting results.

Decision Making

The well-being of the group, harmony, and consensus are extremely important, and decisions take time. Usually, the person who makes a final decision will not be at the meeting at which the proposal is laid out. Having things go smoothly is more important than articulating personal opinions, and telling "inconvenient" truths or being "too honest" must be avoided for fear of making others uncomfortable. "Yes" has a variety of meanings: it can mean "yes," "maybe," or even "highly unlikely."

Women

In the Philippines, women have long been treated more equally than in other Asian countries. The ideal Filipina is modest, shy, self-effacing, and loyal. Aggressive women who interact freely with men are not admired by women in this culture. Women are not essentially viewed as inferior, and hold positions of authority in business, politics, government, and law, with more visibility and power than in many other Asian nations. Foreigners should be aware that Philippine culture is conservative, especially when it comes to public interactions between men and women.

Meetings

Meetings should be set up far in advance (ideally by a third party who knows you and the Filipinos who will attend), and should be confirmed when you reach the Philippines. When a meeting is set, a common question is, "Is that Filipino time or Western time?" Filipino time will generally mean the meeting will start half-an-hour to an hour late. Even in the best of circumstances, traffic (particularly bad in Manila) and weather (sudden tropical cloudbursts) often make the most punctual people late.

Business Attire

Filipinos dress well for business and judge others by their clothes. Dress neatly, carefully, tastefully, and wear quality clothing. The weather will probably be warm, but men should wear a jacket and tie. Follow the lead of your host in removing the jacket once a meeting has begun. Women should wear a business suit or matching ensemble, preferably with stockings. Filipinas are quite fashion-conscious, and this is a culture where foreign women who are similarly inclined can indulge themselves. But avoid extremes in clothing or jewelry. Off-hours tip: do not wear shorts on the street, and avoid sandals (or you will be labeled a "hippie").

Cultural Cautions

DO'S

- Be aware of the crucial importance of *hiya* to Filipinos.
- Be aware of how important Filipinos regard owing favors and being in someone's social debt.
- Treat Filipinos as individuals, and always be respectful, friendly, and interested in them.

DON'TS

- Never do or say anything that will cause a Filipino to suffer *hiya*.
- Never do or say anything that might be felt as ridicule, hurt someone's feelings, or be seen as a lack of respect.

CUSTOMS

- Filipinos believe that a personal relationship based on mutual trust is a must for doing business.
- The use of third parties to initiate relationships and propose ventures helps avoid embarrassment or insult for everyone involved.
- The massive bureaucracy slows virtually every project. One traditional way to speed things up is a small bribe *(lagay)*. But this can lead to ethical questions and legal problems, and the government is trying to change this old way of doing business. Another way to facilitate business matters is to work with a Filipino who is adept at navigating the cumbersome Philippine bureaucracy. An associate who understands the system and can function well within it will be of invaluable help.
- Business cards are not as important as or exchanged with the same rituals as in other Asian nations. You may offer your card upon first meeting someone, or cards may be exchanged at the end of the meeting. Do not be surprised if the person you're meeting has not brought a card.
- Business gifts are appropriate if you're meeting someone with whom you have an important and established relationship. In other circumstances, they are not necessary or expected.

OBSERVATIONS

- The Philippines has the world's third largest English-speaking population, yet its culture has more in common with Asia than the West. There are more than 90 spoken languages and dialects, and a similar number of indigenous tribal groups.
- Customs can differ from region to region, and among people of different religions. The biggest differences occur mainly in rural areas and places with large Muslim populations. When doing business in outlying areas, be aware of the cultural material discussed throughout this section. When dealing with Muslims, be particularly aware of different social customs, dietary prohibitions, and the role of women.

NEGOTIATIONS

- Filipinos are known as tough, savvy negotiators, but this will probably be overshadowed by other cultural considerations. They will be extremely polite and very aware of others' comfort.
- Philippine groups act together, with the senior member doing most, if not all, of the speaking.
- Direct confrontation should be avoided. Difficult issues will often be postponed or completely avoided until a way can be found to work them out.
- Your group should be unified. Voice any doubts, criticisms, or disagreements only among yourselves, in private meetings. Speaking up with "interesting alternatives" or contradictory ideas will confuse the Philippine team.
- The person who will ultimately make the decision will probably not be at the meeting, so do not push for an immediate, final answer. This will only make everyone uncomfortable.
- It is important to have your agreement (or proposed agreement) written down, to help prevent misunderstandings, embarrassment, or conflict that can severely strain relationships.

Legal Matters

LEGAL BRIEFS

Legal System

The Philippines is basically a civil code country. Much of its legislation, particularly its commercial and business laws, are patterned after those of the United States.

Intellectual Property Rights

Patents Philippine patent law is based on US patent law, and the concepts and principles are fundamentally the same. Patents may be obtained for inventions, industrial designs, and utility models. The term of a patent is 17 years beginning from the date the patent is granted. It takes from two to three years to obtain patent registration. Foreigners may apply for a Philippine patent provided their country of citizenship grants by law substantially similar privileges to Philippine citizens seeking or holding patents.

Trademarks The trademark law is patterned after the US Lanham Act. To qualify for registration, a mark must be in actual use in commerce in the Philippines for not less than two months before the filing date. However, national treatment is accorded to citizens of countries that are members of the International Union for the Protection of Industrial Property (Paris Union). This allows registration in the Philippines of a mark registered in the applicant's home country, regardless of actual use in the Philippines. Trademark registration is effective for 20 years.

Copyright By law, copyrights are acquired and protected from the moment of creation without need for any other requirement or formality. Copyrights may be registered for most literary and artistic works, as well as computer programs and scientific models and designs. However, with respect to certain works such as books, periodicals, lectures, sermons, collections of literary, scholarly or artistic works, and sound recordings, registration and deposit are required in order to recover damages for infringement. Even without prior registration and deposit of a work, the creator may seek an injunction against any infringement and have the infringing copies and devices impounded. The copyright term is the lifetime of the creator plus 50 years after death.

Trade secrets No codified laws specifically protect trade secrets, but general provisions of the Civil Code and the Philippine criminal statutes protect these secrets and similar confidential information.

Business Registration

The Corporations Code and the Foreign Investments Act require foreign entities intending to do business in the Philippines to secure a license from the Philippine Securities and Exchange Commission (SEC). Enterprises engaged in certain activities may also be required to secure authorizations from other government agencies that regulate the particular industries, such as banking, insurance, mining, and natural resources. An enterprise that engages in certain preferred business activities and seeks to take advantage of special tax and other incentives must register with the Board of Investments. Technology transfer agreements must be registered with the Technology Transfer Registry of the Bureau of Patents, Trademarks, and Technology Transfer, which is part of the Department of Trade and Industry.

Contracts and Dispute Resolution

Parties have broad freedom to contract, and the contract terms are generally binding on them. However, there are specific instances in which the law requires that a document be executed or formalities observed for the contract to be valid or enforceable in court. Because of considerable exposure to the US legal system, contracts are becoming longer, more detailed, and closer in style and scope to those commonly used in the US. Lawsuits are still the predominant means used to settle contract disputes, although litigation is protracted and expensive. The Rules of Court provide for discovery procedures but these are not widely used. Arbitration clauses are becoming more common in contracts between Filipino and foreign parties, but arbitration and other methods of alternative dispute resolution are not yet widely practiced, except in connection with labor disputes.

Notaries

A notary public is authorized to administer oaths and to authenticate written documents, such as deeds of conveyance. As a general rule, acknowledgment of a document is not necessary for its validity. An acknowledged document, however, has a greater evidentiary value because it is deemed to have been executed publicly, and thus it does not need further proof of due execution and authenticity.

Labor

All workers are guaranteed the fundamental right to form and join unions. Although the right to strike is implicit, voluntary modes of dispute settlement are encouraged. At all stages of a labor dispute, the parties will make concerted efforts to amicably settle through conciliation and mediation. Collective bargaining is recognized as the ideal system for determining pay rates. Minimum wage rates are fixed on a regional basis by the Regional Tripartite Wage Boards of the Department of Labor and Employment.

Source: Angara Abello Concepcion Regala & Cruz, Makati, Metro Manila

- **Corporations** The corporation is the predominant form of business entity, and Philippine corporation and securities laws are patterned after those of the US. It takes from two weeks to one month to obtain a certificate of incorporation from the SEC, but "express lane" standard forms are available, which can be processed in one to three days.

- **Maximum workweek** Normal work hours should not exceed 8 hours per day. Employers must provide workers a rest period of 24 consecutive hours after every six consecutive normal work days. In practice, many white-collar workers work five days a week. There are 12 paid holidays per year. An employee who has completed the first year in service is entitled to a five day leave with pay.

- **Employee right to work** An employee's security of tenure is constitutionally protected, and an employee cannot be dismissed except for cause. In case of doubt, disputes are often resolved in favor of the employee.

- **Monopolies** Combinations and conspiracies in restraint of trade are prohibited. Penalties for violations include forfeiture of business property and personal criminal liability for business principals.

- **International agreements** The Philippines is a member of ASEAN, APEC, GATT/WTO, Pacific Economic Cooperation Conference, Asian Productivity Organization, and Convention on the Recognition and Enforcement of Foreign Arbitral Awards.

LEGAL CONTACTS

Angara Abello Concepcion Regala & Cruz
5th Floor Accra Building
122 Gamboa Street
Legaspi Village
Makati, Metro Manila
Tel: (2) 817-0966 Fax: (2) 816-0119

V.E. Del Rosario & Partners
Rasadel Bldg.
1011 Makati, Metro Manila
Tel: (2) 818-6011/3, 877-876/7
Fax: (2) 818-0194

Feria, Feria Lugtu & La Ó
Ferlaw Bldg.
366 Cabildo St.
1002 Intramuros, Metro Manila
Tel: (2) 479-182, 478-040, 407-196
Fax: (2) 530-0582

Gozon Defensor & Parel Law Offices
15th Fl., Sagittarius Condominium
H.V. de la Costa St.
Salcedo Village
Makati, Metro Manila
Tel: (2) 816-3716/9 Fax: (2) 817-0696

Laurel Law Offices
15th Fl., JMT Corporate Condominium
Ortigas Center
Pasig, Metro Manila
Tel: (2) 634-2711 Fax: (2) 633-8680

Puno and Puno Law Offices
5th Fl., Hongkong Bank Center
San Miguel Ave.
Pasig, Metro Manila
Tel: (2) 631-1261 Fax: (2) 631-2517

Quisumbing Torres & Evangelista Law Office
Pacific Star Bldg.
Makati Ave., cor. Sen. Gil J. Puyat Ave.
Makati, Metro Manila
Tel: (2) 817-3016 Fax: (2) 817-4432

Romulo, Mabanta, Buenaventura, Sayoc & de los Angeles
4th Fl., King's Court I Bldg.
2129 Pasong Tamo
Makati, Metro Manila
Tel: (2) 815-3011 Fax: (2) 810-3110

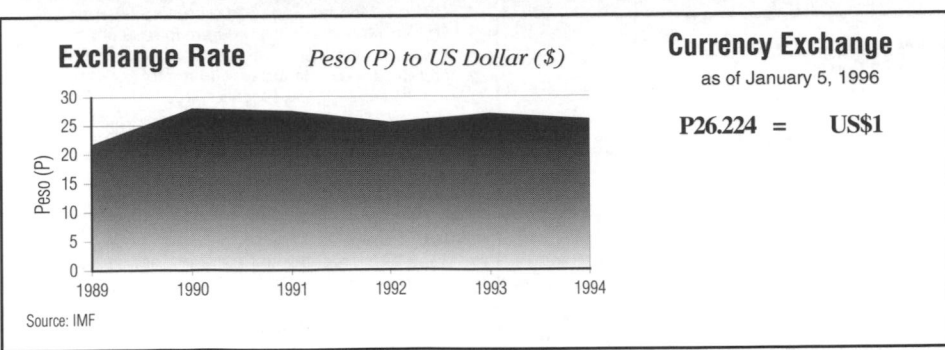

Exchange Rate *Peso (P) to US Dollar ($)*

Peso (P): 0, 5, 10, 15, 20, 25, 30
Years: 1989, 1990, 1991, 1992, 1993, 1994

Source: IMF

Currency Exchange
as of January 5, 1996

P26.224 = US$1

Currency

The currency in use is the Philippine peso (P).

Foreign Exchange

Authorized banks can exchange foreign currency. Recent laws passed by the Philippines make it possible to sell and purchase foreign currency outside the banking system. Nonresidents can open accounts in the Philippines without approval from the Central Bank, but the accounts can only be credited with pesos or convertible foreign currencies.

Capital Transfers

Authorized banks can sell foreign exchange for invisible payments, even without prior approval from the Central Bank. The only exceptions to this rule are for payments related to any kind of foreign loan or investments requiring documentation from the Central Bank. All profits and dividends accruing to nonresidents can be effected directly through commercial banks without prior approval from the Central Bank. There are no surrender requirements for invisibles proceeds, and they may be used without restriction.

Investment Incentives

There are several incentives for firms engaged in government-preferred activities, including an income tax holiday, tax and duty exemption on imported capital equipment and accompanying spare parts, and tax credit on domestic capital equipment. Investments in less-developed areas are automatically entitled to additional incentives, including 100 percent foreign ownership and large deductions from taxable income.

Investment Restrictions

While investment liberalization has been substantial, barriers to foreign entry remain for a variety of reasons. Depending on the industry or activity, foreign ownership is heavily regulated or restricted outright.

TAXATION

Taxation requires sophisticated knowledge of complex rules and regulations specific to each country. The information presented here is from the Ernst & Young Corporate Tax Guide and Directory, available from the Ernst & Young accounting office in your country, or from:

Punongbayan & Araullo
Mail Address:
POB 7573
Domestic Airport
Post Office Lock Box
1300 Domestic Road
Pasay City, Metro Manila
Philippines
Street Address:
6th Floor, Vernida IV Bldg.
Alfaro St., Salcedo Village
1200 Makati, Metro Manila
Philippines
Tel: (2) 810-9741, 812-6091
Telex: 22078 Ans bk PNA PH
(Via Philcom-RCA)
Fax: (2) 810-9748

At a Glance

Corporate Income Tax Rate (%) (a)	35
Capital Gains Tax Rate (%)	35
Branch Tax Rate (%)	35
Withholding Tax (%)	
Dividends (b)(c)	0
Interest on Peso Deposits (b)(d)	20
Royalties from Patents, Know-how, etc. (b)	20
Branch Remittance Tax	15
Net Operating Losses (Years)	
Carryback	0
Carryforward	0

(a) Certain Philippine-source income of foreign corporations is taxed at preferential rates.
(b) If the recipient is a nonresident foreign corporation, the final withholding tax rate is generally 35%.
(c) Dividends paid to nonresident foreign corporations are subject to a 15% rate if certain conditions are met.
(d) Interest received by nonresidents on loans to Philippine residents is subject to a 20% final withholding tax.

Money Matters

BITS AND PIECES

- **Corporate income tax** All resident companies are taxed on their worldwide income. Resident foreign companies, however, created under foreign laws and engaged in trade or business in the Philippines, are taxed on net taxable income derived from the Philippines. All other nonresident companies are considered nonresident foreign corporations and are taxed only on gross income derived from the Philippines.
- **Regulations** All investments are regulated by the comprehensive Omnibus Investments Code of 1987. The Board of Investments (BOI) is responsible for implementing the code, bringing Philippines incentive schemes into line with those of other countries in the Association of Southeast Asian Nations (ASEAN).
- **Capital gains** In most cases, capital gains are taxed the same way as ordinary income.
- **Foreign tax relief** Tax credits are available to resident companies for income and taxes paid or owing to any country.
- **Capital transfers** All inward transfers must be registered with the Central Bank. There are no exceptions to this rule.
- **Gold** All forms of gold can, at the request of the owner and with consent of the Central Bank, be sold to the Central Bank.

BANKS

Bank of America, NT&SA (USA)
BA-Lepanto Bldg.
8747 Paseo de Roxas
Makati, Metro Manila
Tel: (2) 815-5000, 815-8046
Fax: (2) 815-5895

Bank of Tokyo (Japan)
5th Fl., Ayala Bldg.
Makati, Metro Manila
Tel: (2) 892-1976   Fax: (2) 816-0413

Citibank, NA (USA)
Citibank Center Bldg.
8741 Paseo de Roxas
Makati, Metro Manila
Tel: (2) 815-7000   Fax: (2) 815-7703

Security Bank and Trust Company
SBTC Bldg.
6778 Ayala Ave.
Makati, Metro Manila
Tel: (2) 818-7677   Fax: (2) 816-4213

Solidbank Corporation
Solidbank Bldg.
Cor. Juan Luna and Dasmariñas Streets
Binondo, Metro Manila
Tel: (2) 831-2821

Union Bank of the Philippines
SSS Makati Bldg.
Ayala Ave.
Makati, Metro Manila
Tel: (2) 892-0011   Fax: (2) 818-6058

United Coconut Planters Bank
Makati Ave.
Makati, Metro Manila
Tel: (2) 818-8361   Fax: (2) 818-6863

Philippine National Bank (PHILNABANK)
PNB Bldg.
257 Escolta St.
Escolta, Metro Manila
Tel: (2) 402-051
Fax: (2) 496-091

Bank of the Philippine Islands
BPI Bldg.
Ayala Ave.
Makati, Metro Manila
Tel: (2) 818-5541
Fax: (2) 715-8434

Far East Bank and Trust Company
FEBTC Bldg.
Muralla St.
1002 Intramuros, Metro Manila
Tel: (2) 401-020/1

Business Travel

	LH 1906	MADRID	935	113-3
	LH 1022	STUTTGART HBF.	935	-
	AF 1701	LYON	940	683-6
	AV 822	HELSINKI	940	113-3
	AA 071	SFRANCISCO-DALLAS	945	731-7

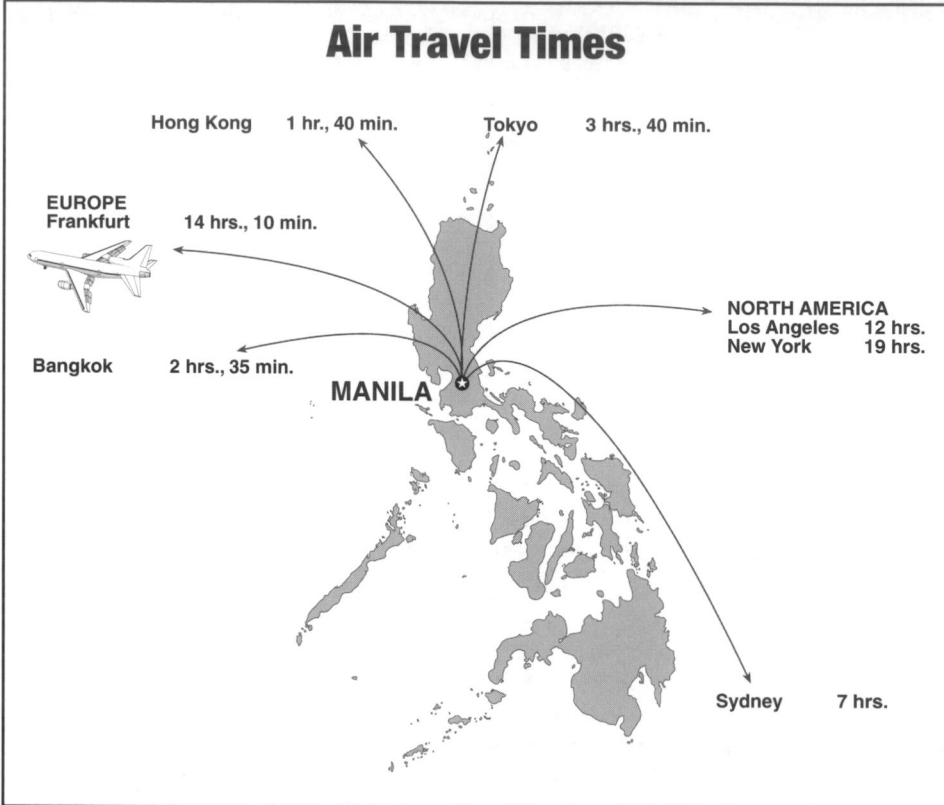

Air Travel Times

Hong Kong — 1 hr., 40 min.

Tokyo — 3 hrs., 40 min.

EUROPE Frankfurt — 14 hrs., 10 min.

NORTH AMERICA
Los Angeles — 12 hrs.
New York — 19 hrs.

Bangkok — 2 hrs., 35 min.

MANILA

Sydney — 7 hrs.

COMMUNICATIONS

Telephones Telephone service is not well-developed. International calls can be quickly connected, but local service is not reliable or available. Businesspeople should use messengers, who are readily available, for conducting local business in the Philippines.
Fax Fax service is available at large hotels, but the poor telephone system often renders it unusable. Telex service is recommended for business communication instead of faxing services.
Post office Post offices are located throughout the major cities and service is generally fine. Home mail delivery is Monday through Saturday. Post offices also offer telegram service. Stamps can be purchased at hotels and stores.
TV/Radio Manila has five commercial radio stations and many others exist throughout the country. There are five major television networks and 33 broadcasting stations.

BEST TRAVEL BOOKS

Culture Shock, a Guide to Customs and Etiquette, Philippines. 250 pages.
Importing from the Philippines, A buyer's manual. 204 pages.
Philippines Business. World Trade Press, San Rafael, Calif.
Lonely Planet Travel Survival Guide, Philippines. Packs a great deal of information into a small package, clearly written for the traveler who desires a deep appreciation for the culture and the people. 550 pages, 16 color.
The Travellers Guide to Philippines Customs and Manners. Elizabeth Devine & Nancy Braganti. An invaluable guide for people not wanting to put foot in mouth.

TELEPHONE NUMBERS

If you are calling from outside the Philippines you will need to add the country code [63] and any other international dialing requirements from within your country.
- Operator 144
- Directory 144
- International Operator 108
- Police 166
- Emergency 911
- Tourist Police .... (2) 501660
- Fire Manila .... (2) 5811176
- Fire Makati .... (2) 8162553
- First Aid/Ambulance .... (2) 596061
- Tourism Information .... (2) 501660
- Dentist .... (2) 83225413
- Manila Chamber of Commerce .... (2) 498321
- Philippine Chamber of Commerce .... (2) 817-6981
- Chamber of International Trade .... (2) 712-0193
- Department of Trade and Industry .... (2) 818-5701
- Limousine Service .... (2) 506-601
- DHL International .... (2) 885-511
- Federal Express .... (2) 810-5372
- Cultural Center .... (2) 832-1125
- Foreign Investments Assistance .... (2) 818-1831
- Bureau of Customs .... (2) 484161
- Foreign Affairs Ministry .... (2) 502081
- Philippine Airlines .... (2) 818-01111
- Philippine National Railway .... (2) 210-011

Credit Card Information
Lost or stolen credit cards (call collect to the US, regardless of which country the card was issued in).
- Amex .... [1] (919) 333-3211
- Diner's Club .... [1] (303) 799-1504
- MasterCard .... [1] (314) 275-6690
- Visa .... [1] (410) 581-7931

Travelogue

WORKWEEK

Offices Monday-Friday 9:00 am to 5:00 pm.
Banks Monday-Friday 9:00 am to 3:00 pm.
Government Monday-Friday 9:00 am to 5:00 pm.
Retail Monday-Saturday 9:00 am to 7:30 pm.

HOLIDAYS

Holidays 1996
January 1 New Year's Day
April 4 Maundy Thursday
April 5 Good Friday
April 9 Bataan and Corregidor Day and Heroism Day
May 1 Labor Day
June 12 Independence Day
August 4th Sunday National Heroes' Day
November 1 All Saints' Day
November 30 Bonifacio Day
December 25 Christmas
December 30 Rizal Day

VISA AND PASSPORT

A valid passport and an onward ticket are required for entry to the Philippines.

DEPARTURE FORMALITIES

A departure tax of P220 will be collected from all travelers. A visa is not required for stays up to 21 days.

IMMUNIZATION

International certificates of vaccination are required if you are arriving from an infected area. International certificate of vaccine for yellow fever required if you are transiting or arriving from infected area within 6 days. Cases of cholera have been reported. Vaccinations recommended include cholera, malaria, polio, tetanus, typhoid. Travelers remaining in the Philippines longer than 6 months require a valid AIDS clearance certificate.

TIPPING

Taxi: optional but appreciated, 10 percent. Porters: 10 pesos per piece. Hotels, restaurants: 10 percent. Doorman: 10 pesos. Small services: 5 pesos.

CRIME

Crime is common and a serious matter in the Philippines. The violence between Philippine Christians and Muslims creates a presence of military rebels and activities that can be dangerous, with the most common targets being government officials, missionaries, military personnel, and American residents. Guerrilla armies do exist making travel to the Bicol region and the Quezon Province dangerous. The Mindanao Region, the Samar Islands, and the ARMM can also be dangerous. Do not travel off paved highways at night.

INFRASTRUCTURE

Manila International Airport is one of the best facilities in the Pacific. International direct flight service is available to many countries. Manila Domestic Airport shares runways with the international airport but the passenger terminal is located across from the airport. Philippine Airlines is suggested for all inter-island travel. Taxis are available from the airport to downtown. Purchase tickets at the terminal counters. Buses also operate to and from the airport with fares collected before you board. Rental cars are available throughout Manila and at the airport and any valid driver's license is accepted. Large hotels do provide shuttle service. Chauffeur-driven cars can also be rented for the day. Taxis are inexpensive and metered and can be hailed from the street or arranged by telephone for pick up. Most are driven recklessly and are poorly maintained. Do not accept any offer for a flat fee and always insist the meter be used. Buses are reasonable but very often crowded and routes are usually confusing to travelers. Metro Rail is Manila's light rail system.

NATIONAL TOURIST OFFICE

Department of Tourism
DOT Bldg.
T.M. Kalaw St.
Rizal Park, Manila
Tel: (2) 599-031/048
Fax: (2) 521-7274

Contents

GOVERNMENT AGENCIES

Asset Privatization Trust
10th Fl., BA-Lepanto Bldg.
8747 Paseo de Roxas
Makati, Metro Manila
Tel: (2) 861-619, 815-9201/5

Bangko Sentral ng Pilipinas (BSP)
(Central Bank of the Philippines)
A. Mabini St., cor. Vito Cruz St.
Malate, Metro Manila
Tel: (2) 507-051, 593-380/1, 595-263, 582-372
Fax: (2) 522-3987, 597-363

Bases Conversion Development Authority
2nd Fl., Rufino Center
Ayala Ave., cor. Herrera St.
1226 Makati, Metro Manila
Tel: (2) 813-5383, 864-006/9
Fax: (2) 813-5424/7

Board of Investments (BOI)
Industry and Investments Bldg.
385 Sen. Gil J. Puyat Ave.
1200 Makati, Metro Manila
Tel: (2) 818-1831, 868-403, 867-895, 875-602
Fax: (2) 8191887, 851166

Board of Investments (BOI)
Investment and Marketing Department
Industry and Investments Bldg.
385 Sen. Gil J. Puyat Ave.
Makati, Metro Manila
Tel: (2) 868-403, 816-127, 875-602
Fax: (2) 819-1793, 819-1816, 819-1887, 851-166

Board of Investments One-Stop Action Center
(BOI-OSAC)
Industry and Investments Bldg.
385 Sen. Gil J. Puyat Ave.
1200 Makati, Metro Manila
Tel: (2) 815-0702, 858-8322, 815-3731, 867-884
Fax: (2) 810-9728, 761-2165

Bonded Export Marketing Board
Ground Fl., Industry and Investments Bldg.
385 Sen. Gil J. Puyat Ave.
Makati, Metro Manila
Tel: (2) 856-127, 818-1831/9
Fax: (2) 810-9728

Bureau of the Animal Industry (BAI)
Visayas Ave.
Diliman
Quezon City, Metro Manila
Tel: (2) 966-883

Bureau of Air Transportation
Old MIA Rd.
Pasay City, Metro Manila
Tel: (2) 832-3047, 831-8078, 832-3308
Fax: (2) 833-1577

Bureau of Customs
Port Area
Manila
Tel: (2) 530-0966, 484-161/9
Fax: (2) 474-421/4, 530-0966, 818-2971

Bureau of Domestic Trade Promotion
2nd. Fl., Trade and Industry Bldg.
361 Sen. Gil J. Puyat Ave.
Makati, Metro Manila
Tel: (2) 817-5132, 817-5322
Fax: (2) 810-9363

Bureau of Export Trade Promotion
Department of Trade and Industry
5th Fl., New Solid Bldg.
357 Sen. Gil J. Puyat Ave.
Makati, Metro Manila
Tel: (2) 817-5298, 817-5203, 818-5701
Fax: (2) 817-4923, 819-1816

Bureau of Fisheries and Aquatic Resources
Arcadia Bldg.
Quezon Ave.
Quezon City, Metro Manila
Tel: (2) 965-498

Bureau of Food and Drugs
DOH Compound
Alabang

Muntinlupa, Metro Manila
Tel: (2) 842-4583, 807-0751
Fax: (2) 842-4603

Bureau of Forest Development
Visayas Ave.
Diliman
Quezon City, Metro Manila
Tel: (2) 964-826

Bureau of Internal Revenue
National Internal Revenue Bldg.
Diliman
Quezon City, Metro Manila
Tel: (2) 991-683, 965-644
Fax: (2) 922-4894

Bureau of International Trade Relations
Department of Trade and Industry
361 Sen. Gil J. Puyat Ave.
Makati, Metro Manila
Tel: (2) 817-8087   Fax: (2) 818-7846

Bureau of Patents, Trademarks and Technology Transfer
Department of Trade and Industry
361 Sen. Gil J. Puyat Ave.
Makati, Metro Manila
Tel: (2) 815-4919, 818-3109, 818-3944, 882-350
Fax: (2) 818-4145

Bureau of Plant Industry
Department of Agriculture
692 San Andres
Malate, Manila
Tel: (2) 571-726, 571-776, 586-201
Fax: (2) 521-7650

Bureau of Product Standards
3rd Fl., Trade and Industry Bldg.
361 Sen. Gil J. Puyat Ave.
Makati, Metro Manila
Tel: (2) 817-5527, 817-5339, 817-9602
Fax: (2) 817-9870

Bureau of Telecommunications
A. Roces Ave.
Quezon City, Metro Manila
Tel: (2) 964-391

Bureau of Trade Regulation and Consumer Protection
Department of Trade and Industry
2nd Fl., Trade and Industry Bldg.
361 Sen. Gil J. Puyat Ave.
Makati, Metro Manila
Tel: (2) 817-5280, 817-5340, 863-431, 818-5701 to 35
Fax: (2) 810-9363

Center for International Trade Expositions and Missions
ITC Complex
Roxas Blvd., cor. Sen. Gil J. Puyat Ave.
Pasay City, Metro Manila
Tel: (2) 831-2201/9, 832-5001, 832-3982
Fax: (2) 832-3965

Center for Labor Relations Assistance
2nd Fl., Trade and Industry Bldg.
361 Sen. Gil J. Puyat Ave.
Makati, Metro Manila
Tel: (2) 817-5180, 866-878
Fax: (2) 817-5180

BUSINESS AND TRADE ORGANIZATIONS

Cebu Chamber of Commerce and Industry
Room 104, WDC Bldg.
Osmena Blvd.
6000 Cebu City
Tel: (32) 99-312, 99-689

Chamber of International Trade
Ground Fl., Peralas Bldg.
646 Quezon Ave.
Quezon City, Metro Manila
Tel: (2) 712-0193

Confederation of Philippine Exporters
Room S-324, PICC-CCP Complex
Roxas Blvd., Metro Manila
Tel: (2) 832-0309, 831-9844

Employers Federation of the Philippines (ECOP)
4th Fl., ECC Bldg.
355 Sen. Gil J. Puyat Ave.
Makati, Metro Manila
Tel: (2) 816-3813   Fax: (2) 858-576

Makati Business Club
2nd Fl., Princess Bldg.
104 Esteban St.
Legaspi Village
Makati, Metro Manila
Tel: (2) 816-2658, 816-2660, 812-3812, 812-3753
Fax: (2) 816-2658, 812-3813

Manila Chamber of Commerce
410 Shurdut Bldg.
Intramuros, Metro Manila
Tel: (2) 498-321

Philippine Industrial Estates Association PHILEA Desk
Ground Fl., Industry and Investments Bldg.
385 Sen. Gil J. Puyat Ave.
Makati, Metro Manila
Tel: (2) 818-1831/9
Fax: (2) 810-9728

Philippine Chamber of Commerce
7th Fl., ODC International Plaza
219 Salcedo St.
Legaspi Village
Makati, Metro Manila
Tel: (2) 817-6981

Philippine Chamber of Commerce and Industry
Ground Fl., Secretariat Bldg., East Wing
CCP Complex
Roxas Blvd.
Pasay City, Metro Manila
Tel: (2) 833-8591/
Fax: (2) 833-8895

WORLD TRADE CENTER

World Trade Center Metro Manila
15th Fl., Solidbank Bldg.
Paseo de Roxas
1200 Makati, Metro Manila
Tel (2) 819-7232, 819-7297
Fax: (2) 819-7205

BUSINESS ORGANIZATIONS

American Chamber of Commerce of the Philippines
Corinthian Plaza, 2nd Fl.
Paseo de Roxas
1299 Makati, Metro Manila
Tel: (2) 818-791
Fax: (2) 816-6359
Mailing address: POB 1578, MCC, Manila

Canadian Chamber of Commerce and Industry
Ground Fl., InterBank Bldg.
Paseo de Roxas
Makati, Metro Manila
Tel: (2) 812-8568

Euro Info-Office
3rd Fl., King's Court II Bldg.
2129 Don Chino Roces Ave.
Makati, Metro Manila
Tel: (2) 811-223
Fax: (2) 818-8030

European Chamber of Commerce of the Philippines
5th Fl., Kings Court II Bldg.
Pasong Tamo
Makati, Metro Manila
Tel: (2) 854-747, 866-995/8, 854-4747
Fax: (2) 815-2688

Federation of Filipino-Chinese Chambers of Commerce and Industry, Inc.
6th Fl., Federation Center Bldg.
Muelle de Binondo St.
Manila
Tel: (2) 474-921/5   Fax: (2) 530-1369

Philippine-US Business Council
5 E. Rodriguez Jr. Ave., cor. Pasig Blvd.
Pasig, Metro Manila
Tel: (2) 693-8576

US-ASEAN Council
Thomas Jefferson Bldg.
395 Sen. Gil J. Puyat Ave. Ext.
Makati, Metro Manila
Tel: (2) 818-4336

NEWSPAPERS

Philippine News Agency
Media Center
Maharlika Broadcasting System
Bohol Ave.
3005 Quezon City, Metro Manila
Tel: (2) 976-661

Philippine Information Agency
Visayas Ave.
Diliman
Quezon City, Metro Manila
Tel: (2) 921-7941

Asian Wall Street Journal
Dow Jones Publishing Co. (Asia)
GPOB 9825
Hong Kong
Tel: [852] 2573-7121   Fax: [852] 2834-5291

Business World
Business World Publishing Corp.
4th Fl., Diamond Motor Bldg.
Ortigas Ave.
Greenhills
San Juan, Metro Manila
Tel: (2) 799-291, 793-934

Malaya
People's Independent Media, Inc.
C.C. Castro Bldg.
38 Timog Ave.
Quezon City, Metro Manila
Tel: (2) 983-271/6

Manila Bulletin
Bulletin Publishing Corp.
Cor. Muralla and Recoletos Streets
Intramuros, Metro Manila
Tel: (2) 473-621

Manila Chronicle
Manila Chronicle Publishing Corp.
371A Bonifacio Drive
Port Area, Metro Manila
Tel: (2) 810-6941/4   Fax: (2) 481-085

Manila Times
La Vanguardia Publishing Co.
Cor. Scout Santiago and Ojeda Streets
Quezon City, Metro Manila
Tel: (2) 964-448

Morning Times
Zulueta St.
POB 51
Cebu City, Cebu
Tel: (32) 77-032

People's Journal
Philippines Journalists Inc.
Times Journal Bldg.
Railroad St., cor. 19th and 20th Streets
Port Area, Metro Manila
Tel: (2) 486-872

Philippine Daily Inquirer
POB 2050
1099 Manila
Tel: (2) 700-620/9

RADIO AND TELEVISION

Department of Transportation and Communications
3rd Fl., Philcomcen Bldg.
Ortigas Ave.
Pasig, Metro Manila
Tel: (2) 631-8761/3, 631-8666, 721-3781
Fax: (2) 632-9985

National Telecommunications Commission
VIBAL Bldg.
Epifanio de los Santos Ave. cor. Times St.
Quezon City, Metro Manila
Tel: (2) 924-4042, 924-4008, 981-160
Fax: (2) 921-7128

ABS-CBN Broadcasting Corporation
Mother Ignacia Ave.
Quezon City, Metro Manila
Fax: (2) 921-5888

Banahaw Broadcasting Corporation
Capitol Hills, Diliman
3005 Quezon City, Metro Manila
Tel: (2) 961-109

Far East Broadcasting Co.
POB 1
0560 Valenzuela, Metro Manila
Tel: (2) 292-1152
Fax: (2) 292-4724, 359-9490

Maharlika Broadcasting System
Media Center
Sgt. Esuerra Ave.
3005 Quezon City, Metro Manila
Tel: (2) 922-0880

Nation Broadcasting Corporation (NBC)
NBC Tower
Epifanio de los Santos Ave.
Guadalupe
1200 Makati, Metro Manila
Tel: (2) 819-5673
Fax: (2) 819-7234

Philippines Broadcasting Service (PBS)
Bureau of Broadcast Services
Office of the Press Secretary
4th Fl., Philippine Information Agency Bldg.
Visayas Ave.
Quezon City, Metro Manila
Tel: (2) 924-2607
Fax: (2) 924-2745

Radio Philippines Network
Broadcast City
Capitol Hills, Diliman
Quezon City, Metro Manila
Tel: (2) 977-661
Fax: (2) 984-322

AD AGENCIES

AB Communications
20th Fl., Pacific Star Building
Sen. Gil J. Puyat Ave., cor. Makati Ave.
Makati, Metro Manila
Tel: (2) 815-8466/8
Fax: (2) 815-8493

Ace/Saatchi & Saatchi Advertising
9th Fl., Feliza Bldg.
108 Herrera St.
Legaspi Village
Makati, Metro Mila
Tel: (2) 810-1901 to 20
Fax: (2) 812-5035

Dentsu, Young & Rubicam, Alcantara/Manila
704 Pablo Ocampo Sr. St.
Manila 1072
Tel: (2) 574-681/9
Fax: (2) 521-8129

Jimenez/DMB&B
23rd Fl., Pacific Star Bldg.
Sen. Gil J. Puyat Ave., cor. Makati Ave.
Makati, Metro Manila
Tel: (2) 815-8318
Fax: (2) 815-8333

Lintas Manila
PO Box MCC 1081
Makati, Metro Manila
Tel: (2) 811-1111
Fax: (2) 811-0130

Taipan Bozell
2nd Fl., DPSI Business Center
210 N. Garcia St., Bel Air II
Makati, Metro Manila
Tel (2) 894-5157
Fax: (2) 594-5159

ACCOUNTING FIRMS

Coopers & Lybrand
c/o Carlos J. Valdes
MCPOB 2431
Makaki, Metro Manila
Tel: (2) 857-706

Dia Murillo Dalupan
POB 3119
Manila 1099
Tel: (2) 864-325 Fax: (2) 817-5766

KMPG Fernandos Santos & Lopez
MCPOB 1659
Makati, Metro Manila
Tel: (2) 812-8331

Laha, Manabat, Salgado & Co.
MCPOB Box 3483
Makati, Metro Manila
Tel: (2) 818-9492 Fax: (2) 816-6595

Punongbayan & Araullo
6th Floor, Vernida IV Bldg.
Alfaro St.
Salcedo Village
Makati, Metro Manila 1200
Tel: (2) 810-9741, 812-6091

SGV & Co.
POB 589
Manila 1099
Tel: (2) 819-3011 Fax: (2) 810872

SyCip, Gorres, Velayo & Co.
6760 Ayala Ave.
Makati, Metro Manila
Tel: (2) 819-3011 Fax: (2) 819-0872

Joaquin Cunanan and Company
8th Floor, BA-Lepanto Bldg.
8747 Paseo de Roxas
Makati, Metro Manila
Tel: (2) 818-7622/6, 818-9103/5
Fax: (2) 815-3514

Alas Group
(A member of Horwath International)
POB 2839 MCC
Manila
Tel: (2) 810-1701 Fax: (2) 812-463

INTERNET ADDRESSES

Usenet group(s):
soc.culture.filipino

Philippine Business and Development
http://www.iphil.net/rp/busdev/index.html

The Philippines
http://www.dlsu.edu.ph/othersites/pinas/pinas.html

Philippines Embassy in the UK
http://turnpike.net/metro/latimer/philemb/philemb.html

Philippine Business OnLine
http://is.eunet.ch/astarte/pbo/quick.html

Philippine WWW Pages
http://www.moz.com.com/SCF/SCF.html

Poland

Republic of Poland

Economy

Overview

In 1994 the Polish economy continued its strong recovery from the recession of the year before. Most of the trends seen in recent years continued, with the industrial sector output pulling along the rest of the economy. Agricultural output was depressed by drought for the second time in three years. Inflation remained high, but did decline, as did the trade deficit. However, progress on privatization and other structural reforms has been slow and uncertain. Most subsidies and controls on the prices of consumer goods have been eliminated. However, with a return of the Communists to power in the recent elections, the future of Poland's economic policy is uncertain.

Trade

A few remaining state-owned trading companies compete with private traders, but few restrictions are placed on foreign trade. Germany, Russia and Italy are Poland's largest trading partners. Remarkably, a major component of Poland's economic recovery has been the sale of goods to nonresidents visiting Poland. Estimates of this trade range as high as 9.5 billion zloty (US$4 billion a year), about five percent of GDP. Because of the lower price of gasoline in Poland there is essentially no cost for Germans living within 300 kilometers to come shopping. For the last three years, Germans have traveled across the border to Poland by the millions to buy food, clothing, and gasoline. In 1994, it became evident that Russians were also engaging in this trade. Receipts from this trade are the largest source of the increase in Poland's foreign exchange reserves seen since mid-1993.

Sectors

Agriculture Agricultural output again suffered from drought in 1994, after having recovered in 1993 from the 1992 drought which had caused a decline of nearly 12 percent. Inefficient and undercapitalized, this sector still accounts for only seven percent of GDP, while employing about one-quarter of the Polish labor force.

Industry Manufacturing contributed the most to economic growth in 1993, accounting for 50 percent of GDP. While it still dominates the Polish economy, other industrial sectors are now emerging.

Services Poland's banking system is being restructured, and banks now set their own lending and deposit rates, but banking and accounting services are still inefficient by world standards. However, rates of growth in many of the service industries have begun to rise, and they should soon begin to modernize as a result. It is estimated that the import of services accounts for more than 20 percent of total imports.

Trends

Poland's GDP grew at an estimated rate of 4.5 percent in 1994. Opportunities will continue to emerge as privatization of state industry, which has been slow to date, continues—assuming the new administration does continue such policies. The prospect for real economic growth and the tremendous size of the Polish market are the main draws for foreign companies doing business in Poland. Most multinationals believe that Poland is the best market in Central and Eastern Europe for their products and/or investments. The rate of inflation (almost 600 percent in 1990), continues to decline, and remained at an annual rate of about 27 percent throughout 1994.

At a Glance

THE COUNTRY

Location Eastern Europe, bordered on the north by the Baltic Sea, and on the south by Slovakia and the Czech Republic.
Terrain The majority of Poland is mountainous, marked by a glaciated region and a narrow region with bays and lakes.
Climate Only the southern areas are humid. Westerly winds cool much of the country. The summers are cool and the winters range from moderately cold to cold. Rainfall averages from 50cm to 135cm.

THE PEOPLE

Population 38,500,000
Ethnic composition
Poles 98%
Significant minorities include Ukrainians, Lithuanians, Belorussians, Germans, and Gypsies.
Religious composition
Roman Catholic 95%
Russian Orthodox and Protestantism are also widely practiced.
Languages spoken Polish is the official language, but English, French, German, and Russian are also understood to varying degrees.
Education and literacy Virtually the entire population is literate. All primary and secondary and most university education is free.
Labor force
Total 17,500,000
By occupation: agriculture 27%, trade, transport, and comunications 15%, industry and contruction 32%, government and other 25%.

COUNTRY FACTS

Political and legal The political and legal systems are currently being transformed. Power is divided between a president and a parliament. The judiciary is supervised by the Ministry of Justice; all lawyers are employed by the state.
Telephone All communication services are government owned and operated. There are over 4.5 million telephones; international service is readily available from the cities. International country code: [48]; city codes: Crakow (Krakow) (12), Warsaw (22) or (2).
Transportation The major transportation system is Poland's railroad. Highways are extensive but in poor condition. The major ports are in Szczecin, Gdynia, and Gdansk, and are in good condition. The Okecie International Airport in Warsaw is Poland's major airport, and the only one with international service.
Environment The main government agencies responsible for the environment are the Institute for Environmental Planning and the Ministry of Administration, Regional Economy, and Environmental Protection. Almost 75 percent of Poland's forests have been damaged. Water pollution in the Baltic Sea is 10 times higher than ocean waste would indicate. Current issues are pollution from industrial waste and gas emissions.
Media 27 AM, 27 FM, and 40 television stations. There are 45 daily newspapers, most with political orientations.
Health The government is aiming for complete socialization. There are private practices, but all health professionals must spend some time serving the state.

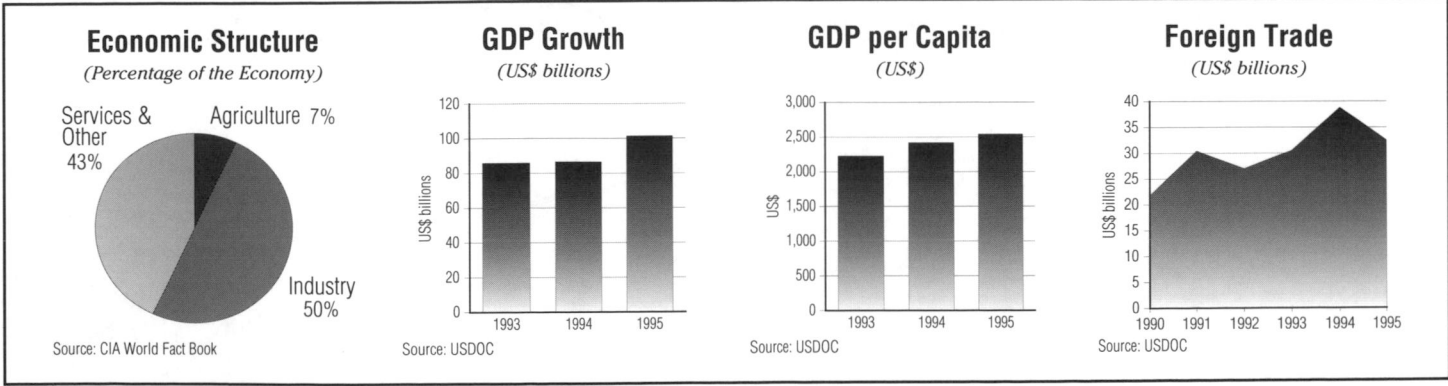

Economic Structure
(Percentage of the Economy)

Services & Other 43%
Agriculture 7%
Industry 50%

Source: CIA World Fact Book

GDP Growth
(US$ billions)

1993, 1994, 1995

Source: USDOC

GDP per Capita
(US$)

1993, 1994, 1995

Source: USDOC

Foreign Trade
(US$ billions)

1990 1991 1992 1993 1994 1995

Source: USDOC

Baltic   Sea

Pomeranian Bay

Gulf of Gdansk

Russia

Lithuania

* A province has the same name as its capital except where noted.

15°

54°

Slupsk

Gdynia
Gdansk

Koszalin

Elblag

Tczew

Swinoujscie

Suwalki

Szczecin

Stargard Szczecinski

Walcz

Chojnice

Olsztyn

Pila

Swiecie
Grudziadz

Gorzow

Notec

Bydgoszcz

Thrun

Ostroleka
Lomza

Bialystok

Narew

Gorzow Wielkopolski

Wisla

Cieckanow

Kostrzyn

Poznan

Wloclawek

Plock

Bug

Belarus

Warsaw

Siedlce

Konin

Warta

Warszawa

Biala Podlaska

Zielona Gora

Leszno

Kalisz

Lodz

Skierniewice

Ger.

Neisse

Lubin

Legnica

Jelenia Gora

Sieradz

Piotrkow Trybunalski

Tomaszow Mazowiecki

Pulawy

Radom

Lublin

Chelm

51°

Piotrkow

Oder

Wroclaw

Walbrzych

Opole

Kielce

Ostrowiec Swietokrzyski

Zamosc

Elbe

Czech Republic

Klodzko

Czestochowa

Tarnobrzeg

Stalowa Wola

Bytom

Katowice

Rzeszow

Oswiecim

Krakow

Przemysl

Bielsko-Biala

Tarnow

Bielsko

Nowy Targ

Nowy Sacz

Krosno

San

Ukraine

18°

Slovakia

21°

24°

Poland

★ National capital
◉ Regional capital
● Secondary city

—— Primary road
······· Railroad
—— Province border
▬▬ International border

| 0 | 50 | 100 | 150 km |
| 0 | 50 | | 100 mi |

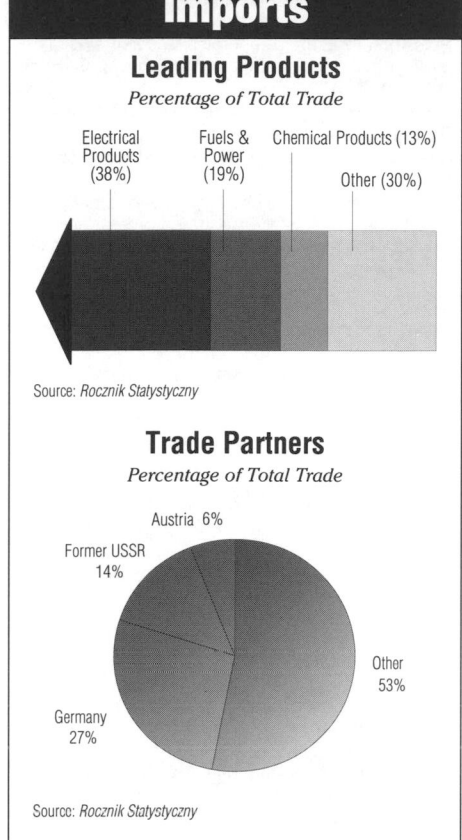

Foreign Trade

Imports

Leading Products
Percentage of Total Trade

Electrical Products (38%)   Fuels & Power (19%)   Chemical Products (13%)   Other (30%)

Source: *Rocznik Statystyczny*

Trade Partners
Percentage of Total Trade

Austria 6%
Former USSR 14%
Germany 27%
Other 53%

Source: *Rocznik Statystyczny*

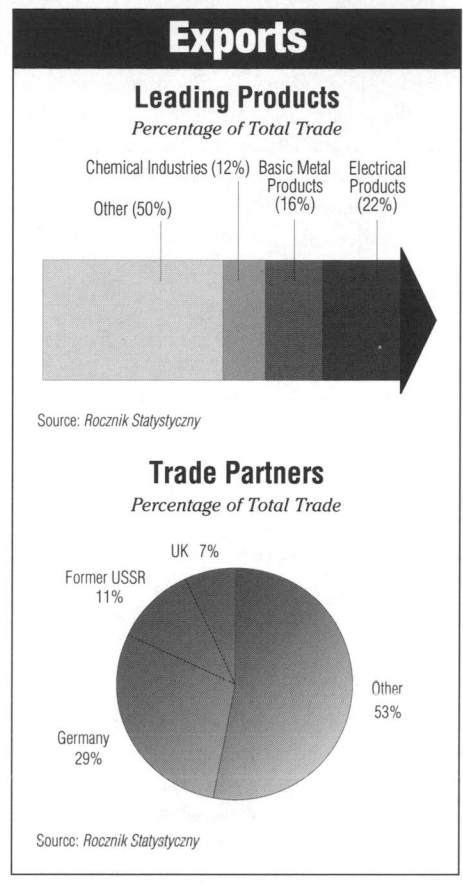

Exports

Leading Products
Percentage of Total Trade

Chemical Industries (12%)   Basic Metal Products (16%)   Electrical Products (22%)   Other (50%)

Source: *Rocznik Statystyczny*

Trade Partners
Percentage of Total Trade

UK 7%
Former USSR 11%
Germany 29%
Other 53%

Source: *Rocznik Statystyczny*

Opportunities

FOR IMPORTING TO POLAND
- computers
- consumer electronics
- aircraft
- yellow corn
- boring and sinking machinery
- chicken
- wheat
- fuel, power
- food
- chemicals

FOR EXPORTING FROM POLAND
- hams
- casein
- berry juices
- lamps
- agricultural tractors

GROWTH SECTORS
- manufacturing
- commercial construction
- communications
- retail trade

GOVERNMENT PROCUREMENT
- motorway and bridge construction equipment
- telecommunications services
- power supplies
- airport construction equipment
- navigation lighting systems
- air pollution control equipment
- water - waste management treatment equipment

Trade News

RULES AND REGULATIONS

- **Regulations law** Customs, taxes, and foreign investment regulations are in place in Poland. Follow-up amendments have reduced bureaucracy and government interference, modified tax incentives, and terminated restrictions of profit repatriation. Some permits are still necessary; while the application process can be cumbersome and tedious, it has been simplified.

- **Import restrictions and licenses** Strategic goods, police and military products, radioactive elements, weapons, transportation equipment, and chemicals require special licenses or concessions. Imports of beer, wine, gas, cigarettes, and certain agricultural and food products—dairy, poultry, tobacco—are also licensed. A permit is necessary to sell imported alcoholic products. A Phytosanitary Import Permit issued by Plant Quarantine Inspection Service is required for the import of all live plants, and fresh fruits and vegetables into Poland. Prohibited for import are two-stroke engine cars; automobiles, racing cars, and vans older than 10 years; trucks older than six years; commercial vehicles and farm machinery older than three years; and some high-proof liquors.

- **Tariffs, import taxes, and customs valuation** Poland follows the harmonized tariff system which classifies products and forms the basis for duty rates on imports. Tariff rates have changed several times since their implementation and are still changing. There is a general 22 percent value-added tax (VAT) and significant excise taxes apply to certain products.

- **Customs duties** Customs duties apply to all products imported into Poland, and range from zero to 90 percent, with the average between eight to 12 percent. Customs duty codes provide different rates for the same commodities depending on their point of export. There are basic, autonomous, preferential, and special customs rates. In addition to customs tariffs, all commodities imported into Poland are subject to an obligatory five percent import tax.

- **Quotas** Quotas have been applied within certain industries including the automotive, computer and pharmaceutical sectors. In some cases, the quotas are targeted to products originating from specific export regions and in others they have been assessed to help protect local industry. Gasoline, diesel fuel, heating oils, wine, cigars, and cigarettes are subject to import quotas.

- **Trade and investment barriers** Poland has passed a law on copyrights to combat wide-spread piracy especially of video and sound recordings.

- **Export licenses** are required for products such as petroleum products, metals, soil products, plastics, polyvinyl chloride, synthetic rubber and fiber, chipboards, preserved and half-tanned hides, munitions, and internationally controlled strategic goods. The export of live geese and goose eggs is prohibited.

FREIGHT FORWARDERS

C. Hartwig
Forwarding Agent for Rail, Air, Sea, River Transport
Poznanska 15
POB 375
00-950 Warsaw
Tel: (2) 229-60-31
Telex: 814601

Spedrapid
Polish-Czech Forwarding Company
Zgoda 8
POB 201
81-361 Gdynia
Tel: (58) 21-60-85
Fax: (58) 21-66-14

Business Culture

Greetings and Courtesies

It is the custom in Poland to shake hands upon meeting, and on departure. Be wary of shaking hands over a threshold, for Poles consider that bad luck. Business cards, in both your language and Polish, are exchanged with all participants in meetings. It is also invaluable to obtain letters of introduction. In both business and formal settings, use a person's professional title and surname; first names are used only after a close relationship has been established. An invitation into a Polish home is rare, and an honor. Guests normally bring flowers to the host, in an odd number and never red roses. Toasting is customary at both informal and formal dinners and guests are welcome to reciprocate. It is rude in Poland to begin eating before everyone has been served.

Business Ethic and Framework

The main reason for any Polish success in business is the Poles' geniality which turns businesspeople into friends. Poles are willing to assist on any level, while attempting to acquire management skills and gain experience in international business. Although traditional ineffective methods are bowing to more progressive methods of doing business, patience is still essential with Polish businesspeople. The human connection is an important component of business relations in Poland; Polish businesspeople insist on trust and confidence in their prospective partners before they sign any agreement. Foreign businesspeople should be willing to take the time and effort necessary to build a good relationship with their Polish associates, for only then will they be amenable to discussing business. Courtesy demands that foreign businesspeople make contact with the highest levels of Polish organizations; if possible, with the person actually in charge. Poles see it as an insult to do otherwise.

Decision Making

The Polish spirit is composed of self reliance and individualism. In addition, most Poles are blunt; if they don't like the way negotiations are proceeding, they will not hesitate to tell a foreign visitor what they think. Poles have survived war, loss of territory, and submission to outside governments. They enter the decision-making process fearless. The details of an agreement are important to Poles; every point must be spelled out and explained. Decisions by committee continue to be a deeply rooted tradition that prolongs conclusion of all agreements. Once a decision has been made, it is easily overturned. Poles will make a decision only when they feel right about a deal—and no sooner.

Women

An old-world mentality toward working women continues to fill the workplace in Poland. Although women in Poland are architects, factory managers, and high-level bureaucrats, and are represented in almost every other profession in the work force, male chauvinism is still alive. Polish women do have equal access to higher education, however. The credibility of professional women has been given a boost by Poland's Prime Minister Suchock, and this indicates that their presence in high levels of business and government will increase. Members of the younger generations are more willing to accept women in positions of power.

Meetings

Prior appointments are necessary for doing business in Poland. Any communication to plan meetings with Polish business partners should be done by fax or telex; those methods are more reliable than the undependable Polish mail system. A further impediment is the telephone system in Poland, which also remains inefficient. Foreign businesspeople should expect confusion with meetings to be the norm. Appointments are sometimes suspended or canceled without notice; the wrong people may even arrive. It is important to leave early for meetings, since Polish transportation is notoriously slow. Presentations in Poland should be thoroughly prepared. Poles are aggressive and encourage competition in their business dealings. In Poland, no agreement is final until signed and even then agreements can easily fall apart due to changed circumstances or a decrease in the level of trust.

Business Attire

Appropriate business dress in Poland consists of dark business suits of a conservative cut; understated dresses for women are acceptable. Conservative business attire is suitable for both formal and informal Polish functions. Women, especially, should dress conservatively. While always neatly attired, Poles are not especially fashion conscious, and an ensemble of the latest design might just look "weird" to them.

Cultural Cautions

DO'S

- Good topics of conversation include Poland and its history, your country, your family and your activities, and the solidarity movement.
- Poles greatly appreciate foreign visitors being familiar with their national heroes like Chopin, Copernicus, and Pope John Paul II.
- It is essential to confirm meetings several times.
- Be patient. Everything in Poland takes longer.
- It is best to adopt a considerate, yet reserved attitude.
- Request permission to photograph people or formerly forbidden objects like airports, borders, and railways. Confiscation of photography equipment is still a possibility.

DON'TS

- Don't discuss German or Russian involvement in World War II.
- Poles find it rude for others to chew gum during a conversation.
- Don't use first names unless invited to do so.
- It is considered very rude to ask someone to stop smoking in Poland.

CUSTOMS

- People usually stand about an arm's length from each other when conversing. There is usually no touching while speaking in business, except among good friends.
- Hard liquor, particularly Cognac, is ingrained into Poland's lifestyle. You may be offered several glasses, even at business meetings.
- Flicking one's finger against one's neck usually means an invitation for a drink. It is usually done only between close friends, however, and otherwise considered rude.
- Polish is the official language and the native tongue of the Poles.
- Poles tend to speak softly.
- The Catholic religion is widely practiced throughout the country.
- When dining, the hands should be visible and above the table at all times. Do not begin eating until everyone has been served, and empty your glass only if you want a refill.
- Polish men may kiss a woman's hand when greeting, but foreign visitors are not expected to do the same.
- Common business hours are between 8:00 am and 6:00 pm.

OBSERVATIONS

- Public transportation is efficient and inexpensive.
- Poles generally do not take a lunch break at work, but work nonstop until closing time. Only then do they eat, which can be disturbing to foreign visitors who are used to lunch breaks.
- Poles do not hesitate to speak out and tell foreign visitors what they think, even when doing so may cause problems.
- Don't rush off after eating. Poles love talking late—often very late—into the night.

NEGOTIATIONS

- Negotiating tactics differ little from those of other European nations.
- Protocol is important in business and professional relations.
- When conducting business in Poland, be prepared to spend some time developing a good personal relationship. Only then will Poles discuss business.
- The best months for doing business in Poland are September through May. Try to avoid June, July, and August, the months when Polish businesspeople take their vacations.
- Be ready for pointed but affable negotiations, at which Poles are expert.

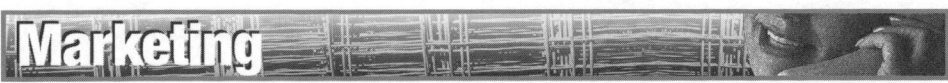

Overview

Poland offers a number of marketing opportunities for all types of companies, both big and small. A personal approach is a must; don't expect to find success through the post office or the telephone, both of which can be unreliable. Patience is also necessary; profits will probably be a long time coming because most Poles tend to take their time before making big decisions. A wait of six months to a year or even longer is not unheard of. Seminars are probably the best way of making one's products known in Poland, although charges tend to be high. Mass media is opening up to advertising, but it may not actually reach many people.

Distribution

Although a number of private companies are becoming more powerful, most foreign trade goes through the government at some level. Although bureaucracy was a much greater problem under Communist rule, it still is a major factor. Prepare for a mountain of red tape before getting your products to their source.

Agents, Distributors, and Partners

There are 11 major state agencies in Poland that accept foreign representation, and a number of smaller ones that deal with specific industries. It is possible to do business without an agent, however, and several companies have found considerable success with this method. Study the country before beginning any relationship with an agent; several have set up office without substantial capital or recourses. Branch offices, technical information offices, or a technical project office can be established in Poland, but only to big manufacturing companies and companies already executing or intending to sign a long-term cooperation agreement with a Polish industrial enterprise. Licenses are valid for one year but can be renewed easily and indefinitely. Technical offices are restricted only to the provision of technical information and services concerning delivered machinery and equipment. They are not liable for personal or income tax.

Selling Techniques

The most important initial step is to identify the Foreign Trade Enterprise which deals with the item concerned and to supply it with a regular flow of literature and sample quotations. It is difficult to do business in Poland without regular, personal visits to commercial contacts; the post office is rarely used and can not be trusted to do an efficient job anyway. Visiting Poland for personal meetings is absolutely essential, but initial approaches may be made by correspondence and trade literature (preferably addressed to an individual official rather than an organization). Participation, even on a modest scale, at the Poznan Trade Fair is a useful and relatively easy way of identifying likely end-users. Correspondence is usually in English, although promotional literature should always be in Polish. German and French is also used in businesses, but this should not be assumed.

Advertising

Advertising can be placed through the Foreign Trade Publicity and Publishing Enterprise (AGPOL), and technical journal advertising can be arranged through the technical publications section of the Chief Technical Organization (WCT-NOT). Direct mail publicity is very popular with advertisers. Newspapers are more popular than radio or television, and print advertising is more successful than broadcast ads. The most popular newspapers in Poland include: *The Trybuna Ludu*, the publication of the Polish United Workers' Party, *the Rzeczpospolita,* published by the government, and *Zycie Warszawy,* Warsaw's daily newspaper. AGPOL and the Polish Chamber of Foreign Trade publish numerous trade papers, which can be an excellent advertising source. The Naczelna Organizacja Techniczna (NOT) publishes a number of technical and particular-industry periodicals, and Wydawnictwa Komunikacyjne publishes 13 technical journals concerning transport and communications. The Poznan International Trade Fair is the most popular exhibition event, lasting eight days and with 50 countries represented. There are also a number of smaller trade shows specializing in a particular field, such as medical, agriculture, publishing, or computers.

Service and Customer Support

Service is a must. Poles appreciate customer support and in many cases they will ask prior to purchasing how much service they will get after purchasing the product. Again, personal visits are a must. Poland is a relatively small country, and any mistakes you make could come back to haunt you. It is recommended and may even be a must to have an agent in the country whose job is solely service, depending on the good. Electronics and technological items will most likely require a great deal of after-sales service.

Marketing in Poland

MARKETING TIPS

- **Prices** All prices should be quoted in sterling or US dollars.
- **Language** All advertising material should be in Polish. Although many companies do have foreign language speakers, your best bet would be to translate your material.
- **Post** The post office is used frequently in Poland, but is not very reliable. The time taken for surface and air mail to reach Poland can vary between three days to three weeks, depending on weather conditions, etc.
- **Buying seasons** While there are no set buying periods for capital goods, especially those for large projects, there is some tendency for orders under negotiation in any one year to be settled by September or October.
- **Advice enterprises** Foreign sellers often utilize Polish advice enterprises to provide them with information regarding manufacturing specifications and consumer preferences.
- **Hard currency** Many enterprises have the right to retain an element of their hard currency earnings for their own import needs.
- **Terms of payment** Confirmed letters of credit are recommended, but exporters are advised to contact their bank.

AD AGENCIES

BBDO Warsaw
ul. Balonowa 20
02-635 Warsaw
Tel: (22) 449292
Fax: (22) 443529

Biuro Reklamy S.A.
Ul. Flory 9
00-586 Warsaw
Tel: (2) 622-6404
Fax: (2) 622-5252

Euro RSCG
Plac Powstancow Warszawy 9
00-039 Warsaw
Tel: (22) 268281
Fax: (22) 274413

GGK Warsaw
ul. Bagatela 10/10
00-585 Warsaw
Tel: (2) 625-6615
Fax: (2) 625-7959

Leo Burnett Warsaw
Sp. Z.O.O. ul. Zwyciezcow 18
03-912 Warsaw
Tel: (22) 178420

Parintex
ul. Zurawia 45
00-680 Warsaw
Tel: (2) 625788
Fax: (2) 614322

Publicis, FCB Poland
ul. Wiertnicza 107
00-952 Warsaw
Tel: (2) 642-4920
Fax: (2) 642-3486

Saatchi & Saatchi Adv. MC
ul. Moliera 6
00-076 Warsaw
Tel: (22) 269491
Fax: (22) 263803

Young & Rubicam Poland
ul. Madalinskiego 101A
02-506 Warsaw
Tel: (22) 2452456
Fax: (22) 245-2534

GOVERNMENT AGENCY

Ministry of Post and Telecommunications
pl. Malachowskiego 2
00-940 Warsaw
Tel: (2) 26-67-36, 26-65-56
Fax: (2) 26-48-40, 26-73-66

Legal

Legal System

Poland is a civil code country. Its laws are based on the French and German legal systems. The judiciary is supervised by the Ministry of Justice, which also oversees the training and practice of lawyers. The prosecutor-general, independent of the ministry, is appointed by the Council of State. He then appoints the prosecutors on the lower levels. The Supreme Court, the highest judicial organ, functions primarily as a court of appeal. Its judges are elected by the Council of State for five-year terms. Poland is still creating many business laws, because free enterprise is such a new idea to many companies in the country.

Intellectual Property Protection

Patents and trademarks Patent law is administered by the patent office. Patents are registered for a 15-year term from the date of filing. Foods and chemical products can not be patented, but the processes of manufacturing such products are patentable. Trademark protection is extended for 10 years from the date of filing, and applications may be renewed for additional 10-year periods. Trademark protection is extended to foreign firms, provided that Polish firms receive the same protection in the foreign company's country of origin. Application for trademark renewal should be made before the expiration of the registration. Manufacturers and traders are strongly advised to patent their inventions in Poland. Patent and trademark protection is weak but the government is currently drafting legislation to more forcefully protect intellectual property.

Copyrights The Polish government recently passed the Copyright Law, covering many domestic copyrights with or without registration. Registration continues for 50 years after the creator's death. Poland refused to sign the Geneva Convention on Phonograms. Protection is sparse and piracy is still a problem.

Trade secrets Recent laws passed in Poland define trade secret violations, but do not prescribe penalties.

Business Registration

Registration for foreign businesses that wish to incorporate in Poland has been relaxed in recent years, and it now is the same for foreign and domestic companies. Nevertheless, many foreign businesses and investors have complained about the difficulties in completing bureaucratic requirements and subsequent delays when dealing with Poland. Have patience; getting permits can take months. Businesses may need to obtain permits to operate in certain sectors, such as legal services or real estate. While the majority of licenses are approved, a substantial number are still refused. Patience, local advice, and personal contacts are a must.

Contracts and Dispute resolution

Most oral contracts in Poland are valid, but the law stipulates that some agreements must be in writing. Nevertheless, always try to get every contract in writing. Many Polish businesspeople think that "yes" is a subjective phrase. Enforcement through litigation is not an easy process because Poland's commercial code was written before World War II; several foreign businesses are lobbying the government to update it. It is unlikely that Polish courts will accept without review the decisions of a foreign court. Disputes are generally settled amicably among the parties, although formal arbitration is not yet common.

Notaries

Notaries public act within the scope of authority granted by law. They are considered to be persons of public trust and have a number of responsibilities in Poland, including the preparation of deeds and certificates.

Labor

Poland has a well-educated labor force with relatively low labor costs. All workers have the legal right to establish trade unions and to join any union they choose. Unions can strike, but must first go through a lengthy bureaucratic process. Polish laws allow employers to challenge a pending strike through several alternative means, including legal action. Unions and management councils currently set wages in ad hoc negotiations. The Polish legal code specifies minimum safety conditions for workers. Compulsory labor does not exist in Poland, although it is not prohibited by law. Child labor laws prohibit the employment of children under the age of 14 and permit the employment of persons aged 14 to 18 only if they have completed basic schooling. If there are potential hazards on the job, the minimum age of employment is 18. The government and unions negotiate a national minimum wage every three months. Labor strife has become a rare occurrence in recent years.

Legal Matters

LEGAL BRIEFS

- **Foreign investment laws** All foreign investors and businesses must comply with domestic laws. They must also obtain permission to be involved in some activities.
- **Secured interests** Secured interests in property are recognized and enforced, but there are some idiosyncrasies to the Polish system. For example, there is no method for recording liens.
- **Competition** Theoretically, competitive equality is applied to private enterprises in competition with state-owned enterprises. In practice, public enterprises are often favored for government contracts.
- **Monopolies** The government's anti-monopoly office is responsible for tracking and eliminating monopolistic practices.
- **Union consolidation** The trade union act of 1949 consolidated the existing unions into the Central Council of Labor Unions.
- **Communist judges** Most judges are holdovers from the Communist era who lack extensive legal training. A 1993 law allows the Ministry of Justice to recall a judge determined by a disciplinary commission to have failed to exercise "court independence." This law is currently being challenged before the Constitutional Tribunal.
- **Appellate courts** Legislation was recently passed reestablishing intermediate-level appellate courts for the first time since before World War II. These courts will consider procedural issues only.
- **Constitutional tribunal** A constitutional tribunal also offers opinions on legislation and exercises no real authority of judicial review.
- **International agreements** Poland is a member of GATT/WTO; ATA Carnet Convention; and the Convention on the Recognition and Enforcement of Foreign Arbitral Awards.

LEGAL CONTACTS

Amhurst Brown Colombotti
ul. Koszykowa 59 M.6
00-660 Warsaw
Tel: (22) 29-16-84
Fax: (2) 6213289

Baker & McKenzie
Jur Gruszczynski Law Office
ul. Dluga 26/28
00-238 Warsaw
Tel: (2) 637-2217
Fax: (2) 637-2216

Boesbeck, Barz & Partner
ul. Wspolna 25
00519 Warsaw
Tel: (2) 62-83-029

Dickinson, Wright, Moon, Van dusen & Freeman, Sp. z o.o.
46 Wilcza Street, 4th Floor
00-679 Warsaw
Tel: (22) 299-241
Fax: (2) 628-4107

Kalwas & Partners Law Office
Piekna 3 St.
00-539 Warsaw
Tel/Fax: (2) 621-29-34

Kubiak, Lukowicz, Zielinski Solicitors
13 Mazowiecka Str.
00-052 Warsaw
Tel: (22) 26-71-39
Fax: (22) 26-83-19

Norr, Stiefenhofer & Lutz
Kancelaria Adwokacka Sp. Z O.O.
ul. Nowogrodzka 50
00-950 Warsaw
Tel: (2) 6216232

Wardynski & Partners
Aleje Ujazdowskie 12
00-478 Warsaw
Tel: (2) 622 04 00
Fax: (2) 628 90 40

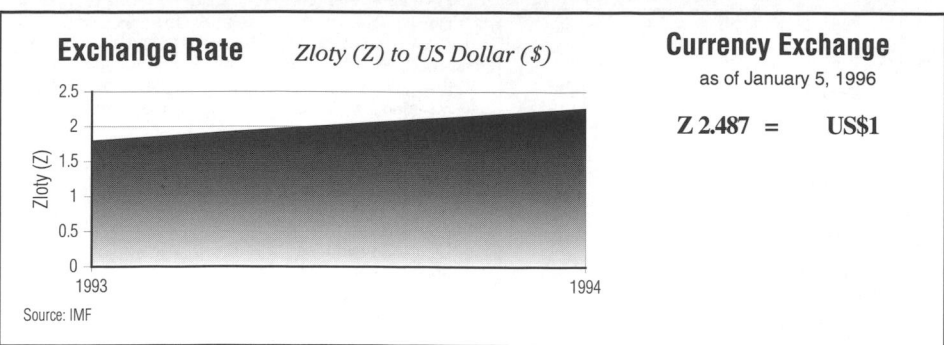

Exchange Rate
Zloty (Z) to US Dollar ($)

Source: IMF

Currency Exchange
as of January 5, 1996

Z 2.487 = US$1

Currency

The currency of Poland is the zloty (Z or Zl). The zloty is divided into 100 groszy.

Foreign Exchange

The Parliament controls all foreign exchange policies. Regulations are carried out by the Minister of Finance in the form of general foreign exchange permits or by the president of the National Bank of Poland (NBP) in the form of individual permits. Currency can be exchanged at foreign exchange banks, customs offices, and post offices. Nonresidents can open convertible currency accounts ("C" accounts) at all foreign exchange banks. These accounts can be credited with any funds brought into Poland, transfers from other "C" accounts, and with any amount of convertible currency acquired in Poland. Nonresidents can also open zloty accounts, the same accounts available to residents, but these accounts can only be credited with zlotys earned in Poland and foreign exchange converted at the official exchange rate.

Capital Transfers

All invisibles payments from merchandise transactions are permitted freely. Approval is required for any other invisibles payment. Any profits from direct investments can be transferred abroad up to a maximum annual amount of 10 percent. The Minister of Finance can permit transfers in excess of 50 percent of the surplus.

Investment Incentives

Poland has encouraged foreign investment in an attempt to join the European Economic Union (EU). All foreign investment regulation is governed by the Foreign Investment Act. Any level of foreign ownership is allowed, up to 100 percent, except for a few sectors. There is no screening of foreign investments. There are a few requirements that all investors must comply with, regardless of origin.

Investment Restrictions

Some sectors, including management of seaports and airports, real estate agency sales and services, and defense industries, require a permit for investment. Under broadcasting legislation, a foreign investor can not own more than 33 percent of a broadcasting enterprise. The acquisition of real estate by a foreign entity requires a permit from the Ministry of Interior. Non-farm real estate may be purchased outright, but foreign entities may only lease farmland for a maximum of 99 years.

Money Matters

BITS AND PIECES

- **Corporate income tax** Any companies with a registered office or seat or place of management in Poland is taxed on worldwide income. All other businesses are taxed on income from Poland only.
- **Capital gains** In general, capital gains are treated as part of a company's profits and taxed at the regular corporate rate.
- **Foreign tax relief** Poland usually agrees to exempt foreign-source income from taxes. Foreign taxes are credited against Polish tax in certain circumstances.
- **Investment concessions** Concessions are available for any investment over ECU 2 million a year.
- **Gold** Residents can hold gold in any form, but any trading is subject to permission from foreign exchange authorities.

BANKS

Amerbank
ul. Marszalkowska 115
00-102 Warsaw
Tel: (22) 248-505
Fax: (22) 249-981

Citibank
ul Senatorska 12
00-082 Warsaw
Tel: (2) 635-8116
Fax: (2) 635-5527

Bank Depozytowo-Kredytowy SA
ul. Chopina 6
20-928 Lublin
Tel: (81) 217-12
Fax: (81) 713-153

Bank Handlowy w Warszawie SA
(Commercial Bank SA)
ul. Chalubinskiego 8
00-950 Warsaw
Tel: (22) 300-100
Fax: (22) 300-113

Bank Polska Kasa Opieki SA
90-950 Lodz
Tel: (42) 361-470
Fax: (42) 367-772

Bank Rozwoju Eksportu SA
(Export Development Bank SA)
Plac Bankowy 2
00-950 Warsaw
Tel: (2) 635-5926
Fax: (2) 635-2713

Bank Zachodni SA
ul. Ofiar Oswiecimskich 41/43
50-950 Wroclaw
Tel: (71) 446-621
Fax: (71) 441-982

Enterprise Credit Corporation
ul. Towarowa 25
00-869 Warsaw
Tel: (2) 323-508, 321-332, 321-359
Fax: (2) 327-542

Polish-American Enterprise Fund
ul. Nowy Swiat 6/12
00-950 Warsaw
Tel: (22) 625-2017, 625-2069
Fax: (22) 625-7933

Pomorski Bank Kredytowy SA
Pl. Zolnierza Polskiego 16
70-952 Szczecin
Tel: (91) 334-769
Fax: (91) 533-114

Powszechny Bank Gospodarczy SA
Al. J. Pilsudskiego 12, (Pekao, SA)
ul. Traugutta 7/9
00-950 Warsaw
Tel: (2) 269-211
Fax: (22) 275-807

Powszechny Bank Kredytowy SA
ul. Nowy Swiat 6/12
00-950 Warsaw
Tel: (22) 661-7777
Fax: (22) 296-988

TAXATION

Taxation requires sophisticated knowledge of complex rules and regulations specific to each country. The information presented here is from the Ernst & Young Corporate Tax Guide and Directory, available from the Ernst & Young accounting office in your country, or from:

Ernst & Young
ul. Wspolna 62
00-684 Warsaw
Poland
Tel: (2) 625 5477, (22) 295241
Telex: 817914 ernst pl
(39) 12 08 03 (Satellite Phone)
Fax: (22) 29 42 63

At a Glance

Corporate Income Tax Rate (%)	40
Capital Gains Tax Rate (%) (a)	0/40
Representative Office Tax Rate (%)	40
Withholding Tax (%)	
Dividends (b) (c)	20
Interest (c)(d)	20
Royalties (c)	20
Net Operating Losses (Years)	
Carryback	0
Carryforward	3

(a) Certain capital gains are tax-exempt.
(b) Imposed on payments made in Poland and abroad.
(c) The rate of this tax may be reduced by a tax treaty.
(d) This rate applies only to interest transferred abroad.

Business Travel

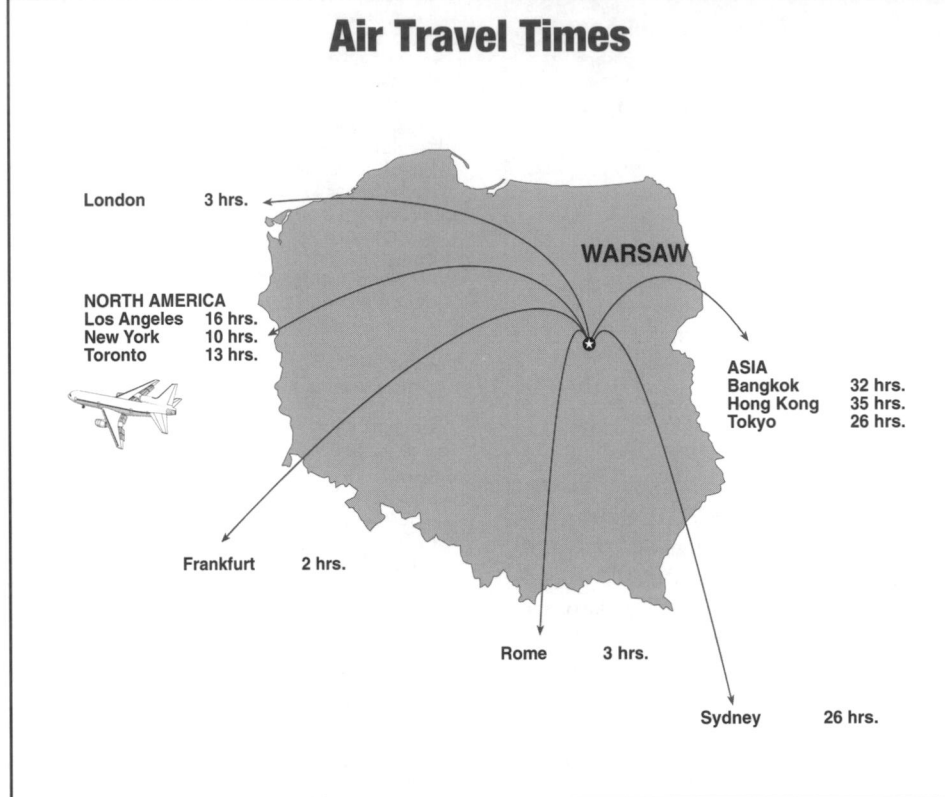

Air Travel Times

London   3 hrs.

WARSAW

NORTH AMERICA
Los Angeles   16 hrs.
New York   10 hrs.
Toronto   13 hrs.

ASIA
Bangkok   32 hrs.
Hong Kong   35 hrs.
Tokyo   26 hrs.

Frankfurt   2 hrs.

Rome   3 hrs.

Sydney   26 hrs.

COMMUNICATIONS

Telephones Poland's telephone system has greatly improved in recent years. Direct dialing around the world is fast, but because the Polish system is still rotary dial, some link-up services are limited. Public pay phones are unreliable.

Fax Many large hotels and business centers have fax machines, and Warsaw's main post office has 24-hour fax service. Fax capabilities are generally very good, depending on the quality of the sending or receiving signal.

Post office Large towns usually have one post office open 24 hours. Stamps are available at post offices, hotels, and kiosks. The green mailboxes are for local mail, blue for airmail, and red for all classes. International mail delivery is unreliable. Photocopying is not readily available in Poland.

BEST TRAVEL BOOKS

Poland: A Travel Survival Kit, Krzysztof Dydynski. Illustrated, 528 pages, Lonely Planet Publications.
Do's and Taboo's Around the World. The Bestselling Guide to International Behavior. Edited by Roger Axtell, compiled by the Parker Pen Company. The ultimate guide to international behavior, now completely updated and expanded. Helpful, fun to read!
The Real Guide: Poland, Mark Salter and Gordon McLachlan. Prentice Hall
Poland Travel Guide, Marc Heine. Hippocrene Books.

USEFUL TELEPHONE NUMBERS

If you are calling from outside Poland, you will need to add the country code [48] and any other international dialing requirements from within your country.

- Warsaw Radiotaxi 9624
- Operator 900
- International Operator 901, 902
- Local Directory 911
- Ambulance 999
- Fire 998
- Police 997
- Road Service 981, 854
- Pharmacy 24 hour .... (22) 321-392
- Warsaw Local Train Information .... (22) 200-361
- International Train Information .... (22) 257-554
- Railway.. (22) 244-400
- Avis: Airport .... (2) 650-4872
- Eurocar .... (22) 246-9896
- Hertz .... (22) 229-3896
- Central Bank .... (22) 200-321
- Media/Foreign Bureaus .... (2) 628-0001
- Radio/TV .... (22) 478-100
- Chamber of Commerce .... (22) 260-221

Credit Card Information
Lost or stolen credit cards (call collect to the US, regardless of which country the card was issued in).

- Amex ....[1] (919) 333-3211
- Diner's Club................................[1] (303) 799-1504
- MasterCard ....[1] (314) 275-6690
- Visa ....[1] (410) 581-7931

Travelogue

WORKWEEK

Offices Monday-Friday 8:00 am to 4:00 pm.
Banks Monday-Saturday 9:00 am to 4:00 pm.
Government Monday-Saturday 9:00 am to 3:00 pm.
Retail Monday-Saturday 11:00 am to 9:00 pm.
In addition, some institutions consider one Saturday per month a workday.

HOLIDAYS

Holidays 1996
January 1 New Year's Day
April 8 Easter Monday *
May 1 Labor Day
May 3 Constitution Day
June 6 Corpus Christi Day
August 15 Assumption
November 1 All Saints' Day
November 11 Independence Day
December 25 Christmas
December 26 Boxing Day
*Date varies from year to year.

VISA AND PASSPORT

Foreigners must have a valid passport, but a visa is not required for stays up to 90 days. Visitors must register at a hotel or with local authorities within 48 hours of arrival.

DEPARTURE FORMALITIES

A customs declaration form, stamped by Polish officials upon entering Poland, must be retained by the traveler and presented upon departure. Polish law prohibits the export of Polish currency (zlotys).

IMMUNIZATION

No vaccinations are required for travel to Poland unless you are arriving from an infected area.

TIPPING

Tip taxi drivers about 10 percent. Restaurants include a service charge of 10 to 15 percent, but diners usually round off the bill for the waiter and add another 10 percent if entertainment was provided.

CRIME

Petty crime is common and increasing in tourist areas, particularly in and around public transportation. Warsaw has a serious crime problem, with prevalent car thefts and break-ins, street crimes, and residential burglaries. Violent crime is rare but on the rise. Watch for illegal currency transactions affecting unsuspecting visitors.

INFRASTRUCTURE

Poland is a moderately developed nation with tourist facilities not up to date in all areas. Air transportation is excellent to and from Poland and transportation within Poland includes convenient flight and rail systems. Rental cars are abundant but heavy traffic makes driving between cities hazardous; reserve well in advance. Taxi service is reasonably good in most cities. Coach cars can be rented. Purchase tickets ahead of time for buses and trams. Train service is the main means of long-distance travel within Poland. A PolRailPass is very affordable. The subway is open for transit and is still under some construction. Sea ports are modern.

NATIONAL TOURIST OFFICES

Center for Tourist Information
ul. Mazowiecka 7
Warsaw
Tel: (22) 266-448
Agencja CIT Mufa
Pl. Zamkowy 1-13
Warsaw
Tel: (2) 635188

GOVERNMENT AGENCIES

Central Customs Office
ul. Swistokrzyska 12
00-916 Warsaw
Tel: (22) 20-0311
Fax: (22) 27-3427

Central Statistical Office
Al Niepodleglosci 208
00-925 Warsaw
Tel: (22) 25-3231
Fax: (22) 25-9078

Ministry of Communication
Plac Masachowskiego 2
00-940 Warsaw ?
Tel: (22) 26-1411, 26-1071
Fax: (22) 26-4840

Ministry of Internal Affairs
ul. Rakowiecka 2 b
02-517 Warsaw
phone: (48-22) 21-0251

Ministry of Land Use and Construction
ul. Wspolna 2
00-926 Warsaw
Tel: (22) 661-8111
Fax: (22) 628-5887, 295-389

Ministry of Transport and Shipping
ul Chalubinskiego 4/6
00-928 Warsaw
Tel: (22) 244-411
Fax: (22) 300-089

Ministry of Environmental Protection
ul. Wawelska 52/54
00-922 Warsaw
Tel: (22) 250-001
Fax: (22) 253-355

Ministry of Agriculture and Food Economy
ul. Wspolna 30
00-930 Warsaw
Tel: (2) 628-5745
Fax: (2) 292-894

Ministry of Finance
ul. Swietokrzyska 12
00-490 Warsaw
Tel: (2) 694-5555
Fax: (2) 266-352

Ministry of Foreign Economic Relations
Pl. Trzech Krzyzy 5
00-507 Warsaw
Tel: (2) 693-5000, 628-6125
Fax: (2) 628-6808, 625-4944

Ministry of Industry and Trade
ul. Wspolna 2/4
00-921 Warsaw
Tel: (22) 21-0351
Fax: (22) 21-2550

Ministry of Privatization
ul. Krucza 36
00-525 Warsaw
Tel: (2) 628-9531
Fax: (2) 625-1114

The State Foreign Investment Agency
Aleja Roz 2
00-559 Warsaw
Tel: (2) 621-0623 x149
Fax: (2) 621-8427

Ministry of Culture and Art
ul. Krakowski Przedmiescie 15/17
00-950 Warsaw
Tel: (22) 623-10-00
Fax: (22) 226-19-22

Ministry of Health and Social Welfare
ul. Miodowa 15
00-923 Warsaw
Tel: (22) 231-21-44
Fax: (22) 229-50-43

Polish Patent Office
Al. Niepodlegsosci 188/192
02-555 Warsaw
Tel: (22) 25-8001
Fax: (22) 25-0581

Polish Telecomunication S.A.
Plac Masachowskiego 2
00-940 Warsaw
Tel: (22) 27-4363
Fax: (22) 26-5633

BUSINESS AND TRADE ORGANIZATIONS

Polish Distributors Federation
ul. Okrezna 2
00-916 Warsaw
Tel: (22) 409-154
Fax: (22) 427-986

ARS POLONA
(Books, Periodicals and Printing Services)
ul. Krakowski Przedmiescie 7
POB 1001
00-068 Warsaw
Tel: (2) 226-12-01, 226-47-60
Telex: 813498

BALTONA
(Sale of Goods in Free Zones Outside Poland)
ul. Pulaskiego 6
POB 365
81-963 Gdynia
Tel: (58) 220-23-57

CEPELIA
(Export of Artistic and Folk Handicrafts)
ul. Lucka
00-950 Warsaw
Tel: (2) 220-50-01
Telex: 813671

CIECH
(Pharmaceutical Dyestuffs, Pesticides, Photochemicals, Fertilizers, Plastics, Rubber)
ul. Jasna 12
POB 271
00-950 Warsaw
Tel: (2) 226-90-01 through 09
Telex: 814561

CONFEXIM
(Textile Goods)
ul. Kosciuszki 123
POB 78
90-950 Lodz
Tel: (42) 36-35-22
Telex: 886877

M. CZARNECKI SA
(Representation of Foreign Firms in Poland)
ul. Marszalkowska 87
POB 215
00-950 Warsaw
Tel: (22) 28-02-96
Fax: (22) 29-59-43

DAL
(Industrial Cooperation, Barter and Compensation)
ul. Marszalkowska 82
POB 25
00-517 Warsaw
Tel: (22) 28-42-51
Telex: 81483

DYNAMO
(Import-Export and Barter, Representation of Foreign Firms in Poland)
ul. Stawki 2
00-950 Warsaw
Tel: (2) 635-68-34
Fax: (2) 635-68-38

PAGED
(Timber and Wood Products)
Trzech Drzyzy 18
POB 991
00-950 Warsaw
Tel: (2) 229-52-41
Telex: 814221

POLIMAR
(International Trading Company)
ul. Stawki
POB 151
00-950 Warsaw
Tel: (22) 39-77-80

POLSERVICE
(Patents, Licenses and Technical Services)
ul. Chaolubinskiego
00-613 Warsaw
Tel: (22) 30-05-22
Fax: (22) 30-00-76

SCORIMPEX
(Skins and Hides, Leather and Fur Garments and Footwear)
ul. Piotrkowska 148/150
POB 133
90-950 Lodz
Tel: (42) 36-38-33, 36-25-29
Telex: 885251

TEXTILIMPEX
(Textiles, Clothing and Knitwares)
ul. Tragutta 25
POB 320
90-950 Lodz
Tel: (42) 36-16-38
Telex: 886471

TORIMEX
(Consumer Goods)
ul. Nowogrodzka 25/41
POB 394
00-691 Warsaw
Tel: (22) 21-66-52
Telex: 813611

Foreign Investor's Chamber of Industry and Commerce
Krakowskie Przedmiescie 47/51
00-071 Warsaw
Tel: (22) 31-1764 , 27-2234
Fax: (22) 26-8593

Foundation for Polish Exports
ul. Kròlewska 27
00-060 Warsaw
Tel: (22) 27-6810
Fax: (22) 27-6810

BUSINESS ORGANIZATIONS

National Chamber of Commerce of Poland
ul. Trebacka 4
00-916 Warsaw
Tel: (22) 260-221
Fax: (22) 274-673

American Chamber of Commerce in Poland
Plac Powstancow Warszawy 1
00-950 Warsaw
Tel: (22) 263-960
Fax: (22) 265-131

Business Foundation
ul. Krucza 38/42, Room 117
00-512 Warsaw
Tel: (2) 621-993
Fax: (2) 621-9761

Small Business Chamber
ul. Smocza 27
01-048 Warsaw
Tel: (22) 380-172
Fax: (22) 383-553

Business Center Club
Palac Bramy 2
00-136 Warsaw
Plac Zelaznej Bramy 2
Tel: (2) 625-3037
Fax: (2) 621-8420

CONSULTING FIRMS

Alcat Communications
ul Karlowicza 9a
0(22) 501 Warsaw
Tel: (22) 484-640
Fax: (22) 486-782

Arthur Andersen
ul. Nowy Swiat 6/12, 4th Floor
00-400 Warsaw
Tel: (22) 625-1164
Fax: (22) 625-1208

Company Assistance Ltd.
ul. Podwale 13
00-950 Warsaw
Tel: (22) 635-8650
Fax: (22) 317-920

Coopers & Lybrand
ul. Mokotowska 49
00-950 Warsaw
Tel: (22) 660-0666
Fax: (22) 660-0572

Deloitte & Touche
ul. Grzybowska 80/82
00-844 Warsaw
Tel: (22) 661-5300
Fax: (22) 661-5350

Ernst & Young
ul. Wspolna 62
00-844 Warsaw
Tel: (22) 295-241, 625-5477
Fax: (22) 294-263

Price Waterhouse
ul. Emilii Plater 28
00-688 Warsaw
Tel: (22) 630-3030
Fax: (22) 630-3040

LEGAL CONTACTS

National Council of the Polish Bar Association
ul. Swietojerska 16
00-202 Warsaw
Tel: (2) 635-4062
Fax: (2) 635-2709

Legal Information Centre
Polish Chamber of Commerce
ul Trebacka 4
00-950 Warsaw
Tel: (22) 261842

NEWSPAPERS

Czas Krakowski
ul. Rynek Kleparski
31-150 Krakow
Tel: (12) 225355
Telex: 0322491
Fax: (12) 217502

Dziennik Baltycki
Targ Drzewny 3/7
80-886 Gdansk
Tel: (58) 313560
Fax: (58) 313560

Dziennik Lodzki
ul. Sienkiewicza 315
90-113 Lodz
Tel: (42) 364-585
Fax: (42) 322-832

Express Wieczorny
Al. Jerozolimskie 125/127
02-017 Warsaw
Tel: (2) 628-5231
Fax: (22) 416-920
Fax: (71) 35756

Gazeta Poznanska
ul. Grunwaldzka 19
60-782 Poznan
Tel: (61) 665-568
Fax: (61) 665-568

Gazeta Robotnicza
ul. Podwale 62
50-010 Wroclaw
Tel: (71) 35756

Gazeta Współczesna
15-950 Bialystok
POB 193 ul. Suraska 1
Tel: (85) 23241

Gazeta Wyborcza
ul. Nowy Swiat 27
00-029 Warsaw
Tel: (22) 269-081
Fax: (22) 261-434

Sztandar Mlodych
ul. Wspolna 61
02-015 Warsaw
Tel: (2) 628-7661
Fax: (2) 628-2049

Rzeczpospolita (daily)
Pl. Starynkiewicza 7
02-015 Warsaw
Tel: (22) 298-614
Fax: (22) 214-658

Zycie Warszay
Al. Armii Ludowej 3/5
00-575 Warsaw
Tel: (2) 625-6990
Fax: (22) 252-829

STOCK EXCHANGE

Warsaw Stock Exchange
Nowy Swiat 6/12
00-495 Warsaw
Tel: (2) 628-3232
Fax: (2) 628-8191

RADIO AND TELEVISION

Polish Radio S.A.
Al. Niepodleglosci 77/85
00-950 Warsaw
Tel: (22) 45-9110
Fax: (22) 44-5280

Polish Television S.A.
ul. J.P. Woronicza 17
00-950 Warsaw
Tel: (22) 44-6260
Fax: (22) 43-0141

PERIODICALS

Forum
ul. Sniadeckich 10
00-678 Warsaw
Tel: (22) 256150

Gazeta Bankowa
Pankiewicza 3
00-696 Warsaw
Tel: (2) 6287272, 625-5908
Fax: (22) 212653, (2) 625-5836

Morze (Maritime)
ul. Widok 10
00-023 Warsaw
Tel: (22) 273551
Fax: (22) 273551

Panorama
Rynek 13
40-003 Katowice
Tel: (32) 538595
Fax: (32) 538374
Telex: 0315212

Polish Business Voice
ul. Rutkowskiego 26/12
00-020 Warsaw
Tel/Fax: (22) 275-155

Polish Foreign Trade
ul. Kierbedzia 4
00-957 Warsaw
Tel: (22) 416-061
Fax: (22) 405-607

Polityka
(Politics)
ul. Dubois 9
00-182 Warsaw
Tel: (2) 6353091
Fax: (2) 6351797
Telex: 812546

Poradnik Gospodarski (Agriculture)
ul. A. Mickiewicza 33
60-837 Poznan
Tel: (61) 46001

Przeglad Tygodniowy
ul. Bracka 22
00-950 Warsaw
Tel: (22) 271889
Fax: (22) 279128
Telex: 816400

Przeglad Tygodniowy
POB 992
00-950 Warsaw
ul. Bracka 22
Tel: (22) 271889
Fax: (22) 279128
Telex: 816400

Przekrój
ul. Reformacka 3
31-012 Kraków
Tel: (12) 221833
Fax: (12) 214929
Telex: 0322733

Res Publica Nowa
POB 856
00-950 Warsaw 1
ul. Smolna 12
Tel: (22) 264817
Fax: (22) 262329

Rynki Zagraniczne
Polish Chamber of Foreign Trade
00-950 Warsaw
Tel: (22) 260-042
Fax: (22) 274-673

Sport
40-053 Katowice
ul. Mlynska 1
Tel: (32) 53995
Fax: (32) 537138
Telex: 0312436

INTERNET ADDRESSES

Usenet group(s):
soc.culture.polish

Polish Homepage
http://info.fuw.edu.pl/poland.html

Business Opportunities in Poland
http://www.wtinet.com/wti/pe.htm

Polish Network Resources
http://info.fuw.edu.pl/pzs/pzs.html

Government of Poland
http://www.urm.gov.pl/

Poland Country Guide
http://ciesin.cl.uw.edu.pl/poland/poland-home.html

Portugal

Portuguese Republic

Economy

Overview

The government's economic goal is to modernize Portuguese markets, industry, and infrastructure, and train and educate its work force in order to match the productivity and income levels of its more advanced EU partners. Although Portugal has made great strides toward modernization and privatization, its per capita GDP is still only about two-thirds the EU average. A severe recession in 1993 undermined economic development efforts, but the government was able to maintain exchange rate stability and as a result inflation was reduced and the economy has showed recovery through 1994 and 1995. While market forces are increasingly important, and the government has embarked on an extensive privatization program, public expenditures still account for 52 percent of GDP, several points higher than the OECD average. The administration is currently focusing on infrastructure development in anticipation of further economic growth in the medium term.

Trade

Portugal is an open economy, in which foreign trade comprises 50 percent of GDP. It currently has no programs designed to directly subsidize exports. However, EU grants to modernize Portuguese industry and agriculture may indirectly achieve this result. Portugal has largely harmonized its trade regime with that of the EU, and its main trading partners are now Western European countries (with EU countries accounting for over 70 percent of all trade) and the United States.

Sectors

Agriculture Since 1960, the proportion of the labor force engaged in agriculture has dropped from 42 to 20 percent. Agriculture production now contributes only seven percent of the country's GDP. Portugal imports a substantial share of its food and animal feed.

Industry Industrial employment has risen from 21 to 35 percent of the labor force since 1960 and industry now contributes 44 percent of GDP. Major products are textiles, clothing, cork products, electronic equipment, canned seafood, olive oil, and assembled automobiles. Portugal also has large shipbuilding and repair yards. Portuguese domestic industry is relatively unsophisticated, however, and needs to adjust to survival-threatening competition from the EU if it expects to continue to grow.

Services Service industries account for 49 percent of GDP, and include general commerce, banking, and finance, housing, and government services. Tourism has expanded rapidly and now earns more than five percent of GDP.

Trends

With the PSD (Partido Socialista Democratico—a "center" party) holding an absolute majority in the national legislature, the next few years should see a continuity in national government policy. The primary objective of Portugal's economic policy is to achieve convergence with its more advanced EU partners; that is, to make Portuguese economic fundamentals resemble more closely those of other economies in the Union. This entails maintaining a growth rate which is higher than the EU average. A continued flow of the EU Structural Funds Program will make this outcome possible.

At a Glance

THE COUNTRY

Location Southwestern Europe, bordering the North Atlantic Ocean west of Spain.
Terrain Mountainous north of the Tagus River, rolling plains in south.
Climate Varies from north to south. Hot summers in Central Portugal, warm and dry in the south, and cool and rainy in the north.

THE PEOPLE

Population 10,500,000
Ethnic composition Homogeneous Mediterranean stock with a small black African minority.
Religious composition
Roman Catholic 97%
Protestant denominations 1%
Other 2%
Languages spoken Portuguese.
Education and literacy Education has been compulsory since 1911. An estimated 83 percent of the population age 15 and over can read and write.
Labor force
Total: 4,600,000
By occupation: services 45%, industry 35%, agriculture 20%.

COUNTRY FACTS

Political and legal Portugal is a parliamentary democracy with a legal system based on civil law. The Constitutional Tribunal reviews legislation. Anyone 18 years and older can vote. Portugal accepts compulsory International Court of Justice judgments.
Telephone Service is generally good and is available to most international points. There are almost 2.7 million telephones. International country code: [351]. Selected city codes: Lisbon (1), Porto (2).
Transportation There are world-wide connections for air travel to and from Portugal. Domestic air services fly to Porto, Faro in the Algarve, and several provincial cities. Railroads and buses reach all points in the country. Lisbon has good inexpensive taxi, bus, subway, and streetcar service.
Environment Air and water pollution pose significant environmental problems, particularly in the urban areas. Desertification of the land and industrial pollution are the other problems threatening Portugal's wildlife and agriculture. Current issues include soil erosion, water pollution—especially in the coastal areas—and air pollution from industrial emissions.
Media The government-owned television network broadcasts on two channels reaching 1.8 million television sets. Radio broadcasts are either government or religious networks operating from 57 AM and 66 FM stations and serving the nation's 2.2 million radios. There are 28 daily newspapers published in Portugal with a variety of affiliations.
Health The public health sector is extremely large, with annual expenditures of 579 billion escudos (US$3.9 billion). Life expectancy is 72 years for males and almost 79 years for females. The fertility rate is 1.46 children per woman with 66 percent of married women (ages 15 to 49) using contraception.

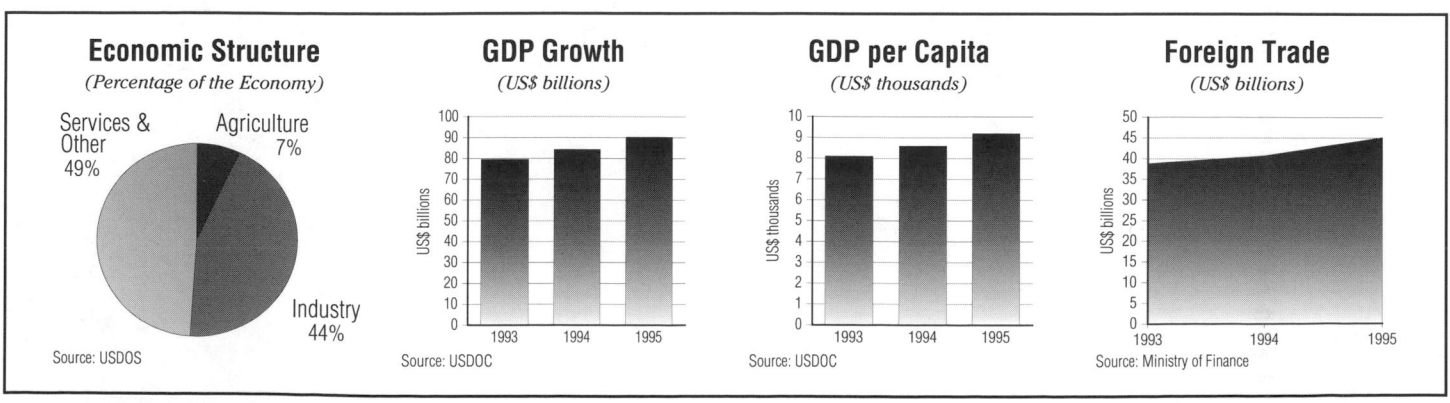

Economic Structure
(Percentage of the Economy)
Services & Other 49%
Agriculture 7%
Industry 44%
Source: USDOS

GDP Growth
(US$ billions)
Source: USDOC

GDP per Capita
(US$ thousands)
Source: USDOC

Foreign Trade
(US$ billions)
Source: Ministry of Finance

North

Atlantic

Ocean

Spain

42°

Rio Minho
Valença
Rio Lima
Viana do Castelo
Braga
Guimarães
Fafe
Porto
Rio Tamega
Chaves
Bragança
Vila Real
Rio Douro

Viseu
Aveiro
Rio Mondego
Guarda
Covilhã
Figueira da Foz
Coimbra
Rio Tezere

40°

Leiria
Tomar
Abrantes
Castelo Branco
Rio Tejo
Caldas da Rainha
Tagus
Santarém
Portalegre
Mora
Estremoz
Vendas Novas
Lisbon
Almada
Barreiro
Setúbal
Alcácer do Sal
Evora
Rio Sado
Grândola
Moura
Sines
Beja
Serpa
Rio Guadiana
Rio Chança

38°

Vila Real de Santo António
Portimão
Tavira
Lagos
Sagres
Faro
Golfo de Cádiz

10° 8° 6°

Portugal

⊛ National capital
◉ Region capital
● Secondary city
— Primary road
---- Railroad
— Administrative border
━ International border

0 25 50km
0 25 50mi

Districts are named after their respective capitals. The Azores districts of Angra do Heroismo, Horta, and Ponta Delgada, and the Madiera Islands district of Funchal are not shown.

Foreign Trade

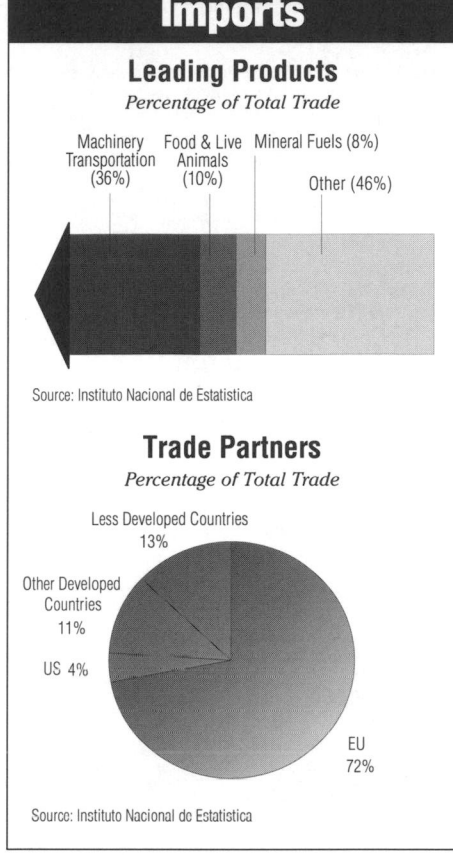

Imports

Leading Products
Percentage of Total Trade

Machinery Transportation (36%)
Food & Live Animals (10%)
Mineral Fuels (8%)
Other (46%)

Source: Instituto Nacional de Estatistica

Trade Partners
Percentage of Total Trade

Less Developed Countries 13%
Other Developed Countries 11%
US 4%
EU 72%

Source: Instituto Nacional de Estatistica

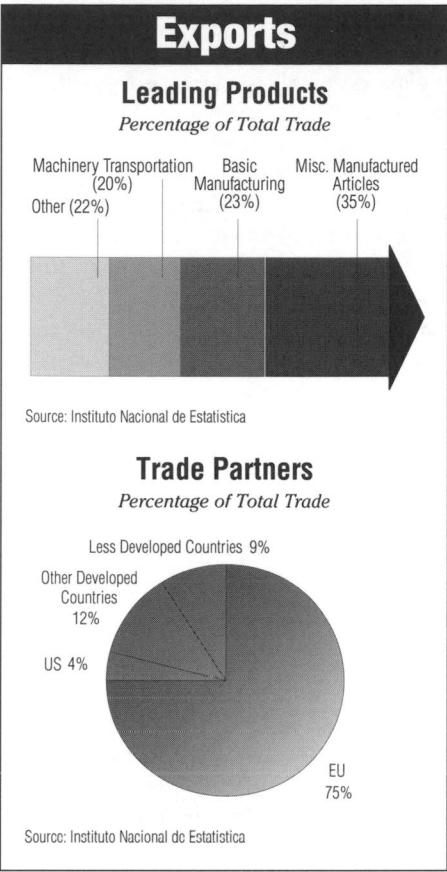

Exports

Leading Products
Percentage of Total Trade

Machinery Transportation (20%)
Other (22%)
Basic Manufacturing (23%)
Misc. Manufactured Articles (35%)

Source: Instituto Nacional de Estatistica

Trade Partners
Percentage of Total Trade

Less Developed Countries 9%
Other Developed Countries 12%
US 4%
EU 75%

Source: Instituto Nacional de Estatistica

Opportunities

FOR IMPORTING TO PORTUGAL
- environmental pollution control
- waste management
- telecommunications
- health systems
- medical equipment
- computers and peripherals
- computer software
- textile reconversions
- transport equipment
- agricultural products
- chemicals
- petroleum
- textiles

FOR EXPORTING FROM PORTUGAL
- cotton textiles
- cork
- paper products
- canned fish
- wine
- timber
- timber products
- resin
- machinery
- appliances

GROWTH SECTORS
- basic consumer manufactures
- textiles
- cork products
- automobiles

GOVERNMENT PROCUREMENT
- highway construction equipment
- municipal sanitation and machinery
- upgrading individual business
- engineering services

Trade News

RULES AND REGULATIONS

- **Trade news** Don't underestimate Portugal's trading power. The country is one of the most accessible markets in the world in key growth areas, especially considering its relatively small overall size. Its location in relation to Europe and Asia is also a key to its importing strength.

- **Import restrictions** Certain products require special documents: food products need a certificate of health in Portuguese; electric materials need a certificate of conformity to EU directives; grapes, alcoholic beverages, and tobacco need a certificate of authenticity. Certificates of origin may also be required if the origin can in any way be attributed to a country subject to quantitative or other restrictions. These and other regulations will probably delay any import, possibly by weeks.

- **Import licenses** Because Portugal is a member of the EU, the majority of imported products have been liberalized. There are certain agricultural products which require import licenses called "import certified" and international import certificates are required for strategic/dual-use products (products that may be used for both military and civilian purposes). For dual-use products, a certificate of delivery may also be required. There are also licenses required for the import of textile products and some industrial products from certain countries. Applications for import licenses should be submitted to the General Directorate of External Commerce. Tobacco, alcoholic beverages, and automobiles are still subject to some import controls, generally resulting from specific bilateral agreements.

- **Special Import provisions** Advanced rulings on tariff classifications can be obtained upon requests made in writing to customs at Oporto or Lisbon. No phone calls will be accepted.

- **Export controls** Since May 1988, Portugal adopted EC directive regarding exportation. Presently, Portuguese exporters need to obtain an export declaration before they ship their merchandise. Recently approved implementation of simplified export proceedings has begun.

- **Prohibited imports** Following EU Customs codes, Portugal has no prohibited imports; however, some products are subject to very strict controls such as strategic products, wildlife, hazardous articles, nonsport firearms, and ammunition.

- **Entry and re-export** Foreign merchandise landed in Portugal must be declared for importation or temporary entry into the EU territory within a period of 45 days if landed by sea, or 20 days if landed by air or from land.

- **Import payments** Import declarations are valid for six months for customs clearance purposes. Generally, all imports are allowed into Portugal, but declarations are required for products under European Union surveillance. A few industrial imports are subject to restrictions only when they originate in Third World countries.

- **Regulations system** Portugal is currently transposing EU single market directives into a national law easing regulations. Barriers to trade, capital, and labor movements are progressively diminishing, although there will still be remnants of them for some time.

- **Red tape** Prepare for a good deal of red tape or bureaucratic hassles when dealing with Portugal. The red tape has improved since the introduction of the foreign investment regime, but several businesses find the bureaucracy excessive. Some businesses believe entry costs would be reduced with the introduction of a one-stop registration entity.

GOVERNMENT AGENCY

Dirreccao Geral das Alfondegas
Director General of Customs
Rua da Alfandega
1100 Lisbon
Tel: (1) 87-87-85
Fax: (1) 87-83-35

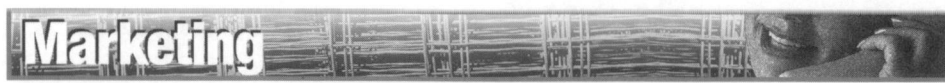

Overview

Portugal is an old country where modernization and traditional values coexist. Modern sales techniques are generally accepted and effective, but many business people still consider personal contact and a handshake stronger than any paper agreement. Because the Portuguese economy is growing quickly, consumers have witnessed overall purchasing power increases every year; and they are therefore inclined to buy on impulse. The Lisbon area has the highest purchasing power in the country but suffers already from traffic congestion and rising costs. Oporto has the most dynamic industrial development in Portugal and is also an area of high purchasing power. Oporto is now connected to Lisbon by a new motorway and a new bridge over the Douro river. The coastal region between these two cities, and the area extending into Braga and Setubal, is the predominate location of a large majority of Portuguese industries. While state-owned monopolies are being eliminated, certain sectors will continue to remain government-controlled, such as mail, water distribution, sewage, rail service, airport and port authorities, armaments, and telecommunications.

Distribution

Portugal is a small country with its population mostly concentrated on the Atlantic coast. Most sales channels serve the entire territory. Major industries, as well as the head offices of large corporations, are located in the Lisbon region, as are the headquarters of most financial institutions. The major distribution centers are Lisbon in the south and Oporto in the north; though the regional centers of Braga, north of Oporto, and Setubal, south of Lisbon, have grown into their own in recent years. However, many large importers and wholesalers have branch sales offices, or sub-agents and dealers, in other principal cities and towns, including those of the Portuguese islands Madeira and the Azores.

Agents, Distributors, and Partners

Foreign firms interested in selling in Portugal generally start by appointing an agent or a distributor. Most manufacturing exporters are commonly represented in the market through exclusive importers or distributors who may appoint sub-distributors and dealers. Distributors who operate a sales network covering the entire country expect exclusive representation agreements and tend to be quite specialized in their respective market segments. A foreign seller offering a wide range of products may require representation by different local firms chosen each for its particular products. Some large retail stores, which were rare in the past, import directly. These are becoming more common and an increasingly attractive option to foreign sellers.

Selling Techniques

The institutional buyer is quality-conscious and very sensitive to pricing. For consumer goods, the decisive selling factors may be a combination of price, quality, trademark, or the product's innovative features. Direct sales, hypermarkets, and commercial malls are changing the purchasing habits of the population. Franchising is a relatively new word in the Portuguese commercial vocabulary, but since 1989 franchising has brought a new vigor to the retail market. As with many European countries, Portugal does not have any legislation about franchising. The first franchises to get the attention of Portuguese consumers were non-food stores, especially clothing; next were food stores, then cosmetics, and now other businesses are making their appearance in the most important cities and towns. Direct marketing comprising door-to-door sales, mail order sales, and television sales have become increasingly popular in Portugal. The scope of direct marketing as a sales instrument expands every year to new areas of activity, such as on-line grocery shopping, fresh-baked goods, office supplies, and computer accessories.

Advertising

All common advertising media is available in Portugal. Newspapers, magazines, television, billboards, cinema, and more recently, advertising in automatic bank teller machines, are the most popular methods. Market research services are performed by a number of firms, but only a few offer complete services. There are several agencies with foreign capital participation. Trade shows are an effective means for product promotion, and Portugal hosts several specialized international trade shows each year.

Service and Customer Support

New suppliers to the Portuguese market should devote adequate effort to the sales support, product services, and after-sales maintenance required to develop product awareness. Local wholesalers expect foreign sellers to provide adequate after-sales service support that they can pass on to customers. Portuguese consumers have come to expect a reasonable level of product service and support, representative of their present purchasing patterns, which tend to favor higher quality, modern products.

Marketing in Portugal

MARKETING TIPS

- **Post office** A great deal of marketing and promotional literature is sent through the mail. Transit time is two to four days. Surface mail takes about three weeks.
- **Market growth** The Portuguese economy is expected to grow in the near future, as the country integrates into the EU. This translates to a number of new and growing markets for investors. Thoroughly study the potential markets before investing any time or money.
- **Improving wages** After several years of losing ground, real wages are beginning to recover. Business profits are also expected to be strong since productivity gains are larger than real wage increases.
- **Telephones** Telephone service is improving but still far from international standards. Fax machines are new in the country and are used only sparingly.

AD AGENCIES

Saatchi & Saatchi Advertising
Rua Dr. Eduardo Neeves, No. 9-2
1000 Lisbon
Tel: (1) 793-7105
Fax: (1) 793-8337

J. Walter Thompson Publicidade S.A.
Av. Eng. Duarte Pacheco
Amoreiras - Torre 2, 15th Fl.
1000 Lisbon
Tel: (1) 693-136
Fax: (1) 388-1311

Wunderman Cato Johnson Portugal
R. Soares de Passos, Bloco 2, R/C
1300 Lisbon
Tel: (1) 364-6690
Fax: (1) 364-6790

Young & Rubicam (Portugal)
Av. Duque d'Avila 26-5 Andar
1000 Lisbon
Tel: (1) 355-7161
Fax: (1) 539-077

MARKET RESEARCH FIRMS

A.C. Nielsen Co.
Rua D. Filipa Vilhena 38-3
1000 Lisbon
Tel: (1) 793-7342
Fax: (1) 793-7287

Ecotel Portugal - Estudos de Mercado SA
Av. Almirante Reis 59-4
1100 Lisbon
Tel: (1) 352-0931
Fax: (1) 352-6559

E M Estudos de Mercado Lda. (ESEO)
Rua dos Anjos 66-1
1100 Lisbon
Tel: (1) 57-8777
Fax: (1) 57-86-77

**Marketing, Organizacao e Formacao Lda.
(MARKTEST)**
Rua de Sl Jose 183-2
1100 Lisbon
Tel: (1) 342-3212
Fax: (1) 346-0894

**Estudos de Mercado Lda.
(NEDRO-NIELSEN-ESEO)**
Rua D. Filipa Vilhena 38
1000 Lisbon
Tel: (1) 793-7342

**Marketing e Estudos de Mercado Lda. 9
(PLURITESTE)**
Rua do Campo 98-4E
1200 Lisbon
Tel: (1) 342-3491
Fax: (1) 342-3491

**Meios de Publicidade e Estudos de Mercado S.A.
(TEAM)**
Av. Dq. D'Avila 24-1
1000 Lisbon
Tel: (1) 57-75-33
Fax: (1) 315-1919

Business Culture

Greetings and Courtesies

Most men greet by enthusiastically hugging and slapping each other's backs. Women who know each other well greet with a kiss on both cheeks. A firm handshake with eye contact is an important custom when first meeting and departing. Business cards are essential in Portuguese business; make sure you always have them available in both English and Portuguese. Use titles with the last name until invited to do otherwise; first names are usually only used among close friends. Titles include *Senhor, Senhora, Senhorita, Doutor* (for anyone with a university degree), and *Engenheiro* or *Arquitecto* for those in the appropriate technical fields. Most Portuguese are very reserved; you will not see the extensive gestures their Spanish neighbors favor. Even in the more outgoing areas, it takes time to establish friendships. Portuguese also respect manners; a simple "please" or "thank you" will go a long way to establishing a relationship. Although English is widely used and spoken, especially in urban areas and tourist spots, try to communicate in Portuguese. Learning even a few words and phrases is greatly appreciated. When talking to Portuguese, avoid conversations about politics and the government. It is also impolite to appear too inquisitive in your conversations. Some popular topics of conversation are family, pleasing aspects of Portugal, sports, and personal interests.

Business Ethic and Framework

The Portuguese businessperson is usually conservative and formal, and at the same time courteous and gracious. Business style is restrained but not formal and Portuguese businesses prefer careful preparation and clear terms. Individualism is important, but emphasis in terms of respect and deference is usually placed on age, seniority, educational background, and financial standing. The contract has always been honored and respected in law and by a centuries-old tradition of keeping international agreements.

Meetings and Decision Making

Avoid making appointments between noon and 3:00 pm; all offices are closed. Prior appointments are essential, especially for government visits. You should arrive to meetings on time, even though the host will usually take a casual approach to being timely. It is best to take a conservative approach to meetings, and be sure to check all dates and times accordingly. Business rarely takes place during dinner. Don't be surprised if meetings run late; people and relationships are thought of as more important here than ending a discussion prematurely. Before going to the first meeting, try to find someone who supports your position within the Portuguese company who can lobby for you. Face-to-face meetings are more popular than those over the telephone. Meetings usually begin with casual, friendly conversation and are often held in old, intimate coffee houses. Business discussions often take place during long lunches. Portuguese businesspeople prefer to consider a proposal carefully before accepting anything. Opinions will usually come quicker than decisions.

Women

Women working outside the home, at least in urban areas, are becoming more common. Female business managers are most common in the cities; rural areas still cling to conservative ideas. Throughout the country, however, the emphasis still remains on women as homemakers with absolute authority in domestic matters. As Portugal emerges into a democracy, women are slowly acquiring positions of power. They still hold many entry level jobs in businesses, though even this is a step up from a few years ago. Men still remain dominant in much of the culture, though foreign businesswomen should be treated with respect. Street theft can be a problem, and women should be sure to hold handbags tightly, especially in the urban areas.

Business Attire

Dress in a conservative suit with a topcoat or raincoat during the winter. Lisbon's streets are mostly cobblestone; bring sturdy, comfortable shoes. Men wear suits to work, though sport jackets are gaining popularity. Because of the usually pleasant temperatures, cotton summerwear will prove the most comfortable. Laundering services are expensive compared with other Western European countries. Appropriate dress is highly recommended when visiting official buildings or restaurants. It is considered unacceptable to walk around the streets in shorts or bikini tops. Theft is a problem, particularly in Lisbon, and businesspeople should be advised not to appear too much like a tourist.

Cultural Cautions

DO'S

- Gratuities are often included in the check, but an additional tip of 10 percent is customary.
- Beckon someone by waving all the fingers with the palm up.
- When visiting a family at home, guests should wait outside the door until invited inside.

DON'TS

- When offered refreshments, never refuse.
- When eating, keep your elbows off the table and your hands out of your lap.
- Never interrupt any conversation, especially when an elder is speaking.
- Avoid pointing an index finger at anyone. This could be interpreted as a rude gesture.

CUSTOMS

- You need not bring a gift when invited to dinner. Instead, take the hosts to dinner to reciprocate.
- Dinner is served first to the guest; the hostess or host will eat only when everyone else is served. Always leave some food on the plate when finished.
- Almost all products have fixed prices, and bargaining is not appropriate.
- Elders are always shown great respect.
- A host often toasts the guest with *"A Sua Saude"* (to your health); the guest should respond with thanks.
- Business is largely suspended the weeks before and after Easter and for two weeks before and after Christmas.
- When the host opens the door for a guest after dinner, this is a signal for the guest to leave.

OBSERVATIONS

- Portuguese restaurants do not readily accept checks. Traveler's checks are more widely accepted, but don't be surprised if they are refused as well.
- The water in Portugal is overall drinkable, but bottled water is inexpensive and safer.
- A driver's license, proof of insurance, and automobile papers are documents necessary to drive.
- Never leave valuables in the car. Instead, open the glove compartment and leave the seats tipped in the forward position to demonstrate that there is nothing in your automobile worth stealing. If possible, park in front of a police station, a busy cafe, or under a bright street light.
- Because of the large numbers of French migrant workers, French is well-understood in many areas. English is understood in urban areas, particularly Lisbon and Algarve. The Portuguese language is related to Spanish, and Spanish speakers will notice that their questions may be understood, but they will usually be answered in Portuguese.
- Here is a glossary of common hand gestures: shaking a pinched earlobe while raising the eyebrows means something is exceptionally good; pulling the lower eyelid slightly down with the forefinger can mean "how clever you are" or "you're kidding;" the thumb rubbing rapidly against the first two fingers indicates money; and rocking the hand with fingers spread and palm down means "more or less."

NEGOTIATIONS

- Take a conservative, low-pressure approach to negotiations. Clearly communicate prices and delivery dates, making sure these are understood.
- If faced with an ultimatum, don't be afraid to walk away rather than accept less than face value. The Portuguese will look upon such a decision with respect, and it will show them you mean business and are a thorough negotiator. Although it may not equal success this time, it will probably help you in future negotiations.

Legal

Legal System

Portugal's laws are a based civil code system patterned primarily on other Western laws. The judicial wing has a great deal of independence from other branches of the government and does not suffer any other kind of political pressure.

Intellectual Property Rights

Patents Patents are granted for a 20-year period and are not renewable. If patents are not worked within a three-year period (dating from notice of the grant), the patent is subject to compulsory licensing. Requests for patents are subject to approval by the Industrial Property Bureau of the Ministry of Industry and Energy. Food, chemicals, and pharmaceutical products and processes are patentable, yet products not providing new industrial results are not.

Trademarks Trademarks on all products are registered in Portugal by foreign and domestic firms with the Institute of Industrial Property (INPI). Trademarks are registered for a 10-year period, and are renewable for additional 10-year periods. Flags, coats of arms and heraldic insignias, official marks or stamps, and generally public marks are not granted protection. Industrial designs and models are offered protection rights for one year which are renewable indefinitely.

Copyrights Portugal is a party to the Berne Convention for the Protection of Artistic and Literary Works. Copyrights are protected for the life of the author and for 50 years following the author's death. Registration is made with the Bureau of Literary, Scientific, and Artistic Property. The Portuguese Association of Software Producers (ASSOFT) has conducted an aggressive public awareness campaign including raids of large companies and seizures of illegal software. Enforcement problems remain, however, and are exacerbated by long delays in concluding court cases.

Trade secrets Trade secret violations have been a problem, although the government has promised to put a stop to them. Court decisions are slow, however, and they can be costly to the plaintiff. The best way to protect against trade secret violations in Portugal is to stipulate against any possible violations and provide for the penalties in the initial contract. This has proved a successful step in the past and will be upheld by the court.

Business Registration

To form a public corporation or a quota company a foreign enterprise must first gain approval from the Portuguese Institute of Foreign Trade (ICEP)). There are no residency requirements for establishing either type of company. The branch is one of the simplest forms of business organizations for foreign entities to organize. Branches must comply with Portuguese laws regarding the establishment and operation of business organizations, although they do not have their own legal standing. Registering as a subsidiary provides an incorporated company with its own separate legal standing for sales purposes.

Contracts and Dispute Resolution

Portugal is a member of the International Center for the Settlement of Investment Disputes. Recently there have been very few investment disputes involving foreign investors, except for one case involving a company which was prevented from developing land for a hotel because the land was subsequently declared part of a natural reserve. Since 1985, the company has been seeking compensation through the Portuguese legal system. The courts have been very quick to reach business dispute verdicts, and the decisions are, for the most part, respected.

Labor

Portugal has the lowest hourly wage rates in Western Europe. There is a good pool of skilled and unskilled workers to draw from, and increased industrialization and improved technology are being accompanied by an increase in skilled workers. Workers are not required to join a union, but about 55 percent of the labor force is unionized. Contractual agreements, negotiated between employers and employee representatives, are the rule in almost all business sectors. The average workweek is 42 hours with a maximum of 44 hours. Salaries are usually paid by the month. Labor contracts with foreigners must be registered at the Ministry of Labor and Social Security (Ministério do Trabalho e Segurance Social). Businesses may employ foreigners only if their entire staff numbers more than five, and at least 90 percent of the existing staff is Portuguese. Portugal has several laws regarding worker safety and basic labor rights. Workers in Portugal take a somewhat casual attitude toward work. Decisions are often made at the last minute and there is little sense of urgency. Productivity remains low compared to other European countries, although this is not entirely attributable to the local work ethic. Companies establishing operations in Portugal will probably have to devote some time to worker training. There have been almost no instances of political violence stemming from labor.

Source: José Miguel Júdice, Lisbon

Legal Matters

LEGAL BRIEFS

- **Diminishing laws** Trade, capital, and labor barriers are liberalizing as Portugal transposes EU single market directives into national law.
- **Tax reform** A major tax reform in 1989 brought the Portuguese tax system closer to those found in other EU countries.
- **Software** Recent legislation improving the protection of copyright law has also increased the sale of computer software.
- **Labor laws** Portugal is a member of the International Labor Organization (ILO). The government generally adheres to the ILO conventions protecting labor rights. The major shortcoming in this regard are violations of minimum age requirements.
- **Foreign employees** Although Portugal welcomes foreign labor, at least 90 percent of the employees of resident companies must be Portuguese.
- **Public sector advantages** There are competitive advantages for state entities operating in airline transport and telecommunications.
- **Court delays** Despite legal improvements, many cases are delayed by lack of a trained staff and little money.
- **EU changes** As Portugal applies EU standards to its markets, several barriers to trade, capital, and labor movements are progressively diminishing.

LEGAL CONTACTS

José Miguel Júdice
R. Silva Carvalho, 234
1250 Lisbon
Tel: (1) 380-0700 Fax: (1) 388-2176

Abreu, Cardigos & Partners
Rua Marques De Sa Da Bandeira 8, R/C
1000 Lisbon
Tel: (1) 353 2555
Fax: (1) 353 6347

Artur Reis e Sousa Advogado
Avenida Fontes Pereira de Melo, 25-6th D
1000 Lisbon
Tel: (1) 529627
Fax: (1) 522186

Borges Neto e Associados
Rua D. Joao V, N 11-1 Esq
1200 Lisbon
Tel: (1) 387 4848
Fax: (1) 387 4950

Mateus Andrade Dias e Associados
Rua Antonio Maria Cardoso, N 25-4
1200 Lisbon
Tel: (1) 3468134
Fax: (1) 3473746

M.P. Barrocas & Associados
Av. Fontes Pereira de Melo, 15-7th Floor
1000 Lisbon, Portugal
Tel: (1) 522156
Fax: (1) 576202

Pena, Machete & Associados
Av. Miguel Bombarda, 61-5
1000 Lisbon
Tel: (1) 3157719
Fax: (1) 52 56 28

Ronald Charles Wolf
Travessa Do Ferreiro, 23 - 5D
1200 Lisbon
Tel: (1) 396475
Fax: (1) 6163439

Teixeira De Freitas & Jardim Fernandes
Praca Joao do Rio, N 8 - 5 DT
1000 Lisbon
Tel: (1) 8461921
Fax: (1) 8461927

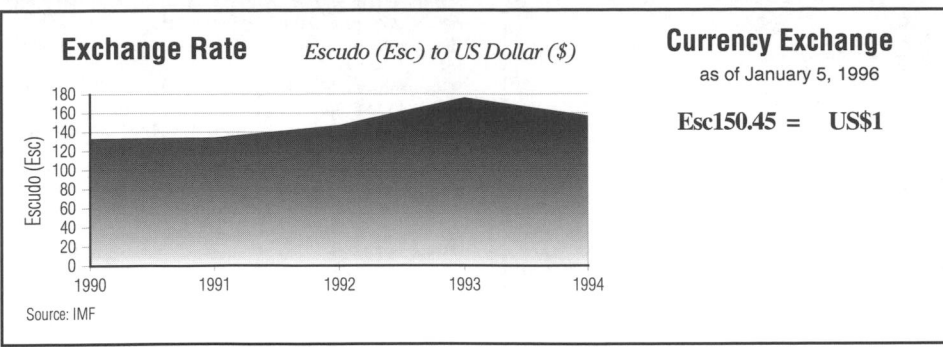

Exchange Rate — Escudo (Esc) to US Dollar ($)

Source: IMF

Currency Exchange

as of January 5, 1996

Esc150.45 = US$1

Currency

The currency in use is the Portuguese escudo (Esc). Portugal participates in the exchange rate and intervention system (ERM) of the European Monetary System (EMS), and maintains a spot exchange rate between the Portuguese escudo and the currencies of other participants of the ERM.

Foreign Exchange

There are no exchange controls. Banks are allowed to exchange foreign currency with themselves and with residents and nonresidents at free market rates of exchange. The degree of foreign exchange risk banks can take must fall within the limits established by the Banco de Portugal.

Capital Transfers

There is no difference in Portugal between resident and nonresident accounts. Nonresidents can open accounts in any currency. Issuing of securities by nonresidents in a foreign capital market requires prior authorization from the Minister of Finance.

Investment Incentives

Portugal actively seeks foreign investment, and nonresidents can invest in most sectors open to private investment. There are some restrictions to foreign investment in certain strategic areas. All investment incentives are open to both residents and nonresidents. Competition between public and private entities has been reduced recently, but government agencies still have a hold on airline transport and telecommunication businesses.

Investment Restrictions

The bureaucracy has improved recently, but several business have still complained about the excessive red tape involved in establishing a business.

TAXATION

Taxation requires sophisticated knowledge of complex rules and regulations specific to each country. The information presented here is from the Ernst & Young Corporate Tax Guide and Directory, available from the Ernst & Young accounting office in your country, or from:

Ernst & Young
Mail Address:
Apartado 1137
1003 Lisboa Codex, Portugal
Street Address:
Edificio República
Avenida da República, 90-3
1600 Lisboa, Portugal
Tel: (1) 791 20 00
Cable: Ernstaudit, Lisbon, Portugal
Fax: (1) 795 75 85

At a Glance

Corporate Income Tax Rate (%)	
Corporate Income Tax (a)	36
Municipal Surcharge	(b)
Capital Gains Tax Rate (%) (a)	36
Withholding Tax (%)	
Dividends	
Paid to Residents (c)(d)	30
Paid to Nonresidents (c)(g)	30
Interest	
Shareholders' Loans	
Resident Shareholders (d)	15
Nonresident Shareholders(g)	20
Bonds Issued by Companies	
Resident Holders(d)(e)	25
Nonresident Holders (e)(f)(g)(h)	20
Government Bonds (i)	20
Bank Deposits	
Resident Depositors (d)	20
Nonresident Depositors	20
Royalties	
Paid to Residents (d)	15
Paid to Nonresidents (g)	15
Branch Remittance Tax	0
Net Operating Losses (Years)	
Carryback	0
Carryforward	5

(a) Corporate income tax (I.R.C.) applies to resident companies and nonresident companies with permanent establishments in Portugal.
(b) Municipal surcharge of up to 10% on the corporate income tax.
(c) Includes 5% substitute inheritance tax.
(d) Income must be declared and is subject to the normal tax rates. Amounts withheld may be credited to I.R.C.
(e) The rate is 20% on interest from government bonds.
(f) Applicable to interest from private and public company debentures.
(g) These rates may be reduced by tax treaties.
(h) Applies to bonds issued after October 15, 1994. A 25% withholding tax applies to bonds issued on or before that date.
(i) Interest on certain government bonds traded on the stock exchange and paid to nonresidents not operating in Portugal through a permanent establishment may in certain circumstances be exempt from tax.

Money Matters

BITS AND PIECES

- **Capital gains** All capital gains derived from the sale of fixed assets and from the sale of financial assets are included in taxable income subject to corporate income taxes.
- **Foreign tax relief** Foreign-source income is taxable in Portugal unless a double tax treaty applies. In that case, the foreign tax can be credited against the Portuguese tax liability.
- **Relief for losses** All losses can be carried forward for five years, but no carryback is allowed.
- **Capital transactions** There are no restrictions or controls on transactions, and no distinction is made between capital transfers with residents of EU member countries and residents of countries not affiliated with the EU.
- **Gold** Residents can hold, buy, and sell gold in any form without restriction.
- **Payments for invisibles** There are no restrictions for any invisibles payments.
- **Escudo** The escudo is divided into 100 centavos. The symbol, $, is written between the escudo and centavo units. For example, 50$30 means 50 escudos and 30 centavos. One thousand escudos is called a conto.
- **Credit cards** Credit cards are accepted in major urban hotels and restaurants but seldom anywhere else.
- **Money exchange** Exchanging money and establishing banking relations do not pose any particular problems. Automatic Teller Machines (ATMs) are becoming more popular throughout the country. Be sure to check with your bank or credit card company to see if it belongs to a network that has ATMs in Portugal. Some banks can even give cash advances on some credit cards over the counter.
- **Income tax and worldwide income** Residents of Portugal are liable for income tax on worldwide income. Individuals who spend 183 days or more in Portugal during a calendar year, or who spend less time but possess a house in the country are considered a resident for that year. Income tax is assessed on a resident's worldwide income and a nonresident's Portuguese income. Unless legally separated, the income of spouses and dependents is aggregated.
- **Social security** Social security contributions are levied at 11 percent on employees and 24.5 percent on employers. Foreign employees working temporarily in Portugal are exempt from social security contributions, however, if they are covered by comparable security schemes in their home country.
- **Professional taxes** *Imposto profissional*, or professional taxes, are levied on income, whether in cash or in kind, from services performed in Portugal. Taxpayers with no more than one means of employment are not obliged to file a Professional Tax return unless they receive a cash bonus or benefit. In most cases, the Professional Tax is deducted from salaries at progressive rates of up to 20.5 percent.
- **Foreign employee's benefits** Under the foreign investment code, the salaries of foreign nationals working in Portugal for less than three years can be remitted abroad net of taxes and living expenses, without any type of restriction or regulation.
- **Treaty** Portugal has a double-taxation treaty with the UK.
- **Corporate tax** The basic rate of corporate tax is 36.5 percent. Nonresident firms are subject to taxes of up to 25 percent on royalties, dividends, and interest income, as well as remuneration obtained in their capacity as members of statutory organizations.

CENTRAL BANK

Banco de Portugal
Rua do Comercio, 148
1100 Lisbon
Tel: (1) 36-52-91
Tel: (1) 36-48-43

Business Travel

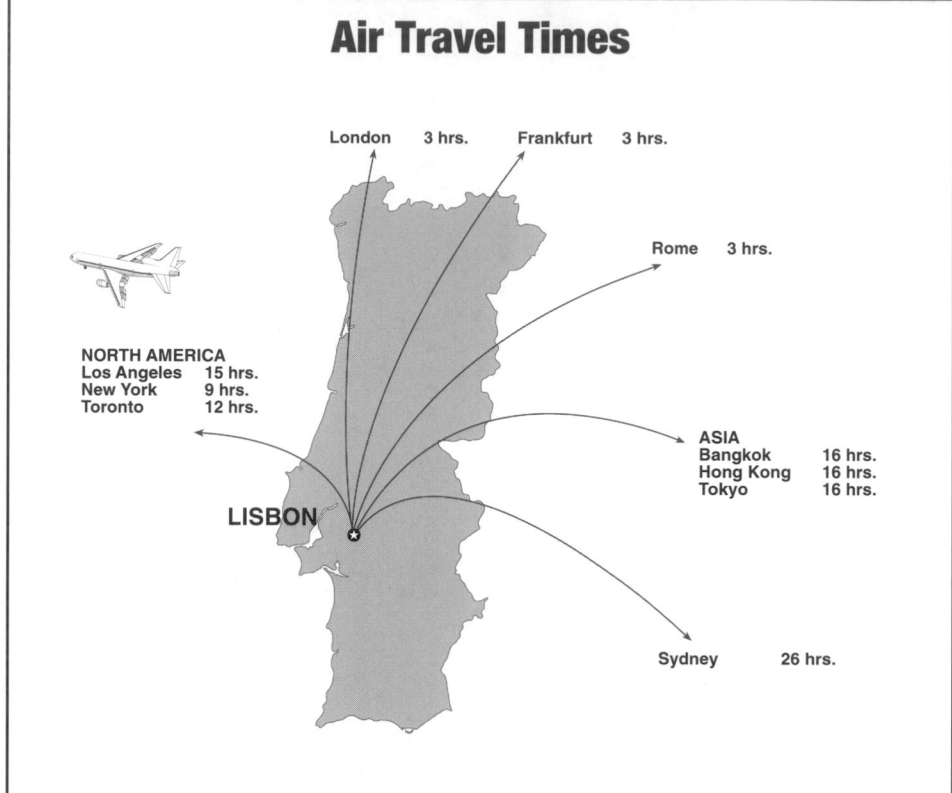

Air Travel Times

London   3 hrs.   Frankfurt   3 hrs.

Rome   3 hrs.

NORTH AMERICA
Los Angeles   15 hrs.
New York   9 hrs.
Toronto   12 hrs.

ASIA
Bangkok   16 hrs.
Hong Kong   16 hrs.
Tokyo   16 hrs.

LISBON

Sydney   26 hrs.

COMMUNICATIONS

Telephones The government-owned telephone system is improving but is not up to European standards. International calls are least expensive when dialed direct from a phone booth. Phone booths are marked "Credifone" and located at phone offices, post offices, and on the street. More phone booths accept magnetic cards than coins; cards can be purchased at places listed in the phone booth.

Fax All major hotels have fax equipment.

Post office Regular mail service, surface and air parcel post are available to most foreign destinations. Mailboxes on the street are round and red. Portuguese stamps need glue, available in pots at the post office. Telegrams, the most reliable means of communication, can be sent from most post offices, marked with a CTT sign.

BEST TRAVEL BOOKS

Birnbaum's Portugal, Alexandra M. Birnbaum. Birnbaum Travel Guides Series. Illustrated, 432 pages, Harper Collins.

Do's and Taboo's Around the World. The Bestselling Guide to International Behavior. Edited by Roger Axtell, compiled by the Parker Pen Company. The ultimate guide to international behavior, now completely updated and expanded. Helpful, fun to read!

Portugal: Cadogan Guides, David J. Evans. Illustrated, 424 pages, Globe Pequot.

Portugal: A Traveller's Guide, Ian Robertson. Illustrated, J. Murray UK.

Fodor's Europe, Best of 31 Countries. Contains information on historical towns, great culture, scenic coastal countryside.

Berlitz Business Travel Guide, Europe. Concise economic details, successful trip planning, background information on people and cities, useful facts and addresses.

USEFUL TELEPHONE NUMBERS

If you are calling from outside Portugal, you will need to add the country code [351] and any other international dialing requirements from within your country.

- Directory Assistance 118
- Emergency/Ambulance 115
- Operator/Directory 12
- International Operator Europe 099
- International Operator 098
- Information/Weather 16
- Time 15
- Telegram 10
- Local Operator 142
- Computer Rentals .... (1) 879947
- Graphic Design Studio .... (1) 836951
- DHL ....(1) 808520
- Federal Express .... (1) 807647
- Police .... (1) 3466141
- First Aid .... (1) 665342
- Fire .... (1) 606060
- Pharmacy 24 hour .... (1) 2416118
- Lisbon Taxi..(1) 815-50-61
- Central Bank .... (1) 3462931
- Media/ Foreign Bureaus .... (1) 8683715
- Radio/TV .... (1) 3475065
- Chamber of Commerce .... (1) 3427179

Credit Card Information
Lost or stolen credit cards (call collect to the US, regardless of which country the card was issued in).
- Amex ....[1] (919) 333-3211
- Diner's Club..............................[1] (303) 799-1504
- MasterCard ....[1] (314) 275-6690
- Visa ....[1] (410) 581-7931

Travelogue

WORKWEEK

Offices Monday-Friday 9:00 am to 1:00 pm and 3:00 pm to 7:00 pm; and half day Saturday.

Banks Monday-Friday 8:30 am to 3:00 pm; and Saturday 9:00 am to 12:00 noon.

Government Monday-Friday 9:30 am to 12:30 pm and 2:30 pm to 6:00 pm.

Retail Monday-Friday 9:00 am to 1:00 pm and 3:00 pm to 6:00 pm; and Saturday mornings.

Modern shopping centers called "Commercial Centers" are open daily from 10:00 am to 11:00 pm.

HOLIDAYS

Holidays 1996
January 1 New Year's Day
February 20 Carnival Day *
April 5 Good Friday *
April 7 Easter Sunday *
April 25 Liberty Day
May 1 Labor Day
June 6 Corpus Christi*
June 10 National Day
August 15 Assumption Day
October 5 Proclamation of the Republic
November 1 All Saints' Day
December 1 Independence Day
December 8 Immaculate Conception
December 25 Christmas
*Dates vary from year to year. In addition, every town has a patron saint whose feast day is a local holiday, and August is vacation month.

VISA AND PASSPORT

Foreigners must have a valid passport, but a visa is not required for stays up to 60 days.

DEPARTURE FORMALITIES

A traveler can leave Portugal with the same amount of foreign currency that was brought in. There are no other departure formalities.

IMMUNIZATION

No inoculations are required unless you are arriving from an infected area, but a typhoid shot and polio booster are recommended.

TIPPING

Restaurants will add service charge and tax, but extra tipping is customary: five to 10 percent for the waiter, and something for special service from the maitre d', captain, and busboy. Taxi drivers get 10 percent. Room service waiters: five to 10 percent of the bill. Tipping to all service people in Portugal is very appreciated and somewhat expected.

CRIME

The Portuguese crime rates are generally lower than the rest of Europe. Theft from parked cars is the major problem, particularly in underground parking lots. Take caution in dimly lit urban areas at night, avoid wandering off main streets. Pickpocketing and pursesnatchings are common.

INFRASTRUCTURE

Portugal is moderately developed, with tourist facilities widely available. Telecommunications available include long distance calling, cellular telephones, videoconferencing and internet services, and electronic mail services. The national bus company, Rodoviaria, reaches almost all towns; the trains are less comfortable, less frequent, less extensive, and generally slower. The metered taxis, black with green roofs, are the best way for business travelers to get around; be sure to enter and leave taxis on the payment side, not the street, to avoid being ticketed. Trams are available but are slow and unreliable as a means of transportation. In Portugal, you will find easy access to public transportation.

NATIONAL TOURIST OFFICE

Tourist office
Palacio Foz
Praca dos Restuadores
Lisbon
Tel: (1) 3466307

GOVERNMENT AGENCIES

Ministerio das Financas
Ministry of Economy and Finance
Av. Infante D. Henrique, 1
1100 Lisbon
Tel: (1) 888-4675

Ministerio da Industria e Energia
Ministry of Industry
Rua da Horta Seca, 15
1200 Lisbon
Tel: (1) 52-54-19

Ministerio do Emprego e Seguranca Social
Ministry of Labor
Praca de Londres, 2
1000 Lisbon
Tel: (1) 847-0430
Fax: (1) 80-11-12

Secretaria de Estado da Integracao Europeia
Secretariat of European Integration
Av. Visconde Valmor, 66-6
1000 Lisbon
Tel: (1) 76-05-30
Fax: (1) 86-73-73

Secretaria de Estado de Agricultura
Secretary of State for Agriculture
Praca de Commercio
1100 Lisbon
Tel: (1) 346-3151
Fax: (1) 32-03-71

Secretaria de Estado do Comercio Externo
Secretary of State for Foreign Trade
Av. da Republica, 79
1000 Lisbon
Tel: (1) 793-4049
Fax: (1) 793-2831

Secretaria de Estado das Pescas
Secretary of State for Fishing
Av. Brasilia, (Alges, Praia)
1400 Lisbon
Tel: (1) 61-63-61
Fax: (1) 61-65-16

Direccao Geral das Alfandegas
Director General of Customs
Rua da Alfandega
1100 Lisbon
Tel: (1) 87-87-85
Fax: (1) 87-83-35

Laboratorio Nacional de Engenharia e Tecnologia Industrial
(High-Tech Laboratory)
Rua de S. Pedro de Alcantara, 70
1200 Lisbon
Tel: (1) 346-8856
Fax: (1) 32-46-36

Secretaria do Estado das Obras Publicas
(Secretary for Public Works)
Rua da Prata 8, 2
1100 Lisbon
Tel: (1) 87-85-41
Fax: (1) 87-18-73

Secretaria do Estado da Habitacao
(Secretary for Housing)
Rua da Prata, 8 - 3
1100 Lisbon
Tel: (1) 87-85-41
Fax: (1) 87-57-09

Secretaria de Estado dos Transportes
(Secretary for Transports)
Praca do Comercio
1100 Lisbon
Tel: (1) 87-71-41
Fax: (1) 87-97-41

Dirrecao General dos Portos
(Director General for Ports)
Av. Elias Garcia, 103
1000 Lisbon
Tel: (1) 76-61-35
Fax: (1) 77-25-17

Instituto National de Estatistica
National Institute of Statistics
Av. Antonio Jose de Almeida
1078 Lisbon Codex
Tel: (1) 847-0050
Fax: (1) 848-9480

Junta Nacional de Investigao Cientifica e Tecnologica
National Scientific and Technology Research Board
Rua de D. Carlos, I, 126
1200 Lisbon
Tel: (1) 67-90-21
Fax: (1) 60-74-81

Direccao de Servicos de Direitos de Autor
Copyright Office
Palacio Foz - Restauradores
1000 Lisbon
Tel: (1) 37-34-81
Fax: (1) 37-34-82

Secretaria de Estado da Industria
Secretary for Industry
Rua da Horta Seca, 15
1200 Lisbon
Tel: (1) 346-3091
Fax: (1) 346-9816

Secretaria de Estado da Energia
Secretary for Energy
Rua da Horta Seca, 15
1200 Lisbon
Tel: (1) 346-3091
Fax: (1) 346-9816

Conselho, Gestao e Investimentos, S.A.
Av. Fontes Pereira de Melo, 43- r/c Esq
1000 Lisbon
Tel: (1) 55-99-76, 56-27-93

Direccao-Geral do Comercio Externo
Directorate-General of External Commerce
Av. da Republica, 79
1600 Lisbon
Tel: (1) 73-30-02, 73-37-30 993
Telex: 13418

Servico de Estrangeiros
Rua Conselheiro Jose Silvestre Ribeiro, 22 - Carnide
1600 Lisbon
Tel: (1) 714-1027
Telex: 18353

Instituto Financeiro de Apoio ao Desenvolvimento da Agricultura e Pescas
Rua D. Estefania, 77
1000 Lisbon
Tel: (1) 57-53-49, 57-55-77 049
Telex: 13022

Direccao-Geral da Industria
Av. Conselheiro Fernandes Sousa, 11
1100 Lisbon
Tel: (1) 65-91-71, 65-91-61

Direccao-Geral de Turismo
Av. Antonio Augusto de Aguiar, 86
1000 Lisbon
Tel: (1) 575-5086, 575-5068
Fax: (1) 55-69-17

Companhia de Seguros de Credito
Av. da Republica, 58
1000 Lisbon
Tel: (1) 76-01-31, 76-34-68

Registo Nacional das Pessoas Colectivas
Av. Oscar Monteiro Torres, 39-A
1600 Lisbon
Tel: (1) 73-50-34
Telex: 62555

Instituto de Apoio as Pequenas e Medias Empresas e ao Investimento
Industrial Small Business Institute
Rua Rodrigo da Fonseca, 73/73-AQ; (57,2)
1200 Lisbon
Tel: (1) 52-54-19
Fax: (1) 52-09-00

REMEMBER
- When you telephone (or fax) to Portugal from another country you must always include the country code [351] before the numbers given.
- When you send mail to Portugal, be sure to write PORTUGAL in capital letters on its own line below the addresses given.

Madeira Development Company
Rua Imperatriz D. Amelia
POB 4164
9052 Fuchal Codex
Madeira, Portugal
Tel: (91) 2-54-66
Fax: (91) 2-89-50

BUSINESS AND TRADE ORGANIZATIONS

Associacao Comercial de Lisbon
Rua das Portas de Santo Antao, 89
1100 Lisbon
Tel: (1) 32-71-79
Fax: (1) 32-43-04

Associacao Comercial do Porto
Palacio da Bolsa
Rua Ferreira Borges
4000 Porto
Tel: (2) 2-44-97

Associacao Industrial Portuguesa
Praca das Industrias
1399 Lisbon Codex
Tel: (1) 362-0130
Fax: (1) 362-9048

Associacao Industrial Portuense
Av. da Boavista, 2671
4100 Porto
Tel: (2) 67-22-57, 67-22-75

Confederacao dos Agricultores de Portugal
Calcada Ribeiro Santos, 19 - r/c
1200 Lisbon
Tel: (1) 67-68-20, 67-51-71

Confederacao do Comercio Portugues
Rua Saraiva de Carvalho, 1 -2
1200 Lisbon
Tel: (1) 66-85-39, 66-85-52

Confederacao da Industria Portuguesa
Av. 5 de Outubro, 35 -1
1000 Lisbon
Tel: (1) 54-74-54

American Chamber of Commerce in Portugal
Rua D. Estefania, 155-5
1000 Lisbon
Tel: (1) 57-25-61, 57-82-08
Telex: 42356

DIRECTORIES AND STATISTICAL YEARBOOKS

TOP Export of Portugal
English-Portuguese
Jovitur, Lda.
Av. Infante Santo, 23 3 B
1300 Lisbon

Estatisticas Industrias
(Industrial Statistics)
Annuario Estatistico
(Statistical Yearbook)
Estatisticas do Comercio Externo
(Foreign Trade Statistics)
Instituto Nacional de Estatistica
Av. Antonio Jose de Almeida
1000 Lisbon

NEWSPAPERS

Diário de Aveiro
Av. Dr Lourenco Peixinho 15-5 A
3800 Aveiro
Tel: (34) 24601
Telex: 37489
Fax: (34) 22635

Correio do Minho
Palácio de Exposicões e Desportos
Apdo 290
4703 Braga Codex
Tel: (053) 74087
Telex: 32337

Diário do Minho
Rua de Santa Margarida 4A
4719 Braga Codex
Tel: (53) 613414
Fax: (53) 613415
Telex: 32340

Diário de Coímbra
Rua da Sofia 179 ou Estrada de Eiras
3000 Coímbra
Tel: (39) 25461
Fax: (39) 492-128
Telex: 52147

Diário do Sul
Apdo 37
Travessa de Santo André 8
7001 Évora Codex
Tel: (66) 23144
Fax: (66) 741252

Notícias d'Évora
Rua do Raimundo 41-43
7002 Évora Codex
Tel: (66) 22348

Diário de Leiria
Av. Heróis de Angola 76-3-C
2400 Leiria
Tel: (44) 33881
Fax: (44) 812498
Telex: 65264

A Capital
Travessa do Poco da Cidade 26
Lisbon Codex
Tel: (1) 3465908
Fax: (1) 3463497
Telex: 12386

Correio da Manha
Rua Mouzinho da Silveira 27
1200 Lisbon
Tel: (1) 527636
Fax: (1) 3528256
Telex: 42439

Diário de Notícas
Av. da Liberdade 266
1200 Lisbon
Tel: (1) 561151
Fax: (1) 536627
Telex: 12379

Journal do Dia
Praceta da Tabaqueira Lote A 5
Porta B
Matinha
1900 Lisbon
Tel: (1) 8583421
Fax: (1) 8584421
Telex: 15558

Público
Rua Amilear Cabral
Lote 1
Quinta do Lambert
1700 Lisbon
Tel: (1) 7599135
Fax: (1) 7587638
Telex: 65205

PERIODICALS

Activa
R. Marcos Portugal 18
Algés
1495 Lisbon
Tel: (1) 4105570
Fax: (1) 4107050

Africa Hoje
Rua Joaquim António de Aguia 45-5 Esq.
1000 Lisbon
Tel: (1) 557175
Fax: (1) 3557667
Telex: 42487

Anglo-Portuguese News
Apdo 113
2765 Estoril
Lisbon
Tel: (1) 2443115
Telex: 66973

Autories
Av. Duque de Loule 31
1098 Lisbon Codex
Tel: (1) 578320
Fax: (1) 530257

Autosport
Av. Infante D. Henrique 334
1800 Lisbon
Tel: (1) 851052
Fax: (1) 8518990

Avante
Rua Soeiro Pereira Gomes
1699 Lisbon
Tel: (1) 769725

A Bola
Travessa da Queimada 23
r/c E. 2 D.
1294 Lisbon Codex
Tel: (1) 3463981
Fax: (1) 3464503
Telex: 12880

Brotéria-Revista de Cultura
Rua Maestro António Taborda 14
1200 Lisbon
Tel: (1) 3961660
Fax: (1) 3956629

Casa & Jardim
Rua da Misericórdia 137
S/L Esq.
1200 Lisbon
Tel: (1) 3472127
Fax: (1) 3421490
Telex: 62609

Colóquio/Artes
Av. de Berna 45
1000 Lison
Tel: (1) 7935131
Fax: (1) 7935139
Telex: 63768

Colóquio/Letras
Av. de Berna 56-3
1093 Lisbon Codex
Tel: (1) 7935131
Fax: (1) 7935139
Telex: 63768

Correio da Madeira
Rua do Carmo 19-3 Dto.
9000 Funchal
Tel: (91) 20738

Cosmopolitan
Rua Marcos Portugal 16A
Alges
1495 Lisbon
Tel: (1) 4105570

O Diabo
Rua Alexandre Herculano 7-5 Esq.
1100 Lisbon
Tel: (1) 572367
Fax: (1) 570263
Telex: 64331

RADIO AND TELEVISION

RDP-Radiodifusao Portuguesa, EP
Eng. Duarte Pacheco 5
1000 Lisbon
Tel: (1) 3872041
Fax: (1) 653468
Telex: 15649

RDP-Radio Portugal International
Rua de Sao Marcal 1
1200 Lisbon
Tel: (1) 3475065
Fax: (1) 3474475
Telex: 43247

RDP/Acores
Rua Dr Aristides Moeira da Mota 33
9500 Ponta Delgada
Sao Miguel
Azores
Tel: (96) 22045
Fax: (96) 27996
Telex: 82139

RDP/Madeira
Rua dos Netos 27
9000 Funchal
Madeira
Tel: (91) 29155
Fax: (91) 27740
Telex: 72111

RDP/Norte (Northern Zone)
Rua Candido dos Reis 74-1
4099 Porto Codex
Tel: (2) 320163
Fax: (2) 320188
Telex: 22449

RDP/Centro (Central Zone)
Rua Dr José Alberto dos Reis
3049 Coímbra Codex
Tel: (39) 716623
Fax: (39) 724253
Telex: 52280

Rádio Renascenca (RR)
Rua Capelo 5
1294 Lisbon Codex
Tel: (1) 3474270
Fax: (1) 3422658
Telex: 13030

Correio da Manha-Radio
Rua Tierno Galvan
Torre 3
Amoreiras, 7
Sala 706
1200 Lisbon
Tel: (1) 658385
Fax: (1) 659963
Telex: 65905

Estacao Rádio da Madeira
CP 450
Pico dos Barcelos
Funchal
Madeira
Tel: (91) 64395

Posto Emissor de Radiodifusao do Funchal
Rua Ponte de S. Lázaro 3
Funchal
Madeira
Tel: (91) 227249
Fax: (91) 221797
Telex: 72519

Radio Press
Rua das Merces 58/62
4200 Porto
Tel: (2) 4102348
Fax: (2) 493150
Telex: 28979

INTERNET ADDRESSES

Usenet group(s):
soc.culture.portuguese

Portuguese Home Page
http://s700.uminho.pt/homepage-pt/

Romania

Economy

Overview

Although Romania is committed to the development of a market economy, five years after the overthrow of Communism its economy remains largely socialized. The government owns most industry, all natural resources, and 10 percent of agricultural lands. The development of a private sector has started to modify the structure of the economy. Private enterprises have secured 35 percent of GDP, though basic industries have seen little change, and the expectations are that they will remain under state control for the foreseeable future. Overall, the progress of privatization in Romania has been disappointing so far.

Trade

Over the past few years, Romania has made significant progress bringing its trade regulations and standards in line with international practices in order to stimulate foreign trade. The Romanian economy cannot function without a series of vital imports. Over 60 percent of the country's imports are raw materials (mainly oil and gas), and it is also a net importer of minerals, machinery, and other necessary capital inputs. Romania exports metals, transportation equipment (including automobiles to China and Latin America), wood and wood items, textiles and apparel, leather goods, and glassware. Its major trading partners are Germany, Russia, Italy, Iran, and France.

Sectors

Agriculture Agriculture is a source of substantial potential national wealth for Romania, and presently accounts for 18 percent of GDP. It could easily meet domestic demand for food, and also generate substantial surpluses for exports. Major sectors include grains, fruit trees, and viticulture, as well as animal husbandry.

Industry Industrial enterprises contribute 44 percent of Romania's GDP, of which nearly 60 percent is in the manufacture of industrial machinery and equipment. Other major sectors include oil and gas, chemicals, mining equipment, and machine building. All of Romania's industry sectors are well developed, with the exception of some high-technology areas such as computers and electronics.

Services The services sector is still comparatively small in Romania, contributing only 38 percent of GDP. However, as compared with the situation existing before 1990, the progress achieved by this sector has been extraordinary. The newly emerging private companies are imparting new dynamism to the service sector, particularly in retail trade, hotels and restaurants, tourism, banking and insurance, legal advice, and health care.

Trends

The Romanian Government has projected an average seven percent annual growth rate for industry between now and the end of the century. As economic recovery progresses, growth is expected to be especially strong in sectors such as coal mining and machine building. The highly trained labor force and the low salary scale in Romania will assure a considerable comparative advantage in the years ahead. For the next several years, however, Romania's economic performance, and thus its demand for imports, will continue to be constrained by the slow pace of privatization and the decline of its traditional heavy industries.

At a Glance

THE COUNTRY

Location Eastern Europe, north of the Balkan Peninsula; bounded on the north and northeast by Ukraine and Moldova.
Terrain The Carpathian Mountains cover much of the country. The Transylvanian Basin is a hilly region dissected by wide, deep valleys.
Climate Moderate and humid; can get extremely cold in the winter and moderately warm in the summer. Temperatures decrease toward the high elevations in the northwest.

THE PEOPLE

Population 22,800,000
Ethnic composition
Romanians.. 89.5%
Hungarians 7.1%
Gypsies and other minorities 2.9%
Religious composition
Romanian Orthodox Church 87%
There are 13 other recognized denominations, including Roman Catholicism and the Reformed Church of Romania.
Education and literacy Almost 97 percent of the population can read and write. Education is compulsory for four years in rural areas, and seven years in the cities; children are offered free education between the ages of seven and 15. Admission to an advanced institution depends on a variety of factors, including the student's social background.
Labor
Total..10,000,000
By occupation: agriculture 29.8%, industry 35.2%, trade and transportation 14.8%, construction 4.6%, and other sectors 15.6%.

COUNTRY FACTS

Political and legal A new constitution was written in November 1991, but many ideas are still similar to the Soviet-era documents. Government is centralized and secretive. Power is divided between a president and legislature. The courts are theoretically independent but in practice are still partly controlled by the government.
Telephone There are 2.3 million telephone subscribers. International service is available but may be difficult in rural areas. International country code: [40].
Transportation Railroads provide the majority of transportation. Most of the roads are in poor condition; less than half are paved. Otopeni International Airport, near Bucharest, is the principal international air terminal. Only the Danube and Prut rivers are suitable for inland navigation.
Environment The National Council for Environmental Protection is the main environmental agency. Industrialization has caused water and air pollution. Most environmental laws have not been enforced. Radioactivity from the Chernobyl nuclear site and earthquakes have contributed to the environmental damage.
Media There are 12 AM and 5 FM radio stations, and 13 television stations. There are 34 daily newspapers with a combined annual circulation of 3.6 million.
Health All health concerns are regulated by the Ministry of Public Health and Social Welfare. Almost all medical services are public. Life expectancy is 70 years for both males and females.

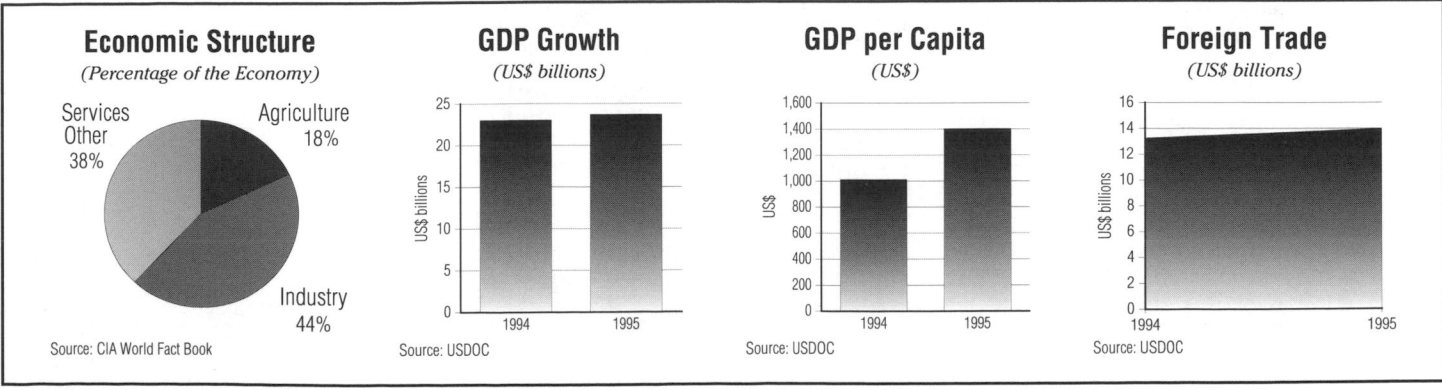

Economic Structure
(Percentage of the Economy)

Services Other 38%
Agriculture 18%
Industry 44%

Source: CIA World Fact Book

GDP Growth
(US$ billions)

Source: USDOC

GDP per Capita
(US$)

Source: USDOC

Foreign Trade
(US$ billions)

Source: USDOC

Business Travel

LH 1906	MADRID	935	113-3	
LH 1022	STUTTGART HBF.	935	-	
AF 1701	LYON	940	683-6	
AY 822	HELSINKI	940	113-3	
AA 071	SFRANCISCO-DALLAS	945	731-7	

COMMUNICATIONS

Telephones Local telephone service is automatic and fairly dependable. International calls can be delayed, but connections are generally good (expect 2-5 hour wait for overseas phone lines). The cost per minute of international phone service rises as the call gets longer. International calls can be placed from major hotels.
Fax Major hotels offer fax and telex service, post office also provides this service.
Post office Mail service in and out of Romania is slow and unreliable.

BEST TRAVEL BOOKS

Romanian Travel Pack, Hugo's Language Courses Series, 128 pages including cassette. Hunter Publishing Inc.
Berlitz Business Travel Guide, Europe. Concise economic details, successful trip planning, background information on people and cities, useful facts and addresses.
Fodor's Europe, Best of 31 Countries. Contains information on historical towns, great culture, scenic coastal countryside.
Do's and Taboo's Around the World. The Bestselling Guide to International Behavior. Edited by Roger Axtell, compiled by the Parker Pen Company. The ultimate guide to international behavior, now completely updated and expanded. Helpful, fun to read!

USEFUL TELEPHONE NUMBERS

If you are calling from outside Romania, you will need to add the country code [40] and any other international dialing requirements from within your country.

- Police 955
- Ambulance/Emergencies 961
- Fire 981
- International Calls 971
- Directory Assistance (Institutions)..................... 930
- Directory Assistance (A-L) 931
- Directory Assistance (M-Z)................................ 932
- Train Timetable 952
- Taxi 953
- Time 958
- Romanian Automobile Club (ACR) 927
- Tarom Airline .... (1) 6594185
- ONT Carparti Car Rental....................... (1) 6145160
- Hertz.. (1) 6502595
- Chamber of Commerce and Industry ...... (1) 139883
- Ministry of Foreign Affairs .... (1) 166850
- Central Bank .... (1) 6140262
- Media/Foreign Bureau .... (1) 6182878

Credit Card Information
Lost or stolen credit cards (call collect to the US, regardless of which country the card was issued in).

- Amex .... [1] (919) 3333211
- Diner's Club.................................... [1] (303) 7991504
- MasterCard .... [1] (314) 2756690
- Visa .... [1] (410) 5817931

Travelogue

WORKWEEK

Offices Monday-Friday 8:00 am to 12:30 pm and 1:00 pm to 4:00 pm; Saturday 8:00 am to 12:30 pm.
Banks Monday-Friday 9:00 am to noon.
Government Monday-Friday 8:00 am to 12:30 pm and 1:00 pm to 4:00 pm; Saturday 8:00 am to 12:30 pm.
Retail Monday-Friday 8:00 am to 5:00 pm.

HOLIDAYS

Holidays 1996
January 1-2 New Year's
April 14 Orthodox Easter*
May 1-2 Labor Day*
December 1 National Day
December 25 Christmas
*Dates vary year to year.

VISA AND PASSPORT

Foreigners must have a valid passport and visa. Visas can be obtained in advance from the Romanian Embassy in the traveler's country of residence. Visas may also be obtained at border crossings, but the cost is slightly higher.

DEPARTURE FORMALITIES

Foreigners must have a Romanian visa and an exit form (talon de iesire—a small white paper obtained on entering the country and placed inside the passport) to leave Romania. No more than 5,000 Romanian lei may be exported. Up to US$50,000 cash may be exported, so long as it was declared on entry. Customs regulations prohibit the export of some items. Tourists should save all receipts for presentation to customs authorities.

IMMUNIZATION

Only visitors arriving from infected areas need vaccination certificates, but it is suggested that polio and hepatitis vaccinations be current.

TIPPING

Tipping is generally about 10 percent in Romania. Taxi: 5-10 percent. Hotels, nightspots, restaurants, barbers, beauticians: 5 percent. US dollars are readily accepted for tips.

CRIME

Crimes against tourists are a rising problem in Romania. Thefts are most likely to occur on trains and at train stations.

INFRASTRUCTURE

Tourist facilities are not yet up to Western European standards but are being upgraded. All major cities have airline service nearby and taxi service is readily available at the airports. A domestic and international rail system serves Romania well and the extensive domestic highway network is now being upgraded. Trains are good but book far in advance. The road system is relatively good but service conditions are not reliable. Taxis are inexpensive, but hard to get.

NATIONAL TOURIST OFFICE

Carpati National Travel Agency
Gen. Magheru Calea 7
Bucharest
Tel: (1) 6145160

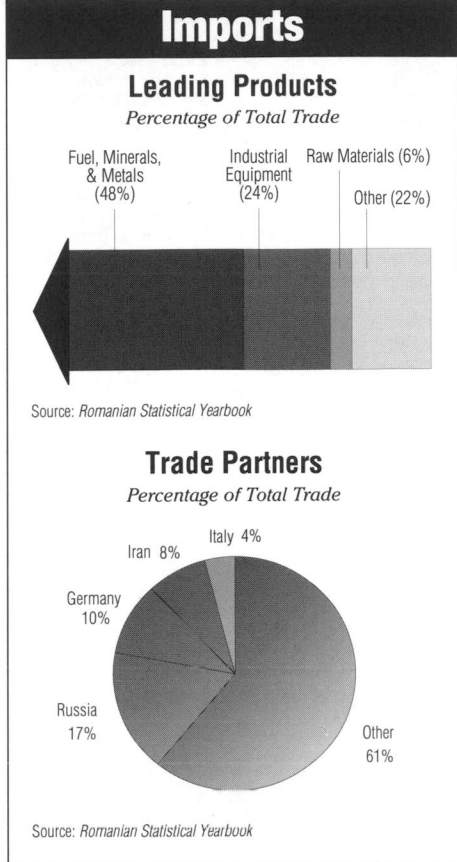

Imports

Leading Products
Percentage of Total Trade

Fuel, Minerals, & Metals (48%)
Industrial Equipment (24%)
Raw Materials (6%)
Other (22%)

Source: *Romanian Statistical Yearbook*

Trade Partners
Percentage of Total Trade

Iran 8%
Italy 4%
Germany 10%
Russia 17%
Other 61%

Source: *Romanian Statistical Yearbook*

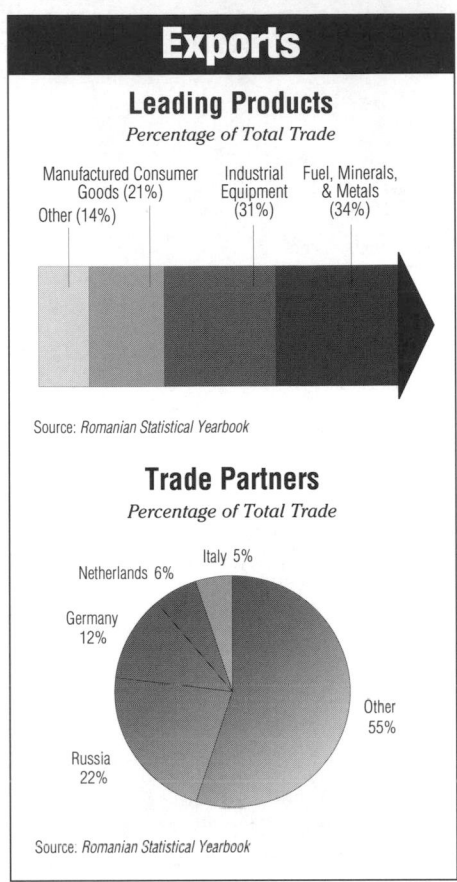

Exports

Leading Products
Percentage of Total Trade

Manufactured Consumer Goods (21%)
Other (14%)
Industrial Equipment (31%)
Fuel, Minerals, & Metals (34%)

Source: *Romanian Statistical Yearbook*

Trade Partners
Percentage of Total Trade

Netherlands 6%
Italy 5%
Germany 12%
Russia 22%
Other 55%

Source: *Romanian Statistical Yearbook*

Opportunities

FOR IMPORTING TO ROMANIA
- clothing, pharmaceuticals, vegetables
- consumer and mechanical goods
- electronic equipment
- machinery, transformers, aluminum, rail vehicles

FOR EXPORTING FROM ROMANIA
- agriculture and livestock
- furniture

GROWTH SECTORS
- agriculture
- textile and apparel
- medical industry

Trade News

RULES AND REGULATIONS
- **Import licenses** Import licenses are requested for sanitary and safety standards. Some special approvals are necessary for toxic explosives and arms.
- **Tariffs and taxes** The Romanian market is quite open, requiring no special conditions for access or necessary operation. Romania adopted an 8-tiered customs tariff in 1993. This tariff is similar to the International Harmonized System of tariff nomenclature. The weighted average of customs duty is 11 percent with notable exceptions for fuels and ores for which the taxation is zero or between three and 10 percent. Duties applied to industrial equipment are about 15 percent ad valorem. Various ores, coal, chemical products, and machine tools are not dutiable. Tariffs are considerably higher for such items as cigarettes, furs, carpets, fuels, vehicles, and photographic equipment and supplies.

Legal

Legal System

Romania's legal framework is in flux. Several gaps remain, including the absence of a modern bankruptcy code. Romanian contract law follows many of the concepts in the French and Italian civil codes.

Intellectual Property Rights

Patents Patents are recognized and protected by the State Office for Inventions and Trademarks. Applications must be written in Romanian. The law also recognizes rights for drawings and industrial models. Patent laws are similar to those of other Eastern European countries.

Trademarks Rights in registered trademarks last for 10 years and may be renewed. Application is made to the State Office for Inventions and Trademarks. If no objections are filed, the process takes at least three months to complete.

Copyrights A new copyright law is being considered by the Romanian Parliament. The stated intent is to create standards that are consistent with those of the European Union. Presently, pirated copies of audio and videotapes are marketed openly and no protection for computer software exists.

Business Registration

Trade companies may be founded as general partnerships, limited joint-stock companies, or limited partnerships. There are no laws that directly inhibit foreign business from forming an entity in Romania.

Contracts and Dispute Resolution

Few legal specialists are qualified to interpret the commercial implications of recent legal developments in Romania. There is little experience in Western methods of negotiating contracts; once contracts are concluded, there are often no means of enforcing them. Contracting parties are free to use arbitration to settle disputes. Arbitration can be undertaken in accordance with the terms of the parties' contract, as the courts will make every effort to uphold such clauses.

Legal Matters

LEGAL BRIEFS
- **Corporations** The corporate entity is unknown in Romania. The most popular form of business is a "trade company."
- **Employee right to work** The right to work is guaranteed by Romania's constitution.
- **Notaries** State-appointed notaries will certify documents, deeds, and other instruments. While Romanian law does not specifically provide for affidavits, such documents may be used as evidence concerning private international law relations. Affidavits must be authenticated by the proper foreign authorities, the diplomatic mission in the respective country's consular office in Romania, and the Romanian Ministry of Foreign Affairs.
- **Labor** Workers have the right to form and join unions and to bargain collectively. The right to strike is specifically guaranteed. Current legislation stipulates that labor unions are independent bodies, free from government or political control. Employer financial difficulties often result in nonpayment or deferral of wages. Workplace health and safety legislation is pending. The standards that do exist are not well enforced. Foreigners may be employed in managerial and specialty positions only.
- **Legal protection** Expect a large amount of red tape and the need to deal with overlapping authorities in all transactions. Corruption can be a problem. Foreigners have the same fundamental rights as citizens with a few exceptions. Their rights are also protected by a number of international agreements.
- **International agreements** Romania is a member of GATT/WTO; CISG; Convention on the Recognition and Enforcement of Foreign Arbitral Awards; and ATA Carnet Convention; it is a candidate to become a member of the EU.

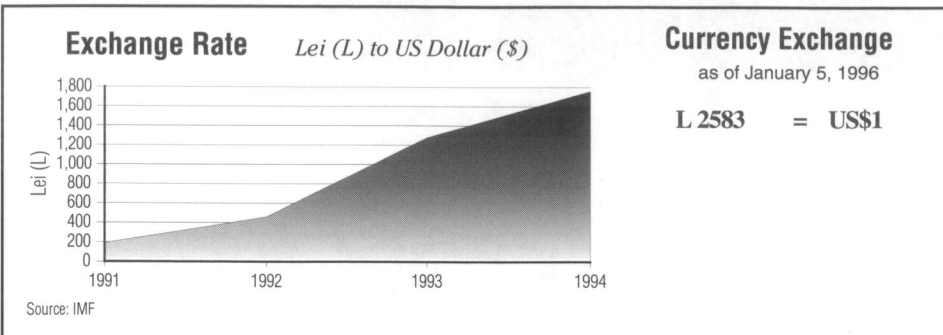

Exchange Rate — *Lei (L) to US Dollar ($)*

Lei (L): 1,800 / 1,600 / 1,400 / 1,200 / 1,000 / 800 / 600 / 400 / 200 / 0

1991 1992 1993 1994

Source: IMF

Currency Exchange
as of January 5, 1996

L 2583 = US$1

Currency

The currency of Romania is the Romanian leu (L), the plural of which is the lei.

Foreign Exchange

The National Bank of Romania (NBR) controls all rules and regulations concerning foreign currency exchange. Domestic commercial banks are authorized to conduct foreign exchange transactions. They are also permitted to have foreign banks as correspondents or to borrow directly abroad with NBR authorization.

Capital Transfers

The maximum amount of foreign currency nonresidents can bring into Romania is the equivalent of US $50,000. There are no restrictions on invisibles payments, but commercial banks must verify that the transfer is for current account purposes. Any large transfer of currency must be made through an authorized bank.

Investment Incentives

Romania recently has fine tuned legislation to attract foreign investment. Nonresident investors have free access to domestic markets and are allowed to participate in the country's privatization programs. They can own up to 100 percent of enterprises and can assign their contractual obligations and their rights to other investors, domestic and foreign. There are a number of tax incentives for foreign investors, including a two- to five-year tax holiday and reductions in succeeding years. Special provisions are available for large investments, including an exemption from customs duties on raw materials and machinery for seven years, and from income tax for five years from the date a profit begins.

Investment Restrictions

Although Romania has been very open to foreign investment, some barriers still exist. Foreign investors complain bitterly of the excessive time it takes to secure the necessary documents required to conduct business in Romania. Many foreign investors have taken on a local Romanian partner to get through the bureaucracy, although even that does not guarantee success. Corruption is also a major problem which serves to hinder foreign investment.

Money Matters

BITS AND PIECES

- **Corporate income tax** Resident companies, registered in Romania, are subject to tax on their worldwide income. Nonresident companies are subject to tax on income from Romania only.
- **Capital gains** All capital gains are included in taxable income and taxed at the regular tax rates.
- **Foreign tax relief** Foreign taxes can be credited against Romanian taxes.
- **Capital transfers** All inward and outward transfers of capital must be authorized by the NBR.
- **Gold** The NBR can purchase or sell gold in any manner. It authorizes certain people to hold gold or engage in transactions.
- **Import payments** All imports are subject to tariffs, ranging from zero to 60 percent. The average tariff rate is around 13 percent. An import surcharge is imposed on some items.
- **Export payments** Some exports are subject to quotas. All proceeds must be kept in accounts opened at authorized banks, but accountholders are free to use balances in these accounts.

BANKS

National Bank of Romania
Str. Lipscani Nr. 23-25
Bucharest
Tel: (1) 615-2750
Fax: (1) 312-3831

Agrobank
Str. Smardan Nr. 3
Bucharest
Tel: (1) 613-5520
Fax: (1) 312-0340

Anglo-Romanian Bank
Bd. D.Cantemir Nr.1
Bucharest
Tel: (1) 450-4606

Banca Comerciala "Ion Tiriac"
Str. Doamnei Nr.12
Bucharest
Tel: (1) 638-7560, 312-5878
Fax: (1) 613-4858

Banca Comerciala Romana
Bd. Republicii Nr. 14
Bucharest
Tel: (1) 614-5680, 614-3213
Fax: (1) 615-7560

Banca Pentru Mica Industrie Si Libera
Calea Plevnei Nr. 46-48
Bucharest
Tel: (1) 312-0034, 312-0031
Fax: (1) 613-0788

Bucharest Bank
Bd. Dimitrie Cantemir Nr. 1
Bucharest
Tel: (1) 321-1521
Fax: (1) 321-1520

Credit Bank
Str. Corbeni Nr. 30
Bucharest
Tel: (1) 211-5114, 211-4161

French-Romanian Bank
Bd. N. Balcescu Nr. 11
Bucharest
Tel: (1) 311-2812, 312-1358
Fax: (1) 311-2813

Post Bank
Bd. Libertatii Nr.14 Bl.104
Bucharest
Tel: (1) 312-2772
Fax: (1) 400-1362

Romanian Bank for Foreign Trade
Calea Victoriei Nr.22-24
Bucharest
Tel: (1) 614-9190, 615-7603
Fax: (1) 638-4040

TAXATION

Taxation requires sophisticated knowledge of complex rules and regulations specific to each country. The information presented here is from the Ernst & Young Corporate Tax Guide and Directory, available from the Ernst & Young accounting office in your country, or from:

Ernst & Young Romania
B-dul Maresal Averescu 8-10
Sector 1, Cod 71316
Bucharest, Romania
Tel: (1) 3128703, 6652540
Fax: (1) 3128703

At a Glance

Corporate Income Tax Rate (%)	38
Capital Gains Tax Rate (%)	38
Branch Tax Rate (%)	44.2
Withholding Tax	
Dividends (a)	10
Interest (b)	
Royalties from Patents, Know-how, etc. bc)	20
Branch Remittance Tax	10
Net Operating Losses (years)	
Carryback	0
Carryforward	5

(b) Applicable to residents and nonresidents.
(c) Applicable to nonresidents.

Overview

As Romania moves through the early and unstable stages of progress toward a free market economy, doing business there presents a complex and difficult situation for the foreigner. The new private sector has experienced rapid growth, mostly in trade and services, and that has been mainly in small and medium-sized companies. (Utilities, transportation, and large manufacturing remain state enterprises.) Additionally, over 30,000 commercial firms have entered the field of foreign trade following the 1990 abolition of the government monopoly of foreign trade. For the most part, these new trading companies focus on consumer goods.

Agents and Distribution

The choice of a local partner is a critical step. Because the Romanian situation is complex and difficult (for foreigners and locals alike), prospective traders must invest sufficient time on their own to satisfy themselves that the selected Romanian firm is fully capable and reliable. Fortunately, well qualified technical expertise and capability exists. Romanian specialists are very skilled although they have been isolated for nearly two decades from the mainstream of technical knowledge.

Selling Techniques

Alternate selling methods such as franchising and direct marketing are only just beginning to appear in Romania. Due to the relatively low purchasing power of Romanian consumers, and the vagaries of local authorities, many of these selling methods are not presently viable.

Advertising and Customer Support

Accompanying Romania's moves to a market economy has been a growth in the advertising field. Key to this growth are increased quantity and quality of media, the development of domestic professional advertising agencies, and the arrival of branches of international agencies. Romanians are often convinced of their own skills despite the fact that they lack experience and knowledge of Western business practices. The firm entering business in Romania should pay attention to correcting these attitudes in its operations by providing a solid foundation of training for foreign associates and employees.

Marketing in Romania

MARKETING TIPS

- **Important qualities** Quality and price but especially payment considerations are the most important factors in determining who will succeed in doing business in Romania. Like all former East European countries, Romania is cash poor. A seller's willingness to grant long-term credit arrangements and to consider barter transactions and such concepts as processing contracts will put it in a favorable competitive position.
- **Media** TV is the predominant medium followed by radio, press, outdoor advertising, and movie advertising. TV is dominated by the state-owned TVR, but there exist two smaller networks, CNN among them, and several small independent stations in major cities. Movie and billboard ads are growing in use and importance.
- **Financing and credit** Business financing is extremely limited due to a shortage of capital and virtually no local sources of credit.
- **Special competitive factors** Sellers should consider extending credit and providing unorthodox financing (barter, for example).
- **Business and commercial code** Due to the lack of business law, business practices are governed largely by custom and favor of the authorities, making access to local knowledge an essential condition of business.
- **Absence of distribution system** Due to the lack of wholesaling and retailing systems, the foreign supplier will have to establish its own system through association with local partners.
- **Price controls abolished** Freedom in pricing products is now established; the few remaining price controls apply exclusively to a limited number of products manufactured by state-owned companies.
- **Business climate** Entering into business with local partners remains risky.

Business Culture

Greetings and Courtesies

Romanians consider entertaining guests to be an honor, but it is rare for foreign guests to be invited into a Romanian home. It is customary to bring gifts to business associates in Romania, perhaps inexpensive pens or lighters imprinted with your company's logo. When dining, several toasts are exchanged and guests are expected to contribute. Romanian hosts will want you to stay for dinner as long as possible. Don't be in a rush to leave.

Business Ethic and Framework

Doing business in Romania can be a frustrating experience, but patience may pay off. Bitter toward Communists, Romanians have eagerly embraced the free market system, and display a new excitement in their business dealings, especially when compared to previous years when strong new businesses were rare.

Meetings and Decision Making

Meetings in Romania should be held on a one-to-one basis. They are often distrustful, even of other Romanians. Foreign businesspeople are often told what the Romanian thinks they want to hear rather than the facts as they exist. Prepare for a lengthy meeting. Business presentations should be filled with facts and figures and organized to speed the decision-making process. Commonly, no one wants to carry responsibility, and decisions are passed from office to office with the plea, "It's not my problem."

Women

Women in Romania are treated with extreme respect and courtesy. Romania maintains traditional attitudes toward women, and women attempting to work as professionals have to work hard to prove themselves in order to be treated equally. Most Romanian women are very common in the workplace under the new economy due to financial need. Foreign women may run into resistance in conducting business with Romanian males, but a firm, professional attitude should hold sway.

Cultural Cautions

DO'S

- Compliment your Romanian hosts and associates generously.
- Good topics of conversation are sports, travel, music, fashion, and books.

DON'TS

- Refrain from discussing politics, the economy, or any negative aspects of Romania.
- It is considered impolite to yawn without covering the mouth.
- It is insulting to refuse a gift in Romania.
- Avoid asking questions about Romanians' personal life and family.

CUSTOMS

- It is best to wear a conservative business suit, dark in color, for meetings in Romania. Romanians frown on casual dress for business. A dress and suit with necktie are appropriate for all Romanian occasions.
- Romanians no longer avoid controversial opinions.

OBSERVATIONS

- It is better for a visitor to let their hosts lead conversation into areas formerly not open for discussion.

NEGOTIATIONS

- Romanians are known as "hard bargainers."
- Foreign businesspeople should establish parameters at the start of negotiations, making clear what they will and will not do. Do not waver from that position.
- Romanians are willing to take risks in negotiations, a legacy of their Byzantine and Turkish trading traditions.
- Promises in Romania are not always kept.
- Credit terms are major elements of any deal.

GOVERNMENT AGENCIES

The Government of Romania
General Secretariate
Piata Victoriei Nr.1, Bucharest
Tel: (1) 614-3400, 733-7660
Fax: (1) 659-2019

Supreme Court of Justice
Calea Rahovei Nr. 4, Bucharest
Tel: (1) 312-0920
Fax: (1) 613-0882

Ministry of Foreign Affairs
Aleea Modrogan Nr.14, Bucharest
Tel: (1) 633-4060, 401-633-4742
Fax: (1) 312-7589

Ministry of Commerce
Str. Apolodor Nr.17, Bucharest
Tel: (1) 614-1141, 781-6287
Fax: (1) 312-2342

Ministry of Agriculture and Food Industry
Bd. Republicii Nr.24, Bucharest
Tel: (1) 614-4020, 615-4412
Fax: (1) 613-0322

Ministry of Waters, Forests and Environment Protection
Bd. Libertatii Nr.12, Bucharest
Tel: (1) 631-6146, 781-3488
Fax: (1) 312-4227

Ministry of Research and Technology
Str. Mendeleev Nr. 21-25
Tel: (1) 650-5095, 650-2080
Fax: (1) 312-1410

Ministry of Communications
Bd. Libertatii Nr.14, Bucharest
Tel: (1) 400-1100, 400-1103
Fax: (1) 400-1742

Commission for Citizenship Problems
Bd. Mihail Kogalniceanu Nr. 33, Bucharest
Tel: (1) 614-4400

General Custom Department
Str. Nicolae Iorga, Bucharest
Tel: (1) 659-2080, 650-7280
Fax: (1) 650-5894

Ministry of Education
Str. General Berthelot, Nr. 28-30, Bucharest
Tel: (1) 615-7430, 614-2680
Fax: (1) 615-7736

Ministry of Finance
Str. Apolodor Nr. 17, Bucharest
Tel: (1) 781-3100
Fax: (1) 781-4360

Ministry of Industries
Calea Victoriei Nr.152, Bucharest
Tel: (1) 650-5020, 650-4190
Fax: (1) 650-3029

Ministry of Labour and Social Protection
Str. Demetru I. Dobrescu Nr. 2, Bucharest
Tel: (1) 615-0200, 617-0160
Fax: (1) 613-8764

Ministry of the Interior
Str. Domnita Anastasia Nr. 3-5, Bucharest
Tel: (1) 614-3535, 679-4545
Fax: (1) 312-1500

Ministry of Transports
Bd. Dinicu Golescu Nr. 38, Bucharest
Tel: (1) 617-7140, 617-1880, 617-2060

National Agency for Privatization
Str. Ministerului, Nr. 2-4, Bucharest
Tel: (1) 615-0200, 617-0160
Fax: (1) 312-0809

National Commission for Statistics
Bd. Libertatii Nr. 16, Bucharest
Tel: (1) 781-3100, 614-3371
Fax: (1) 312-4873

Office for Consumers Protection
Str. Elev Stefanescu Stefan Nr. 9, Bucharest
Tel: (1) 642-2553, 642-5496

Office for Inventions and Trade Marks
Str. Ion Ghica Nr. 5, Bucharest
Tel: (1) 615-9066
Fax: (1) 312-3819

Romanian Development Agency
Bd. Magheru Nr.7, Bucharest
Tel: (1) 312-5160, 312-5161
Fax: (1) 312-0371, 613-2415

GENERAL TRADE ASSOCIATIONS

AUTODACIA
(Automobiles)
POB 81, 0300 Pitesti
Tel: 634978 Telex: 18396

DANUBIANA
(Export of Chemicals, Auto Tires, Yarns and Plastics)
Boulevard Republicii 10, Bucharest
Tel: (1) 6156051

ELECTRONUM
(Electronic Equipment and Computer Technology)
Str. Alexandru Sahia 33, Bucharest
Tel: (1) 6137081 Telex: 11547

GEOMIN
(Mining and Geological Cooperation)
Calea Victoriei 220, Bucharest
Tel: (1) 6592930

METALIMPORTEXPORT
(Metals)
Str. Mendeleev 21-25, Bucharest
Tel: (1) 6596825 Telex: 11515

MINERALIMPORTEXPORT
(Minerals)
Boulevard Republicii 16, Bucharest
Tel: (1) 6139167 Telex: 11873

CHAMBERS OF COMMERCE

The Chamber of Commerce and Industry of Romania
Bd. Nicolae Balcescu Nr. 22, Bucharest
Tel: (1) 312-1312
Fax: (1) 312-2091

National Register of Commerce
Bd. Expozitiei Nr. 4, Bucharest
Tel: (1) 312-7845, 312-7847
Fax: (1) 312-9661

Romexpo S.A.
(Fairs and Exhibitions)
Bd. Marasti Nr.65-67, Bucharest
Tel: (1) 223-1160, 223-1181
Fax: (1) 312-8400, 222-6169

Chamber of Commerce and Industry Bacau County
Str. Libertatii 1
5500 Bacau
Tel: (34) 146262 Fax: (34) 171070

Chamber of Commerce and Industry Bihor County
Str. General Magheru 7
3700 Oradea
Tel: (59) 117381 Tel/Fax: (59) 117178

Chamber of Commerce and Industry Brasov County
B-dul Eroilor 5
2200 Brasov
Tel: (68) 117046 Fax: (68) 150333

Chamber of Commerce and Industry Cluj County
Piata Unirii 2
3400 Cluj-Napoca
Tel: (64) 111351 Fax: (64) 112214

Chamber of Commerce and Industry Constanta County
Str. Mircea cel Batran 84, Bl. MF1
8700 Constanta
Tel: (41) 665494 Fax: (41) 3122401

Chamber of Commerce and Industry Dolj County
Str. Ion Maiorescu 10
1100 Craiova
Tel: (51) 118876 Fax: (51) 112652

Chamber of Commerce and Industry Galati County
Str. Mihai Bravu 46
6200 Galati
Tel: (36) 415505 Fax: (36) 414750

Chamber of Commerce and Industry Iasi County
B-dul Copou 4
6600 Iasi
Tel: (32) 112170 Fax: (32) 112170

Chamber of Commerce and Industry Mures County
Str. Tusnad 5
2200 Tirgu Mures
Tel: (65) 168121 Fax: (65) 169219

Chamber of Commerce and Industry Prahova County
Str. Republicii 2, Intr. B, Cam. 424
2000 Ploiesti
Tel: (44) 143427 Fax: (44) 112552

Chamber of Commerce and Industry Satu Mare County
Piata 25 Octombrie No. 1
3900 Satu Mare
Tel: (61) 714036 Fax: (61) 715058

Chamber of Commerce and Industry Sibiu County
Str. Telefoanelor 1
2400 Sibiu
Tel: (69) 416447 Fax: (69) 411831

Chamber of Commerce and Industry Timis County
Piata Victoriei 3
1900 Timisoara
Tel: (56) 190766 Fax: (56) 190311

MARKET RESEARCH FIRMS

Aromar
Tel: (1) 6150658, 6153923

Institute of World Economy
Blvd. Carol I No. 12, Bucharest
Tel: (1) 6141653 Fax: (1) 3110759

Research Team Romania SRL
Str. Iancu de Hunedoara 2, Bl. H6, Ap. 31
Tel: (1) 6598895 Fax: (1) 3110672

FOREIGN BANKS

Chemical Bank (USA)
Bd. Republicii Nr.16, Bucharest
Tel: (1) 312-0325, 312-1075
Fax: (1) 615-8414

Frankfurt-Bucharest Bank (Germany)
Calea Victoriei Nr. 22-24, Bucharest
Tel: (1) 613-1030, 312-0908
Fax: (1) 613-0040

MISR-Romanian Bank (Egypt)
Str. G.Enescu Nr.4, Bucharest
Tel: (1) 312-0564, 312-0908
Fax: (1) 312-0893

Societe Generale (France)
Bd. N. Balcescu Nr. 16, Bucharest
Tel: (1) 638-2494, 312-0060

RADIO & TELEVISION STATIONS

Romanian Radio
Temisana Str.
Bucharest
Tel: (1) 3123640

Romanian Television
Calea Dorobanti 191
Bucharest
Tel: (1) 6331593 Telex: 11251/2

INTERNET ADDRESSES

Usenet group(s):
soc.culture.romanian

The Romanian WWW Home Page
http://www.info.polymtl.ca/zuse/tavi/www/rom_eng.html

US Romanian Embassy
http://www.embassy.org/romania/

Russia

Russian Federation

Economy

Overview

Russia has endured a period of economic and political change following the dissolution of the USSR. Once heavily reliant on revenues from exports to other republics of the former USSR, the effects of the disruption of these traditional trade ties, and its own delay in implementing economic reforms, have resulted in a real GDP decline of between 40 and 50 percent in the past four years. Russia has traditionally focused on the promotion of heavy industry to run its economy, and has made good use of its abundant and diverse supply of natural resources. It needs now to focus on continued market reforms and infrastructure development.

Trade

Russia has experienced a sharp decline in the total value of its foreign trade since the break-up of the Soviet Union. Germany is its largest trading partner, followed by China, and the United States. Russia continues to run an overall trade surplus, due to increased trade on international markets and the drop in imports as a result of new import taxes. The slow process of transforming itself from a planned to a market economy, and finding new trading partners for marginally competitive goods, is resulting in declining output, and this trend is likely to continue in the short to medium term.

Sectors

Agriculture Agricultural output has declined in the past few years but this sector continues to play an important role in the Russian economy, employing 13 percent of the population. Russia has begun, slowly, to privatize this sector, but over 90 percent of its agricultural land remains under the control of former state collectives and the state continues to purchase much of the agricultural output at non-market prices.

Industry Heavy industry has long been the driving force behind Russia's economy and although output has fallen rapidly, largely due to the decline of military-related industries, its dominance continues. It suffers from aging technology, machinery, and facilities, however, as well as from a lack of competitiveness. The production of consumer durables is one area showing an increase in output due to rising demand on the domestic market. Russia has the greatest mineral reserves in the world and the mining of coal, petroleum, iron ore, copper, and iron alloys will play an increasingly important role in the future.

Services Russia has a well-developed, if somewhat outdated, services sector which should continue to grow and modernize as the country continues its economic transformation.

Trends

The Russian government is continuing its large-scale privatization plan, has agreed to the terms of the GATT Uruguay Round Agreement, and is actively encouraging foreign investment. It is, nonetheless, experiencing difficulties in creating a stable business environment sufficient to attract foreign investors. Part of this might be due to the serious problems of crime and corruption in business and a labor force which is unsuited to Russia's changing economy. Though both export and import levels continue to fall, consumer demand for low-cost products is increasing, and this should provide increasing opportunities for foreign businesses as the economy recovers.

At a Glance

THE COUNTRY

Location Northern Asia, between Europe and the North Pacific Ocean.
Terrain Broad plain with low hills west of the Urals; vast coniferous forest and tundra in Siberia; uplands and mountains along southern borders.
Climate Ranges from steppes in the south through humid continental in much of European Russia; subarctic in Siberia to tundra climate in the polar north.

THE PEOPLE

Population 149,600,000
Ethnic composition
Russian 81.5%
Tatar 3.85%
Ukrainian 3%
Chuvash 1.2%
Bashkir, Byelorussian, Moldavian 2.4%
Other 8.1%
Religions Russian Orthodox, Muslim, Jewish, Roman Catholic, Protestant, Buddhist, Other.
Languages spoken Russian (official); more than 140 other languages and dialects.
Education and literacy Russia can boast a 100 percent literacy rate for ages five though 49. Education is mostly state funded and compulsory for 10 years. State-funded stipends are available for higher education.
Labor force
Total: 75,000,000
By occupation: production and economic services 83.9%, government 16.1%

COUNTRY FACTS

Political and legal Russia is a federation of 21 autonomous republics. The legal system is based on civil law, with judicial review of legislative acts.
Telephone Russia's telephone system is inadequate, particularly international connections. There are 164 telephones per 1,000 people and 11,000,000 unfilled applications for telephone service. International country code: [7]. Selected city codes: Moscow (095), (501), and (502), St. Petersburg (812), Minsk (0172).
Transportation Russia's transportation system has fallen into disrepair. That which still functions operates beyond its capacity and is subject to frequent delays.
Environment Current issues include air pollution from heavy industry, emissions of coal-fired electric plants, and transportation in major cities. Deforestation, soil erosion, and soil contamination from improper application of agricultural chemicals are major problems.
Media All broadcasting is controlled by the state. There are over 1,000 AM, FM, and short wave radio stations which reach 98.6 percent of the population, and 310 television stations. There are about 750 daily newspapers with a total annual circulation of 133,979,000.
Health Life expectancy varies greatly; females average 74 years while men average 62 years. The live birth rate is 16 children per 1,000 people.

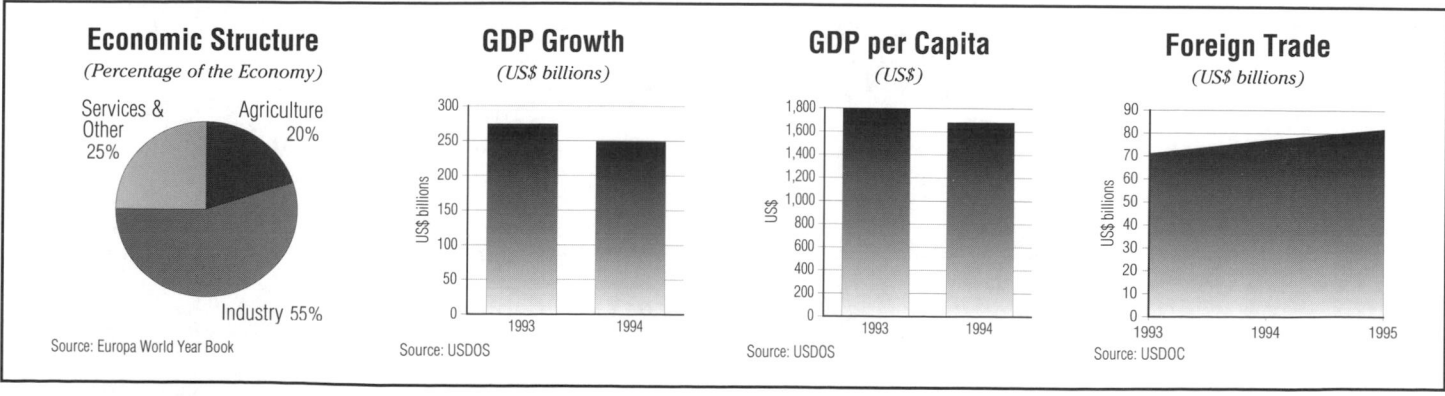

Economic Structure
(Percentage of the Economy)

Services & Other 25%
Agriculture 20%
Industry 55%

Source: Europa World Year Book

GDP Growth
(US$ billions)

Source: USDOS

GDP per Capita
(US$)

Source: USDOS

Foreign Trade
(US$ billions)

Source: USDOC

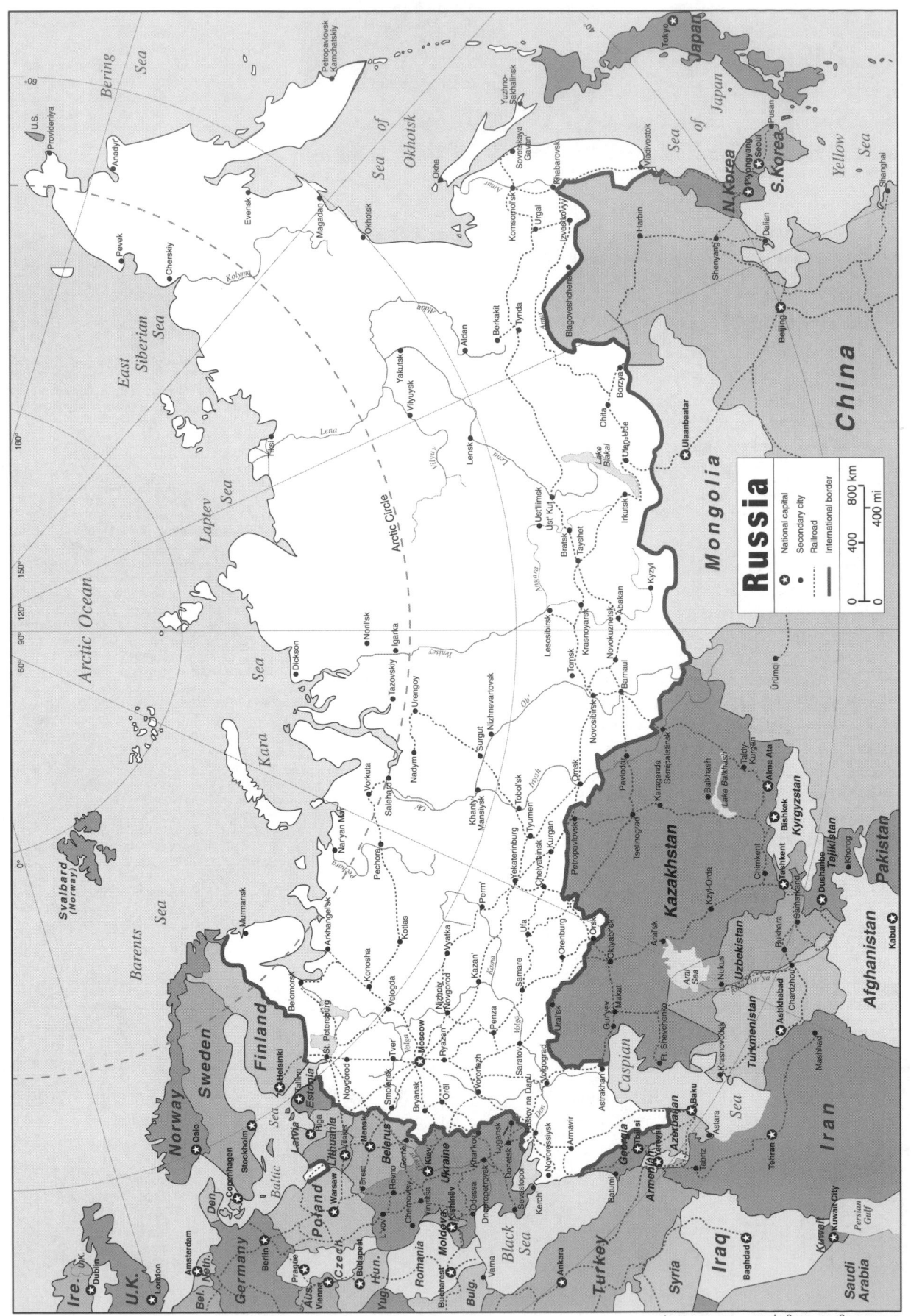

©1994 Magellan GeographixSMSanta Barbara, CA

Foreign Trade

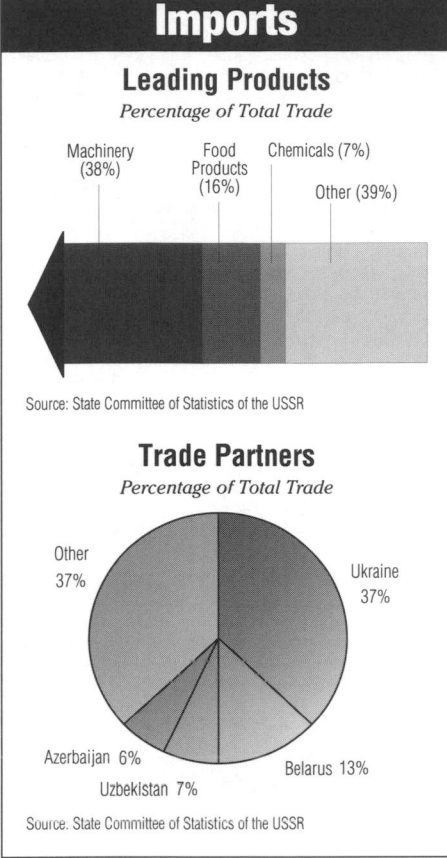

Imports

Leading Products
Percentage of Total Trade

Machinery (38%)
Food Products (16%)
Chemicals (7%)
Other (39%)

Source: State Committee of Statistics of the USSR

Trade Partners
Percentage of Total Trade

Other 37%
Ukraine 37%
Azerbaijan 6%
Uzbekistan 7%
Belarus 13%

Source: State Committee of Statistics of the USSR

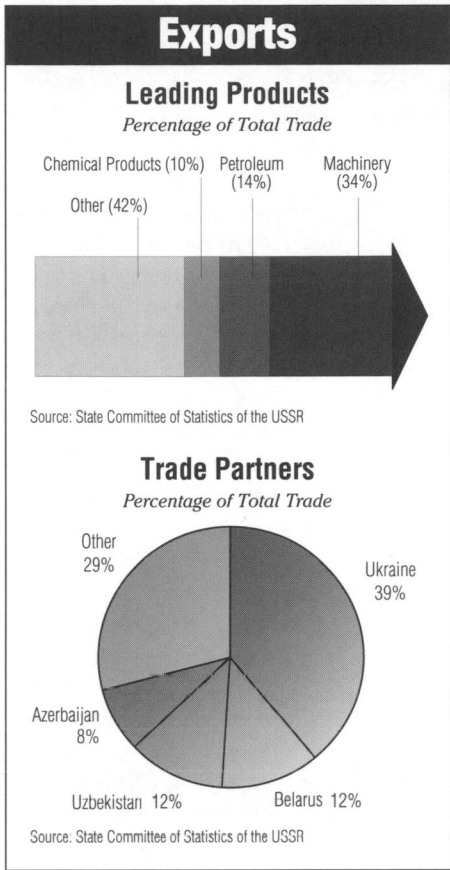

Exports

Leading Products
Percentage of Total Trade

Chemical Products (10%)
Petroleum (14%)
Machinery (34%)
Other (42%)

Source: State Committee of Statistics of the USSR

Trade Partners
Percentage of Total Trade

Other 29%
Ukraine 39%
Azerbaijan 8%
Uzbekistan 12%
Belarus 12%

Source: State Committee of Statistics of the USSR

Opportunities

FOR IMPORTING TO RUSSIA
- machinery and equipment
- chemicals
- consumer goods
- grain
- meat
- sugar
- semifinished metal products

FOR EXPORTING FROM RUSSIA
- natural resources
- petroleum and petroleum products
- natural gas
- woods and wood products
- metals
- chemicals
- military manufactures

GROWTH SECTORS
- food and clothing
- foodstuff
- capital equipment - food processing machinery
- residential construction
- home appliance and home electronics
- building materials
- construction equipment
- manufacturing equipment

GOVERNMENT PROCUREMENT
- civil aviation
- civil shipbuilding and harbor modernization
- telecommunications
- global navigation system
- international space station engineering services and equipment

Trade News

RULES AND REGULATIONS

- **Trade news** In the breakup of the Soviet Union, Russia lost a number of key ports, which has led to overcrowding at the St. Petersburg port. The transportation infrastructure leaves much to be desired.

- **Import licenses** Import licenses are required for importation of various goods including combat and sporting weapons; self-defense articles; explosives; military and ciphering equipment; radioactive materials and waste, including uranium; strong poisons and narcotics; precious metals; alloys; and stones.

- **Tariffs and import taxes** Import tariffs have been raised several times. The latest increase was introduced on March 15, 1994, with an effective date of July 1, 1994. The new duty schedule proposes a mean import tariff of 13 to15 percent, which is several times higher than that levied by most Western countries. Recently, the Russian government announced plans to lower some tariffs.

- **Other import tariffs** Excise tax applies to a number of "luxury" goods, such as alcohol, cigarettes, and cars (20-250 percent).

- **Customs duties** Companies are required to pay customs duties on most goods imported into Russia. The import duty is calculated as a percentage of the value of the imported goods as established for customs purposes. Most tariffs range from 7.5 to 15 percent. The Russian government raises import tariffs to increase federal revenue and encourage domestic production. Import duties are waived by the Russian government under certain conditions.

- **Value-added tax** A value-added tax (VAT) is added on most goods sold in Russia including goods imported into Russia. The VAT, which is eventually passed down to the consumer, is levied in Russia at a standard rate of 23 percent. The VAT on imported goods is calculated as a percentage of the sum of the customs value of the good, the import tariff, and the excise tax. In addition to import tariffs and the VAT, some goods imported into Russia are subject to an excise duty. They are imposed at relatively high rates on imported goods that are viewed as luxuries, primarily alcoholic beverages and automobiles. Excise taxes range from 35 to100 percent.

- **Trade barriers** There are no significant legal barriers to the import market, but there are a number of factors which discourage trade. Hindrances to trade include: ownership and jurisdictional disputes, financial illiquidity of a majority of Russian firms, lack of a normal commercial market, absence of a commercial legal framework, high cost and general difficulty of doing business, severe infrastructure problems (telecom, roads, banking system, ports, etc.), payment arrears and frozen accounts, frequent changes in government and firm personnel, high taxes which frequently change, frequent changes in the import and export regime, lack of systematic and accessible credit information, and mounting crime and corruption.

- **Export controls** Russia continues to levy export duties on commodities for which domestic prices are kept below world market levels. The export of weapons, military equipment, and dual-use materials and technology will continue to require a license.

- **Export payments** Export duties are levied on a number of products, and range up to 30 percent. Duties are payable when the goods cross the border, but payments can be postponed for up to 60 days if a bank guarantee for the payment is provided.

GOVERNMENT AGENCIES

Ministry of Foreign Economic Relations
32/34, Smolenskaya-Sennaya Ploshchad
Moscow 121200
Tel: (095) 244-3690
Fax: (095) 244-1600

State Customs Committee
1a, Komsomolskaya Ploshchad
Moscow 107842
Tel: (095) 975-3289
Fax: (095) 975-4823

Overview

The stereotype of Russia as a homogeneous market dominated by state-owned outlets that service unsophisticated customers has collapsed along with the former USSR. As Russia progresses toward a free-market economy, it must streamline its distribution channels and strengthen its customer base. Many opportunities await in this potentially huge market.

Distribution

While Russia has historically been a difficult market to crack, the fall of Communism and the birth of free enterprise have created several openings for foreign businesses. The privatization of the Russian retail sector has created a rapid proliferation and diversification of retail outlets. Choosing an effective sales channel is the key to introducing any product into the Russian market. Such channels are becoming increasingly more product and customer specific. Direct sales are currently the most popular approach for suppliers of capital goods and industrial equipment. Russian end-users of these types of products are predominately large state-owned or recently privatized enterprises. Large firms marketing to Russian enterprises typically operate from an office located in a major city, either Moscow, St. Petersburg, or Vladivostok. Moscow is by far the most popular location for representative offices, although other cities are becoming more popular, especially as the push moves away from the previously Communist center of Moscow and into the other, more market-oriented, cities. Smaller suppliers of capital goods often find it more cost-effective to use intermediary organizations, such as commission agents or trading companies.

Agents, Distributors, and Partners

Since many distributors are limited to main cities, suppliers generally market their products through distributorships by establishing a representative office, then identifying Russian firms capable of acting as distributors. In a few product categories (apparel, office equipment, and personal computers), foreign suppliers can choose from a small but growing number of existing Russian distributors, who service their foreign suppliers by placing products on store shelves and directly handling customs procedures and obligations. Some suppliers, especially small and medium-sized firms seeking a cost effective alternative to establishing a representative office in Russia, use intermediary organizations such as commission agents, export management companies, and export trading companies. These agents often possess their own office and sales personnel, can perform a number of marketing services on behalf of foreign suppliers, make sales calls to prospective end-users, exhibit the supplier's products at trade shows and exhibitions, and negotiate sales contracts. Agents should understand right away that, while Moscow should be used as a base of operations, most sales will be made in other cities, or "in the field." Russia's industrial zones, like cities in the Urals region, Siberia, the Far East, and the Northwest/St. Petersburg region, will have many more potential buyers than Moscow. These areas used to depend on Moscow for direction, but with the fall of the Communist government, the enterprises are largely independent of any central government control and often do not even have permanent representatives in Moscow. Consider establishing a base in one of these cities.

Selling Techniques

Because Russia is such a large country and the geographic dispersion of buyers is so vast, frequent air travel by sales representatives to visit prospective buyers is a necessity. Foreign firms importing automobiles, home electronics, and fast food have succeeded through franchised dealerships, providing the foreign seller with the greatest possible control over the marketing of its products. A small but increasing number of firms have entered into joint venture arrangements to manufacture and sell finished goods, although joint ventures remain risky in this emerging market.

Advertising

The number of Western and Russian advertising agencies is growing rapidly despite, or perhaps due to, the lack of a regulatory system. Currently, television, radio, print, and billboard advertising are used for consumer goods and financial services markets. Trade exhibitions remain a useful marketing tool for the foreign exporter.

Service and Customer Support

Because the Western standards for quality and service are new to Russia, foreign sellers must train and supervise their distributors or partners. Russians will usually consider price before after-sales service when deciding on a product. However, with the recent influx of foreign goods from which to choose, Russians will increasingly look for superior product support and service.

Marketing in Russia

MARKETING TIPS

- **Special support** Foreign suppliers must provide considerable hands-on training for distributors, as well as supervision thereafter to insure that the distributor upholds the quality standards of the seller and its products, and to make certain that the goods actually reach the market segment targeted by the seller.

- **Undeveloped commercial and tax codes** The majority of commercial regulations are contained in thousands of presidential, governmental, and ministerial decrees resulting in overlapping and conflicting laws.

- **Pricing** Low per capita income, lack of competition for certain products and excessive competition for others, and high inflation make pricing exceptionally difficult.

- **Distributor proliferation** Beware. Many of these recently formed Russian distributors have comparatively short track records, and their experience is often limited to specific regional centers like Moscow and St. Petersburg. Many suppliers have chosen to market products through authorized distributorships they create from scratch. This obviously entails greater expense than utilizing existing networks, but it is much safer and allows the supplier to establish a distribution network capable of handling larger product volumes.

- **Government purchases** Despite the nearly complete disintegration of the former Soviet Union's centralized trading regime, the federal and regional Russian government organizations still make direct purchases of foreign goods, especially pharmaceuticals and medical equipment.

AD AGENCIES

BBDO Marketing
Moscow, 109017
Sartomonetny Preulok, 31
Tel: (095) 231-3906
Fax: (095) 238-3088

Dentsu Inc.
Moscow, 21059
Moscow Office, Hotel Slavyanskaya Bus. Center
South Wing Berezhkovskaya
Naberezhnaya 2
Tel: (095) 941-8112

Friedmann & Rose
119034 Moscow
4/8 3rd Obydensky Per., Ste. 2
Tel: (095) 202-9800

McCann-Erickson Russia
103473, Moscow
1st Volkonski Pereulok 10
Tel: (095) 926-4088
Fax: (095) 926-4089

Young & Rubicam/Sovero
Moscow 123610
Ctr. for Int'l. Trade
Office 1404A
12 Krasnopresnenskaya Nab
Tel: (095) 253-2185

MARKET RESEARCH CONTACTS

JSK Mosvneshinform
Moscow 129278
2/1, Pavla Korchagina Ul.
Tel: (095) 282-3286, 205-1423
Fax: (095) 283-4785, 205-7873

Ministry of Foreign Economic Relations National Market Research Institute
Moscow 119285
4, Pudovkina Ul.
Tel: (095) 147-0153, 147-4366
Fax: (095) 143-8664

INFORCOM
Moscow 103031
26, Bld. 7, 5, Moskvina Ul.
Tel: (095) 925-6644
Fax: (095) 975-2679

 **Business Culture**

Greetings and Courtesies

Russians like to shake hands and give their name when meeting with visitors for the first time. While conversing with Russians, it is proper to maintain direct eye contact. Looking away is considered rude. Russians give a high priority to addressing others using correct titles. Failure to use a title is impolite and Russians find it offensive. To determine associates' correct titles, refer to their business cards. Business cards should be printed in both your language and in Russian. Offering your card with both hands serves as an introduction in Russia; present cards to everyone in a meeting. Appropriate gifts for Russians include fine books, chocolates, desk accessories, tokens from your country, or an item with your company logo. Other gifts that are appreciated are items that are currently unavailable in Russia. Heavy drinking is ingrained in the Russian style of doing business; sweets and cookies are also often offered at business meetings.

Business Ethic and Framework

 Russians have a work ethic that drives them to persevere with an agenda until completion once discussions have begun. Even though privately owned businesses are increasing, most businesses in Russia are still government owned. That means miles of red tape and endless waiting along with a fair amount of corruption. It takes an abundance of patience, as well as flexibility, to do business in Russia. The increase in development of private enterprise demonstrates that Russian business people are hard-working, disciplined, and quick learners. The stimulus of a free market is erasing the former work ethic of struggling to meet deadlines after months of inactivity. Russians prefer to have a brief social conversation before beginning any meeting.

Decision Making

 Be prepared for a long wait before your Russian associates come to a decision. Decisions in Russia are most commonly made by committees, and are made slowly; the committee must deliberate carefully on each issue and consensus will be vigorously sought. Russians insist on building a personal relationship with foreign visitors before any agreements are reached. Russians dislike what they consider a Western attitude about business: expecting success and a check after only a few hours of work.

Women

 Communism, if nothing else, helped to break down many of the barriers between Russian men and women. However, Russian society has traditionally been divided in terms of sex and class and this tradition dies hard. Many Russian men will not accept women in positions of power, although younger Russian men seem more willing. Women now hold nearly all positions in Russian business, such as architects, managers, and high-level bureaucrats. Many older women in Russia hold jobs traditionally held by men—a necessity because so many Russian men died in World War II. Women may retire at age 55 in Russia, while men must wait until they are 60 years old. Foreign businesswomen should not experience difficulty in Russia so long as they approach each encounter in a no-nonsense manner.

Meetings

 Russian hospitality is recognized worldwide. This hospitality extends to business meetings. Russian hosts often take foreign guests out on the town. Dinner, floor shows, and lots of drinking are all part of Russian business entertainment. But setting up a meeting in Russia can be a daunting task. Because of a scarcity of secretaries, it is impossible to leave messages and difficult to arrange meetings in Russia. It is advisable to confirm a meeting several times before the appointment; having written confirmation is also a good idea. Appointments in Russia often go awry. It is common for meetings to get postponed or canceled without notice. Incredibly, the wrong people will sometimes arrive for your meetings. It may be necessary to employ an interpreter for a meeting in Russia in order to avoid mistakes. An interpreter should never be seated at the head of a table—or between you and your Russian associate. Talk to your associate, not to the interpreter.

Business Attire

 Conservative business suits are appropriate for all occasions, including formal evening functions. Russians judge others quickly by what they wear, and the first thing they notice is the type of shoe being worn. Shoes are a status symbol in Russia; good ones should be worn in business situations. Avoid excessive jewelry or flashy clothing. Russians will often notice a high-quality watch; if you have one, wear it.

Cultural Cautions

DO'S

- Be punctual. Promptness is valued in Russian society.
- Turn and face people when you need to pass them, especially in an auditorium or theater.
- Learn a few phrases in Russian, it will endear you to your Russian hosts.
- Become familiar with the nationality map of Russia.

DON'TS

- Avoid talking about the negative aspects of Soviet or Russian history.
- Avoid the OK sign, it's a vulgar gesture in Russian society.
- Never cut into a line of people. Long and orderly lines are part of Russian daily life.
- Do not refuse an invitation to a Russian home; and take a gift when you go.
- Do not ask for a drink, wait until one is offered.
- Do not refuse second helpings of food when offered; it can be considered an insult.
- Do not litter and never drop anything, even a scrap of paper, in the street. It's offensive to Russians—and it's illegal.
- Do not take anyone's word at face value.
- Russians consider it rude to ask someone to stop smoking.

CUSTOMS

- Russians are reluctant to show positive feelings in public, preferring to express frustration with Russian daily life.
- The Russian host, not the guest, always initiates a toast.
- Out of habit, Russians answer "no" to any question. Persistence may be needed to obtain the final answer.
- Russians enjoy giving and receiving gifts. They appreciate anything with a western flair, such as: blue jeans, cassettes of pop music, and T-shirts. Do not bring large quantities of these items to Russia, however. You may be accused of trading on the black market.
- Russians often demonstrate affection for friends and family with a slap on the back and a hug. During business, however, Russians are formal and will not tolerate physical affection.
- Although Russians have feared foreigners in the past, now they welcome foreign business and the prosperity and democratic values the people bring to Russia.

OBSERVATIONS

- To speak or understand Russian is an advantage and makes an important impression on the people of Russia.
- Russians tend to have a good sense of humor.
- Letters of introduction are helpful.
- Transportation in Russia can be sluggish.
- Expect a long wait when dining out in Russia, perhaps two hours or more.

NEGOTIATIONS

- Russian negotiators are always thoroughly prepared. Your business presentations should be organized, articulate, and supported with facts and figures.
- Russian businesspeople can be shrewd negotiators. They are especially good in negotiating barter arrangements—they've had to be.
- Russians are excellent strategists. Expect much scheming and emotional outbursts.
- Negotiations can be rather lengthy and usually involve socializing.
- Russia's legal system is still in a state of change. While the government has promised to develop a modern, codified system of business law, this will not happen overnight. Consult a local attorney before any legal transaction.

Legal

Legal System

Russia's current constitution took effect in 1992. Its laws are still being created and revised, and enforcement is a key problem. Basically, Russia is a federation and follows a civil law tradition. The legal system is currently in a state of flux, a result of the fall of Communism. A presidential decree orders state enterprises to settle any inter-enterprise debt and instructs the government to establish a system of promissory notes to handle any remaining debt. Another presidential decree threatens unprofitable and corrupt state enterprises with direct state control or liquidation.

Intellectual Property Rights

Patents Russian law protects inventions, industrial designs, and utility models. Patents are protected for 20 years (10 years for designs). Formal patent examination is performed within two months after filing, but the process may take several years. The Russian government may use patented industrial property without the patent holder's consent, but will pay commensurable royalties. While Russian law provides remedies for infringement, Russian courts are unlikely to actively enforce a patent holder's rights on the assumption that other remedies are usually sufficient to prevent infringement, especially if personal or small-scale infringement occurs.

Trademarks Trademarks are protected only if they are registered with the Russian Patent Agency. No rights arise from prior use. Once registered, a trademark must be used in Russia within five years or it is subject to cancellation. Protection lasts for 10 years and may be renewed.

Copyrights Copyrights are not dependent on registration but it is best to register works. The term of protection is for the life of the author plus 50 years. Russia has acceded to the Universal Copyright Convention (UCC) and has indicated its interest in joining the Berne Convention for the Protection of Literary and Artistic Works. Some items—such as folk art—cannot be copyrighted. Russia has enacted separate legislation for the protection of computer software, yet reverse engineering is permitted.

Business Registration

Private joint stock companies for profit are allowed in Russia. All enterprises must register with the state and keep registration current. Enterprises must show that they are duly organized and are organized in compliance with law. Russian law allows a government agency to deny registration to a prospective organization only if legal requirements have been violated, but in practice local authorities sometimes make registration difficult and tedious for private entrepreneurs. A substantial number of permits, licenses, and lease or occupancy agreements must be secured before operations get underway.

Contracts and Dispute Resolution

The Russian concept of contract varies from that of Western European civil law and Anglo-American common law. In fact, the term "contract" was not defined in Russian law until 1994. A Russian contract is one that establishes, alters, or terminates civil rights and obligations. The obligations are determined by the civil code, which the contract must refer to in each specific case. As in any country, a breach of contract dispute can be complicated and time consuming. The civil code provides general remedies for a breach of civil rights, including contractual rights. Russian courts favor awards of specific performance because a party in breach is often not financially able to pay damages. Russia has not yet drafted a corporation law.

Notaries

Notaries function in the civil law tradition and require formal legal education. Among their many duties, they authenticate documents and signatures.

Labor

The majority of Russia's work force is suited to the needs of the Soviet-era command economy and ill-suited to needs of an emerging market economy. Unemployment continues to grow steadily, reaching nearly eight percent of the work force in early 1995. In addition, another five percent of the work force are underemployed, forced to work short weeks, or on extended furloughs. Russian labor law regulates labor relations at all enterprises in which employment must be formalized through the use of employment contracts or collective labor agreements. A labor collective (Russia has maintained former socialist terms for nonexecutive employees) has certain inalienable rights. Employees have the right to join unions and to seek collective bargaining. Minimum wages have been set by law but most employee salaries tend to be higher. Most of the "official" labor unions, formerly the Communist trade unions, operate in a subservient role to enterprise management, in much the same way they did in Soviet times. Workers have little confidence in trade unions and most feel powerless to challenge management.

Legal Matters

LEGAL BRIEFS

- **Corporations** The most popular enterprises are joint stock companies.
- **Workweek** Russia follows a 40-hour workweek for most positions, with holiday and overtime pay considered. Employees are entitled to four weeks of vacation per year.
- **Right to work** Employees have a right to work, and 30 day notices of termination are common.
- **Legal enforcement** Uneven implementation of laws creates further complications; various officials, branches of government, and jurisdictions interpret and apply regulations with little consistency and the decisions of one may be overruled or contested by another.
- **Political violence** The political climate in Moscow is currently stable but unpredictable over the medium to long term.
- **Crime** Crime has become one of the most frequently cited concerns of foreign (and Russian) business, particularly those involved with large amounts of cash and goods.
- **Legislative changes** Keeping up with legislative changes and presidential decrees is a daunting task.
- **Bureaucracy** The fears of some Russian officials that foreigners will purchase Russian assets at below-market rates can impede bureaucratic approval.
- **Corruption** A major concern of foreign investors is corruption at all levels.
- **International agreements** Russia is a member of GATT/WTO and Convention Abolishing the Requirement of Legalization for Foreign Public Documents.

LEGAL CONTACTS

Baker & McKenzie
Moscow
Pushkin Plaza
(C/- Perestroika JV)
No. 7 Bolshoi
Gnezdnykovsky Pereulok
Tel: (095) 200-6167
Fax: (095) 200-0203

Beiten Burkhardt Mittl & Wegener
103001 Moscow
ul. Alekseja Tolstovo D.30/1
Tel: (095) 202 37 60
Fax: (095) 202 37 60

Clifford Chance
Moscow 103051
ul. Sadovaya-Samotechnaya 24/27 2nd Floor
Tel/Fax: (501) 258-50-51

Dameu Legal Adviser
103009 Moscow
Stratnoi Boulevard
4, Building 1, Suite 70
Tel: (095) 209-52-83
Fax: (095) 209-52-33

Hogan & Hartson L.L.P.
119048 Moscow
33/2 Usacheva Street
Building 3
Tel: (095) 245-5190
Fax: (095) 245-5192

Macleod Dixon
Moscow 109017
Larushensky Perulok 15
Tel: (501) 231-5833
Fax: (501) 882-4058

Rodgers, Miller, Ellison & Holt P.C.
Nastasinsky 2 R. 303
103798, GSP, Moscow
K-6 Centre
Tel: (095) 200-3400
Fax: (095) 209-3757

Scheele, Schwartz, Zielcke & Partner
103808 Moscow
Nem. Dantchenko 3
Tel: (095) 292-8595

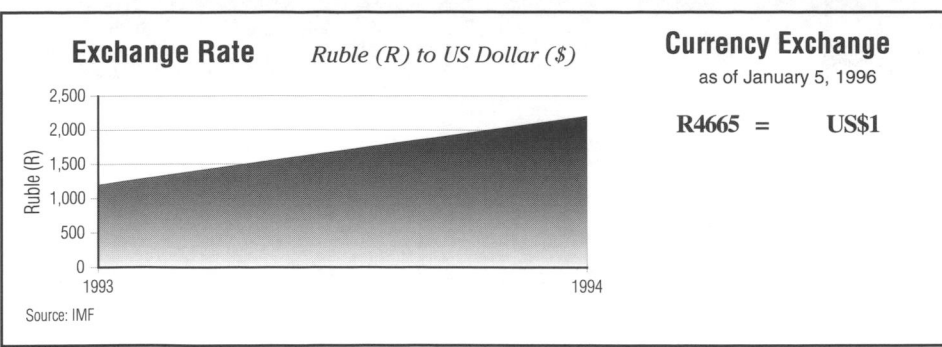

Exchange Rate — Ruble (R) to US Dollar ($)

Currency Exchange
as of January 5, 1996

R4665 = US$1

Source: IMF

Money Matters

BITS AND PIECES

- **Foreign tax relief** Foreign withholding taxes can be credited against Russian tax imposed on the same income, and limited to the amount of Russian tax on the income.
- **Capital gains** All capital gains are included in taxable income and taxed at regular rates.
- **Reserve funds** Companies are required to create a tax-deductible reserve fund, up to a maximum of 25 percent of their contributed capital.
- **Capital transfers** All capital transfers of residents, except repayment of foreign loans, must be authorized by the CBR.
- **Gold** Domestic trade in gold is not permitted. Exportation of gold requires authorization of the government.
- **Control** The responsibility for regulating foreign trade and exchange transactions is shared by the CBR, the Ministry of Finance, the Ministry of Foreign Economic Relations, the Federal Service of the Russian Federation for Foreign Exchange and Export Control, the State Tax Service, and the State Customs Committee. Most government issues are the responsibility of several groups.

Currency

The currency in use is the ruble (R), which is divided into 100 kopeks.

Foreign Exchange

Exchange authority is shared by a number of groups, including the Central Bank of Russia (CBR) and the Ministry of Finance. Most of the responsibility lies with the CBR, and it has delegated exchange transaction power to authorized banks. The ruble is a nonconvertible currency outside the territory of the Commonwealth of Independent States.

Capital Transfers

Nonresidents can transfer income from investments without restrictions. Most proceeds from invisibles are surrendered. The 1991 Investment Code prohibits the nationalization of foreign investments except following legislative action and where deemed to be in the national interest.

Investment Incentives

The government has tried to encourage foreign investment, and nonresidents are cautiously optimistic about doing business in Russia. There are no restrictions on payments for invisibles, and residents can purchase foreign exchange for all invisibles payments from authorized banks. Russian law offers few incentives to foreign investors. Those set out in the 1991 investment law, including certain tax benefits, have never been implemented, or have been largely eliminated or superseded by subsequent laws and decrees. Nevertheless, most companies already established in Russia feel the opportunities there far outweigh the risks. Few established foreign companies are leaving and many continue to demonstrate an interest in Russia's rich geological and human resources, and its high-technology markets.

Investment Restrictions

There have been many difficulties creating an attractive climate for investors. Tariff rates fluctuate and there is a great deal of economic and political uncertainty. In addition, commercial laws are being continually changed and modified, and bureaucratic requirements can be confusing to investors. Economic and political uncertainty serve as disincentives to companies looking for investment opportunities. Bureaucratic requirements can be confusing and burdensome to investors and bureaucratic discretion may be capricious in awarding tenders or development rights to companies.

BANKS

Vneshtorgbank (Bank for Foreign Trade)
Moscow 107078
9, Academika Sakharova Ul.
Tel: (095) 204-6441, 204-6484
Fax: (095) 207-1066, 238-6924

Sberbank (Savings Bank)
Moscow 109644
18/6, B. Androniyevskaya Ul.
Tel: (095) 298-1152
Fax: (095) 298-1713

International Moscow Bank
Moscow 103009
5/6, Pushkinskaya Ul.
Tel: (095) 292-9632, 963-8341
Fax: (095) 292-9873, 975-2214

Inkombank
Moscow 117420
14/1, Nametkina Ul.
Tel: (095) 332-0678, 332-0699
Fax: (095) 331-8833

Moscow Business Bank
Moscow 103780
15, Kuznetskiy Most
Tel: (095) 921-8582
Fax: (095) 924-0490

Rossiyskiy Credit Bank (Russian Credit Bank)
Moscow 125252
7 Peschanaya Ul.
Tel: (095) 195-9096, 943-7560, 943-7572
Fax: (095) 198-7717, 943-7535

Tokobank
Moscow 107078
POB 29
7, Ul. Mashi Poryvaevoy
Tel: (095) 204-9100, 204-7208
Fax: (095) 975-2578 Satellite Fax: (502) 956-3138

Dialogbank (US-Russia Joint Venture)
Moscow 103012
4, Staropansky Per.
Tel: (095) 288-8771, 288-9625, 288-9309
Fax: (095) 288-9352, 923-6556

Uralvneshtorgbank
Yekaterinburg 620219
7, Generalskaya Ul.
GSP-626
Tel: (3432) 57-38-69
Fax: (3432) 44-49-72

Gosbank Russian Federation
Moscow 117049
4 Zhitnaya Ul.
Tel: (095) 237-3065

Rosveneshtorgbank
Foreign Trade Bank of Russia
Moscow 103031
Kuznetsky Most 16
Tel: (095) 925-5231

TAXATION

Taxation requires sophisticated knowledge of complex rules and regulations specific to each country. The information presented here is from the Ernst & Young Corporate Tax Guide and Directory, available from the Ernst & Young accounting office in your country, or from:

Ernst & Young Vneshaudit/Vneshconsult
103062 Moscow
Podsosensky Pereulok 20/12
Russia
Tel: (095) 927-0569, 917-3322
     (095) 917-3121, 917-1701
     (502) 2204687 (Satellite Phone)
Telex: 612130 VNESH SU
Fax: (095) 917-3607
     (502) 2204682

At a Glance

Corporate Profits Tax Rate (%)	38
Capital Gains Tax Rate (%)	38
Branch Tax Rate (%)	38
Withholding Tax (%)	
Dividends	15
Interest	15
Royalties from Patents, Know-how, etc.	20
Payments of Other Russian-Source Income to Foreign Companies	20
Branch Remittance Tax	0
Net Operating Losses (Years)	
Carryback	0
Carryforward	5

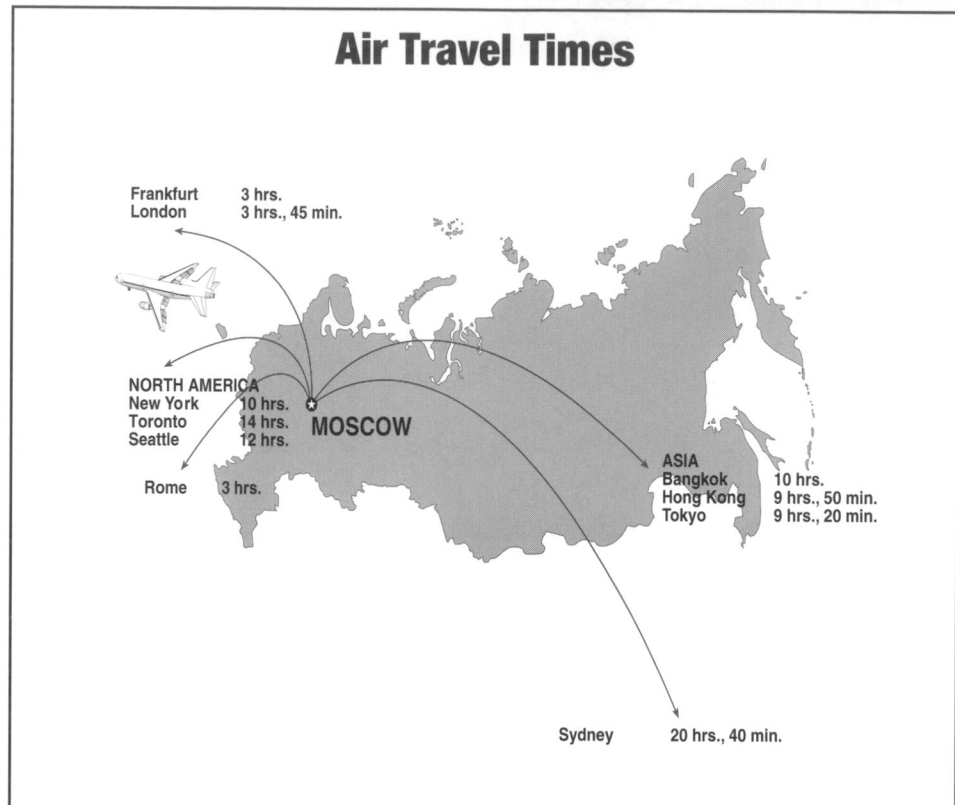

Air Travel Times

Frankfurt   3 hrs.
London   3 hrs., 45 min.

NORTH AMERICA
New York   10 hrs.
Toronto   14 hrs.
Seattle   12 hrs.

MOSCOW

Rome   3 hrs.

ASIA
Bangkok   10 hrs.
Hong Kong   9 hrs., 50 min.
Tokyo   9 hrs., 20 min.

Sydney   20 hrs., 40 min.

COMMUNICATIONS

Telephones Telephones are unreliable, whether calling into, within, or out of Russia. Direct international calls can be made from telegraph offices and hotel rooms. Dial 8, wait for the tone, then dial 10 and the country code. You can make intercity calls from homes, telegraph offices, hotel rooms, or special phone booths. Dial 8, wait for the tone, then dial the city code.

Fax Central post offices, major hotels, and business centers are equipped to send and receive faxes.

Post office Postal service is undependable in Russia, particularly for incoming mail. For faster delivery, write the address in Russian and follow the Russian sequence: country, city plus index number, street, house number, addressee's name. Parcels can be mailed only from specifically designated post offices and must be brought in unwrapped.

BEST TRAVEL BOOKS

Russia, Insight Travel Guides, Windows on the World Series. Illustrated, 350 pages. Houghton Mifflin Co.

Russia, Insider's Guide Series. Illustrated, 224 pages, Hunter NJ Publishing Inc.

Moscow-Saint Petersburg Handbook: Including the Golden Ring. Illustrated, 250 pages. Moon Publications, California.

Fodor's A Travel Guide, Russia and the Baltic Countries. Tourist oriented, excellent source of city details.

Do's and Taboo's Around the World. The Bestselling Guide to International Behavior. Edited by Roger Axtell, compiled by the Parker Pen Company. The ultimate guide to international behavior, now completely updated and expanded. Helpful, fun to read!

Russia Survival Guide, Paul Richardson. The definitive guide to doing business and travel in Russia. Lonely Planet Publications.

USEFUL TELEPHONE NUMBERS

If you are calling from outside Russia, you will need to add the country code [7] and any other international dialing requirements from within your country.

- Moscow Fire 01
- Moscow Police 02
- Moscow Ambulance 03
- Local Information 05
- Russian Information 09
- Time 100
- Photocopy Store Moscow . (095) 2511208; 2511215
- Translation Moscow .... (095) 2187218; 3600874
- USP Courier Service St. Petersburg . (812) 2986950
- Granatpost JV Courier .... (095) 3122693
- Chamber of Commerce Moscow ...... (095) 2997612
- Train Information Moscow .... (095) 9214513
- International Calls 07, (095) 2719020
- Long Distance Operator 8196
- Pharmacy, St. Petersburg .... (812) 3112077
- Telegrams .... (095) 9272002
- Moscow Airport Information .... (095) 1555005
- Moscow Train Information................ (095) 9214513
  Russian Railway .... (095) 2621628

Car Rental
- Avis .... (095) 5785676
- Hertz .... (095) 5787532
- InNis .... (095) 1555021
- Mosrent .... (095) 2480251
- Rozec-Car .... (095) 2415393

Credit Card Information
Lost or stolen credit cards (call collect to the US, regardless of which country the card was issued in).
- Amex ....[1] (919) 333-3211
- Diner's Club................................[1] (303) 799-1504
- MasterCard ....[1] (314) 275-6690
- Visa ....[1] (410) 581-7931

Travelogue

WORKWEEK

Offices Monday-Friday 9:00 am to 6:00 pm.
Banks Monday-Friday 9:30 am to 1:00 pm.
Government Monday-Friday 9:00 am to 6:00 pm.
Retail Monday-Saturday 11:00 am to 8:00 pm, closed one hour for lunch.

HOLIDAYS

Holidays 1996
January 2 New Year's
January 7 Orthodox Christmas
March 8 International Women's Day
May 1 International Labor Day
May 2 Spring Day
May 9 Victory Day
June 12 Independence Day
November 7 Revolution Day
By custom, the Monday preceding a public holiday on a Tuesday is taken as an additional public holiday, in which case the preceding Saturday is the working day.

VISA AND PASSPORT

Foreigners traveling to Russia need a valid passport. Foreigners also need a Russian visa, which must be obtained prior to arriving in Russia, and visitors need to register through their hotel or sponsor if the visit will exceed three days. Exit dates stamped on the visa must be strictly observed.

DEPARTURE FORMALITIES

All foreigners need an exit visa to depart Russia. For short stays, the exit visa is issued with the entry visa; for longer stays it must be obtained by the sponsor after the traveler's arrival. The customs declaration form that was received upon entering the country must be retained to show when you exit the country. Russia's changing customs laws are inconsistently enforced. Any item worth more than 300,000 rubles is subject to a 600 percent duty. Items of historical or cultural value may be exported only with written approval of the Ministry of Culture and payment of 100 percent duty. Caviar must be accompanied by a receipt from a store licensed to sell to foreigners. Rubles cannot be exported from Russia.

IMMUNIZATION

Travelers should have all immunizations up to date, particularly diphtheria and typhoid. Malaria and cholera vaccinations are advised if traveling near Azerbaijan and Tadjikistan. Certificates for smallpox and cholera inoculations are required of travelers from infected countries. Foreigners planning to stay beyond 90 days must produce a certificate showing they do not carry the AIDS virus.

TIPPING

Tipping is officially discouraged but is appreciated by small services. Taxi: 10 to 15 percent. Porters: 50 kopeks per bag. Hotels: none. Restaurants: 10 to 15 percent. Barbers, beauticians: five to 10 percent.

CRIME

Crime in Moscow and Saint Petersburg is often targeted against foreigners. Robberies, pickpocketing, and muggings, sometimes by groups of children, are common in tourist areas. Travelers are safer in groups organized by reputable tour agencies. Russian businesspeople have a reputation for dishonesty.

INFRASTRUCTURE

Efficient metro systems deliver citizens around the big cities, marked above ground by a fluorescent red M. Russia also has a comprehensive system of buses, trolleys, and taxis, as well as trains that are efficient, comfortable, and spacious. The subway or metro is the recommended mode of urban transportation in Russia. It is fast, clean, and reliable.

NATIONAL TOURIST OFFICE

Intourist
16 Prospekt Marksa
Moscow
Tel: (095) 203-6962

GOVERNMENT AGENCIES

Committee on Economy and Finance
St. Petersburg
16, Vosnessenskiy Prospekt
Tel: (812) 319-9666, 319-9658, 319-9554

Ministry of Agriculture
Moscow
Orlikov Pereulok, 1/11
Tel: (095) 207-4243
Fax: (095) 207-8362

Minister of the Economy
Moscow
Krasnopresnenskaya Nab. 2
Tel: (095) 205-4595
Fax: (095) 205-4318

Ministry of Finance
Moscow
Ulitsa Ilinka 9, Entrance 1
Tel: (095) 923-3456
Fax: (095) 925-0889

Ministry of Foreign Affairs of the Russian Federation
Nakhodka
24, Nakhodkinskiy Prospekt
Tel: (42366) 570-21

Ministry of Agriculture and Food Production
107802 Moscow
Orilkov per. 3
Tel: (095) 208-1760, 207-4243, 204-4307

Ministry of Economics
103881 Moscow
Neglinnaya ul. 23
Tel: (095) 292-9139, 292-8644

Ministry of Ecology and Natural Resources
Moscow
Tel: (095) 252-2305

Ministry of Foreign Economic Relations
Moscow 121200
32/34 Smolenskaya-Sennaya Ploshchad
Tel: (095) 244-3690
Fax: (095) 244-1600

Ministry of Fuel and Energy
103074 Moscow
7, Kitaysky Proezd
Tel: (095) 220-5252
Fax: (095) 220-5656

Ministry of Science and Technology Policy
Moscow
Tel: (095) 229-2501

Ministry of Transportation
Moscow
Sadovo-Samotechnaya ul. 10
Tel: (095) 200-0803, 200-0095

Moscow Registration Chamber
Moscow 103009
Mokhovaya Ul., 11, Bld. 8-E
Tel: (095) 132-0500
Tel/Fax: (095) 202-2787

State Committee for Statistics
Moscow
ul. Kirova 59
Tel: (095) 228-1633

State Duma
Committee for Economic Policy
Moscow
2, Georgiyevisky Pereulok
Tel: (095) 292-4260   Fax: (095) 292-4622

State Investment Corporation
103685 Moscow
35, Myasnitskaya Ul.
Tel: (095) 925-6796 Fax: (095) 207-6936

Ministry of Culture
103693 Moscow
Kitaisky Proezd 7
Tel: (095) 220-4500

Ministry for Press and Information
121811 Moscow
ul. Kachalova 12
Tel: (095) 290-5366

WORLD TRADE CENTERS

World Trade Center Moscow
123610 Moscow
A/O "SOVINCENTR"
12, Krasnopresnenskaya nab.
Tel: (095) 256-6303
Fax: (095) 253-9471

World Trade Center Novosibirsk
Siberia
28, Krasny Prospekt
630099 Novosibirsk
Tel: (3832) 23-37-35, 98-02-03
Fax: (3832) 23-63-35, 23-37-35

World Trade Center St. Petersburg
192007 St. Petersburg
Tambowskaya Str. 12A
Tel: (812) 112-9272
Fax: (812) 112-8631

BUSINESS AND TRADE ORGANIZATIONS

Council for Trade and Economic Cooperation
121248 Moscow
3, Naberezhnaya Shevchenko
Tel: (095) 243-5514, 243-5470
Fax: (095) 230-2467

American Chamber of Commerce
121151 Moscow
Suite 737, Slavyanskaya-Radisson Hotel
2, Berezhkovskaya Nab.
Tel: (095) 941-8435
Fax: (095) 941-8437

Khabarovsk Territory Chamber of Commerce and Industry
680000 Khabarovsk
113, Shevronova Ulitsa
Tel: (4212) 33-03-11, 33-11-30
Fax: (4212) 33-03-12

Magadan Territory Chamber of Industry and Commerce
6, Gorkiy Street
Magadan
Tel: (41322) 25-132

Primorskiy Territory Chamber of Commerce and Industry
Vladivostok
13A, Okeanskiy Prospekt
Tel: (4232) 26-96-30
Fax: (4232) 22-72-26

Russian Chamber of Commerce and Industry
103684 Moscow
6, Ilyinka Ul.
Tel: (095) 929-0286, 929-0260, 929-0261, 929-0262,
Fax: (095) 929-0356

Yakutsk Chamber of Industry and Commerce
Yakutsk
15, Kirova Ulitsa
Republic of Sakha, 677000
Tel: (41122) 20-382, 60-124

NEWSPAPERS

Den (Day)
103662 Moscow
Tsvetnoy bul. 30
Tel: (095) 200-35-98

Glasnost (Openness)
103132 Moscow
Novaya pl. 14
Tel: (095) 206-40-37

Izvetiya (News)
103791 Moscow
Pushkinskaya pl. 5
Tel: (095) 209-91-00
Telex: 411121
Fax: (095) 230-23-03

Krasnaya Zvezda (Red Star)
123826 Moscow
Khoroshevskoye shosse 38
Tel: (095) 941-21-58
Fax: (095) 941-40-57

Kuranty (Chimes)
103009 Moscow
ul. Stankevicha 12
Tel: (095) 203-06-10
Fax: (095) 292-55-15

Moskovskaya Pravda (Moscow Pravda)
123846 Moscow
ul. 1905 goda 7
Tel: (095) 259-82-33
Fax: (095) 259-63-60

Nezavisimaya Gazeta (The Independent Newspaper)
Moscow
ul. Myasnitskaya 13
Tel: (095) 925-94-63

Pravda (Truth)
125867 Moscow
ul. Pravdy 24
Tel: (095) 257-37-86
Telex: 411209
Fax: (095) 200-22-91

Rossiiskiye Vesti (Russian News)
103379 Moscow
ul. Bolshaya Sadovaya 8
podyezd 4
Tel: (095) 209-98-22
Fax: (095) 209-98-22

PERIODICALS

Ekonomika i Zhizn (Economics and Life)
101462 Moscow
Bumazhny proyezd 14
Tel: (095) 250-57-93
Fax: (095) 212-30-93

Finansy (Finances)
103050 Moscow
ul. Tverskaya 22B
Tel: (095) 299-43-33
Fax: (095) 299-93-06

Kommersant
Moscow
Khoroshovskoye Shosse 41
Tel: 095) 941-09-00

Mir Daidzhest Pressi
Business World Press Digest
191180 St. Petersburg
POB 55

Mirovaya Ekonomika i Mezhdunarodniye Otnosheniya
(World Economy and International Relations)
Moscow
Profsoyuznaya ul. 23
Tel: (095) 128-08-83
Fax: (095) 31-07-27
Telex: 411687

Rossiisky Ekonomishesky Zhurnal (Russian Economic Journal)
109542 Moscow
Ryazanksy pr. 99
Tel: (095) 377-25-56

Voprosy Ekonomiki (Problems of Economics)
117218 Moscow
ul. Krasikova 27
Tel: (095) 129-04-44
Fax: (095) 310-70-01

Ekho Planety (Echo of the Planet)
103009 Moscow
Tverskoy bul. 10-12
Tel: (095) 202-69-96
Fax: (095) 290-66-45

Mezhdunarodnaya Zhizn (International Life)
103064 Moscow
Gorokhovsky per. 14
Tel: (095) 265-37-81

Novoye Vremya (New Times)
103792 Moscow
pl. Pushkina 5
Tel: (095) 229-88-72
Fax: (095) 200-41-92
Telex: 411164

RADIO AND TELEVISION

All-Russian State Television and Radio Broadcasting Company
125124 Moscow
ul. Yamskovo Polya 19/21
Tel: (095) 250-05-11
Telex: 411252
Fax: (095) 250-01-05

BANKS

Central Bank of the Russian Federation
Moscow
4 Zhitnaya ul.
Tel: (095) 237-30-65

Rosvneshtorgbank
Bank of Foreign Trade of the Russian Federation
103031 Moscow
Kuznetsky most 16
Tel: (095) 925-52-31
Telex: 414726
Fax: (095) 973-20-96

Commercial Bank Industriaservis
127811 Moscow
Miusskaya pl. 7
Tel: (095) 251-60-04
Telex: 412731
Fax: (095) 258-54-01

Commercial Credobank
113035 Moscow
Osipenko 15 kor. 2 podyezd 4
Tel: (095) 220-34-35

Commercial Conversion Bank (Conversbank)
109017 Moscow
Bolshaya Ordynka 24/26
Tel: (095) 239-26-20
Fax: (095) 233-25-40

Stroisevzapbank Commercial Innovation Bank
117916 Moscow
ul. Stroiteley 8 kor. 2
Tel: (095) 930-61-21
Fax: (095) 930-12-77
Telex: 111849

Stocoopbank Co-operative Bank Stolichny
113005 Moscow
Pyatnitskaya ul. 72
Tel: (095) 928-76-83

International Moscow Bank
103009 Moscow
ul. Pushkinskaya 5/6
Tel: (095) 292-96-32
Fax: (095) 975-22-14
Telex: 412284

St. Petersburg Innovation Bank
191194 St. Petersburg
ul. Chaykovskovo 24
Tel: (812) 279-03-33

St. Petersburg Industrial and Construction Bank
191011 St. Petersburg
Nevsky pr. 38
Tel: (812) 110-46-38
Fax: (812) 310-61-73
Telex: 121345

COMMODITY EXCHANGES

Baikal Commodity Exchange (BCE)
670000 Ulan-Ude
23 ul. Sovetskaya
kom. 37
Tel: (30122) 2-26-81
Fax: (30122) 2-26-81

Konversia Commodity and Raw Materials Exchange
140056 Moscow
6 ul. Sovetskaya
Tel: (095) 551-01-88
Fax: (095) 175-24-94

Khabarovsk Commodity Exchange (KHCE)
680037 Khabaraovsk
66 Karl Marx Street
Tel: (81422) 33-65-60
Fax: (81422) 33-65-60

Komi Commodity Exchange (KOCE)
167610 Suktyvkar
Komi Republic
16 October Prospekt
Tel: (82122) 2-32-86
Fax: (82122) 3-84-43

Kuzbass Commodity and Raw Materials Exchange (KECME)
650043 Kemrovo
7 ul. Yermaka
Tel: 26-85-02

Kuznetsk Commodity and Raw Materials Exchange (KCME)
650079 Novokuznetsk
2 ul. Nevskovo
Tel: (83843) 42-15-29
Fax: (83843) 42-22-75

Moscow Commodity Exchange (MCE)
129223 Moscow
pr. Mira
Russian National Exhibition Center
Pavillion 4
Tel: (095) 188-95-38
Fax: (095) 188-95-83

Moscow Commodity Exchange of Building Materials (ALISA)
117334 Moscow
45 Leninsky pr.
Tel: (095) 137-00-06
Fax: (095) 137-67-23

Petrozavodsk Commodity Exchange (PCE)
185028 Petrozavodsk
31 Kranaya ul.
Tel: (7) 80-57
Fax: (7) 80-57

Russian Commodity and Raw Materials Exchange (RCME)
103070 Moscow
ul. Myasnitskaya 26
Tel: (095) 262-80-80
Fax: (095) 262-57-57

Russian Commodity Exchange of the Agro-Industrial Complex (ROSAGROBIRZHA)
Moscow
11 Volokolamskoye shosse
Tel: (095) 209-52-25

Siberia Commodity Exchange (SCE)
630106 Novosibirsk 25
Krasny pr.
Tel: (8383-2) 22-30-95
Fax: (8383-2) 22-03-90

Tyumen Commodity Exchange (TCE)
625016 Tyumen
106 Melnikaytskaya ul.
Tel: (3452) 24-04-75
Fax: (3452) 22-34-96

Ural Commodity Exchange (UCE)
620012 Yekaterinburg
23 pr. Kosmonavtov
Tel: (3432) 55-69-61
Fax: (3432) 51-53-64

LEGAL CONTACTS

Beiten Burkhardt Mittl & Wegener
103001 Moscow
ul. Alekseja Tolstovo D.30/1
Tel: (095) 202 37 60
Fax: (095) 202 37 60

Dameu Legal Adviser
103009 Moscow
Stratnoi Boulevard
4, Building 1, Suite 70
Tel: (095) 209-52-83
Fax: (095) 209-52-33

Hogan & Hartson L.L.P.
119048 Moscow
33/2 Usacheva Street
Building 3
Tel: (095) 245-5190
Fax: (095) 245-5192

Macleod Dixon
Moscow 109017
Larushensky Perulok 15
Tel: (501)231-5833
Fax: (501) 882-4058

Rodgers, Miller, Ellison & Holt P.C.
103798, GSP, Moscow K-6 Centre
Nastasinsky 2 R. 303
Tel: (095) 200 3400
Fax: (095) 209 3757

Scheele, Schwartz, Zielcke & Partner
NEM. Dantchenko 3
103808 Moscow
Tel: (095) 292-8595

INTERNET ADDRESSES

Usenet group(s):
alt.current-events.russia
soc.culture.russia
soc.culture.russian

Russian News
http://solar.rtd.utk.edu/friends/news/news.html

Russian Economic Resource Center
http://www.eskimo.com/~bwest/rerc.html

Russian Business, Trade and Investment
http://www.zpub.com/rtc

Russian Online Resources
http://www.ed.ac.uk/~esge11/russlist.html

City Net - Russia
http://www.city.net/countries/russia/

Galaxy - Russia
http://galaxy.einet.net/galaxy/Community/World Communities/Europe/Russia.html

Saudi Arabia

Kingdom of Saudi Arabia

Economy

Overview

The discovery and exploitation of the largest oil reserves in the world and the use of its substantial oil revenues to develop industry and infrastructure have helped Saudi Arabia to rapidly transform itself from an undeveloped economy to a modern industrial state. As a country that relies heavily on oil it is subject to the effects of wide price fluctuations. The government has thus sought to diversify the economy through a series of five-year plans; although oil production continues to dominate, industry and agriculture account for an increasingly greater share of economic activity. The economy has slowed somewhat in recent years, due to the government's emphasis on developing a sturdy and sophisticated infrastructure which will support diversified development for the long term.

Trade

Saudi Arabia's foreign trade has declined somewhat in recent years, as oil prices have dropped and other export markets have not yet developed enough to make up the difference. The US is the largest source of both its imports and exports, followed by Japan, France, Italy, and Germany. Saudi Arabia's traditionally high trade surpluses are almost entirely the result of trade in petroleum—accounting for over 90 percent of total exports. Saudi Arabia currently continues to run a large trade surplus, but it will have to focus its efforts on the development of other products and markets in order to maintain its favorable balance of trade.

Sectors

Agriculture Saudi Arabia has traditionally been an agricultural country, but the importance of this sector declined following the tremendous boom in the oil industry. The country is currently a net importer of food, and agriculture has become an important focus for development. Although only one percent of the land is suitable for agriculture, output has expanded rapidly in this sector in the past few years, particularly in wheat, vegetables, fruit, and livestock. Still, Saudi Arabia will be a net importer of food for the foreseeable future, and import opportunities should continue to be favorable.

Industry Industry is dominated by the oil sector, accounting for 75 percent of total government revenues. Oil production has fallen considerably from the highs of the 1970s and early 1980s but Saudi Arabia remains the leading oil producer and exporter in the world. The government's current five-year plan emphasizes the need to continue the ongoing diversification of the economy, and the non-oil manufacturing sector has experienced strong growth recently as a result. The main growth areas include metal mining, electronic components, aircraft repair, plastics, processed foods, fertilizers, and cement.

Services Due to Saudi Arabia's vast wealth, services industries are well developed and are major contributors to GDP.

Trends

Saudi Arabia is seeking to integrate more closely with the world trading system, and has thus undertaken a program of diversification and, on a lesser scale, liberalization of its economy. The world should expect products other than oil to emerge from Saudi Arabia in the future, and its wealthy population should continue to provide ready markets for a variety of imported goods and services.

At a Glance

THE COUNTRY

Location Middle East, between the Red Sea and the Persian Gulf.
Terrain Primarily desert with rugged mountains in the southwest.
Climate Arid, with great extremes of temperature in the interior; hot and humid along the coast.

THE PEOPLE

Population 16,900,00
(Note: 12.3 million Saudis, 4.6 million foreign nationals)
Ethnic composition
Arab 90%
Afro-Asian 10%
(Note: Does not include foreign nationals in Saudi Arabia)
Religious composition
Sunni Muslim 85%
Shiite Muslim 15%
Languages spoken Arabic.
Education and literacy Education is free at all levels, including college and post-graduate work. The literacy rate for males at 73 percent is significantly greater than females at 48 percent, who nonetheless constitute 43 percent of students.
Labor force..5,000,000
By occupation: government 34%, industry 28%, service and commerce 22%, agriculture 16%.
(Note: Only 5% of the labor force is female)

COUNTRY FACTS

Political and legal Saudi Arabia is a monarchy and is governed according to Sharía (Islamic law). The country is divided into 14 administrative regions called emirates. Saudis do not hold voting rights or privileges. All courts are controlled by the government.
Telephone The telephone systems are modern with direct connections to the US, other Arab countries, and Western Europe. Nearly two million telephones are in use. International country code: [966]. Selected city codes: Jeddah (2), Mecca (2), Riyadh (1).
Transportation Women are forbidden to drive in Saudi Arabia. There are many domestic and international flights scheduled daily; taxis and rental cars are available in all major cities.
Environment The government has not given priority to environmental protection but has recently become concerned with desertification of agricultural land. Extensive seawater desalination facilities have become necessary to counter the depletion of underground water resources. Up to six million barrels of oil dumped in surrounding waters during the Persian Gulf War dealt a serious blow to coastal areas.
Media The broadcasting stations—43 AM, 13 FM, and 80 TV—are regulated by the government. Newspapers are privately owned; however, criticism of the fundamental principles of Islam and basic institutions, including the royal family, is forbidden.
Health Important advances have improved immunization coverage and provided better regional health care coverage though it is still largely inadequate. Malnutrition is a major disease, dysentery attacks all ages and classes, and trachoma is common. Life expectancy has improved to 69 years and the infant mortality rate stands considerably above those of other middle-income countries.

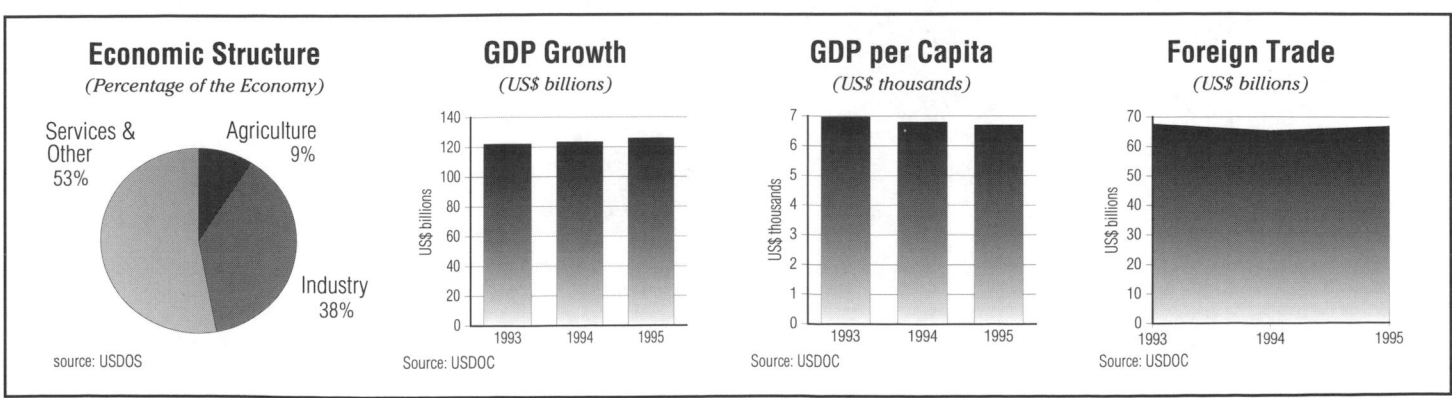

Economic Structure
(Percentage of the Economy)

Services & Other 53%
Agriculture 9%
Industry 38%

source: USDOS

GDP Growth
(US$ billions)

1993, 1994, 1995

Source: USDOC

GDP per Capita
(US$ thousands)

1993, 1994, 1995

Source: USDOC

Foreign Trade
(US$ billions)

1993, 1994, 1995

Source: USDOC

Beirut
Mediterranean **Lebanon**
Sea Haifa **Damascus**
Israel
Tel Aviv
Yafo
Jerusalem **Amman**
Dead Sea

Syria

Bakhtaran
Kashan

Afghanistan

Birjand

Baghdad
Karbala
Al Hillah
An Najaf
Al Amarah
Khorramabad
Dezful
Esfahan

Iran

Kaf Turayf
Elat Al **Jordan**
Aqabah
Haql Al Bi'r
Al **Al Jawf**
Qurayyaa
Tabuk

Ar'ar
Sakakah
Rafha

Iraq
Euphrates
Al Basrah
Abadan
Ahvaz
Bandar-e
Khomeyni

Kuwait
Kuwait

Yazd

Kerman

Zahedan

Sa'idabad

Shiraz
Bandar-e
Bushehr

Tabuk
Duba Tayma

Al Hududash Shamaliyah
Jubbah
Baq'a
Hafar al Batin
King Khalid
Military City

Ra's al Khafji

Persian

Bandar-e Abbas
Strait of Hormuz

Ha'il

Al Madinah

Al Wajh

Umm Lajj

Buraydah
Unayzah

Al Qasim
Rumah

Al Jubayl
Ad Dammam
Dhahran

Bahrain
Manama

Ra's al Khaymah
Dubayy
Al Fujayrah
Oman

*Gulf of
Oman*

Egypt
Mina
Berenice

Yanbu
al Bahr
Medina
Al Madinah
Afif

Qatar
Doha

Ad Dawadimi

Riyadh
(Ar Riyad)
Al Kharj

As Salwa

Gulf

Abu Dhabi

Suhar

Al
Buraym
Muscat

**United Arab
Emirates**

Al
Hufuf

Harad

Boundary Undefined

Red

Badr
Hunayn

Halaban
Zalim

Ar Riyad

Sur

Makkah

Mecca
(Makkah)
Jiddah
At Ta'if

Sudan

Ranyah

Ash Sharaqiyah

Oman

60°

Port Sudan

**Al
Bahah**
Qalat
Bishah

Al Lidam
As Sulayyil

Sea

Al Qunfudhah

'Asir

Abha
Khamis Mushayt

Najran

Boundary Undefined

Salalah

18°

Jizan
Jizan
Najran

Ash Sharawrah

36°

Kassala
Ak'ordat
Mits'iwa
Asmera

Saywun

Sayhut

Yemen

Al Mukalla

*Arabian
Sea*

Sanaa

Al Hudaydah
Zabid
Ibb
Ta'izz
Al Mukha
Lahij
Aseb
Aden

Ethiopia

Djibouti

Gonder

Dese

Djibouti

Gulf of Aden

Berbera

Somalia

42°

48°

54°

© 1994 Magellan Geographix SM Santa Barbara, CA

Saudi Arabia

✪	National capital
●	Secondary City
⊠	Airfields
●━●━●	Crude Oil pipeline
═══	Primary road
········	Railroad
━ ━ ━	1967 Cease Fire line
─ ─ ─	1949 Armistice line
········	Emirate border
━━━━	International border
────	Administrative line

0   300 km
0   200 mi

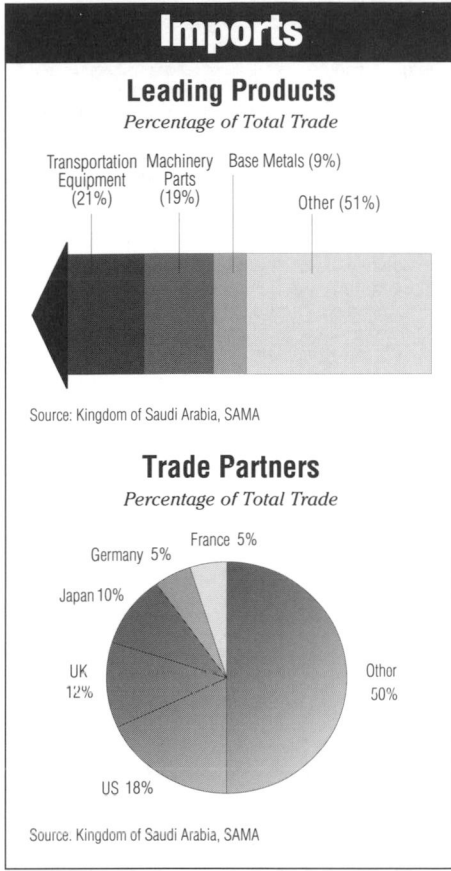

Imports

Leading Products
Percentage of Total Trade

Transportation Equipment (21%)
Machinery Parts (19%)
Base Metals (9%)
Other (51%)

Source: Kingdom of Saudi Arabia, SAMA

Trade Partners
Percentage of Total Trade

Germany 5%
France 5%
Japan 10%
UK 12%
US 18%
Other 50%

Source: Kingdom of Saudi Arabia, SAMA

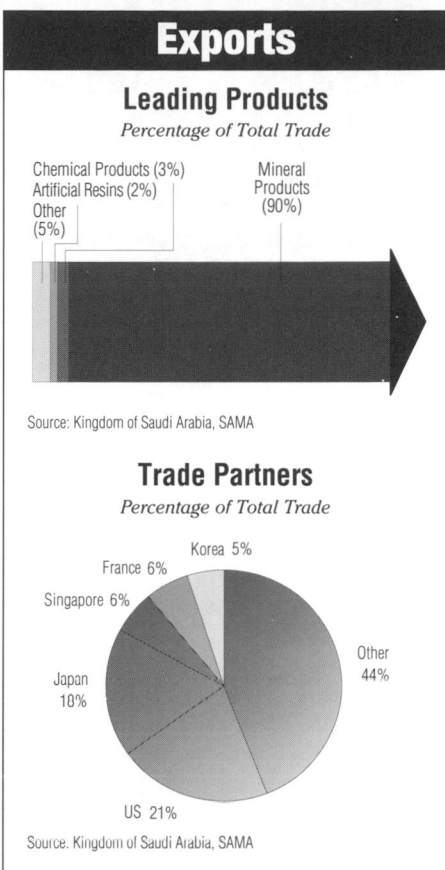

Exports

Leading Products
Percentage of Total Trade

Chemical Products (3%)
Artificial Resins (2%)
Other (5%)
Mineral Products (90%)

Source: Kingdom of Saudi Arabia, SAMA

Trade Partners
Percentage of Total Trade

Korea 5%
France 6%
Singapore 6%
Japan 10%
US 21%
Other 44%

Source: Kingdom of Saudi Arabia, SAMA

Opportunities

FOR IMPORTING TO SAUDI ARABIA
- machinery and equipment
- chemicals
- foodstuffs
- motor vehicles
- textiles
- furniture
- consumer goods (high end)
- computers, peripherals, and software

FOR EXPORTING FROM SAUDI ARABIA
- petroleum
- petroleum products

GROWTH SECTORS
- construction
- agriculture
- building
- high technology

GOVERNMENT PROCUREMENT
- broadcasting equipment
- telecommunications services and equipment
- electric power
- road construction services and equipment

Trade News
RULES AND REGULATIONS

- **Import licenses** The importation of certain articles is either prohibited or requires special approval from competent authorities. In addition, import of the following products requires special approval by Saudi authorities: agricultural seeds, live animals and fresh and frozen meats, books, periodicals, movies and tapes, religious books and tapes, chemicals and harmful materials, pharmaceutical products, wireless equipment, horses, products containing alcohol, natural asphalt, and archaeological artifacts.

- **Tariffs and import taxes** Saudi Arabia does not impose any direct import taxes. Customs duties vary from zero to 30 percent applied on the cost, insurance, and freight value (CIF) as follows: sugar, rice, soybean meal, livestock, fresh or frozen meat, corn and barley, tea, coffee, and cardamom are exempt. A 30 percent duty rate is applied on tobacco. A 20 percent tariff is applied on the following: some biscuits, candies, table eggs, poultry meat, dairy products, paints, bleach, cleaning products, desert coolers, aluminum (rods, pipes, structures, drums, boxes), mineral water, dry batteries, salt, lubricating oils, electric cables, oxygen and ethylene gas, plastic household equipment and utensils, wood products, including furniture, steel, cement, and soap. Other items carry a 12 percent customs duty. In accordance with the Unified Economic Agreement between the Gulf Cooperation Council states (GCC: Saudi Arabia, United Arab Emirates, Bahrain, Oman, Qatar, and Kuwait) products manufactured in any one of these member states will be exempt from customs duties when exported to any of the GCC states provided that 51% of the factory equity is owned by a GCC national.

- **Non-tariff barriers** In practice, some non-tariff barriers remain. The Statute for Protection and Encouragement of National Industries provides certain privileges to protect local industry by way of limiting or prohibited imports of competitive products, or raising customs duties from 12 to 20 percent on the imports of competitive products. This "infant industry" protection is usually given only when the local supplier is able to meet 50 percent of local requirements with no loss in the quality of the product, though exceptions exist. In addition, licensed manufacturers may apply for and receive an exemption of duty on imported raw materials and components.

- **Customs valuation** All merchandise moving through Saudi customs ports is appraised by the Department of Customs of the Ministry of Finance. Import valuation is primarily used for collection of import duties and often does not reflect the actual transaction value. Saudi customs valuation procedures are not GATT-consistent, nor are they based on invoice value. Minimum prices are used, which is contrary to GATT. Customs agents rely on their own experience and local prices, as well as some contact with manufacturers, to assess import tariffs.

- **Export controls** Saudi exporters need to submit a copy of their commercial registration which indicates they are allowed to export. They are also required to submit a certificate of origin of Saudi products (issued by the Ministry of Commerce). Certain items such as antiques, Arabian horses, livestock, or subsidized items need special approval to export. Exports of oil, petroleum products, natural gas and wheat all require export licenses.

- **Prohibited imports** Imports from Israel are banned entirely. In addition, products produced by companies on the Damascus boycott list or shipped on vessels on this list are also banned. Importation of the following products is also prohibited by law: weapons, alcohol, narcotics, pork, pornographic materials, distillery equipment, and certain sculptures. There are health and sanitation regulations on all imported foods. The Ministry of Commerce has issued a number of directives aimed at preventing outdated goods from entering the kingdom.

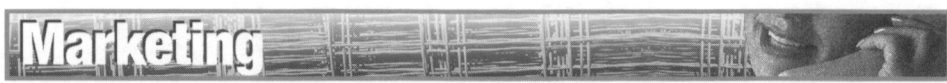

Overview

Foreign managers have had a strong influence introducing advanced selling techniques to the Saudi Arabian market, which until a few years ago relied primarily on word-of-mouth and age-old buying patterns. Advertising and public relations firms are multiplying, and the Saudis have become selective and sophisticated clients. A large portion of the upper- and middle-classes were educated in the United States or Europe, and like to display their knowledge of world affairs by discussing them at length as an introduction to business negotiation. Foreign sellers must be prepared to provide the latest and best equipment, technology, or methods, as the Saudis have no real interest in buying anything second-best. Sales meetings are usually conducted at a leisurely pace, over tea and coffee, although details of transactions can be handled by facsimile, and no serious commitment is likely to be made without a face-to-face discussion.

Distribution

There are three major marketing regions in Saudi Arabia: the Western Region with its commercial center of Jeddah; the Central Region where the capital city Riyadh is located, and the Eastern Province where the oil and gas industry is most concentrated. Each has its distinct business community and cultural flavor, and there are few truly national companies dominant in more than one region. Many companies import goods directly for their own use or for direct sale to consumers. New suppliers may find it advantageous to appoint different agents or distributors for each region, mindful of the fact that the distributorships must generally be exclusive with respect to either product line or geographic region.

Agents, Distributors, and Partners

Foreign suppliers are not required to appoint a local Saudi agent or distributor to sell to Saudi companies, but are required to find a Saudi partner before they are allowed to engage in trade within the kingdom. Saudi nationals receive strong preference in sales to government agencies and state corporations. Also, obtaining a business visa for Saudi Arabia requires sponsorship by a Saudi national. Consequently, the prospective supplier may find it best to establish local representation, especially for product lines requiring strong sales and service efforts. The most direct and widely used method is simply to appoint an agent or distributor who can set up the seller's office under its own commercial registry and obtain the required visas for the supplier's personnel.

Selling Techniques

Franchising is one of the fastest growing methods of selling in Saudi Arabia, due to the Saudis' desire to own their own businesses and also their appreciation for Western business methods. Franchising opportunities exist in the fast-food industry, office temporary services, mail and package services, printing services, and convenience stores. Competition is particularly fierce among United States, European, and local franchises in the car rental, laundry and dry cleaning, and auto maintenance businesses. Direct marketing is not often used because personal relations between vendors and customers are more important than in the West, and also because many forms of direct selling are unacceptable to the Islamic culture. Direct mail cannot be used because the Saudi postal system does not deliver mail to the home.

Advertising

Advertising, once a minor aspect of sales, has grown since the recent lifting of a ban on televised commercials. Most companies now use various forms of media, as well as traditional trade promotion events. The Saudi Ministry of Information supervises radio and television broadcasts and screens the contents in accordance with strict moral and religious standards. Television commercials are broadcast on two government channels (one Arabic, one English) during limited periods of the day. Newspaper advertising is carried by both the Arabic and English language press, but is less effective due to a low readership. Trade promotion through exhibits is a cornerstone of industrial and wholesale selling. Five to 10 trade events are held in each of the kingdom's three major cities between September and June.

Service and Customer Support

Brand loyalty and established preferences are less noticeable than in many other countries. Consequently, above average sales service and customer support are indispensable to winning and maintaining new clients. Saudis view a foreign firm's physical presence as a tangible sign of long-term commitment. Many Saudi distributors handle numerous product lines, making it difficult to promote all products effectively. In consequence, Saudi agents typically expect the supplier to assume many of the market development costs. Foreign suppliers often detail a salesperson specifically to the Saudi distributor to provide marketing, training, and technical support.

Marketing in Saudi Arabia

MARKETING TIPS

- **Financing and credit** Financing has become a leading consideration in purchasing, especially for investment goods and repeat orders.
- **Government purchases** Government spending accounts for 40 percent of GDP. However, payment delays of 6 to 15 months due to recent financial setbacks have become common and can pose problems to foreign suppliers.
- **Special support required** Government contracts require equipment suppliers to commit to providing maintenance and spare parts for three years.
- **Terminating agency agreements** Terminating a distributorship agreement can be very difficult. Therefore, time is well-spent in making the proper selection the first time.

CONSULTING FIRMS

Al-Saif Management and Economic Consultants
PO Box 60944
Riyadh 11555
Tel: (1) 4651982
Fax: (1) 4644668

Consultancy & Research Center
PO Box 7188
Riyadh 11462
Tel: (1) 4793321, 4792673
Fax: (1) 4794122

Business Consultants International Group
PO Box 91450
Riyadh 11633
Tel: (1) 4786154, 4784275
Fax: (1) 4783794

The Consulting Center for Finance and Investment
PO Box 2462
Riyadh 11451
Tel: (1) 4782525
Fax: (1) 4768021

Arthur D. Little International
PO Box 3266
Riyadh 11471
Tel: (1) 4770153, 4770227
Fax: (1) 4770134

AD AGENCIES

Akeel/Saatchi & Saatchi Advertising
POB 20927
Jeddah 21465
Tel: (2) 6510665
Fax: (2) 6513959

Bozell Orientations Advertising Group
POB 12617
Jeddah 21483
Tel: (2) 6512036
Fax: (2) 6519584

Afkar Promoseven Saudi Arabia
POB 20675
Jeddah 21465
Tel: (2) 6724119
Fax: (2) 6701957

MEMAC - United
POB 7868
Jeddah 21472
Tel: (2) 6514269
Fax: (2) 6517749

Business Culture

Greetings and Courtesies

Greetings are effusive, eloquent, and elaborate. Saudis pride themselves on their way with words; they will lavish praise and compliments upon greeting one another. There is also a great deal of touching and hand holding, sometimes even a quick kiss on the cheek (even between men). They love to visit and talk with one another, so greetings are rarely curt; be prepared to stop and visit for a while. If the Saudi is accompanied by a female do not greet or offer your hand; you will probably not even be introduced to her. Saudis are very status conscious; if a Saudi has a title, he expects to be called by it, and foreigners meeting titled Saudis are at a distinct disadvantage unless they hold equivalent titles or rank.

Business Ethic and Framework

The influence of Islam is everywhere and is felt continuously. Men quote the Koran in business discussions, and the government letterhead carries the Islamic creed. Yet Saudi Arabia has made a tremendous effort to keep pace with the twentieth century; and it has had the resources to do so. The result is a combination of ultramodern high-tech and ancient tradition. Family loyalties remain the most powerful force; family cohesion and solidarity are the sources of a Saudi man's all-important courage and honor. It is honorable to display loyalty to the family, and to do work that does not dirty the hands. But loss of honor means loss of all status; so anything—even lying or killing—is sometimes justified in order to save a man's honor. Job security and advancement are generally based on loyalty and family or friendship ties rather than technical competence or managerial performance.

Decision Making

Decision making by Saudis is highly personalized and is based on the principles of the Bedouin *majlis*. The Saudi manager will consult with several people to gain a consensus; and he will give the greatest credence to those he trusts most as friends, and will consider their opinions over those of experts. In family-controlled businesses, positions of responsibility are built around individuals with whom the senior executive feels comfortable. Delegated authority is frequently reassigned to reward individuals who happen to be in favor at the moment. There is very little teamwork, group cohesion, or company loyalty; and decisions once made are frequently overturned seemingly on a whim.

Women

Generally, a woman has only half the legal rights of a man. A Saudi woman's place is still in the home, and Saudi women are segregated from all men except those in her family. Women are not allowed to drive cars and cannot even take taxis alone. Women are separated from men at all formal gatherings, and they are not allowed to work without the consent of their male guardians, and in any event cannot work in places where they might come into contact with men. This is changing, however slowly. Several women have started women's banks; and women control over a third of the kingdom's wealth. Foreign businesswomen will get very little accomplished in Saudi Arabia; it is best simply to acknowledge this and send a man instead.

Meetings

It is difficult for a foreign businessman to obtain access to senior Saudi business and government managers without the help of another influential Saudi; after he does gain access, he must court the Saudi aggressively. Only after several visits to the Saudi's office, and innumerable cups of coffee will the Saudi discuss business, and then only if he trusts the foreigner. Junior level managers should never be sent to business meetings with senior Saudi businesspeople who may look upon this as a slight. A business meeting with Saudi executives is a test of patience. Meetings are generally delayed by the late arrival of the Saudis, who profusely greet each other prior to getting down to business. Coffee is brought in and there is a long period of discussion devoted to non-work related subjects. Even after the meeting starts, it is likely to be constantly interrupted as the Saudis take telephone calls and greet others who enter the room to talk about different subjects.

Business Attire

Saudis are officially discouraged from wearing Western attire in the kingdom and usually wear their traditional dress. The men wear loose fitting robes and head pieces; women wear black cloaks or capes over their heads and clothing covers their entire bodies. Foreigners should not try to imitate this dress, but should dress in conservative clothing suitable to doing business in their own country.

Cultural Cautions

DO'S

- Every businessperson should visit a *suq*, the Saudi traditional market bazaar.
- Saudi law requires that Arabic be used in correspondence with the government.
- Speak softly, make points subtly or indirectly, and maintain an attitude of politeness, even if your Saudi companion is having a temper tantrum.
- Make prior appointments for business meetings and try to arrive at the appointed hour.
- Be prepared to eat a tremendous amount of food if invited to a business associate's home for a meal. Proper appreciation of a meal is shown by eating large quantities.

DON'TS

- Do not try to accomplish any business during the annual 100-day fast and pilgrimage period.
- Foreign males should not attempt to enter into conversation with a Saudi female; this is more for her protection than the foreigners'.
- Sensible foreigners do not attempt to drive in Saudi Arabia. It is dangerous!
- Do not pull your hand away sharply if a Saudi businessperson walking with you takes your hand and holds it as you go. This is a sign of friendship, nothing more.

CUSTOMS

- Saudis stop whatever it is they are doing at the noon call to prayer and resume several hours later after the mid-afternoon call to prayer.
- A guest's coffee cup is refilled until he signals that he does not want any more by holding the cup out and shaking it from side to side.
- Bluntness is considered rude.
- Revenge for any insult or slight is considered a Saudi's right, tradition, and duty.
- It is customary for a Saudi to evade the truth rather than risk controversy which could lead to confrontation.
- Saudis may offer you their possessions if you admire them; they will be offended if you refuse the offer.

OBSERVATIONS

- There is limited social interaction between Saudis and foreigners at the same class level, and virtually none between class levels.
- Saudis consider family profiteering and unrecorded business payments normal business practices.
- If a Saudi wants to convince someone that he intends to do something, he states his intentions several times. If he merely agrees to do something, it might be nothing more than a polite form of evasion.
- Saudis are extremely sensitive and susceptible to having their feelings hurt. They do not like to be contradicted, corrected, or argued with, even in the most pleasant, well-meaning manner. Any critical comment will be taken as an insult.
- Saudis will crowd the personal space that Westerners normally leave for each other, and will stand toe-to-toe and stare directly into the eyes of whomever they talk to.

NEGOTIATIONS

- Many Saudis are offended when foreigners request that contracts be put in writing; they feel that verbal agreements should suffice; in Saudi Arabia they often do.
- Negotiations proceed slowly, and only after a Saudi hears something in the general conversation that appeals to him can a foreign executive prepare an outline which will form the basis for developing a proposal.
- Negotiations are best approached from a very personal basis, motivated equally by the desire to enrich the friendship and to further business interests.
- Saudi executives refuse to share information and rarely provide foreigners with any indication as to how the negotiations are proceeding.

Legal

Legal System

Saudi Arabia is a monarchy with a council of ministers. All laws are issued by the king.

Intellectual Property Protection

Patents Saudi Arabia recently passed the Regulations Act, protecting foreign and domestic patents. Saudi Arabia has had a Patent Law since 1989 and the Patent Office accepts applications, but it has not yet issued a patent. Saudi Arabia is not a member of any major international patent treaties, so it is unclear how much protection patent holders can expect. Once issued, patents last for 15 Hejira years from the date of issue.

Trademarks Trademarks not in dispute can be registered a minimum of 30 days after the application is filed.

Copyrights Saudi Arabian laws protect foreign and domestic copyrights, provided that the works are published, acted, or shown for the first time in Saudi Arabia. However, whether copyright protection is available in practice for foreign works is unclear because virtually none are published or presented first in Saudi Arabia. Protection for sound and audiovisual works is for a term of 25 Hejira years after the date of publication. For other copyrights, protection lasts until 50 Hejira years after the creator's death. There is no mention of computer software protection. Copyright violators are subject to fines, and if a business is found guilty, the penalty may be to shut it down for 15 days. The Saudi government maintains that this will be sufficient to extend protection to foreign works. The Saudi government has taken actions to enforce foreign copyrights, and pirated material has been seized or forced off the shelves of a number of stores. Overall, however, piracy remains a problem.

Trade secrets No specific laws protect trade secrets; however they are often protected by contract. All disputes must be handled through the Board of Grievances.

Business Registration

All companies must be registered with the companies section of the Ministry of Commerce. Branch offices of wholly foreign-owned entities are required to obtain a foreign capital investment license. Any foreign-owned business making multiple public sector contracts may obtain a Representative Office License, allowing the business to establish an office and supervise the various business ventures within Saudi Arabia. Foreign businesses can obtain a Technical and Scientific Services Office License from the Ministry of Commerce, allowing them to establish an office, offer technical and scientific services, and undertake research.

Contracts and Dispute Resolution

Foreign companies require a Saudi agent or partner to enter into a contract with a Saudi business. The agent must be a Saudi national. Most disputes are handled through arbitration. Companies must get approval from the President of the Council of Ministers, who will pick a neutral arbitrator to help decide the case. Dispute settlement in Saudi Arabia continues to be time-consuming and uncertain. Even after a decision is reached in a dispute, effective enforcement of the judgment can still take years. Some firms investing in Saudi Arabia include in their contracts a foreign arbitration clause, but such clauses are not allowed in government contracts without a decision by the Saudi Council of Ministers.

Notaries

Notaries public are highly important officials who have the same qualifications as judges and are well versed in Shari'a law. They approve numerous mortgage and real estate documents.

Labor

Recruitment of expatriate labor is regulated jointly by the Ministry of Interior and the Ministry of Labor and Social Affairs. In general, the government encourages the recruitment of Muslim workers, either from Muslim countries or from countries such as India and Sri Lanka with sizable Muslim minorities. The largest groups of foreign workers now come from Pakistan, the Philippines, and India. The Ministry of Labor and Social Affairs regulates most labor-related issues, including health and safety provisions. The Ministry also attempts to ease disputes between management and labor before litigation occurs. Labor unions are not permitted in Saudi Arabia. Written labor contracts are often used, but oral ones are also enforced. There are stiff penalties for terminating an employee without "valid reason"—usually three to five months' salary as termination damages. The Saudi government does not adhere to the ILO Convention protecting worker rights.

Legal Matters

LEGAL BRIEFS

- **Language** All documents, agreements, and correspondence must be in Arabic.
- **Monopolies** Saudi Arabia does not regulate monopolies or restrictive trade practices.
- **Law reports** All statutes and most ministerial resolutions are published in the official newspaper of record, *Umm Al-Qura*.
- **Maximum workweek** Employees can work a maximum of 48 hours per week, not including breaks and meals. During the fasting month of *Ramadan*, the maximum workweek is 36 hours. The government grants 15 vacation days for employees who have at least one year of service.
- **Attorneys** Saudi litigants have an advantage over foreign parties in almost any investment dispute, because of their first-hand knowledge of Saudi law and culture and the relatively amorphous dispute settlement processes. Foreign partners involved in a dispute find it advisable to hire local attorneys with knowledge of Saudi legal practices in the area of dispute.
- **Litigation problems** In several cases, disputes have caused serious problems for foreign investors. For instance, Saudi partners have blocked foreigners' access to exit visas, forcing them to remain in Saudi Arabia against their will. In cases of alleged fraud, foreign partners may also be jailed to prevent their departure from the country, while awaiting police investigation or adjudication of the case.
- **Bankruptcy laws** The country does not have a written bankruptcy law, but there are provisions in the law dealing with liquidations and the appointment of receivers.
- **Political violence** There have been no incidents over the past few years involving politically motivated damage to projects and/or installations. Saudi Arabia is not exceptionally politicized and civil disturbances in the short term are not likely.
- **Technology protection** There is no specific protection for semiconductor chip layout design; however, it would be protected under the Patent Law and the Copyright Law.
- **Competition** The Saudi Government does not have a specific policy nor laws which foster competition.
- **Labor laws** Saudi labor law forbids union activity, strikes, and collective bargaining. There is no forced or compulsory labor, however. Any required overtime, over and above the usual five-and-one-half to six-day week is compensated, normally at time and a half rates. The minimum age for employment is 13.
- **Western expatriates** Westerners comprise less than two percent of the labor force, and the percentage is slowly dropping as they are replaced by Saudis and less expensive expatriates from Third World countries.
- **Saudi workers vs. expatriates** Effective September 1985, the Ministry of Labor and Social Affairs is required to certify that there are no qualified Saudis for a particular job, before it can be filled by an expatriate worker.
- **Policies** Saudi tax and labor laws and policies tend to favor high-tech transfers and the employment of Saudis, which may not be the most efficient use of investment resources. Saudi health and safety laws and policies are not used to distort or impede the efficient mobilization and allocation of investments. Bureaucratic procedures are not streamlined or transparent, but Saudi red tape can generally be overcome with persistence.
- **International agreements** Saudi Arabia is a member of OPEC the Arab League; and the Convention on the Recognition and Enforcement of Foreign Arbitral Awards.

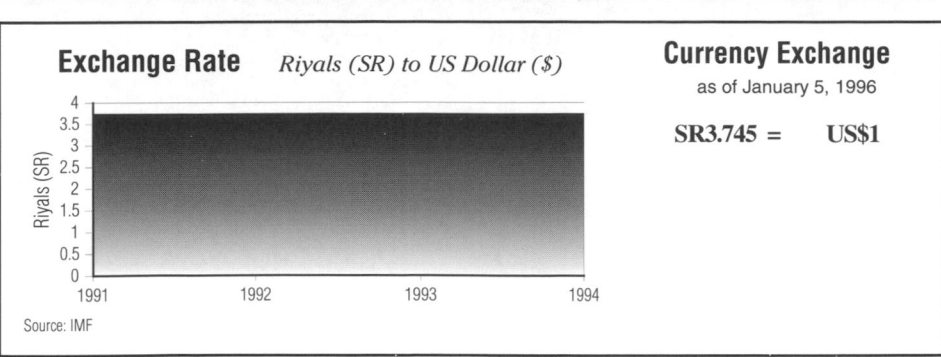

Exchange Rate *Riyals (SR) to US Dollar ($)*

Source: IMF

Currency Exchange
as of January 5, 1996

SR3.745 = US$1

Money Matters

BITS AND PIECES

- **Capital gains** All capital gains are treated as ordinary income and taxed at regular rates.
- **Foreign tax relief** Saudi Arabia provides no relief for foreign taxes paid.
- **Income losses** There are no provisions under Saudi Arabia's tax regulations for carryforward or carryback of losses.
- **Foreign vs. domestic capital** Approved foreign capital carries the same economic weight as domestic capital, with the same privileges.
- **Gold** Residents are free to hold, purchase, and sell gold in any form.

BANKS

Arab National Bank
POB 56921
Riyadh 11564
Tel: (1) 402-9000
Fax: (1) 402-7747

Saudi French Bank
POB 56006
Riyadh 11554
Tel: (1) 404-2222
Fax: (1) 404-2311

Saudi American Bank
POB 833
Riyadh 11421
Tel/Fax: (1) 477-4770

Saudi Arabian Monetary Agency
POB 2992
Riyadh 11461
Tel: (1) 478-7400
Fax: (1) 441-1384

Saudi Hollandi Bank
POB 1467
Riyadh 11431
Tel: (1) 406-7888, 401-0288
Fax: (1) 403-1104

Saudi British Bank
POB 9084
Riyadh 11413
Tel: (1) 405-0677
Fax: (1) 405-0660

United Saudi Commercial Bank
POB 25895
Riyadh 11476
Tel: (1) 478-4200, 478-8075
Fax: (1) 478-3197

Al-Rajhi Investment and Banking Corporation
POB 28
Riyadh 11411
Tel: (1) 405-4244
Fax: (1) 405-2950

Riyad Bank
POB 229
Riyadh 11411
Tel: (1) 401-4000, 402-4011
Fax: (1) 404-2705

The Saudi Investment Bank
POB 3533
Riyadh 11481
Tel: (1) 477-8433
Fax: (1) 477-6781

Saudi Cairo Bank
POB 11222
Jeddah 21453
Tel: (2) 632-3044
Fax: (2) 632-3044 x 548

National Commercial Bank
POB 3555
Jeddah 21481
Tel: (2) 644-6644
Fax: (2) 644-6644 x 3254

Islamic Development Bank
POB 5925
Jeddah 21432
Tel: (2) 636-1400
Fax: (2) 636-6871

Currency

The currency of Saudi Arabia is the Saudi riyal (SR), divided into 100 halalas.

Foreign Exchange

Rates of the riyal with other currencies are decided by the Saudi Arabian Monetary Agency.

Capital Transfers

There are no restrictions or regulations placed upon proceeds from or payments for invisibles. There has been no evidence of any property expropriation in the past, nor are there any recent policy shifts that would lead one to assume there would be any in the future.

Investment Incentives

There are a number of incentives for foreign investors, including the provision of land and buildings in industrial estates at nominal rents. Resident companies do receive some favoritism, however. Only foreign-owned companies are subject to a corporate income tax, and only Saudi companies can engage in internal trading and actually own land.

Investment Restrictions

All proposals for new investments, mergers, or acquisitions must go through a licensing process set up by the Ministry of Industry and Electricity. For investments with government participation, the process is simple. For purely private ventures, however, the process can be very time-consuming. All license applications must be accompanied by a variety of forms, including an outline of the venture's proposed capital structure and any plans for training residents for technical and managerial positions. Any investors or potential investors must have a Saudi sponsor to obtain a business visa, and businesswomen often face difficulties when requesting visas. Under the 1969 labor and working person regulations, 75 percent of a firm's work force and 51 percent of its payroll must be Saudi, unless an exemption has been obtained from the Ministry of Labor and Social Affairs. Saudis represent only about a third of the estimated seven million workers in Saudi Arabia, however, so few firms have been able to meet these requirements. Foreign firms are under constant pressure to employ more Saudis.

TAXATION

Taxation requires sophisticated knowledge of complex rules and regulations specific to each country. The information presented here is from the Ernst & Young Corporate Tax Guide and Directory, available from the Ernst & Young accounting office in your country, or from:

Whinney, Murray & Co.
Mail Address:
P.O. Box 2732
Riyadh 11461, Saudi Arabia
Street Address:
4th and 5th Floors
Building 2
Abanumay Commercial Centre
Salah Eddin Alayoubi Street
Malaz, Riyadh, Saudi Arabia
Tel: (1) 477 6272
Cable: Ernstaudit, Riyadh
Telex: 401348 Ans bk ERNST SJ
Fax: (1) 477 6352

At a Glance

Corporate Income Tax Rate (%) (a)	45
Capital Gains Tax Rate (%) (a)	45
Branch Tax Rate (%) (a)	45
Withholding Tax (%)	
Dividends	0
Interest	(b)
Royalties from Patents, Know-how, etc. (b)	
Branch Remittance Tax	0
Net Operating Losses (Years)	
Carryback	0
Carryforward	0

(a) Rates lower if profits do not exceed SR 1 million.
(b) Withholding tax is imposed on payments to nonresidents. In general, the normal corporate income tax rates are applied to a deemed profit element of at least 15%. However, certain types of payments are taxed on 100% deemed profit.

Business Travel

	LH 1906	MADRID	935	113-3
	LH 1022	STUTTGART HBF.	935	-
	AF 1701	LYON	940	683-6
	AY 822	HELSINKI	940	113-3
	AA 071	SFRANCISCO-DALLAS	945	731-7

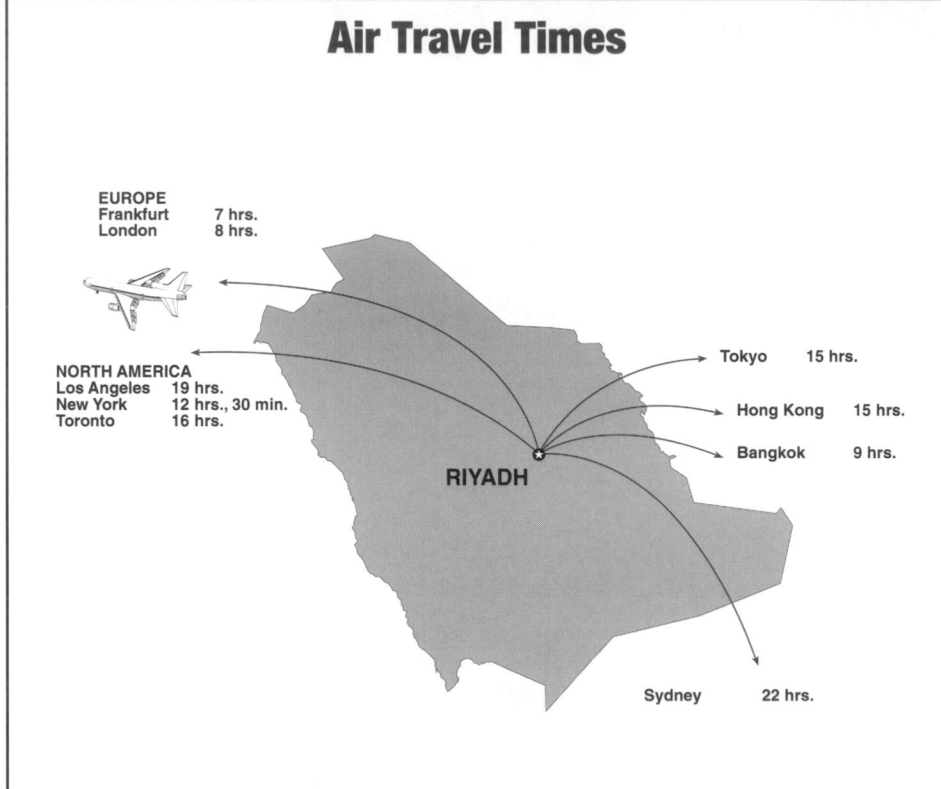

Air Travel Times

EUROPE
Frankfurt   7 hrs.
London   8 hrs.

NORTH AMERICA
Los Angeles   19 hrs.
New York   12 hrs., 30 min.
Toronto   16 hrs.

RIYADH

Tokyo   15 hrs.
Hong Kong   15 hrs.
Bangkok   9 hrs.
Sydney   22 hrs.

COMMUNICATIONS

Telephones Saudi Arabia has one of the most modern telephone systems in the world. More than 100 countries can be dialed direct from almost all hotels and businesses. Public coin-operated telephones are readily available in big cities.
Fax Major hotels in big cities offer public fax services in their business centers. Public telex facilities are available at most hotels.
Post office Most internal mail service is routed to post office boxes and takes two days by air. International air mail is expedient, but surface mail is slow. Parcel delivery is expensive and unreliable. Stamps are bought at post offices.

BEST TRAVEL BOOKS

Saudi Arabia Pocket Guide. Berlitz Editors Pocket Guides Series. Berlitz Publishing Co., Inc.
Hippocrene Companion Guide to Saudi Arabia. Gene Lindsay.
Understanding Arabs, a Guide for Westerners. Margaret Nydell.
The Traveler's Guide to Middle Eastern and North African Customs and Manners. Elizabeth Devine and Nancy Braganti.
Middle East, Lonely Planet on a Shoestring. Details, details, details! 126 maps.
Do's and Taboo's Around the World. The Bestselling Guide to International Behavior. Edited by Roger Axtell, compiled by the Parker Pen Company. The ultimate guide to international behavior, now completely updated and expanded. Helpful, fun to read!

USEFUL TELEPHONE NUMBERS

If you are calling from outside Saudi Arabia, you will need to add the country code [966] and any other international dialing requirements from within your country.

- Police Riyadh, Jeddah 999
- Ambulance 997
- Fire 998
- Local Operator 905
- International Operator 901
- Directory Information 905
- International Information 900
- Photocopying Jeddah.........(2) 643216; (2) 6314149
- Secretarial Jeddah .... (2) 6434115
- Translation Jeddah .... (2) 6434115
- Photocopy Riyadh ....(1) 4764520; (1) 4021022
- Translation Riyadh .... (1) 4785962
- Chamber of Commerce Jeddah .... (2) 6423535
- Chamber of Commerce Riyadh .... (1) 11421
- Airport Jeddah .... (2) 6855527
- Airport Riyadh .... (1) 2211100
Car Rental
- Avis .... (1) 6511668
- Budget .... (1) 6532680
- Europcar .... (1) 6317231
Credit Card Information
Lost or stolen credit cards (call collect to the US, regardless of which country the card was issued in).
- Amex .... [1] (919) 3333211
- Diner's Club................................. [1] (303) 7991504
- MasterCard .... [1] (314) 2756690
- Visa .... [1] (410) 5817931

Travelogue

WORKWEEK

Offices Saturday-Wednesday 8:30 am to 12:30 pm and 2:00 pm to 7:30 pm.
Banks Saturday-Wednesday 8:30 a.m to noon and 5:00 pm to 7:00 pm; Thursday 8:30 am to 11:30 am.
Government Saturday-Wednesday 7:30 am to 2:30 pm.
Retail Saturday-Wednesday 8:30 am to 12:30 pm and 2:00 pm to 7:30 pm.
Friday is the Muslim Sabbath and Thursday is a weekly holiday for most offices. Hours are limited during Ramadan and the Haj (pilgrimage) period.

HOLIDAYS

Holidays 1996
January * Leilat al Meiraj
February 19-23 Id-Al-Fitr/Ramadan
April 26-30 Id-Al-Adha/Hajj or Pilgrimage to Mecca
June/July * Muharram Islamic New Year
June/July * Ashoura
September/August * Mouloud Birth of the Prophet
Not all religious days are public holidays. Businesses customarily close for seven days for observance of the end of Ramadan and the Feast of the Sacrifice, occurring in late May or early June. Religious days are based on the lunar calendar, and exact dates are announced by the royal palace upon the sighting of the moon or at the beginning of the month. Check with a Saudi embassy or consulate for precise information on holidays when making travel plans.

VISA AND PASSPORT

A passport is required that is valid for at least six months beyond the estimated stay in Saudi Arabia. UK and Gulf Cooperation Council citizens do not require visas. All others must obtain visas in advance; business visas require a letter of guarantee, itinerary, and an invitation from your sponsor. Women applying for business visas require special authorization.

DEPARTURE FORMALITIES

There are no restrictions to bringing or taking out Saudi or foreign currencies other than the Israeli Shekel, which is prohibited. Foreign currency must be declared, however. Gold, silver, and Saudi Arabian bank notes require a permit from the Monetary Agency.

IMMUNIZATION

Visitors arriving from countries infected with yellow fever need evidence of vaccination. During the Haj (pilgrimage) period, meningitis AC vaccination is required of arriving visitors. Malaria prophylaxis is recommended and cholera, smallpox, typhoid, and typhus inoculations are recommended but not required.

TIPPING

No tipping is necessary on airport-authorized taxis. Porters should be tipped SR5-10. Tipping is not expected but is appreciated in other service establishments.

CRIME

Petty crime is virtually unknown because of the stern Islamic laws. Foreigners can be arrested and detained for activity that is legal in their own country, such as cursing or possessing alcohol.

INFRASTRUCTURE

Cities in Saudi Arabia are modern. First class hotels have amenities and business support facilities but are in short supply during the religious pilgrimage (Haj) period. Public transportation is excellent and domestic air travel is popular, but you must have a letter from your sponsor to travel around Saudi Arabia. Yellow taxis can be hailed on the street or summoned by a doorman; negotiate fares before the trip starts. Intracountry travel between cities is excellent; with taxis, car rental, trains, buses, and domestic air travel it is easy to get from one place to the next.

NATIONAL TOURIST OFFICE

Saudi Tourist and Travel Bureau
P.O. Box 863
Jeddah 21421
Tel: (2) 6443005

GOVERNMENT AGENCIES

Saudi Ports Authority
PO Box 5162
Riyadh 11188
Tel: (1) 4050005
Fax: (1) 4059974

General Organization for Technical Education and Vocational Training
PO Box 7823
Riyadh 11472
Tel: (1) 4052620
Fax: (1) 4065876

General Organization for Grain Silos and Flour Mills
PO Box 3402
Riyadh 11471
Tel: (1) 4643500
Fax: (1) 4631943

King Abdul Aziz City for Science and Technology
PO Box 6086
Riyadh 11442
Tel: (1) 4883555
Fax: (1) 4883118

Ministry of Agriculture and Water
PO Box 2639
Riyadh 11195
Tel: (1) 4016666
Fax: (1) 4030030

Ministry of Commerce
PO Box 1774
Riyadh 11162
Tel: (1) 4012229
Fax: (1) 4038421

Ministry of Education
Riyadh 11148
Tel: (1) 4042888, 4042952
Fax: (1) 4037229

Ministry of Finance and National Economy
PO Box 6902
Riyadh 11177
Tel: (1) 4050080, 4050000
Fax: (1) 4059202

Ministry of Foreign Affairs
Riyadh 11124
Tel: (1) 4067777, 4416836
Fax: (1) 4020100

Ministry of Health
PO Box 21217
Riyadh 11176
Tel: (1) 4012220, 4012392
Fax: (1) 4026395

Ministry of Higher Education
Riyadh 11153
Tel: (1) 4415555
Fax: (1) 4419004

Ministry of Industry and Electricity
PO Box 5729
Riyadh 11127
Tel: (1) 4776666, 4772722
Fax: (1) 4773973

Ministry of Labor and Social Affairs
Riyadh 11157
Tel: (1) 4771480, 4787166
Fax: (1) 4771480

Ministry of Municipalities and Rural Affairs
Riyadh 11136
Tel: (1) 4415434
Fax: (1) 4421934

Ministry of Planning
PO Box 1358
Riyadh 11183
Tel: (1) 4013333, 4023462
Fax: (1) 4014224

Ministry of Public Works and Housing
Riyadh 11151
Tel: (1) 4022036, 4022268
Telex: 400415 MINPUB SJ

Saudi Arabian Basic Industries
PO Box 5101
Riyadh 11422
Tel: (1) 4012033
Fax: (1) 4012045

Saline Water Conversion Corporation
PO Box 5968
Riyadh 11432
Tel: (1) 4631111
Fax: (1) 4631952

Saudi Arabian Public Transport Company
PO Box 10667
Riyadh 11443
Tel: (1) 4545000
Fax: (1) 4542100

Saudi Arabian Standards Organization
PO Box 3437
Riyadh 11471
Tel: (1) 4793332
Fax: (1) 4731826

Saudi Consolidated Electric Company, Central Province
PO Box 57
Riyadh 11411
Tel: (1) 4031033
Fax: (1) 4051191

Saudi National Shipping Company
PO Box 8931
Riyadh 11492
Tel: (1) 4785454
Fax: (1) 4778036

Saudi Arabian Railway Organization
PO Box 37
Dammam 31241
Tel: (3) 8348888
Fax: (3) 8713456

Ministry of Communications
PO Box 3813
Rlyadh 11178
Tel: (1) 4043000, 4042928
Fax: (1) 4055705

Ministry of Information
PO Box 843
Riyadh 11161
Tel: (1) 4013440, 4014440
Fax: (1) 4068544

Ministry of Posts, Telephone and Telegraph
Riyadh 11112
Tel: (1) 4631152, 4040288
Fax: (1) 4058458

BUSINESS AND TRADE ORGANIZATIONS

Saudi Consulting House
PO Box 1267
Riyadh 114314
Tel: (1) 4484588, 4484688
Fax: (1) 4481234

Arab Petroleum Investments Corpn
POB 448
Dhahran Airport 31932
Tel: (3) 8647400
Fax: 8945076
Telex: 870068

General Investment Fund (Public Investment Fund)
c/o Ministry of Finance and National Economy
Airport Rd.
Riyadh 11177
Tel: (1) 4050000
Telex: 401021

National Agricultural Development Co. (NADEC)
POB 2557
Riyadh 11461
Tel: (1) 4783488
Telex: 403681

Royal Commission for Jubail and Yanbu
POB 5964
Riyadh 11432
Tel: (1) 4794445
Telex: 401386 (English) 404560 (Arabic)

Saudi Consulting House (SCH)
POB 1267
Riyadh 11431
Tel: (1) 4484533
Telex: 401152

Saudi Fund for Development (SFD)
POB 1887
Riyadh 11441
Tel: (1) 4640292
Fax: 4647450
Telex: 401145

Saudi Industrial Development Fund (SIDF)
POb 4143
Riyadh 11149
Tel: (1) 4774002
Fax: 4790165
Telex: 401065

CHAMBERS OF COMMERCE

Riyadh Chamber of Commerce and Industry
PO Box 596
Riyadh 11421
Tel: (1) 4040044
Fax: (1) 4021103

Council of Saudi Chambers of Commerce and Industry
PO Box 16683
Riyadh 11474
Tel: (1) 4053200
Fax: (1) 4024747

Jeddah Chamber of Commerce and Industry
PO Box 1264
Jeddah 21431
Tel: (2) 6515111
Fax: (2) 6517373

Chamber of Commerce and Industry for the Eastern Province
PO Box 719
Dammam 31421
Tel: (3) 8571111
Fax: (3) 8570607

Federation of Arab Gulf Chambers of Commerce
PO Box 2198
Dammam 31451
Tel: (3) 8265943

Abha Chamber of Commerce and Industry
POB 722
Abha
Tel: (7) 2271818
Fax: (7) 2271919
Telex: 905001

Al-Ahsa Chamber of Commerce and Industry
POB 1519
Horuf 31982
Tel: (93) 5820458
Fax: (93) 5875274
Telex: 861230

Ar'ar Chamber of Commerce and Industry
POB 440
Ar'ar
Tel: (4) 6626544
Fax: (4) 6624581
Telex: 812058

Al-Baha Chamber of Commerce and Industry
POB 311
al-Baha
Tel: (7) 7254116
Fax: (7) 7270308
Telex: 731048

Ha'il Chamber of Commerce and Industry
POB 1291
Ha'il
Tel: (6) 5321060
Fax: (6) 5331366
Telex: 311086

Islamic Chamber of Commerce and Industry
Riyadh
Tel: (1) 532339
Telex: 25533

Al-Jizan Chamber of Commerce and Industry
POB 201
al-Jizan
Tel: (7) 3223763
Fax: (7) 3223507
Telex: 911065

Al-Jouf Chamber of Commerce and Industry
POB 585
al-Jouf
Tel: (4) 6249060
Fax: (4) 6240108
Telex: 821065

Al-Majma' Chamber of Commerce and Industry
POB 165
al-Majma' 11952
Tel: (6) 4320268
Fax: 4322655
Telex: 447020

Mecca Chamber of Commerce and Industry
POB 1086
Mecca
Tel: (2) 5744202
Fax: 5741684
Telex: 540011

Medina Chamber of Commerce and Industry
POB 443
Airport Rd.
Medina
Tel: (4) 8225190
Fax: 8268965
Telex: 570009

Najran Chamber of Commerce and Industry
POB 1138
Najran
Tel: (7) 5222216
Fax: 5223926
Telex: 921066

Qassim Chamber of Commerce and Industry
POB 444
Buraydah
Qassim
Tel: (6) 3814000
Fax: 3812231
Telex: 301060

Al-Qurayat Chamber of Commerce and Industry
POB 416
Al-Qurayat
Tel: 6423034
Fax: 6423172

Tabouk Chamber of Commerce and Industry
POB 567
Tabouk
Tel: (4) 4222736
Fax: 4227387
Telex: 681173

Ta-if Chamber of Commerce and Industry
POB 1005
Ta'if
Tel: (2) 7464624
Fax: 7380040
Telex: 751009

Union of Arabian Chambers of Commerce and Industry
POB 112837
Riyadh
Tel: (1) 814269
Telex: 20347

Yanbu Chamber of Commerce and Industry
POB 58
Yanbu
Tel: (4) 3224257
Fax: 3226800

ADVERTISING AGENCIES

Akeel/Saatchi & Saatchi Advertising
301 Adham Commercial Centre
Jeddah

Bozell Orientations Advertising Group
Adham Commercial Center
Jeddah

Horizon Advertising (Jeddah)
Al Taher Bldg., 2nd Fl.
Jeddah

Impact/BBDO
Ali Reza Tower
Jeddah

The Rowland Company
301 Adham Commercial Center
Jeddah

Zeead DMB&B
3rd Fl., AliReeza Tower
Jeddah

NEWSPAPERS

Arab News
POB 4556
Jeddah 21412
Tel: (2) 6691888
Fax: 6671650
Telex: 604397

Al-Bilad (The Country)
POB 6340
Jeddah 21442

Al-Jazirah (The Peninsula)
POB 354
Riyadh 11411
Tel: (1) 4025555
Fax: (1) 4021795
Telex: 401479

Al-Madina al-Munawara (Medina-The Enlightened City)
POB 807
Jeddah
Tel: (2) 6880344
Telex: 601356

An-Nadwah (The Council)
Jarwal Sheikh Sayed Halabai Bldg.
Mecca
Tel: (2) 5427868
Telex: 401205

Okaz
POB 1508
Jeddah 21412
Tel: (2) 6722630
Telex: 401360

Ar-Riyadh
POB 851
Riyadh
Tel: (1) 4420000
Telex: 401664
Fax: 4417580

Saudi Gazette
POB 5576
Jeddah
Tel: (2) 6722630
Telex: 600920

Al-Yaum (Today)
POB 565
Dammam
Tel: (3) 8331906
Telex: 801109

RADIO AND TELEVISION

Saudi Arabian Broadcasting Service
c/o Ministry of Information
POB 570
Riyadh
Tel: (1) 4014440
Fax: (1) 4025253
Telex: 4025253

Saudi Aramco FM Radio
Bldg. 3030 LIP
Dhahran
Tel: (3) 8762818
Fax: (3) 8740238
Telex 801120

Saudi Arabain Government Television Service
POB 570
Riyadh 11421
Tel: (1) 4014440
Fax: (1) 4044192
Telex: 401030

Dhahran HZ-22 TV, Channel 3 TV
Bldg. 3030 LIP
Dhahran
Tel: (3) 8754634
Fax: (3) 8750238
Telex: 801120

INTERNET ADDRESSES

Usenet group(s):
soc.culture.arabic

royal Embassy of Saudi Arabia
http://imedi.saudi.net/

US–Saudi Arabian Business Council
http://www.us-saudi-business.org/

Arab Net–Saudi Arabia
http://www.arab.net/welcome.html

Senegal

Republic of Senegal

Economy

Overview

After several decades of serious economic difficulties and periods of political instability, Senegal's economy has stabilized in recent years with the help of considerable international aid. As a country of few other natural resources, it is overwhelmingly reliant on agriculture and consequently remains vulnerable to such variable factors as world commodity price fluctuations and drought. In the past decade, the government has had some success with its program of economic liberalization which provides for increased incentives to the industrial and agricultural sectors, and which also seeks to streamline many government operations. Although the economy has experienced modest growth in recent years, long-term prospects depend largely on continued adherence to its economic reform program.

Trade

Senegal's foreign trade account has been characterized in recent years by a significant trade imbalance. France is the largest source of both its imports and exports, followed by other EU countries, the Côte d'Ivoire and Nigeria. Over the past four years Senegal's trade deficit has increased by over 40 percent due to a combination of poor export performance and increasing imports. High domestic costs have had an adverse effect on the competitiveness of Senegal's exports, and in 1994—in response to advice from international institutions—it devalued its currency by 50 percent against the French franc. The government hopes this move will stimulate export growth and reduce domestic demand for imports.

Sector

Agriculture Senegal is primarily an agricultural country; almost 70 percent of its population is engaged in some form of food production. This sector relies heavily on groundnut (peanut) production, which accounts for 50 percent of agricultural output and engages 65 percent of cultivated land. Earnings from agriculture have not been consistent due to the predominance of this one crop, weather conditions and fluctuating world prices. As a result the government is attempting to diversify this sector, particularly into rice and tomato cultivation. The fishing industry has significantly increased its export earnings in recent years and the potential for future growth in this area is good.

Industry Major advances have been made in industry in recent years and Senegal now has one of the largest industrial sectors in West Africa. Phosphate production is a leading foreign currency earner and this sub-sector is experiencing renewed growth as a result of increasing prices worldwide. The government is also pursuing the development of agroindustries.

Services Senegal's services sector does not yet provide much potential to foreign traders.

Trends

Despite making steady economic progress, Senegal continues to rely heavily on foreign aid. The government is proceeding with its economic reform program which includes privatization of state enterprises, reduction of government subsidies, the lowering of inflation, and tighter budget controls. It is also focusing on increasing export competitiveness by reducing the costs of production, increasing private sector incentives and simplifying regulations. Moderate growth in real GDP is expected in the short to medium term and opportunities for foreign exporters remain positive but limited in this small market.

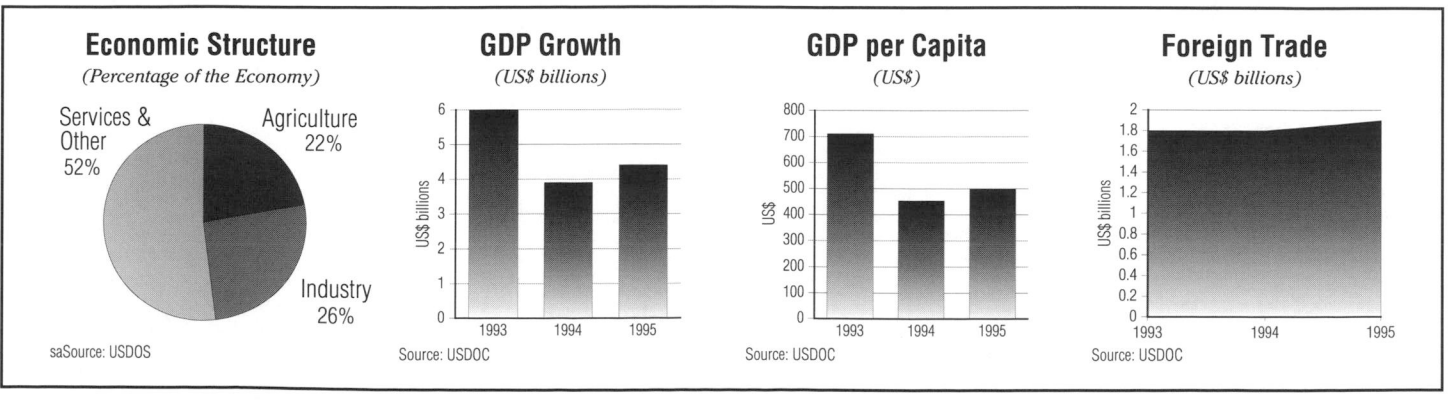

Economic Structure
(Percentage of the Economy)

Services & Other 52%
Agriculture 22%
Industry 26%

saSource: USDOS

GDP Growth
(US$ billions)

1993 1994 1995

Source: USDOC

GDP per Capita
(US$)

1993 1994 1995

Source: USDOC

Foreign Trade
(US$ billions)

1993 1994 1995

Source: USDOC

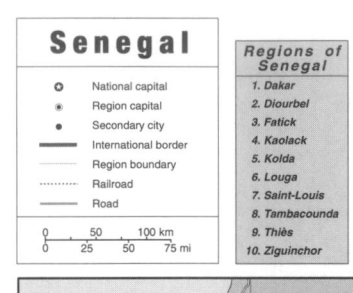

©1992 Magellan Geographix^{SM}Santa Barbara, CA (800) 929-4627

Travelogue

WORKWEEK

Offices Monday-Friday 8:00 am or 9:00 am to noon and 3:00 pm to 6:00 pm; Saturday 8:00 am or 9:00 am to noon.
Banks Monday-Friday 8:00 am to 11:15 am and 2:30 pm to 4:00 pm.
Government Monday-Friday 8:00 am to noon and 2:30 pm to 6:00 pm.
Retail Monday to Saturday 8:00 am to noon and 2:30 pm to 6:00 pm.

HOLIDAYS 1996

Holidays 1996
January 1 New Year's Day
April 4 Senegalese National Day
April 8 Easter Monday
May 1 Labor Day
May 16 Ascension Day
August 15 Assumption Day
November 1 All Saints' Day
December 25 Christmas Day
In addition, Muslim holidays including Korite, Tabaski, Tamkharit, and Mawlud are observed on dates that vary with the lunar calendar.

VISA AND PASSPORT

Visitors must have a valid passport and an onward or return ticket; a visa is not required for stays less than 90 days.

DEPARTURE FORMALITIES

Foreign currency may not be exported from Senegal without an express authority from the Office des Changes of the Banque Centrale des Etats de Afrique de Ouest. Foreign currency must be declared upon arrival to be exported upon departure. Visitors who work in Senegal must have an income tax clearance certificate to leave the country.

IMMUNIZATION

Evidence of a vaccination for yellow fever within the past 10 years is mandatory at the port of entry. Malaria prophylaxis is also recommended.

TIPPING

Taxis are all metered, and no additional tip is given above the amount indicated on the meter. Hotel bills usually include a service charge. In restaurants and bars, tip no more than 10 percent of the bill.

CRIME

Street crime is moderate in Senegal, but there are pickpockets, thieves, and scam artists in crowded areas.

INFRASTRUCTURE

Senegal has a relatively well-developed infrastructure, especially compared to other countries in West Africa. Facilities of varying quality for tourists are widely available. Roads in the interior are rough, but there are better roads in the coastal region and between most of the larger towns. Rail travel is not recommended although it is a popular mode of travel for the locals. Buses and good taxi service are available.

NATIONAL TOURIST OFFICE

Ministry of Tourism and Air Transport
97, ave. André Peytavin
Immeuble Kébé - ext.
PO Box 4049
Dakar
Tel: 225376, 211380
Fax: 229413

COMMUNICATIONS

Telephone International calls to most countries can be dialed directly. Local services are adequate and the government is currently implementing an expansion program.
Fax Fax services are available at some major hotels and businesses.
Post office Most post offices are centrally located. Postal service is relatively reliable. Stamps can be purchased at major hotels.

BEST TRAVEL BOOKS

The Gambia and Senegal. Insight Guides Series, 1993. Houghton Mifflin.
Meet Me in West Africa: The Ivory Coast, Togo and Senegal, Judith Rothberg. Vantage Press, Inc.
Africa on A Shoestring, Lonely Planet. Filled with useful information.
Do's and Taboo's Around the World. The Bestselling Guide to International Behavior. Edited by Roger Axtell, compiled by the Parker Pen Company. The ultimate guide to international behavior, now completely updated and expanded. Helpful, fun to read!

USEFUL TELEPHONE NUMBERS

If you are calling from outside Senegal you will need to add the country code [221] and any other international dialing requirements from within your country.
Airlines
- Air Afrique 252084
- Air Algerie 252059
Car Rental
- Avis 51713
- Europcar 51136
- Police 17
- Hospital 252135
Credit Card Information
Lost or stolen credit cards (call collect to the US, regardless of which country the card was issued in).
- Amex .... [1] (919) 333-3211
- Diner's Club .... [1] (303) 799-1504
- MasterCard .... [1] (314) 275-6690
- Visa .... [1] (410) 581-7931

Foreign Trade

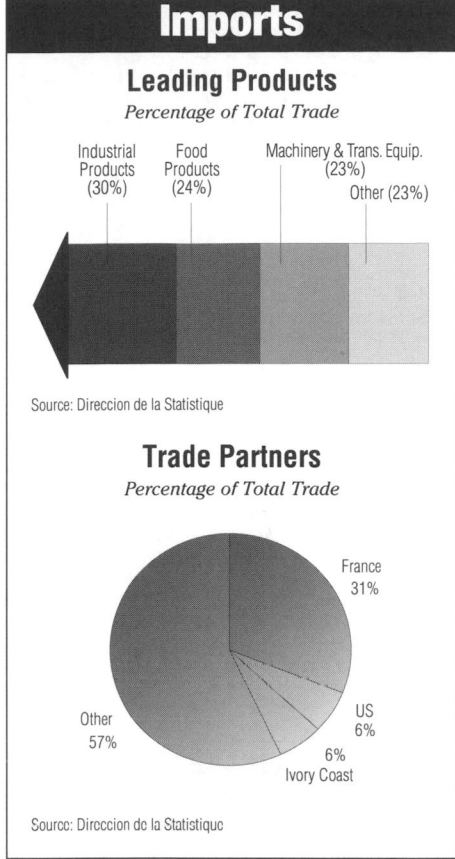

Imports

Leading Products
Percentage of Total Trade

- Industrial Products (30%)
- Food Products (24%)
- Machinery & Trans. Equip. (23%)
- Other (23%)

Source: Direccion de la Statistique

Trade Partners
Percentage of Total Trade

- France 31%
- US 6%
- Ivory Coast 6%
- Other 57%

Source: Direccion de la Statistique

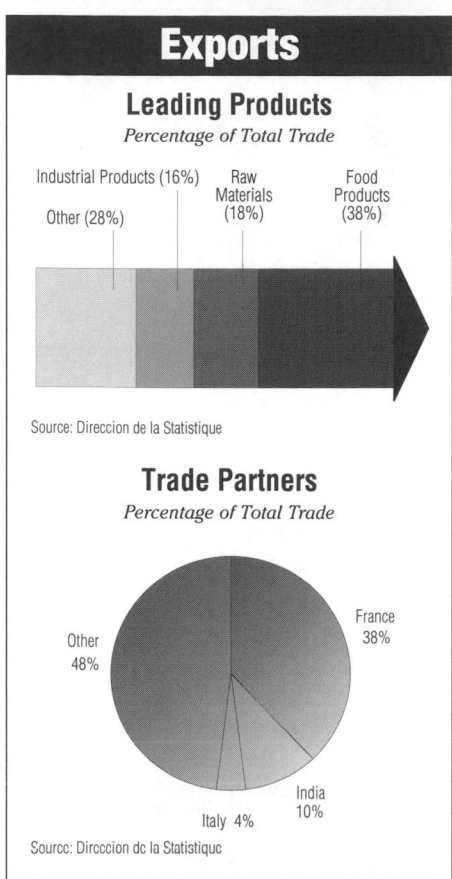

Exports

Leading Products
Percentage of Total Trade

- Industrial Products (16%)
- Other (28%)
- Raw Materials (18%)
- Food Products (38%)

Source: Direccion de la Statistique

Trade Partners
Percentage of Total Trade

- France 38%
- India 10%
- Italy 4%
- Other 48%

Source: Direccion de la Statistique

Opportunities

FOR IMPORTING TO SENEGAL

- asbestos, cement, paints, chemical fertilizers
- beer, flour, soft drinks, confectionery
- clothing, footware, textiles
- commercial vehicle assembly

FOR EXPORTING FROM SENEGAL

- groundnut, fish, cotton
- mining - iron ore, phosphates

GROWTH SECTORS

- tourism
- industry, especially phosphate production
- agriculture and agroindustries

Trade News

RULES AND REGULATIONS

- **Agents** Senegal has a few technically qualified agents and competition for their services is high.
- **Import licenses** Import licenses are not required for most goods originating in the European Community and the franc area.
- **Tariffs and import taxes** Customs duty is 15% for goods originating from countries admitted under the preferential minimum tariffs. This includes Britain and other EU countries. The rate for goods originating from ECOWAS (CEDEAO) countries is five percent. Pharmaceutical products, books, brochures, fertilizers, herbicides, fungicides, insecticides, seeds and domestic gas are now exempted from customs duty.
- **Fiscal tax** Senegal applies an import tax to imported goods irrespective of country of origin.

Legal

Legal System

Senegal is a civil code country using mainly the rudiments of the French legal system.

Intellectual Property Rights

Senegal is a member of the African Organization for the Intellectual Property Rights (OAPI), which has established among its member states a common system for obtaining protection for patents, trademarks, and industrial designs. All registration accomplished in one of those fourteen states in accordance with the law of this or that state, or registered at the head office of the OAPI located in Yaounde, is considered as a local registration in each state member of the OAPI. All foreign filers have to make their registration directly to the head office of the OAPI through a proxy chosen in one of the member states.

Patents On average it takes 18 months to obtain patent registration. Patents are protected for 20 years. An annual charge is levied during this period.

Trademarks Trademark registration has to be accomplished at the office of the Clerk of the Civil Court who has to pass it on to the head office of the OAPI. The recording of the trademark by the OAPI protects it for 20 years from the date of application.

Copyrights The Senegalese Office of Authors Rights has the role of enforcing copyright obligation.

Business Registration

Foreign and domestic private entities are permitted to establish and own businesses and to engage in most forms of remunerative activity. Local majority is necessary only in a few specially protected areas, such as fishing. A maximum 10-day deadline has been fixed for responding to applications for authorization to conduct business. If all requirements are fulfilled a response is given within one month. The services provided by the government are free of charge.

Source: Etude Konate & Preira

Legal Matters

LEGAL BRIEFS

- **Contracts and dispute resolution** If required, arbitration is carried out according to agreements concerning the protection of investments between Senegal and the state of origin of the private person or legal entity. In the absence of such agreements, arbitration is governed by the model rules on arbiter procedure adopted by the UN International Law Commission. Business disputes are usually settled by lawsuit, and litigation is readily resorted to.
- **Notaries** Notary publics perform many of the same functions as lawyers, including forming companies and filing all documents related thereto. Only a notary can authenticate the articles of companies and do legal advertising.
- **Intellectual property rights** Local statutes recognize reciprocal protection for authors or artists who are nationals of countries adhering to the 1971 Paris Convention of Intellectual Property Rights.
- **International agreements** Senegal is a member of the World Intellectual Property Organization and also of the Berne Copyright Convention. Senegal has signed and ratified the treaty for the harmonization of business law in the franc zone.
- **Companies** Joint stock and limited liability companies are common organizations in business.
- **Trademark renewal** Trademarks may be renewed indefinitely by subsequent registrations. On average it takes six months to obtain the registration.

LEGAL CONTACT

Etude Konate & Preira
44, rue Carnot, BP 9002
Dakar
Tel: 22-86-60 Fax: 23-38-64

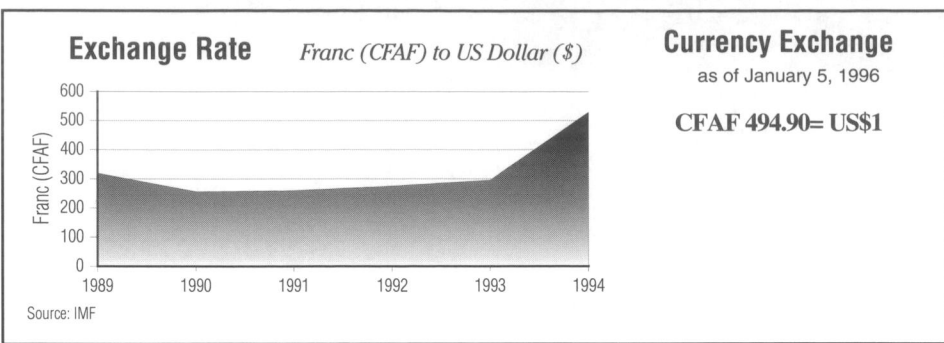

Exchange Rate
Franc (CFAF) to US Dollar ($)

Franc (CFAF): 600, 500, 400, 300, 200, 100, 0
Years: 1989, 1990, 1991, 1992, 1993, 1994

Source: IMF

Currency Exchange
as of January 5, 1996

CFAF 494.90= US$1

Currency

The currency in use is the CFA franc (CFA or CFAF).

Foreign Exchange

Foreign exchange controls exist for transactions outside the franc zone (a monetary zone that includes France and its former overseas colonies). Banks may charge an exchange commission on the purchase or sale of foreign exchange. There are no taxes on the purchase or sale of foreign exchange. Forward cover against exchange rate risk is available to residents for certain categories of imports.

Capital Transfers

Payments for invisibles to France, Monaco, and Operations Account countries are freely allowed; payments to other countries are subject to approval. Payments for invisibles related to trade are permitted if the basic trade transaction has already been approved or does not require authorization. Proceeds from invisibles with France, Monaco, and Operations Account countries may be retained. Foreign currency received from other countries must be surrendered within one month of the due date or date of receipt.

Investment Incentives

The government of Senegal actively solicits foreign interest and investment, and has stopped its practice of participating in foreign investment projects. There is no discrimination against businesses conducted or owned by foreign investors, and there are no barriers regarding 100 percent ownership of businesses by foreign investors in most areas.

Investment Restrictions

In order to qualify for investment incentives, small and medium-sized firms are required to invest at least CFA five million (US$8,600), to employ at least three Senegalese nationals full-time, and to keep regular accounts in a standard format.

TAXATION

Taxation requires sophisticated knowledge of complex rules and regulations specific to each country. For more detailed information we suggest you refer to the Ernst & Young Corporate Tax Guide and Directory, available from the Ernst & Young accounting office in your country, or from:

FFA Ernst & Young
22, rue Ramez Bourgi
B.P. 2085
Dakar, Senegal
Tel: 23-33-80, 23-58-85
Telex: 090 600 GA 51220
Fax: 23-80-32

- **Note:** Foreign tax credits are not allowed, income subject to foreign tax that is not exempt from Senegalese tax under the territoriality principle is taxable net of the foreign tax. A tax treaty with France is in effect, which provides a tax credit for French taxes paid on dividends.

At a Glance

Corporate Income Tax Rate (%)(a)	35
Capital Gains Tax Rate (%)(b)	35
Branch Tax Rate (%)(a)	35
Withholding Tax (%)	
Dividends, Directors' Fees and Nondeductible Expenses (c)	16
Interest	16
Royalties from Patents, Know-how, etc.	20
Payments to Nonresidents for Certain Services and Activities (d)	20
Branch Remittance Tax (e)	10
Net Operating Losses (Years)	
Carryback	0
Carryforward (f)	3

(a) The minimum tax is CFAF 500,000 (CFAF 1 million if annual turnover exceeds CFAF 500 million a year).
(b) The tax may be deferred or reduced if the proceeds are used to acquire new fixed assets in Senegal within three years or in the event of a merger.
(c) Special rules apply to certain dividends. Nondeductible expenses include foreign head office overhead, interest paid to shareholders more than two percentage points above a standard rate set by the central bank, interest on loans in excess of the capital stock amount, and gifts and liberalities.
(d) This tax is imposed on technical assistance fees and certain other payments to nonresident companies and nonresident individuals that do not carry on a trade or business in Senegal. The rate is 15% for payments to French individuals or corporations.
(e) This rate applies unless modified by a tax treaty.
(f) Losses may be carried forward three years, losses attributable to depreciation may be carried forward indefinitely.

Money Matters

BITS AND PIECES

- **Common currency** The CFA franc is issued by the Central Bank of West African States (BCEAO), and is common to Benin, Burkina Faso, Côte d'Ivoire, Mali, Niger, Senegal, and Togo.
- **Nonresident accounts** Regulations concerning nonresident accounts are based on French regulations. Nonresident accounts may not be credited with CFA bank notes, French bank notes, or Operations Account country bank notes.
- **Travel** Residents traveling to countries that are in the franc zone but not members of the WAMU may take out bank notes, other than CFA franc notes, up to CFA 2 million. Residents traveling to countries outside the franc zone are limited to CFA 500,000 for tourist travel and CFA 75,000 per day for business travel.
- **Capital movement** There are no exchange controls on capital movements between Senegal and France, Monaco and Operations Account countries. Capital transfers to other countries are subject to approval, although capital receipts are freely permitted.
- **Nonresident travelers** Nonresident travelers must declare all foreign exchange upon entry.
- **Imports payments** Import transactions must be domiciled with an authorized bank if the value is more than CFA 500,000. Authorization entitles the importer to purchase the required exchange. Importers may not acquire foreign exchange until the contractual date of payment.
- **Export payments** Proceeds from exports must be collected within 120 days of the arrival of the goods at their destination, and repatriated through BCEAO less than one month after due date. Export payments more than CFA 500,000 must be domiciled with an intermediary bank.

BANKS

Banque Centrale des Etats de l'Afrique de l'Ouest (BCEAO)
Ave Abdoulaye Fadiga
BP 3108
Dakar
Tel: 23-16-15
Fax: 23-93-35

Banque Internationale pour le Commerce et l'Industrie du Senegal (BICIS)
2 ave Roume
BP 392
Dakar
Tel: 23-10-33
Fax: 23-37-07
Telex: 21642

BIAO-Senegal
1 place de l'Independeance
BP 129
Dakar
Tel: 23-10-00
Fax: 23-20-05

Credit Lyonnais Senegal (CLS)
17 blvd Pinet-Laprade
Angle rue Huart
BP 56
Dakar
Tel: 23-10-08
Fax: 23-84-30
Telex: 21622

Credit National du Senegal (CNS)
7 ave Roume
BP 319
Dakar
Tel: 23-34-86
Fax: 23-72-92
Telex: 61283

Societe Generale de Banques au Senegal SA (SGBS)
19 ave Roume
BP 323
Dakar
Tel: 23-10-60
Fax: 23-90-36
Telex: 21801

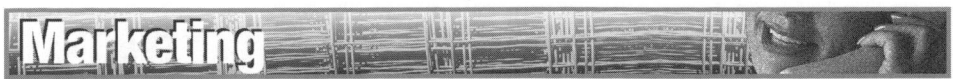

Marketing

Overview

The French influence remains strong in Senegal: government business documents are published in French, and French trading companies remain dominant on the commercial scene. The capital city, Dakar, is the hub of economic activity and the largest consumer market, with 25 percent of the population. There are a few large retail stores in the largest cities but the bulk of retail sales occur through traditional merchants and street markets. Authorized prices set by the government apply to household commodities. Other prices are free and determined according to supply and demand.

Agents and Distribution

Foreign suppliers may employ an agent, appoint a dealer or a distributor, or establish a branch office or subsidiary; each of these approaches has been used by exporters to Senegal. Dakar is the principal distribution center. Distribution occurs both by modern methods and through more traditional means, based on family or political relationships. The more traditional distributors are mainly local, deal in a limited range of goods, and carry very small inventories. The modern sector is dominated by a few French-owned import-export firms that cover all aspects of trade from importing to retailing, but their number is decreasing. Existing alongside these companies are extremely competitive small-scale traders specializing in wholesale and retail of consumer goods.

Advertising

Advertising is available in many media, from newspapers, magazines, and TV and radio, to billboards; and the rates are modest. The local newspapers are published in French with ethnic inserts. Several European magazines and newspapers are available. Various trade organizations publish bulletins and newsletters. However, the reading public is small and limited to Dakar. As with Third World countries elsewhere, sponsoring a sports team, local band, or musical performer is an effective advertising strategy. Local advice should be obtained before planning an advertising or marketing effort.

Marketing in Senegal

MARKETING TIPS

- **Price controls** The government exercises price controls on selected products, mainly agricultural products and household foodstuffs.
- **Undeveloped distribution channels** Distribution is accomplished by importers and merchants; there is no separate distribution industry.
- **Selling techniques** Traditional face-to-face selling is the prevalent practice.
- **Service and customer support** Due to poorly developed infrastructure and general inaccessibility, product support and customer service are not highly expected.
- **Franchising** Franchising does not yet exist in Senegal.
- **Direct marketing** Western-style direct marketing is impractical due to the many small villages and the lack of modern communications and delivery methods. Door-to-door selling is limited to low-value consumer products sold with informal credit arrangements.
- **Market centers** Sandaga, a sprawling unregulated market in the center of Dakar, is the capital's major selling point for manufactured goods ranging from textiles, footwear, and cosmetics to high-tech stereo equipment.
- **Government and marketing** The government plays an important role in the markets by establishing prices and controlling distribution channels. The government also controls the distribution of commodities it deems to be of strategic value, such as edible oils, sugar, and rice. The government and state enterprises are significant purchasers of equipment and supplies; nearly all such contracts are awarded through competitive bidding.
- **Prices** Prices are of three kinds: administered, authorized, and free, depending on the product to be sold.

Business Culture

Greetings and Courtesies

Senegalese greetings are distinguished by a very long handshake—to be maintained during a full discussion of your health, your family, your general state of inner peace, and the weather. This is a formality; always respond that everything is fine. All handshakes should be of a very gentle grip. When a man is greeting a Senegalese woman, he should wait for her to extend her hand first.

Business Ethic and Framework

Senegal is 95 percent Muslim, a feature that sets the tone for the nation's business climate as well as its general culture. Business is conducted primarily in French, though English-speaking businessmen are fairly common. The local language is Wolof. A patient approach is necessary for doing business in Senegal; the Senegalese will want to take their time getting to know you. A cardinal rule of the Senegalese business culture is to refrain from any displays of anger, no matter how frustrating your business endeavors may be.

Decision Making

Decisions come slowly in Senegal due to a combination of protracted bureaucracy, a social climate which involves an inordinate amount of elaborate greetings and protocol, and a year-round searing heat. Expect any important final decisions to come from the top people in a firm or agency. Never attempt to reach a business decision over the phone, regardless of the person's prominence.

Women

Women are surprisingly well-represented in significant and powerful positions in Senegal's business community. Foreign companies sending a businesswoman there can feel secure that she will treated with respect. In accordance with the Muslim foundation of Senegal, a foreign businesswoman should avoid an aggressive manner, and conduct herself with modesty and discretion at all times.

Cultural Cautions

DO'S

- Always socialize before getting down to business.
- Senegalese appreciate conversations about economics.

DON'TS

- Topics of conversation to avoid include politics and religion.
- If invited by a Senegalese to a restaurant, don't offer to pay. This will seem rude and insulting.

CUSTOMS

- When in a Senegalese house, never walk by an adult without greeting him or her.
- Meetings should always be scheduled for the cooler morning hours.
- Be prepared for meetings to accommodate interruptions in accordance with the Muslim daily prayer schedule.

OBSERVATIONS

- Punctuality standards are typically loose for the region, though Senegalese businessmen are accommodating and reliable about setting and keeping basic appointments.
- If you are dealing with government officials, be prepared for slow progress involving many meetings and a great deal of red tape. Low-paid ministry officials can expedite the process, however, and gifts are common to gain their assistance.
- The French style of attire is prevalent in the Senegalese business community. Men dress conservatively and elegantly in two- and three-piece suits, while women wear skirts and dresses—though pants are acceptable. Women, should not wear tight or low-cut outfits, or short skirts that show their legs.

NEGOTIATIONS

- Always set appointments at least a week in advance of your arrival, then reconfirm them.

GOVERNMENT AGENCIES

Ministry of Agriculture and Water Resources
Immeuble Adfministratif
Dakar
Tel: 23-10-88
Telex: 3151

Ministry of Communications
58 blvd de la Republique
Dakar
Tel: 23-10-65
Fax: 21-41-04

Ministry of Culture
Immeuble Administratif
Dakar
Tel: 23-10-88
Telex: 482

Ministry of the Economy, Finance and Planning
Centre Comptable Andre Peytavin
Rue Charles Laisne et ave Carde
BP 462
Dakar
Tel: 22-65-50
Telex: 61203

Ministry of Energy, Mines and Industry and of Trade and Crafts
122 bis ave Andre Peytavin
BP 4037
Dakar
Tel: 22-99-94
Fax: 22-55-94
Telex: 61149

Ministry of Equipment, of Road, Rail and Maritime Transport and Fisheries
Immeuble Communal
Blvd du General de Gaulle
Dakar
Tel: 21-42-01
Telex: 3151

Ministry of Foreign Afairs and Senegalese Abroad
Place de l'Independance
Dakar
Tel: 21-62-84
Telex: 482

Ministry of Health and Social Welfare
Immeuble Administratif
Dakar
Tel: 23-10-88
Telex: 482

Ministry of Housing and Town Planning
Ave Andre Peytavin
BP 4028
Dakar
Tel: 23-91-27
Fax: 22-56-01

Ministry of the Interior
Rond-point de la Republique
Dakar
Tel: 21-41-51
Telex: 3351

Ministry of Tourism and Air Transport and of the Environment and Nature Conservation
23 rue Calmette
BP 4049
Dakar
Tel: 21-11-26

TRADE ASSOCIATIONS

Mission Francaise de Cooperation
BP 2014
Dakar
Telex: 3103

Societe de Developpement Agricole et Industriel (SODAGRI)
Immeuble Fahd, 9e etage
Blvd Djily Mbaye x Macodou Ndiaye
BP 222
Dakar
Tel: 21-04-26
Fax: 22-54-06

Societe de Development des Fibres Textiles (SODE-FITEX)
Km 4.5
blvd. du Centenaire de la Commune de Dakar
BP 3216
Dakar
Tel: 32-47-50
Fax: 21-01-53

Societe d'Exploitation des Ressources Animales du Senegal (SERAS)
Km 2.5, blvd du Centenaire de la Commune de Dakar
BP 14
Dakar
Tel: 32-31-78
Fax: 32-06-90

Societe Nationale d'Amenagement et d'Exploitation des Terres du Delta du Fleuve Senegal et des Vallees du Fleuve Senegal et de la Faleme (SAED)
Route de Khor
BP 74
Saint-Louis
Tel: 61-15-33
Fax: 61-14-63
Telex: 75124

Societe Nationale de Commercialisation des Oleagineux du Senegal (SONACOS)
Immeuble SONACOS
32-36 rue du Dr Dalmette
BP 639
Dakar
Tel: 23-1052
Fax: 23-88-05
Telex: 51418

Societe Nationale d'Etudes et de Promotion Industrielle (SONEPI)
Derriere Residence Seydou Nourou Tall
Ave Bourguiba Prolongee
BP 100
Dakar
Tel: 25-21-30
Fax: 24-65-65
Telex: 61178

Societe Nouvelle des Etudes de Developpement en Afrique (SONED-AFRIQUE)
Immeuble SONACOS
32-36 rue Calmette
BP 2084
Dakar
Tel: 23-94-57
Fax: 23-42-31
Telex: 51464

CHAMBERS OF COMMERCE

Chambre de Commerce, d'Industrie et d'Agriculture de la Region de Dakar
1 place de l'Independance
BP 118
Dakar
Tel: 23-71-89
Telex: 61112

Chambre de Commerce, d'Industrie et d'Artisanat de la Region de Diourbel
BP 7
Diourbel
Tel: 71-12-03

Chambre de Commerce et d'Industrie de la Region du Kaolack
BP 203
Kaolack
Tel: 41-20-52
Telex: 7474

Chambre de Commerce de la Region de Louga
BP 26
Louga
Tel: 67-11-14

Chambre de Commerce, d'Industrie et d'Agriculture de la Region de Saint-Louis
rue Bisson Nord
BP 19
Saint-Louis
Tel: 61-10-88

Chambre de Commerce, d'Industrie et d'Agriculture Region de Tambacounda
BP 127
Tambacounda
Tel: 81-10-14

Chambre de Commerce, d'Industrie et d'Agriculture de la Region de Thies
Ave Lamine-Gueye
BP 3020
Thies
Tel: 51-10-02

Chambre de Commerce, d'Industrie et d'Artisanat de la Region de Ziguinchor
BP 26
Ziguinchor
Tel: 91-13-10

NEWSPAPERS

Le Soleil
Route du Service geographique
BP 92
Dakar
Tel: 32-46-92
Fax: 32-03-81

Sud au Quotidien
Immeuble Fahd
BP 4130
Dakar
Tel: 22-53-93
Fax: 22-52-90

PERIODICALS

Afrique Nouvelle
9 rue Paul Holle
BP 283
Dakar
Tel: 22-51-22

Construire l'Afrique
BP 3770
Dakar
Tel: 56-07-90
Fax: 54-19-61

Le Democrate
10 rue de Thiong
Dakar

Senegal d'Aujourd'hui
58 blvd de la Republique
BP 4027
Dakar

RADIO AND TELEVISION

Societe Nationle de Radiodiffusion Television Senegalaise (RTS)
BP 1765
Dakar
Tel: 21-78-01
Fax: 22-34-90

INTERNET ADDRESSES

Usenet group(s):
soc.culture.african

AdminNet Senegal
http://cri.ensmp.fr/~scherer/adminet/world/sn/

Trade Point Dakar
http://www.unicc.org/untpc/incubator/sen/tpdak/welcome.html/

Singapore

Republic of Singapore

Economy

Overview

A highly strategic location in one of the world's major shipping lanes, a government dedicated to free trade and industrial development, and a strong work ethic all have helped Singapore to attain its position as a major economic power in Southeast Asia. As a country with virtually no natural resources it has focused on imports of raw materials and exports of high-tech, high value-added goods to achieve a level of economic importance greater than its small size would suggest. This largely export-led economy is continuing to grow and long-term prospects are positive.

Trade

Singapore is heavily reliant on foreign trade; gross earnings from foreign trade are nearly five times the value of its GDP. The US is its largest trading partner and the largest source of its exports, followed by Japan and Malaysia. Singapore's economy is one of the most open in the world and this, combined with an affluent population and its role as a gateway to Southeast Asia, makes it a very attractive trading market.

Sectors

Agriculture The agricultural sector has limited resources and the main activities include the cultivation of vegetables, pork, and poultry. Singapore needs to import most of its food and this means agricultural imports should continue to flourish, especially high-value consumer oriented food products.

Industry Industrialization has fueled Singapore's economic transformation since its separation from Malaysia in 1965. Petroleum refining is the largest sub-sector in terms of the total value of production but rapid expansion is continuing in the areas of electronics, electrical and transportation machinery, food products, and textiles. Electronics is the fastest growing sub-sector and although it faces strong competition from other Asian countries, the government is concentrating on increasing labor productivity in order to remain competitive in the low-cost, high-tech markets.

Services Singapore has a very strong services sector that should continue to prosper as the Southeast Asian economies expand. Financial services is the largest sub-sector and although it has experienced dramatic growth in the past year this trend is not likely to continue in the short to medium term. Tourism remains strong and should maintain its contribution to GDP even as financial services growth slows.

Trends

Singapore's economy remains buoyant and the recent increase in foreign investment in the manufacturing sector underlines the world's optimistic outlook for the tiny country's future. The government is actively investing in the fast-growing economies of South and East Asia, and is looking particularly to China for investment opportunities. It is also focusing on maintaining competitiveness through increased productivity, and it is continually developing new products and markets to drive growth of the export-led economy. Singapore has the third highest per capita income in Southeast Asia and this makes it is an excellent market for imports of high-value consumer goods. External demand continues to be the foundation for growth and the general recovery in its main export markets should ensure the continued growth of Singapore's economy.

At a Glance

THE COUNTRY

Location Southeastern Asia, between Malaysia and Indonesia.
Terrain Lowland; gently undulating central plateau contains water catchment area and nature preserve.
Climate Tropical; hot, humid, rainy; no pronounced rainy or dry seasons. Thunderstorms occur on 40 percent of all days (67 percent of days in April).

THE PEOPLE

Population 2,900,000
Ethnic composition
Chinese.. 76.4%
Malay 14.9%
Indian 6.4%
Other... 2.3%
Religions Buddhist, Taoist, Muslim, Hindu, Christian.
Languages spoken English, Mandarin and other Chinese dialects, Malay, Tamil.
Education and literacy Nearly 90 percent of the adult population can read and write. Literacy is more than 90 percent for Singaporeans under 35 years of age.
Labor force
Total:...1,500,000
By occupation: financial, business, and other services 30.2%, manufacturing 28.4%, commerce 22.0%, construction 9.0%, other 10.4%.

COUNTRY FACTS

Political and legal Singapore is a republic with a parliamentary system of government. Political authority rests with the prime minister and the cabinet.
Telephone Singapore's telephone system is among the most efficient in Southeast Asia; facilities are modern and comprehensive, providing high-quality communications with the rest of the world. International Country Code: [65].
Transportation Buses, taxis, and subways run efficiently through most parts of the country. Automobile traffic is regulated with permits. Taxis also have special requirements for motoring into downtown zones from the suburbs. International flight connections are excellent.
Environment Air pollution from transportation vehicles in the urban areas, along with industrial pollution, limited water supply, and limited land availability which presents waste disposal problems are the major environmental issues.
Media The ratio of 45.59 telephones per 100 population rates among the highest in East Asia. Radio and television stations are government-owned and operated. Newspapers, however, are privately owned and published daily in English, Chinese, and Malay. While freedom of the press is guaranteed by law, the International Press Institute has on various occasions cited Singapore for interference with press freedom. Movies, theater productions, and magazines are censored for sexual content.
Health Singaporeans enjoy one of the highest health levels in all of Southeast Asia. High standards in housing, sanitation, water supply, and hospitals are attributable to this achievement. One hundred percent of the population has access to safe drinking water and nutritional standards are among the highest in Asia.

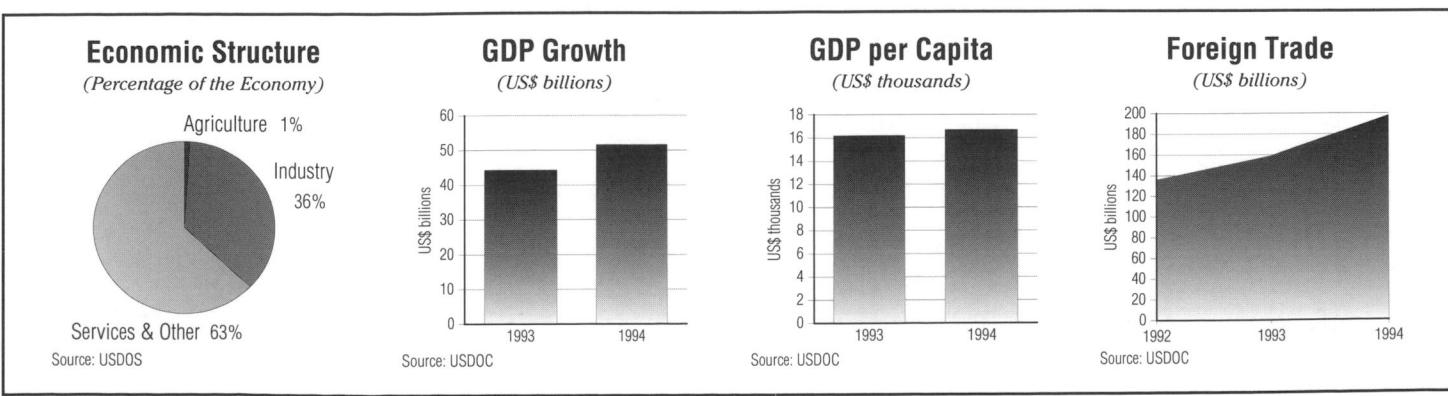

Economic Structure
(Percentage of the Economy)
Agriculture 1%
Industry 36%
Services & Other 63%
Source: USDOS

GDP Growth
(US$ billions)
1993 1994
Source: USDOC

GDP per Capita
(US$ thousands)
1993 1994
Source: USDOC

Foreign Trade
(US$ billions)
1992 1993 1994
Source: USDOC

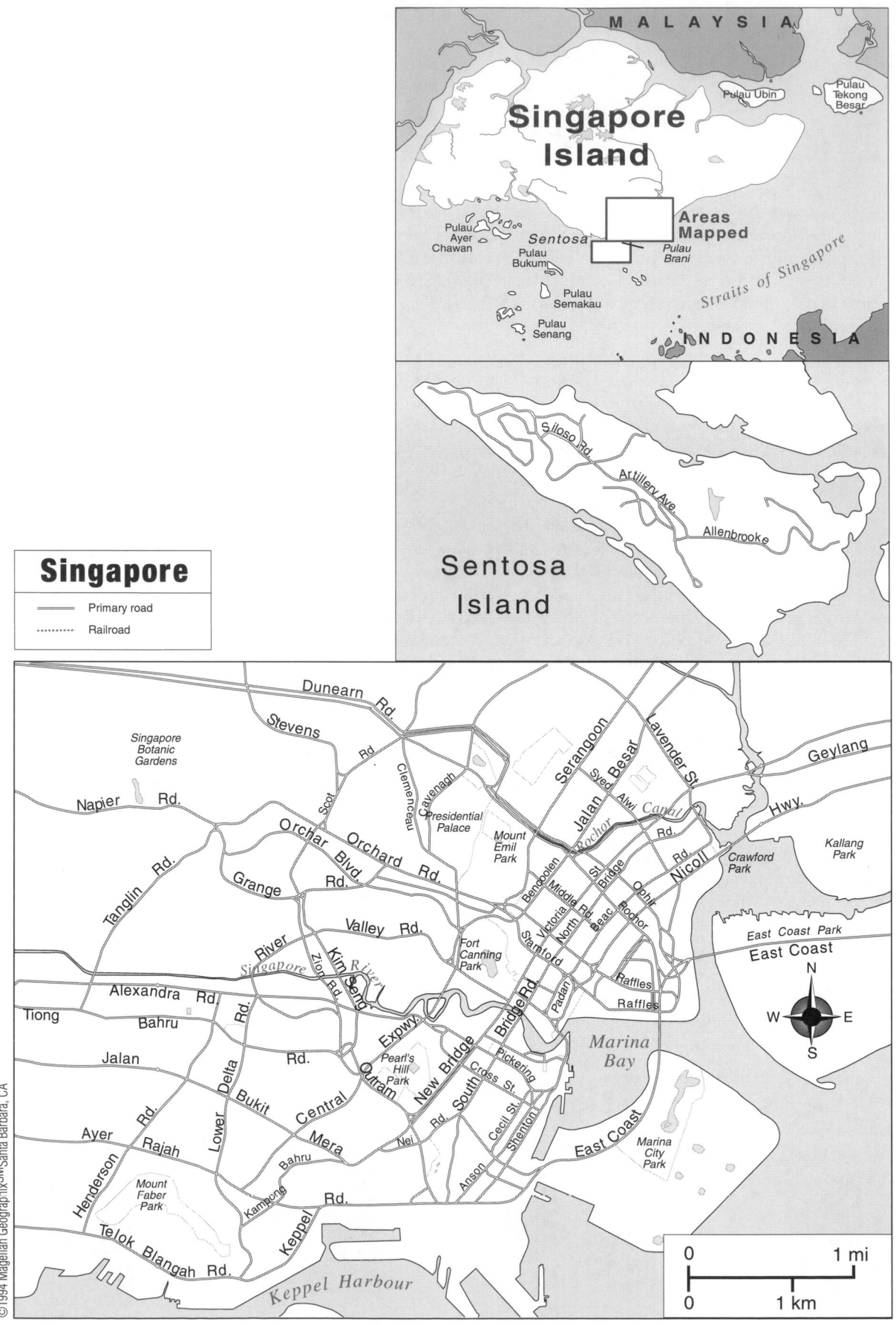

Foreign Trade

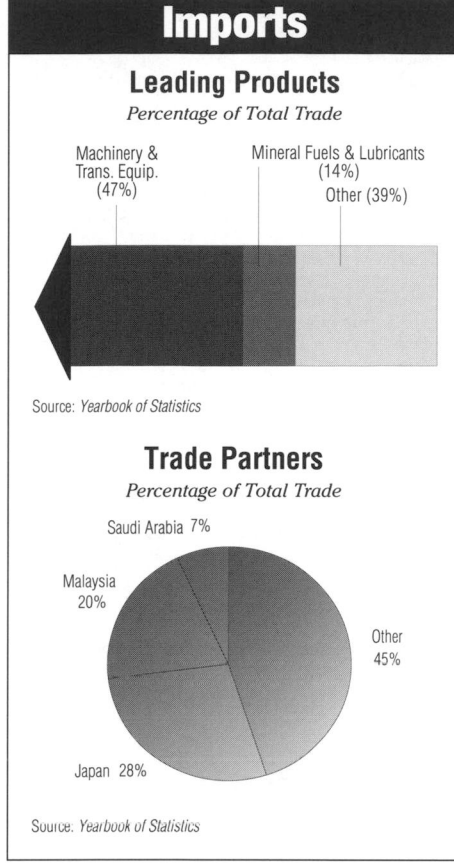

Imports

Leading Products
Percentage of Total Trade

Machinery & Trans. Equip. (47%)
Mineral Fuels & Lubricants (14%)
Other (39%)

Source: *Yearbook of Statistics*

Trade Partners
Percentage of Total Trade

Saudi Arabia 7%
Malaysia 20%
Japan 28%
Other 45%

Source: *Yearbook of Statistics*

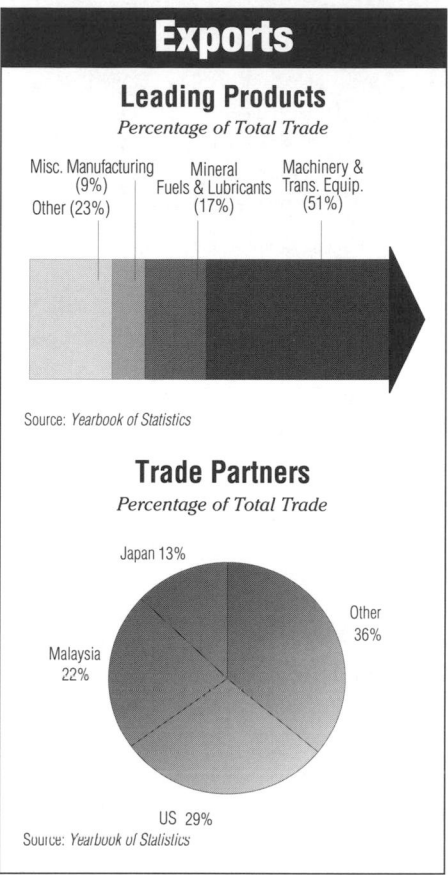

Exports

Leading Products
Percentage of Total Trade

Misc. Manufacturing (9%)
Other (23%)
Mineral Fuels & Lubricants (17%)
Machinery & Trans. Equip. (51%)

Source: *Yearbook of Statistics*

Trade Partners
Percentage of Total Trade

Japan 13%
Malaysia 22%
Other 36%
US 29%

Source: *Yearbook of Statistics*

Opportunities

FOR IMPORTING TO SINGAPORE
- aircraft and avionics equipment
- computer hardware, software, and peripherals
- drugs and pharmaceuticals
- electrical machinery
- electronic components
- electronics industry test equipment
- food processing and packaging equipment
- laboratory scientific instruments
- medical and dental equipment and supplies
- office machines and supplies
- petroleum products
- printing and graphic arts equipment
- refrigeration equipment
- robotics and automation equipment
- security and safety equipment
- skin care products
- sporting and recreational goods
- telecommunications products

FOR EXPORTING FROM SINGAPORE
- chemicals
- clothing
- computers and peripherals
- electronics
- fabricated metal products
- foods
- freshwater ornamental fish
- household appliances
- jewelry
- machinery and equipment
- office and data machines
- oil and refined petroleum products
- orchids
- printed materials and paper products
- stationery products
- telecommunications equipment
- wood and timber products

GROWTH SECTORS
- cinematography
- franchises
- pharmaceuticals
- professional services: accounting, banking and financial, medical, management and consulting, information and tax services
- ship repair and conversion
- sports and leisure items

GOVERNMENT PROCUREMENT
- airport and seaport facilities
- aviation equipment
- biotechnology products for health care and agriculture
- construction of public housing, schools, and hospitals
- environmental protection goods and services
- petrochemicals
- roadway construction and expansion
- telecommunication products

Trade News
RULES AND REGULATIONS

- **Regulation** The Singapore Trade Development Board (STDB), which is part of the Ministry of Trade and Industry (MTI), has jurisdiction over all aspects of foreign trade. Anyone importing or exporting products in Singapore must register with STDB and obtain a central registration number. The CR number can be applied for in person, by fax, or by mail.

- **Import restrictions** Singapore currently has no import quotas, and almost all products—except those controlled for health, safety, or security reasons—can be imported without restriction. Controlled products include rice, film and video, and telecommunications equipment. Importation of animal and plant products needs permission from the Primary Production Department. Importation of chemicals and pharmaceuticals needs permission from the Ministry of Health.

- **Tariff limits** Only a few categories of imports are subject to tariffs, which are minimal. Such categories include alcohol, clothing, motor vehicles, petroleum products, sugar, tobacco, and wood furniture.

- **Tariffs** Singapore's tariffs are minimal; 96 percent of goods enter Singapore duty-free. Singapore still maintains significant tariffs on cigarettes, alcoholic beverages, automobiles, and gasoline to discourage their use.

- **Fines and penalties** Singapore has a reputation for a very stable, if authoritarian, political climate. Importation of prohibited goods, falsification of documents, and/or illegal possession of goods may result in imprisonment, fines, and seizure of goods.

- **Export controls** The only substantial export controls are those imposed by other nations that require Singapore to limit its own exports of certain products such as, for example, textiles.

- **Trade organizations** Singapore's primary affiliation is with the Association of Southeast Asian Nations (ASEAN), a developing regional trade block. It is also a contracting member of GATT/WTO.

- **Export payments** Some exports originating in Singapore are subject to restrictions and other nontariff barriers from destination countries.

- **Market access barriers** Singapore maintains some market access restrictions in the services sector.

- **Export subsidies** Singapore does not subsidize exports although it does actively promote them. The government offers significant incentives to attract foreign investment, almost all of which is in export-oriented industries.

- **Duties** The government introduced a consumption-based tax, the Goods and Services Tax (GST) as part of its long-term move to reduce taxes on earnings. The GST of three percent (fixed for five years) is levied on all domestic consumption of goods and services, with certain exceptions, and on imports of goods into Singapore.

- **Import declaration** Importers are required to present an import declaration for all imports.

- **Marking and labeling** Labels are required on all imports of food, drugs, liquors, paints, and solvents, and must specify the country of origin. Prepackaged foods must be labeled in English.

- **Abandoned and re-exported goods** Dutiable goods on which duties have not been paid may be re-exported without payment of duty only if they are moved under customs control and checked out at the port of boundary station.

- **Additional documentation** Documents required by customs authorities for air and surface shipments out of Singapore include the commercial invoice, the bill of lading, the air waybill for air freight, export declaration, packing lists, and insurance documents.

Overview

Singapore markets are receptive, open, and straightforward. Product quality is important, and price competition is severe. The Singapore retail sector is modern, sophisticated, and well-developed. Retailers and supermarkets generally charge slotting or listing fees for shelf space. The supplier may also be expected to provide an extra discount for any chiller or freezer space, if it is required. Suppliers should note that the small size of the market dictates that most importers cannot handle single-product containers and must depend on foreign consolidators. The government contract system is considered to be fair and transparent.

Distribution

Distribution and sales channels are simple and direct. Imported goods are usually distributed through established trading firms that have branches in Singapore and throughout Singapore's marketing area. These firms offer sales, after-sales servicing, and technical and engineering assistance. The after-sales support is of primary importance to foreign manufacturers in gaining consumer confidence. Therefore, care should be taken when selecting an agent. Foreign firms may co-locate company representatives with a Singapore trading firm. The company representative is responsible for before- and after-sales supervision of agents and distributors. This is a valuable function since a large trading company may represent product lines of several hundred foreign suppliers involving several thousand items. Singapore trading companies offer many services. They will maintain spare parts inventories, provide maintenance services, sell or process indent orders, and market to both wholesalers and retailers. Most consumer goods are imported by mass stocking distributors who resell part of their purchases to retailers, and retain the balance for sale in their own retail outlets. Processed and pre-packaged food products are imported by more than 300 trading firms, both large and small. Almost all fruit imports are overseen by the Singapore Fruit Exchange, which is an agglomeration of hundreds of small and large fruit handlers; it controls more than 80 percent of the market. The remaining fruit is imported directly by supermarkets.

Agents, Distributors, and Partners

Since most industrial goods are sold through agents (though some are also imported by stocking distributors, and food products are also imported by agents who act in a second capacity as distributors) a good agent and/or distributor is essential and highly recommended. There are very few firms that act solely as agents or importers. Thankfully, finding a prospective agent is easy. Singaporean firms are aggressive about seeking new products to market and usually respond enthusiastically to new opportunities. The Singapore Registry of Companies and Businesses publishes an excellent guide that walks the first-time registrant through the process of establishing an office.

Selling Techniques

Selling techniques vary according to industry and product, but are comparable to the techniques used in any other sophisticated market. Price, quality, and service are the main selling factors in Singapore. Prospective exporters should be aware that competition is fierce, and bargaining is extensively practiced, even in the commercial and industrial sectors where buyers often want a discount and vendors, therefore, inflate initial prices to offset customary reductions. The deciding factor is often simply predicated on after-sale services. Franchising is growing in popularity because many cash-rich Singaporean firms are looking for new growth opportunities and are interested in establishing franchising outlets.

Advertising

Advertising is widely used in marketing in Singapore. There are several advertising and public relations firms that provide a complete range of public relation services. Product modification and market identification is a possible means to develop an association with either the manufacturer or the local distributor and the product. Foreign suppliers are also welcome to buy advertisement space in local newspapers. Here again, it is often useful to obtain the services of a local advertisement firm to format an advertisement in order to ensure that its marketing approach conforms to local customs and preferences. Overall, most forms of advertising familiar to exporters are available in Singapore. The type of promotion will, of course, depend on the product and the target market. Flyers, billboards, store displays, television, radio, and newspapers are all effective marketing techniques. Market research is also recognized as an essential and effective marketing tool and is utilized with increasing frequency in Singapore.

Service and Customer Support

Good sales support and customer service are vital in Singapore. The market is so price competitive that support or customer service can make the difference between success and failure. Newcomers to this market should bear this in mind and plan accordingly.

Marketing in Singapore

MARKETING TIPS

- **Agent relations** There are very few trading firms that act solely as agents or importers.
- **Need for local attorney** Foreign legal firms cannot practice law in Singapore.
- **Credit terms** Standard credit terms are 30-60-90 days.
- **Small market size** Suppliers should note that most importers cannot handle single-product containers and must depend on (foreign) consolidators.
- **Special competitive factors** Pricing is extremely competitive, with service or after-sale support usually deciding the sale.
- **Communications.** Singapore is a major telecommunications center. International direct dial telephone is available to most countries. The local telephone system is fully automated. Singapore is linked to other countries by satellite communications, telefax, telegraph, and telegram services. Telecom, the Telecommunication Authority of Singapore, has an electronic telex exchange; its international telex service extends to more than 200 countries.
- **Trade fairs** Some of the more popular trade fairs include: the Asia Supermarket, for equipment and services for sale or use by wholesalers and retailers in the supermarket industry, usually held in September; and the Asian International Gift Fair, for corporate gifts, character merchandise, and consumer electronic devices, usually held in late Spring or early Summer.
- **Popular products** Products are bought for enjoyment as well as necessity in Singapore. Almost as many people own a television as own a refrigerator, and over 75 percent of the population owns a video-cassette recorder.
- **Direct marketing** Direct marketing is by far the most popular means of marketing, not only for consumer products like auto parts and accessories, but also among industries that want to avoid middlemen costs. Some advantages include a direct access to large consumer markets, but there are also disadvantages, such as extreme competition from other producers, because such stores market a large number of products.
- **Television and radio marketing** Rising family incomes make radio and television a very popular medium for advertising. The Singapore Broadcasting Corporation (SBC) is listened to by more than 70 percent of the population.
- **Publication advertising** Advertising in more popular foreign publications also reaches the Singapore market. Foreign consumer, news, and trade magazines have a wide circulation, particularly among the more affluent international business and professional customers, many headquartered in Singapore.
- **Planning** Planning is always a good idea; you can't succeed in marketing by accident, especially not in Singapore. Sometimes, however, the plan may be to use a shotgun approach.
- **Distributions** Increase the distributions of promotional brochures and technical data to potential buyers. That way, when your agent makes personal sales calls, his clients and potential customers won't be completely in the dark.
- **Demonstrations** Hold many demonstrations of your products. They are invaluable to customers.
- **Promptness** Be on time. Competition is so fierce that any delays will probably jeopardize your sales. If possible, stockpile your products in Singapore to ensure that your agent has a steady supply.
- **Agent help** Let your agent know you're backing him with whatever it takes. Make it easy to request help.

MARKETING CONTACT
Direct Marketing Association of Singapore
100 Beach Rd., #27-05, Shaw Towers
Singapore 0718
Tel: 29704385
Fax: 2998308

Business Culture

Greetings and Courtesies

Singapore is home to Chinese, Malays, and Indians, and people's behavior is shaped by their specific cultural backgrounds. Chinese lower their eyes slightly as a sign of respect upon meeting someone. Staring into the eyes of a Chinese might make them uncomfortable. Handshaking is the accepted greeting. Chinese usually shake hands very lightly, and a handshake may last as long as ten seconds. Face, a measure of one's dignity, is crucial to Chinese. Chinese are enormously sensitive to maintaining face in everything they do. Saying or doing anything that causes someone to lose face can instantly destroy a relationship and any business that might result from it. Never insult or criticize someone in front of others. Don't make fun of a Chinese, even if only as a joke. Malays are the second biggest ethnic group in Singapore. Primarily Muslims, they live by the teachings of the Koran. Their moral code is called *budi*, and is based on courtesy and respect (especially for elders and parents). When meeting foreigners, Malays often shake hands. You should wait for a Malay to initiate a handshake. If they don't, smile and slightly nod. Indians are the third largest group in Singapore's business world. Many Indians are Muslims, and follow the same code of behavior as Malays.

Business Ethic and Framework

The business arena is dominated by Chinese Singaporeans. Chinese behavior is largely determined by Confucianism, which teaches respect for superiors, duty to family, loyalty to friends, humility, sincerity, and courtesy. Among coworkers, people of higher status and age are respected by those beneath them, and deferred to in speech and action. Older foreign businesspeople are likely to be treated more seriously than younger ones. Never is business approached or treated as an issue separate and apart from the larger context of the personal relationships involved.

Decision Making

Consensus is very important to Singaporeans and they will probably require time for private discussion before making a decision. Chinese try to avoid saying no, for fear of causing embarrassment or losing face. Instead of directly saying no, they are likely to say something is inconvenient or suggest something else. They may also tell you what they think you want to hear, as a way of being polite. Pushing a matter after you've received an evasion will probably cause embarrassment, nor should you push for an immediate answer. Consensus will never be reached in the company of foreigners because all issues will not be voiced.

Women

Women are increasingly common in management positions, but Singapore is a very conservative society. All interactions between men and women should be completely professional. Any compliments should concern a woman's work, not her looks. Commenting on a woman's looks might be regarded as flirting, which is taboo and might cost a woman her job. When men and women meet, the man should let the woman initiate a handshake. If she doesn't, he should smile and nod. Most public physical contact between men and women is taboo. When foreign women deal with Malay men, they should dress conservatively, behave formally, avoid touching men (even foreign men) in front of Malays, and keep a proper distance.

Meetings

Asians are more at ease as a group than as individuals; they become uncomfortable when people speak for themselves or make statements that are not in harmony with the stated group view. One person, preferably your group's senior member, should be your spokesperson; avoid conflicting statements from other team members. It is a good idea to send a list of your representatives before the meeting, and to include their rank in your company. You should also request a similar list. Your team leader should enter the room first. Group leaders sit opposite each other, with others in descending order of importance. Small talk will come first. Business is addressed after people feel comfortable with each other. The head of the host team will deliver a short welcome speech, then turn the floor over to visitors. Asians prefer to hear a proposal as a broad overview, and then respond to issues point by point.

Business Attire

The tropical climate is hot and humid all year long. During winter, expect intense thunderstorms and torrential rain. Suits are standard, but should be of tropical-weight materials. Jackets are often discarded, so pick your shirts carefully. Women should dress very conservatively.

Cultural Cautions

DO'S

- Be aware of the importance of face in all your dealings with Singaporean Chinese.
- Be aware of Singapore's cultural mix. There is no one Singaporean mentality. To relate best to people, know if they are Chinese, Malay, or Indian, and learn about their specific cultures.
- The government is a powerful presence and exerts much control over people's lives. Social behavior is strictly regulated. Be familiar with and obey all laws. Behavior like spitting, dropping cigarettes, and not flushing a public toilet can result in heavy fines. Recently, the government banned the sale of chewing gum.

DON'TS

- Never do or say anything that could cause a Chinese to lose face.
- Never give government officials expensive gifts. Don't give any gift to an official unless the two of you have a strong personal relationship. The government feels gifts can result in corruption.
- Never kiss or hug someone of the opposite sex in a business situation.
- When entertaining Malays, never offer alcohol, pork, or meat not properly prepared.
- Don't give Malays or Indians anything with your left hand, or gesture toward someone with your left hand. The left hand is considered unclean.

CUSTOMS

- Gifts are important among Chinese, expressing friendship, symbolizing hopes for success, and showing appreciation. Do not give very expensive gifts, unless they are for a long-time associate who has been of great help. You can give one gift to an entire company. If one gift is given, it should be presented to the senior person. If you give several gifts, be sure they are all of equal value and don't omit anyone with whom you have a relationship.
- Business cards are important. When dealing with Chinese, a formal exchange of cards follows handshakes. It can be helpful to have your card printed with Chinese text on one side. If possible, get expert advice on the specific Chinese characters, as some ideograms are considered more favorable than others. Among Chinese, cards are given and received with both hands. Hold the card by the corners, between thumb and forefinger. When receiving a card, do not just put it in your pocket. Take a few moments to study the card, and respond to it with the proper respect.
- Malays believe the head is sacred. Do not touch the head of a Malay child (or adult).
- Muslims are forbidden contact with dogs, and consider pictures of dogs improper. Do not give a Muslim child a stuffed toy dog or anything printed with images of dogs.

OBSERVATIONS

- Singapore has the greatest concentration of ethnic Chinese in Southeast Asia. Since this group is a strong presence throughout the region, forming relationships with Singaporean Chinese is one of the best ways to become established in Southeast Asia.
- Many Indians do not approve of alcohol and tobacco.

NEGOTIATIONS

- Singaporeans are shrewd negotiators who can be both subtle and aggressive. Tactics include getting angry as a means of intimidation, flattery to get you off-guard, prolonging negotiations to wear you down, and seeming to not care about a deal, then suddenly making excessive demands.
- A common tactic is delaying major negotiations until you are about to leave the country, then making unreasonable demands.
- Be prepared to walk away. You will gain more from making it clear that you would rather have no deal at all than a bad deal.

Legal

Legal System

Singapore's civil and commercial law is based principally on English law although it has borrowed from India, Australia, and Malaysia as well.

Intellectual Property Rights

Patents Protection for patents was formerly available in Singapore for patents already registered through the British Patent Office or the European Patent Office. The patent law has been completely revised with the 1995 adoption of the Patent Act, bringing Singapore's patent protection more into line with international standards. Legal protections are adequately enforced.

Trademarks A trademark application takes approximately two years to process by the Registry of Trademarks. A trademark may be registered in any of 37 classes. Registration in one class will give protection only in that class. If a trademark is not registered but has acquired recognition through usage, the owner can seek a civil legal remedy against infringement.

Copyrights Until mid-1987, the UK Imperial Copyright Act applied in Singapore. In 1987, Singapore's own Copyright Act came into force. While based primarily on the Imperial Act, the new Act made a number of innovations. For example, it extends protection and criminal sanctions to computer software. Singapore strictly polices computer piracy. Protection for corporate copyrights is 50 years; for individuals, protection is for life plus 50 years.

Trade secrets Employee confidentiality is commonly protected under individual employment contracts. No specific law protects trade secrets.

Business Registration

Every entity that conducts business in Singapore must obtain clearance to use a specific business name and must then register with the Registrar of Companies and Businesses (RCB). Some entities must additionally obtain a license from a separate authority that regulates the particular industry or activity. For example, firms offering financial services must obtain approval from the Monetary Authority of Singapore, and certain manufacturers must be licensed by the Registrar of Manufactures. However, the term "conduct" is used in a technical sense to include activities related to the entity's primary business and undertaken frequently or at least on a regular basis. A business that carries on only limited activities in Singapore need not register.

Dispute Resolution

Singapore has a highly developed legal and court system. The courts actively encourage parties to settle their disputes through negotiation. The route to final adjudication is a relatively short one because the courts actively participate in moving cases along without unnecessary delay. The courts award compensatory damages or specific performance as appropriate. Various mechanisms are available to enforce court judgments and orders effectively.

Arbitration is governed by the Arbitration Act and is the main alternative to court proceedings. Many contracts provide for arbitration. The courts will almost always require parties to these agreements to arbitrate. The Singapore International Arbitration Centre was established with the aim of becoming a regional center for arbitration of commercial disputes. Interest in mediation and other alternative dispute resolution mechanisms is on the rise.

Notaries

Notaries are appointed by the Attorney General. A notary public may administer oaths or affirmations to confirm the due execution of any document, affidavit, or statutory declaration for use in any court or place outside Singapore, or any documents made by a master or crewmember of any vessel with respect to matters concerning that vessel. All such documentation must be in English or translated into English by a recognized High Court translator.

Labor

In general, no child under age 14 can be employed, except that a child who is older than 12 may be employed in nonindustrial, light work suited to the child's capacity. There is no minimum wage rate. Termination of employment is permitted with adequate notice, which is specified by law with respect to a particular industry or occupation. An employer who fails to meet the statutory notice guidelines may be required to pay some termination compensation. Employees have the right to join a registered trade union and to participate in union activities. A strike can only be commenced after a majority of the union members have consented by secret ballot.

Source: Chor Pee & Company, Singapore

Legal Matters

LEGAL BRIEFS

- **Fast entry** Presence can be quickly established by organizing a representative office. Such an office is limited, however, to the conduct of liaison and promotional activities; it cannot carry on business.
- **Preferred entity** The entity most commonly formed in Singapore—by foreign and domestic interests alike—is the private company limited by shares, which can be incorporated within two weeks of the approval of its name by the Registry of Companies. Minimum paid capital is S$20,000; minimum number of directors is two (all natural persons and one ordinarily a resident of Singapore); and 100-percent foreign ownership is permitted. The minimum cost of setting up a company, including registration fees, legal fees, and filing fees, is about S$3,500.
- **Maximum workweek** The law provides for a maximum workday of 8 hours and a workweek of 44 hours. Overtime pay must be paid for work in excess of those hours, and cumulative overtime may not exceed 72 hours per month.
- **Tax incentives** A number of incentives are set out in the Economic Incentives (exemption from tax) Act and are administered by the Economic Development Board. Singapore has recently introduced a goods and services tax of three percent. Compulsory registration is required with the GST department if annual turnover is over S$1 million. There are no capital gains taxes.
- **Legal advice** It is wise to hire local counsel in forming or registering a business in Singapore.
- **Joint ventures** Joint ventures are usually temporary enterprises, formed by two or more parties for the purpose of completing a specific project. They may be formed by either individuals or corporations.
- **Local managers** All foreign businesses are required to hire a resident manager to oversee operations, and branches of foreign corporations must employ at least two resident agents to be responsible for the company's actions and liabilities. They may be foreigners but they must be resident in Singapore.
- **Takeovers and mergers** The Code on Takeovers and Mergers supplements the statutory provisions in the Companies Act. The aim is to mandate good business principles and sound practices regarding takeovers and mergers. Investments by way of takeovers or mergers of companies listed on the Stock Exchange of Singapore (SES) are not unusual, but they must comply with the provisions laid down in the listing manual of the SES. Final approval comes from the Securities Industry Council, which together with the MAS, regulates the industry.
- **Political violence** There has been no politically motivated violence in Singapore for the past 24 years. Tough internal security laws give the government wide-ranging powers to keep in check any instability or civil disturbance.
- **Wages** Wages are higher than in most developing and newly industrializing countries in East Asia.
- **Labor-management relations** There has only been one strike in Singapore since 1978, and labor-management relations are excellent. Industrial disputes are usually settled through mediation by the government.
- **Unions** Only about 15 percent of Singapore's work force is unionized.
- **International agreements** Singapore is a member of GATT/WTO; ASEAN; International Convention on the Settlement of Investment Disputes between States and Nationals of other States; New York Convention on the Recognition and Enforcement of Foreign Arbitral Awards; Convention on the Taking of Evidence Abroad in Civil or Commercial Matters; Patent Cooperation Treaty; Paris Convention; and Budapest Treaty; and ATA Carnet Convention.

LEGAL CONTACT

Chor Pee & Company
50 Raffles Place
18th Floor, Shell Tower
Singapore 0104
Tel: 220-1911 Fax: 224-4118

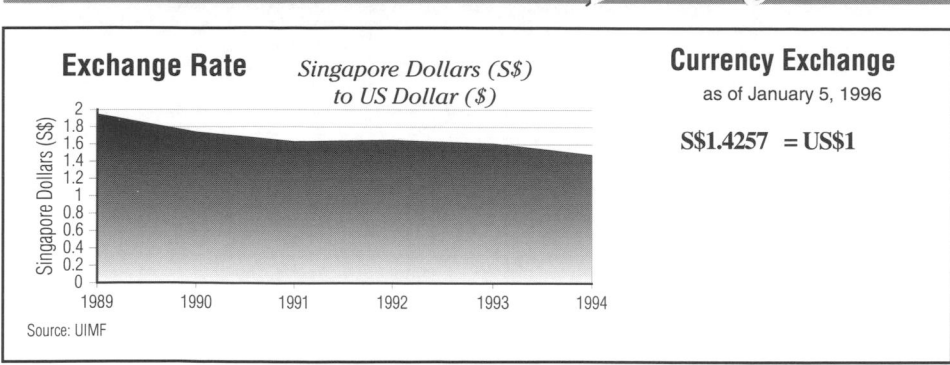

Source: UIMF

Money Matters

BITS AND PIECES

- **Corporate income tax** All companies, resident and nonresident, are taxed on all domestic income and income outside Singapore if received in Singapore.
- **Capital gains** There is no taxation of capital gains in Singapore.
- **Anti-avoidance legislation** The Singapore Revenue Commission can substitute prices if transactions with a foreign affiliate are entered into at an artificial price.
- **Capital transfers** There are no restrictions or requirements regarding capital transfers.
- **Gold** Residents and nonresidents alike can hold, buy, or sell gold freely.
- **Capital flows** The government imposes no restrictions on international capital flows into or out of Singapore.
- **Internationalizing the currency** The Monetary Authority of Singapore (MAS) requires all foreign and domestic banks to observe its policy of discouraging the internationalization of the Singapore dollar.
- **Incentive schemes** Some incentive schemes in Singapore include the Product Development Assistance Scheme to encourage local product design and enhance Singapore's technological base, and the Research and Development Assistance Scheme, designed to encourage medium-term research and development projects.

Currency

The currency of Singapore is the Singapore dollar (S$), which is divided into 100 cents.

Foreign Exchange

There are no formal exchange regulations, but the Monetary Authority of Singapore (MAS) is responsible for all exchange matters. All foreign currency futures are traded at the Singapore International Monetary Exchange. Banks can hedge their rate risk through a forward foreign exchange transaction. There are no taxes on purchases or sales of foreign exchange.

Capital Transfers

There are no differences between resident and nonresident accounts. Nonresidents can bring in or take out any amount of currency without requirements or restrictions. There are no restrictions or regulations for payments for invisibles. Receipts don't need to be surrendered and may be disposed of freely.

Investment Incentives

Singapore has one of the world's most open investment regimes. The primary government agency promoting foreign investment is the Economic Development Board (EDB). It locates sectors with a high potential to contribute to the economy and assists foreign and domestic firms investing in new technology, training, and product development activities. Some incentive schemes include the Product Development Assistance Scheme and the Research and Development Assistance Scheme. Government policies encourage local firms to form strategic partnerships with multinational corporations, especially in high-technology activities. Several multinationals consider Singapore the gateway to the fast expanding South and East Asian markets. Investment regulations are transparent and the bureaucracy is not oppressive.

Investment Restrictions

Foreign companies face restrictions in some sectors, including banking and insurance. In banking, for example, the 22 foreign banks with full licenses cannot open new branches, freely relocate existing ones, or operate off-premise automatic teller machines. With one exception, the Stock Exchange of Singapore (SES) restricts membership to firms with a maximum of 49 percent foreign equity. The seven completely foreign-owned "international members" of the SES have limited voting rights and limited input into SES policy decisions.

BANKING CONTACTS

Bank of Singapore Ltd.
101 Cecil St. #01-02, Tong Eng Bldg.
Singapore 0106
Tel: 2239266, Fax: 2247407, Telex: 24179

Chung Khiaw Bank Ltd.
10 Anson Rd. #01-01, International Plaza
Singapore 0207
Tel: 2228622, Telex: 22027

DBS Bank (Development Bank of Singapore)
6 Shenton Way, DBS Bldg.
Singapore 0106
Tel: 2201111, Fax: 2211306, Telex: 24455

Monetary Authority of Singapore (MAS)
MAS Bldg., 10 Shenton Way
Singapore 0207
Tel: 2255577, Fax: 2299229, Telex: 28174

Bank of America
78 Shenton Way #19-00
Singapore 0207
Tel: 2236688
Fax: 223310

Hongkong and Shanghai Banking Corporation
21 Collyer Quay #19-00
Hong Kong Bank Bldg.
Singapore 0104
Tel: 5357655
Fax: 2250663

Overseas-Chinese Banking Corp. Ltd.
2 Shenton Way #01-01, ICB Bldg.
Singapore 0106
Tel: 2211711, Fax: 5337955, Telex: 21209

Overseas Union Bank Ltd.
1 Raffles Place, OUB Centre
Singapore 0104
Tel: 5338686, Fax: 5332293, Telex: 24475

Singapore Merchant Banker's Association
24 Raffles Pl. #16-02, Clifford Centre
Singapore 0104
Tel: 5327565, Fax: 5323390

The Association of Banks in Singapore
10 Shenton Way, #12-08, MAS Bldg.
Singapore 0207
Tel: 2244300, Fax: 2241785, Telex: 29291

United Overseas Bank Ltd.
1 Banham St. #01-00, UOB Bldg.
Singapore 0104
Tel: 5339898, Fax: 5342334, Telex: 21539

TAXATION	At a Glance		
Taxation requires sophisticated knowledge of complex rules and regulations specific to each country. The information presented here is from the Ernst & Young Corporate Tax Guide and Directory, available from the Ernst & Young accounting office in your country, or from: Ernst & Young Mail Address: P.O. Box 384 Singapore 9007, Singapore Street Address: 10 Collyer Quay #21-01 Ocean Building, Singapore 0104 Tel: 5357777 Cable: Ernstaudit, Singapore Telex: RS22172 Ans bk ERNST Fax: 5327662	Corporate Income Tax Rate (%) (a) 27		
	Capital Gains Tax Rate (%)....................................0		
	Branch Tax Rate (%) (a)......................................27		
	Withholding Tax (%)		
	Dividends..0		
	Interest..27		
	Royalties from Patents, Know-how, etc...............27		
	Branch Remittance Tax 0		
	Net Operating Losses (Years)		
	Carryback 0		
	Carryforward ....Unlimited		
	(a) Numerous tax exemptions and reductions are available.		

Business Travel

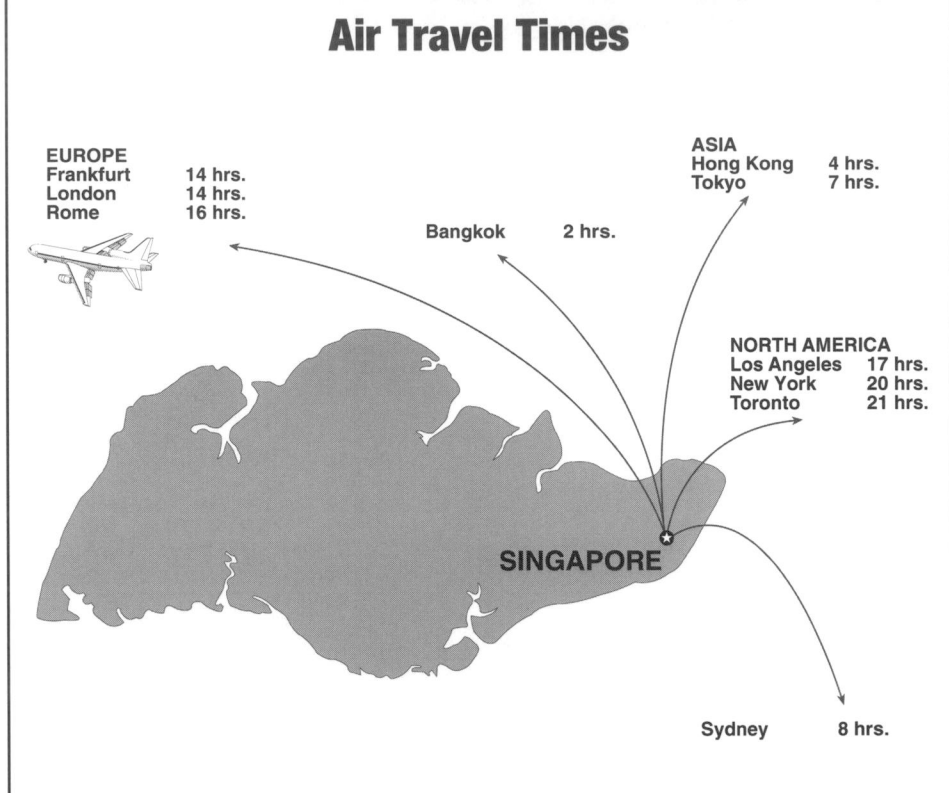

Air Travel Times

EUROPE
Frankfurt 14 hrs.
London 14 hrs.
Rome 16 hrs.

Bangkok 2 hrs.

ASIA
Hong Kong 4 hrs.
Tokyo 7 hrs.

NORTH AMERICA
Los Angeles 17 hrs.
New York 20 hrs.
Toronto 21 hrs.

SINGAPORE

Sydney 8 hrs.

COMMUNICATIONS

Telephones The phone system in Singapore is highly advanced and operates 24 hours a day. International direct dial connects to major cities around the world. Public phones are very common. Station-to-station calls, credit card calls, and collect calls can easily be made to and from Singapore. Hotels will charge an additional 80 percent for calls made overseas. To avoid this use international phones at the airport or post offices.

Fax Fax service is also widely available with state-of-the-art equipment. All hotels offer this service and telegram and telex services.

Post office Postal service is very reliable, particularly from the large hotels.

BEST TRAVEL BOOKS

Malaysia, Singapore, & Brunei, Lonely Planet Travel Survival Kit. Over 400 pages of useful information.
Fielding Worldwide, The Adventurer's Guide to the Wonders of Malaysia and Singapore. 300 pages.
All-Asia Travel Guide, Southeast Asia, Volume One. Far Eastern Economic Review.
Culture Shock, A Guide to Customs and Etiquette, Singapore & Malaysia.
The Travellers Guide to Asian Customs and Manners. Elizabeth Devine & Nancy Braganti. An invaluable guide for people not wanting to put foot in mouth.
Wall Street Journal Guide to Business Travel, Hong Kong and Singapore.
Four Dragons Guidebook. The indispensable guide to Hong Kong, Singapore, Thailand, Taiwan. Volume One. Fredric M. Kaplan.
Insight Pocket Guides, Singapore.

TELEPHONE NUMBERS

If you are calling from outside Singapore you will need to add the country code [65] and any other international dialing requirements from within your country.

- Ministry of Trade and Industry 225-9911
- Local Directory 103
- Time of Day 1711
- Telecom Customer Service 734-3344
- Post Office Information 533-0234
- DHL International 334-8911
- Federal Express 743-2626
- Singapore Immigration Department 530-1182
- Bus Information 287-2727
- SABS Taxi Service 250-0700
- Singapore Commuter 474-7707
- Limousine 2353111
- Chauffeur 2233668
- Avis - Airport 5428855
- Hertz 7344646
- National (Hong Seh Motors) 3888444
- Thrifty 5427288
- Police 999
- Ambulance/Fire/Emergency 995
- Singapore Chamber of Commerce 337-8381
- Commercial Services and Library 338-9722
- Customs and Excise Department.............. 272-8222
- Economic Development Board.................. 336-2288

Credit Card Information
Lost or stolen credit cards (call collect to the US, regardless of which country the card was issued in).
- Amex ....[1] (919) 333-3211
- Diner's Club.................................[1] (303) 799-1504
- MasterCard ....[1] (314) 275-6690
- Visa ....[1] (410) 581-7931

Travelogue

WORKWEEK

Offices Monday-Friday 9:00 am to 1:00 pm, 2:30 pm to 5:00 or 6:00 pm. Saturday 9:00 am to noon.
Banks Monday-Friday 10:00 am to 3:00 pm. Saturday 9:30 a.m. to 11:30 p.m.
Government Monday-Friday 9:00 am to 1:00 pm, 2:00 pm to 5:00 pm. Saturday 8:00 am to 1:00 pm.
Retail Monday-Saturday 9:00 am to 6:00 pm. It is common for stores relying on tourists to stay open later in the evenings.

HOLIDAYS

Holidays 1996
January 1 New Year's Day
January 21, February 19 Chinese New Year's
February 21 Hari Raya Puasa*
April 5 Good Friday*
May 1 Singapore Labor Day
April/May Vesak Day *
June/July Hari Raya Jaji *
August 9 Singapore National Day
October Deepavali *
December 25 Christmas
*Dates vary from year to year.

VISA AND PASSPORT

Visas are not required for stays up to 90 days. A 14-day visitor permit is issued upon arrival, which can be extended for an additional 14 days with proof of adequate funds and an onward ticket. It is forbidden to bring chewing gum into Singapore.

DEPARTURE FORMALITIES

An airport departure tax will be collected for all travelers on international and domestic flights. Export permits are necessary for valuable jewelry, weapons, or animals. There are no limits set on the amount of Singapore and foreign notes, traveler's checks; and letters of credit brought into or out of the country.

IMMUNIZATION

No proof of vaccination is required unless you have come from an infected area within the past six days. African and South American countries may be considered infected.

TIPPING

Tipping is prohibited at the airport and in most hotels and restaurants. It is not customary to tip taxi drivers, though it will not be refused by the driver.

CRIME

Incidents of crime are minimal with the worst threat being a pickpocket. Be aware that jaywalking, spitting, chewing gum, and not flushing in a public restroom are all punishable by fines of S$500. Caning is mandatory for males convicted of vandalism and immigration violations.

INFRASTRUCTURE

Changi International Airport has been rated the best in the world. Taxi and bus service is available between downtown and the airport. City buses are easy to use and inexpensive, generally crowded at rush hour, but faster than taxis because they drive in special bus lanes. Exact fare is paid as you board. Keep the ticket issued in order to return it to the driver at the end of the ride. Express trains and buses run to Kuala Lumpur and Bangkok. The preferred means of transportation is by taxi though taxis are no longer inexpensive. They are strictly regulated by the government so all will be equipped with meters. There are extra charges for additional passengers, luggage, travel in the downtown Restricted Zone, and travel between midnight and six am. The subway system is called the MRT and is clean and well lighted. One line runs north-south and the other runs east-west. Maps are easy to read and service is frequent.

NATIONAL TOURIST OFFICE

Singapore Tourist Promotion Board
36-04 Raffles City Towers
250 North Bridge St.
Tel: 3396622
Fax: 3399423

GOVERNMENT AGENCIES

Civil Aviation Authority of Singapore
PO Box 1
Singapore 9181
Tel: 5421122
Fax: 5421231

Construction Industry Development Board
National Development
Annex A, 3rd Storey
9 Maxwell Road
Singapore 0106
Tel: 2256711
Fax: 2257301

Customs & Excise Department
1 Maritime Square #03-01 & #10-01
World Trade Centre
Singapore 0409
Tel: 2728222
Fax: 2779090

Economic Development Board
250 North Bridge Rd. #24-00
Raffles City Tower
Singapore 0617
Tel: 3362288
Fax: 339607

Information Communication Institute of Singapore
1 Hillcrest Rd. #08-00
Singapore
Tel: 4676000
Fax: 4676601

Ministry of Communications
460 Alexandra Rd., PSA Bldg. #39-00
Singapore 0511
Tel: 2707988
Fax: 2799734

Ministry of Community Development
512 Thomson Rd., MCD Bldg.
Singapore 1129
Tel: 2589595

Ministry of Defence
3 Maritime Sq. #04-00
Singapore 1024
Tel: 4741155
Fax: 7620112

Ministry of Education
Kay Siang Rd.
Singapore 1024
Tel: 4739111
Fax: 4756128

Ministry of Finance
8 Shenton Way, Treasury Bldg.
Singapore 0106
Tel: 2259911
Telex: 34371

Ministry of Finance
Central Procurement Office
Depot Road
Singapore 0410
Tel: 2721655
Fax: 2790524

Ministry of Finance
Registry of Companies & Businesses
10 Anson Rd. #05-01/15
Singapore 0207
Tel: 2278551
 Fax: 2251676

Ministry of Foreign Affairs
250 North Bridge Rd. #07-00
Raffles City Tower
Singapore 0617
Tel: 3361177
Fax: 3394330

Ministry of Health
16 College Rd., College of Medicine Bldg.
Singapore 0316
Tel: 2237777
Fax: 2241677

Ministry of Health
Pharmaceutical Dept.
2 Jalan Bukit Merah
Singapore 0316
Tel: 2213014
Fax: 2226797

Ministry of Information and the Arts
Department of Information
460 Alexandra Rd., PSA Bldg.
Singapore 0511
Tel: 2707988
Fax: 2799784

Ministry of Information and the Arts
Department of the Arts
512 Thompson Rd., MCD Bldg.
Singapore 1129
Tel: 2589595
Fax: 3506118

Ministry of Labour
18 Havelock Rd. #07-01
Singapore 0105
Tel: 5341511
Fax: 5344840

Ministry of the Environment
40 Scotts Rd., Environment Bldg.
Singapore 0922
Tel: 7327733
Fax: 7319456

Ministry of Trade and Industry
#33-00 Treasury Bldg.
Singapore 0106
Tel: 2259911
Fax: 3209260

National Computer Board
71 Science Park Dr., NCB Bldg.
Singapore 0511
Tel: 7782211
Fax: 7789641

Port of Singapore Authority
460 Alexandra Rd., PSA Bldg.
Singapore 0511
Tel: 2747111
Fax: 2744677

Singapore Broadcasting Corporation
Caldecott Hill, Andrew Rd.
Singapore
Tel: 2560401

Singapore Trade Development Board
230 Victoria St. #07-00
Bugis Junction Office Tower
Singapore 0718
Tel: 3376228
Fax: 3376898, 3376838

Telecommunication Authority of Singapore
31 Exeter Rd. #05-00 Comcentre
Singapore 0923
Tel: 7343344, 7387788
Fax: 7328428, 7330073

WORLD TRADE CENTER

World Trade Centre Singapore
1 Maritime Square #09-72
Singapore 0409
Tel: 3212783, 3212103, 3212791
Fax: 2740721

BUSINESS AND TRADE ORGANIZATIONS

Association of Small & Medium Enterprises
Blk. 139, Kim Tian Rd. #02-00
Singapore 0316
Tel: 2712566
Fax: 2711257

Federation of Merchants' Association
25 Genting Rd. #08-01
Singapore
Tel: 7417822

International Business Women's Association
c/o C K Woo & Company
Orchard PO Box 23
Singapore 9123

Tel: 3384070

International Procurement Management Association of Singapore
111 North Bridge Rd. #20-03
Peninsula Plaza
Singapore 0617
Tel: 7384210
Fax: 3389609

Singapore Chinese Chamber of Commerce & Ind.
47 Hill St. #09-00
Singapore 0617
Tel: 3378381
Fax: 3390605

Singapore Federation of Chambers of Commerce & Industry
47 Hill St. #03-01, SCCCI Bldg.
Singapore 0617
Tel: 3389761/2
Fax: 3395630

Singapore Indian Chamber of Commerce
101 Cecil St. #23-01, Tong Eng Bldg.
Singapore 0106
Tel: 2222505
Fax: 2231707

Singapore International Chamber of Commerce
6 Raffles Quay #05-00, Denmark House
Singapore 0104
Tel: 2241255
Fax: 2242785

Singapore Malay Chamber of Commerce
10 Anson Rd. #24-07, International Plaza
Singapore 0207
Tel: 2211066, 2230347
Fax: 2235811

Singapore Manufacturers' Association
20 Orchard Rd., SMA House
Singapore 0923
Tel: 3388787
Fax: 3385385

Air-conditioning & Refrigeration Association
58 Kensington Park Rd.
Singapore 1955
Tel: 2885491

Bankers' Association [Singapore Merchant]
24 Raffles Pl. #16-02, Clifford Centre
Singapore 0104
Tel: 5327565
Fax: 5323390

Book Exporters & Importers Council
c/o Chopmen Publisher
865 Mountbatten Rd. #05-28/29
Katong Shopping Centre
Singapore
Tel: 3441495
Fax: 3440180

Building Materials Suppliers' Association [Singapore]
426 Race Course Rd.
Singapore 0821
Tel: 2984660

Computer Society [Singapore]
71 Science Park Dr.
Singapore
Tel: 7783901
Fax: 7788221

Contractors Association Ltd. [Singapore]
1 Bt. Merah Lane 2, Construction House
Singapore 0315
Tel: 2789577
Fax: 2733977

Direct Marketing Association of Singapore
100 Beach Rd. #27-05, Shaw Towers
Singapore 0718
Tel: 2970438
Fax: 2998308

Electrical Contractors Association [Singapore]
315 Outram Rd. #10-09A, Tan Boon Liat Bldg.
Singapore 0316
Tel: 2263216
Fax: 2237568

Electronic Industries in Singapore [Association of]
470 North Bridge Rd. #03-09
Singapore
Tel: 3374643
Fax: 3399341

Freight Forwarders Association [Singapore]
7500A Beach Rd. #13-314, The Plaza
Singapore 0719
Tel: 2964645
Fax: 2922504

Furniture Manufacturers' & Traders' Association
16C 4/F., Geylang Lor 37, NTWU Bldg.
Singapore 1438
Tel: 7441600, 7441421
Fax: 7452917

Granite Quarry Owners & Employers Association
141 Cecil St. #05-00, Tung Ann Association Bldg.
Singapore 0106
Tel: 2211560

Grocer's Association [Singapore]
33A Lor 15 Geylang
Singapore
Tel: 7451821

Industrial Automation Association [Singapore]
151 Chin Swee Rd. #03-13, Manhattan House
Singapore 0316
Tel: 7346911
Fax: 235572

Marine Industries [Association of Singapore]
1 Maritime Sq. #09-50, World Trade Centre
Singapore 0409
Tel: 2707883
Fax: 2731867

Medical Practitioners of Singapore [Assn of]
Alumni Medical Centre
2 College Rd.
Singapore 0316
Tel: 2230901

Microcomputer Trade Association
211 Henderson Rd. #01-01
Singapore
Tel: 2782855

Pharmaceutical Industries [Singapore Assn of]
30 Shaw Rd., 5/F., Roche Bldg.
Singapore 1336
Tel: 2868277
Fax: 2802167

Rattan Industry Association [Singapore]
12 Lor 24A Geylang
Singapore
Tel: 7441853

Ready-Mixed Concrete Association of Singapore
Blk. 1 Thomson Rd. #03-332E
Singapore
Tel: 2568359

Real Estate Developers' Association of Singapore
190 Clemenceau Ave. #07-01
Singapore Shopping Centre
Singapore 0923
Tel: 3366655
Fax: 3372217

Restaurant Association of Singapore
11 Dhoby Ghaut #04-03, Cathay Bldg.
Singapore 0922
Tel: 3383774
Fax: 3390903

Rubber Association of Singapore
79 Robinson Rd. #14-01, CPF Bldg.
Singapore 0106
Tel: 2219022
Fax: 2241641, 2215316

Shipping Association [Singapore National]
456 Alexandra Rd. #02-02, NOL Bldg.
Singapore 0511
Tel: 2733574, 2783464
Fax: 2745079 Telex: 24021

Ship Suppliers [Singapore Association of]
1 Colombo Court #07-19
Singapore 0617
Tel: 3367755
Fax: 3390329

Textile & Garment Manufacturers' Association of Singapore
47 Beach Rd. #06-01/02
Singapore
Tel: 3372022
Fax: 3389179

NEWSPAPERS

Asian Wall Street Journal
2/F. AIA Bldg., 1 Stubbs Rd.
GPO Box 9825
Hong Kong
Tel: 25737121
Fax: 28345291

Business Times
Times House
390 Kim Seng Rd.
Singapore 0923
Tel: 7370011
Fax: 7335271

International Herald Tribune
7/F. Malaysia Bldg., 50 Gloucester Rd.
Wanchai, Hong Kong
Tel: 28610616
Fax: 28613073

New Paper
News Centre
82 Genting Lane
Singapore 1334
Tel: 7444875
Fax: 7449949

Shin Min Daily News
(Chinese)
News Centre
82 Genting Lane
Singapore 1334
Tel: 7444875
Fax: 7449949

The Straits Times
Singapore Newspaper Services Pte. Ltd.
Circulation Department
82 Genting Lane
Singapore 1334
Tel: 7444875

PERIODICALS

ASEAN Business Quarterly
Asia Research Pte. Ltd.
PO Box 91, Alexandra Post Office
Singapore

ASEAN Economic Bulletin
Institute of Southeast Asian Studies
Heng Mui Keng Terrace
Singapore 0511
Tel: 7780955
Fax: 7781735

Asian Finance
3rd Fl., Hollywood Center
233 Hollywood Road
Hong Kong
Tel: 28155221
Fax: 28504437

Economic Bulletin
Singapore International Chamber of Commerce
6 Raffles Quay #05-00, Denmark House
Singapore 0104
Tel: 2241255
Fax: 2242785

Singapore Business
Times Trade Directories Pte. Ltd.
Times Centre, 1 New Industrial Rd.
Singapore 1953
Tel: 2848844
Fax: 2881186

Singapore Economic Review
Department of Economics and Statistics
University of Singapore
Singapore 0511
Tel: 7723941
Fax: 7752646

Singapore Management Review
Singapore Institute of Management
3/F., Thong Teck Bldg.
Scotts Rd.
Singapore 0922
Tel: 7378866

AD AGENCIES

CR & Grey Advertising
No. 20 Maxwell Rd.
#02-01 Maxwell House
Singapore 0106, Singapore
Tel: 225-0998
Fax: 225-6995

DDB Needham Worldwide Pte. Ltd.
11A/B Stanley St.
0106 Singapore
Tel: 323-4811
Fax: 323-4822
Telex: 22247

Dentsu, Young,& Rubicam
The Concourse, #30-00
300 Beach Rd.
Singapore 0719
Tel: 295-4816
Fax: 294-0864

McCann-Erickson (Singapore) Private Limited
03-00 Int'l. Bldg.
360 Orchard Rd.
Singapore 0923
Tel: 7379911
Fax: 7371455
Telex: 21663

Ogilvy & Mather
Ste. 11-01, World Trade Ctr.
One Maritime Sq.
Singapore 0409
Tel: 2738011 Fax: 2742156

INTERNET ADDRESSES

Usenet group(s):
soc.culture.singapore

Singapore Online Guide
http://www.ncb.gov.sg:80/sog/sog.html

Asia ONE Media Page
http://www.asia1.com.sg/

Singapore Trade Development Board
http://www.tdb.gov.sg/

Singapore ONLINE (TM)
http://www.singapore.com/

Singapore Business Times
http://www.asia1.com.sg/bt/pages/bt.html

Singapore International Chamber of Commerce
http://www1.usa1.com/~ibnet/sicchp.html

Slovakia

Slovak Republic

Economy

Overview

Slovakia faces the considerable challenge of moving toward a modern market economy. To do so it must create new government institutions and rebuild its declining industrial base with limited resources. Slovakia contributed only 25 percent of the former Czechoslovakia's GDP and its disadvantaged economy has contracted further as a result of the demise of the USSR. Between 1991 and 1993 total industrial production fell by over 50 percent, and exports to its primary market, the Czech Republic, have declined by over one third. Although GDP has declined less rapidly in the past two years, Slovakia's negative growth rates are expected to continue in the short to medium term. Future growth depends on further market liberalization and the government is placing much emphasis on its strategic location between Western and Eastern Europe as a means to promote business.

Trade

In the past two years Slovakia has experienced a significant decline in the total value of its foreign trade. Eastern European nations are the primary markets for its exports, and it buys the majority of its imports from the same sources. Unfortunately, most of these economies are themselves struggling, and are unable to provide the markets necessary to support Slovakia's desired export growth. The Czech Republic is the largest single source of both its imports and exports, followed by the CIS republics, Germany, Poland, and Austria. Although foreign trade is critical to economic growth, Slovakia is right now concerned primarily with developing its domestic economy.

Sectors

Agriculture Slovakia is traditionally an agricultural country and this sector continues to play a central role in its economy. It is largely self-sufficient in food production and its principal agricultural goods include wheat, barley, potatoes, hops, sugar beets, and livestock.

Industry Industry has become the primary contributor to Slovakia's GDP and a major source of employment in the country, despite a sharp fall in production in recent years. Much of the decline is attributed to the breakup of the Eastern Bloc and output has fallen rapidly in traditionally strong subsectors such as the armaments industry. Major industries include coal, construction, chemicals, clothing, steel, iron ore, copper, plastics, and resins. Many firms are being privatized, but they will have to contend in the short run with the problems of aging machinery and technology in order to compete in international markets.

Services Much of the services sector remains underdeveloped as the country focuses on rebuilding industry and sustaining agricultural output.

Trends

The Slovak government has been more reluctant than its Czech Republic neighbor to fully embrace open market policies. Efforts to privatize part of its state-owned and controlled economy have met with some success but they have also resulted in lower output, unemployment, and inflation. Little or no growth is expected in the short term and long-term prospects depend on the success of market liberalization and the government's ability to attract foreign investment.

At a Glance

THE COUNTRY

Location Eastern Europe; shares boundaries with Poland on the north and Ukraine on the east.
Terrain Rugged mountains in the central and northern part of the country, and lowlands in the south; several lakes and valleys in the north.
Climate Continental, with hot summers and cold winters. Rainfall averages 49 cm, although it can exceed 200 cm annually in the north.

THE PEOPLE

Population 5,400,000
Ethnic Composition
Slovak.. 85%
Hungarians 11.5%
Romany (gypsies)................................... 1.5%
Ruthenians... 1%
Czechs 1%
The Gypsy population in eastern Slovakia is sizeable and underreported.
Religious composition
Roman Catholic 74%
Other major churches include the Slovak Evangelical Church of the Augsburg Confession and the Orthodox Church.
Languages Slovak is the official language. Some minority languages may be used for official business.
Education and literacy Estimated adult literacy is 99 percent. Education is compulsory for 10 years, until the age of 18. Slovakia also has 13 universities.
Labor force
By occupation: agriculture 11%, industry 43%, and unemployed 14.5%.

COUNTRY FACTS

Political and legal The 1992 constitution calls for a 150-member legislature. The courts are constitutionally independent from other branches of government, and are beginning to separate into commercial, civil, and criminal branches. The Constitutional Court is the highest judicial body, and reviews both the constitutionality of laws and the decisions of lower courts.
Telephone Local and long distance telephone, telegraph, and telex services are available. International dialling code: [42]. City codes: Bratislava (7), Presov (91).
Transportation There are over 3,600 kilometers of railroads. Roads are available and in moderate condition. Slovakia relies on the Danube for transportation of goods. Air service is primarily through Ivanka Airport at Bratislava.
Environment Slovakia suffers from air, water, and land pollution, mostly caused by industry and mining. Sulfur dioxide emissions were reported at the highest levels in Europe. Current issues are deforestation (75 percent of the trees are affected), acid rain, and erosion.
Media There is one radio station, Slovak Radio Bratislava, and one television station, Slovak Television. There are 12 major daily newspapers in Bratislava and one each in Kosice and Banská Bystrica. Most are published by the government.
Health More than 90 percent of children are immunized for various diseases, including tuberculosis and polio. Life expectancy is 72 years for both males and females.

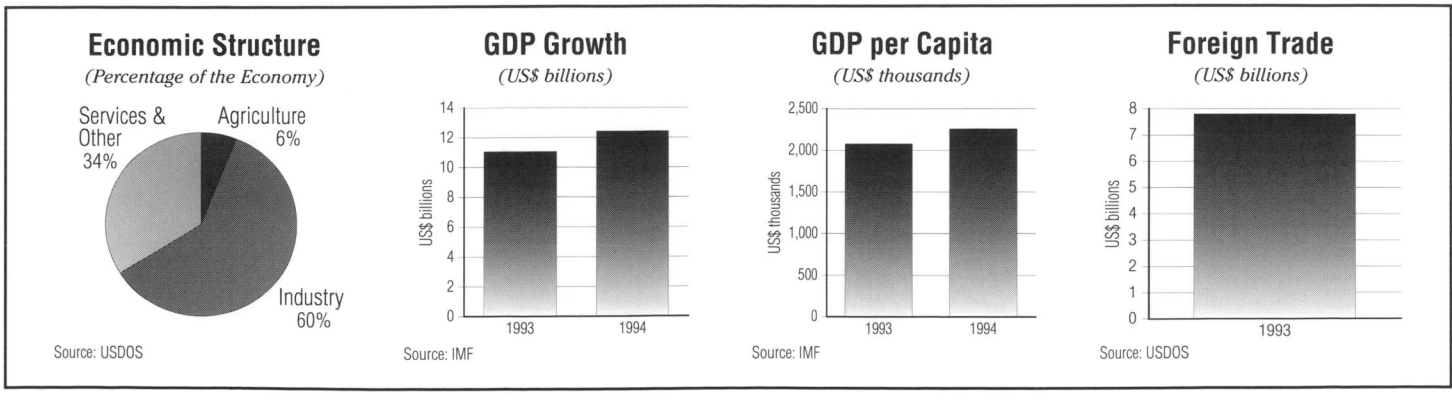

Economic Structure
(Percentage of the Economy)
Services & Other 34%
Agriculture 6%
Industry 60%
Source: USDOS

GDP Growth
(US$ billions)
1993 1994
Source: IMF

GDP per Capita
(US$ thousands)
1993 1994
Source: IMF

Foreign Trade
(US$ billions)
1993
Source: USDOS

COMMUNICATIONS

Telephones Dialing out from Slovakia may require international operator. International calls are easiest at the post office or from telephones with a globe on top. Pay phones require deposit of coin or phone card for dial tone. The mobile phone dialing prefix is 0901.

Fax Facsimile services are available at larger hotels for both faxing and telegraph. Faxes may be sent or received at Slovak Telecommunications, Jaroslova Str.1, Bratislava.

Post office The mail service is quite modern. Stamps can be purchased at post offices and major hotels.

BEST TRAVEL BOOKS

The Czech Republic and Slovakia. Fodor's Travel Publications.

Language, Values and the Slovak Nation, Tibor Pichler and Januarya Gasparikova, eds., 1993. Cultural Heritage and Contemporary Change Series, Volume 5, Council for Research in Values and Philosophy.

Fodor's A Travel Guide, The Czech Republic and Slovkia. An indispensable guide for travelers who know that there's more to these two republics than irresistible Prague. 500 pages.

Berlitz Business Travel Guide, Europe. Concise economic details, successful trip planning, background information on people and cities, useful facts and addresses.

NATIONAL TOURIST OFFICES

InterHotels Tourist Service (ITS)
Kocelova 9
Bratislava
Tel: (7) 202 82 15
Fax: (7) 215 772

Bratislava Information Service (BIS)
Panska 18
Bratislava
Tel: (7) 333 715, 334 370

USEFUL TELEPHONE NUMBERS

If you are calling from outside Slovakia, you will need to add the country code [42] and any other international dialing requirements from within your country.

- International Dialing Information 0139
- Int'l Operator 0131, 0132, 0133, 0134, 0135
- Inter-city operator 0108
- Police 158
- Fire 150, 490444
- Ambulance 155, (7) 494949
- Directory Assistance 120, 121
- Telegrams 127
- Lost Property Department .... (7) 34611
- Tourist Information .... (7) 333715, 334370
- InterHotels Tourist Service (ITS) .... (7) 2028215
- Translations .... (7) 334415
- Railroad .... (7) 2044484, 498275
- Taxi .... (7) 302111

Credit Card Information
Lost or stolen credit cards (call collect to the US, regardless of which country the card was issued in).

- Amex ....[1] (919) 333-3211
- Diner's Club ....[1] (303) 799-1504
- MasterCard ....[1] (314) 275-6690
- Visa ....[1] (410) 581-7931

INFRASTRUCTURE

Slovakia is a moderately developed European nation undergoing profound economic and political changes. Tourist facilities are not as developed as those found in Western Europe and many of the goods and services taken for granted in other European countries are not yet available. Rail services are available for travel.

CRIME

Slovakia has a low rate of violent crime. However, there has been an increase in street crime such as pickpocketing, especially at night near major tourist sites.

Travelogue

WORKWEEK

Government Monday-Friday, 8:30 am to 7:30 pm. Saturday and Sunday closed.
Banks Monday-Friday, 8:00 am to 6:00 pm.
Commerce and Industry Monday-Friday, 8:30 am to 6:30 pm. Closed Saturday and Sunday.
Retail Monday-Friday, 9:00 am to 5:00 pm.

HOLIDAYS

Holidays 1996
January 1 New Year's Day
April 7-8 Easter Sunday and Monday
May 1 International Labor Day
July 5 Cyril and Methodius Day
September 15 Virgin Mary Day
November 1 All Saints Day
December 25-26 Christmas
In addition, commerce and public transport virtually close down the week between Christmas and New Year's.

VISA AND PASSPORT

Visas are not required for stays up to 30 days for US and Western European citizens. Canadian citizens must get a visa in advance (Can$50). Foreigners must have a valid passport, onward tickets, and sufficient daily funds (at least US$15 for every day they plan to spend in the country).

IMMUNIZATION

No International vaccination certification is required unless you are arriving from an infected area.

TIPPING

Taxi: 10 percent. Porters: SK30 per piece. Hotels: none. Restaurants: five to 15 percent. Barbers, beauticians: five to 10 percent. Small Services: SK20.

Foreign Trade

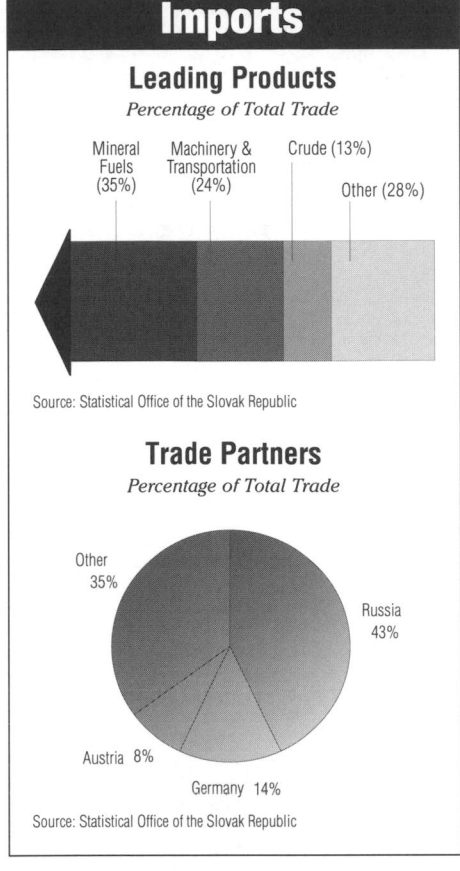

Imports

Leading Products
Percentage of Total Trade

Mineral Fuels (35%)
Machinery & Transportation (24%)
Crude (13%)
Other (28%)

Source: Statistical Office of the Slovak Republic

Trade Partners
Percentage of Total Trade

Other 35%
Russia 43%
Austria 8%
Germany 14%

Source: Statistical Office of the Slovak Republic

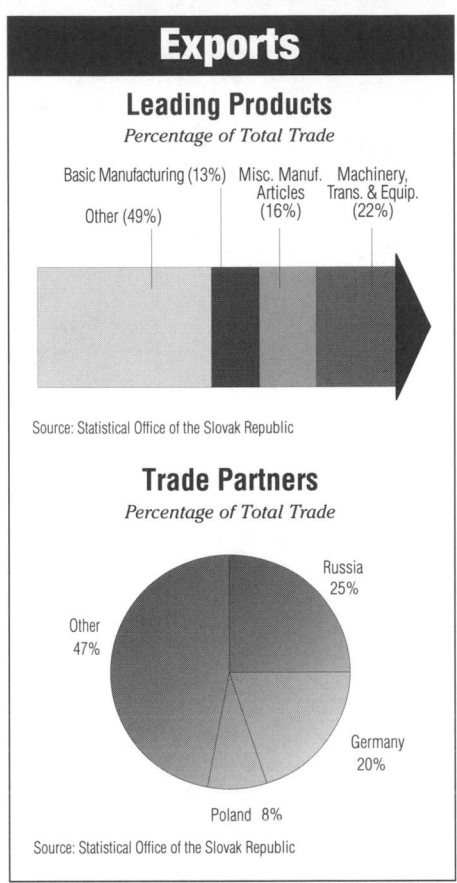

Exports

Leading Products
Percentage of Total Trade

Basic Manufacturing (13%)
Misc. Manuf. Articles (16%)
Machinery, Trans. & Equip. (22%)
Other (49%)

Source: Statistical Office of the Slovak Republic

Trade Partners
Percentage of Total Trade

Russia 25%
Other 47%
Germany 20%
Poland 8%

Source: Statistical Office of the Slovak Republic

Opportunities

FOR IMPORTING TO SLOVAKIA
- machinery and transport equipment
- fuels
- lubricants

FOR EXPORTING FROM SLOVAKIA
- agricultural products
- chemicals, minerals, metals, fuels
- machinery and transport equipment

> ### GROWTH SECTORS
> - agriculture
> - construction
> - telecommunications

Trade News

RULES AND REGULATIONS
- **Trade news** Customs procedures are not intrinsically complicated or burdensome. The basic form required is the "Unified Customs Declarations" which conforms to EU standards. Occasional problems have arisen in individual cases, usually due to the unfamiliarity of one or more parties with the new procedures.
- **Import licenses** Import licenses are governed by the 1991 decree of the former Czechoslovak Ministry of Foreign Trade, which remains valid under Slovak law. The decree divides commodity items into "general" and "specific" categories for the purpose of licensing. For most of the approximately 100 groups of items in the "general" category, obtaining a license is a formality.

Legal

Legal System

The newly constituted government of Slovakia is implementing primarily a civil code system. However, with laws changing rapidly, the judicial system is hard pressed to determine which laws are currently applicable.

Intellectual Property Rights

The Slovak Republic's intellectual property laws were enacted in the 1990s and therefore are some of the most advanced in Eastern Europe.

Patents The law offers broad protection for inventions, industrial designs, and rationalization proposals. It encompasses integrated circuit layout designs and product and process protection. Licenses and assignments must be made by written contract. To take effect with respect to third parties, licenses and assignments must be registered.

Trademarks Trademark protection is available, but the legislation is based on "first to register" rather than "first to use," which poses potential difficulties for foreign investors.

Copyrights Protection is available for traditionally copyrighted creations, and also for computer programs, databases, and sound recordings.

Trade secrets The Slovakian government is currently considering legislation to greater protect trade secrets, but the current laws do little to protect companies against trade secret violations.

Dispute Resolution

Negotiation and settlement may be the best means of dispute resolution at present. The court process is likely to be subject to substantial delays. Arbitration is available, and the process is expected to improve with the enactment of a new law in this area. Certain disputes that must be brought before agencies other than the courts may not be submitted to arbitration.

Legal Matters

LEGAL BRIEFS
- **Business entities** Most often, foreign businesses expand their operations into Slovakia through a registered branch or subsidiary company established there.
- **Commercial freedoms** The rights to engage in enterprise and other economic activity and to protect intellectual property are guaranteed by the constitution.
- **Labor** Unions exist, but they are not strong because job shortages are creating high employment demand. For this same reason, strikes are rare.
- **Government unions and strikes** Members of the military cannot join unions. Judges, prosecutors, firefighters, and members of the police force are prohibited from striking.
- **Contracts** Commercial contracts tend to be straightforward. They address the issues without excess words.
- **Bankruptcy** Under Slovakia's new bankruptcy law, a board of creditors (maximum of seven) formed upon court recommendation can take control of enterprises in bankruptcy proceedings; the board has three months to work out a recovery program before liquidation occurs.
- **International agreements** CISG; New York Convention on the Recognition and Enforcement of Foreign Arbitral Awards; and Convention on the Taking of Evidence Abroad in Civil or Commercial Matters.
- **Business registration** A business is generally required to register if it conducts systematic business activity in the country; that is, if a sales representative visits regularly. Application for registration is submitted to the Slovak Commercial Register.

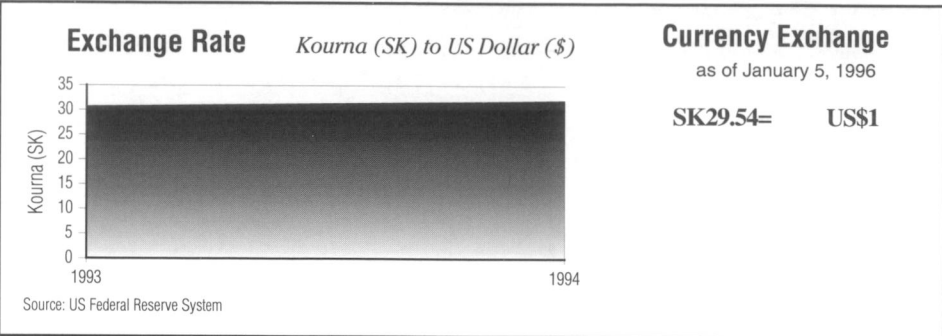

Exchange Rate

Kourna (SK) to US Dollar ($)

Source: US Federal Reserve System

Currency Exchange
as of January 5, 1996

SK29.54=   US$1

Money Matters

BITS AND PIECES

- **Corporate income tax** Resident companies are subject to tax based on worldwide income. Nonresident companies are subject only to income from the Slovak Republic.
- **Capital gains** All capital gains are included with other taxable income and taxed at the regular income tax rate.
- **Foreign tax relief** Tax credits are available to resident companies for income earned abroad. The credit is the lower of the Slovak corporate tax payable on the foreign income and the foreign tax paid.
- **Equity participation** There is no limit on equity participation by nonresidents.
- **Gold** Residents must sell gold, except for gold coins, to financial institutions dealing in foreign exchange within 30 days of acquisition. In most cases, nonresidents must have a foreign exchange license to export gold.
- **Export Payments** Some exports, including certain food items, are subject to fees.
- **Import Payments** All imports are subject to an ad valorem import tariff, ranging from 0 to 15 percent with a few exceptions. The Slovak Republic gives preferential treatment to imports from developing countries. They benefit from a duty exemption and a 75 percent reduction from the applicable customs duties. Advance payments for imports are restricted to 15 percent for any import more than K1 million.
- **Government procurement** No "buy Slovak" law exists, but the government is careful the pace of economic reform doesn't threaten the concerns of local producers.
- **Privatization** The government has made it clear that some sectors (telecommunications, energy) will not be privatized in the short run.
- **Tax concerns** Holding companies are subject to a 15 percent withholding tax on intra-group dividend payments. Since dividends are paid from after-tax profits, they are doubly taxed.
- **Expatriates** Expatriates employed in Slovakia are not exempted from (relatively high) social security and health insurance payments even when they remain covered under their home-country system.
- **Privatization** About 9,500 small enterprises, including 6,500 retail shops, have been privatized. Large-scale privatization has been repeatedly delayed by political changes within the government, as well as by bureaucratic barriers.
- **Commercial code** The code adopted in Czechoslovakia in 1992 remains valid in Slovakia.
- **Taxes** A new tax system was introduced in 1993, with later modifications. Taxes are measured by the calendar year and consist of a value-added tax of 25 percent on most items and 6 percent on basic foodstuffs and essentials.
- **Additional taxes** Some other taxes to consider: an excise tax, a personal income tax of 15 to 47 percent, a corporate income tax of 45 percent, and taxes on real estate, auto registration, inheritance, gifts, etc.
- **Wage controls** Selective wage controls were successfully implemented in loss-making enterprises and the energy and finance sectors. Most private enterprises are exempt from these controls.
- **Price controls** About 96 percent of all price controls have been removed. Controls on food, energy, heat, and a few other necessary sectors remained but were phased out in December 1995 with periodic price increases during the next two years to bring prices to market levels.

GOVERNMENT AGENCY

Ministry of the Economy
Mierová 19
827 15 Bratislava
Tel: (7) 299-8111
Fax: (7) 368-093

Currency

The currency of the Slovak Republic is the Slovak koruna or crown (SK or K), the plural of which is the koruny. The crown is divided into 100 halierov, or hellers (h).

Foreign Exchange

The National Bank is responsible for all exchange controls and regulations in coordination with the Ministry of Finance. The koruna is internally convertible and may move toward full convertibility by the year 2000. There are two types of nonresident accounts in the Slovak Republic, one for domestic currency and the other for foreign currency. Domestic currency accounts are granted only in exceptional cases, and all payments abroad from these accounts require a permit from the National Bank. Foreign currency accounts are usually granted to nonresidents.

Capital Transfers

There is no limit on equity participation by nonresidents. Credits can be obtained from foreign banks with the approval of the Central Bank. In most cases, the exportation and importation of domestic currency is restricted, but there are no requirements for importing or exporting foreign currency. Residents must repatriate all foreign exchange more than the equivalent of SK 5,000 that was acquired abroad and sell it to a bank or deposit it in a private foreign exchange account. There are no restrictions for collecting proceeds from invisibles. There are no restrictions or regulations for most payments for invisibles. A permit is required in most instances for any payments relating to family maintenance, education, and medical treatment. Transfers of inherited assets abroad are allowed to all countries. Companies registered in Slovakia may earn hard currency but must deposit it in crown accounts; they may purchase hard currency for business reasons, subject to some limitations.

Investment Incentives

Slovakia has taken a positive stance toward foreign investment, although in practice some obstacles exist. There are no significant barriers to the participation of foreign equity or personnel.

Investment Restrictions

Foreign citizens cannot own land in Slovakia, but may form legal entities in Slovakia that are permitted to purchase land.

TAXATION

Taxation requires sophisticated knowledge of complex rules and regulations specific to each country. The information presented here is from the Ernst & Young Corporate Tax Guide and Directory, available from the Ernst & Young accounting office in your country, or from:

Ernst & Young Co Consulting
Riecna 1
814 99 Bratislava
Slovak Republic
Tel: (7) 330 793, 331 000
Fax: (901) 700-258 (Satellite link)

At a Glance

Corporate Income Tax Rate (%)	40
Capital Gains Tax Rate (%)	40
Branch Tax Rate (%)	40
Withholding Tax (%) (a)	
Dividends (b)	15
Interest Paid by Financial Institutions (c)	0/15/25
Royalties (d)	25
Income from Media (e)	10
Rental Income from Leases (f)	1
Other Income	25
Net Operating Losses (Years)	
Carryback	0
Carryforward	5

(a) Rates may be reduced by treaty.
(b) Applicable to residents and nonresidents.
(c) The 0% rate applies to interest on hard currency accounts, the 15% rate applies to interest paid to residents, and the 25% rate applies to interest paid to nonresidents.
(d) Applicable to nonresidents only. For resident companies, royalties are included in taxable income and subject to tax at the regular corporate income tax rate of 40%.
(e) Applicable to income of up to SK 3,000 a month received by authors for contributions to newspapers, radio, and television.
(f) This withholding tax is imposed on gross rent if the lease includes a right to purchase the leased asset. Other rental payments are subject to a 25% withholding tax.

Marketing

Overview

Slovakia has emerged from four decades of communist rule and is eager to play catch up with the rest of the world. The people are well-read and enjoy just about anything that is Western. The economy is currently tight, and spending money isn't easily found. The government still controls many of the sectors, and they will probably not be privatized any time soon, so many buyers will probably be employees of the government. If enthusiasm is any indication, however, the people of Slovakia will ensure that some excellent markets open up there in the near future.

Agents and Distribution

Agents are very useful. Most are located in the urban areas, and although the rural areas are beginning to open up with the appearance of Western technology, most marketing should center around the cities.

Selling Techniques

Any business in Slovakia will require a personal business trip—probably several. The best months to travel are between September and May. Giving presents is good manners in Slovakia; a bottle of whiskey or cognac, cigarettes, instant coffee, an odd number of flowers, or small articles of clothing are usually appreciated. Never offer a Slovak cash, though; it could be seen as a bribe. Bring plenty of promotional brochures, flyers, and other pieces of literature.

Advertising

Advertising is similar to many other European countries. Advertising agencies are available and can be very helpful, especially considering the rather large government bureaucracy which may have to be navigated through. A number of foreign publications are available and are widely read by Slovakians. *The Prague Post* is an English-language weekly paper containing news, business information, and entertainment listings. *The Prague Business Week* is another weekly business publication, featuring business news, market reports, company news, and coverage of local financial developments.

Marketing in Slovakia

MARKETING TIPS

- **A lawyer can help** Hire a lawyer with a knowledge of English to guide you through the tangle of new regulations.
- **Patience** Nothing worthwhile in Slovakia happens quickly. Slovaks will agree to do many things for a visitor, but don't expect anything to happen quickly. Also, it will be necessary to follow up over and over again. Be prepared to reinvest profits first. A common complaint from Slovak businesspeople is that some foreigners "arrive on Monday, have meetings on Tuesday, and expect to take their money out on Wednesday."
- **Mail** Mail service has improved recently, and is reasonably efficient and inexpensive these days. Mail from North America takes about 6 to 10 days, mail going to North America occasionally arrives within four to five days. Since there are separate windows for many services, make sure you are in the correct line.
- **Initial contacts** The first business contact should not be limited only to senior management. Gaining the support of middle management and labor is critical to the success of negotiations.
- **Phones and faxes** Telephone systems are not very dependable, and faxes are rarely used for advertising or other marketing devices.
- **Languages** Language used to be a major barrier, but it has eased recently. Slovaks speak Slovak but German is the second language of most businesspeople there. A growing number of younger people speak English also.
- **Czechoslovakia vs. Slovakia** Be careful not to use the word "Czechoslovak" instead of Slovak in any marketing literature or meetings. Slovakia has its own culture and identity, and many Slovaks are extremely sensitive about this.

Business Culture

Greetings and Courtesies

Slovaks will greet foreign visitors warmly. It is customary to shake hands with everyone at an initial meeting. Men normally wait for women and older people to extend their hands first. Courtesy requires that you use a proper title when addressing Slovaks, along with their surnames. Gifts are given at most social and business meetings. Learning a few phrases of the Slovak language will go a long way in breaking down the natural reserve of your Slovak host.

Business Ethic and Framework

The citizens of Slovakia are committed to democracy and freedom, things Slovaks have been without for decades. The pace of life is slow in Slovakia, and this is reflected in their way of doing business. Slovaks are punctual, however, and expect their foreign visitors to be also.

Meetings and Decision Making

Preparing for a meeting in Slovakia means planning far in advance. It is also important to arrive on time although, upon your arrival, expect to find a message requesting that the meeting be delayed. Slovaks are serious about business, but they won't respond to an aggressive approach on the part of foreign business associates. Slovaks know how to use their charm and hospitality to their advantage. They are, however, reluctant to show their feelings. Sometimes Slovaks will feign agreement with visitors because they are reluctant to firmly say "no." Slovaks would rather respond with "we shall see."

Women

Many Slovak women hold down full-time jobs and have full responsibility of their homes, leaving little time for other pursuits. There is a significant disparity in wages, favoring men over women. Women in Slovakia receive paid maternity leave for three years.

Cultural Cautions

DO'S

- Bring a gift to your host. This could include: wine, whiskey, cognac, quality chocolates, or odd number of flowers, but not red roses.
- Double-check everything. A lot of confusion exists about new rules and the situation constantly changes.

DON'TS

- Don't discuss politics or religion, socialism, or the break up of Czechoslovakia.
- Avoid taking photographs in museums or art galleries.
- Be careful to avoid a patronizing attitude with your Slovak business partners.
- Do not expect success to come quickly.
- Avoid voicing your opinions.

CUSTOMS

- Toasting is proper, but wait for the host to initiate.
- Avoid putting your elbows on the dining table.
- Slovaks rarely entertain business associates in their homes.

OBSERVATIONS

- Slovaks are not "touchers," especially in business situations.

NEGOTIATIONS

- Take proposals with a grain of salt. Slovaks may agree to something even if there is only a small chance of success, or even when they can't do something.
- Initial business contacts should not be limited to senior management. Middle management and labor support are crucial to the fulfillment of negotiations.

GOVERNMENT AGENCIES

Ministry of Agriculture, Water and Forestry
Dobrovicova 12
812 66 Bratislava
Tel: (7) 490-581
Fax: (7) 578-34

Ministry of Construction and Public Works
Spitalska 8
816 44 Bratislava
Tel: (7) 441-111
Fax: (7) 367-054

Ministry of the Economy
Mierova 19
827 15 Bratislava
Tel: (7) 299-861
Fax: (7) 230-122

Ministry of Education and Science
Hlboká 2
813 30 Bratislava
Tel: (7) 492-002
Fax: (7) 497-792

Ministry of Environment
Hlboka 2
812 35 Bratislava
Tel: (7) 492-451
Fax: (7) 311-368, 311-384

Ministry of Finance
Stefanoviça ul. c. 5
813 08 Bratislava
Tel: (7) 497-541 Fax: (7) 498-042

Ministry of Foreign Relations
Stromová ul. 1
PO Box 87/15
810 05 Bratislava
Tel: (7) 370-4210, 370-4242 Fax: (7) 376-364

Ministry of Health
Spitalska 6
813 05 Bratislava
Tel: (7) 574-82
Fax: (7) 575-08, 598-04

Ministry of Labor and Social Affairs
Spitálska 4-6
816 43 Bratislava
Fax: (7) 512-58

Ministry of Privatization
Drienova 24
820 09 Bratislava
Tel: (7) 234-332
Fax: (7) 294-548

Ministry of Transport, Posts, and Telecommunications
Mileticova 19
820 06 Bratislava
Tel: (7) 672-36, 674-67
Fax: (7) 254-800

Office of the Government of the Slovak Republic
Slobody 1
842 18 Bratislava
Tel: (7) 415-1111
Fax: (7) 492-795

BUSINESS AND TRADE ORGANIZATIONS

Drevounia
(Wood Products and Furniture)
ul. Dr. V. Clementisa 10
Bratislava 82610

Hudroconsult Bratislava
(Engineering Consultant for Industrial, Agricultural, Transport, and Water Management Projects)
Radlinskeho ul. 37
Bratislava 81543

Slovak Chamber of Commerce and Industry
Mileticova 1
821 08 Bratislava
Tel: (7) 62016
Fax: (7) 69892

Slovak National Agency for Foreign Investment and Development
Manesovo nam. 2

816 01 Bratislava
Tel: (7) 847-219
Fax: (7) 849-806

Interal
(Information and Publicity Agency for Foreign Products)
Kalininova 17
Bratislava 85254

Intercoop
(Handicrafts, Folk Art, Wines, and Food Products)
ul. Dr. V. Clementisa 10
Bratislava 82608

LEGAL CONTACTS

Blaha, Erben, Novak & Partners
Benediktiho 5
811 05 Bratislava
Tel: 42/7/498754
Fax: 42/7/498754

Cechova, Hrbek
Marianska No. 3
811 08 Bratislava
Tel: 42-7-232 033
Fax: 42-7-321 254

Edmont Prekopp
Laurinska 8
814 99 Bratislava 1
Tel: (202) 335-896
Fax: (202) 331-723

Squire, Sanders & Dempsey
Mudronova 37
811 05 Bratislava
Tel: (202) 315-370
Fax: (202) 313-918

Flassik & Flassikova & Valentova & Vasova
Stetinova 5
811 06 Bratislava
Tel: 42 7 315 860
Fax: 42 7 335 022

BANKS

Narodna Banka Slovenska
(National Bank of Slovakia)
Gorkeho 14
818 54 Bratislava
Tel: (7) 319-1111
Fax: (7) 364-721

Investincna a Rozvoyjva Banka
(Investment and Development Bank)
Sturova 5
818 55 Bratislava
Tel: (7) 389-1111
Fax: (7) 363-484

Istrobanka
Laurinska 1
810 00 Bratislava
Tel: (7) 397-111
Fax: (7) 331-744

Priemyselna Banka
(Industrial Bank)
Bozeny Nemcovej 30
040 61 Kosice
Tel: (95) 35326
Fax: (95) 30311

Slovenska Kreditna Banka
(Slovak Credit Bank)
nam. SNP 13
814 99 Bratislava
Tel: (7) 455-111
Fax: (7) 321-021

Tatra Banka
Vajanskeho nab. 5
810 06 Bratislava
Tel: (7) 452-111
Fax: (7) 334-656

Vfseobecna Uverova Banka
(General Credit Bank)
nam. SNP 19
818 56 Bratislava
Tel: (7) 364-843
Fax: (7) 367-087

STOCK EXCHANGES

Bratislavska medzinarodna komoditna burza (BMKB)
Bratislava International Commodity Exchange
Zahradnicka 153
Bratislava
Tel: (7) 211-454
Fax: (7) 213-585

Burza cennych papierov Bratislava (BCPB)
Securities Exchange Bratislava
Cukrova 14
Bratislava
Tel: (7) 305-11
Fax: (7) 335-725

NEWSPAPERS

Hospodarske Noviny (Economic News)
Pribinova 25
810 11 Bratislava
Tel: (7) 324-026
Fax: (7) 210-3609

Pravda
Pribinova 25
810 11 Bratislava
Tel: (7) 367-503
Fax: (7) 210-4759

Vecernik
Pribinova 25
819 16 Bratislava
Tel: (7) 325-085
Fax: (7) 210-4521

PERIODICALS

Deak-Avizo
Teslova 26
821 02 Bratislava
Tel: (7) 627-10
Fax: (7) 672-39

Express
Pribinova 25
819 05 Bratislava
Tel: (7) 210-4031
Fax: (7) 325-185

Extra S
Halkova 11
831 03 Bratislava
Tel: (7) 369-715
Fax: (7) 325-154

RADIO AND TELEVISION

Slovensky Rozhlas (Radio)
Mytna 1
811 06 Bratislava
Tel: (7) 493-174

Slovensky Televizia (Television)
Mlynska dolina 28
845 45 Bratislava
Tel: (7) 725-948
Fax: (7) 725-227

INTERNET ADDRESSES

Mailing lists:
bit.listserv.slovak-l
soc.culture.Czecho-Slovak

Slovakia Home Page
http://www.tuzvo.sk/homepage.html

Eunet Slovakia
http://www.eunet.sk/slovakia/

EUNet Slovakia
http://www.eunet.sk/slovakia/

Slovakia Home Page
http://www.tuzvo.sk/homepage.html

South Africa

Republic of South Africa

Economy

Overview

South Africa continues its herculean attempt to rebuild its economy after several years of international isolation resulting from its apartheid policies. An apparently stable political regime has undertaken an ambitious five-year program to rebuild, develop, and liberalize private industry in an effort to alleviate massive unemployment and reduce the vast disparities in income between blacks and whites. Foreign investors have responded positively, if cautiously. The South African stock market has recently shown signs of life, and it continues to rise, spurred by both domestic and foreign buying. Export markets are growing as the world takes note of the high quality of many South African goods. The current economic revival is being led by an increase in gold exports and substantial recovery in the agricultural sector.

Trade

South Africa's foreign trade has historically been characterized by inward-looking and protective policies, but the lifting of UN sanctions in 1993 and the stabilization of political conditions have resulted in a marked increase in overall trade. The US is the largest source of both its imports and exports, followed by Germany, the UK, and Japan. Although significant import barriers are still in place, they are being slowly reduced. Total trade should increase significantly as the world discovers the high quality and price competitiveness of many South African goods.

Sectors

Agriculture Although only 15 percent of its arable land is suitable for agriculture, South Africa is a net exporter of food, producing a wide variety of products such as fruits, wine, tobacco, sugarcane, and corn. Substantial increases in output have put agriculture at the forefront of economic recovery and a government shift toward free market policies will result in greater growth to this previously protected sector.

Industry South Africa has long exploited the mining of its rich natural resources to become the world's largest producer and exporter of gold. It is also a major world player in the value-added processing of minerals to produce products such as alloys and stainless steel. Although the manufacturing industry is a world leader in many specialized sectors, including synthetic fuels and mining equipment and machinery, much of South Africa's industrial plant needs to be upgraded to support export expansion; this means imports of industrial machinery should flourish in the near term.

Services Tourism has already boomed, and shows signs of becoming a major contributor to overall GDP. The financial sector and institutions in South Africa are highly sophisticated and include an effective and growing stock exchange, developing markets, and banks and financial institutions with the ability to handle sophisticated international financial transactions.

Trends

Although the economy is beginning to recover from a five-year recession and the government has embarked on its Reconstruction and Development Program, South Africa faces many long-term problems, not the least of which is the continuing need to redress the inequities of apartheid, which, though abolished, continues to place a drain on the country's resources. However, the government has made, and continues to make progress, and its long-term prospects are positive.

At a Glance

THE COUNTRY
Location Southern Africa, at the extreme southern tip of the continent.
Terrain Vast interior plateau rimmed by rugged hills and narrow coastal plain.
Climate Mostly semiarid; subtropical along coast; sunny days, cool nights.

THE PEOPLE
Population 43,900,000
Ethnic composition
African (black) 75.2%
White 13.6%
Colored (mixed race) 8.6%
Asian (Indian) 2.6%
Religions Predominantly Christian; traditional African, Hindu, Muslim, Jewish.
Languages spoken Eleven official languages, including Afrikaans, English, Ndebele, Pedi, Sotho, Swati, Tsonga, Tswana, Venda, Xhosa, Zulu.
Education and literacy Seven years of education are compulsory for all children, but this is not currently enforced; an estimated two million school-age children do not attend school. About 76 percent of the population can read and write.
Labor force
Total: 13,400,000
By occupation: services 35%, agriculture 30%, industry 20%, mining 9%, other 6%.

COUNTRY FACTS
Political and legal The Republic of South Africa maintains an executive system of government under the 1993 transitional constitution. It has a bicameral parliament and a legal system based on Roman-Dutch law and English common law.
Telephone South Africa is the telecommunications leader on the African continent with approximately 5.3 million telephones—84 percent of the network having already become digital. Telkom SA provides connections to 220 international destinations, 218 which can be direct dialed. International Country Code: [27]. Selected city codes: Cape Town (21), Durban (31), Johannesburg (11), Pretoria (12).
Transportation The transport infrastructure—airlines, railroads, luxury tour buses, and rental cars—is well-developed. The renowned Blue Train is one of the most luxurious passenger railway services in the world. International airlines offer regularly scheduled flights to and from the country.
Environment Agricultural runoff and urban discharge contaminating rivers, acid rain, soil erosion, and desertification pose a considerable threat to the quality of South Africa's environment. The excessively rapid population growth adds to the problems South Africa faces. Current issues are the lack of arterial rivers or lakes which requires extensive water control and conservation measures.
Media South African radio and television broadcasts, with the exception of some independent radio stations and subscription television services, are controlled by the South African Broadcasting Corporation.
Health The standard of community health is high, with areas of highly specialized medical care comparable to those in the developed world. Life expectancy for men is 62 years and for women almost 68 years.

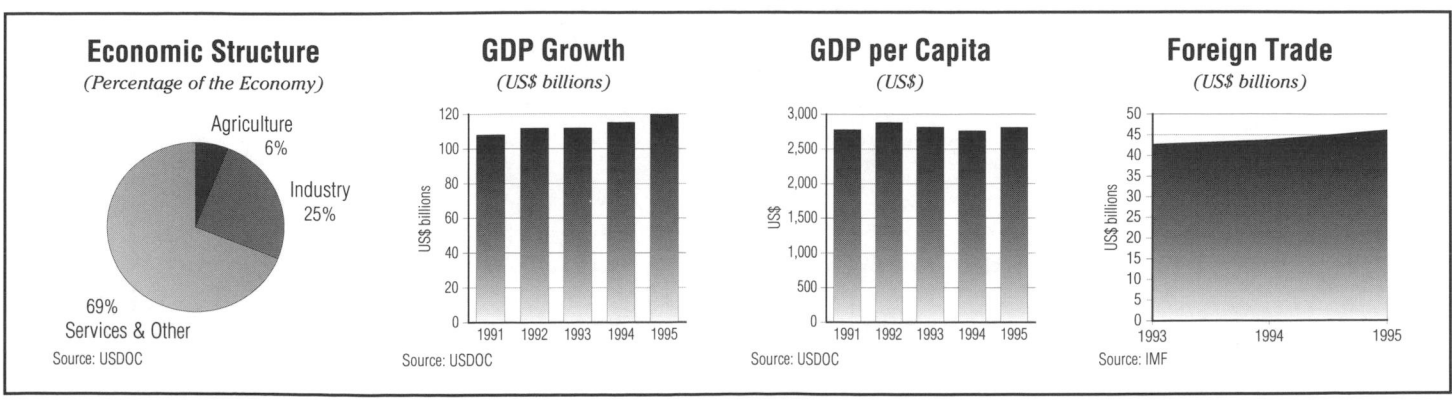

Economic Structure
(Percentage of the Economy)
Agriculture 6%
Industry 25%
Services & Other 69%
Source: USDOC

GDP Growth
(US$ billions)
1991 1992 1993 1994 1995
Source: USDOC

GDP per Capita
(US$)
1991 1992 1993 1994 1995
Source: USDOC

Foreign Trade
(US$ billions)
1993 1994 1995
Source: IMF

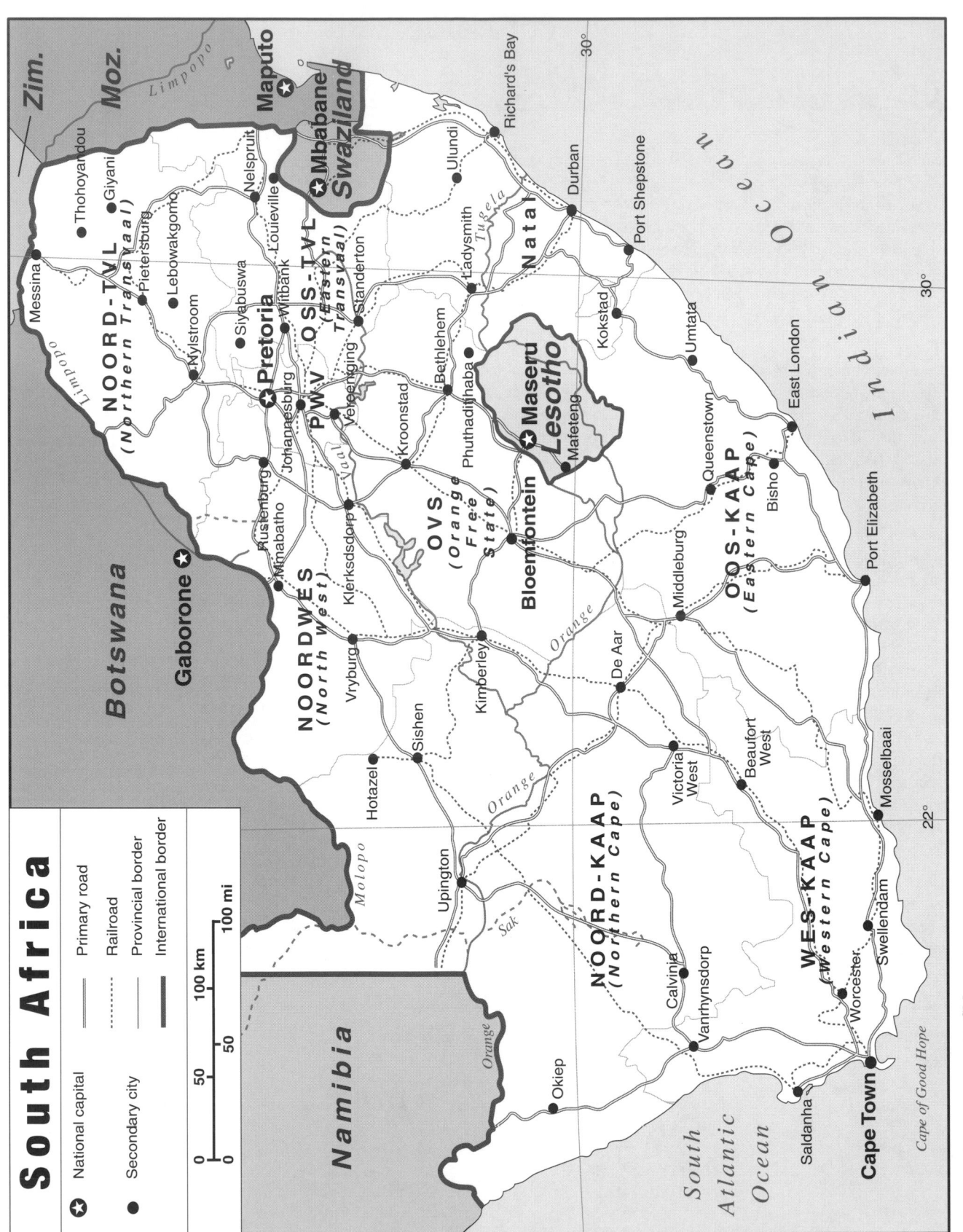

South Africa

⭐	National capital	—	Primary road
●	Secondary city	⋯	Railroad
		—	Provincial border
		▬	International border

Scale: 0 — 50 — 100 km / 0 — 50 — 100 mi

Zim.
Moz.
Limpopo
Maputo
Mbabane
Swaziland
Thohoyandou
Giyani
Nelspruit
Louieville
Richard's Bay
30°
Messina
Pietersburg
Lebowakgomo
Nylstroom
NOORD-TVL
(Northern Transvaal)
Siyabuswa
Witbank
O S S - T V L
(Eastern Transvaal)
Standerton
Ulundi
Ladysmith
Tugela
Natal
Durban
Port Shepstone
Pretoria
P W V
Johannesburg
Vereeniging
Bethlehem
Phuthaditjhaba
Maseru
Lesotho
Mafeteng
Kokstad
Umtata
East London
30°
Botswana
Gaborone
Rustenburg
Mmabatho
Klerksdorp
Kroonstad
Vaal
O V S
(Orange Free State)
Bloemfontein
Queenstown
Middleburg
O O S - K A A P
(Eastern Cape)
Bisho
Port Elizabeth
NOORDWES
(North West)
Vryburg
Kimberley
De Aar
Orange
Hotazel
Sishen
Beaufort West
Mosselbaai
22°
Molopo
Namibia
Upington
Sak
Victoria West
NOORD-KAAP
(Northern Cape)
Calvinia
Vanrhynsdorp
WES-KAAP
(Western Cape)
Worcester
Swellendam
Orange
Okiep
Saldanha
Cape Town
Cape of Good Hope
Indian Ocean
South Atlantic Ocean

©1994 MAGELLAN Geographix SM Santa Barbara, CA

Foreign Trade

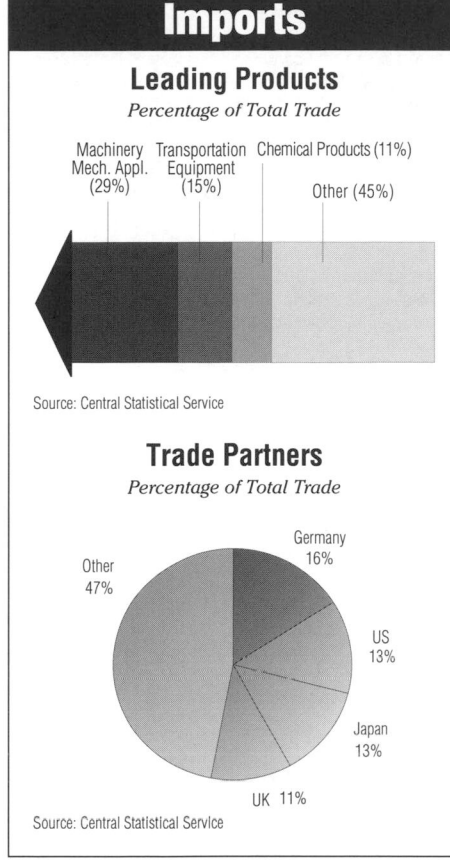

Imports

Leading Products
Percentage of Total Trade

Machinery Mech. Appl. (29%)
Transportation Equipment (15%)
Chemical Products (11%)
Other (45%)

Source: Central Statistical Service

Trade Partners
Percentage of Total Trade

Germany 16%
US 13%
Japan 13%
UK 11%
Other 47%

Source: Central Statistical Service

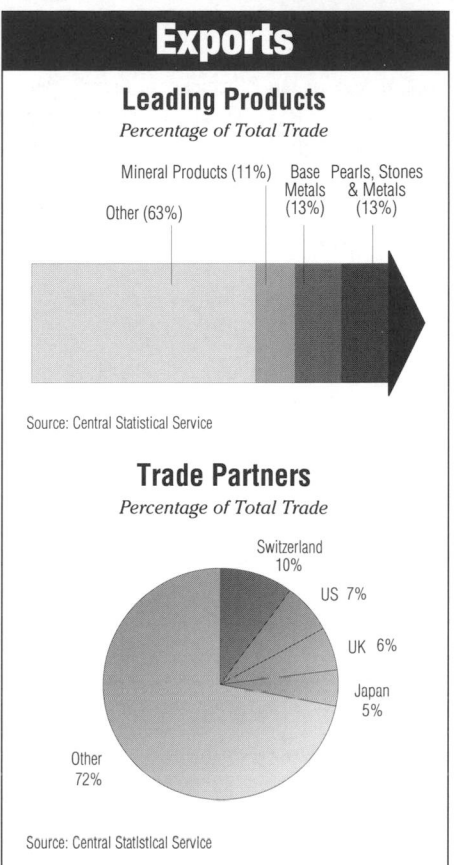

Exports

Leading Products
Percentage of Total Trade

Mineral Products (11%)
Base Metals (13%)
Pearls, Stones & Metals (13%)
Other (63%)

Source: Central Statistical Service

Trade Partners
Percentage of Total Trade

Switzerland 10%
US 7%
UK 6%
Japan 5%
Other 72%

Source: Central Statistical Service

Opportunities

FOR IMPORTING TO SOUTH AFRICA

- machinery
- mining equipment and transportation equipment
- automobiles
- transportable medical equipment
- aircraft parts
- rice
- office machinery equipment
- housing (building supplies)
- cost-effective technology
- electrification

FOR EXPORTING FROM SOUTH AFRICA

- gold
- industrial metals
- minerals and metals (ferro alloys, stainless steel)
- agricultural products
- coal
- commodities
- food

GROWTH SECTORS

- informal sectors: education/training, job creation, small business assistance
- mining (gold, diamond, coal)
- processing of minerals
- railway rolling stock
- synthetic fuels
- mining industry
- gas and water
- service sectors
- telecommunications (cellular services)
- electricity generation
- defense industry

GOVERNMENT PROCUREMENT

- advanced office equipment and machinery
- road construction equipment
- industrial plant equipment

Trade News

RULES AND REGULATIONS

- **Duty free** Many goods enter duty free, while those subject to duty generally pay at a rate between five and 25 percent.
- **Value-added tax (VAT)** A VAT of 14 percent is payable on nearly all imports. However, goods imported for use in manufacturing or resale by registered traders may be exempt from VAT.
- **Excise tax** Specific excise duties are levied on beverages, tobacco and tobacco products, mineral waters, some petroleum products, and motor vehicles. Ad valorem excise duties are levied on office machinery photographic film, and luxury consumer goods such as cosmetics, home entertainment products, and motorcycles.
- **Rebates** Various tariff rebates exist for cases in which the imported commodity will be used in a subsequent domestic manufacturing or other value-added process.
- **Import permits (licenses)** South Africa is signatory to the Tokyo Round Agreement on import licensing procedures. Some goods imported require an import permit which the South African importer obtains from the Directorate of Import and Export Control within the Department of Trade and Industry. Products requiring permits include: consumer goods (foodstuffs, clothing, fabrics, footwear, and books), wood, paper products, motor and aviation fuels, and refined petroleum products. Products which do not require permits include: raw materials, and other products for industrial purposes, new spare parts, and assemblies and materials imported as original equipment for the manufacture of motor vehicles. Permits are only required for specific categories of goods and are obtainable from the Director of Import and Export. Importers must possess an import permit prior to the date of shipment. Failure to produce a required permit could result in the imposition of penalties.
- **Quotas** South Africa does not maintain any formal import quotas.
- **Tariff rates** Liberalization is due in South Africa's outmoded protective trade regime which uses high tariffs to combat competitive imports. South Africa protects infant industries through high tariffs, which range from five to 50 percent on luxury goods to as high as 100 percent for automobiles. Any South African producer may petition for tariff protection; approval is more likely where the producer has a major share of the domestic market and can show that foreign competition is eroding the company's market dominance. In the short to medium term, there may be continuing market access problems with some products, but the overall trend should be toward trade liberalization.
- **Import surcharge** The import surcharge was originally imposed as a means to restore the country's deteriorating balance of payments. The surcharge is levied on the customs value (f.o.b.) of the imported goods. The government would like to eliminate the surcharge entirely in the future when the country's balance of payments is strong enough. (Zero percent on essential foods, agricultural implements, manufacturing, etc; 15 percent on aircraft, vehicles, earthmoving equipment, software, etc; and 40 percent luxury consumer goods, i.e., TVs, tape recorders, video machines, antiques).
- **GATT** Currently, 90 percent of South Africa's tariff rates are GATT-bound; this percentage will increase 10 percent as Uruguay Round obligations are implemented.
- **Barter/countertrade** The South African Government has no laws, regulations, or published policies regarding barter/countertrade. It views countertrade as a second-best alternative to be engaged in only when normal trade cannot be conducted.

Marketing

Overview

South Africa is the African continent's largest and most developed economy. It is highly diversified with a modern infrastructure and a strong financial sector. Approximately 90 percent of the population is located in areas surrounding the interior cities of Johannesburg and Pretoria and the three coastal port cities of Cape Town, Durban, and Port Elizabeth. The ports are large, modern, and support a well-developed import and export industry. Johannesburg is the hub for the commercial, financial, and transportation industries. The influence of powerful state corporations—a legacy of the 1980s—is being reduced but remains important. The government still regulates the prices of many goods through the Price Control Act. It also employs its own purchasing standards and price preferences in a schedule based on the percentage of local content in order to encourage the development of local industry.

Distribution

South Africa offers foreign suppliers a wide variety of methods to distribute and sell their products, such as using an agent or distributor, selling through established wholesalers or dealers, selling directly to retailers, or establishing a branch or subsidiary with its own sales force. Slightly less than 50 percent of merchandise sales pass through both a wholesaler and retailer, 40 percent of sales are from the manufacturer directly to the retailer, and 10 percent of merchandise purchases are bought by consumers directly from the producer or importer. Sales agents are often used for the distribution of consumer goods, as well as for the distribution of some industrial raw materials, especially when products are highly competitive or lack a large market. It is common to appoint a single agent capable of providing national coverage, either through one office or a network of branch offices. Capital equipment is often best handled by distributors who buy on their own account and carry a wide range of spare parts and accessories. Leading distributors often have branches throughout South Africa and sell to both wholesalers and retailers.

Agents, Distributors, and Partners

Once contacts are established, it is advisable to visit the country, since firsthand knowledge of the market and society is useful. Moreover, such a visit provides the opportunity for a personal appraisal of the prospective agent or distributor. Exporters should carefully research the reputation and financial references of any potential representative, and always when appointing a distributor. Also, foreign sellers should take care to find out if the distributor handles a competing product, as some exporters have been approached by major South African corporations whose holding companies market products directly competing with those of the foreign seller. It is important to maintain close contact with the local agent in order to track changes in importing procedures and to ensure that the agent is effectively representing the market interests of the foreign seller.

Selling Techniques

Although selling goods via agents through the traditional wholesale distribution system is the normal practice, many Western sellers of consumer goods now sell directly to retail organizations, such as consumer corporations, department stores, chain stores, and cooperative groups of independent retailers, assuming the functions of wholesale buying, selling, and warehousing. Franchising is currently one of the most promising areas for growth; there are presently more than 100 franchisers with a total of some 3,000 outlets. Although the fast-food industry is the largest franchiser, the service sector (such as automobile servicing) exhibits promise for future growth. A recent phenomenon in South Africa is the rise of hypermarkets which sell large quantities of almost all consumer goods on a self-serve basis. These hypermarkets, located in suburban shopping centers, have disrupted the traditional distribution chain by purchasing directly from manufacturers and bypassing wholesalers.

Advertising

Advertising is sophisticated in South Africa, uses all the usual media, and is provided by local full-service agencies. Allied services such as comparison shopping and market research are readily available. During the 1980s fast-moving consumer goods accounted for most advertising expenditures; the 1990s have seen an escalation in social advertising, in which public service organizations are the clients and social services campaigns are the products.

Service and Customer Support

In South Africa's very competitive marketplace, it is essential that foreign sellers provide adequate servicing, spare parts and components, and qualified service personnel. In most cases, services should be available locally because delays often lead purchasers to seek alternative suppliers. The prospective exporter should place appropriate emphasis on quality of performance, product, and after-sale service.

Marketing in South Africa

MARKETING TIPS

- **Special competitive factors** The government still plays a central economic role through state corporations producing goods as near monopolies, although this influence is being reduced through privatization.
- **Pricing** Price controls on many goods remain in effect under the Price Control Act.
- **Government** Government purchasing is a significant factor in the economy. Procurement is highly centralized and nearly all of it is done through competitive bidding. Although the procedure favors products of local manufacture, foreign bidders are not precluded.
- **Telephone** Phone services in South Africa are among the best in Africa. International service is available from all major cities and a number of rural areas, as well. Faxes are also available in cities.
- **Postal service** Postal services are up to Western standards. Incoming mail usually reaches its target within one week. Mail should be used for communication with agents, and not for any marketing campaign.
- **Changes in sales techniques** Shopping center hypermarkets which sell all kinds of consumer goods have appeared recently and threaten to displace smaller retailers.
- **Traveling with promotional items** In most cases, sales duty, import surcharges, and customs duty are payable on samples carried by visitors for use in taking orders. Refunds for such charges are usually made on the re-export of such items.
- **Buying by tender** Official buying authorities, including mining companies, obtain most of their requirements by tender.

AD AGENCIES

Grey Advertising
PO Box 2146
Sandton 2146
Tel: (11) 444-1400
Fax: (11) 444-4530

J. Walter Thompson Co. So. Africa (Pty.) Ltd.
PO Box 3939
Johannesburg 2128
Tel: (11) 806-8000
Fax: (11) 806-8010

McCann-Erickson South Africa (Pty.) Ltd.
PO Box 10663
Johannesburg 2128
Tel: (11) 803-3510
Fax: (11) 803-4222

Saatchi & Saatchi Klerck & Barrett
PO Box 650831
Benmore, Johannesburg 2010
Tel: (11) 883-4672
Fax: (11) 884-4336

Sussens Mann Tyson Ogilvy & Mather PR (Pty.)
PO Box 3077
Sandton 2146
Tel: (11) 886-7153
Fax: (11) 886-7676

Wunderman Cato Johnson
Nissan House, 3rd Fl.
15 Alice Lane
Sandhurst, Sandton 2146
Tel: (11) 881-9111
Fax: (11) 881-9387

MARKET RESEARCH CONTACT

South Africa Marketing Research Association
POB 91879
Auckland Park 2006
Tel: (11) 482-1419
Fax: (11) 726-3639

Business Culture

Greetings and Courtesies

The handshake is the standard greeting in South Africa. When a black and a white person shake hands, as well as two blacks, the "African" handshake is used: start with a standard handshake, then slip your hand up around the other person's thumb, then return to the standard grip. Two white people shaking hands will exchange only the standard handshake; do not attempt the African style. Among good friends, men will often hug, women will exchange kisses on the cheek. Titles, such as Doctor, Professor, or Judge, as well as Mister, Mrs., and Advocate (for a lawyer) should always be used when applicable. Use first names only after the South African uses yours. In initial conversation, do not ask about an Afrikaaner's marital status or family, as they tend to be reserved about discussing such matters.

Business Ethic and Framework

While South Africa remains a high-powered industrial juggernaut, the richest and most productive nation in the history of Africa, the recent abolition of its apartheid policies has brought significant changes to every aspect of its society, with more on the way. The business framework, however, remains for the most part a direct reflection of the conservative, austere, and highly motivated character of the Afrikaaner himself. Standards of punctuality, efficiency, and reliability in South African business rival those of Germany or Japan. Further, despite the recent, and continual, expansion of the business community to include more blacks, Indians, and Asians, the defiant isolation of the ruling Afrikaaners during South Africa's apartheid years has produced a marked insularity, an "us and them" character within their business world that precludes easy access by foreigners. Patience and dignified deportment, however, will allow you to demonstrate your integrity and so gain their trust.

Decision Making

Once a bond of trust is established, business will proceed quickly and without interruptions. Tough, protracted bargaining is not a feature of the South African culture. Decisions come from the top people in a South African company, and thus it is recommended that you send a high-ranking member of your company to the initial meetings. When a South African businessperson does make a decision, he will want a ready response. Patience is more than a virtue in South Africa, it is a must; the phrase "just now" means "in a short while," not "immediately."

Women

The attitude of South Africa's business community towards women remains decidedly chauvinistic and male oriented. There are very few women in senior management positions, and women are generally excluded from decision-making processes. In meetings, women of equal or even superior rank are often expected to make tea. A foreign businesswoman, however, can expect to be treated with respect, providing she is not overly aggressive or indiscreet. South Africans have become accustomed to dealing with Western businesswomen in positions of authority.

Meetings

Meetings start on time, are scheduled for any part of the day, and are preceded by a brief but important period of personal conversation. Foreign businesspeople should be thoroughly prepared in advance, with graphics and visual aids, if possible. Business lunches and dinners are common, but they are for the most part social events. The real business takes place in meetings. Don't be surprised if blacks don't rise when introduced, although this is changing as blacks gain more stature in this society. This gesture does not apply when women are being greeted. At an initial meeting, send someone fairly senior in your company's hierarchy; this will make negotiations a little smoother.

Business Attire

Standard Western business attire is the norm in South Africa. For meetings, businessmen wear a suit and tie; women a suit or conservative dress. In summer (December through March), the acceptable business "uniform" is a khaki shirt and Bermuda shorts. For casual dress in cities, both women and men may wear shorts or jeans. Keep in mind the Boer farmers in rural communities are very conservative. In those areas, women should not wear low-cut tops or short shorts. In other areas, people are used to seeing women in halter tops and sleeveless dresses. Proper attire when visiting someone's home can vary widely, so be sure to ask what you should wear; sometimes people sit around the pool and eat outdoors.

Cultural Cautions

DO'S

- South Africans will not enjoy last minute attempts for meetings. Make appointments at least two months in advance of your arrival.

DON'TS

- Avoid profanity, as South Africans retain a puritanical manner which is easily offended. Also avoid any gestures or movements that could be construed as offensive.
- Avoid critical discussions of South Africa's politics and ethnic tensions.
- Never criticize the country and its people. South Africans have been subjected to so much criticism regarding apartheid that they are very touchy and may take extreme offense to any type of criticism, no matter how subtle. People who live outside cities are especially sensitive to criticism.
- South Africans are very proud of their culture and heritage. Be careful not to compare South Africa to other countries.
- Never refer to black South Africans as *karrirs,* as this is a very offensive and derogatory term.
- Do not bring any material which could be considered pornographic, including such magazines as *Playboy.*

CUSTOMS

- Business cards, in English, are crucial. Bring a healthy supply.
- There are different greetings, depending on the culture you are meeting (*Sakubona* from the Zulu, *Molo* from the Xhosa, etc.), but English greetings such as "Hello" and "Good morning" are frequently heard.
- Waving from a distance is accepted, unlike other African countries.
- Avoid scheduling meetings on national holidays. Each religion also observes its own holidays, so advance preparation is advised.
- People often entertain at home, and the style is usually casual. Offer to bring something, such as wine, beer, or dessert.
- South Africa has the highest technological advances in Africa. Computers, faxes, telexes, and photocopying facilities are widely available.
- One final word of caution: Among some cultures, it is not polite to gesture with your left hand.

OBSERVATIONS

- South Africa is still very conservative in regards to women in social and business settings. Be aware that it is customary in South Africa for a man to precede a woman through a door.
- Feel free to use the word "white," but don't use the term "non-white" to refer to other groups in the country.
- Don't plan on paying your South African host back for meals, entertaining, etc; it's not customary, and be sure not to push the matter at all, or your host may take offense. Plan to entertain your hosts when they come to your country.

NEGOTIATIONS

- There are many places to find a South African business contact, including the South African Chamber of Commerce in Johannesburg. Many times contacts are made through word of mouth. Treasure every personal business contact you can make; it may come in very handy.

Legal

Legal System

Roman-Dutch law constitutes an important part of South African law, but many areas have been refashioned on English lines by legislative and judicial actions. The courts operate independently of the executive and bicameral parliament.

Intellectual Property Rights

Patents Protection and enforcement of patent rights are not a problem for the term of the patent, but patent rights are construed strictly. An infringement exists if the essence of the protected invention is pirated. A product made by a patented process or apparatus is also protected by the patent.

Trademarks Statutory and common law trademark protection is afforded in South Africa. Although the statutes were originally intended to create a registration system to record existing rights and facilitate enforcement, they have developed into a system of substantive law that has created rights existing independently of the common law. However, the common law rights are in many ways broader in scope than those created by statute. Furthermore, the protection afforded by the statutory rights is strictly limited to the goods or services with respect to which the trademark is registered, while the common law rights are not subject to any such absolute limitation.

Copyrights The law of copyright currently protects the following broad categories: literary, musical and artistic works, sound recordings, cinematograph films, broadcasts (television and sound), program-carrying signals, published editions and computer programs. No formalities are prescribed for acquisition of copyright in these works; provided that the works meet certain conditions, copyright exists automatically.

Business Registration

Every company incorporated outside South Africa that establishes a place of business in the republic must within 21 days after establishment file with the Registrar of Companies in Pretoria certain prescribed documents, including a list containing details of its directors, distinguishing between directors resident in the republic and nonresident directors. When registering the memorandum of that company, the Registrar distinguishes the registration from those of companies incorporated in the republic. External companies are obliged also to comply with the provisions of the Companies Act, including the submission of statutory returns and the filing of annual financial statements pertaining to the South African operation and the country of incorporation with the Registrar of Companies.

Contracts and Dispute Resolution

Although disputes between corporate contracting parties frequently result in litigation, contract terms that provide for alternative mechanisms for dispute resolution are becoming increasingly common. Dispute resolution may or may not be made subject to the Arbitration Act, depending on the wishes of the parties. The Alternative Dispute Resolution Association of South Africa (ADRASA) also provides mediation and arbitration services for the resolution on a more informal and expeditious basis of commercial disputes.

Notaries

The legislature and the courts both place special reliance on notarial acts. Certain documents, including servitudes and long leases over land, must by law be prepared and attested by a notary. Formal documents executed in the Republic of South Africa for use outside its borders must be authenticated before they will be recognized in the countries where used. Notaries are authorized to provide such a service, but authentication is not the exclusive preserve of notaries. Notaries may also act as commissioners of oaths.

Labor

Workers have the legal right to associate freely in unions. The trade union movement in South Africa is very strong, and total person-days lost to strikes remains high. Most labor negotiations see some sort of industrial action before they are finally concluded. The right to strike is recognized and is exercised freely. A new Labor Relations Bill is currently being negotiated between government, business, and labor. This would result in a sweeping streamline of current labor laws, and is designed to repair the country's reputation for labor strife. The proposed law would limit workers' right to strike, provide for communication forums between workers and employers, and set up a state-funded panel to handle disputes.

Source: Silberbauers Incorporated, Cape Town

Legal Matters

LEGAL BRIEFS

- **Commercial court** Recent changes to South Africa's judicial system include the establishment of the Commercial Court in Johannesburg.
- **Mining** A major effort is under way to reform the current mining law in favor of nationalization.
- **EU cooperation** South Africa has signed a framework partnership agreement which will form the basis for a permanent cooperation accord with th EU.
- **Unions** Despite poor economic conditions and work force reductions, trade union membership in South Africa continues to increase and presently exceeds as many as three million workers. At the end of 1991, 200 trade unions with a total membership of 2.75 million were registered with the Department of Manpower. An estimated 300,000 workers belong to some 47 unregistered trade unions. Total union membership represents approximately 45 percent of the employed.
- **Labor bargaining** Tough bargaining distinguishes labor negotiations. The time between the tabling of initial demands at the negotiating table and final settlement can often be two to three months, indicating that employers sometimes spend nearly 25 percent of the year locked in the wage-bargaining process.
- **Labor growth** The National Manpower Commission calculates that, in the past 10 years, formal employment opportunities have grown less than one percent, creating just 500,000 jobs. In contrast the labor supply has grown by an average of 2.8 percent per year.
- **Dispute resolution groups** South Africa is not a member of the International Center for the Settlement of Disputes (Washington Convention) but is a member of the New York Convention of 1958 on the Recognition and Enforcement of Foreign Arbitral Awards.
- **Political violence** South Africa has been one of the most violent societies in the world. Some factors contributing to the violence include competition for resources, ethnic conflict, and the influence of elements in the security forces who oppose the democratic process. In an effort to get a grip on this situation, the South African National Defense Force has been brought in to assume the role of maintaining order in selected townships.
- **International agreements** South Africa is a member of GATT/WTO; Southern African Development Community (GADC); New York Convention on the Recognition and Enforcement of Foreign Arbitral Awards; and ATA Carnet Convention.

LEGAL CONTACTS

Silberbauers Incorporated
Southern Life Centre
8 Riebeek Street
POB 921
8000 Cape Town
Tel: (21) 419-9040 Fax: (21) 214-348
Bowman Gilfillan Hayman Godrey Inc.
JCI House, 12th Floor
28 Harrison Street
POB 2439
Johannesburg 2000
Tel: (11) 836-2811
Fax: (11) 836-6909
Edward Nathan & Friedland Inc.
23rd Floor, Sanlamsentrum
206/214 Jeppe Street
POB 3370
Johannesburg 2000
Tel: (11) 337-2100
Fax: (11) 333-6942
D.M. Kisch Inc.
Syfrets Park
23 Girton Road
Parktown
POB 668
Johannesburg 2000
Tel: (11) 484-4122/9
Fax: (11) 484-2653/4 (24 hours)

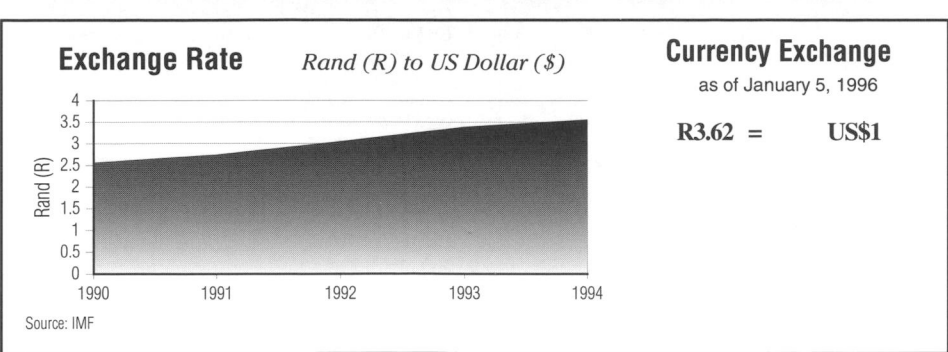

Exchange Rate — Rand (R) to US Dollar ($)

Source: IMF

Currency Exchange
as of January 5, 1996

R3.62 = US$1

Currency

The currency of South Africa is the South African rand (R), which is divided into 100 cents.

Foreign Exchange

The South African Treasury controls all exchange licenses, but has delegated this authority to the Reserve Bank and to authorized dealers throughout South Africa. There are different types of nonresident accounts, depending on whether the nonresident is a member of the Common Monetary Area. All nonresident accounts are subject to exchange control restrictions, but can be opened in any currency.

Capital Transfers

Travelers can import any amount of foreign currency. There are established limits for some invisibles payments. All proceeds must be surrendered within seven days of the date of accrual unless an exemption is obtained. There are no restrictions on the reinvestment of profits and earnings.

Investment Incentives

South Africa is open to foreign investment. It offers a substantial market with growth potential, access to other markets in Africa, and labor costs lower than in Western industrialized countries (although production levels are also lower). All foreign and domestic investment is considered equal. Foreign investors are allowed 100 percent ownership of a company. There is very little screening of nonresident investment. The only major incentive for foreign investors is access to domestic financing and a two-tiered foreign exchange system with a special exchange rate for nonresidents.

Investment Restrictions

Some sectors, including the automotive industry, have specific performance requirements for foreign investors. There are very few restrictions for investors, although the labor and legal problems currently gripping the country could become problems for potential investors. There are a few areas reserved for domestic ownership, primarily those already dominated by state enterprise or related to national security.

Money Matters

BITS AND PIECES

- **Company tax** Company tax is imposed on income from South Africa only.
- **Capital gains** Capital gains are not subject to tax.
- **Foreign tax relief** Unilateral relief is granted through a credit for foreign taxes paid on income deemed to be from a South African source.
- **Capital transfers** All inward transfers are freely permitted, but outward capital transfers require the approval of the Reserve Bank.
- **Gold** Only authorized dealers, monetary authorities, and registered gold producers can hold, buy, and sell gold for any more than numismatic purposes.
- **Excise tax** Specific excise duties are levied on alcoholic and nonalcoholic beverages, tobacco and tobacco products, mineral waters, some petroleum products, and motor vehicles. Ad valorem excise duties are levied on office machine, photographic film, and luxury consumer goods such as cosmetics, home entertainment products, and motorcycles.
- **Tariff rebates** Various rebates and relief of duties exist for cases in which the imported commodity will be used in a subsequent domestic manufacturing or other add-value process. The importer must consult the Import Control Act to determine whether the potential imports are eligible for rebate or relief of customs duty and surcharge.
- **Regulations** Traders are subject to exchange control approval, administered by the South African Reserve Bank. This is only a formality. Advance payment for imports is severally limited under South African Reserve Bank Exchange Control regulations, however. The Ministry of Trade and Industry is empowered to regulate, prohibit, or ration imports to South Africa in the national interest, though most goods may be imported to South Africa without restrictions.
- **Export controls/restrictions** A number of products are subject to export control and licenses, including strategic goods (exhaustible resources), agricultural products administered by control boards, metal waste and scrap. Diamonds for export must be registered with the Diamond Board. Only ostriches and their fertilized eggs are subject to complete export prohibition. Export prohibitions on any product are difficult to enforce. To benefit from export incentives, firms must be registered with and approved by the Department of Trade and Industry.
- **Import payments** Importers are automatically granted exchange to pay for current imports upon presenting to their bank the proof of importation. A permit is also occasionally required. Import tariffs are levied at varying rates, from five to 40 percent.
- **Export payments** In most cases, all exports proceeds must be surrendered within six months of the date of shipment or seven days of the date of accrual. Authorized dealers can grant credit to exporters for up to 12 months.

BANKING CONTACTS

African Bank
ABSA Towers, 19th Floor
160 Main Street
Johannesburg 2001
Tel: (11) 3303222 Telex: 489399
Fax: (11) 3303511

Registrar of Financial Institutions
Private Bag X238
Pretoria 0001
Tel: (12) 325-2550

Rand Merchant Bank Ltd.
25 Fredman Drive
POB 786273
Sandton 2199
Tel: (11) 8833622 Telex: 427602
Fax: (11) 7838651

South African Reserve Bank
Church Square
POB 427
Pretoria 0001
Tel: (12) 313-3911 Fax: (12) 313-3917
Telex: 322425

TAXATION

Taxation requires sophisticated knowledge of complex rules and regulations specific to each country. The information presented here is from the Ernst & Young Corporate Tax Guide and Directory, available from the Ernst & Young accounting office in your country, or from:

Ernst & Young
Mail Address:
POB 2322
Johannesburg 2000
South Africa
Street Address:
Ernst & Young House
4 Pritchard Street
Johannesburg, South Africa

At a Glance

Corporate Income Tax Rate (%) (a)(b)	35
Capital Gains Tax Rate (%)	0
Branch Tax Rate (%) (a)(b)	35
Withholding Tax (%)	
Dividends	15
Interest	0
Royalties from Patents, Know-how, etc. (c)	12
Branch Remittance Tax	0
Net Operating Losses (Years)	
Carryback	0
Carryforward	Unlimited

(a) A secondary tax on companies at a rate of 25% is also imposed.
(b) Gold mining companies are taxed under a special formula with a marginal rate of 58% or under a dual-rate system—company tax at a marginal rate of 43% and the secondary tax on companies.
(c) Applicable to companies that are resident outside South Africa and to nonresident individuals.

Business Travel

LH 1906	MADRID	935	113-3
LH 1022	STUTTGART HBF.	935	--
AF 1701	LYON	940	683-6
AY 822	HELSINKI	940	113-3
AA 071	SFRANCISCO-DALLAS	945	731-7

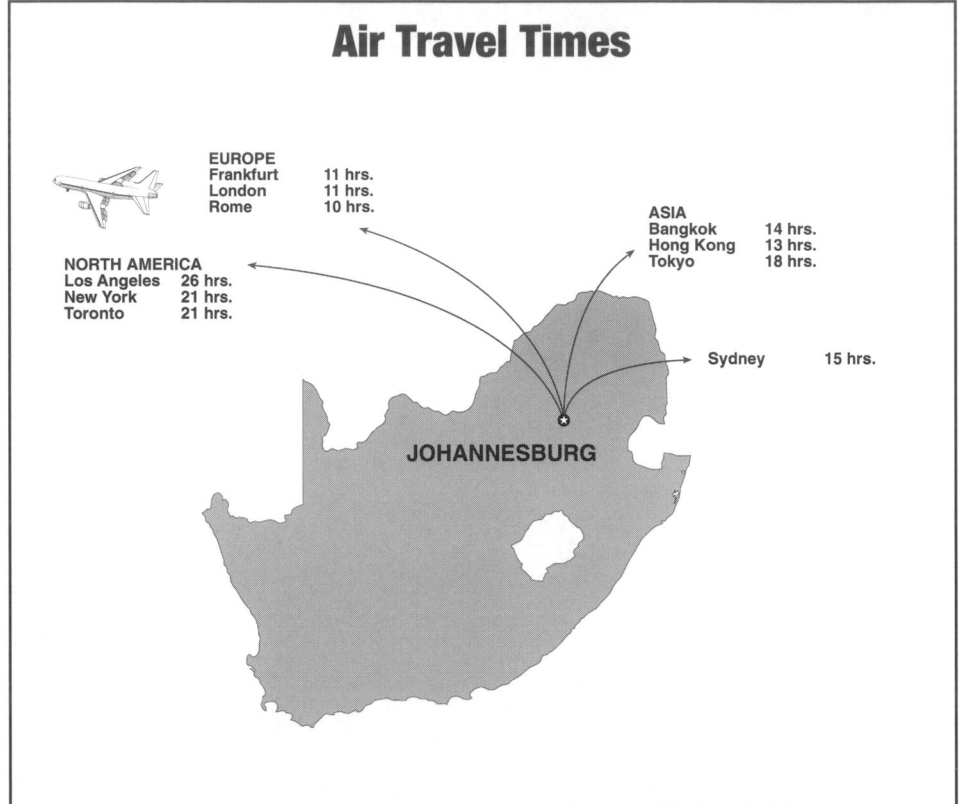

Air Travel Times

EUROPE
Frankfurt   11 hrs.
London   11 hrs.
Rome   10 hrs.

NORTH AMERICA
Los Angeles 26 hrs.
New York   21 hrs.
Toronto   21 hrs.

ASIA
Bangkok   14 hrs.
Hong Kong   13 hrs.
Tokyo   18 hrs.

Sydney   15 hrs.

JOHANNESBURG

COMMUNICATIONS

Telephones Telephone communications are generally good. Direct dialing works within and between cities. Many overseas calls can be dialed direct, but some international calls take several hours to place. Cellular phones are becoming popular.

Fax Fax machines are increasingly common and available in most businesses, government offices, and major hotels.

Post office International mail is dependable; surface mail takes about four times longer than air mail.

BEST TRAVEL BOOKS

The Travel Guide to South Africa, Les De Villiers et al. 256 pages, Business Books International.

South Africa, Lesotho and Swaziland: A Travel Survival Kit. Illustrated, 560 pages. Lonely Planet Publications.

South Africa Pocket Guides. Berlitz Editors Pocket Guides Series, illustrated, 144 pages. Berlitz Publishing Co., Inc.

Culture Shock, A Guide to Customs and Etiquette, South Africa.

Do's and Taboo's Around the World. The Bestselling Guide to International Behavior. Edited by Roger Axtell, compiled by the Parker Pen Company. The ultimate guide to international behavior, now completely updated and expanded. Helpful, fun to read!

USEFUL TELEPHONE NUMBERS

If you are calling from outside South Africa, you will need to add the country code [27] and any other international dialing requirements from within your country.
- South African Railways .... (11) 773893
- Local Information/Directory 1023
- Long Distance Information/Directory 1025
- Taxi Capetown .... (12) 4197777
- Taxi Johannesburg .... (12) 725333
- Taxi Pretoria .... (12) 3258072
- Blue Train .... (11) 7737361
- South African Transportation Services (11) 7734791
- Tourist Office .... (12) 3300188
- Police 10111
- Emergency 999
- Fire Capetown .... (21) 46141
- Fire Johannesburg .... (12) 3312222
- Fire Pretoria .... (12) 3232781

Credit Card Information
Lost or stolen credit cards (call collect to the US, regardless of which country the card was issued in).
- Amex ....[1] (919) 333-3211
- Diner's Club.................................[1] (303) 799-1504
- MasterCard ....[1] (314) 275-6690
- Visa ....[1] (410) 581-7931

Travelogue

WORKWEEK

Offices Monday-Friday 9:00 am to 5:00 pm.
Banks Monday-Friday 9:00 am to 3:30 pm (except Wednesday, 9:00 am to 1:00 pm). Saturday 9:00 am to 11:00 am.
Government Monday-Friday 9:00 am to 3:30 pm (except Wednesday, 9:00 am to 1:00 pm). Saturday 9:00 am to 11:00 am.
Retail Monday-Friday 8:30 am to 5:00 pm. Saturday, 8:30 am to 1:00 pm.

HOLIDAYS

Holidays 1996
January 1 New Year's Day
April 5 Good Friday*
April 8 Easter Monday
April 27 Independence Day
May 1 Workers' Day
May 31 Republic Day
September 2 Settlers' Day *
October 10 Kruger Day
December 25 Christmas Day
December 26 Day of Goodwill
*Dates vary from year to year.

VISA AND PASSPORT

All visitors to South Africa require valid passports. Foreigners except UK citizens need visas, which should be obtained in advance and are usually good for up to 36 months.

DEPARTURE FORMALITIES

Export of foreign currency is limited to the amount declared upon arrival. South African currency can be exported up to R200 per person.

IMMUNIZATION

An international health certificate is required and yellow fever vaccinations are required of visitors from infected areas. Anti-malaria premedication is recommended and should be taken.

TIPPING

No tipping is necessary (unless for exceptional service) at hotels or restaurants that add a 10 percent service charge. If no service charge was added, tip 10 to 15 percent. Porters get about R2; other attendants and taxi drivers about 10 percent; tour and safari guides a little more.

CRIME

Street crime affecting foreigners has increased, especially in urban areas. Do not carry large amounts of cash or walk alone at night. Avoid leaving valuables within sight in cars.

INFRASTRUCTURE

Major hotels, reliable public transportation, and numerous car rental agencies serve South Africa. Domestic air travel is inexpensive and preferred for traveling the great distances that separate major cities. Inner-city transportation is usually by taxi, which cannot be hailed on the street but can be called from restaurants and hotels. Rail, air travel, coach and rental cars are available.

NATIONAL TOURIST OFFICES

Tourist Office
Munitoria Bldg.
Pretoria
Tel: (12) 3137694
Satour
Carlton Centre
Johannesburg
Tel: (11) 3315241

Contacts

GOVERNMENT AGENCIES

Department of Trade and Industry
Private Bag x84
Pretoria 0001
Tel: (12) 310-9791
Fax: (12) 322-0298

Director General of National Education (& Sports/ Recreation)
Private Bag X122
Pretoria 0001
Tel: (12) 314-6001
Fax: (12) 325-2768

Minister of Agriculture
Private Bag X116
Pretoria 0001
Tel: (12) 21-7670
Fax: (12) 21-7219

Minister of Environmental Affairs & Tourism
Private Bag X883
Pretoria 0001

Minister of Finance
Private Bag X115
Pretoria 0001
Tel: (12) 323-8911
Fax: (12) 323-3262

Minister of Health
Private Bag X399
Pretoria 0001
Tel: (12) 328-4773
Fax: (12) 325-5526

Minister of Mineral & Energy Affairs
Private Bag X646
Pretoria 0001
Tel: (12) 322-8695/6
Fax: (12) 322-8699

Minister of National Housing
Private Bag X645
Protoria 0001
Tel: (12) 44-1879
Fax: (12) 343-8934

Minister of Post, Telecommunications & Broadcasting
Private Bag X882
Pretoria 0001
Tel: (12) 319-8000
Fax: (12) 319-8020

Minister of Public Enterprises
POB 55711
Pretoria 0001
Tel: (12) 44-2369
Fax: (12) 44-5848

Minister of Public Works
Private Bag X65
Pretoria 0001
Tel: (12) 324-1510
Fax: (12) 325-6398

Minister of Sports & Recreation
Private Bag X869
Pretoria 0001
Tel: (12) 21-1781/2
Fax: (12) 21-8493

Minister of Transport
Private Bag X193
Pretoria 0001
Tel: (12) 328-3084/5
Fax: (12) 328-3194

Minister of Welfare & Population Development
Private Bag X399
Pretoria 0001
Tel: (12) 328-4600
Fax: (12) 325-7071

Post Master General
Private Bag X860
Pretoria 0001
Tel: (12) 319-8012
Fax: (12) 319-8020

Water Affairs & Forestry
Private Bag X313
Pretoria O001
Tel: (12) 299-2944
Fax: (12) 326-2630

WORLD TRADE CENTER

World Trade Centre Johannesburg
World Trade Centre Building
World Trade Centre Avenue
Kempton Park 1620
Jurgens Park
Tel: (11) 883-3737
Fax: (11) 975-9415

BUSINESS AND TRADE ORGANIZATIONS

South African Foreign Trade Organization
POB 782706
Sandton 2146
Tel: (11) 883-3737
Fax: (11) 883-6569

Association for the Promotion of the Western Cape
POB 1678
Cape Town 8000
Tel: (21) 45-3201
Fax: (21) 45-3751

Agricultural and Veterinary Chemicals Association
POB 1995
Halfway House
Tel: (11) 805-2079, 805-2070
Fax: (11) 805-2222

Computer Users Industry Council of South Africa
5 Alexandra Avenue
Halfway House Box
1688 Halfway House
Tel: (11) 805-3151

Motor Industries Federation
POB 2940
Randburg 2125
Tel: (11) 789-2542

Motion Picture Association
POB 52867
Saxonwold 2132
Tel: (11) 880-5885
Fax: (11) 880-5493

South African Direct Marketing Association
POB 85370
Emmarentia 2029
Tel: (11) 482-1419
Fax: (11) 726-3807

Computing Services Association
Private Bag 34
Auckland Park 2006
Tel: (11) 726-5300
Fax: (11) 726-8421

Business Equipment Association
POB 3277
Randburg 2125
Tel: (11) 789-3805
Fax: (11) 789-3327

National Clothing Federation of South Africa
POB 75755
Gardenview 2047
Tel: (11) 622-8125
Fax (11) 622-8316

Council of Southern African Banks
POB 61380
Marshalltown 2107
Tel: (11) 838-5833
Fax: (11) 833-1072

The South African Association of Consulting Engineers
POB 1644
Randburg 2125
Tel: (11) 787-5944
Fax (11) 789-5264

Electrical Engineering & Allied Industries Association
POB 1338
Johannesburg 2000
Tel: (11) 833-6033
Fax (11) 838-1522

The Grocery Manufacturers' Association of South Africa
POB 34
Randburg 2125
Tel: (11) 886-3008
Fax: (11) 886-5375

Chamber of Mines
5 Hollard Street
POB 809
Johannesburg
Tel: (11) 838-8211
Fax: (11) 834-1884

Black Association of Travel Agents of South Africa
POB 11435
Marine Parade
Durban 4060
Tel: (31) 37-6433/4
Fax: (31) 37-3805

Foundation for African Business & Consumer Organizations
POB 8785
Johannesburg 2000
Tel: (11) 832-1911
Fax: (11) 836-5920

South African Black Franchisers Association
POB 80
Meadowlands 1851
Tel: (11) 939-2121
Fax: (11) 939-2013

South African Import and Export Association
POB 9736
Johannesburg 2000
Tel: (11) 839-1385/6
Fax: (11) 839-1386

African Industrial Development Corporation
POB 1280
Edenvale 1610
Tel: (11) 609-4053
Fax: (11) 452-6403

Business Opportunity Centre
POB 828
Auckland Park 2006
Tel: (11) 839-2750/1
Fax: (11) 839-1897

CHAMBERS OF COMMERCE

American Chamber of Commerce in Southern Africa
POB 62280
2107 Marshalltown
Tel: (11) 788-0265/6
Fax: (11) 880-1632

South African Chamber of Business
POB 91267
Auckland Park 2006
Tel: (11) 482-2524
Fax: (11) 726-1344

Johannesburg Chamber of Commerce and Industry
Private Bag 34
Auckland Park 2006
Tel: (11) 726-5300
Fax: (11) 726-8421

Durban Regional Chamber of Business
POB 1506
Durban 4000
Tel: (31) 301-3699
Fax: (31) 301-3699

Cape Town Chamber of Commerce
POB 204
Cape Town 8000
Tel: (21) 23-2323
Fax: (21) 24-1878

National African Federated Chamber of Commerce & Industry
Private Bag X81
Soshanguve 0152
Tel: (1214) 3204/6
Fax: (1214) 2024

FREIGHT FORWARDERS

South African Association of Freight Forwarders
Private Bag 34
Auckland Park
Johannesburg
Tel: (11) 726-4019
Fax: (11) 726-3415

STOCK EXCHANGE

Johannesburg Stock Exchange
POB 1174
Johannesburg 2000
Tel: (11) 8336580
Telex: 487663

LEGAL CONTACTS

Goldman Judin and Werner
1st Floor, Village Walk
Maude Street
Johannesburg 2146 (Sandton)
Tel: (11) 883 5667/8
Fax: (11) 883 5669

Lindsay, Keller & Partners
6th Floor, JHI House
11 Cradock Avenue, Rosebank
Johannesburg 2196
Tel: (11) 880-8980
Fax: (11) 880-9182

Mallinick, Ress, Richman & Closenberg
2 Long Street
Cape Town 8001
Tel: (21) 419-4411
Fax: (21) 217-207

Moss-Morris Inc.
20th Floor, Office Tower
Sandton City, Fifth Street
Sandton
Johannesburg 2000
Tel: (11) 884-9367
Fax: (11) 884-7949

Webber Wentzel Bowens
60 Main Street
Johannesburg 2001
Tel: (11) 832-2636
Fax: (11) 834-6701

Werksmans
22 Girton Road
Parktown
POB 927
Johannesburg 2000
Tel: (11) 488-0000
Fax: (11) 484-3100, 484-3200

NEWSPAPERS

Bureau of Information
Private Bag X745
Pretoria 0001
Tel: (12) 3142911
Fax: (12) 3233831

Directorate of Publications
Private Bag X9069
Cape Town 8000
Tel: (21) 456518
Fax: (21) 456511

South African Media Council
POB 31559
Braamfontein
Tel: (11) 4032878
Fax: (11) 4032879

The Argus
POB 56
Cape Town 8000
Tel: (21) 4884911
Fax: (21) 4884075
Telex: 527383

Die Burger
POB 692
Cape Town 8000
Tel: (21) 4062222
Fax: (21) 4062913
Telex: 527751

Cape Times
POB 11
Cape Town 8000
Tel: (21) 4884911
Fax: (21) 4884717

Daily Dispatch
33 Caxton St.
POB 131
East London 5200
Tel: (431) 430010
Fax: (431) 435159
Telex: 250678

Eastern Province Herald
POB 1117
Port Elizabeth 6000
Tel: (41) 5047911
Fax: (41) 554966
Telex: 243351

Evening Post
POB 1121
Port Elizabeth 6000
Tel: (41) 5047911
Fax: (41) 554966
Telex: 243351

Oosterling
52 Cawood St.
POB 525
Port Elizabeth 6000
Tel: (41) 542431
Fax: (41) 545166

RADIO AND TELEVISION

South African Broadcasting Corporation (SABC)
Private Bag X1
Auckland Park 2006
Tel: (11) 7149111
Fax: (11) 7143106
Telex: 424116

Channel Africa Radio
POB 91313
Auckland Park 2006
Tel: (11) 7142600

SABC-Television
Private Bag X41
Auckland Park 2006
Tel: (11) 7149111
Fax: (11) 7145005
Telex: 424116

BUSINESS PERIODICALS

South African Builder
Emdon Publishing
POB 1123
Pinegowrie 2123
Tel: (11) 886-0208
Fax: (11) 789-5223

Financial Mail
Times Media Publications
POB 9959
Johannesburg 2000
Tel: (11) 497-2711
Fax: (11) 834-1686

Finance Week
Finance Week Pty Ltd.
Private Bag 78816
Sandton 2146
Tel: (11) 444-0555
Fax: (11) 444-0424

Franchise Digest
Franchise Association of Southern Africa
POB 31708
Braamfontein 2017
Tel: (11) 403-3468
Fax: (11) 403-1279

Enterprise Magazine (Black Business)
POB 91845
Auckland Park 2006
Tel: (11) 483-3863
Fax: (11) 483-3194

Chem Data
CSIR
POB 395
Pretoria 0001
Tel: (12) 841-2911
Fax: (12) 86-2869

Computer Week
Systems Publishers Pty Ltd.
Private Bag X8
Craighall 2196
Tel: (11) 789-1808
Fax: (11) 789-4725

Computing South Africa
Thomson's Publications
POB 56182
Pinegowrie 2123
Tel: (11) 789-2144
Fax: (11) 789-3196

INTERNET ADDRESSES

Usenet group(s):
soc.culture.south-africa

South African Reserve Bank
http://www.resbank.co.za/

African National Congress Homepage
http://www.anc.org.za/

Independent Online News Service
http://www.independent.co.za/news/

Index South Africa
http://minotaur.marques.co.za/index.htm

Virtual South Africa
http://africa.com/

TravelNet
http://os2.iaccess.za/travel/index.htm

South Korea
Republic of Korea

Economy

Overview

A devastated, largely agrarian economy in the early 1950s, South Korea has grown to become one of the developing world's biggest success stories. Exports remain very strong, and even though imports are rising at an even faster rate, the economy shows no signs of overheating. Korea's business environment is dominated by *chaebol*, large conglomerates that set the tone for businesses nationwide. South Korea has a reputation for protectionism and for an environment that favors domestic competitors at the expense of outsiders. South Korea is also losing the labor cost edge that enabled it to develop so rapidly, and it is now trying to revamp its economy to focus on higher-value-added products in order to compete in a global economy in which even lower cost competitors are challenging its dominance.

Trade

Major exports include apparel, semiconductors, ships and boats, imaging equipment, man-made fabrics, and iron and steel plates. Imports include crude oil, semiconductors, petrochemicals, iron and steel, computer equipment, and lumber. South Korea's main trading partners include the US—which accounts for nearly 25 percent of its total trade—Japan, Hong Kong, Germany, Singapore, and Saudi Arabia.

Sectors

Agriculture South Korea is traditionally an agricultural society, but the sector's relative input is declining because of the rise in the contributions of the industrial and service sectors. Accounting for less than 10 percent of GDP, agriculture continues to employ about 17 percent of the work force.

Industry Employing only slightly more than 25 percent of the work force, industry provides somewhat less than half of GDP, and has been the engine driving growth in the economy for the past decade. The main activities include machinery, transportation equipment, chemicals, textiles, iron and steel production, and food processing. South Korea is focusing on higher-value-added production as it loses cost competitiveness in traditional low- and mid-range manufacturing.

Services Growing more rapidly than the economy as a whole, the service sector already employs more than half of the work force and contributes nearly 50 percent of GDP. Productivity has been low, primarily because of overregulation, but deregulation of these industries could spur substantial growth. Tourism is growing, and provides an ever greater contribution to the GDP.

Trends

Aggressive trading practices, booming manufacturing sectors, and a healthy currency are bright spots in South Korea's economic future. Major impediments to continued economic success in South Korea include its obsolete infrastructure, stringent controls, and waning cost competitiveness. The government has announced that a major goal will be improvement of roads, airports, and the telecommunication industry. South Korea's poor reputation for attracting foreign investment and the number of complaints from foreign firms regarding South Korea's exclusionary business practices could hurt the country's chances of moving ahead economically, at least at the rapid pace of recent years. While its labor force is an asset, South Korea has a shortage of skilled, technical workers and is fast becoming overpriced in the international market.

At a Glance

THE COUNTRY
Location Eastern Asia, between North Korea and Japan.
Terrain Mostly hills and mountains, wide costal plains in the west.
Climate Temperate climate; its four seasons are like that of the eastern US.

THE PEOPLE
Population 45,000,000
Ethnic composition
Koreans make up almost 100 percent of the population.
Religious composition
Mayahana Buddhism 7.5%
Traditional Protestant 6.9%
The majority of Koreans believe in varying mixtures of Taoism, Confucianism, Buddhism, Christianity, Ch'ondogyo, and local animism.
Languages spoken Korean is the official language, although English is widely taught in schools.
Education and literacy Six years are compulsory and free to the public, and secondary schools are available. Almost 87 percent of students are enrolled in secondary schools. About 99.1 percent of males over the age of 15 can read and write, and 93 percent of females.
Labor force
Total: 20,000,000
By occupation: services and other 52%, mining and manufacturing 27%, agriculture, fishing, forestry 21%.

COUNTRY FACTS
Political and legal Republic, with powers shared between the president and the legislature. Political parties: Government party—Democratic Liberal Party (DLP), Opposition parties—New Democratic Union (DDU) and Democratic Party (DP).
Telephone Excellent domestic and international services. There are over 14 million telephone lines. International country code [82]. City codes: Seoul (2), Taegu (53).
Transportation International airports serve Seoul (Kimpo), Pusan (Kimhae), and Cheju Island. Extensive intercity air, rail, and bus service is available. There is an excellent network of local bus, taxi, and, in Seoul, subway services.
Environment The Korean Peninsula is rich in varieties of plant life typical of temperate regions. Warm temperate vegetation, including camellias and other broadleaved evergreens, predominate. Current issues include air pollution in large cities, water pollution from the discharge of sewage, and industrial effluents.
Media Press censorship still exists, and reporters critical of the government have been harassed. There are 39 daily newspapers, half published in Seoul. The six major newspapers have a combined circulation of eight million. There are 79 AM, 46 FM, and 256 TV stations. Many periodicals exist.
Health Services are fair to good in most major cities. Most Korean physicians have been trained in Western medicine and hospital services are adequate. Outside of the major hotels, water generally is not potable. Life expectancy of men is 67 years, of women, 73 years.

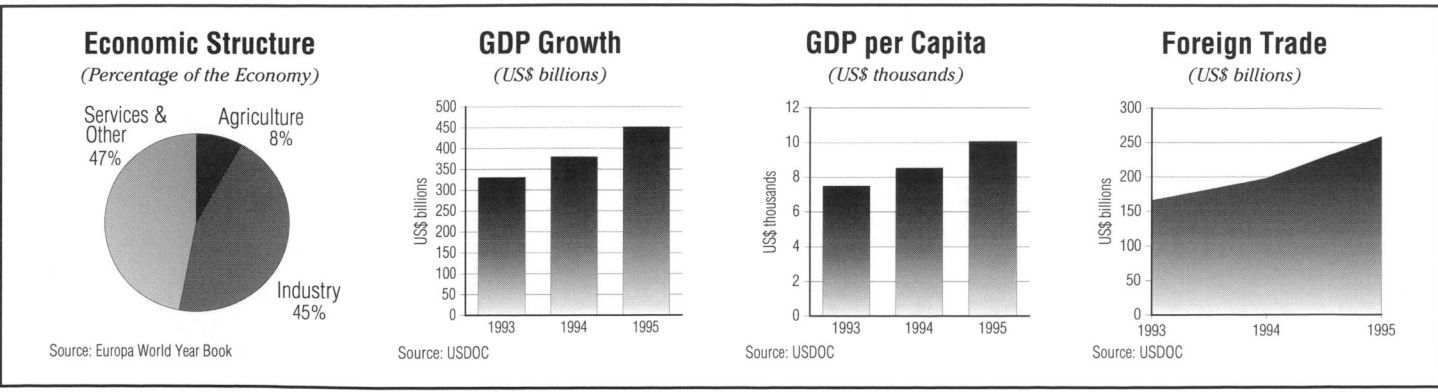

Economic Structure
(Percentage of the Economy)

Services & Other 47%
Agriculture 8%
Industry 45%

Source: Europa World Year Book

GDP Growth
(US$ billions)

Source: USDOC

GDP per Capita
(US$ thousands)

Source: USDOC

Foreign Trade
(US$ billions)

Source: USDOC

South Korea

☆	National capital
⊙	Administrative capital
●	Secondary city
───	International boundary
·········	Administrative boundary
───	Primary road
───	Secondary road
·········	Railroad
─ ─ ─	Demarcation line
▬▬▬	Demilitarized zone
⚓	Primary ports
⊠	Airfields

0   25   50   75 km
0   25   50 mi

Administrative Notes

*The South Korean Province of Kyonggi is administered from Seoul.

*The South Korean Province of Kyongsang-bukto is administered from Taegu.

*The South Korean Province of Kyongsang-namdo is administered from Pusan.

*The South Korean City of Kwangju is an individual Province, and the administrative Capital of Cholla-namdo Province.

©1995 Magellan GeographixSMSanta Barbara, CA

P'yongyang
Onch'on
Namp'o-si
Tae-ri
Namp'o
Majon-ni
Kosan
Yonsan
T'ongch'on
Kangwon
Kosong
Hwanghae-bukto
Sep'o
Kansong
Sinch'on
Sariwon
Ich'on
P'yonggang
Changyon-up
P'yongsan
Hwanghae-namdo
Haeju
Kaesong-si
Hwach'on
Kangwon
Inje
Yangyang
Ongjin
Kaesong
Yonch'on
Kyonggi
Ch'unch'on
Kangnung
Munsan
Uijongbu
Kukch'on
Soul-t'ukpyolsi
Hongch'on
Kimp'o
Yangp'yong
Inch'on-Jikhalsi
Seoul
Yoyang-ni
Pukp'yong-ni
Inch'on
Suwon
Yoju
Wonju
Hwangji-ri
P'yongt'aek
Ansong
Chech'on
Sosan
Chungju
Tanyang
Ch'onan
Ch'ungch'ong-bukto
Yongju
Yong-yang
Hongsong
Ch'ongju
Yech'on
Ch'ungch'ong-namdo
Kongju
Poun
Chomch'on
Andong
Yongdok
Taech'on
Kam-gang
Taejon
Sangju
Uisong
Kyongsang-bukto
Yongdong
Kimch'on
Kunsan
Iri
P'ohang
Chonju
Chinan
Yongch'on
Kyongju
Cholla-bukto
Taegu
Chongup
Anui
Hapch'on
Onyang
Ulsan
Namwon
Namji-ri
Yangsan
Yonggwang
Kyongsang-namdo
Chinju
Kimhae
Kwangju
Masan
Pusan
Yongsanp'o
Sunch'on
Samch'onp'a
Cholla-namdo
Yosu
Koje-do
Mokp'o
Posong
Kangjin
Chin
Wando
Kohung
Chindo
Cheju
Cheju
Cheju-do

Sea of Japan
Ullung-do
South Korea
130°
37°
38°
36°
34°
Korea Strait
Western Channel
Eastern Channel
Shushi
Tsushima
Iki
Japan
Sasebo
126°
128°
130°

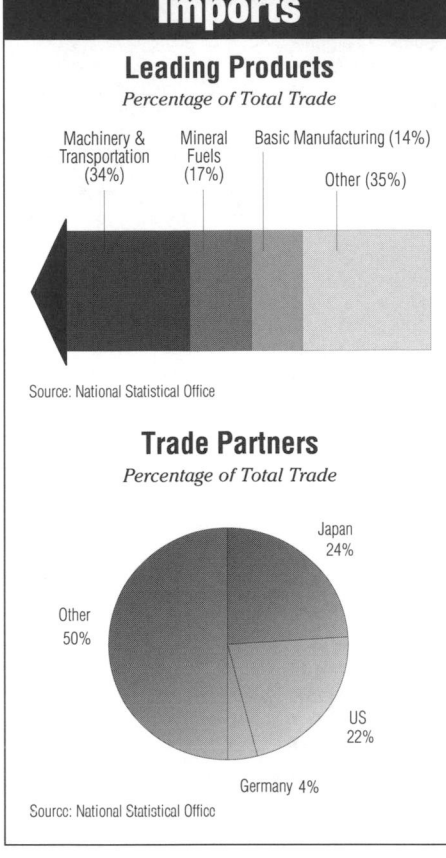

Imports

Leading Products
Percentage of Total Trade

Machinery & Transportation (34%)
Mineral Fuels (17%)
Basic Manufacturing (14%)
Other (35%)

Source: National Statistical Office

Trade Partners
Percentage of Total Trade

Japan 24%
Other 50%
US 22%
Germany 4%

Source: National Statistical Office

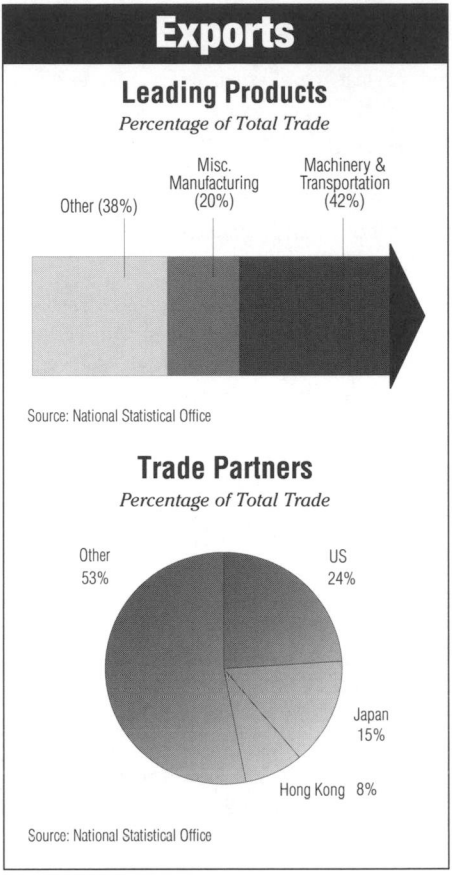

Exports

Leading Products
Percentage of Total Trade

Other (38%)
Misc. Manufacturing (20%)
Machinery & Transportation (42%)

Source: National Statistical Office

Trade Partners
Percentage of Total Trade

Other 53%
US 24%
Japan 15%
Hong Kong 8%

Source: National Statistical Office

Opportunities

FOR IMPORTING TO SOUTH KOREA

- automotive parts and service equipment
- computer hardware, software, and peripherals
- cosmetics and toiletries
- drugs and pharmaceuticals
- electronic components
- electronics industry production and test equipment
- films, videos, and audio recordings
- food processing and packaging equipment
- household consumer goods: dishwashers, ovens, refrigerators, washers and dryers
- industrial process control equipment
- laboratory instruments
- machine tools and metalworking equipment
- medical equipment
- pollution control equipment
- pulp and paper processing equipment
- refrigeration equipment
- telecommunications equipment

FOR EXPORTING FROM SOUTH KOREA

- agricultural products: ginseng, leaf tobacco, leather, seafood
- automobiles
- chemical products
- computers and peripherals
- consumer electronics: musical instruments, microwave ovens, radios, television sets
- cookware
- electronic components
- footwear
- home appliances: air conditioners, ovens, refrigerators, washers and dryers
- iron and steel
- machine tools, semiconductors
- ships
- sporting goods and recreational equipment
- textiles and apparel
- toys
- turbines, generators, and other machinery

GROWTH SECTORS

- advertising services
- building projects
- cable television
- information services
- real estate
- retail distribution
- securities market
- telecommunications services
- travel and tourism

GOVERNMENT PROCUREMENT

- construction of new industrial zones for traditional and high-technology products
- environmental protection
- electrical power systems
- road and railway construction and expansion
- telecommunications products

Trade News

RULES AND REGULATIONS

- **Regulation** The Ministry of Trade and Industry (MTI) governs most aspects of South Korea's foreign trade. It sets trade policy, issues trading and import licenses, and regulates import restrictions.
- **Trading license** Those wishing to conduct export or import business in South Korea must register with and obtain a license from the MTI. Traders are classified into two groups: Class A traders are specialized traders whose activities are not restricted. Class B traders are small- and medium-sized enterprises whose activities are restricted.
- **Import license** In addition to a trading license, importers must have a specific license for every import transaction. Licenses for unrestricted commodities are issued automatically on application to the South Korea Exchange Bank or any Class A foreign exchange bank or branch.
- **Import restrictions** Most raw materials, capital goods, and consumer goods are not restricted. Certain agricultural products, luxury items, and domestically produced goods are restricted or prohibited. About 376 items are classified as restricted. Restrictions are scheduled to be phased out by July 1, 1997, in accordance with GATT.
- **Trading companies** Korean general trading companies (GTCs), known in South Korea as *chaebol*, are modeled after the highly successful large-scale Japanese trading firms. GTCs act as a liaison between buyer and seller and are eligible for, among other things, preferential measures regarding importation of raw materials and participation in international tenders.
- **Tariffs** Tariff rates for imported raw materials and manufactured goods were to be reduced from an average of 13 percent in 1988 to 7.9 percent in 1993. Not all reductions have taken place and some rates have actually been raised, though the general trend is to reduce tariff rates so that they equal the rates of the world's developed economies.
- **Export policies** South Korea is liberalizing its export policies by allowing more local agents and distributors to act as buyers and sellers of Korean goods. Traders must register with and obtain a license from MTI. Inspection of products leaving South Korea may be either voluntary or mandatory depending on product.

FREIGHT FORWARDERS

Customs Brokers Association
209-9, Nonhyon-dong, Kangnam-gu
Seoul
Tel: (2) 547-9714/6
Fax: (2) 549-7813

Korea International Freight Forwarders Association
80, Chockson-dong, Chongno-gu
Seoul
Tel: (2) 783-8000
Fax: (2) 733-7249

Korean Shippers Council
Rm. 4404, KWTC Bldg.
159, Samsung-dong, Kangnam-gu
Seoul
Tel: (2) 551-5383/5
Fax: (2) 551-5231

American President Lines Ltd.
14/F., Daehan Fire Ins. Bldg.
51-1, Namchang-dong, Chung-gu
Seoul
Tel: (2) 772-0701
Fax: (2) 756-9688/9

Dongwoo Express International Co., Ltd.
9/F., Sejong Bldg.
100, Tanglu-dong, Chongno-gu
Seoul
Tel: (2) 739-9801
Fax: (2) 737-7254

Overview

South Korea is one of the world's most dynamic economies. Per capita wealth has been growing; and the wealthier Koreans get, the more processed food they eat, the more reference and educational books they read, and the more color televisions, computers, stereo systems, washing machines, and microwave ovens they buy. Despite government threats of tax audits against Koreans traveling abroad who bring back too many foreign purchases, Koreans continue to travel, and spend, at record rates. Impediments to trade include the language barrier, petty bureaucratic obstruction, nontransparent regulations, and a morass of exclusive and monopoly tie-ins and other relations with the *chaebol*.

Distribution

Foreign manufacturers can enter this market through agents, branch offices, joint ventures, and subsidiaries. Most consumer goods enter through the major cities: Seoul or Inchon in the north, Taejon in the central region, or Pusan in the south. A complex network of small family-run outlets, which are all but incomprehensible to the foreigner, handle most retail distribution. The many large department stores in Seoul and Pusan may provide the fastest way for an overseas firm to present its goods to consumers. General merchandise stores, chain stores, shopping centers, and high-volume discount stores have recently been generating interest. Midrange and upscale department store sales are growing, as are purchases made using credit cards. The distribution system is gradually being overhauled and streamlined, which can only benefit foreign companies.

Agents, Distributors, and Partners

Registered traders and offer agents are the best means for outsiders seeking to enter the Korean market. Registered traders are importers and wholesalers licensed by the government who buy and sell for their own accounts. These firms make all arrangements and process all paperwork. However, they often handle goods from firms in many countries and can rarely give a product the attention the foreign company desires. Most offer agents are branches of firms based in the US, Hong Kong, and Japan. Most generally give more personal attention to promoting their customers' products; however, few have the influence and connections found at the large registered trading firms. Door-to-door sales forces handle a range of items from books and cutlery to water purifiers and yogurt drinks. Joint ventures are permitted, but tend to be controlled by *chaebol*-related Korean partners.

Selling Techniques

Adapt products to Korean tastes and conditions. Stay in close contact with business partners and customers and consistently display a firm commitment to the Korean market. Frequent visits by parent company representatives, bringing local representatives to the home company for development updates, and frequent demonstrations and exhibitions are all ways to tie distributors to the products they handle. Geographic proximity and technical sophistication have made Japanese products the standard by which Koreans tend to judge other products, although they are amenable to accepting other products, provided the others demonstrate sufficient advantages in features or pricing.

Advertising

All major international advertising agencies maintain a presence in Korea, and several local agencies are both internationally oriented and familiar with the concerns of foreign firms seeking to place products in the Korean market. Newspapers receive the largest share of advertising expenditures; there are 39 dailies, including specialized financial and foreign language papers, and some weeklies. Television time purchased before January 1990 can be held indefinitely by the purchaser. This "permanent time" is sold on a weekly basis regardless of client or product seasonality. There is fierce competition for the remaining spots, usually sold in 15-second blocks. Nearly 800 cinemas run commercial advertising. Seoul has a world-class 55-story structure and exhibition hall complex, the Korea World Trade Center; shows there attract an international and regional clientele, as well as a nationwide audience.

Service and Customer Support

After-sales service ranks just below product features as a selling point. Although a tradition of self-reliant improvisation in servicing remains, heavy competition among foreign suppliers to provide professional service has become a much more important part of selling. Prospective competitors must measure themselves against Japanese firms, which set the standard for customer service. High-quality training programs—and the actual provision of engineers to install and trouble-shoot specialized equipment—are methods used by outsiders seeking to offer superior service in Korean markets.

Marketing in Korea

MARKETING TIPS

- **Franchises** The franchising business is developing rapidly; it currently includes fast food restaurants, retailing, hotels, automotive parts and service, travel, and amusement.

- **Choosing partners** Koreans are extremely nationalistic and often operate with hidden agendas that favor the local partner; foreign outfits must exercise care when selecting a Korean partner to make sure that both parties understand the expectations of the other and that the necessary community of interest exists to properly promote the foreign product.

- **Government markets** Tenders are handled through the Office of Supply of the Republic of South Korea (OSROK). Bids must be made through a registered Korean agent. Awards are made to the lowest bidder, but there is room for negotiation based on specifications, schedules, and other considerations.

- **Work with your agent** Visit often; demonstrate your products thoroughly; provide promotional literature in Korean and to the local agent's specifications; work on follow-up and support in sales dealing with sales leads; and be sure you deliver on time.

AD AGENCIES

Adworld International
1031-28, Sadang 1-dong, Tongjak-gu
Seoul
Tel: (2) 585-5744 Fax: (2) 581-6626

Cheil Bozell, Inc.
5/F., Jung-Dong Bldg.
15-5, Jung-Dong, Choong-gu
Seoul 100-120
Tel: (2) 773-5321 Fax: (2) 773-7990

Dae Hong Advertising Inc.
(Affil. with DDB Needham Worldwide)
1, Kongpyong-dong, Chongno-gu
Seoul
Tel: (2) 724-8114 Fax: (2) 735-7112

J. Walter Thompson Korea Ltd.
Dongwon Bldg.
41-4, 2-ka, Myungryun-dong
Chongro-ku
Seoul 110-522
Tel: (2) 745-8663 Fax: (2) 745-8662

Jin Advertising Co., Ltd.
50-10, 2-ga, Chungmu-ro, Chung-gu
Seoul
Tel: (2) 275-7001 Fax: (2) 277-0040

Korad, Ogilvy & Mather
Samtan Bldg.
947-7, Daechi-dong, Kangnam-ku
Seoul
Tel: (2) 564-0066 Fax: (2) 565-2676/77

Korea First Advertising Co., Ltd.
108-2, Ryong-dong, Chongno-gu
Seoul
Tel: (2) 730-9711 Fax: (2) 739-5672

Nara Advertising Inc.
28-1, Chamwon-dong, Socho-gu
Seoul
Tel: (2) 549-0691 Fax: (2) 549-0690

Oricom Inc.
105-7, Nonhyon-dong, Kangnam-gu
Seoul
Tel: (2) 510-3114 Fax: (2) 542-3966

Saatchi & Saatchi/Ye-Eum
7/F., Iljin Bldg.
50-1, Dohwa-dong, Mapo-ku
Seoul
Tel: (2) 707-9700 Fax: (2) 707-9800, 707-9840

Samhee Communications Inc.
(Affil. with Lintas Worldwide)
34, Sosomun-dong, Chung-gu
Seoul
Tel: (2) 774-3232 Fax: (2) 756-667

Union Advertising Inc.
(Affil. with Grey Pacific)
22, Chong-dong, Chung-gu
Seoul
Tel: (2) 739-2951 Fax: (2) 736-42185

Business Culture

Greetings and Courtesies

Koreans are extremely polite, friendly, and formal in business dealings. Face, a measure of one's dignity, is crucial to Koreans. They are enormously sensitive to maintaining face in everything they do. Saying or doing anything that causes someone to lose face can instantly destroy a relationship and any business that might result from it. Never insult or openly criticize someone in front of others, no matter how subtle you think the criticism may be. Koreans generally bow to each other, but with foreigners handshaking is now the accepted greeting. In very formal situations, and if dealing with an older person, bowing is appropriate. If you are not sure whether to bow or shake hands, allow the Koreans to take the lead. Business cards are important. At the first meeting, handshakes or bows are followed by a formal exchange of cards, with text in Korean on one side. When receiving a card, do not just put it in your pocket. Take a few moments to study the card, and respond to it with the proper respect.

Business Ethic and Framework

Koreans are generally highly disciplined and hard-working, but they can also be distrustful of outsiders and extremely nationalistic. Korean behavior is largely determined by Confucianism, which teaches respect for superiors, duty to family, loyalty to friends, humility, sincerity, and courtesy. Workers generally respect the companies they work for and are driven to help their business succeed. Among coworkers, people of higher status and age are respected by those beneath them, and are deferred to in speech and action. Business friends trust and respect each other, and help each other succeed. Employees work hard and are generally efficient and productive. Management styles are a combination of Confucianism and Western behavior, depending on an individual's background. Generally, business is conducted formally, with great value placed on punctuality, efficiency, and thriftiness.

Decision Making

Koreans make it a point never to act as individuals but to have group cohesion. Before any action is taken or a decision made, there must be consensus from everyone involved. This is reached by circulating written memos that must receive everyone's approval. Koreans try not to say no or deliver bad news. If a project or negotiation develops problems, no one will want to admit there are difficulties and it may be necessary to look for subtle signs that something has gone wrong.

Women

Women are regarded as second-class citizens. Korean women are generally employed only as secretaries, no matter how much education they have or what kind of abilities they demonstrate. However, foreign businesswomen should experience few problems. Nevertheless, they are expected to be highly professional, appropriate, and neither aggressive nor confrontational. Women may generally go on the streets and dine alone, but may feel more comfortable if escorted.

Meetings

Business meetings are very formal. Arrange the time and place well in advance, and be sure to be punctual. Before a meeting, mail or fax the subjects and issues under discussion and include as much detail as possible. Koreans generally are not sure how to behave at a first meeting until everyone's status is determined. Questions about one's education, parents, place of birth, or age all help to determine status. Koreans are more at ease as a group than as individuals, and become uncomfortable when people speak as individuals instead of as a group, or when they make statements that are not in harmony with the stated group view. One person should be designated as your group's spokesman. This should be the group's senior member. Koreans will judge the seriousness of your dealings by the status of your representatives in your company. It is a good idea to send them a list of these representatives before the meeting, and to include their rank in your company. You should also request a similar list.

Business Attire

Koreans dress formally and usually wear three-piece suits for business. You will probably be judged by the quality of your attire, so your best clothes are most appropriate. Accessories and jewelry such as rings and watches will also be taken into account and admired by your Korean business counterparts, but avoid excessively expensive or showy jewelry or ornaments.

Cultural Cautions

DO'S

- Be aware of the importance of face in all your dealings with Koreans.
- Always treat people with the respect to which their position entitles them.
- Thank people for a job well-done or praise them in front of their superiors for their good work.
- In South Korea, business relationships are personal relationships. To create a good business relationship, establish a personal connection that demonstrates your respect and trustworthiness. It could pay off in the end.

DON'TS

- Never do or say anything that could cause someone to lose face.
- Do not insult or harshly criticize someone in front of others.
- Don't make fun of someone, even as a playful joke.
- If things go wrong, never single out one person for blame. They will lose face and you will destroy your relationship with them.

CUSTOMS

- Gift giving is common, expected, and part of doing business. Bribery is common, too. Giving a gift of money to individuals in the company will often accomplish a lot. But bribes are officially illegal and it is difficult to know how much to give or when. Your Korean business counterparts will often hint about gifts.
- Accounting procedures are most irregular in South Korea. Manipulating financial records to show a profit or instill investor and consumer confidence is common. Be extremely cautious when checking a company's finances.

OBSERVATIONS

- Business dealings can be made easier by hiring a Korean advisor or consultant.
- Koreans prefer to deal with the same person, and treat every interaction as a personal one. The same individual should always represent your company and be prepared to hold that position at least three years.
- In South Korea, the value of a written contract is tied to the personal relationship of those who sign it. Further, if one of these people is relocated or quits his job, Koreans will tend to view the contract as cancelled unless it is negotiated again. Be sure everyone understands all aspects of the contract before agreeing to it.
- Business matters involve enormous red tape, and all documents are subject to revision by anyone who reviews them. It is extremely important to maintain personal relationships with everyone involved in a deal.

NEGOTIATIONS

- Outsiders are not given the same respect as other Koreans.
- Be prepared for almost anything, including intimidation, unrealistic promises, and strategies that obviously benefit the Koreans.
- In South Korea, a common business tactic is to delay major negotiations until you're about to leave the country, then try to place unreasonable demands and conditions on your proposal.
- If you have a product that Koreans want and cannot get elsewhere, emphasize its value; it will be appreciated.
- Be prepared to walk away. You will gain more from making it clear that you would rather have no deal at all than a bad deal.
- Don't give things away. This will be viewed as a sign of weakness. Every agreement must be reached by give and take. Always get something for everything you give.
- Sometimes even a signed agreement does not mean negotiations are finished. Koreans will always seek a better deal and will sometimes sign an agreement they do not intend to keep.

Legal

Legal System

With the introduction of the Western legal system around 1900, South Korea adopted a continental civil law system with a set of codes: civil, commercial, criminal, and civil procedure. The common law of the US has been quite influential upon the Korean legal system and practice.

Intellectual Property Rights

Patents and Trademarks South Korea is a first-to-file jurisdiction. It is necessary to file first in order to claim a patent or trademark, regardless of who was first to create the underlying mark, product, or procedure. On average, it takes four years to have a patent registered in the Korean Industrial Property Office (KIPO). For a trademark, the average period is one and a half years. Certain disputes related to patents or trademarks are subject to a unique administrative adjudication. Complaints related to a grant or rejection of registration are heard by administrative judges at the KIPO. An appeal is taken by an appellate board in the same office. An aggrieved party in these administrative trials may only seek a final judgment in the Supreme Court. In 1998, however, a patent court will be established and take appeals from the initial administrative trial. Infringements of trade secrets are forbidden under the Unfair Competition Prevention Act (UCPA). UCPA also prohibits the use of marks which may confuse one's business with the business of a competitor. The scope of trademark protection is relatively narrow in South Korea. Famous foreign trademarks may invoke these UCPA provisions only if they are proven to be "well-organized" and utilized in Korea.

Copyrights and Computer Software No registration is required for protection of a copyright. Registration, however, is necessary to perfect a transfer or pledge of a copyright. Also, registration creates a presumption that the registrant is the author of the registered work and that the work is first published on the date of publication stated in the registration. Computer programs are protected under the Computer Program Protection Act.

Trade Secrets There is no legislation directed specifically to the protection of trade secrets.

Business Registration

Foreign business operations in South Korea require governmental approval under the Foreign Capital Inducement Act (FCIA). The FCIA also provides certain tax benefits. Foreign business presence in South Korea may take the form of a branch office, joint venture corporation, or wholly owned subsidiary. Although most businesses are now open to foreign investment, certain business areas are either not open, or only partially open, to foreigners. Business names, seals, business activities by minors, managerial positions, and details relating to corporate matters must be registered into the Commercial Register. If a foreign company intends to engage in commercial transactions in Korea, it must register the full name and permanent residence of at least one representative resident in Korea, and the governing law under which the entity was incorporated.

Contracts and Dispute Resolution

Korean businesspersons are generally not accustomed to a finely-tuned agreement with provisions against all possible contingencies. In other words, the spirit of a contract is more important than the letter. However, an increasing number of firms are willing and able to draft such lengthy contracts, which is what many Western businesspeople seem to prefer. Koreans prefer to have disputes settled privately, without intervention of public institutions such as a court or institutional arbitration body.

Notaries

Documents authenticated by notaries bear a strong presumption of authenticity when introduced as evidence in court. Additional legal effects of notarized documents are set forth in individual statutes. Law offices with at least three attorneys (not individual attorneys) may apply for and receive authority to act as notaries.

Labor

Minimum employment conditions are set forth by the Labor Standards Act. An employer must make a matching contribution for employees into the national medical insurance and the national pension plans. Employees may not be dismissed unless the dismissal is for good cause. Such good cause is narrowly construed by the court, and dismissing employees for restructuring or downsizing purposes is not easy. Notable is the statutory severance pay system. Any employee who has worked for at least one year is entitled to severance pay in the amount of one month's salary for each year of service. Although labor unions are constitutionally protected, their collective activities, such as strikes, must comply with the statutes prescribing procedural requirements for such collective actions.

Source: Lee & Ko, Seoul

Legal Matters

LEGAL BRIEFS

- **Courts' protection of legal rights** The principal remedy for breach of contract in South Korea is requiring specific performance, through which the non-breaching party may be restored to the position as if no breach had occurred. Unlike common law countries, however, Korean courts rarely issue an order like an injunction.

- **Damages** Whether based on a contractual or tort claim, damages are only compensatory. No punitive damages are recognized and evidence supporting the damages are subject to rather strict review.

- **Real property** In South Korea, a building constitutes a real property separate from the land on which it stands. Acquisition of land by a foreign company requires governmental approval, although the acquisition of a building does not.

- **Antitrust** Under the Monopoly Regulation and Fair Trade Act (MRFTA), a monopoly or an attempt to monopolize is not condemned. Generally, companies are only prohibited from engaging in Unfair Trade Practices as set forth by the Fair Trade Commission (FTC), which is in charge of antitrust enforcement under the MRFTA. Companies with dominant position in a market have obligations not to abuse their market power. International business agreements should comply with the Fair Trade Guidelines prescribed by the FTC. Standard form contracts are also subject to the FTC review. In addition to the activities of the FTC, individuals may claim damages for antitrust violation.

- **Bankruptcy** Korean companies seldom file a bankruptcy. Petitions for corporate reorganization are granted to limited types of cases in order to prevent abuses.

- **Civil disputes** Commercial disputes can be adjudicated in a civil court. A lawsuit should be considered a last resort, however, signaling the end of a business relationship. Disputes can also be taken to the Korean Commercial Arbitration Board (KCAB), who can act as an intermediary to a settlement or appoint a mediator.

LEGAL CONTACTS

Lee & Ko
17th & 18th Fl., Marine Center Main Bldg.
118, 2-ka, Namdaemun-ro, Chung-ku
C.P.O. Box 8735
Seoul 100-770
Tel: (2) 753-2151
Fax: (2) 753-0373/5

Bae, Kim & Lee
Shin-a Bldg.
39-1, Seosomun-dong, Chung-ku
Seoul 100-752
Tel: (2) 317-4114
Fax: (2) 757-2267, 755-7676

Central International Law Firm
5th Fl., Korea Reinsurance Bldg.
80, Soosong-dong, Chongro-ku
Kwangwhamoon P.O. Box 356
Seoul 110-140
Tel: (2) 735-5621/6, 735-5072/4
Fax: (2) 733-5206/7

Hwang Mok Park & Jin
6th Fl., Peeres Bldg.
222, 3-ka, Chungjung-ro, Seodaemun-ku
Seoul 120-013
Tel: (2) 365-6251/5
Fax: (2) 365-3369/70

Kim & Chang
Seyang Bldg.
223, Naeja-dong, Chongro-ku
Seoul 110-053
Tel: (2) 737-4455
Fax: (2) 737-9091/3

Korean Bar Association
1553-1, Seocho-dong
Seocho-ku
Seoul 137-070
Tel: (2) 522-3763/4
Fax: (2) 522-3767

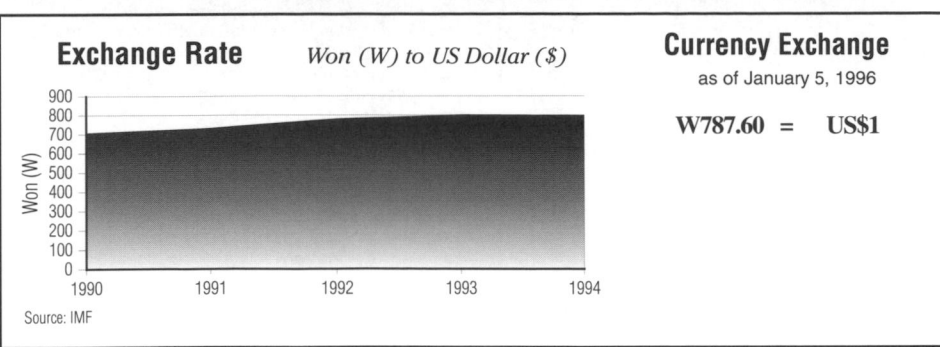

Exchange Rate — *Won (W) to US Dollar ($)*

Won (W): 900, 800, 700, 600, 500, 400, 300, 200, 100, 0

1990 1991 1992 1993 1994

Source: IMF

Currency Exchange
as of January 5, 1996

W787.60 = US$1

Currency

The currency in use is the Korean won (W).

Foreign Exchange

The exchange rate between the won and the US dollar is determined daily on the basis of a weighted average of interbank rates. The exchange rate of the won against other currencies is determined by the corresponding exchange rates of the US dollar. Buy and sell rates offered by foreign exchange banks are established by supply and demand conditions. No taxes are paid on foreign exchange transactions. A foreign exchange bank may conduct all foreign exchange transactions. The exchange market is strictly regulated by the Bank of Korea. Foreign exchange banks, and branch offices of foreign banks in Korea, may offer international banking and foreign exchange services.

Capital Transfers

Nonresidents may open a foreign currency deposit account with a foreign exchange bank; remittances and withdrawals from these accounts may be made freely. Approval is not required to remit funds abroad, or for payments for any approved transaction. Nonresidents may hold won accounts, and residents may hold foreign currency deposit accounts. Special permission is required to export more than two million won, or more than US$10,000 in foreign currency. Nonresidents, when leaving the country, may acquire foreign exchange up to the amount for which they have proof of conversion.

Investment Incentives

Foreign investment in 261 categories of high technology is eligible for an increasing range of tax reductions. The range of incentives was recently broadened to include complete waiver of certain taxes. The Korean government also has a number of programs to encourage research and development by private sector organizations.

Investment Restrictions

The government ceased imposing performance requirements on new foreign investment as of July 1989, and eliminated all preexisting requirements in December, 1992. The Korean idea of performance requirements is rather limited, however. It does not include foreign equity ownership restrictions, offshore financing restrictions, or work visa policies forcing local hiring, all of which continue in force.

Money Matters

BITS AND PIECES

- **Double taxation** Tax credits are given for corporate taxes paid to foreign governments, although the relief cannot exceed the lesser of the tax paid abroad or the Korean tax amount equivalent to the ratio of the income from foreign sources to the total taxable income. If the foreign tax credit is limited in this way, the excess may be carried forward for five tax years.
- **Foreign borrowing** Authorization is required for foreign borrowing by firms other than banks. Regulations on foreign borrowing have been tightened.
- **Banking system** There are 14 nationwide commercial banks, 10 regional banks, 52 foreign bank branches, and six specialized banks.
- **Credit** Credit is often in short supply, and domestic companies have better access to local funding. The government maintains strict controls over interest rates, capital inflow, and the money supply. The demand for won is often unable to be fully met.
- **Financial reform** In 1993, a five-year financial sector reform program was announced to loosen foreign exchange and capital controls, eliminate government credit schemes, and deregulate the interest rates.
- **Repatriation** Repatriation of funds is usually not limited, but South Korea may do so if the international balance of payments is threatened, or because an excessive fluctuation in the interest or exchange rates occurs.
- **Investment categories** The Foreign Capital Inducement Act (FCIA) categorizes business activities as either open, conditionally restricted, or closed to foreign investment.
- **Investment restrictions** There are currently 150 sectors restricted to foreign investment, including 24 in the agricultural sector, 12 in the manufacturing sector, and 114 in the services sector; 43 sectors are partially open to foreign investors, but only those satisfying certain conditions. The Ministry of Finance recently announced that all but 91 sectors will be open by the year 1997, and only seven categories will limit foreign participation to joint venture investment.
- **Investment application** A host of laws, regulations, and changing policies make for a challenging business environment. Korean law also does not permit direct investment through a merger with or acquisition of an existing domestic firm.
- **Public support** The Korean public generally supports foreign investment as beneficial to the national economy. There are no significant non-governmental groups that oppose foreign investment, although consumer groups have from time to time spoken out against imports, arguing that what they see as "luxury" goods may encourage social unrest or that foreign agricultural products are a threat to public health.

BANKS

Commercial Bank of Korea Ltd.
111-1, 2-ka, Namdaemun-no, Chung-ku
Seoul 100-792
Tel: (2) 754-3920, 775-0050
Fax: (2) 754-9203, 753-5264 Telex: 24611

Export-Import Bank of Korea
16-1, Yoido-dong, Yongdeungpo-ku
Seoul 150-010
Tel: (2) 784-1021 Fax: (2) 784-1030 Telex: 26595

Korea Development Bank
10-2, Kwanchul-dong, Chongno-ku
Seoul 110-111
Tel: (2) 733-2121, 733-4141 Fax: (2) 733-4768 Telex: 27463

Korea Long Term Credit Bank
15-22, Yoido-dong, Yongdeungpo-ku
Seoul 150-010
Tel: (2) 782-0111 Fax: (2) 784-7310 Telex: 26342

Bank of America NT & SA (USA)
8/F., Sunghwa Bldg.
192-18, Kwanhoon-dong, Chongno-ku
Seoul 110-300
Tel: (2) 733-2455 Fax: (2) 738-0624 Telex: 23294

TAXATION

Taxation requires sophisticated knowledge of complex rules and regulations specific to each country. For more detailed information we suggest you refer to the Ernst & Young Corporate Tax Guide and Directory, available from the Ernst & Young accounting office in your country, or from:

Young Wha
Accounting Corporation
P.O. Box 338
Seoul, Republic of Korea
Tel: (2) 783-1100, 785-0981/5
Telex: K24263 Ans bk ATYOUNG K
Fax: (2) 783-5890, 785-6991

- Domestic corporations are taxed on worldwide income. A foreign corporation is taxed on Korean-source income only.

At a Glance

Corporate Income Tax Rate(%)(a)	30
Capital Gains Tax Rate(%)(a)(b)	20
Branch Tax Rate(%)(a)	30
Withholding Tax(%)	
Dividends (c)	0
Interest (a)(c)	20
Royalties from Patents, Know-how, etc. (c)	0
Branch Remittance Tax	0
Net Operating Losses (Years)	
Carryback	0
Carryforward	5

(a) A 7.5% surtax is also levied.
(b) Capital gains are included in ordinary taxable income. A special 20% surtax is also levied on income from transfers of property, this rate increases to 40% if ownership is not registered.
(c) These rates apply to payments to domestic corporations and foreign corporations with a place of business in Korea. For foreign corporations that do not have a place of business in Korea, there is a 2% withholding tax on leasing income, 20% from personal services income, and 25% from interest income; and the lesser of 25% of the net gain or 10% of the gross amount of any gain from a transfer of securities or shares.

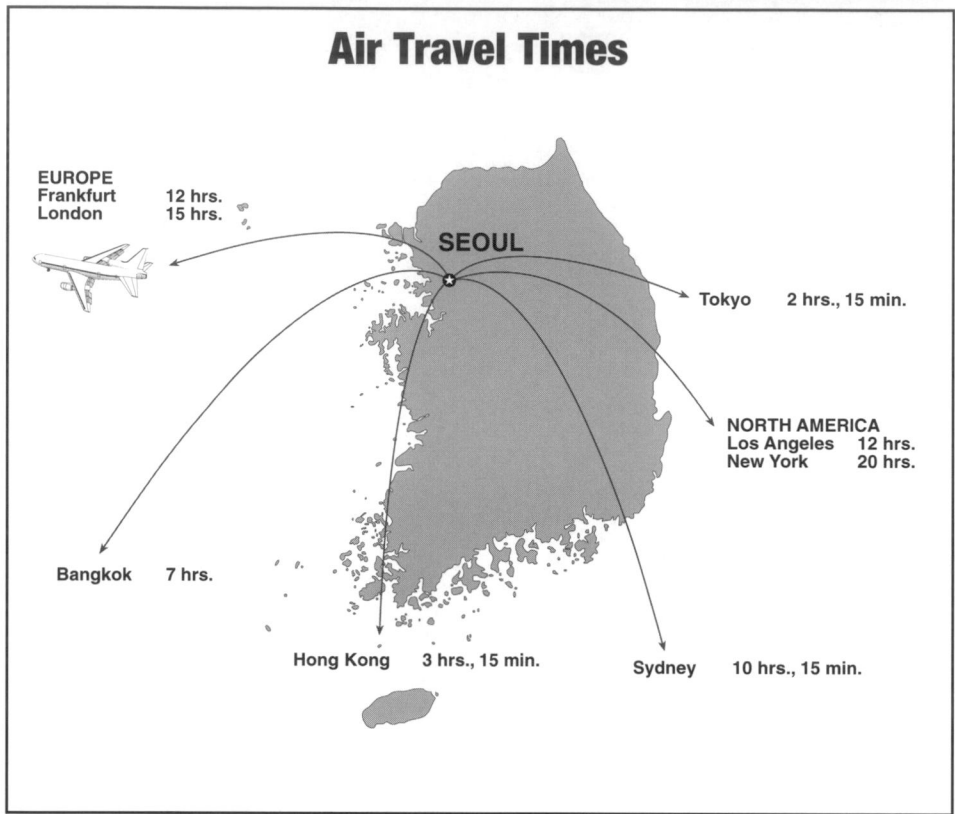

Air Travel Times

EUROPE
Frankfurt   12 hrs.
London   15 hrs.

SEOUL

Tokyo   2 hrs., 15 min.

NORTH AMERICA
Los Angeles   12 hrs.
New York   20 hrs.

Bangkok   7 hrs.

Hong Kong   3 hrs., 15 min.

Sydney   10 hrs., 15 min.

COMMUNICATIONS

Telephones Telephone service in South Korea is modern and first-rate. Public phones are color coded: orange for local calls and gray and blue for local or long-distance. Any call can be made from card phones. Cards can be purchased at banks, telephone offices, post offices, and shops near phone booths.
Fax Fax machines are in wide use in South Korea and are available at most major hotels.
Post office The postal service is efficient, fast, and inexpensive. Most major hotels have postal services.

BEST TRAVEL BOOKS

The best source of information is the Korean National Tourism Corp. **Travel Manual Korea, Travelers' Korea,** and **Facts About South Korea** are available from its offices and are very informative.
Fodor's Korea, edited by Julie Tomazs. New York: **Fodor's Travel Publication**. 275 pages. Tourist and activity oriented, but has excellent hotel and restaurant information and maps.
Korea, by Geoff Crowther and Choe Hyung Pun. Hawthorn, Victoria, Australia: Lonely Planet Publication. 265 pages. Geared to budget travelers, but packed with cultural, practical, and "survival" information.
The Korea Guidebook, by Kyung Cho Chung, Phyllis Haffner, and Fredric M. Kaplan. Boston: Houghton Mifflin Company. 608 pages. A detailed, insightful guide with the bonus of a 100-page "Doing Business in Korea" section.
Culture Shock, A Guide to Customs and Etiquette, Korea.
The Travellers Guide to Korean Customs and Manners. Elizabeth Devine & Nancy Braganti. An invaluable guide for people not wanting to put foot in mouth.
Far Eastern Economic Review, All Asia Travel Guide, Volume 2. The best guide available for the business traveller.

USEFUL TELEPHONE NUMBERS

If you are calling from outside Korea, you will need to add the country code [82] and any other international dialing requirements from within your country.

- Domestic collect calls 114
- International operator 0077
- International collect calls 007
- International directory information 0074
- Overseas Telegraph 1156
- Police 112
- Fire 119
- Ambulance/Fire 119
- Subway ....(2) 744-2400
- Railroad ....(2) 755-2111
- Taxi ....(2) 414-0150; 331-1238
- Weather 735-0365
- KNTC Kimpo Airport Info.....(2) 665-0088, 665-0988
- KNTC Kimhae Airport Info....................(51) 98-1100
- Seoul Tourist Center ....(2) 731-6337, 735-8688
- Tourist Complaint Center ....(2) 735-0101
- Traffic Complaint Center ....(2) 777-5000
- Lost and Found ....(2) 755-4400

Credit Card Information
Lost or stolen credit cards (call collect to the US, regardless of which country the card was issued in).

- Amex ....[1] (919) 333-3211
- Diner's Club................................[1] (303) 799-1504
- MasterCard ....[1] (314) 275-6690
- Visa ....[1] (410) 581-7931

Travelogue

WORKWEEK

Offices Monday-Friday 8:30 am to 7:00 pm.
Banks Monday-Friday 9:30 am to 4:30 pm, and Saturday until 1:30 pm.
Government Monday-Friday, 9:00 am to 6:00 pm, and Saturday, until 1:00 pm. From November to February offices close at 5:00 pm.
Retail Generally open from 10:30 am to 7:30 pm daily, closing one day during the week.

HOLIDAYS

Holidays 1996
January 1-2 New Year's Day
January 30-February 1 Lunar New Year's*
March 1 Independence Movement Day
April 5 Arbor Day
May 8 Buddha's Birthday*
May 5 Children's Day
June 6 Memorial Day
July 17 Constitution Day
August 15 Independence Day
September 8, 9, 10 Thanksgiving Day*
October 3 National Foundation Day
December 25 Christmas Day.
*Dates are based on a lunar calendar and vary each year.

VISA AND PASSPORT

A valid passport is required for visits of up to 90 days. Nationals from Western Europe (except Ireland) and several African, American (except US), and Asian countries do not require visas. Most others can enter the country for 14 days with a confirmed return ticket. Visas for longer stays must be obtained from a consulate prior to entry.

DEPARTURE FORMALITIES

Foreign currency exceeding the equivalent of US$5,000 will be confiscated and duties will have to be paid on items such as jewelry and camera equipment unless a full declaration is made upon entry to Korea. Receipts are necessary to reconvert won back to your local currency in amounts exceeding US$500.

IMMUNIZATION

Vaccinations are not required for entry unless a traveler is arriving from an area infected with yellow fever or cholera.

TIPPING

Tipping is not common in Korea. Restaurants and hotels add service charges to their bills, but small tips are appropriate for porters, taxi drivers who help with baggage, and guides who are especially helpful. Otherwise, a sincere thank you will do.

CRIME

Tourists have little to worry about in South Korea as the most prevalent type of crime is white-collar crime. Street crime is not common.

INFRASTRUCTURE

South Korea has highly developed air, bus, train, taxi, hotel, and telecommunication industries.

NATIONAL TOURIST OFFICE

Korean National Tourism Corporation
CPO Box 903
Seoul 100-609
Tel: (2) 757-6030

GOVERNMENT AGENCIES

Customs Administration
71, Nonhyun-dong, Kangnam-gu
Seoul 135-00
Tel: (2) 542-7141
Telex: 24346, 24716

Fisheries Administration
541, 5-ga Namdaemun-no, Chung-ku
Seoul
Tel: (2) 777-8271
Telex: 24719

Inchon Maritime & Port Authority
1-17, 7-ga, Hang-dong, Chung-ku
Inchon 160
Tel: (32) 883-4061

Industrial Property Administration
58-3 Socho-dong, Kangnam-ku
Seoul
Tel: (2) 568-5830/2, 568-8151

Korea Maritime & Port Authority
112-2, Inui-dong, Chongno-ku
Seoul 110
Tel: (2) 744-4030

Korean Overseas Information Services
82-1, Sejong-no, Chongno-ku
Seoul
Tel: (2) 720-4817, 739-4481, 739-4483
Telex: 23203

Ministry of Agriculture, Forestry and Fisheries
1, Jungang-dong
Gwachon City, Kyonggi Province
Tel: (2) 503-7209, 503-7208
Telex: 24759

Ministry of Communications
100, Sejong-no, Chongno-ku
Seoul 110-777
Tel: (2) 750-2811, 750-2800
Telex: 24819

Ministry of Construction
1, Jungang-dong
Gwachon City, Kyonggi Province
Tel: (2) 503-7312
Fax: (2) 503-7409

Ministry of Culture
82-1, Sejong-no, Chongno-ku
Seoul 100-050
Tel: (2) 736-7946
Fax: (2) 736-8513

Ministry of Education
77, Sejong-no, Chongno-ku
Seoul 110-760
Tel: (2) 720 3053, 720 3570
Fax: (2) 736-3402
Telex: 24758

Ministry of Energy and Resources
1, Jungang-dong
Gwachon City, Kyonggi Province
Tel: (2) 503-9611, 503-9605
Telex: 23472

Ministry of Finance
1, Jungang-dong
Gwachon City, Kyonggi Province
Tel: (2) 503-9211, 503-9206
Fax: (2) 503-9324
Telex: 23243
Foreign Investment Advice Office
Tel: (2) 503-7171
Foreign Investment Information Center
Tel: (2) 503-9259
Foreign Investment Promotion Division
Tel: (2) 503-9276
One-Stop Service Office
Tel: (2) 503-9258

Ministry of Foreign Affairs
77, Sejong-no, Chongno-ku
Seoul
Tel: (2) 720-2687, 738-9601
Telex: 24651

Ministry of Government Administration
77-6, Sejong-no, Chongno-ku

Seoul
Tel: (2) 720-4351
Telex: 24803

Ministry of Labor
1, Jungang-dong
Gwachon City, Kyonggi Province
Tel: (2) 503-9700
Fax: (2) 503-9771
Telex: 24718

Ministry of National Defense
101, Huam-dong, Yongsan-ku
Seoul
Tel: (2) 754-3843

Ministry of Public Information
82-1, Sejong-no, Chongno-ku
Seoul 110-050
Tel: (2) 720-4728, 720-1456
Telex: 23203

Ministry of Science and Technology
1, Jungang-dong
Gwachon City, Kyonggi Province
Tel: (2) 503-7609
Fax: (2) 503-7673
Telex: 24230

Ministry of the Environment
7-16, Sincheon-dong, Songpa-ku
Seoul
Tel: (2) 421-0217, 422-0282, 423-0282
Fax: (2) 421-0280

Ministry of Trade and Industry
1, Jungang-dong
Gwachon City, Kyonggi Province
Tel: (2) 503-9405
Fax: (2) 503-9496
Telex: 24478

Ministry of Trade and Industry
Consultation Office for Overseas Companies
Rm. 524, Bldg. 3, Govt. Complex II
Gwachon City, Kyonggi Province
Tel: (2) 500-2539, 507-2152
Fax: (2) 503-9655

Ministry of Transportation
168, 2-ka, Bongnae-dong, Chung-ku
Seoul
Tel: (2) 392-9801, 392-7606
Fax: (2) 392-9809
Telex: 24778

Ministry of Transportation
Maritime and Port Administration
112-2, Inui-dong, Chongno-ku
Seoul
Tel: (2) 774-4030
Telex: 26528 HANGMAN

Ministry of Transportation
National Railroad Administration
168 2-ga, Pongnai-dong, Chung-ku
Seoul
Tel: (2) 392-0078
Telex: 24802 KHRAIL

Office of Supply of the ROK
520-3, Bangpo-dong, Kangnam-gu
Seoul, Rep. of Korea
Tel: (2) 533-9656
Telex: OSROK K23244, 23703

Pusan Maritime & Port Authority
1116-1, Jwachun-dong, Dong-ku
Pusan
Tel: (51) 633-2620

GENERAL TRADE ORGANIZATIONS

Andong Chamber of Commerce
139-5, Wunheung-dong, Kyung-buk
Andong
Tel: (571) 2-2643
Fax: (571) 2-6519

Customs Friendship Association
62-13, Nonhyon-dong, Kangnam-gu
Seoul
Tel: (2) 544-3032
Fax: (2) 549-8711

Korea Chamber of Commerce & Industry
45, 4-ka, Namdaemun-ro, Chung-ku
Seoul
Tel: (2) 316-3114
Fax: (2) 757-9475
Telex: 25728

Korea Export Buying Offices Association
Rm. 3102, KWTC Bldg.
159, Samsung-dong, Kangnam-gu
Seoul
Tel: (2) 551-3195/8

Korea Foreign Trade Association
159-1, Samsung-dong, Kangnam-gu
Seoul
Tel: (2) 551-5114
Fax: (2) 551-5100

Korea Marketing Association
45, Namdaemunno 4-ga, Chung-gu
Seoul
Tel: (2) 753-5011
Fax: (2) 752-8074

Korea Productivity Center
122-1, Chockson-dong, Chongno-gu
Seoul
Tel: (2) 739-5868
Fax: (2) 736-0322

Seoul Chamber of Commerce
45, 4-ka, Namdaemun-ro, Chung-ku
Seoul
Tel: (2) 757-0757
Fax: (2) 776-8213

Small & Medium Industry Promotion Corporation
24-3, Youido-dong, Yongdungpo-gu
Seoul
Tel: (2) 783-9611/8
Fax: (2) 784-9230

FOREIGN BUSINESS ORGANIZATIONS

American Chamber of Commerce in Korea
Rm. 307, Westin Chosun Hotel
87, Sogong-dong, Chung-gu
Seoul
Tel: (2) 753-6471, 752-3061
Fax: (2) 755-6577

British Chamber of Commerce in Korea
13/F., Naewoi Bldg.
9-1, Ulchiro 2-ga, Chung-gu
Seoul
Tel: (2) 757-5143
Fax: (2) 757-7444

French Chamber of Commerce & Industry in Korea
6/F., 22, Chong-dong, Chung-gu
Seoul
Tel: (2) 584-8813

International Executive Service Corporation
Rm. 601, Leema Bldg.
146-1, Susong-dong, Chongno-gu
Seoul
Tel: (2) 733-1021
Fax: (2) 733-1028

Italian Trade Commission
Rm. 311, KCCI Bldg.
45, Namdaemunno 4-ga, Chung-gu
Seoul
Tel: (2) 779-0811/3
Fax: (2) 757-2927

Japan Chamber of Commerce & Industry
6/F., KCCI Bldg.
45, Namdaemunno 4-ga, Chung-gu
Seoul
Tel: (2) 755-6672
Fax: (2) 755-2415

Japan External Trade Organization (JETRO)
7/F., The Korea Press Center Bldg.
25, 1-ka, Taepyung-ro, Chung-ku
Seoul
Postal add: CPO Box 8499, Seoul
Tel: (2) 739-8657, 739-4503
Fax: (2) 739-4658

Korea-US Economic Council, Inc.
Rm. 4304, KWTC Bldg.
159, Samsung-dong, Kangnam-gu
Seoul
Tel: (2) 551-3366
Fax: (2) 551-3365

Korean-German Chamber of Commerce & Industry
10/F., KCCI Bldg.
45, Namdaemunno 4-ga, Chung-gu
Seoul
Tel: (2) 776-1546/9
Fax: (2) 756-7828

INDUSTRY-SPECIFIC ORGANIZATIONS

Agriculture & Fishery Marketing Cooperation
191, Hangangno 2-ga, Yongsan-gu
Seoul
Tel: (2) 795-8201/5
Fax: (2) 790-5265, 798-7513

Apparel Sub-Material Association [Korea]
2A-1, KOEX Bldg.
159, Samsung-dong, Kangnam-gu
Seoul
Tel: (2) 551-6000/2
Fax: (2) 551-6006

Automobile Manufacturers Association [Korea]
8/F., 63 Bldg.
Youido-dong, Yongdungpo-gu
Seoul
Tel: (2) 782-1360/1
Fax: (2) 782-0464

Bedding Goods Industry Cooperative [Korea]
159-1, Samsung-dong, Kangnam-gu
Seoul
Tel: (2) 551-1919
Fax: (2) 551-1918

Book Binding Industry Cooperative [Korea]
614-7, Ahyon-dong, Mapo-gu
Seoul
Tel: (2) 362-7182

Chemical Fibers Association [Korea]
80, Chokson-dong, Chongno-gu
Seoul
Tel: (2) 734-1191/4
Fax: (2) 738-0111

Coal Mining Industry Cooperative [Korea]
10-2, Youido-dong, Yongdungpo-gu
Seoul
Tel: (2) 784-7821/7

Construction Equipment Association [Korea]
44-1, Youido-dong, Yongdungpo-gu
Seoul
Tel: (2) 783-4001/3
Fax: (2) 734-7959

Deep Sea Fisheries Association [Korea]
6/F., Samhomulsan Bldg.
Yangjae-dong, Socho-gu
Seoul
Tel: (2) 589-1621/4
Fax: (2) 589-1030/1

Electric Power Corporation [Korea]
167, Samsung-dong, Kangnam-gu
Seoul
Tel: (2) 550-3114
Fax: (2) 550-5982

Electronic Industries Association of Korea
5/F., Danwoo Bdlg.
850-22, Pangbae-dong, Sochu-gu
Seoul
Tel: (2) 553-0941/7, 553-8725
Fax: (2) 555-6195

Foods Industry Association [Korea]
1002-6, Pangbae-dong, Socho-gu
Seoul
Tel: (2) 585-7062
Fax: (2) 586-4906

Forestry Association [National Federation of]
111-5, Samjon-dong, Songpa-gu
Seoul
Tel: (2) 416-9416
Fax: (2) 416-7381
Tel: (2) 215-8838/9
Fax: (2) 215-9729

Garment Industry Cooperative [Korea]
105-238, Kongdok-dong, Mapo-gu
Seoul
Tel: (2) 717-3191, 715-8998
Fax: (2) 718-3192

Glass Industry Cooperative [Korea]
53-20, Taehyon-dong, Sodaemun-gu
Seoul
Tel: (2) 364-7799
Fax: (2) 312-8838

Iron and Steel Association [Korea]
51-8, Susong-dong, Chongno-gu
Seoul
Tel: (2) 732-9231/5
Fax: (2) 739-1090

Paper Industry Cooperative [Korea]
831, Yoksam-dong, Kangnam-gu
Seoul
Tel: (2) 567-5912/3
Fax: (2) 567-6984

Petrochemical Industry Association [Korea]
1-1, Yonji-dong, Chongno-gu
Seoul
Tel: (2) 744-0116 Fax: (2) 743-1887

Pharmaceutical Traders Association [Korea]
Rm. 1801, KWTC Bldg.
159, Samsung-dong, Kangnam-gu
Seoul
Tel: (2) 551-1841
Fax: (2) 551-1850

Stainless Steel Pipe Industry Cooperative [Korea]
4/F., Cheil Bldg.
58-85, Mullae-dong 3-ga, Yongdungpo-gu
Seoul
Tel: (2) 679-1932
Fax: (2) 633-0379

NEWSPAPERS

Asian Wall Street Journal
Dow Jones Publishing Co. (Asia)
2/F. AIA Bldg.
1 Stubbs Rd.
GPO Box 9825
Hong Kong
Tel: [852] 2737121
Fax: [852] 2345291

International Herald Tribune
7/F. Malaysia Bldg.
50 Gloucester Rd.
Wanchai, Hong Kong
Tel: [852] 2610616
Fax: [852] 2613073

Asiaweek
Asiaweek Ltd.
199 Des Voeux Road
Central, Hong Kong
Tel: [852] 2155662
Fax: [852] 2155903

Economic Bulletin
Economic Planning Board
1, Jungang-dong
Gwachon City, Kyonggi Province
Tel: (2) 503-9020
Fax: (2) 503-9033

Korea Trade & Business
KOTRA
KWTC Bldg.
159-1, Samsung-dong, Kangnam-gu
Seoul
Tel: (2) 551-4181
Fax: (2) 551-4477

RADIO AND TELEVISION

Korea Broadcasting Commission (KBC)
14-15/F., Press Center
25, Taepyung-ro 2-ka, Chung-ku
Seoul
Tel: (2) 735-2640
Fax: (2) 722-5296
Government body which oversees television
programming and advertising.

Korean Broadcasting System (KBS)
18 Youido-dong, Yongdungpo-gu
Seoul 150-010
Tel: (2) 781-1000
Operates a national network of radio stations and two
national television networks.

Munhwa TV-Radio Broadcasting Corp. (MBC)
31, Youido-dong, Yongdungpo-gu
Seoul 150-728
Tel: (2) 780-0114

Seoul Broadcasting System (SBS)
10-2, Youido-dong, Yongdungpo-gu
Seoul
Tel: (2) 320-0114

ACCOUNTING FIRMS

Arthur Andersen & Co.
Anjin Accounting Corporation
5/F., Samwhan Camus Bldg.
17-3, Yoido-dong, Youngdeungpo-ku

KMPG San Tong & Co.
7/F., Koreana Bldg.
61-1, 1-ka Taipyung-ro, Chung-ku
Seoul 100-101
Postal add: CPO Box 7144, Seoul 100-671
Tel: (2) 733-2345
Fax: (2) 733-5317

STOCK EXCHANGE

Korean Securities Dealers Association
34, Youido-dong, Yongdungpo-gu
Seoul
Tel: (2) 783-5391/5
Fax: (2) 785-1513

Korean Stock Exchange
33, Yoido-dong, Youngdeungpo-gu
Seoul 150-010
Tel: (2) 783-3371

INTERNET ADDRESSES

Usenet group(s):
soc.culture.korean

South Korea Information
http://sunsite.sut.ac.jp/asia/korea/korea.html

WWW Servers in South Korea
http://flower.comeng.chungnam.ac.kr/sharon/www-
server-in-korea-eng.html

Information Sources in South Korea
http://comp.kbsc.re.kr/korea_info_server.html

City Net - South Korea
http://www.city.net/countries/south_korea

Spain

Kingdom of Spain

Economy

Overview

Despite long periods of political upheaval and economic paralysis, Spain has utilized rapid industrial growth, widespread mechanization of agriculture, and a successful transition to democracy to establish itself as an important European economy. As a country rich in mining and land resources, it has focused on building a strong manufacturing base and developing a wide array of agricultural produce for export. The economy is now emerging from recession but full recovery is dependent on continuing export growth and on increased revenues in the tourism sector. The government has acknowledged those priorities and stated its intention to pursue them.

Trade

In the past two decades the Spanish economy has been very receptive to imported goods and this has lead to a serious imbalance in its foreign trade account. European Union nations are the primary markets for its exports and it buys the majority of its imports from the same sources. France is its largest trading partner, followed by Germany, Italy, and the US. Spain's traditionally high trade deficits have been reduced somewhat by a slowdown in the economy, providing a much needed adjustment in the balance of trade. Increased competitiveness of Spanish goods due to devaluation of the peseta and revival in the economies of its main trading partners are providing the impetus for a slow but steady recovery.

Sectors

Agriculture Spain is traditionally an agricultural nation, but since joining the EU in 1986 agriculture has become less important to its economy. This sector is becoming increasingly vulnerable to competition from other European producers, and has suffered from the effects of EU agricultural policies, which do not favor its most competitive producers.

Industry Industry has been the primary growth sector of the Spanish economy for the past four decades. Spain is looking to the manufacturing sector, particularly export-oriented industries, to provide the impetus for further economic expansion. Increased competitiveness and renewed growth in the economies of its European partners should see a gradual increase in output from these sectors. Traditional subsectors such as iron and steel, textiles, chemicals, automobiles, coal, zinc, and petroleum continue to be the central focus for productive output.

Services Spain is primarily a service nation and over 50 percent of the population is employed in this sector. Revenues from tourism and related services are heavily relied upon to counteract large trade deficits and this sector has the best growth prospects in the short term.

Trends

Spain continues to run a high trade deficit but it is currently undergoing a slow export-led recovery. As external competition increases, Spain needs to address the problems of its restrictive business and labor laws, as well as its high unemployment rate. The weak peseta is leading to some relief in the external trade imbalance as export volumes rise and increased tourism receipts give a welcome lift to its current account. Spain continues to show strong growth, and long-term prospects are good, assuming the government continues its pursuit of market liberalization and export expansion.

At a Glance

THE COUNTRY

Location Southwestern Europe, bordering the North Atlantic Ocean and the Mediterranean Sea, between Portugal and France.
Terrain Mountainous with high plateaus.
Climate Temperate; clear hot summers and cold winters in interior. Dry; temperate in northwest area. Moderate and cloudy along coast.

THE PEOPLE

Population 39,300,000
Ethnic composition Mediterranean and Germanic composite.
Religious composition
Roman Catholic 99%
Other sects 1%
Languages spoken Spanish (official), Catalan 17%, Galician 7%, Basque 2%.
Education and literacy Spanish society is highly literate—97 percent of the population 15 years of age and older can read and write. Education is compulsory until 16 years of age.
Labor force
Total:...14,600,000
By occupation: services 53%, industry 24%, agriculture 14%, construction 9%.

COUNTRY FACTS

Political and legal Spain is a constitutional monarchy whose independence dates back to 1492. Its legal system is based on civil law with regional applications; it does not accept compulsory International Court of Justice jurisdiction. All citizens may vote at 18 years of age or older.
Telephone Domestic and international telephone services are generally adequate and readily available. There are over 15 million telephones in Spain. International country code: [34]. Selected city codes: Madrid (1), Barcelona (3), Seville (5), Granada (58), Pamplona (48).
Transportation Public transportation is inexpensive and widely used. Taxis are abundant and fares are reasonable. Air and rail facilities connect to most cities in Spain and to most major cities throughout Europe. Rental cars are available and major highways are good; however be advised that gas prices are among the highest in Europe. There are over 1,000 kilometers of inland waterways, but they are of little economic importance.
Environment Pollution of the Mediterranean Sea from untreated sewage and effluents from the offshore production of oil and gas is currently a major environmental problem in Spain. Both deforestation and desertification have become problems due to unplanned cutting and soil erosion.
Media The government owns and operates or supervises Spanish radio and television services. There are over 500 radio stations for 12.1 million radios. There are an estimated 15 million television sets for the four state-owned television networks. There are more than 100 daily newspapers—Sunday editions are particularly popular.
Health Health care is the largest public sector in Spain. Sanitary conditions and facilities meet European standards. Life expectancy of males is 74 years; of females, 81 years.

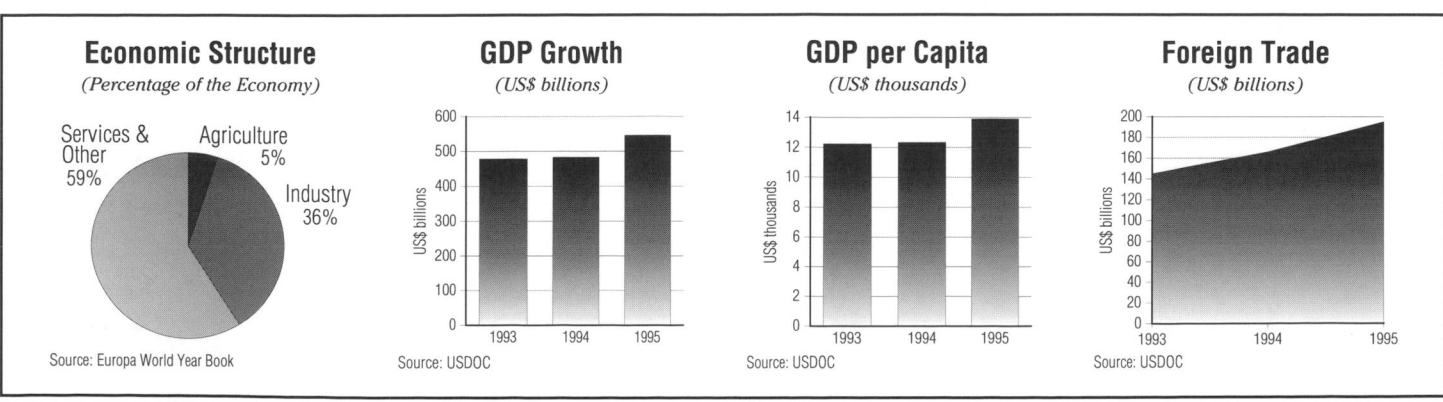

Economic Structure
(Percentage of the Economy)

Services & Other 59%
Agriculture 5%
Industry 36%

Source: Europa World Year Book

GDP Growth
(US$ billions)

Source: USDOC

GDP per Capita
(US$ thousands)

Source: USDOC

Foreign Trade
(US$ billions)

Source: USDOC

Spain

- ★ National capital
- ◉ Provincial capital
- ● Secondary city
- Primary road
- Railroad
- Administrative border
- International border

| 0 | 50 | 100km |
| 0 | 50 | 100mi |

Provinces of Spain

1	La Coruña	26	Madrid
2	Lugo	27	Guadalajara
3	Ovieda	28	Teruel
4	Santander	29	Tarragona
5	Vizcaya	30	Cáceres
6	Guipúzcoa	31	Toledo
7	Pontevedra	32	Cuenca
8	Orense	33	Castellón
9	León	34	Badajoz
10	Palencia	35	Ciudad Real
11	Burgos	36	Albacete
12	Alava	37	Valencia
13	Navarra	38	Huelva
14	Zamora	39	Córdoba
15	Valladolid	40	Jaén
16	Segovia	41	Murcia
17	Soria	42	Alicante
18	Logroño	43	Cádiz
19	Zaragoza	44	Sevilla
20	Huesca	45	Málaga
21	Lérida	46	Granada
22	Barcelona	47	Almeria
23	Gerona	48	Baleares
24	Salamanca	49	Santa Cruz de Tenerife
25	Ávila	50	Las Palmas

©1994 Magellan GeographixSMSanta Barbara, CA

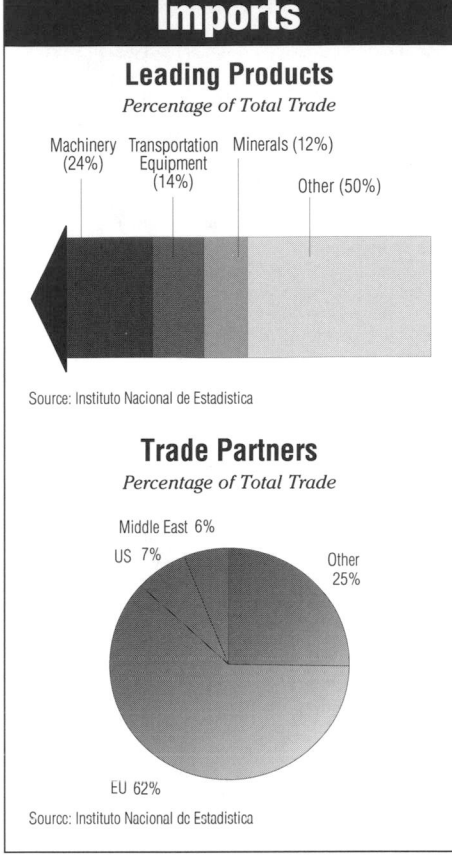

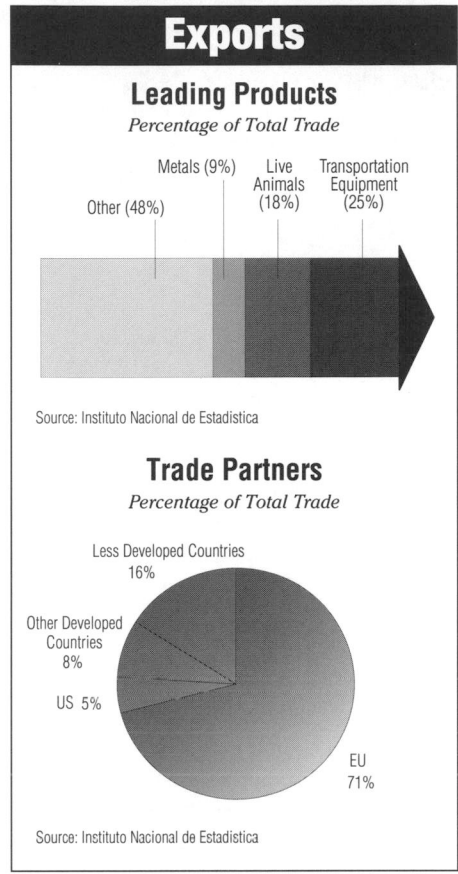

Opportunities

FOR IMPORTING TO SPAIN
- petroleum/fuels
- aircraft
- chemicals
- machinery
- transportation equipment
- fish
- sorghum
- telecommunications equipment
- medical equipment
- franchising
- computer software

FOR EXPORTING FROM SPAIN
- automobiles
- fruits
- minerals
- metals
- clothing
- footwear
- textiles
- semi-finished manufactured goods
- foodstuffs
- machinery

GROWTH SECTORS
- airport construction
- seaport facilities
- railroads
- automobiles
- tourism
- steel
- chemicals
- rubber products
- textile industry (shoes, leather goods, clothing)

GOVERNMENT PROCUREMENT
- road construction equipment and engineering services
- railroad construction equipment
- airport construction
- water treatment
- hydraulics
- television transmission equipment
- water treatment facilities
- telecommunications (including mobile telephone licensing)

Trade News

RULES AND REGULATIONS

- **Trade news** Spain is one of the industrial world's most energy import-dependent economies. After two years of recession, the Spanish economy seems to be undergoing a slow export-led recovery. Lower consumer consumption decreased demand for imports and allowed a much needed reduction of the current trade deficit, which had skyrocketed during the 1980s. Export growth was strong in late 1993; it was linked to the incipient recovery in the economies of Spain's largest trading partners and an increased competitiveness of Spanish products.

- **Regulations** Spain's social-democratic government exercises influence in the economy more through regulations than through direct ownership. In fact, during 1993 the government began partial privatization of several major firms, a process that is expected to continue.

- **Local competition** Local competition diminishes in those markets that require high technology. Domestic competition is high in consumer goods such as apparel, footwear, and textiles. Local companies are strong manufacturers of industrial products, such as metal-working equipment, automotive products, and aerospace parts and pieces. There is also strong competition in insurance and financial services.

- **Export restrictions** Pharmaceutical certificates are required. Illicit narcotics and drugs are banned, as are explosives, fire weapons, defense equipment and materials, tobacco, and gambling material. EU regulations on hormones ban US beef and feed products along with US cattle imports.

- **Import licenses/quotas** Spain was obligated under its EU accession agreement to transform its structure of formal and informal import restrictions for industrial products into a formal system of import licenses and quotas. Importers apply for import licenses at the Spanish General Register of the Department of Commerce or any of its regional offices. The license application must be accompanied by a commercial invoice that includes freight and insurance, the CIF price, net and gross weight, and invoice number. Licenses once granted are normally valid for six months.

- **Import authorization** Import authorization is used to control imports which are subject to quotas. Special import provisions are cleared by customs agents or brokers who handle the necessary formalities on behalf of the importing firm or individual. A bill of lading, or original invoice with a copy, a certificate of origin, and an import declaration are required for most clearances through Customs for products which will remain in Spain.

- **Tariff rates** Spanish tariffs for EU countries are zero since January 1, 1993, while third-country goods, including the US and Japan, receive the EU's Common External Tariff. Since 1988, Spain has used the Harmonized System of tariff nomenclature for applying duties. Spain has adhered to the GATT code since 1963. It subscribes to the Multilateral Trade Negotiations (MTN) codes on technical barriers to trade, subsidies, and customs valuation. Spain has a wide range of commercial treaties with Eastern Europe and the former Soviet Union. These set categories of goods to be traded over a specific number of years. Most food products are subject to high duties or variable import levies which generally preclude access into the Spanish market.

- **Export control** Exports are regulated by Organic Law and Royal Decree. The Royal Decree establishes both the regulations and the COCOM list applicable, as well as the procedures to follow.

GOVERNMENT AGENCY

Ministry of Industry, Trade, and Tourism
Ministerio de Industria
Comercio y Turismo
Paseo de la Castellana 160
250 Madrid
Tel: (1) 3494000

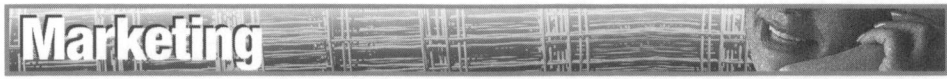

Overview

Spain is less European, more Latin in style, and relationships are very important. Spanish business is sometimes more important than price or quality, especially in large account sales. Decision making is different than in most industrial nations; it is centralized in the chief executive, who will take action only after the issue has been reviewed by many different departments. Consequently, an initial 'yes' means only that the firm will study the proposal, not that it will buy the product. The Basque Country, part of Spain's north coast, and Catalonia, which includes Barcelona, have long traditions as autonomous regions with their own official languages and customs. There are 15 other autonomous regions with lesser and varying degrees of autonomy and cultural identity.

Distribution

The Spanish market is really a set of regional markets joined to two major hubs: Madrid and Barcelona. The majority of agents, distributors, foreign subsidiaries, and government-controlled entities operate from these two hubs. Dealers, branch offices, or government offices located elsewhere will almost invariably obtain supplies from their Madrid or Barcelona contacts rather than by importing directly. The Madrid hub principally serves the central, southern, and western parts of Spain, while Barcelona serves the north and east. Barcelona also serves the Balearic Islands off the Mediterranean coast, and the enclave cities of Ceuta Melilla in North Africa. Madrid is the center for banking, administration, transportation, and the headquarters for international companies. Barcelona and Bilbao are the primary industrial centers as well as being the principal ports.

Agents, Distributors, and Partners

Most foreign firms sell their products in Spain through distributors. Agents and distributors are generally exclusive, covering the entire country. Although the majority of distributors have their head offices in Madrid or Barcelona, many are located in Bilbao, Valencia, and several other industrial cities where a particular industry may be concentrated. Distributors generally have sub-offices, enabling them to cover other parts of the country. The key to a foreign firm's success in Spain is to appoint a competent agent or establish an effective subsidiary in either Madrid or Barcelona. Personal relationships are important and will often determine the quality of attention and effort provided by an agent or distributor. Foreign sellers should therefore invest considerable time establishing close personal ties with their local agents.

Selling Techniques

New selling techniques are becoming very popular. Vending machines have sprouted up all over Spain in the last decade. Selling techniques, once modified to allow for local tastes, are very similar to those of other Western countries. Franchising has seen sustained growth since the mid-1970s due to the continued rise in the standard of living, as well as better training and performance of retail trade professionals. Continued growth is expected as the markets become more segmented and require more retail specialization. Likewise, direct marketing has grown in recent years and is expected to grow at a compound rate of 15 percent through 1997. While mail order buying is growing rapidly, it lags far behind that seen in other European Union countries. The fastest growing segment of direct marketing is telemarketing. Large and well-known distribution companies are entering the mail order business, and increased sophistication of the national telephone company brightens telemarketing's future.

Advertising

Print media and radio are currently the principal advertising methods, but television is fast becoming predominant. Until 1989, the state television system TVE was the only national network. In that year the government authorized the creation of commercial television and issued licenses to three new private channels which have since won 55 percent of viewer time. Antena 3TV, one of the three private channels, currently reaches 82 percent of Spanish territory and is the audience leader. Spain has a well-developed chain of radio stations; the majority of Spaniards obtain their news from radio, not television. Billboards are common in urban areas, but are prohibited along main roads. Advertising may be placed directly with the media, and there are no standard rates for placing or creating advertisements. Spanish agencies compete strongly for multinational and foreign clients.

Service and Customer Support

Consumer satisfaction is not a big issue in Spain. Foreign distribution companies introduced this concept, and only recently have consumer groups begun to appear. However, a new product liability law was passed in 1994 that effectively protects consumers. Demand among Spanish consumers for product service is growing fast although customer service is not so important; many shops do not even allow returns. Only large department stores and new, usually foreign, retailers have a return policy.

Marketing in Spain

MARKETING TIPS

- **Distribution channels** Distribution is organized around two hub cities: Madrid and Barcelona.
- **Financing and credit** EU firms compete in offering generous financing, an essential element of doing business in Spain.
- **Government purchasing** There is no central agency for public-sector purchases; each central or regional government agency or state-owned company purchases independently.
- **Pricing** Products and services in Spain are subject to a VAT, currently at 15 percent. Prices must also reflect financing costs occasioned by the customary deferred payment terms.
- **Payment policies** Commercial payments are based on 90-day terms; larger firms often negotiate or impose terms up to six months. The government regularly defers all payments, up to as much as one year.
- **Special competitive factors** Western European companies, and increasingly Japanese firms, provide formidable competition to new entrants in the Spanish market.
- **Changes in sales techniques** Direct marketing is increasing, and is expected to grow at a compound rate of 15 percent through 1997.

AD AGENCIES

Bassat, Ogilvy & Mather S.A.
Avenida Josep Tarradellas
no. 123, First Floor
08029 Barcelona
Tel: (3) 4192929
Fax: (2) 4194962

Conquest Europe
Av. Brasil, 7-10
28020 Madrid
Tel: (1) 5566043
Fax: (1) 5556588

D'Arcy Masius Benton & Bowles, Madrid S.A.
Lagasca 88, 7th Fl.
28001 Madrid
Tel: (1) 4314811
Fax: (1) 5773897

Grey Direct/Madrid
Paseo de la Castellana 91
Planta 11
28046 Madrid
Tel: (1) 597-1750
Fax: (1) 556-6542

McCann-Erickson S.A.
Rosano Pino 5
28020 Madrid
Tel: (1) 5710200
Fax: (1) 5701116
Telex: 42303

Saatchi & Saatchi Advertising
Paseo de la Castellana 89
Planta 11-A
28046 Madrid
Tel: (1) 5561200
Fax: (1) 5550442
Telex:42930

Vitruvio/Leo Burnett
Planta 27
Plaza de Pablo Ruiz
Torre Picasso S/N
28020 Madrid
Tel: (1) 5561120
Fax: (1) 5565705

Wunderman Cato Johnson, S.A.
Raimundo Fernandez Villaverde
65-9 pta
Edificio Windsor
28003 Madrid
Tel: (1) 5555954
Fax: (1) 5561694

Business Culture

Greetings and Courtesies

Public display of affection, such a kiss on the cheek, is for family and friends only; visitors should not initiate such contact. Close male friends exchange an *abrazo*, or hug. Female friends greet and part with a slight embrace. For the first meeting and departure, shake hands with everyone present, even children. Spaniards stand and sit closely, using frequent hand and arm gestures, and often interrupt each other. Address people by their titles, such as *Señor*, *Señorita*, or *Señora*; *Don* and *Doña* show greater respect. First names are used between close friends and young people; in business circles you will probably not be asked to call someone by their first name.

Business Ethic and Framework

When dealing with Spaniards, agreements usually start with an oral understanding, followed by a handshake and a contract. The letter of the contract will be strictly fulfilled, and Spaniards expect the same in return. Spanish people are usually very direct; they will tell you exactly what is on their mind. Manners are important, but the Spanish make it a point not to be too stiff or formal. Collaboration is more often an opportunity to voice opinions rather than a path to decisions. Spaniards trust friends and family the most, and nepotism is common.

Decision Making

Family ownership has been common in Spain for decades, centuries in some cases. Ownership structures have become complicated; you may think you are dealing with a decision maker but you probably are not. Spanish businesspeople will present their own views often, but will rarely be convinced with other arguments. Confrontation should be avoided at all costs; admitting an error is one of the worst mistakes you can make. Decisions are slow; they come from a central authority figure less impressed by facts than by intuition. Sharing the burden of decision making is seen as a sign of weakness. The best leader is an autocrat who cares for his people—the patron—but who stands essentially alone. Spaniards are generally conservative, and will resist any risky decisions. Many younger managers are trying to implement Western methods, but it is still not always possible to get access to the decision maker. In that case, help the person with whom you can build a relationship to persuade the decision maker.

Women

Many women in Spain, especially in the larger cities of Madrid and Barcelona, are career oriented and proud of their business success in middle management or above. Social and educational status often determines the role women play in business. Female professionals include lawyers, doctors, scientists, professors, and executives. The macho attitude is a fast-fading cliche, so women executives may not appreciate doors being held open for them. Foreign businesswomen should encounter very little difficulty in accomplishing their business in Spain.

Meetings

Punctuality is important only if attending a bullfight. Many businesspersons do not arrive at the office until 11:00 am and take lunch at 5:00 pm; yet they will stay at their desks until 8:00 or 9:00 pm. Frequent interruption of meetings by phone calls or a personal aside are entirely normal. Prior appointments are absolutely necessary, but do not schedule meetings between 12:30 and 4:30 pm. The predominant air at meetings is informality; meetings are extremely casual. Small talk will occupy at least the first half hour of a meeting; do not begin to discuss business until your host extends the invitation. Spaniards tend to be friendly, individualistic, and stoic. They tend to rely on both verbal and nonverbal communication; sometimes what you say isn't as important as what you don't say. Their advice is meant to correct a visitor's errors. The focus of most meetings is the present; though the *mañana* attitude is no longer dominant, Spaniards prefer to live for the moment and let the future take care of itself.

Business Attire

Spaniards are usually modest, but take pride in social position and personal appearance; affluence and standing are reflected in the quality of one's clothes. Men usually avoid bright or contrasting colors; women strive to be stylish and children are dressed as well as possible. Business dress is essentially conservative, but becomes more informal the further west you go; European styles predominate.

Cultural Cautions

DO'S

- Conversation should include sports, travel, history, and politics.
- The host or hostess will stand when offering a toast, speak a little, and finish with *"Salud"* (health) when everyone stands.
- When dining, keep elbows off the table and hands out of your lap.
- If you are presented with a gift, open it immediately.

DON'TS

- Dahlias and chrysanthemums are associated with death; do not bring them to a host's home, nor take any flowers in bunches of 13.
- Do not speak of high taxes, religion, family, or Spain's neutrality during World War II. Also avoid comparing Spanish and American politics. Say nothing negative about bullfighting, which is regarded as more of an art than a sport.
- Leaving food on the plate is an insult, especially at a host's home.
- The US "okay" sign is considered obscene here. The "thumbs up" is regarded as supportive of the Basque separatist movement.
- Don't yawn or stretch in public.
- Crossing the legs is considered improper for women.
- Avoid showing avarice in a business deal. Everyone wants to make a profit, but it isn't talked about.

CUSTOMS

- The main meal of the day is between 1:30 and 4:30 pm, followed by a siesta.
- Spaniards usually entertain in restaurants; an invitation to their home is a mark of special favor and the guest should bring a wrapped gift for the hostess of chocolates, pastry, or wine and candy for the children.
- Dinner is usually not eaten until late in the evening; often later than ten.
- At meals, women and older persons are seated and served first.
- Adults who eat while walking are thought rude.

OBSERVATIONS

- Your host may interrupt you; credit eagerness, not rudeness.
- Business cards should be printed in Spanish and English, and exchanged at the end of meetings.
- If someone digresses, they will be annoyed if you try to lead them back to business. Don't take the lead.
- Criticism is an exercise of rank and is almost always taken personally; honor is always a consideration.
- Spaniards will not say "no" directly; a typical negative response might be, "We'll let you know."
- Though they love to talk, Spaniards will usually understate their achievements.

NEGOTIATIONS

- Nationals will be pleased by a visitor's attempt to speak Spanish, although it is a good idea to have an interpreter present at formal negotiations.
- Remember that the Spanish will want to get everything they can out of a deal.
- Approach negotiations formally, with a thoroughly prepared but low-key presentation. Modesty and understatement are highly valued; boasting is not.
- Eye contact is crucial; lack of it is considered a sign of dishonesty.
- The Spanish will not instantly come to the point; they want their visitors to deduce their meaning from significant clues.
- Superlatives and drama flavor Spanish conversation; these indicate a speaker's interest.
- Delivery dates are rarely taken literally, and quality checks are regarded with resentment.
- Bargaining is rare, since the agreed-upon price is usually treated as fair.
- Doing someone a favor can earn a friend for life.

Legal System

Spain is a parliamentary democracy with several Western traditions. The judicial system is independent from other branches of government.

Intellectual Property Protection

Patents Patents must be registered with the Spanish Office of Patents and Trademarks to be considered valid. Most applications are registered quickly. Spain is party to several international patent and industrial property conventions.

Trademarks Trademarks must be registered with the Spanish Office of Patents and Trademarks to be considered valid. To register a particular designation as a trade name, the designation must be the name or style of the person wishing to register it.

Copyrights Spain recently modified its copyright laws, giving more power to creators to protect their work. Copyrights last for 60 years following the death of the author. Spain is a member of several international copyright conventions, and has signed a number of agreements with other countries, giving foreign copyrights more power. The Business Software Alliance (BSA) estimates that 80 percent of PC software in use has been copied illegally. The government recently passed legislation allowing unannounced civil search procedures that permit software developers having a reasonable suspicion of an infringement of their copyright to get a judge to allow a search of the alleged wrongdoer's premises without warning.

Trade secrets Trade secrets are protected by several laws in Spain. Injunctions regarding trade secret violations are relatively easy to file and will be prosecuted.

Business Registration

All companies must be constituted by public deed subscribed before a notary public and entered in the Mercantile Registry. A company acquires the status of a legal entity only on registration. If the founders are foreign, they must present to the Registrar a certificate (issued by their consular officers) that they have the necessary legal capacity in accordance with the laws of their own countries to constitute the company. Most foreign companies must be listed as a contractor with the Ministry of Finance.

Contracts and Dispute Resolution

Spanish companies typically follow contract terms to the letter. Contracts are not valid unless they are written and contain such information as the amount and type of work, the different people involved, and the date for completion of the work. Disputes are handled through Spanish courts, and judgments must be registered with a notary public to be valid.

Notaries

Notaries are very important in Spain. Many documents must be approved by a notary to be considered valid, including the deeds of constitution for all kinds of companies and all contracts affecting real estate. Several types of affidavits and powers of attorney must be executed before a notary to have full effect.

Labor

Workers have basic labor rights, including effective occupation, free syndication, collective bargaining, assemblage, and the right to strike. Every four years Spanish workers elect delegates to represent them before management. If a certain proportion of those delegates are union-affiliated, those unions form part of the workers' committees. Dues-paying union membership is among the lowest in the EU (generally estimated at about 10 percent of the work force), but unions are involved in negotiating collective agreements for over half of the work force. The minimum working age is 16. Employment discrimination based on age, race, religion, politics, and language is prohibited. Basic employment agreements need not be in writing, but either party may request a written contract. Special employment agreements must be in writing, including at-home work contracts, part-time contracts, and contracts for the performance of a specific job. Large employers generally have individual collective agreements, but in industries characterized by smaller companies, collective agreements are often industry-wide or regional. Spain's two unemployment indexes vary by as much as five percentage points and neither is generally accepted as precisely accurate. What is clear is that Spain continues to have a real unemployment problem, among the worst in the European Union. The right to strike is guaranteed in the constitution and has been interpreted to include general strikes called to protest government policy.

Legal Matters

LEGAL BRIEFS

- **Business entities** The most popular business entity established in Spain is the Sociedad Anónima (S.A.), which offers limited liability in most instances.
- **Employee taxes** All taxes and social security contributions to be paid by employees cannot be paid by employer.
- **Maximum workweek** A workweek cannot exceed 40 hours, and yearly remunerated vacations are set at a minimum of 30 weekdays.
- **Government contracts** Government contracts are decided by means of competitive bidding and in certain cases by direct negotiation.
- **Recent strikes** There have been several labor strikes in recent years, the most recent being a one-day nationwide strike held collectively by Spanish trade unions on January 27, 1994, to protest the government's proposed labor market reform legislation.
- **Labor law problems** Employers have long criticized Spanish labor law (much of which originated in the Franco era) as unusually inflexible and with very high severance payments, thus discouraging new hiring.
- **Employment statistics** The Active Population Survey (EPA) indicated over 15 million Spaniards in the work force at the end of 1993. National Employment Institute (INEM) unemployment figures for year-end 1994 (the most recent available) reveal a static employment situation, with unemployment rates maintaining at about 18 percent.
- **Regulatory system** Spain has modernized its commercial laws and regulations following its 1986 entry into the EU. Local regulatory framework compares favorably with other major European countries. Bureaucratic procedures have been streamlined and most red tape eliminated. Labor law and regulations are the exception; although there has been new legislation implemented in May 1994 liberalizing some labor procedures.
- **Private ownership** Private ownership is protected by the constitution. Spanish law establishes clear rights to private ownership.
- **Recent disputes** There have been no major disputes involving foreign investment interests and the Spanish government in recent history. In any case, legislation establishes mechanisms to solve such disputes if they ever arise.
- **Political violence** Spain is involved in a long-running campaign against Basque Fatherland and Liberty (ETA), a terrorist organization founded in 1959 and dedicated to promoting Basque independence. ETA regularly targets Spanish government officials, members of the military and security forces, and moderate Basques for assassination. The group has carried out numerous bombings against Spanish government facilities and economic targets. In recent years, the Spanish government has had more success in controlling ETA due in part to increased security cooperation with French authorities.
- **International agreements** Spain is a member of CISG; Convention on the Granting of European Patents; New York Convention on the Recognition and Enforcement of Foreign Arbitral Awards; Convention on the Service Abroad of Judicial and Extrajudicial Documents in Civil or Commercial Matters; Convention on the Taking of Evidence Abroad in Civil or Commercial Matters; and ATA Carnet Convention.

LEGAL CONTACTS

Clifford Chance
Paseode la Castellana 110
Madrid 28046
Tel: (1) 562-76-74 Fax: (1) 562-49-93

Despacho Melchor de las Heras Abogados, SC
José Abascal, 58
28003 Madrid
Tel: (1) 442-1077 Fax: (1) 441-1472, 442-8476

Consejo General de Abogacia Esponola
Calle de Serrano No. 9
Madrid 28001
Tel: (1) 5227711
Fax: (1) 4319365

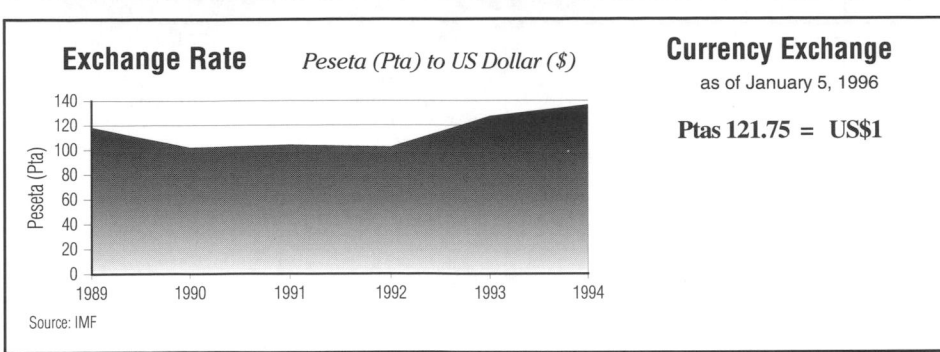

Exchange Rate
Peseta (Pta) to US Dollar ($)

Peseta (Pta) — 1989, 1990, 1991, 1992, 1993, 1994

Source: IMF

Currency Exchange
as of January 5, 1996

Ptas 121.75 = US$1

Money Matters

BITS AND PIECES

- **Capital gains** Capital gains are usually treated as normal income and taxed at the regular corporate tax rate.
- **Relief for losses** Tax losses can be carried forward and offset against future taxable income for five fiscal years. Carrying back losses is not permitted.
- **Debt-to-equity rules** Any interest paid on loans from foreign-related parties in excess of 2:1 debt-to-equity is treated as dividends.
- **Financial assets** Nonresidents can freely purchase any kind of financial asset and contract all types of commercial credit without restriction. All transactions must be reported to the Bank of Spain.
- **Gold** Any acquisition of gold must be authorized by the Directorate-General of Foreign Trade.
- **Import payments** Foreign exchange in the appropriate currency to pay for authorized imports is granted freely.
- **Export payments** There are no restrictions for export payments, but some goods require prior authorization from the Directorate-General of Foreign Trade, regardless of destination.
- **Spanish rules** Trade and investment are influenced largely by Spain's obligations to European Union. Nonetheless, legislation is too rigid by Western Standards.

Currency

The currency of Spain is the Spanish peseta (P or Pta). Spain participates in the exchange rate and intervention system (ERM) of the European Monetary System (EMS), and maintains a spot exchange rate between the Spanish peseta and the currencies of other participants of the ERM.

Foreign Exchange

The Ministry of Economy and Finance, through the Directorate-General of External Transactions, handles all exchange control regulations, including verification and remaining administrative authorization for importing or exporting currency. The Bank of Spain regulates all commercial banks' activities and nonresident accounts. Nonresidents can open accounts in Spain and deposit any amount of currency, domestic and foreign. All nonresident accounts are subject to reporting requirements.

Capital Transfers

Exporting more than the equivalent of one million pesetas in notes must be declared, and more than the equivalent of five million pesetas requires authorization. Importing more than the equivalent of one million pesetas in notes must be declared only when they are intended to be used for investment or banking purposes. There are no restrictions for proceeds of invisibles, but importing more than the equivalent of one million pesetas must be declared. There are no restrictions for invisible payments, but authorization is required for exporting more than Ptas five million.

Investment Incentives

The Spanish government has set up new regulations and foreign exchange to attract foreign investment. Nonresidents can own up to 100 percent of equity, except in a few strategic sectors. All EU-resident companies receive the same treatment as Spanish companies in some areas, including national defense and broadcasting.

Investment Restrictions

There are very few investment restrictions in Spain. Once an investment is made, it must also be registered, to verify the purpose of the investment. Requirements for registration are, however, simple and straightforward.

BANKS

Argentaria
Corporacion Bancaria de España
Paseo de Recolestos, 10
28004 Madrid
Tel: (1) 537-70-00

Banco Central Hispano
Alcala, 49
28014 Madrid
Tel: (1) 522-40-40
Fax: (1) 521-97-03

Banco de España
Alcala, 50
28014 Madrid
Tel: (1) 338-50-00

Banco Guipuzcoano
Avda. de la Libertad 21
20004 San Sebastian
Tel: (43) 418100
Fax: (43) 426828

Banesto
Paseo de la Castellana, 7
28046 Madrid
Tel: (1) 338-10-00

Bankers Trust Company
Paseo de la Castellana 31
28046 Madrid
Tel: (1) 538-75-00

Chase Bank España
C/ Peonias 2, planta 7
28042 Madrid
Tel: (1) 321-91-00

Chemical Bank España
Paseo de la Castellana, 51
28046 Madrid
Tel: (1) 349-28-00

Citibank España, S.A.
Avenida de Europa, 19
Parque Industrial La Moraleja
Alcobendas
Madrid
Tel: (1) 663-11-00

Morgan Guaranty Trust of New York
Jose Ortega y Gasset, 29
28006 Madrid
Tel: (1) 435-60-41
Fax: (1) 577-58-14

New York Chemical Bank
Paseo de la Castellana, 51
28046 Madrid
Tel: (1) 349-28-00

TAXATION	At a Glance	
Taxation requires sophisticated knowledge of complex rules and regulations specific to each country. The information presented here is from the Ernst & Young Corporate Tax Guide and Directory, available from the Ernst & Young accounting office in your country, or from: **Ernst & Young** Tax/Legal Torre Picasso Pza. Pablo Ruiz Picasso 28020 Madrid, Spain Tel: (1) 572-72-00 Fax: (1) 572-74-00, 572-72-38, 572-73-72	Corporate Income Tax Rate (%) (a)	35
	Capital Gains Tax Rate (%) (b)	35
	Branch Tax Rate (%)	35
	Withholding Tax (%)	
	Dividends (b)	25
	Interest	25
	Royalties from Patents, Know-how, etc.	25
	Branch Remittance Tax	25
	Net Operating Losses (Years)	
	Carryback	0
	Carryforward	5
	(a) Other rates apply to specified entities.	
	(b) Certain capital gains are exempt from tax.	
	(d) Certain interest is exempt from tax.	

Business Travel

LH 1906	MADRID	935	113-3
LH 1022	STUTTGART HBF.	935	-
AF 1701	LYON	940	683-6
AY 822	HELSINKI	940	113-3
AA 071	SFRANCISCO-DALLAS	945	731-7

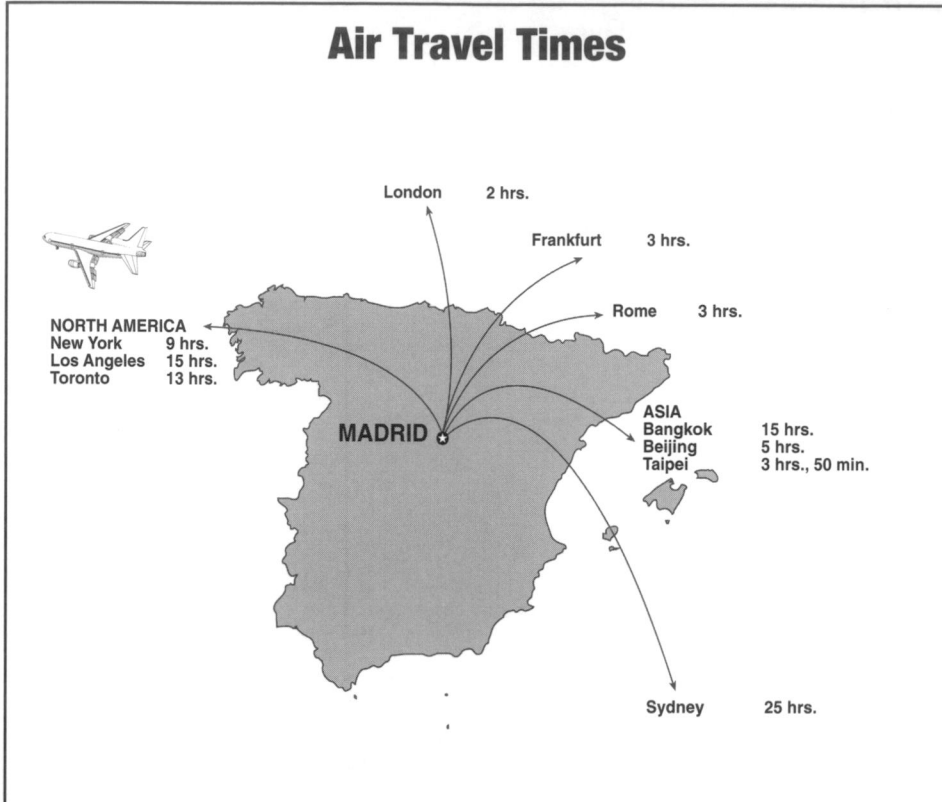

Air Travel Times

London   2 hrs.

Frankfurt   3 hrs.

Rome   3 hrs.

NORTH AMERICA
New York   9 hrs.
Los Angeles   15 hrs.
Toronto   13 hrs.

MADRID

ASIA
Bangkok   15 hrs.
Beijing   5 hrs.
Taipei   3 hrs., 50 min.

Sydney   25 hrs.

COMMUNICATIONS

Telephones The telephone system is inadequate, and service can be unreliable. Long distance calls can be made from booths marked *Telefonica*, located at convenient spots in major cities, or from coin-operated public phones in restaurants, cafes, hotels.

Fax Domestic and overseas fax services are readily available.

Post office The postal service is inefficient and unreliable. Long delays can occur while packages are cleared or opened for censorship, and pilferage is common. Air mail must be clearly marked and have the correct postage or it will be sent by much slower surface mail. Mail sent from post offices is safer than mail dropped in boxes.

BEST TRAVEL BOOKS

Fodor's Spain: The Complete Guide Including Mallorca, Ibiza and the Canary Islands, Fodor's Travel.
Frommer's Spain. Frommer's Comprehensive Travel Guide Series, illustrated, 564 pages, Prentice Hall General Reference and Travel.
Birnbaum's Spain, Alexandra M. Birnbaum ed., Birnbaum Travel Guides Series. Illustrated, 608 pages. Harper Collins Publishers, Inc.
Berlitz Business Travel Guide, Europe. Concise economic details, successful trip planning, background information on people and cities, useful facts and addresses.
Culture Shock, A Guide to Customs and Etiquette, Spain.
Do's and Taboo's Around the World. The Bestselling Guide to International Behavior. Edited by Roger Axtell, compiled by the Parker Pen Company. The ultimate guide to international behavior, now completely updated and expanded. Helpful, fun to read!

USEFUL TELEPHONE NUMBERS

If you are calling from outside Spain, you will need to add the country code [34] and any other international dialing requirements from within your country.

- Local Operator 003
- Operator 0
- Directory Information 003
- International Calls 07
- Madrid and Barcelona Police 091
- Madrid Ambulance .... (1) 252-2792
- Barcelona Ambulance .... (1) 302-3333
- International Telegrams .... (1) 222-6300
- Domestic Telegrams .... (1) 222-6200
- Chamber of Commerce and Industry ... (1) 429-3193
- Ministry of Industry .... (1) 458-8010
- State Railroad (Madrid) .... (1) 733-3000
- Ambulance 5222222
- Fire Madrid 080; (1) 2323232
- Fire Barcelona .... (31) 335353
- Pharmacy 098

Credit Card Information
Lost or stolen credit cards (call collect to the US, regardless of which country the card was issued in).

- Amex .... [1] (919) 333-3211
- Diner's Club............................... [1] (303) 799-1504
- MasterCard .... [1] (314) 275-6690
- Visa .... [1] (410) 581-7931

Travelogue

WORKWEEK

Offices Monday-Friday 9:00 am to 1:30 pm and 3:00 pm to 6:00 pm. (July and August, 8:30 am to 2:00 or 2:30 pm.)
Banks Monday-Saturday 8:30 am to 2:30 pm.
Government Monday-Friday 9:00 am to 1:00 pm.
Retail Monday-Saturday 9:00 am to 1:00 pm and 4:00 pm to 8:00 pm.

HOLIDAYS

Holidays 1996
January 1 New Year's Day
January 6 Epiphany
April 4 Holy Thursday
April 5 Good Friday
April 8 Easter Monday
August 15 Assumption Day
October 12 National Day
November 1 All Saints' Day
December 6 Constitution Day
December 8 Immaculate Conception
December 25 Christmas
In addition, each region has fiestas and holidays with varying dates.

VISA AND PASSPORT

Foreigners must have a valid passport, but a visa is not required for tourist stays of up to 90 days. Citizens of EU countries need a valid National Identify card from their home state to enter. US, Australia, and New Zealand citizens need a valid passport and are given an authorized three-month stay, which can be renewed for three additional months.

DEPARTURE FORMALITIES

Travelers can export the equivalent of US$4,700 in foreign money not exchanged and up to 100,000 ptas.

IMMUNIZATION

No immunization is required except for travelers entering from infected areas, but typhoid, paratyphoid, polio, tetanus is recommended for travelers who expect to be in the major cities.

TIPPING

Tip an additional five to10 percent above a restaurant service charge. Taxi drivers in cities get 5 to10 percent. In metered taxis from the airport, tip a driver to Madrid 10 percent of the fare and a driver to Barcelona 5 to 10 percent of the fare. Hotel desk clerks and doormen get 100 ptas, porters 50 ptas per bag, and maids 200 ptas per week.

CRIME

Spain has a very low rate of violent crime, but petty crimes are often directed against tourists who are caught off guard. Watch for thieves and con artists working with an accomplice who distract the travelers' attention by soliciting good will or offering unsolicited assistance.

INFRASTRUCTURE

Tourist facilities are widely available, including good hotels, an excellent subway system (Metro), taxis (recognized by the letters SP for *servicio publico*) which are metered. Car rental agents operate throughout Spain. There are two classes of trains. Buses offer reliable transportation but can be crowded. The motorways in Spain are safe but if anyone is injuried in an automobile accident, a jail sentence can be given.

NATIONAL TOURIST OFFICES

Ministry of Tourism
Plaza San Juan de la Cruz 1
28003 Madrid
Tel: (1) 456-1144

Madrid Convention Bureau
Tel: (1) 588-2900
Fax: (1) 588-2930

GOVERNMENT AGENCIES

Ministry of Agriculture, Fisheries and Food
Paseo Infanta Isabel, 1
28014 Madrid
Tel: (1) 347-5000
Fax: (1) 468-6888 Telex: 47062

Ministry of Culture
Plaza del Rey, 5/n
28071 Madrid
Tel: (1) 532-5089
Fax: (1) 531-9212 Telex: 27286

Ministry of Economy and Finance
Alcalà, 9
28014 Madrid
Tel: (1) 522-1000
Fax: (1) 522-4916, 531-4805
Telex: 48387

Ministry of Education and Science
Alcalà, 34
28014 Madrid
Tel: (1) 522-1100
Fax: (1) 521-3775, 522-9256

Ministry of Health and Consumer Affairs
Paseo del Prado, 18 y 20
28071 Madrid
Tel: (1) 420-0000
Fax: (1) 429-3526
Telex: 22608

Minister of Industry and Energy
Paseo de la Castellana, 160
28071 Madrid
Tel: (1) 349-4000
Fax: (1) 457-8066
Telex: 42112

Ministry of Labor and Social Security
Nuevos Ministerios
Augustin de Bethencourt, 4
28071 Madrid
Tel: (1) 553-6000
Fax: (1) 553-0271

Ministry of Public Works, Environment and Transportation
Paseo de la Castellana, 67
28071 Madrid
Tel: (1) 533-1600
Fax: (1) 533-6577

Secretariat of State for International Cooperation and Latin America
Plaza de la Provincia, 1
28071 Madrid
Tel: (1) 366-4800
Fax: (1) 366-7358

Secretariat of State for Relations with the European Union
Francisco Silvela, 82
28071 Madrid
Tel: (1) 356-7001
Fax: (1) 361-4852

Consejo Asesor de Exportación
Secretaría de Estado de Comercio
Dirección General de Comercio Exterior
Paseo de la Castellana 162
28046 Madrid
Tel: (1) 583-6011
Fax: (1) 563-1823

Empresa Nacional del Gas SA
State Gas Company
Avda América 38
28028 Madrid
Tel: (1) 384-5000
Fax: (1) 256-8530

Instituto Nacional de Hidrocarburos
Oil, Gas and Petrochemical Companies
Paseo de la Castellana, 89
28046 Madrid
Tel: (1) 456-5300
Telex: 48162

Instituto Nacional de Industria
National Industrial Institute
Plaza del Marqués de Salamanca, 8
28071 Madrid
Tel: (1) 575-7650
Fax: (1) 575-5641

WORLD TRADE CENTERS

World Trade Center Barcelona
Urgell 240, 6 A
08036 Barcelona
Tel: (3) 439-45-34
Fax: (3) 439-73-96

World Trade Center Bilbao
Alameda de Urquijo 10, 1º D
48008 Bilbao
Tel: (4) 415-70-55
Fax: (4) 415-77-79

World Trade Center Madrid, S.A.
Paseo de la Habana, 26
3rd Floor, Suite #4
28036 Madrid
Tel: (1) 411-61-45
Fax: (1) 562-40-04

World Trade Center Sevilla
Edificio World Trade Center
Isla de la Cartuja
41092 Sevilla
Tel: (5) 448-82-22
Fax: (5) 446-21-73

World Trade Center Valencia, S.A.
Av. de las Ferias, 2 (Edificio Hotel)
46035 Valencia
Tel: (6) 390-11-16
Fax: (6) 390-08-83

BUSINESS ORGANIZATIONS

American Chamber of Commerce
Av. Diagonal 477
08036 Barcelona
Tel: (3) 405-12-66
Fax: (3) 405-31-24

Camara Oficial de Comercio e Industria de Madrid
Huertas 13
28012 Madrid
Tel: (1) 538-35-00
Fax: (1) 538-36-77

Consejo Superior de Camaras de Comercio, Industria y Navegacion
Higher Council of Chambers of Commerce
Claudio Coello 19
28006 Madrid
Tel: (1) 575-34-00
Fax: (1) 435-23-92

BANKS

Bank of America, S.A.E.
Capitan Haya 1
28020 Madrid
Tel: (1) 455-66-00

Banco de Bilbao-Vizcaya
Paseo de la Castellana, 81
28046 Madrid
Tel: (1) 374-80-00

Banco de Madrid
Carrera de San Jeronimo, 13
28014 Madrid
Tel: (1) 429-24-43

Banco de Santander
Paseo de la Castellana 75
28046 Madrid
Tel: (1) 435-04-55

Banco Hipotecario de España
Paseo de Recoletos, 10
28001 Madrid
Tel: (1) 575-46-00

Banco Popular Espanol
Alcala, 26
28014 Madrid
Tel: (1) 435-36-20

REMEMBER
- When you telephone (or fax) to Spain from another country you must always include the country code [34] before the numbers given.
- When you send mail to Spain, be sure to write SPAIN in capital letters on its own line below the addresses given.

Caja de Madrid
Plaza de Celenque, 2 - 2da.
28013 Madrid
Tel: (1) 532-00-00

LEGAL CONTACTS

Baker & McKenzie
Pinar 18
Madrid 28006
Tel: (1) 411-3062
Fax: (1) 262-2425

Stephenson Harwood
Fernando El Santo 15-3
Madrid 28014
Tel: (1) 319-1212
Fax: (1) 319-1940

J & B Cremades & Asociados
Goya 18
28001 Madrid
Tel: (1) 431 83 54
Fax: (1) 576 97 94

Despacho Jimenez De Parga Abogados Asociados
Paseo De Gracia 96
08008 Barcelona
Tel: (3) 215 03 66
Fax: (3) 487 17 41

Folchi & De Pascual y Asociados
3rd Floor, Corcega 302-304
08008 Barcelona
Tel: (3) 415 00 32
Fax: (3) 218 59 50

Estudio Legal, Abogados
C/ Velazquez 51
28001 Madrid
Tel: (1) 578 06 43
Fax: (1) 431 21 52

Cuatrecasas
Paseo De Gracia 111
08008 Barcelona
Tel: (3) 290 55 00
Fax: (3) 290 55 67

Despacho Melchor De Las Heras
Jose Abascal 58, 4a Planta
28003 Madrid
Tel: (1) 442 10 77
Fax: (1) 442 60 45

J & A Garrigues
Antonio Maura 16
28014 Madrid
Tel: (1) 521 21 51
Fax: (1) 521 70 16

Uria & Menéndez
Hermosilla 30
28001 Madrid
Tel: (1) 586 04 00
Fax: (1) 586 04 04

Gomez-Acebo & Pombo
Castellana 164
28046 Madrid
Tel: (1) 582 91 00
Fax: (1) 582 91 14

Bufete AF
Vallehermoso, 50 C.P.
28015-Madrid
Tel: (1) 593 00 72
Fax: (341) 594 28 ?

PERIODICALS

Actualidad Económica
Recoletos 1, planta 7
28001 Madrid
Tel: (1) 337-3220
Fax: (1) 383-2218

Dinero
O'Donnell 12
28009 Madrid
Tel: (1) 409-6345

El Economista
Conde de Aranda 8
28001 Madrid
Tel: (1) 411-0653
Fax: (1) 411-0752

El Mundo Financiero
Hermosillo 93
Apdo 6.119
28001 Madrid
Tel: (1) 577-3376
Fax: (1) 577-8981

El Nuevo Lunes
Plaza de España 18
Torre de Madrid, planta 32, of. 4
28008 Madrid
Tel: (1) 247-3101

El Nuevo Lunes de la Economía y la Sociedad
Plaza de España 17, planta 7, of. 3
28008 Madrid
Tel: (1) 541-0134
Fax: (1) 248-0406

Información Comercial Española
Paseo de la Castellana 162, planta 16
28046 Madrid
Tel: (1) 349-3965
Fax: (1) 349-3634

Más
Juan de Austria 6
28010 Madrid
Tel: (1) 445-7454

Mercado
Valentín San Narciso 14
28018 Madrid
Tel: (1) 303-5484
Fax: (1) 303-4598

Pronto
Avda. Gran Vía Carlos III 124, planta 5
08034 Barcelona
Tel: (3) 280-0088
Fax: (3) 280-5555

Tribuna de Actualidad
Eladio Lopez Vilches 18
28033 Madrid
Tel: (1) 383-2218

RADIO AND TELEVISION

Radio Nacional de España (RNE)
Casa de la Radio
Prado del Rey
28023 Madrid
Tel: (1) 346-1000
Fax: (1) 518-3240

RTVE (Radiotelevision Española)
Casa de la Radio
Prado del Rey
28023 Madrid
Tel: (1) 581-7000
Fax: (1) 346-2064

Televisión Española
Prado del Rey
Apdo 26002
28023 Madrid
Tel: (1) 711-0400

AD AGENCIES

Bassat, Ogilvy & Mather S.A.
Av. Josep Tarradellas, No. 123, 1st Fl.
08029 Barcelona
Tel: (3) 4192929
Fax: (3) 4194962

Conquest Europe
Av. Brasil, 7-10?28020 Madrid
Tel: (1) 5566043
Fax: (1) 5556588

D'Arcy Masius Benton & Bowles, S.A.
Lagasca 88, 7th Fl.
28001 Madrid
Tel: (1) 4314811
Fax: (1) 5773897

Grey Advertising
Paseo de la Castellanan 91, Planta 11
28046 Madrid
Tel: (1) 5971750
Fax: (1) 5566530

J. Walter Thompson S.A.
Arapiles 13
28015 Madrid
Tel: (1) 4487500, 4487600
Fax: (1) 5941031

McCann-Erickson S.A.
Rosario Pino 5
28020 Madrid
Tel: (1) 5710200
Fax: (1) 5701116

Saatchi & Saatchi Advertising
Paseo de la Castellana 89, Planta 11-A
28046 Madrid
Tel: (1) 5561200
Fax: (1) 5550442

Vitruvio/Leo Burnett
Planta 27, Plaza de Pablo Ruiz
Torre Picasso s/n
28020 Madrid
Tel: (1) 5561120
Fax: (1) 5565705

Wunderman Cato Johnson
Raimundo Fernandex Villaverde 65-9 pta.
Edificio Windsor
28003 Madrid
Tel: (1) 555-5954
Fax: (1) 5561694

Young & Rubicam
Raimundo Fernandez Villaverde 65
Edificio Windsor, 10th Fl.
28003 Madrid
Tel: (1) 5563113
Fax: (1) 5560473

NEWSPAPERS

ABC
Juan Ignacio Luca de Tena 7
28027 Madrid
Tel: (1) 339-9000
Fax: (1) 320-3680

Diario 16
Basauri 17, Edif. Valrrealty
La Florida
28023 Madrid?
Tel: (1) 558-9800
Fax: (1) 558-9896

Diario de Cádiz
Ceballos 1
Apdo 57
11003 Cádiz
Tel: (56) 226605
Fax: (56) 320011
Telex: 76009

El Mundo
Sanchez Pacheco 61
28002 Madrid
Tel: (1) 586-4800
Fax: (1) 519-5192

El País
Zona Franca
Sector B
Calle D
08004 Barcelona
Tel: (3) 4010500
Fax: (3) 3353925
Telex: 97940

El Periodico
Consell de Cent 425–427
08009 Barcelona
Tel: (3) 265-5353
Fax: (3) 484-6512

Expansion de la Actualidad Economica Diaria
Recoltos 1, planta 5
28001 Madrid
Tel: (1) 337-3220
Fax: (1) 575-6502

Gaceta de los Negocios
(Business and finance)
O'Donnell 12
28009 Madrid
Tel: (1) 586-3300
Fax: (1) 577-6233

Iberian Daily Sun
(English language)
Zurbano 74
28010 Madrid
Tel: (1) 442-7700
Fax: (1) 442-7854

La Region Internacional
Menendez Pelayo 3, planta 1
28009 Madrid
Tel: (1) 577-5685
Fax: (1) 275-2053

La Vanguardia
Pelayo 28
08001 Barcelona
Tel: (3) 3015454
Fax: (3) 3185587
Telex: 54530

INTERNET ADDRESSES

Usenet group(s):
soc.culture.spain

Embassy of Spain (Ottawa, Canada)
http://www.docuweb.ca/SiSpain/

EUNet Spain
http://www.eunet.es/

Info About Spain
http://www.uji.es/mapes/spain_info.html

The Webfoot's Guide to Spain
http://www.webfoot.com/travel/guides/spain/spain.html

Sri Lanka

Democratic Socialist Republic of Sri Lanka

Economy

Overview

An emphasis on free markets, privatization, and promoting and developing its export markets has considerably changed Sri Lanka's business climate in recent years. Its primary resources are agricultural and, although agriculture remains central to the Sri Lankan economy, it has increasingly focused on the manufacturing sector to propel the economy. The wholesale and retail trades have also grown significantly in recent years. Although the level of state participation in the economy has been significantly reduced, the public sector is still large. However, the government has committed to further privatization as part of its ongoing, overall liberalization of the economy, and rates of growth should rise accordingly.

Trade

The government's economic policy is aimed at the promotion of exports and the control of import growth. As such, Sri Lanka has experienced strong export-led growth in the past few years that has significantly increased the total value of its foreign trade. Developed countries are the primary markets for its exports, and it buys almost half its imports from eastern Asian countries. The US isis the primary destination country for its exports, followed by Germany and the UK. Recent increases in Sri Lanka's trade deficit are primarily the result of increasing demand for machinery and equipment, which augurs well for future economic expansion.

Sectors

Agriculture Sri Lanka has traditionally been an agricultural country and this sector remains central to the health of the economy, employing almost 50 percent of the population and contributing 27 percent of GDP. While output is often affected by drought conditions and other climatic factors, there has recently been high output of its main export commodities—tea and rubber. Together with coconuts, these account for over 30 percent of total export earnings. Sri Lanka imports large quantities of rice, wheat, and sugar.

Industry Although mechanized industry is still in the early stages of development, it is a principal growth area in Sri Lanka's economy. Textiles and garments currently account for almost half of total export earnings, but moves are being made to expand the assembly industry and ultimately move into the full production of electrical and electronic goods.

Services Sri Lanka's once robust tourist industry has been adversely affected by the unstable political situation existing since the early 1980s. However, with political stability returning, tourism is once again making an important contribution to the economy. Along with this recovery comes growth in other service industries, which should all fare well as increased political stability brings greater prosperity.

Trends

Sri Lanka has experienced strong growth in recent years, and is continuing on the road to a market-oriented private sector economy. The government is actively promoting private enterprise, deregulating industries, and encouraging foreign investment. Recent growth rates in the main export industries are expected to continue and the government hopes to broaden its industrial base in the long term. If the political situation remains stable, Sri Lanka should continue to post positive growth rates in the near term.

At a Glance

THE COUNTRY

Location An island located in the Indian Ocean; lies south and slightly east of the southernmost point of India.

Terrain The south-central part is a rough plateau. Coastal plains are in the north. Numerous rivers and streams flow seaward in all directions from the central mountain area.

Climate Mostly tropical and monsoonal; varies from warm in the coastal plains and lowlands to temperate in the hill and mountain regions. Has no summer or winter but only rainy and dry seasons.

THE PEOPLE

Population 17,400,000
Ethnic composition
Sinhalese 74%
Sri Lankan Tamils 12%
Sri Lankan Moors... 7%
Indian Tamils 6%
Malays and other minorities................................. 1%
Religious composition Buddhism is the predominant religion, but there are also substantial numbers of Hindus, Muslims, and Christians.

Languages spoken Sinhala is the official language, although Tamil is also recognized as a national language.

Education and literacy More than 88 percent of adults can read. Education is compulsory for 10 years, and all schools including universities are free. The educational system has been separated by language: one in Sinhalese and the other in Tamil.

Labor force
Total...5,900,000
By occupation: agriculture 50%, industry and commerce 19.6%, services 14.4%.

COUNTRY FACTS

Political and legal Power is divided between the president and the legislature. Civil laws are based on Roman-Dutch system; criminal laws are based on the British system. Muslims have their own laws for some situations. Courts are independent from government control.

Telephone The government owns and operates all telephone and telegraph systems. More than half of all telephones are in Colombo. International country code: [94]. City codes: Colombo Central (1), Galle (9), Kotte (1).

Transportation Highways are expensive to travel on and many are in poor condition. All railroads are owned and operated by the state. Colombo is one of the world's great artificial harbors. The principal international airport is Katunayaka, north of Colombo.

Environment Deforestation has caused erosion, destruction of wildlife habitats, and reduction of water flow; about 58,000 hectares of forestland were lost each year between 1981 and 1985.

Media The government operates broadcasting services in Sinhala, Tamil, and English. Two television broadcasting stations began in 1992. Censorship has been imposed, primarily from the National Press Council.

Health The government provides medical service free to almost everyone, but care is hampered by a shortage of trained personnel and limited funds.

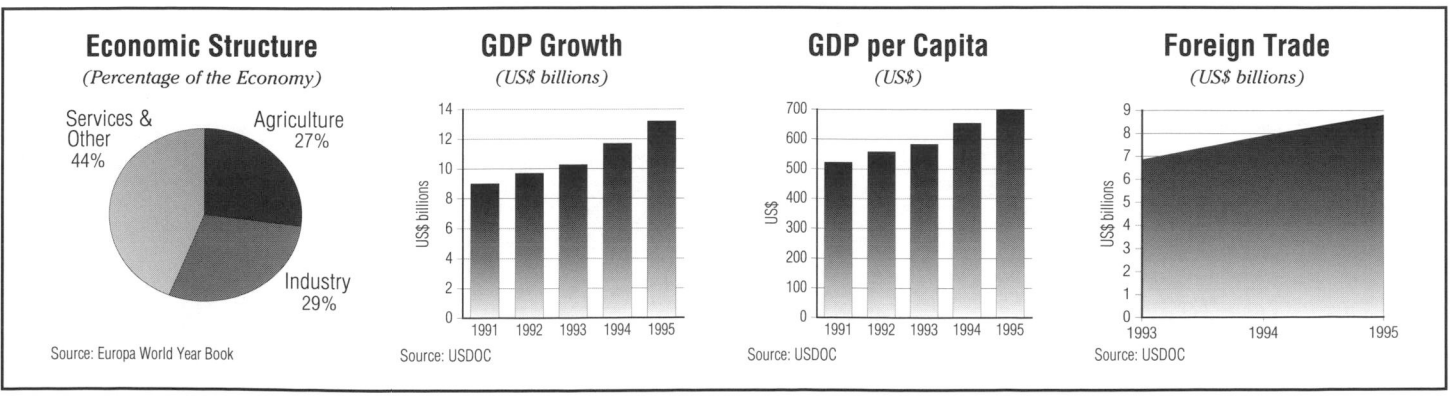

Economic Structure
(Percentage of the Economy)

Services & Other 44%
Agriculture 27%
Industry 29%

Source: Europa World Year Book

GDP Growth
(US$ billions)

Source: USDOC

GDP per Capita
(US$)

Source: USDOC

Foreign Trade
(US$ billions)

Source: USDOC

Business Travel

Travelogue

WORKWEEK
Offices Monday-Friday 8:30 am to 5:00 pm with one hour for lunch.
Banks Monday-Friday 9:00 am to 3:00 pm and some until 5:30 pm.
Government Monday-Friday 8:30 am to 6:15 pm.
Retail Monday-Friday 10:00 to 8:30 pm and some until 10:00 pm.

HOLIDAYS
Holidays 1996
February 4 Independence Day
April 5 Good Friday
April Eid Al-Adha*
May 1 May Day
May 22 National Heroes' Day
July 28 Holy Prophet's Birthday
June 30 Special Bank Holiday
December 25 Christmas
December 31 Special Bank Holiday
Sri Lankan holidays are observed by four religions: Buddhism, Hinduism, Islam, and Christianity. Many holidays and festivals with varying dates are not listed above and can be ascertained through a Sri Lankan embassy or consulate. When making travel plans check ahead for dates.
*Dates change; some are based on lunar sightings.

VISA AND PASSPORT
Foreigners must have a valid passport, onward ticket, and sufficient daily funds. A tourist visa for stays up to 90 days or a business visa for up to 30 days may be obtained upon entry. Foreigners entering Sri Lanka on a tourist visa cannot change the status of their visa.

DEPARTURE FORMALITIES
Amounts exceeding US$5000 that have been declared on arrival but not spent in Sri Lanka may be exported on departure.

IMMUNIZATION
Yellow fever and cholera immunizations are needed for travelers arriving from infected areas. Anti-malaria medication is advised.

TIPPING
A tip on top of a 10 percent service charge is customary, though not obligatory in hotels. Restaurants, nightspots: 15 percent. Small services: 10 percent.

CRIME
Petty street crime, such as purse snatching and pickpocketing, is common on crowded local transportation. Travel is restricted in some areas due to armed conflicts arising from political instability.

INFRASTRUCTURE
Several five-star hotels offer good accommodations for business travelers, but tourist facilities may be basic outside the capital and major tourist areas. All parts of the island are accessible by roadway, and taxis and motorized tri-shaws are abundant. The telecommunications system is being constantly improved.

NATIONAL TOURIST OFFICE
Sri Lanka Ceylon (SLTB)
78 Steuart Place Galle Road
Colombo 3
Tel: (1) 437059 or
Airport: (1) 452411

COMMUNICATIONS
Telephones The telecommunications system is being upgraded. International direct dialing is available and cellular phones are becoming increasingly common.
Fax International telex and facsimile services are available to major cities connected to the global network. Telegraph and cable services are good and available round the clock in Colombo.
Post office International mail and speedy courier services are available and reliable.

BEST TRAVEL BOOKS
Sri Lanka: A Travel Survival Kit. John Noble and Susan Forsyth. Illustrated, 212 pages, Lonely Planet Publications.
Sri Lanka. Insight Guides Series. Houghton Mifflin.
Sri Lanka Pocket Guide. Pocket Guides Series, Berlitz Publishing Co.
Culture Shock, A Guide to Customs and Etiquette, Sri Lanka.
The Travelers Guide to Sri Lanka Customs and Manners. Elizabeth Devine & Nancy Braganti. An invaluable guide for people not wanting to put foot in mouth.
Far Eastern Economic Review, All Asia Travel Guide Volume 3. The best guide available for the business traveller.
Insight Pocket Guides, Sri Lanka.

USEFUL TELEPHONE NUMBERS
If you are calling from outside Sri Lanka, you will need to add the country code [94] and any other international dialing requirements from within your country.
- Central Telegraph Office .... (1) 432424
- Ceylon Chamber of Commerce .... (1) 4217457
- National Chamber of Commerce.............. (1) 25271
- Women's Chamber of Commerce .... (1) 1699475
- Department of Commerce .... (1) 1430068
- State Trading Corporation .... (1) 126981
Credit Card Information
Lost or stolen credit cards (call collect to the US, regardless of which country the card was issued in).
- Amex .... [1] (919) 333-3211
- Diners' Club................................. [1] (303) 799-1504
- MasterCard .... [1] (314) 275-6690
- Visa .... [1] (410) 581-7931

Foreign Trade

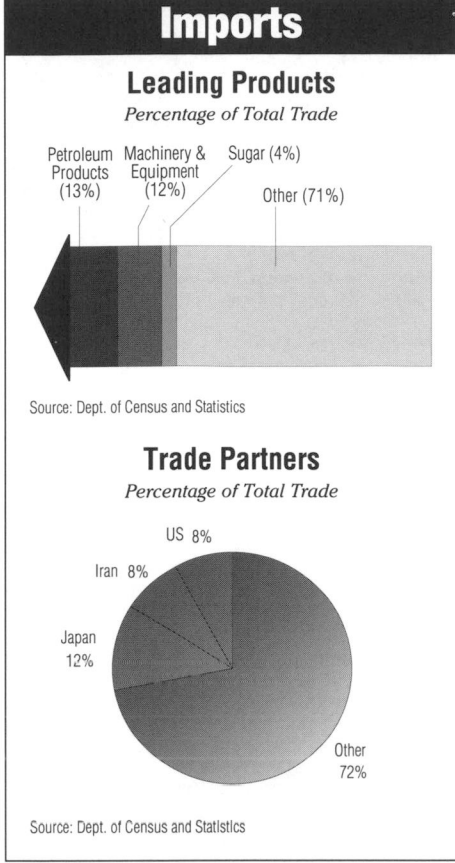

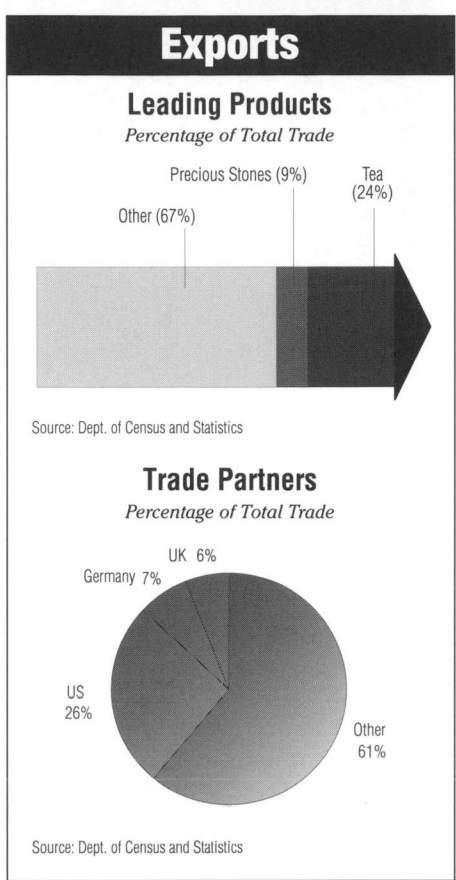

Imports

Leading Products
Percentage of Total Trade

Petroleum Products (13%)
Machinery & Equipment (12%)
Sugar (4%)
Other (71%)

Source: Dept. of Census and Statistics

Trade Partners
Percentage of Total Trade

US 8%
Iran 8%
Japan 12%
Other 72%

Source: Dept. of Census and Statistics

Exports

Leading Products
Percentage of Total Trade

Precious Stones (9%)
Tea (24%)
Other (67%)

Source: Dept. of Census and Statistics

Trade Partners
Percentage of Total Trade

UK 6%
Germany 7%
US 26%
Other 61%

Source: Dept. of Census and Statistics

Opportunities

FOR IMPORTING TO SRI LANKA
- machinery, transport equipment, building materials
- petroleum and chemicals
- sugar, wheat and wheat flour, textiles

FOR EXPORTING FROM SRI LANKA
- textiles and apparel
- minor agricultural products, food and beverages, tea
- petroleum products, rubber

GROWTH SECTORS
- agriculture, forestry and fishing
- mining and quarrying
- manufacturing
- construction

Trade News

RULES AND REGULATIONS
- **Tariffs** Sri Lanka has a four-band import schedule based on the harmonized system of classification. The four rate bands are 10, 20, 35, 45 percent. Most consumer goods and agricultural products are at 45 percent. Imports for most export-oriented industries are either entered duty free or entitled to duty rebates. The government will further reduce import duties by bringing down the highest nominal band to 35 percent.
- **Import taxes** In addition to import duties there are a number of other taxes applicable to imports. The government of Sri Lanka adopted a value-added tax (VAT) system in April 1995, which is likely to actually replace most of these taxes.

Legal

Legal System

Roman Dutch law is the foundation of Sri Lanka's legal system and still is applied when other laws or judicial decisions do not apply. Both English law and Roman Dutch law apply in contracts and delict torts. Sri Lanka continues to review and revise its laws and statutes to promote a competitive business environment.

Intellectual Property Rights

Patents Application is made with the Registry of Patents and Trademarks. Patents are limited to 15 years and industrial designs to five years. However, patents must be renewed annually to ensure that they are being exploited.

Trademarks Sri Lanka recognizes both trademarks and service marks. The exclusive right to a mark is acquired by registration. Protection also is available to well known marks not registered in Sri Lanka. Trademarks must be registered with the Registry of Patents and Trademarks and are valid for 10 years. They may be renewed.

Copyrights Copyrights are not registered. A work is protected automatically by operation of law. Original literary, artistic, and scientific works are protected. At present, copyright protection is not extended to computer programs, databases, and semiconductor layout designs.

Trade secrets Trade secrets are not protected under the current law.

Business Registration

A company may be incorporated in Sri Lanka by filing its memorandum and articles of association with the Registrar of Companies in Colombo.

Labor

Most permanent full-time workers are covered by laws pertaining to minimum hours of work, minimum wage, leave, the right of association, and safety and health standards.

Legal Matters

LEGAL BRIEFS
- **Statutory law** Sri Lankan commercial law is almost entirely statutory.
- **Courts** The court system is free from government interference. Procedures exist for enforcing foreign judgments.
- **Property interests** Secured interests in property are recognized and enforced. A reliable registration system exists for recording property.
- **Employment of foreigners** In general, Sri Lankan law prohibits the employment of foreigners unless they offer specialized skills not available locally.
- **Provident funds** All employers are required to make provident fund contributions of 10-12 percent for their staff. A further three percent contribution to the employees' trust fund is also payable.
- **Employment laws** There are regulations on minimum recruitment age, working hours, holidays, leave, maternity benefits, social security, and workers' compensation.
- **International agreements** Sri Lanka is a member of Berne Copyright Convention and World Intellectual Property Organization.

LEGAL CONTACTS

John Wilson & Assistants
365 Dam Street
Colombo 12
Tel: (1) 324579 Fax: (1) 699165

Julius & Creasy
No. 22 3/1 22 3/2 Sir Baron Jayatilaka Mawatha
Hongkong & Shanghai Bank Building
POB 154
Colombo
Tel: (1) 422601/5 Fax: (1) 445553

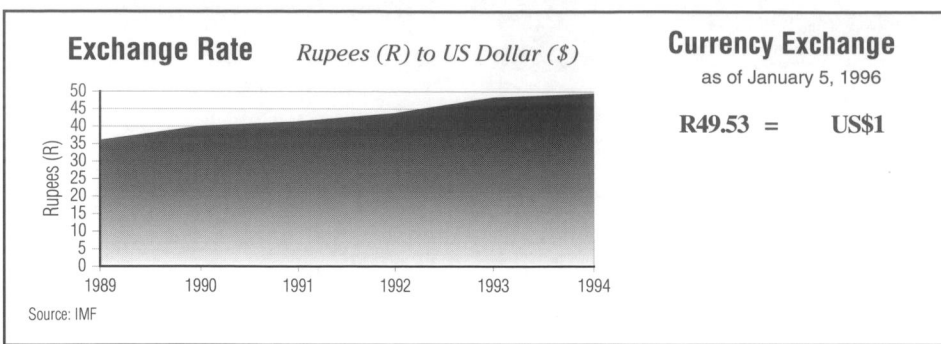

Exchange Rate *Rupees (R) to US Dollar ($)*

Rupees (R): 50, 45, 40, 35, 30, 25, 20, 15, 10, 5, 0

1989   1990   1991   1992   1993   1994

Source: IMF

Currency Exchange
as of January 5, 1996

R49.53 = US$1

Currency

The currency of Sri Lanka is the Sri Lankan rupee (R), which is divided into 100 cents.

Foreign Exchange

The Central Bank of Sri Lanka announces the daily spot buying and selling rates of the rupee against the US dollar for transactions with the commercial banks. The commercial banks provide a forward exchange market in which rates for current transactions are freely determined.

Capital Transfers

All remittances of foreign exchange in Sri Lanka must normally be made through commercial banks, authorized to carry out operations in foreign currencies in accordance with the exchange control procedures prescribed by the Controller of Exchange. Proceeds from the sale or liquidation of investments in projects along with the capital appreciation, may be remitted in full. Expatriates leaving Sri Lanka for residence in the country of their permanent domicile are permitted to transfer in full assets representing their retirement funds and savings.

Investment Incentives

The Board of Investments offers incentives which include: preferential tax at 15 percent per annum for a period of 20 years; duty-free imports of plant, machinery, raw material, and other project-related goods as approved by the BOI; exemption from turnover tax and excise duty for imports of export companies; 15 percent income tax on expatriate incomes; free transferability of shares. The BOI also offers several incentive programs, including a tax holiday of five years for the growing and processing of agricultural products, and substantial preferential tax rates for several years thereafter.

Investment Restrictions

Foreign investment is restricted in shipping and travel agencies; freight forwarding; professional services; education; mass communication; telecommunications; supply of water; mining; deep sea fishing; timber-based industries; tea, rubber, and coconut industries.

TAXATION

Taxation requires sophisticated knowledge of complex rules and regulations specific to each country. The information presented here is from the Ernst & Young Corporate Tax Guide and Directory, available from the Ernst & Young accounting office in your country, or from:

Ernst & Young
Mail Address:
P.O. Box 101
Colombo 10, Sri Lanka
Street Address:
201 De Saram Place
Colombo 10, Sri Lanka
Tel: (1) 697363 through 697367
Cable: Ernstaudit, Colombo
Telex: 21620 Ans bk TYCO CE
Fax: (1) 697369

At a Glance

Corporate Income Tax Rate (%) (a)	35
Capital Gains Tax Rate (%) (b)	
Branch Tax Rate (%) (a)	35
Withholding Tax (for Payments Out of Sri Lanka)	
Dividends (%) (c)(d)	15
Interest (%)	15
Royalties from Patents, Know-how, etc. (%)	15
Branch Remittance Tax 1/9 of taxable profit or 1/3 of taxable remittances, whichever is lower	
Net Operating Losses (Years)	
Carryback (e)	0
Carryforward	Unlimited

(a) An income tax surcharge of 15% is also levied through the 1994-95 fiscal year.
(b) Rates vary depending on holding period.
(c) An advance company tax is also payable on the distribution of a dividend.
(d) This tax, also known as the Dividend Tax at Source, is imposed on the gross dividend and, in general, is also imposed on dividends paid to residents.
(e) Three years on the cessation of a business

Money Matters

BITS AND PIECES

- **Corporate income tax** Resident companies are taxed on worldwide income. Nonresident companies are taxed on income from Sri Lanka only.
- **Foreign tax relief** Foreign tax relief is available under various agreements. Generally, tax payable is allowed as a credit against any foreign tax.
- **Relief for losses** Losses are considered deductible if, had there been a profit instead of a loss, such profit would have been assessable. Such losses can be carried forward indefinitely. Losses can be carried back for three years on cessation of a business.
- **Gold** Any imports or exports of gold require licenses from the Controller of Imports and Exports.
- **Foreign participation** Foreign participation can be up to 100 percent of equity in Sri Lankan companies in most sectors.
- **Preferential treatment** The export sector, tourism, and infrastructure projects such as telecommunications, transport, housing, and hospital projects enjoy preferential investment treatment.
- **Expropriation** The Sri Lankan government has not expropriated any foreign investments since 1978.
- **Accounting** Accounting standards are not mandated by law, other than for publicly quoted companies. Auditors' opinions are not mandatory even for statements of publicly quoted companies.
- **Stock exchange** The Colombo Stock Exchange, while small by larger emerging market standards, is one of the most efficient in the region. It has a fully computerized clearing and settlement system.
- **Capital outflow** Sri Lanka does not encourage domestic investment in other countries.
- **Turnover tax** Sri Lanka imposes a turnover tax on a number of selected luxury items. The basic rate of 20 percent applies to packaged soups; record-players; television sets; fax machines; and cameras. An even higher rate of 40 percent applies to electrical household appliances (except refrigerators); non-industrial air conditioners; and cordless telephones. In addition, there is a progressive tax on net wealth.
- **Liberalization of controls** The government is expected to liberalize exchange controls in an effort to stimulate foreign investment and encourage greater foreign participation in the economy overall.
- **Guarantees** The Sri Lankan government provides safeguards for foreign investment by way of investment protection agreements, which guarantee protection against nationalization and expropriation; free transfer of profits, capital and other fees; and the timely settlement of investment disputes.

BANKS

ABN-AMRO Bank
41 Jandhipathi Mawatha
Colombo 1
Tel: (1) 423637/9, 423361 Fax: (1) 447843

American Express Bank Ltd.
45 Janadhipathi Mawatha
Colombo 1
Tel: (1) 431288/9, 323366 Fax: (1) 448295

ANZ Grindlays Bank Ltd.
37 York Street
Colombo 1
Tel: (1) 446150/7, 432286/8 Fax: (1) 446158

Bank of Oman Ltd.
67 Sir Chittampala A. Gardiner Mawatha
Colombo 2
Tel: (1) 447216 Fax: (1) 447220

Bank of Ceylon
4 Bank of Ceylon Mawatha
Colombo 1
Tel: (1) 446790, 544333 Fax: (1) 445798

Banque Indosuez
Janadhipathi Mawatha
Colombo 1
Tel: (1) 436181/5, 445509/10

Commercial Bank
21 Bristol Street
Colombo 1
Tel: (1) 447516, 430420 Fax: (1) 449889

Marketing

Distribution

International trade is centered in the capital city and chief port, Colombo, which handles more than 90 percent of all imports and exports. While hundreds of trading firms are involved in domestic distribution, only 20 to 30 of the largest also engage in international trade. There are many medium to small importers, but only a few private sector importers have branches or distribution points elsewhere in the country. Most importers simply wholesale directly to regional buyers, either wholesale distributors or retail outlets. Inland transport is dominated by independent trucking companies.

Agents, Distributors, and Partners

A foreign company may transact business in Sri Lanka through either a branch or a representative office, which it must register as a foreign company under Sri Lanka's companies act. Because the largest trading houses represent many foreign principals, the medium or small firms often make better representatives. However, if products require stocking, servicing, or spare parts, larger firms are the better choice due to their better developed distribution channels. Most foreign firms active in Sri Lanka select their local agents on the basis of financial stability. Most agent sales are conducted on a commission basis.

Selling Techniques

Price is the most important sales factor but companies with wide distribution enjoy a competitive edge and can get away with charging slightly more because they can provide better service. Franchising is allowable but not yet common, and is so far dominated by US fast-food operations. Joint ventures have become popular in recent years, particularly for export projects.

Advertising

Newspapers, magazines, radio, and TV all accept advertising. There are several English -anguage newspapers as well as ones in Sinhala and Tamil. International periodicals are readily available. Until recently both radio and TV were government monopolies, with tightly controlled programming and advertising, but the private sector now operates several radio and TV stations, all of which accept advertising.

Marketing in Sri Lanka

MARKETING TIPS

- **Trade news** The government has deregulated most sectors, eliminated most price and quota controls, liberalized the issuance of import licenses, terminated export taxes, privatized many state-run firms, and it actively promotes inward investment in almost all fields. Nonetheless, import and pricing decisions are frequently vetoed and argued by the Cabinet.
- **Government sales** Selling to the government is crucially dependent on identifying and recruiting a reliable and well-connected agent.
- **TV and radio advertising** Advertising through the mass media is becoming increasingly important as new TV channels and radio stations are opened.
- **Service and customer support** New suppliers to the Sri Lanka market should devote adequate effort to sales support, product service, and after-sales maintenance in order to establish and maintain a reputation for reliability.

AD AGENCY

Grant McCann-Erickson
660 Galle Rd.
Colombo 3
Tel: (1) 580971
Fax: (1) 580978

MARKET RESEARCH FIRMS

Agro Skills Ltd.
77/1 Isipathana Mawatha
Colombo 5
Tel: (1) 584124 Fax: (1) 584124
Resource Organization and Management International Ltd.
1 6th Lane, Galle Road
Colombo 3
Tel: (1) 575233 Fax: (1) 575233

Business Culture

Greetings and Courtesies

The traditional greeting among Sri Lankans is the *namaste*, formed by placing the palms together under the chin and bowing the head slightly. When meeting foreigners, the accepted greeting is the handshake. Strong handshakes with firm grips are common. Sri Lankan women will shake hands with foreign men, but do not embrace or kiss a woman. Titles are very important to Sri Lankan businesspeople. If a person has a title be sure to use it. Do not use first names until you know someone fairly well.

Business Ethic and Framework

People's religion and ethnic group will shape their behavior. Fate is an important belief to many Sri Lankans. They will do the best they can, but they firmly believe that the outcome is in the hands of God. General business attire is informal; suits are not required. A long-sleeved shirt and tie will be adequate. Women should wear a two- or three-piece outfit suitable for business. Never wear a sleeveless dress or blouse.

Meetings and Decision Making

Make appointments in advance, and reconfirm meetings upon arriving. Sri Lankans value punctuality, but may keep visitors waiting for several minutes. Visitors are usually offered tea, which is the national drink. It is polite to compliment the quality of the tea. Decisions are made slowly. Sri Lankans like to know people before doing business with them. Impatience will be seen as rude.

Women

Sri Lanka was the first country to have a woman prime minister. Women can expect to be taken seriously and respected. Sri Lankans often smile as a way of saying thank you, but smiling too freely in public might be perceived as flirting. Sri Lankan businesspeople, both men and women, are accustomed to and comfortable with dealing with females in management or decision-making positions.

Cultural Cautions

DO'S

- Hospitality is very important. If your host offers you a gift, accept it graciously.
- Be relaxed during conversations. Sri Lankans tend to think that foreigners are always in a hurry.

DON'TS

- The head is considered sacred. Do not touch a person's head (not even a child's).
- Do not touch another person with your feet or shoes. If this happens accidentally, apologize.
- Don't beckon to someone with the index finger.
- Women must never touch a Buddhist monk, offer to shake a monk's hand, or even hand anything directly to a monk.

CUSTOMS

- Business cards are exchanged upon meeting someone, but no elaborate response is expected.
- A caste system is still in effect in Sri Lanka. If you invite someone to sit and they are embarrassed or reluctant, do not push the issue.
- If you smoke, extinguish your cigarette before a meeting.
- The two main religious and political groups—Tamils and Sinhalese—have a lot of tension between them. The issues should not be discussed.

NEGOTIATIONS

- Sri Lankans shake their heads left to right to show agreement, and nod the head up and down to indicate no. If you are confused about what is meant, get a spoken answer.
- Be patient. Impatience will be seen as rude; high-pressure tactics will be resisted and resented.
- Many Asians view foreigners as always being in a hurry, and encourage them to sign an agreement without proper time to study the details.

GOVERNMENT AGENCIES

Board of Investment of Sri Lanka
PO Box 1768
Colombo 1
Tel: (1) 422407 Fax: (1) 447995

Ceylon Electricity Board
50 Chittampalam A. Gardiner Mawatha
Colombo 2
Tel: (1) 530423

Department of Commerce
"Rakshana Mandiraya" Vauxhall Street
Colombo 2
Tel: (1) 430068, 329733 Fax: (1) 430233

Department of Immigration & Emigration
Chaithiya Road
Colombo 1
Tel: (1) 436354 Fax: (1) 437040

Department of Inland Revenue
Sir Chittampalam A. Gardiner Mawatha
Colombo 2
Tel: (1) 421241 Fax: (1) 430816

Ministry of Finance
Galle Face Secretariat
Colombo 1
Tel: (1) 433349 Fax: (1) 433349

Ministry of Foreign Affairs
Republic Building
Colombo 1
Tel: (1) 325371 Fax: (1) 446091

Ministry of Handloom & Textile Industry
375 "Vilasitha Niwasa" Havelock Road
Colombo 6
Tel: (1) 508032/3/4 Fax: (1) 503211

Ministry of Industries, Science and Technology
48 Sri Jinaratana Road
Colombo 2
Tel: (1) 27551 Telex: 21248

Ministry of Ports and Shipping
45 Leyden Bastian Road
Colombo 1
Tel: (1) 423487

Ministry of Post & Telecommunication
C.T.O. Building, Lotus Road
Colombo 1
Tel: (1) 422591/2/3 Fax: (1) 541531

Ministry of Power and Energy
C.E.B. Bldg. Sir Chittampalam A. Gardiner Mawatha
Colombo 2
Tel: (1) 422051 Fax: (1) 422066

Ministry of Tourism and Rural Industrial Development
45 St. Michael's Road
Colombo 3
Tel: (1) 540221

Secretariat for Infrastructure Development and Investment
87 Horton Place
Colombo 7
Tel: (1) 696947 Fax: (1) 696952

Securities and Exchange Commission of Sri Lanka
73 W A D Ramanayake Mawatha
Colombo 2
Tel: (1) 438250

STOCK EXCHANGE

Colombo Stock Exchange
2nd Floor Mackinnons Building, York Street
Colombo 1
Tel: (1) 446581 Fax: (1) 445279

TRADE AND BUSINESS ORGANIZATIONS

Agricultural Development Authority
38, D.R. Wijewardene Mawatha
Colombo 10
Tel: (1) 34355

American Chamber of Commerce of Sri Lanka
Colombo Hilton Hotel, Lotus Road
Colombo 1
Tel: (1) 544644 Fax:(1) 544657

Building Materials Corporation
541, Sri Sangaraja Mawatha
Colombo 2
Tel: (1) 26701

Ceylon Chamber of Commerce
50 Nawam Mawatha
Colombo 2
Tel: (1) 421745/6/7 Fax: (1) 449352

Ceylon Shipping Corporation
6, Sir Baron Jayatilleke Mawatha
PO Box 1718
Colombo 1
Tel: (1) 328772 Fax: (1) 447547

Cooperative Wholesale Establishment
440, Union Place
Colombo 2
Tel: (1) 596081

Insurance Corporation of Sri Lanka
Rakshana Mandiraya
21, Vauxhall Street
PO Box 1337
Colombo 2
Tel: (1) 435301 Fax: (1) 547742

National Chamber of Commerce
2nd Floor, Y.M.B.A. Building PO Box 1375
Colombo 1
Tel: (1) 325271 Fax: (1) 445409

Sri Lanka Export Development Board
115 Sir Chittampalam A. Gardiner Mawatha
Colombo 2
Tel: (1) 438512, 438515 Fax: (1) 438404

Sri Lanka State Trading Corporation
68/70, York Street
Colombo 1
Tel: (1) 26981

Women's Chamber of Commerce & Industry
32 1/1 Castle Street
Colombo 8
Tel: (1) 699475 Fax: (1) 695913

MARKET RESEARCH FIRMS

Lanka Asia Management Systems Co. (Pvt) Ltd.
Hotel Lanka Oberoi, Suite 340
77 Steuart Place
Colombo 3
Tel: (1) 437437, 421171 Fax: (1) 437437 x341

Lanka Market Research Bureau Ltd.
3rd Floor, 228 Galle Road
Colombo 4
Tel: (1) 500525 Fax: (1) 500437

Teams (Pvt) Ltd.
PO Box 262
Colombo
Tel: (1) 686429 Fax: (1) 686947

BANKS

Central Bank of Sri Lanka
Janadhipathi Mawatha
Colombo 1
Tel: (1) 421191 Fax: (1) 440353

Citibank N.A.
67 Dharmapala Mawatha
Colombo 7
Tel: (1) 449061 Fax: (1) 445487

Deutsche Bank
86 Galle Road
Colombo 3
Tel: (1) 447062/6, 438057 Fax: (1) 447062

Emirates Bank International Ltd.
64 Lotus Road
Colombo 1
Tel: (1) 323467, 447436

Habib Bank Ltd.
140-142 2nd Cross Street
Colombo 11
Tel: (1) 328713, 446041 Fax: (1) 430890

Habib Bank AG Zurich
118 Keyzer Street
Colombo 11
Tel: (1) 446041/8

Hatton National Bank
10 R.A. de Mel Mawatha
Colombo 3
Tel: (1) 421885, 430908 Fax: (1) 446312

Hongkong & Shanghai Banking Corporation Ltd.
24 Sir Baron Jayatilleke Mawatha
Colombo 1
Tel: (1) 325435/8, 446591/9 Fax: (1) 438585

Indian Bank
22 Baili Street
Colombo 1
Tel: (1) 323402/3, 447163

Indian Overseas Bank
45 Janadhipathi Mawatha
Colombo 1
Tel: (1) 324422/4

Muslim Commercial Bank Ltd.
8 Leyden Bastian Road
Colombo 1
Tel: (1) 448765/6, 440567/8 Fax: (1) 448764

Overseas Trust Bank Ltd.
39 Bristol Street
Colombo 1
Tel: (1) 447655/8, 447133

Peoples Bank
75 Sir Chittampalam A. Gardiner Mawatha
Colombo 2
Tel: (1) 324188, 326429 Fax: (1) 447671

Public Bank Berhad
324 Galle Road
Colombo 3
Tel: (1) 576288 Fax: (1) 573958

Sampath Bank
55 D.R. Wijewardana Mawatha
Colombo 10
Tel: (1) 448291, 434431 Fax: (1) 434217

Seylan Bank Ltd.
33 Sir Baron Jayatilleke Mawatha
Colombo 1
Tel: (1) 437901/7, 446517 Fax: (1) 433072

Standard Chartered Bank
17 Janadhipathi Mawatha
Colombo 1
Tel: (1) 326671/4, 433302 Fax: (1) 432522

State Bank of India
16 Sir Baron Jayatilleke Mawatha
Colombo 1
Tel: (1) 326133/5, 439404/6

LEGAL CONTACT

Murugesu & Neelakandan
75 3/1 Hemas Building (3rd Floor)
York Street
Colombo 1
Tel: (1) 445254
Fax: (1) 445255

INTERNET ADDRESSES

Usenet group(s):
soc.culture.sri-lanka

Sri Lanka Home Page
http://vicnet.net.au/~slanka/slhome.html

Welcome to Sri Lanka!
http://arachnic.es.cf.ac.uk/Sri_Lanka/

Sweden

Kingdom of Sweden

Economy

Overview

A high level of cooperation between government and private industry, a highly skilled work force, and a concentration on high quality engineering have helped Sweden become one of the world's most advanced industrialized nations. As a country rich in timber, iron ore, and hydropower it has focused on these resources as the foundation for its industrialized export-oriented economy. After achieving this favorable position, however, the Swedish economy has been troubled in recent years by a deep recession, from which it is only now emerging.

Trade

Sweden has traditionally relied on international markets to absorb its productive output, and foreign trade remains vital to its economy. Germany is the largest source of both its imports and exports, followed by the UK, the US, and Denmark. The recent significant increases in the value of Swedish imports result more from the devaluation of the Swedish krona than from a major increase in domestic demand for imported products. The decline in currency value has made Swedish products more competitive on international markets and has created an export-led recovery which should continue in the short term.

Sectors

Agriculture Sweden has the largest timber reserves in Western Europe and, although it is not a major employer, forestry remains important to the economy, accounting for 20 percent of the total value of exports. Major products include paper, wood pulp, timber, and furniture. Agriculture accounts for just over three percent of GDP and most production in this sector is for the domestic market. Although it is self-sufficient in many agricultural products, substantial import opportunities exist for consumer oriented non-domestic food products.

Industry Industry is the underlying strength of the Swedish economy. Privately owned firms account for 90 percent of industrial output, and mechanical engineering makes up a large proportion of industrial output. Swedish industrialists have taken full advantage of abundant, high quality raw materials to become world renowned producers of steel, aluminum, copper, lead, automobiles, ships, and aircraft. Sweden also consistently produces high-quality, high-tech goods in its highly automated factories.

Services Sweden is primarily a service nation, but growth in this sector has been curtailed by a recent, deep recession. Tourism-related services are expected to take advantage of the relative price competitiveness caused by the devaluation of the krona, and the general recovery of worldwide economies.

Trends

Export-led growth arising from increased price competitiveness in international markets continues to pull Sweden out of recession. The government is focusing on strict monetary controls to curb the growing budget deficit, and the urgent need to address record unemployment levels remains a priority. In spite of the relatively higher cost of imports due to currency devaluation, there are substantial opportunities to sell to the domestic market, particularly in the area of high tech products such as computers, medical equipment, electronic components, and pollution control equipment. Economic growth is expected to continue at a steady pace, and long-term prospects are very positive.

At a Glance

THE COUNTRY

Location A Nordic state in Northern Europe, bordering the Baltic Sea, between Norway and Finland.
Terrain Mostly flat or gently rolling lowlands, mountains in the west.
Climate Temperate in the south with cold, cloudy winters and cool, partly cloudy summers. Subarctic in the north.

THE PEOPLE

Population 8,800,000
Ethnic composition White, Lapp (Sami), foreign born, or first-generation immigrants predominantly make up the population. There are also Finns, Yugoslavs, Danes, Norwegians, Greeks, and Turks.
Religious composition
Evangelical Lutheran 94%
Roman Catholic 1.5%
Pentecostal 1%
Other.. 3.5%
Languages spoken Swedish is the official language, although there are also small Lapp- and Finnish-speaking minorities. Immigrants speak native languages.
Education and literacy
Almost 99 percent of the population over 15 can read and write.
Labor force
Total..4,500,000
By occupation: community, social, and personal services 38.3%, mining and manufacturing 21.2%, commerce, hotels, and restaurants 14.1%, banking, insurance 9%, communications 7.2%, construction 7%, and agriculture, fishing, and forestry 3.2%.

COUNTRY FACTS

Political and legal Sweden is a democracy ruled by a parliament chosen by general election and a prime minister who appoints a cabinet. The highest legal body is the Supreme Court, and it can review the constitutionality of legislation.
Telephone Sweden has excellent domestic and international facilities available; there are over 8.2 million telephones, and satellites make mobile phone systems possible. The country code is [46]. Selected city codes: Stockholm (8), Goteborg (31), Malmo (40).
Transportation Railroads are a major source of transportation; there are over 12,000 kilometers of rail stretched across the country. Only about one-third of the 205,000 kilometers of highway is paved. Small steamers and barges can navigate through over 2,000 kilometers of inland waterways. There are a number of major airports with international service.
Environment Only seven percent of the land is arable, and more than 1,100 square miles have been irrigated. Ice floes in the surrounding waters can interfere with navigation, especially in the Gulf of Bothnia. Soil and lakes are being damaged by acid rain, and the North and Baltic Seas are being polluted.
Media There are a number of broadcast stations available: five AM, 360 FM, and 800 (mostly repeaters) television stations.
Health Life expectancy of males is 78 years; of females, 81 years. The birth rate is 13.5 births per 1,000 citizens (1994).

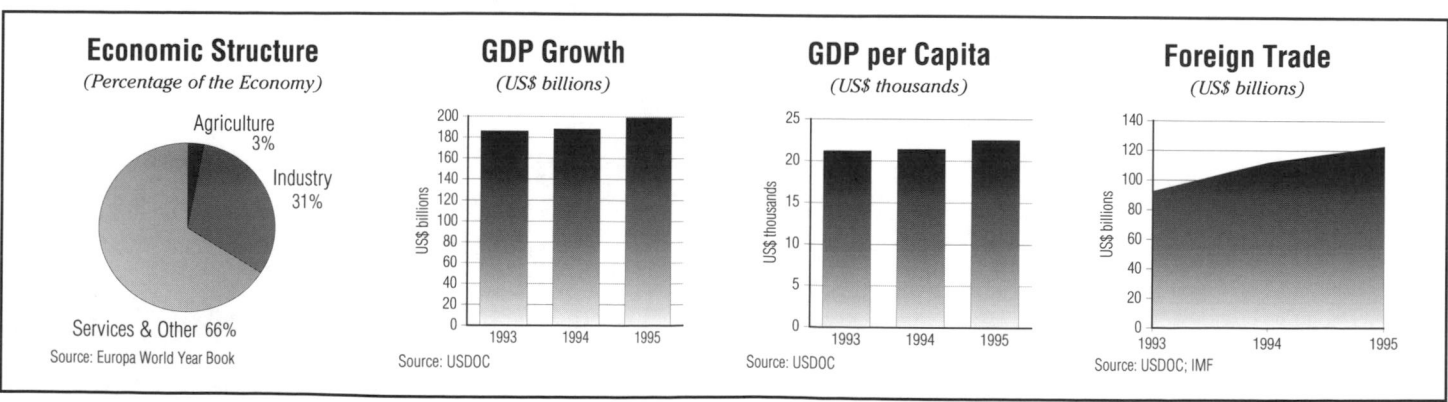

Economic Structure
(Percentage of the Economy)

Agriculture 3%
Industry 31%
Services & Other 66%

Source: Europa World Year Book

GDP Growth
(US$ billions)

1993 1994 1995

Source: USDOC

GDP per Capita
(US$ thousands)

1993 1994 1995

Source: USDOC

Foreign Trade
(US$ billions)

1993 1994 1995

Source: USDOC; IMF

Sweden

- ✪ National capital
- ◉ Region capital
- ● Secondary city
- —— Primary road
- ···· Railroad
- —— Administrative border
- ━━ International border

0 50 100 km
0 50 100 miles

Länners of Sweden

1 Malmöhus Län
2 Kristianstads Län
3 Blekinge Län
4 Hallands Län
5 Kronobergs Län
6 Kalmar Län
7 Gotlands Län
8 Jönkopings Län
9 Alvs Borgs Län
10 Skara Borgs Län
11 Östergötlands Län
12 Göteborgs Och Bohus Län
13 Värmlands Län
14 Örebro Län
15 Södermanlands Län
16 Stockholms Län
17 Uppsala Län
18 Västmanland Län
19 Kopparbergs Län
20 Gälveborgs Län
21 Jämtlands Län
22 Västernorrlands Län
23 Västerbottens Läns
24 Norrbottens Län

Russia

Norwegian Sea

Arctic Circle

Kirkenes

Kiruna
Malmberget
Jokkmokk
Boden
Luleå
Piteå
Storuman
Skellefteå
Vilhelmina
Lycksele
Umeå
Örnsköldsvik
Östersund
Ånge
Härnösand
Sundsvall
Hudiksvall
Mora
Falun
Gävle
Borlänge
Oslo
Uppsala
Västerås
Karlstad
Stockholm
Örebro
Södertälje
Mellerud
Nyköping
Mariestad
Motala
Norrköping
Vänersborg
Linköping
Uddevalla
Falköping
Göteborg
Borås
Jönköping
Västervik
Visby
Nässjö
Oskarshamn
Varberg
Varnamo
Kalmar
Halmstad
Växjö
Halsingborg
Karlskrona
Lund
Kristianstad
Copenhagen
Malmö
Ystad

Finland

Helsinki
Tallinn
Estonia
Riga
Latvia
Lithuania

Gulf of Bothnia
Gulf of Finland
Aland Islands
Baltic Sea
Gotland

Denmark
North Sea
Skagerrak
Kattegat

Foreign Trade

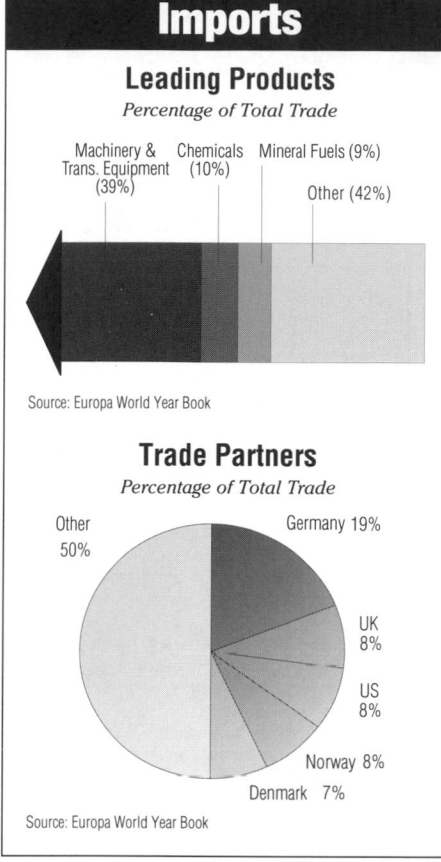

Imports

Leading Products
Percentage of Total Trade

Machinery & Trans. Equipment (39%)
Chemicals (10%)
Mineral Fuels (9%)
Other (42%)

Source: Europa World Year Book

Trade Partners
Percentage of Total Trade

Other 50%
Germany 19%
UK 8%
US 8%
Norway 8%
Denmark 7%

Source: Europa World Year Book

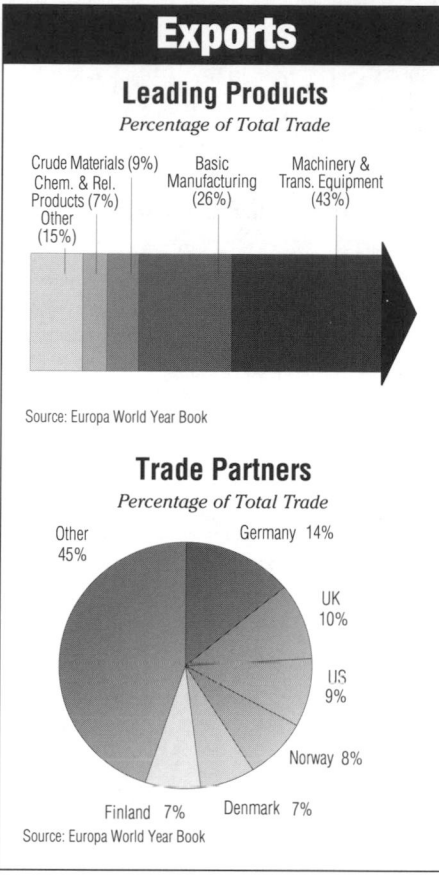

Exports

Leading Products
Percentage of Total Trade

Crude Materials (9%)
Chem. & Rel. Products (7%)
Other (15%)
Basic Manufacturing (26%)
Machinery & Trans. Equipment (43%)

Source: Europa World Year Book

Trade Partners
Percentage of Total Trade

Other 45%
Germany 14%
UK 10%
US 9%
Norway 8%
Denmark 7%
Finland 7%

Source: Europa World Year Book

Opportunities

FOR IMPORTING TO SWEDEN

- agricultural products
- machinery and transportation equipment
- engineering and chemical products
- textiles, finished goods
- construction materials
- computers, high-tech products, telecommunications
- aircraft and parts
- airport and ground support equipment
- electronic components
- defense industry equipment
- medical equipment
- recreational equipment, travel and tourism services
- pollution control equipment
- furs
- foodstuffs, snack products, tobacco, and wine

FOR EXPORTING FROM SWEDEN

- machinery and equipment
- precision instruments
- metal products
- foodstuffs
- textiles
- clothing

GROWTH SECTORS

- restructuring and modernization of industry
- private industry
- mechanical engineering
- chemicals and energy (mainly oil)

GOVERNMENT PROCUREMENT

- self-service systems for convenience goods
- roads and railways
- ports
- railway links
- air navigation equipment
- conventional power stations
- repairs of nuclear power plants
- rebuilding ports
- purification and waste-treatment equipment
- hospitals
- schools

Trade News

RULES AND REGULATIONS

- **EU** Customs procedures, including the classification and valuation of imported goods, are governed by EU rules.
- **Import restrictions** There are some safety and other regulations that effectively bar the import of certain merchandise, such as products harmful to public order, health, or safety.
- **Import licenses** Licenses are required for only a few commodities.
- **Agricultural products** Certain agricultural products are subject to import fees which are imposed as a result of a Swedish government program designed to support agriculture.
- **Tariff rates** Sweden has one of the lowest tariff levels in the world, averaging less than 5 percent ad valorem on finished goods and about 3 percent on semimanufactures. Most raw materials are imported duty free. The tariff structure is a single-column tariff using the Harmonized System of Classification. Import duties apply to all countries receiving most-favored-nation (MFN) treatment. Most raw materials, basic chemicals, pharmaceuticals, newsprint, and pig iron are duty free. Certain items, mainly machinery not produced in Sweden, are admitted duty free.
- **Free trade zones** Sweden has foreign trade zones with bonded warehouses in the ports of Stockholm, Gothenburg, and Malmo. Goods may be stored for an unlimited time in these zones without customs clearance, but they may not be consumed or sold on a retail basis. Permission may be granted to use these goods as materials for industrial operations within a free trade zone. The same tax and labor laws apply to foreign trade zones as to other workplaces in Sweden.
- **Temporary entry** Commercial samples, advertising materials, film, and medical and professional equipment may be brought into the country for a short period duty-free.
- **Surcharges** Customs surcharges are not levied. However, most all imports are subject to a VAT and some products are subject to special taxes.
- **Exchange control** There are no foreign exchange restrictions in Sweden as they were removed in 1991. Commercial transactions are not restricted either.
- **Sanitation certificates** Certificates are necessary for goods that can bring in contagious animal or vegetable diseases.
- **Excise tax** Motor vehicles, alcoholic beverages, sugar, malt, carbonated beverages, tobacco, and fuels are many of the items the Swedish government applies an excise tax upon.
- **Additional taxes** Luxury items, gifts, real estate transfers, and capital distributions are subject to additional taxes.

SHIPPING FIRMS

Eff John International
POB 29091
100 52 Stockholm
Tel: (8) 666-34-00

Ferm International Ship Management AB
POB 39
440 60 Skärhamn
Tel: (304) 67-10-70
Fax: (304) 67-11-10
Telex: 2428

Nordström & Thulin AB
Skeppsbron 34-36
POB 1215
111 82 Stockholm
Tel: (8) 613-19-00
Fax: (8) 21-22-28
Telex: 17907

Stena AB
405 19 Göteborg
Tel: (31) 85-80-00
Fax: (31) 12-06-51
Telex: 2559

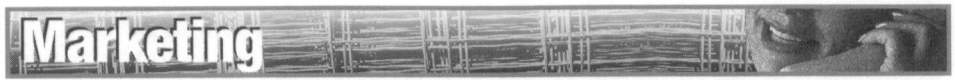

Overview

Sweden is a diverse, affluent, and ready market for a wide variety of foreign goods and services. The government leaves business to private enterprise, and all forms and types of businesses operate in the country. Stockholm is the capital and business center, with a population of more than 1.5 million. The central offices of most businesses with dealings in the Nordic and Baltic regions are headquartered here.

Distribution

Sweden's major distribution centers are Stockholm, Goteborg, and Malmo. Its distribution structure has undergone substantial changes, and is currently characterized as highly efficient. The Federation of Swedish Commerce and Trade is the principal organization for private wholesale and import trade. Its membership includes more than 50 trade associations, representing 1,200 member firms for all types of goods. Approximately two-thirds of all Swedish imports are purchased through wholesalers/importers; the remaining one-third are direct purchases by Swedish firms and retail organizations.

Agents, Distributors, and Partners

Swedish commercial agents are organized under the Federation of Commercial Agents of Sweden. The Federation, in collaboration with organizations in the other Nordic countries, has developed a new, comprehensive form for agency agreements. Normally, an exclusive agent or distributor is appointed to cover the entire country. Often the agent or distributor represents several foreign firms. Suppliers seeking an agent in Sweden should plan to visit the country in order to make a firsthand appraisal of the relative merits of prospective agents. Close contact between the principal and the agent or distributor is very important and should be developed early.

Selling Techniques

Franchising is one of the fastest growing methods of doing business in Sweden; it is especially popular in the fast-food and auto service industries. Good franchise opportunities exist in the home improvement sector, apparel retailing, and business services. Companies considering franchising in Sweden are strongly encouraged to conduct a careful legal study of any franchising agreement. Sweden has comprehensive franchise laws, and they are specific to the country; foreign franchisors will probably have to adjust their forms and formats accordingly. Several franchising consultants are available in Sweden to help companies get started. To meet the needs of the Swedish market, franchisers should be prepared to modify their products or adapt their marketing policy in order to compete fully in this market.

Exporters of consumer goods may find it advantageous to sell directly to department stores, consumer cooperatives, chains, and other retail outlets. Telephone marketing is still pretty rare, but mail-order sales and TV-shop sales are growing. Direct marketing is also used in the retailing of books and magazines.

Joint ventures have recently gained acceptance, and several foreign sellers operate joint ventures with Swedish partners. Joint ventures are not legal entities, and a legal vehicle must be formed to pursue the project.

Trade fairs and exhibitions should not be overlooked. Each year, there are three major trade fair venues in Sweden, and together they have approximately two million visitors.

Government procurement at the national level is established by legislative acts, whereas local governments and state-owned companies are completely free to set their own purchasing policies, which are generally based on purely business considerations, and make no distinction between domestic and foreign suppliers.

Advertising

All types of media are available in Sweden, and advertising plays a major role in Sweden's commercial life. Daily newspapers and other publications are the most important media for advertising, consuming over half of the total advertising expenditures. The Swedish are avid readers. There are several major metropolitan papers in Stockholm, Goteburg, and Malmo, and there are several daily papers with nationwide distribution. Direct mail is another important form of advertising, accounting for about 30 percent of all advertising spending. Other forms of advertising, useful for certain types of products, are point-of-sale, cinema, and posters and billboards.

Service and Customer Support

To compete in the Swedish markets suppliers should provide a high-quality product, dealer support, product service, and after-sale support. Local agents and distributors expect the principal's full support concerning promotional efforts, technical information, and advertising materials.

Marketing in Sweden

MARKETING TIPS

- **European Union** Sweden is pursuing membership in the European Union, having agreed on its terms for accession in 1994.
- **Local government purchases** Local government procurement has become increasingly significant and in some cases offers American companies excellent trading opportunities. However, procurements are open to many countries and local governments are free to adopt their own procurement procedures. Generally, no distinction is made between domestic and foreign suppliers or contractors. The normal procedures for inviting bids is through circular letters addressed to firms known to be reputable and reliable.
- **Health care purchases** Sweden purchases quite a bit of health care equipment, and the purchase orders are relatively large. Their medical facilities are modern; therefore new equipment purchases are ongoing.
- **Population distribution** The northern two-thirds of Sweden is sparsely populated, but it has many large industrial plants for forest products, mining, and hydroelectric power, along with other types of companies. Major population centers are Sundsvall, Skelleftea, Lulea, and Umea.
- **Continental connection** A bridge is to be built in the near future to connect Malmo and the Danish capital, Copenhagen, and thus southern Sweden with the Continent.
- **Agency contracts** The Federation of Commercial Agents of Sweden, in collaboration with organizations in the other Nordic countries, has developed a new contract form for agency agreements which should be used.
- **Agency agreements** may include provisions for a choice of law. Swedish law applies by default to the resolution of all disputes if a specific law is not chosen. There are no statutory requirements for renewal and no limitation on the period of the agreement, and contracts may be for fixed or indefinite terms. Indefinite-term agreements terminate when either party chooses.

AD AGENCIES

The Blomquist Agencies
Wallingatan 12, Box 1512
111 85 Stockholm
Tel: (8) 200856
Fax: (8) 208608

Hall & Cederquist/Young & Rubicam
Kaptensgatan 6, Box 5477
114 57 Stockholm
Tel: (86) 657100
Fax: (86) 638266
Telex: 10342

J. Walter Thompson Sweden AB
Kungsgatan 26, 5th Fl.
111 83 Stockholm
Tel: (8) 234600
Fax: (8) 241580
Telex: 17984

Lintas Stockholm
Grev Turegatan 11 A
Sturegallerian
S11446 Stockholm
Tel: (8) 6795740
Fax: (8) 6113810

McCann-Erickson AB
Nybrogatan 11
Box 5511
114 85 Stockholm
Tel: (8) 6651975
Fax: (8) 6606563

Wunderman Cato Johnson
Riddargatan 19
Box 14104
Stockholm
Tel: (8) 6604270
Fax: (8) 6674368

 **Business Culture**

Greetings and Courtesies

The Swedish are reserved but friendly. They adhere to formality in addressing others; first names are rarely used. Correct forms of address are Herr (Mr.), Fru (Mrs.), and Froken (Miss), followed by the last name. Always use the formal address followed by the last name unless you are invited to do otherwise. The common greeting is a firm handshake, and be sure to shake hands when parting as well. When answering their phones, the Swedish use last names only, often concluding the call without a "good-bye." While their mannerisms seem abrupt to some foreigners, don't take offense, for truly, no offense is intended. In business, the Swedish are always driven to be as efficient as possible. Punctuality in both business and social occasions is a concept that is beyond courtesy; it's an essential practice. In Sweden, being early is often considered as rude as being late and one should never arrive more than five minutes before or after the scheduled time. While the exchange of business gifts is not a Swedish custom, a bottle of wine or champagne to celebrate a special occasion is a thoughtful gesture (there's a high tax on alcohol and perfume in Sweden; you may wish to bring in your quota if you anticipate occasions of celebration are in the offing). Tasteful gifts representative of your company will always be received with appreciation.

Business Ethic and Framework

Sweden's business environment is formal and highly reserved. Third party introductions are your best method of entry into the community. It is wise to have appointments scheduled before arriving in Sweden as cold calls and drop-ins are not welcome and meet with little success. Trade show attendance and the local Chambers of Commerce may facilitate appropriate introductions for you. If you do attempt self-introduction by way of a letter, be certain to provide substantial amounts of background information regarding you, your firm, and your purpose of a business alliance. Time is a valued commodity in Sweden's corporate ranks, where there is much business to transact and few executives to carry out the work. You will be expected to be efficiently prepared, succinct, and to the point during each phase toward concluding a successful relationship.

Decision Making

Swedish bureaucracy leaves little room for individualism and decision making is usually an executive team effort. The entire process takes time, given the constraints of bureaucracy in place. Be patient. Executives rarely take responsibility for a final decision without the consent of their associates. You are more likely to meet with success if you maintain this protocol: prepare your offering well in advance and provide plenty of details; state precisely what it is you want in the beginning and do not quibble or try to alter your proposition along the way; do not plan to engage in a bout of bargaining. Your Swedish associates like to get things right the first time and are not amenable to last-minute revisions.

Women

While women are found in every kind of occupation in Sweden's work force, they have yet to make a remarkable appearance in high levels of management. The nature of the Swedish economy encourages dual wage-earning families. Working mothers are given flexible work hours so they can maintain both career and family, and the *hemmaman* (house husband) is now an acceptable role for men.

Meetings

The importance a Swedish corporation places on your meeting will determine the number and level of rank of the executives they send to attend. On your part, advise your Swedish counterparts in advance of who will be attending from your firm and do not bring anyone unannounced. You will have to send your agenda and any pertinent materials in advance. Your Swedish associates do not like surprises; they prefer to work from a fixed agenda and once the agenda is set it will be difficult to change it in any way during the meeting. Advance preparedness on your part is essential.

Business Attire

Dress is generally conservative; however, there is variance from industry to industry and company to company. Subdued colors are recommended and ties are normally worn with sport jackets. Women's attire is generally conservative as well. Skirts and blouses are considered appropriate.

Cultural Cautions

DO'S

- Make eye contact often, especially during meetings. However, avoid excessive hand gestures when possible.
- Exercise good posture and your Swedish counterparts will admire you.
- The Swedish appreciate people who know the cultural differences among Sweden, Norway, Denmark, and Finland.
- If a dinner guest in a Swedish home, take your hostess flowers. Unwrap flowers before presenting them to the hostess.

DON'TS

- If you are providing the entertainment, try not to out-do your Swedish associates.
- Littering is especially frowned upon in Sweden. Don't litter.
- Avoid any discussion of religion, politics, and taxes.
- Do not criticize Swedish culture.
- Never try to barge into the middle of a line of waiting people.
- Do not put your hands in your pockets when talking; it is considered rude.

CUSTOMS

- In Sweden there are very stringent laws enforced which limit the amount of money that can be spent when entertaining guests or clients. While it is common to be invited out to dine, extravagant entertaining is not looked upon favorably in business.
- Swedes are usually calm and reserved; they rarely gesture while talking.
- The Swedish practice the European style of eating, and the person who comes to the table with both good form and manners is appreciated. Upon finishing a meal, place knife and fork together (fork tongs up) diagonal through the center of your plate.
- Toasting is frequently done in Sweden. The host is the first person to make the toast. You should never toast anyone senior in age until they toast you, and never lift your glass until the host has said "skoal."
- If you are seated on your hostess' left, you should make a toast to her during dessert. If you are on her right, you should give a small speech of appreciation.
- If you are privileged to be guest of honor it is important to understand this custom: The guest of honor is always the first to leave the party. Other guests feel very uncomfortable leaving a party before the guest of honor.

OBSERVATIONS

- First meetings are more for getting to know one another than for formal business discussions. Cards are normally exchanged during introductions, so have several available.
- Business lunches are often conducted within offices, and business is discussed during the meal, which usually lasts about two hours.
- The Swedish are known to exercise local pride—that is, they speak pridefully of their towns and regions—and it is wise to avoid praising one area or region over another.

NEGOTIATIONS

- Swedish business practitioners avoid conflict at all cost. They require that the details of your offer or proposal be worked out well before any form of negotiation takes place, and in fact, before you make your presentation.
- Swedes do not like to haggle over price. Your best strategy is to be well prepared regarding your bottom line before you reach a negotiation stage, therefore avoiding this situation.
- Negotiators should be alert to any abrupt shifts in the conversation. Issues will have to be worked out with diplomacy.
- Keep discussions formal and businesslike, and avoid aggressive behavior.

Legal System

The constitutional monarchy of Sweden follows the continental European law tradition and is strongly dependent on statutory law. It is a civil code country; parliament and the king are separate in functions from the judiciary.

Intellectual Property Rights

Patent Law Registration of a patent takes an average of four years. An application is opened for public inspection before registration. To acquire registration as a patent an invention must be considered new and must differ essentially from what is known before the application filing date for registration. Regarding infringement, Swedish law contains a doctrine of equivalence. An infringement can result in damages as well as in criminal charges.

Trademarks It takes on average one year to register a trademark (designating the goods or services) or a trade name (designating the business). A trademark or a trade name may be protected through registration or if the symbol has become established through actual use on the market. An infringement of an exclusive right to a trademark or a trade name may result in damages as well as criminal charges.

Copyright Law Authors, artists and photographers have a constitutional right to their intellectual work. The Copyright Act is harmonized with the Copyright Acts in Denmark, Norway, and Finland. The Copyright Act protects works of literal and artistic character that have achieved original character. The requisite "originality" is present when the work has risen to a "modicum of creativity" in relation to what already exists. Copyright protection is effective until the end of the seventieth year after the death of the author or artist.

Business Registration

For the most part, foreign companies and individuals are not restricted in establishing or acquiring businesses in Sweden. The few exceptions include such areas as banking and finance, insurance, and stockbrokers, which need approval from appropriate state authorities. Companies and branch offices of foreign companies are registered at the Patent and Registration Office. For branch offices a managing director must be appointed, and the director or a deputy must be resident within the European Economic Community. For companies registered in Sweden the managing director and half the board of directors must be residents within the European Economic Community. Acquisitions of Swedish companies and businesses must in most cases be reported to the Competition Authority. If an acquisition is deemed to abuse free competition, the agreement on acquisition can be declared void. Business operations in Sweden must also register with the income and VAT authorities.

Contracts and Dispute Resolution

Contracts in Sweden are generally short. Adherence to contract terms is important, and business disputes are quite rare. Freedom of contract is a basic principle in Swedish law. Several statutes, such as the Contracts Act and the Sale of Goods Act, supplement standard written contracts unless the parties agreed otherwise. The Swedish courts will normally respect the content of a contract, whether written or oral. However, the Contracts Act provides that a contract or condition in a contract can be adjusted if found unfair by the court. Most disputes are settled through negotiations. Major contract disputes are normally settled in arbitration because Swedish courts adjudicate cases very slowly. Sweden has a strong tradition as a country of arbitration in international bilateral agreements. Swedish courts and arbitrators normally make strong efforts to reach a settlement between disputing parties. A strong incentive for parties to settle disputes is that normally the losing party in a litigation or arbitration is summoned to pay all costs of the winning party and for the arbitrators.

Notaries

Documents submitted to Sweden authorities and courts must generally be in Swedish. Notaries and certified translators can prepare and authenticate such documents.

Labor

Workers and trade unions hold significant sway. Large sectors of the employment force bargain collectively, and the use of collective agreements concerning employment contracts is widespread. Generally, a worker cannot be laid off for reasons other than a shut down of the business. The main principle in such situations is also that the last worker employed is the first to go.

A lay-off can be declared void by a court of law and the employer can be sued for damages. Workers have a constitutional right to strike.

Source: Advokatbyrån Frie AB, Stockholm, Sweden

Legal Matters

LEGAL BRIEFS

- **Business entities** The favored business entity is the limited share capital company. Minimum share capital is SKr100,000. Formation costs of such a company are generally approximately SKr10,000.
- **Maximum workweek** The maximum workweek is 40 hours. Workers are entitled to a minimum of 25 days of paid vacation. Considering national holidays, a year consists of 220 work days.
- **Forced labor** Forced or compulsory labor is prohibited by law and does not exist.
- **Child labor** Compulsory nine-year education ends at age 16, and full employment is normally permitted at that age under supervision of local municipal or community authorities. In effect, however, very few 16- or 17-year old children are employed, except in part-time or summer jobs. Those under age 18 may work only during daytime and under a foreman's supervision.
- **Minimum wage** There is no minimum wage law, but there is substantial assistance available for social welfare entitlements to supplement those with low wages.
- **Workweek** The standard workweek is 40 hours or less. The amount of overtime is regulated, as are minimum rest periods.
- **International agreements** Sweden is a member of EU; GATT/WTO; CISG; New York Convention on the Recognition and Enforcement of Foreign Arbitral Awards; Convention on the Taking of Evidence Abroad in Civil or Commercial Matters; Convention on the Service Abroad of Judicial and Extrajudicial Documents in Civil or Commercial Matters; ATA Carnet Convention.
- **Legal costs** The losing party in litigation or arbitration is liable to pay the costs of the winning party.

LEGAL CONTACTS

Advokatbyrån Frie AB
POB 55547
102 04 Stockholm
Tel: (8) 660 04 60
Fax: (8) 665 78 88

Advokatfirman Tisell & Co AB
POB 7324
103 90 Stockholm
Tel: (8) 614 22 00
Fax: (8) 611 22 55

Advokatfirman Vinge KB
POB 1703
111 87 Stockholm
Tel: (8) 614 30 00
Fax: (8) 611 90 37

Arbitration Institute of the Stockholm Chamber of Commerce
POB 16050
103 21 Stockholm
Tel: (8) 613 18 00
Fax: (8) 411 24 32

Baker & McKenzie Advokatbyrå KB
POB 26163
100 41 Stockholm
Tel: (8) 676 77 00
Fax: (8) 24 89 20

Lagerlöf & Leman Advokatbyrå AB
POB 5402
114 84 Stockholm
Tel: (8) 665 66 00
Fax: (8) 667 68 83

Mannheimer Swartling Advokatbyrå
POB 1650
111 86 Stockholm
Tel: (8) 613 55 00
Fax: (8) 613 55 01

Swedish Bar Association
POB 27321
102 54 Stockholm
Tel: (8) 459 03 00
Fax: (8) 660 07 79

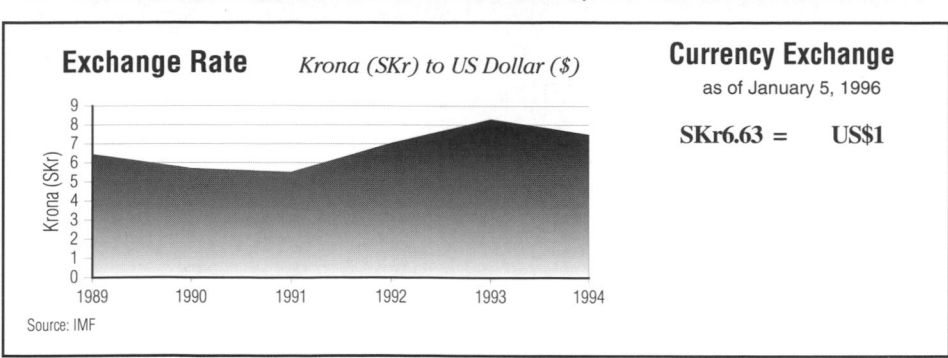

Exchange Rate *Krona (SKr) to US Dollar ($)*

Krona (SKr): 9 8 7 6 5 4 3 2 1 0

1989   1990   1991   1992   1993   1994

Source: IMF

Currency Exchange
as of January 5, 1996

SKr6.63 = US$1

Currency

The currency of Sweden is the krona (plural kronor), SKr or Kr, which is divided into 100 are.

Foreign Exchange

The Swedish authorities do not maintain margins in respect of exchange transactions, and spot and forward exchange rates are determined on the basis of demand and supply conditions in the exchange market. There are no taxes or subsidies on purchases or sales of foreign exchange. Authorized banks may at any time buy and sell any foreign currency on a spot or forward basis against another foreign currency or kronor.

Capital Transfers

All capital transactions are free from restriction. For tax control and statistical purposes, however, residents depositing funds in foreign bank accounts or transacting through such an account must report the amount to the Swedish National Tax Board and to the Central Bank.

Investment Incentives

The Swedish government provides many kinds of incentives to research and development programs through the National Board for Industrial and Technical Development to promote further growth of its country. The government also pursues a regional development policy in order to generate more employment in certain areas of the country, and there is a wide range of regional support which provides incentives for investing in these areas. Loans are available on favorable terms, and a range of more regional supports, including location and employment grants, reduced payroll taxes, low-rent industrial parks, and economic free zones, are also available. Such support has not been affected by Swedish membership in the EU. Regional development support is concentrated in the lightly populated northern two-thirds of the country.

Investment Restrictions

Sweden has made many fundamental changes to its foreign investment regime, which have significantly liberalized its investment climate and opened the country to foreign participation. There nevertheless remain a number of practical impediments to direct investment in Sweden. These include a fairly extensive, though non-discriminatory, system of concessions and authorizations needed to engage in many activities, and the dominance of a few, very large players in certain sectors.

TAXATION

Taxation requires sophisticated knowledge of complex rules and regulations specific to each country. For more detailed information we suggest you refer to the Ernst & Young Corporate Tax Guide and Directory, available from the Ernst & Young accounting office in your country, or from:

Ernst & Young
Box 3143
103 62 Stockholm, Sweden
Tel: (8) 613 90 00
Fax: (8) 791 75 11 (Tax)

• Swedish companies can generally claim a credit against tax liability for comparable taxes paid abroad. However, some tax treaties may override internal foreign tax credit rules, and exempt foreign source income from Swedish tax.

At a Glance

Corporate Income Tax Rate (%)	28
Capital Gains Tax Rate (%)(a)	28
Branch Tax Rate (%)	28
Withholding Tax (%)	
Dividends (b)	30
Interest	0
Royalties from Patents, Know-how, etc. (c)	0
Branch Remittance Tax	0
Net Operating Losses (Years)	
Carryback	0
Carryforward	Unlimited

(a) There is no special assessment for capital gains, but certain rules apply to the calculation of the amount of capital gains and losses.
(b) This rate is applicable to nonresidents.
(c) Royalties paid to nonresidents are not subject to withholding tax, but are taxed at the normal corporate rate of 28%.

Money Matters

BITS AND PIECES

• **Dividends** Dividends from Swedish companies on shares held as business assets are tax exempt. Dividend distribution on portfolio shares, and on shares held as current assets, are taxable.

• **Social security taxes** Employers must pay a social security contribution on salaries and wages of 32.86%. Employees pay 3.95% on amounts up to SKr 267,750.

• **South Africa** Prohibition of trade with South Africa was lifted as of September 1, 1993.

• **Securities transactions** Transactions in securities may be carried out freely. Prior to 1993, capital transactions had to be carried out through an authorized currency dealer, and foreign securities had to be purchased or sold through a security trading institution authorized by the Riksbank. Effective January 1, 1993, the prohibition on depositing funds in foreign accounts, or executing transactions through these accounts, was lifted.

• **Expropriation** Private property is only expropriated for public purposes, in a non-discriminatory manner, and in accordance with established principles of international law.

• **Conversion policy** A subsidiary or branch may transfer fees to a parent company outside of Sweden for management services, research expenditures, etc. In general, yields on invested funds, such as dividends and interest receipts, may be freely transferred. A foreign-owned firm may also raise foreign currency loans both from its parent corporation and credit institutions abroad.

• **Gold** There are no special regulations on trading in gold.

BANKS

Bohusbanken
Ostra Hamngt. 32
POB 11055
404 22 Goteborg
Tel: (31) 10-79-00
Fax: (31) 15-87-03
Telex: 27200

Gota Bank
Sveavagen 14
10377 Stockholm
Tel: (8) 790-40-00
Fax: (8) 790-40-61
Telex: 19420

JP Bank
Klarabergsviadukten 70
107 81 Stockholm
Tel: (8) 700-47-00
Fax: (8) 11-06-86
Telex: 14439

Nordbanken
Smalandsgt. 17
105 71 Stockholm
Tel: (8) 614-70-00
Fax: (8) 20-08-46
Telex: 12399

Ostgota Enskilda Bank
Storgt. 23, POB 328
581 03 Linkoping
Tel: (13) 11-65-00
Fax: (13) 21-36-45
Telex: 50052

Svenska Handelsbanken
Kungstradgardsgt. 2
106 70 Stockholm
Tel: (8) 701-10-00
Fax: (8) 611-50-71

Swedbank (Sparbanken Sverige AB)
Brunkebergstorg 8
105 34 Stockholm
Tel: (8) 22-23-20

The Swedish Central Bank
Brunkebergstorg 11
103 37 Stockholm
Tel: (8) 787-00-00
Fax: (8) 21-05-31

Business Travel

LH 1906	MADRID	935	113-3
LH 1022	STUTTGART HBF.	935	-
AF 1701	LYON	940	683-6
AY 822	HELSINKI	940	113-3
AA 071	SFRANCISCO-DALLAS	945	731-7

Air Travel Times

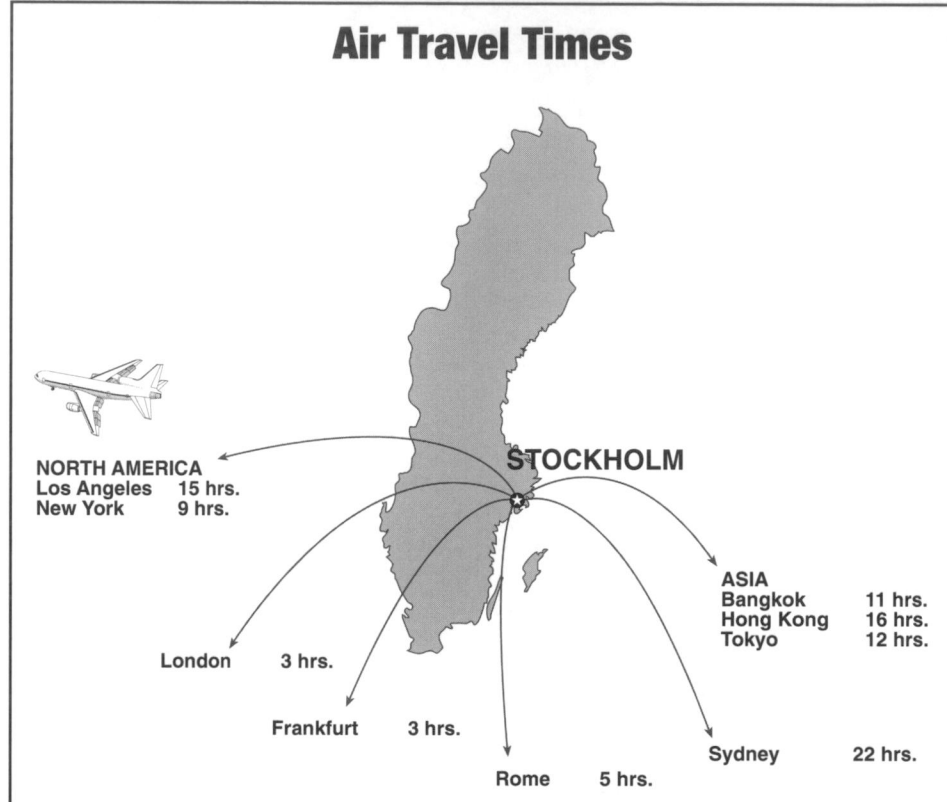

STOCKHOLM

NORTH AMERICA
Los Angeles   15 hrs.
New York   9 hrs.

London   3 hrs.

Frankfurt   3 hrs.

Rome   5 hrs.

ASIA
Bangkok   11 hrs.
Hong Kong   16 hrs.
Tokyo   12 hrs.

Sydney   22 hrs.

COMMUNICATIONS

Telephones The Swedish telephone system is very reliable. Direct dial service is usually available and excellent. The plentiful public telephone booths, where overseas calls can be made, are green rectangular boxes. The SOS button should be used only for emergencies.
Fax Fax service is widely available in Sweden.
Post office Mailboxes are yellow with blue crowns and post horns. Stamps can be purchased at post offices, news kiosks (pressbyran), and hotel desks.

BEST TRAVEL BOOKS

Sweden, Fodor's Staff. Fodor's Travel Publications. The ins and outs of travel in Sweden.
Sweden, Visitors Guide Series. Illustrated, 256 pages, Hunter Publishing Inc.
Sweden, Insight Guides Series. Houghton Mifflin. Valuable and informative, easy to read.
Fodor's Europe, Best of 31 Countries. Contains information on historical towns, great culture, scenic coastal countryside for the busy traveler.
Do's and Taboo's Around the World. The Bestselling Guide to International Behavior. Edited by Roger Axtell, compiled by the Parker Pen Company. The ultimate guide to international behavior, now completely updated and expanded. Helpful, fun to read! Helpful information for the business traveler.
Europe Berlitz Business Travel Guide. Useful facts, addresses, words and phrases and background information on people and cities. Concise economic details on each country. Berlitz Publishing Company.
Multinational Travel Companion for the Executive. Twenty third edition. Strand Publishing Company, Inc. Travel tips world-wide.'

USEFUL TELEPHONE NUMBERS

If you are calling from outside Sweden, you will need to add the country code [46] and any other international dialing requirements from within your country.
- Local Information... 90140
- International Information 242800
- Operator 001
- International Operator 018; 0018; 011
- Local Directory 07975
- Domestic Directory 90140
- Swedish Tourist Board .... (8) 7892000
- Swedish Customs .... (8) 7897300
- Swedish Chamber of Commerce .... (8) 7838500
- Ministry of Industry .... (8) 7631000
- Avis .... (8) 946030
- Budget .... (8) 946055
- Hertz .... (8) 240720
- InterRent .... (8) 946210
- Kemwell .... (8) 946140
- Central Bank .... (8) 7870000
- Medical .... (8) 449200
- Pharmacy 24 hour .... (8) 248280
- Convention Bureau .... (8) 7361500
- Stock Exchange .... (8) 6138800
- Chamber of Commerce .... (8) 6131800

Credit Card Information
Lost or stolen credit cards (call collect to the US, regardless of which country the card was issued in).
- Amex .... [1] (919) 333-3211
- Diner's Club................................. [1] (303) 799-1504
- MasterCard .... [1] (314) 275-6690
- Visa .... [1] (410) 581-7931

Travelogue

WORKWEEK
Offices Monday-Friday 9:00 am to 5:00 pm or 6:00 pm.
Banks Monday-Friday 9:30 am to 3:00 pm; Thursday to 6:00 pm.
Government Monday-Friday 9:00 am to 4:00 pm or 5:00 pm.
Retail Monday-Friday 9:00 am to 5:00 pm or 6:00 pm; Saturday 9:00 am to 2:00 pm or 4:00 p.m.

HOLIDAYS
Holidays 1996
January 1 New Year's Day
January 6 13th Day of Christmas
April 5 Good Friday
April 8 Easter Monday
May 1 Labor Day
May 16 Ascension Day
May 26 Whit Monday
June 21 Midsummer Day
November 5 All Saints' Day
December 24-26 Christmas
Offices are also closed on Midsummer Eve, Christmas Eve, and New Year's Eve. Government and many business offices generally close at 1:00 p.m. on the day before major holidays. Many companies close down completely for vacation in July.

VISA AND PASSPORT
Foreigners must have a valid passport. A tourist or business visa is not required for stays up to 90 days, beginning on entry to the Nordic area: Sweden, Norway, Denmark, Iceland, and Finland.

DEPARTURE FORMALITIES
No more than 6,000 Swedish kroner may be taken out. Kr1,000 notes should not be exported, because they are not exchangeable at foreign banks.

IMMUNIZATION
Sweden has no vaccination requirements unless you are arriving from an infected area.

TIPPING
A service charge of 15 percent for hotel rooms and 13 percent in restaurants will be added to your bill in most situations. In addition, the small change is generally left for the waiter or bartender. Tip taxi drivers 10 percent, cloakroom attendants Kr3–5, porters Kr3 per bag. Barbers are not tipped; however, in most cases hairdressers are. Nightspots are tipped between 15 and 20 percent.

CRIME
Sweden has a low crime rate. Violent crime is rare, but theft ranging from pickpocketing to burglary does occur, particularly in public areas or vacant residences. Keep an eye on personal belongings and luggage at airports as well as keeping valuables out-of-sight in automobiles to avoid break-ins.

INFRASTRUCTURE
Sweden has a well-developed business infrastructure. Hotels are well managed and comfortable. The transportation network includes efficient trains and a vast bus system, as well as a good selection of car rentals. International and domestic air transportation is widely available. Rail service throughout Sweden, Denmark, Finland and Norway can be purchased with a Nordic Tourist Ticket which allows 21 days of unlimited travel by train. Modern subways are found in many cities and run until 2 am. Long-distance buses, taxis, and car rentals are other available means of transportation. Arterial roads criss-cross Sweden; driving violations are strictly observed. There are many narrow, cobble-stone streets.

NATIONAL TOURIST OFFICE
Swedish Tourist Board
Sverigehuset, Kungstradgarden
(POB 7473)
10392 Stockholm
Tel: (8) 7892000

GOVERNMENT AGENCIES

Ministry of Agriculture
Drottninggatan 21
103 33 Stockholm
Tel: (8) 763-10-00
Fax: (8) 20-64-96

Ministry of Education
Drottninggatan 16
103 33 Stockholm
Tel: (8) 763-10-00
Fax: (8) 723-11-92

Ministry of the Environment and Natural Resources
Tegelbacken 2
103 33 Stockholm
Tel: (8) 763-10-00
Fax: (8) 24-16-29

Ministry of Finance
Rödbodgatan 6
103 33 Stockholm
Tel: (8) 763-10-00
Fax: (8) 24-39-05

Ministry of Foreign Affairs
Gustav Adolfstong 1
POB 16121
103 23 Stockholm
Tel: (8) 786-60-00
Fax: (8) 723-11-76

Ministry of Health and Social Affairs
Jakokbsgatan 26
103 33 Stockholm
Tel: (8) 763-10-00
Fax: (8) 723-11-91

Ministry of Housing, Culture and Immigration
Jakokbsgatan 26
103 33 Stockholm
Tel: (8) 763-10-00
Fax: (8) 21-68-13

Ministry of Industry and Commerce
Fredsgatan 8
103 33 Stockholm
Tel: (8) 763-10-00
Fax: (8) 411-36-16

Ministry of Labor
Drottninggatan 21
103 33 Stockholm
Tel: (8) 763-10-00
Fax: (8) 20-98-59

Ministry of Transport and Communications
Vasagatan 8-10
103 33 Stockholm
Tel: (8) 763-10-10
Fax: (8) 11-89-43

Statens Energiverk
(Swedish National Energy Commission)
Liljeholmsvägem 30
117 87 Stockholm
Tel: (8) 744-9500

Televerket
(Swedish Telecommunications Administration)
Márbackagatan 11
123 86 Farsta
Tel: (8) 713-10-00
Fax: (8) 713-33-33

WORLD TRADE CENTER

World Trade Center Stockholm
POB 70354
107 24 Stockholm
Tel: (8) 700-45-00
Fax: (8) 21-06-81

BUSINESS AND TRADE ORGANIZATIONS

Exparträdet (Trade Council)
Stargt. 19
POB 5513
114 85 Stockholm
Tel: (8) 783-85-00
Fax: (8) 662-90-93

Företagarnas Riksorganisation (Federation of Private Enterprises)
Vegagt. 14
113 93 Stockholm
Tel: (8) 610-17-00
Fax: (8) 33-10-20

Grossisförbundet Svensk Handel (Federation of Swedish Commerce and Trade)
Grevgt. 34
POB 16383
103 27 Stockholm
Tel: (8) 666-11-00
Telex: 19673
Fax: (8) 662-74-57

Kommerskolleguim
(Board of Trade)
POB 1209
111 82 Stockholm
Tel: (8) 791-05-00

Handelskammaren i Jönköpings Län
Elmiavägen
554 54 Jönköping
Tel: (36) 16-03-10
Telex: 70164
Fax: (36) 12-95-79

Handelskammaren i Karlstad
Pihlgrensgt. 7
652 26 Karlstad
Tel: (54) 11-00-22
Fax: (54) 18-60-02

Mellansvenska Handelskammaren
POB 296
801 04 Gävle
Tel: (26) 10-54-30
Fax: (26) 14-38-72

Norrbotten Handelskammaren
Storgt. 7
951 35 Luleå
Tel: (920) 122-10
Fax: (920) 94-857

Handelskammaren för Örebro och Västmanlands Län
Köpmangt. 5
702 10 Örebro
Tel: (19) 11-22-23
Telex: 73152
Fax: (19) 11-77-50

Östsvenska Handelskammaren
Stora Torget 8
621 56 Visby
Tel: (0498) 24-81-20
Fax: (0498) 27-18-17

Stockholms Handelskammare
V. Trägärdsgt. 9
POB 16050
103 22 Stockholm
Tel: (8) 613-18-00
Telex: 15638
Fax: (8) 11-24-32

Sveriges Kemiska Industrikontor (Kemikontoret) (Association of Swedish Commercial Agents)
POB 12705
112 94 Stockholm
Tel: (8) 783-80-00
Telex: 19990
Fax: (8) 663-63-23

Sydsvenska Handelskammaren
Skeppsbron 2
211 20 Malmö
Tel: (40) 73-550
Telex: 33388
Fax: (40) 11-86-09

Västernorrlands och Jämtlands Läns Handelskammare
Kyrkogt. 26
852 31 Sundsvall
Tel: (60) 17-18-80
Fax: (60) 486-40
Telex: 71263

Västsvenska Handelskammaren
POB 5253
402 25 Göteborg
Tel: (31) 83-59-00
Telex: 27430
Fax: (8) 83-59-36

TRANSPORTATION FIRMS

Stena AB
405 19 Göteborg
Tel: (31) 85-80-00
Telex: 2559
Fax: (31) 12-06-51

Transatlantic Shipping Co.
403 36 Göteborg
Tel: (3) 64-50-00
Telex: 2300

United Tankers AB
POB 8806
402 71 Göteborg
Tel: (31_ 79-30-00
Telex: 21060
Fax: (31) 79-31-12

Wallenius Lines
Swedenborgsgt. 19
POB 17086
104 62 Stockholm
Tel: (8) 772-05-00
Fax: (8) 640-68-54
Telex: 19010

TRADE FAIR

Malmö Trade Fair
POB 19015
200 73 Malmö
Tel: (40) 80-030
Telex: 32256
Fax: (40) 19-25-20

NEWSPAPERS

Norvästra Skänes Tidningar
262 83 Ängelholm
Tel: (431) 84-000
Fax: (431) 82-065

Ljusnan, Tidning för Hälsingland
POB 1059
821 12 Bollnäs
Tel: (278) 13-000
Telex: 81003

Boräs Tidning
POB 224
501 04 Boräs
Tel: (33) 17-80-00
Fax: (33) 10-14-36

Smälands-Tidningen
POB 261
575 23 Eksjö
Tel: (381) 13-200
Fax: (381) 12-215

Eskilstuna-Kuriren med Strenganäs Tidning
POB 366
631 05
Eskilstuna
Tel: (16) 15-60-00
Fax: (16) 11-63-04

Hallands Nyheter
311 81 Falkenberg
Tel: (346) 29-000
Fax: (346) 29-120

Dala-Demokraten
POB 825
791 29 Falun
Tel: (23) 47-500
Fax: (23) 25-814

Arbetarbladet
POB 287
801 04
Gävle
Tel: (26) 15-93-00
Fax: (26) 18-52-70

Göteborgs-Posten
Polhemsplatsen 5
405 02 Göteborg
Tel: (31) 62-40-00
Fax: (31) 80-27-69
Telex: 21581

Helsingborgs Dagblad
POB 822 251 08 Helsingborg
Tel: (42) 17-50-00
Fax: (42) 17-50-01
Telex: 72291

Hudiksvalls Tidning
POB 91
824 01 Hudiksvall
Tel: (650) 154-00
Fax: (650) 156-10
Telex: 71569

Barometern med Oskarshamns-Tidningen
POB 620
391 26 Kalmar
Tel: (480) 59-100
Fax: (480) 86-406
Telex: 43051

Kristianstadsbladet
POB 537
291 25 Kristianstad
Tel: (44) 18-55-00
Fax: (44) 12-62-76

Arbetet
POB 125
201 21 Malmö
Tel: (40) 20-50-00
Fax: (40) 10-15-81
Telex: 32182

Skaraborgs Läns Allehanda
POB 407
541 28 Skövde
Tel: (500) 46-75-00
Fax: (500) 48-05-82

Aftonbladet
Arenav. 63
105 18 Stockholm
Tel: (8) 725-20-00
Fax: (8) 600-01-77
Telex: 17138

Sundsvalls Tidning
Trädgärdsgt. 27-29
851 72 Sundsvall 3
Tel: (60) 19-70-00
Fax: (60) 11-97-94

Upsala Nya Tidning
POB 36
Danmarksgt. 28
751 03 Uppsala
Fax: (18) 12-95-07
Telex: 76035

PERIODICALS

Aktuellt för Kontor
POB 6903
102 39 Stockholm
Tel: (8) 669-08-20
Fax: (8) 668-85-41

Arbetsmiljö
Birger Jarlsgt. 124
POB 5970
114 89 Stockholm
Tel: (8) 16-67-40
Fax: (8) 15-67-57

Byggnadsarbetaren
POB 19013
104 32 Stockholm
Tel: (8) 728-48-00
Fax: (8) 728-49-80

Dagens Lantbruk
POB 1321 171 25 Solna
Tel: (8) 735-53-65

Dina Pengar
POB 1712
111 87 Stockholm
Tel: (8) 24-54-25
Fax: (8) 10-34-75

Ny Teknik
Klara Södrakyrkogt. 1
106 12 Stockholm
PRO-Pensionären
POB 3274
103 65 STockholm
Tel: (8) 701-67-00
Fax: (8) 20-33-58

Skog & Säg
Säbi, Box 394
551 15 Jönköping
Tel: (36) 19-86-00

Vi och vär Landsbydg
POB 1246
111 82 Stockholm
Tel: (8) 23-61-80

AD AGENCIES

Bates September AB, Jarnvagsgatan 14
POB 1043
251 10 Helsingborg
Tel: (18) 9300
Fax: (13) 9700

Liberg & Co.
Limhanmsvagen 54
Box 20051
20074 Malmo
Tel: (40) 77460
Fax: (40) 910806

Almen Direct
Eriksbersgatan 27
Box 7852
103 99 Stockholm
Tel: (8) 6142580
Fax: (8) 6781046

Andren & Werne Leo Burnett
Kungs Gatn 49
Box 476
101 29 Stockholm
Tel: (8) 613300
Fax: (8) 6130005

Burson-Marsteller AB
World Trade Ctr.
Klarabergsviadukten 70
Box 70361
10724 Stockholm
Tel: (8) 7005500
Fax: (8) 7005501

RADIO AND TELEVISION

Sveriges Riksradio AB
Oxensteirnsgt. 20
105 10 Stockholm
Tel: 8) 784-00-00
Fax: (8) 66072-57

Sveriges Television AB
105 10 Stocklhom
Tel: (8) 784-00-00
Fax: (8) 660-43-27

TV3
Storängskroken 10
115 79 Stockholm
Tel: (8) 664-44-00

STOCK EXCHANGE

Stockholm Stock Exchange Ltd
Källargränd 2
POB 1256
111 82 Stockholm
Tel: (8) 613-88-00
Fax: (8) 10-81-10
Telex: 13551

INTERNET ADDRESSES

Usenet group(s):
soc.culture.nordic

Swedish Corporations
http://www.netg.se/Oppen/Foretagsinfo/UKindex.html

Information about Sweden
http://www.westnet.se/sweden/

Swedish News
http://salk.edu/~magnus/swnews.html

Stockholm Stock Exchange
http://www.xsse.se/eng/

Swedish Railways
http://www.docs.uu.se/~rolandb/SJ/index.html

Swedish Government Agencies
http://www.sunet.se/sweden/
government_agencies.html

Switzerland

Swiss Confederation

Economy

Overview

A highly developed industrial sector, a skilled labor force and a minimum of state intervention have helped Switzerland to become one the world's most affluent countries. It has focused on its high quality manufacturing and services sectors to maintain its renowned strength and stability. Having experienced recession in the past few years the economy is now beginning to grow again and long-term prospects are positive.

Trade

Switzerland relies heavily on international trade to absorb its production, and its consistently high performing export sector has usually sustained the economy even in times of recession. Germany is its largest trading partner, followed by France, Italy, and the US. Switzerland traditionally runs a trade deficit in goods, which is more than offset by trade in the invisible services sector, but in 1993 it recorded its highest goods trade surplus of the century. Although imports are now returning to previous levels, the goods trade surplus trend is expected to continue in the short-term, and long-term prospects are extremely positive.

Sectors

Agriculture This sector has been declining in importance for some time and is now largely sustained by government subsidies. Switzerland is 65 percent self sufficient in food, though it imports a large quantity of high-value agricultural produce. Other agricultural products remain protected by high tariffs. Pressure from consumers and compliance with the GATT Uruguay Round Agreement are slowly providing greater access to these markets.

Industry A reputation for high quality and astute business expertise has helped Swiss industry to establish a broad base in many of the world's markets. Machinery, including metals and electronics, has traditionally been the strongest performer, but lack of price competitiveness has resulted recently in declining production. The chemical industry continues to grow and prospects are particularly good in the area of pharmaceuticals.

Services Switzerland is primarily a service nation and the strong economy should ensure further growth in this area. It is one of the world's top financial centers, and banking and insurance are the largest subsectors; the general increase in world trade offers excellent growth opportunities for its commercial banks. Tourism has been strong and stable for quite some time in both exports and imports, making this an important market for tourism-related services.

Trends

Switzerland's strong economy and stable currency provide an excellent platform for future growth. The government has agreed to reform its agricultural sector, making it more market oriented and accepting of foreign goods. A receptive business climate with very few barriers to imports, and an affluent population make this market attractive to foreign sellers, particularly in the area of high-tech consumer goods. Switzerland's economic and political stability should ensure continued growth throughout the long term.

At a Glance

THE COUNTRY

Location West-central Europe; bounded on the north by the Federal Republic of Germany and on the south by Italy.

Terrain Much of the country is mountainous, the Jura Mountains in the northwest, and the Alps in the south. There are fertile plains and hills running between the two mountain ranges.

Climate Temperate but varies with altitude, wind exposure, and other factors. The Alps are generally cold, with winter averages near or below freezing, but some other areas of the country are warm and moist with no frost.

THE PEOPLE

Population 6,900,000
Ethnic composition Much of the Swiss population is derived from Germans, French, and Italians.
Religious composition
Roman Catholic 47.6%
Protestant 44.3%
Other 8.1%
Languages
German 65%
French... 18%
Italian 12%
Romansch... 1%
Other... 4%
Education and Literacy Adult illiteracy is virtually nonexistent. Primary education is free. There are 26 educational systems, based on cultural and language needs.
Labor force
Total...3,500,000
By occupation: industrial sector 34%, agriculture and fishing 6%, construction 9.2%, and services 60%.

COUNTRY FACTS

Political and legal A federal union governed by the Federal Assembly, the legislature, Federal Council, and the executive branch. The judiciary is independent from other branches of government.

Telephone The telephone and telegraph systems are government-owned and operated. All electronic media and electronic mail are the province of Radio Suisse, a public corporation. International country code: [41]. City codes: Berne (31), Geneva (22), Zürich (1).

Transportation A majority of the railroad system is owned by the government. The roads are extensive and in excellent condition. Airports in Zürich, Geneva, and Basel have international flight capabilities.

Environment Switzerland was one of the first countries to pass environmental legislation, and provisions for environmental protection are incorporated in the constitution. Forests have been damaged from acid rain and air pollution and the government is taking measures to protect further damages.

Media Broadcasting is controlled by the Swiss Broadcasting Corporation (SBC), an autonomous corporation controlled by the government. Independent radio stations have been operating since 1983. Switzerland has the world's third highest number of newspapers per 1,000 citizens.

Health Health standards and medical care are excellent. Switzerland is one of the major producers of specialized pharmaceutical products. Life expectancy is 78 years for males and females.

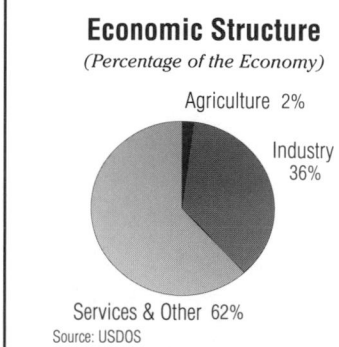

Economic Structure
(Percentage of the Economy)

Agriculture 2%
Industry 36%
Services & Other 62%

Source: USDOS

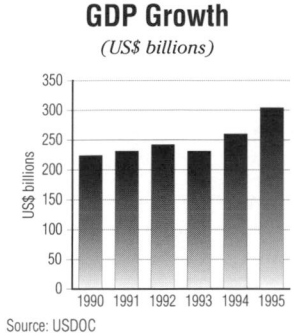

GDP Growth
(US$ billions)

Source: USDOC

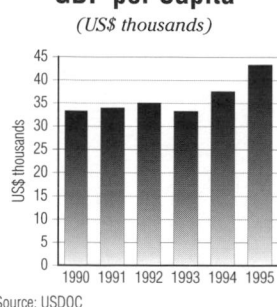

GDP per Capita
(US$ thousands)

Source: USDOC

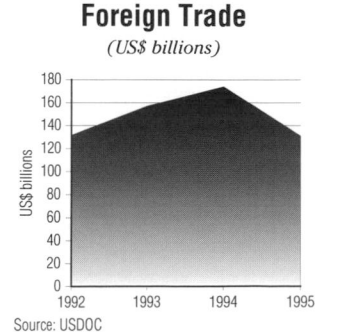

Foreign Trade
(US$ billions)

Source: USDOC

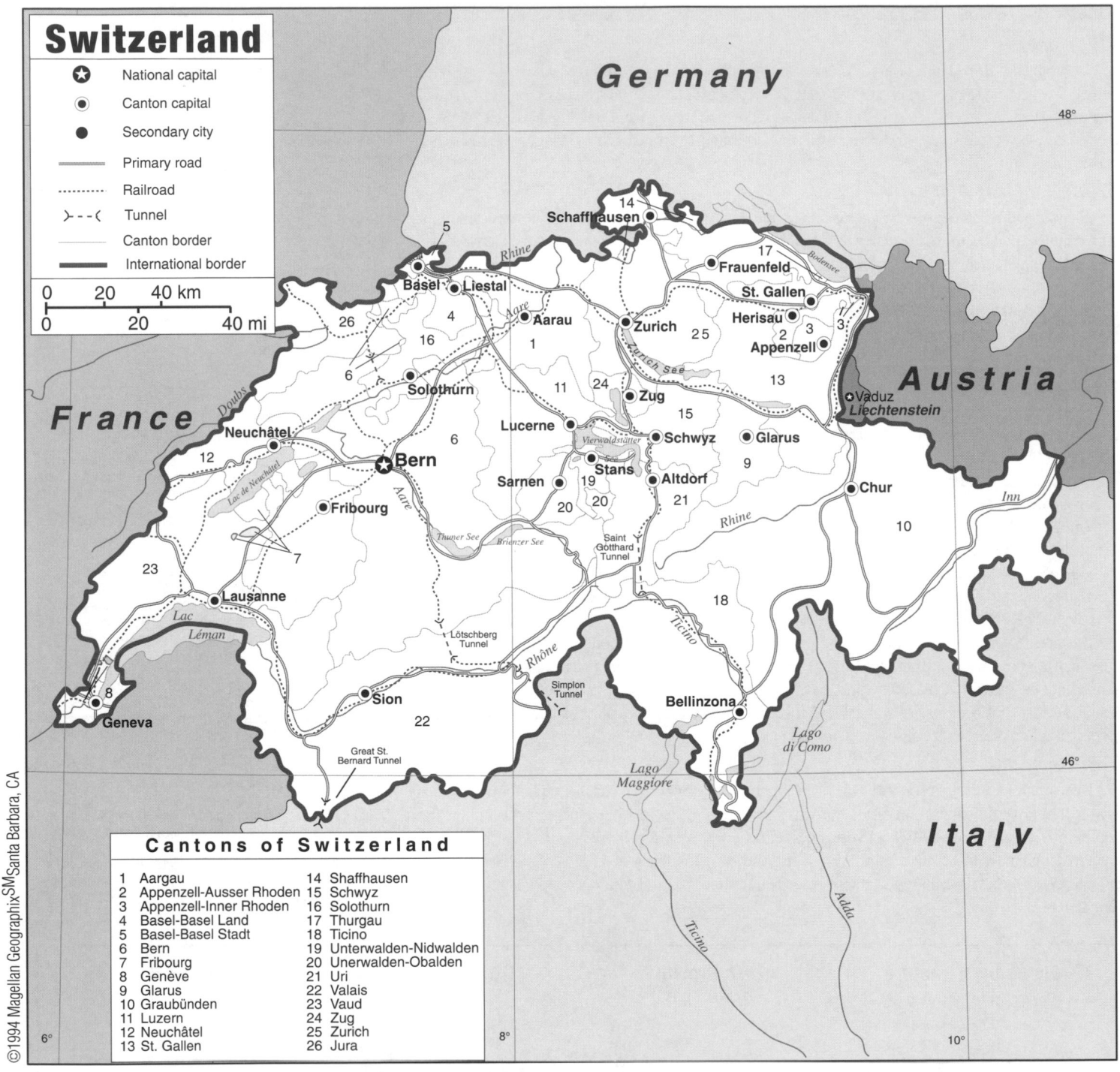

Switzerland

★	National capital
⊙	Canton capital
●	Secondary city
—	Primary road
····	Railroad
)--(	Tunnel
—	Canton border
▬	International border

0   20   40 km
0   20   40 mi

Germany

France

Austria

Italy

Schaffhausen
Frauenfeld
St. Gallen
Herisau
Appenzell
Basel   Liestal
Aarau
Zurich
Vaduz
Liechtenstein
Solothurn
Zug
Neuchâtel
Lucerne
Schwyz
Glarus
Bern
Sarnen
Stans
Altdorf
Fribourg
Chur
Lausanne
Saint Gotthard Tunnel
Lötschberg Tunnel
Sion
Simplon Tunnel
Great St. Bernard Tunnel
Geneva
Bellinzona

Rhine
Aare
Zurich See
Doubs
Lac de Neuchâtel
Aare
Thuner See
Brienzer See
Vierwaldstätter See
Rhine
Inn
Rhône
Ticino
Lac Léman
Lago Maggiore
Lago di Como
Ticino
Adda
Bodensee

48°
46°
6°   8°   10°

Cantons of Switzerland

1	Aargau	14	Shaffhausen
2	Appenzell-Ausser Rhoden	15	Schwyz
3	Appenzell-Inner Rhoden	16	Solothurn
4	Basel-Basel Land	17	Thurgau
5	Basel-Basel Stadt	18	Ticino
6	Bern	19	Unterwalden-Nidwalden
7	Fribourg	20	Unerwalden-Obalden
8	Genève	21	Uri
9	Glarus	22	Valais
10	Graubünden	23	Vaud
11	Luzern	24	Zug
12	Neuchâtel	25	Zurich
13	St. Gallen	26	Jura

©1994 Magellan GeographixSMSanta Barbara, CA

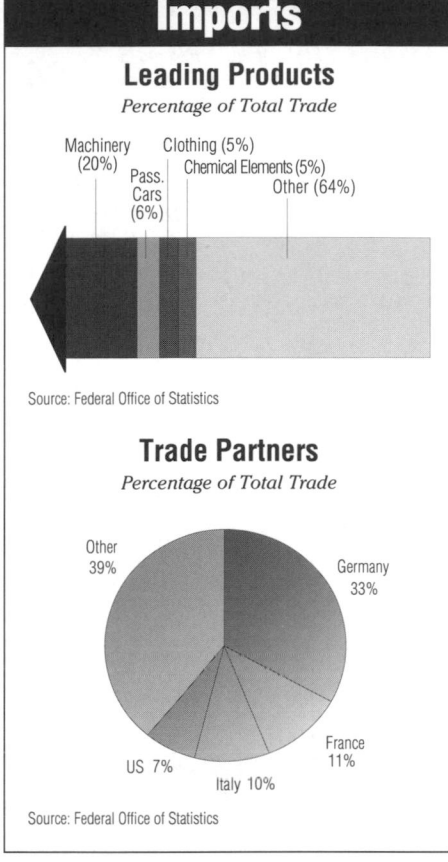

Imports

Leading Products
Percentage of Total Trade

Machinery (20%)
Pass. Cars (6%)
Clothing (5%)
Chemical Elements (5%)
Other (64%)

Source: Federal Office of Statistics

Trade Partners
Percentage of Total Trade

Other 39%
Germany 33%
France 11%
Italy 10%
US 7%

Source: Federal Office of Statistics

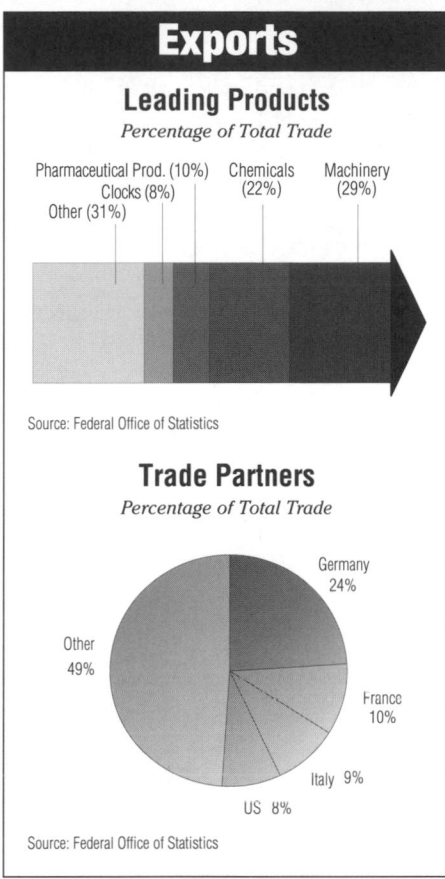

Exports

Leading Products
Percentage of Total Trade

Pharmaceutical Prod. (10%)
Clocks (8%)
Other (31%)
Chemicals (22%)
Machinery (29%)

Source: Federal Office of Statistics

Trade Partners
Percentage of Total Trade

Germany 24%
Other 49%
France 10%
Italy 9%
US 8%

Source: Federal Office of Statistics

Opportunities

FOR IMPORTING TO SWITZERLAND

- computer software
- computers and peripherals
- telecommunication equipment
- travel and tourism services
- aircraft and parts
- electronic components
- medical equipment
- pollution control equipment
- laboratory scientific instruments
- analytic process control instruments
- quality control instruments (non-chemical)
- renewable energy equipment
- raw materials
- gold
- works of art
- measuring/testing equipment
- packaging equipment

FOR EXPORTING FROM SWITZERLAND

- watches
- clocks
- art and antiques
- medicaments and other medicinal products
- textile machinery
- leather machinery
- organic-inorganic compounds
- heterocyclic compounds
- engineering skills
- marketing skills

GROWTH SECTORS

- manufacturing
- private banking
- insurance
- chemical industry
- agriculture

GOVERNMENT PROCUREMENT

- Metro-construction of a high-speed, magnetic underground passenger transportation system, valued at some $8.3 billion
- Upgrade of air traffic control systems

Trade News

RULES AND REGULATIONS

- **Trade news** Imports are blocked by a variety of complex import rules and regulations. Pressure from consumers and trading partners in the GATT will result in new market access opportunities for exporters when the Uruguay Round reforms begin to be implemented.

- **Import restrictions** Strictly speaking, there are no prohibited imports in legal, commercial trade with Switzerland. The Swiss method of controlling unwanted imports is through the imposition of restrictions, quotas, and other rules and regulations.

- **Import licenses, quotas, and regulations** These are required only for a limited number of products, and generally fall into two categories—measures for the protection of the country's agriculture, and measures of state control.

- **Agriculture** Switzerland imposes quantitative restrictions in order to insure the country's food supply in the event that supplies from abroad are cut off. Products affected by these restrictions include cattle, meat, milk, dairy products, indigenous fresh fruits and vegetables, seasonal cut flowers, cereals and forage products, and wine and grape juice. These products subject to quota may not be imported without an import license, and licenses are granted only to importers established in Switzerland. The system of import licensing for agricultural products will be significantly modified following implementation of the GATT reforms for agriculture. Switzerland will continue to block trade through high tariffs, however.

- **Special import licenses** Special import licenses are also required for certain products which are not subject to quotas, but which are covered by special regulations concerned with public health, plant health, quarantine (plants), and veterinary; regulations concerning the protection of species, safety measures, price control measures (for certain textile products); and measures for protection of the Swiss economy and public morality. Such import licenses are also issued only to persons and firms domiciled in Switzerland.

- **Tariff rates** Customs duties on imports are, with few exceptions, based on weight rather than on value. In many instances, especially with high-value, low-weight products, customs duties are almost negligible. With tariff rates averaging about 3.2% in the industrial goods sectors, Switzerland's tariff policy favors the development of trade.

- **Statistical tax** In addition to customs duties, there is a three percent statistical tax on the total customs duty payable. This fee is designed to cover the cost of preparation of the relevant foreign trade statistics.

- **Additional duties** Additional duties are charged on certain goods such as beer, grain used in the preparation of brewing malt, some alcoholic beverages, raw materials for distilling, and motor fuels. Certain products used as fuel are subject to countervailing duties.

- **Export restrictions** The February 1992 Nonproliferation Ordinance placed controls on exports of material and technology related to weapons of mass destruction, including those on the Nuclear Suppliers Group dual-use list as well as annexes for the MTCR list and chemical and biological equipment. The government is now at work on further tightening its export control laws.

FREIGHT FORWARDERS

Swiss Freight Forwarders' Association
POB 63
4002 Basel

Suisse-Atlantique
Société de Navigation Maritime SA
7 chemin Messidor
CP 4140
1002 Lausanne
Tel: (21) 3182201
Fax: (21) 3182279
Telex: 454101

Marketing

Overview

Despite its small size, Switzerland's diverse culture and language make it impossible to apply a single marketing strategy to the whole country. A number of large international trading and transit companies operate in Switzerland. Licensing can be a successful and profitable market entry strategy for foreign firms. The structure of retail trade has responded to a trend toward concentration and vertical integration. The number of independent retailers has decreased, giving way to an increasing number of self-service and discount stores, supermarkets, chain stores, and department stores. These stores do not specialize, but deal in a wide range of products.

Distribution

Distribution in Switzerland varies according to product type, source of manufacture, and distribution sites. In each case it is necessary to determine the appropriate approach.

Capital goods manufacturers may export directly where contracts with a limited number of customers represent appreciable shares of the market. However, a company new to the Swiss market or one whose product requires training for use and after-sales service would be well-advised to engage the services of a technically qualified Swiss agent with a good knowledge of the market. Swiss buyers of raw materials often use specialized importers, although large orders may be made directly from producers overseas. Exporters of consumer goods may deal with a wholesaler, who is in most cases also the importer. Many Swiss wholesalers are also importers, and they generally expect exclusive regional or national rights for the imported product. Wholesalers maintain stocks of products and provide quality control, transport, warehousing, and financing. Associations of wholesalers have been created for various sectors to protect sector interests and compete effectively with other forms of distribution. In response to the competition from integrated retail operations, individual retailers have established organizations to take care of wholesale purchasing, importing, and other services. Functioning as cooperatives, most of these buying groups and associations deal in consumables such as foodstuffs, textiles, shoes, pharmaceuticals, toys, and hardware.

Agents, Distributors, and Partners

Manufacturers and suppliers of consumer goods may deal with a wholesaler, employ a representative agent, or sell directly to buying offices of large retail chains. Many foreign sellers prefer to deal with representative agents in order to retain control over the distribution of their products.

Selling Techniques

New-to-market suppliers are urged to participate in established trade shows to give their products commercial exposure. Swiss buyers tend to rely on trade shows as a principal means of finding new products. Indeed, it is more difficult to arrange personal meetings with prospective Swiss business partners or representatives if the company has not already shown its commitment to the Swiss market by participating in these events. Retail sales techniques are similar to those in Western Europe. More than 200 franchises operate in the Swiss market. Franchising has long been practiced by the automotive trade and is a well-established distribution and retail system for the clothing industry. Franchising has also experienced an increase in the service and catering sectors. Direct marketing is growing in Switzerland, and electronic shopping and telemarketing are becoming more widely exploited. Mail order has won increasing acceptance, and mail order firms can expect continued growth.

Advertising

It is generally advisable to use the services of a Swiss advertising consultant. Serious and tasteful presentations are hallmarks of Swiss advertising. Advertising spending in Switzerland is one of the world's highest on a per capita basis. The Swiss Broadcasting Company holds a monopoly on the production and broadcast of radio and television programming. There are three television stations, each catering to the German-, Italian-, and French-speaking populations. Advertising on Swiss television is similar to the rest of Europe, presented in blocks of time, rather than interspersed between programs. Television advertising is subject to certain restrictions and several products are banned from advertising on TV. Radio advertising is limited to local radio stations.

Service and Customer Support

Supplier should provide detailed product information. Providing rapid and efficient quality service and after-sales support is absolutely essential. The Swiss expect that products will work correctly and that manufacturers will readily repair what is broken. If foreign suppliers are not prepared to do this, they will, quite simply, not make sales in this country.

Marketing in Switzerland

MARKETING TIPS

- **Advertising** Swiss advertising is more sedate than in many other sophisticated markets.
- **Establishing business relationships** The first order given to a new supplier is often regarded by the buyer as a trial order.
- **Trade shows** Exhibiting at trade shows is essential to a new firm or new product entering the market in Switzerland.
- **Price controls** There are some controls of prices for selected agricultural products and pharmaceutical products.
- **Quality** Swiss business partners demand the highest quality support and service from foreign suppliers.
- **Agents** Swiss law provides for two types of representatives: Commission agents, who are independent agents and may represent several firms, and salaried salespeople working for specific Swiss distribution firms.
- **Language and cultural diversity** Switzerland comprises three language districts which are: Italian, French, and German.

MARKET RESEARCH FIRMS

Consulink & Partner
Bucholzstrasse 24
3066 Stettlen-Bern
Tel: (31) 931-66-44
Fax: (31) 931-66-44

Heini Rutz Consulting
International Marketing
Johannisburgstrasse 16
8700 Kuesnacht-Zürich
Tel: (1) 910-55-74
Fax: (1) 910-37-63

AC Nielsen SA Buchrain
PO Box 3967
6002 Luzern
Tel: (41) 30-44-44
Fax: (41) 33-17-07

Battelle-Europe
Geneva Research Centers
7 route de Drize
1227 Carouge-Geneva
Tel: (22) 30-07-07
Fax: (22) 343-67-32

IHA - GMF
Institut fuer Marktanalysen AG
Obermattweg 9
6062 Hergiswil
Tel: (41) 95-91-11
Fax: (41) 95-91-23

Admerca AG
Marketing Consultants
Arosastrasse 25
8008 Zürich
Tel: (1) 422-41-77
Fax: (1) 422-97-77

Trimedia Communications AG
Birmensdorferstrasse 55
PO Box 1153
8036 Zürich
Tel: (1) 466-51-11
Fax: (1) 466-51-55

Swiss Volksbank
Head Office
Weltpoststrasse 5
PO Box 5323
3001 Bern
Tel: (31) 32-81-11
Fax: (31) 32-79-14

Bank Leu AG
Bahnhofstrasse 32
PO Box 553
8022 Zürich
Tel: (1) 219-11-11
Fax: (1) 219-36-45

 **Business Culture**

Greetings and Courtesies

Switzerland is a multilingual, multicultural country, distinct for its regional differences, and greetings there vary accordingly. While English is a predominant language of business, the national languages of German, French, and Italian are also widely spoken. A handshake followed by a polite greeting ("Pleased to meet you") is correct form. In the German region, the address includes *Herr* (Mr.), *Frau* (Mrs.) and *Fraulein* (Miss) followed by the last name only. If the male individual bears a degree or professional title it is appropriate to say *"Herr Doktor"* or *"Herr Professor"* and exclude the last name. However, when addressing professional women you do use the last name; e.g., *"Frau Doktor Schmidt."* In the French speaking region, use the terms *Monsieur* (Mr.), *Madame* (Mrs. or Ms.), or *Mademoiselle* (Miss) followed by the last name. In the Italian speaking region, use the terms *Signor* (Mr.), *Signora* (Mrs.), or *Signorina* (Miss) followed by the last name. Do not use first names unless invited to do so. Exchanges of gifts upon first meeting is not a custom. As a relationship grows, a gift of fine cognac is always appreciated. Likewise, a box of fine chocolates to be shared by the staff is a thoughtful gesture.

Business Ethic and Framework

 The Swiss are hard working and extremely formal in business. Third party introductions are very important. Banking and accounting firms can be helpful resources for introductions to people and opportunities in Switzerland. Scheduled appointments are necessary as the Swiss are not receptive to cold calls or to seeing anyone without an appointment. However, it is important to investigate regional differences in order to know specific business practices throughout Switzerland. Quality products and services are essential, more important than price, and the highest standards and quality will be expected from any venture that approaches the Swiss business community. Hard sell techniques are counterproductive and aggressive sales tactics should be avoided. The rank and status of the visiting representatives is not important to the conducting of business, provided the representative is technically competent and has the authority to conclude an agreement.

Decision Making

 In larger corporations, decision by consensus among top management is the norm. In smaller firms, a single top manager may render a decision. In either case, and regardless of regional differences, the key to effecting a decision swiftly will depend how well you've presented your program for introducing a high-quality product/service into the Swiss marketplace. Additionally, your Swiss colleagues will place some amount of weight on the longevity of your firm as well as the history of its market performance.

Women

 Until recently, women have not had an interest in pursuing corporate management—or so it is said. Having achieved the right to vote as late as 1971, women's roles are rapidly changing. Many women are found at mid-level management positions in banking, insurance, public relations, and advertising. Some have more recently moved into engineering positions. Many Swiss firms have instituted equal opportunity programs to see that women have a chance to advance. Women with families are also increasingly joining the work force, taking part-time jobs or job-sharing. Many companies are receptive to such arrangements and continue to treat the women professionally.

Meetings

 The Swiss do not like to mix business with pleasure and they prefer to have meetings take place in the office. Business lunches are few and usually celebrate the success of a completed business transaction. Keeping in mind there are regional differences, generally speaking, the Swiss prefer to get to the point of a purpose and they try to avoid preliminary small talk. Introductions will be made and business cards exchanged. In Switzerland, the host determines when to conclude a presentation, and it is their prerogative to schedule subsequent meetings. You will not be thought aggressive to ask your host for a follow-up meeting or to inquire about the decision-making process. Eye contact during meetings conveys interest and respect.

Business Attire

 Business suits should be conservative. Dark blue or pin stripes are acceptable, and double breasted or three piece suits are preferred over sport jackets and slacks. Ties of sober color and design are appropriate. Women in business should avoid low necklines, costume jewelry, and bright colors. Skirts and blazers or suits and dresses are appropriate.

Cultural Cautions

DO'S

- Exchanging business cards is a ritual in Switzerland. Take plenty along. If invited to a Swiss home, send flowers in advance. Always send an odd number of flowers, and avoid sending red flowers, which are associated with passion.
- Be sensitive to regional language and cultural differences. Make certain not to confuse the language with the people. All nationals are "Swiss" and proud of it.

DON'TS

- Excessive displays of wealth, and "show-off" behavior of any kind, is considered to be impolite.
- Don't bring attorneys to initial business meetings, especially when dealing with small firms that won't understand their role.
- Never smoke at the dinner table.
- Don't ask personal questions of your Swiss counterparts—questions of age, job, family, or personal life are inappropriate. The Swiss are very private people.

CUSTOMS

- One favorite Swiss saying claims that if someone is late, he is either not wearing a Swiss watch or didn't take a Swiss train.
- Good posture is a must in Switzerland. Crossing your legs in public is accepted but don't stretch them out or slouch in your chair.
- When standing in line, there will probably be a great deal of pushing and shoving.
- When dining at a restaurant, don't be surprised if strangers seat themselves at your table. It is not necessary to strike up a conversation.
- The best compliment guests can give at dinner is to take second helpings of the food.
- The Swiss value nature, beauty, hard work, sobriety, thrift, independence, tolerance, punctuality, cleanliness, orderliness, and a sense of responsibility. This politically neutral country is made up of 26 member states, known as cantons, and the entire confederation celebrates the diversity of its cultures. Each canton exhibits a sense of local pride and it would be a mistake to enter debates favoring one region over another.
- One passionately felt Swiss motto goes: "Unity, yes; uniformity, no."

OBSERVATIONS

- The Swiss take great pride in their wine and it is the wise guest who shows a similar appreciation. Discussing the different wine regions in Switzerland makes for good conversation during a meal. Also, when visiting a Swiss home, it is customary to leave a tip for household staff in the tray by the coat room. One other caution when treated to a "home cooked" Swiss meal: don't use too much salt and pepper, if any. You may insult the cook.
- The elderly are very respected. Many people will go out of their way to help them out, giving up a seat on the bus or carrying luggage or bags.
- The Swiss give hundreds of hours during their lifetime for military training in Switzerland's small professional army. Technically, every Swiss man in the army serves several weeks of military service each year. However, it is best to avoid discussing issues relating to military service, as well as issues of politics, money, religion, and weight watching.

NEGOTIATIONS

- Negotiations will vary according to Switzerland's regions and the individual firms you are dealing with. As advised above, avoid bringing attorneys to initial meetings. Once basic agreement has been reached, however, an attorney's presence will not invite mistrust.
- In general, Swiss approach negotiations with a knowledgeable straightforwardness, and negotiations will usually proceed accordingly.
- Avoid high pressure tactics and conditional displays during negotiations; it will make the Swiss uncomfortable.

Legal

Legal System

Switzerland is a federal state, meaning that government is divided between the federal level and the 26 individual cantons. Some tasks are within the joint competence of the canton and federal governments. Most private laws (such as statutes governing persons, family, succession and estate, real estate, contract and commercial codes, corporations, and negotiable instruments) are federal. Civil and criminal procedure, as well as court organization, largely remain matters for the cantons. Switzerland is a civil code country; the private laws largely derive from Roman tradition and, thereafter, principally from Germanic legal concepts.

Intellectual Property Rights

Switzerland has one of the best regimes in the world for the protection of intellectual property, and protection is afforded equally to foreign and domestic rightsholders.

Patents Patent protection is very broad, and Switzerland recognizes and protects valid patents from most countries. If filed in Switzerland, a patent application must be made in one of the country's three official languages, and must be accompanied by detailed specifications and if necessary by technical drawings. The duration of a patent is 20 years, and is not renewable beyond this time.

Trademarks Switzerland recognizes well-known trademarks and has established simple procedures to register and renew all marks. The initial period of protection is 20 years. Trademark infringement is very rare. It is now possible to register a service trademark in Switzerland.

Copyrights The new Copyright Act improved a regime that was already strong, and introduced special provisions for the protection of computer software. Infringement is considered a criminal offense. The term of protection is life plus 70 years.

Business Registration

With some exceptions, physical persons or legal entities conducting a business activity with commercial structures must be registered with the Registry of Commerce of the canton where the business is incorporated. The Swiss branch of a foreign company must also be registered in Switzerland. It must appoint a representative with Swiss domicile. A simple office representation does not need to be registered. For certain commercial activities, such as banking and insurance, an official authorization is needed and such activities could be subject to official surveillance.

Contracts and Dispute Resolution

The Swiss Code of Obligations finds its inspiration mainly in German law. The fundamental principle is freedom to contract. Swiss courts often deal with the performance of national or international contracts. In cases of urgency, injunctions or attachment orders can be obtained to protect assets relevant to a matter in dispute. If a debtor has no domicile in Switzerland, Swiss law also allows a creditor to attach assets of the debtor found within the Swiss jurisdiction. The order is granted on the unilateral request of the claimant, who must show *prima facie* evidence of the claim and often post a bond as security. Effective January 1997, a new federal law on Debt Enforcement and Bankruptcy will place more restrictions on the attachment of the assets of a debtor domiciled outside Switzerland. Numerous arbitration proceedings take place in Switzerland. The recent Federal Act on Private International Law contains a chapter devoted to international arbitration. It is a very modern and liberal law on arbitration, well adjusted to the particular needs of parties in the commercial field, and specifically designed to efficiently resolve disputes.

Notaries

In Switzerland, notaries draft and execute various deeds. They also authenticate signatures and the contents of deeds. Certain deeds, such as deeds for transferring real estate or corporate bylaws, must be executed in the presence of a notary.

Labor

By international comparison, Swiss labor law does not offer great protection to employees. The employer can fairly easily terminate an employment agreement, provided the legal notice requirements are met and a short trial period is allowed. An employee cannot usually challenge a termination, except to show that the conditions for termination were not met or that the termination was abusive; the remedy is to compel the employer to pay an indemnity to the employee, but not to rehire. Swiss law has no minimum wage requirement, but in many fields the trade unions have negotiated collective employment agreements with employers associations to provide for minimum wages and other guarantees. The federal government can declare such collective agreements to be binding.

Source: Poncet Turrettini Amaudruz & Neyroud

Legal Matters

LEGAL BRIEFS

- **Banking secrecy** Banks are subject to surveillance by the Federal Banking Commission. Banking secrecy is protected and its violation is a criminal offense. However, it cannot be invoked in cases of domestic or foreign criminal proceedings. Bankers and financial intermediaries are obligated to know the identity of both the contracting party and the beneficial owner of the funds that they receive in trust. A bank account cannot be opened simply in the name of an offshore company or a third party without simultaneously disclosing the identity of the beneficial owner.

- **Business entities** A joint stock company is the usual legal entity to conduct business. The minimum capital is SwF100,000 (approximately US$86,000) out of which 50 percent has to be paid in at the time of incorporation. The board of directors can be composed of one or more members. However, the majority must be Swiss nationals domiciled in Switzerland.

- **Arbitration** Parties and the arbitrators retain a large extent of freedom to organize arbitral proceedings, as long as they observe some essential principles, such as a written arbitration clause, independence of the arbitrators, equality of the parties, and due process. Remedies against an arbitral award are limited and can be, in case of international arbitration, waived in advance.

- **Data protection** The Federal Act on Data Protection has now been enacted. It provides for protection of data stored and used on individuals and corporations, including guidelines processing, maintaining, and accessing such data. It also authorizes an individual to access personal data. Cross-border data flow can be illegal if the recipient's country does not offer equal protection.

- **International agreements** Switzerland is a member of CISG; New York Convention on the Recognition and Enforcement of Foreign Arbitral Awards; Convention Abolishing the Requirement of Legalization for Foreign Public Documents; ATA Carnet Convention.

LEGAL CONTACTS

Poncet Turrettini Amaudruz & Neyroud
8-10 rue de Hesse
1204 Geneva
Phone: (22) 660-0460
Fax: (22) 665-7888

Bernheim, Ming, Halperin et Ducret-Burger
5, Avenue Leon-Gaud
1206 Geneva
Tel: (22) 347 71 51
Fax: (22) 347 68 31

Borel & Barbey
2, Rue de Jargonnant
1207 Geneva
Tel: (22) 736.11.36
Fax: (22) 736.45.88

Combe, De Bavier & De Senarclens
37, quai Wilson
1211 Geneva
Tel: (22) 741 01 01
Fax: (22) 741 01 27

Froriep Renggli
4, Rue Charles-Bonnet
1206 Geneva
Tel: (22) 347 1818

Hornung & Levy
16 Boulevard Des Tranchees
POB 345
1211 Geneva 12
Tel: (22) 789 0011

Keppeler, Maurer, Kroo & Spirgi
32, route De Lalagnou
1208 Geneva
Tel: (22) 735.26.28

Lalive & Partners
6, Rue de L'Athenee
1205 Geneva
Tel: (22) 319 87 00

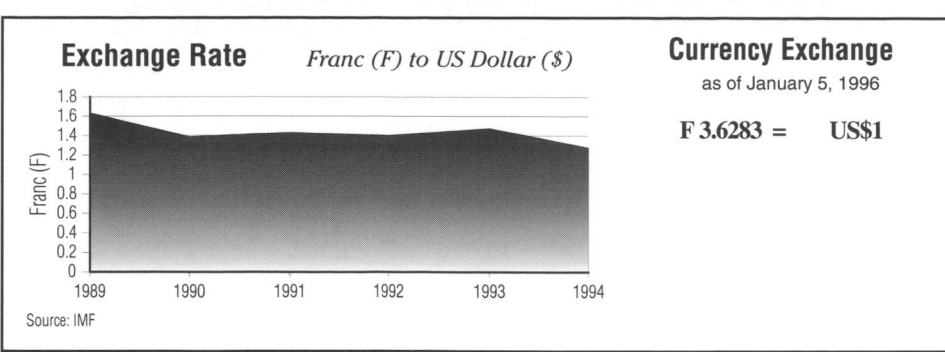

Exchange Rate
Franc (F) to US Dollar ($)

Franc (F): 1.8, 1.6, 1.4, 1.2, 1, 0.8, 0.6, 0.4, 0.2, 0
Years: 1989, 1990, 1991, 1992, 1993, 1994

Source: IMF

Currency Exchange
as of January 5, 1996

F 3.6283 =   US$1

Money Matters

BITS AND PIECES

- **Principality of Liechtenstein** For purposes of import and export, the Principality of Liechtenstein is included in the Swiss customs territory. However, Liechtenstein is considered a foreign country for purposes of bank supervision.
- **Foreign investment** The Swiss government has a relaxed attitude toward foreign investment, and attempts to maintain a condition that is favorable to both Swiss and foreign investors. The country enjoys economic and political stability and an efficient capital market.
- **Stock exchanges** There are stock exchanges in Zürich, Geneva, and Basel, and an electronic options/futures exchange in Zürich. The exchanges are regulated only in Basel and Zürich.
- **Purchase of property** Current law restricts foreigners' right to purchase Swiss real estate. A new law is under discussion that would make it unnecessary for foreigners to acquire authorization before purchasing residential or commercial property.
- **Foreign banks** Foreign banks play a major role in the Swiss banking community, and comprise nearly 40 percent of the total number of banking institutions.
- **Financial services** Specialized financial institutions exist for the clearing of funds and securities. The postal check system is used by individuals for settling local currency denominated obligations. Specialized services are available and are also offered by the major banks.

BANKS

Banca del Gottardo
Viale S. Francini 8
6901 Lugano
Tel: (91) 28111
Fax: (91) 239487
Telex: 841051

Bank Lue Ltd
Bahnhofstr. 32
8001 Zürich
Tel: (1) 2191111
Fax: (1) 2193197
Telex: 812174

Credit Suisse
Paradeplatz 8
PO Box 590
8021 Zürich
Tel: (1) 333-11-11
Fax: (1) 332-55-55

Migros Bank AG
Seidengasse 12
8023 Zürich
Tel: (1) 2298111
Fax: (1) 2111244
Telex: 813034

Neue Aargauer Bank
Hauptstr. 1
5200 Brugg
Tel: (56) 327111
Fax: (56) 421160
Telex: 825108

Swiss Bank Corporation
Aeschenplatz 6
4002 Basel
Tel: (61) 288-20-20
Fax: (61) 288-45-76

Union Bank of Switzerland
Regional Management North America
Bahnhofstrasse 45
PO Box 645
8021 Zürich
Tel: (1) 234-11-11
Fax: (1) 236-71-07

United Overseas Bank SA
11 quai des Bergues
1201 Geneva 1
Tel: (22) 7319841
Fax: (22) 7323002
Telex: 412100

Currency

The currency of Switzerland is the Swiss franc (F or SwF), divided into 100 centimes.

Foreign Exchange

Exchange rates are determined, in principle, on the basis of underlying demand and supply conditions in the exchange markets. However, the Swiss National Bank reserves the right to intervene if and when circumstances warrant—and it does not hesitate to do so. Residents and nonresidents may freely negotiate foreign exchange contracts with banks in all currencies, in respect of both commercial and financial transactions.

Capital Transfers

There is complete freedom of transfer of investment income, royalties, and repatriation of capital. There are no Swiss government policies or laws that regulate or limit the inflow or outflow of capital.

Investment Incentives

The government does not offer large-scale incentives to prospective investors, and those that exist are open to foreign and domestic investors alike. The principal incentives provided by the federal government consist of low-interest loans to promote the hotel and catering/restaurant industry in mountain regions. Sometimes the cantons offer more substantial benefits, especially in the more rural areas. The most common incentives are subsidies or loans by cantons for the development of industrial sites; guarantees on bank loans; capital loans at below-market interest rates; grants for facilities conducting research and development activities; and subsidies to defray certain investment costs. Exemptions from taxes on profits and capital gains are also offered.

Investment Restrictions

National treatment is granted to foreign investors, with the exception of national security areas such as hydroelectric and nuclear power, operation of oil pipelines, transportation of explosive materials, operation of airlines, and marine navigation. The law also limits the freedom of foreigners to purchase real estate, and makes such purchases subject to government approval.

TAXATION

Taxation requires sophisticated knowledge of complex rules and regulations specific to each country. For more detailed information we suggest you refer to the Ernst & Young Corporate Tax Guide and Directory, available from the Ernst & Young accounting office in your country, or from:

ATAG Ernst & Young AG
Bleicherweg 21
P.O. Box 5272
8022 Zürich
Switzerland
Tel: (1) 286-31-11
Telex: 815515 Ans bk ATAG CH
Fax: (1) 286-31-47

- Corporate tax is based on total worldwide earnings, but income from a Swiss company's foreign establishment is excluded from taxation. Companies outside of Switzerland are liable for Swiss taxes on their Swiss establishments.
- Several treaties are in force to avoid double taxation situations.

At a Glance

Corporate Income Tax Rate (%)(a)	10 to 27
Capital Gains Tax Rate (%)(b)	—
Branch Tax Rate (%)(a)	10 to 27
Withholding Tax (%)	
Dividends (b)	35
Interest (c)	35
Royalties from Patents, Know-how, etc.	0
Branch Remittance Tax	0
Net Operating Losses (Years)(d)	
Carryback	0
Carryforward	7

(a) Varies according to canton. Federal income tax, at a maximum rate of 9.8%, is additional.
(b) Taxes are levied at both the federal and cantonal level, and are calculated based on specific situations.
(c) A federal tax is imposed on bank interest and interest from publicly offered bonds, debentures, and other written instruments of indebtedness issued by a Swiss borrower, but not on commercial loans or loans from foreign parents to Swiss subsidiaries.
(d) For federal tax purposes, losses may be carried forward seven years. The carryforward period varies among cantons, but the period is typically between five and seven years. Losses may not be carried back under federal or cantonal law.

Business Travel

LH 1906	MADRID	935	113-3
LH 1022	STUTTGART HBF.	935	-
AF 1701	LYON	940	683-5
AY 822	HELSINKI	940	113-3
AA 071	SFRANCISCO-DALLAS	945	731-7

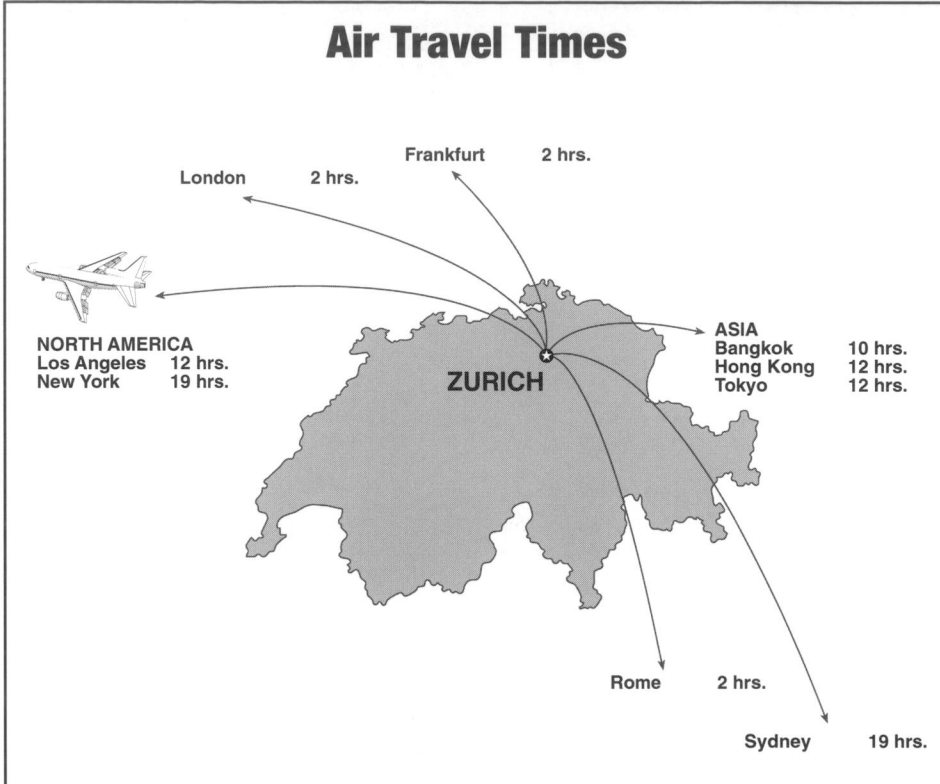

Air Travel Times

London   2 hrs.
Frankfurt   2 hrs.

NORTH AMERICA
Los Angeles   12 hrs.
New York   19 hrs.

ZURICH

ASIA
Bangkok   10 hrs.
Hong Kong   12 hrs.
Tokyo   12 hrs.

Rome   2 hrs.

Sydney   19 hrs.

COMMUNICATIONS

Telephones The Swiss telephone system is among the most modern, comprehensive, and reasonably priced in the world, with rare service problems and direct dialing to most countries available. Public booths are less expensive than hotels, which add a hefty service charge.

Fax Facilities for faxing are widely available in offices, larger hotels, and post offices.

Post office The postal system is excellent for local and international mail that is properly zip-coded. The postal code for Switzerland (CH) may precede the zip code on mail sent from outside Switzerland; for example: 2100 Geneva. Stamps can be purchased at post offices and hotel desks.

BEST TRAVEL BOOKS

Frommer's Switzerland and Liechtenstein. Illustrated, Prentice Hall General Reference and Travel.

Fielding's Switzerland and the Alpine Region, Margaret Zellers, Travel Guide Series, 724 pages. Fielding Worldwide Inc.

Switzerland: The Smart Traveler's Guide to Zürich, Basel and Geneva. Holt, Henry and Co., Inc., 224 pages.

Fodor's A Travel Guide, Switzerland.

Travel Guide, Switzerland, Lonely Planet. Goes beyond cuckoo and chocolates to find there's much more to the real Switzerland. 352 pages, 20 color pages.

Fodor's Europe, Best of 31 Countries. Contains information on historical towns, great culture, scenic countryside.

Multinational Travel Companion for the Executive. Twenty–third edition. Strand Publishing Company, Inc. Travel tips worldwide.'

USEFUL TELEPHONE NUMBERS

If you are calling from outside Switzerland, you will need to add the country code [41] and any other international dialing requirements from within your country.

- Directory Assistance 111
- Long Distance Assistance 114
- Telegrams 110
- Roadway Assistance 140
- News 167
- Time 161
- Road Conditions 163
- Emergency Road Assistance 140
- Weather Conditions.. 162
- Central Taxi Dispatch 141
- Police 117
- Fire 118
- Ambulance 144
- Tourist Office, Basel............................(41) 2615050
- Tourist Office, Bern .... (31) 221212
- Tourist Office, Geneva .... (22) 3105031
- Tourist Office, Zürich............................ (1) 2114000
- Convention Bureau, Zürich .... (1) 2881111

Airlines
- Lufthansa (Zürich) ....(1) 286-70-00
- Swissair (Zürich) ....(1) 258-34-34
- United (Zürich) ....(1) 155-95-55

Car Rental
- Avis, Zürich .... (1) 2417070
- Budget, Zürich....................................... (1) 2092670
- Europcar, Zürich.................................... (1) 2715656
- Hertz, Zürich.. (1) 2428484

Credit Card Information
Lost or stolen credit cards (call collect to the US, regardless of which country the card was issued in).
- Amex...[1] (919) 333-3211
- Diner's Club...............................[1] (303) 799-1504
- MasterCard ....[1] (314) 275-6690
- Visa ....[1] (410) 581-7931

Travelogue

WORKWEEK

Offices Monday-Friday 8:00 am to noon and 2:00 pm to 6:00 pm, with some taking shorter lunches and closing earlier.

Banks Monday-Friday 8:30 am to 4:30 pm.

Government Monday-Friday 7:30 or 8:30 am to 5:30 or 6:00 pm, with some taking up to two hours for lunch.

Retail Monday-Friday 8:00 am to 12:15 pm and 1:30 pm to 6:30 pm, often closed Monday morning. Saturday 8:00 am to 4:00 pm.

HOLIDAYS

Holidays 1996
January 1-2 New Year's and Baerzelistag Days
April 5 Good Friday*
April 8 Easter Monday*
May 16 Ascension Day
May 26 Whit Monday
August 1 Swiss National Day
Dec 25 Christmas
Dec 26 Boxing Day
*Dates change from year to year.
Additional holidays are observed locally.

VISA AND PASSPORT

A valid passport is required; a visa is generally not required for tourist or business stays up to 90 days. However, it is advised to check with your consulate first as there are many exceptions. Passports must be good for six months beyond the intended stay. All travelers must hold onward tickets, valid travel documents, and sufficient funds.

DEPARTURE FORMALITIES

No restrictions apply to the export of Swiss currency and there are no other departure formalities.

IMMUNIZATION

No vaccinations or immunizations are required unless the traveler has passed through an infected area before entering Switzerland. The air is thin in Switzerland, bring along any medications you may need. Take special care in the mountains, helicopter rescues are expensive.

TIPPING

Taxi rates usually include the tip; if not, 10-15 percent is expected. All Swiss restaurants include tips and service fees in the bills, and no additional tip is expected. Washroom attendants do not generally get a tip. Doormen and small services are generally tipped in the range of F1.

CRIME

Switzerland's rate of violent crime is low, but petty crime occurs at peak tourist periods and in areas frequented by crowds, tourists, or drug users and dealers. Do not neglect personal security.

INFRASTRUCTURE

Switzerland's business infrastructure is excellent. The air, road, and rail networks are efficient and well maintained. Frequent rail service is readily available and all railways are electric. The larger trains have restaurants or buffet cars, others have snack foods. Train service is considered excellent. Taxis can be hailed on the street or ordered by phone and are metered. Taxis are not available for drivers for hire. Telecommunications and tourist facilities are outstanding. Car rental is available; however motoring can be fast on the main roads. The autobahn speed limit is 75 mph (120 kph), other roads have posted speed limit signs. Traffic drives on the right, front seat belts must be fastened. Emergency services and up-to-date road information can be had by calling The Touring Club Suisse and the Automobile Club Suisse. Before crossing an Alpine pass be sure to inquire about road conditions.

NATIONAL TOURIST OFFICE

Swiss National Tourist Office
Bellariastrasse 38
8038 Zürich
Tel: (1) 288-11-11
Fax: (1) 288-12-05

GOVERNMENT AGENCIES

Bundesamt fuer Aussenwirtschaft
Federal Office of External Economic Affairs
Bundeshaus Ost
3003 Bern
Tel: (31) 322-22-11
Fax: (31) 322-23-30

Bundesamt fuer Industrie, Gewerbe und Arbeit
Federal Office of Industry, Trade and Work
Bundesgasse 8
3003 Bern
Tel: (31) 322-29-44
Fax: (31) 322-27-49

Bundesamt fuer Konjunkturfragen
Federal Office for Economic Policy
Belpstrasse 53
3003 Bern
Tel: (31) 322-21-33
Fax: (31) 372-41-02

Bundesamt fuer Umwelt, Wald und Landschaft
Environmental Protection Agency
Hallwylstrasse 4
3003 Bern
Tel: (31) 322-93-11
Fax: (31) 322-70-54

Bundesamt fuer Gesundheitswesen
Federal Office of Health
Bollwerk 27
3001 Bern
Tel: (31) 322-95-11
Fax: (31) 322-95-07

Bundesamt fuer Statistik
Federal Office for Statistics
Schwarztorstrasse 96
3003 Bern
Tel: (31) 323-60-11
Fax: (31) 323-60-61

Federal Office of Telecommunication
Zukunftsstrasse 44
2501 Biel
Tel: (32) 28-55-11
Fax: (32) 28-55-55

Eidg. Zollverwaltung
Federal Customs Office
Monbijoustrasse 40
3003 Bern
Tel: (31) 322-65-11
Fax: (31) 322-78-72

WORLD TRADE CENTERS

World Trade Center Basel
Isteinerstrasse 53
4021 Basel
Tel: (61) 691-20-29
Fax: (61) 686-21-82

World Trade Center Geneva
10, Route de l'Aéroport
PO Box 306
1215 Geneva 15
Tel: (22) 798-99-89
Fax: (22) 791-08-85

World Trade Center Lausanne
PO Box 476
Avenue de Gratta-Paille 2
1000 Lausanne 30 Grey
Tel: (21) 641-11-11
Fax: (21) 641-11-10

World Trade Center Lugano
One World Trade Center
6982 Lugano-Agno
Tel: (91) 50-21-11
Fax: (91) 51-21-01

World Trade Center Zürich
Siewerdtstrasse 8
8050 Zürich
Tel: (1) 316-13-35
Fax: (1) 316-13-94

BUSINESS AND TRADE ORGANIZATIONS

Vorort des Schweizerischen Handels und Industrievereins
Union of Commerce and Industry Associations
Mainaustrasse 49
8034 Zürich
Tel: (1) 382-23-23
Fax: (1) 382-23-32

Schweizerische Zentrale fuer Handelsfoerderung
Swiss Office for Trade Promotion
Stampfenbachstrasse 85
8035 Zürich
Tel: (1) 365-51-51
Fax: (1) 365-52-21

Vereinigung des Schweizerischen Import und Grosshandels
Federation of Importers and Wholesalers
PO Box 656
4010 Basel
Tel: (61) 271-33-85
Fax: (61) 272-30-39

Verband Schweizerischer Transit und Welthandelsfirmen Transit and World Trade Confederation
PO Box 526, Aeschenvorstadt 4
4010 Basel
Tel: (61) 272-72-00
Fax: (61) 272-80-90

Verband des Schweizerischen Versandhandels
Mail Order Association
Brandenbergstrasse 30
8304 Wallisellen
Tel: (1) 830-16-02
Fax: (1) 830-16-08

Verein schweizerischer Metallwarenfabrikanten
Metal Product Manufacturers Association
Gartenstrasse 3
6304 Zug
Tel: (42) 21-61-34
Fax: (42) 21-88-43

Schweizerische Normen-Vereinigung
Standards Association
Muehlebachstrasse 54
8008 Zürich
Tel: (1) 254-54-54
Fax: (1) 254-54-74

Schweizer Automatik Pool
Electronics, Automation Equipment & Computer Manufacturers & Distributors Association
c/o ATAG Ernst & Young AG
PO Box 5272
8022 Zürich
Tel: (1) 286-31-11
Fax: (1) 202-92-83

ProTelecom
Telecommunication Association
Laupenstrasse 18a
3001 Bern
Tel: (31) 382-44-44
Fax: (31) 382-33-31

Information, Communication, Software and Business Organization Association
Badenerstrasse 356
8040 Zürich
Tel: (1) 492-48-48
Fax: (1) 492-35-09

Verband Schweiz. Firmen fuer Arzt und Spitalbedarf Medical and Hospital Supply Association
Monbijoustrasse 8
3011 Bern
Tel: (31) 382-44-24
Fax: (31) 382-46-20

Schweiz. Ingenieur und Architekten Verein
Society of Engineers and Architects
Selnaustrasse 16
8039 Zürich
Tel: (1) 283-15-15
Fax: (1) 201-63-35

REMEMBER

- When you telephone (or fax) to Switzerland from another country you must always include the country code [41] before the numbers given.
- When you send mail to Switzerland, be sure to write SWITZERLAND in capital letters on its own line below the address given.

Swiss Textile Federation
PO Box 4838
8022 Zürich
Tel: (1) 201-57-55
Fax: (1) 201-01-28

Swiss Franchise Association
Pilatusstrasse 55
6003 Lucerne
Tel: (41) 22-20-02
Fax: (41) 22-20-04

Schweizerische Bankvereinigung
Swiss Banking Association
PO Box 4182, Aeschenplatz 7
4002 Basel
Tel: (61) 295-93-93
Fax: (61) 272-53-82

Schweizerischer Bauernverband
Laurstr. 10
5200 Brugg
Tel: (56) 325111
Fax: (56) 415348

Schweizerischer Gewerbeverband
Schwarztorstr. 26
3007 Berne
Tel: (31) 257785

Schweizerischer Handels-und Industrie-Verein
Börsenstr. 26
8001 Zürich
Tel: (1) 2212707
Fax: (1) 2119092
Telex: 813294

Zentralverband schweizerischer Arbeitgeber-Organisationen
Florastr. 44
8034 Zürich
Tel: (1) 3830758
Fax: (1) 3833980

CHAMBERS OF COMMERCE

Swiss-American Chamber of Commerce
Talacker 41
8001 Zürich
Tel: (1) 211-24-54
Fax: (1) 211-95-72

Berner Handelskammer
Chamber of Commerce of Bern
Gutenbergstrasse 1
3001 Bern
Tel: (31) 382-17-11
Fax: (31) 382-17-15

Chambre de Commerce et de l'Industrie de Geneve
Bd du Theatre 4
1211 Geneve 11
Tel: (22) 311-53-33
Fax: (22) 310-03-63

Zentralschweizerische Handelskammer
Kapellplatz 2
6002 Luzern
Tel: (41) 51-68-65
Fax: (41) 51-52-88

Chambre Neuchateloise du Commerce et de l'Industrie
Rue de la Serre 4
2001 Neuchatel
Tel: (38) 25-75-41
Fax: (38) 24-70-92

Camera di Commercio del Cantone Ticino
Corso Elvezia 16
6901 Lugano
Tel: (91) 23-50-31
Fax: (91) 22-03-41

Zurcher Handelskammer
Chamber of Commerce of Zürich
Bleicherweg 5
8022 Zürich
Tel: (1) 221-07-42
Fax: (1) 211-76-15

NEWSPAPERS

Aargauer Tagblatt/ Brugger Tagblatt/Frejämter
Tagblatt
Bahnhofstr. 39
5001 Aarau
Tel: (64) 266161
Telex: 981146

Basler Zeitung
Hochbergerstr. 15
4002 Basel
Tel: (61) 661111
Telex: 962140

Der Zürichbieter
Poststr. 2
8303 Bassersdorf
Telex: 55202

La Regione
Via Ghiringhelli 9
6500 Bellinzona
Tel: (92) 254141
Fax: (92) 261056

Berner Tagwacht
Monbijoustr. 61
3001 Berne
Tel: (92) 254141
Fax: (92) 261056

Berner Zeitune
Nordring
Postfach 1147
3001 Berne
Tel: (31) 414646
Telex: 233888

Bieler Tagblatt/Seeländer Bote
Freiestr. 9-13
2501 Bienne
Telex: 934568

Bündner Tagblatt
Hartbertstr. 7
7001 Chur
Tel: (81) 221423
Fax: (81) 222309
Telex: 851310

Le Démocrate
6 route de Courroux
2800 Delémont
Tel: (66) 221751
Fax: (66) 226821

La Suisse
15 rue des Savoises
1211 Geneva 11
Tel: (22) 7085050
Telex: 427666

Der Rheintaler
Auerstr. 17
9435 Heerbrugg
Tel: (71) 723503
Fax: (71) 723527

Luzerner Neuste Nachrichten
Zürichstr. 5
6002 Lucerne
Tel: (41) 391515
Telex: 868133

St Galler Tagblatt
Fürstenlandstr. 122
9001 St Gallen
Tel: (71) 297711
Telex: 77537

Solothurner Zeitung
Postfach 748
4501 Solothurn
Tel: (65) 247247

Berner Oberländer
Seestr. 42
3700 Spiez
Tel: (33) 544444
Fax: (33) 547894

Zürcher Oberländer
8620 Wetzikon
Tel: (1) 9333333
Telex: 875547
Fax: (1) 9323232

Der Landbote
Garnmarkt 1
8401 Winterthur
Tel: (52) 2134051
Fax: (52) 2127518
Telex: 896417

Blick
Dufourstr. 23
8021 Zürich
Tel: (1) 2596262
Telex: 817300

PERIODICALS

Die Alpen
Thorackerstr. 3
3074 Muri
Tel: (031) 9515787
Fax: (031) 9511570

Bilanz
Edenstr. 20
8021 Zürich
Tel: (1) 2077221
Fax: (1) 2015916
Telex: 816765

Finanz und Wirtschaft
Weberstr. 8-10
Postfach 913
8021 Zürich
Tel: (1) 2411134
Fax: (1) 2911490
Telex: 812386

L'Hebdo
3 Pont Bessieres
1005 Lausanne
Tel: (21) 203611
Fax: (21) 203617

Management Zeitschrift: Journal for Management and Industrial Engineering
Zürichbergstr/Revue Suisse pour l'organisation industrielle
Zürichbergstr. 18
8028 Zürich
Tel: (1) 2610800
Fax: (1) 2612468
Telex: 815065

NEWS AGENCIES

Schweizerische Depeschenagentur AG (SDA)
Swiss News Agenciy
Länggassstr. 7
3012 Berne
Tel: (31) 243333
Fax: (31) 238538
Telex: 911500

Agence France-Presse (AFP)
Bureau C-14
Palais des NAtionas
1211 Geneva 10
Tel: (22) 7321120
Fax: (22) 734488292
Telex: 22210

Inter Press Service (IPS)
Bureau C504
Palais des Nations
1211 Geneva 10
Tel: (22) 7346011
Telex: 22442
Fax: (22) 7342430

DIRECTORIES AND YEARBOOKS

Swiss Financial Yearbook
Elvetica Edizioni SA
PO Box 134
6834 Morbio
Tel: (91) 43-50-56
Fax: (91) 43-76-05

Trade Associations listing
Schwabe & Co. AG Verlag
PO Box 254
4132 Muttenz
Tel: (61) 461-27-61
Fax: (61) 461-25-00

STOCK EXCHANGES

Basel Stock Exchange
Börsenkammer des Kantons Basel-Stadt
Aeschenplatz 7
4002 Basel
Tel: (61) 2720555
Telex: 962524
Fax: (61) 2720626

Berne Stock Exchange
Berner Börsenverein
Aarbergergasse 36
3011 Berne
Tel: (31) 224042
Fax: (31) 225309

Bourse Suisse de Commerce
Bahnhofquai 7
8023 Zürich
Tel: (1) 2112870
Fax: (1) 2112872

INTERNET ADDRESSES

Usenet group(s):
soc.culture.swiss

Swiss FirmIndex Online
http://www.firmnet.ch/firmindex

Swiss Info
http://www.swissinfo.ch/index_e.html

Geneva Guide International
http://is.eunet.ch/GenevaGuide/

Swiss Home
http://www.swisshome.ch/swisshome/

Welcome to Switzerland
http://heiwww.unige.ch:80/switzerland/

Swiss Phone Directory
http://etb.eunet.ch/cgi

Syria

Syrian Arab Republic

Economy

Overview

Syria's developing state-run economy grew rapidly in the 1970s but for the past decade growth has been hampered by the heavy burdens of defense expenditure, shortages in foreign exchange, adverse climatic conditions, and inefficient state enterprises. Although it continues to rely heavily on agriculture and on light manufacturing industries, the discovery of large oil reserves in the mid-1980s means petroleum exports now play a key role in the economy. In the past three years the economy has been boosted by substantial foreign aid resulting from its participation against Iraq in the Gulf War, more favorable weather conditions, and some degree of economic deregulation.

Trade

Syria's ongoing transition to a market economy has resulted in an increase in the total value of foreign trade. Developed countries are the primary markets for its exports, and it buys more than half its imports from the same sources. EU countries are the largest source of both its imports and exports, followed by the former countries of the Soviet Union, Iran, and Libya. Syria's traditional trade deficit narrowed somewhat in the past decade but has once again begun to widen due to rising import levels resulting from import liberalization measures, greater private sector investment, and increased availability of foreign exchange.

Sectors

Agriculture Syria has traditionally been an agricultural country and this remains the most important sector of its economy, accounting for 27 percent of GDP and engaging more than 35 percent of the population. In the past few years the agricultural sector has recovered from serious drought and it has once again become the economy's leading growth area. Although the government has recognized the need to undertake major land irrigation schemes, progress to date has been slow due to high costs and a declining water supply. Principal crops include wheat, barley, cotton, tobacco, and various fruits and vegetables.

Industry This mainly state-run sector experienced rapid growth in the 1960s, displacing agriculture as the main generator of wealth. In recent years, however, most industries have suffered from declining output. Petroleum has become the leading industry since the discovery of large oil reserves; oil production has increased fourfold in the past decade. Textiles make up the largest manufacturing subsector, and the development of a thriving phosphate production sector has helped to diversify Syria's industrial base.

Trends

Syria's economy is slowly changing in response to implementation of reforms leading to a market system; its growing private sector could play an important role in the future if the government continues with economic reforms already underway. The country continues to face serious difficulties such as rising unemployment, declining water supplies, and inefficiency in state-run industries. Syria's future economic fortunes still largely depend on continued foreign aid, favorable climatic conditions, and a rise in international oil prices, although continued diversification should reduce this reliance in the future. The ongoing liberalization of its economy should lead to greater opportunities for foreign enterprises to sell to the domestic market.

At a Glance

THE COUNTRY

Location Syria is situated in southwest Asia, at the eastern end of the Mediterranean Sea.

Terrain Syria's geography ranges from the narrow coastal plain along the Mediterranean shore to the mountain regions.

Climate The climate varies from the Mediterranean type in the west to extremely arid desert conditions in the east. Rainfall averages about 75 cm (30 in) on the coast, 125 cm (50 in) in some mountain areas, and less than 25 cm (10 in) in the eastern 60 percent of the country. In dry years, rainfall may be reduced by half.

THE PEOPLE

Population 14,300,000
Ethnic composition
Arabs 90%
Kurds 9%
Armenians Turkomans, Circassians, Assyrains, and Jews make up the balance.
Religious composition
Sunni Muslims 74%
Alawis 12%
Christians.. 10%
Druze 3%
There are also a small number of Jews, and other Muslim sects.

Languages spoken Arabic is the official language, although English and French are usually understood. Some other common languages include Armenian and Kurdish.

Education and literacy Literacy: 78% males, 51% females. Education is compulsory for six years.

Labor force
Total:... 3,700,000
By occupation: services (including government) 36%, agriculture 32%, industry and commerce 32%.

COUNTRY FACTS

Political and legal Ruled by the People's Council, a 173-member legislature, and the president. The judicial system is a combination of Ottoman, French, and Islamic laws.

Telephone Telecommunications services are available for local and international calls. Telegraph service is available. International country code [963], city code: Damascus (11).

Transportation The Syrian national railway system, growing road systems (although inadequate), ports, and airlines are available.

Environment The coastal plain is highly cultivated and the little wild growth found is mainly of the brushwood type. Wildlife includes common animals to the eastern Mediterranean region, together with typical desert species. Thick forest has been drastically reduced. Current issues: much of Syria's natural vegetation has been depleted by farming, livestock grazing, and cutting of trees for firewood and construction.

Media All communications facilities are owned and operated by the government. The Syrian Broadcasting Service transmits on medium wave and shortwave, and broadcasts in Arabic and 10 foreign languages. Syrian Arab TV has two stations.

Health Intestinal and respiratory diseases associated with poor living conditions are still common today, particularly in rural areas. Average life expectancy is 67 years.

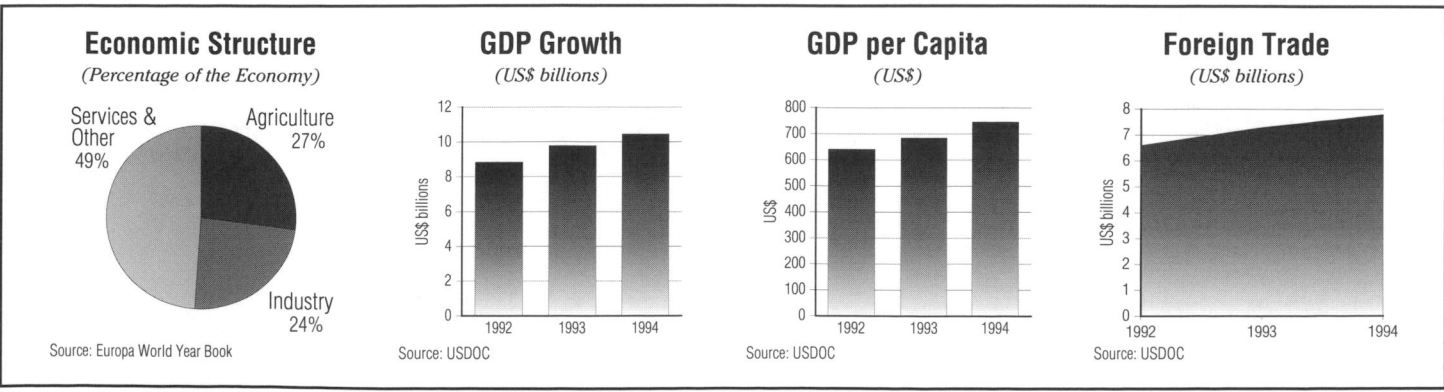

Economic Structure
(Percentage of the Economy)
Services & Other 49%
Agriculture 27%
Industry 24%
Source: Europa World Year Book

GDP Growth
(US$ billions)
Source: USDOC

GDP per Capita
(US$)
Source: USDOC

Foreign Trade
(US$ billions)
Source: USDOC

Business Travel

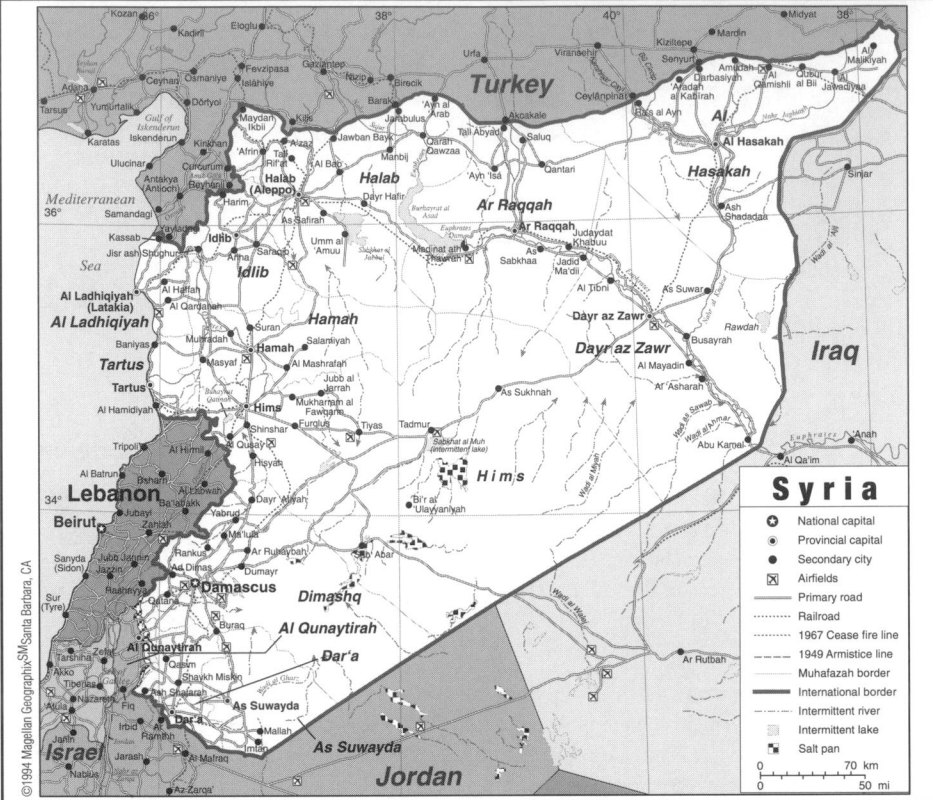

COMMUNICATIONS

Telephone Telephone service is very good within Syria, although limited in some remote areas. Use the telephone office on Avenue An-Nasa or hotels for international and long distance calls. It may take a couple of hours to provide long distance calls at the telephone office. Public telephones are in hotels and telephone offices. Pay phones require a deposit of 25 piastres for a dial tone.

Fax Telex, fax, and telegram services are available, expensive, and time consuming to send. It can take up to a couple of hours for connections; major hotels and post offices may be faster.

Post office Stamps can be purchased at post offices and major hotels.

BEST TRAVEL BOOKS

Discovery Guide to Syria, David Claymore, 224 pages, illustrated. Published by Immel Publishing UK, State Mutual Books and Periodicals.

Syria: A Travel Survival Kit, Damien Simonis. Illustrated, 272 pages. Lonely Planet Publications.

Culture Shock, A Guide to Customs and Etiquette, Syria.

Do's and Taboo's Around the World. The Bestselling Guide to International Behavior. Edited by Roger Axtell, compiled by the Parker Pen Company. The ultimate guide to international behavior, now completely updated and expanded. Helpful, fun to read!

Multinational Travel Companion Executive. Travel tips worldwide. Easy to read, clear, concise. Strand Publishing Company, Inc.

Saudi Arabia. Hippocrene Companion Guide by Gene Lindsey. A complete guide to traveling through Saudi Arabia and surrounding countries. Informative and interesting. 369 pages, 30 pages on Syria.

USEFUL TELEPHONE NUMBERS

If you are calling from outside Syria, you will need to add the country code [963] and any other international dialing requirements from within your country.

- Operator Information 95, 97
- Railways 215815
- Roads 3143, 555406
- Police 93
- Radio/TV .... (11) 720700
- Railway .... (11) 215815
- Shipping .... (11) 226350
- Chamber of Commerce .... (11) 331127
- Ministry of Foreign Affairs .... (11) 411922
- Ambulance 90
- Fire 91
- Tourist Police .... (11) 447160, 552741

Hotels, Damascus

- International de Damas .... (11) 212400
- Meridien .... (11) 718730
- Sheraton .... (11) 229300
- Sultan .... (11) 225768

Restaurants, Damascus

- Ali Baba .... (11) 119881
- Toit de Damas .... (11) 718730

Credit Card Information

Lost or stolen credit cards (call collect to the US, regardless of which country the card was issued in).

- Amex .... [1] (919) 333-3211
- Diner's Club .... [1] (303) 799-1504
- MasterCard .... [1] (314) 275-6690
- Visa .... [1] (410) 581-7931

Travelogue

WORKWEEK

Offices Saturday-Thursday 9:00 am to 2:00 pm and 4:00 pm to 7:00 pm.

Banks Saturday-Thursday 8:00 am to 2:30 pm.

Government Saturday-Thursday, 8:00 am to 2:30 pm.

Retail Saturday-Thursday 9:00 a.m. to 2:00 pm and 4:00 pm to 7:00 pm.

HOLIDAYS 1996

Holidays 1996
January 1 New Year's Day
February 20-22 Eid Al-Fitr**
Mar 8 Revolution Day
April 7 Western Easter
April 17 Independence Day
April 30-May 3 Eid Al-Adha**
May 1 Labor Day
May 6 Martyr Day
May 18 Moslem New Year**
July 28 Prophet's Birthday
October 6 Tishreen War
December 25 Christmas Day
Muslim holidays, particularly Eid-al-Fitr, Eid al-Adha, the birth of Mohammad, and Ashura are observed on dates that vary according to the lunar calendar.

VISA AND PASSPORT

A valid passport and a visa are required for travel to Syria. Consult with your embassy or consulate for changes and exceptions. Business travelers must carry a letter from their company indicating purpose of the visit and letter of invitation from their sponsor. Visas are not issued if there is proof you have been or will be going to Israel. All valuables must be registered upon arrival. Onward tickets, valid travel documents, and sufficient funds are required by all visitors. Entry to Syria is restricted from travelers coming from Israel, South Korea, and Chinese residents of Taiwan.

DEPARTURE FORMALITIES

All valuables that were not registered upon arrival may be confiscated. Export of foreign currency is limited to the amount declared upon arrival. Syrian pounds will not be exchanged for convertible currency so do not purchase more currency than you expect to spend while visiting Syria.

IMMUNIZATION

Travelers arriving from infected areas need yellow fever vaccination certificates. Malaria suppressants are recommended. AIDS certification for short-term visitors is not yet required. Peel fruits and vegetables, avoid raw fish and meat, and do not drink unpasteurized milk while in Syria. Heat exhaustion is a common complaint among visitors as is dehydration; drink plenty of bottled water only.

TIPPING

Taxis: 10 percent. Hotels, restaurants: 10 percent is usually added to bill, but additional 10 percent to waiting staff is appreciated. Barbers and beauticians: 10 percent.

CRIME

Smuggling and corruption run rampant. Take intelligent safety precautions in Syria by avoid leaving valuables within sight in automobiles and keeping a close watch on personal belongings. If involved in an automobile accident, be sure to notify your embassy or the police.

INFRASTRUCTURE

An adequate system of roads and railways serves Syria, but public transportation is inefficient. Buses are the most common form of public transport; service taxis that run along set routes operate in the larger cities and travel between cities.

NATIONAL TOURIST OFFICE

Ministry of Tourism
Rue Victoria
Damascus
Tel: (11) 215916
Telex: 411672

Foreign Trade

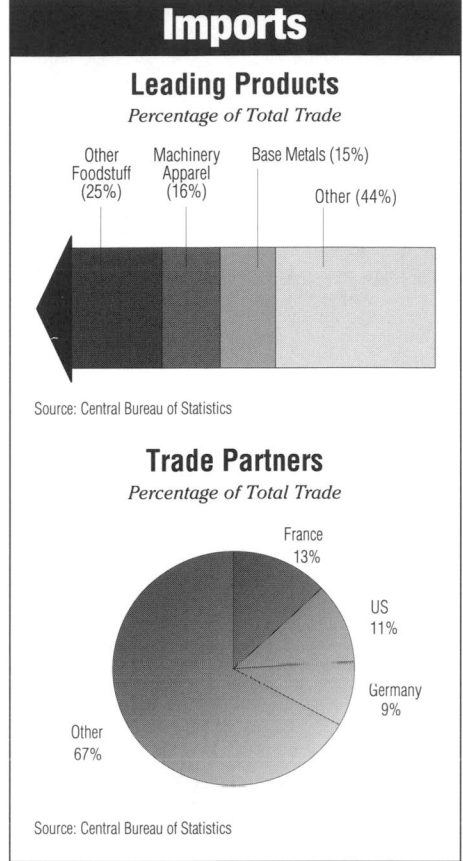

Imports

Leading Products
Percentage of Total Trade

Other Foodstuff (25%)
Machinery Apparel (16%)
Base Metals (15%)
Other (44%)

Source: Central Bureau of Statistics

Trade Partners
Percentage of Total Trade

France 13%
US 11%
Germany 9%
Other 67%

Source: Central Bureau of Statistics

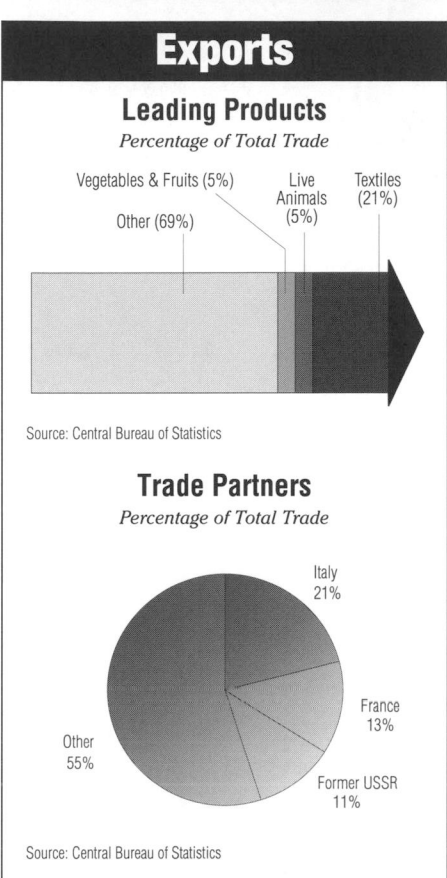

Exports

Leading Products
Percentage of Total Trade

Vegetables & Fruits (5%)
Other (69%)
Live Animals (5%)
Textiles (21%)

Source: Central Bureau of Statistics

Trade Partners
Percentage of Total Trade

Italy 21%
France 13%
Former USSR 11%
Other 55%

Source: Central Bureau of Statistics

Opportunities

FOR IMPORTING TO SYRIA
- electrical power generation equipment
- computers, peripherals, and software
- telecommunications equipment
- food processing equipment
- silo storage facilities

FOR EXPORTING FROM SYRIA
- cereals
- petroleum and products
- synthetic fabrics

GROWTH SECTORS
- cereals and grains
- computers
- crude oil
- vegetables and fruits

Trade News

RULES AND REGULATIONS
- **Government monopolies** The government maintains a monopoly on the importation of strategic goods such as wheat and flour.
- **Regulatory agency** The Ministry of Economy and Foreign Trade is responsible for import licensing.
- **Licensing** Although any commodity not produced locally can be imported, actual licensing is governed by a number of considerations; raw materials and equipment that promote industrial and agricultural development tend to receive favorable consideration, whereas luxury consumer items are discouraged.
- **Free trade zones** Free trade zones are located in Damascus, Aleppo, and in the ports of Latakia and Tartus. There is also a free zone near the border town of Dar'a, which is a joint venture between Syria and Jordan.

Legal

Legal System

Syria's legal system is based partly on French law and partly on Syrian statutes. Shari'ah courts apply Islamic law in cases involving personal status. The Druzes and non-Muslim communities have their own religious courts.

Intellectual Property Rights

Patents Patents are issued for 15-year terms, provided the invention has been utilized within two years after the patent was granted.

Trademarks Syria has trademark protection, and local courts are likely to give plaintiffs fair hearings, but any financial awards are usually in Syrian pounds.

Copyrights There is very little copyright protection in Syria.

Trade secrets There is no compulsory licensing provision, but international rights might be recognized by treaty.

Business Registration

Government approval is required for all business ventures or investments. All investment applications must also be approved through the Higher Council for Investment.

Contracts and Dispute Resolution

All contracts with Syrian businesses should be written. Magistrates determine whether a dispute should be sent to trial.

Labor

Syrian law allows workers to form trade unions. Strikes are not prohibited, except in the agricultural sector, but in practice they are effectively discouraged. In the public sector, unions do not normally bargain collectively on wage issues, but union representatives participate with employers to establish wages.

Legal Matters

LEGAL BRIEFS
- **Labor disputes** Labor-management relations are generally amicable, and most labor disputes are settled informally.
- **Child labor** Children under age 12 are not permitted to work, and parental permission is required for children under age 16. All children are forbidden to work at night.
- **Minimum wage** There is no nationally regulated minimum wage for permanent employees.
- **International Agreements** Syria is a member of CISG, Paris Convention for the Protection of Industrial Property; New York Convention on the Recognition and Enforcement of Foreign Arbitral Awards.

LEGAL CONTACTS

Law Offices of Dr. Moustafa al-Sayed
We Bahsa Str.
POB 11317
Damascus
Tel: (11) 221 9177 Fax: (11) 224 1251

Law Offices of Arab consultants
Port Said Street-Nahhas Building
5th Floor
POB 254
Damascus
Tel: (11) 2217577 Fax: (11) 33 12 581

Ghazi S. Ghazzi
Bureau of Legal Services
Tivi & Silo Building
69 Salhie Street
POB 4238
Damascus
Tel: (11) 229798 Fax: (11) 229798

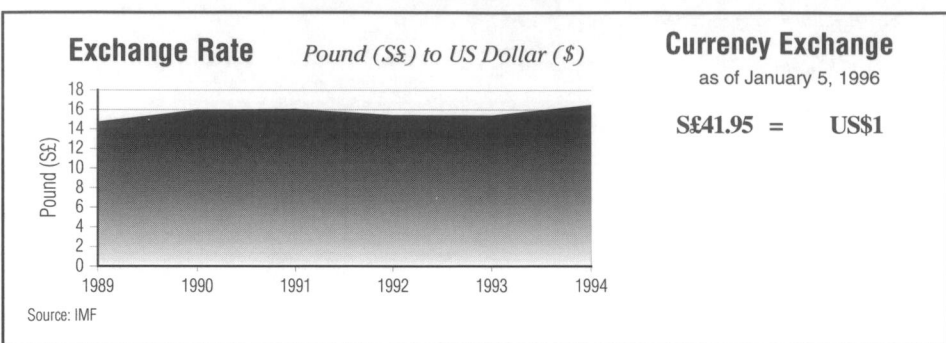

Exchange Rate — *Pound (S£) to US Dollar ($)*

Pound (S£): 18, 16, 14, 12, 10, 8, 6, 4, 2, 0

1989 1990 1991 1992 1993 1994

Source: IMF

Currency Exchange

as of January 5, 1996

S£41.95 = US$1

Money Matters

BITS AND PIECES

- **Banking system** The banking system is controlled by the government, and includes the five banks and the central bank listed below.
- **Finance** Syrian traders usually finance imports from their own resources or their own credit. Documentary transactions for imports must be through a letter of credit at the Commercial Bank.
- **Payment terms** Syrian importers may require a "free of payment" or "180-day credit facilities" clause to be added to pro forma invoices and bills of lading. The importer will then pay through an offshore bank, cash in advance, or through letter of credit; the bill of lading is then sent to the Commercial Bank of Syria. Exporters should avoid delayed payment or "cash against documents" mechanisms, since the Commercial Bank of Syria does not have authority to release funds under these clauses, and the importer would be able to walk away from the contract even after shipment has been made. Exporters are advised to sell goods under "cash in advance" or "confirmed irrevocable letters of credit" unless a good rapport with the importer has been established beforehand.
- **Eximbank** Eximbank financing and insurance is unavailable. Also, the World Bank will not fund projects in Syria.
- **Nonresident accounts** Nonresident Syrian pound accounts may be credited with the proceeds of foreign currencies sold to the Commercial Bank. These accounts may be used for payments to exporters for exports to the country of the account holder, and for expenses within Syria. Nonresidents may also open accounts in convertible foreign currencies.
- **Reconversion of currency** Nonresidents leaving the country may not reconvert Syrian currency into foreign exchange.

Currency

The currency of Syria is the Syrian pound, S£, which is divided into 100 piastres.

Foreign Exchange

The pound is pegged to the US dollar. The exchange rate system consists of four rates: the official rate, which applies to government and official transactions; the rate in neighboring countries, which is determined by the Central Bank, and applies to all public and private capital inflows and receipts from tourists; the airline rate, which applies to purchases of airline tickets by nonresidents; and the promotion rate, which is used only for payments of allowances to certain residents overseas.

Capital Transfers

All inward and outward capital transfers by both the public and private sectors take place at the rate in neighboring countries. The exportation of capital requires the approval of the Exchange Office, as does most borrowing abroad. Capital may be repatriated after five years from the project completion date. Expatriates are permitted to transfer abroad 50 percent of their salaries, and 100 percent of severance pay.

Interest rates are fixed by law. Most rates have not changed in the last several years, even though current real interest rates are negative, which exerts additional inflationary pressures in the economy.

Investment Incentives

Companies that receive licenses under the new investment law are accorded duty free privileges for the import of capital goods and materials necessary for the project, including vehicles. They are also entitled to a tax holiday for the first five years of operation.

Prospects for Syrian private sector investment and imports continue to improve, spurred by economic reforms, including an investment encouragement law. Recent liberalization actions of the Syrian government permit private exporters to retain some foreign exchange export earnings to finance permitted imports for manufacturing inputs, as well as other listed products.

Investment Restrictions

All applications for investment must be vetoed through the Higher Council for Investment. Although no definitive criteria for approving investment is spelled out in the law, the council is more likely to approve a project if it maximizes the use of local resources; creates jobs; boosts exports; utilizes advanced technologies; or advances the government's development plans. In addition, there are several disincentives to investment. Foreign firms have a difficult time receiving timely and complete recovery of normal business and exploration costs incurred, and negotiations to resolve disputed costs can be lengthy. The government requires export licenses to be obtained for every single item imported, and then re-exported, regardless of value. Finally, foreign companies must obtain temporary permits from the government for each item of equipment intended for temporary use and subsequent re-export, and these can be difficult to obtain.

BANKS

Agricultural Bank
BP 5325
Rue Euphrates
Damascus

Central Bank of Syria
POB 2254
Altajrida al-Mughrabia Sq.
Damascus
Tel: (11) 224800
Telex: 11007

Commercial Bank of Syria
BP 933
Place Yousuf al-Azmeh
Damascus
Tel: (11) 218890
Telex: 411002

Industrial Bank
BP 7578
29 Rue May Damascus
Damascus
Tel: (11) 228200

Popular Credit Bank
BP 2841
Rue Fardoss
Dar al-Mohandessin Blvd.
6th Floor
Damascus
Tel: (11) 114260

Real Estate Bank
BP 2337
Rue al-Furat
Damascus
Tel: (11) 218602
Telex: 419171

Overview

Syria's worth as a market has fluctuated with its political alliances, which have changed more swiftly than the country's sand dune configurations. Since 1991, however, Syria has slowly been edging up to a market system. Private ventures are usually small and family owned; when they are beneficial to its needs, the government is fond of forming joint ventures with them (sometimes forcefully).

Distribution and Agencies

Agents and distributors representing international firms have, until recently, been able to service their clientele from their central offices. The population has recently grown; and the government's economic reform program has caused the private sector to keep pace with the growing population. While some companies prefer to continue their former practices, many have contracted sub-agents.

Syrian businesses often order directly from overseas firms without using an agent or distributor. However, developing a long-term presence usually requires an agent or distributor who can promote products, follow leads, and offer customer service. Many Syrian businessmen prefer to keep their agent relationships private in order to avoid paying income taxes; Syrian agents therefore usually request agreements not be disclosed to the government.

Selling Techniques and Advertising

With the expansion of product availability, the Syrian consumer market has become increasingly competitive. Advertising, both on television and in newspapers, has become more widely used, and several private advertising and public relations firms have been opened. Employing desktop publishing techniques, they have raised the quality of advertising production standards considerably. Newspapers charge foreigners top rates, as do television programmers. The government-controlled Arab Institution for Advertising supervises all advertising. The trade press is negligible, and there are no radio stations in Syria. Trade shows are a growing forum; recent events have included exhibitions on computer and electronic equipment. Shows on hotel and tourism equipment, and construction equipment are planned in advance.

Marketing in Syria

MARKETING TIPS

- **Direct marketing**   Direct marketing does not exist nor have any companies been opened to do this type of marketing.
- **Joint ventures**   Syrian businesspeople are very open to joint ventures projects.
- **Best price**   Offering your best price from the start is wise as Syrians are good at bargaining deals that can be time consuming. To avoid lengthy negotiations, offer your best price from the start.
- **Trade events**   Trade shows and the Syrian government's annual International Fair in August are good places to meet prospective clients in Syria.
- **Customer service**   Offering responsive, reliable customer service can establish strong reputations which will lead to future sales. Here again, is where agents or distributors can provide a significant edge.
- **Pricing**   Syrian consumers are heavily price conscious and have been known to purchase mediocre quality goods, simply because they carried the best price.
- **Government purchases**   Government agencies follow a practice called "breaking the price." After financial tender envelopes are opened, bidders are invited to participate in a meeting attended by the purchasing agency and all tenderers at which each bidder is invited to revise his price downward. Such meetings can become an open auction, and the company with the lowest original bid sometimes does not win the contract.
- **Business environment**   Syria's business environment is not friendly; having integrity from the start is a good reputation builder and builds confidence with the markets you are aiming for.

Business Culture

Greetings and Courtesies

Syrians are friendly, talkative, and hospitable people, though they can sometimes be cautious when it comes to Westerners, because the government policy toward the West often changes. The standard greeting is the handshake, which is acceptable when meeting men and women. However, a man should let a woman initiate a handshake. If she does not, smile and nod slightly. Sometimes Syrians will greet people with a warm embrace, and greetings are often accompanied by questions about one's health or family. If a person has a title, be sure to use it.

Business Ethic and Framework

People, family ties, and personal relationships are placed above business. Fate is also an important part of Syrian culture. One does the best one can; but the outcome is ultimately in the hands of God. Class distinctions often determine a person's opportunities and influence their attitude toward getting ahead in life.

Meetings and Decision Making

Be on time, but expect the person you're meeting to be late. It's possible that when you arrive your Syrian associate will be with other people. Syrians commonly discuss business with several friends and associates at the same time. Generally, business will not be addressed until a fair amount of time is taken up with polite, social small talk. Decisions are made slowly, so don't push for faster action or impose a deadline.

Women

Many Syrian women are well-educated, but the opportunities open to them are limited to fields such as teaching and social services. Foreign women should be prepared for the restrictions this conservative Muslim society places on women. Behave with discretion at all times. Do not make prolonged, direct eye contact with Syrian men. Being professional, poised, and self-confident will help in business, but male colleagues may be taken more seriously and given more respect. In general, it is probably not wise to send a female to conduct business in Syria.

Cultural Cautions

DO'S

- Eat food with the right hand only. Use the right hand or both hands to give and receive things. Using the left hand alone is offensive.
- Syrians are very proud of their long history and rich culture. Demonstrating knowledge of and respect for these subjects will be very much appreciated.
- Accept all simple gestures of hospitality. If you must refuse such a gesture, be sure to give a polite explanation.

DON'TS

- Avoid conversation about local or national politics, and do not bring up the subject of Israel.
- Don't point the soles of your shoes at someone, and do not gesture at someone with your feet.
- Muslims are forbidden contact with dogs, and consider pictures of dogs improper. Do not give a Muslim child a toy dog or anything printed with images of dogs.

CUSTOMS

- Public displays of affection between men and women (even if married) are highly offensive.
- Standard attire is a conservative suit. Women should wear tasteful, very conservative clothing. Women should never wear a sleeveless dress or blouse.

OBSERVATIONS

- The Syrian government is an authoritarian socialist regime that is nationalistic, leery of the West, and anti-Israel. It is an active, powerful force in the day-to-day lives of Syrians, and the policies in effect when you travel to Syria will have a strong impact on the outcome of your visit.
- In Syria, business relationships are personal relationships. To establish a good business relationship, establish a personal relationship that demonstrates your good faith and honor.

GOVERNMENT AGENCIES

Ministry of Agriculture and Agrarian Reform
29 rue Ayar
Damascus
Tel: (11) 113613

Ministry of Communications
nr. Majlis ash-Sha'ab
Damascus
Telex: 411993

Ministry of Economy and Foreign Trade
Damascus
Tel: (11) 113513

Ministry of Electricity
Boite Postal 4900
41 rue al-Jamhourieh
Damascus
Tel: (11) 227981

Ministry of Finance
Boite Postal 13136
Rue Jule Jamal
Damascus
Tel: (11) 2239624

Ministry of Industry
Place Yousuf Ahmad
Damascus
Tel: (11) 115647

Ministry of Information
Ave. al-Mazzeh
Immeuble Dar al-Baath
Damascus
Tel: (11) 6664600

Ministry of Petroleum and Mineral Wealth
Rue Moutanabba
Damascus
Tel: (11) 116783

Ministry of Public Works and Water Resources
Rue Saadallah Jabri
Damascus

Ministry of Supply and Internal Trade
Opposite Majlis ash-Sha'ab
Damascus
Tel: (11) 720604

Ministry of Tourism
Rue Victoria
Damascus
Tel: (11) 2215916

Ministry of Transport
Boite Postal 134
Rue About Roumaneh
Damascus
Tel: (11) 336801

GOVERNMENT-RUN ORGANIZATIONS

General Organization for Phosphates and Mines
Boite Postal 228
Homs
Tel: (31) 20405

General Organization for the Textile Industries
Boite Postal 620
Rue Fardoss
Damascus
Tel: (11) 116200

CHAMBERS OF COMMERCE

Aleppo Chamber of Commerce
BP 1261
Rue al-Moutanabbi
Aleppo
Tel: (21) 38236
Telex: 331012

Federation of Syrian Chambers of Commerce
Boite Postal 5909
Rue Mousa ben Nousair
Damascus
Tel: (11) 3337344

Aleppo Chamber of Industry
Boite Postal 1859
Rue al-Moutanabbi
Aleppo
Tel: (21) 339812

Damascus Chamber of Commerce
Boite Postal 147
Rue Mou'awiah
Damascus
Tel: (11) 211339
Fax: (11) 2225874

Damascus Chamber of Industry
Boite Postal 1305
Rue Harika Mou'awiah
Damascus
Tel: (11) 2215042

Alkalamoun Chamber of Commerce
POB 2507
Bucher A. Mawla St
Damascus
Fax: 778394
Telex: 411061

Syrian Chamber of Commerce
POB 5909
Damascus
Tel: (11) 3377344

TRANSPORTATION

Damascus International Airport
Damascus
Tel: 963-430405

Latakia General Port Company
Latakia Baghdad Street
POB 220
Latakia, Syria

Syrian Railways
BP 182
Aleppo
Tel: (11) 213900
Fax: (11) 228480
Telex: 331009

Syrian General Authority for Maritime Transport
BP 730
2 rue Argentina
Damascus
Tel: (11) 226350
Telex: 411012

Ismail, A.M., Shipping Agency Ltd
BP 74
rue du Port
Tartous
Tel: (43) 20543

Sea Transport Agency
BP 78
Kamilieh Quarter
Harbour St
Latakia
Tel: (412) 33964
Telex: 510044

Syrian Navigation Company
BP 314
rue Baghdad
Latakia
Tel: (412) 316356
Telex: 451028

Syro-Jordanian Shipping Co.
BP 148
Rue Port Said
Latakia
Tel: (412) 316356
Telex: 451002

Tabalo, Muhammad Abd ar-Rahman
BP 66
Rue al-Mina Tartous
Tel: (43) 20906
Telex: 470008

RADIO AND TELEVISION

Directorate-General of Broadcasting and Television
Place Omayyad
Damascus
Tel: (11) 720700
Telex: 411138

ADVERTISING

Arab Advertising Organization
BP 2842-3034
28 rue Moutanabbi
Damascus
Tel: (11) 225219
Fax: (11) 220754
Telex: 411923

INTERNET ADDRESSES

Usenet group(s):
soc.culture.syria

Syria Online
http://ourworld.compuserve.com/homepages/syria.htm

Syria's WWW sites
http://www.iii.com/~hajeri/syria.html

Taiwan

Republic of China

Economy

Overview

A government dedicated to industrial development, a strong work ethic, and the successful promotion of foreign investment over the past four decades have helped Taiwan achieve one of the highest growth rates of any country in the world. A country with few natural resources, it initially concentrated on export-oriented, labor-intensive industries, and subsequently moved toward the promotion of high-tech industries. Continued growth in this area, however, requires skilled and expensive labor, and Taiwan's economy has slowed somewhat as companies relocate to lower-cost production centers offshore. Although Taiwan continues to grow, it is now doing so at a more moderate rate.

Trade

Taiwan has relied heavily on foreign trade as the driving force behind its rapid economic development. The US is its largest trading partner and the largest destination for its exports, followed by Japan, Hong Kong, and Germany. While the economy remains export-oriented, the growth of exports has slowed considerably in the past couple of years, and the government is now undertaking efforts to diversify its export markets and to identify new opportunities.

Sectors

Agriculture Taiwan has traditionally been an agricultural country, but production in recent years has not kept pace with growth in the industrial sector. Although only 25 percent of its land is suitable for agriculture, this sector is highly productive and Taiwan exports high quantities of pork, as well as vegetables, sugar, tea, and rice. Taiwan imports large amounts of wheat but imposes high tariffs on agricultural products which makes this a difficult market for importers. Taiwan has a large fishing fleet and exports a variety of products including tuna, eel, and shrimp; deep sea fisheries are playing an increasingly important role in this sector.

Industry Industry has been at the core of Taiwan's rapid economic development, and it continues to be central to the economy. Declining competitiveness has resulted in a shift away from labor-intensive industries to high-tech industries which are more capital intensive. The government is seeking now to increase its technological capacities in order to produce high value-added textile products.

Services Economic prosperity has resulted in a major expansion in services and this sector is continuing to grow. The government is increasingly looking to this sector to propel the economy as production moves offshore. Tourism has picked up in recent years, and should continue to grow in the near term.

Trends

Taiwan continues to broaden its economic base in order to reverse the slowing rate of growth it has seen in the past few years. State enterprises still account for 30 percent of its economy and the government has vowed to pursue a policy of privatization and to reduce its role in the economy. Although the government is moving toward a more liberalized economy, high import tariffs are still in place and certain agricultural imports remain banned. Future development is becoming increasingly dependent on domestic demand, and the impending accession to the GATT/WTO should result in better opportunities for foreigners to sell to this affluent market.

At a Glance

THE COUNTRY

Location Eastern Asia, off the southeastern coast of China, between Japan and the Philippines.
Terrain Eastern two-thirds mostly rugged mountains; flat to gently rolling plains in west.
Climate Tropical; marine; rainy season during southwest monsoon (June-August); cloudiness is extensive and persistent all year.

THE PEOPLE

Population 21,300,000
Ethnic composition
Taiwanese 84%
Mainland Chinese 14%
Aborigine... 2%
Religious composition
Mixture of Buddhist, Confucian, and Taoist 93%
Christian.. 4.5%
Other.. 2.5%
Languages spoken Mandarin Chinese (official), Taiwanese, Hakka dialects.
Education and literacy Taiwan enjoys one of the world's highest literacy rates because of its emphasis on education. About 91 percent of the population is literate. In 1985, about 25 percent of the population attended school, reflecting the relative youthfulness of the island's population. All children receive nine years of free and compulsory education.
Labor force
Total:...7,900,000
By occupation: industry and commerce 53%, services 22%, agriculture 15.6%, civil administration 7%, other 2.4%.

COUNTRY FACTS

Political and legal Multiparty democratic regime; some of the ruling party in Taipei claim to be the government of all China. Universal suffrage is allowed for those citizens 20 years of age or older.
Telephone Best developed telecommunication system in Asia outside of Japan. Domestic telephone rates are moderate; however, international calls dialed from Taiwan can be expensive. International country code: [886]. Selected city codes: Taipei (2), Kaohsiung (7).
Transportation Rental cars are available in Taiwan. There is an extensive bus system, inexpensive taxis, and comfortable passenger express trains to get around the island. Regularly scheduled international and domestic air service is also available.
Environment Water pollution from industrial emissions and untreated sewage is a significant problem in Taiwan. Drinking water is likely to be contaminated outside of the larger hotels and urban centers. Air pollution complicated by a high pollen count is another serious problem.
Media There are about 200 radio stations broadcasting in 14 languages and dialects. There are an estimated 8.6 million radios, 6.3 million television sets, and 232 daily newspapers in Taiwan. Viewpoints diverging from KMT positions are rarely seen thereof.
Health As a result of improved living conditions and mass vaccinations, significant strides have been made in controlling epidemic diseases. Hepatitis is a major problem and high pollen counts combined with air pollution can cause discomfort for people with asthma and allergies. Life expectancy is 75 years of age.

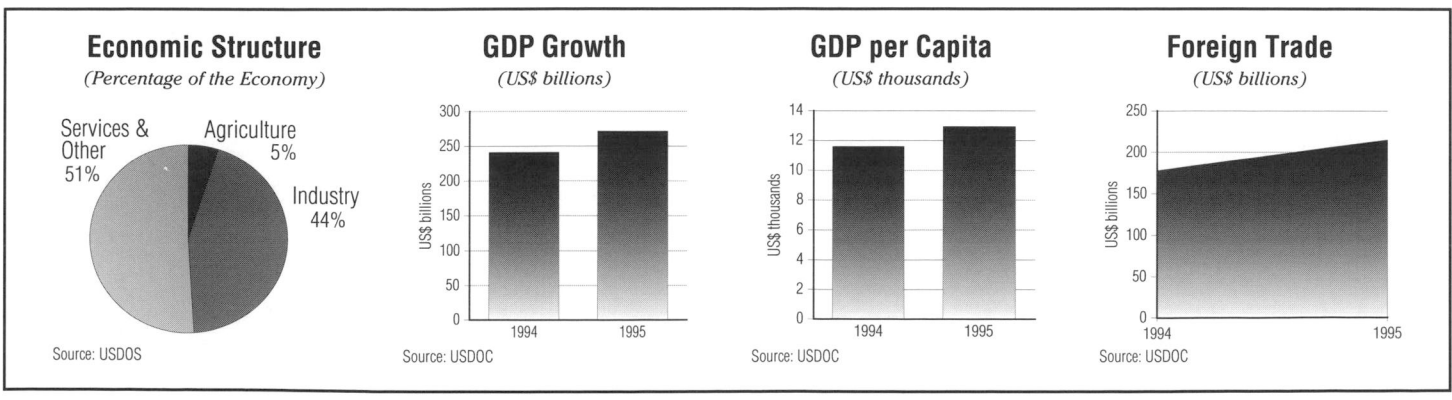

Economic Structure
(Percentage of the Economy)

Services & Other 51%
Agriculture 5%
Industry 44%

Source: USDOS

GDP Growth
(US$ billions)

Source: USDOC

GDP per Capita
(US$ thousands)

Source: USDOC

Foreign Trade
(US$ billions)

Source: USDOC

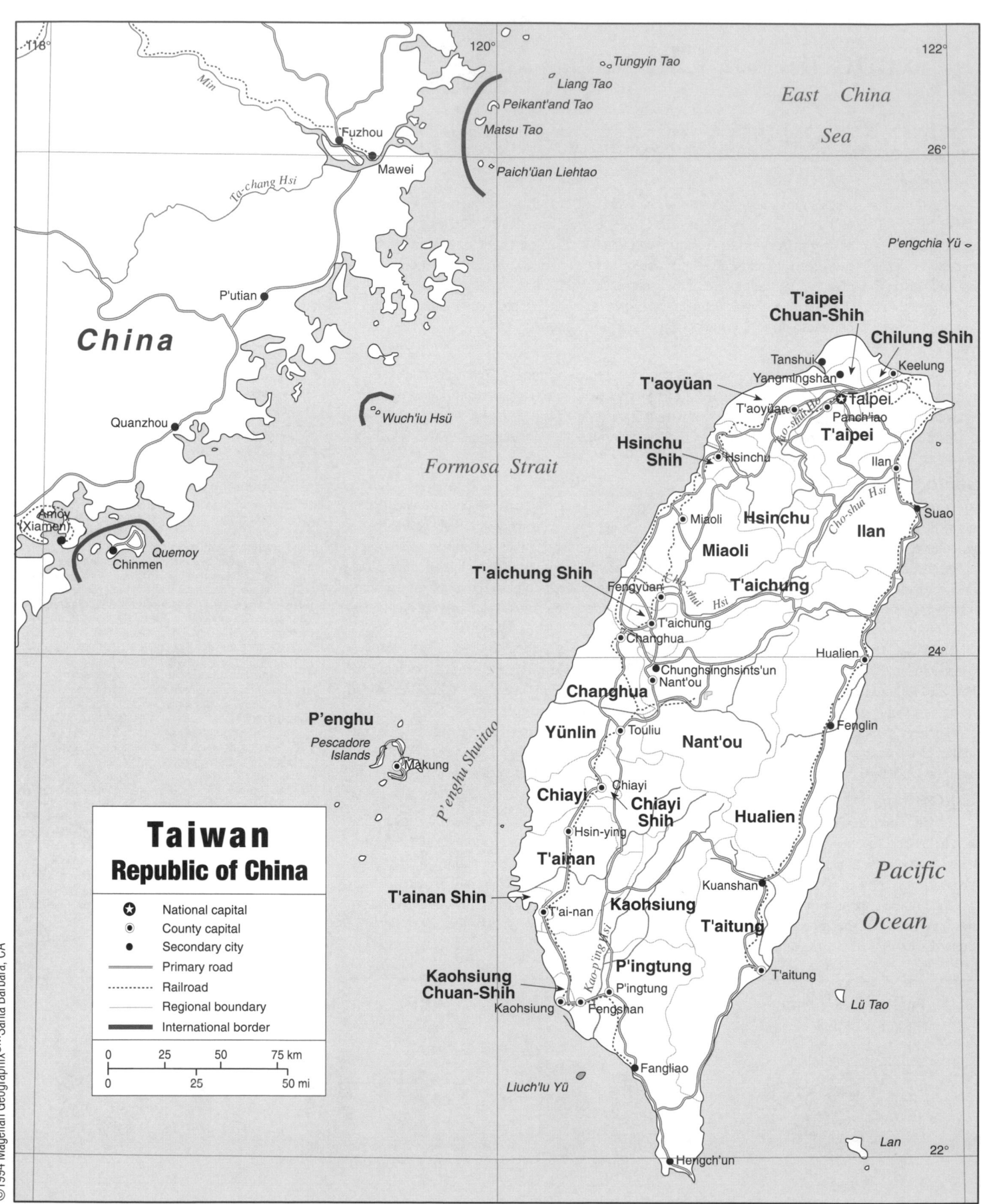

Taiwan
Republic of China

- ⊛ National capital
- ⊙ County capital
- ● Secondary city
- Primary road
- ⋯⋯ Railroad
- Regional boundary
- International border

| 0 | 25 | 50 | 75 km |
| 0 | 25 | | 50 mi |

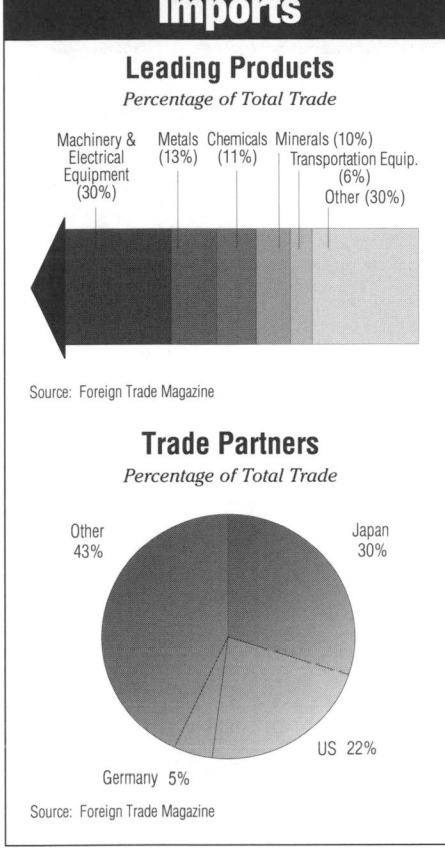

Imports

Leading Products
Percentage of Total Trade

Machinery & Electrical Equipment (30%)
Metals (13%)
Chemicals (11%)
Minerals (10%)
Transportation Equip. (6%)
Other (30%)

Source: Foreign Trade Magazine

Trade Partners
Percentage of Total Trade

Other 43%
Japan 30%
US 22%
Germany 5%

Source: Foreign Trade Magazine

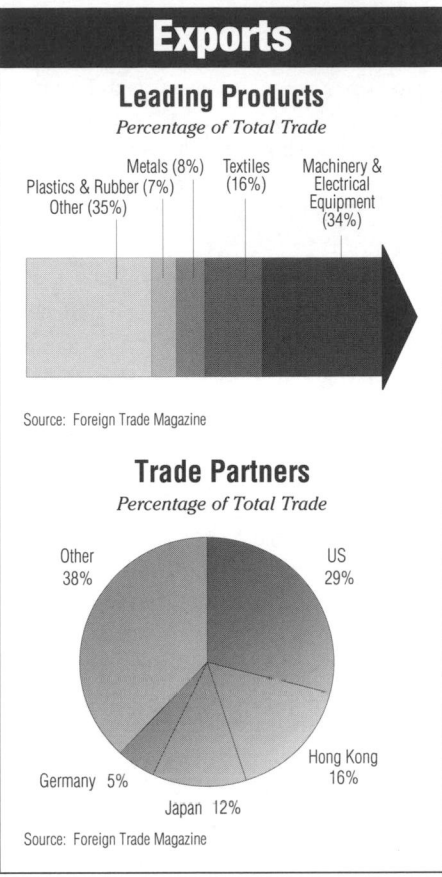

Exports

Leading Products
Percentage of Total Trade

Metals (8%)
Textiles (16%)
Machinery & Electrical Equipment (34%)
Plastics & Rubber (7%)
Other (35%)

Source: Foreign Trade Magazine

Trade Partners
Percentage of Total Trade

Other 38%
US 29%
Hong Kong 16%
Japan 12%
Germany 5%

Source: Foreign Trade Magazine

Opportunities

FOR IMPORTING TO TAIWAN

- air conditioning and refrigeration equipment
- automobiles, parts, and accessories
- building supplies
- computer hardware, software, and peripherals
- cosmetics and toiletries
- electronic components
- engineering plastics
- food and beverages, especially high-value items
- household consumer goods: color television sets, microwave ovens
- industrial organic chemicals
- industrial process controls
- integrated circuits
- laboratory scientific instruments
- medical equipment and supplies
- pollution control equipment
- semiconductor manufacturing equipment
- telecommunications equipment
- toys, games, and sporting goods

FOR EXPORTING FROM TAIWAN

- auto parts
- clocks and watches
- clothing
- computer products
- decorative giftware and housewares
- electronic components
- footwear
- furniture
- hand tools
- jewelry
- machine tools
- metalworking machinery
- musical instruments
- photographic equipment
- plastic and rubber products
- plastics processing machinery
- woodworking machinery
- toys, games, and sporting goods

GROWTH SECTORS

- avionics
- biotechnology
- financial services
- franchising
- machine tools
- real estate
- traditional products (sporting goods, plastic products, electronic goods) made of advanced composite materials

GOVERNMENT PROCUREMENT

- building construction
- electrical power generator
- distributors and transformers
- environmental protection goods and services
- petrochemical facilities and processing equipment
- road and railway construction and expansion
- telecommunication products

Trade News

RULES AND REGULATIONS

- **Regulation** The Board of Foreign Trade (BOFT), an agency of the Ministry of Economic Affairs (MOEA), administers imports and exports, issues licenses, conducts inspections, monitors the operation of registered importers and exporters, and classifies products. Taiwan is not a party to GATT, but in September 1992, a working party was set up to consider Taiwan's application for membership. Acceptance is expected, at which point Taiwan will be required to reduce its current import barriers.

- **Import channels** Products enter Taiwan through three channels: public trading agencies; end-users, such as manufacturers and public utilities; and private traders operating on commission. Most goods should be shipped. Air transport is reserved for products of high value relative to weight or goods that are urgently needed or are perishable.

- **Restrictions** Although Taiwan has already deregulated much of the import process, restrictions or special certifications do apply to certain products, including some agricultural goods, cosmetics, medical equipment, spirits, tobacco products, and toxic chemicals.

- **Tariffs, duties, and other charges** Tariffs on agricultural products and industrial goods are relatively high, despite announcements in 1988 to decrease rates over a four-year period. Tariff rates will be subject to GATT regulations when Taiwan becomes a party to the agreement. Harbor dues, commodity tax, and value-added tax may apply to imported goods. Some import machinery and capital equipment can be imported duty free if foreign investment approval (FIA) is obtained. Raw materials and other goods processed through an export processing zone may also be imported duty free.

- **Export controls** Traditionally a cumbersome process in Taiwan, exportation of goods has recently become more efficient—with the help of export processing zones. Although a number of goods remain tightly controlled, restrictions continue to be eased. Currently 70% of all products designated as permissible to export require no export license.

FREIGHT FORWARDERS

Air Tiger Express Co., Ltd.
133, Chung Hsiao E. Rd.
Sec. 5, Taipei
Tel: (2) 7643196, 7672145
Fax: (2) 7660224

Airlife Freight (Taiwan) Corp.
PO Box 55-617
Taipei
Tel: (2) 7647711/6
Fax: (2) 7606868

Allport Express Inc.
4/F., 391, Shin Yi Rd.
Sec. 4, Taipei
Tel: (2) 7582108, 7586499
Fax: (2) 7294105

American President Lines, Ltd.
5/F., 245 Tun Hwa S. Rd.
Sec. 1, Taipei
Tel: (2) 7764531
Fax: (2) 7772570

Anlun Transportation Co.
PO Box 63-142
Taichung
Tel: (4) 2956779
Fax: (4) 2963213

Barwil Agencies Inc.
11/F., 148 Sung Chiang Rd.
Taipei
Tel: (2) 5368222
Fax: (2) 5431972

Cargolux Airlines International SA
11/F., 131 Min Sheng E. Rd.
Sec. 3, Taipei
Tel: (2) 7139858
Telex: 21546 LAIFU

Overview

Taiwan is well-known as an industrial dynamo that has been racking up export success for more than 20 years. What is less well known is that the dynamo has produced a booming domestic consumer market. As an importer of foreign goods, Taiwan represents a huge market, and its affluent consumers can afford the high quality and relatively high prices of North American and European consumer goods. Taiwan is a land of small businesses and traders who import from all over the world—its economic strength derives not from its handful of giant conglomerates, but from the mulitudinous small-to-medium-sized firms who sell to its large population.

Distribution

Distribution policy varies depending on the type of product and the end-user, but all distribution channels are changing rapidly under the pressures of new demands from sophisticated Taiwan consumers, intensified competition from foreign and domestic rivals, and the introduction of new technology in distribution. Consumer distribution in Taiwan is dominated by a vast number of small, independent retailers who are served by a network of wholesalers, but large retail operations, such as hypermarkets and chains, are changing the face of Taiwan's retail market.

Agents, Distributors, and Partners

Finding a good local partner, whether an agent, distributor, or joint-venture partner, is essential to entering the Taiwan market. Taiwan firms prefer the partnering form of an agency relationship. Although some firms are willing to act as distributors, there is a fear that firms seeking distributors are not serious about the market and will not support their distributor. If a foreign firm insists on maintaining a distributor relationship, it had best be prepared to expend time and resources proving its dedication to this market. In general, foreign sellers are better served here by entering into the closer agency agreements. The Taipei Importers and Exporters Association has more than 100,000 members and is well equipped to help foreign exporters find an agent among its members.

Selling Techniques

The most important consideration for Taiwan industrial buyers is initial price. Taiwan businesspeople are notoriously short-term oriented and foreign firms are frequently frustrated by the fact that most Taiwan firms do not consider the life-cycle cost of a product when making a purchase. Most Taiwan firms will pay a higher price for a product only if they see an immediate payoff somehow, although this attitude is slowly changing. After price, the next most important considerations are quality of the goods and after-sales service. In contrast to the industrial market, Taiwan consumers in many cases prefer to pay more for goods they purchase. Conspicuous consumption is rampant in Taiwan society, and consumers are extremely brand-conscious. Franchising is new to Taiwan, but the concept suits the spirit of the people, and franchises other than fast-food outlets are fast appearing. Direct marketing is undeveloped; with the exception of a few multi-level marketing firms (Avon, for example), direct marketing methods such as mail-order, television sales, and telemarketing are still very rare. There are over 50 department stores, mostly concentrated in the large cities; the bulk of the floor space is rented out to concessionaires who pay rent and a fixed percentage of either their gross or net income. Specialty chain stores are only now beginning to appear, most of them foreign, and they are gaining market share rapidly. The Taiwan government often purchases directly from vendors, both local and foreign.

Advertising

There are more than two dozen advertising agencies that can help prepare and place advertisements but these agencies are mainly managers of campaigns developed by foreign agencies and rarely create material on their own. Taiwan is less reliant on TV and radio advertising than are Western nations. Newspapers are the favored medium for advertising, accounting for almost 40 percent of advertising spending. Television is the next largest, and growing, although television sets are not as common as in Japan or in Western countries. There are three TV networks, regulated by the Government Information Office, which supervises program and advertising content and allocates time for commercials. Other media are cinemas, outdoor advertising, and direct mail. Industrial trade fairs are effective for product promotions, but are meaningful only if the show includes the firm's product category.

Service and Customer Support

Taiwan buyers, both industrial and consumer, expect a very high level of after sales service and support, and they usually look to their immediate seller, and ultimately to the foreign firm's agent or distributor, to get it. As such, foreign sellers in this market must be prepared to provide fast, reliable, and efficient service, including technical training and delivery of spare parts.

Marketing in Taiwan

MARKETING TIPS

- **Distribution channels** Taiwan agents and distributors strongly prefer a joint venture or full partnership relationship.
- **Special competitive factors** Consumers are extremely brand-conscious.
- **Unfamiliar sales techniques** Franchising is new to Taiwan and direct marketing is extremely rare.
- **Product promotion** Participation in major trade shows and advertising in Taiwan trade journals and industry newspapers is an important preliminary to sales visits.

AD AGENCIES

ARZ International Co., Ltd.
2/F., 5, Alley 1, Lane 61
Ruei An St.
Taipei
Tel: (2) 7849111
Fax: (2) 7554022, 7556840

Ball Partnership Agency, Ltd.
10/F., 85 Jen Ai Rd.
Sec. 4, Taipei
Tel: (2) 7751950, 7417934
Fax: (2) 7417934

Bozell/CCAA
4/F., No. 26, Nanking E. Rd.
Sec. 3, Taipei
Tel: (2) 5063101
Fax: (2) 5070060

Brain Advertising Co., Ltd.
5-7/F., 208 Nanking E. Rd.
Sec. 3, Taipei
Tel: (2) 7413131
Fax: (2) 7721579

BSB Taiwan Company Limited
6/F., Chant Bldg., 120 Chien Kou N. Rd.
Sec. 2, Taipei
Tel: (2) 5055305
Fax: (2) 5055332

DDB Needham Worldwide Inc.
4/F., Quantas House, #1 Lin Shen S. Rd.
Taipei
Tel: (2) 3951995
Fax: (2) 3951998

Denstu Inc.-Taipei
11/F., 167 Tun Hua N. Rd.
Taipei
Tel: (2) 7191911
Fax: (2) 7120439

Dentsu, Young & Rubicam/Taipei
6/F., 146 Sung Chiang Rd.
Taipei
Tel: (2) 5219322
Fax: (2) 5219249

Hwa Wei & Grey Advertising Co.
12/F., 180 Nanking E. Rd.
Sec. 4, Taipei
Tel: (2) 7113181
Fax: (2) 7810476

International Advertising Agency Ltd.
4/F., 73 Fu Hsing N. Rd.
Taipei
Tel: (2) 7526211
Fax: (2) 7526210

J. Walter Thompson Limited
18/F., Union Century Bldg., 163 Keelung Rd.
Sec. 1, Taipei
Tel: (2) 7469028
Fax: (2) 7664166

Lintas Taiwan
Rm. 501, Lotus Bldg., 136 Jen Ai Rd.
Sec. 3, Taipei
Tel: (2) 7015299
Fax: (2) 7015129

McCann-Erickson Taiwan Co.
4/F., Ming Tai Bldg., 1 Jen-Ai Rd.
Sec. 4, Taipei 10649
Tel: (2) 7517561
Fax: (2) 7411513

Business Culture

Greetings and Courtesies

A handshake is the accepted greeting. Upon meeting someone, Chinese lower their eyes slightly as a sign of respect. Staring into the eyes of a Chinese might make them uncomfortable. Face (*mianzi*), a measure of one's dignity, is crucial in Taiwan. Taiwanese are enormously sensitive to maintaining face in everything they do. Saying or doing anything that causes someone to lose face can instantly destroy a relationship and any business that might result from it. Never insult or openly criticize someone in front of others. Do not treat someone as a person of lowly rank if their position in their company is high. A person's face is also their company's face. The relationship you develop with a person represents your relationship with his entire company.

Business Ethic and Framework

Dwarfed by and staunchly opposing the People's Republic of China, Taiwan regards business with the rest of the world as crucial to its survival, economically and politically. Taiwanese businessmen are generally practical and shrewd. Work is one of their most prized virtues, and they are willing to work ten or more hours each day. Taiwanese prefer to have their own business rather than be employed by a large corporation. This has resulted in thousands of small-scale, family-owned companies, and potential partners are plentiful. But it also means that business rivalries can be intensely personal and sometimes vicious. Taiwanese behavior is largely determined by Confucianism, which teaches respect for superiors, duty to family, loyalty to friends, humility, sincerity, and courtesy. Among coworkers, people of higher status and age are respected by those beneath them, and deferred to in speech and action. Older businesspeople are likely to be treated more seriously than younger ones.

Decision Making

Consensus is very important to Taiwanese and they will probably require time for a private discussion before they make a decision. Taiwanese try to avoid saying no, for fear of causing embarrassment or losing face. Instead of directly saying no, they are likely to say something is inconvenient or they might suggest something as an alternative. This is a way of being polite, and pushing a matter after you've received an evasive response will probably cause embarrassment and will probably not close a deal.

Women

Taiwanese are used to doing business with women, and women visiting Taiwan can expect to be treated fairly and respectfully. However, except for the fashion and cosmetic industries, it is not usual for a woman to be the senior member of a business group. If your senior representative is a woman, you might consider including a man to "balance" your group. Women should not be overly aggressive or feel they have to "assert" themselves to be respected by Taiwanese businessmen. They do not; in fact, aggressiveness will be looked on with distaste.

Meetings

Taiwanese are more comfortable as a group than as individuals. They become uncomfortable when people speak as individuals, or make statements that are not in harmony with the stated group view. One person, preferably your group's senior member, should be designated as your spokesman. Taiwanese will assume all major communications come from him, and accept what he says as the position of your company. It is a good idea to send a list of your representatives before the meeting, and to include their rank in your company. You should also request a similar list from the Taiwanese. Your team will be led into a room in which the Taiwanese team is already present. The team leader should enter first. Teams sit across a table, leaders opposite each other and others seated in descending order of importance. Small talk will come first. Business is addressed after people feel comfortable with each other. The head of the host team will deliver a short welcome speech, then turn the floor over to the visitors. Your senior team member should speak for your company; avoid conflicting statements from other team members. When talking, your spokesman should address the Taiwanese senior representative. Taiwanese prefer to hear a proposal as a broad overview, and then respond to specific issues or questions point by point.

Business Attire

Except for formal situations, Taiwanese do not put much emphasis on dress style, which sets them apart from other East Asians. They will, however, expect you to wear a Western business suit, conservatively cut and of dark color. Summers in Taiwan are hot and humid, so lightweight materials will be more comfortable.

Cultural Cautions

DO'S

- Be aware of the importance of face in all your dealings with Taiwanese.
- Always treat people with the respect to which their position entitles them.
- Be aware of all favors done for you and gifts you are given. Find a way to reciprocate in kind.
- In Taiwan, business relationships are personal relationships. To establish a good business relationship, establish a personal relationship that demonstrates your respect and trustworthiness.

DON'TS

- Don't make fun of someone, even as a playful joke.
- Avoid mentioning the People's Republic of China. If it does come up in conversation, refer to it as mainland China.
- Taiwanese are aware of and sensitive to their polluted environment. Do not bring it up.

CUSTOMS

- Humility is valued highly in Confucianism. Taiwanese are often so polite and humble that they appear to be self-effacing.
- Taiwanese are extremely courteous to foreigners. This often includes arranging every detail of a guest's visit, and refusing to let a guest spend any money at all.
- Business cards are important. At first meetings, handshakes are followed by a formal exchange of cards. Always carry plenty of cards, ideally with Chinese text on one side. If possible, get expert advice on the specific Chinese characters, as some ideograms are considered more favorable than others. Cards are given and received with both hands.
- Gifts are important, expressing friendship, symbolizing hopes for success, and showing appreciation. Do not give very expensive gifts, unless they are for a long-time associate who has been of great help. In a business situation, business-related items (pens, paperweights) are appropriate. If one gift is given, it should be given to the senior person.
- For wrapped gifts, gold or red are appropriate colors. White and black are colors of mourning.

OBSERVATIONS

- Business dealings can be made easier by having a Taiwanese advisor or consultant.
- Taiwanese prefer to deal with the same person, and treat every interaction as a personal one. The same individual should always represent your company. If they leave their job, they should personally introduce their replacement to the Taiwanese associates.
- If you are importing goods produced in Taiwan, you will be negotiating a relatively standard purchasing agreement. if you are dealing with the Taiwanese government, negotiations will be more involved and the key issue will be the quality of your goods or services.

NEGOTIATIONS

- Taiwanese are savvy, shrewd negotiators. Their tactics are both subtle and aggressive. Often, they will wine and dine potential business associates as a way of gaining an advantage.
- Negotiating tactics include getting angry as a means of intimidation, flattery to get you off-guard, and prolonging negotiations to wear you down.
- A common tactic is delaying major negotiations until you are about to leave the country, then making unreasonable demands.
- Extensive entertaining, particularly at night, is sometimes used to make visitors less alert at the negotiating table.
- Be prepared to walk away. You will gain more from making it clear that you would rather have no deal at all than a bad deal.
- Taiwanese law states that a contract is legally binding. Nevertheless, some Taiwanese still consider a contract only a loose, general commitment to do business.

Legal System

Taiwan is a civil code country; its laws are based on the Germanic legal tradition with influences from other Asian countries. In recent years, Taiwan has adopted highly developed commercial laws to encourage its expanding industrialization, largely relying on US and European systems. Taiwan's national government is divided into five yuans: executive, legislative, judicial, examination, and control.

Intellectual Property Rights

Laws against infringement exist, but enforcement can be difficult. Developing personal contact and trust with a Taiwan business counterpart remains the best way to protect these property rights.

Patents Foreign patent holders can register in Taiwan if their home country has a treaty with Taiwan or offers reciprocal protection to Taiwanese nationals. In the absence of these, a foreign owner may negotiate a patent protection agreement with a Taiwanese organization and seek approval from the Ministry of Economic Affairs. Protection extends to utility models. The novelty will be examined under strict rules before registration is permitted. Approved patent applications will be published in the Patent Gazettes. The period of protection varies from five to 18 years depending on the item patented.

Trademarks Registration of trademarks in Taiwan is essential if protection is desired. The first person who registers is the owner of the mark, regardless of actual use. Foreign owners can register marks if their home countries have treaties, extend reciprocal rights, or are deemed friendly to Taiwan. Transliteration of a trademark is considered a separate mark and should be registered independently. Registration is made to the National Bureau of Standards and lasts for 10 years from the date of registration. Renewals are allowed for indefinite 10-year periods so long as the mark remains in use.

Copyrights Foreign copyright holders may obtain protection in Taiwan only if the work is first published there or the foreign person's home country affords reciprocal rights to Taiwanese nationals. Protection extends to traditional works, plus sound recordings, video tapes, computer programs, maps, and scientific, technical, and engineering design drawings. The protection term runs for the author's life plus 30 years. However, it is limited to 30 years for works copyrighted in the name of a private entity, the government, or any public agency. This limit also applies to motion pictures, video tapes, sound recordings, compilations, photographic works, computer programs, and translations of literary works. Assignments must be registered to be enforceable. A copyright owner may prosecute and recover damages from an infringer of a registered or unregistered copyright, although remedies are limited for unregistered works.

Business Registration

All firms, regardless of structure, must be registered with the Commercial Registry before beginning operations in Taiwan. No firms may engage in activities outside those for which it has been registered. For certain activities, special permission or licenses must be obtained from the government, a process that must be completed before registration. These areas include banking, insurance, brokerage, construction, trust and investment, venture capitalizing, travel agency, shipping, publishing, pharmaceuticals, and air freight fowarders. Foreign companies that seek to establish a branch office and do business in Taiwan must also apply for recognition with the Ministry of Economic Affairs and must obtain a branch license from the municipal or provincial government of the district where the branch will be located.

Contracts and Dispute Resolution

Most principles of contract law are consistent with European and US concepts. Written and oral contracts are considered binding in most cases. Lawsuits are best avoided. Many Taiwanese consider a lawsuit to be an insult. Moreover, civil trials have no juries, delays are inevitable, and judges have substantial powers and corruption is a possibility. Disputes should be resolved through negotiation if at all possible.

Notaries

Notarial offices are set up as special divisions within the local district courts. Notaries will on request issue certificates or otherwise authenticate private documents for a fee.

Labor

The law regulates basic working conditions, minimum wages, work hours, labor agreements, child labor, and benefits. A fixed-term agreement is permitted for temporary jobs and can be terminated without advance notice. In contrast, an employment agreement for a job that will last for an indefinite term can be terminated only for a cause allowed by statute and only after advance notice and remittance of severance pay, which is usually one year's pay. Children under age 16 may not work more than eight hours a day. Unions can be formed within an industry or workshop where there are more than 30 workers who are older than age 20. Six national unions and many local unions exist. Union members have a right to strike, provided that a dispute with management cannot otherwise be resolved in mediation.

Legal Matters

LEGAL BRIEFS

- **Business entities** Foreign companies may do business through representative offices, which also require approval, but registration requirements are fewer.

- **Maximum workweek** Workers must generally be allowed one day off in every seven days. A work day is typically eight hours, and breaks are mandatory. An employee who has not taken the mandated rest days must be allowed special vacation time. If no vacation days are taken, the employee is entitled to additional wages for those vacation days.

- **Monopolies** Unfair competition laws are strong and are administered by the Fair Trade Commission. Price-fixing, boycotts, and unfair trade and commercial practices are all prohibited and will be challenged. Violators may be subject to treble damages and significant criminal penalties. Combinations of companies that could become a monopoly must be approved first by the FTC. Penalties for failing to file with the FTC are stiff: divestiture, compulsory disposition of assets, cessation of business, and fines.

- **International agreements** Taiwan is a member of Convention on Settlement of Investment Disputes between States and Nationals of Other States.

LAW FIRMS

Anglo-American Law Office
12/F., 71 Jen Ai Rd.
Sec. 2, Taipei
Tel: (2) 3921843

Baker & McKenzie
15/F., Hung Tai Center
168 Tun Hwa N. Rd.
Taipei
Tel: (2) 7126151 Fax: (2) 7169250

Cheng Chang & Associates Law Offices
3/F.,-7, 2 Fu Hsing N. Rd.
Taipei
Tel: (2) 7415091   Fax: (2) 7415090 Telex: 20963

Dong & Lee, Attorneys at Law
9/F., 141 Jen Ai Rd.
Sec. 3, Taipei
Tel: (2) 7764612 Fax: (2) 7411686

Far East United Law Office
4/F., 176 Chung Hsiao E. Rd.
Sec. 1, Taipei
Tel: (2) 3928811 Fax: (2) 3214414

Formosa Transnational Attorneys at Law
15/F., 136 Jen Ai Rd.
Sec. 3, Taipei
Tel: (2) 7557366 Fax: (2) 7556486

Howe & Lloyd
8/F.-A, 230 Hsin Yi Rd.
Sec. 2, Taipei
Tel: (2) 3416000 Fax: (2) 3915972

Hua, Kao, Juo & Lin Lawyers
11/F., 296 Kuang Fu S. Rd.
Taipei
Tel: (2) 7764621 Fax: (2) 7764623

Huang & Partners Attorneys and Counsellors-at-Law
10/F., 683 Min Sheng E. Rd.
Taipei
Tel: (2) 7135172 Fax: (2) 7120480

Jones, Day, Reavis & Pogue
7/F., 2 Tun Hwa S. Rd.
Sec. 2, Taipei
Tel: (2) 7046808/9 Fax: (2) 7046791

Kaplan, Russin, Vecchi & Parker
Rm. 901, 9/F., 205 Tun Hwa N. Rd.
Taipei
Tel: (2) 7128956/7 Fax: (2) 7134711

Lee & Li, Attorneys-at-Law
7/F., 201 Tun Hwa N. Rd.
Taipei
Tel: (2) 7153300 Fax: (2) 7133966 Telex: 11651

Liang & Associates Attorneys-at-Law
12/F.-2, 76 Tun Hwa S. Rd.
Sec. 2, Taipei
Tel: (2) 7556595 Fax: (2) 7082946

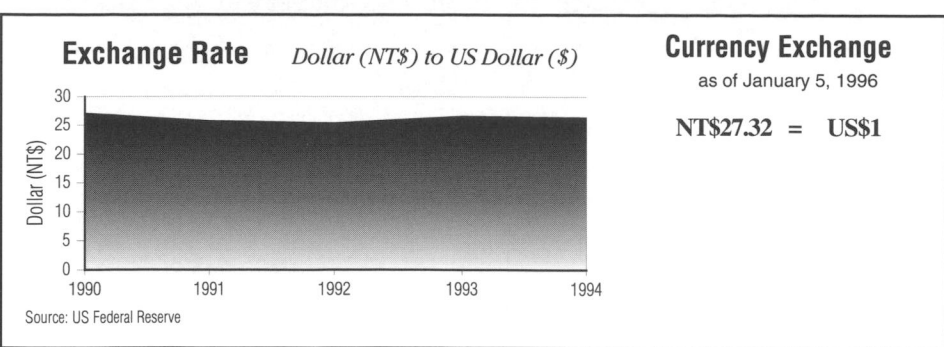

Exchange Rate *Dollar (NT$) to US Dollar ($)*

Dollar (NT$) — 1990, 1991, 1992, 1993, 1994

Source: US Federal Reserve

Currency Exchange
as of January 5, 1996

NT$27.32 = US$1

Currency

The currency of Taiwan is the New Taiwan dollar (NT$), which is divided into 100 cents.

Foreign Exchange

There are no foreign exchange limits for trade transactions, insurance, or authorized investments. Foreign exchange issues are administered by the Central Bank, the Ministry of Finance, and the Ministry of Economic Affairs. Only authorized financial entities are allowed to deal in foreign exchange, and the only transactions allowed are those involving direct commercial exchanges. There is no market for speculative activity or other financial transactions, and individuals and businesses cannot hold free foreign exchange balances for their own uses. There is a thriving black market for foreign exchange, mostly operated through gold shops in Taipei.

Capital Transfers

There are technically no foreign exchange limitations on the repatriation of capital and profits from investments in Taiwan provided that the initial investment was approved and registered with Taiwanese authorities. Most other non-trade-related transactions involving payment or remittances by foreign or resident individuals or entities have a US$5 million annual limit per account. Remittances of amounts greater than US$1 million require a 10-working-day waiting period.

Investment Incentives

Taiwan offers a number of incentives to encourage investment, including accelerated depreciation and tax credits for investment in pollution control systems, production automation and energy conservation. Equipment for research and development purposes can be brought into Taiwan duty-free. Other incentives include interest-free or low-interest loans for developing new and/or leading products, and a broad five-year tax holiday for new investments.

Investment Restrictions

Most export performance, local content requirements, and foreign ownership limits have been removed, though a number of restrictions on foreign institutional investment and banking remain in place. Foreign investment is prohibited in such industries as agriculture, cigarette manufacturing, liquor distilling, and a few other industries. Foreign ownership is restricted in a few necessary industries.

TAXATION

Taxation requires sophisticated knowledge of complex rules and regulations specific to each country. For more detailed information we suggest you refer to the Ernst & Young Corporate Tax Guide and Directory, available from the Ernst & Young accounting office in your country, or from:

Diwan, Ernst & Young
9th Floor
Taipei World Trade Center
International Trade Building
333, Keelung Road, Sec. 1
Taipei, Taiwan, ROC 10548
Tel: (2) 720-4000, 720-1560
Fax: (2) 757-6050, 757-6469 (Tax)

At a Glance

Corporate Income Tax Rate (%)(a)	25
Capital Gains Tax Rate (%)(a)(b)	25
Branch Tax Rate (%)(a)	25
Withholding Tax (%)	

Dividends	
Paid to Residents	15
Paid to Nonresident Corporations (c)	25
Paid to Nonresident Individuals (c)	35
Interest (d)	10/20
Royalties from Patents, Know-how, etc. (d)	15/20
Branch Remittance Tax	0
Net Operating Losses (Years)	
Carryback	0
Carryforward	5

(a) Corporate income taxes are progressive. No tax is assessed for total net income of less than NT$50,000, 15% is assessed on total net income of more than NT$50,000 but less than NT$100,000, and 25% on total net income of more than NT$100,000.
(b) Effective January 1, 1990, income taxation of securities transactions was suspended, but a securities transaction tax of 0.3% (0.1% on bonds and other securities authorized by competent authority) is imposed.
(c) This rate may be reduced to 20%, if the investment is approved by the ROC government pursuant to the Statute for Investment by Foreign Nationals or the Statute for Investment by Overseas Chinese. A nonresident corporation is a foreign corporation without a branch office or fixed place of business in the ROC.
(d) The 20% rate applies to payments to nonresidents.

Money Matters

BITS AND PIECES

- **Foreign tax relief** Tax credits are granted for foreign income tax paid by domestic enterprises, but it may not be more than the additional amount of the ROC tax that would result from including the foreign-source income in the enterprise's total income.
- **Repatriation** Investors must acquire approval from the Ministry of Economic Affairs to repatriate capital or profits overseas if the amount is more than that specified by the exchange control limits.
- **Banking system** Taiwan has a Central Bank, 33 domestic banks, eight business banks, and 37 foreign banks. Domestic, business, and foreign banks all have several branch offices. Other financial institutions also exist for specific sectors, such as farming and fishing.
- **Financing** Importers usually arrange their own financing, but assistance is available in certain circumstances, such as for high technology items, and imports of natural resources and raw materials.
- **Method of payment** The most widely used payment process is the bank-to-bank letter of credit. Some other methods include open account, documents against payment, and documents against acceptance.

BANKS

Central Bank
The Central Bank of China
2 Roosevelt Rd.
Sec. 1, Taipei
Tel: (2) 3936161 Fax: (2) 3973750 Telex: 21532

Chang Hwa Commercial Bank Ltd.
57 Chung Shan N. Rd.
Sec. 2, Taipei
Tel: (2) 5362951 Telex: 11323, 11695, 24604

Hua Nan Commercial Bank Ltd.
38 Chungking S. Rd.
Sec. 1, Taipei
Tel: (2) 3713111 Fax: (2) 3315737

Overseas Chinese Commercial Banking Corp.
8 Hsiang Yang Rd.
Taipei
Tel: (2) 3715181 Fax: (2) 3814056, 3315098

Shanghai Commercial & Savings Bank, Ltd.
16 Jen Ai Rd.
Sec. 2, Taipei
Tel: (2) 3933111 Fax: (2) 3928391

Taipei Bank
50 Chung Shan N. Rd.
Sec. 2, Taipei
Tel: (2) 5425656 Fax: (2) 5231235

United World Chinese Commercial Bank
65 Kuan Chien Rd.
Taipei
Tel: (2) 3125555 Fax: (2) 3318263

Bank of Taiwan
120 Chung King S. Rd.
Sec. 1, Taipei 10036
Tel: (2) 3147377/88 Fax: (2) 38114139

Export-Import Bank of the Republic of China
8/F., 3 Nan Hai Rd.
Taipei
Tel: (2) 3210511 Fax: (2) 3940630 Telex: 26044

Farmers Bank of China
85 Nanking E. Rd.
Sec. 2, Taipei
Tel: (2) 5517141 Fax: (2) 5975794

First Commercial Bank
30 Chungking S. Rd.
Sec. 1, Taipei
Tel: (2) 3111111, 3613611 Fax: (2) 3315739

Bank of America N.T. & S. A. (USA)
205 Tun Hwa N. Rd.
Taipei
Tel: (2) 7154111 Fax: (2) 7132850

Banque Nationale de Paris (France)
7/F., 214 Tun Hwa N. Rd.
Taipei
Tel: (2) 7161167 Fax: (2) 7152027 Telex: 22000

Business Travel

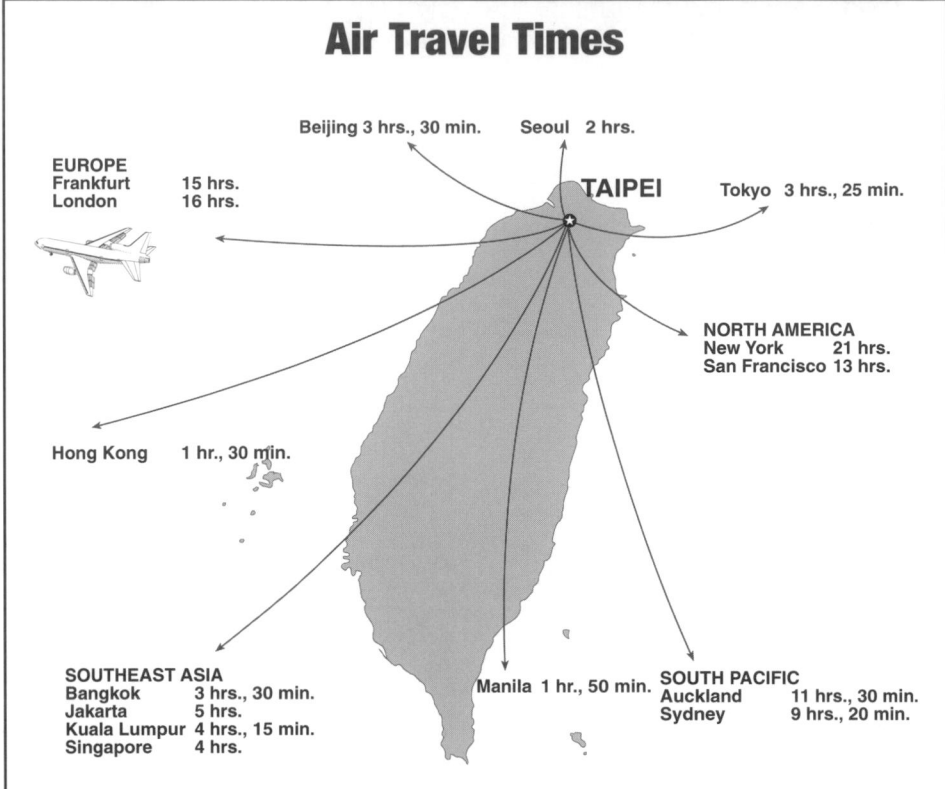

Air Travel Times

Beijing 3 hrs., 30 min.   Seoul 2 hrs.

TAIPEI

EUROPE
Frankfurt   15 hrs.
London   16 hrs.

Tokyo 3 hrs., 25 min.

NORTH AMERICA
New York   21 hrs.
San Francisco 13 hrs.

Hong Kong   1 hr., 30 min.

SOUTHEAST ASIA
Bangkok   3 hrs., 30 min.
Jakarta   5 hrs.
Kuala Lumpur 4 hrs., 15 min.
Singapore   4 hrs.

Manila 1 hr., 50 min.

SOUTH PACIFIC
Auckland   11 hrs., 30 min.
Sydney   9 hrs., 20 min.

COMMUNICATIONS

Telephones Taiwan's telephone system is modern, and direct dialing to many other countries is available from most cities. When using public phones, look for newer ones as older pay phones will go dead without warning when your money runs out. Newer phones have digital displays, especially useful for making long-distance calls. Some public phones take phone cards that are available in train stations and shops with public phones. On weekdays long-distance rates are 40 percent cheaper after 6 p.m. and 70 percent cheaper after 11 p.m.

Fax Fax machines are very popular in Taiwan, and almost every hotel and business has fax capability.

Post office Postal service is reliable and efficient, with a variety of delivery services available. Main post offices are open 24-hours in large cities. Mail can be posted from mailboxes—green for regular mail and red for air mail, aerograms, 24-hour delivery, and "express" service.

BEST TRAVEL BOOKS

Culture Shock, A Guide to Customs and Etiquette, Taiwan.
The Travelers Guide to Taiwan Customs and Manners. Elizabeth Devine & Nancy Braganti. An invaluable guide for people not wanting to put foot in mouth.
Far Eastern Economic Review, All Asia Travel Guide Volume 2. The best guide available for the business traveller.
Four Dragons Guidebook. The indispensable guide to Hong Kong, Singapore, Thailand, Taiwan. Volume One. Fredric M. Kaplan.
Do's and Taboo's Around the World. The Bestselling Guide to International Behavior. Edited by Roger Axtell, compiled by the Parker Pen Company. The ultimate guide to international behavior, now completely updated and expanded. Helpful, fun to read!

USEFUL TELEPHONE NUMBERS

If you are calling from outside Taiwan, you will need to add the country code [886] and any other international dialing requirements from within your country.

- Information Hot Lines .... (2) 7173737
- Overnight Mail ....(2) 7576666, (2) 7136321
- Messenger Service .... (2) 5715256
- Secretarial Services .... (2) 7382022
- Police 118
- Taipei Police......................................(2) 556-6007
- Kaohsiung Police ....(7) 221-5796
- Tainan Police ....(6) 222-9704
- Taichung Police..................................(4) 220-3032
- Foreign Affairs Police ....(2) 381-7475, 381-8341
- Fire 119
- Weather... 166 or 107
- Information (English speaking) ....(2) 311-6796
- Telegram or Telex ....(2) 344-2779, 344-3781
- International Operator 100
- Time 117
- Centers for Disease Control........[1] (404) 332-4559

Car Rental
- Budget .... (2) 8312906
- Central .... (2) 8819545
- Hertz .... (2) 8211333
- VIP .... (2) 7131111

Credit Card Information
Lost or stolen credit cards (call collect to the US, regardless of which country the card was issued in).
- Amex ....[1] (919) 333-3211
- Diner's Club................................[1] (303) 799-1504
- MasterCard ....[1] (314) 275-6690
- Visa ....[1] (410) 581-7931

Travelogue

WORKWEEK

Offices Monday-Friday, 9:00 am to 5:00 pm, and Saturdays until 12:00 pm.
Banks Monday-Friday, 9:00 am to 3:30 pm, and Saturdays until 12:00 pm.
Government Monday-Friday, 8:30 am to 12:30 pm and 1:30 to 5:30 pm. Saturdays until 12:30 pm.
Retail A majority of small shops are open daily from 6:00 am until 10:00 pm. Other shops open from 10:00 am to 10:00 pm.
The Chinese take lunch and lunchtime naps; it is common in Taiwan to offset their early rising and late bedtime routines.

HOLIDAYS

Holidays 1996
January 1 Founding of Republic
February Chinese New Year *
March 12 Death of Sun Yat-sen
March 29 Youth Day
April 4 Women's and Children's Day
April 5 Sweeping of the Tombs
May Dragon Boat Festival *
September 28 Confucius's Birthday
October 10 Double Ten Day
October 25 Taiwan Restoration Day
October 31 Chiang Kai-shek's Birthday
November 12 Sun Yat-sen's Birthday
December 25 Constitution Day.
*Dates vary each year.

VISA AND PASSPORT

A passport is required for all visitors. Visas are not required for stays up to 14 days, provided that the traveler is in possession of a passport valid for at least six months and a return or onward ticket. Visas for stays of up to two months are free of charge, but must be obtained prior to entry.

DEPARTURE FORMALITIES

Only US$5,000 worth of foreign currency may be taken out of Taiwan unless it is declared upon arrival, and no more than NT$8,000 can be imported or exported. Visitors leaving from Chiang Kai-Shek International Airport at Taoyaun are subject to a US$12 departure tax.

IMMUNIZATION

No international certificates of vaccination are required unless you are arriving from an infected area. Recommended vaccinations include hepatitis, influenza, polio, tetanus, and typhoid.

TIPPING

Tipping is officially discouraged and can be considered an insult, use discretion. Taxi: none. Porters, NT$20 per piece. Hotels, restaurants: 10 percent plus a 5 percent VAT generally included in bill. Small services: NT$10.

CRIME

Taiwan's overall crime rate is low. Burglary and theft are the crimes that most often affect foreigners, but street crimes are rare. People are normally quite honest in Taiwan.

INFRASTRUCTURE

Taiwan boasts an excellent infrastructure. Taxis, hotel shuttles, car rentals, city buses, and intercity buses are usually air-conditioned, crowded but clean, relatively inexpensive and available. Trains link major cities. Roads are twisted and somewhat confusing even to those who can read Chinese. Buses require exact change. Hotels are modern, comfortable, and air-conditioned; the best hotels have restaurants, nightclubs, and swimming pools within.

NATIONAL TOURIST OFFICE

Tourism Bureau
290 Chunghsiao Rd.
Sec. 4, Taipei
Tel: (2) 7218541
Fax: (2) 7735487

GOVERNMENT AGENCIES

Central Trust of China
49 Wu Chang Street
Section 1, Taipei, Taiwan
Tel: (2) 311-1151
Fax (2) 311-8107

Civil Aeronautics Administration
Sungshan Airport
Taipei
Tel: (2) 5142458
Fax: (2) 7175828

Council for Economic Planning and Development, Executive Yuan
9/F., 87 Nanking E. Rd.
Sec. 2, Taipei
Tel: (2) 5225300, 5513522
Fax: (2) 5519011

Council for Labor Affairs, Executive Yuan
5/F., 232 Min Shen E. Rd.
Sec. 3, Taipei
Tel: (2) 7182512
Fax: (2) 5149240/2

Council of Agriculture, Executive Yuan
37 Nan Hai Rd.
Taipei
Tel: (2) 3812997
Fax: (2) 3812991

Council of Cultural Planning and Development
102 Aikuo E. Rd.
Taipei
Tel: (2) 3518030
Fax: (2) 3222937

Department of Health
100 Aikuo E. Rd.
Taipei
Tel: (2) 3210151
Fax: (2) 3122907

Directorate General of Budget, Accounting & Statistics, Executive Yuan
1 Chung Hsiao E. Rd.
Sec. 1, Taipei
Tel: (2) 3915231

Directorate General of Post
55 Chinshan S. Rd.
Sec. 2, Taipei
Tel: (2) 3969111
Fax: (2) 3911209

Directorate General of Telecommunications
31 Aikuo E. Rd.
Taipei
Tel: (2) 3443601
Fax: (2) 3223738

Environmental Protection Administration, Executive Yuan
1 Hsiang Yang Rd.
Taipei
Tel: (2) 3117722
Fax: (2) 3116071

Fair Trade Commission, Executive Yuan
8-12/F., 150 Tun Hwa N. Rd.
Taipei
Tel: (2) 5455501
Fax: (2) 5450107

Foreigners' Service Center
Taipei Municipal Police Headquarters
96 Yen Ping S. Rd.
Taipei
Tel: (2) 3818341

Government Information Office
Executive Yuan
2 Tien Chin St.
Taipei
Tel: (2) 3419211, 3228888
Fax: (2) 3920923, 3416252

Inspectorate General of Customs
85 Hsinsheng S. Rd.
Sec. 1, Taipei
Tel: (2) 7413181
Fax: (2) 7114166

International Cooperation Department
15 Foochow St.
Taipei
Tel: (2) 3918198
Fax: (2) 3213275

Department of Reconstruction
2 Szewei 3rd Rd.
Kaohsiung
Tel: (7) 3368333

Kaohsiung Export Processing Zone
2 Chung 1st Rd.
Kaohsiung
Tel: (7) 8217141/9
Fax: (7) 8310897

Keelung Harbour Bureau
Port Building Keelung
Tel: (2) 4236911
Fax: (2) 4284811/2

Ministry of Economic Affairs
15 Fu Chou St.
Taipei
Tel: (2) 3212200
Fax: (2) 3919398

Ministry of Economic Affairs
Anti-Counterfeiting Committee
1 Hu Kou St.
Taipei
Tel: (2) 3510271, 3210561
Fax: (2) 3212827

Ministry of Economic Affairs
Board of Foreign Trade
1 Hu Kou St.
Taipei
Tel: (2) 3510271, 3510286
Fax: (2) 3315387, 3513603, 3517080

Ministry of Economic Affairs
Bureau of Commodity Inspection and Quarantine
4 Tsi Nan Rd.
Sec. 1, Taipei
Tel: (2) 3512141
Fax: (2) 3932324
Telex: 27247

Ministry of Economic Affairs
Industrial Development and Investment Commission
10/F., 7 Roosevelt Rd.
Sec.1, Taipei
Tel: (2) 3947213
Fax: (2) 3926835

Ministry of Economic Affairs
Industrial Development Bureau
41-3 Hsin Yi Rd.
Sec. 3, Taipei
Tel: (2) 7541255
Fax: (2) 7030160

Ministry of Economic Affairs
International Cooperation Department
15 Fu Chou St.
Taipei
Tel: (2) 3918198
Fax: (2) 3213275

Ministry of Economic Affairs
Investment Commission
8/F., 7 Roosevelt Rd.,
Sec. 1, Taipei
Tel: (2) 3513151
Fax: (2) 3963970

Ministry of Economic Affairs
Kaohsiung Export Processing Zone Administration
600 Chiachang Rd., Nantze
Kaohsiung
Tel: (7) 3611212
Fax: (2) 3614348

Ministry of Economic Affairs
Medium and Small Business Administration
3/F., 368 Fu Hsing N. Rd.
Sec. 1, Taipei
Tel: (2) 7049470
Fax: (2) 7054409

REMEMBER
- When you telephone (or fax) to Taiwan from another country you must always include the country code [886] before the numbers given.
- When you send mail to Taiwan, be sure to write TAIWAN in capital letters on its own line below the addresses given.

Ministry of Education
5 Chungshan S. Rd.
Taipei
Tel: (2) 3513111
Fax: (2) 3966803
Telex: 10894

Ministry of Finance
2 Ai Kuo W. Rd.
Taipei
Tel: (2) 3228000
Fax: (2) 3965829

Ministry of Finance
Inspectorate General of Customs
4/F., 131 Nanking E. Rd.
Sec. 3 Taipei
Tel: (2) 7169219

Ministry of Finance
National Tax Administration
547 Chung Hsiao E. Rd.
Sec. 4, Taipei
Tel: (2) 7631313
Fax: (2) 7617698, 7644520

Ministry of Foreign Affairs
2 Chieh Shou Rd.
Taipei
Tel: (2) 3119292
Fax: (2) 3144972
Telex: 11299

Ministry of Justice
130 Chungking S. Rd.
Sec. 1, Taipei 10036
Tel: (2) 3146871
Fax: (2) 3896759

Overseas Chinese Affairs Commission
30 Kungyuan Rd.
Taipei
Tel: (2) 3810039
Fax: (2) 3313392

Taichung Harbour Bureau
Harbour Building, Wuchi
Taichung District
Tel: (4) 6562611

Steel Corporation [China]
5/F., 25 Jen Ai Rd.
Sec. 4, Taipei
Tel: (2) 7216411
Fax: (2) 7210393

WORLD TRADE CENTERS

World Trade Center Kaohsiung
Southeast Bldg.
21st Wu-Fu 3rd Rd., 10/F.
Kaohsiung

World Trade Center Taichung
60 Tienpao St.
Taichung 40706
Tel: (4) 2542271
Fax: (4) 2542341

BUSINESS AND TRADE ORGANIZATIONS

Committee of International Technical Cooperation
185 Hsinghai Rd.
Sec. 2, Taipei
Tel: (2) 7375647
Fax: (2) 7350736

Import-Export Association of Taipei
5/F., 350 Sung Chiang Rd.
Taipei
Tel: (2) 5813521/7
Fax: (2) 5423704

Taichung Chamber of Industry
8, Shih Fu Rd.
Taichung
Tel: (4) 2263613
Fax: (4) 2297398

Taipei Chamber of Commerce
6/F.-1, 602 Tun Hwa S. Rd.
Taipei
Tel: (2) 7542572

Taiwan Chamber of Commerce
4/F., 158 Sung Chiang Rd.
Taipei
Tel: (2) 3113144, 3114152
Fax: (2) 5211980

Taiwan Importers & Exporters Association
14/F., 2 Fu Hsing N. Rd.
Taipei
Tel: (2) 7731155 Fax: (2) 7731159
8/F.-3, 202 Nanking E. Rd.
Sec. 5, Taipei 10573
Tel: (2) 7666661/2
Fax: (2) 7625722

ACCOUNTING FIRMS

Taipei Accountants Association
9/F., 1 Nan Hai Rd.
Taipei
Tel: (2) 3945290
Fax: (2) 3972573

Diwan, Ernst & Young
17/F., Cathay Chung
Cheng Bldg., 2 Chung Cheng Rd.
Sec. 3, Kaohsiung
Tel: (7) 2240011
Fax: (7) 2220198

Peat, Marwick, Mitchell & Co.
12/F., 367 Fu Hsing N. Rd.
Taipei
Tel: (2) 7138001, 7138582
Fax: (2) 7150947
Telex: 23184 PMMTPE

T.N. Soong & Co. (Arthur Andersen)
12/F., Hung Tai Century Tower
156 Min Sheng E. Rd.
Sec. 3, Taipei
Postal address: PO Box 1539, Taipei
Tel: (2) 5459988
Fax: (2) 5459966

T.N. Soong & Co. (Arthur Andersen)
28/F., Long Bon World Trade Bldg.
160 Taichun Kan Rd.
Sec. 1, Taichung
Tel: (4) 3280055
Fax: (4) 3280700

AD AGENCIES

Series/DMB&B Tokyu
2/F.-1, No. 8, Alley 3, Lane 303, Nanking E. Rd.
Sec. 3, Taipei
Tel: (2) 7186336
Fax: (2) 7186334

Taiwan Advertising Co., Ltd.
10/F., 91 Nanking E. Rd.
Sec. 3 Taipei
Tel: (2) 5069201
Fax: (2) 5079244

DIRECTORIES & YEARBOOKS

Asian Computer Directory
Washington Plaza
1st Fl., 230 Wanchai Road
Wanchai, Hong Kong
Tel: [852] (2) 8327123
Fax: [852] (2) 8329208

Bankers Handbook For Asia
Datalino Asia Pacific Inc.
3rd Fl., Hollywood Center
233 Hollywood Road
Hong Kong
Tel: [852] (2) 8155221
Fax: [852] (2) 8542794

Financial & Investment Yearbook ROC
China Economic News Service
555 Chunghsiao East Road
Section 4, Taipei
Tel: (2) 7681234
Fax: (2) 7632303

International Tax and Duty Free Buyers Index
Pearl & Dean Publishing, Ltd.
9/F., Chung Nam Bldg., 1 Lockhart Rd.
Hong Kong
Tel: [852] (2) 8660395
Fax: [852] (2) 2999810

Kompass Register Of Taiwan Industry And Commerce
Trade Winds, Inc.
No. 7, Lane 75, Yungkang St.
Taipei
Tel: (2) 3922718
Fax: (2) 3964022

NEWSPAPERS

Asian Wall Street Journal
Dow Jones Publishing Co. (Asia)
2/F., AIA Bldg., 1 Stubbs Rd.
GPO Box 9825
Hong Kong
Tel: [852] 25737121
Fax: [852] 28345291

Central Daily News
260 Pa Teh Rd.
Sec. 2, Taipei
Tel: (2) 7763322

China News
11/F., 110 Yen Ping S. Rd.
Taipei
Tel: (2) 3887931
Fax: (2) 3815859

Financial Times
Rm. 625A, 209 Sung Chiang Rd.
Taipei
Tel: (2) 7310376

PERIODICALS

Taiwan Trade Opportunities
China External Trade Development Council
4-8/F., CETRA Tower, 333 Keelung Rd.
Sec. 1, Taipei 10548
Tel: (2) 7255200
Fax: (2) 7576653

Trade Winds Weekly: The Asian Weekly for International Traders
Trade Winds, Inc.
No. 7, Lane 75, Yungkang St.
Taipei
Postal address: PO Box 7-179, Taipei
Tel: (2) 3932718
Fax: (2) 3964022

Journal Of The Chinese Chemical Society
Chinese Chemical Society
PO Box 609
Taipei
Tel: (2) 6226149

Taiwan Computer
United Pacific International, Inc.
PO Box 81-417
Taipei
Tel: (2) 7150751
Fax: (2) 7125591

Taiwan Sugar
Taiwan Sugar Corporation
Rm. 606, 25 Pao Ching Rd.
Taipei 100

Target Machinery & Hardware (TMH)
United Pacific International, Inc.
PO Box 81-417
Taipei
Tel: (2) 7150751
Fax: (2) 7169493

Tien Hsin Chi Shu
31 Aikuo East Road
Taipei 106
Tel: (2) 3443601
Fax: (2) 3223738

Trade Winners, Computers & Communications:
Including Electronics & Components Information
PO Box 7-250
Taipei
Tel: (2) 7333988
Fax: (2) 7333990

Travel News Asia
Far East Trade Press, Ltd.
2/F Kai Tak Commercial Bldg.
317 Des Voeux Rd.
Central, Hong Kong
Tel: [852] 25453028
Fax: [852] 25446979

Travel Trade Gazette Asia
Asian Business Press Pte., Ltd.
100 Beach Rd., #26-00 Shaw Towers
Singapore 0718
Tel: [65] 2943366
Fax: [65] 2985534

Travel Trade Gazette Asia
Asian Business Press Pte., Ltd.
100 Beach Rd., #26-00 Shaw Towers
Singapore 0718
Tel: [65] 2943366
Fax: [65] 2985534

What's New in Computing
Asian Business Press Pte., Ltd.
100 Beach Rd., #26-00 Shaw Towers
Singapore 0718
Tel: [65] 2943366
Fax: [65] 2985534

RADIO & TELEVISION STATIONS

Broadcasting Corporation of China (BCC)
53 Jen Ai Rd.
Sec. 3, Taipei
Tel: (2) 7710150
Fax: (2) 7113169

China Television Company
120 Chung Yang Rd.
Nankang District
Taipei
Tel: (2) 7838303

INTERNET ADDRESSES

Usenet group(s):
soc.culture.taiwan

Taiwan Virtual Library
http://peacock.tnjc.edu.tw/taiwan-wwwvl.html

Tradepoint Taiwan
http://tradepoint.anjes.com.tw/

The Republic of China Yearbook 1995
http://www.taipei.org/Yearbook95/index.htm

Taiwan Government Page
http://gio.gov.tw/info/index_e.html

WWW Sites in Taiwan
http://peacock.tnjc.edu.tw/NEW/welcome_mosaic.html

Asia Resources - Taiwan
http://silkroute.com/silkroute/asia/rsrc/country/

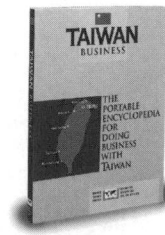

Thailand

Kingdom of Thailand

Economy

Overview

The Thai economy is strong and well-diversified. An emphasis on developing a free, competitive, export-oriented economy has helped Thailand to shift from a predominantly agricultural nation to one of the developing world's fastest growing industrialized economies. Despite the fact that 60 percent of the population is engaged in agriculture, this sector is declining in importance in terms of its contribution to GDP, and the rapidly growing manufacturing, trade, and services sectors now account for two-thirds of GDP. Thailand is now an important producer of a wide range of food products and manufactured goods.

Trade

Thailand has seen a major increase in the total volume and value of its foreign trade due to the rapid growth of its manufacturing sector and the emergence of an increasingly affluent population. Japan is its largest trading partner overall, and the largest source of its imports, followed by the US, Singapore, Germany, and Malaysia. Thailand's recent trade deficits do not reflect poor export performance, but rather result from the high quantity of capital machinery imported as a result of large-scale foreign investment and modernization in the manufacturing sector.

Sectors

Agriculture Thailand has traditionally been an agricultural country, and the processing and export of its agricultural produce, especially rice, has been central to its economy. Although this sector employs almost 60 percent of the work force, its relative importance as a contributor to the country's GDP has declined due to the dramatic growth in industry. Heavy reliance on the rice crop means this sector is vulnerable to fluctuations in world prices and climatic factors, and the government has begun to implement programs to promote more scientific methods in agriculture.

Industry Industry has made the largest contribution to Thailand's economy over the past two decades. The industrial sector has undergone rapid diversification, and the strengthening of the yen has contributed to growth as Japanese companies relocated their manufacturing operations to Thailand. Thailand continues to focus on industrial growth, and has recently liberalized investment regulations to attract both foreign and domestic funds to further this end.

Services This sector is Thailand's most important source of foreign exchange and a major contributing factor in its balance of payments surplus. Tourism continues to expand at a rapid pace, and financial and related services show steady growth in keeping with the increasing wealth of the nation. The financial system is undergoing liberalization and deregulation to make it more efficient and to attract the funds needed to support the country's fast-growing economy.

Trends

The economic boom of recent years has placed a severe strain on Thailand's infrastructure, and the government will have to contend with traffic congestion, acute shortages of professional staff and skilled labor, and the growing economic disparity between Bangkok and the rest of the nation. Thailand has addressed these problems and states its commitment to sustain growth, reduce pollution, diversify trade, and provide a viable infrastructure. Overall, long-term prospects look excellent.

At a Glance

THE COUNTRY
Location Southeastern Asia, bordering the Gulf of Thailand, between Burma (Myanmar) and Cambodia.
Terrain Varies from densely forested to swampy to mountainous.
Climate Tropical with three distinct seasons: hot, rainy, and cool.

THE PEOPLE
Population 59,000,000
Ethnic composition
Thai.. 75%
Chinese.. 14%
Other... 11%
Religious composition
Buddhist... 95%
Muslim 4%
Christian, Hindu, and Other 1%
Languages spoken Thai (official), English, regional and ethnic dialects.
Education and literacy Six years of education are compulsory beginning at age seven. Attendance is around 96 percent, resulting in a literacy rate of 93 percent of the population over age 15, a huge increase from 1947 when literacy was estimated at 44 percent. Education is important to Thailand; it accounts for 16 percent of total government expenditures.
Labor force
Total:...33,000,000
By occupation: agriculture 58%, government and services 24%, industry 15%, other 3%.

COUNTRY FACTS
Political and legal Though nominally a constitutional monarchy, Thailand has been ruled for the most part of this century by its military. The legal system is a combination of Thai and Western laws and Islamic law is applicable in Muslim dominated areas.
Telephone Over 1 million telephones connect almost all principle towns. In remote areas service can be erratic. International service is good. International country code: [66]. Selected city codes: Bangkok (2), Chanthaburi (39), Chiang Mai (53).
Transportation Direct flights to many international cities are readily accessible. Within cities, buses, taxis, rental cars, and three-wheeled samlors (called Dukduks) are available for hire. Local transportation in small towns is often more by pedicabs. Railways present another transportation option. Roadways vary in quality from good to unpaved. Bangkok traffic jams are legendary.
Environment While distinctive forms of plants and animal life can be abundantly found, the nation's environment is increasingly under threat. Water, noise, and air pollution are severe in parts of Thailand. Some wildlife species, like the Javan rhinoceros, have become extinct through illegal hunting and trapping.
Media There are over 40 daily newspapers published in Bangkok, including four in English and eight in Chinese. Outside of Bangkok, newspapers are published weekly and semiweekly, but not daily.
Health Conditions have steadily improved since the 1960s but hepatitis is still fairly common and the AIDS epidemic has begun to have a major impact on the local population. The Thai Government estimates between 200,000-400,000 HIV carriers in Thailand.

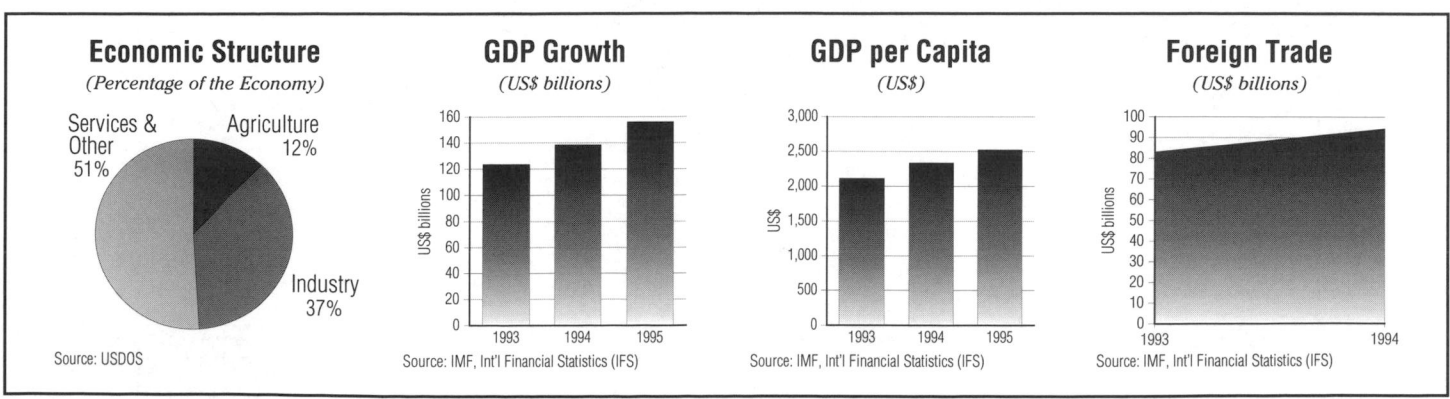

Economic Structure
(Percentage of the Economy)

Services & Other 51%
Agriculture 12%
Industry 37%

Source: USDOS

GDP Growth
(US$ billions)

Source: IMF, Int'l Financial Statistics (IFS)

GDP per Capita
(US$)

Source: IMF, Int'l Financial Statistics (IFS)

Foreign Trade
(US$ billions)

Source: IMF, Int'l Financial Statistics (IFS)

Provinces of Thailand

1 Ang Thong
2 Buriram
3 Chachoengsao
4 Chai Nat
5 Chaiyaphum
6 Chanthaburi
7 Chiang Mai
8 Chaing Rai
9 Chon Buri
10 Chumphon
11 Kalasin
12 Kamphaeng Phet
13 Kanchanaburi
14 Khon Kaen
15 Krabi
16 Krung Thep Mahanakhon
17 Lampang
18 Lamphun
19 Loei
20 Lop Buri
21 Mae Hong Son
22 Maha Sarakham
23 Nakhon Nayok
24 Nakhon Pathom
25 Nakhon Phanom
26 Nakhon Ratchasima

27 Nakhon Sawan
28 Nakhon Si Thammarat
29 Nan
30 Narathiwat
31 Nong Khai
32 Nonthaburi
33 Pathum Thani
34 Pattani
35 Phangnga
36 Phatthalung
37 Phayao
38 Phetchabun
39 Phetchaburi
40 Phichit
41 Phitsanulok
42 Phra Nakhon SiiAyutthaya
43 Phrae
44 Phuket
45 Prachin Buri
46 Prachuap Khiri Khan
47 Ranong
48 Ratchaburi
49 Rayong
50 Roi Et
51 Sakon Nakhon
52 Samut Prakan
53 Samut Sakhon
54 Samut Songkhram
55 Saraburi
56 Satun
57 Sing Buri
58 Sisaket
59 Songkhla
60 Sukhothai
61 Suphan Buri
62 Surat Thani
63 Surin
64 Tak
65 Trang
66 Trat
67 Ubon Ratchathani
68 Udon Thani
69 Uthai Thani
70 Uttaradit
71 Yala
72 Yasothon

Thailand

⊕ National capital
⊙ Provincial capital
● Secondary city
········ Railroad
─── Primary road
━━━ International boundary
─── Province boundary

| 0 | 50 | 100 | 150 | 200 km |
| 0 | 50 | | 100 | 150 mi |

Foreign Trade

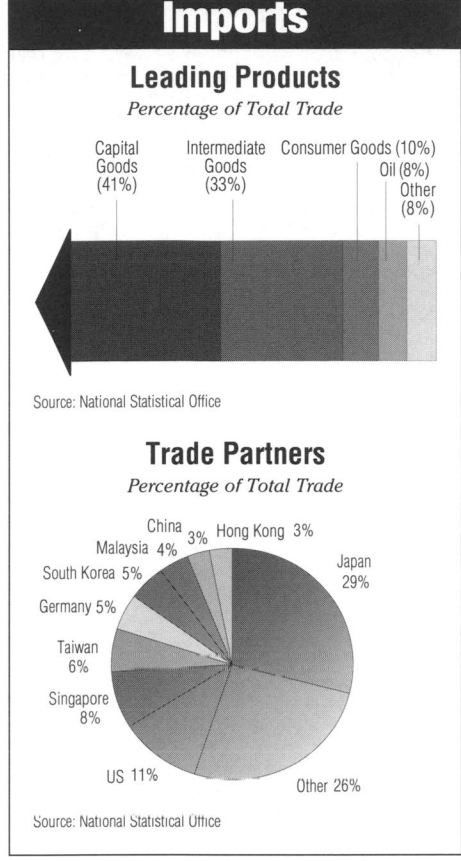

Imports

Leading Products
Percentage of Total Trade

Capital Goods (41%)
Intermediate Goods (33%)
Consumer Goods (10%)
Oil (8%)
Other (8%)

Source: National Statistical Office

Trade Partners
Percentage of Total Trade

China 3%
Hong Kong 3%
Malaysia 4%
South Korea 5%
Germany 5%
Taiwan 6%
Singapore 8%
US 11%
Japan 29%
Other 26%

Source: National Statistical Office

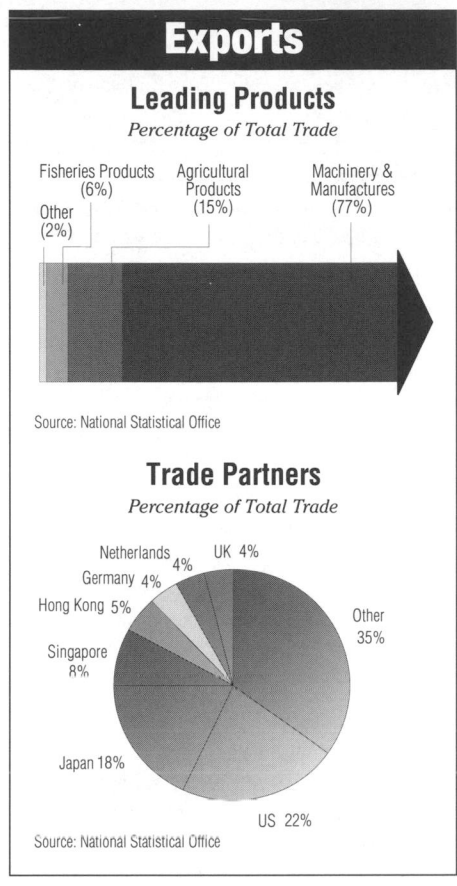

Exports

Leading Products
Percentage of Total Trade

Fisheries Products (6%)
Other (2%)
Agricultural Products (15%)
Machinery & Manufactures (77%)

Source: National Statistical Office

Trade Partners
Percentage of Total Trade

Netherlands 4%
UK 4%
Germany 4%
Hong Kong 5%
Singapore 8%
Other 35%
Japan 18%
US 22%

Source: National Statistical Office

Opportunities

FOR IMPORTING TO THAILAND
- machinery and parts
- petroleum
- iron and steel
- chemicals
- vehicles and parts
- consumer oriented products with good retail potential (fresh fruit—apples, grapes, pears)
- jewelry
- fish preparations
- electrical appliances
- fertilizers and pesticides

FOR EXPORTING FROM THAILAND
- textiles
- footwear
- fishery products
- computers and parts
- jewelry
- rice
- tapioca products
- rubber

GROWTH SECTORS
- manufacturing
- wholesale consumer goods
- retail trade and services industries
- agriculture
- tourism
- mining
- foreign investment
- construction
- computer and electronic industries
- garment and footwear
- furniture and other wood products
- canned food
- toys
- gems
- jewelry

GOVERNMENT PROCUREMENT
- refinery equipment
- telephone lines and equipment
- mass transit system, new rail
- regional centers
- highway development and expansions
- new ports development and expansions
- new central government administrative city
- Eastern Seaboard project (an alternate deep-sea port on Thailand's southern peninsula)
- economic development along the Thai-Malaysian border
- electricity generation
- skilled personnel/education
- solid waste water treatment

Trade News

RULES AND REGULATIONS

- **Regulations** Thailand continues to make major steps toward improving both its regulatory and enforcement regimes. Under current Thai regulations, only persons of Thai nationality may be licensed in many professional services, including accounting, architecture, engineering, and construction management.

- **Import restrictions** Imports of only a few products, including aerosol mixtures of vinyl chloride monomers (for health reasons), and products constituting trademark infringements, are actually banned by Thailand. However, imports of a larger number of items require licenses from various Thai ministries, and licenses to import some of these products may not be routinely available.

- **Import licenses** The Thai Ministry of Commerce requires import licenses on certain raw materials, petroleum, industrial, textile, and agricultural products. While licensing requirements have been dropped on a number of items in recent years, licenses are still required for some 37 categories of items. In the food products area, licensing requirements remain for powdered skim milk, fresh milk, potatoes, soy beans and soy bean oil, refined sugar, and corn for animals. Many of these licensing requirements will be eliminated as Thailand completes the adjustments necessary to conform to its GATT Uruguay Round commitments. Food and pharmaceutical product importers are also required to apply for import licenses from the Thai Food and Drug Administration. The licensing process is time consuming and costly, requiring disclosure of proprietary information. Products imported in bulk and products imported in sealed containers (consumer-ready packaged) require laboratory analysis. Some 39 items must be registered as "specific controlled food items." Although the Thai Food and Drug Administration has made efforts to streamline the registrations process, it usually requires three months or more to complete.

- **Tariff rates** Thailand's present imports regime maintains significant tariff barriers on most products, with current duty rates in the 30-60 percent range for a majority of the products on which duties are collected. However, duty exemptions are routinely granted to firms with investment promotion privileges, and rebates of import duties on raw materials are routinely granted upon export of the finished product. Major steps taken to reduce and simplify import tariffs over the past few years and at present are increasing substantially the import market opportunities. However, competition from foreign and Thai firms is quite stiff. Thailand is making major import duty reductions on many manufactured goods.

- **Barriers** There are few barriers to trading with Thailand. Executing distributorship agreements and setting up offices in Thailand are not difficult tasks. Local lawyers usually can complete the paperwork easily and quickly.

- **Quota** Thailand's quota program for the export of textiles and apparel is administered by the Department of Foreign Trade of the Ministry of Commerce.

- **Export restrictions** Thailand maintains few restrictions on exports, and most are related to national security, environmental protection, and cultural concerns or pursuant to trade agreements (international commodity agreements, agreements governing the textile and apparel trade, subsidies, and dumping, etc.).

FREIGHT FORWARDER

SGS Far East Limited
994 Sol Thonglor Sukhumvit Road
Bangkok 10110
Fax: (2) 381 1994
Telex: 82806 SGSBKK TH

GOVERNMENT AGENCY

Customs Department
At Narong Roag
Khlong Toey
Bangkok 10110

Marketing

Overview

Thailand is one of the fastest growing, most attractive markets for foreign sellers to explore. The Thai people enjoy a fair amount of personal freedom, they are relatively wealthy, eager to try innovative products, and well-inclined to purchase imports from the West. Perhaps most attractive is the fact that a huge percentage of the people live in Bankok, a sprawling metropolis offering every imaginable service and product. Bangkok is also the center from which to service the rest of the country, making it easy for foreign sellers to locate their Thai operations. Western sellers to the Thai market will face stiff competition from Japanese and Taiwanese companies, but can make a favorable impression by emphasizing Western brand names and state-of-the-art features.

Distribution

There are three primary types or methods of importation and distribution. The first category includes large, well-established companies trading with strong financial resources, large sales volumes, and extensive commercial presence in multiple industry sectors. In certain subsectors, where the market is very specialized, these large import/distribution companies use sub-dealers or agents to concentrate their efforts, as is common in the defense industry where personal relationships are very important. These large firms often will propose marketing or production joint ventures, when imports to Thailand reach a sufficient level to arouse the interest of a large local firm. The second type of importer are the smaller agents and distributors who generally specialize in one line of business in which they have well-established contacts and market knowledge. The third group consists of small, new start-up companies that are trying to expand into the import/ distribution business. Direct marketing is also increasing and is expected to take off in the near future. Thais are becoming receptive to franchising, both as customers and as partners.

Agents, Distributors, and Partners

New market entrants should appoint an established agent/distributor with strong technical expertise as well as the essential good contacts and knowledge of the local market. In Bangkok there are several reputable local consultants qualified to design market entry strategies and select partners. Frequent contact is important, especially at the beginning, to build a good working relationship and insure that both parties are pursuing similar goals. Thai investors who are considering franchisers are primarily concerned with payback periods and high franchise fees; it seems the best way to enter this market is through joint ventures.

Selling Techniques

Foreign firms should choose their market niches carefully, and constantly upgrade and improve their product offerings. To differentiate products from local and other foreign competition, foreign sellers should emphasize quality, new product and technology enhancements, and customer service. Foreign marketing executives should visit Thailand often and meet with their local agents and customers as a way to build confidence and further local relationships. It is often beneficial to bring engineers to Thailand on rotating assignments to assist local representatives with training and to accompany local sales engineers on client visits. Successful firms will provide ongoing marketing and technical advice and assistance together with attractive financing arrangements. Established European and Japanese companies often use aggressive credit terms and financing to win an edge over new competition.

Advertising

Exporters buying local advertising space are advised to select an agency that is knowledgeable about the cultural characteristics of the Thai people. Advertising and product promotions are important tools in Thailand. Food and consumer products should be advertised and special promotions should be conducted at local stores, hotels, and entertainment centers. To promote industrial products, it is advisable to translate product literature and technical specifications into the Thai language, advertise in trade journals, and present technical seminars.

Service and Customer Support

Exporters to Thailand must ensure that their products meet local expectations of high quality and customer service. New entrants to Thai markets are wise to invest in training programs to implement a marketing and technical support staff, and exporters of machinery should also arrange training for agents and customers back at their home factories, as well as donate equipment to promote training on their machines.

Marketing in Thailand

MARKETING TIPS

- **Competitive factors** Japanese and Taiwanese manufacturers import most of their capital machinery from abroad.
- **Pricing** Price competition is severe. Local Thai manufacturers will cut prices to the bone to compete, and will draw on local knowledge and life-long relationships for advantage. Market research will be needed to develop a pricing policy.
- **Product and service** Thais have become used to the Japanese emphasis on service and quality.
- **Government purchases** The key to successful bidding for government contracts is to have a reputable local representative with good access to the procuring agency and knowledge of specific requirements and practice. Local representatives are an accepted and legitimate part of the bidding process.

CONSULTING FIRMS

Agrisource
36/11-12 #21, Soi Lang Suan
Ploenchit Road
Bangkok 10330
Tel: (2) 253-5858
Fax: (2) 253-5858

The Brooker Group Ltd.
2nd Fl., Zone D, Rm. 201/2
Queen Sirikit National Convention Center
60 New Rachadapisek Road
Klongtoey
Bangkok 10110
Tel: (2) 229-3111
Fax: (2) 229-3127

Business Advisory Thailand
2nd Fl., SMC Building
285 Sukhumvit Road (near Asoke)
Bangkok 10110
Tel: (2) 253-6291/2, 253-6295
Fax: (2) 254-4576

Business International Dataconsult
Orient Research Ltd.
54 Soi Santipharp, Nares Road
Bangkok 10500
Tel: (2) 236-2780, 233-5606
Fax: (2) 236-8143

Coopers & Lybrand
8th Fl., Sathorn Thani Building
90/14-16 N. Sathorn Road
Bangkok 10500
Tel: (2) 236-5227/8/9, 236-7814
Fax: (2) 237-1201

Deemar Co Ltd.
29/5 Soi Saladaeng 1, Saladaeng Road
Bangkok 10500
Tel: (2) 234-4520/1, 234-4721
Fax: (2) 236-7747

Development Services Ltd.
130/13 Soi Orapin (Soi 12)
Rama VI Road
Bangkok 10400
Tel: (2) 279-9500, 279-2913
Fax: (2) 278-3722

JP Rooney & Associates Group
4th Fl., Panunee Building
518/3 Ploenchit Road
POB 11-1238
Bangkok 10330
Tel: (2) 252-0177, 251-9832
Fax: (2) 251-2323, 254-7343

KPMG Peat Marwick Suthee
9th Fl., Sathorn Thani Building II
92 North Sathorn Road
Bangkok 10500
Tel: (2) 236-6161/2/3/4, 236-7877/8
Fax: (2) 236-6165

Business Culture

Greetings and Courtesies

The traditional greeting among Thais is the *wai*, which signifies "Hello," "Thank you," and "I'm sorry." One places the palms together, fingers extended at chest level, and bows slightly. The higher the hands are placed, the greater the respect, but the fingers are not placed above eye level. When meeting foreigners, the accepted greeting is the handshake. This applies to both men and women. Thais address each other by using the first name preceded by *Khun*. Surnames are used in formal situations. On formal occasions, foreigners can address Thais by using their last name, preceded by Mr., Mrs., or Miss. Titles are important, and if someone has a title use it when greeting them. Thais are extremely courteous and respectful of others. Thailand is often called the "Land of Smiles." Thais tend to be reserved, and feel it is improper to criticize others. They value a sense of humor, laughter, and a genial attitude.

Business Ethic and Framework

The Thai expression, *Mai Pen Rai* (never mind) sums up their attitude toward almost everything. They are by no means lazy or uncaring, but life is to be enjoyed. Problems and reversals are not to be taken too seriously, and they are generally happy with who they are and what they have. Respect is extremely important in Thai culture. Speaking loudly or publicly expressing anger is considered improper behavior and can result in a loss of respect. Showing proper respect is especially important when dealing with older people.

Decision Making

Decisions are made slowly. Thai respect for rank and authority demands that all documents, requests, and proposals must travel up the entire chain of command before they reach the actual decision maker. Thais generally look for some sort of compromise before coming to a decision, even in situations where it may seem no compromise is necessary. They will go to great lengths to avoid giving an outright "no," and believe it is not possible to be too polite. Decisions are made at the top, and subordinates shield high-level executives so they do not have to deal with situations they are not prepared for.

Women

Thai women have long been active and highly visible at all levels of business, and are treated the same as men. Foreign women can expect to be treated with respect and taken seriously, but will find they are more easily accepted if they speak softly. Women should never touch a Buddhist monk, offer to shake his hand, or hand anything directly to him. If a woman must hand something to a monk, she should give it to a man. If no man is around, she should place it on a table or on the ground, and the monk will pick it up. Women should be very careful about their handbags on the street (pursesnatchers often use motorcycles), avoid wearing jewelry in the street, and not go to nightclubs alone. At night, always take taxis (these should be hotel taxis, never unofficial taxis) and if a driver engages you in conversation, say you are married and have children.

Meetings

Punctuality is not a high priority, but arriving on time for a meeting will earn you respect. However, do not be surprised if your Thai associate is late. The pace is relaxed. Thais often make personal phone calls or run errands during the business day. Your first meeting could be a business lunch, at which business might not be discussed at all. Thais like to take time to get to know their potential business partners. When talking business, don't ask questions that require a direct response or a judgment such as, "What do you think of this product?" Such bluntness, and its potential for confrontation, will make a Thai uncomfortable and could be considered impolite. If Thais laugh for seemingly no reason, they are embarrassed and it is best to change the subject.

Business Attire

Thais are extremely neat, and consider appearance to be very important. Dress formally. For men, a dark suit, tie, and polished shoes are recommended. Thailand is hot and humid, so natural fibers that breathe (cotton, linen) will be more comfortable. Women should wear tasteful, conservative dresses (never sleeveless). Stockings are not necessary because of the intense heat. If you wear makeup, full eye makeup is suggested. During the rainy season (June through November), men should bring extra pants because your clothes will be splashed at the ankles.

Cultural Cautions

DO'S

- Always be respectful, courteous, and polite.
- Be extremely respectful when visiting any temple. You will be expected to remove your shoes, so be sure your socks do not have holes.
- Treat all images of Buddha with absolute respect. Don't touch images or statues of Buddha.

DON'TS

- Never say or do anything that in any way shows disrespect for the Royal Family.
- Do not openly express anger, even by raising your voice. Thais find such behavior contemptible.
- The head is considered sacred. Do not touch a person's head or pass something over it, even a child's.
- Never point the soles of your feet at a Thai, a picture of the Royal Family, or an image of Buddha. The feet are the lowliest part of the body. Also, do not point to or gesture at someone with your feet.
- Don't place your arm over the back of a chair in which someone is sitting. It offends Thais.
- Don't slap a Thai on the back or arm, even as a friendly or affectionate gesture.
- Women must never touch a Buddhist monk or offer to shake their hand.
- Do not take any image of the Buddha out of the country. There are serious penalties.

CUSTOMS

- It is offensive to cross one's legs when sitting, especially in the presence of an older person.
- Business cards are important. If possible, have them printed in your language on one side, and in Thai on the other. When given a card, do not just put it in your pocket. Take a moment to review it and treat it with the proper respect.
- Gifts may be given, but should not be too expensive. Appropriate presents include good quality pens, flowers, a box of chocolates, or a basket of fruit, and may be delivered to the office.

OBSERVATIONS

- The King and Queen are revered to the point of adoration, and Thais take great offense at any negative remarks about their royal leaders. There are strict laws regarding how royalty may be referred to. People are subject to arrest—and deportation—for saying or writing anything offensive to the royal family.
- Almost everyone in Thailand has a nickname. Do not be surprised if you are given one too.
- Thailand means "Land of the Free." Thais are immensely proud of the fact that their country has never been colonized by a foreign power.
- The American musical play "The King and I" has never been performed in Thailand because it is considered offensive to a ruler. A Thai may mention it, but do not bring it up yourself.
- The best months for travel to Thailand are November through March. April and May are peak vacation times, and May through October is monsoon season.

NEGOTIATIONS

- Do not raise your voice, hit the table, or in any other way openly express anger.
- Don't seek or expect direct answers, and avoid direct confrontation.
- If things get difficult, or an argument seems to be developing, Thais will make a joke or change the subject. Go along with this shift, or the situation will only get worse.
- If Thais start making excuses or suddenly have difficulty with the language, they are trying to say no.
- Thais find it difficult to deal with a direct negative answer. If you have to say no to something, do so in a polite, nonconfrontational way.
- A senior-level Thai might say they have to check with someone else at a higher level, even when this other person does not in fact exist. This is another way of saying no.

Legal System

The legislature is independent from the executive branch of the Thai government. Judges are appointed and removed by the King on recommendation of a judicial commission. The Constitutional Tribunal interprets the Constitution.

Intellectual Property Protection

Although Thailand has long had laws protecting intellectual property rights, it has come under intense pressure from the international community to expand protection, eliminate abuses, and increase enforcement of these laws. Its legislation is under review and is being revised in an effort to comply.

Patents Patents last for 20 years from the filing date for an invention and 10 years for a design. No product produced by a process protected by a Thai patent can be imported into the country without a special license. Thailand is not a party to any international convention, but priority may be claimed from a basic patent application if the applicant's home country accords the same right to a Thai national. In cases of infringement, the burden of proof will be on the defendant.

Trademarks All trademarks must be registered with the Department of Intellectual Property. They must include photographs or drawings of the product. A trademark is only valid if the proprietor or the proprietor's agent has an office or other place of business in Thailand that the registrar can contact. Trademark law also covers service marks and certification marks. It provides restrictions and stiff penalties for violation.

Copyrights Original works do not need to be registered to be considered copyrighted in Thailand, but works can be recorded with the Department of Intellectual Property, Ministry of Commerce. Copyright lasts for 50 years after the author's death. Penalties for infringement include fines and imprisonment up to one year. The government is currently drafting legislation to protect computer programs and performers' rights.

Business Registration

All businesses must be registered, with information including name and address of the company and names of all the owners or board members. Registration materials must be filed with the Department of Commercial Registration at the Thai Ministry of Commerce.

Contracts and Dispute Resolution

Most contracts can be made orally. Contracts regarding mortgages, company formation, and the sale of immovable property must be written or they are void. Any disputes must be sent to the defendant before the case can be brought to court. Disputing parties usually attempt to achieve a settlement at this point, rather than undertaking costly legal proceedings. Almost always, companies usually try to settle disputes informally before taking the case to court, and mediation and conciliation is commonly utilized. If a dispute is decided by the courts, the process tends to be lengthy.

Labor

Comprehensive labor regulations stipulate hours of work, sick leave, minimum wages, compensation, and other basic conditions with which employers must comply. Depending on the type of job, maximum working hours range from 42 to 54 hours a week. For the purposes of the law, a day means not more than nine hours for commercial work, eight hours for industrial or transport work, and seven hours for work described as hazardous. Employers must contribute to a workers compensation fund at rates varying depending on the level of risk involved. Employers, employees, and the government must each contribute 1.5 percent of an employee's wages to the social security scheme to provide compensation for injury, illness, disability, death, and childbirth. The law also provides for unemployment benefits.

The Labor Relations Act defines the procedures for negotiations between employees and employers. In the event of a labor dispute, the dissenting party must give its demands in writing to the other party. If direct negotiation fails, the case is referred to the Labor Dispute Mediation Office. Disputes in certain essential services, such as railways, telecommunications, and waterworks are handled by the Labor Relations Committee, whose decision is final. Workers are permitted to form associations and unions, although they must be registered with the Labor Department Registrar and may not operate until a license has been issued. Labor union membership is restricted to Thai nationals who are employed by the same employer or who do similar work in the same province. While unions are permitted to strike, the Thai labor movement is not militant. Less than two percent of the work force is unionized, although about 10 percent of the industrial work force belong to unions.

Legal Matters

LEGAL BRIEFS

- **Maximum workweek** Employees may work a maximum of 48 hours per week for standard industrial work.
- **Judgments** All judgments are in writing, and must be rendered on completion of trial. Thailand is not party to any treaties for the enforcement of foreign judgments. They may be submitted as evidence of infringement, however.
- **Child labor** The employment of children under the age of 13 is prohibited and there are restrictions on the employment of children and youths through the age of 18.
- **Environmental legislation** Laws against pollution are becoming stricter in accordance with environmental targets set out in the seventh development plan. However, the enforcement of Thailand's approximately 70 environmental laws is made difficult by an inefficient bureaucracy comprising some 35 different agencies, as well as by a lack of funds.
- **Professional services** Only persons of Thai nationality may be licensed in many professional services, including accounting, architecture, engineering, construction management, brokerage services, and legal services.
- **Intellectual property protections** Thailand has announced its intention to bring its copyright regime into conformity with international standards, and to provide protection through administrative measures for certain pharmaceutical products not eligible for full patent protection under Thai law.
- **International agreements** Thailand is a member of ASEAN, Berne Convention; New York Convention on the Recognition and Enforcement of Foreign Arbitral Awards.

LEGAL CONTACTS

Anek & Associates
Suite 1901-1902 Wall Street Tower
33/96 Surawong Road, Bangrak
Bangkok 10500
Tel: (2) 234-6900
Fax: (2) 236-5835

Marut Bunnag International Law Office
Central Chidlom Tower, 9th Floor
22 Soi Somkid, Ploenchit Road
Bangkok 10300
Tel: (2) 254-0860 to 254-0864
Fax: (2) 254-0865

Inter Consultants Law & Accounting Associates
399/48 Thonglor 21 Lane
Sukhumvit 55 Road, Klongtoey
Bangkok 10110
Tel: (2) 931-2077
Fax: (2) 381-2687

Ukrit Mongkolvavin Law Office
10 Sukhumvit 5
Bangkok 10110
Tel: (2) 255-4015

Russin & Vecchi
Sathorn City Tower
175 South Sathorn Road, 18th Floor
Bangkok 10120
Tel: (2) 679-6005
Fax: (2) 679-6041

Tilleke & Gibbins
Tilleke & Gibbins Building
64/1 Soi Ton Son, Ploenchit Roadd
Bangkok 10330
Tel: (2) 254-2640-58
Fax: (2) 254-4304

Vickery & Worachai Ltd.
16th Floor, Diethelm Tower A
93/1 Wireless Road
Bangkok 10330
Tel: (2) 256-6311
Fax: (2) 256-6317

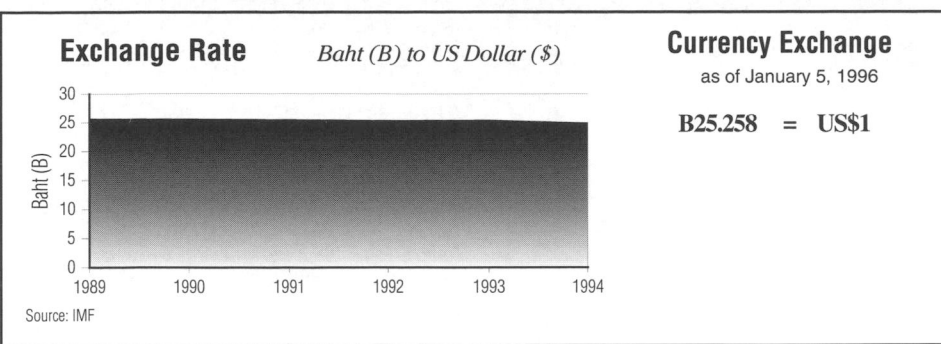

Exchange Rate
Baht (B) to US Dollar ($)

Source: IMF

Currency Exchange
as of January 5, 1996

B25.258 = US$1

Currency

The currency of Thailand is the Thai baht (B), which is divided into 100 santang.

Foreign Exchange

Exchange control is administered by the Bank of Thailand, which delegates responsibility for approving most transactions to authorized banks. The external value of the baht is determined on the basis of the relationship of the baht to a weighted basket of currencies of Thailand's major trading partners and on other considerations. There are no taxes or subsidies on purchases or sales of foreign exchange. Foreign exchange transactions are carried out between commercial banks and customers and among the commercial banks.

Capital Transfers

Capital investments in Thailand through equity participation or portfolio investments are permitted freely. Foreign capital may be brought into the country and loans contracted without restriction, but proceeds must be surrendered to authorized banks or deposited in foreign currency accounts with authorized banks in Thailand within 15 days of receipt. Repatriation of investment funds, loan repayments, and interest payments may be made without restriction.

Investment Incentives

The Thai government encourages foreign direct investment as a means of promoting economic development, employment, and technology transfer. It offers several investment incentives including a 50 percent reduction of import duties on imported machinery; reduction of import duties of up to 90 percent on imported raw materials and components; exemption from corporate income taxes; and exclusion from taxable income of dividends derived from promoted enterprises during the income tax holiday.

Thailand gives permission to bring in foreign nationals to undertake investment feasibility studies; to bring in foreign technicians and experts to work under promoted projects; and to own land for carrying out promoted activities.

Thailand also guarantees against nationalization and competition by new state enterprises.

Investment Restrictions

Thailand has greatly liberalized its investment restrictions, but foreign ownership is still limited to a minority interest in several sectors; land ownership is restricted; and registration of certain types of investment is required.

TAXATION

Taxation requires sophisticated knowledge of complex rules and regulations specific to each country. For more detailed information we suggest you refer to the Ernst & Young Corporate Tax Guide and Directory, available from the Ernst & Young accounting office in your country, or from:

Ernst & Young
POB 1047
Bangkok 10501
Thailand
Tel: (2) 264-0777, 661-9190
Fax: (2) 264-0790, 661-9192

- Thai resident companies are subject to corporate income tax on worldwide income. Branches of foreign companies are subject to taxes on income derived from Thailand sources only.

At a Glance

Corporate Income Tax Rate (%)	30
Capital Gains Tax Rate (%)	30
Branch Tax Rate (%)	30
Withholding Tax (%)	
Dividends	10
Interest (a)	15
Royalties from Patents, Know-how, etc.	15
Branch Remittance Tax	10
Net Operating Losses (Years)	
Carryback	0
Carryforward	5

(a) Interest on some foreign currency loans brought into Thailand between May 1, 1979, and February 28, 1990, is exempt.

Money Matters

BITS AND PIECES

- **Double taxation** Thailand has made double taxation agreements with 26 countries. Foreign tax relief is limited to either the amount of foreign or Thai tax, whichever is the lowest. Taxes paid in nontreaty countries may not be credited against Thai tax, but may be used as a deductible expense for income tax purposes.

- **Related-party transactions** Existence of a related party has no bearing to income tax, if charges are reasonable. Payments made to related parties are deductible, so long as they are for the purpose of generating income for the paying company. However, these types of transactions are subject to scrutiny to determine whether they are reasonable.

- **Loans** Loans may be taken without restriction, but must be surrendered to an authorized bank or deposited in a foreign currency account within 15 days.

- **Expropriation** Private property can be expropriated for public purposes in accordance with Thai law, which provides for due process and compensation.

- **Gold** Residents may hold and domestically negotiate gold jewelry, gold coins, and unworked gold. Purchases or sales of gold on commodity futures exchanges are prohibited. Imports and exports of gold other than gold jewelry are prohibited unless a license has been obtained from the Ministry of Finance.

BANKS

Bank of America, Bangkok Branch
2/2 Wireless Road
Bangkok 10330
Tel: (2) 251-6333
Fax: (2) 253-1905

Bank of Asia Public Company Ltd.
191 South Sathorn Road
Khet Sathorn
Bangkok 10120
Tel: (2) 287-2211/3
Fax: (2) 213-2652, 287-2973/4

Bank of Thailand
POB 154
273 Thanon Samsen
Bankgkhunprom
Bangkok 10200
Tel: (2) 281-3322, 282-3322
Fax: (2) 280-0626

Chase Manhattan Bank
20 North Sathorn Road, Silom
965 Rama I Road, Bangrak
Bangkok 10500
Tel: (2) 234-5992/5
Fax: (2) 234-8386

Citibank N.A.
6th Fl., 127 South Sathorn Road
Bangkok 10120
Tel: (2) 213-2000 through 2007, 213-2441/2
Fax: (2) 213-2527, 213-2530

Krung Thai Bank Ltd.
35 Sukhumvit Road
Bangkok 10110
Tel: (2) 255-2222, 250-0861
Fax: (2) 255-9391/7

Siam City Bank Ltd.
1101 New Petchburi Road
GPOB 488
Bangkok 10400
Tel: (2) 253-0200/9, 208-5000
Fax: (2) 253-7061, 253-1240

Siam Commercial Bank Ltd.
1060 New Petchburi Road
GPOB 1644
Bangkok 10400
Tel: (2) 256-1234
Fax: (2) 253-6697, 254-3359

Thai Farmers Bank Ltd.
400 Phaholyothin Road
Bangkok 10400
Tel: (2) 273-1199, 270-1122
Fax: (2) 270-1144/5

Business Travel

	LH 1906	MADRID	935	113-3
	LH 1022	STUTTGART HBF.	935	-
	AF 1701	LYON	940	683-6
	AY 822	HELSINKI	940	113-3
	AA 071	SFRANCISCO-DALLAS	945	731-7

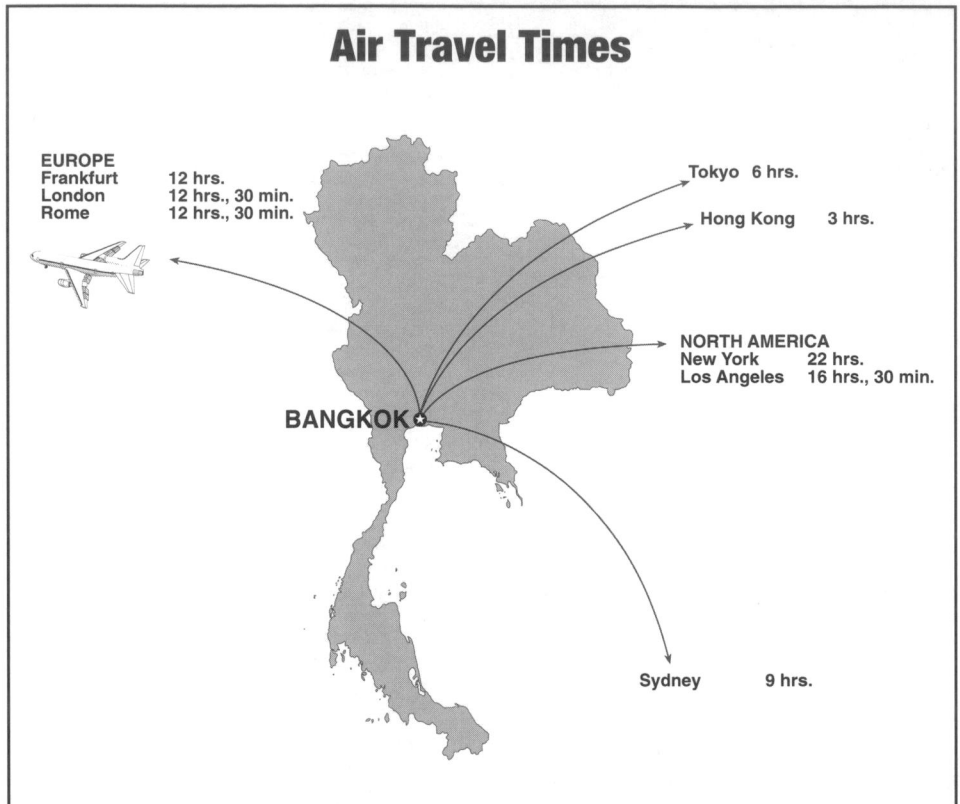

Air Travel Times

EUROPE
Frankfurt   12 hrs.
London   12 hrs., 30 min.
Rome   12 hrs., 30 min.

Tokyo 6 hrs.

Hong Kong   3 hrs.

NORTH AMERICA
New York   22 hrs.
Los Angeles   16 hrs., 30 min.

BANGKOK

Sydney   9 hrs.

COMMUNICATIONS

Telephones Telephone service is very good in the cities of Thailand. International calls may be placed from hotels or post offices, which are slower but less expensive, and can be dialed direct or through the operator.
Fax Most hotels, businesses, and post offices now have fax facilities.
Post office Thailand's mail service is excellent.

BEST TRAVEL BOOKS

Thailand, Indochina and Burma Handbook. Joshua Eliot, 800 pages. Passport Books, NTC Publishing Group.
Knopf Guide to Thailand, Knopf Guide Staff. Alfred A.Knopf, Inc.
Baedeker's Thailand, Karl Baedeker. Prentice Hall General Travel and Reference.
Fodor's Travel Guide, Thailand.
All-Asia Travel Guide, Southeast Asia, Volume One Thailand, Travel Survival Kit, Lonely Planet. Cummings knows his way around this country like a Buddhist monk knows his way around a temple. 700 pages, 16 color.
Culture Shock, A Guide to Customs and Etiquette, Thailand.
The Travellers Guide to Thailand Customs and Manners. Elizabeth Devine & Nancy Bgaranti. An invaluable guide for people not wanting to put foot in mouth.
Four Dragons Guidebook. The indispensable guide to Hong Kong, Singapore, Thailand, Taiwan. Volume One. Fredric M. Kaplan.
Insight Pocket Guides, Thailand. "I can't think of another book which so effectively captures the essence of a country."
Do's and Taboo's Around the World. The Bestselling Guide to International Behavior. Edited by Roger Axtell, compiled by the Parker Pen Company. The ultimate guide to international behavior, now completely updated and expanded. Helpful, fun to read!

USEFUL TELEPHONE NUMBERS

If you are calling from outside Thailand, you will need to add the country code [66] and any other international dialing requirements from within your country.

- Directory Assistance 13
- Long Distance 100
- Tourist Police 195
- Police, Fire, Ambulance 191
- Bangkok Tourist Police 1699
- Highway Police 195
- International Assistance 100
- Bangkok Railway Terminus .... (2) 2337010
- Hua Lampong Station .... (2) 2233762
- Airport Hotel .... (2) 5661020
- Bangkok Center .... (2) 2351780
- Secretarial Services .... (2) 233-9293
- Translation Services .... (2) 233-7714
- Office Secretariat .... (2) 251-5396
- Ambulance .... (2) 252-2171
- Tourist assistance .... (2) 281-5051
- Fire 199 (2) 2460199
- Ambulance .... (2) 2522171
- Missing Persons Bureau .... (2) 2823892
- Pharmacy .... (2) 2983749

Courier Services
- DHL .... (2) 260-7600
- TNT Express .... (2) 249-5702
- CSS Courier .... (2) 253-0098

Credit Card Information
Lost or stolen credit cards (call collect to the US, regardless of which country the card was issued in).
- Amex .... [1] (919) 333-3211
- Diner's Club .... [1] (303) 799-1504
- MasterCard .... [1] (314) 275-6690
- Visa .... [1] (410) 581-7931

Travelogue

WORKWEEK

Offices Monday-Friday 8:00 am to 5:00 pm; some Saturday mornings.
Banks Monday-Friday 8:30 am to 3:30 pm.
Government Monday-Friday 8:30 am to noon and 1:00 pm to 4:30 pm.
Retail Monday-Sunday 10:00 am to 7:00 pm.
Retail stores often stay open later for tourists.

HOLIDAYS

Holidays 1996
January 1 New Year's Day
January-February Chinese New Year *
April 6 King Rama I Memorial Day and Chakri Day
April 12-14 Songkran Days
May 1 Labor Day
May 5 Coronation Day
May Visakha Puja Day *
July 1 Midyear Holiday
August 12 Queen's Birthday
July - August Buddhist Lent *
October 24 Chulalongkorn Day
December 5 King's Birthday
December 10 Constitution Day
In addition, the last Monday in May and August is a bank holiday.
* Dates vary year to year and are based on the lunar calendar.

VISA AND PASSPORT

Only a valid passport is required for a 15-day visit, if you arrive at an international airport. You may be asked to show an onward ticket or equivalent cash. For longer stays or overland entry, obtain a visa in advance.

DEPARTURE FORMALITIES

To export Buddha images or antiques of archaeological value, you will need a license from the Bangkok National Museum (Tel: (2) 224-1370). You may not take out more than US$10,000 in undeclared foreign money or B500 in Thai currency.

IMMUNIZATION

Vaccination certificates are required of travelers from areas infected with cholera or yellow fever. Typhoid and polio vaccinations and malaria tablets are recommended.

TIPPING

Most restaurants and hotels add a 10 percent service charge, so tipping is optional. Tip porters US$.40 per bag and give hotel staff US$.80 for extra service. Never tip taxi drivers.

CRIME

Foreigners are susceptible to petty theft and con games by natives pretending to offer assistance or hospitality. Normal safety precautions should be taken when traveling through Thailand. The punishment for smuggling narcotics is the death penalty and is strictly enforced for all nationalities.

INFRASTRUCTURE

Thailand has experienced a large growth rate, and though the infrastructure has not kept up, it does offer excellent hotels for business travelers. The roadways and mass transit infrastructure are being improved and telecommunications are struggling to keep pace with demand. Flying is the easiest way to get around the country, but the modern, quick, reasonably priced, and comfortable rail system is the most enjoyable way if you have more time. Buses, taxis, pedicabs and boats are typical transportation modes in Thailand but can be a hassle to get. There are too many vehicles and not enough roads in Thailand.

NATIONAL TOURIST OFFICE

Tourism Authority of Thailand
4 Ratchadamnoen Nok Ave.
10100 Bangkok
Thailand
Tel: (2) 282-1143

Contacts

GOVERNMENT AGENCIES

Office of the Board of Investment
555 Vipavadee Rangsit Road
Bangkok 10900
Tel: (2) 537-8111, 537-8155
Fax: (2) 537-8177
Telex: 72435BINVEST TH

Engineering Institute of Thailand
Chulalongjkorn University
Henry Dunant Road
Bangkok 10330
Tel: (2) 218-6794/9
Fax: (2) 251-2506

Office of the Board of Control of the Engineering and Architectural Professions
Ministry of Interior
Visuthikasat Road
Bangkok 10200
Tel: (2) 281-1421
Fax: (2) 282-2161

Commodity Trade Division
Department of Foreign Trade
Ministry of Commerce
Rajadamnoen Klang Road
Bangkok 10200
Tel: (2) 282-7315
Fax: (2) 282-0827

Department of Foreign Trade
Sub-division of Foreign Trade Services
Application for Import Permit
Rajadamnoen Road
Bangkok 10200
Tel: (2) 282-0824
Fax: (2) 282-0825

Public Warehouse Organization (Or-Kor-Sor)
Government Importing Agent
Ministry of Commerce
Maharaj Road
Bangkok 10200
Tel: (2) 222-8830, 222-8821

Drug Control Division
Food and Drug Administration Ministry of Public Health
Bangkok 10200
Tel: (2) 282-6392, 282-4856
Fax: (2) 281-8199

Food Control Division
Food and Drug Administration Ministry of Public Health
Bangkok 10200
Tel: (2) 282-6520, 281-8330, 282-6539
Fax: (2) 281-8199

Division of Manufacturing and Import Facilities Control
Food and Drug Administration
Sam Sen Road
Bangkok 10200
Tel: (2) 282-4180 through 4185

Product Registration Section
Food Control Division
Food and Drug Administration
Sam Sen Road
Bangkok 10200
Tel: (2) 282-4180 through 4185, 281-8330
Fax: (2) 281-8199

Division of Food Analysis
Department of Medical Sciences
6th Fl., Building 5
693 Bamrung Muang Road
Yot-Se, Bangkok 10100
Tel: (2) 223-9873

Agricultural Regulatory Division
Department of Agriculture
Chatuchak
Bangkok 10900
Tel: (2) 579-8516
Fax: (2) 579-4129, 579-3576

Disease Control Division
Department of Livestock Development
Phyathai Road
Bangkok 10400
Tel: (2) 252-5967

Veterinary Control Post
Rm. 308, 3rd Fl.
CARGO Building, Don-Muang Air Port
Bangkok 10900
Tel: (2) 535-1425, 535-1546, 535-1210

Veterinary Control Post
Klong-Toey Port
Bangkok 10110
Tel: (2) 249-1221

Telephone Organization of Thailand
89 Chaengwattana, Donmuang
Bangkok 10210
Tel: (2) 505-1112

WORLD TRADE CENTER

World Trade Center Bangkok
World Trade Center Complex, 7th Floor
4 Rajdamri Road
Bangkok 10330
Tel: (2) 255-9500
Fax: (2) 253-4488

BUSINESS AND TRADE ORGANIZATIONS

American Chamber of Commerce in Thailand
7th Fl., Kian Gwan Building
140 Wireless Road
Bangkok 10330
Tel: (2) 251-9260/1
Fax: (2) 255-2454
Telex: 82778 KGCOM TH, 82827

Thai Chamber of Commerce
150 Rajbopit Road
Bangkok 10200
Tel: (2) 225-0086
Fax: (2) 225-3372
Telex: 72093 TCCTH

Trogot, The Board of Trade of Thailand
150 Rajbopit Road
Bangkok 10200
Tel: (2) 221-0555, 221-1827
Fax: (2) 225-3995

The Federation of Thai Industries
394/14 Samsen Road, Dusit
Bangkok 10330
Tel: (2) 280-0951 through 0958
Fax: (2) 280-0959
Telex: 72202 INDUSTI TH

Thai Contractors Association
110 Wireless Road, Pathumwan
Bangkok 10330
Tel: (2) 255-3991/2, 255-3386/7
Fax: (2) 255-3990

The Consultant Engineers Association of Thailand
c/o R.K.V. Engineering Consultant Co., Ltd.
11/1 Sukhumvit 30 Road
Bangkok 10110
Tel: (2) 258-4838/9
Fax: (2) 259-8177

Forest Industry Organization
76 Thanon Ratchadamnoen Nok
Bangkok 10200
Tel: (2) 282-3243

National Economic and Social Development Board
962 Thanon Krung Kasem
Bangkok 10100
Tel: (2) 282-1151
Fax: (2) 280-4085

AD AGENCIES

Amex Team Advertising Ltd.
276 A1 Bldg.
Raintree Office Garden
Rama 1X Rd.
Huay Kwang
Bangkok 10310
Tel: (2) 719-6444
Fax: (2) 719-6431

REMEMBER

- When you telephone (or fax) to Thailand from another country you must always include the country code [66] before the numbers given.
- When you send mail, be sure to write THAILAND in capital letters on it sown line below the addresses given.

BBDO Asia Pacific
1535-1537 Town in Town
Srivara Rd.
Ladprao 86
Bangkok 10310
Tel: (2) 559-3169
Fax: (2) 559-3170

Leo Burnett Ltd. Thailand
37 Soi Somprasong 3
Petchburi Rd.
Bangkok 10400
Tel: (2) 255-2356
Fax: (2) 253-9189

DDB Needham Worldwide Ltd. (Thailand)
511 Sri Ayudhya Rd.
Bangkok 10400
Tel: (2) 247-7352
Fax: (2) 247-7352

Dentsu, Young & Rubicam/Bangkok
19th-20 Fls.
Grand Amerine Tower
1550 New Petchburi Rd.
Bangkok 10310
Tel: (2) 207-0808
Fax: (2) 207-0818/0819

Grey Thailand Ltd.
Park Avenue, Home Office 2
5th Floor, 446/54-58
Sukhumvit 71, Klongton
Bangkok 10110
Tel: (2) 381-5454
Fax: (2) 711-1227/1226

Lintas Thailand
6th Fl. Sathorn Thani Bldg.
N. Sathorn Rd.
Bangkok 10500
Tel: (2) 236-0266
Fax: (2) 236-9248

McCann-Erickson (Thailand) Ltd.
5th & 6th Fl., Sethiwan Tower
139 Pan Rd.
Bangrak
Bangkok 10500
Tel: (2) 266-6211
Fax: (2) 237-3009

Ogilvy & Mather Ltd.
10th Fl., Silom Center
2 Silom Rd.
Bangkok 10500
Tel: (2) 233-8355
Fax: (2) 237-1546

Padorr & Associates
127/16 Soi 3, Petchburi Rd.
Rajvithi
Bangkok 10400
Tel: (2) 215-7324
Fax: (2) 215-7324

Prakit/FCB
167 Sukhumvit 62
Sukhumvit Rd.
Bangchak, Prakanong
Bangkok 10250
Tel: (2) 713-2216
Fax: (2) 332-8522

Saatchi & Saatchi Advertising Ltd.
25/F Sathorn City Tower
175 S. Sathorn Rd.
Khwaeng Thungmahamek Khet Sathorn
Bangkok 10120
Tel:(2) 679-5200
Fax: (2) 679-5210
Thai Hakuhodo Co. Ltd.
12th Fl., Dietheim Tower bldg., 93/1
Wireless Road
Bangkok 10330
Tel: (2) 256-7005
Fax: (2) 256-7017
J. Walter Thompson Company Limited
Srivikorn Bldg., 12th Fl.
18-8 Asoke Rd.
Bangkok 10110
Tel: (2) 258-0364
Fax: (2) 2589303
Wunderman Thailand
Grand Amarin Tower, 19th Fl., 19th Fl.
1550 New Petchburi Rd.
Bangkok 10310
Tel: (2) 207-0809
Fax: (2) 207-0811

NEWSPAPERS

Ban Muang
1 Soi Pluem-Manee
Thanon Vibhavadi Rangsit
Bangkok
Tel: (2) 513-0230
Daily Mirror
15/22 Thanon Lardprao 104
Bangkok
Tel: (2) 538-0220
Daily Nes
1/4 Thanon Vibhavadi Rangsit
Bangkok
Tel: (2) 579-0010
Dao Siam
60 Mansion 4
Thanon Rajdamnern
Bangkok
Tel: (2) 222-6001
Khao Panich
Daily Trade News
22/77 Thanon Ratchadapisek
Bangkok
Tel: (2) 511-5066
Krungthep Turakij Daily
44 Moo 10
Thanon Bangna-Trad
Bangna
Prakanong
Bangkok
Tel: (2) 392-0051
Fax: (2) 391-1486
Telex: 20326
Matichon
12 Thanon Thedsaban Naruban
Bangken
Bangkok
Tel: (2) 589-0020
Siam Daily
192/8-9 Soi Vorapong
Thanon Visuthikasat
Bangkok
Tel: (2) 281-7422
Siam Rath
12 Mansion 6
Thanon Visuthikasat
Bangkok
Tel: (2) 222-3629
Thai
423-425 Thanon Chao Khamrop
Bangkok
Tel: (2) 223-3175
Thai Rathj
1 Thanon Vibhavadi Rangsit
Bangkok
Tel: (2) 271-0217

Bangkok Post
Bangkok Post Bldg.
136 Soi Na Ranong
off Thanon Sunthorn Kosa
Klongtoey
Bangkok 10110
Tel: (2) 240-93700
Fax: (2) 240-3790
Telex: 82833

PERIODICALS

Bangkok Weekly
533-539 Thanon Sri Ayuthaya
Bangkok 10400
Tel: (2) 245-6138
Fax: (2) 247-3410
Mathichon Weekly Review
12 Thanon Thedsaban Naruban
Bangken
Bangkok
Satri Sarn
83/35 Arkarntrithosthep 2
Thanon
Prachathipatai
Bangkok 10300
Tel: (2) 281-9136
Siam Rath Weekly Review
Mansion 6
Thanon Rajdamnern
Bangkok 10200
Skul Thai
58 Soi 36
Thanon Sukhumvit
Bangkok 10110
Tel: (2) 258-5861
Fax: (2) 258-9130
Wattachak
88 Thanon Bangkoknoi-Nakornchaisri
Talingchan
Bangkok 10170
Tel: (2) 434-0330
Fax: (2) 435-0440
Telex: 72177
Bangkok Post Weekly Review
136 Soi Na Ranong
off Thanon Sunthron Kosa
Klongtoey
Bangkok 10110
Tel: (2) 240-3700
Fax: (2) 240-3790
Telex: 82833
Business Times
Thai Bldg.
Thanon Phra Ram IV
Bangkok 10110
Dara Thai
9-9/1 Sriukson
Thanon Chuapleung
Thangmahamek Yannawa
Bangkok 10120
Tel: (2) 249-1576
Dichan
1400 Thai Bldg.
Thanon Phra Ram Si
Bangkok
Tel: (2) 243-0351
Lalana
44 Moo 10
Thanon Bangna-Trad
Bangna
Bangkok 10260
Tel: (2) 314-1400
Fax: (2) 317-1409
Bangkok 30
139-41 Rimklongprapa Dusit
Bangkok 10800
Tel: (2) 587-8029
Fax: (2) 586-9110
Chao Krung
12 Mansion 6
Thanon Rajdamnern
Bangkok 10200

Grand Prix
129-133
Rim Klong Prapa
Thanon Prachachuen
Bangkok 10800
Tel: (2) 585-6714
Fax: (2) 587-6567
The Investor
Pansak Bldg.
4th FLoor
138/1 Thanon Petchburi
Bangkok 10400
Tel: (2) 282-8166
Kasikorn
Dept. of Agriculture
Bangken
Bangkok 10900
Tel: (2) 579-5369
The Lady
77 Thanon Phra Ram V
Bangkok
Look East
52/38 Soi Saladaeng 2
12/F Silom Condominium
Thanon SIlom
Bangkok 10500
Tel: (2) 233-3401
Fax: (2) 236-6764

RADIO AND TELEVISION

Radio Thailand (RTH)
National Broadcasting Services of Thailand
Government Public Relations Dept.
236 Thanon Vibhavadi Rangsit
Bangkok 10400
Tel: (2) 277-9125
Fax: (2) 277-0122
Telex: 72167
Ministry of Education Broadcasting Service
Centre for Innovation and Technology
Ministry of Education
Bangkok
Tel: (2) 246-0026
Bangkok Broadcasting & TV Co. Ltd. (Channel 7)
998/1 Soi Sirimitr, Phaholyothin, Talad Mawchid
POB 456
Bangkok 10900
Tel: (2) 278-1255
Fax: (2) 270-1976
Telex: 82730
Bangkok Entertainment Co. Ltd. (Channel 3)
2259 Thanon Petchburi Tadmai
Bangkok 10310
Tel: (2) 3145416
Fax: (2) 253-9978
Telex: 82616
The Royal Thai Army Television HSA-TV
Thanon Phaholyothin
Sanam Pao
Bangkok 10400
Tel: (2) 2798854
Fax: (2) 279-0430

STOCK EXCHANGE

Stock Exchange of Thailand (SET)
Sinthon Bldg.
2nd Floor
132 Thanon Witthayu
Bangkok 10330
Tel: (2) 254-0960
Fax: (2) 254-3040

INTERNET ADDRESSES

Usenet group(s):
soc.culture.thai
World Trade Bank Projects in Thailand
http://emailhost.ait.ac.th/Asia/wb-reps/wb-th.html
Department of Export Promotion
http://www.nectec.or.th/bureaux/dep/index.html
Country Information - Thailand
http://emailhost.ait.ac.th/Asia/infoth.html
Thailand Internet Industrial Directory
http://www.sino.net/thai/commerce/thaiprod.html
General Info on Thailand
http://sunsite.au.ac.th/thailand/thailandhome.html

Trinidad & Tobago

Republic of Trinidad & Tobago

Economy

Overview

Rich in oil and natural gas, Trinidad and Tobago became one of the Western hemisphere's most prosperous nations during the oil boom of the 1970s. However, an overreliance on this industry and its subsequent contraction means the economy is only now emerging from a long and painful recession. The government is moving toward a market-oriented economy and is concentrating on attracting foreign investment and on privatizing state enterprises. Control of government expenditure, market diversification and the support and commitment of one of the best educated populations in the developing world should ensure moderate growth in the long-term.

Trade

Trinidad and Tobago is only now beginning to recover from the collapse in oil prices over a decade ago which considerably lowered the total value of its foreign trade. The US is the largest source of its imports and the biggest buyer of its exports, followed by nations of the Caribbean Community (CARICOM), the UK and Venezuela. As part of its economic liberalization program import controls have been lifted and foreign ownership of service enterprises is welcomed. However a sluggish economy is still dampening domestic demand for imports.

Sectors

Agriculture Although agriculture employs 10 percent of the population, it contributes only two percent to total GDP. Still, the government plans to increase production in this sector and to diversify into non-traditional agricultural products for export. The dominant sugar sector is suffering from declining profitability already; therefore there has been a shift toward increasing production in cash crops such as rice, citrus, coffee, and vegetables.

Industry Petroleum and natural gas have been the driving forces behind Trinidad and Tobago's economy for the past four decades. A steady decline in oil production has been countered by an aggressive oil exploration campaign, and natural gas is beginning to play an increasingly important role in the economy. Reserves of natural gas are plentiful and it is expected to be the new foundation for growth for many decades to come. Other important industries include production of chemicals, fertilizers, iron, steel, and wood and related products.

Services Trinidad and Tobago has one of the highest per capita incomes in Latin America and this has sustained a strong service sector. Fifty-two percent of the population is engaged in service industries, chief of which are banking, insurance, trading companies, and distributors and tourism. Past resistance to tourism has been lifted and strong growth is expected in this sector.

Trends

Trinidad and Tobago is experiencing slow but steady growth, due largely to its efforts to move toward a market-oriented economy. The government is concentrating its efforts on ongoing privatization of state enterprises, a disciplined fiscal policy, and an emphasis on attracting foreign investment. The government is still dependent on the energy sector to drive the economy until the effects of its diversification program come into play.

At a Glance

THE COUNTRY
Location British West Indies off the coast of Venezuela.
Terrain Plains and low mountains.
Climate Tropical with a rainy season (June through December).

THE PEOPLE
Population 1,200,000
Ethnic composition
African.. 40%
East Indian... 40%
Mixed 18%
European 1%
Chinese and Other.. 1%
Religious composition
Roman Catholic 30%
Hindu 24%
Anglican 11%
Muslim 6%
Presbyterian.. 3%
Other.. 26%
Languages spoken English, French patois, Hindi, and other dialects.
Education and literacy About 97 percent of the population 10 years of age and over is literate. Education is compulsory for eight years.
Labor force
Total:.. 505,100
By occupation: services 52%, agriculture 10%, manufacturing, mining, and quarrying 15%, construction and utilities 13%

COUNTRY FACTS
Political and legal A former crown colony of Britain, Trinidad and Tobago gained independence in 1962. It is a parliamentary democracy with the highest court of appeal being the Privy Council in London. Universal suffrage is enjoyed by those 18 and older.
Telephone Trinidad maintains telephone services with all major countries of the world. As of 1991 there were over 200,000 telephones. Country code: [1]. Area code for all points: (809).
Transportation Two international airports, a dozen smaller airfields, a large sea port, and 8,000 km of roads make Trinidad a fairly accessible destination. However, large sections of Tobago are either inaccessible by road or are connected by treacherous and/or poorly surfaced roads.
Environment Although oil spillage is the major factor, mining, farming activities, and sewage all contribute to Trinidad and Tobago having a serious water pollution problem. The famed marshlands and mangroves still exist on the west coast of Trinidad at the Caroni Bird Sanctuary where flocks of scarlet ibis are known to roost.
Media There are two AM and four FM radio stations, five television stations and four daily newspapers. Freedom of the press is both guaranteed by the constitution and respected in practice. There are an estimated 400,000 television sets and over 600,000 radios on these islands.
Health Improvements in sanitation have resulted in impressive health benefits. Death rates from malaria, tuberculosis, typhoid, and syphilis have substantially decreased. Average life expectancy is 71 years. Infant mortality rate is 1 percent.

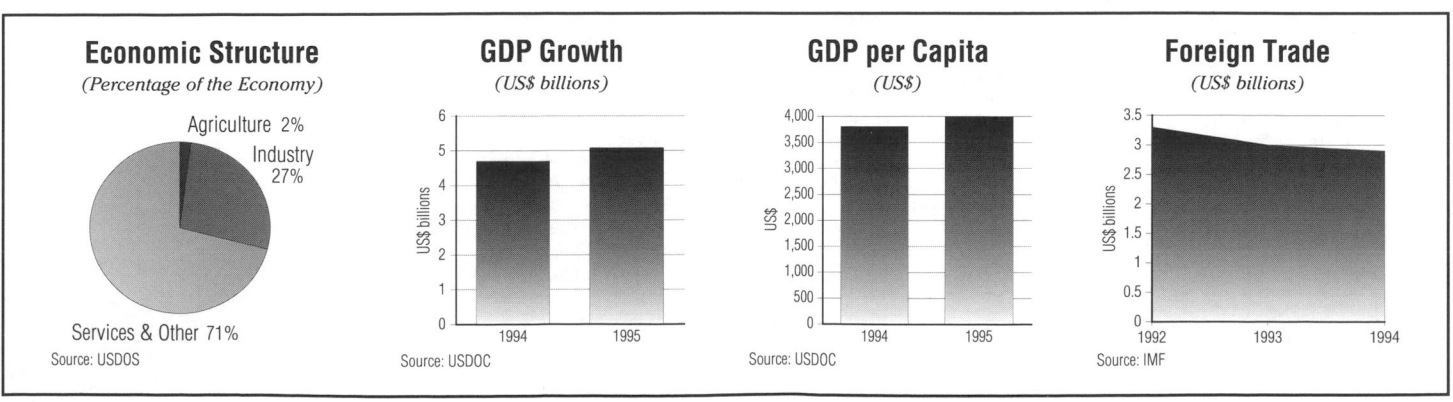

Economic Structure
(Percentage of the Economy)

Agriculture 2%
Industry 27%
Services & Other 71%

Source: USDOS

GDP Growth
(US$ billions)

Source: USDOC

GDP per Capita
(US$)

Source: USDOC

Foreign Trade
(US$ billions)

Source: IMF

Business Travel

		LH 1906	MADRID	935	113-3
		LH 1022	STUTTGART HBF.	935	-
		AF 1701	LYON	940	683-6
		AY 822	HELSINKI	940	113-3
		AA 071	SFRANCISCO-DALLAS	945	731-7

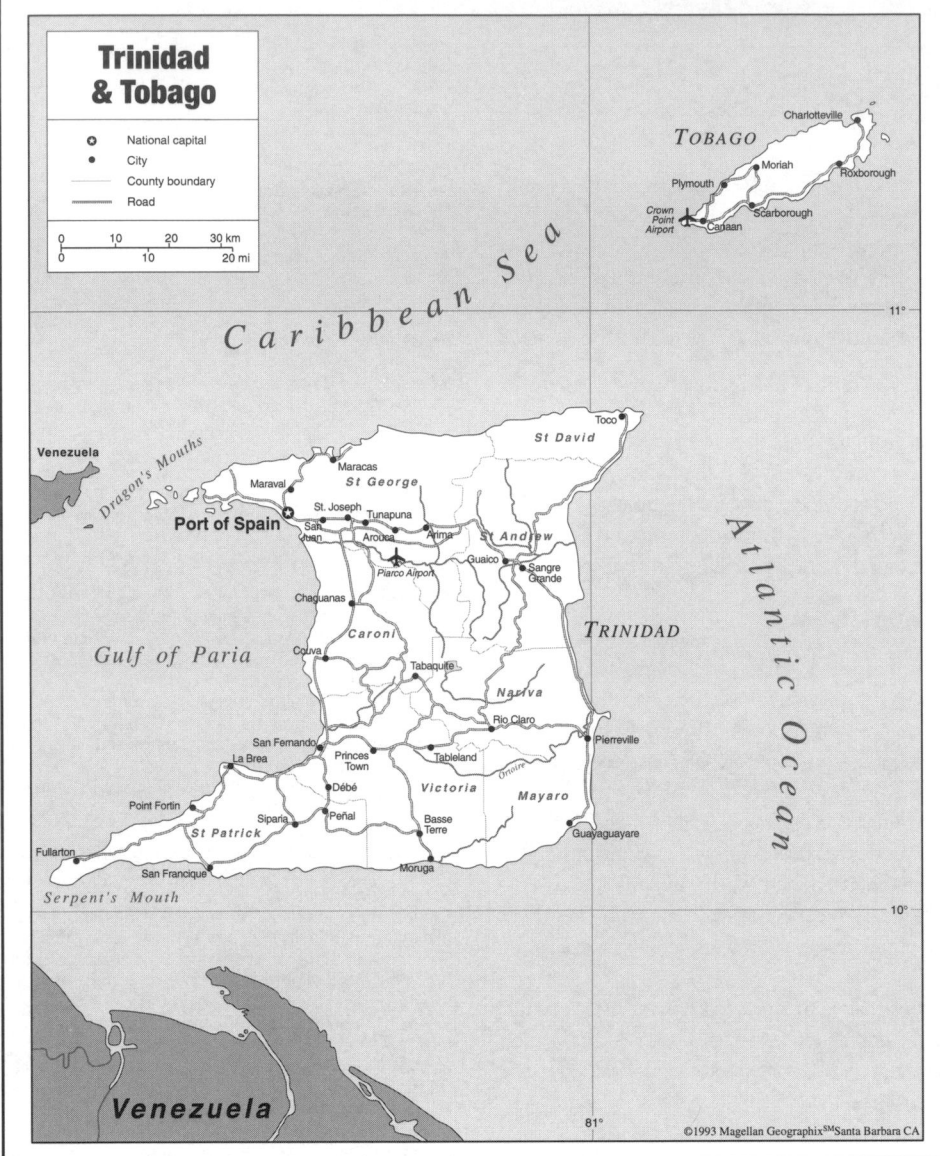

Trinidad & Tobago

⊙ National capital
• City
    County boundary
    Road

0   10   20   30 km
0   10   20 mi

Travelogue

WORKWEEK

Offices Monday-Thursday 8:00 am to 2:00 pm, Friday 9:00 am to noon and 3:00 pm to 5:00 pm.
Banks Monday-Friday 9:00 am to 3:00 pm.
Government Monday-Thursday 8:00 am to 2:00 pm, Friday 9:00 am to noon and 3:00 pm to 5:00 pm.
Retail Monday-Thursday 8:00 am to 2:00 pm, Friday 9:00 am to noon and 3:00 pm to 5:00 pm.

HOLIDAYS

Holidays 1996
January 1 New Year's Day
April 5 Good Friday
April 8 Easter Monday
June 19 Labour Day
August 1 Emancipation Day
August 31 Independence Day
September 24 Republic Day
December 25 Christmas Day
December 26 Boxing Day
In addition, most businesses are closed on Carnival Monday and Tuesday, preceding Ash Wednesday.

VISA AND PASSPORT

Foreigners must have a valid passport and an ongoing or return ticket. Visas are not required for North American and most European citizens. Nationals of Australia, India, New Zealand, Nigeria, Papua New Guinea, Sri Lanka, Tanzania, and Uganda must apply in advance for visas.

DEPARTURE FORMALITIES

The immigration card filled out on arrival must be returned upon departure. A departure tax of TT$75 (US$17.65) is imposed on every passenger more than five years old. It must be paid in local currency.

CRIME

The crime rate is increasing, including violent crime. Generally, Tobago is safer than Trinidad. Avoid major public beaches and the downtown streets of Port-of-Spain, Trinidad at night.

TIPPING

Tipping is not expected, but is appreciated by all service providers.

INFRASTRUCTURE

Trinidad and Tobago has a well-developed infrastructure, with paved roads and highways, and goods and services are available in even the most remote areas.

TOURIST OFFICES

National Tourist Office
134-138 Frederick St.
Port-of-Spain, Trinidad
Tel: (809) 623-1932

National Tourist Office
Scarborough Hall
Scarborough, Trinidad
Tel: (809) 639-2125

Trinidad & Tobago Hotel and Tourism Assoc.
The Travel Centre
Uptown Mall
44-58 Edward St.
Port-of-Spain, Trinidad
Tel: (809) 624-3928

COMMUNICATIONS

Telephones Telecommunications networks are reliable and most overseas calls can be dialed direct.
Fax Fax service is generally available at hotel desks.
Post office Open 24 hours and easily found.
Media There are two AM and four FM radio stations, five television stations, and four daily newspapers. Freedom of the press is both guaranteed by the constitution and respected in practice. There are an estimated 400,000 television sets and over 600,000 radios on these islands.

BEST TRAVEL BOOKS

Trinidad and Tobago. Insight Guides Series. Houghton Mifflin.
Masquerade: Introduction to Trinidad and Tobago, Jeremy Taylor. Caribbean Guides Series, illustrated, 144 pages. Hunter Publishing, Inc.

USEFUL TELEPHONE NUMBERS

If you are calling from outside Trinidad and Tobago, you will need to add the country code [1] and any other international dialing requirements from within your country.

• Police 999
• Fire/Ambulance 990
• Port-of-Spain General Hospital .... (809) 623-2951
• BWIA .... (809) 627-BWIA
• American Airlines .... (809) 664-4661
• United Airlines .... (809) 627-7000

Credit card information:
Lost or stolen credit cards (call collect to the US, regardless of which country the card was issued in).

• Amex .... [1] (919) 333-3211
• Diner's Club .... [1] (303) 799-1504
• MasterCard .... [1] (314) 275-6690
• Visa .... [1] (410) 581-7931

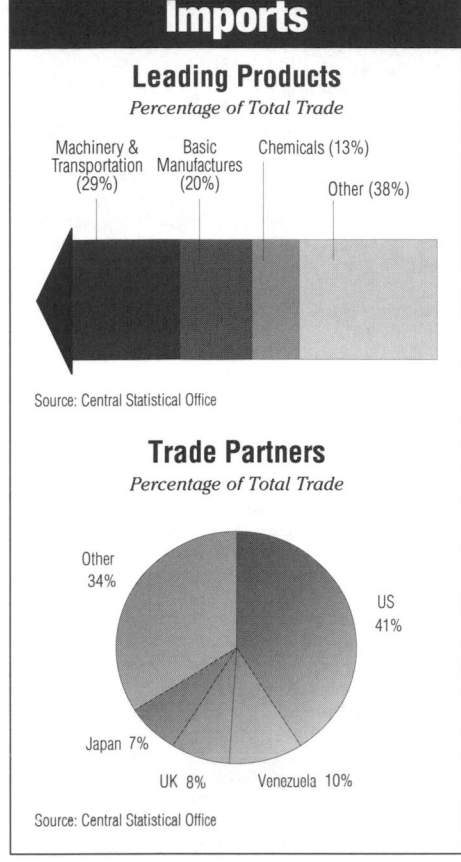

Imports

Leading Products
Percentage of Total Trade

Machinery & Transportation (29%)
Basic Manufactures (20%)
Chemicals (13%)
Other (38%)

Source: Central Statistical Office

Trade Partners
Percentage of Total Trade

Other 34%
US 41%
Japan 7%
UK 8%
Venezuela 10%

Source: Central Statistical Office

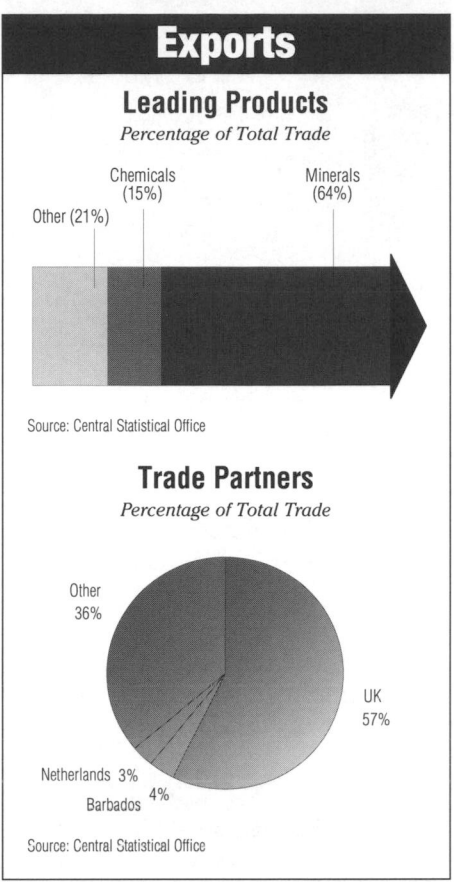

Exports

Leading Products
Percentage of Total Trade

Chemicals (15%)
Minerals (64%)
Other (21%)

Source: Central Statistical Office

Trade Partners
Percentage of Total Trade

Other 36%
UK 57%
Netherlands 3%
Barbados 4%

Source: Central Statistical Office

Opportunities

FOR IMPORTING TO TRINIDAD & TOBAGO
- oil and gas extraction and processing equipment
- industrial and electrical machinery
- paper products, computers and peripherals
- cars, automotive parts and accessories, light vessels

FOR EXPORTING FROM TRINIDAD & TOBAGO
- crude oil and oil (not crude), petroleum products
- ammonia, mineral or chemical fertilizers

GROWTH SECTORS
- wood and related products
- printing and publishing
- iron-carbide plants
- finance and financial services
- insurance and real estate
- transportation and distribution services

Trade News

RULES AND REGULATIONS
- **Import restrictions** Most manufactured products no longer require import licenses, although imports of certain agricultural products are still controlled. Policy changes to make Trinidad & Tobago more attractive to foreign investors have been implemented, including revisions of tax and tariff rates and removal of import restrictions on nearly all products.
- **Import licenses** Only sugar, poultry parts, left-hand drive vehicles, small boats, and firearms remain on the "Negative List" of products requiring an import license.
- **Tariff rates** Imports are subject to the CARICOM common external tariff (CET) which, for dutiable items, now stands at five to 35 percent of CIF value. Further reductions will be made in yearly stages to five to 20 percent by January 1, 1998.

Legal

Legal System

Trinidad & Tobago operates as a parliamentary democracy with the highest court of appeal being the Privy Council in London.

Intellectual Property Rights

Copyrights A copyright is valid for a period of 50 years. Current copyright protection officially complies with the revised Bern and Universal copyright conventions. However, the laws are not enforced. Video rental outlets are replete with pirated videos and operate openly.

Patents The existing law on patent protection establishes a registration system with no form of examination of patentable subject matter, novelty, inventive step, or industrial applicability. Patents are currently valid for a period of 14 years and may be extended for subsequent periods of seven years. Although the existing law is outdated, infringement of patents is not a discernible problem.

Trademarks Trademarks can be registered for a period of 14 years, and renewed by application before the expiration of the registration for an unlimited number of 14-year periods. Counterfeiting of trademarks is not a widespread problem.

Business Registration

Foreign companies must register with the Registrar of Companies within one month of establishing a place of business in Trinidad and Tobago. Certified copies of the company's charter, list of directors, and authorized local representative must be filed. The Registrar must approve the name of any proposed company with limited liability and the name of the company must include the word "limited."

Labor

Workers have the right to join unions and to bargain collectively. Anti-union discrimination is prohibited by law. Occupational health and safety standards are in place and state inspectors monitor these conditions.

Legal Matters

LEGAL BRIEFS
- **Child labor** Children under the age of 12 years are not allowed to work, and children between the ages of 12 and 14 years are permitted to work only in family businesses. General employment is permitted after 14 years.
- **Minimum wage** Trinidad and Tobago has a minimum wage rate for gas station employees, domestic assistants, retail-sales personnel and hotel workers. There is no national or general minimum wage.
- **Workweek** The standard workweek is 40 hours with no cap on overtime.
- **New technologies** Larger firms in Trinidad and Tobago are scrupulous about obtaining legal computer software while many smaller firms are believed to use wholly or partially pirated software.
- **Joint ventures** Joint ventures are not considered as distinct legal entities. These arrangements should always be negotiated by an attorney as the rights and obligations of all parties are limited to those set forth in the agreement.
- **Incorporation** Incorporation proceedings grant the status of limited or unlimited liability and perpetual succession to the entity incorporated.
- **Local attorney** A local attorney is recommended in establishing any type of business arrangement.

LEGAL CONTACT
Messrs. Desmond Allum and Gregory Delzin
Trinity Chambers
98 Duke St.
First Floor
Port-of-Spain, Trinidad

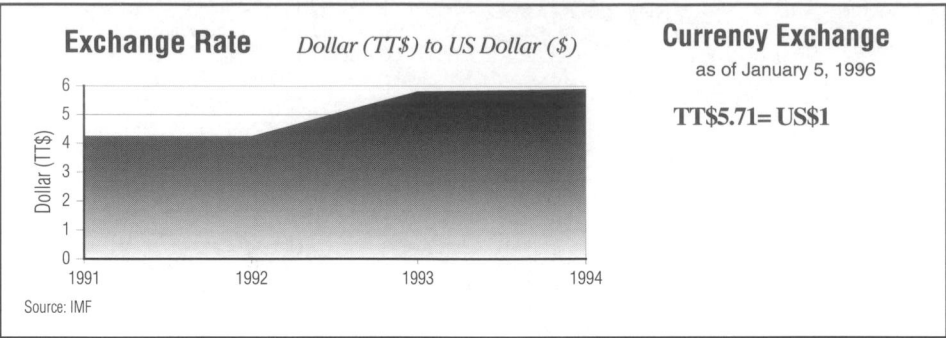

Exchange Rate *Dollar (TT$) to US Dollar ($)*

Dollar (TT$): 6, 5, 4, 3, 2, 1, 0

1991   1992   1993   1994

Source: IMF

Currency Exchange
as of January 5, 1996

TT$5.71= US$1

Currency

The currency of Trinidad and Tobago is the Trinidad and Tobago dollar (TT$), which is divided into 100 cents.

Foreign Exchange

The exchange rate of Trinidad and Tobago is determined by supply and demand. Banks are allowed to conduct foreign exchange transactions with the public without limitations. The authority to administer exchange control is vested in the Central Bank. Commercial banks can purchase foreign currency notes from the public, though it does not repatriate Trinidad and Tobago currency.

Capital Transfers

Exchange controls of foreign currency and securities have been removed. The repatriation of capital dividends, interest, and other distributions and gains on investment may be freely transacted. Capital transfers abroad do not require prior approval.

Investment Incentives

The government of Trinidad and Tobago offers several investment incentives, including: investment allowances, export allowances, tax holidays, industrial and factory buildings, training subsidies, market development grants and accelerated depreciation allowances. Incentives vary according to the specific industry invested in. There are some special additional incentives: enterprise operations in a regional development sector are eligible for a five-year tax credit equal to 15 percent of taxable profit; duty-free concessions are offered on plant, machinery, equipment, raw materials, and components for operations established in the free-trade zone; and direct financial assistance in the form of reduced rate loans.

Investment Restrictions

Foreign direct investment is actively encouraged by the government of Trinidad and Tobago in all sectors. Generally, there are no official restrictions on investment and most disincentives to investment have been removed. Performance requirements are prohibited by law. However, while foreigners may own 100 percent of the share capital in a private company, a license is required to own more than 30 percent of the share capital of a public company. Also foreign ownership of land is limited to one acre for residential purposes and five acres for trade purposes without a license. Waivers of these limitations are freely given, however.

TAXATION

Taxation requires sophisticated knowledge of complex rules and regulations specific to each country. For more detailed information we suggest you refer to the Ernst & Young Corporate Tax Guide and Directory, available from the Ernst & Young accounting office in your country, or from:

Ernst & Young
P.O. Box 158
Port-of-Spain, Trinidad
Tel: (809) 623-1105
Cable: ERNYOUNG, Trinidad
Fax: (809) 623-1314

At a Glance

Corporate Income Tax Rate (%)(a)	38
Short-Term Capital Gains Tax Rate (%)(b)	38
Branch Tax Rate (%)(a)	38
Withholding Tax (%)(c)	
Dividends (d)	10/15
Interest (e)	20
Royalties from Patents, Know-how, etc. (e)	20
Branch Remittance Tax (f)	10
Net Operating Losses (Years)	
Carryback	0
Carryforward	Unlimited

(a) A business levy is also imposed.
(b) Capital gains are usually not subject to tax, but may require a balancing adjustment. Short-term capital gains are subject to tax.
(c) These withholding taxes apply to payments to nonresidents only.
(d) The 10% rate applies to dividends paid to corporations owning 50% or more of the voting power of the distributing company. The 15% rate applies to other dividends.
(e) This rate is applicable to payments to both companies and individuals.
(f) This rate is applicable to remittances of profits to overseas head offices.

Money Matters

BITS AND PIECES

- **Capital market** Trinidad and Tobago has a well-developed capital market. All standard credit instruments are available, including a small, but well-developed stock market.

- **Free zones** A free-zone/port is located at the Point Lisas Industrial Estate. Additional free zones are also being considered. Any business may request free-zone status on an ad hoc basis at any agreed-upon site.

- **Borrowing** There are no restrictions on borrowing by foreign investors, but the availability of local project financing is limited. Local financing is expensive, and interest rates may exceed 20 percent. Because of high interest rates, larger importers often use self financing.

- **Expropriation** No expropriatory actions have been taken since the mid-1980s, and all prior expropriations were justly compensated.

- **Negotiable incentives** The government encourages, through negotiable incentives, projects that generate employment and foreign exchange, provide training and/or technology transfer, boost exports or reduce imports, and generally contribute to the welfare of the country.

- **Screening** Foreign investment is screened only for eligibility for government incentives and assessment of environmental impact.

- **Investment registration** Investment registration procedures have been streamlined and now permit investors to submit a single application for all the licenses, approvals, concessions, and tax benefits necessary to implement a proposed investment project.

- **Double taxation** Trinidad and Tobago maintains treaties with many of its trading partners which eliminate the double taxation of income.

- **Foreign currency accounts** Foreign currency accounts denominated in foreign currency may be maintained at local banks by residents and nonresidents.

- **Gold** One party to any transaction involving gold must be an authorized bank, and gold may not be taken out of the country.

BANKS

The Bank of Commerce, Trinidad & Tobago Ltd.
72 Independence Square
Port-of-Spain, Trinidad
Tel: (809) 625-2711 through 2718 Fax: (809) 627-0904

The Bank of Nova Scotia, Trinidad & Tobago Ltd.
Park & Richmond Streets
Port-of-Spain, Trinidad
Tel: (809) 625-3566 Fax: (809) 625-5633

Citibank (Trinidad & Tobago) Ltd.
12 Queen's Park East
Port-of-Spain, Trinidad
Tel: (809) 625-1046/7/8/9 Fax: (809) 624-8131

Citicorp Merchant Bank Ltd.
74 Independence Square
Port-of-Spain, Trinidad
Tel: (809) 623-4665/6/7 Fax: (809) 624-8131

Republic Bank Ltd.
PO Box 1153, Republic House
11-17 Park Street
Port-of-Spain, Trinidad
Tel: (809) 625-3611 through 3619
Fax: (809) 623-0371

The Royal Bank of Trinidad & Tobago Ltd.
PO Box 287
3B Chancery Lane
Port-of-Spain, Trinidad
Tel: (809) 623-4291/2/3 Fax: (809) 625-3764

Central Bank of Trinidad and Tobago
Central Bank Tower
Eric Williams Plaza
Independence Square
PO Box 1250
Port-of-Spain, Trinidad
Tel: (809) 625-4835 Fax: (809) 627-4696
Telex: 22532

Marketing

Overview

As the economy recovers, the pent up demand of these relatively savvy consumers is creating healthy markets for many consumer goods. There are few restrictions and marketing practices from all over the world are practiced here.

Distribution and Agents

There is no specific legislation regulating representatives, distributors, or franchisers. Parties are virtually free to form their own contractual terms, and royalties and commission rates are not regulated and may be freely agreed to by the parties concerned. The most common agency agreements are as follows:

Sales agency agreement A typical sales agency describes the extent of the agent's field of operations and the extent to which the principal accepts limitations on their freedom of action. The agreement gives the agent an opportunity to exploit markets, but allows the principal to withdraw exclusivity under stated conditions.

Marketing agency agreement In a marketing agreement, no authority is vested in the agent to contract on behalf of the principal. In an appropriately drawn marketing agency agreement, an overseas supplier will not be deemed to be trading within Trinidad and Tobago and incurs no tax liability on sales of its product.

Distributory agreement This typically includes terms on the extent of the territory of the distributor, the extent of his protection from competition from the manufacturer's products supplied to others, the distributor's limits to supply outside the territory.

Selling Techniques

Local and international franchises are quite common and include fast-food outlets, retail establishments, and service providers. As an alternative to a franchise agreement, the foreign franchisor may enter into a "master license" agreement, which delegates most franchisor responsibilities to a local representative. Trinidad and Tobago has no laws specifically governing advertising or other forms of trade promotion.

Marketing in Trinidad and Tobago

MARKETING TIPS

- **Advertising** Businesses in Trinidad and Tobago use newspapers, radio, and television to advertise their products.
- **Pricing** Businesses are generally free to price products at whatever price meets their marketing objectives. However, prices of sugar, schoolbooks, and some pharmaceuticals are controlled.
- **Sales, service, and customer support** There are no regulations governing sales, service, or customer support, but all companies doing business in Trinidad and Tobago are required to have registered in the country an agent or representative who can be held liable for legal disputes.
- **Government procurement** Government procurement practices are generally open and fair, and apply national treatment in their bidding procedures.

MARKET RESEARCH FIRMS

Caribbean Market Research Ltd.
19 Stanmore Avenue
Port-of-Spain, Trinidad
Tel: (809) 623-6857
Fax: (809) 623-6857

Market Facts & Opinions Ltd.
37 Victoria Square South
Corner of Duke and Melbourne Streets
Port-of-Spain, Trinidad
Tel: (809) 627-8417, 627-8524
Fax: (809) 625-7913

Business Culture

Greetings and Courtesies

Handshakes are common for both men and women, both when meeting and upon departing. Friends may embrace, and women friends may hold each other by the shoulders and kiss. Business cards should be printed in Spanish. At social events, the host will usually make individual introductions.

Business Ethic and Framework

Trinidadians are generally considered to be relatively informal, although they are nevertheless concerned with formal dignity, hierarchy, and class. Values emphasize the importance of the personal relationship, and time and effort is taken to establish a personal relationship as a prerequisite to a business relationship. Men should wear conservative business suits and women should wear conservative suits or dresses.

Meetings and Decision Making

Make appointments for meeting well in advance, but reconfirm shortly before. Meetings generally do not begin punctually, although you should be on time. Business lunches are relatively common, but only as a means to further the development of the social bond. Actual decisions are almost always made at a high level of authority. Although you should approach senior people, they will wish to match you with someone of similar rank. It is important to cultivate personal relationships with these peers, because the quality of these relationships may strongly influence the actual decision maker.

Women

Although women in Trinidad and Tobago generally occupy a somewhat secondary status in this traditionally male-dominated society, many operate businesses and may be accorded considerable personal freedom. Trinidadian women are becoming more common and more accepted in business in general, and foreign businesswomen should experience few problems.

Cultural Cautions

DO'S
- Learn something about Trinidad and Tobago's history and culture—your interest will be appreciated, as will attempts to speak Spanish.

DON'TS
- Race, religion, politics, and the economic situation—other than the tourist economy—are topics best avoided.

CUSTOMS
- People tend to stand quite close together; attempts to increase the space between persons in conversation may be viewed as evasive and even insulting.
- Small gifts are given frequently and are usually unwrapped immediately.
- It is considered polite to refuse anything offered a few times before ultimately accepting.

OBSERVATIONS
- Trinidadians are generally offended by evidence of what they consider aggressiveness and greed.
- Although appointments are generally required, you may be able to schedule them on short notice because of the relative informality that prevails.
- Because of the tropical climate, most business is conducted earlier in the day.

NEGOTIATIONS
- Trinidadians present a united front during negotiations, deferring to the senior member.
- Allow negotiations to remain open-ended, so that confrontation can be avoided and talks can be allowed to fade away if agreement cannot be reached.
- Agreements should be written; although historically, contracts have consisted of schematic outlines, Trinidadians now expect somewhat more detailed documents.

GOVERNMENT AGENCIES

Investments Division
Ministry of Finance
Level 15
Eric Williams Finance Building
Eric Williams Plaza
Independence Square
Port-of-Spain, Trinidad
Tel: (809) 627-9700, 627-9672
Fax: (809) 625-4755

Tourism and Industrial Development Company of Trinidad and Tobago
10-14 Phillips St.
Port-of-Spain, Trinidad
Tel: (809) 623-1932/4
Fax: (809) 625-4755

Trinidad and Tobago Free Zones Company Limited
Albion Court, 2nd floor West
61 Dundonald Street
Port-of-Spain, Trinidad
Tel: (809) 625-4749
Fax: (809) 625-4755

World Trade Information Centre
10 - 14 Phillips Street
Port-of-Spain, Trinidad
Tel: (809) 623-6022/3, 623-3591/2
Fax: (809) 624-0050

Ministry of Energy and Energy Industries
Riverside Plaza
PO Box 96
Besson Street
Port-of-Spain, Trinidad
Tel: (809) 623-4241
Fax: (809) (809) 623-2726

Ministry of Labor, Employment, and Cooperatives
Level II, Riverside Plaza
Besson Street
Port-of-Spain, Trinidad
Tel: (809) 623-4241, 627-3308

Ministry of Planning and Development
Eric Williams Finance Building, 14th Floor
Eric Williams Plaza
Independence Square
Port-of-Spain, Trinidad
Tel: (809) 627-9700, 627-9675, 627-8389

Ministry of Public Utilities
Sacred Heart Building
16-18 Sackville Street
Port-of-Spain, Trinidad
Tel: (809) 627-8378, 623-6331
Fax: (809) 625-2793

Ministry of Trade, Industry, and Tourism
Riverside Plaza, 15th Floor
Besson Street
Port-of-Spain, Trinidad
Tel: (809) 623-2931
Fax: (809) 623-8488

Ministry of Works and Transport
Level 5, Salvatori Building
Frederick Street
Port-of-Spain, Trinidad
Tel: (809) 623-8705
Fax: (809) 625-4512

Shipping Corporation of Trinidad and Tobago
12th and 13th Floors, Central Bank Tower
Eric Williams Plaza
Independence Square
PO Box 852
Port-of-Spain, Trinidad
Tel: (809) 623-6771
Telex: 22385

Trinidad and Tobago Tourism Development Authority
134-138 Frederick Street
PO Box 222
Port-of-Spain, Trinidad
Tel: (809) 623-1932
Fax: (809) 623-3848

WORLD TRADE CENTER

World Trade Center Trinidad and Tobago
PO Box 1273
Port-of-Spain, Trinidad
Tel: (809) 669-2320, 664-4101/2, 664-8047, 664-8049
Fax: (809) 669-2319

BUSINESS AND TRADE ORGANIZATIONS

Trinidad and Tobago Manufacturers Association
8 Stanmore Avenue
Port-of-Spain, Trinidad
Tel: (809) 623-1029, 623-1030 Fax: (809) 623-1031

Trinidad and Tobago Hotel and Tourism Association
Trinidad Hilton
PO Box 243
Port-of-Spain, Trinidad
Tel: (809) 624-3065
Telex: 22319

American Chamber of Commerce of Trinidad and Tobago
Hilton International
Upper Arcade
Port-of-Spain, Trinidad
Tel/Fax: (809) 627-8570

Trinidad and Tobago Chamber of Commerce and Industry
Hilton International, Rms. 950-952
POB 499
Port-of-Spain, Trinidad
Tel: (809) 627-1461
Fax: (809) 627-4376

South Trinidad Chamber of Industry and Commerce Inc.
Suite 313
Cross Shopping Centre
San Fernando, Trinidad
Tel: (809) 657-9077, 652-5613
Fax: (809) 652-3347

AD AGENCIES

Aleong & Agostini
38 Maraval Rd.
Port-of-Spain, Trinidad
Tel: (809) 622-1980
Fax: (809) 628-6606

Hernandez/FCB
Long Circular Mall Level 4
Port-of-Spain, Trinidad
Tel: (809) 622-6411
Fax: (809) 628-2800

Lonsdale
10 Herbert St.
Port-of-Spain, Trinidad
Tel: (809) 622-6280
Fax: (809) 628-0210

McCann-Erickson (Trinidad) Ltd.
81-83 Abercromby St.
Port-of-Spain, Trinidad
Tel: (809) 623-8807
Fax: (809) 623-7282

NEWSPAPERS

Trinidad Guardian
22-24 St. Vincent St.
Port-of-Spain, Trinidad
Tel: (809) 623-8871
Fax: (809) 623-8871

Daily Express
35 & 37 Independence Square
Port-of-Spain, Trinidad
Tel: (809) 623-1711
Fax: (809) 627-1451

Newsday
Chacon House
19-21 Chacon St.
Port-of-Spain, Trinidad
Tel: (809) 623-4929
Fax: (809) 625-8362

TELEVISION STATIONS

Trinidad and Tobago Television (TTT)
Television House
Maraval Road
Port-of-Spain, Trinidad
Tel: (809) 622-4141
Fax: (809) 622-0344

Caribbean Communications Network (CCN)
Independence Square
Port-of-Spain, Trinidad
Tel: (809) 623-1711

Audio Visual Media (AVM)
Lady Young Road
Morvant
Tel: (809) 674-1333
Fax: (809) 638-3883

LEGAL CONTACTS

Mssrs. Desmond Allum and Gregory Delzin
Trinity Chambers
98 Cuke Street, First Floor
Port-of-Spain, Trinidad

De Nobriga, Inniss and Company
90 Edward Street
Port-of-Spain, Trinidad
Tel: (809) 623-4802

Fitzwilliam, Stone, Furness-Smith and Morgan
36 Pembroke Street
Port-of-Spain, Trinidad
Tel: (809) 623-1618/9; 2425/6; 0606
Fax: (809) 623-0605

Gift and Company
1 Bacolet Street
Scarborough, Tobago
(809) 639-3187; 639-2212

Hamel-Smith & Company
19 St. Vincent Street
Port-of-Spain, Trinidad
Tel: (809) 623-4237/9

Hobsons
13-17 Keate Street
San Fernando, Trinidad
Tel: (809) 652-3801/3

T.M. Kelshall & Company
11 St. Vincent Street
Port-of-Spain, Trinidad
Tel: (809) 623-4218/9

Montano & Co.
126 Edward Street
Port-of-Spain, Trinidad
Tel: (809) 624-8088
Fax: (809) 627-7897

Pollonais & Blanc
POB 350
62 Sackville Street
Port-of-Spain, Trinidad
Tel: (809) 623-8505

INTERNET ADDRESSES

Usenet group(s):
soc.culture.caribbean

Welcome to Trinidad and Tobago!
http://www.tidco.co.tt

Trinidad and Tobago
http://www.webobj.com/Trinidad

The Republic of Trinidad and Tobago - Unofficial Homepage
http://caribbean-www.lcs.mit.edu/caribbean-www/islands/tnt/

Tunisia

Republic of Tunisia

Economy

Overview

Tunisia has recently embarked on a successful program of economic reform, and its strong links with major European markets have provided a good foundation for sustained economic growth. It continues to rely on oil, phosphates, agriculture, and tourism, and its largely successful efforts to move toward an export-oriented market economy have focused on increasing efficiency and expanding trade in these areas. It is a country of enormous economic potential, with large areas that could be brought under irrigation, and untapped petroleum resources.

Trade

Tunisia's emerging economy has greatly benefited from efforts to liberalize foreign trade. Countries of the EU are the primary purchasers of its exports, and it buys most of its imports from the EU as well. France is its major trading partner, followed by Italy, Germany, Spain, and Belgium. Tunisia has traditionally run a trade deficit, but recent strong export performance and increased demand from its European trading partners have resulted in an improvement in the balance of trade. The continuing removal of trade restrictions on imports makes this a promising market for foreign traders.

Sectors

Agriculture Tunisia is traditionally an agricultural country, and this remains an important sector - employing about 25 percent of the population and making a significant contribution to GDP. A wide variety of crops are produced, including olives, oranges, tomatoes, and grapes; almost half of its productive land is used for livestock. A small but developing fishing industry is likely to become of increasing importance in the future.

Industry The government has focused on providing incentives for the establishment of export-oriented industries, and these are expected to play an increasingly important role in Tunisia's economy. While not as rich in natural deposits as some of its neighbors, exports of crude oil, natural gas, phosphates, and iron ore play an important role in foreign trade. Other important sectors include the manufacture of textiles and footwear in which there is substantial foreign investment.

Services Tunisia's growing tourism market is its most important service industry and its greatest source of foreign exchange. The government is committed to developing and expanding this sector, and many opportunities for foreign investors are available.

Trends

After the early successes of its structural adjustment program, Tunisia is continuing on the road to an open market economy. The government seems committed to reducing its role in the economy by privatizing more industries and by allowing easy access to foreign currency for import/export transactions. With over 60 percent of the population under the age of 25, the high level of unemployment and underemployment is a chronic problem which needs to be addressed. However, the continuing emphasis on creating a vibrant export-oriented economy should result in high GDP growth rates. Although further reductions in tariffs and subsidies need to be made, the ongoing reforms are opening up significant opportunities for exporters.

At a Glance

THE COUNTRY

Location Northern coast of Africa, southeast of Libya and west of Algeria on the Mediterranean Sea.
Terrain South is semi-arid or desert. Arable land in north and along central coast.
Climate Moderate along coast. Hot in the interior. Rainy winters.

THE PEOPLE

Population 8,500,000
Ethnic composition
Arab-Berber 98%
European 1%
Other.. 1%
Religious composition
Muslim 98%
Christian 1%
Jewish and Other... 1%
Languages spoken Arabic (official) and French.
Education and literacy Nine years compulsory education with Arabic the language of instruction in early grades but later replaced by French. Based on the French model and to a lesser extent Islamic influence, Tunisia's literacy rate is about 65 percent.
Labor force
Total:...2,500,000
By occupation: services 41%, industry 34%, agriculture 24%, other 1%.
(Note: an estimated 50 percent of workers are unemployed or underemployed)

COUNTRY FACTS

Political and legal Tunisia gained independence from France in 1956 and became a republic in 1957. It grants universal suffrage at age 20. Known as a leader in the Arab world in the promotion of equal status for women under the law.
Telephone Tunisia has well-developed postal, telephone and telegraph systems which are government operated, link all major cities, and are well above the African average. International country code: [216]. Selected city codes: Bizerte (2), Tunis (1).
Transportation There are over 2,100 kilometers of railroads, the main transportation system in Tunisia. Highways are extensive but mostly in disrepair, and only about half are paved. The main ports are Bizerte, Gabes, Sfax, Sousse, Tunis, and Zarzis. There are 14 major airports.
Environment Erosion is a major problem threatening 76 percent of the nation's land area. Overcrowding and poor sanitation are major problems in cities. Pollution from industry and farming threatens the country's limited water supply. Current issues include toxic and hazardous waste disposal, water pollution from untreated sewage, water scarcity, deforestation, desertification.
Media Government broadcasts in Arabic, French, and Italian on the government owned Tunisian Radio-Television-Broadcasting (ERTT). There are seven AM, eight FM, and 19 TV stations. Censorship prevents criticism of high-government officials or state institutions.
Health Conditions have improved significantly in recent years although diet and sanitation continue to be a problem. Epidemics have virtually disappeared and contagious diseases have been considerably reduced. Average life expectancy is 68 years.

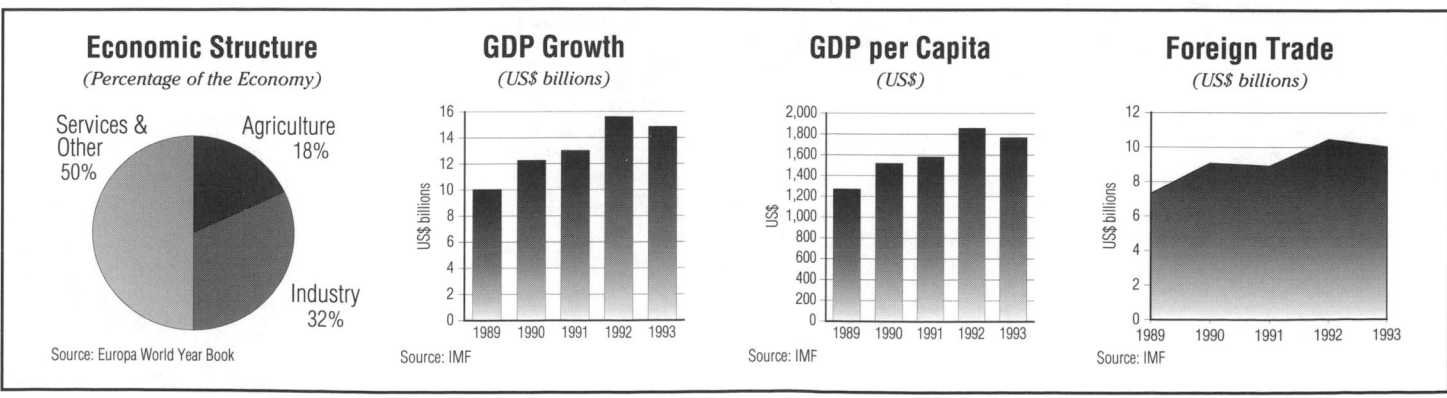

Economic Structure
(Percentage of the Economy)

Services & Other 50%
Agriculture 18%
Industry 32%
Source: Europa World Year Book

GDP Growth
(US$ billions)

US$ billions
16, 14, 12, 10, 8, 6, 4, 2, 0
1989 1990 1991 1992 1993
Source: IMF

GDP per Capita
(US$)

US$
2,000, 1,800, 1,600, 1,400, 1,200, 1,000, 800, 600, 400, 200, 0
1989 1990 1991 1992 1993
Source: IMF

Foreign Trade
(US$ billions)

US$ billions
12, 10, 8, 6, 4, 2, 0
1989 1990 1991 1992 1993
Source: IMF

Business Travel

	LH 1906	MADRID	935	113-3
	LH 1022	STUTTGART HBF.	935	
	AF 1701	LYON	940	683-6
	AY 822	HELSINKI	940	113-3
	AA 071	SFRANCISCO-DALLAS	945	731-7

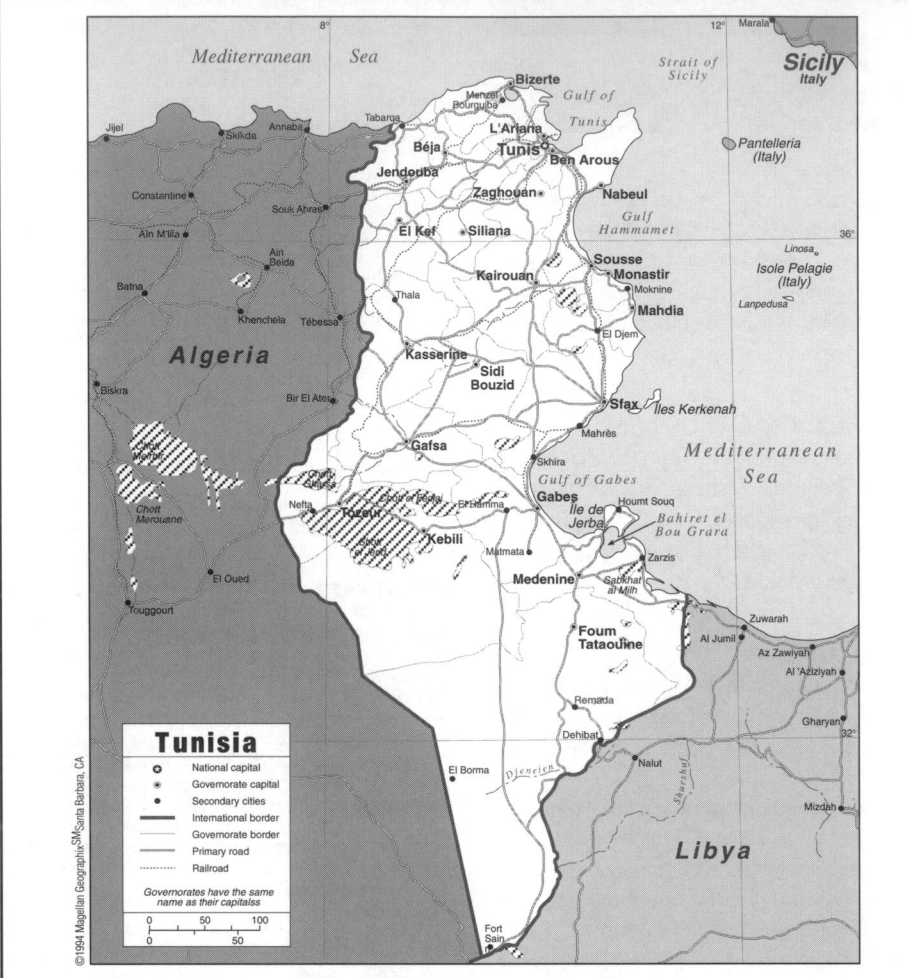

Tunisia
- ⊙ National capital
- ◉ Governorate capital
- ○ Secondary cities
- —— International border
- ······ Governorate border
- —— Primary road
- ---- Railroad

Governorates have the same name as their capitals

0   50   100

©1994 Magellan GeographixSMSanta Barbara, CA

Travelogue

WORKWEEK
Offices Monday-Thursday 8:30 am to 1:00 pm and 3:00 pm to 5:45 pm; Friday and Saturday 8:30 am to 1:30 pm, mornings only in summer.
Banks Monday-Thursday 8:00 am to 11:00 am and 2:00 pm to 4:00 pm; Friday 8:00 am to 11:00 am and 1:00 pm to 3:00 pm, mornings only in summer.
Government Monday-Thursday 8:30 am to 1:00 pm and 3:00 pm to 5:45 pm; Friday and Saturday 8:30 am to 1:30 pm, mornings only in summer.
Retail Monday-Friday 8:00 am to 12:30 pm and 2:30 pm to 6:00 pm; Saturday 8:00 am to 12:00 pm. (In summer, Monday-Saturday 7:00 am to 1:00 pm.)

HOLIDAYS
Holidays 1996
January 1 New Year's Day
February 20-21 Aïd Esseghir El-Fitr*
Mar 20 Independence Day
Mar 21 Youth Day
April 9 Martyr's Day
April 29-30 Aïd El Kebir El-Idha*
May 1 Labor Day
May 19 Ras El Am El-Hejri*
July 25 Republic Day
July 28 Mouled*
August 13 Women's Day
November 7 Constitution Day
In addition, Ramadan (March or April) and the Feast of the Sacrifice (June or July) are observed by Muslims. The exact dates depend on the sighting of the moon and can be ascertained from a Tunisian embassy or consulate prior to departure.
*Dates vary year to year and are based on the lunar calendar.

VISA AND PASSPORT
All visitors need a valid passport, but visas are generally not required for stays up to three or four months.

DEPARTURE FORMALITIES
Local currency may not be exported. With proper documentation, up to D100 may be reconverted into hard currency upon departure.

IMMUNIZATION
An international vaccination certificate is required of travelers coming from infected areas. Recommended immunizations include polio, diphtheria, tetanus, and gamma globulin for hepatitis.

TIPPING
Small tips are offered everywhere. Restaurant bills include service charges, and extra tipping is expected in hotels on top of the service charge. In taxis, tip 10 percent unless the fare was negotiated and includes the tip. Car parkers wearing official badges get M100-200; unofficial parkers get less. Maids get DT1 per day, porters M500 per suitcase.

CRIME
Violent crime is rare, but watch for the occasional pickpockets and pursesnatchers. Women traveling alone may be verbally harassed; travel with other people and stay on the main roads and in well-traveled areas. Always keep valuables out of sight in locked cars. Traveler's checks are advised over carrying large amounts of cash.

INFRASTRUCTURE
Domestic flights are fast and relatively inexpensive. Trains are improving, but foreigners are advised to stick to first class rail travel. Long distance buses serve most cities. Two types of taxis serve Tunis: metered petit taxis for up to four passengers within city limits, and unmetered grand taxis for longer trips with negotiated fares. Car rental is expensive, but the road system is extensive and well maintained. Tunis offers a few luxury hotels and many others suitable for business travelers.

COMMUNICATIONS
Telephones For Africa, the Tunisian telecommunications system is modern and efficient. Direct dialing is available for many international calls, which can be placed from hotels or from cubicles in post offices marked PTT.
Fax Post offices in major cities offer fax services.
Post office Postal service is inexpensive and reasonably efficient. Express mail (*rapide poste*) expedites mail to its destination in less than four days. Stamps are available at post offices (marked PTT), major hotels, and tobacco shops (*tabacs*).

BEST TRAVEL BOOKS
Tunisia. Barnaby Rogerson and Rose Baring. Cadogan Guides Series, illustrated, 384 pages. Globe Pequot.
Baedeker's Tunisia. Baedeker's Series. Illustrated, 448 pages. Prentice Hall General Reference and Travel.
Morocco, Algeria and Tunisia: A Travel Survival Kit. Geoff Crowther and Hugh Finlay, 486 pages. Lonely Planet Publications.
North African Handbook. The ideal practical guide. Updated annually.
Africa on A Shoestring, Lonely Planet. Filled with useful information.

USEFUL TELEPHONE NUMBERS
If you are calling from outside Tunisia, you will need to add the country code [216] and any other international dialing requirements from within your country.
- Police/Emergency 197
- Fire 198
- International Operator 0117
- Ministry of Foreign Affairs .... (1) 661-874
- Airport Information.................... (1) 235-000 x 33-45
- Road Safety Information .... (1) 235-427
- Union of Industry, Commerce and Art.... (1) 780-366
- Police for Foreigners .... (1) 262-088
- National Railways Office .... (1) 340-166
- Ambulance .... (1) 491286
- Doctor .... (1) 341250

Credit Card Information
Lost or stolen credit cards (call collect to the US, regardless of which country the card was issued in).
- Amex .... [1] (919) 333-3211
- Diner's Club................................ [1] (303) 799-1504
- MasterCard .... [1] (314) 275-6690
- Visa .... [1] (410) 581-7931

NATIONAL TOURIST OFFICE
Office National du Tourismo Tunisien (ONTT)
1 Ave. Mohamed V
1001 Tunis
Tel: (1) 341-007

Foreign Trade

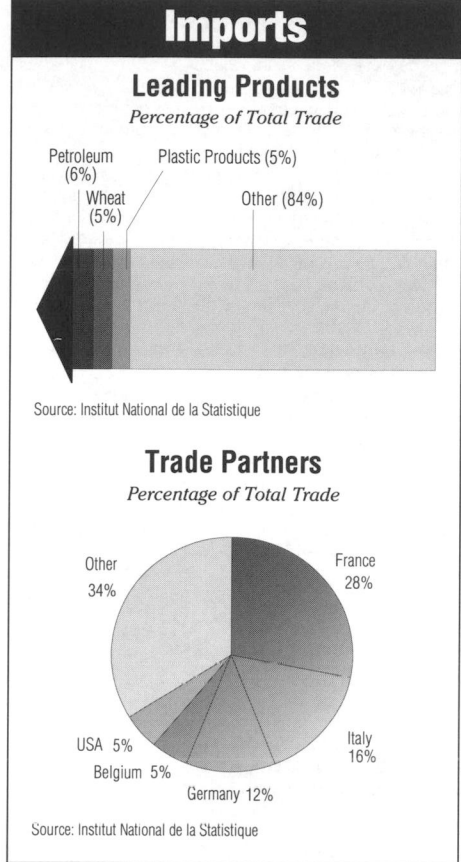

Imports

Leading Products
Percentage of Total Trade

Petroleum (6%)
Wheat (5%)
Plastic Products (5%)
Other (84%)

Source: Institut National de la Statistique

Trade Partners
Percentage of Total Trade

- France 28%
- Italy 16%
- Germany 12%
- Belgium 5%
- USA 5%
- Other 34%

Source: Institut National de la Statistique

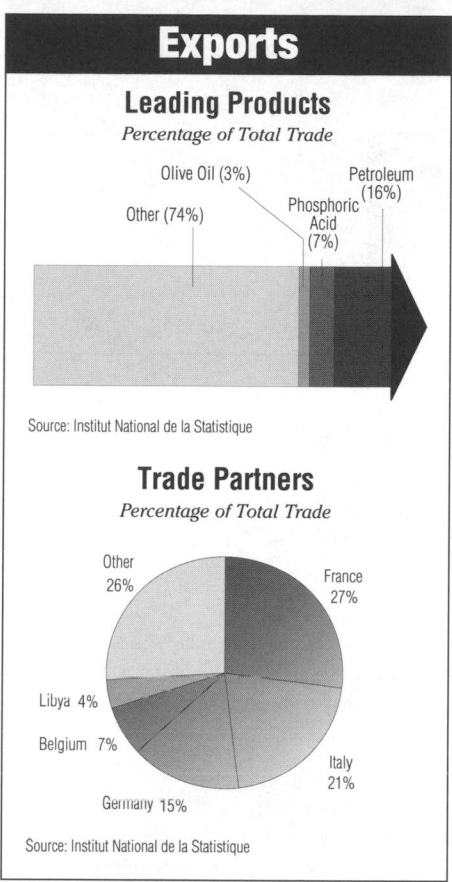

Exports

Leading Products
Percentage of Total Trade

Olive Oil (3%)
Other (74%)
Phosphoric Acid (7%)
Petroleum (16%)

Source: Institut National de la Statistique

Trade Partners
Percentage of Total Trade

- France 27%
- Italy 21%
- Germany 15%
- Belgium 7%
- Libya 4%
- Other 26%

Source: Institut National de la Statistique

Opportunities

FOR IMPORTING TO TUNISIA

- filtering, earth moving, and mechanical equipment
- industrial and telecommunications equipment
- consumer and industrial goods
- food

FOR EXPORTING FROM TUNISIA

- agricultural products
- hydrocarbons, phosphates, and chemicals

GROWTH SECTORS

- tourism services
- non-food product manufacturing
- agriculture
- fishing
- non-manufacturing industries

Trade News

RULES AND REGULATIONS

- **Import licenses** Non-tariff barriers in the form of import licenses are required on certain products, particularly durable consumer goods. For such products, an importer must obtain a license from the Ministry of National Economy specifying the product, quantity, and amount of foreign exchange needed.

- **Tariff rates** All taxes now remaining on imports also apply to locally produced goods and are not considered to be tariff barriers. Imports are subject to a maximum tariff rate of 43 percent and some products have additional duties up to 30 percent. Goods are also subject to a two dinar per declaration customs formality fee. There is an imposed temporary supplemental duty on certain imports which compete with locally produced goods.

Legal

Legal System

Tunisia is a civil code country. Its law is based on the French Napoleonic code.

Intellectual Property Rights

Patents Applications are submitted to the National Institute for Standardization and Industrial Property (NISIP). Tunisia laws provide excellent protection. Patents are issued for periods of five, 10, and 20 years, depending on the patented item. Applications are not examined for novelty, only for proper format. If patents are not exploited within three years, they may be revoked.

Trademarks Copyrights are registered with NISIP and last 25 years, with options to renew. No trademark examination or publication takes place, thus no opposition process is available.

Copyrights Protection has recently been upgraded to cover modern techniques for creating intellectual property. Organisme Tunisiene de Protection des Droits D'Auteur is the agency responsible.

Business Registration

The general procedure for business registration requires submission of a written proposal, which must be approved by Guichet Unique. The firm must also register with appropriate tax authorities and the Records Office of the Court in the local district of the enterprise. The local Chamber of Commerce must be notified, and an establishment notice must be published in the official commercial journal.

Labor

Workers have the right to form unions, bargain collectively, and strike. For strikes, 10 days advance notice must be given. The law prohibits retribution against strikers. Labor disputes are usually handled through conciliation panels. The government must approve collective bargaining agreements and publish them in official journals. Child labor restrictions exist. Minimum wages have kept pace with the cost of living and are roughly D130 dollars a month in industry and D4.50 per day for agriculture.

Legal Matters

LEGAL BRIEF

- **Maximum workweek** Depending on the sector, the maximum workweek is 40 or 48 hours, with one 24-hour rest period. Industrial employees tend to work the longest, followed by agricultural workers.

- **International agreements** Tunisia is a member of several international organizations, including: GATT/WTO; WIPO; Arab League; OAU; New York Convention on the Recognition and Enforcement of Foreign Arbitral Awards. It also has a trade and cooperation agreement with the EU.

- **Trademark piracy** Due to lax enforcement, copyright piracy exists, but it is usually on a small scale, by small-time operators. As a result, the government has recently made changes to copyright laws and promised more enforcement.

- **Business approval** The Guichet Unique will not approve applications to register a business unless a credit source within Tunisia has already been established.

- **Labor laws** Tunisia's labor laws are generally good for both labor and management; they protect workers without imposing burdensome restrictions on employers.

- **Child labor** Tunisian law provides that children under the age of 15 (13 for agricultural employment) may not work.

- **Bankruptcy laws** Bankruptcy laws differ wildly throughout the country, depending on what region you're in. Study the different inflections of each sector.

- **Inspection** Regional labor inspectors examine firms about once every two years to ensure compliance.

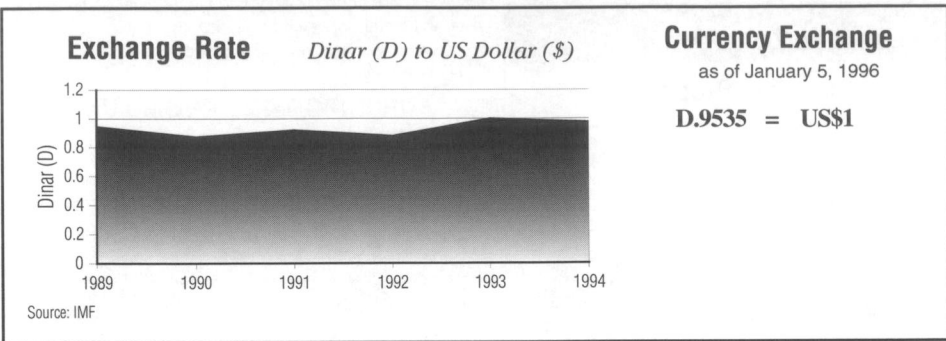

Exchange Rate
Dinar (D) to US Dollar ($)

Source: IMF

Currency Exchange
as of January 5, 1996

D.9535 = US$1

Money Matters

BITS AND PIECES

- **Repatriation** The sale or liquidation of invested capital carried out with foreign exchange transferred from abroad may be repatriated, even if the proceeds exceed the initial value.
- **Credit** Credit is generally allocated on market terms. Foreign investors are able to get credit on the local market. There are a growing number of financial instruments available in Tunisia.
- **Stock market** There is a growing interest in stocks and bonds. There are several mutual funds; and two merchant banks have recently been established.
- **Capital investment** There are several capital controls in place. Capital investors must obtain the approval of the Central Bank before investing in Tunisia. Indirect investment through a mutual fund is allowed.
- **Banking system** The Tunisian banking system is open and modern. It is composed of 12 commercial banks, eight development banks, one savings bank, five portfolio management institutions, three leasing companies, and seven off-shore banks.
- **Expropriation** The government does not expropriate property by eminent domain. Just compensation is offered at the time of expropriation.
- **Gold** Five denominations of commemorative gold coins are legal tender but do not circulate. Residents may acquire and hold gold in any form, though the Central Bank has a monopoly over the importation and exportation of monetary gold.

BANKS

Arab Tunisian Bank
9 rue Hedi Nouira
Tunis
Tel: (1) 351-155 Fax: (1) 342-852

Banque Centrale de Tunisie
Central Bank of Tunisia
Rue Hedi Nouira
Tunis
Tel: (1) 340-588 Fax: (1) 340-615

Banque du Sud
111 Avenue de la Liberte
Tunis
Tel: (1) 289-400 Fax: (1) 780-686

Banque de Tunisie
3 Avenue de France
Tunis
Tel: (1) 340-544 Fax: (1) 352-321

Banque Franco Tunisienne
13 rue D'Alger
Tunis
Tel: (1) 342-100 Fax: (1) 352-055

Banque International Arabe de Tunisie
70-72 Avenue Habib Bourguiba
Tunis
Tel: (1) 340-722 Fax: (1) 340-680

Banque Nationale Agricole
Rue Hedi Nouira
Tunis
Tel: (1) 791-200 Fax: (1) 793-031

Citibank
3 Avenue Jugurtha
Tunis
Tel: (1) 790-066 Fax: (1) 785-556

Credit Foncier et Commercial de Tunisie
13 Avenue de France
Tunis
Tel: (1) 340-511 Fax: (1) 349-909

Societe Tunisienne de Banque
Rue Hedi Nouira
Tunis
Tel: (1) 340-377 Fax: (1) 340-009

Union Bancaire Pour le Commerce et L'Industrie
79 Rue Jamel Abdenasser
Tunis
Tel: (1) 340-644 Fax: (1) 340-644

Union International de Banques
65 Avenue Habib Bourguiba
Tunis
Tel: (1) 347-000 Fax: (1) 353-090

Currency

The currency of Tunisia is the Tunisian dinar (D or TD), which is divided into 1,000 millimes (M).

Foreign Exchange

The exchange value of the dinar is determined according to a basket of currencies. The buying and selling rates for foreign currencies are fixed daily by the Central Bank. The dinar is commercially convertible for all bona fide trade and investment operations.

Capital Transfers

It is illegal to take Tunisian bank notes and coins in or out of the country. There are some restrictions imposed on foreign exchange transactions, but nonresidents are exempt from most of them. Foreign investors may transfer returns on direct or portfolio investments at any time and without prior authorization. This applies to both principal and capital in the form of dividends or interest.

Investment Incentives

There is no discrimination against foreign investors either at the time of the initial investment or later. There are no discriminatory or excessively onerous visa, residence, work permit, or other requirements inhibiting foreign investors. Foreign firms have the same investment incentives as Tunisian ones, and incentives are found mostly in the free trade zones. Companies operating in the free zones are exempt from taxes and customs duties, except social security taxes for employees who opt for the Tunisian social security system. Free zone companies may also choose between resident and nonresident status, depending on the foreign contribution to the company's capital. Nonresident status has some advantages, including guaranteed transfer of foreign currency capital invested in a free zone and the income derived from it; all payments made within the free zone may be made either in foreign currency or in convertible dinars; and any commercial relationship between companies located in the free zone and those located outside Tunisia, and between companies within the free zone itself, is not subject to control.

Investment Restrictions

Generally, government authorization is required if foreign ownership exceeds 50 percent of a service company, and there is no national treatment in the agricultural sector. Foreign ownership of land is prohibited.

TAXATION

Taxation requires sophisticated knowledge of complex rules and regulations specific to each country. For more detailed information we suggest you refer to the Ernst & Young Corporate Tax Guide and Directory, available from the Ernst & Young accounting office in your country, or from:

AMC
95, rue de Palestine
1002 Tunis, Tunisia
Tel: (1) 788-306, 787-920
Fax: (1) 782-212

- Tunisia's unified investment code provides for an exemption of 35 percent of reinvested profits and income from personal or business income tax. The code also provides for reduction of customs duties and suspensions of the value-added tax on capital goods.

At a Glance

Corporate Income Tax Rate (%)	35
Capital Gains Tax Rate (%)	35
Branch Tax Rate (%)	35
Withholding Tax (%)	
Dividends	0
Interest (a)	15
Royalties (a)(c)	15
Gross Rents (b)	15
Management Fees (a)	5
Branch Remittance Tax	0
Net Operating Losses (Years)	
Carryback	0
Carryforward	3

(a) This rate applies to payments received by both residents and nonresidents.
(b) This rate applies to payments to nonresidents only.
(c) The following types of payments to nonresidents are subject to the 15% withholding tax: copyright royalties; payments for use of and proceeds from sales of patents, trademarks, designs, models, plans, formulas, manufacturing processes, and movies; payments for use of industrial, commercial, agricultural, harbor, or scientific equipment; payments for industrial, commercial, or scientific information; or payments for technical or economic studies.

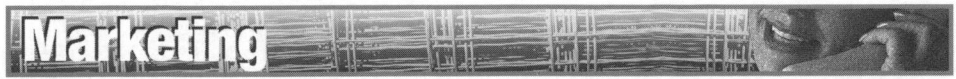

Marketing

Overview

Despite official discouragement, there is considerable consumer demand from the 60 percent of the population under the age of 25 who have developed a taste for a wide variety of Western consumer goods.

Distribution

Tunisia's distribution channels are similar to those in many developed countries, providing options for wholesale or retail marketing. Most activity occurs in the major coastal cities: Tunis, Sfax, Sousse-Monastir, and Bizerte. Almost any type of good can be found, either in retail markets, through one of thousands of small-scale shops, or at the dozens of huge, open-air markets.

Agents, Distributors, and Partners

A local agent is invaluable when confronted with bureaucratic obstacles, multi-layered customs regulations, and essential translation services. Knowing who to sell to and what to sell usually spells the difference between success and failure. A list of reliable agents is available at most embassies.

Advertising

French is Tunisia's main commercial language, so campaigns must not ignore this fact. Most businesses advertise in the press, especially in the French daily, *La Presse*. Arabic newspapers carry advertising but not reproductions of the human face or form. Two television channels accept advertising. Cinemas and outdoor sites are available, and international trade fairs are also popular with advertisers. Several agencies in Tunis can provide a full range of services for a multinational firm's needs.

Service and Customer Support

A major complaint Tunisians have about overseas products is the lack of after-sales service. The US firm Caterpillar is an excellent example of a company maintaining a large market share through its firm commitment to extensive service. After-sales service can often make the difference between success and failure in Tunisia.

Business Culture

Greetings and Courtesies

Frequent handshakes (the right hand only) are the most common gesture of greeting and departure. Address others with a title and their surname. Tunisians tend to be very punctual and time tends to be very important to them. Don't take this rule lightly: it could mean the difference between success and failure.

Business Ethic and Framework

Tunisian culture has survived invasions and conquests from East and West, developing a resiliency which promotes accommodation and economic growth and produces a sound business attitude. Too often, those unfamiliar with this nation think being Islamic makes people too unworldly to operate in a pro-Western world; but this is far from correct. The Tunisian businessman combines a basically conservative attitude with vast patience. He approaches business with an evenhanded attitude not found in some neighboring countries. There are powerful pro-Western forces in this culture which have opened trade practices to the US and EU countries; in turn, those influences affect the ways of doing business. Wear a lightweight, conservative suit in summer, and medium weight clothing with a topcoat from November to March.

Women

Businessmen will, if necessary, deal with foreign female executives, but prefer to finalize terms with men. Legal equality between the genders, such as equal rights in divorce and child custody, is vigorously supported by the government. A few women serve at various levels of government service. Political decision making is centralized, however, and women's influence is limited here. Practically, and especially in rural areas, women are largely in the position they occupied centuries ago in the West: keepers of hearth and home. A woman's honor is zealously guarded, first by her family and then by her husband.

Marketing in Tunisia

MARKETING TIPS

- **Direct marketing opportunities** Direct marketing offers the chance to avoid the sometimes lengthy process of looking for a suitable representative. However, it requires a local presence to adequately keep track of details.
- **Import restrictions** There are two agricultural products which face import barriers. First, cotton imported from the United States and certain other non-Arab countries is subject to a 17 percent duty, while that from Egypt, Syria, and other major Arab-world suppliers is duty free. Second, Tunisia prohibits the importation of American meat which has been treated with hormones.
- **Franchising** Franchising is new to Tunisia, but some are being introduced to the communities, especially US fast-food franchises. There is growing interest in the idea and many Tunisian entrepreneurs are seeking contacts with foreign companies.
- **Direct marketing** For companies with a local presence, direct marketing offers many cost advantages and is fairly well accepted in Tunisia.

MARKET RESEARCH CONTACT

International Executive Service Corps
15 rue Aziza Othmana
Mutuelleville
Tunis
Tel: (1) 795-733
Fax: (1) 792-72

GOVERNMENT AGENCY

Institut National de la Normalisation et de la Propriete Industrielle
(Industrial Standards and Ownership Authority)
Cite El Khadra
Tunis
Tel: (1) 785-922
Fax: (1) 781-563

Cultural Cautions

DO'S

- If invited to a *hammam* (the Tunisian bath, often mistakenly called a "Turkish bath" in the West), accept; little business is openly discussed here, but your host will use this time to assess your character.
- When entering a house, remove your shoes.

DON'TS

- Men should bring women to business talks or social event only if the women are specifically invited. Western women should cover their arms, legs, head, and body, and avoid all talk from emancipation points of view.

CUSTOMS

- Print business cards in English-Arabic, French-Arabic, or English-French; present them with both hands after being introduced.
- If invited to a home, bring a wrapped, high-quality gift such as a specially bound book or a memento from your country. Don't bring cologne.
- Over-praising an article requires that it be given to the guest.

OBSERVATIONS

- Tunisians will not openly express disapproval, but rather will make a carefully-worded suggestion for an alternate possibility.

NEGOTIATIONS

- Tunisian style combines endless politeness with a smiling and pleasant firmness.
- Terms will be repeatedly questioned in an effort to be certain they are the best possible; questions will be indirect and courteously phrased, but always with the same goal: to test and reaffirm. Price is a paramount concern, but no deals exist without slowly established trust.

Contacts

GOVERNMENT AGENCIES

Ministere de la Cooperation Internationale et de l'Investissement Exterieur
149 Avenue de la Liberte
Tunis
Tel: (1) 798-522
Fax: (1) 799-069

Ministere de l'Economie Nationale
37 rue Kheireddine Pacha
Tunis
Tel: (1) 780-594
Fax: (1) 781-782

Ministere du Plan et du Developement Regional
Place Ali Zouaoui
Tunis
Tel: (1) 353-550
Fax: (1) 351-666

Ministere des Finances
Place du Gouvernement
La Kasbah
Tunis
Tel: (1) 566-210
Fax: (1) 563-959

Ministere de l'Environnement et de L'Amenagement du Territoire
Centre Urbain Nord
Tunis
Tel: (1) 704-000
Fax: (1) 702-431

Ministere des Affaires Sociales
(Office des Tunisiens a l'Etrangr)
23 rue de Khartoum
Tunis
Tel: (1) 782-455
Fax: (1) 780-967

Ministere de l'Agriculture
30 Rue Alain Savary
Tunis
Tel: (1) 681-654
Fax: (1) 890-391

Ministere du Tourisme et de l'Artisanant
Avenue Mohamed V
Tunis
Tel: (1) 341-077
Fax: (1) 350-997

Ministere des Transports
Zone Montplaisir
Avenue Mohamed V
Tunis
Tel: (1) 781-824
Fax: (1) 790-149

Direction General du Commerce Exterieur
(Foreign Trade Department of Ministry of National Economy)
Rue D'Irak
Tunis
Tel: (1) 283-427
Fax: (1) 890-531

Agence de Promotion de L'Industrie
(Ministry of National Economy Agency for the Promotion of Industry)
rue de Syrie
Tunis
Tel: (1) 792-144
Fax: (1) 782-482

Agence Fonciere Industrielle
(Ministry of National Economy Agency for Allocation of Land for Industrial Use)
2 rue Badii Ezzamen
Cite Mahrajane
Tunis
Tel: (1) 286-111
Fax: (1) 783-303

Societe Tunisienne D'Electricite et du Gaz
(State Electricity and Gas Company)
38 rue Kamel Ataturk
Tunis
Tel: (1) 341-311
Fax: (1) 341-401

Societe Nationale D'Exploitation et de Distribution Des Eaux
(State Water Company)
23 rue Jawaher Lel Nehru
Montfleury
Tunis
Tel: (1) 493-700
Fax: (1) 491-876

Office National D'Assainissment
(State Sanitation Agency)
32 rue Hedi Nouira
Tunis
Tel: (1) 343-200
Fax: (1) 350-411

Direction General des Telecommunications
(Telecommuncations Department of the Ministry of Communications)
Boulevard du 9 Avril
Tunis
Tel: (1) 561-933
Fax: (1) 564-357

Tunisair
(State Airline)
Boulevard du 7 Novembre
Tunis
Tel: (1) 700-100
Fax: (1) 700-008

Direction General des Douanes
(Bureau of Customs)
rue Ich-Bilia
Tunis
Tel: (1) 333-600
Fax: (1) 353-255

Centre de Promotion des Exportations
(State Agency for Export Promotion)
28 rue Ghandi
Tunis
Tel: (1) 350-344
Fax: (1) 353-683

WORLD TRADE CENTER

Tunis World Trade Center
6, Avenue Mohamed Ali Akid 1003
Cite Olympique Tunis
Tel: (1) 783-155
Fax: (1) 784-744

STOCK EXCHANGE

Bourse des Valeurs Mobilieres de Tunisie
(Stock Exchange)
19 Bis rue Kamel Ataturk
Tunis
Tel: (1) 252-649
Fax: (1) 347-256

BUSINESS AND TRADE ORGANIZATIONS

Tunisian-American Chamber of Commerce
15 rue Aziza Othmana
Mutuelleville
Tunis
Tel: (1) 288-316
Fax: (1) 799-851

Office des Céréales
(Cereals Industry)
30, rue Alain Savery
Tunis
Tel: (1) 790-351
Fax: (1) 789-573

Office du Commerce de Tunisie
(Tunisian Trade Board)
1, rue de Syrle
1060 Tunis
Tel: (1) 682-901
Telex: 14177

Office National des Mines
(Mining)
26, rue d'Angleterre
Tunis
Tel: (1) 253-122
Telex: 12004

Office National des Pêches
(Marine and Fishing Authority)
Le Port, La Goulette
Tunis
Tel: (1) 275-093
Telex: 12388

Office des Terres Domaniales
(Agricultural Production and Management of State-Owned Lands)
43, rue d'Iran
Tunis
Tel: (1) 280-322
Telex: 13566

Société Générale des Industries Textiles
(Textile Industry)
Bir Kassaa, Ben Arous
Tunis
Tel: (1) 297-100
Telex: 12444

Société Tunisienne de l'Electricité et du Gaz
(Electricity and Natural Gas)
38, rue Kemal Atatürk
BP 190
1080 Tunis
Tel: (1) 341-311
Fax: (1) 349-981
Telex: 14020

INTERNET ADDRESSES

Tunisia's WWW sites
http://www.liii.com/~hajeri.html

The Tunisian WWW Home Page
http://www.nt.e-technik.uni-erlangen.de/~younes/tunisian_home/tunisia.html

Turkey
Republic of Turkey

Economy

Overview

Free market principles and export-led growth strategies adopted in the 1980s have helped Turkey make a dramatic shift from a state-directed, insular market to one of the world's most open and fastest growing economies. Although agriculture remains at the core of the economy, employing more than half the total labor force, industry and tourism have been the driving forces behind Turkey's recent economic success. After achieving such rapid growth, however, the economy in now in the midst of a serious downturn, although this is more a crisis of confidence in the government's abilities than it is a serious economic imbalance. In general, long-term prospects remain very good.

Trade

An economic orientation toward Western countries has significantly increased the total value of Turkey's foreign trade. Major western markets are the primary destinations of its exports, and it buys a high percentage of its imports from developed countries. Germany is the largest source of both its imports and exports, followed by the US and Italy. A growing middle-class represents a substantial market for consumer goods, and imported machinery will be required in a variety of industries to facilitate continued export growth. The slowing economy has contained export and import levels in the short run, but a full recovery is expected.

Sectors

Agriculture Agriculture is at the core of Turkey's economy, engaging 55 percent of its work force and contributing 25 percent of its exports. Diversity in regional climates permits the production of a wide range of crops including cotton, tobacco, grains, fruits, and vegetables. Though sometimes prone to drought conditions, Turkey's soil is highly productive, making it one of the few countries self-sufficient in food in the 1980s. Extensive government irrigation projects should enable this sector to continue to play an important role in Turkey's foreign trade.

Industry Industry has been the driving force behind Turkey's rapid economic expansion. The apparel industry is the largest sector for exports, followed by iron and steel, and other textile products. Turkey's present goal is to widen its manufacturing and industrial bases, which should create good markets for raw materials and industrial machinery.

Services Although a potential financial center linking Europe and Asia. Turkey does not yet have the ability to provide modern, sophisticated financial or business services. Tourism, however, has increased in the past few years, providing many new opportunities in this and related areas.

Trends

Continuing its policy of export-led growth, the government is looking to exploit its proximity to Central Asian markets by establishing joint ventures with foreign partners in the region. Potential membership in the European Union has helped Turkey to focus on liberalizing its economy in order to bring it up to Western standards. The determination to modernize its economy augurs well for substantial growth in exports, and presents excellent opportunities to sell to the growing domestic market. Turkey's extremely liberal foreign trade provisions should continue to draw capital from around the world.

At a Glance

THE COUNTRY

Location Southwestern Asia, bordering the Mediterranean Sea and Black Sea, between Bulgaria and Iran.
Terrain Mostly mountainous with a high central plateau and a narrow coastal plain.
Climate Temperate; hot, dry summers with mild wet winters; harsher weather in the interior.

THE PEOPLE

Population 62,000,000
Ethnic composition
Turkish 80%
Kurdish 20%
Religious composition
Muslim 99.8%
Other.. 0.2%
Languages spoken Turkish (official), Kurdish, and Arabic.
Education and literacy The literacy rate is 90 percent for males and 71 percent for females. Education is compulsory and free for children aged six to 14; however inadequate distribution and number of schools and teachers only allow for two-thirds of school-aged children to receive an education.
Labor force
Total:..20,800,000
By occupation: agriculture 48%, services 32%, industry 20%.
(Note: about 1,800,000 Turks work abroad).

COUNTRY FACTS

Political and legal Turkey is a republican parliamentary democracy. The legal system was derived from various continental legal systems. Voting is allowed for men and women 21 years of age and older.
Telephone International and domestic telephone service is generally dependable. There are about 7,500,000 telephones. International country code: [90]. Selected city codes: Istanbul (212) and (216), Ankara (312).
Transportation More than 20 scheduled airlines connect Turkey with all parts of the world. Local buses, share cabs, and minibuses (dolmus) provide satisfactory local transportation, although they can be crowded. Taxis are readily available. Although main roads are fairly good in and between large centers, drivers should exercise extreme care due to heavy truck and other traffic, and unpredictable drivers. Night driving in the countryside should be avoided because of poorly lit vehicles on the highway.
Environment Dumping of chemicals (including mercury) and detergents have severely contaminated the country's water supply. Soil erosion, deforestation, and air pollution are the current environmental problems with which Turkey must deal. In addition, Turkey is subject to severe earthquakes.
Media The state operates AM and FM radio stations as well as television broadcasts. There are 9.2 million radio sets and 10 million registered television sets. There are a number of independent newspapers published in Turkey.
Health Free medical treatment is available to all Turkish citizens and public health standards in larger cities approach those in the US. Turkish law requires that at least one pharmacy must be open in a neighborhood at all times. Life expectancy is 70 years and the fertility rate is 3.2 children per woman.

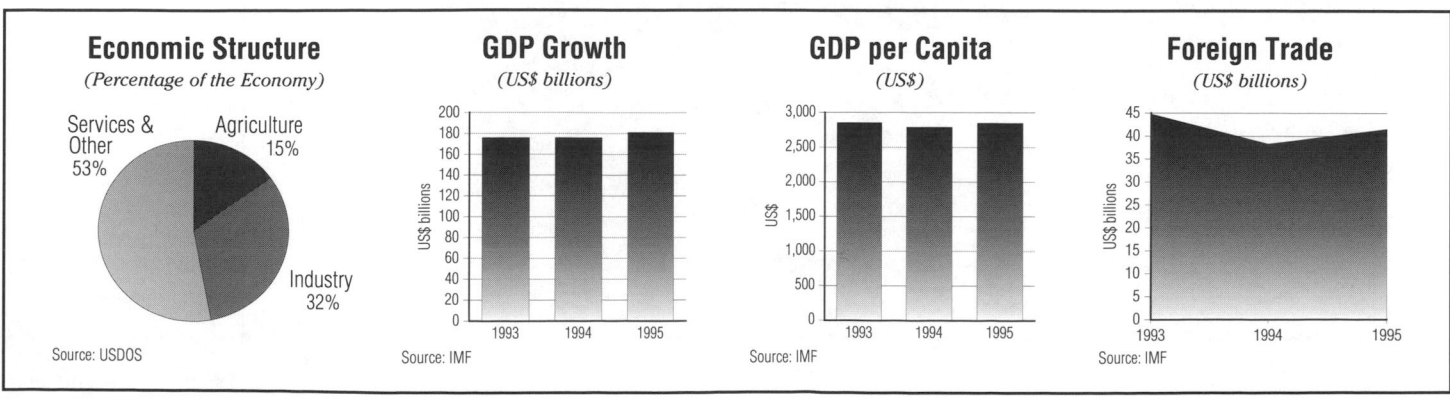

Economic Structure
(Percentage of the Economy)

Services & Other 53%
Agriculture 15%
Industry 32%

Source: USDOS

GDP Growth
(US$ billions)

1993 1994 1995
Source: IMF

GDP per Capita
(US$)

1993 1994 1995
Source: IMF

Foreign Trade
(US$ billions)

1993 1994 1995
Source: IMF

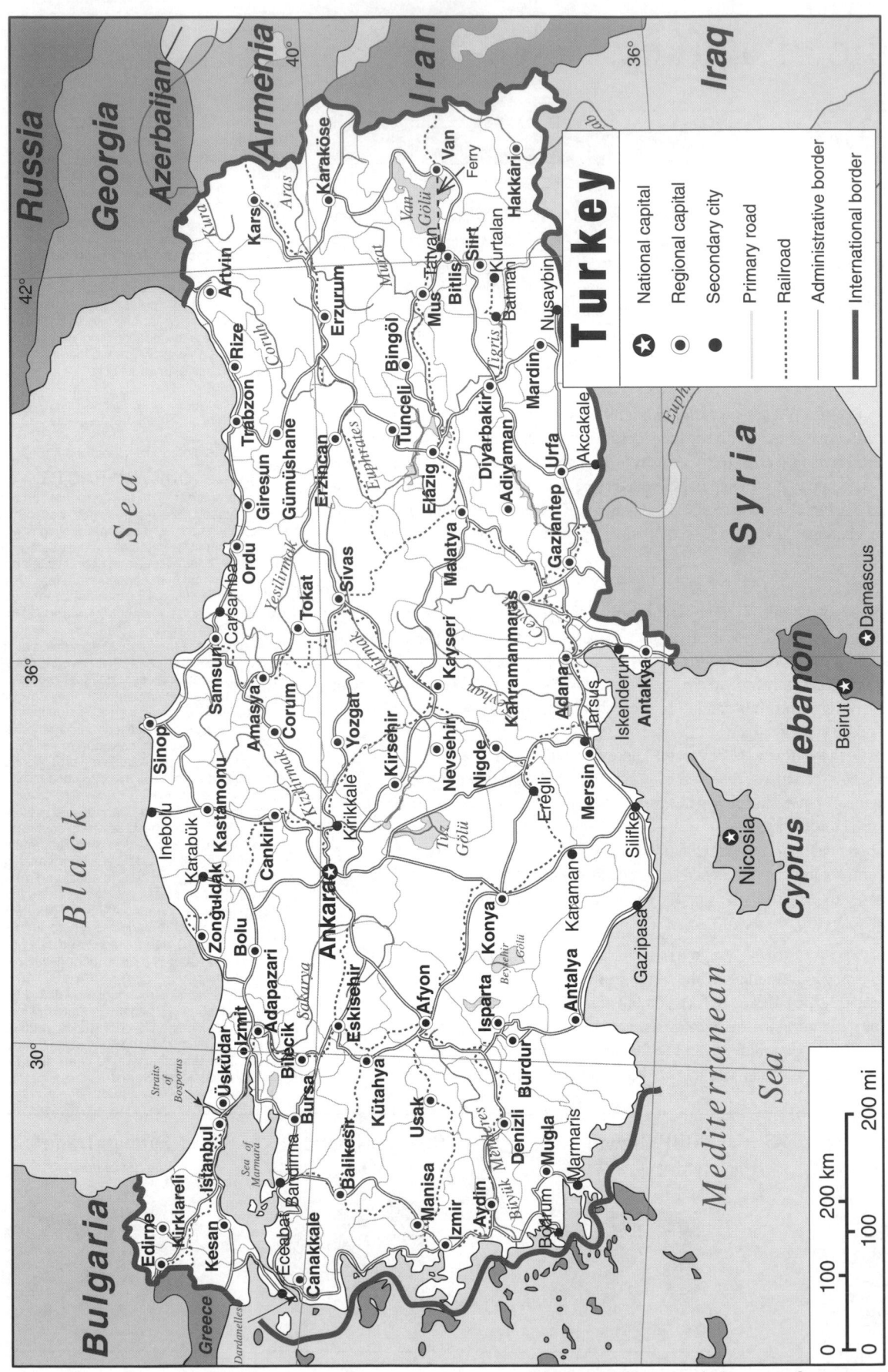

Turkey

- ⊛ National capital
- ⊙ Regional capital
- ● Secondary city
- —— Primary road
- ···· Railroad
- —— Administrative border
- ▬▬ International border

Foreign Trade

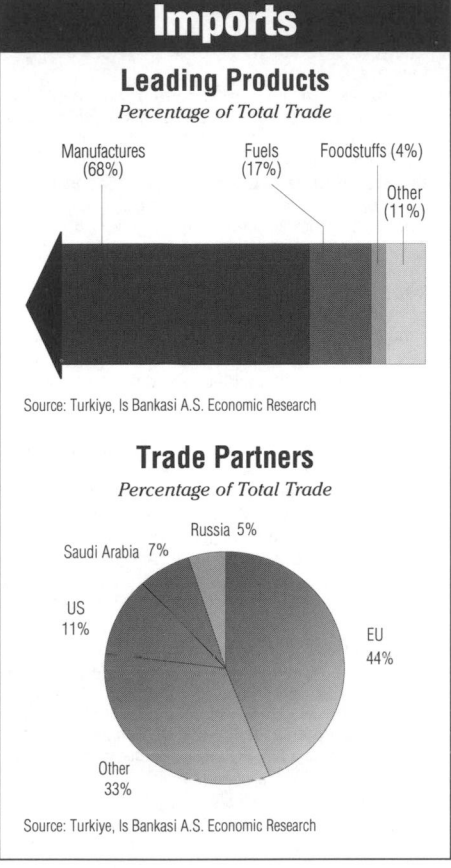

Imports

Leading Products
Percentage of Total Trade

Manufactures (68%)
Fuels (17%)
Foodstuffs (4%)
Other (11%)

Source: Turkiye, Is Bankasi A.S. Economic Research

Trade Partners
Percentage of Total Trade

Russia 5%
Saudi Arabia 7%
US 11%
EU 44%
Other 33%

Source: Turkiye, Is Bankasi A.S. Economic Research

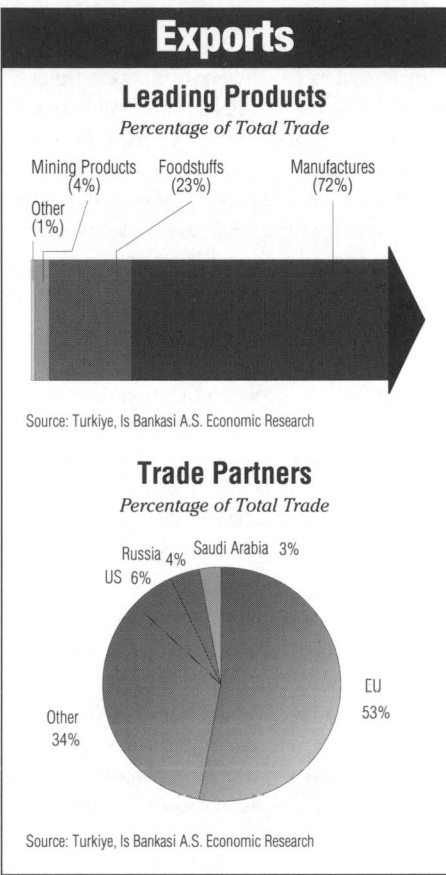

Exports

Leading Products
Percentage of Total Trade

Mining Products (4%)
Foodstuffs (23%)
Manufactures (72%)
Other (1%)

Source: Turkiye, Is Bankasi A.S. Economic Research

Trade Partners
Percentage of Total Trade

Russia 4%
Saudi Arabia 3%
US 6%
EU 53%
Other 34%

Source: Turkiye, Is Bankasi A.S. Economic Research

Opportunities

FOR IMPORTING TO TURKEY
- petroleum
- pharmaceuticals
- dyes
- iron
- steel
- machinery
- plastics
- rubber
- transport vehicles

FOR EXPORTING FROM TURKEY
- unmanufactured tobacco
- textile products/apparels
- petroleum oils
- ferroalloys
- cotton
- cement
- raisins
- nuts
- leather
- glass
- ceramics

GROWTH SECTORS
- food processing
- textiles
- basic metals
- chemicals
- petrochemicals

GOVERNMENT PROCUREMENT
- power generations projects
- telecommunication projects
- industrial chemicals
- architectural/construction/engineering services
- BOT's (Built-operate-transfer projects)
- new power plants

Trade News

RULES AND REGULATIONS

- **Import licenses** All importers must obtain a general import license valid for one year from the Undersecretariat of Foreign Trade (UFT). The general license specifies the classifications of the products that the importer is allowed to import. There are no restrictions on obtaining a general import license.

- **Import permission certificates** All importers are required to obtain an import permission certificate for each type of item to be imported. Without an import permission certificate, a bank cannot issue foreign exchange for payment. Import certificates are obtained from the Central Bank, commercial banks, or from the UFT (or other appropriate government agency). Goods cannot be cleared through customs without a separate certification for each eight-digit customs tariff code product.

- **Royalties** For imports of motion pictures, full-video cassettes and their brochures, and advertisements, an import certificate is issued by banks. Only the actual cost of the item is considered, not the royalty costs.

- **Tariff rates** Turkey has been an Associate Member of the European Union (EU) since 1964. Industrial exports from Turkey enter the EU duty free; industrial products from the EU and the European Free Trade Association (EFTA–Austria, Finland, Iceland, Norway, Sweden, and Switzerland) enjoy lower customs tariff rates than those from other countries.

- **Tariff exemptions** Capital goods, some raw materials, imports by government agencies and enterprises, and products for investments with incentive certificates are exempt from import fees.

- **Export restrictions** Turkey was a member of CO-COM and has actively participated in the planning discussions for a COCOM-successor regime. Since Turkey is not a major producer or exporter of dual-use or other sensitive technologies, the country's export control inspection and licensing infrastructure is dispersed and only loosely linked, involving the Ministries of Foreign and Industrial Affairs, Customs, and the Treasury, and participation by expert scholars and technicians from academia on an ad hoc basis. However, talks are underway within the government to consolidate appropriate export control and nonproliferation experts from the various ministries into one nonproliferation agency attached to the Ministry for Foreign Affairs. Legislation has been drafted to this effect, but has not yet been submitted to Parliament.

- **Temporary entry** Materials may be temporarily imported into Turkey without payment of duties and tax if they are to be used in the production or manufacture of a product that is to be exported. The importer gives security in the form of a bank guarantee in the amount of applicable duties and taxes. Temporary admission of goods intended for re-export in their original form is permissible free of import duties and taxes with the approval of the Undersecretariat for Foreign Trade.

- **Samples** Samples with no commercial value are admitted duty free. Samples with commercial value may be imported into Turkey under the temporary importation system.

- **After-sales service** Products that require after-sales service such as motor vehicles, household electrical goods, office equipment, heaters, gas-fired burners, lathes, and wireless equipment require an import permission certificate from the Ministry of Industry and Commerce. In order to obtain such a certificate, importers must guarantee that they will establish a spare-parts network and maintenance capability in each of the seven geographic areas of Turkey.

GOVERNMENT AGENCY

Dis Ticaret Mustesarligi Ithalat Genel Mudurlugu
Undersecretariat of Foreign Trade, General Directorate of Imports
Eskisehir Karayolu, Inonu Bulvari
06510 Emek, Ankara
Tel: (312) 212-8724 Fax: (312) 212-8765

Marketing

Overview

Despite the recent fall in imports, foreign firms have found Turkey generally to be one of the more attractive emerging markets. Marketing in Turkey is characterized by the absence of a developed business infrastructure, and emphasis is placed instead on personal contacts. In fact, it is virtually impossible to surmount complicated bureaucratic requirements, language obstacles, and purchasing transactions without a competent and trustworthy local agent. But opportunities abound for foreign sellers who recognize that Turkey is still developing with regards to Western marketing methods and standards, and that they therefore may have to initially offer low prices and alternative payment methods in order to get their foot in the door. Turkey has a large, and increasingly affluent population, it has historically acted as a gateway between East and West, and Turkish consumers are extremely open to the purchase of foreign goods and services. It promises good payoffs in the long run.

Distribution

Marketing of most foreign products in Turkey is through foreign suppliers' agents or distributors. Depending on the location of the products' consumers or end-users, most distributors have a dealer network throughout the country or in areas where the product is most used. Commission agents make periodic sales calls on their customers, usually accompanied by their foreign principals. Distributors maintain separate regional or nationwide dealer networks, depending on the distribution and sales patterns of the particular product.

Agents, Distributors, and Partners

Unless a foreign seller's interest is large enough to warrant opening an office in the country, the most effective means of selling in Turkey is through a reliable and qualified local representative. It is strongly recommended that sole agents or distributors be appointed, either for the whole country or for specifically designated areas or product types. In cases where a large volume of government business is expected, it is essential either to appoint an Ankara firm or an Istanbul firm with a branch office in the capital due to complicated bureaucratic procedures and language barriers. Turkish companies prefer to establish joint ventures. But whatever the arrangement, a foreign firm should carefully investigate the reputation and possible conflicting interests of any prospective agents before signing an agreement.

Selling Techniques

Once a foreign seller appoints an agent, the agent or distributor expects and should receive the principal's full support in regard to literature, technical information, and advertising material. Possible government buyers and potential private-sector dealers should receive catalogs and other literature imprinted with the name and address of the local agent or distributor. Both agents and their principals, whenever possible, should periodically visit existing and potential customers, since personal contact in Turkey is paramount. In larger Turkish cities, international trade promotional events such as fairs, exhibits, and seminars are a common method of sales promotion. These fairs are also opportunities for foreign sellers to assess existing competition and survey potential markets, since all major foreign and local suppliers participate in these events. Catalogs from the events can serve as trade lists for a specific product or sector. A common and very effective marketing practice used by European principals is to invite the agent to the principal's country every year for an annual sales meeting.

Government purchases The Turkish government procurement system is often frustrating and inconsistent, but it does not discriminate against foreign suppliers. In government tenders, state organizations give particular importance to the way proposals are prepared and to their adherence to administrative and technical specifications. Price, quality, and financial credit terms and length of repayment period are the most important factors in purchasing decisions.

Advertising

Advertising on television and in newspapers is highly effective. In Turkey there are 10 major television channels and four general circulation newspapers, all headquartered in Istanbul. Chambers of commerce and industry, various associations, and trade publications also serve as channels for advertising. Advertising collateral, such as catalogs, product brochures, and posters should be considered a central component of any advertising effort, and not merely an adjunct to mass media advertising.

Service and Customer Support

Foreign sellers are expected to provide service centers and training for their products. It is advantageous to establish an office in Turkey with servicing facilities, spare parts, and equipment in the country's major centers. After-sales service is very important for many products; customers expect it and the government attempts to insure it through special import requirements on these items.

Marketing in Turkey

MARKETING TIPS

- **Personal contact** Frequent personal contact is essential at all levels of solicitation in Turkey.
- **Local agent** Local Turkish representatives are necessary, whatever the form of the importer's business presence.
- **Pricing** Price is the most important consideration in government tenders. Private-sector buyers emphasize quality, but they are also affected by both price and financing arrangements.
- **Barriers to trade** Lack of domestic financing, vagaries of the government purchasing plans, convoluted bidding procedures for government contracts, and a duty structure favoring European Union products all pose difficulties to foreign sellers.
- **Trade fairs** Exhibits, seminars, and trade fairs remain important marketing activities, and can be found in large urban centers throughout the year.
- **Promotional and product support** Agents expect to be supported with marketing and sales promotional literature, and local facilities for product service and maintenance.
- **Agency agreements** Agency agreements under Turkish law are private contracts between two parties, and their stipulations vary according to mutual consent. There are no fixed commission rates.
- **Franchising** The franchising sector has grown and diversified tremendously in the past few years, extending into smaller towns from urban centers, and expanding from fast foods to apparel and retail operations.
- **Direct marketing** Unless a foreign firm has established an office in Turkey, direct marketing from the firm's home country is not recommended. In fact, it is virtually impossible to surmount complicated bureaucratic requirements, language obstacles, and purchasing transactions without a competent local agent.
- **Joint ventures** Especially in large urban centers, a highly sophisticated joint venture infrastructure exists in terms of legal support, as well as financial or consultancy services which may be required by foreign investors or joint venture partners.

AD AGENCIES

Cenajans Grey
Osmanli Sokak No. 19
80090 Taksim
Istanbul
Tel: (212) 251-74-84
Fax: (212) 711-1227, 711-1226

Grafika: Lintas A.S.
POB 729 Sisli
80220 Istanbul
Tel: (212) 28-52-325
Fax: (212) 27-64-098

Manajans Thompson Reklam Isleri A.S.
Buykdere Cad. 191
Levent
80509 Istanbul
Tel: (212) 279-2900
Fax: (212) 282-6477
Telex: 813.430

Markom/Leo Burnett A.S.
Perlhan Sokak No. 126
Sisli Istanbul
Tel: (212) 234-2708
Fax: (212) 246-0842
Telex: 27572

Pars-McCann
Buyukdere Caddesi
Ecza Sokak, No. 6
80498 Istanbul
Tel: (212) 2796585
Fax: (212) 2702627
Telex: 26946

Saatchi & Saatchi Advertising
19 Mayis Caddesi
Nova Baran Plaza
80220 Istanbul
Tel: (212) 6226280

Business Culture

Greetings and Courtesies

Shake hands with all present, including wives and children, when arriving and departing. Use the title and surname until told otherwise, first names are reserved only for close friends. The first name followed by *bey* (sir) or *hanim* (madam) shows special respect, as does *Haj* for those who have made the pilgrimage to Mecca (it can be placed either before or after a name). When meeting friends or strangers, say *Merhaba* (Hello) or *Nasilsiniz* (How are you?). A reply to the second greeting is, *Iyiyim, teshekur ederim* (Fine, thanks). When greeting a close friend of the same sex, and sometimes the opposite sex, Turks clasp hands and kiss both cheeks. Turkish businesspeople tend to be generous and hospitable, even toward strangers. They enjoy lively conversation and socializing, especially in restaurants, but they tend to be private in regards to family and family matters. An invitation to a Turkish home should be considered and honor and will likely be a fairly formal affair.

Business Ethic and Framework

Turks are proud of their traditions and history but are also tolerant of other ways. They consider themselves neither Europeans nor Arab but a distinct ethnic and cultural group. Businesspeople will align themselves much more closely with Europe than the Middle Eastern world. Turks have incorporated elements from both hemispheres into their culture, and they are proud of modern features they have adopted as well. Everyone works long hours here; they expect contracts to leave the quality of the product unquestioned and focus on an equitable price. Importers here are price- and credit-conscious. The best strategy is to offer the lowest possible price initially to make the sale. New companies in particular have to develop distribution patterns to be successful in Turkey. Confirmed letters of credit are always safest when dealing with new overseas accounts. The center of Turkish culture is the family, but Turks are convinced money helps keep the family together. Companies are often treated as extended families.

Decision Making

Turks are known to haggle before agreeing to almost any proposal. You are expected to haggle back; to do otherwise could be considered an insult. Almost all business contacts here adopt the attitude of, "Let's see if we can be friends; if so, we can do business." Then the haggling begins, often designed to test the new friend's strength. It is better to walk away from a deal than to agree to something out of intimidation alone. Although Turks will often consult others before making a decision, a clear decision will be made, and you will get a definite answer to your proposal. Decisions are made as much on personal relationships and subjective feelings as they are on business practicalities. Thus, proposals couched in personal terms, rather than on strictly business principles, will sometimes be looked on more favorably.

Women

Turkish women often find themselves torn between Western ideas of equality and their more traditional Muslim roles. Thanks to the country's 90 percent literacy rate, those roles are rapidly changing and women are given more equality. The justice system still denies a woman's right to own property, and some crimes against women go unpunished. (In a recent unusual incident, a Turkish woman and her daughter were killed by their male relatives because the men considered the women's clothing immodest.) Nearly all city girls are sent to religious school as adolescents. Many women work in the city, some in the same firm as their husbands. Women are teachers, hold editorial posts on Turkey's major newspapers, and make up nearly 20 percent of the lawyers—not to mention holding the highest positions in government.

Meetings

Make appointments well in advance. Turkish businesspeople tend to be on time, so strive for punctuality. Light conversation over Turkish coffee (the strongest blends in this part of the world) or tea begins most business discussions; avoid rushing the pace. Meetings can run late, but be patient; trying to speed the meeting to a quick ending is considered rude. Most Turkish businessmen and younger government officials speak French, English, and German, but several businesses hire a translator or agent to expedite their business in the country.

Business Attire

Turks often judge others by the way they dress; make conservative choices. Western styles are common; European fashions are especially popular among young people. Women should have arms, knees, and shoulders covered, as well as the head if entering a mosque.

Cultural Cautions

DO'S

- Conversation can include Western lifestyle, sports (especially soccer) and hobbies, professions, family, and fashion.

DON'TS

- Keep your hands off your hips and out of your pockets when speaking.
- Avoid talking about religion, racial strife (especially with the Kurds), Communism, the Cyprus-Greece incident, and human rights abuses; all are intertwined in this culture. Bad news should stay a private matter.
- Never point the sole of your shoe or foot at another person.
- Women should avoid crossing their legs when facing another person; it is a sign of sexual desire.
- Adults do not eat or smoke on the street.
- Since nearly all Turks are Muslims, never use the left hand for any purpose in public; this is the toilet hand and to use it is a deadly insult. Use the right hand or both.

CUSTOMS

- Visitors are rarely invited to mosques; if you are, remove your shoes before entering. In rural areas, people remove shoes before entering a home, but this is no longer an urban custom.
- Hospitality is abundant, almost overwhelming.
- An invitation to a Turkish businessperson's home is a mark of a special favor. Bring flowers, candy, or pastries. If you know that the family serves alcoholic beverages, take wine.
- Turks love to entertain with long, lavish lunches or dinners. Whoever invites, pays.
- Modest gifts are given at the consummation of a successful deal and at the New Year.
- Guests are served before family and friends. Eating with fingers is common, but take your cue from the host. Always compliment the host or hostess after dinner.
- The ninth lunar month is Ramadan; some business entities operate only in the morning, and many not at all.
- A downward nod means yes; a backward nod followed by "tsk" means no.
- The end of harvest is the time for weddings in both city and country.

OBSERVATIONS

- In the world of Islam, religion is inseparable from culture, though Turks do not practice the Islam of many Muslim states, since Turkish society is secular. One application of this concept is how Turks treat a foreign company's desire for a firm deadline. Muslims regard the future as Allah's province, and consider involvement with it as dangerous. The visitor should work with broad outlines rather than insist on specifics.
- The most popular form of entertainment is restaurant dining.
- Turkey is very open to Western ideas and technology, more so than its Middle Eastern neighbors.
- Fundamentalists have a greater challenge than in other Muslim countries; *Penthouse* and *Playboy* have been published in Turkish editions.
- The further south or east one goes, the more rural, traditional, and poor the country becomes, although more than 60 percent of Turks live in cities and towns.
- Despite modern changes, many Turks think of the three legs of their culture as, "I am a Turk, a Muslim, and a man."

NEGOTIATIONS

- Contractual provisions need to be general.
- Determining when a reference to Allah's will is sincere or a delaying tactic is difficult.
- Haggling is endemic to the Turkish population, and they expect it of those with whom they do business. Be prepared to do so.

Legal System

The republic of Turkey adopted the civil code system after the 1923 collapse of the Ottoman Empire. The commercial, civil, penal, and administrative codes bear strong similarities to the relevant codes of Germany, Switzerland, Italy, and France respectively. Turkish courts are divided into three: civil courts for civil and commercial disputes; criminal courts, which enforce solely penal laws; and administrative courts for matters involving the state. The Yargitay is the court of appeals for civil and criminal decisions. The country's highest court is the constitutional court.

Intellectual Property Rights

Protection of intellectual property rights does not generally meet Western standards, despite recent modifications to intellectual property laws (including the trademark act, the patent act, and the intellectual property code).

Copyrights Turkey has only very recently amended its copyright law. The new law, which came into effect on June 12, 1995, significantly improves protection for most copyright protected media. Fines are also substantially increased. When it is fully implemented the law should have a significant impact on the current widespread, unauthorized copying and sale of foreign-copyrighted books, tapes, and software. The Cinema, Video, and Music Works Law, although recently revised, has helped reduced piracy of these items, but enforcement has been problematic and penalties are not harsh enough to act as a deterrent.

Patents The new patent bill is weakened by the absence of pipeline protection and its broad compulsory licensing provisions. An agreement with the EU allows Turkey to postpone introduction of patent protection for pharmaceuticals until 1999.

Trademarks A trademark law has been drafted and may be implemented in the near future. Counterfeiting of foreign trademarked products is currently widespread.

Trade secrets There is currently no Turkish law specifically protecting trade secrets.

Business Registration

Application for the establishment of a new company, opening a branch office, or initiating participation in an existing company is made in writing to the General Directorate of Foreign Investment of the Undersecretariat for Foreign Trade (GDFI). Permission from the GDFI must be granted before the foreign investor can commence doing business.

Contracts and Dispute Resolution

The Turkish Code of Obligations is based on the Swiss Code of Obligations. Parties to a contract are free to reach any agreement with respect to a particular subject matter provided that their agreement does not violate public policy or any mandatory provisions of law. Special codes have been enacted to control certain types of transactions, such as leasing and insurance. Arbitration is a reliable alternative to litigation for dispute resolution. Foreign court judgments and arbitration awards are recognized and enforceable in Turkey. ICC arbitration is a forum to resolve disputes arising from international transactions that involve Turkey. Turkey is a party to many multilateral and bilateral treaties on procedural aspects of cross-border arbitration.

Labor

Under Turkish labor law all workers have the right to associate freely and form representative unions. Turkish government bars military personnel, teachers, police, and civil servants from organizing unions, but constitutional amendments granting all categories of employees the right to form unions and expanding the right to strike is under consideration. An arbitration board settles disputes in cases where strikes are forbidden. However, labor-management relations are generally good. Employers are obliged by law to negotiate in good faith with unions that have been certified as bargaining agents. The law specifies a series of steps which a union must take before it may legally strike, and a similar series of steps before an employer may engage in a lockout. Strikes are usually of short duration and almost always peaceful. The incidence of strikes decreased markedly in 1994 —down by 27 percent from 1993.

Current legislation forbids full-time employment of children under 15. The law also requires that schoolchildren of age 13 and 14 who work part-time must have their working hours adjusted to accommodate school requirements. The constitution also prohibits children from engaging in physically demanding labor, such as underground mining, and from working at night.

Source: Duygun Yarsuvat & Ömür Yarsuvat Law Offices, Istanbul

Legal Matters
LEGAL BRIEFS

- **Business entities** Turkish law provides for stock corporations, limited liability companies, and partnerships. A stock corporation is identified by the initial "A"; a limited liability company, with "Ltd. ti"; and a partnership, with "Komandit" or "Kollektiv Ortaklik." Liaison offices or representative offices are available to those who want to explore the country's business potential without committing more than operational expenses.
- **Stock corporations** Most foreign investors establish or acquire an interest in a stock corporation. The management of a stock corporation is carried out by its board of directors. Officers run the daily business operations.
- **Trade regulation** Only after heavy pressure from other nations has Turkey agreed to adopt legislation on trade regulation and consumer protection. Nevertheless, trade regulation is up to international standards. Antitrust and unfair competition laws are similar in scope to those of the United States and the EU, while the consumer rights law is in line with EU legislation.
- **Legal environment** Turkish courts are not biased against non-Turkish parties in a litigated dispute. The laws afford the same protection to all persons regardless of race, religion, or origin. However, litigation and enforcement of any judgment can take considerable time because of the heavy workload of the courts. Two- to three-year long-litigation is quite common and should be expected in international litigation.
- **International covnetions and agreements** GATT/WTO; NATO; OECD; EU; Convention on the Service Abroad of Judicial and Extrajudicial Documents in Civil or Commercial Matters; Convention on the Recognition and Enforcement of Foreign Arbitral Awards; Convention Abolishing the Requirement of Legalization for Foreign Public Documents; ATA Carnet Convention.
- **Work safety** Laws regarding work safety are weak throughout the country. Some occupational safety and health regulations and procedures are mandated by law. Limited resources and lack of safety awareness often result in inadequate enforcement, however.
- **Compulsory labor** The constitution prohibits forced or compulsory labor and it does not exist.
- **IPR infringement** Trademark lawyers generally believe that the relevant laws are adequate, but that the criminal justice system, overwhelmed by more serious crimes, is not willing to devote the effort necessary to prosecute offenders. Counterfeiters are generally small operations rather than large companies.
- **Unfair competition** A law on the prevention of unfair competition came into force in 1989 which protects industry against unfair competition due to dumped or subsidized imports.
- **Foreign investment** Turkish foreign investment legislation does not allow companies special privileges or to become monopolies.
- **Labor law jurisdiction** The laws are effectively enforced only in organized industrial and service sectors.
- **Maximum hours of work** Labor laws are very structured in Turkey. The law provides for a nominal 45-hour work week and limits the overtime that employers may request.
- **Non-wage benefits** Most workers in Turkey receive nonwage benefits such as transportation, meal allowances, and vacation time that can last as long as two weeks.

LEGAL CONTACT
Duygun Yarsuvat & Ömür Yarsuvat Law Offices
Haci Adil Sokak 44
2. Levent
80620 Istanbul
Tel: (212) 282-4503
Fax: (212) 282-7910

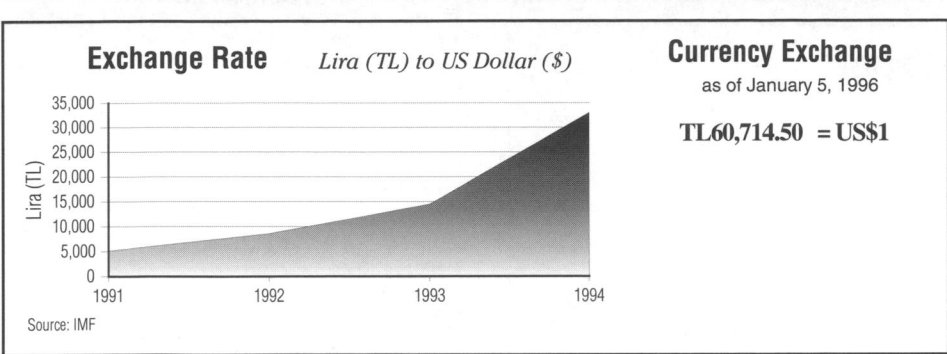

Exchange Rate — Lira (TL) to US Dollar ($)

Source: IMF

Currency Exchange
as of January 5, 1996

TL60,714.50 = US$1

Currency

The currency of Turkey is the Turkish lira (TL).

Foreign Exchange

Administration of exchange controls is delegated to the Central Bank, which regulates all matters related to foreign exchange operations. The lira is fully convertible and the exchange rate is determined by the market. The Central Bank intervenes in money markets to dampen short-term exchange rate fluctuations and to provide liquidity during extraordinary events.

Capital Transfers

Nonresidents may open accounts denominated in foreign exchange and liras with authorized commercial banks. The holders may dispose of such accounts at their discretion. Turkish law guarantees the free transfer of profits, fees, and royalties, and repatriation of capital. There are no limitations on the inflow or outflow of funds for remittances.

Investment Incentives

Turkey provides investment incentives including subsidized credit facilities, and exemptions on corporate and value-added tax, customs fees, and duties. Investment incentives are clearly specified in regulations and are available on a national treatment basis. Investment incentives are greater in less developed regions and eligibility depends on minimum value. Turkey annually issues a list of investment incentives. Current incentives include: corporate tax exemptions; customs duties exemptions; refund of VAT and VAT deferral; land allocation; exemption from building and construction taxes; discounts on electricity charges; soft loans; and special credits.

Investment Restrictions

Turkey imposes few restrictions on investments. However, nonresidents investing in Turkey must import capital in kind or in foreign exchange. Foreign investors must bring in a minimum of US$50,000 in capital. Treasury screens foreign investments, although proposals are routinely granted.

TAXATION

Taxation requires sophisticated knowledge of complex rules and regulations specific to each country. For more detailed information we suggest you refer to the Ernst & Young Corporate Tax Guide and Directory, available from the Ernst & Young accounting office in your country, or from:

Ernst & Young
YonetimDanismanligi A.S.
Yildiz Posta Caddesi 26/16 K:5
Yesil Apartmani B Blok
Esentepe, Istanbul
Turkey
Tel: (212) 274-9966, 274-9967
Fax: (212) 274-9293

At a Glance

Corporate Income Tax Rate (%)(a)	25
Capital Gains Tax Rate (%)(a)	25
Branch Tax Rate (%)(a)	25
Withholding Tax (%)(b)	
Dividends (c)	10/20
Interest from Private Sector Bonds (d)(e)	10/20

Other Interest	0
Royalties from Patents, Know-how, etc. (d)	25
Professional Fees	
Petroleum-Exploration Activities (d)(f)	5
Other Activities (d)(f)	20
Salaries (d)	25
Progress Billings on Long-Term Construction and Repair Contracts (d)(g)	5
Payments on Financial Leases (d)	1
Real Estate Rental Payments (d)	20
Branch Remittance Tax (c)	20
Net Operating Losses (Years)	
Carryback	0
Carryforward (h)	5

(a) A 7% surtax is levied on the corporate income tax.
(b) A 7% surtax is imposed on all withholding taxes.
(c) Profits derived from group B securities investment funds are subject to a 10% withholding tax, regardless of whether profits are distributed. (Group A securities investment funds and investment companies derive profits from transactions involving their operating portfolio, where at least 25% of the portfolio consists of stock certificates. Group B describes investment funds and companies that are not specified by Group A.) A 20% withholding tax is imposed on after-tax profits of all companies, including branches of foreign companies, regardless of whether profits are distributed. Dividends are not subject to a separate withholding tax.

Money Matters

BITS AND PIECES

- **Foreign investment** There are no performance requirements imposed as a condition for establishing, maintaining, or expanding an investment. There are no requirements that nationals own shares in investments by foreigners, that the share of foreign equity be reduced over time, or that the investor transfer technology on certain terms. Investors need not purchase from local sources.

- **Free Trade Zones** There are six free trade zones in Turkey: Mersin, Antalya, Aegean, Trabzon, and two in Istanbul. These areas are tax free, and foreign-owned firms enjoy the same opportunities and treatment as Turkish entities. More free zones are planned.

- **Import instruments** Letters of credit are typically used for private-sector transactions, and are always irrevocable and usually confirmed. As Turkish importers develop long-term contacts, suppliers are usually willing to accept cash against documents and goods shipments. Deferred payment is not common, except in supplier financing situations.

- **Banking system** There are approximately 67 banks, in Turkey, 12 investment and development banks and 55 commercial banks. Banks may engage in regular banking, securities brokering, and other businesses. The Turkish banking system has been restructured to comply with Western standards.

- **Stock market** Foreign investors have access to Turkey's developing capital markets, including the Istanbul Stock Exchange. Established in 1986, the Istanbul Stock Exchange is still quite small, and cannot yet support the country's capital needs.

- **Credit** Credit is allocated on market terms to any qualified borrower, whether foreign or domestic.

- **Gold** The Central Bank is authorized to import gold into Turkey and to conduct purchase and sale transactions with the public without restriction. The exportation and importation of gold are allowed within a framework established in the export and import regimes.

- **Restricted sectors** Equity participation by foreign shareholders is limited to 49 percent in the following sectors: aviation, insurance, and broadcasting.

- **Foreign direct investment** Foreign direct investment is viewed favorably by almost all non-governmental groups. However, some politicians and trade unions oppose block sales of state economic enterprises to foreigners.

- **Expropriation** Expropriations must be for public purpose and non-discriminatory. Compensation must be reasonably prompt, adequate, and effective. As a practical matter, the Turkish government occasionally expropriates private property for public works or for state enterprise industrial projects.

BANKS

Akbank T.A.S.
Sabanci Center, 4. Levent
80745 Istanbul
Tel: (212) 270-3355 Fax: (212) 269-7383

Citibank, N.A.
Ataturk Bulvari No. 177
06680 Kavaklidere, Ankara
Tel: (312) 417-5060 Fax: (312) 418-4549

T.C. Ziraat Bankasi
Gazi Mustafa Kemal Bulvari
Sihhiye, Ankara
Tel: (312) 310-3747

Koc-Amerikan Bank
Ataturk Bulvari, Zafer Ishani 58/1
Kizilay, Ankara
Tel: (312) 418-1804 Fax: (312) 425-3237

Turkiye Is Bankasi A.S.
Ataturk Bulvari No. 191
06680 Kavaklidere, Ankara
Tel: (312) 428-1140 Fax: (312) 425-0750

Yapi ve Kredi Bankasi A.S.
Yapi Kredi Plaza A Blok
Buyukdere Caddesi
80620 Levent, Istanbul
Tel: (212) 280-1111 Fax: (212) 280-1670

Business Travel

	LH 1906	MADRID	935	113-3
	LH 1022	STUTTGART HBF.	935	
	AF 1701	LYON	940	683-6
	AY 822	HELSINKI	940	113-3
	AA 071	SFRANCISCO-DALLAS	945	731-7

Air Travel Times

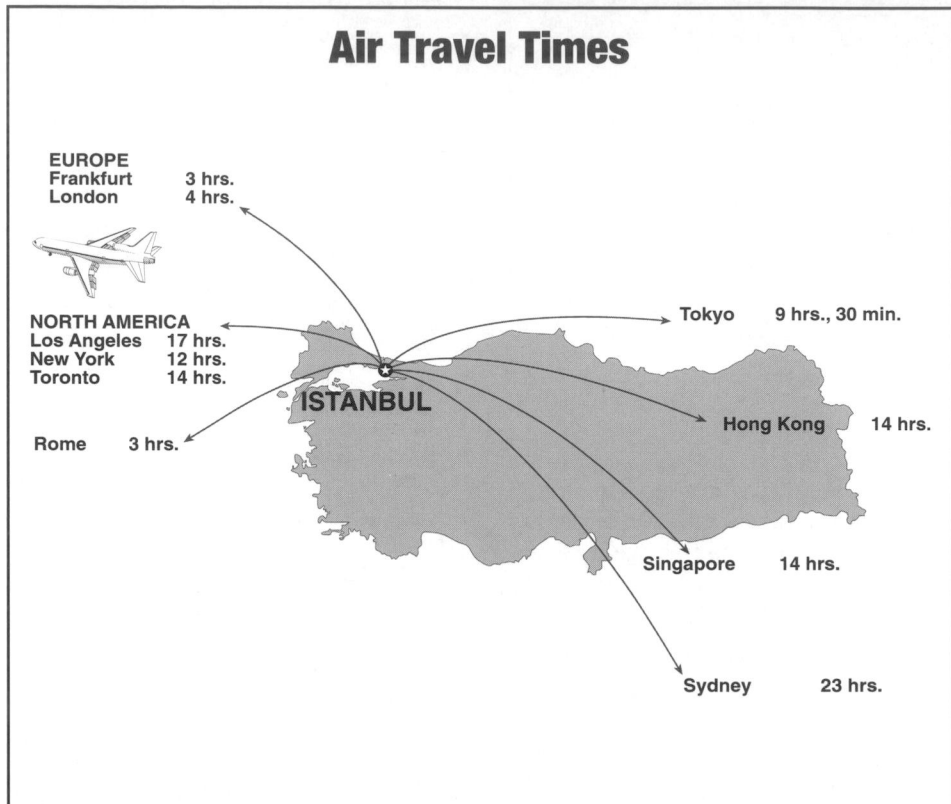

EUROPE
Frankfurt   3 hrs.
London   4 hrs.

NORTH AMERICA
Los Angeles 17 hrs.
New York   12 hrs.
Toronto   14 hrs.

Rome   3 hrs.

ISTANBUL

Tokyo   9 hrs., 30 min.

Hong Kong   14 hrs.

Singapore   14 hrs.

Sydney   23 hrs.

COMMUNICATIONS

Telephones The telephone system in Turkey is good and the Turkish government's PTT operates all of the telephone service. Direct dial is available, but some service may be unreliable. Public phones require a *jeton* coin.

Fax Most international correspondence is done by fax.

Post office The PTT also manages the postal service. Airmail takes approximately one week for delivery worldwide. The express mail service, Acele Posta Servisi, for letters and small packages reaches over 70 countries.

BEST TRAVEL BOOKS

Turkey, Travel Survival Kit, Lonely Planet. Provides invaluable information and is highly recommended. 752 pages.

Fodor's A Travel Guide, Turkey. Tourist oriented, excellent source of city details, filled with maps, language sections, cultural and historical information.

Middle East On a Shoestring, **Lonely Planet** Details, details, details! 126 maps.

Fodor's Europe, Best of 31 Countries. Contains information on historical towns, great culture, scenic coastal countryside.

Do's and Taboo's Around the World. The Bestselling Guide to International Behavior. Edited by Roger Axtell, compiled by the Parker Pen Company. The ultimate guide to international behavior, now completely updated and expanded. Helpful, fun to read!

Berlitz Business Travel Guide, Europe. Concise economic details, successful trip planning, background information on people and cities, useful facts and addresses.

USEFUL TELEPHONE NUMBERS

If you are calling from outside Turkey, you will need to add the country code [90] and any other international dialing requirements from within your country.

- US Consulate/Istanbul .... (212) 251-3602
- Tourism Police .... (212) 5285369
- Ankara Police .... (212) 1341756
- Istanbul Police .... (212) 52852369
- Izmir Police.................................... (232) 218652
- DHL .... (212) 2750800
- First Aid 112
- Istanbul Ataturk Airport.................... (212) 6636460
- Avis, Istanbul................................. (212) 2577670
- Budget, Istanbul .... (212) 2539200
- Hertz, Istanbul .... (212) 2344300
- Ankara Chamber of Commerce .... (312) 3104810
- Istanbul Chamber of Commerce .... (212) 5114150
- Fax .... (212) 5262197
- Izmir Chamber of Commerce .... (232) 144355
- Turkish Businessmen's Association.. (212) 1307474
- Export Promotion Center................. (212) 11772223
- Touring and Automobile Club........ (212) 282787415
- Istanbul Airlines.............................. (212) 5703400
- Turkish Airlines............................... (212) 5477300
- National Railway Authority .... (212) 527-0050
- Ankara Hotel .... (212) 18306680
- Merit Oteli .... (212) 2317760
- Kent Oteli .... (212) 1355050

Credit Card Information
Lost or stolen credit cards (call collect to the US, regardless of which country the card was issued in).
- Amex ....[1] (919) 333-3211
- Diner's Club..............................[1] (303) 799-1504
- MasterCard ....[1] (314) 275-6690
- Visa ....[1] (410) 581-7931

Travelogue

WORKWEEK

Government Monday-Friday 8:30 am to 12:30 pm, 1:30 pm to 5:30 pm.

Business Monday-Friday 8:30 am to 12:30 pm, 1:30 pm to 5:30 pm.

Banks Monday-Friday 8:30 am to noon, 1:30 pm to 5:00 pm.

Retail Monday-Saturday 9:00 am to 1:00 pm, 2:00 pm. to 7:00 pm.

During the summer months in the Aegean and Mediterranean regions many offices close in the afternoon.

HOLIDAYS

Holidays 1996
January 1 New Year's Day
February 19-22 Sugar Holiday
April 23 National Sovereignty and Children's Day
April 28-May 2 Sacrifice Holiday
May 19 Ataturk Memorial, Youth and Sports Day
August 30 Zafer Bayrami-Victory Day
October 28-29 Turkish Independence Day (from 1 pm on October 28.)

VISA AND PASSPORT

New visa regulations are in effect for visiting Turkey. Many visitors are required to obtain visas before entering Turkey. Those with standard passports may obtain visas from any Turkish Consular Office or at the border crossing point. Anyone with diplomatic or official passports must also obtain a visa before entering Turkey.

DEPARTURE FORMALITIES

Any unauthorized purchase or removal of antiquities or cultural artifacts is strictly forbidden.

IMMUNIZATION

International certificate of vaccination is not required unless you are arriving from an infected area.

TIPPING

For taxi drivers it is not necessary to tip though it is customary to round up the cab fare. Hotel bellboys should be tipped five percent of your room price.

CRIME

In major cities such as Istanbul there are reports of pickpockets and muggings. Some bars and nightclubs may seriously overcharge tourists. Travel to eastern Turkey, except for the Black Sea Coast, can be dangerous. The terrorist attacks that occur here do include civilian targets. It is advised to remain in city centers at night if traveling in the eastern provinces. In the southeastern provinces are incidents of terrorist attacks against military and civilians.

INFRASTRUCTURE

Many international airlines have frequent flights to Turkey. Turkish Airlines has daily flights between major cities and flies to many cities worldwide. Istanbul's Ataturk International Airport, 24 km southwest of the city, has bus and taxi service to downtown. Airport buses are operated by Turkish Airlines. Public transportation is available in cities but business travelers are advised to travel by taxis because fares are low. Good quality apartments are available in Istanbul for very reasonable rents. Six months' to one year's rent is commonly expected in advance. When traveling by car use extreme care due to heavy traffic and unpredictable drivers. Avoid driving at night as vehicles are poorly lit. For information on traveling by car, contact Turkey's Touring and Automobile Club. Rental cars cannot be driven across the border. The railway system has express trains that link Istanbul, Ankara, and Izmir. Luxury buses operate between Istanbul and Ankara. For city buses, purchase tickets at kiosks before boarding.

NATIONAL TOURIST OFFICE

Ministry of Tourism
Ismet Inonu Bulvan 91, Sok. No. 5
Ankara
Tel: (312) 212-8300

Contacts

GOVERNMENT AGENCIES

Devlet Planlama Teskilati
State Planning Organization
Tel: (312) 230-8720
Fax: (312) 231-3498

Hazine Mustesarligi Banka ve Kambiyo Genel Mudurlugu
Undersecretariat of Treasury, General Directorate of Banking and Foreign Exchange General Directorate
Eskisehir Karayolu, Inonu Bulvari
06510 Emek, Ankara
Tel: (312) 212-8871
Fax: (312) 212-8775

Devlet Istatistik Enstitusu
State Institute of Statistics
Necatibey Caddesi No. 114
06100 Ankara
Tel: (312) 417-6440
Fax: (312) 418-5027

Turk Standartlari Enstitusu Standart Hazirlama Baskanligi
Turkish Institute of Standards, Standards Preparation Department
Necatibey Caddesi No. 112
06100 Bakanliklar, Ankara
Tel: (312) 417-0020
Fax: (312) 425-4399

Ihracati Gelistirme Merkezi
Export Promotion Center
Mithatpasa Caddesi No. 60
Kizilay, Ankara
Tel: (312) 417-2223
Fax: (312) 417-2233

Bayindirlik ve Iskan Bakanligi
Ministry of Public Works and Settlement
Vekaletler Caddesi No. 1
Bakanliklar, Ankara
Tel: (312) 417-9260
Fax: (312) 418-0406

Ulastirma Bakanligi
Ministry of Communications and Transportation
Bahcelievler Son Durak
Emek, Ankara
Tel: (312) 212-4632
Fax: (312) 212-4187

Posta-Telgraf-Telefon Genel Mudurlugu
PTT General Directorate
Samsun Yolu
06101 Aydinliklar, Ankara
Tel: (312) 313-1130
Fax: (312) 313-1153

Tarimsal Uretim Gelistirme Genel Mudurlugu
General Directorate of Agricultural Production Development
Milli Mudafaa Caddesi No. 20
Kizilay, Ankara
Tel: (312) 417-8400
Fax: (312) 425-2016

Enerji ve Tabii Kaynaklar Bakanligi
Ministry of Energy and Natural Resources
Konya Yolu
06100 Bestepe
Ankara
Tel: (312) 213-6601
Fax: (312) 223-6984

Saglik Bakanligi
Ministry of Health
Refik Saydam Institute of Health
Ankara
Tel: (312) 435-5680
Fax: (312) 435-0546

Environmental Health and Health Units Dept.
Mithatpasa Caddesi
06410 Sihhiye, Ankara

Cevre Bakanligi (MOE)
Ministry of Environment
Eskisehir Yolu 8. Km.
Ankara
Tel: (312) 285-3283
Fax: (312) 286-2271

Milli Egitim Bakanligi
Ministry of National Education
Bakanliklar, Ankara
Tel: (312) 425-5330
Fax: (312) 417-7027

WORLD TRADE CENTERS

World Trade Center Ankara
Akay Caddesi No 10 06640
Tahran Caddesi No 30 06700
Ankara
Tel: (312) 417-4083, 417-2134
Fax: (312) 417-8571, 418-8655

World Trade Center Istanbul
Atatürk Hava Limani Yani, Çobançesme Kavsagi
PO Box 40
34830 Havalimani, Istanbul
Tel: (212) 573-0099, 573-3979, 574-5459
Fax: (212) 526-2197

BUSINESS AND TRADE ORGANIZATIONS

Dis Ekonomik Iliskiler Kurulu
Foreign Economic Relations Board
Odakule, Beyoglu, Istanbul
Tel: (212) 243-4180
Fax: (212) 243-4184

Investment Promotion Department
Ataturk Bulvari No. 149
06640 Bakanliklar, Ankara
Tel: (312) 417-8667
Fax: (312) 417-9711

Yabanci Sermaye Koordinasyon Dernegi
Association for Foreign Capital Coordination
Barbaros Bulvari, Morbasan Sokak
Koza Is Merkezi B Blok/Kat 1
80700 Besiktas, Istanbul
Tel: (212) 272-5094
Fax: (212) 274-6664

Yem Sanayicileri Dernegi
Food Industrialists Association
Tuna Caddesi, Halk Sokak 20/7
Yenisehir, Ankara
Tel: (312) 431-1685
Fax: (312) 431-2704

Otomotiv Sanayii Dernegi
Automotive Manufacturers' Association
Atilla Sokak No. 6
81190 Altunizade, Istanbul
Tel: (216) 318-2994
Fax: (216) 321-9497

Reklamcilar Dernegi
Advertising Firms' Association
Yildiz Cicegi Sokak No. 19
80630 Etiler, Istanbul
Tel: (212) 257-8873
Fax: (212) 257-8870

Turkiye Bilisim Dernegi
Informatics Association of Turkey
Selanik Caddesi No. 17/4
06650 Kizilay, Ankara
Tel: (312) 418-4755
Fax: (312) 425-4817

Turkiye Insaat ve Tesisat Muteahhitleri Birligi
Association of Construction Contractors
Ahmet Mithat Efendi Sokak 21/2
96550 Cankaya, Ankara
Tel: (312) 439-1712
Fax: (312) 439-4621

Elektronik Cihaz Imalatcilari Dernegi
Electronic Equipment Manufacturers'Association
Yildiz, Barbaros Bulvari
Sahir Kesebir Sokak 34
80700 Besiktas, Istanbul
Tel: (212) 266-0290
Fax: (212) 272-4711

Cevre Teknolojisi Uygulayicilari Dernegi
Association of Practitioners of Environmental Technology
Irfan Bastug Caddesi, Yuva Apt. 3/10
80280 Gayrettepe, Istanbul, Ankara
Tel: (212) 272-2904
Fax: (212) 272-2904

Tabibler Odasi
Chamber of Medical Doctors
Turkocagi Caddesi 17, Kat 3
Cagaloglu, Istanbul
Tel: (212) 522-1911
Fax: (212) 522-7374

Seluloz ve Kagit Sanayicileri Vakfi
Paper and Paper Pulp Industrialists' Foundation
Buyukdere Caddesi No. 81
Kurgu Is Hani Kat 8, Daire 15
80300 Mecidiyekoy, Istanbul
Tel: (212) 266-9524
Fax: (212) 266-9524

Turkiye Giyim Sanayicileri Dernegi
Turkish Clothing Manufacturers' Association
Yildiz Posta Caddesi
Dedeman Is Hani 48/8
80700 Gayrettepe, Istanbul
Tel: (212) 274-2525
Fax: (212) 272-4060

Turkiye Seyahat Acentalari Dernegi
Travel Agents Association of Turkey
Cumhuriyet Caddesi No. 3
80230 Elmadag, Istanbul
Tel: (212) 245-8950
Fax: (212) 252-3183

Turizm Yatirimcilari Dernegi
Tourism Investors Association
Inonu Caddesi 48, Isik Apt. Kat 3
Gumussuyu, Istanbul
Tel: (212) 245-5545
Fax: (212) 245-6031

CHAMBERS OF COMMERCE

Union of Chambers of Commerce, Industry, Maritime Commerce and Commodity Exchanges of Turkey
Ataturk Bulvari No. 149
06640 Bakanliklar, Ankara
Tel: (312) 418-3360
Fax: (312) 418-3268

Ankara Chamber of Commerce
Sehit Tegmen Kalmaz Caddesi No. 30
06050 Ulus, Ankara
Tel: (312) 310-4810
Fax: (312) 310-8436

Ankara Chamber of Industry
Ataturk Bulvari 193/4
Kavaklidere, Ankara
Tel: (312) 417-1200
Fax: (312) 417-2060

Istanbul Chamber of Commerce
Ragip Gumuspala Caddesi No. 84
34378 Eminonu, Istanbul
Tel: (212) 511-4150
Fax: (212) 526-2197

Istanbul Chamber of Industry
Mesrutiyet Caddesi 118
80050 Tepebasi, Istanbul
Tel: (212) 252-2900
Fax: (212) 249-3963

Deniz Ticaret Odasi
Chamber of Maritime Commerce
Meclisi Mevusan Caddesi No. 22
80154 Sali Pazari; Istanbul
Tel: (212) 252-0130
Fax: (212) 293-7935

Izmir Chamber of Commerce
Ataturk Caddesi No. 126
35210 Pasaport, Izmir
Tel: (232) 441-7777
Fax: (232) 483-7853

Aegean Chamber of Industry
Cumhuriyet Bulvari No. 63
Izmir
Tel: (232) 484-4330
Fax: (232) 483-9937

CONSULTING FIRMS

International Business Services A.S.
Abdi Ipekci Caddesi, Kizilkaya Apt. 59/4
80200 Macka, Istanbul
Tel: (212) 231-0481
Fax: (212) 231-6614

Arthur Andersen & Co. (YALIM A.S.)
Arjantin Caddesi No. 17/6
06700 Kavaklidere, Ankara
Tel: (312) 468-4081
Fax: (312) 468-4291

Denet Touche Ross
Denet Mali Danismanlik A.S.
Buyukdere Caddesi No. 121
Ercan Han, Kat 4-6
80300 Gayrettepe, Istanbul
Tel: (212) 275-9690
Fax: (212) 272-3323

BANKS

Turkiye Garanti Bankasi A.S.
Buyukdere Caddesi No. 63
80670 Maslak, Istanbul
Tel: (212) 285-4040
Fax: (212) 286-0135

Iktisat Bankasi T.A.S.
Buyukdere Caddesi No. 165
80496 Zincirlikuyu, Istanbul
Tel: (212) 274-1111
Fax: (212) 274-7028

Turk Ticaret Bankasi A.S.
Yildiz Posta Caddesi No. 2
80280 Gayrettepe, Istanbul
Tel: (212) 288-5900
Fax: (212) 288-6113

STOCK EXCHANGE

Istanbul Menkul Kiymetler Borsasi (IMKB)
Rihtim Cad. 245
Eren Han
Tophane, Karakoy
80030 Istanbul
Tel: (1) 2524800
Fax: (1) 2524915
Telex: 22748

NEWSPAPERS

Yeni Adana
Abiodinpasa Cad. 56
Adana
Fax: (322) 593655

Ankara Ticaret
Ruzgarli Sok. O.V. Han 2/6
Ankara
Tel: (312) 4182832
Telex: 42308

Ankara Ulus
Ruzagrli Gayret Sok. 1
Ankara
Tel: (312) 3091774

Belde
RuzGarli Gayret Sok. 7/1
Ankara
Tel: (312) 3106820

Turkish Daily News
Tunus Cad. 50/A-7
06680 Kavaklidere
Ankara
Tel: (312) 4282957
Fax: 4278890

Turkiye Ticaret Sicili
Karanfil Sok. 56
Bakanliklar
Ankara

Apoyevmatini
Istiklal Cad.
Suriye Pasaji 348
Nryohlu
Istanbul
Tel: (212) 2437635

Bugun
Medyua Plaza Basin Ekspres Yolu
34540 Gunesli
Istanbul
Tel: (212) 5504850

Cumhuriyet
Turkocagi Cad. 39
34334 Cagaloglu
Istanbul
Tel: (212) 5120505
Fax: (212) 5138595
Telex: 22246

Dunya
Narlibahce Sok. 15
34440 Cagaloglu
Istanbul
Tel: (212) 5120190
Fax: (212) 5138595
Telex: 23822

Hurriyet
Babiali Cad. 15-17
34360 Cagaloglu
Istanbul
Tel: (212) 5120000
Fax: (212) 5120026
Telex: 22249

Jamanak
Istiklal Cad.
Narmalli Yurdu
Beyoglu
Istanbul
Tel: (212) 2435639

Milliyet
Nuruosmaniye Cad. 65
Istanbul
Tel: (212) 5114410
Fax: (212) 5138742
Telex: 22884

Gunluk Ticaret
Dolskxsfr Dok. 5
PK 507
Istanbul
Tel: (212) 2444736

Atakan Sok. 14
Mecidekoy
Istanbul
Tel: (212) 2752200
Fax: (212) 2752200
Telex: 26924

Alaykosku Cad
Eryilmaz Sok. 13
Cagaloglu
Istanbul
Tel: (212) 5285000
Telex: 22284

Cobancesme
Kalendar Sok. 21
Yenibosna
Istanbul
Tel: (212) 5511477
Fax: (212) 5512822

Gazi Osman
Pasa Bul. 5
Izmir
Tel: (232) 254400

PERIODICALS

Adalet Dergisi
Adalet Bakanligi
Ankara
Tel: (312) 4192199

Bayrak Dergisi
Necatibey Cad.
Karakimseli Han 56
Ankara
Tel: (4) 3241476
Fax: (4) 3107248
Telex: 44401

Mimarlik
Konur Sok. 4
Kizilay
Ankara
Tel: (312) 4173727
Fax: (312) 4180361

Resmi Kararlar Dergisi
Adalet Bakanligi Egitim Dairesi Baskanligi
06659 Bakanliklar, Ankara
Tel: (312) 4192199
Fax: (312) 4173954

Teknik ve Uygulama
Konur Sok. 4/4
06442 Kizilay
Ankara
Tel: (312) 4182374

Turkish Review
Ataturk Bul. 203
06688 Kavaklidere, Ankara
Tel: (312) 4671180
Fax: (312) 4682100
Telex: 42384

Tekstil ve Muhendis
Elmasbahceler Mah. Sabunevi Sok
Muhendisler Is Hani 19, Kat. 2
16230 Bursa
Tel: (224) 538018
Fax: (224) 525514

Archaeology and Art Magazine
Hayriye Cad. 3/5 Corlu Apt.
80060 Beyoglu , Istanbul
Tel: (212) 2456838
Fax: (212) 2456877

Istanbul Key
Halaskargazi Cad. 364
Sisli Meydani
Istanbul
Tel: (212) 2314631
Telex: 27800

Presence
Pangalti
Olcek Sok. 82
80230 Istanbul
Tel: (212) 2408801
Fax: (212) 2408801

RADIO AND TELEVISION

Turkiye Radyo Televizyon Kurumu (TRT)
Nevzat Tandogan Cad. 2
Kavaklidere
Ankara
Tel: (312) 4282230

INTERNET ADDRESSES

Usenet group(s):
soc.culture.turkish
clari.world.mideast.turkey

Turkish Ministry of Foreign Affairs Homepages
http://www.mfa.gov.tr/

Discover Turkey
http://www.missouri.edu/~c584540/index.html

Republic of Turkey HomePage
http://home.imc.net/turkey/index.htm

Turkish Daily News
http://www.eecs.nwu.edu/~yusuf/turkey/trknws/

Republic of Turkey Home Page
http://home.imc.net/turkey/

Ukraine

Economy

Overview

After gaining independence from the Soviet Union in 1992, Ukraine is now poised to transform itself from a centrally planned economy to one based on free markets. A country rich in natural resources, it focused in the past on large-scale agricultural production and on developing heavy industry—much of this built with inexpensive material inputs and energy supplies from Russia, now no longer available. It desperately needs now to modernize and restructure, and make its products competitive with the rest of the world. So far, however, the Ukrainian government has failed to construct a feasible economic plan; a serious decline in industrial production, energy resource problems, a collapse in foreign trade links, and a growing budget deficit have been the result. The government has now undertaken a new economic reform program but negative growth rates continue and long-term prospects remain uncertain.

Trade

Ukraine has experienced a significant decline in the total value of its foreign trade in the past five years. The former countries of the Soviet Union are its major trading partners, followed by Germany, China, and Austria. Most of its trade is with developed countries, although serious economic decline in recent years has resulted in a collapse in the export market, which in turn has resulted in a shortage of hard currency for imports. Although it is actively seeking to increase its foreign trade, the lack of infrastructure, its undeveloped banking system, and its general inexperience trading in an open market have hampered efforts so far. Foreign traders must have a long-term business outlook to trade here.

Sectors

Agriculture Ukraine has traditionally been an agricultural country. As part of the Soviet Union, Ukraine contributed 25 percent of total sugar, grain, and vegetable production and over 20 percent of dairy and meat output. Since independence, agricultural output has suffered a sharp decline but this sector remains one of the best prospects for Ukraine's economic future.

Industry Manufacturing and industry have been at the core of Ukraine's economy for the past seven decades and continue to be of vital importance, accounting for 43 percent of GDP and employing over one-third of the population. With the collapse of the Soviet Union, Ukraine's industry lost its inexpensive material and energy supply, and its outdated, oversized, energy-intensive sector is currently producing at only two-thirds of its 1990 level.

Services The service sector is not yet well-developed, although tourism and related services have shown some life in recent years.

Trends

Ukraine continues to experience serious economic deterioration and the downsizing, restructuring, and modernizing of its economy remain the government's most pressing and difficult future objectives. Although there has been some public resistance to market reforms, the government has committed itself to expediting the privatization process, lifting export and currency controls, reforming the tax and banking systems, and reducing the budget deficit. Increased opportunities to sell to this large domestic market depend largely on the success of the government's long-term economic policies.

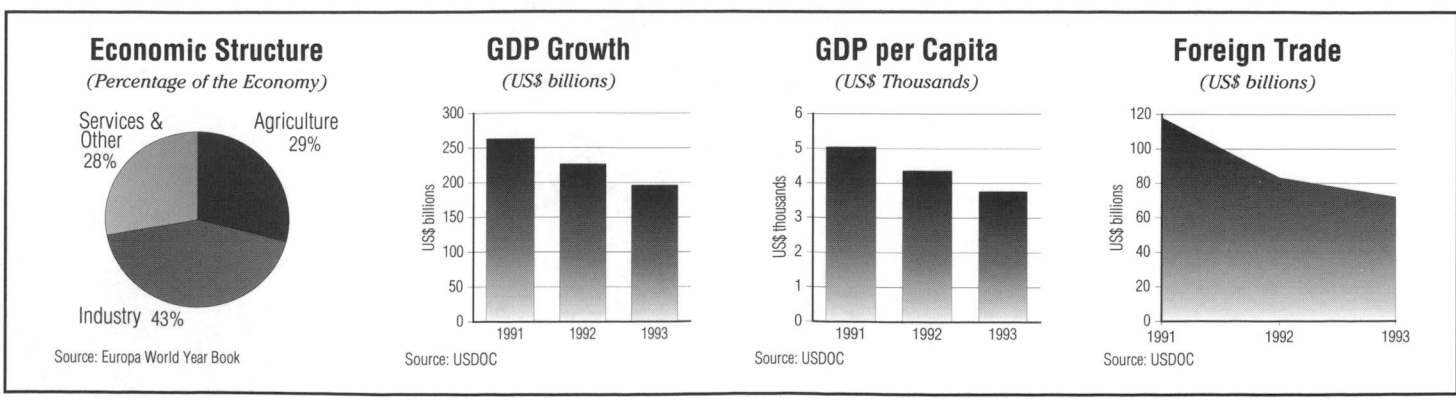

Economic Structure
(Percentage of the Economy)

Services & Other 28%
Agriculture 29%
Industry 43%

Source: Europa World Year Book

GDP Growth
(US$ billions)

Source: USDOC

GDP per Capita
(US$ Thousands)

Source: USDOC

Foreign Trade
(US$ billions)

Source: USDOC

Business Travel

LH	1906	MADRID	935	113-3
LH	1022	STUTTGART HBF.	935	-
AF	1701	LYON	940	683-6
AY	822	HELSINKI	940	113-3
AA	071	SFRANCISCO-DALLAS	945	731-7

COMMUNICATIONS

Telephones Telephone service is improving but is still fairly cumbersome. International calls can be placed through an operator but can take hours to connect. Direct dialing is available to Europe, Israel, and North America.

Fax Fax machines are becoming more widespread in Ukraine, but the quality of the machines is generally low. Businesspersons might want to bring their own.

Post office Mail delivery is maddeningly slow. Service can be sped up by addressing mail in a familiar language or format (country, city with index number, street, house number, name). Mailboxes are hard to find, but major hotels have reliable postal facilities.

BEST TRAVEL BOOKS

Multinational Travel Companion Executive Travel Tips World Wide.

NATIONAL TOURIST OFFICE

Intourist
Vul. Hospitalna 12
Kiev
Tel: (44) 2253051

USEFUL TELEPHONE NUMBERS

If you are calling from outside Ukraine, you will need to add the country code [380] and any other international dialing requirements from within your country.

- Kiev Airport ....(44) 267-243
- Fire 01
- Police 01
- Ambulance/Emergency 03
- Operator 08, 09
- International .... (44) 2719020
- Taxi 058
- Ukartour .... (44) 2125570
- Intourist .... (44) 2253051
- DHL .... (44) 224-7577
- Federal Express .... (44) 261-7987
- Translation Services .... (44) 290-4022
- Ukrainian Chamber of Commerce ..... (44) 244-7344
- Aeroflot.............................. (44) 721-201 or 956-701
- Kiev central bus station ..... (44) 634-127 or 637-180

Credit Card Information
Lost or stolen credit cards (call collect to the US, regardless of which country the card was issued in).

- Amex .... [1] (919) 333-3211
- Diner's Club................................[1] (303) 799-1504
- MasterCard ....[1] (314) 275-6690
- Visa ....[1] (410) 581-7931

Travelogue

WORKWEEK

Offices Monday-Friday 9:00 am to 6:00 pm.
Banks Monday-Friday 9:30 am to 1:00 pm.
Government Monday-Friday 9:00 am to 6:00 pm.
Retail Monday-Saturday 11:00 am to 8:00 pm, with department stores open 8:00 am to 9:00 pm. Food stores are open 8:00 am to 8:00 pm, and until 7:00 pm on Sundays.

HOLIDAYS

Holidays 1996
January 1 New Year's Day
January 7 Orthodox Christmas
March 8 International Women's Day
May 1-2 International Solidarity Days
May 8-9 Victory Days
August 24 Independence Day
November 7-8 Revolution Days

VISA AND PASSPORT

Passports and visas are required. Visas should be obtained in advance from Ukrainian embassies or consulates (those acquired in Ukraine can cost as much as US$150). A letter of invitation from a person, company, or organization in Ukraine, or a tour company voucher is currently required to obtain a visa. The visa's duration will be determined by this letter. Travelers who arrive without a visa must obtain one either at the border point or within 24 hours of arrival at a local "Visas, Permits, and Passport Department" office of the Ministry of Internal Affairs (VVIR). In-transit visas (good for 72-hours) are issued at most major airports and checkpoints. All foreigners visiting Ukraine are required to register their passports with local law enforcement authorities. Registration is automatic when visitors check into a hotel. Private visitors must have their hosts, relatives, or landlords register their passport at the local VVIR office. A US$10 fee is usually charged. Foreigners staying three working days or less need not register. Visitors who do not register may experience delays when leaving Ukraine.

DEPARTURE FORMALITIES

Visitors leaving Ukraine from Kiev or Odessa airports will not pay a departure tax.

IMMUNIZATION

International certificate of vaccination is not required unless you are arriving from an infected area.

TIPPING

Tipping is officially discouraged, but is still appreciated. Taxi: 10 to15 percent. Hotels: 10 to15 percent. Restaurants: 5 to10 percent. Barbers and beauticians: 5 to10 percent. Airport porters are rare, but if one is found, they should be tipped.

CRIME

Crime is a growing problem in the Ukraine, with the violent crime rate increasing. Westerners and their residences are commonly targeted by the local criminal element.

INFRASTRUCTURE

The train, bus, metro, and taxi industries in Ukraine are developed and reliable. Domestic air travel and telecommunications can be unpredictable. Taxi rides are negotiated between driver and passenger. Train transportation is the mode of choice, but make reservations in advance. Subways (Metro) are fast, clean and reliable. Buses and trolleys are another reliable mode of transportation in Ukraine.

Foreign Trade

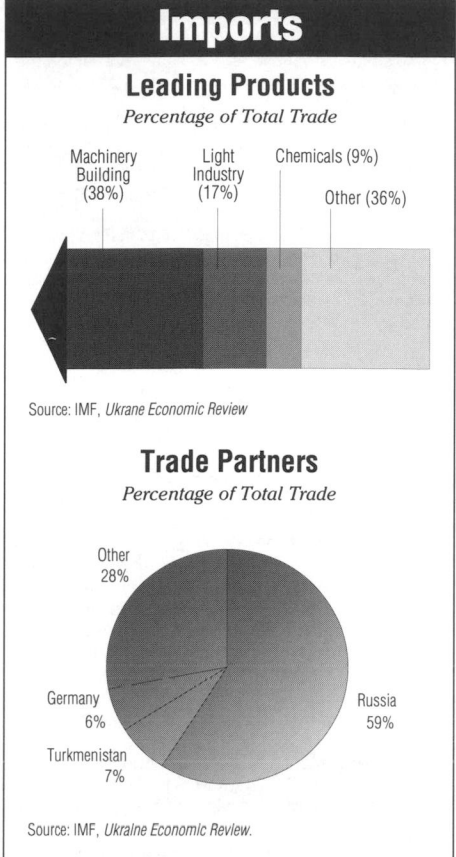

Imports

Leading Products
Percentage of Total Trade

Machinery Building (38%)
Light Industry (17%)
Chemicals (9%)
Other (36%)

Source: IMF, *Ukrane Economic Review*

Trade Partners
Percentage of Total Trade

Other 28%
Germany 6%
Turkmenistan 7%
Russia 59%

Source: IMF, *Ukraine Economic Review.*

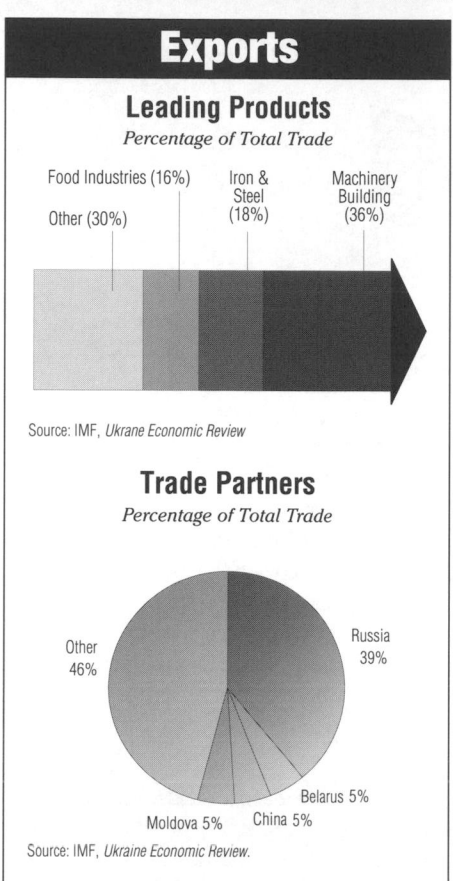

Exports

Leading Products
Percentage of Total Trade

Food Industries (16%)
Other (30%)
Iron & Steel (18%)
Machinery Building (36%)

Source: IMF, *Ukrane Economic Review*

Trade Partners
Percentage of Total Trade

Other 46%
Russia 39%
Belarus 5%
China 5%
Moldova 5%

Source: IMF, *Ukraine Economic Review.*

Opportunities

FOR IMPORTING TO UKRAINE

- maize
- wheat
- pesticides
- agricultural machinery
- specialized machinery and equipment
- ADP equipment

FOR EXPORTING FROM UKRAINE

- inorganic chemical elements
- pig iron
- iron and non-alloy steel
- non-ferrous base metals

GROWTH SECTORS
- agricultural
- food processing industry
- capital good toward military production

Trade News

RULES AND REGULATIONS

- **Regulations** Certifications standards and documentation from the country of origin are necessary for any type of importing into Ukraine.
- **Import restrictions** Imported goods are not considered to have legally entered Ukraine until they have been processed through the port of entry and been cleared by Ukrainian customs officials. Imports to Ukraine are required to meet the certification standards of the country of origin. In cases where Ukrainian standards are not established, country of origin standards may prevail.
- **Import licenses** Duties on goods imported for resale are subject to import license requirements. However, the requirements are currently being revised and may soon change.

Legal

Legal System

Ukraine follows a civil code tradition. Though the last Soviet constitution is still effective, a new constitution is being drafted. Of concern is Ukraine's underdeveloped judicial system that makes contracts, regulations, and statutes difficult to enforce.

Intellectual Property Rights

Patents and trademarks Most technology is patentable with the exception of pharmaceuticals and chemical processes. No provisions for opposition proceedings exist. Currently, trademarks are protected for 20 years and are renewable. But trademarks not used within five years of registration can be revoked.

Copyrights Ukraine has agreed to respect and protect literary works, artistic works, sound recordings, and computer software. The country intends to adhere to the Berne Convention.

Trade secrets Trade secrets are not specifically protected by law, either commercial or civil.

Business Registration

Businesses must register with appropriate authorities. Trade exporters must register with the Ministry of External Economic Relations of Ukraine.

Contracts and Dispute Resolution

Contracts are deemed executable if all parties are agreed on all significant conditions and terms—that is, those conditions that are recognized by law or required for performance.

Labor

Foreigners working in the Ukraine have rights and duties equal to that of Ukrainian citizens. Where international contracts or agreements in which Ukraine participates provide provisions other than that found in Ukrainian labor legislation, the rules of the international agreement or contract will apply in court. In Ukraine, the labor contract is the indisputable basis for the establishment of labor relations.

Legal Matters

LEGAL BRIEFS

- **Maximum workweek** Employees have a legal right to work. General grounds of employee termination are many and are found in Article 36 of the Labor Code of Ukraine.
- **Legal protection** Because of the changing law, speedy conclusions to legal disputes cannot be expected. A growing number of US law firms are operating in Ukraine.
- **Notaries** The legal function and office of the notary is established by law and state. Private notaries are available. Notaries certify rights and facts of legal importance and perform other notarial acts in order to make documents trustworthy and give them a presumption of validity.
- **Right to strike** The right to strike is protected by law, except for the military, police, and continuing process plants. Although political strikes are considered illegal, some workers who go on strike make political demands along with economic ones.
- **Child labor** The minimum employment age is 18, although children aged 15 to 17 can be employed by businesses with governmental permission.
- **Minimum wage** A minimum wage has been established, but, due to hyperinflation, it is generally significantly below the cost of living.
- **Trade agreements** Ukraine is negotiating membership in the CIS, and has joined all the major multilateral financial organizations.

LAW FIRM

Robinson, Lake, Lerer & Montgomery
Kiev
30 Karl Libkchnet Ulitsa
Tel: (44) 293-6393
Fax: (44) 293-2462

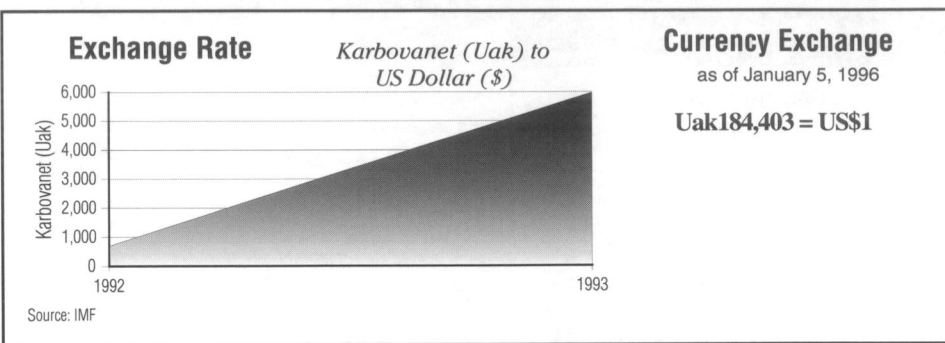

Exchange Rate — *Karbovanet (Uak) to US Dollar ($)*

Currency Exchange
as of January 5, 1996

Uak184,403 = US$1

Source: IMF

Currency

The currency of Ukraine is the karbovanet (Uak). There are no coins.

Foreign Exchange

The National Bank of Ukraine (NBU), in consultation with the Council of Ministers, sets the official exchange rate of the karbovanets against the US dollar. The official rates for all other convertible currencies are determined weekly based on market rates. In addition to the official exchange rate, there are three other rates in effect: the administered rate, which is applied to the proportion of foreign currency export proceeds that must be surrendered to the NBU; the auction exchange rate, which is determined at the most recent weekly auction conducted by the NBU; and the rate for cash transactions for individuals at commercial banks, which is freely determined and quoted on a daily basis by commercial banks. There are no taxes or subsidies on purchases or sales of foreign exchange.

Capital Transfers

Residents and nonresidents may open and operate foreign currency deposits under certain conditions. The opening and operation of accounts in domestic currency by nonresidents is prohibited. Foreign investors may, after paying taxes and fees, transfer abroad without restriction dividends, profits, and other foreign exchange assets obtained legally in connection with their investments.

Investment Incentives

While the Ukraine government officially welcomes and encourages foreign investment it is in no position to offer incentives in this regard. It does, however, grant tax relief to enterprises established with foreign capital investments; the nature of the relief depends on the activity of the enterprise, its turnover, and the proportion of foreign equity capital ownership. Additional tax relief may be granted for investments in priority sectors or in special economic zones. Several Western countries maintain programs offering low-interest loans, funding capital, etc., to traders interested in pursuing investment opportunities in the Ukraine.

Investment Restrictions

Restrictions to foreign investment revolve primarily around the uncertainties of the economy and the rapidly changing bureaucracy, which makes it difficult to know about, let alone comply with, investment rules and regulations.

Money Matters

BITS AND PIECES

- **Economic crisis** Although Ukraine rapidly became a member of the IMF, the EBRD, and the IBRD, the government's economic mismanagement and failure to implement economic reforms have prevented the development of any significant bilateral or multilateral financial assistance programs.
- **Capital flight** Ukraine's failure to implement economic reforms has resulted in a disastrous flight of much-needed capital, along with rampant inflation fed by a loose monetary policy, and a severe shortage of hard currency.
- **Privatizations** Due to the lack of an institutional infrastructure to deal with asset valuation during hyperinflation, spontaneous and somewhat unregulated privatization projects are being orchestrated by enterprise managers and workers collectives—often at prices that will not withstand any scrutiny.
- **Taxes** The Ukrainian tax structure includes a 40 percent tax on hard currency earnings of domestic enterprises, which proves to be a strong disincentive to Ukrainian enterprises with export potential.
- **Non-convertibility** One of the fundamental financial problems encountered in the Ukrainian market is the non-convertibility of the Ukrainian karbovanets, popularly known as the coupon.
- **Official exchange rates** A set of official exchange rates is published by the NBU every Friday and is maintained for the following week. The official exchange rates are used for transactions with the government, including, in particular, mandatory surrender of foreign currency export proceeds to the government.
- **Foreign exchange licensing** Commercial banks must be licensed by the NBU to engage in foreign exchange transactions. There are about 40 commercial banks licensed to engage in international transactions and to hold foreign exchange accounts abroad.
- **Sources of foreign exchange** Importers have three sources of foreign exchange: they may use their foreign exchange holdings at domestic commercial banks; they may tender for foreign exchange at the weekly auction; or they may apply to the Tender Committee for foreign exchange allocations. (The Tender Committee also decides allocations of foreign exchange obtained through mandatory surrender of export proceeds.)
- **Repatriation** Firms must repatriate all of their foreign exchange proceeds from exports to domestic commercial bank accounts within 30 days of shipment, and sell, within five days of repatriation, 50 percent of the foreign currency export proceeds.
- **Gold** The NBU grants permission to commercial banks to export and import gold and other monetary metals. Other residents are required to obtain a license from the Ministry of Finance to deal in precious metal and stones.

BANKS

Joint-Stock Bank Inko
Kiev 252021
Mechnikova 10
Tel: (44) 432-45-66 Fax: (44) 294-87-90

Kiev Narodny Bank
Kiev-1
Sofiyevska 1
Tel: (44) 228-39-45 Fax: (44) 229-35-55

National Bank of Ukraine
Kiev 252001
vul. Institutska 9
Tel: (44) 293-38-22 Fax: (44) 293-16-97

Ukrainian Innovation Bank
Kiev 252601
Institutska 12A
Tel: (44) 228-76-37 Fax: (44) 229-02-75

Ukrainian Export-Import Bank
Kiev 252001
Khrecshchatik 8
Tel: (44) 226-27-45 Fax: (44) 29-80-82

<table>
<tr><td colspan="2">TAXATION</td></tr>
<tr><td colspan="2">Taxation requires sophisticated knowledge of complex rules and regulations specific to each country. For more detailed information we suggest you refer to the Ernst & Young Corporate Tax Guide and Directory, available from the Ernst & Young accounting office in your country, or from:</td></tr>
<tr><td colspan="2">Ernst & Young Ukraina
Kiev 254053
3/7 Kiyanovsky Pereulok
Ukraine
Tel: (44) 212-3564, 212-0150, 212-1941, 212-0222
Fax: (44) 212-5225</td></tr>
</table>

At a Glance	
Corporate Income Tax Rate (%)	30
Capital Gains Tax Rate (%)	30
Branch Tax Rate (%)	30
Withholding Tax (%)	
Dividends	15
Interest	15
Royalties	15
Freight	6
Other Ukrainian-Source Income	15
Branch Remittance Tax	0
Net Operating Losses (Years)	
Carryback	0
Carryforward	0

The government has taken steps to normalize its tax structure to comply with Western standards. The current system includes an ad valorem tax, enterprise income tax, excise taxes, and personal income taxes. The tax structure also includes a 40% tax on hard currency earnings of domestic enterprises. Companies with foreign capital investments are granted some tax relief, depending on the nature of the enterprise and proportion of foreign capital.

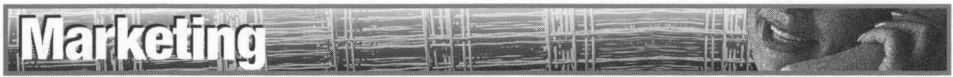

Overview

Ukraine is faced with several problems that hinder the marketing of foreign products, and could be a nightmare for foreign businesses. Hyperinflation—nearly 30 percent a month–overthrows most economic reforms almost before they've begun, and the heavy industry sector is oversized, outdated, energy-intensive, heavily polluting, and geared almost exclusively toward military production. Faced with such problems, why should foreign investors chart a path through this marketing morass? First, Ukraine is a brand-new market for a wide variety of products and services; companies which enter now and endure through the rough times the next few years will surely have secured an unassailable hold in their sectors. Second, restructuring and reform offers equal opportunity; small and medium-sized companies' chances for success are equal to the multinational giants'. The challenges are formidable, yet foreign firms are making money in Ukraine. Ukrainians are eager to survive this painful transition period, and are determined to make their new market economy a success. They are therefore open to new products and marketing methods, however unfamiliar to Ukraine they might initially be.

Agents, Distributors, and Partners

Very few Ukrainians have traveled beyond the borders of the former USSR, and this makes for a distorted view of foreigners. Look for partners in the younger generations; although they are unfamiliar with Western methods, and currently unskilled at marketing measures, they believe they have much to gain by making wise decisions and working hard. They are eager and ambitious, and sometimes know how to take advantage of the opportunities the current unsettled and undeveloped markets present.

Advertising

Newspapers include four major dailies published in Ukrainian and the *Kiev Times* published in English; these are the sources for most advertising. The BBC launched its radio service in June 1992 but does not carry ads. Ukrainian consumers have not yet been bombarded with advertising and it can be a very effective means of gaining customers–out of curiosity if nothing else. A majority of Ukrainian households have radios and they listen to them often. Try advertising on this medium.

Business Culture

Greetings and Courtesies

Ukrainians have a heritage of extraordinary hospitality. Although entertaining can be difficult in Ukraine, guests are welcomed warmly. Shake hands upon meeting with Ukrainians, and when departing from them. In both business and formal settings, a person's professional title and surname are used in Ukraine; only after a close relationship has been established is a first name used. Ukrainians often entertain in their homes and it is proper to bring gifts to your hosts.

Business Ethic and Framework

Glasnost has clearly become the most typical feature of everyday life in Ukraine, and has encouraged contention among its citizens. Ukrainians are not obsessed with their jobs, as in other parts of the world. Workers often arrive at their jobs late or not at all; they take long lunch breaks and then leave early. Ukrainians expect their friendships, with the responsibilities and trusts they entail, to extend to business relationships as well.

Meetings and Decision Making

Because of Ukraine's poor telephone system, all meetings should take place face-to-face. Decisions are made only after a lengthy process. Ukrainians find it easier to say "no" than to take responsibility for their decisions. On the other hand, many younger businesspeople are eager to form alliances with more experienced foreigners, and may therefore make unfounded claims, more in hope of what they expect from the future than from blatant deception.

Women

Women have a strong influence in Ukrainian culture, and are recognized as important contributors in Ukrainian society. Careers in Ukraine are delineated by sex, with certain professions reserved for men. Ukrainian women do not tolerate any injustice and they generally will quite aggressively stand up for their rights.

Marketing in Ukraine

MARKETING TIPS

- **Marketing relationships** Ukraine must look at least partly to the markets of the EU, though membership is too far in the future to depend on for the short term. Various Western market advisors suggest a number of conditions, including rapid price liberalization, budget balancing, and privatization that might provide a balance to economic chaos, and Ukraine is slowly acting on some of these proposals.
- **Agricultural markets** Ukraine has well-developed agricultural markets, but no chemicals or machinery to maintain and expand them. They eagerly seek out manufacturers and sellers of these products.
- **Exclusive agreements** Beware. Capitalism and the free market are still new concepts to many Ukrainian businesspeople, and if you are offered any type of "exclusive" arrangement with a Ukrainian distributor, it may not be true. Many Ukrainians, in both the private and public sectors, have been known to make "exclusive" agreements with several Western partners.
- **Agency agreements** Beware. Contract principles are not well-developed and are in any event often ignored. This has become such a problem that many Western businesspeople have insisted on a clause stipulating arbitration of any disagreements in Stockholm, Sweden.
- **Black market** Many current Ukrainian entrepreneurs have had years of training in the black market and can offer valuable expertise and contacts which would otherwise be unavailable to Western businesspeople through normal bureaucratic channels.
- **Radio/TV** A US-Ukrainian joint venture broadcasting company, Ukrainian-American Broadcasting (UAB), is the first non-government television and radio company in Ukraine and is moving toward 24-hour programming, including commercials. The UAB is becoming increasingly popular.

Cultural Cautions

DO'S

- Have a few toasts in mind ahead of time. You will need them.
- It is important to arrive on time to Ukrainian meetings.
- Letters of introduction can help in initiating business in Ukraine.

DON'TS

- Do not refer to Ukraine as "White Russia" or "Little Russia." They were names used by the former Soviet Union and are a sensitive subject.

CUSTOMS

- Be forewarned: Ukrainians stand close when conversing.
- Ukrainians may give unsolicited advice about your looks, your clothing, and the state of your health. Don't be offended; they are only concerned for your welfare.
- More important to Ukrainians than jobs and careers are family and friends.

OBSERVATIONS

- The mass media is mistrusted in Ukraine, and regarded as biased toward certain positions.
- Second helpings will be offered at dinner in Ukraine, but remember food is in short supply and must not be wasted.

NEGOTIATIONS

- A question will often be answered by a question, rather than a straight answer.

Contacts

GOVERNMENT AGENCIES

Ministry of Agricultural Policy Issues and Foodstuffs
Kiev 252001
Khreshchatick ul. 24
Tel: (44) 226-34-66, (44) 228-47-74
Fax: (44) 229-87-56, 229-33-60, 293-20-93

Ministry of Economic Affairs
252008 Kiev
vul. M. Hrushevskoho 12/2
Tel: (44) 293-4465

Ministry of Education
Kiev 252001
Kreshchatik ul. 34
Tel: (44) 226-31-52
Fax: (44) 216-79-09, 274-50-53

Ministry of Energy and Electrification
Kiev 252001
Khreshchatil ul. 30
Tel: (44) 226-30-27
Fax: (44) 224-40-21, 220-18-85

Ministry of Environmental Protection
Kiev 252001
Kreshchatik ul. 5
Tel: (44) 228-06-44
Fax: (44) 229-83-83

Ministry of Finance
Kiev 252008
Grushevskogo 12/2
Tel: (44) 226-20-44
Fax: (44) 226-25-17

Ministry of Foreign Affairs
252018 Kiev
Mykhaylivska pl. 1
Tel: (44) 21-2833
Fax: (44) 226-3169

Ministry of Health
Kiev
ul. Shotta Rustavelli 9
Tel: (44) 226-26-23, 293-01-08
Fax: (44) 293-20-93

Ministry of Labor
Kiev 252004
Pushkinska 28
Tel: (44) 226-24-45
Fax: (44) 224-59-05

Ministry of Statistics
Kiev 252023
Shota Rustaveli ul. 3
Tel: (44) 226-20-21
Fax: (44) 227-42-66

Ministry of Transportation
Kiev 252113
Prospekt Peremogy 57
Tel: (44) 269-44-15
Fax: (44) 446-40-05

State Committee for Customs Control
Kiev 252034
Reitarska ul.
Tel: (44) 229-89-51, 225-42-30
Fax: (44) 225-40-79

State Committe for Light Industry
Kiev 252023
Kuibysheva ul. 8/10
Tel: (44) 226-21-05
Fax: (44) 220-65-98

State Committee for Promotion of Small Businesses
Kiev 252008
Sadova ul. 3
Tel: (44) 293-13-22
Fax: (44) 293-34-49

State Ukraine Information Agency
Kiev 252001
Lenina ul. 8/16
Tel: (44) 226-32-30

NEWSPAPERS

Demokratychna Ukraina
25047 Kiev-47
Democratic Ukraine
pr. Peremohi 50
Tel: (44) 441-85-46

Holos Ukrainy
252047 Kiev 7
Voice of Ukraine
vul. Nesterova 4
Tel: (44) 441-89-46
Fax: (44) 224-72-54

News from Ukraine
252055 Kiev
Vul. Artema 91

Nezavizimost
252047 Kiev
Peremohy pr. 50
Tel: (44) 441-83-33

Pravda Ukrainy
252047 Kiev 47
Peremohy pr. 50
Tel: (44) 225-51-42

Rabochaya Gazeta/Robitnycha Hazeta
Kiev 47
pr. Pobedy 50
Tel: (44) 441-86-57
Fax: (44) 446-02-98

Silski Visti
Kiev 47
Peremohy pr. 50
Tel: (44) 441-83-33

Uryadoviy Kuryer
252008 Kiev
vul. Sadova 1
Tel: (44) 293-55-09

Vecherniy Kyiv
252136 Kiev
Vul. Marshala Hrechka 13
Tel: (44) 434-61-09

Za Vilnu Ukrainu
290000 Lviv
Vul. Voronovo 3
Tel: (322) 72-89-04
Fax: (322) 72-95-27

Zemlia i Volia
Lviv-58
Vul. 700-richya Lviva 63
kv. 213
Tel: (322) 59-96-71

COMMODITY EXCHANGES

Kiev Universal Commodity Exchange
252015 Kiev
vul. Leyptsihska 1A
Tel: (44) 290-27-14
Fax: (44) 47-72-84

BUSINESS AND TRADE ORGANIZATIONS

Congress of Business Circles of Ukraine
252601 Kiev
vul. Prorizna 15
Tel: (44) 228-64-81
Fax: (44) 229-52-84

Ukranian Chamber of Commerce and Industry
254655 Kiev
vul. V. Zhytomyrska 33
Tel: (44) 212-33-53
Fax: (44) 229-52-84

Ukrimpex
252054 Kiev
vul. Vorovskoho 22
Tel: (44) 216-21-74
Fax: (44) 216-29-96

PERIODICALS

Barvinok
252119 Kiev
vul. Degtyarivska 38-44
Tel: (44) 211-04-98

Berezil
310078 Kharkiv
vul. Chernyshevskoho 59
Tel: (572) 43-41-84

Dnipro
252119 Kiev
vul. Degtyarivska 38-44
Tel: (44) 213-98-79

Donbass
340055 Donetsk
vul. Artema 80A
Tel: (0622) 93-82-26

Dzvin
290005 Lviv
vul. Vatutina 6
Tel: (322) 72-36-20

Kiev
252025 Kiev
vul. Desyatinna 11
Tel: (44) 229-02-80

Lyudina i Svit
254025 Kiev
10 Rylsky provulok
Tel: (44) 228-23-87

Malyatko
252119 Kiev
vul. Degtyarivska 38-44
Tel: (44) 213-98-91

Nauka i Suspilstvo
252047 Kiev
Peremohy pr. 50
Tel: (44) 441-8-10

Novini Kinoekranu
25233 Kiev
vul. Saksahan skoho 6
Tel: (44) 227-47-07

Obrazotvorche Mistetstvo
252015 Kiev
vul. Yanvarskovo Vosstaniya 21 kor. 20
Tel: (44) 290-47-51

Odnoklassnnik
254119 Kiev
vul. Degtyarivska 38-44
Tel: (44) 211-02-78

Perets
252047 Kiev
vul. P. Nesterova 4
Tel: (44) 441-82-14

Politika i Chas
252025 Kiev
vul. Desiatynna 4-6
Tel: (44) 229-75-73

RADIO & TELEVISION

State Teleradio Company
Kiev 252001
Kreshchatik ul. 26
Tel: (44) 226-31-44

INTERNET ADDRESSES

Usenet group(s):
alt.current-events.ukraine

Global Ukraine
http://www.gu.kiev.ua/

United Arab Emirates

Economy

Overview

The UAE's economy is influenced to a great extent by a single commodity—oil. Since its formation in 1971, oil revenues have transformed the seven emirates from a largely arid and sparsely populated region into a prosperous, modern economy. However, fluctuations in the strength and stability of oil prices have led to uneven development in other sectors, especially the agriculture, tourism, transport and communications industries. Diversification away from total dependence on oil has therefore become one of the government's top priorities. Some progress has been made, and the government continues to invest heavily in these and other industries.

Trade

Oil and gas have enabled the UAE to maintain a favorable balance of trade for many years. Japan is the principal destination for UAE exports, although other Asian nations are gaining in importance. Japan is also the UAE's most important import source, followed by the US, the UK, and Germany. The UAE imports mainly machinery and transport equipment, as well as a substantial amount of food and live animals. It imports 90 percent of the products it consumes.

Sectors

Agriculture Although not yet a sector of any importance, the government is working to develop a sustainable agricultural industry. However, neither the climate nor the limited water supply is conducive to this endeavor. Currently, cultivation consists primarily of dates, although the emirates are growing more vegetables and fruits each year.

Industry The petroleum industry has single-handedly transformed the United Arab Emirates' economy. It has proven oil reserves estimated at 100 billion barrels with gas reserves estimated to be over two hundred trillion cubic feet; at the present rate of production these supplies would last well over 100 years. Major expansions of both oil and gas production are currently underway in Abu Dhabi, its most resourceful region.

Services Due to its wealth and relatively relaxed social standards, the UAE serves as a strong financial center for the region. Banking and other financial services are sophisticated and widely available. The government is also actively developing the tourist industry, which should provide many opportunities for related services industries.

Trends

The future of the United Arab Emirates' economy will continue to be determined to a large extent by oil prices. Despite its extensive oil and gas reserves authorities are beginning to look at ways to diversify the economy, especially in Dubai whose mature oil fields are expected to be the first to cease production. Almost a third of its imports are re-exported and its re-export trade is expanding as businesses seek out new markets. Its strategic location ensures that it will remain a major trading center in the Arabian Gulf region. Its relatively liberal social standards should continue to draw Western investment seeking to take advantage of the affluence of the region.

At a Glance

THE COUNTRY

Location Middle East, on the Persian Gulf between Oman and Saudi Arabia.
Terrain Largely desert with some mountainous areas.
Climate Hot, humid, low annual rainfall. Cooler in eastern mountains.

THE PEOPLE

Population 1,900,000
Note: UAE nationals constitute a minority, the majority of the population are Palestinians, Egyptians, Jordanians, Yemenis, Omanis, Iranians, Pakistanis, Indians, and Filipinos residing in the UAE on a temporary basis.
Ethnic composition
South Asian 50%
Other Arab 23%
Emirian (UAE nationals) 19%
Other.. 8%
Religious composition
Muslim (mostly Sunni) 96%
Other.. 4%
Languages spoken Arabic (official), Persian (Farsi), English, Hindi, and Urdu.
Education and literacy Education is compulsory from ages six to 12. High standards and enormous strides in education have resulted in a 60 percent literacy rate amongst Emirians.
Labor force
Total: 650,000
By occupation: industry and commerce 85%, agriculture 5%, services 5%, government 5%.
Note: 85 percent of the work force is comprised of foreign nationals.

COUNTRY FACTS

Political and legal The United Arab Emirates is a loose federation of seven emirates, each with a leader, and a 40-member legislative council (consultative only). The ruler of Abu Dhabi, whose emirate produces the most oil, is the president of the UAE. There are no political parties or suffrage. While secular laws are now being introduced, Islamic law remains predominant in the judicial system.
Telephone Telecommunications systems are modern and comprehensive. International country code: [971]. Selected city codes: Abu Dhabi (2), Ajman (6), Al Ain (3), Dubai (4), Fujairah (70), Jebel Dhana (52), Khawanij (48), Sharjah (6).
Transportation Air transportation is critical to the region, and the UAE has 26 usable airports; 22 with permanent-surface runways. There are also over 2,000 km of highways, the majority in good condition. The main ports are Al Fujayrah, Khawr Fakkan, Mina' Jabal Ali, and Mina' Khalid.
Environmental Fresh water is quickly becoming a rarity because of desalination plants. Desertification is also a major problem, as is beach pollution from oil spills.
Media There are eight AM, three FM, and 12 television stations.
Health No unusual precautions in food and drink are required. Water is potable. Malaria is a possible danger in some areas. Many Western-trained doctors practice in the UAE. The affluence of the country ensures modern and plentiful medical services and supplies. Life expectancy is about 70 years for males and 74 years for females. The fertility rate is 4.6 children per woman.

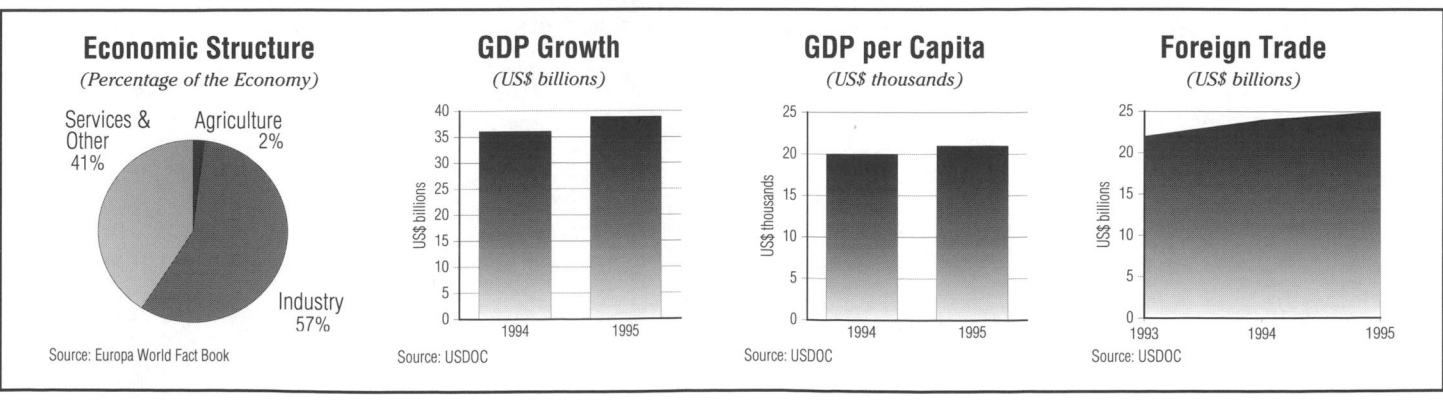

Economic Structure
(Percentage of the Economy)
Services & Other 41%
Agriculture 2%
Industry 57%
Source: Europa World Fact Book

GDP Growth
(US$ billions)
Source: USDOC

GDP per Capita
(US$ thousands)
Source: USDOC

Foreign Trade
(US$ billions)
Source: USDOC

Business Travel

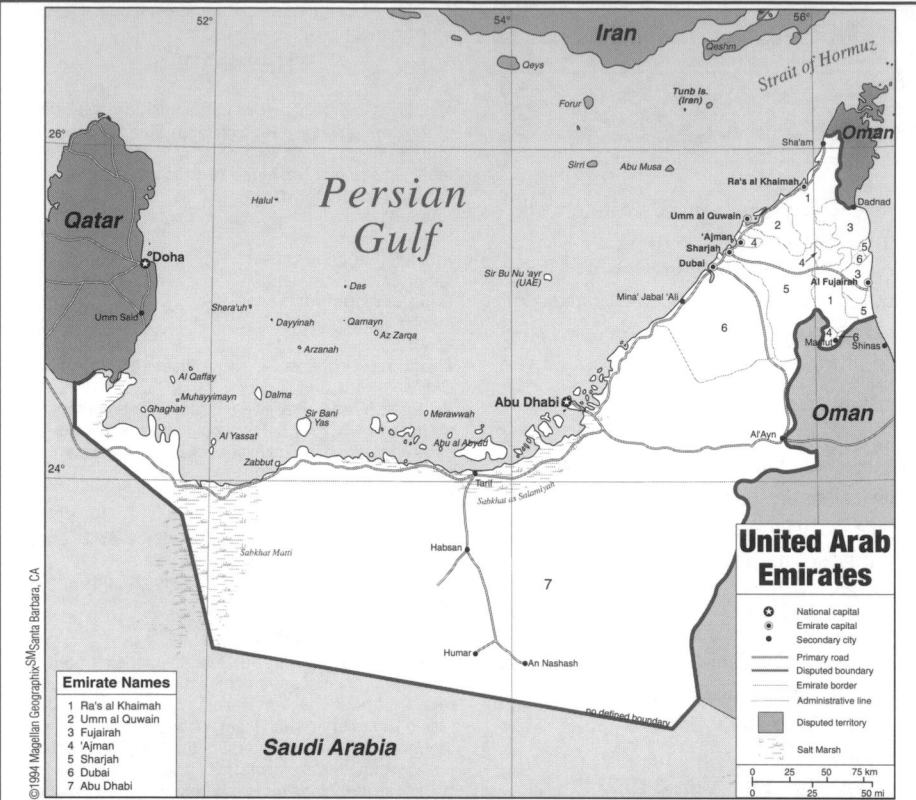

COMMUNICATIONS

Telephones The telephone system in the UAE is modern but can be time consuming. Direct dial is available to the UK and US. Other international calls must be operator assisted and can take hours to go through.
Fax Fax and telex facilities are available in larger hotels and at offices of the government telephone organization, Emirtel.
Post office Postal service is generally efficient, although it can be unpredictable. There is no home delivery in UAE; all mail is delivered to post office boxes.

BEST TRAVEL BOOKS

The Traveler's Guide to Middle Eastern and North African Customs and Manners. Elizabeth Devine & Nancy Braganti. How to converse, dine, tip, bargain, dress, make friends, and conduct business while in the Middle East and North Africa.
Multinational Travel Companion Executive. Twenty Third Edition. Travel tips world-wide. Strand Publishing Company, Inc.
Saudi Arabia. Hippocrene Companion Guide. Gene Lindsey, Hippocrene Books, New York. Fully explores Saudi Arabia and surrounding countries.

USEFUL TELEPHONE NUMBERS

If you are calling from outside the United Arab Emirates, you will need to add the country code [971] and any other international dialing requirements from within your country.

- Hilton International Abu Dhabi .... (2) 661900
- Al Ain Intercontinental Al Ain .... (3) 34034
- Carlton Tower Dubai .... (4) 22711
- Operator 100
- International Operator 150; 160
- Airport Information .... (2) 224222
- Police Emergency 999
- Ambulance 998
- Fire 997

Car Rental
- Avis .... (2) 245219
- Budget .... (2) 757178
- Europcar .... (2) 757183

Credit Card Information
Lost or stolen credit cards (call collect to the US, regardless of which country the card was issued in).
- Amex .... [1] (919) 333-3211
- Diner's Club............................... [1] (303) 799-1504
- MasterCard .... [1] (314) 275-6690
- Visa .... [1] (410) 581-7931

Travelogue

WORKWEEK

Offices Saturday-Wednesday 8:00 am to 1:00 pm and 4:00 pm to 7:00 pm, and Thursday until noon.
Banks Saturday-Thursday, 8:00 am to noon.
Government Saturday-Wednesday 8:00 am to 2:00 pm, and Thursday until noon.
Retail Monday-Wednesday 8:00 am to 1:00 pm and 4:00 pm to 6:00 pm, Thursday 8:00 am to noon. Hours for retail vary.
In the summer, hours begin and end one hour earlier for businesses and government offices.

HOLIDAYS

Holidays 1996
January 1 New Year's Day
January 1 Ascension of the Prophet**
February 19-21 Eid Al-Fitr*
April 27 Waqfa Arafat*
April 28-30 Eid Al-Adha*
May 1 Labor Day
May 18 Islamic New Year*
July 28 Birth of the Prophet*
August 6 Sh. Zayed Accession Day
December 2-3 National Day
*Dates are based on a lunar calendar and vary each year.

VISA AND PASSPORT

Visitors to the United Arab Emirates need valid passports and visas. To obtain work or residence permits, an AIDS test is required after arrival. A visitor must be invited by a sponsor. Major hotels sponsor tourist and business travelers which are collected at airports or ports of entry. Note that if your passport shows any signs of travel to Israel you will be denied entry to the UAE.

DEPARTURE FORMALITIES

There are no departure formalities for the United Arab Emirates.

IMMUNIZATION

International certificate of vaccination not required unless you are arriving from an infected area. International certificate of vaccine for cholera is required if you are arriving from an infected area within five days; yellow fever within six days. Vaccinations for hepatitis, malaria, polio, tetanus, and typhoid are advised.

TIPPING

Most hotel and restaurant bills include a 10 percent service charge, especially in the northern emirates. If a restaurant does not include service charge, tip 10 to 15 percent. Porters are tipped Dh2 per bag, and taxi drivers are not tipped.

CRIME

Due to the UAE's strict discipline measures, crime is generally not a problem for travelers in the emirates.

INFRASTRUCTURE

The United Arab Emirates has developed hotel, air, taxi, and telecommunication systems. Roads can be highly congested, Dubai has extremely narrow streets and speeding is common. Taxis are the best way of getting around, are less expensive, and are often faster than air between Abu Dhabi and Dubai. There is no rail system nor any domestic air transportation network, despite the fact that all the emirates have modern airports.

TOURIST OFFICE

Ras al-Khaimahj Information and Tourism Dept.
141 Ras al-Khaimah
Dubai
Tel: (4) 7751151
Sharjah Department of Tourism
POB 8
Sharjah
Tel: (6) 581111
Fax: (6) 581167

Foreign Trade

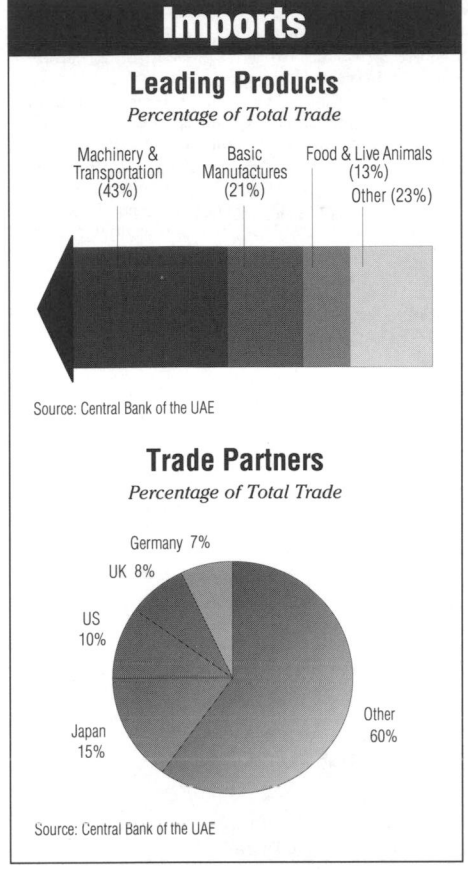

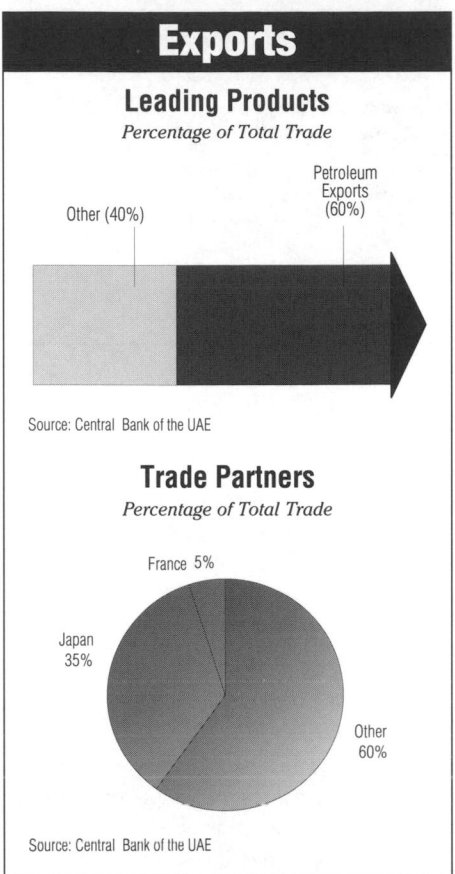

Opportunities

FOR IMPORTING TO THE UAE
- live animals, live trees and plants
- meat, fish and crustaceans
- diary products, fruits, vegetables, coffee, tea, spices
- milling industry products

FOR EXPORTING FROM THE UAE
- petroleum products
- oil

GROWTH SECTORS
- crude oil
- manufacturing
- construction
- financial services

Trade News

RULES AND REGULATIONS
- **Tariff rates** Each emirate operates its own customs authority, but tariffs and general policies are coordinated through a national committee. Tariffs are very low ranging from zero to four percent. Duties are assessed on a CIF basis.
- **Exports** All goods exported from the UAE must have proper documentation issued by the Ministry of Economy and Commerce and the various Chambers of Commerce in the respective individual emirates.
- **Temporary entry** Goods may be imported duty free and stored in any of several free zones in the UAE. There is no provision for duty free entry of parts or components which are intended for the manufacture of products which are subsequently exported.

Legal

Legal System

The United Arab Emirates (UAE) is ruled by *sheikhs*, and laws are passed down by ruling families.

Intellectual Property Protection

Patents The UAE recently passed a patent law, but it has not yet been implemented. No significant measures have been taken against violators. Pirated computer software dominates the UAE market.

Trademarks The UAE has not enforced any of the trademark laws it recently passed.

Copyrights Most foreign copyright laws are ignored.

Trade secrets The legal system in the UAE tends to favor domestic businesses, and it is difficult for foreign companies to get an injunction for trade secret violations.

Business Registration

Registration tends to be lengthy and difficult. Companies must have 51 percent UAE ownership, except on major project or defense contracts where no local company is able to provide the goods or services. Companies must be registered with the Chamber of Commerce and the local emirate government.

Contracts and Dispute Resolution

Businesses in the UAE prefer a wide range of contracts, from simple and short to long and detailed. There have been several contractor disputes but few investment disputes. Many disputes have eventually been handled through arbitration, but resolution can be difficult and uncertain.

Labor

The Ministry of Labor regulates all expatriate labor; all such employment contracts must be registered. There is no minimum wage. Organization and collective bargaining is not allowed, and public sector strikes are a criminal offense. Lack of respect for employees exists, but overall labor-management relations are relatively good.

Legal Matters

LEGAL BRIEFS
- **JAFZ** The Jebel Ali Free Zone (JAFZ) is a haven for nonresident businesses. Foreigners can own up to 100 percent of a company.
- **Arbitration** The Abu Dhabi Commercial Conciliation and Arbitration Center was created by the government to accelerate commercial disputes.
- **New laws** If parties agree to arbitration, it is enforceable, and no one can file a claim with a court if arbitration has already decided the issue.
- **Bankruptcy** The UAE recently wrote the Federal Commercial Code, including its first legislation on bankruptcy. The code governs the procedures and effects of bankruptcy much more closely than before.
- **Branch offices** Branch offices may be established but local sponsorship is required.
- **IPR** The UAE is not a party to any significant international patent, copyright, or trademark conventions, and these rights are not generally protected in the country.
- **Labor** The labor law sets out a schedule of end-of-service gratuities for private companies, starting with 21 days' pay for each year of service.

LEGAL CONTACTS

Clifford Chance
18th Floor, Dubai World Trade Centre
POB 9380
Dubai
Tel: (4) 314333 Fax: (4) 313990, 314565

Kudsi Fox and Gibbons
POB 46010
Abu Dhabi
Tel: (2) 322858 Fax: (2) 331586

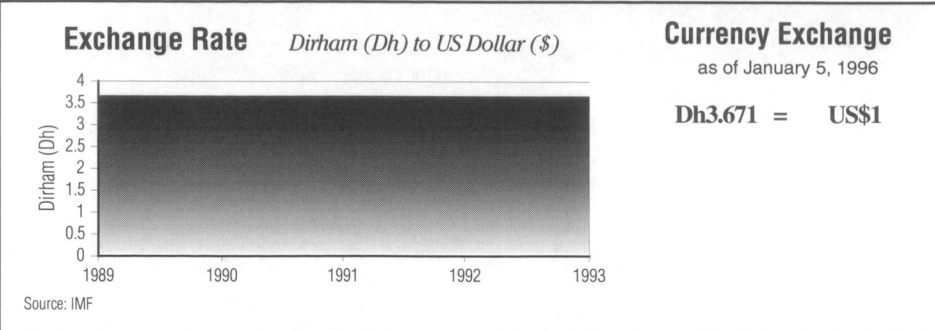

Exchange Rate *Dirham (Dh) to US Dollar ($)*

Source: IMF

Currency Exchange

as of January 5, 1996

Dh3.671 =   US$1

Money Matters

BITS AND PIECES

- **Bank notes** Travelers may take out and bring in any amount in foreign or domestic bank notes.
- **Prescription of currency** All settlements with Israel are prohibited. No other prescription of currency requirements are in force.
- **Accounts** Distinction is drawn between accounts held by residents and those held by nonresidents, and different rules and requirements apply thereto.
- **Gold** Residents and nonresidents may freely purchase, hold, and sell gold in any form, at home or abroad. They may also, without a permit, import and export gold in any form, but only licensed parties may import gold for trade purposes.

Currency

The currency of the United Arab Emirates is the dirham, (Dh), which is divided into 100 fils.

Foreign Exchange

The dirham has been pegged to the US dollar at a stable rate since 1980. All currencies are traded freely at market determined rates, and no license is required to change money. The currency of Israel, however, cannot be bought or sold in the UAE. There are no taxes or subsidies on purchases or sales of foreign exchange.

Capital Transfers

There is neither exchange control legislation nor an exchange control authority in the UAE. No exchange controls are imposed on capital receipts or payments by residents or nonresidents.

Investment Incentives

Incentives are given to foreign investors in the free zones, but there are no other incentives for investments outside the free zones. The laws and regulations governing foreign investment are generally favorable to foreign investment, but they are still evolving, and foreign investors are advised to contact their embassy or commercial advisement department to obtain the most current investment information. There are no specific significant government financed or subsidized industrial research and development programs in the UAE. While the government offers subsidies for manufacturing firms, these are only available to those with at least a 51 percent local ownership.

Investment Restrictions

Companies established in the UAE are required to have a minimum of 51 percent UAE national ownership. However, profits may be apportioned differently. Branch offices of foreign companies are required to have a national agent unless the foreign company has established its office pursuant to an agreement with the federal or an emirate government. All general partnership interests must be owned by UAE nationals. Foreign projects must be managed by a national or have a board of directors with a majority of UAE nationals. Suppliers, contractors, or tenderers with respect to federal projects must either be UAE nationals or a company in which at least 51 percent of the share capital is owned by UAE nationals.

BANKS

Citibank, NA
Khalid Ibn Al Walid Street
Dubai
Tel: (4) 522100 Fax: (4) 524942

American Express Bank Ltd.
POB 3304
Dubai
Tel: (4) 223236 Telex: 46245

Abu Dhabi Commercial Bank
POB 5550
Dubai
Tel: (4) 228141

Bank of Oman Limited
POB 1250
Dubai
Tel: (4) 229131 Fax: (4) 226061

Central Bank of the United Arab Emirates
POB 854
Abu Dhabi
Tel: (2) 652220 Fax: (2) 6668483

Bank of the Arab Coast Ltd.
POB 5536
Deira, Dubai
Tel: (4) 223101 Telex: 46177

Commercial Bank of Dubai
POB 2668
Deira, Dubai
Tel: (4) 523355 Fax: (4) 520444

Investment Bank for Trade and Finance PLC
POB 1885
Sharjah
Tel: (6) 355391 Fax: (6) 546683

Middle East Bank Ltd.
POB 5547
Deira, Dubai
Tel: (4) 256256 Fax: (4) 255322

National Bank of Abu Dhabi
POB 4
Abu Dhabi
Tel: (2) 335262 Fax: (2) 336078

National Bank of Dubai Ltd.
POB 777
Dubai
Tel: (4) 222241 Fax: (4) 215939

National Bank of Fujairah
POB 887
Fujairah
Tel: (9) 224518 Fax: (9) 224516

National Bank of Ras al-Khaimah PSC
POB 5300
Ras al-Khaimah
Tel: (7) 221127 Fax: (7) 223238

National Bank of Sharjah
POB 4
Sharjah
Tel: (6) 547745 Fax: (6) 543483

National Bank of Umm al-Qaiwain Ltd.
POB 800
Umm al-Qaiwain
Tel: (6) 655225 Fax: (6) 655440

Lloyds Bank PLC
POB 3766
Dubai
Tel: (4) 375005 Fax: (4) 375026

TAXATION

Taxation requires sophisticated knowledge of complex rules and regulations specific to each country. For more detailed information we suggest you refer to the Ernst & Young Corporate Tax Guide and Directory, available from the Ernst & Young accounting office in your country, or from:

Ernst & Young
POB 136, Abu Dhabi
United Arab Emirates
Tel: (2) 322224
Cable: Ernstaudit, Abu Dhabi
Telex: 22672 Ans bk ERNST EM
Fax: (2) 342968

At a Glance

Corporate Income Tax Rate (%)(a)	0
Capital Gains Tax Rate (%)(a)	0
Branch Tax Rate (%)(a)	0
Withholding Tax (%)(a)	0

(a) The Federal Ministry does not impose any taxes, however, the individual emirates promulgate their own corporate tax laws. Generally, taxes are imposed only on oil and gas producing companies based on individual concession agreements.

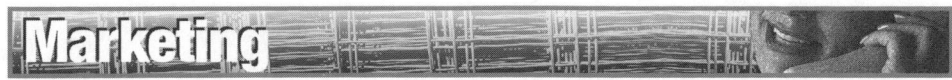

Overview

The commercial trading position of the UAE has traditionally been that of middleman or trader acting as a conduit for goods from large manufacturers in Africa, the Middle East, and Asia.

Distribution

Foreign firms have many paths to trade in the UAE. They can sell directly to end-users; sell through a nonexclusive retailer; appoint an agent or distributor; establish a company presence; or license or franchise products to a local firm. Many food importers are also distributors, wholesalers, and retailers who know the region and trade patterns well.

Agents, Distributors, and Partners

The UAE makes no distinction between agents and distributors, calling both commercial agents. All agents must register with the Ministry of Economy and Commerce. An agent may only be terminated for cause, determined by a government committee which has a history of ruling in favor of agents. Even if the ruling is for the foreign firm, compensation is usually required for the agent. Only UAE nationals or companies wholly owned by UAE nationals can register as local agents, who are granted automatic exclusivity for the geographic territory defined in the agreement (usually an entire emirate). Joint ventures with foreign firms require local majority ownership, which prescribes profit and loss distribution; the license for the joint venture need not be published.

Selling Techniques and Advertising

Franchising agreements are growing rapidly, although only UAE citizens may be franchisees. Direct marketing has not proved particularly effective, except for orders from large businesses for their own use. Many sellers advertise in the two English daily newspapers, the *Gulf News* and *Khaleej Times*, and in the several weekly and monthly English magazines; all are effective consumer market vehicles. Many Arabic and Third World publications are also available. Radio and television are broadcast in English, Arabic, and Hindi. Any firm new to this market needs to conduct careful research into this culture's values, which adhere to the nation of Islam, when preparing promotional campaigns.

Marketing in the United Arab Emirates

MARKETING TIPS

- **Selling techniques** From late September through May, except for the holy month of Ramadan, the UAE hosts an almost continuous series of major trade exhibitions and conferences.
- **Quality** It is important to stress quality if your goods are higher priced than products from other regions. Gulf consumers recognize high quality and are willing to pay a premium for such products.
- **Middle- and lower-class consumers** These markets are served through small stores and shops in traditional *souks*, or bazaars.

AD AGENCIES

Bozell Prime
POB 13872
Dubai
Tel: (4) 824824
Fax: (4) 824008

Fortune Promoseven
POB 6834
Dubai
Tel: (4) 669686
Fax: (4) 669873

Lintas Gulf
POB 60798
Dubai
Tel: (4) 317080
Fax: (4) 314784

TMI
POB 4327
Dubai
Tel: (4) 215342
Fax: (4) 282009

Business Culture

Greetings and Courtesies

Businesspeople are generally friendly and open. They embrace or shake hands when meeting and departing, and several times in between. Businesspeople will quickly give much more information about themselves than in the West. Family and social connections are important, more so than personal accomplishments. Expect several invitations to have coffee and meals. Titles are used often, and anyone with an M.D. or Ph.D. must be addressed as "Dr." ("*duktoar*" for a man, "*duktoara*" for a woman).

Business Ethic and Framework

UAE culture is somewhat "dualist," with both modernist and traditionalist ways of thinking present at the same time. Businesspeople usually believe that many things in life are controlled by fate, and that the inherent personalities of women and men are vastly different. Honor is often more important than facts; rarely will an Arab admit an error. All beliefs and laws are based on the Islamic creed, even for the minority of people who are not Muslim. Bureaucrats are given a great deal of power; connections with government officials are invaluable.

Meetings and Decision Making

Good personal relationships and contacts are the most important factors in business with Arabs. Faith and friendship are used to decide most issues, sometimes even overriding reasoning. Regulations or decisions can be changed in view of someone's personal situation. Businesspeople have a hard time saying "no," and if your question doesn't get an answer you should take it as a negative response.

Women

Women can be professionals, but they still acknowledge their place in the family structure and believe in the need to guard their reputation carefully. At social events, if a woman is unmarried or her husband is not present, she should be reserved. Most women veil their faces, at least partially, in public.

Cultural Cautions

DO'S

- Always be hospitable. If you bring food back into the office, be sure to bring enough for everyone.
- Inquire about your colleagues' health or well-being. The gesture will be appreciated.

DON'TS

- You will be asked out repeatedly. While it is okay to decline occasionally, to turn down too many offers is seen as a slight.
- Avoid familiarity with members of the opposite sex. The public display of intimacy between men and women is strictly forbidden by the Arab social code.

CUSTOMS

- A person's dignity, honor, and reputation are of paramount importance.
- The most popular form of entertainment is conversation, and Arabs enjoy long discussions over meals or coffee.
- Loyalty to one's family takes precedence over personal needs. Social class and family background are the major determining factors of personal status.
- Friendship is very important; Arabs place high value on good friendships, and friends will do a lot for each other.

OBSERVATIONS

- A great deal of respect is given to elders. Arabs tend to believe that wisdom increases with age.
- Supervisors constantly praise their employees, to reassure them that their hard work is noticed.
- Arabs stand closer to each other than in other countries. Men often hold hands and kiss each other on the cheek, both signs of friendship. It is also common to touch someone repeatedly during a conversation.
- Don't press a sensitive issue. If you don't get a direct answer, it is probably best to move on.

GOVERNMENT AGENCIES

Ministry of Agriculture and Fisheries
POB 213
Abu Dhabi
Tel: (2) 662781

Ministry of Communications
POB 900
Abu Dhabi
Tel: (2) 651900 Fax: (2) 668675

Ministry of Economy and Commerce
POB 901
Abu Dhabi
Tel: (2) 215455 Fax: (2) 215339

Ministry of Education
POB 295
Abu Dhabi
Tel: (2) 213800

Ministry of Electricity and Water
POB 1672
Abu Dhabi
Tel: (2) 6950575 Fax: (2) 690064

Ministry of Finance and Industry
POB 443
Abu Dhabi
Tel: (2) 726000 Fax: (2) 773301

Ministry of Foreign Affairs
POB 1
Abu Dhabi
Tel: 92) 652200 Fax: (2) 668015

Ministry of Health
POB 848
Abu Dhabi
Tel: (2) 214100 Fax: (2) 215422

Ministry of Information and Culture
POB 17
Abu Dhabi
Tel: (2) 463100, 453000 Fax: (2) 452504

Ministry of Labor and Social Affairs
POB 809
Abu Dhabi
Tel: (2) 651890 Fax: (2) 665889

CHAMBERS OF COMMERCE

Federation of U.A.E. Chambers of Commerce & Industry
POB 3014
Abu Dhabi
Tel: (2) 214000 Fax: (2) 339210

Abu Dhabi Chamber of Commerce and Industry
POB 662
Abu Dhabi
Tel: (2) 214000 Fax: (2) 215867

Ajman Chamber of Commerce and Industry
POB 662
Ajman
Tel: (6) 422177 Fax: (6) 427591

Ras Al Khaimah Chamber of Commerce and Industry
POB 87
Ras Al Khaimah
Tel: (77) 33511 Fax: (77) 30233

Sharjah Chamber of Commerce and Industry
POB 580
Sharjah
Tel: (6) 541444 Fax: (6) 541119

Umm Al Qaiwan Chamber of Commerce and Industry
POB 436
Umm Al Qaiwan
Tel: (6) 69215 Fax: (6) 667056

WORLD TRADE CENTER

Dubai World Trade Center
POB 9292
Dubai
Tel: (4) 314200 Fax: (4) 313493, 3064089

PETROLEUM COMPANIES

International Petroleum Investment Company
POB 7528
Abu Dhabi
Tel: (2) 336200 Fax: (2) 216045

Abu Dhabi Gas Industries Co
POB 665
Abu Dhabi
Tel: (2) 651100 Fax: (2) 6047414

Abu Dhabi National Oil Company
POB 898
Abu Dhabi
Tel: (2) 666000 Fax: (2) 722244

Abu Dhabi Drilling Chemicals and Products Ltd.
POB 46121
Abu Dhabi
Tel: (2) 730400 Fax: (2) 730725

Supreme Petroleum Council
POB 26555
Abu Dhabi
Tel: (2) 666000 Fax: (2) 661469

Abu Dhabi Oil Company Ltd.
POB 630
Abu Dhabi
Tel: (2) 661100 Fax: (2) 665965

Amerada Hess Oil Corporation of Abu Dhabi
POB 2046
Abu Dhabi
Tel/Fax: (2) 779500

Total Abu al-Bukhoosh Oil Company Ltd.
POB 4058
Abu Dhabi
Tel: (2) 335566 Fax: (2) 322948

Zakum Development Company
POB 6808
Abu Dhabi
Tel: (2) 661700 Fax: (2) 669448

DUGAS-Dubai Natural Gas Company Ltd.
POB 4311
Dubai
Tel: (4) 46234 Fax: (4) 46118

Dubai Petroleum Company
POB 2222
Dubai
Tel: (4) 442990 Fax: (4) 462200

Emirates Petroleum Products Co. (Pvt.) Ltd.
POB 5589
Dubai
Tel: (4) 372131 Fax: (4) 375990

NEWSPAPERS

Akhbar Dubai (Dubai News)
Department of Information
Dubai Municipality
POB 1420
Dubai

Al-Ittihad
POB 17
Abu Dhabi
Tel: (2) 461600 Telex: 22984

Emirate News (Daily)
POB 791
Abu Dhabi
Tel: (2) 451446 Fax: (2) 453662

Khaleej Times (Daily)
POB 3082
Abu Dhabi
Tel: (2) 336000 Fax: (2) 336424

UAE and Abu Dhabi Official Gazette
POB 899
Abu Dhabi

UAE Press Service Daily News
POB 2035
Abu Dhabi
Tel: (2) 44292

Gulf News (Daily)
POB 6519
Dubai
Tel: (4) 447100 Fax: (4) 441627

BUSINESS PERIODICALS

Dubai Annual Trade Review
POB 516
Dubai
Tel: (4) 531076 Fax: (4) 531959

Abu Dhabi Chamber of Commerce Review (Monthly)
POB 662
Abu Dhabi
Tel: (2) 214000 Telex: 22449

Trade and Industry (Monthly)
POB 1457
Dubai
Tel: (4) 221181 Fax: (4) 211646

UAE Digest (Monthly)
POB 6872
Sharjah
Tel: (6) 354633 Fax: (6) 354627

RADIO & TELEVISION STATIONS

Abu Dhabi Radio
POB 63
Abu Dhabi
Tel: (2) 451000 Fax: (2) 451155

Dubai Radio and Colour Television
POB 1695
Dubai
Tel: (4) 370255 Telex: 45605

UAE Radio and Television-Dubai
POB 1695
Dubai
Tel: (4) 370255 Fax: (4) 371079

UAE TV-Abu Dhabi
POB 637
Abu Dhabi
Tel: (2) 452000 Fax: (2) 451470

UAE Television-Sharjah
POB 111
Sharjah
Tel: (6) 361111 Fax: (6) 541755

FREIGHT FORWARDERS

Orient Transport Company
POB 984
Abu Dhabi
Telex: 23539 OTCADH EM

Danzas Commercial Delegation
POB 1579
Dubai
Telex: 46398 SOTIM EM

OTC Pte. Ltd.
POB 2370
Dubai
Fax: (4) 245855 Telex: 47586 OSNA EM

International Shipping Agencies
POB 5162
Ras-al-Khaimeh
Fax: (7) 29499 Telex: 99226 ISARAK EM

INTERNET ADDRESSES

Usenet group(s):
soc.culture.arabic

Arab.net
http://www.arab.net/welcome.html

Omnibus–Emirates
http://www.nresults.com/uae

The United Arab Emirates
http://ns2.emirates.net.ae/uae/

United Kingdom

United Kingdom of Great Britain and Northern Ireland

Economy

Overview

Close proximity to large continental European markets, a flexible labor force, and its reputation as a global financial center, have helped the United Kingdom maintain its position as one of the world's leading economies. Much of its wealth was established by virtue of its strong tradition as a trading nation, and international trade continues to be of vital importance to its economy. Having experienced two major recessions in the past two decades, the government has now placed a strong emphasis on the privatization of industry, free trade, and minimum government intervention in the marketplace; these are beginning to see returns in the efficiency and growth potential of the UK's economy.

Trade

The United Kingdom is likely to be the only major EU country to increase the total value of its foreign trade in the near term. EU countries are the primary markets for its exports, and it buys the majority of its imports from other developed Western countries. Germany is the largest source of both its imports and exports, followed by the US, France, and the Netherlands. The size and growth potential of its economy and the ease of doing business here make this an important import market. The UK has maintained its relatively recent role as a crude oil exporter and significant increases in productivity in the manufacturing sector have given it a cost advantage that is likely to increase export growth overall.

Sectors

Agriculture The UK has a highly mechanized and intensive agricultural sector employing just one percent of the work force. Climatic factors limit production to just over 50 percent of its food requirements, mainly in the livestock and dairy sectors. This means it is a major market for agricultural imports––especially high-value, consumer-oriented products.

Industry Industry continues to be the backbone of the UK's economy. Recent government policies to privatize national industries and redeploy resources in this sector have resulted in increased productivity and competitiveness in world markets. Major industries include industrial plant equipment, chemicals, crude oil, and motor vehicles. However, the increasing influx of foreign-owned companies is resulting in a greater emphasis on high-technology, export-oriented industries.

Services Primarily a service nation, this sector accounts for 65 percent of GDP and modest growth is expected as the economy continues to strengthen. It is an international financial center and the deregulation of the financial services sector has significantly increased its competitiveness in this area. The UK continues to draw tourists from all over the world, and tourism is a healthy contributor to GDP.

Trends

The UK's modest economic recovery continues and consumer confidence appears to be returning with the leveling of unemployment, and decreasing rates of interests and inflation. The expanding domestic market is attracting larger import volumes but significant export growth is being curtailed by a slowdown in the economies of its major EU trading partners. The government's strong role in developing a stable business environment and attracting foreign investment has ensured significant growth in the short term while its long-term prospects will be increasingly linked to the fortunes of its EU partners.

At a Glance

THE COUNTRY

Location Western Europe, bordering on the North Atlantic Ocean and the North Sea, between Ireland and France.
Terrain Mostly rugged hills and low mountains, level to rolling plains.
Climate Temperate; prevailing southwest winds. More than half of all days are overcast.

THE PEOPLE

Population 58,000,000
Ethnic composition
English 81.5%
Scottish 9.6%
Irish 2.4%
Welsh 1.9%
Other... 2.8%
Religious composition
Anglican 46%
Roman Catholic 16%
Other... less than one percent
(Note: The UK does not include a religion question on its census form).
Languages spoken English, Welsh, and Scottish form of Gaelic.
Education and literacy The UK is a highly literate society. Education is compulsory for 12 years and attendance is nearly 100 percent. 99 percent of the population over 15 years of age can read and write.
Labor force
Total..29,000,000
By occupation: services 72%, manufacturing and engineering 18%, mining and energy 5%, construction 4%, agriculture 1%.

COUNTRY FACTS

Political and legal The United Kingdom is a constitutional monarchy; however its constitution is unwritten. Instead, law is based on statute, common law, and "traditional rights." There are three separate branches of government and two main political parties (Labor and Conservative). There are several levels of courts, including magistrates' courts, county courts, and the highest legal body, the House of Lords.
Telephone Public telephones are plentiful in cities, and are often found in hotels and post offices. Many Western European cities can be reached by direct dialing. The distinctive red phone booths are slowly being replaced with modern looking cubicles. For information anywhere in Britain, dial either 142 or 192. For the operator, dial 100. Country code: [44].
Transportation London is a major international destination. The UK has extensive transportation routes by air, rail, and bus. Buses (coaches) are excellent and most are economical. Rental cars are readily available. Travel between points is quick and easy.
Environment Air pollution is caused by sulfur dioxide emissions from power plants. There is also water pollution from large-scale disposal of sewage at sea.
Media The UK has one of the most advanced media systems in the world. There are 225 AM, 525 FM, and 207 television stations.
Health There are generally good medical facilities. Living conditions are generally excellent, with no health hazards. Life expectancy is 74 years for males and 77 years for females. Birth rates are 1.83 children per woman. The UK has a national health system.

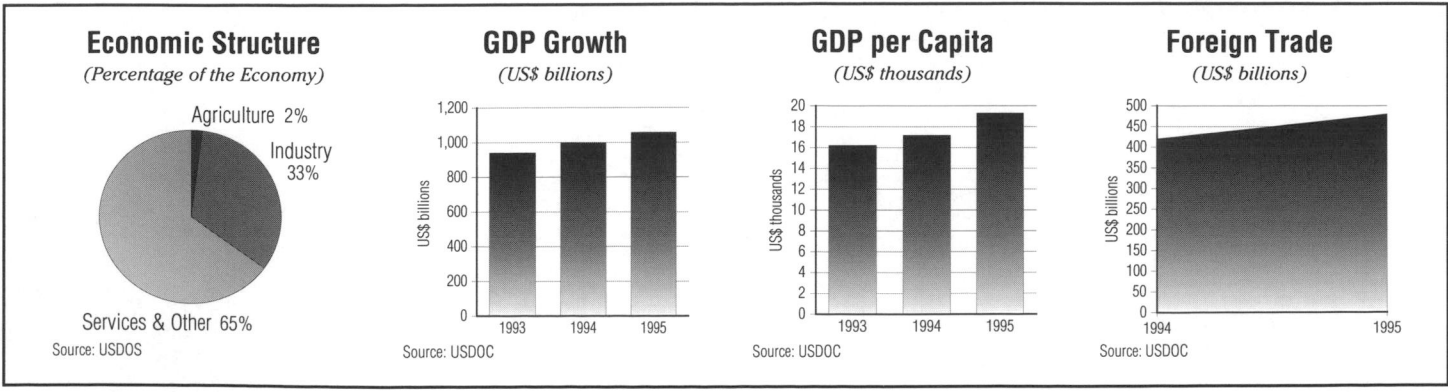

Economic Structure
(Percentage of the Economy)

Agriculture 2%
Industry 33%
Services & Other 65%

Source: USDOS

GDP Growth
(US$ billions)

US$ billions — 1993, 1994, 1995

Source: USDOC

GDP per Capita
(US$ thousands)

US$ thousands — 1993, 1994, 1995

Source: USDOC

Foreign Trade
(US$ billions)

US$ billions — 1994, 1995

Source: USDOC

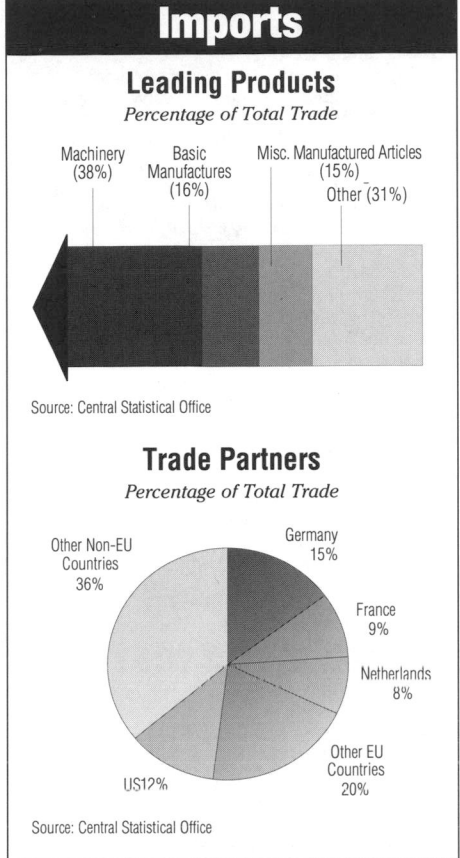

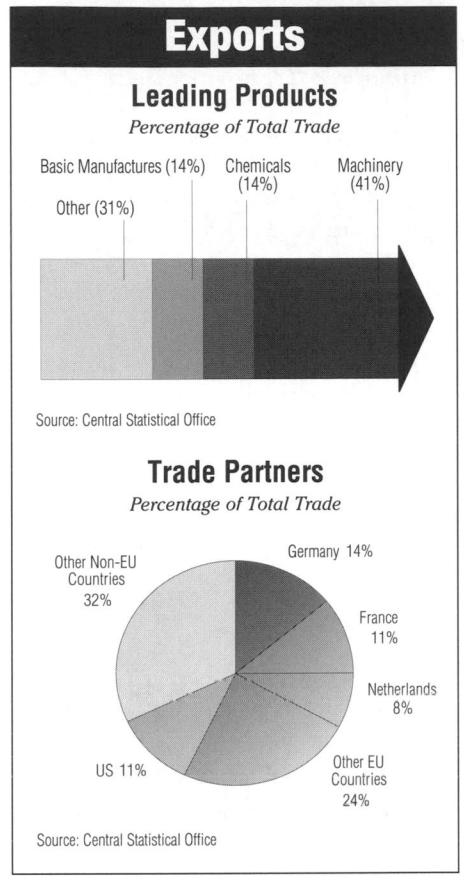

Opportunities

FOR IMPORTING TO THE UNITED KINGDOM

- aircraft and parts, defense equipment
- computer software, computer and peripherals
- oil and gas field machinery and services
- telecommunications services
- general consumer goods, books, toys and games
- automotive parts and service
- packaging materials
- hotel and restaurant equipment
- biotechnology, industrial chemicals
- building products, electrical power systems
- apparel, cosmetics, and toiletries
- telecommunications, security and safety equipment
- medical equipment and pharmaceuticals
- laboratory, scientific, and pollution control equipment
- sporting goods and recreational equipment
- forest products

FOR EXPORTING FROM THE UNITED KINGDOM

- cheese
- cocoa and cocoa products
- fruits
- vegetables
- textiles
- apparel
- medical equipment
- machinery
- semifinished goods
- sugar and confectioneries
- cereals

Trade News

RULES AND REGULATIONS

- **Tariff policy** The United Kingdom is a member of the European Union which provides for common external tariffs, a common agricultural policy, a joint transportation policy, and the free movement of goods, labor, and capital within and between its member nations.
- **Raw materials** Most raw materials enter duty free or at low rates of duty, while rates on most manufactured goods fall within a range of five to seven percent.
- **Other rates** Imports of textiles face duties of up to 15 percent; and electronic products reach 14 percent.
- **Customs charges** Customs charges are payable in British pounds sterling at the time the goods are cleared through customs. However, importers can arrange with customs to defer payment of certain duties and other charges for a 30-day period, provided that adequate security is given.
- **Value-added tax** The United Kingdom applies a valued-added tax on most goods and services, whether domestically produced or imported. The VAT is imposed as a flat rate and is applied on the CIF duty-paid value of the goods and services.
- **Declaration** Whatever the length of stay, all goods for commercial use, professional effects, any prohibited goods, and everything in excess of duty-free allowances must be declared at the time of entry.
- **Import restrictions** Prohibited imports include AM citizen band radio, devices that project toxic, noxious, or harmful substances, counterfeit currency, and certain types of pornography.
- **Import licenses** Only a very limited range of goods are subject to import licenses. These include firearms and explosives and controlled drugs.
- **Product standards** The ongoing EU harmonization of product standards, labelling, testing, and certification requirements will substantially simplify foreign sellers' ability to enter European markets.
- **Temporary entry** Importers must give a security for the amount of duty payable in the form of either a bond or cash deposit, which is released or refunded upon re-exportation of the goods. The time limit for re-exportation normally ranges from 6 to 12 months from the date of importation, but extensions of time may be obtained from the customs authorities.

TRANSPORTATION FIRMS

Associated Container Transportation (Services) Ltd.
Richmond House
Terminus Terrace
Southampton SO9 1GG
Tel: (1703) 634433
Telex: 477622
Fax: (1703) 330940

N.J. Goulandris Ltd.
The Aadelphi
John Adam Street
London WC2N 6AP
Tel: (171) 930-1277
Telex: 883157

P & O Containers Ltd.
Beagle House
Braham Street
London E1 8EP
Tel: (171) 488-1313

Souter Shipping Ltd.
Clayton House
Regent Centre
Gosforth
Newcastle upon Tyne
NE3 3HW
Tel: (191) 285-0621
Telex: 53186

Stephenson Clarke Shipping Ltd.
Europe House
World Trade Centre
London E1 9AJ
Tel: (171) 709-9188
Fax: (171) 265-0929

GROWTH SECTORS

- agriculture
- construction
- energy/water
- financial services
- manufacturing

GOVERNMENT PROCUREMENT

- heavy construction equipment and services
- telecommunications equipment
- pollution control equipment and services
- medical equipment

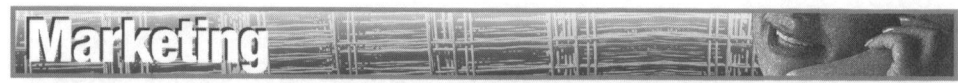

Overview

Companies interested in trading with the United Kingdom should approach it as an integral part of the European market, a US$4 trillion market of 370 million consumers. The improved business climate alone is expected ultimately to increase imports of goods and services. Additionally, the Single Market is projected to add 1.8 million jobs and produce a US$260 billion increase in demand for goods and services in the block, and will eventually force European companies to become more competitive since they will no longer be guaranteed protected home markets. Recent developments in the UK economy—including further deregulation of the telecommunications market, which is already more liberal than any other European country, as well as plans to privatize all or part of the railroads, the postal system, the prison system, and air traffic control—offer attractive joint venture possibilities for foreign businesses.

Distribution

As one of the world's most active trading nations, the UK has a well-developed network of distribution channels, which tend to vary according to product group, ranging from the branch office of a foreign seller to large import houses that purchase abroad and sell on their own account. Between these two extremes are sales agents, specialized importers, brokers, and importing distributors. The distinction between the types is not clear cut and considerable variation exists even within a product group. Larger United Kingdom businesses frequently buy directly from overseas suppliers. A recent development is the appearance of organizations, referred to as importers/factors, that take care of the pricing, warehousing, distribution, and factoring of large quantities of import goods.

Agents, Distributors, and Partners

Distributors are of the two traditional types: wholesalers and brokers, often called commission wholesalers. Generally, firms new to the market of the UK find it more convenient to appoint one distributor to cover the whole country. Then, when they become more established, they often appoint other regional distributors in order to achieve even greater market penetration. Business may be carried on through a broker, general commission agent, or other independent agent, or through a salesman not authorized to conclude contracts. Recent changes to British law have increased regulation of the principal-agent relationship. Foreign sellers should determine their legal responsibilities and the most advantageous distribution channel with the help of knowledgeable legal advice in the UK.

Selling Techniques

Recently, independent wholesalers have faced increasing competition from large-scale retail organizations that have direct access to manufacturers and are, therefore, able to promote sales through their own retail outlets and mail order. As a result, only a portion of the trade in consumer goods now passes through wholesalers. This change has stimulated the creation of new forms of wholesale organizations for the benefit of both wholesalers and retailers. Smaller retailers, as a defense against the larger ones, have joined organizations incorporating one or more wholesalers. Through these organizations they benefit from the economics of bulk purchasing and cooperative sales promotion schemes without the loss of independence. Other widely accepted selling techniques in the UK are franchising, joint-venture, licensing agreements, and direct marketing.

Advertising

The advertising industry is highly developed and provides a full-range of advertising and market research services. Of the US$12 billion in annual advertising expenditures, 60 percent goes to newspaper advertisements and 31 percent to commercial television. With their immense circulation and deep penetration throughout the country, the 130 national daily and Sunday papers are extensively used by manufacturers, retailers, and professional advertising agencies. Television advertising is conducted through the stations of the Independent Broadcasting Authority (IBA). The IBA is a quasi-government corporation that contracts with independent stations that provide programs. It is important that print and other advertising or direct marketing promotions designed for other English-speaking markets be examined by an advertising agency or direct marketing house to modify the materials for legal and cultural differences in this area.

Service and Customer Support

Larger distributors expect foreign manufacturers will already have their products adapted for local sale and use. Sales service and after-sales product service and maintenance is expected, and consumers will generally not deal with sellers who cannot or do not provide these services. Adequate supplies of replacement parts and accessories should be maintained in the country, and foreign sellers should develop reliable and timely distribution systems for these inventories.

Marketing in the UK

MARKETING TIPS

- **European Union** Trade and marketing practices within the UK are continually changing to conform to those of the Union.
- **Telecommunications** The telecommunications industry is more liberal than that of any other EU country; foreign vendors of network services are able to compete with domestic ones.
- **Privatization** Privatization of state industries continues, and provides many opportunities for foreign sellers.
- **Computer products** Computer and other high-tech marketing practices have changed dramatically in recent years, evolving to resemble those of the United States.
- **Profit margins** Retailers in the UK have tended to demand higher profit margins than those on the rest of the continent.
- **Distribution methods** Methods vary widely according to merchandise type and market size.
- **Pricing** A value-added tax of 17.5 percent is charged on the majority of goods sold and this should be factored into pricing decisions.
- **Government** Both central and local governments increasingly buy services previously provided in-house. Most departments are subject to the GATT MTN procurement code and must not discriminate against bidders from GATT signatory countries.

AD AGENCIES

Bates Communications
121-141 Westbourne Terrace
London W26JR
Tel: (171) 262-0828
Fax: (171) 402-3070

BMP DDB Needham Worldwide Ltd.
12 Bishop's Gridge Rd.
London W2 6AA
Tel: (171) 258-3979
Fax: (171) 402-4871

D'Arcy Masius Benton & Bowles Ltd.
2 St. James Square
London SW1Y 4JN
Tel: (171) 839-3422
Fax: (171) 839-5329

Grey Communications Group Ltd.
215-227, Great Portland St.
London, W1N 5HD
Tel: (171) 636-3399
Fax: (171) 637-7473

Saatchi & Saatchi Advertising
80 Charlotte St.
London W1A 1AQ
Tel: (171) 636-5060
Fax: (171) 637-8489
Telex: 261580

MARKETING ASSOCIATIONS

Association of Household Distributors
3 Brunswick Square
Gloucester GL1 1UG
Tel: (1452) 387070
Fax: (1452) 300912

Data Protection Registry
Wycliffe House, Water Lane
Wilmslow, Cheshire SK9 5AF
Tel: (1625) 530086
Fax: (1625) 524510

Direct Mail Information Service
5 Carlisle Street
London W1V 5RG
Tel: (171) 494-0483
Fax: (171) 494-0455

Direct Mail Services Standards Board
26 Eccleston Street
London SW1W 9PY
Tel: (171) 824-8651
Fax: (171) 824-8574

Business Culture

Greetings and Courtesies

English is spoken in the UK, but each country (England, Ireland, Scotland, and Wales) has different idioms, many of which are different from those used in the United States. In the business community it is considered bad form to address anyone by a first name. The correct form includes Mr., Mrs., Miss, Dr., Professor, etc., followed by the last name. When introduced to a knight, "Sir" is followed by both first and last names. e.g. Sir John Ferguson, after which you would address him, "Sir John" in both speaking and writing—never Sir Ferguson. His wife would be addressed as Lady Ferguson always, without using the first name. Shaking hands is the standard form of greeting throughout the UK. Always wait for the woman to extend her hand first. An exchange of business gifts might take place on very special occasions, but in general the British do not expect gifts or practice the custom. If gift-giving is your preferred method of showing appreciation, keep it tasteful and modest in price so as not to be construed as a bribe. Otherwise, it is perfectly acceptable to treat British colleagues to dinner, or an evening at the theater. The English tend to be formal and conservative. Suspicious of extremes, the British do not appreciate emotional or overt enthusiastic displays, but prefer calm reserve in both behavior and emotion.

Business Ethic and Framework

Offices throughout the United Kingdom are formal and third party introductions are important. Most senior corporate executives comprise a tightly knit network and it can be difficult to penetrate the net. The British are suspicious of individuals or corporations with whom they are unfamiliar. Gaining access by way of top bank officials, accounting firms, or introductions by members of the diplomatic corps may be helpful. Self-introductions by way of letter should include appropriate background materials, proper references, and a clear statement of intent. Advance appointments are essential; cold calls and drop-ins are considered impolite. Be prepared: the British look down on conceived "Get rich quick" plans; nonetheless, proposals should emphasize short-term benefits over long-term goals of more than 10 years.

Decision Making

The decision-making process depends on the type of business or corporate entity with which you deal. In family-dominated firms, decisions are made by the chairman or CEO. Other institutes exercise a more decentralized system, authorizing particular departments or profit-centered subsidiaries to render decisions in accord with their own operations, often without first reporting to the board. Finally, there are those entities where the board is the supreme decision-making body, and in most of Britain's firms executives and non-executives share board responsibilities while representatives of both shareholders and non-shareholders lend their expertise and status to the corporation.

Women

British women now comprise 45 percent of the work force, and their numbers are growing. Though there is still disparity between the pay accorded their male counterparts, women are advancing to management positions in the UK. Women are competitive in business and are taken very seriously. Treat them as you would any business colleague.

Meetings

Meetings open and close with polite courtesies and informal conversation. In between, be prepared with details and facts, presented in a logical format. The British prefer a soft, understated sales presentation to aggressive hard-sell tactics. Answer questions directly and with as much information or statistics as are available on your topic. Though an advance agenda and other materials are required to be in place before the scheduled meeting, do not assume your British colleagues have familiarized themselves with the materials. Bring extras along just in case. Additionally, immediately follow up your meeting with a letter outlining points discussed and how you intend to proceed with your proposal.

Business Attire

Dark or pinstripe suits of quality fiber are appropriate for men. Pay special attention to the tie you wear, as striped ties, depending on their colors, may well depict membership in a private club or school. Laced shoes rather than loafers are worn in business. Women who wish to be taken seriously in business need to dress accordingly—that is, stylish but conservative. Low necklines, short skirts, or slacks are inappropriate forms of attire. Jewelry should be simple and elegant.

Cultural Cautions

DO'S

- Good manners are essential for doing good business in the UK. Say "please" and "thank you" as often as is appropriate. Remove hats when entering a building.
- British English is different from American English, so be prepared to modify your language accordingly. The British will often not understand American idioms.
- Be prepared for invitations and dress properly for the occasion. British entertain readily and often rather formally. Certain events involve certain dress codes. Check with the concierge at your hotel if uncertain.

DON'TS

- Persons from Scotland are Scots or Scotsmen, not Scotch or Scotchmen.
- Avoid talking about politics, royal gossip, and religion.
- Don't question the British assumption that British television is the best in the world. (Better yet, avoid any behavior indicating that British moral superiority is questionable.)
- Don't stare at someone in public. Privacy is highly respected in the UK.
- Never barge your way into the middle of a line of people.
- When addressing a group in Wales, avoid rubbing your nose, standing with your hands in your pocket, or shuffling your feet.
- Upon meeting the Queen of England, do not speak to her first. She must speak to you first. Wait until the Queen extends her hand to you and never initiate the greeting on your own.
- Nothing is a bigger turn off to businesspeople than continuing to discuss business over drinks and dinner.

CUSTOMS

- The British are subtle and less straightforward than are those from many other Western cultures. They are reluctant to be direct for fear of offending anyone.
- Loud conversations in public are looked down upon.
- The Loyal Toast is an important ritual throughout the UK. At the end of a dinner party, Port is always served. Traditionally, it is passed to the left and guests serve themselves. (If you don't drink Port, fill your glass with water.) When everyone is served the host/hostess will make a brief after-dinner speech at the end of which all guests raise their glasses and speak the words "The Queen" before sipping.

OBSERVATIONS

- It is important not to confuse the names Great Britain and the United Kingdom. Great Britain refers only to England, Scotland, and Wales. The United Kingdom also includes Northern Ireland.
- If you are going to smoke, always offer a cigarette to others in your group before smoking.
- Men should always cross their legs at the knees; women usually cross their legs at the ankles.
- Women in business do encounter a few obstacles while entertaining. British men are somewhat embarrassed about having a woman pick up the check. Women should make arrangements in advance with the maitre'd on how the bill is to be paid to avoid embarrassing her guests.

NEGOTIATIONS

- The British can be extremely tough negotiators, so be prepared.
- Bringing an attorney too early into negotiations is a sign of distrust.
- Be well prepared and able to answer direct questions about your product and your proposal.
- Oral agreements followed by a handshake are legally binding if entered into with a British executive empowered to make a deal. Legally, written agreements confirm those made orally and are usually in broad outline form. Only major agreements receive full legal attention and result in complex documents.

Legal

Legal System

England and Wales England and Wales have common law jurisdiction subject to the supremacy of the European Court of Justice.

Scotland Part of the UK, Scotland is developing to match economic and social changes, drawing influence from the Canon and Roman law as practiced by the Italians, Dutch, and French.

Intellectual Property Rights

Trademarks Both trade and service marks may be protected by registration in the UK under the Trade Marks Act 1994. Registration gives the proprietor the exclusive right to use the mark in relation to the goods for which the mark is registered. That right will be infringed by any other person who, without permission, uses the same or a confusingly similar mark in relation to the same goods or services. To be protected, either mark must be registered at the Patents Office. The duration is seven years initially and 14 years for successive applications. The registration process takes about 12 months. Registration is not a prerequisite for protection, and not all trade marks are registrable. Common law rights in marks can be acquired through use. Their use by third parties can be prevented by means of an action for 'passing off.'

Copyright An original literary, dramatic or artistic work is protected by statute from the date of creation for the life of the author plus 50 years (but as a result of an EC Directive currently being implemented this period is being extended to 70 years). Computer programs are also protected by copyright. There is no need for registration to obtain copyright protection other than for registered designs.

Patents Applications for the grant of a patent are made to the Patent Office in London and must satisfy criteria of being both novel and capable of industrial or agricultural use. If granted, a patent will last for 20 years. As a piece of incorporeal moveable property, a patent may be sold or licensed, and can be used as security for a loan. If rights protected by a patent are infringed, the holder may obtain a remedy by way of interdict and/or damages or payment of profits. He may also seek delivery or destruction of any items which infringe the patent. Registration is slow but is effective from the date of application.

Business Registration

England and Wales An overseas corporation establishing a place of business or a branch must register with the Registrar of Companies within one month of commencing business. There are ongoing filing requirements. Information provided to the Registrar of Companies is public information. The costs of registering a place of business are small (and principally involve legal fees). A branch or place of business with employees must also register with the Income Tax and Social Security Authorities.

Scotland A company incorporated outside Great Britain establishing a place of business in Scotland must comply with the national and European registration requirements. Company and branch particulars must be submitted to the Register of Companies in Edinburgh within one month of the opening.

Contracts and Dispute Resolution

A contractual document is generally considered to contain all terms and conditions of the agreement. Arbitration is gaining popularity, as it is seen as a cheaper, faster, and more satisfactory method of dispute resolution than court action. Many contracts with overseas parties appoint an arbitration body and rules to deal with disputes. In any dispute the loser will usually be ordered to pay the winner's costs.

England and Wales Companies do not hesitate to sue if an informal approach to a dispute fails.

Scotland Litigation is viewed as a last resort; parties generally make great effort to resolve disputes informally.

Notaries

England and Wales No laws require notarization of documents, and notaries are not widely used.

Scotland Notaries frequently attest and authenticate powers of attorney to be used abroad, as required by many foreign legal systems.

Labor

Employees who satisfy certain requirements are given the right not to be "unfairly dismissed" by their employers. Statutes also gives most employees who have been dismissed by reason of redundancy after being employed for at least two years the right to a redundancy payment from the employer. The law provides broad protections to workers. Foreign workers require work permits. A permit is granted only for a specific job with a specific employer; no change of employment (which includes taking a different job because of a transfer or promotion) is permitted without approval of the Department of Employment. Some foreign employees may need a visa before entering the UK. Application for an employment visa is made to UK government representatives in the country of departure.

Sources: For the UK, Radcliffes & Co., London. For Scotland, Gray & Connochie, Aberdeen

Legal Matters

LEGAL BRIEFS

- **Jurisdiction** The Brussels convention of September 27, 1968, has been ratified and its rules of jurisdiction are enforced in the district of Scotland. The Court of Session has the power to determine questions relating to heritable or moveable property situated in Scotland (including intellectual property requiring registration).

- **Legislation** Despite having its own legal system, Scotland's statutes tend to emanate from the UK parliament in London. These in turn may be superseded by EU legislation, which is frequently the case in the spheres of employment and sex discrimination in particular. Recent developments have been swift and far reaching, requiring constant awareness of new law from a number of sources.

- **Young persons** The age of legal capacity in Scotland is now 16 years. However, a person under the age of 21 years may apply to the court in order to set aside a transaction which was entered into between the ages of 16 and 18, if it was considered prejudicial to him. Ratification of a transaction upon reaching the age of 18 years will preclude any such applications.

- **Authentication** Although notaries are not much used in England, certain matters must however be authenticated and/or sworn before a solicitor or other appropriate legal officer.

- **Registration** A branch or place of business with employees must also register with the Income Tax and Social Security Authorities, but there is no general system of licensing.

- **Different areas** Laws may be wildly different depending on which area of the United Kingdom you are in.

- **Contracts** Because contracts tend to be lengthy and detailed, many common words and phrases whose meanings are universally understood are included in each one.

- **Remedies** Courts will generally award damages rather than specific performance of a contract except in cases where damages are not an adequate remedy. Injunctions, especially those granted before the full hearing of a dispute takes place, are an increasingly valuable and relatively quick remedy in appropriate cases.

LEGAL CONTACTS

Radcliffes & Co.
5 Great College Street
London SW1P 3SJ
Tel: (171) 222-7040
Fax: (171) 222-6208

Gray & Connochie
106-108 Crown Street
Aberdeen AB9 1BF
Tel: (1224) 586-201
Fax: (1224) 575-098

Baker & McKenzie
Aldwych House
Aldwych
London WC2B 4JP
Tel: (171) 242-6531
Fax: (171) 831-8611

Clifford Chance
200 Aldersgate Street
London EC1A 4JJ
Tel: (171) 600-1000
Fax: (171) 600-5555

Fox and Gibbons
2 Old Burlington Street
London W1X 2QA
Tel: (171) 439-8271
Fax: (171) 734-8843

Stephenson Harwood
One, St. Paul's Churchyard
London EC4M 8SH
Tel: (171) 329-4422
Fax: (171) 606-0822

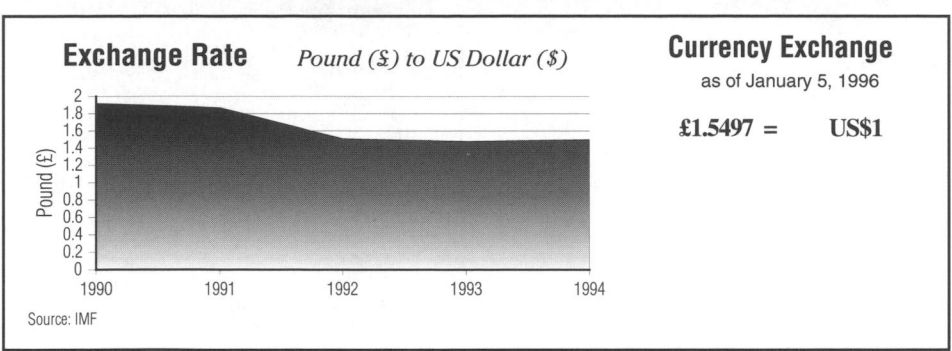

Exchange Rate *Pound (£) to US Dollar ($)*

Pound (£): 2, 1.8, 1.6, 1.4, 1.2, 1, 0.8, 0.6, 0.4, 0.2

1990   1991   1992   1993   1994

Source: IMF

Currency Exchange
as of January 5, 1996

£1.5497 =   US$1

Currency

The currency of the United Kingdom is the pound sterling (£), which is divided into 100 pence (p).

Foreign Exchange

Spot and forward exchange rates are determined based on supply and demand conditions, although the authorities may intervene in the event of undue fluctuations in the exchange rate. Banks may accept foreign currency deposits without restriction and are permitted to offer foreign exchange to both residents and nonresidents at free market rates. The UK has a large foreign exchange market, and there are no restrictions on the amount of foreign currency which is available. The financial market is transparent and flexible, and the financial institutions are sound. Queuing for foreign exchange is unnecessary.

Capital Transfers

There are no restrictions on inward or outward investments, and transfers of profits, payments of dividends, loan principal and interest, and royalties are unlimited. Capital may be repatriated freely. Repatriation of earnings is not restricted.There are no restrictions on capital transfers by either residents or nonresidents.

Investment Incentives

The UK does not discriminate between nationals and foreigners in the formation and operation of British companies. Financial assistance to a maximum of 25 percent of eligible costs may be granted for exceptional projects which meet certain criteria. Special incentives are available for investment in "assisted areas" which are considered to be in need of new industry to revitalize their economies. These incentives consist of Regional Selective Assistance, Regional Enterprise Grants (for firms with fewer than 25 employees), and Central Government Subsidized Rent, which grants free rent periods.

Investment Restrictions

Restrictions are few, though the government does have the power to prohibit the takeover by nonresidents of certain manufacturing operations which might be vital to national interests.

TAXATION

Taxation requires sophisticated knowledge of complex rules and regulations specific to each country. For more detailed information we suggest you refer to the Ernst & Young Corporate Tax Guide and Directory, available from the Ernst & Young accounting office in your country, or from:

Ernst & Young
Becket House
1 Lambeth Palace Road
London SE1 7EU
England
Tel: (171) 928 2000
Cable: Ernstaudit, London, SE1
Telex: 885234 Ans be ERNS LO G
Fax: (171) 928 1345

- The Foreign Income Dividend (FID) permits UK companies to specify that some dividends be paid out of foreign income.
- Resident companies are subject to corporate tax on worldwide profits. Foreign taxes may be credited against the corporate tax imposed on the same profits. There are numerous tax treaties in place to protect foreign nationals against double taxation.

At a Glance

Corporate Income Tax Rate (%)(a)	33
Capital Gains Tax Rate (%)(b)	33
Branch Tax Rate (%)	33
Withholding Tax (%)	
Dividends (c)	0
Interest (d)	25
Royalties from Patents, Know-how, etc. (e)	25
Branch Remittance Tax	0
Net Operating Losses (Years)	
Carryback	3
Carryforward	Unlimited

(a) A small companies rate of 25% may apply if taxable profits are less than 300,000 Pounds Sterling. Rules are in force to prevent businesses from taking advantage of this rate by fragmenting into smaller companies.
(b) Capital gains are subject to tax at the standard corporate tax rate. Capital gains tax is generally not levied on nonresidents.
(c) Advance corporate tax at 20/80 is payable. The UK's partial imputation system of corporate tax specifies that a company making a distribution must pay 20/80 of the distribution as advance corporation tax, which is offset against the tax liability for the accounting period in which the distribution is paid.
(d) This rate applies to payments to residents other than banks, and to nonresidents.
(e) This rate applies to payments to residents and nonresidents.

Money Matters
BITS AND PIECES

- **Screening** The UK does not operate any investment screening mechanisms.
- **Local participation** There are no requirements for joint ventures or local management participation or control.
- **Reciprocity** In the financial services sector the government can restrict or prohibit investment from foreigners whose governments do not offer national treatment of UK persons and businesses.
- **Expropriation** Expropriation is alien to UK traditions and there is no established practice relating to the grant of compensation. Nationalization requires an act of parliament.
- **Special incentives** To attract investment to the Development Areas where new industries and additional employment are needed, the government has programs providing special graduated benefits, such as grants toward capital expenditures on new premises and on capital equipment, tax allowances, training assistance, and special wage premiums.
- **Tax treaties** A comprehensive series of tax treaties protects a foreign national against double taxation.
- **Credit** Foreign investors are able to obtain credit in the local market at normal market terms, and a wide range of credit instruments are available to all investors, domestic and foreign alike.
- **Gold** Gold bullion and gold coins are not subject to any type of control. Gold sovereigns and Britannias are considered legal tender but do not circulate. There is a free gold market in London in which gold bars are freely traded.

BANKS

ANZ Grindlays Bank PLC
Minerva House
POB 7
Montague Close
London SE1 9DH
Tel: (171) 378-2121

Bank of England
Threadneedle Street
London EC2V 8DQ
Tel: (171) 601-4444

Citibank, NA
Cottons Centre
Hay's Lane
POB 199
London SE1 2QT
Tel: (171) 234-5678
Fax: (171) 234-2398

Lloyds Bank PLC
71 Lombard Street
London EC3P 8JH
Tel: (171) 626-1500
Telex: 888301

Midland Bank PLC
27 Poultry
London EC2P 2BX
Tel: (171) 260-8000
Telex: 8811822

National Westminster Bank PLC
41 Lothbury
London EC2P 2BP
Tel: (171) 726-1000
Telex: 888388

Standard Chartered PLC
1 Aldermanbury Square
London EC2V 7SB
Tel: (171) 280-7500
Telex: 885951

Bank of America International Ltd.
1 Watling Street
POB 262
London EC4P 4BX
Tel: (171) 634-4000
Telex: 884552

West Merchant Bank Ltd.
33-36 Gracechurch Street
London EC3V 0AX
Tel: (171) 623-8711
Fax: (171) 626-1610

Business Travel

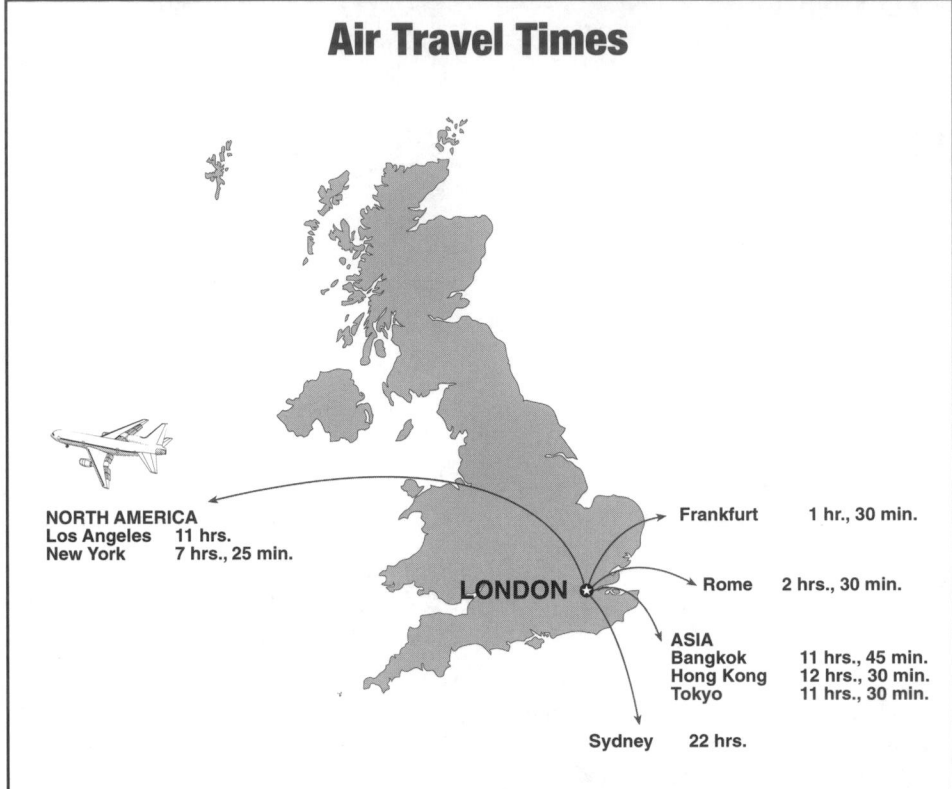

Air Travel Times

NORTH AMERICA
Los Angeles   11 hrs.
New York   7 hrs., 25 min.

LONDON

Frankfurt   1 hr., 30 min.

Rome   2 hrs., 30 min.

ASIA
Bangkok   11 hrs., 45 min.
Hong Kong   12 hrs., 30 min.
Tokyo   11 hrs., 30 min.

Sydney   22 hrs.

COMMUNICATIONS

Telephones   The phone system in Britain is excellent. If calling from a pay phone wait for the other party to answer before depositing coins.

Fax   Fax machines are available in most offices, large hotels, and post offices. All telegrams are subject to a 15 percent VAT charge.

Post office   Stamps are only sold at post offices, where lines are frequently long. There are 2 classes of letters, first and second class. Letters under 20g that are sent to Europe from England automatically go air mail.

TV/Radio   The BBC is the largest broadcasting system in Britain, with two television and five radio stations, and is owned by the government.

BEST TRAVEL BOOKS

Do's and Taboo's Around the World. The Bestselling Guide to International Behavior. Edited by Roger Axtell, compiled by the Parker Pen Company. The ultimate guide to international behavior, now completely updated and expanded. Helpful, fun to read!

Berlitz Business Travel Guide, Europe. Concise economic details, successful trip planning, background information on people and cities, useful facts and addresses.

USEFUL TELEPHONE NUMBERS

If you are calling from outside the UK, you will need to add the country code [44] and any other international dialing requirements from within your country.

- Emergency 999
- Time 123
- International Operator 0051
- London Taxi ....(171) 286-6010
- US Embassy ....(171) 499-9000
- Fax ....(171) 409-1637
- Immigration Department ....(181) 686-0688
- British Tourist Office ....(171) 849-9000
- Foreign and Commonwealth Office..(171) 233-3000
- British Airways.................................(181) 759-2525
- United Airlines ....(181) 990-9900
- DX Express/Birmingham ....(121) 454-2479
- Citadel Couriers/Edinburgh ....(131) 228-2800
- QED Messenger/Glasgow................(141) 248-2440
- A to Z Messenger/ London...............(171) 254-2000
- British Chambers of Commerce ....(171) 240-5831
- Scottish Chambers of Commerce ....(141) 204-2121
- British Overseas Trade Board..........(171) 215-5365
- Department of Trade ....(171) 215-7877
- Industry Department for Scotland ....(141) 221-9833
- Focus Information Services..............(171) 937-0050
- Customs and Excise ....(171) 620-1313

Credit Card Information

Lost or stolen credit cards (call collect to the US, regardless of which country the card was issued in).

- Amex ....[1] (919) 333-3211
- Diner's Club................................[1] (303) 799-1504
- MasterCard ....[1] (314) 275-6690
- Visa ....[1] (410) 581-7931

Travelogue

WORKWEEK

Government   Monday-Friday 10:00 am to 1:00 pm, 2:00 pm to 5:00 pm.
Business   Monday-Friday 9:00 am to 5:00 pm.
Banks   England and Wales: Monday-Friday 9:30 am to 3:30 pm. Scotland: Open to 7:00 pm on Thursdays.
Retail   Monday-Saturday 9:00 am to 5:30 pm.
Post Office   Monday-Saturday 9:00 am to 8:00 pm.

HOLIDAYS

Holidays 1996
January 1 New Year's Day
April 5 Good Friday*
April 8 Easter Bank Holiday*
May 1 May Day
May 27 Spring Holiday
August 26 Summer Bank Holiday
December 25 Christmas Day
December 26 Boxing Day*
*Dates vary each year. Regional holidays exist.

VISA AND PASSPORT

Anyone entering the United Kingdom must have a valid passport. No visas or entry permits are required for stays up to six months. If the visitor's stay exceeds three months, anyone over 16 years of age should register with the local British police. In London, you are required to register at the Aliens Registration Office. Regulations are currently undergoing proposals for change which may restrict foreign nationals from residing in the United Kingdom. Contact the nearest British consulate to inquire about work permits.

DEPARTURE FORMALITIES

There are no departure formalities for the United Kingdom. There are no restrictions regarding currency.

IMMUNIZATION

No immunizations are required. For pets and livestock there are strict quarantine restrictions. No inoculations are necessary unless coming from an infected area.

TIPPING

10 percent for taxi drivers. Hotel and restaurant bills generally include VAT and service, but it's nice to ask. If tip is not included, waiters get 15 percent. Hotel porters: 50p per bag. Hairdressers: 10 percent.

CRIME

Incidents of violent crime are usually low and firearms are strictly controlled. Report the theft of a passport immediately to the local police or the nearest embassy. Political demonstrations are generally peaceful but there are incidents of terrorism related to the political conflict with Northern Ireland. A current cease-fire remains in effect.

INFRASTRUCTURE

The UK is a center for international travel. Tourist facilities throughout the United Kingdom are well developed, including luxury accommodations. Foreign investment is encouraged and British participation is not required. There are now three international airports near London. Use the Tube (underground subway) for the quickest transportation to central London. Airline buses, double-decker buses, and taxis are also available to London. An extensive rail system, operated by British Rail, connects all parts of the United Kingdom. The Chunnel is now in operation connecting England and France. In urban centers, taxis can be hailed from the curb or hired by telephone. In general public transportation is excellent.

TOURIST OFFICE

London Tourist Board and Convention Bureau
26 Grosvenor Gardens
London SW1
Tel: (171) 730-3488

GOVERNMENT AGENCIES

British Overseas Trade Board
Kingsgate House
66-74 Victoria Street
London SW1E 6SN
Tel: (171) 215-5000

Department of Trade and Industry
London House
19 Old Court Place
London W8 4PF
Tel: (171) 215-2501
Fax: (171) 215-8451

Department of Trade and Industry
123 Victoria Street
London SW1H 0NN
Tel: (171) 215-5000

Consumer Affairs Division 1A
Department of Trade and Industry
10-18 Victoria Street
London SW1H ONN
Tel: (171) 215-3258

Central Office of Information
Hercules Road
London SE1 7DU
Tel: (171) 928-2345

Central Statistical Office
Great George Street
London SW1P 3AQ
Tel: (171) 270-3000

Department of Employment
Caxton House
12 Tothill Street
London SW1H 9NA
Tel: (171) 273-3000

Department of the Environment
2 Marsham Street
London SW1P 3EB
Tel: (171) 276-0900, 276-3000

Department of Health
Richmond House
79 Whitehall
London SW1
Tel: (181) 066-5544

Consumer Affairs Division 1A
Department of Trade and Industry
10-18 Victoria Street
London SW1H ONN
Tel: (171) 215-3258

Patent and Trademarks Office
Hazlitt House
45 Southhampton Buildings
London WC2A 1AR
Tel: (171) 438-4726

The House of Commons
Houses of Parliament
London SW1A 0AA
Tel: (171) 219-3000

Ministry of Agriculture, Fisheries and Food
Whitehall Place
London SW1A 2HH
Tel: (171) 270-3000
Fax: (171) 270-8125

Department of Transport
2 Marsham Street
London SW1P 3EB
Tel: (171) 276-3000
Fax: (171) 276-0818

HM Customs and Excise
New King's Beam House
22 Upper Ground
London SE1 9PJ
Tel: (171) 620-1313

Board of Inland Revenue
Somerset House
London WC2R 1LB
Tel: (171) 438-6622

Associated British Ports
150 Holborn
London EC1N 2LR
Tel: (171) 486-6621
Telex: 23913

British Ports Federation
Victoria House, Vernon Place, 7th Floor
London WC1B 4LL
Tel: (171) 242-1200
Telex: 295741

British Railways Board
PO Box 100
Euston House
24 Eversholt Street
London NW1 1DZ
Tel: (171) 928-5151
Fax: (171) 922-6994

British Telecommunication Plc.
81 Newgate street
London EC1A 7AJ

British Waterways Board
Greycaine Road
Watford
Herts WDZ 45R
Tel: (923) 226422
Fax: (923) 226081

Forestry Commission
231 Corstorphine Road
Edinburgh EH12 7AT
Tel: (131) 334-0303
Fax: (131) 334-3047

Office of Population Censuses and Surveys
Head Office, St. Catherines House
10 Kingsway
London WC2B 6JP
Tel: (171) 242-0262
Fax: (171) 242-0262, 242-2167

Office of Telecommunications
Export House
Ludgate Hill
London EC4M 7JJ
Tel: (171) 822-1600
Fax: (171) 822-1643

Public Record Office
Ruskin Avenue
Kew, Richmond
Surrey TW94DU
Tel: (81) 876-3444
Fax: (81) 878-8905

Radiotelecommunications Agency
Waterloo Bridge House
Waterloo Road
London SE1 8UA
Tel: (171) 215-5000
Fax: (171) 928-5746

Water Services Association
1 Queen Anne's Gate
London SW1H 9BT
Tel: (171) 222-8111
Telex: 918518

WORLD TRADE CENTERS

Cardiff World Trade Center, Wales
Cardiff International Arena, Mary Ann Street
Cardiff, CF1 2EQ
Tel: (1222) 234-900
Fax: (1222) 234-901

World Trade Centre Liverpool
Brunswick Enterprise Center
Brunswick Business Park
Liverpool L3 4BD
Tel: (151) 709-4759, 707-2756
Fax: (151) 709-2843

BUSINESS AND TRADE ORGANIZATIONS

British Standards Institution
Linford Wood
Milton Keynes
Buckinghamshire MK14 6LE
Tel: (190) 822-0022

REMEMBER
- When you telephone (or fax) to the United Kingdom from another country you must always include the country code [44] before the numbers given.
- When you send mail to the United Kingdom, be sure to write UNITED KINGDOM or UK in capital letters on its own line below the addresses given.

Confederation of British Industry
Centre Point
103 New Oxford Street
London WC1A 1DU
Tel: (171) 379-7400

Office of Fair Trading
Field House, Bream's Buildings
London EC4A 1PR
Tel: (171) 242-2858
Fax: (171) 268-8800

British Exporters Association
16 Dartmouth St.
London, SW1H 9BL
Tel: (171) 222-5419

Institute of Export
64 Clifton St.
London, EC2A 4HB
Tel: (171) 247-9812
Fax: (171) 377-5343

Aluminum Federation
Broadway House, Calthorpe Rd.
Five Ways
Birmingham, B15 1TN
Tel: (121) 456-1103
Fax: (121) 456-2274

Association of the British Pharmaceutical Industry
12 Whitehall
London SW1A 2DY
Tel: (171) 930-3477
Fax: (171) 930-3290

Brewers' Society
42 Portman Sq.
London W1H 0BB
Tel: (171) 486-4831
Fax: (171) 935-3991

British Clothing Industry Association
British Apparel and Textiles Centre
7 Swallow Place
Oxford Circus
London W1R 7AA
Tel: (171)408-0020
Fax: (171) 493-6276
Telex: 25149

British Footwear Manufacturers Federation
Royalty House
72 Dean St.
London W1V 5HB
Tel: (171) 437-5573
Fax: (171) 494-1300

British Printing Industries Federation
11 Bedford Row
London WC1R 4DX
Tel: (171) 242-6904
Fax: (171) 405-7784

Dairy Trade Federation
19 Cornwall Terrace
London NW1 4QP
Tel: (171) 486-7244
Fax: (171) 487-4734
Telex: 262027

Food and Drink Federation
6 Catherine St.
London, WC2B 5JJ
Tel: (171) 836-2460
Fax: (171) 836-0580
Telex: 299388

Glass and Glazing Federation
44-48 Borough High St.
London SE1 1XB
Tel: (171) 403-7177
Fax: (171) 357-7458

Producers Alliance for Cinema and Television (PACT)
Gordon House, Greencoat Place
London SW1P 1PH
Tel: (171) 233-6000
Fax: (171) 233-8935

Society of Motor Manufacturers and Traders
Forbes House, Halkin St.
London SW1X 7DS
Tel: (171) 235-7000
Fax: (171) 235-7112
Telex: 21628

The Sugar Bureau
Duncan House, Dolphin Sq.
London, SW1V 3PW
Tel: (171) 828-9465

Timber Trade Federation
Clareville House 26-27
Oxendon St.
London, SW1Y 4EL
Tel: (171) 839-1891
Fax: (171) 930-0094

United Kingdom Petroleum Industry Association
9 Kingsway
London, WC2B 6XH
Tel: (171) 240-0289
Fax: (171) 379-3102

Leather Producers' Association
Leather Trade House
King's Park Rd., Moulton Park
Northampton, NN3 1JD
Tel: (1604) 494131
Fax: (1604) 648220
Telex: 317124

National Metal Traders Federation
Fleming House
Renfrew St.
Glasgow, G3 6TG
Tel: (41) 332-0826
Telex: 779433

British Furniture Manufacturers Association
30 Harcourt St.
London, W1H 2AA
Tel: (171) 724-0854

British Hospitality Association
40 Duke St.
London, W1M 6HR
Tel: (171) 499-6641
Fax: (171) 355-4596
Telex: 296619

CHAMBERS OF COMMERCE

American Chamber of Commerce in the UK
75 Brook Street
London W1Y 2EB
Tel: (171) 493-0381

Association of British Chambers of Commerce
9 Tufton Street
London SW1P 3QB
Tel: (171) 222-1555

British American Chamber of Commerce
8 Staple Inn, Holborn
London WC1V 7QH
Tel: (171) 404-6400
Fax: (171) 404-6828

International Chamber of Commerce
14-15 Belgrave Square
London SW1X 8PS
Tel: (171) 823-2811

The Developing Countries Trade Agency (DECTA)
Bank House, Sutton Court Rd.
Sutton, Surrey, SM1 4SP
Tel: (181) 643-3311
Telex: 948116 Fax: (081) 643-8030

London Chamber of Commerce and Industry
Swan House, Queen St.
London, EC4
Tel: (171) 248-4444
Fax: (171) 489-0391
Telex: 888941

NEWSPAPERS

The Guardian
119 Farringdon Road
London EC1R 3ER
Tel: (171) 278-2332
Fax: (171) 837-2114

The Independent
40 City Road
London EC1Y 2DB
Tel: (171) 253-1222
Fax: (171) 956-1431

The Observer
Chelsea Bridge House
Queenstown Road
Battersea, London SW8 4NN
Tel: (171) 627-0700
Telex: 888963

The Sun
1 Pennington Street
Wapping, London E1 9BD
Tel: (171) 782-4000
Telex: 267827

The Times
1 Pennington Street
Wapping, London E1 9XN
Tel: (171) 782-5000
Fax: (171) 488-3242

Newspaper Publishers' Association
34 Southwark Bridge road
London SE1 9EU
Tel: (171) 928-6928
Fax: (171) 928-2067

BUSINESS PERIODICALS

The Banker (Monthly)
FT Business Information Ltd.
Greystoke Place
Fetter Lane
London EC4A 1ND
Tel: (171) 405-6969

Direct Marketing International (Monthly)
Detailextra Ltd.
3 Bridgefoot
Market Deeping
Peterborough PE6 8AA
Tel: (1778) 380065
Fax: (1778) 380075

Direct Marketing World
Charterhouse Communications Ltd.
Boundary House
91-93 Charterhouse Street
London EC1N 6HR
Tel: (171) 250-0649
Fax: (171) 250-0637

Direct Response Magazine
P.R. Magazines Ltd.
4 Market Place
Hertford SG14 1EB
Tel: (1992) 501177
Fax: (1992) 500387

The Economist
25 St. James's Street
London SW1A 1HG
Tel: (171) 839-7000
Telex: 24344

Euromoney
Nestor House
Playhouse Yard
London EC4V 5EX
Tel: (171) 779-8888
Fax: (171) 779-8506

Investors Chronicle
Greystoke Place
Fetter Lane
London EC4A 1ND
Tel: (171) 405-6969
Fax: (171) 405-5276

Management Today
22 Lancaster Gate
London W2 3LY
Tel: (171) 413-4566
Fax: (171) 413-4138

Precision Marketing
Centaur Communications Ltd.
St. Giles House

50 Poland Street
London W1V 4AX
Tel: (171) 494-0300
Fax: (171) 287-9715

Accountancy Age.
32-34 Broadwick St.
London, W1A 2HG
Tel: (171) 439-4242
Fax: (171) 437-7001
Telex: 23918

Campaign
Haymarket Publications Ltd.
30 Lancaster Gate
London, W2 3LY
Tel: (171) 413-4036
Fax: (171) 652-3122
Telex: 8954052

Computer Weekly
Reed Business Publishing Ltd.
Quadrant House, The Quadrant
Sutton, Surrey, SM2 5AS
Tel: (181) 652-3122
Fax: (181) 652-4695

Computing
NU Publications
BV VNU House
32-34 Broadwick St.
London, W1A 2HG
Tel: (171) 439-4242
Fax: (171) 437-7001
Telex: 23918

Crops
Reed Farmers Publishing
Quadrant House, The Quadrant
Sutton, Surrey, SM2 5AS
Tel: (181) 652-4080
Fax: (181) 652-8928

Economic Journal
University of York
Heslington, York, Y01 5DD
Tel: (1904) 433575
Fax: (1904) 433433

Farmers Weekly
Reed Business Publishing Ltd.
Quadrant House, The Quadrant
Sutton, Surrey, SM2 5AS
Tel: (181) 652-4911
Fax: (181) 652-4005
Telex: 892084

What Personal Computer
33-39 Bowling Green Lane
London, EC1R 0DA
Tel: (171) 837-1212
Fax: (171) 833-9592

RADIO & TELEVISION STATIONS

Independent Television Commission
33 Foley Street
London W1P 7LB
Tel: (171) 255-3000

Radio Authority
Holbrook House
14 Great Queen Street
London WC2B 5DG
Tel: (171) 430-2724
Fax: (171) 405-7064

BBC
BBC Broadcasting House
London W1A 1AA
Tel: (171) 580-4468

INTERNET ADDRESSES

Usenet group(s):
soc.culture.uk
uk.events
UK Pages
http://www.neosoft.com/~dlgates/uk/ukindex.html
BBC Online
http://www.bbcnc.org.uk/
UK Guide
http://www.cs.ucl.ac.uk/misc/uk/intro.html
Foreign & Commonwealth Office
http://www.fco.gov.uk/
UK Department of Trade and Industry
http://www.dti.gov.uk/

United States

United States of America

Economy

Overview

An open, vibrant economic climate, an entrepreneurial spirit, and innovative manufacturing and industrial sectors have helped the US to become the most powerful economy in the world. As a country rich in resources it has focused on upgrading its broad industrial base and developing its highly sophisticated services sector to maintain its position as the world's largest economy. Although its markets are now maturing and growth rates in certain industries have slowed substantially, the US remains one of the world's most efficient markets, offering extensive opportunities to traders from all over the world.

Trade

The US is the world's leading nation in terms of the total value of foreign trade. Canada is its largest trading partner and the largest source of both its imports and exports, followed by Japan, Mexico, China, and Germany. The US suffers from a continual and widening trade deficit, but this is more the result of its relatively open market and a population that is highly receptive to imported goods than it is a result of poor export performance. In an effort to reverse its trade imbalance the government has placed increasing pressure on trading partners to allow greater access to American goods.

Sectors

Agriculture Although agriculture represents just over two percent of GDP, the US is the most productive agricultural economy in the world. Its agricultural industry is highly efficient, and relies to a large extent on modern mechanization. The US traditionally runs a trade surplus on agricultural products, exporting mainly oilseeds, vegetables, fruits and nuts, wheat, cotton, feed grains, and rice.

Industry Industry has been the foundation of the US's spectacular economic development over the past century. While production of low-tech consumer goods has suffered recently due to a lack of price competitiveness, manufacturing continues to thrive, and exports from this sector have increased by more than 100 percent in the past decade. The US benefits from a broad manufacturing and industrial base producing a variety of goods such as food products, transportation equipment, chemicals, industrial machinery, electrical equipment, petroleum, and coal. The economy is increasingly moving towards the production of high-tech products, particularly in the area of electronics and computer technology. US high-tech products are seen as industry leaders worldwide.

Services The US is increasingly becoming a service nation; this sector accounts for over 50 percent of the nation's GDP and employment. The US is the world's largest financial center and the provision of financial services is currently the economy's leading growth area. Other major sub-sectors include wholesale and retail trade, energy, communications services, and transportation.

Trends

Although its economy is experiencing relatively healthy growth, the US continues to run large trade and budget deficits. Recognizing the need to increase exports, the government is paying increasing attention to developing regional trade alliances. Still, import volumes are increasing at a faster rate than exports, providing excellent opportunities to sell to this affluent market. As overseas markets expand, export growth should accelerate accordingly.

At a Glance

THE COUNTRY

Location Central North America, between Mexico and Canada.
Terrain Varies widely from mountain ranges to coastal regions and large plains areas.
Climate Varies from cold and snow in the north to hot and humid in the southeast.

THE PEOPLE

Population 258,300,000
Ethnic composition
White.. 78%
African American 10%
Hispanic 8%
Other.. 4%
Religious composition About 80 percent of the population is Christian. A substantial number say they are not religious, and smaller groups follow religions such as: Judaism, Eastern Orthodox, Buddhism, Hinduism, and Islam.
Languages spoken There is no official language. English is the most common, especially in business and government, but a number of foreign languages are spoken in various areas.
Education and literacy Education is compulsory throughout the country through age 16. Colleges include junior or community colleges, offering two-year degrees, four-year colleges and universities, and graduate or professional schools.
Labor force
Total...129,500,000
By occupation: managerial/professional 27.1%; technical, sales, and administrative 30.9%; services 13.8%; manufacturing, mining, and transportation 25.5%; farming, fishing, and forestry 2.87%

COUNTRY FACTS

Political and legal The high legal body is the Supreme Court, appointed by the president and approved by the legislature. The courts are free from political pressure.
Telephone One of the most advanced telephone systems in the world. There are a number of long distance companies offering international service. Calls can be made from urban and rural areas. The country code is [1]; area codes can be obtained from an operator.
Transportation The United States claims to have the most sophisticated transportation systems in the world. There are a number of major airports with international service, high quality road systems, and several inland waterways.
Environment The government has passed much legislation to preserve the environment, including the Clean Air Act Amendments of 1970 and 1990, and the Endangered Species Act of 1973. Current issues include "acid rain," precipitation contaminated by fossil fuel wastes, and finding adequate facilities for solid waste disposal.
Media All electronic communications systems are privately owned but regulated by the Federal Communications Commission. Approximately 98 percent of all US households own at least one television set. Cable is also becoming quite powerful, with 57.6 million subscribers. There are 1,570 daily newspapers in the US.
Health Healthcare is among the most advanced in the world. The system is privatized, and services can be costly.

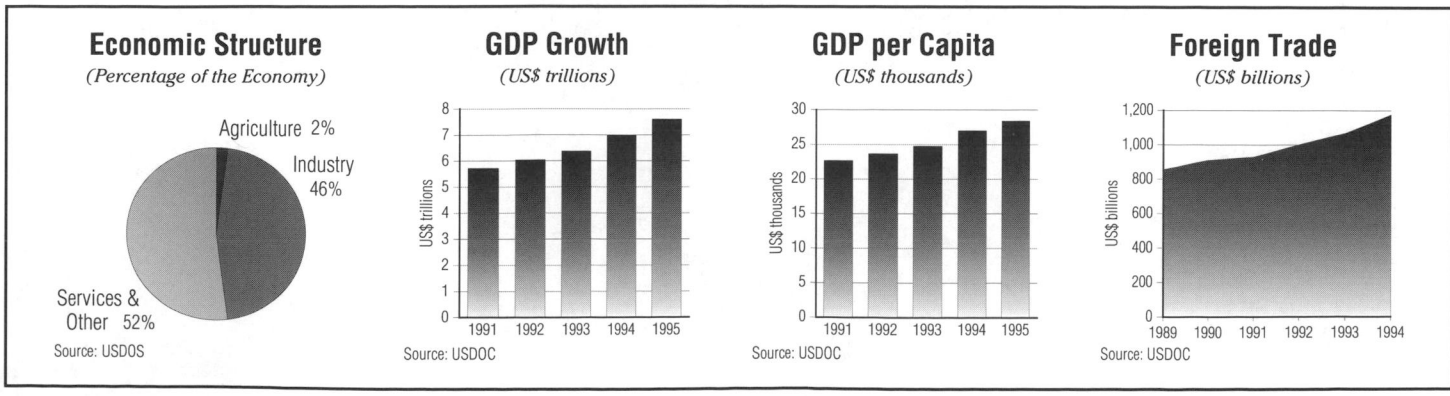

Economic Structure
(Percentage of the Economy)
Agriculture 2%
Industry 46%
Services & Other 52%
Source: USDOS

GDP Growth
(US$ trillions)
1991 1992 1993 1994 1995
Source: USDOC

GDP per Capita
(US$ thousands)
1991 1992 1993 1994 1995
Source: USDOC

Foreign Trade
(US$ billions)
1989 1990 1991 1992 1993 1994
Source: USDOC

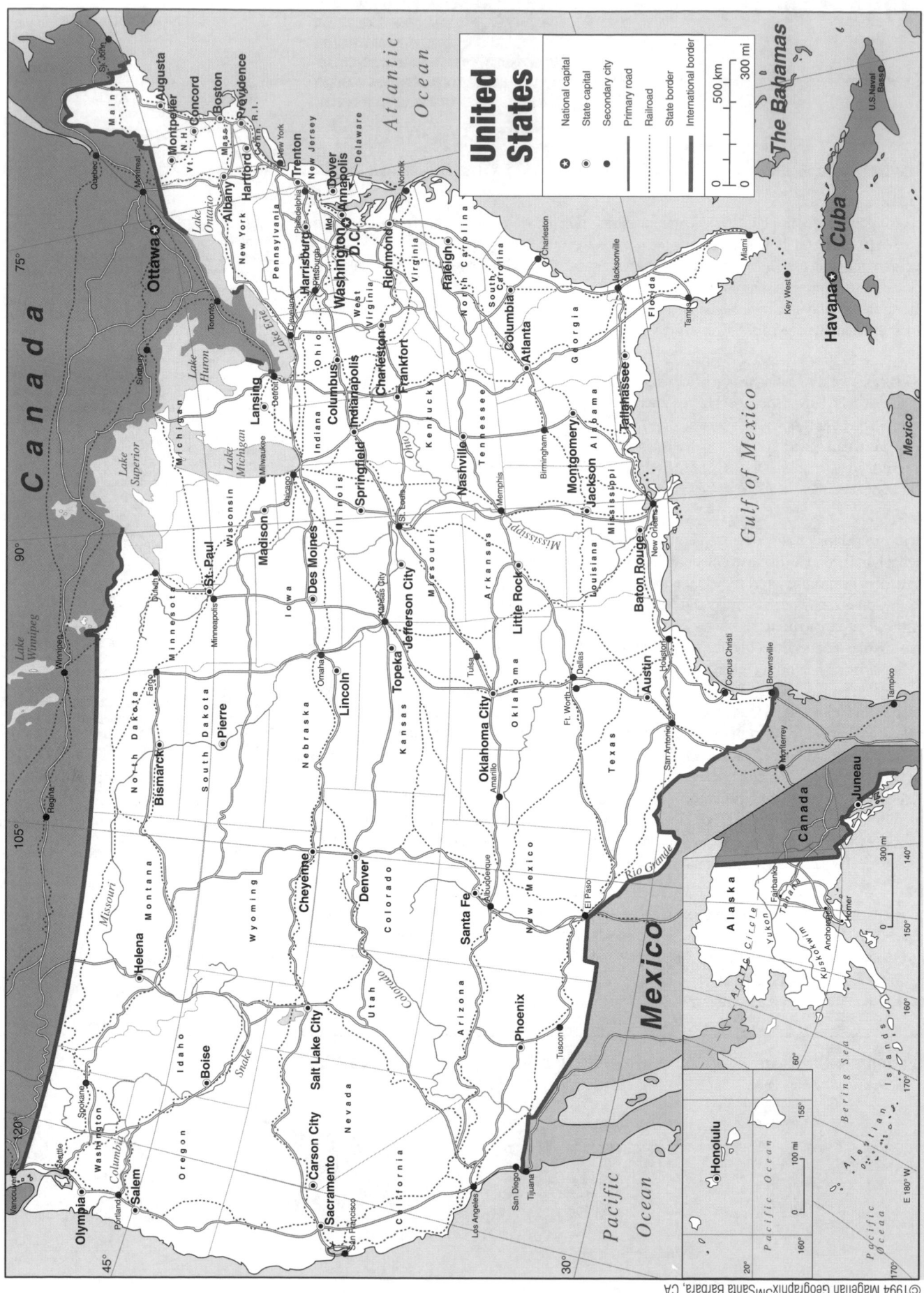

United States

⊕	National capital	
⊙	State capital	
•	Secondary city	
	Primary road	
	Railroad	
	State border	
	International border	

300 mi
500 km

Foreign Trade

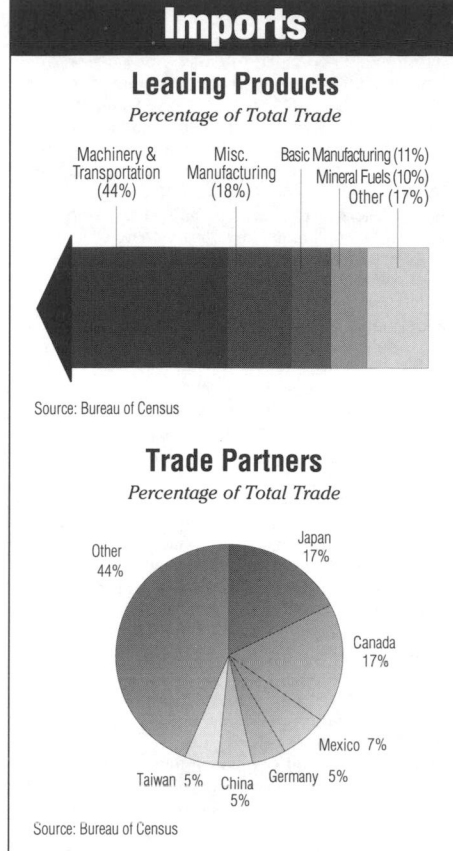

Imports

Leading Products
Percentage of Total Trade

Machinery & Transportation (44%)
Misc. Manufacturing (18%)
Basic Manufacturing (11%)
Mineral Fuels (10%)
Other (17%)

Source: Bureau of Census

Trade Partners
Percentage of Total Trade

Other 44%
Japan 17%
Canada 17%
Mexico 7%
Germany 5%
China 5%
Taiwan 5%

Source: Bureau of Census

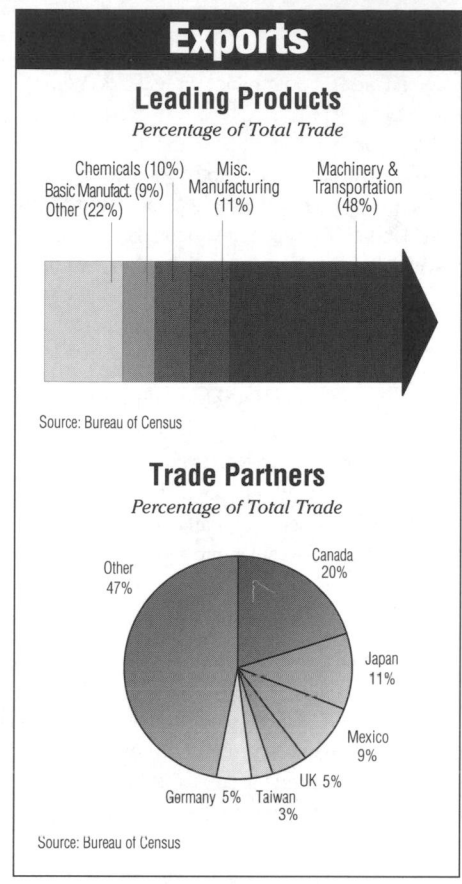

Exports

Leading Products
Percentage of Total Trade

Chemicals (10%)
Basic Manufact. (9%)
Other (22%)
Misc. Manufacturing (11%)
Machinery & Transportation (48%)

Source: Bureau of Census

Trade Partners
Percentage of Total Trade

Other 47%
Canada 20%
Japan 11%
Mexico 9%
UK 5%
Taiwan 3%
Germany 5%

Source: Bureau of Census

Opportunities

FOR IMPORTING TO THE USA

- clothing
- computer equipment
- construction materials and equipment
- environmental protection equipment
- food, especially ethnic foods, coffee, fish
- footwear
- furniture
- household appliances
- jewelry
- leather goods
- lubricants and fuels
- machine tools
- sporting and recreational goods
- stereos
- television sets
- toys
- vehicles and parts
- videocassette recorders

FOR EXPORTING FROM THE USA

- analytic and optical instruments
- clothing
- computer hardware, software, and peripherals
- electrical machinery
- electronic components
- environmental technologies and services
- food and beverages
- leather hides
- medical, surgical, and dental equipment
- metalworking equipment
- organic and inorganic chemicals
- paper and paperboard
- pharmaceuticals
- business consulting, engineering, financial, and legal services
- textiles
- vehicles and parts
- wood and lumber

GROWTH SECTORS

- business services
- construction services
- electronic information services
- energy resources
- financial services
- insurance
- high-technology products
- real estate development

GOVERNMENT PROCUREMENT

- chemicals and cleaning compounds
- clothing
- computers and office machines
- defense equipment and supplies
- electronic products and components
- furniture
- professional services
- scientific instruments
- vehicles and parts

Trade News

RULES AND REGULATIONS

- **Regulation** The US Customs Service, an agency within the Department of the Treasury, administers all regulations. Customs collects duties, taxes, and fees; administers some navigation laws and treaties; enforces inspection; protects against criminal trade; and oversees other government trade departments.

- **Import restrictions** The US is the world's largest importer of goods. However, any item deemed to adversely affect the US economy, security, consumer health and well-being, or domestic plant and animal life may be restricted. Restrictions include limits on the ports where products may enter, and product requirements. Many products must meet mandatory technical and safety standards.

- **Import quotas** Quotas are established by the US Congress, presidential proclamation, and agency directives, and enforced by US Customs. Quotas may refer to either absolute quantity of goods or to quantities of goods imported at reduced tariff rates.

- **Import licenses** Some products are not easily imported and need special licenses or permits. They include arms and armaments, alcoholic beverages, food, dairy products, vehicles, textiles, and toys.

- **Tariff rates** Tariff rates are assigned according to country of origin and the 10,000 product classifications in the Harmonized Tariff Schedule of the US (HTSUS). With the exception of preferential duties available as a result of specific treaties, the US applies tariffs on a nondiscriminatory basis for countries granted most-favored nation (MFN) status.

- **Export licensing** Licenses are needed for exports destined for places other than US territories or Canada. There are two types of licenses: (1) general licenses, for most goods; and (2) individual validated licenses (IVLs), for weapons, high-technology products that have the potential to be used against the US or its allies, and goods in short supply. The US Department of Commerce administers the licenses.

TRANSPORTATION FIRMS

A.W. Fenton Co., Inc.
6565 Eastland Road
Cleveland, OH 44124
Tel: (216) 243-5900
Fax: (216) 826-0515

Air Express Int'l
PO Box 1231
120 Tokeneke Road
Darien, CT 06820
Tel: (203) 655-7900
Fax: (203) 655-5779

Circle International
260 Townsend St.
San Francisco, CA 94107
Tel: (415) 978-0600

Global Transportation Services
7550 24th Ave. South, Suite 144
Minneapolis, MN 55450
Tel: (612) 727-1091
Fax: (612) 727-1428

Japan Freight Consolidators
1039 Hillcrest Blvd.
Inglewood, CA 90301
Tel: (213) 776-3160
Fax: (213) 215-0789

Panalpina, Inc.
Harborside Financial Center
Plaza Two, 34 Exchange Place
Jersey City, NJ 07302
Tel: (201)451-4000
Fax: (201) 451-8572

Yusen Air and Sea Service (USA), Inc.
60 East 42nd St. Rm. 1915
New York, NY 10165
Tel: (212) 983-1170
Fax: (212) 490-6497

Sea-Land Service, Inc.
PO Box 2555
Elizabeth, NJ 07207
Tel: (908) 603-2144
Fax: (908) 603-2831

Overview

US markets are extremely diverse, with demands ranging from raw materials to the most sophisticated products. Markets are increasingly splintered into regional and demographic sub-markets. While it is difficult to import some products into the US, the biggest marketing problem is the level of competition importers face once they get there. Foreign sellers should pay particular attention to the risk of product liability lawsuits, which are more common than elsewhere. Personal contact is helpful, but not critical, to building a commercial relationship in the United States. Due to the great distances separating major US cities, telephone contact is usually sufficient and, indeed, the United States is more oriented toward communication than transportation. A personal visit should be made once an ongoing and profitable relationship has been achieved.

Distribution

Marketing and distribution channels are not monolithic, centralized, nor federally regulated and are generally open to new entrants. Therefore, exporters to the United States can choose existing distribution channels or set up their own. By doing business through a US distributor a foreign seller can avoid the pitfalls from starting at the beginning of this tremendous and complex market. Nevertheless, there are alternatives to hiring an agent or distributor. Without establishing a single or defined channel a foreign seller may either: (1) bid on government projects or procurement contracts; (2) market directly to businesses or consumers; (3) exhibit at trade shows, fairs, or conventions; or (4) enter into a joint venture with a local company.

Agents, Distributors, and Partners

In the United States, the distribution of bulk commodities, capital goods, and consumer goods is handled through wholesale distributors. In contrast, motor vehicles and parts are distributed and sold primarily through each manufacturer's network of franchised dealers. Wholesalers or distributors are either merchant wholesalers who purchase goods and take full title to them, or commission wholesalers who function as agents or brokers, selling goods to which the supplier retains title and responsibility. Foreign sellers should weigh the advantages of dealing with wholesalers directly or using US agents or partners.

Selling Techniques

To sell successfully in the United States a comprehensive marketing plan is essential. This plan should consider the nature of the particular US market and its developing trends. Recently, marketing has moved from a nationwide approach toward customized regional and local plans. Exporters should note this trend and consider modifying their products for sale to specific regions or customer groups. Initial marketing efforts should concentrate on a specific market or region by establishing the product in the market, building long-term relationships with distributors and customers, and finally, achieving repeat sales before attempting to maximize profits. Test-marketing to a targeted group through US specialists can show the market potential of a product without a heavy investment. The exporter should consider alternative selling methods, such as telemarketing, direct sales through television shopping channels, and specialty catalog sales, all of which are rapidly gaining popularity. The marketing plan should include follow-up methods to measure the effectiveness of specific marketing efforts.

Advertising

Most advertisers conduct advertising through agencies. Large, full-service advertising agencies still dominate the business, but are experiencing increased competition from regional agencies and public relations firms. The first-time advertiser in US markets will find an overwhelming variety of advertising channels and methods. The traditional channels of periodicals, radio, and television have spawned numerous innovative alternatives on both national and local levels. Cable television and regional and specialty periodicals are becoming increasingly useful in reaching specially targeted audiences. Don't overlook the Internet; it is becoming the hot, new medium for businesses to advertise their goods.

Service and Customer Support

US businesses emphasize on-time delivery and try to adhere to the general principle of "no surprises," when at all possible. The trader should insure delivery on time, even if it requires the expense of a courier service. "No surprises" means that delays, mistakes, and other bad news should be communicated immediately to the other party; failure to do so will elevate irritation to anger. US vendors, as well as consumers, are demanding higher levels of customer support and product service. Foreign sellers to the United States should heed the fact that US business is intent on achieving what is termed "Total Quality Management."

Marketing in the United States

MARKETING TIPS

- **Deliver on time** Wholesale and retail customers attach much importance to on-time or early delivery. Do not promise what you cannot deliver, and make sure to deliver goods by the promised date and time.
- **Think segmentation** Market your products and services to segments of the national markets, such as regions, sub-populations, demographic groups, and "niche" (highly specialized) markets.
- **Be alert to increasing change and diversity** Institutions, buying habits, advertising channels—all are changing in the US. Markets are fragmenting, ethnic minorities are increasing in numbers and importance, and self-identified groups are proliferating.
- **Safety and quality standards** Imports into the US must satisfy some of the most stringent standards and regulations in the world. Additionally, US consumers are accustomed to choosing from the best and cheapest of the world's goods.
- **A litigious society** The US houses more lawyers and launches more suits than any other country—many of them product-related. Exporters to the US should pay particular attention to avoiding lawsuits by customers injured while using defective products.
- **Honesty** Foreign businesses should regard the US proverb, "Honesty is the best policy," as the accepted US business practice. Secret dealing or the offer of gifts, bribes, or special considerations will jeopardize business and government relations.
- **Pricing** Price competition is severe with commodity items. On the other hand, US consumers often regard imported luxury, specialty, or stylish goods as fashionable and high-quality, and will be less sensitive to price.
- **The US has many governments** Satisfying the Federal (national) laws and regulations is not sufficient; states and even cities are allowed to regulate business and to set taxes.
- **Maintenance** US consumers expect excellent maintenance and service of products. Indeed, the law imposes warranties in many instances requiring that products work as they are advertised or intended.

AD AGENCIES

Bates USA
The Chrysler Bldg.
405 Lexington Ave.
New York, NY 10174
Tel: (212) 297-7000 Fax: (212) 986-0270

Bozell Worldwide, Inc.
40 W. 23rd. St.
New York, NY 10010
Tel: (212) 727-5000 Fax: (212) 727-2436

Chiat/Day Inc. Advertising
340 Main St.
Venice, CA 90291
Tel: (310) 314-5000 Fax: (310) 396-1273

Grey Advertising Inc.
777 Third Ave.
New York, NY 10017
Tel: (212) 546-2000 Fax: (212) 546-1495

J. Walter Thompson Co.
466 Lexington Ave.
New York, NY 10017
Tel: (212) 210-7000 Fax: (212) 210-7066

Ogilvy & Mather Worldwide, Inc.
309 W. 49th St.
New York, NY
Tel: (212) 237-4000 Fax: (212) 237-5123

Young & Rubicam Inc.
285 Madison Ave.
New York, NY 10017
Tel: (212) 210-3000 Fax: (212) 490-9073

Saatchi & Saatchi
275 Hudson St.
New York, NY 10014-3620
Tel: (212) 463-2000 Fax: (212) 463-9855

Business Culture

Greetings and Courtesies

The US is the world's fourth largest country and its society is complex. In addition, many minority groups living throughout the country retain their own cultures. US businesspeople are generally outgoing and pleased with their high standard of living. However, one should be careful not to attach special importance to this geniality. Gestures and invitations that can signal intimacy in other cultures might be nothing more than someone "just being friendly." The accepted greeting is smiling, making eye contact, and shaking hands. Handshakes are generally firm and brief, with a rapid, simple up-and-down motion. Greetings can be followed by general questions about your trip, your health, or the weather. Such questions are a form of politeness. Long, detailed answers are not expected or especially wanted. After this quick, often superficial exchange, the next topic will be business.

Business Ethic and Framework

Individualism and a competitive spirit are highly valued. The individual is placed above the company, community, and even family; people are encouraged to think for themselves, act on their beliefs, and establish their own identity. However, being part of a team is also important. These apparent opposites are often reconciled by creating teams of people chosen for their individual strengths, and building the team through the contributions of each person. The concept of everyone's right to pursue any effort is basic to the US psyche. Freedom also means the freedom to compete; competition is open and sometimes brutal. Many common business expressions come from terms used in sports and war.

Decision Making

A common US expression is "time is money." Except for situations involving large corporations, US businesspeople are generally results-oriented, prefer to make quick decisions, and move fast to put their decisions into action. In smaller businesses, one person could be the sole decision maker for the entire company and might make a decision immediately without even consulting others.

Women

Men hold the vast majority of management positions, but the US has more women in higher-levels jobs than any other country. Women expect to be treated seriously and with the respect to which their position entitles them. Failure to do this will be insulting. A woman may not respond at the moment, but she will probably express her displeasure to her colleagues later. Businesswomen are as open and direct as men. This should not be viewed as anything more than being friendly. Foreign women can expect to be treated the same as men, but exactly how a woman is dealt with will depend on the US person she is encountering. Sexual discrimination is against the law and is not openly practiced, but private biases do exist. If a woman encounters discrimination, it will be more a reflection of the person discriminating than of their company.

Meetings

Schedules are busy and work days are full, so meetings start on time. US business culture tends to be informal, with an emphasis on getting things done. Generally, businesspeople are informal and direct, sometimes to the point of being confrontational. They will usually get down to business quickly, so as not to waste time. Talk will be open and fast-paced. People might interrupt each other or finish sentences for someone else. They will freely give their own opinions, suggest and debate different ideas or approaches, and contradict senior group members. Control and efficiency are important. US people want to be informed of new developments and changes, good or bad, so they can deal with them. Holding something back might be viewed as dishonesty. US people value directness about intentions, and what can or can not be done. Evasions, even as a form of politeness, will be seen as irresponsibility or dishonesty.

Business Attire

Standard attire is a business suit, especially when dealing with large companies. However, as in everything else, individuality is accepted. Being neatly dressed and well-groomed is most important. There is generally more latitude when dealing with smaller companies or in rural areas, where ties are not as essential or suits may not be expected. Minimal attire is a jacket and tasteful pants, shirt, and shoes. Women should dress professionally and, for best results, conservatively when conducting business. Avoid extremes in fashion, and excessive jewelry, heavy makeup, or accessories.

Cultural Cautions

DO'S

- Be straightforward, honest and sincere, yet also be yourself. Fitting into what you think is a US personality will be difficult, and could seem like insincerity. This will do more harm than good.
- Colleagues, subordinates, and the spouse of an associate might express their opinion about what they see or hear. Listen to everyone respectfully, even if they are not directly "part of the deal."
- The US has several large ethnic populations. Some prefer to be treated as you would treat anyone in the larger business world. Others want to be seen as different. Be sensitive to this situation and treat ethnic minorities as you would treat anyone else unless they indicate that they want to be treated differently.

DON'TS

- Don't agree to something if it isn't true or can't be done.
- Don't take a US person's open criticism of their country as an invitation that you can say the same things. In the US, everyone criticizes the government—but will be just as quick to defend it.

CUSTOMS

- Business cards are exchanged casually and informally. They are usually filed away or pocketed with only a quick glance or not read at all, unless a name, address, or phone number is being verified. While this would be considered impolite or disrespectful in many cultures, in the US stopping a conversation to examine a business card might be viewed as rude.
- US people will often entertain visitors by inviting them to their home or taking them to a restaurant or club. Immediate reciprocity is not expected (especially from a foreigner), but might be anticipated on a visit to that person in their own country.
- Direct eye contact is common, and is a sign of openness and honesty.

OBSERVATIONS

- The US is very large, and customs vary from region to region. The South tends to be the most different—more relaxed and proud of its gracious hospitality.
- Business environments vary not only from region to region but also with the size of a company. Large corporations are more bureaucratic, conservative, formal, and slower to reach decisions. Smaller companies tend to be more casual, faster, and have executives who are more accessible.
- US people tend to think in clear-cut generalities and overlook subtle shadings. Thus, they are likely to view people from other continents as one, treating all Asians or all Europeans the same and ignoring the differences between the cultures of individual countries. This is not meant to be insulting, and can usually be changed if politely pointed out.

NEGOTIATIONS

- US people tend to negotiate openly and directly, clearly stating what they want. They may be less clear about what they are willing to give up. If you are not sure about anything, ask a direct question.
- US people generally do not haggle over prices. When they hear a price they often accept that figure, and might respond immediately if it is too high. Responding by changing the price might raise questions about your honesty and the general good faith or your negotiations.
- Tactics depend largely on the personality of the individual with whom you are dealing. Other factors include how big a company is, and how much international experience they have.
- One common tactic is to use two different negotiators. One will be aggressive, difficult, and present excessive demands. The other will be friendly, easygoing, and pleasant. After dealing with the "bad" one, you will probably be more open and agreeable to what the "good" one proposes.
- Another tactic is for a company to start with what appears to be a large demand, and then gradually give up points that appear to be big but are in fact minor.

Legal

Legal System

The US is a federal democratic republic, politically divided into 50 states, each of which has a sovereign government and its own legal system.

Intellectual Property Rights

Patents A patent application describing the invention in detail and stating specifically what the inventor believes is new and patentable is filed with the US Patent and Trademark Office in Washington, DC. Generally, a patent will be granted for the invention if the invention is novel, useful, and not obvious to a person of ordinary skill in the relevant art. Utility patents are granted for a term of 17 years; design patents for 14 years. Upon expiration of a patent term, the right to exclude others also expires, and anyone may use the invention without permission. A foreign patent does not protect intellectual property in the US, although by reason of certain formal conventions and treaties to which the US and a number of countries are signatories, owners of intellectual property rights in such foreign countries may obtain certain benefits that could not otherwise be accorded to them by the intellectual property laws of the US.

Trademarks Rights in and to trademarks and service marks are acquired by the first person, company, or other entity that actually uses the mark in an ongoing business on goods or in connection with the performance of services. Although a trademark or service mark need not be registered to be protected, because rights are acquired by the mere use of a mark with goods or services, federal registration gives notice to unwitting infringers that a mark is owned. Registration of trademarks used in a particular state may be obtained by filing an application with such state. After a trademark has been used in interstate commerce, federal registration may be obtained by completing an application with the US Patent and Trademark Office. Trademarks are granted for renewable terms of 10 years.

Copyrights A copyright automatically arises when a work is created. To maintain copyright protection, an appropriate notice should be placed on the work when published and copyright registration should be obtained from the US Copyright Office. The term of copyright protection is the author's lifetime plus 50 years.

Trade secrets Laws precluding the misuse of trade secrets have been enacted by individual states, and vary from state to state.

Business Registration

Each state has its own codified business and commercial laws pursuant to which commercial enterprises may be organized and registered.

Contracts and Dispute Resolution

Contracts in the US can be complex and lengthy documents, especially for trade, investment, and real estate matters. The contract negotiation process is primarily a function of whether the parties have a prior working relationship and whether they can negotiate and operate on an equal basis.

Resolving disputes through lawsuits in the US tends to be a costly, lengthy, and an often acrimonious proposition. Certain industries, such as the construction trades and the medical insurance field, have increasingly utilized alternative dispute resolution processes, such as arbitration and mediation, instead of litigation to resolve differences. Under arbitration, the parties to a contract agree in advance to submit their disputes to arbitration and agree on a method of selecting an arbitrator or arbitrators from an approved group of recognized authorities. Mediation can be used in conjunction with arbitration and for other matters in any stage of litigation.

Notaries

Notaries play a fairly restrictive role in the US, where their function is to authenticate signatures on documents, and little special training is required to become a notary. In the US, attorneys usually perform the more technical functions allocated to notaries elsewhere.

Labor

Subject to a few broad limitations, labor agreements are freely made between employers and employees. Workers have the right to join unions and bargain collectively, and they exercise this right freely. Federal and state laws have restricted what had been, under the at-will doctrine, the absolute right of an employer to discharge employees with or without cause, with or without notice, and with or without compensatory payments. Several laws favoring employees now govern terminations, including those requiring advance notice and termination payments. Federal law sets a minimum wage, although it is generally not sufficient to support a family. Although there are few limitations on the maximum number of hours an employee can work, in most case overtime pay must be paid for all hours in excess of a stated maximum per week or day.

Source: For Puerto Rico, SIERRA/SERAPION, Hato Rey

Legal Matters

LEGAL BRIEFS

- **Attorneys** Attorneys licensed to practice in foreign countries are generally permitted to act as consultants in the US, but may not practice law unless specifically licensed by the applicable state bar association or board.
- **Choice of law** In determining whether to apply the laws of its state or the laws of another state, a court will characterize the issue between the parties to a particular body of law, such as torts, contracts, property, or some other field, and will apply the laws of its own state for that subject accordingly.
- **Consumer credit** Federal and state laws generally require that contracts or agreements involving consumer credit or debt clearly disclose such items as the amounts of the loan or debt, together with all finance charges, late charges, other fees and allowances, and due dates.
- **Shareholder liability** If a corporate shareholder deals at arm's length with the corporation, respecting it as a separate entity, the shareholder generally is not liable for acts of the corporation and is responsible only for fulfilling the shareholder's promises, if any, to pay in additional capital.
- **Foreign investment** The laws affecting foreign investment are diverse and complex, but a foreign business in the US is free from many of the governmental licensing and other restrictions found in other countries.
- **Interest** State laws generally specify the maximum rate of interest which may be charged for a loan or forbearance of money, goods, or items. State provisions also typically prohibit usury, the rate or amount of interest that exceeds the highest rate of interest allowed by law.
- **Monopolies** US antitrust law seeks to encourage competition by prohibiting monopolistic practices and unreasonable restraints on trade. When a foreign corporation sets up a US subsidiary, the foreign corporation itself may become subject to US antitrust laws.
- **Sole proprietorships** No special laws govern the organization or operation of this form of business enterprise, in which an individual person is the direct owner of the assets of the business and is wholly responsible for its liabilities.

LEGAL CONTACTS

Baker and McKenzie
One Prudential Plaza
130 E. Randolph Dr.
Chicago, IL 60601
Tel: (312) 861-8000 Fax: (312) 861-2898

Carlsmith Ball Wichman Case & Ichiki
555 South Flower St., 25th Fl.
Los Angeles, CA 90071-2326
Tel: (213) 955-1200 Fax: (213) 623-0032

Cravath, Swaine & Moore
825 Eighth Ave.
New York, NY 10019
Tel: (212) 474-1000 Fax: (212) 474-3700

Fulbright & Jaworski
1301 McKinney, Suite 5100
Houston, TX 77010
Tel: (713) 651-5151 Fax: (713) 651-5246

Pillsbury Madison & Sutro
255 Bush St.
San Francisco, CA 94104
Tel: (415) 983-1000 Fax: (415) 983-1600

Skadden, Arps, Slate, Meagher & Flom
919 Third Ave.
New York, NY 10022
Tel: (212) 735-3000 Fax: (212) 735-2000

White & Case
1555 Ave. of the Americas
New York, NY 10036
Tel: (212) 819-8200 Fax: (212) 354-8113

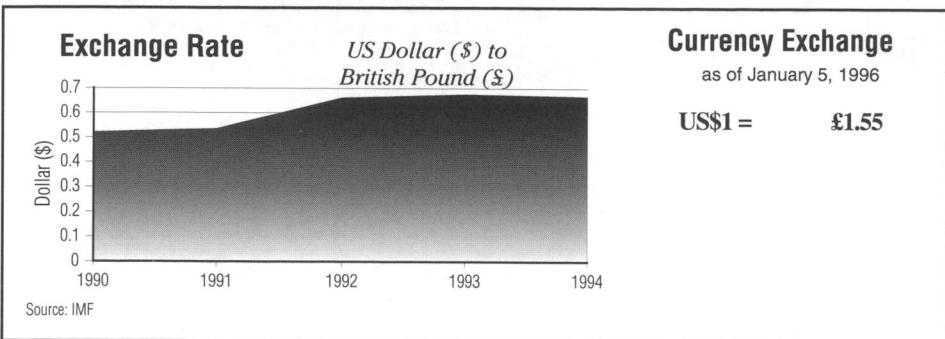

Exchange Rate

US Dollar ($) to British Pound (£)

Source: IMF

Currency Exchange

as of January 5, 1996

US$1 =   £1.55

Currency

The currency of the United States is the US dollar; its symbol is $, and the principal subdivision is 100 cents.

Foreign Exchange

The United States has no foreign exchange control restrictions and all US banks are permitted to accept foreign currency deposits. US authorities do not maintain margins with respect to exchange transactions, and spot and forward exchange rates are determined on the basis of supply and demand conditions in the exchange markets. There are no taxes or subsidies on purchases or sales of foreign exchange.

Capital Transfers

There are no restrictions on foreign exchange payments, except those imposed under the Department of Treasury regulations involving transactions with certain countries. Otherwise, all payments may be made in any currency without restriction. Transfer and payments abroad may be made freely, except payments to countries under sanctions. The proceeds from exports are not subject to foreign exchange controls.

Investment Incentives

The US maintains numerous foreign free trade zones which serve as secured areas outside of customs territories for the purpose of attracting and promoting international trade and commerce. Foreign sellers can forward their products to these zones to be held for an unlimited period while awaiting favorable market conditions in the US or in neighboring countries without being subject to customs entry, payment of duties, or posting of bonds. In addition, various state and local governments offer incentives to attract foreign investment.

Investment Restrictions

For the most part, foreign interests may own unlimited equity in a US business enterprise. However, foreign investors are subject to US laws that regulate transactions made within the US, and certain restrictions are imposed on investments that affect vital national resources or security interests, including radio communications, domestic air transportation, banking and insurance, energy resources, nuclear materials, and ownership of some agricultural land.

TAXATION

Taxation requires sophisticated knowledge of complex rules and regulations specific to each country. The information presented here is from the Ernst & Young Corporate Tax Guide and Directory, available from the Ernst & Young accounting office in your country, or from:

Ernst & Young LLP
787 Seventh Ave.
New York, NY 10019
Tel: (212) 773-3000
Cable: Ernstaudit, New York
Telex: 7607796 Ans bk ERNSTAUDIT NY
Fax: (212) 977-9359, 773-5116, 773-5582, 773-5583, 773-5584

At a Glance

Corporate Income Tax Rate (%) (a)	35
Capital Gains Tax Rate (%)	35
Branch Tax Rate (%) (a)	35
Withholding Tax (%) (b)	
Dividends (c)	30
Interest (c)(d)	30
Royalties from Patents, Know-how, etc. (c)	30
Branch Remittance Tax (e)	30
Net Operating Losses (Years)	
Carryback	3
Carryforward	15

(a) In addition, many states levy income or capital-based taxes. An alternative minimum tax is imposed .
(b) Rates may be reduced by treaty.
(c) Applicable to payments to nonresidents.
(d) Interest on certain "portfolio debt" obligations issued after July 18, 1984 and noneffectively connected bank deposit interest are exempt from withholding.
(e) This is the branch profits tax.

Money Matters

BITS AND PIECES

- **Capital payments** Whether incoming or outgoing, by residents or nonresidents, capital payments are not restricted.

- **Investments** Investments involving ownership interest in banks are subject to federal and state banking laws and regulations, but inward and outward direct or portfolio investments are generally free of approval requirements.

- **Gold** Gold may be freely bought, held, or sold in any form, domestically or abroad, with the exception of certain sanctioned countries. Commercial banks may deal in gold bullion and gold coins. A license is not required by importers, exporters, refiners, or processors of gold. US gold coins are legal tender at face value. Commercial imports of gold jewelry are free of quantitative restrictions, but are subject to an import duty. There is no duty on gold ore, bullion, or coins, although all forms must be declared to customs.

- **Black market** Because there are no exchange controls there is no black market in US currency within the country. Business transactions will almost always be conducted through the financial system.

BANKS

Australia and New Zealand Bank Group
120 Wall St.
New York, NY 10005
Tel: (212) 820-9805

Banca Commerciale Italiana
1 William St.
New York, NY 10004
Tel: (212) 607-3500

Bank of America, NT&SA
555 California St.
PO Box 37000
San Francisco, CA 94137
Tel: (415) 624-3456
Fax: (415) 624-0412

Chase Manhattan Bank
1 Chase Manhattan Plaza
New York, NY 10081
Tel: (212) 552-2222
Fax: (212) 552-3875

Chemical Bank
270 Park Ave.
New York, NY 10017
Tel: (212) 270-6000

Citibank, NA
399 Park Ave.
New York, NY 10043
Tel: (212) 559-1000
Fax: (212) 559-5138

First National Bank of Chicago
One First National Plaza
Chicago, IL 60670
Tel: (312) 732-4000

First Union National Bank of Florida
225 Water St.
POB 2080
Jacksonville, FL 32202
Tel: (904) 361-2265
Fax: (904) 361-6197

NationsBank
901 Main St.
POB 831000
Dallas, TX 75283-1000
Tel: (214) 508-6262
Fax: (214) 880-9074

Republic National Bank of New York
452 Fifth Ave.
POB 423
New York, NY 10018
Tel: (212) 525-5000

Wells Fargo, NA
464 California St.
San Francisco, CA 94163
Tel: (415) 477-1000

Business Travel

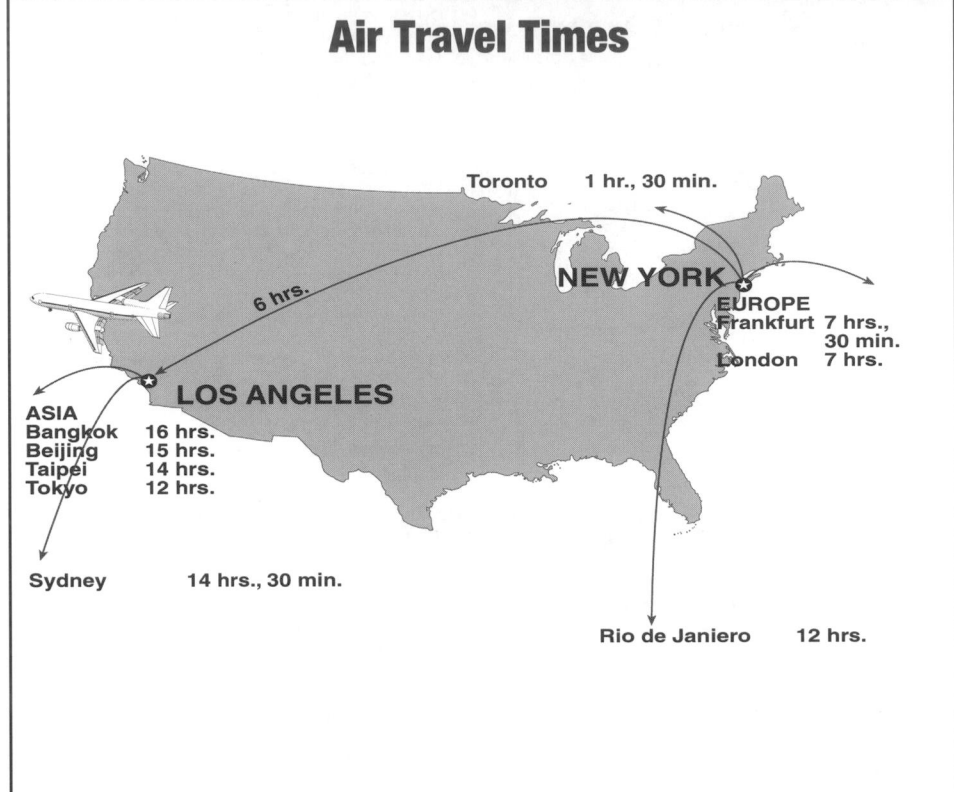

Air Travel Times

Toronto   1 hr., 30 min.

NEW YORK

6 hrs.

EUROPE
Frankfurt   7 hrs., 30 min.
London   7 hrs.

LOS ANGELES

ASIA
Bangkok   16 hrs.
Beijing   15 hrs.
Taipei   14 hrs.
Tokyo   12 hrs.

Sydney   14 hrs., 30 min.

Rio de Janiero   12 hrs.

COMMUNICATIONS

Telephones Service in the US is efficient and modern. Direct dialing is available to just about anywhere. Hotels add substantial surcharges to calls, so public phones are a better bet. They are often subject to vandals, however, so finding a working one may be a challenge. Public phones only take coins or use credit or phone cards and can be found on streets, at service stations, and in hotels and public buildings.

Fax Fax services are available at most hotels and businesses and at photocopy shops. With the popularity of fax, telegrams and telexes are not used as often in the US as elsewhere.

Post office The postal service is fast, efficient, and reliable. Various services are available from the post office (overnight or two-day delivery). Most post offices are open from 8:00 am to 5:00 pm, with some Saturday hours at larger branches. Stamps can be purchased at some supermarkets or in post offices lobby vending machines, and letters can be mailed from the dark blue mailboxes found on many streets.

BEST TRAVEL BOOKS

Birnbaum's United States for Business Travelers 95, New York: Harper Perennial, 1994. 1,014 pages. Focuses on the top 42 business destinations and supplies maps for each. Lists available business services as well as tourist information. Updated annually.

Fodor's USA: The Complete Guide to the Best of Everything in All Fifty States, New York: Fodor's Travel Publications. 1,072 pages. Tourist-oriented but has more than 100 maps and a wide range of information.

Frequent Travelers to Major Cities, New York: Prentice Hall Travel, 1994. Geared to the business traveler, this book contains many detailed maps and useful telephone numbers.

Culture Shock, A Guide to Customs and Etiquette, United States.

USEFUL TELEPHONE NUMBERS

If you are calling from outside the United States, you will need to add the country code [1] and any other international dialing requirements from within your country. (800) numbers are toll-free for use in the US and Canada.

- Local Operator 0
- Long-Distance Operator 00
- International Access Code 011
- Local Directory Assistance 411
- Emergencies 911
- Long-Distance Assistance...1 (area code) 555-1212

Courier Services
- Federal Express .... (800) 238-5355
- DHL .... (800) 225-5345
- UPS .... (800) 662-7389

Airlines
- American .... (800) 433-7300
- Delta .... (800) 221-1212
- Northwest .... (800) 225-2525
- United .... (800) 241-6522

Car Rental
- Budget .... (800) 527-0700
- Dollar .... (800) 800-4000
- Hertz .... (800) 654-3131

Bus and Train
- Greyhound Bus (National) .... (800) 231-2222
- Amtrak Train (National) .... (800) 872-7245

Credit Card Information
Lost or stolen credit cards
- Amex .... (919) 333-3211
- Diner's Club..................................... (303) 799-1504
- MasterCard .... (314) 275-6690
- Visa .... (410) 581-7931

Travelogue

WORKWEEK

Offices Monday-Friday 9:00 am to 5:00 pm with a half hour to hour lunch break around noon.
Banks Monday-Friday 9:00 am to 5:00 pm. Some banks have morning hours on Saturdays as well.
Government Monday-Friday 9:00 am to 5:00 pm.
Retail Most stores open daily by 10:00 am and are open until 6:00 or 7:00 pm, but close earlier on Sundays.

HOLIDAYS

Holidays 1996
January 1 New Year's Day
January 15 Martin Luther King Jr. Day*
February 19 Presidents' Day*
May 27 Memorial Day*
July 4 Independence Day
September 2 Labor Day*
October 14 Columbus Day*
November 11 Veterans Day
November 28-29 Thanksgiving*
December 25 Christmas
*Dates vary each year.

VISA AND PASSPORT

Passports and visas are needed by all travelers to the United States except those from Canada, Mexico, and the 22 nations that participate in the Visa Waiver Pilot Program (VWPP). Tourist and business visas are available at US embassies and consulates. Business visitors should also have a letter stating intent and length of stay from the US company they are visiting. Citizens from countries in the VWPP need only a passport, a return ticket, and proof of solvency for a 90-day stay. Canadian and Mexican visitors do not need return tickets. A valid 10-year passport is necessary to enter the US. Visitors cannot bring in meat or meat products, seeds, plants, or fruits. Carrying illegal drugs is punishable.

DEPARTURE FORMALITIES

There are no departure formalities for the United States.

IMMUNIZATION

No immunizations are required for entry to the United States unless you are arriving from an infected area.

TIPPING

Tipping is an important supplement to service industry salaries in the US. Waiters, taxi drivers, hairdressers, and bartenders are tipped 15 percent of the bill. Porters are tipped US$.50 to US$1 per bag, and coat-checkers and airport van drivers should be tipped US$1.

CRIME

The crime rate is higher in larger cities, but it is most prevalent in certain areas. Street crime is an issue for tourists, especially in tourist areas, so safeguard money and valuables. Rental cars are increasingly becoming targets for criminals in some areas; check with your rental agency to see if they remove stickers identifying the car as rented.

INFRASTRUCTURE

Air, train, bus, taxi, hotel, telecommunication, and rental car industries are highly developed in the US. Large cities such as Los Angeles, New York City, Chicago, and San Francisco all have bus systems that are dependable and are in use 24 hours a day, however, safety is sometimes a concern. Highway speed limits are 55 miles per hour. Rush-hour traffic in larger cities can be time consuming; avoid being on the roads early mornings and from 4:00 pm to 7:00 pm. Monday-Friday. Amtrak trains travel throughout the US, as do the Greyhound bus lines.

NATIONAL TOURIST OFFICE

United States Travel and Tourism Administration
US Dept. of Commerce, Room 1865
Washington, DC 20230
Tel: (202) 377-0136 Fax: (202) 377-8887
State tourism offices, city tourist bureaus, and local chambers of commerce are the best places for information about where you are visiting. The US is not known for accurate, centralized information.

GOVERNMENT AGENCIES

Agency for International Development (AID)
Main State Bldg.
2201 C St. NW
Washington, DC 20523
Tel: (202) 663-1449, 647-1850 Fax: (202) 647-1770

Bureau of Alcohol, Tobacco and Firearms (BATF)
650 Massachusetts Ave. NW
Washington, DC 20226
Tel: (202) 927-7777, 927-8500 Fax: (202) 927-7862

Bureau of Export Administration (BXA)
14th St. and Constitution Ave. NW
Washington, DC 20230
Tel: (202) 482-2000, 482-2721 Fax: (202) 482-2387

Bureau of International Organization Affairs
2201 C St. NW
Washington, DC 20520
Tel: (202) 647-3686, 647-6400 Fax: (202) 647-6510

Bureau of Land Management
1849 C St. NW
Washington, DC 20240
Tel: (202) 208-3100, 501-5717 Fax: (202) 208-5902

Bureau of Mines
810 7th St. NW
Washington, DC 20241
Tel (202) 208-3100, 501-9649 Fax: (202) 501-3716

Bureau of Oceans and International Environmental and Scientific Affairs
2201 C St. NW
Washington, DC 20520
Tel: (202) 647-3686, 647-4000 Fax: (202) 647-0217

Consumer and Public Liaison
1000 Independence Ave. SW, CP-60
Washington, DC 20585
Tel: (202) 586-5373 Fax: (202) 586-0539

Commodity Futures Trading Commission
2033 K St. NW
Washington, DC 20581
Tel: (202) 254-6387, 254-8630 Fax: (202) 254-6265

Consumer Product Safety Commission (CPSC)
Washington, DC 20207
Tel: (301) 504-0500, 504-0580 Fax: (301) 504-0124

Customs Service
1301 Constitution Ave. NW
Washington, DC 20229
Tel: (202) 927-6724, 927-6724 Fax: (202) 927-1393

Department of Agriculture (USDA)
14th St. and Independence Ave. SW
Washington, DC 20250
Tel: (202) 720-8732, 720-2791 Fax: (202) 720-2166

Department of Commerce (DOC)
Main Commerce Bldg.
14th St. and Constitution Ave. NW
Washington, DC 20230
Tel: (202) 482-2000 Fax: (202) 482-4576

Department of Defense (DOD)
The Pentagon
Washington, DC 20301
Tel: (703) 697-5737

Department of Education
400 Maryland Ave. SW
Washington, DC 20202
Tel: (202) 708-5366, 401-1576 Fax: (202) 401-0596

Department of Energy (DOE)
1000 Independence Ave. SW
Washington, DC 20585
Tel: (202) 586-5000, 586-5575 Fax: (202) 586-4403

Department of Health and Human Services
200 Independence Ave. SW
Washington, DC 20201
Tel: (202) 619-0257, 690-6867 Fax: (202) 690-6274

Department of Housing and Urban Development (HUD)
HUD Bldg.
451 7th St. SW
Washington, DC 20410
Tel: (202) 708-1422, 708-1420 Fax: (202) 708-0299

Department of the Interior
Main Interior Bldg.
1849 C St. NW
Washington, DC 20240
Tel: (202) 208-3100, 208-3171 Fax: (202) 208-5048

Department of Justice (DOJ)
Main Justice Bldg.
10th St. and Constitution Ave. NW
Washington, DC 20530
Tel: (202) 514-2000, 514-2007 Fax: (202) 514-0468
10th St. and Pennsylvania Ave. NW
Washington, DC 20535
Tel: (202) 324-3000, 324-3691 Fax: (202) 324-4705

Department of Labor (DOL)
200 Constitution Ave. NW
Washington, DC 20210
Tel: (202) 219-5000, 219-7316 Fax: (202) 219-6161

Department of State
Main State Bldg.
2201 C St. NW
Washington, DC 20520
Tel: (202) 647-3686, 647-4000 Fax: (202) 647-0464

Department of the Treasury
Main Treasury Bldg.
15th St. and Pennsylvania Ave. NW
Washington, DC 20220
Tel: (202) 622-2000

Department of Transportation
Department of Transportation (DOT)
400 7th St. SW
Washington, DC 20590
Tel: (202) 366-4000, 366-5580 Fax: (202) 426-4508

Environmental Protection Agency (EPA)
401 M St. SW
Washington, DC 20460
Tel: (202) 260-2090, 260-2080
Fax: (202) 260-0500 (Enforcement)

Export-Import Bank of the United States (Eximbank)
811 Vermont Ave. NW
Washington, DC 20571
Tel: (202) 566-8990 Fax: (202) 566-7524

Federal Aviation Administration (FAA)
800 Independence Ave. SW
Washington, DC 20591
Tel: (202) 366-4000, 267-8521 Fax: (202) 267-5047

Federal Communications Commission (FCC)
1919 M St. NW
Washington, DC 20544
Tel: (202) 632-7106, 632-7000 Fax: (202) 653-5402

Federal Energy Regulatory Commission (FERC)
825 N. Capitol St. NE
Washington, DC 20426
Tel: (202) 208-0200, 208-1371 Fax: (202) 208-2106

Federal Grain Inspection Service (FGIS)
PO Box 96454
Washington, DC 20090
Tel: (202) 720-8732, 720-5091 Fax: (202) 205-9237

Federal Highway Administration (FHA)
400 7th St. SW
Washington, DC 20590
Tel: (202) 366-4000, 366-0660 Fax: (202) 366-7239

Federal Railroad Administration (FRA)
400 7th St. SW
Washington, DC 20590
Tel: (202) 366-4000, 366-4043 Fax: (202) 366-7009

Federal Trade Commission (FTC)
6th St. and Pennsylvania Ave. NW
Washington, DC 20580
Tel: (202) 326-2000, 326-2222 Fax: (202) 326-2050

Federal Transit Administration (FTA)
400 7th St. SW
Washington, DC 20590
Tel: (202) 366-4000, 366-4043 Fax: (202) 366-3472

Fish and Wildlife Service (FWS)
1849 C St. NW
Washington, DC 20240
Tel: (202) 208-3100, 208-5634 Fax: (202) 208-6965

Food and Drug Administration (FDA)
5600 Fishers Lane
Rockville, MD 20857
Tel: (301) 443-1544, 443-3170 Fax: (301) 443-5930

Food and Drug Administration
Small Manufacturers Assistance
5600 Fishers Lane
Rockville, MD 20857
Tel: (301) 443-6597 Fax: (301) 443-8818

Food and Drug Administration
Center for Devices and Radiological Health
12720 Twinbrook Parkway
Rockville, MD 20857
Tel: (301) 443-4690 Fax: (301) 443-3193

Food Safety and Inspection Service (FSIS)
14th St. and Independence Ave. SW
Washington, DC 20250
Tel: (202) 720-8732, 720-9113 Fax: (202) 690-4437

Foreign Agricultural Service (FAS)
14th St. and Independence Ave. SW
Washington, DC 20250
Tel: (202) 720-8732, 720-9115 Fax: (202) 690-1595

Foreign Trade Zones Board
Main Commerce Bldg.
Washington, DC 20230
Tel: (202) 482-2862 Fax: (202) 482-0002

Immigration and Naturalization Service (INS)
425 Eye St. NW
Washington, DC 20536
Tel: (202) 514-4316 Fax: (202) 514-3296

International Trade Administration (ITA)
14th St. and Constitution Ave. NW
Washington, DC 20230
Tel: (202) 482-2000 Fax: (202) 482-5933

Maritime Administration
400 7th St. SW
Washington, DC 20590
Tel: (202) 366-4000, 366-5807 Fax: (202) 366-3890

National Highway Traffic Safety Administration (NHTSA)
400 7th St. SW
Washington, DC 20590
Tel: (202) 366-4000, 366-9550 Fax: (202) 366-2106

National Institute of Standards and Technology
Bldg. 101, #A1134
Gaithersburg, MD 20899
Tel: (301) 975-2000, 975-2762 Fax: (301) 869-8972

National Telecommunications and Information Administration
Main Commerce Bldg.
Washington, DC 20230
Tel: (202) 482-1551 Fax: (202) 482-1635

Animal and Plant Health Inspection Service
PO Box 96464
Washington, DC 20090
Tel: (202) 720-2791, 720-2511 Fax: (202) 720-3054

Center for Food Safety and Applied Nutrition
200 C St. SW
Washington, DC 20204
Tel: (202) 205-5850 Fax: (202) 205-5025

Occupational Safety and Health Administration (OSHA)
200 Constitution Ave. NW
Washington, DC 20210
Tel: (202) 219-8151, 219-7162 Fax: (202) 219-6064

Office of Hazardous Materials Safety
400 Seventh St. SW
Washington, DC 20590
Tel: (202) 366-0656 Fax: (202) 366-3753

Office of International Economic Affairs
200 Constitution Ave. NW #S5325
Washington, DC 20210
Tel: (202) 219-7597 Fax: (202) 219-5071

Office of International Economics & Policy
The Pentagon, Rm. 4B-938
Washington, DC 20301-2100
Tel: (703) 697-3248 Fax: (703) 695-0054

Patent and Trademark Office
Washington, DC 20231
Tel: (703) 557-3158, 308-4357

Social Security Administration
6401 Security Blvd.
Baltimore, MD 21235
Tel: (410) 965-8882, 965-7700 Fax: (410) 965-1344

Technology Administration
14th St. and Constitution Ave. NW
Washington, DC 20230
Tel: (202) 482-0137 Fax: (202) 482-4817

Travel and Tourism Administration
Main Commerce Bldg.
Washington, DC 20230
Tel: (202) 482-1904 Fax: (202) 482-4279

US International Development Cooperation Agency
Main State Bldg.
2201 C St. NW
Washington, DC 20523
Tel: (202) 647-1850, 647-9620 Fax: (202) 647-1770

Internal Revenue Service (IRS)
1111 Constitution Ave. NW
Washington, DC 20224
Tel: (202) 622-5000, (800) 829-1040

Interstate Commerce Commission (ICC)
12th St. and Constitution Ave. NW
Washington, DC 20423
Tel: (202) 927-5350, 927-6000 Fax: (202) 927-5728

National Labor Relations Board (NLRB)
1717 Pennsylvania Ave. NW
Washington, DC 20570
Tel: (202) 632-4950, 254-8064 Fax: (202) 254-6781

Office of the US Trade Representative
600 17th St. NW
Washington, DC 20506
Tel: (202) 395-3230 Fax: (202) 395-3911

Overseas Private Investment Corp. (OPIC)
1100 New York Ave. NW
Washington, DC 20527
Tel: (202) 457-7200, 336-8799 Fax: (202) 408-9859

Securities and Exchange Commission (SEC)
450 5th St. NW
Washington, DC 20549
Tel: (202) 272-2650 Fax: (202) 272-7050

Small Business Administration (SBA)
409 3rd St. SW
Washington, DC 20416
Tel: (202) 205-6740, 205-7713 Fax: (202) 205-7064

US International Trade Commission (ITC)
500 E St. SW
Washington, DC 20436
Tel: (202) 205-2000, 205-1000 Fax: (202) 205-1819

US Postal Service (USPS)
475 L'Enfant Plaza SW
Washington, DC 20260
Tel: (202) 268-2020, 268-2284 Fax: (202) 268-6980

US Trade and Development Agency
State Annex 16
Washington, DC 20523
Tel: (703) 875-4357 Fax: (703) 875-4009

BUSINESS AND TRADE ORGANIZATIONS

American Association of Exporters and Importers
11 West 42nd St.
New York, NY 10036
Tel: (212) 944-2230 Fax: (212) 382-2606

American Society of International Executives
122 C St. NW, Suite 740
Washington, DC 20001
Tel: (202) 783-0051

International Trade Facilitation Council
3144 Circle Hill Rd.
Alexandria, VA 22305
Tel: (703) 548-1234

International Traders Association
The Mellinger Company
6100 Variel Ave.
Woodland Hills, CA 91367
Tel: (818) 884-4400

National Association of Export Companies
PO Box 1330, Murray Hill Station
New York, NY 10156
Tel: (212) 725-3311 Fax: (212) 725-3312

National Cooperative Business Association
1401 New York Ave. NW, #1100
Washington, DC 20005
Tel: (202) 638-6222 Fax: (202) 638-1374

National Customs Brokers and Forwarders Association of America (NCBFAA)
One World Trade Center, Suite 1153
New York, NY 10048
Tel: (212) 432-0050 Fax: (212) 432-5709

National Foreign Trade Council (NFTC)
1625 K St. NW
Washington, DC 20006
Tel: (202) 887-0278 Fax: (202) 452-8160

National Industrial Council
1331 Pennsylvania Ave. NW, #1500N
Washington, DC 20004
Tel: (202) 637-3053 Fax: (202) 637-3182

Small Business Exporters Association (SBEA)
4603 John Taylor Court
Annandale, VA 22003
Tel: (703) 642-2490 Fax: (703) 750-9655

United States Council for International Business
1212 Ave. of the Americas, 21st Floor
New York, NY 10026
Tel: (212) 354-4480 Fax: (212) 575-0327

US Chamber of Commerce
International Division
1615 H St. NW
Washington, DC 20062
Tel: (202) 463-5460 Fax: (202) 463-3114

US Business and Industrial Council
220 National Press Bldg.
14th and F Streets NW
Washington, DC 20045
Tel: (202) 662-8744 Fax: (202) 662-8754

CHAMBERS OF COMMERCE

Chicago Association of Commerce & Industry
200 North LaSalle St.
Chicago, IL 60601
Tel: (312) 580-6900 Fax: (312) 580-0046

Columbus Area Chamber of Commerce
PO Box 1527
Columbus, OH 43216
Tel: (614) 221-1321 Fax: (614) 469-8250

District of Columbia Chamber of Commerce
1411 K St. NW, Suite 603
Washington, DC 20005
Tel: (202) 347-7201

Greater Boston Chamber of Commerce
600 Atlantic Ave., 13th Floor
Boston, MA 02210-2200
Tel: (617) 227-4500

Greater Dallas Chamber of Commerce
1201 Elm St., Suite 2000
Dallas, TX 75270
Tel: (214) 746-6739

Greater Detroit Chamber of Commerce
600 West Lafayette Blvd.
Detroit, MI 48226
Tel: (313) 964-4000 Fax: (313) 964-0531

Greater Houston Partnership
1100 Milan St., 25th Floor
Houston, TX 77002
Tel: (713) 658-2416

Greater Miami Chamber of Commerce International Economic Development
Omni Complex
1601 Biscayne Blvd.
Miami, FL 33132
Tel: (305) 350-7700 Fax: (305) 3374-6902

Greater Philadelphia Chamber of Commerce
1234 Market St., Suite 1800
Philadelphia, PA 19107-3718
Tel: (215) 972-3990 Fax: (215) 972-3900

Greater San Diego Chamber of Commerce
402 W. Broadway, Suite 1000
San Diego, CA 92101-3585
Tel: (619) 232-0124 x391 Fax: (619) 234-0571

Greater Seattle Chamber of Commerce
Trade and Transportation Division
600 University Ave., #1200
Seattle, WA 98101
Tel: (206) 389-7307

Greater Washington Board of Trade
1129 20th St. NW
Washington, DC 20036
Tel: (202) 857-5900

Indianapolis Chamber of Commerce
320 N. Meridean St., Suite 928
Indianapolis, IN 46204
Tel: (317) 464-2200 Fax: (317) 464-2233

International Commerce Division
404 South Bixel St.
Los Angeles, CA 90017
Tel: (213) 629-0602 Fax: (213) 629-0708

New York Chamber of Commerce
1 Battery Park Plaza
New York, NY 10004
Tel: (212) 493-7400 Fax: (212) 344-3344

San Francisco Chamber of Commerce
San Francisco World Trade Association
465 California St., 9th Floor
San Francisco, CA 94104
Tel: (415) 392-4511, x 801/822 Fax: (415) 392-0485

INTERNET ADDRESSES

Usenet group(s):
soc.culture.usa

FedWorld Home Page
http://www.fedworld.gov/index.html#usgovt

Internet Business Directory
http://ibd.ar.com/

Purchases Over the Internet: Discussions
http:search.mccmedia.com/menus/22931.html

CommerceNet
http://www.commerce.net/information/information.html

The Company Corporation
http://www.service.com/tcc/home.html

Foreign Exchange Rates
http://www.dna.lth.se/cgi-bin/rates

Tourism Offices Worldwide Directory
http://www.mbnet.mb.ca/lucas/travel/tourism-offices.html

The USA CityLink Project
http://www.NeoSoft.com:80/citylink

Hotels and Travel on the Internet
http://www.webscope.com/travel/hompage.html

Uruguay

Republic of Uruguay

Economy

Overview

A combination of prolonged social and political stability, a high standard of education and the exploitation of prime agricultural land have helped Uruguay to achieve one of the highest standards of living in Latin America. As a country whose main natural resource is its fertile soil, it has focused on building strong agriculture and agroindustry sectors, though its highly developed services sector has become the dominant force in the economy. In the past few decades, however, economic growth has stagnated due to persistent inflation, excessive state regulation, and inefficient state-run monopolies in important industries.

Trade

Uruguay relies heavily on foreign trade to drive its economy. Latin American countries are the primary markets for its exports, and it buys most of its imports from the same sources. Brazil is the largest source of both its imports and exports, followed by Argentina, the US, and Germany. Agriculture plays a central role in Uruguay's foreign trade; although it makes up only 11 percent of GDP it accounts for over 50 percent of total exports. While overall wealth has declined in the past three decades, the country's population is one of the most affluent in Latin America, making it a relatively good market for imports. However, a strengthening peso and a decline in overseas markets are containing export growth resulting in a widening of its trade deficit.

Sectors

Agriculture Uruguay has traditionally been an agricultural country and this sector remains important to the economy as a major source of foreign exchange. Agricultural products make up more than half of its export total, and inputs to this sector make major contributions to an agricultural-based industry. Raising livestock is the main agricultural activity, primarily for the production of meat, hides, and wool.

Industry Industry accounts for 25 percent of GDP. A large proportion of this sector is devoted to the transformation of raw imports to produce such products as leather goods, textiles, and processed meat. The production of consumer goods for local consumption has suffered due to increasing competition and the rising peso.

Services Tourism is the third most important industry in Uruguay, though it has recently suffered from the rising peso and financial hard times in nearby Argentina. It is expected to recover somewhat as the Argentine economy stabilizes. Uruguay also has a well-developed financial services sector.

Trends

Although its economy is relatively affluent and basically healthy, Uruguay's economic growth remains flat and its trade deficit continues to widen. The government is slowly carrying out a program of economic reform that includes privatization of state enterprises, reduction of inflation, and reform of the financial and social security systems. Uruguay took a significant step towards strengthening regional economic ties by joining Brazil, Argentina, and Paraguay in establishing the Southern Cone Common Market (Mercosur) in 1991. This should result in increased economic integration with its larger neighbors and could form the basis for improved growth rates in the future.

At a Glance

THE COUNTRY

Location Uruguay is situated in the southeastern part of South America.
Terrain The general character of the land is undulating hills, with a few forest areas along the banks of the numerous streams.
Climate The climate is temperate; the average temperature in June, the coolest month, is about 15°C (59°F) and the average for January, the warmest month is 25°C (77°F). The weather is transitional between the weather of the humid Argentine pampas and that of southern Brazil. Rainfall is evenly distributed throughout the year and averages about 109 cm (43 in) in Montevideo to 127 cm (50 in) farther north.

THE PEOPLE

Population 3,200,000
Ethnic composition
White and European origin 88%
Spanish, Italian, Portuguese, English, and other
  Europeans 8%
Mulattos and Blacks.. 4%
Religious composition
Roman Catholic 78%
Protestant 5%
Jewish 2%
Languages spoken Spanish is the official language, although Brazilero, a Portuguese-Spanish mix, is common along the Brazilian frontier.
Education and literacy Adult literacy is 96%. Education in elementary, secondary, and technical schools and at the University of the Republic in Montevideo is free. Elementary education, which is compulsory, lasts six years.
Labor force
Total: 1,400,000
By occupation: manufacturing 22%, government 20%, commerce 17%, agriculture 13%, utilities, construction, transport, and communications 12%.

COUNTRY FACTS

Political and legal Uruguay is run by a republic government with political parties such as Colorado, Blanco (National), Broad Front Coalition, New Space Party.
Telephone The state owns the telegraph and telephone services. International country code: [598]. City code: Montevideo (2).
Transportation Highways have surpassed railways as the principal means of conveyance for passengers and freight. Montevideo is the major Uruguayan port. Carrasco airport is used by most international carriers.
Environment Uruguay is primarily a grass-growing land, and the vegetation is essentially a continuation of the Argentine pampas. Forest areas are relatively small. Large animals have virtually disappeared from the eastern regions.
Media Uruguay has 110 radio stations and 33 television stations. The number of radio receivers is about 1,880,000 and the number of television sets is 750,000. There are 33 daily newspapers with 6 dailies in Montevideo.
Health The government traditionally has placed great emphasis on preventive medicine and on the sociological approach to public health problems. Life expectancy is 72 years.

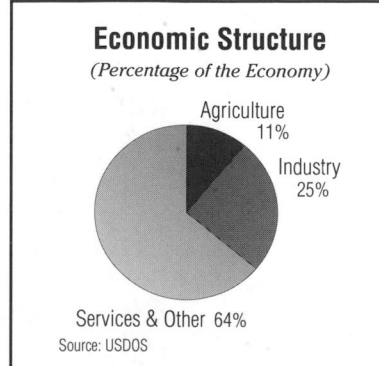

Economic Structure
(Percentage of the Economy)

Agriculture 11%
Industry 25%
Services & Other 64%

Source: USDOS

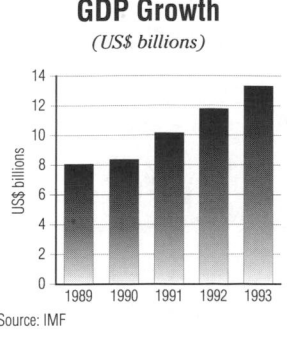

GDP Growth
(US$ billions)

Source: IMF

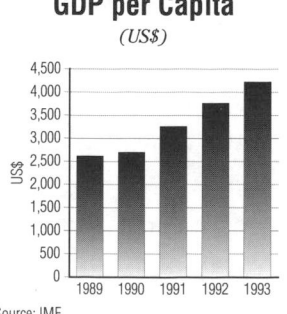

GDP per Capita
(US$)

Source: IMF

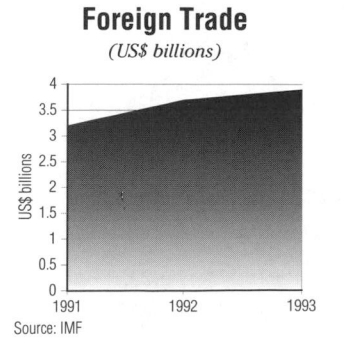

Foreign Trade
(US$ billions)

Source: IMF

Uruguay

- National capitol
- Secondary city
— Road
···· Railroad
Department capitals are noted with bold type

0   20   40   60 km
0   20   40 mi

Monte Caseros · Bella Union
Artigas · Quaraí
Artigas
Belén
Santana do Livramento
Concordia · **Salto**
Salto
Arapey Grande
Daymán
Rivera
Corrales
Rivera
Tacuarembó
Aceguá
Paysandú
Piedra Sola
Quequay Grande
Tacuarembó
Paysandú · Guichon
Tres Arboles
Km 329
Melo
Jaguarão
Cerro Largo
Río Branco
Concepción del Uruguaa
Young
Paso de los Toros
Placido Rosas
Río Negro
Embalse del Río Negro
Santa Clara de Olimar
Treinta y Tres
Negro
Fray Bentos
Mercedes
Soriano
Yi
Durazno
Sarandí Del Yi
Treinta-y-Tres
Cebollati
Durazno
Laguna Mirín
Dolores
José Pedro Varela
Trinidad
Flores
San Salvador
Cardona
Florída
Lavalleja
Rocha
Xui
Nueva Palmira
Carmelo
Santa
San José
Florida
Colonia
San José de Mayo
Santa Lucía
Lucía
Minas
Rocha
Cabo Polonia National Park
Colonia del Sacramento
Juan Lacazz
Canelones
Canelones
Maldonado
Buenos Aires
Las Piedras
Pando
La Paloma
Argentina
Río de la Plata
Montevideo
Maldonado
Punta del Este
Atlantic Ocean

Brazil

©1994 Magellan Geographix℠Santa Barbara, CA

© Copyright 1996 by World Trade Press. All Rights Reserved.

Foreign Trade

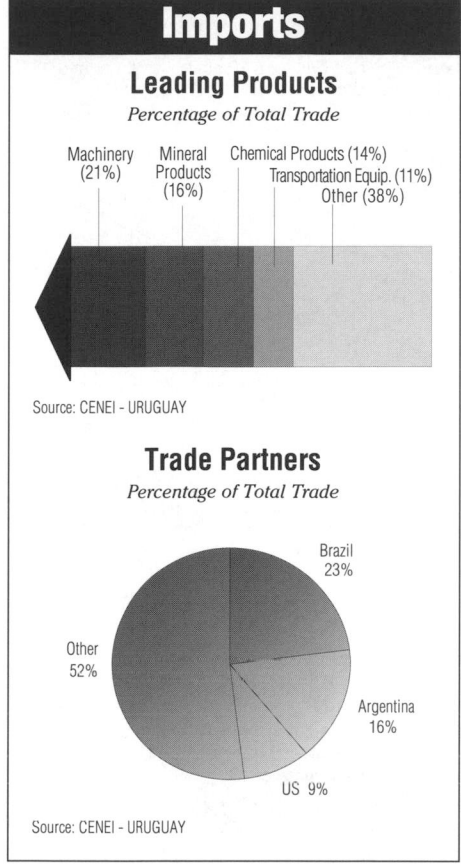

Imports

Leading Products
Percentage of Total Trade

Machinery (21%)
Mineral Products (16%)
Chemical Products (14%)
Transportation Equip. (11%)
Other (38%)

Source: CENEI - URUGUAY

Trade Partners
Percentage of Total Trade

Brazil 23%
Argentina 16%
US 9%
Other 52%

Source: CENEI - URUGUAY

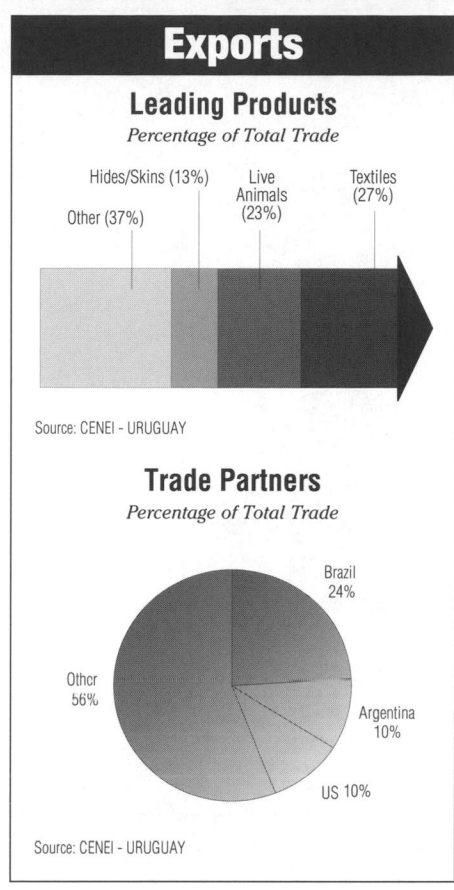

Exports

Leading Products
Percentage of Total Trade

Hides/Skins (13%)
Live Animals (23%)
Textiles (27%)
Other (37%)

Source: CENEI - URUGUAY

Trade Partners
Percentage of Total Trade

Brazil 24%
Argentina 10%
US 10%
Other 56%

Source: CENEI - URUGUAY

Opportunities

FOR IMPORTING TO URUGUAY
- fuels
- chemicals
- machinery
- metals
- plastics
- vehicles
- minerals
- equipment
- consumer goods

FOR EXPORTING FROM URUGUAY
- meat
- livestock
- wool
- hides
- leather
- wool products
- fish
- rice
- furs

Trade News

RULES AND REGULATIONS

- **Import licenses** Certain imports require special licenses or customs documents. Among these are drugs, certain medical equipment and chemicals, firearms, radioactive materials, fertilizers, vegetable materials, frozen embryos, livestock, bull semen, anabolics, sugar, seeds, hormones, meat, and vehicles.

- **Registration** Except for the above, import licenses are not generally required; however, all imports are subject to registration prior to the placing of orders abroad. Registrations are generally valid for 180 days, within which period goods must be cleared through customs.

- **Tariff rates** The top tariff rate has been lowered from 24 percent to 20 percent. Tariffs for products from Mercosur member countries (Brazil, Argentina, and Paraguay) have been virtually eliminated. There are no plans for further reductions of tariffs on products from other countries at this time.

- **Tariff exemptions** The only exemptions to tariff regulations, in the context of anti-dumping legislation, are reference prices and minimum export prices, fixed in relation to international levels and in line with commitments assumed under GATT. These are applied to neutralize unfair trade practices which threaten to damage national production activity or delay the development of such activities, and are primarily directed at Argentina and Brazil.

- **Export tax** Greasy wool; meat; beef; horse; dry, salted, and pickled hide;, and livestock are subject to an export tax of 5%.

- **Services** Few significant restrictions exist in services.

- **Government procurement** A government decree establishes that in conditions of equal quality or adequacy to the function, domestic products will have preference over foreign ones. Among foreign bidders, preference will be given to those who offer to purchase Uruguayan products.

- **Industrial free zones** Industrial free zones operate in a restriction-free environment, with no duties or taxes payable on industrial or commercial activities taking place therein. The exemption within the zones applies not only to import tariffs and other customs duties, but also to corporate income taxes, wealth taxes, and consumption taxes.

GOVERNMENT AGENCIES

Ministerio de Ganaderia, Agricultura y Pesca
Ministry of Agriculture
Constituyente 1476
11200 Montevideo
Tel: (2) 40-41-55/9; 48-45-97 Fax: (2) 49-96-23

Ministry of Economy and Finance
Colonia 1089, Piso 3
11100 Montevideo
Tel: (2) 92-10-17 Fax: (2) 92-12-77

Ministry of Foreign Affairs
Avenida 18 de Julio 1205
11100 Montevideo
Tel: (2) 92-10-06/7/8 Fax: (2) 92-13-27

Comision Administradora de las Zonas Francas
Avenida Libertador
Brig. General Lavalleja 1623
11 Montevideo
Telex: FFPAL UY

GROWTH SECTORS
- agricultural production
- industrial engineering
- industrial machinery
- agriculture products

GOVERNMENT PROCUREMENT
- expertise and equipment for construction and operation of the sewage and waste supply
- telecommunications - mobile telephone systems
- ground transportation vehicles and equipment

Business Travel

Air Travel Times

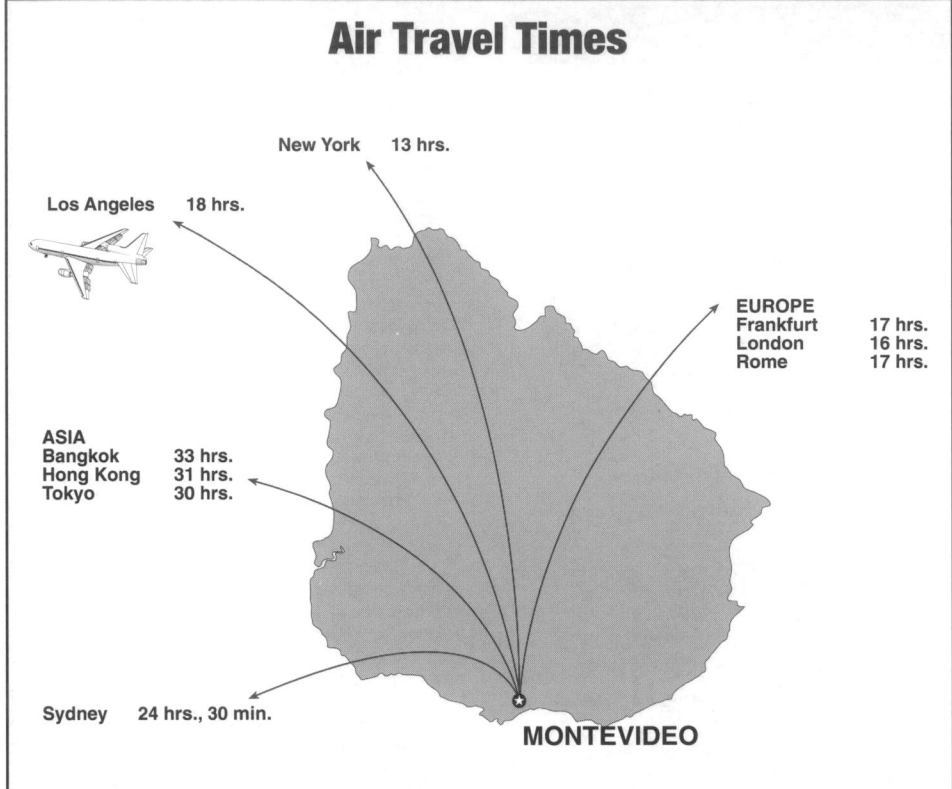

New York   13 hrs.

Los Angeles   18 hrs.

EUROPE
Frankfurt   17 hrs.
London   16 hrs.
Rome   17 hrs.

ASIA
Bangkok   33 hrs.
Hong Kong   31 hrs.
Tokyo   30 hrs.

Sydney   24 hrs., 30 min.

MONTEVIDEO

COMMUNICATIONS

Telephones Phone services are adequate. Use AN-TEL for 24 hour telephoning for both direct dial and international calling with discounted rates between 10 pm and 7 am.
Fax services are available at major hotels.
Post office Stamps can be purchased at post offices. Valuables in the mail service are often opened and stolen. The main post office is at Buenos Aires 451.

BEST TRAVEL BOOKS

Argentina, Uruguay & Paraguay: A Travel Survival Kit by Wayne Bernhardson and Marla Massolo. Lonely Planet Publications. 606 pages. Written for the budget traveler but has good practical information. This guide gives all the essentials—indispensable.
The Travelers Guide to Uruguay Customs and Manners. Elizabeth Devine & Nancy Braganti. An invaluable guide for people not wanting to put foot in mouth.
Do's and Taboo's Around the World. The Bestselling Guide to International Behavior. Edited by Roger Axtell, compiled by the Parker Pen Company. The ultimate guide to international behavior, now completely updated and expanded. Helpful, fun to read!
South American Handbook. Chicago: Passport Books. Indispensible—updated annually.

USEFUL TELEPHONE NUMBERS

If you are calling from outside Uruguay, you will need to add the country code [598] and any other international dialing requirements from within your country.
- Operator 12
- International Operator 218
- US Embassy ....(2) 23-60-61
- Fax .... (2) 488611
- Roadway Assistance .... (2) 911251
- Foreign Consulates 442
- Omnibus Colonia .... (2) 5231
- Tourist Ministry .... (2) 989105
- Hospital .... (2) 4057
- Police 890
- Ambulance/First Aid .... (2) 40111
- General Information 214
- Time 6
- Montevideo Airport .... (2) 602261

Car Rental
- Avis .... (2) 608129
- Avis Airport .... (2) 617005
- Budget .... (2) 916363
- Hertz .... (2) 907957

Credit Card Information
Lost or stolen credit cards (call collect to the US, regardless of which country the card was issued in).
- Amex...[1] (919) 333-3211
- Diner's Club................................[1] (303) 799-1504
- MasterCard ....[1] (314) 275-6690
- Visa ....[1] (410) 581-7931

Travelogue

WORKWEEK

Offices Monday-Friday 8:30 am to 12:30 pm and 7:00 pm to 10:00 pm.
Banks Monday-Friday mornings only.
Government Monday-Friday 7:30 am to 1:30 pm.
Retail Monday-Friday, 8:30 am to 12:30 pm and 7:00 pm to 10:00 pm.

HOLIDAYS

Holidays 1996
January 1 New Year's Day
January 6 Ephiphany
February 27-28 Carnival
April 4 Holy Thursday*
April 5 Good Friday*
April 19 Landing of the 33 "Orientales"
May 1 Labor Day
May 18 Battle of Las Piedras
June 19 Artigas Day
August 25 Independence Day
October 12 Columbus Day
November 2 All Saints' Day
December 25 Christmas
*Dates vary each year.

VISA AND PASSPORT

A passport is required of all travelers. A visa is not required for stays of up to three months for most nationals. For customs requirements, please contact the nearest Uruguayan embassy.

DEPARTURE FORMALITIES

There are no departure formalities for Uruguay. You can bring out of Uruguay what you bring in.

IMMUNIZATION

International certificate of vaccination is not required unless you are arriving from an infected area. Bring plenty of suntan lotion if you are bound for the beach; it gets very hot in Uruguay.

TIPPING

Taxi: 10 percent. Porters: 50 centesimo per piece. Hotel, restaurants, nightspots: 15 to 20 percent included in bill. A small additional tip is expected. Barbers and beauticians: 10 percent. Services: 20 centesimos.

CRIME

Street crimes such as pickpocketing are increasing, along with teenage muggings, but generally these events are not common.

INFRASTRUCTURE

Montevideo is the only large city, with the remaining urban population living in approximately 20 towns. Towns are extremely compact, walking is encouraged. Airports are being updated, though air travel can often be suspended. Buses, car and motorbike rentals, and ferry transportation are popular. Boat services can be crowded, with limited space for luggage. Uruguay drivers can be rather ruthless so drive carefully on the winding and hilly terrained roads. Police take bribes for traffic violations.

NATIONAL TOURIST OFFICE

Tourist Office
19 de Abril 250
Montevideo
Tel: (2) 2001

Marketing

Overview

Uruguay has, despite official pronouncements, resisted the free-market reforms and privatizations undertaken by its neighbors. The younger generation has largely departed for greener pastures, mostly in Brazil and Argentina; those left behind are adverse to change, and seem to prefer a generous social system to the workings of competitive markets. Such a group does not make for avid consumers, but trade nonetheless shows interesting, surprising turns. Due to the large government bureaucracy, the public sector is the biggest buyer in Uruguay, particularly of capital goods, but it purchases a significant quantity of consumer goods as well. Well-developed social programs and a comprehensive pension scheme ensure that wealth is fairly evenly distributed throughout the country, so there is little diversity in purchasing tastes. A product, once accepted, will generally sell well for quite a while throughout most of the country.

Distribution and Agents

Direct representation, either through a distributor or an agent resident in Uruguay, is essential. A substantial part of the importing business is controlled by large merchant houses in Montevideo. These merchant houses have their own traveling salespeople who visit the towns of the interior. Merchant houses are the only enterprises really equipped to hold stocks of merchandise as inventory for future sales. They will usually handle a variety of merchandise and cover the entire country.

Selling Techniques and Advertising

Uruguayans rely heavily on advertising to launch a new product. However, the volume of sales that can be expected from this small market does not justify great expense on advertising. Most of the important daily newspapers are published in the capital of Montevideo, where more than 45 percent of the country resides. Several regional newspapers are available in other cities, as are the main Buenos Aires papers. There are approximately 40 radio stations in Montevideo and more than 60 outside the capital. Four television stations transmit from Montevideo; 16 others serve various regions. All the above feature advertising. Agencies in Montevideo are the best source for data regarding merchandising campaigns.

Marketing in Uruguay

MARKETING TIPS

- **Buying seasons** There are no special buying seasons; due to the moderate climate normal trade continues throughout the year.
- **Agencies** There is no special agency legislation and it is not necessary for an agency agreement or contract to be legalized. No compensation is payable on termination of an agency agreement unless specifically provided for in the contract.
- **Mercosur** Despite its proximity and surface similarities, the Uruguayan market is quite different from its neighbors, Argentina and Brazil; it deserves special, individualized attention.
- **Local visits** Local representatives appreciate visits from their principals, and such visits should be planned in advance and last at least two or three days. The personal touch is of extreme importance here.
- **Government procurement** Most government buying is by public tender and foreign firms wishing to tender for government contracts must work through a properly established local representative. Generally speaking, tenders are not accepted directly from foreign countries.

AD AGENCIES

Corporation/Thompson
Convencion 1343-8
Edif. La Torre
Montevideo
Tel: (2) 923434
Fax: (2) 920719

Empresas Ogilvy & Mather
Cataluna 3137
11600 Montevideo
Tel: (2) 475477
Fax: (2) 475476

Business Culture

Greetings and Courtesies

Handshakes are customary for men and women, both when arriving and leaving. Male and female friends may kiss each other on the cheek. Present your business card (in Spanish) upon introductions. At social events, it is acceptable to say a collective good-bye, except to individuals with whom you have had an extensive conversation.

Business Ethic and Framework

Uruguayan businesspeople are cosmopolitan, sophisticated, and Eurocentric; executives in particular are noted for their strong work ethic. Initial business encounters are usually quite formal in this otherwise relaxed society. The country adheres faithfully to the general Latin precept that business relationships are based on personal relationships.

Meetings and Decision Making

Prior appointments are important, and should be made two weeks in advance. Meetings are conducted in a very formal, generally European manner. However, punctuality is relatively unimportant and minor delays on your part are acceptable. Although Uruguayan business is largely international and sophisticated in style and outlook, authority remains narrowly concentrated, and actual decisions are almost always made at a high level.

Women

Uruguayan businesswomen are becoming more common and more accepted in general, although their presence remains rare in the upper levels of management. In general, foreign businesswomen should experience few problems. Although women may walk and dine alone, many will feel more comfortable if escorted, and should take a taxi if venturing out after dark. Conservative suits or dresses are acceptable for business occasions; formal wear is seldom required.

Cultural Cautions

DO'S

- Learn something about Uruguay's history and culture—your interest and any attempts to speak Spanish will be appreciated.
- Sports—particularly football (soccer)—and international current events are a good topic of conversation; family topics are usually reserved until after you are better acquainted with your Uruguayan counterpart.

DON'TS

- Avoid race, religion, and politics in conversation.

CUSTOMS

- It is customary to send a small gift (candy or flowers) ahead of time when invited to a meal at a home.
- Titles are important, and business associates are addressed by their title and surname.

OBSERVATIONS

- Much entertaining is done at restaurants, with the guests being invited to the host's home afterward for coffee.

NEGOTIATIONS

- To avoid misunderstandings, be sure you know who has the authority to make a decision, and the procedures and time frames that must be considered.
- Uruguayans present a united front during negotiations, deferring to the senior member.
- Allow negotiations to remain open-ended, so that confrontation can be avoided and talks can be allowed to fade away if agreement cannot be reached.
- Agreements should be reduced to writing. Although contracts have historically consisted simply of schematic outlines, Uruguayans now expect more detailed documents.

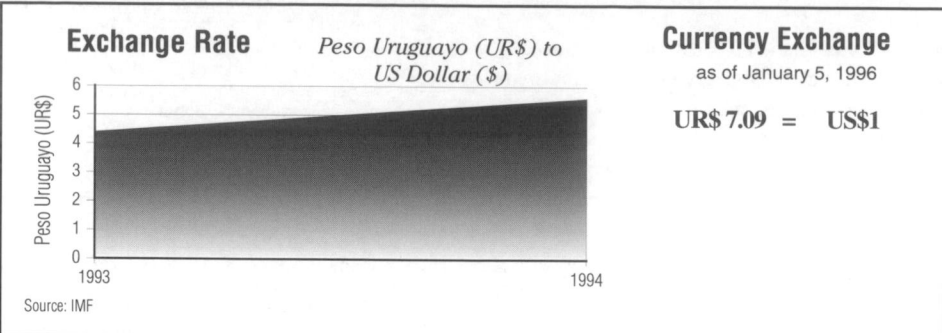

Exchange Rate

Peso Uruguayo (UR$) to US Dollar ($)

Source: IMF

Currency Exchange

as of January 5, 1996

UR$ 7.09 = US$1

Currency

The currency of Uruguay is the peso uruguayo (UR$), which is divided into 100 centesimos.

Foreign Exchange

Exchange transactions are carried out through authorized banks, financial houses, exchange houses, and the Central Bank. Any person or firm may conduct exchange transactions in the market, provided this does not become a customary business. The Central Bank intervenes to ensure that the exchange rate remains within preset limits, but it allows market rates to float freely within these limits. There are no other foreign exchange controls. The peso is freely convertible into US dollars and for any transaction, and much of the economy is based on the dollar.

Capital Transfers

Inward and outward private capital transfers by either residents or nonresidents may be made freely, with the exception of certain limited inward and outward transfers. There are no surrender or repatriation requirements or restrictions on capital or profits.

Investment Incentives

In theory, Uruguay welcomes foreign investment, and there are few restrictions on such. Foreign banks are very active in off-shore banking, and there are no significant restrictions on professional services such as law, medicine, or accounting. Also, travel and ticketing services are unrestricted to foreign investment.

Investment Restrictions

There have been significant limitations on foreign equity participation in certain sectors of the economy. Investment in areas regarded as strategic—including electricity, hydrocarbons, banking, railroads, telecommunications, and the press—require government authorization.

Money Matters

BITS AND PIECES

- **Mercosur** Uruguay has been the beneficiary of large inflows of capital, primarily from its neighbors and Mercosur partners Argentina and Brazil.
- **Price controls** Price controls are limited to a small set of products and services for public consumption such as bread, milk, passenger transportation, utilities, and fuels.
- **Taxes** The government relies heavily on consumption taxes (value-added and excise) and taxes on foreign trade (export taxes and tariffs) for its general revenues.
- **Gold** Residents and nonresidents may freely purchase, hold, and sell financial gold with a fineness of not less than 0.9 in Uruguay or abroad. Gold for industrial purposes is subject to the general policy that governs the exportation, importation, and trading of goods.

BANKS

American Express Bank, SA
Rincon 473
Montevideo
Tel: (2) 960092
Fax: (2) 962245
Telex: 22055

Banco Central del Uruguay
Avda Juan P. Fabini esq.
Florida Montevideo
Tel: (2) 917117
Fax: (2) 921634
Telex: 26659

Banco de la Republica Oriental del Uruguay
Calle Cerrito 351 y Zabala
Montevideo
Tel: (2) 950157
Fax: (2) 962064
Telex: 26990

Banco Hipotecario del Uruguay
Avda Fernandez Crespo 1508
Montevideo

Banco Comercial
Cerrito 400
Casilla 34
Montevideo
Tel: (2) 960541
Fax: (2) 953569
Telex: 26911

Bank of America NT & SA
25 de Mayo 552
Montevideo
Tel: (2) 960938
Telex: 820

Central Bank of Uruguay
Avenida Juan P. Fabini esq. Florida
Montevideo
Tel: (2) 91-71-17
Telex: 6659

Centrobanco
25 de Mayo 528
Montevideo
Tel: (2) 960423
Telex: 26626

First National Bank of Boston
Zabala 1463
Montevideo
Tel: (2) 960127
Fax: (2) 962209
Telex: 22433

Lloyds Bank (BLSA) Ltd.
Zabala 1500
Casilla 204
Montevideo
Tel: (2) 960976
Fax: (2) 961262
Telex: 26632

TAXATION

Taxation requires sophisticated knowledge of complex rules and regulations specific to each country. For more detailed information we suggest you refer to the Ernst & Young Corporate Tax Guide and Directory, available from the Ernst & Young accounting office in your country, or from:

Cr. Ricardo Villamarzo y Asociados
Avda. 18 de Julio 984, 4th Floor
Palacio Brasil
POB 1303
11100 Montevideo
Uruguay
Tel: (2) 92-31-47
Cable: Nitram
Fax: (2) 92-13-31

- Corporations are taxed on income derived from all activities performed, property situated, or economic rights used in Uruguay.
- Capital gains are considered as ordinary income, and taxed at the customary corporate tax rate.

At a Glance

Corporate Income Tax Rate (%)	30
Capital Gains Tax Rate (%)	30
Branch Tax Rate (%)	30
Withholding Tax (%)	
Dividends (a)(b)	30
Interest	0
Royalties (a)	30
Technical Assistance Payments (a)(c)	30
Branch Remittance Tax (b)	30
Net Operating Losses (Years)	
Carryback	0
Carryforward	3

(a) Applicable to nonresidents. A nonresident corporation is defined as a corporation not incorporated in Uruguay.
(b) Dividends and branch remittances are subject to withholding taxes of 30 percent, if the funds are considered taxable income in the beneficiary's country, and if a tax credit is in place for the tax withheld in Uruguay. Dividends paid to residents are tax-exempt.
(c) Technical assistance payments are tax-exempt if taxed in the beneficiary's country, and if no tax credits for the tax withheld in Uruguay have been granted.

Legal

Legal System

Uruguay is a civil code country. Judicial power is vested in the Supreme Court of Justice. The judiciary is structurally independent of the executive branch. The Congress is the legislative branch.

Intellectual Property Rights

Patents Uruguay approves patents for new discoveries or inventions, new industrial products, and new methods to achieve an industrial result or product. Patents are granted for 15 years, without extensions. Annual payments are required to keep the registration active. A patent must be used within five years, plus a two-year extension; otherwise any interested person may obtain a license to use it. A foreign patent not exercised may be revalidated in Uruguay three years after it was granted in the country of origin. Improvements on an existing patent may be eligible for a separate patent on the improvement only, but consent of the owner of the principal patent is required to exercise the subsidiary patent right.

Trademarks An applicant for a trademark should address the National Center of Industrial Property. To register a foreign trademark, the owner must present a certificate of inscription from the country of origin. The certificate must be accompanied by eight copies of the trademark, a description stating how the trademark will be used, a receipt for the payment of the tax, and a power of attorney if the petition is made by an agent. Uruguay law contains a long list of exceptions that cannot be used as trademarks.

Copyrights A copyright applies to any literary, scientific, or artistic creation, including software, books, pictures, maps, music, theatrical works, screenplays, paintings, drawings, and sculptures. It comprises the right to alienate, publish, reproduce, translate, execute, and circulate in any manner. Copyright protection is granted following an announcement in the official newspaper. Inscription must be requested within two years after the initial publication of the work in Uruguay, or within three years if the work is published abroad and the author is Uruguayan. Protection runs for the author's life plus 40 years.

Trade Secrets A few laws protect trade secrets, but it is still difficult to get an injunction against violators, and trials are usually lengthy.

Business Registration

All corporate documents and respective authorizations must be recorded in the Public Register. If a corporation is established by public subscription, promoters must draw up a prospectus. It must be approved by the administrative authority and recorded at the Register of Commerce. An organization meeting must be called after the subscription period, to decide on issues such as the report of promoters and evaluation of contributions other than money.

Contracts and Dispute Resolution

Businesses in Uruguay prefer written contracts, although verbal ones will stand up in court. Contracts can and should be made through legal representatives. For a contract to exist, Uruguayan law requires parties who have capacity to contract, valid consent, licit object, lawful cause, and licit form. Mercantile contracts are governed by the commercial code, supplemented by the civil code. Parties may stipulate that contracts will be governed by foreign legislation and jurisdiction, provided there is a justified reason. The stipulation is not valid if the contracts refer to matters within the exclusive jurisdiction of Uruguayan courts, such as contracts to be performed in Uruguay.

Notaries

Notaries execute a number of documents in Uruguay, and must have their signatures on file. To become a notary, one must be a Uruguayan citizen and pass a special course. There are also age and personality requirements that must be met. Documents executed abroad are accepted in Uruguay if executed in accordance with the laws of the respective country and properly legalized to be effective in Uruguay. Powers of attorney granted abroad must also be translated and notarized in Uruguay. Notaries maintain a protocol or register containing all documents executed before them.

Labor

The Constitution guarantees the right of workers to organize freely and encourages the formation of unions. Labor unions are independent of government or political party control. Employees have the right to strike. Collective bargaining takes place on a plant-wide or sector-wide basis, with or without government mediation, as the parties wish. Forced or compulsory labor is prohibited by law. There is a legislated minimum wage, set by the Price and Wage Commission, and workers are protected by health and safety standards, which are generally adhered to in practice. The ratio of work hours to work stoppages in Uruguay is relatively low.

Legal Matters

LEGAL BRIEFS

- **Business entities** Entities with limited liability are popular. Limited partnerships are comprised of "comanditados" who are jointly liable without limitation for partnership debts, and "comanditarios" whose liability is limited to the amount of their contribution. The name "comanditarios" cannot appear in the firm name under penalty of joint liability. Limited liability companies can be formed by a minimum of two partners and a maximum of 50.

- **Public contracts** Contracts with government, state agencies, and state enterprises are subject to special rules.

- **Foreign judgments** Foreign judgments that resolve disputes are accepted in Uruguay courts, but only if they meet Uruguay legal requirements. For example, they must be rendered by a court with subject matter jurisdiction, comply with due process, be duly legalized, and be translated into Spanish.

- **Workweek** The standard workweek is 48 hours in six days, with overtime compensation for work in excess of 48 hours.

- **Minimum age** Children as young as 12 may be employed if they have a work permit. Children under the age of 18 may not perform dangerous, fatiguing, or night work, apart from domestic employment.

- **Forced labor** Forced or compulsory labor is prohibited by law and in practice and there is no evidence of its existence.

- **Assignments** As toward third persons an assignee of a credit is not considered as owner until the debtor is notified, which may be effected by exhibiting the credit document, which must bear a note signed by the assignor and designate the assignee.

- **Corporations** Corporations are designated by name accompanied by words "Sociedad Anonima" or abbreviation "S.A." At least two shareholders are required for organization and continued legal existence of corporation.

- **International agreements** Uruguay is a member of GATT/WTO; OAS.

LEGAL CONTACTS

Posadas, Posadas & Vecino
Juncal 1305-21st Floor
Montevideo
Tel: (2) 96-2202
Fax: (2) 96-2429

Bado, Kuster, Zerbino & Rachette
Paysandu 935, Piso 3
1100 Montevideo
Tel: (2) 92-0395
Fax: (2) 92-5950

Estudio Juridico DM (Duran & Muxi)
Misiones 1305, Piso 1
11000 Montevideo
Tel: (2) 95-4386
Fax: (2) 96-2755

Esdudio Dr. Mezzera
Plaza Independecia 811, Piso 1
11100 Montevideo
Tel: (2) 92-9020
Fax: (2) 92-2415

Olivera & Peirano
Misiones 1424, Piso 2
11000 Montevideo
Tel:(2) 95-9820, 96-5859
Fax: (2) 96-5863

GOVERNMENT AGENCIES

Ministry of Economy and Finance
Colonia 1089, 3º
Montevideo
Tel: (2) 921017
Fax: (2) 921277

Ministry of Education and Culture
Reconquista 535
11000 Montevideo
Tel: (2) 95-01-03
Fax: (2) 98-64-15

Ministry of Foreign Affairs
Colonia 1206
Montevideo
Tel: (2) 921007
Fax: (2) 921327

Ministry of Housing, Territorial Planning and the Environment
Zabala 1427
11000 Montevideo
Tel: (2) 95-02-11, 95-04-21
Fax: (2) 96-29-14 Fax: (2) 96-29-14

Ministry of Industry, Energy and Mines
Rincón 747
11000 Montevideo
Tel: (2) 90-02-31, 91-29-42
Fax: (2) 92-12-45

Ministry of the Interior
Mercedes 993
Montevideo
Tel: (2) 989024
Fax: (2) 900502

Ministry of Labor and Social Security
Juncal 1511, Piso 4
11000 Montevideo
Tel: (2) 96-26-81
Fax: (2) 96-37-67

Ministry of Livestock, Agriculture and Fisheries
Avenida Constituyente 1476
11200 Montevideo
Tel: (2) 40-41-55 through 9, 48-45-97
Fax: (2) 49-96-23

Ministry of Public Health
Avenida 18 de Julio 1892
11200 Montevideo
Tel: (2) 40-01-01, 40-01-04
Fax: (2) 48-53-60

Ministry of Public Works and Transport
Rincon 575
Montevideo
Tel: (2) 963197
Fax: (2) 963122

Ministry of Tourism
Avenida del Libertador Brigadier General Lavalleja 1409, Piso 5/6
11100 Montevideo
Tel: (2) 90-41-48, 91-32-43
Fax: (2) 80-93-97

Ministry of Transportation and Public Works
Rincón 561
11000 Montevideo
Tel: (2) 95-73-86, 95-75-44
Fax: (2) 90-26-83

CHAMBERS OF COMMERCE

Chamber of Industries
Avda Libertador Brig. Gral Lavalleja 1670, 1º
Montevideo
Tel: (2) 901941

National Chamber of Commerce
Edif. de la Bolsa de Comercio
Misiones 1400, Casilla 1000
11000 Montevideo
Tel: (2) 961277

Chamber of Commerce for Local Products
Avda Gral Rondeau 1908
11800 Montevideo
Tel: (2) 940644
Fax: (2) 940673

Inter-American Council of Commerce and Production
Edif. de la Bolsa de Comercio
Misiones 1400
11000 Montevideo
Tel: (2) 961277

WORLD TRADE CENTER

World Trade Center Montevideo
Hidalgos 527 Of. 802
11300 Montevideo
Tel: (2) 70-19-88, 70-74-64
Fax: (2) 71-56-00

BUSINESS AND TRADE ORGANIZATIONS

Board of Foreign Commerce
Cuareim 1384
Montevideo
Tel: (2) 90-11-28, 90-39-68, 90-30-41

International Trade Consortium
Rio Negro 1394 Of. 703
Montevideo 11800
Tel: (2) 921090, 922212

Export Trade de Uruguay
Caramuru 6092
Montevideo 11400
Tel: (2) 605217

Uruguayan Exporters Union
Rincon 454 Fl. 2
Montevideo 11000
Tel: (2) 961117
Fax: (2) 961116

Camara de Industriea
Avenida Libertador
Brig. General Lavalleja 1672
Montevideo
Telex: 22575 PROCOEX UY

Importers and Wholesalers Association
Misiones 1400
Montevideo

Trade Chamber
Misiones 1400
Montevideo
Tel: (2) 955763

AD AGENCIES

Grey-Diciembre
Boulevard Artigas 1913
Montevideo
Tel: (2) 400066
Fax: (2) 484924

Impetu, Asociada A Lintas Worldwide
Colonia 924, Piso 8
Montevideo
Tel: (2) 920544
Fax: (2) 921942

McCann-Erickson Corp. (S.A.)
Avda. Luis P. Ponce 1529
Montevideo 11600
Tel: (2) 789531
Fax: (2) 789491

Viceversa/Young & Rubicam
Rio Branco 1494
Montevideo
Tel: (2) 924710
Fax: (2) 921992

NEWSPAPERS

El Dia
Avda 18 de Julio
Montevideo

El Diario
Rio Negro 1028
Montevideo
Tel: (2) 920348
Fax: (2) 921326

El Diario Espanol
Cerrito 551-555
Apdo 899
Montevideo

Diario Oficial
Florida 1178
Motevideo

Gaceta Comercial
Juncal 1391
11000 Montevideo
Tel: (2) 920348
Fax: (2) 962596

La Manana
Rio Negro 1028
Montevideo
Tel: (2) 920348
Fax: (2) 921326

El Pais
Michelini 1287
Montevideo
Tel: (2) 912175

Boletin Comercial
Colon 1580
Montevideo

Indice Industrial-Anuario de la Industria Uruguaya
Sarandi 456
Montevideo
Tel: (2) 951963

Marketing S
Duvimioso Terra 1157
Casilla 10529
Montevideo
Tel: (2) 412174

RADIO AND TELEVISION

Administracion Nacional de Telecomunicaciones (ANTEL)
Avda Daniel Fernandez Crespo 1534
Montevideo
Tel: (2) 404585
Fax: (2) 486071

Asociacion Nacional de Broadcasters Uruguayos (ANDEBU)
Calle Yi 12264
Montevideo
Tel: (2) 900053

Monte Carlo TV Color
Paraguay 2253
Casilla 5019
Montevideo
Tel: (2) 944591
Fax: (2) 942001

SAETA TV - Canel 10
Dr. Lorenzo Carnelli 1234
Montevideo
Tel: (2) 402120
Fax: (2) 409771

SODRE - Servicio Oficial de Difusion Radiotelevision y Espectaculos
Blvd. Artigas 2552
Montevideo
Tel: (2) 806448

INTERNET ADDRESSES

Usenet group:
soc.culture.uruguay

República Oriental del Uruguay
http://bilbo.edu.uy/uruguay.html

Uruguay on the Internet
http://www.latinworld.com/countries/uruguay

Venezuela

Republic of Venezuela

Economy

Overview

Venezuela has endured a number of political and economic crises which have shaken both foreign and domestic business confidence in the country. In the past year it has suffered a major banking collapse, a huge devaluation of its currency, and skyrocketing inflation. However, after reform and liberalization measures were employed in late 1994, it is now operating in an austere and fiscally responsible manner. GDP has not yet recovered, but the government is making every effort to draw foreign investment and encourage domestic industries to become competitive in international markets.

Trade

Venezuela's petroleum industry continues to be the dominant factor in its foreign trade account. The US is the largest source of both its imports and exports, followed by Colombia, which profited from a recent trade agreement, and Japan. Venezuela's recent trade surpluses have resulted more from shrinking import levels due to economic crises, than from overall growth. The government is committed to increasing Venezuela's trade with its regional partners, as well as expanding its trading contacts globally. Recent reforms, including the removal of many barriers to foreign investment, have moved Venezuela toward a more diversified, competitive, and export-oriented economy.

Sectors

Agriculture This sector accounts for only five percent of GDP, and employs about six percent of the labor force. Agricultural imports are significant, and wheat imports in particular will continue to be important not only for domestic consumption but also for the production of products for export.

Industry The petroleum industry is the driving force behind Venezuela's economy, and is by far the single largest contributor to government revenues. Until recently, emphasis was placed on crude oil exports but a shift has now been made to the marketing of oil products. Much of the hydrocarbon sector has been opened up to foreign investment and large petrochemical joint ventures have been established. Mineral exports are expected to double over the next five years due to newly implemented projects.

Services Although tourism continues to contribute significantly to GDP, the financial and currency crises have seriously hampered development of other services industries. The financial markets are in chaos, banks have not yet recovered from the crisis of 1994, and many other service providers have suffered as a result.

Trends

Venezuela's rich natural resources and its industrious population give it a strong foundation for long-term growth. It will, however, have to recover from the banking debacle and currency crisis of 1994 before it can make any real progress toward sustained growth. The government has made positive efforts toward rescuing the economy, although this has often been at the expense of civil rights and social stability. It has also reversed itself on many market-oriented reforms. However, strong ties with trading partners in the region should aid its efforts, and there may well be plenty of opportunity for foreign participation in the near future.

At a Glance

THE COUNTRY

Location Northern South America, bordering the Caribbean Sea between Colombia and Guyana.
Terrain Varies from mountainous to plains.
Climate Tropical; hot, humid to moderate depending on the elevation.

THE PEOPLE

Population 20,600,000
Ethnic composition
Mestizo 67%
White.. 21%
Black... 10%
Indian 2%
Religious composition
Roman Catholic 96%
Protestant 2%
Other.. 2%
Languages spoken Spanish (official) and numerous Indian dialects.
Education and literacy Nine years of schooling is compulsory. About 90 percent of the population can read and write.
Labor force
Total:.. 7,500,000
By occupation: services 58%, industry 36% and agriculture 6% (1985).

COUNTRY FACTS

Political and legal Venezuela is a federal republic governed by an executive, legislative, and judicial branch. The president decides the size and makeup of the cabinet. The executive branch drafts most legislation, which is then debated by the legislature. The Congress can override any presidential veto. The legal system is based on Napoleonic code. All courts are part of the federal system. The justices of the Supreme Court are appointed by Congress. There is universal suffrage at 18 years of age.
Telephone Telecommunications are modern and rapidly expanding. There are more than 1,400,000 telephones in the country. International electronic mail can be sent and received in Venezuela. International country code: [58]. Selected city codes: Caracas (2), Maracay (43), San Cristobal (76), Bolivar (85), Valencia (41).
Transportation While Venezuela has an extensive road system, it is often poorly maintained. Only 31,000 of the 81,000 kilometers of highway are paved. With the exception of air service, the transportation sector has not kept pace with the country's growth, and falls behind international standards. There are a number of major airports that have international service. Caracas has a modern subway but the rest of the nation is serviced by only one functioning rail line.
Environment Only three percent of the land is arable; more than 2,600 square miles of land is irrigated. Venezuela is subject to floods, rockslides, mudslides, and periodic drought. Current issues: sewage pollution of Lago de Valencia; oil and urban pollution; soil degradation; and urban and industrial pollution, especially along the Caribbean coast.
Media There are 181 AM stations but no FM, and 59 television stations.
Health Life expectancy is 70 years for males and 76 for females. Infant mortality rates are high at 27 deaths per 1,000 births.

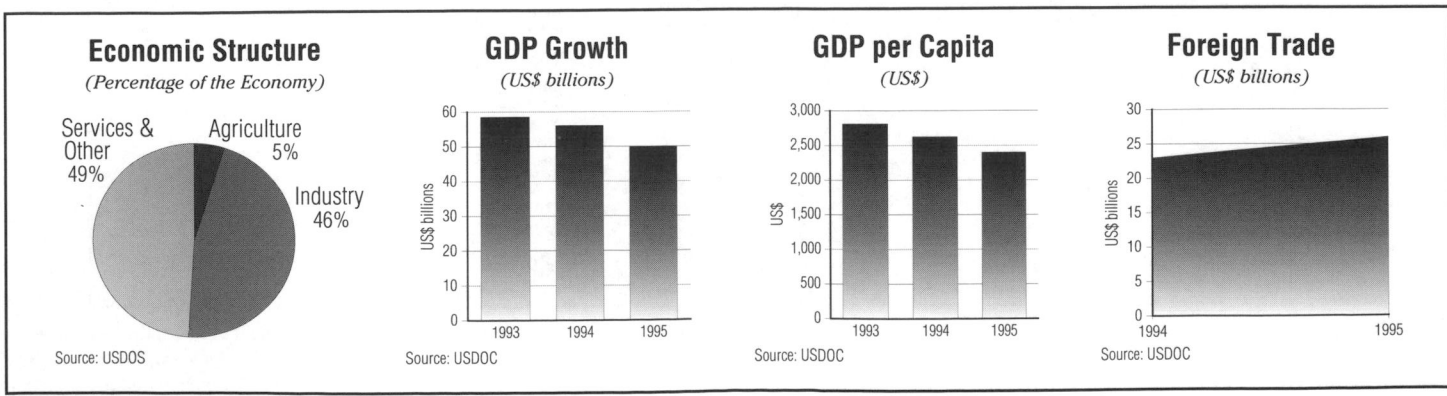

Economic Structure
(Percentage of the Economy)
Services & Other 49%
Agriculture 5%
Industry 46%
Source: USDOS

GDP Growth
(US$ billions)
1993, 1994, 1995
Source: USDOC

GDP per Capita
(US$)
1993, 1994, 1995
Source: USDOC

Foreign Trade
(US$ billions)
1994, 1995
Source: USDOC

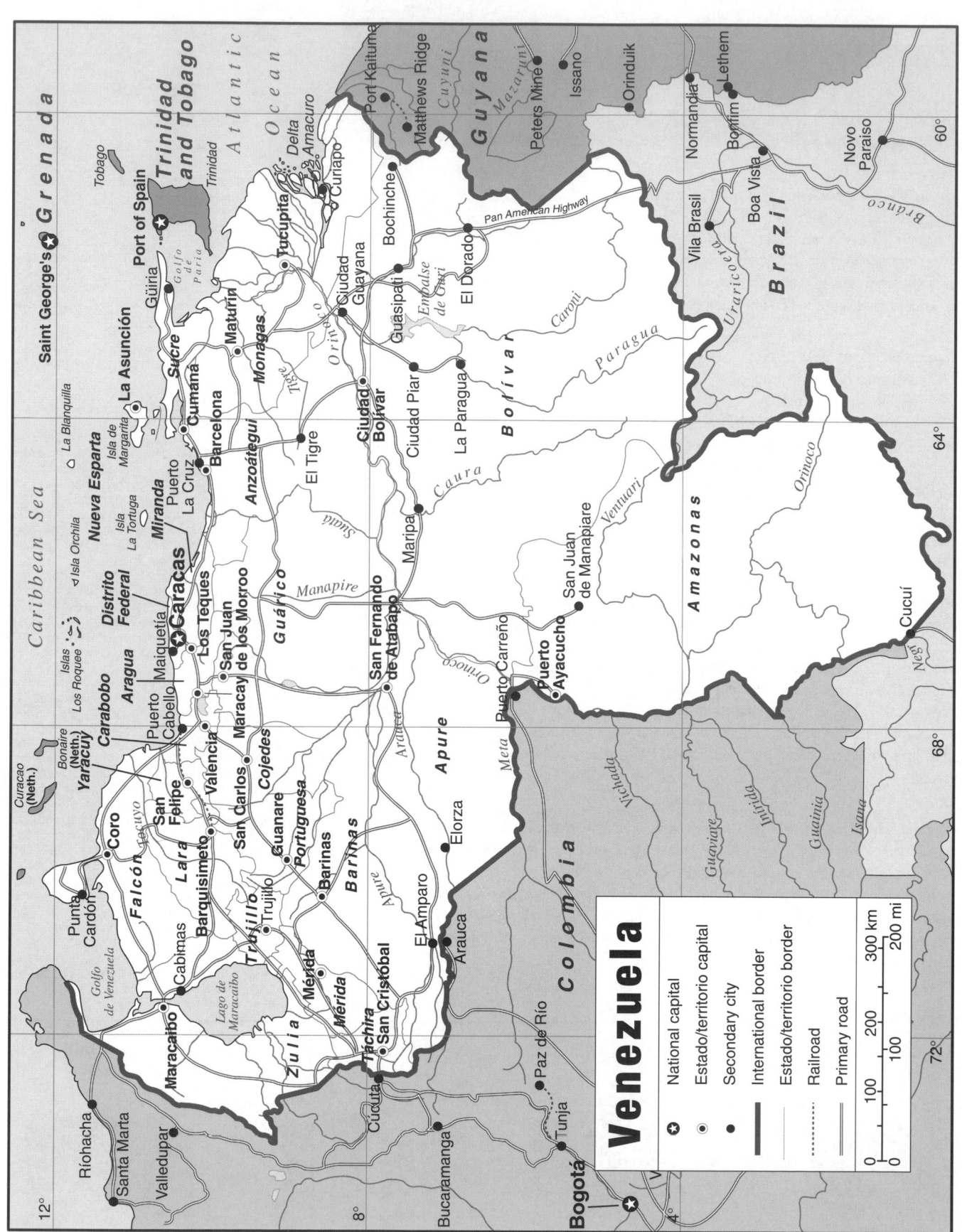

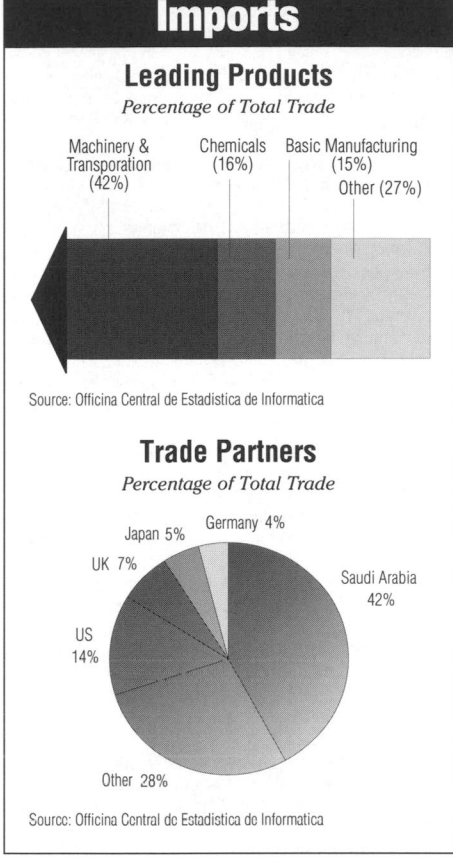

Foreign Trade

Imports

Leading Products
Percentage of Total Trade

Machinery & Transporation (42%)
Chemicals (16%)
Basic Manufacturing (15%)
Other (27%)

Source: Officina Central de Estadistica de Informatica

Trade Partners
Percentage of Total Trade

- Japan 5%
- Germany 4%
- UK 7%
- Saudi Arabia 42%
- US 14%
- Other 28%

Source: Officina Central de Estadistica de Informatica

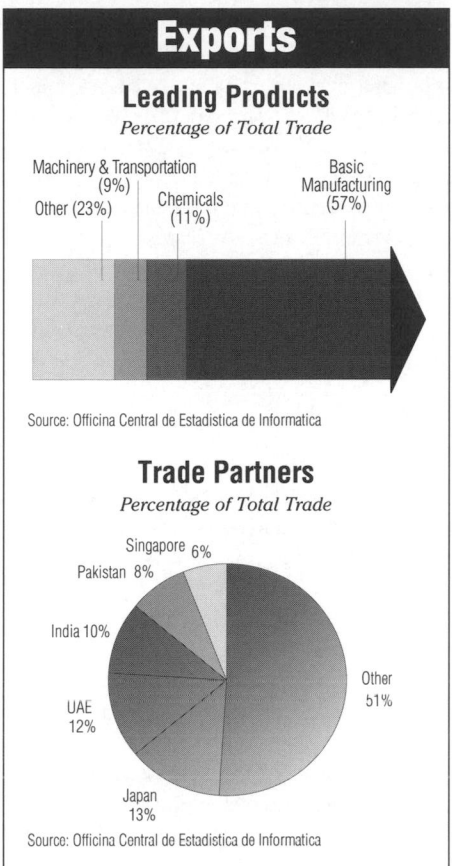

Exports

Leading Products
Percentage of Total Trade

Machinery & Transportation (9%)
Other (23%)
Chemicals (11%)
Basic Manufacturing (57%)

Source: Officina Central de Estadistica de Informatica

Trade Partners
Percentage of Total Trade

- Singapore 6%
- Pakistan 8%
- India 10%
- UAE 12%
- Japan 13%
- Other 51%

Source: Officina Central de Estadistica de Informatica

Opportunities

FOR IMPORTING TO VENEZUELA
- electrical machinery and equipment
- transportation equipment (cars, trucks, parts)
- chemicals
- minerals and mineral products
- wheat and feed grains
- health and beauty products
- high fashion clothing

FOR EXPORTING FROM VENEZUELA
- petroleum
- natural gas
- hydroelectric power
- iron ore
- coal
- bauxite

GROWTH SECTORS
- hospital and health system modernization
- improved prisons
- improved highways
- improved water distribution
- improved housing

GOVERNMENT PROCUREMENT
- infrastructure
- housing
- medical care
- construction equipment
- medical equipment
- security and safety equipment

Trade News

RULES AND REGULATIONS

- **Regulations** Customs requires that all documents be in Spanish. The Venezuelan Standards Agency (COVEININ) has established almost 300 obligatory standards that apply to imported products. In such cases, customs authorities require a Venezuelan certificate of compliance. The certification can be obtained with a letter confirming compliance granted by a recognized standards institute in the country of origin.

- **Trading companies** The government of Venezuela owns and operates an extensive portion of the country's domestic product.

- **Import restrictions** At this time, imports of used autos, used clothing, and used tires are prohibited. Products such as cigarette paper, bank notes, weapons of war and certain explosives can only be imported by government agencies. Weapons for private use, such as shotguns, sporting rifles, air rifles, non-military pistols, and commercial explosives can only be imported through a company owned by the Ministry of Defense (CAVIM), which can delegate authority to import on its behalf.

- **Import licenses** Licenses have generally been eliminated, but a number of products still require them, including arms and explosives. Import certificates are required for certain products subject to special supervision, such as phytosanitary certificates for grains, seeds, and plants. Medicines, foods, and cosmetics require registration by the Ministry of Health.

- **Tariff rates** All imports are assessed a one percent customs handling charge. The import duties are calculated on the CIF value of the shipment. Venezuela has adopted the harmonized tariff schedule. Duties range from 0 to 20 percent, with a few exceptions such as automobiles which carry a duty of 35 percent. All imports also face a 12 percent luxury tax (alcoholic beverages, cigarettes, vehicles priced between US$22-44,000, and jewelry.) A 20 percent luxury tax is charged on commercial cable television services, vehicles priced above US $44,000, motorcycles of more than 500 cc, pleasure boats, coin-operated games, furs, and satellite dishes.

- **Capital goods** The re-export of capital goods is normally not allowed, unless the owner has made prior arrangements to the effect that the equipment is to be used in Venezuela only for a specific project and is not to stay in the country.

- **Temporary entry** Venezuela allows the import of merchandise on a temporary basis for exhibitions, cultural purposes, demonstrations, scientific purposes, or specific contracts. The importer must request permission for temporary entry, providing an exact description of the merchandise, its number or volume, its value, and its expected date of re-export. Normally, temporary entry permits are granted for a maximum stay of up to six months. The one percent customs handling charge must be paid and is not reimbursable.

- **Export restrictions** In rare cases controls can be applied by the Foreign Trade Institute (ICE), but these are usually in cases where the control avoids a domestic shortage.

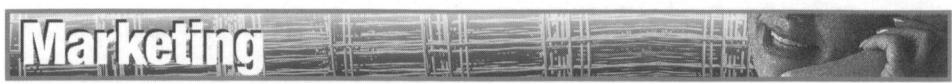

Overview

In theory, it is relatively easy for a foreign seller to enter the Venezuelan market. Registration procedures are fairly straightforward, and no specific business licenses are required for local entities to import foreign products. The business infrastructure, including telephone service, is becoming more developed, and office space and trained personnel are readily available. However, the cost of doing business in Venezuela is relatively high, because of steep tariffs and the many levels of commissioned agents involved. Also, the current administration has recently clamped down on and seriously inhibited the workings of a free market. It has become one of the largest purchasers of goods and services. Purchases by government agencies are ruled by a complex system of laws, decrees and regulations—and there is no specific agency in charge of government procurement or which provides guidance to foreign sellers. Moreover, government officials are not permitted to conduct business in any language except Spanish. Thus, foreign sellers who have a reliable and well-connected agent in Venezuela have a much better chance of success than those who do not.

Distribution

All channels are open to foreign sellers: manufacturer's representatives or commission agents, wholesale import distributors, import retailers, or direct sales. The Venezuelan commercial code does not restrict business activities to specific modes of operation and any combination of channels are common. Wholesalers often are retailers at the same time. Many retailers handle their own imports, placing orders through commission agents, or purchasing directly from the foreign manufacturers, or from exporters. Venezuelan companies tend to place repeated small orders, and to hold small inventories. Foreign companies requiring minimum orders, or even minimum annual sales, will encounter strong resistance from prospective representatives or agents.

There are numerous malls, though large department stores are few, and only in the past few years have discount stores appeared in Venezuela. Franchises are allowed and are slowly becoming more common; however, in the long run franchises will probably be successful only if they bring technology, services, or systems unavailable in Venezuela. The formation of joint ventures by forming a new company with local capital or by buying into an existing local company is quite common, and there are few restrictions or regulations governing them.

Agents, Distributors, and Partners

With a large pool of many potential customers, an agent with access to all of them is the best method of covering the market. Agents in Venezuela provide a wide spectrum of services and commissions vary widely depending on the nature of the product and the work or time required by the agent. The use of agents where there are multiple levels of customers may be the most practical and efficient means of covering the market. Wholesalers or distributors do not generally have sales forces; they rely instead on advertising. Venezuela has no set of laws or regulations which protect a local agent. On the other hand, placing Venezuelan citizens on the company's payroll can be unexpectedly costly in case of separation, since in that case they are entitled to all benefits of the very generous labor laws.

Selling Techniques

Direct marketing through television commercials, newspaper inserts, house visits, or street vendors is common in Venezuela. Mail orders are impossible due to the very poor postal system. Placing orders by phone with delivery by messenger is becoming popular, and several companies insert catalogs in newspapers. As the telephone system continues to improve, direct marketing by phone will become more common. Providing materials in Spanish is key to successful selling.

Advertising

There are numerous advertising companies in Caracas, including subsidiaries of well-known foreign agencies. Daily newspapers are the most common form of advertising, even for machinery or industrial equipment. Television and radio commercials are often used to promote consumer goods. Billboards, distribution of leaflets, newspaper inserts, and in-store promotions are also used. Trade shows are numerous and well-attended, and serve as an excellent vehicle to finding an agent or distributor.

Service and Customer Support

It is extremely important that prospective agents or distributors provide technical information and maintenance requirements, especially if a product is new to the market. Maintaining an adequate stock of spare parts is also considered essential. An agent might request training at the exporter's factory, since the average Venezuelan business does not have sales engineers or specialists and some form of specialized expertise will often be required.

Marketing in Venezuela

MARKETING TIPS

- **Legal complexities** Contracting a local law firm is advisable before entering into any business relationship, especially one with the Venezuelan government.
- **Price controls** In an effort to control inflation, the government has placed price controls on an increasing number of products, particularly foods, pharmaceuticals, and services.
- **Product pricing** For other than controlled products, pricing is pretty much left to market and competitive forces. Generally, pricing is what the market will bear, and mark-ups of 100 percent or more are not uncommon.
- **Special competitive factors** The cost of doing business in Venezuela is high, partly because of expensive labor fringe benefits, and salaries for personnel with English language abilities or technical aptitude.
- **Franchise payments** Franchise payments, royalties and patents, and technical assistance agreements must be registered with the Superintendent of Foreign Investment.
- **National treatment** Joint ventures and wholly owned subsidiaries of foreign companies are treated the same as Venezuelan firms.
- **Establishing an office** A business must first be registered with the Venezuelan Commercial Registry to be legally established.
- **Coordinating or reporting offices** The opening and operating of a coordinating or reporting office is not considered foreign investment or a business activity as long as the office does not sell and is being financed from the home office.
- **Price-fixing** Price-fixing among manufacturers or dealers is prohibited by law, and heavy fines can be levied on violators.
- **Contract changes** When dealing with the government, it is advisable to insist that all contract change requests be made in writing, and that any subsequent agreement related thereto be reduced to writing and signed by an authorized representative.

AD AGENCIES

Leo Burnett Venezuela, C.A.
Centro Plaza, Torre B
Niveles 7, 8YA
Avenida Francisco deMiranda
Caracas 1062
Tel: (2) 283-7066
Fax: (2) 283-8764

Fischer-Grey
Edificio OficenroLos Ruices Piso 2
Caracas 1070
Tel: (2) 238-0062
Fax: (2) 234-3874, 239-9711

Ghersy Bates
Av. Principal Los Ruices Diego Cisnero
Dentro Empresarial Autana Caracas, 10-11-A
Tel: (2) 237-5147
Fax: (2) 237-5437

Zulia MTS Bates
Av. 21 Esq. Calle 71
Maracaibo
Tel: (43) 518553
Fax: (43) 518459

McCann-Erickson Publicidad, S.A.
Torre la Primera
Av. Francisco de Miranda
50163 Caracas
Tel: (2) 2011511
Fax: (2) 9530702

J. Walter Thompson De Venezuela C.A.
Apartado 952
Caracas
Tel: (2) 913544
Fax: (2) 927183

Franklin Whaite & Associates S.A.
Apartado de Correos
66.026 Caracas
Tel: (2) 9593633
Fax: (2) 9593407

Business Culture

Greetings and Courtesies

Handshakes are customary among both men and women, both when arriving and leaving. Male friends may hug and female friends may kiss each other on the cheek, and even acquaintances may touch (but only men with men and women with women). If you are not introduced by your host, it is acceptable to introduce yourself in both business and social contexts. Always say good-bye to everyone when leaving a social event.

Business Ethic and Framework

Venezuelans are considered to be among the more demonstrative South Americans, although Venezuelan business and social culture is based on correct, often strongly hierarchical but personal relationships that recognize personal dignity. To Venezuelans, work is not the most important part of life, but they do adhere strictly to the forms that govern what is nevertheless one of life's more important spheres. Appropriateness is critical, and Venezuelans value tactfulness and sensitivity as much as they dislike overt aggressiveness. However, they can be quite direct and have few cultural inhibitions about saying "no."

Decision Making

Authority remains rather narrowly concentrated and actual decisions are almost always made at a high level. You should approach senior people, but expect that Venezuelans will want to know your standing within the hierarchy and will generally wish to match you with someone of similar rank, despite the fact that only their senior people will actually be able to approve agreements. Cultivate these peer relationships, because the quality of these relationships may strongly influence the actual decision maker even when your immediate counterpart is not the one making the decision.

Women

Although women generally occupy a secondary status in male-dominated Venezuela, many operate businesses and may be accorded considerable freedom. Venezuelan women are becoming more common and more accepted in business in general, although their presence remains rare in the upper levels of business hierarchies. In general, foreign businesswomen should experience few problems. Nevertheless, foreign businesswomen are expected to be highly professional, appropriate, and neither aggressive nor confrontational. Although women may generally go on the streets and dine alone, many will feel more comfortable if escorted, and all should take a taxi if venturing out after dark.

Meetings

Introductions and contacts are imperative. If you do not have a mutual business acquaintance to introduce you, consult with your embassy for a referral. Appointments should be made at least two weeks in advance and reconfirmed the day before. Venezuelans may or may not be punctual, but they expect you to be. Because of their international experience, Venezuelans have become accustomed to dealing directly with business issues; however, because business relationships are founded on personal relationships, several meetings and perhaps more than one trip may be required to conclude an agreement. Business entertaining is fairly common, with the business lunch being an institution, but one that is usually initiated by the Venezuelan party. Business is seldom discussed directly at business dinners, which are more social in tone. Invitations to a home are rare, and much entertaining is done at restaurants, hotels, or clubs. Spouses are seldom included; remember that even polite attention to someone else's spouse can be misinterpreted.

Business Attire

Foreign businessmen are expected to wear rather formal, conservatively fashionable, dark, lightweight suits. Foreign businesswomen should wear elegant suits or dresses, with stockings (although Venezuelan women generally do not) and heels. Formal wear is seldom needed (in case it is, a tuxedo is necessary; and cocktail dresses are worn for both formal and less-formal occasions). A suit and tie or a dress is appropriate for social occasions, such as an invitation to dinner. For less formal social occasions, conservative resort-type wear is suitable; jeans are worn, but often with jackets, which are ubiquitous. Neither men nor women should wear shorts, and women should avoid anything revealing. Flashy accessories or jewelry and excessive makeup should be avoided, but Venezuelans are fashion conscious and tend to judge people by their dress, and particularly by the quality of their accessories.

Cultural Cautions

DO'S

- Sports—football (soccer) and baseball are the most popular and are a good topic of conversation.
- Maintain good posture and eye contact throughout a meeting—to do otherwise may be interpreted as a sign of disrespect.

DON'TS

- Avoid race, religion, politics, and the recent economic situation as topics of conversation. Family questions or comments should also be avoided.
- Keep your feet flat on the floor; do not prop them on a piece of furniture.

CUSTOMS

- Personal spacing is quite close; attempts to increase spacing between yourself and a speaker may be interpreted as aloofness, disinterest, or rudeness. You are expected to remain close, focusing on the other person and what he has to say.
- Always ask for business cards; they may not be given freely. Your cards should be in Spanish, and it is a courtesy to translate other materials as well.
- Titles are important, and business associates are addressed by their title and surname (first names are used only among close friends in Venezuela).
- Coffee is almost always offered; you should accept to acknowledge hospitality.
- As a courtesy, acknowledge the staff with *buenos días* when entering a shop or office—expect a collective response—and say *adios* when leaving.
- If invited out for a meal or other social occasion, flowers are an appropriate gift. Orchids—the national flower—are appreciated.
- Any business-related gifts should be neither too expensive nor too cheap. Imported whisky (Scotch) or cognac are appropriate, while items with your company logo are not. Handkerchiefs symbolize sad events and knives symbolize the severing of a relationship: neither would be appropriate gifts.
- Dinner parties may not begin until 11:00 pm and seldom break up before midnight at the earliest.
- At formal meals wait until everyone has been served before beginning. You do not have to finish everything on your plate, nor will you have to fend off offers of second helpings.
- The person who issues the invitation pays, although men always pay for women. There may be two separate checks—one for food and one for drinks.
- Thank you notes are used for most occasions.

OBSERVATIONS

- Let the Venezuelans set the tone for initial interactions—if they respond in Spanish, plan to deal in Spanish. Language may be seen as a measure of seriousness and willingness to meet them halfway.
- Stay at the best hotels and entertain at the best—usually French—restaurants to garner prestige.
- Venezuelans tend to be emotional and express their individuality in a highly structured, conservative manner. Always acknowledge the dignity and individuality of the person you are dealing with, while remaining correct in your own behavior.
- Men drink whisky (Scotch), mixed drinks—often with rum—wine, or beer before dinner. It is considered inappropriate for women to drink distilled liquor and déclassé for them to drink beer.

NEGOTIATIONS

- Venezuelans are offended by absolute alternatives and may view compromise as a loss of face; you must be careful how you couch your proposals to avoid an all-or-nothing situation, or even when compromising.
- Formal negotiations may have to be recessed and the sticking points pursued in a less formal atmosphere, such as over dinner. In particularly difficult situations, a third party intermediary may be needed.
- Follow up all oral communications in writing; something that does not exist in writing may not exist at all.

Legal

Legal System

Venezuela's legal system is based on civil law, with strong influence from French and Italian civil codes.

Intellectual Property Rights

Patents An application for patent registration is filed with the Industrial Property Register of the Ministry of Development. Applications are processed slowly, averaging four to five years. Opposition to registration may be made by any interested party based on a variety of grounds.

Trademarks Trademark law provides protection for well-known trademarks, prohibits the coexistence of similar marks, and provides for cancellation of trademark registrations for nonuse within the Andean Pact for three years or on the basis of bad faith. The application process for a trademark is the same as for a patent. Use of a trademark is not a requirement to obtain a registration certificate, but it is necessary to avoid future cancellation of the mark. Protection granted to well-known trademarks has been supported by a recent Supreme Court decision. Trademark piracy is common in the clothing, toy, and sporting goods areas and enforcement remains poor.

Copyrights Protection is granted throughout the author's life and 50 years after death. No formality is necessary for the use and exercise of intellectual rights, but filing with the Intellectual Production Register is recommended to obtain public recognition of the existence of the intellectual work and the presumption of ownership. Although infringements of the regulations are severely sanctioned, control over pirate sales is still insufficient. Computer software, satellite signals, and cable television are covered under Venezuela's Copyright Law.

Trade Secrets The law affords some protection to trade secrets and valuable information, but these rights are best assured by contractual undertakings.

Business Registration

In general, foreign capital, technology transfers, and patents and trademarks use and exploitation contracts must be registered with the Superintendency of Foreign Investments of the Finance Ministry. Representative offices do not require approval or incorporation. All operations must comply with Venezuelan tax regulations.

Contracts and Dispute Resolution

Business relationships may be conducted with or without written contracts, but written contracts are important to Venezuelan businesses. A contract is the formal agreement between the parties and should cover all aspects of the negotiation, including dispute resolution. Disputes are usually resolved through negotiations and out-of-court settlements to avoid the inconvenience of a lawsuit. Litigation is only considered as a last resort. Foreign companies are rarely involved in lawsuits because most contracts provide for alternative dispute resolutions. The parties may choose to arbitrate a disagreement before a national or international arbiter of their choice. Procedures and rules of arbitration are also at the option of the parties. If a lawsuit is brought, a Venezuelan court may order specific performance, monetary damages, and attorney fees.

Notaries

Notaries provide evidence to authenticate the signature and date of execution of all documents drafted by the parties and signed before the notary. Venezuelan notaries do not draft documents. Documents filed before notaries and most documents filed with public offices must be translated into Spanish by a duly authorized translator. The public must have access to notary records. Venezuelan consulates perform notarial duties as well as document legalization.

Labor

Worker's rights are strongly protected by the constitution and labor laws. Labor unions or associations may be legally organized by workers to bargain collectively, and both Venezuela's Constitution and its labor law recognize and encourage the right of unions to exist. About 25 percent of the national labor force is unionized. Children between the ages of 12 and 14 may work if given special permission by the National Institute for Minors or the Labor Ministry. Children between the ages of 14 and 16 may work if given permission by their legal guardians. Although severance payments are burdensome for Venezuelan corporations, labor costs are still comparatively lower than in other countries. Minimum wage and other compensatory bonuses are established and adjusted regularly by presidential decrees because of the current economic situation. All employees must be registered with and contribute to Social Security.

Source: d'Empaire, Reyna, Bermúdez y Asociados, Caracas

Legal Matters

LEGAL BRIEFS

- **Business entities** Corporations are the most usual business vehicle, although partnerships and other structures are also used for certain contracts. Investors are advised to obtain local legal advice when selecting the type of corporation and completing the incorporation procedure. Incorporation by promoters or administrators requires the filing of articles of incorporation and bylaws with the Mercantile Registry.
- **Maximum workweek** A maximum of eight working hours per day is established by law. Employees have a right to annual paid vacations and official holidays. The statutory vacation period varies with length of employment. Corporations may establish collective holidays.
- **Legal environment** The judicial system works slowly and faces continuing charges of corruption.
- **Organic Labor Law** The Organic Labor Law limits foreign employment in companies with 10 or more employees, to 10 percent of the payroll. Renumeration for foreign workers must not exceed 20 percent of total wages paid.
- **IPR piracy** Piracy of intellectual property rights of all sorts is common and pirated copies are sold on the domestic market as well as exported to a number of countries in the region, including the US.
- **Union activities** The law prohibits employers from interfering with the formation of unions or with their activities and from stipulating as a condition of employment that new workers must abstain from union activity or must join a specified union.
- **Forced labor** There is no forced or compulsory labor in Venezuela.
- **Minimum wages** Venezuela has both urban and rural minimum wage rates.
- **Overtime** Overtime may not exceed two hours daily, 10 hours weekly, or 100 hours annually and may not be paid at a rate less than time-and-a-half.
- **Workplace safety** The law requires that work places must maintain sufficient protection for health and life against sickness and accidents, and it imposes fines from one-quarter to two times the minimum salary for first infractions.
- **International agreements** Venezuela is a member of GATT/WTO; OAS; ALADI; Andean Pact; Inter-American Convention on International Commercial Arbitration.

LEGAL CONTACTS

d'Empaire, Reyna, Bermúdez y Asociados
Centro Plaza, Torre "D"
Nivel 18
1RA Transversal Los Palos Grandes
Caracas
Tel: (2) 285-0044 Fax: (2) 285-5922, 283-4529

Federacion de Colegios de Abogados de Venezuela
Esquina de Veroes, Edificio America
Piso 9, Oficina 911-912
Caracas

Anzola Boveda Raffalli y Rodriguez
Torre Britanica, Piso 10
Av. Jose Felis sosa, Altamira Sur.
Caracas 1062
Tel: (2) 263-2003 Fax: (2) 263-4286

Baker & McKenzie
Edificio Aldemo, Afenida Venezuela, Urb El Rosal
Caracas
Tel: (2) 9530833 Fax: (2) 9537094

Escritorio Calcano-Vetancourt
Edificio Seguros Venezuela, 7th Floor
Avenida Francisco De Miranda
Campo Alegre
POB 12
Caracas 1010-A
Tel: (2) 953.04.44 Fax: (2) 953.21.70

Muci-Abraham & Asociados
Edificio Banco Lara, Piso 7
Avenida Principal La Castellana
Caracas 1060
Tel: (2) 261-4544 Fax: (2) 265-3916

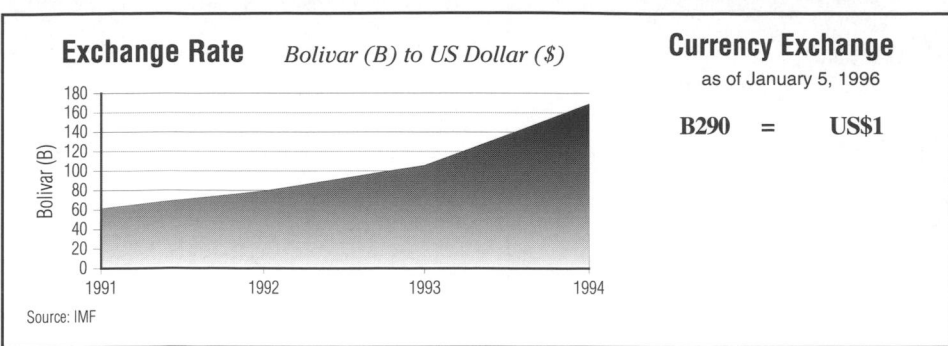

Exchange Rate *Bolivar (B) to US Dollar ($)*

Bolivar (B): 180, 160, 140, 120, 100, 80, 60, 40, 20, 0
Years: 1991, 1992, 1993, 1994

Source: IMF

Currency Exchange

as of January 5, 1996

B290   =   US$1

Currency

The currency of Venezuela is the bolivar (B).

Foreign Exchange

The exchange rate of the bolivar is determined by supply and demand, although the Central Bank, as the largest seller of foreign exchange, greatly influences the actual exchange rate. Resident commercial banks and exchange houses are designated as authorized foreign exchange dealers.

Capital Transfers

Foreign investors may repatriate 100 percent of profits and capital, including proceeds from the sale of shares or liquidation of the company, and there are no restrictions on the reinvestment of profits.

Investment Incentives

Investment incentives take the form of tax credits or exemption from customs duties. Incentives are available to both domestic and foreign companies and encourage production for the export market.

Investment Restrictions

Although there are few legal restrictions, disincentives to invest arise from current government policies, including the imposition of price and foreign exchange controls.

TAXATION

Taxation requires sophisticated knowledge of complex rules and regulations specific to each country. For more detailed information we suggest you refer to the Ernst & Young Corporate Tax Guide and Directory, available from the Ernst & Young accounting office in your country, or from:

Perez-Mena, Everts, Baez, Morales & Asociados
Av. Francisco de Miranda
Edif. Mene-Grande
Piso 2, Los Palos Grandes
Caracas, Venezuela
Tel: (2) 209-4011, 209-4222
Cable: Ernstaudit, Caracas, Venezuela
Telex: 23216 Ans bk ERNST VC
Fax: (2) 285-0386, 285-5378

- Venezuelan corporations are taxed on income from Venezuelan sources. A Venezuelan corporation is one that has been incorporated in Venezuela, regardless of the shareholders' nationality.
- Foreign corporations are subject to corporate tax on income earned in Venezuela.

At a Glance

Corporate Income Tax Rate (%)(a)	34
Capital Gains Tax Rate (%)(a)	34
Branch Tax Rate (%)(a)	34
Withholding Tax (%)	
Dividends	0
Interest	
Paid to Residents	
Individuals (%)	3
Corporations (%)	5
Paid to Nonresidents	
Individuals (%) (b)	34
Corporations (%) (c)	0
Royalties	
Paid to Residents (d)	0
Paid to Nonresidents	
Individuals (%) (e)	34
Corporations (f)	—
Professional Fees	
Paid to Residents	
Individuals (%)	3
Corporations (%)	5
Paid to Nonresidents (%) (g)	34
Rents	
Paid to Residents	
Individuals (%)	3
Corporations (%)	5
Paid to Nonresidents	
Individuals (%)	20
Corporations (%)	5
Technical Assistance	
Paid to Residents	0
Paid to Nonresidents (%) (h)	34
Technological Services	
Paid to Residents	0
Paid to Nonresidents (%) (i)	34
Net Operating Losses (Years)	
Carryback	0
Carryforward	3

(a) This is the minimum progressive rate, and applies to income more than Bs 3 million. Petroleum companies are subject to a 67.7% income tax; mining activities are taxed at 60%.
(b) Withholding tax is imposed on 95% of the gross payment.
(c) Withholding tax rates generally carry a maximum rate of 34% and are applied to 95% of the gross payment.
(d) Residents consider royalties to be ordinary income.
(e) Royalties are taxed at 90% of gross receipts.
(f) Withholding taxes have a maximum rate of 34%.
(g) Professional fees paid to nonresidents are taxed at 90% of gross receipts.
(h) Technical assistance payments to nonresidents are taxed at 30% of gross receipts.
(i) Technological services payments to nonresidents are taxed at 50% of gross receipts.

Money Matters

BITS AND PIECES

- **Gold** Venezuelan gold coins are legal tender but do not circulate. Gold coins, medallions, and bars are freely negotiated among authorized dealers.
- **Banking** Banking and financial services, and insurance and reinsurance sectors are now open to 100 percent foreign ownership.
- **Capital flight** Although capital may freely leave the country, the government has implemented a fixed foreign exchange rate of the local currency against the US dollar, as well as indirect foreign exchange controls in order to stem capital flight.
- **Repatriation** Although foreign investors, in both capital and direct investment, are guaranteed the right to repatriate dividends and capital, foreign companies have in practice been unable to do so since the imposition of currency controls in mid-1994.
- **Unofficial transactions** Currency transactions conducted outside the official system are illegal and carry heavy penalties.
- **Expropriation** There have been no uncompensated expropriations in the recent past, and none are expected.

BANKS

Banco Central de Venezuela
Esq. de Carmelitas
Apartado Postal 2017
Caracas 1010
Tel: (2) 801-5111
Fax: (2) 861-0084, 81-88-72

Banco de Venezuela
Esquina de Sociedad
Torre Banco de Venezuela
Caracas
Tel: (2) 501-2202, 501-2220
Fax: (2) 501-2217

Banco Exterior
Ave. Urdaneta, Urapal a Rio
Edif. Banco Exterior
Caracas
Tel: (2) 501-0111
Fax: (2) 574-4755

Banco Industrial de Venezuela, CA
Avenida Universidad, esq. Traposos
Apartado 2054
Caracas 1010
Tel: (2) 545-9222

Banco Internacional
Ave. Urdaneta, Esq. Animas
Edif. Banco Internacional
Caracas
Tel: (2) 408-7111

Banco Mercantil
Ave. Andres Bello, No. 1
Edif. Mercantil
Urb. San Bernardino
Caracas
Tel: (2) 507-1111, 507-2111

Banco Provincial
Ave. Vollmer, con Ave. Este 0
Centro Financiero Provincial
Urb. San Bernardino
Caracas
Tel: (2) 574-8522

Banco Union
Ave. Universidad
Chorro a Dr. Diaz
Torre Grupo Union
Caracas
Tel: (2) 501-7111, 501-7866

Banco Venezolano de Credito
Monjas a San Francisco, Sur 2
Edif. No. 7
Caracas
Tel: (2) 801-1111
Fax: (2) 541-2557

Citibank
Carmelitas a Altagracia
Edif. Citibank
Caracas
Tel: (2) 81-96-01

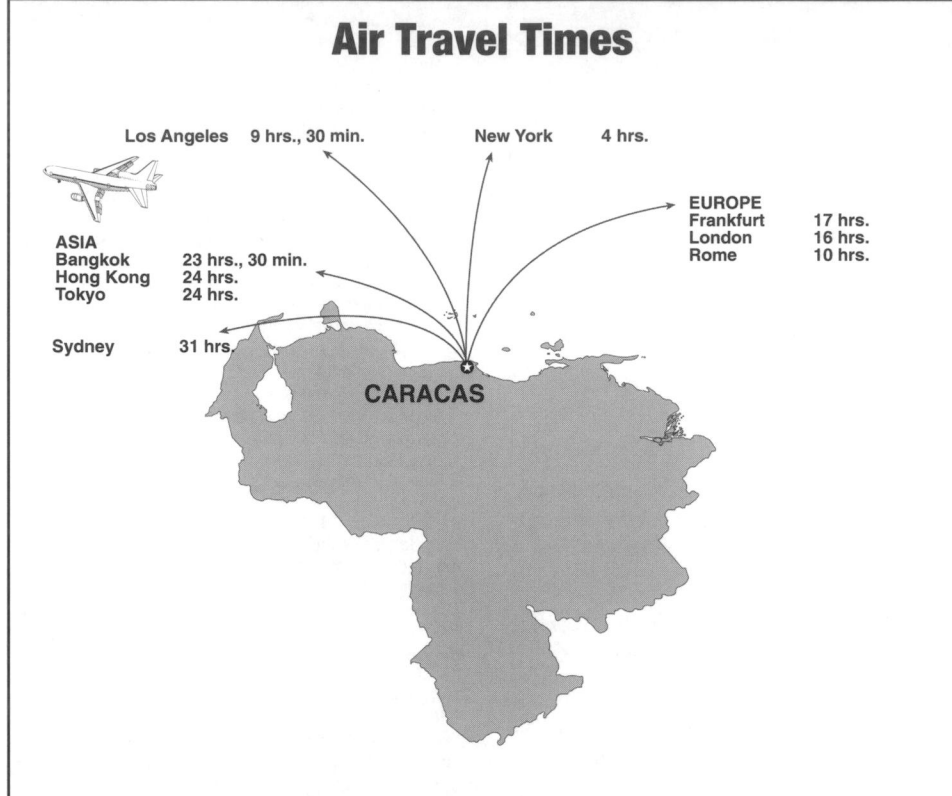

Air Travel Times

Los Angeles   9 hrs., 30 min.   New York   4 hrs.

EUROPE
Frankfurt   17 hrs.
London   16 hrs.
Rome   10 hrs.

ASIA
Bangkok   23 hrs., 30 min.
Hong Kong   24 hrs.
Tokyo   24 hrs.

Sydney   31 hrs.

CARACAS

COMMUNICATIONS

Telephones The phone system is improving though remains difficult to rely on. A busy signal does not necessarily mean the line is busy, nor does a ringing sound mean the phone of the intended party is ringing. Lines get crossed frequently and not all exchanges are digitized.

Fax The most efficient, immediate communication is by fax, which is widely available.

Post office Local mail delivery is not dependable. Use an international courier for papers and documents only. Any other items will be delayed at Customs. Messengers are available for delivery within urban areas.

BEST TRAVEL BOOKS

Lonely Planet, Travel Survival Kit, Venezuela. This new title rounds out Lonely Planet's coverage of South America written by our resident South American author.

The Travellers Guide to Latin America Customs and Manners. Elizabeth Devine & Nancy Braganti. An invaluable guide for people not wanting to put foot in mouth.

Venezuela Alive. The best practical guide to Venezuela on the market.

Do's and Taboos Around the World, The Bestselling Guide to International Behavior. Edited by Roger Axtell, compiled by The Parker Pen Company. The ultimate guide to international behavior, now completely updated and expanded. Helpful, easy to read.

NATIONAL TOURIST OFFICE

Corporacion de Turismo de Venezuela
Centro Capriles, 7º
Plaza Venezuela
Apdo 50200
Caracas
Tel: (2) 781-8370

USEFUL TELEPHONE NUMBERS

If you are calling from outside Venezuela, you will need to add the country code [58] and any other international dialing requirements from within your country.

- Caracas Taxi .... (2) 769122
- Railway System/Caracas ....(2) 41-6141
- Hotel Tamanaco ....(2) 91-4555
- Hotel Eurobuilding ....(2) 907-1111
- Hotel Caracas Hilton ....(2) 503-5000
- US Embassy/Caracas ....(2) 285-2222
- Express mail...(2) 916-694
- DHL/Caracas.......................................(2) 263-2122
- Federal Express/Caracas.....................(2) 781-8520
- International operator 0051
- Airline/shipping information/Caracas......(2) 32-1170
- Chamber of Commerce/Caracas ....(2) 571-3222
- Chamber of Commerce/Maracaibo ......(61) 91-3255
- Ministry of Development.......................(2) 422-8008

Car Rental
- Avis ....(2) 261-1477
- Budget ....(2) 283-4333
- Hertz ....(2) 952-1846

Credit Card Information
Lost or stolen credit cards (call collect to the US, regardless of which country the card was issued in).
- Amex ....[1] (919) 333-3211
- Diner's Club................................[1] (303) 799-1504
- MasterCard ....[1] (314) 275-6690
- Visa ....[1] (410) 581-7931

Travelogue

WORKWEEK

Government Monday-Friday 7:30 am to 3:30 pm, or 9:30 pm to 5:30 pm.

Business Monday-Friday 8:00 am to noon and 2:00 pm to 6:00 pm.

Retail Monday-Saturday 9:00 am to 1:00 pm and 3:00 pm to 7:00 pm.

Metro system Monday-Sunday 5:30 am to 11:00 pm.

Factories Monday-Friday 7:30 am to 4:30 pm, closed December 25 to January 15.

Banks Monday-Friday 8:30 am to 1:30 pm, 2:00 pm to 4:30 pm.

HOLIDAYS

Holidays 1996
January 1 New Year's Day
January 10 Ephiphany*
February 27-28 Carnival*
March 19 St. Joseph*
April 4 Maundy Thursday*
April 5 Good Friday *
April 19 Signing of Independence
May 1 Labor Day
May 29 Ascension*
June 26 Corpus Christi*
June 24 Battle of Carbobo
June 29 Sts. Peter & Paul*
July 5 Independence Day
July 24 Bolivar's Birthday
August 15 Assumption
October 12 Columbus Day
October 30 All Saints' Day
December 8 Immaculate Conception*
December 25 Christmas Day
In addition to the holidays listed here are many additional bank holidays during which businesses remain open. Factories are closed December 25 through January 15 for the New Year's season.
*Dates vary from year to year.

VISA AND PASSPORT

All visitors must have a valid passport and visa or tourist card. Tourist cards are issued on the flight to Venezuela. Visitors with business visas will be required to pay local income taxes if the stay exceeds 180 days. Carry your passport at all times. To obtain a business visa for up to one year, you must receive prior authorization from the Venezuelan government.

DEPARTURE FORMALITIES

An exit tax of Bs2,000 is required of all visitors when leaving. It must be paid in local currency.

IMMUNIZATION

Smallpox vaccinations are required if the traveler is arriving from an infected area. Tetanus, yellow fever vaccinations, and malaria prophylaxis are recommended.

TIPPING

Restaurants have a ten percent service charge; leave an additional five to ten percent if the service is good. Do tip taxi drivers, porters, hairdressers, tour guides, parking and cloakroom attendants, ushers, and maids.

CRIME

Cross border violence occurs. Pickpockets are common in crowded bus and subway stations. Barrios and isolated urban parks are dangerous, lock cars. Thieves are common and aggressive in urban areas.

INFRASTRUCTURE

In Caracas, the Metro subway is dependable, economical, and efficient but limited to east-west routes through the city. Buses and taxis are also available. All taxis have yellow license plates, avoid those without. Airport buses are available and run hourly. Be aware for car travel that roads can be poorly marked and congested in urban areas.

REMEMBER
- When you telephone (or fax) to Venezuela from another country you must always include the country code [58] before the numbers given.
- When you send mail to Venezuela, be sure to write VENEZUELA in capital letters its own line below the addresses given.

GOVERNMENT AGENCIES

Comision Nacional de Telecomunicaciones
National Telecommunications Commission
Calle Veracruz con Cali
Edif. MTC, Las Mercedes
Caracas
Tel: (2) 92-66-11, 92-63-33
Fax: (2) 92-77-80

Corporacion Venezolana de Turismo
Venezuelan Tourism Corporation
Torre Oeste, Piso 37
Parque Central
Caracas
Tel: (2) 574-1268, 573-6408
Fax: (2) 573-8983

Instituto de Comercio Exterior
Foreign Trade Institute
Avenida Libertador - Sector La Florida
Centro Comercial Los Cedros -Penthouse
Caracas 1050
Tel: (2) 762-3810, 762-1118, 762-3082
Fax: (2) 762-3885, 71-60-61

Ministerio de Agricultura y Cria
Ministry of Agriculture
Av. Lecuna, Torre Este
Piso 14, Parque Central
Caracas
Tel: (2) 599-0445/9
Fax: (2) 574-7305

Ministerio de Educacion
Ministry of Education
Esq. de Salas, Edif. Sede del Ministerio de Educacion
Piso 20
Caracas
Tel: (2) 562-9198, 562-9238
Fax: (2) 562-0175

Ministerio de Hacienda
Ministry of Finance
Edif. Centro Simon Bolivar
Torre Norte, Piso 6
Caracas
Tel: (2) 483-1380, 483-5462
Fax: (2) 41-57-71

Ministerio de Relaciones Exteriores
Ministry of Foreign Relations
Av. Urdaneta, Esq. de Conde a Carmelitas
Edif. MRE, Piso 2
Caracas
Tel: (2) 834-305, 824-305, 824-484
Fax: (2) 831-376, 836-526

Ministerio de Relaciones Interiores
Ministry of the Interior
Av. Urdaneta, Esq. Carmelitas
Frente al Banco Central de Venezuela
Caracas
Tel: (2) 575-0010, 834-110, 834-334
Fax: (2) 861-1967

Ministerio de Sanidad y Asistencia Social
Ministry of Health and Social Assistance
Edif. Centro Simon Bolivar
Torre Norte, Piso 8
Caracas
Tel: (2) 41-43-42, 41-26-86

Ministerio del Ambiente y de los Recursos Naturales Renovables
Ministry of the Environment and Renewable Natural Resources
Edif. Centro Simon Bolivar
Torre Sur, Piso 18
Caracas
Tel: (2) 408-1001, 408-1412, 408-1162
Fax: (2) 483-2445

Ministerio del Trabajo y Desarrollo Social
Ministry of Labor and Social Development
Torre Sur, Piso 5
Edif. Centro Simon Bolivar
Caracas
Tel: (2) 483-1881, 41-86-17
Fax: (2) 483-5940

Ministerio de Transporte y Comunicaciones
Ministry of Transportation and Communications
Av. Lecuna, Torre Oeste, Piso 51
Parque Central
Caracas
Tel: (2) 509-1004/2
Fax: (2) 574-3043

Oficina Central de Estadistica e Informatica
Central Statistics and Informatics Office
Avenida Boyaca, Edif. Fundacion La Salle, Mariperez
Caracas
Tel: (2) 782-1133
Fax: (2) 782-2243

Venezuelan Standards Agency
Ave. Andres Bello
Edif. Torre Fondocomun, Piso 12
Caracas
Tel: (2) 575-4111 x235, 576-3701
Fax: (2) 574-1312, 576-3701

WORLD TRADE CENTER

World Trade Center Caracas
4ta. Avenida de Los Palos Grandes
Con Romulo Gallegos
Edificio "La Torre del Parque"
Piso 9, Los Palos Grandes
Caracas 1060
Tel: (2) 285-2255, 285-4647, 285-7707, 285-8109
Fax: (2) 285-0302, 286-4435

BUSINESS AND TRADE ORGANIZATIONS

Asociacion de Fabricantes de Cortes de Calzados
Calle Mexico No. 15
Entre Calles El Cristo Y Magallanes - Catia
Caracas 1030
Tel: (2) 89-29-45, 89-71-44

Asociacion de Supermercados y Afines
Ave. Principal de los Ruices
Centro Empresarial Los Ruices
Piso 1, Ofic. 116
Caracas 1071
Tel: (2) 234-4490, 35-75-58
Fax: (2) 238-0308

Asociacion Nacional de Hoteles de Venezuela
Parque Central Edif. San Martin
Nivel Oficina 2, Ofc. 201
Caracas 1010
Tel: (2) 574-5672, 574-3994, 574-5494
Fax: (2) 574-4094

Asociacion de Industriales de las Artes Graficas
Ave. Principal con 2a Transversal de los Cortijos de Lourdes
Edif. Centro Empresarial Senderos
Piso 1, Ofic. 107-B
Caracas
Tel: (2) 239-3322, 239-3543
Fax: (2) 239-3921

Asociacion Nacional Pequena y Mediana Industria de Calzado y Similares
7ma. Avenida - Entre Calles Bolivar y Peru -Catia
Edif. El Llanero, Piso 1, Mezzanina No. 5
Caracas 1030
Tel: (2) 871-2039, 89-64-31

Asociacion Textil Venezolana
Edif. Karam, Piso 5, Ofic. 503
Ibarras a Pelota, Av. Urdaneta
Caracas
Tel: (2) 561-6851, 561-6922

Asociacion Venezolana de Exportadores
Association of Exporters
Centro Comercial Concresa
Piso 2, Oficina 435
Redoma de Prados del Este
Caracas 1080
Tel: (2) 979-4542, 979-2524   Fax: (2) 979-5096

Asociacion Venezolana de Productores de Pulpa
Papel y Carton
Edif. Camara de Industriales, Piso 6
Esq. Puente Anauco
Caracas 1010
Tel: (2) 572-5398

Camara Venezolana de Empresas de Informatica
Venezuelan Association of Hardware and Software
Av. Sucre, Torre Centro Parque Boyaca
Piso 8 Oficina 81
Los Dos Caminos
Caracas
Tel: (2) 283-7036, 283-2777, 283-7945
Fax: (2) 283-703

Camara Venezolana de la Industria de Alimentos
Av. Principal de Los Ruices
Centro Empresarial
Piso 5, Of. 510, Los Ruices
Caracas
Tel: (2) 239-9818, 239-0918
Fax: (2) 238-3268

Camara Venezolana de Joyeros y Relojeros
Venezuelan Jewelry Chamber
Padre Sierra a Munoz
Oficentro Padre Sierra
Piso 1 -Local E
Caracas 1010
Tel: (2) 83-80-87, 835-5951
Fax: (2) 483-7640, 483-3663

Colegio de Arquitectos de Venezuela
Av. Colegio de Arquitectos
La Urbina Norte
Caracas
Tel/Fax: (2) 241-3143

Confederacion Nacional de Asociaciones de Productores Agropecuarios
National Confederation of Agricultural Producers
Edif. Casa de Italia
Planta Baja
Av. La Industria
San Bernardino
Caracas
Tel: (2) 571-4035
Fax: (2) 573-4423

Consejo Nacional de Informatica, Telecomunicaciones y Electronica
Ave. Sucre, Torre Centro Parque Boyaca
Piso 19, Ofic. 192, Los Dos Caminos
Caracas
Tel: (2) 283-5511, 283-5346
Fax: (2) 283-5511

Consejo Venezolano de la Industria
Venezuelan Industry Council
Esq. Puente Anauco
Edif. Camara de Industriales
Mezzanina, La Candelaria
Caracas 1011
Apartado Postal 14255 (Caracas 1011)
Tel: (2) 573-0222
Fax: (2) 571-5491

Federacion Venezolana de Camaras y Asociaciones de Comercio y
Produccion
Venezuelan Federation of Chambers and Associations
Av. El Empalme
Edif. Fedecamaras - Penthouse
Urb. El Bosque
Caracas 1050
Apartado Correos 2568 (Caracas 1010-A)
Tel: (2) 731-1711/3, 731-1845
Fax: (2) 74-20-97

Instituto de Comercio Exterior
Foreign Trade Institute
Centro Comercial Los Cedros
Avenida Libertador, Piso 2
Apdo 51852
Caracas 1050
Tel: (2) 729-960
Fax: (2) 716-061

CHAMBERS OF COMMERCE

Camara de Comercio de Caracas
Caracas Chamber of Commerce
Av. Andres Eloy Blanco (Este 2) - No. 215
Edif. Camara de Comercio de Caracas - Piso 8
Urbanizacion Los Caobos
Caracas 1050
Tel: (2) 571-3222, 571-2742
Fax: (2) 571-0050

Camara Venezolano-Americana de Comercio e Industria
Venezuelan-American Chamber of Commerce
Torre Credival - Piso 10 - Oficina A
Segunda Av. de Campo Alegre
Caracas 1060
Apartado Postal 5181 (Caracas 1010-A)
Tel: (2) 263-0833, 267-2076
Fax: (2) 265-0764

RADIO & TELEVISION STATIONS

Cámara Venezolana de la Industria de Radiodifusion
Apartado 3955
Tel: (2) 31-2653
Telex: 29281

Cámara Venezolana de la Televisión
Edificio Torre La Previsora, 7,
Cruce Avenida Abraham Lincoln con Las Acacias
Sabana Grande
Apartado 60423
Chacao, Caracas
Tel: (2) 781-4608

Radio Nacional
Apartado 3979
Caracas 1010

Radio Caracas Television (RCTV)
2a Transversal Los Cortijos de Lourdes
Apartado 70734
Caracas
Tel: (2) 239-6622
Telex: 21340

Televisora Andina de Mérida-TAM
Palacio Arzobispal
Plaza Bolivar
Apartado 222
Mérida
Tel: (74) 52-5758
Telex: 74287

Televisora Nacional
Apartado 3979
Caracas

Venevision-Channel 4
Apartado 6674
Caracas 1010
Tel: (2) 782-4444
Telex: 21144

Venezolana de Television-Canal 5 y 8
Avenida Montecristo
Los Ruices
Apartado 2739
Caracas
Tel: (2) 34-4998
Fax: (2) 239-2675

NEWSPAPERS

El Diario de Caracas
Avenida Principal de Boleita Norte
Apartado 76478
Caracas 1070-A
Tel: (2) 239-1722
Telex: 29193

El Mundo
Torre de la Prensa
Puente Trinidad a Panteon
Apartado 1192
Caracas
Tel: (2) 81-4931
Telex: 21173

El Nacional
Edificio El Nacional
Puente Nuevo a Puerto Escondido
Apartado 209
Caracas
Tel: (2) 483-9133
Fax: (2) 41-2365

El Universal
Edificio El Universal
Avenida Urdaneta esq. de Animas
Apartado 1909
Caracas
Tel: (2) 561-7511
Telex: 21263

The Daily Journal
Avenida Fuerzas Armadas
Crucecita a San Ramon
Apartado 1408
Caracas 1010-A
Tel: (2) 562-1122
Telex: 26499

BUSINESS PERIODICALS

Agricultura Venezolana (twice monthly)
Apartado 8373
Caracas 101

Bohemia Venezolana (Weekly)
Edificio Bloque Dearmas
Final Avenida San Martin cruce con Avenida La Paz
Apartado 575
Caracas
Tel: (2) 443-1066
Telex: 22683

Business Venezuela (twice monthly)
Apartado 5181
Caracas 1010-A
Tel: (2) 63-0833
Fax: (2) 32-0764

Economia Venezolana
Apartado 8373
Caracas

Número (Monthly)
Apartado 75570
El Marqués
Caracas1070
Tel: (2) 283-7731
Fax: (2) 283-4277

DIRECTORY

Venezuelan Exporters Directory
Editora Ferga, Ca
Avenida Francisco de Miranda
Torre Bazar Bolivar
Piso 5, Of. 501
El Marquez
Apartado 16044
Caracas 1011-A
Tel: (2) 239-1564
Fax: (2) 34-1008

BANKS

Avenida Universidad
esq. Traposos
Apartado 881
Caracas 1010-A
Tel: (2) 545-5033
Fax: (2) 545-9574

Banco Caracas
Avenida Urdaneta
Veroes a Sta. Capilla, No. 4
Caracas
Tel: (2) 801-6511

Banco Consolidado
Plaza La Castellana
Ave. Los Chaguaramos y Blandin
Torre Consolidada
Urb. La Castellana
Caracas
Tel: (2) 206-3333

Banco del Caribe
Dr. Paul a Salvador de Leon
Caracas
Tel: (2) 505-5511, 505-5711

Banco de la Construccion, CA
Edificio Banco de la Contrución
Venida Urdaneta, esq. Platanal
Apartado 6719
Caracas
Tel: (2) 408-8111
Telex: 21602

LAW FIRMS

Bufete Rodriguez Machado
Edificio Mene Grande, 15 Piso (Penthouse)
Avenida Francisco De Miranda
Urbanizacion Los Palos Grandes
Apartado 792
Caracas 1010
Tel: (2) 283-5667
Fax: (2) 285-5969

Rodriguez & Mendoza
Edf. Parque Cristal
Torre Este, Piso 11
Av. Francisco De Miranda, Los Palos Grandes
POB 6260 Caracas 1010-A
Caracas 1062
Tel: (2) 285-4944
Fax: (2) 285-1379

Escritorio Siso
3era. Avenida De Campo Alegre
Quinta San Luis
POB 60770
Caracas 1060
Tel: (2) 263-2544
Fax: (2) 261-5966

Travieso Evans Hughes Arria Rengel & Paz
Centro Plaza, Torre A, 20th Floor
Avenida Francisco De Miranda, Los Palos Grandes
Caracas 1062l
Tel: (2) 285-2322
Fax: (2) 283.7798

CONSULTING FIRMS

Arthur D. Little de Venezuela, C.A.
Avenida Los Chaguaramos
Centro Gerencial Mohedano, Piso 12
Ofic. A y B
La Castellana
Caracas
Tel: (2) 261-8840, 261-4472 Fax: (2) 261-5249

Booz-Allen & Hamilton de Venezuela, S.A.
Avenida Francisco de Miranda
Edif. Parque Cristal, Piso 14
Torre Oeste
Urb. Los Palos Grandes
Caracas
Tel: (2) 285-3522 Fax: (2) 285-5462

Datos CA
Edificio Luz Electrica
Avenida JM Vargas
Santa Fe
Caracas
Telex: 28078 DATCA VC

Dun & Bradstreet, C.A.
Ave. Principal Colinas de Bello Monte
Edif. Centro Cristobal, Pisos 8 y 9
Colinas de Bello Monte
Caracas
Tel: (2) 752-9322, 751-9935 Fax: (2) 751-5235

Ronai & Asociados, S.R.L.
Ave. Gloria con Ave. Golf
Residencias La Pradera
Urb. El Bosque
Caracas
Tel: (2) 731-2408, 731-3964 Fax: (2) 731-3954

The Gallup Organization
Calle Santa Cruz
Quinta La Mora
Urb. Chuao
Caracas
Tel: (2) 92-83-83

INTERNET ADDRESSES

Usenet group(s):
soc.culture.venezuela

Guide to Venezuela
http://www.ve.net/

Venezuela on the Internet
http://www.latinworld.com/countries/venezuela

Venezuelan Embassy, Washington DC
http://venezuela.mit.edu/embassy/

Vietnam

Socialist Republic of Vietnam

Economy

Overview

Vietnam is only now beginning to recover from the effects of the prolonged military actions, civil war, and political upheavals over the past 50 years. It has moved from an insular, largely self-sufficient economy to one that actively seeks foreign participation. Nearly every sector remains in the developmental stage, although the government has invested heavily in projects aimed toward sustained long-term economic growth.

Trade

Vietnam's foreign trade patterns have been seriously disrupted by political conflicts resulting in international isolation over the past few decades. Japan is its leading trading partner, followed by Hong Kong, Singapore, and France; although the list is rapidly expanding. Vietnam's consistent trade deficits result from difficulties in substantially increasing exports, and from its heavy reliance on imports of raw materials and capital goods in order to sustain its present output levels. The government has taken the first steps toward market reform, and foreign traders are beginning to respond enthusiastically.

Sectors

Agriculture   Vietnam is primarily an agricultural nation and this sector accounts for 40 percent of GDP, although it continues to employs more than 65 percent of the population. The government has placed an increasing emphasis on improving agricultural productivity; while it has met with some modest success, shortages of farm equipment and fertilizers have curtailed overall growth. Rice remains the principal crop, and the staple diet of the population, but Vietnam is becoming increasingly dependent on cash crops such as tea, coffee, and rubber to develop its economy further. The legacy of partition has resulted in a greater emphasis on collective agriculture in the north while the south continues to be more oriented toward small, family farms.

Industry   While there have been some increases in output in recent years, manufacturing has not yet become a significant sector in the Vietnam economy. It is characterized primarily by inefficiency and low productivity. Production of petroleum, a major export commodity, has increased but most areas of heavy industry in the north—such as steel and cement—have gone into decline. The south focuses on textiles and food processing but these too have been operating below capacity, and continue to rely too heavily on imported machinery and raw materials.

Trends

Vietnam continues to suffer from serious economic difficulties—including stagnant or declining output, poor quality of production, and unemployment rates of nearly 25 percent. Major improvements in the quality of industrial and manufacturing output are needed before it can become a true competitor in world markets. However, the government has committed to develop greater domestic sources of consumer goods, and to orient its economy toward international trade. It has substantially improved international relations with several important trading nations, and looks poised to take advantage of the tremendous growth in Southeast Asia. Vietnam is beginning to attract foreign investment from the West and further success in this area could lead to a major boost for its flagging economy.

At a Glance

THE COUNTRY
Location   Southeastern Asia, bordering the South China Sea, between Laos and the Philippines.
Terrain   Varies from mountainous to coastal delta.
Climate   Tropical to monsoon.

THE PEOPLE
Population 73,100,000
Ethnic composition
Vietnamese.. 85-90%
Chinese, Muong, Thai, Khmer, and Other....... 10-15%
Religious composition   Buddhism, Hoa Hao, Cai Dai, Christian, Animism, Islam.
Languages spoken   Vietnamese, French, Chinese, Khmer, and tribal languages (Mon-Khmer and Malayo-Polynesian).
Education and literacy   A strong emphasis on education has resulted in Vietnam's high literacy rates; 88 percent of the population over 15 years of age can read and write. Literacy is still low among the Montagnard groups. All education facilities are administered by the government, with an effort toward applied sciences and vocational training. Vietnam sends a number of students to the Soviet Union and other countries under bilateral technical assistance programs. The government's efforts to improve school facilities and educational infrastructure have been hampered, however, by the high birth rates and continuing economic problems.
Labor force
Total:...32,000,000
By occupation: agriculture 65%, industrial and services 35%.

COUNTRY FACTS
Political and legal   Vietnam is a communist state with a legal system based on communist legal theory and French civil law. Most policy is set by the Politburo and carried out by the Secretariat. The most powerful legislative bodies are the State Council and the Council of Ministers; most of whose members also are involved with the Communist Party Central Committee. There is only one political party, the Vietnamese Communist Party, which is the most important political institution. Government policy is largely the prerogative of the communist leadership.
Telephone   Obsolete switching equipment is a serious problem in Vietnam. The inadequate telephone system is a major constraint on the business sector. Telephone availability is mostly limited to the better hotels. International country code: [84]. Selected city codes: Hanoi (4), Ho Chi Minh City (8).
Transportation   While 85,000 km of highways exist, only 9,400 km are paved. Other transportation options include over 3,000 km of rail, over 17,000 km of navigable inland waterways, and 100 airports. Airplanes are best for long-distance travel. Seagoing craft ply inland rivers.
Environment   Beware of flooding. Much of the delta region is seasonally flooded; a complex system of dikes and levees has been installed to fight the waters. The north has a monsoon climate.
Health   Life expectancy is an average 62 years for males; 66 years for females. Death rate is eight per 1,000 citizens; birth rate is 33 births per 1,000 citizens.

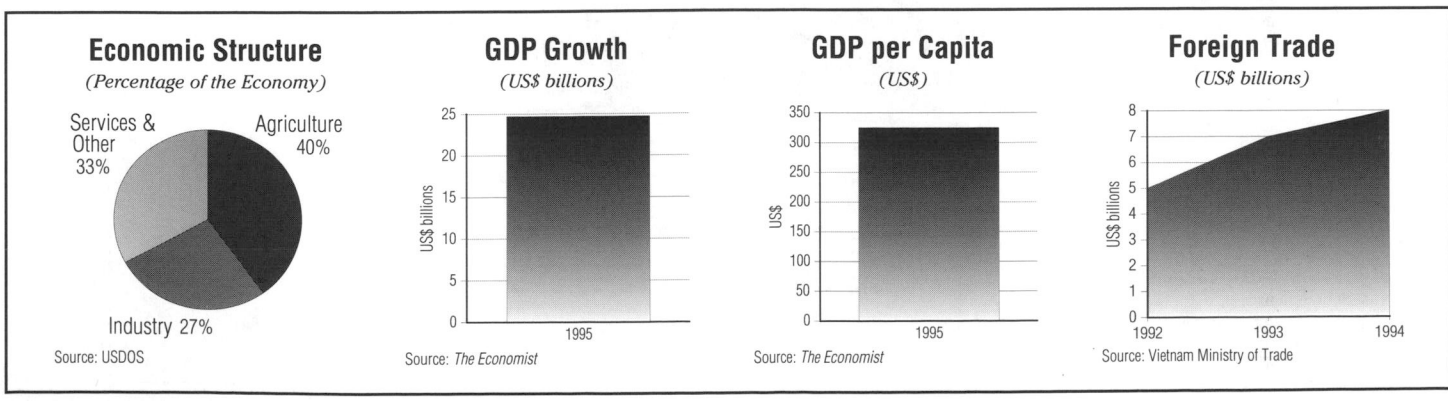

Economic Structure
(Percentage of the Economy)
Services & Other 33%
Agriculture 40%
Industry 27%
Source: USDOS

GDP Growth
(US$ billions)
1995
Source: *The Economist*

GDP per Capita
(US$)
1995
Source: *The Economist*

Foreign Trade
(US$ billions)
1992   1993   1994
Source: Vietnam Ministry of Trade

Vietnam

- National capital
- Province capital
- Secondary city
- International border
- Province boundary
- Railroad
- Road

©1994 Magellan Geographix℠Santa Barbara, CA

0 50 100 150 km
0   50   100 mi

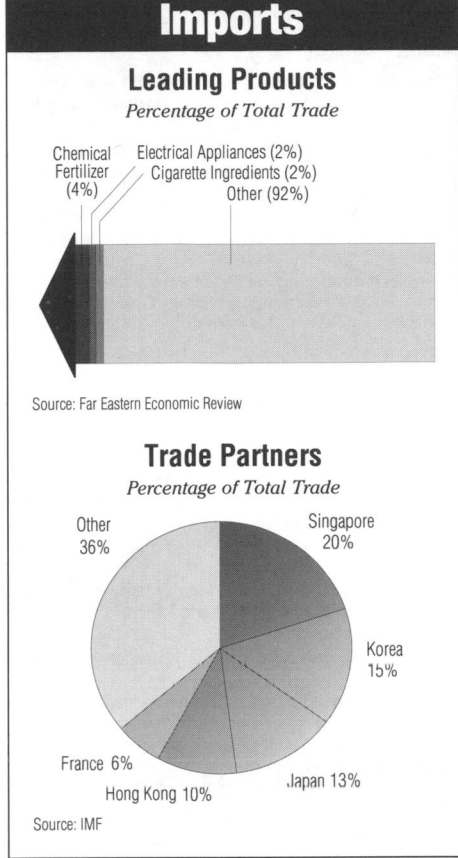

Imports

Leading Products
Percentage of Total Trade

Chemical Fertilizer (4%)
Electrical Appliances (2%)
Cigarette Ingredients (2%)
Other (92%)

Source: Far Eastern Economic Review

Trade Partners
Percentage of Total Trade

- Other 36%
- Singapore 20%
- Korea 15%
- Japan 13%
- Hong Kong 10%
- France 6%

Source: IMF

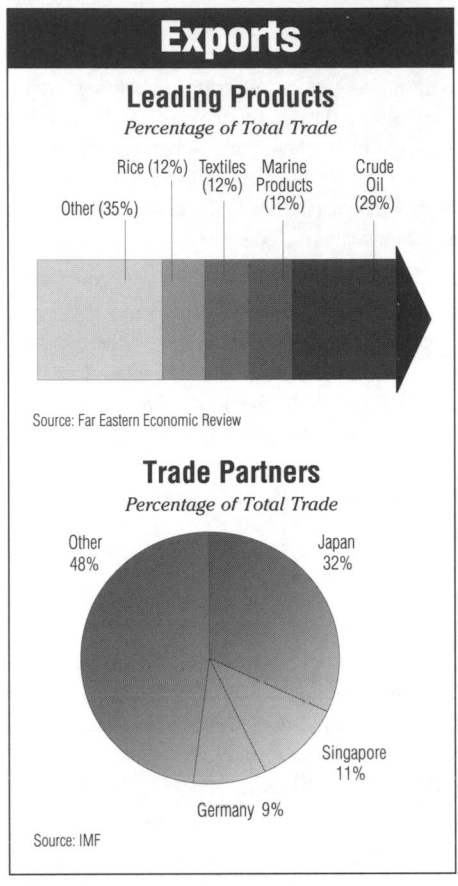

Exports

Leading Products
Percentage of Total Trade

Rice (12%)
Textiles (12%)
Marine Products (12%)
Crude Oil (29%)
Other (35%)

Source: Far Eastern Economic Review

Trade Partners
Percentage of Total Trade

- Other 48%
- Japan 32%
- Singapore 11%
- Germany 9%

Source: IMF

Opportunities

FOR IMPORTING TO VIETNAM

- petroleum
- good quality used equipment (not more than 10 years old)
- steel products
- road building equipment, scaffolding
- machinery for construction of high-rise buildings
- chemicals
- fertilizers
- medicines
- raw cotton
- bath soap
- cosmetics
- construction equipment and building materials
- medical products and pharmaceuticals
- condoms
- dental equipment
- processed food stuffs

FOR EXPORTING FROM VIETNAM

- agricultural products
- handicraft products
- seafood
- rubber
- wood flooring
- coffee
- coal
- tea
- rice

GROWTH SECTORS

- construction
- heavy industry
- energy production
- telecommunications
- agricultural cash-crop production

GOVERNMENT PROCUREMENT

- Most of the infrastructure in Vietnam is dilapidated after many years of warfare. There is a huge volume of reconstruction to be undertaken to rehabilitate and upgrade the existing infrastructure.
- industrial production equipment
- sophisticated construction machinery
- regular supplies of construction materials

Trade News

RULES AND REGULATIONS

- **Regulations** The primary target of economic reform was the commodity sector whereby government rules and regulations were to be de-emphasized in favor of marketplace forces. As a result, light industry and agriculture exports are seen as the most promising targets for investment.
- **Import licenses** As a general rule, a foreign company may not carry out trading activities directly on the Vietnamese market unless it is licensed to do so by the State Committee for Cooperation and Investment (SCCI) under the foreign investment law. If you do not have a license, you will have to carry out your trading activities indirectly by appointing an agent or a distributor to sell the goods in Vietnam. The advantage of being licensed as a vehicle under the foreign investment laws lies in the fact that it enables you to trade directly in Vietnam by selling the goods in return for a profit on the market. An import license is needed to import construction equipment.
- **Product specific licenses** The Ministry of Foreign Trade issues specific licenses for specific products.
- **Quotas** The Ministry of Trade has been known in certain cases to grant approval to foreign companies for the establishment of branch offices for trading in Vietnam, but only where the goods sought to be traded are manufactured in Vietnam. These instances are, however, dictated largely by policy considerations and it would be difficult to secure approval to open a trading branch until the branch office regulations have been enacted by the Ministry of Trade. Foreign companies should be aware that no Vietnamese party may import goods into Vietnam unless they possess an import license allowing importation of that particular brand of goods. Depending on the type of import category that the goods fall under, there may also be quota restrictions or special approvals from various ministries.
- **Barriers** The Vietnamese market is promising, but difficult and corrupt. Ports are crowded, unmaintained, and there is not enough equipment to move imported items. Some shipments can sit for weeks before being cleared for distribution.
- **An Giang** An Giang province is actively seeking foreign investment for several large-scale projects, including agricultural development, animal husbandry, and construction. It offers many incentives and liberal trade policies in order to attract the level of investment necessary to meet its goals.
- **Coffee exports** A new, flat rate tax on exported coffee has lowered the price of coffee, boosted coffee exports, and discouraged tax evasion. Vietnam is looking to become a major supplier of coffee worldwide.

GOVERNMENT AGENCIES

Department of Customs
51 Nguyen Van Cu
Hanoi
Tel: (2) 263910

Ministry of Trade
31 Trang Tien
Hanoi

FREIGHT FORWARDERS

Interdean Ltd. Vietnam
52A Nguyen Binh Khiem
Hanoi
Tel: (4) 244480
Fax: (4) 241508

Sea Land
5-7 Nguyen Hue
D1 Ho Chi Minh City
Tel: (8) 225324
Fax: (8) 292493

Transpo Vietnam
25A Phan Dinh Phung
Hanoi
Tel: (4) 231632
Fax: (4) 231679

Overview

Vietnam is a rich land full of well-educated, industrious, poor people. However, its growing middle- and upper-classes are increasingly creating demand for consumer products. Although marketing foreign products here remains difficult due to changing and as yet uncertain rules, regulations, and distribution channels, many foreign sellers have already found their niches in the rapidly growing consumer goods markets. The swiftest expanding markets are in hotels and tourism, petroleum development, telecommunications, and low-tech manufacturing such as textiles and garments. Hanoi's first international standard supermarket opened in 1994; it is a joint venture with a Japanese chain.

Distribution

The best strategy is to begin locally, dealing with one province or municipality at a time. Provincial authorities continue to gain power from the central government, and courting them lays the basis for long-term future support. Goods enter through the underdeveloped ports of Da Nang, Haiphong, and Ho Chi Minh City (formerly Saigon). Hanoi is the capital and has a major international airport, along with Ho Chi Minh City. Other major outlets are rare but some are slowly emerging. Many foreign sellers are having good luck setting up distribution systems in the outlying provinces, where the people's committees are smaller and sometimes more manageable. Dong Nai and Ba Ria Vung Tau provinces have both liberalized their foreign investment and distribution processes.

Agents, Distributors, and Partners

Companies entering this market need to adopt a long-term approach. Government permission is required for everything including a representative or branch office (even though these are not considered investments in the country). Firms trying to operate without a Vietnamese agent or partner will encounter massive roadblocks, including virtually non-navigable licensing procedures in many of the provinces. A local partner's capital contribution is usually in the form of land-use rights, since foreigners cannot own land in Vietnam. Local partners can also contribute invaluable aid in the form of personal contacts and ready-made relationships—an absolute necessity to doing business in Vietnam.

Selling Techniques

Personal contact in Vietnam is vital to business; investors must not be discouraged if initial letters and faxes are not answered. Keep trying. Successful telephone contact followed by a personal visit or two are customary to beginning any business relationship, especially here. Foreign sellers should also be prepared for long delays, while there is seemingly no action being taken on their proposal. It may just be grinding through the bureaucracy. Companies should routinely double their estimate of time and costs; and then be willing to wait yet longer. Only firms willing to wait as Vietnam develops in the next few years stand a chance of making a profit.

Advertising

Advertising was illegal until 1990, and any product promotion was limited to trade fairs and similar government sponsored and controlled venues. However, in the past few years, advertising has really taken off as firms have moved to take advantage of a release of pent-up demand. Billboards are the most popular form of advertising, followed by the printed media. There are several dailies and periodic journals published in Vietnamese; the only daily English paper is the *Saigon Newsreader*. The *Saigon Echo* is a significant French daily. Other publications in English include the quarterly *Vietnam Foreign Trade*, the monthly *Vietnam Courier,* and the weekly *Saigon Times*. Notable business magazines are *Vietnam Today*, *The Vietnam Investment Review*, and *Vietnam Economic Times*. All of these accept advertising. The national radio service broadcasts in Vietnamese, with external service in several languages. Most of the main cities have television stations. Sanctions are imposed on soft pornography or any promotions which glorify the Western way of life, although these are being significantly relaxed.

Service and Customer Support

Shipments must include a full-range of replacement parts, and companies need to include technical training for a Vietnamese partner and staff. Foreign companies should consider bringing key people from their plants in other nations and be prepared to conduct on-site classes. It is difficult to find trained technical staff from the local population to service foreign equipment and this remains a significant barrier to the success of many foreign operations. As a practical matter, every office should be supplied with its own generator to offset frequent power shortages and brownouts.

Marketing in Vietnam

MARKETING TIPS

- **Boom city** The per capita income of Ho Chi Minh City is 2.8 times higher than the national average, drawing many foreign sellers eager to sell to the growing middle class there.
- **Trade fairs** Vietnam sponsors many trade fairs and exhibitions throughout the year, most of them in Hanoi or Ho Chi Minh City.
- *Doi Moi* *Doi Moi* (renovation) has brought more money in people's pockets, more people doing business, and a better quality of life overall.
- **Value added** Many opportunities exist in increased exploitation and processing of natural resources, such as coffee and rubber.
- **Western products** Many firms are already profiting from the Vietnamese attraction to Western products and the quality and fashion-statement status that is associated with them.
- **Family consumption** An average Vietnamese family will spend about 50 percent of its income on food, with an additional 30 percent on other expenses, leaving about 20 percent as disposable income.
- **Advertising** Advertising expenditures are rising fast in Vietnam, and television is the best way to reach this growing market, despite recent large price rises. Prices are still reasonably affordable.
- **Foreign commercials** Foreign commercials are usually not compatible for Vietnam, though many international advertisers run their commercials as is. Television advertising should be made in Vietnam, using local specialists.
- **Cowboy consultants** There are scores of business consultants in the major cities of Vietnam, but many of them have no actual experience in the country, and virtually no personal contacts - both of which are critical to the success of a foreign operation just getting started in the Vietnamese market. Research carefully and obtain referrals before hiring somebody.

CONSULTING FIRMS

Ashta International, Inc.
29 Han Thuyen
Hanoi
Tel: (4) 261236
Fax: (4) 261237

Craft Corp.
25 Phan Dinh Phung
Hanoi
Tel: (4) 231496
Fax: (4) 238185

FISC
12 Nam Ky Khoi Nghia
D1, Ho Chi Minh City
Tel: (8) 291100
Fax: (8) 298434

Investip
1 Bis Yet Kieu
Hanoi
Tel: (4) 264707
Fax: (4) 268737

John Bailey & Associates
3 Phan Chu Trinh
Hanoi
Tel: (4) 258958
Fax: (4) 260639

Kingship Limited
17 Hang Chuoi
Hanoi
Tel: (4) 247230
Fax: (4) 260262

Pham Tran & Assoc.
8 Tran Hung Dao
Hanoi
Tel: (4) 265524

Quangnam-Danang Investment Cons'y
452 Ong Ich Khiem
Danang
Tel: (51) 25077
Fax: (51) 25852

Business Culture

Greetings and Courtesies

The accepted greeting is shaking hands (both when saying hello and good-bye). Vietnamese often shake with both hands to show respect for a person. They also bow the head slightly as they shake hands to show respect. If an elderly person does not extend their hand first, the proper greeting is a slight bow. In general, women tend to bow their head rather than shake hands. When meeting a woman, shake hands only if she initiates the gesture. Otherwise smile and nod slightly.

Business Ethic and Framework

Vietnamese are hard-working and efficient, but are still recovering from decades of war, coping with the reunification of a nation that is in many ways still two separate countries, and living in a communist economy that is slowly (and often chaotically) introducing free enterprise. Generally speaking, the will to do business is certainly present but the experience and wherewithal may be lacking. Efficient business laws are not yet in place, guidelines and regulations change constantly, and standardized international accounting practices have yet to be instituted. In some instances, agreements have been dissolved after foreign companies believed they had been negotiated and agreed to in good faith; the Vietnamese have no problems with changing agreements at will. Such incidents are caused by inexperience and the turmoil that comes with a society and culture in flux, rather than from any malicious intent. But these problems do exist and anyone engaging in business in Vietnam should be prepared for them.

Decision Making

Politeness and modesty are key elements of Vietnamese behavior. Vietnamese try to avoid direct confrontation and will often talk around a sensitive subject, relying on the other person to understand what they are really saying. Though they are punctual for meetings, Vietnamese also seem to be in no hurry when it comes to decisions or accomplishing things. In addition, the people you meet might not have the authority to make decisions. When negotiating, determine that the person you are dealing with actually has decision-making authority. Also, it is important to speak with everyone who has any power over your efforts, including the appropriate local party and government officials.

Women

Women are prominent in business and government, and foreign woman can expect to be treated with respect and taken seriously. The north is more conservative and traditional than the south and woman doing business there should make an extra effort to be professional and dress conservatively. Be prepared to deal with women in all capacities and at all levels. Treat them professionally, as business associates rather than as women.

Meetings

Be on time—punctuality is important to the Vietnamese. Meetings are a combination of socializing and formal interaction. First meetings might begin with casual talk over coffee or tea, in a generally informal atmosphere. However, business is not treated lightly and Vietnamese do not welcome jokes or an inappropriately casual attitude. A smile might be a sign of amusement or happiness, but it may also mean embarrassment, frustration, anxiety, or anger. If you are meeting with more than one person, determine who the senior person is, approach them immediately, and give them your card (introducing yourself through an underling is considered insulting). You will probably need an interpreter. Choose one carefully, and be sure they are familiar with the nuances of both Vietnamese and your language. Your Vietnamese associates will probably have their own interpreter, but relying on this person might mean taking a risk, as some interpreters exaggerate their expertise.

Business Attire

Business dress is casual, but conservative. Suits are worn during the winter, spring and autumn, but during summer both businesspeople and government opt for simply a shirt and tie. The north is more conservative, and women should avoid low necklines or hemlines that rise above the knee. Modest gold jewelry and a quality watch will count in your favor. However, avoid overly expensive jewelry or showy ornaments. In the north, temperatures and weather vary with the seasons; the south is generally hot and humid all year long. April and May are the hottest months, and are also the times when the humidity is highest.

Cultural Cautions

DO'S

- Vietnamese value personal relationships in business. Take the time to let your Vietnamese associate get to know you. This will initially slow things down, but will ultimately be worth the effort.
- To establish a good business relationship, establish a personal relationship that demonstrates your respect and trustworthiness.
- Always treat people with the respect to which their position entitles them, and always be polite.

DON'TS

- The head is considered sacred. Do not touch a person's head (not even a child's).
- Do not point the soles of your feet at someone. The feet are the lowliest part of the body. Also, do not point to or gesture at someone with your feet.
- Don't cross your legs while seated. It is considered impolite.
- Don't brag about your success or boast about your accomplishments. To Vietnamese, modesty is an important virtue.

CUSTOMS

- Vietnamese smoke heavily you will probably be offered a cigarette. Accept this gesture whether you smoke or not. If you do not smoke, simply put the cigarette on the table in front of you after taking it. Your Vietnamese associates will take note of this and not offer you another.
- Gifts are appreciated by Vietnamese (as are favors) and will often be repaid by helping to make business go faster and easier. Appropriate gifts include a carton of cigarettes (555 and Marlboro are popular) or quality whisky (such as Johnny Walker).

OBSERVATIONS

- Business dealings can be made easier by having a Vietnamese advisor or consultant.
- Vietnam is a communist country, but private investment is being encouraged and the government has introduced the concept of *doi moi* (renovation). This policy includes private enterprise, an openness to international trade, and more personal freedoms. To stimulate new ventures, a foreign investment code has been enacted. Anyone attempting to do business in Vietnam should become familiar with this code, as well as other laws and regulations pertaining to business.
- Vietnam is not only a bureaucracy, it is a state-run bureaucracy. Officials have wide discretionary power, so it is very important to have good relationships with anyone who has any influence over your business efforts.
- Vietnam is undergoing massive changes that can impact on business in a number of ways—usually negatively and unexpectedly. Virtually anything can happen and does, so plan accordingly.
- Be prepared for difficulties arising from decaying infrastructure, unfamiliarity with modern business practices, and a general lack of experienced managers, entrepreneurs, and businesspeople.
- To the Vietnamese, the war with the US (the "American War") is already history. In general, Vietnamese are not anti-American, and have put that war behind them.
- Vietnam is a long-term investment of time, money, resources, and energy, and should be approached as such. It will take considerable effort to bring any venture to fruition and there will probably be numerous setbacks along the way.

NEGOTIATIONS

- A common tactic is delaying major negotiations until you're about to leave the country, then making unreasonable demands.
- Be prepared to walk away. You will gain more from making it clear that you would rather have no deal at all than a bad deal.
- Be patient. Many Asians view foreigners as always being in a hurry, and encourage them to sign an agreement without proper time to study the details.

Legal

Legal System

Vietnam is a developing civil code country employing a combination of Asian, French, and socialist legal traditions.

Intellectual Property Rights

Patents Patents are granted to protect inventions and utility solutions. Registration of patents generally takes 18 months, and certain provisions of the registration process serve to limit patent protection in Vietnam. Patent owners are required to exhaust all administrative remedies with the National Office of Intellectual Property before bringing an action for infringement to court.

Trademarks Despite laws which protect trademark holders, owners of trademarks must remain alert and active to protect their rights from infringement. Under a revised registration system, the first to file an application is considered the legal owner of the trademark. As a result, some investors have found their trademarks appropriated by enterprising local firms. Vietnam does not give special status to trademarks registered in the applicant's home country, except under the provisions of the Paris Convention and the Madrid Union, which Vietnam has ratified.

Copyrights There is, as yet, only rudimentary recognition and enforcement of copyrights in Vietnam. Publication and trading in copied and counterfeit goods is pervasive. Vietnam has not yet ratified the Berne and Universal Copyright Conventions which provide international protection of copyrights and worldwide recognition of the assignment of copyrights. However, inclusion of computer software as one of the protected categories in a new, national copyright law should ease some of the fears of foreign companies considering importing sophisticated software into Vietnam.

Trade Secrets There is no trade secret law. Only by registering a patent of industrial design can technology owners secure some degree of legal protection.

Business Registration

All foreign investment activities must be licensed by the State Committee for Cooperation and Investment (SCCI). Investment incentives apply. Local capital contribution is largely limited to land use rights. The investment licensing process remains bureaucratic, although improvements have been made during the past two years. However, there is overlapping jurisdiction and many registration documents must be filed several times in different places. Most business activity is highly regulated. It is prudent to identify and establish an individual dialogue with the relevant government bodies early in the licensing process. Representative offices are popular, but are prohibited from engaging in business activity for profit. At this time, and with some limited exceptions, there is no legal form in Vietnam equivalent to the branch office, but, in the future, the branch is expected to become more recognized as restrictions are liberalized.

Contracts and Dispute Resolution

Contract law is still in its formative stage. The law is silent or is not sufficiently clear in some key areas. Much of the law on contract may be changed as a result of a new civil code expected to be passed in the near future. In the meantime, parties wishing to enter into contracts are advised to draft agreements dealing with all possible contingencies, rather than relying on the law to resolve issues. There are new arbitration rules, but the single most significant consideration for settling disputes in Vietnam presently is to avoid them altogether. Vietnam is still struggling with the complexities of transforming a socialist economy into a quasi market-based economy, and its undeveloped legal system cannot yet fully accommodate Western-styled commercial litigation or disputes.

Notaries

Notaries certify documents and their activities are regulated by law. The notary public office of a city or province is the authority empowered to certify the authenticity of a document and verify the conformity and legality of a document, as well as the identity and capacity of the signatores. Spoken and written language used in performing notary work must be Vietnamese; however, foreigners may utilize an interpreter. Certified translations of documents exists.

Labor

Foreign companies and joint ventures are required to sign collective or individual labor agreements with their employees. The labor agreement must cover the following subjects: salary, working conditions, safety and health issues, social welfare insurance, discipline and reward system, and termination and dispute resolution. Foreign enterprises are encouraged to hire Vietnamese employees. The minimum industrial wage is set at US$35 per month in the large cities. Employers and employees contribute to social insurance and other benefits.

Source: Russin & Vecchi, Ho Chi Minh City

Legal Matters

LEGAL BRIEFS

- **Land ownership** Private ownership of land is not permitted in Vietnam. All land is legally owned by the people and administered by the state. Restrictions on the transfer and the mortgage of land still pose a serious limitation to raising capital for projects. Foreign enterprises investing in Vietnam may use land either by leasing it or by entering into a relationship with a local partner who secures land use rights from the government.
- **Working hours** The maximum workweek for all employees is 48 hours: eight hours per day from Monday to Saturday. Employees working for one year are eligible to receive 12 days paid vacation in addition to five paid national holidays.
- **Foreign investment** The four forms of foreign direct investment permitted in Vietnam are: joint venture company, business cooperation contract, 100 percent foreign-owned enterprise, and build-operate-transfer project. The joint venture company is the favored business entity, comprising approximately 70 percent of all foreign investment in Vietnam.
- **Management of joint ventures** Because of the requirements of Vietnam's Foreign Investment Law, even foreign investors with a 70 percent interest do not have total control. For example, some fundamental decisions such as borrowing, discharging key personnel, etc., require unanimous board approval.
- **New laws** Vietnam has become a law factory, and productivity is increasing. There are over 7,000 legal documents at the central level, with another 55,000 at the provincial and city level.
- **Commercial dispute resolution** The Standing Committee of National Assembly has issued an ordinance which sets out guidelines for the conduct of economic disputes, including disputes that involve foreign parties.
- **Land law** A new law sets out a legal regime for the registration of house ownership and provides that expatriates residing in Vietnam may be allowed to buy houses through a state agency. However, if an expatriate house owner leaves the country for more than 90 days and does not exercise certain listed rights, he/she will lose the house to the state.
- **Labor** The Vietnamese labor code is one of the longest legal instruments in Vietnam. It contains provisions dealing with recruitment, trial periods of employment, forms of employment, labor agreements, the right to strike, and termination and dispute resolution. The code specifically applies to foreign invested enterprises and representative offices which employ staff in Vietnam.
- **Companies law** The companies law could soon be revised and strengthened due to pressure by foreign investors. Without a cohesive set of laws regulating all forms of companies, the establishment of a stock exchange will be impossible, and this hampers foreign investment.

LEGAL CONTACTS

Russin & Vecchi
OSIC Building, 6/F
8 Nguyen Hue Street
Ho Chi Minh City
Tel: (8) 824-3029, 824-3114 Fax: (8) 824-3114

Clifford Chance
52 Nguyen Binh Khiem
Hanoi
Tel: (4) 229-182 through 186 Fax: (4) 229-190

Baker & McKenzie
41 Ly Thai to Street
Hoan Kiem District
Hanoi

Chor Pee & Co.
96 Ba Trieu Street
Hoan Kiem District
Hanoi
Tel: (4) 228 787 Fax: (4) 251 875

Freehill Hollingdale & Page
34A Quang Trung Street
Hanoi
Tel: (4) 227 839 Fax: (4) 227 909

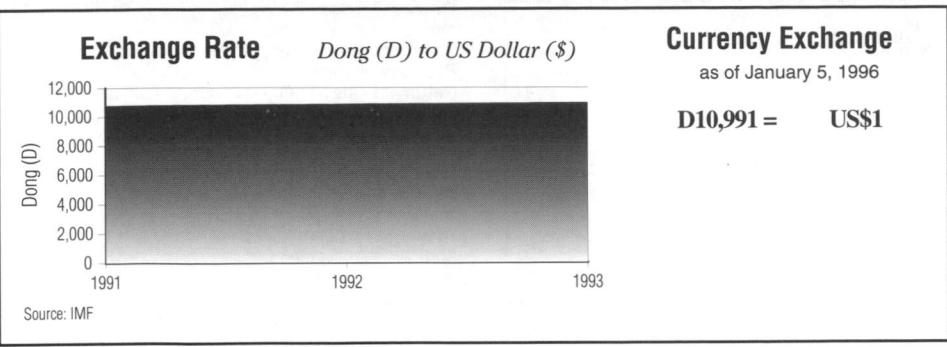

Exchange Rate *Dong (D) to US Dollar ($)*

Source: IMF

Currency Exchange
as of January 5, 1996

D10,991 =   US$1

Currency

The currency of Vietnam is the dong (D or VND).

Foreign Exchange

All foreign exchange transactions take place at the rate established at foreign exchange trading floors located at the branches of the State Bank of Vietnam in Hanoi and Ho Chi Minh City. Businesses that need foreign exchange for their import needs or debt payment obligations are allowed to submit their bids to the market seven days before the due date of payment.

Capital Transfers

Nonresidents are permitted to maintain nonresident accounts either in foreign currencies or in convertible dong; however, they may not open interest-yielding bank accounts in dong. Nonresidents can freely reconvert into foreign currency and transfer abroad unused balances in Vietnamese currency. Foreign currency deposited in a bank may be withdrawn for payments or transferred to other units or individuals.

Investment Incentives and Restrictions

Restrictions are few and Vietnam offers many incentives for foreign investors. However, in application, the incentives are hard to come by and Vietnam's cumbersome bureaucracy acts to restrict many investment opportunities.

Money Matters

BITS AND PIECES

- **Licensing** All trade transactions require a license from the Ministry of Trade.
- **Surrender requirements** Earnings are subject to several different surrender requirements under Decision No. 188 of the Council of Ministers, although this is not strictly enforced. In practice, the Council tolerates full retention of foreign exchange receipts.
- **Reporting requirements** Foreign trade organizations and firms engaged in international trade must submit plans for imports and exports to the State Planning Committee. The committee may request revisions every three months.
- **Trade transactions** International trade settlements are executed primarily by the Bank of Foreign Trade and a few authorized commercial banks.
- **Foreign investment** Three forms of foreign investment are provided for: contracted business cooperation, joint ventures between a foreign investor and Vietnamese enterprise; or firms wholly owned by foreign investors. There is a 50- to 70-year limit on enterprises with foreign capital. For smaller projects, foreign investment licenses are granted by the State Committee for Cooperation and Investment; provincial authorities must be consulted for larger projects.
- **Exchange rates** The official exchange rate does not fluctuate between the close of one transaction day and the opening of the next.
- **Foreign-invested businesses** Most foreign-invested businesses must be self sufficient in foreign exchange. Income in foreign currency, whether earned from export or in Vietnam must be sufficient to cover foreign currency expenditures, including the remittance of profits overseas.
- **Tax incentives** Projects falling into investment encouragement areas benefit from tax reductions, falling to as little as 10 percent for infrastructure projects in remote areas.
- **Gold** Gold may be brought into the country, provided that required customs declarations are made and a customs tariff is paid. Nonresidents are entitled to export gold up to the amount they brought in.

BANKS

ANZ Bank
14 Le Thai To
Hanoi
Tel: (4) 258190 Fax: (4) 258188/189

Bank of America
51 Ly Thai To
Hanoi
Tel: (4) 250003 Fax: (4) 260772

Bangkok Bank Ltd.
117 Nguyen Hue
D1 Ho Chi Minh City
Tel: (8) 223416 Fax: (8) 223421

Banque Indosuez
1 Ba Trieu
Hanoi
Tel: (4) 265323 Fax: (4) 265322

Deutsche Bank
25 Tran Binh Trong
Hanoi
Tel: (4) 268554 Fax: (4) 268652

Firstvina Bank
3-5 Ho Tung Mau
Ho Chi Minh City
Tel: (8) 291566/581 Fax: (8) 291583

Hong Kong Bank
4th Floor, Textimex Bldg.
10 Hguyen Hue
D1, Ho Chi Minh City
Tel: (4) 251266 Fax: (4) 230530

State Bank of Vietnam
47-49 Ly Thai To
Hanoi
Tel: (4) 52831 Telex: 411244

Thai Military Bank
11 Ben Chuong Duong
D1 Ho Chi Minh City
Tel: (8) 241500

TAXATION

Taxation requires sophisticated knowledge of complex rules and regulations specific to each country. For more detailed information we suggest you refer to the Ernst & Young Corporate Tax Guide and Directory, available from the Ernst & Young accounting office in your country, or from:

Ernst & Young
61 Trang Thi
Hanoi, Vietnam
Tel: (4) 265595
Fax: (4) 265596
or
Ernst & Young
22A Nguyen Van Troi
Q. Phu Nhuan
Ho Chi Minh City, Vietnam
Tel: (8) 447655
Fax: (8) 447960
or
Ernst & Young IndoChina Ltd.
15/F Hutchison House
10 Harcourt Road
Central, Hong Kong
Tel: (852) 2846-9888
Fax: (852) 2877-0578,
    (852) 2629-3887

- Other significant taxes include a value-added tax for a limited range of items, turnover tax, consumption tax, levies on petroleum production and consumption, social insurance contributions, and land rents.

At a Glance

Corporate Income Tax Rate (%)(a)	
Companies with Foreign-Owned Capital (b)	10/15/20/25
Companies without Foreign-Owned Capital	25/35/45
Capital Gains Tax Rate (%)(c)	10/15/20/25
Branch Tax Rate (%)(d)	-
Withholding Tax (%)	
Dividends (e)	5/7/10
Interest (f)	-
Royalties (g)	5/10/15
Payments to Contractors (h)	4/8
Remittance Tax (i)	5/7/10
Net operating Losses (Years)	
Carryback	0
Carryforward	5

(a) Companies are classified as either domestic companies or companies with foreign-owned capital.
(b) For petroleum and mining companies, the State Committee for Cooperation and Investment (SCCI) determines the tax rate, which may exceed 25%. These companies are subject to a resource tax.
(c) Gains derived from sales of fixed assets are treated as taxable profits, and subject to normal profits tax rates.
(d) Foreign companies may not establish branches in Vietnam.
(e) These are rates under the remittance tax.
(f) Vietnam does not withhold tax on interest. Tax may be levied on interest paid to residents of countries with which Vietnam has double tax treaties.
(g) The 5% rate is for royalties paid to Vietnamese and foreign individuals for technology transfers more than VND 2 million. The 10% rate applies to royalties paid under contracts for terms of less than five years. The 15% rate applies to royalties paid to entities under contracts with terms of more than five years.
(h) Contractor tax is a final withholding tax on gross contract fees of foreign companies doing work and earning income in Vietnam from contracts with Vietnam based organizations.
(i) The Remittance Tax is applied to profits remitted to foreign investors.

Business Travel

	LH	1906	MADRID	935	113-3
	LH	1022	STUTTGART HBF.	935	
	AF	1701	LYON	940	683-6
	AY	822	HELSINKI	940	113-3
	AA	071	SFRANCISCO-DALLAS	945	731-7

Air Travel Times

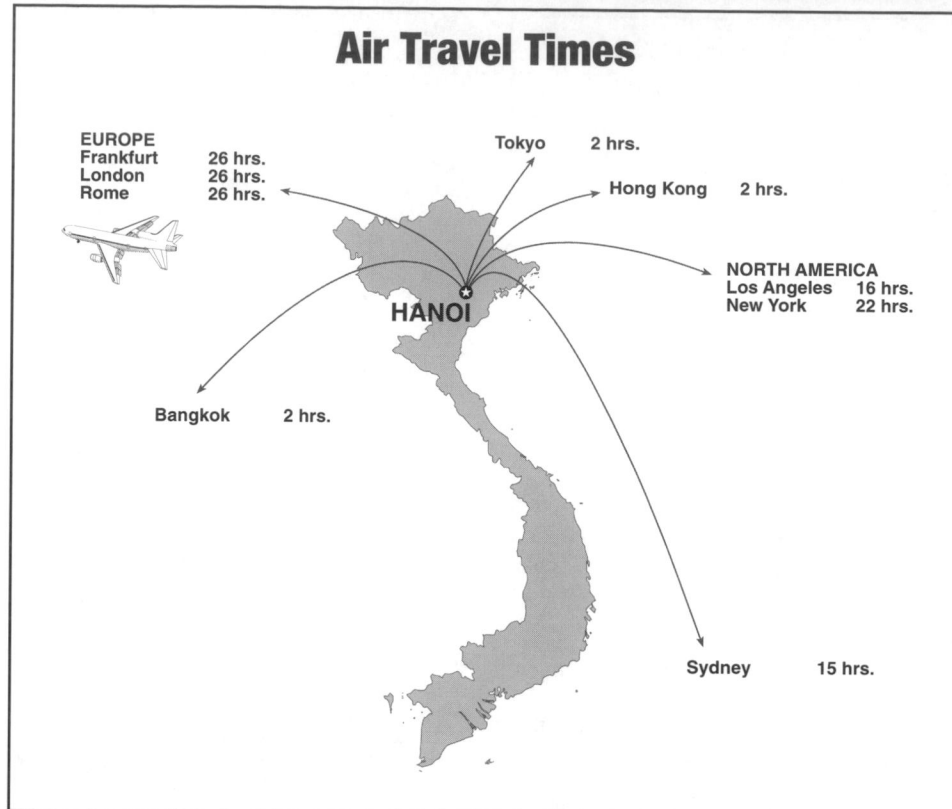

EUROPE
Frankfurt 26 hrs.
London   26 hrs.
Rome   26 hrs.

Tokyo   2 hrs.

Hong Kong   2 hrs.

NORTH AMERICA
Los Angeles 16 hrs.
New York   22 hrs.

HANOI

Bangkok   2 hrs.

Sydney   15 hrs.

COMMUNICATIONS

Telephones International calls can be made from major hotels or post offices. Domestic long-distance calls are made by dialing 01 followed by the area code and number.
Fax Telex and fax services are available at post offices and major hotels, but reaching other countries can be difficult from remote areas.
Post office Postal services are adequate and reasonably efficient. Post offices are open seven days a week, from early morning to evening and faxes can be sent and many consumer goods bought there.

BEST TRAVEL BOOKS

The Vietnam Guidebook, Barbara M. Cohen, 1993. Eurasia Travel Guides Series, illustrated, 496 pages. Houghton Mifflin.
Vietnam: A Travel Survival Kit, Daniel Robinson and Robert Storey. Illustrated, 454 pages, Lonely Planet Publications.
Vietnam Business Guide, Lewis B. Sckolnick, ed. Illustrated, 250 pages. Rector Press Ltd.
All-Asia Travel Guide, Southeast Asia, Volume One.
Culture Shock, A Guide to Customs and Etiquette, Vietnam.
Vietnam, Fielding Worldwide. Wink Dulles. The adventurous, up-to-the-minute guide to the world's newest tourist destination.
Vietnam Risks, Rewards, Regulations. Terence Lim, Guo Lih Chyi. Cassia Communications, Singapore.

USEFUL TELEPHONE NUMBERS

If you are calling from outside Vietnam, you will need to add the country code [84] and any other international dialing requirements from within your country.
• Vietnam Airlines ....(4) 21130
• Saigon GPO DHL ....(8) 96203
• Hanoi GPO DHL ....(4) 57124
• Fuji Cab Ho Chi Minh City ....(8) 252-452
• Mansfield Toserco ....(4) 269-444
• Car Rental Service Co. ....(8) 254-074
• Saigon Tourist Car Rental Co. ....(8) 295-925
• Saigon Auto Salon ....(8) 291-505
Credit Card Information
Lost or stolen credit cards (call collect to the US, regardless of which country the card was issued in.)
• Amex ....[1] (919) 333-3211
• Diner's Club................................[1] (303) 799-1504
• MasterCard ....[1] (314) 275-6690
• Visa ....[1] (410) 581-7931

Travelogue

WORKWEEK

Offices Monday-Friday 7:30 am to 4:30 pm; Saturday mornings.
Government Monday-Friday 7:30 am to 4:30 pm; Saturday mornings.
Retail Monday-Friday 7:30 am to 4:30 pm; Saturday mornings.
Many offices close for an hour or two at lunch time.

HOLIDAYS

Holidays 1996
January 1 New Year's Day
January-February Lunar New Year*
April 30 Reunification Day
May 1 Labour Day
September-October Mid-Autumn Festival*
*Dates vary according to lunar calendar.

VISA AND PASSPORT

Visitors to Vietnam need a valid passport and a visa obtained in advance. Business travelers need a specific business visa. Visitors must register with police within 48 hours, but hotels will complete this process instead; bring two visa photographs. Visitors who do not register are fined about US$20 upon departure.

DEPARTURE FORMALITIES

The copy of the customs form issued to you when you arrive in Vietnam must be presented upon departure. You cannot take out more cash than you brought in.

IMMUNIZATION

Inoculations are recommended for tetanus, diphtheria, meningitis, and polio, as well as malaria treatments. A Japanese encephalitis inoculation is recommended. Bring anti-mosquito lotion and anti-diarrhea tablets in case of infestation and stomach ailments due to drinking water, which should only be bottled or boiled water. Only use ice cubes from major hotels.

TIPPING

Not expected, but certainly appreciated, and becoming increasingly common. Ten percent is adequate, almost more than Vietnamese make in one day.

CRIME

Petty theft is common. The pickpockets in Saigon are brazen and will steal the eyeglasses right off your face. Watch shopkeepers' measurements and avoid 'freelance bankers' on the streets; customers are commonly swindled. Never leave luggage unattended, even for a minute. Police must be paid for assistance (bribery.) It is questionable if it is even worth calling for help as they are not all that helpful. However, in general, it is no worse than the crime in other Asian countries.

INFRASTRUCTURE

Vietnam has modern hotels with amenities, but the infrastructure is generally antiquated. Domestic air service and rental cars are available for internal travel, and taxis are becoming increasingly available in the cities. Look for taxis in stalls; they are hard to come by on the street. The remains of this war-torn country leave roads much to be desired. There are no international trains in Vietnam but trains serve all coastal areas. Travel by ferry or boats on rivers can be slow, short distances can take hours, even all day. Local travel guides are advised as not all visitors are allowed in certain areas.

NATIONAL TOURIST OFFICE

Vietnam National Administration of Tourism
80 Quan Su St.
Hanoi
Tel: (4) 253314

GOVERNMENT AGENCIES

Ministry of Agriculture and Food Industry
Bach Thao
Hanoi
Tel: (4) 259670

Ministry of Construction
37 Le Dai Hanh
Hanoi
Tel: (4) 268271

Ministry of Culture and Information
51 Ngo Quyen
Hanoi
Tel: (4) 253231

Ministry of Education and Training
49 Dai Co Viet
Hanoi
Tel: (4) 692250

Ministry of Energy
18 Tran Nguyen Han
Hanoi
Tel: (4) 257232

Ministry of Finance
8 Phan Huy Chu
Hanoi
Tel: (4) 253983

Ministry of Foreign Affairs
1 Ton That Dam
Hanoi
Tel: (4) 258201
Telex: 258201

Ministry of Forestry
123 Lo Duc
Hanoi
Tel: (4) 253236/7

Ministry of Heavy Industry
54 Hai Ba Trong
Hanoi
Tel: (4) 267867

Ministry of Labor, Invalids, and Social Affairs
12 Ngo Quyen
Hanoi
Tel: (4) 253875

Ministry of Light Industry
7 Trang Thi
Hanoi
Tel: (4) 253831

Ministry of Fisheries
57 Ngoc Khanh
Hanoi
Tel: (4) 254714, 256396

Ministry of Justice
25A Cat Linh
Hanoi
Tel: (4) 255316

Ministry of Public Health
138A Giang Vo
Hanoi
Tel: (4) 262970

Ministry of Science, Technology and Environment
39 Tran Hung Dao
Hanoi
Tel: (4) 252731/2

Ministry of Transportation and Communications
80 Tran Hung Dao
Hanoi
Tel: (4) 254070

State Cooperation and Foreign Investment Committee
56 Quoc Tu Giam
Hanoi
Tel: (4) 256893

State Inspection Commission
218 Doi Can
Hanoi
Tel: (4) 256893

FOREIGN TRADE CORPORATIONS

Agrexport
(Vietnam National Agricultural Produce Export-Import Corp)
6 Trang Tien
Hanoi
Tel: (4) 254234
Fax: (4) 259170

Agrimex
(Vietnam National Agricultural Products Corp)
59 Ly Tu Trong
District 1
Ho Chi Minh City
Tel: (8) 224710
Fax: (8) 291349

Airimex (General Civil Aviation Import-Export and Forwarding Co)
Gia Lam Airport
Hanoi
Tel: (4) 271513
Fax: (4) 259222

Animex (National Livestock and Poultry Import-Export Corp)
379 Minh Khai
Hanoi
Tel: (4) 264011
Fax: (4) 263645

Artexport-Hanoi (National Handicrafts and Art ARticles Export-Import Corp)
31-33 Ngo Quyen St.
Hanoi
Tel: (4) 252760
Fax: (4) 259275

Barotex (National Bamboo and Rattan Export-Import Corp)
37 Ly Thuong Kiet
Hanoi
Tel: (4) 256428
Fax: (4) 262387

Centrimex (South-Central Export-Import Co)
48 Tran Phu Rd.
Nha Trang City
Tel: (58) 221239

Coalimex (National Coal Export-Import and Material Supply Corp)
47 Quang Trung
Hanoi
Tel: (4) 255684

Cocenex (Central Production Import-Export Corp)
80 Hang Gai
Hanoi
Tel: (4) 254535
Fax: (4) 294306

Confectimex
(The Vietnam Foreign Trade Co for Garments)
32 Trang Tien
Hanoi
Tel: (4) 253604
Fax: (4) 257554

Constrexim
(National Construction Materials and Technique Export-Import Corp)
39 Nguyen Dinh Chieu
Hanoi
Tel: (4) 263448
Fax: (4) 262701

Cosevina
(Overseas Vietnamese Service and Export-Import Co)
102 Nguyen Hue
District 1
Ho Chi Minh City
Tel: (8) 291506
Fax: (8) 291024

Cultureimex
(State Enterprise for the Export and Import of Works of Art and other Cultural Commodities)
22B Hai Ba Trung
Hanoi
Tel: (4) 252226
Fax: (4) 259224

Foreign Trade Arbitration Committee
33 Ba Trieu
Hanoi
Tel: (4) 252961
Fax: (4) 256446

Genecofov
(General Co of Food of Vietnam)
64 Ba Huyen Thanh Quan
District 3
Ho Chi Minh City
Tel: (8) 293366
Fax: (8) 295428

Generalexim
(National General Export-Import Co)
46 Ngo Quyen
Hanoi
Tel: (4) 246009
Fax: (4) 259894

Intimex
(National Foreign Trade Enterprise)
96 Tran Hung Dao
Hanoi
Tel: (4) 256240
Fax: (4) 259259

Lipaco
(National Essential Oils, Aromatics and Cosmetic Complex Enterprises)
171-175 Ham Nghi
District 1
Ho Chi Minh City
Tel: (8) 297336
Fax: (8) 297384

Machinoimport
(National Machinery Export-Import Corp)
8 Trang Thi
Hanoi
Tel: (4) 52703
Fax: (4) 54050

Marine Supply
(Marine Technical Materials Import-Export and Supplies)
276A Danang Rd
Haiphong
Tel: 246539

Mecanimex
(National Mechanical Products Export-Import Co)
54 Hai Ba Trung
Hanoi
Tel: (4) 257459

Minexport (National Minerals Export-Import Corp)
35 Hai Ba Trung
Hanoi
Tel: (4) 255265
Fax: (4) 253326

Packexport (National Packaging Technology and Import-Export Co)
31 Hang Thung
Hanoi
Tel: (4) 262792
Fax: (4) 269227

Petechim (National Petroleum Import-Export Corp)
194 Nam Ky Khoi Nghia
District 3
Ho Chi Minh City
Tel: (8) 52603
Fax: (8) 52903

Printimex (National Printing Materials and Equipment Export-Import Corp)
175 Nguyen Thai Hoe
Hanoi
Tel: (4) 232581
Fax: (4) 259254

Rubexim (National Rubber Export-Import Corp)
64 Truong Dinh
District 3
Ho Chi Minh City
Tel: (8) 297171
Fax: (8) 297341

Seaprodex (National Sea Products Export-Import Corp)
87 Ham Nghi
District 1
Ho Chi Minh City
Tel: (8) 291333
Fax: (8) 290146

Technimex (Technology Export-Import Corp)
70 Tran Hung Dao
Hanoi
Tel: (4) 256751
Fax: (4) 256209

Trxtimex (National Textiles Export-Import Corp)
25 Ba Trieu
Hanoi
Tel: (4) 257700
Fax: (4) 262268

Tocontap (National Sundries Export-Import Corp)
36 Ba Trieu
Hanoi
Tel: (4) 254191
Fax: (4) 255917

Trade Service Co (TSC)
79 Ba Trieu
Hanoi
Tel: (4) 264259
Fax: (4) 266649

Vegetexco (National Vegetables and Fruit Export-Import Crop)
Trung Tu
Dong Da
Hanoi
Tel: (4) 263396
Fax: (4) 263926

Vietcochamber
33 Ba Trieu
Hanoi
Tel: (4) 252961
Fax: (4) 256446

Vietrans (National Foreign Trade Forwarding and Warehousing Corp)
13 Ly Nam De
Hanoi
Tel: (4) 254913
Fax: (4) 255829

Vietranscimex (National Transport and Communication Export-Import Corp)
22 Nguyen Van Troi
Phu Nhuan District
Ho Chi Minh City
Tel: (8) 442993
Fax: (8) 445240

Vimedimex (Medical Products Export-Import Corp)
246 Cong Quynh
Ho Chi Minh City
Tel: (8) 298441
Fax: (8) 225953

Vinacafe (National Coffee Export0Import Corp)
5 Ong Ich Khiem
Hanoi
Tel: (4) 262382
Fax: (4) 256422

Vinachemex (Chemicals Export-Import Co)
4 Pham Ngu Lao
Hanoi
Tel: (4) 2256377

Vinacimex (National Union of Cement Factories)
108 Le Duan
Hanoi
Tel/Fax: (4) 263748

Vinacontrol
54 Tran Nhan Tong
Hanoi
Tel: (4) 253840
Fax: (4) 253844

Vinafim (Film Import, Export and Film Service Corp)
73 Nguyen Trai
Dong Da
Hanoi
Tel: (4) 244566

Vinafood (National Food Export-Import Corp)
40 Hai Ba Trung
Hanoi
Tel: (4) 256771

Vinexad
(National Foreign Exhibition and Advertising Agency)
9 Dinh
Hanoi
Tel: (4) 255546
Fax: (4) 255556

Xunhasaha (State Enterprise for Export and Import of Books, Peridicals and other Cultural Commodities)
32 Hai Ba Trung
Hanoi
Tel: (4) 252313

LAW FIRMS

Mandel, Ngo & Partners
Business Center
Hotel Pullman Metropole
15 Ngo Quyen Street
Hanoi
Tel: (4) 269975
Fax: (4) 244809

Pollak & Co., Ltd.
76 Hang Trong
Hanoi
Tel: (4) 254971
Fax: (4) 260260

Simeon & Associates
13 Tran Hung Dao
Hanoi
Tel: (4) 251 558
Fax: (4) 251 514

Sinclair Roche & Temperley
16 Nguyen Truong To
Ba Dinh District
Hanoi
Tel: (4) 250002
Fax: (4) 260770

White & Case
Representative Office
57 Nguyen Du Street
Hai Ba Trung District
Hanoi
Tel: (4) 227-575
Fax: (4) 227-297

PERIODICALS

Khoa Hoc Ky Thuat King Te The Gioi (World Science, Technology and Economy)
5 Ly Thuong Kiet
Hanoi
Tel: (4) 252931

Thuong Mai (Commerce**)**
100 Lo Duc St.
Hanoi
Tel: (4) 263150

ACCOUNTANTING FIRMS

Cooper and Lybrand
43 Ngo Quyen
Hanoi
Tel: (4) 251215
Fax: (4) 251737

Bourne Griffiths (Vietnam) Ltd.
Lieu Giai
Ba Dinh District
Hanoi
Tel: (4) 347082
Fax: (4) 349142

Ernst & Young
61 Trang Thi
Hanoi
Tel: (4) 265595
Fax: (4) 265596

KPMG
2A Nguyen Dinh Chieu
Hanoi
Tel: (4) 228128
Fax: (4) 258999

Price Waterhouse
38A Trieu Viet Vuong
Hanoi
Tel: (4) 228985/86
Fax: (4) 228992

NEWSPAPERS

Hanoi Moi
44 Le Thai To
Hanoi
Tel: (4) 253067

Nhan Dan
71 Hang Trong
Hanoi
Tel: (4) 254231

Quan Doi Nhan Dan
7 Phan Dinh Phung
Hanoi
Tel: (4) 254118

Vietnam News
79 Ly Thuong Kiet
Hanoi
Tel: (4) 2546943

Saigon Giai Phong
432 Xo Viet Nghe Tinh
Ho Chi Minh City
Tel: (4) 295942

RADIO AND TELEVISION

Voice of Vietnam
58 Quan Su
Hanoi
Tel: (4) 257272
Fax: (4) 255765

Central Television
Giang Vo
Hanoi
Tel: (4) 243188

INTERNET ADDRESSES

Usenet group(s):
soc.culture.vietnamese
Vietnam Information
http://sunsite.nus.sg/SEAlinks/vietnam-info.html
Vietnam Links
http://radon.gas.uug.arizona.edu/~don/vietlink.html

Zimbabwe

Republic of Zimbabwe

Economy

Overview

Zimbabwe, formerly Rhodesia, gained its independence fairly recently from the UK—in 1980. Although progress has been made, the country's economy continues to struggle with the problems typically associated with post-colonial countries—a heavy reliance on agriculture, declining colonial infrastructure, ambivalence toward foreign investment, and an unskilled native work force. Though rich in natural resources, Zimbabwe continues to regulate its economy strictly, which has resulted in poor market incentives for local businesses. The introduction of Zimbabwe's Economic Structural Adjustment Program in 1991 has seen a gradual shift to an open market economy, accompanied by a steady growth in GDP.

Trade

Zimbabwe's restrictive controls on both internal and external business have resulted in a slow growth rate in its foreign trade. Developed countries are the primary markets for its exports, and it buys the vast majority of its imports, predominantly machinery and transportation equipment, from its partners. South Africa is its largest trading partner followed by Germany, the UK, and the United States. Zimbabwe relies heavily on agriculture, but production in this sector has fluctuated widely, resulting in uneven growth over the years.

Sectors

Agriculture The heart of the Zimbabwe economy, agriculture employs 75 percent of the population, supplies 40 percent of the exports, and represents 20 percent of GDP. The government has devoted substantial efforts toward promoting modern equipment and technology and providing education in order to increase the efficiency of this important sector, and to make producers competitive in international markets.

Industry This sector is largely agro-based, although there is also a substantial industry associated with mining. The government is actively promoting investment in manufacturing, an effort that has begun to provide greater access to much needed raw materials and up-to-date machinery. Moderate, long-term growth is expected, but rising interest rates are expected to reduce growth in the short term.

Services Tourism is an important sector in the Zimbabwe economy, although it is still in the early developmental stages. The government is committed to growth in this area, however, and other service industries should benefit as a result. At present, however, most other service industries serve only local markets.

Trends

Zimbabwe is a country in transition, though it faces formidable difficulties in moving to a market-oriented, economically successful independent state. An unemployment level of 35 percent and high inflation rates remain its most serious problems. It will also have to reduce the current high level of government expenditures dedicated to noninfrastructure projects. Increased access to foreign exchange and government incentives to foreign investors in the mining industry should draw much-needed capital to the country in the near future.

At a Glance

THE COUNTRY

Location South Central Africa, between the Zambezi River on the north and the Limpopo River on the south.
Terrain Most of Zimbabwe is rolling plateau. The highveld is a central ridge forming the country's watershed, with streams flowing to the Limpopo and Sabi rivers.
Climate Moderate tropical temperatures, relatively low humidity. Most rain falls in the higher eastern elevations, which are also cooler than other areas. A summer rainy season from November to March is followed by a drier transitional season with lower temperatures.

THE PEOPLE

Population 11,000,000
Ethnic composition
African.. 97.6%
European 2%
Asian and of mixed race .... less than 1%
Religious composition
Protestants... 17%
Roman Catholics.. 9%
Other Christian churches 14%
There are also substantial minorities of Muslims, Hindus, and Baha'is.
Languages spoken English, the official language, is widely spoken. Also Shona and Ndebele.
Educations and literacy Adult literacy rates are 73.7 percent for men and 60.3 percent for women. Africans and non-Africans are educated under the same system, regulated by the Ministry of Education.
Labor force
Total...3,100,000
By occupation: agriculture 74%, transport and services 16%, mining and manufacturing 10%.

COUNTRY FACTS

Political and legal Power is vested in a parliamentary and executive branch. The legal system is based on Roman-Dutch law and has also been influenced by the system of South Africa. The judiciary is independent from other branches of government.
Telephone The Ministry of Information, Posts, and Telecommunications controls telephone and telegraph services. International service is available primarily in urban areas. International country code: [263]. City codes: Bulawayo (9), Harare (4), Mutare (20).
Transportation The public corporation, National Railways of Zimbabwe, operates the country's railroads. Roads are in generally poor condition; only 15,000 km of the more than 85,000 km of highway are paved. The principal airports are in Harare and Bulawayo; both receive international flights.
Environment Only the largest of Zimbabwe's rivers have a year-round water flow. The most serious environmental problems include erosion of agricultural lands and deforestation. Air and water pollution from transportation vehicles and mining are on the rise.
Media Radio broadcasts over two AM and three FM channels, and government produced television programs are broadcast from Harare and Bulawayo. There are two daily papers and more than 40 magazines published in Zimbabwe.
Health All health services are the responsibility of the Ministry of Health. About 85 percent of the population has access to health care services. Safe water is available to about 84 percent of the population, but only about 40 percent have adequate sanitation.

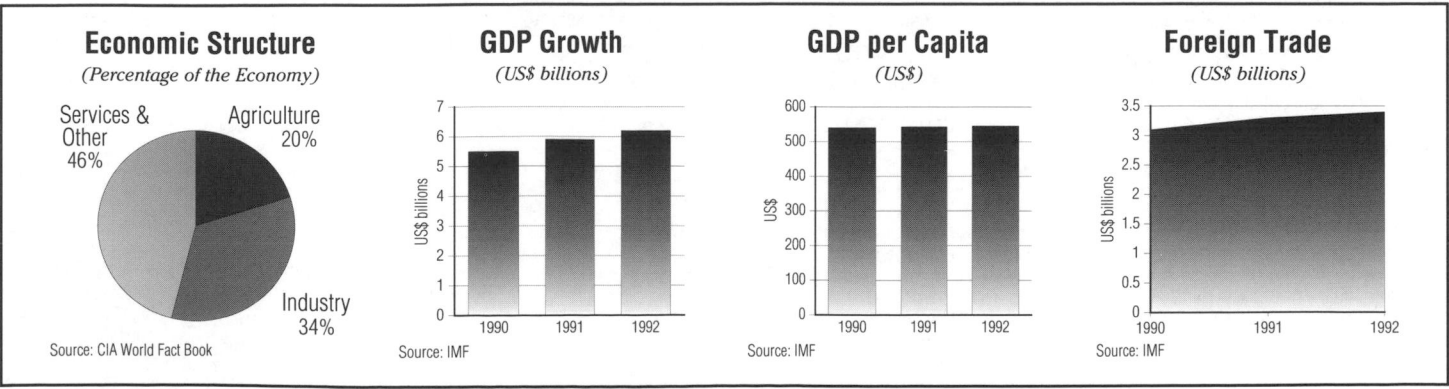

Economic Structure
(Percentage of the Economy)

Services & Other 46%
Agriculture 20%
Industry 34%

Source: CIA World Fact Book

GDP Growth
(US$ billions)

1990 1991 1992

Source: IMF

GDP per Capita
(US$)

1990 1991 1992

Source: IMF

Foreign Trade
(US$ billions)

1990 1991 1992

Source: IMF

Zimbabwe

○ National capital
● Secondary city
━━ International border
···· Province border
─── Primary road
···· Railroad

0   50   100 km
0 25   50   75 mi

© 1992 Magellan Geographix℠ Santa Barbara, CA

Travelogue

WORKWEEK

Government Monday-Friday 7:45 am to 4:45 pm.
Business Monday-Friday 8:00 am to 4:30 pm.
Banks Monday-Tuesday and Thursday-Friday 8:00 am to 3:00 pm. Wednesday to 1 pm. Saturday 8:30 am to 11 am.
Retail Monday-Friday 8:00 am to 5:00 pm. Saturday 8:00 am to 1:00 pm.

HOLIDAYS

Holidays 1996
January 1 New Year's Day
April 5 Good Friday
April 8 Easter Monday
April 18 Independence Day
May 1 Workers' Day
May 25 Africa Day
August 11 Heroes' Day
August 12 Defense Forces Day
December 25 Christmas Day
December 26 Boxing Day

VISA AND PASSPORT

All visitors must have valid travel documents, enough money for their stay, and a return ticket or enough money to purchase one. For a stay of less than six months most travelers need a passport, but no other documentation is usually required. Nationals of certain countries must obtain visas; the visa requirements change from time to time. Visas can take at least several weeks to receive. With a few exceptions, visas are not required for visits of less than three months.

DEPARTURE FORMALITIES

An airport departure tax of US$20 will be collected.

IMMUNIZATION

Anti-malarial tablets are recommended, particularly if you are traveling to low-lying areas. Begin taking them before arrival. Do not swim in or drink untreated water. Tap water is generally safe in urban areas, but caution is always advisable. AIDS has currently infected 10 to 20 percent of the population. Foreign travelers from areas infected with yellow fever or cholera must show inoculation certificates to enter the country.

TIPPING

For restaurants, 10 percent is sufficient. Porters should receive a tip based on the number of bags handled, about 50 cents per bag. Hotel maids should receive Z$5 when you check out of the hotel. Taxi drivers should receive 10 percent of the fare.

CRIME

Street crime is rare in Zimbabwe; walking alone at any time of the day in urban areas is usually safe. Women should be cautious at night. The most common theft is of car parts because of the country's shortage of cars and parts. Check with Zimbabwe officials before traveling to isolated areas.

INFRASTRUCTURE

Well-developed roads and railways help create an excellent surface transportation system. This country serves as a railroad hub for cargo throughout southern Africa. Taxi service is available in Harare and all major towns but is expensive. Inquire at your hotel about the best taxi service. City buses are crowded and routes are confusing. If you plan to travel by car, remember to drive on the left. All vehicles must be insured. Air travel connects with southern and eastern Africa and many European countries. Harare International Airport is located 15 km from downtown. The most economical transportation to the city is the airport bus run by Air Zimbabwe. For air travel within the country, Air Zimbabwe is the most reliable, with daily flights to most large towns. Air travel is certainly faster and often cheaper than bus or train travel between cities.

NOTE

All non-Zimbabwean residents, by law, must pay for their hotel accommodations in foreign currency, such as US dollars, UK pounds, or South African rands.

COMMUNICATIONS

Telephones The telecommunications system is being upgraded and does not yet offer advanced services such as cellular and paging. Domestic telephone service is fairly reliable but not many homes have service. International links exist to neighboring and more than 150 overseas countries. Public pay phones often are out of order. Locating the ones that work is easy—look for the line of waiting callers. International calls are best placed through a hotel. Getting through to some overseas countries can take substantial time; usually the operator will place the call and then contact you when the line connects. An earth satellite station has been built at Mazowe, promising greater access to international communications.

Fax Fax machines are uncommon, but most hotels and post offices have telex service. Banks and travel agencies may have fax services available.

Post office The postal service in Zimbabwe is reliable and economical. Airmail requires approximately five days for international delivery.

TV/Radio Radio Zimbabwe is owned by the government and broadcasts on AM and FM channels. Two television stations operate in the evenings.

BEST TRAVEL BOOKS

Africa on a Shoestring. Lonely Planet. Filled with informative tips, essential travel facts, places to go, things to do throughout the African continent.
Travel Survival Kit, Zimbabwe, Botswana & Namibia. Lonely Planet. Specific to the region, briefs travelers on the history, culture, people, geography, sights, and accommodations. Includes photographs and maps.
The Travelers' Guide to African Customs & Manners. St. Martin's Press. Tips on traveling, communications, transportation, and legal issues that visitors to Africa should know before landing in the country.

USEFUL TELEPHONE NUMBERS

If you are calling from outside Zimbabwe, you will need to add the country code [263] and any other international dialing requirements from within your country.

- Air Zimbabwe .... (4) 52681, 737011
- National Railways .... (4) 700011
- Express Motorways .... (4) 702221
- Echo Car Hire .... (4) 702221
- Europcar .... (4) 2634
- Hertz .... (4) 720351
- Impexo Rent-a-Car .... (4) 728732
- Rixi Taxi Services .... (4) 707707
- Creamline Taxis .... (4) 703333
- Meikles Hotel .... (4) 795655
- Impexo Tours .... (4) 705780

Credit Card Information
Lost or stolen credit cards (call collect to the US, regardless of which country the card was issued in).

- Amex ....[1] (919) 333-3211
- Diner's Club ....[1] (303) 799-1504
- MasterCard ....[1] (314) 275-6690
- Visa ....[1] (410) 581-7931

NATIONAL TOURIST OFFICES

Tourism House
Cnr. 4th Street/Jason Moyo Avenue
PO Box 8052
Causeway
Harare
Tel: (4) 79-3666/9, 70-6511
Telegrams: ZIMTOUR

Department National Parks and Wild Life Management
Harare Travel Center Booking Office
PO Box 8151
Causeway
Harare
Tel: (4) 70-6077

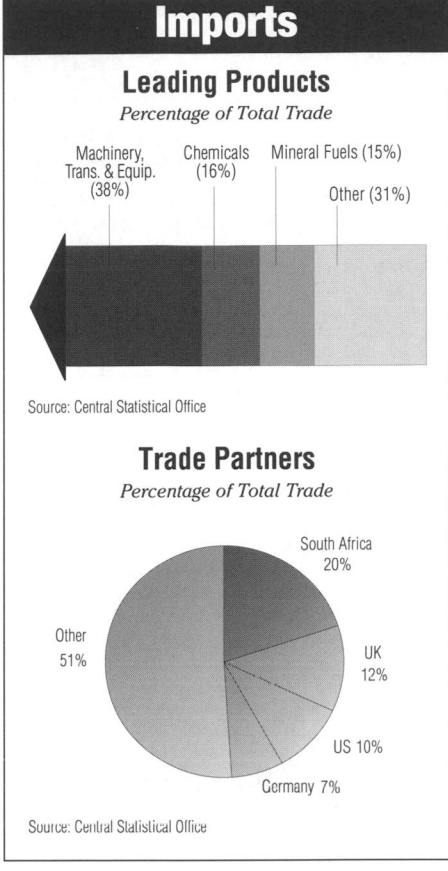

Imports

Leading Products
Percentage of Total Trade

Machinery, Trans. & Equip. (38%)
Chemicals (16%)
Mineral Fuels (15%)
Other (31%)

Source: Central Statistical Office

Trade Partners
Percentage of Total Trade

South Africa 20%
Other 51%
UK 12%
US 10%
Germany 7%

Source: Central Statistical Office

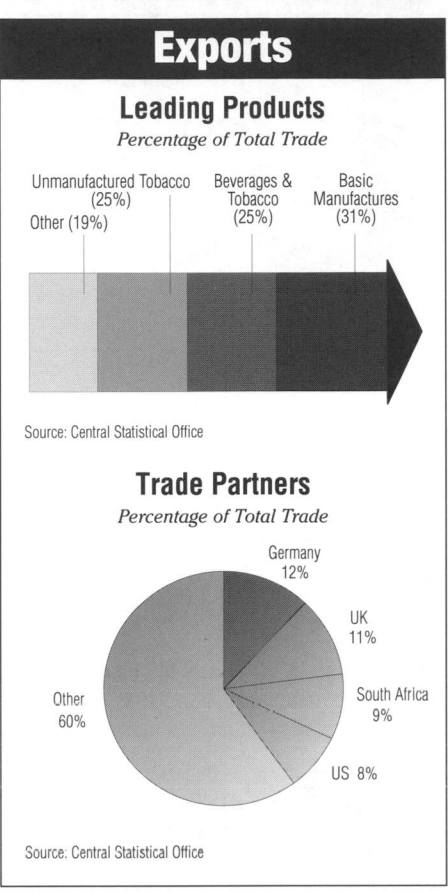

Exports

Leading Products
Percentage of Total Trade

Unmanufactured Tobacco (25%)
Other (19%)
Beverages & Tobacco (25%)
Basic Manufactures (31%)

Source: Central Statistical Office

Trade Partners
Percentage of Total Trade

Germany 12%
UK 11%
Other 60%
South Africa 9%
US 8%

Source: Central Statistical Office

Opportunities

FOR IMPORTING TO ZIMBABWE
- agricultural, industrial, and mining equipment
- construction materials and equipment
- engineering services
- franchising

FOR EXPORTING FROM ZIMBABWE
- agricultural products: tobacco, cotton, sugar, coffee and corn (maize)
- clothing
- nickel and ferrochrome
- oilseed

GROWTH SECTORS
- construction and agricultural machinery
- data processing equipment and software
- fertilizers
- general manufactured products
- industrial and transportation equipment
- pharmaceuticals

Trade News

RULES AND REGULATIONS
- **Regulation** The primary regulatory agencies are the MTC and MIT. A trade liberalization program, begun in the early 1990s, has largely removed trade restraints. Foreign exchange controls on trade-related transactions have been eliminated except for restrictions on capital controls. Most price controls have been abolished.
- **Import restrictions** Export firms acquire import rights based on foreign exchange earnings and are permitted to use this privilege to import goods except those on a small negatives list. Import rights may be sold. Licenses are valid for 12 months from issue and are issued with no geographical restriction. Importers are free to choose country of supply. Licenses are issued on an FOB basis and do not cover invisibles.

Legal

Legal System

A parliamentary democracy, Zimbabwe derives its law from Roman-Dutch heritage, with influence from South Africa. The judiciary is independent of the executive and legislative branches.

Intellectual Property Rights

Protection is provided by statute. There are public registries for trademarks, designs, and patents. Applications for registration should be made through a local agent. Patent protection is 20 years, trademark is 10 years, copyright is generally 50 years. Registrations are renewable.

Business Registration

Companies and private business corporations are registered and regulated pursuant to the Companies Act. Listed public companies are additionally regulated by the rules of the Zimbabwe Stock Exchange. A central registry of companies is operated in Harare. Shop and trading licenses are generally required for most businesses. These licenses are usually obtained from local authorities. Businesses must register with a number of other authorities as well, including the National Social Security Authority and the Accident Prevention and Compensation Scheme.

Contracts and Dispute Resolution

Written contracts are essential, and disputes are best resolved by negotiation between the parties.

Labor

Guidelines for industry-wide wages are set by the government. All industries except domestic and agricultural are represented in annual contract negotiations by a union or industry council. Public sector employees are subject to different laws than private sector workers. Government regulations control work hours, benefits, and health and safety conditions. The pensions and benefits scheme is compulsory. Employees have a right to strike with advance notice.

Legal Matters

LEGAL BRIEFS
- **Business entities** Subsidiaries and branches of foreign companies may be set up in Zimbabwe. Limited liability companies are popular, and recent legislation has authorized private business corporations, which are similar to South African closed corporations.
- **Antitrust practices** Zimbabwe has no commission regulating monopolies, but public demand is growing for the creation of one. The Zimbabwe Stock Exchange regulates dealings in securities that are listed on it.
- **Labor-management relations** The Office of Labor Relations maintains a cadre of Labor Relations Officers, each of whom is assigned to monitor conditions at particular firms and respond to worker grievances. If a Labor Relations officer cannot resolve a dispute between the management and workers committee at the plant level, then the case is sent to the Regional Hearings Officer, and onward to the National Labor Tribunal, if necessary.
- **Collective bargaining** The government encourages both workers and employers to organize at the industry level, and to bargain collectively.
- **Minimum wage** The law does provide for a minimum wage, but it is not adequate to support a family.
- **Work safety** There are no specific safety standards for the work environment.
- **International agreements** UN, GATT/WTO, British Commonwealth, Nonaligned Movement, Association of Southern African States, Southern African Development Community, World Bank, International Monetary Fund, Organization of African Unity, Preferential Trade Area, African Regional Industrial Property Organization, Berne Convention, Paris Convention.

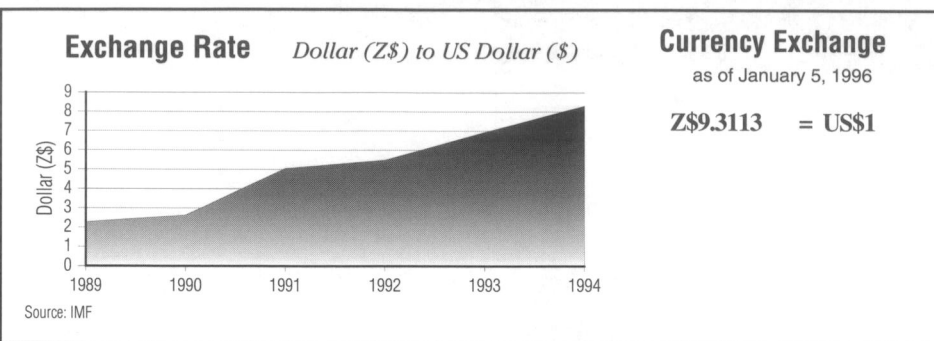

Exchange Rate *Dollar (Z$) to US Dollar ($)*

Dollar (Z$) — 9, 8, 7, 6, 5, 4, 3, 2, 1, 0

1989 1990 1991 1992 1993 1994

Source: IMF

Currency Exchange
as of January 5, 1996

Z$9.3113 = US$1

Currency

The currency in use is the Zimbabwe dollar (Z$), which is divided into 100 cents.

Foreign Exchange

Government controls over foreign exchange transactions have been substantially reduced, although many broad controls are still in place over the import and export of goods, remittances of business profits, and investments by companies with nonresident ownership. The Zimbabwe dollar's exchange rate is determined by a trade-weighted basket of currencies, with the US dollar as the intervention currency.

Capital Transfers

Foreign investments since September 1979 may be repatriated up to the value of the capital invested less dividends transferred abroad. Repatriation of capital invested before September 1979 is prohibited.

Investment Incentives

The Zimbabwe Investment Centre, created in 1990 to increase the country's export earnings, has authorized millions of dollars in projects in the past six years. Nearly 60 percent of the projects approved by the ZIC were joint ventures, and one-fifth were entirely foreign-owned. A wholly foreign-owned company that qualifies as an export-oriented project may repatriate 100 percent of its after-tax profits. Special incentives are available for mining companies.

Investment Restrictions

Foreign investment is restricted in the following areas: primary food and cash crop production; fishing; poultry farming; tourism; transport (but not air); retail and wholesale; barber and beauty shops; bakeries; and tobacco production. The ZIC scrutinizes proposals for establishing new businesses, expanding businesses with foreign exchange components, and acquiring interests in Zimbabwean businesses.

TAXATION

Taxation requires sophisticated knowledge of complex rules and regulations specific to each country. For more detailed information we suggest you refer to the Ernst & Young Corporate Tax Guide and Directory, available from the Ernst & Young accounting office in your country, or from:

Ernst & Young
P.O. Box 62
Harare, Zimbabwe
Tel: (4) 75-1808
Cable: Ernstaudit
Telex: 24273 ZW
Fax: (4) 79-1240

• Licensed investors in special export processing zones are exempt from income tax on profits for five years; branch profits tax; capital gains tax; shareholders tax; tax on interest, remittances, fees, and royalties; customs duty; and sales tax.

At a Glance

Corporate Income Tax Rate (%) (a)(b)	40
Capital Gains Tax Rate (%) (c)	10/30
Branch Tax Rate (%)(d)	48.4
Withholding Tax (%)	
Dividends(%) (e)	20
Interest	
Paid by Banks and Other	
Financial institutions (%) (f)(g)	30
Paid by Building Societies (%) (f)(g)	20
Paid by Others (%) (h)	10
Royalties (%)	20
Remittances (%) (i)	20
Fees (%) (j)	20
Branch Remittance Tax	0
Net Operating Losses (Years)	
Carryback	
Carryforward (k)	6

(a) This rate will be reduced from 40% to 37.5% for the year ending March 31, 1996, and subsequent years.
(b) A 10% rate applies for five years to approved manufacturers in growth areas, effective April 1, 1994.
(c) The 10% rate applies to capital gains on securities listed on the Zimbabwe Stock Exchange. Other capital gains carry the 30% rate.
(d) This rate combines the 40% corporate income tax rate and the 8.4% branch profits tax.
(e) This tax applies to dividends paid to shareholders other than resident corporations.
(f) Interest paid by post office banks and interest on building society class C shares are tax-exempt.
(g) This withholding tax only applies to residents, but the special tax rate applies to all taxpayers.
(h) This tax applies only to nonresidents.
(i) Final tax imposed on remittances transferred from Zimbabwe by nonresidents for technical, managerial, administrative, or consulting expenditures incurred outside Zimbabwe in connection with trade carried on in Zimbabwe.
(j) This tax applies to payments by residents to nonresidents for technical, managerial, administrative, consulting, or directors' fees.
(k) Mining losses can be carried forward indefinitely.
Income tax applies to all amounts derived from Zimbabwean sources. Certain types of incomes are exempt.

Money Matters

BITS AND PIECES

• **Personal foreign currency** Foreign currency and traveler's checks may be imported with no restrictions, but must be sold or exchanged through authorized dealers. Travelers departing from Zimbabwe may take as much as Z$250 and as much as the equivalent of Z$250 in foreign bank notes. Nonresidents may take any traveler's checks they had when they entered, less the amount sold to dealers.

• **Nonresident money transactions** Payments by nonresidents to residents must be made in denominated currencies. There are 17 freely convertible denominated currencies, including Deutsche marks, Japanese yen, and US dollars. Nonresidents may open accounts on approval of the exchange control authorities. A nonresident account may hold foreign currencies, and may be used for payments to residents and nonresidents or payments abroad. Residents and nonresidents are permitted to open foreign currency accounts, although funds withdrawn and converted into local currency may not be redeposited.

• **Preferential trade area** Member countries participating in the Preferential Trade Area for Eastern and Southern African States (PTA) can use national currencies for day-to-day payments during transaction periods of two calendar months, with net balances settled in convertible currencies.

• **Foreign exchange allowances** The foreign exchange allowance for import-related business travel is Z$600 per day, with a maximum of Z$6,000 per trip and an annual maximum of Z$12,000. For export-related business travel, exchange allowance is Z$700 per day, Z$8,000 per trip and Z$16,000 per year.

BANKS

African Development Bank
The Harare Regional Office of the African
Development Bank
2nd Floor
Batanai Gardens
PO Box 8404
Causeway
Harare

ANZ Grindlays Bank PLC
Ottoman House
1st Floor
59 Samora Machel Avenue
PO Box 300
Harare
Tel: (4) 795871 Fax: (4) 702270

Barclays Bank of Zimbabwe Limited
Box 1279
Harare
Tel: (4) 729811

First Merchant Bank of Zimbabwe Limited
Box 2786
Harare
Tel: (4) 703071 Fax: (4) 738810

Institute of Bankers of Zimbabwe
PO Box UA521
Harare
Tel: (4) 706277

Merchant Bank of Central Africa Ltd.
Old Mutual Centre, 14th Floor
PO Box 3200
Harare
Tel: (4) 738081 Fax: (4) 708005

Standard Chartered Bank Zimbabwe Limited
P.O. Box 373
Harare
Tel: (4) 752864 Fax: (4) 752860

Standard Chartered Merchant Bank
Box 60
Harare
Tel: (4) 708585 Fax: 72566

Syfrets Merchant Bank Ltd.
Nimbank House
46 Speke Avenue
PO Box 2540, Harare
Tel: (4) 794581 Fax: (4) 704741

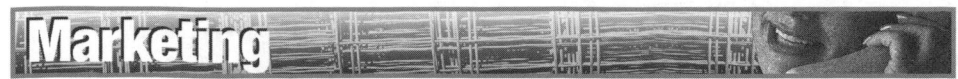

Distribution Overview

Zimbabwe remains a country in transition. Traders new to this nation need to be aware that, despite significant reforms, considerable initial effort and patience are necessary when entering this small but promising market. Most foreign firms select agents and distributors based on their established sales channels and ability to provide after-sales service.

Selling Techniques

Direct sales are occasionally used, but personal contact with local representatives has created the strongest ongoing business and sustained market penetration. Clear operating instructions, product displays, sample handouts, and frequent personal visits are vital tools for successful sales in Zimbabwe.

Advertising

The press is the most popular advertising medium. There are two daily newspapers, some weeklies, and several trade, technical, and business magazines. Radio and television broadcasts are operated by the government-owned Zimbabwe Broadcasting Corporation, which accepts fewer ads. Cinema advertising is effective. Outdoor displays are restricted to transit facilities, except for neon and other signs owned by commercial establishments. In Harare, the capital, there are several agencies that offer a full range of sales promotion and market services. Most local distributors expect their suppliers to provide advertising and promotional support, particularly when introducing a new product or brand name.

Service and Customer Support

Foreign exchange is often unavailable, so plant facilities and equipment often have to be used beyond their usual lifespan. Importers need to be prepared to furnish after-sales service and spare parts; this is a significant factor in long-term success.

Marketing in Zimbabwe

MARKETING TIPS

- **Setting up** Office and residential accommodations are excellent, and the cost of living is among the lowest in the world.
- **Language** English is widely spoken.
- **Government contracts** There is a tendency to award government and public sector contracts to locally owned firms.
- **Franchising** Franchising is still not widely established, but it is growing exponentially.

MARKET RESEARCH FIRMS

Human Resources (Pvt) Ltd.
PO Box 3426
Harare
Tel: (4) 793166

Imani Development Ltd.
PO Box 88
Harare
Tel: (4) 308134

Lever Bros. (Pvt) Ltd.
PO Box 950
Harare
Tel: (4) 61941

Lintas: Worldwide Zimbabwe
PO Box 3684
Harare
Tel: (4) 704336, 751597

Mike Rossouw Marketing Consultants (Pvt) Ltd.
PO Box 2184
Harare
Tel: (4) 735725

Probe Market Research (Pvt) Ltd.
PO Box 4381
Harare
Tel: (4) 792734

Greetings and Courtesies

A handshake is the standard greeting to be maintained while an often lengthy discussion ensues concerning your family and health. Only very good friends hug on greeting, and women and girls often curtsy. It is considered rude to look elders in the eye when greeting them. Refrain from using a Zimbabwean's last name until he or she has used yours.

Business Ethic and Framework

Business negotiations are conducted in English within most of Zimbabwe's burgeoning commercial community. Personal relationships are essential in maneuvering through the network of companies and government agencies, and a good deal of socializing must be expected before progress is achieved. Standards of punctuality are fairly high, although many meetings are usually necessary to work through the layers of bureaucracy, regulations, and decision makers. Meetings are always preceded by tea and conversation. Business lunches and dinners are very important and comprise a good deal of the "business meetings."

Decision Making

Progress is slow in arriving at important final decisions, as everyone seems to require the authorization of someone else. Accountability can be lost in the shuffle. Persistence and patience are essential here. In general, decision making is a group process, and everybody involved must reach some sort of consensus. For this reason, it is especially important to establish and maintain excellent relationships with business contacts at all levels—each one of them may help to facilitate a positive outcome.

Cultural Cautions

DO'S

- Always treat elders with great respect; this is one of Zimbabwe's most basic values.
- Plan your appointments well in advance.
- Bring a good supply of business cards (in English) because getting new ones printed is difficult in Zimbabwe.

DON'TS

- Refrain from displays of public affection and intimacy.
- Avoid discussions of politics and economic conditions.
- Avoid setting meetings during the month of June since business comes to a standstill during this cool month of the year.

CUSTOMS

- Very few women are found in significant positions in the Zimbabwean business world. Foreign businesswomen can expect to be treated with more respect if they appear to be married and conduct themselves with modesty and restraint.
- Zimbabweans are completely Westernized in their dress. For business attire men wear a suit and tie, women a suit or dress. Avoid fancy clothes in the rural areas because locals will stereotype you as a "rich foreigner."

Contacts

GOVERNMENT AGENCIES

Department of Customs & Excise
Head Office
PO Box 8015
Causeway, Customs House
corner South Ave./Angwa Street
Harare
Tel: 79-0801

Electricity Supply Authority
Electricity Centre
PO Box 377
25 Samora Machel
Avenue Central
Harare

Ministry of Coordinating Regional and International Organizations
Club Chambers, 9th Floor
Baker Avenue
Causeway
Harare

Ministry of Education and Culture
Ambassador House, 14th Floor
Union Avenue
PO Box 8022
Causeway
Harare
Tel: (4) 73-4050 Telex: 26430

Ministry of Energy, Water Resources and Development
Private Bag 7712
Makombe Building, Block 3
Leopold Takawira Avenue/Herbert Chitepo Avenue
Causeway
Harare
Tel: (4) 70-7861 Telex: 22141

Ministry of Environment and Tourism
Private Bag 7753
Karigamombe Centre, 14th Floor
Causeway
Harare
Tel: (4) 79-4455, 70-4707 Telex: 2141

Ministry of Finance, Economic Planning and Development
Private Bag 7705
Munhumutapa Building, Ground Floor
Causeway
Harare
Tel: (4) 72-2101, 79-4571 Telex: 22141

Ministry of Foreign Affairs
Munhumutapa Building, 1st Floor
Samor Machel Avenue
PO Box 4240
Causeway
Harare
Tel: (4) 72-7005, 79-4681

Ministry of Industry and Commerce
Private Bag 7708
Causeway
Harare
Tel: (4) 70-2731

Ministry of Information, Posts and Telecommunications
PO Box 8232
Liquenda House, 9-11th Floors
Baker Avenue
Causeway
Harare
Tel: (4) 70-3091, 70-3891
Telex: 24142

Ministry of Transport and Energy
PO Box 8109
Kaguvi Building
Central Avenue
Causeway
Harare
Tel: (4) 70-0991, 70-7121, 79-2695

Zimbabwe Investment Center
Box 5950
Harare
Tel: (4) 79-0991 Fax: (4) 70-8976

BUSINESS AND TRADE ORGANIZATIONS

Bulawayo Chamber of Commerce
PO Box 1292
8th Avenue
Bulawayo
Tel: 69769

Confederation of Zimbabwean Industries
Box 3794
Industry House
109 Rotten Row
Harare
Tel: (4) 73-9833 Fax: (4) 70-2873

Harare Chamber of Commerce
6th Floor, PO Box 1934
Equity House
Rezende Street
Harare
Tel: (4) 708611

Industrial Development Corporation
PO Box 8531
Causeway
Harare
Tel: (4) 70-6971 Fax: (4) 79-6028

Small Enterprises Development Corporation
Corner Manica Road/Angwa Street
Harare
Tel: (4) 705198

Trade Fair Zimbabwe
PO Famona Showgrounds
Hillside Road
Famona, Bulawayo
Tel: 6-4911 Telex: 3273 ZIFTA ZW

Zimbabwe National Chamber of Commerce (ZNCC)
PO Box 1934
Equity House, 6th Floor
Rezende Street
Harare
Tel: 70-8611 Telex: 2531 CHACOM ZW

ZimTrade
Box 2738
Harare
Tel: (4) 73-1020 Fax: (4) 70-6930

MARKETING BOARDS

Agricultural Marketing Authority
PO Box 8094
Causeway, Royal Mutual House, 4th Floor
45 Baker Avenue
Harare
Tel: (4) 73-0944 Telex: 22586

Cotton Marketing Board of Zimbabwe
Kurima House
PO Box 2697, 89 Baker Avenue
Harare
Tel: (4) 700531

Dairy Marketing Board
Head Office
PO Box 587
Harare
Tel: (4) 705701

Tobacco Marketing Board
PO Box UA214
Harare
Tel: (4) 66311 Telex: 24656

Grain Marketing Board of Zimbabwe
Kurima House
PO Box 2697, 89 Baker Avenue
Harare
Tel: (4) 700531

RADIO & TELEVISION

Zimbabwe Broadcasting Corporation
PO Box HG444
Highlands
Harare
Tel: (4) 707222 Fax: (4) 795698

NEWSPAPERS

The Chronicle
PO Box 585
Bulawayo
Tel: 65471 Telex: 3059

Daily Gazette
PO Box 66070
Kopje
Harare
Tel: (4) 738722

The Herald
PO Box 396
Harare
Tel: (4) 795771
Fax: (4) 791311

BUSINESS PERIODICALS

Commerce (Monthly)
PO Box 1683
Harare

Economic Review (2X/year)
c/o Zimbabwe Banking Corporation
PO Box 3198
Harare
Tel: (4) 735010
Fax: (4) 735600

The Financial Gazette (Weekly)
PO Box 66070
Kopje
Harare
Tel: (4) 738722

Quarterly Guide to the Economy (Quarterly)
First Merchant Bank of Zimbabwe Ltd.
FMB House
67 Samora Machel Avenue
PO Box 2786
Harare
Tel: (4) 703071
Fax: (4) 738810

FREIGHT FORWARDERS

Air Express International
PO Box 1521
Harare
Tel: (4) 705307/8/9

WTC Freight Zimbabwe (Pvt.) Ltd.
PO Box 4156
Harare
Tel: (4) 790981

Zimbabwe Shipping & Forwarding Agents
PO Box 77 Bulawayo
Tel: (4) 71202

The Herald
PO Box 396
Harare
Tel: (4) 795771
Fax: (4) 791311

INTERNET ADDRESSES

Usenet group(s):
soc.culture.zimbabwe

ZimWEB
http://www.mother.com/~zimweb/

Zimbabwe Focus
http://cy.co.za/atg/stbroz.html